HANDBOOK OF LATIN AMERICAN STUDIES: No. 54

A Selective and Annotated Guide to Recent Publications in Art, History, Literature, Music, Philosophy, and Electronic Resources

VOLUME 55 WILL BE DEVOTED TO THE SOCIAL SCIENCES: ANTHROPOLOGY, ECONOMICS, GEOGRAPHY, GOVERNMENT AND POLITICS, INTERNATIONAL RELATIONS, AND SOCIOLOGY

EDITORIAL NOTE: Comments concerning the *Handbook of Latin American Studies* should be sent directly to the Editor, *Handbook of Latin American Studies*, Hispanic Division, Library of Congress, Washington, D.C. 20540.

HANDBOOK OF LATIN AMERICAN STUDIES: NO. 54

HUMANITIES

Prepared by a Number of Scholars
for the Hispanic Division of The Library of Congress

DOLORES MOYANO MARTIN, *Editor*
P. SUE MUNDELL, *Assistant Editor*

1995

UNIVERSITY OF TEXAS PRESS   *Austin*

International Standard Book Number 0-292-751907
International Standard Serial Number 0072-9833
Library of Congress Catalog Card Number 36-32633
Copyright © 1995 by the University of Texas Press
All rights reserved
Printed in the United States of America

Requests for permission to reproduce material
from this work should be sent to
Permissions, University of Texas Press
Box 7819, Austin, Texas 78713-7819.

First Edition, 1995

The paper used in this publication meets
the minimum requirements of American National
Standard for Information Sciences—Permanence
of Paper for Printed Library Materials,
ANSI Z39.48-1984. ∞

CONTRIBUTING EDITORS

HUMANITIES

Barbara von Barghahn, *George Washington University*, ART
María Luisa Bastos, *Lehman College, CUNY*, LITERATURE
Judith Ishmael Bissett, *Miami University, Ohio*, LITERATURE
Alvaro Félix Bolaños, *Tulane University*, LITERATURE
John Britton, *Frances Marion University*, HISTORY
Francisco Cabanillas, *Bowling Green State University*, LITERATURE
Sara Castro-Klarén, *The Johns Hopkins University*, LITERATURE
Don M. Coerver, *Texas Christian University*, HISTORY
Harold Colson, *University of California, San Diego*, ELECTRONIC RESOURCES
Noble David Cook, *Florida International University*, HISTORY
Edith B. Couturier, *National Endowment for the Humanities*, HISTORY
Edward Cox, *Rice University*, HISTORY
Joseph T. Criscenti, *Professor Emeritus, Boston College*, HISTORY
Marshall Eakin, *Vanderbilt University*, HISTORY
Luis Eyzaguirre, *University of Connecticut*, LITERATURE
Fernando García Núñez, *University of Texas at El Paso*, LITERATURE
Magdalena García Pinto, *University of Missouri, Columbia*, LITERATURE
Dick Gerdes, *University of New Mexico*, LITERATURE
María Cristina Guiñazú, *Lehman College-CUNY*, LITERATURE
Linda B. Hall, *University of New Mexico*, HISTORY
Michael T. Hamerly, *University of Guam*, HISTORY
Robert Haskett, *University of Oregon*, HISTORY
José M. Hernández, *Professor Emeritus, Georgetown University*, HISTORY
Kathleen Higgins, *University of Iowa*, HISTORY
Rosemarijn Hoefte, *Royal Institute of Linguistics and Anthropology*, HISTORY
Carlos R. Hortas, *Hunter College-CUNY*, LITERATURE
Regina Igel, *University of Maryland*, LITERATURE
Nils P. Jacobsen, *University of Illinois*, HISTORY
William H. Katra, *University of Wisconsin-Eau Claire*, LITERATURE
Norma Klahn, *University of California, Santa Cruz*, LITERATURE
Pedro Lastra, *State University of New York at Stony Brook*, LITERATURE
Asunción Lavrin, *Arizona State University at Tempe*, HISTORY
Maria Angélica Guimarães Lopes, *University of South Carolina*, LITERATURE
Carol Maier, *Kent State University*, TRANSLATIONS
Teresita Martínez-Vergne, *Macalester College*, HISTORY
David McCreery, *Georgia State University*, HISTORY
Naomi Hoki Moniz, *Georgetown University*, LITERATURE
José M. Neistein, *Brazilian-American Cultural Institute, Washington*, ART
José Miguel Oviedo, *University of Pennsylvania*, LITERATURE

Daphne Patai, *University of Massachusetts-Amherst*, LITERATURE
Anne Pérotin-Dumon, *Pontificia Universidad Católica de Chile*, HISTORY
Richard A. Preto-Rodas, *University of South Florida*, LITERATURE
René Prieto, *Southern Methodist University*, LITERATURE
José Promis, *University of Arizona*, LITERATURE
Jane M. Rausch, *University of Massachusetts-Amherst*, HISTORY
Oscar Rivera-Rodas, *University of Tennessee, Knoxville*, LITERATURE
Bélgica Rodríguez, *Organization of American States*, ART
Humberto Rodríguez-Camilloni, *Virginia Polytechnic Institute and State University*, ART
Armando Romero, *University of Cincinnati*, LITERATURE
Kathleen A. Ross, *Duke University*, TRANSLATIONS
Enrique Sacerio-Garí, *Bryn Mawr College*, LITERATURE
William F. Sater, *California State University, Long Beach*, HISTORY
Susan M. Socolow, *Emory University*, HISTORY
Saúl Sosnowski, *University of Maryland*, LITERATURE
Robert Stevenson, *University of California, Los Angeles*, MUSIC
Barbara A. Tenenbaum, *The Library of Congress*, HISTORY
Juan Carlos Torchia Estrada, *Organization of American States*, PHILOSOPHY
Lilián Uribe, *Central Connecticut State University*, LITERATURE
Marie Louise Wagner, *Georgetown University*, HISTORY
Kathy Waldron, *Citibank, N.A., Miami*, HISTORY
Stephen Webre, *Louisiana Tech University*, HISTORY
Raymond Williams, *University of Colorado*, LITERATURE
Stephanie Wood, *University of Oregon*, HISTORY
Winthrop R. Wright, *University of Maryland*, HISTORY

SOCIAL SCIENCES

Juan del Aguila, *Emory University*, GOVERNMENT AND POLITICS
Benigno Aguirre-López, *Texas A&M University*, SOCIOLOGY
Amalia Alberti, *Independent Consultant, San Salvador*, SOCIOLOGY
G. Pope Atkins, *University of Texas at Austin*, INTERNATIONAL RELATIONS
Melissa H. Birch, *Washburn University*, ECONOMICS
Eduardo Borensztein, *International Monetary Fund*, ECONOMICS
Jacqueline Braveboy-Wagner, *The City College-CUNY*, INTERNATIONAL RELATIONS
Roderic A. Camp, *Tulane University*, GOVERNMENT AND POLITICS
William L. Canak, *Middle Tennessee State University*, SOCIOLOGY
César Caviedes, *University of Florida*, GEOGRAPHY
Marc Chernick, *Johns Hopkins University*, GOVERNMENT AND POLITICS
Harold Colson, *University of California, San Diego*, ELECTRONIC RESOURCES
Lambros Comitas, *Columbia University*, ANTHROPOLOGY
David W. Dent, *Towson State University*, GOVERNMENT AND POLITICS
Clinton R. Edwards, *University of Wisconsin-Milwaukee*, GEOGRAPHY
Gary S. Elbow, *Texas Tech University*, GEOGRAPHY
Malva Espinosa, *Instituto Latinoamericano de Estudios Transnacionales, Santiago*, SOCIOLOGY
Gary Feinman, *University of Wisconsin-Madison*, ANTHROPOLOGY
Damián Fernández, *Florida International University*, INTERNATIONAL RELATIONS

Magnus Mörner, *Göteborgs Universitet, Sweden,* SCANDINAVIAN LANGUAGES
Małgorzata Nalewajko, *Academia de Ciencias de Polonia, Warszawa, Poland,*
POLISH LANGUAGE

Special Contributing Editors

Marie Louise Bernal, *Library of Congress,* SCANDINAVIAN LANGUAGES
Christel Krause Converse, *College Park, Md.,* GERMAN LANGUAGE
Barbara Dash, *Library of Congress,* RUSSIAN LANGUAGE
Georgette M. Dorn, *Library of Congress,* GERMAN AND HUNGARIAN LANGUAGES
George J. Kovtun, *Library of Congress,* CZECH LANGUAGE
Vincent C. Peloso, *Howard University,* ITALIAN LANGUAGE
Juan Manuel Pérez, *Library of Congress,* GALICIAN LANGUAGE
Iêda Siqueira Wiarda, *Library of Congress,* SPECIAL MATERIAL IN PORTUGUESE
LANGUAGE,
Hasso von Winning, *Southwest Museum, Los Angeles,* GERMAN MATERIAL ON MESO-
AMERICAN ARCHAEOLOGY

CONTENTS

HISTORY

LITERATURE

EDITOR'S NOTE

I. GENERAL AND REGIONAL TRENDS

Unlike most 20th-century upheavals in Latin America, the most important revolution of the last ten years has been silent rather than explosive, secretive rather than public, and frankly, almost ignored, an unparalleled technological leap that has led to the astonishing electronic resources available today for the study of the region. During the past decade, "Latin America has progressed from being a minor presence in most computerized databases to serving as perhaps the top Third World and Western Hemisphere arena for improved bibliographic and full-text coverage, new product development, and electronic networking" (p. 3). Between 1989 and 1993, four major Latin American databases of unprecedented bibliographic and news strength, referred to as "the four tigers" (p. 6), emerged outside of commercial channels to form the present electronic core of our field. In order of appearance, these are the databases and their coverage: 1) for current newspaper and journal article abstracts: *INFO-SOUTH*, University of Miami North-South Center; 2) for electronic news: *Latin America Data Base* or *LADB*, University of New Mexico, Albuquerque; 3) for journal citations: the *Hispanic American Periodical Index* or *HAPI Online*, University of California, Los Angeles; and 4) for citations and scholars' annotations of books, book chapters, journal articles, proceedings' papers, online databases, computer files, etc.: the *Handbook of Latin American Studies* or *HLAS*, Library of Congress (p. 6–9).

In order to help assist this revolution's casualties—those affected by an ever-increasing sense of "information overload"—we are proud to introduce in this volume a new chapter, whose first installment is entitled: "Electronic Resources on Latin America: a Decade of Progress and Promise." After *HLAS 54*, the chapters will alternate, according to volume, between "Electronic Resources in the Social Sciences" and "Electronic Resources in the Humanities." We are also pleased to recognize the author of this new chapter, Harold Colson of the University of California, San Diego, as one of the most astute, well informed, and articulate observers of this remarkable phenomenon. I highly recommend this chapter to all *HLAS* users and contributors.

As we anticipated in the last humanities volume (see *HLAS 52*, p. xvii), publications sponsored by the various Quincentennial commissions in Spain and Latin America continue to figure prominently in this *Handbook*, particularly in the colonial history and literature chapters. The commemoration of this date, notes one contributor, has generated a remarkably high number of negative interpretations of Columbus' voyage as a prelude to genocide (p. 735). On the other hand, scholars that take a less oppositional view are exemplified by Anthony Pagden and his exceptionally fine study *La caída del hombre natural* (item **5355**), a work which is far more complete than the English original, according to the author. Pagden's work is a rich, multifaceted and sophisticated examination of the earliest interpretations of the New World, of those first "ethnographies" European observers wrote about their

American subjects. On the other hand, another contributor laments Pagden's pessimistic view of the efforts of Europeans to interpret the New World (p. 126). Another major work is David Brading's *The first America* (item **941**), a "monumental study of the origins, evolution and demise of a distinctive Creole national identity in Spanish America" that lasted from the early colonial period to the middle of the 19th century (p. 126).

Other valuable studies are Inga Clendinnen's skeptical analysis of both the European and indigenous sources, "Fierce and Unnatural Cruelty: Cortés and the Conquest of Mexico" (item **3572**); the special Quincentennary supplement issued by *The Journal of Latin American Studies* and edited by Tulio Halperín-Donghi, Victor Bulmer-Thomas, and Laurence Whitehead which "contains an unusually perceptive group of articles that encompass major trends throughout the region" (p. 127); Rolena Adorno's illuminating and perceptive interpretations of various colonial texts such as her reading of Cabeza de Vaca's *Naufragios* (item **3519**), her analysis of early chroniclers within the context of Spanish censorship (item **3557**), her reappraisal of Bartolomé de las Casas (item **3518**), her examination of how the treatment of indigenous populations influenced Spanish writings about Indians in the 16th century (items **3559** and **3558**), and her reflections on the significance and importance of Spanish concepts such as "war," "chivalry," and "civilized," and what they meant to the 16th-and 17th-century Europeans and Americans (items **3560** and **3516**). Finally, we should note Gordon Brotherston's *Book of the Fourth World: reading the Native Americans through their literature* (item **3462**), described in this volume as "a masterpiece on the literatures of the American Indians, a book that the field has been striving towards for many years and which has finally found its proper form in this comprehensive, informed, intelligent, and sensitive study of the classics of the Fourth World" (p. 461).

Additional colonial works annotated in this volume that deserve special mention are: the inspired and insightful *Religion in the Andes* by Sabine MacCormack (item **2256**); "the most significant and certainly the most enjoyable and . . . stimulating" study of colonial Chile, *La invención del Reino de Chile* by Giorgio Antei (item **2457** and p. 298); a major database compiled and edited by Manuel Lucena Balmoral, *Fuentes para el estudio de la fiscalidad colonial . . . : la producción del oro en el Nuevo Reino de Granada a través de las Cajas Reales: 1651–1701* (item **2293**); a fine *Catálogo de pintura colonial en Chile* by Luis Mebold Köhnenkamp which fills an important void while setting high standards (item **187** and p. 40); and the seven-volume series, *Arte novohispano* (items **161, 150, 106, 160, 107, 151, 121,** and p. 23). Finally, the most important article on colonial South America is probably Noble David Cook's masterful work, "Migration in Colonial Peru" (item **2371** and p. 297).

We should also note the fine contribution of two scholars who in 1992 produced the first two journals entirely dedicated to Hispanic-American colonial studies: 1) *Colonial Latin American Review,* an annual publication edited by Raquel Chang-Rodríguez at the Department of Romance Languages, The City College of New York;[1] and 2) *Colonial Latin American Historical Review,* a quarterly edited by Joseph P. Sánchez at the University of New Mexico's Spanish Colonial Research Center.[2]

Major themes of the national period that have attracted much attention over the last decade also continue in this *Handbook,* and authors are increasingly shedding more light than heat on these subjects. Examples are new economic histories that are more rigorous and less ideological, fresher and more useful approaches to regional history, and finally, greater sophistication and more scholarly standards in studies of Afro-Latin populations and Latin American women.

Although many excellent economic studies of the colonial period continue to be featured in this *Handbook*, it is mostly economic histories of the national period that are noted by contributors. One historian remarks that "Mexico's recent economic and financial problems have provoked greater interest" in the country's economic and business history, as exemplified by Stephen Haber's excellent overview of economic development problems in modern Mexico (item **1509** and p. 185). Another interesting work that offers "broad new insights into the rise of Peru's modern economy" is Alfonso Quiroz's major study of the nation's credit institutions and markets between the mid-19th and mid-20th centuries (item **2768**). Quiroz "reevaluates the era of export growth before the World Depression as beneficial for Peru's development, but ironically views increasing State interventionism in subsequent decades as fostering rather than impeding oligopolization" (p. 364). Major contributions to the economic history of Chile are "the late Harold Blakemore's splendid monograph on the British nitrate railroad" (item **2830**), José Bengoa's "superb two volumes" on the agrarian sector and the relationship between Chilean *patrón* and *inquilino* (item **2828**), and the volume edited by José Garrido which is a detailed history of Chile's agrarian reform (item **2855** and p. 383). Economic histories of Venezuela are also more regional, with the best examples being Germán Galué's major study of the origins of Maracaibo's coffee-related commerce (item **2590**), and José Murguey Gutiérrez's survey of the impact of railroads on the economic development of Trujillo (item **2596** and p. 343). For Costa Rica, we have the first study of popular consumption patterns in Patricia Jiménez Vega's work (item **1789**) and for El Salvador, an excellent survey of its 19th-century economic history by Héctor Lindo Fuentes (item **1746** and p. 219). In the Caribbean, the economics of slavery continues to attract considerable attention, as in William Darity Jr.'s "strident plea for an appreciation of the central role of the slave trade and slavery in Britain's industrialization" (item **1997** and p. 241). Finally, and most markedly, we find that in Brazil "regional studies . . . with an economic orientation form a notable segment of recent publications" (p. 422). Among them we can single out Mattoso's "magisterial" work on Bahia (item **3368**), Bittencourt's on Espírito Santo (item **3164**), Mott's on Sergipe (item **3377**), Pesavento's on Rio Grande do Sul (items **3393** and **3391**), and Hering's on Santa Catarina (item **3314**).

The strong and lasting trend in regional studies which we have been noting for the last decade and the past five humanities volumes (i.e., *HLAS 44*, 1982, through *HLAS 52*, 1992) continues in *HLAS 54* but with a more sophisticated approach. This is especially the case in Mexico, where there has been a "retreat from the *microhistoria*" that has dominated regional history since the 1968 publication of *Pueblo en vilo* by Luis González y González. Scholars are "still studying localities, but they are looking at them in ways that other researchers, interested in national themes, can use more easily to provide important collaborative or contrary data" (p. 183). Examples of these new approaches range from Mexico where, in the words of one contributor, "two extraordinary scholars, Mario Cerutti (items **1348** and **1330**) and Jean Meyer (items **1395** and **1394**), have greatly advanced the study of particular regions" (p. 183), to Peru where a collaborative volume on Arequipa constitutes the first *general* "history of a city and department outside of Lima written by professional historians" (item **2759** and p. 364).

Interest in the history of epidemics and public health continues in works such as Saúl Franco Agudelo's "extensive treatment of malaria and the medical responses to this dreaded disease" (item **868** and p. 126), and three exemplary articles by Marcos

Cueto that "demonstrate the great value of studying Peruvian health policies during the past century" (items **2718, 2719,** and **2717**). These works "combine detailed information about epidemics with issues concerning the extension of State power to various regions and localities, and with popular conceptions regarding science, disease and governmental interference in local affairs" (p. 364).

Another decade-long trend that continues unabated in this *Handbook* is interest in the history of Latin American populations and individuals of African descent. In the field of Afro-Brazilian history, several noteworthy publications are featured in this volume, such as Horacio Gutiérrez's work on the international traffic in child slaves (item **3202**), Oracy Nogueira's biography of the black physician and politician Alfredo Casemiro de Rocha (1855–1933, see item **3383**), George Reid Andrews' and Kim Butler's "studies of Afro-Brazilian political mobilization" (items **3231** and **3250**), and George Reid Andrews' "important study of race relations and racial inequality" in Brazil (item **3232** and p. 422). In Costa Rica, "recent interest has focused on the black West Indian workers of Limón and their struggles against both the United Fruit Company and mainstream *tico* racism" (items **1738, 1715,** and **1740** and p. 219). In the British Caribbean, "some of the most impressive publications address the dynamics of post-slavery societies" (p. 241). For example, "Robert Stewart's excellent work explores the role of religion in post-emancipation conflicts in Jamaica" (item **2105**) and various other studies "elucidate the plight of plantation workers in this crucial transitional period when planters still sought to control labor as they had so effectively during slavery" (items **1977, 1993, 1980, 2096,** and p. 242). In the French Caribbean, we have a history of "the fascinating transformation of Guadeloupe slaves into overseas citizens of the French Republic" (item **2002** and p. 243). On the Dutch Caribbean, the most important works are Alex van Stipriaan's study of Suriname's plantations and slavery which will be the standard work for many years to come (item **2106**) and a fascinating effort by historian Ben Scholtens and three anthropologists to trace and describe Saramaka rituals, a project that required the authors to enter Suriname's interior, a region immersed in civil war (item **2217** and p. 244). In Cuba, among the best books are the outstanding volumes on Afro-Cuban culture by Jorge and Isabel Castellanos (items **1799** and **1800**). Finally, and once again in Brazil, the rise of writers of African descent continues in literature as well. The persistence of the *Quilombhoje* movement (see *HLAS 52:4581*) attests to the vitality of both black studies and of Afro-Brazilian writing exemplified by the short stories of Eustáquio José Rodrigues (item **4797**) and Anatólio Alves de Assis (item **4765**).

In the field of women's studies, some of the most interesting and innovative work has been studies of women, family, gender, and sexuality in Brazil. Alida Metcalf, for example, makes a major contribution to the understanding of settlement patterns and family history (item **3209**), Ronaldo Vainfas' "history of sexuality and morality in colonial Brazil is also an impressive addition to the literature of this period" (item **3226**), and finally, Dain Borges has produced a fine study of the family in Bahia from 1870–1945 (item **3246** and p. 422). In Mexico, Edith Couturier's examination of an aristocratic widow is one of the more substantive works on women's history (item **1213**), while Ana María Atondo Rodríguez's study of child prostitution in colonial Mexico is among the most intriguing (item **1149** and p. 159). For Venezuela, Elías Pino Iturrieta has produced one of the more interesting books of the biennium, a tantalizing history of promiscuity, bigamy, and sodomy entitled *Contra lujuria castidad: historias de pecado . . .* (item **2280** and p. 297), and Ermila Troconis de Veracoechea "has written a pioneering history of the role of women of all classes and races in the evolution of Venezuelan society" (item **2605** and p. 343). In Argentina, Raúl A. Molina's *La familia porteña* (item **2548**) is particularly important because of the extensive quotes from marriage and divorce records otherwise lost forever (p. 298). Other historians are examining the impact of the concept of "honor" on the lives and status of upper- and lower-class women (p. 395). Finally, as the field of women's studies continues to grow so does the number of female historians in and of Latin America.

A similar development is also evident in the field of literature, where women's studies parallels the continuing emergence of many female writers of the first rank. This is especially true of recent poetry in Peru, where for a long time the only major female poet was the excellent Blanca Varela. In contrast, "today Varela is surrounded by women of various generations and artistic tendencies who have added a new dimension to Peruvian poetry" (p. 584). The following items constitute a small sample of works by these remarkable women writers: M. Alvarez (item **4290**), A.M. Gazzolo (item **4359**), and G. Pollarolo (item **4422**). Likewise in the Spanish Caribbean, "women writers are a major reason for the high quality of Puerto Rican literature" (p. 520). Among the youngest Puerto Rican poets is Mayra Santos Febre (items **4180** and **4448**), and among the more established are Olga Nolla (item **4409**) and Etnairis Rivera (item **4432**). And, of course, the fiction writer Rosario Ferré continues as "the leading Puerto Rican writer of her time" (p. 521). In Brazil, established women poets like Olga Savay, Hilda Hilst, and Stella Leonardos have been joined by many younger women following in the wake of Cora Coralina (item **4769**) and Adélia Prado (see *HLAS 52:5028* and p. 664). Magdalena García Pinto's collection of "long, frank, and thoughtful interviews" with Latin American women writers is probably the best of its kind (item **3474** and p. 461). And, at long last we can welcome the fact that Latin American women writers, "until recently woefully undertranslated," are finally becoming available to the English-reading public (p. 677).

II. OBITUARIES

LEWIS U. HANKE (1905–1993)

It is with deep sadness that we note the passing of Lewis Hanke, founder of the *Handbook* and in a very real sense, by extension, the father of Latin American studies in the United States. A tireless researcher and prolific writer, Hanke's scholarly contribution was prodigious.[3] We miss him sorely, yet his legacy, the *Handbook of Latin American Studies*, remains and will remain a vibrant reminder of his time with us. In his memory, Hanke's four children, Joanne Hanke Schwarz, Jonathan G. Hanke, Susan H. Abouhalkah, and Peter S. Hanke, have graciously provided the Hispanic Division with funds to undertake further dissemination of the *Handbook* via the Internet.

III. CLOSING DATE FOR VOLUME 54

The closing date for works annotated in this volume was mid-1993. Publications received and cataloged at the Library of Congress after that date will be annotated in the next humanities volume, *HLAS 56*.

IV. ELECTRONIC ACCESS TO THE *HANDBOOK*

Beginning with volume 50 (1990), the bibliographic records for the *Handbook's* print edition have been created online at the Library of Congress, thereby creating a cumulative, annotated database. The verified records corresponding to each published edition from volume 50 onward are now available in a variety of formats:

on tape from the Library's Cataloging Distribution Service; online via the Research Library Group's Eureka service; and on CD-ROM from the National Information Services Corporation in Baltimore, Maryland. In addition, the *Handbook's* complete working file (which covers volumes 50 onward and contains records in various stages of the editorial process) is available via the Internet by gophering to marvel.loc.gov. Furthermore, as of October 1995, the entire retrospective set (volumes 1–53) will be available on CD-ROM from the University of Texas Press.[4] The electronic conversion of these prior volumes was made possible by the exceptional good will and financial support of the Fundación MAPFRE América in Madrid: the foundation's president, Ignacio Hernando de Larramendi, and *HLAS* conversion team members Joaquin van den Brule, Anunciada Colón, Luis De Palma, Javier Alverez, Jesús Luis Domínguez, and José Manuel Rute, as well as Daniel Restrepo Manrique, Ignacio González Casanovas, and many others without whose assistance this project would have remained a pipe dream. We gratefully acknowledge their long hours, incredible energy, and absolute devotion to this joint endeavor. In addition, we are also extremely appreciative to Richard Ekman, Secretary and Program Officer for the Andrew W. Mellon Foundation of New York, for his moral support and the Mellon Foundation's financial assistance for this project. We also wish to acknowledge the major role played by the Hispanic Division's new chief, Georgette M. Dorn, in the retrospective conversion effort. Her assistance was crucial in securing the necessary institutional and financial support, and as usual, her impeccable advice was extremely helpful in our effort to improve the research value of the electronic *Handbook.* We are grateful to Harvard University Press, University Press of Florida, and especially Joanna Hitchcock, the director of the University of Texas Press, for granting us permission to convert their respective print volumes to electronic format. Finally, we owe a great deal to Donald C. Curran and Ellen Hahn, our managers at the Library of Congress until Fall 1995, for their unwavering support.

V . CHANGES IN VOLUME 54

Changes in Coverage

This *Handbook* completes the implementation of changes recommended by the *Handbook's* Advisory Board in 1992, changes which were taken to help tailor the *Handbook* to accomplish its most essential mission: assisting humanistic and social science researchers of Latin America. For instance, the separate "Bibliography and General Works" sections painstakingly prepared over the years by Ann Hartness of the University of Texas at Austin and Lionel V. Loroña of The New York Public Library have been eliminated. Instead, works of a bibliographic nature will be reviewed by the contributor responsible for the specific discipline to which the bibliography refers. We hope that this change will assist the *Handbook's* users in locating specialized bibliographies of interest to them. The section on precolumbian art has also been eliminated; relevant publications on this topic will now be annotated by the *Handbook's* archaeologists.

Readers will also note that as of this volume the *Handbook* has reduced its coverage of literary criticism: this policy change recommended by the *Handbook's* Advisory Board was implemented to allow more space for inclusion of original Latin American literary works (e.g., prose, poetry, drama, etc.), for which the *Handbook* continues to be probably the single most comprehensive and major annotated bibliography. For works of literary criticism on Latin America readers are urged to consult the *MLA International Bibliography of Books and Articles on the Modern Lan-*

guages and Literatures, an annual multivolume work published by the Modern Language Association of America, and the *Hispanic American Periodicals Index (HAPI)* published by the University of California, Los Angeles. The *Handbook* has also eliminated the chapter devoted to linguistics, a field which generates numerous bibliographies and is no longer served by inclusion in the *Handbook.*

Finally, we must mention the decline in the output of the Brazilian publishing industry during the last several years. This trend, attributable in part to Brazil's economic woes during this biennium, is reflected in the reduced number of Brazilian titles annotated below. We are optimistic that this trend will be reversed in the near future.

Electronic Resources

As mentioned above, this volume does inaugurate one new section, that on "Electronic Resources," a topic whose constantly changing and ethereal nature requires a separate section written by a specialist able to stay abreast of advances in this wide-ranging field. Harold Colson of the University of California at San Diego has completed this chapter for *HLAS 54.*

History

The Mesoamerican ethnohistory section was annotated by Stephanie Wood and Robert Haskett of the University of Oregon. John Britton of Francis Marion University (Florence, South Carolina) covered works of a general historical nature. The section on the national period of Central American history was prepared by David McCreery of Georgia State University. Teresita Martínez-Vergne of Macalester College (St. Paul, Minnesota) joined the group of contributors collaborating on the Caribbean, the Guianas, and the Spanish Borderlands, annotating works on Puerto Rican history. Materials on modern Bolivia and colonial Brazil were covered by Marie-Louise Wagner of Georgetown University and Kathleen Higgins of the University of Iowa, respectively.

Literature

Dick Gerdes of the University of New Mexico collaborated with Raymond Williams to prepare the section on Andean literature, annotating works of fiction as well as literary criticism for Bolivia, Ecuador, and Peru. Two new contributors joined the group collaborating on the Spanish American poetry section: Francisco Cabanillas of Bowling Green State University (Bowling Green, Ohio) annotated works of poetry from the Hispanic Caribbean, and Lilián Uribe of Central Connecticut State University covered Argentina, Paraguay, and Uruguay. The Brazilian poetry section was completed by Naomi Hoki Moniz of Georgetown University. Mario Rojas of Catholic University assumed responsibility for the Spanish American drama section, and Kathleen Ross of New York University joined the group of contributors working on literature in translation.

Special Contributing Editors

Christel Krause Converse, a historian of Latin America, has agreed to annotate works in German.

Subject Index

The *Handbook* uses Library of Congress Subject Headings (LCSH) when they are consistent with usage among Latin Americanists. Differences in practice, however, make adaptation of LCSH headings necessary: 1) the *Handbook* index uses only two levels, while LC headings usually contain more; and 2) *Handbook* practice is to prefer a "subject-place" pattern, while LC practice generally uses a "place-subject" pattern. Automation of the *Handbook* has required that the subject index be compiled with two audiences in mind: users of the print edition of the *Handbook* and users of the online *Handbook* database. It has also demanded that index terms, once established, remain as stable as possible. Work has begun towards a complete thesaurus of *Handbook* subject index terms. In the meantime, cross references are included from subject terms used in *HLAS 48-HLAS 53* to new terms used in this volume. Finally, since the *Handbook* is arranged by subject, readers are encouraged to consult the table of contents for broad subject coverage.

VI. ACKNOWLEDGMENTS

During the past eighteen months the workload of the *Handbook* staff has nearly doubled as a result of our undertaking several exciting yet time-consuming projects to make the *Handbook* data more readily available electronically. In addition to coordinating and assisting the Fundación MAPFRE América with the retrospective conversion of volumes 1–49, the Assistant Editor and an energetic new temporary *Handbook* employee, Assistant to the Editor for Internet Access Randolf M. Wells, have also undertaken the merging of the current and retrospective *Handbook* databases for mounting on the World Wide Web. Because of these additional projects, much of the burden of editing volume 54 fell to Senior Assistant to the Editor David Dressing, an invaluable member of the *Handbook* team during the past four years who graciously agreed to postpone his graduate school plans to help see us through this crunch. Were it not for David's exemplary assistance, the publication of this volume would have been greatly delayed. We are deeply indebted to him for the dedication he has shown to the *Handbook* over the years. We also wish to express our appreciation to Ann Mulrane and Amy Puryear who took on additional responsibilities during this period. Despite the extra efforts of these *Handbook* staff members, we have had to eliminate temporarily one of the three proofing cycles each volume undergoes in order to expedite the publication of this volume. We expect to return to our regular level of editorial oversight once the two electronic conversion projects are completed.

Dolores Moyano Martin, Editor
P. Sue Mundell, Assistant Editor

1   Department of Romance Languages (NAC 5/2232), Convent Ave. at 138th Street, The City College, New York, NY 10031.
2   Zimmerman Library, Spanish Colonial Research Center, Univ. of New Mexico, Albuquerque, NM 87131.
3   See the Dedication and Editor's Note in *HLAS 50* for additional information about Hanke's exceptional contribution to Latin American studies.
4   To order the *HLAS/CD* contact the University of Texas Press, P.O. Box 7819, Austin TX 78713. Tel.: 512-471-7233; Toll free: 800-252-3206; Fax: 512-320-0668..

HANDBOOK OF
LATIN AMERICAN STUDIES:
No. 54

ELECTRONIC RESOURCES ON LATIN AMERICA: A Decade of Progress and Promise

HAROLD COLSON, *Head of Public Services and Latin American Librarian, International Relations and Pacific Studies Library, University of California, San Diego*

THE FIELD OF LATIN AMERICAN STUDIES is in the midst of profound and quickening advances in scholarly information dissemination via electronic means, a virtual revolution in technologies, resources, and linkages that has already transformed our capabilities for seeking and obtaining knowledge about the region. During the past decade, Latin America has progressed from being a minor presence in most computerized databases to serving as perhaps the top Third World and Western Hemisphere arena for improved bibliographic and full-text coverage, new product development, and electronic networking. Specifically, in response to market demands for more news and business information from and about Latin America, many leading commercial files and systems have begun to strengthen their regional coverage. In addition, our community can now draw upon a small but increasingly powerful set of new databases that focus on Latin American affairs and stress current news and much-needed core bibliographic coverage. Finally, the diffusion of compact disc technology and Internet connectivity throughout the hemisphere is helping bring many heretofore isolated resources to the electronic mainstream.

This contribution will examine the recent evolution and present state of the computerized database environment for Latin American studies, surveying representative sources available as of early 1994 rather than citing every known product. Given that the global database market includes over 8,000 separate files (up from 300 in 1979), and that most of these products likely contain at least some references, texts, or data on Latin America, it would be rather impractical to attempt a comprehensive inventory of all relevant "electronicana." [1] Furthermore, chapters in subsequent *Handbook* volumes will treat social sciences and humanities databases in greater detail, and the existing surveys of Latin Americanist resources online can be tapped for additional background and leads. Of particular note as starting points are the works by Colson and Stern (item **10**) and Levison (item **17**). The former describes the database scene for Latin American studies as it existed through early 1990, highlighting key products across several disciplines and formats. In order to help make room for annotations of new files, databases listed in Colson and Stern's article will not be annotated in this chapter unless they have changed significantly in the past few years. Levison's article reviews various resources in news, business, and current affairs, the areas of most substantial expansion since 1990.

The online database industry emerged in the 1960s from various US government-funded projects to provide computerized bibliographic storage and retrieval for burgeoning technical literatures in medicine, aerospace, education, and other fields of national policy interest. Once allied with contemporaneous advances in mainframe computing power and global packet-switching links, these large files of abstracts formed the cores of the commercial database systems that went online to the public (principally university libraries and the defense-industrial-scientific research community) in the early 1970s. Early vendors (or "hosts") such as Dialog, ORBIT, and BRS provided subscribers with remote, interactive, and fee-based access to growing collections of bibliographic files or databases, largely in scientific and technical fields. Eventually, however, the commercial market expanded beyond its sci-tech beginnings to include major discipline-based indexing tools in the social sciences and humanities, along with large numbers of law- and business-related databases and computerized newspapers, magazines, newswires, and newsletters. In addition, the late 1980s witnessed the rise of the CD-ROM (compact disc-read only memory) format as a convenient and often less-expensive alternative to the dial-up database for storage and retrieval of bibliographic and text files. Among other advantages, compact disc databases offer purchasers unlimited local use for a set cost, unlike the per-minute and per-citation pricing that effectively bars some individuals and institutions from taking full advantage of most online systems. Many databases originally available only via remote connection were quickly brought out in CD-ROM versions, and the disc medium has given several specialty files an electronic outlet that was denied by the market-driven calculations of the major online systems. Although dial-up session rates and CD-ROM purchase prices vary considerably, many database investments pay for themselves by saving time otherwise expended on tedious and sometimes fruitless manual searches through indexes, newspapers, and other publications. Most databases enable users to generate customized retrieval sets that cannot be produced using counterpart print resources, and many key products (e.g., library union catalogs, some new article indexes, and wire services) are produced only in computerized form.

The present contours of mainline database coverage for Latin America are much changed from 1980, when Veenstra compiled his pioneering list of "Data Bases Relating to Latin American Studies" (item 27), but they remain substantially similar to the portraits offered at the close of the 1980s. The leading commercial systems continue to provide online versions of familiar disciplinary abstracting and indexing tools, including *Historical Abstracts, MLA International Bibliography, Sociological Abstracts, Psychological Abstracts, Journal of Economic Literature, Index of Economic Articles, United States Political Science Documents, Art Index, Religion Index, ERIC,* and *Geographical Abstracts.* These resources provide varying levels of Latin Americanist content, with the largest numbers of records found in the history and literature files. In addition, attractive multidisciplinary coverage of the region is available through such files as *Social SciSearch, PAIS International, Dissertation Abstracts Online, Social Science Index,* and *Arts & Humanities Search.* Of these, *PAIS* deserves special commendation, for it pioneered strong regional content by providing article citations from some 100 important but otherwise unindexed Latin American journals in economics, political science, and related policy fields. A noteworthy companion product with similar Latin Americanist strength is the new *IntlEc* CD-ROM (item 52), which indexes global journals and research report series in international economics, development, and finance.

One recent trend concerning bibliographic databases has been the rise of new distribution channels, products, search interfaces, and pricing options through nonprofit library consortia such as the Online Computer Library Center (OCLC), the Research Libraries Group (RLG), and the Colorado Alliance of Research Libraries Systems (CARL Systems). OCLC has some 40 standard and specialty databases on its EPIC and FirstSearch systems, including an exclusive mega-catalog representing over 30 million book, periodical, map, score, recording, and manuscript holdings in member libraries worldwide (item **62**). On the basis of total Latin Americanist entries, this online union catalog or "WorldCat" ranks as the largest available anywhere, as these sample subject heading retrievals attest: "Mexico," 182,388 items; "Argentina," 69,511; "Latin America," 65,824; "Guatemala," 20,847; and "Ecuador," 19,188. The new *Article1st* database (item **31**) is another OCLC exclusive that provides citations from over 15,000 leading journals and magazines, principally from North America and Europe but with considerable coverage of Latin American topics. In similar fashion, the Eureka system from RLG contains a massive library union catalog with over 23 million records (items **68**), along with unique research files like *Anthropological Literature* (item **29**) and *Index to Foreign Legal Periodicals* (item **47**). CARL Systems offers *UnCover* (item **71**), a database providing article indexing and tables of contents for some 14,000 periodicals received by its contributing libraries. Like CD-ROM products, these systems are intended for direct access by students, faculty, and other "end users" unfamiliar with the usual arcana of traditional online command syntax, so the database interfaces feature more on-screen prompts and menus than are found on their commercial predecessors. In addition, the systems offer flat-fee or "subscription" pricing that helps take the financial worry out of large-scale or time-consuming searches, and gives institutions the freedom to offer widespread, unmediated access. FirstSearch, Eureka, and *UnCover* also offer easy online links to allied document delivery services, enabling users to request fax or mail delivery of specific items for a fee.

When used together, the mainline bibliographic files can help lead searchers to much published information on Latin America, with cumulative strength that may be characterized as very good for books, excellent for recent periodicals published in North America and Europe, and fair to poor for periodical articles from Latin America. The years covered by available bibliographic databases differ considerably; most files reach back at least through the early 1980s, and a few have retrospective depth back to the 1960s and beyond. In most cases, the files are updated with additional records on weekly, monthly, or quarterly schedules. Given the bibliographic nature of these files, actual retrieval is accomplished primarily through searches for author names or words from titles, abstracts, or subject headings (often called "descriptors"). Both *Social SciSearch* and *Arts & Humanities Search* have the special feature of cited reference searching, which permits the retrieval of articles based on their bibliographic references to previous works. Many of the commercial files listed above have also been issued in CD-ROM versions, and most are available via dial-up from virtually every college, university, government, and major public library in the US.

Although bibliographic databases formed the initial core of the commercial online industry, they were joined and eventually surpassed in number by products containing entire articles and other complete texts rather than mere citations. These "full-text" files consist primarily of online legal resources (e.g., legislation, regulations, court rulings, law reviews) along with thousands of computerized newspapers, magazines, newswires, newsletters, and transcripts covering general news, national and international events, government and law, and especially business. Leading full-text vendors include WESTLAW and LEXIS for legal information, NewsNet for newsletters, Dow Jones News/Retrieval for business, and NEXIS, Dialog, Data-Times, Data-Star, and FT Profile for newspapers and other publications in many topical areas. Full-text databases are generally updated daily or weekly, with some wire service files refreshed several times per day for very current access to breaking stories. In many cases, the electronic works are available on their host systems before the print versions of the same titles reach subscribers, and long runs of specific publications can be searched to display articles mentioning certain names, words, or phrases anywhere in the text. Signing up with one or more of the full-text vendors can thus give institutions access to a large and timely "virtual library" of specialized publications, many of which would be too expensive or even impossible to acquire in print form.

Interestingly, one of the oldest computerized publications is the well-known Latin American Newsletters Ltd. family of weekly and monthly reports on the region, but through most of the 1980s Latin America was largely a marginal or background presence in the world of full-text newspapers, wire services, magazines, and such. Certainly, online coverage of Latin American affairs could be found on full-text electronicana ranging from *The New York Times* and *The Economist* to the *BBC Summary of World Broadcasts* and the Inter Press Service newswire, but nearly all of the available publications were generalist sources produced in North America or Europe. It was not until sufficient "northern" political and later economic attention shifted to Latin America in the late 1980s that the region began to receive dedicated coverage by the full-text market. Nowadays, owing to hemispheric developments in free trade, integration, privatization, and environmental protection, Latin America is perhaps the top global arena for improving full-text information coverage, with major database hosts and producers seeking to fill the gaps for timely political, economic, and business news and information on the region by bringing additional files and publications online. Among the specialty publications that have appeared online within the past few years are such titles as *Environment Watch: Latin America, Mexico Trade and Law Reporter, Latin Finance, Latin American Telecom Report, LDC Debt Report/Latin American Markets, Americas Trade and Finance,* and *Brazil Watch.* Although nearly all established and new full-text coverage is still provided by North American and European sources, there have been a few arrivals from south of the Rio Grande. For example, the powerful *PROMT* business database (item **64**) now provides English-language abstracts of stories appearing in several leading trade journals, general newspapers, and business dailies from Argentina and Brazil. Likewise, regional newswires such as Notimex (item **61**) from Mexico and the Spanish-language feed from Agence France-Presse have appeared on some hosts.

The present boomlet of improved bibliographic and full-text coverage for Latin America is an encouraging development for librarians and researchers who struggled through the prior lean years, but the commercial progress outlined above actually trailed some crucial database undertakings from the government and academic sectors. Between 1989 and 1993, four major Latin Americanist databases of unprecedented bibliographic and news strength debuted outside commercial channels to form the present electronic core for our field. In order of appearance, they were *INFO-SOUTH* for current newspaper and magazine article abstracts, *Latin America Data Base* for electronic news, *HAPI Online* for journal article citations, and the *Handbook of Latin American Studies* for book and article annotations. Offering direct access to scholars and libraries along with budget-friendly pricing, these new electronic resources filled major gaps in existing database coverage of Latin America, brought key area studies resources closer to the researcher's work space, and attracted considerable attention from commercial online systems eager to offer improved regional content. Indeed, without the pacesetting contributions of these "four tigers" of the Latin American database world, there would be little cause for this *Handbook* chapter, for the overall *coyuntura electrónica* would likely be as mixed and pessimistic as it was in the last published review before *INFO-SOUTH* and the rest appeared.

The *INFO-SOUTH Latin American Information System* (item **49**) offers selective indexing and abstracting for articles appearing in over 1,500 periodicals dealing with contemporary political, economic, social, and business affairs in Latin America and the Caribbean. Although some earlier online products treat certain academic journals relating to Latin America, *INFO-SOUTH* is the first system to provide basic coverage of current newspapers and magazines from the region, long the richest yet least accessible periodicals of all. At the present time, *INFO-SOUTH* staff abstract selected articles from approximately 60 newspapers and magazines published in some 20 Latin American and Caribbean countries large and small, along with items published in hundreds of additional sources from Europe and throughout the Americas. With the bulk of its 75,000 records drawn from news sources, *INFO-SOUTH* offers initial "one-stop shopping" for published information on current affairs across Latin America, although the delays inherent in periodical receipt and processing mean that it cannot provide yesterday's or even last week's articles from, say, Argentina or Mexico. Nevertheless, for recent background information drawn from important but previously untapped regional news publications, *INFO-SOUTH* has no peer. Coverage dates back to 1988, with new records added weekly. Drawing from its in-house paper archive of every item selected for database treatment, the Miami operation also offers a responsive, relatively inexpensive, and quite essential article delivery service for individuals and institutions wanting more than just the online abstracts.

Like the very first online databases covering aerospace and medicine, *INFO-SOUTH* was conceived and built with funding from the US government, and it operates today largely on the basis of federal support. The Foreign Relations Authorization Act for fiscal years 1988 and 1989 called for the Dept. of State to lead an effort for "the establishment of a Latin American and Caribbean Data Base" with online bibliographic features not "significantly duplicative of existing services." The Congressional sponsor of this provision noted that rapid access to Latin American information is "one key to successfully advancing our own national interests," but that "much of the information we need for adequate analysis is not readily available." By collecting timely and hitherto elusive information for government agencies, business and industry, the scholarly community, and the general public, he continued, a specialty Latin American and Caribbean database "offers immense potential for contributing to sounder decisions in areas of public policy, private investment, trade, and finance." [2] The Univ. of Miami garnered the million-dollar contract for this bibliographic project, entered the first records online in Sept. 1988, and unveiled *INFO-SOUTH* to the Latin Americanist community in a hotel suite at the 1989 Latin American Studies Association (LASA) conference in Miami. Over two years later, online industry leader Dialog added *INFO-SOUTH* to its repertoire of some 400 files in a rather belated commercial move to ameliorate the Latin American information gap.

The government-university role in the development of *INFO-SOUTH* is significant in at least three ways. First, federal sponsorship has helped keep the price of a direct, unlimited subscription to the system well within the grasp of most institutions with strong interests in Latin America, unlike the costly per-minute rates associated with many commercial databases. Second, given the stated legislative intent and an original customer base heavy with federal agencies, *INFO-SOUTH* first concentrated on providing Latin American information with operational relevance to policymakers and analysts in the Washington community, the "political, economic, and social" triad so pronounced in its early literature. (More recently, Miami staff have begun adding business-related abstracts in response to needs from their growing corporate clientele.) Third, the commercial database industry was slow to provide increased Latin American coverage on its own, demonstrating a long-held bias against area studies resources as being market losers. Indeed, the industry did not really warm to the Latin American scene until the early 1990s, when obvious market opportunities, rising customer demands, and attractive off-the-shelf files made the region too compelling to resist any longer.

The second key online arrival was the *Latin America Data Base*, produced by the Latin American Institute of the Univ. of New Mexico, which debuted in 1986 as a set of topical electronic newsletters on current regional affairs. By 1991 the newsletter issues were available as a unified searchable file (item **54**), and today *LADB* stands out as the most commercially widespread Latin Americanist resource of all, with loads on Dialog, DataTimes, NEXIS, NewsNet, and other major hosts. *LADB* staff members monitor diverse print, newswire, and radio reports from Latin America to produce three timely and original electronic updates on political and economic events in the region, namely *Chronicle of Latin American Economic Affairs*, *Notisur: Latin American Political Affairs*, and *Sourcemex: Economic News & Analysis on Mexico*. A fourth title, *Central America Update*, ran for several years before its coverage was picked up elsewhere. Each weekly issue usually contains the equivalent of around 8–10 single-spaced pages of text, loaded with so many detailed reports, texts, summaries, and analyses as to be unmatched in the English-language press. The complete database now includes over 20,000 articles dating back to 1986, making *LADB* a virtual newspaper of record for recent events in the region. Like *INFO-SOUTH*, the *LADB* products can be acquired via direct subscription at rates substantially lower than those charged by the commercial resellers.

Next on the scene was the online version of the *Hispanic American Periodicals Index* (item **46**) from the Latin American Center at the Univ. of California, Los Angeles (UCLA). *HAPI* is a standard annual print index for Latin American studies, providing citations to articles, book reviews, documents, original literary works, and other materials appearing in some 400 key humanities and social science journals. Despite its considerable value to the Latin Americanist community, the first attempt to place a computerized version of *HAPI* on a national online system failed owing to unfavorable market projections made by the candidate vendor (area studies resources have low use, the company said in 1984). In Sept. 1991, however, *HAPI Online* was introduced to the world as part of the UCLA library catalog system, and a second avenue opened in 1993 with its debut as a Eureka database from RLG. With over 180,000 citations dating back to 1970, *HAPI Online* forms the largest body of journal citations from and about Latin America yet to appear in computerized form, and ranks as one of the strongest database sources for articles on Latin American history, literature, and arts. The present online rush toward better Latin American coverage is concentrated in current politics, business, news, and related areas, so *HAPI Online*, a few disciplinary files, and the library union catalogs are virtually the only resources with retrospective strengths in the humanities. Like its companions from Florida and New Mexico, *HAPI Online* is available at moderate prices attuned to the academic user market.

The fourth and potentially largest "tiger" is the *Handbook of Latin American Studies* itself (items **45**), which gained general distribution in 1993 when the Library of Congress released several of its databases for direct (and free) outside use. Although *HLAS* citations are subsumed in a general Library of Congress file rather than being treated as a separate database, there are simple search techniques that will retrieve only *Handbook* entries from the millions of records online. In addition to the obvious advantage of rapid author and word searchability, the online *Handbook* is more up to date and contains even more entries than its print counterpart: works selected for annotation by contributors as well as citations of works not annotated by them for the print edition are both posted to the database well before the print volumes are available. As of early 1994 the online *Handbook* contains over 40,000 citations [3] dating back through volume 50, although the prospective mother of all Latin Americanist databases resides in the more than 213,000 book, article, and chapter entries still offline in the prior volumes dating from 1935–89. Nevertheless, the young *HLAS* database is developing into a central resource for the entire Latin American studies field, with free global connectivity, [4] equitable coverage for humanists and social scientists, unique access to book chapters and many journals not treated elsewhere, and greater size and currency over the print edition. In addition to its Library of Congress load, *HLAS* is available on the Eureka online system from RLG and the two-disc *Latin American Studies* CD-ROM from National Information Systems Corporation (item **55**; the NISC set also includes *INFO-SOUTH*, *LADB*, and *HAPI*, among other databases).

The principal remaining sectors of the present Latin Americanist database field are: 1) statistical files; and 2) Internet resources, both of which will be treated in more detail by the next volume of the *Handbook*. This arrangement will afford these resources a proper review within their social sciences milieu, plus give the young but superheated Internet arena another year to coalesce. Briefly, therefore, statistical databases for the study of Latin America are largely issued by national government agencies, international organizations, econometric firms, and financial information services, with data generally available from the producer via network connection, magnetic tape, diskette, or, in some cases, CD-ROM. Among the most accessible general files of interest to Latin Americanists are the International Monetary Fund's *International Financial Statistics*, the World Bank's *World Tables*, and the US Dept. of Commerce's *National Trade Data Bank* (item **60**), although hundreds of additional numeric databases exist at costs ranging from free through moderate to exorbitant. As mentioned before, there are also excellent directories of global databases that can lead interested researchers to relevant files in various formats.

The rise and global expansion of the Internet during the early 1990s ranks as one of the most portentous developments ever in the young life of the electronic database field, offering wonderful opportunities for enhanced information retrieval as readily as it poses unprecedented challenges of description and education. Given the tremendous present growth and change in the Internet sector it can be difficult for network beginners and veterans alike to comprehend and manage the terrible beauty that faces them through the computer screen, and extracting pertinent Latin Americana from the millions of retrievable items on the net remains a tricky proposition. Nevertheless, the power of the Internet is already undeniable and irresistible, and will become even more so as new players, services, resources, and tools join the infrastructure. Insofar as a substantial review of the Internet will appear in the next *Handbook* volume, this section will only highlight some key network pointers or gateways, starting with Tuss' helpful review of leading user handbooks (item **25**) and Molloy's introductory list of Latin Americanist resources (item **20**). Perhaps the best starting point for guided Latin Americanist forays across the Internet is the UT-LANIC system (item **73**) provided by the Institute of Latin American Studies at the Univ. of Texas, a system which organizes many far flung resources into convenient topical and geographic menus. Databases accessible through UT-LANIC and similar servers include research library catalogs with strong Latin American holdings, periodical indexes, news archives, texts of treaties and other documents, national and international statistics, government reports, literary texts, economic working papers, and much more. In addition, most of the bibliographic and full-text databases cited above, including the four Latin Americanist tigers, are available on the Internet, although generally with password controls as appropriate to screen out unlicensed users. (*HLAS* and *UnCover*, however, are open to all at no charge.) A fee-based but highly affordable Internet system that offers strong Latin American news and conferencing content is PeaceNet (item **63**).

This survey of major database resources for Latin American studies has necessarily been heavy with North American and European sources, insofar as the first, and for many years the only, available files were produced and stored in those regions. Of course, Latin America was not without its own computerized resources and networks, but the files were largely scientific in content or difficult to access remotely. Since the late 1980s, however, the database scene in Latin American has fairly erupted with new and promising releases, facilitated and encouraged in large part through the parallel diffusion of CD-ROM technologies and Internet connectivity throughout much of the region. Both developments offer distribution outlets for specialty electronic resources from Latin America that stand little chance of placement on the established commercial hosts. Among the first (1988) Latin American CD-ROM databases to appear on the market was Multiconsult's one-disc package of several bibliographic files from the Univ. Nacional Autónoma de México, including the major *CLASE, BIBLAT,* and *PERIODICA* indexes from the Centro de Información Científica y Humanística (item **36**). Dozens of other hitherto inaccessible national and local databases from Mexico and elsewhere followed on compact disc during the next five years, with Mexico's Univ. de Colima emerging as a regional leader in CD-ROM mastering and production (items **40, 33, 34, 35,** etc.). Many Latin American discs contributed new depth to core periodical indexing on themes ranging from art to Central American politics, and some files brought massive collections of full-text newspaper articles and legal materials online for the very first time. One pathbreaking CD-ROM was the *CDPRESS* archive of over 200,000 complete articles selected from some 60 Mexican national and state newspapers (item **38**), later followed by separate disc products containing *El Financiero* (item **43**) and *El Norte* (item **50**). Another promising Mexican release was *Códice 90* (item **39**), offering computerized results and cartography from the most recent national census of population and housing. Statistical information from Latin America is poorly represented online, but the compact disc medium's portability, reasonable cost, and high storage capacity may serve to attract other key numeric products from appropriate national and international agencies. For example, the United Nations Economic Commission for Latin America and the Caribbean (ECLAC) has already issued a CD-ROM containing certain of its bibliographic databases (item **51**), and there are statistical files in Santiago that could receive similar treatment. Finally, we may eventually enjoy disc-based collections of manuscript and archival images. The Univ. de Colima released a CD-ROM in 1993 with full-text finding aids from the Mexican national archives (item **30**), and various pilot projects have been undertaken in Latin America, Spain, and the US to reproduce actual historical papers in computerized image form.

Internet connections are available in some form within many Latin American countries, giving local investigators access to global research tools while bringing some heretofore isolated materials to the attention of Latin Americanists worldwide. It should be stressed that the Internet arena defies inventories of more than daily currency, but there are some representative products from Latin America that deserve mention at this early juncture. Among the open Internet resources are library catalogs, periodical indexes, news publications, research reports, statistics, and discussion group archives. The UT-LANIC server offers a convenient gateway to many of these files, but other pathways are available to the enterprising Internet explorer. One recent Internet arrival that complements the various Latin Americanist article databases noted above is *CLASE* (Citas Latinoamericanas en Ciencias Sociales e Humanidades) from UNAM. This large periodical index (over 85,000 citations from 1,000 journals dating back to 1979) was first released in 1988 on the pioneering Multiconsult CD-ROM (item **36**), but online access through the Internet offers greater currency and prospects for reaching more users. In a similar fashion, the powerful *Delphi en Español* database system (item **41**), featuring real-time wire feeds and news from across Latin America, gave its subscribers an Internet access option in 1993. Perhaps most promisingly of all, text and image repositories of some Mexican newspapers have been connected to the Internet, and electronic distribution of certain Latin American dailies is also on the horizon.

The last decade has witnessed promising changes in the database environment for Latin American studies. Throughout most of the 1980s, Latin America was treated in scattered, uneven, and rather unsatisfactory fashion by an assortment of commercial bibliographic files. Except for library cataloging databases and a few disciplinary files, most available resources had little content from Latin America, with regional newspaper and magazine articles virtually unreported online. Likewise, the existing full-text resources were mostly generalist publications emanating from North America and Europe, leaving the exemplary BBC radio broadcasts database as perhaps the only source of primary news from Latin America. Beginning in 1988, however, Latin American studies underwent a remarkable turnaround in online power, as crucial specialty databases emerged from government and academic channels, established commercial resources responded to market demands for more current information on Latin America, and new information technologies and networks brought scholars closer to electronic resources from across the hemisphere and beyond. These recent developments have given us a greatly improved position for the study of Latin America through electronic means, but continued progress in all sectors is required to fulfill the promise of our present boom. Still, considering where we stood only five or six years ago, these are the best of times for online Latin Americana.

Notes
1 See the essay by Martha E. Williams (item 5) for statistical compilations and trend analyses on the world database industry.
2 *133 Congressional Record*, H5005, June 16, 1987.
3 As of April 1995, the *Handbook* database contained just over 59,000 records.
4 To access the *Handbook* via the Internet using the Library of Congress gopher, point to Marvel.Loc.Gov on port 70, and the main menu will appear. Select "Library of Congress Online Information Systems," and then select "Connect to LOCIS." Once in LOCIS, select the "LC Catalog" and then select "Books Cataloged since 1968." For documentation, from the main menu choose "LC Online Systems," choose "Quick Search Guides to LOCIS," and then select the Handbook guide.

DIRECTORIES

1   The CD-ROM Directory . . . with Multimedia CD's. Vol. 11, 1994- . London; Washington: TFPL Publishing.

Often considered the leading reference for the CD-ROM and multimedia industries, this annual volume treats 6,000 titles covering every interest area. Interestingly, the directory itself is also available as a semiannual CD-ROM database.

2   CD-ROMs in Print. 1993- . Compiled by Regina Riga. Westport, Conn.: Meckler.

Lists just over 3,500 research, educational, recreational, and technical disc products on the world market. Published annually.

3   Fuente, Julia de la et al. Directorio de bases de datos de América Latina y el Caribe: DIBALC. Coordinación de Elsa Barberena Blásquez. México: UNAM, Facultad de Filosofía y Letras, 1992. 144 p.: indexes.

Two decades of Latin American achievement in database development are recognized in this welcome volume, also known as DIBALC. Most of the 659 files are available only within the producing institution or country, and thus do not appear in other print directories.

4   Fulltext Sources Online. 1994- . Needham, Mass.: BiblioData.

Gives location and coverage details for over 4,500 journals, newspapers, newsletters, and newswires available in full-text form on leading commercial hosts. Covers titles in science, technology, medicine, law, finance, business, general news, and other areas. Published twice a year.

5   Gale Directory of Databases. 1993- . Edited by Kathleen Young Marcaccio. Detroit: Gale Research.

This semiannual compilation describes some 8,400 bibliographic, full-text, directory, and numeric databases from across the globe. Online files are treated in Vol. 1, with CD-ROM products and other "portables" listed in Vol. 2. Includes geographic and subject indexes along with a review of database industry trends. An excellent resource that provides additional details on just about every database and host system mentioned in this chapter.

6   The Latin American information base. Compiled by Kinloch C. Walpole, Jr. Gainesville, Fla.: Latin American Information Base; Latin American Database Interest Group, 1993. 2 computer disks (3 1/2").

Electronic "database of databases" from and about Latin America lists many private or noncommercial files not available through online vendors. The program files can be downloaded from the UT-LANIC server. Also contained in the second *Bancos bibliográficos latinoamericanos* CD-ROM from Univ. de Colima, Mexico.

7   Manual of online search strategies. Edited by C.J. Armstrong and J.A. Large. 2nd ed. New York: G.K. Hall; Toronto: Maxwell Macmillan Canada, 1992. 699 p.: bibl., indexes.

Excellent handbook on databases and applicable search techniques in major academic fields. Contributors introduce the database environments in their disciplines and describe relevant files on the principal North American and European commercial systems and beyond. Shows many sample searches.

SURVEYS AND REVIEWS

8   Ainsworth, Shirley. Mexican information resources in electronic format. (*in* The Bowker annual: library and book trade almanac. Edited by Catherine Barr. 39th ed. New Providence, NJ: R.R. Bowker, 1994, p. 75–90, bibl., tables)

Thorough and timely survey of online, CD-ROM, diskette, and Internet resources by librarian at El Colegio de México. Provides annotated entries for dozens of products containing newspaper articles (citations, texts, and images), statistics, laws and regulations, company listings, journal articles, library holdings, and more. Includes publisher and distributor contact information.

9   Annis, Sheldon. New Internet-based information tools for Latin America. (*in* Latin America: the emerging information power. Washington: Special Libraries Assn., 1993, p. 21–29)

An outline of author's online tour through the Internet using the common "gopher" utility to find and organize Latin Americanist resources. Gives Internet addresses for 19 relevant information sites in the US, Mexico, Ecuador, and Chile. Includes a review of networking developments and prospects in Latin America.

10   Colson, Harold and **Peter Stern.** Databases: essay. (*in* Latin America and the Caribbean: a critical guide to research sources. Edited by Paula H. Covington. New York: Greenwood Press, 1992, p. 139–153)

First broad assessment and inventory of major database resources for the study of Latin America, completed in early 1990 on the cusp of the present area studies information wave. Includes annotated entries for some 60 remote and CD-ROM files with bibliographic and full-text information on Latin America, along with a review essay strong on useful background, trends, and analysis. Valuable as a baseline survey of relevant electronic resources.

11   Colson, Harold. Latin America online: business and current affairs. (*in* ONLINE/CD-ROM Conference. Proceedings. Weston, Conn.: ONLINE, Inc., 1991, p. 40–43)

Examines *INFO-SOUTH, LADB, HAPI Online, Delphi en Español,* and selected general databases with good bibliographic and full-text coverage. Concludes that, despite recent progress, the online market still lacks searchable versions of major newswires from Latin America and needs broader, deeper, and timelier coverage of local periodicals, including full-text versions of key general and business newspapers.

12   Colson, Harold. Latin American studies online: status and outlook. (*in* Seminar on the Acquisition of Latin American Library Materials, *33rd, Berkeley, California, 1988.* Latin American frontiers, borders, and hinterlands: research needs and resources. Edited by Paula Covington. Albuquerque, N.M.: SALALM; Univ. of New Mexico, 1990, p. 471–478)

Written for a Latin Americanist audience in the Summer of 1988 just after word of INFO-SOUTH preparations reached the field. Reviews the advantages, strengths, weaknesses, and prospects of existing online coverage of Latin America, with a focus on the few regionalist products such as the *Amerique Latine* abstract database from France, the *Latin American Newsletters* collection, and the early *LADB.*

13   Colson, Harold. Searching Latin America online: social sciences and humanities. (*Database Search.,* 4:6, June 1988, p. 20–24, bibl., table)

Written for an audience of online search specialists, this article discusses Latin American coverage across several general files and a few regionalist ones, nearly all of which are still operational. Written while *HAPI* and *HLAS* were offline and just before the *INFO-SOUTH* project was announced, it laments that Latin America lacks the convenience and power of a good area studies file, and that existing online coverage of foreign-language resources ranges from barely adequate to very poor. Indicative of the mixed state of coverage at the time and the pessimism regarding improvements from the commercial sector.

14   Durniak, Barbara Ammerman. Latin American information online: *INFO-SOUTH.* (*Online/Weston,* 15:6, Nov. 1991, p. 67–68)

First substantial review of *INFO-SOUTH* written by a librarian and online searcher.

15   Fryxell, David A. Everything you ever wanted to know about Latin America (and more). (*Link-Up/Minneapolis,* 10:7, Jan./Feb. 1994, p. 10–11)

Enthusiastic look at the *LADB* family of electronic publications, highlighting ease of use and strengths in underreported news, analysis, and statistics.

16   Hernández, Nicolás, Jr. Latin American databases: technological resources for scholars in the nineties. (*in* CALICO Annual Symposium, *Williamsburg, Va., 1993.* Proceedings. Durham, N.C.: Duke Univ., 1993, p. 70–72)

Examines *INFO-SOUTH, LADB, HAPI Online,* and *HLAS,* along with files from UNAM.

17   Levison, Andrew. Latin America online: best databases for news, business and current affairs. (*Database/Weston,* 16:6, Dec. 1993, p. 14–28, bibl., tables)

Cover story in leading online industry magazine, written by a database columnist-consultant, signals present Latin American information boom. Uses test searches to draw revealing statistical comparisons across several commercial files, mostly of the full-text variety. Also covers *INFO-SOUTH, LADB, HAPI Online,* and *HLAS.* Sidebars address Internet resources, databases from Latin America, and searching in an international affairs library. Presently stands as the top review of news-oriented sources and recent Latin Americanist arrivals.

18   Levison, Andrew and **Heberto Reynel Iglesias.** The online industry in Mexico. (*Online/Weston,* 17:3, May 1993, p. 116–119, tables)

Useful introduction to database usage and production in Mexico, which has one of the most developed online sectors in all of Latin America. Describes databases from SECOBI, UNAM, Univ. de Colima, and other players. Telecommunications problems and high costs for access to foreign databases give CD-ROM products a dominant role in the Mexican market.

19   Miller, Rory and **Patricia Noble.** Information technology for Latin Americanists. Liverpool, England: Society for Latin American Studies; Advisory Council on Latin American and Iberian Information Resources, 1994. 44 p.: bibl., glossary, index.

Handy booklet is perhaps the first guide to treat broad range of computerized and networked resources of interest to academic researchers in the Latin American studies field. Although written from a British context, work highlights many key resources and techniques applicable to Latin Americanists everywhere. Topics include electronic mail, newsgroups and conferences, online library catalogs, bibliographic databases, data archives, electronic journals and texts, and various Internet information tools such as ftp, gopher, archie, WAIS, and WWW.

20   Molloy, Molly. Internet resources for Latin American studies. (*Coll. Res. Libr. News,* 54:7, July/Aug. 1993, p. 395–399)

Annotated guide to selected Internet discussion groups, text files, servers, and more.

21   O'Leary, Mick. *INFO-SOUTH* fills foreign data gap. (*Inf. Today,* 9:6, June 1992, p. 13–14)

Positive assessment by leading online columnist written soon after the database appeared on Dialog.

22   Rodríguez, Ketty. The information search in Latin America: an analysis of Latin American databases. (*Libri/Copenha-*

gen, 43:3, July/Sept. 1993, p. 245–262, bibl., tables)

Perceptive look at information resources (print, online, CD-ROM) in the developed world and in Latin America views local databases in the context of reducing information dependency, filling coverage gaps, and overcoming economic and technological barriers to development. Cites several database projects in Latin America.

23   Stern, Peter. Coaxing the historian into the new information age. (*Colon. Lat. Am. Rev.,* 1:1/2, 1992, p. 201–221)

Insightful, wide-ranging, and sometimes provocative journey through the electronic marketplace informs as it calls for greater use of established and rising resources. History and the humanities have been neglected and underutilized as fields for computerized database research, but librarian-historian-online specialist Stern weaves together relevant opportunities and projects ranging from commercial files, *RLIN,* and *HAPI Online* to electronic newsletters, archival digitization, and Internet-based communications.

24   Stern, Peter. Databases in the humanities and social sciences: an update and review of border research. (*in* Seminar on the Acquisition of Latin American Library Materials, *33rd, Berkeley, California, 1988.* Latin American frontiers, borders, and hinterlands: research needs and resources. Edited by Paula Covington. Albuquerque, N.M.: SALALM Secretariat, General Library, Univ. of New Mexico, 1989, p. 461–470)

Considers rise of online databases, available files for historical and frontier studies, usage of such electronic resources by humanities and social science scholars, and prospects for Latin Americanists in the online revolution. Author presages emerging roles of CD-ROM databases, end-user systems, and scholarly electronic networks in bringing more information power to scholars at affordable prices.

25   Tuss, Joan. Roadmaps to the Internet: finding the best guidebooks for your needs. (*Online/Weston,* 18:1, Jan. 1994, p. 14–26, bibl., ill.)

Internet has spawned a mini-boom in published guides, primers, directories, handbooks, and yellow pages, which a visit to almost any bookstore clearly demonstrates. Tuss evaluates 11 books on the Internet and lists many more in print on the way. Available publications generally have little in the way of Latin Americanist advice, but they do describe techniques and tools that can lead you to relevant resources.

26   **Valk, Barbara G.** HAPI Online: a basic resource for Latin American research. (*DLA Bull.*, 12:3, Winter 1992, p. 3–6, ill., tables)

Decription of *HAPI* database for users in the University of California system following its debut within the MELVYL catalog system in late 1992. Discusses database scope, subject terminology, searching methods, display commands, and other features.

27   **Veenstra, John G.** Data bases relating to Latin American studies. (*in* Seminar on the Acquisition of Latin American Library Materials, *25th, Albuquerque, N.M., 1980.* Library resources on Latin America: new perspectives for the 1980s. Edited by Dan C. Hazen. Madison, Wis.: SALALM Secretariat, Univ. of Wisconsin-Madison, 1981, p. 307–312)

Perhaps the first published inventory of electronic Latin Americana, drawn largely from emerging general bibliographic files on Dialog, BRS, and other early commercial vendors. The accompanying conference panel summary (p. 30) notes "the increasing importance of on-line data bases, and the rapid increase in the number of such bases available to the public."

DATABASES AND SYSTEMS

28   ***ABI/Inform.*** 1974- . Louisville, Ky.: UMI; Data Courier.

Indexes and abstracts around 1,200 international periodicals in business, management, economics, finance, and other fields, with coverage beginning in 1971. Over 500 titles now in full-text. Covers trade magazines as well as scholarly journals, but virtually no Latin American periodicals. Updated weekly. Available on Dialog, OCLC's EPIC, and RLG's Eureka. CD-ROM version also available. Some business school libraries have a disc version with article images online.

29   ***Anthropological Literature.*** 1994- . Cambridge, Mass.: Tozzer Library, Harvard Univ.

A recent arrival to the online scene with over 80,000 citations to articles and essays in anthropology, archaeology, ethnohistory, folklore, linguistics, and related fields since 1984. Substantial Latin American content. Corresponds to a print and microfiche index with the same title. Updated quarterly. Available on RLG's Eureka. Also available on CD-ROM from G.K. Hall.

30   **ARGENA.** Colima, Mexico: Centro Nacional Editor de Discos Compactos, Univ. de Colima; México: Archivo General de la Nación, 1993. Computer laser optical disc (4 3/4 in.)

CD-ROM describing 322 groups of documents in the Mexican national archives. Also includes bibliographic references, tables, illustrations, and other information.

31   ***Article1st.*** 1990- . Dublin, Ohio: OCLC Online Computer Library Center.

New index to some 15,000 magazines and scholarly journals, mostly from North America and Europe. A convenient source for broad coverage of Latin America in English-language periodicals. One of the few article indexes updated on a daily basis. Available on OCLC's EPIC and FirstSearch.

32   **Bancos bibliográficos latinoamericanos y de el Caribe I.** Colima, Mexico: Centro Nacional Editor de Discos Compactos, Univ. de Colima, 1991. 1 computer laser optical disc (4 3/4 in.)

A one-disc collection of 50 assorted databases from Cuba, Costa Rica, Ecuador, Colombia, and Mexico. Topics range from humanities to agriculture to technology.

33   **Bancos bibliográficos latinoamericanos y de el Caribe II.** Colima, Mexico: Centro Nacional Editor de Discos Compactos, Univ. de Colima, 1993. 1 computer laser optical disc (4 3/4 in.)

Published with support from UNESCO, this CD-ROM contains 83 databases from 71 institutions in 14 Latin American countries plus Spain and the US.

34   **Bancos bibliográficos mexicanos I.** Colima, Mexico: Centro Nacional Editor de Discos Compactos, Univ. de Colima, 1989. 1 computer laser optical disc (4 3/4 in.)

The first CD-ROM database collection from the now-prolific Colima operation, produced with support from the Mexican government. This disc contains 16 specialty bibliographic databases compiled by UNAM, CONACYT, and Colima itself. Topics include education, economics, political campaigns, health, and more.

35 Bancos bibliográficos mexicanos II.
Colima, Mexico: Centro Nacional Editor de Discos Compactos, Univ. de Colima, 1990. 1 computer laser optical disc (4 3/4 in.)
This second Colima disc unites 22 Mexican databases covering Mexican literature, population and demography, health care, and other topics.

36 *Bibliografía Latinoamericana = Latin American Bibliography.* 1988- . México: Centro de Información Científica y Humanística, UNAM.
This CD-ROM collection first appeared in 1988 and the present disc contains over 250,000 article citations in several databases, including *CLASE* (Latin American journals in social sciences and humanities), *BIBLAT* (articles by Latin Americans or about Latin America in foreign periodicals), *PERIODICA* (Latin American science and technology journals), and *MEXINV* (articles by Mexicans). Covers some 8,200 worldwide periodicals since 1978. *CLASE, BIBLAT,* and *PERIODICA* are now available for direct on-line access over the Internet.

37 *CD-DIS: A.I.D.'s Development Information System,* 1992- . Arlington, Va.: LTS Corp.; U.S. Agency for International Development, Center for Development Information & Evaluation.
CD-ROM provides descriptions of USAID projects, citations to project and technical reports, and texts of selected agency publications since 1974. A source for identifying specialized development-related studies about Latin America. Updated quarterly.

38 CDPress. 1991- . Xalapa, Veracruz: CdRom de México.
Subtitled *La prensa nacional y estatal en disco compacto* and produced in conjunction with the Centro de Estudios Agrarios, this CD-ROM was perhaps the first full-text newspaper database to come out of Latin America. The initial six discs contain more than 200,000 articles selected from Mexican newspapers in the Distrito Federal and the states of Chiapas, Chihuahua, Jalisco, Michoacán, Morelos, Nuevo León, Puebla, and Veracruz, many of which are difficult to obtain in paper let alone electronically. A powerful resource for research on Mexican affairs.

39 Códice 90: XI censo general de población y vivienda, 1990; resultados definitivos. Aguascalientes, Mexico: Instituto Nacional de Estadística, Geografía e Informática (INEGI), 1992. 1 computer laser optical disc (4 3/4 in.) plus 3 instruction leaflets.
This first CD-ROM from the Mexican national statistical agency (INEGI) provides final results from the 1990 general census of population and housing. Offers more than 26,000 variables at the national, state, municipal, and local levels. Includes computerized census cartography.

40 CRIES CD-ROM. Managua: Coordinadora Regional de Investigaciones Económicas y Sociales, 1993. 1 computer laser optical disc (4 3/4 in.)
Released in 1993 as the first bibliographic CD-ROM from Central America, provides 12 databases of political, economic, and social information. Includes indexes of Nicaraguan newspapers (1979–92) and regional publications on Central American politics, economics, and international relations. Many of these sources are not indexed on other computerized products.

41 *Delphi en Español.* 1988- . Miami Beach, Fla.: Innovative Telematics.
The US node of a Latin American news, business, and conferencing system, featuring real-time feeds of Agence France-Presse, ACAN-EFE, and other Spanish-language newswires. Includes gateways to commercial databases and access to Delphi nodes in Argentina and other Latin American countries. Excellent, inexpensive source for very current news from Latin America. System recentlry renamed ITINET.

42 Ecuador. México: Multiconsult, S.C., 1990. Computer laser optical disc (4 3/4 in.)
Contains over 30,000 records for holdings in the general library of the Pontificia Univ. Católica del Ecuador. An early example of Latin American library database publishing using the young CD-ROM format.

43 *El Financiero.* 1993- . México: CD-ROM de México.
Premiere disc of this full-text newspaper database provides almost 12,000 articles published Jan.-March 1993. Articles from *El Financiero* are also on the *CDPress* discs (see item **38**), but coverage here is much more complete. Updated monthly.

44 *Geobase.* 1980- . Norwich, England: Elsevier; Geo Abstracts.

Contains around 500,000 abstracts to worldwide literature in the earth sciences, including geography, natural resources, demography, ecology, development, and environment. Online counterpart to *Geographical Abstracts* and other bibliographic tools. Updated monthly. Available on Dialog.

45 *Handbook of Latin American Studies.* Vol. 50, 1990- . Washington: Hispanic Division, Library of Congress.

Contains published and unpublished bibliographic entries from the *Handbook* beginning with volume 50 (1990), although the citations themselves treat works published back through the middle of the 1980s. The most current online version is available as part of the Books file in the Library's online catalog, which can be reached directly or via UT-LANIC and many other Internet routes. Also on RLG Eureka and the *Latin American Studies* CD-ROM set (item **55**). A retrospective CD-ROM containing volumes 1–53 of the *Handbook* will be available from the Univ. of Texas Press by the end of 1995.

46 *HAPI Online.* 1991- . Los Angeles: UCLA Latin American Center.

Database version of the printed *Hispanic American Periodicals Index* treats some 400 social sciences and humanities journals relating to Latin America, the US-Mexico borderlands and Hispanics in the US. Broad coverage and retrospective depth make this a core resource for our area studies field. Updated monthly between Oct. and June. Available directly from UCLA, via RLG's Eureka, and on the *Latin American Studies* CD-ROM set (item **55**).

47 *Index to Foreign Legal Periodicals.* 1985- . Berkeley, Calif.: American Assn. of Law Libraries.

A recent online arrival that indexes articles from over 450 legal periodicals. Subject focus is international law, comparative law, and municipal law in countries outside the US, British Isles, and Commonwealth. Holds over 70,000 records, with many pertaining to Latin America. Print version dates back to 1960. Updated quarterly. Available on RLG's Eureka and CD-ROM.

48 *Index to the Foreign Broadcast Information Service (FBIS) Daily Reports.* 1989- . New Canaan, Conn.: NewsBank/Readex.

CD-ROM index to *Daily Report: Latin America* and the other regional series issued in paper and microfiche by the US Foreign Broadcast Information Service since 1975. Searches headlines and subjects but does not contain the full report texts, which are available electronically only within federal government circles. Updated monthly.

49 *INFO-SOUTH Latin American Information System.* 1988- . Coral Gables, Fla.: North-South Center, Univ. of Miami.

The first commercially available bibliographic database on current affairs in Latin America and still virtually the only file to abstract major newspapers and news magazines from the region. Selection emphasizes contemporary economic, political, social, and business developments in the region. A powerful and unmatched resource for Latin Americanists, both as a recent news monitor and as a research base. Updated weekly. Available directly from the producer and on Dialog. Part of the *Latin American Studies* CD-ROM set (see item **55**).

50 *InfoMéxico.* 1993- . Monterrey: InfoSel.

InfoSel, part of *El Norte* publishing house, released this bibliographic and full-text CD-ROM database in 1993. Disc contains over 600,000 citations to Mexico-related articles in the national and foreign press, including over 20 Mexican newspapers and magazines. Articles from *El Norte* itself are available in full-text form. Except for the *Proyecto Cero* compilation (item **65**), no other database indexes Mexican newspapers as far back as 1986. Updated quarterly.

51 **Información para el desarrollo.** Santiago: Comisión Económica para América Latina y el Caribe, s.d. Computer laser optical disc (4 3/4 in.).

Contains three bibliographic databases, namely *DOCPAL* for population studies, *CLAPAN* for economic and social planning literature, and *CEPAL* for the agency's own publishing output. Over 70,000 citations altogether. Like many Latin American databases, it uses the Mini-Micro CDS/ISIS search system distributed throughout the developing world by UNESCO.

52 *IntlEc CD-ROM: the Index to International Economics, Development, and Finance.* 1992- . Washington: Joint Bank-Fund Library; Alexandria, Va.: Chadwyck-Healey.

Indexes some 2,000 journals and research paper series dating from 1981 and onwards located in the International Monetary Fund-World Bank library. Strong coverage of publications from developing areas, unlike most other periodical indexes. Includes nearly 15,000 citations dealing with Latin America and the Caribbean, making this a useful complement to *PAIS, HLAS, HAPI,* and *Economic Literature Index.* Updated quarterly.

53   KOMPASS México. México: INFO-TEC, 1993. Computer laser optical disc (4 3/4 in.)

One of the first company directories for a Latin American country to appear on CD-ROM. This database describes around 20,000 industrial and commercial enterprises in Mexico. KOMPASS International is a leading publisher of national business directories.

54   *Latin America Data Base.* 1991- . Albuquerque: Latin American Institute, Univ. of New Mexico.

A family of electronic newsletters covering current political and economic affairs across Latin America. Provides convenient full-text access to unique news reports, summaries, chronologies, statistics, and analyses drawn from regional wire services, radio broadcasts, newspapers, and other sources. Each component newsletter is updated weekly. LADB is available directly from the producer and on most major online services, including Dialog, NEXIS, NewsNet, DataTimes, and Dow Jones News/Retrieval. Such broad distribution on these systems is a commercial affirmation of its primacy as a news source on Latin America. Also available on *Latin American Studies* CD-ROM (item **55**).

55   *Latin American Studies.* Vol. 1–2. 1992- . Baltimore, Md.: National Information Services Corp.

This CD-ROM set offers several important Latin Americanist databases. Vol. I contains *HLAS, HAPI,* and the catalog of the Benson Latin American Collection at the Univ. of Texas at Austin; Vol II includes *INFO-SOUTH, LADB,* and *World Law Index.* A powerful portable resource on Latin America, but the semiannual updating weakens the timely value of *LADB* and *INFO-SOUTH.*

56   *Latin American Taxation Data Base.* 1993- . Amsterdam: International Bureau of Fiscal Documentation.

Contains comprehensive current information on tax systems in Latin American countries. Includes texts of relevant legislation and descriptions of economic and political systems, treaties, forms of business organization, and more. Updated semiannually.

57   *Legislación al día: DIALEX.* 1991- . Colima, Mexico: Univ. de Colima, Centro Editor de Discos Compactos; México: Archivo General de la Nación; Secretaría de Educación Pública; Consejo Nacional de Ciencia y Tecnología.

Published by Colima for the AGN, this CD-ROM indexes over 360,000 legal dispositions published in the *Diario Oficial de la Federación* through 1990.

58   Legislación federal mexicana. México: Cámara de Diputados del H. Congreso de la Unión; Colima, Mexico: Univ. de Colima, 1992. Computer laser optical disc (4 3/4 in.)

This Colima compact disc contains the complete texts of 222 Mexican laws passed between 1917–92. Other information about the Mexican legislature is also included.

59   LILACS. 1988- . São Paulo: Centro Latino-Americano e do Caribe de Informação em Ciencias da Saude.

Distributed since 1988, this is one of the first Latin American CD-ROM databases treating Latin American literature in health sciences and health-related environmental and policy topics. Sponsored by the Pan American Health Organization. Contains over 75,000 abstracts. Updated quarterly.

60   *The National Trade Data Bank: NTDB.* 1990- . Washington: U.S. Dept. of Commerce, Economics and Statistics Administration, Office of Business Analysis.

Born from the Omnibus Trade and Competitiveness Act of 1988, the two NTDB discs offer dozens of textual and statistical databases from US government agencies. The files include data on US foreign trade by commodity and country, reports on overseas markets and economic conditions, and other publications designed to help increase exports by American firms. Many of the government reports treat Latin American nations and received very limited public distribution before 1990. One of the most popular and widely disseminated CD-ROM databases issued by the US government. Updated monthly. Also available via Internet.

61 *Notimex.* 1992- . México: Agencia
Mexicana de Noticias.
English-language stories from the offical Mexican news agency are carried full-text
on DataTimes, Dow Jones, and NEXIS. A CD-
ROM product from NISC compiles Spanish-
language stories with semiannual updating.

62 *OCLC Online Union Catalog.* 1968- .
Dublin, Ohio: OCLC Online Com-
puter Library Center.
Known as "WorldCat" on the OCLC
FirstSearch system, this database provides
searchable library catalog records for
30 million recent and historical items held by
institutions in North America, Europe, and
Asia. Although hundreds of individual library
catalogs are available on the Internet, OCLC
enables one to search through the combined
holdings of thousands of member collections
in a single operation. Coverage is best for
items cataloged in the last two or three decades, but many libraries have added retrospective records covering centuries of prior publishing output. Updated daily. Available only
from OCLC.

63 *PeaceNet.* 1986- . San Francisco: Institute for Global Communications.
One of four IGC computer communications networks offering low-cost electronic
mail, global conferencing, and information resources for individuals and nongovernmental
organizations in the Americas and beyond. A
good source for very current news and documentation in peace issues, environmental
protection, human rights, social justice, and
related areas. Companion networks are
EcoNet, ConflictNet, and LaborNet.

64 *PROMT.* 1972- . Foster City, Calif.:
Predicasts.
Contains nearly 3 million citations,
with abstracts and selected full-text, to
worldwide trade and business sources on
companies, products, and industries. Information is drawn from more than 1,200 periodical
publications ranging from newspapers and industry magazines to electronic services like
LADB. PROMT is becoming a strong source
for specialized reports on business, finance,
trade, and economics in Latin America. Updated weekly. Available on Dialog, Data-Star,
NEXIS, and FT Profile.

65 **Proyecto Cero.** Xalapa, Mexico: CD-
ROM de México, 1991. 1 computer
laser optical disc (4 3/4 in.)

This precursor to CDPress unites 9
Mexican newspaper article databases on one
disc. There are state databases on Jalisco, Michoacán, Morelos, Tabasco, and Veracruz covering 1987 through early 1991, with another
Jalisco file offering citations from 1940–80.
Other files cover church affairs, human
rights, and agriculture-forestry-commercial
fishing. Over 184,000 entries, mostly summaries but with some texts.

66 **Red latinoamericana en ciencias de la
comunicación.** Colima, Mexico: Centro Nacional Editor de Discos Compactos,
Univ. de Colima, 1992. 1 computer laser optical disc (4 3/4 in.)
Collection of databases published on
CD-ROM by Colima for institutions in the
communicactions studies network. Contains
nine bibliographic databases from Ecuador,
Brazil, Peru, Uruguay, Mexico, and Spain.

67 *Reuter Textline.* 1980- . London:
Reuters.
Formerly available only through the
producer's own system, this global abstract
and full-text file is now loaded on Dialog,
NEXIS, and Data-Star. Contains more than
5 million entries culled from some 2,000
newspapers, journals, magazines, and newswires. A good source for current and background coverage of Latin American news. Updated daily.

68 *RLIN.* 1974- . Mountain View, Calif.:
Research Libraries Group.
An online bibliographic database representing the combined holdings (over 23 million records) of more than 200 RLG member
libraries. Like the competing OCLC database,
it includes cataloging records for books, periodicals, theses, manuscripts, sound recordings, audiovisuals, scores, computer files, and
more. Available from RLG in its original,
command-language mode and in a friendlier
Eureka version. Updated daily.

69 *SICE: Foreign Trade Information System.* 1983- . Washington: General Secretariat, Organization of American States.
Intended to provide foreign trade information to the private and public sectors
within OAS member countries, this database
includes over 7 million online records with
trade data, tariff schedules, company directories, regulations, prices, and more. Coverage
is best for the US and parts of Latin America

(Mexico, Brazil, Colombia, and the Southern Cone), with new coverage planned for Europe and Japan. Updating varies by file.

70   SINF. 1990- . México: Dirección General de Información, UNAM.

This compact disc provides some 170,000 citations (with summaries) to articles appearing in six Mexican national newspapers: *Excelsior, El Universal, UnomásUno, La Jornada, El Financiero,* and *El Nacional.* Coverage includes politics, economics, law, education, science, culture, media, disasters, sports, and more. Along with *INFO-SOUTH, CDPress,* and *InfoMéxico,* this is one of the few electronic sources for (partial) indexing of Mexican newspapers. Disc now issued as BINFHER (Banco de Información Hemerográfica).

71   UnCover. 1988- . Denver, Colo.: The UnCover Company.

This article index debuted on the Internet in 1988 as a solely electronic product (no print equivalent) from the Colorado Alliance of Research Libraries. It now contains over 3 million citations from around 14,000 periodicals held by contributing libraries. A convenient source for articles on Latin America from a wide variety of scholarly, popular, and trade periodicals, mostly in English. Open for free access from the Internet. Updated daily.

72   United Nations Conference on Environment and Development, *Rio de Janeiro, 1992.* Earth summit = Sommet planète terre = Cumbre para la tierra. Ottawa, Ont.: International Development Research Centre; New York: United Nations Publications, 1993. 1 computer laser optical disc (4 3/4 in.) plus 1 introductory manual (50 p.)

Searchable text and image archive of official, primary source documents from the 1992 UN Conference on Environment and Development (UNCED) in Rio de Janeiro. Includes preparatory conference papers, national environmental reports, research papers, NGO documents, offical statements and conventions, and *Agenda 21.* Many materials are unavailable through other database sources. Search interface available in English, Spanish, or French.

73   UT-LANIC. 1993- . Austin: Institute of Latin American Studies, Univ. of Texas.

Univ. of Texas' Latin American Network Information Center (LANIC) serves as a gateway to many Internet resources of value to Latin Americans and Latin Americanists. Connecting to UT-LANIC gives users access to hundreds of remote catalogs and databases organized by subject and country. Some files are held directly on the UT-LANIC server itself, including a database of news from Mexico, US Agency for International Development statistics, a database of databases on Latin America, and directories of Latin Americanist resources on the Internet.

74   Venezuela en disco compacto. México: Multiconsult, S.C., 1989. Computer laser optical disc (4 3/4 in.)

Early catalog of holdings (over 190,000 items) in Venezuelan libraries developed by the Instituto Autónomo Biblioteca Nacional y de Servicios de Bibliotecas in Caracas. Published by Multiconsult soon after its pioneering *Bibliografía latinoamericana* CD-ROM for UNAM. Venezuelan library collections are now searchable on the Internet through the Biblioteca Nacional's SAIBIN union catalog.

75   *World Law Index, Part I: Index to Hispanic Legislation.* 1976- . Washington: Hispanic Law Division, Library of Congress.

Contains some 50,000 summaries of national laws, decrees, and regulations in Latin America, Spain, Portugal, the Philippines, and Lusophone Africa. Updated quarterly. Available on the Library's public catalog, via RLG's Eureka, and as part of the *Latin American Studies* CD-ROM (see item **55**).

JOURNAL ABBREVIATIONS

ABI/INFORM.   ABI/INFORM. UMI/Data Courier. Louisville, Ky.

Anthropol. Lit./Online.   Anthropological Literature. Tozzer Library. Cambridge, Mass.

Article1st/OCLC.   Article1st. OCLC Online Computer Library Center. Dublin, Ohio.

Bibl. Latinoam./CD-ROM.   Bibliografía Latinoamericana-Latin American Bibliography. Centro de Información Científica y Humanística, Univ. Nacional Autónoma de México. México.

CD-DIS/Arlington. CD-DIS. United States Agency for International Development, Development Information Services Clearinghouse. Arlington, Va.

CD-ROM Dir. CD-ROM Directory. TFPL Publishing. London.

CD-ROMs Print. CD-ROMs in Print. Meckler. Westport, Conn.

CDPress. CDPress. CD-ROM de México. Xalapa, Mexico.

Coll. Res. Libr. News. College and Research Libraries News. Assn. of College and Research Libraries. Chicago, Ill.

Colon. Lat. Am. Rev. Colonial Latin American Review. Simon H. Rifkind Center for the Humanities, Dept. of Romance Languages, City College of New York. New York.

Database Search. Database Searcher. Meckler Pub., Westport, Conn.

Database/Weston. Database. Online, Inc., Weston, Conn.

Delphi Esp./Online. Delphi en Español. Innovative Telematics. Miami Beach, Fla.

DLA Bull. DLA Bulletin. Univ. of California, Division of Library Automation. Berkeley.

Financiero/CD-ROM. El Financiero. CD-ROM de México. México.

Fulltext Sources Online. Fulltext Sources Online. Bibliodata. Needham Heights, Mass.

Gale Dir. Databases. Gale Directory of Databases. Gale Research. Detroit.

Geobase/Online. Geobase. Elsevier/Geo Abstracts.

HAPI Online. HAPI Online. UCLA Latin American Center. Los Angeles.

HLAS/Online. Handbook of Latin American Studies. Hispanic Division, Library of Congress. Washington.

Index FBIS Dly. Rep./CD-ROM. Index FBIS Daily Report. NewsBank/Readex. New Canaan, Conn.

Index Foreign Leg. Period. Index to Foreign Legal Periodicals. American Association of Law Libraries. Berkeley, Calif.

Inf. Today. Information Today. Learned Information, Inc., Medford, N.J.

INFO-SOUTH/Online. INFO-SOUTH Latin American Information System. North-South Center, Univ. of Miami. Miami, Fla.

InfoMéxico/CD-ROM. InfoMéxico. InfoSel. Monterrey, Mexico.

IntlEc CD-ROM. IntlEc CD-ROM: the Index to International Economics, Development and Finance. Joint Bank-Fund Library. Washington.

LADB/Online. Latin America Data Base. Latin American Institute, Univ. of New Mexico. Albuquerque.

Lat. Am. Stud./NISC. Latin American Studies. National Information Services Corporation. Baltimore, Md.

Lat. Am. Tax. Data Base. Latin American Taxation Data Base. International Bureau of Fiscal Documentation. Amsterdam.

Libri/Copenhagen. Libri. Munksgaard. Copenhagen.

LILACS/CD-ROM. LILACS. Centro Latino-Americano e do Caribe de Informação em Ciencias da Saude. São Paulo.

Link-up/Minneapolis. Link-up. On-Line Communications. Minneapolis, Minn.

Natl. Trade Data Bank. National Trade Data Bank. U.S. Dept. of Commerce, Economics and Statistics Administration, Office of Business Analysis. Washington.

Notimex/CD-ROM. Notimex. Agencia Mexicana de Noticias. México.

OCLC Online Union Cat. OCLC Online Union Catalog. OCLC Online Computer Library Center. Dublin, Ohio.

Online/Weston. Online. Online, Inc., Weston, Conn.

PeaceNet. PeaceNet. Institute for Global Communications. San Francisco, Calif.

PROMT/Online. PROMT. Predicasts. Foster City, Calif.

Reuter Textline. Reuter Textline. Reuters. London.

RLIN/Online. RLIN. Research Libraries Group. Mountain View, Calif.

SICE/Online. SICE: Foreign Trade Information System. General Secretariat, Organization of American States. Washington.

SINF/CD-ROM. SINF. Dirección General de Información, Univ. Nacional Autónoma de México. México.

UnCover/Online. UnCover. The UnCover Co., Denver, Colo.

UT-LANIC. UT-LANIC. Institute of Latin American Studies, Univ. of Texas. Austin.

World Law Index I. World Law Index, Part I: Index to Hispanic Legislation. Hispanic Law Division, Library of Congress. Washington.

ART

SPANISH AMERICA
Colonial
General, Middle America, and the Caribbean

BARBARA VON BARGHAHN, *Professor of Art History, George Washington University*

THE MAJORITY OF ENTRIES THIS YEAR must be perceived as significant contributions to the history of art. Not only were many books published with substantially improved color reproduction, but also the quality of research was clearly evident by the documentation of sources, select bibliographies, and informative notes.

While the scope of subjects ranged from studies of principal monuments to encyclopedic volumes focusing upon specific periods of art in New Spain, particularly impressive was the attention given to neglected areas, such as iconography, portraiture, and stylistic crosscurrents with the motherland.

The handsome seven-volume series *Arte Novohispano* should be highlighted because of the overall excellent coverage of topics and superb color plates (items **106, 107, 121, 150, 151, 160,** and **161**). Also noteworthy were the illuminating studies of renowned edifices, such as the Cathedral of Morelia (item **125**), the Cathedral of Oaxaca (item **131**), the Cathedral of Mexico (item **159**), Santa Prisca in Taxco (item **156**), San Agustín de Acolman (item **148**), and San Nicolás Tolentino de Actopan (item **109**). Some publications about viceregal paintings in museums and ecclesiastical institutions deserve singular comment because of the lucid essays and excellent plates: Museo Nacional del Virreinato (item **101**), Querétaro (item **167**), San Luis Potosí (item **111**), Hidalgo (item **164**), Michoacán (item **116**), and Guatemala (item **172**). Current publications also include important investigations about the *tilma* of the "Virgin of Guadalupe" (items **132** and **120**).

There are rich mines for research that remain a *desideratum* for the future. For instance, monographs with sharp color plates that would serve to define the sources and stylistic evolution of key artists who formed the Mexican School of painting are long overdue. In addition, as there are now sufficient encyclopedic texts, it is time to chronologically cluster and assess paintings by renowned masters and their disciples. Resolving problems in connoisseurship may be a challenging task, but current scholarship indicates it can be accomplished. With respect to illustration captions, one would welcome more daring in assigning reasonable dates to retables by preeminent artists, and attention should be directed to providing at least approximate sizes. Furthermore, bilingual publications would accelerate dissemination of knowledge about colonial Mexican art in the US.

Artistic crosscurrents between Middle America and other colonial centers in the New World remain to be addressed. Since members of religious orders—unconfined by geographic parameters—travelleled between the viceroyalities established by Spain, a shift towards comparative analysis might bear fruit. In addition, there are too few iconographic studies of art commissioned by these eruditc patrons who did maintain contact with humanist Seville.

The entries for this year are of such exceptional merit that this brief essay cannot do justice to the surfeit of commendable texts which have been published recently. As in *HLAS 52*, due to the *Handbook's* space limitations the great majority of applicable journal articles could not be included here. Readers are encouraged to consult the many pertinent essays appearing in vols. 59–64 of the *Anales del Instituto de Investigaciones Estéticas* (México: Univ. Nacional Autónoma de México, 1988–1993). These scholarly articles should be checked because they encompass the macrocosmic areas of vital research which will eventually be presented in monographic form.

In completing this review of recently published books and articles, the contributing editor gratefully acknowledges the assistance of Mr. Christopher Wilson, PhD candidate in art history at George Washington University.

GENERAL

76   Arellano, Fernando. El arte hispanoamericano. Caracas: Univ. Católica Andrés Bello, 1988. 413 p., 64 p. of plates: bibl., ill. (some col.)

Popular edition of general survey of colonial art and architecture in Spanish America. Chap. 1 discusses European stylistic terminology used throughout the text with mixed results and offers sketchy account of precolumbian cultures that flourished in ancient America. Visual material is limited to 128 color and b/w photographs of uneven quality, and does not adequately reflect the book's scope. Duplicate photograph of the interior of Jesuit church of San Pedro is, in one instance, identified as an ancient Mayan monument! [H. Rodríguez-Camilloni]

77   Bayón, Damián and Murillo Marx. History of South American colonial art and architecture: Spanish South America and Brazil. New York: Rizzoli, 1992. 442 p.: bibl., ill. (some col.), index.

Faithful English translation of monumental work originally published in Spanish in 1989 (see *HLAS 52:153*). This is a comprehensive overview of colonial South American architecture, painting, and sculpture from Panama to Chile, including Brazil. Useful catalogs of principal monuments with additional historical data and individual bibliographical references follow Pts. 1 and 2 by Bayón and Pt. 3 by Marx. The 891 excellent illustrations provide impressive visual survey

of art and architecture of the period. [H. Rodríguez-Camilloni]

78   Bernabeu Albert, Salvador *et al.* Historia urbana de Iberoamérica. v. 1; v. 2, pt. 1–2. Dirección científico de Francisco de Solano. Coordinación de María Luisa Cerrillos. Madrid: Consejo Superior de los Colegios de Arquitectos de España, 1987–1990. 3 v.: bibl., ill. (some col.), maps. (Testimonio)

First two volumes of a projected monumental five-volume urban history of Latin America undertaken by the Comisión Nacional Quinto Centenario. An impressive team of specialists from Spain and Latin America collaborated on the project, including Salvador Bernabeu, Alvaro Gómez Ferrer, Ramón Gutiérrez, Jorge Enrique Hardoy, Alfonso Jiménez, Carlos Malamud, Juan Antonio Tineo, Pedro Vives and others. Vol. 1 deals with origins of Latin American cities up to 1573, focusing on precolumbian settlements and European foundations that marked the earliest period of conquest and colonization; vol. 2, published in two separate parts, addresses the "baroque city," which focuses on urbanization patterns in the Americas between 1573–1750. Even though many chapters can be read as self-contained case studies, they complement each other well and provide a comprehensive multidisciplinary approach to the subject. High quality visual material such as color maps and other graphics specially produced for this publication as well as reproductions of historic documents and contemporary photographs make this an invaluable permanent contribution. [H. Rodríguez-Camilloni]

79 Bonet Correa, Antonio. El urbanismo en España e Hispanoamérica. Madrid: Cátedra, 1991. 218 p.: bibl., ill. (Ensayos Arte Catedra)

Thirteen important previously published essays collected in one volume. Well-written and thoroughly documented, book emphasizes morphological analysis of urban centers in Spain and Spanish America dating mostly from the 16th-18th centuries. Only the final three essays deal with specific Spanish American topics: the development of the plaza mayor in Spanish American cities; the city of León Viejo in Nicaragua; and the nunnery of Santa Catalina in Arequipa, Peru. Good b/w illustrations complement the text. [H. Rodríguez-Camilloni]

80 Calderón Quijano, José Antonio. Los estudios en España sobre la historia de la arquitectura militar y las fortificaciones americanas, 1939-1989. (*Rev. Indias*, 50:188, enero/abril 1990, p. 109-126, appendix)

General review of bibliography devoted to history of military architecture and fortifications in the Americas from 1939-89. The 215 titles in the appendix are an indispensable checklist of publications on the subject. [H. Rodríguez-Camilloni]

81 Castedo, Leopoldo. Historia del arte iberoamericano. v. 1, Precolombino; El arte colonial. Madrid: Alianza Editorial, 1988. 1 v.: bibl., ill. (some col.), index.

First of two-volume work devoted to general history of Latin American art and architecture from precolumbian times to present. Supersedes author's 1969 one-volume *A History of Latin American Art and Architecture* (see *HLAS 32:211*) with a more effective discussion of the material by thematic chapters and more illustrations. Spanish colonial period is covered in the second-longer-part of this volume (p. 189-444), and reflects the author's first-hand familiarity with the many monuments and works of art presented. The topic's scope, however, imposes severe limitations and the free use of European stylistic labels remains controversial. B/w photographs and a few better color plates are not fully integrated with the text, but generally are found close to where they are mentioned. Up-to-date bibliography broken down by chapters

offers important suggestions for further reading. [H. Rodríguez-Camilloni]

82 Chiappero, Rubén Osvaldo. Capítulos indianos: aproximación a símbolos del arte hispanoamericano. Santa Fe, Argentina: Amaltea, 1991. 145 p.: bibl., ill.

This popular edition of short essays deals with Latin American colonial art and architecture topics. Relies on secondary sources and makes no new contribution to the subject matter. Careless pagination has resulted in the duplication of p. 12-23 and the omission of p. 60-71. Some essays are illustrated with fine drawings by Hugo Lazzarini. [H. Rodríguez-Camilloni]

83 La ciudad hispanoamericana: el sueño de un orden. Madrid: Centro de Estudios Históricos de Obras Públicas y Urbanismo, Ministerio de Obras Públicas y Urbanismo, 1989. 302 p.: bibl., col. ill.

Handsome companion catalog to exhibition of same title held at the Museo Español de Arte Contemporáneo of Madrid (1989). Text is divided into two parts. Pt. 1 corresponds to the catalog and describes the seven major themes: the territory, the inhabitants, the colonization, the pattern, the past history, the colonial city, and evolution and permanence. Pt. 2 covers critical studies on Spanish American cities by various authors including José Alcina Franch, José Luis García Fernández, Pedro A. Vives, Guillermo Céspedes del Castillo, María Concepción García Saiz, Josefa Vega Janino, Ignacio González Tascón, Ramón Gutiérrez, Jorge E. Hardoy and Catalina Romero. Informative essays are lavishly illustrated with stunning color photographs and color reproductions of historic plans from the Archivo General de Indias in Seville. Fine contribution to history of town planning in Spanish America from its beginnings to the present. [H. Rodríguez-Camilloni]

84 Exposición de Puertos y Fortificaciones en América y Filipinas. Dos ejemplos de fortificaciones españolas en la Exposición de Puertos y Fortificaciones en América y Filipinas. Juan Manuel Zapatero. Madrid: Comisión de Estudios Históricos de Obras Públicas y Urbanismo, 1985. 50 p.: bibl., ill. (some col.) (Biblioteca CEHOPU)

Handsomely-illustrated catalog documents two three-dimensional scale models of the fortifications Castillo de San Lorenzo el Real in Chagre, Panama, and Castillo San Felipe in Puerto Cabello, Venezuela, constructed for a 1985 exhibition in Madrid under the direction of José Mañas Martínez. Also reprints two critical studies by Juan Manuel Zapatero, making this publication an important supplement to the general exhibition catalog (see item 91). [H. Rodríguez-Camilloni]

85   Gutiérrez, Ramón et al. Cabildos y ayuntamientos en América. Mar del Plata, Argentina: IAIHAU; Azcapotzalco, Mexico: Univ. Autónoma Metropolitana-Azcapotzalco; México: Tilde, 1990. 134 p.: bibl., ill.

Eight well-documented studies by different authors trace history of building type that served as seat of municipal government in Spanish American colonial cities. Significant examples from Argentina, Cuba, Chile, Mexico, and Uruguay are dicussed in different chapters illustrated with b/w photographs and reproductions of plans and archival drawings. [H. Rodríguez-Camilloni]

86   López, Santiago Sebastián. Diffusion of the counter-reformation doctrine. (*in* Temples of gold, crowns of silver: reflections of majesty in the Viceregal Americas. Curated by Barbara von Barghahn. Washington: George Washington Univ., 1991, p. 57–79, facsims., plates, photos)

Well-written essay considers ecclesiastical doctrine of the Counter-Reformation as the basic instrument of conversion for New World missionaries. Also examines the role of colonial religious paintings as didactic tools in this conversion process. Author discusses several popular iconographic themes at length and illustrates them with examples from Mexico and Perú, providing meaningful comparisons of parallel developments at different points in time. Wherever possible, literary and visual sources used by colonial artists are carefully noted by the author. [H. Rodríguez-Camilloni]

87   López-Yarto, Amelia and María Concepción García Sáiz. El arte americano en las publicaciones periódicas españolas. (*Rev. Indias*, 49:187, sept./dic. 1989, p. 697–705)

General review of the literature on Latin American art and architecture during the colonial period and since independence published in Spanish periodicals. Study provides a valuable complement to Amelia López-Yarto's "Bibliografía del Arte Americano en las Revistas Españolas" (see item 92). [H. Rodríguez-Camilloni]

88   Mogollon Cano-Cortes, Pilar. Repercusiones del arte mudéjar en América. (*in* Simposio Hispano-Portugués de Historia del Arte, 5th, *Valladolid, Spain, 1989.* Actas. Coordinación de Juan José Martín González. Valladolid, Spain: Univ. de Valladolid, 1990, p. 173–177)

Comparative study of better-known examples of *mudéjar* architecture in Spain and Spanish America. Examples are discussed only in general terms and there are no illustrations. [H. Rodríguez-Camilloni]

89   Palmer, Gabrielle G. and Donna Pierce. Cambios: the spirit of transformation in Spanish colonial art. Santa Barbara, Calif.: Santa Barbara Museum of Art; Univ. of New Mexico Press, 1992. 149 p.: bibl., ill. (some col.), index, col. maps.

Exhibition catalog commemorating the Quincentenary documents art and decorative arts in Mexico and South America during the Viceregal period. Perceptive introduction by Jacinto Quirarte emphasizes the uniqueness of the artistic heritage of the Americas. Essays include: "The Changing Face of Spanish Colonial Art in South America," by Gabrielle G. Palmer; and "Metamorphasis in Spanish Colonial Art [of New Spain]," by Donna Pierce. All 119 works in the exhibition are reproduced in excellent color photographs accompanied by factual information and critical commentaries. [H. Rodríguez-Camilloni]

90   Pizarro Gómez, Francisco Javier. La iconografía del Nuevo Mundo y su repercusión en las artes españolas y portuguesas. (*in* Simposio Hispano-Portugués de Historia del Arte, 5th, *Valladolid, Spain, 1989.* Actas. Coordinación de Juan José Martín González. Valladolid, Spain: Univ. de Valladolid, 1990, p. 215–226, ill.)

Brief study examines how early descriptions of the New World in chronicles and other written accounts were translated into fantastic allegorical images by European artists from the 16th-18th centuries. The dissemination of these images via woodcuts, engravings, and other printed sources helped perpetuate misconceptions about the Americas and their indigenous populations, who came to be regarded as mysterious and highly exotic. [H. Rodríguez-Camilloni]

91   Puertos y fortificaciones en América y Filipinas. Madrid: Comisión de Estudios Históricos de Obras Públicas y Urbanismo, 1985. 465 p.: bibl., ill. (some col.), indexes. (Biblioteca CEHOPU)

Impressive catalog published in conjunction with the exhibition held in Madrid in 1985 under the auspices of CEHOPU. A seminar on the same topic was held in June, 1984 in Madrid (for the seminar's proceeding see *HLAS 50:190*). In addition to the exhibition catalog of 138 panels reproduced in full color, text includes 12 illustrated essays by renowned scholars such as Pedro Suárez Bores, Pedro Vives, Juan Manuel Zapatero, and María Concepción García Sáiz. For related work, see item **84.** [H. Rodríguez-Camilloni]

92   Relaciones artísticas entre España y América. Madrid: Consejo Superior de Investigaciones Científicas: Centro de Estudios Históricos, Depto. de Historia del Arte Diego Velázquez, 1990. 481 p.: bibl., ill., indexes.

Impressive anthology of original research conducted 1987–89 by 11 distinguished scholars led by Enrique Arias Anglés. Different aspects of artistic relations between Spain and her American colonies are explored in iconographic studies that deal with paintings, sculpture, and architecture from the 16th-19th centuries. The 20th century is represented in a chapter that analyzes the I Bienal Hispanoamericana de Arte held in Madrid between Oct. 12, 1951 to April 27, 1952. Book concludes with an extremely useful bibliography of articles on Spanish American art published in Spain from 1836–1989. [H. Rodríguez-Camilloni]

93   Ruiz Mateos, Aurora. Arquitectura civil de la Orden de Santiago en Extremadura: la casa de la encomienda; su proyección en Hispanoamérica. Badajoz, Spain: Consejería de Educación y Cultura de la Junta de Extremadura, Excma. Diputación Provincial de Badajoz, 1985? 318 p.: bibl., ill.

This model of archival research was originally written as a doctoral dissertation under the direction of José María de Azcárate. Study surveys 28 *encomiendas* pertaining to the military order of St. James the Great in Extremadura, Spain and 87 buildings dating

between 1480–1798 distributed in 47 towns of the region. Whenever possible, a detailed history and analysis of the buildings is complemented by contemporary photographs and carefully reconstructed plans, sections and axonometric drawings. The *casa de encomienda* served as residence of the *Comendador* and was the likely source of inspiration for the layout of several colonial houses in Spanish America, particularly in Mexico and Peru. Exhaustive archival documentation either summarized or fully transcribed is also provided in microfiche format as an aid for future studies. [H. Rodríguez-Camilloni]

94   Stroessner, Robert J. Beyond the pillars of Hercules: Spanish colonial painting from the New World. (*in* Temples of gold, crowns of silver: reflections of majesty in the Viceregal Americas. Curated by Barbara von Barghahn. Washington: George Washington Univ., 1991, p. 16–33, facsims., plates, photos)

Overview of development of Latin American colonial art and architecture aimed at the general public stresses its diversity and complexity and the serious need for its re-evaluation and conservation. Author correctly points out that "even though Spanish colonial art spread over a vast area of the globe and embraced a cultural heritage shared by over one fifth of the world's population, it remains the least known, understood or appreciated area of world art." [H. Rodríguez-Camilloni]

95   Viñuales, Graciela María. Patrimonio arquitectónico: aportes a la cultura nacional y americana. Buenos Aires: Instituto Argentino de Investigaciones de Historia de la Arquitectura y del Urbanismo, 1990. 104 p.

Anthology of articles and conference papers previously delivered by the author deal with history and theory of restoration and preservation of historic monuments in Latin America. Offers important recommendations for professional training in the field, methods of recording historic buildings, the use of traditional construction material, and effective strategies for preservation work following seismic disasters. [H. Rodríguez-Camilloni]

96   Von Barghahn, Barbara and **Evelyn Figueroa.** Colonial centers for devotional sculpture: artists and techniques. (*in* Temples of gold, crowns of silver: reflections of majesty in the Viceregal Americas. Curated by

Barbara von Barghahn. Washington: George Washington Univ., 1991, p. 136–153, photos)

General overview of Spanish American colonial religious sculpture, with particular emphasis on examples from Guatemala and Ecuador. Of special interest is information on materials and techniques used by different artists. [H. Rodríguez-Camilloni]

97 Von Barghahn, Barbara. A crucible of gold: the "rising sun" of monarchy in the blending of cultures. (*in* Temples of gold, crowns of silver: reflections of majesty in the Viceregal Americas. Curated by Barbara von Barghahn. Washington: George Washington Univ., 1991, p. 34–56, facsims., plates, photos)

Suggestive study deals with various aspects of political authority, religious ritual, and secular pageantry portrayed in selected examples of Spanish and Spanish American colonial art. Iconographic reading of several artistic programs permits valuable insights into the mentality of the Spanish Golden Age and a better understanding of why the experiences of Spaniards in the New World were regarded by contemporaries of Charles V as the fulfillment of a messianic destiny. Frequent references to Roman Antiquity and classical mythology reinforced the Spanish Crown's claim to that rich cultural heritage symbolized by the Pillars of Hercules emblem and the Holy Roman Emperor's adopted motto *Plus Ultra.* According to the author, in the Spanish American colonies the Crown and the Church became the Pillars of Hercules, "the mortar and the pestle constituting a 'Crucible of Gold.' " [H. Rodríguez-Camilloni]

98 Von Barghahn, Barbara. From the tower of David to the citadel of Solomon: mirrors of virtue for a Viceregal "silver age." (*in* Temples of gold, crowns of silver: reflections of majesty in the Viceregal Americas. Curated by Barbara von Barghahn. Washington: George Washington Univ., 1991, p. 154–179, photos)

Analytical study investigates iconography of the Virgin Mary and diffusion of her cult under different titles throughout Spanish America during the colonial period, including the Virgin of the Rosary, the Virgin of Guadalupe, the Virgin of Pomata, and the Virgin of Valanera. Comparisons of paintings by Spanish and colonial artists reflect different approaches to the subject matter and local pre-

ferences. *The Virgin of Cerro Mountain* painted around 1720 in Potosí, Bolivia, for example, offers a striking amalgam of precolumbian and European iconography. The concluding section, "A Matriach's Legacy," considers the impact of the portrait of Queen Isabella I of Castile on representations of the Virgin in Spanish America. [H. Rodríguez-Camilloni]

99 Von Barghahn, Barbara. Imaging the cosmic goddess: sacred legends and metaphors for majesty. (*in* Temples of gold, crowns of silver: reflections of majesty in the Viceregal Americas. Curated by Barbara von Barghahn. Washington: George Washington Univ., 1991, p. 93–115, facsims., photos)

Well-illustrated study investigates several iconographic themes in Spanish American colonial painting, including the Immaculate Conception and the representation of Christian saints. Author also speculates on impact that royal portraits by Iberian court artists may have had upon Spanish American "dressed statue" icons of the Virgin and discusses several works of art that show how Andean rituals were melded to Catholic doctrines during the colonial period. [H. Rodríguez-Camilloni]

MEXICO

100 Ahued Valenzuela, Salvador. El libro del histórico y virreinal Colegio Apostólico de Propaganda Fide de Nuestra Señora de Guadalupe de Zacatecas y Convento Franciscano del siglo XVIII. Guadalajara, México: S. Ahued Valenzuela, 1991. 189 p.: bibl., col. ill.

Author surveys architectural features of the institution (now a museum) and discusses numerous Mexican colonial paintings housed there. Although many photographs are blurred and present inaccurate color, the book reproduces images of extraordinary colonial treasures. One chapter is dedicated to the Gallery of Viceregal Art which contains works by such masters as Miguel Cabrera and Cristóbal de Villalpando.

101 Alarcón Cedillo, Roberto M. *et al.* Pintura novohispana: Museo Nacional del Virreinato, Tepotzotlán. Tepotzotlán, México: Asociación de Amigos del Museo Nacional del Virreinato, 1992. 1 v.: bibl., ill. (some col.).

The museum houses some of the finest

examples of Mexican colonial painting and this collection catalog is one of the best available resources for the study of art of New Spain, covering works from the 16th, 17th, and beginning of the 18th centuries. Each of the 233 works is reproduced in a color photograph of excellent quality and accompanied by an iconographic explanation. Also includes introductory essays which discuss history of painting in New Spain, as well as iconographic and technical considerations of works produced during the colonial period.

102 Altamirano R., Hugo. La ciudad de Oaxaca que conoció Morelos. Oaxaca: s.n., 1992. 52 p.: bibl., ill. (some col.), maps.

Fine study of 19th-century Oaxaca around the time that General D. José María Morelos y Pavón led his army against the Spanish troops of Simón Gutiérrez de Villegas on Nov. 25, 1812. B/w photographs and plans of the city are informative.

Andrews, Anthony P. The rural chapels and churches of early colonial Yucatán and Belize: an archaeological perspective. See *HLAS 53:247.*

103 El arte de la platería mexicana, 500 años: noviembre 1989-febrero 1990. Mexico: Centro Cultural Arte Contemporáneo, 1989. 595 p.: bibl., ill. (some col.)

Very informative work on viceregal silver in New Spain from the 16th-19th centuries. In addition to splendid color plates, text includes useful material on mining and on the silversmith profession. A total of 130 entries for sacred and secular metal works are accompanied by a classification of 80 marks illustrated in b/w. Numismatic designs, medals, swords, and tableware are also included in the exhibition catalog.

Baños Ramos, Eneida. Elementos de juegos de pelota mexicas en la Ciudad de México, D.F. See *HLAS 53:269.*

104 Bargellini, Clara. La arquitectura de la plata: iglesias monumentales del centro-norte de México, 1640-1750. Mexico: UNAM, Instituto de Investigaciones Estéticas; Spain: Turner, 1991. 450 p.: bibl., 239 ill. (some col.), index, map.

Volume explores parish churches in north-central Mexico. Pt. 1 addresses single and triple nave churches, their architects, and the sculptural decoration of the façades. Pt. 2

discusses the history and structure of nine churches with each chapter covering one church. Final section contains photographs of excellent quality.

105 Bargellini, Clara *et al.* Homenaje a Federico Sescosse: un hombre, un destino y un lugar. Zacatecas, Mexico: Gobierno del Estado de Zacatecas, 1990. 140 p., 46 p. of plates: bibl., ill. (some col.)

Volume is a tribute to Federico Sescosse and his work of restoring the colonial monuments of Zacatecas. Pt. 1 surveys his life and work, while Pt. 2 consists of nine essays about various aspects of Mexican colonial art. The essays address such topics as the depiction in paintings of costumes worn by St. Michael the Archangel, and the iconography of a Baroque portal of the sanctuary of Guadalupe in Zacatecas.

106 Bérchez, Joaquín. Arquitectura mexicana de los siglos XVII y XVIII. Presentación de René Taylor. México: Grupo Azabache, 1992. 290 p.: bibl., ill. (some col.). (Arte novohispano; 3)

Superb color plates of monuments of Mexican architecture from the Baroque to the neoclassical period. Excellent analysis of building façades, both ecclesiastical and civil, is enhanced by relevant discussions concerning interior ornamentation. Photographs that show details of decorative elements are particularly impressive.

107 Burke, Marcus B. Pintura y escultura en Nueva España: el barroco. Presentación de Virginia Armella de Aspe. México: Grupo Azabache, 1992. 196 p.: bibl., col. ill. (Arte novohispano; 5)

Comprehensive study of painting and sculpture in New Spain from 1640-1790 presents an array of superb color plates. Cogent discussions about stylistic sources provide an excellent foundation for author's examination of individual masters who flourished during the Baroque epoch.

108 Cómez Ramos, Rafael. Arquitectura y feudalismo en México: los comienzos del arte novohispano en el siglo XVI. México: Univ. Nacional Autónoma de México, 1989. 183 p.: bibl., ill. (Cuadernos de historia del arte; 47)

Compact volume explores medieval Castilian legacy of images and ideas in 16th-century architecture of New Spain, with particular focus on symbolism of structure, both palatine and ecclesiastic. Excellent notes, bibliography, b/w photographs, and elevation drawings are of scholarly interest.

109 Convento de San Nicolás Tolentino de Actopan, Hidalgo. Coordinación y fotografía de José Manuel Rivero Torres. Textos de Juan Manuel Menes Llaguno. Pachuca de Soto, Mexico: Coordinación de Turismo, Cultura y Recreación, 1987. 53 p.: bibl., col. ill.

The 16th-century Convento de San Nicolás Tolentino is especially significant for its open chapel and for the murals which decorate the interior walls of the *Sala de Profundis* and the staircase. Book provides history and descriptions of the structure as well as vivid color photographs.

110 Los conventos del siglo XVI en el Estado de Hidalgo. Pachuca, Mexico: Gobierno del Estado de Hidalgo, Secretaría de Turismo, Cultura y Recreación, 1987? 267 p.: bibl., ill. (some col.)

Architectural study is accompanied by truly outstanding color photographs. Each viceregal edifice is introduced by a brief discussion of its history and distinguishing qualities. One of the most handsome texts to appear on the subject of convent architecture in Hidalgo in recent years.

111 Everaert Dubernad, Luis. Tres grandes colegios de la Nueva España. Fotografía de Bob Schalkwijk. Edición de Mario de la Torre. México: Grupo Aluminio, 1990. 156 p.: bibl., ill. (some col.).

Volume treats three significant educational institutions in Mexico which originated during the viceregal period: the Jesuit Colegio de San Ildefonso; the Colegio de las Vizcaínas; and the Palacio de Minería. Color photographs include colonial patios, staircases, libraries, and vestibules, as well as spectacular views of commissioned murals by José Clemente Orozco, Diego Rivera, Fernando Leal, and Jean Charlot. Opens with a poem by Octavio Paz ("Nocturno de San Ildefonso," 1940).

112 Fachadas de México. México?: INFONAVIT, 1989. 191 p.: col. ill.

Picture book contains predominately color plates illustrating palatine architecture of the precolumbian period, viceregal houses and post-independence residences.

113 Fernández, Miguel Angel. El vidrio en México. México: Centro de Arte Vitro, 1990. 279 p.: bibl., ill. (some col.).

Well-illustrated study of the history of glass from the colonial period to the 20th century. Volume covers a range of subjects: viceregal windows; inlaid furniture and mirrors; ecclesiastical decoration; paintings on glass; ornamental and utilitarian vessels; dynasties of artisans. Includes an especially interesting analysis of glass as represented in 18th-century still life and genre works depicting the diverse castes. Invaluable catalog of specialists in glass (1553–1909) is presented as an appendix.

114 Fuentes Aguirre, Jorge. La Catedral de Santiago de Saltillo: una fé transformada en monumento. Fotografía de Enrique Salazar e Híjar. Saltillo, Mexico: Amigos del Patrimonio Cultural de Saltillo, 1991. 175 p.: bibl., ill. (chiefly col.).

Volume studies the magnificant cathedral of Santiago de Saltillo in Nueva Vizcaya province. Begun in 1745 and dedicated in 1800 to St. James the Elder (Santiago el Mayor), this church has dramatic portals characterized by Solomonic columns and *estípites*. The interior is distinguished by an exquisite "Altarpiece of St. Joseph" with polychromed statues and a large painting of "The Two Trinities" by José de Alcíbar. A "Holy Family with Sts. Joachim and Ana," also by Alcíbar, and a "Virgin of Carmen" attributed to Miguel Cabrera, are among the church's finest treasures.

115 García López, Ricardo. La obra franciscana en San Luis Potosí: aspecto histórico y patrimonio cultural. San Luis Potosí, Mexico: Univ. Autónoma de San Luis Potosí, 1986. 87 p., 46 leaves of plates: bibl., ill.

Study of Franciscan evangelization and art, accompanied by b/w photographs, complements major volumes by Francisco de la Maza (item **124**) and Rafael Morales Bocardo. Text presents information about sculpture in the Convent of San Luis and paintings ascribed to Antonio de Torres (sacristy and choir, 1719–21), Francisco Martínez, and Miguel Cabrera.

116 González Galván, Manuel. Arte virreinal en Michoacán. Fotografías de Judith Hancock. Introducción de Elisa Vargas

Lugo de Bosch. México: Frente de Afirmación Hispanista, 1978. 300 p.: bibl., ill.

Features excellent b/w photographs by Judith Hancock Sandoval, each accompanied by a brief descriptive paragraph. Book is divided into sections which consider the following aspects of colonial art and architecture in Michoacán: sculpted crucifixes; crosses; and baptismal fonts; Plateresque and Baroque styles of architecture; decorated ceilings; and colonial monuments in Morelia and Pátzcuaro.

117 Guía de edificios antiguos de Guadalajara. Edición de Ramón Mata Torres. Fotografía de Víctor Arauz. Mexico: Litográfica Sally, 1988. 70 p.: ill.

B/w photographs of religious and civil edifices built in Guadalajara during the colonial period and the 19th century. On the page facing each photograph, author includes a brief history of the architectural monument.

118 Gutiérrez Zamora, Angel Camiro. La imagen histórica de la Virgen de Guadalupe. México: Editorial Diana, 1990. 196 p.: bibl., ill. (some col.).

Study of miraculous image of the Virgin of Guadalupe uses results of infrared photography to argue that the original *tilma* of Juan Diego has been altered by overpainting. Author also investigates pigments preserved on the image.

119 Historia del arte mexicano. v. 5–8, Arte colonial. 2a ed. México: SEP; Salvat, 1986. 4 v.: bibl., ill. (some col.).

These four volumes each contain scholarly essays by prominent authorities on Mexican colonial art history as well as numerous color plates. Vol. 5 focuses on colonial architecture: patronage by monastic orders (Franciscan, Dominican, Augustinian, Carmelite); the heritage of precolumbian Mexico; and urbanization of viceregal cities. Vol. 6 centers on evolution of Mexican architecture from Baroque period to the 18th century, examining: the cathedrals; convents of New Spain; the genesis of the Baroque; variations in religious architecture in Mexico, Hidalgo, and Guerrero; 17th-18th century architecture in Puebla, Tlaxcala, and Veracruz; Baroque structures in Chihuahua, Nuevo León, Coahuila, Zacatecas, Durango, and San Luis Potosí; and Baroque churches in the

Southeast. Vol. 7 examines both architecture and painting in New Spain from the 16th-17th centuries: Baroque architecture in Querétaro, Guanajuato, and Aguascalientes; viceregal buildings in Michoacán, Jalisco, Nayarit, Sinaloa, and Colima; the Baroque in Argamasa; Jesuit missions in Sonora and Baja California; civil architecture in New Spain; haciendas; public works; viceregal mural painting; Mannerist painting; and Baroque painting ca. 1650. Vol. 8 focuses on painting, sculpture, and the decorative arts in New Spain, including: 18th-century painting; portraiture; 16th-17th century sculpture and altarpieces; the fine arts (silver, jewelry, featherwork, furniture); industrial arts (ceramics, iron, crystal, lacquer, textiles); colonial engravings; and parish churches.

120 Imágenes guadalupanas, cuatro siglos: noviembre 1987-marzo 1988. México: Centro Cultural/Arte Contemporáneo, 1987. 379 p.: bibl., ill. (some col.).

Abundantly-illustrated catalog explores iconography of the Virgin of Guadalupe in Mexican art from the 16th-20th centuries. Includes representations in painting, engraving, *enconchados*, sculpture, jewelry, photography, and other media.

121 López Guzmán, Rafael J.; Lazaro Gila Medina; Ignacio Henares Cuéllar; and Guillermo Tovar de Teresa. Arquitectura y carpintería mudéjar en Nueva España. Presentación de Sergio Zaldívar Guerra. México: Grupo Azabache, 1992. 190 p.: bibl., ill. (some col.). (Arte novohispano; 7)

Vibrantly-illustrated text contains important information regarding Moorish design in Mexican colonial architecture. Investigation of carved wooden ceilings includes material about urbanization, organization of carpentry guilds, the concept of *mudéjar* in treatises, and the evolution of *artesonado* from the Renaissance to the early Baroque.

122 Mangino Tazzer, Alejandro. La restauración arquitectónica: retrospectiva histórica en México. 2. ed. México: Editorial Trillas, 1991. 276 p.: bibl., ill., index.

Pt. 1 concerns theory of preserving monuments of Mexico from the precolumbian epoch to the 20th century. Pt. 2 discusses international conservation documents and legal matters involved in the restoration of monuments under the national patrimony. Pt. 3 presents a technical discussion of the criteria and processes for restoration.

123 Martínez del Río de Redo, Marita. El retrato civil en la Nueva España: Museo de San Carlos, octubre 1991-enero 1992. México: Museo de San Carlos, 1992. 73 p.: bibl., col. ill.

Exhaustive exhibition catalog examines secular art in New Spain from the 16th-18th centuries. Color illustrations and detailed entries serve to amplify knowledge about formal portraiture as it evolved during the viceregal period. Most paintings pertain to the upper class, and collectively, they elucidate aspects of pre-independence society in a manner similar to the genre series of *Castas*. While the ultimate sources for these splendid portraits may be found in Hapsburg and Bourbon palatine art, sitters are portrayed in fashionable finery that has a distinctively Mexican opulence.

Matos Moctezuma, Eduardo. La plaza en el México antiguo. See *HLAS 53:203.*

124 Maza, Francisco de la. Arquitectura de los coros de monjas en Puebla. Selección y prólogo de Mercedes Meade de Angulo. Puebla, Mexico: Gobierno del Estado de Puebla; México: Instituto de Investigaciones Estéticas, UNAM, 1990. 104 p.: bibl., ill.

For communities of cloistered nuns in the Viceroyalty of New Spain, the choir was the center of prayer life within the convent. Author discusses the lives of cloistered nuns in colonial Mexico, and then proceeds to investigate the history and decoration of choirs in 11 convents. Although the photographs are tinted with purple, they reveal that the choirs remain adorned with wondrous treasures of colonial art.

125 Mazín, Oscar; Herón Pérez Martínez; and Elena I. Estrada de Gerlero. La Catedral de Morelia. Coordinación de Nelly Sigaut. Introducción de Clara Bargellini. Fotografía de Vicente Guijosa. Zamora, Mexico: Colegio de Michoacán; Morelia: Gobierno del Estado de Michoacán, 1991. 439 p.: bibl., ill. (some col.), index.

Comprehensive study of the architecture and decoration over several centuries of the illustrious Cathedral of Valladolid in Michoacán. In 1740, the Sevillian Gerónimo de Balbas served as the major architect of the project. His Borromini-style Baroque façade totally changed the complexion of the old Cathedral of Morelia (ca. 1585). Several talented builders, painters, and craftsmen completed the structure. Well over half this text reproduces significant historical records pertaining to the new Cathedral's erection and ornamentation.

126 México colonial. Oviedo, Spain: Caja de Ahorros de Asturias, 1990. 147 p.: bibl., ill. (some col.), maps. (Dos culturas '92)

Exceptional volume on viceregal art from the Museo de América, presented by the Caja de Ahorros de Asturias, is a reprint of a 1989 exhibition catalog. Contains well-documented essays by Spanish scholars.

127 Mogilner, Mark. Edificaciones del Banco Nacional de México: seis virreinales y una contemporánea. Fotografía de Mark Mogilner. México: Fomento Cultural Banamex, 1988. 191 p.: ill. (some col.).

Vibrantly illustrated plans and sectional drawings of secular palaces of the viceregal era, including Mexico City residences that belonged to the Marquis of Jaral, the Counts of San Mateo de Valparaíso, and Agustín de Iturbide. Other buildings in the text include: the House of the Count of Valle de Suchil (Durango, Durango); the House of La Canal (San Miguel de Allende, Guanajuato); the House of Diezmo (Morelia, Michoacán); and the House of Francisco de Montejo (Mérida, Yucatán).

128 Montejano y Aguiñaga, Rafael. Santa María de Guadalupe en San Luis Potosí: su culto, su santuario, su calzada y sus santuarios. México: Ediciones Paulinas, 1982. 481 p.: bibl., ill.

Exhaustive study traces history of the Santa María de Guadalupe sanctuary from its origin in the 17th century to the 20th century. Study is well-documented with extracts from historical texts and inventories, but the few b/w photographs are of poor quality.

129 Monterrosa Prado, Mariano and Leticia Talavera. La pintura mural de los conventos franciscanos en Puebla: estudio iconográfico. Mexico: Gobierno del Estado de Puebla, 1990. 1 v.: bibl., ill.

Murals of religious themes and decorative motifs such as grotesqueries, garlands, and illusionistic architectural frames adorned the interiors of 16th century Franciscan monasteries in Puebla. This iconographic study of the murals reproduces drawings of entire compositions and of minute details, and provides explanations of various subjects and motifs.

130 Mora, María Elvira. La plástica en el paso de la colonia al México independiente. Colaboración de María Elvira Mora y Clara Inés Ramírez. México: Comisión Nacional para las Celebraciones del 175 Aniversario de la Independencia Nacional y 75 Aniversario de la Revolución Mexicana, 1985. 63 p.: bibl., ill. (Serie de cuadernos conmemorativos; 57)

Study of Mexican art and architecture from end of 18th to early 19th century consists of brief chapters illustrated with b/w photographs. Chapters cover the Academy of San Carlos, neoclassical architecture, painting, sculpture, and engraving.

131 Mullen, Robert James. La arquitectura y la escultura de Oaxaca, 1530s-1980s. Traducción de Juan I. Bustamante. México?: Tule; Codex, 1992. 2 v.: bibl. index.

Important investigation of colonial churches, monasteries, and civil architecture in Oaxaca is well documented and very informative. (Abbridged English ed. will be published in 1995 by Arizona State University.) Vol. 1 examines architecture in city of Oaxaca, including: introduction and lengthy discussion of the Cathedral (1544–1752); analysis of Dominican, Jesuit, Augustinian, and Franciscan monasteries; parish churches; and civil architecture. Vol. 2 covers the surrounding towns.

Muriel, Josefina. Las instituciones de mujeres: raíz de esplendor arquitectónico en la antigua ciudad de Santiago de Querétaro. See item **1252.**

132 Museo Colonial del Carmen (México). Catálogo de pintura del Museo de El Carmen. México: PROBURSA, 1987. 135 p.: bibl., ill. (some col.).

Catalog includes photographs and brief iconographic explanation of Mexican colonial paintings housed in the museum, originally a Discalced Carmelite monastery. Many of the paintings portray subjects associated with the Carmelite order. There are outstanding representations of the Virgen of Carmen, of Santa Teresa de Jesús (the 16th-century foundress of the Carmelite reform), and of Teresa's close friend and co-reformer, San Juan de la Cruz.

133 Navarrete, Carlos. La fuente colonial de Chiapa de Corzo: encuentro de historias. Chiapas, Mexico: Gobierno del Estado, 1991. 81 p.: bibl., ill. (some col.), map. (Chiapas eterno)

Called Chiapa de Indios during the colonial era, this small town in the region of Chiapas has very original fountains. The most important basin is "La Pilona," erected in 1562 by Fray Rodrigo de León. The fountain in the form of a *mudéjar* chapel with eight archs supporting the cupola betrays influences from gothic Castile. This well documented study includes an excellent bibliography.

134 Obras maestras del arte colonial: exposición homenaje a Manuel Toussaint, 1890–1990; catálogo. México: Instituto de Investigaciones Estéticas; Museo Nacional de Arte, 1990. 158 p.: bibl., ill. (some col.).

Catalog of an exhibition of Mexican colonial art held in honor of Toussaint, a pioneering scholar in this field. Work includes photographs and iconographic explanations of 61 paintings, sculptures, and decorative objects which reveal the grandeur of Mexican viceregal art. Essay by Elisa Vargas Lugo de Bosch surveys Toussaint's scholarly investigations.

135 El Palacio de Minería. 4. ed. México: Sociedad de Ex-alumnos de la Facultad de Ingeniería, UNAM, 1988. 231 p.: bibl., ill. (some col., some folded).

Monograph devoted to a project designed by Mantel Tolsa and built between 1797–1813 in Mexico City. First study to detail importance of this historic landmark includes texts written by different specialists. [B. Rodríguez]

136 Los palacios de la Nueva España, sus tesoros interiores: Museo de Monterrey, noviembre 1990-marzo 1991, Museo Franz Mayer, abril 1991-junio 1991. México: Ediciones e Impresiones Gant, 1990. 129 p.: bibl., ill. (some col.).

Well-illustrated exhibition catalog explores interior decoration of Mexican viceregal palaces. Concentrates on furniture, sculpture, painting, silver, porcelain (most was imported to Mexico from Asia), and other decorative objects. Final section includes essays on *enconchados* (panels inlaid with mosaics of shells), feather paintings, and Philippine ivory carvings imported to New Spain.

137 Pérez Salazar, Francisco. El grabado en la ciudad de Puebla de los Angeles. Ed. facsímilar. Puebla, Mexico: Gobierno del Estado de Puebla, 1990. 68 p.: ill.

First published in 1933, Pérez Salazar's study surveys engravings produced in Puebla de Los Angeles from the 17th-19th centuries. Subjects of the engravings include representations of heraldic devices, depictions of the funerary monuments erected after the death of a monarch, and portrayals of the Virgin and single figures of saints.

138 Pintura mexicana y española de los siglos XVI al XVIII. Madrid: Sociedad Estatal Quinto Centenario, 1991. 91 p.: ill. (chiefly col.).

Catalog for exhibition held at the Palacio Nacional de Exposiciones (Madrid), this volume is magnificently illustrated with color plates and an essay each on Mexican Painting (Meade) and Spanish Painting (Pérez Sánchez). Catalog entries and brief biographies for identified artists would have enhanced the text.

139 Prado Núñez, Ricardo and **Rafael Barquero Díaz Barriga.** Taxco virreinal y sus capillas. Chilpancingo, Mexico: Instituto Guerrerense de Cultura, 1991. 110 p.: bibl., ill. (some col.).

Volume examines chapels erected in the colonial city of Taxco, Guerrero, during the viceregal period. Book complements monumental studies by Manuel Toussaint such as *Tasco: su historia, sus monumentos . . .* (México, 1932), and contains good descriptions of each edifice's history and architectural style, color plates of the façades, and useful plans.

140 La Quinta Casa de Correos: crónica del servicio postal en México. México: Secretaría de Comunicaciones y Transporte, Servicio Postal Mexicano, 1990. 179 p.: bibl., ill. (some col.).

This richly illustrated volume surveys the construction and architectural decoration of the Quinta Casa de Correos, inaugurated on Feb. 17, 1907. The book also examines the history of Mexico's postal system from precolumbian times through the 20th century.

141 Ramírez de Alba, Horacio. La construcción en el Estado de México: un estudio técnico con referencia histórica. Zinacantepec, Mexico: El Colegio Mexiquense; Toluca: Gobierno del Estado de México, 1991. 240 p.: bibl., ill.

Highly technical study examines different facets of construction in Mexico from precolumbian times to the 20th century. Volume presents drawings of buildings and plans of pyramids, bridges, aqueducts, towers, arched patios, and building façades in effort to analyze their systems of structural support.

142 Ramírez Montes, Guillermina. Pedro de Rojas y su taller de escultura en Querétaro. Querétaro, México: Dirección de Patrimonio Cultural, Secretaría de Cultura y Bienestar Social del Gobierno del Estado de Querétaro, 1988. 113 p.: bibl., ill. (some col.). (Documentos de Querétaro; 7)

Publication investigates the art and impact of Pedro de Rojas (1699–1773), and presents important documentary information. Larger photographs would have been desirable for the significant retables discussed: "Nuestra Señora del Sagrario" (La Parroquia de Cadereyta, Querétaro); "St. Anne" (Church of San Agustín Salamanca, Guanajuato); "St. Joseph" (Church of Santa Rosa de Viterbo, Querétaro); and "St. Rose of Lima" (Church of St. Clare, Quéretaro).

143 Rangel, Magdalena E. de. La Casa de los Azulejos: reseña histórica del Palacio de los Condes del Valle de Orizaba. Fotografías de Sebastián Saldívar. México: San Angel Ediciones, 1986. 131 p., 10 p. of plates: bibl., ill. (some col.).

Historical survey of the House of Tiles in Mexico City, a major monument of viceregal architecture. Volume includes color photographs of the interior and exterior, as well as photographic details of the tiles which adorn the façade.

144 Rangel, Magdalena E. de. El Palacio de los Condes de Heras Soto: sede del Centro Histórico de la Ciudad de México. México: Depto. del Distrito Federal, 1984. 194 p., 22 p. of plates (some folded): bibl., ill. (some col.). (Col. Distrito Federal; 5)

Exhaustive study of one of the most beautiful examples of Mexican Baroque architecture, whose restoration began in 1978. [B. Rodríguez]

145 Reyes Valerio, Constantino. El pintor de conventos: los murales del siglo XVI en la Nueva España. México: Instituto Nacional de Antropología e Historia, 1989. 187 p.: bibl., ill. (Col. científica; 173. Serie Historia)

Thorough examination of artists who painted murals that adorn the walls of 16th-century monasteries in Mexico. Author focuses on contributions of indigenous artists in the creation of the murals, and includes how they were converted to Christianity and taught to paint Christian subjects.

146 Robles García, Nelly M.; **Marcelo Leonardo Magadán;** and **Alfredo Moreira Quirós.** Reconstrucción colonial en Mitla, Oaxaca. México: Escuela Nacional de Conservación, Restauración y Museografía, Instituto Nacional de Antropología e Historia, 1987. 78 p.: bibl., ill. (Cuaderno de trabajo; 1)

Author uses archaeological and literary evidence in attempt to reconstruct appearance of colonial structures in Mitla. Volume is illustrated with photographs and plans and surveys the results of research. Includes discussion of the method of investigation.

147 Salazar de Garza, Nuria. La capilla del Santo Cristo de Burgos en el ex-Convento de San Francisco. México: Instituto Nacional de Antropología e Historia, Secretaría General de Desarrollo Social, Depto. del Distrito Federal, 1990. 143 p. (Col. Divulgación)

Book focuses on history and decoration of the Chapel of Santo Cristo de Burgos in the former Convent of St. Francis in Mexico City. Author discusses retables placed in the chapel during the 18th century, and includes selection of historical documents pertaining to the foundation and decoration of the chapel.

148 San Agustín de Acolman. México: Teléfonos de México, 1990. 134 p.: ill. (some col.)

Exquisitely illustrated study of the Augustinian monastery at Acolman, one of the most important viceregal structures, built under the auspices of Fray Francisco de la Cruz and six Augustinian friars who arrived at San Juan de Ulúa on May 26, 1533. After a critical discussion of the arrival of the order to New Spain, volume comprehensively investigates the Monastery of San Agustín de Acolman, from the architecture of the cloisters to the unique decoration of the murals and altarpieces in the Church.

149 Santín, Rosalía and **Sergio Nava Rodríguez Gil.** El ex-Convento del Carmen de Morelia: hoy Instituto Michoacano de Cultura. Morelia, Mexico: Instituto Michoacano de Cultura, Patrimonio Artístico y Cultural, 1988. 61 p.: bibl., ill.

Brief study focuses on history of the Carmelites in Valladolid (Morelia), and includes useful information about Fray Juan de la Madre de Dios' arrival in New Spain (1585) with 11 Carmelite monks. Pivitol role of the cofradia dedicated to Our Lady of Carmen is discussed with respect to the colonial convent, which dates about 1619–1735. Several views of the structure are captured in very good b/w photographs.

150 Sartor, Mario. Arquitectura y urbanismo en Nueva España, siglo XVI. Presentación de Carlos Chanfón Olmos. México: Grupo Azabache, 1992. 286 p.: bibl., ill. (some col.). (Arte novohispano; 2)

Well-documented volume discusses: urbanization based on utopian ideals of the city and society; civil structures; religious edifices; and stylistic analysis of architectural decoration. Includes sumptuous illustrations with color plates and floor plans.

151 Sebastián, Santiago. Iconografía e iconología del arte novohispano. Presentación de José Pascual Buxó. México: Grupo Azabache, 1992. 179 p.: bibl., col. ill., map. (Arte novohispano; 6)

Book explores origins of imagery in New Spain, including topics such as: the allegorical perception of the Church; the Virgin Mary and Christ; hagiography of religious orders; images of death; humanist iconography, such as the liberal arts; emblems; and the representation of Indians in New Spain and Europe. A fascinating study, accompanied by color plates.

152 Secretos de maques, y charoles, y colores &. Traducido del francés al castellano por Francisco Vicente Orellana, año 1755. México: Dirección de Restauración del Patrimonio Cultural, INAH-SEP, 1980. 94 p.: bibl., ill.

Reproduction of manuscript dated 1755 discussing technical aspects of painting such as preparation and application of varnishes and lacquers. Little is known about its provenance or the original author.

153 Sentíes R., Horacio. La Villa de Guadalupe: historia, estampas y leyendas. Colaboración fotográfica especial de Armando Salas Portugal. México: Ciudad de México Librería y Editora, 1992. 308 p.: bibl., ill. (some col.), map.

Volume discusses history and monuments of Guadalupe and contains excellent photographs of churches and civil architecture. In the section on the Museo Guadalupano, there are photographs of paintings by such major masters as Miguel Cabrera, Baltasar de Echave Ibia, and Juan Correa, as well as brief biographies of artists whose works are in the museum.

154 Sescosse, Federico. Las fuentes perdidas. Zacatecas, Mexico: Sociedad de Amigos de Zacatecas, 1991. 58 p.: bibl., ill.

Informative study examines civic architecture of Zacatecas, specifically the important fountains that once stood in its plazas. Contains useful photographs and engravings.

155 Sotomayor, Arturo. La ciudad antigua de México: siglos XVI-XX. Realización y diseño de Beatrice Trueblood. México: Bancomer, 1990. 227 p.: bibl., ill., index, (some col.), maps.

Lavishly illustrated volume opens with maps of Mexico City that can be superimposed to achieve a perception of urbanization from the 16th-20th centuries. Provides useful historical chronology from 1519–1897. Subsequent chapters focus on evolution of the cityscape and societal changes from the Spanish conquest to the Victorian age.

156 Taylor, René et al. Santa Prisca restaurada. Introducción de Javier Wimer. Chilpancingo, Mexico: Gobierno Constitucional del Estado de Guerrero, 1990. 255 p.: bibl., ill. (some col.), index. (Biblioteca del sur)

Informative, lavishly-illustrated volume builds on the monumental study by Elisa Vargas Lugo (see *HLAS 38:328*). Eight essays provide a comprehensive, well-documented analysis of the 18th-century Church of San Sebastián and Santa Prisca (Taxco). Text with numerous color plates focuses on salient aspects of Baroque decoration at Santa Prisca and is a significant contribution to Mexican colonial art history.

157 Tepeapulco. Dirección de Ricardo García Sainz. México: Diesel Nacional, S.A. 1992. 196 p.: bibl., col. ill., maps.

Author discusses colonial churches and monasteries in the Tepeapulco region, northeast of Tenochtitlán, from the Spanish conquest to the 20th century. The study covers architectural styles and ornamentation and includes color plates with details taken from Aztec codices.

158 Tovar de Teresa, Guillermo. Bibliografía novohispana de arte. v. 1, Impresos mexicanos relativos al arte de los siglos XVI y XVII. v. 2, Impresos mexicanos relativos al arte del siglo XVIII. Prólogo de José Pascual Buxó. México: Fondo de Cultura Económica, 1988. 2 v.: ill. (Biblioteca americana)

These two volumes form a catalog of books pertaining to art printed in Mexico during the colonial period. Author reproduces frontispiece of each book, and then presents a description of its contents, as well as an explanation of portions which deal with art. In many cases, lengthy passages from original text are included. Valuable tool for scholars of Mexican colonial art.

159 Tovar de Teresa, Guillermo and **Jaime Ortiz Lajous.** Catedral de México, Retablo de los Reyes: historia y restauración. México: Secretaría de Desarrollo Urbano y Ecología, 1985. 109 p.: bibl., ill.

Superb study of the "Retable of the Kings," the altarpiece of the Cathedral of Mexico created by Gerónimo de Balbas. Completed by 1724, the retable and its paintings by Juan Rodríguez Juárez have been recently restored by the Secretaría del Patrimonio Nacional. Building on prior investigations by Manuel Toussaint and Justino Fernández, text includes new documents from the "Enrique Cervantes" collection. Precise floor plans, iconographical scheme of the paintings, excellent plates, and analysis of the restoration are admirable features of the book.

160 Tovar de Teresa, Guillermo. Pintura y escultura en Nueva España, 1557–1640. Presentación de Jorge Alberto Manrique. México: Grupo Azabache, 1992. 256 p.: bibl., ill. (some col.). (Arte novohispano; 4)

Monumental analysis of painting and

sculpture in New Spain accompanied by stunning color plates. Among recent studies, this well-documented book most succinctly explains the assimilation of Spanish images and ideas during the 16th century and the artistic evolution of early Mexican Baroque style.

161 **Tovar de Teresa, Guillermo; Miguel León Portilla;** and **Silvio Zavala.** La utopía mexicana del siglo XVI: lo bello, lo verdadero y lo bueno. México: Grupo Azabache, 1992. 108 p.: bibl., ill. (some col.), maps. (Arte novohispano; 1)

Study of early decades of viceregal Mexico contains excellent color plates and an introduction by Octavio Paz. Describes Viceroy de Mendoza's utopian vision for building New Spain's capital city, as well as the philosophical impact of learned authorities such as Fray Juan de Zumárraga, the scholar of Erasmus, and Vasco de Quiroga, an admirer of St. Thomas More.

162 **Tres siglos de pintura religiosa en San Luis Potosí.** San Luis Potosí, Mexico: Pro San Luis Monumental, 1991. 306 p.: bibl., col. ill.

Richly illustrated volume investigates paintings of 17th-19th centuries now housed in various collections in San Luis Potosí. Volume describes paintings in institutions such as the Cathedral, the Monastery of San Francisco, the Monastery of the Discalced Carmelites, and the Casa de la Cultura.

163 **Vargas Lugo de Bosch, Elisa** and **José Guadalupe Victoria.** Un edificio que canta: San Agustín de Querétaro. Querétaro, Mexico: Ediciones del Gobierno del Estado de Querétaro, 1989. 96 p.: bibl., ill. (Documentos de Querétaro; 14)

Study of 18th-century monastery of St. Augustine in Querétaro is divided into two sections. The first surveys the monastery's history in a series of brief chapters, while the second investigates architecture and sculptural decoration of the church and cloister and proposes an iconographic interpretation of the subjects represented.

164 **Velázquez Chávez, Agustín.** La pintura colonial en Hidalgo en tres siglos de pintura colonial mexicana: con nuevos datos sobre pinturas en los estados de Aguascalientes, Durango, Guanajuato, Hidalgo, Jalisco,

México, Michoacán, Morelos, Nayarit, Oaxaca, Puebla, Querétaro, San Luis Potosí, Sonora, Tlaxcala, Zacatecas y la Ciudad de México. Pachuca de Soto, Mexico: Gobierno del Estado de Hidalgo, Coordinación de Turismo, Cultura y Recreación, 1986. 638 p.: bibl., ill. (some col.).

This valuable resource for study of art in viceregal Mexico consists of 478 photographs, many of them in color, of Mexican colonial paintings ranging from 16th-century murals in Franciscan and Augustinian monasteries to 18th-century secular portraits. Author also includes biographies of Mexican colonial artists and lists locations of their known works.

165 **Victoria, José Guadalupe** *et al.* Estudios acerca del arte novohispano: homenaje a Elisa Vargas Lugo. México: Univ. Nacional Autónoma de México, Coordinación de Humanidades, 1983. 188 p.: bibl., ill., maps.

This volume's 18 essays on various aspects of art in the Viceroyalty of New Spain are a tribute to the distinguished and prolific scholar of Mexican colonial art, Elisa Vargas Lugo. Most deal with architecture, but some essays address topics such as the representation of the Holy Family, with Joaquín and Anna, in a painting in the Cathedral of Mexico City and sculpture production in 16th-century Mexico.

166 **Villegas, Víctor Manuel** *et al.* Valenciana y el churrigueresco. Guanajuato, Mexico: Univ. de Guanajuato, 1990. 204 p.: bibl., facsims., ill. (some col.), indexes.

Under the patronage of Don Antonio Obregón y Alcocer, Viscount of La Mina and Count of Valenciana, the Church of San Cayetano was built in the Churrigueresque style (1765-88). This oversize text presents sectional drawings, plans, and a discussion about artists of Guanajuato who worked on the project. The iconography of interior decoration is deftly handled, as is the examination of elements constituting the Spanish Churrigueresque style.

167 **Wright, David** *et al.* Querétaro, ciudad barroca. Coordinación general de Juan Antonio Isla Estrada. Coordinación editorial de diseño y fotografías de José Manuel Rivero Torres. Prólogo de Carlos Arvizu García. Querétaro, Mexico: Dirección de Patrimonio Cultural, Secretaría de Cultura y Bienestar Social, Gobicrno dcl Estado dc Querétaro, 1988. 236 p.: bibl., ill. (some col.).

Study focuses on art and architecture created in Querétaro during the 17th-18th centuries. First essay provides historical context by exploring daily life in Querétaro during the Baroque era. Civil and religious architecture are each investigated in illustrated essays, and Rogelio Ruiz Gomar has contributed a survey of the Baroque paintings which adorn the city's buildings. Of particular interest is the essay on retables, which includes fascinating photographic details of the canvases that were inserted into these elaborate altarpieces.

168 Yanez Díaz, Gonzalo. Espacios urbanos del siglo XVI en la región Puebla Tlaxcala. Puebla, Mexico: Gobierno del Estado de Puebla, Univ. Autónoma de Puebla: Comisión Puebla V Centenario, 1991. 497 p.: bibl., ill., maps. (Col. V centenario)

Comprehensive investigation of colonial urbanization in Puebla-Tlaxcala focuses on ancient Mesoamerican, medieval Spanish, and classical Renaissance designs as the primary sources for spatial integration of city plazas with churches, convents, palaces, and other civic structures. Author's dissection of the complex manner in which town planning evolved to meet demands of colonial society will be of considerable assistance to scholars. Includes extensive notes, a complete bibliography, and good illustrations.

CENTRAL AMERICA
AND THE CARIBBEAN

169 Binney, Marcus; John Harris; and Kit Martin. Jamaica's heritage: an untapped resource; a preservation proposal. Edited by Marguerite Curtin. Kingston: Mill Press; Tourism Action Plan, Ltd.; Jamaica National Heritage Trust, 1991. 88 p.: ill. (some col.), maps.

Volume addresses traditionally neglected topic of Jamaica's historical areas of Port Royal, Falmouth, Spanish Town, New Seville, and Río Bueno, and its art and social customs. Text includes color illustrations and covers from Spanish settlement until the 20th century.

170 García de Benedictis, Ana Virginia and **Juan Rafael Quesada Camacho.** Centenario de la parroquia San Joaquín de Flores, 1888–1988. San José: Comisión Nacional de Conmemoraciones Históricas, 1990. 64 p.: ill., maps, photos.

Brief history of village of San Joaquín also reproduces texts of archival documents dating from the 19th-20th centuries which pertain to the region's development. Maps and plans are included as well as a section of b/w photographs, notably images of the Church of San Joaquín de Flores.

171 Lara Roche, Carlos. San José en el arte colonial guatemalteco. Guatemala: Sociedad Centroamericana de Investigaciones y Divulgación de San José, 1989. 161 p.: bibl., ill. (some col.).

Brief, specific iconographical study of colonial statues and paintings in Guatemala. Contains information relevant to the veneration of St. Joseph, such as impact of Bethlemite order founded by Fray Pedro de San José de Betancourt.

172 Monteforte Toledo, Mario *et al.* Las formas y los días: el barroco en Guatemala. Madrid: Sociedad Estatal Quinto Centenario; Turner Libros, 1989. 249 p., 75 p. of plates: bibl., ill. (some col.), indexes. (Col. Encuentros: Serie Textos)

Authors provides historical context by exploring the structure of Guatemalan colonial society, and then investigate painting, sculpture, retables, and architecture produced in that region. There are some excellent color photographs, particularly of magnificent polychromed wooden sculpture which distinguished Guatemala as an important center of artistic production during the colonial period.

173 Peña, Dionicio de Jesús. La ciudad amurallada: Santo Domingo colonial. Santo Domingo: Editora Alfa y Omega, 1992. 30 p., 32 p. of plates: bibl., ill. (some col.), maps.

Volume examines colonial Santo Domingo through color plates of ecclesiastical and civic architecture, a black and white engraving of the old city surrounded by walls, and a plan that indicates key urban monuments. Although discussions of specific buildings are brief, they provide historical information about one of the most important colonial ports of the New World.

174 Pérez Montás, Eugenio. Carimos: monumentos y sitios del Gran Caribe = monuments and sites of the greater Caribbean. Traducción al inglés de Francisco Díaz Morales. Santo Domingo: Museo de las Casas Reales, 1989. 358 p.: ill. (some col.). (Casas Reales; 2. etapa, no. 20)

Volume consists of 33 articles that deal with history of architecture in the Caribbean and the conservation of monuments. Author treats topics such as housing traditions in Barbados and the legacy of Andrea Palladio in the Caribbean.

175 Pintura y escultura hispánica en Guatemala. Coordinación de J. Haroldo Rodas E. Guatemala: H. Rodas Estrada, 1992. 179 p.: bibl., ill., index.

Important reference book which should be consulted by specialists. Product of intense research about colonial artists working in Guatemala, book includes clear description of trajectory of such art from the se-

lection of material to the art market. [B. Rodríguez]

176 Trujillo Pardo, Carmen; Miriam Méndez-Plasencia; and Margarita Suárez García. Museo de Arte Colonial. La Habana: Editorial Letras Cubanas, 1985. 105 p.: chiefly ill.

Museum of Colonial Art catalog briefly describes the institution's history and its various rooms. Museum's collection of architectural elements, furniture, porcelain, and other decorative objects is illustrated in b/w photographs.

177 Velarde B., Oscar A. El arte religioso colonial en Panamá. Panamá: Instituto Nacional de Cultura, Dirección Nacional de Patrimonio Histórico, Proyecto de Desarrollo Cultural, PNUD, UNESCO, 1990. 98 p.: bibl., ill.

Considering dearth of material available about colonial art of Panama, this small book is worthy for its information about churches and religious art.

South America

HUMBERTO RODRIGUEZ-CAMILLONI, *Associate Professor and Director, Henry H. Wiss Center for Theory and History of Art and Architecture, College of Architecture and Urban Studies, Virginia Polytechnic Institute and State University*

THE EXTRAORDINARY STIMULUS PROVIDED by the celebration of the Quincentennial of the discovery of the Americas continues to be reflected in the quality and quantity of publications reviewed for this volume of *HLAS*. Any attempt at a bibliographical summary will inevitably do little justice to the many important contributions made by different scholars; thus only selected highlights can be presented here. In general, the high standard of scholarship noted for the previous biennium is maintained and it is most gratifying to observe that more and more studies guided by new methodological approaches are permitting a fuller understanding and greater appreciation of the rich Spanish American colonial cultural heritage.

Current research trends reveal a preference for thematic, iconographic, and comparative studies. The emphasis is therefore no longer on stylistic classification, but on a more serious investigation about the special distinctive qualities of colonial art and architecture. Notable examples of this approach are found in the excellent essays compiled in *Relaciones artísticas entre España y América* (item **92**) and in the exibition catalogs *Cambios: the spirit of transformation in Spanish colonial art* (item **89**) and *Temples of gold, crowns of silver: reflections of majesty in the Vicere-*

gal Americas (Washington: George Washington Univ., 1989; many of this catalog's individual articles are annotated separately below).

By far the largest number of titles deal with architecture, urbanism, and painting, even though there are some outstanding works on other subjects. The scope ranges from the encyclopedic multivolume, multiauthored *Historia urbana de Iberoamérica* (item **78**) and the *History of South American colonial art and architecture*, a general survey by Damián Bayón and Murillo Marx (item **77**), to the single-monument monograph such as Graziano Gasparini and Carlos F. Duarte's *Historia de la Catedral de Caracas* (item **196**). Histories of individual cities and their cultural heritage are well represented by *Potosí, patrimonio cultural de la humanidad* (item **232**) and Carlos Martínez's *Santafé: capital del Nuevo Reino de Granada* (item **201**).

The Spanish government has continued to sponsor a number of fine books emphasizing cross-cultural relations between the Old and New Worlds. In some cases, these have been associated with handsome exhibitions held both in Spain and America at one time or another under the auspices of the Comisión de Estudios Históricos de Obras Públicas y de Urbanismo (CEHOPU). Two noteworthy examples are *Puertos y fortificaciones en América y Filipinas* (item **91**), the well-illustrated catalog for the exhibition held in Madrid in 1985, and *La ciudad hispanoamericana: el sueño de un orden* (item **83**) which accompanied the 1989 exhibition at Madrid's Museo Español de Arte Contemporáneo, an exhibition which travelled to Washington to the OAS's Art Museum of the Americas in Oct. 1992.

In Latin America, banks and other private institutions have made possible the publication of many high quality books on art and architecture. Special mention should be made here of the deluxe series by El Sello Editorial in Bogotá, Colombia which will contribute to the dissemination of information on the artistic treasures of major Latin American cities during the Spanish colonial period. So far, *Tesoros de Tunja* (item **200**) and *Tesoros de Quito* (item **241**) have been released, but other volumes are expected to follow. Beautifully designed and illustrated with exquisite color photos (including some foldouts), these books are themselves truly works of art.

Several titles devoted to non-religious architecture are indicative of a new focus being placed on military and residential buildings. Gabriel Guarda's *Flandes indiano: las fortificaciones del Reino de Chile, 1541–1826* may be singled out as a definitive study on the subject (item **183**). The result of many years of archival research, it is a model of scholarly work lavishly illustrated with many full color reproductions of historic maps and drawings. On the other hand, Aurora Ruiz Mateos' *Arquitectura civil de la Orden de Santiago en Extremadura: la casa de la encomienda; su proyección en Hispanoamérica* (item **93**) focuses on the typology of the little-known *casa de encomienda* and presents a research methodology that should prove valuable for similar studies throughout Spanish America.

Luis Mebold Köhnenkamp's *Catálogo de pintura colonial en Chile* (item **187**) is a *catalogue raisonné* that sets a high standard for future publications on Spanish colonial painting while filling an important void in the literature on the subject. With painstaking care, the author discusses the colonial paintings housed in Santiago's convents, including their present state of conservation. Most important, perhaps, it presents a model research methodology and makes available for the first time a rich corpus of works virtually unknown to the scholarly community.

Escultura en el Perú (item **214**) is an exceptional book largely devoted to Spanish colonial sculpture in the cities of Lima, Trujillo, Cusco, and Arequipa. It is the most comprehensive study on the subject to date since Harold E. Wethey's pioneer work *Colonial architecture and sculpture in Peru* (Cambridge, 1949). Through authoritative texts and spectacular color plates, scholars now have the opportunity to appreciate the special qualities of this art in all its glory for the first time. A future volume will examine the development of colonial sculpture in other important centers, presumably including Cajamarca, Ayacucho and Huancavelica. As more inventories of colonial sculpture are completed in the different Latin American countries (items **190, 199,** and **223**), it is likely that more publications will address this topic in the future.

Titles devoted to the decorative arts deal primarily with silversmiths and their work. Among these is Carlos F. Duarte's *El arte de la platería en Venezuela* (item **195**), an exhaustive study on the subject. With a complete biographical catalog of silversmiths active in Caracas and other cities of Venezuela from 1567–1810, this book is an indispensable reference for future studies.

Recent symposia that need to be recorded here include the two sessions on "Iberian American Architecture from the 16th through the 18th Centuries" held at the Society of Architectural Historians meeting (*Albuquerque, N.M., April 1992*) and the International Colloquium of the History of Art (*17th, Zacatecas, Mexico, Sept. 1993*). While not restricted to Spanish American colonial topics, both of these meetings gathered groups of renowned scholars from around the world who presented a cross-section of the state of the art of current research in the field. The Zacatecas colloquium stressed the theme of "Comparative Visions: Art, History and Identity in the Americas," thus offering unique cross-cultural perspectives within the hemisphere. It is hoped that the proceedings from this important event will soon be published by the Univ. Nacional Autónoma de México's Instituto de Investigaciones Estéticas.

Finally, I should like to remember in a special way the names of a few distinguished colleagues and friends whose recent deaths have left significant voids in the field: Mario Chacón Torres (Bolivia, d. 1984); Jorge Bernales Ballesteros (Peru, d. 1991); Jesús Lámbarri Bracesco (Peru, d. 1991); and Jorge Hardoy (Argentina, d. 1993). Many of their valuable contributions have been reviewed in this and other volumes of *HLAS* and have been widely acclaimed by the international scholarly community. As a modest token of appreciation and gratitude, I dedicate this section to their memory.

CHILE, ARGENTINA, PARAGUAY, AND URUGUAY

178 El arte de las misiones jesuíticas: agosto-septiembre, año de MCMLXXXV. Catálogo de Claudia L. de Caamaño y Horacio L. Botalla. Buenos Aires: Municipalidad de la Ciudad de Buenos Aires, Secretaría de Cultura, 1985. 88 p.: maps.

Popular guide to 1985 exhibition held at the Museo Municipal de Arte Hispanoamericano "Isaac Fernández Blanco" in Buenos Aires. Main text consists of six separate studies by Juan Pedro Franze, Ramón Gutiérrez, Werner Hoffmann, Adolfo Luis Ribera, and Daisy Rípodas Ardanaz, who provide an overview of the historic importance of the Jesuit missions in Paraguay and Argentina during the 17th-18th centuries. Analysis and interpretation focuses on a selection of sites with extant architectural remains and examples of the high quality religious art produced there. A complete list of the architectural fragments, sculptures, paintings, and ornaments in the exhibition is included, but only four items are reproduced in b/w photographs.

179 Barbieri, Sergio and Iris Gori. La reedificación de la Iglesia de la Compañía como Matriz de Salta, 1791–1800. (*Invest. Ens.*, 39, enero/dic. 1989, p. 423–430)

Documentation from the Archivo del Arzobispado in Córdoba sheds new light on the reconstruction of the former Jesuit church in Salta from 1791–1800. The magnitude of the project can be appreciated by the work of painters Tomás Cabrera and Isidoro Paiva, master carpenters Francisco Salguero, Manuel Grande, and Francisco Bravo, and other artisans. The church functioned as Iglesia Matriz until its destruction by an earthquake in 1844.

180 Cruz de Amenabar, Isabel. Arte y sociedad en Chile, 1550–1650. Santiago: Ediciones Univ. Católica de Chile, 1986. 318 p.: bibl., ill. (some col.)

Social history of art of colonial Peru and Chile is based largely on the secondary sources listed in the abundant footnotes and extensive bibliography. Text is a bit disjointed and occasionaly reads like a catalog of different topics, but nonetheless contains a wealth of information useful for future studies. Author focuses on colonial painting and sculpture, and though there are only 24 illustrations, they include some important and little-known works of art of early colonial Chile. Text ends abruptly with a description of a portrait painting, but author intends to write a second volume.

181 Gallardo, Rodolfo; Alejandro Moyano Aliaga; and David Malik de Tchara. Las capillas de Córdoba. Buenos Aires: Academia Nacional de Bellas Artes, 1988. 114 p.: bibl., ill. (Estudios de arte argentino; 3)

Good survey of 14 selected rural churches of Córdoba prov. represents an important corpus of regional architecture dating from the 17th-18th centuries. Author presents each monument's history in chronological order, supported by documentation from the Archivo Histórico and the Archivo del Arzobispado in Córdoba. A section of b/w photographs and measured drawings of five of the churches follows the text.

182 Goulão, María José. Ourives portugueses na região do Rio de la Plata nos séculos XVII, XVIII e XIX. (in Simposio Hispano-Portugués de Historia del Arte, 5th, Valladolid, Spain, 1989. Actas. Coordinación de Juan José Martín González. Valladolid, Spain: Univ. de Valladolid, 1990, p. 127–137, photos)

Original research documents work of Portuguese silversmiths active in Argentina between the 17th-19th centuries. Illustrated examples of their work are primarily from the silver collection of the Museo Municipal de

Arte Hispanoamericano "Isaac Fernández Blanco" and other private collections in Buenos Aires. Footnotes provide a useful guide to other bibliographical sources.

183 Guarda, Gabriel. Flandes indiano: las fortificaciones del Reino de Chile, 1541–1826. Santiago: Ediciones Univ. Católica de Chile, 1990. 425 p.: bibl., ill. (some col.), index, maps.

Definitive study of Chilean fortifications during the colonial period by a distinguished Chilean historian. Author provides detailed accounts of design and construction of fortifications in Valdivia, Chiloé, Valparaíso, and other locations, all supported by a wealth of visual and written archival documentation. Fine quality color photographs of each complement historic maps and drawings, many reproduced here in color for the first time. Includes complete references in notes, an exhaustive bibliography, and a useful glossary of technical terms. A model of scholarship and an indispensable reference for future studies.

184 Gutiérrez, Ramón. La transición del barroco al neoclasicismo en la Cuenca del Plata: la obra de José Custodio de Sa y Faría. (Bol. Mus. Inst. Camón Aznar, 48/49, 1992, p. 141–162, facsim., maps)

Detailed account of the life and professional career of Portuguese architect and military engineer José Custodio de Sa y Faría (c. 1728–92), whose designs in Brazil, Paraguay, Argentina, and Uruguay marked a decisive turning point toward development of neoclasicism in the region. Text discusses history of selected religious buildings and fortifications designed by Sa y Faría for both the Portuguese and Spanish colonial governments.

185 Las iglesias antiguas de Córdoba. Textos de Rodolfo Gallardo. Fotos de Sergio Barbieri. Buenos Aires: Fundación Banco de Boston, 1990. 102 p.: bibl.

Fine survey of major religious monuments in Córdoba dating from the 17th-19th centuries. In separate chapters illustrated with excellent b/w photographs, author discusses the Cathedral, La Compañía, San Francisco, La Merced, Santo Domingo, Santa Catalina, San José, San Roque and Nuestra Señora de Pilar. Text combines factual information with a sensitive appreciation of the rich artistic and architectural heritage of the city.

186 Kubler, George. Sistemas misionales entre los Indios Pueblo, los Guaraníes y en California. (*An. Arquit.*, 4:4, 1992, p. 171–180)

Important, well-documented comparative study of Spanish colonization in New Mexico, California, and Paraguay. Author shows that though defensive considerations were a major issue in each case, there were marked differences in the missionary systems used by the Franciscan, Dominican, and Jesuit Orders from the 16th-18th centuries. List of major bibliographic sources complements the notes.

187 Mebold Köhnenkamp, Luis. Catálogo de pintura colonial en Chile: obras en monasterios de religiosas de antigua fundación. Consultores, Isabel Cruz O., Gabriel Guarda, y Hernán Rodríguez V. Santiago: Ediciones Univ. Católica de Chile, 1987. 387 p.: ill. (some col.).

Deluxe catalogue raisonné of colonial paintings housed in convents in Santiago. General introduction discusses scope of Gabriel Guarda's work and is followed by an important chapter in which author fully outlines methodology of this ambitious project. Each work is carefully described and includes present state of conservation. Wherever possible, iconographic sources and cross references with similar works in other collections are noted. Excellent b/w and color plates (some are detail enlargements) make available a rich corpus of pictorial works previously unaccessible to most scholars. Indispensable reference for future studies.

188 Morquio Blanco, Luis. La estancia de Dn. Juan de Narbona: historia de una estancia colonial. Montevideo?: L. Morquio Blanco, 1990. 210 p.: bibl., ill., maps.

Historical account of the hacienda of don Juan de Narbona built between 1732–38, considered to be the oldest standing colonial building in Uruguay. Narrative focuses on the life and times of the famous owner-builder, whose businesses and professional activity extended into Buenos Aires. Final chapters discuss social prominence enjoyed by Narbona's descendants during the 19th century.

189 Paniagua Pérez, Jesús. Las pinturas murales del convento de La Concepción de Cuenca, Ecuador. (*Cuad. Arte Colon.*, 7, mayo 1991, p. 109–128, ill.)

Good study of little-known mural paintings that decorate walls and ceilings of the refectory and *De Profundis* room adjacent to main cloister of La Concepción in Cuenca. Discussion focuses on iconography of the representation and describes the technique of the anonymous painter, believed to have executed the work during the first half of the 18th century.

190 Patrimonio artístico nacional: inventario de bienes muebles. v. 2, Provincia de Salta. Buenos Aires: Academia Nacional de Bellas Artes, 1988–1991. 1 v.: bibl., ill. (some col.), indexes.

Second volume in series follows the format of the first volume on Corrientes prov. (see *HLAS 48:365*). Features a catalogue raisonné of painting, sculpture, furniture, and decorative arts in the religious monuments and private collections of the Salta prov. Fieldwork was again conducted by Iris Gori and Sergio Barbieri, under the direction of Héctor H. Schenone. The 1,018 works included in the survey (most of which are reproduced in b/w or color photographs) represent an important corpus of Spanish colonial art and will serve as a basis for future studies. Vol. three will cover Jujuy prov.

191 Sebastián, Santiago. Lectura iconográfica de la versión guaraní del libro del Padre Nieremberg: de la diferencia entre lo temporal y eterno. (*Bol. Mus. Inst. Camón Aznar*, 48/49, 1992, p. 309–328, photos)

Iconographic study of engravings from the 1705 Guaraní edition of the book on morals by Spanish Jesuit, Juan Eusebio Nieremberg (1595?-1658). A comparison with engravings by Dirk Bouttats in the Spanish edition (Antwerp, 1684) shows that edition as the main, but not the exclusive source, of iconographic inspiration. On the other hand, the greatest originality in the Guaraní edition is found in its representation of fantastic demons, which may have been inspired by the native artist's fear of the Paraguayan jungle.

192 Soiza Larrosa, Augusto. La Capilla de la Caridad de Montevideo y el arquitecto español Miguel Estévez, 1798. (*Bol. Hist. Ejérc.*, 279/282, 1990, p. 197–241, bibl., facsims., ill., index, map, tables)

Author provides complete documentation on history of the construction of La Caridad chapel (formerly Capilla de la Santísima Virgen María y del Patriarca San José), part of the Montevideo hospital complex of the same name. Evidence shows that the Spanish architect don Miguel Estévez Díaz, "Maestro Mayor de las Reales Obras," designed the chapel in 1798. Despite its later transformations, it remains the third oldest building from the Spanish colonial period in Montevideo.

193 Vega Castillos, Uruguay R. El fuerte de San Miguel. (*Bol. Hist. Ejérc.*, 267/270, 1984, p. 99–132, ill.)

Well-documented history of the San Miguel fort located in Uruguay's Rocha dept. Study covers its Spanish and Portuguese founding in 1734 and 1737, respectively, and its later transformations throughout the 19th century. Concludes with detailed chronology and description of the restoration works undertaken during the present century.

194 Zumel Menocal, Lucio. Las ruinas de San José de Lules, monumento nacional de la República Argentina. (*in* Simposio Hispano-Portugués de Historia del Arte, *5th, Valladolid, Spain, 1989.* Actas. Coordinación de Juan José Martín González. Valladolid, Spain: Univ. de Valladolid, 1990, p. 291–295, photos)

Strictly descriptive account of architectural remains of San José de Lules, a former Jesuit church and school in Tucumán prov. The original church dates from the 17th century, but was greatly modified by the Dominicans during the next two centuries. Nonetheless, author argues for the preservation of this important national historic landmark.

COLOMBIA AND VENEZUELA

195 Duarte, Carlos F. El arte de la platería en Venezuela: período hispánico. Caracas: Fundación Pampero, 1988. 438 p.: bibl., ill. (some col.), index.

Definitive work by the foremost authority on the subject. Almost two decades of painstaking archival research were devoted to this monumental effort which demonstrates the importance and extraordinary quality of silverwork in Venezuela during the Spanish colonial period. Duarte documents the artistic activity of some 294 silversmiths in Caracas from 1567–1810 and reveals that, both qualitatively and quantitatively, this city rivaled production of other centers in Mexico and Peru. Study is illustrated with 218 color

and b/w photographs of selected works, accompanied by informative captions. Provides complete biographical catalog of silversmiths active in Caracas and other cities of Venezuela with individual archival references. Indispensable reference for the study of colonial silver work in Venezuela and elsewhere in Spanish America.

196 Duarte, Carlos F. and **Graziano Gasparini.** Historia de la Catedral de Caracas. Caracas: Ediciones Armitano, 1989. 238 p.: bibl., ill. (some col.), index.

Elegant monograph on the Cathedral of Caracas by two leading authorities provides a comprehensive history of its original construction and subsequent transformations up to the present. Thoroughly discusses important issues of chronology and attribution pertaining to architecture and works of art within the Cathedral in light of documentary evidence from the Archivo del Cabildo Eclesiástico and other historic archives. Excellent visual material consists of architectural plans as well as historic and contemporary b/w and color photographs. In the tradition of the finest Armitano art books. Definitive study and essential reference for Spanish colonial architecture in Venezuela.

197 Duarte, Carlos F. El maestro de pintor y dorador, José Lorenzo Zurita. (*Armitano Arte*, 13, abril 1988, p. 43–64, bibl., photos.)

Author discusses the life and artistic career of distinguished Creole mulatto painter, José Lorenzo Zurita (c. 1695–1753), in light of the recent discovery of several works signed by him. The discovery permits a better appreciation of Zurita's contribution to colonial painting in Caracas during the first half of the 18th century, and will facilitate identification of other works by Zurita and his circle. Concludes with a useful cronology of his life.

198 Gómez Hurtado, Alvaro and **Francisco Gil Tovar.** Arte virreinal en Bogotá = Colonial art in Bogotá. Bogotá: Villegas Editores, 1987. 199 p.: col. ill.

Important book devoted to colonial religious art in Bogotá celebrates the city's 450th foundation anniversary. Good quality color photographs depict selected artistic treasures from various museum and private collections. Unusual trilingual text in Spanish, English, and Portuguese. Alvaro Gómez Hurtado's introductory essay, "American Art and Identity" is followed by Francisco Gil Tovar's critical study, "The Conquest, Conversion to Christianity and Art." Though not integrated with the text, illustrations by themselves are a valuable corpus of visual material.

199 Inventario del patrimonio cultural de Antioquia. v. 2, Coleciones de Santa Fe de Antioquia. Prólogo de Manuel Mejía Vallejo. Investigación y textos de Gustavo Vives Mejía. Fotografías de Hernán Bravo Restrepo. Medellín, Colombia: Secretaría de Educación y Cultura de Antioquia, Dirección de Extensión Cultural, 1988. 1 v.: bibl., ill., index.

Vol. 2 catalogs the collections of paintings, sculpture, silverwork, pottery, furniture, and decorative arts housed in major religious buildings and public museums of Santa Fé de Antioquia. Extensive captions describe individual works in general terms. Media, measurements, artist (if known), and approximate date are given. Small b/w photographs are only used as visual references. Also includes section with biographical summaries of principal artists.

200 Iriarte, Alfredo. Tesoros de Tunja. Fotografía de Germán Montes y Santiago Montes. Bogotá: Sello Editorial, 1989. 141 p.: col. ill.

Deluxe publication inaugurates a new series by El Sello Editorial devoted to dissemination of colonial artistic treasures of major Latin American cities. Spectacular color plates (often an entire page) reveal the splendor of Tunja's art and architecture. Volume features all of the city's famous houses and churches and their works of art, which can be appreciated in detail perhaps for the first time. Text is aimed at the general public and provides sensitive narrative that takes the reader on a wonderful journey of discovery. All in all, an unusual effort that sets a high qualitative standard.

201 Martínez, Carlos. Santafé: capital del Nuevo Reino de Granada. Bogotá: Banco Popular, 1988. 302 p.: ill. (some col.).

Monumental study of colonial Bogotá, written by the dean of Colombian urban historians on occasion of the city's celebration of its 450th anniversary. Detailed chapters are devoted to the city's founding, its morphol-

ogy and growth across time, its administrative and economic history, and its architecture and urban spaces. Text is complemented with fine maps and plans drawn by Carlos Pérez and Alfonso Tamayo, and handsome perspective drawings by Camilo Santamaría. Book concludes with transcription of three important historic documents concerning the conquest of the New Kingdom of Granada.

202 Mateus Cortés, Gustavo. Nuevos apuntes para la historia del patrimonio artístico de Tunja, con el acta de fundación y el título de ciudad. Tunja, Colombia: Magister en Historia, Escuela de Posgrado de la Facultad de Educación, Univ. Pedagógica y Tecnológica de Colombia, 1989. 96 p.: ill. (Nuevas lecturas de historia, 0121–165X; 8)

Brief, evocative guide to historic monuments and artistic treasures of the colonial Tunja written on occasion of the celebration of the 450th anniversary of its foundation. Handsome pen-and-ink drawings by Willie Hostos depict exterior views of the most representative monuments.

203 Oribes y plateros en la Nueva Granada: exposición. Banco de la República, Museo de Arte Religioso, Bogotá, mayo-julio 1990. Bogotá: Banco de la República, 1990. 91 p.: bibl., ill. (some col.).

Elegant catalog published for exhibition of colonial gold and silver works held at the Museo de Arte Religioso in Bogotá. Critical studies by Marta Fajardo de Rueda, Luis Duque Gómez, and Jaime Gutiérrez Vallejo document the work of several distinguished colonial goldsmiths and silversmiths whose names have been recorded in archival documents. Provides insights on actual use of many of the art objects in the liturgy of the Catholic Church. Color photographs showing selected details complement b/w photographs of the descriptive catalog.

204 Revelaciones: pintores de Santafé en tiempos de la colonia: Museo de Arte Religioso, febrero-marzo de 1989, Bogotá, Colombia. Bogotá: Museo de Arte Religioso, 1989. 69 p.: bibl., ill. (some col.).

Exhibition catalog documents restoration of 38 religious paintings from private collections and historic monuments in Bogotá. Individual essays by Marta Fajardo de Rueda, Lucía Cadavid, Jaime Guiérrez and Helena Weisner discuss the history of colonial paintings in Bogotá, history of the city, iconography of the religious images, and restoration of the paintings, respectively. Color reproductions are of uneven quality, but all 38 paintings are included. Book concludes with a list of biographical profiles of the artists represented and a guide to related works of art located elsewhere in the city.

PERU, ECUADOR, AND BOLIVIA

205 Arequipa. Dirección de José Antonio de Lavalle. Texto de Patricio Ricketts Rey de Castro. Leyendas de Mariano Felipe Paz Soldán. Traducción para el português de Vera Moyna. Fotografía de Billie Hare. Rio de Janeiro, Brasil: Spala Editora, 1988. 341 p.: col. ill.

More of a literary account of the geography, history and rich cultural heritage of Arequipa dept. and its capital, the "White City of the Andes," than a history of art. More importantly, though, the book offers unparalleled photographs (394 spectacular color plates) depicting the land, people, and the distinctive art and architecture of Arequipa, an invaluable visual resource for many disciplines.

206 Arnaiz, José Manuel. Cosme de Acuña y la influencia de la escuela madrileña de finales del S. XVIII en América. (*Academia/Madrid*, 73, 20 semestre 1991, p. 136–177)

Well-documented study of the life and artistic career of Spanish painter Cosme de Acuña (1758-c. 1814) updates earlier research by M. Ossorio y Bernard (1883–84), F.J. Sánchez Cantón (1985), and Claude Bédat (1973, 1989). Author gives special attention to Acuña's training and subsequent teaching at the Academia de San Fernando in Madrid and his appointment in 1786 as professor (*director de pintura*) at the new Real Academia de San Carlos in Mexico City. Identification of a number of religious paintings by him and his followers in the church of Santa Teresa, Cochabamba, attests to the extent of his influence in Bolivia during the latter part of the 18th century.

207 Bernales Ballesteros, Jorge. Arquitectos y escultores de las tierras del Duero en el Virreinato del Perú: siglos XVI y XVII. (*in* Simposio Hispano-Portugués de Historia del Arte, *5th, Valladolid, Spain, 1989*. Actas.

Coordinación de Juan José Martín González. Valladolid, Spain: Univ. de Valladolid, 1990, p. 33–42)

Short biographies highlight work of selected Castilian and Portuguese architects and sculptors in the Viceroyalty of Perú during the 16th and 17th centuries. Documentation, drawn primarily from the Archivo de Indias in Seville and secondary sources, shows the cosmopolitan make-up of the artistic community in colonial Peru.

208 Casaseca Casaseca, Antonio. Pintura cuzqueña en el Museo de Salamanca. Valladolid, Spain: Junta de Castilla y León, Consejería de Cultura y Bienestar Social, 1989. 49 p.: bibl., col. ill. (Monografías del Museo de Salamanca; 1)

Analytical study and catalog of eight paintings from the Cuzco School depicting *ángeles arcabuceros* (archangels with muskets) acquired by the Museum of Salamanca in 1974–75. Author argues convincingly for the originality of this popular iconographic theme in Cusco and the Altiplano region of Peru and Bolivia in paintings from the second half of the 17th to the first half of the 18th century. Relies on the questionable term "mestizo" for their stylistic classification. Good reproductions attest to the richness of color and decorative detail characteristic of these works.

209 Chacón Torres, Mario. El convento de Santa Teresa en Potosí. (*Hist. Boliv.*, 4: 1, 1984, p. 33–44, appendix)

Improved version of article first published in 1983 issue of the same journal. Text concentrates on the history of the convent of Santa Teresa in Potosí, whose original foundation was approved in 1684. Also provides a room-by-room description of the institution and its works of art, but does not include illustrations.

210 Chacón Torres, Mario. Iconografía de Vicente Bernedo. Potosí, Bolivia: Editorial Potosí; Casa Nacional de la Moneda, 1988. 78 p.

Posthumous publication of brief, sensitive biography and iconography of the dominican Fray Vicente Bernedo (1562–1619), whose exemplary religious life based on prayer and service to the poor in Potosí remains legendary even today. Author presents nearly two dozen engravings and paintings from South America and Europe, demonstrating that Bernedo was a popular iconographic theme throughout the 17th and 18th centuries. B/w plates are of uneven quality.

211 Damian, Carol. The Virgin and Pachamama: images of adaptation and resistance. (*SECOLAS Ann.*, 23, March 1992, p. 125–137, plates)

Much too brief essay examines the possible survival during colonial period of indigenous myths and religious beliefs in the guise of signs and symbols included in Christian representations by the Cuzco School of painting. Ideas presented are sketchy and the evidence is very sparse, but article indicates that the topic was covered fully in author's doctoral dissertation.

212 Dean, Carolyn S. Ethnic conflict and Corpus Christi in colonial Cuzco. (*Colon. Lat. Am. Rev.*, 2:1/2, 1993, p. 93–120, bibl. plates)

Original research based on author's doctoral dissertation proposes a new interpretation of the famous series of paintings from the Cuzco School representing the procession of Corpus Christi. Beyond their obvious religious content, the paintings are viewed as sociopolitical statements reflecting the traditional rivalry between Inca and non-Inca (Cañari and Chachapoya) indigenous groups, who were residents of Cusco's Santa Ana parish.

213 Durán Montero, María Antonia. La entrada en Lima del Virrey D. García Hurtado de Mendoza, Marqués de Cañete. (*Rev. Dep. Hist. Arte*, 3, 1990, p. 57–61)

Paper of talk delivered at a 1980 congress organized by the Centro de Estudios Hispanoamericanos in Seville documents 1590 festivities in Lima associated with the arrival of the new viceroy, García Hurtado de Mendoza, Marqués de Cañete. Text includes description of the triumphal arch designed by the Augustinian Fray Mateo de León, which was erected on this occasion.

214 Escultura en el Perú. Lima: Banco de Crédito del Perú, 1991. 409 p.: bibl. (Col. Arte y tesoros del Perú)

Monumental work corresponds to vol. 18 of the acclaimed art book series originally conceived by José Antonio de Lavalle. Six critical essays by prominent scholars Jorge Bernales Ballesteros, Ricardo Estabridis Cárdenas, Teresa Gisbert, José de Mesa, Jesús

Lámbarri Bracesco, Luis Enrique Tord, and Alfonso Castrillón Vizcarra trace the development of sculpture in the colonial Peruvian cities of Lima, Trujillo, Cusco, and Arequipa. This is the most comprehensive study on the subject to date, superseding Wethey's *Colonial architecture and sculpture in Peru* (see *HLAS 15:580*). Excellent color plates permit an appreciation of the outstanding works of figural sculpture, retables, choir stalls, and pulpits created during the period. Final chapter is devoted to monumental and funerary sculpture in Lima during the 19th and 20th centuries, a topic that remains virtually unexplored. Without doubt, this volume fills a significant void in the artistic literature of Spanish America and will be an indispensable reference.

215 Flores Ochoa, Jorge; Elizabeth Kuon Arce; and Roberto Samanez Argumedo. De la evangelización al incanismo: la pintura mural del sur andino. (*Histórica/Lima*, 15:2, dic. 1991, p. 165–203, bibl., ill.)

Authors survey extant and destroyed examples of mural painting from colonial and modern times in the Cusco and Puno regions and preview their major book on the topic (Lima: Banco de Crédito del Perú, 1993). Discussion of the iconography reveals that mural painting, often intended for a more restricted audience, exhibits a greater freedom of expression than commonly found in easel painting. As such, it can be viewed as a closer reflection of social and political aspirations at a particular time.

216 García Mahiques, Rafael. Gemidos, deseos y suspiros: el programa místico de Santa Catalina de Arequipa. (*Bol. Mus. Inst. Camón Aznar*, 48/49, 1992, p. 83–113, photos)

Well-illustrated study examines iconography of the series of canvas paintings that decorate the walls of the Naranjos cloister of Santa Catalina convent in Arequipa. Two 17th-century Flemish emblem books, Hermann Hugo's *Pia desideria* (Antwerp, 1624) and Benedictus van Haeften's *Schola cordis* (Antwerp, 1629) are identifed as visual sources that inspired the anonymous colonial paintings.

217 Gisbert, Teresa. The Andean gods throughout Christianity. (*in* Temples of gold, crowns of silver: reflections of majesty in the Viceregal Americas. Curated by

Barbara von Barghahn. Washington: George Washington Univ., 1991, p. 80–92, facsims., plates, photos)

Sensitive iconographic study examines selected themes of Spanish colonial art in the Andean regions of Peru and Bolivia that show a syncretism of precolumbian and Christian beliefs. In the absence of an indigenous system of writing, the author correctly points out, "the Andean thought, Christian and Precolumbian, [was] expressed in outlines, signs and relationships that transmit [ted] knowledge about ancient Andean myths as well as Christian dogmas." Well-chosen illustrations help support many of the key points made in the text.

218 Gisbert, Teresa. Historia de la vivienda y los asentamientos humanos en Bolivia. México: Instituto Panamericano de Geografía e Historia, 1988. 243 p.: bibl., ill., maps. (Pub.; 431)

Pioneer study on Bolivian dwelling types and settlement patterns predominantly covers precolumbian times, but also includes Indian towns and major cities founded after the Spanish conquest. Separate chapters are devoted to rural architecture and the Jesuit missions of Mojos and Chiquitos in the eastern region of Bolivia. Most valuable are the many maps and architectural drawings assembled for this publication. B/w photographs, however, have not reproduced well due to the poor quality of the paper.

219 Gisbert, Teresa. La imagen del Paraíso en la pintura cuzqueña. (*Bol. Mus. Inst. Camón Aznar*, 48/49, 1992, p. 115–139, photos)

Analytical essay considers the garden populated by exotic flora and fauna as a symbol of heavenly paradise in Cusco School paintings and architectural examples from the Altiplano region around Lake Titicaca. Contemporary written sources and *kero* representations suggest parallels with precolumbian myths that may have contributed to the appeal of this theme for Indian artists.

220 Gisbert, Teresa. La pintura mural andina. (*Colon. Lat. Am. Rev.*, 1:1/2, 1992, p. 109–145, bibl., photos)

Important, well-documented study of selected examples of mural painting from precolumbian times through the 19th century in the Cusco region of Peru and the Lake Titica-

ca and Potosí regions of Bolivia. Gisbert proposes a tentative stylistic and chronological classification according to the following scheme: 1) precolumbian; 2) pre-Toledan (before 1570); 3) renaissance and Mannerism (1580–1630); Baroque (textile and figurative styles); 5) symbolic representation of Paradise and the cardinal virtues; and 6) Inca renaissance and popular painting. Special attention is given to the discussion of some recurrent iconographic themes and their possible meanings.

221 Gonzáles Gamarra, F. La Pinacoteca del Museo Nacional de Historia: informe de F. Gonzáles Gamarra sobre la restauración de sus fondos, Lima, 1930. (*Bol. Lima*, 19:81, mayo 1992, p. 13–18)

Report on the restoration of the collection of paintings in the Museo Nacional de Historia undertaken from 1920–30 includes a reference to four anonymous works from the Cuzco School: 1) *Portrait of Bishop Mollinedo y Angulo* (1.17 x 2.07 m.); 2) *Portrait of Charles III, King of Spain* (0.99 x 1.17 m.); 3) *Virgin and Child* (0.68 x 0.95 m.); and 4) *Holy Family* (0.47 x 0.35 m.).

222 Heredia Moreno, María del Carmen. Las ordenanzas de los plateros limeños del año 1633. (*Arch. Esp. Arte*, 64:256, oct./dic. 1991, p. 489–501)

Essay analyzes ordinances that applied to silversmiths that were approved by municipal authorities of Lima in 1633. This important document, which consists of ten articles, was the legislation which controlled and protected work of goldsmiths and silversmiths in the viceregal capital for nearly 150 years. Author points out similarities and differences with contemporary legislation from Seville and Madrid.

223 Inventario y catalogación del patrimonio artístico mueble: Arequipa. Lima: Instituto Nacional de Cultura, 1989. 135 p.: bibl., ill. (some col.) (Inventario del patrimonio artístico mueble; 2)

Book follows format of first volume in the series: *Inventario del Patrimonio Mueble de Cajamarca* (Lima, 1986). Provides comprehensive photographic survey of altarpieces, paintings and sculptures in the major religious monuments of colonial Arequipa, including the Cathedral, La Compañía, Santo Domingo, San Francisco, Orden Terciaria

Franciscana, Santa Rosa and La Recoleta. Small, poor quality b/w photographs are useful only as visual reference. Basic data on each work of art includes subject matter, medium, measurements, location and state of conservation.

224 Jurado Noboa, Fernando. Plazas y plazuelas de Quito. Quito: Banco Central del Ecuador, 1989. 251 p.: bibl., ill. (Col. Sociedad Amigos de la Genealogía; 39)

Significant contribution to Quito's urban history is based on original archival research. Expanding on the author's previous work, *Calles de Quito* (1989), this study presents a detailed account of the city's plazas and plazuelas ranked by size and their development across time. Wherever possible, the owners of individual properties have been carefully recorded and the exact location of buildings facing the squares indicated in separate schematic plans. Even though no bibliography is included, the footnotes give a guide to some primary and secondary sources.

225 Louzao Martínez, Francisco Javier. Platería colonial en la colegiata coruñesa: un atril quiteño de principios del siglo XVIII. (*Arch. Esp. Arte*, 65:258, abril/junio 1992, p. 235–238, ill.)

Brief note documents 18th-century silver missal stand from colonial Quito in the Real Colegiata de Santa María del Campo, La Coruña. Archival sources suggest that this may be the only surviving piece from the silver collection once owned by Don Antonio Fernández de Fraga which was shipped to Spain in 1730 according to the donor's last wishes.

226 Martín, Cristina Esteras. Luis de Lezana, platero del Cuzco. (*Bol. Mus. Inst. Camón Aznar*, 48/49, 1992, p. 31–60, photos)

Biographical essay documents the artistic career of cusqueño silversmith Luis de Lezana, which extended from at least 1665 until 1713, possibly the year of his death. Author has discovered extant works by this artist in Spain and South America, particularly in several parish churches near Cusco and in private collections in Lima. Consistent high quality of Lezana's silverwork in both its technical refinement and originality of design is eloquent testimony of advanced development of his art during the colonial period.

227 Mattos-Cárdenas, Leonardo. El urbanismo y sus modelos en el área andina, 1532–1632. (*Rev. Rev. Interam.*, 19:1/2, primavera/verano 1989, p. 5–63, bibl., maps, photos)

Important essay examines several theoretical models that may have inspired the layout of Spanish colonial towns in the Viceroyalty of Peru from 1532–1632. Abundant contemporary written and visual sources are used to support author's arguments. Proposes typology of city plans based on actual examples. Good bibliography and illustrations, even though these are not integrated with the text.

228 Mesa, José de and **Teresa Gisbert.** La pintura en los museos de Bolivia. La Paz: Editorial Los Amigos del Libro, 1991. 281 p.: bibl., ill. (some col.). (Col. Descubra Bolivia)

Revised and enlarged edition of the book *Museos de Bolivia* originally published in 1969. Text offers descriptive and analytical catalog of pictorial collections at the Museo Nacional de Arte, Museo de la Catedral and Museos Municipales in La Paz; the Museo de La Moneda and Museo de Santa Teresa in Potosí; and the Museo Charcas and Museo de la Catedral in Sucre. Most works date from the colonial period, but the 19th-20th centuries are also represented. In each case, authors have made an effort to reflect the findings of most recent scholarly research. B/w illustrations are useful as visual references, while the color reproductions are of better quality. The final chapter provides a useful brief history of paintings in Bolivia.

229 Ortiz de Zevallos Paz-Soldán, Carlos. Torre Tagle. Lima: Fondo de Promoción Turística, 1989. 64 p.: ill. (some col.).

New edition of tourist guide of the most famous 18th-century urban palace in Lima, first published in 1973. Provides reliable historic information and brief room-by-room descriptions. Small but generally good quality color photographs replace the former b/w illustrations showing overall views and details of the architecture and works of art in the building.

230 Pastor, Mercedes. Tradition and ceremony: the colonial art of Viceregal Peru. (*in* Temples of gold, crowns of silver: reflections of majesty in the Viceregal Americas. Curated by Barbara von Barghahn. Washington: George Washington Univ., 1991, p. 128–135, facsim., map, photos)

Brief, superficial view of traditions and ceremonies in precolumbian and colonial Peru. Parallel celebrations of Corpus Christi and Inti Raymi in Cusco, for instance, are only discussed in very general terms.

231 Potosí: catalogación de su patrimonio urbano y arquitectónico. La Paz: Instituto Boliviano de Cultura, 1990. 249 p.: bibl., ill., maps.

Comprehensive catalog of historic monuments of Potosí and surrounding areas compiled by a team of professionals under the expert coordination of architects Teresa Gisbert and Luis Prado. Text reproduces 126 actual inventory forms used in the field survey and provides basic historic and descriptive information on each monument. Small b/w photographs vary in quality, but excellent location maps and measured floor plans are included. The final chapters transcribe existing municipal legislation on historic preservation and list monuments that need to be preserved.

232 Potosí, patrimonio cultural de la humanidad. Potosí, Bolivia: Compañía Minera del Sur, 1988. 257 p., 5 folded leaves of plates: bibl., ill. (some col.)

Deluxe edition celebrates Potosí, recently named "Monument of the Americas" by the OAS and entered in the World's Heritage List by UNESCO. Four chapters by different authors offer a general history of the city, emphasizing the colonial silver mining industry that made it so famous. Of special interest is the fine chapter devoted to architecture, painting, and sculpture of colonial Potosí by renowned Bolivian art historians José de Mesa and Teresa Gisbert. The final chapter on colonial mining by Juan Fernández includes handsome foldout measured drawings of the Pampa Ingenio and the Casa de La Moneda. Excellent reproductions of historic documents and beautiful color photographs greatly enhance this quality publication.

233 Proaño, Luis Octavio. La Merced, arte e historia. Quito: R. Rivadeneira Palacios, 1989. 363 p.: bibl., ill.

Detailed history of construction of the church and convent in Quito based on original archival research. Text is descriptive rather than analytical, but provides comprehensive overview of architectural elements and major works of art that were commissioned by religious authorities of the Mercedarian order at different times during the colonial period. B/w photographs generally did not reproduce well on the poor quality printed paper.

234 Ramos Sosa, Rafael. El Monumento Pascual de la Catedral de Lima: siglos XVI-XVIII. (*Cuad. Arte Colon.*, 7, mayo 1991, p. 99–108, ill.)

Original research on temporary monuments erected inside the Cathedral of Lima during the yearly celebration of Holy Week and Easter Sunday. Like the *catafalques* constructed after the death of a Spanish monarch, these monuments grew in size and importance during the colonial period and were often commissioned to important architects or sculptors. Author also shows that on various occasions an original *catafalque* was slightly modified and later reused as a Maundy Thursday monument and viceversa.

235 Rodríguez Camilloni, Humberto. The *retablo*-façade as transparency: a study of the frontispiece of San Francisco, Lima. (*An. Inst. Invest. Estét.*, 62, 1991, p. 111–122)

Detailed examination of a number of non-Hispanic European sources which may have inspired the design of the frontispiece of the San Francisco church in Lima. Author analyzes its central iconographic theme, which is a key to the understanding of the entire composition. Also proposes idea that the architect, Constantino de Vasconcelos, may have intended the frontispiece to serve as a transparency or preview of the main altar.

236 Rodríguez Moreno, Oswaldo A. Museo del Convento La Concepción: catálogo de su colección permanente de arte religioso. 2. ed. rev. Riobamba, Ecuador: Edit. Pedagógica Freire, 1986. 33 p.: bibl., ill., map.

Popular tourist guide to the museum of religious art housed in the convent of La Concepción in Riobamba. Brief, descriptive text accompanies poor quality b/w photographs.

237 Rowe, John Howland. El plano más antiguo del Cuzco. (*Histórica/Lima*, 14: 2, dic. 1990, p. 367–377, bibl.)

Short, important study brings to light the oldest known plan of Cusco, which dates from 1643 and which the author discovered in 1987 in the Archivo Arzobispal de Lima. Carefully drawn and painted with watercolors, the document is a rare visual record of the western section of Cusco corresponding to the parishes of Santa Ana and the Hospital de los Naturales. Since the plan predates the devasting earthquake of 1650, it provides invaluable information on buildings that were standing at the time.

238 San Cristóbal Sebastián, Antonio. Fray Cristóbal Caballero y la portada de La Merced de Lima. (*Anu. Estud. Am.*, 48, 1991, p. 151–203)

New documentation discovered by the author in the Archivo General de la Nación in Lima permits a more accurate appreciation of the artistic career of the distinguished Mercedarian sculptor and architect during the second half of the 17th century. Close comparisons with other works by Caballero strongly suggest that he was also the designer of the famous frontispiece of La Merced in Lima begun in 1697. Selected relevant documents are transcribed in an appendix.

239 San Cristóbal Sebastián, Antonio. Vigencia actual de la obra *Colonial architecture and sculpture in Peru,* de Harold Wethey. (*Rev. Dep. Hist. Arte*, 3, 1990, p. 147–168, bibl.)

Retrospective critical review of Harold E. Wethey's pioneer book (see *HLAS 15: 580*) points out its strengths and weaknesses. Wethey's shortcomings are perhaps judged a bit too harshly in the light of significant advances in scholarship during the last three decades. Bibliography lists selected major publications on Peruvian colonial art and architecture since 1949.

240 Stastny M., Francisco. Jardín universitario y *Stella Maris:* invenciones iconográficas en el Cuzco. (*in* International Congress of Americanists, *44th, Manchester, England, 1982.* Actas. México: Instituto de Investigaciones Estéticas, UNAM, 1987, p. 141–162, plates)

Reprint of important, well-documented iconographic study published in *Historia y Cultura* (see *HLAS 48:381*). Author argues convincingly for the originality of the theme of the university garden as developed by the Cuzco School of painting, and explains its meaning in terms of the traditional

rivalry between the University of San Antonio Abad and the School of San Bernardo.

241 Tesoros de Quito. Bogotá: El Sello Editorial, 1990. 142 p.: bibl., col. ill.

Second volume in this deluxe series (see also item **200**) features the major religious monuments of Quito and their artistic treasures. In every respect, it continues the high standard set by the first volume, including an impressive collection of color plates that show full views and details of the works of art to best advantage. Informative text by Carlos de la Torre Reyes incorporates selected passages from the writings of well-known Ecuadorian art historians, such as José Gabriel Navarro and José María Vargas.

242 Vandevivere, Ignace. El uso popular de las fuentes flamencas en la pintura colonial hispanoamericana. (*in* Simposio Hispano-Portugués de Historia del Arte, *5th, Valladolid, Spain, 1989.* Actas. Coordinación de Juan José Martín González. Valladolid, Spain: Univ. de Valladolid, 1990, p. 285)

Brief, intelligent note proposes a reevaluation of the use of Flemish prints in colonial painting. Rather than providing a Flemish stylistic influence as such, the prints are viewed predominantly as a vehicle for transmission of new Christian signs and symbols among an indigenous population, whose pictorial tradition privileged the two-dimensional surface as the popular medium for the display of a visual language.

243 Villasís Endara, Carlos. Navarro, el arte de la investigación: semblanza biográfico-crítica. Quito: Editora la Económica, 1988. 214 p.: bibl., ill.

Unpretentious, small publication pays an important tribute to the Ecuadorian José Gabriel Navarro (1883–1965), a pioneer in the field of Ecuadorian art history. Author discusses Navarro's contribution toward a better appreciation of Ecuadorian art and architecture, particularly of the colonial period, within the historic context of his generation. A list of his publications, including little-known articles, will be of great value to all scholars.

244 Von Barghahn, Barbara. The colonial paintings of Leonardo Flores. (*Lat. Am. Art Mag.*, 5:2, 1993, p. 47–49, ill.)

Brief, sensitive article highlights work

of Leonardo Flores (1650–1710?), a famous Creole painter from La Paz active in the Altiplano region around Lake Titicaca. The consistently high quality of Flores' paintings has contributed to his ranking as one of the top artists of his generation. As the author points out, "altering classic compositions with a distinctive lexicon of images and ideas, the magnificent paintings of Bolivian Leonardo Flores exemplify the alloy that was forged by the jolting encounter of two diverse cultures."

19th and 20th Centuries

BELGICA RODRIGUEZ, *Associate Professor of Latin American Art, Universidad Central de Venezuela; Director, Art Museum of the Americas, Organization of American States*

DUE TO THE RECENT BOOM in Latin America art, publications in the field have increased. For instance, for *HLAS 52* I had the opportunity to review more than 200 items while for this volume I looked at more than 300. Using a systematic selection process, I narrowed these original 300 items down to 200 which I carefully reviewed; from that group 130 were ultimately selected for inclusion here. Due to the *Handbook's* space limitations not all the worthwile publications could be included; I tried to cover the most representative. As I wrote in my introduction to *HLAS 52*, the Latin American bibliography can no longer be considered minor in comparison to other regions: the artistic development of the region has spurred more books, catalogs, and other publications. Mexico is the country with the most entries, followed by Argentina, Chile, Colombia, and Venezuela. Other countries and regions, namely Ecuador, Peru, Central America, and the Caribbean are also well represented, with interest in the latter two continuing to grow. In terms of theoretical reflection and aesthetic proposals, there are a few important books which enrich the field: *Hacia una teoría americana del arte* (item **245**); *De la plástica cubana y caribeña* by Yolanda Wood (item **314**); and *Modernidade: vanguardas artísticas na América Latina* compiled by Ana Maria de Moraes Belluzzo (item **251**).

Both the development and promotion of Latin American art require the field to support and improve its publications. Unfortunately current publications are directed almost solely at Spanish-speaking specialists; there are very few bilingual or English-language editions. This situation has handicapped art historians and art critics outside of Latin America who do not speak Spanish. Perhaps this lack of interest in the Spanish language is indicative of a more general lack of interest in the culture of the so-called Third World. To counteract this trend, it is important that Latin American art critics and historians begin to publish consistently in languages other than Spanish. Another problem which complicates dissemination of our research is the poor publications distribution system within Latin America: it is difficult to find or buy an artistic publication outside the country of its publication. It is high time to address this problem and form networks to alleviate it.

Notwithstanding the above, the number of entries seen and reviewed for this edition afford optimism as to the development of Latin America's artistic publications. One very informative and relevant publication is *La peinture de l'Amérique latine au XXe siècle: identité et modernité* (item **247**) by Damián Bayón and Roberto Pontual, two distinguished Latin American scholars who address the subject from a new historical and theoretical position, that of identity and modernity. Another important publication is Romualdo Grughetti's *Nueva historia de la pintura y la escultura en la Argentina: de los orígenes a nuestros días* (item **316**), an exhaustive study which gives a comprehensive history of both painting and sculpture in Argentina. I would also like to mention Luis Camnitzer's *New art of Cuba* (item **306**), an English-language treatise on Cuban art, both inside and outside the country, which is well documented, illustrated and written.

In conclusion it can be said that Latin American publications on art have been improving continually. My main criticism is that, as in *HLAS 52,* most of the monographs treat the region in isolation, without first building a framework from which to understand Latin American art in relation to other parts of the world. Scholars and art historians have started to address this question; I hope that the next biennium will see these works in published form.

GENERAL

245 Acha, Juan; Adolfo Colombres; and **Ticio Escobar.** Hacia una teoría americana del arte. Prólogo de Adolfo Colombres. Buenos Aires: Ediciones del Sol, 1991. 260 p.: bibl., ill. (Serie antropológica)

Collection of essays by three authors delivered at congresses and seminars makes for an uneven structure. Nevertheless, book does address principal theoretical problems of visual creation in Latin America and builds a theory that justifies its art as outcome of a specific cultural context. One of the most important books on the subject written to date.

246 Ades, Dawn *et al.* Arte en Iberoamérica, 1820–1980: Palacio de Velázquez, 14 de diciembre de 1989–4 de marzo de 1990. Madrid: Turner, 1989? 362 p.: bibl., ill. (some col.). (Col. Encuentros: Serie Catálogos)

Catalog of exhibit fails to show Latin American development during 1820–1980. Essays include little that is new and are mostly devoted to Mexico. Nevertheless, the catalog is an important biographical and bibliographical source for specialists and has excellent color illustrations.

247 Bayón, Damián and **Roberto Pontual.** La peinture de l'Amérique latine au XXe siècle: identité et modernité. Paris: Mengès, 1990. 224 p.: bibl., ill. (some col.), index.

Pontual covers Brazil and the rest of Latin America is handled by Bayón. Very well written book provides historical and artistic facts, some of which are analyzed in terms of identity and modernism. Work is important for researchers and specialists, as it discusses Latin American art as a whole as well as its particular manifestations as national act. Numerous color and b/w reproductions.

248 Bienal de Pintura del Caribe y Centroamérica, 1st, Santo Domingo, 1992. Catálogo. Santo Domingo: Galería de Arte Moderno, 1992? 290 p.: ill.

Important catalog of first effort to present complete survey of paintings from all Central American and Caribbean countries. Paintings reproduced in b/w. Laudable attempt to promote a group of artists that should be better known.

249 Castedo, Leopoldo. Historia del arte iberoamericano. v. 2, Siglo XIX; Siglo XX. Madrid: Alianza Editorial, 1988. 1 v.: bibl., ill. (some col.), indexes.

Author's revision of work written more than 20 years ago and based on research completed in 1960s. Provides superficial historic view of 19th- and 20th-century Latin American art and architecture in short monographs for each country, the shortest ones devoted to Peru, Bolivia and Ecuador. Lacking in methodology but very well illustrated.

250 Mito y magia en América: los ochenta. Curadores, Miguel Cervantes y Charles Merewether. Museografía de Miguel Cervantes, Walter Hopps y John Peters. Registro de Jeffery J. Pavelka. Monterrey, Mexico: MARCO, 1991. 394 p.: bibl., ill. (some col.).

Catalog's confusing introduction overemphasizes "myth and magic" as the only important features of Latin American art. Superficial essays try to demonstrate that the region's art iconography derives from *santería* folklore, and other popular beliefs in magic. Very limited approach.

251 Modernidade: vanguardas artísticas na América Latina. Organização de Ana Maria de Moraes Belluzzo. Colaboração de Aracy Amaral *et al.* São Paulo: Memorial

Editora UNESP, 1990. 319 p.: bibl., ill. (some col.). (Cadernos de cultura; 1)

Compilation of scholarly essays address Latin American art and the avant garde. Authors analyze artistic and cultural relations, issues of national identity, and the aesthetic confrontation between international artistic centers and Latin America. Includes very important documents and manifestos on the subject. Few b/w reproductions.

252 Nuestras raíces: muestra de arte iberoamericano. México: Consejo Nacional para la Cultura y las Artes; Instituto Nacional de Antropología e Historia, 1991. 143 p.: col. ill.

Catalog with excellent color reproductions of precolumbian and colonial art from different countries and cultures presents panoramic view in terms of ceramics, paintings, and sculptures, especially in wood. Somewhat irrelevant texts are still useful as short introductions to the works.

253 Nueva arquitectura en América Latina: presente y futuro. Edición de Antonio Toca. México: Ediciones G. Gili, 1990. 284 p.: bibl., ill. (Arquitectura latinoamericana)

Interesting theoretical essays by various authors address questions of architectural development, its possibilities, and its projections in Latin America. Authors analyze the field and assess its state in various countries and estimate projections into the future. Includes good reproductions.

254 Segre, Roberto; Eliana Cárdenas; and **Lohania Aruca.** Historia de la arquitectura y del urbanismo III: América Latina y Cuba. La Habana: Ediciones ENSPES, 1981? 354 p.: bibl., ill.

Although poorly printed and synthetic, this small textbook mostly devoted to Cuba provides clear and precise discussion of subject. Ranges from precolumbian cultures to Cuban urbanism (1940–58).

255 El surrealismo entre Viejo y Nuevo Mundo: 6 marzo-22 abril 1990: Sala de Exposiciones de la Fundación Cultural Mapfre Vida. Madrid: Quinto Centenario, 1990. 346 p.: bibl., ill. (some col.). (Col. Encuentros: Serie Catálogos)

Large catalog of important exhibit explores conceptual relationship and images of Surrealism in the Canary Islands, the Caribbean, Mexico, and New York. Emphasizes exodus of European artists to Latin America during World War II. Works and personal memorabilia of artists are richly illustrated in color and b/w.

MEXICO

256 Alamilla, Miguel Angel et al. Aparición de lo invisible: pintura abstracta contemporánea en México, septiembre-enero, Sala José Juan Tablada, México, D.F., 1991–1992. México: Museo de Arte Moderno, 1991. 111 p.: bibl., col. ill.

Important catalog concerns contemporary group of painters in the tradition of Mexican abstract art. Includes references to each artist, resumés, personal photos, and color reproductions.

257 Alva Martínez, Ernesto and **Sara Schara Ickowics.** Color en la arquitectura mexicana. México: COMEX, 1992. 203 p.: bibl., col. ill.

Examination of Mexican architects' use of color hypothesizes that color is not the product of theoretical knowledge but of artistic intuition and a "continuation of being Mexican." Color illustrations show buildings, interiors, and aspects specific to their relation to setting and landscape.

258 Anguiano, Raúl. Raúl Anguiano: una vida entregada a la plástica y catálogo de la exposición de pinturas, dibujos, estampas, tapices, esculturas y cerámicas en el Instituto Cultural Cabañas, Guadalajara, Jalisco, México, del 15 de octubre al 30 de noviembre de 1985. Textos de homenaje de Emmanuel Palacios, Raúl Anguiano, y Xavier Moyssén. Guadalajara: Instituto Cultural Cabañas, 1985. 124 p.: ill. (some col.). (Col. Homenajes)

Critics and specialists contribute important texts to this catalog which illustrates artist's paintings, drawings, textiles, sculptures, graphic work, and ceramics. Includes chronological notes on his life and work, as well as color and b/w illustrations.

259 Aurrecoechea, Juan Manuel and **Armando Bartra.** Puros cuentos: la historia de la historieta en México, 1874–1934. México: Consejo Nacional para la Cultura y las Artes; Museo Nacional de Culturas Populares: Grijalbo, 1988. 291 p.: bibl., ill. (some col.), index.

Excellent study on Mexican comic strip drawings and caricatures shows Mexican history from their perspective. Thoroughly illustrated in b/w, work also encompasses sources and influences on Mexican comics. Vol. 1 of projected two.

260 Borràs, Maria Llüísa. Fernando García Ponce. Introducción de Dore Ashton. México: Fomento Cultural Banamex, 1992. 265 p.: bibl., col. ill.

Excellent compilation of texts place the artist in the so-called generation of "rupture." In his short life, García Ponce created works well represented by good color reproductions. In the 1960s he explored new ways of painting that set him apart from Mexican nationalist realism.

261 Cano Manilla, Ramón. Homenaje a Ramón Cano Manilla. Textos de Abel Ramírez Ramírez y Loida Fernández. Fotografía de Rafael Doniz, Joaquín de la Cruz y Carlos Santamaría Ochoa. Ciudad Victoria, México: Gobierno del Estado de Tamaulipas: Instituto Tamaulipeco de Cultura, 1989. 108 p.: bibl., ill. (some col.).

Short biography of Cano's life includes excellent color illustrations and descriptions of his work, as well as chronological notes. Some of his mural paintings were taken as important symbols for the Mexican people's education because of their moral and pedagogical intent.

262 Cardoza y Aragón, Luis. Carlos Mérida: color y forma. México: Consejo Nacional para la Cultura y las Artes; Ediciones Era, 1992. 211 p.: bibl., ill. (some col.). (Galería: Colección de arte mexicano)

Anthology of author's published texts includes excellent chronology of Mérida's life and work, but accompanying texts offer no new insights into an already well-known artist. Excellent color reproductions show Mérida's stylistic development (1911–82) in graphic terms.

263 Chapa Martínez, Roberto. Diálogos con Federico Cantú. Monterrey, Mexico: Univ. Autónoma de Nuevo León, Centro de Información de Historia Regional, 1988. 56 p., 54 leaves of plates: bibl., ill. (Serie Biblioteca de Nuevo León; 3)

Consists of interviews with the artist and a biographical introduction. Cantú talks about his life, work, and contemporary fellow artists. Interesting information on a particular period in Mexican art. B/w illustrations.

264 Chávez Morado, José. José Chávez Morado: su tiempo, su país; obra plástica. Guanajuato, Mexico: Gobierno del Estado de Guanajuato, 1988. 215 p.: bibl., ill. (some col.).

Exhaustive exhibit of work by well-known Mexican artist. Includes good documentation; color and b/w illustrations; references to his easel painting, mural painting, sculpture and graphic work; special chronological information on his monumental works; and reproduction of some of his writings.

265 Clausell, Joaquín. Joaquín Clausell, 1866–1935. México: Editorial MOP, 1988. 27 p., 94 p. of plates: bibl., col. ill.

Description of artist's life and his creative process as impressionist painter. Exhaustive bibliography and color illustrations follow thematic sequence. Lacks formal analysis of paintings but makes for good reading.

266 Conde, Teresa del et al. Pablo O'Higgins: hombre del siglo XX. Presentación de Gonzalo Celorio. México: Difusión Cultural, UNAM, 1992. 142 p.: bibl., ill.

Useful texts shed light on artist's personality and his graphic and mural paintings, which had enormous influence on Mexican art during first decade of 20th century. Includes good color and b/w reproductions.

267 Corzas, Francisco. Francisco Corzas. México: Univ. Autónoma Metropolitana, 1985. 137 p.: bibl., ill. (some col.).

Luxury edition includes excellent color and b/w illustrations, valuable texts written prior to the artist's death, and important analysis of his work.

268 De Micheli, Mario. Siqueiros. México: Secretaría de Educación Pública/Cultura, 1985. 100 p.: bibl., ill. (some col.).

Historical and analytical study of several periods of Siqueiros' creative life. Easy to read, the book offers a wide range of information. Color and b/w illustrations.

269 Díaz Morales, Ignacio. Ignacio Díaz Morales habla de Luis Barragán. Conversación con Fernando González Gortázar. Guadalajara, Mexico: Editorial Univ. de Guadalajara, 1991. 93 p.: ill., index. (Col.

Fundamentos: Serie Arquitectura y urbanismo)

Interview with Díaz Morales about Barragán's life and work provides important information on aspects of Mexican architecture. Interesting and passionate text in which one architect speaks of another who was his close friend. Includes b/w illustrations.

270 Drewes, Michael. Carl Gangolf Kaiser, 1837–1895: und seine Tätigkeit als Hofarchitekt Maximilians von Mexiko. (*Mitt. Inst. Österr. Gesch.forsch.*, 101:2/4, 1993, p. 383–403, facsim., ill., maps)

Using 40 recently discovered documents, author revises his previous views concerning the role of Maximilian's imperial architect. Provides insight into management of Mexican public buildings during Hapsburgs' short reign in Mexico. Of interest to art historians. [G.K. Converse]

271 La Escuela Mexicana de Escultura: maestros fundadores; Museo del Palacio de Bellas Artes, marzo-abril 1990. México: Instituto Nacional de Bellas Artes; Consejo Nacional para la Cultura y las Artes, 1990. 167 p.: bibl., ill.

Illustrated catalog-exhibit about group of unknown sculptors who followed a nationalist trend in their work during the first two decades of the 20th century. Includes short and clear introduction, notes on each artist's work and life, critical anthology, and bibliography. Valuable document.

272 Felguérez, Manuel. Manuel Felguérez: muestra antológica. México: Secretaría de Educación Pública; Instituto Nacional de Bellas Artes, 1987. 98 p.: bibl., ill. (some col.).

Publication encompasses Felguérez's art from his first figurative painting to his abstract-constructive work. Includes excerpts of relevant criticism and analysis of his work as well as important statements by the artist. Color and b/w illustrations.

273 Fernando Gamboa, embajador del arte mexicano. México: Consejo Nacional para la Cultura y las Artes, 1991. 115 p.: ill.

Interesting and informative book is also homage to Gamboa, who devoted much time towards developing museums and related fields in Mexico. Reproduces articles, notes, and catalogs published in the 1940s. Provides insights into Gamboa as professional and individual.

274 Gerzso, Gunther. Exposición retrospectiva de Gunther Gerzso, enero/marzo de 1981. Monterrey, Mexico: Museo de Monterrey, 1981? 1 v.: bibl., ill. (some col.).

Catalog of retrospective exhibit of Gerzso's work. Introduction includes analysis of and quotations from the artist. Excellent color reproductions.

275 Gironella, Alberto. Tren de vida. México: Festival Internacional Cervantino, 1990. 57 p.: ill. (chiefly col.).

Catalog for exhibit of Gironella's works (1954–90). A short essay introduces the painter's personality. Of interest chiefly because of good color reproductions.

276 Goeritz, Mathias. Mathías Goeritz: un artista plural; ideas y dibujos. Edición y prólogo de Graciela Kartofel. México: Consejo Nacional para la Cultura y las Artes, 1992. 161 p.: ill.

Artist's ideas and drawings form nucleus of book. Includes reproductions of Goeritz's published and manuscript texts, essays, manifestoes, criticism, and some concrete poems. Color illustrations of drawings (1942–90). Good source on the artist's personality.

277 Herner de Larrea, Irene; Gabriel Larrea; and Rafael Angel Herrerías. Diego Rivera, Paraíso Perdido en Rockefeller Center. Prólogo de Carlos Sirvent. México: EDICUPES, 1986. 216 p., 24 p. of plates: bibl., ill. (some col.).

Exhaustive study of social content of Rivera's mural at Rockfeller Center. Reproduces newspaper clippings and other printed material on the story of the mural's creation, completion, and destruction.

278 Historia del arte mexicano. v. 1–4, Arte prehispánico. v. 5–8, Arte colonial. v. 9–12, Arte del siglo XIX. v. 13–16, Arte contemporáneo. 2a ed. México: SEP; Salvat, 1986. 16 v.: bibl., ill. (some col.).

These 16 vols., published under the coordination of Jorge Alberto Manrique, provide the most comprehensive history of Mexican art, from prehispanic to contemporary period. Important contribution for art critics and specialists. Color and b/w illustrations.

279 Hurlburt, Laurance P. The Mexican muralists in the United States. Foreword by David W. Scott. Albuquerque: Univ. of New Mexico Press, 1989. 320 p., 8 p. of plates: bibl., ill. (some col.), index.

Valuable and thorough study on subject that needs further research. Author documents very well this period in the history of Mexican muralism. Very good b/w illustrations.

Iturriaga de la Fuente, José N. Litografía y grabado en el México del XIX. v. 1. See item **1379.**

280 **Larrosa, Manuel.** Mario Pani, arquitecto de su época. Prólogo y edición de Louise Noelle. México: UNAM, Impr. Universitaria, 1985. 177 p.: bibl., ill. (one col.), maps.

Describes and analyzes work of Mario Pani, an important architect in the development and modernization of Mexico City. His work (1936–78) was a turning point in Mexican architecture and in the modern history of the country. Beginning with his Hotel Reforma (1936), Pani built many of the city's important modern buildings, including the University City completed in 1952. Excellent b/w illustrations.

281 **Luis Barragán: ensayos y apuntes para un bosquejo crítico.** México: El Museo Rufino Tamayo, 1985. 131 p.: bibl., ill., plans.

Series of critical essays about well-known Mexican architect explore his attitude towards creation of a Mexican vernacular architecture. Includes bibliography, chronological notes, and b/w illustrations of drawings.

282 **Luna Arroyo, Antonio.** Jorge González Camarena en la plástica mexicana. México: UNAM, Coordinación de Humanidades, 1988. 337 p.: ill. (some col.).

Solid text about artist's life and work, especially his relationship with Mexican muralism. Author attempts to cover many aspects of his artistic production and existential beliefs including a bio-psycho-social study of his life. Color and b/w illustrations.

283 **Modernidad y modernización en el arte mexicano, 1920–1960.** México: Museo Nacional de Arte, 1991. 184 p.: bibl., ill. (some col.).

Explores important period in modernization of Mexican art and in the development and renovation of the nation's culture (1920–60). Critical texts by intellectuals and artists, reproduction of works (color and b/w), and heterogeneous materials all stress significance of these 40 years.

284 **Museo José Luis Cuevas (México).** Museo José Luis Cuevas. México: Secretaría de Educación Pública, Depto. del Distrito Federal; Fondo de Cultura Económica; Banca Serfín, 1992. 231 p.: ill. (some col.).

New museum, inaugurated in beautiful building in Mexico City's historical center, will display a permanent exhibit of Cuevas' work. Museum also includes additional galleries for temporary exhibits of other Latin American artists. Full color illustrations.

285 **Noelle, Louise.** Arquitectos contemporáneos de México. México: Editorial Trillas, 1989. 171 p.: bibl., ill.

Dictionary of Mexican architects includes biography, dates, commentaries on works, and bibliography. B/w illustrations of buildings, plans and maquettes. Good reference guide on subject.

286 **Orozco, José Clemente.** J.C. Orozco en el Instituto Cultural Cabañas: 340 obras de caballete. Guadalajara, México: Instituto Cultural Cabañas del Gobierno del Estado de Jalisco, 1983. 155 p.: ill. (some col.).

Bilingual catalog illustrates various manifestations of Orozco's art: caricature, murals, portraits, and graphic work. Includes two short texts: a poem devoted to the artist's life; and a more analytical essay that examines his caricatures. Exhaustive chronology with b/w photos but few color illustrations.

287 **Paz, Octavio** and **Manuel Alvarez Bravo.** Instante y revelación. Edición de A. Muñoz. México: Fondo Nacional para Actividades Sociales, 1982. 100 leaves: chiefly ill.

Beautiful publication includes short introductory text by Octavio Paz and selection of lonely photographs by well-known Mexican artist Manuel Alvarez Bravo. Some photos feature poems by Paz.

Peden, Margaret Sayers. Out of the volcano: portraits of contemporary Mexican artists. See item **3767.**

288 **Pérez de Salazar y Solana, Javier.** José María Velasco y sus contemporáneos: una muestra de la pintura mexicana académica de la segunda mitad del siglo XIX y principios del XX, época de J.M. Velasco. Monterrey: PERPAL, 1982. 242 p.: bibl., col. ill.

Comprehensive reference work in encyclopedia style covers academic painting in

Mexico from the middle of the 19th through the early 20th century, concentrating mainly on prominent artists. Includes short biographical notes on each artist, extensive bibliography, reproduction of documents, a short history of Real Academia de San Carlos, and a panoramic view of Mexico since Independence. Color illustrations.

289 La polémica del arte nacional en México, 1850–1910. Recopilación de Daniel Schávelzon. México: Fondo de Cultura Económica, 1988. 368 p.: bibl., ill. (Sección de obras de historia)

Compilation of articles about art and architecture defined as *neoindigenista, indigenista* or *prehispanista*, which author proposes to call *neoprehispánica.* Complete panorama of Mexico's cultural development, from prehispanic times to the 19th century (National School). Provides good introduction to important segment of Mexican culture. Good b/w illustrations.

290 Posada, José Guadalupe. Monografía: las obras de José Guadalupe Posada, grabador mexicano, con introducción de Diego Rivera. Edición de Frances Toor, Paul O'Higgins y Blas Vanegas Arroyo. México: Ediciones Toledo; Instituto Nacional de Bellas Artes; Aguascalientes, Mexico: Instituto Cultural de Aguascalientes, 1991. 208 p.: ill.

Bilingual monograph includes good illustrations of graphic works which have survived the artist. Text by Diego Rivera. Interesting contribution towards a deeper understanding of Posada's work.

291 Revueltas, Fermín. Fermín Revueltas. Investigación, textos y selección de material de Judith Alanís. Fotografía de Flor Garduño. México: Celanese Mexicana, 1984. 1 v. (unpaged): ill. (some col.).

Describes how artist's life and work are connected to the country's historical and cultural development. Texts show Revueltas' significance in the movement called *Estridentismo* which included important Mexican intellectuals and artists during first decades of 20th century. Color illustrations show works from 1928 to his mural paintings of 1932–34.

Schaefer, Claudia. Textured lives: women, art, and representation in modern Mexico. See item **3771.**

292 Siqueiros, David Alfaro. Me llamaban El Coronelazo. 2a ed. México: Grijalbo, 1987. 613 p., 32 p. of plates: ill., index. (Testimonios)

Witty and ironical memories and testimonies by Siqueiros narrate his life as artist and political figure, as well as Mexico's cultural and political life during that period.

293 Tibol, Raquel. Gráficas y neográficas en México. México: Secretaría de Educación Pública; Univ. Nacional Autónoma de México, 1987. 302 p.: bibl., ill. (Foro 2000)

Author describes and analyzes development of graphic art from its arrival with Rinate de Prevost to Orozco, Posada, and the Taller de Gráfica Popular through recent artists like Zalce, Moreno Capdevila, and Jesús Martínez. Based on author's previously published texts. B/w illustrations.

294 Tibol, Raquel. Hermenegildo Bustos: pintor de pueblo. 2. ed. México: Consejo Nacional para la Cultura y las Artes; Ediciones Era, 1992. 199 p.: bibl., ill. (some col.), map. (Galería. Col. de arte mexicano)

Excellent catalog and text on Bustos' work provides profound insights into his life and work. Solid research on 19th-century artist who mostly painted portraits and ex-votos. Excellent b/w illustrations.

295 Toussaint, Manuel. Saturnino Herrán y su obra. 2. ed. facsimilar. México: UNAM, Instituto de Investigaciones Estéticas; Instituto Cultural de Aguascalientes; Instituto Nacional de Bellas Artes, 1990. 36 p., 59 leaves of plates: ill. (some col.).

Second ed. of important text by Toussaint, one of the first studies on Herrán's work, especially of his portraits, still-lifes and landscapes. Narrative prose offers general view of artist's life and work during first decade of 20th century. Emphasizes its "Mexican essence."

CENTRAL AMERICA

296 Fiallos Salgado, Raúl. Datos históricos sobre la plástica hondureña. Tegucigalpa?: Litografía López, 1989. 129 p.: bibl., ill. (some col.).

General history of Honduran art set within the historical, economical, and sociocultural changes undergone by the country. Author does not treat the aesthetic aspects of

Honduran art. Includes interesting information and b/w illustrations.

297 Herrera, Fabio. Fabio Herrera, serigrafías, 1991 = Fabio Herrera's screen prints, 1991. San José: Premia Editores, 1991. 46 p.: bibl., ill. (some col.). (Andrómeda)

Uninteresting study describes Herrera's graphic work and silkscreens from 1991. Includes biographical notes, bibliography, and color and b/w illustrations.

298 López Rojas, Evaristo and **Longino Becerra.** Gregorio Sabillón: vida y trayectoria artística. Tegucigalpa: Baktun Editorial, 1991. 44 p.: bibl., ill. (some col.).

Text in catalog-type book describes life and artistic development of Sabillón, an Honduran figurative painter who lives in Spain. Important in that it provides information on one of many artists who are little-known throughout Latin America. Color and b/w reproductions.

299 Méndez Dávila, Lionel. Elmar Rojas. Estudio introductorio por Edward J. Sullivan. Guatemala: Armitano Editores; Galería Ambiente Ediciones, 1993? 230 p.: ill. (some col.).

Luxury edition with excellent full color illustrations analyzes work of well-known Guatemalan painter. Interesting texts, written in literary terms, place Rojas' painting within a local context. Includes short references to his life.

300 I Bienal de Arte Pictórico Cervecería Nacional, Panamá 1992. Coordinación de Irene Escoffery and Mónica E. Kupler. El Dorado, Panama: Cervecería Nacional; Museo de Arte Contemporáneo, 1992. 112 p.: plates.

Interesting catalog of exhaustive exhibit of Panamanian art provides overview of the nation's contemporary art. Includes important information and color and b/w illustrations.

301 Recinos, Efraín. Efraín Recinos y su obra: exposición, homenaje. Guatemala: Fundación Paiz, 1991. 1 v.: ill. (some col.).

Catalog of exhibit dedicated to important and polifacetic Guatemalan artist. Text mostly devoted to his architectural works, also includes two interviews with him as well as notes and comments by intellectuals

and other artists. Color illustrations of his architecture and two paintings.

302 Sancho, José. José Sancho. Introducción de Bélgica Rodríguez. Ecazú, Costa Rica: J. Sancho, 1991. 1 v.: ill. (some col.).

Series of eight pamphlets about the artist's sculpture. Introduction, written by Bélgica Rodríguez, traces development of artist's work through the pamphlets. Good color and b/w illustrations.

THE CARIBBEAN

303 Amelia Peláez: fulgor de las islas: XIX Festival Internacional Cervantino. México: SRE; Gobierno del Estado del Guanajuato, 1991? 85 p.: bibl., ill. (some col.).

Catalog of exhibit held at Museo Nacional de La Habana. Introductory text analyzes work of Peláez, an important artist in both the Cuban and international context. Offers good information on her life with b/w personal photos. Color plates illustrate her work from 1926–67.

304 Antonín Nechodoma: umbral para una nueva arquitectura caribeña. Edición de Enrique Vivoni Farage y María del Pilar González Lamela. Río Piedras, Puerto Rico: Archivo de Arquitectura y Construcción de la Univ. de Puerto Rico, Escuela de Arquitectura, 1989. 105 p.: bibl., ill.

Catalog documents exhibition on restoration of Casa Roig, a national landmark and museum in Humacao, Puerto Rico. Provides many personal and professional references to architect Antonio Nechodoma, designer of Casa Roig and other Puerto Rican buildings. Useful research on the island's architecture.

305 Arte contemporáneo dominicano. Santo Domingo: Instituto Dominicano de Cultura Hispánica, 1987? 72 p.:

Interesting directory of Dominican artists includes short biographies and photos of each as well as additional interesting information.

306 Camnitzer, Luis. New art of Cuba. Austin: Univ. of Texas Press, 1993. 1 v.: bibl., index.

Exhaustive treatise on contemporary Cuban art published in English is very well written and documented. Provides clear dis-

cussion of several issues important for understanding Cuban art today. Recommended to
students, specialists, and art critics interested
in Latin American art. B/w illustrations.

307 Jamaican heritage in architecture. London: Berger Paints Jamaica, 1990.
75 p.: ill.

Interesting catalog covers Jamaican
buildings (private residences, schools,
churches and public buildings) prior to 1910.
It was published "in response to the need to
increase public awareness of the island's rich
architectural heritage." Introduction by architect Errol Alberga includes excerpts from academic paper. B/w illustrations.

308 La Habana en Madrid. Madrid: Centro
Cultural de la Villa, 1989? 64 p.:
col. ill.

Catalog of comprehensive exhibit of
Cuban art (e.g., painting, sculpture, ceramic,
photography, graphic work, and textile design). Includes list of artists and short introductory notes about the development of Cuban visual art.

309 Lam, Wifredo. Wifredo Lam, 1902–
1982: obra sobre papel; colección Museo Nacional, Palacio de Bellas Artes, La Habana; junio-octubre 1992, Fundación Cultural
Televisa, AC. Coordinación y edición de Lucía García-Noriega *et al.* México: Centro Cul-
tural/Arte Contemporáneo, 1992. 127 p.:
bibl., ill. (some col.).

Catalog of Lam's works on paper de-
posited at the Museo Nacional, Palacio de
Bellas Artes, La Habana, covers period from
Paris sojourn to his return to Cuba in 1940s.
Excellent color reproductions feature per-
sonal style and artistic quality of his work.

**310 Museo Nacional de Bellas Artes
(Cuba).** La Habana: salas del Museo
Nacional de Cuba, Palacio de Bellas Artes. In-
troducción de Miguel Luis Núñez Gutiérrez.
Fotografía de Gerhard Murza. La Habana: El
Museo Nacional de Bellas Artes, 1990. 184 p.:
chiefly col. ill.

Catalog of museum's permanent collection which consists of antique art, European and Cuban painting. Provides introduction to museum's history, the collection, and
biographical notes on its artists. Color reproductions of the works exhibited are accompanied by technical information as well as thematic and artistic descriptions of each work.

**311 El paisaje dominicano: pintura y
poesía.** Pintura de Jeannette Miller.
Poesía de Freddy Gatón Arce. Santo Domingo: BHD, 1992. 104 p.: ill. (some col.).

Provides valuable research and good information from 19th century through present.
Includes analysis of several conceptual issues.
Four periods of nation's landscape painting
appear in color illustration.

Rigau, Jorge. Puerto Rico, 1900: turn-of-the-
century architecture in the Hispanic Caribbean, 1890–1930. See item **1833.**

312 Tolentino, Marianne de. Cándido Bidó:
pintor de su tierra. v. 1–2. Santo Domingo: C. Bidó, 1989–1990. 2 v.: bibl., ill.
(some col.).

Bilingual edition in two volumes includes good color and b/w illustrations. Vol. 1
is devoted to the painter's subject matter,
analyzing each work extensively and insert-
ing text by other authors to highlight Bidó's
personality and work. Second article by Juan
Bosch consists of a biography and synopsis of
Bidó's creative development.

313 Vargas, Fernando. Dionisio Blanco: las
pinturas enigmáticas = the enigmatic
paintings. Santo Domingo: s.n., 1991. 143 p.:
ill. (some col.).

Bilingual publication describes artist's
life and analyzes his artistic production in the
context of his country's art. Excellent color
and b/w illustrations.

314 Wood, Yolanda. De la plástica cubana y
caribeña. La Habana: Editorial Letras
Cubanas, 1990. 213 p.: bibl., ill. (Letras cubanas. Giraldilla)

Condensed and useful short book
about society and artistic development consists of two parts: 1) architecture and urbanism in Havana; and 2) several notes and articles that analyze Cuba's artistic avant-garde
since the 1900s. Includes important historical
background concerning artistic changes despite the Machado dictatorship. Easy to read.

SOUTH AMERICA
Argentina

315 Badii, Líbero. Obra pictórica. Buenos
Aires: Emecé Editores, 1991. 118 p.: ill.
(some col.).

Interesting and well illustrated book

with color and b/w reproductions of Badii's work. Includes autobiographical contribution in which artist expresses his vision of art and life, makes statements about his painting style, and describes his overall understanding of art. Documents Badii's thoughts and feelings about creation and communication.

316 Brughetti, Romualdo. Nueva historia de la pintura y la escultura en la Argentina: de los orígenes a nuestros días. Buenos Aires: Ediciones de Arte Gaglianone, 1991. 284 p.: bibl., ill. (some col.).

Includes good research on development of Argentine painting and sculpture. Examines the problems conveyed by Argentine art and provides general historical information. Divided into two sections: 1) from prehistoric times to 1940s generation including beginning of abstract movement in 1945; and 2) the 1945–50 period. Few b/w illustrations.

317 Bustamante, Bárbara. Escultura argentina siglo XX. Fotografías de Lutz Matschke. Coordinación de María del Carmen Carbi. Buenos Aires: A.M.C. Ediciones, 1991. 206 p.: ill.

For each artist, this bilingual ed. provides description of sculptor's works, short commentary and biography, personal memorabilia, and one illustration of his work. Provides useful general information.

Cirvini, Silvia. Mendoza: la arquitectura de la reconstrucción posterremoto, 1861–1884. See item **2934.**

318 Gutiérrez Zaldívar, Ignacio. Soldi. Buenos Aires: Zurbarán Ediciones, 1991. 139 p.: bibl., ill. (some col.).

Valuable and beautifully illustrated publication on Soldi includes excellent study of his work as well as chronology, notes, and additional materials important for understanding his evolution within Argentine art.

319 Irigoyen, Adriana and **Ramón Gutiérrez.** Nueva arquitectura argentina: pluralidad y coincidencia. Bogotá: ESCALA, 1990. 221 p.: bibl., ill. (some col.). (Col. SomoSur; 8)

Well-written, illustrated, and interesting book on Argentine domestic architecture, specifically housing and malls, depicts new architectural approach to such buildings as well as influences of traditions, climates, nature, etc.

320 The Journal of Decorative and Propaganda Arts. v. 18, 1992– . Miami, Fla.: Wolfson Foundation of Decorative and Propaganda Arts.

Outstanding issue (241 p.) entirely devoted to architecture and decorative styles of Argentina from 1875–1945, a period when the nation was reinventing itself, according to editor P. Johnson. Includes splendid photographs, illustrations, and 12 articles devoted to the following subjects: the Bariloche style by Levisman Clusellas; Héctor Basaldúa's stage designs by E. Basaldúa; Buenos Aires' 1930s architecture by G. Whitelow; Francisco Salamone's urban art by A. Bellucci; Argentine social realism by M. Pacheco; master *fileatadores* of Buenos Aires by M. Estenssoro; Argentine high fashion by E. Moreira; interview with José María Peña by E. Shaw; and two articles by Peña, on public sculpture and art-noveau stained glass. Separate section (119 p.) includes Spanish translation of all articles. [Ed.]

321 Livingston, Rodolfo. Arquitectura y autoritarismo. Buenos Aires: Ediciones de la Flor, 1991. 244 p.: ill.

Compilation of articles on architecture and authoritarianism published in Argentine newspapers and magazines (1980–90). Study of specific examples of buildings and city plans, especially those developed during the last military regime. Describes the relationship between architecture vis-à-vis human beings in Buenos Aires. Criticizes disorder and lack of understanding on the part of the military regime to handle the problem. Author's analysis applies to other Latin American countries as well.

322 Pérez, Elba. Distéfano. Buenos Aires: Banco Tornquist/Crédit Lyonnais, 1991. 142 p.: bibl., ill. (some col.).

Text sheds light on this Argentine artist's paintings, drawings, and sculptures through analysis of his output (1965–91). Full color illustrations and good choice of materials.

323 Squirru, Rafael F. El artista y su tiempo. Buenos Aires: Ediciones Fundación Rozenblum, 1991. 280 p.: ill.

Compilation of author's articles written in an accessible and pleasant style discusses both universal and Argentine art as well as his theoretical concepts about aesthetics and artistic ethics. Provides good information on Argentine contemporary art. B/w reproductions.

324 Squirru, Rafael F. *et al.* Kosice. Buenos Aires: Ediciones de Arte Gaglianone, 1990. 206 p.: bibl., ill. (some col.).

Monograph on important Argentine artist is very well illustrated in color and b/w. Includes important research and analysis of Kosice's work, written by several specialists, as well as his own explanations of "Hydrospatial City," luminic sculptures, and his manifestos and participation in launching the Buenos Aires Madi Group. Short introduction by Squirru.

325 Whitelow, Guillermo. Héctor Basaldúa. Buenos Aires: Academia Nacional de Bellas Artes; Fondo Nacional de las Artes, 1980. 65 p.: ill. (some col.). (Monografías de artistas argentinos)

Important study includes short and clear text in which author analyzes Basaldúa's life and work. Profusely illustrated in color and b/w. Includes vast collection of memorabilia (e.g., letters, personal photos, etc.) as well as biographical synthesis and account of his paintings and set designs.

Bolivia

Gómez-Martínez, José Luis. Bolivia, un pueblo en busca de su identidad. See item **2798.**

326 Prada, Teresa de. Bolivian artists' guide = Guía de artistas bolivianos. La Paz: Quipus, 1991? 1 v.: col. ill.

Bilingual guide to Bolivian artists includes short biographical notes and some color illustrations. Although providing scant information, book is still useful because it takes notice of these relatively obscure artists.

Chile

327 Bravo, Claudio. Claudio Bravo: pinturas y dibujos; Museo de Monterrey, 25 de marzo/5 de mayo 1982. Monterrey, Mexico: El Museo de Monterrey, 1982? 1 v.: ill. (some col.).

Catalog of exhibit of paintings and drawings by this internationally known Chilean artist. Short introduction only superfi-

cially analyzes Bravo's important work but the biography and color and b/w illustrations illustrate his artistic development.

328 Burón, Ximena. Ximena Burón. Santiago: Fundación Andes, 1989. 1 v.: col. ill.

Part of *Monographs of Chilean Artists*, an excellent series published by the Andes Foundation. Includes good color reproductions, is very well printed, and offers information on Burón's life and work.

329 Cruz de Amenabar, Isabel. Seis pintores chilenos: de fines del siglo XIX y principios del siglo XX. Santiago?: Editorial Antártica, 1990. 64 p.: bibl., col. ill. (Col. Museo Nacional de Bellas Artes)

Study of six landscape painters who are part of the Chilean Museum of Fine Arts' collection: Onofre Jarpa (1849–1940), Thomas Somerscales (1842–1947), Alberto Orrego Luco (1845–1931), Alfredo Helsby (1862–1933), Pablo Burchard (1873–1974), and Enrique Lynch (1864–1936). Includes color reproductions of paintings by each artist, biographies, and short chronological notes.

Diener Ojeda, Pablo *et al.* Rugendas, América de punta a cabo: Rugendas y la Araucanía. See item **645.**

330 Eliash, Humberto and **Manuel Moreno.** Arquitectura y modernidad en Chile, 1925–1965: una realidad múltiple. Santiago: Ediciones Univ. Católica de Chile, 1989. 198 p.: bibl., ill., maps. (Serie Arte/arquitectura)

Study of emergence of modernism in Chilean architecture consists of seven important chapters. Chronological notes address continued impact of earthquakes on urban renewal, a fact which has determined the particular style of the nation's architecture. Reevaluates some buildings and analyzes 40 years of the relationship between architecture and the nation's physical and cultural contexts, such as its social, cultural, and technological development. Includes b/w illustrations.

331 Encuentro Arte Industria, 3rd, Santiago, 1989. Tercer Encuentro Arte Industria, 1989. Coordinación general de Lily Lanz. Santiago: Sociedad de Fomento Fabril (SFF), 1989. 80 p.: ill. (some col.).

Important catalog of "Arte-Industria" exhibit devoted to interaction between art and industry. Many artworks exhibited were originally funded and supported by industry, which played a role in the development and realization of Chilean art. Color illustrations.

332 Ivelić, Milan and **Luisa Ulibarri.** Intimidades: 20 artistas visuales chilenos. Santiago: Editorial La Puerta Abierta, 1989. 119 p.: ill. (some col.).

As the word "intimacy" in the title indicates, book offers personal and close look at "the present situation in Chilean art" of a group of artists almost unknown outside the country: Ernesto Banderas, Julio Palazuelos, Verónica Rojas, Enrique Zamudio, Nancy Gewold, Angela Riesco, Elisa Aguirre, Carlos Fernández, Luis Mandiola, Hugo Marín, Ricardo Mesa, Francisca Núñez, Jaime León, Inés Harnecker, Odette Sansot, Ulrich Welss, Roberto Dannemann, Omar Gatica, Sergio Lay and Enrique Matthey.

333 Larraín Arroyo, Consuelo. Marta Colvin: el signo ancestral de América en la piedra. Santiago: Depto. del Extensión Cultural, Ministerio de Educación, 1989. 24 p. (Col. Diapolibros)

Analysis of different periods in the creative life of this Chilean sculptor. Provides information about her life and work, excerpts from criticism, and series of color slides. Important for art critics and specialists.

334 Matta Echaurren, Roberto Sebastián. Exposición Matta uni verso. Ministerio de Educación de Chile, Ministerio de la Cultura de Venezuela. Santiago?: Enersis, 1991. 1 v.: bibl., ill. (some col.).

Important catalog of exhibit of remarkable Chilean artist. Known internationally, Matta began his artistic career in 1933 in the surrealist movement in Paris. Introductory text offers full and detailed account of his life and work. Good color reproductions of paintings (1955–91).

335 Munizaga, Gustavo. Estructura y ciudad. Dibujos de Andrés Fernández *et al.* 2a. ed. Santiago: Ediciones Univ. Católica de Chile, Vicerrectoría Académica, Comisión Editorial, 1985. 147 p.: bibl., ill.

Compilation of results of research conducted by author on the "application of systems of movement and the collective form in urban design." Uses his investigations of systems and typologies with wealth of diagrams and illustrations in order to explain develop-

ment of architecture and urbanism in Santiago.

336 Ossa Puelma, Nena. Grandes maestros de la pintura chilena. Santiago: Fundación de Bellas Artes, 1989. 63 p.: ill. (some col.). (Col. Museo Nacional de Bellas Artes)

Short introduction to the work and environment of these master painters: Pedro Lira Rencoret, Juan Francisco González, Alfredo Valenzuela Puelma, and Alberto Valenzuela Llanos. Includes biographical notes on each artist and color illustrations.

Vicuña, Cecilia. Unravelling words & the weaving of water. See item **4988.**

Colombia

337 Arango, Silvia. Historia de la arquitectura en Colombia. Bogotá: Centro Editorial y Facultad de Artes, Univ. Nacional de Colombia, 1990. 291 p.: bibl., ill., index.

Good study based on exhaustive and solid research of Colombian architecture. Author revised text and works from 1985 exhibit and included additional material. B/w illustrations.

338 Ariza, Gonzalo. Gonzalo Ariza. Textos de Ana María Escallón *et al.* Reproducciones fotográficas de Oscar Monsalve. Bogotá: Villegas Editores, 1989. 239 p.: bibl., ill. (some col.).

Series of texts discusses different aspects of this landscape painter's work. Provides complete illustrations of works (1937–88), but lack of chronological order makes it difficult to follow his stylistic development. Nevertheless, an important publication.

339 Caballero, Luis. Luis Caballero, retrospectiva de una confesión: Biblioteca Luis-Angel Arango, mayo-julio de 1991. Bogotá: Banco de la República, 1991. 79 p.: bibl., ill. (some col.).

Interesting and very well illustrated catalog of retrospective exhibit devoted to Caballero. Texts and biographical information illuminate the work of this important Colombian artist.

340 Grau, Enrique. Enrique Grau, artista colombiano. Texto de Donald B. Goodall *et al.* Bogotá: Amazonas Editores, 1991. 253 p.: bibl., ill. (some col.).

Excellent and interesting publication

in which three specialists analyze Grau's life and works. Periods of his long creative life serve as good examples of the development of Colombian art. Includes extensive chronology that places Grau's work within the art of his time. Full color and b/w illustrations.

341 Hoyos, Ana Mercedes. Ana Mercedes Hoyos, de la luz al palenque. Texto de Eduardo Serrano. Bogotá: Ediciones Alfredo Wild, 1990. 123 p.: bibl., ill. (some col.).

Exhaustive monograph analyzes Hoyos' work across her different periods, from Pop to geometric abstract paintings through her famous still-lives of today. Important for understanding Hoyos' work. Includes wealth of quotations from articles by editor Serrano, Hoyos herself, and late critic Marta Traba. Richly illustrated.

342 Jiménez, Darío. Darío Jiménez: exposición antológica, 1938–1980; Biblioteca Luis-Angel Arango, XXX aniversario, salas de exposición, marzo-abril de 1987. Bogotá: Banco de la República, 1987. 91 p.: ill. (some col.).

Exhibit catalog analyzes his work and life within Colombia's artistic context. Reproduces artist's texts and important chronological notes with information on Colombian art. Color and b/w reproductions.

343 Núñez Borda, Luis. L. Núñez Borda, el pintor de Bogotá. Investigación para la biografía del artista y localización de su obra pictórica de María Cristina Iriarte. Fotografía de Danilo Vitalini y Miguel A. García. Bogotá?: Litográficos de Escala, 1988. 116 p.: col. ill., index.

Study of artist known as "the painter of Bogotá" describes his life and work, the latter as a "testimony to the city's spirit and the traditions of the capital and its surroundings." This interesting artist who painted his landscape within Colombian context towards the end of the 19th century and beginning of the 20th was relatively unknown. Includes analysis of individual works and full illustrations in color.

344 Oberndorfer, Leni. Pedro Nel Gómez, pintor, escultor y amante: una crónica. Medellín: Secretaría de Educación y Cultura de Antioquia, 1991. 2 v. (878 p.): ill. (some col.). (Col. Ediciones especiales; 6)

Interesting two-volume compilation of documentation about the life and work of important Colombian artist (e.g., letters, criticism, Nel Gómez's comments and statements, etc.). Personal views of author Oberndorfer are occasionally imposed because of her particular analytical approach.

345 Obregón, Alejandro. Alejandro Obregón, pintor colombiano = Alejandro Obregón, peintre colombien. Coordinación de Soffy Arboleda de Vega et al. Traducción de Jean Pierre Larousse. Bogotá: Ministerio de Relaciones Exteriores: Instituto Colombiano de Cultura, 1985. 159 p.: bibl., ill. (some col.).

Catalog of retrospective exhibit at Bogotá's National Museum. Articles by different authors offer great diversity of opinions about Obregón's work. Some are plain nonsense such as "Musicality in A.O.;" others are of definite interest such as those written by the late Marta Traba. Color illustrations depict Obregón's artistic progress, from first portraits to his 1980s abstract landscapes.

346 Panesso, Fausto. Arte y parte: cuatro décadas en el arte colombiano. v. 1. Fotografías de Olga Lucía Jordán. Bogotá?: Ediciones Gamma, 1990. 1 v.: col. ill.

Luxurious edition includes beautiful color illustrations and articles on each of 21 individuals selected. Neither a history nor anthology, work is designed to promote the artists and their works.

347 Rayo, Omar. Omar Rayo. Bogotá: Bolivar Seguros, 1990. 170 p.: ill. (some col.).

Beautiful publication illustrated with works completed between 1964–90. Through artist's images the reader can follow Rayo's artistic development. With the exception of Cobo Borda's article, other texts add little of interest about Rayo's artistic and historical importance.

348 Rojas, Carlos. Carlos Rojas: una constante creativa. Bogotá: Museo de Arte Moderno de Bogotá, 1990. 1 v.: col. ill.

Catalog includes extensive interview revealing the depths of Rojos' work and the complexity of the creative act. Clear texts address significance of Rojas' artistic production. Very well illustrated in color.

349 Saldarriaga Roa, Alberto. Arquitectura y cultura en Colombia. Bogotá: Univ. Nacional de Colombia, 1986. 159 p.: bibl., ill.

Concise and well-written book draws together various essays by Saldarriaga Roa analyzing Colombian architecture, its background, motifs, and impact on the country's cultural development. Proposes interesting new system for analysis of architecture. Includes b/w illustrations and good bibliography.

350 Salmona, Rogelio. Rogelio Salmona: arquitectura y poética del lugar. Análisis crítico de Germán Téllez. Traducción de Susana Cowles de Restrepo. Bogotá: Facultad de Arquitectura, Univ. de los Andes: ESCALA, 1991. 348 p.: ill. (some col.). (Col. SomoSur; 11)

Valuable bilingual publication dedicated to leading Colombian architect. Important analysis of Salmona's creations follows his own opinions on architecture as an "architecture of reality." Editor's analysis and full descriptions enhance our understanding of Salmona's work. Well illustrated in color and b/w.

351 Serrano, Eduardo. Andrés de Santa María: pintor colombiano de resonancia universal. Investigación y supervisión de Myriam Acevedo. Bogotá: Museo de Arte Moderno de Bogotá: Novus Ediciones, 1988. 250 p.: bibl., ill. (some col.), index.

Extensive analysis of artist regarded as the founder of Colombian modernism. Includes detailed chronology of his life and work, description of various creative periods, and historic context in which he developed his art. Handsomely illustrated in color.

Ecuador

352 Almeida, Enrique. El arte genial de Víctor Mideros: centenario de su nacimiento, 1888–1988. Quito: Tall. Gráf. del Instituto Andino de Artes Populares del Convenio Andrés Bello, 1988. 156 p.: bibl., ill.

Although book's first part contains series of repetitive and casual reflections on art, philosophy, and beauty, second part covers Mideros' life and art in an interesting manner.

Bock, Sophie. Quito, Guayaquil: identificación arquitectural y evolución socio-económica en el Ecuador, 1850–1987. See *HLAS 53:5240.*

353 Castro y Velázquez, Juan. Pintura costumbrista ecuatoriana del siglo XIX: de la colección Castro y Velázquez. Quito: Centro Interamericano de Artesanías y Artes Populares, 1990. 47 p.: bibl. (Cuaderno de cultura popular; 16)

Short introduction to a well-worked topic which deserves further dissemination. Includes references to *costumbrista* artists, mostly anonymous individuals who worked in small formats in Quito during the last years of 19th and beginning of the 20th centuries. Text offers information on ethnic groups such as the population of Otavalos and Quito. No illustrations.

354 100 artistas del Ecuador. Dirección de Inés María Flores. Introducción de Hernán Rodríguez Castelo. Textos de Inés María Flores y David Andrade Aguirre, basados en artículos originales publicados en Revista Diners por Hernán Rodríguez Castelo *et al.* Quito: Dinediciones, 1990. 285 p.: bibl., col. ill.

Compilation of texts by different Ecuadorian specialists published in *Diners Magazine.* Important contribution to Ecuadorian contemporary art despite book's lack of cohesion. Includes short biography of each artist and color illustrations.

355 Llamazares Martín, Vicente. Quito. Madrid: Instituto de Cooperación Iberoamericana: Quinto Centenario, 1989. 234 p.: bibl., col. ill. (Col. Ciudades iberoamericanas)

Excellent monograph on this beautiful colonial city provides information on its history, people, customs, and landscape. Includes very well written texts and excellent color illustrations.

356 Moya Tasquer, Rolando and **Evelia Peralta.** Arquitectura contemporánea: nuevos caminos en Ecuador. Quito: TRAMA, 1991. 183 p.: bibl., ill. (Serie Historia)

Analyzes new Ecuadorian architecture according to country's social and economic evolution and its interaction with international architecture. Clear, short, and analytical texts discuss subject. Includes b/w illustrations and discussion of buildings as well as references to important Ecuadorian architects.

357 Ribadeneira de Cásares, Mayra. Tigua: arte primitivista ecuatoriano. Ecuador?: Centro de Arte Exedra, 1990. 70 p.: col. ill.

Interesting catalog-book on the naif painters of Tigua, Ecuador. Uses original approach to address their artistic expression. Includes excellent color illustrations and information about these artists.

Peru

358 Doblado, Juan Carlos. Arquitectura peruana contemporánea: escritos y conversaciones. Lima: Arquidea Ediciones, 1990. 119 p.: ill.

Useful publication divided into two sections: 1) general articles in which author analyzes Peruvian architecture (postmodernism, Latin American identity, etc.); and 2) series of interviews with architects whose observations aid understanding of the development of contemporary Peruvian architecture. No illustrations.

359 Moll, Eduardo. Luis Palao Berastain, 1943. Lima?: Braedt, 1990. 144 p.: ill. (some col.).

Monograph with good color illustrations includes enough analytical text for understanding Palao Berastain's watercolors. Unfortunately author does not establish the relation between this artist and Peruvian art. Of interest to scholars interested in Palao Berastain.

360 Moll, Eduardo. Tilsa Tsuchiya, 1929–1984. Lima: Editorial Navarrete, 1991. 127 p.: ill. (some col.).

Discusses life and paintings of Tsuchiya, who has recently achieved international recognition. Chronological notes and author's comments provide good information about her creative process. Fully illustrated in color, plus personal photos in b/w.

361 Salazar Bondy, Sebastián. Una voz libre en el caos: ensayo y crítica de arte. Lima: Jaime Campodónico/Editor, 1990. 296 p.: ill.

Interesting compilation of general observations about Peruvian, Latin American and European art includes critical analyses of specific art works and related matters.

362 Szyszlo, Fernando de. Fernando de Szyszlo. Bogotá: E.A. Wild, 1991. 233 p.: col. ill. (chiefly ill.), index.

English version of Spanish original includes beautiful color reproductions, Szyszlo's reflections about his own painting

and Peruvian art, and chronological notes. Important work for specialists in which various authors attempt to analyze Szyszlo's work. Unfortunately, prose sounds more like poetry than art criticism.

363 Tola, José. José Tola: 1969–1991. México: Premià Editora, 1991. 1 v.: bibl., ill.

Informative book about Tola's life and work consists of miscellaneous materials (e.g., texts, letters, quotations from several sources, commentaries, interviews, etc.). Overall, this useful book conveys the importance and complexity of Tola's work and his motivation as an artist. Very well illustrated in color and b/w.

364 Tord, Luis Enrique. Jorge Vinatea Reinoso. Lima: Banco del Sur del Perú, 1992. 219 p.: bibl., chiefly ill. (some col.).

Book is a tribute to life and work of Vinatea Reinoso, a painter who died very young but whose work is considered among the most important in Peruvian art. Moving letters, criticism, commentaries and text place him within the socioeconomic and cultural context of the time in Peru. Includes short thematic descriptions of paintings and good color illustrations.

365 Tord, Luis Enrique. Teodoro Núñez Ureta: pintura mural. Estudio y comentarios de Teodoro Núñez Ureta. Lima: Banco Industrial del Perú, 1989. 151 p.: bibl., ill. (some col.) ;

Monograph on Peru's most important muralist reproduces Núñez Ureta's own texts on his ideas about murals. His subjects are landscapes with patriotic or moral themes as well as scenes of everyday life. Includes explanation of these works as well as color illustrations of his murals in Lima, Tarma and Arequipa, in which the influence of Mexican muralism is noticeable. Important attempt to incorporate him into the development of Latin American muralism.

366 Zevallos, Andrés. Tres pintores cajamarquinos: Mario Urteaga, José Sabogal, Camilo Blas. Fotografía de Alois Eichenlaub. Cajamarca, Perú: Asociación Editora Cajamarca, 1991. 112 p.: bibl., ill. (some col.).

Interesting book on three artists responsible for fostering the development of Peruvian art includes short introduction on art and culture in Cajamarca as well as artistic and biographical notes on each painter. Color and b/w illustrations of works and personal photos of artists.

Uruguay

367 Fonseca, Gonzalo. Gonzalo Fonseca. Montevideo: Ministerio de Educación y Cultura, Museo Nacional de Artes Plásticas y Visuales, 1990. 55 p.: ill. (some col.).

Trilingual catalog of exhibit at the 44th Venice Biennial (Spanish, English, Italian). Introduction by Angel Kalenberg provides deep insights into Fonseca's work. Includes many illustrations in color and b/w.

368 Hernández, Anhelo. Matto: pinturas y esculturas. Fotografías de Alfredo Testoni y Danielle Chappard. Montevideo: Impr. AS, 1991. 53 p.: ill. (some col.).

Unfortunately, book's text is very confusing and fails to place Matto's important work within the context of Latin American and international art. This Uruguayan artist works in the tradition of the great Joaquín Torres García, an artist who developed his own theory of aesthetics. Includes bilingual, exhaustive chronology, and excellent color and b/w illustrations.

369 Lucchini, Aurelio. El concepto de arquitectura y su traducción a formas en el territorio que hoy pertenece a la República Oriental del Uruguay. Montevideo: Univ. de la República, Facultad de Arquitectura, Instituto de Historia de la Arquitectura, 1986. 1 v.: bibl., ill. (some folded).

Historiographic handbook offers view of Uruguayan architecture from introduction of neoclassic style, eclecticism, and rationalism through more recent developments in the late 19th century. Interesting work establishes a strong connection between Uruguayan and European architecture. Includes b/w illustrations.

Venezuela

370 Abinade, José. El color humano: 20 pintores venezolanos. Caracas: Academia Nacional de la Historia, 1990. 170 p. (El Libro menor; 167)

Consists of useful interviews and commentaries on a number of Venezuelan artists covering aspects of their professional and private lives. Indeed, more than a study of their art, this is a personal assessment of their minds and souls. No illustrations.

371 Esteva Grillet, Roldán. Desnudos no, por favor y otros estudios sobre artes plásticas venezolanas. Caracas: Alfadil Ediciones, 1991. 219 p.: ill. (Col. Trópicos; 32)

Compilation of author's very well written, brisk, and to-the-point essays on Venezuelan art (1984–88) published in catalogs, art magazines, and newspapers. Essays cover various topics and contemporary artists and provide useful historical information and analysis of their works. B/w illustrations only.

372 Noriega, Simón. El realismo social en la pintura venezolana, 1940–1950. Mérida, Venezuela: Univ. de Los Andes, Consejo de Publicaciones, 1989. 138 p.: bibl., ill. (some col.).

Addresses important decade in development of Venezuelan art (1940–50). Author treats *realismo social* as a very important movement and although some theoretical observations are polemical, he does open debate for further analysis and revision of the opinions of other Venezuelan specialists. Important study includes extensive chronology and short biographies of artists. Some b/w and color reproductions.

373 Otero Rodríguez, Alejandro. Saludo al siglo XXI. Caracas: Armitano Editor, 1989. 126 p.: ill. (chiefly col.).

Beautiful book, very well printed and illustrated in full color shows the late Otero's research on computer art and is specifically related to IBM's computerized design of his gigantic sculpture Torre Solar. Includes other computerized images of Otero's kinetic sculptures.

374 Pedro Centeno Vallenilla. Caracas: Armitano Editores: Museo de Arte Contemporáneo de Caracas Sofía Imber, 1991. 133 p.: bibl., ill. (some col.).

Good catalog of a Centeno Vallenilla retrospective exhibit. Analyzes his works within national and international contexts as well as in terms of the artist's own life. Monograph reveals the artist's importance in Venezuela's artistic development. Color and b/w reproductions.

375 Premio Eugenio Mendoza: mención escultura. 5. ed. Caracas: Sala Mendoza, 1990. 30 p.: ill.

Catalog of sculptors awarded this important prize. Lacks relevant texts but includes good color reproductions of participating artists: Milton Becerra, Ricardo Benaím, Eugenio Espinoza, José Gabriel Fernández, Mayleen García, Luis Lartitegui, Oscar Machado, Carlos Medina, Marcos Salazar, Antonieta Sosa, Nelson Varela, and Carlos Mendoza.

BRAZIL

JOSE M. NEISTEIN, *Executive Director, Brazilian-American Cultural Institute, Washington*

ONE THIRD OF ALL WORKS ANNOTATED for this volume cover 20th-century Brazilian art, a fact which attests both to the overwhelming number of authors and publishers attuned to modern and contemporary creativity as well as to the cultural vitality of the country. Scholars also contributed interesting and valuable publications to the criticism and history of Brazilian art. On the other hand, publications about cartoons, comic strips, and Afro-Brazilian and Indian traditions have declined to such an extent that there are no annotations on these topics in this volume.

Insofar as important inventories of the Brazilian patrimony are concerned, two items should be singled out, one for Pernambuco (item **378**) and the other on Espírito Santo (item **376**). On the colonial period, we welcome an in-depth study of Albert Eckhout (item **384**); a monograph on São Paulo's Luz Monastery and its Sacred Art Museum (item **383**), and a Brazilian edition of some of English art historian John Bernard Bury's best essays on colonial Brazil (item **382**). There are two publications of special interest for the 19th century: Jorge Getulio Veiga's *Chinese export porcelain in private Brazilian collections* (item **390**) and José Roberto Teixeira Leite's *Pintores negros do oitocentos* (item **388**).

Among the many worthwhile publications on the 20th century, one should mention the comparative study of São Paulo's Week of Modern Art and New York's Armory Show (item **392**) and the political appraisal of Portinari's work (item **398**), both long overdue publications. The role played by the Brazilian upper classes in the development of modern art is sharply examined by Durand (item **397**), while the encompassing study by Walter Zanini of The Santa Helena Group is another relevant contribution (item **408**), as is Ronaldo Brito's monograph on Sérgio Camargo (item **395**).

Arquitetura moderna no Rio de Janeiro is an outstanding research source (item **416**); Pierre Verger's *Centro Histórico de Salvador: 1946–1952* is the best photography book on the subject to date (item **412**); and *Minas dos Inconfidentes* (item **411**) may well be the most beautiful book of photography on colonial Minas in many years. *Fontes e chafarizes do Brasil* also gathers exceptionally beautiful photographs (item **417**). Last but not least, *Retratos do Brasil* is an outstanding contribution to the history of political caricature in Brazil (item **421**).

REFERENCE AND THEORETICAL WORKS

376 **Achiamé, Fernando.** Catálogo de bens culturais tombados no Espírito Santo. Organizado por Fernando Antônio de Moraes Achiamé, Fernando Augusto de Barros Bettarello e Fernando Lima Sanchotene. São Paulo: Vitória, Brasil: Massao Ohno Editor, 1991. 190 p.: ill. (some col.), map.

Accurate description of principal buildings (18th through 20th centuries) in Espírito Santo state includes civilian, military, and religious architecture. Provides references to issues of conservation and is illustrated with b/w photographs.

377 Arlégo, Edvaldo. Olinda, patrimônio natural e cultural da humanidade = Olinda, world's natural and cultural heritage. Recife, Brazil: Edições Edificantes, 1990. 155 p.: bibl., ill.

Set of chronicles about life and traditions in Olinda as well as personal views on the traditional architecture of one of the most representative colonial sites in Brazil. Midway between history and travel guide.

378 Inventário do patrimônio cultural do Estado de Pernambuco: Sertão do São Francisco. Recife, Brazil?: FUNDARPE, Governo do Estado de Pernambuco, Secretaria de Turismo, Cultura e Esportes de Pernambuco, 1987. 282 p.: bibl., ill., maps.

Exhaustive inventory covers all aspects of architecture in Pernambuco by using representative buildings for each category and period of Pernambucan history: rural, urban, civilian, religious, and military. Includes wealth of material for future in-depth research. Photos in b/w, maps, charts, and elevations.

379 Morais, Frederico. Panorama das artes plásticas: séculos XIX e XX. 2a. ed. rev. São Paulo: Instituto Cultural Itaú, 1991. 164 p.

Pt. 2 of this book, devoted to Brazil, is of special interest to this *HLAS* chapter. Succint and informative.

380 O Museu Histórico Nacional. São Paulo: Banco Safra, 1989. 365 p.: ill. (some col.).

Rio de Janeiro's Museum of National History opened in 1922 to celebrate the centennial of Brazil's independence. Its holdings encompass artifacts, documents, and art and decorative objects related to the entire history of Brazil, as well as a specialized library. Best of its kind in the country, the museum is housed in a large military building (or arsenal) built in the 1770s, with later additions. This well printed book contains best available examples for each category of the museum's collections. Informative texts.

381 Oliveira, Franklin de. Morte da memória nacional. 2a. ed., rev. e ampliada. Rio de Janeiro: Prefeitura da Cidade do Rio de Janeiro, Secretaria Municipal de Cultura, Turismo e Esportes, Fundação Rio/RIOARTE: Topbooks, 1991. 178 p.: bibl. (Biblioteca carioca)

Highly controversial and provocative,

Oliveira's essays were first published in 1964. His vehement condemnation of Brazil's lack of artistic and cultural preservation, its insufficient official support, and how this threatens the national memory is as strong today as it was 30 years ago. In these 13 essays, Oliveira points out major preservation issues throughout the nation.

Santos, Sydney M.G. dos. O legado de Vicente Licínio Cardoso: as leis básicas da filosofia da arte. See item **5490.**

COLONIAL PERIOD

Bayón, Damián and **Murillo Marx.** History of South American colonial art and architecture: Spanish South America and Brazil. See item **77.**

382 Bury, John. Arquitetura e arte no Brasil colonial. Organização de Myriam Andrade Ribeiro de Oliveira. Tradução de Isa Mara Lando. São Paulo: Nobel, 1991. 219 p.: bibl., ill.

John Bernard Bury (1917-) is a relatively little-known English art historian who has contributed excellent studies on the art and architecture of colonial Brazil. This set of texts includes such essays as: "The Twelve Prophets of Congonhas do Campo," "Jesuit Architecture in Brazil," and "As Igrejas Borromínicas no Brasil." Significant additon to the bibliography of art on colonial Brazil.

383 Museu de Arte Sacra, Mosteiro da Luz. São Paulo: Editora Artes, 1987. 180 p.: bibl., ill. (some col.).

Luz Monastery, continuously occupied by the Order of the Immaculate Conception, is the sole extant colonial building in São Paulo. Still in its original form, it was built by Frei Antônio de Sant'Anna Galvão in 1774 and has been declared a national treasure. Its architecture offers one of the finest examples of "taipa" construction, a primitive "castiço" mode of building. Since 1969 the Luz Monastery has also housed the Sacred Art Museum of the São Paulo Metropolitan Curia, one of the finest of its kind in Brazil as attested by excellent color photographs. Includes very good essays on various aspects of the extensive Brazilian holdings.

384 Valladares, Clarival do Prado. Albert Eckhout: a presença da Holanda no Brasil, século XVII; revisão crítica e atualidade. Verbetes científicos de Luiz Emygdio de

Mello Filho. Rio de Janeiro: Edições Alumbramento, 1989. 141 p.: bibl., ill. (chiefly col.).

Since the 1960s, there has been an increasing interest in the Dutch occupation of the Brazilian Northeast, especially the eight years of Count João Maurício de Nassau-Siegen's rule in Pernambuco in the 1600s. This splendid book is the result of exhaustive archival research in The Netherlands, Portugal, Spain, and Brazil as well as of study of relevant exhibitions such as that of the Museum of Modern Art of Rio de Janeiro (1968), two exhibitions at The Hague and Siegen (1979), and one at the Imperial Palace in Rio de Janeiro (1987). Includes excellent critical review and stunning color reproductions.

385 Viotti, Hélio Abranches and **Murillo Moutinho.** Anchieta nas artes. 2a. ed. ampliada. São Paulo: Edições Loyola, 1991. 186 p.: bibl., ill. (some col.). (Monumenta anchietana—obras completas; 15)

Life of Jesuit José de Anchieta (1534–97), Apostle of Brazil, is interwoven with Brazil's own historical origins. He catechized and defended the Indians, supported the preservation of the country's territory, founded colleges that were the nation's first cultural centers, and is usually regarded as the founder of Brazilian literature. Book consists of anthology of how Anchieta's life and works have influenced Brazilian art over the centuries. Rich iconography encompasses Jesuitic art throughout Brazil.

19TH CENTURY

386 Benedito Calixto: memória paulista. São Paulo: Pinacoteca, 1990. 122 p.: bibl., ill. (some col.).

Special focus on the "paulista" side of Calixto's production. Of particular interest are the essays: "Calixto e a Iconografia Paulistana," by B.L. de Toledo; "Benedito Calixto como Documento," by Ulpiano T.B. de Menezes; and "B.C.: Memória Paulista," by Dalton Sala. Color reproductions are fine but too small in format.

387 Kaiser, Gloria and **Robert Wagner.** Thomas Ender, Brasilien-Expedition 1817: Aquarelle aus dem Kupferstichkabinett der Akademie der bildenden Künste Wien; Hispanic Division, Library of Congress, Washington DC 1993, Biblioteca Nacional, Rio de Janeiro, Saguão Nobre 1994: Handbuch

und Katalog = Thomas Ender, Expedição ao Brasil 1817: aquarelas do gabinete de gravuras da Academia de Artes Viena. Graz: Akademische Druck- u. Verlagsanstalt, 1994. 103 p.

Metternich sent an expedition to Brazil on the occasion of Dom Pedro I's marriage to Princess Leopoldine, who became Empress of Brazil. Thus, Austria became very important to Brazil politically, scientifically, and culturally. Thomas Ender joined the expedition as its artist and produced 782 drawings and watercolors of exquisite beauty and of great documentary interest, 40 of which are reproduced in this handsome publication. Excellent texts and color reproductions.

388 Leite, José Roberto Teixeira. Pintores negros do oitocentos. Edição de Emanoel Araújo. São Paulo: Edições K; Motores MWM Brasil, 1988. 246 p.: bibl., ill. (chiefly col.).

From the 1840s to the early 20th century there was a considerable number of active black painters in Brazil, a fact that was little known in Brazil itself. Some were very fine artists such as Estevão Silva, Firmino Monteiro, Pinto Bandeiro João, and Artur Timóteo da Costa. This well documented study includes a good introduction and illustrations. Most welcome book that is long overdue.

389 Prado, João Fernando de Almeida. O artista Debret e o Brasil. São Paulo: Companhia Editora Nacional, 1990. 159 p.: ill. (Brasiliana; 386)

Reprint of classic account about Jean Baptiste Debret, a member of the French Artistic Mission sent to Imperial Brazil in 1816.

390 Veiga, Jorge Getulio and **Carlos Eduardo de Castro Leal.** Chinese export porcelain in private Brazilian collections. London: Distributor, Han-Shan Tang, 1989. 344 p.: bibl., ill. (some col.), map.

Jorge Getulio Veiga's magnificent collection contains "Imperial" Chinese export porcelain pieces as well as the "Mail Service" of Brazil's Bragança court, also called "Porcelana da Companhia das Indias." These were commissioned porcelain service sets featuring European engravings, coats of arms, armorial shields, etc., and were exported from Asia to Europe along with Blanc-de-Chine, Celadon, and the whole range of blue-and-white chinaware. Some Brazilian private collections contain some of the finest examples of porcelain and china that came to Brazil in the 18th and 19th centuries. Volume may well be the best record of such Brazilian holdings to date. Very fine color plates.

20TH CENTURY

391 Acervo, masterpieces, Banco Chase Manhattan. Rio de Janeiro: Editora Index, 1989. 118 p.: col. ill.

Chase Manhattan Bank has been a consistent collector of Brazilian art since the early 1960s. This handsomely designed and printed book features the stars of this wide-ranging collection.

392 Bastos, Eliana. Entre o escândalo e o sucesso: a Semana de 22 e o Armory Show. Campinas, Brasil: Editora da Unicamp, 1991. 198 p.: bibl., ill. (Col. Repertórios)

Long-overdue and most welcome comparative study of São Paulo's "Week of Modern Art" and New York's "Armory Show." This remarkable study updates Mário de Andrade's and Walt Kuhn's historical prophecies as well as Oswald de Andrade's ideas on material progress and the new artistic and cultural order. Eliana Bastos sharply underscores the contradictions and shows how roles played by Dona Olívia Guedes Penteado and Mrs. Mabel Dodge were stunningly similar.

Bayón, Damián and **Roberto Pontual.** La peinture de l'Amérique latine au XXe siècle: identité et modernité. See item **247.**

393 BR 80: pintura Brasil década 80. São Paulo: Instituto Cultural Itaú, 1991. 109 p.: col. ill.

Overview of Brazilian painting in the 1980s, supported by Instituto Cultural Itaú, covers output of representative artists in their 20s or early 30s. Includes major trends and a dozen insightful essays by different critics who introduce the groups by their regional or artistic orientation. Fine color reproductions.

394 Brill, Alice. Samson Flexor: do figurativismo ao abstracionismo. São Paulo: K; MWM; EDUSP, 1990. 261 p.: bibl., ill. (some col.).

One of Brazil's most representative abstract painters, Samson Flexor was born in Rumania and lived in Paris before settling in Brazil. Through his entire life, he conducted a running dialogue with different masters of abstract art. Alice Brill focuses on this dialogue, on Flexor's own convictions, and the balance he struck between the emotional and the rational. Insightful book contains a wealth of information and excellent color reproductions.

395 Brito, Ronaldo. Camargo. São Paulo: Edições Akagawa, 1990. 265 p.: bibl., ill. (some col.).

In addition to his works with nuclei of elements that propose a cosmos close to the absurd and the aleatory, Camargo also produced reliefs with few and sometimes only one element. Camargo is certainly one of the best, most energetic and elegant sculptors of Brazil, and this book does him justice. Brilliant text by Ronaldo Brito. Excellent b/w and color photographs.

396 A cor e o desenho do Brasil = Drawing and colour in Brazil. São Paulo: Mauro Ivan Marketing Editoral, 1984? 82 p.: ill. (some col.).

Catalog of travelling exhibition of Brazil's finest living artists, each one illustrated with three works and biographical data. Includes five insightful, critical essays.

397 Durand, José Carlos. Arte, privilégio e distinção: artes plásticas, arquitetura e classe dirigente no Brasil, 1855/1985. São Paulo: Editora Perspectiva; Editora da Univ. de São Paulo, 1989. 307 p.: bibl., ill. (Estudos; 108: Sociologia da arte)

Examines, from a political scientist's viewpoint, role of the Brazilian upper classes in the introduction of international influences and the fostering of national talents within Brazil's art scene. Author's analysis of the various Mecenases and the ups-and-downs of the art market in Paris and São Paulo constitutes an enlightening evaluation that furthers our understanding of modern art in Brazil. A sparkling, welcome contribution.

398 Fabris, Annateresa. Portinari, pintor social. São Paulo: Editora Perspectiva; Secretaria de Estado da Cultura; Editora da Univ. de São Paulo, 1990. 147 p.: bibl., ill. (Col. Estudos; 112: Arte)

Deliberately partial approach to Portinari's work establishes the artist's style in all its phases, and then assesses the ideological element of his output. Particularly interesting are the issues related to the contradictions between the "official painter" and the progressive artist during the *Estado Novo* era.

399   Flavio-Shiró. Flavio-Shiró. Rio de Janeiro: Salamandra, 1990. 189 p.: ill. (chiefly col.).

Born in Japan and raised in Brazil, Flavio-Shiró has lived in Paris for the past 35 years. He remains one of the few Japanese-Brazilian artists who has never been part of an artistic "movement." His work has developed in a uniquely recognizable pattern defined by the universe of memory, childhood images and perceptions. His work reflects his biography as does this book, rich in color reproductions and valuable texts.

400   Galvão, Roberto. Uma visão da arte no Ceará = A vision of arts in Ceará. Fortaleza, Brasil: Indústria Del Rio, 1987. 123 p.: bibl., ill (some col.).

Author points out artistic consequences of French and Dutch competition with the Portuguese in colonial Ceará. Also reviews the 19th century. The book's main thrust, though, is Ceará's contribution to 20th-century Brazilian art, with Antônio Bandeira, Aldemir Martins and Sérvulo Esmeraldo as but a few among many fine examples Good color reproductions.

401   Martins, Aldemir. Aldemir Martins. São Paulo: Empório Cultural, 1990. 1 v. (unpaged): ill. (Col. Branco e preto; 1)

Visual travelogue of great artistic interest is comprised of pencil drawings in a small format. J. Klintowitz's introductory essay is appropriately titled "Aldemir Martins: a Saudade e a Reconstrução do Mundo."

402   Mendonça, Casimiro Xavier de. Jeanete Musatti. São Paulo: Ex Libris, 1991. 142 p.: bibl., col. ill.

One of the finest artists in Brazil to work with boxes, Mussati is the tropical counterpoint to Joseph Cornell. Her historical and artistic characters have a direct link to her personal experiences and her boxes are autobiographical. As in the case of Rembrandt, her accumulation of accessories plays a major role. Insightful, sensitive essays by Casimiro Xavier de Mendonça. Excellent color reproductions.

403   Morais, Frederico. Felícia Leirner: a arte como missão. São Paulo: Museu Felícia Leirner, 1991. 103 p.: bibl., ill. (some col.), map.

Incisive study by Frederico Morais on one of the most expressive Brazilian sculptors of our century underscores Leirner's relationship to surrealism. Splendid b/w and color photographs.

404   Mulher e arte. Belo Horizonte: Núcleo de Estudos e Pesquisas sobre a Mulher, Univ. Federal de Minas Gerais, 1988. 119 p.: bibl., ill. (Cadernos do Núcleo de Estudos e Pesquisas sobre a Mulher; 6)

Broad spectrum of essays includes several of special interest: "Mulher Artista, Mulher Arteira; Pagu," and "A Presença da Mulher no Movimento Modernista de Belo Horizonte, no Início do Século."

405   Scliar, Carlos. Scliar: a persistência da paisagem: uma aventura moderna no Brasil: Museu de Arte Moderna do Rio de Janeiro, setembro-outubro de 1991. Rio de Janeiro: Museu de Arte Moderna, 1991. 186 p.: ill. (some col.).

From cubism and Morandi, Carlos Scliar inherited discipline, elegance, simplicity, and impeccable technique. Catalog was published for the exhibition at the Museum of Modern Art in Rio de Janeiro which celebrated Scliar's 50 years in art. His work synthesizes old and new, past and present. The exhibition gathered the best works from every period of the artist's output. Includes statements by many critics, fellow artists, and the artist himself, as well as biographical data.

406   Segall, Lasar. O desenho de Lasar Segall. São Paulo: Museu Lasar Segall, Instituto Brasileiro do Patrimônio Cultural; Brasilia: Secretaria de Cultura da Presidência da República, 1991. 169 p.: bibl., ill.

Lasar Segall's multifaceted talents also include drawing. This book, designed to celebrate the centennial of Segall's birth, is entirely devoted to his output in charcoal, pencil, grafite, China ink, blue ink and pen, brush and pen, sepia, white gouache, etc. Insightful text by Mário de Andrade.

407   Segall, Lasar. Lasar Segall e o Rio de Janeiro: dezembro 1991, Museu de Arte Moderna do Rio de Janeiro. Curadoria, Museu Lasar Segall, Instituto Brasileiro do Patrimônio Cultural, IBPC. Rio de Janeiro: Museu de Arte Moderna do Rio de Janeiro, 1991. 167 p.: bibl., ill. (some col.).

In Segall's words, "Brazil revealed to

me the miracle of color and light. I felt that in this country everything seems lighter and higher, elevating us from earth. Teaches joy. . . . " The city of Rio in particular made a great impact on Segall as he went on to become one of the greatest Brazilian artists of this century. He was originally from Lithuania via Germany. Informative, insightul texts. Rich iconography, in color and b/w.

408 Zanini, Walter. A arte no Brasil nas décadas de 1930–40: o Grupo Santa Helena. São Paulo: Nobel: EDUSP, 1991. 190 p.: bibl., ill. (some col.), index.

The Santa Helena Group, which sprang up in 1935 in a spontaneous and unnoticed manner, was comprised of artists who already knew each other. It was made up mainly of immigrant proletarians, mostly Italians who lived in São Paulo. Their group awareness led them to become a Familia Artística Paulista, with common interests being landscape and urban habitat. Book offers an excellent account of their background, history, and accomplishments.

PHOTOGRAPHY

409 Lima, Solange Ferraz de *et al.* Fotografia: usos e funções no século XIX. Organização de Annateresa Fabris. São Paulo: Editora da Univ. de São Paulo, 1991. 298 p.: bibl., ill. (Texto & arte; 3)

Essays of special interest to this *HLAS* chapter are: "O Circuito Social da Fotografia" which focuses on 19th-century Brazil; "A Representação da Natureza na Pintura e na Fotografia Brasileiras do Século XIX;" and "Pictorialismo e Imprensa: o Caso da Revista *O Cruzeiro*, 1928–1932."

410 Mariani, Anna. Paisagens, impressões: o semi-árido brasileiro. Textos de Euclides da Cunha, Antonio Medina Rodrigues, Manuel Correa de Andrade. São Paulo: Companhia das Letras, 1992. 93 p.: chiefly col. ill., maps.

Consists of photography of documentary and artistic value on Brazil's semi-arid regions. Between the rain and the drought there is a profusion of color tones.

411 Minas dos Inconfidentes. Coordenação editorial de Anna Gomes Ferreira. Fotografia de Miguel Aun. Texto de Francisco Iglésias. São Paulo: EP&C Editoração Publica-

ções & Comunicações, 1988. 143 p.: bibl., chiefly col. ill.

The manifold Minas dos Inconfidentes can be the Minas of gold civilization, the Minas of colonial oppression, the Minas of poets, the Minas of 18th-century townscapes. Book focuses on sites related to the late 18th-century political conspiracy against the Portuguese Crown. Fine text and breathtaking color photographs.

412 Verger, Pierre. Centro histórico de Salvador: 1946 a 1952. São Paulo: Corrupio, 1989. 1 v.: bibl., chiefly ill.

Through his photographs, taken over a 40-year period, Verger penetrated deeply into the soul of the city of Salvador, in Bahia. A humanistic scientist, he shows the confluence of memory and future. Book is of extraordinary cultural, documentary, and artistic value.

CITY PLANNING, ARCHITECTURE, AND LANDSCAPE ARCHITECTURE

413 Os decoradores = The decorators. Rio de Janeiro: Spala Editora, 1991. 182 p.: col. ill.

Book of aesthetic, artistic, and cultural value pays homage to the creativity and talent of Brazilian interior decorators and architects. Richly illustrated with excellent color photographs. Introduces each designer with short biography and an evaluation of his or her artistic features.

414 Figueiredo, Guilherme and **Riva Bernstein.** Patrimônio histórico do Rio de Janeiro. Rio de Janeiro?: Edições Europa, 1988. 1 portfolio (unpaged): bibl., col. ill.

Handsome portfolio includes reproductions of Riva Bernstein's watercolors of Rio's most picturesque views and its architectural past. Provides extensive introduction and notes by Guilherme Figueiredo.

415 Sánchez, Fernanda *et al.* Arquitetura em madeira: uma tradição paranaense. Curitiba: Scientia et Labor, 1987. 20 p., 41 leaves of plates: bibl., ill., map. (Série Novo autor)

Polish immigrants in Paraná towards the end of the 19th century built "casas polacas" on the outskirts of Curitiba, thus establishing a local tradition of wood architecture. Special text introduces this style, which is further illustrated by a variety of examples and basic technical features.

416 Xavier, Alberto; Alfredo Britto; and Ana Luiza Nobre. Arquitetura moderna no Rio de Janeiro. Rio de Janeiro: RIOARTE; Fundação Vilanova Artigas; São Paulo: Editora Pini, 1991. 315 p.: bibl., ill., maps.

Good cross-section of Rio's modern architecture covers public and private buildings in virtually all categories. Provides descriptions, elevation plans, and photographs as well as various glossaries and indexes. Selection consists of 200 buildings spread over six decades and is an important source to understand Modernism and its consequences for Brazilian architecture.

MISCELLANEOUS

417 Fontes e chafarizes do Brasil = Founts and fountain heads of Brazil. São Bernardo do Campo, Brazil: Mercedes-Benz do Brasil, 1991. 144 p.: bibl., col. ill.

In Brazil, large-scale use of water for urban purposes began in 1870, though installations for water use date back to colonial days. Churches and monastic buildings were notable for their water systems, and the art of making *chafarizes* reached its highest level during the Imperial period in the 19th century. Most have decayed over the years, but now many are being restored. This book's lavish photographs reproduce many Brazilian founts and fountain heads, most of them of cultural value and artistic beauty. Includes fine historical and analytical texts. Excellent color photographs.

418 Gráfica: arte e indústria no Brasil; 180 anos de história. São Paulo: Bandeirante S.A. Gráfica e Editora, 1991. 175 p.: bibl., ill. (some col.), index.

Of particular interest to this chapter are examples of layout and printing of 19th-century lithographic posters, family magazines, and commercial labels, as well as 20th-century offset printing of catalogs, newspapers, posters, programs, magazines, book covers, film posters, etc. Also includes best examples of Brazilian commercial and industrial graphics of cultural and artistic value as well as many good color reproductions.

419 Martins, Carlos; Julio Bandeira; Vera Beatriz Siqueira; and Neyde Gomes de Oliveira. Rio de Janeiro, Capital B'Além Mar, na coleção dos Museus Castro Maya. Rio de Janeiro: Centro Cultural Banco do Brasil-Museu, 1994. 67 p.: photos.

Exhibition was divided into two parts: 1) "Rio de Janeiro of the Traveller-Reporters: Images of a Tropical Court;" and 2) "Urban History: Space, Culture and Society." Basically, this is a European view of the tropical reality and richness of Brazil, a nation-to-be. Includes handsome reproductions of originals by J.B. Debret, Rugendas, Chamberlain, Vidal, and Count of Clarac.

420 Pinturas & pintores: Rio antigo. Coordenação geral de Paulo Berger. Rio de Janeiro: Livraria Kosmos Editora, 1990. 251 p.: col. ill. (some folded), index.

Attributes the outstanding quality of Rio's individual iconography to Rio's being the richest of Brazilian cities, the national capital from 1750–1960, and a place of legendary beauty. Book reflects the extraordinary wealth of prints, drawings, watercolors, and paintings produced in that period that drew from the city's architecture, natural scenery, and everyday life. Well researched and illustrated, this volume is a sheer delight. Includes biographical data on all of the many artists.

421 Retratos do Brasil: a oposição na República através da caricatura. Rio de Janeiro: Biblioteca Nacional, 1990. 1 portfolio (13 leaves, 94 leaves of plates): chiefly ill.

Excellent contribution to the history of political caricature in Brazil. Includes many and good quality b/w reproductions.

JOURNAL ABBREVIATIONS

Academia/Madrid. Academia: Boletín de la Real Academia de Bellas Artes de San Fernando. Madrid.

An. Arquit. Anales de Arquitectura. Secretariado de Publicaciones de la Univ. de Valladolid. Valladolid, Spain.

An. Inst. Invest. Estét. Anales del Instituto de Investigaciones Estéticas. Univ. Nacional Autónoma de México. México.

Anu. Estud. Am. Anuario de Estudios Americanos. Consejo Superior de

Investigaciones Científicas; Univ. de Sevilla, Escuela de Estudios Hispano-Americanos. Sevilla, Spain.

Arch. Esp. Arte. Archivo Español de Arte. Consejo Superior de Investigaciones Científicas, Centro de Estudios Históricos. Madrid.

Armitano Arte. Armitano Arte: Revista Venezolana de Cultura. Ernest Armitano. Caracas.

Bol. Hist. Ejérc. Boletín Histórico del Ejército. Montevideo.

Bol. Lima. Boletín de Lima. Revista Cultural Científica. Lima.

Bol. Mus. Inst. Camón Aznar. Boletín del Museo e Instituto Camón Aznar. Museo e Instituto de Humanidades Camón Aznar. Zaragoza, Spain.

Colon. Lat. Am. Rev. Colonial Latin American Review. Simon H. Rifkind Center for the Humanities, Dept. of Romance Languages, City College of New York. New York.

Cuad. Arte Colon. Cuadernos de Arte Colonial. Museo de América; Ministerio de Cultura. Madrid.

Hist. Boliv. Historia Boliviana. Cochabamba, Bolivia.

Histórica/Lima. Histórica. Pontificia Univ.

Católica del Perú, Depto. de Humanidades. Lima.

Invest. Ens. Investigaciones y Ensayos. Academia Nacional de la Historia. Buenos Aires.

J. Decor. Propag. Arts. The Journal of Decorative and Propaganda Arts. Wolfson Foundation of Decorative and Propaganda Arts. Miami, Fla.

Lat. Am. Art Mag. Latin American Art Magazine. Latin American Art Magazine Inc., Scottsdale, Ariz.

Mitt. Inst. Österr. Gesch.forsch. Mitteilungen des Instituts für Österreichische Geschichtforschung. Vienna.

Rev. Dep. Hist. Arte. Revista del Departamento de Historia del Arte. Univ. de Sevilla. Spain.

Rev. Indias. Revista de Indias. Consejo Superior de Investigaciones Científicas, Instituto Gonzalo Fernández de Oviedo. Madrid.

Rev. Rev. Interam. Revista/Review Interamericana. Inter-American Univ. Press. Hato Rey, Puerto Rico.

SECOLAS Ann. SECOLAS Annals. Southeastern Conference on Latin American Studies; West Georgia College. Carrollton, Ga.

HISTORY

ETHNOHISTORY
Mesoamerica

ROBERT HASKETT, *Associate Professor of History, University of Oregon*
STEPHANIE WOOD, *Assistant Professor of History, University of Oregon*

AS WE TOOK UP THE TASK of evaluating recent works in Mesoamerican ethno-history, it soon became clear that our predecessor's prognostication was correct: the quality and quantity of serious scholarship has indeed grown exponentially. Some of this can probably be attributed to the interest created by the 500th anniversary of the first Columbus voyage. Few of the works described here consciously invoke that event, or the celebrations and condemnations connected with its commemoration. Yet surely heightened awareness of cultural contact, conflict, change, and modification invoked by the Quincentenary is at least partly responsible for the quickened production of thoughtful documentary analyses (items **490** and **585**), the publication, transcription, translation, and interpretation of a rich body of codices and colonial-era indigenous language documents (items **431, 455, 450, 511, 571, 462,** and **576**), and the new readings of such durable sources as Sahagún's multifaceted work (items **426** and **562**).

The cultures of the Maya and the Nahuas (most prominently the Mexica, still often referred to as the Aztecs) before, during, and after the Iberian invasion have continued to receive the lion's share of scholarly attention. New levels of sophistication have been reached for the Nahua in the interpretation of ritual, religious ideology, and the historical and political implications of so-called "mythic" versions of the past, above all in the work of Inga Clendinnen (item **452**), Miguel León-Portilla (item **515**), and the collection of essays in editor David Carrasco's *To change place* (item **577**). For the Maya, Linda Schele's and David Freidel's outstanding book, *A forest of kings* (item **564**), is a beautifully realized example of innovative sociocultural interpretation based on a rich mix of archaeological, linguistic, and ethnohistorical data. Other investigators have concentrated on trade and tribute (items **434** and **496**), land (item **513**), nutrition and health (item **542**), and the crucial subject of prehispanic state formation and ordering, with Susan Schroeder's striking readings of Chimalpahin (items **565** and **566**) and Ross Hassig's penetrating look at precontact Mesoamerican militarism (item **492**) of great significance.

Concern with the myriad consequences of the Spanish invasion is still growing. More and more authors present interpretive syntheses based on the extensive use of mundane indigenous-language documentation such as petitions, testaments, and the like (items **488** and **539**). The major fruit of this analytical vine is James Lockhart's superb *The Nahuas after the conquest* (item **518**), the most thoroughgoing indigenous-centered reconstruction of Nahua culture currently available and likely to be regarded as a "new Gibson." Nothing comparable for the greater Maya region (nor for Oaxaca, for that matter) has appeared in the last few years, but a body of dynamic thematically- or regionally-focused inquiries have (items **445, 497,** and **529**), such as Kevin Gosner's revisionist study of the Tzeltal revolt in Chiapas (item **478**). This revolt turned, in part, on frustrated Tzeltal efforts to redefine and control their own experience of Catholicism. A significant number of thought-provoking articles probe the indigenous reaction to, and participation in, the process of religious conversion and education (items **443, 453, 460, 484, 509,** and **584**). All of these investigations have wider implications for the understanding of indigenous peoples' concepts of themselves, their communities, and their relationships to the Spanish system as a whole.

The more obvious emergence of two comparatively new areas of emphasis in the field also should be highlighted. One group of authors takes us into the lives of women, at the moment mainly those living before the conquest, examining among other things issues of gender and sexuality (items **432** and **441**): Louise Burkhart's thoughtful work on Nahua concepts of domesticity is an excellent example (item **442**). A second body of work pays greater attention to what might be termed Mesoamerica's *periphery,* including the Tarascan region, the Isthmus of Tehuantepec, and Mexico's far north, with the output of two investigators into the sociocultural implications of the cacao industry—William R. Fowler for the Pipil of El Salvador (item **469**) and Janine Gasco for Socunusco (item **474**)—worthy of special attention.

In closing, we want to make readers aware of two new journals which are potential venues for serious ethnohistorical scholarship: the *Colonial Latin American Historical Review* and the *Colonial Latin American Review.* It should also be noted that we have reviewed four meaty volumes of the significant journal *Estudios de Cultura Náhuatl* which have appeared since the publication of *HLAS 52.* Combined with the wealth of excellent material that has crossed our desks in the preparation of this section, this is all evidence for a dynamic field of scholarship showing every indication of exciting growth in multiple directions.

422 Acuña, René. Códice Fernández Leal. Instituto de Investigaciones Filológicas, UNAM. Tlalpan, Mexico: Ediciones Toledo, INAH, 1991. 63 p.: bibl., ill. (1 col.), index.

Careful revisionist study of the origin, dating, and contents of this important early postconquest codex, which author concludes is from a Nahua rather than Mixtec tradition. Some useful comparisons with the *Códice Porfirio Díaz* are made.

423 El álbum de la mujer: antología ilustrada de las mexicanas. v. 1, Epoca prehispánica. Edición de Enriqueta Tuñón Pablos. México: Instituto Nacional de Antropología e Historia, 1991. 4 v.: bibl., ill. (Col. Divulgación)

Brief anthology of primary selections and secondary articles grouped around the themes of life cycle, social mores, and public roles for prehispanic Nahua women. Contem-

porary authors include Iris Blanco, Miguel León-Portilla, Alfredo López Austin, Eduardo Matos, Jacques Soustelle, and Luis Vargas.

424 Alcalá, Jerónimo de, *Fray.* La relación de Michoacán. Versión paleográfica, separación de textos, ordenación coloquial, estudio preliminar y notas de Francisco Miranda. México: Secretaría de Educación Pública, 1988. 372 p.: bibl. (Cien de México)

Careful transcription of this key account, introduced by an essay in which Miranda makes a case for Alcalá as the compiler of the *Relación,* discusses the text itself, and provides observations on its historical and cultural context.

425 Anawalt, Patricia Rieff. The emperors' cloak: Aztec pomp, Toltec circumstances. (*Am. Antiq.,* 55:2, April 1990, p. 291–308, ill., map)

Analyzes imperial tribute in textiles,

specifically those produced with a certain tie-dye design, as they were linked to Mexica rulers' claims to Toltec heritage (and the legitimation of their authority). Innovative methodology with significant conclusions.

426 Anderson, Arthur J.O. La *Salmodia* de Sahagún. (*Estud. Cult. Náhuatl,* 20, 1990, p. 17–38)

Admirable study of Sahagún's 1583 Nahuatl *Salmodia Christiana,* used to teach biblical verses set to music. Includes transcriptions and translations of several Psalms and discusses how the work was intended to capitalize on a perceived indigenous facility for learning ceremonial music rooted in pre-existing ritual traditions.

427 Arnold, Philip P. Eating landscape: human sacrifice and sustenance in Aztec Mexico. (*in* To change place: Aztec ceremonial landscapes. Edited by David Carrasco. Boulder: Univ. Press of Colorado, 1991, p. 219–232, bibl., facsims.)

Thought provoking interpretation of the meaning of child sacrifice in the "Atl Cahualo" ceremony, staged during the height of the dry season. The ceremony is viewed as a ritual exchange between Tlaloc and humanity and is closely associated with imagery of earth, water, wood, and food.

428 Aveni, Anthony F. Mapping the ritual landscape: debt payment to Tlaloc during the month of Atlacahualo. (*in* To change place: Aztec ceremonial landscapes. Edited by David Carrasco. Boulder: Univ. Press of Colorado, 1991, p. 58–73, bibl., map, table)

Exacting survey of sites associated with the Atlacahualo ritual, showing spatial and ritual links between Tenochtitlan's ceremonial center and sacred points outside the city which would have been on its horizon. Author explains how ritual ties between center and periphery incorporated the natural world into the urban environment.

429 Barba de Piña Chan, Beatriz. Buscando raíces de mitos mayas en Izapa. Campeche, Mexico: Univ. Autónoma del Sudeste, 1988. 172 p.: bibl., ill., map.

Treatment of the ways in which the decorative art of Mayan ceremonial centers such as Izapa transmitted politically-charged religious ideology to the masses. Author also argues for a direct relationship between the graphic representation of myth at Izapa with texts such as the Popul Vuh.

430 Barlow, Robert Hayward. Obras de Robert H. Barlow. v. 2, Tlatelolco: fuentes e historia. v. 3, Los mexicas y la Triple Alianza. Edición de Jesús Monjarás-Ruiz, Elena Limón y María de la Cruz Paillés H. México: Instituto Nacional de Antropología e Historia; Puebla, Mexico: Univ. de las Américas, 1989–1990. 2 v.

Projected seven-volume monographic series contains Barlow's often pathbreaking works. Vol. 2 completes Barlow's "Tlatelolco Cycle" and includes the Nahuatl text and a Spanish translation of the previously unpublished "Anales de Juan Miguel (Anales de Tlatelolco y Azcapotzalco, 1519–1662)." Vol. 3 assembles Barlow's works dealing with the expansion and organization of the Mexica empire, including several heretofore unavailable essays examining the conquests of specific rulers and an article entitled "Método que se propone para establecer una cronología [de la historia del Valle de México]."

Baroni Boissonas, Ariane. La formación de la estructura agraria en El Bajío colonial, siglos XVI y XVII. See item **1196.**

431 Baudot, Georges and **Tzvetan Todorov.** Relatos aztecas de la conquista. México: Consejo Nacional para la Cultura y las Artes, 1990. 483 p.: bibl., ill., maps.

Editors present key indigenous accounts of the conquest of Mexico and provide insightful commentary. New translations of relevant portions of three Nahuatl texts are included (Book XII of the *Florentine Codex,* the *Anales Históricos de Tlatelolco,* and the *Códice Aubin*) as well as transcriptions of three Spanish-language texts (Muñoz Camargo's *Historia de Tlaxcala,* the *Códice Ramírez,* and Durán's *Historia*).

432 Bauer, Arnold J. Millers and grinders: technology and household economy in Meso-America. (*Agric. Hist.,* 64:1, Winter 1990, p. 1–17)

Excellent, often descriptively entertaining essay examines the persistence of traditional maize processing technology in Mesoamerica. Bauer addresses implications for women who spent long hours every day over the metate and the comal, while surveying the subject through the early 20th century.

433 Baumann, Roland. Tlaxcalan expression of autonomy and religious drama in the sixteenth century. (*J. Lat. Am. Lore,* 13 : 2, 1987, p. 139–153)

Interpretive discussion of apparently Catholic religious theater staged in Tlaxcala by its indigenous citizens demonstrates ways in which it was orchestrated to convey unsuspected (by Spaniards) meanings and to serve noble and corporate ends, including the quest for privileged status.

434 Berdan, Frances F. Economic dimensions of precious metals, stones, and feathers: the Aztec State society. (*Estud. Cult. Náhuatl,* 22, 1992, p. 291–323, bibl., maps, tables)

Excellent study of the economic importance of luxury items in Aztec Mexico highlights means of procurement, elaboration, distribution, and consumption. The author contends that tribute was not the major source for most of these goods, thus adding a significant dimension to our understanding of the precontact imperial economy.

435 Boone, Elizabeth Hill. Migration histories as ritual performance. (*in* To change place: Aztec ceremonial landscapes. Edited by David Carrasco. Boulder: Univ. Press of Colorado, 1991, p. 121–151, bibl., facsims.)

Well-argued thesis that the Mexica migration story should be viewed as a rite of passage, a ritual performance propelling the migrants from the status of humble Chichimeca to a chosen imperial people.

436 Borah, Woodrow. Yet another look at the Techialoyan Codices. (*in* Land and politics in the Valley of Mexico: a two-thousand-year perspective. Edited by H.R. Harvey. Albuquerque: Univ. of New Mexico Press, 1991, p. 209–221)

Thought-provoking discussion of ongoing debate surrounding interpretations of Nahuatl-language Techialoyan Codices (heavily pictorial documents written on native paper) and primordial titles (mainly prose written on European paper) enshrining local views of corporate history and property holding.

437 Broda, Johanna. The sacred landscape of Aztec calendar festivals: myth, nature, and society. (*in* To change place: Aztec ceremonial landscapes. Edited by David Ca-rrasco. Boulder: Univ. of Colorado Press, 1991, p. 74–120, bibl., maps, tables)

Wide-ranging study of ritual-spatial linkages emphasizes the astronomical alignments of sites on the periphery of Tenochtitlan.

438 The broken spears: the Aztec account of the conquest of Mexico. Edited and with an introduction by Miguel León Portilla. Expanded and updated ed. Boston: Beacon Press, 1992. 196 p.: bibl., ill., index.

Welcome new edition of this indispensable collection of indigenous accounts of the Spanish conquest. Klor de Alva's forward highlights the fundamental significance of the documents, not only for students of the conquest of Mexico, but for those seeking to understand broader issues of conquest and foreign domination. León-Portilla has added a new section entitled "Aftermath," which contains translations of revealing Nahuatl language texts dating from the Spanish era, the Mexican Revolution, and the late 20th century.

439 Brotherston, Gordon and **Ana Gallegos.** El *Lienzo de Tlaxcala* y el *Manuscrito de Glasgow:* Hunter 242. (*Estud. Cult. Náhuatl,* 20, 1990, p. 117–140)

Fine descriptive analysis of lengthy pictorial document with close affinity to the *Lienzo de Tlaxcala* which is appended to a copy of Diego Muñoz Camargo's 1585 *Descripción de la ciudad y provincia de Tlaxcala* held in the Univ. of Glasgow's Hunter Collection. Authors situate documents in Tlaxcala's ongoing efforts to attain privileges from the crown and to redefine themselves in the face of the dislocations of the conquest (see also item **527**).

440 Brumfiel, Elizabeth M. Agricultural development and class stratification in the southern valley of Mexico. (*in* Land and politics in the Valley of Mexico: a two-thousand-year perspective. Edited by H.R. Harvey. Albuquerque: Univ. of New Mexico Press, 1991, p. 42–62, maps, tables)

Careful ethnohistorical and archaeological analysis of sociopolitical implications of *chinampa* agriculture on Lake Chalco's Xico Island. Author demonstrates that the Mexica State made its nobility an arm of imperial expansion by granting nobles *chinampa* tracts in outlying areas, thus encouraging the spread of urban-oriented cultivation.

441   Brumfiel, Elizabeth M. Weaving and cooking: women's production in Aztec Mexico. (*in* Engendering archaeology: women and prehistory. Edited by Joan M. Gero and Margaret W. Conkey. Oxford: Basil Blackwell Ltd., 1991, p. 224–251)

Significant article challenges the static, idealized, even politically-charged, male-generated picture of women as primarily cooks and weavers in the ethnohistorical literature. Archaeological evidence suggests that these traditional pursuits were both more important and more complex than generally portrayed.

442   Burkhart, Louise M. Mujeres mexicas en "el frente" del hogar: trabajo doméstico y religión en el México azteca. (*Mesoamérica/Antigua*, 12:23, junio 1992, p. 23–54, facsims.)

Excellent study recovers Mexica attitudes towards the status of women by focusing on the religious ideology of domestic tasks. Author argues persuasively that Spanish-influenced interpretations of Nahua culture obscured indigenous concepts which saw the female role in the home as crucial and complementary to male activities on the battlefield.

443   Burkhart, Louise M. A Nahuatl religious drama of c. 1590. (*Lat. Am. Indian Lit. J.*, 7:2, Fall 1991, p. 153–171, bibl.)

Perceptive analysis of the earliest extant Nahuatl religious play furthers knowledge of Nahua mediation of the Christianization process. Burkhart shows in detail how the native translator modified this drama, based on a Spanish original, to more closely harmonize it with indigenous concepts.

444   Carlson, Robert S. and **Martin Prechtel.** The flowering of the dead: an interpretation of Highland Maya culture. (*Man/London*, 26:1, March 1991, p. 23–42, bibl.)

Examines Maya concepts that link the renewal of nature to the transformation and rebirth of human beings and ably relates these to the theme of cultural survival. Thus, the authors provide more persuasive evidence for the ability of indigenous people to be actors in, rather than merely victims of, conquest and colonialism.

445   Carmagnani, Marcello. El regreso de los dioses: el proceso de reconstitución de la identidad étnica en Oaxaca, siglos XVII y XVIII. México: Fondo de Cultura Económica, 1988. 263 p.: bibl., map. (Sección de obras de historia)

Sophisticated study of the reconstitution of ethnic identities among the indigenous people of Oaxaca in the aftermath of the Spanish conquest, particularly in the late colonial period. Carmagnani's thought-provoking analysis, based on a wealth of archival material, develops themes related to religious and secular concepts of space and territoriality, economic systems (including the roles of cofradias and *hermandades*), and sociopolitical hierarchy.

446   Carrasco, David. The sacrifice of Texcatlipoca: to change place. (*in* To change place: Aztec ceremonial landscapes. Edited by David Carrasco. Boulder: Univ. Press of Colorado, 1991, p. 31–57, bibl.)

Evocative analytical recreation of the importance of movement through space, physical transformations, and shifting public appearances, or, in other words "changing place," during the preparation of the Tezcatlipoca impersonator and his eventual sacrifice at the festival of Toxcatl.

447   Carrasco, Pedro. Los mayeques. (*Hist. Mex.*, 39:1, julio/sept. 1989, p. 123–166, bibl.)

Exacting discussion of the term *mayeque*, usually translated as "dependent agricultural laborer," but actually a social designation whose precise meaning continues to be debated. Surveying the 16th-century colonial record, Carrasco attempts to trace its origins and geographic specificity, and to separate postconquest influences from probable prehispanic meanings.

448   Carrasco, Pedro *et al.* Los pueblos de indios y las comunidades. Introducción y selección de Bernardo García Martínez. México: El Colegio de México, Centro de Estudios Históricos, 1991. 304 p.: bibl. (Lecturas de historia mexicana; 2)

Handy compilation of ethnohistorical essays reprinted from *Historia Mexicana* covers the 16th-19th centuries and reaches from the Yucatán to Apache territory. Corporate concerns outweigh individual, and the use of Spanish-language sources prevails, but these articles nevertheless are the product of eminent scholars and have enduring value.

449 Carrasco, Pedro. The territorial structure of the Aztec empire. (*in* Land and politics in the Valley of Mexico: a two-thousand-year perspective. Edited by H.R. Harvey. Albuquerque: Univ. of New Mexico Press, 1991, p. 93–112, tables)

Investigation of the Triple Alliance empire's internal structure and the mechanisms holding it together, from the manipulation of dynasties in conquered *altepetl* to the resettlement of people from the Valley of Mexico in newly obtained areas. This innovative work uncovers a much higher degree of imperial political integration than is often pictured.

450 Castillo, Cristóbal del. Historia de la venida de los mexicanos y otros pueblos e Historia de la conquista. Traducción y introducción de Federico Navarrete Linares. México: Instituto Nacional de Antropología e Historia, Proyecto Templo Mayor: GV Editores: Asociación de Amigos del Templo Mayor, 1991. 226 p.: bibl. (Col. Divulgación)

Critical edition of the surviving fragments of the two histories written by Castillo includes a lengthy introduction by editor. Transcriptions of the Nahuatl originals are presented in parallel with Spanish translations. Welcome new edition of an underutilized source for precontact and conquest history.

451 Charlton, Thomas H. Land tenure and agricultural production in the Otumba region, 1785–1803. (*in* Land and politics in the Valley of Mexico: a two-thousand-year perspective. Edited by H.R. Harvey. Albuquerque: Univ. of New Mexico Press, 1991, p. 223–263, maps, tables)

Careful examination of the varying quality and uses of properties held by indigenous communities, native elites, and those renting parcels from towns in the late-colonial Otumba region. Evidence points to a distinct lack of egalitarianism in their distribution that is traced to the prehispanic era.

452 Clendinnen, Inga. Aztecs: an interpretation. Cambridge; New York: Cambridge Univ. Press, 1991. 398 p.: bibl., ill. (some col.), index, maps.

Important interpretation of late precontact Mexica culture. Author presents a probing and at times lyrical analysis of the meaning and functions of human sacrifice and other ritual observances. She emphasizes ways in which the majority, both men and women, may have been touched by, and participated in, ceremonial religious observances at the level of the local shrine, the neighborhood, and the home.

453 Clendinnen, Inga. Ways to the sacred: reconstructing "religion" in sixteenth century Mexico. (*Hist. Anthropol.*, 5, 1990, p. 105–141, bibl.)

Sophisticated analysis searches for the essence of postconquest indigenous religiosity, through study of the persistence, the refashioning, and the evolution of sacred ritual. Clendinnen's sources allow her to establish precontact practices and beliefs more securely than those of the Spanish era, but the article as a whole provides valuable interpretative tools for other interested scholars.

454 Cline, S.L. A cacicazgo in the seventeenth century: the case of Xochimilco. (*in* Land and politics in the Valley of Mexico: a two-thousand-year perspective. Edited by H.R. Harvey. Albuquerque: Univ. of New Mexico Press, 1991, p. 265–274)

Significant study of sociopolitical fortunes of the Xochimilcan Cerón y Alvarado cacicazgo from the early Spanish era to 1686. Cline reconstructs relationships between the family's dynastic fortunes and their landholding strategies, and factors in the role of gender in estate maintenance.

455 *Codex Chimalpopoca:* the text in Nahuatl; with a glossary and grammatical notes. Edited by John Bierhorst. Tucson: Univ. of Arizona Press, 1992. 210 p.: bibl.

For annotation, see English-language companion volume (item **500**).

456 Coe, Michael D. Breaking the Maya code. New York: Thames and Hudson, 1992. 304 p.: bibl., ill., index.

Marvelous account of the often torturous path leading to recent breakthroughs in the decipherment of Maya texts. Writing with a novelist's verve, Coe produces a gripping book that is at once a kind of intellectual history, a study of the linguistic analysis of Maya glyphs, and a cautionary tale for scholars who fail to keep an open mind about new theories, methodologies, and perspectives.

457 Coloquio de Documentos Pictográficos de Tradición Náhuatl, *1st, México,* 1983. Primer Coloquio de Documentos Pictográficos de Tradición Náhuatl. Presentación de Carlos Martínez Marín. México: Instituto de Investigaciones Históricas, UNAM, 1989. 280 p., 82 p. of plates: bibl., ill. (Serie de cultura náhuatl: Monografías; 23)

Collection of 21 essays, originally presented in 1983, covers wide range of significant topics connected with the interpretation of pre- and postcontact pictorial documents and artifacts from central Mexico. Authors address themes such as glyphic interpretation, history, symbolism, tribute, land tenure, land measure, and indigenous elements found in 16th-century Catholic Church decoration. Among documents receiving repeated and sometimes revisionist attention are the *Matrícula de tributos*, the *Códice Mendoza*, and the *Códice Aubin*.

458   Comercio, comerciantes y rutas de intercambio en el México antiguo. Recopilación de Lorenzo Ochoa. México: SECOFI, 1989. 219 p.: bibl., ill. (some col.)

Collection of previously-published articles, mostly from the late 1970s and early 1980s, but useful for their thematic unity. Contributors include such noted scholars as Pedro Carrasco, Edward E. Calnek, and Román Piña Chan.

Cortés Alonso, Vicenta. La imagen del otro: indios, blancos, y negros en el México del siglo XVI. See item **1212.**

459   Davis, Wade and **Andrew T. Well.** Identity of a New World psychoactive toad. (*Anc. Mesoam.*, 3:1, Spring 1992, p. 51–59, bibl., photos)

Article debunks idea that the Maya ingested venom from the highly-toxic large toad, *Bufo marinus*, as a hallucinogen. Rather, the authors believe the Maya used dried venom from *Bufo alvarius*, a similar toad from Sonora, whose venom can be safely smoked to produce hallucinations, and which was obtained through long-distance trading.

460   Dehouve, Danièle. El discípulo del Silo: un aspecto de la literatura náhuatl de los Jesuitas del siglo XVIII. (*Estud. Cult. Náhuatl*, 22, 1992, p. 345–379)

Well-executed discussion and analysis of a late colonial Jesuit text, written in parallel Latin, Spanish, and Nahuatl. The discussion sheds light on evangelistic literature as it evolved beyond the much-studied works of the 16th century.

461   Díaz Fleury, Luis. Los metales y las piedras preciosas en el mundo Azteca. (*in* Jornadas de Historiadores Americanistas, *1st, Santafé, Spain, 1987*. América: hombre y sociedad. Presentación de Joaquín A. Muñoz Mendoza. Granada, Spain: Diputación Provincial de Granada, 1988, p. 141–154, bibl.)

Examines ethnohistorical and linguistic evidence to determine the exact nature of metallurgical knowledge of precontact peoples of central Mexico. Some relevant comparisons with European techniques of the same period are drawn as well.

462   Documentos tlaxcaltecas del siglo XVI en lengua náhuatl. Introducción, paleografía, traducción y notas de Thelma D. Sullivan. México: Univ. Nacional Autónoma de México, 1987. 350 p.: bibl., ill. (Serie antropológica; 55: Lingüística)

Sullivan transcribes and translates 11 Nahuatl-language records held by the Tlaxcalan State Archive (six lawsuits concerning land, two criminal cases, and three testaments). Also included is an excellent description of the archive, helpful discussions of the linguistic and paleographic idiosyncracies of the documents, and a valuable vocabulary of key Nahuatl terms.

463   Dürr, Eveline. Der Aufstand der Tzeltal, 1712–1713: Analyse einer Revitalisationsbewegung im kolonialen Mesoamerkia. Münster: Lit, 1991. 394 p.: bibl., ill., map. (Ethnologische Studien; 17)

Research based on extensive colonial documentation and secondary literature on messianic, nativistic, and charismatic movements. Author analyzes Tzeltal rebellion of 1712–13 within the framework of micro- and macro-sociological effects caused by imposition of a new order on individuals and societal structures. [C.K. Converse]

464   Elzey, Wayne. A hill on a land surrounded by water: an Aztec story of origin and destiny. (*Hist. Relig.*, 31:2, Nov. 1991, p. 105–149)

Densely argued interpretation of a legend from Durán's *Historia* in which Huitzilopochtli flees in defeat back to his other Coatlicue at Azlan. Author asserts that the ramifications of this story modify traditional notions about the Mexica worldview and gender ideology, and suggests possible links with the later account of the Virgin of Guadalupe.

465 Estrada Lugo, Erin Ingrid Jane. El *Códice Florentino:* su información etnobotánica. Montecillo, Mexico: Colegio de Postgraduados, Institución de Enseñanza e Investigación en Ciencias Agrícolas, 1989. 399 p.: bibl., ill. (some col.)

Detailed, computer assisted realization of the vast amount of ethnobotanical information contained in the *Florentine Codex.* Most valuable for its numerous detailed tables which identify and arrange plants by scientific name, by taxonomy, by use, and by other important criteria.

466 Evans, Susan T. El sitio Cerro Gordo: un asentamiento rural del período azteca en la Cuenca de México. (*Estud. Cult. Náhuatl,* 19, 1989, p. 183–215, bibl., maps, tables)

Well documented study of a prehispanic rural community in the vicinity of Teotihuacan, ably using archaeological and ethnohistorical data to fashion a socioeconomic profile.

467 Florescano, Enrique; Alfredo López Austin; Pedro Carrasco; and Georges Baudot. Debate: mito e historia en la memoria nahua. (*Hist. Mex.,* 39:3, enero/marzo 1990, p. 607–725, bibl., ill.)

Five articles address and expand upon recent examinations of history and myth in Mesoamerican texts. Theoretical debate centers on interpretive issues raised by postconquest renditions of Mexica origins, migration, and rise to imperial status. Collectively, authors' thoughtful positions, which range from proposing the dissection of these sources as myth to seeing them as some combination of myth and history, may not definitively settle the issue, but represent a major contribution nonetheless.

468 Florescano, Enrique. La nueva imagen del México antiguo. (*Vuelta/México,* 15:173, abril 1991, p. 32–38, photo)

Insightful discussion of trends in the study of ancient Mexico concentrates on important approaches developed during the last thirty years. Florescano highlights Schele and Freidel's *A Forest of Kings* (see item **564**) as the culmination of these scholarly tendencies.

469 Fowler, William R., Jr. The living pay for the dead: trade, exploitation, and social change in early colonial Izalco, El Salvador. (*in* Ethnohistory and archaeology: approaches to postcontact change in the Americas. Edited by J. Daniel Rogers and Samuel M. Wilson. New York: Plenum Press, 1993, p. 181–199, bibl.)

Well-researched study of the impact of conquest, depopulation, and the exploitative practices of lay and religious Spanish residents on the Pipil of 16th-century cacao-producing Izalco. Suggests many significant parallels with events and trends in more frequently studied parts of Mesoamerica.

470 Freidel, David A. and Linda Schele. Kingship in the late preclassic Maya lowlands: the instruments and places of ritual power. (*Am. Anthropol.,* 90:3, Sept. 1988, p. 547–568)

Authors suggest the origin of *ahaw* (the institution of kingship) and some of its dimensions, sustaining their arguments with material empirical evidence, such as glyphic texts, colonial documentation, and archaeological data.

471 Galarza, Joaquín. In amoxtli, in tlacatl = el libro, el hombre; códices y vivencias. México: Aguirre y Beltrán Editores, 1987. 262 p.: bibl., ill., maps.

Collection of lectures (methodological and often autobiographical) related not only to understanding the Mesoamerian past via indigenous pictorials and texts but also to combining this with modern ethnographic field work. Examines selected codices, revisits the ongoing Techialoyan controversy, and discusses Nahuatl study in Milpa Alta.

472 García, José Miguel. Consideraciones sobre la escritura zapoteca. (*in* Jornadas de Historiadores Americanistas, *1st, Santafé, Spain, 1987.* América: hombre y sociedad. Presentación de Joaquín A. Muñoz Mendoza. Granada, Spain: Diputación Provincial de Granada, 1988, p. 57–65, bibl., ill.)

Nicely done piece in which author identifies phonetic elements in precontact Zapotec glyphic inscriptions and addresses the puzzling lack of evolution in Zapotec writing which, once it reached a level of incipient phoneticism in the Classic period, never advanced farther.

473 García Cook, Angel and B. Leonor Merino Carrión. El cultivo intensivo: condiciones sociales y ambientales que lo originan. (*in* Agricultura indígena: pasado y presente. Coordinación de Teresa Rojas Rabiela. México: Ediciones de la Casa Chata, 1990, p. 69–87)

Short, well-crafted examination of the connections between the environment, population growth, and societal complexity, and the elaboration and intensification of agriculture in the precontact Puebla-Tlaxcala region.

474 Gasco, Janine. Socioeconomic change within native society in colonial Soconusco, New Spain. (*in* Ethnohistory and archaeology: approaches to postcontact change in the Americas. Edited by J. Daniel Rogers and Samuel M. Wilson. New York: Plenum Press, 1993, p. 163–180, bibl., graphs, maps)

Solid work based on both archival and archaeological data drawn mainly from the town of Ocelocalco. Author examines links between the cacao industry, increasing (but never complete) social leveling within native society, and the development of a unique relationship between individual indigenous people and Spaniards in colonial Soconusco.

Gómez-Pompa, Arturo; José Salvador Flores; and **Mario Aliphat Fernández.** The sacred cacao groves of the Maya. See *HLAS 53:191.*

475 Gonzalbo Aizpuru, Pilar. Historia de la educación en la época colonial: el mundo indígena. México: Colegio de México, Centro de Estudios Históricos, 1990. 274 p.: bibl., index. (Serie Historia de la educación)

Extensively documented investigation into Spanish approaches toward educating New Spain's indigenous population highlights class and gender-based structures of instruction, political implications, and how the native elite sought to gain from a colonial education.

476 Gosner, Kevin. Caciques and conversion: Juan Atonal and the struggle for legitimacy in post-conquest Chiapas. (*Americas/Francisc.*, 49:2, Oct. 1992, p. 115–129)

Excellent examination of abortive 1584 idolatry investigation into activities of Juan Atonal, an elite town officer of Chiapa de Indios. Atonal and others attempted to maintain their status and authority, partially endangered by competing Spanish clergy, by practicing shamanism and participating in or leading clandestine cults which had clear prehispanic overtones.

477 Gosner, Kevin. Conceptualización de comunidad y jerarquía: enfoques recientes sobre la organización política maya

colonial en el altiplano. (*Mesoamérica/Antigua*, 12:22, dic. 1991, p. 151–165)

Well-executed critical discussion of recent revisionist work centered on the sociopolitical nature of colonial highland Maya communities. Gosner suggests that earlier arguments that the Maya elite lost their grip on local power were incorrect and offers thoughtful consideration of the nature of colonial *parcialidad* and its relation to the precontact *calpul* or *chinamitl.*

478 Gosner, Kevin. Soldiers of the Virgin: the moral economy of a colonial Maya rebellion. Tucson: Univ. of Arizona Press, 1992. 227 p.: bibl., index, maps.

Praiseworthy study of the Tzeltal Revolt of 1712 in highland Chiapas. In his often revisionist analysis, author identifies underlying causes of the unrest and sees denunciations by the Catholic clergy of a popular religious cult dedicated to an apparition of the Virgin to a young Maya girl as a more immediate catalyst.

479 Graulich, Michel. Las brujas de las peregrinaciones aztecas. (*Estud. Cult. Náhuatl*, 22, 1992, p. 87–98)

Thoughtful interpretation of the conflict between Malinalxochitl, portrayed as a fearful sorceress, and her brother Huitzilopchtli during the Mexica migration. Author sees her as a feminine agent redolent of symbols of passivity and rootedness in the earth who attempts to oppose the active force of her brother and deter the Mexica from their ultimate goal.

480 Graulich, Michel. L'inauguration du temple principal de Mexico en 1487. (*Rev. Esp. Antropol. Am.*, 21, 1991, p. 121–143, bibl., ills.)

Author systematically reviews references to human victims, numbering from 20,000 to 80,000, sacrificed by Aztec priests for inauguration of the Great Temple (1487). Graulich also considers: 1) philological interpretation of original sources; 2) technical feasibility of thousands of executions in four days, with sanitary problems raised by blood and bodies; and 3) the proportions of what are known to be large defeated populations subjected to Aztec practices of capture and sacrifice. Concludes authoritatively that such high estimates cannot be discarded. [A. Pérotin-Dumon]

481 Graulich, Michel. Tozoztontli, Huey Tozoztli et Toxcatl: fêtes aztèques de la moisson et du milieu du jour. (*Rev. Esp. Antropol. Am.*, 14, 1984, p. 127–164, bibl., tables)

Study based on author's previous works on feast days in Aztec solar calendar, which had become increasingly out of phase with their corresponding seasons. Graulich discusses scholarly interpretations of rituals and deities associated with four agrarian celebrations as they can be reconstituted for early 16th century. [A. Pérotin-Dumon]

482 Guzmán Betancourt, Ignacio. "Policía y "barbarie" de las lenguas indígenas de México, según la opinión de gramáticos e historiadores novohispanos. (*Estud. Cult. Náhuatl*, 21, 1991, p. 179–218)

Lengthy inquiry into the ethnocentrism displayed by major colonial Spanish grammarians and historians as they described the "good" and "bad" characteristics of the main indigenous languages, especially Nahuatl. Author links linguistic prejudices to wider cultural biases and briefly compares Eurocentrism to what might be called Nahuacentrism, or Nahua attitudes toward other ethnic groups.

Guzmán Böckler, Carlos. Donde enmudecen las conciencias: crepúsculo y aurora en Guatemala. See *HLAS 53:5083.*

483 Haly, Richard. Bare bones: rethinking Mesoamerican divinity. (*Hist. Relig.*, 31:3, Feb. 1992, p. 269–304)

Ingenious argument, bound to be controversial, examines perceptions of Nahua religious ideology. Haly argues that Ometeotl, long seen as a dualistic creator deity, was really created by the Spanish and by later scholarly misinterpretation of oral tradition and myth. Omitecutli, skeletal "Bone Lord," is identified as the true creator of life.

484 Harris, Max. Disguised reconciliations: indigenous voices in early Franciscan missionary drama in Mexico. (*Radic. Hist. Rev.*, 53, Spring 1992, p. 13–25)

Intriguing reinterpretation of two Nahua-acted missionary dramas staged under Franciscan sponsorship in 1539: *The conquest of Rhodes* in Mexico City and *The conquest of Jerusalem* in Tlaxcala. Author uncovers subtle indigenous manipulation of the performances which injected them with "hidden transcripts of . . . dissent" about the justice of the Spanish conquest.

485 Hartau, Claudine. Herrschaft und Kommunikation: Analyse aztekischer Inthronisationsreden aus dem Codex Florentinus des Fray Bernardino de Sahagún. Hamburg: Wayasbah, 1988. 246 p.: bibl. (Wayasbah publication; 12)

Uses in-depth analysis of speeches and prayers by Aztec ruler and priests to reconstruct purely normative ideological presentations. These do not reflect actual power structures but illustrate rhetorical strategies used to legitimize the ruler and to induce acceptable social behavior. Texts (in German translation) include admonitions to practice agriculture and avoid use of hallucinogens and wine. [C.K. Converse]

486 Harvey, H.R. The Oztoticpac lands map: a reexamination. (*in* Land and politics in the Valley of Mexico: a two-thousand-year perspective. Edited by H.R. Harvey. Albuquerque: Univ. of New Mexico Press, 1991, p. 163–185, maps, tables)

Study of landholding patterns at early postconquest Oztoticpac, near Texcoco, is based on an important early cadastral map. By perceptively interpreting its pictorial and written data, and completing a groundbreaking interpretation of conventions of land measurement, the author is able to reconstruct significant configurations of class-based property holding.

487 Haskett, Robert Stephen. The Indian municipality of Cuernavaca in the colonial period. (*in* Reunión de Historiadores Mexicanos y Norteamericanos, 7th, Oaxaca, Mexico, 1985. Memorias. México: Univ. Nacional Autónoma de México, 1992, v. 1 La ciudad y el campo en la historia de México, p. 115–126, tables)

Brief, detailed examination of officer career patterns, social concepts, marital alliances, and other personal attributes of Cuernavaca's indigenous ruling group, mainly during the 17th and 18th centuries. Based on this analysis, author establishes the persistence of a stratified native elite to Independence.

488 Haskett, Robert Stephen. Indigenous rulers: an ethnohistory of town government in colonial Cuernavaca. Albuquerque: Univ. of New Mexico Press, 1991. 294 p.: bibl., ill., index, map.

Careful study of the nature and evolution of indigenous municipal governments in the Cuernavaca jurisdiction of the Cortés Marquesado del Valle. Author uses a large variety of Nahuatl-language records and more traditional Spanish-language documents to chart the ruling group's adaptation of imposed political, social, economic, and cultural forms.

489 Haskett, Robert Stephen. "Our suffering with the Taxco tribute:" involuntary mine labor and indigenous society in central New Spain. (*HAHR*, 71:3, Aug. 1991, p. 447–475, tables)

Detailed treatment of the impact of labor at Taxco on indigenous tribute workers, most from the Cuernavaca region. Utilizing Nahuatl-language materials whenever possible, author examines internal pressures, responses, and dislocations experienced by men and women involved in the labor drafts.

490 Haskett, Robert Stephen. Visions of municipal glory undimmed: the Nahuatl town histories of colonial Cuernavaca. (*CLAHR/Albuquerque*, 1:1, Fall 1992, p. 1–36)

Analysis of non-professional, Nahuatl-language town histories, known as primordial titles, from Cuernavaca and surrounding communities. Through a combination of linguistic and historical analysis, author recovers elements of an elite Nahua worldview, including their attitudes towards the Spanish State, and their perceptions of the nature of the corporate group.

491 Hassig, Ross. Aztec and Spanish conquest in Mesoamerica. (*in* War in the tribal zone: expanding states and indigenous warfare. Edited by R. Brian Ferguson and Neil L. Whitehead. Santa Fe, N.M.: School of American Research Press, 1992, p. 83–102)

Skillful analytical comparison between Aztec and Spanish empire-building as it was played out in Mesoamerica explains the nature of, the reasons for, and consequences of their differing imperial strategies and techniques.

492 Hassig, Ross. War and society in ancient Mesoamerica. Berkeley: Univ. of California Press, 1992. 337 p., 16 p. of plates: bibl., ill., index, maps.

Exemplary study of war and militarism within the context of the rise and fall of several distinct Mesoamerican sociopolitical systems highlights interrelationships between social organization, economic imperatives, technological innovation, and military capacity. Author concludes that the cultural exchange inherent in what he sees as a cyclical process of empire building gradually created the culture now known as Mesoamerica.

493 Hernández Rodríguez, Rosaura. El Valle de Toluca: época prehispánica y siglo XVI. Toluca, Mexico: Colegio Mexiquense; Ayuntamiento de Toluca, 1988. 159 p.: appendices, bibl., ill., index.

Updated ed. makes more accessible author's 1952 thesis, which is especially useful for its presentation of prehispanic ethnic and geographical information. Appendices consist of 17 documents (dating 1547–1603, the earliest one in Nahuatl) from the Hospital de Jesús collection, Archivo General de la Nación.

494 Herr Solé, Alberto. El Archivo Angel María Garibay Kintana de la Biblioteca Nacional. (*Estud. Cult. Náhuatl*, 22, 1992, p. 180–222, tables)

Produced in honor of the 100th anniversary of Garibay's birth, this is a useful description of his extensive works held at Mexico's national library.

495 Heyden, Doris. Dryness before the rains: Toxcatl and Tezcatlipoca. (*in* To change place: Aztec ceremonial landscapes. Edited by David Carrasco. Boulder: Univ. Press of Colorado, 1991, p. 188–202, bibl., facsims.)

Well crafted analysis of the meanings of imagery and ritual connected with Tezcatlipoca during the Toxcatl festival, associated with the end of the dry season and the onset of the rains and growing season.

496 Hicks, Frederic. Subject states and tribute provinces: the Aztec empire in the northern Valley of Mexico. (*Anc. Mesoam.*, 3:1, Spring 1992, p. 1–10, bibl., map)

Reconstruction of subject states and tribute provinces of the Triple Alliance in the northern part of the Valley of Mexico argues that, in the same general area, tribute from some communities would flow to the imperial capitals and from others to local rulers.

497 Hill, Robert M. Colonial Cakchiquels: highland Maya adaptations to Spanish rule, 1600–1700. Fort Worth, Texas: Harcourt

Brace Jovanovich, 1992. 175 p.: bibl., ill., index, map. (Case studies in cultural anthropology)

Well written reconstruction of 17th-century Cakchikel culture and its links to the prehispanic past. Author seeks to understand the Cakchikels' "tenacity and success" in surviving many demands related to their incorporation into the Spanish empire.

498 Hill, Robert M. The Pirir papers and other colonial period Cakchiquel-Maya testamentos. Nashville, Tenn.: Vanderbilt Univ., 1989. 109 p., 1 leaf of plates: bibl., ill., map. (Vanderbilt Univ. publications in anthropology; 37)

Well crafted study of four Cakchikel testaments stresses information about family organization and relationships. Hill complements his excellent description and analysis with parallel Cakchikel, English, and Spanish versions of the texts.

499 Historia de la religión en Mesoamérica y áreas afines: primer coloquio. Edición de Barbro Dahlgren de Jordán. México: Instituto de Investigaciones Antropológicas, UNAM, 1987. 303 p., 1 folded leaf of plates: ill. (Serie antropológica; 78: Etnología/historia.)

Collection of essays, some of which warrant special attention: Blas R. Castellón discusses historical cycles of Quetzalcoatl and Huitzilopochtli; Noel Morelos García links Teotihuacan state-building and a growing synthesis of discrete agricultural deities with the single figure of Tlaloc; and Yólotl González insightfully discusses Mexica deity taxonomy.

500 History and mythology of the Aztecs: the *Codex Chimalpopoca*. Translated by John Bierhorst. Tucson: Univ. of Arizona Press, 1992. 238 p.: bibl.

This English-language volume and its Nahuatl companion (item **455**) facilitate access to the two principal components of the so-called *Codex Chimalpopoca:* the *Annals of Cuauhtitlán* (a chronicle of the Chichimec migration through the time of the Spanish landfall) and the Legend of the Suns creation epic. They were originally written down in 1570 and 1558 respectively, but derive from older oral and pictorial traditions. Bierhorst's explanatory notes, glossary, concordance of nouns and titles, and subject guide to ethno-

graphic material enhance the considerable utility of these valuable primary sources. Ideally these two volumes should have been combined into a single, bilingual edition. For another English translation of the Legend of the Suns, without the Nahuatl text, see item **525.**

501 Hodge, Mary G. Land and lordship in the Valley of Mexico: the politics of Aztec provincial administration. (*in* Land and politics in the Valley of Mexico: a two-thousand-year perspective. Edited by H.R. Harvey. Albuquerque: Univ. of New Mexico Press, 1991, p. 113–139, map, tables)

Careful investigation of political subordination finds that elites of states subject to the Triple Alliance who were assigned land and tribute incomes outside of their home communitities became less dependent on their own tributaries and more closely linked to their new imperial patrons. At the same time their local power was diminished when outsiders were given access to provincial resources.

502 Horn, Rebecca. The sociopolitical organization of the *corregimiento* of Coyoacán. (*in* Reunión de Historiadores Mexicanos y Norteamericanos, *7th, Oaxaca, Mexico, 1985.* Memorias. México: Univ. Nacional Autónoma de México, 1992, v. 1, La ciudad y el campo en la historia de México, p. 103–113)

Perceptive study of colonial Coyoacán, based on Nahuatl and Spanish sources, demonstrates marked persistence of precontact sociopolitical organization despite the area's proximity to Mexico City. However, the situation was not static, and over time older structures were modified in a number of important ways.

503 Huehuehtlahtolli = Testimonios de la antigua palabra. Estudio introductorio de Miguel León Portilla. Transcripción del texto náhuatl y traducción al castellano de Librado Silva Galeana. México: Secretaría de Educación Pública; Fondo de Cultura Económica, 1991. 242 p.: bibl., ill.

Discussion and translation of significant socialization manual first compiled under the direction of Fray Andrés de Olmos and reconstructed from partial copies held by the John Carter Brown Library and the Univ. of Pennsylvania. The original Nahuatl is given only for the first book of the document, and readers are referred to a facsimile published in 1988 by the Mexican Comisión Nacional Conmemorativa del V Centenario del Encuentro de Dos Mundos for the entire native-language text.

504   The Indian community of colonial Mexico: fifteen essays on land tenure, corporate organizations, ideology, and village politics. Edited by Arij Ouweneel and Simon Miller. Amsterdam: CEDLA, 1990. 321 p.: bibl., ill., maps. (Latin America studies; 58)

Vital collection of essays explores topics listed in the subtitle and emphasizes crucial importance of land as a mechanism of corporate (and individual) identity and survival. Significant work on confraternities is also presented. Contributing authors include Ursula Dyckerhoff, Bernardo García Martínez, Stephanie Wood, Wayne S. Osborne, Robert Haskett, Danièle Dehouve, D.A. Brading, Serge Gruzinski, Asunción Lavrin, William B. Taylor, and Eric Van Young.

505   Jansen, Maarten. The search for history in Mixtec codices. (*Anc. Mesoam.*, 1:1, Spring 1990, p. 99–112, bibl., facsims.)

Interesting study of the evolution of studies of Mixtec codices makes extensive use of illustrations. Author's special concerns are issues of geography, religion, and historical chronology as presented in the documents.

506   King, Mark B. Poetics and metaphor in Mixtec writing. (*Anc. Mesoam.*, 1:1, Spring 1990, p. 141–151, bibl., facsims.)

Explores poetic symbolism in Mixtec codices, centered especially on the Vienna Codex. Author identifies and translates brief pictographic "captions" which seem to have had a syllabic function and could convey poetic passages heavy with ideological and cultural meaning.

507   Klein, Herbert S. Family and fertility in Amatenango, Chiapas, 1785–1816. (*in* Reunión de Historiadores Mexicanos y Norteamericanos, 7th, Oaxaca, Mexico, 1985. Memorias. México: Univ. Nacional Autónoma de México, 1992, v. 1, La ciudad y el campo en la historia de México, p. 127–132)

Reconstruction of 319 family histories carefully asssembled from birth, death, and marriage registers from the late colonial Tzeltal community of Amatenango. Author finds

that Tzeltal women married at a very young age, resulting in prolonged fertility and marked population growth, which in turn may have been rooted in a solid subsistence base.

508   Klor de Alva, J. Jorge. Colonizing souls: the failure of the Indian Inquisition and the rise of penitential discipline. (*in* Cultural encounters: the impact of the Inquisition in Spain and the New World. Berkeley: Univ. of California Press, 1991, p. 3–22, bibl., ill., tables)

Probing analysis of the failure of the Inquisition and its spectacular public punishments as productive tools for the acculturation of central New Spain's indigenous peoples. Instead, author convincingly demonstrates how confession, religious instruction, and various forms of physical and spiritual punishment meted out by the parish clergy had a much more profound and long-lasting effect.

509   Klor de Alva, J. Jorge. Religious rationalization and the conversions of the Nahuas: social organization and colonial epistemology. (*in* To change place: Aztec ceremonial landscapes. Edited by David Carrasco. Boulder: Univ. Press of Colorado, 1991, p. 233–245, bibl., table)

Excellent analysis of competing indigenous and Spanish Catholic religious constructs suggests a three-phase sequence of "sociocultural transformations." Using this scheme, author posits a trajectory of incomplete conversion and explains why Christian concepts established themselves within a basically native belief system, rather than the opposite.

510   Klor de Alva, J. Jorge. Sin and confession among the colonial Nahuas: the confessional as a tool for domination. (*in* Reunión de Historiadores Mexicanos y Norteamericanos, 7th, Oaxaca, Mexico, 1985. Memorias. México: Univ. Nacional Autónoma de México, 1992, v. 1, La ciudad y el campo en la historia de México, p. 91–101)

Innovative portrayal of Christian confession as a means of social control. Just as importantly, author suggests that questions posed in Nahuatl-language confessionals hold vital information about indigenous sexuality, worldviews, the psychological impact of epidemics, internal political relations, and even land use.

511 **Krippner-Martínez, James.** The politics of conquest: an interpretation of the *Relación de Michoacán.* (*Americas/Francisc.,* 47:2, Oct. 1990, p. 177–197)
Excellent analysis of this extremely important text, identified as having two authorial voices, one indigenous, the other Franciscan. Article identifies the sociocultural and political implications behind these voices and scrutinizes concepts of gender as they related to male elites' efforts to make sense of their conquest and subjugation.

512 **Krug, Frances Mary.** The Indian municipality within a Spanish urban conquest: seventeenth century Puebla. (*in* Reunión de Historiadores Mexicanos y Norteamericanos, *7th, Oaxaca, Mexico, 1985.* Memorias. México: Univ. Nacional Autónoma de México, 1992, v. 1, La ciudad y el campo en la historia de México, p. 59–67)
Investigation of Puebla's indigenous municipality, which originated from the use of forced labor from Tlaxcala to build and expand the city. By mining the *Códice Gómez de Orozco, 1524–1691,* rich Nahuatl-language annals, the author is able to reconstruct the establishment and organization of three self-governing indigenous *altepetl* in Puebla.

513 **Land and politics in the Valley of Mexico: a two thousand-year perspective.** Edited by H.R. Harvey. Albuquerque: Univ. of New Mexico Press, 1991. 325 p.: bibl., ill., index, maps.
Anthology of cutting-edge contributions pursues interconnected themes of land and sociopolitical structure beyond the level of empire and great estate to the strata of the region, the *altepetl,* and the humble agricultural community. For contributions of special ethnohistorical merit, see items **436, 440, 449, 451, 454, 486, 501, 544, 566,** and **581.**

514 **León-Portilla, Ascensión H. de.** Tepuztlahcuilolli = Impresos en náhuatl: historia y bibliografía. México: Univ. Nacional Autónoma de México, Instituto de Investigaciones Históricas e Instituto de Investigaciones Filológicas, 1988. 2 v.: bibl., ill. (Serie de cultura náhuatl: Monografías; 22)
Indispensable reference work on the Nahuatl language. Vol. 1 offers an historical overview of the activities and products (grammars, vocabularies, texts, linguistic and historical analyses, etc.) of scholars from the 16th-20th centuries. Vol. 2 is an annotated

bibliography of works published in Nahuatl or about the language.

515 **León Portilla, Miguel.** The Aztec image of self and society: an introduction to Nahua culture. Introduction by J. Jorge Klor de Alva. Salt Lake City: Univ. of Utah Press, 1992. 248 p.: bibl., ill., index.
Beautifully-written study examines the synthesis of Mexica concepts about their origins, the nature of their society, and sociopolitical ordering as rendered in native language texts. Author also explores competing ideological visions, including the "martial-mystical view of the cosmos" considered the creation of the Mexica *Cihuacoatl* Tlacaelel, and the somewhat more resistive and more peaceful worldview enunciated by such figures as Nezehualcoytl of Texcoco.

516 **Ligorred Perramón, Francisco de Asís.** Literatura maya: de los jeroglíficos al alfabeto latino. (*Bol. Am.,* 30:38, 1988, p. 189–207, bibl.)
Views Maya colonial texts and precontact glyphic inscriptions as literary as well as historical and religious tracts. Author finds elements of cultural resistance embodied in postconquest texts, and discusses form and content of the *Ritual de los Bacabes,* the *Cantares de Dzitbalché,* and ten known books of *Chilam Balam.*

517 **Lockhart, James.** Complex municipalities: Tlaxcala and Tulancingo in the sixteenth century. (*in* Reunión de Historiadores Mexicanos y Norteamericanos, *7th, Oaxaca, Mexico, 1985.* Memorias. México: Univ. Nacional Autónoma de México, 1992, v. 1, La ciudad y el campo en la historia de México, p. 45–57)
Well-crafted comparative study of the structure of two *altepetl* of central Mexico, based largely on extensive Nahuatl-language records. Lockhart analyzes in detail such things as *cabildo* representation, rotation of officers among the *capulli* or *tlaxilacalli* (subunits) of each municipality, and officer career patterns. A version of this article also appears in item **519.**

518 **Lockhart, James.** The Nahuas after the conquest: a social and cultural history of the Indians of central Mexico, sixteenth through eighteenth centuries. Stanford, Calif.: Stanford Univ. Press, 1992. 650 p.: bibl., ill., index.

Magnificent study of post-conquest Nahua society and culture makes innovative use of a great variety of Nahuatl-language source materials to fashion the most detailed and intimate view of postconquest Nahua society available. The book, which presents compelling multi-stage model of cultural continuity and change, will long serve as a methodological model for those seeking to understand the ways in which indigenous people confronted and mediated the sociocultural pressures of invasion and foreign domination.

519 Lockhart, James. Nahuas and Spaniards: postconquest central Mexican history and philology. Stanford, Calif.: Stanford Univ. Press; Los Angeles: UCLA Latin American Center Publications, 1991. 1 v.: bibl. (Nahuatl studies series; 3)

Collection of 13 excellent articles, five of which have never before appeared in print, presents the author's innovative interpretation and reconstruction of postconquest Nahua society. The heart of the book contains a series of ethnohistorical studies based heavily on Nahuatl-language sources, and includes several painstaking transcriptions and English translations of representative Nahuatl texts (two other articles deal mainly with Spaniards).

520 Lockhart, James. Postconquest Nahua society and concepts viewed through Nahuatl writings. (*Estud. Cult. Náhuatl*, 20, 1990, p. 91–116, bibl.)

Admirable summary of Lockhart's interpretive scheme of the evolution of Nahua society under Spanish rule, richly illustrated with case studies. Author links cultural trends with three distinct stages in linguistic adaptation.

521 López Austin, Alfredo. The myth of the half-man who descended from the sky. (*in* To change place: Aztec ceremonial landscapes. Edited by David Carrasco. Boulder: Univ. Press of Colorado, 1991, p. 152–157, bibl.)

Brief, intriguing study considers how a Texcocan origin myth was manipulated, contending that over time it became more and more historical in content and structure.

522 Lovell, W. George. Disease and depopulation in early colonial Guatemala. (*in* International Congress of Ameri-

canists, *46th, Amsterdam, 1988.* "Secret judgments of God:" Old World disease in colonial Spanish America. Edited by Noble David Cook and W. George Lovell. Norman: Univ. of Oklahoma Press, 1992, p. 49–83)

Careful analysis of well known published sources, such as the *Annals of the Cakchiquels*, and a significant number of archival documents seeks to definitively link Maya depopulation and specific disease episodes from the early 16th through early 17th centuries.

523 Maldonado Jiménez, Druzo. Cuauhnáhuac y Huaxtepec: Tlalhuicas y Xochimilcas en el Morelos prehispánico. Cuernavaca, Mexico: Univ. Nacional Autónoma de México, Centro Regional de Investigaciones Multidisciplinarias, 1990. 293 p.: bibl., ill., maps.

Richly detailed, regional ethnohistorical study of two important precontact Nahua states. Author's painstaking reconstruction of Cuauhnahuac and Huaxtepec's sociopolitical structure and history, as well as their external economic and political relations, significantly complements the more numerous studies of the Valley of Mexico during the same period.

524 El manuscrito *Can Ek:* descubrimiento de una visita secreta del siglo XVII a Tah Itzá (Tayazal), última capital de los maya itzáes. Transcripción y comentario de Grant Jones. Introducción de George E. Stuart. Washington: National Geographic Society; México: Instituto Nacional de Antropología e Historia, 1991. 72 p. (Col. Divulgación)

Description, commentary, and transcription of four surviving folios of a document which narrates previously unknown visit in or around 1695 of three Franciscian friars and ten Maya sacristans to Tah Itzá in an attempt to convert its ruler, Can Ek. Document adds important new insights into Spanish contacts with the "rebel" Maya state.

525 Markman, Roberta H. and **Peter T. Markman.** The flayed God: the Mesoamerican mythological tradition: sacred texts and images from pre-Columbian Mexico and Central America. San Francisco, Calif.: Harper San Francisco, 1992. 456 p., 16 p. of plates: bibl., ill. (some col.), index, maps.

Collection of numerous plastic, pictorial, and written examples of Mesoamerican mythic tradition arranged topically around themes such as creation, fertility, and ruler-ship. A first-rate interpretive commentary accompanies the illustrations and texts, the latter of which include a full English translation of Nahuatl-langauge *Leyenda de los Soles* prepared by Willard Gingerich. For another English translation of the *Leyenda* see item **500.**

526 Márquez Morfín, Lourdes. La dieta
        maya prehispánica en la costa yuca-
teca. (*Estud. Cult. Maya,* 18, 1991, p. 359–
394)

Detailed analysis of the nature of the lowland Maya diet takes into account ecological and social variables. Much of the discussion centers on the coastal region of the Yucatan and highlights the great importance of fish as a major source of protein. Issues of nutrition are also addressed.

527 Martínez, Andrea. Las pinturas del
        Manuscrito de Tlaxcala. (*Estud. Cult.
Náhuatl,* 20, 1990, p. 141–162)

Examines the *Lienzo de Tlaxcala* and provides highly detailed discussion of interrelationships between early surviving postconquest documents pertaining to Tlaxcala's history. Situates documents in Tlaxcala's ongoing efforts to attain privileges from the crown and to redefine themselves in the face of the dislocations of the conquest (see also item **439**).

528 Martínez, Hildeberto. Tepeaca en el
        siglo XVI: tenencia de la tierra y orga-
nización de un señorío. México: Centro de Investigaciones y Estudios Superiores en Antropología Social, 1984. 230 p.: bibl., ill., maps. (Ediciones de la Casa Chata; 21)

Solidly crafted study of Tepeaca investigates the evolution of its internal sociopolitical organization, as well as the landholdings of a number of important ruling families. Author uncovers persistence of essentially precontact class-related structures of land tenure and the organization of labor.

529 Megged, Amos. Accommodation and
        resistance of elites in transition: the
case of Chiapas in early colonial Mesoamerica. (*HAHR,* 71:3, Aug. 1991, p. 477–500)

Very well done study, based on an impressive amount of primary research and focused mainly on Chiapa de Indios and Zinacatlan, of complex ways in which local Maya elites dealt with the imposition of Spanish control, some choosing to cooperate, others to resist.

530 Menegus Bornemann, Margarita. Del
        señorío a la república de indios: el caso
de Toluca, 1500–1600. Prólogo de Mariano Peset. Madrid: Ministerio de Agricultura, Pesca y Alimentación, Secretaría General Técnica, 1991. 271 p.: bibl., maps. (Serie Estudios; 62)

Examines destruction of the *señorío indígena* and the formation of *repúblicas de indios* among the Matlatzinca communities of the Toluca Valley in the 16th century. Author pays particular attention to jurisdictional adjustments, tribute rearrangements, and, above all, the fate of corporate landholdings.

531 Menegus Bornemann, Margarita. La
        propiedad indígena en la transición,
1519–1577: las tierras de explotación colectiva. (*in* Mundo rural, ciudades y población del Estado de México. Coordinación de Manuel Miño Grijalva. Toluca, México: El Colegio Mexiquense; Instituto Mexiquense de Cultura, 1990, p. 43–68, bibl., tables)

Systematically executed study focuses on the 16th-century Valley of Toluca and explores shifts in indigenous community land tenure and use. Author identifies pattern in which colonial-era changes in tribute production, as well as the mounting need to fund local political and Church functions, forced the increasing reallocation of lands away from subsistence cultivation.

532 The Mesoamerican ballgame. Edited
        by Vernon L. Scarborough and David R.
Wilcox. Tucson: Univ. of Arizona Press, 1991. 404 p.: bibl., ill., index.

Interdisciplinary collection of 16 essays from a conference held at Tucson in 1985 explores the history, functions, and meanings of the Mesoamerican ballgame. The volume's scope permits a multi-regional reconstruction of the game, and demonstrates its underlying, pan-regional character. While all the offerings are of high quality, articles by Jeffrey K. Wilkerson, Vernon L. Scarborough, Lee A. Parsons, John W. Fox, Marvin Cohadas, Linda Schele and David A. Freidel, and Susan D. Gillespie will be of special interest to ethnohistorians.

533 Monaghan, John. Performance and the
        structure of the Mixtec codices. (*Anc.
Mesoam.,* 1:1, Spring 1990, p. 133–140, bibl., facsims)

Preliminary study, focused mainly on

the Vienna Codex, suggests that Mixtec codices were intended to be read or performed in public. The size and arrangement of figures in the codices seem to represent poetic couplets or triplets, a structure which the author maintains can be related to modern Mixtec prayer and chant.

534   Monnet, Jérôme. Mexcaltitán, territorio de la identidad mexicana: la creación de un mito de origen. (*Vuelta/México,* 15:171, feb. 1991, p. 25–30, photos)

Intriguing discussion identifies the community of Mexcaltitán, situated in a lake in Nayarit state, as the legendary Aztlán. Article considers how Mexcaltitán has become a centerpiece of the modern "myth" of Mexican national identity, moving from status as "cradle of the Mexica" to "cradle of the Mexicans."

535   Motolinía, Toribio, Fray. El libro perdido: ensayo de reconstrucción de la obra histórica extraviada de Fray Toribio. Trabajo realizado en el Seminario de Historiografía Mexicana de la Univ. Iberoamericana, dirigido por Edmundo O'Gorman. México: Consejo Nacional para la Cultura y las Artes, 1989. 648 p.: bibl., index. (Quinto centenario)

Significant reconstruction of an extensive lost historical work thought to have been written by Motolinía. O'Gorman and his collaborators have painstakingly and plausibly compiled the present, indexed work by drawing from the well-known *Historia,* and the *Memoriales,* as well as references to, and apparent quotations from, the "lost book" found in such sources as Zorita's *Relación de la Nueva España.*

536   Navarrete Pellicer, Sergio. Las transformaciones de la economía indígena en Michoacán: siglo XVI. (*in* Agricultura indígena: pasado y presente. Coordinación de Teresa Rojas Rabiela. México: Ediciones de la Casa Chata, 1990, p. 109–127)

Well-done study explores the impact of postconquest labor systems, crops, and livestock on the indigenous population of Michoacán. Author discusses how indigenous peoples reacted to new introductions, adopting some, but resisting others which threatened to push native crops off of the best lands.

537   Nicholson, Henry B. The Octli cult in late pre-Hispanic Central Mexico. (*in* To change place: Aztec ceremonial landscapes. Edited by David Carrasco. Boulder:

Univ. Press of Colorado, 1991, p. 158–187, bibl., facsims., photo)

Detailed, richly-illustrated discussion of the nature and significance of the Octli cult, based on a careful analysis of important pictorial and native language sources.

538   Noguez, Xavier. Cuáuhyotl y Ocelóyotl: un problema de status adscritos y adquiridos en la sociedad mexica prehispánica. (*Hist. Mex.,* 39:2, oct./dic. 1989, p. 355–386, bibl.)

Careful examination of sources such as Sahagún and Durán traces Nahuatl terms for eagle and ocelot in both the natural world and social categories to better understand the relative status associated with such concepts, whether given at birth or acquired during life.

539   Offutt, Leslie S. Levels of acculturation in northeastern New Spain: San Esteban testaments of the seventeenth and eighteenth centuries. (*Estud. Cult. Náhuatl,* 22, 1992, p. 409–443)

Excellent analysis of 39 Nahuatl testaments from the Tlaxcalan colony of San Esteban de Nueva Tlaxcala, in Saltillo. Author identifies important linguistic and material patterns which signal a growing awareness and impact of Spanish culture over time.

540   Olivier, Guilhem. Conquérants et missionnaires face au *péché abominable*: essai sur l'homosexualité en mésoamérique au moment de la conquête espagnole. (*Caravelle/Toulouse,* 55, 1990, p. 19–51, bibl.)

Presents novel research on neglected topic of homosexuality in precolumbian Mesoamerica. Author critically surveys both Spanish and indigenous sources to reveal male homosexual behavior associated with deities, rituals, and transvestite figures in communities. Apparently, marginal regions were more tolerant of homosexuality, its repression coinciding with rise of centralized power. [A. Pérotin-Dumon]

541   O'Mack, Scott. Yacateuctli and Ehecatl-Quetzalcoatl: earth-divers in Aztec Central Mexico. (*Ethnohistory/Society,* 38:1, Winter 1991, p. 1–33, bibl., ill.)

Multi-faceted essay links for the first time two patron deities of merchants with diving waterfowl, symbols of "mediation and acquisition" associated with an earth-diver who obtained subaqueous mud in order to create the earth and, by extension, the island Tenochtitlan-Tlatelolco.

542 Ortiz de Montellano, Bernard. Aztec medicine, health, and nutrition. New Brunswick: Rutgers Univ. Press, 1990. 308 p.: bibl., ill., index.

Notable study examines Mexica medical practices and ideologies (including their influences on colonial and more modern techniques), and the interrelated themes of diet, nutrition, and the health of the general population. Author also explores concepts of the human body, disease causation, the susceptibility of the human population to sickness, and the efficacy of curing practices. Presents a convincing argument for the potential richness of the Mexica diet (and the concomitant absence of any need to practice large-scale cannibalism to obtain protein).

543 Paddock, John. Señoríos indígenas del Valle de Oaxaca, 1200–1600. (*in* Reunión de Historiadores Mexicanos y Norteamericanos, *7th, Oaxaca, Mexico, 1985.* Memorias. México: Univ. Nacional Autónoma de México, 1992, v. 1, La ciudad y el campo en la historia de México, p. 25–35)

Succinct study of rulership in the community of Macuilxochitl centers on the postconquest genealogical *Mapa de Macuilxochitl* (c. 1580). Author analyzes this document in conjunction with similar records such as the *Codex Nuttall,* and uncovers ethnic complexity within Zapotec ruling lines and in society itself.

544 Parsons, Jeffrey. Political implications of prehispanic *chinampa* agriculture in the Valley of Mexico. (*in* Land and politics in the Valley of Mexico: a two-thousand-year perspective. Edited by H.R. Harvey. Albuquerque: Univ. of New Mexico Press, 1991, p. 17–41, maps, tables)

Well-crafted piece uses archaeological data and postcontact documentary sources to contrast the tight, nuclear system created by Teotihuacan to manage its empire with Tenochtitlan's imperial strategy of fostering swampland drainage and intensification of *chinampa* agriculture, and hence the growth and dispersion of the population.

545 Pastor, Rodolfo. Ideología y parentesco en el señorío mixteco según las fuentes del siglo XVI. (*in* Origen y formación del estado en Mesoamérica. Edición de Andrés Medina, Alfredo López Austin y Mari Carmen Serra. México: Univ. Nacional Autónoma de México, 1986, p. 85–111)

Analysis of sociopolitical ideologies and structures among precontact Mixtecs, based heavily on the interpretation of codices from or containing information about the Mexica.

Peniche Rivero, Piedad. Sacerdotes y comerciantes: el poder de los mayas e itzas de Yucatán en los siglos VII a XVI. See *HLAS 53:212.*

546 Pérez Zevallos, Juan Manuel and **Ludka de Gortari Krauss.** Indice de documentos para la historia indígena en la Huasteca. Tlalpan, Mexico: Gobierno del Estado de Hidalgo: CEHINHAC; CIESAS, 1987. 232 p.: ill., index.

Useful annotated index of documents related to colonial Huastecan indigenous communities held by the Archivo General de la Nación in Mexico City. Indexes the following *ramos:* Congregaciones, Indios, General de la Parte, Mercedes, Tributos, and Tierras. Introduction provides brief descriptions of contents of municipal and parish archives of the Huasteca itself, few of which have much in the way of colonial materials.

547 Pérez Zevallos, Juan Manuel. Las reducciones y la agricultura en la Nueva España, 1599–1604. (*in* Agricultura indígena: pasado y presente. Coordinación de Teresa Rojas Rabiela. México: Ediciones de la Casa Chata, 1990, p. 143–163)

Balanced exploration of *congregación* and indigenous agriculture in various ecological zones. Author discusses why some communities might have benefitted from the shift, while others did not, and explores resistance offered by some towns faced with threats to their traditional lands and agricultural practices.

548 Pohl, John M.D. and **Bruce E. Byland.** Mixtec landscape perception and archaeological settlement patterns. (*Anc. Mesoam.,* 1:1, Spring 1990, p. 113–131, bibl., facsims., maps)

Compelling analysis of place signs and geographical representations in Mixtec codices, as well as related data from modern ethnographic studies, site surveys, and archaeological evidence. Authors explore the impact of perceptions of landscape on settlement patterns, and concepts of the internal and external ordering of states.

549 Pollard, Helen Perlstein. The construction of ideology in the emergence of the prehispanic Tarascan state. (*Anc. Me-*

soam., 2:2, Fall 1991, p. 167–179, bibl., ill., maps, table)

Well-researched article discusses the connection between the emergence of the Tarascan state in 1300 and the creation of a new religion serving to legitimate the new entity and its rulers. Author argues that this religion was much more systematically constructed and based more heavily on pre-existing Tarascan traditions than has sometimes been thought.

550 Pollard, Helen Perlstein. Taríacuri's legacy: the prehispanic Tarascan state. Introduction by Shirley Gorenstein. Norman: Univ. of Oklahoma Press, 1993. 1 v.: bibl., index. (The Civilization of the American Indian series; 209)

Excellent study of a society too often ignored by Mesoamericanists, the Tarascan state and empire, in tradition said to have been founded by the cultural hero Taríacuri. Author situates her examination of the sociopolitical and ideological nature of this state and its religion in a thoroughgoing analysis of both the archaeological and ethnohistorical record, taking into account the effects of ecology and geography on human population and the economy.

551 Prem, Hanns J. Disease outbreaks in central Mexico during the sixteenth century. (*in* International Congress of Americanists, *46th, Amsterdam, 1988*. "Secret judgments of God:" Old World disease in colonial Spanish America. Edited by Noble David Cook and W. George Lovell. Norman: Univ. of Oklahoma Press, 1992, p. 20–48)

Meticulous study of specific disease episodes which challenges more traditional notions by arguing that the greatest loss of life was abrupt and took place at the time of conquest, with recurring outbreaks, but gradually lessening loss of life characterizing the century which followed.

552 Quezada, Noemí. Congregaciones de indios en el Valle de Toluca y zonas aledañas. (*in* Mundo rural, ciudades y población del Estado de México. Coordinación de Manuel Miño Grijalva. Toluca, México: El Colegio Mexiquense: Instituto Mexiquense de Cultura, 1990, p. 71–90, bibl.)

Discusses colonial *congregación* programs in the Valley of Toluca and adjacent areas, employing primary sources and reconstructing both Spanish goals and the *de facto* process, including indigenous responses to the programs which led to their moderation.

Quezada, Noemí. Sexualidad y magia en la mujer novohispana, siglo XVIII. See item **1180.**

553 Redmond, Elsa M. and **Charles S. Spenser.** The prehistoric city and state of Monte Albán: a view from its frontier. (*in* Reunión de Historiadores Mexicanos y Norteamericanos, *7th, Oaxaca, Mexico, 1985*. Memorias. México: Univ. Nacional Autónoma de México, 1992, v. 1, La ciudad y el campo en la historia de México, p. 3–24)

Authors use both archival and archaeological data to examine role of militarism in the formation and maintenance of the Zapotec state. Also discuss use of frontier garrisoning, resettlement of conquered people, and exchange of such things as tribute and agricultural techniques.

554 Reff, Daniel T. Disease, depopulation, and culture change in northwestern New Spain, 1518–1764. Salt Lake City: Univ. of Utah Press, 1991. 330 p.: bibl., index, maps.

Meticulously-researched presentation challenges long-accepted characterizations rooted in late colonial Jesuit accounts of the region's native people as "barbaric" hunter-gatherers living in small, dispersed populations. Reff employs new archaeological discoveries and information from neglected 16th-century Spanish accounts to convincingly demonstrate that, at the point of contact, the peoples of the northwest, though not culturally homogenous, lived in more settled and more sophisticated polities than previously believed, many of them with distinct affinities to better-known central Mesoamerican communities.

555 Rivera Dorado, Miguel. Un punto de vista sobre el mito central del Popol Vuh. (*Rev. Esp. Antropol. Am.*, 18, 1988, p. 51–74, bibl.)

Painstaking analysis links the myth of the divine heros Huanahpú and Ixbalanqué in the Popul Vuh to Maya cosmogany and the origin and travels of the sun, moon, and Venus.

556 Rodríguez-Shadow, María. El estado azteca. Toluca, Mexico: Univ. Autónoma del Estado de México, 1990. 255 p.: bibl. (Col. Historia; 7)

Analyzes how the Mexica elite maintained state and class power and legitimacy by means of ideology and sociopolitical control, including State-sponsored mechanisms of repression.

557 Rodríguez-Shadow, María. La mujer azteca. 2a. ed. Toluca, Mexico: Univ. Autónoma del Estado de México, 1991. 287 p.: bibl., ill. (Col. Historia; 6)

Explores varied roles played by women of precontact Tenochtitlan. Based on an interpretation of Spanish and indigenous-language colonial accounts, the author considers impact of social class, ethnicity, age, and gender ideology. This is an expanded and updated version of the 1988 edition.

558 Rodríguez V., María J. Enfoques y perspectivas de los estudios sobre la condición femenina en el México antiguo. (*Mesoamérica/Antigua*, 11:19, junio 1990, p. 1–11)

Useful critical discussion of trends in the study of precontact Mexica women from the 1940s-80s.

559 Rojas, José Luis de. La organización del imperio mexica. (*Rev. Esp. Antropol. Am.*, 21, 1991, p. 145–169, bibl., map, table)

Thoughtful examination of the complex structure of the Mexica empire relies heavily on *relaciones geográficas*, plus chronicles and tribute documents. Author argues for greater study and understanding of the empire's evolution, rather than focusing on its nature at time of contact with Spaniards.

560 Rojas, José Luis de. El Xoconochoco: ¿una provincia aislada del imperio? (*Rev. Esp. Antropol. Am.*, 19, 1989, p. 91–107, bibl., maps, tables)

Well executed study of Soconusco and its incorporation into the Mexica empire. Author shows that the region was conquered and maintained as an imperial province, despite its geographical isolation, because of its utility as a source of cacao and as a key point of exchange for luxury products from Guatemala.

561 Rojas Rabiela, Teresa. La agricultura prehispánica de Mesoamérica en el siglo XVI. (*in* Mundo rural, ciudades y población del Estado de México. Coordinación de Manuel Miño Grijalva. Toluca, Mexico: El Colegio Mexiquense; Instituto Mexiquense de Cultura, 1990, p. 17–40, bibl., ill.)

Accessible overview of agricultural practices during the time of the Spanish conquest, with special focus on the Toluca region. Author is especially interested in delineating the geographic spread and specificity of various agricultural systems, as well as the implements and techniques used to exploit them.

562 Sahagún, Bernardino de. Breve compendio de los ritos idolátricos que los indios de esta Nueva España usaban en tiempo de su infidelidad. Edición de María Guadalupe Bosch de Souza y Guillermo Rousset Banda. 2. ed. México: Lince Editores, 1990. 69 p.: bibl., facsim.

Facsimile, with modern annotated transcription, of this significant Spanish-language work by Sahagún (c. 1570) which presents a summary of material about Nahua deities, religious practices, and beliefs. Editor Bosch provides a brief introductory discussion about Sahagún, the historical context of the work, and its contents.

563 Sanders, William T. The population of the Central Mexican symbiotic region, the Basin of Mexico, and the Teotihuacan Valley in the sixteenth century. (*in* The native population of the Americas in 1492. Edited by William M. Denevan. Madison: Univ. of Wisconsin Press, 1992, p. 85–150, graphs, map, tables)

Lengthy, detailed, revisionist demographic study adds important new dimension to the ongoing controversy over the population of precontact central Mesoamerica. Sanders' careful calculations provide population figures generally much lower than those which have been widely accepted.

564 Schele, Linda and David Freidel A. A forest of kings: the untold story of the ancient Maya. New York: Morrow, 1990. 542 p., 16 p. of plates: bibl., ill. (some col.), index.

Beautifully-written exploration of Maya history from preclassic through classic times, based on the imaginative use of a wide range of archaeological, linguistic, and ethnohistorical evidence. Authors center on experiences of several important Maya states and, often in a revisionist manner, treat a number of significant themes such as: the shift of warfare from ritual combat to political conquest; changing definitions of rule; and strategies adopted by the rulers of Chichén

Itza (who are identified as Maya rather than central Mexican) to deal with political crises facing them with the fall of most major classic-era centers.

565 **Schroeder, Susan.** Chimalpahin & the kingdoms of Chalco. Tucson: Univ. of Arizona Press, 1991. 264 p.: bibl., ill., index.

Detailed reconstruction of the organization of a significant sub-imperial region, precontact Chalco, assembled from the Nahuatl texts of indigenous historian Chimalpahin. Especially important are discussions of the meanings of entities such as *altepetl* and titles such as *quauhlatoani*.

566 **Schroeder, Susan.** Indigenous sociopolitical organization in Chimalpahin. (*in* Land and politics in the Valley of Mexico: a two-thousand-year perspective. Edited by H.R. Harvey. Albuquerque: Univ. of New Mexico Press, 1991, p. 141–162, facsim., map, tables)

Masterful analysis of Chimalpahin's 17th-century Nahuatl-language writings centers on an examination of *altepetl* structure and organization.

567 **Schroeder, Susan.** The noblewomen of Chalco. (*Estud. Cult. Náhuatl*, 22, 1992, p. 45–86, bibl., map, tables)

Illuminating analysis of roles of Chalcan noblewomen in the writings of Chimalpahin. Author demonstrates importance of royal women in establishing ruling lineages, in inter-dynastic marriages, and in legitimating dynastic succession, patterns which were maintained beyond the conquest through at least the end of the 16th century.

568 **Schwaller, John Frederick.** Constitution of the Cofradía of Tula, Hidalgo, 1570. (*Estud. Cult. Náhuatl*, 19, 1989, p. 217–244)

Worthwhile discussion, transcription, and translation of a 16th-century cofradia register. Schwaller's commentary aids the reader in discovering significant details about the internal religious life of the community, as well as nuances in relationships between resident Spaniards and the indigenous population.

569 **Schwaller, John Frederick.** Guías de manuscritos en náhuatl = Guides to Nahuatl manuscripts: the Newberry Library (Chicago), the Latin American Library (Tulane University), the Bancroft Library (Berkeley). México: Univ. Nacional Autónoma de México, Instituto de Investigaciones Históricas, 1987. 73 p.: bibl.

Essential guide to the Nahuatl-language manuscripts held in these three key repositories. Schwaller provides concise descriptions of the indexed materials, an illuminating discussion of the types of documents, and a history of each collection. For another version of this guide see *HLAS 50:559*.

570 **Schwaller, John Frederick.** Guías de manuscritos en náhuatl conservados en The John Carter Brown Library (Providence, Rhode Island) y The Benson Latin American Collection (Univ. of Texas, Austin). (*Estud. Cult. Náhuatl*, 21, 1991, p. 311–337)

Extremely useful descriptive guide to Nahuatl holdings of these two repositories, sure to remain the basic key to the collections for years to come.

571 **El Señorío de San Esteban del Saltillo: voz y escritura nahuas, siglos XVII y XVIII.** Recopilación de Eustaquio Celestino Solís. Saltillo, Mexico: Archivo Municipal de Saltillo, 1991. 193 p.: bibl.

Transcription and translation of twenty-one 17th- and 18th-century Nahuatl testaments and petitions from this Tlaxcalan immigrant municipality, now found in Saltillo's Municipal Archive (with the exception of one petition, currently in Mexico's National Archive). Worthwhile publication enhanced by straightforward commentary provided by the translator.

572 **Smith, Mary Elizabeth** and **Ross Parmenter.** The Codex Tulane. New Orleans: Middle American Research Institute, Tulane Univ., 1991. 142 p., 13 plates: bibl., ill., index, maps. (Publication; 61)

Publication, with commentary, of this 16th-century pictorial genealogical codex from the Mixtec region of southern Puebla state uncovers important pre- and postcontact dynastic information, as well as the means by which the document came to be presented as a land "map" in an early 19th-century lawsuit.

573 **Sociedad Mexicana de Antropología. Mesa Redonda, *19th, 1985?*** La validez teórica del concepto Mesoamérica. México: Instituto Nacional de Antropología e Historia: Sociedad Mexicana de Antropología, 1990. 218 p.: bibl., maps. (Col. científica; 198. Serie Antropología)

Participants and commentators of this multi-disciplinary round-table consider the validity of the concept of Mesoamerica from its first use by Kirchhoff in 1943 to the present.

574 Spores, Ronald. Tututepec: a postclassic-period Mixtec conquest state. (*Anc. Mesoam.*, 4:1, Spring 1993, p. 167–174, bibl., tables)

Thoughtful preliminary study of the evolution and organization of the centralized, multi-ethnic Tututepec empire of southern Oaxaca which rose to importance under the leadership of ruler 8 Deer and persisted to the Spanish conquest. Author makes some telling comparisons between the Oaxacan and Tarascan empires.

575 Stiles, Neville; Jeff Burnham; and James Nauman. Los consejos médicos de Dr. Bartoloache sobre las pastillas de fierro: un documento colonial en el náhuatl del siglo XVIII. (*Estud. Cult. Náhuatl*, 19, 1989, p. 269–287)

Useful discussion, transcription, and translation of a late-colonial Nahuatl document written to serve the purposes of a Spanish physician reveals his view of native inferiority and tendency to drunkenness. Notable is the authors' inclusion of a catalog of Nahuatl terms for specific types of maladies mentioned in the original document.

Swann, Michael M. Migration, mobility, and the mining towns of colonial northern Mexico. See item **1325.**

576 El título de yax y otros documentos quichés de Totonicapán, Guatemala. Edición facsimilar, transcripción, traducción y notas de Robert M. Carmack y James L. Mondloch. México: Instituto de Investigaciones Filológicas, Centro de Estudios Mayas, UNAM, 1989. 224 p.: bibl., ill., maps. (Fuentes para el estudio de la cultura maya; 8)

Informative commentaries by the editors complement this presentation of facsimiles, transcriptions, and Spanish translations of several important colonial *títulos*: the Quiche-language *Título de Yax*, the *Título de Pedro Velasco*, the *Título de Cristóbal Ramírez*, the *Título de Paxtocá*, and the *Título de Caciques.* Scholars of the so-called primordial titles of central Mexico will find the present volume a very useful comparative tool.

577 To change place: Aztec ceremonial landscapes. Edited by David Carrasco. Boulder: Univ. Press of Colorado, 1991. 254 p.: bibl., ill., index.

Superb collection of 16 essays ranges from discussions of new archaeological revelations from the Templo Mayor and associated sites, to innovative studies of the conception and meaning of ceremonial space, and concludes with richly nuanced reflective works on related themes from the precontact through modern periods. The unifying topic of the volume is the issue of ritual transformation in thought, action, movement, and physical place. For individual essays see items **427, 428, 435, 437, 446, 495, 509, 521,** and **537.**

578 Tschohl, Peter. Es setzte sich auf den Thron Calizto, der nur 80 Tage regierte. (*Mexicon/Berlin*, 15:6, Dec. 1993, p. 115–118, bibl., tables)

In his examination of three controversial theories scrutinizing the anomaly of a Spanish name appearing during the precolumbian period in the *Anales de Cuauhtitlan*, Tschohl concludes that empirical reliance on the exact pattern of the physical evidence must take precedence over theoretical considerations. [C.K. Converse]

579 Vollmer, Gunter. Esopo para mexicanos o el intento de enseñar a indígenas una vida prudente. (*in* Jornadas de Historiadores Americanistas, *2nd, Granada, Spain, 1988.* América: encuentro y asimilación. Edición de Joaquín A. Muñoz Mendoza. Granada: Diputación Provincial de Granada, 1989, p. 97–108, appendix, bibl.)

Explores the perhaps surprising use of Aesop's Fables, translated into Nahuatl, as a tool for teaching European values.

580 Weeks, John M. Defining variability in colonial lowland maya domestic groups. (*Rev. Esp. Antropol. Am.*, 21, 1991, p. 171–219, bibl., map, tables)

Detailed analysis of a 1615 house-by-house census from the Campeche communities of Cheusih and Sahcabchen yields a picture of great variation in the size and composition of households, and explores issues related to kinship and residence patterns. Inclusion of transcriptions of the census is extremely useful.

581 Williams, Barbara J. The lands and political organization of a rural tlaxilacalli in *Tepetlaoztoc*, c. A.D. 1540. (*in* Land and politics in the Valley of Mexico: a two-thousand-year perspective. Edited by H.R. Harvey. Albuquerque: Univ. of New Mexico Press, 1991, p. 187–208, ill., maps, photos, tables)

Important analysis of several key early-colonial Nahuatl-language texts from the rural *tlaxilacalli* of Tepetlaoztoc, in the Texcoco region. Author uses the texts to construct a fresh discussion of the organization and land tenure situation of a small rural community just before and immediately after the Spanish conquest.

582 Williams, Barbara J. La producción y el consumo de maíz: un estudio preliminar de Tlanchiuhca, Tepetlaoztoc. (*in* Agricultura indígena: pasado y presente. Coordinación de Teresa Rojas Rabiela. México: Ediciones de la Casa Chata, 1990, p. 209–226, tables)

Useful though brief analysis of two early colonial codices, the *Códice de Santa María Asunción* and the *Códice Vergara*, focuses on local indigenous soil taxonomy and maize production. Interested scholars will find the many tables presented in the article of great use.

583 Witschey, Walter R.T. Maya inheritance patterns: the transfer of real estate and personal property in Ebtun, Yucatán, Mexico. (*Estud. Cult. Maya*, 18, 1991, p. 395–416, appendix)

Informative outline of inheritance patterns pays close attention to the impact of gender, as revealed in the collection of land-related documents known as the *Titles of Ebtun*. Includes appendix with summaries of the relevant documents.

584 Wood, Stephanie. Adopted saints: Christian images in Nahua testaments of late colonial Toluca. (*Americas/Francisc.*, 47:3, Jan. 1991, p. 259–293, tables)

Detailed investigation of the worship of Catholic saints in 17th- and 18th-century indigenous households in a central Mexican valley, based on 170 wills in Nahuatl. Some attention to changes from the 16th century, to gender issues, to private cofradias, and to the growing importance of the Virgin of Guadalupe.

585 Wood, Stephanie. The cosmic conquest: late-colonial views of the sword and cross in central Mexican *Títulos*. (*Ethnohistory/Society*, 38:4, Spring 1991, p. 176–195, bibl.)

Exploration of retrospective indigenous views of the Spanish conquest of central Mexico drawn from unorthodox community histories in Nahuatl written down in the 17th and 18th centuries. These records show surprising acceptance of colonial structures and religion, but also highlight the growing competition over resources between the indigenous community and the Spanish settler.

586 Wood, Stephanie. Don Diego García de Mendoza Moctezuma: a Techialoyan mastermind. (*Estud. Cult. Náhuatl*, 19, 1989, p. 245–268)

Effort to answer some of the nagging questions that continue to plague the study of the unorthodox Techialoyan manuscripts points to the possible involvement of a member of the Mendoza Moctezuma family, notorious for creative cacique genealogies. Appended is a Spanish translation of a tentative addition to the Techialoyan corpus.

587 Wright, David. Conquistadores otomíes en la Guerra Chichimeca. Querétaro, Mexico: Dirección de Patrimonio Cultural, Secretaría de Cultura y Bienestar Social, Gobierno del Estado de Querétaro, 1988. 107 p.: bibl., ill., indexes. (Documentos de Querétaro; 6)

Useful description, analysis, and transcription of two related late 17th- or early 18th-century documents (apparently related to the genre of primordial titles) found in the Tierras collection of Mexico's Archivo General de la Nación, originally used in lawsuit by the cacique don Diego García de Mendoza.

588 Zavala, Silvio Arturo. El servicio personal de los indios en la Nueva España. v. 4, Suplemento a los tres tomos relativos al siglo XVI. México: Colegio de México, Centro de Estudios Históricos, 1989? 1 v.: bibl., indexes.

Continues author's important project of commentaries and summaries of primary records about labor service extracted by Spaniards from New Spain's indigenous peoples. Vol. 4 supplements materials from the first three vols. and also includes digests of records held in such repositories as the Archivo Notarial del Estado de Puebla, as well as discussions of relevant secondary literature.

589 Zeitlin, Judith Francis and **Lillian Thomas.** Spanish justice and the Indian cacique: disjunctive political systems in sixteenth-century Tehuantepec. (*Ethnohistory/Society*, 39 : 3, Summer 1992, p. 285–315, bibl.)

Sophisticated study of tensions and transformations within indigenous society implicit in the collision of Isthmus Zapotec and Spanish concepts of political rule and justice as played out in a 1553 suit brought against don Juan Cortés, traditional ruler of Tehuantepec.

South America

NOBLE DAVID COOK, *Professor of History, Florida International University*

THE QUINCENTENNIAL OF THE ENCOUNTER between peoples of the two hemispheres has resulted in careful reexamination of the nature and impact of European expansion. There has been a subsequent flood of scholarly and popular discourse in which both specialists and novices have engaged in often heated debate over the meaning of contact. The reevaluation has not led to a new synthesis, but it has sharpened our understanding of the uneasy relation between Old and New World peoples in the context of a changing environment.

One consequence has been the appearance of new critical editions of basic texts, such as the English translation of Bernabé Cobo (item **629**) and, more importantly for scholars, Laura González and Alicia Alonso's new edition of Polo de Onde-gardo's *Relación* (item **766**); María del Carmen Martín Rubio's edition of the narrative of Inca descendant Diego de Castro Tito Cusi Yupanqui (item **721**); Henrique Urbano and Ana Sánchez's version of a chronicle by Juan de Santa Cruz Pachacuti Yanqui Salcamaygua, a south Andean native voice (item **600**); and Urbano and Pierre Duviols' text of Cristóbal de Molina (item **732**). Numerous other new multivolume or facsimile editions of the early chronicles have been published in Spain and America, and will serve the public well.

Another result is the publication of volumes of the collected work of seasoned scholars, and the publication of conference results. Waldemar Espinosa Soriano's important but scattered chapters on Ecuadorian ethnohistory (item **653**), Tom Zuidema's focused evaluation of Inca Cusco (item **837**), and the late Thierry Saignes' seminal work on conflict on the Chiriguano frontier (item **787**) are important materials for students and specialists alike. Heraclio Bonilla's conference series on early contact (item **634**) and on the 19th-century Andean world (item **599**), Raquel Thiercelin's massive set covering a broad range of peoples and places (item **638**), and Segundo Moreno and Frank Salomon's collection on the Andes (item **781**) set high standards for edited works.

A third consequence is the appearance of new documentary collections and catalogs that will facilitate continued investigations. Research tools range from Diana Bonnett Vélez's catalog of Quito materials (item **612**) to Thomas Welch's Inca bibliography (item **830**). Some new tribute lists, verging on censuses, have appeared, including John Murra's for 1569–70 Valles de Sonqo (item **827**), Cristóbal Landázuri's for 1551–59 Chillos (item **828**), and Raimund Schramm's for 1560 Cochabamba (item **678**). Collections of Amazonian material have also come to light (items **594** and **690**).

Although we have not yet seen a new synthesis, some work does stand out. Colombia and Ecuador have seen close attention, and some good results, including Luis Fernando Calero's excellent overview (item **619**) and Carlos Castaño Uribe's study of the Carib (item **624**). For the central Andes, we have Norman Meiklejohn's excellent evaluation of the Christianization of the Aymara (item **726**), Erick Langer's perceptive studies of 19th-century Bolivia (items **703, 704,** and **705**), Luis Miguel Glave Testino's work on rural Cusco over a long chronological period (items **676** and **677**), a similarly broad temporal coverage by Jorge Zevallos Quiñones for north coastal Lambayeque (item **834**), and Teodoro Hampe Martínez's focus on the early central valleys (items **684** and **685**). In the transitional zone, Xavier Izko has examined inter-ethnic conflict along the southeastern frontier of the Inca empire (items **698** and **699**). For Paraguay, Branislava Susnik has made a variety of important contributions (items **807, 808,** and **809**), while in Argentina, Meinrado Hux prepares biographical surveys of caciques (item **691, 692,** and **693**), Kristine L. Jones examines a discrete Mapuche example (item **700**), and Tom Dillehay studies societal relations (item **647**). Work continues in Chile on the uneasy frontier relationship and the role of missionaries, with serious contributions by Jorge Pinto Rodríguez (items **764** and **765**) and others.

Some important contributions have been made in the fields of ethno- and archaeoastronomy; they include the work of Edmundo Magaña on northern South America, and Mariusz Ziolkowski and Robert Sadowski on the Andean Highlands (items **814** and **835**). All regions of South America have seen significant ethnohistorical scrutiny, although the weakest coverage seems to run in a band from the Eastern Llanos of Venezuela into, and including, the Guyana Highlands, and the north bank of the Amazon as far as its mouth. Nádia Farage's important contribution on the Roraima district is an exception (item **657**).

590 Acre: história e etnologia. Organização de Marco Antonio Gonçalves. Rio de Janeiro: Núcleo de Etnologia Indígena, Laboratório de Pesquisa Social, DCS, IFCS, UFRJ, 1991. 343 p.: bibl., ill., maps.

Important ethnographic/historical work on little studied region (entities examined include Kampa, Apuriña, Kulina, Masko, Machineri, Jamamadi, Kaxinaua, Arara-Shauanaua, Poyanaua, Yaminaua, Katukina, Amawaka, Nukini). Excellent bibliography.

591 Adorno, Rolena. The genesis of Felipe Guamán Poma de Ayala's *Nueva corónica y buen gobierno.* (*Colon. Lat. Am. Rev.,* 2:1/2, 1993, p. 53–92, bibl., facsims.)

Author uses *Y no ay remedio . . .* (Lima: Centro de Investigación y Promoción Amazónica, 1991, edited by Elías Prado Tello and Alfredo Prado Tello), a recently published document held in family hands which sheds light on the Chupas area of Huamanga from 1550s-1650s, to place the native chronicler in local society and clarify his perspectives. Also illuminates concepts of *yanacona, mitmaq,* and *forastero.*

592 Adorno, Rolena. Retórica y resistencia pictóricas: el grabado y la polémica en los escritos sobre el Perú en los siglos XVI y XVII. (*in* Imágenes de la resistencia indígena y esclava. Edición de Roger Zapata. Lima: Editorial Wari, 1990, p. 33–77, bibl.)

Fascinating account of the earliest published texts of the conquest of Tawantinsuyu with pictorial images. Author points out the substantial impact of "picture" over word and the possible influence on Guamán Poma de Ayala.

593 Aguiló, Federico. Tipología religiosa andina: ensayo lingüístico y simbológico. La Paz: Editorial Los Amigos del Libro, 1988. 96 p.: bibl. (Col. Lingüística; NA 575)

Short, provocative analysis of "high" (Inca State) religious terminology and variations: Aymara, Puquina, and various Quechua dialects. Focuses especially on meaning of the "I" term (as found in Illapa, Inti, and so forth).

594 Albis, Manuel María. Curiosità della foresta d'Amazzonia e arte di curar senza medico: un quaderno di viaggio colombiano del 1854 conservato nella Biblioteca Nazionale Universitaria di Torino. Edizione, traduzione e note di Alberto Guaraldo; con saggi e testi di commento di Silvia Benso *et al.* Torino, Italy: Segnalibro, 1991. 248 p.: bibl., ill. (some col.) (Popoli e culture delle Americhe; 3)

Publication of document found in the National Library, University of Turin, under the title, *Curiosidades de la montaña i medico den casa por el presbiterio Manuel Maria Albis año de 1854.* Editors include the Spanish original, an Italian translation, and articles by specialists. Work describes the Caquetá district of the Colombian Amazon, and useful medicines.

595 Aldazabal, Verónica Beatriz. La identificación de los Mocetene a través de las fuentes. (*Amazonía Peru.*, 8:16, 1988, p. 69–77, bibl., map)

Author identifies Beni region ethnic entity following 17th century.

596 Alonso Sagaseta, Alicia. Las momias de los Incas: su función y realidad social. (*Rev. Esp. Antropol. Am.*, 19, 1989, p. 109–135, bibl., ills., map, table)

Finds the word *bulto* employed by the chroniclers of Peru could mean three things: looks at the meaning as "mummy" of the Inca, along with the duties of the royal *panaca,* or lineage (except the heir, who will establish a new line). Examines the role of those involved in the care of *wakas,* including the ceremonies and rituals associated with their cult, both daily as well as the more important annual festivals. Also evaluates role of *wakas* of the Incas as mediators, and the socioeconomic function of the *panacas.* Useful overview that calls for more profound analysis of the Inca ancestor cults.

597 Amodio, Emanuel. Invasión y defensa de los resguardos indígenas en el oriente de Venezuela, 1770–1850. (*Montalbán/ Caracas,* 23, 1991, p. 267–308, bibl.)

Examines land rights of Kari'ñas (Caribs) from late 18th to mid-19th century. In the 18th century ownership of large land units became concentrated. Independence accelerated

the tendency, but natives frequently resorted to violent resistance to restrict the process.

598 Anders, Martha B. Historia y etnografía: los *mitmaq* de Huánuco en las visitas de 1549, 1557 y 1562. Lima: Instituto de Estudios Peruanos, 1990. 98 p.: bibl., ill. (Col. mínima; 20)

Author presents another view of precontact Andean society based on the last years of Inca administration. Tragically, both Anders and archaeologist Margarita Pérez Zegarra perished in an Aug. 1990 accident on the Panamerican highway between Lima and Chincha Baja.

599 Los Andes en la encrucijada: indios, comunidades y estado en el siglo XIX. Recopilación de Heraclio Bonilla. Quito: Ediciones Libri Mundi Enrique Grosse-Luemern; FLACSO-Sede Ecuador, 1991. 495 p.: ill., maps. (Ensayo)

Series of important articles by specialists. Pt. 1 centers on internal structure of communities and pt. 2 on their relation to the State. Includes contributions by H. Bonilla. E. Tandeter, X. Izko, E.D. Langer, A. Diez Hurtado, C. Contreras, L.M. Glave, G. Rodriguez Ostria, M. Moscoso, S. Palomeque, G.R. Valarezo, and F.E. Mallon.

600 Antigüedades del Perú. Edición de Henrique Urbano y Ana Sánchez. Madrid: Historia 16, 1992. 271 p.: bibl., ill. (Crónicas de América; 70)

Editors have provided a readily-available and solidly edited version of two chronicles: the *Relación anonima* and Juan de Santa Cruz Pachacuti Yanqui Salcamaygua's *Relación de antiguedades.* . . .

601 Araya, José M. and **Eduardo A. Ferrer.** El comercio indígena: los caminos al Chapaleofú. Tandil, Argentina: Univ. Nacional del Centro de la Provincia de Buenos Aires: Municipalidad de Tandil, 1988. 75 p.: bibl., ill.

Author stresses evolution of trade links between Mapuche and Spanish cattlemen and merchants in late-18th and early-19th century. The focal point was the trade fair of Chapaleofú.

602 Areces, Nidia R.; Cristina I. De Bernardi; and Griselda B. Tarrago. Blancos e indios en el corredor fluvial paranaense. (*Anuario/Rosario,* segunda época, 1989/90, p. 341–363)

Applies model of social articulation proposed by Leopoldo Bartolomé to 16th century Spanish-Indian relations of mid-Paraná.

603 Arellano, Carmen and Albert Meyers. Testamento de Pedro Milachami, un curaca cañari en la región de los Wanka, Perú, 1662. (*Rev. Esp. Antropol. Am.*, 18, 1988, p. 95–127, bibl., map)

This last will (from Zevallos notarial records in Huancayo), plus commentary by the authors, allows for comprehensive view of a wealthy central Andean curaca in mid-17th century. Noteworthy is the fact that a Cañar chieftain had become head administrator of Lurinhuanca.

604 Arnaud, Expedido. A legislação sobre os índios do Grão Pará e Maranhão nos séculos XVII e XVIII. (*Bol. Pesqui. CEDEAM*, 4:6, jan./junho 1985, p. 34–72, bibl.)

Synopsis of laws dealing with native Americans in one sector of Brazil.

Barragán Romano, Rossana. Espacio urbano y dinámica étnica: La Paz en el siglo XIX. See *HLAS 53:2886.*

605 Barrios Pintos, Aníbal. Los aborígenes del Uruguay: del hombre primitivo a los últimos charrúas. Montevideo: Librería Linardi y Risso, 1991. 191 p.: bibl., ill., maps.

One of the few competent works on the subject.

606 Barros, Edir Pina de. Política indigenista, política indígena e suas relações com a política expansionista no II império em Mato Grosso. (*Rev. Antropol./São Paulo*, 30/31/32, 1987/88/89, p. 183–223, bibl., tables)

Useful introduction to Brazilian-Indian contacts in Mato Grosso during mid-19th century.

607 Bauer, Brian S. The development of the Inca state. Foreword by Gary Urton. Austin: Univ. of Texas Press, 1992. 185 p.: bibl., ill.

Author rejects traditional view of evolution of Inca state based on a literal reading of colonial chroniclers. He attempts to establish an archaeologically-based chronological sequence based on investigations in the Paruro district of Cusco. Finds "Inca" influences to be regional, earlier, and more pervasive than previously believed, and questions utility of "history" of conquests of Pachacuti Inca Yupanqui in explaining rise of State.

608 Beltrán Peña, Francisco and Lucila Mejía Salazar. La utopía mueve montañas: Alvaro Ulcué Chocué. Bogotá: Editorial Nueva América, 1989. 284 p.: bibl., ill. (Antropología; 5)

Authors examine life and thought of Paez "prophet," Alvaro Ulcué Chocué (1943–84), and provide some ethnohistorical background, but work is mostly sociological.

Bengoa C., José. Quinquén: cien años de historia pehuenche. See *HLAS 53:5387.*

609 Beozzo, José O. et al. Política indigenista de la Iglesia en la colonia. Recopilación de Juan Bottasso. Quito: Ediciones Abya-Yala; Roma, Italia: Movimientos Laicos para América Latina, 1991. 339 p.: bibl., ill. (Col. 500 años; 38)

Geographically broad coverage of Church-Indian relations includes the following relevant chapters: Francesca Cantú, "Descubrimiento del Nuevo Mundo y Visión Utópica en el Siglo XVI;" Luis Fernando Botero V., "La Iglesia y el Indio en la Colonia: una Lectura a los Sínodos Quitenses de 1570, 1594 y 1596;" and Domingo Llanque Chana, "Criterios y Métodos Misionales en los Siglos XVI-XVII en la Evangelización del Perú."

610 Bermúdez Páez, Alvaro E. Etnohistoria de Subachoque: siglos XVI-XVII. (*Rev. Colomb. Antropol.*, 29, 1992, p. 81–117, appendix, bibl., map, tables)

Author examines Muiscas of Subachoque Valley, and includes list of important documents in the National Archive in Bogotá.

611 Bonavia, Duccio. Perú, hombre e historia. v. 1, De los orígenes al siglo XV. Lima: EDUBANCO, 1991. 1 v.: bibl., ill. (some col.), maps.

Fine synthesis of Peru's history prior to Inca expansion.

612 Bonnett Vélez, Diana. La Sección Indígenas del Archivo Histórico de Quito, siglos XVI-XVIII: documento. Quito: FLACSO; Abya-Yala, 1992. 100 p. (Guías de investigación)

Valuable catalog (organized topically) for ethnohistorical researchers.

613 Bouroncle Carreón, Alfonso. Contribución al estudio de las aymaras y otros ensayos. Lima: Ed. Literatura y Arte, 1990. 139 p.: bibl.

Anthology of marginal importance brings together published and unpublished work of Arequipeña physician and writer.

614 Bouysse-Cassagne, Thérèse *et al.* Tres reflexiones sobre el pensamiento andino. La Paz: Hisbol, 1987. 231 p.: bibl., ill. (some col.) (Biblioteca andina; 1)

Compilation of three important and useful articles includes: "Pacha: en Torno al Pensamiento Aymara" by T. Bouysse-Cassagne and O. Harris; "Entre Ch'axwa y Muxsa: para una Historia del Pensamiento Político Aymara" by T. Platt; and "Aproximaciones a una Estética Andina: de la Belleza al Tinku" by V. Cereceda.

615 Bravo Guerreira, María Concepción. Estrategia indígena en las campañas de la conquista del Perú. (*in* Jornadas de Historiadores Americanistas, 2nd, Granada, Spain, 1988. América: encuentro y asimilación. Edición de Joaquín A. Muñoz Mendoza. Granada: Diputación Provincial de Granada, 1989, p. 73–86)

Argues rightly that ease of Spanish conquest of Tawantinsuyu came with native complicity, fratricidal strife among the many sons of the last Incas, and a willingness to ally with outsiders to gain the throne. Traditional ethnic animosity was also a factor.

616 Bray, Warwick. Emblems of power in the chiefdoms of the New World. (*in* Circa 1492: art in the age of exploration. Edited by Jay A. Levenson. Washington: National Gallery of Art; New Haven: Yale Univ. Press, 1991, p. 535–539, photos, maps)

Brief account of relationship of gold artifacts and myth among contact period Sinú, Muisca, Tairona, and greater Chiriqui.

617 Brown, Michael Fobes. Beyond resistance: a comparative study of utopian renewal in Amazonia. (*Ethnohistory/Society,* 38:4, Fall 1991, p. 388–413, bibl.)

Important examination of five case studies of milenarianism points out that movements may have preceeded and been independent of European influence.

Brüning, Hans Heinrich. Fotodokumente aus Nordperu von Hans Heinrich Brüning, 1848–1928 = Documentos fotográficos del norte del Perú de Juan Enrique Brüning, 1848–1928. See item **2703.**

Caillavet, Chantal. Les chefferies préhispaniques du nord de l'Equateur: formes d'habitat et organisation territoriale. See *HLAS 53: 764.*

618 Caillavet, Chantal. Producción textil indígena y la integración en el mercado colonial: la etnia otavalo—Ecuador—en el siglo XVI. (*in* International Congress of Americanists, *45th, Bogotá, 1985.* Etnohistoria e historia de las Américas. Bogotá: Ediciones Uniandes, 1988, p. 213–218, bibl.)

Author evaluates importance of production, manufacturing, and distribution of cotton "mantas."

619 Calero, Luis Fernando. Pastos, quillacingas y abades, 1535–1700. Bogotá: Banco Popular, 1991. 220 p. (Biblioteca Banco Popular: Col. Textos universitarios)

Thorough ethnohistorical reconstruction based on extensive archival investigation. Author concentrates on economic and social concerns, and carefully uses extant *visitas.*

620 Cañedo-Argüelles Fabrega, Teresa. Población indígena en el Alto Paraná: variantes de un proceso de adaptación; siglos XVI y XVII. (*in* Jornadas de Historiadores Americanistas, *1st, Santafé, Spain, 1987.* América: hombre y sociedad. Presentación de Joaquín A. Muñoz Mendoza. Granada, Spain: Diputación Provincial de Granada, 1988, p. 127–137, maps)

Excellent study of uneasy interethnic relations between the Guaraní and Spanish populations of Corrientes, Argentina.

621 Carril, Bonifacio del. Los indios en la Argentina, 1536–1845. Buenos Aires: Emecé Editores, 1992. 156 p.: bibl., ill.

Illustrations, drawings, paintings, and photographs depict native peoples of Argentina. Volume begins with works by Ulrich Schmidel, Francis Drake, and Hendrik Ottsen (ca. 1536–99), continues with 18th-century images of Jesuit missions by Florián Paucke and Martin Dobrizhoffer, and finishes with the first photographic depictions. Useful for both ethnohistorians and anthropologists.

622 Casamiquela, Rodolfo M. *et al.* Del mito a la realidad: evolución iconográfica del pueblo tehuelche meridional. Viedma, Argentina: Fundación Ameghino, 1991. 290 p.: bibl., ill., index.

Critical text profusely-illustrated with drawings, paintings, and photographs depicting the Tehuelche.

623 Casanova Guarda, Holdenis. Misión y etnocentrismo en la Araucania, siglo XVIII. (*Actas Colomb.*, 2:5, 1992, p. 47–55)
Author examines differences between Jesuit-Franciscan conversion methods along the Chilean frontier.

624 Castaño Uribe, Carlos. Configuración cultural de los Karib en Colombia: algunos comentarios e hipótesis. (*Rev. Esp. Antropol. Am.*, 14, 1984, p. 205–226, bibl., ill., map)
Good overview of Karib evolution in Colombia. Author argues that the group originated between the Alto Zingú and Tapajoz (Brazil). Slowly and sporadically they ascended the Magdalena, settling on crests above tributaries and building oval residences (*malocas*). Early Karib society was largely egalitarian, with war leader and shaman assuming leading roles during crises.

625 Chaim, Marivone M. Política indigenista em Goiás no século XVIII. (*Rev. Antropol./São Paulo*, 30/31/32, 1987/88/89, p. 175–181, table)
Brief overview of Pombaline Indian settlements in Goiás.

626 Chaumeil, Jean-Pierre. De Loreto à Tabatinga: d'une frontière l'autre; antagonisme sur l'Amazone au XIXe siècle et après. (*Homme/Paris*, 122/124, avril/déc. 1992, p. 355–375, bibl., photos, maps, tables)
Foreign travelers in the 19th century viewed the Brazilian settlement Tabatinga as "civilized" but characterized the Peruvian settlement as backward, despite their relative similarity. Author attempts to fathom reasons for such divergent characterizations.

627 Chevalier, François. Servidumbre de la tierra y rasgos señoriales en el Alto Perú hispánico: apuntes comparativos sobre los yanaconas. (*Histórica/Lima*, 13:2, dic. 1989, p. 153–170, bibl.)
Brief discussion of legal evolution of Yanacona.

Cipolletti, María Susana. Un manuscrito tucano del siglo XVIII: ejemplos de continuidad y cambio en una cultura amazónica. See item **2326.**

628 Classen, Constance. Literacy as anti-culture: the Andean experience of the written word. (*Hist. Relig.*, 30:4, May 1991, p. 404–421)
Andeans have been marginalized because theirs is a world of speech, not writing; yet to write will destroy Andean culture.

629 Cobo, Bernabé. Inca religion and customs. Translated and edited by Roland Hamilton. Foreword by John Howland Rowe. Austin: Univ. of Texas Press, 1990. 279 p.: bibl., index, maps.
English translation (based on manuscript originals in Seville) of the important last part of the Jesuit historian's examination of Andean religion and society. Useful for the classroom.

630 Coloma Porcari, César. Don Francisco Chuquihuanca Ayulo: ¿el último Inca? (*Bol. Lima*, 11:66, nov. 1989, p. 5–13)
Documents in hands of Chuquihuanca (1905) dating from 16th and 18th centuries suggest his family descended from Huayna Capac. Includes transcriptions.

631 Combès, Isabelle. El "testamento" chiriguano: una política desconocida del post-1892. (*Bull. Inst. fr. étud. andin.*, 20:1, 1991, p. 237–251, bibl., maps)
The 1892 execution of the last Chiriguano "prophet" ended the group's stubborn bid for independence, though the group itself still persists.

632 Combès, Isabelle. Yaci: mythes et représentations tupi-guarani de la lune. (*Homme/Paris*, 31:120, oct./déc. 1991, p. 5–19, bibl.)
Based on 16th-century accounts, examines the importance of the moon in Tupi-Guarani belief, especially the link between the lunar calendar and rituals of cannibalism.

633 Conlazo, Daniel. Los indios de Buenos Aires, siglos XVI y XVII. Buenos Aires: Búsqueda-Yuchán, 1990. 127 p.: bibl., ill. (Col. Desde Sudamérica)
Brief, competent introduction to the indigenous groups of Argentina stresses the period before the 1680s.

634 Los conquistados: 1492 y la población indígena de las Américas. Recopilación de Heraclio Bonilla. Bogotá: Tercer Mundo Editores; Ecuador: FLACSO, 1992. 450 p.: bibl., tables.
Volume contains several significant ethnohistorical contributions: Bonilla's "1492 y la Población Indígena de los Andes" overviews population trends and social and economic consequences of colonialism; Roberto Choque's "Los Aymaras y la Cuestión Colo-

nial" focuses particularly on the role of resistance to outside domination; Enrique Urbano's "Sincretismo y Sentimiento Religioso en los Andes" examines the impact of the Counterreformation on religious conformity in the Andes and the legacy of local devotions; R. Tom Zuidema's "El Encuentro de los Calendarios Andino y Español" studies the Inca division of the year into the dry and wet seasons; Manuel Burga's "El Corpus Christi y la Nobleza Inca Colonial: Memoria e Identitad" focuses on the Cusco celebrations.

635 Coronel Feijoo, Rosario. El valle sangriento de los indígenas de la coca y el algodón a la hacienda cañera jesuita: 1580–1700. Quito: Facutad Latinoamericana de Ciencias Sociales, Sede Ecuador: ABYA-YALA, 1991. 172 p.: bibl., ill., maps. (Col. Tesis: Historia; 4)

Valuable examination of causes and impact of the shift from Amerindian cultivation of Chota valley products to Jesuit sugar plantations with African slave labor.

636 Costales, Piedad Peñaherrera de and **Alfred Costales Samaniego.** Los llactaios. Quito: Ediciones Abya-Yala: Centro de Investigaciones para la Educación Popular, 1987? 253 p.: bibl.

Authors overview native resistance and rebellion in colonial Quito.

637 Crivelli Montero, Eduardo A. Malones: ¿saqueo o estrategia?; el objetivo de las invasiones de 1780 y 1783 a la frontera de Buenos Aires. (*Todo es Hist.*, 283, enero 1991, p. 6–32, bibl., facsims.)

Well-documented study argues that Indian attacks on Buenos Aires were intended to force authorities into recognizing their sovereignty and way of life; they were not carried out solely for pillage and revenge.

638 Cultures et sociétés, Andes et Méso-Amérique: mélanges en hommage à Pierre Duviols. v. 1–2. Études recueillies par Raquel Thiercelin. Aix-en-Provence: Univ. de Provence, Service des publications, 1991. 2 v. (834 p.): bibl., ill.

As with most festschrifts, these volumes include articles of true worth, as well as some which are less substantial. Volumes cover the entire Americas from contact to the present century. Those on the Andean world worthy of special consideration are: Michel Adnès, "Là et Maintenant, Domingo de Santo Tomás"; Rolena Adorno, "La Visión del Visitador y el Indio Ladino;" Xavier Albó, "El Thakhi o 'Camino' en Jesús de Machaqa;" Annabelle Arnoux, "De Quelques Représentationes Plastiques de Viracocha;" Josep M. Barnadas, "Miquel Serra i Coll (?1586): un Canonge Lascasista Catalanà a América?;" Francois Bourricaud, "Yawar Fiesta: Violence et Autodestruction;" Chantal Caillavet, "Samson dans les Andes ou du Bon Usage de la Chevelure: Représentations Autochtones et Coloniales;" Teresa Gisbert, "La Cuatripartición Andina y la Relación Pachacamac-Viracocha;" Eduardo Guillén Guillén, "Dos Notas Históricas y un Documento Inédito;" Teodoro Hampe Martínez, "Control Moral y Represión Ideológica: la Inquisición en el Perú, 1570–1820;" John V. Murra, "Le Débat sur l'Avenir des Andes en 1562;" Franklin Pease G.Y., "Nota sobre la Noticia del Perú;" Deborah A. Poole, "Time and Devotion in Andean Ritual Dance;" Thierry Saignes, "Idolatir sans Extirpateur: Chamanisme et Religion dans les Andes Orientales; Pelechuco, 1747;" Henrique Urbano, "Pachamama o la Madre Devoradora: el Sacrificio de Kilku Warak'a alias Alencastre;" Gary Urton, "The Stranger in Andean Communities;" and Tom R. Zuidema, "Batallas Rituales en el Cuzco Colonial."

639 D'Altroy, Terence N. and **Ronald L. Bishop.** The provincial organization of Inka ceramic production. (*Am. Antiq.*, 55:1, Jan. 1990, p. 120–138, bibl., ill.)

Authors use archaeological evidence to argue that Inka ceramic production was largely local, with little long-distance transport.

640 D'Altroy, Terence N. Provincial power in the Inka empire. Washington: Smithsonian Institution Press, 1992. 272 p.: bibl., ill., index.

This massive effort sets a new standard. Examines archaeological and postcontact documentary evidence on Xauxa and Wanka peoples of upper Mantaro Valley to elucidate Inca expansion into region. Uses hegemonic-territorial model in comprehensive analysis of control at provincial level.

641 Dantas, Beatriz Góis. História de grupos indígenas e fontes escritas: o caso de Sergipe. (*Rev. Antropol./São Paulo*, 30/31/32, 1987/88/89, p. 469–479, bibl.)

Author examines attempts to recreate past through state documents. This article evaluates an 1850 land law, questioning the impact of miscegenation and loss of community lands in an attempt to explain why Indians of Sergipe seemed to disappear after 1850s.

642 Dearborn, D.S.P. and R.E. White. Quartering the year in Tawantinsuyu. (*in* International Congress of Americanists, *45th, Bogotá, 1985.* Rituales y fiestas de las Américas. Bogotá: Ediciones Uniandes, 1988, p. 60–64)

Studies of Pisac and Machu Picchu remains indicate that Incas knew astronomy and could tell the solstices. However, evidence suggests that they could only tell the equinox by count, not by observation.

643 Dejo, Juan. Guamán Poma Ayala y la lógica andina de la conciliación. (*Apuntes/Lima*, 26, primer semestre 1990, p. 77–92, bibl.)

Evaluates conciliation and understanding as one aspect of Guamán Poma's work, indicating that certain elements were part of Andean practice.

644 Delgado Díaz del Olmo, César. El diálogo de los mundos: ensayo sobre el Inca Garcilaso. Arequipa, Perú: UNSA, 1991. 499 p.: bibl.

Fascinating and fresh attempt to enter the mind of the mestizo author. Very impressive effort, especially in light of the difficulties of access to new sources.

645 Diener Ojeda, Pablo *et al.* Rugendas, América de punta a cabo: Rugendas y la Araucanía. Santiago: Editorial Aleda, 1992. 183 p.: bibl., ill.

Series of reflections on the work of a 19th-century artist who depicted the Araucanians. Potential ethnohistorical value.

646 Diez Hurtado, Alejandro. Las comunidades indígenas en el Bajo Piura, Catacaos y Sechura en el siglo XIX. (*in* Los Andes en la encrucijada: indios, comunidades y Estado en el siglo XIX. Quito: Ediciones Libri Mundi, 1991, p. 169–198, bibl., graph, map, tables)

Focus on productive activities, land and water, political and social status, and role of cofradías.

647 Dillehay, Tom D. Keeping outsiders out: public ceremony, resource rights, and hierarchy in historic and contemporary Mapuche society. (*in* Wealth and hierarchy in

the intermediate area. Edited by Frederick W. Lange. Washington: Dumbarton Oaks Research Library and Collection, 1992, p. 379–422, bibl., maps, photos, tables)

Dillehay uses ethnohistorical sources to examine kinship, societal ranking, shamanism, and resource rights in central Chile, emphasizing wealth, elites and hierarchies over time. Land is the principal wealth, women are the main exchange commodity, and "prestige goods the binding contractual elements" (p. 385). This "must read" is an excellent overview of the present state of knowledge of Mapuche society.

648 Dillehay, Tom D. El rol del conocimiento ancestral y las ceremonias en la continuidad y persistencia de la cultura mapuche. (*in* Congreso Internacional de Americanistas,*45th, Bogotá, 1985.* Rituales y fiestas de las Américas. Bogotá: Ediciones Uniandes, 1988, p. 27–38, maps)

Author attributes the Mapuche's cultural persistence to ceremonial tradition and a close relation to (and knowledge of) their ancestors.

649 Documentos inéditos sobre la historia de Caldas, Chocó y Risaralda. Transcripción y recopilación de Víctor Zuluaga Gómez. Pereira, Colombia: Univ. Tecnológica de Pereira, 1988. 155 p.

Author transcribes a series of 17th to early 20th-century materials relating to ethnic groups and focuses on their treatment by Europeans.

650 Documentos sobre a Amazônia: início do séc. XIX. Edición de Arthur Cézar Ferreira Reis. (*Rev. Inst. Estud. Bras.*, 362, jan./março 1989, p. 132–151)

Series of early 19th-century documents are of some marginal ethnographic value.

651 Durand, José. Garcilaso Inca jura decir verdad. (*Histórica/Lima*, 14:1, julio 1990, p. 1–25, bibl.)

Author rejects a solely literary reading of Garcilaso, emphasizing rather his strengths in historical presentation.

652 Ellefsen, Bernardo. Matrimonio y sexo en el incario. Cochabamba, Bolivia: Editorial Los Amigos del Libro, 1989. 430 p.: bibl., ill. (Enciclopedia boliviana)

Author uses chroniclers and early colonial dictionaries and grammers to systematically examine marriage, especially of Inca elite.

653 Espinoza Soriano, Waldemar. Etnohistoria ecuatoriana: estudios y documentos. Quito: Ediciones ABYA-YALA, 1988. 396 p.: bibl., ill.

Compilation of an important series of previously published but largely inaccesible articles on Ecuadorian themes.

654 Estévez, Juan José. Pincén: vida y leyenda. La Plata, Argentina: Tall. Gráf. del Estado y Boletín Oficial de la Provincia de Buenos Aires, 1991? 268 p.: bibl., ill.

The "popular" format of this publication, with its drawings and poetry, is deceiving. It is, nonetheless, a biographical study of one of the most important late 19th-century Pampas Puelche native leaders, based on solid archival research and oral history.

655 Estrella, Eduardo. El pan de América: etnohistoria de los alimentos aborígenes en el Ecuador. 2a ed. Quito: Ediciones ABYA-YALA, 1988. 390 p.: bibl., ill.

Important contribution on indigenous nutrition and food sources contains good historical data and includes medicinal uses of plants.

656 Etnohistoria del Amazonas. Coordinación de Peter Jorna, Leonor Malaver, y Menno Oostra. Quito: Ediciones ABYA-YALA; Roma: MLAL, Movimiento Laicos para América Latina, 1991. 288 p.: bibl., maps. (Col. 500 años; 36)

Editors note that most recent works are based on cultural ecology and structuralist models, leading to a certain methodological impasse. The articles in this volume include: J.H. Parra on lower Putumayo tribes of Siona, Kofán, Ingano and Huitoto; M. Oostra on the white in oral tradition (Miriti-Paraná); M. Schafer on interchange between Ashéninga and Asháninca in central Peruvian jungle; E. Frank on concept of "ethnicity" in anthropological studies; M.S. Cipolletti on ethnographic information in 1779–91 *Comisión de Límites al Amazonas*; P. Faulhaber on myth among Tefé; O. Sampaio Silva on "border" Amazonian natives between Brazil and neighbors; N. Díaz Martínez on Mbya (Guarani) migration; C.F. Matallana and J. Schackt on oral history of Jurumi (Miriti-Paraná River); A. Gómez on impact of rubber collection in Colombian Amazon, 1870–1930; P. Jorna on Cambeba del Solimes; L. Malaver on impact of Indian-white contacts in Amazonia; and N.L. Whitehead on long-term impact of contact on señores of Epuremei in Guayanas.

657 Farage, Nádia. As muralhas dos sertões: os povos indígenas no rio Branco e a colonização. São Paulo: Paz e Terra, 1991. 197 p.: bibl., ill., maps.

Fundamental work on the peoples of the Roraima district of Brazil's northern frontier with Guyana; focuses on the 18th century.

658 Faria, Francisco C. Pessoa. Os astrônomos pré-históricos do Ingá. São Paulo: Instituição Brasileira de Difusão Cultural, 1987. 114 p.: bibl., ill. (Biblioteca História, explorações e descobertas; 34)

Author speculates on a possible astronomical meaning for petroglyphs at Ingá in Paraiba state.

659 Fauria, Carme. Avance y límites del imperio inca en la costa norte. (*Bol. Am.*, 31:39/40, 1989/90, p. 27–51, bibl.)

Traces late Inca efforts at expansion into north Andean coast and suggests that one of their reasons was to gain access and control of *mullu* shells.

660 Fernández-Maquieira, B. Sara Mateos. Un modelo de conversión franciscana: las misiones del Pangoa, siglos XVII y XVIII. (*Amazonía Peru.*, 20, dic. 1991, p. 35–48)

Halting Franciscan efforts between Ene and Perené began in 1673, with myths of abundant peoples and mineral wealth, perhaps even fostered by friars. Control was directed from Ocopa until Juan Santos Atahualpa uprising.

661 Fernández Villegas, Oswaldo. Las capullanas: mujeres curacas de Piura siglos XVI-XVII. (*Bol. Lima*, 11:66, nov. 1989, p. 43–50, bibl., maps, tables)

Reviews role of women chiefs in transitional north coastal Peru and notices that the practice extended to interior Ayabaca.

662 Fernández Villegas, Oswaldo. Un curaca de la sierra central del Perú: siglo XVII. (*Bol. Lima*, 13:78, nov. 1991, p. 49–55, appendix, bibl., graph)

Author uses 1811 copies of 17th-century documents found in district archive of Piura to trace claims of Chupaca chiefs (Mantaro Valley) to Inca Huayna Cápac, indicating the importance of Indian elite's efforts to secure recognition.

663 Fernández Villegas, Oswaldo. Curacazgos de la costa norte: Piura. (*Bol. Lima,* 10:60, nov. 1988, p. 45–47, map, tables)
Based on series of important documents in Archivo Departmental de Piura, author constructs tentative list of chiefs of Catacaos, Sechura, and Piura from precontact to early 19th century. Noteworthy are a number of female chiefs, known as *capullanas.*

664 Fernández Villegas, Oswaldo. La huaca Narihualá: un documento para la etnohistoria de la costa norte del Perú. (*Bull. Inst. fr. étud. andin.,* 19:1, 1990, p. 103–127, ill., map)
Mid-17th century case of grave robbing in Piura permits analysis not only of site (contemporary excavation included), but also activities of "huaqueros."

665 Fernández Villegas, Oswaldo. Unión étnica en el curacazgo de Narihuala, costa norte del Perú, siglo XVIII. (*Bol. Lima,* 19:81, mayo 1992, p. 43–48, bibl., photos)
Record of legal conflict over rights in the 18th century allows for reconstruction of relations between ethnic lords; here lineages were linked to retain control.

666 Fleischmann, Ulrich; Mathias Rohrig Assunção; and Zinka Ziebell-Wendt. Os Tupinamba: realidade e ficção nos relatos quinhentistas. (*Rev. Bras. Hist.,* 11:21, set. 1990/fev. 1991, p. 125–145)
Author reevaluates cannibalism of Tupinamba based on the historical accounts of Hans Staden, André Thevet, Jean de Léry and Gabriel Soares de Sousa. Argues caution in analysis of 16th-century notices because there was frequent borrowing.

667 Flores Espinoza, Javier F. Hechicería e idolatría en Lima colonial, siglo XVII. (*in* Coloquio Internacional del Grupo de Trabajo Historia y Antropología Andinas, *2nd, Quito, 1990.* Poder y violencia en los Andes. Edición de Henrique Urbano y Mirko Lauer. Cusco, Peru: Centro de Estudios Regionales Andinos Bartolomé de Las Casas, 1991, p. 53–74, bibl.)
Excellent study of Indians in Lima and the impact of the Inquisition.

668 Forgues, Roland. Nueva visión hispánica de los mitos americanos: el caso viracocha. (*Edad Oro,* 10, primavera 1991, p. 105–116, bibl.)

Idea of creator deity evolved in 16th-17th century Andes as consequence of political and missionary ends. This native American fall into idolatry justified Spanish conquest.

669 Fossa Falco, Lydia. Leyendo hoy a Cieza de León: de la Capacocha a la Capac Hucha. (*Bol. Lima,* 13:73, enero 1991, p. 33–41, bibl., tables)
Points out implicit ethnocentrism of chronicler in text of chapter 29 of the *Señorío de los Incas.*

670 Fossa Falco, Lydia. "Pucara:" una clave lingüística para leer a Cieza de León. (*Bol. Lima,* 11:64, julio 1989, p. 45–54, appendix, bibl., tables)
Author examines chronicler's use of the word *pucara,* which Cieza equates with "castile," or "fortress." In the author's view, this use represents Cieza's late medieval Spanish mind-set that prohibited him from truly understanding the nature of the Andean world.

671 Fuentes, Aldo. Historia y etnicidad en la Amazonía Peruana: el caso de los Chayahuita. (*Amazonía Peru.,* 9:17, 1989, p. 61–77, bibl.)
Examination of continuity and change in interethnic relations in a provincial village of Alto Amazonas (Loreto Depto.) from 17th century, when village was Christianized by Jesuits.

Gallois, Dominique Tilkin. Migração, guerra e comércio: os waiãpi na Guiana. See *HLAS 53:1092.*

672 García Jordán, Pilar. Problemática de la incorporación de las selvas amazónicas a los estados nacionales latinoamericanos, siglos XIX-XX: algunas reflexiones sobre el caso peruano. (*Bol. Am.,* 32:41, 1991, p. 261–271)
Author surveys changing relations between Church and State in early national Peru in the context of Amazonian expansion. The State was interested in establishing control in the Amazon and was willing to expend its own meager resources, though private investment also proved critical.

673 Garraín Villa, José Luis. Algunos apuntes sobre el testamento de Pedro Cieza de León. (*in* Coloquios Históricos de Extremadura, *18th, Trujillo, Spain, 1989.* Cáceres,

Spain: Institución Cultural El Brocense, 1991, p. 91–103)

Reviews aspects of Cieza's will and its relation to the town of Llerena.

674 Ginóbili de Tumminello, María Elena. Aportes científicos de los salesianos: observaciones etnológicas y etnográficas de la obra inédita del P. Lino Carbajal. Bahía Blanca, Argentina: Archivo Histórico Salesiano de la Patagonia Norte; Viedma, Argentina: Fundación Ameghino, 1990. 71 p.: bibl., map. (Documentario patagónico; 2)

Good introduction to native peoples of the Argentine pampas.

675 Glave, Luis Miguel. Un curacazgo andino y la sociedad campesina del siglo XVII: la historia de Bartolomé Tupa Hallicalla, curaca de Asillo. (*Allpanchis/Cusco,* 21:33, 1989, p. 11–39, bibl.)

Various documents permit Glave to reconstruct aspects of leader's career. Good example of type of effort needed to deepen our understanding of the curaca group.

676 Glave, Luis Miguel. Trajinantes: caminos indígenas en la sociedad colonial, siglos XVI/XVII. Lima: Instituto de Apoyo Agrario, 1989. 461 p.: bibl., ill. (Serie Tiempo de historia; 6)

One of most useful works on Andean commerce and exchange among native peoples in early colonial era. Author examines roads, storage facilities, coca exchange, the 17th-century "crisis," as well as women in the economy.

677 Glave, Luis Miguel. Vida—símbolos y batallas: creación y recreación de la comunidad indígena; Cusco, siglos XVI-XX. México: Fondo de Cultura Económica, 1992. 315 p.: bibl., ill., maps. (Sección de obras de historia)

Mature and balanced ethnohistorical analysis of the Canas district of southern Peru. Author uses excellent archival sources, in particular censuses, to weave the origin of communities, pointing out reasons for the endurance of indigenous peoples in Cusco region.

Gomes, Mércio Pereira. Os índios e o Brasil: ensaio sobre um holocausto e sobre uma nova possibilidade de convivência. See *HLAS 53: 1093.*

678 Gonzales, Juan. Visita de los yndios churumatas e yndios charcas de Totora que todos están en cabeza de Su Magestad, 1560. Transcripción e introducción de Raimund Schramm. La Paz: MUSEF, 1990. 63 p.: bibl. (Serie Fuentes primarias)

Published *visita* gives early ethnohistorical information on Cochabamba district.

679 Guallart Martínez, José María. Entre pongo y cordillera: historia de la etnia aguaruna-huambisa. Lima: Centro Amazónico de Antropología y Aplicación Práctica, 1990. 258 p.: bibl., ill.

Written from view of native peoples residing in northeastern Peru. Although personal interviews were conducted and some isolated local archives were consulted, this work is of little use for the professional.

680 Guarda, Gabriel. Los cautivos en la guerra de Arauco. (*Bol. Acad. Chil. Hist.,* 54:98, 1987, p. 93–157, bibl.)

Extensive overview of Spanish captives taken during the long conflict on the Chilean colonial frontier. Author examines 331 colonial cases, looking at variables such as sex, occupation, those who were ransomed, miscegenation, and Spaniards who voluntarily joined the natives. Very important are the brief biographical sketches of those taken captive and released by 1833.

681 Guibovich del Carpio, Lorgio A. Macate a través de la historia. Lima: Editorial y Publicaciones Guibodelcar; Ediciones y Distribuciones Palma, 1988. 264 p.: bibl., ill., map.

Based on work in municipality of Macate, Huaylas, as well as in major depositories in Lima, author recreates town's past, from preincaic period to mid-20th century.

682 Guibovich Pérez, Pedro. Cristóbal de Albornoz y el *Taki Onqoy.* (*Histórica/ Lima,* 15:2, dic. 1991, p. 205–236, bibl.)

New information on career of extirpator of idolatries.

683 Guibovich Pérez, Pedro. Los libros del curaca de Tacna. (*Histórica/Lima,* 14: 1, julio 1990, p. 69–84, bibl.)

Santiago Ara (d. 1793), a curaca who studied law at Univ. de Chuquisaca, was active in Audiencia of Charcas. His library consisted of 100 volumes.

684 Hampe Martínez, Teodoro. Notas sobre la encomienda real de Chincha en el siglo XVI. (*Fénix/Lima,* 32/33, 1987, p. 80–95, tables)

Carefully examines tribute and population data for an especially important coastal sector. Finds rapid decline toward 1625.

685   Hampe Martínez, Teodoro. Sobre tierras y riego en el Valle de la Magdalena a fines del siglo XVII. (*Histórica/Lima,* 14:1, julio 1990, p. 85–92, bibl.)
Document found in Archivo General de Indias in Seville sheds additional light on control and distribution of water in Lima district.

686   Heckenberger, Michael. A conquista da Amazônia. (*Ciênc. Hoje,* 15:86, nov./ dez. 1992, p. 62–67, bibl., ill., maps, table)
Brief overview argues that the Europeans who first descended the Amazon in the 16th century encountered densely settled regions under strong political leadership. These populations declined rapidly as a consequence of enslavement and disease. Author rejects low population densities for the Amazon postulated by Betty Meggers (1954).

687   Hernández, Max *et al.* Entre el mito y la historia: psicoanálisis y pasado andino. Lima: Ediciones Psicoanalíticas Imago, 1987. 199 p.: bibl., index.
Suggestive and stimulating cooperative effort by four Andean specialists who evaluate Inca myth and "history" on basis of "Western" psychological systems.

688   Hidalgo Lehuedé, Jorge and **Guillermo Focacci.** Multietnicidad en Arica, s. XVI: evidencias etnohistóricas y arqueológicas. (*Chungará/Arica,* 16/17, oct. 1986, p. 137–147, bibl., table)
Exploitation of Arica's valuable resources, especially marine, led to a very complex ethnic picture in region.

689   Hidalgo Lehuedé Jorge and **Patricia Arevalo F.** Atacama antes y después de la rebelión de 1781: siete documentos inéditos del Archivo General de la Nación Argentina. (*Chungará/Arica,* 18, agosto 1987, p. 91–100, bibl.)
Non-native reaction to Bourbon reforms set the stage for Indian insurrection that took place.

690   Hortegón, Diego *et al.* La gobernación de los quijos, 1559–1621. Introducción de Cristóbal Landázuri. Recopilación de MARKA, Instituto de Historia y Antropología Andina. Iquitos, Perú: IIAP; CETA, 1989. 464 p., 2 leaves of plates: bibl., ill., indexes. (Monumenta amazónica: A; 1)
Compilation of early documents

largely from Spanish archives focuses on conquest, settlement, and rebellion among the Quijos. Rich ethnohistorical source.

691   Hux, Meinrado. Caciques huilliches y salineros. Buenos Aires: Ediciones Marymar, 1991. 222 p.: bibl., ill. (Col. Patagonia)
Biographical studies of major chiefs of Río de la Plata. Useful reference.

692   Hux, Meinrado. Caciques pamparanqueles. Buenos Aires: Ediciones Marymar, 1991. 159 p.: ill., maps. (Col. Patagonia)
Biographical sketches of 18th- and 19th-century caciques of Ranqueles in central Argentine pampas.

693   Hux, Meinrado. Caciques pehuenches. Buenos Aires: Ediciones Marymar, 1991. 72 p.: bibl., ill., maps. (Col. Patagonia)
Continuation of author's efforts to provide basic bio-bibliography for Argentina.

694   Inca storage systems. Edited by Terry Y. LeVine. Norman: Univ. of Oklahoma Press, 1992. 385 p.: bibl., ill., indexes, maps.
Fundamental work on subject is exceptionally well-organized and brings together the following specialists: T.N. D'Altroy, T.K. Earle, J.E. Snead, C. Morris, J.R. Topic, C.E. Chiswell, C.A. Hastorf, and H.A. Lennstrom. Contributors examine various aspects of food storage, from architectural issues to the botanical, from Inca times to present. Far more comprehensive than the title suggests, the book is, as the editor points out, really "about financing an empire" (p. 3).

695   Los incas y el antiguo Perú: 3000 años de historia. v. 1–2. Madrid: Ayuntamiento de Madrid, Concejalía de Cultura: Centro Cultural de la Villa de Madrid: Quinto Centenario, 1991. 2 v.: bibl., ill. (some col.). (Col. Encuentros: Serie Catálogos)
Profusely illustrated volumes contain introductory surveys by specialists.

696   Inda C., Lorenzo. Historia de los urus: comunidad Irohito Yanapata. La Paz: HISBOL; Radio San Gabriel, 1988. 35 p.: ill. (Biblioteca de autores étnicos)
Contemporary oral history of an Uru, as written down by community member, refers to events as early as 1675. Facsimile edition of handwritten text with frequent drawings add value to this personal work.

697 Os indios d'Aldeia dos Anjos: Gravataí, século XVIII. Porto Alegre, Brasil: Escola Superior de Teologia e Espiritualidade Franciscana, 1990. 96 p.: indexes. (Col. Fontes; 5)

Transcription of documents includes lists and information on residents of former Tupi-Guaraní mission, which was concentrated by the Portuguese in Rio Grande do Sul under military governorships of José Marcelino de Figueiredo (1769–80) and Sebatião Xavier da Veiga Cabral (1780–1801).

698 Izko, Xavier. Los *ayllus* de Sakaka y Kirkyawi, Bolivia: dos fronteras étnicas en litigio, s. XVI-XX. (*Data/La Paz*, 1, 1991, p. 85–111, bibl.)

Important examination of evolution of interethnic conflict, between *ayllu*, local lords, and moiety, as part of dynamic of south Andean political development. Presents case study of a conflict between two *ayllus* based on inspections of 1593, 1646 (stemming from Crown "recognitions" of land titles), and 1895. For related work see item **699**.

699 Izko, Xavier. Fronteras étnicas en litigio: los ayllus de Sakaka y Kirkyawi, Bolivia, siglos XVI-XX. (*in* Los Andes en la encrucijada: indios, comunidades y estado en el siglo XIX. Quito: Ediciones Libri Mundi, 1991, p. 63–131, bibl., map, tables)

First-rate analysis of interethnic conflict during poorly studied 19th century. For related work see item **698**.

700 Jones, Kristine L. Calfucurá and Namuncurá: nation builders of the pampas. (*in* The human tradition in Latin America: the nineteenth century. Edited by Judith Ewell and William H. Beezley. Wilmington, Del.: Scholarly Resources, 1989, p. 175–186, bibl.)

Excellent study of Mapuche leader and his son and a pellucid description of European-Indian relations on the Argentine frontier.

701 Klauer, Alfonso. Tahuantinsuyo, el cóndor herido de muerte. Lima: Distribuidora Selecciones del Perú; IMPROFFSET, 1990. 180 p.: bibl., ill., maps.

In this popular account, author argues that the Inca empire could not have sustained itself, for the elite had subjected local peoples to unwanted domination. Ease of Spanish conquest was the result of lingering animosities to Inca rule.

Ladeira, Maria Inês and **Gilberto Azanha.** Os índios da Serra do Mar: a presença Mbyá-Guarani em São Paulo. See *HLAS 53:1095*.

702 Lagrange, Jacques. Le roi français d'Araucanie. Préface de Son Altesse royale, le prince d'Araucanie. Le Bugue, France: PLB, 1990. 67 p.: bibl., ill. (Col. Fleur de lys)

Biographical sketch of a curious 19th-century French soldier of fortune "elected" king of Araucania and Patagonia.

703 Langer, Erick D. Andean rituals of revolt: the Chayanta Rebellion of 1927. (*Ethnohistory/Society*, 37:3, Summer 1990, p. 227–253)

Interpretive essay examines two rituals performed during southern Bolivian uprising: a ritualized trial of an estate owner; and a more dangerous act of cannibalism of a detested *hacendado*. Legislation of 1870 had abolished the native community, and pressure from outsiders on Indian lands soon increased. Colonial tribute continued in the guise of the *contribución territorial*, and abuses led to Indian revolts. Langer argues "Andean tradition permits cannibalism of powerful but evil individuals under special circumstances of war or in ritual battles (p. 243)."

704 Langer, Erick D. Mandeponay: Chiriguano Indian chief in the Franciscan missions. (*in* The human tradition in Latin America: the nineteenth century. Edited by Judith Ewell and William H. Beezley. Wilmington, Del.: Scholarly Resources, 1989, p. 280–295, bibl.)

Adept native caudillo in Bolivia (1868–1904) tried to maintain ethnic identity of people while Bolivia was beginning process of modernization.

705 Langer, Erick D. Persistencia y cambio en las comunidades indígenas del sur de Bolivia en el siglo XIX. (*Data/La Paz*, 1, 1991, p. 61–83, map, tables)

Case study of ecologically-diverse (from *puna* to hot valleys) Chuquisaca region covers provinces of Yamparáez, Tomina and Cinti. Author explores why communities were able to persist in the face of expansion of haciendas, in which frequent land disputes sometimes resulted in violence. National legislation of 1874 and 1880, based on classical liberal ideals of creating an independent landholding class of native farmers, led to increasing pressures after 1880. Larger entities were more successful in resisting encroachments.

Larico Yujra, Mariano. Yo fui canillita de José Carlos Mariátegui: (auto)biografía de Mariano Larico Yujra. See item **2749.**

706 León Solis, Leonardo. Maloqueros y conchavadores en Araucanía y las Pampas, 1700–1800. Prólogo de John Lynch. Temuco, Chile: Ediciones Univ. de la Frontera, 1990. 245 p.: bibl. (Serie Quinto centenario; 7)

Major contribution based on extensive examination of European and American documentary collections traces native-European relations on Chile-Argentine frontier.

707 Lerche, Peter. Häuptlingstum Jalca: Bevölkerung und Ressourcen bei den vorspanischen Chachapoya Peru. Berlin: D. Reimer, 1986. 229 p.: bibl., ill.

Author uses archaeological and ethnohistorical data as well as observations of current subsistence farming to examine changing settlement patterns and resource utilization in the Upper Marañón and Central Huallaga regions during the precolumbian period. Emphasizes impact of significant ecological changes during and after the Inca conquest. [C.K. Converse]

708 López Avila, María Imelda. Expresiones de la vida espiritual y colonial de los muiscas en el siglo XVI. (in Historia y culturas populares: los estudios regionales en Boyacá. Recopilación de Pablo Mora Calderón y Amado Guerrero Rincón. Boyacá, Colombia: Instituto de Cultura y Bellas Artes de Boyacá, Centro de Investigación de Cultura Popular, 1989, p. 73–81, bibl.)

Brief survey of religious beliefs of Muiscas after initial introduction of Christianity.

709 López-Baralt, Mercedes. Icono y conquista: Guamán Poma de Ayala. Madrid: Hiperión, 1988. 483 p.: bibl., ill., port. (Libros Hiperión; 102)

Attempt to enter the mind of Guamán Poma, in order to understand the meaning of his text. Author borrows from ethnohistory, iconography, semiotics, comparative literature, and history of ideas to probe relation between visual and written texts. She finds that the physical layout of visual images depict Andean structures. Other themes explored include: the picture as Andean narrative; liter-

ary culture in Golden Age Spain; impact of Tridentine reforms on Peru; symbolic structures in Guamán Poma's drawings; text's relation to the "art of memory"; the cultural use of his depiction of "vices" and "virtues;" and the relevance to polyculturalism.

710 López-Baralt, Mercedes. El retorno del inca rey: mito y profecía en el mundo andino. La Paz: HISBOL, 1989. 118 p.: bibl., ill. (Breve biblioteca de bolsillo; 11)

More accessible edition of earlier published work (see *HLAS 50:677*).

711 Lorandi, Ana María and **Roxana Boixadós.** Etnohistoria de los valles calchaquíes en los siglos XVI y XVII. (*Runa/Buenos Aires*, 17/18, 1987/88, p. 263–419, bibl.)

Important study of peoples (Pular and Calchaqui, plus various sub-groups) in northwest Argentina that long resisted Spanish control. Uses archaeological and documentary evidence.

712 Lorandi, Ana María. Evidencias en torno a los Mitmaqkuna incaicos en el N.O. argentino. (*Anthropologica/Lima*, 9:9, 1991, p. 213–237, bibl., map)

Author uses incomplete data, but persuasively argues case for Inca settlement in north Andean Argentina, which persisted under Spanish.

713 Lorandi, Ana María and **Cora V. Bunter.** Reflexiones sobre las categorías semánticas en las fuentes del Tucumán colonial: los valles Calchaquíes. (*Histórica/Lima*, 14:2, dic. 1990, p. 281–315, bibl.)

Evaluation of colonial texts (to late 17th century) provides ethnographic information on native residents of region. Data not nearly as detailed as for Peru.

714 Lorandi, Ana María. La resistencia y rebeliones de los Diaguito-Calchaquí en los siglos XVI y XVII. (*Cuad. Hist.*, 8, dic. 1988, p. 99–124, bibl.)

Balanced survey of almost continuous resistance to Spanish domination by groups in northwest Argentina.

715 Magaña, Edmundo. Astronomía wayana y tarëno: Guyana Francesa, Surinam, norte de Brasil. (*Am. Indíg.*, 48:2, abril/junio 1988, p. 447–461, bibl.)

Studies astronomical knowledge of two groups, examining mythology, calendar, and star formations.

716 Mahn-Lot, Marianne. Les Incas vus par Cieza de León au-milieu du XVIe siècle. (*Rev. hist./Paris*, 578, avril/juin 1991, p. 321–326)

Brief evaluation of Cieza's work on Incas.

717 Málaga Medina, Alejandro. Reducciones toledanas en Arequipa: pueblos tradicionales. Arequipa, Peru: Biblioteca de Autores Arequipeños; PUBLIUNSA, 1989. 244 p.: bibl., ill.

Reprint of earlier works on Viceroy Francisco de Toledo's Indian settlements in Arequipa district.

718 Mamani Condori, Carlos B. Taraqu, 1866–1935: masacre, guerra y "renovación" en la biografía de Eduardo L. Nina Qhispi. La Paz: Ediciones Aruwiyiri, 1991. 172 p.: bibl., ill. (Serie Agresión colonial y resistencia indígena)

More than a biographical study of a single individual, this work encompasses eight Bolivian Altiplano *ayllus*, from the time of the sale of communal lands by Gen. Melgarejo (1864–71). Central figure was born in 1887. Encroachments on communal lands led to resistance, culminating in revolt. Author insightfully examines the 1920 Taraqu rebellion, and the broader role of Nina Qhispi.

719 Mandrini, Raúl José. Notas sobre el desarrollo de una economía pastoril entre los indígenas del suroeste bonaerense: fines del siglo XVIII y comienzos del XIX. (*Etnía/Olavarría*, 34/35, 1989/90, p. 67–87, bibl.)

Persuasively argues that native peoples of area between Tandil and Ventana can be classified as true nomadic pastoralists, based largely on description provided in 1822 diary of Pedro A. García.

720 Mannheim, Bruce. The Inca language in the colonial world. (*Colon. Lat. Am. Rev.*, 1:1/2, 1992, p. 77–108, bibl.)

Important evaluation of the extension by Spaniards of the Quechua language throughout the southern Andes. The spread of Quechua ended the linguistic diversity characteristic of the region even under the Incas, who had used their own language for administration.

721 Martín Rubio, María del Carmen. En el encuentro de dos mundos, los incas de Vilcabamba: instrucción del inga Don Diego de Castro Tito Cussi Yupangui, 1570. Prólogo de Francisco Valcárcel B. Madrid: Ediciones Atlas, 1988. 241 p.: bibl., ill. (En conmemoración del V centenario del descubrimiento de América; 2)

New critical edition of important source.

722 Martín Rubio, María del Carmen. Historia de Maynas, un paraíso perdido en el Amazonas: descripción de Francisco Requena. Prólogo de Róger Rumrrill. Madrid: Ediciones Atlas, 1991. 113 p.: bibl., ill., maps. (En conmemoración del V centenario del descubrimiento de América; 4)

Critical edition of geographical writings of colonial governor of Maynas in the late 18th century includes excellent biographical study.

723 Martínez C., José Luis. Los grupos indígenas del Altiplano de Lípez en la subregión del Río Salado. (*Chungará/Arica*, 16/17, oct. 1986, p. 199–201, bibl.)

Documents contacts among indigenous peoples of Northern Chile between the Atacama coast and Potosí.

724 Martínez C., José Luis et al. Interetnicidad y complementariedad: dinámicas de las estrategias de supervivencia de los atacameños en el siglo XVII. (*Histórica/Lima*, 15:1, junio 1991, p. 27–42)

Author uses parish registers and archival material in Argentina and Bolivia to suggest that internal distribution of resources in desert region follows possible "Andean models" delineated in the north, and that interethnic distributions based on complementarity are more societally-determined than ecological.

725 Martínez Garnica, Armando. Un caso de alteración aurífera colonial en el Bajo Magdalena. (*Boletín/Bogotá*, 23, enero/abril 1989, p. 47–59, ill., table)

Author demonstrates process and significance of lowering gold content in tribute items. Based on a 1555 unpublished report (AGI, Justicia 587A), refers to encomienda of Juan de Azpeleta, including Malibúes of Zimpieguas, Nicao, and Tamalameque in the present dept. of César.

726 Meiklejohn, Norman. La Iglesia y los lupaqas de Chucuito durante la colonia. Cusco, Peru: Centro de Estudios Rura-

les Andinos Bartolomé de las Casas; Puno, Peru: Instituto de Estudios Aymaras, 1988. 284 p.: bibl. (Archivos de historia andina; 7)
Best work on subject, based on extensive archival research. Author provides balanced and fresh insights on activities of first Dominicans, then Jesuits, on shores of Lake Titicaca.

727 Meneses, Georgina. Tradición oral en el imperio de los Incas: historia, religión, teatro. San José: Editorial Depto. Ecuménico de Investigaciones, 1992. 189 p.: bibl., ill. (Col. Análisis)
Survey based on works prior to the 1980s. Following balanced introduction to Inca civilization, author examines genesis of dramatic art (role of religion, forms of communication, language, choirs and dance, literature), then the formal theater (historical and political use, tragedy and comedy, depictions of the "Death of Atahuallpa," "Yauri Tito Inca," and "Ollantay").

728 Meseldzic de Pereyra, Zivana. Higiene y cosmética entre los antiguos peruanos. (*Bol. Lima,* 19:81, mayo 1992, p. 23–31, bibl., ill.)
Surveys bathing, soaps, skin ointments, insect repellents, body painting, and dental hygiene in Andes on basis of chroniclers and modern studies.

729 Michieli, Catalina Teresa. La sociedad huarpe: sus relaciones con la tenencia de la tierra y los recursos económicos. (*Chungará/Arica,* 16/17, oct. 1986, p. 195–198, bibl.)
Author examines landholding patterns and use in Cuyo region of Argentina from 16th century.

730 Millones, Luis. Mesianismo e idolatría en los Andes centrales. (*in* Estructuras sociales y mentalidades en América Latina: siglos XVII y XVIII. Compilación de Torcuato S. Di Tella. Buenos Aires: Fundación Simón Rodríguez, 1990, p. 147–205, bibl., map)
Selection of four previously published works (1971–87) on religious movements and idolatry from *Taki Onqoy* in 1560s to Arequipa in early 19th century.

731 Millones, Luis. El texto andino: las muchas lecturas. (*Cuad. Am.,* 6:33, mayo/junio 1992, p. 78–90, bibl.)
Evaluates shifting patterns in the understanding of basic "texts" of Andean world during past half-century.

732 Molina, Cristóbal de and Cristóbal de Albornoz. Fábulas y mitos de los Incas. Edición de Henrique Urbano y Pierre Duviols. Madrid: Historia 16, 1989. 199 p.: bibl. (Crónicas de América; 48)
Competent and accessible new critical edition of important source.

733 Molinari Morales, Tirso Anibal and Jaime Ríos Burga. Patria, nación y mesianismo inca en las ideologías de los procesos anti-coloniales en el Perú, 1780–1814. Lima: Univ. de Lima, Facultad de Ciencias Humanas, 1990. 165 p.: bibl. (Cuadernos de historia; 10)
Authors search for origins of nationalism in late 18th and early 19th century, focusing on role of caciques and Andean messianism.

734 Monteiro, John Manuel. Alforrias, litígios e a desagregação da escravidão indígena em São Paulo. (*Rev. Hist./São Paulo,* 120, jan./julho 1989, p. 45–57)
From a study of wills and manumission documents, author argues that Indian slavery was under pressure in São Paulo from 1690–1730, as evidenced in the growing number of poor freed natives. Discovery of gold led to continual efforts to maintain freedom from forced labor.

735 Monteiro, John Manuel. De índio a escravo: a transformação da população indígena de São Paulo no século XVII. (*Rev. Antropol./São Paulo,* 30/31/32, 1987/88/89, p. 151–174, bibl.)
Focuses on three aspects of Indian slavery: capture and transport; legal justification by regime; and social relations between slave and master—characterized by paternalism and violence.

736 Mora Penroz, Ziley. La Araucanía, mística antigua para la grandeza de Chile. Temuco, Chile: Z. Mora Penroz, 1988. 243 p.: bibl., ill. (some col.).
Uneven anthology of excerpts from printed works on the Mapuche.

737 Morales Gómez, Jorge. Ethohistoria guane. (*in* Historia y culturas populares: los estudios regionales en Boyacá. Recopilación de Pablo Mora Calderón y Amado

Guerrero Rincón. Boyacá, Colombia: Instituto de Cultura y Bellas Artes de Boyacá, Centro de Investigación de Cultura Popular, 1989, p. 83–90, bibl., maps)

Brief ethnohistorical survey of Colombian group on northern border of Muiscas.

738 Mott, Luiz Roberto de Barros. Conquista, aldeamento e domesticação dos índios Gueguê do Piauí, 1764–1770. (*Rev. Antropol./São Paulo*, 30/31/32, 1987/88/89, p. 55–78, bibl.)

Following overview of contacts with diverse Piauí peoples to 1763, author uses important documents in Arquivo do Estado do Piauí to reconstruct fate of the settled group.

739 Motta Zamalloa, Edmundo. De morenos y cruceros: religión popular, intercambio y cosmovisión andina. Lima: Univ. Nacional Mayor de San Marcos, Seminario de Historia Rural Andina, 1987. 206 p.: bibl., ill., indexes, map.

Another important work supported by Pablo Macera's group. Author focuses on relations between the coast and the Highlands in the Tacna region. Main theme is popular religion, with attention given to the "dance of the morenos" and the religious festivals of the crosses.

740 Moya Espinoza, Reynaldo. Historia pre-hispánica de la región Grau. Sullana, Peru: Sietevientos Editores; Maza Editores, 1992. 194 p.: ill., maps. (Serie El Revés de los médanos; 4)

Brief ethnohistory of northernmost region (Paita to Piura) of Peru's Pacific coast by dedicated non-specialist.

741 Mróz, Marcin. Paracronología dinástica de los Incas según Guamán Poma de Ayala. (*in* International Congress of Americanists, 45th, Bogotá, 1985. Rituales y fiestas de las Américas. Bogotá: Ediciones Uniandes, 1988, p. 65–78, tables)

Argues that native chronicler used a *quipu* to establish Inca chronology.

742 Mujica, Don Martín Joseph de. Testimonios y documentos: abusos de varias clases de mitas y carácter perezoso del Yndio. (*Bol. Lima*, 13:78, nov. 1991, p. 7–14, photo)

Author continues publication of document which outlines indigenous abuses in Guamanga district into the first decade of the 19th century.

743 Muratorio, Blanca. The life and times of Grandfather Alonso, culture and history in the upper Amazon. New Brunswick, N.J.: Rutgers Univ. Press, 1991. 295 p.: bibl., ill., index, maps. (Hegemony and experience)

Insightful combination of oral history of Quichua-speaking Rucuyaya Alonso and the cultural history of the people of the Napo province, Ecuador. Rejects "official" view that the Upper Napo Quichua were effectively acculturated in the colonial era and became submissive receptacles of western Christianity. Valuable and perceptive analysis.

744 Murra, John V. La etnohistoria. (*in* La etnohistoria en Mesoamérica y los Andes. México: Instituto Nacional de Antropología e Historia, 1987, p. 159–175, bibl.)

Review of state of research in Andean ethnohistory when this paper was presented at the International Congress of Americanists Meeting (43rd, Vancouver, Canada, 1979).

745 Nueva historia del Ecuador. v. 1–2, Epoca aborigen. Edición de Enrique Ayala Mora. Quito: Corporación Editora Nacional; Grijalbo, 1983–1991. 2 v.: bibl., ill. (some col.)

First two volumes in this projected 15-volume series (see item **2679**) edited by Enrique Ayala Mora. Written under supervision of Segundo Moreno, vols. 1–2 provide fine chronological overview by specialists. Contributors include E. Salazar, J.G. Marcos, J. Echeverria Almeida, S. Moreno and U. Oberem.

746 Oberem, Udo. La "reconquista" de Manco Inca: su eco en el territorio de la actual República del Ecuador. (*Antropol. Ecuat.*, 4/5, 1986/87, p. 95–102, bibl.)

The uprising of Manco in Lima and Cusco extended to Ecuador in mid-1536. At the same time, the Cañaris assisted the Spanish in lifting the attack on Lima.

747 Ocampo López, Javier. Los fundamentos geo-históricos en la formación de los pueblos de Boyacá. (*in* Historia y culturas populares: los estudios regionales en Boyacá. Recopilación de Pablo Mora Calderón y Amado Guerrero Rincón. Boyacá, Colombia: Instituto de Cultura y Bellas Artes de Boyacá, Centro de Investigación de Cultura Popular, 1989, p. 127–142, bibl.)

Examines geographical factors in evolution of Spanish-native relations in district, especially Tunja.

748 Opresión colonial y resistencia indígena en la alta Amazonía. Recopilación de Fernando Santos Granero. Quito: CEDIME; FLACSO, Sede Ecuador, 1992. 184 p.: bibl., maps. (Serie Amazonía)

Series of important articles includes: Ramírez Montenegro, "Dominación y Resistencia Indígena en la Amazonia Noroccidental, Siglos XVI-XVIII;" Garcés Dávila, "La Economía Colonial y su Impacto en las Sociedades Indígenas: el Caso de la Gobernación de Quijos, Siglos XVI-XVII;" Ruiz Mantilla, "Jumandi: Rebelión, Anticolonialismo y Mesianismo en el Oriente Ecuatoriano, Siglo XVI;" Santos Granero, "Anticolonialismo, Mesianismo y Utopía en la Sublevación de Juan Santos Atahuallpa, Siglo XVIII;" Lehm Ardaya, "Efectos de las Reducciones Jesuíticas en las Poblaciones Indígenas de Maynas y Mojos;" and Melgar Ortiz, "Formas de Dominación Indígena de Chiquitos, Siglos XVI-XVIII."

749 Padrón Farve, Oscar. El censo Guaraní misionero de 1832. (*Bol. Hist. Ejérc.*, 283/286, 1992, p. 97–122, ill., map, tables)

Argues for substantial impact of mission Guaraní on Uruguay. This count (names of individuals by village, in categories of men, women, boys, girls) which was taken before forced move under President Rivera, lists some 859 people living in 11 villages, with females constituting 63.5 percent.

750 Paez Constela, Roberto. Balsas de cueros de lobo en la segunda mitad del siglo XIX: antecedentes cuantitativos para el norte de Chile. (*Chungará/Arica*, 16/17, oct. 1986, p. 421–428, appendix, bibl., graphs)

Author attempts to establish number of such *balsas* on the Chilean seacoast from naval records. These craft were used for fishing and the transport of goods and people.

751 Palacio Asensio, José Luis. Nucanchic huiñai huiñai causai: nuestro pasado bajo Río Napo ecuatoriano. Quito: Editor FCUNAE, 1989. 298 p.: bibl., ill.

Popularized historical overview of various ethnic entities of Ecuadorian Amazon.

752 Palacios, Silvio and **Ena Zoffoli.** Gloria y tragedia de las misiones guaranies: historia de las reducciones jesuíticas durante

los siglos XVII y XVIII en el Río de la Plata. S.l.: Mensajero, 1991. 433 p.

Competent survey especially strong in areas of medicine and architecture.

753 Paraiso, Maria Hilda B. Os Botocudo em Bahia, Minas Gerais, e Espírito Santo. (*Dédalo/São Paulo*, 28, 1990, p. 63–95, bibl.)

Attempts survey from 16th century to present, with focus on social organization and interethnic relations.

754 Paraiso, Maria Hilda B. Os índios de Olivença e a zona de veraneio dos coronéis de cacau da Bahia. (*Rev. Antropol./São Paulo*, 30/31/32, 1987/88/89, p. 79–109, bibl.)

Historical overview of group of Tupiniquin of Ilhéus followed by closer examination of exploitative economic relations with Brazilians in the 19th and 20th centuries.

755 Parejas Moreno, Alcides J. and **Virgilio Suárez Salas.** Chiquitos: historia de una utopía. Santa Cruz, Bolivia: Cordecruz; Univ. Privada de Santa Cruz, 1992. 332 p.: bibl., ill. (some col.), maps.

Thorough examination of the Chiquitana and their interaction with the European world from 1592–1767 while under the domination of the Jesuit mission system stresses settlement pattern and religious and secular architecture. For historian's comment see item **2442.**

756 Parra Morales, Trinidad. Los muzos, un pueblo extinguido. Bogotá: Ediciones Tercer Mundo, 1985. 71 p.: bibl., ill.

Introductory overview of Muzos, based largely on published documents, but with brief archival research. Author stresses reasons for their demise, especially exploitation and disease.

757 Patterson, Thomas Carl. The Inca empire: the formation and disintegration of a pre-capitalist state. New York: Berg; St. Martin's Press, 1991. 211 p.: bibl., index, maps. (Explorations in anthropology)

Author emphasizes rise of the Inca state and role of repression of subjected ethnic entities in the process. The Spanish successfully adopted and continued the practice to maintain domination.

758 Paz, Gustavo L. Resistencia y rebelión campesina en la Puna de Jujuy, 1850–1875. (*Bol. Inst. Hist. Ravignani*, 4, 1991, p. 63–89)

Serious evaluation of one of last Argentine Andean native uprisings.

759 Pease G.Y., Franklin. La conquista española y la percepción andina del otro. (*Histórica/Lima*, 13:2, dic. 1989, p. 171–196, bibl.)

Pease examines the divergent perceptions of self and "other" of both Spaniards and Andeans in the context of the initial relationship.

760 Pease G.Y., Franklin. Perú, hombre e historia. v. 2, Entre el siglo XVI y el XVIII. Lima: EDUBANCO, 1992. 1 v.: bibl., ill. (some col.), maps.

Lavishly illustrated overview of colonial era by foremost scholar emphasizes indigenous relations with Europeans. Includes a fine bibliography and thorough discussion of historiographical issues.

761 Pease G.Y., Franklin. Las primeras versiones españolas sobre el Perú. (*Colon. Lat. Am. Rev.*, 1:1/2, 1992, p. 65–76)

Review of first European reports of Peru, from letters to chronicles, notes their deficiencies and emphasizes an unfolding understanding of Tawantinsuyu.

762 Pérez, Pablo Fernando. El comercio e intercambio de la coca: una aproximación a la etnohistoria de Chicamocha. (*Boletín/Bogotá*, 27, 1990, p. 15–35, bibl., photos, tables)

Author investigates local extent and impact of coca production beginning with 1602 Boyacá, Colombia inspection. Argues unlikehood of two annual harvests in 17th century. Concludes that groups practiced a control of microzones, not dissimilar to the central Andes, and that coca production was stimulated through colonial tribute requirements.

763 Perich Slater, José. Extinción indígena en la Patagonia. Punta Arenas, Chile: Tall. Gráf. Uteau y González, 1985. 183 p.: bibl., ill., map.

Non-specialist attempts to explain extinction of various Tierra del Fuegan groups (Ona, Yaghan, Alacaluf). Personal experience is no substitute for systematic research.

764 Pinto Rodríguez, Jorge. Etnocentrismo y etnocidio: franciscanos y jesuitas en la Araucanía, 1600–1900. (*in* CEHILA, *16th, Santo Domingo, 1989.* Sentido Histórico del V Centenario, 1492–1992. Edición de Gui-

llermo Meléndez. San José: Editorial Depto. Ecuménico de Investigaciones, 1992, p. 105–123, bibl.)

Brief overview of work of two principal orders among Mapuche. Finds most Europeans ethnocentric, tending towards ethnocide.

765 Pinto Rodríguez, Jorge *et al.* Misioneros en la Araucanía, 1600–1900: un capítulo de historia fronteriza en Chile. vols. 1–2. Bogotá: Consejo Episcopal Latinoamericano, 1990. 2 v.: bibl., ill. (Col. V centenario; 38)

First vol. of this important compilation includes articles, while vol. 2 contains documents. J. Pinto Rodriguez presents historical overview of missions on Chilean frontier; H. Casanova Guarda examines missions of Colegio de Propaganda Fide Chillán (1756–1818); and S.M. Uribe Gutiérrez studies Capuchines in Araucanía in period 1848–1901.

766 Polo de Ondegardo. El mundo de los incas. Edición de Laura González y Alicia Alonso. Madrid: Historia 16, 1990. 173 p.: bibl. (Crónicas de América; 58)

One of the many early reports of discoverers reprinted to coincide with the Quincentenary. This accessible and well-edited version is one of the most important works by Polo de Ondegardo.

767 Porro, Antonio. Mitologia heróica e messianismo na Amazônia seiscentista. (*Rev. Antropol./São Paulo*, 30/31/32, 1987/88/89, p. 383–389, bibl.)

Brief overview to present.

768 Powers, Karen M. Resilient lords and Indian vagabonds: wealth, migration, and the reproductive transformation of Quito's chiefdoms, 1500–1700. (*Ethnohistory/Society*, 38:3, Summer 1991, p. 225–249)

Important examination of the impact of migration in the northern Andes. By looking at a single lineage, the Hatis of Latacunga, Powers focuses on the adaptive strategy of curacas. Here is another case of a successful curaca family securing almost astounding "wealth." By skillful absorption of migrants (particularly those who had fled native communities to avoid mita and tribute requirements) and balanced redistribution, some chieftains were able to retain power and maintain "Andean society" in spite of mounting colonial exactions. Persuasive arguments that warrant close consideration.

769 Presta, Ana María. Ingresos y gastos de una hacienda jesuítica altoperuana: Jesús de Trigo Pampa Pilaya y Paspaya, 1734–1767. (*Anu. IEHS*, 4, 1989, p. 85–114, appendix, bibl., graphs, map)

Excellent study based on hacienda accounts in document in Archivo Histórico de Potosí. Lands extended from tropical valleys to the highland punas, with revenues from textile production, aguardiente, livestock, and rental of land and mills.

770 Puente Brunke, José de la. Un documento de interés en torno al tributo indígena en el siglo XVI. (*Histórica/Lima*, 15:2, dic. 1991, p. 265–313, bibl., tables)

Important summary of tribute report of Viceroy Francisco de Toledo (1575) for La Plata, La Paz, Cusco, Arequipa, Huamanga, Trujillo, Piura, Guayaquil and Puerto Viejo. Original is located in Marqués del Risco Collection., Univ. de Sevilla (mss 330/122, document 60).

Querejazu Lewis, Roy. Bolivia prehispánica. See *HLAS 53:669.*

771 Ramírez de Jara, María Clemencia. Los Quillacinga y su posible relación con grupos prehispánicos del oriente eucatoriano. (*Rev. Colomb. Antropol.*, 29, 1992, p. 27–61, bibl., maps)

Author suggests inhabitants of Sibundoy Valley in northeast Nariño and Almaguer migrated into Colombia from Ecuador along eastern slopes of Andes, bringing tropical forest cultural practices.

772 Ramón Valarezo, Galo. El poder y los norandinos: la historia en las sociedades norandinas del siglo XVI. Quito: Centro Andino de Acción Popular, 1990. 256 p.: bibl., ill., maps. (Cuaderno de discusión popular; 23)

Carefully balanced survey of northern Andean political entities, particularly the Pastos and Litas, and their incorporation first into Tawantinsuyu, then the Spanish colonial state. Includes discussion of historiographical issues and a useful bibliography.

773 Randall, Robert. The mythstory of Kuri Qoyllur: sex, *seqes*, and sacrifice in Inca agricultural festivals. (*J. Lat. Am. Lore*, 16:1, Summer 1990, p. 3–45, bibl., ill.)

This seminal article analyzes the love story of messenger Kilaku Yupanki and Kuri Qoyllor, a daughter of Waskar Inca. At a deeper level, author presents challenging evaluation of Inca cosmology, particularly as it relates to the agricultural cycle. Very significant and potentially the "last" contribution of Randall (1945–90).

774 Rappaport, Joanne. Imágenes míticas, pensamiento histórico y textos impresos: los paeces y la palabra escrita. (*in* International Congress of Americanists, *45th, Bogotá, 1985*. Rituales y fiestas de las Américas. Bogotá: Ediciones Uniandes, 1988, p. 103–112, bibl.)

Study of a non-literate indigenous group of the Cauca dept. of Colombia argues they do possess an historical consciousness, though distinct from that of literate cultures.

775 Ravagnani, Oswaldo Martins. Aldeamentos Goianos em 1750: os jesuítas e a mineração. (*Rev. Antropol./São Paulo*, 30/31/32, 1987/88/89, p. 111–132, bibl., map)

Studies impact of mining on native peoples of Goiás. Once hunted by slavers, with the arrival of mines, the Indians were forced off their lands, and neither the Jesuits nor the state were able to protect them.

776 Ravagnani, Oswaldo Martins. Eu te batizo: em nome da servidão; a catequese dos Xavante. (*Rev. Antropol./São Paulo*, 30/31/32, 1987/88/89, p. 133–149, bibl.)

Author evaluates efforts of various religious efforts among one tribe in Goias-Mato Grosso from mid-18th century contact to present. Aim of Church, state and landowners was to make natives tractable.

777 Ravines, Rogger. Hongos comestibles del antiguo Perú. (*Bol. Lima*, 13:73, enero 1991, p. 23–24, ill.)

Notes terms for mushrooms in Felipe Guamán Poma de Ayala, as well as four early colonial dictionaries. Attempts identification based on modern analysis.

778 Ravines, Rogger. Parecer sobre las misiones a los chiriguanas del p. Juan de Atienza. (*Bol. Lima*, 12:70, julio 1990, p. 19–22)

Transcription of Atienza's report follows brief biographical sketch.

779 Ravines, Rogger. Testamentos de mujeres indígenas: siglo XVII. (*Bol. Lima*, 13:75, mayo 1991, p. 7–10)

Published transcriptions of early 18th-century wills found in notarial section of Archivo Departamental de Cajamarca, one by native upper-class woman, the other an illegitimate mestiza, show richness of documentation for study of "people without a voice."

780 Rebolledo, Loreto. Comunidad y resistencia: el caso de Lumbisí en la colonia. Quito: FLASCO; Abya-Yala, 1992. 321 p.: bibl. (Col. Tesis: Historia; 5)

Microhistory of native peoples of Cumbayá and their reaction to Spanish domination. Author examines ecological foundations, social and political organization, tribute and mobility, and patterns of land tenure in a thorough and important archival based regional study.

781 Reproducción y transformación de las sociedades andinas, siglos XVI-XX: simposio auspiciado por el Social Science Research Council. v. 1–2. Recopilación de Segundo Moreno Y. y Frank Salomon. Quito: Ediciones ABYA-YALA; Roma: MLAL, Movimiento Laicos para América Latina, 1991. 2 v. (693 p.): bibl., ill. (Col. 500 años; 41–42)

Important collection of largely new articles on Andean ethnohistory. Contributors include: F. Salomon, G. Urton, S. MacCormack, D.W. Gade, T. Saignes, X. Albó, C. Caillavet, T. Abercrombie, C.S. Assadourian, L.M. Glave, C. Fonseca Martel and E. Mayer, K. Spalding, G. Ramón Valarezo, B. Larson, J. Lockhart, S.E. Moreno, M. Burga, T. Gisbert, S. Rivera, and R. Cerrón-Palomino.

782 Río, Mercedes del. Estrategias andinas de supervivencia: el control de recursos en Chaqui, siglos XVI-XVIII. (*Anu. IEHS,* 4, 1989, p. 53–84, appendix, graphs, map, tables)

Author surveys an indigenous group northeast of La Plata, in order to further evaluate Murra's model of control of resources.

783 Río, Mercedes del. Simbolismo y poder en Tapacarí. (*Rev. Andin.,* 8:1, julio 1990, p. 77–113, bibl., tables, maps)

Thorough examination of political and economic power of García Mamani, a Soras curaca of Tapacari (Bolivia) through *quipu*-based will and other documents of late 16th century.

784 Rostworowski, María de Diez Canseco. La región del Colesuyu. (*Chungará/Arica,* 16/17, oct. 1986, p. 127–135, bibl.)

The Colesuyu section of the Inca empire, inhabited by *yungas,* fishermen, and Highland ethnic enclaves, extended from Camaná to Tarapacá, and occupied a distinct category from the "four quarters."

785 Rowe, John Howland. Machu Picchu a la luz de documentos de siglo XVI. (*Histórica/Lima,* 14:1, julio 1990, p. 139–154, appendix, bibl.)

No mention can be found of the site in the chroniclers, but known documents refer to "Picchu" (in encomienda of Hernando Pizzaro, Aria Maldonado) before Bingham's "discovery." Bingham seems to have ignored these in order to claim discovery of lost city of Vilcabamba.

786 Rozas Bonuccelli, Fernando. Plantas alimenticias en el antiguo Perú. Lima: Consejo Nacional de Ciencia y Tecnología, 1989. 175 p.: bibl., ill.

New survey of precontact plants available in Peruvian Andes includes botanical description, range, soil, propagation, harvest data, uses, and nutritional data.

787 Saignes, Thierry. Ava y karai: ensayos sobre la frontera chiriguano, siglos XVI-XX. La Paz: Hisbol, 1990. 272 p.: bibl., ill., index, maps. (Biblioteca andina; 9)

Some previously published articles, here organized and substantially revised into coherent overview of uneasy Chiriguano relation with the "enemy." Work illuminates nature of cultural persistence in spite of constant pressure.

788 Saignes, Thierry. Entre 'bárbaros' y 'cristianos:' el desafío mestizo en la frontera chiriguano. (*Anu. IEHS,* 4, 1989, p. 13–51, map, table)

Significant work on mestizo role as intermediary on frontier of eastern Charcas, culturally located between the Andes and Paraguay. Author offers new insights into dynamics of social order in Chiriguano territory.

789 Sala i Vila, Nuria. El levantamiento de los pueblos de Aymaras en 1818. (*Bol. Am.,* 31:39/40, 1989–90, p. 203–226)

Studies South Andean situation following suppressed 1814 Cuzco revolt. Notes that the impact of crop shortages (1816–17), a "general epidemic," and reintroduction of Indian tribute abolished by the Cortes of Cádiz all contributed to localized 1818 uprising.

790 Sala i Vila, Nuria. Mistis e indígenas: la lucha por el control de las comunidades indígenas en Lampa, Puno, a fines de la colonia. (*Bol. Am.*, 32:41, 1991, p. 35–66)

Important examination of tensions within Andean society, particularly commoner-curaca, in critical period from suppression of Túpac Amaru revolt to Independence.

791 Salzano, Francisco M. *et al.* História dos índios no Brasil. Recopilación de Manuela Carneiro da Cunha. São Paulo: Fundação de Amparo à Pesquisa do Estado de São Paulo; Companhia das Letras; Secretaria Municipal de Cultura, Prefeitura do Município de São Paulo, 1992. 611 p.: bibl., ill., index, maps.

Well-illustrated college level introduction by regional specialists includes useful bibliography.

792 Sánchez, Ana. La aparición de la Virgen en la doctrina de Acoria: Huamanga, 1688. (*Rev. Esp. Antropol. Am.*, 20, 1990, p. 105–134, bibl.)

Document (transcription included) from Archivo Arzobispal de Ayacucho allows insight into popular religious culture. Aparition followed damaging earthquake of 1687.

793 Sánchez, Ana. Mentalidad popular frente ideología oficial: el Santo Oficio en Lima y los casos de hechicería, siglo XVII. (*in* Coloquio Internacional del Grupo de Trabajo Historia y Antropología Andinas, *2nd, Quito, 1990.* Poder y violencia en los Andes. Edición de Henrique Urbano y Mirko Lauer. Cusco, Peru: Centro de Estudios Regionales Andinos Bartolomé de Las Casas, 1991, p. 33–52, graphs)

Useful introduction to topic with mix of primary and secondary sources.

794 Sánchez, Sandra and **Gabriela Sica.** La frontera oriental de Humahuaca y sus relaciones con el Chaco. (*Bull. Inst. fr. étud. andin.*, 19:2, 1990, p. 469–497, bibl., maps)

Concentrates on period 1595–1650 and the various ethnic entities in transitional area of Zenta Valley to north of Jujuy, Argentina.

795 Sánchez-Albornoz, Nicolás. Territorio y etnia: la comunidad indígena de Santa Cruz de Oruro, Collao, en 1604. (*Hist. Mex.*, 39:1, julio/sept. 1989, p. 167–179, bibl., tables)

Census of 1604 found in Archivo General de la Nación in Buenos Aires permits full description of population structure, migration, and local economy of south Andean community.

Santos, Sílvio Coelho dos. Indios e brancos no sul do Brasil: a dramática experiência dos xokleng. See *HLAS 53:1108.*

796 Schaedel, Richard P. Cosmic interrelationships and perceptions: regulatory or controlling? (*in* International Congress of Americanists, *45th, Bogotá, 1985.* Rituales y fiestas de las Américas. Bogotá: Ediciones Uniandes, 1988, p. 19–26, bibl.)

Theoretical overview of evolution of Quechua and Aymara ethnology-ethnohistory.

797 Schaedel, Richard P. Interrelaciones y percepciones cósmicas andinas: ¿regulatorias o de control? (*Histórica/Lima*, 15:1, junio 1991, p. 63–91, bibl.)

Author surveys development of field of Andean ethnohistory and then focuses on issue of relationship between cosmology and regulation and control.

Schindler, Helmut. Bauern und Reiterkrieger: die Mapuche-Indianer im Süden Amerikas. See *HLAS 53:1228.*

798 Schmelz, Bernd. Lope de Atienza, Missionar und Ethnograph: sein Werk "Compendio historial del estado de los indios del Perú" (1572–75) als ethnohistorische Quelle. Bonn: Holos, 1987. 106 p.: bibl. (Mundus Reihe Alt-Amerikanistik; 1)

Provides excellent biographical information and suggests, by analysis of key textual selections, that Atienza's work can provide valuable information on Indian life. Also evaluates Atienza's perception of the "native."

799 Schreiber, Katharina Jeanne. Wari imperialism in Middle Horizon Peru. Foreword by Jeffrey R. Parsons. Ann Arbor: Museum of Anthropology, Univ. of Michigan, 1992. 332 p.: bibl., ill. (Anthropological papers; 87)

Excellent overview of the Wari focuses on provincial center of Jincamocco and attempts to explain Wari's relatively rapid expansion and quick demise.

800 Sebill, Nadine. Ayllus y haciendas: dos estudios de caso sobre la agricultura colonial en los Andes. La Paz: HISBOL, 1989.

143 p.: bibl., ill. (Serie Alternativas étnicas al desarrollo; 1)

Author effectively analyzes the visita of Chaqui in 1609–11 to study foundations of society and economy. Also reviews its relation to hacienda (1595–98) of Llanqueuma in La Paz district.

801 Seed, Patricia. "Failing to marvel:" Atahualpa's encounter with the word. (*LARR*, 26:1, 1991, p. 7–32)

Author, like Sabine G. MacCormack (*HLAS 52:2166*), sees importance in Atahualpa's "rejection" of the Bible at Cajamarca in accounts of the Spanish conquest. Concludes that "it was the kind of story about the other that the narrator wished to tell that determined how the book . . . landed on the ground . . . " Seed, however, interprets Guamán Poma and Garcilaso de la Vega "as situated ambiguously between Spanish and Quechua traditions," unlike MacCormack who views them as Andean. For literary critic's comment see item **3551**. [M.T. Hamerly]

802 Silverman-Proust, Gail P. Tawa Inti Qocha, símbolo de la cosmología andina: concepción Q'ero del espacio. (*Anthropologica/Lima*, 6:6, 1988, p. 9–42, bibl., ill.)

Designs woven in cloth depict duality, quadruplicate organization, and ecological zoning in Cusco region.

803 Simposio sobre Etnohistoria Amazónica, Mérida, Venezuela, 1985. Los meandros de la historia en Amazonía: memorias del Simposio. Recopilación de Roberto Pineda-Camacho y Beatriz Alzate Angel. Quito: Abya-Yala; MLAL, 1990. 354 p.: bibl., maps. (Col. 500 años; 25)

Important series of articles focusing on larger Amazon basin includes: E.J. Langdon on conquest of Siona del Putumayo; G. Rivas and A. Oviedo on colonization of Colombian upper Amazon (1535–95); I. Bellier on the Payaguas; M. Useche on Upper Orinoco, Casiquiare and Río Negro; P. and F. Grenand on peoples of the coast of Amapá; M.L. Carneiro da Cunha and E.B. Viveiros de Castro on Tupinamba; S. Benchimol on Mura Indians (1738); R. Pineda on violence in the Bajo Caquetá; M. Benavides on metal tool use among Ashaninka in Peruvian jungle; Y. Mora de Jaramillo on river commerce in southern Colombia; and A. Zarzar on the Nahua (Pano-speaking group of Peruvian Amazon).

804 Solano, Francisco de. Los nombres del Inca Garcilaso: definición e identidad. (*Anu. Estud. Am.*, 48, 1991, p. 121–150)

Garcilaso used four different names during his life. Most writers have viewed these changes as successive states of mind. However, Solano points out that such practices were not unusual in the 16th century, and continues by examining the Inca's preoccupation with genealogy.

805 Sotomayor, María Lucía. Organización socio-política de las cofradías. (*Rev. Colomb. Antropol.*, 29, 1992, p. 155–189, bibl.)

Lay brotherhoods link the Church as an institution with native parishioners. Because of paucity of data they have not received the scholarly attention they deserve, but here we have a solid start based on the community of Cuitiva of Sogamoso (Boyacá) in second half of 18th century.

806 Stanish, Charles. Ancient Andean political economy. Austin: Univ. of Texas Press, 1992. 195 p.: bibl., ill., index, maps.

Author suggests methodology for testing models of political economy in the southern Andes, and applies test of zonal complementarity in the Moquegua drainage. Intent is to take models of Murra and Rostworowski and "develop a framework capable of interpreting both of these seemingly opposing models into a single, consistent approach" (p. 5).

807 Sušnik, Branislava. Etnohistoria del Paraguay: etnohistoria de los Chaqueños y de los Guaraníes: bosquejo sintético. (*Supl. Antropol.*, 23:2, dic. 1988, p. 7–50, bibl.)

Excellent introduction to major ethnic entities by leading specialist. Also published in *América Indígena* (Vol. 44, No. 3, julio/sept. 1989).

808 Sušnik, Branislava. Una visión socio-antropológica del Paraguay del siglo XIX. v. 1. Asunción: Museo Etnográfico Andrés Barbero, 1992. 1 v.

Continuation of author's massive study (see item **809**), with shift in emphasis to social and economic history in the half century following independence.

809 Sušnik, Branislava. Una visión socio-antropológica del Paraguay del siglo XVIII. Asunción: Museo Etnográfico Andrés Barbero, 1991. 143 p.: bibl., index, map.

Examination focuses on pre- and post-1740 Paraguay, with stress on changes in second period that led to rural homogeneity, new socio-racial policy, decline of native hostility, and formation of a national identity. (See also item **808**.)

810 Szemiński, Jan. Yana Wara Inka a iñaqa ñusta. (*Estud. Latinoam.*, 13, 1990, p. 169–179, table)

Perceptive attempt to delineate nature of one group of non-Cusco Inca women on basis of Guamán Poma text and early and modern dictionaries.

Taylor, Anne Cristine. La invención del Jívaro: notas etnográficas sobre un fantasma occidental. See *HLAS 53:1303.*

811 Téllez Lúgaro, Eduardo and **Osvaldo Silva Galdames.** Atacama en el siglo XVI: la conquista hispana en la periferia de los Andes Meridionales. (*Cuad. Hist.*, 9, dic. 1989, p. 45–69, maps)

Excellent evaluation of early Spanish attempts to penetrate Atacama desert region, and the natives' strong and relatively continuous resistance.

812 Tellez Lúgaro, Eduardo. Producción marítima, servidumbre indígena y señores hispanos en el partido de Atacama: un documento sobre la distorsión colonial del tráfico entre el litoral atacameño y Potosí. (*Chungará/Arica*, 16/17, oct. 1986, p. 159–165, bibl.)

Late 16th-century document points out extent of exchange between the northern Chilean coast and the Highland around Potosí.

813 Thiemer-Sachse, Ursula. Derecho de los indígenas a utilizar el agua de riego. (*in* Peruanistas contemporáneos II: temas, métodos, avances. Edición de Wilfredo Kapsoli E. Lima: Consejo Nacional de Ciencia y Tecnología (CONCYTEC), 1989, p. 67–81)

Author reviews a handful of early colonial descriptions of native irrigation rights and concludes that the Spanish caused major disruptions.

814 Time and calendars in the Inca Empire. Edited by Mariusz S. Ziólkowski and Robert M. Sadowski. Oxford, England: B.A.R., 1989. 213 p.: bibl., ill., maps. (BAR international series; 479)

Includes papers first presented at the 1985 Bogotá sessions of the 45th International Congress of Americanists as well as new works by Duviols, Dearborn and Schreiber, Ziólkowshi, and Ziólkowski and Sadowski. Very important contribution to the debate over Inca concepts of time, calendar, measurement, and record.

815 Tovar Pinzón, Hermes. Formaciones sociales prehispánicas. 2a. ed., ampliada y corr. Bogotá: Editorial El Búho, 1990. 160 p.: bibl., ill.

Author's revision of 1974 study, *Notas sobre el modo de producción precolombino*, attempts a synthesis of precolumbian social organization of high civilization areas in the Americas.

816 Triana Antorveza, Adolfo. Contribución a la historia de la Provincia de Neiva: el caso del Caguán. (*Rev. Colomb. Antropol.*, 29, 1992, p. 119–154, bibl., map, table)

Study of uneasy relationship between Dujos in Caguán and community of Neiva (on upper Magdalena River), from contact to present century.

817 Urbano, Henrique. Clases sacerdotales y sociedades andinas. (*in* International Congress of Americanists, *45th, Bogotá, 1985*. Rituales y fiestas de las Américas. Bogotá: Ediciones Uniandes, 1988, p. 90–102, bibl.)

Author examines native priests and covers themes such as symbolism, mythic-codynastic conflict, and religious practices.

818 Urbano, Henrique. Los héroes Wiracocha y la Constelación de Orión: simbolismo ternario andino y calendarios agrícolas. (*in* International Congress of Americanists, *45th, Bogotá, 1985*. Rituales y fiestas de las Américas. Bogotá: Ediciones Uniandes, 1988, p. 79–87, bibl.)

Suggests link between Wiracocha myths and belt of Orion (Chacana), associated with calendar and beginnings of rainy season.

819 Urton, Gary. Calendrical cycles and their projections in Pacariqtambo, Peru. (*in* International Congress of Americanists, *45th, Bogotá, 1985*. Rituales y fiestas de las Américas. Bogotá: Ediciones Uniandes, 1988, p. 168–181, bibl., tables)

Author describes local knowledge of astronomical events and the ritual agricultural calendar. Also shows how astronomical knowledge is passed on and is used to explain the social and economic universe of villagers.

820 Vainfas, Ronaldo. Colonialismo e idolatrias: cultura e resistência indígenas no mundo colonial ibérico. (*Rev. Bras. Hist.*, 11:21, set. 1990/fev 1991, p. 101–124)

Attempts classification of idolatry from early 16th century and describes its relation to material life and indigenous struggles. This preliminary effort to make sense of various native religious movements and to trace their relationships merits examination.

821 Valencia Llano, Alonso. Resistencia militar indígena en la gobernación de Popayán. Cali: Univ. del Valle, 1991. 190 p., 3 leaves of plates: bibl., maps (some col.). (Col. Interés general)

Comprehensive examination of Spanish attempts to subjugate the Cauca district, and the almost continuous native resistance. In addition to early rebellion of encomienda Indians, there was constant conflict on the mining frontier, as well as war with the Pijaos.

822 Vargas, Javier. Matrimonio, familia y propiedad en el Imperio Incaico: contribución al estudio de la historia del derecho peruano. Lima: Cultural Cuzco, 1988. 114 p.: bibl.

Surveys subject on basis of several accounts of chroniclers.

823 Viertler, Renate Brigitte. A duras penas: um histórico das relações entre índios Bororo e "civilizados" no Mato Grosso. São Paulo: FFLCH-USP, 1990. 212 p.: bibl., maps. (Antropologia; 16)

Good evaluation of interaction of Bororo with outside world based on ethnographic and historical investigation first conducted during thesis research.

Viertler, Renate Brigitte. Mito, rito e condições de sobrevivência entre os índios Bororo do Mato Grosso: esboço para uma abordagem interdisciplinar do fenômeno mítico. See *HLAS 53:1115.*

824 Villalobos R., Sergio. Los pehuenches en la vida fronteriza: investigaciones. Santiago: Ediciones Univ. Católica de Chile, 1989. 269 p.: bibl., ill.

Valuable overview of rarely studied

group examines both Chilean and Argentine evidence. Author stresses survival strategies.

825 Villasante Cervello, Mariella. Biblioteca Nacional: Archivo de Manuscritos Virreynato; Selva Peruana. (*Amazonía Peru.*, 10:19, 1990, p. 113–190)

Copies of card catalog entries for documents relating to the Amazon Basin.

826 Viola, Alfredo. Reducción de San Francisco Solano de los Remolinos. (*Hist. Parag.*, 28, 1991, p. 119–145)

Author documents peaceful settlement of some 800 Mbocovies on edge of Paraguay River in Chaco in 1776.

827 Visita de los valles de Sonqo en los yunka de coca de La Paz, 1568–1570. Edición a cargo de John V. Murra. Madrid: Instituto de Cooperación Iberoamericana: Quinto Centenario: Instituto de Estudios Fiscales, 1991. 687 p.: bibl., ill., indexes, maps. (Monografías Economía quinto centenario)

Visita contains complete ethnographic information on names, ages, status, holdings. Edition includes articles, but there is a documentary foundation for a whole series of studies. Data are comparable to that found in the *visita* of Huanuco in 1562 and of Collaguas in 1591.

828 Visita y numeración de los pueblos del Valle de los Chillos, 1551–1559. Recopilación de Cristóbal Landázuri N. Quito: MARKA; ABYA-YALA, 1990. 313 p.: bibl., indexes, map. (Fuentes para la historia andina; 1)

Well-edited colonial inspection includes two complementary articles: Landázuri, "El Cacicazgo y la Encomienda: Anotaciones en torno a la Visita de 1559 al Valle de los Chillos;" and Salomon and Grosboll, "Nombres y Gente en el Quito Incaico: Recuperación de un Proceso Histórico Indocumentado a través de la Antroponimia y la Estadística," originally published in *American Anthropologist* (Vol. 88, 1986). The *visita* contains excellent economic and demographic data.

829 Vitar, Beatriz. Las relaciones entre los indígenas y el mundo colonial en un espacio conflictivo: la frontera tucumano-chaqueña en el siglo XVIII. (*Rev. Esp. Antropol. Am.*, 21, 1991, p. 243–278, bibl.)

Author examines Spanish expansion from Tucumán into regions of the Chaco populated by indigenous tribes. The rise of cattle ranching in the 18th century spurred Spanish penetration of the Lowlands east of the Highland mining centers. Frequent native attacks provided the pretext for Spanish military *entradas*, especially the one in 1710. Spanish ability to control the peoples of the Chaco depended on native cultural characteristics.

830 **Welch, Thomas L.** and **René L. Gutié-rrez.** The Incas: a bibliography of books and periodical articles. Washington: Columbus Memorial Library, Organization of American States, 1987. 145 p.: indexes. (Hipólito Unanue bibliographic series; 1)

Useful bibliography includes 1,116 items and an index.

831 **Wright, Robin M.** Uma história de re-sistência: os heróis Baniwa e suas lutas. (*Rev. Antropol./São Paulo,* 30/31/32, 1987/88/89, p. 355–381, bibl.)

Study of the Hohodene, a Baniwa group living in northwest Amazonia on Alto Rio Negro. Through origin myth and examination of mid-19th century Baniwa "messiah" Venâncio Christu, author shows how myth and legend reinforce cultural resistance to outside domination.

832 **Zapater Equioíz, Horacio.** La búsqueda de la paz en la guerra de Arauco: Padre Luis de Valdivia. Santiago: Editorial Andrés Bello, 1992. 230 p.: bibl., ill., map.

Modern evaluation of career of Jesuit Valdivia's missionary efforts on Chilean frontier emphasizes his advocacy of peaceful relations during the early 17th century.

833 **Zapater Equioíz, Horacio.** Confederación bélica de pueblos andinos, amazónicos, cordilleranos, durante el dominio español. (*Chungará/Arica,* 16/17, oct. 1986, p. 167–171, bibl.)

Argues *Titu Cusi* resistance in 1560s included Chiriguanos, Calchaquies, Omaguacas, Casavindos, Chichas, and Apatamas. Rebellion of 1658 was also widespread.

834 **Zevallos Quiñones, Jorge.** Los cacicazgos de Lambayeque. Trujillo, Peru: Gráfica Cuatro, 1989. 138 p., 1 folded leaf of plates: ill., maps.

Valuable contribution based on local public and private archives as well as National Archive in Lima. Provides ethnohistorical data on some 20 North Peruvian coastal political entities.

835 **Ziólkowski, Mariusz S.** and **Robert M. Sadowski.** La arqueoastronomía en la investigación de las culturas andinas. Quito: Banco Central del Ecuador: Instituto Otavaleño de Antropología, 1992. 378 p.: bibl., ill., maps. (Col. Pendoneros; 9)

One of best works on subject includes updated sections of previous work by the two specialists. Topics examined include site orientation, problem of reconstruction of lunar and solar calendars, correlation of Inca-European dates, analysis of Quechua, Aymara, and Yunga terminology relating to time and astronomical events. Provides tables indicating dates of sky events visible in Andes (solar and lunar eclipses, meteor showers, comets).

836 **Ziólkowski, Mariusz S.** Los cometas de Atawallpa: acerca del papel de las profecías en la política del Estado Inka. (*Anthropologica/Lima,* 6:6, 1988, p. 87–109, appendices, bibl.)

Attempts to link known astronomical events with historical events of questionable date in "contact" period Peru.

Ziólkowski, Mariusz S. El culto estatal del imperio Inca. See *HLAS 53:896.*

837 **Zuidema, Reiner Tom.** Reyes y guerreros: ensayos de cultura andina. Lima: FOMCIENCIAS, 1989. 563 p., 11 p. of plates: bibl., ill., maps. (Grandes estudios andinos)

Spanish-language compilation of some of most important contributions of Zuidema from 1967–83, useful since originals are often difficult to locate.

838 **Zúñiga Ide, Jorge.** Evolución de los géneros de vida de un sector costero del norte semi-árido de Chile. (*Chungará/Arica,* 16/17, oct. 1986 p. 437–446, bibl.)

Northern Chilean fishing, hunting, collecting groups surviving off marine resources persisted in difficult environment into 18th century.

GENERAL HISTORY

JOHN BRITTON, *Professor of History, Francis Marion University*

THE SUBSTANTIAL INCREASE in the number of items in the "General History" section was largely the result of Quincentenary-related publications in Latin America, Spain, the US, and Great Britain. While the quality of these publications varied widely, and scholarly circumspection sometimes capitulated to ideological and political purposes, overall this crop of books and articles brought forth a healthy harvest.

There is a temptation to concentrate on studies of the first encounter of Europe and America, but such an approach would do a disservice to those authors who, after years of research and writing on important but non-Quincentenary topics, saw their work reach the printed page in this biennium. Therefore, this essay will cover the full range of historical writing customary for the General section of the Handbook.

Two outstanding monographs that reach into the wider realm of Latin American history were Saúl Franco Agudelo's extensive treatment of malaria and the medical responses to this dreaded disease (item **868**) and Pablo Emilio Pérez-Mallaína-Bueno's social and cultural history of the everyday lives of 16th-century sailors (item **1033**). A large outpouring of books on the influence of particular Spanish regions and ethnic groups in America included Lutgardo García Fuentes' exemplary study of the role of the Basques in the colonial iron and steel industry (item **975**).

Three works of considerable importance appeared in the field of intellectual history. Anthony Pagden's stimulating but pessimistic evaluation of European intellectuals' efforts to deal with New World cultures contains a disturbing message for students of any area or region (item **902**). David Brading's monumental study of the origins, evolution and demise of a distinctive Creole national identity in Spanish America extends from the early colonial period to the middle of the 19th century and concentrates on Mexico and Peru (item **941**). Luis Vitale courageously ventures onto dangerous ground with his challenging thesis concerning the construction of a theoretical framework drawn uniquely from, and applicable to, the Latin American historical experience (item **919**).

The controversy that surrounded the Quincentenary was often disruptive, but it also produced some enlightenment about the encounter and its consequences as well as the continued relevance of events from a half millennium ago. Kirkpatrick Sale wrote perhaps the most extensive condemnation of the European conquest and colonization (item **908**), a piece especially of merit for its sharply focused statement of that position. Steven Stern's article brought together a rare combination of erudition, analytical thinking, tempered judgement, and brevity to view this era from a balanced historical and political perspective (item **1067**). From a very promising and much more specialized approach, Luis Ramos Gómez authored four articles on the complex relationships between Columbus and native Americans with an emphasis on the point of view of the latter (items **1041, 1042, 1044,** and **1043**). Valerie Flint probed the ideas and ideals of Columbus in a highly readable exploration of his "imaginative landscape" (item **972**).

In addition to the works of Ramos and Stern, several articles made especially valuable contributions to the difficult process of synthesis: José López Piñero's work on Nicolás Monardes was a solid contribution to colonial medical history (item **1006**); Allan Kuethe and Lowell Blaisdell added depth to the understanding of the

Bourbon era in Spain and colonial America (item **996**); Juan Ortega y Medina continued to provide his penetrating insights in a study of 19th-century cultural imperialism (item **1095**); Carlos Newland wrote an impressive synthesis of trends in 19th-century primary schooling (item **1094**); Florencia Mallon made a highly successful venture into the field of comparative history with her study of Indian communities and the State in Mexico and the Andes (item **887**); and Emília Viotti da Costa brought much-needed academic perspective to a review essay in the changing field of post-Cold War labor history (item **1103**).

Three edited publications brought together informed and important short pieces that contributed to the understanding of the larger aspects of Latin American history: 1) the conference proceedings from the 4th Jornadas de Historiadores Americanistas, entitled *América: religión y cosmos* (item **881**; 2) John Verano and Douglas Ubelaker's in-depth volume on disease and demography (item **864**); and 3) the special Quincentenary supplement to *The Journal of Latin American Studies*, edited by Tulio Halperín Donghi, Victor Bulmer-Thomas, and Laurence Whitehead, which contains an unusually perceptive group of articles that encompass major trends throughout the region (items **859, 873, 887, 1008, 1060, 1067,** and **1098**).

This biennium also marked the appearance of *Latin America and the Caribbean: a critical guide to research sources*, an especially useful research guide edited by Paula Covington containing a valuable group of historiographical and bibliographical essays by David Block (item **936**), Paula Covington (item **860**), Lyman L. Johnson and Susan Socolow (item **993**), Frank Safford (item **907**), and Richard Slatta (item **916**).

GENERAL

839 **Agustinos en América y Filipinas: actas del congreso internacional, Valladolid, 16–21 de abril de 1990.** v. 1–2. Edición de Isacio R. Rodríguez. Valladolid, Madrid: s.n., 1990. 2 v. (1150 p.): bibl., ill.

Proceedings of April 1990 congress on the history of the Augustinians in the Americas and Asia. A dozen of the contributions concern the Philippines, Japan, and China. The remaining 32 deal with the Americas, with topics ranging from theology to the founding of missions. Much of the research is from published sources and some from archival materials.

840 **Alberti Manzanares, Pilar.** La mujer indígena americana en *Revista de Indias*. (*Rev. Indias*, 49:187, sept./dic. 1989, p. 683–690, bibl.)

Brief summary of and comment on seven articles on Indian women published in the *Revista de Indias* from 1948–85.

841 **Alvarez, L. Alonso** *et al.* Os intercambios entre Galicia e América Latina: economía e historia. Coordinación de L. Alonso Alvarez. Santiago, Spain: Univ. de Santiago de Compostela, 1992. 191 p.: bibl., ill. (Cursos e congresos de Santiago de Compostela; 72. Publicacións en economía; 36)

History of economic relations between Galicia and Latin America from 1760s-1860s and during the late 20th century (mainly 1980s). One chapter examines Galician immigration to Latin America (1900–30). Well-documented and includes many statistical tables and graphs. [J.M. Pérez]

842 **Alzugaray, Juan José** *et al.* Los vascos y América: ideas, hechos, hombres. Coordinación de Ignacio de Loyola Arana Pérez. Madrid: Gela; Espasa-Calpe/Argantonio, 1990. 403 p.: bibl., ill., maps (some col.). (Biblioteca del V Centenario. Gran enciclopedia de España: Monografías)

Wide-ranging collection of 47 articles and essays on the Basque presence in the Americas, both North and South. Glossy pages with several illustrations.

843 **América entre nosotros: exposición itinerante.** v. 1. Madrid: Quinto Centenario, 1989. 1 v.: ill., maps (some col.) (Col. Encuentros)

Multi-authored set of a dozen general essays on Latin American history from the prehispanic period to 20th century intended to reach a popular audience.

844 Aragón y América. Coordinación de José A. Armillas Vicente y Domingo Buesa Conde. Zaragoza, Spain: Crealibros; Diputación General de Aragón, 1991. 444 p.: bibl., col. ill.

Multi-authored survey of Aragonese role in Americas from conquest through 19th century emphasizes biography including sketches of Felix de Azara, Antonio Amar y Borbón, and José Martí.

845 Avni, Haim. Judíos en América: cinco siglos de historia. Madrid: Editorial MAPFRE, 1992. 328 p.: bibl., index. (Col. América, crisol de pueblos; 1. Col. MAPFRE 1492)

Superb synthesis of the Jewish experience in the Western Hemisphere from Argentina to Canada. Avni emphasizes social history—especially immigration and community formation—and also includes salient political, diplomatic, and economic factors. Episodes of antisemitism are placed within relevant contexts.

846 Ballán, Romeo et al. Misioneros de la primera hora: grandes evangelizadores del Nuevo Mundo. Lima: Editorial Sin Fronteras, 1991. 288 p.: ill., maps.

Collection of 34 short essays intended for a general readership on the efforts of missionaries to convert and defend Indians and Africans throughout the colonial and modern eras in Spanish and Portuguese America. The writings of (some contributors Ballán, Enrique Dussel, Fernando Zolli, Oscar Rodríguez Maradiaga) often reflect a somewhat temperate version of liberation theologians' views of the relationship between large institutions and the masses.

847 Ballesteros Gaibrois, Manuel. Historia de América. Madrid: Ediciones Istmo, 1989. 706 p.: bibl., ill., index, maps (some col.). (Colegio Universitario de Ediciones Istmo; 8)

New ed. of a 1946 work (see *HLAS 13: 1173*) with a 63 p. appendix and a new introduction by José Gómez-Tabanera.

848 Barnadas, Josep María. Els catalans a les Indies, 1493–1830: buròcrates, clergues, professions liberals; assaig de panorama. v. 1–3. Barcelona, Spain: Generalitat de Catalunya, Comissió Amèrica i Catalunya, 1992. 3 v.: bibl., index. (Col. Joan Orpí)

Vol. 1 consists of an historical (mainly biographical) survey of the role of Catalans in the history of America. Vol. 2 contains a lengthy bibliography, and vol. 3 is a biographical registry of 3,461 names.

849 Block, David. History: general bibliography. (*in* Latin America and the Caribbean: a critical guide to research sources. Edited by Paula H. Covington. New York: Greenwood Press, 1992, p. 291–319)

Useful annotated listing of basic research tools (guides, periodicals, etc.) for Latin American history. Of special value is the section on "Resources," which includes descriptions of several archives in the US.

850 Cagiao, Pilar. Instituciones no oficiales gallegas a través de la acción de los emigrantes: otra imagen de América. (*in* La formación de la imagen de América Latina en España, 1898–1989. Madrid: Organización de Estados Iberoamericanos para la Educación, la Ciencia y la Cultura (OEI), 1992, p. 331–345, bibl.)

Short essay examines image of America that Galician immigrants disseminated in Spain and, particularly, in Galicia. Author explores two aspects of the process: 1) personal correspondence to family in Galicia; and 2) a genuine interest of Galician immigrants in promoting education and culture in Galicia, leading to the creation of nongovernmental institutions dedicated to that purpose. The author mentions the example of the 1926 founding in Santiago de Compostela of the *Biblioteca America* through the efforts of a Galician immigrant in Buenos Aires, Argentina. [J.M. Pérez]

851 Campesinos: kleine boeren in Latijns-Amerika vanaf 1520 [Campesinos: small holders in Latin America since 1520.] Edited by Arij Ouweneel. Amsterdam: Thela, 1993. 483 p.: appendix, bibl., graphs, ill., map, table

Volume includes 18 articles in Dutch by one American and 17 Dutch historians, sociologists, social geographers, political scientists, and anthropologists who discuss history of indigenous peoples and peasants in Guatemala, Mexico, Peru, the Andes, Paraguay, Chile, and the Caribbean. [R. Hoefte]

852 Canedo, Lino Gómez. Los gallegos en el gobierno, la milicia y la Iglesia en América. A Coruña, Spain: Xunta de Galicia,

Consellería de Relacións Institucionais e Portavoz do Goberno, Comisionado Director do V Centenario, 1991. 209 p.: bibl., col. ill. (Col. Galicia e América)

Description of Galicians in Spanish colonial administration by this pioneer of Galician studies in America. Book includes brief biographical sketches and career highlights of Galicians identified by the late Gómez Canedo. Includes an index of names and is profusely annotated. [J.M. Pérez]

853 Castañeda, Paulino and **Juan Marchena.** La jerarquía de la Iglesia americana, 1500–1850. (*Hisp. Sacra,* 40, julio/dic. 1988, p. 701–730, graphs, tables)

Extensive study of Latin American bishops includes geographical and social origins, secular versus regular backgrounds, and academic training. Nice balance between statistics and prose explanations.

854 Caudillos: dictators in Spanish America. Edited, with an introduction and notes, by Hugh M. Hamill. Norman: Univ. of Oklahoma Press, 1992. 373 p.: bibl., ill., index, map.

Thorough reworking of the editor's *Dictatorship in Spanish America* (see *HLAS 28:404a*) includes a new introduction and new selections on political and sociological theory as well as articles based on more recent research.

855 Coll i Alentorn, Miquel *et al.* Encuentro con América. Barcelona: Editorial Herder, 1988. 167 p.: bibl.

Collection of diverse conference presentations by diplomats, academics, and other public figures on the meaning of the first "encounter with America."

856 Coloquio de historia canario-americana. v. 5, pts. 3–4. Las Palmas, Spain: Ediciones del Excelentísimo Cabildo Insular de Gran Canaria, 1982. 2 v.

Pt. 3 contains wide range of articles in Spanish discussing archival sources while pt. 4 articles in Spanish, English, and French examine the history of the Canary Islands and the Atlantic islands in general from the 14th to the 19th centuries.

857 Comas i Güell, Montserrat. Els fons americans de la Biblioteca-Museu Balaguer, de Vilanova i la Geltrú. (*in* Jornades d'Estudis Catalano-Americans, *4th, Barce-*

lona, Spain, 1990. Actes. Barcelona: Generalitat de Catalunya, Comissió Amèrica i Catalunya, 1992, p. 71–75, bibl.)

Short article briefly describes founding of the Biblioteca-Museu Balaguer and its collections, which include books from the 15th to the 18th centuries, newspapers (18th-19th centuries), manuscripts, etc., all with American themes. Efforts are underway to prepare and publish a guide to the library's collections. [J.M. Pérez]

858 Congreso Internacional sobre los Dominicos y el Nuevo Mundo, *2nd, Salamanca, Spain, 1990.* Actas. Edición de José Barrado. Salamanca: Editorial San Esteban, 1990. 1037 p.: bibl., ill., index. (Los Dominicos y América; 6)

Large collection of articles on various phases of the work of the Dominican order in Latin America with heavy emphasis on the early colonial period. Contributions by both religious and secular historians.

859 Cortés Conde, Roberto. Export-led growth in Latin America, 1870–1930. (*J. Lat. Am. Stud.,* 24, Quincentenary Supplement 1992, p. 163–179)

Carefully-considered review of analyses of export-oriented economies, mainly Argentina, Brazil, and Mexico. Cortés Conde rejects the Prebisch-Singer perspective that favored inward-looking industrialization but concludes that the export-directed growth of the period, while impressive, also contained serious problems. Based on an overview of major monographs by historians and economists.

860 Covington, Paula H. General bibliography. (*in* Latin America and the Caribbean: a critical guide to research sources. Edited by Paula H. Covington. New York: Greenwood Press, 1992, p. 1–55)

Useful annotated bibliography of research guides, bibliographies, biographies, dictionaries, encyclopedias, dissertation guides, Latin American studies guides, published library catalogs, and abstracts and indexes for periodicals. Organized with general works listed first, followed by country-by-country listings.

861 Crow, John Armstrong. The epic of Latin America. 4th ed. Berkeley: Univ. of California Press, 1992. 961 p.: bibl., ill., index, map.

Revised version of a standard college text. Crow's appreciation of social and cultural history remains vital and perceptive, and he has added material on Central America, Argentina, and Latin American-US relations in the troubled 1980s.

862 Cuart Moner, Baltasar. De Bolonia a las Indias: los colegiales de San Clemente en la administración americana durante el siglo XIII (sic). (*Rev. Univ./Alcalá*, 7, 1991, p. 170–189)

Scholarly analysis of the American colonial careers of Univ. of Bologna graduates during the 18th (not 13th) century.

863 Delval, Raymond. Les Musulmans en Amérique latine et aux Caraïbes. Préface de Frédéric Mauro. Paris: L'Harmattan, 1992. 299 p.: bibl., ill., maps. (Recherches & documents: Amériques latines)

Work is first comprehensive study on 612,000 Muslims living today in Latin America and the Caribbean, one-third of them in Brazil. Traces their historical roots: Iberian colonization and trade of Sudanese slaves; 19th-century indentured labor force from what are today India and Pakistan; mass labor migrations from Central Europe, 1880–1940; recent exiles from Palestine and Lebanon. By country, gives size of community and its socio-occupational make-up and location, showing that Caribbean communities of Trinidad and Tobago, Guyana, and Suriname are the liveliest. Important acquisition for all libraries. [A. Pérotin-Dumon]

864 Disease and demography in the Americas. Edited by John W. Verano and Douglas H. Ubelaker. Washington: Smithsonian Institution Press, 1992. 294 p.: bibl., ill., index.

Twenty-five specialized studies examine infectious diseases in the Western Hemisphere from the preconquest period to the early 19th century. Includes a thoughtful introductory essay and a carefully-reasoned conclusion by the editors.

865 Durán Luzio, Juan. Bartolomé de las Casas ante la conquista de América: las voces del historiador. Heredia, Costa Rica: EUNA, 1992. 349 p.: bibl. (Col. Guayabo)

Challenging historical and literary analysis begins by explaining three crucial texts by Las Casas and proceeds to an exploration of the effects of Las Casas' writings on French essayist Michel de Montaigne and Nicaraguan poet Ernesto Cardenal.

866 Encuentro Internacional Quinto Centenario, San Juan, 1990. Impacto y futuro de la civilización española en el Nuevo Mundo: actas. Madrid?: Associación de Licenciados y Doctores Españoles en Estados Unidos, 1991. 660 p.: bibl. (Col. Encuentros: Serie Seminarios)

Unusually wide range of topics are covered in over 70 contributions, some scholarly and others mainly "thought-pieces." Subjects vary from Columbus, Cervantes, Carlos Fuentes, and technology transfer.

867 Escandell Bonet, Bartolomé. Baleares y América. Madrid: Editorial MAPFRE, 1992. 440 p.: bibl., ill., index, col. maps. (Col. Las Españas y América; 2. Col. MAPFRE 1492)

Specialized study uses biographical, economic, and sociological angles to explore influence of the Balearic Islands in Spanish America.

868 Franco Agudelo, Saúl. El paludismo en América Latina. Guadalajara, México: Editorial Univ. de Guadalajara, 1990. 288 p.: bibl., ill., map. (Col. Fin de milenio: Serie Medicina social)

Important study of the persistence of malaria in Latin America. Drawing from a variety of medical, sociological, and historical sources, the author explores the "chaotic world" of the mosquito, the impact of increasing sea and air travel, the work of the Rockefeller Foundation, and possible alternatives in public health policy.

869 500 Jahre Mestizaje in Sprache, Literatur und Kultur. Herausgegeben von Sonja M. Steckbauer und Kristin A. Müller. Salzburg: Univ. Salzburg, Institut für Romanistik, 1993. 180 p.

Proceedings of a 1992 international conference on Latin Amerian culture and literature held at Salzburg Univ. contains 8 individual contributions. Two examine general aspects concerning *mestizaje* and the multicultural shape of the region (Martin Lienhard, Rafael Gutiérrez Girardot), and three more focus on the *mestizo* image in contemporary narrative by Cortázar, Posse, and Scorza (Ernst Rudin, Karl Kohut, Lieselotte Engl).

Diverse and valuable collection of Latin Americanist studies from the Germanic scholarly milieu. [T. Hampe-Martínez]

870 García Añoveros, Jesús María. La monarquía y la Iglesia en América. Valencia?: Asociación Francisco López de Gómara, 1990. 301 p.: bibl. (La Corona y los pueblos americanos; 6)

Historical survey of the Catholic Church in Spanish America and its relationship with the Spanish crown from conquest to independence. García Añoveros sees a unique experience for the Church in America, but does not cast this exceptionality in the same terms as used by the "liberation theology" historians like Enrique Dussel.

871 Grafton, Anthony; April Shelford; and Nancy Siraisi. New worlds, ancient texts: the power of tradition and the shock of discovery. Cambridge, Mass.: Harvard Univ. Press, 1992. 282 p.: bibl., ill., index.

Insightful study of the impact of the voyages of discovery on European thought from 1450 to 1700 based on research in the manuscript collections of the New York Public Library. Emphasizes a complex evolution as opposed to a sudden revolution in the minds of Goro Dati, Francis Bacon, Jean Blaeu, Bartolomé de Las Casas, Bernardino de Sahagún and other thinkers as they grappled with new information in the context of the dominant European intellectual traditions.

872 Haber, Stephen H. Industrial concentration and the capital markets: a comparative study of Brazil, Mexico, and the United States, 1830–1930. (*J. Econ. Hist.*, 51: 3, Sept. 1991, p. 559–580, bibl., tables)

Important synthesis of history of capital formation in the textile industries of these three nations. Based on a thorough survey of the secondary literature, Haber concludes that the key factors were the presence of large and active banking institutions and government policies that allowed banks to engage in venture investments.

873 Halperín Donghi, Tulio. Backward looks and forward glimpses from a Quincentennial vantage point. (*J. Lat. Am. Stud.*, 24, Quincentenary Supplement 1992, p. 219–254)

Thoughtful analysis of the importance of the State in Latin America from colonial era through today. Author employs a healthy historical skepticism in his evaluation of the projections for a diminished State role in the "new world order." For version in Spanish, see *Revista de Occidente*, (vol. 131, abril 1992, p. 7–36).

874 Harwich Vallenilla, Nikita. Histoire du chocolat. Paris: Editions Desjonquères, 1992. 292 p.: bibl., ill., index, map, photos.

This volume, the best in a series devoted to history of tropical crops, some of which shaped tastes and created empires, deals with an indigenous food staple that Europeans adopted as an exotic hot beverage. Economist-historian shows how cacao export engendered cycles of prosperity and crisis in national economies of Venezuela, Ecuador and Brazil. [A. Pérotin-Dumon]

875 Hernández, Prócoro. Els catalans i el món indígena americà. Barcelona: Generalitat de Catalunya, Comissió Amèrica i Catalunya, 1992. 151 p.: bibl., ill. (Col. Joan Orpí)

Short three-part book on Catalans in the New World. Pt. 1 is a brief overview from discovery to present. Pt. 2 focuses on specific topics such as Catalans in Jesuit missions of Paraguay, Catalans in Alta California, etc. Pt. 3 focuses on Catalan Latin Americanists, including a brief biographical description and major works. Sources are listed for each section. [J.M. Pérez]

876 Hernández Sánchez-Barba, Mario. Castilla y América. Madrid: MAPFRE, 1992. 361 p.: bibl., index. (Col. Las Españas y América; 1. Col. MAPFRE 1492)

Broad, thematic survey of the contributions of Castile and Castilians to American history including demography, linguistics, government, urbanization, and social hierarchies as well as some stimulating theses on the impact of Castilian *mentalidades* in America.

877 Historical dictionary of the Spanish Empire, 1402–1975. Edited by James Stuart Olson *et al.* New York: Greenwood Press, 1992. 702 p.: bibl., index.

Single-volume reference tool with brief but apt entries and good balance among political, economic, and social topics. Focus is on the period from conquest to independence and written in clear style suited for undergraduates. Some longer entries contain bibliographies.

878 Istoriía Latinskoĭ Ameriki: dokolumbova ėpokha — 70-e gody XIX veka [The history of Latin America: the precolumbian epoch to the 1870s]. Redakt͡sionnaiā kollegiía, Nikolaĭ Matveevich Lavrov. Moskva: Izd-vo Nauka, 1991. 518 p.: bibl., ill., index.

In textbook treatment, scholars from the Institute of Latin American Studies and Moscow State Univ. offer a panorama of early Latin American history, including development of each of the major nations and a discussion of 19th-century Russian relations. Comprising 29 narrative chapters and a lengthy bibliography of Soviet and Western sources, this volume is the first of a planned multi-volume set on *The history of Latin America*, part of the Institute of World History's ongoing series of regional histories. Name index and contents appear in Russian and Spanish. [B. Dash]

879 Jiménez Codinach, Estela Guadalupe. The Hispanic world, 1492–1898: a guide to photoreproduced manuscripts from Spain in the collections of the United States, Guam and Puerto Rico = El mundo hispánico, 1492–1898: guía de copias fotográficas de manuscriptos españoles existentes en los Estados Unidos de América. Washington: Library of Congress: U.S. Government Printing Office, 1994. 1060 p.: bibl., ill. (some col.), index, maps.

Valuable reference tool contains a comprehensive listing of photoreproduced manuscripts from Spain in US libraries. The manuscript collections are listed by state and contain helpful information such as archive addresses and phone numbers as well as descriptions of the collections and many individual documents.

880 Jornadas de Historia de la Medicina Hispanoamericana, 2nd, Cádiz, Spain, 1986. Anales. Cádiz: Servicio de Publicaciones de la Univ. de Cádiz, 1989? 267 p.: bibl., ill.

Collection of a wide range of studies of the medical history of Spanish America covers topics from the colonial period to early 20th century. Final section includes studies of the 19th century evolution of specializations such as pediatrics, anesthesiology, and ophthalmology to urology.

881 Jornadas de Historiadores Americanistas, 4th, Santafé, Spain, 1990. América: religión y cosmos. Granada, Spain: Junta de Andalucía, Diputación Provincial de Granada; Sociedad de Historiadores Mexicanistas, 1991. 442 p.: bibl., ill., maps. (Textos del descubrimiento)

Scholars from both Europe and America contribute 26 articles on the religious and cosmological aspects of Indian America from northern Mexico to Andean South America. These studies span centuries from the precolumbian period to present and include topics such as the ceremonial practices of the preclassic Maya, the image of Quetzalcoatl in Mesoamerican religion, the political legitimacy of the Sapa Inca, attitudes toward death in 18th century New Spain, and survivals of native religion and medicine into the last decades of the 20th century.

882 Jornades d'Estudis Catalano-Americans, 2nd, Barcelona, Spain, 1986. Jornades. Barcelona: Comissió Catalana del Cinquè Centenari del Descobriment d'America, 1987. 510 p.: bibl., ill., index.

Fairly well-focused collection of articles on trade patterns in Spanish America and Catalonia'a expanding role in this commerce during the 18th and 19th centuries. The last section covers the independence period and Catalan trading activities in the Caribbean through the final years of Spanish domination in Cuba and Puerto Rico.

883 Kahle, Günter. Lateinamerika in der Politik der europäischen Mächte, 1492–1810. Köln: Böhlau Verlag, 1993. 102 p.: bibl., table.

Both the nature of its primary sources (treaties, reports, memories) and its interpretive viewpoint make this work a fine compendium of diplomatic history. Kahle, professor emeritus at Cologne University, reviews the Western Hemisphere's position in the political horizons of Spain, Portugal, France, England, and Holland from the late 15th century up to the Wars of Independence. Well-written, useful manual for beginning students of colonial Latin America. [T. Hampe-Martínez]

884 Keen, Benjamin. A history of Latin America. v. 1, Ancient America to 1910. v. 2, Independence to present. 4th ed. Boston: Houghton Mifflin, 1991. 2 v.: bibl., ill., index, maps.

Now available in both a single volume and a two volume set, this fourth ed. of the standard college textbook contains some revisions on ancient America, Columbus, colonial labor conditions, the role of women in Latin America, and the impact of the drug trade in Colombia.

885 Latin American military history: an annotated bibliography. Edited by David G. LaFrance and Errol D. Jones. New York: Garland, 1992. 734 p.: map. (Garland reference library of the humanities; 1024. Military history bibliographies; 12)

A dozen leading scholars of military history assembled bibliographies in their areas of specialization. The short but pithy introductions to each of the 12 sections are especially valuable.

886 Lepkowski, Tadeusz. Historia de América Latina en Polonia, 1968–1988: temas, problemas, métodos. (*Estud. Latinoam.*, 12, 1989, p. 283–297)

Refreshingly frank assessment of the study of Latin American history in Poland. A marginal activity among Poland's professional historians, its study reflects an "institutionalized Marxism."

Lovell, W. George. Mayans, missionaries, evidence and truth: the polemics of native resettlement in sixteenth-century Guatemala. See *HLAS 53:2696.*

887 Mallon, Florencia E. Indian communities, political cultures, and the State in Latin America, 1780–1990. (*J. Lat. Am. Stud.*, 24, Quincentenary Supplement 1992, p. 35–53)

Stimulating essay in comparative history explores differences between Mexico's mestizo polity and ethnic politics of the Andean states of Bolivia and Peru. Also contains important insights on the history of revolution in Indo-mestizo Latin America in the 20th century. Extensive, informative footnotes.

888 Martín Rodríguez, Manuel and **Antonio Malpica Cuello.** El azúcar en el encuentro entre dos mundos. Traducción de T. Cartwright. Madrid: Asociación General de Fabricantes de Azúcar de España, 1992. 287 p.: bibl., ill. (some col.), maps (some col.).

General history of sugar in Spain, Latin America, and the Caribbean from the medi-

eval period to end of 19th century covers agricultural, technological, and economic aspects. The original Spanish text is followed by an English translation. Based largely on secondary sources.

889 Mauro, Frédéric. Histoire du café. Paris: Editions Desjonquères, 1991. 249 p.: bibl., ill. (Col. Outremer)

History of coffee production throughout the world is designed for lay reader. Author, an authority on colonial Brazil, traces development of coffee industry in that country since 18th century. Notes that in Spanish America and the Caribbean coffee often replaced cacao and was a complement to sugar. [A. Pérotin-Dumon]

890 Mena, José María de. Así fue el imperio español: anécdotas, personajes, hazañas. 2. ed. Barcelona: Plaza & Janes, 1992. 211 p., 16 p. of plates: bibl., ill.

Small book on a very large topic. Stretching from the 13th century to the 20th, this fast-paced survey has more to offer the general reader than the scholar. Approximately 2/3 of the text covers Spanish America.

891 Mesquita Samara, Eni de. Mulheres das Américas: um repasse pela historiografia Latino-Americana recente. (*Rev. Bras. Hist.*, 11:21, set. 1990/fev. 1991, p. 227–239, bibl.)

Review essay on selected books and articles in Portuguese and English on the role of women in Latin America focuses on women's involvement in struggles for various forms of power. Publication dates range from 1951–89.

892 Meyer, Jean A. Historia de los cristianos en América Latina: siglos XIX y XX. México: Vuelta, 1989. 389 p.: bibl. (La Reflexión)

Broad but succinct overview of the history of the Catholic Church in Latin America also includes a chapter on growth of Protestantism. Text combines interpretive narratives of the role of religion in individual countries with provocative analytical generalizations.

893 Meyer, Jean Lauren. Histoire du sucre. Paris: Editions Desjonquères, 1989. 335 p.: bibl., ill. (Col. Outremer)

Introduction to development of sugar agriculture and industry throughout the world is helpful for understanding how sugar shaped the fate of colonial Caribbean as well as its role in 19th- and 20th-century economies of tropical Latin American countries. [A. Pérotin-Dumon]

894 Morales Padrón, Francisco. Andalucía y América. Sevilla, Spain: Ediciones Guadalquivir, 1988. 182 p.: bibl. (Biblioteca Guadalquivir; 2)

, General historical account of the interaction of Andalusia and America emphasizes the early colonial period. A chapter on 20th century Andalusian scholars specializing in American studies gives a brief but valuable portrait of a neglected area of intellectual history.

895 Mörner, Magnus. Ensayos sobre historia latinoamericana: enfoques, conceptos y métodos. Quito: Corporación Editora Nacional, 1992. 240 p.: bibl. (Biblioteca de Ciencias Sociales: 37)

Useful compendium of recently published articles and chapters in anthologies by versatile senior Latin Americanist covers historiography, problematics of social history, comparative history, the Túpac Amaru rebellion, and travel accounts as sources. [M.T. Hamerly]

896 Mörner, Magnus. Region and State in Latin America's past. Baltimore: Johns Hopkins Univ. Press, 1993. 142 p.: bibl., ill., index, maps. (Johns Hopkins symposia in comparative history)

Original contribution in historical sociology on the interaction of the nation State with various regions from the colonial period to the early 20th century. Mörner uses case studies from the Jesuit Guarani missions, early national Venezuela, the Quebra Quilos movement in Brazil, and European immigration to Argentina. Much-needed contribution in the exploration of the connections between regional history and the history of central governments.

897 Mörner, Magnus. Social and political legacies of emancipation of slavery in the Americas. (*Ibero-Am./Stockholm*, 22:1, 1992, p. 3–30, bibl., table)

General overview of recent literature on impact of emancipation and some thoughtful guiding questions for researchers. Covers Latin America, the Caribbean, and the US.

898 Murray, D.R. Slavery and the slave trade: new comparative approaches. (*LARR*, 28:1, 1993, p. 150–161)

Review article examines nine books published between 1988–91 by authors such as Philip Curtin and Alan Watson. Author draws on his firm grasp of the historiography of slavery from Frank Tannenbaum's work in the 1940s onward.

899 Navarro Azcue, Concepción. Parámetros históricos de la regionalización américana. (*Rev. Complut. Hist. Am.*, 17, 1991, p. 11–37)

Author discusses geographical theory and the nature of historical regions, and then includes case studies ranging from New Spain in the 16th century to several examples from later Latin American history.

900 Núñez Jiménez, Antonio. Reportaje del descubrimiento. Génova: F. Pirella, 1989. 179 p.: bibl., ill., index.

Interesting, often speculative approach to the evaluation of Columbus' role includes judgements of Martí, Bolívar, Marx, and several other major figures.

901 Núñez Seixas, Xosé M. O galeguismo en América, 1879–1936. Coruña, Spain: Ediciós do Castro, 1992. 325 p.: bibl. (Historia)

This is the first of the many books written on Galician nationalism that deals with that theme as manifested in America, mainly the Southern Cone. Author contends that many of the civic associations founded by Galicians in America for the purpose of helping immigrants and providing them with a sense of "Galicia" in America, later became extremes of Galician nationalism and pride, particularly in places like Argentina, where there was a large intellectual community. Book is profusely annotated and the author consulted many unpublished sources and collections, many of them private. [J.M. Pérez]

902 Pagden, Anthony. European encounters with the New World from Renaissance to romanticism. New Haven: Yale Univ. Press, 1993. 216 p.: bibl., ill., index.

Intellectual history of European response to the Americas from Columbus and Las Casas to Diderot and Humboldt. Pagden's pessimistic appraisal of Europe's quest to understand the nature of society and the individual in the New World flows from an effective blending of anthropology and philosophy. This penetrating examination of a crucial interaction in world history is necessary reading for anyone interested in the intellectual bases for modern imperialism.

903 Palma, Norman. Reflexiones sobre la destrucción de las Indias: ensayo. Bogotá: Indigo Ediciones, 1992. 69 p.: bibl.

Brief, critical philosophical discussion of the value system that supported the conquest and its persistence to the present.

904 Pérez Vidal, José. Aportación de Canarias a la población de América: su influencia en la lengua y en la poesía tradicional. Las Palmas, Spain: Cabildo Insular de Gran Canaria, 1991. 188 p.: bibl., ill., maps. (Col. Alisios; 1)

Scholarly overview of the migration of Canary Islanders to America followed by brief discussions of their settlement, organized by island and region (e.g., Santo Domingo and Texas). The last half of the book is a linguistic analysis of their contribution to the development of the Spanish language, folklore, and poetry in America with special attention to Mexico.

905 Pérez Vila, Manuel et al. Guía histórica de la nación latinoamericana. v. 1–2. Caracas: Fundación Bicentenario de Simón Bolivar; Instituto de Altos Estudios de América Latina, 1991. 2 v.: bibl., ill.

Effort to build a Latin American history emphasizes the region's geopolitical and cultural unity. This thesis works for the colonial period (vol. 1), but variations and diversity emerge thereafter (vol. 2).

906 Presencia de la Merced en América: actas del I Congreso Internacional, Madrid, 30 de abril-2 de mayo de 1991. v. 1–2. Edición de Luis Vázquez Fernández. Madrid: Revista Estudios, 1991. 2 v. (1323 p.): bibl., ill., maps.

Variety of studies on the history of the Mecedarian order in the Americas from the early colonial years to modern era. Most of the authors are members of the order.

907 Safford, Frank. History, 1750–1850: essay. (in Latin America and the Caribbean: a critical guide to research sources. Edited by Paula H. Covington. New York: Greenwood Press, 1992, p. 343–376)

Extensive bibliographical survey util-

izes a new periodization: the recognization of a "middle period" in Latin American history. Emphasizes research trends since 1960s and includes an annotated bibliography of reference works.

908 Sale, Kirkpatrick. The conquest of paradise: Christopher Columbus and the Columbian legacy. New York: Knopf; Random House, 1990. 453 p.: bibl., index, maps.

Polemical discussion by leftist social critic of effects of the European arrival to and colonization of America. Although Columbus is the central figure in this book, author's arguments go far beyond his role as an individual. Sale is critical of the personality and actions of the historical explorer but directs his most devastating criticism at the legacy of conquest and Columbian images that have emerged over five centuries. From these points of departure Sale launches his attack on European imperialism.

909 Sauer, Carl Ortwin. The early Spanish Main. New foreword by Anthony Pagden. Berkeley: Univ. of California Press, 1992. 306 p.: bibl., index, maps.

Reprint of 1966 ed. (see *HLAS 28: 448a*).

910 Scheina, Robert L. Unexplored opportunities in Latin American maritime history. (*Americas/Francisc.*, 48:3, Jan. 1992, p. 397–406)

Author discusses military, technical, economic, and biographical aspects of maritime history with useful comments regarding the location and value of primary sources.

911 Segundo, Juan Luis. El legado de Colón y la jererquía de verdades cristianas. (*in* América, 1492–1992: contribuciones a un centenario. Edición de José Joaquín Alemany. Madrid: Univ. Pontificia Comillas, 1988, p. 107–127)

Wide-ranging discussion of the conquest, the colonial Catholic Church, and the place of liberation theology in the Church's recent history.

912 Seiler, Otto J. Südamerikafahrt: deutsche Linienschiffahrt nach den Ländern Lateinamerikas, der Karibik und der Westküste Nordamerikas im Wandel der Zeiten. Herford, Germany: E.S. Mittler, 1992. 265 p.: bibl., ill. (some col.), index.

While volume is addressed to the general reader, the documentation and especially photographs and illustrations from the archives of Hapag-Lloys, Hamburg-Süd, and various other maritime and German state archives provide valuable background and information on German-Latin American shipping from 1830s to present. [C.K. Converse]

913 Simposio de CEHILA, 16th, Santo Domingo, 1989. Sentido histórico del V centenario, 1492–1992. Edición de Guillermo Meléndez. San José: Editorial Depto. Ecuménico de Investigaciones, 1992. 214 p.: bibl. (Col. Historia de la Iglesia y de la teología)

Collection of essays presents the conquest and subsequent colonial relations from various perspectives of dominated groups. Present-day implications of conquest and continuing issues associated with imperialism are major themes in many of these essays. Contributors include Enrique Dussel, Jorge Pinto Rodríguez, and Eduardo Hoornaert.

914 Simpósio Internacional A Revolucão Francesa e seu Impacto na América Latina, São Paulo, 1989. A Revolução Francesa e seu impacto na América Latina. Organição de Osvaldo Coggiola. São Paulo: Nova Stella; EDUSP; Brasília: Conselho Nacional de Desenvolvimento Científico e Tecnológico, 1990. 371 p.: bibl. (Biblioteca da república)

Collection of 28 essays by mostly Brazilian authors range from research articles with footnotes to brief "thought pieces." Though the approaches are diverse, most of the essays deal with some form of intellectual history.

915 Slatta, Richard W. Historical frontier imagery in the Americas. (*in* Seminar on the Acquisition of Latin American Library Materials, *33rd, Berkeley, California, 1988.* Latin American frontiers, borders, and hinterlands: research needs and resources. Edited by Paula Covington. Albuquerque, N.M.: SALALM; Univ. of New Mexico, 1990, p. 5–25)

Sweeping survey of the salient histories of North and South American frontiers with special attention to the conflict between farms and ranches. Informative footnotes.

916 Slatta, Richard W. History since 1850: essay. (*in* Latin America and the Caribbean: a critical guide to research sources. Ed-

ited by Paula H. Covington. New York: Greenwood Press, 1992, p. 377–405)

Carefully-crafted, concise, topical, historiographical essay emphasizes economic and social themes. An annotated bibliography is arranged by country.

917 Sport and society in Latin America: diffusion, dependency, and the rise of mass culture. Edited by Joseph Arbena. New York: Greenwood Press, 1988. 162 p.: bibl., index. (Contributions to the study of popular culture, 0198–9871; 20)

Collection of well-researched, thought-provoking essays on an important area in popular culture that deserves serious academic attention. Each essay places sport within a larger social, cultural, and/or political framework.

918 Tolentino Dipp, Hugo. Los mitos del Quinto Centenario. Santo Domingo: Editora Alfa y Omega, 1992. 165 p.

Non-scholarly polemic condemns the Spanish Conquest and five related "myths:" "the encounter of two cultures," the Columbus legacy, the civilizing mission of Spain, the conversion of the native Amerians, and the Dominican Republic's Hispanic identity.

919 Vitale, Luis. Introducción a una teoría de la historia para América Latina. Buenos Aires: Planeta, 1992. 317 p.: bibl.

Bold attempt to construct a series of coherent, interconnected generalizations about Latin American history to set it apart from the "Eurocentric model." More than a series of overly abstract theses, the book connects theory to concrete historical experiences. Vitale's approach rejects the monocausality implicit in much Marxist writing, and opts for a flexible approach that places social, ideological, ecological, and political factors alongside the economic.

920 Werz, Nikolaus. Handbuch der deutschsprachigen Lateinamerikakunde. Freiburg i. Br.: Arnold-Bergstraesser-Inst.; Arbeitsgemeinschaft Deutsche Lateinamerika-Forschung; 1992. 890 p. (Freiburger Beiträge zu Entwicklung u. Politik; 11)

Vademecum for those interested in the development of Latin American studies outside the Western Hemisphere. Contains 25 review essays concerning various scientific approaches to Latin America that have been used in Germany. The contributions, alphabetically arranged by discipline, cover from archaeology and architecture to tropical ecology and zoology. Some of the lengthiest essays concern the fields of art history (Hans Haufe), cultural anthropology (Hanns-Albert Steger), history (Horst Pietschmann), linguistics (Wolf Dietrich), literature (Karl Kohut), and music (Max Peter Baumann). In addition, two complementary essays deal with the Latin Americanist tradition in Austria and Switzerland. [T. Hampe-Martínez]

921 Zea, Leopoldo. Hispano-América siglo XIX, ruptura y reencuentro. (*in* Jornadas de Historiadores Americanistas, *2nd, Santafé, Spain, 1989.* América: encuentro y asimilación. Edición de Joaquín A. Muñoz Mendoza. Granada: Diputación Provincial de Granada, 1990, p. 157–164)

Interpretive essay views 1898 as Spain's turning point from its imperial past which then opened the way for a cultural rapproachement with Spanish America.

COLONIAL

Adorno, Rolena. The intellectual life of Bartolomé de las Casas. See item **3518.**

922 Aguirre, Angel. Inculturación misionera de los Agustinos en América. (*Rev. Agust.,* 33:102, sept./dic. 1992, p. 1229–1251)

Interesting attempt to define a new expression—"inculturation" (as distinct from acculturation)—to explain the missionary process as practiced by Augustinians and Franciscans in New Spain. In this theory, inculturation is more sensitive to local needs and is less overwhelming.

923 Alberro, Solange. Elogio de la vagancia en la América colonial: las andanzas de Francisco Manuel de Quadros en Perú, Nueva Granada y Nueva España, 1663. (*Colon. Lat. Am. Rev.,* 1:1/2, 1992, p. 161–173, bibl.)

Fascinating case study of an opportunistic Franciscan friar. An uncommon look at picaresque side of colonial society in the persona of a marginalized creole who flitted from continent to continent and from town to town. [M.T. Hamerly]

924 Albi, Julio. La defensa de las Indias, 1764–1799. Madrid: Instituto de Cooperación Iberoamericana, Ediciones Cultura Hispánica, 1987. 253 p., 8 p. of plates: bibl., ill.

Study of the Bourbon defense system

for Spain's American empire stresses the conflicts with the British in the Caribbean and North America. Author combines his own archival research with a broad reading of monographs in Spanish and English.

925 Alcina Franch, José. El mundo indígena americano a la llegada de los españoles: ¿evolución o historia? (*in* Jornadas de Historiadores Americanistas, *1st, Santafé, Spain, 1987.* América: hombre y sociedad. Presentación de Joaquín A. Muñoz Mendoza. Granada, Spain: Diputación Provincial de Granada, 1988, p. 81–96, bibl.)

Interpretive synthesis of earlier works in anthropology, archaeology, and history on precolumbian cultures. Alcina emphasizes the complexity and diversity of indigenous America as the result of the interaction of historical events and evolutionary change.

926 La América de los virreyes. v. 1. Cádiz: V Centenario del Descubrimiento y Evangelización de América, Delegación Diocesana de Cádiz-Ceuta, 1990. 1 v.: bibl., ill.

Five very general essays on various aspects of life in colonial Spanish America cover government, science and culture, and art. Its limited scholarly apparatus and broad generalizations diminish book's value for serious researchers.

Anadón, José. Historiografía literaria de América colonial. See item **3562.**

927 Los Andaluces y América. Prólogo de Manuel Chaves. Introducción y coordinación de Antonio Domínguez Ortiz. Madrid: Gela; Espasa-Calpe/Argantonio, 1991. 328 p.: bibl., ill. (some col.), maps. (Gran enciclopedia de España y América: Monografías)

Fifteen of these 17 essays explore Andalusia's impact on colonial Spanish America. The focus on art and culture is bolstered by color illustrations that include reproductions of historic maps and works of art, and photographs of metal work and architecture. A fluid style and convenient bibliographies suit this work for a broad readership.

928 Andrés Martín, Melquiades. Dinero, cultura y espiritualidad en torno al descubrimiento y evangelización. Bogotá: Consejo Episcopal Latinoamericano, 1990. 250 p.: bibl. (Col. V centenario; 39)

Book of five essays provides historical vignettes of the era of discovery and conquest. The first essay is a documented study of the financial sources for Columbus' first voyage. The remaining four explore the intellectual and religious climate of Spain and the work of the Franciscans in America.

929 Ayala, Manuel José de. Diccionario de gobierno y legislación de Indias. t. 4–11. Edición y estudios de Marta Milagros del Vas Mingo. Madrid: Instituto de Cooperación Iberoamericana; Ediciones de Cultura Hispánica, 1989–1993. 8 v.: bibl., ill., index.

Reedition of 1936 Altamira edition of work by colonial jurist includes useful indexes. These eight most recent volumes cover topics from *comisarios* to *preferencias*.

930 Barceló F. de la Mora, José Luis and **José Luis Barceló Mezquita.** Summa Colombina: diccionario enciclopédico de Colón. Madrid: Sociedad Estatal Quinto Centenario: Progensa, 1990. 512 p.: ill., maps.

Single vol. reference work probably intended for popular consumption. Interesting illustrations, but lacks footnotes and bibliography.

931 Batista, Juan. La estrategia española en América durante el siglo de las luces. Madrid: Editorial MAPFRE, 1992. 284 p.: bibl., index, maps. (Col. Armas y América; 1. Col. MAPFRE 1492)

Sweeping synthesis of Spain's 18th-century efforts to hold its empire from Florida to the Nootka Sound to the Juan Fernández Islands to the Malvinas Islands. Author includes discussions of the contributions of strategic analysts such as the Marqués de Santa Cruz as well as the implementation of defense policies and the conduct of war.

932 Baudot, Georges. La Corona y la fundación de los reinos americanos. Valencia, Spain: Asociación F. López de Gómara, 1992. 224 p.: bibl. (La Corona y los pueblos americanos; 5)

Broad survey of 16th-century Spanish America with the crown as the centerpiece. Solid version of history "from the top down" in which Baudot traces the impact of the crown at various levels in the political, economic, and cultural life of the American colonies.

933 Baudot, Georges. Cosmogonía indígena de América y encuentro de dos mundos. (in Constelaciones de modernidad: anuario conmemorativo del V centenario de la llegada de España a América. México: Univ.

Autónoma Metropolitana Unidad Azcapotzalco, 1990, p. 29–48)

Impressive attempt to grasp the cosmogonical, philosophical, and perceptual problems of the Indians in the face of the European conquest.

934 Baudot, Georges. La frontera imaginada: fronteras políticas y fronteras imaginarias en la fundación de la América virreinal. (in Congreso Internacional sobre Fronteras en Iberoamérica Ayer y Hoy, *1st, Tijuana, Mexico, 1989.* Memoria. Edición de Alfredo Félix Buenrostro Ceballos. Mexicali: Univ. Autónoma de Baja California, 1990, t. 1, p. 33–45)

Historical sketch of 16th-century myths and legends concerning imaginary lands and peoples of America from Cibola to Paititi and the impact of these notions on the Spanish mind. Uses both archival and published sources.

935 Biblioteca Nacional (Spain). Catálogo de manuscritos de América existentes en la Biblioteca Nacional. Edición de Julián Paz. Revisión de Clotilde Olarán y Mercedes Jalón. 2a. ed. Madrid: Ministerio de Cultura, 1992. 529 p.: index.

Revised and expanded version of the catalog originally edited by Julián Paz and published in 1944. The 1992 ed. contains 1,610 listings accompanied by brief descriptions of the manuscripts and a 59-page alphabetical index.

936 Block, David. Themes and sources for missionary history in Hispanic America. (in Seminar on the Acquisition of Latin American Library Materials, *33rd, Berkeley, California, 1988.* Latin American frontiers, borders, and hinterlands: research needs and resources. Edited by Paula Covington. Albuquerque, N.M.: SALALM; Univ. of New Mexico, 1990, p. 62–71)

Effective and informative discussion of recent scholarship on colonial missions.

937 Borah, Woodrow. The historical demography of aboriginal and colonial America: an attempt at perspective. 2nd. ed. (in The native population of the Americas in 1492. Edited by William M. Denevan. Madison, Wisc.: Univ. of Wisconsin Press, 1992, p. 13–34)

Historiographical survey of demographical studies of native Americans in the colonial period by one of the major figures in the field. Although somewhat dated (original was written in 1965), Borah has provided a few revisions and a two-page addendum on works in the 1970s.

938 Borah, Woodrow. Introduction. (*in* International Congress of Americanists, *46th, Amsterdam, 1988.* "Secret judgments of God:" Old World disease in colonial Spanish America. Edited by Noble David Cook and W. George Lovell. Norman, Oklahoma: Univ. of Oklahoma Press, 1991, p. 3–19)

Sophisticated overview of research and research problems in the study of epidemic disease including explanations of "virgin soil epidemics" and disease origins. The last section contains ideas for the direction of future research.

939 Bordejé y Morencos, Fernando de. Tráfico de Indias y política oceánica. Madrid: Editorial MAPFRE, 1992. 341 p.: bibl., ill., index. (Col. Mar y América; 1. Col. MAPFRE 1492)

Historical survey of Spain's imperial trade and naval policies from the early 1500s to the late 1700s. Based on published monographs and also considerable archival research. Especially strong coverage of the last half of the 16th century.

940 La botánica en la Expedición Malaspina, 1789–1794: Pabellón Villanueva, Real Jardín Botánico, octubre-noviembre 1989. Madrid: Turner, 1989. 218 p.: bibl, ill. (some col.) (Col. Encuentros: Serie Catálogos)

Lavish catalog of 264 water colors of flora drawn and painted during the Malaspina Expedition and exhibited at the Real Jardín Botánico in 1989 in commemoration of the Expedition's 200th anniversary. Includes eight essays by prominent scholars on the expedition's scientists, especially Antonio Pineda and Tadeo Haenke, and their work. See also item **4083.** [M.T. Hamerly]

941 Brading, David A. The first America: the Spanish monarchy, Creole patriots, and the liberal State, 1492–1867. Cambridge, England: Cambridge Univ. Press, 1991. 761 p.: bibl., ill., index.

Important work in intellectual and political history set within a comparative framework. Brading explores the texts of major commentators over more than three cen-

turies to trace the idea of Creole national identity in Spanish America with emphasis on New Spain/Mexico and Peru. Study incorporates the complex interactions of the State, the Church and native Americans within Creole efforts to devise a cohesive polity and culture.

942 Bravo, Concepción. Cincuenta años de edición y estudios de fuentes documentales y crónicas de Indias en España. (*Rev. Indias,* 50:188, enero/abril 1990, p. 9–49, appendix)

Thoughtful discussion of works often neglected in historiographical studies. Includes well-organized and extensive bibliography.

943 Bruit, Héctor H. América Latina: quinhentos anos entre a resistencia e a revolução. (*Rev. Bras. Hist.,* 10:20, março/agosto 1990, p. 147–171)

Provocative essay emphasizes a "silent" resistance to conquest and colonial domination as a central theme in Latin American history. Conceptual framework based on Foucault.

944 Buelna Serrano, Elvira. Modernidad y contramodernidad de la Compañía de Jesús. (*in* Constelaciones de modernidad: anuario conmemorativo del V centenario de la llegada de España a América. México: Univ. Autónoma Metropolitana Unidad Azcapotzalco, 1990, p. 49–78, bibl.)

Brief, pointed essay on the internal divergences within and external influences on the Jesuits in the two centuries leading up to their expulsion from America. Emphasizes the differences between their innovative activities in the Americas and their conservative "anti-modern" position in Spain.

945 Calderón de Cuervo, Elena. Las cartas de Amerigo Vespucci: hacia la conceptualización discursiva del Nuevo Mundo. (*Cuad. Am.,* 6:33, mayo/junio 1992, p. 91–107, bibl.)

Textual analysis of Vespucci's writings with the main purpose of providing insights into the motives and ideas of the Italian navigator and writer as they were shaped by his historical environment. Calderón de Cuervo sees these texts as a successful exercise in the "rhetoric of persuasion" through which Vespucci won acceptance for himself and his version of the New World.

946 Carabias Torres, Ana María. Excolegiales mayores en la administración española y americana durante el reinado de Felipe V. (*Rev. Univ./Alcalá,* 7, 1991, p. 55–93, graphs, tables)

Preliminary investigation of the contribution of Spanish universities to the colonial bureaucracy includes a list of 210 officials.

947 Casas, Bartolomé de las. De regia potestate. Edición de Jaime González Rodríguez. Introducción de Antonio-Enrique Pérez Luño [and] Quaestio theologalis. Edición de Antonio Larios y Antonio García del Moral. Madrid: Alianza, 1990. 488 p.: bibl., index. (Obras completas; 12)

Vol. 12 of a 14 vol. ed. of the writings of Las Casas. Both works in this volume are accompanied by useful introductions and editorial commentary. According to the editors, this publication contains the first edited version of *Quaestio theologalis.*

948 Casas, Bartolomé de las. De unico vocationis modo. Edición de Paulino Castañeda Delgado y Antonio García del Moral. Madrid: Alianza, 1990. 708 p.: bibl., index. (Obras completas; 2)

Second vol. in a series of Las Casas' complete works. Introductory essays cover historiographical themes. Textual footnotes provide additional commentary.

949 Casas, Bartolomé de las. The devastation of the Indies: a brief account. Translated from the Spanish by Herma Briffault. Introduction by Bill M. Donovan. Baltimore: Johns Hopkins Univ. Press, 1992. 138 p.: bibl., ill.

Paperbook ed. of the 1974 translation with a 1992 introduction by Donovan.

950 Casas, Bartolomé de las. In defense of the Indians: the defense of the Most Reverend Lord, Don Fray Bartolomé de las Casas, of the Order of Preachers, late Bishop of Chiapa, against the persecutors and slanderers of the peoples of the New World discovered across the seas. Translated and edited by Stafford Poole. Foreword by Martin E. Marty. DeKalb: Northern Illinois Univ. Press, 1992. 385 p.: bibl., ill.

Long-awaited translation of Las Casas' crucial work successfully combines scholarship and readability. Translator Poole modernized the text by moving citations from the body of the work into footnotes and also

added a "translator's commentary" for observations of value to scholars.

951 Casas, Bartolomé de las. Witness: writings of Bartolomé de las Casas. Edited and translated by George William Sanderlin. Foreword by Gustavo Gutiérrez. Maryknoll, N.Y.: Orbis Books, 1992. 182 p: bibl.

Republication of the 1971 anthology with revisions in the original introduction and a 1992 foreward by Gutiérrez.

952 Castañeda, Carmen. Student migration to colonial urban centers: Guadalajara and Lima. (*in* Migration in colonial Spanish America. Edited by David J. Robinson. Cambridge: Cambridge Univ. Press, 1990, p. 128–142, graphs, maps, tables)

Comparative study of college student migration to Guadalajara, Mexico during the 1700s and to Lima, Peru between 1587 and 1621. Illuminates relationships between spatial and social mobility and the pull attraction of cities. [M.T. Hamerly]

953 Cerezo Martínez, Ricardo. La proyección marítima de España en la época de los Reyes Católicos. Madrid: Ministerio de Defensa, Instituto de Historia y Cultura Naval, 1991. 337 p.: bibl., ill., index, maps. (Historia de la Marina española)

General treatment of the Spanish navy from medieval times into the early 16th century includes political, economic, and scientific dimensions as well as naval history.

954 Colón, Fernando. The life of the Admiral Christopher Columbus: by his son Ferdinand. Translated, annotated, and with a new introduction by Benjamin Keen. 2nd ed. New Brunswick, N.J.: Rutgers Univ. Press, 1992. 398 p.: bibl., ill., index, maps.

Republication of the 1959 ed. with only a few "trifling changes in the preface" and some revisions in the translation. The introduction, "Christopher Columbus in History: Images of the Man and his Work, 1492–1992," is a 46-page essay that places Fernando Colón's biography in its historical and historiographical context and includes some of the most recent works on the early colonial period.

955 Columbus, Christopher. The Columbus papers: the Barcelona letter of 1493, the landfall controversy, and the Indian guides; a facsimile edition of the unique copy

in the New York Public Library. Edited by
Mauricio Obregón with a new English translation by Lucia Graves. New York: Macmillan, 1991. 85 p.: bibl., ill. (some col.).
    Reproduction of the Barcelona letter
along with an English translation. Obregón's
able introductory text includes a defense of
Morison's conclusions concerning the Columbus expedition's first landfall at San
Salvador.

956   Columbus, Christopher. El primer
        viaje de Cristóbal Colón. Edición de Ju-
lio F. Guillén y Tato. Madrid: Editorial Naval,
1990. 213 p.: bibl., ill. (some col.) (Hombres,
hechos e ideas; 23)
    Reprint of 1945 ed. of Columbus' diary
of his first voyage with brief introduction and
annotation by the editor.

**957   Columbus documents: summaries of
        documents in Genoa.** Translated by
Luciano F. Farina. Edited by Luciano F. Farina
and Robert W. Tolf. Detroit, Mich.: Omni-
graphics, 1992. 195 p.: index.
    Descriptive and evaluative guide to 179
archival documents pertaining to the life of
Christopher Columbus. A brief introduction
and an extensive 55-page index enhance the
usefulness of this impressive work.

958   Comadrán Ruiz, Jorge. Los sacerdotes
        criollos y las prelaturas indianas dur-
ante el período hispánico. (*Rev. Hist. Am. Argent.*, 15:29, 1989, p. 75–136, appendix, bibl.)
    Author argues that American-born
elites were able to succeed in colonial civil or
Church administration. Nonetheless, because
Creoles tended not to enjoy the *mayorazgo,*
they often voluntarily chose to forego careers
which would involve moving far from their
native region, choosing instead to tend their
local economic interests. Includes a brief
catalog of 216 Creoles who rose to rank of
bishop. [SMS]

**959   Congreso Internacional sobre los Do-
        minicos y el Nuevo Mundo, 3rd, Gra-
nada, Spain, 1990.** Actas. Madrid: Editorial
Deimos, 1990. 850 p.: maps.
    Contains a wide variety of scholarly ar-
ticles and preliminary research projects most
of which concern colonial Spanish America.
Includes studies of Francisco Ximénez's early
18th-century work on Maya ethnography and
the relations between Dominicans and encomenderos in Tucumán during early 1600s.

**960   Congreso Internacional sobre los Fran-
        ciscanos en el Nuevo Mundo, 3rd, La
Rábida, Spain, 1989.** Actas. Madrid: Editorial
Deimos, 1989. 1286 p.: bibl., ill., index.
    Proceedings of a 1989 Congress on
Franciscan history includes 29 studies on a
variety of topics—from a listing of records relating to Franciscans in the books of registry
in the AGI (1551–1650) to several studies of
missionary activity ranging from Mexico to
Mosquitia to Paraguay.

**961   Cook, Noble David and W. George
        Lovell.** Unraveling the web of disease.
(*in* International Congress of Americanists,
46th, Amsterdam, 1988. Secret judgements of
God: Old World disease in colonial Spanish
America. Edited by Noble David Cook and
W. George Lovell. Norman: Univ. of Oklahoma Press, 1991, p. 213–242)
    Convenient, clearly-expressed, ex-
tended definitions of the major epidemic diseases that spread through the native American population in the Spanish colonial period.
Also includes discussion of "the causal chain
of disease." Drawn from the basic monographic studies.

962   Cortés Alonso, Vicenta. Fuentes docu-
        mentales de América en España. (*Rev.
Indias*, 49:187, sept./dic. 1989, p. 601–612)
    Valuable listing of guides, inventories,
and catalogs for archives published in Spain
from 1939–89, including state and regional
archives.

963   Cro, Stelio. Montaigne y Pedro Mártir:
        las raíces del buen salvaje. (*Rev. Indias,*
50:190, sept./dic. 1990, p. 665–685)
    Comparative analysis of texts by Mon-
taigne and Martyr. Cro's main thesis is that
Montaigne relied more on the writings and,
to some extent, the ideas of Martyr in the development of the notion of the "noble savage" than the works of the Spanish
chroniclers.

964   Davidson, Basil. Columbus: the bones
        and blood of racism. (*Race Cl.*, 33:3,
Jan./March 1992, p. 17–25)
    Accusatory discussion of Columbus as
"the father of the slave trade in the Americas." More anti-imperialist ideology than
scholarship.

965   Delgado Barrado, José Miguel. Las rela-
        ciones comerciales entre España e In-
dias durante el siglo XVI: estado de cuestión.

(*Rev. Indias,* 50:188, enero/abril 1990, p. 139–150)

Useful historiographical study emphasizes the need for additional research in 16th-century trade and trade policies.

966 Duviols, Jean-Paul. Théodore de Bry et ses modèles français. (*Caravelle/Toulouse,* 58, 1992, p. 7–16, plates)

Interpretive study of the origins and evolution of De Bry's works on the Americas.

967 Escobedo Mansilla, Ronald. Historiografía española sobre hacienda indiana, 1940–1989. (*Rev. Indias,* 50:188, enero/abril 1990, p. 127–137)

Well-organized review of the scholarship in Spain on colonial finance emphasizes recent publications.

Espiritualidad barroca colonial: santos y demonios en América. See item **1156.**

968 Esteva Fabregat, Claudio. La corona española y el indio americano. v. 1. Valencia, Spain: Asociación Francisco López de Gómara, 1989. 1 v.: bibl. (La Corona y los pueblos americanos; 4)

Interesting perspective on the conquest written by an anthropologist with a firm grasp of native American culture and the legislation, policies, and politics of the Spanish colonial system.

969 Fernández Gaytán, José. Don Pedro Porter y Cassante, navegante, descubridor, gobernador de Chile y almirante de la Mar del Sur. (*Rev. Hist. Naval,* 10:39, 1992, p. 75–96, bibl., ill.)

Biography of lesser-known 17th-century naval officer who discharged several important offices, including those of explorer of the Gulf of California, Admiral of the South Sea Fleet, and interim Captain General of Chile. [M.T. Hamerly]

970 Figueras, Antonio. Los dominicos en las luchas de América. Guatemala: Convento de Santo Domingo, 1988. 285 p.: bibl., index.

Previously unpublished 1944 manuscript is obviously dated by more recent studies, but has historiographical value because of time and circumstances of original writing.

971 Fisher, John. Trade, war and revolution: exports from Spain to Spanish America, 1797–1820. Liverpool, England: Institute of Latin American Studies, Univ. of

Liverpool, 1992. 145 p.: appendices, bibl. (Monograph Series; 16)

Heavily quantitative study of Spanish exports to America based on the registers of departures in the Archivo General de Indias. The statistics reveal the decline of trade during the uncertain war years of the late 18th century and the growing importance of regional ports in the Americas.

972 Flint, Valerie I.J. The imaginative landscape of Christopher Columbus. Princeton, N.J.: Princeton Univ. Press, 1992. 233 p.: bibl., ill. (some col.), index.

Careful exploration of the "mental world" of Columbus covers his study of maps, his known reading, and his exposure to "sea stories." Flint emphasizes Columbus' fascination with the Far East and the dominant influence of medieval Christianity in his worldview.

973 Galera Gómez, Andrés. La Ilustración española y el conocimiento del Nuevo Mundo: las ciencias naturales en la Expedición Malaspina, 1789–1794; la labor científica de Antonio Pineda. Madrid: Centro de Estudios Históricos, Consejo Superior de Investigaciones Científicas, Depto. de Historia de la Ciencia, 1988. 277 p.: bibl., ill. (some col.), index. (Publicaciones del C.S.I.C. conmemorativas del V centenario del descubrimiento de América)

Notwithstanding title, this fine book examines the scientific and other labors of naturalist Antonio de Pineda, one of the Malaspina Expedition's principal scientists. Exceptionally well-researched. [M.T. Hamerly]

974 Gámez Amián, Aurora. Las grandes compañías malagueñas para el comercio con América, 1785–1794. (*Rev. Indias,* 51:191, enero/abril 1991, p. 58–96, appendices, graphs, tables)

Detailed statistical study of the brief flurry of trade between private companies of the port of Málaga and the Spanish colonial ports in America, mainly Veracruz.

975 García Fuentes, Lutgardo. Sevilla, los vascos y América: las exportaciones de hierro y manufacturas metálicas en los siglos XVI, XVII y XVIII. Madrid?: Fundación BBV; Laida, 1991. 331 p.: bibl., ill.

Well-researched study of the role of Basques in Spain and the Spanish empire. The text goes beyond the production and trade of iron and other metals to provide insights into this important sector of the colonial economy. Balanced blend of quantitative material and analytical narrative.

976 Garrido, Pablo María. Presencia de los Carmelitas de Castilla en la evangelización de América. (*Hisp. Sacra*, 43, enero/junio 1991, p. 205–226)

Highly specialized study of the work of the Carmelite order emphasizes biographical sketches.

977 Gelman, Jorge Daniel and **Carlos Malamud.** La economía colonial americana en los siglos XVII y XVIII: la consolidación en las élites locales. (*Rábida/Huelva*, 11, marzo 1992, p. 48–57)

Well-organized essay on the rise and consolidation of regional elites within the Spanish empire. A convergence of imperial and regional elite interests made for a "marriage of convenience" that enabled the system to survive this crucial period. Mentions the names of some authors of secondary works in the text, but there are no footnotes.

978 Gil, Juan. La almoneda de la *Victoria*. (*Anu. Estud. Am.*, 45:1, 1988, suplemento, p. 105–116)

Detailed description of the condition of and the 1523 sale of the *Victoria*, the surviving ship of the Magellan expedition's circumnavigation of the globe.

979 Gil, Juan. Historiografía española sobre el descubrimiento y descubrimientos. (*Rev. Indias*, 49:187, sept./dic. 1989, p. 779–816)

Survey of Spanish historical treatments of the discovery period written since the Spanish Civil War. Organized around three main themes: 1) Columbus and his voyages; 2) exploration of the Atlantic, including Vespucci; and 3) exploration of the Pacific, including Magellan. Brief but valuable comment on the difficult environment for historical research in Spain during the 1940s.

980 Gran Canaria e Indias durante los primeros Austrias: documentos para su historia. Recopilación de Manuel Lobo Cabrera. Canarias: Comisión de Canarias para la Conmemoración del V Centenario del Descubrimiento de América, 1990. 540 p.: bibl., index.

These extracts from the notarial archive of Las Palmas are accompanied by a thorough 57-page index and an informative introduction that includes a description of the archive.

981 Gruzinski, Serge. L'Amérique de la conquête: peinte par les Indiens du Mexique. Paris: Unesco; Flammarion, 1991. 238 p.: bibl., ill. (some col.), index, maps.

Study of the Spanish conquest as it appeared in the visual works of Indian artists. Profusely illustrated with numerous reproductions of the original works (many in color) accompanied by extensive commentaries and their historical accounts.

982 Guarda, Gabriel. Los laicos en la cristianización de América. Santiago: Ediciones Univ. Católica de Chile, 1987. 187 p.: bibl., ill. (Investigación)

Well-constructed survey of the role of lay members of the Catholic Church in the colonial period based on scholarly monographs, published documents, and archival material. Effective combination of biography, historical sociology, and religious history. Most examples of general tendencies are drawn from New Spain, Peru, and Chile.

983 Guerra, François-Xavier. La revolución francesa y su recepción en el mundo hispánico. (*Cuad. CENDES*, 12, sept./dic. 1989, p. 123–152)

Thought-provoking general essay explores "the echoes" of revolutionary acts of the 1780s and 1790s and the influence of the idea of the nation as a broadly-inclusive sociopolitical unit.

984 Gutiérrez, Gustavo. Dios o el oro en las Indias: siglo XVI. Salamanca, Spain: Ediciones Sígueme, 1989. 162 p.: bibl. (Pedal; 204)

Provocative, somewhat polemical explanation of the theology of Bartolomé de las Casas particularly as applied in his defense of the Indians.

985 Gutiérrez Escudero, Antonio. América: descubrimiento de un mundo nuevo. Madrid: Ediciones Istmo, 1990. 358 p.: bibl., maps. (Col. La Historia en sus textos)

Book of selected documents on the first encounter prefaced with an extended introduction by Gutiérrez Escudero.

986 Hardoy, Jorge E. Localización y causas de abandono de las ciudades hispanoamericanas durante las primeras décadas del siglo XVI. (*in* Nuevas perspectivas en los estudios sobre historia urbana latinoamericana. Buenos Aires: Instituto Internacional de Medio Ambiente y Desarrollo América Latina, 1989, p. 9–39)

Analytical discussion of the reasons for the founding and survival of cities such as Santo Domingo and the failure and abandonment of locations such as Darién. Among other critical factors, Hardoy identifies the presence of large Indian populations, proximity to valuable resources, and the relations between Spaniards and local population.

987 Hehrlein, Yacin. Mission und Macht: die politisch-religiöse Konfrontation zwischen dem Dominikanerorden in Peru und dem Vizekönig Francisco de Toledo, 1569–1581. Mainz, Germany: Matthias-Grünewald-Verlag, 1992. 173 p.: bibl. (Walberberger Studien der Albertus-Magnus-Akademie: Theologische Reihe; 16)

Study based on extensive research in Spanish, Peruvian, and Italian archives. Emphasizes extent and ruthlessness of Viceroy Francisco de Toledo's victory over the Dominican order. While Spanish power was enhanced, the still powerful Dominicans lost their position in the secular arena. [C.K. Converse]

988 Hernández Sánchez-Barba, Mario. La monarquía española y América: un destino histórico común. Madrid: Ediciones Rialp, 1990. 197 p. (Libros de historia; 32)

Broad, interpretive essay on the administrative-legal role of the Spanish monarchy as the focal point of the Spanish empire. Lacks bibliography and other scholarly apparatus.

989 Herren, Ricardo. La conquista erótica de las Indias. Barcelona: Planeta, 1991. 268 p., 8 p. of plates: bibl., ill., index, maps. (Memoria de la historia; 53. Episodios)

Well-written account of the sexual activism of Spanish conquistadores among native American women during the first 40 years after conquest. Effective synthesis based on secondary works and published sources but lacks a feminist analytical perspective.

990 Higuera, Gonzalo. La conquista de América, el derecho internacional y los derechos humanos. (*in* América, 1492–1992: contribuciones a un centenario. Edición de José Joaquín Alemany. Madrid: Univ. Pontificia Comillas, 1988, p. 7–42)

Explains Francisco de Vitoria's views and his role as one of the first major commentators on human rights in an international context.

991 Hijano Pérez, María de los Angeles. El municipio iberoamericano en la historiografía española. (*Rev. Indias,* 50:188, enero/abril 1990, p. 83–94, bibl.)

Forthright appraisal of the relative lack of work in this area includes suggestions for increasing the scholarly effort in Spain.

992 La imagen del Indio en la Europa moderna. Sevilla: Consejo Superior de Investigaciones Científicas, Fundación Europea de la Ciencia, Escuela de Estudios Hispano-Americanos, 1990. 514 p.: bibl., ill., index. (Publicaciones de la Escuela de Estudios Hispano-Americanos de Sevilla; 353)

Valuable collection of articles on an important topic. Written by an international array of scholars, these articles include analyses of a variety of 16th- and 17th-century European perspectives on native Americans.

993 Johnson, Lyman L. and **Susan M. Socolow.** Colonial history: essay. (*in* Latin America and the Caribbean: a critical guide to research sources. Edited by Paula H. Covington. New York: Greenwood Press, 1992, p. 321–342)

Succinct historiographical essay covers the last 25 years of publications in colonial history. Authors emphasize social and economic history and include an annotated bibliography.

994 Kaspar, Oldrich. Fuentes para el estudio de la historia de viajes de los misioneros checos, moravos y silesios de la Compañía de Jesús al Nuevo Mundo en los siglos XVII y XVIII conservadas en Archivo General de Indias de Sevilla. (*Rev. Indias,* 52:194, enero/abril 1992, p. 165–180)

Impressive historiographical and archival discussion of a highly specialized topic.

995 Klor de Alva, J. Jorge. Colonialism and postcolonialism as (Latin) American mirages. (*Colon. Lat. Am. Rev.,* 1:1/2, 1992, p. 3–23, bibl.)

Provocative essay maintains that the terms "colonial" and "postcolonial" are anachronistic when applied to preindependence core areas of Latin America. Author argues that while indigenous peoples were "colonized," places like Mexico—in which native-born Spaniards, mestizos, and mulattoes were in the majority—did not resemble later "colonies" established by industrializing European nations in which small groups of transplanted foreigners controlled large native populations. [R. Haskett and S. Wood]

996 Kuethe, Allan J. and **Lowell Blaisdell.** French influence and the origins of the Bourbon colonial reorganization. (*HAHR*, 71: 3, August 1991, p. 579–607)

Carefully-researched article is a basic revision of the Bourbon reform in Spanish colonial history. Focusing on commercial policy, the authors conclude that the Spanish government acted under its own terms and in its own interest in the reform of the colonial system. Based on archival research.

997 Laboa, Juan María and **José A. Almandoz.** Presencia eclesiástica en la historia y colonización de América: razones y logros. (*in* América, 1492–1992: contribuciones a un centenario. Edición de José Joaquín Alemany. Madrid: Univ. Pontificia Comillas, 1988, p. 165–188)

Response to the critiques of the role of Spanish Catholicism by Vargas Llosa and Octavio Paz asserts the importance of clerics in the defense of native Americans. Includes some historiographical commentary.

998 Labrador, Carmen. Política educativa de España en América, 1790–1795. (*in* América, 1492–1992: contribuciones a un centenario. Edición de José Joaquín Alemany. Madrid: Univ. Pontificia Comillas, 1988, p. 231–270, appendix)

Study gives several examples of change in educational policy including the founding of schools of navigation, a medical amphitheater in Lima, and a "colegio" for American youth in Granada. The last half of the article covers the expansion of the periodical press in America.

999 Langue, Frédérique. Bibliografía minera colonial. (*Anu. Estud. Am.*, 45:1, 1988, suplemento, p. 137–162, bibl.)

Listing of scholarly works in Spanish and English includes sections on general studies of mining and region-by-region listings of specialized studies.

1000 Lavrin, Asunción. Misión de la historia e historiografía de la Iglesia en el período colonial americano. (*Anu. Estud. Am.*, 46:2, 1989, suplemento, p. 11–54)

Comprehensive survey of scholarly writing on the Catholic Church includes histories written in the colonial period as well as the 19th and 20th centuries. Includes commentary on the early religious chronicles and more recent specialized studies of the regular orders, the Inquisition, missionary work, and general Church histories.

1001 Lazar, Moshe. Scorched parchments and tortured memories: the "Jewishness" of the Anussim—crypto-Jews. (*in* Cultural encounters: the impact of the Inquisition in Spain and the New World. Berkeley: Univ. of California Press, 1991, p. 176–206)

Author combines secondary works with archival sources to reconstruct the scattered writings together with poems, songs, and other oral traditions used by the Anussim to preserve their culture in the face of difficult conditions. Lazar emphasizes the role of women in this process.

1002 Levaggi, Abelardo. Juzgados y jueces de Indias en Canarias, siglo XVII: una contribución al estudio del contrabando americano. (*Publ. Inst. Estud. Iberoam.*, 8:6, 1989, p. 97–118)

Archival sources support this discussion of the legal and organizational foundations and eventual corruption of the judgeships located on the Canary Islands.

1003 Levaggi, Abelardo. Notas sobre la vigencia de los derechos indígenas y la doctrina indiana. (*Rev. Complut. Hist. Am.*, 17, 1991, p. 79–91)

Brief, terse overview of the Spanish discussion and debates concerning the rights of native Americans from Las Casas to Solórzano y Pereya.

1004 Lira Montt, Luis. La concesión de títulos de Castilla a los habitantes en Indias. (*Bol. Acad. Chil. Hist.*, 54:98, 1987, p. 169–197)

Well-organized examination of royal concessions of land to the colonial aristocracy concentrates on the late 18th century. Includes royal requirements for such concessions. Based on archival research.

1005 López Medel, Tomás. Colonización de América: informes e testimonios, 1549–1572. Dirección de Luciano Pereña. Madrid: Consejo Superior de Investigaciones Científicas, 1990. 378 p. (Corpus Hispanorum de pace; 28)

Collection of documents from the career of Tomás López who served the Spanish Crown in various positions in Guatemala, New Spain, and New Granada from the 1540s–60s. A reform-minded official, López wrote letters and reports that frequently criticized existing practices and advocated change. Brief but helpful introduction.

1006 López Piñero, José M. Las "nuevas medicinas" americanas en la obra— 1565-1574—de Nicolás Monardes. (*Asclepio/ Madrid*, 42:1, 1990, p. 3–67, bibl., table)

Excellent combination of biography and medical history portrays Monardes' European introduction of "new medicines" from America. Extensive footnotes and bibliography.

1007 Lucena Giraldo, Manuel and **Juan Pimentel Igea.** Los "Axiomas políticos sobre la América" de Alejandro Malaspina. Aranjuez, Spain: Doce Calles; Madrid: Sociedad Estatal Quinto Centenario, 1991. 202 p.: bibl., ill. (some col.) (Theatrum naturae: Serie El Naturalista y su época)

New ed. of Malaspina's critical report on the state of Spain's American empire in the late 18th century accompanies introductory essays that provide biographical background and historical context.

Lucena Salmoral, Manuel. América 1492: retrato de un continente hace quinientos años. See *HLAS 53:158.*

1008 Lynch, John. The institutional framework of colonial Spanish America. (*J. Lat. Am. Stud.*, 24, Quincentenary Supplement 1992, p. 69–81)

Impressive synthesis of the history of Spanish colonial administration casts the role of governmental institutions in their political and social contexts. Emphasis on the assertion of the "absolutist state" by the Bourbons after 1750.

1009 Madariaga, Salvador de. Vida del muy magnífico señor don Cristóbal Colón. 9. ed. Buenos Aires: Editorial Sudamericana, 1991. 542 p.: bibl., ill., index, maps.

Reprint of the 1940 ed. (see *HLAS 6: 2819*).

1010 Maddison, Francis. Tradition and innovation: Columbus' first voyage and Portuguese navigation in the fifteenth century. (*in* Circa 1492: art in the age of exploration.

Edited by Jay A. Levenson. Washington: National Gallery of Art; New Haven: Yale University Press, 1991, p. 89–94, ill.)

Historical explanation of the development of navigational instruments during the era of discovery was written to accompany an exhibit at the National Gallery of Art in Washington.

1011 Mahn-Lot, Marianne. La "liberté" de l'Indien d'Amérique aux XVIe et XVIIe siècles et la politique de regroupement. (*Rev. hist./Paris*, 575, juillet/sept. 1990, p. 77–87)

Brief overview of Spanish policy towards Indians with emphasis on the Church's efforts to protect Indian communities.

1012 Manzano Manzano, Juan. Colón y su secreto: el predescubrimiento. 3. ed. Madrid: Ediciones de Cultura Hispánica, 1989. 927 p., 19 p. of plates (some folded): bibl., ill., index, maps (some col.) (Col. colombina; 3)

Third ed. of 1976 work with new prologue in which the author responds to recent critical commentary on his thesis that Columbus was the first European to find South America.

1013 Manzano Manzano, Juan. Cristóbal Colón: siete años decisivos de su vida, 1485–1492. 2. ed. Madrid: Ediciones de Cultura Hispánica, 1989. 612 p., 15 leaves of plates: bibl., ill., index. (Col. colombina; 2)

Second ed. of a 1964 work with a new epilogue by the author on recent studies of Columbus. For comments on original see *HLAS 28:433a.*

1014 Martín Acosta, María Emelina. Estado de la cuestión sobre la avería en la historiografía española y americanista: la Avería de 1602. (*Rev. Indias*, 50:188, enero/abril 1990, p. 151–160)

General discussion of works on the *avería* with some detailed commentary on policy formation in the early 1600s.

1015 Martínez de Salinas Alonso, María Luisa. Contribución al estudio sobre los arbitristas: nuevos arbitros para las Indias a principios del siglo XVII. (*Rev. Indias*, 50: 188, enero/abril 1990, p. 161–169)

Brief discussion of Spain's monetary and tax policies in a crucial period of colonial economic history. Based on monographs recently published in Spain.

1016 Martínez Gracia, Valentín. Fray Pedro de Gante, primer maestro del continente iberoamericano. Valencia, Spain: Union Misional Franciscana, 1989. 90 p.: bibl., ill. (Franciscanos en el Nuevo Mundo; 5)

Brief, sympathetic sketch of the life of the Franciscan priest.

1017 Martínez Shaw, Carlos. Comercio colonial ilustrado y periferia metropolitana. (*Rábida/Huelva*, 11, marzo 1992, p. 58–72)

Analysis of the effects of free trade on the Spanish imperial economy. Largely a synthesis of recently published monographs as reflected in extensive and informative footnotes.

1018 Martinic D., Zvonimir. La italianidad de Colón. (*Actas Colomb.*, 2:4, 1991, p. 19–47, facsim.)

Review of several theories regarding the birthplace of Columbus. The author accepts Genoa as the most widely supported by historians.

1019 McAlister, Lyle N. Spain and Portugal in the New World, 1492–1700. Minneapolis: Univ. of Minnesota Press, 1984. 585 p., 8 p. of plates: bibl., index, maps. (Europe and the world in the Age of Expansion; 3)

Comprehensive synthesis of modern historical scholarship on the first two centuries of the Spanish and Portuguese empires in America. McAlister discusses disputed areas such as the nature of the economies of 17th-century New Spain and Peru in a balanced yet penetrating analysis. This text also contains proportional treatments of social, cultural, and political factors. The 50-page bibliographic essay is a boon for scholars.

1020 Meza Villalobos, Néstor. Estudios sobre la conquista de América. Santiago: Editorial Universitaria, 1989. 181 p.: bibl. (Col. El Saber y la cultura)

Reprint of 1971 ed. (see *HLAS 36: 1597*).

1021 Migration in colonial Spanish America Edited by David J. Robinson. Cambridge, England; New York: Cambridge Univ. Press, 1990. 399 p.: bibl., ill., index, maps. (Cambridge studies in historical geography; 16)

Collection of 14 well-researched scholarly articles introduced by the editor. The authors represent several disciplines and their research covers a large cross section of colonial society. One of the patterns that emerges in these studies is the Indians' use of migration as an active and sometimes strategic response to Spanish colonial institutions and policies.

1022 Molina Martínez, Miguel. La leyenda negra. Madrid: NEREA, 1991. 317 p.: bibl., index.

Balanced study of a controversial topic includes selected writings of the leading historians involved.

1023 Monasterio de Santa María de la Rábida (Spain). Los franciscanos y el Nuevo Mundo. Sevilla: Guadalquivir, 1992. 165 p.: bibl., col. ill.

Descriptive text and illustrations accompany an exposition of artifacts of Franciscan history from the discovery and colonization periods at the convent of La Rábida.

1024 Montero, Aristónico et al. Los dominicos en la evangelización del Nuevo Mundo. Madrid: Institutos Pontificios de Filosofía y Teología, 1992. 368 p.: bibl., ill., maps. (Publicaciones de los Institutos Pontificios de Filosofía y Teología: Serie II, Teología/misionología; 9)

Most of the eight essays in this multi-authored, multi-faceted book deal with missionary activities of the Dominicans in colonial Latin America (also includes their activity in the Philippines, Japan, and some modern theology). Essays cover Dominican linguistic work among native Americans, education, and two modern perspectives on the work of Las Casas.

1025 Montero, José. Los virreyes españoles en América. Barcelona, España: Mitre, 199?. 367 p.: bibl.

Personal sketches predominate in this heavily biographical study. Little comment on or analysis of institutional, social, or economic factors.

1026 Mörner, Magnus. Migraciones a Hispanoamérica durante la época colonial. (*Anu. Estud. Centroam.*, 48:2, suplemeto 1991, p. 3–25, bibl.)

Comprehensive commentary on scholarly studies of colonial migration published since Mörner's 1975 historiographical article.

New Iberian world: a documentary history of the discovery and settlement of Latin

America to the early 17th century. v. 3, Central America and Mexico. See item **1677**.

1027 O'Gorman, Edmundo. En torno a la conmemoración del descubrimiento de América. (*in* Jornadas de Historiadores Americanistas, *1st, Santafé, Spain, 1987*. América: hombre y sociedad. Presentación de Joaquín A. Muñoz Mendoza. Granada, Spain: Diputación Provincial de Granada, 1988, p. 13–16)

This discussion of the purposes of commemorative exercises as opposed to the study of history has obvious implications for the quincentennial.

1028 O'Gorman, Edmundo. La invención de América. (*in* Jornadas de Historiadores Americanistas, *1st, Santafé, Spain, 1987*. América: hombre y sociedad. Presentación de Joaquín A. Muñoz Mendoza. Granada, Spain: Diputación Provincial de Granada, 1988, p. 99–108)

Tightly-focused restatement of O'Gorman's provocative assessment of the discovery of America as a philosophical and historical revolution in which Columbus plays more an instrumental than a cognitive role.

1029 Oliva Melgar, José María. El monopolio de Indias en los siglos XVI y XVII: plata y mitos en un sistema imperial. (*Rábida/Huelva*, 11, marzo 1992, p. 34–47, tables)

Interpretive study of the basic organization and implementation of the Spanish monopoly in America with special emphasis on the control of precious metals. Includes commentary on the conclusions of Borah, A.G. Frank, Chaunu, Lynch, Brading, and others. Lacks footnotes and bibliography.

1030 Ortadó i Maymó, Josep Maria. Catalunya, la nació descobridora d'Amèrica. Barcelona?: s.n., 1992. 107 p.: bibl., ill., map.

Slim volume attempts to expand on conjectural evidence to prove that Columbus was a Catalan native.

1031 Peralta, Germán. Los mecanismos del comercio negrero. Lima: Kuntur Editores; CONCYTEC' Interbanc, 1990. 391 p.: bibl.

Thorough study of the commercial, financial, and governmental aspects of the slave trade in Latin America from 1595–1640. The first two sections contain a narrative-analytical approach while the third is largely statistical. Based on extensive archival research.

1032 Pérez, Juan Manuel. Evangelio y libertad: primeros dominicos en América. Cusco, Peru: Centro Bartolomé de Las Casas, 1990. 170 p.: bibl.

Emphasis on role of an early ally of Las Casas, Father Pedro de Córdoba, who used his authority to advocate peaceful conversion of native Americans.

1033 Pérez-Mallaína Bueno, Pablo Emilio. Los hombres del océano: vida cotidiana de los tripulantes de las flotas de Indias, siglo XVI. Sevilla, Spain: Sociedad Estatal para la Exposición Universal Sevilla '92, 1992. 256 p.: plates

Impressive combination of primary research, thematic organization, and lucid prose explores both the "daily life" of mariners and their social origins, standards of living, and ship-board discipline. One innovative section covers the "horizontes mentales," including religiosity and superstition.

1034 Phillips, Carla Rahn. Los Tres Reyes, 1628–1634: the short life of an unlucky Spanish galleon. Minneapolis: Univ. of Minnesota Press, 1990. 72 p.: bibl., ill., index, map.

Succinct, well-researched account of the brief career of a single Spanish galleon from its construction in the royal shipyard at Zorroza near Bilbao to its sinking off the port of Cartagena. This galleon was involved in the reassertion of Spanish naval power in the Caribbean just after Piet Heyn's capture of the Spanish treasure fleet in 1628. Interesting details but only slight attention to larger historical trends.

1035 Pino, Fermín del. Edición de crónicas de Indias e historia intelectual, o la distancia entre José de Acosta y José Alcina. (*Rev. Indias*, 50:190, sept./dic. 1990, p. 861–878)

Analysis of José de Acosta's views of the Indian. Author contrasts Acosta's approach to this subject with that of Las Casas. Continuation of a debate between Del Pino and José Alcina.

1036 Pino, Fermín del. La Renaissance et le Nouveau Monde: José d'Acosta, jésuite anthropologue, 1540–1600. (*Homme/Paris*, 122/124, avril/déc. 1992, p. 309–326, bibl.)

Author of seminal *Natural and moral history of the Indies* (1590), Acosta precursed modern anthropology by guiding his own generation and generations to come in the right direction regarding the origins and "evolution" of Amerindians. [M.T. Hamerly]

1037 Pinto Rodríguez, Jorge. Los cinco gremios mayores de Madrid y el comercio colonial en el siglo XVIII. (*Rev. Indias,* 51: 192, mayo/agosto 1991, p. 293–326, table)
Impressive account of the disruptive impact of the arrival of the Madrid-based guilds in Peru and New Spain, the hostile response of local merchants, and the ultimate demise of these enterprises. Based on archival research.

1038 Ponce Leiva, Pilar. Publicaciones españolas sobre cabildos americanos, 1939–1989. (*Rev. Indias,* 50:188, enero/abril 1990, p. 77–81, appendix)
Very brief commentary concentrates on the writings of Constantino Bayle and Guillermo Lohmann Villena.

1039 Primeras cartas sobre América, 1493– 1503. Edición de Francisco Morales Padrón. Sevilla: Secretariado de Publicaciones, Univ. de Sevilla, 1990? 255 p.: bibl. (Col. de bolsillo; 105)
Letters from Columbus, Vespucci, and nine other early voyagers to America are accompanied by a 60-page editor's introduction and explanatory footnotes.

500 años: ¿holocausto o descubrimiento? See item **1070.**

1040 Ramón, Armando de; Juan Ricardo Couyoumdjian; and **Samuel Vial.** Historia de América. v. 1, La gestación del mundo hispanoamericano. Santiago: Editorial A. Bello, 1992. 1 v.: bibl., ill., maps.
Vol. 1 of a projected multi-volume history of Spanish America intended for university students and the general public includes a tripartite organization: native American civilizations; the encounter and conquest; and the colonial period up to 1763. Authors maintain an appropriate balance of geographical, political, economic, social, religious, and cultural factors to make for a comprehensive text.

1041 Ramos, Luis. El papel del indígena en el primer plan colonizador español de América. (*in* Jornadas de Historiadores Americanistas, *1st, Santafé, Spain, 1987.* América: hombre y sociedad. Presentación de Joaquín A. Muñoz Mendoza. Granada, Spain: Diputación Provincial de Granada, 1988, p. 109–125)

Author examines the text of Columbus' diary and letters to determine his perception of the native Americans on the first voyage. Concludes that Columbus preferred peaceful incorporation of natives into the Catholic Church and Spanish trade.

1042 Ramos Gómez, Luis J. La aportacion de la *Revista de Indias* al estudio del inicio de la colonización española de América: del descubrimiento a la conquista armada, octubre de 1492 a abril de 1494. (*Rev. Indias,* 49:187, sept./dic. 1989, p. 691–696)
Outlines plans for the study of the first phase of Spanish colonization of America with an emphasis on the perspective of the native American. Includes some historiographical commentary.

1043 Ramos Gómez, Luis J. Los dos pactos sellados por Guacanagarí y Cristóbal Colón en diciembre de 1492. (*Rev. Esp. Antropol. Am.,* 20, 1990, p. 67–91, bibl.)
Detailed examination of the relationship between Columbus and Guacanagarí based on a close reading of the primary sources. Article is a major part of the author's continuing study of the interaction of native Americans and the early Spanish explorers.

1044 Ramos Gómez, Luis J. El sometimiento del cacique de Port de Paix, Haití, a los Reyes Católicos en el primer viaje de Cristóbal Colón, diciembre de 1492. (*Rev. Esp. Antropol. Am.,* 19, 1989, p. 137–152, bibl.)
Extended explanation of the circumstances surrounding the agreement between Columbus and the native American leader on the northwestern coast of Hispaniola.

1045 Ramos Pérez, Demetrio *et al.* Hispanoamérica. v. 4. Caracas: Academia Nacional de la Historia de Venezuela, 1988? 1 v.: bibl., ill. (some col.), index. (Historia general de América; 14. Período colonial)
Continuation of a multi-volume history of the Americas. Vol. 4 deals with the Spanish conquest, the demographic and social history of the Spanish Empire, and Indian labor and African slavery in Spanish America. Comprehensive and well-organized.

1046 Ramos Prieto, Domingo A. Geografía y frontera en cronistas e historiadores del siglo XVI americano. (*in* Jornadas de Historiadores Americanistas, *2nd, Granada, Spain, 1988.* América: encuentro y asimilación. Edición de Joaquín A. Muñoz Mendoza. Granada: Diputación Provincial de Granada, 1989, p. 189–210, map)

Study of modern conceptions of the frontier applied to 16th century chroniclers. Ramos Prieto concludes that chroniclers did not use an intellectual framework similar to modern conceptions, but that their observations concerning geographical space and cultural zones contain much of value for contemporary research.

1047 Ransby, Barbara. Columbus and the making of historical myth. (*Race Cl.,* 33:3, Jan./March 1992, p. 79–86)

Sharp polemical attack on "the popular myths surrounding Columbus (that) serve as subtle, and sometimes not so subtle, justifications for both male supremacy and white supremacy."

Rieu-Millán, Marie Laure. Los diputados americanos en las Cortes de Cádiz: igualdad o independencia. See item **1097.**

1048 Rivera Pagán, Luis. Evangelización y violencia: la conquista de América. San Juan: Editorial CEMI, 1990. 449 p.: bibl., ill.

Sharply critical evaluation of the Spanish conquest and its accompanying theological rationalizations. Challenging perspective that concentrates on debates about the conquest and the theological and secular assumptions behind these debates.

1049 Robinson, David J. Introduction: towards a typology of migration in colonial Spanish America. (*in* Migration in colonial Spanish America. Edited by David J. Robinson. Cambridge: Cambridge Univ. Press, 1990, p. 1–17, ill., map)

Introductory essay on the complex processes of population movement includes various historical contexts for migrations and the different types of forced and voluntary migrations.

1050 Romano, Ruggiero. Entre encomienda castellana y encomienda indiana: una vez más el problema del feudalismo americano, siglos XVI-XVII. (*Anu. IEHS,* 3, 1988, p. 11–39)

Extended definition of feudalism followed by the application of this concept to the encomienda. Romano argues that the encomienda was a feudal institution and also makes several pointed historiographical comments.

1051 Rumeu de Armas, Antonio *et al.* Hernando Colón y su época. Sevilla: Real Academia Sevillana de Buenas Letras, 1991. 107 p.: (Publ. de la Real Academia Sevillana de Buenas Letras: Monografías)

Six essays on the life and times of Hernando Colon focus not only on his work as his father's biographer but also as a collector of manuscripts and books.

1052 Saiz Diez, Félix. Los Colegios de Propaganda Fide en Hispanoamérica. Prólogo de Julián Heras. 2. ed. Lima: CETA, 1992. 373 p.: bibl., ill. (Serie V centenario, franciscanos evangelizadores del Perú; 3)

New ed. of work originally published in 1969 has no changes in the text but does include an updated bibliography and additional documents in the appendix (for original ed., see *HLAS 32:2079*).

1053 Sala Catalá, José. La ciencia y la técnica en las expediciones de límites hispano-portuguesas: su proyección internacional. (*in* Congreso Internacional sobre Fronteras en Iberoamérica Ayer y Hoy, *1st, Tijuana, Mexico, 1989.* Memoria. Edición de Alfredo Félix Buenrostro Ceballos. Mexicali: Univ. Autónoma de Baja California, 1990, t. 1, p. 46–51, bibl.)

Brief, carefully-reasoned discussion of Spanish and Portuguese efforts to resolve boundary disputes in 18th-century South America. Author addresses the semantic and historical debates surrounding the terms frontier, borderland, and boundary.

1054 Santos Hernández, Angel. Acción misionera de los jesuitas en la América meridional española. (*in* América, *1492–1992:* contribuciones a un centenario. Edición de José Joaquín Alemany. Madrid: Univ. Pontificia Comillas, 1988, p. 43–106)

Convenient summary of Jesuit missionary activities derived largely from monographs and other published sources. Extensive footnotes are valuable. Much emphasis on the Paraguayan missions.

1055 Sanz Tapia, Angel. El impuesto del 1% sobre la plata de Indias, 1779–1792. (*Anu. Estud. Am.,* 48, 1991, p. 235–281, graphs, tables)

Detailed quantitative study of the implementation of the silver tax in several Spanish ports and the government's use of this income. Based on archival research.

1056 Schama, Simon. They all laughed at Cristopher Columbus. (*New Repub.,* Jan. 6 & 13, 1992, p. 30–40)

Acerbic, critical review essay on Quincentennial books and the Quincentennial exhibit at the National Gallery of Art. Schama sees the exhibit as an example of "massive cultural bloat" and is disappointed by most of the books under review except for the biography of Columbus by Felipe Fernández-Armesto and the historical-literary analysis of the Europeans' early perceptions of America by Stephen Greenblatt.

1057 Schwaller, John Frederick. The clash of cultures. (*LARR,* 27:3, 1992, p. 227–243)

Review essay covers nine books published between 1987–90 that deal with the interaction of Indians and Europeans in the colonial period. High quality summaries and commentaries, especially on the works by Anthony Pagden.

1058 Searle, Chris. Unlearning Columbus: a review article. (*Race Cl.,* 33:3, Jan./March 1992, p. 67–77)

Essay encompasses fiction, biography, and history, all evaluated in terms heavily critical of Columbus and the arrival of the Europeans in the Americas.

1059 Seed, Patricia. Colonial and postcolonial discourse. (*LARR,* 26:3, 1991, p. 181–200)

Review essay explores historical and anthropological studies and literary criticism that treat problems of perspective and textual bias concerning issues such as the relationship between the imperial centers and their colonial wards. Seed's command of the literature is impressive (Derrida, Said, and Taussig, for example). Analysis will be provocative for deconstructionists and non-deconstructionists alike.

1060 Sempat Assadourian, Carlos. The colonial economy: the transfer of the European system of production to New Spain and Peru. (*J. Lat. Am. Stud.,* 24, Quincentenary Supplement 1992, p. 55–68)

Author argues that the period from 1570–1620 was critical for the Spanish Crown's imposition of a European system of mercantile production in its major American colonies in order to "maximize shipments of silver to the metropolis." Among the results

of this process was the growth of the Europeanized sectors of the colonial economy including not only mining but also textiles and agriculture. Author gives considerable attention to the impact of these changes on the indigenous economic sector.

1061 Sempat Assadourian, Carlos. Fray Bartolomé de las Casas, obispo: la naturaleza miserable de las naciones indianas y el derecho de la Iglesia; un escrito de 1545. (*Hist. Mex.,* 40:3, enero/marzo 1991, p. 387–451, bibl.)

Lengthy essay introduces two previously unpublished documents (included in an appendix) relevant to the relationship between Bartolomé de las Casas and Francisco Marroquín. Author explores the circumstances surrounding Las Casas' work in Chiapas, the context of Church politics in the 1540s, and the place of these two documents in this period.

1062 Serrano Mangas, Fernando. Naufragios y rescates en el tráfico indiano durante el siglo XVII. Lima: Seglusa Editores; Marina de Guerra del Perú, Fondo de Publicaciones, Dirección General de Intereses Marítimos, 1991. 142 p.: bibl., ill., maps.

An account of the shipwrecks that plagued the Spanish treasure fleet in the 17th century and of efforts to recover sunken cargoes. Study concentrates on navigational and engineering aspects and has little to say about the economic and political consequences of these disasters. Based on archival research.

1063 Serrano y Sanz, Manuel. Los amigos y protectores aragoneses de Cristóbal Colón. Barcelona: Riopiedras Ediciones, 1991? 487 p.: bibl.

This new edition of a 1918 publication adds a 233-page appendix of 599 documents. Serrano y Sanz wrote a biographical and sociological study of those who supported Columbus while he struggled to gain favor in the Spanish court. Most of these supporters, including Luis de Santangel, were descendants of *conversos.*

1064 Serrera Contreras, Ramón María. Tráfico terrestre y red vial en las indias españolas. Barcelona: Lunwerg, 1992. 336 p.: bibl., col. ill.

Extensive and impressive synthesis of the history of land transportation systems in the Spanish Empire based on secondary works and some archival research. Numerous maps and illustrations are nicely reproduced (many in color) from original documents and drawings.

1065 Solano, Francisco de. Ciudades hispanoamericanas y pueblos de indios. Madrid: Consejo Superior de Investigaciones Científicas, 1990. 423 p.: bibl. (Col. Biblioteca de América; 2)

Collection of author's previously published studies on the urbanization process as it impacted both major cities and the *pueblos de indios* in the Spanish colonies. Solano's original introductory essay gives a broad perspective on this important topic.

1066 Stern, Peter. Coaxing the historian into the new information age. (*Colon. Lat. Am. Rev.*, 1:1/2, 1992, p. 201–221, bibl.)

Low-keyed, practical discussion of online database potential for colonialists including the "extraordinarily secretive" project in the Archivo General de Indias, databases available in the US, and "some modest proposals" to spread the use of new research technologies.

1067 Stern, Steven J. Paradigms of conquest: history, historiography, and politics. (*J. Lat. Am. Stud.*, 24, Quincentenary Supplement 1992, p. 1–34)

Carefully-considered scholarly appraisal of the controversies surrounding Columbus and the European arrival in the Americas. Rather than personalities and ideologies, Stern concentrates on the historical interaction of Europeans and active (not passive) native Americans as the appropriate, if complex, focus of attention. Footnotes cite a wealth of studies from several disciplines. Exemplary work of calm, deliberate analysis on a subject that often elicits overly-heated exchanges.

1068 Stevenson, Michael. Columbus and the war on indigenous peoples. (*Race Cl.*, 33:3, Jan./March 1992, p. 27–45)

Attack on the European conquest of America which was, in the author's view, the beginning of an imperial "total war" against native Americans.

1069 Thornton, John K. Africa and Africans in the making of the Atlantic world, 1400–1680. Cambridge; New York: Cambridge Univ. Press, 1992. 347 p.: bibl., index, 5 maps. (Studies in comparative world history)

Challenging examination of the role of Africans in the Americas both outside and within the institution of slavery. Employing the methodologies of modern social and economic history, author concludes that through independent African-based trade, the persistence of African religion and culture, and resistance to slavery, Africa and the Africans were active as well as passive participants in the history of the Atlantic world.

1070 500 años: ¿holocausto o descubrimiento? Recopilación de Juan Rafael Quesada Camacho y Magda Zavala. San José: Editorial Universitaria Centroamericana, 1991. 387 p. (Col. Rueda del tiempo)

Interesting collection of over 100 short, strongly-worded polemical pieces mostly from the Costa Rican popular press on issues surrounding the Quincentenary.

1071 Vaquer, Onofre. ¿Dónde nació Cristóbal Colón? Palma de Mallorca, Spain: El Tall Editorial, 1991. 89 p.: bibl., ill. (El Calaix d'El Tall; 4)

Exploration of the evidence concerning Columbus' birthplace with the most extensive discussion centering on Majorca.

1072 Varela Marcos, Jesús. Estado de la cuestión sobre comercio castellano-americano por Santander, 1765–1778. (*Rev. Indias*, 50:188, enero/abril 1990, p. 171–182, bibl.)

Historiographical survey of the development of free trade between the American colonies and the port of Santander. Includes both general, macro-economic studies and specialized works on the port city.

1073 Varinas, Gabriel Fernández de Villalobos, Marqués de. Estado eclesiástico, político y militar de la América, o grandeza de Indias. Edición y estudio preliminar de Javier Falcón Ramírez. Madrid: Instituto de Cooperación Iberoamericana; Sociedad Estatal Quinto Centenario; Instituto de Estudios Fiscales, Ministerio de Economía y Hacienda, 1990. 772 p.: bibl. (Monografías Economía quinto centenario)

Late-17th-century account of challenges confronting the Spanish Empire in America. An informed, thoughtful introduction alerts the reader to the colorful career and, at times, extremist positions taken by Fernández de Villalobos.

1074 **Vásquez de Espinosa, Antonio.** Compendio y descripción de las Indias Occidentales. v. 1–2. Edición de Balbino Velasco Bayón. Madrid: Historia 16, 1992. 2 v. (1127 p.): bibl. (Crónicas de América; 68)

New ed. of the early-17th century travel account by the Carmelite writer includes a biographical and historiographical appraisal of Vásquez Espinosa and his work written especially for this edition by Balbino Velasco.

1075 **Vázquez, Josefina Zoraida.** La imagen del indio en el español del siglo XVI. Veracruz, Mexico: Univ. Veracruzana, 1991. 150 p.: bibl.

Well-developed exploration of Spanish attitudes towards those whom they conquered and ruled during the 16th century, based primarily on the work of Gonzalo Fernández de Oviedo and on the *Relaciones Geográficas de Indias*, the latter of which are valuable because they portray a variety of opinions and date from later in the century. [R. Haskett and S. Wood]

1076 **Vidales, Carlos.** Corsarios y piratas de la Revolución Francesa en las aguas de la emancipación hispanoamericana. (*Ibero-Am./Stockholm*, 19:2, 1989, p. 3–18)

Swedish sources provide information on the operations of French pirates—many based on the Swedish-controlled island of San Bartolome—in the Spanish Caribbean during the Wars for Spanish American Independence.

1077 **Vives, Pedro A.** Las Indias del Rey y las colonias de España: siglos XVI y XVII. (*Rábida/Huelva*, 11, marzo 1992, p. 9–21, bibl., graphs, table, photo)

Taking as his point of departure the Recopilación de Leyes of 1681, Vives examines the shifting interplay between the Spanish Crown and the American colonies in politics, finance, and economics.

1078 **Vornefeld, Ruth M.** Spanische Geldpolitik in Hispanoamerika, 1750–1808: Konzepte und Massnahmen im Rahmen der bourbonischen Reformpolitik. Stuttgart, Germany: F. Steiner, 1992. 300 p.: appendix, bibl., ill. (Vierteljahrschrift für Sozial- und Wirtschaftsgeschichte. Beihefte, 0341–0846; Nr. 102)

Well-conceived dissertation originally submitted to Bonn University (1991) explores the projects and dispositions of monetary reform in 18th-century Spanish America. Vornefeld examines monetary policies within the framework of Bourbon administrative reforms in Indies, and in relation to fiscal outputs, regional markets, and social tensions in the colonies. Excellent thoretical approach, though lacking complementary quantitative evidence. [T. Hampe-Martínez]

1079 **Wendt, Astrid.** Kannibalismus in Brasilien: eine Analyse europäischer Reiseberichte und Amerika-Darstellungen für die Zeit zwischen 1500 und 1654. Frankfurt, Germany; New York: P. Lang, 1989. 245 p.: ill. (European university studies. Series XIX, Antropology-Ethnology. Section B, Ethnology; 15)

Not a study of cannibalism as much as an analysis of interpretations, responses to, and judgments of reports of cannibalism by Portuguese, Germans, French, English and Dutch explorers in the 16th and 17th centuries. Such interpretations often reflected shared the political and religious beliefs as well as the level of economic development of the explorers' nations at the time. [C.K. Converse]

1080 **Wright, A.D.** The institutional relations of Church and State in the overseas Iberian territories. (*Hisp. Sacra*, 40, julio/dic. 1988, p. 693–699)

Brief synthesis of the difficulties in relations between the Catholic Church and the Spanish and Portuguese governments in the early colonial period. Drawn from secondary sources and the Archivio Segreto Vaticano.

1081 **Zavala, Silvio Arturo.** Diseño de América. (*Mem. Acad. Mex. Hist.*, 33, 1989/90, p. 5–13, maps, plates)

Brief commentary on the Waldseemüller maps and their depiction of America.

1082 **Zavala, Silvio Arturo.** Examen del título de la conmemoración del V Centenario del descubrimiento de América. (*in* Jornadas de Historiadores Americanistas, *1st, Santafé, Spain, 1987.* América: hombre y sociedad. Presentación de Joaquín A. Muñoz Mendoza. Granada, Spain: Diputación Provincial de Granada, 1988, p. 17–21)

Broad overview of the historical environment of Columbus' first voyage with emphasis on the Spanish and Portuguese contributions to the age of discovery.

INDEPENDENCE AND
19TH CENTURY

1083 Barahona, Renato. The Basques and the loss of the American colonies, 1810–1840: approach to a problem. (*RIEV/San Sebastián*, 39:36, 1991, p. 23–34)

Preliminary scholarly evaluation of the disruptive impact of Spanish American independence on the Basque region.

1084 Buisson, Inge. Frauen in Hispanoamerika in Reiseberichten von Europäerinnen, 1830–1853. (*Jahrb. Gesch.*, 27, 1990, p. 227–257)

Interesting but sketchy contribution to the study of 19th-century women's history uses contemporary observations from three European women, with divergent philosophies, of women in Peru, Mexico, and Cuba. [C.K. Converse]

1085 Claro T., Regina. La revolución francesa y la independencia hispanoamericana. (*Rev. Chil. Humanid.*, número especial, 1989, p. 73–92, bibl.)

Brief overview of this complex subject emphasizes the influence of ideas.

1086 Clayton, Lawrence A. William Russell Grace: merchant adventurer. (*in* The human tradition in Latin America: the nineteenth century. Edited by Judith Ewell and William H. Beezley. Wilmington, Del.: SR Books, 1989, p. 189–203, bibl.)

Well-written biographical sketch of the Irish-American entrepreneur who built the Grace company operations in 19th-century Peru. Presented in a style suitable for undergraduates with a short but thorough commentary on sources.

1087 Díaz Moreno, José María. Actitud de la Iglesia en los paises de expresión española: en torno a la independencia. (*in* América, 1492–1992: contribuciones a un centenario. Edición de José Joaquín Alemany. Madrid: Univ. Pontificia Comillas, 1988, p. 271–338)

Author examines the Catholic Church's "fluctuations" in response to the emergence of independent nations in Spanish America from 1810 to the 1830s. The most extensive section concerns the responses of the Holy See in Rome.

1088 Gleijeses, Piero. The limits of sympathy: the United States and the independences of Spanish America. (*J. Lat. Am. Stud.*, 24:3, Oct. 1992, p. 481–505)

Author finds more suspicion and antipathy than sympathy in relations between the leaders of Latin American independence movements and the US Administrations from Jefferson to John Quincy Adams. Based on archival research and a broad reading of monographs.

Istoriíà Latinskoĭ Ameriki: dokolumbova ėpokha — 70-e gody XIX veka [The history of Latin America: the precolumbian epoch to the 1870s]. See item **878.**

1089 Izard, Miquel. América Latina, siglo XIX: violencia, subdesarrollo y dependencia. Madrid: Editorial Síntesis, 1990. 175 p.: bibl., maps. (Historia universal contemporánea; 6)

General history of Latin America from independence to 1898 emphasizes conflict between oligarchs and the masses, and the problems of economic dependence. Not a typical chronological text—each chapter is a thematic essay with examples from various countries.

1090 López-Ocón Cabrera, Leoncio. Las relaciones científicas entre España y la América Latina en la segunda mitad del siglo XIX: un balance historiográfico. (*Rev. Indias*, 50:188, enero/abril 1990, p. 305–333)

Study of the efforts of Spanish scientists and scientific institutions to develop working relationships with Latin American scientists. Employs a broad definition of science that includes biology and the social sciences.

1091 Lucena Giraldo, Manuel and **Maria del Mar Flores.** Una aproximación a la Colección Bauza. (*Rev. Indias*, 50:189, mayo/agosto 1990, p. 547–584, bibl.)

Descriptive listing of manuscripts, maps, and charts in the collection of Felipe Bauza, head of the Spanish *Depósito Hidrográfico* in the early 19th century. Includes a brief history of the Bauza Collection and how it ended up in the British Museum.

1092 Mas Chao, Andrés. Apuntes para un estudio de las causas y desarrollo de la independencia de hispanoamérica. (*Rev. Hist. Mil.*, 67, 1989, p. 79–117, bibl.)

Author attempts to reinterpret Spanish American independence movements by emphasizing a growing *criollo* sense of frustration with the imperial bureaucracy and the breakdown of communication within the empire. The bibliography is sparse and no foot-notes are included.

1093 Moreno Alonso, Manuel. Las *Conversaciones americanas sobre España y sus Indias* de Blanco White. (*Anu. Estud. Am.*, 45:1, 1988, suplemento, p. 79–104)

Penetrating explication of the circumstances surrounding the writing of Blanco White's "Conversaciones" along with a reprinting of the document.

1094 Newland, Carlos. La educación elemental en Hispanoamérica: desde la independencia hasta la centralización de los sistemas educativos nacionales. (*HAHR*, 71:2, May 1991, p. 335–364, tables)

Broad overview of published studies on 19th-century primary education in Spanish America. Analysis is especially strong on the rise and fall of the Lancastrian system and the centralization of education under the control of the expansive national governments of the late 19th century.

1095 Ortega y Medina, Juan A. Monroísmo historiográfico y arqueológico. (*in* Jornadas de Historiadores Americanistas, *2nd, Granada, Spain, 1989*. América: encuentro y asimilación. Edición de Joaquín A. Muñoz Mendoza. Granada: Diputación Provincial de Granada, 1990, p. 165–177)

Challenging evaluation of US and British historical and archaeological writing on precolumbian and Hispanic America during the first half of the 19th century. Author emphasizes the works of Prescott and Stephens and finds strong elements of aggressive imperialism in their observations.

1096 Revuelta González, Manuel. Las misiones de los jesuitas españoles en América y Filipinas durante el siglo XIX. (*in* América, 1492–1992: contribuciones a un centenario. Edición de José Joaquín Alemany. Madrid: Univ. Pontificia Comillas, 1988, p. 339–390, appendices, table)

Extensive archival research supports this account of the return of the Jesuit order to Latin America in the 19th century.

1097 Rieu-Millán, Marie Laure. Los diputados americanos en las Cortes de Cádiz: igualdad o independencia. Madrid: Consejo Superior de Investigaciones Científicas, 1990. 438 p.: bibl., index. (Biblioteca de historia de América; 3)

Well-executed, full-scale scholarly treatment drawn from archival sources and integrated with published monographs. Covers social and economic backgrounds of delegates as well as their political and ideological positions. Rieu-Millán also explains the *criollo's* positions on the issues of Indian tribute, the opening of the colonial economy, federalism versus centralism, and the rising movements for independence.

1098 Safford, Frank. The problem of political order in early republican Spanish America. (*J. Lat. Am. Stud.*, 24, Quincentenary Supplement 1992, p. 83–97)

Critical examination of various schools of thought on the cause of political disorder in the early 19th century. Author tends to see economic structure as carrying more explanatory weight than either cultural or ideological factors.

1099 Sevilla Soler, Rosario. Hacia el estado oligárquico: Iberoamérica, 1820–1850. (*Rábida/Huelva*, 11, marzo 1992, p. 88–102)

Interesting study of ideological, political, economic, and social factors that formed the "oligarchic state" in the first three decades after independence is based on extensive reading of monographs published in Spanish and includes informative footnotes.

1100 Waddell, David Alan Gilmour. Anglo-Spanish relations and the recognition of Spanish American independence. (*Anu. Estud. Am.*, 48, 1991, p. 435–462)

Detailed study of British-Spanish diplomacy in the 1820s based on British and Spanish archives. Waddell places his subject in its full international context including the Monroe Doctrine and continued British support for the Portuguese in Brazil.

20TH CENTURY

1101 Andújar, Manuel *et al.* El exilio de las Españas de 1939 en las Américas: adónde fue la canción? Coordinación de José María Naharro-Calderón. Barcelona: Anthropos, Editorial del Hombre, 1991. 431 p.: ill. (Memoria rota. Exilios y heterodoxias; 22. Estudios)

Insightful introduction followed by 26 essays on Spanish migration to the Western Hemisphere in the wake of the Spanish Civil War. Emphasizes biographical sketches of ordinary people as well as the more famous such as Juan Ramón Jiménez, Ramón Sender, and Luis Buñuel.

1102 Castillo-Cárdenas, Gonzalo. Between authoritarianism and liberation: the politics of middle class protestantism in Latin America. (*in* MACLAS: Latin American essays. Edited by Alvin Cohen. Bethlehem, Penn.: Middle Atlantic Council of Latin American Studies; Lehigh Univ., 1992, v. 5, p. 96–115, bibl.)

Exploration of and commentary on the unpublished memoirs of Alexander Allan, a Scotch missionary in Colombia from 1910–46. Valuable for the insights into missionary work, social change, and the conflict between authoritarianism and liberation from a Protestant perspective.

1103 Costa, Emília Viotti da. Estructuras versus experiencia: novas tendências na história do movimiento operário e das classes trabalhadoras na América Latina; o que se perde e o que se ganha. (*ANPOCS BIB*, 29, 1990, p. 3–16, bibl.)

Incisive survey of recent trends in Latin American labor history emphasizes the discord between "structuralists" and "culturalists." Author also explores the impact of the crisis of the left (communism, in particular) on the study of the working class.

1104 Deutsch, Sandra McGee. Gender and sociopolitical change in twentieth-century Latin America. (*HAHR*, 71:2, May 1991, p. 259–306)

Analytical survey of secondary works on gender roles in politics in four putatively revolutionary situations: Mexico, 1919–1934; Argentina, 1946–1955; Cuba, 1959-; and Chile, 1970–1973. Author finds contradictory government policies and limited progressive change for women except in Carrillo's Yucatán, Castro's Cuba, and, to a limited extent, Allende's Chile.

1105 Greenleaf, Floyd. The Seventh-Day Adventist church in Latin America and the Caribbean. Berrien Springs, Mich.: Andrews Univ. Press, 1992. 2 v.: bibl., index.

Author admits that he has written a sympathetic account of the expansion of the church told mainly from institutional-administrative perspective. Though narrow in focus, the book has two strengths: 1) Greenleaf's thorough footnoting; and 2) his extensive use of church archives.

1106 Halperín Donghi, Tulio. El presente entra en la historia: para una visión retrospectiva del último tercio de siglo latinoamericano. (*in* Jornadas de Historiadores Americanistas, 2nd, Granada, Spain, 1989. América: encuentro y asimilación. Edición de Joaquín A. Muñoz Mendoza. Granada: Diputación Provincial de Granada, 1990, p. 447–463)

Interpretive essay on Latin American political and economic trends in the context of the end of the Cold War and the growing influence of the new international economic and political order. Author emphasizes the prevalence of diversity and uncertainty within the Western Hemisphere.

1107 Hellman, Judith Adler. Making women visible: new works on Latin American and Caribbean women. (*LARR*, 27:1, 1992, p. 182–191)

Review essay of six recent books on women and contemporary political and economic change. Although author views these works in a positive light, she concludes "that women were invisible for so long that the attempt to bring to light the complexities and nuances of their changing economic and political condition is proving to be a highly challenging task."

1108 Knight, Alan. Social revolution: a Latin American perspective. (*Bull. Lat. Am. Res.*, 9:2, 1990, p. 175–202, bibl.)

Bold, thought-provoking essay in comparative history in which the author compares the Mexican, Bolivian, and Cuban revolutions within the larger framework of similar European and Asian movements. Knight emphasizes outcomes and long-term consequences over causation and stresses the uniqueness of each revolution rather than uniform patterns.

1109 La-tin Mei-chou, ti san chüan [History notes of Latin America]. v. 3. Edited by Li Ch'un-hui, Su Chen-hsing, and Hsu Shih-ch'eng. Beijing: The Commercial Press, 1993. 697 p.: appendices, bibl., maps, plates, tables

First and only full-length work published to date in China on the contemporary history of Latin America is a continuation of this pioneering multivolume set. Vol. 3 summarizes the history of Latin America from the end of WWII to the end of the 1980s. Work is representative of research and achievements of the Institute of Latin American Studies, Chinese Academy of Social Sciences. Editors and authors include a noted professor of Latin American history, as well as the Institute's director, deputy director, and other senior research fellows. [Mao Xianglin]

1110 Latin America since 1930: Spanish South America. Edited by Leslie Bethell. Cambridge, England; New York: Cambridge Univ. Press, 1991. 919 p.: bibl., index, maps. (The Cambridge history of Latin America; 8)

This eighth of a proposed ten-volume history of Latin America contains exceptionally high-quality historical syntheses within a balanced framework of political, economic, and social events and trends. Coverage extends into the late 1980s and, in the case of Colombia, the election of 1990.

1111 Livi Bacci, Massimo. Inmigración y desarrollo: comparación entre Europa y América. Barcelona: Fundación Paulino Torras Domènech, 1991. 41 p.: bibl. (Itinera cuadernos; 3)

Transcript of an address by Livi-Bacci stresses current immigration issues and, particularly, North America's "positive ideology" toward immigration in contrast to Europe's "negative ideology."

1112 Luna, Lola G. Desarrollo y cambios en la situación de las mujeres latinoamericanas, s. XX. (in Jornadas de Historiadores Americanistas, 2nd, Granada, Spain, 1989. América: encuentro y asimilación. Edición de Joaquín A. Muñoz Mendoza. Granada: Diputación Provincial de Granada, 1990, p. 277–289)

Important survey of recent trends in women's history and the expansion of institutional commitments to broaden and deepen research and publication in this field. For related article, see the following item.

1113 Luna, Lola G. Mujeres latinoamericanas: historiografía, desarrollo y cooperación. (Bol. Am., 32:41, 1991, p. 151–163)

Based on the author's "Desarrollo y cambios en la situacion de las mujeres latinoamericanos, s. XX" (see item **1112**).

1114 Mauro, Frédéric. Les études historiques françaises sur L'Amerique Latine, 1945–1990. (Cah. Am. lat., 9, 1990, p. 99–110)

Frank and perceptive discussion of the intellectual and institutional frameworks for the study of Latin American history in France. Explores channels for scholarly publication and the promotion of collaborative work among scholars.

1115 Meyer, Jean A. Les protestantismes en Amerique Latine: une perspective historique. (Cah. Am. lat., 9, 1990, p. 7–21, bibl.)

Based on a chapter from the author's book *Historia de los cristianos en América Latina* (item **892**). Emphasizes the spread of Protestant influences after 1929 with special attention to Argentina, Chile, and Brazil.

1116 Miller, Francesca. Latin American feminism and the transnational arena. (in Women, culture, and politics in Latin America. Berkeley: Univ. of California Press, 1990, p. 10–26)

Pioneering study of the activities and ideas of Latin American feminists who participated in international conferences from 1898 to the 1947 Primer Congreso Interamericano de Mujeres in Guatemala. From both published and archival sources.

1117 Nunn, Frederick M. The time of the generals: Latin American professional militarism in world perspective. Lincoln: Univ. of Nebraska Press, 1992. 349 p.: bibl., index.

Incisive analysis of the mentalities and ideologies of Latin America's "professional militarists" from 1964–89. Nunn's research draws heavily from military journals to deal with a period in which archives and interviews remain elusive. His conclusions, expressed in world-wide comparative perspective, find militarism most rampant in Argentina, Brazil, Chile, and Peru. He also examines the uniquely Latin American social and cultural context behind persistent military adventurism in politics, a sequel to the author's *Yesterday's soldiers* (see *HLAS 46: 1911*).

1118 Yamamoto, Atsuko. Noguchi Hideyo shirarezaru kiseki: Merí Roretta Dajisu to no deai. Tokyo: Yamate Shobo Shinsha, 1992. 325 p.: bibl., ill., maps.

Book traces research and life of world-famous Japanese bacteriologist, Hideyo Noguchi (1876–1928) in Mexico, Panama, Ecuador, Peru, and Brazil in first quarter of the 20th century. Noguchi lived in Latin America for 10 years and left many achievements. He is one of the first Japanese scientists who exercised much influence on the progress of Latin American medical science. [K. Horisaka]

1119 Zea, Leopoldo. Latinoamérica en el contexto internacional. (*in* Jornadas de Historiadores Americanistas, 2nd, Granada,

Spain, 1989. América: encuentro y asimilación. Edición de Joaquín A. Muñoz Mendoza. Granada: Diputación Provincial de Granada, 1990, p. 13–20)

Speculative essay on the future of Latin America based on the current international situation. Zea sees closer ties with Europe by way of Spain and Portugal and a consequent diminishing of US influence.

MEXICO
General and Colonial Period

ASUNCION LAVRIN, *Professor of History, Arizona State University at Tempe*
EDITH B. COUTURIER, *National Endowment for the Humanities*

LOCAL HISTORY, HISTORICAL DEMOGRAPHY, and social and economic history provide the most engaging materials in Mexican historiography this biennium. The reorganization of local archives inspired academic interest in microhistory as well as popular local histories that fill the general readers' need for non-academic records of their past. The pre-1992 publication rush that called for sweeping reassessments of the past also yielded a good number of historiographical essays, specialized bibliographies on notable historical figures, and reissues of significant historical works. These works represent solid scholarship and make historical sources more accessible to students at different levels of interest. The reissue of Zavala's studies on colonial labor (item **1195**) and of Gerhard's three volumes on Mexican historical geography (item **1162**) are excellent examples of this output. A series of documents on Hernán Cortés, culled from many sources, hold a special place of their own in the general historiography (item **1153**).

Worth noting as indexes to recent scholarship in topical history are the essays in the two-volume selection of works presented at the Conference of Mexican and Unites States Historians (*8th, San Diego, 1990*). It gathers 60 essays on a variety of topics and all students of Mexican history should consult it (item **1130**).

The opening of local archives and emphasis on local or regional studies continue to benefit mostly the history of the central core of Mexico and Yucatán, areas that attract the bulk of historiographical attention. Since the late 1980s demography and the study of class or special groups within colonial society have displaced the study of landholding patterns and issues of economic productivity which characterized the 1960s and 70s. Demographic studies attempt to grasp the larger meaning of population changes, the connection between population movements, economic cycles, and regional economies. Important efforts in those directions are by Thomas Calvo for Guadalajara (item **1204**) and Garavaglia and Grosso for Tepeaca (item **1221**).

The essays included in David J. Robinson's book on Spanish American migration add significant nuances to topics related to that historical process: for instance, Rodney Watson offers a reinterpretation of indigenous migrations in Chiapas (item **1277**). The need to tie reliable demographic data to larger socioeconomic issues leads Ouweneel to delineate his own theoretical framework for future studies (item

1255). Whether on a large or a local scale, demographic studies are taking an important lead in colonial historiography.

Economic and credit studies are enriched with solid monographs focused on the late 18th-century, relying on more easily quantifiable data than any other period. The sweeping view of Bourbon economic forces provided by Richard Garner is worth special attention as a useful grand synthesis of major trends in agriculture, mining, trade, and royal economic policies (item **1159**).

Social history continues to furnish the greatest variety of topical studies. The Seminar on the Study of Mentalities provides another volume of essays exploring the nature of sexual behavior in New Spain (item **1187**), broadening the boundaries of gender studies. Couturier's study of an aristocratic widow is the most substantive work on women's history (item **1213**), while the most intriguing is on colonial prostitution (item **1149**).

On ecclesiastical history, several essays on the Inquisition inject new material into this all-time favorite. Other studies introduce such new themes as the foundation of nunneries, episcopal administration, and popular colonial religious beliefs. Colonial elites and their role as power-yielders within local socety and as members of local institutions receive a good share of attention, especially for Michoacán, Yucatán and Veracruz. Important contributions in this aspect of social history are those by Juárez Nieto (item **1235**), Martínez Ortega (item **1246**), González Muñoz (item **1227**), and Jackie R. Booker (item **1202**). Himmerich Valencia takes us back to the first historical elite, the postconquest encomenderos, in a useful group profile (item **1232**).

Works on indigenous communities, their stake in local interests, and their role in colonial society continue to offer an important counterbalance to studies of the elite in the historiography of colonial Mexico. The internal politics of indigenous communities, an unusual monographic topic, is probed by Escobar Ohmstede in *Los problemas de elección del cabildo indígena en Yahualica: 1787–1792* (item **1216**), but the more traditional topics such as tribute and labor continue to be sources for strong scholarly studies.

Land ownership patterns and hacienda studies, much reduced in scale since the 1970s, are represented here with several important regional works proposing reinterpretations of postulated trends. For Puebla, see Rik Hoekstra's views in *Profit from the wastelands* (item **1233**) and for Yucatán, see García Bernal's erudite essays on 17th-century hacienda formation and cattle ranching which add new dimensions to the study of indigenous communities (items **1222** and **1223**).

The Bourbon reforms and the independence period are represented by Jiménez Codinach's solid analysis of Mexican and British relations (item **1381**) and by several specialized essays on counterrevolution and international espionage. [AL]

In the works annotated for this biennium, the field of northern history appears to have reached a new stage in sophistication and quality of work. The historical outline of northern New Spain is beginning to incorporate some of the economic and social complexities gleaned during the last 40 years from research on the central and southern regions. Outstanding among the books is Weber's volume (item **1326**), both for the combination of extensive original research and interpretation. As in the case of many articles annotated for this section, the book is notable for its incorporation of new viewpoints on the Indians and their relationship to newcomers. While focused on the north, Weber's discussion of the general issues surrounding the colonization process provides new insights for colonial Mexican history.

Among the shorter works annotated here, literature on the missions has produced the largest number of works of special note. Representative of these works are studies of three scholars with very different points of view: Robert Jackson (item **1304**), Cynthia Radding (item **1315**), and Susan Deeds (item **1296**). The substantial work of Jean Meyer is also to be noted (item **1311**). José Cuello's study of slavery and encomienda (item **1294**) joins other works on labor, often subsumed under the discussions of the missions.

Social and economic studies of mining have inspired much research. Michael Swann focuses on varieties of population patterns (item **1325**); Cramaussel illuminates an important question on the forms of mining *reales*, helping us to understand the differences between their appearances and those based on conventional plans executed for other towns and cities (item **1293**); Peter Bakewell contributes to the continuing debate on economic growth as related to silver production (item **1288**). The history of Zacatecas has inspired a number of important works; especially notable among these are two works by Frédérique Langue (items **1236** and **1237**).

Work inspired by regional congresses addressing the differences within the northern regions has been reflected in many contributions for the period covered here; because of space considerations, many of these works have not been annotated, but the general high quality of the research is notable. Among many other serious studies of land tenure—noting the wide variety in colonial economic organization—mention should be made of Salvador Alvarez (item **1285**). Finally, the decline in the number of meritorious works on the northern regions noted four years ago seems to have been definitively reversed for the 1990s with the appearance of many significant works based on extensive research in primary sources. [EBC]

GENERAL

1120 Alves, Abel A. Nature and bodies, land and labor: Mexico's colonial legacy. Meadville, Penn. Allegheny College; Akron, Ohio: Univ. of Akron, 1991. 63 p. (Latin American issues)

Broadly conceived essay links Mexico's present-day society and political practices to her past. Author establishes comparisons between land tenure patterns, food sources, and resulting policies to control both during colonial and post-independence periods. [AL]

1121 Amerlinck, María Concepción et al. Historia y cultura del tabaco en México. Prólogo de Fernando Benítez. México: Tabamex, Secretaría de Agricultura y Recursos Hidráulicos, 1988. 293 p.: bibl., ill. (some col.).

Richly illustrated work by a number of scholars touches on ancilliary subjects such as art history, changes in production, legislation, and manufacture of tobacco. [EBC]

1122 Archivo General de la Nación (Mexico). Catálogo de textos marginados novohispanos: Inquisición, siglos XVIII y XIX. México: Archivo General de la Nación, 1992. 792 p.: indexes.

Excellent archival guide lists unusual inquisitorial sources in prose and poetry such as personal letters, autobiographies, theological writings, satirical poems, witchcraft investigations, etc. Annotations to each entry render this source invaluable for researchers. [AL]

Barrios Castro, Roberto. México en su lucha por la tierra: de la independencia a la Revolución, 1521–1987. See item **1453**.

Bastian, Jean-Pierre. La heterodoxia religiosa en la historiografía mexicanista, 1968–1988. See item **1454**.

1123 Borah, Woodrow. Cinco siglos de producción y consumo de alimentos en el México Central. (*Mem. Acad. Mex. Hist.,* 31, 1979/89, p. 117–144)

Reviews food production and consumption in Mexico from preconquest to 20th century. Considers availability, varieties of staple food, and changes in production and consumption. [AL]

1124 Cabrera Ypiña, Octaviano and **Matilde Cabrere Ypiña de Corsi.** Historia de la Hacienda de San Diego: municipio de Río Verde, S.L.P. México: Editográfica Guadalajara, 1989. 180 p.: ill.

Dilettante history of a hacienda held by same family for 200 years includes biographical vignettes of family members. Lacks footnotes or bibliography, but obviously based on reliable historical sources. [AL]

1125 Campos Rodríguez, Patricia. Catálogo del archivo de la Basílica Colegiata de Guanajuato, 1605–1977. México: Instituto Nacional de Antropología e Historia, 1981. 285 p.: bibl., ill. (Col. científica; 101: Catálogos y bibliografías)

Archive holdings include incomplete series of baptismal books (1605–1976); matrimonial information (1778–1976); marriage records (1669–1977); religious confirmations (1742–1974); burials (1669–1972); account books for the parish of Guanajuato (1680–1977); and books recording church social activities for 19th and 20th centuries. [AL]

1126 Castañeda, Carmen. Teorías, métodos y fuentes en las investigaciones de historia regional: el caso de la región de Guadalajara. (*in* La region histórica. Caracas: Fondo Editorial Tropykos, 1991, p. 21–40, table)

Author reviews five major historical works on the Guadalajara region and assesses their contribution toward expanding the concept of region itself and our historical knowledge of the area under study. [AL]

1127 Centro de Estudios de Historia de México. Archivo Histórico. Centro de Estudios de Historia de México Condumex: fondos virreinales que se conservan hasta la fecha en su Archivo Histórico: lista en orden cronológico desde 1491 hasta 1821. Compilación de Josefina Moguel Flores. México: Centro de Estudios de Historia de México, 1991. 85 p.

Very useful guide to this important collection includes listings far beyond 1821. [AL]

1128 Cincuenta años de historia en México: en el cincuentenario del Centro de Estudios Históricos. v. 2. Coordinación de Alicia Hernández Chávez y Manuel Miño Grijalva. México: Colegio de México, Centro de Estudios Históricos, 1991. 1 v: bibl., ill.

This volume contains selection of 23 articles published in *Historia Mexicana* on culture, education, and political organization. Those dealing with culture are all on the colonial period; education and politics focus on 19th and 20th centuries. No information on vol. 1 is included. [AL]

1129 Con el sello de agua: ensayos históricos sobre Tlacotalpan. Coordinación de Gema Lozano y Nathal. México: Instituto Veracruzano de Cultura; México: Instituto Nacional de Antropología e Historia, 1991. 259 p.: bibl., ill.

Thirteen historical essays on Tlacotalpan result from concerted effort to rescue town's municipal archives. Documents dating from between 1766 and 1973 permitted works on a variety of topics such as indigenous rebellions, restoration of lands, history of primary schools, and tobacco and sugarcane workers in early 20th century. A good example of local history. [AL]

1130 Conference of Mexican and United States Historians, 8th, San Diego, Calif., 1990. Five centuries of Mexican history = Cinco siglos de historia de México. Edited by Virginia Guedea and Jaime E. Rodríguez. México: Instituto de Investigaciones Dr. José María Luis Mora; Irvine: Univ. of California at Irvine, 1992. 2 v.

These 60 papers delivered by Mexican and North American historians examine following topics: the Old World, the New World (mostly the conquest period), faith, culture, political processes, the economy, society, the countryside, and the frontiers. Of generally high quality, collection serves as a weathervane of current historical research in both countries. Several European historians also participated. Recommended. [AL]

1131 Estudios históricos sobre desastres naturales en México: balance y perspectivas. Coordinación de Virginia García Acosta. México Centro de Investigaciones y Estudios Superiores en Antropología Social, 1992. 76 p.: bibl.

Five short, provocative essays focus on new field of disaster studies, so appropriate for earthquake-prone Mexico. Important key to new trend. [B. Tenenbaum]

1132 Ethnology of the Alta California Indians. Edited with an introduction by Lowell John Bean and Sylvia Brakke Vane. New York: Garland Pub., 1991. 2 v.: bibl., ill., maps. (Spanish borderlands sourcebooks; 3–4)

Valuable collection of articles and sources on the California Indians dates from 1883–1987. Includes many difficult to find materials. [EBC]

1133 Guanajuato: historiografía. Coordinación de José Luis Lara Valdez. León, Mexico: Colegio del Bajío, 1988. 263 p.: bibl., ill., maps.

Twelve essays indicate sources for the study of Guanajuato and the historiography of the city, as well as several monographs on local history. Essays result from a state-wide seminar carried out in 1987. Although the quality of the works is uneven, sections on sources and historiography are useful research tools. [AL]

1134 Historia general de Michoacán. v. 1, Escenario ecológico, época prehispánica. v. 2, La Colonia. v. 3, El siglo XIX. v. 4, El siglo XX. Coordinación de Enrique Florescano. Morelia, Mexico: Gobierno del Estado de Michoacán, Instituto Michoacano de Cultura, 1989. 4 v.: bibl., ill., maps (some col.).

Four-volume set of coffee-table books on history of Michoacán was written by a team of historians. Beautiful illustrations and readable text for the general public. [AL]

1135 Iturriaga de la Fuente, José N. Anecdotario de viajeros extranjeros en México: siglos XVI-XX. México: Fondo de Cultura Económica, 1988–1990. 3 v: bibl. (Sección de obras de historia)

Three-volume compilation of foreign visitors' (some were also settlers) impressions of Mexico between 16th and 20th centuries. Collection tells as much about the travelers as about Mexico. These vignettes make entertaining reading for the non-specialist while introducing some historical figures for the more academic-oriented reader. [AL]

1136 Jarquín Ortega, María Teresa. Guía del archivo parroquial de Metepec. Zinacatepec, Mexico: Colegio Mexiquense, 1991. 142 p.

Guide to parish records of a Franciscan evangelization area that was first organized under the direction of Bishop Juan de Palafox. Most holdings are in *incomplete* series, but with long year cycles that permit demographic serial work. Among the series are: baptismal books (1673–1990); deaths (1646–1974); confirmations (1822–1989); marriages (1722–1989); marriage information (1813–1982); confraternities (1647–1776), and archconfraternities (1893–1945). [AL]

1137 Lafaye, Jacques and **James Lockhart.** A scholarly debate: the origins of modern Mexico: *indigenistas* vs. *hispanistas.* (*Americas/Francisc.*, 48:3, Jan. 1992, p. 315–330)

Two well-known scholars argue their case for indigenous and Spanish influence on the formation of contemporary Mexico. The two offer credible bases for accepting the blend of both in Mexican culture and history. [AL]

1138 Nebel, Richard. Santa María Tonantzin, Virgen de Guadalupe: religiöse Kontinuität und Transformation in Mexiko. Immensee, Switzerland: Neue Zeitschrift für Missionswissenschaft, 1992. 372 p. (NZM Supplementa; 40)

Solid piece of research examines cult of the Virgin of Guadalupe and its social and ideological repercussions throughout Mexican history. Nebel analyzes the Guadalupe phenomenon from both a historical and theological perspective, thus emphasizing the process of cultural assimilation resulting from Virgin's appeal for dialogue and mutual comprehension between Aztecs and Spaniards (and their respective descendants). Extensive and informative survey is based solely on printed materials. [T. Hampe-Martínez]

1139 Orosa Díaz, Jaime. Historia de Yucatán. 8. ed. Mérida, Mexico: Univ. Autónoma de Yucatán, 1988. 341 p.: bibl., ill., map.

Popular general history of Yucatán. [AL]

1140 Palomera, Esteban J. La obra educativa de los jesuitas en Guadalajara, 1586–1986: visión histórica de cuatro siglos de labor cultural. Guadalajara, Mexico: Instituto de Ciencias; México: Univ. Iberoamericana, Depto. de Historia, 1986. 402 p.: bibl., ill., ports.

Linear and narrative history of Jesuit educational institutions in Guadalajara is particularly strong for 19th and 20th centuries. [AL]

1141 Ríos de la Torre, Guadalupe and **Marcela Suárez Escobar.** Reglamentarismo, historia y prostitutas. (*in* Constelaciones de modernidad: anuario conmemorativo del V centenario de la llegada de España a América. México: Univ. Autónoma Metropolitana Azcapotzalco, 1990, p. 127–150)

Using attitudes toward prostitutes as example, authors note that colonial humanists tried to control and redeem whereas positivists tended to control and stigmatize. The fascinating statistics on medical exams taken from archives of the Secretaría de Salud make article worthwhile. [B. Tenenbaum]

1142 Rojas, Beatriz. Camotlán: cómo nació un conflicto entre Jalisco y Nayarit. (*Secuencia/México*, 22, enero/abril 1992, p. 5–40, bibl., facsims., map, table)

Detailed study examines long-standing boundary dispute between Jalisco and Nayarit which continues into the present. Well documented. [AL]

1143 Ruiz, Ramón Eduardo. Triumphs and tragedy: a history of the Mexican people. New York: W.W. Norton, 1992. 512 p.: bibl., index.

Grand view of Mexican history is narrated in vibrant language for the general reader. Ruiz underlines struggle of the underdog against the plutocrats and politicians. Although the political is emphasized, this chronicle of the saga of a people fighting against almost unbeatable odds interweaves economic, cultural, and social commentary as well. Emphasis is on 19th and 20th centuries; the latter is, for the author, "one of the most creative" in Mexican history. [AL]

1144 Segundo catálogo de tesis sobre historia de México. II Addenda. Investigación de Cecilia Greaves. Coordinación de Berta Ulloa y Anne Staples. México: Comité Mexicano de Ciencias Históricas, 1987. 1 v.

Continues the useful catalog (see *HLAS 50:119*) of doctoral dissertations and master's theses on Mexican history produced in Mexican and US universities. [AL]

COLONIAL
General

1145 Aguirre Beltrán, Gonzalo. Orizaba: nobles criollos, negros esclavos e indios de repartimiento. (*Palabra Hombre*, 72, oct./dic. 1989, p. 39–66, bibl.)

Article presents history of the family of the counts of Orizaba throughout colonial period. [AL]

1146 Alberro, Solange. Les Espagnols dans le Mexique colonial: histoire d'une acculturation. Paris: A. Colin, 1992. 131 p.: bibl. (Cahiers des annales; 43)

Opens a totally new topic for inquiry and research: Spanish acculturation to the New World and indigenous influence. Alberro poses questions on use of food and drink, superstitions, new forms of personal behavior, and artistic expression of the Spaniards and

their descendants to suggest that acculturation was an ongoing process worth investigating in depth to challenge popular belief that it is restricted to imitation of the conquerors by the conquered. [AL]

1147 El álbum de la mujer: antología ilustrada de las mexicanas. México: Instituto Nacional de Antropología e Historia, 1991. 4 v.: bibl., ill. (Col. Divulgación)

Useful anthology contains excerpts from writings on women by several authors. Editorial work has passages arranged to illustrate stages of women's lives as well as gender-bound themes such as fertility, education, sexual morality, fashion, and others. Introductory remarks paint a broad picture of colonial women. [AL]

1148 Arenas Frutos, Isabel. Aspectos culturales de la historiografía cortesiana en España, 1940–1989. (*Rev. Indias*, 50:188, enero/abril 1990, p. 277–288)

Bibliographical review lists works on Cortés in poetry, theater, music, and painting. [AL]

1149 Atondo Rodríguez, Ana María. El amor venal y la condición femenina en el México colonial. México: Instituto Nacional de Antropología e Historia, 1992. 357 p.: bibl. (Col. Divulgación)

Study of formal and informal prostitution in New Spain is based largely on cases extracted from ecclesiastical or inquisitorial sources, and legal matter. Informative in an anecdotal manner. Useful social history. [AL]

1150 Baudot, Georges and **María Agueda Méndez.** La Revolución Francesa y la Inquisición mexicana: textos y pretextos. (*Caravelle/Toulouse*, 54, 1990, p. 89–105, bibl.)

Catalogs types of texts on France or the French Revolution that came under inquisitorial ban. Texts were mostly political, but also included were reports on Haitian revolt, praise for the Revolution, and religious satire, all expressions of a political counterculture. [AL]

1151 Brading, David A. La devoción católica y la heterodoxia en el México borbónico. (*in* Espiritualidad barroca colonial: santos y demonios en América. México: Univ. Iberoamericana, 1994, p. 17–40)

General overview of religious life and

customs in New Spain and the role of religious institutions in fostering such expression. Magic, sermons, confraternities, and the role of some missionary institutions are mixed together in a study that lacks a central theme, offering only glimpses of people and their religious practices. [AL]

Bustos, Gerardo. Libro de las descripciones: sobre la visión geográfica de la Península de Yucatán en textos españoles del siglo XVI. See *HLAS 53:2718.*

1152 **Castro Gutiérrez, Felipe.** Profecías y libelos subversivos contra el reinado de Carlos III. (*Estud. Hist. Novohisp.,* 11, 1991, p. 85–96)
　　Using Inquisition documents, author finds evidence of support for exiled Jesuits including poems, prophecies, and stories. Points out genuine anger at the Bourbon State and Charles III. [EBC]

1153 **Documentos cortesianos.** Edición de José Luis Martínez. México: Fondo de Cultura Económica, 1990–1992. 4 v.: bibl., ill., indexes. (Sección de obras de historia)
　　These four volumes of documents for the study of Hernán Cortés contain a significant body of valuable documentary sources for graduate students and investigators. Editor has inserted brief guidelines and information on sources and historical actors. The volumes cover Cortés' life and deeds from 1518–48. Polished edition in fine paper with illustrations. [AL]

1154 **Durand-Forest, Jacqueline de.** Hernández y la botánica mexicana. (*Caravelle/Toulouse,* 55, 1990, p. 53–64)
　　Delineates the life and work of Francisco Hernández, physician to Philip II and capable botanist of New Spain, whose original manuscripts have disappeared but whose work was used by many others for 200 years. [AL]

1155 **La educación de la mujer en la Nueva España: antología.** Edición de Pilar Gonzalbo Aizpuru. México: Ediciones El Caballito; Secretaría de Educación Pública, 1985. 155 p.: ill. (Biblioteca pedagógica)
　　Sixteen passages from colonial sources, mostly didactic in nature, guide reader to the models of feminine behavior. [AL]

1156 **Espiritualidad barroca colonial: santos y demonios en América.** Coordinación de Clara García Ayluardo y Manuel Ramos Medina. México: Univ. Iberoamericana,

Depto. de Historia, 1994. 155 p. (Manifestaciones religiosas en el mundo colonial americano; 1)
　　Essay collection considers 17th-century religion in Spanish America. Though largely focused on Mexico, an essay on Santa Rosa de Lima and another on the nature of religion for blacks and whites in Cartagena broaden its scope. Essays illustrate new trends in ecclesiastical history, which focus more on nature of religon than on religious institutions. [AL]

1157 **Flores Hernández, Benjamín.** "Pelear con el Cid después de muerto:" las *Apologías y discursos de las conquistas occidentales* de Bernardo Vargas Machuca, en controversia con la *Brevísima relación de la destrucción de las Indias,* de Fray Bartolomé de las Casas. (*Estud. Hist. Novohisp.,* 10, 1991, p. 45–105)
　　Detailed study examines little-known work of an author who contested De las Casas' interpretation of the Spanish conquest. Written early in the 17th century, the work did not receive royal approval for publication. Of bibliographical interest. [AL]

1158 **García Acosta, Virginia.** Los precios del trigo en la historia colonial de México. México: Centro de Investigaciones y Estudios Superiores en Antropología Social, 1988. 161 p.: bibl., ill. (Ediciones de la Casa Chata; 25)
　　Using records left by bakers as they bought wheat, preserved by the Tribunal de Fiel Ejecutoria, work studies price of wheat for period 1741–1812. Wheat prices, like those for other products, rose steeply in late 18th century. [AL]

1159 **Garner, Richard L.** and **Spiro E. Stefanou.** Economic growth and change in Bourbon Mexico. Gainesville: Univ. Press of Florida, 1993. 354 p.: bibl., ill., index, map. (University of Florida social sciences monograph; 80)
　　Colony-wide analysis of 18th-century Mexican economy covering agricultural production, tithe revenues, supply and demand, market mechanisms, mining production, manufacturing, internal and foreign trade, credit, and government policies concludes that growth did not stimulate any fundamental change in the economic structure. Intensive and engaging, work is rich source of information and an exciting challenge for economic and social historians. [AL]

1160 Gerhard, Peter. A guide to the historical geography of New Spain. Rev. ed. Norman: Univ. of Oklahoma Press, 1993. 484 p.: bibl., index, maps.
See item **1162.**

1161 Gerhard, Peter. The north frontier of New Spain. Rev. ed. Norman: Univ. of Oklahoma Press, 1993. 456 p.: bibl., ill., index, maps.
See item **1162.**

1162 Gerhard, Peter. The southeast frontier of New Spain. Rev. ed. Norman: Univ. of Oklahoma Press, 1993. 219 p.: bibl., index, maps.

Long-awaited publication of revised editions of three classic historical and geographical reference sourcebooks for colonial Mexico. Author ably mixes history and geography to provide solid information on native cultures, the conquest, government and *encomiendas,* church activities and administration, and population changes for all the important administrative divisions of New Spain. For the other two titles see items **1160** and **1161.** [AL]

1163 Gonzalbo Aizpuru, Pilar. El curriculum oculto en los colegios novohispanos de la Compañía de Jesús. (*in* Constelaciones de modernidad: anuario conmemorativo del V centenario de la llegada de España a América. México: Univ. Autónoma Metropolitana, Unidad Azcapotzalco, 1990, p. 79–98)

Outlines and briefly discusses main guidelines of Jesuits' educational objectives. [AL]

1164 González Claverán, Virginia. La expedición científica de Malaspina en Nueva España, 1789–1794. México: Colegio de México, Centro de Estudios Históricos, 1988. 528 p., 4 p. of plates: bibl., ill. (some col.), index.

Exhaustive, archival-based study examines Alejandro Malaspina's scientific expedition to New Spain. [AL]

1165 Gortari Rabiela, Hira de. Julio-agosto de 1808: "La lealtad mexicana." (*Hist. Mex.,* 39:1, julio/sept. 1989, p. 181–203, bibl.)

Examines brief period of loyalty to the Spanish Crown prior to break between staunch royalists and reformists. [AL]

1166 Greenleaf, Richard E. Historiography of the Mexican Inquisition: evolution of interpretations and methodologies. (*in* Cul-

tural encounters: the impact of the Inquisition in Spain and the New World. Berkeley: Univ. of California Press, 1991, p. 248–276)

Useful and challenging review examines main historiographical trends, mostly from 1960s to present, on study of the Inquisition. Author undertakes a chronological and thematic approach to cover the variety of writers and topics under study, and ends with a discussion of his own revisionist opinion and those of other interpreters of the Inquisition. [AL]

1167 Guzmán, Eulalia. Una visión crítica de la historia de la conquista de México-Tenochtitlán. México: Univ. Nacional Autónoma de México, Instituto de Investigaciones Antropológicas, 1989. 206 p. (Serie antropológica; 97: Etnología)

Printed version of taped lectures given by controversial "historian" Eulalia Guzmán in 1960 is of historiographical interest. [AL]

1168 Hampe Martínez, Teodoro. Esbozo de una transferencia política: asistentes de Sevilla en el gobierno virreinal de México y Perú. (*Hist. Mex.,* 41:1, julio/sept. 1991, p. 49–81, bibl.)

Author examines training of the men appointed as viceroys of Mexico and Peru, focusing especially on those who held *both* posts. The training, designed for royal officers in Seville, did not yield positive results for the performance of administrative duties as viceroys. Interesting approach to institutional history. [AL]

1169 Hordes, Stanley M. The Inquisition and the crypto-Jewish community in colonial New Spain and New Mexico. (*in* Cultural encounters: the impact of the Inquisition in Spain and the New World. Berkeley: Univ. of California Press, 1991, p. 207–217)

Reviews cycles of inquisitorial activities against crypto-Jews in New Spain throughout the colonial period. Suggests that New Mexico was the target of early and late colonial crypto-Jewish migration. [AL]

1170 Kicza, John. Migration to major metropoles in colonial Mexico. (*in* Migration in colonial Spanish America. Edited by David J. Robinson. Cambridge: Cambridge Univ. Press, 1990, p. 193–211)

Explores patterns of migration to main cities (mostly Mexico City) as represented by occupational groups such as merchants, bureaucrats, professionals, craftsmen, and unskilled workers. Provides premises for further study. [AL]

1171 Langue, Frédérique. Les français en Nouvelle-Espagne à la fin du XVIIIe siècle: médiateurs de la révolution ou nouveaux créoles? (*Caravelle/Toulouse*, 54, 1990, p. 37–60, bibl.)
Considers migration of French revolutionary ideas to New Spain. These ideas, especially the concept of a new motherland, were attractive to both French migrants and *criollo* intellectuals in New Spain. However, French revolutionary ideas were insufficient to end loyalty to Spain. [AL]

1172 Laserna Gaitán, Antonio Ignacio. Las unidades de medida agrarias en Nueva España durante el siglo XVIII. (*in* Jornadas de Historiadores Americanistas, 2nd, Granada, Spain, 1988. América: encuentro y asimilación. Edición de Joaquín A. Muñoz Mendoza. Granada: Diputación Provincial de Granada, 1989, p. 211–233, tables)
Reviews and discusses problem posed by variety of surface measurements used in colonial period. Author eulogizes work of several 18th-century Mexican mathematicians and attempts to disentangle contemporary interpretations of colonial measurements. [AL]

1173 Lozano Armendares, Teresa. Los juegos de azar: ¿una pasión novohispana? (*Estud. Hist. Novohisp.*, 11, 1991, p. 155–181)
Examines colonial legislation prohibiting and regulating gambling. Chronicles attempts to sell monopolies and prohibit certain games, and includes discussion of establishment of the lottery. Based in part on *bandos* preserved in Mexico's Archivo General de la Nación. [EBC]

1174 Martínez, José Luis. Hernán Cortés. México: Univ. Nacional Autónoma de México; Fondo de Cultura Económica, 1990. 1015 p.: bibl., ill., index. (Sección de obras de historia)
Latest effort to rewrite a contemporary biographical synthesis of Mexico's conqueror. Based on an extensive bibliography, Martínez succeeds in compiling much information on aspects of Cortés' life often overlooked in briefer works. Iconographic and bibliographic surveys of literary works about Cortés complement historical information. Author assumes a middle ground in his judgment of

Cortés' actions. Though a definitive study of the conqueror still eludes scholars, this volume is an informative and commendable attempt. [AL]

New Iberian world: a documentary history of the discovery and settlement of Latin America to the early 17th century. v. 3, Central America and Mexico. See item **1677.**

1175 Newson, Linda A. Explicación de las variaciones regionales de las tendencias demográficas en la América española colonial: el caso de México. (*Hist. Mex.*, 41:4, abril/junio 1992, p. 517–549, bibl.)
Broad survey examines factors that caused uneven regional demographic changes throughout colonial period. Posits that diseases, the intensity of Spanish colonization, and the use of labor and natural resources must be taken into consideration. [AL]

1176 Pérez Herrero, Pedro. Los beneficiarios del reformismo borbónico: metrópoli *versus* élites novohispanas. (*Hist. Mex.*, 41:2, oct./dic. 1991, p. 207–264, bibl., graphs, tables)
Another contribution to debate on 18th-century economic growth, work recommends a reevaluation of treasury figures to account for inflation, escalating administrative costs, and other variables. Concludes that period of greatest prosperity was first half of 18th century; that reforms benefited regional elites through creation of new administrative positions; and that actions of the Crown at end of the period convinced upper class that connection with Spain no longer provided benefits. [EBC]

1177 Pietschmann, Horst. Consideraciones en torno al protoliberalismo, reformas borbónicas y revolución: la Nueva España en el último tercio del siglo XVIII. (*Hist. Mex.*, 41:2, oct./dic. 1991, p. 167–205, bibl.)
Detailed study examines administrative, political, and practical effects of establishment of *intendencias.* Among other considerations, argues that use of Gálvez kin network for principal positions was motivated less by nepotism than by desire to assure success of the reforms. [EBC]

1178 Pietschmann, Horst. Revolución y contrarevolución en el México de las reformas borbónicas: ideas protoliberales y liberales entre los burócratas ilustrados novohispanos, 1780–1794. (*Caravelle/Toulouse*, 54, 1990, p. 21–35, bibl.)

Summary review considers political struggle among "enlightened" and traditionalist administrators in Spain and New Spain. Loyalty to Spain and preservation of power prevailed over liberalizing influences of the Enlightenment and the French Revolution. [AL]

1179 Quezada, Noemí. The Inquisition's repression of *curanderos*. (*in* Cultural encounters: the impact of the Inquistion in Spain and the New World. Berkeley: Univ. of California Press, 1991, p. 37–57, ill., tables)

Investigation of the ideology and procedures of New Spain's Holy Office in its attempts to control certain practices of *curanderos*. Author provides an ethnic profile of the *curanderos* and discusses practices most likely to draw the attention of the Inquisition authorities. [R. Haskett and S. Wood]

1180 Quezada, Noemí. Sexualidad y magia en la mujer novohispana, siglo XVIII. (*An. Antropol.*, 26, 1989, p. 261–295, bibl.)

Well executed study of the ways in which some women—Spanish, *casta*, or indigenous—relied on magic in an attempt to manipulate norms of sexuality and marital customs, often in reaction to tensions imposed by orthodox Spanish gender ideology. [R. Haskett and S. Wood]

1181 Reher, David Sven. ¿Malthus de nuevo?: población y economía en México durante el siglo XVIII. (*Hist. Mex.*, 41:4, abril/junio 1992, p. 615–664, bibl., graphs, tables)

Uses demographic, economic, and ethnic data to explain late 18th-century crisis. Underlines significance of population growth, lack of technological change, and decline in agricultural production as factors having a negative influence on poorer sectors of the population. [AL]

1182 Reher, David Sven. Population et économie dans le Mexique du XVIIIe siècle: une analyse des fluctuations annuelles. (*Population/Paris*, 46:5, sept./oct. 1991, p. 1185–1205, bibl., tables)

Studies effect of price of corn on demographic fluctuations in late 18th-century New Spain. Author finds that Mexican demographic pattern resembles that of northern Europe. Based on price series and population data published by several authors. [AL]

1183 La Revolución Francesa en México. Coordinación de Solange Alberro, Alicia Hernández Chávez, y Elías Trabulse. México: El Colegio de México; Centro de Estudios Mexicanos y Centroamericanos, 1992. 287 p.: bibl.

Fifteen worthwhile essays examine impact of French Revolution on Mexican politics and thought. Of particular note are Trabulse on diffusion of French Enlightenment materialism in Mexico, Carlos Herrejón Peredo on how Mexicans understood that phenomenon, and Andrés Lira on its depiction in the works of Justo Sierra. [B. Tenenbaum]

1184 Rubial García, Antonio and **Clara García Ayluardo.** La vida religiosa en el México: un acercamiento bibliográfico. México: Univ. Iberoamericana, Depto. de Historia, 1991. 137 p.

Very useful and up-to-date bibliography includes all aspects of Mexican ecclesiastical history. Lists contemporary and historical printed works only; no reference to archival sources. [AL]

1185 Sarabia Viejo, María Justina. Bibliografía de México en la época colonial. (*Anu. Estud. Am.*, 46:2 suplemento, 1989, p. 91–122, bibl.)

Continuation of an extensive annotated bibliography on colonial Mexico (see *HLAS 52:979*). [AL]

1186 Sarabia Viejo, María Justina. Historiografía española en torno a Hernán Cortés, 1940–1989. (*Rev. Indias*, 50:188, enero/abril 1990, p. 265–276)

Useful survey considers historical output on Hernán Cortés over the last 50 years. Among themes included are: biographies, documentation relative to his times and his family, military activities, his relations with the indigenous peoples, and his colonizing ventures. [AL]

1187 Seminario de Historia de las Mentalidades y Religión en México Colonial (México). El placer de pecar & el afán de normar. México: Instituto Nacional de Antropología e Historia; Editorial J. Mortiz, 1988. 378 p.: bibl., col. ill. (Contrapuntos)

Eight authors explore nature of sexual behavior in New Spain. Analytical studies of religious and lay legislation define licit and illicit relations, while studies of actual cases illustrate praxis of sexual relations and mean-

ing of sexual behavior. Of special interest is
Solange Alberro's study of sexuality and domesticity among New Spain's Jews. [AL]

**1188 Simposio de Historia de las Mentalida-
des, 3rd, México?, 1991?** Familia y
poder en Nueva España: memoria. México:
Instituto Nacional de Antropología e Historia, 1991. 193 p.: bibl., ill. (Col. científica;
228. Serie Historia)

Includes 14 case studies of colonial
families and one religious order, with a
cameo quality for fine detail. Studies provide
additional information on well-known patterns rather than breaking new ground. [AL]

1189 TePaske, John Jay. La crisis financiera
del virreinato de Nueva España a fines
de la colonia. (Secuencia/México, 19, enero/
abril 1991, p. 123–140, bibl., graphs, ill.)

Traces fiscal profile of the Royal Ex-
chequer in New Spain during last 30 years of
the colony. Underlines desperate fiscal situation of the colony despite peak collection
years prior to 1810. [AL]

1190 Torre Villar, Ernesto de la. Los descubridores de la Nueva España. (in Jornadas de Historiadores Americanistas, 2nd,
Granada, Spain, 1988. América: encuentro y
asimilación. Edición de Joaquín A. Muñoz
Mendoza. Granada: Diputación Provincial de
Granada, 1989, p. 379–393)

Presents synthetic review of works of
José Antonio de Villaseñor y Sánchez and
Juan José de Eguiara y Eguren, 18th-century
"rediscoverers" of New Spain's physical and
intellectual wealth. [AL]

1191 Trabulse, Elías. Crítica y heterodoxia:
ensayos de historia mexicana. Guadalajara, Mexico: Univ. de Guadalajara/Xalli,
1991. 157 p.: bibl. (Reloj de sol)

Essays (some previously published)
written by notable intellectual historian lack
internal unity, but writing is crisp and ideas
reveal a deep knowledge of the colonial period. [AL]

**1192 Viqueira, Carmen and José Ignacio Ur-
quiola.** Los obrajes en la Nueva España,
1530–1630. México: Consejo Nacional para la
Cultura y las Artes, 1990. 374 p.: bibl., ill.
(Regiones)

Revisionist collection of essays brings
together a reinterpretation of labor legislation
in textile factories, and factual information

on costs of production (salaries, productivity,
etc.). Viqueira proposes that obraje legislation did not reflect mercantilist policies, but
an adjustment to New Spain's industrial
needs in light of demographic decline.
Thought-provoking work merits serious attention from specialists. [AL]

**1193 Zaballa Beascoechea, Ana de and
Josep-Ignasi Saranyana.** La discusión
sobre el joaquinismo novohispano en el siglo
XVI en la historiografía reciente. (Quinto
Cent., 16, 1990, p. 173–189)

Refutes thesis that Joachinite millenarian thought was a key component of early
Franciscan evangelizers such as Fray Martín
de Valencia. Author questions Phelan, Baudot, Bataillon, and others, leading into an interesting revisionist debate. [AL]

1194 Zahino Peñafort, Luisa. La cuestión indígena en el IV Concilio Provincial
Mexicano. (Relaciones/Zamora, 45, invierno
1990, p. 5–31)

Interesting essay examines recommendations of the IV Concilio Provincial Mexicano (1771) for the indigenous population.
Negative opinions on indigenous people held
by key figures, criticism raised regarding behavior of the clergy, and proposed new recommendations on adoption of the Spanish language reflected the mixed message contained
in royalist policy of Charles III. [AL]

1195 Zavala, Silvio Arturo. Estudios acerca
de la historia del trabajo en México:
homenaje del Centro de Estudios Históricos a
Silvio Zavala. Edición de Elías Trabulse. México: El Colegio de México, Centro de Estudios
Históricos, 1988. 272 p.: bibl., index.

Notable historian is honored by this reissue of the eight introductory essays to his
monumental history of labor in Mexico. Two
other shorter essays are included. Useful
reading for advanced students of Mexican colonial history. [AL]

Central and South

1196 Baroni Boissonas, Ariane. La formación de la estructura agraria en El Bajío
colonial, siglos XVI y XVII. México: SEP,
1990. 229 p.: bibl., ill., maps. (Cuadernos de la
Casa Chata; 175)

Well researched study of the formation
and evolution of agricultural systems in the

Bajío and their reliance on the migration of sedentary indigenous peoples into the area to offset, at least in part, the region's lack of a settled precontact agrarian population. Author shows that many of the migrants lived in new, ethnically diverse indigenous communities, often with lands of their own. [R. Haskett and S. Wood]

1197 Baudot, Georges. Fray Toribio Motolinía denunciado ante la Inquisición por Fray Bernardino de Sahagún en 1572. (*Caravelle/Toulouse*, 55, 1990, p. 13–17)

Briefly discusses meaning of Sahagún's denunciation of his *correligionario* whom Baudot identifies as Fray Toribio de Motolinía. Baudot corrects his previous interpretation of this incident and indicates Sahagún's despair of achieving a true conversion among the Indians. [AL]

1198 Baudot, Georges. La pugna franciscana por México. México: Alianza Editorial Mexicana; Consejo Nacional para la Cultura y las Artes, 1990. 338 p.: bibl. (Los Noventa; 36)

Collection of previously published essays are enriched by inclusion of a series of little-known documents. Author sees Franciscans pursuing a relentless political enterprise to dominate the process of Amerindian religious and intellectual conversion. [AL]

1199 Belanger, Brian C. Between the cloister and the world: the Franciscan Third Order of colonial Querétaro. (*Americas/Francisc.*, 49:2, Oct. 1992, p. 157–177)

Traces history of the Third Order (of religious lay people) from an organization devoted to the traditional function of dispenser of charity to operators of an educational institution. Details aspects of Order's history, practices and problems. [EBC]

1200 Bermúdez G., Gilberto. La formación de las haciendas en la región de Jalapa, 1580–1630. (*Palabra Hombre* 67, julio/sept. 1988, p. 67–74, bibl., map)

Brief account of 11 haciendas focuses on ownership and assets. [AL]

1201 Booker, Jackie R. Needed but unwanted: black militiamen in Veracruz, Mexico, 1760–1810. (*Historian/Honor Society*, 55:2, Winter 1993, p. 259–276, photo, tables)

Reviews story of blacks and mixed-blood militiamen in Veracruz and compares it to their experience in other areas of Spanish and Portuguese America. Includes data on recruitment, salaries, performance, and relations with white militiamen. Informative. [AL]

1202 Booker, Jackie R. Veracruz merchants, 1770–1829: a mercantile elite in late Bourbon and early independent Mexico. Boulder, Colo.: Westview Press, 1993. 191 p.: bibl., index, maps. (Dellplain Latin American studies; 29)

Detailed examination of merchants in Veracruz during late colonial period. Author documents social, economic, and policy issues, as well as the political problems faced by this group during transition to and after Independence. Important contribution to study of social elites. [AL]

1203 Bribiesca Sumano, María Elena and **Guadalupe Yolanda Zamudio Espinosa.** Catálogo de protocolos de la notaría no. 1, Toluca. v. 1–3, 6. Toluca de Lerdo, México: Ediciones del Gobierno del Estado de México, 1984–1993? 4 v.: facsims., indexes. (Documentos del Estado de México)

According to volume subtitles, Vols. 1–3 cover notarial transactions in Toluca and surrounding towns from 1566–1633, 1566–1633 [i.e., 1560–1631], and 1610–1626, respectively. Vol. 6 covers 1617–75. Despite considerable gaps and incomplete information, all the volumes are a rich source for social history and an excellent guide for research. Annotations are well done and complemented by name and subject indexes and a glossary.

1204 Calvo, Thomas. Demografía y economía: la coyuntura en Nueva Galicia en el siglo XVII. (*Hist. Mex.*, 41:4, abril/junio 1992, p. 579–613, bibl., tables, graphs)

Ties demographic movements in Guadalajara and vicinity to mining and agricultural changes in 17th century, pointing to decline of the former and increasing importance of the latter. [AL]

1205 Campo del Pozo, Fernando. Fray Alonso de Veracruz y los privilegios de los religiosos en Indias. (*Rev. Agust.*, 33:102, sept./dic. 1992, p. 1283–1315)

Provides explanation of the privileges held by the friars during conquest of the New World as recorded by Fray Alonso de la Veracruz, a key figure in the process of evangelization and an expert in canon law. Based on a manuscript available at the John Carter Brown Collection (Providence, R.I.). [AL]

1206 Castañeda, Carmen. El impacto de la Ilustración y de la Revolución Francesa en la vida de México, finales del siglo XVIII: 1793 en Guadalajara. (*Caravelle/Toulouse*, 54, 1990, p. 61–87, bibl.)

This study of inquisitional investigation and exile to Spain of theologian Juan Antonio Montenegro posits that many young members of the Mexican elite were influenced by French revolutionary ideas. [AL]

1207 Castañeda, Carmen and **María de la Luz Ayala.** Universidad y comercio: los dominios de la elite de Guadalajara, 1792–1821. (*in* Congreso de Historia Regional Comparada, *2nd, Ciudad Juárez, Mexico, 1990.* Actas. Edición de Ricardo León García. Ciudad Juárez, Mexico: Univ. Autónoma de Ciudad Juárez, 1991, p. 217–240, appendices, tables)

Presents prosopographic study of two groups of the colonial provincial elite. [AL]

1208 Castro Gutiérrez, Felipe. Movimientos populares en Nueva España: Michoacán, 1766–1767. México: Univ. Nacional Autónoma de México, 1990. 158 p.: bibl., maps. (Serie Historia novohispana; 44)

Narrative analysis examines Michoacán's popular disturbances in 1766–67. Author sees clear social and ethnic roots in this significant but ultimately ineffective insurgency against Spanish rule. [AL]

1209 Cervantes, Fernando. The devils of Querétaro: scepticism and credulity in late seventeenth-century Mexico. (*Past Present*, 130, Feb. 1991, p. 51–69)

Interesting essay concerns midcolonial theological discourse. A series of female demoniac possessions pitted Propaganda Fide Franciscans against the Inquisition. At bottom lay a theological quandary about the power of God and the efficacy of the devil. [AL]

1210 Colección de documentos para la historia de Nayarit. v. 1, Los albores de un nuevo mundo. Recopilación de Thomas Calvo. Guadalajara, Mexico: Univ. de Guadalajara; México: Centre d'études mexicaines et centraméricaines, 1989. 1 v.: bibl.

One of five volumes of selected documents on Nayarit, a backwater area in New

Spain. Documents have been extracted from archival sources in Guadalajara, Mexico, and Spain, and from printed sources. They cover the 16th-17th centuries and deal with a variety of social and economic issues affecting Indians and Spaniards. Well-chosen selection useful for graduate students and researchers. [AL]

1211 Colección de documentos para la historia de Nayarit. v. 2, Nuevas mutaciones. Recopilación de Jean A. Meyer. Guadalajara, Mexico: Univ. de Guadalajara; México: Centre d'études mexicaines et centraméricaines, 1990. 1 v.

Second volume in documentary history of Nayarit comprises archival samples on demography, agriculture, land tenure, taxes, pastoral visits, and daily life. [AL]

1212 Cortés Alonso, Vicenta. La imagen del otro: indios, blancos, y negros en el México del siglo XVI. (*Rev. Indias*, 51:192, mayo/agosto 1991, p. 259–292, appendix, ill., table)

Author uses the Osuna Codex for a meticulous study of the representation of the three races involved in early formation of New Spain. She argues that indigenous perception of themselves and "others" is a valuable source of information on that period. [AL]

1213 Couturier, Edith. Una viuda aristócrata en la Nueva España del siglo XVIII: la Condesa de Miravalle. (*Hist. Mex.*, 41:3, enero/marzo 1992, p. 327–363, bibl.)

Traces life, family connections, and economic and personal interests of María Magdalena Dávalos y Orosco, Countess of Miravalle. Work is good example of use of biography to illustrate social mores and meaning of gender in colonial society. [AL]

Davis, Clint. Water control and settlement in colonial Mexico's first frontier: the *bordo* system of the Eastern Bajío. See *HLAS 53:2726.*

1214 Dubernard Chauveau, Juan. María de Estrada, la heroina de la conquista. Cuernavaca, Mexico: s.n., 1989. 78 p.: ill.

Provides heavily padded but still brief account of María de Estrada, early settler in Cuba and participant in the conquest of Mexico. [AL]

1215 Eisman Lasaga, Carmen. El manuscrito de Fray Pedro de Vera (1603) en la biblioteca del Palacio Real de Madrid. (*Rev. Agust.*, 33:102, sept./dic. 1992, p. 1317–1374)

Editor claims that this manuscript is a more accurate version of a 1603 description of Augustinian province of Michoacán than the work published in 1891. Provides useful introductory editorial comments and annotations to the text. [AL]

1216 Escobar Ohmstede, Antonio. Los problemas de elección del cabildo indígena en Yahualica, 1787–1792. (*in* Encuentro de Investigadores de la Huasteca, *4th, Tlalpan, Mexico, 1988?.* Cuextecapan, lugar de bastimentos. Coordinación de Agustín Avila Méndez y Jesús Ruvalcaba Mercado. México: SEP, 1991, p. 32–41)

Microstudy looks at political manipulation of elections in an indigenous community in late 18th century. Reveals tensions and antagonism among indigenous factions, parish priest, and Spanish officials. Narrative history. [AL]

1217 Escobar Olmedo, Armando Mauricio. Catálogo de documentos michoacanos en archivos españoles. v. 1. Morelia, Mexico: Univ. Michoacana de San Nicolás de Hidalgo, 1989. 1 v.

Carefully edited guide lists documents on Michoacán preserved in Spanish archives and available in microfilm in Michoacán. This volume provides information on selections from the Archivo General de Indias in Seville. Annotations on the archives and the sources are very useful. [AL]

1218 Fernández Márquez, Antonio and **Rocío Sánchez Rubio.** Trujillanos en Nueva España: proceso inquisitorial contra Alonso Ramiro de Hinojosa, 1597. (*in* Coloquios Históricos de Extremadura, *18th, Trujillo, Spain, 1989.* Actas. Cáceres, Spain: Institución Cultural El Brocense de la Excma. Diputación Provincial de Cáceres, 1991, p. 63–72)

Inquisitional records unveil details in life of two migrants to New Spain in late 16th century. This case study illustrates their economic and social interests, and behavioral problems. [AL]

1219 Galve, Gelvira de Toledo, *Condesa de.* Two hearts, one soul: the correspondence of the Condesa de Galve, 1688–96. Edited, annotated, and translated by Meredith D. Dodge and Rick Hendricks. Albuquerque: Univ. of New Mexico Press, 1993. 272 p.

The correspondence of one of Sor Juana's noble friends, a subject of many of Sor Juana's poems, is of interest to colonialists. Useful addition to the limited number of women's letters. [AL]

1220 Gálvez, José de. Informe sobre las rebeliones populares de 1767 y otros documentos inéditos. Edición de Felipe Castro Gutiérrez. México: Univ. Nacional Autónoma de México, 1990. 122 p.: appendices, bibl., index. (Serie Historia novohispana; 43)

Includes selection of 14 unabridged documents on the Gálvez visit to New Spain in 1767. [AL]

1221 Garavaglia, Juan Carlos and **Juan Carlos Grosso.** El comportamiento demográfico de una parroquia poblana de la colonia al México independiente: Tepeaca y su entorno agrario, 1740–1850. (*Hist. Mex.,* 40:4, abril/junio 1991, p. 615–671, bibl., graphs, maps, tables)

Presents carefully crafted demographic overview of the town of Tepeaca from 1740–1850. Population became increasingly *mestiza* and prone to emigration. While the Spanish group increased in size, it became older in age. [AL]

1222 García Bernal, Manuela Cristina. La pérdida de la propiedad indígena ante la expansión de las estancias yucatecas: siglo XVII. (*in* Jornadas de Andalucía y América, *8th, Univ. Hispanoamericana Santa María de la Rábida, Sevilla, Spain, 1988.* Propiedad de la tierra, latifundios y movimientos campesinos en Andalucía y América: actas. Sevilla, Spain: Escuela de Estudios Hispanoamericanos, C.I.C.S.; Univ. Hispanoamericana Santa María de la Rábida, 1991, p. 56–90)

Author proposes that usurpation of indigenous land in Yucatán was occurring before the 18th century through royal grants or land sales by indigenous peoples in times of demographic crisis. Uses examples of well-developed 17th-century haciendas and cattle *estancias*, and of easy transfer of land prevalent in that century through *mercedes* and title fixing, to support her thesis and change interpretation of land ownership in the peninsula. [AL]

1223 García Bernal, Manuela Cristina. Un posible modelo de explotación pecuaria en Yucatán: el caso de la propiedad de Tziskal-Chacsinkin. (*Anu. Estud. Am.,* 48, 1991, p. 283–348, tables)

Intensive study of a Yucatecan cattle

ranch throughout the colonial period provides detailed information on legal aspects of property transfers, economic cycles in the property's life, incorporation of further lands, chantries, indigenous labor, administrative problems, etc. Thorough coverage is based on archival research. [AL]

1224 García Bustamente, Miguel. El comercio negrero en el Piedemonte de Veracruz: Xalapa, Córdoba y Orizaba, 1595–1690. (*HISLA/Lima*, 13/14, 1989, p. 25–37, bibl., graphs, tables)

Useful study examines African slave trade on circum-Caribbean coast of Mexico. Slaves were destined for sugar mills. Author furnishes statistical information on provenance, price, and gender. [AL]

1225 García-Lomas, Cristina. Las huestas de Hernán Cortés. (*in* Jornadas de Historiadores Americanistas, *1st, Santafé, Spain, 1987*. América: hombre y sociedad. Presentación de Joaquín A. Muñoz Mendoza. Granada, Spain: Diputación Provincial de Granada, 1988, p. 155–180)

Engaging essay examines the men who followed Cortés and the nature of his "army" in order to illustrate the type of men who conquered the New World. Author establishes that there was no professional "army" in the 1520s, and proceeds to analyze sociological profile of Cortés' men, the behavior of the group, and relationship between the captain and his men. [AL]

1226 González González, Enrique. El rechazo de la Universidad de México a las reformas ilustradas, 1763–1777. (*Rev. Univ./Alcalá*, 7, 1991, p. 94–124)

Author argues that university faculty lacked interest in modernizing scientific teaching. Local and metropolitan efforts to update medical teaching were successfully blocked in an example of resistance to the Enlightenment. [AL]

1227 González Muñoz, Victoria and **Ana Isabel Martínez Ortega.** Cabildos y elites capitulares en Yucatán: dos estudios. Sevilla, Spain: Escuela de Estudios Hispano-Americanos de Sevilla, Consejo Superior de Investigaciones Científicas, 1989. 289 p.: bibl., index. (Publicaciones de la Escuela de Estudios Hispano-Americanos de Sevilla; 344. Col. Dos colores)

Two separate studies of the municipal

council of the main cities in Yucatán (Mérida, Valladolid, and Campeche) cover 1650–75 and 1700–25 respectively. Authors analyze economic, social, and political power of *cabildo* members, their endogamic connections, and the institution of *repartimiento* in this area. Important contribution. [AL]

1228 Grañen Porrúa, Isabel. El ámbito sociolaboral de las imprentas novohispanas, siglo XVI. (*Anu. Estud. Am.*, 48, 1991, p. 49–94, photos, table)

Relates establishment of first printing houses in Mexico City. Surveys needs of these businesses, their labor force, the role of women as owners, and the most important books published during 16th century. [AL]

1229 Greenleaf, Richard E. *et al.* Gonzalo Gómez, primer poblador español de Guayangareo, Morelia: proceso inquisitorial. Morelia, Mexico: Fimax Publicistas, 1991. 288 p.

Contains complete reproduction of inquisitorial process carried out against Morelia's first Spanish settler, accused of Judaization. Introduction by two notable historians provides biographical data of historical figures, and explains situation of Jews in New Spain as well as the inquisitorial process. [AL]

1230 Gutiérrez Rodríguez, Víctor. El colegio novohispano de Santa María de Todos Santos: alcances y límites de una institución colonial. (*Estud. Hist. Soc. Econ. Am.* 9, 1992, p. 23–35)

Author points out the relative research neglect of *colegios*, centers of higher education in Spain and Spanish America. Outlines the story of Santa María de Todos Santos in Mexico and its rivalry with the university over privileges. [AL]

1231 Haskett, Robert Stephen. "Our suffering with the Taxco tribute:" involuntary mine labor and indigenous society in central New Spain. (*HAHR*, 71:3, August 1991, p. 447–475)

Surveys indigenous labor demand and supply for Taxco silver mines throughout colonial period. Balanced analysis based on archival sources provides many useful insights. [AL]

1232 Himmerich y Valencia, Robert. The *encomenderos* of New Spain, 1521–1555. Foreword by Joseph P. Sánchez. Austin:

Univ. of Texas Press, 1991. 348 p.: bibl., ill., index, maps, tables.

Profiles first *encomienda* holders of New Spain. Traces their social and regional origins in Spain, and their integration into New Spain's early society through settlement and marriage. Includes mini-biographies of 506 *encomenderos*. Maps and tables enhance usefulness of this compact guide to New Spain's first elite. [AL]

1233 Hoekstra, Rik. Profit from the wastelands: social change and the formation of haciendas in the Valley of Puebla, 1570–1640. (*Rev. Eur.*, 52, June 1992, p. 91–123, graphs, maps, tables)

Proposes reinterpretation of changes in land ownership and formation of haciendas in late 16th-century Puebla. Demographic depletion and subsequent shifts, tribute reforms, redefinition of legal notion of ownership, and land grants to Spaniards were key factors in the creation of a hacienda system. Based on archival research. [AL]

1234 Jarquín Ortega, María Teresa. Formación y desarrollo de un pueblo novohispano: Metepec en el Valle de Toluca. Metepec, Mexico: Colegio Mexiquense; H. Ayuntamiento de Metepec, 1990. 367 p.: bibl., ill., index, maps.

Microhistory of town of Metepec, near Toluca, focuses mainly on 16th and 17th centuries. Examines civil administration, land tenure, labor, and religious affairs. Thorough work based on archival sources. [AL]

1235 Juárez Nieto, Carlos. Oligarquía y poder político en Valladolid de Michoacán, 1790–1810. (*An. Mus. Michoacano*, 2, 1990, p. 45–72)

Analyzes elite society in Valladolid in late 18th century, underlining family networks and individual roles of notable members of economic, political, and religious upper crust. [AL]

1236 Langue, Frédérique. Mineros y poder en Nueva España: el caso de Zacatecas en vísperas de la independencia. (*Rev. Indias*, 51:192, mayo/agosto 1991, p. 327–341)

Surveys economic expansion of mining in Zacatecas in 1780s, and ascent of a new economic and political elite. This elite became involved in an internal power struggle which author suggests was a forerunner of 19th-century political rivalries. [AL]

1237 Langue, Frédérique. Trabajadores y formas de trabajo en las minas zacatecanas del siglo XVIII. (*Hist. Mex.*, 40:3, enero/marzo 1991, p. 463–506, bibl.)

Reevaluation and analysis of sociology of mine labor and entrepreneurs in 18th century explains fate of *partido*, and collapse of a varied system of workers and owners into wage laborers and substantial owners in 19th century. Significant contribution to economic and labor history. [EBC]

1238 Lerdo de Tejada, Juan Antonio. Cartas a un comerciante español, 1811–1817. Prólogo y notas de Carmen Blázquez Domínguez. Xalapa, Mexico: Univ. Veracruzana; Instituto Veracruzana de Cultura, 1989. 189 p. (Col. UV rescate; 31)

Contains series of letters exchanged between Juan Antonio Lerdo de Tejada—merchant in Veracruz and father of Miguel Lerdo de Tejada, president of Mexico—and his business correspondent in Mexico City, between 1811 and 1817. Rich in financial and political information. Originals are in the manuscript collection of Columbia University. [AL]

1239 Lipsett-Rivera, Sonya. Indigenous communities and water rights in colonial Puebla: patterns of resistance. (*Americas/Francisc.*, 48:4, April 1992, p. 463–483, maps, tables)

Interesting study examines 65 litigation incidents for control of water resources by Spanish and indigenous peoples in the Puebla region in the 18th century. Active and passive resistance methods are examined, and author stresses importance of these activities owing to demographic increases, greater demand for land and irrigation, and an economy strained by competition from other agricultural regions. [AL]

1240 Lipsett-Rivera, Sonya. Water and bureaucracy in colonial Puebla de los Angeles. (*J. Lat. Am. Stud.*, 25:1, Feb. 1993, p. 25–44, map, tables)

Thorough study examines Puebla's water supply, revealing allocation and distribution policies for private and public customers. [AL]

1241 Lockhart, James. Españoles entre indios: Toluca a fines del siglo XVI. (*in* Haciendas, pueblos y comunidades: los valles de México y Toluca entre 1530 y 1916. México: Consejo Nacional para la Cultura y las Artes, 1991, p. 52–116)

Reprints important article which originally appeared in 1974 (see *HLAS 40:2502*). An English-language version of this essay is included in Lockhart's *Nahuas and Spaniards: postconquest Central Mexican history and philology* (see item **519**). [R. Haskett and S. Wood]

1242 Lohmann Villena, Guillermo. Notas sobre la presencia de la Nueva España en las cortes metropolitanas y de cortes en la Nueva España en los siglos XVI y XVII. (*Hist. Mex.*, 39:1, julio/sept. 1989, p. 33–40, bibl.)

Brief essay examines inconclusive attempts of the Cabildo de México to organize the local *cortes* and pay tribute to the Crown for this privilege. Similar attempts to have American representatives in the Spanish *cortes* came to naught, since the taxation implicit in the granting of such a privilege discouraged the colonists. [AL]

1243 López Ramírez, María del Carmen. El desagüe de Huehuetoca. (*in* Jornadas de Historiadores Americanistas 2nd, *Granada, Spain, 1989*. América: encuentro y asimilación. Edición de Joaquín A. Muñoz Mendoza. Granada, Spain: Diputación Provincial de Granada, 1990, p. 63–86, tables)

Main contribution of this essay is data from a little-known manuscript relating accounts of cost and financing of Mexico City's drainage between 1607 and 1777. [AL]

1244 Loreto López, Rosalva. Familias y conventos en Puebla de Los Angeles durante las reformas borbónicas: los cambios del siglo XVIII. (*Anu. IEHS*, 5, 1990, p. 31–50, tables)

Very general study looks at changes in nuns' investments and lifestyle in 17th-century Puebla. Data on convents of Santa Catalina and Santa Inés are welcomed. [AL]

1245 Malvido, Elsa. Migration patterns of the novices of the Order of San Francisco in Mexico City, 1649–1749. (*in* Migration in colonial Spanish America. Edited by David J. Robinson. Cambridge: Cambridge Univ. Press, 1990, p. 182–192, graph, maps, tables)

Traces demographic changes experienced by the Franciscan Order novices throughout mid-colonial period. Retreat from missionary activities and acceptance of Mexican-born novices changed nature of Order's membership. [AL]

1246 Martínez Ortega, Ana Isabel. Estructura y configuración socioeconómica de los cabildos de Yucatán en el siglo XVIII. Sevilla, Spain: Excma. Diputación Provincial de Sevilla, 1993. 363 p.: bibl., index. (Sección V centenario del descubrimiento)

Thorough and solid study examines *cabildos* of the Yucatán's three main cities: Mérida, Valladolid, and Campeche. Topics included are: social composition and economic power of *cabildo* members; sale of positions; endogamy, family, and networks; and effect of Bourbon intendants on the institution. Based on archival research, work provides important information on the Yucatán power elite. [AL]

1247 Mazín, Oscar. Entre dos majestades: el obispo y la Iglesia del Gran Michoacán ante las reformas borbónicas, 1758–1772. Zamora, Mexico: Colegio de Michoacán, 1987. 305 p.: bibl., ill., index, maps.

Solid monograph examines tenure of Pedro Anselmo Sánchez de Tagle, Bishop of Michoacán between 1758–72. Surveys key topics such as parish secularization, restructuring of tithes, relations with ecclesiastical *cabildo*, foundation of schools, and patronage of charity institutions. A different type of ecclesiastical history, work examines interaction of Church and State by presenting activities of a prelate amidst the Bourbon reforms which generated numerous policy confrontations. [AL]

1248 Meade, Joaquín and **Rafael Almanza.** Los agustinos en San Luis Potosí. Introducción, transcripción, y notas de Rafael Montejano y Aguiñaga. San Luis Potosí, Mexico: Archivo Historico del Estado de San Luis Potosí, 1989. 150 p.: bibl., ill., index.

Reprint of Joaquín Meade's history of the Augustinian Order in Potosí, last published in 1965. [AL]

1249 Menegus Bornemann, Margarita. La organización económico-espacial del trabajo indígena en el valle de Toluca, 1530–1630. (*in* Haciendas, pueblos y comunidades: los valles de México y Toluca entre 1530 y 1916. México: Consejo Nacional para la Cultura y las Artes, 1991, p. 21–51, maps, tables)

Surveys provenance and nature of indigenous labor employed in the mines and public works of the Toluca Valley. Although based on printed sources, this synthesis is useful for graduate students. [AL]

1250 Mora Cañada, Adela. La Universidad de México a través de su hacienda en 1700. (*Estud. Hist. Soc. Econ. Am.*, 9, 1992, p. 59–80, table)

Microstudy looks at income and expenses of the Univ. de México, filling a gap in available knowledge of the university's finances. [AL]

1251 Moreno de los Arcos, Roberto. New Spain's Inquisition for Indians from the sixteenth to the nineteenth century. (*in* Cultural encounters: the impact of the Inquisition in Spain and the New World. Berkeley: Univ. of California Press, 1991, p. 23–36, bibl., ill.)

Briefly discusses the several stages of ecclesiastical control over indigenous religious practices prior to establishment of the Inquisition, and exclusion of these practices from subjection to that institution. [AL]

1252 Muriel, Josefina. Las instituciones de mujeres: raíz de esplendor arquitectónico en la antigua ciudad de Santiago de Querétaro. (*Estud. Hist. Novohisp.*, 10, 1991, p. 141–172, photos)

Surveys the foundation of nunneries and schools for women in Querétaro, underlining the value of the churches, paintings, and altars as among the best in colonial architecture. [AL]

1253 Musset, Alain. Congregaciones y reorganización del espacio: el caso del acueducto de Tenango, siglo XVI. (*in* Mundo rural, ciudades y población del Estado de México. Coordinación de Manuel Miño Grijalva. Toluca, México: El Colegio Mexiquense; Instituto Mexiquense de Cultura, 1990, p. 147–163, ill., map)

Underscores importance of water supply for some arid indigenous towns of central Mexico, and provides a case study of construction of the aqueduct of Tenango built by the indigenous people for their town under Dominican direction. [AL]

1254 Navas-Sierra, J. Alberto. Gran Bretaña, Napoleón, Fernando VII y la pretendida regencia en México en 1808. (*Rev. Indias*, 46: 178, julio/dic. 1986, p. 509–559, bibl.)

Detailed narrative relates British-supported plan to create a Bourbon regency in Mexico during estrangement of Ferdinand VII from the Spanish throne. A failed plot, incident reveals complexities of international affairs during that period. [AL]

1255 Ouweneel, Arij. Growth, stagnation, and migration: an exploration analysis of the *tributario* series of Anáhuac, 1720–1800. (*HAHR*, 71:3, August 1991, p. 531–577, graphs, maps, tables)

Author searches for reliable data to verify demographic changes in the Mexico City and Puebla areas. Using tribute collection data, author proposes that migration, urbanization, proto-industrialization, and even changes in ethnic affiliation among migrants are key factors in the study of demographic changes. [AL]

1256 Pérez Verdía, Luis. Historia particular del Estado de Jalisco. Guadalajara, México: Editorial Univ. de Guadalajara, 1988- . 3 v.: ill. (Col. facsimilar)

Facsimile edition (first ed., 1910) of a standard colonial history of Jalisco state by notable 19th-century historian Luis Pérez Verdía. Of historiographical interest. [AL]

1257 Pescador, Juan Javier. Inmigración femenina, empleo y familia en una parroquia de la ciudad de México: Santa Catarina, 1775–1790. (*Estud. Demogr. Urb.*, 5:3, sept./ dic. 1990, p. 729–754, bibl., graphs, maps, tables)

Demographic analysis looks at Santa Catarina parish in Mexico City, 1775–1790. Female population imbalance is explained by migration responding to employment opportunity in services and manufacturing. [AL]

1258 Prem, Hanns J. Disease outbreaks in central Mexico during the sixteenth century. (*in* International Congress of Americanists, *46th, Amsterdam, 1988.* "Secret judgements of God": Old World disease in colonial Spanish America. Edited by Noble David Cook and W. George Lovell. Norman: Univ. of Oklahoma Press, 1991, p. 20–48, map, tables)

Author uses native and contemporary sources to review all major 16th-century epidemics, questioning nature of the diseases and postulating an "abrupt" rather than a gradual process of depopulation once an epidemic began. [AL]

1259 Rabell, Cecilia. Matrimonio y raza en una parroquia rural: San Luis de La Paz, Guanajuato, 1715–1810. (*Hist. Mex.*, 42:1, julio/sept. 1992, p. 3–44, bibl., graphs, tables)

Meticulous study examines marriage patterns across the four predominant ethnic groups in a rural community of central New Spain. Author finds exogamy was more frequent in first half of 18th century, while illegitimacy declined throughout the century. Very useful for comparative studies. [AL]

1260 Ragon, Pierre. Les Indiens de la découverte: evangélisation, mariage et sexualité; Mexique, XVIe siècle. Paris: Harmattan, 1992. 255 p.: bibl., ills., tables. (Col. Recherches et documents Amériques latines)

Careful study examines enforcement of Christian marriage canons by theologians and missionaries in 16th-century Mexico. Author surveys indigenous response and assesses their difficulties in assimilating Western Christian concepts regarding this basic sacrament. [AL]

Ramírez Rancaño, Mario. El sistema de haciendas en Tlaxcala. See item **1572.**

1261 Ramos Medina, Manuel. Imagen de santidad en un mundo profano: historia de una fundación. México: Univ. Iberoamericana, Depto. de Historia, 1990. 248 p.: bibl.

Lucid account relates foundation of Reformed Carmelites in Spain and their transfer to New Spain. Author focuses on 17th-century convent of San José (or Santa Teresa la Antigua) in Mexico City. Elements of this history include bishops and their financial and patronage interest in establishment of the Carmelite convent, chaplains, patrons, and relations with the world outside the convent. A long chapter on interior life of the convent characterizes San José as the spiritual elite among feminine convents in Mexico City. [EBC]

1262 Rasmussen, Jørgen Nybo. Fray Jacobo Daciano. 1. ed. en español Zamora, México: El Colegio de Michoacán, 1992. 290 p.: bibl., ill., index, maps.

Work is translation from Danish of a biography of Jacobus de Dacia, a Franciscan friar and son of a Danish king who was especially renowned for his advocacy of ordination for indigenous peoples. [EBC]

1263 Rico Medina, Samuel. Los predicamentos de la fe: la Inquisición en Tabasco, 1567–1811. Villahermosa, Mexico: Gobierno del Estado de Tabasco, 1990. 194 p.: bibl., ill. (Lo de entonces)

Author surveys activities of the Inquisition in Tabasco, dwelling on transgressions

of the faith, sexual ethics, and wayward priests. Work is based on primary sources and helps to expand our data pool on gender relations. [AL]

1264 Rojas, José Luis de. Consideraciones sobre el tributo en Michoacán en el siglo XVI. (*Relaciones/Zamora*, 42, primavera 1990, p. 5–21, tables)

Studies system of indigenous tribute in Michoacán from 1528–70, focusing on textiles and their role in fulfilling tax obligations. [AL]

1265 Rubial García, Antonio. Los santos milagreros y malogrados de la Nueva España. (*in* Espiritualidad barroca colonial: santos y demonios en América. México: Univ. Iberoamericana, 1994, p. 107–124)

Reviews three proposed but failed beatification candidates. Relates proposed models of sanctity upheld in 17th-century Mexico, their political implications, and what they reveal about period's spirituality and its expression. [AL]

1266 Ruiz Abreu, Carlos. Comercio y milicias de Tabasco en la colonia. Villahermosa, Mexico: Gobierno del Estado de Tabasco; ICT Ediciones, 1989. 386 p.: appendices, bibl., ill., maps. (Lo de entonces)

Brief account looks at trade and contraband in late colonial Tabasco. Best parts of this work are the documentary appendices, especially a 1766 militia census comprising fully one-third of the volume. [AL]

1267 Ruiz Medrano, Ethelia. Gobierno y sociedad en Nueva España: segunda audiencia y Antonio de Mendoza. Zamora, Mexico: El Colegio de Michoacán; Gobierno del Estado de Michoacán, 1991. 407 p.: bibl., maps.

In-depth examination of 1535–50 period, and the administrations of the Second Audiencia and Viceroy Mendoza. Author analyzes policies adopted for solving problems of land tenure and allocation of indigenous labor. Also studies entrepreneurial activities of one powerful *oidor* to illustrate activities of first settlers in their search for financial gain. Serious and useful study based on archival sources. [AL]

1268 Salafranca Ortega, Jesús F. La Diócesis de Oaxaca en vísperas de la insurgencia. (*in* Jornadas de Historiadores Americanistas, 2nd, Granada, Spain, 1989. América: encuentro y asimilación. Edición de Joaquín A. Muñoz Mendoza. Granada: Diputación Provincial de Granada, 1990, p. 51–62)

Detailed report relates pastoral visits of Oaxaca's Bishop Antonio Bergoza y Jordán (1800–03) and the new tax scheme for indigenous peoples recommended during his prelacy. [AL]

1269 Salazar de Garza, Nuria. La vida común en los conventos de monjas de la ciudad de Puebla. Puebla, Mexico: Gobierno del Estado de Puebla, Secretaría de Cultura, 1990. 156 p. (Bibliotheca angelopolitana; 5)

Succinct account examines process of ecclesiastical reform of nunneries from 1768–75. Long quotations from primary sources are joined by short narrative paragraphs. No bibliography. [AL]

1270 Santos Carrera, Moisés and Jesús Alvarez Hernández. Historia de la cuestión agraria mexicana: estado de Guerrero; épocas prehispánica y colonial. Chilpancingo, Mexico: Univ. Autónoma de Guerrero; México: Centro Estudios Históricos del Agrarismo en México, s.d. 203 p: bibl.

Studies litigation over land ownership in Guerrero, mostly in 18th century. Presented as a struggle between indigenous communities and Spaniards. Based on archival sources. [AL]

1271 Sepúlveda, Juan Ginés de. Historia del Nuevo Mundo. Introducción, traducción y notas de Antonio Ramírez de Verger. Madrid: Alianza, 1987. 231 p.: bibl., maps. (Alianza universidad; 495: Historia)

Modern translation from original Latin of Sepúlveda's De orbe novo, first printed in 1781. This history of the conquest of Mexico based on the best contemporary sources and written in Renaissance Latin complements Sepúlveda's Historia de Carlos V. [AL]

1272 Soto Pérez, José Luis. Fuentes documentales para la historia de la provincia franciscana de Michoacán en el siglo XVIII. (Arch. Ibero-Am., 52:205/208, 1992, p. 81–106)

General description of Franciscan Archives of the province of Michoacán, which are located in Celaya and contain a rich collection of documents for history of Franciscans in Mexico. Holdings of the Franciscan Archives cover entire span of Mexican history

and should be very helpful for study of the order. [AL]

1273 Thibon-Marey, Placer. Sur les pas de Sahagún au XVIIe siècle: Hernando Ruiz de Alarcón. (Caravelle/Toulouse, 56, 1991, p. 5–13)

Discusses survival of prehispanic Aztec beliefs and rituals as gathered in 1620s by Hernando Ruiz de Alarcón and compared with earlier observations by Fray Bernardino de Sahagún. [AL]

1274 Torre Villar, Ernesto de la. Diego Antonio Bermúdez de Castro en la historiografía novohispana. (Hist. Mex., 39:2, oct./dic. 1989, p. 387–416, bibl.)

Capable analysis looks at one of the least-known historians of the city of Puebla. [AL]

1275 Torre Villar, Ernesto de la. Eguiara y Eguren, orador sagrado. (Estud. Hist. Novohisp., 10, 1991, p. 173–188)

Presents intellectual profile of Juan José de Eguiara y Eguren, a prolific 18th-century religious preacher. Surveys and evaluates his contribution to that genre in his over 400 sermons. [AL]

1276 Torre Villar, Ernesto de la. La teología en Nueva España: apuntamientos. (Mem. Acad. Mex. Hist., 34, 1991, p. 5–61)

Lists main theologians of New Spain and their key works. Includes Univ. de Mexico and main regular orders. Valuable as a reference. [AL]

1277 Watson, Rodney. Informal settlement and fugitive migration amongst the Indians of late-colonial Chiapas, Mexico. (in Migration in colonial Spanish America. Edited by David J. Robinson. Cambridge: Cambridge Univ. Press, 1990, p. 238–278, graphs, tables)

Excellent study examines population movements and changes in Chiapas throughout colonial period. Based on archival sources, author concludes that indigenous migrations were an adaptation to colonial circumstances and an extension of preconquest agricultural patterns. [AL]

1278 Whitmore, Thomas M. Disease and death in early colonial Mexico: simulating Amerindian depopulation. Boulder, Colo.: Westview Press, 1992. 261 p.: bibl., ill., index, map. (Dellplain Latin American studies; 28)

Gives computer-based estimate of indigenous depopulation in central Mexico after the conquest. Considers data contemporary to the events as well as present-day data and models. Heavily mathematical approach yields credibility to estimates of great losses in the population throughout 16th century. Not easy to read. [AL]

1279 Widmer S., Rolf. Política sanitaria y lucha social en tiempos de viruelas: corona, comercio y communidades indígenas en Tehuantepec, 1795–96. (*Relaciones/Zamora,* 44, otoño 1990, p. 33–74, bibl., map, tables)
Studies sanitary policies adopted by royal officials during 1795 smallpox epidemics in Tehuantepec region. Policy design and enactment and Indian local resistance are discussed and interpreted as a struggle of economic interests. [AL]

1280 Wobeser, Gisela von. La Inquisición como institución crediticia en el siglo XVIII. (*Hist. Mex.,* 39:4, abril/junio 1990, p. 849–879, bibl., tables)
Informative study examines income and investments of the Inquisition, especially during 18th century. Loans, liens, and credit policy changes are carefully described. Banking relationship between merchants and Inquisition in early 19th century is of special interest. [AL]

1281 Wood, Stephanie. Gañanes y cuadrilleros formando pueblos: región de Toluca, época colonial. (*in* Mundo rural, ciudades y población del Estado de México. Coordinación de Manuel Miño Grijalva. Toluca, Mexico: El Colegio Mexiquense; Instituto Mexiquense de Cultura, 1990, p. 93–143, bibl., maps, tables)
Reviews formation of townships in agricultural and mining areas of Toluca during 17th and 18th centuries. Author stresses struggle between permanent hacienda residents, non-resident workers, and established communities to obtain recognition as communities. [AL]

1282 Yuste López, Carmen. El Conde de Tepa ante la visita de José de Gálvez. (*Estud. Hist. Novohisp.,* 11, 1991, p. 119–131)
Francisco de Viana, Conde de Tepa, a wealthy *montañés,* may have influenced Viceroy Antonio de Bucareli to oppose establishment of *intendencias.* Tepa's reasons may have derived from his own personal economic interests. [EBC]

North and Borderlands

1283 Adams, David Bergen. Las colonias tlaxcaltecas de Coahuila y Nuevo León en la Nueva España: un aspecto de la colonización del norte de México. Saltillo, Mexico: Archivo Municipal de Saltillo, 1991. 303 p.: bibl., ill., map.
Translation of a 1970 dessertation chronicles and analyzes impact of Tlaxcalan colonies on northern Mexico. Provides information on both Tlaxcalans' relationships with other migrants and their interaction with other indigenous groups. [EBC]

1284 Alvarez, Salvador. Chiametla: una provincia olvidada del siglo XVI. (*Trace/México,* 22, déc. 1992, p. 5–23, bibl., tables)
Clarifies establishment of Pacific coast frontier of New Spain in the 16th century, noting that this was New Spain's first boundary with contested regions to the north. [EBC]

1285 Alvarez, Salvador. Tendencias regionales de la propiedad territorial en el norte de la Nueva España, siglos XVII y XVIII. (*in* Congreso de Historia Regional Comparada, 2nd, Ciudad Juárez, Mexico, 1990. Actas. Edición de Ricardo León García. Ciudad Juárez, Mexico: Univ. Autónoma de Ciudad Juárez, 1991, p. 141–179, graph, maps, tables)
Points out relative neglect of hacienda studies for the north since 1952 publication of Francois Chevalier's *La formation de grandes domaines au Mexique* (see HLAS 18: 1747a). Attempts to redress this gap through study of *composiciones* issued for northwestern Nueva Vizcaya in relation to variety of previous land tenure arrangements and social organization of the population. [EBC]

1286 Arbeláez, María Soledad. The Sonoran missions and Indian raids of the eighteenth century. (*J. Southwest,* 33:3, Fall 1991, p. 366–386, appendix, tables)
Preliminary findings regarding effects of Apache and Seri raids on Jesuit missions demonstrate that object of the raids was to take tamed horses (and not necessarily other livestock), an action which could frustrate Jesuit aim of achieving self-sufficiency. [EBC]

1287 Baegert, Jacob. Noticias de la península americana de California. Notas introductorias de W. Michael Mathes y Raúl Antonio Cota. Traducción del alemán de Pedro R.

Hendrichs. 2. ed. La Paz, Mexico: Gobierno del Estado de Baja California Sur, 1989. 262 p.: bibl., index, map. (Serie Cronistas; 3)

Second edition of a 1942 translation (see *HLAS 8:233*) relates German Jesuit's description of Baja California in the middle of the 18th century. [EBC]

1288 Bakewell, Peter. La periodización de la producción minera en el norte de la Nueva España durante la época colonial. (*Estud. Hist. Novohisp.*, 10, 1991, p. 31–43)

New estimates of silver production in New Spain demonstrate that there was a 25 percent reduction in silver production from 1635–70 (compared with the period 1615–35). Postulates that silver production steadily increased in 18th century due to improved beneficiation techniques and employment of explosives to uncover new veins of silver. [EBC]

1289 Barco, Miguel del. Historia natural de la Antigua California. Introducción de Miguel León-Portilla. Madrid: Historia 16, 1989. 317 p.: bibl. (Crónicas de América; 53)

Well-annotated edition of scientific treatise of this 18th-century Jesuit includes biographical and critical introduction. [EBC]

1290 Barrazza Arévalo, Héctor. La población negra en el sur de Coahuila. (*in* Congreso de Historia Regional Comparada, *2nd, Ciudad Juárez, Mexico, 1990.* Actas. Edición de Ricardo León García. Ciudad Juárez, Mexico: Univ. Autónoma de Ciudad Juárez, 1991, p. 191–214, bibl., graphs, tables)

Notarial transactions, parish records and a census reveal existence of a number of slaves and a significant Afro-mestizo population in Parral and surrounding areas. Notes drop in slave prices in last half of 18th century. [EBC]

1291 Benignos Acuña, Clemencia *et al.* Mil tres textos sobre la historia de la Frontera Norte. México: Comité Mexicano de Ciencias Históricas, 1986. 445 p.

Comprehensive annotated bibliography, divided by states and including onomastic index, lists materials to be found in Mexican repositories. [EBC]

1292 Cramaussel, Chantal. Evolución de las formas de dominio del espacio colonial: las haciendas de la región de Parral. (*in* Congreso de Historia Regional Comparada, *2nd, Ciudad Juárez, Mexico, 1990.* Actas. Edición de Ricardo León García. Ciudad Juár-

ez, Mexico: Univ. Autónoma de Ciudad Juárez, 1991, p. 115–140, appendix, map)

Solidly researched study examines land ownership process in Durango-Chihuahua region. Author uses data for entire colonial period to propose three major periods in process of land tenure and labor definition. Identifies *latifundia* growth after 1700. [AL]

1293 Cramaussel, Chantal. La urbanización primitiva del real de Parral. (*Trace/ México*, 22, déc. 1992, p. 37–53, bibl., maps, tables)

Important study deals with urban geography of mining towns. Points out that streets and house lots in Parral followed pre-existing patterns based on central role of water for beneficiation of silver. [EBC]

1294 Cuello, José. The persistence of Indian slavery and *encomienda* in the northeast of colonial Mexico, 1577–1723. (*J. Soc. Hist.*, 21:4, Summer 1988, p. 683–700)

Analyzes and compares labor systems in Saltillo and Nuevo León. Discovers that Spanish and Mexican settlers had an interest in preserving the hunter-gatherer bands of indigenous peoples in order to have seasonal labor available. [EBC]

1295 Curiel, Gustavo. Cuatro inventarios de bienes de particulares del real y minas de San José del Parral, siglo XVIII. (*in* Congreso de Historia Regional Comparada, *2nd, Ciudad Juárez, 1990.* Actas. Edición de Ricardo León García. Ciudad Juárez, Mexico: Univ. Autónoma de Ciudad Juárez, Mexico, 1991, p. 249–279, map, tables)

Documents contain valuable data about elite material culture and an introductory explanation. [EBC]

1296 Deeds, Susan M. Mission villages and agrarian patterns in a Nueva Vizcayan heartland, 1600–1750. (*J. Southwest*, 33:3, Fall 1991, p. 345–365, map)

Historical study of various localities reveals that decline in indigenous population by end of 17th century was decisive factor in loss of lands by both missions and villages. Forced labor, aggression against indigenous properties, and increase in non-indigenous population vitiated viability of indigenous villages and missions. [EBC]

1297 Flagler, Edward K. Las relaciones interétnicas entre los navajos y los españoles de Nuevo México. (*Rev. Esp. Antropol. Am.*, 18, 1988, p. 129–157, bibl., map)

Detailed study recounts effects of 18th-century wars and treaties on relationships among missionaries, Spaniards, Navajos and other Indian groups. Describes adaptations made by Navajos in their evolution from a small population of hunter-gatherers to an expanding group based on sheep breeding and other borrowed cultural traits, combined with elements of their own precontact culture. [EBC]

1298 González de la Vara, Martín. La visita eclesiástica de Francisco Atanasio Domínguez al Nuevo México y su relación. (*Estud. Hist. Novohisp.*, 10, 1991, p. 267–288, bibl.)

Places in historical context the 1775 Franciscan *visita*. Quotes liberally from the account, which has never been published in Spanish. Author adds valuable information on history of the missions and concerns of Franciscans. Provides biographical materials on the *visitador.* [EBC]

1299 González Rodríguez, Luis. Testimonios sobre la destrucción de las misiones tarahumares [i.e., tarahumaras] y pimas en 1690. (*Estud. Hist. Novohisp.*, 10, 1991, p. 189–235, bibl.)

Publication of crucial parts of extensive letters written by Jesuits and others describing 1690 rebellion is combined with author's narrative materials and biographical and ethnographic observations. [EBC]

1300 El Gran Nayar. Investigación y compilación de Jean A. Meyer. Guadalajara, Mexico: Univ. de Guadalajara; México: Centre d'Etudes Mexicaines et Centraméricaines, 1989. 291 p.: bibl., maps. (Col. de documentos para la historia de Nayarit; 3)

Collection and transcription of documents about Nayarit begins with 1709 and continues through end of colonial period, with special emphasis on indigenous peoples. As arranged, collection makes a coherent story. [EBC]

1301 Guest, Francis F. Principles for an interpretation of the history of the California missions, 1769–1893. (*Hisp. Sacra*, 40, julio/dic. 1988, p. 791–805)

In a spirited defense of work of Franciscan friars, author urges that 18th-century Spanish context be considered. Replies to some of the recent arguments critical of treatment of indigenous peoples. [EBC]

1302 Hilton, Sylvia L. La alta California española. Madrid: Editorial MAPFRE, 1992. 366 p.: bibl., indexes, map. (Col. España y Estados Unidos; 7. Col MAPFRE 1492)

Useful work grounded in a thorough review of secondary sources includes social, political, and military history. [EBC]

1303 Jackson, Robert H. La colonización de la Alta California: un análisis del desarrollo de dos comunidades misionales. (*Hist. Mex.*, 41:1, julio/sept. 1991, p. 83–110, bibl., tables)

See item **1305.**

1304 Jackson, Robert H. La dinámica del desastre demográfico de la población india en las misiones de la Bahía de San Francisco, Alta California, 1776–1840. (*Hist. Mex.*, 40:2, oct./dic. 1990, p. 187–215, graphs, tables)

Comparative demographic analysis of northern California missions indicates that their high mortality rates were due not to epidemics but to enclosure of residents in small spaces, syphilis, and cultural shock. Draws comparisons with missions in southern California. [EBC]

1305 Jackson, Robert H. Population and the economic dimension of colonization in Alta California: four mission communities. (*J. Southwest*, 33:3, Fall 1991, p. 387–439, appendices, tables)

Based on extensive quantitative research, these two articles (see also item **1303**) on California missions conclude that indigenous population supported the *presidios*— and, by extension, the cost of the Spanish conquest and colonization—with both their labor and the crops produced by the missions. [EBC]

1306 Jiménez-Pelayo, Agueda. El impacto del crédito en la economía rural del norte de la Nueva Galicia. (*HAHR*, 71:3, Aug. 1991, p. 501–529, graphs, tables)

Excellent study examines sources of credit, means of acquisition and disposal of capital destined for credit, and circulation of such funds. Diachronic study of 18th century sheds light on the pulse of this important aspect of the economy. [AL]

1307 Jiménez-Pelayo, Agueda. Problemas de tierra de comunidades indígenas en el norte de la Nueva Galicia en la época colonial. (*Yearbook/CLAG*, 15, 1989, p. 87–95, bibl., map)

Microstudy examines indigenous land tenure issues in northern Nueva Galicia, an agricultural region close to Zacatecas. Author studies land grant process, struggle for land control among indigenous peoples, and indigenous/Spanish relations. Based on archival research. [AL]

1308 McCaa, Robert. Gustos de los padres, inclinaciones de los novios y reglas de una feria nupcial colonial: Parral, 1770–1814. (*Hist. Mex.*, 40:4, abril/junio 1991, p. 579–614, bibl., graph, tables)

Author uses Parral data for 1770–1814 period to analyze issue of parental consent or dissent to marriages and several variables affecting marriage choices in that area. [AL]

1309 McCaa, Robert. Marriage, migration, and settling down: Parral, Nueva Vizcaya, 1770–1778. (*in* Migration in colonial Spanish America. Edited by David J. Robinson. Cambridge: Cambridge Univ. Press, 1990, p. 212–237, appendix, map, tables)

Marriage registrations are linked to several late 18th-century censuses to establish settlement patterns of newly-formed families. Author's analysis includes occupation, gender, region of birth, and other variables. Ends with assessment of changes in technology of census use and of richer analytical possibilities of computer-generated data. Pithy work. [AL]

1310 Merrill, William L. La indoctrinación religiosa en la tarahumara colonial: los informes de los visitadores Lizasoain y Aguirre al final de la época jesuítica. (*in* Congreso de Historia Regional Comparada, *2nd, Ciudad Juárez, Mexico, 1990.* Actas. Edición de Ricardo León García. Ciudad Juárez, Mexico: Univ. Autónoma de Ciudad Juárez, 1991, p. 283–302, graphs, table)

Explores reason behind various degrees of religious conversion and Christian practice among the Tarahumaras by using communion as index of familiarity with Christianity. Considers factors such as indigenous willingness to practice Christianity, missionary's period of residence, differing views among contemporary reporters, etc. [AL]

1311 Meyer, Jean A. Las misiones jesuitas del Gran Nayar, 1722–1767: aculturación y predicación del Evangelio. (*Trace/México*, 22, déc. 1992, p. 86–101, bibl.)

Important essay uses material about Jesuit missions among the Cora and other groups of Nayarit region to analyze process of conversion. Points out that while Jesuits sought to change marriage and social customs among the indigenous peoples, they respected varieties of religious experiences. [EBC]

1312 Meyer, Michael C. Public health in northern New Spain. (*Estud. Hist. Novohisp.*, 11, 1991, p. 135–153)

Chronicles efforts to improve water supplies, clean up excrement from public places, and contain spread of yellow fever. Especially valuable for account of introduction of smallpox vaccine. [EBC]

1313 Offutt, Leslie S. Hispanic society in the Mexican northeast: Saltillo at the end of the colonial period. (*J. Southwest*, 33:3, Autumn 1991, p. 322–344, appendix)

New vision of Saltillo as the prototype of a northern city uses two characteristics to establish likenesses to southern and central New Spain. Author observes the similar characteristics of merchants, and finds resemblances in patterns of land tenure. She disputes idea of dominance of huge *latifundia* in all of the northern regions. [EBC]

1314 Piñera Ramírez, David. Ocupación y uso del suelo en Baja California: de los grupos aborígenes a la urbanización dependiente. México: Centro de Investigaciones Históricas, UNAM-UABC, 1991. 221 p.: bibl.

History of Baja California based on study of systems of land tenure integrates social and economic data with analysis of agrarian property legislation. [EBC]

1315 Radding, Cynthia. La economía misional y la subsistencia indígena en Sonora, siglo XVIII. (*Trace/México*, 22, déc. 1992, p. 59–71, bibl., tables)

Studies economic balance between Jesuit mission and indigenous village, especially in terms of local economy and trade. Looks at practice of using surplus for constructing ecclesiastical buildings and evangelization as well as for construction of indigenous community houses and celebration of festivals. Notes existence of three separate economies: indigenous, mission, and mercantile. Expulsion of the Jesuits strengthened private sector. [EBC]

1316 Radding, Cynthia. Población, tierra y la persistencia de comunidad en la provincia de Sonora, 1750–1800. (*Hist. Mex.*, 41:

4, abril/junio 1992, p. 551–577, bibl., tables, map)

As a result of indigenous migration, ethnic distinctions became subordinate to control over land in 18th-century Sonora. Concludes that indigenous communities were not closed corporations, as mining and agricultural wage labor made possible the privatization of land. [EBC]

1317 Radding, Cynthia. Las reformas borbónicas en la provincia de Sonora: el régimen de propiedad en la sociedad colonial. (*Noroeste Mex.*, 10, 1991, p. 51–57, bibl., ill.)

Studies work of *visitadores* Gallardo and Gálvez, and infers that certain measures had the effect of reducing amount of land available to indigenous peoples and also resulted in opening of formerly settled areas to nomadic intrusions. [EBC]

1318 Río, Ignacio del. A la diestra mano de las Indias: descubrimiento y ocupación de la Baja California. México: Instituto de Investigaciones Históricas, UNAM, 1990. 108 p.: bibl. (Serie Historia novohispana; 42)

Essay looks at attractions and difficulties of discovery and settlement of Baja California, with special attention to work of the Jesuits. [EBC]

1319 Río, Ignacio del. Colonialismo y frontera: la imposición del tributo en Sinaloa y Sonora. (*Estud. Hist. Novohisp.*, 10, 1991, p. 237–265)

Studies legislation and limitations in practice on collection of tribute. Concludes that local people may have benefited more from the tribute than did the government in Mexico City or Spain. [EBC]

1320 Río, Ignacio del. Proceso y balance de la reforma tributaria del siglo XVIII en Sonora y Sinaloa. (*in* Simposio de Historia y Antropología de Sonora, *13th, Hermosillo, Mexico, 1989.* Memoria. Coordinación de Juan Manuel Romero Gil. Hermosillo, Mexico: Instituto de Investigaciones Históricas, Univ. de Sonora, 1989, v. 1, p. 161–178)

Detailed and precise article examines establishment and collection of tributes among indigenous groups in Sonora and Sinaloa after Gálvez's visit in 1769. Author establishes reluctance shown by indigenous peoples to pay taxes and the meager results obtained from actual collection. Based on archival sources. [AL]

1321 Salmón, Roberto Mario. Indian revolts in northern New Spain: a synthesis of resistance, 1680–1786. Lanham, Md.: Univ. Press of America, 1991. 145 p.: bibl., ill., index, map.

Extraordinarily lucid account, based on archival materials as well as secondary sources, examines relations among indigenous peoples, settlers, and missionaries that led to rebellions on the frontier. [EBC]

1322 San José de Gracia y San Antonio de Arrona: economía y sociedad en dos haciendas mineras de Sinaloa en el siglo XVIII. Investigación en equipo bajo la dirección de María Encarnación Rodríguez Vicente. Madrid: Univ. Autónoma de Madrid, 1989. 291 p.: bibl., ill. (Col. de estudios; 15)

The result of team work, this excellent monograph on two mining haciendas in Sinaloa focuses on a variety of economic and social topics: personality of the owners, cost and profit of production, the labor force, the mines as centers of trade, human settlement and resources, and daily life. Based on extensive (13,000 p.) inheritance litigation between 1771–97. [AL]

1323 Sandos, James A. Christianization among the Chumash: an ethnohistoric perspective. (*Am. Indian Q.*, 15:1, Winter 1991, p. 65–89, bibl.)

In an impassioned denunciation of treatment of indigenous peoples in Franciscan missions in California, author claims that 1824 rebellion resulted from friars' abuse of the people. [EBC]

1324 Simmons, Marc. The last conquistador: Juan de Oñate and the settling of the far southwest. Norman: Univ. of Oklahoma Press, 1991. 208: bibl., ill., index. (The Oklahoma western biographies; 2)

Popular history based on primary sources narrates biography of Oñate, representing him as emblematic of the ideal conquistador. Provides insights into late 16th- and 17th-century politics in Spain, New Spain, and New Mexico. [EBC]

Swann, Michael M. Migrants in the Mexican North: mobility, economy, and society in a colonial world. See *HLAS 53:2758.*

1325 Swann, Michael M. Migration, mobility, and the mining towns of colonial northern Mexico. (*in* Migration in colonial Spanish America. Edited by David J. Robinson. Cambridge: Cambridge Univ. Press, 1990, p. 143–181, graph, maps, tables)

Population study of Parral and three other mining centers for which censuses exist reveals complex patterns of labor recruitment and migration reflecting history of each center, center's age at time of census, and ethnic segregation of new arrivals. Article brings together ethnographic materials and history. Valuable and complex study. [EBC]

1326 Weber, David J. The Spanish frontier in North America. New Haven, Conn.: Yale Univ. Press, 1992. 579 p.: bibl., ill., index, maps. (Yale Western Americana series)

Volume is perhaps the most important contribution since Bolton to the history of contested regions among the indigenous, Anglo, and Hispanic worlds. Combines narration and analysis of principal historic questions. Readable book is also useful for a clear and searching analysis of colonial experience both on the frontier and in central New Spain. [EBC]

Independence, Revolution, and Post-Revolution

BARBARA A. TENENBAUM, *Mexican Specialist, Hispanic Division, Library of Congress; Editor in Chief, Encyclopedia of Latin-American History*
DON M. COERVER, *Professor of History, Texas Christian University*
LINDA B. HALL, *Professor of History, University of New Mexico, Albuquerque*

INDEPENDENCE TO REVOLUTION

One of the glories of annotating materials on Mexico from 1810 to 1910 is the wealth and variety of studies published in each biennium. This period in particular was characterized by a multiplicity of superb articles in every aspect of the field. Well over 200 separate items were reviewed, most of which were meritorious and deserving of notice. Space limits, however, dictated careful selection and reflection, as well as the creation of specific criteria for inclusion in the section. Obviously, each must represent a contribution to the field, but this standard by itself could not weed out many items since, with few exceptions, they all had something new to say. Not even the previous criteria such as use of footnotes or primary sources were sufficient to exclude works with superlative illustrations or outstanding bibliographies. In many cases, then, the critical deciding vote became the nebulous judgment of whether scholars would be enriched by knowing about a particular work.

This biennium marked a true watershed in the development of Mexican historiography in Mexico itself. Happily we saw a retreat from the *microhistoria* that has characterized the field since the 1968 publication of *Pueblo en vilo* by Luis González y González. Scholars are still studying localities, but they are looking at them in ways that other researchers, interested in national themes, can use more easily to provide important collaborative or contrary data. The group of books and articles under review here—ranging from documents from Nayarit to village life in Michoacán to railroad building in Yucatán—amply demonstrates the change. Further, researchers are going to the regions to look at how national phenomena were carried out in *el campo.* This is particularly true of Knowlton's investigation into aspects of the reform in Michoacán (item **1382**), Thomson's for Sierra de Puebla (item **1427**), and Velasco Toro's for Veracruz (item **1436**).

Two extraordinary scholars, Mario Cerutti (items **1348** and **1330**) and Jean Meyer (items **1395** and **1394**), have greatly advanced the study of particular regions.

Cerutti has spearheaded work on 19th-century Nuevo León and has assembled one of the most productive teams in the field while Jean Meyer has worked individually on Nayarit. In fact, during this biennium Cerutti has published five major articles and has edited one book. Although only one of the articles has been annotated here, it would be worthwhile to draw readers' attention to his other important accomplishments on Spaniards in the economy of northern Mexico; [1] the liberal press during the Reform; [2] the role of Monterrey in the northeast; [3] and trade across the Río Bravo during the war years 1855–67, this last deserving an English translation and publication. [4]

Although political histories led the way, works concentrating on the economy were not far behind. Particularly noteworthy was the relative paucity of the basic political biographies that tended to hagiography, together with the increasing sophistication shown in studies of art as historical representation, intense examinations of previously accepted 19th-century statistics, and burgeoning forays into constitutional questions, disaster problematics, ecology, and public health.

The biennium also saw the publication of many stunning "picture books" on interesting and/or important themes. These included: Octavio Chávez's *La charrería: tradición mexicana*, on Mexico's first national sport; [5] Ramón Valdiosera's *3000 años de moda mexicana*, with wonderful illustrations of Mexican "fashions;" [6] and *México: un libro abierto*, a history of the development of books and the publishing industry produced expressly for the 1992 Frankfurt Book Fair. [7] The photo series *Veracruz, Imágenes de su Historia*, [8] added two new volumes this biennium: t. 6, *Los tuxtlas*, and t. 7, *Xalapa*. And for *Fotografías del Nayar y de California, 1893–1900*, Jean Meyer gathered together interesting photos of the indigenous peoples and archaeology of Nayarit and California taken by León Diguet, French ethnographer and contemporary of Carl Lumholtz. [9]

The only discordant note in what was otherwise a glorious biennium for the field was the disappearance of the excellent *Boletín de Fuentes para la Historia Económica de México* edited by Carlos Marichal and published by the Centro de Estudios Históricos at El Colegio de México. We can only hope it will be reinstated. [BAT]

REVOLUTION AND POST-REVOLUTION

Interest in regional history remained strong during the last biennium. State studies included Mexico (item **1444**), Chiapas (items **1456** and **1457**), Tabasco (item **1465**), Chihuahua (item **1503**), Puebla (item **1523**), Michoacán (item **1455**), Yucatán (item **1524**), and Oaxaca (item **1588**). Guerrero Miller provided an interesting comparative study of three Huastecan leaders caught up in the centralization process (item **1506**), while everybody's favorite cacique—Saturnino Cedillo—came in for additional scrutiny (items **1528** and **1537**). Benjamin and Wasserman have compiled an excellent collection of regional studies relating to the first two decades of the revolutionary period (item **1567**).

Agrarian studies maintained their prominent place and took a variety of forms in the last biennium. The multivolume *Historia de la cuestión agraria mexicana* (item **1515**) issued installments dealing with the crucial period from 1934–50. Roberto Barrios Castro—former secretary-general of the Confederación Nacional Campesina—provided an "official" perspective on agrarian history (item **1453**), while Hubert Carton de Grammont described the "vacillating" agrarian policies of Calles (item **1505**). The classic work of Antonio Díaz Soto y Gama on Zapata was reprinted (México: Instituto Nacional de Estudios Históricos de la Revolución Mexicana,

1987), while Armando Ayala Anguiano, questioning the Zapata legend and its political exploitation, fired away at a long line of self-styled agrarian reformers (item **1451**). John Gledhill traveled to Michoacán to file a grim microhistorical report on the status of agrarian reform (item **1500**) and Angel Gutiérrez also described the agrarian history of that state (item **1508**). Noé G. Palomares Peña analyzed three case studies of the impact of agrarian reform on foreign landholdings in Chihuahua (item **1563**). Finally, Alan Knight revised both traditional and revisionist interpretations of agrarian history in discussing the destruction of the great haciendas (item **1519**).

Mexico's recent economic and financial problems have provoked greater interest in economic and business history. Stephen Haber's excellent article provides a good overview of economic development problems in modern Mexico (item **1509**), and the role of the central government has attracted considerable attention (items **1472, 1474, 1549,** and **1570**). Anderson (item **1447**), Haynes (item **1510**), and Sariego Rodríguez (items **1590** and **1591**) pursue different approaches in discussing the impact of foreign investment. Also important are individual studies by Bortz (item **1459**), Camp (item **1464**), and Topik (item **1603**).

The papal visit to Mexico in 1979 has brought renewed interest in Church history and Church-State relations, with studies of the latter ranging from the Madero era (item **1482**) to the Salinas de Gortari Administration (item **1546**). The Cristero Rebellion still attracts considerable interest with works by Mendoza Barragán (item **1545**), Ortoll (items **1559** and **1558**), and Slawson (item **1595**) included below. Gerald O'Rourke's state-level study clearly demonstrates that the end of the Cristero rebellion did not automatically mean an end to Church-State conflict (item **1556**). Historiographical articles have also appeared by Bastian (item **1454**), Blancarte (item **1458**), Negrete (item **1554**), and Ramírez Ceballos (item **1571**).

Labor history continues its tradition of multivolume works with the latest volume in *La Clase Obrera en la Historia de México* series, in which Juan Felipe Leal and José Villaseñor examine the political and economic situation of labor in the late Porfiriato and early revolutionary era (item **1526**). At the opposite end of the time frame, Kevin Middlebrook (item **1607**) describes the increasingly uneasy relationship between workers and the State in the crisis years of the 1980s. Case studies of the work force are provided by Mario Camarena and Susana Fernández (item **1463**), Gema Lozano y Nathal (item **1532**), and Concepción Méndez and Rodolfo Huerta (item **1544**).

Enrique Krauze's two latest installments in the *Biography of Power* series (items **1521** and **1522**) deal with two of the most important and controversial revolutionary figures: Calles and Cárdenas. Both volumes are balanced and make good use of extensive illustrations. These works will be of interest to the specialist as well as the general reader.

Carlos González Herrera, University of New Mexico, assisted in the assembling and evaluation of materials. [DMC and LBH]

Notes

   1   Mario Cerutti, "Españoles, Gran Comercio y Brote Fabril en el Norte de México, 1850–1910." (*Siglo XIX,* 1:2, feb. 1992, p. 49–93).
   2   Mario Cerutti, "Poder Regional, Gobierno Central y Periodismo Liberal en México en los Años de la Reforma." (*Humanitas* [Monterrey], 23, 1990, p. 223–246).
   3   Mario Cerutti, "Monterrey y Su Ambito Regional: 1850–1910; Referencia Histórica y Sugerencias Metodológicas." (*La Palabra y el Hombre,* 72, oct./dic. 1989, p. 17–37).
   4   Mario Cerutti and Miguel González Quiroga, "Guerra y Comercio Entorno al Río

Bravo, 1855–1867: Línea Fronteriza, Espacio Económico Común." (*Historia Mexicana*, 40:2, oct./dic. 1990, p. 217–297).
  5 México: Instituto Mexiquense de Cultura, 1991.
  6 México: EDAMEX; Cámara Nacional de la Industria del Vestido, 1992.
  7 México: Consejo Nacional para la Cultura y las Artes, 1992.
  8 See *HLAS 52:1200*.
  9 México: Centro de Estudios Mexicanos y Centroamericanos de la Embajada de Francia en México; Instituto Nacional Indigenista, 1991.

INDEPENDENCE TO REVOLUTION

1327 Aboites Aguilar, Luis. Poder político y "bárbaros" en Chihuahua hacia 1845. (*Secuencia/México*, 19, enero/abril 1991, p. 17–32, bibl., ill.)
  Reflective article relates difficulties of administering a state like Chihuahua which was incapable of protecting its borders from incursions by indigenous peoples and other neighbors to the north.

1328 Acevedo, Esther. Las imágenes de la historia: memoria y destrucción. (*Mem. Mus. Nac. Arte*, 3, 1991, p. 27–41, ill., photos)
  Enlightening study relates Maximilian's attempts to give Mexico a monument to its history.

1329 Adleson, S. Lief. Clase y comunidad: los estibadores de Tampico, 1880–1911. (*in* Comunidad, cultura y vida social: ensayos sobre la formación de la clase obrera. México: Instituto Nacional de Antropología e Historia, 1991, p. 299–319)
  An important initial study elucidates both evolution of Tampico and history of stevedores in that important port. Hopefully, this will prompt more research in these two interesting areas.

1330 Agua, tierra y capital en el noreste de México: la región citrícola de Nuevo León, 1850–1940. Edición de Mario Cerutti. Monterrey, Mexico: Facultad de Filosofía y Letras, Univ. Autónoma de Nueva León, 1991. 247 p.: bibl., ill., maps.
  Includes five important essays on the citrus-growing region of Nuevo León. Of special interest is Sieglin's study on water and capital accumulation.

1331 Aguilar Aguilar, Gustavo. Los Almada y los Redo en Sinaloa: origen de dos grandes fortunas. (*Clío/Sinaloa*, 4, sept./dic. 1991, p. 3–6, ill.)
  Short but significant account of accu-

mulation of two fortunes in Sinaloa during the Porfiriato could provide important material for general and long-awaited study of capital formation nationwide.

1332 El álbum de la mujer: antología ilustrada de las mexicanas. v. 3–4. México: Instituto Nacional de Antropología e Historia, 1991. 2 v.: bibl., ill. (Col. Divulgación)
  Valuable collection of statements about women in 19th century includes lively illustrations.

1333 Alvarado, Lourdes. Porfirio Parra y Gutiérrez: semblanza biográfica. (*Estud. Hist. Mod. Contemp. Méx.*, 11, 1988, p. 183–199)
  Short biography of Porfirio Parra, successor of Barreda in promotion of Mexican positivism and author of an examination of the Mexican character *Pacotillas* (1900).

Alves, Abel A. Nature and bodies, land and labor: Mexico's colonial legacy. See item **1120.**

1334 Los años de crisis de hace cien años: Colima, 1880–1889. Dirección de José Miguel Romero de Solís. Colima, Mexico: Univ. de Colima; H. Ayuntamiento de Colima, 1988. 397 p.: bibl., ill., map.
  Nine fascinating essays focus on small state of Colima over a single decade, examining such relevant topics as a yellow fever epidemic, the Catholic Church, female education, the beginning of statistical record-keeping, and public hygiene.

1335 Arteta, Begoña. Destino manifiesto: viajeros anglosajones en México, 1830–1840. Azcapotzalco, Mexico: Coordinación de Extensión Universitaria, Unidad Azcapotzalco, Univ. Autónoma Metropolitana; México: Ediciones Gernika, 1989. 146 p. (Col. Ensayos; 23)
  Compilation of travelers' impressions of Mexico concerning important subjects like the Church, the Army, women, and the fate of Texas and California. Although assembled

with a Mexican nationalist bias, still an interesting collection.

1336 Baranda, Marta and **Lía García Verástegul.** Estado de México, una historia compartida. México: Gobierno del Estado de México, Instituto de Investigaciones José María Luis Mora, 1987. 390 p.: bibl., maps.

Historical synthesis of the state of Mexico between 1810 and 1910 has both political and economic focus. [A. Lavrin]

1337 Barrios Castro, Roberto and **Constantino López Matus.** El Istmo de Tehuantepec en la encrucijada de la historia de México. México: Editorial Libros de México, 1987. 299 p.: bibl., ill., maps.

Excellent reference work examines significant but little studied subject. Contains information on ethnic groups, documents on Tadeo Ortiz and his relations with the national government, and material on various plans to build an interoceanic canal in Tehuantepec.

1338 Bastian, Jean-Pierre. Los disidentes: sociedades protestantes y revolución en México, 1872–1911. México: Fondo de Cultura Económica; El Colegio de México, 1989. 373 p.: bibl., index.

Thanks to this important Swiss scholar, historians of Mexico have been learning about Protestants, not simply in the north but throughout the country, even in Yucatán. A fascinating work of research. Highly recommended.

Belmonte Guzmán, María de la Luz. La organización territorial de Veracruz en el siglo XIX. See *HLAS 53:2715.*

1339 Benson, Nettie Lee. The provincial deputation in Mexico: harbinger of provincial autonomy, Independence, and federalism. Austin: Univ. of Texas Press, 1992. 225 p.: bibl., ill., index, maps. (Special publication/Institute of Latin American Studies, Univ. of Texas at Austin)

Long-awaited updated English version of extremely important work (see *HLAS 20: 2810*) examines Mexico's transition from colony to republic through vehicle of the provincial deputation.

1340 Blázquez Domínguez, Carmen and **Ricardo Corzo Ramírez.** La Iglesia en Veracruz: inicios de la restauración republicana,

1867–1869. (*Palabra Hombre*, 72, oct./dic. 1989, p. 205–251, bibl.)

Important look at the Church in Veracruz includes interesting information about eventual erection of the diocese in 1863.

1341 Bock, Berry. Patronage op de 19de eeuwse Mexicaanse hacienda [Patronage on the 19th-century Mexican hacienda]. (*Anthropol. Verkenn.*, 11:2, 1992, p. 8–22, bibl.)

From a cultural perspective, author provides insight into social history of hacienda workers, arguing that such a perspective can best explain interrelationships between demographics, economic change, modernization, and social behavior. Uses theoretical model based on concept of normative economics to analyze complexities of these interrelationships. [R. Hoefte]

1342 Briseño Senosiain, Lillian; María Laura Solares Robles; and **Laura Suárez de la Torre.** Valentín Gómez Farías y su lucha por el federalismo, 1822–1858. México: Instituto de Investigaciones José María Luis Mora; Guadalajara, Mexico: Gobierno del Estado de Jalisco, 1991. 450 p.: appendices, bibl.

Extensive, well-researched biography of Gómez Farías includes a documental appendix. Good reference work, but not the definitive study.

1343 Buchenau, Jürgen. Up against the big stick: Mexico's challenge to US hegemony in Central America, 1906–1910. (*SECOLAS Ann.*, 23, March 1992, p. 70–80)

Posits new argument based on archival material that Mexico sought to keep US out of Central America in 1909 and that this opposition provoked State Department's abandonment of Don Porfirio the following year.

1344 Buve, Raymond. Political patronage and politics at the village level in Central Mexico: continuity and change in patterns from the late colonial period to the end of the French Intervention. (*Bull. Lat. Am. Res.*, 11:1, Jan. 1992, p. 1–28, bibl.)

Provides good but flawed start on understanding relations in Mexican countryside from 1780–1867. Would have been better if a concrete case study had anchored hypothesis of emergence of village cacique as powerful figure. Recommended.

Cárdenas Noriega, Joaquín. Mi generación: de Madero a la dedocracia: remembranzas, vivencias, reflexiones históricas. See item **1468.**

1345 Carreño A., Gloria. El presidio del mineral del monte: un caso de trabajo forzado en la minería, 1850–1874. (*in* Congreso de Historia Regional Comparada, *2nd, Ciudad Juárez, Mexico, 1990.* Actas. Edición de Ricardo León García. Ciudad Juárez, Mexico: Univ. Autónoma de Ciudad Juárez, 1991, p. 491–502)

Interesting article looks at contracts between government and the mines for convict labor. Would have been more significant if production figures could have been incorporated.

1346 La casa de citas: en el barrio Galante. Recopilación de Ava Vargas. Prólogo de Carlos Monsiváis. México: Grijalbo; Consejo Nacional para la Cultura y las Artes, 1991. 86 p.: chiefly photos (some col.).

This book of photos of prostitutes is an important contribution to history of Mexican sexuality from 1900–20. Contains provocative introductions by both Vargas (mainly on the photography) and Monsiváis (on sexuality), but both ignore the obvious—that in a country so obsessed with race, the sepia and other photographic tones make women with Indian faces look remarkably white-skinned.

1347 Ceballos Ramírez, Manuel. La democracia cristiana en el México liberal: un proyecto alternativo, 1867–1929. (*in* Coloquio de Antropología e Historia Regionales, *8th, Zamora, Mexico, 1986.* El nacionalismo en México. Edición de Cecilia Noriega Elío. Zamora, Mexico: El Colegio de Michoacán, 1992, p. 205–220)

Identifies seven stages of relationship between Catholicism and the Mexican State: 1) secularization (1867–92); 2) conciliation (1892–1903); 3) recuperation (1903–11); 4) participation (1911–14); 5) anticlericalism (1914–18); 6) new recuperation (1918–26); and 7) conflict (1926–29). Also discusses Catholic project for societies enamored of "modernity." Recommended.

1348 Cerutti, Mario and **Rocío González Maíz.** Autonomía regional y Estado nacional a mediados del siglo XIX: Santiago Vidaurri y el liberalismo "de la frontera," 1846–1867. (*in* Coloquio de Antropología e Historia Regionales, *8th, Zamora, Mexico, 1986.* El

nacionalismo en México. Edición de Cecilia Noriega Elío. Zamora, Mexico: El Colegio de Michoacán, 1992, p. 551–561)

Wonderfully concise piece summarizes much of Cerutti's work on Santiago Vidaurri, the caudillo of Nuevo León. Paper demonstrates importance of Cerutti's research for understanding the Mexican nation in 19th century. Must reading.

1349 Cervantes Bello, Francisco Javier. Los militares, la política fiscal y los ingresos de la Iglesia en Puebla, 1821–1847. (*Hist. Mex.,* 39:4, abril/junio 1990, p. 933–950, bibl., tables)

Major contribution to our understanding of public finance and the Church covers period from Independence to the Mexican-American War. Highly recommended.

1350 Chowning, Margaret. The contours of the post-1810 depression in Mexico: a reappraisal from a regional perspective. (*LARR,* 27:2, 1992, p. 119–150, appendices, bibl., tables)

Thoughtfully argues that as seen in Michoacán, 1821–80 period was not one of universal and continued economic depression. Author finds considerable sustained recovery and entrepreneurial risk-taking from 1830s onward. Highly recommended.

1351 Coerver, Don M. From confrontation to conciliation: Church-State relations in Mexico, 1867–1884. (*J. Church State,* 32:1, Winter 1990, p. 65–80)

Succinctly argues that Díaz's conciliatory attitude toward the Church began with his first administrations in 1870s, and that enforcement of reform laws was left up to the states. Also contains interesting tidbits about Protestants in Mexico in 1880s.

1352 La conciencia nacional y su formación: discursos cívicos septembrinos, 1825–1871. Recopilación y prólogo de Ernesto de la Torre Villar, con la colaboración de Ramiro Navarro. México: Univ. Nacional Autónoma de México, 1988. 346 p.

Although volume does not contain all *discursos* of the *septembrinos,* this collection is a godsend for historians of political culture and ideology. Recommended.

Congreso de Historiadores Duranguenses, *1st, Durango, Mexico, 1985.* Ponencias. See item **1480.**

1353 Correspondencia de la Guerra de Castas: epistolario documental, 1843–1866. Recopilación de Fidelio Quintal Martín. Mérida, Mexico: Ediciones de la Univ. Autónoma de Yucatán, 1992. 135 p. (Mérida, la de Yucatán y el Quinto Centenario)

Important work adds to our understanding of a movement generally considered to be outside the scope of conventional historical sources.

1354 Costeloe, Michael P. The Central Republic in Mexico, 1835–1846: *hombres de bien* in the age of Santa Anna. Cambridge, England; New York: Cambridge Univ. Press, 1993. 324 p.: bibl., index. (Cambridge Latin American studies; 73)

Author uses the *hombres de bien* (civilian professionals) as a focus for politics in centralist years 1835–1846, as seen in Mexico City. Wealth of sources.

1355 Díaz, María Elena. The satiric penny press for workers in Mexico, 1900–1910: a case study in the politicisation of popular culture. (*J. Lat. Am. Stud.*, 22:3, Oct. 1990, p. 497–526, appendix, ill.)

Contends that popular "penny press" purchased by working class supported a vigorous democratic, liberal, and sometimes anti-US working-class consciousness. Regrettably does not indicate place of publication or distribution patterns of examples used.

1356 Díaz y de Ovando, Clementina. Memoria de un debate, 1880: la postura de México frente al patrimonio arqueológico nacional. México: Univ. Nacional Autónoma de México, 1990. 97 p.: ill., index. (Divulgación/ Instituto de Investigaciones Estéticas; 3)

Innovative work by highly creative scholar examines beginning of Mexican national archaeology through debate about whether French archaeologist Désiré Charnay would be permitted to export his finds.

1357 El Distrito Federal de dos leguas, o, cómo el Estado de México perdió su capital. Recopilación de Gerald L. McGowan. Toluca de Lerdo, Mexico: Gobierno del Estado de México, Secretaría de Finanzas; Zinacantepec, México: El Colegio Mexiquense, 1991. 260 p.: bibl., maps. (Fuentes para la historia del Estado de México; 1)

Will be of interest to those who need more than O'Gorman provides on how state of México became separated from the Distrito Federal.

1358 Domínguez Medina, Martha. Colección Pablo Herrera Carrillo. Mexicali, Mexico: Centro de Investigaciones Históricas, UNAM-UABC, 1991. 1 v.: bibl. (Catálogos e inventarios; 2)

Catalog describes collection of documents assembled by lawyer and antiquarian about history of Mexicali and Baja California from 19th to mid-20th centuries. [EBC]

1359 Espacio y perfiles. Recopilación de Carlos Contreras Cruz. Puebla, Mexico: Univ. Autónoma de Puebla, Instituto de Ciencias, Centro de Investigaciones Históricas y Sociales; Consejo Mexicano de Ciencias Sociales; H. Ayuntamiento de Puebla, 1989. 317 p.: bibl., ill., maps. (Historia regional mexicana del siglo XIX; 1)

Extremely valuable collection of articles examines entrepreneurs and the economy in 19th century. Recommended.

Estadistas, caciques y caudillos. See *HLAS 53:4942.*

1360 Ferrer Muñoz, Manuel. Guerra civil en Nueva España, 1810–1815. (*Anu. Estud. Am.*, 48, 1991, p. 391–434, map)

Synthetic review of main events of the wars preceding Mexican Independence, events which the author believes constituted a large civil war. [A. Lavrin]

1361 Flores Clair, Eduardo. Conflictos de trabajo de una empresa minera: Real del Monte y Pachuca, 1872–1877. México: Instituto Nacional de Antropología e Historia, 1991. 237 p.: bibl., ill. (Serie Historia. Col. Divulgación)

Helpful study looks at operations as well as labor disputes of one of the most studied mines in world history. Good companion to Chávez Orozco, Couturier, Ladd, Randall, and Rankin, among others.

1362 Florescano, Enrique. El nuevo pasado mexicano. México: Cal y Arena, 1991. 229 p.: bibl.

Although published in 1991, this work by Mexico's leading historiographer demonstrates how fast the field is changing. Expect a major revision in 2001, if not sooner.

1363 Florescano Mayet, Sergio. El agua y la industrialización de Xalapa y su región durante el siglo XIX. (*Palabra Hombre*, 70, abril/junio 1989, p. 175–192, ill., tables)

Brief essay looks at fight over water

rights in Jalapa. Could have used more information about water needs for industrialization versus for simple subsistence. Nevertheless, begins what will come to be an important debate.

1364 French, William E. Prostitutes and guardian angels: women, work, and the family in Porfirian Mexico. (*HAHR*, 72:4, Nov. 1992, p. 529–553)

Outlines campaign launched in Chihuahua state to induce working class to adopt middle-class values. Measures included restriction of prostitution, promotion of female education, and enactment of anti-alcohol laws.

1365 Galeana de Valadés, Patricia. Las relaciones Iglesia-Estado durante el Segundo Imperio. México: Instituto de Investigaciones Históricas, UNAM, 1991. 206 p.: bibl. (Serie Historia moderna y contemporánea; 23)

Although based mostly on secondary sources and letters, work is one of the first objective accounts of a major aspect of the French Empire in Mexico.

1366 Gamboa Ojeda, Leticia. Mercado de fuerza de trabajo e industria textil: el centro-oriente de México durante el Porfiriato. (*Siglo XIX*, 1:1, oct. 1991, p. 9–36)

Fascinating survey of conditions for textile workers includes valuable insights on company stores and importance of migration. Important contribution.

1367 Gidi Villarreal, Emilio and Carmen Blázquez Domínguez. El poder legislativo en Veracruz. v. 1, 1824–1917. Xalapa?: Gobierno del Estado de Veracruz, 1992. 1 v.: bibl., ill. (Veracruz en la cultura)

Good addition to current literature on elections and the legislative process includes lists of members of Veracruz legislature during Porfiriato.

1368 El Gobernador Bernardo Reyes y sus homólogos de la frontera norte. Recopilación de David Piñera Ramírez. Monterrey, Mexico: Fondo Editorial de Nuevo León, 1991. 394 p.: bibl. (Col. Los trabajos y los días)

Title is somewhat misleading: work is less about Reyes than about his fellow northern governors. Contains a few useful essays.

1369 Gómez Izquierdo, José Jorge. El movimiento antichino en México, 1871–1934: problemas del racismo y del naciona-

lismo durante la Revolución Mexicana. México: Instituto Nacional de Antropología e Historia, 1991. 183 p.: bibl., ill., maps. (Serie Historia. Col. Divulgación)

Groundbreaking study explores Mexican sentiments against Chinese immigration, which began as early as 1871. Research improves considerably after the Revolution.

González, Luis. The cultural modernization of Mexico, 1857–1958. See item **1502.**

1370 González de la Lama, Renée. Tres aspectos de la modernización liberal en Veracruz, 1873–1896. (*Palabra Hombre*, 72, oct./dic. 1989, p. 163–176, bibl.)

Useful discussion of *jarocho* participation in sale of communal landholdings, compulsory public education, and centralization of political power. Good case study that could be employed to examine these phenomena nationwide.

1371 González Montes, Soledad. Trabajo femenino y expansión de las relaciones capitalistas en el México rural a fines del porfiriato: el distrito de Tenango del Valle, Estado de México, 1900–1910. (*in* Haciendas, pueblos y comunidades: los valles de México y Toluca entre 1530 y 1916. México: Consejo Nacional para la Cultura y las Artes, 1991, p. 270–299, graph, map, tables)

A close examination of change in workforce in Tenango, state of Mexico, shows that growth of sugar industry in Morelos from 1900–10 lured men away from the fields, with their places being taken by women. This displacement resulted in the general impoverishment of the population.

González Navarro, Moisés. The social transformation of Mexico, 1867–1940. See item **1504.**

1372 González Pedrero, Enrique. País de un solo hombre: el México de Santa Anna. v. 1, La ronda de los contrarios. México: Fondo de Cultura Económica, 1993. 1 v.: bibl., ill. (some col.), maps. (Sección de obras de historia)

Just when historians thought it was safe to write about 19th-century Mexico as if it were inhabited by someone other than Antonio López de Santa Anna, this lavish first volume appears. Surprisingly, author puts his subject in a Western Hemispheric context (to the point of discussing Bolívar), and provides a substantial bibliography and beautiful illustrations. Even so, volume is not worth its hefty purchase price and would be better suited to library consultation.

1373 González Sierra, José. La rica hoja: San Andrés y el tabaco a fines del XIX. (*Palabra Hombre*, 72, oct./dic. 1989, p. 179–203)

Although limited to in-depth analysis of a single *jarocho* town (San Andrés), article is one of few studies concerned with Mexican tobacco industry.

1374 González y González, Luis. 75 años de investigación histórica en México. (*in* México, setenta y cinco años de revolución. México: INEHRM; Fondo de Cultura Económica, 1988, v. 4, p. 651–704, bibl.)

Useful bird's-eye survey of Mexican historiography over last 100 years is based mostly on work of Mexican historians. [A. Lavrin]

1375 Gorriño, Manuel María. El doctor Gorriño y Arduengo: su proyecto para la primera constitución potosina, 1825. Presentación, comentarios y notas de Jesús Motilla Martínez. Ed. facsimilar, 1. ed. San Luis Potosí, Mexico: Casa de la Cultura de San Luis Potosí; Consejo Estatal para la Cultura y las Artes, 1990. 54 p.: bibl., facsims., plates.

Brief volume contains introduction to and discussion of a plan for a constitution for San Luis Potosí state. Historians fascinated by evolution of government systems will find this useful. Includes facsimile of the text of the constitution.

1376 Grosso, Juan Carlos. Organizaciones y conflictos laborales en México a fines del siglo XIX: el caso de los trabajadores textiles de Puebla. (*Anuario/Rosario*, 14, 1989/90, p. 137–164)

In-depth look at 1884 textile strike in Puebla includes excellent information on evolution of Mexican working class. Recommended.

Haber, Stephen H. Assessing the obstacles to industrialization: the Mexican economy, 1830–1940. See item **1509.**

1377 Herrera Canales, Inés. Mercurio para refinar la plata mexicana en el siglo XIX. (*Hist. Mex.*, 40:1, julio/sept. 1990, p. 27–51, bibl., graphs)

Significant addition to our understanding of Mexican mining industry includes new information on competition between European and California mercury monopolies. Regrettably does not examine effect of competition on mining production.

Imágenes de Guadalajara a través de un siglo. See item **1516.**

1378 Iparraguirre, Hilda. La historia social y los sin historia: nuevas perspectivas de análisis y hemerográficas para el estudio del proceso de proletarización. (*Rev. Hist./Neuquén*, 2, nov. 1991, p. 53–61, bibl.)

Interesting and provocative synopsis (with misleading title) tells history of working class in Moroleón, Guanajuato, without recourse to Marxist jargon. Particularly useful for non-labor historians.

1379 Iturriaga de la Fuente, José N. Litografía y grabado en el México del XIX. v. 1. México: Telmex, 1993. 1 v: bibl., ill. (some col.).

Gorgeous and rare compilation of works by the most important graphic artists, mostly foreigners, working in Mexico in first half of 19th century includes good bibliography.

1380 Jáuregui Frías, Luis Antonio. La mecánica de un pronunciamiento: la disolución del Constituyente de 1842. (*Palabra Hombre*, 73, enero/marzo 1990, p. 208–226, bibl.)

Agrees with Costeloe (see *HLAS 52: 1160*) that *pronunciamientos* against Constituent Congress of 1842 were part of an orchestrated campaign.

1381 Jiménez Codinach, Estela Guadalupe. La Gran Bretaña y la independencia de México, 1808–1821. Traducción de Mercedes Pizarro Suárez e Ismael Pizarro Suárez. México: Fondo de Cultura Económica, 1991. 392 p.: bibl., ill. (Sección de obras de historia)

Shows that in key years 1808–13 British sought to impede Mexican independence. Also demonstrates variety of interests involved in independence movement on both sides of the Atlantic.

1382 Knowlton, Robert J. La división de las tierras de los pueblos durante el siglo XIX: el caso de Michoacán. (*Hist. Mex.*, 40:1, julio/sept. 1990, p. 3–25, bibl.)

Demonstrates that sale of communal property of Michoacán began sooner, and was infinitely more complicated, than previously thought. Good companion to Bazant, Berry, and Powell on this issue.

1383 Lanz Cárdenas, José Trinidad. La contraloría y el control interno en México: antecedentes históricos y legislativos. 2. ed. México: Secretaría de la Contraloría General de la Federación; Fondo de Cultura Económica, 1993. 674 p.: bibl., ill.

Fascinating look at establishment and organization of the Mexican financial apparatus is particularly helpful for post-revolutionary period.

1384 Lavalle Argudín, Mario. La Armada en el México independiente. México: Instituto Nacional de Estudios Históricos de la Revolución Mexicana; Secretaría de Marina, 1985. 448 p.: bibl., ill.

This first substantial basic history of Mexican navy, a subject almost never studied, is good starting point for future in-depth research.

1385 Loete, Sylvia K. Aspects of modernization on a Mexican hacienda: labour on San Nicolás del Moral, Chalco, at the end of the nineteenth century. (*Rev. Eur.*, 54, 1993, p. 45–64, bibl., graphs)

Analyzes labor policy of hacienda owner José Solórzano y Mata during the Porfiriato. Reconstructs an agricultural year, and focuses on hacienda management's efforts to modernize and resulting impact on paternalistic labor relations. [R. Hoefte]

1386 Luca de Tena, Torcuato. Ciudad de México: en tiempos de Maximiliano. Barcelona: Planeta, 1989. 183 p.: bibl., ill. (some col.), index. (Ciudades en la historia)

Semi-scholarly contribution to history of the city includes lots of pictures and a good bibliography.

1387 Ludlow, Leonor. El Banco Nacional Mexicano y el Banco Mercantil Mexicano: radiografía social de sus primeros accionistas, 1881–1882. (*Hist. Mex.*, 39:4, abril/junio 1990, p. 979-1027, bibl., tables)

Highly recommended seminal article on banking in 1880s is a must for those interested in the Porfiriato and in French finance as well.

1388 MacGregor, Josefina. México y España: del porfiriato a la revolución. México: Instituto Nacional de Estudios Históricos de la Revolución Mexicana, Secretaría de Gobernación, 1992. 243 p.: bibl., ill (Col. Sociedad)

Without much archival research, volume focuses on both diplomatic relations between the countries and activities of Spaniards in Mexico.

Mallon, Florencia E. Alianzas multiétnicas y problema nacional: los campesinos y el Estado en Perú y México en el siglo XIX. See item **2754.**

1389 Martínez M., Lucía. Un empresario en el valle de México: Iñigo Noriega Laso, 1867–1913. (*in* Haciendas, pueblos y comunidades: los valles de México y Toluca entre 1530 y 1916. México: Consejo Nacional para la Cultura y las Artes, 1991, p. 300–317, table)

Relates creation of agribusiness in the Chalco and elsewhere through efforts of Spanish immigrant Iñigo Noriega Laso.

1390 Matabuena Peláez, Teresa. Algunos usos y conceptos de la fotografía durante el Porfiriato. México: Univ. Iberoamericana, 1991. 166 p.: bibl., ill. (some col.).

This major contribution, showing the many ways photographs were used during the Porfiriato, is important both as a history of photography in Mexico and worldwide and as social history. An important advance.

1391 Mayo, John. Imperialismo de libre comercio e imperio informal en la costa oeste de México durante la época de Santa Anna. (*Hist. Mex.*, 40:4, abril/junio 1991, p. 673–696, bibl.)

Important article revisits British consul Eustaquio Barron's activities on the west coast, arguing against Platt's informal empire thesis (see *HLAS 51:1714*). Contends British Navy protected smuggling activities.

1392 McGowan, Gerald L. El estado del Valle de México, 1824–1917. Zinacantepec, Mexico: El Colegio Mexiquense; Toluca, Mexico: Gobierno del Estado de México, 1991. 101 p.: bibl., maps. (Fuentes para la historia del Estado de México; 2)

Presents timely analysis of changes in jurisdictional status of state of Mexico as it is continually absorbed by the Distrito Federal.

1393 Mentz, Brígida von. La historia social del México del siglo XIX y el estudio de algunos aspectos de la estratificación social en Sultepec a fines del siglo XIX. (*in* Mundo rural, ciudades y población del Estado de México. Coordinación de Manuel Miño Grijalva. Toluca, México: El Colegio Mexiquense: Instituto Mexiquense de Cultura, 1990, p. 167–188, bibl., table)

Fully developed picture of Sultepec, a mining center in present-day state of Morelos, contains interesting statistics and observations on literacy rates.

1394 Meyer, Jean A. De cantón de Tepic a estado de Nayarit, 1810–1940. Guadalajara, Mexico: Univ. de Guadalajara; México: Centre d'études mexicaines et centraméricaines, 1990. 297 p.: ill., maps. (Col. de documentos para la historia de Nayarit; 5)

Fifth volume (for volume 4, see item **1395**) in series of documental collections on history of this small Pacific coast state. Volumes will be useful for studies of west coast trade and for examination of social phenomena and revolutionary movements nationwide.

1395 Meyer, Jean A. La tierra de Manuel Lozada. Guadalajara, Mexico: Univ. de Guadalajara; México: Centre d'études mexicaines et centraméricaines, 1989. 402 p.: bibl. (Col. de documentos para la historia de Nayarit; 4)

See item **1394**.

1396 Moreno Rivas, Manuel. Socialismo en Topolobampo: apuntes para la historia. Guadalajara, Mexico: Editorial Agata, 1992. 358 p.: bibl., ill., maps (2 folded).

Fascinating story of the Credit Foncier company's socialist colony of Topolobampo, Sonora, founded by North American Albert Kimsey Owen. Also examines its effect on the Díaz government during period 1886–95.

1397 Olmo Calzada, José Luis del et al. Molino del Rey: historia de un monumento. Coordinación de María Elena Salas Cuesta. Fotografía de Ramón Enríquez Rodríguez e Ignacio Borja Aldana. México: Instituto Nacional de Antropología e Historia, 1988. 144 p.: bibl., ill. (Col. científica; 170. Serie Antropología física)

Pioneering effort combines detailed discussion of battle with an analysis of its commemorative monument. Recommended.

1398 Olveda, Jaime. La oligarquía de Guadalajara: de las reformas borbónicas a la reforma liberal. México: Consejo Nacional para la Cultura y las Artes, 1991. 457 p.: bibl. (Regiones)

This well-researched and long-awaited

prosopographical study of the movers and shakers of the second largest city of Mexico sheds considerable light on forces that shaped the early republic.

1399 Olveda, Jaime. Proyectos de colonización en la primera mitad del siglo XIX. (*Relaciones/Zamora*, 42, primavera 1990, p. 23–47)

Misnamed article emphasizes struggle for religious toleration in order to facilitate immigration.

1400 Orozco, Víctor. Notas sobre las relaciones de clase en Chihuahua durante la primera fase de las guerras indias. (*in* Congreso de Historia Regional Comparada, 2nd, Ciudad Juárez, Mexico, 1990. Actas. Edición de Ricardo León García. Ciudad Juárez, Mexico: Univ. Autónoma de Ciudad Juárez, 1991, p. 369–382)

Weak article discusses persistence of slave conditions for indigenous peoples in the north and consequent reluctance of these peoples to defend property held by the powerful.

1401 Ortiz Figueroa, Jesús. La tenencia de la tierra en Tijuana según fuentes documentales, 1880–1900. (*Meyibó/Tijuana*, 3:7/8, 1988, p. 39–52)

Poorly written but informative article looks at development of what has come to be known as the San Diego/Tijuana metropolitan area.

1402 Ortiz Peralta, Rina. El abasto de la sal para la minería: las salinas de Tepopoxtla, 1849–1900. (*Hist. Mex.*, 41:1, julio/sept. 1991, p. 111–133, bibl., tables)

Provides important insights on salt production and mining, and on success of moneylenders' attempts to diversify their portfolios.

1403 Parcero, María de la Luz. Condiciones de la mujer en México durante el siglo XIX. México: Instituto Nacional de Antropología e Historia, 1992. 239 p.: bibl. (Col. científica; 264. Serie Historia)

Author presents a vast amount of information on a newly-emerging subject. Good complement to her *La mujer en el siglo XIX en México: bibliografía* (see *HLAS 50:1176*).

1404 Pérez Escutia, Ramón Alonso. Aspectos de la vida preinsurgente de Hidalgo: hacendado, litigante y administrador. Prólogo de Gerardo Sánchez Díaz. Morelia, Mexico: Centro de Estudios Sobre la Cultura Nicolaita; Univ. Michoacana de San Nicolás de Hidalgo, 1991. 289 p.: bibl., col. ill.

Volume primarily contains documents, but does provide much new evidence about this very litigious priest who had strong ties to many of those who would be affected by his movement. Fascinating look at the "Padre de la Patria" before his heroic deeds.

1405 Pérez Toledo, Sonia and **Herbert S. Klein.** La población de la ciudad de Zacatecas en 1857. (*Hist. Mex.*, 42:1, julio/sept. 1992, p. 77–102, appendix, bibl., graphs, map, tables)

Interesting analysis of a provincial migration with a greater number of female emigrants than male demonstrates usefulness of provincial census records.

1406 Pi-Suñer, Antonia. La presencia española en México en la época de la reforma, 1854–1860. (*in* Jornadas de Historiadores Americanistas, *2nd, Santafé, Spain, 1989. América: encuentro y asimilación.* Granada, Spain: Diputación Provincial de Granada, 1990, p. 107–118)

Article about Spaniards mentions their activity in industry and moneylending, but fails to note their impact on the Reform itself.

1407 Piñera Ramírez, David. Los orígenes de Ensenada y la política nacional de colonización. Baja California, Mexico: Univ. Autónoma de Baja California; Gobierno del Estado de Baja California; Grupo Cultural Septentrión, 1991. 194 p.: bibl., ill.

Interesting and well-researched work examines founding of Ensenada, as an extension of the US economy, by Mexico's Compañía Internacional. Also valuable for information on the Porfiriato on the frontier.

1408 Pitner, Ernst. Maximilian's lieutenant: a personal history of the Mexican campaign, 1864–7. Translated and edited by Gordon Etherington-Smith. Note on the Mexican background by Don M. Coerver. Albuquerque: Univ. of New Mexico Press, 1993. 201 p.: bibl., ill., index, maps.

This useful source for evaluating French empire's impact on Mexico gives an interesting European perspective on things Mexican, few of which passed muster.

1409 El Porfiriato en Sinaloa. Recopilación de Gilberto López Alanís. Culiacán, Mexico: Dirección de Investigación y Fomento de Cultura Regional del Gobierno del Estado de Sinaloa, 1991. 234 p.: bibl. (Historia y región; 3)

Collection of conference papers presented in 1989. Particularly noteworthy are those by Aguilar and Ibarra on the banks of Sinaloa and Valencia on local empresarios.

1410 Primer centenario del ferrocarril en San Luis Potosí, 1888–1988. San Luis Potosí, Mexico: Archivo Histórico del Estado de San Luis Potosí, 1991. 122 p.: bibl.

Six informative essays examine relationship between little-studied city of San Luis Potosí and positive contributions made by its railroad. Worthwhile contribution.

1411 Pueblos, villas y ciudades de Michoacán en el porfiriato. Coordinación de Gerardo Sánchez Díaz. Morelia, Mexico: Univ. Michoacana de San Nicolás de Hidalgo, Consejo de la Investigación Científica, Instituto de Investigaciones Históricas, 1991. 241 p.: bibl., ill. (some col.), maps.

Stimulating collection of essays on a variety of towns and small cities in Michoacán at end of 19th century evokes a fascinating microcosm of life outside main centers during the period. Valuable contribution.

1412 Radkau, Verena. Hacia la construcción de lo "eterno femenino." (*Pap. Casa Chata*, 6:8, 1991, p. 23–34, bibl.)

Weakly-researched discussion examines Mexican belief in biological inferiority of women during the Porfiriato, even on the part of such luminaries as Molina Enríquez.

1413 Rankine, Margaret E. The Mexican mining industry in the nineteenth century with special reference to Guanajuato. (*Bull. Lat. Am. Res.*, 11:1, Jan. 1992, p. 29–48, bibl., tables)

Author uses figures from La Luz in Guanajuato, already producing prodigiously in the 1840s, to challenge assumption that mines didn't return to productivity until 1849.

1414 Ratz, Konrad. Maximilian in Querétaro: der Untergang des Zweiten Mexikanischen Kaiserreiches. Graz, Austria: Akademische Druck- u. Verlagsanstalt, 1991. 424 p.: bibl., facsims., photos.

Contains facsimiles of documents relating to critical four months prior to execution of Emperor Maximilian in 1867, as well as photographs of imperial and republican personalities. Outstanding materials drawn from Mexican, Austrian, and Belgian archives vividly illustrate a dramatic episode in Mexican history. [C.K. Converse]

1415 Reyes G., Juan Carlos. El mercado "De la Madrid": un ejemplo de arquitectura porfirista en Colima. Colima, Mexico: Univ. de Colima, 1991. 72 p.: bibl., ill. (Cuadernos de historia regional)

Short, interesting chapter in growing field of history of architecture in the Porfiriato. Author notes that using foreign-born architects and materials often brought cachet to a project.

1416 Riguzzi, Paolo. México, Estados Unidos y Gran Bretaña, 1867–1910: una difícil relación triangular. (*Hist. Mex.*, 41:3, enero/marzo 1992, p. 365–436, bibl.)

Lengthy description examines triangular relation between Mexico and the two English-speaking powers. Provides much more subtle depiction of Britain's relationship than that of the US with its complicated regional peculiarities.

1417 Rodríguez O., Jaime E. La paradoja de la independencia de México. (*Secuencia/México*, 21, sept./dic. 1991, p. 7–17, bibl., ill.)

Important comparison of US and Mexican independence experiences concludes that independence wars bequeathed Mexico a militarized country and a loss of respect for national institutions.

1418 Rodríguez O., Jaime E. The struggle for the nation: the centralist-federalist conflict in Mexico. (*Americas/Francisc.*, 49: 1, July 1992, p. 1–22)

Offers much-needed explanation of why New Spain did not disintegrate into separate nations, instead opting for federalist solution in 1824. Worthwhile.

1419 Romero Gil, Juan Manuel. Minería y sociedad en el noroeste porfirista. (*Siglo XIX*, 1:1, oct. 1991, p. 37–73)

Stimulating article shows how the development of new technologies and an important change in Mexican law which devolved subsoil rights to concessionaries paid big dividends in expansion of mineral production in the northwest to 1910. Recommended.

1420 Sa, Na and Chang Yu-ling. Lun Mo-hsi-ke hua ch'iao she hui ti pien chien [On the changes in the overseas Chinese community in Mexico]. (*Hua ch'iao hua jen li shih yen chiu*, 1, 1989, p. 32–39)

Surveys the formation, development and decline of the overseas Chinese community in Mexico from 1880s through 1930s, analyzing historical backgrounds and social causes, and assessing role of Chinese citizens and emigrés in modern Mexico. [Mao Xianglin]

1421 Salinas Novoa, Carlos. Francisco García Salinas: gobernante modelo, modelo de gobernante: Zacatecas, 1824–1835. Zacatecas, Mexico: Legislatura del Estado de Zacatecas, Gobierno del Estado de Zacatecas, 1991. 199 p.: bibl.

Biography studies one of the most important defenders of federalism and anticlericalism in early republican Mexico. Although dependent on secondary sources, work pulls together interesting material on both García Salinas and Zacatecas.

1422 Schenk, Frank. La distribución de la propiedad de tierras en México hacia 1900: más falacias estadísticas; el caso del distrito de Sultepec, Estado de México. (*in* Jornadas de Historiadores Americanistas, 2nd, Santafé, Spain, 1989. América: encuentro y asimilación. Granada, Spain: Diputación Provincial de Granada, 1990, p. 231–258, appendix, graph, tables)

Important article supporting both Guerra (see *HLAS 50:1162*) and Meyer (see *HLAS 50:1174*) attacks generally held belief that haciendas had swallowed up most of available land during the Porfiriato. Shows that Meyer's estimates of 10–20 percent are accurate for district of Sultepec (state of México). Also valuable for discussion of statistical fallacies in general. Highly recommended.

1423 Skerritt Gardner, David. La "modernidad" y el "progreso" en el campo: el corredor central del estado de Veracruz en el siglo XIX. (*Palabra Hombre*, 72, oct./dic. 1989, p. 111–135, tables)

Interesting article examines how agricultural processes which evolved nationwide functioned in central corridor of Veracruz.

Shows that "modern" haciendas often allowed workers to grow subsistence crops on land they would come to regard as their own.

1424 **Sobarzo, Alejandro.** Deber y conciencia: Nicolás Trist, el negociador norteamericano en la guerra del 47. México: Editorial Diana, 1990. 269 p.

Superficial work looks at a crucial figure who deserves better treatment. No scholarly apparatus at all; thus reader is left in doubt about origin of the information.

1425 **Tapia Méndez, Aureliano** and **Luis Avila Blancas.** Fray José María de Jesús Belaunzarán y Ureña. Monterrey, Mexico: Producciones al Voleo-El Troquel, 1988. 119 p.: bibl., ill.

Biography of important cleric is somewhat pedestrian, but nevertheless makes significant contribution to a highly neglected field.

1426 **Thompson, Angela.** To save the children: smallpox inoculation, vaccination, and public health in Guanajuato, Mexico, 1797–1840. (*Americas/Francisc.*, 49:4, April 1993, p. 431–455, tables)

Through the window of a vaccination campaign, the careful reader can learn much about how the State functioned in a crucial area. Interesting contribution to growing field of history of epidemics and public health. Recommended.

1427 **Thomson, Guy P.C.** Popular aspects of liberalism in Mexico, 1848–1888. (*Bull. Lat. Am. Res.*, 10:3, 1991, p. 265–292, bibl.)

Provides very important critique of present understanding of national support for the Reform among indigenous peoples and mestizos. Using data from Morelos and Sierra de Puebla, Thomson argues that villagers understood political events and supported liberalism as a way of maintaining their lands and way of life.

Topik, Steven. Metrópoles macrocéfalas: uma comparação entre a primazia do Rio de Janeiro e a da Cidade do México entre 1800 e 1910. See item **3443.**

1428 **Toussaint Alcaraz, Florence.** Escenario de la prensa en el Porfiriato. México: Fundación Manuel Buendía; Colima, Mexico: Univ. de Colima, 1989. 108 p.

Provides useful overview for research-

ers who use newspaper sources, as well as a short examination of the press itself. Recommended.

1429 **Trabulse, Elías.** José María Velasco: un paisaje de la ciencia en México. Toluca, Mexico: Instituto Mexiquense de Cultura, 1992. 332 p.: bibl., ill. (some col.), index.

If you thought Velasco was a landscape painter who liked trains, read this expert exhibition catalog and think again. In the hands of Trabulse, Mexico's foremost historian of science, Velasco becomes the vehicle for discussing development of natural history as an intellectual discipline. Excellent work certain to provoke much discussion.

Ulloa, Berta. Conflict threatening Mexico's sovereignty: the continuing crisis, 1867–1940. See item **1605.**

1430 **Valdés Aguilar, Rafael.** Epidemias en Sinaloa: una aproximación histórica. Culiacán, Mexico: Dirección de Investigación y Fomento de Cultura Regional del Gobierno del Estado de Sinaloa, 1991. 159 p.: bibl. (Serie Historia y región; 4)

Modest examination looks at epidemic disease in Sinaloa from cholera in 1830s to AIDS today. Alerts reader to obscure sources.

1431 **Vanderwood, Paul J.** Santa Teresa: Mexico's Joan of Arc. (*in* The human tradition in Latin America: the nineteenth century. Edited by Judith Ewell and William H. Beezley. Wilmington, Del.: SR Books, 1989, p. 215–232, bibl.)

Cult in Tomochic, Chihuahua, led by visionary Teresa Urrea became focus of a rebellion in 1892 which was quelled by federal troops. Fine article, although title comparison to the "Maid of Orleans" seems overdrawn.

1432 **Vázquez, Josefina Zoraida.** El *Foreign Office*, California, Texas y la guerra con Estados Unidos. (*Mem. Acad. Mex. Hist.*, 34, 1991, p. 95–118)

Fills in important gaps concerning British reaction to Mexican offers of Texas lands for debt reduction. Also supplies interesting notes on British reaction to Mexican-American War.

1433 **Vázquez, Josefina Zoraida.** El impacto de familia: intentos mexicanos para la integración hispanoamericana, 1830–1847. (*Rev. Indias*, 51:193, sept./dic. 1991, p. 545–570)

Provocative contribution relates how Mexico tried to reverse process by which four Spanish American viceroyalties became a multitude of separate nations.

1434 Vázquez Mantecón, Carmen; Alfonso Flamenco Ramírez; and Carlos Herrero Bervera. Las bibliotecas mexicanas en el siglo XIX. México: SEP, Dirección General de Bibliotecas, 1987. 254 p.: bibl., ill., index. (Historia de las bibliotecas en México; 2)

Important contribution to history of culture and education focuses mainly on the capital.

1435 Vega, Josefa. Los primeros préstamos de la Guerra de Independencia, 1809–1812. (*Hist. Mex.*, 39:4, abril/junio 1990, p. 909–931)

Exciting new research about loans to Spanish Crown during crucial years of independence wars leads to interesting possibilities about connections between fiscal drain and movement toward insurgency.

1436 Velasco Toro, José. La política desamortizadora y sus efectos en la región de Papantla, Veracruz. (*Palabra Hombre*, 72, oct./dic. 1989, p. 137–162, tables)

Shows how idea of breaking up indigenous communal property had substantial and longstanding roots in Veracruz. Also relates indigenous peoples' efforts to maintain their property through lawsuits and armed uprisings, and finally through concept of *condueñazgo* (large lots of collective property), a process which was ongoing until at least 1892. Good companion to Knowlton (see item **1382**), and highly recommended.

1437 Viajeros anglosajones por Jalisco: siglo XIX. Recopilación de José María Muriá y Angélica Peregrina. México: Instituto Nacional de Antropología e Historia, Programa de Estudios Jaliscienses, 1992. 375 p.: bibl. (Col. Regiones de México: Serie Historia)

Collection is useful for its wide variety of observations on Jalisco. Important material for emerging field of tourism and travel literature.

1438 Walker, David W. Homegrown revolution: the Hacienda Santa Catalina del Alamo y Anexas and agrarian protest in eastern Durango, Mexico, 1897–1913. (*HAHR*, 72:2, May 1992, p. 239–273)

Details not only development of revolutionary activity but also daily life on the hacienda and estate finance.

1439 Wells, Allen. All in the family: railroads and henequen monoculture in the Porfirian Yucatán. (*HAHR*, 72:2, May 1992, p. 159–209, graphs, map, tables)

Fascinating article demonstrates how even railroad-building responded to local ways: Yucatecan paternalism, monoculture, and debt-peonage all affected construction. A model study.

REVOLUTION AND POST-REVOLUTION

1440 Abascal, Salvador. Lázaro Cárdenas, presidente comunista. v. 1, Hasta el 31 de diciembre de 1935. México: Editorial Tradición, 1988. 1 v.: bibl.

The author-editor, a prolific writer and former *sinarquista* leader, takes a predictably negative view of events of early Cárdenas presidency. Approximately one-half of work is devoted to pre-1934 period.

1441 El agrarismo de la Revolución Mexicana. Edición de Margarita Menegus Bornemann. Prólogo de Juan Maestre Alfonso. Madrid: Instituto de Cooperación Iberoamericana, Ediciones de Cultura Hispánica, 1990. 124 p.: bibl. (Antología del pensamiento político, social y económico de América Latina; 9)

Brief introduction to topic is followed by collection of documents relating primarily to pre-1917 period. Documents are organized around pronouncements by Zapata, Carranza, and Villa.

1442 Aguilar Mora, Jorge. Una muerte sencilla, justa, eterna: cultura y guerra durante la Revolución Mexicana. México: Ediciones Era, 1990. 439 p.: bibl.

Romanticized history adds some interesting details to our knowledge of the Mexican Revolution in the north.

1443 Agustín, José. Tragicomedia mexicana. v. 1, La vida en México de 1940 a 1970. México: Planeta, 1990. 1 v: ill. (Espejo de México; 5)

Novelist-essayist turns his hand and wry sense of humor to recent history with unpredictable results. Although organized around presidential administrations, gives considerable attention to social, intellectual, and cultural developments. Vol. 2 will cover period 1970–88.

1444 Alanís Boyso, Rodolfo. El Estado de México durante la Revolución Mexicana, 1910–1914. Toluca, Mexico: Gobierno del Estado de México, Secretaría de Administración, 1985. 217 p.: bibl., ill.

Gives overview of political, military, economic, and social affairs for state of México from 1910 to mid-1914. Maderista phase of Revolution had little impact on state, with Revolution being "imported" by the *Zapatistas*. Armed struggle in state had little effect at national level but led to political instability and economic depression.

1445 Albro, Ward S. Always a rebel: Ricardo Flores Magón and the Mexican Revolution. Fort Worth: Texas Christian Univ. Press, 1992. 219 p.: bibl., ill., index.

Excellent work examines exile activities of Ricardo Flores Magón and growing anarchist content of his revolutionary pronouncements, especially after 1908. See also item **1534.**

1446 Alonso, Jorge. En busca de la convergencia: el Partido Obrero Campesino Mexicano. México: Centro de Investigaciones y Estudios Superiores en Antropología Social, 1990. 442 p.: bibl. (Ediciones de la Casa Chata; 33)

Study of disunity of Mexican left from 1940–64 focuses on Partido Obrero Campesino Mexicano (POCM). The POCM was founded in 1950 as a Marxist-Leninist-Stalinist party dedicated to establishing socialism in Mexico. The POCM tried—mostly unsuccessfully—to promote unity among leftist groups and merged itself out of existence in 1963.

1447 Anderson, Fred. The giant that came to Hermosillo. (*J. Southwest,* 34:2, Summer 1992, p. 187–205)

Focusing on opening of a major assembly plant in Hermosillo by Ford Motor Company (the "giant"), author describes recent efforts at industrialization in a state that was traditionally agricultural. Includes discussion of local, state, federal, and Ford development strategies.

1448 Arenal Fenochio, Jaime del. El nacionalismo conservador mexicano del siglo XX. (*in* Coloquio de Antropología e His-

toria Regionales, *8th, Zamora, Mexico, 1986.* El nacionalismo en México. Zamora, Mexico: El Colegio de Michoacán, 1992, p. 329–354, bibl.)

Explores conservative branch of nationalist thought based in Hispanism, Roman Catholicism, and especially anti-communism. Five authors are carefully discussed: Toribio Esquivel Obregón, Carlos Pereyra Gómez, José Vasconcelos, Manuel Herrera y Lasso, and Alfonso Junco.

1449 Asesinato en Coyoacán: antología. Edición de Patricia Ortega Ramírez. Prólogo de José Woldenberg. México: El Nacional, 1990. 340 p.: ill.

Collection of articles from Mexico City newspaper *El Nacional* deals with events leading up to assassination of Leon Trotsky in Aug. 1940, and with the assassination itself.

1450 Avila Espinosa, Felipe Arturo. El pensamiento económico, político y social de la Convención de Aguascalientes. Aguascalientes, Mexico: Instituto Cultural de Aguascalientes; México: INEHRM, 1991. 234 p.: bibl. (Contemporáneos)

Fine and much needed discussion considers practical and ideological frameworks of various factions within Mexican revolutionary movement. Three solid introductory chapters discuss background to actual meetings, with balance of book devoted to Convention of Aguascalientes itself and further evolution of the conventionist movement.

1451 Ayala Anguiano, Armando. Zapata y las grandes mentiras de la Revolución Mexicana. México: Editorial Diana, 1991. 230 p.

Provoked by outpouring of laudatory speeches and writings about Zapata and agrarian reform in connection with 75th anniversary of the Revolution, author focuses on agrarianism and political uses of Zapata legend. Author questions sincerity of long line of agrarian reformers from Obregón to contemporary "UNAMized intellectuals" and government bureaucrats.

1452 Barrientos, Herlinda; María Dolores Cárdenas; and Guillermo González Cedillo. Con Zapata y Villa: tres relatos testimoniales. México: Instituto Nacional de Estudios Históricos de la Revolución Mexicana, Secretaría de Gobernación, 1991. 153 p.: ill. (Testimonio)

Three individuals who participated in the Revolution offer their vivid recollections.

1453 Barrios Castro, Roberto. México en su lucha por la tierra: de la independencia a la Revolución, 1521–1987. México: Costa-Amic Editores, 1987. 290 p.: bibl., ill.

General survey of agrarian history from Spanish conquest to administration of Miguel de la Madrid features lengthy quotations from various decrees, plans, and reports. Most of volume is devoted to post-1910 period. Author served as head of the Depto. de Asuntos Agrarios y Colonización under President López Mateos and as secretary-general of the Confederación Nacional Campesina.

1454 Bastian, Jean-Pierre. La heterodoxia religiosa en la historiografía mexicanista, 1968–1988. (*Cristianismo Soc.*, 27:101, 1989, p. 47–58, bibl.)

Author examines recent historiography of religious heterodoxy which he defines as a "break from the dominant and monopolizing religious norms." Connection between religious heterodoxy and social change has been at the center of much of the literature. Works on colonial period and 19th century are also included. See also items **1458, 1554,** and **1571.**

1455 Bautista Zane, Refugio. Educación y revolución en Michoacán: la gubernatura del general Lázaro Cárdenas, 1928–1932. Chapingo, Mexico: Dirección de Difusión Cultural, 1991. 29 p. (Serie Contextos; 3)

Laudatory work describes Cárdenas' efforts at reform as governor. Author maintains that constitutional reforms of 1917 had scarcely begun in the state when Cárdenas became governor, and that his governorship represented a small-scale version of program later implemented at the national level. Emphasizes role played by state labor organization formed by Cárdenas (the Confederación Revolucionario Michoacana del Trabajo—CRMT), and leading part played by students and teachers in that organization.

1456 Benjamin, Thomas. ¡Primera viva Chiapas! Local rebellions and the Mexican revolution in Chiapas. (*Rev. Eur.*, 49, Dec. 1990, p. 33–53, maps)

Excellent article analyzes regional variation in the Revolution. Author demonstrates that two major rebellions during period 1910–20 (one supposedly *maderista*, the other supposedly *villista*) reflected primarily local concerns and actually represented disagreements between elite groups in the state. The *villista* revolt easily turned into an *obregonista* movement in 1920 when it suited local needs.

1457 Benjamin, Thomas. A rich land, a poor people: politics and society in modern Chiapas. Drawings by Alberto Beltrán. Albuquerque: Univ. of New Mexico Press, 1989. 350 p.: bibl., index.

Political history centers on persistence of elite control despite national political upheavals that periodically influence state politics. Much emphasis is on governors whose modernization schemes benefited local elite. Fundamental problems of labor and land that characterized late Porfiriato persist to present and contribute to growing violence and repression.

1458 Blancarte, Roberto. La Iglesia Católica en México desde 1929: introducción crítica a la producción historiográfica, 1968–1988. (*Cristianismo Soc.*, 27:101, 1989, p. 27–42)

As title indicates, author is more concerned with general environment influencing historiography than with detailed review of the literature. Author identifies reasons behind cyclical interest in Church history and marks 1979 visit of Pope John Paul II to Mexico as a division point. Much of discussion is based on concept that *modus vivendi* between Church and State started to change as early as 1950. See also items **1554, 1571** and **1454.**

1459 Bortz, Jeffrey. The effect of Mexico's postwar industrialization on the U.S.-Mexico price and wage comparison. (*in* U.S.-Mexico relations: labor market interdependence. Stanford, Calif.: Stanford Univ. Press, 1992, p. 214–234, tables)

Excellent comparative study looks at wages and prices during 1939–85 period. Concludes that Mexico's postwar industrialization did not raise Mexican wages in relation to US wages and therefore could not end push-effect of differential wages on migration from Mexico to US.

1460 Brondo Whitt, E. La campaña sobre Zacatecas. Zacatecas, Mexico: Gobierno del Estado de Zacatecas, 1990. 94 p.: ill., map. (Serie Zacatecas en la Revolución; 1)

Participant relates buildup to and Battle of Zacatecas in June 1914 which led to major victory for forces of Pancho Villa over those of Victoriano Huerta. See also item **1473**.

1461 Brown, Jonathan Charles. Oil and revolution in Mexico. Berkeley: Univ. of California Press, 1992. 453 p.: bibl., ill., index.

Excellent, even-handed treatment of evolution of Mexican oil industry to 1920 focuses on foreign-owned oil companies. The industry's growth resulted both from injections of foreign expertise and capital, and Mexico's own economic restructuring. The "primacy of Mexico's social heritage" meant that Mexicans at all levels attempted to "manage" process of modernization brought by oil companies. Extensively researched and convincingly revisionist, work is one of the best of the biennium.

1462 Calles, Plutarco Elías. Correspondencia personal. v. 1. Introducción, selección y notas de Carlos Macías. Hermosillo, Mexico: Gobierno del Estado de Sonora; Instituto Sonorense de Cultura; México: Fideicomiso Archivos Plutarco Elías Calles y Fernando Torreblanca; Fondo de Cultura Económica, 1991. 1 v.: bibl., index. (Vida y pensamiento de México)

Important publication brings together hundreds of letters, telegrams, and personal documents written by or addressed to Calles himself. Documentation focuses on growth of the State in Mexico (1919–35), aspects of Mexican cultural life (1924–35), and Calles family correspondence (1919–45). Carlos Macías provides excellent guide to the materials in his introduction.

1463 Camarena, Mario and **Susana A. Fernández.** Los obreros-artesanos en las fábricas textiles de San Angel, 1920–1930. (*in* Comunidad, cultura y vida social: ensayos sobre la formación de la clase obrera. México: Instituto Nacional de Antropología e Historia, 1991, p. 173–199, tables)

Focuses on workers' response to transition to modern industrial production in five large factories, in what was still technically an agricultural area. Emphasis is on efforts of skilled workers to protect their artisan traditions from increasing mechanization. See also item **1544**.

1464 Camp, Roderic Ai. Entrepreneurs and politics in twentieth-century Mexico. New York: Oxford Univ. Press, 1989. 306 p.: bibl.

Using data on 200 leading entrepreneurs, author concludes that exchange of personnel between public and private sectors is relatively low, and that influence of entrepreneurial group on government policy has been declining since 1980 as influence of labor has increased. His new information confirms importance of family-run corporations and conglomerates in Mexican economy. For political scientist's comment see *HLAS 53:3300*.

1465 Canudas, Enrique. Trópico rojo: historia política y social de Tabasco: los años garridistas, 1919–1934. Villahermosa, Mexico: Gobierno del Estado de Tabasco, ICT Ediciones, 1989. 2 v. (Lo de entonces)

Political history of Tabasco centers on controversial activities of Tomás Garrido Canabal—governor, federal senator, secretary of agriculture under Cárdenas, and leader of the anticlerical "Camisas Rojas." See also item **1466**.

1466 Caparroso V., Amado Alfonso. Tal cual fue Tomás Garrido Canabal. México: Editorial Libros de México, 1985. 598 p.: ill.

Laudatory biography of controversial Tabascan politician is written by close friend and political associate wishing to refute the "black legend" that has grown up around "el hombre del Sureste." See also item **1465**.

1467 Cárdenas García, Nicolás. La reconstrucción del Estado mexicano: los años sonorenses, 1920–1935. México: Unidad Xochimilco, División de Ciencias Sociales y Humanidades, UNAM, 1992. 176 p.: bibl. (Breviarios de la investigación; 18)

Examines political struggle and practice of power from 1920–35. Reconstruction of the Mexican State was not a product of political consensus but rather the result of a flexible policy of political alliances in which regional *caciques*, military chiefs, and the US were principal players. Sonoran dynasty consistently favored economic development over social reform.

1468 Cárdenas Noriega, Joaquín. Mi generación: de Madero a la dedocracia: remembranzas, vivencias, reflexiones históricas. México: Editorial Pac, 1987. 225 p.: bibl.

Personal reflections on course of the Revolution from 1910 to mid-1980s is interspersed with lengthy digressions into colonial period and 19th century. Author adopts a conservative, conspiracy-driven interpretation with a motley crew of villains composed of Yankees, Masons, Protestants, and Marxists.

1469 Carr, Barry. Marxism and communism in twentieth-century Mexico. Lincoln: Univ. of Nebraska Press, 1992. 437 p.: bibl., index.

Good historical survey of Partido Comunista Mexicana (PCM), and of Mexican left as a whole, emphasizes a number of relationships: between Mexican communism and other leftist traditions; between Mexican left and the official party; between PCM and the Comintern; and between PCM and the Communist Party of the US. Book is organized around "important episodes" in evolution of the left, such as the Cárdenas Administration and the student rebellion of 1968.

La casa de citas: en el barrio Galante. See item **1346.**

1470 Castañeda Batres, Oscar. Revolución Mexicana y Constitución de 1917, 1876–1938. 2. ed. México: M.A. Porrúa, 1989. 429 p.: bibl., ill. (Documentos para la historia del México independiente; 3)

Appproximately one-fourth of work is made up of two essays, one covering the Porfiriato and the other the period 1906–38. Remainder of book consists of documents relating to the two periods, including full text of the Constitution of 1917.

Ceballos Ramírez, Manuel. La democracia cristiana en el México liberal: un proyecto alternativo, 1867–1929. See item **1347.**

1471 Cedeño del Olmo, Manuel. Estado y partidos políticos en el período constitucional de la Revolución Mexicana, 1916–1920. Tabasco, Mexico: Univ. Juárez Autónóma de Tabasco, Centro de Investigación de la División de Ciencias Sociales y Humanidades, 1988. 226 p.: bibl.

Traces development of four key political parties, the social and economic forces influencing them, and their relationship to the emerging government during Carranza Administration. Parties discussed are: Partido Liberal Constitucionalista, Partido Coopera-

tista Nacional, Partido Laborista Mexicano, and Partido Nacional Agrarista.

1472 Cerda González, Luis. La influencia del sector externo en el proceso de industrialización mexicano durante los primeros años posrevolucionarios. (*Estud. Hist. Mod. Contemp. Méx.,* 11, 1988, p. 233–261, tables)

After discussion of methodology and Porfirian background, author traces Mexico's "extraordinary weakness" with respect to changes in foreign trade and the ensuing effect on industrialization process and government policy between 1920–40. The world depression beginning in 1929 accelerated trend toward industrial production based on import substitution.

1473 Cervantes, Federico and **Raúl E. Puga.** Como fue el ataque a Zacatecas. v. 1–2. Zacatecas?: Gobierno del Estado de Zacatecas, 1990–1991. 2 v.: ill., photos. (Serie Zacatecas en la Revolución; 3)

Vol. 1 is a brief, useful account by a participant. Vol. 2 consists of a collection of mediocre magazine articles relating to key Battle of Zacatecas in June 1914 between forces of Pancho Villa and those of Victoriano Huerta. See also item **1460.**

1474 Chabat, Jorge. Mexico's foreign policy in 1990: electoral sovereignty and integration with the United States. (*J. Interam. Stud. World Aff.,* 33:4, Winter 1991, p. 1–25)

Assesses "economization" of Mexico's foreign policy under Miguel de la Madrid and Carlos Salinas. Includes discussion of free trade agreement, drug traffic, and bilateral problems arising from Mexico's electoral process.

1475 Chávez Montañez, Armando B. Diccionario de hombres de la Revolución en Chihuahua. Ciudad Juárez, México: Univ. Autónoma de Ciudad Juárez; Meridiano 107 Editores, 1990. 232 p.: bibl. (Semanario)

Useful reference work focuses primarily on those who fought in Villa's División del Norte.

1476 Chenaut, Victoria. Migrantes y aventureros en la frontera sur. México: Secretaría de Educación Pública; CIESAS, 1989. 113 p.: bibl., ill., maps. (Frontera)

This study of Quintana Roo-Belize border region encompasses considerable time span (1830s-1980s) and range of topics (Caste War to illegal immigration).

1477 Chezem, Curtis G. The Mexican automobile battle. (*J. West*, 30:4, Oct. 1991, p. 45–51, ill.)

Well-illustrated account describes May 1916 gun battle between small group of *villistas* and three carloads of members of the Pershing Expedition under command of George S. Patton who later indicated that the incident influenced his thinking about armored warfare.

1478 Comisión Nacional para las Celebraciones del 175 Aniversario de la Independencia Nacional y 75 Aniversario de la Revolución Mexicana. Así fue la Revolución Mexicana. v. 1, Crisis del porfirismo. v. 2, Caída del antiguo régimen. v. 3, Madero y el tiempo nuevo. v. 4, La lucha constitucionalista. v. 5, El triunfo de la Revolución. v. 6, Conjunto de testimonios. v. 7, La Revolución día a día. v. 8, pts. 1–2, Los protagonistas. México: Consejo Nacional de Fomento Educativo, 1985. 8 v. in 9: bibl., ill. (some col.), index, maps.

Multivolume, multiauthored work examines early years of the Revolution. Vols. 1–5 provide analytical narrative from Porfirian background to Constitutional Convention of 1916–17. Vol. 6 is a collection of documents ranging from Díaz-Creelman interview to articles of the Constitution of 1917. Vol. 7 provides chronology of notable events from 1904 to early 1917. Vol. 8 contains biographical essays on the "protagonists" of early revolutionary period. Very well illustrated, especially with maps and diagrams. Intended for general public but also useful for the specialist.

1479 Concurso Estatal de Ensayo sobre la Historia de las Ligas de Comunidades Agrarias y Sindicatos Campesinos, 1st, México, 1987. Historia de las ligas de comunidades agrarias y sindicatos campesinos. México: Confederación Nacional Campesina; Centro de Estudios Históricos del Agrarismo en México, 1988. 6 v.: bibl., ill.

Collection of 34 essays focuses on state-level efforts to organize rural workers based on geographical location. Vol. 1 covers Centro Norte (Aguascalientes, San Luis Potosí, Zacatecas); Vol. 2, Centro (Michoacán, Guanajuato, México, Querétaro); Vol. 3, Cen-

tro Sur (Distrito Federal, Morelos, Tlaxcala, Guerrero); Vol. 4, Norte (Baja California, Nuevo León, Durango, Chihuahua); Vol. 5, Sureste (Oaxaca, Tabasco, Chiapas, Quintana Roo, Yucatán); Vol. 6, Golfo Central (Veracruz, San Luis Potosí).

1480 Congreso de Historiadores Duranguenses, 1st, Durango, Mexico, 1985. Ponencias. Durango, Mexico: Univ. Juárez del Estado de Durango, Instituto de Investigaciones Históricas, 1990. 393 p.: bibl., maps. (Serie Memoria; 2)

Papers from 1985 congress cover wide range of themes, some relating to pre-Revolutionary period.

1481 Congreso Internacional sobre la Revolución Mexicana, San Luis Potosí, Mexico, 1990 Memoria. San Luis Potosí, Mexico: Gobierno del Estado de San Luis Potosí; México: Instituto Nacional de Estudios Históricos de la Revolución Mexicana, Secretaría de Gobernación, 1991. 2 v.: bibl., ill.

Papers presented in connection with 80th anniversary of promulgation of Plan of San Luis Potosí cover broad range of topics, from Church-State relations to art and revolution.

1482 Correa, Eduardo J. El Partido Católico Nacional y sus directores: explicación de su fracaso y deslinde de responsabilidades. México: Fondo de Cultura Económica, 1991. 220 p.: bibl.

Reprint of work written in 1914 but not published until 1939. Author was a *maderista* and key figure in the Partido Católico Nacional (PCN), directing its newspaper *La Nacional.* The PCN—founded in May 1911—showed early political strength but later suffered from its association with Huerta regime. Excellent introduction by Jean Meyer.

1483 Cosio, Marie Eugénie Zavala de. Los antecedentes de la transición demográfica en México. (*Hist. Mex.*, 42:1, julio/sept. 1992, p. 103–128, graphs, tables)

Traces demographic transition of Mexico from late-19th to mid-20th century. Begins with declining mortality due to modern medicine and public health programs; examines a period of declining mortality and increasing fertility; and finally enters a period when both mortality and fertility are declining. Trends are compared and contrasted on urban/rural basis.

Cuéllar Vázquez, Angélica. Proceso de industrialización. See *HLAS 53:4934.*

1484 Diccionario histórico y biográfico de la Revolución Mexicana. v. 2. México: Instituto Nacional de Estudios Históricos de la Revolución Mexicana, Secretaría de Gobernación, 1990. 1 v.: bibl.

Major reference work organized by groupings of states was published in honor of 80th anniversary of the Revolution. Time period covered is 1890–1920. Includes biographies, military actions, political groups, publications, conventions/congresses, plans and manifestos, and popular songs and other cultural manifestations of the Revolution. Vol. 2 deals with Chiapas, Chihuahua, the Distrito Federal, and Durango.

1485 Dios, Jesús Ezequiel de. José Domingo, el idealista. Villahermosa, Mexico: Gobierno del Estado de Tabasco; ICT Ediciones, 1989. 159 p.: bibl., ill. (Los que escriben la historia)

Studies Tabascan revolutionary figure José Domingo Ramírez Garrido, who served as a military leader under political thinker and writer Salvador Alvarado. Includes numerous photos, but none of subject, attesting to the book's general level of organization.

Domínguez Medina, Martha. Colección Pablo Herrera Carrillo. See item **1358.**

1486 Encinas Blanco, Angel. Lo que no se ha dicho de la matanza de Villa en San Pedro de la Cueva. (*in* Simposio de Historia y Antropología de Sonora, *13th, Hermosillo, Mexico, 1989.* Memoria. Coordinación de Juan Manuel Romero Gil. Hermosillo, Mexico: Instituto de Investigaciones Históricas de la Univ. de Sonora, 1989, v. 1, p. 475–491, bibl.)

Revisionist work looks at massacre carried out by *villista* troops at town of San Pedro de la Cueva during Villa's disastrous Sonora campaign in late 1915. Emphasis is on survivors of the massacre. See also *HLAS 40: 2759.*

1487 El exilio español en México. Madrid: Ministerio de Cultura, Dirección General de Bellas Artes, 1983? 88 p.: ill. (some col.).

Catalog accompanies 1983–84 Madrid exhibition depicting Spanish exile activities in Mexico from fall of the Spanish Republic in 1939 through the 1970s.

1488 La expropiación petrolera vista por la prensa mexicana, norteamericana e inglesa, 1936–1940. Recopilación de Alicia Gojman de Backal. México: Petróleos Mexicanos, 1988. 426 p.: bibl.

Work commemorates 50th anniversary of oil expropriation and creation of Pemex. After a brief historical introduction, most of work is devoted to collection of articles taken from newspapers primarily in Mexico and the US. More than just a Pemex public relations piece.

1489 Felipe Carrillo Puerto. Prólogo y selección de Berenice Lacroix Macosay. México: Depto. del Distrito Federal, 1985. 160 p.: ill., ports. (Col. Conciencia cívica nacional; 13)

Brief biography of Yucatecan revolutionary is followed by a much more extensive collection of poems, articles, and documents mostly dealing with his execution.

1490 Fell, Claude. José Vasconcelos: los años del águila, 1920–1925; educación, cultura e iberoamericanismo en el México postrevolucionario. México: Univ. Nacional Autónoma de México, 1989. 742 p.: bibl. (Serie Historia moderna y contemporánea; 21)

Provides detailed examination of Vasconcelos' philosophy and educational reforms he pursued as head of Universidad Nacional and secretary of education in early 1920s.

1491 Flores Magón, Ricardo. Correspondencia de Ricardo Flores Magón, 1904–1912. Recopilación e introducción de Jacinto Barrera Basols. Puebla, Mexico: Univ. Autónoma de Puebla, 1989. 462 p.: indexes. (Col. Historia)

Correspondence, often including replies, is taken from archives of Secretaria de Relaciones Exteriores. Introduction explains context of and provenance of correspondence.

Florescano, Enrique. El nuevo pasado mexicano. See item **1362.**

1492 Fuentes Aguirre, Armando. Madero, caudillo civil de la Revolución. México: Patronato del Instituto Nacional de Estudios Históricos de la Revolución Mexicana, 1973. 159 p.: port. (Biblioteca del Instituto Nacional de Estudios Históricos de la Revolución Mexicana; 62)

Slim volume aims at refuting "black legend" view of Madero as naive, indecisive, manipulated figure distracted by his vegetarian and spiritist views.

1493 Gall, Olivia. Trotsky en México: y la vida política en el período de Cárdenas, 1937–1940. México: Ediciones Era, 1991. 423 p.: bibl. (Col. Problemas de México)

Work integrates Trotsky into his Mexican milieu better than any previous study of the exile. Objectivity is lacking, however.

1494 García Cantú, Gastón. Idea de México. México: Consejo Nacional para la Cultura y las Artes; Fondo de Cultura Económica, 1991. 6 v.: bibl., ill., indexes. (Vida y pensamiento de México)

Series of linked essays which discuss US-Latin American relations, with special focus on Mexico, from beginning of 19th century to Bush presidency.

1495 García Díaz, Bernardo. Santa Rosa y Río Blanco. Copias fotográficas de Adrián Mendieta Pérez. Jalapa Enríquez, Mexico: Gobierno del Estado de Veracruz, Archivo General del Estado, 1989. 167 p.: bibl., ill., maps. (Veracruz, imágenes de su historia; 2)

Graphic history depicts migrations, urbanization, and labor organization connected with two major textile factories established in 1890s in state of Veracruz. Narrative covers through 1930s.

1496 Garciadiego Dantan, Javier. Higinio Aguilar: milicia, rebelión y corrupción como *modus vivendi*. (*Hist. Mex.*, 41:3, enero/marzo 1992, p. 437–488, ill.)

Fascinating study examines improbable military career of a man for whom militarism, rebellion, and corruption became a way of life. A "folkloric opportunist and typical counter-revolutionary," Aguilar started his rebellious career in 1869 by opposing Juárez regime and ended it in 1920s contesting Sonoran dynasty of Obregón and Calles.

1497 Garrido, Luis Javier. El nacionalismo priísta. (*in* Coloquio de Antropología e Historia Regionales, *8th, Zamora, Mexico, 1986*. El nacionalismo en México. Edición de Cecilia Noriega Elío. Zamora, Mexico: El Colegio de Michoacán, 1992, p. 259–274)

Discusses changing visions of Mexican nationalism, from the reinstitutionalizing government and later the official party of 1917 through the De la Madrid presidency.

1498 Garza Madero de Suárez, Elena. Gustavo y Francisco Madero: dos raíces, un ideal: historia oral y epistolaria. Monterrey, Mexico: Gobierno de Nuevo León, Secretaría de Administración, Dirección de Acción Cívica y Editorial, 1991. 200 p., 7 p. of plates: bibl., ill.

Family portrait of the Maderos by Gustavo's granddaughter includes reminiscences by Gustavo's daughter as well as limited selection of family correspondence.

1499 Gilly, Adolfo. Los dos socialismos mexicanos. (*in* Coloquio de Antropología e Historia Regionales, *8th, Zamora, Mexico, 1986*. El nacionalismo en México. Edición de Cecilia Noriega Elío. Zamora, Mexico: El Colegio de Michoacán, 1992, p. 355–371)

Extremely general discussion and analysis of ideas of State-building within Mexican left from the Revolution through student uprising of 1968. The "two socialisms" refer to an agrarian socialism on the one hand, and a more Marxist workers' socialism on the other.

Glantz, Margo. The family tree: an illustrated novel. See item **5061.**

1500 Gledhill, John. Casi nada: a study of agrarian reform in the homeland and Cardenismo. Albany: Institute for Mesoamerican Studies, State Univ. of New York at Albany, 1991. 420 p.: bibl. (Studies on culture and society; 4)

Examines impact of land reform on Guaracha hacienda in state of Michoacán. Transformation from hacienda to collective *ejido* to individual *ejido* has brought little material benefit to *ejiditarios*, and more recent reforms in 1980s did little to change "the structure of inequality within the *ejido*." Rural struggle now is between neo-Liberals and neo-Cardenists.

1501 Gómez Arias, Alejandro and **Víctor Días Arciniega.** Memoria personal de un país. México: Grijalbo, 1990. 293 p.: ill., index. (Testimonios)

Memoirs of distinguished journalist include episodes from his childhood, his famous friendship with Frida Kahlo, his active defense of university autonomy in 1929, and his collaboration with *Excelsior* editor Julio Scherer. Ends with discussion of political events of 1988 and of prospects for the party of Cuauhtémoc Cárdenas.

Gómez Izquierdo, José Jorge. El movimiento antichino en México, 1871–1934: problemas del racismo y del nacionalismo durante la Revolución Mexicana. See item **1369.**

1502 González, Luis. The cultural modernization of Mexico, 1857–1958. (*in* Modernization and Revolution in Mexico: a comparative approach. Edited by Omar Martínez Legorreta. Tokyo: United Nations Univ., 1989, p. 66–77)

Author identifies four phases in Mexico's modernization, focusing on last two: era of "liberal culture" (1856–1910); and the Revolution (1910–1958). Author does not see revolutionary phase as a radical break from preceding period and views modernization as essentially an elite activity.

1503 González Herrera, Carlos. La política chihuahuense de los años veinte: el gobierno de Ignacio C. Enríquez, 1920–1923. (*Nóesis/Juárez,* 5:2, julio/dic. 1990, p. 89–113)

Excellent study examines Ignacio Enríquez's tenure as governor of Chihuahua in immediate aftermath of the Revolution. Clearly illustrates success of his conciliatory and pragmatic policies, which led to fragile but real social consensus and relative peace within the state.

1504 González Navarro, Moisés. The social transformation of Mexico, 1867–1940. (*in* Modernization and Revolution in Mexico: a comparative approach. Edited by Omar Martínez Legorreta. Tokyo: United Nations Univ., 1989, p. 1–19)

Good overview for the general reader gives equal attention to pre-Revolution and post-Revolution periods. General themes include: landholding, industrialization, the peasantry, workers and unionization, Church-State relations, and education.

González y González, Luis. 75 años de investigación histórica en México. See item **1374.**

1505 Grammont, Hubert Carton de. Calles y el agrarismo mexicano a principios de los 30: organización gremial de los pequeños propietarios. (*Caravelle/Toulouse,* 56, 1991, p. 37–52)

Examines "vacilating" agrarian policies pursued by Calles, whom author sees as caught between economic conviction that larger landholdings represented Mexico's agri-

cultural future and political need to maintain peasant support through further land distribution. Calles followed an "Italian fascist" approach in reorganizing rival economic interests in agrarian sector and subordinating them to federal policy.

1506 Guerrero Miller, Alma Yolanda. Cuesta abajo: declinación de tres caciques huastecos revolucionarios: Cedillo, Santos y Peláez. Presentación de Octavio Herrera Pérez. México: M.A. Porrúa, Grupo Editorial, 1991. 119 p.: bibl., ill.

Comparative study examines three Huastecan *caciques* (Saturnino Cedillo, Manuel Peláez, and Gonzalo Santos), their role in centralization of power in the post-revolutionary State, and their responses to the centralized government which they helped create. Author concludes that the case studies do not justify establishment of a "model" for decline of *cacique* power. See also items **1537, 1528,** and *HLAS 50:1213, HLAS 52:1301,* and *HLAS 52:1302.*

1507 Guilpain Peuliard, Odile. Felipe Angeles y los destinos de la Revolución Mexicana. Prólogo de Adolfo Gilly. México: Fondo de Cultura Económica, 1991. 241 p.: bibl. (Sección de obras de historia)

Excellent work combines emotional intensity and historical rigor to provide readable and comprehensive biography of this important revolutionary figure. Includes penetrating prologue by Adolfo Gilly.

1508 Gutiérrez, Angel; José Napoleón Guzmán Avila; and Gerardo Sánchez Díaz. La cuestión agraria: revolución y contrarrevolución en Michoacán: tres ensayos. Morelia, Mexico: Univ. Michoacana de San Nicolás de Hidalgo, 1984. 71 p.: bibl. (Col. Historia nuestra; 6)

Three essays relate to state agrarian history, only one of them dealing exclusively with revolutionary period. This latter essay covers the 1917–26 period, focusing on activities of governors Pascual Ortiz Rubio and Francisco José Múgica Velázquez.

1509 Haber, Stephen H. Assessing the obstacles to industrialization: the Mexican economy, 1830–1940. (*J. Lat. Am. Stud.,* 24:1, 1992, p. 1–32)

Carefully argued article shows that, in contrast to Europe and US, Mexico experienced an industrial lag during the period.

From 1830–80 the lag was caused by factors external to firms, whereas between 1880–1910 hindrances were largely internal. From 1910–30 internal constraints, combined with new external problems including political instability, slowed industrial growth even further. Production began to pick up only in the mid-1930s.

1510 Haynes, Keith A. Dependency, postimperialism, and the Mexican Revolution: an historiographic review. (*Mex. Stud.*, 7:2, Summer 1991, p. 225–251)

Critiques three popular views of the Revolution: 1) the Revolution as not really revolutionary; 2) the Revolution as the first modern, popular social revolution; and 3) the "dependency" interpretation. Author is particularly interested in revising dependency interpretation in favor of a "postimperialist" view (a class analysis of international corporate expansion).

1511 Hernández Enríquez, Gustavo Abel. Historia moderna de Puebla. v. 1, 1917–1920, Gobierno del doctor Alfonso Cabrera Lobato. Puebla, Mexico: G.A. Hernández Enríquez, 1986. 1 v: bibl., ill., index.

Examines events during Administration of Alfonso Cabrera Lobato, constitutionalist governor who served from July 1917 to May 1920. While author consulted a variety of sources, he leans heavily on newspaper accounts, especially *El Universal.* For vols. 2–3, see item **1512.**

1512 Hernández Enríquez, Gustavo Abel. Historia moderna de Puebla. v. 2, 1920–1924, el período de la anarquía constitucional. v. 3, 1925–1926, la contrarrevolución en Puebla. Puebla, Mexico: G.A. Hernández Enríquez, 1988. 2 v: bibl., ill., indexes.

Vol. 2 is basically a political history organized around chaotic succession of governors (14 in all) during Obregón presidency. Author also devotes a chapter to analyzing "class struggle" involving peasants, workers, and the wealthy. Vol. 3 deals with a brief period (1925–26) but a broader range of topics. Political focus is on the governor, Claudio Nabor Tirado, a mediocre conservative willing to follow orders of Calles. Also gives considerable attention to economic and social factors. Heavy dependence on newspaper sources, as in vol. 1, which covers the Admin-

istration of Dr. Alfonso Cabrera Lobato (see item **1511**).

1513 Hibino, Barbara. Cervecería Cuauhtémoc: a case study of technological and industrial development in Mexico. (*Mex. Stud.*, 8:1, Winter 1992, p. 23–43)

Interesting study examines evolution of a business firm which deviated from the foreign dependency model of many of its contemporaries. Using domestic capital and its own technology, Cervecería Cuauhtémoc was able to compete successfully in both domestic and international markets and became the foundation for some of the most important industrial groups in Mexico (Alfa, Visa, Vitro).

1514 Hinds, Harold E. and **Charles M. Tatum.** Not just for children: the Mexican comic book in the late 1960s and 1970s. Westport, Conn.: Greenwood Press, 1992. 245 p.: bibl., ill., index. (Contributions to the study of popular culture: 0198-9871; 30)

Highly informative and readable work, with good historical introduction, looks at comic-book phenomenon in Mexico. Recommended for its insights into Mexican culture.

1515 Historia de la cuestión agraria mexicana. v. 5, pts. 1–2, El cardenismo [por Everardo Escárcega López *et al.*] v. 6, El agrarismo y la industrialización de México, 1940–1950 [por Sergio de la Peña y Marcel Morales Ibarra]. México: Siglo Veintiuno Editores; Centro de Estudios Históricos del Agrarismo en México, 1989? 3 v.

Vol. 5 deals with "watershed" years of agrarian reform under Cárdenas. Agrarian reform is depicted as part of a broader program to transform entire country. Counterreform activities are also discussed. Vol. 6 deals with 1940–50 period and describes conflict between agrarianism inherited from Cárdenas years and official policy of promoting industrialization.

1516 Imágenes de Guadalajara a través de un siglo. Guadalajara, Mexico: H. Ayuntamiento de Guadalajara 89–92, Comisión de Planeación Urbana, 1990. 51 p.: bibl., ill., map. (Col. Cuadernos de la ciudad)

Photographic comparison/contrast between late 19th-century and late 20th-century Guadalajara includes limited accompanying narrative.

1517 Joseph, Gilbert M. and **Allen Wells.** The rough-and-tumble career of Pedro Crespo. (*in* The human tradition in Latin America: the twentieth century. Edited by William H. Beezley and Judith Ewell. Wilmington, Del.: Scholarly Resources, 1987, p. 27–40)

Studies local Yucatecan leader who served as a linking figure between Maya and dominant Spanish-speaking society. Initially allied with Díaz government, personal grievances led him to become active in *maderista* movement.

1518 Karetnikova, Inga and **Leon Steinmetz.** Mexico according to Eisenstein. Albuquerque: Univ. of New Mexico Press, 1991. 200 p.: bibl., ill., index, map.

Describes great Russian filmmaker Sergei Eisenstein and his failed efforts in early 1930s to capture essence of Mexico in his never-completed film *¡Que Viva México!.* For a literary figure's vision of same period see item **1616.**

1519 Knight, Alan. Land and society in revolutionary Mexico: the destruction of the great haciendas. (*Mex. Stud.,* 7:1, Winter 1991, p. 73–104)

Provides excellent evaluation of traditional and revisionist interpretations of nature of the hacienda, role of the peasantry, and nature of agrarian reform. Author offers some revision of both traditional and revisionist views. Emphasizing a sociopolitical rather than economic focus, he concludes that 30 years of agrarian reform led to destruction of the great haciendas and reconstitution of the Mexican peasantry.

1520 Knight, Alan. Racism, revolution, and *indigenismo:* Mexico, 1910–1940. (*in* The idea of race in Latin America, 1870–1940. Edited by Richard Graham. Austin: Univ. of Texas Press, 1990, p. 71–113, photos)

Excellent study of role played by "race" and racism in the Revolution. Author examines shifting concept of race and discusses the need to distinguish between race and ethnicity. According to author, the Revolution had no "self-conscious Indian project," and Indians were the "objects," not the "authors," of *indigenismo.* This official "Indianness" was at odds with Mexico's social reality.

1521 Krauze, Enrique. Lázaro Cárdenas, general misionero. Investigación iconográfica de Aurelio de los Reyes. México: Fondo de Cultura Económico, 1987. 222 p.: bibl., ill. (Biografía del poder; 8)

Balanced, extensively illustrated political biography of the Revolution's most controversial president provides good coverage of Cárdenas' post-1940 activities.

1522 Krauze, Enrique. Plutarco E. Calles: reformar desde el origen. Investigación iconográfica de Aurelio de los Reyes. México: Fondo de Cultura Económica, 1987. 154 p.: bibl., ill. (some col.). (Biografía del poder; 7. Tezontle)

Author provides a popular view of the "Jefe Máximo."

1523 LaFrance, David G. and **Guy P.C. Thomson.** Juan Francisco Lucas: patriarch of the Sierra Norte de Puebla. (*in* The human tradition in Latin America: the twentieth century. Edited by William H. Beezley and Judith Ewell. Wilmington, Del.: Scholarly Resources, 1987, p. 1–13, bibl.)

Fascinating discussion makes clear the enduring significance of local leadership in Mexican countryside despite enormous political upheaval in nation as a whole from time of the Revolution of Ayutla until Lucas' death in 1917.

1524 Land, labor & capital in modern Yucatán: essays in regional history and political economy. Edited by Jeffery T. Brannon and Gilbert M. Joseph. Tuscaloosa: Univ. of Alabama Press, 1991. 322 p.: bibl., ill., index, map.

Interdisciplinary collection of essays is divided into three parts. Pt. 1 deals with expansion of commercial agriculture and its impact on traditional Mayan society. Pt. 2 focuses on intensification of commercial agriculture and enclave development in late 19th century. Pt. 3 assesses revolutionary challenges to henequen monoculture.

Lanz Cárdenas, José Trinidad. La contraloría y el control interno en México: antecedentes históricos y legislativos. See item **1383.**

1525 Lara Pardo, Luis. De Porfirio Díaz a Francisco I. Madero: la sucesión dictatorial de 1911. Ed. facsimilar. México: Comisión Nacional para las Celebraciones del 175 Aniversario de la Independencia Nacional y

75 Aniversario de la Revolución Mexicana, 1985. 285 p. (La biblioteca de obras fundamentales de la independencia y la Revolución)

Reprint of work first published in New York in 1912. Author was medical doctor turned journalist who wrote in exile in 1911. He is critical of both Díaz and Madero but reserves his greatest criticism for Madero whom he compares unfavorably with a list of 19th-century Mexican rulers.

1526 Leal, Juan Felipe and **José Villaseñor.** En la Revolución, 1910–1917. México: Siglo Vientiuno Editores, 1988. 382 p.: maps. (La clase obrera en la historia de México; 5)

Excellent study examines political activities, economic situation, and organizational efforts of workers during late Porfiriato and early years of the Revolution. Most of the attention is on 1910–13 period.

Leal, Juan Felipe. El Estado y el bloque en el poder en México. See *HLAS 53:3343.*

1527 León García, Ricardo. Bancos chihuahuenses durante el Porfiriato, 1880–1916. (*Nóesis/Juárez,* 5:2, julio/dic. 1990, p. 5–32)

Explores development and role of banking and credit systems in modernizing society of Chihuahua.

1528 Lerner, Victoria. Génesis de un cacicazgo: antecedentes del cedillismo. México: Coordinación General de Estudios de Posgrado, UNAM, 1989. 318 p.: bibl., ill., maps. (Col. Posgrado; 5)

Author explores two themes related to the domination of San Luis Potosí state politics by durable *cacique* Saturnino Cedillo: 1) situation of various social classes (*hacendados,* small proprietors, peasants); and 2) changes in political system and situation. Emphasis is on 1914–20 period of "revolutionary transition." See also items **1537, 1506,** *HLAS 50:1213, HLAS 52:1301,* and *HLAS 52:1302.*

1529 Lida, Clara Eugenia; José Antonio Matesanz; and **Beatriz Morán Gortari.** La Casa de España en México. México: Colegio de México, 1988. 201 p.: bibl., index. (Jornadas; 113)

Provides detailed account of institution sponsored by Cárdenas to support refugee intellectuals from Spain's civil war. The Casa had a brief history, from its establishment in 1938 to its transformation into El Colegio de México in 1940.

1530 Loaeza, Soledad. Clases medias y política en México: la querella escolar, 1959–1963. México: Colegio de México, Centro de Estudios Internacionales, 1988. 427 p.: bibl.

Studies conflict within and outside the PRI over 1959 government effort to impose required textbooks on all schools. Set against background of Cardenista/Alemanista split, Catholic middle-class opposition to the policy provided cover for business opposition to the PRI on labor matters, and ultimately led to modification of textbook policy.

1531 López Alanís, Gilberto. Culiacán, 1920. Culiacán, Mexico: Dirección de Investigación y Fomento de Cultura Regional del Gobierno del Estado de Sinaloa, 1990. 157 p.: bibl. ill. (Historias municipales)

Detailed municipal chronology is organized on a monthly basis. Companion piece to author's *Culiacán, 1910: un cabildo ante la revolución* (1986).

1532 Lozano y Nathal, Gema. La negra, loca y anarquista Federación Local de Trabajadores del Puerto de Veracruz. (*Antropol. Soc.,* 30, abril/junio 1990, p. 10–19, bibl., photos)

Examines activities of Federación Local de Trabajadores del Puerto de Veracruz (FLTV) in 1923. This anarcho-syndicalist collection of workers' organizations was plagued by internal disagreements, financial difficulties, organizational problems, and competition from other workers' movements such as the local communist party.

1533 Ludlow, Leonor. Las demandas de la derecha clerical, 1917–1940. (*in* Coloquio de Antropología e Historia Regionales, 8th, Zamora, Mexico, 1986. El nacionalismo en México. Zamora, Mexico: El Colegio de Michoacán, 1992, p. 313–327)

Focuses on role of Catholic Church in intellectual construction of Mexican nationalism.

1534 MacLachlan, Colin M. Anarchism and the Mexican Revolution: the political trials of Ricardo Flores Magón in the United States. Foreword by John Mason Hart. Berkeley: Univ. of California Press, 1991. 185 p.: bibl., index.

Excellent study examines legal problems experienced by Ricardo Flores Magón and his associates in trying to operate from exile in the US. See also item **1445**.

1535 Madero, Gustavo A. Gustavo A. Madero: epistolario. Selección y prólogo de Ignacio Solares. México: Editorial Diana, 1991. 239 p.: ports.

Compiles letters and telegrams written or received by Gustavo Madero between 1898–1913, most of which are communications with his wife. Writings are particularly good in relating stresses of the *maderista* period.

1536 Manzano Añorve, María de los Angeles. Cuajinicuilapa, Guerrero: historia oral, 1900–1940. México: Ediciones Artesa, 1991. 119 p.: bibl., ill.

Oral history of a municipality in Costa Chica section of Guerrero state focuses primarily on agriculture and agrarian reform.

1537 Martínez Assad, Carlos R. Los rebeldes vencidos: Cedillo contra el Estado cardenista. México: Fondo de Cultura Económica, 1990. 252 p., 16 p. of plates: bibl., ill. (Sección de obras de historia)

Latest addition to literature on cacique of San Luis Potosí examines late stages of Cedillo's career and the forces that supported and opposed his continuation in power. Cedillo ultimately became an anachronism in a political system that was becoming increasingly centralized and presidential. See also items **1506 1528**, *HLAS 50:1213*, *HLAS 52: 1301*, and *HLAS 52:1302*.

1538 Martínez C., Leonardo. Hacia una reconsideración de la historia del periodismo en México. (*Rev. Mex. Cienc. Polít. Soc.*, 36:139, enero/marzo 1990, p. 31–44)

Presents interesting but inconclusive speculations about status of history of Mexican journalism, using as examples the newspapers *El Imparcial* and *El Universal*.

1539 Matute, Alvaro. Notas sobre la historiografía positivista mexicana. (*Secuencia/México*, 21, sept/dic. 1991, p. 49–64, bibl., ill.)

Author defines the term "positivism" in relation to historical studies, and analyzes the works of several Mexican historians (ranging from Vicente Riva Palacio to Emilio Rabasa) for their positivist content.

1540 Medin, Tzvi. El sexenio alemanista: ideología y praxis política de Miguel Alemán. México: Ediciones Era, 1990. 207 p.: bibl. (Col. Problemas de México)

After providing a background chapter on "complex legacy" of Cárdenas years and "rectifications" of the Avila Camacho Administration, author furnishes excellent overview of Alemán presidency. Topics covered include: restructuring of political power, Alemán's economic policy, culture and education, and foreign affairs. Author concludes that Alemán had a well-defined ideology and plan when he assumed office and was successful in implementing them.

1541 Mellinger, Phil. "The men have become organizers:" labor conflict and unionization in the Mexican mining communities of Arizona, 1900–1915. (*West. Hist. Q.*, 23:3, Aug. 1992, p. 323–347, ill.)

Focuses on disagreement within labor movement over whether to include or exclude Mexican and Mexican-American miners in organizing efforts by Western Federation of Miners. By 1915 inclusionists had gained control, implementing a policy that the union's national headquarters had been supporting for almost a decade. Includes connection with activities in northern Mexico.

1542 Melzer, Richard. The Lone Eagle in Mexico: Charles A. Lindbergh's less famous record-setting flight of 1927. (*J. West*, 30:1, Jan. 1991, p. 30–36, ill.)

Well-illustrated article chronicles Lindbergh's flight from Washington to Mexico City in Dec. 1927 and subsequent impact on Mexico/US relations.

1543 Méndez, Jesús. Foreign influences and domestic needs in intellectual institution building: the gestation of the Casa de España/Colegio de México. (*SECOLAS Ann.*, 21, March 1990, p. 5–23)

Author places establishment of the Casa/Colegio in broader context of long-term desire for university reform and intellectual institution building, rather than in Cárdenas' immediate educational policies and desire to aid Spanish exiles. Interest in a "Spanish model" of university reform dates to late Porfiriato.

1544 Méndez G., Concepción and **Rodolfo Huerta G.** La vida social de los trabajadores en la fábrica de papel San Rafael, 1890–

1930. (*in* Comunidad, cultura y vida social: ensayos sobre la formación de la clase obrera. México: Instituto Nacional de Antropología e Historia, 1991, p. 75–92)

Using two stages of development—1890-1914 and 1918–30—authors discuss evolution of work force and working conditions at a paper factory in a rural area of Mexico state. Revolutionary disturbances forced suspension of factory operations between 1914–18. See also item **1463**.

1545 Mendoza Barragán, Ezequiel. Testimonio cristero: memorias del autor. Presentación de Jean A. Meyer. Prólogo de Juan Landerreche Obregón. México: Editorial Jus, 1990. 427 p.: bibl., ill.

Compelling and vivid memoir is written by dedicated member of Cristero movement. Narrative begins in 1922 and continues through early 1940s. Includes chronology and useful commentaries by Jean Meyer.

1546 Metz, Allan. Mexican Church-State relations under President Carlos Salinas de Gortari. (*J. Church State*, 34:1, Winter 1992, p. 111–130)

Early (perhaps premature) study of relationship between Salinas Administration and the Catholic Church covers period to July 1991. Author foresees growing Church-State cooperation but little prospect for change in constitutional restrictions on the Church.

1547 Un México a través de los Prieto: cien años de opinión y participación política. Recopilación de Luis Prieto Reyes, Guillermo Ramos y Salvador Rueda Smithers. Jiquilpan de Juárez, Mexico: Centro de Estudios de la Revolución Mexicana Lázaro Cárdenas, 1987. 699 p., 1 leaf of plates: ill.

"Collective autobiographies" of seven members of the Prieto family (among which the most famous was Jorge Prieto Laurens) cuts across four generations and almost a century. The Prieto family faithfully reflects transformation of Mexican political life from the Porfiriato to student upheavals of the 1960s and 1970s.

1548 México, un pueblo en la historia. v. 5, Nueva burguesía: 1938–1957 [de] Teresa Aguirre *et al.*. v. 6, El ocaso de los mitos: 1958–1968 [de] Ilán Semo. v. 7, Fin de siglo [de] Américo Saldívar. v. 8, El otro México: 1600–1985 [de] David R. Maciel y Juan

Gómez-Quiñones. Coordinación de Enrique Semo. Puebla, Mexico: Univ. Autónoma de Puebla; México: Editorial Nueva Imagen, 1990? 4 v.: bibl., ill.

Multivolume, multiauthored work uses historical materialism as its point of departure. Vol. 5 covers 1938–57, while Vol. 6 treats 1958–68. Vol. 7 deals primarily with 1969–78 period, although there is some treatment of 1980s. Vol. 8 discusses Mexican movement to, and role in, area north of the Río Bravo from 1600 to 1985, although most of attention is on 20th century.

1549 Meyer, Lorenzo. The political modernization of Mexico, 1867–1940. (*in* Modernization and Revolution in Mexico: a comparative approach. Edited by Omar Martínez Legorreta. Tokyo: United Nations Univ., 1989, p. 27–39)

Balanced overview for the general reader examines changes in functions and structures of power. Main theme is concentration of political power, particularly in the presidency, and resulting impact on Mexico's economic development.

1550 Meyer, Lorenzo. Su Majestad Británica contra la Revolución Méxicana, 1900–1950: el fin de un imperio informal. México: Colegio de México, Centro de Estudios Internacionales, 1991. 579 p., 16 leaves of plates: bibl., ill., index.

Outstanding overview of Mexican-British relations in first half of 20th century focuses on diplomatic and economic relations. Based heavily on British diplomatic archives.

1551 Meyers, William K. Pancho Villa and the multinationals: United States mining interests in *villista* Mexico, 1913–1915. (*J. Lat. Am. Stud.*, 23:2, 1991, p. 339–363)

Excellent discussion examines Villa's interaction with mining interests during period in which his movement dominated much of northern Mexico.

1552 Muriá, José María. Ensayos de historiografía jalisciense. Guadalajara, Mexico: Univ. de Guadalajara/Xalli, 1990. 93 p. (Reloj de sol)

Collection of essays previously published in diverse sources deals with historiography of Jalisco. Topics include ethnohistory, pamphleteering, and historians of Guadalajara.

1553 Necoechea G., Gerardo. Familia, comunidad y clase: los inmigrantes mexicanos en Chicago, 1916–1930. (*in* Comunidad, cultura y vida social: ensayos sobre la formación de la clase obrera. México: Instituto Nacional de Antropología e Historia, 1991, p. 201–267)

Author traces formation of Mexican community in Chicago during 1920s. Development of a sense of community was not just a reaction to oppressive conditions; it was also the product of interaction of kinship, nationality, and class consciousness arising out of a common work experience.

1554 Negrete, Marta Elena. Comentarios a la ponencia: "La Iglesia Católica en México desde 1929 . . . " (*Cristianismo Soc.*, 27: 101, 1989, p. 43–46)

Reply to Blancarte's entry (see item **1458**) mostly reiterates his main points. See also items **1571** and **1454**.

1555 Ochoa Serrano, Alvaro. La violencia en Michoacán: ahí viene Chávez García. Morelia, Mexico: Gobierno del Estado de Michoacán; Instituto Michoacano de Cultura. 1990. 327 p.

Collection of documents and articles deals with revolutionary bandit from Michoacán. Includes short introductory essay by the compiler.

1556 O'Rourke, Gerald. La persecución religiosa en Chihuahua, 1913–1938. Chihuahua, Mexico: Editorial Camino, 1991. 250 p.: bibl., ill. (Col. Centenario; 12)

Examines Church-State conflict that developed in Chihuahua due to efforts to implement anticlerical provisions of Constitution of 1917, especially licensing of priests. Gives particular attention to activities of Rodrigo Quevedo, last *callista* governor of the state.

1557 Ortega Arenas, Juan. México al final del siglo XX. México: Editorial Claridad, 1987. 599 p.: bibl., ill. (México, historia y realidad; 2)

After a lengthy historical overview, author discusses Mexican situation in late 20th century from a Marxist perspective. It is not a pretty sight with the masses being exploited by monopolies, transnational imperialists, and the national bourgeoisie.

1558 Ortoll, Servando. La campaña militar en Colima durante la Revolución Cristera, 1926–1929. (*in* Congreso de Historia Regional Comparada, 2nd, Ciudad Juárez, Mexico, 1990. Actas. Edición de Ricardo León García. Ciudad Juárez, Mexico: Univ. Autónoma de Ciudad Juárez, 1991, p. 450–460)

Brief discussion examines factors which made Cristero Rebellion difficult to extinguish in Colima. Author concludes that it was to financial and personal advantage of the leaders of government to keep rebellion alive, but also points out the almost total lack of coordination among the military forces in attacks on the rebels.

1559 Ortoll, Servando. Reportes consulares e historiografía del fenómeno cristero. (*Secuencia/México*, 21, sept./dic. 1991, p. 83–94, bibl., ill.)

Author examines how historiography of Cristero Rebellion was influenced by reports of three diplomatic officials: Ernest Lagarde, French chargé in Mexico City; George Rublee, personal assistant to US Ambassador Dwight Morrow; and Miguel Cruchaga Tocornal, Chilean Ambassador to Mexico. Author discusses interpretations proposed by Jean Meyer and David Bailey, and offers his own revisionist views.

1560 Osorio, Rubén. Pancho Villa, ese desconocido: entrevistas en Chihuahua a favor y en contra. Prólogo de Friedrich Katz. Chihuahua, Mexico: Gobierno del Estado de Chihuahua, 1991. 250 p., 8 p. of plates: bibl., ill.

Valuable collection comprises 24 interviews completed between 1970–90, with sympathizers as well as enemies of Pancho Villa. Each includes short introduction describing interview setting. Provides information on Villa's personality and ideology, and on nature of his movement.

1561 Otero, Gerardo. The new agrarian movement: self-managed, democratic production. (*Lat. Am. Perspect.*, 16:4, Fall 1989, p. 28–59, bibl., table)

Examines background and formation of the Coalición de Ejidos Colectivos de los Valles del Yaqui e El Mayo in Sonora. Author views workers involved as neither peasants nor agricultural proletarians but rather as "agricultural semiproletarians" locked in a struggle with state organizations and a "ferocious agrarian bourgeoisie."

1562 Palomares Peña, Noé G. El poder del Estado e de los hacendados chihuahuenses en la distribución de la tierra, 1923–1939: el caso de la empresa norteamericana Palomas. (*Nóesis/Juárez,* 5:2, julio/dic. 1990, p. 63–88)

Case study illustrates ability of US owners to significantly delay expropriation of large latifundios in the wake of the Revolution.

1563 Palomares Peña, Noé G. Propietarios norteamericanos y reforma agraria en Chihuahua, 1917–1942. Ciudad Juárez, Mexico: Univ. Autónoma de Ciudad Juárez, 1991. 165 p.: bibl., maps. (Estudios regionales; 4)

Author examines impact of state and federal agrarian reform activities on three major North American properties founded during the Porfiriato: the Palomas Land and Cattle Company, the Cargill Lumber Company, and the Hearst-owned hacienda San José de Babícora. Diplomatic pressure, economic needs, and legal action permitted the three landholdings to retain most of their property during period studied.

1564 Pansters, Wil. Patronage en politieke modernisering in Mexico, 1930–1940 [Patronage and political modernization in Mexico, 1930–1940]. (*Anthropol. Verkenn.,* 11:2, 1992, p. 64–79, bibl.)

Analyzes political structure of two regional power groups and function of clientelism to show that political modernization processes did not undermine clientelism and personalism. Concludes that different principles of organization (clientelism, institutionalization, and bureaucratization) provide useful insights into workings of Mexican political system. [R. Hoefte]

1565 Pastor, Robert. Post-Revolutionary Mexico: the Salinas opening. (*J. Interam. Stud. World Aff.,* 32:3, Fall 1990, p. 1–22)

Examines economic and political reforms undertaken by Salinas. Author sees two pivotal issues: 1) will economic reforms work?; and 2) will political reforms wait?

1566 Piccato, Pablo. Congreso y Revolución: ensayo. México: Instituto Nacional de Estudios Históricos de la Revolución Mexi-

cana, Secretaría de Gobernación, 1991. 171 p.: bibl.

Studies 1912–13 congressional debates over establishing a parliamentary form of government. Supporters of parliamentary government were not closely connected to revolutionary factions and viewed proposed system as a way of preventing civil war.

1567 Provinces of the Revolution: essays on regional Mexican history, 1910–1929. Edited by Thomas Benjamin and Mark Wasserman. Albuquerque: Univ. of New Mexico Press, 1990. 390 p.: bibl., index, maps.

Includes 12 essays that focus on the Revolution. Six involve regional case studies, and six are devoted to general analysis. Concluding historiographical essay by Benjamin is particularly useful.

1568 Py, Pierre. Francia y la Revolución Mexicana, 1910–1920, o, La desaparición de una potencia mediana. Traducción de Ismael Pizarro Suárez y Mercedes Pizarro Suárez. México: Centro de Estudios Mexicanos y Centroamericanos; Fondo de Cultura Económica, 1991. 307 p.: bibl., ill.

Using a Mexican time frame, author traces French policy with and in Mexico. This policy reflected rivalry with Germany as well as need to take into account the positions of the US and England. Additional problems arose as policy pursued by French colony in Mexico diverged from official French policy. Outbreak of war in 1914 forced France to completely subordinate its Mexican diplomacy to that of the US. Based on extensive research in French and Mexican archives.

1569 Quiroz Flores, Sonia. El Archivo Plutarco Elías Calles como fuente para la historia de la banca en México. (*Bol. Fuentes Hist. Econ. Mex.,* 5, sept./dic. 1991, p. 47–52, photo)

After relating history and general organization of Calles archive, author discusses its value for financial and economic history of Mexico, especially for period 1920–37. Strong points include financial correspondence, banking legislation, and regional and sectoral economic reports.

1570 Ramírez, Miguel D. Mexico's economic crisis: its origins and consequences. New York: Praeger, 1989. 149 p.: bibl.

Good blend of political and economic

history explains Mexico's 1980s economic/financial crisis. Author examines government's development policy since 1940, placing much of the blame for crisis of 1980s on irresponsible fiscal policies of 1970s.

1571 Ramírez Ceballos, Manuel. La historiografía mexicanista y la Iglesia Católica, 1968–1988. (*Cristianismo Soc.*, 27: 101, 1989, p. 15–26)

Author sees three elements influencing recent historiography of the Mexican Church: 1) internal reform arising from Vatican II; 2) the professionalization of history; and 3) recent developments in Mexican history. See also items **1458, 1554,** and **1454.**

1572 Ramírez Rancaño, Mario. El sistema de haciendas en Tlaxcala. México: Consejo Nacional para la Cultura y las Artes, 1990. 292 p.: bibl. (Regiones)

Thorough study examines system of land ownership in Tlaxcala and its dismantling by the revolution. Author follows process through 1980s, underlining politics of land tenure throughout time. [A. Lavrin]

1573 Ramos, Marta. La élite militar revolucionaria en México: sus orígenes socioculturales y ligas personales. (*Estud. Hist. Mod. Contemp. Méx.*, 11, 1988, p. 219–231)

Author analyzes "sociocultural characteristics" of highest-ranking military leaders at end of 1914, and concludes that most did not fit folkloric view of illiterate commoners risen to leadership. Most had above-average educations, owned property, and were locally influential, thereby justifying their classification as members of an "elite."

1574 Ravelo Lecuona, Renato. La revolución zapatista de Guerrero. v. 1, De la insurrección a la toma de Chilpancingo, 1910–1914. Chilpancingo, Mexico: Univ. Autónoma de Guerrero, 1990. 1 v.: bibl., ill.

Detailed study analyzes origins and development of peasant movement in Guerrero. Projected two-volume work: vol. 1 covers up to taking of Chilpancingo by Zapatista forces in March 1914.

1575 Reuter, Peter and David Ronfeldt. Quest for integrity: the Mexican-U.S. drug issue in the 1980s. (*J. Interam. Stud. World Aff.*, 34:3, Fall 1992, p. 89–155)

Provides excellent examination of role of drug enforcement in recent US/Mexican relations. Authors believe that US government is upset by doubts primarily about integrity of Mexico's drug control effort, rather than its effectiveness. US government has not sufficently taken into account lengthy history of smuggling along the border and Mexico's preoccupation with national sovereignty.

1576 La Revolución en las regiones: memorias. Guadalajara, Mexico: Instituto de Estudios Sociales, Univ. de Guadalajara, 1986. 2 v.: bibl., ill.

Collection of essays presented at Univ. of Guadalajara in 1984 deals with regional aspects of the Revolution. "El Norte," "El Sur," and first part of "El Centro" are included in vol. 1; vol. 2 continues with "El Centro" and also covers "El Golfo" and "El Occidente."

1577 La Revolución Mexicana a través de sus documentos. México: Univ. Nacional Autónoma de México, 1987. 4 v.: bibl., ill., indexes.

Collection of documents includes brief introductions placing them in historical context. The term *document* is interpreted very broadly to include correspondence, historical critiques, excerpts from major works, and revolutionary plans. Vol. 1 deals primarily with immediate Porfirian background; Vol. 2 is devoted to election of 1910; Vol. 3 covers period from outbreak of the Revolution to Madero's becoming president in November of 1911; Vol. 4 covers presidency of Madero.

1578 The revolutionary process in Mexico: essays on political and social change, 1880–1940. Edited by Jaime E. Rodríguez O. Los Angeles: UCLA Latin American Center Publications; Irvine, Calif.: Univ. of California-Irvine, Mexico/Chicano Program, 1990. 331 p.: bibl., ill., index. (UCLA Latin American studies; 72)

Collection of essays is from a series of symposia centered on concept of the Revolution as evolutionary process rather than radical departure. Mildly revisionist, most of essays are limited by region, topic, or time period.

1579 Richardson, William Harrison. *Meksikanistika:* five decades of Soviet historical writings on Mexico. (*Mex. Stud.*, 8:1, Winter 1992, p. 45–86)

Reviews Soviet historical scholarship on Mexico since 1940 using Soviet periodization. Marxist-Leninist ideology not only provided framework for historical interpretation, but also determined to a great extent the topics for research (revolutionary movements being of prime interest). Publication problems and limited travel funds have hampered Mexican studies, and post-1985 reforms in Soviet Union have not yet worked their way into historical scholarship.

1580 Rivera, Antonio G. La revolución en Sonora. Prólogo de Manuel González Ramírez. 2. ed. Hermosillo, Mexico: Gobierno del Estado de Sonora, 1981. 471 p., 32 p. of plates: bibl., ill. (Publicaciones del Gobierno del Estado de Sonora 1979–1985)

Unrevised second ed. (first ed., México: 1969) of a classic study covers Mexican Revolution until 1920.

1581 Rocha Islas, Martha; Marcela Tostado Gutiérrez; and Enriqueta Tuñón Pablos. Una ciudad destruida: apuntes para la reconstrucción de su historia. México: Dirección de Estudios Históricos, Instituto Nacional de Antropología e Historia, 1987. 2 v.: ill. (Cuaderno de trabajo; 52)

Detailed chronology of impact of Mexico City earthquake of Sept. 1985 is organized around 26 themes, including water, gas, debt negotiations, business activity, sports and leisure, and education.

1582 Rodríguez García, Rubén. La Cámara Agrícola Nacional Jalisciense: una sociedad de terratenientes en la Revolución Mexicana. México: Instituto Nacional de Estudios Históricos de la Revolución Mexicana, 1990. 126 p.: bibl. (Regiones)

Examines state society of agricultural landowners from establishment in 1899 through early 1920s. The group played a key role in helping landowners defend their properties against the military and legal attacks of the revolutionaries. Although maintaining that it was non-political, the group utilized its governmental connections at all levels to defend its interests.

1583 Rodríguez Kuri, Ariel. El discurso del miedo: *El Imparcial* y Francisco I. Madero. (*Hist. Mex.*, 40:4, abril/junio 1991, p. 697–740, bibl.)

Provides detailed account of role played by *científico* newspaper *El Imparcial* as voice of the opposition to Madero regime from May 1911 to Jan. 1913. Author sees paper as first example of "metropolitan press"

in Mexico and as a rallying point for Porfirian elite in absence of an organized political party to express their views.

1584 Rodríguez Lapuente, Manuel. Breve historia gráfica de la Revolución Mexicana. 2. ed. México: GG, 1987. 197 p.: ill.

Emphasis of work is on the "graphic:" good illustrations, adequate accompanying text, and brief captions. Time frame covered is from Porfirian background through Calles Administration.

1585 Romero-Castilla, Alfredo. The regional impact of the Meiji Restoration and the Mexican Revolution. (*in* Modernization and Revolution in Mexico: a comparative approach. Edited by Omar Martínez Tegorreta. Tokyo: United Nations Univ., 1989, p. 111–127)

Strained comparison looks at impact of the two movements on their respective regions, particularly as "models." Author concludes that Meiji restoration did not serve as a successful model, while Mexican Revolution was in no position to present itself as a model.

1586 Ruibal Corella, Juan Antonio. Calles, hombre de su tiempo. Hermosillo, Mexico: Impresora La Voz de Sonora, 1989. 208 p.: bibl., ill.

Favorable biography of the "Jefe Máximo" published in conjunction with 60th anniversary of founding of the official party gives little attention to post-1928 period.

Sa, Na and **Chang Yu-ling.** Lun Mo-hsi-ke hua ch'iao she hui ti pien chien [On the changes in the overseas Chinese community in Mexico]. See item **1420.**

1587 Sánchez García, Alfonso. Ocaso y final del círculo rojinegro. Toluca, Mexico: Univ. Autónoma del Estado de México, 1991. 76 p.: bibl., ill. (Col. Historia; 10)

Author chronicles political fortunes of the Partido Socialista del Trabajo which dominated politics in the state of Mexico in the 1920s and 1930s.

1588 Sánchez Silva, Carlos. Crisis política y contrarrevolución en Oaxaca, 1912–1915. México: Instituto Nacional de Estudios Históricos de la Revolución Mexicana, 1991. 196 p.: bibl. (Regiones)

Focuses on rise and fall of Miguel Bolaños Cacho (governor of Oaxaca, 1912–14), and reorganization of power after his overthrow. Author refutes view that he was a mere reflection of Huerta dictatorship, maintaining that the governor was pursuing a counterrevolutionary agenda from the start of his administration. Overthrow of Bolaños Cacho meant return to power of old-line supporters of Porfirio and Félix Díaz.

1589 Sandos, James A. Rebellion in the borderlands: anarchism and the Plan of San Diego, 1904–1923. Norman: Univ. of Oklahoma Press, 1992. 237 p.: bibl., ill., index, maps.

Veteran Borderlands historian takes extended look at the Plan of San Diego, in the process revising even some of his own earlier views. Sandos believes that the Plan can be best understood in context of "frontier radicalism" rather than as expression of Mexican revolutionary factionalism or international intrigue.

1590 Sariego Rodríguez, Juan Luis. Enclaves y minerales en el norte de México: historia social de los mineros de Cananea y Nueva Rosita, 1900–1970. México: Centro de Investigaciones y Estudios Superiores en Antropología Social, 1988. 430 p.: bibl., ill., maps. (Ediciones de la Casa Chata; 26)

Traces evolution of two different mining enclaves (copper in Sonora, coal in Coahuila) through three different stages: 1) formation of the enclaves (1890–1930); 2) rise of labor movement and involvement of the State in mining matters (1930–50); and 3) "Mexicanization" of mining and dissolution of enclaves (1950–70). In three-sided struggle involving labor, management, and government, workers receive most of the attention.

1591 Sariego Rodríguez, Juan Luis. Interpretaciones sobre la historia contemporánea de la minería en Chihuahua. (*in* Congreso de Historia Regional Comparada, *2nd, Ciudad Juárez, Mexico, 1990.* Actas. Edición de Ricardo León García. Ciudad Juárez, Mexico: Univ. Autónoma de Ciudad Juárez, 1991, p. 510–523, tables)

Examines relationship between social and economic development in the state, with particular emphasis on workers.

1592 Schulze, Karl-Wilhelm. Konzept und realität der agrarpolitik Pancho Villas auf dem Hintergrund der Sozial- und Landverhältnisse in Chihuahua während des Porfi-

riats und der Revolution. (*Jahrb. Gesch.*, 30, 1993, p. 279–325)

Uses Chihuahua's historical agrarian and property records as well as extensive material drawn from Mexico's Oral History Program to write a revisionist paper emphasizing Pancho Villa's role as a rational agrarian revolutionary. [C.K. Converse]

1593 Serrano Alvarez, Pablo. La política pública regional en el gobierno de Lázaro Cárdenas, 1934–1940. Colima, Mexico: Univ. de Colima, 1991. 46 p.: bibl., ill., maps. (Cuadernos de historia regional)

Examines regional planning aspects of Cárdenas' Six-Year Plan. Aimed at promoting national political and economic integration, Cárdenas' regional planning had uneven impact on both an intra-regional and inter-regional basis, an inequality that was accentuated in subsequent presidential administrations.

1594 Shao, Lixin. Reflections on democratic revolutions in Mexico and China. (*in* Modernization and Revolution in Mexico: a comparative approach. Edited by Omar Martínez Legorreta. Tokyo: United Nations Univ., 1989, p. 151–159)

Author compares Chinese Revolution of 1911 with both Mexican independence movement and Revolution of 1910. Major differences between revolutions lay in agrarian reform and in revolutionary attitude toward foreign interests. See also *HLAS 52:1258.*

1595 Slawson, Douglas J. The National Catholic Welfare Conference and the Church-State conflict in Mexico, 1925–1929. (*Americas/Francisc.*, 49:1, July 1990, p. 55–93)

Analyzes role played by NCWC, especially its general-secretary, the Rev. John Burke, in settlement of Church-State controversy under Calles. Author maintains that Burke made as important a contribution as did US Ambassador Dwight Morrow in resolution of the conflict.

1596 La Soberana Convención Revolucionaria en Aguascalientes, 1914–1989. Aguascalientes, Mexico: Instituto Cultural de Aguascalientes, 1990. 205 p.: bibl., ill.

Proceedings from a series of conferences commemorating 75th anniversary of the Soberana Convención Revolucionaria at Aguascalientes includes contemporary political speeches, conference papers, documents, a chronicle of the Convention, and extensive illustrations (uncaptioned).

1597 Sociedad Sonorense de Historia. Simposio. 2nd, Hermosillo, Mexico, 1989 [and] 3rd, Hermosillo, Mexico, 1990. Memoria. Hermosillo, Mexico: Estado Sonora, Instituto Sonorense de Cultura; Sociedad Sonorense de Historia, 1991. 243 p.: bibl. (Memoria; 2)

Although many of the papers in this collection are of largely regional interest and based on well-known secondary sources, collection includes several notable works: an essay by Danna Levi Rojo and Adriana Konzevik Crabib examines social and educational backgrounds of Coahuila's revolutionary elite; María de las Mercedes Lelo de Larrea's paper studies failure of Calles' railroad policy; and Juan José Gracida's synthesizes Sonora's role in the Revolution.

1598 Soto, Shirlene Ann. Emergence of the modern Mexican woman: her participation in Revolution and struggle for equality, 1910–1940. Denver, Colo.: Arden Press, 1990. 199 p., 16 p. of plates: bibl., index, map, ports. (Women and modern revolution series)

Examines role of women in both the revolutionary movement and in women's rights movement. Author places development of women's organizations against broader background of the Revolution.

1599 Tanaka, Michiko. The peasants and the nation-state in Japan, Mexico, and Russia, 1860–1940. (in Modernization and Revolution in Mexico: a comparative approach. Edited by Omar Martínez Legorreta. Tokyo: United Nations Univ., 1989, p. 78–110)

Compares process of nation-state formation in three countries with a long agrarian tradition and which followed the "Western model" in their development. Focus is on policies affecting peasants, with most attention devoted to 19th century.

1600 Taylor, Lawrence Douglas. Revolución mexicana: guía de archivos y bibliotecas: México-Estados Unidos. México: Instituto Nacional de Estudios Históricos de la Revolución Mexicana, 1987. 272 p.: bibl., index.

Useful guide lists archives, libraries, and personal collections. Most of work is devoted to sources in Mexico City, but sections on regional and local archives in Mexico and on institutions in US are also included.

1601 Tenorio, Mauricio. Viejos gringos: radicales norteamericanos en los años treinta y su visión de México. (*Secuencia/México*, 21, sept./dic. 1991, p. 95–117, bibl., ill.)

Examines "rediscovery" of Mexico in 1930s by radical North American writers, especially Joseph Freeman and Frank Tannenbaum. Author sees "rediscovery" as resulting primarily from changes in US rather than from new developments in Mexico. Consequently, discussion centers on political-intellectual environment in US rather than on Mexican factors that were incorporated into a new "vision of Mexico."

1602 Terrones Benítes, Adolfo. Toma de Durango de 18 de junio de 1913. Durango, Mexico: Editorial del Supremo Tribunal de Justicia, 1988. 108 p.: ill., maps. (Cuaderno; 11)

Compilation of magazine articles written in 1956 deals with military activities leading up to and the actual taking of Durango by forces under the command of *villista* general Tomás Urbina. Author was a participant in the fighting and later became a revolutionary general.

Topik, Steven. Los lazos que ataron: Brasil y Méjico en la economía mundial, 1880–1910. See item **3442.**

1603 Topik, Steven. La Revolución, el Estado y el desarrollo económico en México. (*Hist. Mex.*, 40: 1, julio/sept. 1990, p. 79–144, bibl.)

Revisionist view of traditional interpretation that the Revolution was necessary to prepare the way for "nationalistic, interventionist, developmentalist" State that would emerge in 1930s and 1940s. Topik persuasively argues that roots of developmental interventionism lay in "third phase" of the Porfiriato (1897–1910), and supports his thesis by comparing Mexican experience with that of Brazil which did not experience a similar revolution.

1604 Trueba Lara, José Luis. La xenofobia en la legislación sonorense: el caso de los chinos. (*in* Simposio de Historia y Antropología de Sonora, *13th, Hermosillo, Mexico, 1989.* Memoria. Coordinación de Juan Manuel Romero Gil. Hermosillo, Mexico: Instituto de Investigaciones Históricas de la Univ. de Sonora, 1989, v. 1, p. 341–373, bibl.)

Examines anti-Chinese measures enacted by Sonora government in 1920s and early 1930s. Measures fell into several categories: outright prohibition of Chinese immigration; restrictions on marriages between Chinese and Mexicans; creation of Chinese barrios; laws limiting commercial activity; and labor regulations.

1605 Ulloa, Berta. Conflict threatening Mexico's sovereignty: the continuing crisis, 1867–1940. (in Modernization and Revolution in Mexico: a comparative approach. Edited by Omar Martínez Legorreta. Tokyo: United Nations Univ., 1989, p. 40–65)

Survey of US/Mexican relations intended for general reader gives equal attention to pre-Revolutionary and post-Revolutionary periods.

1606 Ulloa, Berta. La Revolución más allá del Bravo: guía de documentos relativos a México en archivos de Estados Unidos, 1900–1948. México: El Colegio de México, 1991. 310 p.: ill., index.

Useful guide is divided into three general categories: libraries; historical societies; and university collections. Work is necessarily limited in scope, covering only five libraries, one historical society, and six university collections. Includes description as well as list of materials. Materials cover period 1900–48.

1607 Unions, workers, and the State in Mexico. Edited by Kevin J. Middlebrook. San Diego: Center for U.S.-Mexican Studies, Univ. of California, San Diego, 1991. 249 p.: bibl. (U.S.-Mexico contemporary perspectives series; 2)

Collection of essays focuses on relationship between workers (union and nonunion) and the State in crisis years of 1980s. General impression is that economic decline of last decade has broken down harmony between working class and the government, with growing dissatisfaction apparent even in ranks of government's traditional ally, the Confederación de Trabajadores de México.

1608 United States-Mexico border statistics since 1900. Edited by David E. Lorey. Los Angeles: UCLA Latin American Center

Publications, 1990. 475 p.: bibl., ill., index. (Statistical abstract of Latin America: Supplement series; 11)

Extensive collection contains quantitative data relating to the "border," which includes those Mexican and US states along the international boundary. Most of the work is comprised of statistical tables, and little of the data extends beyond 1980. For 1990 update see item **1609.**

1609 United States-Mexico border statistics since 1900: 1990 update. Edited by David E. Lorey. Los Angeles: UCLA Latin American Center Publications, 1993. 137 p.: bibl., ill., index. (Statistical abstract of Latin America: Supplement series; 13)

Update of work annotated in item **1608.**

1610 Uribe Salas, José Alfredo and **Alvaro Ochoa Serrano.** Emigrantes del oeste. México: Consejo Nacional para la Cultura y las Artes, 1990. 164 p.: bibl. (Regiones)

Collection of documents on migration of Michoacanos to US between 1877–1934 includes two excellent introductory essays by the editors.

Valdés Aguilar, Rafael. Epidemias en Sinaloa: una aproximación histórica. See item **1430.**

1611 Vargas, Zaragosa. Armies in the fields and factories: the Mexican working classes in the midwest in the 1920s. (*Mex. Stud.*, 7:1, Winter 1991, p. 47–71)

Describes Mexican migration into and within US midwest, focusing on four main "employment sectors:" sugar beets, railroads, steel mills, and auto work. Author sees immigrants as making a successful transition from traditional agricultural work to industrial employment.

1612 Vigencia del cardenismo. Coordinación de Fernando Carmona. México: Instituto de Investigaciones Económicas, UNAM; Editorial Nuestro Tiempo, 1990. 183 p.: bibl. (Col. Pensamiento político de México)

Five authors offer essays identifying "principal ingredients" of *cardenismo.* Tone of work is set by one essayist who describes Cárdenas as "more than a superman."

1613 Vinyes, Fernando. México: diez veces llanto. Presentación de Manuel F. Molés. Madrid: Espasa-Calpe, 1991. 305 p.: ill. (Col. La Tauromaquia; 36)

Anecdotal account of Mexican bull-fighting in 20th century is organized around careers of 10 prominent bullfighters. While author disclaims any interest in presenting a "glossary of tragedies," his subjects tend to meet violent (though not always predictable) ends. Well-illustrated with numerous character studies of other bullfighters.

1614 Visión histórica de la frontera norte de México. v. 3. Coordinación de David Piñera Ramírez. Mexicali, Mexico: Univ. Autónoma de Baja California, Centro de Investigaciones Históricas UNAM-UABC, 1987. 1 v.: ill., maps, ports., tables.

Multiauthored work takes both topical and chronological look at northern border. Pt. 1 uses chronological approach employing three time periods: 1910–34, 1934–45, and 1945-present. Pt. 2 discusses contemporary topics such as regionalism, economic activity, migration, and urban development.

1615 Zermeño Padilla, Guillermo. Toribio Esquivel Obregón: del hombre público al privado: "Memorias" a la sombra de la re-volución. (*Secuencia/México,* 21, sept./dic. 1991, p. 65–81, bibl., ill.)

Provides introduction to soon-to-be-published memoirs of Esquivel Obregón—educator, lawyer, journalist, and public figure. Esquivel Obregón's public life lasted less than five years, beginning in 1909 as a supporter of anti-reelectionism of Madero and culminating in a brief stint (five months) as Huerta's Ministro de Hacienda. He belonged to that group who came of age in late Porfiriato, who thought of "revolution" in strictly political terms.

1616 Zogbaum, Heidi. B. Traven: a vision of Mexico. Wilmington, Del.: SR Books, 1992. 255 p.: bibl., index, map. (Latin American silhouettes)

Examines popular literary figure of 1920s and 1930s whose fictional works reflected the "struggle of a European anarchist confronted with the Mexican Revolution." Traven's works exhibited his changing attitude toward the Revolution (uncritical support to disillusionment) as well as influence of developments in his native Germany.

CENTRAL AMERICA

STEPHEN WEBRE, *Professor of History, Louisiana Tech University*
DAVID MCCREERY, *Professor of History, Georgia State University*

THE ANTICIPATED BOOM in Central American historical studies has yet to arrive, but important works continue to appear. As in the past, the region's most developed historical production still originates from Costa Rica. In Nicaragua, the effects of the Sandinista Front's 1990 electoral defeat are not yet clear, but some of the more "politically engaged" foreign scholars have already turned to other interests; it is likely now that economic problems there will have a greater impact on academic work than political conditions. For Guatemala, with several significant exceptions, serious historical investigation and writing continue to be largely the work of outsiders, a condition due in part to scarcity of resources as well as to the dangers inherent in certain kinds of research.

Meanwhile, recent work on Honduras by a new generation of national historians is promising, and there is hope that in El Salvador a successful peace settlement will result in an atmosphere once again conducive to scholarly endeavors. Belize and Panama remain the stepchildren of Central American historiography, but several significant works have come out on the latter. An important event was the July 1992 Primer Congreso Centroamericano de Historia, held in Tegucigalpa and attended by approximately 200 scholars representing every Central American country except Belize, plus the US, Canada, Mexico, and several European countries. A successful second congress took place in Guatemala City in August 1994.

New studies of the colonial period are few in number but of generally high quality. Particularly important are works on early Costa Rican society by Eugenia Ibarra Rojas (item **1663**) and Claudia Quirós Vargas (item **1680**), while the appearance in Spanish of Germán Romero Vargas' thesis on 18th-century Nicaragua is a major event (item **1681**). Of significance, too, is Bernardo Belzúnegui Ormazábal's study of the agrarian question in the period immediately preceding independence (item **1647**). No specialist should ignore new essays by Christopher Lutz and George Lovell (item **1671**) and by Lovell and William Swezey (item **1669**) which substantially reconceptualize the human geography of Spanish Guatemala. Researchers will benefit also from new reference works, such as Lawrence Feldman's exhaustive guide to 16th-century Guatemalan encomiendas (item **1655**) and Gustavo Palma's first-rate edition of the so-called Gavarrete index to Guatemalan land records (item **1633**). Among foreign scholars active in colonial studies, North Americans remain prominent, but Spaniard Jesús María García Añoveros continues to be productive (items **1657, 1658,** and **1659**), and Mexican Mario Humberto Ruz has emerged as a distinctive voice, exploring unusual topics in unfamiliar archives (items **1682, 1683,** and **1684**).

There are several important new works on national period topics. For Guatemala, Piero Gleijeses' new book on the 1945–54 decade offers a revisionist view of that controversial period (item **1730**), while Héctor Lindo Fuentes has published an excellent survey of the 19th-century economic history of El Salvador (item **1746**). Nicaraguan historiography has been ill-served in the past, but now Jeffrey Gould's oral history of rural popular resistance (item **1734**) and the collaborative project directed by Orlando Núñez on the Sandinistas' struggle for survival in the 1980s (item **1707**) set new standards. Students of Costa Rica continue to generate many first-rate monographs, including Marc Edelman's look at *latifundismo* in Guanacaste province (item **1716**) and Claudio Antonio Vargas' examination of Church-State relations (item **1788**). Also impressive on Costa Rica are synthetic treatments, such as those by Iván Molina on the pre-coffee economy (item **1635**) and Orlando Salazar Mora on liberalism (item **1770**).

Studies of rural society figure prominently in the historical literature on Central America. The long tradition of such works on Guatemala continues with Norman Schwartz, who combines participant observation and archival research to explain changes in the northern Petén region (item **1777**), and with David McCreery (items **1749** and **1750**), Piero Gleijeses (item **1728**), and Susan Berger (item **1697**), all of whom survey the impact of the State on the countryside. Also, the productivity of Costa Rican scholars remains undiminished, as is evident in recent works on such topics as tobacco (item **1629**), sugar (item **1687**), small settler agriculture (item **1773**), and land privatization (items **1708** and **1769**).

Organized labor, both urban and rural, is receiving increased attention, notably in new studies of recent events in Guatemala by José Fernández (item **1719**), and in El Salvador by Rafael Guidos Véjar (item **1735**). Useful, too, are books on the early history of unionism in Panama by Hernando Franco Muñoz (item **1725**) and Ricaurte Soler (item **1781**). In Costa Rica, recent interest has focused on the black West Indian workers of Limón and their struggles against both the United Fruit Company and mainstream *tico* racism (items **1715, 1738,** and **1740**), but Marielos

Aguilar Hernández looks also at the failure of Costa Rican unions to develop as an autonomous force (item **1690**). Less rigorous are Ramón Amaya-Amador and Rigoberto Padilla Rush's study of the 1954 Honduran banana strike (item **1691**), and the volume compiled by Armando Amador on Nicaragua's unions before 1979 (item **1779**).

Among personal accounts to appear recently, two important ones from Nicaragua are the memoirs of Tomás Borge, a founder of the FSLN (item **1700**), and oral histories of individuals involved in the Sandinista Revolution as recorded by Denis Lynn Daly Heyck (item **1745**). From El Salvador's decade of revolutionary turmoil come Marta Harnecker's revealing interviews with FMLN leaders (item **1737**), Francisco Mena Sandoval's story of his conversion from army officer to rebel (item **1752**), and the remembrances of the crew of Radio Venceremos (item **1747**). Costa Rica offers more standard fare. Politicians putting their own spin on history include two ex-presidents, Rodrigo Carazo (item **1706**) and the late "Don Pepe" Figueres (items **1720** and **1721**).

Traditional concerns of politics and economics continue to dominate historical writing on Central America, but some new topics are attracting scholars, primarily in Costa Rica. Recent studies examine popular consumption patterns (item **1789**) and education (items **1693** and **1780**) in Costa Rica, literate culture in Guatemala (item **1649**) and Costa Rica (item **1755**), attitudes toward death in Costa Rica (item **1676**) and in Panama (item **1627**), and the construction of nationalism and a nationalist discourse in Costa Rica (item **1762**), Guatemala (item **1761**), and Honduras (items **1621, 1717,** and **1718**). And finally, two radically different approaches to the use of photographic images as historical documentation come from Guatemala (items **1692** and **1754**).

GENERAL

1617 Acuña Ortega, Víctor H. and **Iván Molina Jiménez.** Historia económica y social de Costa Rica, 1750–1950. San José: Editorial Porvenir, 1991. 214 p.: bibl., ill. (Col. Debate)

Compiles six solidly researched essays on socioeconomic history published at different times during the 1980s, together with a short bibliographical essay. Meant as a text for classroom use, work provides a useful introduction to historiographical debates in Costa Rica.

1618 Arellano, Jorge Eduardo. Nueva historia de Nicaragua. v. 1. Managua: Fondo Editorial CIRA, 1990. 125 p.: bibl., facsims., maps, photos.

First of six volumes planned to survey Nicaraguan history from its beginning to the Sandinista Revolution. Present volume covers from the earliest evidence of human habitation through the population catastrophe of the 16th century. Extensive notes, bibliography, and documentary appendices enrich a rather spare, didactic text.

1619 Arellano, Jorge Eduardo and **Ascención Oviedo Estrada.** Nuevos estudios sobre el "padre indio" Tomás Ruiz, 1777–18—. León, Nicaragua: Biblioteca Pbro. Dr. Tomás Ruiz; Banco Central de Nicaragua, 1989. 32 p.: bibl., ill.

Father Tomás Ruiz's claim on the Nicaraguan historical imagination is due to the fact he was the first Indian to receive a doctorate, was the founder of Univ. de León, and, as a participant in the so-called conspiracy of Belén (1813), was a precursor of Central American independence. Work includes a heavily documented biographical sketch, with textual analysis of two of Ruiz's sermons. Two separate essays, one by each of the authors.

1620 Argueta, Mario. Diccionario histórico-biográfico hondureño. Tegucigalpa: Editorial Universitaria, 1990. 205 p. (Col. Realidad Nacional; 29)

Approximately 165 detailed biographical sketches of prominent Honduran personalities, mostly from 19th and 20th centuries, and mostly political figures (including party

officials, military officers, and labor leaders).
Some important names missing (e.g. Poli-
carpo Bonilla), but valuable reference tool.

1621 Barahona, Marvin. Evolución histórica
de la identidad nacional. Tegucigalpa:
Editorial Guaymuras, 1991. 292 p.: bibl.,
maps. (Col. Códices)

Selective, interpretive history of colonial through early 20th-century Honduras
finds a "heterogeneous, multiracial, and pluricultural" society. The majority of Hondurans
are impoverished mestizos marginalized by
elites who have failed to build a solid State
because of recurring outside interventions.

1622 Bolland, O. Nigel. Colonialism and resistance in Belize: essays in historical
sociology. Benque Viejo del Carmen, Belize:
Cubola Productions; ISER; SPEAR, 1988. 218
p.: bibl., ill., index.

Many of these essays examining Beli-
zean social and economic development from
the beginning of European and African presence to national independence (1981) have
been previously published elsewhere. Most
cover familiar topics such as slavery, Creole
culture, and race relations, but two studies on
British-Maya relations shed light on a hitherto seldom addressed problem.

1623 Calatayud, Liduvina. Guía del Archivo
Diocesano de León. (*Bol. Nicar. Bibliogr. Doc.*, 66, marzo/abril 1991, p. 93–106)

Brief description of cathedral archives
of León, Nicaragua. Holdings include colonial
municipal and intendancy records, in addition to diocesan records from 1685 to the
20th century. Collection is important, because so much of Nicaragua's historical documentation has been lost or destroyed.

1624 Casaus Arzú, Marta. Guatemala: linaje
y racismo. San José: FLASCO, 1992.
343 p.: bibl., ill. (3 folded).

Uses prosopography and detailed genealogical reconstructions based on published
material and interviews to study formation of
dominant economic, social, and political
elites in Guatemala. Racism against indigenous minority is seen as key to elite ideology,
justifying continuing minority domination.

Central America. See *HLAS 53:5069.*

1625 Díez de Arriba, Luis. Historia de la
Iglesia de Guatemala. t. 1, Período colonial. t. 2, Crisis. Guatemala City?: s.n.,
1988–1989. 2 v.

Chronological and institutional history
of the Guatemalan Catholic Church from the
colonial period to the 1920s. Episodic, unan-
alytic, and with little information on sources,
it does reproduce many document fragments.
A serious history of this important institution remains to be written.

1626 Espino, Rodrigo and **Raúl Martínez.**
Panamá. México: Instituto de Investigaciones Dr. José María Luis Mora, 1988. 193
p. (América Latina. Centroamérica y el
Caribe)

Brief general account of Panama's history from early days of Spanish rule to independence from Colombia (1903), with emphasis on the 19th century.

Fallas, Luis Carlos. Orígenes del capitalismo
dependiente en Costa Rica: aspectos fundamentales del desarrollo socio-económico
costarricense desde el período precolombino
hasta el siglo XIX o primera fase de la República. See *HLAS 53:5077.*

1627 Figueroa Navarro, Alfredo. Testamento
y sociedad en el Istmo de Panamá: siglos XVIII y XIX. Panamá: Impr. Roysa, 1991.
207 p.: bibl., ill., maps.

Detailed quantitative study of more
than 2,000 wills reveals regional differences
and changes over time in the origins, wealth,
and literacy of the population, as well as in
death rites. Contains much material on
slaves and free blacks. Most of book consists
of tables and graphs.

1628 Fuchs, Jochen. Costa Rica: von der
Conquista bis zur "Revolution;" historische, ökonomische und soziale Determi-
nanten eines konsensualistisch-neutralis-
tischen Modells in Zentralamerika. Erstausg.,
1. Aufl. Berlin: Schelzky & Jeep, 1991. 357 p.:
bibl., maps.

Costa Rica's evolution into a Central
American "Switzerland" is a historical accident largely due to geographic, demographic,
and economic factors, all of which facilitated
the development of consensus politics. Unfortunately, author detects no structural components that could serve as a model for democratic development in other countries. While
author recognizes the nation's uniqueness he
uses an almost dialectical approach in order
to demolish myths surrounding Costa Rican
development. [C.K. Converse]

1629 González García, Yamileth. Continuidad y cambio en la historia agraria de Costa Rica. San José: Editorial Costa Rica, 1989. 307 p.: bibl., maps.

Extensively researched history of 16th to 19th century rural Costa Rica focuses on the problems of the subsistence economy and the operation of the tobacco monopoly in late colonial and post-independence years. Shows that sales of Church and community properties in the 19th century did not result in "rural equality" but instead allowed dominant elites to gain control of resources needed for coffee production.

1630 Hale, Charles R. Relaciones interétnicas y la estructura de clases en la costa atlántica de Nicaragua. (*Estud. Soc. Centroam.*, 48, sept./dic. 1988, p. 71–91, bibl.)

Introductory social history of Nicaragua's Caribbean coast focuses on succession of dominant ethnic groups. Mosquito Indians gave way to English-speaking blacks (Creoles), who by the end of the 19th century gave way in turn to mestizo migrants from interior highlands. Each hierarchical arrangement was reinforced by dominant group's connection to an external power.

1631 Historia general de Costa Rica. v. 1, El surgimiento de un territorio [de] Luis Guillermo Brenes Quesada; El mundo de nuestros aborígenes [de] Carlos Humberto Aguilar Piedra {et al.(v. 2, El descubrimiento y la conquista [de] Francisco Rivas Ríos; La colonia [de] Carlos Meléndez Chaverri; La mayólica—arqueología colonial [de] Floria Arrea Sierman. v. 3, Hacia la formación del Estado nacional, 1821–1870 [de] Marina Volio Brenes *et al.* v. 4, Costa Rica, 1870–1949: la República liberal [de] Ana María Botey Sobrado y Vladimir de la Cruz. v. 5, Costa Rica, 1949-hoy: la Segunda República [de] Eugenio Rodríguez Vega *et al.* Suplemento, Actas de Independencia. Dirección de Vladimir de la Cruz. San José: Euroamericana de Ediciones Costa Rica, 1988–1989. 6 v.: bibl., ill. (some col.), maps.

Ambitious, richly illustrated multivolume history of Costa Rica by recognized specialists includes detailed maps and up-to-date bibliographies. Companion facsimile volume reproduces documents related to independence. Largely celebratory popular synthesis from the isthmian country with the most advanced historiographic tradition.

1632 Incer Barquero, Jaime. Nicaragua, viajes, rutas y encuentros, 1502–1838: historia de las exploraciones y descubrimientos, antes de ser Estado independiente, con observaciones sobre su geografía, etnia y naturaleza. San José: Libro Libre, 1990. 638 p.: bibl., ill., index, maps. (Col. V centenario. Serie Raíces)

Early Nicaragua as reconstructed from the observations and experiences of conquerors, explorers, missionaries, pirates and other travelers, with emphasis on increasing knowledge of country's physical features and native population.

1633 Indice general del archivo del extinguido Juzgado Privativo de Tierras depositado en la Escribanía de Cámara del supremo gobierno de la República de Guatemala. Segunda parte que comprende el índice alfabético general. Edición de Gustavo Palma Murga. México: CIESAS; Centro de Estudios Mexicanos y Centroamericanos, 1991. 504 p.: bibl.

Publication of the so-called "Indice de Gavarrete" is a major event. Named after José Juan de Mata Gavarrete y Cabrera (1829–1882) who compiled it in manuscript in 1863, it is an alphabetical guide by place name to extant colonial and early national Guatemalan land records now housed in Archivo General de Centroamérica. Editor provides informative introduction and, where appropriate, adds comments and modern archival citations to Gavarrete's entries. Although title describes index as "second part," first part, if it ever existed, is now lost, and alphabetical guide is thought to be complete.

1634 Móbil, José A. and Ariel Déleon Meléndez. Guatemala, su pueblo y su historia. v. 1. Guatemala: Serviprensa Centroamericana, 1991. 1 v.: bibl., ill., maps.

First installment of projected two volume survey of Guatemalan history, addressed to students and general readers. Opens with origin of solar system and concludes with separation from Mexico (1823). Much detail on prehispanic period, and on institutional, social, and economic aspects of colonial era. Extensive bibliography of secondary sources, but no index.

1635 Molina Jiménez, Iván. Costa Rica, 1800–1850: el legado colonial y la génesis del capitalismo. San José: Editorial de la Univ. de Costa Rica, 1991. 403 p.: bibl., ill., maps. (Col. Historia de Costa Rica)

Based on extensive research, this impressive synthesis effectively refutes the idea that rural areas were characterized by an impoverished and closed economy before coffee, and identifies the basis for the expansion and diffusion of coffee after 1830. Ends with a useful bibliographic essay. This lightly footnoted work is intended for general audience.

1636 Osorio Osorio, Alberto. Chiriquí en su historia, 1502–1903. Ed. conmemorativa del V Centenario del Descubrimiento de América. Panamá: Litografía ENAN, 1988. 2 v.: bibl.

Work on Panama's western province from discovery to national independence (1903) emphasizes political events and institutional developments, with extensive citations to archival sources.

1637 Oyuela, Irma Leticia de. Historia mínima de Tegucigalpa: vista a través de las fiestas del patrono San Miguel a partir de 1680 hasta fines del siglo XIX. Tegucigalpa: Editorial Guaymuras, 1989. 107 p.: bibl., ill. (Col. Códices: ciencias sociales)

Brief history of the Honduran capital, from its origins as a mining camp in the 16th century. Cult of local patron St. Michael the Archangel is theme throughout, but scope of study is broader than the subtitle suggests. Author laments Tegucigalpa's loss of distinctiveness due to effects of modernization.

1638 *Paraninfo: Revista del Instituto de Ciencias del Hombre Rafael Heliodoro Valle,* Vol. 1, No. 1, mayo 1992- . Tegucigalpa: Instituto de Ciencias del Hombre Rafael Heliodoro Valle.

New academic journal founded to commemorate centennial of Honduran writer Rafael Heliodoro Valle (1891–1959). Of interest to historians are 16th-century documents from Sevilla's Archivo General de Indias, article by Olga Joya on difficulties of early Church in Honduras, and essay by Marcos Carías on Valle himself.

1639 Pérez Brignoli, Héctor. Migration and settlement in Costa Rica, 1700–1850. (*in* Migration in colonial Spanish America. Edited by David J. Robinson. Cambridge: Cambridge Univ. Press, 1990, p. 279–294, graphs, maps, tables)

Essay stresses importance, until comparatively recently, of constantly expanding settlement frontier in accounting for Costa Rica's historical distinctiveness. Using parish records, in particular baptisms, author examines 150-year period, ending approximately with consolidation of coffee culture. Concludes that western half of Central Valley was already the most dynamic area of Costa Rica.

1640 Pinto Soria, Julio César. Guatemala: de la historiografía tradicional a la historiografía moderna. (*Polít. Soc./Guatemala,* 25/28, junio 1989/junio 1991, p. 159–186)

Extended essay on Guatemalan historiography, inspired by author's dissatisfaction with recent general history by Francis Polo Sifontes (see *HLAS 52:1365*). Citing many key scholarly works, author assesses development of field and sketches future agenda in terms of both topics to be studied and approaches to be taken.

1641 Riekenberg, Michael. Zum Wandel von Herrschaft und Mentalität in Guatemala: ein Beitrag zur Sozialgeschichte Lateinamerikas. Köln; Wien: Böhlau Verlag, 1990. 134 p.: bibl.

Provocative attempt to apply theories of German sociologist Norbert Elias to historical evolution of Guatemala, with particular regard to role of *mentalité* as agent of social discipline. Sees 19th century as key to evolution of despotic, violent society.

1642 Rubio Sánchez, Manuel. Monografía de la Ciudad de Antigua, Guatemala. Guatemala: Tip. Nacional, 1989. 1 v.: bibl. (Col. Guatemala; 49: Serie Francisco Vela; 2)

Useful study of Antigua emphasizes little-studied period following city's destruction by 1773 earthquake. Long quotations from primary sources and extensive documentary appendices enrich present volume, which closes with independence from Spain (1821).

1643 Stone, Samuel Z. The heritage of the conquistadors: ruling classes in Central America from the Conquest to the Sandinistas. Foreword by Richard E. Greenleaf. Lincoln: Univ. of Nebraska Press, 1990. 241 p.: bibl., ill., index.

Following his earlier work on Costa Rica, Stone argues here that although many of Central American elites are descended from the same few conquistadors, they have developed different ruling styles in different .

countries depending on local availability of land, labor, and capital. Scarcity bred democracy while abundance fostered dictatorship. For sociologist's comment see *HLAS 53: 5116*.

COLONIAL

1644 Acuña León, María de los Angeles and **Doriam Chavarría López.** Endogamia y exogamia en la sociedad colonial cartaginesa, 1738–1821. (*Rev. Hist./San José*, 23, enero/junio 1991, p. 107–144, tables)

Matrimonial records are used to trace intra-racial and inter-racial marriage and gradual formation of racially mixed population in late colonial Cartago, Costa Rica.

1645 Arellano, Jorge Eduardo. Granada durante la época colonial. (*Bol. Nicar. Bibliogr. Doc.*, 66, marzo/abril 1991, p. 9–18)

Brief sketch, based on familiar sources, of early history of Granada, Nicaragua. Founded in 1525, Granada was important port and trade fair site serving Caribbean until earthquake and pirate raids of the late 17th century.

1646 Ares Queija, Berta. Tomás López Medel: de figura mal conocida a autor mutilado; notas acerca de una edición fallida. (*Rev. Indias*, 51:193, sept./dic. 1991, p. 633–642)

Specialist in field offers bitingly negative evaluation of recent Spanish edition of works of Tomás López Medel, Oidor de Guatemala (1549–1555) and an important source for mid-16th century history.

1647 Belzúnegui, Bernardo. Pensamiento económico y reforma agraria en el Reino de Guatemala, 1797–1812. Guatemala: Comisión Interuniversitaria Guatemalteca de Conmemoración del Quinto Centenario del Descubrimiento de América, 1992. 434 p.: bibl., ill., index.

Examination of land, labor, and economic ideas in late colonial Guatemala covers more than modest title suggests. Useful are studies of *repartimiento* labor, and sale and *composición* of state land under Bourbons. Concludes with detailed review of various agrarian reform proposals advanced but never put into effect.

1648 Bertrand, Michel. Une fondation à double inconnue: réflexions autour de la naissance de San Pablo Rabinal. (*in* Vingt

études sur le Mexique et le Guatemala réunies à la mémoire de Nicole Percheron. Toulouse, France: Presses Universitaires du Mirail, 1991, p. 337–347, bibl.)

Review of historical debate concerning founding date and original location of Rabinal, gateway to Guatemala's Verapaz region and established, according to tradition, by Bartolomé de las Casas himself.

1649 Carillo Padilla, José Domingo. Las lecturas en Santiago de Goathemala, 1770–1780. (*Estudios/Guatemala*, 2, sept. 1989, p. 53–75, appendix, bibl., tables)

Pioneering essay uses data from estate inventories to describe book ownership and reading tastes in late colonial Guatemala. Smallness of sample (31 cases in single decade) makes conclusions tentative, but significant in field where little has been done.

1650 Crónicas de viajeros: Nicaragua. v. 1. Introducciones y notas de Jaime Incer Barquero. San José: Libro Libre, 1990 1 v.: bibl. (Col. V centenario. Serie Raíces)

Columbian Quincentenary project extracts from early accounts of discovery and exploration of Nicaragua, featuring words of Christopher and Ferdinand Columbus, Bartolomé de las Casas, Gil González Dávila, Pedro Mártir de Anglería, Gonzalo Fernández de Oviedo, Francisco Hernández de Córdoba, and others.

1651 Cruz Reyes, Víctor C. *et al.* El convento mercedario de las Minas de Tegucigalpa, 1650–1830. Tegucigalpa: Instituto Hondureño de Antropología e Historia, 1989. 50 p.: bibl., ill., maps, tables.

Informative contribution on neglected topic. Broader in scope than title suggests, briefly surveys Mercedarian missionization activity in colonial Honduras. Based on extensive research in primary documentation.

1652 Documentos coloniales de Chiapas en el Archivo General de Centroamérica. Guatemala: Archivo General de Centro América, 1986. 63 p.: bibl.

Partial inventory of documents relating to colonial Chiapas found in Guatemala City's Archivo General de Centroamérica. Entries provide date, brief description, and archival classification number.

1653 Documentos coloniales de Honduras. Recopilación de Héctor M. Leyva. Tegucigalpa: Centro de Publicaciones Obispado de Choluteca; Centro de Estudios Históricos y Sociales para el Desarrollo de Honduras, 1991. 349 p.: bibl., index. (Col. Padre Manuel Subirana; 3)

Well-chosen collection of 47 documents on colonial Honduras, drawn largely from Seville's Archivo General de Indias and Guatemala City's Archivo General de Centroamérica. Many periods and topics are represented. Valuable feature is appendix listing 238 additional documents published elsewhere, with full bibliographic citations.

1654 Enríquez Macías, Genoveva. Nuevos documentos para la demografía histórica de la Audiencia de Guatemala a finales del siglo XVII. (*Mesoamérica/Antigua*, 17, junio 1989, p. 121–183, bibl., tables)

Two important documents from the Archivo General de Indias: a 1684 tax apportionment listing virtually all indigenous communities in the Audiencia; and a reasonably complete 1685 census of Nicaragua conducted by Oidor don Antonio de Navia Bolaño. With introduction and notes.

1655 Feldman, Lawrence H. Indian payment in kind: the sixteenth-century encomiendas of Guatemala. Culver City, Calif.: Labyrinthos, 1992. 92 p.: bibl., index, maps.

Indispensable reference, intended "to provide a geographical, economic and demographic framework" (p. ix) for study of early colonial Guatemala. Compilation of extant references to 16th-century encomiendas, specifying names of encomenderos, tribute assignments, and numbers of tributaries where available. Detailed maps, analytical tables, and content and source notes add value. Information is usefully organized by both colonial and modern place names and jurisdiction.

1656 Fortune, Armando. Composición étnica y mestizaje en el Istmo de Panamá durante la colonia. (*in* Congreso de la Cultura Negra de las Américas, *1st, Cali, Colombia, 1976. Actas.* Bogotá: Fundación Colombiana de Investigaciones Folclóricas, 1988, p. 103–115)

Conventional overview of race mixture in colonial Latin America, with occasional reference to Panama and several questionable assertions. Based on familiar secondary sources.

1657 García Añoveros, Jesús María. Las misiones franciscanas de la Mosquitia nicaragüense. (*in* Congreso Internacional sobre

los Franciscanos en el Nuevo Mundo, *3rd, La Rábida, Spain, 1989.* Actas. Dirección de Paulino Castañeda. Madrid: Editorial Deimos, 1989, p. 885–922, bibl., tables)

Useful overview of Franciscan activities in Central America during 17th century. Title is misleading, because article explicitly omits missions to Mosquitia, which author treated in previous study (see *HLAS 52:1384*).

1658 García Añoveros, Jesús María. Problemas en el cumplimiento de las obligaciones cristianas de los indígenas del corregimiento del Valle de Guatemala, 1687. (*Rev. Indias*, 50:190, sept./dic. 1990, p. 687–739)

Extended analysis, with long quotations from original, of 1687 inquiry into state of formal Catholic observance and local, or popular, religion in pueblos of central Guatemalan highlands, carried out by vigorously assertive Bishop Fray Andrés de las Navas y Quevedo (1682–1701).

1659 García Añoveros, Jesús María. Visitas pastorales en las diócesis del reino de Guatemala, 1752–1791. pt. 2. (*Hisp. Sacra*, 42, enero/junio 1991, p. 227–326, maps)

Description and analysis of pastoral inspection tours undertaken by colonial bishops, whose records provide valuable historical documentation on population, economic activities, spiritual life, and "moral" conditions. Present installment includes *visitas* to Guatemala and El Salvador by Pedro Cortés y Larraz (1768–70), which is well known and has been extensively studied; and to Chiapas by Fray Juan Manuel García de Vargas y Rivera (1771–74) and Francisco Polanco (1777–78). On Bishop García de Vargas, see also item **1660**.

1660 García Vargas y Rivera, Manuel. Relaciones de los pueblos del Obispado de Chiapas, 1772–1774. Introducción, paleografía y notas de Jorge Luján Muñoz. San Cristóbal de Las Casas: Patronato Fray Bartolomé de Las Casas, 1988. 51 p.: map.

Records of two pastoral visits to towns of diocese of Chiapas during early 1770s, rich in data on population, crops, and religious organization. Also published in *Mesoamérica* (Antigua, Vol. 11, No. 19, junio 1990, p. 114–168).

1661 Gasco, Janine. Población y economía en el Soconusco durante el siglo XVI: el ejemplo del pueblo de Guilocingo, 1582. (*Mesoamérica/Antigua*, 2:20, dic. 1990, p. 249–265, maps, tables)

Unusually detailed census data from 16th-century Guilocingo (modern Pueblo Nuevo Comaltitlán in Chiapas, Mexico) permits tentative conclusions on demographic, social, and economic history of early Soconusco, including household size and structure, ethnicity, migration, distribution of wealth (cacao trees), cacao production, and tribute system.

1662 Gasteazoro, Carlos Manuel. Introducción al estudio de la historia de Panamá: fuentes de la época hispánica. Prólogo de Celestino Andrés Aráuz. 2a. ed. Panama: Editores Manfer, 1990. 157 p.: bibl., ill., maps.

Welcome event. New edition of classic reference work describes and evaluates principal published and unpublished sources for history of colonial Panama. Introduction places author's own career in historical perspective and provides update on works published since guide first appeared in 1950s.

1663 Ibarra Rojas, Eugenia. Las sociedades cacicales de Costa Rica: siglo XVI. San José: Editorial de la Univ. de Costa Rica, 1990. 246 p.: bibl., ill., maps. (Col. Historia de Costa Rica)

Sees Costa Rica's indigenous population at moment of conquest as more numerous and more socially and culturally complex than previously thought. Ethnographically detailed study treats settlement patterns, production, trade, and social and political organization, and attempts to explain rapid disintegration of indigenous world following European contact. Based on familiar published primary sources, plus recent anthropological and archaeological research.

1664 Incer Barquero, Jaime. Grupos indígenas de Nicaragua en los siglos XVI y XVII. (Bol. Nicar. Bibliogr. Doc., 69, sept./oct. 1991, p. 1–12, bibl., facsim., ill., maps)

Straightforward description of native groups inhabiting Nicaraguan territory in first centuries of Spanish era, based on familiar printed sources, a study of toponyms, and the sparse extant archaeological literature.

1665 Langebaek, Carl Henrik. Cuna long distance journeys: the result of colonial interaction. (Ethnology/Pittsburgh, 30:4, Oct. 1991, p. 371–380)

Interesting account of Cuna integration beginning in 17th century into the international market economy through contact with non-Spanish Europeans. Panama's Cuna resisted domination from Spain and migrated to Caribbean coast to escape it, coming into closer contact with British, French, and Dutch traders.

1666 Leiva Vivas, Rafael. Tráfico de esclavos negros a Honduras. Tegucigalpa: Editorial Guaymuras, 1982. 157 p.: bibl., ill.

Episodic account of African slavery in colonial Honduras, with emphasis on role in sugar and mining industries and settlement of Caribbean coast, based on extensive archival research. Useful work on a frequently overlooked question.

1667 Lovell, W. George. Conquista y cambio cultural: la sierra de los Cuchumatanes de Guatemala, 1500–1821. Traducción de Eddy Gaytán. Antigua, Guatemala: Centro de Investigaciones Regionales de Mesoamérica; South Woodstock, Vt.: Plumsock Mesoamerican Studies, 1990. 270 p.: bibl., ill., index, maps. (Serie monográfica, 0252–9971; 6)

More than a simple translation of same author's *Conquest and survival in colonial Guatemala: a historical geography of the Cuchumatán Highlands, 1500–1821* (1985; see HLAS 48:2238). Incorporates much new material and represents evolution of author's thinking since appearance of English-language original.

1668 Lovell, W. George. Disease and depopulation in early colonial Guatemala. (*in* International Congress of Americanists, *46th, Amsterdam, 1988.* "Secret judgments of God": Old World disease in colonial Spanish America. Edited by Noble David Cook and W. George Lovell. Norman: Univ. of Oklahoma Press, 1991, p. 49–83, map, tables)

Contribution to ongoing debate. For 16th-century Guatemala, extant historical evidence permits direct correlation of major declines in native population with outbreaks of epidemic diseases originating in Old World.

1669 Lovell, W. George and William R. Swezey. Indian migration and community formation: an analysis of *congregación* in colonial Guatemala. (*in* Migration in colonial Spanish America. Edited by David J. Robinson. Cambridge: Cambridge Univ. Press, 1990, p. 18–40, maps, tables)

Consideration of conquest-imposed origin of Guatemalan towns. Authors call for greater attention to *chinamit* (or *parcialidad*) rather than *pueblo de indios* as basic unit of highland Maya society, and for more nuanced application of Eric Wolf's famous model of closed corporate community. Emphasizing movement of peoples, authors conclude "colonial Maya communities . . . were fluid and dynamic, not static or fixed" (p. 39).

Lovell, W. George. Mayans, missionaries, evidence and truth: the polemics of native resettlement in sixteenth-century Guatemala. See *HLAS 53:2696.*

Lovell, W. George. Parish registers in Jacaltenango, Guatemala. See *HLAS 53:2697.*

1670 Luján Muñoz, Jorge. Un jurista y autor ignorado del Reino de Guatemala: Don Antonio de Paz y Salgado. (*Hist. Crít./Tegucigalpa,* 1:6, nov. 1991, p. 5–16)

Introduction to 18th-century Guatemalan writer, popular in his day but now forgotten. This attorney, poet, and author of self-help books was born in Tegucigalpa and died ca. 1750. Also a humorist, his advice to prospective litigants included such witticisms as "a bad settlement is better than a good lawsuit" and "stupid and obstinate [clients] make for rich lawyers."

1671 Lutz, Christopher H. and W. George Lovell. Core and periphery in colonial Guatemala. (*in* Guatemalan Indians and the State, 1540 to 1988. Edited by Carol A. Smith. Austin: Univ. of Texas Press, 1990, p. 35–51, maps)

Important synthesis reconceptualizes spatial dimension of Guatemala's colonial experience. In place of traditional schemes (e.g., ladino east and Indian west), authors propose division into Spanish/ladino core and Indian periphery. Each region had highland and lowland components, and distinctive settlement, landholding, and productive patterns, determined by greater or lesser ecological suitability to wheat, cattle, sugar, indigo, and other Spanish enterprises.

1672 Lutz, Christopher H. Population change in the Quinizilapa Valley, Guatemala, 1530–1770. (*in* Studies in Spanish American population history. Edited by David J. Robinson. Boulder: Westview Press, 1981, p. 175–194, graphs, maps)

Model local study focuses on distinctive group of towns southwest of modern Antigua, Guatemala, traces their origin to forced migrations following the Spanish conquest,

and reconstructs their colonial-period population history.

1673 McCreery, David. Atanasio Tzul, Lucas Aguilar, and the Indian kingdom of Totonicapán. (*in* The human tradition in Latin America: the nineteenth century. Edited by Judith Ewell and William H. Beezley. Wilmington, Del.: Scholarly Resources, 1989, p. 39–58, bibl.)

Famous 1820 rebellion is seen as typical colonial tax revolt rather than evidence of Indian participation in contemporary struggle for independence from Spain.

1674 Meléndez Chaverri, Carlos. El pacífico sur en el proceso colonizador costarricense del siglo XVI y albores del XVII. (*Rev. Arch. Nac.,* 52:1/12, enero/dic. 1988, p. 117–126, bibl.)

Dean of Costa Rican historians complains that scholarly concentration on Central Valley has obscured conquest and colonization of Pacific coast. Focuses on Perafán de Ribera's unsuccessful settlement at Nombre de Jesús (1561) and on opening of mule route to Panama, for which he credits Guatemala Audencia President Alonso Criado de Castilla (1598–1611).

Moberg, Mark. Continuity under colonial rule: the *alcalde* system and the Garifuna in Belize. See *HLAS 53:1033.*

1675 Molina Argüello, Carlos. El Reino de Guatemala en el siglo XVIII. (*Bol. Nicar. Bibliogr. Doc.,* 74, sept./oct. 1992, p. 17–37, ill., maps)

Factual overview of administrative, ecclesiastical, military, and economic organization of Spanish Central America during second half of 18th century. Handy for evolution of internal territorial divisions, but cites no sources.

1676 Moya Gutiérrez, Arnaldo. El rito mortuorio en el Cartago dieciochezco. (*Rev. Hist./San José,* 24, julio/dic. 1991, p. 23–52)

Innovative study of attitudes toward death in 18th-century Costa Rica, based on wills and probate documents. Testamentary provisions reaffirmed dominant ideology, while funerary and memorial observances reflected deceased's place in local social hierarchy.

1677 New Iberian world: a documentary history of the discovery and settlement of Latin America to the early 17th century. v. 3,

Central America and Mexico. Edited, with commentaries by John Horace Parry and Robert G. Keith, with the assistance of Michael Jiménez. New York: Times Books; Hector & Rose, 1984. 1 v.: bibl., ill., index.

First-hand accounts in English translation of discovery, conquest, and colonization of Mexico and Central America, accompanied by introductory essays, glossary, and reproductions of contemporary maps. Familiar sources extracted include works by Fernando Cortés, Pedro de Alvarado, Bernal Díaz del Castillo, Bartolomé de las Casas, Pedro Mártir de Anglería, and many others. Also includes less familiar but representative documents, such as wills, *probanzas*, and cabildo correspondence.

1678 Newson, Linda A. La población indígena de Honduras bajo el régimen colonial. (*Hist. Crít./Tegucigalpa*, 1:6, nov. 1991, p. 17–56, tables)

Condensed Spanish-language version of findings from author's important book on population decline in colonial Honduras (see *HLAS 50:1352*). Also appeared in *Mesoamérica* in 1985 (see *HLAS 48:2223*).

1679 Percheron, Nicole. Producción agrícola y comercio de la Verapaz en la época colonial. (*Mesoamérica/Antigua*, 2:20, dic. 1990, p. 231–248, graphs, maps)

Study of Guatamala's Verapaz region from preconquest to independence reveals dynamic economy characterized by diversified agricultural and artisan activities, and by thriving trade with other regions, including unconquered Lacandón frontier.

1680 Quirós Vargas, Claudia. Historia de Costa Rica. v. 1, La era de la encomienda. San José: Editorial de la Univ. de Costa Rica, 1990. 1 v.: bibl., ill., maps.

Major contribution. Thoroughly documented study of 16th and 17th centuries differs from more traditional accounts in assigning to Costa Rica's indigenous population a central, active role in formation of society and economy.

1681 Romero Vargas, Germán. Las estructuras sociales de Nicaragua en el siglo XVIII. Managua: Editorial Vanguardia, 1988. 544 p.: bibl., ill. (Rescate; 2)

Major contribution, based on extensive archival research. Impressive attempt to describe society in Nicaragua's Pacific high-

lands from 1679–1820. Topics addressed include deterioration of indigenous communities, social and economic basis of domination by Spanish elite, and emergence of mixed-blood marginal groups. Translation of 1976 Sorbonne doctoral thesis.

1682 Ruz, Mario Humberto. Chiapas colonial: dos esbozos documentales. México: Univ. Nacional Autónoma de México, Instituto de Investigaciones Filológicas, 1989. 236 p.: bibl., ill. (Cuaderno / Centro de Estudios Mayas; 21)

Two separate studies, first of which analyzes correspondence of Chiapas bishops in the 16th and 17th centuries. Second is a sketchy history of an Indian hospital at Comitán (founded 1793). Bibliography and documentary appendices enhance usefulness.

1683 Ruz, Mario Humberto. Melodías para el tigre: Pablo de Rebullida y los indios de la Talamanca, 1694–1709. (*Rev. Hist./San José*, 23, enero/junio 1991, p. 59–105, maps)

Backround to 1709 revolt led by cacique Pablo Presbere on Costa Rica's Talamanca frontier, with focus on missionization activities as causal factor. Good use of previously unstudied Vatican records, with sensitivity to both missionary and native points of view.

1684 Ruz, Mario Humberto. Sebastiana de la Cruz, alias "La Polilla," mulata de Petapa y madre del hijo de Dios. (*Mesoamérica/Antigua*, 12:23, junio 1992, p. 55–66)

Perceptive study makes effective use of 1695 case from Inquisition records in Mexico City's Archivo General de la Nación to offer rare look at daily life and religion in Santiago de Guatemala's mulatto community, an important but often overlooked segment of colonial urban population.

1685 Solórzano F., Juan Carlos. Centroamérica a finales de la dominación hispánica, 1750–1821: transformación, desarrollo y crisis de la sociedad colonial. (*Rev. Hist./Managua*, 1:1, enero/junio 1990, p. 37–62)

This useful—although not particularly original—synthesis of late colonial period is drawn from customary secondary sources.

1686 Terga, Ricardo. La mies es abundante. v. 2–4, 6. Guatemala: s.n., 1988. 4 v.: bibl., ill., maps.

"Abundant harvest" of title refers to Spanish culture in Guatemala. Ambitious, but idiosyncratic and somewhat amateurish project identifies Spanish settlers in urban and rural areas of colonial province. Interpretive essays accompany long lists of names, dates, and other data drawn from baptismal registers and other typical sources. Regions covered are Baja Verapaz and central highlands (vol. 2), Zacapa and Acasaguastlán (vol. 3), Chiquimula and Jutiapa (vol. 4), and western highlands (vol. 6).

1687 Torres C., Jeannette María; Margarita Torres Hernández; and Nancy Zúñiga C. La caña de azúcar en Heredia, 1800–1820. Ciudad Universitaria Rodrigo Facio, Costa Rica: CSUCA, Confederación Universitaria Centroamericana, Secretaría General, 1988. 27 p.: bibl. (Cuadernos de investigación; 37)

Authors use wills to look at market production of sugar in late colonial Heredia, Costa Rica and conclude that sugar was area's chief link to the market in these years; processing equipment was held in few hands and generated monopoly rent; and producers violently resisted efforts to enforce state *aguardiente* monopoly.

1688 Ward, Christopher. The defense of Portobelo: a chronology of construction, 1585–1700. (*Ibero-Am. Arch.*, 16:2, 1990, p. 341–386, maps, tables)

Account of fortress construction at colonial Panama's Caribbean port is based on extensive archival research. Sheds light on Spanish strategic thinking and military engineering practices.

Weeks, John M. and Nancy J. Black. Mercedarian missionaries and the transformation of Lenca Indian society in western Honduras, 1550–1700. See *HLAS 53:517*.

NATIONAL

1689 Acker, Alison. Honduras: the making of a banana republic. Boston: South End Press, 1988. 166 p.: bibl., index, maps.

Brief synthesis of recent Honduran history based on published sources argues need for thorough-going revolution akin to Nicaragua and El Salvador. Useful principally because so little is available in English on Honduras.

1690 Aguilar Hernández, Marielos. Clase trabajadora y organización sindical en Costa Rica, 1943–1971. San José: ICES; Editorial Porvenir; FLACSO, 1989. 203 p.: bibl. (Col. Debate)

Based on extensive work in newspapers and interviews, author argues that Costa Rican unions have allowed themselves to be manipulated by State and political parties, and have failed to develop an adequate counter-hegemonic project.

1691 Amaya-Amador, Ramón and Rigoberto Padilla Rush. Memorias y enseñanzas del alzamiento popular de 1954. Tegucigalpa?: Ediciones J.P. Wainwright, 1989. 120 p.: ill.

Popular account of the 1954 strike—here labeled an "uprising"—against the United Fruit Company. Meant for "workers," it was writen by two communist party militants.

1692 Aragón, Magda and Edgar Barillas. Cine e historia social en Guatemala: imágenes de una década—los años treintas. (*Estudios/Guatemala*, 3, dic. 1990, p. 29–85, bibl., photos)

From 1920s to 1950s, Guatemalan government's Tipografía Nacional maintained a film production unit. Some 600 public information (propaganda) documentaries survive on unstable nitrate stock. Authors present selection of stills from era of dictator Jorge Ubico (1931–44), each with two captions: one that states the message the film producers intended to convey, while the other reveals the deeper truth each image communicates about Guatemalan reality in the 1930s.

1693 Araya Pochet, Carlos. La universidad de Costa Rica, 1972–1990: transformación, crisis y perspectivas. (*Rev. Hist./Heredia*, 21/22, enero/dic. 1990, p. 231–261, bibl., tables)

Welcome addition to scant bibliography on higher education in Central America. Focuses on Third University Congress in 1972–73 that led to democratization of university administration, increased enrollments, faculty reforms, and more attention to extension education.

1694 Arguedas Chaverri, Ana Virginia and Martha Ramírez Arias. La actividad cafetalera y el caso de Julio Sánchez Lépiz. San José: Editorial Univ. Estatal a Distancia, 1990. 144 p.: bibl., ill.

Well-documented monograph on activities of progressive Costa Rican coffee grower and rancher from turn-of-the-century to 1930s.

1695 Argueta, Mario. Bananos y política: Samuel Zemurray y la Cuyamel Fruit Company en Honduras. Tegucigalpa: Editorial Universitaria, 1989. 153 p.: bibl., ill., map. (Col. Realidad Nacional; 27)

Balanced, brief survey of Samuel Zemurray/Cuyamel Fruit Company's interventions in Honduran politics, 1911–40s, with appendix of excerpts from earlier writers on the subject. For general reader, not specialist.

1696 Bell, John Patrick. La Asociación General de Agricultores frente a la Reforma Agraria en la Guatemala revolucionaria, 1944–1954. (*Anu. Estud. Centroam.*, 18:1, 1992, p. 17–28, bibl.)

Demonstrates that the AGA moderated its position on land reform over the course of the "revolutionary" decade, from one of absolute rejection of any change to expressed willingness to tolerate reform less drastic than Arbenz's Decree 900.

1697 Berger, Susan A. Political and agrarian development in Guatemala. Boulder: Westview Press, 1992. 251 p.: bibl., index. (Westview special studies on Latin America and the Caribbean)

Guatemalan State has enjoyed more autonomy since 1931 than usually recognized and has sometimes exercised this autonomy to implement policies meant to stimulate agrarian development. Not only have these policies often damaged well-being of majority of population but they have also failed to accomplish stated goals because of budget constraints, bureaucratic and class infighting, and exclusionary politics.

1698 Bibliographical essays. (*in* Central America since Independence. Edited by Leslie Bethell. Cambridge: Cambridge Univ. Press, 1991, p. 327–356)

Eight descriptive and evaluative bibliographic essays which conclude *Central America since Independence* (item **1709**) deal with: "The Aftermath of Independence, 1821-c. 1870;" "The Liberal Era, 1870–1930;" "Crisis and Conflict, 1930 to the Present;" and Guatemala, El Salvador, Honduras, Nicaragua, and Costa Rica since 1930. These essays parallel the chapters of this work—which is comprised of parts of several volumes of *The*

Cambridge History of Latin America—and provide an excellent overview of key publications on the subject.

1699 Bolaños Geyer, Alejandro. William Walker: the gray-eyed man of destiny. v. 3, Nicaragua. v. 4, War of liberation. v. 5, Truxillo. Maps by Julio Velázquez. Lake Saint Louis, Mo.: A. Bolaños-Geyer, 1988–91. 3 v.: bibl., ill., indexes.

Vol. 3 reviews 19th-century Nicaraguan history, then follows Walker from June 1855 to May 1856; vol. 4 covers Walker's presidency from June 1856 until his expulsion from Central America in May 1857; vol. 5 chronicles Walker's repeated and unsuccessful efforts to return to Central America and analyzes his book *The war in Nicaragua* "in the light of . . . . [the] unconscious, irresistible psychological forces [that] led [him] astray." Includes an extensive list of sources. For vol. 1 and 2, see *HLAS 52:1421.*

1700 Borge, Tomás. The patient impatience: from boyhood to guerilla: a personal narrative of Nicaragua's struggle for liberation. 1st Eng. ed. Willimantic, Conn.: Curbstone Press; East Haven, Conn.: INBOOK, 1992. 452 p.

Autobiographical memoirs of the only survivor among founders of the FSLN. A fascinating picture of life in Somoza's Nicaragua and an insider's account of the formation and early struggles of the Sandinistas. Ends with Carlos Fonseca's death in 1976. Also available in Spanish as *La paciente impaciencia* (Managua: Editorial Vanguardia, 1989). For translation specialist's comment, see item **5056.**

1701 Brenes, Lidiette. La nacionalización bancaria en Costa Rica: un juicio histórico. San José: Facultad Latinoamericana de Ciencias Sociales, 1990. 230 p.: bibl.

Nationalization of the Costa Rican banking industry in the late 1940s benefited chiefly the agro-industrial economic elites, while bank credit to the government allowed the maintenance of social programs that undercut popular protest against the effects of unequal accumulation. The early 1980s crisis stimulated a more "neoliberal" approach and a shift toward non-traditional investments.

1702 Brown, Richmond F. Charles Lennox Wyke and the Clayton-Bulwer Formula in Central America, 1852–1860. (*Americas/Francisc.*, 47:4, April 1991, p. 411–445)

Detailed study of British diplomat in

Central America who vigorously opposed US expansion and successfully negotiated territorial and boundary agreements with the isthmian governments in 1859.

1703 Browning, John Dudley. Vida e ideología de Antonio José de Irisarri. Guatemala: Editorial Universitaria de Guatemala, 1986. 282 p., 11 leaves of plates: bibl., ill., index. (Col. Editorial Universitaria; 73)

A detailed study of the thought, long life, and generally unsuccessful political career of this Guatemalan merchant turned journalist and diplomat for Chile and Central America during the Independence period.

Bulmer-Thomas, Victor. Honduras since 1930. See *HLAS 53:3464.*

1704 Burns, E. Bradford. Establishing the patterns of progress and poverty in Central America. (*in* Studies of development and change in the modern world. Edited by Michael T. Martin and Terry R. Kandal. New York: Oxford Univ. Press, 1989, p. 202–215, bibl.)

Brief overview of Central American history focuses on period 1860–1930 and establishment of export monoculture. Author insists scholars must distinguish among "growth," "development," and "modernization" in assessing impact of changes and in setting research agendas.

1705 Camacho Navarro, Enrique. Los usos de Sandino. México: Univ. Nacional Autónoma de México, 1991. 145 p.: bibl. (Nuestra América; 28)

An intellectual history of how various groups, from Somocistas to Sandinistas, have "used" texts and ideas said to be derived from Sandino to buttress interpretations of history and to justify policies.

1706 Carazo, Rodrigo. Carazo: tiempo y marcha. San José: Editorial Univ. Estatal a Distancia, 1989. 666 p.: bibl., ill. (some col.), index.

Personal memoirs of Costa Rican president (1978–82). This Unidad president stresses his efforts to avoid being drawn into the Nicaraguan conflict and to resist the creeping "Central Americanization" of Costa Rica.

1707 Cardenal, Gloria *et al.* La guerra en Nicaragua. Edición de Orlando Núñez. Managua: CIPRES, 1991 526 p.: bibl., ill.

The product of collective research and

writing, this volume is one of the best yet available for understanding the events of the 1980s in Nicaragua, even though it is clearly partisan. It portrays the conflict as the result of both internal and external causes and as one fought by multiclass alliances on both sides, rather than simply as the result of US aggression. Thoroughly researched and footnoted.

1708 Castro Sánchez, Silvia. Estado, privatización de la tierra y conflictos agrarios. (*Rev. Hist./Heredia,* 21/22, enero/dic. 1990, p. 207–230)

Surveys the efforts of the Costa Rican State during the 1850s to promote "progress" through privatization of land, administration of State resources, and participation in land disputes as less-than-partial judge. Brief work is limited almost entirely to legislation.

1709 Central America since independence. Edited by Leslie Bethell. Cambridge; New York: Cambridge Univ. Press, 1991. 366 p.: bibl., ill., index, maps.

Essays by various authors written originally for different volumes of the *Cambridge History of Latin America* are brought together here in a paperback version for classroom use. Organized by country, the focus is on events since 1930. See also item **1698**; for political scientist's comments on individual articles, see *HLAS 53*, items 3403, 3409, 3464, and 3470.

Cerdas Cruz, Rodolfo. Costa Rica since 1930. See *HLAS 53:3409.*

1710 Cerdas Cruz, Rodolfo. Sandino, el APRA y la Internacional Comunista: antecedentes históricos de la Nicaragua de hoy. (*Cuad. Centroam. Hist.,* 7, enero/abril 1990, p. 67–97, tables)

Author suggests that Sandino failed to understand the links between international imperialism and domestic elites because of his own and subordinates' petty bourgeois origins. The International broke with Sandino over his refusal to convert an anti-imperialist uprising into a social revolution.

1711 Contreras, Gerardo and **José Manuel Cerdas.** Los años 40: historia de una política de alianzas. 3a ed. San José: Editorial Porvenir; Instituto Costarricense de Estudios Sociales, 1988. 202 p.: bibl. (Col. Debate)

Thorough history of Costa Rican communist party, from its founding through the

Partido Vanguardia Popular (PVP) period and Calderón alliance, with emphasis on 1942–49. This balanced work does not shrink from admitting party errors.

1712 Dávila Cubero, Carlos. ¡Viva Vargas!: historia del Partido Confraternidad Guanacasteca. San José: Ediciones Guayacán, 1987. 246 p.: bibl., ill.

Treats the formation and activities of a regional opposition party in 1930s Costa Rica. Author sees party as having called attention to Guanacaste's social and economic problems which were addressed after 1948. Based on party documents and newspapers.

1713 Documento de la Prensa Gráfica: el conflicto en El Salvador. San Salvador: Dutriz Hermanos, 1992. 142 p.: ill. (some col.)

Daily account of the conflict in El Salvador from the pages of the newspaper *El Gráfico*. Covers the years from the late 1970s to early 1992 and is generally hostile to the FMLN.

1714 Dosal, Paul J. The political economy of industrialization in revolutionary Guatemala, 1944–1954. (*Can. J. Lat. Am. Caribb. Stud.*, 15:29, 1990, p. 17–36, graphs)

Argues that although Arévalo and Arbenz supported laws and policies intended to promote industrialization, tensions between the political leadership and the industrial bourgeoisie over social reforms hindered industrial development during the revolutionary decade.

1715 Echeverri-Gent, Elisavinda. Forgotten workers: British West Indians and the early days of the banana industry in Costa Rica and Honduras. (*J. Lat. Am. Stud.*, 24:2, May 1992, p. 275–308)

Article compares employment of black West Indians on the Atlantic coasts of Honduras and Costa Rica from the 1870s to the 1930s and makes clear the difficulties faced by workers when they attempted to organize to protect their interests. Based chiefly on British Foreign Office papers.

1716 Edelman, Marc. The logic of the latifundio: the large estates of northwestern Costa Rica since the late nineteenth century. Stanford, Calif.: Stanford Univ. Press, 1992. 478 p.: bibl., ill., index.

Large, "underutilized" haciendas have persisted in Guanacaste because the specific historical "kinds of economic development in

the region have permitted—and in some ways encouraged—both the coexistence of traditional and modern enterprises and the extensive and intensive uses of land within the same haciendas." Extensive utilization originated in the isolation characteristic of the years before 1950 but persists because it minimizes capital risk.

1717 Euraque, Darío A. Notas sobre formación de clases & poder político en Honduras 1870s-1932. (*Hist. Crít./Tegucigalpa*, 1: 6, nov. 1991, p. 59–79, bibl.)

Because local elites remained at the margins of capitalism, represented in Honduras by the banana industry, military caudillos rather than an elite hegemonic bloc controlled the State well into the 20th century. These exercised more "flexibility" when confronted by demands from the lower classes than did the oligarchies of neighboring countries.

1718 Euraque, Darío A. La "reforma liberal" en Honduras y la hipótesis de la "Oligarquía Ausente," 1870–1930. (*Rev. Hist./San José*, 23, enero/junio 1991, p. 7–56, tables)

Late 19th-century reforms in Honduras did not produce a strong State or a locally-controlled export economy, but rather an elite dependent on land speculation, commerce and transport, and office holding. The ultimately-disappointed promise of mining diverted local attention from the creation of a Honduran-owned banana industry.

1719 Fernández, José M. Cambio, organización y conflicto social en el Altiplano indígena de Guatemala. (*in* Jornadas de Historiadores Americanistas, *2nd, Granada, Spain, 1989*. América: encuentro y asimilación. Edición de Joaquín A. Muñoz Mendoza. Granada: Diputación Provincial de Granada, 1990, p. 319–334, bibl.)

Shows how the Guatemalan Comité de Unidad Campesina (CUC) grew out of the peasant leagues, cooperatives, and base communities brought together by the rebuilding efforts following the 1976 earthquake and led by a younger generation of Indians. A good, short piece based on secondary sources.

1720 Figueres Ferrer, José; Guillermo Villegas; and Benjamín Núñez. El espíritu del 48. San José: Editorial Costa Rica, 1987. 347 p.: ill.

These personal memoirs of Partido Liberación Nacional leader and ex-president Don Pepe Figueres regarding 1948 events were written with Guillermo Villegas and Rev. Benjamín Núñez. Co-authors claim to have verified Figueres' account with documentary research, but none is cited.

1721 Figueres Ferrer, José. José Figueres: escritos y discursos, 1942–1962. Selección, prólogo y notas de Alfonso Chase. Ed. homenaje al 80 aniversario de su nacimiento. San José: Editorial Costa Rica, 1989 632 p.: ports.

Collection of the speeches, programs, and writings of a founder of the PLN party and an ex-president of Costa Rica. No analysis.

1722 Fischel Volio, Astrid et al. Historia de Costa Rica en el siglo XX: análisis de su desarrollo institucional. Selección y coordinación de Jaime Murillo. San José: Editorial Porvenir, 1989. 345 p.: bibl., ill. (Col. Ensayos)

Eleven essays by various authors on broadly defined "institutions" meant to "complete" and expand on item **1732**. Particularly useful are the pieces on the political-electoral system, local government, recent demographic trends, and means of communication.

1723 Les Forces politiques en Amérique centrale. Sous la coordination de Alain Rouquié, avec la collaboration d'Hélène Arnaud. Paris: Karthala, 1991. 302 p.: bibl., maps. (Col. Hommes et sociétés)

Country by country summaries of the histories, ideologies, and alliances of political parties, as well as attention to other organized groups involved in political action (e.g., revolutionary groups, the Church, the military, and unions and union confederations). Emphasizes the decade of the 1980s.

1724 Foroohar, Manzar. The Catholic Church and social change in Nicaragua. Albany, N.Y.: State Univ. of New York Press, 1989. 262 p.: bibl., index.

Thoroughly-researched and well-written overview of Church-State relations in 20th-century Nicaragua, with attention to splits within the Church prompted by the rise of Liberation Theology and the FSLN. Epilogue covers post-1979 conflicts. Generally sympathetic to the "people's" church and the FSLN.

1725 Franco Muñoz, Hernando. Blázquez de Pedro y los orígenes del sindicalismo panameño. Panamá: Movimiento Editores, 1986. 165 p.: bibl., ill., ports.

Studies the ideas and activities of an immigrant Spanish anarcho-syndicalist labor organizer in Panama during the 1910s and 1920s. Reproduces some of Blázquez de Pedro's writings.

1726 Gabbert, Wolfgang. Creoles—Afroamerikaner im karibischen Tiefland von Nicaragua. Berlin: Freie Univ. Berlin, 1991. 392 p.: bibl., maps.

Ethnicity rather than race is author's central theme in this social history. Using archives of Moravian Church and interdisciplinary sources, traces distinct development of Nicaragua's African Creoles, shifts in predominance and attitudes vis-à-vis the Mosquito Indians and the central State. [C.K. Converse]

1727 Garrard-Burnett, Virginia. Positivismo, liberalismo e impulso misionero: misiones protestantes en Guatemala, 1880–1920. (*Mesoamérica/Antigua*, 11:19, junio 1990, p. 13–31)

As invited guests of the Reform Liberals after 1871, protestant missionaries worked to reform not only the souls but the "minds, bodies, and spirits" of Guatemala's Indian population. Protestantism meshed with elite social Darwinism and positivism, as well as serving US "spiritual manifest destiny" in Central America.

1728 Gleijeses, Piero. The agrarian reform of Jacobo Arbenz. (*J. Lat. Am. Stud.*, 21:1, Feb. 1989, p. 453–480, bibl.)

Presents evidence that the 1952 agrarian law was drafted almost entirely by the Guatemalan Communist Party (PGT) and shows that for the brief time it was allowed to operate it was an economic success, as even the US embassy acknowledged.

1729 Gleijeses, Piero. The death of Francisco Arana: a turning point in the Guatemalan Revolution. (*J. Lat. Am. Stud.*, 22:3, Oct. 1990, p. 527–552)

Arana was killed by supporters of Arévalo and Arbenz as they attempted to arrest and exile him in order to head off an army coup, a coup Arana himself initially had resisted.

1730 Gleijeses, Piero. Shattered hope: the Guatemalan Revolution and the United States, 1944–1954. Princeton, N.J.: Princeton Univ. Press, 1991. 430 p.: bibl., ill., index.

Based chiefly on interviews, and some limited use of archives, the author argues that Arbenz was quite sympathetic to the Communists and allowed them power in the government beyond what their numbers warranted. Although sympathetic to the reforms, Gleijeses feels that Arbenz misstepped by pushing for radical changes too quickly given the world environment at the time.

1731 Gómez Díez, Francisco Javier. El reformismo jesuítico en Centroamérica: la revista ECA en los años de la guerra fría. (*Anu. Estud. Am.*, 49:1, suplemento 1992, p. 85–104, tables)

Analyzes content of first 20 years of one of the leading journals in Central America devoted to social issues. Finds that during this time the journal argued for genuine, Catholic-based social and economic reform, in alliance with the US, as the necessary antidote to Communism.

1732 Gómez U., Carmen Lila et al. Las instituciones costarricenses del siglo XX. San José: Editorial Costa Rica, 1986. 376 p.: bibl.

Twelve essays of uneven quality by different authors that treat "institutions" such as Freemasonry, primary education, religious tolerance, and the national university in the late 19th century and peasant movements and the decentralization of public administration in the 20th century.

1733 Gould, Jeffrey L. "La raza rebelde:" las luchas de la comunidad indígena de Subtiava, Nicaragua, 1900–1960. (*Rev. Hist./ Heredia*, 21/22, enero/dic. 1990, p. 69–117)

Divisions in Indian community of Subtiava allowed certain groups to make class alliances outside the town that, while "ladinoizing" them in clothing and education, actually broadened and strengthened the community's ethnic identity and helped it maintain this in face of outside pressures.

1734 Gould, Jeffrey L. To lead as equals: rural protest and political consciousness in Chinandega, Nicaragua, 1912–1979. Chapel Hill: Univ. of North Carolina Press, 1990. 377 p.: bibl., ill., index.

Examination of origins and forms of rural protest against effects of capitalist agriculture in 20th-century Nicaragua. Oral history shows Somoza's populist appeals raised popular expectations and schooled peasants in dealing with State, thereby preparing them to support FSLN in 1970s. Important contribution to Nicaraguan rural history.

Guatemalan Indians and the State, 1540 to 1988. See *HLAS 53:939.*

1735 Guidos Véjar, Rafael. El movimiento sindical después de la segunda guerra mundial en El Salvador. (*ECA/San Salvador*, 45:504, oct. 1990, p. 871–892, tables)

Shows how unions were forced by violence of the 1977–82 years to abandon their earlier political participation for "depoliticization" and "bread and butter" unionism.

1736 Handy, Jim. Anxiety and dread: State and community in modern Guatemala. (*Can. J. Hist.*, 26, April 1991, p. 43–65)

Except for 1944–54 period, Indians in rural Guatemala generally have suffered when forced or enticed into interacting with national institutions. The army tends to see even mildly autonomous rural activity as a potential threat to its control and reacts with repression.

1737 Harnecker, Marta. Con la mirada en alto: historia de las Fuerzas Populares de Liberación Farabundo Martí a través de entrevistas con sus dirigentes. Donostia, Spain: Tercera Prensa, 1991. 337 p.: index. (Gakoa liburuak; 10)

Extensive, sympathetic interviews with the leadership of the FMLN, organized more or less chronologically to follow the development of the movement. It is particularly useful for studying the strategies and internal politics of the FMLN, including the murder of Comandante Ana María (Mélida Anaya Montes).

1738 Harpelle, Ronald N. The social and political integration of West Indians in Costa Rica, 1930–50. (*J. Lat. Am. Stud.*, 25:1, Feb. 1993, p. 103–120)

A broad examination of the efforts of the black West Indian community of Limón during the 1930s and 1940s to come to terms with the Costa Rican "white settler" national mythology and the racist demands of the State. Rejects the idea that this population refused to integrate and instead faults West Indians for focusing on assimilation rather than fighting discrimination.

1739 Harrison, Benjamin T. Dollar diplomat: Chandler Anderson and American diplomacy in Mexico and Nicaragua, 1913–1928. Pullman, Wash.: Washington State Univ. Press, 1988. 168 p.: bibl., index.

By analyzing the career of an international lawyer and diplomat who equated US foreign policy with private investment, the author attempts to show that the chief determinants of US policy toward Central America and Mexico in the early 20th century were not economic interests and big business but issues such as the "White Man's Burden," Social Darwinism, morality and Christianity, and isolationism.

1740 Hernández, Carlos. Los inmigrantes de Saint Kitts: 1910, un capítulo en la historia de los conflictos bananeros costarricenses. (*Rev. Hist./San José,* 23, enero/junio 1991, p. 191–240, bibl.)

Interesting article based on Costa Rican sources studies Nov. 1910 strike by black West Indians against the United Fruit Company and against subsequent company efforts to replace them with cheaper workers from St. Kitts. It points up conflicting interests among the strikers and the role of the Costa Rican State in defeating the workers.

1741 Jonas, Susanne. The battle for Guatemala: rebels, death squads, and U.S. power. Foreword by Edelberto Torres Rivas. Boulder, Colo.: Westview Press, 1991. 288 p.: bibl., ill., map. (Latin American perspectives series; 5)

A singularly well-informed study of Guatemalan political history for the years 1970s-1990 written by an author with long experience in the area and based on wide reading and extensive interviews. This is the best treatment currently available of the causes, course, and effects of the horrific violence that has afflicted Guatemala in recent decades.

1742 Karlen, Stefan. Paz, progreso, justicia y honradez: das Ubico-Regime in Guatemala, 1931–1944. Stuttgart: F. Steiner, 1991. 581 p.: bibl., ill., index, maps. (Beiträge zur Kolonial- und Überseegeschichte, 0522–6848; 52)

This very detailed biography of Jorge Ubico is based on established, mainly US sources, with scant attention to Guatemalan archives. Offers little new interpretation.

1743 Kit, Wade. The fall of Guatemalan dictator Manuel Estrada Cabrera: US pressure or national opposition? (*Can. J. Lat. Am. Caribb. Stud.,* 15:29, 1990, p. 105–127)

Convincingly refutes the thesis that US pressure was the primary factor in the overthrow of Guatemalan dictator Manuel Estrada Cabrera in 1920; his fall instead was the result of domestic unrest fed by the Church, urban labor, and the Unionist Party.

1744 Lehoucq, Fabrice Edouard. Class conflict, political crisis and the breakdown of democratic practices in Costa Rica: reassessing the origins of the 1948 Civil War. (*J. Lat. Am. Stud.,* 23:1, Feb. 1991, p. 37–60)

Costa Rica's resort to violence in 1948 was the result of a general breakdown of compromise efforts and of the loss of faith in validity of the electoral system. Calls for additional studies of the relations between class interests, economic change, and political action.

1745 Life stories of the Nicaraguan revolution. Edited by Denis Lynn Daly Heyck. New York: Routledge, 1990. 355 p.: ill.

Short oral-history biographies of Nicaraguans caught up voluntarily or involuntarily in the Sandinista Revolution. Heavily in favor of FSLN sympathizers.

Lindenberg, Marc. Central America: crisis and economic strategy 1930–1985, lessons from history. See *HLAS 53:1908.*

1746 Lindo-Fuentes, Héctor. Weak foundations: the economy of El Salvador in the nineteenth century. Berkeley: Univ. of California Press, 1990. 239 p.: bibl., index.

Well-written account of changes accompanying shift to commercial coffee monoculture in El Salvador after 1860. Demonstrates how elites were able to use political and economic power to manipulate change to their own advantage, while much of population sank into landlessness and poorly-paid wage labor.

1747 López Vigil, José Ignacio. Las mil y una historias de Radio Venceremos. San Salvador: UCA Editores, 1991. 546 p.: ill. (Col. Testigos de la historia; 4)

First-person stories of the operation of FMLN's Radio Venceremos during the late 1970s and 1980s. An unusual and interesting perspective on the war and a contribution to understanding the uses of radio in Latin American revolution.

1748 Luján Muñoz, Jorge. Los partidos políticos en Guatemala desde la Independencia hasta el fin de la Federación. Guatemala?: s.n.; 1989. 80 p.: bibl.

A brief introduction to the postindependence political parties of Guatemala divides the period into the years 1821–26, characterized by considerable fluidity, and those of 1826–40, when membership stabilized and platforms became more polarized.

Más de 100 años del movimiento obrero urbano en Guatemala. v. 1. See *HLAS 53:3457.*

1749 McCreery, David. Hegemonía y represión en la Guatemala rural, 1871– 1940. (*Rev. Hist./Heredia*, 21/22, enero/dic. 1990, p. 37–67, table)

Analyzes expansion of State hegemony in Guatemalan countryside during Liberal era in terms of coercive mechanisms employed to ensure cheap labor for coffee *fincas* and forms of peasant resistance to such demands.

1750 McCreery, David. State power, indigenous communities, and land in nineteenth-century Guatemala, 1820–1920. (*in* Guatemalan Indians and the State, 1540 to 1988. Edited by Carol A. Smith. Austin: Univ. of Texas Press, 1990, p. 96–115, table)

Important revisionist account presents more nuanced view of coffee's impact on Guatemala's highland Indian communities. Liberal legislation notwithstanding, there was no wholesale dissolution of village common lands. Also, violent resistance to State-imposed change became less common, rather than more so, as generally believed.

1751 Mejía, Medardo. Historia de Honduras. v. 5. Tegucigalpa: Univ. Nacional Autónoma de Honduras, Editorial Universitaria, 1989? 1 v.: bibl. (Col. Realidad nacional; 23)

Narrative political history, together with essays on the economy and "races," without sources but interspersed with reproductions of documents. Focuses on late 19th and early 20th centuries and tends to substitute Liberal partisanship for analysis. For previous volumes, see *HLAS 48:2222, HLAS 52: 1467,* and *HLAS 52:1468.*

1752 Mena Sandoval, Francisco Emilio. Del ejército nacional al ejército guerrillero. San Salvador?: Ediciones Arcoiris, 1990? 368 p.

A first-person account by a professional Salvadoran army officer of his life in the military in the 1960s and 1970s, his conversion to the opposition, and his service with the guerrillas in the early 1980s. Episodic and undocumented, but fascinating reading.

1753 Mendieta Alfaro, Róger. Olama y Mollejones. Managua: s.n., 1992. 208 p.: ill.

A detailed remembrance by one of the participants of a 1959 "invasion" of Nicaragua by Conservative party adherents led by Pedro Joaquín Chamorro. The author quotes others involved on both sides but provides no notes or bibliography.

Molina Chocano, Guillermo. Estado liberal y desarrollo capitalista en Honduras. See *HLAS 53:5091.*

1754 Molina F., Diego. Cuando hablan las campanas: álbum fotográfico del ayer. Guatemala: Exploración Cultural de Guatemala en coordinación con Everest de Guatemala, 1989. 111 p.: ill. (some col.).

Charming volume. Text is minimal, but many vintage photographs illustrate life in Guatemala City from mid 19th century through 1930s. Particularly useful for students of urban development, as contains many street scenes and images of structures no longer in existence.

1755 Molina Jiménez, Iván. Documentos: los catálogos de libros como fuente para la historia cultural de Costa Rica en el siglo XIX. (*Rev. Filos./San José*, 30:71, junio 1992, p. 103–116, appendices)

Uses the inventories of the Univ. of Santo Tomás Library in 1859 and of a bookstore in San José in 1858 to argue for the utility of such materials for the reconstruction of cultural history.

1756 El movimiento sindical en Guatemala, 1975–1985. México: Ciencia y Tecnología para Guatemala A.C., 1989. 124 p.: bibl. (Formación y capacitación; 1)

Valuable introduction to a confusing subject in a violent time that examines the labor mobilizations of the late 1970s, the repression of the early 1980s, and efforts to rebuild after 1983. Describes the structures and organization of specific unions and federations and the reasons for the successes and failures of their struggles, based on written materials and interviews.

1757 Muñoz Guillén, Mercedes. El Estado y la abolición del ejército, 1914–1949. San José: Editorial Porvenir, 1990. 228 p.: bibl., ill.

The best historical study to date of a Central American army. Shows that the institution was central to the development of the nation-State in the 19th century but that the growing substitution of the police for internal control and US interventions in regional struggles in the first decades of the 20th century made the declining role for the military clear and opened the way for its abolition in Costa Rica.

Opazo Bernales, Andrés. Costa Rica: la Iglesia Católica y las transformaciones sociales. See *HLAS 53:5100.*

1758 Oyuela, Irma Leticia de. Cuatro hacendadas del siglo XIX: selección de cuatro capítulos de la mujer en la hacienda. Tegucigalpa: Univ. Nacional Autónoma de Honduras, Editorial Universitaria, 1989. 84 p.: bibl. (Col. Letras hondureñas; 42)

Extracted from a promised larger work on the hacienda in 18th- and 19th-century Honduras, the chapters here examine conflicts between the roles traditionally ascribed to women and the economic needs or possibilities of a modernizing economy. Based largely on wills and inventories.

1759 Padilla Vela, Raúl. El fascismo en un país dependiente: la dictadura del general Maximiliano Hernández Martínez. San Salvador: Editorial Universitaria, Univ. de El Salvador, 1987. 72 p. (Cuadernos universitarios; 12)

Short history intended for beginning university students finds the origins of many of El Salvador's current problems (e.g., systematic violation of human rights and institutionalized military rule) in the "martinato." No notes or sources.

1760 Palma Murga, Gustavo. El Estado y los campesinos en Guatemala durante el período 1944–1951. Guatemala: Dirección General de Investigación, Univ. de San Carlos de Guatemala, 1992. 43 p.: bibl.

Brief discussion of peasant-State rela-

tions in Guatemala during "revolutionary" presidency of Juan José Arévalo (1945–51). In spite of political elites' desire to effect significant change in countryside, they accomplished little due to resistance of large propertied interests and urban reformers' own limited knowledge and understanding of peasant population.

1761 Palmer, Steven. Central American union or Guatemalan republic?: the national question in liberal Guatemala, 1871–1885. (*Americas/Francisc.,* 49:4, April 1993, p. 513–530)

Focuses on newspaper journalism and Independence Day speeches to explore the development of a concept of nationalism as a subset of Unionism in the urban political culture of late 19th-century Liberal Guatemala.

1762 Palmer, Steven. Getting to know the Unknown Soldier: official nationalism in Liberal Costa Rica, 1880–1900. (*J. Lat. Am. Stud.,* 25:1, Feb. 1993, p. 45–72)

Innovative exploration of the formation of a nationalist discourse by Costa Rica's coffee Liberals, using the example of the secular beatification of Juan Santamaría, hero of the 1856–57 National War. The Liberals sought the nation's "imagined origins" in the National War to compensate for a missing independence struggle and saw in Santamaría a model subject for the subordinate classes to emulate.

1763 Pinto Aguilar, Rodolfo Mauricio Gerardo. Relación entre Iglesia y Estado durante el gobierno del Presidente Estrada Cabrera, 1898–1920. (*Cult. Guatem.,* 7:1, enero/abril 1986, p. 85–116, bibl.)

Based in part on oral history interviews, describes difficult relationship between Guatemala's Roman Catholic hierarchy and Manuel Estrada Cabrera, Liberal dictator (1898–1920) used to having his own way. Particular emphasis on role of Bishop José Piñol y Batres who spoke out against the regime in its waning years.

1764 Pizzurno Gelós, Patricia. Antecedentes, hechos y consecuencias de la Guerra de los Mil Días en el Istmo de Panamá. Panamá: Ediciones Fomato 16/ GECU; Extension Universitaria, Univ. de Panamá, 1990. 233 p.: bibl.

Looks at the War of a Thousand Days in Panama less in terms of military activities than from the perspective of financing the war and supplying the armies. In the aftermath of the fighting many on the Isthmus counted on construction of the canal to rebuild local economy, so that rejection of the Hay-Herrán Treaty left them no option but independence.

1765 Pompejano, Daniele. Alle radici della questione dello stato in America Centrale, 1821–1871. (*Latinoamerica/Rome*, 12: 42/43, aprile/ott. 1991, p. 72–93, bibl.)

Essay seeks to clarify relationship between hegemonic blocs and sources of power in 19th-century Central America. Concentrates largely on Guatemala, arguing that the Rafael Carrera dictatorship of the 1840s-50s was a product of broad support within powerful sectors of society—the Church, the capital city merchant's, and cochineal oligarchy—despite Carrera's lowly social origins. The demise of cochineal meant significant shifts in alignment of the blocs. The Los Altos region liberals, who competed well in the world coffee market, cancelled out the Church's influence, and a new authoritarian regime under Barrios shifted from conservative to liberal. [V. Peloso]

1766 Revilla Argüeso, Angel. Cultura hispanoamericana en el istmo de Panamá. Panamá: ECU Ediciones; Convento de Santo Domingo, 1987. 383 p.: bibl.

A chronicle of literary and popular culture in Panama, organized into chapters such as "Literature," "Music," "Religion (Catholicism)," and "Superstition." Book contains much information but in a jumbled and fragmented form.

1767 Riekenberg, Michael. Die Rebellion der *montañeses* im Südosten Guatemalas, 1837/38, und der Machtaufstieg Rafael Carreras. (*Ibero-Am. Arch.*, 19:1/2, 1993, p. 37–62)

In this revisionist paper Rafael Carrera emerges as a shrewd leader who, although pro-clerical, derived his support from a broadly based coalition of rural mestizos, indigenous peoples, and municipalities which resisted Liberals' economic policies and centralization efforts. [C.K. Converse]

1768 Rivero Quintero, Francisco. La marca del Zorro. Entrevista de Sergio Ramírez. Madrid: Mondadori España, 1989. 287 p.: maps. (Omnibus)

Sergio Ramírez's account of the revolu-

tionary deeds of Comandante Francisco Rivera Quintero, "El Zorro," a leader of the uprisings in Estelí during the fight against Somoza, and commander on the Northern Front. Based chiefly on video-taped interviews, it is a powerful view of the Sandinista Revolution at the ground level.

1769 Rodríguez, Eugenia and **Iván Molina Jiménez.** Compraventas de cafetales y haciendas de café en el valle central de Costa Rica, 1834–1850. (*Anu. Estud. Centroam.*, 18:1, 1992, p. 29–50, appendix, graphs, maps, tables)

A detailed study based on *protocolo* records of land transactions during the early years after coffee's introduction to Costa Rica. Examines regional differences in the rate and form at which coffee developed, fragmentation and consolidation of coffee land, credit terms and other conditions of sale, and the participation of various groups in the traffic.

1770 Salazar Mora, Orlando. El apogeo de la República Liberal en Costa Rica: 1870–1914. San José: Editorial de la Univ. de Costa Rica, 1990. 308 p.: bibl., ill. (Col. Historia de Costa Rica)

Argues that Costa Rica's Liberal reform was an effort to implement a new model of domination that relied less on simple repression than legitimation through manipulation of civil society and electoral participation. However, fraud and voting restrictions limited its success, as did the State's refusal to address the "social question."

Salisbury, Richard V. Anti-imperialism and international competition in Central America, 1920–1929. See *HLAS 53:4612.*

1771 Salisbury, Richard V. Revolution and recognition: a British perspective on isthmian affairs during the 1920s. (*Americas/Francisc.*, 48:3, Jan. 1992, p. 331–349)

Although by the 1920s Great Britain had conceded hegemony over Central America to the US and generally relied on the North Americans to safeguard British interests in the region, minor differences, typically over recognition of regimes and the need for military intervention, occasionally occurred and had to be resolved.

1772 Salvetti, Patrizia. L'emigrazione italiana in Nicaragua. (*Stud. Emigr.*, 28: 101, marzo 1991, p. 2–26)

Mass immigration failed to develop, but individual Italian immigrants had considerable success in late 19th-century Nicaragua, due chiefly to their superior education and capital resources. After 1912 this success ran up against limits set by the US intervention.

1773 Samper K., Mario. Generations of settlers: rural households and markets on the Costa Rican frontier, 1850–1935. Boulder: Westview Press, 1990. 286 p.: bibl., ill., index, maps. (Dellplain Latin American studies; 26)

Samper carefully documents the process by which merchant capital fostered and then exploited petty commodity production among small-holder settlers in the northwestern part of Costa Rica's central valley, extracting profits through moneylending as well as from processing and export trade monopolies. Concludes with a useful comparative chapter.

1774 Sandino, the testimony of a Nicaraguan patriot: 1921–1934. Compiled and edited by Sergio Ramírez. Edited and translated, with an introduction and additional selections by Robert Edgar Conrad. Princeton, N.J.: Princeton Univ. Press, 1990. 516 p., 16 p. of plates: bibl., ill., index, maps.

Translations of letters, speeches, manifestos, etc. of Augusto C. Sandino, organized chronologically and with a brief historical introduction. The explanatory footnotes that accompany the documents are very helpful.

1775 Schoonover, Thomas David. France in Central America 1820s–1929: an overview. (*Rev. fr. hist. Outre-mer*, 79:295, 2e trimestre 1992, p. 161–197, tables)

Finds that French influence generally declined in Central America after Independence as Great Britain, and then US, gained control of trade and shipping. French activities shifted instead to canal building and investment and after 1900 to culture. Includes an extensive bibliography.

1776 Schoonover, Thomas David. The United States in Central America, 1860–1911: episodes of social imperialism and imperial rivalry in the world system. Durham: Duke Univ. Press, 1991. 253 p.: bibl., index.

A series of case studies of involvement of US individuals and government in Central America illustrates "the rivalry that grew out of the internationalization of laissez-faire competition." Schoonover argues that the goal of the US initially was to alleviate the class tensions generated in North America by rapid capital accumulation ("social imperialism") and then in the 1890s to continue that accumulation in face of international depression.

1777 Schwartz, Norman B. Forest society: a social history of Petén, Guatemala. Philadelphia: Univ. of Pennsylvania Press, 1990. 367 p.: bibl., ill., index, maps.

Model regional history based on archival research, interviews, and participant observation that shows how the Petén developed initially as a stable and relatively egalitarian, if poor, society but began to break up into violent land- and resource-grabbing components in the 1960s and 1970s when roads penetrated the area.

1778 Selser, Gregorio. Panamá: érase un país a un canal pegado. México: Univ. Obrera de México, 1989. 293 p.: bibl.

A fairly standard treatment that intertwines Panama's domestic politics with that country's efforts to regain control of the Canal Zone. Based on a limited number of sources fleshed out by interviews with some of those who worked with Omar Torrijos on the 1977 negotiations.

1779 Un siglo de lucha de los trabajadores de Nicaragua, 1880–1979. Testimonios y compilación de Armando Amador. Managua: Univ. Centroamericana, 1992. 203 p.: bibl.

Relentlessly chronological, unfootnoted, and eager to lay all of Nicaragua's labor woes at the door of "imperialism," this book nevertheless includes useful if fragmented material on Nicaragua's labor movement before 1979.

1780 Silvia H., Margarita. La educación de la mujer en Costa Rica durante el siglo XIX. (*Rev. Hist./San José*, 20, julio/dic. 1989, p. 67–80)

A brief introduction to an interesting topic that suggests that Liberals saw education as important to women's central role as mothers, in order to prepare them to properly socialize children to respect the nation-State.

1781 Soler, Ricaurte. Cuatro ensayos de historia: sobre Panamá y nuestra América. 3. ed. Panamá: Ediciones de la Revista Tareas, 1987. 127 p.: bibl.

One essay examines intellectual currents in the early 20th century Panamanian labor movement and another looks at anti-imperialist thought and action in Panama from the mid-19th century to the 1970s, particularly among the middle classes.

1782 Solís Rivera, Luis Guillermo. Consideraciones históricas en torno a las formaciones político-sociales en un área de colonización reciente: la dinastía de los colonizadores. (*Rev. Arch. Nac.*, 52:1/12, enero/dic. 1988, p. 133–140)

Study of local power structure in municipality of Pérez Zeledón, frontier settlement in southeastern Costa Rica colonized largely after 1880 by migrating peasants. Based on parish records and oral interviews.

1783 Sollis, Peter. The Atlantic Coast of Nicaragua: development and autonomy. (*J. Lat. Am. Stud.*, 21:1, Feb. 1989, p. 481–520, bibl.)

Surveys the periods of British, US, and Somoza hegemony over the Nicaraguan Atlantic coast before discussing the conflicts between local inhabitants and the Sandinistas during the 1980s and subsequent efforts to establish regional autonomy. The author suggests that international concern for the Mosquito has diverted attention from successful Sandinista efforts to accommodate the interests and concerns of various local ethnic groups.

1784 Soto Harrison, Fernando. ¿Qué pasó en los años 40? San José: Editorial Univ. Estatal a Distancia, 1991. 368 p., 32 p. of plates: ill.

A personal memoir, backed by extensive documentation, of the Teodoro Picado presidency in Costa Rica (1944–1948), in which the author was Minister of Government. Pays particular attention to electoral reform.

1785 Taracena Arriola, Arturo. Cochinilla y clases sociales en la Guatemala del siglo XIX. (*in* Vingt études sur le Mexique et le Guatemala: réunies à la mémoire de Nicole Percheron. Toulouse, France: Presses Universitaires du Mirail, 1992, p. 349–367, bibl., ill., maps, tables)

Essay on social and political aspects of cochineal agrees that red dye production in early 19th-century Guatemala allowed country's integration into capitalist world system with little negative impact on indigenous

communities, but claims that, otherwise, crop's "democratic" characteristics have been overemphasized.

1786 Torres Hernández, Margarita. Producción, oficios y migración en San Rafael de Heredia: un análisis del censo poblacional de 1927. (*Rev. Hist./San José*, 24, julio/dic. 1991, p. 89–122, appendices, graphs, map, tables)

Manuscript materials from the 1927 Costa Rican census show a tendency among the children of small landholders either to migrate to less settled areas or to suffer downward mobility into wage labor. Includes extensive statistical appendices.

Vargas, Oscar-René. Elecciones presidenciales en Nicaragua, 1912–1932: análisis sociopolítico. See *HLAS 53:3489.*

1787 Vargas, Oscar-René. La revolución que inició el progreso: Nicaragua, 1893–1909. Managua: Centro de Investigación y Desarrollo ECOTEXTURA; CONSA, 1990. 278 p.: bibl.

Said to be the first of a projected four volumes on Nicaraguan history for 1821–1939, this one deals with the Zelaya years, which the author sees as a period of capitalist accumulation and consolidation, despite persistance of coerced labor. Generally this is simplified Marxist analysis applied to a very limited range of secondary historical sources.

1788 Vargas Arias, Claudio Antonio. El Liberalismo, la Iglesia y el Estado en Costa Rica. San José: Ediciones Guayacán, 1991. 253 p.: bibl.

Excellent analysis of Church-State relations in the 1880s and early 1890s looks first at the "presence" of Church in 19th-century society, then details the internal reorganization of the Church and its conflicts with the State over Liberal laws and Church participation in politics. Sees the conflicts as part of State efforts to gain secular hegemony over the nation and the national territory.

1789 Vega Jiménez, Patricia. De la banca al sofá: la diversificación de los patrones de consumo en San José, 1857–1861. (*Rev. Hist./San José*, 24, julio/dic. 1991, p. 53–87, appendices, tables)

Newspaper advertising reveals that rising coffee income in the 1850s prompted a general growth and diversification of imports and their substitution for local products among Central Valley elites; particularly popular were imported foods and clothing, while foreign textiles were so generalized as to require no advertising.

1790 Wagner, Regina. Los alemanes en Guatemala: 1828–1944. Guatemala: Asociación de Educación y Cultura Alejandro von Humboldt, Comité de Investigaciones Históricas, 1991. 535 p.: bibl., ill., index, maps.

This pioneering work by a German-Guatemalan reflects extensive research, chiefly in German diplomatic archives, and covers all aspects of the immigrants' lives in Guatemala. Largely a compilation of material rather than an analytic history, it will be essential to any future work on the subject.

1791 Webre, Stephen. Central America. (*in* Latin American military history: an annotated bibliography. New York: Garland Publishing, 1992, p. 557–586, bibl.)

Essay with extensive appended bibliography provides overview of development of armed forces in 19th- and 20th-century Central America, description of key primary sources and existing secondary literature, and suggestions for future research.

1792 Woodward, Ralph Lee, Jr. Changes in the nineteenth-century Guatemalan State and its Indian policies. (*in* Guatemalan Indians and the State, 1540 to 1988. Edited by Carol A. Smith. Austin: Univ. of Texas Press, 1990, p. 52–71)

Woodward traces government policies toward the indigenous population from roughly 1800–65, focusing particularly on the Conservative regime headed by Rafael Carrera. He sees period as "a real turning back toward a more feudal, Hapsburg tradition of decentralized government."

THE CARIBBEAN, THE GUIANAS, AND THE SPANISH BORDERLANDS

EDWARD L. COX, *Associate Professor of History, Rice University, Houston*
ANNE PEROTIN-DUMON, *Associate Professor of History, Pontificia Universidad Católica de Chile*
JOSE M. HERNANDEZ, *Professor Emeritus of History, Georgetown University*
ROSEMARIJN HOEFTE, *Deputy Head, Department of Caribbean Studies, Royal Institute of Linguistics and Anthropology, The Netherlands*
TERESITA MARTINEZ-VERGNE, *Associate Professor of History, Macalaster College*

THE BRITISH CARIBBEAN

SCHOLARLY INTEREST IN THE Caribbean has continued unabated over the past few years, and has resulted in the publication of a number of highly commendable works on the region. While slavery continues to attract the attention of scholars, there has been considerable interest in the immediate post-emancipation societies of the British Caribbean. Indeed, some of the most impressive publications address the dynamics of post-slavery societies. In addition, several authors have concentrated on the experiences of Indian immigrants to the colonies in the latter half of the 19th century and working class challenges to planter hegemony in an effort to enhance workers' socioeconomic positions. It is somewhat premature to say whether or not this change in focus is sufficiently great or sustained to constitute a trend in scholarly interest.

As was the case in earlier volumes of the *Handbook*, the economics of slavery again attracted considerable attention. William Darity, Jr., makes a strident plea for an appreciation of the central role of the slave trade and slavery in Britain's industrialization (item **1997**), while Selwyn Carrington calls for further examination of the impact of mature capitalism on the slave trade and slavery (item **1987**). In an extremely important article that is likely to stimulate much scholarly debate, William

Green argues that the *supply* and availability of slaves, rather than the *demands* of sugar growers, stimulated Barbados' sugar revolution (item **2013**). Finally, J.R. Ward (item **1944**) argues that, contrary to previously held views, Jamaican planters were more receptive to the use of the plough in place of the hoe and suggests that though their counterparts throughout the Caribbean might have wished to adopt similar labor-saving devices, the physical condition of the islands was the crucial determinant in their decision-making.

Several excellent pieces address the culture and social institutions of slaves. Michael Mullin (item **1922**) focuses on religion and family life in his examination of the relationship between slave acculturation and the changing nature of slave resistance, while Michael Craton and Gail Saunders (item **1992**) examine the multifaceted nature of resistance among slaves in the Bahamas. David Barry Gaspar (items **1863** and **2009**) reminds us of the resilience of Antigua's slaves amidst the harsh conditions under which they lived, while Winston McGowan (item **2059**) and M.K. Bacchus (item **1970**) explore the efforts of Christian missionaries among slaves in British Guiana.

The transition from slavery to freedom, as well as the experiences of the newly emancipated workers, have received fruitful study. A number of these publications obviously grew out of general interest in and conferences scheduled around the celebration of the 150th anniversary of general slave emancipation. Thomas Holt's *The meaning of freedom: race, labor, and politics in Jamaica and Britain, 1832–1938* (item **2021**) deserves special mention for the insightful analysis it provides of the divergent and changing goals and perceptions entertained by whites and blacks, planters and ex-slaves, residents of both Britain and Jamaica in the 100 years separating two major milestones in British Caribbean history. Robert Stewart's excellent work (item **2105**) explores the role of religion in post-emancipation conflicts in Jamaica. The contributions of Jean Besson (item **1977**), Michael Craton (item **1993**), Nigel Bolland (item **1980**), and Veront Satchell (item **2096**) elucidate the plight of plantation workers in this crucial transitional period when planters still sought to control labor as they had so effectively done during slavery.

The immigration scheme to supply the plantations with workers from overseas, as well as the experiences of these immigrants in the colonies, have been addressed by a number of extremely fine articles. Anand James (item **2029**) concentrates on the politics surrounding and the experiences of liberated Africans who were sent to British Guiana, while Isaac Dookhan (item **1998**), Reuben J. Kartick (items **2033** and **2034**), and Brinsley Samaroo (item **1837**) examine various aspects of the experiences of these migrants in British Guiana and Trinidad.

The most important publications for the 20th century have addressed the discontent of the working class and its efforts to improve to its material conditions. Brackette Williams (item **2234**) provides a rather sophisticated analysis of the problems posed by race and class divisions in Guyana's quest to enhance the meaning of nationhood. Susan Craig's succinct treatment of the Trinidad labor disturbances of 1937 (item **2146**) provides a useful backdrop for Raoul Pantin's work on the 1970 Revolution (item **2197**) and the publication by the editors of the *Daily Express* of the extremely useful first hand stories on the Muslimeen grab for power in 1990 (item **2230**). [ELC]

FRENCH AND DANISH CARIBBEAN

Commemoration of the historic slave insurrection of 1791 in Saint-Domingue has shed important new light on the slave mobilization and the wars of Haiti's independence that were seminal to the formation of the modern Caribbean. Applying a rigorous historical critique David Geggus reexamines the question of voodoo in 18th-century Saint-Domingue (item **1909**) and its significance for the subsequent Haitian Revolution (item **1908**). Marcel Auguste shows how rebels who became soldiers fought in the revolutionary wars (item **1890**), and Frank Moya Pons disentangles the momentuous repercussions of the war on Santo Domingo (item **1921**). The emergence of politics in the revolutionary era, an issue often subsumed under the term "social movement," is discussed by Anne Pérotin-Dumon for free-coloreds and slaves in Guadeloupe (item **1928**). New ground is broken on the Caribbean Enlightenment by James McClellan's work on the scientific activities of Saint-Domingue colonists (item **1917**) and by *Francs-maçons des loges françaises aux Amériques,* a research tool on French colonial free-masons by Elisabeth Escalle and Mariel Gouyon Guillaume (item **1902**).

Another anniversary, that of Columbus' momentous landing in the Bahamas, has stimulated examination of early European colonization. Jean-Pierre Moreau emphasizes Spanish reactions to the arrival of European free-rovers in the Lesser Antilles (item **1869**), while the destiny of Caribs after the European intrusion and the images of them developed in Western literature is the topic of Philip Boucher's *Cannibal encounters* (item **1851**).

Three books convey different facets of the colonial experience in 19th-century Caribbean and Guyana: 1) Josette Fallope's *Esclaves et citoyens,* tracing the fascinating transformation of Guadeloupe slaves into overseas citizens of the French Republic (item **2002**); 2) a welcome reprint of a narrative by Jules Crevaux, a gifted writer, enlightened observer, and the first European to explore the regions at the limits of the Guyana and Amazon Basins in 1870 (item **1994**); and 3) the original memoirs of Jacques-Aimé Péray, a French hat-maker enlisted in the French Navy who turned peddler and shop-keeper in Martinique—memoirs which are wonderfully evocative of a petit-blanc's life in the 1820s (item **2072**).

Probably the most dynamic field has been that of genealogical and family history, best represented by *Généalogie et Histoire de la Caraïbe,* a monthly publication since January 1989. It is tackling issues such as last names conferred to emancipated slaves in Martinique and Guadeloupe (item **1999**), and unearthing new sources with ramifications throughout the whole Caribbean (item **1929**).

As often, a renewal in perspective occurs at the margins of long-studied themes. *Slave society in the Danish West Indies* (item **1811**), artfully compiled from works by the late Neville Hall, shows slave living within a small slaveholding society and a diversified economy. François Nault and Francine Mayer have provided an in-depth study of slave demography in St. Bartholomew, a society whose population was in majority white (item **2062**). On the topic of European commercial interests, economic historians Michael Zeuske and Hermann Kellenbenz have produced fresh research on the rise of the German presence in Haiti, Curaçao and St. Thomas in the early 19th century (items **2128** and **2036**).

The contribution of migrants and minorities to the formation of societies is another emerging theme with relevance beyond the French Caribbean. Zvi Loker provides an anthology of colonial documents on Jews in the Caribbean (item **1818**), and Raymond Delval's *Les Musulmans en Amérique latine et aux Caraïbes,* a country-by-country survey, shows the liveliest Muslim communities to be in Trinidad and Tobago, Guyana, and Suriname (item **863**). In *L'Emigration antillaise en France,* Alain Ancelin offers a rich portrait and thoughtful analysis of Martiniquais and Guadeloupéens immigrants to France after 1962 (item **2132**), a period which Arlette Lameynardie's photographs document with great sensitivity in *Regards sur la Martinique des années soixante* (item **2204**). [APD]

DUTCH CARIBBEAN

Scanning recent work on the history of the Dutch Caribbean leads to the conclusion that there is not much new under the sun. Plantations, slavery, and Maroons continue to top the list of research topics. One of the most important books to appear is by Alex van Stipriaan (item **2106**). Based on extensive archival research, it will be the standard work on Suriname plantations and slavery for many years to come. Let's hope that it will be translated into English so that a wider audience can read Van Stipriaan's magnum opus. Together with Gert Oostindie's case study of a coffee and a sugar plantation from 1720–1870 (see *HLAS 52:1572*), we now have a rather complete picture of the agricultural, economic, and social history of Suriname plantations.

Wim Hoogbergen continues to write about the history of the Maroons. His 1985 dissertation on the Boni Maroon wars from 1757 to 1860 (see *HLAS 50:1582*) serves as the basis for further publications: in 1990 a slighty condensed English translation appeared (see *HLAS 52:1665*), and in 1992 Hoogbergen published a popular account of the Maroon wars in Dutch called *De Bosnegers zijn gekomen!* (item **1911**). Furthermore, Hoogbergen has written many articles on this topic (see *HLAS 53:1012*).

Finally, one of the most fascinating books in the last couple of years is a joint effort by the historian Scholtens and three anthropologists—Wekker, Van Putten, and Dieko—who describe in great detail the extensive rituals following the death of Aboikoni, the *gaama* or paramount chief of the Saramaka. To write *Gaama duumi, buta gaama* (item **2217**) the authors had to overcome numerous obstacles arising from the civil war in the interior of Suriname and the Saramaka's historical distrust of outsiders. Their work was definitely worth the effort. [RH]

PUERTO RICO

Three trends mark the production of works of Puerto Rican history in the past two years. The most evident, and possibly least interesting, is the proliferation of volumes focusing on "events" in the island's history that have captured the attention of the general readership. The second is many authors' continued preference for social and economic themes legitimized by "the new history" of the 1970s and 1980s, and, concomitantly, the exploration of new questions within the framework of traditional political history. Although few Puerto Rican historians have consistently applied new methods of analysis to their work, the third trend—the shift toward postmodernism and cultural studies—is a promising development.

Four events stimulated the production of works related to the island's history. First and foremost was the ill-fated attempt to celebrate Columbus' landfall in 1493, which resulted in a reexamination of the early colonial period—particularly the experiences of subordinate groups—as evidenced in Alegría's account of the travels of a black conquistador (item **1847**); Sued-Badillo's articles on the enslavement of the indigenous peoples and Africans (items **1881** and **1882**); Moscoso's reconstruction of a 16th-century slave uprising (item **1870**); and López Cantos' work on slaves in the 18th century (item **1867**). Also worthy of mention is Sued-Badillo's detailed recording of the activities of the San Juan cabildo in the first half of the 16th century (item **1880**). Secondly, the announcement that a plebiscite intended to definitely settle Puerto Rico's political status would be held in 1991 and the consequent referendum that measured the population's preference regarding association with the US promoted the publication of a number of works of a strictly political nature. Cabán chose to go back to the first decades of the 20th century for insights on Puerto Rico's colonial status (item **2141**); Zapata-Oliveras examined the international dimension (item **2237**); Marrero Betancourt traced the obstacles to self-determination back to the 1930s and 1940s (item **2183**); García-Passalacqua and Rivera Lugo analyzed the most recent developments (item **2161**); while Santiago-Valles challenged the nature of the debate (item **2215**). Similarly, the anniversaries of the births of Eugenio María de Hostos and Pedro Albizu Campos served to encourage writers to rethink the ideological impact of these influential figures. Cassá's "Sociedad e Historia en el Pensamiento de Hostos" (item **1988**) and López Cantos' selection of Hostos' writings (item **2023**) deserve mention. The republication of Hostos' complete works, begun in 1989 by the University of Puerto Rico and the Institute of Puerto Rican Culture (item **2022**), is an exciting prospect for years to come. Ferrao continued his work of demythifying Albizu Campos in two articles which examine his self-defense in 1934–36 and his ties to Catholicism (items **2156** and **2155**); Rodríguez-Fatricelli re-examined Albizu's national-, metropolitan-, and international-based strategies (item **2209**); and Vassallo and Torres Martinó collected various writings on the nationalist leader (item **2134**). Finally, several works on Luis Muñoz Marín and on Arturo Morales Carrión, whose deaths closed a chapter in the island's political and intellectual history, also appeared in this period: Bird Piñero's *Don Luis Muñoz Marín: el poder de la excelencia* (item **2140**); Rosario Natal's *Luis Muñoz Marín: juicios sobre su significado histórico* (item **2179**); and *Arturo Morales Carrión: homenaje al historiador y humanista* (item **1795**).

As a legacy of the "new history" movement, microstudies on the processes related to the island's economic development during the 19th century—such as migration, slave and wage labor, and agricultural production—continued to dominate. Noteworthy among these are Luque de Sánchez's "La Revolución Francesa y su Impacto Inmigratorio" (item **2047**); Martínez-Vergne's *Capitalism in colonial Puerto Rico* and "The Allocation of Liberated African Labour through the Casa de Beneficencia . . ." (items **2057** and **2056**); Negrón Portillo's and Mayo Santana's *La esclavitud urbana en San Juan* (item **2065**); Pérez Vega's "Las Oleadas de Inmigración . . ." (item **2076**); San Miguel's "La Economía de Plantación . . . en Vega Baja" (item **2093**); and Scarano's *Haciendas y barracones . . .* (item **2098**). Town histories sponsored by local history committees generally concentrated on the same themes. See, for example, Camuñas Madera's "Fundación y Crecimiento de Lares . . ." (item **1985**) and Santana Rabell's *Historia de Vega Alta de Espinosa* (item **2095**). However, Colón's urban history of Isabela (item **1991**) and Martínez Fernández's study of the Partido Popular Democrático in 20th-century San Lorenzo (item **2184**) are exceptions to the above-mentioned trend towards economic histories. Two traditional political studies deserve to be mentioned: Arrigoitia's work on José de Diego (item **2137**) and Navarro García's analysis of the governorship of Miguel de la Torre (item **2063**).

Most exciting are the cross-disciplinary explorations into Puerto Rico's early 20th century provided by Ramos' *Amor y anarquía* (item **2142**) and Rigau's *Puerto Rico 1900* (item **1833**). More focused on social processes, but equally concerned with the social construction of meaning are Alvarez Curbelo's "La Mirada en la Tierra . . ." (item **2131**); Rosario Urrutia's "El Combate Prohibicionista . . ." (item **2211**); Schwartz's "The Hurricane of San Ciriaco . . ." (item **2101**); and Zavala's "El Exilio Republicano . . ." (item **2238**). Fully in the realm of cultural studies are Pérez's "La Plena Puertorriqueña . . ." (item **2200**) and Hernández's "The Origins of the Consumer Culture . . ." (item **2169**). [TMV]

CUBA, THE DOMINICAN REPUBLIC, AND THE SPANISH BORDERLANDS

No new trends of any significance are perceptible in the items reviewed here. As usual, the subsection entitled Spanish Borderlands has been graced by a small number of solid works, both monographic and synthetic; and the same can be said of the literature on the colonial period, an area of research that customarily attracts few, but hard-working and dedicated scholars. In contrast, also as in the preceding biennium, the quality of material drops sharply as the focus shifts to the 19th and 20th centuries, especially the latter. The lack of perspective of many of these works of contemporary history is such that one wonders how they would look had they been written 50 years from now, or whether they would have been written at all.

Of course, also as two years ago, there are exceptions to the rule, works that rise above the mass of publications, and that, therefore, deserve special mention. In the Dominican Republic there are at least two that must be so recognized: Frank Moya Pons' study on Dominican import substitution and industrialization policies (item **2191**), and Mu-Kien A. Sang's scholarly biography of Buenaventura Báez (item **2094**).

Cubans, who have published more profusely, have written an even larger number of works that stand out as important contributions. Some of them are indeed outstanding, as the Castellanos' volumes on *Cultura afrocubana*, written by Cubans living in the US (items **1799** and **1800**). Others are perhaps not as exciting, but still must be singled out as truly meritorious. This is the case, for example, of the studies on Cuban railroads (items **1845** and **2061**), two ground-breaking works that complement one another; and such is the case, too, of Fray Manuel Maza's little volume on *El clero cubano y la independencia* (item **2058**), the first impartial attempt that has been made in 60 years to dispel the prejudices that have often obscured the role played by the Catholic Church in the Cuban independence movement. Of comparable value are a small number of works published in Cuba by relatively unknown scholars, among which should be mentioned as examples Gabino La Rosa Corzo's *Los palenques del oriente de Cuba* (item **2038**) and Francisco Pérez Guzmán's introduction to Loynaz del Castillo's memoirs (item **2046**), a noteworthy bibliographical essay.

In closing, reference must be made to the scholarship of non-native historians, some of whom have also produced very serious work. John L. Offner, for instance, has managed to offer new insights into such an exhausted topic as the Spanish American War (item **2066**), and J.C.M. Ogelsby has suggested new ways of interpreting the problem of Cuban independence (item **2067**). Significant studies on these and other topics have also been written by contemporary Spanish scholars who deserve commendation for their careful research as well as for their balance and objectivity. [JMH]

GENERAL

1793 **Albury, Paul.** Paradise Island story. London: Macmillan Caribbean, 1984. 121 p.: bibl., ill. (some col.), maps.

Useful general history of this Bahamian island covers period from mid-17th century to present and is based on both primary and secondary sources. Author shows how the island eventually became a "paradise" for the burgeoning tourist industry of the modern period. [ELC]

1794 **Aldrich, Robert** and **John Connell.** France's overseas frontier: Départements et territoires d'outre-mer. Cambridge; New York: Cambridge Univ. Press, 1992. 357 p.: bibl., ill., index.

Authors examine the institutional framework of French overseas departments or

"D.O.M." that govern Martinique, Guadeloupe and Guyana (and other remnants of former French colonial empire), and their evolution since 1946. This collaborative effort by an economist and a political scientist provides comprehensive historical background from the 17th-century French colonization to decolonization. Their treatment of D.O.M.'s politics, economy, and culture pays equal attention to institutions, processes and records, and to the specifics and commonalities of each "department" or "territory." Last two chapters offer valuable insights on the future of D.O.M.s within the francophone world. Packed with facts (and some factual errors of minor significance) and references, this indepth study, the first in English, is a definitive reference work on the subject. [APD]

1795 Arturo Morales Carrión: homenaje al historiador y humanista. San Juan: Centro de Estudios Avanzados de Puerto Rico y el Caribe, 1989. 302 p.: bibl., ill.

Essays in honor of noted Puerto Rican historian and statesman are written by distinguished colleagues and friends, each an authority in his field of expertise—philosophy, law, linguistics, ethnology, as well as history of education, institutions, and ideas. Articles vary in quality and should be examined separately. Volume also includes biographical information on Morales Carrión. [TMV]

1796 Bégot, Danielle. Les habitations-sucreries du littoral guadeloupéen et leur évolution. (*Caribena/Martinique*, 1, 1991, p. 149–190, bibl., photos, map)

Insightful essay is based on original research on coastal Guadeloupean communication network. Traces 18th-century changes as island's sugar economy moved from Basse-Terre coastal plantations to Grande-Terre inland plantations and as these were gradually replaced by sugar factories. Through four case studies, Bégot pinpoints specific factors in development of coastal plantations and their present vulnerability in a changing environment. [APD]

1797 Blakely, Allison. Blacks in the Dutch color spectrum: lexicography and racial imagery. (*Historian/Honor Society*, 54:4, Summer 1992, p. 657–668, facsims., plates)

Dutch maritime empire serves as case study of evolution of European perceptions of race and color since 16th century. Author concludes that visual depictions illustrate negative images of blacks. In written descriptions, however, attitudes vary greatly over time and from place to place. [RH]

1798 Campbell, Carl C. Colony & nation: a short history of education in Trinidad & Tobago, 1834–1986. Kingston: IRP, 1992. 134 p.: bibl., index.

Extremely useful examination of education in Trinidad and Tobago from slavery to 1980s. Author covers British system, emergence of popular education after slavery, role of technical schools, the reform and expansion of educational opportunities from 1930s, and churches' contribution in educational effort. [ELC]

1799 Castellanos, Jorge and **Isabel Castellanos.** Cultura afrocubana. v. 2, El negro en Cuba, 1845–1959. Miami, Fla.: Ediciones Universal, 1990. 1 v. (Col. Ebano y canela)

This laboriously constructed synthesis of history of Cuban blacks concludes with the year 1959. Authors chose, perhaps wisely, to leave account of events under the Revolution to future historians. A major contribution. [JMH]

1800 Castellanos, Jorge and **Isabel Castellanos.** Cultura afrocubana. v. 3, Las religiones y las lenguas. Miami, Fla.: Ediciones Universal, 1992. 1 v. (Col. Ebano y canela)

Perhaps the most interesting and original volume (thus far) of this comprehensive study of Cuban blacks and their contribution to national culture. Relies heavily on extensive research by the noted Cuban ethnologist Lydia Cabrera. [JMH]

1801 Cepero Bonilla, Raúl. Escritos históricos. La Habana: Editorial de Ciencias Sociales, 1989. 370 p. (Economía)

Includes *Azúcar y abolición* (see *HLAS 15:1665*), one of the most influential revisionist writings published in Cuba in the last few decades. Other works such as *Política azucarera* are much less valuable except as good examples of historical and economic radicalism. [JMH]

1802 Conjonction: Revue Franco-Haitienne. Nos. 188/189 (special), 1991- . Ancienne Cathédrale de Port-au-Prince. Port-au-Prince: Institut français d'Haiti.

Special issue on the old cathedral of

Port-au-Prince looks at its 18th-century architecture and its significance for parishioners. Total destruction of the building during recent political disturbances gives particular value to this collective undertaking initially intended to document restoration program. [APD]

1803 Craton, Michael and **D. Gail Saunders.** Islanders in the stream: a history of the Bahamian people. v. 1, From aboriginal times to the end of slavery. Athens: Univ. of Georgia Press, 1992. 1 v.: bibl., ill., index, maps.

Thorough treatment examines history of the Bahamas from precolumbian times to abolition of slavery in 1838. Addresses adaptation of migrant peoples to life in scattered islands, and emphasizes realities of life for them: slavery, race and class divisions, and, finally, struggle for freedom as precursor to demands for national independence. [ELC]

Delval, Raymond. Les Musulmans en Amérique latine et aux Caraïbes. See item **863.**

1804 Desmangles, Leslie Gérald. The faces of the gods: vodou and Roman Catholicism in Haiti. Chapel Hill: Univ. of North Carolina Press, 1992. 218 p.: bibl., ill., index, map.

Examines folk religion of Haiti: its beliefs, deities and rituals. Religious specialist explains formation of voodoo as a "juxtaposition" of West African traditions and European Catholicism. See also item **1909.** [APD]

1805 Dix ans de publications sur la Guyane, 1979–1989. Cayenne: Comité de la culture, de l'éducation et de l'environnement, 1989. 59 p.: index.

Useful work lists 10 years of publications in French Guiana: scholarly studies, children's books, and scientific research linked to French aerospace experiments. [APD]

1806 Dwarswaard, Esther. De Nederlandse zending onder indianen, in voor-koloniale en koloniale periode: geschriften over en door indianen [Dutch mission to the Indians, in the precolonial and colonial period: writings by and about Indians]. (*Wampum/Leiden,* 11, 1992, p. 83–102, bibl., ill.)

Overview of Dutch missionary activity in New World after 1492 covers major zones of Dutch influence. Discusses what these missionaries have written about their own lives and those of the indigenous peoples. [RH]

First encounters: Spanish explorations in the Caribbean and the United States, 1492–1570. See *HLAS 53:598.*

1807 Franco, José Luciano. Africanos y sus descendientes criollos en las luchas libertadoras, 1533–1895. (*Bol. Arch. Nac./ Cuba,* 4, 1990, p. 1–14)

Summary of involvement of blacks in Cuba's independence movement is helpful, although somewhat hagiographic in tone and not entirely devoid of errors. Author does not mention his sources and demonstrates his usual neglect of analysis. [JMH]

1808 Franco Pichardo, Franklin J. Historia del pueblo dominicano. Santo Domingo: Instituto del Libro, 1992. 2 v.

Very useful survey of Dominican history covers the period of discovery and conquest to post-Trujillo era. Unfortunately author chose not to append a bibliography to his work nor to mention the 2,000 bibliographical references which, according to the cover, back up his narrative. [JMH]

1809 García Muñiz, Humberto and **Betsaida Vélez Natal.** Bibliografía militar del Caribe. Río Piedras: Univ. de Puerto Rico, 1992. 177 p. (Serie Bibliográfica; 1)

Exhaustive, unannotated bibliography of scholarly books and articles, government publications, dissertations, and pamphlets is divided by linguistic region. Covers military, paramilitary, and police forces, as well as foreign presence. [TMV]

1810 Guillermo, Jorge. Cuba: five hundred years of images. Photographs by Brynn Bruyn. New York: Abaris Books; Amsterdam: Thoth, s.d. 143 p.: photos.

Visual history of Cuba uses historical documents and recent photographs, more than 40 of which are full-page and in color. First chapter shows how Cuba might have looked before arrival of Columbus, while the last covers era of US intervention and the start of the republic. [RH]

1811 Hall, Neville. Slave society in the Danish West Indies: St. Thomas, St. John, and St. Croix. Edited by Barry W. Higman. Baltimore: Johns Hopkins Univ. Press, 1992. 287 p.: bibl., index. (Johns Hopkins studies in Atlantic history and culture)

Articles and unpublished material by late historian are artfully assembled and edited by Barry Higman. Result is excellent synthesis on societies with a small slaveholding pattern and a diversified economy. [APD]

1812 Handler, Jerome S. Supplement to *A guide to source materials for the study of Barbados history, 1627–1834.* Providence, R.I.: John Carter Brown Library and Barbados Museum and Historical Society, 1991. 89 p., 3 p. of plates: ill., index.

Contains almost 300 entries on Barbados that were either not included in author's earlier *Guide* (see *HLAS 35:1158*), or that needed additional annotation. Although most entries were published before 1834, author has included some which contain first-hand information applicable to earlier years. Essential for students of Barbados history during slavery. [ELC]

1813 Haraksingh, Kusha R. The Hindu experience in Trinidad. (*in* Indians in the Caribbean. Edited by I.J. Bahadur Singh. New Delhi: Sterling Publishers Private Ltd., 1987, p. 167–184)

Author seeks to discover full meaning of Hindu experience in Trinidad and to ascertain its significance in social and economic change. Argues that " . . . Hindu approach has been able to devise a mechanism to reduce conflict and to foster an accommodation between tradition and a Western setting." [ELC]

1814 Hartog, Johannes. De geschiedenis van twee landen: de Nederlandse Antillen en Aruba: met een recente historische bibliografie. Zaltbommel, The Netherlands: Europese Bibliotheek, 1993. 183 p.: bibl., ill., index, maps.

Richly-illustrated general introduction to history of Dutch Caribbean islands. First half covers precolumbian times to 19th century. Second half deals with 20th-century topics: oil industry, relations with The Netherlands, and constitutional developments. Includes chronology and extensive bibliography. [RH]

1815 Hill, Errol. The Jamaican stage, 1655–1900: profile of a colonial theatre. Amherst: Univ. of Massachusetts Press, 1992. 346 p.: bibl., index.

Excellent study catalogs different groups and companies, including resident amateurs, which performed in colonial Ja-

maica. Contains useful appendices of productions in 1783, and catalog of original Jamaican plays. Extremely useful for cultural/social history, especially for changing values in post-emancipation Jamaica. [ELC]

1816 Huijgers, Dolf and **Lucky Ezechiëls.** Landhuizen van Curaçao en Bonaire [Country houses of Curaçao and Bonaire]. Amsterdam: Persimmons, 1992. 286 p.: appendices, bibl., graphs, photos.

Coffee-table book on country houses of Curaçao and Bonaire describes history and architecture of each house. Introduction gives brief history of Curaçao and island's plantations. Includes more than 350 color photographs. [RH]

1817 Hurault, Jean. Fransen en Indianen in Frans Guiana: eerste kolonisatiepogingen aan het eind van de achttiende eeuw [French and Amerindians in French Guiana: first attempts at colonization in the late eighteenth century]. (*SWI Forum,* 9:1/2, okt. 1992, p. 25–69, bibl., ill., maps)

Summarizes most important historical accounts of colonization attempts in French Guiana in 17th and 18th centuries. Author discusses attempts to settle along the Amazon, Jesuit missions in the coastal areas, and 18th-century assimilation policy. Article closes with brief overview of social and economic condition of the Amerindians in 1992. [RH]

1818 Jews in the Caribbean: evidence on the history of the Jews in the Caribbean zone in colonial times. Compiled by Zvi Loker. Jerusalem: Misgav Yerushalayim, Institute for Research on the Sephardi and Oriental Jewish Heritage, 1991. 411 p.: bibl., facsims., indexes, maps.

Welcome selection of original documents from Caribbean, American and European collections is supplemented by extensive bibliography. Document covers diverse aspects of early Caribbean Jewish communities: settlements, geography of migrations, international trade networks, plantation activities, religious life, and networks. [APD]

Jha, J.C. Hinduism in Trinidad. See *HLAS 53: 1014.*

1819 Keegan, William F. The people who discovered Columbus: the prehistory of the Bahamas. Gainesville: Univ. Press of Florida, 1992. 279 p.: bibl., ill., index. (Ripley P. Bullen series. Columbus quincentenary series)

Arguing that scholars' overreliance on Columbus' journal has contributed to "significant misinterpretations of the prehistoric record," author uses ethnohistorical clarifications, ethnographic accounts of modern populations, and archaeological investigations to provide reinterpretation of precolumbian Bahamian history. [ELC]

1820 Lipsch, Maurice. Amerikaanse flora en fauna in Nederland [American flora and fauna in The Netherlands]. (*Wampum/ Leiden*, 11, 1992, p. 40–61, ill.)

Gives overview of American plants and animals introduced into The Netherlands. In particular, the West India Company and John Maurits van Nassau (the Governor-General of Dutch Brazil) played important roles in transferring knowledge about these new products and animals. [RH]

1821 López Sánchez, José. Ciencia y medicina: historia de la medicina. La Habana: Editorial Científico-Técnica, 1986. 409 p.

Essays are devoted primarily to history of medicine in Cuba. Their value is very uneven: some are truly interesting and even ground-breaking; others, as those dealing with Finlay and his scientific accomplishments, are too politically charged. [JMH]

López Segrera, Francisco. Sociología de la colonia y neocolonia cubana, 1510–1959. See *HLAS 53:5166.*

1822 Martínez Almánzar, Juan Francisco. Manual de historia crítica dominicana. v. 1, 1492–1865. Santo Domingo: Centro de Adiestramiento e Investigación Social; Asociación de Excursionistas Académicos, 1991. 1 v.: bibl., ill., maps.

Modest book, but worthwhile for author's revisionist approach and his novel views of men and events. [JMH]

1823 Mason, Peter. Amerika zonder begin of eind [America without beginning or end]. (*Wampum/Leiden*, 11, 1992, p. 1–15, ill.)

Gives overview of European, especially Dutch, images of indigenous peoples as presented in paintings, literature, and objects deposited in museums. Some of these images

were realistic, while others were symbolic and contrasted civilized Europe with mysterious South America. [RH]

1824 Mesa León, Marisol; Reinaldo Ramos Hernández; and Maylene Gayoso Leiva. Los servicios informativos en el Archivo Nacional de Cuba. (*Rev. Cuba. Cienc. Soc.*, 8:23, mayo/agosto 1990, p. 31–41, bibl., tables)

Useful for anyone planning to do research in the Archivo Nacional de Cuba. [JMH]

1825 Mouren-Lascaux, Patrice. La Guyane. Paris: Karthala, 1990. 186 p., 12 p. of plates: bibl., ill. (Méridiens)

Written by well-informed French high official, work nicely blends socioeconomic data on contemporary situation with history. Stresses contribution of immigrant communities: 18th-century African Maroon slaves, 19th-century Chinese indentured labor, and recent Haitian refugees. [APD]

1826 Mousnier, Mireille and Brigitte Caille. Atlas historique du patrimoine sucrier de la Martinique, XVIIe-XXe s. Paris: L'Harmattan, 1990. 103 p., 16 p. of plates: bibl., ill.

Addition to emerging field of environmental history in Caribbean lists main map collections that document Martinique's sugar economy. Analyzes five maps (1670, 1770, 1820, 1882, and 1955), and traces key changes in sugar plantations, central factories and sugar distilleries, and communications network. Shows that earliest plantations have almost totally disappeared or have been completely altered as they were absorbed into larger production units. [APD]

1827 Mousnier, Mireille. Occupation spatiale des habitations littorales à la Martinique. (*Caribena/Martinique*, 1, 1991, p. 123–146, bibl., photos, maps)

Shows that Martinique communication in 17th and 18th centuries relied upon a network of coastal plantations. These were marginalized in 19th century by development of inland sugar factories; the development of railroad and road networks provided privileged access to the sea for a few. [APD]

1828 Naranjo Orovio, Consuelo and Miguel Angel Puig-Samper Mulero. El legado hispano y la conciencia nacional en Cuba. (*Rev. Indias*, 50:190, sept./dic. 1990, p. 789–808)

Although central theme of article is not entirely divorced from reality, it is too ambitious to be compressed into a 20-page study. As a result, treatment of subject appears deficient and superficial. [JMH]

1829 Orozco, Carla. La educación en la historiografía puertorriqueña. (*Op. Cit./ Río Piedras*, 6, 1991, p. 40–64)

Writings reviewed are grouped into 19th- and 20th-century assessments of trajectory of education. Author concludes that evaluations of public instruction system are indicative of scholars' own political preference (pro-US or nostalgic for Spanish past). [TMV]

1830 Othily, Arthur. Eléments de chronologie Aluku. Cayenne: ORSTOM, Centre de Cayenne, 1988. 16 leaves: bibl. (Série Dynamismes sociaux et développement)

Amateur historian gathered scholarly materials on one of the Boni Maroon groups which lives in today's French Guiana. [APD]

Pérez, Louis A. Cuba and the United States: ties of singular intimacy. See *HLAS 53:4697.*

1831 Pieterse, Evelien. Amerika binnen handbereik [America within reach]. (*Wampum/Leiden*, 11, 1992, p. 16–39, bibl., ill.)

Deals with European fascination for the New World. Because it was too expensive and dangerous for most people to actually cross the Atlantic, the exotic New World was brought to Europe in the form of plants, animals, objects, and people. Article provides several examples of indigenous peoples exhibited in Europe from 16th century to present. [RH]

1832 Poyo, Gerald E. The Cuban experience in the United States, 1865–1940: migration, community, and identity. (*Cuba. Stud.*, 21, 1991, p. 19–36)

Focuses primarily on migration of Cuban tobacco workers to US and their role in Cuban exile communities. Relies heavily on printed sources. [JMH]

1833 Rigau, Jorge. Puerto Rico, 1900: turn-of-the-century architecture in the Hispanic Caribbean, 1890–1930. New York: Rizzoli, 1992. 232 p.: bibl., ill. (some col.), index, maps.

Author defines architectural modernism as a movement parallel to that in litera-

ture. Elements such as exoticism (orientalism), cosmopolitanism, experimentation, "departure from stated precepts [going] hand in hand with recognition of the original sources," opulence, colors, gardens, spatial sequences, praise of urban and rural life appeared both in the poems of Luis Lloréns Torres, Virgilio Dávila, and Evaristo Ribera Chevremont, and in the architecture of Antonín Nechodema, Alfredo Weichers, Juan Bértoli Carderoni, Blas Silva Boucher, and Manuel V. Domenech. Author's narrative weaves together changes in conceptualizations of space, transformations in economy and society due to US political domination, and literary manifestations of reinterpretation of American future with European past. [TMV]

1834 Román, Madeline. El movimiento de mujeres y la politización de la vida cotidiana: algunas reflexiones en torno al problema del poder. (*Rev. Cienc. Soc./Río Piedras*, 27:3/4, sept./dic. 1988, p. 69–80)

Author contends that the intrusion of capitalism into the sphere of reproduction forces new conceptualizations of women's role in working class and in political organizations. Reinforces notion that the personal is political. [TMV]

1835 Sáez, José Luis. La Compañía de Jesús y la devoción popular Dominicana. (*Arch. Hist. Soc. Iesu*, 54:117, enero/junio 1990, p. 93–103)

Author is the foremost historian of Jesuit order in the Caribbean. Article lives up to his high standards of objectivity and scholarship. [JMH]

1836 Salabarría Abraham, Berarda and **Luis Frades Santos.** El archivo nacional de Cuba: balance y perspectiva. (*Rev. Cuba. Cienc. Soc.*, 8:23, mayo/agosto 1990, p. 18–24)

Provides useful information about the Archivo Nacional de Cuba. [JMH]

1837 Samaroo, Brinsley. The Indian connection: the influence of Indian thought and ideas on East Indians in the Caribbean. (*in* Indians in the Caribbean. Edited by I.J. Bahadur Singh. New Delhi: Sterling Publishers Private Limited, 1987, p. 103–121, bibl.)

Author traces how East Indians in the Caribbean have maintained closeness with their ancestral home—through dance, song, films, and religion. Issues a plea for other East Indians both to understand how their ancestors coped with their sojourn in the new land and to give new meaning to their experiences. [ELC]

1838 Scholtens, Ben. Indianen en Bosnegers, een historisch wisselvallige verhouding [Amerindians and Maroons, a historically unstable relationship]. (*SWI Forum*, 9:1/2, okt. 1992, p. 70–98, bibl., ill.)

Discusses relationships between Amerindians and Maroons from 16th century to present. Government policies had a negative influence on these relations. Nonetheless, trade between the two groups occurred and relations were strengthened by migrations in the 19th century. The civil war (1986–92), however, exposed latent animosity between Maroons and Amerindians once again. [RH]

1839 Thompson, Donald and **Annie F. Thompson.** Music and dance in Puerto Rico from the age of Columbus to modern times: an annotated bibliography. Metuchen, N.J.: Scarecrow Press, 1991. 339 p.: indexes. (Studies in Latin American music; 1)

Comprehensive annotated bibliography is organized by type of work: bibliographies; reference material, general histories, and collected essays; biographies, interviews, and eulogies; panoramic surveys of music and dance; chronicles, travel pieces, and early histories; concert music, church music, and music instruction; lyric theater and ballet; traditional folk music and dance; urban music and dance; *danzas;* "La Borinqueña" (national anthem); and miscellaneous. Has subject and author index. [TMV]

1840 Venegas Delgado, Hernán. Métodos, fuentes y procedimientos de la historia regional cubana: algunas ideas. (*Islas/Santa Clara*, 94, sept./dic. 1989, p. 75–85)

Includes interesting discussion of archival sources available in Cuba for historical investigation. [JMH]

1841 Vieira, Jean L. De geschiedenis van de kleding op Aruba: van natuurmens tot een cultureel mozaïek [The history of clothing on Aruba: from natural state to cultural mosaic]. Oranjestad, Aruba: Charuba, 1990. 61 p.: bibl., ill. (some col.).

Provides introduction to clothing, and to clothing, shoe, and hatter industries, from precolumbian times to present. Author pays more attention to daily clothing and accessories of well-to-do classes than to folk traditions. [RH]

1842 Voyage aux iles d'Amérique. Paris: Archives nationales, 1992. 310 p.: bibl., ill., maps.

Catalog of an exhibition to commemorate 1492 anniversary includes annotations of documents and artifacts displayed, as well as thematic essays that throw light on many facets of French colonial Caribbean. [APD]

1843 Wekker, Justus B. Archiefdocumenten verhalen over Indianen [Archival documents tell about Amerindians]. (*SWI Forum*, 9:1/2, okt. 1992, p. 99–127, maps)

Inventory of archival sources in Suriname on social history of Amerindians focuses on contacts between various Amerindian groups and their relationships with Maroons, the government, and the Church. Sources used are the *West-Indisch plakaatboek* (West Indian book of decrees), collected writings of the missionary F. Staëlin, the State Archives of Suriname, and the archives of the Roman Catholic diocese of Paramaribo. [RH]

1844 Wild Majesty: encounters with Caribs from Columbus to the present day: an anthology. Edited by Peter Hulme and Neil L. Whitehead. Oxford, England: Clarendon Press; New York: Oxford Univ. Press, 1992. 369 p.: bibl., ill., index, maps.

Central theme of these narratives is assumptions and ideologies about Caribs embraced by Europeans and their descendants. Includes selections by military leaders, travelers, missionaries, ethnographers, and colonial administrators. [ELC]

1845 Zanetti Lecuona, Oscar and **Alejandro García Alvarez.** Caminos para el azúcar. La Habana: Editorial de Ciencias Sociales, 1987. 417 p.: bibl., ill., maps. (Historia de Cuba)

This is probably the first comprehensive history on Cuban railroads. Despite its sectarianism, this is a serious and carefully researched work. [JMH]

1846 Zanetti Lecuona, Oscar. Los cautivos de la reciprocidad: la burguesia cubana y la dependencia comercial. La Habana: Depto. de Historia de Cuba, Univ. de La Habana; Ministerio de Educación Superior, 1989. 220 p.: bibl.

Attempts to explain historically the development of Cuba's commercial dependence on the US. Although partisan, this is a serious work that cannot be ignored. [JMH]

EARLY COLONIAL

1847 Alegría, Ricardo E. Juan Garrido, el conquistador negro en las Antillas, Florida, México y California c. 1503–1540. San Juan: Centro de Estudios Avanzados de Puerto Rico y el Caribe, 1990. 140 p.: bibl., ill. (some col.)

Book documents life of Juan Garrido, a free black who traveled to America from Africa by way of Lisbon, during early colonial period. Principal source is *probanza* of 1538, asking Crown for favors based on performance during conquest. Author is careful to contextualize many of events in Garrido's life with wide array of secondary literature. Particularly novel is use of Mexican iconography to illustrate participation of Garrido in conquest of Mexico. *Probanza* is included as an appendix. Unfortunately, layout gives impression of an elementary school book. [TMV]

1848 Arranz Márquez, Luis. Repartimientos y encomiendas en la Isla Española: el repartimiento de Albuquerque de 1514. Madrid: Ediciones Fundación García Arévalo, 1991. 640 p.: bibl., ill., index. (Serie documental Fundación García Arévalo; 2)

In addition to new information, work contains illuminating statistics on *encomenderos*, indigenous peoples, caciques, demographic mobility, and social groups. Serious scholarly work is based on just the right combination of primary and secondary sources. [JMH]

1849 Baud, Michiel. A colonial counter economy: tobacco production on Española, 1500–1870. (*Nieuwe West-Indische Gids*, 65:1/2, 1991, p. 27–49, bibl.)

Case study shows one of the many failures of Spanish colonial centralism. Based primarily on secondary sources. [JMH]

1850 Beckles, Hilary. White servitude and Black slavery in Barbados, 1627–1715. Knoxville: Univ. of Tennessee Press, 1989. 218 p.: bibl., ill., index.

Impressive study examines transformation of paternalistic indentured labor into market system of black servitude during early

years of plantation agriculture in Barbados. Author shows how race and color ideologies became intertwined, and how this development affected division of labor in Barbados and other British Caribbean islands. [ELC]

1851 Boucher, Philip P. Cannibal encounters: Europeans and Island Caribs, 1492–1763. Baltimore: Johns Hopkins Univ. Press, 1992. 217 p.: bibl., ill., index. (Johns Hopkins studies in Atlantic history and culture)

This longitudinal study of indigenous peoples from prior to Europeans' arrival in the region up to deportation of last groups in 18th century fills a vacuum in the literature. Demonstrates Caribs' entanglement in Anglo-French colonial rivalry. Last chapter shows image of Caribs in Western thought and literature evolving from "ignoble" to "noble." [APD]

1852 Boucher, Philip P. Les Nouvelles Frances: France in America, 1500–1815, an imperial perspective. Providence, R.I.: John Carter Brown Library, 1989. 122 p.: bibl., ill., index, maps.

Authoritative list of major narratives on early French settlements in the Caribbean is preceded by excellent survey of French colonization. [APD]

1853 Camus, Michel Christian. A Saint-Domingue en 1687. (*Rev. Soc. häiti.*, 47:171, déc. 1991, p. 1–12)

Welcome new publication of official report documents early colonization of Haiti: geography of settlements; economy of tobacco production and hunting feral cattle; and difficult beginning of royal control over buccaneers. [APD]

1854 Camus, Michel Christian. Une note critique à propos d'Exquemelin. (*Rev. fr. hist. Outre-mer*, 77:286, 1990, p. 79–90)

Elucidates some of the mysteries surrounding author of 17th-century bestseller on buccaneers in America entitled *De Americaensche zee-roovers* (Amsterdam: 1678). [APD]

1855 Chauleau, Liliane. Case-pilote, Le Prêcheur, Basse-Pointe: étude démographique sur le nord de la Martinique, XVIIe siècle. Préface de Jean Ganiage. Paris: L'Harmattan, 1990. 188 p.: bibl., ill.

Demographic study of more than 3,000

whites and free coloreds in northern Martinique (1680–1715) is based on parish records and two censuses. Concludes that: 1) women married 10 years younger than men; 2) low birth rate points to underregistration of infant mortality; and 3) rural parishes were relatively spared yellow fever epidemics. [APD]

1856 Dobal, Carlos. El primer apostol del Nuevo Mundo: biografía de Fray Bernardo Boyl, vicario apostólico en América Latina y celebrante de la primera misa. Santiago, Dominican Republic: Univ. Católica Madre y Maestra, 1991. 153 p.: ill. (Col. Estudios)

Makes plausible attempt to vindicate memory of the priest who celebrated the first mass in the New World, a priest whose reputation was tarnished by his troubles with Columbus. Uses some primary sources but draws heavily on several previous books. [JMH]

1857 Fuente García, Alejandro de la. Azúcar y esclavitud en Cuba en el siglo XVII: elementos para un análisis. (*Bol. Arch. Nac./ Cuba*, 2, 1989, p. 44–63, bibl., graphs, tables)

Respectable contribution to our knowledge of early development of Cuba's sugar industry is based on printed and archival sources. [JMH]

1858 Fuente García, Alejandro de la. Esclavos africanos en La Habana: zonas de procedencia y denominaciones étnicas, 1570–1699. (*Rev. Esp. Antropol. Am.*, 20, 1990, p. 135–160, graphs, tables)

As the author points out, much research remains to be done on this subject. This scholarly article, though, is a significant contribution and will be useful to future researchers. [JMH]

1859 Fuente García, Alejandro de la. Los ingenios de azúcar en La Habana del siglo XVII, 1640–1700: estructura y mano de obra. (*Rev. Hist. Econ.*, 9:1, invierno 1991, p. 35–67, bibl., graphs, tables)

Good study examines pre-plantation phase of Cuba's sugar industry. Documents quite satisfactorily differences between exploitation of sugar cane during that period and that which followed. Balanced and well researched. [JMH]

1860 Fuente García, Alejandro de la. Los matrimonios de esclavos en La Habana, 1585–1645. (*Ibero-Am. Arch.*, 16:4, 1990, p. 507–528)

Based primarily on previously neglected materials from ecclesiastical archives, this excellent article is required reading for all those interested in Cuba's population and society in early colonial period. [JMH]

1861 Fuente García, Alejandro de la. El mercado esclavista habanero, 1580–1699: las armazones de esclavos. (*Rev. Indias*, 50: 189, mayo/agosto 1990, p. 371–395, graphs, tables)

Solid piece of scholarship is highly recommended. [JMH]

1862 García del Pino, César and **Alejandro de la Fuente García.** Apuntes sobre la historiografía de la segunda mitad del siglo XVI cubano. (*Santiago/Cuba*, 71, dic. 1988, p. 59–117, appendix, bibl.)

Despite obvious prejudices of the authors, work is excellent bibliographical essay that contains some sharp comments and observations. [JMH]

1863 Gaspar, David Barry. Slave importation, runaways, and compensation in Antigua, 1720–1729. (*in* The Atlantic slave trade: effects on economies, societies, and peoples in Africa, the Americas, and Europe. Edited by Joseph E. Inikori and Stanley L. Engerman. Durham, N.C.: Duke Univ. Press, 1992, p. 301–320, bibl., tables)

Through examination of compensation claims in Antigua, author concludes that while slave importation apparently led to high levels of runaways, masters vigorously prosecuted slaves who absconded because they could rely on local markets for replacements. [ELC]

1864 Haudrere, Philippe. Les premiers colons de Léogane. (*in* Commerce et plantation dans la Caraïbe, XVIIIe et XIX siècles: actes du Colloque de Bordeaux, 15–16 mars 1991. Bordeaux: Centre d'histoire des espaces atlantiques; Maison des pays ibériques, 1992, p. 71–79)

Analysis of oldest parish records kept for colonial Haiti concerning marriage of 2,264 individuals in parish of St. Rose of Léogane (1666–1735) throws light on social origin and life of early colonists. [APD]

1865 Huerga, Alvaro. El Concilio Provincial del Santo Domingo, 1622/3. (*Quinto Cent.*, 16, 1990, p. 101–119)

Solid piece of scholarship examines vicissitudes of this obscure council. [JMH]

1866 Lespagnol, André. Les Malouins dans l'espace caraïbe au début du XVIIIe siècle: la tentation de l'interlope. (*in* Commerce et plantation dans la Caraïbe, XVIIIe et XIXe siècles: actes du Colloque de Bordeaux, 15–16 mars 1991. Bordeaux: Centre d'histoire des espaces atlantiques; Maison des pays ibériques, 1992, p. 9–25, maps, table)

This small port in French Brittany specialized in contraband with Spanish American colonies (1698–1725) after being excluded from the trade monopoly granted by the State to major French Atlantic ports. [APD]

1867 López Cantos, Angel. La vida cotidiana del negro en Puerto Rico en el siglo XVIII: alimentación. (*Rev. Cent. Estud. Av.*, 4, enero/junio 1987, p. 147–155)

Compares 18th-century urban and rural slaves in terms of food consumption and dress. Sources include laws from Archivo General de Indias. Little analysis of motivations of master or slave groups in making legal provisions more flexible. [TMV]

1868 Menezes, Mary Noel. The controversial question of protection and jurisdiction re: the Amerindians of Guyana. (*SWI Forum*, 9:1/2, okt. 1992, p. 7–24, bibl., ill., map)

Discusses Dutch and English colonial policy regarding native inhabitants of (British) Guiana. The Dutch forged a good relationship with the Amerindians because success in trade depended on peace and friendliness. British continued the Dutch policy. [RH]

1869 Moreau, Jean-Pierre. Les Petites Antilles de Christophe Colomb à Richelieu, 1493–1635. Paris: Karthala, 1992. 319 p.: bibl., ill. (some col.), index.

Factual treatment of French, English, and Dutch presence in the Caribbean prior to the founding of colonies fills a lacuna in French literature. Traces maritime movements of northwestern Europeans, their privateering raids against the Spaniards, and interaction with the Caribs. Uses original Spanish documents to describe Spaniards' shrinking presence in the Lesser Antilles. [APD]

Morrissey, Marietta. Slave women in the New World: gender stratification in the Caribbean. See *HLAS 53:1036.*

1870 Moscoso, Francisco. El alzamiento de los esclavos *biohoes* en Puerto Rico, 1564–1569. (*Rev. Cent. Estud. Av.*, 9, julio/dic. 1989, p. 85–94)

Uses *probanza* of Alonso Moreno to examine mid-16th-century uprising by slaves belonging to specific ethnic group. Locates African origins of slaves; reconstructs mode of production in early period; and speculates on motives of witnesses in order to illuminate social and economic aspects of life in 16th century. [TMV]

Oostindie, Gert. Voltaire, Stedman and Suriname slavery. See item **2069.**

1871 Postma, Johannes. The dispersal of African slaves in the West by Dutch slave traders, 1630–1803. (*in* The Atlantic slave trade: effects on the economies, societies, and peoples in Africa, the Americas, and Europe. Durham, N.C.: Duke Univ. Press, 1992, p. 283–299, bibl., tables)

Study delineates destination of slaves transported by Dutch across the Atlantic. Activities are broken down into convenient time spans to facilitate correlation with comparable studies. During 1630–1803 period, Dutch slavers exported approximately 543,000 slaves from Africa, of which 15 percent lost their lives before arrival. Destinations shifted from Brazil to Spanish America and then to the Guianas. [RH]

1872 Ramos Gómez, Luis J. La construcción y destrucción del fuerte de La Navidad en 1493: un ejemplo de conquista y de resistencia. (*in* Encuentros Debate América Latina Ayer y Hoy, *3rd, Barcelona, 1991.* Conquista y resistencia en la historia de América. Coordinación de Pilar García Jordán y Miquel Izard. Barcelona: Publicacions Univ. de Barcelona, 1992, p. 45–60, bibl.)

Author reinterprets available historical evidence to argue that the position of Spaniards left behind in Hispaniola after Columbus' first voyage vis-à-vis the natives was not that of conquerors but of subordinates of the local chiefs. [JMH]

1873 Río Moreno, Justo del and **Lorenzo E. López y Sebastián.** El comercio azucarero de La Española en el siglo XVI: presión monopolística y alternativas locales. (*Rev. Complut. Hist. Am.*, 17, 1991, p. 39–78, bibl., maps)

Focuses on one of the lesser known aspects of the history of sugar. Based on extensive archival research. [JMH]

1874 Rosenblat, Angel. The population of Hispaniola at the time of Columbus. (*in* The native population of the Americas in

1492. Edited by William M. Denevan. Madison: Univ. of Wisconsin Press, 1992, p. 43–66, map)

Author defends his previous calculation of Hispaniola's population at the time of the discovery, apparently with great success. [JMH]

1875 Rossignol, Bernadette and **Philippe Rossignol.** L'origine de la paroisse Saint-François de Basse-Terre à la Guadeloupe. (*Généal. hist. Caräíbe*, 44, déc. 1992, p. 694–698)

Document dating from 1673 that throws light on early history of Basse-Terre, Guadeloupe's capital city, is published in this article. [APD]

1876 Roura, Norma. Una botica de principios del siglo XVII. (*Bol. Arch. Nac./Cuba*, 2, 1989, p. 5–19, bibl., tables)

Provides fascinating description of the stock of an apothecary shop in Havana in early 17th century. [JMH]

1877 Smith, E. Valerie. Early Afro-American presence on the island of Hispaniola: a case study of the "immigrants" of Samaná. (*J. Negro Hist.*, 72:1/2, Winter/Spring 1987, p. 33–41)

Informative and interesting work is based largely on interviews with residents of the area. [JMH]

1878 Sorhegui, Arturo. ¿Como se estructuró bajo la dominación española la primera ocupación del espacio de La Habana? (*Islas/Santa Clara*, 91, sept./dic. 1988, p. 3–19, maps, tables)

Account of pattern of Spanish colonial settlements in western Cuba is clear and concise; however, author unfortunately neglected to identify his sources. [JMH]

1879 St. Domingue, census records and military lists, 1688–1720. Translated and edited by Winston De Ville. Introduction by Thomas Fiehrer. Ville Platte, La.: W. De Ville, 1988. 40 p.: ill., index.

Family historians will make good use of these data on Haiti's earliest settlements (1688–1720), compiled from original sources and arranged systematically according to individuals. Introduction discusses type of sources and their reliability. [APD]

1880 Sued Badillo, Jalil. El cabildo sanjuanero durante la primera mitad del siglo XVI. (*Rev. Juríd. Univ. P.R.*, 60:1, 1991, p. 209–250)

Erudite account of first cabildos on the island explores conflict between Crown and settlers, and describes sources of income, functions, officials, and other institutional matters. [TMV]

1881 Sued-Badillo, Jalil. Christopher Columbus and the enslavement of Amerindians in the Caribbean. (*Mon. Rev.*, 44:3, July/Aug. 1992, p. 71–102)

Indicts Columbus as instrument of nascent capitalist world order. Depicts the Admiral as greedy, self-interested, and ultimately near-sighted. Suggests inevitability of slavery in New World. [TMV]

1882 Sued-Badillo, Jalil. Igreja e escravidão em Porto Rico do século XVI. (*in* Escravidão negra e história da Igreja na América Latina e no Caribe. Petrópolis, Brazil: Editora Vozes Ltda., 1987, p. 67–83, bibl., tables)

Author selected parts of his book *Puerto Rico negro* (see *HLAS 50:1559*) to highlight Church's ideological defense of slavery, its participation in early slave economy (mining and sugar), its collusion with dominant class to preserve hegemony, and resultant resistance on part of Africans. [TMV]

1883 Vega, Bernardo. Los cacicazgos de la Hispaniola. 2. ed. Santo Domingo: Fundación Cultural Dominicana, 1987. 87 p., 2 folded leaves of plates: bibl., maps (some col.).

Unless new documentation is unearthed by investigators, this work might well prove to be the definitive study of indigenous chiefdoms of Hispaniola at the time of Columbus' discovery. [JMH]

1884 Vergé-Franceschi, Michel. Fortunes et plantations des administrateurs coloniaux aux Iles d'Amérique au XVIIe et XVIIIe siècles. (*in* Commerce et plantation dans la Caräíbe, XVIIIe et XIXe siècles: actes du Colloque de Bordeaux, 15–16 mars 1991. Bordeaux: Centre d'histoire des espaces atlantiques; Maison des pays ibériques, 1992, p. 115–142)

Traces formation of a body of French colonial administrators (1635–1791), their training, career antecedents, and social and geographical origins. Provides biographical data on some 70 individuals. Emphasizes tendency of such individuals to acquire properties in territories they governed despite official prohibition. [APD]

1885 Wassén, S. Henry. Notes on a book concerning Dr. Chanca, ship's doctor during Columbus's second voyage to the West Indies in 1493. (° *Arstryck/Göteborg*, 1987/ 1988, p. 45–51, bibl.)

In this interesting bibliographical essay, emphasis is on Dr. Chanca's physiological experiments; however, it also includes an enlightening discussion of the sources for Columbus' second voyage. [JMH]

LATE COLONIAL AND FRENCH REVOLUTIONARY PERIOD

1886 Abénon, Lucien-René and **Mäiotte Dauphite.** Les guadeloupéens réfugiés à Saint Pierre de 1794 à 1796. Carbet, Martinique: Centre d'art Musée Paul Gauguin, 1990. 37 p.: ill., map.

Uses entries in vital records to identify Guadeloupe refugees to St. Pierre of Martinique during the French Revolution. Shows different waves, with climax in 1794–96. [APD]

1887 Adélaïde-Merlande, Jacques. La Caraïbe et la Guyane au temps de la Révolution et de l'Empire, 1789–1804. Paris: Karthala, 1992. 222 p.: bibl., ill. .

Standard account of revolutionary process in Haiti, Lesser Antilles, and French Guyana is notable for its effort to embrace varied settings and to trace repercussions beyond French Caribbean. [APD]

1888 Auguste, Claude B. Les Congos dans la révolution häitienne. (*Rev. Soc. häiti.*, 46:168, déc. 1990, p. 11–42)

Author focuses on contribution of Congo slaves to Haitian wars of independence. The most recent arrivals to Haiti, they practiced voodoo and were frequently Maroons. Author claims they adopted guerrilla tactics before others, but were mostly excluded from officer ranks by rebel leaders who had initially sided with the French. [APD]

1889 Auguste, Claude B. Toussaint Louverture et la Révolution française. (*Jahrb. Gesch.*, 28, 1991, p. 53–83)

Account of Haitian founding father's rise based on original documentation effectively delineates three moments marked by different goals: 1) 1791: fighting on the Spanish side, and later, the French side to achieve emancipation; 2) 1796: dismissing French revolutionary officials and concluding international alliances to seek independence; and 3) 1799: challenging French rule by drafting a constitution and occupying Spanish Santo Domingo to assume full powers. Author sees Toussaint's policy as "continuation of the anti-slavery dynamic" initiated by the French Revolution and arrested by Directoire and Consulat regimes (1795–1801). [APD]

1890 Auguste, Marcel B. L'Armée française de Saint-Domingue: dernière armée de la Revolution. (*Jahrb. Gesch.*, 28, 1991, p. 85–105)

Analyzes composition of the French army in St. Domingue during revolutionary wars (1793–1801): 1) emancipated slaves used as guerrillas; 2) veterans of war against Spain in Santo Domingo; 3) legions of former free coloreds from west and south of St. Domingue; and 4) French veterans from war against England in Lesser Antilles. Insists correctly on unprecedented "indigenization" of this colonial army. [APD]

1891 Barcia, María del Carmen. Influencias múltiples: Cuba y la Revolución Haitiana. (*Univ. La Habana*, 237, enero/abril 1990, p. 47–65)

Focuses on conservative impact on Cuban society of the French that migrated at the time of the Haitian Revolution, while neglecting to analyze influence of the masonic lodges they founded. Based on printed and archival sources. [JMH]

1892 Boisrond Tonnerre. Mémoires pour servir à l'histoire d'Häiti. Port-au-Prince: Editions des Antilles, 1991. 132 p.: bibl. (Col. Connaissance du passé)

Work is welcome reprint of earliest historical narrative on Haitian wars of independence. Introduction about the author—a free colored, a veteran of Dessalines' army, and a high official in the New Republic—explains *Mémoires*' thrust: the epic grandeur of a war which was fought against the horrors of slavery, thereby justifying its extreme violence. [APD]

Brana-Shute, Rosemary. Legal resistance to slavery in eighteenth century Suriname. See *HLAS 53:987.*

1893 Campbell, Carl C. Cedulants and capitulants: the politics of the coloured opposition in the slave society of Trinidad, 1783–1838. Port of Spain: Paria Pub. Co.,

1992. 429 p.: bibl., index. (University series; 1)
Long overdue study considers free coloreds in British Crown Colony who had attained their status under old Spanish laws and culture. When military governors sought to deny them rights previously guaranteed to them, free colored leadership petitioned British government to obtain both clarification of their legal status and improvement in their sociopolitical position. [ELC]

1894 Cauna, Jacques. Les comptes de la sucrerie Fleuriau: analyse de la rentabilité d'une plantation de Saint-Domingue au XVIIIe siècle. (*in* Commerce et plantation dans la Caraïbe, XVIIIe et XIXe siècles: actes du Colloque de Bordeaux, 15–16 mars 1991. Bordeaux: Centre d'histoire des espaces atlantiques; Maison des pays ibériques, 1992, p. 143–167)
Using case of a sugar plantation in 18th-century Saint-Domingue owned by leading merchant house of La Rochelle, author convincingly argues that plantation papers do not reflect all business arrangements and unlawful deals, and therefore constitute incomplete and misleading evidence about owners who were wealthy and socially successful. [APD]

Colón, María Judith. Historia de Isabela y su desarrollo urbano, 1750–1850. See item **1991.**

1895 Commerce et plantation dans la Caraïbe, XVIIIe et XIXe siècles: actes du Colloque de Bordeaux, 15–16 mars 1991. Coordination de Paul Butel. Bordeaux: Centre d'histoire des espaces atlantiques; Maison des pays ibériques, 1992. 260 p.: graphs, maps, tables. (Col. de la Maison des pays ibériques; 52)
Proceedings of a 1991 conference held at Univ. of Bordeaux III include fresh research on 17th-19th century in following areas: 1) contraband network undermining official colonial trade, and war economy of privateering; 2) economy and size of labor migrations of white indentured labor and African slaves; and 3) comparative assessment of investments, management, and profits for Spanish and French colonial plantations. For annotations on specific chapters see items **1866, 1995, 2097, 1899, 2126, 1864, 1884, 1894, 1938** and **1942.** [APD]

1896 Coppolani, Jean-Yves. Des Antillais déportés en Corse à l'époque napoléonienne. (*in* Mourir pour les Antilles: indépend-

ance nègre ou esclavage, 1802–1804. Paris: Editions caraïbéenes; Cayenne: Centre d'études et de recherches caraïbéenes, 1991, p. 189–199)
Work is first research on overlooked aspect of Guadeloupe insurrection of 1802: ex-members of the native revolutionary army deported by the French government to island of Corsica. [APD]

1897 Cottias, Myriam. A note on 18th- and 19th-century plantation inventories from Martinique. (*Nieuwe West-Indische Gids*, 64:1/2, 1990, p. 1–6, bibl., tables)
Identifies 38 female-centered families, representing 55 percent of slaves from lists of two Martinique plantations (1766). Contrasts members from old, stable families with newcomers who, lacking kinship ties, were more frequently sold. [APD]

1898 Crane, Elaine Forman. The socioeconomics of a female majority in eighteenth century Bermuda. (*Signs/Chicago*, 15:2, Winter 1990, p. 231–258)
Author argues that despite preponderance in 18th-century Bermuda of white women who had much control over various aspects of their lives, powerful social forces operated to ensure that these women made no discernible effort to challenge male hegemony in the political and economic realms. [ELC]

1899 Deveau, Jean-Michel. Les affaires Van Hoogwerff à Saint-Domingue de 1773 à 1791. (*in* Commerce et plantation dans la Caraïbe, XVIIIe et XIXe siècles: actes du Colloque de Bordeaux, 15–16 mars 1991. Bordeaux: Centre d'histoire des espaces atlantiques; Maison des pays ibériques, 1992, p. 169–181, table)
At peak era of slave trade for French port of La Rochelle, this merchant of modest Dutch origins invested and lost everything in the slave trade by not diversifying his activities to acquire plantations that would have supplied him with homebound cargoes of sugar and coffee at the best prices. [APD]

1900 Díaz Espada y Fernández de Landa, Juan José. Obispo Espada: ilustración, reforma y antiesclavismo. Selección, introducción y notas de Eduardo Torres-Cuevas. La Habana: Editorial de Ciencias Sociales, 1990. 317 p.: bibl. (Palabra de Cuba)
Author's introduction is followed by a

number of documents produced by Bishop Espada. Author radicalizes to an implausible degree Cuban historiography's traditional view of the Bishop. Clearly, he is not equipped to assess the Bishop's work as a Catholic prelate nor to deal seriously with some recent studies of this aspect of his career. [JMH]

1901 Dreyfus, Simone. Les Réseaux politiques indigènes en Guyane occidentale et leurs transformations aux XVIIIe siècles. (*Homme/Paris,* 122/124, avril/déc. 1992, p. 75–98, bibl.)

Author draws from her own field research on political organization of Caribs from islands and mainland coast and challenges views informed by Lévi-Strauss that the present-day political networks among limited numbers of kinship-based groups were immobile over time. Dreyfus argues that present-day networks differ widely from their previous form, which included occasional war alliances stemming from a belief in achieving identity through sacrificing prisoners. By using Carib networks to expand their trade, European merchants, particularly the Dutch in the 17th century, reoriented Caribs solely toward war and trade and aligned them along two sets of long-term European alliances. [APD]

1902 Escalle, Elisabeth and Mariel Gouyon Guillaume. Francs-Maçons des loges françaises aux Amériques, 1750–1850: contribution à l'étude de la société créole: dépouillement du Fonds maçonnique au département des manuscrits de la Bibliothèque nationale. Paris: Ed. E. Escalle, s.d. 865 p.: index, maps.

Very useful research tool on some 31 French Masonic Lodges established throughout colonial Caribbean offers: 1) analysis of correspondence and membership for each lodge; and 2) identification (origin, profession, etc.) of 4,623 Masons. Throws light on an important colonial organization. [APD]

1903 Fick, Carolyn E. The making of Haiti: the Saint Domingue revolution from below. Knoxville: Univ. of Tennessee Press, 1990. 355 p.: bibl., index.

Looks on revolution of St. Domingue-Haiti as "history from below" and "a clash of opposing forces." Author argues that "what took place from 1791 onward lies in the distrust of the slaves in regard to the white masters and in their hatred of the plantation,"

and that Maroon slaves turned into revolutionary rebels. Contains original research on troops of former slaves that fought in the Saint Domingue South. [APD]

1904 Fick, Carolyn E. The Saint Domingue slave insurrection of 1791: a sociopolitical and cultural analysis. (*J. Caribb. Hist.,* 25:1/2, 1991, p. 1–40)

States main conclusions of a larger study (see item **1903**), focusing on Bois-Câiman ceremony which allegedly sparked slave insurrection of August 1791. Credits ceremony with playing a role in preparation and execution of the insurrection. For another point of view see item **1908**. [APD]

1905 Fouchard, Jean. Plaisirs de Saint-Domingue: notes sur la vie sociale, littéraire et artistique. Port-au-Prince: H. Deschamps, 1988. 125 p.: bibl. (Regards sur le temps passé; 4)

Welcome new edition of a classic describes urban culture (literature, theater, popular entertainment) in late colonial Saint Domingue. This culture has been overlooked by historians due to its total disappearance in subsequent revolutionary process. [APD]

1906 Franco, José Luciano. La independencia de Estados Unidos y la diplomacia española. (*Bol. Arch. Nac./Cuba,* 4, 1990, p. 35–63)

Interesting study is based almost entirely on Spanish archival materials. Author provides much detailed information with minimal analysis. [JMH]

1907 García, Gloria. La exportación de moneda y el comercio de esclavos en Cuba, 1760–1800. (*Rábida/Huelva,* 11, marzo 1992, p. 73–81, tables)

Article is somewhat disappointing regarding treatment of exportation of currency, but provides interesting details about how slave trade was carried out in Cuba during this period. [JMH]

1908 Geggus, David. The Bois-Câiman ceremony. (*J. Caribb. Hist.,* 257:1/2, 1991, p. 41–57)

Geggus uses this meeting's subsequent significance for Haiti to authoritatively disentangle the actual meeting prior to the slave insurrection of northern Saint Domingue. Careful critique of evidence reveals that several slave meetings were fused into a single event which served to crystallize the meaning of Haitian independence for later generations. See also items **1909** and **1904**. [APD]

1909 Geggus, David. Haitian voodoo in the eighteenth century: language, culture, resistance. (*Jahrb. Gesch.*, 28, 1991, p. 21–51)
Examines "religious world of slaves who created Haiti." Careful critique of late printed versions of two voodoo chants leads author to refute Dahomey (Central African Bantu) origins of voodoo, and the assumption that Dahomey religious influence helped forge a national unity prior to the Haitian Revolution by providing ideology and leaders. Author substantiates instead: 1) overwhelming number of Benin (West African Congo) slaves in Saint Domingue by 1780 (particularly in the north where the insurrection took place), whose presence eroded earlier Dahomey influence; 2) ambiguous role of voodoo in colonial times that "may have equally promoted resistance and diffused tensions, or reinforced ethnic divisions;" and 3) leading role of Creoles (who reportedly mocked voodoo) in the insurrection. See also items **1908** and **1904**. [APD]

1910 La Guadeloupe: les Antilles et la Révolution française: itinéraires. Guadeloupe: Office régional du patrimoine guadeloupéen, 1991. 156 p.: col. ill., col. maps.
Contains handsome photographs of places of special relevance for the revolutionary era (1789–1802). [APD]

1911 Hoogbergen, Wim S.M. De Bosnegers zijn gekomen!: slavernij en rebellie in Suriname [The Bush Negroes have arrived! slavery and abolition in Suriname]. Amsterdam: Prometheus, 1992. 349 p.: bibl., ill., index, maps.
History of Boni Maroons in Suriname and French Guiana focuses on 18th-century Boni Maroon wars. Book is a revision of author's dissertation (1985), which was later translated into English (see *HLAS 52:1665*). [RH]

Hoogbergen, Wim S.M. The history of the Suriname Maroons. See *HLAS 53:1011*.

Hoogbergen, Wim S.M. Origins of the Suriname Kwinti Maroons. See *HLAS 53:1012*.

1912 Houdaille, Jacques. Reconstitution des familles de Saint-Domingue, Häiti, au XVIII siècle. (*Population/Paris*, 46:1, jan./fév. 1991, p. 29–40)
Examines parish records for 5,500 persons, born free and emancipated, of all races, from 12 parishes of colonial Haiti (1693–1787). Compares demographic characteristics with those of France. Notes underregistration of infants' births and deaths. [APD]

1913 Kuethe, Allan J. La desregulación comercial y la reforma imperial en la época de Carlos III: los casos de Nueva España y Cuba. (*Hist. Mex.*, 41:2, oct./dic. 1991, p. 265–292, bibl.)
Well-known expert on Charles III's imperial reforms explores the various internal mechanisms that led the Spanish Crown to apply different policy solutions to different areas of the empire. [JMH]

Leton, Collette. Archeologie, patrimoine de la Martinique. See *HLAS 53:610*.

1914 Lore, Françoise and **Jean-Marie Lore.** Les engagements à Nantes vers les îles d'Amérique de 1690 à 1734. Nantes, France: F. et J.-M. Lore, 1987. 103 p., 5 leaves of plates: ill.
Nominative list of 2,827 servants who left from port of Nantes includes geographical origins and occupations. Shows that most came from surrounding regions and that one-third had professional skills (barrel-makers, laborers, and tailors most prominent). Throws light on most important French port to specialize in labor migration, trading in both indentured servants and African slaves for several decades. [APD]

1915 Marrero, Leví. Cuba: economía y sociedad. v. 9–12, Azúcar, Ilustración y conciencia: 1763–1868. Madrid: Editorial Playor S.A., 1986–1989? 4 v.
Most recent volumes in author's massive history of Cuba ends with outbreak of wars of independence. By no means the best work of the series, in general these volumes reflect traditional viewpoints of Cuban historiography and add very little to what is already known about the period. [JMH]

1916 Marx, Jenifer. Pirates and privateers of the Caribbean. Malabar, Fla.: Krieger Pub. Co., 1992. 310 p.: bibl., index.
Valuable work gathers information on an interesting phase of Caribbean history in one volume. Lacks material on impact, if any, that activities of these men, who *operated in* rather than *being of* the Caribbean, had on local society. [ELC]

1917 McClellan, James Edward, III. Colonialism and science: Saint Domingue in
the Old Regime. Baltimore: Johns Hopkins
Univ. Press, 1992. 393 p.: bibl., ill., index, maps.

First work to document scientific research and activity (in physics, botany, etc.) in
Saint Domingue. Author traces its applica-
tions in health, engineering and agronomy by
public officials, scientific societies and individual colonists, and breaks new ground in
knowledge of the urbane and cosmopolitan
culture of the Enlightenment in the Caribbean. [APD]

1918 Mézière, Henri. Le général Leclerc,
1772–1802, et l'expédition de Saint-
Domingue. Préface de Jean-Marcel Champion. Paris: Tallandier, 1990. 286 p., 8 p. of
plates: bibl., ill. (Bibliothèque napoléonienne,
0153–0534)

Biography of general who headed the
1802–04 expedition to reestablish French
control over its colony reveals that Napoleon's plans considerably underestimated
Haitian soldiers' pride and tenacity, and that
yellow fever rather than incapacity of command doomed the expedition. [APD]

1919 Morrissey, Carol Mae. The road to
Bellevue. (*Jam. J.*, 22:3, Aug./Oct.
1989, p. 2–11, bibl., photos, tables)

Offers very fruitful analysis of problems which the mentally ill encountered in
18th- and 19th-century Jamaica, and of belated efforts to construct a new lunatic
asylum. Article provides illumination on island's social conditions up to 19th century.
[ELC]

**1920 Mourir pour les Antilles: indépendance
nègre ou esclavage, 1802–1804.** Direction de Michel L. Martin et Alain Yacou. Paris: Editions caribéennes; Cayenne: Centre
d'études et de recherches caraïbéennes, 1991.
237 p.: bibl.

Short contributions deal mostly with
military dimension of the revolutionary process in Saint Domingue and Guadeloupe
(1789–1802), its human cost, and its impact
on public opinion and collective memory. See
also item **1896.** [APD]

1921 Moya Pons, Frank. The Haitian revolution in Santo Domingo, 1789–1809.
(*Jahrb. Gesch.*, 28, 1991, p. 125–162)

Comprehensive account examines repercussions of Haitian Revolution on neighboring Spanish colony of Santo Domingo,

which was experiencing military conflicts
among the French, English, and Spanish, and
which was repeatedly invaded by Haitian and
French revolutionary leaders. Argues convincingly that just as development of French
Saint Domingue/Haiti had contributed to
economic reactivation of the Spanish colony,
the crisis produced by the slave rebellion in
the French colony provoked Santo Domingo's
ruin. [APD]

1922 Mullin, Michael. Africa in America:
slave acculturation and resistance in
the American South and the British Caribbean, 1736–1831. Urbana: Univ. of Illinois
Press, 1992. 412 p.: bibl., ill., index, maps.
(Blacks in the New World)

Author examines relationship between
slave acculturation and changing nature of
slave resistance at peak of evolution of mature, slave-based plantation societies. Uses
slave resistance to show differences in values
and ways of African and Creole slaves, and
demonstrates implications of these differences for understanding various facets of lives
and experiences of slaves in both regions.
Useful study. [ELC]

1923 Munford, Clarence J. and **Michael
Zeuske.** Black slavery, class struggle,
fear and revolution in St. Domingue and
Cuba, 1785–1795. (*J. Negro Hist.*, 73:1/4,
1988, p. 12–32)

Attempts to show relevance of concept
of the "great fear" (developed by Georges Le-
febvre in connection with the French Revolution) to emergence of the Cuban sugar oligarchy and plantation economy in late 18th century. Based on new materials from French and
Cuban archives. [JMH]

1924 Nicholls, David. Pompée-Valentin Vastey: royalist and revolutionary. (*Rev.
Hist. Am.*, 109, enero/junio 1990, p. 129–143)

Insightful study examines most original thinker in independent, early 19th-
century Haiti. A free colored who joined the
black leaders, Vastey defended system of he-
reditary monarchy and formation of a new national elite. A strident critic of a "colonial
system," he denounced role of slavery in fostering a racist colonial ideology and warned of
danger of a "neo-colonialism" based on economic domination. [APD]

1925 Oostindie, Gert. The economics of Surinam slavery. (*Econ. Soc. Hist. Neth.*,
5, 1993, p. 1–24)

In this essay on economic historiography of Suriname, author lists clichés about economic performance of Surinamese plantations and contrasts these conventional views with recent research. Also discusses theoretical approaches to economics of Suriname slavery, and concludes by reviewing recent demographic research. [RH]

Oostindie, Gert. Voltaire, Stedman and Suriname slavery. See item **2069.**

1926 Peire, Jaime Antonio. Estudio social y económico de los mercedarios de México y el Caribe, 1773–1790. (*Jahrb. Gesch.,* 26, 1989, p. 113–135, tables)

Not too edifying chapter of history of the Catholic Church in colonial Spanish America relies on printed and archival sources. [JMH]

1927 Pérez, Louis A., Jr. Cuba and the United States: origins and antecedents of relations, 1760s-1860s. (*Cuba. Stud.,* 21, 1991, p. 57–82, tables)

Argues that trade and travel during the period served as factors for subsequent integration of economy and culture of Cuba into the US system. [JMH]

1928 Pérotin-Dumon, Anne. The emergence of politics among free coloureds and slaves in revolutionary Guadeloupe. (*J. Caribb. Hist.,* 25:1/2, 1991, p. 100–135)

Considers "local process of politicization in moments when people believed that changes were possible and acted upon that belief." Careful examination of demonstrations, petitions, rumors, and meetings shows free colored and slave males, "each for their own reasons, but together challenging political authority." Argues for new kind of political history of revolutions in the French Caribbean beyond works of 19th-century white Creole and Haitian nationalist historians and current interpretations by social historians. [APD]

1929 Pérotin-Dumon, Anne. Villes et marchands antillais au XVIIIe siècle: le cas de la Guadeloupe. (*Généal. hist. Caräíbe,* 46, fév. 1993, p. 726–729)

Author depicts evolution of Guadeloupe trade throughout 18th century using as examples the careers of four colonial merchants. Commerce on the island ranged from coastal and contraband activities to transatlantic connections with France and entrepôt trade with North America and Dutch and Danish Caribbean islands. [APD]

1930 Pluchon, Pierre. Toussaint Louverture défie Bonaparte: l'adresse inédite du 20 décembre 1801. (*Rev. fr. hist. Outre-mer,* 79:296, 1992, p. 383–389)

In this shrewd diplomatic statement made as an impending military expedition threatened to reduce his autonomy, Haitian leader asserted his beliefs that: 1) France could have no hostile intentions toward Haitians since France alone defended Haiti against English enemies; and 2) his own power was constitutional. [APD]

Postma, Johannes. The dispersal of African slaves in the West by Dutch slave traders, 1630–1803. See item **1871.**

1931 Rossignol, Philippe and **Bernadette Rossignol.** Au Surinam: il y a deux siècles, 1793. (*Généal. hist. Caräíbe,* 50, juin 1993, p. 807–810)

Some 20 private and business letters seized by the French from English ships on their way to Amsterdam, Utrecht, and Le Havre provide lively description of white colonists' successes, hopes, and trials. Contains a list of the collection. [APD]

1932 Rossignol, Philippe; Bernadette Rossignol; and Marcel Favre. Les débuts de la révolte de Saint-Domingue dans la plaine du Cap, vécu par Louis de Calbiac. (*Généal. hist. Caräíbe,* 48, 1993, p. 774–785)

Letter from white planter from Port de Paix to his mother presents dramatic account of horrors of guerrilla warfare and retaliation raids and of shifting alliances between color-based factions as Saint-Domingue/Haiti sank into civil war in 1792. [APD]

1933 Saunders, D. Gail. Slave life, slave society and cotton production in The Bahamas. (*Slavery Abolit.,* 11:3, Dec. 1990, p. 332–350, tables)

Article examines work routines of Bahamian slaves engaged in cotton cultivation from 1783–1834. Includes fruitful discussion of sexual division of labor, and of how fortunes of cotton cultivation affected quality-of-life issues for slaves. Argues that task system encouraged slaves to take initiatives in farming their own grounds and raising animals. Important work. [ELC]

1934 Schüller, Karin. Die Haitianer deutscher Herkunft. (*Jahrb. Gesch.,* 28, 1991, p. 277–284)

Valuable effort gathers scarce data on 18th-century Germanic immigration to

French Caribbean islands that culminated in their little-known military participation in Haiti's war of independence. [APD]

1935 Sheridan, Richard B. Captain Bligh, the breadfruit, and the Botanic Gardens of Jamaica. (*J. Caribb. Hist.*, 23:1, 1989, p. 28–50)

Extremely valuable discussion examines circumstances behind Bligh's bringing breadfruit plant to Jamaica and manner in which it was received and distributed on the island. [ELC]

1936 Sheridan, Richard B. Changing sugar technology and the labour nexus in the British Caribbean, 1750–1900, with special reference to Barbados and Jamaica. (*Nieuwe West-Indische Gids*, 63:1/2, 1989, p. 59–93, bibl., tables)

This important article analyzes impact of technological change on employment, productivity, and welfare of workers in sugar industry. Also looks at availability of capital, access to skilled and unskilled labor, role of the planter class, and changing sugar prices. Concludes that adoption of technological improvements in late 19th century enhanced Barbados' sugar economy while Jamaica's economy became more diversified. [ELC]

1937 Stedman, John Gabriel. Stedman's Surinam: life in eighteenth-century slave society. Edited by Richard Price and Sally Price. Baltimore: Johns Hopkins Univ. Press, 1992. 425 p.: bibl., ill., maps.

Abridged version of complete critical edition (see *HLAS 52:1691*).

1938 Tarade, Jean. Le commerce entre les Antilles françaises et les possessions espagnoles d'Amérique à la fin du XVIIIe siècle. (*in* Commerce et plantation dans la Caraïbe, XVIIIe et XIXe siècles: actes du colloque de Bordeaux, 15–16 mars 1991. Bordeaux: Centre d'histoire des espaces atlantiques; Maison des pays ibériques, 1992, p. 27–43)

In spite of national monopolies in colonial trade, officials encouraged relationships between French Caribbean and Spanish colonies at end of 18th century so that sugar-producer Saint-Domingue would be supplied by Venezuela with timber, cattle, and other food. [APD]

1939 Thornton, John K. African soldiers in the Haitian Revolution. (*J. Caribb. Hist.*, 257:1/2, 1991, p. 58–80)

Argues that participation of African slaves in early military actions was the key to success of the Revolution due to Africans' previous experience in military tactics in Congo and Dahomey. [APD]

1940 Tornero, Pablo. Comercio colonial y proyección de la población: la emigración catalana a Cuba en la época del crecimiento azucarero, 1790–1817. (*Bol. Am.*, 31:39/40, 1989–90, p. 235–264, tables)

Fills a gap in our knowledge of Spanish migration to Cuba in 19th century. Unfortunately, author gives us very little information about social extraction of the immigrants. [JMH]

1941 Venegas Delgado, Hernán. El pensamiento temprano de la Ilustración cubana como expresión de su nacionalidad: Francisco de Arango y Parreño, 1765–1837. (*Islas/Santa Clara*, 90, mayo/agosto 1988, p. 69–73)

Despite his Marxist background, author makes a surprisingly positive appraisal of the work of Arango y Parreño, architect of Cuba's 18th-century sugar revolution. [JMH]

1942 Villiers, Patrick. La course en Martinique et en Guadeloupe pendant la guerre de succession d'Autriche. (*in* Commerce et plantation dans la Caraïbe, XVIIIe et XIX siècles: actes du colloque de Bordeaux, 15–16 mars 1991. Bordeaux: Centre d'histoire des espaces atlantiques; Maison des pays ibériques, 1992, p. 45–64)

Examines privateering in Saint-Pierre, Martinique—the principal French port in the Caribbean—as an alternative to a colonial trade greatly reduced by 18th-century wars. [APD]

1943 Villiers, Patrick. La Marine de Louis XVI. v. 1, Vaisseaux et frégates, de Choiseul à Sartine. Grenoble, France: J.-P. Debbane, 1983. 1 v: bibl., ill.

Well-researched study examines naval and mercantile policy of a French monarchy (1660–1760) increasingly concerned with the French Antilles. Includes much new data and many insights on: 1) naval protection of French commercial shipping lanes across the Atlantic; and 2) war economy based on privateering and contraband in colonial Haiti, Martinique and Guadeloupe. [APD]

1944 Ward, J.R. The amelioration of British West Indian slavery, 1750–1834: technical change and the plough. (*Nieuwe West-Indische Gids*, 63:1/2, 1989, p. 41–58, bibl.)

Argues that use of the plough in place

of hoes in pre-emancipation Jamaica has been grossly underestimated, and that physical conditions in Caribbean islands rather than slavery itself constituted major determinant of mechanization. [ELC]

1945 Yacou, Alain. Esclaves et libres français à Cuba au lendemain de la Révolution de Saint-Domingue. (*Jahrb. Gesch.*, 28, 1991, p. 163–197, tables)

Interesting study examines little-known aspect of migratory flow into Cuba as a result of 1790s Haitian Revolution. [JMH]

SPANISH BORDERLANDS

Alegría, Ricardo E. Juan Garrido, el conquistador negro en las Antillas, Florida, México y California c. 1503–1540. See item **1847.**

1946 Arenas Frutos, Isabel. Auge y decadencia del sistema misional franciscano en Florida durante el primer período español, 1565–1763. (*Anu. Estud. Am.*, 48, 1991, p. 95–120, map)

Contains vital information for history of Florida's evangelization. Makes extensive use of archival sources. [JMH]

1947 Arnaud Rabinal, Juan Ignacio *et al.* Estructura de la población de una sociedad de frontera: la Florida española, 1600–1763 (*Rev. Complut. Hist. Am.*, 17, 1991, p. 93–120, graphs, tables)

Rather than a purely demographic study, work is an approach to the pattern of Florida's population's evolution during the period. One of the first studies of a general character attempted thus far. [JMH]

1948 Buker, George E. The search for the seven cities and early American exploration. (*Fla. Hist. Q.*, 71:2, Oct. 1992, p. 155–168, table)

Fascinating study casts abundant light on medieval myths and legends. [JMH]

1949 Cebrián González, María del Carmen. El obispado de Nueva Orleans. (*Hisp. Sacra*, 40, julio/dic. 1988, p. 777–789)

Useful for historians interested in problems of ecclesiastical administration, work relies heavily on Spanish archival sources. [JMH]

1950 Cook, Noble David. Beyond *The martyrs of Florida:* the versatile career of Luis Gerónimo de Oré. (*Fla. Hist. Q.*, 71:2, Oct. 1992, p. 169–187)

Well-written and researched work, but nevertheless tells us very little about the most important aspect of Oré's career: his work as an apostle and evangelizer. [JMH]

1951 Cusick, James. Across the border: commodity flow and merchants in Spanish St. Augustine. (*Fla. Hist. Q.*, 69:3, Jan. 1991, p. 277–299, tables)

Shows that Saint Augustine, at least during first half of Second Spanish Period, was part of a wide trade network led by Havana and Charleston. Raises important questions for future investigation. [JMH]

1952 Domingo Acebrón, María Dolores. Los deportados de la Guerra de los Diez Años: Cuba, 1868–1878. (*Rev. Indias*, 51:191, enero/abril 1991, p. 143–166, appendices, tables)

Covers an aspect of Cuba's first war of independence that was in need of serious and systematic study. Makes extensive use of archival sources. [JMH]

1953 Franco de Espés Mantecón, Carlos. El negocio americano de un señor aragonés. Zaragoza, Spain: Comisión Aragonesa V Centenario; Diputación General de Aragón, 1990. 128 p.: bibl., ill., map. (Col. Aragón y América; 12)

Describes frustrated effort of one of Ferdinand VII's favorites to seize a large chunk of Florida's territory. Well written and researched. [JMH]

1954 Hann, John H. Heathen Acuera, murder, and a Potano *cimarrona:* the St. Johns River and the Alachua prairie in the 1670s. (*Fla. Hist. Q.*, 70:4, April 1992, p. 451–474)

Author translates and edits recently unearthed record of a 1678 criminal case which reveals existence of heathen Acuera a generation after the Timucua rebellion (1656) and provides information about life in the 1670s from Potano region of present Alachua County east to the St. Johns River. [JMH]

1955 Hann, John H. Political leadership among the natives of Spanish Florida. (*Fla. Hist. Q.*, 71:2, Oct. 1992, p. 188–208)

Makes valuable contribution to a field that only recently has attracted attention of scholars. [JMH]

1956 Hilton, Sylvia L. El Misisipi y la Luisiana colonial en la historiografía española, 1940–1989. (*Rev. Indias*, 50:188, enero/abril 1990, p. 195–212, appendix)

Excellent bibliographical essay is extremely useful as introduction to Spanish historiography on the subject. [JMH]

1957 Hoffman, Paul E. Luisiana. Madrid: Editorial MAPFRE, 1992. 328 p.: bibl., ill., index, map. (Col. España y Estados Unidos; 8. Col. MAPFRE 1492)

Readable and well-researched historical survey of Spanish Louisiana, whose historiography, the author writes, contains a number of gaps. The documentation required to fill them, however, is apparently readily available in Spain. [JMH]

1958 Johnson, Sherry. The Spanish St. Augustine community, 1784–1795: a reevaluation. (*Fla. Hist. Q.*, 68:1, July 1989, p. 27–54)

Informative, well-researched, and very interesting article rejects portrayal of local society by US historians, maintaining rather that Saint Augustine was thoroughly Hispanicized during period in question. [JMH]

1959 Landers, Jane. Gracia Real de Santa Teresa de Mose: a free black town in Spanish colonial Florida. (*Am. Hist. Rev.*, 95: 1, Feb. 1990, p. 9–30)

Serious, scholarly study is historiographically significant for a number of important questions long debated by historians, e.g., the relative severity of British and Spanish slave systems. [JMH]

1960 Milanich, Jerald T. and Charles Hudson. Hernando de Soto and the Indians of Florida. Gainesville: Univ. Press of Florida; Florida Museum of Natural History, 1992. 292 p.: bibl., ill., index, map. (Columbus quincentenary series. The Ripley P. Bullen series)

Authors use interdisciplinary approach to successfully reconstruct De Soto's route through Florida. They have also provided a good deal of information about Florida's native societies in the 16th century. Major contribution to our knowledge of Florida's social geography. [JMH]

1961 Parker, Susan R. Men without god or king: rural settlers of East Florida, 1784–1790. (*Fla. Hist. Q.*, 59:2, Oct. 1990, p. 135–155)

Drastically revises Anglophile conceptualization of the rural settlers as uncivilized and wild orphans of British rule. Carefully written and researched. [JMH]

1962 Peck, Douglas T. Reconstruction and analysis of the 1513 discovery voyage of Juan Ponce de León. (*Fla. Hist. Q.*, 71:2, Oct. 1992, p. 133–154, maps)

Author retraces Ponce de León's voyage using a yacht for the segments of open ocean navigation, and determining remainder of his trajectory by viewing and confirming Ponce de León's log description of geographical landforms encountered. Interesting new approach to the topic. [JMH]

1963 Reitz, Elizabeth J. Dieta y alimentación hispano-americana en el Caribe y la Florida en el siglo XVI. (*Rev. Indias*, 51: 191, enero/abril 1991, p. 11–24, tables)

Solid piece of research emphasizes vital role of domestic animals in success or failure of Caribbean settlements. [JMH]

1964 Romero Cabot, Ramón. Ideología y propaganda expansionista norteamericana y la Florida española. (*Rev. Indias*, 51: 191, enero/abril 1991, p. 121–142)

Author harshly criticizes the ideological justification of US expansionism in the case of the Florida peninsula. Develops themes that deserve further research. [JMH]

1965 Sáinz Sastre, María Antonia. Florida in the XVIth century: discovery and conquest. Madrid: Editorial MAPFRE, 1992. 317 p.: bibl., ill., index, maps. (Series of Spain and the United States; 1. Col. MAPFRE 1492)

Scholarly account and major contribution to history of the discovery and conquest of Florida is based on thorough knowledge of available sources, both primary and secondary. [JMH]

1966 Solís de Merás, Gonzalo. Pedro Menéndez de Avilés y la conquista de la Florida, 1565. Edición y presentación de José Manuel Gómez-Tabanera. Oviedo, Spain: Grupo Editorial Asturiano; Principadolibros, 1990. 259 p.: bibl., ill., maps. (Anaquel cultural asturiano; 2)

Written by Menéndez de Avilés' brother-in-law, work is one of the best sources for study of life and times of the famous *Adelantado de la Florida*. [JMH]

19TH CENTURY

1967 Aguirre, Sergio. Nacionalidad y nación en el siglo XIX cubano. La Habana: Editorial de Ciencias Sociales, 1990. 132 p. (Historia)

Despite their ideological bent and some shortcomings (which author himself acknowledges), the three essays in this book are worthwhile reading, especially the one dealing with attitudes of the Cuban bourgeoisie in the 19th century. [JMH]

1968 Alegría Ortega, Idsa E. Tras los pasos y la música de Ana Otero Hernández. (*Rev. Music. Puertorriq.*, 2, julio/dic. 1987, p. 4–31)

Traditional chronological account relates professional career of well-known 19th-century Puerto Rican pianist. Largely as a result of her perseverance and dedication, she toured major cities of Europe, South America, and the eastern US. Based on meticulous reading of newspaper reviews of her concerts. [TMV]

1969 Austin-Broos, Diane J. Redefining the moral order: interpretations of Christianity in postemancipation Jamaica. (*in* The meaning of freedom: economics, politics, and culture after slavery. Edited by Frank McGlynn and Seymour Drescher. Pittsburgh, Pa.: Univ. of Pittsburgh Press, 1992, p. 221–243, bibl.)

Argues that missionaries created as a new stereotype the Christian black: "a European Christian who happened to be of African descent and historically situated in Jamaica." Thus, important aspect of subsequent religious struggles rested on local resistance to petit-bourgeois forms which Christianity exhibited on the island. [ELC]

1970 Bacchus, M.K. Education in the preemancipation period: with special reference to the colonies which later became British Guiana. (*Transition/Guyana*, 18, 1991, p. 20–49)

Author concludes that although planters initially opposed early 19th-century missionaries' attempts to educate slaves due to fear that workers would become intractable, they eventually supported education because of its potential to promote social stability. [ELC]

1971 Bahamonde Magro, Angel and **José Gregorio Cayuela Fernández.** La creación de nobleza en Cuba durante el siglo XIX. (*Hist. Soc./Valencia*, 11, otoño 1991, p. 57–82, tables)

Excellent study of Spanish policy regarding creation of a nobility class in colonial Cuba is based primarily on records of Spanish notaries public. [JMH]

1972 Barcia, María del Carmen. Burguesía esclavista y abolición. La Habana: Editorial de Ciencias Sociales, 1987. 229 p.: bibl., ill. (Historia de Cuba)

Argues that abolition of slavery in Cuba was conditioned by belated development of the plantation system and Spain's inadequate economic policies. A scholarly work based on primary and secondary sources. [JMH]

1973 Bartlett, Christopher J. Britain and the abolition of slavery in Puerto Rico and Cuba, 1868–1886. (*J. Caribb. Hist.*, 23, 1989, p. 96–110)

Analyzes doubts and misgivings of British governments about putting pressure on Madrid for abolition of slavery during this period. Carefully written and researched. [JMH]

1974 Baud, Michiel. Sugar and unfree labour: reflections on labour control in the Dominican Republic, 1870–1935. (*J. Peasant Stud.*, 19:2, Jan. 1992, p. 301–325, bibl.)

Author takes issue with theories which suppose an essential contradiction between capitalist production and unfree labor relations. He argues that capitalist entrepreneurs tried hard to restrict free wage labor relations. In the Dominican Republic, a system of differential mechanization brought about a rigid separation between unskilled field workers and (semi-) skilled workers. [RH]

1975 Beckles, Hilary. Caribbean antislavery: the self-liberation ethos of enslaved blacks. (*J. Caribb. Hist.*, 22:1/2, 1988, p. 1–19, bibl.)

Asserts that at core of anti-slavery throughout Caribbean were efforts and determination of slaves to obtain freedom by any means necessary. Slaves' efforts to obtain freedom, rather than pleadings of anti-slavery agitators, are placed on center stage. [ELC]

1976 Beckles, Hilary. An economic life of their own: slaves as commodity producers and distributors in Barbados. (*Slavery Abolit.*, 12:1, May 1991, p. 31–47)

Argues that despite hostile environment and oppressive legislation, slaves were able to establish their own vibrant economic culture through exchange of locally-grown crops and small livestock. Although plantation economy prevailed, slaves were virtually in charge of internal marketing system. [ELC]

1977 Besson, Jean. Freedom and community: the British West Indies. (*in* The meaning of freedom: economics, politics, and culture after slavery. Edited by Frank Mc-Glynn and Seymour Drescher. Pittsburgh, Pa.: Univ. of Pittsburgh Press, 1992, p. 183–219, bibl.)

Emergence of free Afro-Caribbean communities was one of most important aspects of aftermath of full emancipation. Examines origin and development of these communities, and central role of customary kin-based land rights in perpetuating free communities in post-emancipation B.W.I. [ELC]

1978 Bibliografiá del presbítero Félix Varela Morales, 1788–1853. Recopilación y anotación de Josefina García-Carranza. Edición de Enildo A. García. New York: Senda Nueva de Ediciones, 1991. 258 p.: ill., indexes. (Literatura y esclavitud; 2. Senda de estudios y ensayos)

Work is perhaps the most complete compilation of Varela's bibliography published thus far. [JMH]

1979 Blow, Michael. A ship to remember: the Maine and the Spanish-American War. New York: Morrow, 1992. 496 p.: bibl., ill., index, maps.

Entertaining book with plausible conclusion examines both the Philippine War and the Spanish-American War. Author exclusively uses English-language printed sources, and narrative is occasionally marred by factual mistakes and excessive adherence to traditional interpretations. [JMH]

1980 Bolland, O. Nigel. The politics of freedom in the British Caribbean. (*in* The meaning of freedom: economics, politics, and culture after slavery. Edited by Frank Mc-Glynn and Seymour Drescher. Pittsburgh, Pa.: Univ. of Pittsburgh Press, 1992, p. 113–146, bibl.)

Views changing social relationships between ex-slaves and ex-masters in 19th-century British Caribbean through political lens in effort to comprehend meaning of freedom for both groups. Examines patterns of coercion and resistance in labor process, and

role of the State in maintaining planter hegemony. [ELC]

1981 Boomgaard, Peter and **Gert Oostindie.** Changing sugar technology and the labour nexus: the Caribbean, 1750–1900. (*Nieuwe West-Indische Gids*, 63:1/2, 1989, p. 3–22, bibl.)

Historiographical discussion examines links between slavery and level of modernization of Caribbean sugar industry. Authors assess often overlooked innovations that were actually achieved, and discuss behavior, with underlying rationale, of both planters and slaves. Suggests topics for further research. [RH]

1982 Brown, Deryck R. The response of the banking sector to the general crisis: Trinidad, 1836–56. (*J. Caribb. Hist.*, 24:1, May 1990, p. 28–64, table)

Extremely useful and original work focuses on an often neglected topic. Examines establishment and operations of the Colonial Bank, the mercantile community's response to it, competition from West India Bank, and finally, crisis engendered by Sugar Duties Act. Banking sector's tardiness in responding to crisis may well have aggravated the situation. [ELC]

1983 Calleia Leal, Guillermo G. La voladura del Maine. (*Rev. Hist. Mil.*, 34:69, 1990, p. 163–196, bibl., facsim., plates)

Interesting discussion considers Spanish point of view concerning cause of the sinking of the *Maine*. Worth reading and pondering. [JMH]

1984 Cambrón Infante, Ascensión. La estancia de Ramón de la Sagra en Cuba, 1822–1835. (*Santiago/Cuba*, 71, dic. 1988, p. 119–151)

Biographical sketch is of limited value. Author appears to know far more about La Sagra than about Cuba. [JMH]

1985 Camuñas Madera, Ricardo R. Fundación y crecimiento de Lares durante la primera parte del siglo XIX. (*Rev. Hist./San Juan*, 7, enero/dic. 1988, p. 95–122)

Argues that displacement of local residents (mostly illiterate) by Europeans (mostly Catalans, Majorcans, and Basques, but also French and Corsicans) was an irreversible fact by 1840. Lares was economic backwater where foreigners with resources found it easy to dominate economics and society. [TMV]

1986 Cancel, Mario R. Sociedades secretas: mito y realidad: el caso de Segundo Ruiz Belvis. (*Horizontes/Ponce*, 34:67, oct./ abril 1991, p. 49–61, appendix)

Explores legal and clandestine activities on part of elite directed at undermining regime of slavery and repressive political climate. Abolitionism and separatism took divergent paths, however. Abolitionist movement failed to incorporate blacks or slaves, and was sidetracked by political struggle in the 1866 Junta de Información. Author argues that Segundo Ruiz Belvis, a leading political figure, participated in these struggles as very much a man of his time. [TMV]

1987 Carrington, Selwyn. The state of the debate on the role of capitalism in the ending of the slave system. (*J. Caribb. Hist.*, 22:1/2, 1988, p. 20–41, bibl.)

Interesting analysis examines major themes, issues, and works on the role of capitalism in decline of slavery. Author calls for further examination of impact of "mature capitalism" on slave trade and slavery. [ELC]

1988 Cassá, Roberto. Sociedad e historia en el pensamiento de Hostos. (*Hómines/ San Juan*, 14:2/15:1, sept. 1990/sept. 1991, p. 23–31)

Author downplays positivist influences and places Hostos with other figures whose positions were "democratic-revolutionary," such as Gómez, Betances, Martí, and Maceo. In condemning history's glorification of power, Hostos advocated a knowledge of history that is political and moral; yet, he accepted industrialist rationalization as formula for progress. [TMV]

1989 Chance, Russell E., Jr. Protest in post-emancipation Dominica: the "Guerre Negre" of 1844. (*J. Caribb. Hist.*, 23:2, Nov. 1989, p. 118–141)

Extremely useful study examines week-long armed protest by free blacks in Dominica opposed to the taking of a census. Census was perceived by blacks as the first step in a process by local authorities to re-enslave them. [ELC]

1990 Child, Jack. The 1889–1890 Washington Conference through Cuban eyes: José Martí and the First International American Conference. (*Rev. Interam. Bibliogr.*, 34: 4, 1989, p. 443–456)

Gives fair assessment of Martí's view of conference. Shows that his writings on the subject were far more balanced than many tend to believe. [JMH]

1991 Colón, María Judith. Historia de Isabela y su desarrollo urbano, 1750–1850. Río Piedras, P.R.: ESMACO, 1988. 231 p.: bibl., graphs, maps, photos.

Urban study examines northwestern town of Isabela, especially after move from site of Tuna to present-day location. Author verifies dominant position of propertied class—landowners and merchants, including slave traders—through sale of land and residences. She also examines physical structures themselves in effort to define social classes. Deliberately ignores productive apparatus and people connected to Isabela—workers, owners, managers, etc. Includes maps, graphs, and photos. [TMV]

Commerce et plantation dans la Caräïbe, XVIIIe et XIXe siècles: actes du Colloque de Bordeaux, 15–16 mars 1991. See item **1895**.

1992 Craton, Michael and **D. Gail Saunders.** Seeking a life of their own: aspects of slave resistance in the Bahamas. (*J. Caribb. Hist.*, 24:1, May 1990, p. 1–27)

Full significance of this study rests on authors' ability to use the Bahamas as a case study for enhancing our understanding of slave resistance in general. Concludes that resistance increased in the last phase of slavery, and that such resistance occurred not necessarily among the most oppressed slaves. [ELC]

1993 Craton, Michael. The transition from slavery to free wage labour in the Caribbean, 1780–1890: a survey with particular references to recent scholarship. (*Slavery Abolit.*, 13:2, Aug. 1992, p. 37–67)

Extremely useful bibliographical essay deals with emergence of "new" societies in post-emancipation Caribbean. Concludes that former slaves and their descendants continued to resist their exploitation in post-emancipation period, and moved, however slowly, "towards a true class consciousness and solidarity." [ELC]

1994 Crevaux, Jules. Le mendiant de l'Eldorado. Préface de Jacques Meunier. Paris: Phébus, 1989. 413 p.: ill. (Le Tour du monde. D'ailleurs, 0180–9687)

Naval physician turned geographer and ethnologist relates his famous voyage of the

1870s. Crevaux was first European to sail up the Maroni and Oyapock rivers at the southern limits of French Guiana near the Brazilian border. His precise and wonderfully evocative descriptions, his enlightened views, and his broad curiosity make this new edition a highly recommended acquisition. [APD]

1995 Daget, Serge. Dans l'illégalité, la traite négrière française vers Cuba et Porto-Rico, 1817–1831. (*in* Commerce et plantation dans la Caraïbe, XVIIIe et XIXe siècles: actes du colloque de Bordeaux, 15–16 mars 1991. Bordeaux: Centre d'histoire des espaces atlantiques; Maison des pays ibériques, 1992, p. 81–98, tables)

Examines illegal introduction of about 25,200 slaves to the Caribbean between 1815–31. Some 130 French ships were fitted out in Bordeaux, Nantes, and Le Havre, but registered Spanish. The ships often declared Martinique and Guadeloupe as their official destination, while using merchant houses in Danish St. Thomas and Dutch St. Eustachius to send slaves to their main market in Cuba, then to Puerto Rico. [APD]

1996 Daget, Serge. Main d'oeuvre et avatars du peuplement en Guyane française, 1817–1863. (*Rev. fr. hist. Outre-mer*, 79:297, 1992, p. 449–474)

Traces series of unsuccessful migration policies involving Chinese, Indian, and African indentured labor, and French convict labor, implemented between 1817–64 following prohibition of slave trade. Only with gold mining in 1870s did development of vast untapped territory of French Guiana really begin. [APD]

1997 Darity, William, Jr. British industry and the West Indies plantations. (*in* The Atlantic slave trade: effects on economies, societies, and peoples in Africa, the Americas, and Europe. Edited by Joseph E. Inikori and Stanley L. Engerman. Durham, N.C.: Duke Univ. Press, 1992, p. 247–279, bibl., tables)

Author bemoans silence of economic historians on importance of slave trade and slavery to Britain's industrialization. Through analysis of theories of economic growth and works of 19th-century writers, he supports Eric Williams' thesis that slave trade and slavery contributed significantly to Britain's industrialization. [ELC]

De Verteuil, Anthony. Eight East Indian immigrants: Gokool, Soodeen, Sookoo, Capildeo, Beccani, Ruknaddeen, Valiama, Bunsee. See *HLAS 53:5134.*

1998 Dookhan, Isaac. The elusive nirvana: Indian immigrants in Guyana and the Des Voeux Commission, 1870–71. (*Rev. Rev. Interam.*, 17:3/4, otoño/invierno 1987, p. 54–89, bibl., table)

Author concentrates on reports of individual who played crucial role in Guyana's legal system and highlights hardships immigration inflicted on the workers, their reaction to the exploitative system, and slow pace of change reluctantly introduced by authorities. [ELC]

1999 Elisabeth, Léo. A propos des noms de famille donnés aux gens de couleur libres. (*Généal. hist. Caraïbe*, 1992, p. 415, 432, and 439; 1993, p. 572–573)

Provides detailed description of legal and social usage in conferring last names on emancipated slaves in Martinique and Guadeloupe (whether transmissible or not), a process that culminated with the abolition of slavery in 1848. Analyzes different categories of names given. (APD)

2000 Emmer, Pieter C. Between slavery and freedom: the period of apprenticeship in Suriname, Dutch Guiana, 1863–1873. (*Slavery Abolit.*, 14:1, 1993, p. 87–113, tables)

Discusses economic, social, medical, demographic, and legal aspects of transition period between slavery and free labor. Emmer compares Suriname apprenticeship with experiences in the British Caribbean and concludes that, despite belated emancipation in Suriname, the two regions followed a similar path in the transition from slavery to apprenticeship. [RH]

2001 Emmer, Pieter C. Immigration into the Caribbean: the introduction of Chinese and East Indian indentured laborers between 1839–1917. (*in* European expansion and migration: essays on the intercontinental migration from Africa, Asia, and Europe. New York: Berg, 1992, p. 245–276, bibl., graph, table)

Very general survey of Chinese and East Indian migration to the Caribbean is based on secondary literature. Discusses demographic aspects, push and pull factors, transportation, reception, settlement on the plantations, and integration. [RH]

2002 Fallope, Josette. Esclaves et citoyens: les noirs à la Guadeloupe au XIXe siècle dans les processus de résistance et d'intégration: 1802–1910. Basse-Terre: Société d'histoire de la Guadeloupe, 1992. 713 p.: bibl., maps. (Bibliothèque d'histoire antillaise; 12)

Comprehensive treatment of Guadeloupe society over a century examines demographic, occupational, cultural, and political aspects of transition from slavery to citizenship. Particularly informative on period 1840–80. Considers: 1) lengthy process of conferring family names on thousands of emancipated slaves; 2) new political dynamic created by male universal electoral franchise and marked by free-colored leadership and clientelism; 3) assimilation policy translated into advance of public education and opening of local civil service; and 4) emergence of socialist ideology in opposition to racism held as being contrary to republican ideal at turn of the century. [APD]

2003 Fernández, Susan. The money and credit crisis in late colonial Cuba. (*Cuba. Stud.*, 21, 1991, p. 3–18)

Makes a positive contribution to the study of a relatively unexplored aspect of Cuba's economic history. [JMH]

2004 Fernández Santalices, Manuel. Bibliografía del P. Félix Varela. Miami, Fla.: Saeta Ediciones, 1991. 1 v.

Work is very useful despite a few important omissions. [JMH]

2005 Ferrer, Ada. Social aspects of Cuban nationalism: race, slavery, and the Guerra Chiquita, 1879–1880. (*Cuba. Stud.*, 21, 1991, p. 37–56)

Central thesis of article cannot be accepted without important reservations and qualifications. [JMH]

2006 Franco, José Luciano. Las conspiraciones de 1810–1812. (*Bol. Arch. Nac./Cuba*, 4, 1990, p. 15–31)

Work is detailed and informative but lacks analysis. No footnotes or mentioning of sources. [JMH]

2007 Frisch, Peter J. La recherche généalogique en Haiti. (*Généal. hist. Caräibe*, 36, mars 1992, p. 530–539)

Important study examines: 1) collections of civil and parish records following Haiti's independence (1804), including their place and state of conservation; and 2) practices related to names and surnames as reflecting a colonial heritage in a new nation. [APD]

2008 Garralda Arizcun, José Fermín. La situación económica en Cuba durante la guerra de los diez años, 1868–1878, en la correspondencia privada del Mayorazgo de Zozaya. (*Prínc. Viana*, 52:194, sept./dic. 1991, p. 99–119)

While not a major contribution, helps for understanding the troubles that Cuba went through during the war. [JMH]

2009 Gaspar, David Barry. Working the system: Antigua slaves and their struggle to live. (*Slavery Abolit.*, 13:3, Dec. 1992, p. 131–155)

Useful study focuses on role of resistance and Antiguan slaves' participation in domestic economy as they sought to carve out niche for themselves despite harsh conditions. [ELC]

2010 González Barrios, René. En el mayor silencio. La Habana: Editora Política, 1990. 225 p.: bibl., ill., ports. (Col. Curujey)

Given the dearth of materials on the subject, this unpretentious study is useful, although author did not or could not consult materials in Spanish archives. [JMH]

2011 González Fernández, Doria. Las manufacturas tabacaleras cubanas durante la segunda mitad del siglo XIX. (*Rev. Indias*, 52:194, enero/abril 1992, p. 129–156)

Shows how concentration preceded foreign penetration in Cuban tobacco industry during period in question. Carefully written and researched. [JMH]

2012 González García, Juan Francisco. La edad de la luz. La Habana: Editora Abril, 1990. 96 p.: bibl., ill., index, maps, plates.

Biographical sketch of the scion of a distinguished Cuban family who died fighting for independence is interesting and well documented. [JMH]

2013 Green, William A. Supply versus demand in the Barbadian sugar revolution. (*J. Interdiscip. Hist.*, 18:3, Winter 1988, p. 403–418, tables)

While accepting Eric Williams' argument of direct, long-term nexus between adoption of staple agricultural products and advent of slavery, author denies that large-scale importation of slaves to Barbados was undertaken in response to expressed *demand* of sugar planters. He concludes, rather, that *supply* of slaves fostered Barbados' sugar revolution. [ELC]

2014 Guerra Díaz, Carmen and **Isabel Jiménez Lastre.** La industria azucarera cienfueguera en el siglo XIX: notas históricas para su estudio. (*Islas/Santa Clara*, 91, sept./dic. 1988, p. 52–76, maps, tables)

Brief but useful account of development of sugar in Cuba's south-central region includes abundant statistical information. [JMH]

2015 Hall, Neville. Apollo Miller, freedman: his life and times. (*J. Caribb. Hist.*, 23: 2, Nov. 1989, p. 196–213)

Extremely useful treatment of a free colored man in St. Thomas, who promoted the business of cock-fighting and was also involved in ice cream catering. Highlights entrepreneurial opportunities available for free coloreds in urban setting. [ELC]

2016 Hanna, W.J. Tourist travel to Jamaica in the 1890s. (*Jam. J.*, 22:3, Aug./Oct. 1989, p. 12–20, bibl., photos)

Through survey of travel books and guides to Jamaica at end of 19th century, author provides extremely useful information on travel conditions, promotional literature, and views of the island. Highly recommended. [ELC]

2017 Hernández Sandoica, Elena. Transporte marítimo y horizonte ultramarino en la España del siglo XIX: la naviera "Antonio López" y el servicio de correos a las Antillas. (*Santiago/Cuba*, 71, dic. 1988, p. 23–57)

Work is by no means a definitive exposé of political connections between the steamship company and the Spanish government. As author herself acknowledges, topic requires further, deeper, and more detailed research. [JMH]

2018 Heuman, Gad. 1865: prologue to the Morant Bay Rebellion in Jamaica. (*Nieuwe West-Indische Gids*, 65:3/4, 1991, p. 107–127, bibl.)

Author discusses island politics and large-scale public meetings which took place in nine months preceding outbreak of the Morant Bay Rebellion in October. [ELC]

2019 Hidalgo Paz, Ibrahím. Incursiones en la obra de José Martí. La Habana: Editorial de Ciencias Sociales, 1989. 240 p.: bibl. (Col. de estudios martianos)

Author uses cult-like approach to Martí characteristic of Cuban writers, but his essays are still somewhat useful for their emphasis on certain lesser known aspects of Martí's life and work. [JMH]

2020 Hira, Sandew. The evolution of the social, economic and political position of the East Indians in Surinam, 1873–1893. (*in* Indians in the Caribbean. Edited by I.J. Bahadur Singh. New Delhi: Sterling Publishers Private Limited, 1987, p. 347–369)

Thoughtful article simultaneously examines position of East Indians in Suriname and larger question as to what factors affected inter-ethnic relations. Despite title, study extends to 1980s. [ELC]

2021 Holt, Thomas Cleveland. The problem of freedom: race, labor, and politics in Jamaica and Britain, 1832–1938. Baltimore, Md.: Johns Hopkins Univ. Press, 1992. 517 p.: bibl., ill., index, maps. (Johns Hopkins studies in Atlantic history and culture)

Stimulating and provocative study examines what the author calls a movement from freedom of individual Jamaicans in 1830s to freedom of the nation-state in 1930s. Pays particular attention to role of British political ideology in intervening century to highlight conflicts which island experienced and the solutions advanced. Worker dissatisfaction found expression in violent outbursts in 1930s, culminating in introduction of measures to complete unfinished agenda of 1830s. [ELC]

2022 Hostos, Eugenio María de. Diario. t. 1, 1866–1869. Prólogo de Gabriela Mora. Ed. crítica. San Juan: Editorial del Instituto de Cultura Puertorriqueña; Río Piedras: Editorial de la Univ. de Puerto Rico, 1989. 290 p.: bibl., ill., indexes. (Obras completas; v. 2, t. 1)

Published to commemorate 150th anniversary of birth of one of most influential Puerto Rican social analysts and political thinkers, volume differs from other editions in that it ends with Hostos' European experience (suggesting that his life in America marks a break). Gabriela Mora writes excellent introduction in which she places diary in genre of intimate journals; provides it with social and political context; and evaluates it as literature. Contains very useful indexes. [TMV]

2023 Hostos, Eugenio María de. Eugenio María de Hostos. Edición de Angel López Cantos. Madrid: Instituto de Cooperación Iberoamericana, Ediciones de Cultura Hispánica, 1990. 187 p.: bibl. (Antología del pensamiento político, social y económico de América Latina; 12)

Introductory essay places Hostos within Krausist and positivist currents of late 19th century. Selections are grouped as follows: moral and social concepts, Spanish America, Cuba and its independence, Puerto Rico and its self-determination. A chronology and listing of Hostos' writings and readings about him are appended. Book is quick, useful reference, available to broad reading public. [TMV]

2024 Huerta Martínez, Angel. El clero cubano y su participación en la enseñanza primaria, 1800–1868. (*Anu. Estud. Am.*, 48, 1991, p. 479–556)

Well researched, balanced, and informative work is a definite contribution to history of primary education in Cuba. [JMH]

2025 Huerta Martínez, Angel. La enseñanza primaria en Cuba en el siglo XIX, 1812–1868. Sevilla, Spain: Excma. Diputación Provincial de Sevilla, 1992. 501 p.: bibl., ill. (Diputación Provincial de Sevilla. Sección Historia. V centenario del descubrimiento de América; 15)

As author points out, Cuban historians may disagree with him but no one will be able to ignore his work which is probably the most exhaustive published thus far on the subject. A major contribution to the knowledge of 19th-century Cuba. [JMH]

2026 Iglesias, Bernardo and **René González.** Presencia extranjera en la Guerra del P95: estudio del Primer Cuerpo del Ejército Libertador. (*Bol. Arch. Nac./Cuba*, 2, 1989, p. 64–87, appendix, map, plate, tables)

Information provided about the number of foreigners that made up this particular unit of the Cuban liberating army would have been even more significant had authors informed us of the total strength of the unit. [JMH]

2027 Indice y extracto de las reales cédulas, órdenes, instrucciones y reglamentos, etcétera de este libro, que abraza todas las correspondientes al año 1824. (*Bol. Arch. Nac./Cuba*, 4, 1990, p. 82–110)

Of use for researchers interested in 19th-century Cuba. [JMH]

2028 Iznaga, Diana. Presencia del testimonio en la literatura sobre las guerras por la independencia nacional, 1868–1898. La Habana: Editorial Letras Cubanas, 1989. 339 p.: bibl. (Ensayo. Giraldilla)

Includes comments on the most important works produced by leading figures of Cuban independence movement. Comments tend to be uncritical, hagiographic, and unmindful of the crucial problems underlying some of the texts. [JMH]

2029 James, Anand. The emigration of liberated Africans to British Guiana, 1841–1852. (*Hist. Gaz.*, 31, April 1991, p. 1–12)

Highlights attitude of British government towards scheme for bringing liberated Africans to British Guiana plantations. Early enthusiasm for scheme was replaced with skepticism by late 1840s, when officials grudgingly admitted that liberated Africans could not solve colony's labor needs. [ELC]

2030 James Figarola, Joel. Acerca del diario de campaña de Carlos Manuel de Céspedes. (*Rev. Bibl. Nac. José Martí*, 82:1/2, 1991, p. 73–88, facsim.)

Historical and literary analysis sharply reflects nature of the first Cuban war of independence once first few rebel successes were over. [JMH]

2031 Johnson, Howard. The emergence of a peasantry in the Bahamas during slavery. (*Slavery Abolit.*, 10:2, Sept. 1989, p. 172–186)

Insightful article places emergence of peasantry or protopeasantry in the Bahamas from 1767 onwards within the larger context of post-emancipation British Caribbean peasantries. Argues that plantation provided institutional framework for development of peasantry by slaves, freed persons, and liberated Africans who generally had a greater degree of autonomy than in other British Caribbean colonies. [ELC]

2032 Johnson, Howard. Friendly societies in the Bahamas, 1834–1910. (*Slavery Abolit.*, 12:3, Dec. 1991, p. 183–199)

Author demonstrates that these societies, established immediately after emancipation, were precursors to labor unions. As did later working-class organizations, they aimed to improve the lot of their members. [ELC]

2033 Kartick, Reuben J. James Crosby: Immigration Agent General. (*Hist. Gaz.,* 35, July 1991, p. 2–10)

Through this brief biography of James Crosby, author sheds light on conflicts between planters and officials as well as on problems which different members of civil service experienced in crucial post-emancipation period in British Guiana. Useful work. [ELC]

2034 Kartick, Reuben J. Joseph Beaumont: Chief Justice of British Guiana, 1863–1868. (*Hist. Gaz.,* 35, Aug. 1991, p. 2–10)

Extremely important article highlights both Gov. Hincks' frequent disputes with various independent-minded officials, and, more importantly, Beaumont's crusade for rights of Indian migrant workers in British Guiana. [ELC]

2035 Kartick, Reuben J. The village policy of Francis Hincks, 1862–1868. (*Hist. Gaz.,* 32, May 1991, p. 1–8)

Examines Governor Hincks' belated efforts to regularize establishment of free villages in British Guiana by ex-slaves who had purchased abandoned estates in post-emancipation era. Concludes that efforts failed because of inadequacy of supervisory mechanism and hesitancy of government to punish recalcitrant minority. [ELC]

2036 Kellenbenz, Hermann. Die Geschäfte des Carl Hopfengärtner in Aux Cayes. (*Jahrb. Gesch.,* 28, 1991, p. 251–275)

Correspondence (1797–1806) of a merchant from Stuttgart based in southern Haiti documents interests of merchants from the Baltic regions of Germany and Scandinavia in Haiti, St. Thomas, and Curaçao, as well as life of a young partner trying to succeed abroad. [APD]

2037 Krakovitch, Odile. Les Antillais et les bagnes de Cayenne: nouvelle approche de la répression dans les Caraïbes. (*Rev. hist./ Paris,* 575, juillet/sept. 1990, p. 89–100)

Drawing from rich sources, establishes geographical origins, rhythm of arrivals, and nature of condemnations for 10,000 convicts

from French colonies (North Africa, Senegal, Reunion Island, Martinique, and Guadeloupe) sent to prison colony of Devil Island (Cayenne) from 1851–55. [APD]

2038 La Rosa Corzo, Gabino. Los palenques del oriente de Cuba: resistencia y acoso. La Habana: Editorial Academia, 1991. 250 p.: bibl., ill., maps.

Highly recommended book worth reading solely for its introductory chapter, in which author makes a critical evaluation of literature on palenques to date. Generally speaking, work is result of exemplary scholarship and rigorous use of new research methods. [JMH]

2039 Lafleur, Gérard. Les immigrés du Matouba au XVIIIe siècle. (*Généal. hist. Caraïbe,* 51, juillet/août 1993, p. 831–834)

Traces origins of a rural parish created in 1765 in the heights surrounding Guadeloupe's capital, Basse-Terre, and area's settlement by German colonists. [APD]

Lamur, Humphrey. Slave religion in Suriname. See *HLAS 53:1017.*

2040 Lamur, Humphrey E. The impact of Maroon wars on population policy during slavery in Suriname. (*J. Caribb. Hist.,* 23: 1, 1989, p. 1–27, maps, tables)

Author argues that measures initiated by government to promote natural increase of plantation slaves failed because of financial consequences of the Maroon wars and removal from plantations of slaves who were recruited to fight for government during the wars. [ELC]

2041 Laviana Cuetos, María Luisa. José Martí: la libertad de Cuba. Madrid: Biblioteca Iberoamericana, 1988. 127 p.: facsims., index, photos

Short biography of Apostle of Cuban Independence is enhanced by numerous color illustrations and photographs. Recommended as a good introduction to Martí's life and work. [JMH]

Le Riverend, Julio. Sistema político y movimientos sociales: Cuba. See *HLAS 53:3648.*

2042 Le Riverend, Julio *et al.* Temas acerca de la esclavitud. La Habana: Editorial de Ciencias Sociales, 1988. 288 p.: bibl. (Historia de Cuba)

Useful collection of essays includes interesting study of José Antonio Saco's methodology and valuable list of manuscripts about slavery extant in Cuba's Biblioteca Nacional José Martí. [JMH]

2043 Le Riverend, Julio. Varela: transición ideológica en pos del futuro. (*Santiago/Cuba*, 71, dic. 1988, p. 5–22)

Although it is possible to argue with more than a few of author's statements about Varela, central theme of article is acceptable to historians of all persuasions. Certainly not a ground-breaking study. [JMH]

2044 Léotin, Marie-Hélène. La révolution anti-esclavagiste de mai 1848 en Martinique. Préface de M. Edmond Mondesir. Illustration de M. Alain Dumbardon. Fort de France: Apal Production, 1991. 34 p.: bibl., ill. (Les Cahiers de l'U.G.T.M. Education)

Contains selected documents on Martinique riots of May 22–23, 1848, that led governor to accelerate process of abolishing slavery. [APD]

2045 Lewis, Rupert. J.J. Thomas and political thought in the Caribbean. (*Caribb. Q.*, 36:1/2, June 1990, p. 46–58, bibl.)

Presents critical evaluation of career and views of a foremost Caribbean 19th-century intellectual whose writings laid the groundwork for self-expression and nationalism in Trinidad. [ELC]

2046 Loynaz del Castillo, Enrique. Memorias de la guerra. La Habana: Editorial de Ciencias Sociales, 1989. 513 p.: ill. (Historia de Cuba)

Work is indispensable source for studies of Cuban wars of independence. Foreword, written by Francisco Pérez Guzmán, is a brilliant historiographical essay written with a rare degree of objectivity. [JMH]

2047 Luque de Sánchez, María Dolores. La Revolución Francesa y su impacto inmigratorio en Puerto Rico. (*Torre/Río Piedras*, 5, número extraordinario, 1991, p. 127–138)

Establishes migratory currents prior to 1815. Explores business activity and concomitant political influence of French emigrés, of whom Spanish officials remained suspicious. [TMV]

2048 Luzón Benedicto, José Luis. Chineros, diplomáticos y hacendados en La Habana colonial: Don Francisco Abella y Raldiris y su proyecto de inmigración libre a Cuba,

1874. (*Bol. Am.*, 31:39/40, 1989–90, p. 143–158)

Interesting account of last-minute attempt by certain Cuban planters to continue importation of Chinese contract laborers after 1874 is based on printed and archival sources. [JMH]

2049 Luzón Benedicto, José Luis; José Baila; and Francisco Sardaña. Estado, etnias y espacio urbano: La Habana, 1878. (*Bol. Am.*, 32:41, 1991, p. 137–150, graphs, tables)

Offers sharp insights into changes that took place in Cuba's social structure during second half of 19th century. [JMH]

2050 Luzón Benedicto, José Luis. El mar en el tráfico chinero: naufragios y amotinamientos. (*in* Encuentros Debate América Latina Ayer y Hoy, *3rd, Barcelona, 1991*. Conquista y resistencia en la historia de América. Barcelona: Publicacions Univ. de Barcelona, 1992, p. 247–259)

Provides solid details of coolie trade between southern China and Havana from 1844–73. Excellent study. [JMH]

2051 Maluquer de Motes Bernet, Jordi. Nación e inmigración: los españoles en Cuba, ss. XIX y XX. Oviedo, Spain: Ediciones Jucar, 1992. 190 p.: bibl., ill. (Cruzar el charco; 1)

Comprehensive survey examines Spanish immigration to Cuba during last century and a half. Uses some materials in Cuban archives, but relies mostly on printed sources. [JMH]

2052 Márquez Macías, Rosario. La búsqueda de un modelo laboral capitalista en la economía cubana: la emigración de colonos canarios, 1852–1855. (*Anu. Estud. Am.*, 48, 1991, p. 557–584, appendix, graphs)

Work is useful as a point of departure for further research. [JMH]

2053 Marshall, Woodville K. Provision-ground and plantation labour in four Windward Islands: competition for resources during slavery. (*Slavery Abolit.*, 12:1, May 1991, p. 48–67)

Author's major conclusion is that provision-ground and internal marketing systems provided slaves with excellent opportunities for independent economic activity, which placed them in conflict with management over land and labor resources. Argues that these experiences affected slaves' attitudes toward plantation labor and toward independent activities in post-slavery period. [ELC]

2054 Martínez de las Heras, Agustín. En la muerte de Gonzalo Castañón: prensa y violencia en la Cuba de 1870. (*Anu. Dep. Hist./Madrid,* 1, 1989, p. 53–76, appendix)

Given the controversial nature of the subject matter, it is almost surprising that article is a balanced and objective account. A solid piece of scholarship. [JMH]

2055 Martínez Fernández, Luis. "Don't die here:" the death and burial of Protestants in the Hispanic Caribbean, 1840–1885. (*Americas/Francisc.,* 49:1, July 1992, p. 23–47, graph, tables)

Scholarly discussion examines extent and importance of Protestants' struggle for funeral and burial rights in Cuba and Puerto Rico during the period. [JMH]

2056 Martínez-Vergne, Teresita. The allocation of liberated African labour through the Casa de Beneficencia: San Juan, Puerto Rico, 1858–1864. (*Slavery Abolit.,* 12:3, Dec. 1991, p. 200–216)

Examines placement of "liberated" Africans with local landowners and further regulations to integrate them as *colonos* (settlers) to argue that State's system of charity reinforced established norms subordinating blacks both socially and economically. Emphasizes that no contradiction seemed to exist between Liberal insistence on liberty and equality and virtual re-enslavement of these men and women under government auspices. [TMV]

2057 Martínez-Vergne, Teresita. Capitalism in colonial Puerto Rico: Central San Vicente in the late nineteenth century. Gainesville, Fla.: Univ. Press of Florida, 1992. 189 p.: bibl., ill., index, map. (Univ. of Florida social sciences monograph; 78)

Well-researched work attempts to correct commonly held views of Puerto Rico's sugar industry in late 19th century. Author shows that demise of San Vicente resulted from limitations of Puerto Rico's economy rather than from difficulties related to the enterprise itself. A significant contribution. [JMH]

2058 Maza Miquel, Manuel. El clero cubano y la independencia: las investigaciones de Francisco González del Valle, 1881–1942.

Santo Domingo: Centro de Estudios Sociales Padre Juan Montalvo; Centro Pedro Francisco Bonó de la Compañía de Jesús en las Antillas, 1993. 276 p.: bibl., ill., maps.

One of the very few serious and impartial studies of connection between Catholic clergy and insurgents during Cuban wars of independence, work is required reading for all those interested in the subject. [JMH]

2059 McGowan, Winston. Christianity and slavery. (*Hist. Gaz.,* 24, Sept. 1990, p. 1–18)

Impressive study relates London Missionary Society's efforts to proselytize slaves in Demerara from 1808–13. Planters opposed missionaries as agents of British antislavery bodies whose teachings would incite slave insurrection. With enthusiastic responses from slaves and support from governors, missionaries overcame obstacles. [ELC]

2060 Moitt, Bernard. Slave resistance in Guadeloupe and Martinique. (*J. Caribb. Hist.,* 25:1/2, 1991, p. 136–159)

Based largely on secondary literature, work explores slave experiences in both Martinique and Guadeloupe during revolutionary era. For a different approach see item **1928.** [AP

Morrissey, Carol Mae. The road to Bellevue. See item **1919.**

2061 Moyano Bazzani, Eduardo L. La nueva frontera del azúcar: el ferrocarril y la economía cubana del siglo XIX. Préambulo de Francisco de Solano. Madrid: Consejo Superior de Investigaciones Científicas, 1991. 404 p.: bibl., ill., maps. (Col. Biblioteca de historia de América; 4)

Based on a well-researched doctoral dissertation, work helps to supplement findings of Zanetti Lecuona and García Alvarez in their pioneering work on Cuban railroads (see item **1845**). [JMH]

2062 Nault, François and Francine M. Mayer. L'abolition de l'esclavage à Saint-Barthélemy vue à travers l'étude de quatre listes nominatives de sa population rurale de 1840 à 1854. (*Rev. fr. hist. Outre-mer,* 79:296, 3e trimestre 1992, p. 305–340, bibl., graphs, maps, tables)

Based on four nominative lists from the period of abolition of slavery (1840–54), this thorough study of the rural population shows: 1) equal white and non-white sectors, the latter evenly distributed among free-coloreds and slaves; 2) a high proportion of adults among slaves but of children among whites, with free-coloreds falling in between; 3) beginning of residential separation between former masters and former slaves, and of migration abroad by whites and coloreds. [APD]

2063 Navarro García, Jesús Raúl. Control social y actitudes políticas en Puerto Rico, 1823–1837. Sevilla, Spain: Excma. Diputación Provincial de Sevilla, 1991. 473 p.: bibl., ill. index. (Diputación Provincial de Sevilla. Sección Historia. V centenario del descubrimiento de América; 11)

Focuses on Puerto Rico to study local impact of absolutist regime of Ferdinand VII (1823–33). Argues that island did not aspire to independence in first decades of 19th century because of ideological control that emanated from Spain in the form of press censorship and educational limitations, and because propertied class benefitted from relaxation of monopoly of commerce. Exhaustively analyzes means used to control nature and distribution of ideas in the colony, but makes no use of vast theoretical literature on the subject. Final chapter projects into liberal transition, rightly emphasizing that changes were not that noticeable. [TMV]

2064 Navarro García, Luis. La independencia de Cuba. Madrid: Editorial MAPFRE, 1992. 413 p.: bibl., ill., index. (Col. Independencia de Iberoamérica; 2. Col. MAPFRE 1492)

Survey of Cuba's long fight for political independence provides helpful Spanish perspective on the Cuban independence movement. Based on secondary sources. [JMH]

2065 Negrón-Portillo, Mariano and Raúl Mayo Santana. La esclavitud urbana en San Juan de Puerto Rico: estudio del Registro de Esclavos de 1872: primera parte. Río Piedras: Centro de Investigaciones Sociales, Univ. de Puerto Rico; Ediciones Huracán, 1992. 137 p.: bibl., ill.

Study is based on *Registro de Esclavos, 1872, Padrón del Barrio de Santo Domingo, 1846,* and *contratos de libertos,* 1873–75. This is the first in a series that proposes to examine slavery in various geographical and economic regions of the island. In this case, authors examine urban slavery in San Juan, specifically conditions under which slaves

worked and lived, and offer profile of a slave family. Findings are placed among major historiographical currents of US and Puerto Rican slave studies. They show sizable number of artisans (13% of 890 cases), many domestics (42%), a high proportion of *coartados* (17.5%), considerably more mulattoes and a few more Africans than in rural areas, and larger degree of autonomy than for agricultural slaves. Authors document breakup of slave families, although they trace efforts to reconstitute after emancipation. Study offers interesting speculations about slaveholders that should be followed up. This research will also benefit from comparisons with free people of color. [TMV]

2066 Offner, John L. An unwanted war: the diplomacy of the United States and Spain over Cuba, 1895–1898. Chapel Hill: Univ. of North Carolina Press, 1992. 306 p.: bibl., ill., index, map.

Revised study of the Spanish-American War is based on multi-archival research. This major contribution maintains that the war was both inevitable and necessary. Neither the US, nor Spain, nor the Cuban nationalists wanted it, but internal politics in each case limited the flexibility needed for diplomatic accommodation. [JMH]

2067 Ogelsby, J.C.M. The Cuban autonomist movement's perception of Canada, 1865–1898: its implication. (*Americas/Francisc.*, 48:4, April 1992, p. 445–461)

Article not only emphasizes significance of Canadian model for Cuban autonomists, but also approaches problem of Cuba's independence from an unusual and refreshing perspective. Well written and researched. A welcome contribution. [JMH]

2068 Olwig, Karen Fog. The struggle for respectability: Methodism and Afro-Caribbean culture on 19th-century Nevis. (*Nieuwe West-Indische Gids,* 64:3/4, 1990, p. 93–114, bibl.)

Contends that while members of rising middle class accepted Methodism's cultural values and practices of respectability as their own and used them as a mark of societal elevation, the lower classes utilized Methodist traditions as an institutional framework to display their identity and seek societal recognition. (For ethnologist's comment see *HLAS 53:1041.*) [ELC]

2069 Oostindie, Gert. Voltaire, Stedman and Suriname slavery. (*Slavery Abolit.*, 14: 2, 1993, p. 1–34)

Compares recent research with traditional, negative representations of Suriname slavery. Author broadens traditional perspective with its one-sided focus on abuse and violence by discussing demography, living and working conditions, and judicial escape hatches. Concludes by reconsidering utility of concept of American slavery as a continuum with variants ranging from harsh to mild. [RH]

2070 Paula, A. F. "Vrije" slaven: een sociaal-historische studie over de dualistische slavenemancipatie op Nederlands Sint Maarten 1816–1863 ["Free" slaves: a social historical study of the dualistic emancipation of slaves on Dutch St. Maarten, 1816–1863]. Zutphen, The Netherlands: Walburg Pers, 1993. 191 p.: bibl., ill., index, maps.

Studies causes and effects of 19th-century slave resistance in St. Maarten. Slaves managed to alter structures of slavery, even though owner-slave relations remained intact. The opportunity to flee to "free" French St. Martin gave Dutch slaves an "independent attitude" and a certain degree of freedom. Author argues that the slaves were "quasi-slaves" from 1848 (French abolition) onward. [RH]

2071 El pensamiento vivo de Máximo Gómez. v. 1. Recopilación de Bernardo García Domínguez. Santo Domingo: Ediciones CEDEE, 1991. 1 v.: bibl.

Includes more than 100 documents from Gómez's archive, two-thirds of which are either little known or have never been published before. [JMH]

2072 Péray, Jacques-Aimé. Le chapelier pirate. Présenté et illustré par Edmond Péray. Paris: Seghers, 1991. 379 p.: ill. (Etonnants voyageurs)

In original memoirs, an old man relates 20 years spent in the French Caribbean in his youth. Both persuasively detailed and witty, provides unique documentation on experience of European immigrants amidst Creole culture in early 19th century. [APD]

2073 Peregrinos de la libertad: documentos y fotos de exilados puertorriqueños del siglo XIX localizados en los archivos y bibliotecas de Cuba. Recopilación y ensayos introductorios de Félix Ojeda Reyes. Río Piedras, P.R.: Instituto de Estudios del Caribe; Editorial de la Univ. de Puerto Rico, 1992. 245 p.: bibl., ill. (some col.), facsims., maps, ports. (Col. caribeña)

Volume provides documentation and photographs surrounding activities of Puerto Rican exiles in Cuba (Ramón Emeterio Betances, Eugenio María de Hostos, Lola Rodríguez de Tió, Juan Rius Rivera, Sotero Figueroa Fernández, Francisco Gonzalo Marín Shaw). Interconnectedness of developments in Spanish Caribbean comes across as underlying theme. Unfortunately, division of book into chapters that deal with each of exiles separately undermines this theme. [TMV]

2074 Pérez, Louis A., Jr. Protestant missionaries in Cuba: archival records, manuscript collections, and research prospects. (*LARR*, 27: 1, 1992, p. 105–120)

Pérez has rendered an invaluable service to researchers interested in Protestant activity in Cuba. [JMH]

2075 Pérez Guzmán, Francisco. Máximo Gómez: la guerra de liberación. La Habana: Editorial de Ciencias Sociales, 1986. 140 p.: bibl. (Historia de Cuba)

Author has worked primarily with printed sources, but he has summarized in one slender volume information that is dispersed in many libraries. [JMH]

2076 Pérez Vega, Ivette. Las oleadas de inmigración sobre el sur de Puerto Rico: el caso de las sociedades mercantiles creadas en Ponce, 1816–1830. (*Rev. Cent. Estud. Av.*, 4, enero/junio 1987, p. 114–123)

Article is summary of author's doctoral dissertation—a prosopographical study of Ponce's commercial class. Confirms traditional understanding that merchants were foreign and landowners were Creole. Good description of activities of a merchant house. Does not provide historiographical context for rich information on advantages and disadvantages of being a merchant. [TMV]

2077 Phillips, Glenn O. The stirrings of the mercantile community in the British West Indies after emancipation. (*J. Caribb. Hist.*, 23: 1, 1989, p. 62–95, tables)

Argues that amidst economic adversity and stress experienced by B.W.I. planters from 1834–67, there arose a mercantile community to position of preeminence by providing finance capital and credit facilities and by engaging in new commercial activities. [ELC]

2078 Pi-Suñer, Antonia. Las relaciones hispano-mexicanas en torno a Cuba en el siglo XIX. (*in* Congreso Internacional sobre Fronteras en Iberoamérica Ayer y Hoy, *1st, Tijuana, Mexico, 1989.* Memoria. Edición de Alfredo Félix Buenrostro Ceballos. Mexicali: Univ. Autónoma de Baja California, 1990, v. 1, p. 111–123)

Balanced and dispassionate account is written from a Mexican perspective. Makes use of materials in Mexican archives. [JMH]

2079 Piqueras Arenas, Josep Antoni and **Enric Sebastià Domingo.** Agiotistas, negreros y partisanos: dialéctica social en vísperas de la Revolución Gloriosa. Valencia, Spain: Edicions Alfons el Magnànim; Institució Valenciana d'Estudis i Investigació, 1991. 376 p.: bibl. (Estudios universitarios; 45)

Although essentially a book about Spanish history, work does deal with connection between Cuban slave interests and Spanish revolutionary experience of 1860s. Author is fully familiar with the most recent Cuban scholarship. [JMH]

2080 Polanco Brito, Hugo Eduardo. La masonería en la República Dominicana. Santiago, República Dominicana: UCMM, 1985. 132 p.: bibl., ill., ports. (Col. Estudios; 111)

Balanced and conciliatory study of Dominican masonry is written by an enlightened prelate. Highly recommended. [JMH]

2081 Portuondo Zúñiga, Olga. El padre de Antonio Maceo, ¿venezolano?: voz de la historia. (*Del Caribe,* 19, 1992, p. 93–97, ill., tables)

Honest and well researched work discusses Cuban hero's family origin. From now on, Maceo's biographers will have to take author's findings into account. [JMH]

2082 Pruna, Pedro M. and **Rosa María González.** Antonio Mestre en la cultura científica cubana del siglo XIX. La Habana: Editorial Academia, 1987. 101 p.: bibl., index.

This first full-fledged biography of important 19th-century figure of Cuban science definitely fills a gap in Cuban historiography. [JMH]

2083 Robert, Karen. Slavery and freedom in the Ten Years' War, Cuba, 1868–1878. (*Slavery Abolit.,* 13:3, Dec. 1992, p. 181–200)

Recommended contribution offers fresh insights into a topic on which writers very frequently merely repeat one another. [JMH]

2084 Robles Muñoz, Cristóbal. La lucha de los independistas cubanos y las relaciones de España con Estados Unidos. (*Hispania/Madrid,* 50:174, enero/abril 1990, p. 159–202)

Based on an impressive scholarly apparatus, work is useful for study of Spanish point of view. However, it includes a number of highly debatable statements. [JMH]

2085 Robles Muñoz, Cristóbal. 1898: diplomacia y opinión. Madrid: Consejo Superior de Investigaciones Científicas, 1991. 389 p.: bibl., index. (Biblioteca de historia; 7)

Although author's style is difficult to read, study is solid and well researched. Shows failure of Spanish diplomacy and paramount influence of Spanish public opinion in denouement of the 1898 Spain/US confrontation. [JMH]

2086 Robles Muñoz, Cristóbal. Reforma moral y conflicto cultural en Santo Domingo, 1862–1865. (*Hisp. Sacra,* 40, julio/dic. 1988, p. 867–889)

Focuses on clash between Spanish ecclesiastical administrators and native clergy as one of the factors in Spain's failure in the Dominican Republic in 1862–65. An illuminating study. [JMH]

2087 Robles Muñoz, Cristóbal. Reformas políticas y pacificación militar en Cuba. (*Hispania/Madrid,* 52:180, enero/abril 1992, p. 173–224)

Focuses on connection between political reform and military pacification as main thrust of Spanish diplomacy during fateful months of 1897. Thoughtful and balanced, but better researched than written. [JMH]

2088 Rodríguez La O., Raúl. "Oscar no es mi único hijo." (*Bol. Arch. Nac./Cuba,* 4, 1990, p. 111–118)

Provides additional documentation of a sad episode of Cuba's Ten Years' War of independence. [JMH]

2089 Rodríguez Pina, Javier. Guerra de castas: la venta de indios mayas a Cuba, 1848–1861. México: Consejo Nacional para la Cultura y las Artes, 1990. 196 p.: bibl.

Work is by no means exhaustive since author used neither Cuban, Spanish, nor some important Mexican archival materials. Written primarily from a Mexican perspective, work nevertheless contributes toward filling a gap in Cuban historiography. [JMH]

2090 Roldán de Montaud, Inés. La Unión Constitucional y la abolición de la esclavitud: las actitudes de los conservadores cubanos ante el problema social. (*Santiago/Cuba*, 73, junio 1989, p. 131–217)
    Casts considerable light on attitude of Cuban politicians and sugar planters toward abolition of slavery. Makes ample use of primary sources. [JMH]

2091 Rose, James G. The strike of 1848. (*Hist. Gaz.*, 23, August 1990, p. 1–15)
    Offers succinct analysis of labor disturbance in British Guiana. Creole workers took action when increased immigration and lower wages led to worsening of their economic position. Planter hegemony increased in wake of aborted strike. [ELC]

2092 Rose, James G. The taxation policy of Sir Henry Light, 1838–1848. (*Hist. Gaz.*, 38, Nov. 1991, p. 2–14)
    Offers cogent analysis of fiscal measures adopted by plantocracy in post-emancipation British Guiana to stifle independence of Creole laborers and ensure that they remained dependent on plantation wage labor. [ELC]

2093 San Miguel, Pedro L. La economía de plantación y la formación de la clase de hacendados en Vega Baja, 1820–1873. (*Rev. Rev. Interam.*, 18:1/2, 1988, p. 45–52)
    Establishes that position of Vega Baja planters was less advantageous than that of foreigners or non-Vega Baja Creoles. Latter had resources to acquire land, slaves, and machinery. [TMV]

2094 Sang, Mu-Kien Adriana. Buenaventura Báez, el caudillo del Sur: 1844–1878. Santo Domingo: Instituto Tecnológico de Santo Domingo, 1991. 442 p.: bibl., index, port.
    Serious and scholarly biography, carefully written and researched, is a major contribution to Dominican historiography. [JMH]

2095 Santana Rabell, Leonardo. Historia de Vega Alta de Espinosa: orígenes, fundación y desarrollo hasta fines del siglo XIX. Santurce, P.R.: Editorial La Torre del Viejo, 1988. 236 p.: bibl., ill.
    Relates history of Vega Alta, especially since separation from Vega Baja at end of 18th century and up to 19th. Argues that stunted economic, demographic, and cultural growth of town was due to preeminence of Hacienda Carmen's owners, limited commercial ties, and out-migration. The "town aristocracy" (cattlemen, lesser landowners, and less-than-successful merchants) was subordinate to the hacienda, but (author suggests) also quite separate from workers, artisans, and the poor. This aristocracy controlled local politics, and some of its members became important figures in island-wide Partido Liberal. [TMV]

2096 Satchell, Veront. "Squatters or freeholders?": the case of the Jamaican peasants during the mid-19th century. (*J. Caribb. Hist.*, 23:2, Nov. 1989, p. 164–177, graph, tables)
    Author disputes earlier conclusions of Gisela Eisner (see *HLAS 28:805a*) that a majority of Jamaican peasants after emancipation were squatters. He concludes rather that they were freeholders who had purchased holdings. Because they lacked land conveyance deeds, however, they were ejected as if they were mere squatters. [ELC]

2097 Saugéra, Eric. L'introduction des noirs aux Antilles et en Guyane française au début du XIXe siècle. (*in* Commerce et plantation dans la Caraïbe, XVIIIe et XIXe siècles: actes du Colloque de Bordeaux, 15–16 mars 1991. Bordeaux: Centre d'histoire des espaces atlantiques; Maison des pays ibériques, 1992, p. 99–113)
    Traces voyages of French slave trading ships that carried some 10,000 slaves to French Caribbean and Guiana from 1793–1810. Voyages were carried out under peculiar circumstances created by abolition of slave trade (1792) and of slavery (1794), followed by reestablishment of both in 1802. [APD]

2098 Scarano, Francisco Antonio. Haciendas y barracones: azúcar y esclavitud en Ponce, Puerto Rico, 1800–1850. Traducción de Mercedes Solís. Río Piedras, P.R.: Huracán, 1993. 286 p.: bibl., ill., maps.
    Excellent translation from the original English (see *HLAS 46:2553*). Work dispels traditional notions of slavery as a benign labor system, and breaks monopoly of political studies in island's historiography. Spanish-speaking scholars of the Caribbean and of labor are fortunate to have this book available. [TMV]

2099 Schmidt, Nelly. Un témoignage original sur Häiti au XIXe siécle: celui de
l'abolitionniste Victor Schoelcher. (*Jahrb.
Gesch.*, 28, 1991, p. 327–341)

Schoelcher's indictment of repressive
and corrupt dictators in the independent republic of 1840s exemplifies method he used
throughout his inquiry into the Caribbean.
He combined a comparative focus, careful
evaluation of his sources, and a commitment
to truth (even when it was unwelcomed by either white Creoles or, as in this case, Haitians and European abolitionists). [APD]

2100 Schuler, Monica. Plantation labourers,
The London Missionary Society and
emancipation in West Demerara, Guyana. (*J.
Caribb. Hist.*, 22:1/2, 1988, p. 88–115)

Utilizing vast trove of material in archives of The London Missionary Society, author discovers tremendous continuity in laborers' attitudes to emancipation both before
and after 1838. While laborers regarded missionaries as agents of social change, colonial
authorities viewed them as mechanisms for
social control. [ELC]

2101 Schwartz, Stuart B. The hurricane of
San Ciriaco: disaster, politics, and soci-
ety in Puerto Rico, 1899–1901. (*HAHR*, 72:3,
Aug. 1992, p. 303–334)

Examines social and economic read-
justments in aftermath of major tropical
storm immediately after US military occupation of island. Insightful analysis of dynamic
between colonial administrators, local elites,
and working class in social construction during an emergency situation. Another welcome addition to effort to demythologize
1898. [TMV]

2102 Shepherd, Verene A. The effects of the
abolition of slavery on Jamaican livestock farms (pens), 1834–1845. (*Slavery
Abolit.*, 10:2, Sept. 1989, p. 187–211, tables)

Drawing heavily on local archival
sources, author sheds light on working conditions for ex-slaves in livestock-rearing sector
of island, as well as on economic fortunes of
the pens. Concludes that although both pens
and plantations experienced harmonious labor relations immediately after abolition,
penkeepers' attempts to classify all appren-
tices as agricultural workers led to strained
relations and the use of migrant laborers.
[ELC]

Sheridan, Richard B. Changing sugar technology and the labour nexus in the British Caribbean, 1750–1900, with special reference to
Barbados and Jamaica. See item **1936.**

**2103 Slaves, sugar, and colonial society:
travel accounts of Cuba, 1801–1899.**
Edited by Louis A. Pérez, Jr. Wilmington,
Del.: Scholarly Resources, 1992. 259 p.: bibl.,
index.

In order to be truly useful, work should
have included a note explaining social and intellectual background of each writer and reasons for selecting each account. It is puzzling,
for example, that *La Havana* by the Countess
of Merlin was excluded. [JMH]

2104 Smith, Raymond T. Race, class, and
gender in the transition to freedom. (*in*
The meaning of freedom: economics, politics,
and culture after slavery. Edited by Frank
McGlynn and Seymour Drescher. Pittsburgh,
Pa.: Univ. of Pittsburgh Press, 1992, p. 257–
290, bibl.)

Author contends that crucial factor for
explaining the social problems experienced
by African-Americans since emancipation
was not slavery itself but rather "the forces
that reproduce the social systems established
after slavery." Author notes that an important
feature of post-emancipation societies was
emergence of a status system combining gender, race, and class. For ethnologist's comment see *HLAS 53:1054.* [ELC]

2105 Stewart, Robert J. Religion and society
in post-emancipation Jamaica. Knoxville: Univ. of Tennessee Press, 1992. 254 p.:
bibl., ill., index, maps.

Impressive study examines role played
by religion, or agents of religion, both European and Afro-Jamaican, in conflicts in post-
emancipation Jamaica. Author argues that in-
ability/unwillingness of officials and religious
leaders to appreciate "worth" of African-
based religions contributed to social and political crisis in island which was still undergoing creolization. Excellent work. [ELC]

2106 Stipriaan, Alex van. Surinaams contrast: roofbouw en overleven in een
Caräíbische plantagekolonie, 1750–1863
[Suriname contrast: exhaustion and survival
in a Caribbean plantation colony, 1750–
1863]. Leiden, The Netherlands: KITLV Uit-
geverij, 1993. 494 p.: bibl., maps, photos, tables. (Caribbean series/Koninklijk Instituut

voor Taal-, Land- en Volkenkunde, 0921–9781; 13)

Noteworthy study demonstrates economic and social differences between coffee, sugar, and cotton plantations. Also focuses on importance of water management in Suriname. Argues that Suriname's plantation economy maintained a precarious balance between survival and exhaustion of soil, capital, and slaves. Based on archival research in England, Suriname, and the Netherlands. [RH]

2107 Stipriaan, Alex van. The Suriname rat race: labour and technology on sugar plantations, 1750–1900. (*Nieuwe West-Indische Gids*, 63, 1989, p. 94–117, bibl., tables)

Addresses whether slavery was an obstacle to efficiency in sugar production, and whether slavery and technical innovation were incompatible. Argues that estates which innovated more rapidly had a better chance of surviving into the next century; thus, sugar production was not hindered by slavery, and assumption that planters or slaves were opposed to innovation is a myth. [RH]

2108 Thésée, Françoise. Le jardin botanique de Saint Pierre, Martinique, 1803–1902. Paris: Editions caribéennes, 1990. 102 p.

Well-written and meticulously researched history of most important botanical garden in the French Antilles offers fascinating description of the plants that were introduced over a century as a result of an active and enlightened policy. [APD]

2109 Thiébaut, Claude. Guadeloupe 1899: année de tous les dangers. Préface du Dr H. Bangou. Paris: Editions L'Harmattan, 1989. 207 p.: bibl., ill., maps.

Contains montage of documents on a series of arsons that took place in Guadeloupe in 1898–99 as first socialist majority was elected to island's council. Work emphasizes: 1) exacerbation of political antagonisms resulting from white planters' accusations linking black socialist leader Hégésippe Légitimus to arsons; 2) impact of US intervention in Cuba which led white planters to consider requesting a similar intervention in Guadeloupe to reestablish order; and 3) firm stance by political and judicial authorities who dismissed whites' accusations about blacks and discarded possibility of US intervention. [APD]

2110 Toledo Sande, Luis. José Martí, con el remo de proa: catorce aproximaciones. La Habana: Centro de Estudios Martianos; Editorial de Ciencias Sociales, 1990. 440 p.: bibl. (Col. de estudios martianos)

Collection of carefully written and researched essays on various aspects of Martí's life and work are of very uneven value, as is usually the case with such anthologies. [JMH]

2111 Tomich, Dale W. *Une petite guinée:* provision ground and plantation in Martinique, 1830–1848. (*Slavery Abolit.*, 12: 1, May 1991, p. 68–91)

Inquiry into legal provisions regulating slave work on provision grounds as opposed to plantation fields leads author to observe a process by which slaves mitigated masters' authority in decades prior to abolition of slavery. [APD]

2112 Tomich, Dale W. Slavery in the circuit of sugar: Martinique and the world economy, 1830–1848. Baltimore, Md.: Johns Hopkins Univ. Press, 1990. 353 p.: bibl., ill. (Johns Hopkins studies in Atlantic history and culture)

Sociologist situates development of Martinique's sugar industry and change in labor conditions in the decades preceding abolition of slavery (1848) within framework of world economic system. [APD]

2113 Tomich, Dale W. Sugar technology and slave labor in Martinique, 1830–1848. (*Nieuwe West-Indische Gids*, 63:1/2, 1989, p. 118–134, bibl.)

Important article contends that planters in Martinique were aware of technological advances, which were introduced on larger plantations when availability of capital permitted. Yet the social implications of slavery delayed full-scale mechanization. [ELC]

2114 Tornero, Pablo. Productividad y rentabilidad de la mano de obra esclava en el desarrollo de la plantación cubana. (*Rev. Indias*, 51:193, sept./dic. 1991, p. 459–480, graphs, tables)

Based on Cuban archival sources, author maintains that slavery, because of its productivity and profitability, was the cornerstone of the Cuban plantation system. [JMH]

2115 Torre Molina, Mildred de la. Valoración del movimiento autonomista por algunos contemporáneos de José Martí. (*Rev.*

Bibl. Nac. José Martí, 81:33, julio/dic. 1990,
p. 79–101)

Retreads traditional paths of Cuban
historiography, which is generally viscerally
anti-autonomist. The contemporaries quoted
and commented upon by author were all leading members of pro-independence movement
and therefore political enemies of autono-
mism by definition. [JMH]

2116 La Trinitaria en su sesquicentenario.
Santo Domingo: Academia Domini-
cana de la Historia, 1988. 130 p.: bibl.

Reprints a number of documents
which are crucial for study of separation of
Dominican Republic from Haiti in 1844.
[JMH]

Trouillot, Michel-Rolph. The inconvenience
of freedom: free people of color and the political aftermath of slavery in Dominica and
Saint-Domingue/Haiti. See *HLAS 53:1062.*

2117 Turner, Mary. Slave workers, subsistence and labour bargaining: Amity
Hall, Jamaica, 1805–1832. (*Slavery Abolit.,*
12:1, May 1991, p. 92–106)

Concludes that in contrast to what
occurred in other parts of Jamaica, ration-
allotment system at Amity Hall hampered
development of bargaining procedures for
slaves. [ELC]

2118 Varia valeriana. Edición de María Teresa Arrarás Mir. San Juan: Instituto de
Cultura Puertorriqueña, 1990. 60 p.

Selection of writings related to Antonio Valero de Bernabé, Puerto Rican general
who fought alongside Bolívar and others in
the wars of independence from Spain. Includes Valero's own narration of his earlier
experiences fighting for Spain in Spain's war
of independence against French domination
(1808–09). Interesting and vivid descriptions
of the horrors of war. [E. Sacerio-Garí]

2119 Venegas Delgado, Hernán. Estudio de
una familia de la oligarquía esclavista
cubana del siglo XIX: los Valle Iznaga. (*Islas/
Santa Clara,* 91, sept./dic. 1988, p. 41–51,
bibl., maps)

Were it not for author's ideological
prejudices, study would be truly useful. [JMH]

2120 Vidales, Carlos. Corsarios y piratas de
la Revolución Francesa en las aguas de
la emancipación hispanoamericana. (*Cara-
velle/Toulouse,* 54, 1990, p. 247–262, bibl.)

New sources from Swedish archives

throw light on little-known role played by
Sweden's Caribbean colony in Spanish-
American wars of independence (1812–25). A
neutral entrepôt, St. Bartholomew was used
by privateers, mostly French, at the service of
Venezuelan and Colombian insurgents. [APD]

2121 Ward, J.R. Emancipation and the planters. (*J. Caribb. Hist.,* 22:1/2, 1988,
p. 116–137, graph, table)

Argues that only by 1830s did British
West Indian planters see emancipation as an
immediate prospect. When it came, most
took compensation money provided by Parlia-
ment to wipe out debts, and held on to their
investment in colonies in hope of improving
economic fortunes. [ELC]

2122 Whitney, Robert. The political
economy of abolition: the Hispano-
Cuban elite and Cuban slavery, 1868–1873.
(*Slavery Abolit.,* 13:2, Aug. 1992, p. 20–36)

Based mostly on secondary sources, focuses on Spanish side of abolition debate.
Maintains that issue of colonial slavery was
closely related to the most critical problems
of Spanish domestic politics. A balanced and
sensible analysis. [JMH]

2123 Wilmot, Swithin. The politics of protest in free Jamaica: the Kingston John
Canoe Christmas riots, 1840 and 1841. (*Caribb. Q.,* 36:3/4, Dec. 1990, p. 65–75)

Unlike most studies of protest in post-
emancipation Jamaica which focus on labor
conflict on estates, author addresses conflict
over leisure and culture. He contends that despite disenfranchisement of most Jamaicans
of African ancestry, disagreements over popular celebrations drew them into political conflicts in which politicians were engaged.
[ELC]

2124 Yáñez Gallardo, Cesar R. La última invasión armada: los contingentes militares españoles a las guerras de Cuba, siglo
XIX. (*Rev. Indias,* 52:194, enero/abril 1992,
p. 107–127)

Includes a number of statistical tables
prepared on the basis of archival data that are
quite useful. There is only an indirect relationship between the two sections into which
article is divided. [JMH]

2125 Zamuel, Hesdie Stuart. Johannes King:
profeet en apostel van het Surinaamse
bosland [Johannes King: prophet and apostle
of the Surinamese hinterland]. Zoetermeer,

The Netherlands: Boekencentrum, 1994. 241 p.: bibl., ill., index, map. (Mission; 6)

Biography of Johannes King, a 19th-century Maroon missionary and pastor. Although influenced by Moravian theology, King was an independent thinker whose ideas combined his African heritage with Moravian doctrine. Finally, author discusses importance of King in areas of faith, contextuality, and ministry of the Gospel. [RH]

2126 Zeuske, Michael. Bajo la bandera prusiana: compañías comerciales, comerciantes y cónsules alemanes en las Antillas, 1815–1860. (*in* Commerce et plantation dans la Caraïbe, XVIIIe et XIXe siècles: actes du colloque de Bordeaux, 15–16 mars 1991. Bordeaux: Centre d'histoire des espaces atlantiques; Maison des pays ibériques, 1992, p. 233–252, tables)

New sources from Prussian and Saxon archives illuminate beginning of German interest in the Caribbean through newly launched merchant companies (1815–25) and a network of consuls, particularly in St. Thomas and the Spanish Caribbean. [APD]

2127 Zeuske, Michael. Kolonialpolitik und Revolution: Kuba und die Unabhängigkeit der Costa Firme, 1808–1821. (*Jahrb. Gesch.*, 27, 1990, p. 149–197)

Scholarly study relates divergent paths followed by Cuba and Venezuela as a result of Spain's imperial crisis early in 19th century. Based on printed as well as archival sources. [JMH]

2128 Zeuske, Michael. Die vergessene Revolution: Haiti und Deutschland in der ersten Hälfte des 19. Jahrhunderts: Aspekte deutscher Politik und Ökonomie in Westindien. (*Jahrb. Gesch.*, 28, 1991, p. 285–325, tables)

Based on original documentation, this comprehensive study details initial German interest in 19th-century Caribbean sparked by the Latin American independence movements. Study examines: activities of companies (1820–50), particularly in coffee imports from Haiti; reports from consuls and merchants based primarily in Curaçao and St. Thomas; impact of Haitian Revolution on German liberals; and voyages of exploration. [APD]

2129 Zips, Werner. Eine afrikansche Gegenmacht in der Karibik. (*Z. Lat.am. Wien*, 40/41, 1991, p. 85–106, bibl.)

Author emphasizes Jamaican Maroon societies' resistance to repression rather than their victimization by Europeans. Also examines spiritual roots of two such societies and their plight vis-à-vis British colonialism as well as an independent Jamaican State. [C.K. Converse]

20TH CENTURY

2130 Abreu, Ramiro J. En el último año de aquella república. La Habana: Editorial de Ciencias Sociales, 1984. 293 p.: bibl. (Historia de Cuba)

Faithfully echoes Castro government's official line on the course of Cuban history prior to the triumph of the Revolution. Relies for the most part on printed sources. [JMH]

2131 Alvarez Curbelo, Silvia. La mirada en la tierra: el imaginario de los propietarios antillanos en la década de los '20. (*Rev. Rev. Interam.*, 18:1/2, 1988, p. 53–63)

Argues that global crisis of 1920s—as it affected Caribbean producers of agricultural exports—resulted in alternative discourse, which equated small landowners with patriotism. This emergent dissident ideology, although it challenged existing balance of power between dominant and subordinate groups, was not revolutionary by any definition. [TMV]

2132 Anselin, Alain. L'émigration antillaise en France: la troisième île. Paris: Karthala, 1990. 293 p.: bibl.

Sociological inquiry looks at 20 years (1962–82) of Guadeloupe and Martinique immigration to France: total number of these immigrants now represents one-third of entire population of the French Caribbean. Biographical sketches convey complexity of human experience and document evolving role of French government immigration agency through several generations of immigrants. Examines immigrants' occupational sectors, levels of income, and geographical location in France. Also analyzes emergence of a new Euro-Caribbean identity among immigrants and their changing perception of gender and race. [APD]

2133 Antología crítica de la historiografía cubana: período neocolonial. Recopilación de Carmen Almodóvar Muñoz. La Habana: Editorial Pueblo y Educación, 1989. 681 p.: bibl., ill.

Were it not for editor's all too obvious political prejudices and biases, book would be an excellent guide to 20th-century Cuban historiography. [JMH]

2134 Arce de Vázquez, Margot et al. Pedro Albizu Campos: reflexiones sobre su vida y su obra y selección de reseñas periodísticas sobre su muerte y entierro. Edición de Ruth Vassallo y José Antonio Torres Martinó. Río Piedras, P.R.: Editorial Marién, 1991. 223 p.: bibl., ill.

Collection of essays by leading public figures, academics, journalists, and followers of Albizu appearing in newspapers and journals during lifetime of "apostle of Puerto Rican nationalism" or on occasions of various commemorative events. Quality and utility of selections vary, precisely because of each author's objectives, scholarly thrust, political views, and proximity to subject matter. [TMV]

2135 Argüelles Espinosa, Luis Angel. Los refugiados mexicanos en Cuba, 1910–1927. (*Palabra Hombre*, 70, abril/junio 1989, p. 117–148, ill., tables)

Informative report examines important aspect of Cuba-Mexico relations at the time of the Mexican Revolution. [JMH]

2136 Aristide, Jean-Bertrand and Christophe Wargny. Aristide: an autobiography. Translated by Linda M. Maloney. Maryknoll, N.Y.: Orbis Books, 1993. 205 p., 8 p. of plates: bibl., ill.

Translated from the French, this portrait of the talented radical priest and of his charismatic role in Haiti's democratization process is based on recorded interviews and directed to a sympathetic audience. [APD]

2137 Arrigoitía, Delma S. José de Diego, el legislador: su visión de Puerto Rico en la historia, 1903–1918. San Juan: Instituto de Cultura Puertorriqueña, 1991. 600 p., 67 p. of plates: bibl., ill. (some col.).

Although author recognizes importance of new historiography (which characterizes De Diego as a nationalist from propertied class with little social consciousness), she defends his image as a gradually radicalized legislator under US domination, whose principal objective was political: Puerto Rico's independence and establishing that Puerto Ricans could govern themselves. She examines his political, economic, cultural, social, and civil

rights bills, all of which were subordinated to and revolved around his political goals. [TMV]

2138 Badejo, Fabian. Claude: a portrait of power. St. Maarten, Netherlands Antilles: International Pub. House, 1989. 186 p.: ill.

Biographical sketch of St. Maarten's long-time politician provides a window on the world of politics in this corner of the Caribbean. [APD]

Bellegarde-Smith, Patrick. Haiti: the breached citadel. See *HLAS 53:3532.*

2139 Bello, Alberto Alfonso and Juan Pérez Díaz. Cuba en España: una gloriosa página de internacionalismo. La Habana: Editorial de Ciencias Sociales, 1990. 275 p.: bibl., ill. (Historia)

One-sided journalistic account looks at Cuban contribution to the cause of the Republic during the Spanish Civil War. For example, work conveniently silences names of those who subsequently abandoned the ranks of the left and became prominent as its opponents. [JMH]

2140 Bird Piñero, Enrique. Don Luis Muñoz Marín: el poder de la excelencia. San Juan?: Fundación Luis Muñoz Marín, 1991. 320 p.

"Autobiographical political chronicle" recounts events as experienced by writer. As insider, author had access to political apparatus, which he observed critically. He does not, however, speculate on motives for Muñoz Marín's shifting political views or personal decisions, a welcome exception to most writings on Muñoz. [TMV]

2141 Cabán, Pedro A. El aparato colonial y el cambio económico en Puerto Rico: 1898–1917. (*Rev. Cienc. Soc./Río Piedras*, 27:1/2, marzo/junio 1988, p. 53–88)

Takes traditional view that turn of century under US domination marked the beginning of capitalism on the island. Explores political underpinnings of system, arguing that present crisis has its roots in early congressional legislation which defined the nature of the colonial state. The factors he considers as relevant and still at play are US geopolitical and strategic interests, differences of opinion among US capitalists, and divisions within the island bourgeoisie.

2142 Capetillo, Luisa. Amor y anarquía: los escritos de Luisa Capetillo. Edición de Julio Ramos. Río Piedras, P.R.: Ediciones Huracán, 1992. 222 p.: bibl., ill. (Col. Clásicos Huracán; 5)

Lengthy introduction places in both historical and literary context the writings of Luisa Capetillo, well-known Puerto Rican anarchist and feminist in first decades of 20th century. Relying heavily on postmodernist analysis, author argues that by appropriating dominant literary discourses of the time, Capetillo transcended limits of the written word and altered its relation to power. In this way, she commented subversively on female sexuality, bourgeois institutions, religion, and everyday happenings. Includes excellent bibliography and biographical notes on Capetillo. [TMV]

Chamberlain, Mary. Renters and farmers: the Barbadian plantation tenantry system, 1917–1937. See *HLAS 53:993.*

Chevannes, Barry. Healing the nation: Rastafari exorcism of the ideology of racism in Jamaica. See *HLAS 53:5133.*

2143 Contín Alfau, Melchor. El Hato Mayor del Rey: reseña histórico-geográfica, tradicional y religiosa. Santo Domingo: Taller, 1991. 219 p.: ill.

Work recounts local history with an international dimension. Those interested in impact of US interventions in the Caribbean must read the chapter on 1917 American occupation of Hato Mayor del Rey. [JMH]

2144 Contrera, Nelio. *Alma Mater:* la revista de Mella. La Habana: Editorial de Ciencias Sociales, 1989. 105 p.: bibl., ill., index. (Historia de Cuba)

Study covers entire collection of *Alma Mater,* from 1922–59. Modest effort with a sectarian tone, but still useful. [JMH]

2145 Córdova, Gonzalo F. Luis Sánchez Morales, servidor ejemplar. San Juan: Editorial Académica, 1991. 261 p.: bibl., ill.

Traditional biography examines key figure in Republican Party in early decades of 20th century. In those years, Córdova suggests, statehood option as we know it began to take shape. Author argues that despite Sánchez Morales' political status preference, he was a true patriot, widely respected by men and women of divergent views. Fits in well

with contemporary political debates on the island. [TMV]

2146 Craig, Susan E. Smiles and blood: the ruling class response to the workers' rebellion of 1937 in Trinidad and Tobago. London: New Beacon Books, 1988. 70 p., 4 p. of plates: bibl., ill.

Succinct treatment looks at socioeconomic conditions in early 20th-century Trinidad and Tobago. Author argues that only marginal reform took place in wake of 1937 labor disturbances and that ruling class hegemony remained intact up to at least the 1950s. [ELC]

2147 Cupull, Adys and **Froilán González.** La CIA contra el Che. La Habana: Editora Política, 1992. 373 p.: ill., index.

The most critical section of this volume, that which deals with involvement of the CIA in Guevara's death, is based entirely on second-hand sources. Credibility of the whole story, as told by authors, is highly doubtful.

2148 Damour, Alix. Häíti, dictature de Prosper Avril. Port-au-Prince?: A. Damour, 1990? 277 p.: ill.

A Haitian journalist denounces repressive rule of General Avril, one of the military dictators that followed the fall of Jean-Claude Duvalier (1986). Author, who views Avril as "working under the *diktat* of western embassies," shows a new awareness of issue of human rights violations. [APD]

2149 Dijk, Frank Jan van. Jahmaica: Rastafari and Jamaican society, 1930–1990. Utrecht, The Netherlands: ISOR, 1993. 482 p.: bibl., maps, table.

Describes and analyzes influence of external factors on process of change and development in the Rastafarian Movement. Emphasizes actions and reactions of wider Jamaican society and their effects on the Movement. Based on newspaper reports, Rastafarian pamphlets, colonial and government records, and interviews. [RH]

2150 Dookhan, Isaac. Military-civilian conflicts in the Virgin Islands during World War II. (*J. Caribb. Hist.,* 24:1, May 1990, p. 89–110)

Concentrating on St. Thomas and St. Croix where military presence existed during the war, author faults both military and local political leaders for failing to take decisive action in face of incipient race-class conflicts. [ELC]

2151 Drakes, Francis M. The People's Association, 1903–1921. (*Hist. Gaz.*, 36, Sept. 1991, p. 2–14)

Succinct treatment of efforts by members of middle class, both East Indians and individuals of African ancestry, in British Guiana to promote economic and political change which would enhance their interests. [ELC]

2152 Drakes, Francis M. The reaction of Sir Frederick Hodgson to the protest of 1905. (*Hist. Gaz.*, 37, Oct. 1991, p. 2–14)

Excellent study of the overreaction of the colonial governor in British Guiana to signs of working-class protest. Governor Hodgson's use of military force, threats, and duplicity suppressed protest, divided workers, and delayed emergence of genuine working class consciousness. [ELC]

2153 Duarte Oropesa, José Antonio. Historiología cubana. v. 4, Desde 1959 hasta 1980: la revolución traicionada. Miami, Fla.: Ediciones Universal, 1993. 1 v. (Col. Cuba y sus jueces)

Despite the bitterness that permeates its pages, the passion that underlies treatment of the subject, and author's judgment of men and events, work is still noteworthy as source of detailed information on the period. [JMH]

Fernández, Ronald. The disenchanted island: Puerto Rico and the United States in the twentieth century. See *HLAS 53:4663.*

2154 Fernández Soriano, Armando. La migración puertorriqueña a Cuba, 1898–1915. (*Rev. Cent. Estud. Av.*, 8, enero/junio 1989, p. 18–26)

Examines Puerto Rican migration to Cuba after US invasion as precursor of larger contingents of Haitians and Jamaicans. Argues that economic and cultural similarities between Puerto Rico and Cuba were obstacles to continued immigration. In addition, asserts that Puerto Rico's status as colony of US tied would-be migrants to Lesser Antilles. [TMV]

2155 Ferrao, Luis A. Pedro Albizu Campos, el Partido Nacionalista y el catolicismo, 1930–1939. (*Hómines/San Juan*, 13:2/14:1, agosto 1989/agosto 1990, p. 224–247)

Author explains Albizu Campos' doctrinaire Catholicism as reaction to Protestantism and Freemasonry and as result of his ties to Irish nationalism formed while at Harvard. Suggests that faction that did *not* prevail within Partido Nacionalista was probably closer to an authentic social justice lay movement. [TMV]

2156 Ferrao, Luis Angel. La persecución y el proceso judicial contra los Nacionalistas, 1934–1936. (*Rev. Hist./San Juan*, 3:7, enero/dic. 1988, p. 123–145)

Author argues that Albizu Campos' self-defense when accused of conspiring to overthrow US government in mid-1930s makes evident his limited revolutionary goals and traditional view of democracy. Based on limited sources. [TMV]

2157 French, Joan. Colonial policy towards women after the 1938 uprising: the case of Jamaica. (*Caribb. Q.*, 34:3/4, Sept./Dec. 1988, p. 38–61, tables, bibl.)

Author argues that colonial policy after 1938 served to blunt the militancy of women who played highly visible roles in 1938 disturbances. Additionally, constitutional advancement which colony achieved in wake of these disturbances likewise denied women equal participation with men. [ELC]

2158 Frente Camagüey. La Habana: Editora Política, 1988. 419 p.: bibl., ill., maps.

Covers some of the most important episodes of Castro's revolutionary war against the Batista dictatorship. Informative and useful, as long as one keeps in mind that this work was commissioned by the Cuban government and the Party. [JMH]

2159 Gaillard, Gusti-Klara. L'expérience häïtienne de la dette extérieure, ou, Une production caféière pillée: 1875–1915. Port-au-Prince: Impr. H. Deschamps, 1990. 174 p.: bibl., ill.

Using interpretive framework of the "Dependency School," well-researched study links decline of custom duties on coffee exports to France (Haiti's main source of income) with rise of domestic political instability, as successive governments proved unable to stop the escalating debt. [APD]

2160 Gaillard, Roger. Les cent-jours de Rosalvo Bobo, ou, Une mise à mort politique. 2. éd. remaniée. Port-au-Prince: R. Gaillard, 1987. 300 p., 8 p. of plates: bibl., ill., index, map. (Les Blancs débarquent; 2)

From a series on modern Haitian political history, this volume examines personality and activities of the well-known leader and medical doctor from northern Haiti. Amid a foreign debt crisis, Bobo's armed uprising against the government was rationale used by US to intervene in 1915. [APD]

2161 García-Passalacqua, Juan M. and **Carlos Rivera Lugo.** Puerto Rico y los Estados Unidos: el proceso de consulta y negociación de 1989 y 1990. Traducción de Cordelia Buitrago Díaz y Betsy López Abrams. Río Piedras: Editorial de la Univ. de Puerto Rico, 1990–1991. 2 v. (162, 380 p.): bibl.

Authors believe that this collection of selected articles illustrates well the consultations and negotiations held between US and Puerto Rico in preparation for plebiscite that was *not* held in 1991. Political parties, the authors assert, must modify their discourse to conform to changing paradigms that have defined US policy toward Puerto Rico, as evidenced in documentation they present. They suggest that plebiscite was not held because, during the preliminary consultations, the statehood option seemed likely to prevail, an option the US could not accept. In authors' opinion, this realization is somewhat of a discovery for many Puerto Ricans. [TMV]

2162 Gautreaux Piñeyro, Bonaparte. El gobierno de Caamaño, 1965: documentos, discursos y decretos. Santo Domingo: Editora Corripio, 1989. 151 p.: ill., facsims.

Includes brief account of Caamaño's government, facsimiles of a number of its decrees, and a dozen of Caamaño's speeches. Most of the decrees concern appointment or dismissal of government officials. [JMH]

2163 González, Raymundo. Peña Batlle y su concepto histórico de la nación dominicana. (*Anu. Estud. Am.*, 48, 1991, p. 585–631)

Presents critical analysis of intellectual evolution of one of the most important representatives of Dominican conservative thought. [JMH]

2164 Guerrero, Miguel. Enero de 1962: ¡el despertar dominicano! 2da. ed. Santo Domingo: Ediciones Mograf, 1991. 294 p.: bibl., ill., index, map. (Col. Historia y cultura)

Journalistic but eminently readable and informative account examines this critical two-week period of contemporary Dominican history. [JMH]

2165 Guerrero, Miguel. Los últimos días de la era de Trujillo. Santo Domingo: Editora Corripio, 1991. 374 p., 20 p. of plates: bibl., ill., index.

Readable and informative journalistic account describes end of Trujillo era. [JMH]

2166 Guevara, Ernesto. A new society: reflections for today's world. Edited by David Deutschmann. Melbourne, Australia: Ocean Press, 1991. 234 p.: bibl., ill., index.

New anthology of Guevara's translated writings is based on two assumptions which reader may or may not share: 1) that Guevara is "one of the most outstanding Marxist thinkers of this century;" and 2) that, as Castro says, "many of his ideas are absolutely relevant today." Book structures Guevara's writings by topic, thus making it easier for reader to consult them. [JMH]

Guevara, Ernesto. Notas para el estudio de la ideología de la Revolución Cubana. See item **5409.**

2167 ¿Hasta cuando las Américas toleran al dictador Castro, el implacable stalinista que continua oprimiendo al pueblo cubano, y amenazando a naciones hermanas?: dos décadas de progresivo acercamiento comuno-católico en la isla-presidio del Caribe. Miami, Fla.: Cubanos Desterrados, 1990. 182 p.: bibl.

Bitter denunciation of the Cuban Catholic Church and its behavior under Castro regime is interesting only because it emanates from an avowed Catholic group, and as a good example of one of the most extreme positions in the debate about Cuban Catholicism. [JMH]

2168 Helg, Aline. Afro-Cuban protest: the Partido Independiente de Color, 1908–1912. (*Cuba. Stud.*, 21, 1991, p. 101–121)

While sound and informative, work tends to view events from perspective of our own times. [JMH]

2169 Hernández, Luis Alberto. The origins of the consumer culture in Puerto Rico: the pre-television years, 1898–1954. (*Cent. Estud. Puertorriq. Bull.*, 3:1, 1990/1991, p. 38–54, bibl.)

Based on premise that technologies are neither independent nor non-ideological, author claims that media are responsible for rapid socioeconomic and cultural changes in Puerto Rico during first half of 20th century.

The media were the "distributional and ideological channels" of expanding capitalism, especially radio after 1922. [TMV]

Hira, Sandew. The evolution of the social, economic and political position of the East Indians in Surinam, 1873–1893. See item **2020.**

2170 **James, C.L.R.** The C.L.R. James Reader. Edited and introduced by Anna Grimshaw. Oxford, England; Cambridge, Mass.: Blackwell, 1992. 451 p.: bibl., index.

Useful collection contains representative writings of this Trinidadian-born man of letters and Pan-African thinker. Includes pieces previously unpublished. Essays shed additional light on thought and career of a brilliant Caribbeanist. Essential reading. [ELC]

2171 **John, George.** Williams, his life and his politics: September 25, 1911-March 29, 1981. Port of Spain: Trinidad Express Newspapers Ltd., 1991. 96 p.: ill. (Express books; 5)

Provides excellent vignettes of life of Eric Williams, former prime minister of Trinidad and Tobago. Especially useful biographical sketch and impressive collection of pictures encapsulates different moods and experiences of individual who dwarfed political stage for 25 years. [ELC]

2172 **Johnson, Peter T.** and **Francisco J. Fonseca.** Cuban serials and primary source collections: a bibliography of microfilm negatives. (*Cuba. Stud.*, 22, 1992, p. 231–246, bibl.)

Bibliography is useful for students of 20th-century Cuba. [JMH]

2173 **Kaplan, S.; R. Moncarz;** and **J. Steinberg.** Jewish emigrants to Cuba, 1898–1960. (*Int. Migr.*, 28:3, Sept. 1990, p. 295–310, tables)

Although some comments made in passing are highly debatable, work is acceptable introduction to the subject.

2174 **Krier, León.** Completar Santurce: estudio preliminar para el plan maestro de un barrio. San Juan: Oficina de Asuntos Urbanos, Oficina del Gobernador, La Fortaleza, 1992. 69 p.: facsims., maps.

Study was commissioned to well-known architect and city planner from Luxembourg by Senate Commission on Urban Affairs in 1988. Argues that Santurce, once an active commercial and residential hub, can be rehabilitated through building three-story multiple-family residences, promoting sense of community, decentralizing authority, and creating green areas. [TMV]

2175 **LaMotta, Gregory.** Working people and the transfer of the Danish West Indies to the United States, 1916–1917. (*J. Caribb. Hist.*, 23:2, Nov. 1989, p. 178–195)

Argues that fledgling labor movement in Danish West Indies strongly supported Denmark's sale of the islands to US in hopes that under US control conditions for the working class would improve. [ELC]

2176 **Léger, Jacques Nicolas.** Le "Carnet" de Jacques Nicolas Léger. (*Rev. Soc. häïti.*, 47:169, mars/juin 1991, p. 66–103; 47:170, sept. 1991, p. 37–81; and 47:171, déc. 1991, p. 35–73)

Private diary written by member of Haiti's educated elite presents day-by-day narration of rise of domestic political crisis and early steps of US assumption of control in early 20th century. General scarcity of public records gives special relevance to this work. [APD]

2177 **Lionet, Christian.** Häïti: l'année Aristide. Paris: L'Harmattan, 1992. 463 p.

This valuable tool for future research examines a turning point in Haiti's democratization: the election of Jean-Bertand Aristide as President in 1990. Based on coverage by French journalist for the major French newspaper *Libération*. Contains abundant factual information and data on key figures and is unusual for its exclusive focus on the national dynamic. [APD]

2178 **López Springfield, Consuelo.** Through the people's eyes: C.L.R. James's rhetoric of history. (*Caribb. Q.*, 36:1/2, June 1990, p. 85–97)

Useful analysis of major writings and ideas of the Caribbean's foremost social critic and political crusader. Author stresses James' versatility and use of history in explaining contemporary issues. [ELC]

2179 **Luis Muñoz Marín: juicios sobre su significado histórico.** Recopilación, presentación y prólogo de Carmelo Rosario Natal. San Juan: Fundación Luis Muñoz Marín, 1990. 110 p.: bibl.

Writings by public figures of all political persuasions compiled upon Muñoz Marín's death. The prologue reopens debate surrounding Muñoz's actions: was the island's material well-being worth its "moral degeneration?" Exposure to dilemmas of the period and contradictions of Muñoz's personality will inevitably lead readers to conclude that Muñoz Marín is still the grand figure of Puerto Rican politics. [TMV]

2180 **Luque Escalona, Roberto.** The tiger and the children: Fidel Castro and the judgment of history. Translated by Manuel A. Tellechea. New Brunswick, N.J.: Transaction Publishers; New York: Freedom House, 1992. 212 p.

Lively attempt to explain rise of Castro's Cuba is written by a well-known Cuban dissident. Along with gross errors, platitudes, and obvious exaggerations, author offers quite a few sharp insights into Cuban situation. For political scientist's comment see *HLAS 53: 3652.* [JMH]

2181 **Malagón Barceló, Javier.** El exilio en Santo Domingo. (*Rev. Eme-Eme*, 15: 84, sept./dic. 1989, p. 3–23)

Personal reminiscences produce a vivid and balanced account of experiences of Spanish exiles who sought refuge in Dominican Republic between 1939–42.

Maluquer de Motes Bernet, Jordi. Nación e inmigración: los españoles en Cuba, ss. XIX y XX. See item **2051.**

2182 **Manley, Michael.** A voice at the workplace: reflections on colonialism and the Jamaican worker. London: A. Deutsch, 1975. 239 p: index.

Written by former trade union organizer who later became prime minister, book is candid portrayal of struggles of Jamaican workers to achieve rights, status, and power in workplace from 1951–74, and of Manley's own involvement in these struggles. Sheds light on Jamaica's class structure. Extremely useful. [ELC]

2183 **Marrero Betancourt, Rosana.** Los proyectos Tydings para la independencia de Puerto Rico y sus efectos. (*Rev. Jurid. Univ. P.R.*, 60:2, 1991, p. 489–566)

Author examines Tydings bills discussed in US Congress during 1930s and 1940s. Concomitant with pro-independence movements on island, the bills destabilized

Puerto Rican politics and made obvious the necessity for self-determination. Nonetheless, the island's political status is still being negotiated in Congress. [TMV]

2184 **Martínez Fernández, Luis.** San Lorenzo: notas para su historia: el comportamiento electoral del municipio durante la era de dominación Popular, 1940–1968. San Juan: Comité Historia de los Pueblos; Oficina Estatal de Preservación Histórica, 1986. 37 p.: bibl., ill., maps.

Author explores why Partido Popular Democrático (PPD) was not popular in San Lorenzo and even lost elections in 1948 and 1960. He concludes that PPD economic program was unattractive to the town's tobacco-based economy because tobacco was grown on small farms (unlike sugar and coffee which were grown on *latifundia*). Religion was also a factor in this conservative town. As it became more profitable to work in sugar and coffee, *sanlorenceños* migrated to US. Even though Partido Nuevo Progresista message had little appeal to urban masses, it was still an alternative to failed PPD development program. [TMV]

2185 **Martínez Villena, Rubén.** Rubén Martínez Villena: el periodista revolucionario: artículos. Edición de Ana Núñez Machín. Santiago de Cuba: Editorial Oriente, 1988. 135 p.: bibl., ill., index.

Anthology of newspaper articles is certain to make the life of researchers easier. [JMH]

2186 **Mathurin, Maggy.** Dechoukay: rêves et bruits de bottes = sonmey ak bri bót yo = sueños y ruidos de botas: Haiti, 1986. Santo Domingo?: Edición GHRAP-CEDEE, s.d. 125 p.: ill. (some col.).

Photographs show popular "uprooting" of repressive figures associated with government of Jean-Claude Duvalier, in year following his downfall (1986). Written from a popular Marxist perspective, commentary omits role of Catholic Church and non-governmental organizations in popular mobilization. [APD]

2187 **Mauvois, Georges B.** Louis des Etages, 1873–1925: itinéraire d'un homme politique martiniquais. Préface de Monchoachi. Photos de Michel Ménil. Paris: Karthala, 1990. 142 p.: bibl., ill. .

Biography of one of Martinique's first

socialist leaders conveys violent political climate of 1920s, in which sugar interests rigged elections and manipulated politicians of all tendencies. [APD]

2188 Michel, Georges. Charlemagne Péralte. Port-au-Prince: G. Michel, 1989. 124 p., 8 p. of plates: bibl., ill.

Summary of life cf leader from northern Haiti famous for leading popular resistance against US occupation was written in honor of 100th anniversary of his birth. Includes chronology and reproductions of photographic and written documents. [APD]

Miranda Peláez, Georgelina and **Irene Bolmey Pavón.** Las Pascuas sangrientas: 1957–1987. See *HLAS 53:3659.*

Moïse, Claude. Constitutions et luttes de pouvoir en Haïti: 1804–1987. v. 1. See *HLAS 53:3539.*

2189 Montenegro González, Augusto. Cuba: vicisitudes de una comunidad eclesial, 1898–1983. (*in* Manual de historia de la Iglesia. v. 10, La Iglesia del siglo XX en España, Portugal y América Latina. Barcelona: Editorial Herder, s.d., 1 v.: bibl.)

Work is easily one of the most balanced and scholarly accounts written regarding trajectory of the Cuban Catholic Church during the national period. Highly recommended. [JMH]

2190 Moya Pons, Frank. Empresarios en conflicto: políticas de industrialización y sustitución de importaciones en la República Dominicana. Santo Domingo: Fondo para el Avance de las Ciencias Sociales, 1992. 433 p.: bibl., index.

Book is based on author's dissertation written at Columbia Univ. under direction of Herbert S. Klein. The dissertation has already spawned articles such as the one also reviewed in this section (see item **2191**). [JMH]

2191 Moya Pons, Frank. Import-substitution industrialization policies in the Dominican Republic, 1925–61. (*HAHR,* 70:4, Nov. 1990, p. 539–577, table)

Careful and well-researched study examines continuing efforts of several Dominican administrations to attract foreign investors. Among other things, article questions dictator Trujillo's alleged economic nationalism, and points to absolute lack of a national industrial class when World War II began. [JMH]

2192 Naranjo Orovio, Consuelo. La actuación de la Falange en Cuba durante la Guerra Civil Española. (*Santiago/Cuba,* 73, junio 1989, p. 109–129)

Study is centered on activities of the Falange, with only brief and often insubstantial references to Cuban response to such activities. Conclusions are a reflection of sources used by the author, which in many cases are openly leftist or pro-Communist. [JMH]

2193 Ocaña R., Antonio. Testimonio para la historia. Santo Domingo: Editora Alfa & Omega, 1991. 432 p.

Collection of mostly personal reminiscences with an obvious political bent is useful for study of 20th-century Dominican Republic. [JMH]

2194 Osa, Enrique de la. Crónica del año 33. La Habana: Editorial de Ciencias Sociales, 1989. 215 p.: bibl., ill. (Ediciones políticas)

Collection of the often distorted views, reminiscences, and highly personal interpretations of men and events from a journalist of the extreme left.

2195 Pacheco, Judas. Abel Santamaría y el Moncada. La Habana: Editora Política, 1983. 230 p.: bibl.

A modest, hagiographical, and politically-inspired biographical sketch of Castro's second-in-command at the time of the Moncada attack. [JMH]

2196 Pamphile, Léon Denius. L'éducation en Haïti sous l'occupation américaine, 1915–1934. Port-au-Prince: Impr. des Antilles, 1988. 316 p.: bibl., index.

Examines system of primary education developed by US occupation authorities as instrument to spread democratic values. As author notes, system was based on a pedagogical tradition foreign to Haiti. [APD]

2197 Pantin, Raoul. Black power day: the 1970 February Revolution: a reporter's story. Santa Cruz, Trinidad and Tobago: Hatuey Productions, 1990. 119 p.: ill.

Well-respected Trinidadian journalist presents gripping account of his experiences and recollections of Black Power protests and demonstrations which culminated in army mutiny. Provides vivid glimpses into mood of country, and of leading political figures. For sociologist's comment see *HLAS 53:3563.* [ELC]

2198 Pantojas-García, Emilio. Puerto Rican populism revisited: the PPD during the 1940s. (*J. Lat. Am. Stud.*, 21:1, Feb. 1989, p. 521–557, tables)

Author's thesis challenges traditional understanding of period of rapid State-sponsored economic and political change. He also disputes more recent interpretations that present political project of Partido Popular Democrático as reflecting goals of a middle class intent on developing an autonomous self-sustained capitalism. In author's words, "Puerto Rican populism [in the form of the early PPD's reformist proposals] articulated the interest not of a local bourgeoisie in formation but of an imperialist bourgeoisie." [TMV]

2199 Peña Batlle, Manuel Arturo. Previo a la dictadura: la etapa liberal. Recopilación, presentación y comentarios de Bernardo Vega. Santo Domingo: Fundación Peña Batlle, 1991. 277 p.: bibl., ill., index. (Obras; 2)

Contains vital documentation for correct interpretation of Peña Batlle's work and thought. [JMH]

2200 Pérez, Jorge. La *plena* puertorriqueña: de la expresión popular a la comercialización musical. (*Cent. Estud. Puertorriq. Bull.*, 3:2, 1991, p. 50–55)

Establishes that origins of *plena* can be found in social protest or denunciation of local evils. But commercial market ignores collective source of this musical production and so dilutes social message. Also, Cuban rhythms were added during 1920s-1940s. Article does not mention racial element (in artists or in audience). [TMV]

2201 Pérez, Louis A., Jr. Cuba-U.S. relations: a survey of twentieth century historiography. (*Rev. Interam. Bibliogr.*, 39:3, 1989, p. 311–328)

Excellent and scholarly guide to vast literature on the subject basically covers US and Cuban materials. A few of author's evaluations are somewhat debatable.

2202 Pérez, Louis A., Jr. Researching United States relations with Cuban Revolution. (*Pac. Hist. Rev.*, 61:1, Feb. 1992, p. 115–120)

Shows conclusively that many years, and perhaps decades, will have to pass before definitive history of US-Cuban revolution relations is written.

2203 Rabkin, Rhoda Pearl. Cuban politics: the revolutionary experiment. New York: Praeger, 1991. 235 p.: bibl., index, map. (Politics in Latin America)

Author set out to write a primarily factual introduction to Cuban politics and has amply succeeded. Book is reasonably well researched, and presentation has been accomplished with intellectual fairness. [JMH]

2204 Regards sur la Martinique des années soixante. Photographies de Arlette Rosa Lameynardie. Textes de Roland Suvélor. Fort-de-France: Editions Exbrayat, 1989. 95 p.: ill.

With just a few photographs of remarkable quality, this album documents better than many studies the remnants of life in Martinique prior to 1960s modernization. Depicts working in the fields, street selling, family gatherings, and mourning the dead. [APD]

2205 Renault, Jean-Michel. Bons baisers de la colonie: la Guadeloupe en 1900. Montpellier, France: Editions du Pélican, 1991. 159 p.: bibl., ill. (some col.).

Felicitous selection of postcards highlights *Belle Époque* in the French Lesser Antilles. Particularly evocative of urban life in Pointe-à-Pitre. [APD]

2206 Rodón Alvarez, Lincoln. 62 años de historia, 1928-1990: autobiografía de Lincoln Rodón. Diagramación y composición de Guillermo J. Jorge. Miami, Fla.: Laurently Pub., 1990. 347 p.: ill., ports.

Useful for period 1928–59, when author was actively involved in Cuban politics. [JMH]

2207 Rodríguez Bonilla, Manuel. La Batalla de La Barranquita. Santo Domingo: Editora Universitaria, 1987. 337 p.: bibl., ill. (Publicaciones de la Univ. Autónoma de Santo Domingo; 560. Col. Historia y sociedad; 73)

Covers the clash between Dominicans and invading Americans in 1916, and efforts made to keep alive the historical record of the battle. Unpretentious work is worth consulting because of its subject matter. [JMH]

2208 Rodríguez-Fatricelli, Carlos. Colonial politics and education: the pan-Americanization of the University of Puerto Rico, 1923-1929. (*Hist. Soc./Río Piedras*, 4, 1991, p. 138–164)

Author argues that Univ. of Puerto Rico began as attempt to make island an inter-American center during chancellorship of Thomas Benner. Uses as examples School of Tropical Medicine, School of Commerce, and Department of Hispanic Studies, all of which were joint efforts with US institutions of higher learning and grant foundations. [TMV]

2209 Rodríguez-Fatricelli, Carlos. Pedro Albizu Campos: strategies of struggle and strategic struggles. (*Cent. Estud. Puertorriq. Bull.*, 4:1, 1991/1992, p. 24–33)

Refutes traditional understanding that Albizu pursued independence through violence when electoral process proved unsuccessful. Author examines national, metropolitan, and international forces to trace strategic trajectory of Partido Nacionalista. [TMV]

2210 Rosado, Marisa. Las llamas de la aurora: acercamiento a una biografía de Pedro Albizu Campos. San Juan: s.n.; Santo Domingo: Editora Corripio, 1992. 246, 193 p.: appendices, bibl., ill.

In this chronological, admiring biography of nationalist leader, author tries to reestablish Albizu as ultimate patriot. Serves as good reference work; collects photographs of personal and political life; and reproduces documents of (somewhat antiquarian) interest. [TMV]

2211 Rosario Urrutia, Mayra. El combate prohibicionista contra "la copa de ron." (*Punto Coma*, 1:2, 1989, p. 47–72)

Author places prohibitionist discourse in political context (1917) and within progressive movement among Puerto Rican upper class, Partido Socialista, Protestant church, and suffragists. She is surprised at extremist positions adopted by both sides. Unfortunately, does not explore economic interests in favor of alcohol consumption. [TMV]

2212 Rúa, Pedro Juan. La encrucijada del idioma: ensayo en torno al inglés oficial, la defensa del español criollo y la descolonización puertorriqueña. San Juan: División de Publicaciones y Grabaciones, Instituto de Cultura Puertorriqueña, 1992. 108 p.

Author traces origins and causes of "English Only" movement in US and its possible effects on Puerto Rico. Book focuses on language as axis of definition of Puerto Rican nationality, both in mainland and island, and

appeals to unity that transcends political ideologies. Author's style and vocabulary are somewhat popular. Quite timely for plebiscite controversy. [TMV]

2213 Ryan, Selwyn D. Revolution and reaction: a study of parties and politics in Trinidad and Tobago, 1970–1981. St. Augustine, Trinidad and Tobago: Institute of Social and Economic Research, Univ. of the West Indies, 1989. 300 p., 8 p. of plates: bibl., ill., index.

Written by one of Trinidad's leading political scientists, book covers period during which Eric Williams' party faced increasing attacks by those disillusioned with post-independence nationalist policies. Argues that temporary economic boom of mid-1970s checked voter discontent and permitted party to win record sixth successive term in 1981. For political scientist's comment see *HLAS 53:3565.* [ELC]

2214 Sáez, José Luis. Papeles del Padre Fuertes, 1871–1926. Santo Domingo: Sociedad Dominicana de Bibliófilos, 1989. 343 p.: bibl., ill. (Col. Quinto centenario: Serie Documentos; 1)

Work is scholarly supplement to author's previously published biography of Father Fuertes, the quiet Spanish priest who spent so many years evangelizing remote province of Barahona. [JMH]

2215 Santiago-Valles, Kelvin. Dancing with colonialism: the current plebiscite debate in Puerto Rico as crisis management. (*Cent. Estud. Puertorriq. Bull.*, 4:2, 1992, p. 12–26)

Denounces "postmodern" rhetoric of three major political parties. Claims current debate over colonial status ignores more important discussion of social and economic effects of colonialism on majority of population. Articulate and convincing argument. [TMV]

2216 Sarría, Pedro. Mi prisionero Fidel: recuerdos del teniente Pedro Sarría. Narrados a Lázaro Barrero Medina. La Habana: Unión de Periodistas de Cuba, 1989. 92 p.: ill.

Reminiscences of the Batista officer who helped to save Castro's life after failure of Moncada attack provide additional information on basically well-known subject. [JMH]

2217 Scholtens, Ben; Gloria Wekker; Laddy van Putten; and Stanley Diko. Gaama duumi, buta gaama: overlijden en opvolging van Aboikoni, grootopperhoofd van de Saramaka Bosnegers [The Paramount Chief is asleep, installation of the Paramount Chief: death and succession of Aboikoni, Paramount Chief of the Saramaka Maroons]. Paramaribo: Afdeling Cultuur Studies-Ministerie van Onderwijs en Volksontwikkeling, 1992. 206 p.: bibl., ill., map, photos.

Detailed and unique description of the extensive series of rituals following the death of *gaama* Aboikoni in 1989. The first chapters provide background on Saramaka society and culture and a biography of Aboikoni. Author documents the rituals associated with the death and succession of a *gaama* in pictures and text. Includes summary in English. [RH]

2218 Silva Gotay, Samuel. El Partido Acción Cristiana: trasfondo histórico y significado sociológico del nacimiento y muerte de un partido político católico en Puerto Rico. (*Rev. Hist./San Juan*, 7, 1988, p. 146–184)

Offers historical overview of position of Catholic Church with respect to US domination and Partido Popular Democrático (PPD). Partido Acción Cristiana united pro-Spanish elements (conceivably favoring independence or autonomy) and annexationists, both opposed to the modernizing populism of PPD (in the form of secular education and birth control). As a party with no class backing and concerned with issues of no real social significance, it was bound to disappear. [TMV]

2219 Silvestrini, Blanca A. Contemporary Puerto Rico: a society of contrasts. (*in* The modern Caribbean. Edited by Franklin W. Knight and Colin A. Palmer. Chapel Hill: Univ. of North Carolina Press, 1989, p. 147–167)

Author traces major political and economic events of 20th century and argues that result of this process is a constantly redefined cultural identity among Puerto Ricans both on the island and in the US. [TMV]

2220 Sims, Harold Dana. Collapse of the house of labor: ideological divisions in the Cuban labor movement and U.S. role, 1944–1949. (*Cuba. Stud.*, 21, 1991, p. 123–147)

Based on confidential central files of the State Dept., study shows that, at the time, US officials were hesitant to purge Cuban labor movement of its Communist leadership. [JMH]

2221 Stolberg, Claus F. British colonial policy and the Great Depression: the case of Jamaica. (*J. Caribb. Hist.*, 23:2, Nov. 1989, p. 142–163, appendix, table)

Author focuses on creation of cooperative enterprise and on attempt at land reform to demonstrate that, in the wake of the Great Depression, Britain adopted modern development policies which represented a partial transition from colonial to post-colonial imperialism. [ELC]

2222 Stoner, K. Lynn. Ofelia Domínguez Navarro: the making of a Cuban socialist feminist. (*in* The human tradition in Latin America: the twentieth century. Edited by William H. Beezley and Judith Ewell. Wilmington, Del.: Scholarly Resources, 1987, p. 119–140, bibl.)

Informative biographical sketch is so sympathetic to Domingo Navarro that the fact that she once volunteered her services as a lawyer to defend Leon Trotsky's murderer is barely mentioned. [JMH]

2223 Stoner, K. Lynn. On men reforming the rights of men: the abrogation of the Cuban adultery law, 1930. (*Cuba. Stud.*, 21, 1991, p. 83–99)

No one will object to central thesis of this article, but some related issues discussed by author are highly debatable. Juridical aspects of problem are neglected. [JMH]

2224 Suggs, Henry Lewis. The response of the African-American press to the United States occupation of Haiti, 1915–1934. (*J. Negro Hist.*, 73:1/4, 1988, p. 33–45)

Reviews diverse reactions of US African-American press to Haiti's occupation. Author notes that the newspaper writings had limited impact among African-American population, which distrusted a press they regarded as bourgeois. [APD]

2225 A survey of Cuban *revistas*, 1902–1958. Compiled and annotated by Roberto Esquenazi-Mayo. Washington: Library of Congress, 1993. 112 p.: bibl., ill., index.

Superb survey of Cuban *revistas* is not merely a bibliographical tool, as Professor Santí states in the introduction, but a literary essay and memoir. Each entry is like a snap-shot of the period in which the *revista* was published. [JMH]

2226 Taibo, Paco Ignacio. La batalla del Che: Santa Clara. La Habana: Editora Política, 1989. 203 p.: bibl. (Col. Curujey)

While not a scholarly work, book is useful for study of important episode of the Cuban Revolution. [JMH]

2227 Tauler López, Arnoldo. Las ideas no se matan. La Habana: Editorial de Ciencias Sociales, 1988. 258 p.: bibl., ill. (Historia de Cuba)

Deals primarily with time Castro spent in Boniato prison after Moncada attack and with attempt of Batista's henchmen to poison him. Based primarily on oral testimony. [JMH]

2228 Tennyson, Brian Douglas. The British West Indies and Mackenzie King's national policy in the 1920s. (*J. Caribb. Hist.*, 24:1, May 1990, p. 65–88)

Argues that Mackenzie King was sincere in his efforts to improve trade relations with the British West Indies, and that this initiative stemmed from his wish to enhance economic conditions in entire region. Though opposed to imperial unity, he wished to foster closer functional cooperation. [ELC]

2229 Thomas, Gordon and **Max Morgan Witts.** The day the world ended. Chelsea, Mich.: Scarborough House, 1991. 306 p.: bibl., ill.

Best modern English-language narrative of 1902 volcanic eruption that annihilated town of Saint-Pierre, Martinique, is based on contemporary press coverage and accounts by witnesses. [APD]

2230 Trinidad under siege, the Muslimeen uprising: 6 days of terror. Port of Spain: Trinidad Express Newspapers, 1990. 126 p.: ill.

Coverage by reporters for one of Trinidad's leading newspapers relates 1990 coup attempt by Muslimeen. Excellent first hand material includes list of persons charged for coup-related crimes and addresses by political leaders. Details grievances of Muslimeen. [ELC]

2231 Valle Ferrer, Norma. Luisa Capetillo: historia de una mujer proscrita. Río Piedras, P.R.: Editorial Cultural, 1990. 150 p.: bibl., ill.

Straightforward, unimaginative biography examines early 20th-century Puerto Ri-

can feminist, anarchist, and labor organizer. Book constantly ties Capetillo's lifestyle to her politics, following anarchist beliefs. Author contextualizes Capetillo's ideas and life cycle, but does not provide a larger framework for her actions. Still, work is principal source for biographical data on major political figure. [TMV]

2232 Vega, Bernardo. La emigración española de 1939 y su impacto sobre los dominicanos. (*in* El destierro español en América: un trasvase cultural. Recopilación de Nicolás Sánchez Albornoz. Madrid: Instituto de Cooperación Iberoamericana; Sociedad Estatal Quinto Centenario, 1991, p. 279–284, bibl.)

Provides good introduction to a subject that deserves further research and development.

2233 Veinticinco años de historia dominicana, 1959–1984. Santo Domingo: Editora Universitaria-UASD, 1987. 221 p. (Publicaciones de la Univ. Autónoma de Santo Domingo; 583. Col. Historia y sociedad; 79)

Some of the most respected Dominican scholars are among the contributors to this interesting multidisciplinary work on the period. [JMH]

2234 Williams, Brackette F. Stains on my name, war in my veins: Guyana and the politics of cultural struggle. Durham, N.C.: Duke Univ. Press, 1991. 322 p.: bibl., ill., index.

Study of multiclass, multiethnic community in Cockalorum, just outside Guyana's capital of Georgetown, concludes that nation-building is impeded in a country where ethnic polarization rather than working class consciousness is the order of the day. For ethnologist's comment see *HLAS 53:1067*. [ELC]

2235 Winocur, Marcos. La burguesía azucarera cubana: estructura capitalista y definición política en la coyuntura insurreccional de 1952–1959. (*Hist. Soc./Valencia*, 11, otoño 1991, p. 83–96, photos)

A one-sided account results from uncritical use of one-sided sources. Author's familiarity with Cuban sugar industry clearly is somewhat limited. [JMH]

2236 Yglesia Martínez, Teresita. The history of Cuba and its interpreters, 1898–1935. Translated by Néstor Capote. (*Americas/Francisc.*, 49:3, Jan. 1993, p. 369–386)

Many of items reviewed by author read as political manifestos rather than historical works, but then that is the nature of much of Cuban historiography. Excellent guide to passions and prejudices underlying Cubans' interpretations of their own history. [JMH]

2237 Zapata-Oliveras, Carlos R. International recognition of the Commonwealth of Puerto Rico. (*Horizontes/Ponce*, 32 : 63/64, oct. 1988/abril 1989, p. 71–95)

Enlightening account of 1950s efforts to get Puerto Rico off United Nations list of territories is based on primary sources. Pertinent to recent debate on status. [TMV]

2238 Zavala, Iris M. El exilio republicano en Puerto Rico: coyuntura histórica. (*in* El destierro español en América: un trasvase

cultural. Recopilación de Nicolás Sánchez Albornoz. Madrid: Instituto de Cooperación Iberoamericana; Sociedad Estatal Quinto Centenario, 1991, p. 267–278)

Author argues that the Spanish Civil War exiles in Puerto Rico (individuals like Juan Ramón Jiménez, Federico de Onís, Samuel Gili Gaya, and the Chilean, Gabriela Mistral) contributed to efforts of intellectuals on island to construct a national culture. Both groups allied to give meaning to certain discursive and linguistic forms under seige by US cultural imperialism. [TMV]

Zips, Werner. Eine afrikansche Gegenmacht in der Karibik. See item **2129.**

SPANISH SOUTH AMERICA
General

MICHAEL T. HAMERLY, *Professor of Library Science, University of Guam*

Ecuador. See item **42.**

2239 Gheerbrant, Alain. The Amazon: past, present, and future. New York: Harry N. Abrams, 1992. 191 p.: bibl., ill. (some col.), index, maps. (Discoveries)

History of the Amazon region as it should be told: without regard for colonial and national period boundaries but taking into account the implications of these boundaries. Magnificently illustrated and elegantly written by the leader of the 1948–50 Orinoco-Amazon Expedition. [MTH]

2240 Girot, Pascal. Resistencia indígena y la evolución de fronteras en el Río Chinchipe, Alto Marañón. (*Rev. Hist./Heredia*, 21/22, enero/dic. 1990, p. 119–148, bibl., tables)

Interesting synthesis and dispassionate analysis of "Jívaro" (i.e., Shuar and Achuar) resistance to Spanish, Ecuadorian, and Peruvian incursions into Chinchipe River Basin (southern Ecuador/northern Peru) from 1600s through 1900s. Emphasizes geopolitical and strategic importance of region from point of view of Spain and modern republics. [MTH]

2241 Gott, Richard. Land without evil: utopian journeys across the South American watershed. London; New York; Verso,

1993. 320 p.: bibl., ill. (some col.), index, maps.

Contemporary accounts of travels into former Jesuit lands (the Pantanal, Upper Paraguay, Chiquitos, and Mojos) with generous quotes from memoirs and recollections of the priests, soldiers, explorers, and settlers who went before. Spell-binding journeys through time as well as space. [MTH]

Latin America since 1930: Spanish South America. See item **1110.**

2242 Stavig, Ward A. The past weighs on the minds of the living: culture, ethnicity, and the rural lower class. (*LARR*, 26:2, 1991, p. 225–246)

More of an historiographic than a review essay. Examines the following four books: Magnus Mörner's *The Andean past* (*HLAS 48:2616*); *The economies of Mexico and Peru during the late colonial period*, edited by Nils Jacobsen and Hans-Jürgen Puhle; *La participación indígena en los mercados surandinos*, edited by Olivia Harris, Brooke Larson, and Enrique Tandeter; and *Resistance, rebellion, and consciousness in the Andean peasant world* (*HLAS 50:737*), edited by Steve J. Stern. The works are evaluated in depth and serve as a springboard for a broad assessment of recent work on postconquest history of Indians and peasants in the Andean region. [MTH]

2243 Vivanco, Carmen et al. Bandoleros, abigeos y montoneros: criminalidad y violencia en el Perú, siglos XVIII-XX. Edición de Carlos Aguirre y Charles Walker. Lima: In-stituto de Apoyo Agrario, 1990. 393 p.: bibl., map. (Serie Tiempo de historia; 7)

Major collection of mostly pioneering essays on social banditry and rural crime in 18th, 19th, and 20th centuries in Peru and Bolivia. For contributions on the colonial period, see items **2414** and **2425**. [MTH]

Colonial Period

MICHAEL T. HAMERLY, *Professor of Library Science, University of Guam*
SUSAN M. SOCOLOW, *Professor of History, Emory University*
KATHY WALDRON, *Citibank International, Miami*

THIS TIME AROUND we have annotated considerably more than 300 items on colonial Spanish South America. Not only has the avalanche of historical studies and published sources precipitated by the Quincentennial continued, but it is also clear that the voluminous output will be with us for some time. For that reason and because scholarly output on Latin America has also increased substantially in the other disciplines, all of the contributing editors to *HLAS* have had to pare their introductory remarks in order to continue to describe and evaluate as many recent and new publications as possible. Reluctantly but inevitably therefore we have had to abandon our customary practice of delineating and commenting on historiographic developments in some depth.

The only new and not quite so new general syntheses that came to our attention during the preceding biennium were Alain Gheerbrant's eminently readable *The Amazon: past, present, and future* (item **2239**) and the new editions of Herbert S. Klein's *Bolivia* (item **2440**) and Brian Loveman's *Chile* (item **2474**). As for the colonial period proper, the most important of the recent general works in our opinion are Sabine MacCormack's inspired as well as insightful *Religion in the Andes* (item **2256**), Isacio Pérez Fernández's truly monumental *Bartolomé de las Casas en el Perú* (item **2259**), and the outstanding volume of essays, *Transatlantic encounters: European and Andeans in the sixteenth century*, edited by Kenneth J. Andrien and Rolena Adorno (item **2261**).

Overall, highly specialized studies or microhistories continue to prevail. That is to say, monograph after monograph, more often than not in considerable detail, on demographic development after demographic development, economic sector after economic sector, ethnic group after ethnic group, institution after institution, personage after personage, pueblo, district or region after pueblo, district or region, social group after social group, etc. continue to be produced. For the most part the corresponding articles and books are more or less well researched and methodologically sound. Some of them are even well written. Unfortunately the tendency to sacrifice inspired interpretation and felicity of style to paradigms and social scientific verbosity also continues. It is not borrowing ideas and approaches from other disciplines that perturbs me but the obfuscation of what might otherwise be lucid scholarship with poorly applied theorems and banal jargon. [MTH]

Turning to colonial Venezuela, among the more interesting of this biennium's bounty are Elías Pino Iturrieta's *Contra lujuria, castidad: historias de pecado en el siglo XVIII venezolano* (item **2280**), tantalizing tales of promiscuity, bigamy, and sodomy, and Edda O. Samudio's able analysis of "Seventeenth-Century Indian Migration in the Venezuelan Andes" (item **2285**). Insofar as neighboring Nueva Granada is concerned, it is good to see an increase in the variety and in the quality of work being done. Perhaps the most significant of the studies noticed in this *Handbook* are Lucena Salmoral's major *Fuentes para el estudio de la fiscalidad colonial . . . la producción de oro en el Nuevo Reino de Granada a través de las cajas reales, 1651–1701* (item **2293**), Rebecca Earle Mond's meticulously researched "Indian Rebellion and Bourbon Reform in New Granada: Riots in Pasto, 1780–1800" (item **2305**), and Pablo Rodríguez's minor but stimulating *Cabildo y vida urbana en el Medellín colonial, 1675–1730* (item **2312**). [KW]

Continuing south, historical output on the former Presidency of Quito remained substantial. Unfortunately much of the work done of late is prosaic albeit important. Notable exceptions are Linda A. Newson's "Old World Epidemics in Early Colonial Ecuador" (item **2339**) and Karen M. Powers' "Resilient Lords and Indian Vagabonds" (item **768**), both of which read well and are well researched, although the Powers pieces (see also item **2341**) are somewhat too social scientific for my taste. Fortunately the largely lackluster monographs are redeemed by: major published sources such as Pedro Fernández de Cevallos' *La ruta de la canela americana* (item **2331**) or the monumental *Relaciones histórico-geográficas de la Audiencia de Quito* (item **2345**); basic sources of data such as Alvaro Jara and John Jay TePaske's *Eighteenth-century Ecuador*, the fourth volume in the benchmark work *The royal treasuries of the Spanish Empire in America* (item **2333**); and such invaluable research guides as Javier Ortiz de la Tabla Ducasse's *Cartas de cabildos hispanoamericanos: Audiencia de Quito, siglos XVI-XIX* (item **2340**).

As for Peru, both upper and lower, so much work is being done that it has become difficult, if not impossible, to remain abreast of the literature. Nearly one fifth of this *Handbook* volume's "Spanish South America: Colonial Period" entries correspond to Lower Peru alone. Very much at the risk of being invidious, the most significant as well as substantial contributions this time around strike me as being: the first vol. in a projected three vol. social history of *La Inquisición de Lima* (item **2364**); José de la Puente Brunke's prize winning *Encomienda y encomenderos en el Perú* (item **2403**); Daniel Restrepo Manrique's model *La Iglesia de Trujillo, Perú, bajo el episcopado de Baltasar Jaime Martínez Compañón* (item **2406**); María Rostworowski de Diez Canseco's fascinating biography of Doña Francisca Pizarro (item **2409**); Carmen Ruigómez Gómez's pioneering study of the Protector of the Indians (item **2411**); and the revisionist reexamination of the Church in the early colonial period, *Evangelización y teología en el Perú* (item **2396**). The best read, however, is Noble David Cook and Alexandra Parma Cook's *Good faith and truthful ignorance* (item **2370**), a book that demonstrates that the marriage between History and the Social Sciences can be fructiferous when entered into and pursued in the proper spirit. And the single most important article is probably Noble David Cook's masterful "Migration in Colonial Peru" (item **2371**).

Output on Upper Peru continues to boom. Potosí no longer looms as large on the scene although among the best of the recent studies is Enrique Tandeter's *Coacción y mercado: la minería de la plata en el Potosí colonial* (item **2451**). Tandeter's book is also available in English as *Coercion and market: silver mining in colonial Potosí, 1692–1826* (Albuquerque: Univ. of New Mexico Press, 1993). Brian Evans' "Death in Aymaya" (item **2433**) and Tandeter's article "Crisis in Upper Peru, 1800–

1805"—available in Spanish too (see item **2452**)—also struck me as exceptionally important. Returning to books, the other most noteworthy appear to have been: Valentín Abecia Baldivieso's wholly new, long since indispensable *Historiografía boliviana* (item **2430**); the well written and illustrated *La ciudad de La Paz* (item **2432**); Alcides J. Parejas Moreno and Virgilio Suárez Salas' exquisite *Chiquitos* (item **2442**); and the impressive proceedings from the Simposio sobre la Importancia de las Misiones Jesuitas en Bolivia (item **2450**).

Turning South again, research on colonial Chile continues in much the same vein as before. On the one hand, some new ground continues to be broken as scholars focus on estates or pueblos heretofore poorly treated, if at all. See for example, Ana María Presta's "Mano de Obra en una Hacienda Tarijeña" in *Agricultura, trabajo y sociedad en América Hispana* (item **2456**). On the other, new editions of old works—often luxurious in keeping with the tone of 1992, such as the opulent edition of Pedro de Valdivia's letters (item **2486**)—are still being produced. The most interesting articles were those published in the aforementioned anthology, *Agricultura, trabajo y sociedad . . .* and in *Estudios sobre la época de Carlos III* (item **2463**). And the most significant book, certainly the most enjoyable and the most stimulating, was Giorgio Antei's *La invención del Reino de Chile* (item **2457**). [MTH]

Crossing the Andes, the onslaught is still with us. Nearly one third of the materials herewithin included focus on the Río de la Plata, or Argentina, Paraguay, and Uruguay during the colonial period. Recent work continues to be dominated by a strong group of economic historians primarily concerned with reconstructing the various sectors of the colonial period economy through a series of highly specialized and minute studies. See especially the contributions of Samuel Amaral (items **2491** and **2492**), Juan Carlos Garavaglia (items **2521** and **2520**), Jorge Daniel Gelman (item **2524**), and Eduardo R. Saguier (items **2568, 2569,** and **2570**). The gaucho versus peasant debate and the role of the frontier discussion have been advanced by Carlos Mayo (items **2545** and **2547**) and Leonardo León Solís (item **2531**). Women have begun to attract some attention. In addition to Mallo's work (item **2536**), Raúl A. Molina's *La familia porteña* (item **2548**) is particularly important inasmuch as he abstracts and quotes extensively from marriage and divorce records otherwise lost forever. And there have been the usual editions of older texts and resumption of publication of critical sources, among the most important of which are the *Cartas anuas de la Provincia Jesuitica del Paraguay* (item **2501**). [SMS]

This *Handbook* marks the farewell appearance of Kathy Waldron as a contributing editor. Kathy has been responsible for colonial Venezuela and Nueva Granada since *HLAS 46.* Many thanks, Kathy, for the many hundreds of untold hours you put in over the last ten years to help make the "Spanish South America: Colonial Period" section comprehensive and perspicacious. To end on a more personal note, it is with considerable sadness that I report the loss of a close friend as well as an outstanding member of the profession, Julio Enrique Estrada Ycaza (1917–1993). Productive to the end notwithstanding the degenerative illness with which he had been afflicted for many years, Estrada Ycaza's last book, coauthored with Clemente Yerovi Indaburu, was *El siglo de los vapores fluviales, 1840–1940* (item **2673**). [MTH]

GENERAL

Alberro, Solange. Elogio de la vagancia en la América colonial: las andanzas de Francisco Manuel de Quadros en Perú, Nueva Granada y Nueva España, 1663. See item **923.**

2244 Andrien, Kenneth J. Spaniards, Andeans, and the early colonial state in Peru. (*in* Transatlantic encounters: Europeans and Andeans in the sixteenth century. Edited by Kenneth J. Andrien and Rolena Adorno.

Berkeley: Univ. of California Press, 1991, p. 121–148, graphs, map)

Important review of policy and economy of early Viceroyalty of Peru, especially during the Toledo years, by a scholar who has elsewhere contributed much to our knowledge of the colonial state in the Andes (see *HLAS 48:2618*). Also an able assessment of state of historiography on 16th-century Ecuador, Peru, and Bolivia. [MTH]

2245 Bakewell, Peter. La maduración del gobierno del Perú en la década de 1560. (*Hist. Mex.*, 39:1, julio/sept. 1989, p. 41–70, bibl.)

Reassesses administrations of Viceroys Conde de Nieva (1561–64) and Lope García de Castro (1564–69). Concludes that important innovations usually attributed to Viceroy Francisco de Toledo (1569–81) such as the *corregimientos de indios* and the *reducciones de indios* were in fact introduced and institutionalized by Nieva and García de Castro in the 1560s. [MTH]

2246 Bayón, Damián and **Murillo Marx.** History of South American colonial art and architecture: Spanish South America and Brazil. New York: Rizzoli, 1992. 442 p.: bibl., ill. (some col.), index.

Superior survey of art and architecture of colonial South America. Most comprehensive account in English since George Kubler and Martin Soria's 1959 *Art and architecture in Spain and Portugal and their American dominions*. Parts one and two by Bayón cover architecture, sculpture, and painting in Spanish South America, including Panamá, and part three by Marx, Ribeiro de Oliveira, Pereira da Silva, and Segawa treat the architecture, sculpture, and painting of colonial Brazil. Both sections include an "Index of Main Monuments," a glossary, and a bibliography. Erudite without being pedantic. Iconographically opulent, there are 891 well-reproduced illustrations, the majority in color. For art historian's assessment of Spanish edition see *HLAS 52:153*. [MTH]

2247 Bradley, Peter T. Society, economy and defence in seventeenth-century Peru: the administration of the Count of Alba de Liste, 1655–61. Liverpool, England: Institute of Latin American Studies, Univ. of Liverpool, 1992. 170 p.: bibl. (Monograph Series; 15)

Detailed examination of administra-

tion of a mid-colonial viceroy, based largely on his correspondence. The monograph takes up disparate and far flung events that the Viceroy concerned himself with such as the loss of flagship *Limpia Concepción* off the coast of Ecuador (1654) and an Indian rebellion in Chile (1655). Important contribution to history of 17th-century Spanish South America. [MTH]

2248 Cano Trigo, José María. Aportaciones de la Armada Española a la geografía de la América del Sur en el siglo XVIII. Huelva, Spain: Univ. Hispanoamericana Santa María de la Rábida, 1992. 76 p.: bibl., ill., maps. (Serie Catálogos)

Brief account and catalog of sailing charts and other maps of coasts and adjacent areas of South America resultant from scientific expeditions of 18th century. Unfortunately majority of the charts and maps are poorly reproduced. [MTH]

2249 Cebrián González, María del Carmen and **Isabel Arenas Frutos.** Situación de la Provincia del Perú a finales del siglo XVI: *La crónica anónima* de 1600. (*Anu. Estud. Am.*, 49:2, 1992, suplemento, p. 11–29, tables)

Outlines Jesuit activities and establishments in Spanish South America circa 1600. Features a prosopographic analysis of Jesuits throughout the viceroyalty. [MTH]

Fernández Gaytán, José. Don Pedro Porter y Cassante, navegante, descubridor, gobernador de Chile y almirante de la Mar del Sur. See item **969.**

2250 Gómez Rivas, León. Don Francisco de Toledo, Comendador de Alcántara, Virrey del Perú: guía de fuentes. (*Anu. Estud. Am.*, 49:1, suplemento 1992, p. 123–171, bibl.)

This important research guide lists all published sources and all known unpublished sources relating to Viceroy Toledo. See also *Francisco de Toledo: disposiciones gubernativas para el Virreinato del Perú*, compiled and edited by María Justina Sarabia Viejo with an introduction by Guillermo Lohmann Villena (Sevilla: Escuela de Estudios Hispano-Americanos, 1986–89; 2 v.) [MTH]

2251 Guilmartin, John F., Jr. The cutting edge: an analysis of the Spanish invasion and overthrow of the Inca empire, 1532–1539. (*in* Transatlantic encounters: Europeans and Andeans in the sixteenth century, 1532–1539. Edited by Kenneth J. Andrien and Rolena Adorno. Berkeley: Univ. of California Press, 1991, p. 40–69)

Stresses importance of "superiority of Spanish arms, strategy, and tactics" in conquest of Tahuantinsuyu without slighting other factors involved. Among the telling points made by Guilmartin is that although the Incas were quick learners as well as capable leaders and able warriors, "they simply did not possess the means to profit from their understanding of the Spaniards' weaknesses and limitations." [MTH]

2252 Helmer, Marie. Cantuta: recueil d'articles parus entre 1949 et 1987. Madrid: Casa de Velázquez, 1993. 550 p.: bibl., ill., maps. (Coll. de la Casa de Velázquez; 39)

Helmer, an Alsacian-born jurist who has devotedly studied the working conditions in the silver mines of Potosí, conveniently collects here 45 essays, notes, and book reviews (all previously published). The book deals mainly with social and economic development in colonial Potosí but focuses also on ethnographic characteristics of Huánuco and Chucuito, contraband and intercontinental trade, rites and ideology in Andean communities, etc. [T. Hampe-Martínez]

2253 Hernández Palomo, Jesús. Las *Cartas Anuas* del Perú en el Archivum Romanum Societatis Iesu: valoración y catálogo, 1603–1765 (*Anu. Estud. Am.*, 48:2, suplemento 1991, p. 27–73)

Lists and describes the contents of the more or less annual reports of Jesuits in Quito, and Lower and Upper Peru to their superiors in Rome from 1603 through 1765. Major sources for study of many aspects of colonial Ecuador, Peru, and Bolivia, not just of the Society of Jesus or of the Catholic Church. Hopefully all of the *Cartas Anuas* will eventually appear in the *Monumenta peruana* (8 vols. to date; Rome, 1954-<1986>) as have those for 1568–1602. [MTH]

2254 Jármy Chapa, Martha de. La expansión española hacia América y el Océano Pacífico. v. 2, La Mar del Sur y el impulso hacia el oriente. México: Distribuciones Fontamara, 1988. 1 v.: bibl., col. maps (Fontamara; 31)

Solid, well-written, panoramic survey of early Spanish activities in the Pacific cov-

ers: voyages of discovery; maritime trade and traffic between New Spain and Peru; trade between New Spain and the Phlippines; Spanish attempts to trade with Japan (in order to supplant the Portuguese); and incursions by English, and then Dutch, pirates and privateers in what had been "Spanish Lake." For vol. 1 of this work, *Un eslabón perdido en la historia: piratería en el Caribe*, see *HLAS 48:2402*. [MTH]

2255 Lavallé, Bernard. Evangelización y explotación colonial: el ejemplo de las doctrinas en los Andes, siglos XVI-XVII. (*Rábida/Huelva*, 11, marzo 1992, p. 22–33, bibl.)

Author draws on numerous examples from different periods and places in what are now Colombia, Ecuador, Peru, and Bolivia to conclude that, by and large, the *doctrinas de indios* were not only mechanisms of exploitation but often family businesses. Although not everyone will concur, Lavallé supports his thesis with solid documentation. [MTH]

2256 MacCormack, Sabine. Religion in the Andes: vision and imagination in early colonial Peru. Princeton: Princeton Univ. Press, 1991. 488 p.: bibl., ill., index, maps.

Reexamines "Andean religion as it was practiced, observed, and remembered during the 16th and 17th centuries." As much an intellectual history of the observers as a reconstruction of beliefs and rituals of the practitioners. A fascinating work that delineates extent to which the authorities upon which modern scholars of the Andean past rely may have seen but not quite understood; yet, at the same time, demonstrates how much may be gleaned from the original *cronistas*. [MTH]

2257 Malaspina, Alessandro. La Expedición Malaspina, 1789–1794. t. 2, Diario general del viaje. pt. 1. Madrid: Ministerio de Defensa, Museo Naval; Barcelona: Lunwerg, 1992. 1 v.: bibl., ill., index, plates.

First ed. of holograph and the first complete ed. of Malaspina's *Diario* as preserved in the Museo Naval (Madrid). This tome takes us from Cádiz to Montevideo, around Cape Horn, up the Pacific coast of the Americas (as far north as Nutka) with numerous stops and observations along the way, and back to Acapulco. Literally transcribed and lavishly illustrated. Includes a name index. For vol. 1 of this magnificent set see *HLAS 52:2008*. [MTH]

2258 Murra, John V. "Nos hazen mucha ventaja:" the early European perception of Andean achievement. (*in* Transatlantic encounters: Europeans and Andeans in the sixteenth century. Edited by Kenneth J. Andrien and Rolena Adorno. Berkeley: Univ. of California Press, 1991, p. 73–89)

The adage, "the more we learn the less we know" (or, the more we realize how much there is to learn) especially applies in the case of early colonial Ecuador, Peru, and Bolivia. Murra reminds us of this in a tantalizing report on his current research on seafaring Chincha and in his masterly review of Domingo de Santo Tomás' efforts to convince the crown and the Council of Indies to abolish the encomienda. On Friar Domingo, see also items **2259** and **2396**. [MTH]

2259 Pérez Fernández, Isacio. Bartolomé de las Casas en el Perú: el espíritu lascasiano en la primera evangelización del Imperio Incaico, 1531–1573. Cusco: Centro de Estudios Rurales Andinos Bartolomé de las Casas, 1988. 712 p.: bibl., ill., index. (Archivos de historia andina; 8)

Monumental monograph explores Las Casas' impact, or what Pérez Fernández appropriately refers to as the impact of the "lascasian spirit," on the spiritual conquest of Quito, and Lower and Upper Peru. Book is solidly reasoned and well-researched and written. Though not all will agree with the author's approach or interpretations, book is rewarding especially for its enormous contribution to knowledge and understanding of Las Casas' close collaborator, Domingo de Santo Tomás, one of the first students of Andean culture. [MTH]

2260 Santistevan, Miguel de. Mil leguas por América: de Lima a Caracas 1740–1741; diario de don Miguel de Santistevan. Edición de David J. Robinson. Bogotá: Banco de la República, 1992. 323 p.: bibl., ill., index, maps. (Col. bibliográfica/Banco de la República. Historia colombiana)

Scholarly edition of private travel diary of Panamanian-born Miguel de Santisteban, who journeyed from Lima to Guayaquil by sea and then from Guayaquil to Caracas by land in 1740–41. Santisteban had a curious eye and an able pen. Well edited and indexed with a solid prefatory study (p. 11–83) by Robinson. [MTH]

2261 Transatlantic encounters: Europeans and Andeans in the sixteenth century. Edited by Kenneth J. Andrien and Rolena Adorno. Berkeley: Univ. of California Press, 1991. 295 p.: bibl., ill., index.

Multidisciplinary, multiauthored volume explores the Andean world, which is increasingly perceived as a very complex and ancient American civilization. The essays also examine the far from simplistic "processes of cultural exchange and transformation that occurred between Andeans and Europeans" during and following the Spanish conquest. An exceptionally important book. For individual essays relevant to this section, see items **2244, 2251, 2258,** and **2354.** [MTH]

2262 Ulloa, Antonio de. Viaje a la América meridional. v. 1–2. Edición de Andrés Saumell. Madrid: Historia 16, 1990. 2 v.: (Crónicas de América; 59A-B)

Moderately-priced ed. of Spanish original of Juan and Ulloa's *A Voyage to South America.* Text is complete but illustrations are not included. Saumell has modernized punctuation and orthography and added numerous explanatory notes. [MTH]

2263 Vizcardo y Guzmán, Juan Pablo. Obra completa. Prólogo de Luis Alberto Sánchez. Bibliografía crítica por César Pacheco Vélez. Edición de Percy Cayo Córdova. Recopilación de Merle E. Simmons. Traducciones de Ana María Juilland. Lima: Banco de Crédito del Perú, 1988. 544 p., 30 p. of plates: bibl., ill., index. (Biblioteca Clásicos del Perú; 4)

Compendium of all known writings of expelled and suppressed Jesuit Vizcardo (also known as Viscardo), author of celebrated *Carta a los españoles americanos,* the *Proyecto para independizar la América Española,* and other essays. Includes previously unpublished correspondence (is covered by Simmons) of this Peruvian-born propagandist and a useful "Bibliografía Crítica." [MTH]

VENEZUELA

2264 Blanco, Jesús. Miguel Guacamaya, capitán de cimarrones. Caracas: Editorial APIGUM, 1991. 62 p.: bibl., ill. (Col. El Otro discurso; 1)

Brief description of the cimarrones of Barlovento, Venezuela's main cacao production area. One fugitive slave, Miguel Guacamaya, organized a successful *cumbre* which functioned for several years until military patrols from Caracas penetrated the region. Not overly detailed but draws connection with Cuban and Dominican slave revolts of same period. [KW]

2265 Castillo Lara, Lucas G. San Cristóbal, siglo XVII: tiempo de aleudar. Caracas: Academia Nacional de la Historia, 1989. 674 p. (Biblioteca de la Academia Nacional de la Historia: Fuentes para la historia colonial de Venezuela; 201)

Adds to earlier work on Tachirense city. Legal disputes reveal competition among rival families for land, cattle and offices, with corrupt judges awarding land rights to powerful groups seeking to consolidate holdings. Descriptive history lacks analysis and conclusion. [KW]

2266 Ferrero Kellerhoff, Inés Cecilia. Capacho: un pueblo de indios en la jurisdicción de la villa de San Cristóbal. Caracas: Academia Nacional de la Historia, 1991. 291 p. (Biblioteca de la Academia Nacional de la Historia: Fuentes para la Historia Colonial de Venezuela; 210)

Institutional history of Capacho, an Indian pueblo that provided mita labor to Spaniards of San Cristóbal. Royal officials forced the transition from personal servitude to tribute in this isolated area where Augustinian missionaries worked. Uses local archives but produces traditional Spanish version of the evolution of *agregaciones* from 1726–1810. [KW]

2267 Gil, Juan. Mitos y utopías del descubrimiento. v. 3, El Dorado. Madrid: Alianza, 1989. 1 v.: bibl., index. (Alianza universidad; 596)

Final vol. of series covers exploration of Orinoco and Amazonas by men in search of El Dorado. This dense study based on chronicles, archival research, and secondary sources relates history of discovery of El Marañón, Paititi and Orinoco where legend of Amazon women arose. Good analysis of the myths which propelled the explorers. [KW]

2268 Gilii, Filippo Salvadore. Ensayo de historia americana. v. 1–3. Traducción y estudio preliminar de Antonio Tovar. 2. ed. Caracas: Academia Nacional de la Historia,

1987. 3 v.: ill., map. (Biblioteca de la Academia Nacional de la Historia: Fuentes para la historia colonial de Venezuela; 71–73.)

Second edition of a work first published 1780–84. For related work see item **2278.** [KW]

2269 González Abreu, Manuel. Dependencia colonial venezolana. 3. ed. Caracas: Univ. Central de Venezuela, Consejo de Desarrollo Científico y Humanístico, 1992. 151 p.: bibl., maps. (Col. Monografías; 27)

Third ed. of a work first published in 1974 is a useful dependency interpretation of the colony/metropolis relation. Book focuses on economic relations of colony whose commerce was monopolized by the Basque trading company. Although recent scholarship develops a more complete interpretation of the economy, this volume is still a useful starting point. [KW]

2270 Gutiérrez, Alberto *et al.* La pedagogia jesuítica en Venezuela, 1628–1767. v. 1–3. Edición de José del Rey Fajardo. San Cristóbal, Venezuela: Univ. Católica del Táchira, 1991. 3 v.: bibl., col. ill.

Three vols. contain articles by noted Jesuit scholars: Alberto Gutiérrez on Loyola and the university; Juan Pacheco on the Universidad Javeriana; José Luis Saez on the university in Española; José del Rey on Venezuelan Jesuit *colegios* and Miguel Bertrán Quera on pedagogy. Well-researched, archival studies are somewhat repetitious of earlier works. Vol. 3 by Fernando Arellano covers Jesuit art in America from 1568–1767 with 100 color prints of churches, statues and paintings. His description of the art is interwoven with historic significance of each print. Despite plethora of Jesuit studies, this one is valuable for its breadth. [KW]

2271 Indice del Archivo Arzobispal de Caracas: Sección Testamentarías. Ordenación, catalogación y microfilmación por Marjorie Acevedo Gómez *et al.* Caracas: Academia Nacional de la Historia, Depto. de Investigaciones Históricas, 1990. 475 p.: index. (Biblioteca de la Academia Nacional de la Historia: Serie Archivos y catálogos; 9)

Index of more than 1,100 wills in the archives of the Archbishopric of Caracas (1600–1879) provides dates, names, and locations. Useful index to major repository of colonial testaments. [KW]

2272 Jornadas sobre el Comercio Vasco con América en el Siglo XVIII y la Real Compañía Guipuzcoana de Caracas en el II Centenario de Carlos III, *Bilbao and San Sebastián, Spain, 1988.* Los vascos y América. Edición de Ronald Escobedo Mansilla, Ana María Rivera Medina y Alvaro Chapa Imaz. Bilbao: Laida, 1989. 477 p.: bibl., ill. (some col.)

Papers presented at a 1988 Bilbao conference on Basque commerce with America in the 18th century include five studies of Basque commercial influence in Peru, Rio de la Plata, Nueva España, North America and the Consulado de Cádiz. Article by José María Mariluz Urquijo on the Compañía de Buenos Aires offers interesting comparisons to the Caracas experience, a topic which occupies the second half of the book. Eight articles by Venezuelan and Spanish historians cover the Compañía Guipuzcoana in detail but most material is not new. [KW]

2273 Ladera de Diez, Elizabeth. Contribución al estudio de la "aristocracia territorial" en Venezuela colonial: la familia Xerez de Aristeguieta, siglo XVIII. Caracas: Academia Nacional de la Historia, 1990. 284 p., 1 folded leaf of plates: bibl., ill., maps. (Biblioteca de la Academia Nacional de la Historia: Fuentes para la historia colonial de Venezuela; 209)

Examines lineage, wealth, inheritance and marriage patterns of the wealthiest Caracas family, whose patriarch, twice married with 16 children, was one of the largest cacao landowners. Well-researched study based upon wills also includes an interesting chapter on elite women as represented by the nine daughters who defied traditional roles. To avoid generalizations based upon one family, work should be consulted along with Robert Ferry's more comprehensive study (see *HLAS 52:2034*). [KW]

2274 Leal Curiel, Carole. El discurso de la fidelidad: construcción social del espacio como símbolo del poder regio, Venezuela—siglo XVIII. Caracas: Academia Nacional de la Historia, 1990. 319 p.: bibl.

Interesting analysis of meaning of objects used at 18th-century public ceremonies. The position and quality of seats, benches, banners, carpets and other items were all indicators of hierarchy, social order, and standing. Symbols of rank were visible and important signs of power which ordered Church-State relations. Useful for those puzzled by the ceremonial detail provided in official colonial records. [KW]

2275 Loreto Loreto, Jesús José. Linajes calaboceños. Caracas: Academia Nacional de la Historia, 1990. 185 p.: ports. (Biblioteca de la Academia Nacional de la Historia: Fuentes para la historia colonial de Venezuela; 207)

Useful but traditional genealogical study of 25 families from the llano city of Calabozo. Most families trace origins to Caracas Valley before migrating to llanos in search of new land. [KW]

2276 Miranda, Francisco de. Colombia. v. 8, El viajero ilustrado. v. 9, Revolución Francesa. Caracas: Ediciones de la Presidencia de la República, 1978–1988. 2 v.: bibl., ill.

Continues re-edition of Miranda's diaries and letters, originally published by Editorial Sur America (1929–50). Introduction by Josefina Rodríguez de Alonso summarizes Miranda's travels in Europe (1788–90), where he met leading merchants, government figures, and intellectuals. Vol. 9 covers Miranda's early negotiations with William Pitt seeking English support for South American independence. After Pitt declined, Miranda turned to France, enlisting in the revolutionary armies in exchange for a committment to support the American cause at a later date. [KW]

2277 Montenegro, Juan Ernesto. Fragmentos del dieciseiseno. Caracas: Contraloría General de la República, 199–? 169 p.: bibl. (Col. Medio siglo de la Contraloría General de la República: Serie Acervo histórico)

Five articles on 16th and 17th-century Venezuela include several accounts of town founding based upon chronicles. The unique section on colonial poetry provides a rare glimpse into the cultural evolution of the new colony. [KW]

2278 Olza Zubiri, Jesús. El padre Felipe Salvador Gilij en la historia de la lingüística venezolana. San Cristóbal, Venezuela: Univ. Católica del Táchira, 1989. 101 p.

Gilij (or Gilii), an Italian Jesuit, spent 18 years in the Orinoco mastering Indian dialects. His works on the Tamanaco and Maipure languages did not survive, but parts are incorporated into *Ensayo de historia americana,* written between 1780–84 (see item 2268). Gilij compared various dialects to differentiate Carib and Maipure lingustic families. Appreciative of linguistic complexity of tribes, he dispels "noble savage" notion. [KW]

2279 Páez, José Antonio. Páez: las razones del héroe. v. 1. Selección, prólogo y notas de Edgardo Mondolfi. Caracas: Monte Avila Editores, 1990. 1 v.: bibl., index. (Biblioteca del pensamiento venezolano José Antonio Páez; 2)

Letters, proclamations and important educational, economic, and social decrees of Páez, the 19th-century Venezuelan caudillo. Documents are from printed sources, primarily Páez's autobiography. Useful but not new. [KW]

2280 Pino Iturrieta, Elías. Contra lujuria, castidad: historias de pecado en el siglo XVIII venezolano. Caracas: Alfadil Ediciones, 1992. 141 p.: bibl. (Col. trópicos; 43)

Good study analyzes the social reaction to the transgressions of two priests and a prominent Creole. Cases involved promiscuity, bigamy, and sodomy. A Franciscan, accused of the latter, was acquitted and then protected by a cedula of perpetual silence. Rare Venezuelan social history. [KW]

2281 Pino Iturrieta, Elías et al. Historia mínima de Venezuela. Venezuela: Fundación de los Trabajadores de Lagoven, 1992. 222 p.

Nine carefully selected essays by prominent historians, including Manuel Pérez Vila, Elías Pino Iturrieta, Manual Rodríguez Campos, Irene Gallad and Ramón J. Velásquez, cover colonial period to the present. Most essays are condensed versions of authors' major works. [KW]

2282 Prato-Perelli, Antoinette da. Las encomiendas de Nueva Andalucía en el siglo XVII: visita hecha por don Fernando de la Riva Agüero, oidor de la Audiencia de Santo Domingo, 1688; traslado y estudio preliminar. v. 1–4. Caracas: Academia Nacional de la Historia, 1990. 4 v.: bibl., ill., maps (some col.) (Biblioteca de la Academia Nacional de la Historia: Fuentes para la historia colonial de Venezuela; 202–205)

Author uses a new source from the AGI, the 1688 *relación* of the *oidor* of the Audiencia of Santo Domingo. He discusses en-

comiendas, Indians, and the economy and reviews the transition period when 40 encomiendas were grouped into nine towns and personal servitude was replaced with tribute. The encomiendas were abolished in the early 18th century. Prato-Perelli, a Swiss anthropologist and historian, is an expert on colonial eastern Venezuela. [KW]

2283 Rodríguez, Manuel Alfredo. La ciudad de la Guayana del Rey. Caracas: Ediciones Centauro/90, 1990. 244 p.: bibl., ill.

Narrative history from 1498–1817 supplements author's two earlier volumes on the post-independence city. Controlling access to the Orinoco, close to Trinidad, and near Portuguese and English territories, Guayana was vital to Spanish control of the region. Very factual but not the definitive work. [KW]

2284 Ruiz, Gustavo Adolfo. Simón Rodríguez: maestro de escuela de primeras letras. Caracas: Academia Nacional de la Historia, 1990. 296 p.: bibl., ill. (Biblioteca de la Academia Nacional de la Historia: Fuentes para la historia colonial de Venezuela; 206)

Famous for being Bolívar's teacher, Simón Rodríguez is well studied. This work concentrates on 1791–95, when he reformed primary education in Caracas. His enthusiasm for Rousseau and the Enlightenment made him suspect in the eyes of conservative cabildo members even though he stopped short of criticizing the governing elite. Covers familiar ground. [KW]

2285 Samudio A., Edda O. Seventeenth-century Indian migration in the Venezuelan Andes. (*in* Migration in colonial Spanish America. Edited by David J. Robinson. Cambridge: Cambridge Univ. Press, 1990, p. 295–312, map, tables)

Migration toward cities and intra-rural migration, both forced and voluntary, was intense. The city of Mérida attracted young and ambitious Indians seeking employment or escape from harsh encomenderos. Author uses *padrones* and *asientos de trabajo* to analyze pueblo population and former residents lost to migration. [KW]

NUEVA GRANADA

2286 Arciniegas, Germán. El caballero de El Dorado. Bogotá: Planeta, 1988. 244 p. (Col. Documento)

Original title was *Jiménez de Quesada* (Bogotá, 1939). Author argues that Cervantes used the explorer and founder of Bogotá as the model for Don Quixote. [KW]

2287 Avellaneda Navas, José Ignacio. Los compañeros de Féderman: cofundadores de Santa Fe de Bogotá. Bogotá: Academia de Historia de Bogotá; Tercer Mundo Editores, 1990. 442 p.: index. (Historia)

Biographies of 120 men who accompanied Federman from Venezuela to central highlands of Nueva Granada. Based on extensive archival material and copious use of chronicles, author concludes that most individuals were from central Spain, averaged 28 years of age, and had seven years experience in the Americas. The men were reasonably educated, of high social class, and stayed to become leaders in the colony. Good index. [KW]

2288 Bell Lemus, Gustavo. Cartagena de Indias: de la colonia a la república. Bogotá: Fundación Simón y Lola Guberek, 1991. 161 p.: bibl., maps. (Col. Historia; 3)

Analyzes transition from late colony to republic, emphasizing changes which failed to yield prosperity. Examines the failure of the Dique Canal venture to improve transportation between the city and the Río Magdalena. [KW]

2289 Deas, Malcolm D.; Efraín Sánchez; and Aída Martínez. Tipos y costumbres de la Nueva Granada: la colección de pinturas formada en Colombia por Joseph Brown entre 1825 y 1841 y el diario de su excursión a Girón, 1834 = Types and customs of New Granada: the collection of paintings made in Colombia by Joseph Brown between 1825 and 1841 and the journal of his excursion to Girón, 1834. Bogotá: Fondo Cultural Cafetero, 1989. 229 p.: ill. (some col.)

Edition of the journal of Joseph Brown, an agent of the Colombian Mining Association who traveled from Bogotá to Girón via Socorro, a route not frequently taken by Europeans. This unique journal covers the period 1825-41 and contains beautiful reproductions of watercolors and prints housed in the Royal Geographical Society of London. [KW]

2290 Díaz del Castillo Z., Emiliano. San Juan de Pasto, siglo XVI. Bogotá: [s.n.], 1987. 333 p.: bibl., ill., map.

Traditional narrative history of founding of Pasto relies on Quito cabildo records

and early chronicles to establish the date of 1537. Pasto, larger than the regional capital of Popayán, served as a starting point for explorers searching for El Dorado. [KW]

2291 Díaz del Castillo Z., Emiliano. Testimonio del Acta de independencia de Cali. Bogotá: CODIDELCAG, 1990. 226 p.: bibl., ill.

First publication of an alleged copy of the testimony to the Act of Independence of July 3, 1810 in Cali. The original manuscript and five other copies were lost, but this account by Joaquin de Cayzedo y Cuero, a leader of the Cali independence movement, survives. Authenticity not verifiable. [KW]

2292 Espinel Riveros, Nancy. Villavicencio, dos siglos de historia comunera, 1740-1940. Villavicencio, Colombia: Gráficas Juan XXIII, 1989. 166 p.: bibl., ill., maps.

Trajectory of a llanero town where little of consequence occured for two centuries. Located at a crossroads in Meta prov., the town remained small and isolated, having originated from a thriving Jesuit cattle hacienda, Apiay, which declined in the 19th century. Study lacks focus, but reveals the precarious existence of a remote town over a 200 year span. [KW]

2293 Fuentes para el estudio de la fiscalidad colonial: las cajas auríferas neogranadinas en el siglo XVII; la producción de oro en el Nuevo Reino de Granada a través de las cajas reales, 1651-1701. Edición de Manuel Lucena Salmoral. Madrid: Univ. de Alcalá de Henares, Dept. de Historia, Area de Historia de America, 1992. 375 p.: bibl., facsims., graphs, maps, tables. (Revista de la Univ. de Alcalá; 8. Estudios de Historia Social y Económica de América.)

Massive study of gold production from 1651-95 uses regional archives to complement AGI holdings. Carefully outlines methodology and evaluates source accuracy, allowing for effects of contraband and official corruption. Region produced 2.5 million *pesos de oro* with cycle of depression 1651-58 and recovery 1678-94. Adds to studies of Venezuela by Arcila Farías and of Mexico, Chile and Peru by TePaske and Klein. [KW]

2294 Glick, Thomas F. Science and independence in Latin America, with special reference to New Granada. (*HAHR*, 71:2, May 1991, p. 307-334, table)

Evaluates role of scientists in independence. Scholastic science, supported by *peninsulares,* had already been challenged by modern scientific thought, backed by Creoles, in colonial universities. Creole scientists, discriminated against by *peninsulares,* became politicized in favor of American autonomy. As active participants in the independence movements, the scientists suffered after the wars as scientific initiative languished in isolation and without support. [KW]

2295 González Joves, Alvaro. Cultura y educación: de la América oculta a Francisco de Paula Santander. Cúcuta, Colombia: Cámara de Comercio de Cúcuta, 1992. 160 p.: bibl., ill.

First part treats status of education in the Cúcuta prov., while the second part covers Santander's presidency and educational reforms. Anticlerical, a follower of utilitarianism, and a firm believer in public education, Santander shared many of the same views as Bolívar on the need for education to promote democratic government. He helped establish a superior school system based upon principles of free, mandatory, universal primary education. He established local schools and a public university, forming the basis for the Colombian educational system, long viewed as more advanced than that of other Latin American countries. [KW]

2296 Hernández Ospino, William José and Carmen Hernández de del Villar. Archivo histórico eclesiástico de la antigua provincia de Santa Marta: índice analítico, 1719–1942. Santa Marta, Colombia: Instituto de Cultura del Magdalena, 1990. 297 p.: ill.

Chronologically arranged list of documents includes some from colonial era but most are from the mid-19th century. One line titles provide guidance to content but thematic index would have been more helpful. [KW]

2297 Herrán Baquero, Mario. El Virrey don Antonio Amar y Borbón: la crisis del régimen colonial en la Nueva Granada. Bogotá: Banco de la República, 1988. 368 p.: bibl. (Col. bibliográfica. Historia colombiana)

New Granada's last viceroy supported public health, sponsored the Botanical Expedition, and promoted development of the eastern llanos, but failed to preserve the

colony for the empire due to his own ineptitude and conflicting admiration of Napoleon. This view is not always shared by historians but author argues that Amar y Borbón could not provide leadership needed to weather imperial crisis brought on by European events. Well-written, objective study based on solid archival work. Balances work done on the revolutionaries by focusing on royalist thought and action. [KW]

2298 Jaramillo Uribe, Jaime. La sociedad neogranadina. 2. ed. Bogotá: Ediciones Uniandes; Tercer Mundo Editores, 1989. 250 p.: bibl. (Ensayos de historia social; 1. Historia)

Now classic work on social history of colonial Colombia. Important chapters on slaves and masters, the indigenous population, and mestizaje and social stratification have stood the test of time. Although expanded, author overlooks new research on slavery, marriage, demographics, and Indian labor so that this study is no longer the avantgarde history it was when published in 1968 as *Ensayos sobre historia social colombiana.* [KW]

Jurado Noboa, Fernando. Esclavitud en la Costa Pacífica: Iscuandé, Barbacoas, Tumaco y Esmeraldas, siglos XVI al XIX. See item **2334.**

2299 Lohmann Villena, Guillermo. Neogranadinos en las órdenes nobiliarias: datos tomados de la obra *Los americanos en las órdenes nobiliarias.* Presentación, comentarios y adiciones de Roberto M. Tisnés Jiménez. Bogotá: Editorial Kelly, 1990. 154 p.: index. (Nueva serie de cultura hispánica; 5)

Extracts and reprints of *neogranadinos* found in Guillermo Lohmann Villena's *Los Americanos en las órdenes nobiliarias* published in 1947. Covers the Orders of Santiago, Calatrava, Alcántara and Montesa. Quick genealogical guide with useful indexes. [KW]

2300 López Medel, Tomás. Visita de la gobernación de Popayán: libro de tributos, 1558–1559. Edición, estudio preliminar y transcripción de Berta Ares Queija. Preámbulo de Francisco de Solano. Madrid: Consejo Superior de Investigaciones Científicas, Centro de Estudios Históricos, Depto. de Historia de América, 1989. 386 p.: bibl., ill. (Col. Tierra nueva e cielo nuevo; 29)

Transcription of the *visita* of López

Medel, *oidor* of the Audiencia de Nueva Granada, recounts Indian tribute roles of Popayán encomenderos. This complete edition with a helpful introduction places the *visita* within the context of New Laws. Francisco Solano leads this team of scholars from the Centro de Estudios Históricos (CSIC, Madrid). [KW]

2301 Mantilla Ruiz, Luis Carlos. El despertar de la conciencia criolla en el Nuevo Reino de Granada: el caso de los franciscanos. Cali, Colombia: Univ. de San Buenaventura de Cali, 1989. 46 p.: bibl. (Publicaciones de la Univ. de San Buenaventura de Cali)

Argues that criollos suffered Spanish prejudices within religious orders and that their struggle to gain acceptance brought awareness of "Americanism." By 1630s, criollos dominated the order but resisted inclusion of mestizos and Indians. Based on archival research and author's previous work on the Franciscans. [KW]

2302 McFarlane, Anthony. Cimarrones y palenques en Colombia: siglo XVIII. (*Hist. Espac.*, 14, junio 1991, p. 53–78)

Originally published in *Journal of Comparative Studies* (Vol. 6, No. 3, 1985). Author explores the ideological basis of 18th-century revolts against the institution of slavery, an aspect missing from earlier rebellions. The palenques, small and short-lived, could not survive, although individuals aspired to freedom as campesinos or miners. [KW]

2303 Meléndez Sánchez, Jorge. Cacao y río: historia del valle de Cúcuta, de San Faustino de los Ríos, de Salazar de las Palmas y de la frontera colombo-venezolana. Bogotá: Gráficas Margal, 1982. 93 p.: bibl., ill.

Brief review of Cúcuta's origins in 1733 as an outgrowth of military excursions against the Motilones. La Compañía Guizpocana introduced cacao to the region, controlled commerce on the Río Zulia, but failed to check the illegal cultivation of tobacco. Disputes between regional cities for control of the area foreshadowed later conflicts between Venezuela and Colombia. [KW]

2304 Meléndez Sánchez, Jorge. La tierra de don Antón: estudio sobre Aguachica colonial. Bogotá: Ediciones Univ. Pedagógica Nacional, 1988? 114 p.: bibl., ill., maps.

Modest history of the humble town of Aguachica, an 18th-century parish situated between Ocaña and the port of Magdalena. It evolved from haciendas owned by Antón García who, like most landowners, was involved in legal disputes with his neighbors. The colonial parish languished until recent times when oil discoveries led to a boom. [KW]

2305 Mond, Rebecca Earle. Indian rebellion and Bourbon reform in New Granada: riots in Pasto, 1780–1800. (*HAHR*, 73:1, Feb. 1993, p. 99–124)

Meticulous research supports conclusion that 1781 and 1800 riots reflected an autonomous region's reaction to tax reform of central government. Pasto Indians resisted taxes for economic reasons and local cabildo, while not encouraging the revolts, shared Indians' antipathy to royal control. [KW]

2306 No hay caciques ni señores. Transcripción e introducción de Hermes Tovar Pinzón. Barcelona: Sendai, 1988? 190 p.: bibl., ill.

Reproduces four documents: a 1560 *visita*; the *relación* of Melchor Pérez de Arteaga (1568); a 1571 *relación* by Gaspar de Puerto Alegre; and a piece on the conquest of Nueva Granada. The latter, previously published, describes Moxa resistance to Europeans' arrival. Good demographic data. [KW]

2307 Nueva historia de Colombia. v. 1, Colombia indígena, conquista y colonia. Bogotá: Planeta, 1990. 1 v.: bibl., ill.

Re-edition of 1978 *Manual de historia de Colombia* which covered the colonial period. This is the introductory vol. to an 8-vol. series which will cover the political history of the republic through 1986 and will include separate volumes on the economy, international relations, education, science and culture. Titled *Colombia indígena, conquista y colonia* and edited by Jaime Jaramillo Uribe, contains 10 essays by top historians such as Juan Friede, Germán Colmenares, Jorge Melo, Javier Ocampo, and Gerardo Reichel-Dolmatoff. Original 1978 essays are not updated but still retain value. [KW]

2308 Oviedo, Basilio Vicente de. Cualidades y riquezas del Nuevo Reino de Granada. Bucaramanga, Colombia: Gobernación de Santander, 1990. 418 p. (Col. Memoria regional; 4)

Detailed accounts of fauna, flora, and town descriptions written by a Creole priest from Boyacá in 1699 are of some use to historians. Educated in Popayán, Oviedo spent his career as a parish priest and wrote 11 volumes of geography and history. One tome survives in Madrid, here re-edited from the 1930 edition. [KW]

2309 Pacheco, Juan Manuel. Los jesuítas en Colombia. v. 3, 1696–1767. Bogotá: s.n., 1989. 3 v.

Concludes series begun with vol. 1 in 1959 and vol. 2 in 1962. Noted historian, José del Rey, completed this last vol. after Pacheco's death in 1986. Definitive study of Jesuits in Colombia. [KW]

2310 Pumar Martínez, Carmen. Don Antonio Amar y Borbón, último virrey del Nuevo Reino de Granada. Borja, Spain: Centro de Estudios Borjanos, Institución Fernando el Católico, 1991. 238 p.: bibl., ill. (Centro de Estudios Borjanos de la Institución Fernando el Católico; 97)

Revisionist study interprets Nueva Granada's last viceroy as neither a weak administrator nor a decadent representative of the monarchy. Uses socioeconomic studies of viceroyalty as overview and places Amar y Borbón in context, arguing that the viceroy surrendered to avoid a slaughter. For a more solid portrait of Amar y Borbón see item **2297.** [KW]

2311 Reportaje de la historia de Colombia: 158 documentos y relatos de testigos presenciales sobre hechos ocurridos en 5 siglos. v. 1, Del descubrimiento a la Era Republicana. Selección y presentación de Jorge Orlando Melo. Bogotá: Planeta, 1989. 1 v.: ill.

Contains original texts which cover traditional themes of exploration and conquest, rebellions and independence, but also touch less common topics such as public celebrations, witchcraft, epidemics and earthquakes. More diverse than most texts of this genre, the work is a useful introduction to original source material. Most documents appear elsewhere but the combination of themes and quality of authors selected makes this volume valuable. For vol. 2, see *HLAS 52:2383*. [KW]

2312 Rodríguez, Pablo. Cabildo y vida urbana en el Medellín colonial, 1675–1730. Medellín, Colombia: Editorial Univ. de Antioquia, 1992. 184 p.: bibl., ill., map. (Col. Clío de historia colombiana; 3)

Well-researched social history of the Medellín cabildo. Dominated by neither merchants nor miners, Creoles nor *peninsulares,* the cabildo reflected the economic and social tensions among leading families who used cabildo positions for prestige rather than for economic gain. Would carrying the study through independence lead to the same conclusions? [KW]

2313 Rodríguez, Pablo. Seducción, amancebamiento y abandono en la colonia. Bogotá: Fundación Simón y Lola Guberek, 1991. 135 p.: bibl., ill. (Col. Historia; 2)

History of the colonial Colombian family, marriage, seduction patterns, and inter-ethnic conflicts over marital partner selection. Concentrates on Medellín and Antioquia, using *juicios de oposición matrimonial* and 26 criminal cases of *amancebamiento.* Concludes that couples out of wedlock were private rebels punished by authorities fearful of any challenge to restrictive norms. Important social history complements Ann Twinam's work (see *HLAS 52:859*). [KW]

2314 Rueda Méndez, David. Introducción a la historia de la esclavitud negra en la Provincia de Tunja: siglo XVIII. Tunja, Colombia: Escuela de Posgrado de la Facultad de Educación, Univ. Pedagógica y Tecnológica de Colombia, 1989. 59 p.: bibl., ill. (Nuevas lecturas de historia; 6)

Brief introduction to slavery in 18th-century Tunja, where slaves only numbered several hundred in a region dominated by Indians. Most were employed in agriculture (where they were crucial for sugar production) and domestic service, and some in mining. The region held fewer slaves proportionally than the North or West zones. [KW]

Safford, Frank. Race, integration, and progress: elite attitudes and the Indian in Colombia, 1750–1870. See item **2657.**

2315 Silva, Renán. Prensa y revolución a finales del siglo XVIII: contribución a un análisis de la formación de la ideología de independencia nacional. Bogotá: Banco de la República, Depto. Editorial, 1988. 188 p.: bibl. (Col. bibliográfica/Banco de la República. Historia colombiana)

Study is based on the *Papel Periódico de la Ciudad de Santa Fé de Bogotá,* published from 1791–97 by the Cuban Manuel del Socorro Rodríguez. Silva analyzes the text of the 265 editions to develop a link between Enlightenment periodicals and burgeoning independence ideals. Of note is the section on the *Papel's* review of the French Revolution with its noted hostility to regicide and class upheaval. Well-done self-contained study, but disconnected from the evolution of the press in New Granada.

2316 Tobar y Buendía, Pedro de. Verdadera histórica relación del origen, manifestación y prodigiosa renovación por sí misma y milagros de la Imagen de la Sacratísima Virgen María Madre de Diós Nuestra Señora del Rosario de Chiquinquirá. Ed. facsimilar de la ed. de 1694. Bogotá: Instituto Caro y Cuervo, 1986. 1 v., 1 leaf of plates: bibl., ill.

Facsimile ed. of work by Fray Pedro de Tobar y Buendía originally published in Madrid in 1694. Author, born in Santa Fé in 1649, became a Dominican and held various ecclesiastic posts in Madrid and New Granada. History of the painting covers a century during which time numerous miracles were attributed to the image. Interesting, folkloric book. [KW]

2317 Triana Antorveza, Adolfo. La colonización española del Tolima: siglos XVI y XVII. Bogotá: FUNCOL-Cuadernos del Jaguar, 1992. 308 p.: bibl., maps. (Cuadernos del jaguar: Serie histórica; 1)

Central Tolima, occupied by Panches, attracted Spanish *entradas* due to its mineral wealth, arable land, and concentrations of population. In 1550, Ibagué was founded and encomiendas were created. Interesting account of Bocanegra-Saajosa and López Matoso families, the established local power bases. [KW]

2318 Vargas Lesmes, Julián. La sociedad de Santafé colonial. Bogotá: CINEP, 1990. 382 p., 11 leaves of plates: bibl., ill.

Ten articles on Bogotá emphasize social development of the colony. Notable contributions include a demographic analysis of population based upon 18th-century *padrones* and a microstudy of the Estrada-Arias family from unusual household records. Family purchases indicate a surprising dependence on imported products to maintain a European life style. [KW]

2319 Villamarín, Juan A. and Judith E. Villamarín. Epidemic disease in the Sabana de Bogotá, 1536–1810. (*in* International Congress of Americanists, *46th, Amsterdam, 1988.* "Secret judgements of God": Old World

disease in colonial Spanish America. Edited by Noble David Cook and W. George Lovell. Norman: Univ. of Oklahoma Press, 1991, p. 113–141, map, tables)

Outlines 14 smallpox, measles, and typhus epidemics between 1537–1810. Early outbreaks of smallpox in 1558 and 1588 may have killed 20 percent of the native population. Mortality was reduced as prevention techniques (including innoculation) were undertaken in 1803. Overview is useful starting point for more detailed work by these two demographers. [KW]

QUITO

2320 Alchon, Suzanne Austin. Native society and disease in colonial Ecuador. Cambridge, England; New York: Cambridge Univ. Press, 1991. 151 p.: bibl., index, maps. (Cambridge Latin American studies; 71)

Examines impact of Old World diseases on New World populations of Ecuador's northern and central Highlands in 16th, 17th, and 18th centuries. Significant study is marred by careless prose, cavalier citations, and unsupported assumptions stated as facts, such as author's statement that the "introduction of smallpox and measels between 1524 and 1533 claimed one-half to two-thirds of [the native population of Highland Ecuador]." Incorporates the author's chapter "Disease, Population, and Public Health in Eighteenth-Century Quito" published in *"Secret judgments of God:" Old World disease in colonial Spanish America* (Norman: Univ. of Oklahoma Press, 1991). For a more sober analysis of nature and consequences of European diseases in early 1500s, see item **2339.** [MTH]

2321 Anda Aguirre, Alfonso. Corregidores y servidores públicos de Loja. Quito: Banco Central del Ecuador, Centro de Investigación y Cultura, 1987. 273 p.: bibl. (Col. histórica; 12)

A veritable "who's who" of corregidores, cabildo members, notaries, and other public officials of 16th, 17th, and 18th century Loja. Author is an assiduous researcher and reliable scholar. [MTH]

2322 Benavides Solís, Jorge. Orígenes de la ciudad en el Ecuador: el caso de Quito. (*Misc. Hist. Ecuat.*, 2:2, 1989, p. 126–137, bibl.)

Reexamines Quito's origins and concludes that as a city it was an Inca/Spanish construct. In other words, the pre-Inca population was disperse albeit dense and a dichomoty between city/countryside did not exist. [MTH]

2323 Borchart de Moreno, Christiana Renate. La imbecilidad y el coraje: la participación femenina en la enconómia colonial, Quito, 1780–1830. (*Rev. Complut. Hist. Am.,* 17, 1991, p. 167–182)

Pioneering, preliminary study of female participation in commercial and manufacturing sectors of Quito's economy during late colonial and independence periods. [MTH]

2324 Bromley, R.J. El comercio precolonial y la transición a un sistema de mercado colonial en la Audiencia de Quito. (*Rev. Ecuat. Hist. Econ.,* 1 : 1, primer semestre 1987, p. 41–58)

Spanish version of "Precolonial trade and the transition to a colonial market system in the Audiencia of Quito" (*Nova americana,* vol. 1, 1978) on which see *HLAS 46 : 2674.*) [MTH]

2325 Castillo Jácome, Julio. Historia de la Provincia de Tungurahua. v. 1–2. Ambato, Ecuador: J. Castillo Jácome, 1990–1991. 2 v.: ill. (some col.), maps.

Written by an autodidact, this is the most comprehensive history of Ambato and its province to date. These first two vols. of a projected ten treat prehispanic and colonial periods but are curiously organized. Vol. 1, for example, opens with a series of vignettes on independence and late colonial periods, continues with long chapters on prehistory, and concludes with sketchy account of first half of colonial period. [MTH]

2326 Cipolletti, María Susana. Un manuscrito tucano del siglo XVIII: ejemplos de continuidad y cambio en una cultura amazónica. (*Rev. Indias,* 52 : 194, enero/abril 1992, p. 181–195)

Author introduces an important ethnohistorical and linguistic find, a 1753 grammar and vocabulary in Encabellado or Tucano recently rediscovered in the New York Public Library. Tucano is presently spoken by the Secoya, believed to be descendants of the Encabellado and who live in same area along the Río Aguarico. [MTH]

2327 Contreras, Carlos. La crisis de la Sierra Central y Norte del Ecuador en la segunda mitad del siglo XVIII. (*Rev. Ecuat. Hist. Econ.,* 1 : 1, primer semestre 1987, p. 17–40, bibl.)

Reevauation of economic crisis in northern and central Highlands during late colonial period, based primarily on data from Archivo General de las Indias. Author argues that fiscal exigencies of Bourbons aggravated an already serious situation. [MTH]

2328 Contreras, Carlos. El sector exportador de una economía colonial: la costa del Ecuador entre 1760 y 1820. Quito: Facultad Latinoamericano de Ciencias Sociales, Sede Ecuador; Abya-Yala, 1990. 192 p.: bibl., ill. (Col. Tesis. Historia; 1)

Licentiate thesis on the export sector of Guayaquil and its district during late colonial period. Adds new information mostly culled from Guayaquil customs records in the Archivo General de la Nación in Lima. Author contributes novel interpretations to ongoing discussion of littoral's first agroexport boom. [MTH]

2329 Cuesta Domingo, Mariano. Los exploradores franciscanos, Domingo de Briera y Laureano de la Cruz. (*in* Congreso Internacional sobre los Franciscanos en el Nuevo Mundo, *3rd, La Rábida, Spain, 1989.* Actas. Dirección de Paulino Castañeda. Madrid: Editorial Deimos, 1989, p. 1139–1177, maps, tables)

Author sketches Franciscan incursions into Encabellado (Tucano) territory in the 1630s, providing historical, demographic, and geographic data. Includes documentary appendix. [MTH]

Demélas, Marie-Danielle and **Yves Saint-Geours.** Jerusalén y Babilonia: religión y política en el Ecuador, 1780–1880. See item **2672.**

2330 Espinosa Fernández de Córdoba, Carlos R. La mascarada del Inca: una investigación acerca del teatro político de la colonia. (*Misc. Hist. Ecuat.,* 2 : 2, 1989, p. 7–39, photos, table)

Detailed analysis of the multifaceted roles the memory of Sapu Inca played in colonial society. In this case the Inca was represented both allegorically in fiestas and iconographically in processions, and also in the person of Don Alonso Arena Florencia Inca, a great grandson of Atahualpa, and corregidor of the Spanish town of Ibarra in the 1660s. [MTH]

2331 Fernández de Cevallos, Pedro. La ruta de la canela americana. Edición de Marcelo Frías y Andrés Galera. Madrid: Historia 16, 1992. 246 p.: bibl. (Crónicas de América; 74)

Publishes important primary source, a long, heretofore ignored *expediente,* spanning years 1775–95, on promotion and exploitation of cinnamon in "the land of Cinnamon" (Canelos) by a vecino of Ambato and the first intendant of Jaén de Bracamoros, Luya, and Chillaos. Introduction recapitulates efforts and schemes to exploit cinnamon throughout Spanish empire and during the entire colonial period, but does not discuss this virtually unknown chapter in economic history of Ecuador. [MTH]

2332 Investigación histórica de la minería en el Ecuador. Recopilación de Maximina Navarro Cárdenas. Quito: Dirección de Industrias del Ejército, 1990? 527 p.

Previously unpublished source materials, largely from the colonial period, for a history of mining in Ecuador. Includes a minimal introduction. [MTH]

2333 Jara, Alvaro and **John Jay TePaske.** The royal treasuries of the Spanish Empire in America. v. 4, Eighteenth-century Ecuador. Durham, N.C.: Duke Univ. Press, 1990. 1 v.: bibl.

Publishes 18th-century *cartas cuentas* of Royal Treasuries of Cuenca (1722–1803), Guayaquil (1714–1804), Jaén de Bracamoros (1762–92), and Quito (1702–1813). Regretably only a handful of 16th and 17th-century treasury accounts from Audiencia of Quito appear to have survived. For the first three vols. of this exceptionally important series, see *HLAS 46:2631.* [MTH]

2334 Jurado Noboa, Fernando. Esclavitud en la Costa Pacífica: Iscuandé, Barbacoas, Tumaco y Esmeraldas, siglos XVI al XIX. Quito: Ediciones ABYA-YALA; Centro Afro-Ecuatoriano; Corporación Ecuatoriana de Amigos de la Genealogía, 1990. 463 p.: bibl., ill, maps. (Col. Historia del negro en el Ecuador y Sur de Colombia; 3. Col. SAG; 58)

Cornucopia of semi-organized notes on demographic, economic, and social aspects of slavery and manumission in what is now southern Colombia and northern Ecuador. Primarily of interest to researchers. [MTH]

2335 Jurado Noboa, Fernando and **Miguel A. Puga.** El proceso de blanqueamiento en el Ecuador: de los Puento a los Egas [de Fernando Jurado Noboa]. Los Puentos en Cayambe y Tabacundo: siglos XVI al XVII [de Miguel A. Puga]. Quito: s.n., 1992. 237 p.: bibl., ill. (Col. Medio milenio; 3)

Two books in one. The first is a genealogical study of Puento, Cabezas, and Egas families. The title accurately captures the relative unimportance of biological *mestizaje* in the cultural and social *mestizaje* of Ecuador. Second book is an ethnohistorical study of the Puentos or caciques of Cayambe and Tabacundo. [MTH]

2336 Jurado Noboa, Fernando. Sancho Hacho: orígenes de la formación mestiza ecuatoriana. Quito: CEDECO; ABYA-YALA, 1990? 414 p.: bibl., ill. (Col. Amigos de la genealogía; 59. Serie Historia social e identidad nacional)

Genealogical study of direct and indirect descendants of "Don Sancho Hacho de Velasco, cacique principal de asiento de Latacunga," a leading member of the native nobility of central Highlands during Spanish conquest and early colonial period. Useful guide to "good" as well as old families of Quito, Latacunga, and Ambato (e.g., the Vergara Diaz, the Martínez, and the Mera). [MTH]

2337 Miranda Ribadeneira, Francisco. Crisis en las misiones y mutilación territorial. Quito: Banco Central del Ecuador, 1986. 200 p.: bibl. (Col. histórica; 10)

Well documented but somewhat tendentious account by Jesuit scholar of alternating efforts by Franciscans and secular clergy to maintain missions in the Oriente after expulsion of Jesuits in 1767. Also concerned with transfer of Governorship and Diocese of Maynas to Viceroyalty of Peru in 1802 and their "devolution" to Quito in 1821. [MTH]

2338 Moreno Egas, Jorge. Quito en 1797. Quito: Centro Ecuatoriano para el Desarrollo de la Comunidad, 1991. 64 p.: bibl., ill. (Serie Historia social e identidad nacional)

Methodologically unsophisticated study of important but heretofore ignored record group, the 1797 lists of communicants of urban parishes of Quito. Unfortunately, the lists are not analyzed in conjunction with parish registers or coeval censuses. [MTH]

2339 Newson, Linda A. Old World epidemics in early colonial Ecuador. (*in* International Congress of Americanists, *46th, Amsterdam, 1988.* "Secret judgments of God": Old World disease in colonial Spanish America. Edited by Noble David Cook and W. George Lovell. Norman: Univ. of Oklahoma Press, 1991, p. 84–112, map, table)

Superior analysis by senior scholar of Old World diseases afflicting Ecuador between 1520s and 1618. Newson is especially concerned with problematics of chronology; identification of diseases including region-specific information; and differential impact of the various epidemics. Maintains that malaria and yellow fever were late arrivals to coast and eastern Lowlands. [MTH]

2340 Ortiz de la Tabla Ducasse, Javier. Cartas de cabildos hispanoamericanos: Audiencia de Quito, siglos XVI-XIX. Edición e introducción de Javier Ortiz de la Tabla Ducasse, Montserrat Fernández Martínez y Agueda Rivera Garrido. Sevilla: Consejo Superior de Investigaciones Científicas, Escuela de Estudios Hispano-Americanos de Sevilla; Asesoría Quinto Centenario, Consejería de Cultura y Medio Ambiente, Junta de Andalucía, 1991. 506 p.: index. (Publicaciones de la Escuela de Estudios Hispano-Americanos de Sevilla; 360)

Detailed calendar of 896 letters from Spanish and Indian cabildos in what are now southern Colombia, Ecuador, and northern Peru to Council of the Indies and the King as found in Audiencia of Quito section of the Archivo General de Indias from 1543 through 1820. Editors list accompanying and parent materials. Well indexed. An exceptionally important research guide. [MTH]

2341 Powers, Karen M. Indian migration in the Audiencia of Quito: crown manipulation and local co-optation. (*in* Migration in colonial Spanish America. Edited by David J. Robinson. Cambridge: Cambridge Univ. Press, 1990, p. 313–323)

Working paper on internal migration in 16th and 17th centuries suggests that heavy labor quotas were largely responsible for out migration. Primarily concerned with manipulation of *forasteros* by Crown and colonials. [MTH]

Powers, Karen M. Resilient lords and Indian vagabonds: wealth, migration, and the reproductive transformation of Quito's chiefdoms, 1500–1700. See item **768.**

2342 Proceso de la creación de la Villa de San Juan de Hambato, 1743–1760. Transcripción de Pedro Arturo Reino Garcés. Ambato, Ecuador: Editorial Pío XII, 1989. 86 p.: ill.

Publishes for first time the *expediente* (the original is in the National Archives of Colombia) on the establishment of Ambato as a villa. Important source for early history of this central Highland town. [MTH]

2343 Ramos Gómez, Luis J. La estructura social quiteña entre 1737 y 1745 según el proceso contra José de Araujo. (*Rev. Indias,* 51:191, enero/abril 1991, p. 25–56)

Fascinating glimpse of shifting alliances and fortunes of prominent members of Quito's elite as revealed by analysis of proceedings initiated by members of local cabildo against President José de Araujo y Río (1736–44), a *limeño.* [MTH]

2344 Ramos Pérez, Demetrio. El cambio de las mentalidades sociales en Quito en la época del despotismo ilustrado. (*Jahrb. Gesch.,* 26, 1989, p. 85–111)

Traces changes in "mentalities" from Hapsburg to Bourbon times, using perceptions of pros and cons of *obrajes* (textile manufacturers) to exemplify transformation from "moralistic and sensitive" to "utilitarian." Somewhat rambling and not altogether convincing. [MTH]

2345 Relaciones histórico-geográficas de la Audiencia de Quito: s. XVI-XIX. Edición, estudio introductorio y transcripción de Pilar Ponce Leiva. Preámbulo de Francisco de Solano. Madrid: Consejo Superior de Investigaciones Científicas, Centro de Estudios Históricos, Depto. de Historia de América, 1991–1992. 2 v.: bibl., index, col. map. (Col. Tierra nueva e cielo nuevo; 30, t. 1–2)

Compendium of 36 heretofore unpublished and 62 previously published *relaciones geográficas* of the Audiencia of Quito from 16th, 17th, 18th, and early 19th centuries. Complete in two vols.; there will not be a third as originally announced. Most of the previously published *relaciones* are newly transcribed. Fundamental set of sources for reconstruction of multiple aspects of prehispanic as well as hispanic past of southern Colombia, Ecuador, and northern Peru. Well introduced and indexed. [MTH]

2346 Requena, Francisco et al. Ilustrados y bárbaros: diario de la exploración de límites al Amazonas, 1782. Edición, introducción y notas de Manuel Lucena Giraldo. Madrid: Alianza Editorial, 1991. 152 p.: bibl., map. (El libro de bolsillo; 1515. Sección Clásicos)

Requena was member of the commission charged with establishing the boundary between Spanish Quito and Portuguese Brazil. This anthology publishes his *Descripción de los varios caminos que dan paso desde la ciudad de Quito al río del Marañón* (1777); *Diario del viaje hecho al río Japurá* . . . (1782); and brief accounts of his other explorations. Well edited with solid introduction and notes. [MTH]

2347 Solís Chiriboga, María Cristina. El Fondo Escribanías Públicas del Cantón Quito: Sección Protocolos, del Archivo Nacional. (*Misc. Hist. Ecuat.*, 2:2, 1989, p. 105–125, bibl.)

Chronological list of record books of 16th- and 17th-century notaries of Quito. Specifies modern assignation, number of extant folios, whether coevally indexed, and current condition of each codex. [MTH]

2348 Super, John C. Compañías y utilidades en el comercio andino temprano: la práctica de los comerciantes de Quito 1580–1610. (*Rev. Ecuat. Hist. Econ.*, 1:1, primer semestre 1987, p. 59–79, tables)

Spanish version of "Partnership and Profit in the Early Andean Trade," on which see HLAS 48:2002. [MTH]

2349 Torre Reyes, Carlos de la. La revolución de Quito del 10 de agosto de 1809. Quito: Banco Central del Ecuador, Centro de Investigación y Cultura, 1990. 621 p.: bibl. (Col. histórica; 13)

Reprint of well-documented, well-written, and well-reasoned study of the beginnings of the independence movement in Ecuador. Originally published in 1961, this ed. includes Jorge Salvador Lara's essay, "Carlos de la Torre y su Historia del 10 de Agosto de 1809" (p. 17–58). [MTH]

2350 Truhan, Deborah L. "Mi ultimada y postrimera boluntad:" trayectorias de tres mujeres andinas; Cuenca, 1599–1610. (*Histórica/Lima*, 15:1, junio 1991, p. 121–155, bibl.)

Author publishes and analyzes last wills and testaments of three Indian women who died in Cuenca in 1599, 1601, and 1610. Article emphasizes how far we are from reconstructing socioeconomic evolution of so-

cial groups in Ecuador but yet exemplifies how much data can be recovered from surviving sources. [MTH]

2351 Uzcátegui Andrade, Byron. Segundo testamento de doña Beatriz Coquilago Ango, nuera del Inca Atahualpa. (*Misc. Hist. Ecuat.*, 2:2, 1989, p. 138–148, bibl., facsims.)

Transcribes second (1602) and apparently last will and testament of a daughter-in-law of Atahualpa. See also author's "Semblanza Documental de la nuera de Atahualpa" (*Museo Histórico*, vol. 55, 1976, p. 177–184.) [MTH]

2352 Villalba F., Jorge. El licenciado Miguel de Ibarra, sexto presidente de la Audiencia de Quito, su gobernador y capitán general, 1550–1608. Quito: Centro de Publicaciones, Pontificia Univ. Católica del Ecuador, 1991. 442 p.: bibl., ill., maps.

Exhaustive biography of sixth president of Audiencia of Quito and a detailed study of almost everything that happened in the colony during his administration (1600–1608). Unfortunately marred by cryptic citations and poor editing. [MTH]

PERU

2353 Adorno, Rolena. The genesis of Felipe Guamán Poma de Ayala's *Nueva corónica y buen gobierno.* (*Colon. Lat. Am. Rev.*, 2:1/2, 1993, p. 53–92, bibl., facsims.)

Author draws on recently published sources of early history of Chupas area to illuminate origins of and viewpoints expressed in *Nueva corónica.* Guamán Poma's people were *mitmaqkuna* and therefore *forasteros.* Furthermore, Guamán Poma and other members of his family were actively involved in land disputes and adverse litigation with the Chupas, resulting in his exile from Huamanga. For ethnohistorian's comment see item **591.** [MTH]

2354 Adorno, Rolena. Images of *indios ladinos* in early colonial Peru. (*in* Transatlantic encounters: Europeans and Andeans in the sixteenth century. Edited by Kenneth J. Andrien and Rolena Adorno. Berkeley: Univ. of California Press, 1991, p. 232–270)

Sophisticated analysis of cultural mestizaje in early colonial Peru. Exemplifies complexities of interaction between Spaniards and Indians as well as perceptions and misperceptions of *indios ladinos* through cogent review of lives and writings of Felipe Guamán Poma de Ayala and Juan de Santa Cruz Pachacuti Yamqui. [MTH]

2355 Aljovín de Losada, Cristóbal. Los compradores de temporalidades a fines de la colonia. (*Histórica/Lima*, 14:2, dic. 1990, p. 183–233, appendices, bibl., tables)

Prosopographic study of buyers of former Jesuit estates. Nearly half of purchasers of haciendas that sold for more than 50,000 pesos were peninsular merchants or Creole merchant/hacendados. Significant contribution to social and economic history of late colonial period. [MTH]

2356 Amancebados, hechiceros y rebeldes: Chancay, siglo XVII. Selección de documentos y estudio de Ana Sánchez. Cusco, Perú: Centro de Estudios Regionales Andinos Bartolomé de las Casas, 1991. 253 p.: maps. (Archivos de historia andina; 11)

Author introduces and publishes eight investigations of incidents of Andean marriage, "witchcraft" and other "idolatrous" practices, and rebellion among Indians in Corregimiento of Chancay in second half of 17th century. Important source for the history of the central coast during middle colonial period, especially for reconstructing aspects of changing Andean religious beliefs and practices. [MTH]

2357 Amich, José; Fernando Pallares; and Vicente Calvo. Historia de las misiones del Convento de Santa Rosa de Ocopa. Edición crítica, introducción e indices de Julián Heras. Iquitos, Peru: CETA; IIAP, 1988. 590 p.: bibl., index. (Monumenta amazónica: B, Misioneros; 3)

History of Franciscan missions throughout Peru's Amazonía from foundation of their *convento mayor* in Ocopa (1724) through early 1900s was begun by Father Amich and finished by Fathers Fernando Pallares and Vicente Calvo. Skillfully edited by Heras, director of Biblioteca del Convento de Ocopa, who has added indices and 21 documentary appendices. [MTH]

Andrien, Kenneth J. Spaniards, Andeans, and the early colonial state in Peru. See item **2244.**

2358 Baciero, Carlos. La ética en la conquista de América y los primeros jesuitas del Perú. (*in* América, 1492–1992: contribuciones a un centenario. Edición de José

Joaquín Alemany. Madrid: Univ. Pontificia Comillas, 1988, p. 129–164)

Analyzes doubts and concerns of first Jesuits in Peru and their mentors at Salamanca concerning legitimacy of Spain's rights to the Indies, of just wars, and of mass conversions. Adds to intellectual history of early colony and of Counter Reformation Spain. [MTH]

Bradley, Peter T. Society, economy and defence in seventeenth-century Peru: the administration of the Count of Alba de Liste, 1655–61. See item **2247.**

2359 Brenot, Anne-Marie. Imaginaire politique et imaginaire economique chez un arbitriste peruvien, Victorino Montero del Aguila: 1696–1755. (*Cah. Am. lat.*, 9, 1990, p. 29–54, bibl., tables)

Maintains that author of unpublished "Estado Político del Reyno del Perú" (1742) was not a precursor of independence as some scholars have asserted, but an advocate of political and economic reforms. Montero del Aguila was simply denouncing bad governors, not the government itself. [MTH]

2360 Burns, Kathryn. Apuntes sobre la economía conventual: el Monasterio de Santa Clara del Cusco. (*Allpanchis/Cusco*, 23:38, segundo semestre 1991, p. 67–95, bibl., table)

Working paper on economic activities of the first and oldest nunnery in Peru. Burns finds that nuns engaged in a much greater variety of activities, including direct management of estates, and played a much more dynamic role in local economy than scholars such as Luis Martín previously noted in *Daughters of the conquistadores* (see *HLAS 46:2626*). [MTH]

2361 Cahill, David P. and **Scarlett O'Phelan Godoy.** Forging their own history: Indian insurgency in the Southern Peruvian Sierra, 1815. (*Bull. Lat. Am. Res.*, 11:2, May 1992, p. 125–167)

Authors survey economic, social, and ideological changes among the Indian peasantry of the bishopric of Cusco (1782–1814) and present a detailed analysis of two local Indian insurrectionary movements that were tied to the urban movement of the Angulo brothers and Mateo Pumacahua in Cusco during 1814 and 1815. Authors consider breakdown of traditional authority structures in Indian communities as the most significant backdrop for these insurrections, but note that within the liberal anti-monarchical conjuncture local peasants developed a project of independence distinct from that of Creoles. Important article based on primary sources. [N. Jacobsen]

2362 Cahill, David P. Independencia, sociedad y fiscalidad: el sur andino, 1780–1880. (*in* Jornadas de Historiadores Americanistas, 2nd, Granada, Spain, 1989. América: encuentro y asimilación. Edición de Joaquín A. Muñoz Mendoza. Granada: Diputación Provincial de Granada, 1990, p. 141–156)

Suggestive essay on displacement of *kurakas* (native leaders) by *gamonales* (Creole hacendados and militia officers) during aftermath of Túpac Amaru rebellion. Examines the long term economic and social ramifications. [MTH]

2363 Cañedo-Argüelles Fabrega, Teresa. La tenencia de la tierra en el sur andino: el Valle de Moquegua, 1530–1825. (*Rev. Indias*, 51:193, sept./dic. 1991, p. 481–503)

Case study of role of land ownership in social and economic history of a rural valley. Among the novel findings, author informs that some Spaniards and mestizos became tributaries, and therefore legal Indians, because the lands acquired by these individuals were subject to tribute. [MTH]

Castañeda, Carmen. Student migration to colonial urban centers: Guadalajara and Lima. See item **952.**

2364 Castañeda Delgado, Paulino and **Pilar Hernández Aparicio.** La Inquisición de Lima. v. 1, 1570–1635. Madrid: Deimos, 1989. 1 v.: bibl., ill.

Comprehensive, detailed, objective, and thoroughly-researched study of Inquisition in Peru treats whole purview of the Holy Office (not just persecution of Jews and protestants), and therefore limns multiple aspects of ordinary life such as bigamy, clerical improprieties, and popular superstition. First of a projected three volumes. [MTH]

2365 Castelli, Amalia. 1663: ¿revuelta social o religiosa? (*Apuntes/Lima*, 26, primer semestre 1990, p. 93–100, bibl.)

Adds another Indian revolt to role call, that of the Repartimiento of Andaxes (Corregimiento of Cajatambo) in 1663. Specific tar-

get of protest was recently founded *obraje* or textile manufactury. [MTH]

2366 Castro-Klarén, Sara et al. El retorno de las huacas: estudios y documentos sobre el Taki Onqoy, siglo XVI. Recopilación de Luis Millones. Lima: Instituto de Estudios Peruanos; Sociedad Peruana de Psicoanálisis, 1990. 450 p.: bibl., index, maps. (Fuentes e investigaciones para la historia del Perú; 8. Biblioteca peruana de psicoanálisis; 2)

New ed. of *Las informaciones de Cristóbal de Albornoz*, originally published by Luis Millones in 1971. This long out-of-print set provides primary sources on manifestations and extirpation of the wide-spread movement of religious and political revolt in the 1560s and 1570s known as *Taki Onqoy* or "dance of disease" in the Cusco and Huamanga areas. Well-edited and indexed, the volume includes several new studies on the movement, the most novel of which is a brief but suggestive essay on psychological aspects of *Taki Onqoy* by a team of ethnohistorians and psychoanalysts. [MTH]

Cebrián González, María del Carmen and **Isabel Arenas Frutos.** Situación de la Provincia del Perú a finales del siglo XVI: *La crónica anónima* de 1600. See item **2249.**

2367 Charney, Paul. The implications of godparental ties between Indians and Spaniards in colonial Lima. (*Americas/Francisc.*, 47:3, Jan. 1991, p. 295–313)

Examines extent of and ways in which *compadrazgo* linked native leaders and Spanish residents in early 17th-century Lima. Also explores the negative impact ties of obligation with outsiders had on *kuracas* and Indian community at large. [MTH]

2368 Coloma Porcari, César. Documentos inéditos para la historia de la Magdalena y el valle de Lima, 1557–1889. (*Hist. Cult./Lima*, 18, 1990, p. 9–109, ill., tables)

Important set of previously unpublished and relatively unknown primary sources for reconstruction of history of Magdalena, now an urban Lima neighborhood, but in colonial times a separate Indian pueblo and Franciscan *doctrina*. Includes several postindependence documents. [MTH]

2369 Contreras, Remedios. Sobre el juicio de residencia del Virrey del Perú Agustín de Jáuregui, 1780–1784. (*Cuad. Hist. Moderna*, 12, 1991, p. 183–203)

Solid case study of review process to which viceroys and other crown appointees were subject. Perhaps most significant aspect of Jáuregui's *residencia* is that no one found fault with him. [MTH]

2370 Cook, Noble David and **Alexandra Parma Cook.** Good faith and truthful ignorance: a case of transatlantic bigamy. Durham: Duke Univ. Press, 1991. 206 p.: bibl., ill., index, maps.

Intriguing tale of Francisco Noguerol de Ulloa, a *de facto* but ultimately not a *de jure* bigamist, who struck it rich in Peru but was not allowed to enjoy his fortune upon return to Spain with a second wife (at least not for some years). An absorbing and rewarding read for its insights into the lifestyles and mentalities of the time. [MTH]

2371 Cook, Noble David. Migration in colonial Peru: an overview. (*in* Migration in colonial Spanish America. Edited by David J. Robinson. Cambridge: Cambridge Univ. Press, 1990, p. 41–61, map)

Authoritative review of what is now known regarding history of migration in colonial Peru and what remains to be researched. Includes tentative typology of migration and overview of types of migrants and migration. Most important article on subject since Rolando Mellafe's seminal "The Importance of Migration in the Viceroyalty of Peru," in *Population and economics,* edited by Paul Depréz (Winnipeg, 1970), p. 303–313. [MTH]

2372 Cook, Noble David. Patrones de migración indígena en el Virreinato del Perú: mitayos, mingas y forasteros. (*Histórica/ Lima,* 13:2, dic. 1989, p. 125–152, bibl.)

Excellent survey of patterns of Indian migration in Lower and Upper Peru throughout the colonial period by a master historical demographer. [MTH]

2373 Dean, Carolyn S. Ethnic conflict and Corpus Christi in colonial Cuzco. (*Colon. Lat. Am. Rev.,* 2:1/2, 1993, p. 93–120, bibl.)

Case study of deep rooted and long standing hostilities between the Cañari and the Chachapoya peoples on one hand and towards the Incas on the other (both of the former allied with the Spaniards against the Incas during the Spanish conquest). Exceptionally important contribution to social as well as ethnic and urban history of the Andes. Re-

minder of the exceptional ethnic diversity of the Andean region. [MTH]

2374 Fernández Alonso, Serena. Iniciativas renovadoras en los cabildos peruanos a fines de la época colonial. (*Rev. Indias,* 51: 193, sept./dic. 1991, p. 505–522)

Revisionist study of impact of Bourbon reforms on local government in late colonial Peru. Maintains that in final analysis intendants strengthened rather than undermined cabildos and municipal autonomy. That was the consequence, but was it the intent? [MTH]

2375 Fernández Alonso, Serena. Selección bibliográfica sobre el Perú virreinal durante el periódo reformista borbónica. (*Historiogr. Bibliogr. Am.,* 49:2, 1992, p. 153–205)

Extensive bibliography of books and articles on 18th- and early 19th-century Peru.

2376 Flores Galindo, Alberto. La ciudad sumergida: aristocracia y plebe en Lima, 1760–1830. 2. ed. Lima: Editorial Horizonte, 1991. 214 p.: bibl., ill. (Historia; 9)

Corrected and revised ed. of *Aristocracia y plebe* (1984). Notable both for its first-rate demographic, economic, and social study of Lima during the late colonial period and for its pioneering history of the urban lower sector. Lamentably "Tito" Flores did not live to add section on "la ciudad sumergida" per se. [MTH]

2377 Garzón Rivera, Emilio. Poder local y violencia en los Andes: un caso en Abancay a fines del siglo XVIII. (*Allpanchis/ Cusco,* 23:38, segundo semestre 1991, p. 129–151)

Analyzes 1782 conflict between corregidor and pastor of Abancay. Author does not attempt to establish model of how rural authorities interacted with one another or exploited their charges, yet ably demonstrates use and misuse of local power. [MTH]

2378 Glave, Luis Miguel. Sociedad campesina y violencia rural en el escenario de la gran rebelión indígena de 1780. (*Histórica/ Lima,* 14:1, julio 1990, p. 27–68, bibl.)

Reexamination of events immediately leading up to Túpac Amaru rebellion. Focuses on realities of daily life and "structural violence" in rebel leader's home province of Canas y Canchis, or Tinta, in the year 1780.

Concludes that "la gente actuaba guiada por sus contradicciones inmediatas." Based almost entirely on archival sources. [MTH]

Gómez Rivas, León. Don Francisco de Toledo, Comendador de Alcántara, Virrey del Perú: guía de fuentes. See item **2250.**

2379 González Sánchez, Carlos Alberto. Repatriación de capitales del Virreinato del Perú en el siglo XVI. Madrid: Banco de España, Servicio de Estudios, 1991. 129 p.: bibl. (Estudios de historia económica, 0213–2702; 20)

Quantitative analysis of disposition of "fortunes" of 16th-century Spaniards who died in Peru (including intestates) and whose recipients resided in the mother country. Suggestive first step towards determining economic and, to a lesser degree, the social success of peninsular emigres during early colonial period. For related article, see item **2422.** [MTH]

Guilmartin, John F., Jr. The cutting edge: an analysis of the Spanish invasion and overthrow of the Inca empire, 1532–1539. See item **2251.**

2380 Hampe Martínez, Teodoro. The diffusion of books and ideas in colonial Peru: a study of private libraries in the sixteenth and seventeenth centuries. (*HAHR*, 73:2, May 1993, p. 211–233, appendices, table)

Masterful synthesis of author's ongoing research on early modern libraries and mentalities. More comprehensive than earlier Spanish version (see *HLAS 52:2154*) in that this digest covers both 16th and 17th centuries. Based on analysis of 24 private collections. [MTH]

2381 Hampe Martínez, Teodoro. Don Pedro de la Gasca, 1493–1567: su obra política en España y América. Prólogo de Juan de Tudela y Bueso. Lima: Pontificia Univ. Católica del Perú, Fondo Editorial, 1989. 426 p.: appendices, bibl.

Exhaustively-researched doctoral thesis and the most comprehensive biography to date of the pacifier of Peru. Includes a documentary appendix almost as long as the text. Major contribution to 16th-century history of both Spain and Peru. [MTH]

Hampe Martínez, Teodoro. Esbozo de una transferencia política: asistentes de Sevilla en el gobierno virreinal de México y Perú. See item **1168.**

2382 Hehrlein, Yacin. Mission und Macht: die politisch-religiöse Konfrontation zwischen dem Dominikanerorden in Peru und dem Vizekönig Francisco de Toledo, 1569–1581. Mainz: Matthias-Grünewald-Verlag, 1992. 173 p.: bibl. (Walberberger Studien der Albertus-Magnus-Akademie: Theologische Reihe; 16)

Reproduction of a history dissertation (Heidelberg Univ., 1991) minutely analyzes the conflict between viceroy Toledo and Dominican *lascasistas* in Peru. Concentrates on three aspects: 1) the expulsion of Dominican missionaries from the Chucuito region; 2) the secularization of San Marcos University, orginally hosted at the Dominican convent in Lima; and 3) the inquisitorial trial against some radical friars charged with "utopic heresy." Valuable and well-documented research on a very specific but important topic in colonial administration. [T. Hampe-Martínez]

2383 Hemming, John. Pizarro: conqueror of the Inca. (*Natl. Geogr. Mag.*, 181:2, Feb. 1992, p. 90–121, ill., maps, photos)

Well written and illustrated introduction to Pizarro and the Spanish conquest of Peru by a leading authority on the subject. For a full account, see Hemming's classic *The conquest of the Incas* (*HLAS 34:1178*). [MTH]

2384 Heras, Julián. Las doctrinas franciscanas en el Perú colonial. (*in* Congreso Internacional sobre los Franciscanos en el Nuevo Mundo, *3rd, La Rábida, Spain, 1989*. Actas. Dirección de Paulino Castañeda. Madrid: Editorial Deimos, 1989, p. 693–720)

Survey of Franciscan missions from foundation, mostly in the 1500s, through their takeover by diocesan clergy in the 1700s and eventual extinction in the 1800s. Includes some new archival data. [MTH]

2385 Hidalgo Lehuedé, Jorge; María Marsilli Cardozo; and Carlos Rodríguez. Composición de tierras en el corregimiento de Arica: la visita de Diego de Baños y Sotomayor en 1643. (*Historia/Santiago*, 25, 1990, p. 175–206, bibl., appendix)

Publishes with spartan introduction mid-17th-century source in literal transcription for study of land titles and usage in Corregimiento of Arica (part of Peru until 1880). Of interest to local scholars and specialists. [MTH]

2386 Historia del Callao. v. 1, pt. 2., Historia, 1615–1826. Callao: Centro de Investigaciones Históricas del Callao, 1990. 162 p.: bibl., ill., maps.

Multiauthored history of Callao. Vol. 1, pt. 1, not seen by this contributor, chronicles the 1500s and early 1600s. Pt. 2 continues the story of the port through its surrender by the royal commander on Jan. 23, 1826. Includes chapter on "demography and economy of colonial Callao" and is well illustrated. Should be consulted as a set, among other reasons because apparently it has a consolidated bibliography. [MTH]

2387 Iwaski Cauti, Fernando. La primera navegación transpacífica entre Perú y Filipinas y su transfondo socio-económico. (*Anu. Estud. Am.*, 47, 1990, p. 123–169)

Fascinating study of beginnings of transpacific trade between Lima and Manila and of machinations of those involved, especially of Gonzálo Ronquillo de Peñalosa, governor of Philippines. Nicely detailed. [MTH]

Jacobsen, Nils. Mirages of transition: the Peruvian Altiplano, 1780–1930. See item **2744.**

2388 Kapsoli Escudero, Wilfredo. Rebeliones de esclavos en el Perú. Colofón de Bernard Lavallé. 2. ed. ampliada. Lima: Ediciones Purej, 1990. 157 p., 4 p. of plates: bibl., ill.

New ed. of original monograph on 18th-century coastal slave rebellions, specifically those of San Jacinto (1768), San José (1779), and Motocachi (1786) in the Nepeña Valley. [MTH]

2389 Laviana Cuetos, María Luisa. Túpac Amaru. Sevilla: Editoriales Andaluzas Unidas, 1990. 165 p.: bibl., ill. (some col.) (Forjadores de América)

Useful introduction to Indian insurrection of 1780–83 and to its principal leader, interpreted à la Boleslao Lewin. [MTH]

2390 León y León Durán, Gustavo. La Perricholi: apuntes histórico genealógicos de Micaela Villegas. Lima: Claire S.A., 1990. 146 p.: bibl., ill., index.

Extensively researched family history of Micaela Villegas y Hurtado de Mendoza, notorious lover of Viceroy Manuel de Amat y Junient, from her grandparents on both sides through her great-great-grandchildren. [MTH]

2391 MacCormack, Sabine. Myth, history and language in the Andes. (*Colon. Lat. Am. Rev.*, 2:1/2, 1993, p. 247–260, bibl.)

Insightful review of recent books on history and languages of what became Peru and on newly published as well as new editions of sources for their study. Perhaps the most important points MacCormack makes are "that the Andean and the Spanish components of Andean history are not so easy to separate" and "that if we are to separate them in any useful sense, we must first endeavour to understand them both." [MTH]

MacCormack, Sabine. Religion in the Andes: vision and imagination in early colonial Peru. See item **2256.**

2392 Melzer, John T.S. Bastion of commerce in the city of kings: the Consulado de Comercio de Lima, 1593–1887 = Bastión de comercio en la ciudad de los reyes: el Consulado de Comercio de Lima, 1593–1887 = Bastion des Handels in der Stadt der Könige: des handelskonsulat von Lima, 1593–1887. Lima: Editorial Concytec, 1991. 201 p.: bibl., ill.

Well-researched survey of the Consulado de Comercio de Lima in English, Spanish, and German. Primarily of interest to specialists. Reads more like notes than an essay. [MTH]

2393 Millones, Luis. Los sueños de Santa Rosa de Lima. (*Historia/Santiago*, 24, 1989, p. 253–266, bibl.)

Excellent analysis of the state of knowledge of this saint, including what may be inferred from her recorded dreams regarding her life and personality. Important contribution to history of private life in Lima. Preview of a full scale, dispassionate biography. [MTH]

2394 Miró Quesada Soto, Aurelio. Fray Lucas de Mendoza: un paraguayo en Lima en el siglo XVII. (*Hist. Parag.*, 23, 1986, p. 49–60)

Biographical sketch of Lucas de Mendoza (1584–1636), an early Paraguayan poet, member of the Augustinian order in Lima, and professor of the Universidad de San Marcos. For related article see item **2560.** [SMS]

Murra, John V. "Nos hazen mucha ventaja:" the early European perception of Andean achievement. See item **2258.**

2395 Neira, Hernán. El espejo del olvido: la idea de América en las *Memorias* de Juan Bautista Túpac Amaru. (*Rev. Indias,* 51: 191, enero/abril 1991, p. 97–120)

Significant study of life and memoirs (Buenos Aires, 1826) of José Gabriel Túpac Amaru's overlooked half-brother, the only family member who survived to tell us what it meant to be an Inca and a member of the hispanized Indian elite during the late colonial period. Significant contribution to history of *mentalités.* [MTH]

Neira Avendaño, Máximo *et al.* Historia general de Arequipa. See item **2759.**

2396 Nguyen, Thai Hop *et al.* Evangelización y teología en el Perú: luces y sombras en el siglo XVI. Lima: Instituto Bartolomé de Las Casas; Centro de Estudios y Publicaciones, 1991. 314 p.: bibl. (CEP; 115)

Remarkable reexamination of the Church's early history in Peru in light of Vatican II, liberation theology, and today's historical cannons and concerns. Includes essays on evangelization efforts of Dominicans, Franciscans, Mercedarians, and Augustinians, on key figures (Bartolomé de Las Casas, Domingo de Santo Tomás, José de Acosta, Guamán Poma de Ayala), and on Andean as well as Christian theology. Also examines catechisms adapted as well as adopted before and after Lima Council III, and role of laity in evangelization in 1500s. [MTH]

2397 Olmedo Jiménez, Manuel. Jerónimo de Loaysa, O.P., pacificador de españoles y protector de Indios. Granada: Univ. de Granada; Salamanca: Editorial San Esteban, 1990. 328 p.: bibl., index. (Biblioteca chronica nova de estudios históricos; 9. Los Dominicos y América; 7)

Solid doctoral thesis on role played by first bishop and archbishop of Lima as a pacifier of Spaniards during the civil wars that followed promulgation of New Laws of 1542 and as a protector of Indians. Somewhat pedantic and apologetic, however. For related work, see item **2411.** [MTH]

2398 O'Phelan Godoy, Scarlett. El "castigo ejemplar al traidor" durante la gran rebelión de 1780–81. (*in* Encuentros Debate América Latina Ayer y Hoy, *3rd, Barcelona, 1991.* Conquista y resistencia en la historia de América. Coordinación de Pilar García Jordán y Miquel Izard. Barcelona: Publicacions Univ. de Barcelona, 1992, p. 167–190, facsims.)

Systematic analysis of violence (especially executions) and its significance as sanctioned and deliberately applied by Túpac Amaru and Túpac Katari against "Spaniards" and "non-Spaniards." Túpac Katari was much less selective than Túpac Amaru in putting people to death. Major contribution to social history of the uprisings. [MTH]

2399 Pease G.Y., Franklin. Las primeras versiones españolas sobre el Perú. (*Colon. Lat. Am. Rev.,* 1:1/2, 1992, p. 65–76, bibl.)

Cogent review of first Spanish accounts of Peru and of its conquest. Among other issues reexamined are authorship of the *Relación Sámano-Xerez* (on which see also *HLAS 44:2641, HLAS 44:2657, and HLAS 46:2630*) and chronology and authorship of Francisco de Xerez's *Verdadera relación de la conquista del Perú.* [MTH]

2400 Peralta Ruiz, Víctor. Fiscalidad y poder regional en el Cusco a fines de la colonia e inicios de la república. (*in* Coloquio Internacional del Grupo de Trabajo Historia y Antropología Andinas, *2nd, Quito, 1990.* Poder y violencia en los Andes. Edición de Henrique Urbano y Mirko Lauer. Cusco, Peru: Centro de Estudios Regionales Andinos Bartolomé de Las Casas, 1991, p. 149–164, bibl.)

Thoughtful and thought-provoking working paper on socioeconomic and political roles of local bureaucracy in rural Cusco during late colonial and early national periods. Focuses particularly on their control over rural rents. [MTH]

Pérez Fernández, Isacio. Bartolomé de las Casas en el Perú: el espíritu lascasiano en la primera evangelización del Imperio Incaico, 1531–1573. See item **2259.**

2401 Presta, Ana María. La tasa toledana del repartimiento de Pairija: un documento inédito del Archivo General de la Nación, Buenos Aires. (*Histórica/Lima,* 15:2, dic. 1991, p. 237–264, bibl.)

Publishes with brief commentary 1577 *tasa* of the Repartimiento of Pairija in the district of Huamanga. An important ethnohistorical and historical demographic source. [MTH]

2402 Puente Brunke, José de la. La burocracia en el Virreinato del Perú: apuntes sobre los siglos XVI y XVII. (*Merc. Peru.,* 501, enero/marzo 1991, p. 49–62)

Author explores financial rewards that tempted members of the Audiencia of Lima and to which many fell prey. Also examines extent to which overlapping jurisdiction and differences in personalities resulted in imbroglios between magistrates and viceroys. [MTH]

2403 Puente Brunke, José de la. Encomienda y encomenderos en el Perú: estudio social y político de una institución colonial. Sevilla: Excma. Diputación Provincial de Sevilla, 1992. 536 p.: bibl., ill. (Publicaciones de la Excma. Diputación Provincial de Sevilla: Sección Historia: V centenario del descubrimiento de América; 14)

Deservedly prize-winning doctoral dissertation. Work is the most detailed, extensively researched and methodologically up-to-date study of the encomienda in Peru to date. Furthermore, it is a social history of those subject to the encomienda and of the *encomenderos* who benefited from it, becoming thereby the principal members of the new elite of the Andes. Among other notable features of this outstanding book on 16th- and 17th-century Peru is De la Puente's jurisdiction-by-jurisdiction reconstruction of encomiendas, who held them, years in which they were regulated (i.e. "tasadas"), number of tributaries, net tribute produced, pensioners who also benefited by them and to what extent, and correponding sources. [MTH]

2404 Ramos, Gabriela. La privatización del poder: Inquisición y sociedad colonial en el Perú. (*in* Coloquio Internacional del Grupo de Trabajo Historia y Antropología Andinas, 2nd, Quito, 1990. Poder y violencia en los Andes. Edición de Henrique Urbano y Mirko Lauer. Cusco, Peru: Centro de Estudios Regionales Andinos Bartolomé de Las Casas, 1991, p. 75–92, appendix)

Not even members of the Holy Office were above the temptation of money. Some actually enriched themselves and the Inquisition by serving as debt collectors, which more or less became a family business. For related work, see Ramos' equally important "La fortuna del Inquisidor: Inquisición y poder en el Perú, 1594–1611," in *Cuadernos para la historia de la evangelización en América Latina* (vol. 4, 1989). [MTH]

2405 Regaldo del Hurtado, Liliana. Improntas socioeconómicas en la evangelización de Vilcabamba. (*Histórica/Lima*, 15:2, dic. 1991, p. 315–335, bibl.)

Author adds a negative chapter to history of Jesuits in Peru. In 1602, Father Juan Font attempted to establish a mission among Indians of the R. Jauja area in order to enrich himself at his charges' expense. [MTH]

2406 Restrepo Manrique, Daniel. La Iglesia de Trujillo, Perú, bajo el episcopado de Baltasar Jaime Martínez Compañón, 1780–1790. v. 1–2. Vitoria-Gasteiz: Eusko Jaurlaritzaren Argitalpen Zerbitzu Nagusia = Servicio Central de Publicaciones del Gobierno Vasco, 1992. 2 v.: bibl. (Amerika eta euskaldunak = América y los vascos; 10)

First vol. of this substantial work (whose cover and spine title appropriately read *Sociedad y religión en Trujillo, Perú, 1780–1790*) is an exquisitely detailed geographic and economic, social and demographic, and ecclesiastical and private life study of northwestern Peru in the 1780s. Vol. 2 publishes many of sources on which vol. 1 is based, notably the "Documentos de la Visita Pastoral" of Bishop Martínez Compañón, and includes a welcome "Catálogo Documentado" of Martínez Campañón's now complete, separately published, but otherwise not indexed iconographic treasure trove, *Trujillo del Perú* (Madrid: Ediciones Cultura Hispánica, 9 v.). [MTH]

2407 Rizo-Patrón, Paul. La nobleza en Lima en tiempos de los Borbones. (*Bull. Inst. fr. étud. andin.*, 19:1, 1990, p. 129–163, bibl., tables)

Essay on titled elite of Lima and "its economic, social, and political behavior" from 1700 to 1821. Chapter from a senior thesis, included here because it incorporates some archival data, especially on economic activities of the nobility. [MTH]

2408 Rodríguez, Manuel Alfredo. El descubrimiento del Marañón. Edición, prólogo y notas de Angeles Durán. Madrid: Alianza Editorial, 1990. 665 p. (Alianza universidad; 654)

Welcome reedition of a classic early history of Jesuit missions to Upper Amazon Basin by a 17th-century Jesuit born in Spain and raised in Quito. Important for coeval perspective and because Rodríguez used numerous sources, including many that have not survived. [MTH]

2409 Rostworowski de Diez Canseco, María. Doña Francisca Pizarro: una ilustre mestiza, 1534–1598. Lima: Instituto de Estudios Peruanos, 1989. 162 p.: bibl., ill. (Serie Historia andina; 14)

Fascinating study of lives (to the extent that available sources permit) and times of daughter of Francisco Pizarro and Quispe Sisa (also known as Inés Huaylas Yupanqui, and therefore a grandaughter of Huayna Cápac), and of two other first generation mestizas. Major contribution to history of families and women in early colonial period. [MTH]

2410 Rostworowski de Diez Canseco, María. Tasa y tributo del curacazgo de Lima. (*Hist. Cult./Lima*, 18, p. 110–113, bibl.)

Publishes with pithy commentary a 1549 tribute schedule of the *Kuraca* of Lima, Gonzalo Taulichuso. Not surprisingly, the encomienda was then assigned to Hernando Pizarro and his spouse (and niece), Francisca. For biography of Francisca see item **2409.** [MTH]

2411 Ruigómez Gómez, Carmen. Una política indigenista de los Habsburgo: el protector de indios en el Perú. Madrid: Instituto de Cooperación Iberoamericana, Ediciones de Cultura Hispánica, 1988. 227 p.: bibl. (Historia)

Well-researched monograph on origins and early years of Protector of the Indians, an office heretofore neglected in Peruvian historiography. Illuminates Habsburg and some of their appointees' efforts to protect and assist "the defeated." For related item see **2397.** [MTH]

2412 Sala Vila, Nuria. La revuelta de Juli en 1806: crisis de subsistencia y economía campesina. (*Rev. Indias*, 51:192, mayo/agosto 1991, p. 343–374, tables)

Coming on the heels of the severe drought and epidemic of 1804–05, the brief revolt by Indian peasants in Juli, led by the town's priests, was directed against the Bourbon reformist project of the Intendant of Puno, Joséf González, who sought to interfere with the privileges and resources of communities and priests in favor of provincial elite interests. Based on solid archival research in the Andes and in Spain. [N. Jacobsen]

2413 Sínodos de Lima de 1613 y 1636. Elaboración de Bartolomé Lobo Guerrero y Fernando Arias de Ugarte. Madrid: Centro de Estudios Históricos del Consejo Superior de Investigaciones Científicas; Salamanca: Instituto de Historia de la Teología Española de la Univ. Pontificia de Salamanca, 1987. 457 p.:

bibl., ill. (Tierra nueva e cielo nuevo; 22. Sínodos americanos; 6)

Reprint of 1754 Lima ed. of Synods of 1613 and 1636. Provisions of Synod of 1613 were still in force in 1754, except as modified by those of 1636 (no synod had been held since) and by edicts of later archbishops. Editors have restored provisions of Viceroy Marqués de Montesclaros from original ed. of the 1613 Synod. Basic sources for study of policies and problematics of the Church in the established colony. Solid introduction by José María Soto Rábanos. [MTH]

2414 Stavig, Ward A. Ladrones, cuatreros y salteadores: indios criminales en el Cusco rural a fines de la colonia. (*in* Bandoleros, abigeos y montoneros: criminalidad y violencia en el Perú, siglos XVIII-XX. Edición de Carlos Aguirre y Charles Walker. Lima: Instituto de Apoyo Agrario, 1990, p. 69–103)

Finds that Indian and mestizo thieves, rustlers, and highwaymen in the provinces of Canas y Canchis and Quispicanchis were delinquents—not social bandits—both before and after the Túpac Amaru rebellion. [MTH]

2415 Tardieu, Jean-Pierre. Evolución del reclutamiento de los negros bozales en la Arquidiócesis de Lima, fin del siglo XVI- siglo XVII. (*HISLA/Lima*, 13/14, 1er y 2do semestre 1989, p. 79–92, bibl., tables)

Quantitative study of slaves from Africa in Archdiocese of Lima between 1583 and 1702. Based on ecclesiastical records, especially parish registers, this study adds more precise date on their origins and confirms Bowser's thesis that the Angola region had become the preferred supply source. [MTH]

2416 Tardieu, Jean-Pierre. Le nouveau David et la réforme du Pérou: l'affaire María Pizarro-Francisco de la Cruz, 1571–1596. Bordeaux, France: Maison des Pays Ibériques, 1992. 268 p.: bibl.

Well-documented analysis of the famous inquisitorial suit which led to the auto-da-fé held in Lima in 1578. The author adopts a psychological interpretation, thus presenting María Pizarro as a neurotic hysteric and her "diabolic" consort, Francisco de la Cruz, as a paranoiac schizophrene. Since religious heterodoxy equaled political subversion at that time, concludes Tardieu, Viceroy Toledo and the Inquisition joined hands to inflict exemplary punishment. Penetrating and lucid contribution to the history of *mentalités*. [T. Hampe-Martínez]

2417 Tardieu, Jean-Pierre. La pathologie ré-hibitoire de l'esclavage en milieu urbain: Lima XVIIème siècle. (*Jahrb. Gesch.*, 26, 1989, p. 19–35, tables)

Studies 64 cases of invoked clauses of guarantee of good health in sale contracts of slaves to establish types, distribution, and demography of maladies among recently acquired slaves. [MTH]

2418 TePaske, John Jay. The costs of empire: spending patterns and priorities in colonial Peru, 1581–1820. (*Colon. Lat. Am. Rev.*, 2:1, Winter 1993, p. 1–33, table)

Overview of expenditures of the Caja Real de Lima. Based on data in vol. 1 of TePaske and Klein's *The royal treasuries of the Spanish Empire in America* (*HLAS 46: 2631*). Able summary of diachronic shifts in viceregal needs and priorities. [MTH]

2419 Tineo, Primitivo. La evangelización del Perú en las instrucciones entregadas al Virrey Toledo, 1569–1581. (*Merc. Peru.*, 502, abril/junio 1991, p. 9–23)

Analyzes instructions issued to Toledo regarding organization of the Church, its evangelizing responsibilities, and tithes. Tineo leaves no doubt that Crown intended to establish and maintain control over regular orders as well as diocesan clergy as soon as expedient. [MTH]

2420 Valcárcel, Carlos Daniel. Tres momentos de Túpac Amaru. (*Hist. Cult./ Lima*, 19, 1990, p. 85–89)

Maintains that although Túpac Amaru began his *cacicazgo* as a loyal subject of the Crown, he became a separatist as well as a revolutionary because his attempts to achieve social reform through peaceful methods were thwarted by "unjust authorities of Cuzco and Lima." [MTH]

2421 Valdizán, Hermilio. Locos de la colonia. Lima: Instituto Nacional de Cultura, 1988. 180 p.: bibl. (El Libro popular)

Originally published more than sixty years ago, this pioneering work on manifestations of mental disorders during the colonial period has stood the test of time and, apparently, not been superceded by a more systematic work. [MTH]

2422 Varón Gabai, Rafael and Auke Pieter Jacobs. Los dueños del Perú: negocios e inversiones de los Pizarro en el siglo XVI. (*Histórica/Lima*, 13:2, dic. 1989, p. 197–242, bibl., tables)

Case study of business enterprises and investments of returning conquistador Hernando Pizarro and his independently wealthy mestiza wife Doña Francisca. Supplements parallel albeit broader work of Ida Altman on *Emigrants and society: Extremadura and Spanish America in the 16th century* (Berkeley: Univ. of California Press, 1989). For English version see HAHR (Vol. 67, No. 4, Nov. 1987, p. 657–695). [MTH]

2423 Vázquez, Juan Teodoro. Crónica continuada de la provincia de San Agustín del Perú. Estudio previo, edición y notas por Teófilo Aparicio López. Zamora, Spain: Ediciones Monte Casino; Valladolid: Editora Estudio Agustiniano 1991. 512 p.: bibl., ill., index.

Continues annals of Augustinian order in Lower and Upper Peru from 1657 through 1721, taking up where Bernardo de Torres and, before him, Antonio de la Calancha left off in *Crónica de la provincia peruana del Orden de los Ermitaños de S. Agustín* (Lima, 1657) and *Corónica moralizada de la Provincia del Perú del Orden de San Agustín* (2 v.: Barcelona, 1639; Lima, 1653). Includes notices of events related to the Order in Chile and Río de la Plata. Basic source for history of the Church and of the Augustinians in Spanish South America. Well-edited edition. [MTH]

2424 Las Visitas a Cajamarca, 1571–72/ 1578: documentos. v. 1–2. Transcripción de Pilar Remy. Lima: Instituto de Estudios Peruanos, 1992. 2 v.: bibl. (Fuentes e investigaciones para la historia del Perú, 1019–4487; 9)

Publishes in literal transcription the *visitas* of 1571/72 and 1578 of Cajamarca. Includes introductory studies by María Rostworowski de Diez Canseco on "etnias forasteras en la visita toledana a Cajamarca" and by Pilar Remy, the transcriber, on "El Documento." Fundamental sources for in-depth study of multiple aspects of late prehispanic and early hispanic history of the Cajamarca region. A minimal table of contents and lack of index make this a difficult work to consult. [MTH]

2425 Vivanco, Carmen. Bandolerismo colonial peruano, 1760–1810: caracterización de una respuesta popular y causas económicas. (*in* Bandoleros, abigeos y montoneros: criminalidad y violencia en el Perú, siglos XVIII-XX. Edición de Carlos Aguirre y Charles Walker. Lima: Instituto de Apoyo Agrario, 1990, p. 25–56)

Schematic study of social banditry on the coast during late colonial period focuses on the characteristics and causes (primarily economic) of brigandage. Not surprisingly, the majority of highwaymen were runaway slaves. [MTH]

2426 Walker, Charles. La violencia y el sistema legal: los indios y el Estado en el Cusco después de la rebelión de Túpac Amaru. (*in* Coloquio Internacional del Grupo de Trabajo Historia y Antropología Andinas, *2nd, Quito, 1990.* Poder y violencia en los Andes. Edición de Henrique Urbano y Mirko Lauer. Cusco, Peru: Centro de Estudios Regionales Andinos Bartolomé de Las Casas, 1991, p. 125–147, bibl., graph)

Essay examines economic, political, and social developments in the wake of, but not necessarily resulting from, the Túpac Amaru rebellion. Author provides a novel analysis of lawsuits brought before the new Audiencia of Cuzco by Indians between 1782 and 1824 for abuses by local authorities. Walker pays special attention to what he refers to as "acceptable" levels of violence. [MTH]

2427 Wightman, Ann. " . . . Residente en esa ciudad . . . ": urban migrants in colonial Cuzco. (*in* Migration in colonial Spanish America. Edited by David J. Robinson. Cambridge: Cambridge Univ. Press, 1990, p. 86–111, tables)

Well-written quantitative analysis of Indian migrants to Cusco in the 1600s uses heretofore unexploited source, the *conciertos de trabajo,* or labor contracts. Wightman is especially concerned with migration's impact on indigenous communities and its role in formation of colonial society. An impressive contribution. [MTH]

2428 Zimmerer, Karl S. Agricultura de barbecho sectorizada en las alturas de Paucartambo: luchas sobre la ecología del espacio productivo durante los siglos XVI y XX. (*Allpanchis/Cusco,* 23:38, segundo semestre 1991, p. 189–225, bibl., map, tables)

Suggestive essay examines impact of Spanish conquest, contemporary population growth, and cultural change on traditional agriculture in the High Paucartambo. The traditional practice of leaving land "fallow" meant/means using it for pastorage on a rotating basis, the extent and timing of which used to be determined communally. [MTH]

ALTO PERU

2429 Abad Pérez, Antolín. Las misiones de Apolobamba, Bolivia. (*in* Congreso Internacional sobre los Franciscanos en el Nuevo Mundo, *3rd, La Rábida, Spain, 1989.* Actas. Dirección de Paulino Castañeda. Madrid: Editorial Deimos, 1989, p. 999-1051, bibl., tables)

Sketches history of little-known Franciscan missions of Apolobamba in *yungas* to the north of La Paz and publishes 21 documents from 1636–1755 relating to their history. [MTH]

2430 Abecia Baldivieso, Valentín. Historiografía boliviana. v. 1, Cronistas y virreyes. La Paz: Empresa Editora Universo, 1991. 386 p.: bibl., index.

Entirely new *Historiografía boliviana,* not just a new ed. of Abecia Baldivieso's well-known 1965 work of the same title. Organized both thematically and chronologically, this vol. assesses writings and lists editions of colonial period chroniclers and other authors. Vol. 2 will do same for independence and national period chroniclers, historians, and other scholars. Indispensable vademecum for all students of Bolivia's past. [MTH]

2431 Acevedo, Edberto Oscar. El letrado Martínez de Escobar en Charcas. (*Invest. Ens.,* 39, enero/dic. 1989, p. 219–244)

Biography of 18th-century Audiencia of Charcas official reviews his legal opinions on issues ranging from education of Indians to disturbances in the Mercedarian convent of Potosí. Author also includes a list of volumes found in Martínez de Escobar's library. [SMS]

2432 Crespo R., Alberto; Mariano Baptista Gumucio; and José de Mesa. La Ciudad de La Paz: su historia, su cultura. La Paz: Alcaldía Municipal, 1989. 638 p.: bibl., ill.

Three works in one vol., each with its own bibliography: 1) solid essay on colonial La Paz (p. 13–133) by Crespo, a professional historian; 2) an equally solid essay on 19th- and 20th-century La Paz (p. 135–300) by Gumucio, a self taught historian; and 3) a substantial essay on cultural history of La Paz from pre-Inca times through present (p. 301–636) by Mesa, an art historian. Well-illustrated. [MTH]

2433 Evans, Brian M. Death in Aymaya of Upper Peru, 1580–1623. (in International Congress of Americanists, *46th, Amsterdam, 1988.* "Secret judgments of God": Old World disease in colonial Spanish America. Edited by Noble David Cook and W. George Lovell. Norman, Oklahoma: Univ. of Oklahoma Press, 1991, p. 142–158, graphs, map, tables)

Model study of state and movement of population of an Altiplano village from 1573 through 1692. Aymaya (Chayanta prov.) is unusual in that its early baptism and burial data have survived albeit only for males. An exceptionally important contribution to early demographic history of the Andes. [MTH]

2434 Evans, Brian M. Migration processes in Upper Peru in the seventeenth century. (in Migration in colonial Spanish America. Edited by David J. Robinson. Cambridge: Cambridge Univ. Press, 1990, p. 62–85, graph, maps, tables)

Analyzes extent to which migration was responsible for changes in distribution of Indian population of Upper Peru between Toledo *tasa* of 1575 and Palata *numeración general* of 1683–1686. Also examines related questions such as "Who were the *originarios* most likely to leave their pueblos?" [MTH]

2435 Fernández Alonso, Serena. Minería peruana y reformismo estatal: las Ordenanzas del Real Banco de San Carlos de la Villa de Potosí. (*Anu. Estud. Am.,* 47, 1990, p. 259–277)

Adds little to well-worked topic of Bourbon efforts to revitalize the Potosí mining industry by facilitating credit and supplies as well as by purchasing silver produced through a *banco de rescate.* [MTH]

2436 Gantier, Joaquín. Juan José de Segovia. Sucre, Bolivia: Banco Nacional de Bolivia, 1989. 202 p.: bibl., ill.

Biography of late colonial judge of Audiencia of Charcas. Reflects original research but is somewhat adulatory. [MTH]

2437 Gato Castaño, Purificación. Tensiones eclesiásticas entre criollos y peninsulares en la Audiencia de Charcas, en el último tercio del siglo XVIII. (*Hisp. Sacra,* 40, julio/dic. 1988, p. 763–776)

Examines and exemplifies competition between Creoles and peninsulars in the 1700s for appointments to ecclesiastical posts and the machinations employed by locals to obtain lucrative appointments for their relatives. Apparently part of larger study in progress. [MTH]

2438 González Casasnovas, Ignacio. Un intento de rectificar el sistema colonial: debates y proyectos en torno a la mita de Potosí a fines del siglo XVII, 1683–1697. (*Rev. Indias,* 50:189, mayo/agosto 1990, p. 431–453)

Covers much the same ground as Jeffrey A. Cole in "Viceregal Persistence Versus Indian Mobility" (see *HLAS 48:2768*), using mostly the same sources. [MTH]

Helmer, Marie. Cantuta: recueil d'articles parus entre 1949 et 1987. See item **2252.**

2439 Klein, Herbert S. Ayllus y haciendas en el mercado boliviano en los siglos XVIII y XIX. (in Estructuras sociales y mentalidades en América Latina: siglos XVII y XVIII. Compilación de Torcuato S. Di Tella. Buenos Aires: Fundación Simón Rodríguez, 1990, p. 87–145, map, tables)

Nothing new except for introduction and conclusion. Chap. 1 originally appeared as "The Structure of the Hacendado Class in Late Eighteenth-Century Alto Peru: the Intendencia of La Paz," (see *HLAS 44:2715*). Chap. 2 first appeared as "Accumulation and Inheritance among the Landed Elite of Bolivia: the Case of Don Tadeo Diez de Medina," see *HLAS 50:1976*). Chap. 3 was first published as "Respuesta Campesina ante las Demandas del Mercado y el Problema de la Tierra en Bolivia: Siglos XVIII y XIX," in *Población y mano de obra en América Latina* (Madrid: Alianza Editorial, 1985), which also focuses on the dept. of La Paz, but extends the time frame through the 1870s. [MTH]

2440 Klein, Herbert S. Bolivia: the evolution of a multi-ethnic society. 2nd ed. New York: Oxford Univ. Press, 1992. 343 p.: bibl., index, maps. (Latin American histories)

Revised and updated edition of standard history of Bolivia includes new chapter on recent developments and substantially augmented bibliography. Country and regional specialists should pay particular attention to the latter, given the extraordinary and continuing flow of publications on Bolivia in past few decades. [MTH]

2441 Minutolo de Orsi, Cristina. Luis de Fuentes y Vargas y la fundación de San Bernardo de la Frontera de Tarija de los Chiriguanaes, 1574. (*Signos Univ.*, 10:19, enero/junio 1991, p. 101–143)

Includes new data on the founder and the foundation of Tarija. Minutolo de Orsi is one of the compilers of *Historia de Tarija: corpus documental*, a five-vol. set (not four, as reported in *HLAS 52:2388*). [MTH]

O'Phelan Godoy, Scarlett. El "castigo ejemplar al traidor" durante la gran rebelión de 1780–81. See item **2398.**

2442 Parejas Moreno, Alcides J. and **Virgilio Suárez Salas.** Chiquitos: historia de una utopía. Bolivia: Cordecruz; Univ. Privada de Santa Cruz de la Sierra, 1992. 332 p.: bibl., ill. (some col.), maps.

Historian Parejas Moreno recapitulates history of Jesuit missions in Chiquitos in loving detail in the first half of this beautiful book, and architect Suárez Salas depicts "El Urbanismo en las Misiones de Chiquitos" in prose and sketches in the second half. Parejas Moreno also concerns himself with the Jesuits' charges, the Chiquitanos. Work includes many photos of people and places, art, architecture, and artifacts, the majority in color. For ethnohistorian's comment, see item **755.** [MTH]

2443 Pereira Fiorilo, Juan. Bolivia, acreedora de Europa. La Paz: Empresa Editora Siglo, 1987. 289 p.: bibl. (Bolivia, historia de su pasado económico; 1)

Volume covers precolumbian and colonial economic history from nationalistic point of view. Contains interesting information on regional economies of the 18th century, but documentation is fragmentary. [M.L. Wagner]

2444 Río, Mercedes del. La tributación indígena en el Repartimiento de Paria, siglo XVI. (*Rev. Indias*, 50:189, mayo/agosto 1990, p. 397–429, graphs, tables)

Detailed, well-documented quantitative study of collection and distribution of Indian tribute in Repartimiento of Paria (east of Lake Poopó) before and after the Toledo *visita*. Particularly concerned with "la circulación del excedente indígena y su destino." [MTH]

2445 Saguier, Eduardo R. La conducción de los caudales de oro y plata como mecanismo de corrupción: el caso del situado asignado a Buenos Aires por las Cajas Reales de Potosí en el siglo XVIII. (*Historia/Santiago*, 24, 1989, p. 287–317, bibl.)

Interesting study examines means by which colonists manipulated transfer of capital from Potosí to Buenos Aires to literally line their own pockets. Work also contributes to ongoing debate as to nature of colonial government: institutionally corrupt?; subject to different standards?; or functionally lax? [MTH]

2446 Saguier, Eduardo R. La crisis minera en el Alto Perú en su fase extractiva: la producción de plata del Cerro del Potosí en la luz de ocho visitas ignoradas de minas, 1778–1803. (*CLAHR/Albuquerque*, 1:1, Fall 1992, p. 67–100, bibl., tables)

Revisionist study of mining profitability at Potosí during late 1700s, based on eight detailed coeval inspections of mines. Argues that decline in production resulted from increased labor costs, not decrease in ore quality. [MTH]

2447 Santamaría, Daniel J. Hacienda y campesinos en el Alto Perú colonial. (*in* Estructuras sociales y mentalidades en América Latina: siglos XVII y XVIII. Compilación de Torcuato S. Di Tella. Buenos Aires: Fundación Simón Rodríguez, 1990, p. 9–86, bibl., tables)

Quantitative study of landed estates, Indian communities, and the landed poor in the *yungas* or eastern valleys, especially Larecaja prov. in the 18th century. Article presents the economic histories of both the Spanish-owned and mostly Indian-worked lands and the Indian-owned and worked lands, including for the most part the *cocales*. Section on Spanish estates (presumably including those owned by mestizos) needs to be placed in demographic and economic context. [MTH]

2448 Santamaría, Daniel J. Población y economía en el pedemonte andino de Bolivia: las misiones de Apolobamba, Mosetenes y Yurakares en el siglo XVIII. (*Rev. Indias*, 50:190, sept./dic. 1990, p. 741–766, graphs, map, tables)

Pioneering study of demographic and

economic aspects of mission pueblos established by Franciscans among forest Aymara of Apolobamba and by Jesuits among Mosetenes and Yurakares. Study was restricted by the limited period (1780–1803) for which data exist. [MTH]

2449 Schramm, Raimund. Archivo histórico de Cochabamba: índice de documentos sobre indios y tierras, siglos XVI, XVII y XVIII. (*Rev. Andin.*, 8:1, julio 1990, p. 187–236, bibl.)

Useful guide to materials in Cochabamba and Mizque sections of Historical Archives of Cochabamba, major sources for the region's ethnohistory. As is often the case, the Cochabamba *expedientes* were bound out of order whereas Mizque *legajos* are in original and therefore chronological order. Includes an "Indice de Personas y Lugares." [MTH]

2450 Simposio sobre la Importancia de las Misiones Jesuitas en Bolivia, *Trinidad, Bolivia, 1987.* Actas. La Paz: Ministerio de Relaciones Exteriores y Culto, Comisión Boliviana de Conmemoración del V Centenario del Descubrimiento de América, Encuentro de Dos Mundos, 1987. 239 p., 13 p. of plates: bibl., ill. (Col. V Centenario; 1)

Symposium on Jesuit activities among Mojos and Chiquitos is impressive for specificity of papers and for presenters' mastery of the sources. These mostly Bolivian scholars make an important contribution to the reconstruction of colonial past of the Beni Dept. [MTH]

Soux, María Luisa *et al.* Apolobamba, Caupolicán, Franz Tamayo: historia de una región paceña. See item **2821.**

2451 Tandeter, Enrique. Coacción y mercado: la minería de la plata en el Potosí colonial, 1692–1826. Buenos Aires: Editorial Sudamericana, 1992. 332 p.: bibl., ill., map. (Col. Historia y cultura)

Exceptionally important work examines interaction between the State, the private sector, Spaniards and Indians in the exploitation of the Red Mountain. Complements related works of Peter Bakewell (*HLAS 48:2766*) and Jeffrey Cole (*HLAS 48:2767*). Quantitative yet eminently readable. Concludes by comparing "la Minería en Nueva España y Potosí durante el Siglo XVIII." Available in English as: *Coercion and market: silver mining in colonial Postosí,*

1692–1826 (Albuquerque: Univ. of New Mexico Press, 1993). Integral history at its best. [MTH]

2452 Tandeter, Enrique. Crisis in Upper Peru, 1800–1805. (*HAHR*, 71:1, Feb. 1991, p. 35–71, graphs, tables)

Sophisticated study of demographic, economic, and social consequences of drought and epidemic years of 1800–05, a severe but heretofore unstudied crisis. Substantively as well as methodologically a very important contribution to history of late colonial Bolivia. Also available in Spanish as: "La crisis de 1800–1805 en el Alto Perú" (in *Data*, La Paz, Vol. 1, 1991, p. 9–49). [MTH]

2453 Thurner, Mark. Guerra andina y política campesina en el sitio de La Paz, 1781: aproximaciones etnohistóricas a la práctica insurreccional a través de las fuentes editadas. (*in* Coloquio Internacional del Grupo de Trabajo Historia y Antropología Andinas, *2nd, Quito, 1990.* Poder y violencia en los Andes. Edición de Henrique Urbano y Mirko Lauer. Cusco, Peru: Centro de Estudios Regionales Andinos Bartolomé de Las Casas, 1991, p. 93–124, bibl.)

Working paper on nature of Andean warfare and "peasant" politics as manifested in 1781 siege of La Paz. Stresses importance of ideology and ritual. Suggestive but somewhat tendentious. [MTH]

Vázquez, Juan Teodoro. Crónica continuada de la provincia de San Agustín del Perú. See item **2423.**

2454 Zulawski, Ann. Frontier workers and social change: Pilaya y Paspaya, Bolivia in the early eighteenth century. (*in* Migration in colonial Spanish America. Edited by David J. Robinson. Cambridge: Cambridge Univ. Press, 1990, p. 112–127, maps, tables)

Primarily an analysis of results of 1725 enumeration of Indian population of Pilaya y Paspaya, a wine producing frontier zone. Examines questions such as why some migrants to the province were better off and better treated by hacendados. Suggests that *forastero* "free" status as opposed to *yanacona* or inherited servile status may be the key. [MTH]

2455 Zulawski, Ann. Mano de obra y migración en un centro minero de los Andes: Oruro, 1683. (*in* Población y mano de obra en

América Latina. Compilación de Nicolás Sánchez-Albornoz. Madrid: Alianza Editorial, 1985, p. 95–114, graphs, tables)

This superior study reconstructs size, age-sex structure, occupations, and origins of Indian population of Oruro as of 1683, using census results of that year, to extent data permit and suggest. Enumeration in question excludes 0–13 year old males and all females. [MTH]

CHILE

2456 Agricultura, trabajo y sociedad en América hispana. Edición de Gonzalo Izquierdo F. Nota preliminar de Félix Fernández Shaw. Santiago: Depto. de Ciencias Históricas, Facultad de Filosofía y Humanidades, Univ. de Chile, 1989. 152 p.: bibl., ill., maps. (Serie Nuevo Mundo, 0716–7571; 3)

Mixed bag of six essays on agriculture, rural labor and society in Meso- and Andean America, and in colonial and early national Chile. Of them, only "Acerca del Origen de la Agricultura en América" is true to the title of the anthology. Most significant and original contributions are those by Ana María Presta on "Mano de Obra en una Hacienda Tarijeña en el Siglo XVII," Guillermo Bravo Acevedo on "La empresa agrícola jesuíta en Chile colonial," and Gonzalo Izquierdo Fernández on "Rasgos utópicos en iniciativas agrarias e industriales durante la primera mitad del siglo XIX en Chile." See also Bravo Acevedo's *Temporalidades jesuitas en el Reino de Chile, 1593–1800* (Madrid: Edit. Univ. Complutense, 1985). [MTH]

2457 Antei, Giorgio. La invención del Reino de Chile: Gerónimo de Vivar y los primeros cronistas chilenos. Bogotá: Instituto Caro y Cuervo, 1989. 294 p., 8 leaves of plates: bibl., ill., index, maps.

Chile owes its origins to the excursions of Valdivia. Also contributing to its creation were Valdivia as epistler and the chroniclers Vivar, Góngora Marmolejo, Mariño de Lobera as completed by Escobar, Ercilla, and, interestingly enough, León Pinelo in his never published *Hazañas de Chile, con su historia.* Antei elucidates their contributions in this eloquent essay. [MTH]

2458 Avila Martel, Alamiro de. La universidad y los estudios superiores en Chile en la época de Carlos III. (*in* Estudios sobre la

época de Carlos III en el Reino de Chile. Santiago: Ediciones de la Univ. de Chile, 1989, p. 171–202, ill.)

Useful survey of origins and early history of the University of Chile. [MTH]

2459 Benavides Courtois, Juan. Arquitectura e ingeniería en la época de Carlos III: un legado de la Ilustración a la Capitanía General de Chile. (*in* Estudios sobre la época de Carlos III en el Reino de Chile. Santiago: Ediciones de la Univ. de Chile, 1989, p. 79–170, ill.)

Well-illustrated, informative review of civil, military, and religious architecture in 18th- and early 19th-century Chile. Emphasizes work of military engineers and the architect Joaquín Toesca, several of whose projects, such as the Palacio de la Moneda (now the seat of the national government), still survive. [MTH]

2460 Bravo Lira, Bernardino. Los hombres del absolutismo ilustrado en Chile bajo Carlos III: formación de una minoría ilustrada alrededor de la administración, la judicatura y el ejército. (*in* Estudios sobre la época de Carlos III en el reino de Chile. Santiago: Ediciones de la Univ. de Chile, 1989, p. 79–170, ill.)

Revisionist study of professional component of elite in late 1700s and early 1800s focuses on individuals rather than groups. Bravo Lira clearly knows his subjects but exaggerates their "exemplary" values and behavior. Also published as "El Absolutismo Ilustrado en Chile bajo Carlos III" in *Boletín de la Academia Chilena de la Historia* (Vol. 55, No. 99, 1988, p. 135–227). [MTH]

2461 Broll C., Julio and Jorge Pinto Rodríguez. Copiapó en el siglo XVIII. Valparaíso, Chile: Instituto de Estudios Humanísticos de la Univ. de Valparaíso, 1988. 146 p.: bibl., ill., maps.

Four separately written but related essays on Corregimiento of Copiapó, a subregion of the Norte Chico, in the second half of 1700s and early 1800s. Two essays by Pinto Rodríguez examine demography and economy of the district, and two others by Broll examine the foundation of the villa and struggle for water between mining and agricultural halves of the valley. For related work see item **2479.** [MTH]

2462 Campos Harriet, Fernando. Alonso de Ribera: gobernador de Chile. 3a. ed. Santiago: Editorial Universitaria, 1987. 208 p.: bibl., ill. (Col. Genio y figura)

Reprint of standard biography of governor of Chile (1601–05 and 1612–17) who played major role in defeating Araucanians. [MTH]

2463 Campos Harriet, Fernando *et al.* Estudios sobre la época de Carlos III en el Reino de Chile. Santiago: Ediciones de la Univ. de Chile, 1989. 372 p.: bibl., ill. (Estudios y documentos para la historia del Reino de Chile)

Anthology of seven essays on governors, culture, and the elite in late colonial Chile. For specific articles see items **2458, 2459, 2460, 2464, 2471, 2473,** and **2475.** [MTH]

2464 Campos Harriet, Fernando. Los gobernadores de Chile bajo Carlos III. (*in* Estudios sobre la época de Carlos III en el Reino de Chile. Santiago: Ediciones de la Univ. de Chile, 1989, p. 79–170, ill.)

Useful summary of what is known about governors of Chile and their administrations during reign of Charles III. Covers Manuel de Amat y Junient (1755–61) through Ambrosio O'Higgins (1788–96), both of whom, it is significant to note, were subsequently promoted to viceregency of Peru. [MTH]

Campos Harriet, Fernando. Historia de Concepción, 1550–1988. See item **2835.**

2465 Camus, Misael. La Iglesia en Chile: siglos XVII y XVIII, según Diego Barros Arana. (*Anu. Hist. Iglesia Chile*, 7, 1989, p. 129–149)

Historiographic study of Barros Arana's treatment of Catholic Church, especially in vols. 5–7 of his *Historia general de Chile.* Camus finds Barros Arana, a 19th-century liberal, excessively anticlerical. [MTH]

2466 Casanueva, Fernando. Smallpox and war in southern Chile in the late eighteenth century. (*in* International Congress of Americanists *46th, Amsterdam, 1988.* "Secret judgments of God": Old World disease in colonial Spanish America. Edited by Noble David Cook and W. George Lovell. Norman, Oklahoma: Univ. of Oklahoma Press, 1991, p. 183–212, maps)

Assesses impact of a 1791 smallpox epidemic on Mapuches and on Spanish settlements in southern Chile. Not surprisingly, Indians were much harder hit than the Spaniards, who took advantage of the situation to occupy the previously impenetrable territory between the Bío-Bío and Chiloé. [MTH]

2467 Cerda Pincheira, Patricia. Las mujeres en la sociedad fronteriza del Chile colonial. (*Jahrb. Gesch.*, 26, 1989, p. 157–171)

Outlines roles played by women in Araucania during colonial period. Maintains that the relative scarcity of "white women" and the nature of local settlements permitted them greater freedom than their counterparts in central Chile. [MTH]

2468 Escobar Quezada, Julio A. Juan Gómez de Almagro, primer alguacil mayor del Reyno de Chile. Chile: Impr. Carabineros de Chile, 1990? 115 p.: bibl.

Amateur biography of first high sheriff of Chile contains some new information on his life and times as found in the Archivo General de Indias. [MTH]

Galería de hombres de armas de Chile. v. 1, Períodos hispánico y de la independencia, 1535–1826. v. 2, Período de la influencia francesa, 1826–1885. v. 3, Períodos de las influencias alemana y norteamericana, 1885–1952. See item **2847.**

2469 Góngora Marmolejo, Alonso de. Historia de todas las cosas que han acaecido en el Reino de Chile y de los que lo han gobernado, 1536–1575. Estudios preliminares por Alamiro de Avila Martel y Lucía Santa Cruz. Santiago: Ediciones de la Univ. de Chile, 1990. 321 p.: bibl., ill.

New ed. of classic chronicle of conquest of Chile. Includes essays by Avila Martel and Santa Cruz on historiography of the conquest and on Góngora Marmolejo. [MTH]

2470 González de Agüeros, Pedro. Descripción historial de Chiloé, 1791. Reedición facsimilar con un apéndice documental. Introducción y notas de Isidoro Vázquez de Acuña. Santiago: Instituto de Investigaciones del Patrimonio Territorial de Chile, Univ. de Santiago, 1988. 427 p.: bibl., ill., maps. (Col. Veritas, 07165293; 3)

Welcome photo-facsimile reprint of detailed late 18th-century description of Chiloé by a Franciscan friar who spent many years there. Original ed. (Madrid, 1791) is a bibliographic curiosity. This ed. is replete with substantial introduction by Vásquez de Acuña, coeval illustrations, and documentary appendix. [MTH]

2471 Guzmán Brito, Alejandro. La cultura jurídico-literaria en Chile durante la época de Carlos III. (*in* Estudios sobre la época de Carlos III en el Reino de Chile. Santiago: Ediciones de la Univ. de Chile, 1989, p. 203–221)

Guzmán Brito finds that criollo lawyers who graduated from the Univ. of San Felipe and practiced in Santiago were not as intellectually and professionally abreast as their European counterparts and thus not as "enlightened." Small sample (the libraries of three individuals) does not warrant generalization, however. [MTH]

2472 Hanisch, Walter. Memorias sobre misiones jesuitas de 1794–1795 [i.e., 1784–1785]. (*Historia/Santiago*, 25, 1990, p. 103–159, bibl., tables, photos)

Publishes two significant sources on state of former Jesuit missions in southern Chile: 1) a 1784 "Relación de las Misiones del Obispado de la Concepción de Chile" by local prelate; and 2) a 1785 "Relación General del Estado de las Misiones de Indios . . . " by the Governor and Captain General of Chile. Introduction is only marginally useful. [MTH]

2473 Lira Montt, Luis. Caballeros chilenos en la Orden de Carlos III, 1780–1830. (*in* Estudios sobre la época de Carlos III en el Reino de Chile. Santiago: Ediciones de la Univ. de Chile, 1989, p. 259–294, ill.)

Thumbnail sketches of 21 distinguished Chilean-born criollos who aspired to and were inducted into the Order of Charles III. [MTH]

2474 Loveman, Brian. Chile: the legacy of Hispanic capitalism. 2nd ed. New York: Oxford Univ. Press, 1988. 451 p.: bibl., index, maps. (Latin American histories)

Substantially revised and updated edition of what has become the standard history of Chile in English. Clearly written and insightful, this work features a substantial (61 p.) annotated guide to the literature on Chile. [MTH]

2475 Millar Carvacho, René. La controversia sobre el probabilismo entre los obispos chilenos durante el Reinado de Carlos III. (*in* Estudios sobre la época de Carlos III en el Reino de Chile. Santiago: Ediciones de la Univ. de Chile, 1989, p. 223–258, ports.)

Another contribution by historian of ideas in colonial Chile on debate between bishops Alday and Espiñeira regarding doctrine of probabilism. The doctrine was often opposed, but never condemned *per se*, because some theologians felt it favored moral laxism. Also probabilism was tainted by association with expelled Jesuits. For related work, see *HLAS 52:2414*. [MTH]

2476 Muñoz Correa, Juan Guillermo. Pobladores de Chile, 1565–1580. Temuco, Chile: Ediciones Univ. de la Frontera, 1989. 336 p.: bibl. (Serie Quinto centenario; 4)

Research notes on all those who appear in earliest extant records of Royal Treasuries of Santiago (1567–77), Valdivia (1574–78), and Concepción (1574–75), totaling 1,711 Spanish, Indian, black, mestizo, and mulatto men and women. [MTH]

2477 O'Donnell y Duque de Estrada, Hugo. El viaje a Chiloé de José de Moraleda, 1787–1790. Madrid: Editorial Naval, 1990. 249 p.: bibl., ill. (some col.), index. (Col. Aula de navegantes; 1. Serie Azul)

Detailed, well-documented and readable account of the 1787–90 hydrographic expedition to Chiloé. Moraleda compiled much data, not just charts and maps during this voyage. [MTH]

2478 Palma Vega, José. La mantención del culto como factor de egreso de recursos económicos de las Iglesias del Corregimiento del Maule en el siglo XVIII. (*Cuad. Acad.*, 1: 1, 1992?, p. 27–32)

Preliminary study of economic aspects of parish life in 1700s, especially what it cost to build and maintain a church. Drawn from records of Augustinian convent of Talca and parish of Pelarco. [MTH]

2479 Pinto Rodríguez, Jorge. La violencia en el corregimiento de Coquimbo durante el siglo XVIII. (*Cuad. Hist.*, 8, dic. 1988, p. 73–98, tables)

Apparently one of only two studies on violence in colonial Chile, article is based on 284 local criminal cases from 1760–1810. The other study is Alamiro de Avila Madrid and Aníbal Bascuñán's pioneering *Notas para el estudio de la criminalidad y la penología en Chile colonial* (Santiago, 1941), which was based on 476 criminal cases heard by the Audiencia of Santiago. [MTH]

2480 Ramírez, Ramón. La alternativa en el gobierno de la Provincia Dominicana de Chile. (*Anu. Hist. Iglesia Chile*, 7, 1989, p. 9–27)

Demonstrates conclusively that practice of alternating rule between peninsulars and Creoles was not introduced into Dominican Province of Chile. The documents summarized redeem an otherwise prosaic contribution. [MTH]

2481 Retamal Avila, Julio and **Osvaldo Silva G.** Prólogo a Chile. Presentación de Oscar Pinochet de la Barra. Santiago: Editorial Salesiana, 1992. 198 p.: bibl. (Col. V centenario Chile)

Well-written survey of prehispanic and colonial Chile includes chapters on economy and society. Intended as a high school text, but also serves as a useful introduction for non-Chileanists. [MTH]

2482 Reyes Ramírez, Rocio de los. Fray Jerónimo de Oré, obispo de Concepción en Chile. (*in* Congreso Internacional sobre los Franciscanos en el Nuevo Mundo, *3rd, La Rábida, Spain, 1989.* Actas. Dirección de Paulino Castañeda. Madrid: Editorial Deimos, 1989, p. 1099–1114)

Well-researched biography of early 17th-century bishop of Concepción. A native of Huamanga and a Franciscan, Oré was an accomplished scholar and able administrator. His *Símbolico católico indiano* (Lima, 1598) is an important linguistic source. [MTH]

2483 Rosales, Diego de. Historia general del Reino de Chile, Flandes indiano. v. 1–2. Revisión de Mario Góngora. 2. ed. integramente rev. Santiago: Editorial Andrés Bello, 1989. 2 v. (1422 p.): bibl., index.

Makes reavailable Góngora's textually definitive 1972 ed. of a major, late 17th-century chronicle of Chile's first century and a half. Largely based on Benjamín Vicuña Mackenna's classic first ed. of the work (1877–1878). [MTH]

2484 Urbina Burgos, Rodolfo. Chiloé y la ocupación de los Llanos de Osorno durante el siglo XVIII. (*Bol. Acad. Chil. Hist.*, 54:98, 1987, p. 219–261, bibl., photos)

Detailed, well-documented study of resettlement of Osorno by *chilotes* in 1795 and of frustated attempts preceding its definitive "repopulation." [MTH]

2485 Urbina Burgos, Rodolfo. La rebelión indígena de 1712: los tributarios de Chiloé contra la encomienda. (*Rev. Tiempo Espacio*, 1, 1990, p. 73–86)

Rescues from archival obscurity major uprising in 1712 of acculturated Indians on the island of Chiloé. Rebellion was provoked by an unusually exigent and cruel encomendero. [MTH]

2486 Valdivia, Pedro de. Cartas de don Pedro de Valdivia: que tratan del descubrimiento y conquista de la Nueva Extremadura. Presentación de Juan Carlos Rodríguez Ibarra. Prólogo e iconografía de Miguel Rojas-Mix. Transcripción y notas de Mario Ferreccio Podestá. Edición de Miguel Rojas-Mix. Madrid: Quinto Centenario; Santiago: Editorial Andrés Bello; Barcelona: Editorial Lumen, 1991. 291 p.: bibl., ill. (some col.) (Extremadura en clave 92)

Opulent ed. of letters of Valdivia regarding discovery and conquest of Chile. Reproduces text of the 12 letters photographically and in literal transcription with explanatory notes. Preceded by two lavishly illustrated introductory essays and followed by 12 scholarly essays on "Old" and New Extremadura, Valdivia, the conquest, his letters, and literature of the conquest. [MTH]

2487 Valladares Campos, Jorge. El padrón de Cauquenes de 1749. (*Bol. Acad. Chil. Hist.*, 55:99, 1988, p. 327–388)

Analyzes but does not aggregate or interpret returns of 1749 census of Cauquenes (capital of former prov. of Maule). Organizes data by families in alphabetical order and within families by head of household, spouse, children, other relatives, retainers, and servants. Includes cross references to parish registers of town. [MTH]

2488 Vallejo Penedo, Juan José. La provincia Agustiniana de Chile en las actas del Capítulo Provincial celebrado en 1647. (*Rev. Agust.*, 33:102, sept./dic. 1992, p. 1375–1398)

Publishes and analyzes minutes of 1647 provincial meeting of Augustinians. [MTH]

2489 Varas Bordeu, María Teresa. Villa de Nuestra Señora de Los Angeles: época fundacional. Santiago: Sociedad Editora e Impresora Multigráfica, 1989. 125 p.: bibl., ill. (some col.)

Short essay on foundation of Los Angeles (1739), the southernmost Spanish settlement in the Central Valley, and a long documentary appendix on establishment and early years of the town. [MTH]

2490 Wever, Natascha. Goudkoorts en giganten: een indruk van de reisverslagen van Hollandse expedities in de Straat van Magalhães en Chili, 1598–1642 [Gold fever and giants: an impression of the travel accounts of Dutch expeditions in the Strait of Magellan and Chile, 1598–1642]. (*Wampum/Leiden*, 11, 1992, p. 62–82)

Overview of the ethnographic information gathered by five Dutch expeditions (1598–1642). All accounts mention the gigantic inhabitants in Patagonia and Southern Chile and speculate about enormous gold deposits. It is difficult to separate fantasy and reality in these reports. [R. Hoefte]

RIO DE LA PLATA

2491 Amaral, Samuel. Comercio libre y economías regionales: San Juan y Mendoza, 1780–1820. (*Jahrb. Gesch.*, 27, 1990, p. 1–67, graphs, tables)

Author studies effects of liberal economic policies on the regional economy of the Río de la Plata interior, challenging the accepted view that the opening of Buenos Aires' port to "free trade," followed by the still freer trade initiated by Independence, spelled the ruin of the "older" interior economies. Amaral closely examines export figures and the production and marketing of wine and aguardiente from Mendoza and San Juan. He concludes that viticulture was always precarious because of climate and animal pests; that there was never a golden age of commerce for this region; that civil war caused more damage to the economy than any other factor; and that many of the contemporary complaints about crisis conditions were nothing more than tactical means used by local producers to further their own corporate interests. [SMS]

2492 Amaral, Samuel. Trabajo y trabajadores rurales en Buenos Aires a fines del siglo XVIII. (*Anu. IEHS*, 2, 1987, p. 33–41)

Amaral's rejoinder to Mayo (see item 2547) based on his analysis of the accounts of a Magdalena estancia (see *HLAS 52:2276*). Author stresses the importance of economic demand in understanding the rural porteño labor market and believes that the vast majority of rural residents worked both for themselves and for large estancias rather than risk moving to the Indian frontier, squatting,

or rustling cattle. In Amaral's eyes, the inhabitants of the pampa were rural peons, rather than free spirited gauchos. [SMS]

2493 Argüelles-Fabrega, Teresa Cañedo. El hispano-guaraní: asimilación y rechazo como factores determinantes de una mentalidad. (*in* Jornadas de Historiadores Americanistas, *2nd, Granada, Spain, 1988.* América: encuentro y asimilación. Edición de Joaquín A. Muñoz Mendoza. Granada: Diputación Provincial de Granada, 1989, p. 333–344, bibl.)

Based solely on secondary sources, author argues that Guaraní family and kin structure could have provided an ideal vehicle for racial harmony between Indians and Spaniards had economic factors not intervened. Nonetheless, racial miscegenation did produce relative racial harmony via the family structure, with mestizos being accepted as Spaniards although there was a clear division between Spaniards and all others. [SMS]

2494 Azara, Félix de. Descripción general del Paraguay. Edición, introducción y notas de Andrés Galera Gómez. Madrid: Alianza Editorial, 1990. 301 p.: bibl. (El Libro de bolsillo; 1499. Sección Clásicos)

New ed. of those portions of Azara's *Geografía física* and his *Viajes* that deal with Paraguay. Azara, an 18th-century Spanish military engineer and naturalist, came to the Viceroyalty of Río de la Plata in 1781 as part of the Boundary Demarcation Commission and remained in the region for 20 years. Important primary source for geography, social history, and ethnohistory. [SMS]

2495 Báez, Cecilio. Historia colonial del Paraguay y Río de la Plata. Asunción: C. Schauman Editor, 1991. 193 p.: bibl., map.

Reprint of a general colonial history of Paraguay (through the reign of Francia) first published in 1926 by the liberal Paraguayan politician, writer and statesman, Cecilio Báez. Báez's attitudes toward the Indians, the clergy, and the law reflect late 19th-century positivism. [SMS]

2496 Baldó Lacomba, Marc. La Ilustración en la Universidad de Córdoba y el Colegio de San Carlos de Buenos Aires, 1767–1810. (*Rev. Univ./Alcalá*, 7, 1991, p. 31–54)

Interesting article argues that an eclectic form of the Enlightenment developed in the Río de la Plata region even before the expulsion of the Jesuits. Nonetheless, the principal schools in the region, the University of Córdoba and the Colegio Carolino of Buenos Aires, failed to modify their curriculum, system of educating and recruiting professors, or administration in spite of specific suggested changes. Provides rich detail on the internal politics of these two institutions. [SMS]

2497 Bertocchi Moran, Alejandro N. Los comandantes del apostadero de Montevideo, 1776–1814. (*Bol. Hist. Ejérc.*, 279/282, 1990, p. 69–95, bibl., facsims., map, table)

Traditional political history reviews commanders of the Montevideo naval station from its inception to the end of the Spanish colonial period. [SMS]

2498 Binayán Carmona, Narciso. Una nueva perspectiva de la conquista. (*Hist. Parag.*, 21, 1984, p. 215–244)

Author defends importance of genealogy in history and argues that most of the Spaniards taking part in the conquest, including those who settled Asunción, were marginal members of the Castilian high nobility. A dubious thesis linked to another argument: that the conquistadors' penchant for fathering illegitimate children comes from Spain's Islamic inheritance. [SMS]

2499 Calvo, Luis María. Santa Fe la Vieja, 1573–1660. Santa Fe: Tall. Graf. SERV-GRAF, 1990. 140 p.: bibl., ill., index, maps.

Interesting urban study of the first city of Santa Fé, founded in 1573 by Juan de Garay and relocated approximately 90 years later. Author discusses technology, use of urban space, architecture and workforce; he also traces, lot by lot, ownership and descriptions of urban property. [SMS]

2500 Cardozo, Efraím. Paraguay de la conquista. Asunción: Lector, 1989. 256 p.

History of 16th-century Paraguay, part of an incomplete general history of the colonial period, by the late dean of Paraguayan historians, Efraím Cardozo (d. 1973). This volume concentrates on political history from the conquest and founding of Asunción to the government of Hernandarias. [SMS]

2501 Cartas anuas de la Provincia Jesuitica del Paraguay, 1632 a 1634. Introducción de Ernesto J.A. Maeder. Buenos Aires: Academia Nacional de la Historia, 1990. 229 p.

Final volume of a series of early 17th-century annual reports sent by the Jesuit Provincial of Paraguay to the Order in Rome. The reports detail Jesuit activities in *colegios* and missions throughout the Río de la Plata region. This report covers 1632–34 and contains brief biographical information on all Jesuits mentioned in the text. Important primary source. [SMS]

2502 Cohan, Clara E. Los marranos en el Paraguay colonial. Asunción: Intercontinental Editora, 1992. 256 p.: bibl., ill.

Author overviews history of "crypto-Jews" in Spain and the Spanish colonies and then shows how the Inquisition confiscated the goods of many Portuguese residents of Asunción who were charged with illegal entry into the region but who were also possibly *marranos*. Includes transcriptions of the trial of a Portuguese barber in 1705 and legal proceedings against Portuguese merchants in 1621. [SMS]

2503 Coria, Luis Alberto. Evolución económica de Mendoza en la época colonial. Dirección de Vidal Linares Benegas. Mendoza, Argentina: Univ. Nacional de Cuyo, Facultad de Ciencias Económicas, 1988. 344 p.: bib., ill.

Detailed overview of the economic history of the Cuyo region uses primary and secondary sources to examine land tenure patterns, production and consumption, labor supply, commerce, and money supply. While Mendoza is seen as a prototypical colonial city, Coria also stresses that its proximity to the Indian frontier and special defense problems were intimately linked to economic and demographic growth. [SMS]

2504 Corrales Elhordoy, Angel. Artillería española en Indias. v. 1, Banda Oriental, 1680–1750. v. 2, Guerra Guaránica. Montevideo: s.n., 1989. 2 v.: bibl., ill., index, maps.

Two-volume history of the Artillery Division of the Spanish Army in the Río de la Plata region. Vol. 1 deals with the Division's role in the founding of Montevideo and the sieges of Colonia. Vol. 2 concentrates on the participation of the Montevideo Artillery Regiment in the Guaraní Wars (1754–56), detailing the strategies, troops, armaments and battles. Both are well illustrated by facsimile reproductions of several interesting maps and documents. [SMS]

2505 D'Alessandro, Graciela and **María Cristina Garra.** Incunables existentes en el Uruguay y primeros libros impresos en el país: catálogo. Montevideo: Ediciones El Galeón, 1991. 114 p.: bibl., ill. (Col. Ensayos bibliográficos; 3)

Catalog of European and Uruguayan incunables existing in Uruguayan collections. "Uruguayan incunables" consist of books and documents published between 1810, the year of the arrival of the printing press in Montevideo, and 1830. [SMS]

2506 Díaz de Guzmán, Ruy. La Argentina. Edición de Enrique de Gandía. Madrid: Historia 16, 1986. 279 p.: bibl. (Crónicas de América; 23)

New ed. of the famous chronicle of the conquest of Río de la Plata written in the early 17th century by the son of one of the original settlers of Asunción. Well annotated and includes a good introductory essay. [SMS]

2507 Doblas, Gonzalo de. Los escritos de d. Gonzalo de Doblas relativos a la Provincia de Misiones, 1785 & 1805. Estudio preliminar de Walter Rela. Montevideo: Ediciones de la Plaza, 1988. 205 p.: bibl.

New ed. of Gonzalo Doblas' two *memorias* (1785, 1805) on the Guaraní mission region. Doblas, appointed Governor of the Concepción district of Misiones in 1781, wrote extensively about the region and its Indian inhabitants, suggesting economic and administrative reforms to encourage development of the region. Important primary source. [SMS]

2508 Dotta, Mario. Breve reseña de los orígenes coloniales del litoral atlántico uruguayo. Montevideo: La Canasta, 1990. 43 p.: bibl.

Brief discussion of the colonial history of Barra de Balizas, a region along the Atlantic coast of present-day Uruguay (Rocha dept.) that was disputed between Spain and Portugal. Lacks map of the area under discussion. [SMS]

2509 Durán Estragó, Margarita. Levantamientos indígenas ante los abusos de la encomienda en Paraguay. (*in* CEHILA, *16th, Santo Domingo, 1989.* Sentido histórico del V Centenario, 1492–1992. Edición de Guillermo Meléndez. San José: Editorial Depto. Ecuménico de Investigaciones, 1992, p. 133–140)

Interesting article uses primary and secondary sources to document a series of Guaraní uprisings (1539, 1543, 1559, 1561–62, 1616, 1657, 1660) which moved from opposition to Spanish treachery to rejection of the *encomienda* system. The last of these rebellions, that of Arecayá, was put down with dramatic bloodletting and the town itself was obliterated, a severe lesson which probably accounts for the end of active Guaraní resistance to the Spanish settlers. [SMS]

2510 Durán Estragó, Margarita. Presencia franciscana en el Paraguay. v. 1–2. Asunción: Univ. Católica, 1987–1988. 2 v.: bibl., ill. (Biblioteca de estudios paraguayos; 19, 24)

Major contribution based on archival documents studies Franciscan institutions in Paraguay. First vol. (475 p.) begins with the establishment of a permanent Franciscan presence in 1575 and studies the reductions, the establishment of convents, seminaries, hospices, parishes and schools. Contains biographical sketches of the major figures and of the Franciscan bishops of Asunción up to 1824, when Francia suppressed the religious orders. Second vol. (165 p.) starts with the return of the Franciscans in 1882, when the order had to begin anew, and covers through the mid-1980s and the contemporary period in which Franciscans and their laity were instrumental in modernizing Catholicism in Paraguay. [G. Dorn]

2511 Durán Estragó, Margarita. Reducciones franciscanas en Paraguay en el s. XVII. (*in* Congreso Internacional sobre los Franciscanos en el Nuevo Mundo, *3rd, La Rábida, Spain, 1989.* Actas. Dirección de Paulino Castañeda. Madrid: Editorial Deimos, 1989, p. 953–976)

Brief overview of some early Franciscan missions in Paraguay (Itá, Caazzapá, Yuty, Itatí, Itapé) and a discussion of Franciscan attitudes toward the encomienda. [SMS]

2512 Ensinck, Oscar Luis. Propios y arbitrios del Cabildo de Buenos Aires, 1580–1821: historia económica de una gran ciudad. Madrid: Instituto de Cooperación Iberoamericana; Sociedad Estatal Quinto Centenario; Instituto de Estudios Fiscales, 1990. 494 p.: bibl. (Monografías Economía quinto centenario)

Detailed study of income and expenses

334 / Handbook of Latin American Studies v. 54

of the Buenos Aires Cabildo from the late
16th century through the first decade of Independence. Author emphasizes the late 18th
century and provides a wealth of data on subjects ranging from prison expenses to funds
spent on welcoming new viceroys. While this
book contains no analysis of municipal funding, there is much material here for social and
economic historians. [SMS]

**2513 Estudios sobre la frontera colonial
pampeana.** Edición de Carlos A. Mayo
y Angela Fernández. Mar del Plata, Argentina:
Univ. Nacional de Mar del Plata, Facultad de
Humanidades, Depto. Historia, Cátedra Historia Americana I, 1986. 28 leaves: bibl.

Three important studies based on primary research examine the late 18th-century
Buenos Aires frontier. Carlos Mayo examines
the social composition and daily life of members of the military companies (*blandengues*)
stationed at Salto, Luján and Zanjón. Mayo
and Amalia Latrubesse de Díaz further explore the daily life of the military outpost of
Zanjón, and in the final study, Mayo presents
work on Spanish renegades including those
who chose to live in Indian society. [SMS]

2514 Ezran, Maurice. Une colonisation
douce, les missions du Paraguay: les
lendemains qui ont chanté. Paris: L'Harmattan, 1989. 316 p.: bibl. (Recherches & documents: Amérique latine)

Generally sympathetic history of the
Jesuit mission saga in Paraguay by a non-
historian, based on writings of Jesuits and
secondary sources. Author sees the Jesuit experience in Paraguay as an example of the
eternal human quest for a utopia. [SMS]

2515 Fernández Cabrelli, Alfonso. Civilismo: un aporte de los primeros pobladores canarios a la idiosincrasia de la gente
oriental. (*Hoy Hist.*, 8:46, julio/agosto 1991,
p. 19–39)

Author hypothesizes that the anti-
militarism, independence, and pugnacious-
ness of Canary Islanders was transmitted to
the original inhabitants of Montevideo, and
thereby explains their on-going opposition to
military power as well as the actions of Artigas, the Uruguayan independence leader.
Though simplistic, the article provides interesting information on jurisdictional disputes
between the Cabildo and military authorities.
[SMS]

2516 Fernández Cabrelli, Alfonso. El misterio de la creación de Santo Domingo
Soriano. (*Hoy Hist.*, 9:50, marzo/abril 1992,
p. 30–38, maps, photos)

Reviews both a 17th- and an 18th-
century map, but fails to determine on which
side of the Río Uruguay the settlement of
Santo Domingo Soriano was originally made.
[SMS]

2517 Ferrer Benimeli, José A. La expulsión
de los jesuitas del Paraguay. (*Rev. Paramillo*, 9/10, 1990, p. 397–415)

Author briefly discusses the geography
of the Paraguayan Jesuit mission zone, examines the 1750 Limits Treaty between Spain
and Portugal, and discusses the politics which
led to the expulsion of the Jesuits from Spanish domains. Book focuses on the reports sent
by the French ambassador in Madrid to the
prime minister, the Duke de Choiseul. Included is the Roda report, echoing Bucareli's
opposition to the Jesuits, which was for-
warded to the French court by the ambassador. [SMS]

2518 Flores G. de Zarza, Idalia. Acción civi-
lizadora y evangelizadora de los franciscanos en la Provincia del Paraguay. (*Hist.
Parag.*, 23, 1986, p. 73–124)

Reviews work of Franciscans in Paraguay based entirely on secondary works.
Stresses their role in the creation of the dio-
cesis of Asunción (1547), as well as their missionary work from the 16th century forward.
[SMS]

2519 Gálvez, Lucía. Mujeres de la conquista.
Buenos Aires: Planeta, 1990. 210 p.:
bibl., ill. (Mujeres argentinas)

Author presents overview of the position of Indian and Spanish women in early colonial settlements of Asunción, Buenos Aires,
Santa Fé, Cuyo, and Tucumán, and then gives
us a popular history of 11 outstanding women
who lived in the difficult conditions of these
early settlements. [SMS]

2520 Garavaglia, Juan Carlos and **Claudia
Wentzel.** Un nuevo aporte a la historia
del textil colonial: los ponchos frente al mercado porteño, 1750–1850. (*Anu. IEHS*, 4,
1989, p. 211–241, appendix, graphs, tables)

Study of the various modes of production of the textile industry (cotton and/or
wool) of Tucumán, Paraguay, the litoral, and
Cuyo, as well as the circuits of commercial-

ization of these products. Authors argue that only two modes of production existed in the region (weaving in Indian villages and domestic rural production), and that neither represented proto-industrialization or nascent capitalism. [SMS]

2521 Garavaglia, Juan Carlos. Producción cerealera y producción ganadera en la campaña porteña: 1700–1820. (*in* Estructuras sociales y mentalidades en América Latina: siglos XVII y XVIII. Compilación de Torcuato S. Di Tella. Buenos Aires: Fundación Simón Rodríguez, 1990, p. 207–240, graphs, map, tables)

Another study by Garavaglia highlightsing the importance of agriculture, especially wheat production, in colonial Buenos Aires. He analyzes tithes paid on grain and animals throughout the region, and by rural sub-regions, both to prove and to refine his thesis: that although production of both cattle and grains grew from the mid-18th century onward, grain production outstripped the cattle industry and generated more taxes in the form of tithes. [SMS]

2522 García, Flavio A. La expedición científica de Malaspina en nuestro medio. (*Rev. Bibl. Nac./Montevideo*, 27, abril 1990, p. 21–33)

Author discusses the Malaspina expedition and its two visits to Montevideo (1789 and 1794), stressing local explorations and local participation. [SMS]

2523 Gato Castaño, Purificación. La educación en el Virreinato del Río de la Plata: acción de José Antonio de San Alberto en la Audiencia de Charcas, 1768–1810. Zaragoza, Spain: Diputación General de Aragón, Depto. de Cultura y Educación, 1990. 374 p.: bibl., ill. (Col. Estudios y monografías; 11)

Lavishly illustrated study of the writings, philosophy, and educational reforms of the enlightened Bishop of Córdoba de Tucumán (1780–85) and Charcas (1785–1804), José Antonio de San Alberto, is based on his pastoral letters and other writings and set against a discussion of the social conditions of the time. San Alberto worked in the fields of clerical education, technical education, and female education. [SMS]

2524 Gelman, Jorge Daniel. Venta al contado, venta a crédito y crédito monetario en América colonial: acerca de un gran

comerciante del Virreinato del Río de la Plata. (*Jahrb. Gesch.*, 27, 1990, p. 101–126, tables)

Interesting article based on the records of the merchant Domingo Belgrano stresses the difference between monetary credit and the sale of goods on credit. Analysis of commercial transactions shows that large-scale merchants depended heavily on credit sales for all operations except sale of real property and slaves. Gelman argues that this double control of commercial transactions (goods and credit) gave the merchants a privileged position when dealing with clients. While the "credit sale" system was a response to the endemic scarcity of money in the colony, he also argues that this problem was in part caused by merchants remitting funds to Europe. Gelman fails to realize that monies sent to Europe were used to fuel the commercial exchange and to repay commercial debts, not to invest in profit-making ventures. [SMS]

2525 González Rodríguez, Jaime. Tribulaciones de un autor residente en América: el caso del Rector de Córdoba Pedro José de Parras, 1777–83. (*Rev. Complut. Hist. Am.*, 17, 1991, p. 139–165)

Detailed discussion of the problems faced by Franciscan friar Pedro José de Parras, rector of the University of Córdoba, in trying to get his manuscript published in Spain. Author finds that while most American intellectuals failed to overcome government obstacles for publishing their works in Spain, Parras, a strong defender of the Crown's right of Royal Patronage, was undermined by opposition within his own order. [SMS]

2526 Heredia, Edmundo A. Cuando Sarratea se hizo revolucionario. Buenos Aires: Plus Ultra, 1986. 107 p.: appendix, bibl., index. (Col. Esquemas históricos; 36)

Brief but informative work describes pre-1812 overseas commercial activities and frustrations of a *porteño* who seemingly had no firm political convictions and who became a revolutionary because the Spanish government acted slowly on his claims against it. Includes documentary appendix. [J. Criscenti]

2527 Heredia Gayán, Alberto Martín. Ascendencia de la familia Heredia Gayán a conquistadores: primeros pobladores e importantes personajes de la época. (*Publ. Inst. Estud. Iberoam.*, 8:6, 1989, p. 37–95, bibl.)

Lengthy discussion of the population,

economy, and society of early Buenos Aires introduces the biographies of several famous ancestors of the Heredia Gayán family. Included are a handful of conquistadors, merchants, military men, bureaucrats and one doctor. [SMS]

2528 Jáuregui Rueda, Carlos. Matrimonios de la Catedral de Buenos Aires. v. 1, 1656–1760. v. 2, 1747–1823. Buenos Aires: Fuentes Históricas y Genealógicas Argentinas, 1989. 533 p.:

Two-vol. transcription of the marriage registers of the Buenos Aires Cathedral, corresponding to books 2–7 of marriages. This is an important source for social historians and demographers, although the compilers have omitted those entries where neither spouse had a last name. We hope that this worthy project of publishing parochial registers continues, but that all records are included. [SMS]

2529 La Rioja: revelaciones documentales acerca de su fundación. Recopilación de Alejandro Moyano Aliaga. Córdoba, Argentina: Junta Provincial de Historia de Córdoba, 1991. 83 p.

The text of seven documents concerning the founding of the city of La Rioja found in the Archivo Histórico de Córdoba. [SMS]

2530 Lanne, Pablo O. ¿Donde asentó Don Pedro de Mendoza la primera Buenos Aires? (*Todo es Hist.*, 288, junio 1991, p. 66–77, facsims., ill., photos)

Popular article uses contemporary reports and depictions to argue that the first settlement of Buenos Aires was not close to the present city, but rather in a gently rolling area further up the Paraná Delta. [SMS]

2531 León Solis, Leonardo. Maloqueros, tráfico ganadero y violencia en las fronteras de Buenos Aires, Cuyo y Chile, 1700–1800. (*Jahrb. Gesch.*, 26, 1989, p. 37–83, tables)

Author discusses the 18th-century Indian wars against the Spaniards, which had been transformed into booty-seeking raids for the Indians. He examines the Indian tribes involved, their invasion routes, and the overall economic and demographic impact of these raids on the frontier of Chile and Río de la Plata. Fine article which demonstrates the increasing cooperation among Indian tribes in undertaking these *maloqueros*. [SMS]

2532 Levaggi, Abelardo. La desamortización eclesiástica en el Virreinato del Río de La Plata. (*Rev. Hist. Am.*, 102, julio/dic. 1986, p. 7–89)

Interesting article traces policy of *desamortización* from its conception and application in Spain to its transfer to the New World, specifically Río de la Plata region. Levaggi presents a wealth of documents to argue that unlike the Mexican case, this legislation did not undermine the economic or social fabric of the region. [SMS]

2533 Lorandi, Ana María. Reflexiones sobre las categorías semánticas en las fuentes del Tucumán colonial: los valles calchaquíes. (*Runa/Buenos Aires*, 17/18, 1987/1988, p. 221–263, map, table)

Arguing for a sensitivity to changing categories in historical documents, author analyzes three sources relating to the Calchaquí Valleys: 1) *probanzas de méritos y servicios* of the conquistadors; 2) letters from the Governor of Tucumán, Felipe de Albórnoz; and 3) the testimony from the trial of Pedro Bohórquez. Finds shifts in ethnic and geographical groupings. [SMS]

2534 Madero, Fernando M. Entre la genealogía y la historia. Buenos Aires: Ediciones del Círculo, 1989. 476 p., 1 leaf of plates: bibl., ill.

Publication of several genealogical and historical articles on 18th- and 19th-century personages by the late Fernando Madero, based on archival research. [SMS]

2535 Maeder, Ernesto J.A. La administración económica de Misiones. (*Invest. Ens.*, 39, enero/dic. 1989, p. 349–388, tables, graphs)

Important study examines the Administración General de Misiones, an agency set up to oversee the ex-Jesuit missions. Author reviews the conditions of the agency's establishment, discusses those charged with the direction of the Administración (whose stated aim was the gradual assimilation of the Indian population) and analyzes the results. In assessing the reasons for agency's failure, he considers problems of policy, personnel, and local market conditions. [SMS]

2536 Mallo, Silvia. La mujer rioplatense a fines del siglo XVIII: ideales y realidad. (*Anu. IEHS*, 5, 1990, p. 117–132)

Interesting discussion of man's idealized vision of late colonial women (as represented in early 19th century newspapers) as contrasted with the ideal expressed by women in testimony contained in Real Audiencia cases, and further contrasted with the reality reflected in these same examples. Author explores the importance of race, social groups, and gender to find that the reality lived by women, especially women in the middle and lower sectors, was far more dynamic than the expressed ideals. [SMS]

2537 Mandrini, Raúl José. Procesos de especialización regional en la economía indígena pampeana, s. XVIII-XIX: el caso del suroeste bonaerense. (*Bol. Am.,* 32:41, 1991, p. 113–136, bibl.)

A leading ethnohistorian of the indigenous groups of the Pampas, Mandrini finds that the inhabitants of the region between the Tandil and Ventana Hills, unlike most other groups, were primarily pastoralists, involved in raising cattle and sheep. Author stresses commercial ties among Indian communities, as well as ties with Chile and Buenos Aires. He notes the wealth of Indian communities beyond the Spanish frontier, and the increasing social differentiation within Indian society. [SMS]

Marco, Miguel Angel de *et al.* Rosario. v. 1, Política, cultura, economía, sociedad: desde los orígenes hasta 1916. See *HLAS 53:2947.*

2538 Márquez de la Plata, José. El Virreinato rioplatense en las vistas fiscales de José Márquez de la Plata. Recopilación de Abelardo Levaggi. v. 1–3. Buenos Aires: Univ. del Museo Social Argentino, 1988. 3 v. (1281 p.): bibl. (Serie V centenario del descubrimiento de América)

Compendium of the legal writings of José Márquez de la Plata, fiscal of the Audiencia of Buenos Aires (1784–1804), is preceded by a solid biographical essay which stresses the complex personal and political alliances in viceregal Buenos Aires, as well as the fiscal's political ideas. Each of Márquez de la Plata's opinions is indexed by the topic. [SMS]

2539 Marquiegui, Dedier Norberto. Estancia y poder político en un partido de la campaña bonaerense: Luján, 1726–1821. Buenos Aires: Fundación Simón Rodríguez; Editorial Biblos, 1990. 111 p.: bibl. (Cuadernos Simón Rodríguez; 18)

Detailed, lengthy, and interesting study of the rise of large *estancieros* in the political, economic, and social arena of Luján. Based on his research with cabildo, parish, and judicial records, Marquiegui believes that the opening of the Buenos Aires market in the years immediately following the French Revolution tended to strengthen the position of large landowners at the expense of middle and smaller property owners. [SMS]

2540 Martínez Martín, Carmen. La expedición del P. Quiroga, S.J., a la costa de los Patagones, 1745–46. (*Rev. Complut. Hist. Am.,* 17, 1991, p. 121–137)

Author reviews the prevailing 16th- and 17th-century misconceptions about the Patagonian region, as well as earlier attempts by the Spanish, English, French, and Dutch to explore the area, but concentrates on the Quiroga visit, which she judges to be the first scientific expedition to the region. The expedition was undertaken by the Jesuits in the hope of setting up missions in the region, but instead they found a shortage of potable water and an Indian population that was difficult to resettle. [SMS]

2541 Martínez Martín, Carmen. Relación de la documentación existente, sobre la provincia del Paraguay, en el Archivo Histórico Provincial de Toledo de la Compañía de Jesús, Alcalá de Henares, Madrid. (*Rev. Complut. Hist. Am.,* 17, 1991, p. 261–263)

Bibliographic note calls attention to several heretofore unlisted documents concerning the Jesuit missions which have been found in a Madrid archive. [SMS]

2542 Martínez Ramos, Roberto. Historia del cuartel de dragones de Montevideo. (*Bol. Hist. Ejérc.,* 279/282, 1990, p. 131–173, index, maps, photos)

History of the building and re-building of a military barracks in 18th- and 19th-century Montevideo. Includes maps and building plans. [SMS]

2543 Massare de Kostianovsky, Olinda. Disputas del Gobernador de Mojos, Lázaro de Ribera, con el Presidente de la Audiencia de Charcas, Don Ignacio Flores. (*Hist. Parag.,* 22, 1985, p. 95–119, bibl.)

Interesting discussion of a late 18th-century feud between Flores, ex-governor of Mojos, Chiquitos and Paraguay who was promoted to the Presidencia of the Audiencia of Charcas, and his successor, Ribera. The dispute began when Flores falsely claimed to be turning non-existent funds over to Ribera, and demonstrates well how local politics and power often undermined the Bourbon reforms. [SMS]

2544 Mayo, Carlos A. Los betlemitas en Buenos Aires: convento, economía y sociedad, 1748–1822. Sevilla: Excma. Diputación Provincial de Sevilla, 1991. 279 p.: bibl. (Publicaciones de la Excma. Diputación Provincial de Sevilla: Sección Historia: V centenario del descubrimiento de América; 13)

Important study of the Bethlehemite monks concentrates on social composition, *mentalité*, and socioeconomic role in colonial Buenos Aires. Mayo documents how the mendicant order was organized, how it perceived itself and its role, and how it financed charitable activities, principally the Santa Catalina hospital. [SMS]

2545 Mayo, Carlos A. Entre el trabajo y el "ocio:" vagabundos de la llanura pampeana, 1750–1810. (*HISLA/Lima*, 13/14, 1er y 2do semestre 1989, p. 67–76, bibl., tables)

As part of an on-going debate on the nature of late colonial rural society and whether most rural inhabitants were peasants or gauchos, Mayo analyzes judicial cases in which rural men were accused of vagabondage. Most were young, white men, usually from nearby rural zones and who tended to own no property. Mayo states that most were part-time vagabonds moving back and forth between employment as *conchabados* and periods of "rest." His solid analysis also suggests that while *estancieros* might have tried to use the judicial system to coerce these men into the labor market, Audiencia judges did not always support their plan. [SMS]

2546 Mayo, Carlos A. Iglesia y esclavitud en el Río de la Plata: el caso de la Orden Betlemita, 1748–1822. (*Rev. Hist. Am.*, 102, julio/dic. 1986, p. 91–102, tables)

Analysis of the treatment of slaves (mostly males) owned by the convent and hospital of Santa Catalina. Author finds that the Bethlemite order neither encouraged nor dissuaded their slaves from marrying. Also looks at working conditions in the hospital and the *estancia* and *chacara* run by the order. [SMS]

2547 Mayo, Carlos A. Sobre peones, vagos y malentretenidos: el dilema de la economía rural rioplatense durante la época colonial. (*Anu. IEHS*, 2, 1987, p. 25–32)

Author continues debate on the nature of the rural economy and workforce of Buenos Aires (see *HLAS 52:2276*), pointing to a basic paradox: the existence of both labor scarcity and an abundance of vagrants. Mayo sees vagabondage resulting partly from the seasonality of the labor demands, but he underlines the freedom of local inhabitants to refuse to enter the labor market, a freedom stemming from the widespread availability of the means of subsistence: an open frontier; clandestine circuits for sale of products; access to land for squatters; and a preindustrial mentality. He suggests that the gauchos existed because land was available. [SMS]

2548 Molina, Raúl A. La familia porteña en los siglos XVII y XVIII: historia de los divorcios en el período hispánico. Buenos Aires: Fuentes Históricas y Genealógicas Argentinas, 1991. 373 p.: bibl.

A history of marriage and divorce within a legal and canonical framework by the late historian Raul Molina (d. 1973). Molina, a conservative Catholic, was the only historian to work with documents in the Archivo de la Curia Eclesiástica, destroyed by fire in 1955. His lengthy quotations from and discussion of cases brought to the ecclesiastical court in Buenos Aires provide a wealth of new information. [SMS]

2549 Molina de Muñoz, Stella. Aportes al estudio de la actividad comercial en las ciudades del Tucumán, 1582–1590. (*Rev. Dep. Hist./Belo Horizonte*, 1:1, 1991, p. 63–73, bibl.)

Modest contribution to work of Garzón Maceda and Assadourian posits that the last decade of the 16th century began a major transformation in the economies of the five cities of Tucumán (Santiago del Estero, Talavera, San Miguel de Tucumán, Córdoba, and Salta). New growth and the entrance of these cities into long-distance trading is credited mainly to increased *potosino* silver production. Unfortunately, the only primary source material used is from Córdoba. [SMS]

2550 Molina Martínez, Miguel and **Francisco José Fernández Segura.** El accitano Pedro de Mendoza y Luján: primer fundador de Buenos Aires. Guadix, Spain: Excmo. Ayuntamiento de Guadix, 1988. 114 p.: bibl., ill.

Brief biography of Pedro de Mendoza, Guadix-born conquistador and founder of the first ill-fated Buenos Aires settlement. Authors append the capitulation granted Mendoza by the Crown in 1534 to undertake the conquest, as well as the inventory of Mendoza's property made after his death in 1537. [SMS]

2551 Moreno, José Luis. Población y sociedad en el Buenos Aires rural a mediados del siglo XVIII. (*Desarro. Econ.*, 29:114, julio/sept. 1989, p. 265–283,bibl., graphs, tables)

Important first attempt to examine rural census of 1744 to determine the characteristics of the local population. Moreno finds that the census listed most rural inhabitants as white; that the gender distribution of the rural population was close to even; that the population was "young"; that large hacendados comprised only five percent of the rural population; and that small and middling landowners involved in mixed ranching and agriculture were an important group in the rural landscape. [SMS]

2552 Moutoukias, Zacharias. Réseaux personnels et autorité coloniale: les négociants de Buenos Aires au XVIIIe siècle. (*Annales/Paris*, 47:4/5, juillet/oct. 1992, p. 889–915)

Author explores importance of personal networks and the social logic of such links to examine the relationship between merchants and bureuaucrats, using as examples three key figures of pre-viceregal Buenos Aires. Moutoukias emphasizes throughout that these complex social networks coexisted with economic power and were often as important. [SMS]

2553 Navarro Floria, Pedro. Ilustración y radicalización ideológica en el Consulado de Buenos Aires, 1755–1810.(*Rev. Indias*, 49:186, mayo/agosto 1989, p. 411–422)

In a chapter from his unpublished doctoral dissertation, author argues that the Consulado de Buenos Aires was in the forefront of Enlightenment thought. Navarro focuses on the institution's interest in the field of information gathering, its establishment of prizes for new scientific advances, and the founding of technical schools to demonstrate the dynamism of the Consulado's secretary, Manuel Belgrano. [SMS]

2554 Necker, Louis. Indios guaraníes y chamanes franciscanos: las primeras reducciones del Paraguay, 1580–1800. Prefacio de Magnus Mörner. Asunción: Centro de Estudios Antropológicos, Univ. Católica, 1990. 279 p.: bibl., ill. (Biblioteca paraguaya de antropología; 7)

Spanish ed. of 1979 French study on Franciscan attempts to convert the Guaraní. Necker examines early missionary attempts which were rejected by the Guaraní, the successful late 16th-century *reducciones*, and the long-lasting Paraná communities which began in the early 17th century and survived the entire colonial period. He concentrates throughtout on the action and reactions of the Guaraní as well as the economic consequences of the missions for both missionized and missionary. Important study which has finally appeared in Spanish. [SMS]

2555 Neyra, Juan Carlos. Prontuario de próceres y traidores. Buenos Aires: Ediciones Cícero, 1990. 367 p.: index.

Contains biographical sketches of those born prior to 1829 who were anti- or pro-Rosas and were praised by liberal historians, or who failed to fight for economic and political independence of Argentina. [J. Criscenti]

2556 Palombo, Guillermo. Los regimientos fijos de Infantería y Dragones de Buenos Aires. (*Publ. Inst. Estud. Iberoam.*, 8: 6, 1989, p. 119–146)

Lengthy and superfluous introduction precedes a rather traditional history of two of the fixed regiments of Buenos Aires, concentrating on military organization, uniforms, and banners. [SMS]

2557 Pastore, Mario. Trabalho forçado indígena e campesinato mestiço livre no Paraguai: uma visão de suas causas baseada na teoria da procura de rendas econômicas. (*Rev. Bras. Hist.*, 11:21, set. 1990/fev. 1991, p. 147–185, bibl.)

Author discusses Indian slavery, *encomiendas*, and free labor in Paraguay and argues that the development and gradual disappearance of forced labor and the growth of a mestizo peasantry were the results of rent-seeking economic behavior on the part of individuals and the State. Author also analyzes the Spanish use of the Indians, using the economic theory of common property. [SMS]

2558 Pérez, Ramón Alberto. El valle legendario de Tucma. Tucumán, Argentina: Ediciones del Cardón, 1985. 180 p.: bibl., ill., maps.

Study of a Diaguita people, the Tucma, whom the author believes were inhabitants of the Tafí Valley. Based on secondary sources. [SMS]

2559 Pistilli S., Vicente. La primera fundación de Asunción: la gesta de Don Juan de Ayolas. Asunción: Editorial El Foro, 1987. 299 p.: bibl., ill.

Study of the first founding of Asunción examines the arrival of Spanish conquistadors in the region. Argues that in his search for a route to the Mar del Sur, Juan de Ayolas founded the site along the Cerro Lambaré. [SMS]

2560 Quevedo, Roberto. En torno a Lucas de Mendoza. (*Hist. Parag.*, 23, 1986, p. 61–74, ill.)

Genealogical study of the forebearers of an early Paraguayan poet. For related article see item **2394.**

2561 Quevedo, Roberto. La mestiza doña Isabel Venegas. (*Hist. Parag.*, 20, 1983, p. 189–219, bibl., ill.)

Study of a Paraguayan-born mestiza, daughter of an Indian woman and a Spanish conquistador, wife of another conquistador, and "mujer principal" of mid-16th-century Asunción. Genealogical information about her children and a transcript of Doña Isabel's will are included. Author underlines the importance of mestizo men and women in early Paraguayan society. [SMS]

2562 Quevedo, Roberto. Saltos del Guairá: un siglo de síntesis histórica, 1524–1632. (*Hist. Parag.*, 21, 1984, p. 173–192, bibl.)

Author overviews repeated Spanish efforts, usually led by expeditions from Asunción, to control the Guairá region, stressing the various attempts to found cities that would provide another Atlantic outlet. Although Spanish settlers managed to establish three settlements (Cuidad Real, Villa Rica, Santiago de Jérez), they were eventually frustrated by *bandeirante* attacks that forced the evacuation of both settlers and Jesuit missions. [SMS]

2563 Quevedo, Roberto. Semblanza y progenie de conquistadores. (*Estud. Parag.*, 15:1/2, dic. 1987, p. 93–129)

Bits and pieces on colonial Paraguayan

figures include the biographies and descendant genealogies of conquistadors Hernan Arias, Felipe de Cáceres, and Bartolomé González, father of the martyr and saint, the Jesuit Roque González. [SMS]

2564 Ramírez Rivera, Hugo Rodolfo E. Don Antonio de Córdoba y la primera expedición científica española reconocedora del Estrecho de Magallanes, 1785–1798: viaje de la fragata Santa María de la Cabeza II y de los paquebotes Santa Casilda y Santa Eulalia de la Real Armada. Santiago: Embajada de España en Chile; Madrid: Comisión Nacional Española de Conmemoración del Quinto Centenario del Descubrimiento de América, 1990. 284 p.: bibl., ill., maps. (Vol. 1 de las Publicaciones de la Embajada de España en Chile)

Study of two late-18th-century expeditions sent under the auspices of the Royal Naval Astronomical Observatory in Cádiz to chart the extreme southern regions of the South American continent, with special emphasis on their contributions to geographical knowledge and cartography. [SMS]

2565 Rodríguez Zía, Jorge L. Visión geopolítica de Juan de Garay. Santa Fe, Argentina: Municipalidad de la Ciudad de Santa Fe, 1987. 141 p.: bibl., ill.

Biography of Juan de Garay, founder of Santa Fé la Vieja and re-founder of Buenos Aires, stresses importance of the Santa Fé project and discusses the conquistadors who accompanied Garay. Includes a helpful detailed chronology of Garay's life and a list of towns founded both successfully and unsuccessfully in the Río de la Plata region up to 1810. [SMS]

2566 Rosal, Miguel A. El transporte hacia Buenos Aires a través de la hidrovía Paraguay-Paraná, 1781–1811. (*Jahrb. Gesch.*, 27, 1990, p. 128–147, graph, tables)

Interesting article examines riverine transportation linking Asunción-Corrientes-Santa Fé-Buenos Aires, and complementing the author's earlier study of land routes (*HLAS 52:2293*). Rosal discusses distances, types of crafts and their value, individual participants in the transportation network, cargo, and transportation charges. He finds that in the interior trade to Buenos Aires, more goods by volume were moved by river than by land. [SMS]

2567 Saban, Mario Javier. Judíos conversos. v. 1, Los antepasados judíos de las familias tradicionales argentinas. Buenos Aires: Editorial Distal, 1990. 1 v.: bibl., ill.

Attempts to identify families started by Portuguese Jews who settled in Spanish colonies of Río de la Plata prior to mid-17th century and were assimilated by end of the colonial period. Genealogical charts are presented for 34 families of Portuguese Jewish origins, and for 40 Portuguese families that might have had Jewish ancestors. [J. Criscenti]

2568 Saguier, Eduardo R. Esplendor y derrumbe de una élite contrarevolucionaria: el clan de los Allende y el ajusticiamiento de Cabeza de Tigre. (*Anu. Estud. Am.*, 48, 1991, p. 349–389)

Author argues that local elites of the interior of the Río de la Plata, weakened because of a series of economic restructurings, first resisted and then incorporated peninsular merchants into their ranks. The newly reformed elite which emerged at the end of the 18th century maintained itself in power until the early 20th century passage of the Saénz Peña Law. Using the case of Córdoba, Saguier discusses the political power of the Allende clan, arguing that familial ties were stronger than any political movement, including the Bourbon reforms. [SMS]

2569 Saguier, Eduardo R. El mercado del cuero y su rol como fuente alternativa de empleo: el caso del trabajo a destajo en las vaquerías de la Banda Oriental durante el siglo XVIII. (*Rev. Hist. Econ.*, 9:1, invierno 1991, p. 103–126, bibl., tables)

Economic analysis juxtaposes costs of producing hides (including information on labor costs, transportation, storage, taxes, and other commercialization costs) with data on the market price of hides and profitability. Saguier believes that rising labor costs made the legal export of hides profitable only in times of peace; during times of war, the cost of trans-Atlantic transportation forced hide producers and merchants to illegal behavior to retain their profit margin. [SMS]

2570 Saguier, Eduardo R. La naturaleza estipendiaria de la esclavitud urbana colonial: el caso de Buenos Aires en el siglo XVIII. (*Rev. Parag. Sociol.*, 26:74, enero/abril 1989, p. 45–54, bibl.)

Discussion of urban and rural slavery in the Río de la Plata points out that the dominant form of porteño slavery was one in which slaves hired themselves out, returning part of their wages to their owner. As a result, porteño slavery was markedly different from other colonial regions, with better treatment and more independence for slaves. Nonetheless, the high cost of slaves coupled with the scarcity of liquid capital restricted wealth formation and the emergence of capitalism. [SMS]

2571 Sánchez Quell, H. Asunción, sembradora de ciudades. (*Hist. Parag.*, 20, 1983, p. 23–42)

After a detailed description of colonial Asunción based chiefly on late 18th-century travelers' reports (especially those of Azara and Aguirre), the author argues that city's dynamic role in providing the impetus for the founding of other cities throughout the Río de la Plata resulted in poverty and exhaustion for the 'mother city.' [SMS]

2572 Santos, Corcino Medeiros dos. O comércio hispano-lusitano do Rio da Prata, na crise do sistema colonial. (*Estud. Ibero-Am./Porto Alegre*, 15:2, dez. 1989, p. 327–346)

Good general article overviews Portuguese-Spanish trade in the Río de la Plata, concentrating on intercolonial commerce in the late 18th century. Author argues that despite periods of conflict between the two Iberian colonies, periods of commercial cooperation were more frequent. [SMS]

2573 Segreti, Carlos S.A. Temas de historia colonial: comercio e injerencia extranjera. Buenos Aires: Academia Nacional de la Historia, 1987. 273 p.: bibl. (Col. de historia económica y social; 7)

Six chapters on the colonial commerce of Buenos Aires stress the effects of Bourbon Reforms, the British entry into Spanish-American markets, and the gradual victory of those merchants in favor of new trading partners over those tied to Spanish suppliers. A solid work. [SMS]

2574 Soaje Pinto, Manuel A. Los Toledo en la conquista del Tucumán. (*Publ. Inst. Estud. Iberoam.*, 8:6, 1989, p. 213–245, bibl.)

Ascendant and descendant genealogy of Captain Fernando de Toledo y Pimentel, a distant relative of the Viceroy of Peru, who served in the late 16th-century conquest of Indians in the Tucumán region. [SMS]

2575 Socolow, Susan M. Parejas bien constituidas: la elección matrimonial en la Argentina colonial, 1778–1810. (*Anu. IEHS*, 5, 1990, p. 133–160)

Spanish version of "Acceptable Partners: Marriage Choice in Colonial Argentina, 1778–1810," on which see *HLAS 52:2302*. [MTH]

2576 Socolow, Susan M. Spanish captives in Indian societies: cultural contact along the Argentine frontier, 1600–1835. (*HAHR*, 72:1, Feb. 1992, p. 73–99, tables)

English version of "Los Cautivos Españoles en las Sociedades Indígenas," on which see *HLAS 52:2303*. [MTH]

2577 Tejerina Carreras, Ignacio G. Introducción al período hispánico en Córdoba. Córdoba, Argentina: Instituto de Estudios Históricos Roberto Levillier, 1990. 132 p.: bibl., ill., maps.

Brief overview of the history of city of Córdoba covers region's precolumbian inhabitants of the region to the institutions, society, culture, and economy of the city, stressing the Spanish Catholic values of the colonial world. [SMS]

2578 300 años de colonia: ciclo conmemorativo. Coordinación de Ernesto Daragnès Rodero. Montevideo: Univ. de la República, 1988. 172 p., 6 leaves of plates: ill. (some col.)

Lavishly illustrated vol. covers past and present of the city of Colonia. Includes solid chapters on the early exploration, first settlement, Portuguese period, Spanish reconquest, urban plan and demography, as well as a chapter on Martín García Island. [SMS]

2579 Velázquez, Rafael Eladio. José Dávalos y Peralta: primer doctor paraguayo en medicina, jefe comunero. (*Hist. Parag.*, 22, 1985, p. 123–239, ill.)

Biography and ascendant-descendant genealogy of Asunción-born Dávalos (1655-c. 1729), the first Paraguayan to earn the degree of Doctor of Medicine. Dávalos practiced medicine for many years in Peru, where he was a professor at the Univ. de San Marcos. Returning to Paraguay, he became an *encomendero* and supporter of Antequera. Author

reproduces the lengthy *probanza* which Dávalos presented to practice in Lima. [SMS]

2580 Velázquez, Rafael Eladio. Transformaciones de la época de la Intendencia en el Paraguay. (*Hist. Parag.*, 20, 1983, p. 75–104)

Overview of late 18th-century Paraguay concentrates on local government (Governor, Lieutenant Governor, cabildo members, and other officials), the social and political economy (agricultural diversification), the abolition of *encomiendas*, military organization, and church re-organization. [SMS]

2581 Velo de Antelo, José María. El gobierno de las Malvinas en el Reinado del Carlos III. (*Cuad. Esc. Dipl.*, 3, segunda época, dic. 1989, p. 45–63)

After the obligatory discussion of sailors who might have visited the Malvinas from the 16th century onward, author traces the French-English-Spanish attempts to claim the islands after 1763. Brief biographic sketch of the island's governors follows. [SMS]

2582 Viola, Alfredo. Origen de los pueblos. (*Hist. Parag.*, 22, 1985, p. 59–94, map)

Discussion of a number of Jesuit missions (San Joaquín, San Estanislao, N.S. de Belén, Timbó) founded to the southeast and northwest of Asunción from 1730s to 1760s stresses that the missionaries were both furthering religious ends as well as helping the Spanish Crown safeguard its territorial jurisdiction. Emphasizes role of Guaraní Indians in convincing other Indian groups (Tobaines, Mbayas, Abipones) to come into the missions. [SMS]

2583 Zapata Gollán, Agustín. Las puertas de la tierra. Santa Fe, Argentina: Univ. Nacional del Litoral, Centro de Publicaciones, 1989. 300 p.: bibl. (Obra completa; 2)

Second vol. of the complete works of Zapata Gollán (1895–1986) contains his previously published studies on the early conquest and settlement of Santa Fé and precolumbian and colonial transportation networks. [SMS]

2584 Zenarruza, Jorge G.C. Jujuy: sus linajes troncales y los a ellos vinculados; los Goyechea. (*Publ. Inst. Estud. Iberoam.*, 8:6, 1989, p. 275–351)

Detailed genealogy of Maestre de

Campo Martín de Goyechea, a late-17th century military man who made his way from the Basque region of Spain to Chile and then to Jujuy, and his descendants. Author finds an unusually high number of prominent individuals related to the Goyechea clan through the female line. [SMS]

2585 Zorraquín Becú, Ricardo. Proyección geopolítica del Virreinato. (*Publ. Inst. Estud. Iberoam.*, 8:6, 1989, p. 353-371)

Overview of the eventual emergence of the Viceroyalty of Río de la Plata is treated as the logical conclusion of a lengthy historical process. [SMS]

19th and 20th Centuries
Venezuela

WINTHROP R. WRIGHT, *Professor of History, University of Maryland, College Park*

VENEZUELAN HISTORIOGRAPHY HAS UNDERGONE a number of significant changes during the past two decades. Despite the fact that the overwhelming majority of books and articles written by Venezuelans still deals with political topics, a growing number of professional historians have produced works on previously overlooked economic and social topics. The titles in this section reflect this trend.

Several excellent economic histories have appeared recently. Among these, Germán Galué offers a major study of the origins of the coffee-related commerce of Maracaibo (item **2590**). In a similar manner, José Murguey Gutiérrez has surveyed the impact of one of Venezuela's few railways on the economic development of the state of Trujillo (item **2596**). The same author has produced an impressive history of the economic and political importance of mining to the development of 19th-century Venezuela (item **2597**). The study by María Elena González Deluca also uses railway building to point out the importance of politics in determining the success of businesses in Venezuela during the late 19th century (item **2594**).

Rounding out the major economic histories, a multivolume documental work put together by Tomás Enrique Carrillo Batalla, *Historia de las finanzas públicas en Venezuela: siglo XX*, provides a rich source of data on 20th-century Venezuelan public finance (see *HLAS 53:2108*).

Three historians have written on social themes of some importance. Ramón Vicente Chacón Vargas' article on epidemics in Caracas during the first half of the 20th century indicts governments for their failure to provide Caracas with sanitary and hygienic conditions beyond those normally associated with rural towns (item **2591**). In a long needed look at gender, Ermila Troconis de Veracoechea has written a pioneering history of the role of women of all classes and races in the evolution of Venezuelan society (item **2605**). A study of immigration from the Canary Islands by Manuel Rodríguez Campos (item **2601**) reveals the slave-like conditions under which most Canarians arrived in Venezuela and the means by which they overcame their servitude and poverty.

Political studies cannot be overlooked entirely. A generation of revisionist historians—shaped by their work on the Castro/Gómez project and by the historical school of the Univ. Central de Venezuela—have reinterpreted the Gómez era. For a volume of essays by the leading members of the group, see Arturo Sosa *et al.* (item **2603**); Yolanda Segnini's treatment of the immediate post-Gómez era demonstrates the direction the revisionists have taken (item **2602**). Two other political works need to be mentioned. Haydée Farías de Urbaneja has completed a solid analysis of the role of the Sociedad Económica de Amigos del País (item **2592**): she makes a cogent argument that between 1830–40 the SEAP did not control Venezuela's governmental policies in spite of the fact that its ranks included many notable members of society. For students of the Betancourt era, Robert Alexander has shared letters from and conversations with Rómulo Betancourt that explain the politician's actions on a number of major issues (item **2586**).

2586 Alexander, Robert Jackson. Venezuela's voice for democracy: conversations and correspondence with Rómulo Betancourt. New York: Praeger Publishers, 1990. 176 p.: bibl., index.

Extraordinary exchange of frank opinions in which Betancourt bares his soul to his North American friend and biographer. Book contains many gems, most of which help to explain the objectives of one of Latin America's leading politicians and political thinkers. Useful for anyone interested in the troubled political history of Venezuela since the 1950s.

2587 Archivo de Rómulo Betancourt. v. 1, 1917–29. Caracas: Editorial Fundación Rómulo Betancourt, 1988. 1 v.: ill., index.

Published in conjunction with the celebration of the 50th anniversary of the founding of Acción Democrática. Includes letters related to Betancourt's activities in exile during 1928 and the actions of his associates, including letters concerning the 1929 fiasco of the "Falke" incident.

2588 Betancourt, Rómulo. Antología política. v. 1. Selección, estudio preliminar y notas de Aníbal Romero, Elizabeth Tinoco, y María Teresa Romero. Caracas: Editorial Fundación Rómulo Betancourt, 1990. 1 v.: bibl., index, port.

Selection of Betancourt's writings from 1928–35 are especially useful for his commentary about movements throughout Latin America, and for understanding his motivations after 1928.

2589 Brito Figueroa, Federico. 30 ensayos de comprensión histórica en el "Suplemento Cultural" de *Ultimas Noticias.* Caracas: Ediciones Centauro, 1991. 559 p.: bibl., ill.

Collection of essays by one of Venezuela's leading Marxist historians, written over a 25-year period. Useful for understanding the complexity of Venezuela's political left and its attitudes toward traditional elites.

2590 Cardozo Galué, Germán. Maracaibo y su región histórica: el circuito agroexportador, 1830–1860. Maracaibo, Venezuela: Editorial de la Univ. del Zulia, 1991. 313 p.: bibl., ill., maps. (Col. Centenario de LUZ; 1)

Major economic study examines origins of Maracaibo's coffee-related commerce. An extensive survey of the city's economic records establishes the regional and international importance of Maracaibo as a major Venezuelan port for the export of agricultural products and the most influential city of Western Venezuela. Useful graphs and charts.

2591 Chacón Vargas, Ramón Vicente. Epidemias de Caracas, 1900–1945. (*Bol. Acad. Nac. Hist./Caracas,* 73:290, abril/junio 1990, p. 51–68, bibl., tables)

Argues that until WWII, Caracas suffered from epidemics usually found in small rural towns that lacked modern sanitary and hygienic facilities. In effect, Caracas provided a decidedly unhealthy environment for its citizens, despite efforts of medical reformers such as Luis Razetti. Neither Castro nor Gómez made significant contributions to the fight against epidemics.

2592 Farías de Urbaneja, Haydée. La autoridad de la Sociedad Económica de Amigos del País en la política gubernamental de 1830–1840. Caracas: Univ. Central de Venezuela, Consejo de Desarrollo Científico y Humanístico, 1991. 153 p.: bibl. (Col. Estudios)

Organized in 1829, the Sociedad Económica de Amigos del País (SEAP) comprised notables of Caracas who sought solutions to Venezuela's most pressing social, economic, and political problems. Influenced by European liberal traditions, they attempted to reform Venezuela's underdeveloped society. Author concludes that despite its membership, SEAP did not control the State. Although highly influential and successful, it could not persuade the government to implement many important reforms. In effect, SEAP gave elites a place to find intellectual solutions, but elites as politicians tended to follow more conservative and specific interest-group policies.

2593 Gabaldón, Eleonora. La ideología federal en la Convención de Valencia, 1858: tiempo y debate. Caracas: Academia Nacional de la Historia, 1987. 461 p.: bibl. (Biblioteca de la Academia Nacional de la Historia: Estudios, monografías y ensayos; 100)

Useful guide to key debates about federalism that took place during 1858 at the constitutional convention held at Valencia. Well-edited, with clear references to central issues.

2594 González Deluca, María Elena. Negocios y política en tiempos de Guzmán Blanco. Caracas: Univ. Central de Venezuela, Consejo de Desarrollo Científico y Humanístico, 1991. 350 p.: bibl., map. (Col. Estudios)

Uses the financing and building of the La Guaira to Caracas Railroad to focus on the relation between Guzmán Blanco's political plans and his desire to modernize. Centralization and modernization worked to his personal benefit. Drawn extensively from the archives of the Fundación Boulton and from correspondence between Guzmán and North American William Pile. In Venezuela, politics determined business decisions.

Historia de las finanzas públicas en Venezuela. See *HLAS 53:2108.*

2595 Méndez S., Herminia. La Iglesia Católica en tiempos de Guzmán Blanco. (*Bol. Acad. Nac. Hist./Caracas*, 74:296, oct./ dic. 1991, p. 107–122, bibl.)

Analysis of repercussions of Guzmán Blanco's efforts to place the Venezuelan Church under the control of the State as part of his scheme to develop the nation according to his liberal doctrine.

2596 Murguey Gutiérrez, José. La construcción de los ferrocarriles en la sección Trujillo del estado Los Andes, 1881–1899. Mérida, Venezuela: J. Murguey Gutiérrez, 1989. 107 p.: bibl., ill.

Solid economic history on the origin and impact of one of Venezuela's few railways on the economy of Trujillo state.

2597 Murguey Gutiérrez, José. La explotación aurífera de Guayana y la conformación de la Compañía Minera de "El Ca-

llao," 1870–1900. Caracas?: Corporación Venezolana de Guayana; MINERVEN, 1989. 208 p.: bibl., ill., index, maps.

Author examines the long-term importance of mining to the economic and political development of 19th-century Venezuela, emphasizing the role of the State in determining mining policies. Includes an impressive amount of economic data, presented clearly in numerous graphs and charts.

2598 Ovalles, Víctor Manuel. El llanero: estudio sobre su vida, sus costumbres, su carácter y su poesía. 2. ed. Caracas: Ediciones Presidencia de la República, 1990. 171 p.: bibl., ill., facsims.

Second ed. of pioneering study on *llaneros* as a regional type first written in 1904 with drawings by César Prieto. Mostly folklore but some historical data. New edition includes an introductory note by Caupolicán Ovalles and essay by José Vicente Abreu comparing Ovalles and Gallegos.

Pino Iturrieta, Elías *et al.* Historia mínima de Venezuela. See item **2281.**

2599 Plaza, Elena. Por el origen de la vida: evolucionismo y creacionismo en Venezuela, 1904–1907. (*Bol. Acad. Nac. Hist./ Caracas*, 74:293, enero/marzo 1991, p. 79–100, bibl.)

Review of the exchange between Dr. Luis Razetti, a leading advocate of evolutionary theory, and the Archbishop of Caracas, Juan Bautista Castro. The author considers this debate one of the most important confrontations in the history of scientific ideas in Venezuela. Castro, who opposed the subordination of the Church to the State, refuted Razetti's position, and in doing so accepted the literal tale in the book of Genesis.

2600 Preussen und Venezuela: Edition der preussischen Konsularberichte über Venezuela, 1842–1850. Edited by Rolf Walter *et al.* Introduction by Hermann Kellenbenz. Frankfurt: Vervuert, 1991. 216 p.: bibl. (Lateinamerika-Studien; 28)

Editor Walter, an expert in German-Venezuelan economic relations, is responsible for the introduction, selection and contextual arrangement of these 19th-century published and unpublished materials on Prussian-Venezuelan relations (i.e., consular records of the Prussian Ministry of Foreign Af-

fairs and Venezuelan diplomatic records).
[C.K. Converse]

2601 Rodríguez Campos, Manuel. La libranza del sudor: el drama de la inmigración canaria en Venezuela entre 1830 y 1859. Caracas: Academia Nacional de la Historia, 1989. 307 p.: bibl. (Biblioteca de la Academia Nacional de la Historia: Fuentes para la historia republicana de Venezuela; 46)

First half of the book presents background and reasons that led Venezuelan governments to encourage immigration of Canary Islanders. Second half treats the conditions that Canary Islanders encountered and how they overcame almost slave-like contracts. From 1830 until Spain recognized Venezuela as an independent nation, the workers received no help from Spanish authorities. Due to Venezuelan attitudes and laws, most failed to improve their lot by moving to Venezuela, remaining as poor there as they had been in the Canaries.

2602 Segnini, Yolanda. Los caballeros del postgomecismo. Caracas: Alfadil Ediciones, 1990. 227 p.: bibl. (Col. Trópicos; 30)

In-depth study of political and intellectual activities in Venezuela following the death of Juan V. Gómez by one of Venezuela's leading revisionists. Offers new interpretations of the López Contreras era, stressing the period's positive growth. Book contains fresh insights and provocative interpretations, and makes extensive use of records from the British Foreign Office.

2603 Sosa, Arturo et al. Gómez, gomecismo y antigomecismo. Caracas: Fondo Editorial de Humanidades y Educación, Univ.

Central de Venezuela, 1987. 201 p. (Col. Obra abierta)

Collection of lectures given by members of a revisionist generation of historians associated with the ongoing Castro/Gómez project at the School of History of the Central Univ. of Venezuela. Thought-provoking essays by Arturo Sosa, Yolanda Segnini, Victor Córdova, Luis Cipriano Rodríguez, Manuel Caballero, Elías Pino Iturrieta, Rodolfo Quintero, and Germán Carrera Damas.

2604 Tosta, Virgilio. El comercio del antiguo estado Zamora y el rol desempeñado por los carros de mulas. (*Bol. Acad. Nac. Hist./Caracas*, 73:291, julio/sept. 1990, p. 61–88)

Explains Ciudad Bolívar's decline in commerce with Zamora state by demonstrating that muleteers carried products to central Venezuelan markets that were previously transportated by river before the advent of modern all-weather roads.

2605 Troconis de Veracoechea, Ermila. Indias, esclavas, mantuanas y primeras damas. Caracas: Academia Nacional de la Historia; Alfadil Ediciones, 1990. 227 p.: bibl. (Col. Trópicos; 25)

Pioneer study of role of women in Venezuela during colonial era through the 19th century. Well-researched, this book combines good analysis with a useful collection of documents. Treats legal, property, and other rights of women of all classes and ethnic groups. Seminal but not definitive.

Zeuske, Michael. Kolonialpolitik und Revolution: Kuba und die Unabhängigkeit der Costa Firme, 1808–1821. See item **2127.**

Colombia and Ecuador

JANE M. RAUSCH, *Professor of History, University of Massachusetts-Amherst*

CAREFULLY-EDITED DOCUMENTARY COLLECTIONS and stimulating general interpretations, both trends noted in *HLAS 52*, remain the salient features of this reporting period. With regard to documents, the Fundación Francisco Paula de Santander, established in 1986, has published nearly 100 volumes of correspondence, diaries, and other documents related to Santander's life and times. Nine of these multivolume collections were annotated in *HLAS 52*, and 12 additional titles are listed here under "Santandereana." Enhanced by introductory essays and methodological notes by well-known historians, these volumes supersede older editions and make accessible materials formerly buried in obscure archives. For a complete description of the Fundación publications, see my essay "The Santander Historical Collection: A Brief Report about a New and Important Documentary Resource" in *Inter-American Review of Bibliography* (Vol. 43, No. 1, 1992).

Nineteenth-century travel accounts by John Steuart (item **2662**) and Rosa Carnegie Williams (item **2626**) have been translated to Spanish. These are the first volumes of a potentially promising documentary series about the history of Bogotá published by the Academia de Historia de Bogotá, an institution created in 1987 as part of the official effort to commemorate the 450th anniversary of the city's founding. Finally, new editions of *Historia contemporánea de Colombia* by Gustavo Arboleda (item **2620**) and *La Iglesia y el Estado en Colombia* by Juan Pablo Restrepo (item **2653**) will make these fundamental but long out-of-print texts available to many libraries.

Noteworthy among the general interpretations is Bushnell's *The making of modern Colombia*, the first one-volume survey of Colombian history to be published in English in many decades (item **2624**). With consummate skill, Bushnell has integrated recent research on Colombian topics into a lively narrative that will appeal both to specialists and undergraduates. Also of interest are essay collections by Colombian scholars Renán Vega Cantor (item **2666**), Alvaro Tirado Mejía (item **2663**), Jorge Orlando Melo (item **2645**), and by members of the Academia Colombiana de Ciencias Económicas (item **2627**). These works span the 19th and 20th centuries and offer fresh approaches to such on-going debates as the evolution of national identity and the origins of La Violencia. For regional history, faculty at the Univ. del Valle continue to lead the way with innovative studies on socioeconomic developments in the Cauca Valley (items **2628** and **2651**), but there are also pioneer works concerning more peripheral provinces such as the island of San Andrés (item **2634**) and the Eastern Llanos (item **2660**). Among several competent biographies, Delpar provides an objective assessment of Soledad Román, the second wife of Rafael Núñez (item **2630**), and investigative journalists Galvis and Donadío paint a convincing portrait of Rojas Pinilla based on an extensive examination of extant archival documents and interviews with his contemporaries (item **2633**).

Labor history, frontier colonization, and La Violencia are other popular topics. Sowell charts the growth of artisan labor organizations and their participation in political activities between 1832–1919 to challenge the traditional conception of a political system monopolized by the elite (item **2661**). His study is complemented by Archila's social history of the working classes in Bogotá, Medellín, Barranquilla, and Barrancabermeja between 1910–45 (item **2621**). The subject of Antioquia's expanding frontier was first explored by geographer James Parsons. Papers presented at a Manizales seminar held in Nov. 1987 reassess the relevance of Antioqueñan colonization in western Colombia (item **2629**), and, when combined with Valencia Llanos' book on the foundation of Manizales (item **2664**), demonstrate that there is still much to learn about settlement dynamics in this region. For the Cundinamarcan province of Sumapaz, see Elsy Marulanda Alvarez's study of frontier expansion from 1870–1965 (item **2643**) and oral accounts of four people who settled there as transcribed by González Arias (item **2636**). On the eastern front, Augusto Gómez traces colonization of the Llanos Orientales from 1870–1970 with an emphasis on the violent interaction between *colonos* and Indians (item **2635**). Two books dealing with La Violencia trace its roots to the late 19th century: Jaramillo Castillo's fascinating analysis of guerrilla units fighting in the War of a Thousand Days (item **2638**); and

Betancourt's investigation of three phases of violence in the department of Valle (item **2623**). Essays on the inter-relationship of La Violencia with political life (item **2658**) and with economic growth and human rights (item **2644**) round out this subgroup. The high quality of these and other works under review is perhaps the strongest testimony that despite ongoing violence and political unrest within Colombia, academic life remains vigorous and productive.

Turning to Ecuador, among the most important entries are four volumes that survey national history from independence to 1960 and form part of the *Nueva historia del Ecuador* edited by Enrique Ayala Mora (item **2679**). Publication of this projected 15-volume series began in 1983 with the goal of providing students and general readers with a synthesis of contemporary scholarship about Ecuador from precolumbian times to the present. The attractive format of the books (each of which contains primary documents, helpful summaries, maps, and bibliographies) makes them excellent introductions to the periods under discussion.

For the 19th century, Gimeno's fine study of Flores' attempt to reestablish a monarchy in 1846 (item **2676**) supplements Mark van Aken's recent biography of Gen. Flores reviewed in the previous Humanities *Handbook* (see *HLAS 52:2436*). Renewed interest in Manuela Sáenz is evident in the heated responses of Ecuadoran and Venezuelan scholars to Densil Romero's novel, *La esposa de Dr. Thorne* (item **2678**). The best works on the 20th century focus on labor history. Pineo analyzes the Guayaquil strike of 1922 (item **2688**), while Gándara Enríquez refutes charges that the military used excessive force to repress the strikers (item **2675**). Ycaza employs a Marxist framework to survey the working class movement from 1935–91 (item **2694**). Finally, Padilla's history of Protestantism in Ecuador breaks new ground on a sociocultural phenomenon that has captured the interest of researchers throughout Latin America (item **2685**).

SANTANDEREANA

2606 Actas de la Diputación Permanente del Congreso de Angostura, 1820–1821. 2. ed. Bogotá: Fundación para la Conmemoración del Bicentenario del Natalicio y el Sesquicentenario de la muerte del Gen. Francisco de Paula Santander, 1989. 365 p.: index. (Biblioteca de la Presidencia)

The Congress of Angostura created a seven-man Permanent Commission (Diputación Permanente) with administrative and judicial authority to administer laws when it was not in session. Meeting three times a week between Jan. 22, 1820 and July 31, 1821, the deputies dealt with state revenues, immigration, and awards of public lands, among other topics. The minutes of these sessions were first published by J.D. Monsalve in 1927. This new edition is based on Monsalve's work and introduced by Arturo Uslar Pietri.

2607 Administraciones de Santander. Recopilación de Luis Horacio López D. Prólogo de Marco Palacios. Bogotá: Fundación para la Conmemoración del Bicentenario del Natalicio y el Sesquicentenario de la Muerte del General Francisco de Paula Santander, 1990. 6 v.: bibl., ill., index. (Biblioteca de la Presidencia)

Compilation of 40 *informes* (annual reports) presented to Congress by the cabinet ministers of interior, finance, and defense (*guerra y marina*). The first 2 vols. cover Santander's years as vice-president of Gran Colombia (1821–27) and the last four when he was president of New Granada (1832–37). Also included are six messages to Congress by Santander, documentation of the 1824 British loan, and an *informe* by Domingo Caicedo who was president in 1831. Marco Palacios' prologue provides a context for evaluating documents.

2608 Archivo Nariño. Recopilación de Guillermo Hernández de Alba. Ordenamiento de Gonzalo Hernández de Alba y Andrés Olivos Lombana. Bogotá: Fundación para la Conmemoración del Bicentenario del Natalicio y el Sesquicentenario de la Muerte del

General Francisco de Paula Santander, 1990. 6 v.: ill., index. (Biblioteca de la Presidencia: Col. Documentos)

Largest and most complete documentary collection published up to now on life and career of Antonio Nariño (1765–1823). Guillermo Hernández de Alba assembled 530 documents from 42 different archives, libraries, and periodicals. The bulk of material covers the years between 1809–15. Gonzalo Hernández de Alba completed the editing after the death of his father.

2609 Causas y memorias de los conjurados del 25 de septiembre de 1828. Introducción de María Isabel Perdomo Pardo y Germán Mejía P. Bogotá: Fundación para la Conmemoración del Bicentenario del Natalicio y el Sesquicentenario de la Muerte del General Francisco de Paula Santander, 1990. 3 v.: index, map. (Biblioteca de la Presidencia. Col. Documentos; 46–48)

Vol. 1 contains transcripts of the trial of over 50 men accused of conspiring to assassinate Bolívar on Sept. 25, 1828. Vol. 2 includes *memorias* and testimonies of 20 men who were either directly implicated in the conspiracy or eye witnesses. Vol. 3 surveys interpretations of events from the 19th century to present with excerpts from works of nine Colombian historians, a poem by Luis Vargas Tejada and a play by José María Samper. When read together with *Proceso seguido al General Santander* (see *HLAS 52:2401*), these volumes provide a solid documental base for assessing a pivotal event in the collapse of Gran Colombia.

2610 Congreso de las Provincias Unidas, 1811–1815. Prólogo de Gonzalo Hernández de Alba. 2. ed. Bogotá: Fundación para la Conmemoración del Bicentenario del Natalicio y el Sesquicentenario de la muerte del General Francisco de Paula Santander, 1988. 2 v.: bibl., index. (Biblioteca de la Presidencia, Administración Virgilio Barco. Documents; 26–27)

Compendium of laws passed by the Congreso de las Provincias Unidas offers insight into the so-called "Patria Boba" era frequently neglected by historians. Collection based on earlier edition published in 1924 by Eduardo Posada. Vol. 1 covers 1811–14; Vol. 2 covers 1814–16 and includes bibliographical sketches of 15 congressmen.

2611 De Boyacá a Cúcuta: memoria administrativa, 1819–1821. Prólogo de Néstor Iván Osuna Patiño. Bogotá: Fundación para la Conmemoración del Bicentenario del Natalicio y el Sesquicentenario de la Muerte del General Francisco de Paula Santander, 1990. 469 p.: index. (Biblioteca de la Presidencia)

Compilation of laws and decrees adopted by Vice-President Santander and his secretaries, Alejandro Osorio and Estanislao Vergara between 1819–21. Documents, originally published in official periodicals such as *Correo del Orinoco*, are arranged chronologically and cover economic, political, educational, military, religious, and judicial matters.

2612 Echeverry Sánchez, Jesús Alberto. Santander y la instrucción pública, 1819–1840. Bogotá: Foro Nacional por Colombia; Medellín: Univ. de Antioquia, 1989. 446 p.: bibl.

History of public instruction from 1819–40 emphasizes gap between policy (as expressed in decrees) and practice (actual teaching in the schools). Points out weaknesses in Santander's programs and identifies sources of opposition to his plans. Part of an ongoing multi-volume interuniversity series. Extensive bibliography.

2613 Los Ejércitos del Rey. Recopilación y prólogo de Alberto Lee López. Bogotá: Fundación para la Conmemoración del Bicentenario del Natalicio y el Sesquicentenario de la Muerte del General Francisco de Paula Santander, 1989. 2 v.: bibl., index. (Biblioteca de la Presidencia)

Correspondence between Viceroy Juan Sámano and Commander José María Barreiro provides insight into the Spanish attempt to retake control of the region. Most of the 649 documents were collected from the Archivo de Indias in Seville. Vol. 1 covers Jan. 25, 1818 to March 11, 1819; Vol. 2 covers March 12, 1819 to Aug. 14, 1819. Prologue by Alberto Lee-López suggests value of the documents. Indexed by name, place, subject, military units, ships.

2614 Escritos sobre Santander. Recopilación de Horacio Rodríguez Plata y Juan Camilo Rodríguez. 2. ed. Bogotá: Fundación para la Conmemoración del Bicentenario del Natalicio y el Sesquicentenario de la Muerte del General Francisco de Paula Santander, 1988. 2 v.: bibl., index. (Biblioteca de la Presidencia, Administración Virgilio Barco)

Compilation of brief essays and speeches by Colombian intellecuals and politicians in praise of Santander. Vol. 1 contains 41 pieces published between 1825–1936. Vol. 2 has 21 pieces published since 1936, many written for the centenary of Santander's death in 1940. Contains a handy chronology of his life and work.

2615 La Gran Colombia y los Estados Unidos de América: relaciones diplomáticas, 1810–1831. Prólogo de Julio Londoño Paredes. Bogotá: Fundación para la Conmemoración del Bicentenario del Natalicio y el Sesquicentenario de la Muerte del General Francisco de Paula Santander, 1990. 2 v.: bibl., ill., index. (Biblioteca de la Presidencia. Col. Documentos; 68–69)

Volume contains 142 documents that trace US-Colombian diplomatic relations between 1819–31, selected by David Bushnell from Cortázar, *Archivo Santander*, and Manning's *Correspondencia diplomática*. Vol. 1 includes two essays written by García Samudio in 1924 on the career of Manuel Torres, minister to Washington (1819–22) and the diplomatic aspects of Santander's regime, 1819–34.

2616 Santander y el Congreso de 1823: actas y correspondencia. Prólogo de Javier Ocampo López. Bogotá: Fundación para la Conmemoración del Bicentenario del Natalicio y el Sesquicentenario de la Muerte del General Francisco de Paula Santander, 1989. 3 v.: index, map. (Biblioteca de la Presidencia. Col. Documentos; 28–30)

Minutes of daily sessions of 1823 Congress and Santander's correspondence to the legislators concerning the matters under consideration. Prologue provides context for documents. Vols. 1 and 2 deal with the Senate; Vol. 3 with the *Cámara.*

2617 Santander y el Congreso de 1824: actas y correspondencia. Prólogo de Javier Ocampo López. Bogotá: Fundación para la Conmemoración del Bicentenario del Natalicio y el Sesquicentenario de la Muerte, 1989. 5 v.: index, map. (Biblioteca de la Presidencia. Col. Documentos; 31–35)

Compilation of minutes of daily sessions of 1824 Congress and Santander's correspondence to the legislators concerning mat-

ters under consideration. Prologue provides context for documents. First three vols. deal with the Senate; the last two with the *Cámara.* Each includes map, chronology, and place, name, and subject indexes.

2618 Santander y el Congreso de 1825: actas y correspondencia. Prólogo de Javier Ocampo López. Bogotá: Fundación para la Conmemoración del Bicentenario del Natalicio y el Sesquicentenario de la Muerte del General Francisco, 1989. 5 v.: index, map. (Biblioteca de la Presidencia. Col. Documentos; 36–40)

Minutes of daily sessions of 1825 Congress and Santander's correspondence to legislators concerning matters under consideration. Prologue provides context for documents. First three vols. deal with the Senate; the last two with the *Cámara.*

COLOMBIA

2619 Albis, Manuel María. Curiosità della foresta d'Amazzonia e arte di curar senza medico: un quaderno di viaggio colombiano del 1854 conservato nella Biblioteca Nazionale Universitaria di Torino. Edizione, traduzione e note di Alberto Guaraldo. Torino, Italy: Il Segnalibro, 1991. 248 p.: col. plates.

Bilingual (Italian-Spanish) edition of an 1854 manuscript recently discovered at the Biblioteca Nazionale in Turin. Author, a parish priest of Garzón (Huila), made several excursions into Putumayo and Caquetá to observe the Andaqui and Macaguaje Indians. Data is ethnological and includes native vocabularies and medical remedies. Nine drawings reproduced from original document. Introductory essays are in Italian only.

2620 Arboleda, Gustavo. Historia contemporánea de Colombia: desde la disolución de la antigua República de ese nombre hasta la época presente. v. 1–12. 2a. ed. Bogotá: Banco Central Hipotecario, 1990. 12 v.:

Political history of years between 1829–61 includes material on many aspects of Colombian society such as legislative acts of each congress and newspapers and books published in each year. Originally published in six volumes between 1918–38. Work is described by Griffin as "the most useful by any Colombian historian for the period," and has long been out-of-print. For this edition Gastón Valencia has divided material into 12 volumes, modernized the spelling and added a biographical note on Arboleda's life and work. Essential acquisition for any research library.

2621 Archila, Mauricio. Cultura e identidad obrera: Colombia, 1910–1945. Bogotá: Cinep, 1991. 475 p.: bibl.

Innovative social history of working class highlights its emergence in Bogotá, Medellín, Barranquilla, and Barrancabermeja. Uses printed sources and nearly 80 oral interviews to discuss daily life, experiences of men and women workers, strikes, union activity, labor legislation, and political participation. Traces transformation of laborers' image from the "pobre" to the "pueblo."

2622 Bergquist, Charles. In the name of history: a disciplinary critique of Orlando Fals Borda's *Historia doble de la costa.* (*LARR*, 25:3, 1990, p. 156–176)

Bergquist responds to Fals Borda's "revolutionary challenge" by analyzing the implications of his *Historia doble de la costa* (see *HLAS 51:4747*) from the perspective of the discipline of history. Concludes that Fals Borda "unwittingly subverts democratic intent" of his multivolume work by "intentionally violating" three basic principles which historians take for granted. Required reading for those trying to come to terms with *Historia doble.*

2623 Betancourt E., Darío and **Martha L. García B.** Matones y cuadrilleros: origen y evolución de la violencia en el occidente colombiano, 1946–1965. Bogotá: UN, Instituto de Estudios Políticos y Relaciones Internacionales; Tercer Mundo Editores, 1990. 217 p.: bibl., ill., maps. (Sociología y política)

Well-researched and well-written article draws on archival and oral testimony to analyze three phases of *La Violencia* in the Valle dept.: 1) colonization and agrarian conflict, 1910–46; 2) conservative violence of guerrilla groups called "pájaros," 1946–57; and 3) bandit groups, 1955–65. Reflects new direction in *Violencia* studies by emphasizing criminal rather than ideological motives.

2624 Bushnell, David. The making of modern Colombia: a nation in spite of itself. Berkeley: Univ. of California Press, 1993. 334 p.: bibl., ill., index, maps.

Leading North American Colombianist draws on five decades of research to write the first one-volume survey of Colombian history published in English in the last 30 years. Argues that Colombians have overcome social, cultural, political, and regional antagonisms to achieve nationhood. Excellent bibliography. Authoritatively and engagingly written. Outstanding introduction to this enigmatic country.

2625 Cacua Prada, Antonio. Salvador Camacho Roldán. Tunja, Colombia: Academia Boyacense de Historia, 1990. 282 p.: bibl., port. (Biblioteca de la Academia Boyacense de Historia: Serie Obras fundamentales; 9)

Pedestrian biography of Camacho Roldán (1827–1900), a businessman, politician, and liberal intellectual who is credited with introducing the study of sociology at the Univ. Nacional in 1882. Includes long excerpts from his numerous writings but lacks footnotes and index. Possible starting point for a more serious study of this important 19th-century figure.

2626 Carnegie-Williams, Rosa. Un año en los Andes, o, Aventuras de una *lady* en Bogotá. Traducción de Luis Enrique Jiménez Llana-Vezga. Bogotá: Academia de Historia de Bogotá; Tercer Mundo Editores, 1990. 158 p., 16 p. of plates: ill. (Col. Viajantes y viajeros)

Diary of English woman who accompanied her husband to Colombia in 1881 and 1882. Includes descriptions of Cartagena, the Magdalena River trip, and Bogotá. Valuable as the only known traveler's account written by a woman that deals with 19th-century Colombia. Helpful introduction by Alfredo Iriarte and translator Luis Enrique Jiménez Llaña-Vezga. Lacks index.

2627 Colmenares, Germán et al. Ensayos de historia económica de Colombia. Bogotá: Legis; ACCE, 1990. 148 p.: (Col. Fondo Editorial)

Nine stimulating essays by members of the Academia Colombiana de Ciencias Económicas. Colmenares, Caballero and Bejarano examine colonial institutions and practices; Ocampo and Misas reassess the 19th century; and Bejarano, Ospina, Escovar, and Consuegra construct theoretical frameworks geared to understanding the Colombian economy in the 1990s.

2628 Colmenares, Germán et al. La independencia: ensayos de historia social. Bogotá: Instituto Colombiano de Cultura, Subdirección de Comunicaciones Culturales,

1986. 186 p.: bibl., ill. (Col. Popular. Col. Autores nacionales; 3a ser., no. 7)

Stimulating essays reflect the cutting-edge of regional historical research being done by the faculty at the Univ. del Valle. Zamira Díaz de Zuluaga compares working conditions of Indians and black slaves in haciendas and mines; Jorge Escorcia analyzes the caste system between 1820–54; Francisco Zuluaga explores the influence of patron-client relations on royalist support and emergence of caudillismo. Germán Colmenares compares regional and population patterns and their long-term social consequences. In a second essay, he argues that historians need to challenge the conclusions of José Manuel Restrepo whose works have long formed the bedrock of studies on early New Granada.

2629 La colonización antioqueña.
FICDUCAL; Gobernación de Caldas. Manizales, Colombia: Impr. Departamental; FIDUCAL; Gobernación de Caldes, 1989. 265 p.: bibl. (Biblioteca de escritores caldenses)

Nine papers presented at seminar held in Manizales in Nov. 1987 reveal the continuing popularity of topic and growing sophistication of research since the publication of James Parsons' *Antioqueñan colonization in Western Colombia* (Berkeley, 1949). Especially notable are Parsons' reflections about his original work and Jaime Jarramillo Uribe's assessment of significance of Antioqueñan colonization within the framework of Colombian national history.

2630 Delpar, Helen. Soledad Romań de Núñez: a president's wife. (*in* The human tradition in Latin America: the nineteenth century. Edited by Judith Ewell and William H. Beezley. Wilmington, Del.: Scholarly Resources, 1989, p. 128–140, bibl.)

Román (1835–1924), the second wife of Rafael Núñez, was a controversial figure in her lifetime. This carefully-crafted biographical sketch emphasizes her defiance of conventional society and argues that her story disproves the widely-held stereotype that Latin American women were completely dominated by their fathers and husbands.

2631 Escobar Rodríguez, Carmen. La revolución liberal y la protesta del artesanado. Bogotá: Fundación Universitaria Autónoma de Colombia, Fondo de Publicaciones; Ediciones Fondo Editorial Suramérica, 1990. 390 p.: bibl.

Tesis de grado examines development of artisan movement in early 19th century from a Marxist perspective, relying mostly on published sources. Author concludes that artisan protest of 1854 was "the first manifestation of urban popular struggles against the power of the landowners, large merchants and nascent dependency to international capitalism" (p. 309). Includes 16 documents and bibliography.

2632 Escorcia S., José. Las vías de comunicación en la provincia de Cartagena: siglo XIX. (*Hist. Espac.*, 14, junio 1991, p. 113–124)

Concise, clearly-written essay discusses the efforts by colonial and 19th-century authorities to break down the geographic isolation of Cartagena from the Colombian interior by establishing direct transit to the Magdalena via the Canal del Dique, building roads, and eventually, a railroad.

2633 Galvis, Silvia and **Alberto Donadío.** El jefe supremo: Rojas Pinilla, en la violencia y el poder. Bogotá: Planeta, 1988. 589 p.: bibl., ill., index. (Espejo de Colombia)

Definitive biography covers career of Rojas up to his overthrow in 1957. Authors, both investigative journalists, combine an exhaustive examination of archival extant documents in Colombia and recently declassified US State Department materials with interviews of key figures of the era. They explain how Rojas and "his closest relatives and collaborators succeeded in squandering in less than four years the most sincere, joyful and unanimous national backing ever given in this century to a Colombian president" (p. 15).

2634 Gaviria Liévano, Enrique. Nuestro archipiélago de San Andrés y la Mosquitia colombiana. Bogotá: Academia Colombiana de Historia; Plaza & Janés/Historia, 1984. 378 p.: bibl., ill., index, maps. (Complemento a la Historia extensa de Colombia; 9)

Study of Colombia's diplomatic efforts to establish sovereignty over the Mosquito Coast and the San Andrés Archipelago. Includes texts of 11 treaties signed between 1825–1972. Prologue by Virgilio Barco discusses the international context as of 1984.

2635 Gómez, Augusto. Indios, colonos y conflictos: una historia regional de los Llanos Orientales, 1870–1970. Bogotá: Siglo XXI Editores; Pontificia Univ. Javeriana; Instituto Colombiano de Antropología, 1991. 411 p.: bibl., ill. (some col.), maps.

History of colonization of the Llanos Orientales since 1870. Anthropologist-historian uses archival materials and oral testimonies to assess impact of settlers from the interior on the indigenous communities and the expansion of cattle ranching on physical environment. Analysis of interethnic conflict especially valuable. See also *Boletin Americanista* (Vol. 31, Nos. 39/40, p. 79) for a summary of this book.

2636 González Arias, José Jairo and Elsy Marulanda Alvarez. Historias de frontera: colonización y guerras en el Sumapaz. Bogotá: Centro de Investigación y Educación Popular, 1990. 236 p.: bibl., ill., maps (some col.)

Transcription of four oral accounts by Sumapaz colonists describes their efforts to settle the land and the impact of *La Violencia* between 1928–57. Introductory chapter by editors provides context for memoirs which offer unique insight into relations between campesino population and guerrillas.

2637 Helguera, J. León and Jo Ann Rayfield. Adolfo León Gómez, 1858–1927: Colombian literateur, social critic and nationalist. (*SECOLAS Ann.*, 22, March 1991, p. 5–16)

An introduction to the life, writings, and ideas of León Gómez who was a Liberal, jurist, and journalist. As editor and contributor to *Sur América* from 1903–27, he emphasized the need for Colombians to develop attitudes, values and habits that would strengthen the country.

2638 Jaramillo Castillo, Carlos Eduardo. Los guerrilleros del novecientos. Bogotá: CEREC, 1991. 416 p.: bibl., ill. (Serie Historia contemporánea y realidad nacional; 29)

Groundbreaking analysis of War of a Thousand Days (1899–1903) based on archival sources and oral tradition. Provides political and economic overview but focuses on characteristic phenomena of irregular guerrilla warfare. Includes chapters on methods of fighting, role of women and children, espionage systems, food and alcohol, folklore, etc., as well as list of 355 guerrilla bands and chronology of all battles. Thorough and fascinating.

2639 Lemaitre, Eduardo. Contra viento y marea: la lucha de Rafael Núñez por el poder. Bogotá: Instituto Caro y Cuervo, 1990.

306 p., 15 leaves of plates: bibl., ill. (Serie La Granada entreabierta; 53)

Renowned Cartagena historian reviews life and work of Núñez between 1863–86 and asserts that he made his most important contributions during this period. Work is based on 40 short essays published weekly in 1975 in *El Diario de la Costa*. Complements *Núñez y la leyenda negra* (Bogotá, 1977) by same author.

2640 Llinás, Juan Pablo. Felipe Angulo y la regeneración. Bogotá: Tercer Mundo Editores, 1989. 235 p.: bibl., index.

Angulo (1854–1912) served as Núñez's minister of hacienda and minister of war in 1884–86 and was later implicated in the so-called "Petit Panama" railroad scandal of 1893. Llinás uses archival and published sources to trace his career, shedding light on some of the murkier aspects of Regeneration.

2641 Londoño V., Patricia. Las publicaciones periódicas dirigidas a la mujer, 1858–1930. (*Bol. Cult. Bibliogr.*, 27:23, 1990, p. 3–23, appendices, ill.)

Author analyzes content of 41 Colombian periodicals directed toward women published between 1858–1956. She charts changing editorial interest from predominantly literary articles in the 19th century to those concerning the "modern woman" between 1910–30 to the varied religious, frivolous, and suffrage movement articles that appeared between 1930–56. Well-written and lavishly illustrated.

2642 Marcucci Vera, César Rolando. General José Ma. Campo Serrano: 1832–1915. Santa Marta, Colombia: Litografía Costa y Mar, 1986. 343 p.: ill.

Detailed biography of major 19th-century political leader from Atlantic Coast. Campo Serrano (1832–1915) was president of Magdalena during the Federation (1863–85) and held numerous positions in Núñez's cabinets during Regeneration. Lacks footnotes but includes many documents concerning his career.

2643 Marulanda Alvarez, Elsy. Colonización y conflicto: las lecciones del Sumapaz. Bogotá: UN, Instituto de Estudios Políticos y Relaciones Internacionales; Tercer Mundo Editores, 1991. 293 p.: bibl., maps. (Sociología y política)

Examination of frontier expansion, development, and consolidation through case study of the occupation and colonization of Sumapaz province from 1870–1965. Author emphasizes conflicts over land, the impact of Law 200 of 1936, and *La Violencia*. Based on extensive archival research including the heretofore untapped Archivo de Los Juzgados de Tierras in Fusagasugá.

2644 Medina, Medófilo. Colombia: violencia política y económica en dos coyunturas; 1945–1950, 1984–1988. (*Síntesis/Madrid*, 9, sept./dic. 1989, p. 240–270, tables)

Insightful comparative analysis of triangular relationship between violence, economic growth, and human rights in two recent periods of Colombian history. Argues that peace is impossible until a collective consciousness develops among the majority of Colombians about the need for national consensus.

2645 Melo, Jorge Orlando. Predecir el pasado: ensayos de historia de Colombia. Bogotá: Fundación Simón y Lola Guberek, 1992. 229 p.: bibl. (Col. Historia; 4)

Nine sparkling essays by leading scholar, all previously unpublished. Topics include Colombian historiography since 1960, colonial culture, the evolution of national identity, history of science, impact of violence, and Colombia's prospect for the future. Well-written and immensely stimulating.

2646 Molina, Gerardo. Gerardo Molina: el magisterio de la política; antología. Edición de Darío Acevedo C. Bogotá: Tercer Mundo Editores, 1992. 419 p.: bibl., ill. (Pensamiento político colombiano)

Anthology of writings on history and political theory by Gerardo Molina (1906–1991), an influential Liberal intellectual, political activist, and leftist presidential candidate in 1982. Includes a prologue by Jorge Orlando Melo, a biographical sketch, and an interview conducted by the editor.

2647 Molina Londoño, Luis Fernando. Empresas y empresarios del siglo XIX en Antioquia: el caso de don Leocadio María Arango. (*Rev. Antioq. Econ. Desarro.*, 32, 1990, p. 60–70, ill.)

Arango (1831–1918) headed the Zancudo Mining Corporation and was one of Antioquia's wealthiest and most influential entrepreneurs of the era. Study based on a university thesis examines his career as busi-

nessman and collector of antiquities. Also considers role of family corporations in Colombian economic history. Excellent bibliography.

2648 Morelli, Sandra. La Revolución Francesa y la administración territorial en Colombia: perspectivas comparadas. Bogotá: Univ. Externado de Colombia, 1991. 348 p.: bibl. (Ordenamiento territorial)

Diachronic study assesses influence of post-Revolutionary French local administrative practices on Colombian constitutions, territorial organization, and legislation from Independence to present. Based on thesis in administrative science presented at Univ. of Bologna. Analysis of recent constitutional change is especially helpful. Includes some data in Italian and French.

2649 Moreno, Pablo. La educación protestante durante la modernización de la educación en Colombia, 1869–1928. (*Cristianismo Soc.*, 29:107, 1991, p. 69–87, bibl.)

Asserts that through the creation of schools between 1869–1928 Protestant missionaries became a permanent force in Colombian society despite the power monopoly exerted by the Catholic Church after adoption of the 1886 Constitution. Serious, pioneering essay on an increasingly important topic.

2650 Ortiz, Alvaro Pablo and **Oscar Lara.** Operación Cobra: historia de una gesta romántica; relato de los acontecimientos ocurridos el 2 de mayo de 1958. Bogotá: Forelia, 1988. 261 p., 12 p. of plates: facsims., ill., ports.

Documents related to failed coup of May 2, 1958 led by Lt. Col. Hernando Forrero who sought to return Rojas Pinilla to power and unseat the caretaker military junta supported by civilian politicians. Editors have assembled statements by protagonists that throw light on an event never fully investigated by the Lleras Camargo Administration.

2651 Pacheco G., Margarita R. La fiesta Liberal en Cali. Cali, Colombia: Ediciones Univ. del Valle, 1992. 204 p.: bibl. (Col. Pensamiento)

Well-documented analysis of Liberal reform era in Cali 1848–54. Argues that elites promoted development of export crops to link local economy to international markets and saw education of popular classes as essential to the process of modernization. Also traces popular response to these efforts.

2652 Reales Orozco, Antonio. Bolívar frente a los médicos y la medicina. Bogotá: Tercer Mundo Editores. 1988. 203 p.: bibl., ill.

Distinguished Barranquilla psychiatrist examines Bolívar's difficult relations with his doctors, the psychosomatic aspects of his physical ailments, the reasons for his wholesale rejection of medical prescriptions, and evaluates the advice given him by Dr. Santiago Gastelbondo two months before his death. Includes biographical data on most of the doctors. Well-written and researched.

2653 Restrepo, Juan Pablo. La Iglesia y el Estado en Colombia. v. 1–2. Prólogo de Fernán González. Ed. tomada de la impresa en Londres en 1885. Bogotá: Banco Popular, 1987. 2 v. (Biblioteca Banco Popular; 132–133)

Classic apologetic work originally published in 1885. Erudite scholar discusses *patronato real*, mortmain, tithes, religious orders, and many other topics as they developed in three eras of Church-State relations: the colony; the Republic before 1861; and the Republic after 1861. Prologue by Fernán González provides political and religious context.

2654 Restrepo Forero, Olga. Sociedades de naturalistas: la ciencia decimonónica en Colombia. (*Rev. Acad. Colomb. Cienc.,* 18:68, mayo 1991, p. 53–64, bibl.)

Sociologist surveys the development of scientific societies between 1830–1930 and discusses the role of their members. She concludes that these associations enhanced the social and political status of members more than they contributed to expansion of scientific investigation. Brief but helpful synthesis.

2655 Reyes, Rafael. Memorias, 1850–1885. Bogotá: Fondo Cultural Cafetero, 1986. 303 p.: ill., maps, ports.

Reyes was a legislator, explorer, diplomat, and dictator-president of Colombia from 1904–09. His memoirs, written in 1911 and published here for first time, provide insight into his career before 1890. Included are accounts of early family life, Amazon explorations, quinine and rubber business ventures, and campaigns in the War of 1885. Prologue by Alvaro Gómez Hurtado.

2656 Rozo Acuña, Eduardo. Bolívar y la organización de los poderes públicos. Bogotá: Editorial Temis, 1988. 218 p.: bibl.

Sophisticated study analyzes evolution of Bolívar's political ideas by systematic comparison of the Constitutions of 1811, 1819, 1821, 1826, 1828, and 1830. Concludes that Bolívar was a creative political thinker, that he rejected monarchy, and that liberty and equality were the unifying concepts in all of his government charters.

2657 Safford, Frank. Race, integration, and progress: elite attitudes and the Indian in Colombia, 1750–1870. (*HAHR,* 71:1, Feb. 1991, p. 1–33)

Uses archival material to examine elite attitudes toward Indians and Afro-Colombians and their incorporation into the dominant Hispanic society. Elites, who regarded the economic backwardness of the Indians as a constraint on progress, sought their integration through division of communal lands and miscegenation. Argues that Afro-Colombians were seen as a threat to social order but endowed with "untapped economic potential."

2658 Sánchez Gómez, Gonzalo. Guerra y política en la sociedad colombiana. (*Anál. Pol.,* 11, sept./dic. 1990, p. 7–27)

Leading historian of *La Violencia* examines the role of war and politics in Colombian life from 1840s to present. Concludes that the State has been the most prominent victim of the strife of the 1980s and adds that, while other Latin American countries are concerned about economic viability, "Colombia is questioning itself about its political viability."

2659 Santana R., Pedro *et al.* Bogotá, 450 años: retos y realidades. Bogotá: Foro Nacional por Colombia; Instituto Francés de Estudios Andinos, 1988. 379 p.: bibl., ill. (Tomo 36 de la Col. Travaux de l'IFEA. Col. Ciudad y democracia)

Six essays by social scientists mark the 450th anniversary of Bogotá's founding. Authors emphasize 20th-century topics such as population growth, development of public services (electricity, water, public transport), and voting patterns within city. Stresses need for political, administrative, and financial restructuring if city is to meet demands of the 21st century. Includes documents that describe Bogotá in 1938 and 1948.

2660 Simposio de Historia de Los Llanos Colombo-Venezolanos, 1st, Villavicencio, Colombia, 1988. Los Llanos: una historia sin fronteras. Bogotá: Academia de Historia del Meta, 1988. 513 p.: bibl., maps.

Twenty-six conference papers, most of high quality, on topics that include: archaeology, ethnohistory, biography, economy, independence era, conflicts and colonization in 19th and 20th centuries, regional studies, and historical methodology. Reflects awakening interest in a region long neglected by scholars.

2661 Sowell, David. The early Colombian labor movement: artisans and politics in Bogotá, 1832–1919. Philadelphia: Temple Univ. Press, 1992. 269 p.: bibl., index, map.

Describes development of artisan labor organizations and traces their political activity between 1832–1919 to show how craftsmen articulated their interests through temporary electoral groups, broad-based demonstrations, mutual aid societies and direct action. Includes stimulating synthesis of recent literature on 19th-century Colombian political history. A related article by Sowell, "The 1893 *Bogotazo*: Artisans and Public Violence in Late Nineteenth-Century Bogotá," appeared in *Journal of Latin American Studies* (Vol. 21, No. 2, May 1989, p. 267).

2662 Steuart, John. Narración de una expedición a la capital de la Nueva Granada y residencia allí de once meses: Bogotá en 1836–37. Bogotá: Academia de Historia de Bogotá; Tercer Mundo Editores, 1989. 264 p.: ill. (some col.) (Col. Viajantes y viajeros)

Steuart was a Scottish entrepreneur who attempted unsuccessfully to establish a hat factory in Bogotá. Good description of life in Bogotá, and along the Magdalena River. Valuable introductions by Pilar Moreno de Angel and the translator, Luis Enrique Jiménez Llaña-Vezga. Illustrated with reproductions of seven watercolors but lacks index.

2663 Tirado Mejía, Alvaro. Sobre historia y literatura. Bogotá: Fundación Simón y Lola Guberek, 1991. 287 p.: (Col. Historia; 1)

Anthology of 22 previously-published essays by leading social historian organized under three headings: "On Colombian History;" "Studies about Antioquia;" and "Newspaper Articles, Prologues and Speeches." Includes "Algunas Características Regionales de Colombia" and "La Revolución en Marcha y la Reforma Constitutional de 1936."

Uribe A., María Victoria. Matar, rematar y contramatar: las masacres de La Violencia en El Tolima, 1948–1964. See *HLAS 53:1265.*

2664 Valencia Llano, Albeiro. Manizales en la dinámica colonizadora, 1846–1930. Manizales, Colombia: Univ. de Caldas, Fondo Editorial, 1990. 342 p., 10 p. of plates: bibl., ill., maps (some col.) (Serie Ciencias sociales y filosofía)

Analysis of the foundation and evolution of Manizales in the context of the colonization of southern Antioquia that began in the mid-19th century. Discusses efforts of Medellín to improve road and rail transportation and explains how some settlers became entrepreneurs. Excellent contribution to study of Colombian frontiers.

2665 Varela B., Edgar. La cultura de la violencia en Colombia durante el s. XIX. Cali, Colombia: Impr. Departamental del Valle, 1990. 119 p.:

Author explores roots of culture of violence in Colombia by examining the way institutions and cultural elements have worked together to legitimize violent political actions in 19th and 20th centuries. Draws on sociological theory and published historical works to explain why some individuals such as Obando and Mosquera were absolved of criminal behavior while others were punished.

2666 Vega Cantor, Renán. Colombia entre la democracia y el imperio: aproximaciones históricas a la turbulenta vida nacional del siglo XX. Bogotá: Editorial El Búho: Editorial Códice, 1989. 322 p.: bibl., ill.

Nine essays offer fresh look at pivotal 20th-century Colombian events such as the Banana Massacre, the war in Leticia and the overthrow of Rojas Pinilla. Working from a Marxist-dependista perspective, Vega Cantor challenges such "castrating myths" as "Olaya Herrera, the genuinely 'nationalist' president." Engagingly written for popular audience. Includes bibliographies and is extensively illustrated with contemporary cartoons. Well worth reading.

2667 Zuluaga R., Francisco U. José María Obando: de soldado realista a caudillo republicano Bogotá: Fondo de Promoción de la Cultura del Banco Popular, 1985. 119 p.: bibl., ill., map. (Biblioteca Banco Popular; 123)

Obando (1795–1861), patriot general,

caudillo of Cauca, vice-president (1831–32), and president (1853–57) is controversial because of unproven accusations that he ordered the assassination of Sucre. Zuluaga critiques previous interpretations and traces his career up to 1832. Obando emerges as a charismatic leader whose actions were shaped by regional conditions and clientelismo. Extensive bibliography of archival and printed sources.

ECUADOR

2668 Achig Subía, Lucas and **Diego Mora Castro.** Exacción tributaria y motines indígenas en el Azuay, 1830–1895. (*Rev. Arch. Nac. Hist. Azuay,* 7, 1987, p. 82–104)

Shows that colonial tithes and taxes on Indians of Azuay persisted throughout the 19th century as a way to maintain the power of State and Church over the natives and to extract the greatest profit from their labor. Uses archival sources to emphasize active and passive resistance of Indians to oppressive levies.

2669 Ayala Mora, Enrique. Historia, compromiso y política: ensayos sobre historiografía ecuatoriana. Quito: Planeta, 1989. 114 p.: (Col. País de la mitad; 10)

Leading scholar analyzes major 19th- and 20th-century works by Ecuadorian historians from the point of view of "relación historia-política-compromiso." Includes 14 short essays addressed to a popular audience. Though some essays are previously published, when taken as a whole, the volume is an important contribution to Ecuadorian historiography.

Bonilla, Heraclio. Lecciones del endeudamiento externo en los países andinos antes de la Primera Guerra Mundial. See item **2701.**

Castillo Jácome, Julio. Historia de la Provincia de Tungurahua. v. 1–2. See item **2325.**

2670 Congreso El Negro en la Historia, *2nd, Esmeraldas, Ecuador, 1990 [and] Jornadas de Historia Social y Genealogía, (11th, Esmeraldas, Ecuador, 1990.)* El negro en la historia: aportes para el conocimiento de las raíces en América Latina. Coordinación de Rafael Savoia. Quito: Centro Cultural Afro-Ecuatoriano, Depto. de Pastoral Afro-Ecuatoriano, 1990. 230 p.: bibl. (Col. SAG; 57. Col. CCA; 2)

Eighteen papers presented at joint 1990 conference held in Esmeraldas. Topics cover colonial and national eras and include biography, genealogy, slavery, and demography. Papers are of uneven quality but reflect continuing interest in recovering the African contribution to Ecuadorian history. For the first conference see *HLAS 52: 2416.*

2671 Cordero Palacios, Octavio. Estudios históricos: selección. Quito: Banco Central del Ecuador; Cuenca: Centro de Investigación y Cultura, 1986. 565 p.: bibl. (Col. histórica; 9)

Reprints three standard works on history of Cuenca and its district. The first is an essay on prehistory of Azuay, the second is Cordero's magnum opus on the short-lived Republic of Cuenca (1820–22), and the third is his sketch of *precursor* Abdón Calderón. [M.T. Hamerly]

2672 Demélas, Marie-Danielle and **Yves Saint-Geours.** Jerusalén y Babilonia: religión y política en el Ecuador, 1780–1880. Quito: Corporación Editora Nacional, 1988. 222 p.: (Biblioteca de ciencias sociales; 21)

Translation of monograph written by two French scholars in 1984. Authors focus on Quito Rebellion (1809–12), the Rocafuerte Administration (1835–43), and dictatorship of García Moreno (1859–75) to demonstrate survival of Catholic tradition from colonial times to late 19th century. Based on archival material collected in Ecuador, Paris, and Madrid.

2673 Estrada Ycaza, Julio and **Clemente Yerovi Indaburu.** El siglo de los vapores fluviales, 1840–1940. Guayaquil, Ecuador: Instituto de Historia Marítima, 1992. 287 p.: bibl., ill.

Unique manual of steam navigation based on memoirs of a former captain. Includes drawings and mechanical specifications of individual ships. Discusses operation problems, crews, and cargo. Interesting contribution to transportation history.

2674 Fazio Fernández, Mariano. El Guayaquil colombiano, 1822–1830. Guayaquil, Ecuador: Banco Central del Ecuador, Subgerencia del Centro de Investigación y Cultura; Archivo Histórico del Guayas, 1988. 453 p.: bibl. (Col. monográfica; 18)

This major contribution traces political evolution of Guayaquil from annexation

by Colombia to definitive separation from Bogotá in 1830. Also examines three aspects of
Guayaquil life in the 1820s: economy and society; religion; press and culture. Includes documents that show development of political process. Based on research in Guayaquil archives.

2675 Gándara Enríquez, Marcos. La semana
trágica de Guayaquil, noviembre de
1922: aproximación a la verdad. Quito: Sociedad Ecuatoriana de Investigaciones Históricas
y Geográficas, 1991. 486 p.: bibl., ill., index.

Army general challenges leftist denunciations of the military repression of massive
1922 labor strike in Guayaquil. After reviewing key descriptions of the events, he states
that the situation "was extremely complicated in its causes, in its brief but intensive
development, and in its consequences"
(p. 292). Appendices include 26 important
documents and excerpts from 23 historians
who have examined the 1922 incident between 1929–90.

2676 Gimeno, Ana. Una tentativa monár-
quica en América: el caso ecuatoriano.
Prólogo de Jaime Delgado Martín y palabras
preliminares de Demetrio Ramos. Quito:
Centro de Investigación y Cultura, Banco
Central del Ecuador, 1988. 496 p.: bibl. (Col.
histórica; 18)

Definitive study of failed expedition of
Gen. Juan José Flores to reestablish a monarchy in 1846 suggests that the scheme was
only the "tip of the iceberg" of monarchial
plots throughout Spanish America. For this
doctoral thesis completed at the Univ. of Valladolid, the author made an exhaustive review of archives in Spain, Ecuador, and Venezuela. Also throws light on Flores' personality
and career.

Jurado Noboa, Fernando and **Miguel A. Puga.**
El proceso de blanqueamiento en el Ecuador:
de los Puento a los Egas [de Fernando Jurado
Noboa]. Los Puentos en Cayambe y Taba-
cundo: siglos XVI al XVII [de Miguel A. Puga].
See item **2335.**

Jurado Noboa, Fernando. Sancho Hacho: orígenes de la formación mestiza ecuatoriana.
See item **2336.**

2677 Luna Tamayo, Milton. Estado: regionalización y lucha política del Ecuador,
1800–1869. (Rev. Arch. Nac. Hist. Azuay, 7,
1987, p. 105–127)

Refutes thesis that Ecuadorian State
was an "accidental geographic space" by examining many factors that contributed to
continuous revolts and civil wars of early national period. Stresses that regional struggle
had local, departmental, and "national" overtones and that its political expressions were
varied according to developments in social
and political life of the country.

Luna Tamayo, Milton. Historia y conciencia
popular: el artesanado en Quito, economía,
organización y vida cotidiana, 1890–1930.
See *HLAS 53:5253.*

2678 Neruda, Pablo et al. En defensa de
Manuela Sáenz: la libertadora del Libertador. Edición de Arturo Valero Martínez.
Selección de textos y coordinación de Carlos
Calderón Chico. Guayaquil, Ecuador: Editorial del Pacífico, 1988? 215 p., 8 leaves of
plates: bibl., ill.

Reactions by 36 Venezuelan and Ecuadorian scholars to Densil Romero's controversial novel *La esposa del Dr. Thorne*, which received a literary prize in 1988 from Spanish
publisher, Tusquets. The Ecuadorian Sociedad Bolivariana condemned the book for "de-
faming the memory of the Quito heroine"
since it focuses exclusively on her sexual activities. Several authors point out that Romero's literary Manuela has little connection
with the historical figure. Cecilia Ansaldo
Briones' thoughtful prologue helps to clarify
issues. Includes bibliography of works about
Sáenz.

2679 Nueva historia del Ecuador. Edición de
Enrique Ayala Mora. Quito: Corporación Editora Nacional; Grijalbo, 1983–1992.
15 v.: ill. (some col.), maps.

This projected 15-volume series provides up-to-date synthesis of recent scholarship on Ecuadorian history from precolumbian times to the present. Series is designed
for students and general readers. Each volume
contains chapters on related topics by recognized specialists. There are also excerpts from
key documents, helpful summaries, maps,
and bibliographies but no indexes. Vols. 1–2
cover "Epoca aborigen" (see item **745**); vols.
3–5 deal with the colonial period (see *HLAS
52:2114*); vols. 6–9 with 19th century (see
items **2680, 2681, 2682,** and *HLAS 52: 2419*);
vol. 10 deals with 20th century (see item
2683), as will vols. 11–13; vol. 14 offers a

chronology of Ecuadorian history; and vol. 15 will make available an anthology of documents.

2680 Nueva historia del Ecuador. v. 6, Independencia y período colombiano. Edición de Enrique Ayala Mora. Quito: Corporación Editora Nacional; Grijalbo, 1989. 1 v.: bibl., ill. (some col.)

Seven essays by six scholars examine the Independence era, emphasizing social movements rather than individual heroic actions. Two general chapters review international setting and Spanish American struggle for independence. The others are specific to Ecuador covering the course of the war; economy and society; Enlightenment; power groups; and Ecuador within Gran Colombia.

2681 Nueva historia del Ecuador. v. 7, Epoca republicana. Edición de Enrique Ayala Mora. Quito: Corporación Editora Nacional; Grijalbo, 1990. 1 v.: bibl., ill. (some col.)

Seven scholars survey 19th-century socioeconomic conditions in the Sierra and on the coast and examine accounts of the principal events between 1830–95, including the founding of the republic, the García Moreno era (1860–75), and progressive era (1875–95). Emphasis is on regional differences and weakness of national institutions.

2682 Nueva historia del Ecuador. v. 8, Epoca republicana. Edición de Enrique Ayala Mora. Quito: Corporación Editora Nacional; Grijalbo, 1990. 1 v.: bibl., ill. (some col.)

Six essays deal with various aspects of 19th-century history including Church-State relations; evolution of Indian communities; literature; art and architecture; Ecuadorian thought; and family, city, and daily life.

2683 Nueva historia del Ecuador. v. 10, Epoca republicana. Edición de Enrique Ayala Mora. Quito: Corporación Editora Nacional; Grijalbo, 1990. 1 v.: bibl., ill. (some col.)

Byron Cardoso Cascate provides an overview of world history between 1920–60 and six other scholars deal with specific aspects of Ecuador's development during this period. Topics covered include the economy; process of industrialization up to 1940; political history 1925–60; the labor movement; 20th-century peasant movements; and culture, art, and ideology.

2684 Osculati, Gaetano. Esplorazione delle regioni equatoriali: lungo el napo ed il fiume delle Amazzoni. Torino, Italy: Il Segnalibro, 1990. 344 p.: facsims., ill., index.

Photofacsimile reprint of second ed. (Milan, 1854) of Italian naturalist's account of his 1846–48 voyage of exploration between Guayaquil, Ecuador and Belém, Brazil. Includes useful introduction by Guaraldo and quality reproductions of his pen and ink sketches and water colors. [M.T. Hamerly]

2685 Padilla J., Washington. La iglesia y los dioses modernos: historia del protestantismo en el Ecuador. Quito: Corporación Editora Nacional, 1989. 455 p.: bibl., maps. (Biblioteca de ciencias sociales; 23)

Pioneering survey of Protestantism from early 19th century to 1980s. Ecuadorian-born author, a Protestant minister, argues that Protestantism must divorce itself from foreign, liberal, capitalist ties and return to basic Christian principals in order to fulfill its mission in Ecuador. Set within broader context of national history; objective in tone, and based on published sources and missionary archives.

2686 Palomeque, Silvia. Cuenca en el siglo XIX: la articulación de una región. Quito: Facultad Latinoamericana de Ciencias Sociales; Abya-Yala, 1990. 296 p.: bibl., ill. (Col. Tesis: Historia; 2)

Argentine historian uses archival material to examine 19th-century economic and social history of Cuenca (including modern provinces of Azuay and Cañar). Three carefully-argued essays analyze data on exports, population movements, and land tenure. Concludes that Cuenca developed in response to its internal dynamics and not those of the neighboring coast.

2687 Pineo, Ronn F. Misery and death in the Pearl of the Pacific: health care in Guayaquil, Ecuador, 1870–1925. (*HAHR*, 70:4, Nov. 1990, p. 609–637, tables)

Case study of Guayaquil health conditions with particular attention to the working class. Balanced approach based on dissertation research. Concludes that although death rates declined between 1870 and 1925, efforts of city officials to improve disease control did not keep pace with needs. Compared with similar tropical ports, Guayaquil was a "disgrace." For Jackson's critique of this article and Pineo's response, see *Hispanic American Historical Review*, Vol. 71, No. 2, May 1991.

2688 Pineo, Ronn F. Reinterpreting labor militancy: the collapse of the cacao economy and the general strike of 1922 in Guayaquil, Ecuador. (*HAHR*, 68:4, Nov. 1988, p. 708–736)

Draws on dissertation research to demonstrate that Nov. 1922 general strike in Guayaquil was a spontaneous response by workers protesting the severe downward slide in their standard of living caused by the collapse of the cacao export economy. Stimulating essay that challenges the widely-held generalization that foreign-born anarchists precipitated Latin America's post WWI strikes.

2689 Ponce Leiva, Pilar. Gabriel García Moreno. Quito: Editorial El Conejo, 1990. 130 p.: bibl. (Col. Ecuador/historia)

Brief but thoughtful biography rejects the myths surrounding García Moreno to present him as "simply a product of his time, his country and his continent" (p. 124). Based on published sources.

2690 Romero y Cordero, Remigio. El ejército en cien años de vida republicana, 1830–1930. Quito?: Centro de Estudios Históricos del Ejército Ecuatoriano, 1991. 491 p. (Biblioteca del ejército ecuatoriano; 1)

History of the Ecuadorian army first published in the journal *Ejército Nacional* in 1930 lacks footnotes or bibliography but does serve as introduction to topic. Second edition features a critical summary of the work by Gen. Marcos Gándara Enríquez.

2691 Valarezo, Galo Ramón. Los indios y la constitución del Estado nacional. (*in* Los Andes en la encrucijada: indios, comunidades y Estado en el siglo XIX. Quito: Ediciones Libri Mundi, 1991, p. 419–455, appendix, bibl., table)

Uses archival data from Cayambe zone to show that Creoles imposed their ideal state over the traditional views of state held by Indians before conquest. By the 19th century Indians had formed their own stateless society within the Ecuadorian republic as a radical way of denying the Creole State. Includes list of 41 Indian rebellions from 1700–1803.

2692 Vega Ugalde, Silvia. Ecuador: crisis políticas y Estado en los inicios de la república. Quito: Facultad Latinoamericana de Ciencias Sociales, Sede Ecuador: ABYA-YALA, 1991. 163 p.: bibl., index. (Col. Tesis: Historia)

Sociopolitical theory covers 1830–45. Uses archival sources to demonstrate that after 1835 there was a clear, conscious attempt by landowners to control the central State apparatus and subordinate to it the Church, army, and local authorities.

2693 Visión actual de José Peralta. Quito: Fundación Friedrich Naumann, 1989. 667 p.: bibl.

Twenty papers presented at 1988 national seminar held in Cuenca. Ecuadorian historians and social scientists explore contemporary assessments of José Peralta (1855–1937), an influential Liberal ideologue, journalist, author, politician, and diplomat. Topics include Peralta's support of lay education, his philosophical works, essays on antiimperialism, and contributions to Liberal thought at the turn of the century.

2694 Ycaza, Patricio. Historia del movimiento obrero ecuatoriano. v. 2, De la influencia de la táctica del Frente Popular a las luchas del FUT. 2a ed. rev. Quito: Centro de Documentación e Información de los Movimientos Sociales del Ecuador, 1984–1991. 1 v.: bibl., ill. (Col. Análisis histórico; 1)

Well-written and researched history of the working class movement from 1935–91 uses Marxist framework. Includes excellent chronology of key events and bibliography.

Peru

NILS P. JACOBSEN, *Associate Professor, University of Illinois, Urbana-Champaign*

HISTORIOGRAPHY ON REPUBLICAN PERU appears to be in a phase of transition. Though no single paradigm or methodology predominates, structuralist and quantitative studies still play a considerable role, often associated with approaches relying on dependency theory, Marxism, or modernization theory. But a younger generation of scholars is slowly and cautiously applying new political, cultural, and intellectual approaches to the study of Peruvian history. The openness and lack of definition of the current intellectual climate has allowed a blending of paradigms and an unorthodox, but often fruitful crossing of topical boundaries. For instance, one work discusses epidemics in conjunction with state-building projects, and another treats specific modern peasant movements along with a historical reconstruction of Indian ethnic identity through collective memory. Thus, some works canvassed in the present volume extend our knowledge on well-studied topics or synthesize knowledge accumulated during the past two decades within now conventional perspectives, while others apply new paradigms or revisionist and, at times, controversial interpretations to well-studied themes. Previously neglected topics of Peru's republican history are also discussed. While some topics noted in preceding *HLAS* volumes as urgently needing attention have finally found their authors (notably the history of public health), others, such as the history of the bureaucracy, the military, gender relations, and taxation, continue to be largely neglected.

The spate of partisan publications on APRA history, so numerous in *HLAS 52* due to the García Administration (1985–90), has abated, although a few previously overlooked titles from the late 1980s are annotated here. Luis Alva Castro's editions of Haya de la Torre's and Luis Alberto Sánchez's articles published in *El Tiempo* of Bogotá during the late 1940s and early 1950s clarify the thought of leading apristas in the crucial transition years of the party's political orientation (items **2738** and **2777**). In the early 1990s, we are seeing more balanced, critical assessments of APRA's impact on Peruvian politics (items **2752** and **2751**), many of which demonstrate the tension between authoritarianism and democracy in Peru's most important social reformist and populist political movement of the 20th century.

"New political history," the attempt to link politics in a more critical manner with its social and ideological implications and the global horizon in which it unfolds, is also addressed in several essays. Peralta Ruiz deftly links State finances in post-independence Cusco with the contest for power between Indian communities, large landholders, and an incipient—largely local and provincial -bureaucracy to show how the rising mestizo class used political offices to gain power and prestige in the countryside (item **2764**). Orrego Penagos traces the social roots of the Civilista Party to the rise of a new republican business elite around the key figure of Domingo Elias, and demonstrates that this earlier *civilismo avant la lettre*, despite its reformism, was hampered from the beginning by its social exclusivism (item **2761**). Chiaramonti suggests the paradox of late-19th-century electoral reforms, which were intended to give greater access to opposition groups in elections, but effectively strengthened oligarchic control on the national and provincial level (item **2712**). Castillo Ochoa's discussion of Sánchez Cerro's political base during the 1930s pinpoints what he views as an exceptional situation, but what in fact has been a recurrent pattern of Peruvian politics over the past 100 years: conservative authoritarian political projects muster considerable popular support (item **2751**).

The War of the Pacific and its aftermath still draws considerable attention, and deservedly so. But rather than focusing on military and diplomatic aspects, historians are now analyzing the profound political, economic, and social ruptures produced by this greatest crisis of the Peruvian polity between the wars of independence and the 1980s (items **2735**, **2754**, **2724**, **2731**, **2708**, and **2706**). This vigorous debate about the very nature of the Peruvian nation-building process began in the early 1980s.

In a broader sense, social movements of various kinds have become a major concern of Peruvianist historians. Husson offers a novel and cogent interpretation of two unusual "Indian rebellions" in the south-central sierra province of Huanta during the 1820s and 1890s, which he views as alliances between Indian peasants and members of the provincial elite against newly rising sociopolitical groups (item **2741**). Several authors offer insights into the broad social movement of peasants and urban indigenista allies that convulsed the southern sierra during the early 1920s. Luis Miguel Glave examines the conflictive construction of collective identities through historical memory in Canas and Espinar provinces and emphasizes that what provincial elites labelled Indian rebellions were often nothing more than the legal and public assertion of citizenship and property rights (item **2730**). In the Altiplano of Puno department, Calisto also finds that "everyday forms of resistance" by Indian peasantry—an influential notion developed for Southeast Asian peasantries by James Scott—were much more common ways of counteracting elite exploitation than militant rebellion (item **2705**). Augusto Ramos Zambrano, though, reminds us that, at least at the height of the southern sierra's broad social movement of the early 1920s, militant local peasant rebellions in the Altiplano could be swift and quite bloody (item **2771**). The accomplished work by Rénique discusses the whole sweep of political and cultural debates and social movements in Cusco from 1895 to the late 1980s, thus placing the upheaval of the early 1920s in a broader context (item **2774**). Rénique chronicles regionalist responses to increasing centralization from Lima, and finds the elite responses becoming weaker after 1930, while popular movements went through several additional militant cycles in the mid- and late 20th century. Simultaneous rural movements in the northern sierra, discussed by Apel, seem to have had a more pragmatic bent than those in the south and were favored by the effective brokerage of socialist politician Hildebrando Castro Pozo (item **2697**).

In contrast to the flourishing of urban labor history in other parts of Latin America, no works related to Peruvian unions, strikes, or factory workers were viewed in this period. Nonetheless, there is growing interest in the insurrectionary potential of another largely urbanized group: high school and university students who have proved such an important constituency for Maoist rebels during the past decades. Nicolás Lynch's critical study of Maoist student leaders at San Marcos University during the 1970s unveils the paradox between their ultra-radical rhetoric and the almost clientelistic political practice of young men who, however sincerely they believed their own speeches, were greatly concerned with upward social mobility and overcoming the sense of alienation from middle class Limeño society they felt due to their modest provincial origins (item **2753**). The benchmark study by Portocarrero and Oliart demonstrates convincingly that during the 1970s and 1980s an intellectually closed, one-dimensional discourse on Peruvian history and society—informed by dependency notions and the lessons of Maoist school teachers—did become widely diffused among school-age youths in Lima and in the provinces (item **2767**). Those who wish to understand the cultural dimensions of Peru's current crisis and the decade-long success of Sendero Luminoso must take those findings into account. In the eastern piedmont of the central Andes, on the other hand, the encounter by an authochtonous ethnic group with MIR guerrillas under Guillermo Lobatón in 1965 produced a very different social movement: the interpretation of the guerrillas as returning ancient cultural heroes, one episode of the recurring Asháninka millenarian movements eloquently chronicled by Brown and Fernández (item **2702**).

In addition to studies of "Indian rebellions" and rural social movements, a number of essays deal with peasants and peasant communities in the Highlands, clearly a topic of still growing interest among historians. Concerns focus on issues of land (items **2715** and **2707**), communal offices and their change through government reforms (item **2721**), State policies towards communities (item **2760**), and the impact of taxation on the communities (items **2764** and **2700**). While the conflict between those who stress the survival of an "Andean" worldview and institutions in the communities, and those focusing on class conflicts and market orientation by peasants continues, there does seem to be a growing agreement that Indian communities were highly adaptable and changing entities, influenced by and responsive to pressures and opportunities in the wider economic and political system. Altamirano's study on the peasant economy in Puno department during the early post-independence period deserves special mention, because he is one of the first Andean-ist historians to highlight the vital role of artesanal crafts for the reproduction of many peasant households (item **2696**).

By contrast, recent publications on coastal agriculture have been scarce, and often merely synthesize or repeat notions developed over the past two decades (items **2695** and **2765**). There are two major exceptions: Gonzales' study of tenant farming in the cotton growing area south of Lima which demonstrates how market forces helped shift a labor regime, born in the 1890s out of labor scarcity, to increasing control and profitability for the landlord (item **2733**); and Gómez Cumpa's painstaking reconstruction of the economic effects of Chilean occupation on the rural economy of Chiclayo during the 1880s (item **2731**).

Among the few works in the present reporting period that deal with urban society, Parker's essay on white-collar employees in early 20th-century Lima stands out (item **2763**). His amply documented thesis suggests that we need to recalibrate our notions of social stratification in Peru's most modern city during a time when presumably the transition to capitalism was in full swing and hence a class-based stratification should have jelled. Parker relies largely on criteria employed by the historical subjects themselves to relate their own standing vis-à-vis that of fellow Limeños, and finds a polarized notion of status based on family honor, education, and "life styles." Although the author does not say so (and might in fact disagree), I would suggest that this polarized notion of social status, between an amorphous and vast underclass and the *gente decente*, was not a direct colonial heritage, but rather grew out of the collapse of the colonial caste society after the mid-19th century. Looking at Lima's society in the same era through the prism of elite and popular culture, Elmore detects a conflictive and ambiguous modernization decades before the massive changes of Leguia's *oncenio* (item **2722**). In the much more conservative urban setting of Cusco during the early post-independence decades, Krüggeler focuses on the surprising permanence of a crucial and insufficiently studied social group, urban artisans (item **2747**). His study further undermines the authority of the dependency approach for provincial societies and highlights strong links between urban and rural economies.

Our understanding of the final phase of slavery in Peru has been furthered by two solid publications. Blanchard's judicious, balanced overview is the first monograph on the institution and its abolition between the 1820s and 1854 (item **2699**). He emphasizes the continued economic importance of slavery even after the end of the slave trade, and suggests that it required an unrelated crisis—the Civil War of 1854–55—to bring about its demise. In contrast, Hünefeldt's more narrowly focused study assigns greater weight to the actions of the slaves themselves in the downfall of Peruvian slavery (item **2740**).

Although there were few studies of immigration in the present reporting period, two deserve mention, one for its controversial thesis, and the other for its suggestive methodology. French geographer Lausent-Herrera's brief overview of the history of Japanese immigration to Peru greatly emphasizes the imperialist and ultra-nationalist goals pursued by the powerful promoters of emigration in Japan as well as by certain ideologues in Peru's Japanese community itself (item **2750**). All along, the author writes, Peru was to have become a Latin American beachhead for a Japanese-controlled interest zone. Hampe Martínez's essay on prominent European immigrants during the 19th century demonstrates the usefulness of parish records to trace the Peruvian trajectory of such newcomers (item **2737**).

Three exemplary articles by Cueto demonstrate the great value of studying Peruvian public health policies during the past century (items **2718, 2719,** and **2717**). They combine detailed information about epidemics with issues concerning the extension of State power to various regions and localities, and with popular conceptions regarding science, disease, and governmental interference in local affairs. These articles show that the study of seemingly technical subjects can throw much light onto the whole fiber of a regional or local society and its reaction to external intervention. During this biennium, the sole study of demographic history of republican Peru is Gootenberg's broad discussion for the 1820s-60s period (item **2734**). Gootenberg carefully analyzes previously unknown population figures for 1827 and highlights the essential stability of the indigenous percentage of Peru's total population between the 1790s and 1876, thus helping to discredit some of the more unreliable and simply imaginative population figures for the period. Yet however much Gootenberg was able to "rationalize" Peru's early republican population history, major problems continue to lurk that will probably only be solved with studies of mortality and natality based on parish records.

A complementary study to Klaiber's important social history of the Catholic Church since independence (item **2746** and *HLAS 52:2489*) is García Jordán's painstakingly researched work on the history of Church-State relations during the first century after independence (item **2727**). This major study offers both more detail than Klaiber on many legislative and ideological battles, and a distinct, rather pessimistic interpretation of the Church's role in the construction of a more inclusive Peruvian polity. Both works will undoubtedly remain crucial reference works for further studies of the Church and religiosity for years to come.

Explicitly economic histories have been sparse during the present reporting period. One outstanding exception is Alfonso Quiroz's major study of Peru's credit institutions and markets between the mid-19th and mid-20th centuries (item **2768**). Influenced by the current neoliberal climate in economic thought, the author reevaluates the era of export growth before the World Depression as beneficial for Peru's development, but ironically views increasing State interventionism in subsequent decades as fostering rather than impeding oligopolization. This work, along with a wealth of data on credit itself, offers broad new insights into the rise of Peru's modern economy.

One further genre of historical writing that had been quite vigorous in the past also seems to have dropped off recently: historical "monographs" of districts, towns, or provinces, often written by untrained local historians, and thus a rich source for insights into popular visions of history. In a more scholarly vein, this biennium includes *Historia general de Arequipa,* the first general history of a city and department outside of Lima written by professional historians (item **2759**). Although uneven in quality, there exists, to my knowledge, no comparable work for any other Peruvian city except Lima. Perhaps this massive volume portends the professionalization of regionally and locally focused historiography in Peru's provinces.

Before closing I would like to mention the stunning volume of photographs by Hans Heinrich Brüning covering the north coast between the 1880s and 1920 (item 2703). Many themes of concern to today's historians are brought to life in these pictures, from everyday life in peasant villages, to work on sugar plantations, civil and religious festivities, and the construction of prominent buildings or structures. Hopefully more such collections of historical photographs can find their way to publication.

Abos-Padilla Urzúa, Ricardo. El tratado secreto Perú-Boliviano visto por diplomáticos de terceros países. See item **2781.**

2695 Alfageme, Augusta. Haciendas y terratenientes azucareros en el siglo XIX. (*Análisis/Lima,* 14, 1990, p. 47–77, bibl.)

Conventional overview of Peru's sugar production and trade during the 19th century. Author stresses the enormous increase in production, the "monopolization" among a handful of very large estates, and the formation of a powerful class of sugar estate owners with increasing influence in politics.

2696 Altamirano, Nelson. La economía campesina de Puno, 1820–1840: repercusiones de la presencia militar y la producción textil. (*Allpanchis/Cusco,* 23:37, primer semestre 1991, p. 93–130, appendices, bibl., tables)

This suggestive revisionist article examines artesanal production and trade, especially that involving textiles. Argues that the industry has been much more important for the subsistence of Indian peasants in the Southern Andes than previously thought. Different production arrangements and trading strategies resulted in significant social differentiation within communities. Conclusions are based on complex calculations of contemporary population, production, and trade statistics.

Amich, José; Fernando Pallares; and **Vicente Calvo.** Historia de las misiones del Convento de Santa Rosa de Ocopa. See item **2357.**

2697 Apel, Karin. Luchas y reivindicaciones de los yanaconas en las haciendas de la sierra piurana en los años 1934–35. (*Bull. Inst. fr. étud. andin.,* 20:2, 1991, p. 353–564)

With the help of organizers from the Socialist Party (Hildebrando Castro Pozo and others), the tenants and sharecroppers of estates in the sierra of Piura dept. negotiated contracts with the landlords that abolished unpaid services and abusive treatment and raised wages. Article is based on research with the yanaconas' claims and contracts.

2698 Aranda de los Ríos, Ramón and **Carmela Sotomayor Roggero.** Sublevación de campesinos negros en Chincha, 1879. Lima: Herrera Editores, 1990. 61 p.: bibl., ill.

Brief, imprecise account of an uprising of black estate workers (ex-slaves) on coastal sugar haciendas south of Lima. Directed against landlord abuses, the uprising occurred in the context of an elite split connected to national dissent over the War of the Pacific.

2699 Blanchard, Peter. Slavery and abolition in early republican Peru. Wilmington, Del.: SR Books, 1992. 247 p.: bibl., index. (Latin American silhouettes)

Despite its declining numbers, slavery remained an important institution after Peru's independence and slave-owners mounted a partially successful campaign to countermand the ameliorative legislation of San Martín and Bolívar. Slave resistance, economic modernization, abolitionists, and international pressure all helped to undermine the institution, but abolition occurred only after a major civil war was fought over other issues. A thoroughly researched, judicious work.

2700 Bonilla, Heraclio. Estado y tributo campesino: la experiencia de Ayacucho. (*in* Los Andes en la encrucijada: indios, comunidades y Estado en el siglo XIX. Quito: Ediciones Libri Mundi, 1991, p. 335–366, bibl., tables)

Author examines the Indian head tax during the first 75 years after independence in Ayacucho dept. and the constant resistance against payment by the Indian peasantry. The head tax meant that Indians carried a large share of the burden of sustaining the political system, while local officials intervened to channel these resources into their own pockets.

2701 Bonilla, Heraclio. Lecciones del endeudamiento externo en los países andinos antes de la Primera Guerra Mundial. (*Rev. Ecuat. Hist. Econ.,* 3:5, primer trimestre 1989, p. 79–92, table)

The level of foreign debt for Andean countries directly corresponds to their integration into world markets. In Peru large foreign debts contributed to the destruction of the country's productive potential. In Ecuador and Bolivia foreign debt remained minimal before World War II.

2702 Brown, Michael Fobes and **Eduardo Fernández.** War of shadows: the struggle for utopia in the Peruvian Amazon. Berkeley: Univ. of California Press, 1991. 280 p.: bibl., ill., index, maps.

Elegantly written history of the impact of and reaction to Western contacts by Asháninka people. The account focuses on the guerrilla campaign of Movimiento de Izquierda Revolucionaria's Túpac Amaru column in Asháninka lands of the central Peruvian Andes during 1965. Authors suggest that this ethnic group repeatedly reinterpreted Western intrusions through millenarian notions, thus expressing the people's fiercely autonomous cultural traditions. The book contains new information on the 1960s guerrilla campaigns.

2703 Brüning, Hans Heinrich. Fotodokumente aus Nordperu von Hans Heinrich Brüning, 1848–1928 = Documentos fotográficos del norte del Perú de Juan Enrique Brüning, 1848–1928. Selección y edición de Corinna Raddatz. Hamburg: Hamburgisches Museum für Völkerkunde, 1990. 144 p.: bibl., chiefly ill.

Excellent edition of Brüning's marvelous photographs taken between the 1880s and 1920. They cover everything from landscape and architecture to ceremonies, work and everyday life in towns, villages and sugar estates, from Piura to Lima. The photographs are preceded by introductory essays on the life and work of Brüning whose importance for northern Peru's ethnohistory has just begun to be appreciated.

2704 Cablegramas chilenos durante la ocupación de Lima, julio-octubre 1881. (*Bol. Lima*, 11:63, mayo 1989, p. 7–16, photos)

This collection of cables sent by Chilean occupation authorities to inform their government about peace negotiations, provisioning of occupation troops, and Peruvian financial and commercial matters affords important glimpses into the mechanics and uncertainties of occupation.

Cahill, David P. Independencia, sociedad y fiscalidad: el sur andino, 1780–1880. See item **2362.**

2705 Calisto, Marcela. Campesinos puneños y resistencia cotidiana, 1900–1930. (*Allpanchis/Cusco*, 23:37, primer semestre 1991, p. 169–202, bibl.)

Non-violent peasant resistance to exploitative demands by large landholders, local authorities, and traders was pervasive in the Peruvian Altiplano during the early 20th century, indicating the limits of elite power in the countryside. Militant rebellion was only a means of last resort but became more widespread after the rise of local indigenista organizations in the 1920s. Based on solid research into primary sources.

2706 Campaña de la Breña: colección de documentos inéditos, 1881–1884. Recopilación de Luis Guzmán Palomino. Lima: Centro de Estudios Histórico-Militares del Perú, 1990. 400 p.: bibl.

Contrary to title, some of these collected documents have been published previously (in contemporary newspapers and books). Document selection is tendentious, seeking to glorify Andrés Avelino Cáceres and denigrate his political adversaries (Iglesias and Piérola). Still, this volume offers much to students of the political and social conflicts that arose during the campaign against the Chilean occupying forces. Documents cover everything from Indian rebellions to party politics and the movement of guerrilla forces.

2707 Cañedo-Argüelles Fabrega, Teresa. Integración de las comunidades campesinas en el Perú contemporáneo: ¿supervivencia o fin? (*Anu. Estud. Am.*, 48, 1991, p. 633–667)

Examination of land tenure, agrarian reform, and the effects of capitalism in a highland community of Moquegua dept. since 1940.

2708 Carpio Muñoz, Juan G. et al. Arequipa en la guerra con Chile. Lima: Editorial y Productora Gráfica Nuevo Mundo, 1991. 259 p.: bibl.

Articles underscore Arequipa's patriotic stand during the War of the Pacific, especially when Lizardo Montero's government was installed in the city (Aug. 1882-Oct. 1883) and during the Chilean occupation (Oct.-Dec. 1883). Includes some new information on acts of resistance against occupiers and popular culture during the war.

2709 Carranza, Luis. La ciencia en el Perú en el siglo XIX: selección de artículos publicados. t. 1. Lima: Editorial Eddili, 1988. 1 v.: bibl., ill.

Selection of papers of Luis Carranza (1843–98), medical doctor, journalist, founder of the "Sociedad Geográfica de Lima," and politician. Works include studies on climate, geography, archaeology, ethnography, politics, and travel descriptions on central Peru. Carranza's scientific work was heavily influenced by positivism and evolutionism.

2710 El caso Haya de la Torre: derecho de asilo. v. 1–2. Recopilación y estudio de Luis Alva Castro y Javier Valle Riestra. Lima: NICOLSA, 1989. 2 v. (675 p.)

Selective, uncritical APRA edition of the diplomatic correspondence and judicial documents relating to Haya de la Torre's exile in the Colombian Embassy in Lima (1949–54).

2711 Cayo Córdova, Percy. Un intento colonizador en el Perú de 1835. (*Apuntes/Lima*, 23, segundo semestre 1988, p. 165–175)

Spanish translation of a report by General William Miller, published in England in 1836, of his 1835 exploration of the piedmont and lowlands east and north of Cusco for the purpose of establishing a military colony. Contains keen ethnographic and natural history observations.

2712 Chiaramonti, Gabriella. Riforma elettorale e centralismo notabilare a Trujillo, Perú, tra Otto e Novecento. (*Quad. Stor.*, 69:3, dic. 1988, p. 903–927)

Electoral reforms of 1892 and 1896 abolished indirect elections and the violence associated with them on the parish level, but created a more centralized and vertical system. Rather than a stronger central State, the regional oligarchy increasingly came to control the electoral machine through the Junta Electoral Nacional and similar bodies on the provincial level. Important article based on research with voting acts in Trujillo prov.

2713 Clayton, Lawrence A. William Russell Grace: merchant adventurer. (*in* The human tradition in Latin America: the nineteenth century. Edited by Judith Ewell and William H. Beezley. Wilmington, Del.: Scholarly Resouces, 1989, p. 189–203, bibl.)

Brief, uncritical biographical sketch of Irish-born businessman (1832–1904) who par-

leyed a life of trade and shipping centered on Peru into the formation of the first inter-American transnational corporation and a successful public career culminating in two terms as mayor of New York.

Coloma Porcari, César. Documentos inéditos para la historia de la Magdalena y el valle de Lima, 1557–1889. See item **2368**.

2714 Comisión para Escribir la Historia Marítima del Perú. Historia marítima del Perú. v. 12, pt. 1, La República 1884–1906. 3. ed., corr. Lima: Instituto de Estudios Histórico-Marítimos del Perú, 1991. 1 v.: bibl., ill., indexes, maps (some col.)

Written by an accomplished academic historian, this is one of the most informative and balanced volumes in the maritime history series. Chapters deal with rebuilding of the Peruvian navy after the War of the Pacific, maritime routes, traffic, ports and shipping lines, and the exploration of and navigation on the Amazon river system, central for late 19th-century development plans. Notes contain much biographical information on navy officers and persons connected with the merchant marine and Amazon explorations.

2715 Contreras, Carlos. Conflictos intercomunales en la Sierra Central, siglos XIX y XX. (*in* Los Andes en la encrucijada: indios, comunidades y Estado en el siglo XIX. Quito: Ediciones Libri Mundi, 1991, p. 199–219, appendix, bibl.)

Indian communities of the central Peruvian Mantaro valley seldom appeared before courts or notaries during the first 50 years after independence, but did so increasingly after 1870. Author analyzes and classifies types of intercommunal conflicts, which were more frequent than conflicts with large landholders, and interprets them largely as a result of increasing commercial and demographic pressures. Through these conflicts and subsequent splintering, the number of communities has steadily risen since the late 19th century.

Contreras, Carlos and **Jorge Bracamonte.** Rumi Maqui en la Sierra Central: documentos inéditos de 1907. See *HLAS 53:1323*.

2716 Cornejo Polar, Jorge. El Estado peruano y la cuestión del pluralismo cultural. Lima: Univ. de Lima, Facultad de Ciencias Humanas, 1991. 216 p.: bibl. (Cuadernos de historia; 13)

Elementary, conventional overview of "cultural" policies (regarding Indians and education) between 1895 and 1985 is based on secondary literature.

2717 Cueto, Marcos. La ciudad y las ratas: la peste bubónica en Lima y en la costa peruana a comienzos del siglo veinte. (*Histórica/Lima*, 15:1, junio 1991, p. 1–26, bibl.)

The 1903 outbreak of bubonic plague in Lima and in most coastal ports led to the organization of an authoritarian sanitary control apparatus by the Peruvian State. Such policies revealed a mistrust of modern science by large parts of population, and a resistance of popular groups to intrusive and damaging State policies. Important article based on primary research.

2718 Cueto, Marcos. Epidemia y sociedad en el Valle de La Convención, 1932. (*Allpanchis/Cusco*, 23:38, segundo semestre 1991, p. 153–187, bibl., tables)

Author analyzes a malaria epidemic in the hot Andean piedmont valleys north of Cusco (1932–33), which left 6–10,000 people dead. Details sluggish and ineffective response of government and large landholders, and blames the nature of the region's colonization and exploitation of laboring tenants for the epidemic's horrendous sweep.

2719 Cueto, Marcos. Sanitation from above: yellow fever and foreign intervention in Peru, 1919–1922. (*HAHR*, 72:1, Feb. 1992, p. 1–22)

A campaign to halt a yellow-fever epidemic on the north coast, largely financed by the Rockefeller Foundation and carried out by US public health experts, was an important part of President Leguía's project to increase State power in the provinces and replicated the authoritarian character of his regime. The campaign, which showed total disregard for cultural traditions of health care, contributed to growing nationalism among professional and common people. Based on extensive primary research.

2720 Descripciones del Callao: textos, planos grabados y fotografías, siglos XVI al XIX. Recopilación de Francisco Quiroz. Callao, Peru: Centro de Investigaciones Históricas del Callao; Instituto Nacional de Cultura, 1990. 238 p.: maps.

Some 40 brief excerpts from the works of chroniclers, scientists, and travellers de-

scribe Callao, 1550–1880. Includes numerous plans and other illustrations of both town and port, some of them rare.

2721 Diez Hurtado, Alejandro. Las comunidades indígenas de Ayabaca: la segunda infancia, 1930–1950. (*Alternativa/Chiclayo*, 17, julio 1992, p. 85–111, bibl., tables)

Official recognition of Indian communities in the northern Peruvian sierra of Piura dept. during the 1930s and 1940s led to profound changes in land tenure and political structure. Article is based on rarely used files presented to the Bureau of Indian Affairs by communities in order to achieve recognition.

2722 Elmore, Peter. Lima: puertas a la modernidad; modernización y experiencia urbana a principios de siglo. (*Cuad. Am.*, 5:6, nov./dic. 1991, p. 104–123)

Thoughtful evocation of cultural change in early 20th-century Lima covers city planning, elite essayistic and fictional writing, popular sports, and music. Author sees a conflictive and partial modernization of Lima's culture antedating Leguía's *oncenio* (1919–31) by a quarter century.

2723 Espinoza Soriano, Waldemar. Cajamarca en la bibliografía histórica regional, nacional e internacional, 1534–1985. (*Bol. Lima*, 10:56, marzo 1988, p. 11–22, bibl.)

Annotated bibliography on the history of Cajamarca from the pre-Incaic era to early 20th century.

2724 Favre, Henri. Remarques sur la lutte des classes au Pérou pendant la guerre du Pacifique. (*Bull. Inst. fr. étud. andin.*, 19:2, 1990, p. 413–430, bibl.)

Based on local sources and collective memory in central highland villages, author postulates that Indian resistance to Chileans during and after War of the Pacific was a social movement and not an expression of nationalism. He underscores the conflict between local notables within the communities and large landholders. Local notables used nationalism as strategy for upward social mobility to legitimize taking resources from hacendados.

2725 Ferreyros, Manuel Bartolomé. Manuel Ferreyros y la patria peruana: epistolario, 1836–1839. Recopilación de Celia Wu Brading. Lima: Pontificia Univ. Católica del Perú, Fondo Editorial, 1991. 363 p.: bibl., 1 port.

Correspondence of important nationalist politician and publicist in exile in Guayaquil during the Peruvian-Bolivian Confederation of Andrés Santa Cruz. Editor's introductory study of Ferreyros' life highlights his influence with key nationalist caudillos such as Gamarra and Salaverry.

2726 García Jordán, Pilar. La cruz y el caucho, o el conflicto permanente: indios, caucheros y frailes en San León del Amazonas en los inicios del siglo XX. (*in* Encuentros Debate América Latina Ayer y Hoy, *3rd, Barcelona, 1991.* Conquista y resistencia en la historia de América. Barcelona: Publicacions Univ. de Barcelona, 1992, p. 301–316, maps)

After sporadic and isolated missionary efforts in the Amazon Lowlands during the 19th century, the Peruvian government approved the creation of three apostolic prefectures in 1898 to administer missionary activities; this was seen as the most effective way to "civilize" tribal Indians. Article focuses on the frustrating experience of Augustinian friars in the northernmost apostolic prefecture, San León del Amazonas. The friars were constantly exploited and undermined by the rubber companies and the missionaries were incapable of halting the horrendous exploitation of the Indians.

2727 García Jordán, Pilar. Iglesia y poder en el Perú contemporáneo, 1821–1919. Cusco, Peru: Centro de Estudios Regionales Andinos Bartolomé de Las Casas, 1991. 393 p.: (Archivos de historia andina; 12)

Most thorough study to date of Church-State relations during the century after independence. Author highlights relatively mild nature of conflict between liberal administrations and the Peruvian episcopate, since both needed one another to sustain their power. She posits the rise of a combative "national Catholicism" since 1870s and the renewed strength of the Church in society and politics since early 1900s after decades of growing weakness due to reasons of ideology, declining revenues, and lack of ordained priests. The work chronicles many legislative battles over Church-State relations, and is an important tool for further research on these issues.

2728 García Jordán, Pilar. Problemática de la incorporación de las selvas amazónicas a los Estados Nacionales Latinoamericanos,

S. XIX-XX. (*in* Jornadas de Historiadores Americanistas. *2nd, Granada, Spain, 1989.* América: encuentro y asimilación. Edición de Joaquín A. Muñoz Mendoza. Granada: Diputación Provincial de Granada, 1990, p. 131–140)

Overview of State and Church missionary policies in Amazonian Lowlands during the 19th century. Even liberal governments supported missions as a means to open rainforest areas inhabited by tribal Indians for economic penetration and State control.

2729 Gargurevich, Juan. Historia de la prensa peruana, 1594–1990. Lima: La Voz Ediciones, 1991. 286 p.: bibl.

Well-known journalist and student of Peruvian press history offers a narrative overview of newspapers and periodicals since colonial period. The work is organized both by historical periods and according to changes in press-orientation and technology. Includes considerable information on press politics and on leading journalists and editors in Lima but little on organization of press enterprises, circulation, or the provincial press.

2730 Glave, Luis Miguel. Los campesinos leen su historia: un caso de identidad recreada y creación colectiva de imágenes; los comuneros canas 1920–1930. (*Rev. Indias,* 50:190, sept./dic. 1990, p. 809–849)

Indian movements and repressive campaigns by local mestizo powerholders in provinces of Canas and Espinar (Cusco dept.) between 1921 and 1931 are viewed as conflictive recreations and renovations of collective identities, based on myths and the communities' historical memories. For the same text with more complete notes and bibliography see Heraclio Bonilla, ed., *Los Andes en la encrucijada: indios, comunidades y Estado en el siglo XIX,* p. 221–73 (Quito: Ed. Libri Mundi, 1991).

2731 Gómez Cumpa, José. Economía agraria de Lambayeque y la guerra, 1879–1886. (*Alternativa/Chiclayo,* 17, julio 1992, p. 113–161, bibl., graphs, tables)

Detailed analysis of effects of Chilean occupation on Lambayeque dept. The heavy forced contributions demanded by occupation authorities, on top of d struction and market dislocations, impoverished Chiclayo's urban and rural economy and contributed to restructuring of agricultural production and land tenure. Based on primary sources.

2732 Gonzáles, Michael J. El control de los hacendados y resistencia de los trabajadores en el norte del Perú, 1880–1921. (*HISLA/Lima*, 13/14, 1er y 2do semestre 1989, p. 39–54, bibl., tables)

Brief overview of north coast sugar haciendas' modernization, labor regime and early labor movements, 1890s-1920s.

2733 Gonzáles, Michael J. The rise of cotton tenant farming in Peru, 1890–1920: the Condor Valley. (*Agric. Hist.*, 65:1, Winter 1991, p. 51–71, tables)

Tenancy and sharecropping developed on south coast cotton estates after the decline of coolie system in the 1890s. Owners reaped increasing profits when cotton prices rose during WWI, but conditions for tenants deteriorated. Cotton tenants moved from individual to organized resistance later than sugar workers. Based on research of correspondence and accounts from an estate near Pisco.

2734 Gootenberg, Paul. Population and ethnicity in early republican Peru: some revisions. (*LARR*, 26:3, 1991, p. 109–157, bibl., tables)

On the basis of an 1827 census, not previously known in its entirety, author develops new estimates for Peru's total population and ethnic composition for the immediate post-independence period. Gootenberg underscores stability of Indian population from 1790s-1860s, and suggests that mestizaje accelerated later than previously thought. Methodologically rigorous discussion of all published demographic data for early republican period.

2735 Guerra, Margarita. La ocupación de Lima, 1881–1883: el gobierno de García Calderón. Lima: Pontificia Univ. Católica del Perú, Dirección Académica de Investigación, Instituto Riva-Agüero, 1991. 355 p., 2 leaves of plates: bibl., index, ports.

Book examines politics and society in Lima from defeat of Peruvian army at Miraflores (Jan. 15, 1881) to capture and deportation of provisional President Francisco García Calderón by Chilean occupation forces (Nov. 6, 1881). Although written from a nationalistic perspective, the book is well-researched and balanced on internal Peruvian political disputes. Author seeks to show García Calderón as honorable and brave political leader, whose popular support, almost nil at the outset of his government, had grown considerably by the time of his removal by Chileans.

2736 Guillén Marroquín, Jesús. La economía agraria del Cusco, 1900–1980. Cusco: Centro de Estudios Rurales Andinos Bartolomé de las Casas, 1989. 415 p.: bibl., ill. (Debates andinos; 16)

Economist provides detailed quantitative study of agricultural production, demand, prices, and credit facilities for Andean and subtropical products in Cusco dept. Author demonstrates the varying conjunctures and structural development of Andean products (wool, meat, cereals) and subtropical products (coffee, cacao, sugar, coca), with some of the latter still experiencing growth after 1950. Andean products did not keep up with demand due to unstable markets, low productivity, adverse government policies and social conflicts. Based on neo-orthodox model highlighting the importance of interregional markets for Cusco's agriculture.

2737 Hampe Martínez, Teodoro. Una dinámica de integración social: inmigrantes europeos y norteamericanos en Lima, siglo XIX. (*Ibero-Am. Arch.*, 17:4, 1991, p. 343–372, bibl., table)

Author uses the records of a Lima parish to trace the history of prominent European and North American immigrants during the 19th century and their marriage to Peruvian women.

2738 Haya de la Torre, Víctor Raúl. Víctor Raúl en *El Tiempo.* v. 1–2. Prólogo de Luis Alberto Sánchez. Colofón de Germán Arciniegas. Recopilación y edición de Luis Alva Castro. Lima: L. Alva Castro, 1988. 2 v. (712 p.): facsim., port.

From 1948–69 Haya de la Torre's articles regularly appeared in Bogotá's *El Tiempo,* published and edited by important friends and supporters of Haya before his exile in the Colombian embassy. The articles cover international politics, cultural issues, and his memories of earlier encounters with important contemporary figures. Articles contain nothing directly on Peruvian politics but help to reveal the evolution of Haya's thought.

2739 Historia de Cajamarca. v. 4, Siglo XIX. Recopilación de Fernando Silva Santisteban *et al.* Cajamarca: Instituto Nacional de Cultura, Cajamarca; Corporación de Desarrollo de Cajamarca, 1989. 1 v.: bibl., ill. (Biblioteca Cajamarca)

Anthology of works on Peru's northernmost Sierra dept. between late colonial period and 1870s includes travel accounts (Humboldt, Stevenson, Maw, Raimondi), political studies, essays on José Galvez and his family, regional newspapers and mining.

2740 Hünefeldt, Christine. Lasmanuelos, vida cotidiana de una familia negra en la Lima del S. XIX: una reflexión histórica sobre la esclavitud urbana. Lima: Instituto de Estudios Peruanos, 1992. 60 p.: bibl. (Col. Mínima; 27)

Brief portrait of slaves in Lima and surrounding valleys during decades leading up to abolition in 1854. Work stresses importance of ties between city and countryside and the slaves' own strategies to achieve freedom as crucial for the decay of Peru's slavery system. Based on thorough research.

2741 Husson, Patrick. De la guerra a la rebelión: Huanta, siglo XIX. Cusco: Centro de Estudios Regionales Andinos Bartolomé de Las Casas; Instituto Francés de Estudios Andinos, 1992. 246 p.: bibl. (Archivos de historia andina; 14. Travaux de l'IFEA; 67)

Analyzes two extraordinary rebellions in the Andean province of Huanta: 1) the "War of the Iquichanos" (1825–27), a monarchist reaction to the recently established republic; and 2) the "Salt Rebellion" (1896–97) against the Piérola Administration, recent victor of a bloody civil war. Author stresses coalition between Indian peasants and members of the provincial elite against newly rising socio-political groups. Suggestive and sophisticated interpretation based on outdated literature.

2742 Jacobsen, Nils. Campesinos y tenencia de la tierra en el Altiplano peruano en la transición de la Colonia a la República. (*Allpanchis/Cusco*, 23:37, primer trimestre 1991, p. 25–92, bibl.)

Essay seeks to bridge the intellectual gap between debates over Bourbon colonial land reform policies and intense struggle to control *altiplano* land in late 18th- and early 19th-century Peru. Asserts that the early independence period Ministry of Hacienda reports reveal that liberal economic policies resulted in advantages to poor and landless peasants over big landlords and other *gamonales* in the struggle to control pasture lands and communal holdings. This interpretation contrasts sharply with received wisdom on the effects of liberal policy. Argues that this was a consequence of the continuation of Bourbon policies by Peruvian liberals and that not until after 1850 did land tenure rulings privilege elites and severely attack communal rights. *Forasteros* gained over *originarios*, a reinterpretation that demands careful attention. [V. Peloso]

2743 Jacobsen, Nils. Civilization and its barbarism: the inevitability of Juan Bustamante's failure. (*in* The human tradition in Latin America: the nineteenth century. Edited by Judith Ewell and William H. Beezley. Wilmington, Del.:SR Books, 1989, p. 82–102, bibl.)

Thought-provoking study of the mestizo political leader of a neglected highlands uprising in 1867, this biographical sketch focuses on the restless personality of the protagonist, his many experiences from Highland businessman to congressional deputy and world traveler. Rising class and ethnic consciousness led Bustamante to severely criticize the social effects of industrialization in Peru. Tax policies eventually forced him to mediate between government and provincial rebels, a position which ended with a commitment to mobilize Puno region uprisings in 1867. Bustamante's intellectual twists and turns, and his mysterious death suggest that this figure deserves further research. [V. Peloso]

2744 Jacobsen, Nils. Mirages of transition: the Peruvian Altiplano, 1780–1930. Berkeley, Calif.: Univ. of California Press, 1993. 481 p.: bibl., graphs, ill., index, maps, tables.

Case study of economic and social developments in the Province of Azángaro, Dept. of Puno. Establishes and examines continuities and changes between the neocolonial period of the late 1700s and the first half of the 1900s, and the wool export cycle period of 1855–1920. This solidly documented, methodologically sound, exceptionally readable study is far-reaching in its findings. [M.T. Hamerly]

2745 Jacobsen, Nils. Taxation in early republican Peru, 1821–1851: policy making between reform and tradition. (*in* América Latina en la Epoca de Simón Bolívar: la Formación de las Economías Nacionales y los Intereses Económicos Europeos, 1800–1850. Edición de Reinhard Liehr. Berlin: Colloquium Verlag, 1989, p. 311–339, tables)

Argues that the conventional view that the Peruvian national treasury was empty because of corruption and neglect is misleading. Notes that revenues rose after the wars of independence and that administration was sound but public expenditures got out of control. Unreformed colonial financial traditions and political struggles among caudillos combined to undermine an otherwise sound tax policy. Based largely on the *Memorias de Hacienda*, this study examines the sources of State revenue. It lays the inability to collect taxes to fears that rigorous enforcement would throttle capital formation and endanger economic recovery after the wars. Regimes turned increasingly to customs duties and capitation taxes to resolve the financial problem of the State, but such sources proved insufficient to cover expenditures. Faults a lack of central state control of spending for raising government deficits before the guano boom. A thoughtful early examination of a critical question. [V. Peloso]

2746 Klaiber, Jeffrey L. The Catholic Church in Peru, 1821–1985: a social history. Washington: Catholic University of America Press, 1992. 417 p.: bibl., index, map.

English version of *HLAS 52:2489..*

2747 Krüggeler, Thomas. El doble desafío: los artesanos del Cusco ante la crisis regional y la constitución del régimen republicano, 1824–1869. (*Allpanchis/Cusco,* 23: 38, segundo semestre 1991, p. 13–65, bibl., tables)

Cusco's urban artisans survived the early post-independence decades despite depressed markets and increased competition from imports because of strong links to the countryside and supplementary income sources. Author explores the broad range of social and economic situations of artisans, and the political weakness of guilds in representing corporate interests. Based on thorough research with primary sources.

2748 Lamas, Gerardo. "Viaje al Cuzco," de Claude Gay. (*Bol. Lima,* 11:63, mayo 1989, p. 23–28, bibl.)

Spanish translation of a brief 1839 account by a noted French naturalist of a journey through the southern sierra.

2749 Larico Yujra, Mariano. Yo fui canillita de José Carlos Mariátegui: (auto)biografía de Mariano Larico Yujra. Edi-

ción de José Luis Ayala. Kollao, Peru: Editorial Periodística S.C.R., 1990. 310 p.: ill.

Author reflects on his life as a communist peasant leader from the Altiplano province of Huancané, his ideas about religion, Andean myths, politics, the relation between races, etc. These lucid memories of an Aymara peasant about social movements and events from the 1920s to 1970s are an important source for ethnohistorical research.

2750 Lausent, Isabelle. Pasado y presente de la comunidad japonesa en el Perú. Lima: IFEA; IEP Ediciones, 1991. 79 p.: bibl. (Travaux de l'IFEA, 0768–424X; 53. Col. Mínima; 23)

Critical overview of Japanese immigration to Peru, migrants' social and economic activities, and their ideological orientation, from initial migration in 1890s to present. Emphasizes goals of emigration companies and other powerful groups in Japan to extend that country's influence over Peru as a source of raw materials; in the post-war period ultranationalist ideologues fostered identification of *nisei* (second generation immigrants) with their country of origin, thus prolonging a certain aloofness of many Japanese Peruvians toward their adopted country.

2751 López, Sinesio et al. Pensamiento político peruano, 1930–1968. Edición de Alberto Adrianzén. Lima: DESCO, 1990. 410 p.: bibl.

Collection of 11 essays and discussions of them by Peruvian social scientists and politicians about key aspects in the formative years of the country's modern political culture, ranging from analysis of ideology and strategy of parties to the thought of leading political writers. Especially noteworthy are Manuel Castillo Ochoa's discussion of Sánchez Cerro's "conservative populism" during the early 1930s; the essays by Ricardo Ramos Tremolada and Gonzalo Portocarrero about Haya de la Torre and APRA's tragic status within Peru's political system; and Carlos Franco's detailed reevaluation of Hildebrando Castro Pozo as one of Peru's most lucid and exemplary modern political and social thinkers/activists.

2752 Luna Vegas, Ricardo. Contribución a la verdadera historia del APRA, 1923–1988. Lima: Editorial Horizonte, 1990. 213 p.: bibl., ill. (Historia; 8)

Author seeks to present an "objective" history of APRA. The book's tone is reflective and it is based on a fairly broad reading of sources and secondary works, but it neglects certain important works. While correcting certain misconceptions and errors, the result is a standard and rather brief text politely critical of APRA from a leftist position.

2753 Lynch, Nicolás. Los jóvenes rojos de San Marcos: el radicalismo universitario de los años setenta. Lima: Zorro de abajo, 1990. 126 p.

Based on extensive interviews with eight student leaders, author undertakes a critical assessment of student politics at San Marcos between 1969 and 1980. Many of the students were isolated, their leaders came from lower class provincial backgrounds, and they felt maladjusted to Lima. Their radical Maoism was marked by an unmediated gap between violent revolutionary rhetoric and policy of concrete demands for students, within a context of upward mobility for their social group.

2754 Mallon, Florencia E. Alianzas multiétnicas y problema nacional: los campesinos y el Estado en Perú y México en el siglo XIX. (*in* Los Andes en la encrucijada: indios, comunidades y Estado en el siglo XIX. Quito: Ediciones Libri Mundi, 1991, p. 457–495, bibl.)

Author analyzes responses of socially and ethnically differentiated local societies to international invasions in Peru's Central Sierra during the 1880s and in Mexico's Sierra de Puebla during the 1860s. Peasant communities were willing to enter multiethnic alliances to defend "patria" and expected full citizenship and inclusion into national polity in return. After defeat of invasion and restabilization of oligarchic regimes, Indian communities were again ethnically isolated and excluded from polity. Conceptually important and controversial work.

2755 Manrique, Nelson. Lanas, circuitos mercantiles, violencia, estructuras de poder, resistencia en el sur peruano. (*in* Encuentros Debate América Latina Ayer y Hoy, *3rd, Barcelona, 1991.* Conquista y resistencia en la historia de América. Coordinación de Pilar García Jordán y Miquel Izard. Barcelona: Publicacions Univ. de Barcelona, 1992, p. 289–299)

Marxist hypothesis explains pervasive violence and gamonalismo in the southern sierra during the wool trade cycle: pre-capitalist merchants required extra economic compulsion to realize a profit.

2756 Martínez Riaza, Ascención. El Perú contemporáneo en la historiografía española, 1940–1988. (*Rev. Indias*, 50:188, enero/abril 1990, p. 227–242, appendix)

Bibliography of titles published in Spain (1940–88) covers history and social science works on republican Peru written by Spaniards, Peruvians, and others.

2757 Morales Stiglich, Guillermo. Haya de la Torre: testimonio de su médico. Lima: Centro de Documentación Andina, 1991. 82 p.: bibl., ill.

Author details Haya's long final illness and his daily life during the last years.

2758 Nałewajko, Małgorzata. La imagen del indio en el Perú durante los años veinte de nuestro siglo: la discusión sobre la integración nacional. (*Jahrb. Gesch.*, 26, 1989, p. 229–259)

Peruvian authors of the 1920s discussing the Indian never defined that term. Most authors ascribed the Indian's "decadence" or "lack of civilization" to social and environmental factors and thus considered a project of national integration feasible.

2759 Neira Avendaño, Máximo et al. Historia general de Arequipa. Arequipa, Peru: Fundación M.J. Bustamante de la Fuente, 1990. 824 p.: bibl., ill., index.

Four prominent regional historians and an archaeologist attempt the first serious comprehensive history of the city and region of Arequipa. Book includes a useful bibliography, but no notes to the text. Chapters vary greatly in quality and style: some offer broad, unsubstantiated interpretive claims while others are simply chronicle-like listings of events, or digests of newspapers. Authors cover prehispanic, colonial, and republican Peru with equal attention. The parts on colonial Peru focus on institutional, ethnohistoric, and social and cultural aspects, while those on the republican era concentrate more on politics and economy, and less on society and culture.

2760 Noéjovich, Héctor Omar. Las relaciones del Estado peruano con la población indígena en el siglo XIX a través de su legislación. (*Histórica/Lima*, 15 : 1, junio 1991, p. 43–62, bibl.)

Formalistic overview of first seven decades of republican legislation concerning Indian communities, citizenship rights, and taxation. Author concludes that under a pseudo-liberal veneer various administrations continued the colonial practices that treated Indians as citizens with diminished rights.

2761 Orrego Penagos, Juan Luis. Domingo Elías y el Club Progresista: los civiles y el poder hacia 1850. (*Histórica/Lima*, 14 : 2, dic. 1990, p. 317–353, bibl.)

The business and political career of Elías (1805–67) serves as backdrop for the discussion of the Club Progresista's ideology and vision of Peru. Author views the club, active during the 1850 presidential campaign on behalf of Elías, as direct precursor to the *civilistas* of the late 1860s and 1870s. Stressing economic development, free trade, popular education, and a moderate anticlericalism, it remained an elitist expression of new commercial and export-agricultural interest lacking a broad social base and disparaging the Indian majority of the country. Suggestive and well-researched article.

2762 Palacios Rodríguez, Raúl. El Perú republicano y moderno, 1868–1968. Lima: Librería Studium Ediciones, 1990. 574 p.: bibl., ill., maps.

Judicious, conventional synthesis emphasizes economic and social themes, at times in unusual detail. Weak for the period after 1930.

2763 Parker, David S. White-collar Lima, 1910–1929: commercial employees and the rise of the Peruvian middle class. (*HAHR*, 72 : 1, Feb. 1992, p. 47–72)

Author reevaluates criteria that define and distinguish white-collar workers in early 20th-century Lima, arguing that honor, education, customs and dress were more important than income and wealth. Even after embracing the modern labor movement, white-collar workers of the 1920s insisted on a strict separateness from blue-collar workers. Important revisionist article based on thorough research.

2764 Peralta Ruiz, Víctor. En pos del tributo: burocracia estatal, elite regional y comunidades indígenas en el Cusco rural, 1826–1854. Cusco, Peru: Centro de Estudios Re-

gionales Andinos Bartolomé de Las Casas, 1991. 159 p.: (Archivos de historia andina; 13)

Ambitious and important study of society and politics in rural post-independence Cusco, the most important regional source of rural fiscal revenue in the young republic. Author centers his analysis on the conflict between: Indian communities; the weak large landholding aristocracy; and the emerging mestizo and Creole local and provincial bureaucracy in charge of collecting Indian and *casta* head taxes. For nearly three decades after 1826 the Indian head tax became the centerpiece of a reconstituted patrimonial "compact" between the Indian communities and local representatives of the State. Based on solid archival research with tax lists and administrative correspondence.

Peralta Ruiz, Víctor. Fiscalidad y poder regional en el Cusco a fines de la colonia e inicios de la república. See item **2400.**

2765 Piel, Jean. Tierra y sociedad: la oligarquía terrateniente del Perú. (*Anu. IEHS*, 2, 1987, p. 283–300)

The hacienda has been the central institution for controlling society and politics in Peru since the colonial period. Large landholders as a class never lost control over the direction of Peruvian politics. During the early 20th century, old and new *latifundistas* merged with foreign and domestic commercial and financial interests to form a solid oligarchy. Monopolization of land and money among this tightly knit oligarchy reached its zenith during the Leguía Administration (1919–30); it was sucessfully challenged only after 1960.

2766 Poloni, Jacques. San Juan de Lurigancho: su historia y su gente; un distrito popular de Lima. Lima: CEP, 1987. 179 p.: bibl., ill., maps.

An unusually well-organized and methodologically-sophisticated local history of a district that has become one of Lima's poor urban neighborhoods since the 1960s. Includes section on urban and rural land tenure and demography.

2767 Portocarrero Maisch, Gonzalo and **Patricia Oliart.** El Perú desde la escuela. Lima: Instituto de Apoyo Agrario, 1989. 236 p.: bibl. (Serie Tiempo de historia; 3)

Two studies examine Peruvian school children's notions of Peruvian history, from the Incas to present. The first traces interpretations of key history textbooks since the mid-19th century. The second presents results of a sociological survey among Peruvian school children of the 1980s about their views of Peruvian history. Authors find that most students share a vulgar dependency view of history, hostility toward foreigners, cynicism about republican Peru, and a glorification of the Inca Empire as the best period in Peru's history. A crucial study to understand the intellectual background of the country's current crisis.

2768 Quiroz, Alfonso W. Domestic and foreign finance in modern Peru, 1850–1950. Pittsburgh, Pa.: Univ. of Pittsburgh Press, 1993. 297 p.: bibl., ill. (Pitt Latin American series)

The most important work on finance in Peru's republican history to date. Author revises conventional dependency notions and suggests a certain degree of autonomy of domestic financial interests. Sees era of export-led growth (1884–1930) as the most dynamic in Peru's economic development and faults era of increasing State intervention (1930–50) with exacerbating oligopolization and inefficiency in nation's economy. In addition to explaining the complexities of domestic and foreign finance, and role of finance in business group formation, the book covers broader issues of economic history.

2769 Quiroz, Alfonso W. Financial development in Peru under agrarian export influence, 1884–1950. (*Americas/Francisc.*, 47: 4, April 1991, p. 447–476, graph)

Peru's domestic financial sector maintained a fragile autonomy between 1884 and 1950. State banking and monetary policies first helped agro-exporters, but since the 1940s, industry and trade gained in priority as credit became more concentrated in Lima, the coast, and the largest enterprises. Suggestive revisionist article based on primary research.

2770 Ramos, Angela. Una vida sin tregua. v. 1–2. Lima: Consejo Nacional de Ciencia y Tecnología; Partido Comunista Peruano; Centro de la Mujer Peruana Flora Tristán, 1990. 2 v.: bibl., ill.

Essays, interviews, poems, and plays by one of Peru's leading 20th-century journalists combine combativeness with elegance,

and wit with contemplation. An associate of José Carlos Mariátegui, Ramos wrote on specific social issues such as vagrancy, prisons, divorce, etc., rather than on broad theories about the essence of Peru.

2771 Ramos Zambrano, Augusto. Tormenta antiplánica [i.e., altipánica]: rebeliones indígenas de la provincia de Lampa, Puno, 1920–1924. Prólogo de Alberto Flores Galindo. Lima: [s.n.], 1990. 126 p.: bibl.

Detailed accounts of four little-known confrontations between Indian peasants and large landholders and local authorities in the livestock raising area of the Altiplano. The confrontations arose in context of the broad Indian insurrectionary movement that swept through most of southern Peru during the early 1920s, with ties to urban *indigenistas.* Based on oral tradition and painstaking research in dispersed archives.

2772 Ravines, Rogger. Notas, testimonios, documentos. (*Bol. Lima,* 12:67, enero 1990, p. 5–19, bibl., photos)

Article includes three previously unpublished letters by General William Miller written in 1823; a thorough analysis of three recently found Chimu vases; and a note on the Mirave petroglyphs, recently discovered in Ilabaya district (Tacna dept.).

2773 Rebaza, Nicolás. Anales del Departamento de La Libertad en la Guerra de la Independencia. Lima: Banco Industrial del Perú, Fondo del Libro, 1989. 373 p.

Third edition of important work originally published in 1898 consists of a province-by-province narration of political and military events, as well as sketches of key royalist and insurgent actors during struggles for independence in the old department of La Libertad (which covered practically the whole of modern northern Peru). Work is based on interviews with participants and painstaking archival research.

2774 Rénique C., José Luis. Los sueños de la sierra: Cusco en el siglo XX. Lima: CEPES, 1991. 413 p.: bibl., map.

Detailed and well-researched account of social and political movements and intellectual debates in Cusco from the Aristocratic Republic (1895–1919) to Alán García's Administration (1985–90). Author stresses regionalist reaction to central State formation and to new economic developments, juxtaposing the programs of the increasingly weak regional elites and those emerging of the popular and radical movements.

2775 Rodríguez Pastor, Humberto. El inmigrante chino en el mercado laboral peruano, 1850–1930. (*HISLA/Lima*, 13/14, 1er y 2do semestre 1989, p. 93–147, bibl., tables)

Author overviews the work done by *coolies* and the types of labor arrangements under which Chinese were employed, and then goes on to describe the geographic and occupational dispersion of Chinese throughout Peru during the early 20th century. Stresses the important contribution of Chinese to Peruvian economic development.

2776 Rodríguez Rea, Miguel Angel and **Silvana Salazar.** Guía de la revista *Historia*, 1943–1945. (*Histórica/Lima*, 13:2, dic. 1989, p. 243–289)

Useful index to a journal edited by Jorge Basadre, which published important historical studies and sources, as well as essays and commentaries on a broad range of contemporary affairs, from politics to art.

2777 Sánchez, Luis Alberto. L.A.S.: crónicas. v. 1. Edición de Luis Alva Castro. Lima: EMI, 1988. 1 v.

Articles published by leading APRA politician and intellectual in *El Tiempo* of Bogotá (1948–49) on political, literary, and broad speculative topics. Contains little on contemporary Peru.

2778 Scherzer, Karl, Ritter von. Así nos vio la Novara: impresiones austríacas sobre Chile y el Perú en 1859. Edición y tradición de Manuel Torres Marín. Santiago: Editorial Andrés Bello, 1990. 166 p.: bibl., ill.

Spanish translation of travel account by Karl Ritter von Scherzer through Chile and Peru in 1859. This was part of the account of the expedition of the Imperial Austrian frigate *Novara* around the world, orginally published in 1861–62.

2779 Sehlinger, Peter J. Páginas trágicas en la historia peruana: las cartas del presidente cautivo Francisco García Calderón desde Chile en 1882. (*Fénix/Lima*, 32/33, 1987, p. 142–149)

First publication of five letters written by Francisco García Calderón in Sept. and Oct. 1882 while in captivity in Santiago, relating details of peace negotiations with the Chilean government and the US mediator, Cornelius Logan.

2780 Urbano Rojas, Jesús and **Pablo Macera.** Santero y caminante: Santoruraj-Ñampurej. Lima: Editorial Apoyo, 1992. 194 p.: ill. (some col.)

Macera, an historian, converses with Urbano Rojas, a master craftsman from Ayacucho who produces intricate miniature altars. They cover his life history, the work process in the craft shops, his travels throughout Peru, and his views on God and the world. A fascinating book and an important ethnohistorical source.

Bolivia

MARIE LUISE WAGNER, *Professorial Lecturer, Georgetown University*

THE TRANSFORMATION OF INDIGENOUS COMMUNITIES in the national period is an important topic in recent scholarship. This year, many good studies contribute to the debate over indigenous resistance to the expansion of the haciendas in different regions (items **2808, 2822, 2818, 2807, 2809, 2799, 2789, 2783,** and **2805**). In addition, the analysis of the role of *campesinos* in the political process indicates a continuing awareness of rural history (item **2786**).

General histories of Bolivia have appeared in an updated edition (item **2801**) and with a radical new interpretation (item **2796**). Antezana's first hand historical account of the MNR from 1949–52 is also noteworthy (item **2782**). Several regional histories help understand the problems of full integration into national policies in modern Bolivia despite limited availability of historical records (items **2817** and **2821**).

Political biographies of Sucre (item **2811**), Tejada Sorzano (item **2792**), Arce (item **2791**), and Paz Estenssoro (item **2802**) are important contributions to Bolivian history, while Barnadas' biography of García Moreno (item **2784**) and Gómez Martínez's analysis of the Bolivian national character (item **2798**) reflect a thorough understanding of intellectual currents.

Gender related issues have appeared recently in historiography (item **2819**) and labor history continues to attract much interest, with two good studies this biennium focusing on the decline of the Bolivian labor movement (items **2806** and **2810**). In military history, material from the archives of the Armed Forces sheds interesting light on the 1932 Battle of Boquerón (item **2813**) and the warfare against Che Guevara (item **2812**).

2781 Abos-Padilla Urzúa, Ricardo. El tratado secreto Perú-Boliviano visto por diplomáticos de terceros países. (*Cuad. Hist.*, 8, dic. 1988, p. 7–33, tables)

Scholarly analysis of US, British, French, German, Italian and Brazilian reaction to treaty of alliance between Bolivia and Peru on Feb. 6, 1873 is based on archival research. Claims that non-involved countries had a more objective view of balance of power in South America.

2782 Antezana Ergueta, Luis. Historia secreta del Movimiento Nacionalista Revolucionario. v. 6, 1949–1952: el sexenio-II. La Paz: Librería Editorial Juventud, 1984–1988. 1 v.: bibl., ill., ports.

Sympathetic description of MNR history from civil war in 1949 to 1952 Revolution. Uses extensive quotes from MNR documents, writings, speeches, and interviews with its leaders, but has only fragmentary bibliographical references. For vol. 4 see *HLAS 50:2255.*

2783 Arze Aguirre, René Danilo. Guerra y conflictos sociales: el caso rural boliviano durante la campaña del Chaco. La Paz: Centro de Estudios de la Realidad Económica y Social, 1987. 303 p.: bibl., index. (Serie Movimientos sociales; 4)

Excellent analysis of social conflicts and destabilization in the Andean and Oriente countryside 1927–35 is based primarily on archival material and interesting interviews with Chaco War veterans. Concludes that unrest during the War reflected increased exploitation by war profiteers and reaction to bandits in the East and Southeast. Important contribution to research on indigenous resistance and rebellion.

2784 Barnadas, Josep María. Gabriel René Moreno, 1836–1908: drama y gloria de un boliviano. La Paz: Ediciones Altiplano, 1988. 269 p.: bibl., index. (Col. Hipótesis)

Well-documented analysis of Moreno's life and *oevre.* Sympathetic to Moreno, author emphasizes his patriotic mission as documentarian, bibliographer, historian, sociologist, and literary critic, and claims that Moreno was a great patriot despite his criticism of Bolivia. Summarizes Moreno's life and work with his subject's own declaration that he was possessed of an "incontestable superioridad moral que dan las penas y trabajos sufridos sin tregua junto con la patria o sobrellevadas ciegamente por la patria."

2785 Bidondo, Emilio A. Alto Perú: insurrección, libertad, independencia; campañas militares, 1809–1825. La Paz: s.n.; Buenos Aires: 549 p.: bibl., maps.

Well-researched account of wars for independence by a military historian is limited in approach but ample in detail. [M.T. Hamerly]

2786 Bolivia, la fuerza histórica del campesinado: con una cronología de Bolivia, América Latina y el Imperio Español, 1492–1983. Recopilación de Fernando Calderón G. y Jorge Dandler. Post-scriptum de Marshall Wolfe. 2a ed. rev. Geneva: Instituto de Investigaciones de las Naciones Unidas para el Desarrollo Social; La Paz: Centro de Estudios de la Realidad Económica y Social, 1986. 632 p.: bibl., ill., maps. (Informe/Instituto de Investigaciones de las Naciones Unidas para el Desarrollo Social; 85.3)

Important multidisciplinary analysis concludes that "los campesinos han sido un grupo social vital en la sociedad, no solo como subordinados sino también como articuladores de modelos alternativos de desarrollo y organización . . . El campesinado ha sido un actor histórico en la política." Contains the following articles: Fernando Calderón y Jorge Dandler, "Movimientos Campesinos y Estado en Bolivia;" Xavier Albó, "Etnicidad y Clase en la Gran Rebelión Aymara/Quechua: Kataris, Amarus y Bases, 1780–1781;" Gonzalo Flores, "Levantamientos Campesinos durante el Período Liberal, 1900–1920;" Jorge Dandler y Juan Torrico, "El Congreso Nacional Indígena de 1945 y la Rebelión de Ayopaya;" Jorge Dandler, "Campesinado y Reforma Agraria en Cochabamba, 1952–1953: Dinámica de un Movimiento Campesino en Bolivia;" Jorge Dandler, "La 'Ch'ampa Guerra' de Cochabamba: un Proceso de Disgregación Política;" Jean Pierre Lavaud, "Los Campesinos Frente al Estado;" Andrew Pearse, "Campesinado y Revolución: el Caso de Bolivia;" Blanca Muñoz, "La Participación de la Mujer Campesina en Bolivia: un Estudio del Altiplano;" Xavier Albó, "Bases Etnicas y Sociales para la Participación Aymara;" Gonzalo Flores, "Estado, Políticas Agrarias y Luchas Campesinas: Revisión de una Década en Bolivia."

Bonilla, Heraclio. Lecciones del endeudamiento externo en los países andinos antes de la Primera Guerra Mundial. See item **2701.**

2787 Botelho Gosálvez, Raúl. Historia de una infidencia diplomática: correspondencia Ríos Gallardo-Fellmann Velarde. La Paz: Empresa Editora Siglo, 1988. 88 p.: bibl., ill., ports.
Relates secret correspondence between Bolivian minister of foreign affairs, José Fellman Velarde, and Chilean special ambassador, Conrado Rios Gallardo, written between 1963–64 in attempt to resume diplomatic relations broken after the 1962 River Lauca incident. Edited by senior Bolivian diplomat.

2788 Cajías, Lupe. Historia de una leyenda: vida y palabra de Juan Lechín Oquendo, líder de los mineros bolivianos. La Paz: Ediciones Gráficas EG, 1988. 453 p., 14 p. of plates: ill. (Col. Tiempo de historia)
Very sympathetic biography of labor leader by Bolivian journalist contains extensive quotes from interviews with Lechín and from documents. Lacks bibliography.

2789 Calderón Jemio, Raúl Javier. Conflictos sociales en el Altiplano paceño entre 1830 y 1860. (*Data/La Paz*, 1, 1991, p. 145–157)
Study based on Univ. of Connecticut doctoral dissertation argues that the population of indigenous communities in the mid-19th century increased despite social conflicts.

2790 Céspedes, Augusto *et al.* Víctor Paz: su presencia en la historia revolucionaria de Bolivia; libro-homenaje en sus 80 años de vida, 1907–1987. Dirección de Guillermo Bedregal. La Paz: Editorial Los Amigos del Libro, Werner Guttentag T., 1987. 233 p.: bibl., ill. (Col. Historia; NA 487)
Festschrift for Víctor Paz Estenssoro by contributors who are mostly members of the MNR includes bibliography of Paz's speeches and writings.

Chassin, Joëlle. Comment rallier les foules à la Révolution? les discours de Juan José Castelli dans l'expédition libératrice du Haut-Pérou, 1810–1811. See item **2929.**

2791 Condarco Morales, Ramiro. Aniceto Arce. La Paz: Amerindia, 1985. 993 p.: bibl., ill., index.
Eulogizing, detailed biography of Bolivian entrepreneur and president (1842–1906). Claims that Arce laid foundations for industrialization with innovations in mining and agricultural sectors and the building of railroads. Stresses Arce's anti-imperialist stand reflected in his emphasis of national control of railways, and argues that Arce is a major nation-builder who consolidated republic. Based largely on extensive archival research, including Arce's personal papers. Contains interesting quotes from documents as well as economic statistics and photographs.

Crespo R., Alberto; Mariano Baptista Gumucio; and José de Mesa. La Ciudad de La Paz: su historia, su cultura. See item **2432.**

2792 Crespo R., Alberto. José Luis Tejada Sorzano: un hombre de paz. La Paz: Librería Editorial Juventud, 1990. 254 p., 16 p. of plates: bibl., ports.
Renowned Bolivian historian provides sound analysis of Sorzano's life and presidency based primarily on his extensive personal archives used here for first time. Good

insight into Bolivian history during first four decades of 20th century. Unfortunately, reference to some sources is fragmentary.

2793 *Feminiflor:* un hito en el periodismo femenino de Bolivia. Recopilación de Luis Ramiro Beltrán. Bolivia: CIMCA, 1987? 151 p.: bibl., ill.

Festschrift for magazine published in Oruro, 1921–23. Contributions include essays on Bolivian journalism in the 1920s and reminiscences by founding members. Emphasis on social justice makes it, according to one of its directors, the precursor of Bolivian female journalism. Contains tables of contents of eight extant issues, a facsimile reprint of No. 24, and photographs.

2794 Fernández, María Elisa. El Mariscal Andrés Santa-Cruz. (*Historia/Santiago,* 24, 1989, p. 215–252)

Sympathetic study of Santa Cruz is based largely on archival material and press reports. Contains useful evaluation of historiography of Santa Cruz from studies by his contemporaries to latest works.

2795 Freemasons. Gran Logia de Bolivia. Apuntes para la historia de la masonería boliviana. La Paz: La Logia de Bolivia, 1991. 157 p.: ill. (some col.)

History of Freemasons from end of 16th century until 1990 is based on collection of documents reprinted in text.

2796 Gallardo Lozada, Jorge. La nación postergada: contribución al estudio de la historia de Bolivia. La Paz: Editorial Los Amigos del Libro, 1984. 520 p. (Enciclopedia boliviana)

Unfootnoted Marxist analysis of Bolivian history from colonial times until 1983 is written by Bolivian activist who was Interior Minister in the revolutionary nationalist government of Gen. Torres, 1970–71.

2797 Gallego, Ferran. Estado, nación, reforma: las paradojas del nacionalismo boliviano en los años treinta. (*Bol. Am.,* 32: 41, 1991, p. 273–286)

Scholarly analysis contrasts strength of reformist nationalism of the Chaco generation with weakness of the Bolivian State. Claims that this nationalism increased at the expense of traditional groups and the socialist left because of the ability of its leaders to build a broad-based alliance.

2798 Gómez-Martínez, José Luis. Bolivia, un pueblo en busca de su identidad. La Paz: Editorial Los Amigos del Libro, 1988. 384 p., 70 p. of plates: bibl., ill. (Col. Enciclopedia boliviana)

Sound analysis of Bolivian national character blames its continuing feudal and personalistic attitude for Bolivia's economic decline and loss of territory after independence. Using primarily artistic expressions by painters, sculptors and writers, especially Guillermo Francovich's *oevre* from the 1920s until present, author concludes that the Chaco generation made for the first time a serious attempt to come to terms with Bolivian reality. This process set in motion an utopic vision that culminated in the 1952 Revolution. But disillusionment with the Revolution led once again to the failure to fully accept Bolivian reality. Includes 70 photographs of Bolivian art.

2799 Grieshaber, Erwin P. Resistencia indígena a la venta de tierras comunales en el departamento de La Paz, 1881–1920. (*Data/La Paz,* 1, 1991, p. 113–145, appendix, photo)

Excellent study of changing patterns of indigenous resistance to expansion of haciendas. In the early 1880s, indigenous communities accepted tribute payments and labor obligations in exchange for access to land. But the subsequent loss of their land and of government protection changed their role in Bolivia's multiethnic society, as mistrust of whites resulted in separatism and violence.

2800 Guevara, Ernesto. El diario del Che en Bolivia: del 7 de noviembre de 1966 al 7 de octubre de 1967. Ilustración y notas según la investigación realizada por Adys Cupull y Froilán González. La Habana: Editora Política, 1988. 478 p.: ill., maps.

Cuban edition of Che's diary features introduction by Fidel Castro, 13 p. of diary previously unpublished in Cuba, and photographs taken on site for this edition, as well as photographs and biographical data of guerrillas of Ñancahuazú.

2801 Guzmán, Augusto. Historia de Bolivia. 7. ed. rev. y actualizada. Cochabamba, Bolivia: Editorial Los Amigos del Libro, 1990. 503 p.: bibl., ill. (Enciclopedia boliviana)

New, slightly revised edition of Bolivian history from 1000 AD until present is written by renowned Bolivian historian. Each chapter is followed by useful summary. For 5th edition see *HLAS 46:3038*.

2802 Guzmán, Augusto. Paz Estenssoro. La Paz: Editorial los Amigos del Libro, 1986. 282 p., 6 p. of plates: bibl., ports. (Obras completas de Augusto Guzmán)

Sympathetic biography of Paz is written by renowned Bolivian historian and writer. Claims that Paz's main motivating force in the 1952 Revolution and the counter-revolution of 1985 was search for stability. Argues that Paz represents the center of the MNR which is not interested in class struggle but rather in the integration of classes and in social justice.

2803 Irurozqui, Marta and **Víctor Peralta Ruiz.** Historiografía sobre la República Boliviana. (*Rev. Indias*, 52:194, enero/abril 1992, p. 11–34, bibl.)

Critical analysis of Bolivian historiography since 1970s focuses on four major themes: 1) changes in economic structure of country; 2) transition from feudalism to capitalism; 3) indigenous resistance to expansion of *latifundios*; and 4) role of elites in regional conformity to national policies.

2804 Irusta Medrano, Gerardo. Memorias de un hombre de armas: revelaciones del Gral. Lucio Añez Ribera. La Paz: Centro de Sistemas, 1990. 294 p.: bibl., ports.

Bolivian journalist relates memoirs of important general representing the Grupo Generacional, apolitical professional officers who played a major role in the coup of Aug. 3, 1981, that led to García Mesas's resignation. Interesting insights into Bolivian armed forces after the Revolution. Useful for military historians despite rather arbitrary organization.

2805 Jáuregui C., Juan H. Conflicto comunidad-hacienda: Pucarani, 1880–1900. (*Data/La Paz*, 1, 1991, p. 159–169, bibl., photo)

Analyzes conflict between haciendas and indigenous communities in Omasuyos prov. that arose from resistance against territorial expansion of haciendas and increasing labor obligations. Stresses indigenous resistance against oppression by mestizo *hacendados* who began to control land and demand services.

2806 Jetté, Christian. De la toma del cielo por asalto a la relocalización: movimiento popular y democracia en Bolivia, 1976–86. La Paz: HISBOL, 1989. 279 p.: bibl. (Serie Movimientos sociales; 5)

Critical analysis of decline of Bolivian labor movement argues that the Central Obrera Boliviana (COB) played vital role in the resignation of Banzer and in democratic consolidation. The labor movement was defeated in 1985 for the following reasons: 1) emphasis on struggle for short-term syndicalist interests and not for political reforms which would have resulted in long-term mass support; 2) inability to build an effective alliance between workers and peasants; and 3) misjudgement of the economic situation and underestimation of the political right. Scholarly, well-documented work.

Klein, Herbert S. Bolivia: the evolution of a multi-ethnic society. See item **2440.**

2807 Klein, Herbert S. La estructura de las haciendas a fines del siglo XIX en Bolivia: las provincias del norte del lago Titicaca. (*Data/La Paz*, 1, 1991, p. 51–61, appendix, graph, tables)

Good, detailed analysis of hacienda expansion at the expense of indigenous communities in the provinces of Omasuyos, Larecaja and Muñecas is based on tax register of 1880.

2808 Langer, Erick D. Andean rituals of revolt: the Chayanta Rebellion of 1927. (*Ethnohistory/Society*, 37:3, Summer 1990, p. 227–253)

A widespread rebellion that mobilized thousands of peasants in Chuquisaca and Potosí depts. resulted in two very different rituals that served to reaffirm Aymara notions of ethnic identity and claims to land: 1) a legalistic transfer of hacienda lands to communities; and 2) the sacrifice, ingestion, and burial of an *hacendado*. The rebels did not espouse egalitarian notions, but rather reactualized their hierarchic colonial vision of dual society. [N. Jacobsen]

2809 Langer, Erick D. Persistencia y cambio en comunidades indígenas del sur boliviano en el siglo XIX. (Ecuador: Ediciones Libri Mundi, 1991, p. 133–167, bibl., map, tables)

Indigenous communities in the south survived relatively unchanged until the 1860s but, unlike Altiplano communities, were not able to resist the expansion of haciendas during the last decades of the century. After 1880, small communities in Chuquisaca desintegrated but larger ones in Oruro and Potosí, despite the loss of land, survived because of their continued access to resources in different ecological zones. In the 1920s, they formed alliances with different ethnic groups and landless hacienda laborers and started the Indigenous Rebellion of 1927. Good contribution to historical research on survival of indigenous communities.

2810 Lazarte, Jorge. Movimiento obrero y procesos políticos en Bolivia: historia de la C.O.B., 1952–1987. La Paz: Tall. Gráf. de Editorial Offset Boliviana, 1989. 289 p.: bibl.

Interesting analysis of the Central Obrera Boliviana's role in the political process is based primarily on COB archival material, newspapers, and interviews by Bolivian sociologist and advisor to COB. Argues that 1987 COB congress showed erosion of the labor movement's strength because of a weak leadership unable to deal with national and syndicalist crises. Good insight into organizational structure of COB, policy formation, financial situation, and interaction with various segments of Bolivian society. Appendix contains document founding COB.

2811 Lofstrom, William Lee. La presidencia de Sucre en Bolivia. Caracas: Academia Nacional de la Historia, 1987. 550 p.: bibl., ill., indexes. (Biblioteca de la Academia Nacional de la Historia. Estudios, monografías y ensayos; 91)

Excellent, well-documented analysis of Sucre's presidency concludes that the main reasons for failure of his reform attempts were: political instability caused by economic problems; erosion of his popularity because of opposition of the Church; hostility of Bolivia's neighbors; and opposition of elite who wanted political power and effectively destroyed all reformist initiatives.

2812 Martínez Estévez, Diego. Ñancahuazú: apuntes para la historia militar de Bolivia. La Paz: Computación y Proyectos, 1989. 301 p., 44 leaves of plates (some folded): ill., maps.

Chronological account by Bolivian officer of military operations against Che Guevara from his arrival in Bolivia in 1966 until his death in 1967. Contains extensive reprints of material from military archives including maps, photographs, orders, statements and captured documents. Interesting insight into military operations.

2813 Marzana, Manuel. La gran batalla: Boquerón, Guerra del Chaco. La Paz: Producciones CIMA, 1991. 312 p.: ill., maps.

Commanding general's chronological account of Battle of Boquerón against overwhelming Paraguayan forces in Sept. 1932 also contains reprints of military orders, troop movements, maps, manifestos and diaries of officers. Useful information on military history.

2814 Moreno, Gabriel René. Gabriel René Moreno, íntimo: 1836–1908. La Paz: Editorial Don Bosco, 1986. 180 p.: ill., index. (Proyecto Cultural Don Bosco)

Collection of unpublished documents and selected letters to and by Moreno (1856–1908) is partly reproduced in facsimile. Contains useful editorial comments.

2815 Murillo Cárdenas, Eliodoro and Gustavo Larrea Bedregal. Razón de Patria, Villarroel y nacionalismo revolucionario. La Paz: Editorial e Impr. Metodista, 1988. 250 p.: ill.

Very subjective account of Razón de Patria (RADEPA) from 1934–46 by two Chaco War veterans. Chronology is inconsistent and appendix contains RADEPA documents but no bibliography.

2816 Pereira Fiorilo, Juan. De la fundación a la Guerra del Salitre. Cochabamba, Bolivia: Editorial Los Amigos del Libro, 1990. 480 p.: bibl, indexes. (Bolivia, historia de su pasado económico; 20.)

Patriotic description of Bolivian economic history from independence until 1884. Contains data on government finances and economic output, but often fails to give exact bibliographical references.

2817 Pinckert Justiniano, Guillermo. Historia de Santa Cruz. v. 1. Santa Cruz, Bolivia: Editorial Universitaria, 1991. 1 v.: bibl., index, maps.

First volume of descriptive history of Santa Cruz (1560–1810). Appendix contains extensive quotations of colonial documents derived from published material and an index of names with biographical data.

Rodríguez, Gustavo and Humberto Solares Serrano. Sociedad oligárquica, chicha y cultura popular: ensayo histórico sobre la identidad regional. See *HLAS* 53 : 5328.

2818 Rodríguez Ostria, Gustavo. Entre reformas y contrarreformas: las comunidades indígenas en el Valle Bajo Cochabambino, 1825–1900. (*Data/La Paz*, 1, 1991, p. 169–210, appendix, bibl., tables)

Author argues that the State played an important role in survival of indigenous communities in Cochabamba until the presidency of Melgarejo. After the 1878 Ley de Exvinculación, landless campesinos and *colonos* became landowners and resisted the growth of the hacienda. Good contribution to studies of political interaction between indigenous communities and State. Article also published as chapter in item **599**, p. 277–334.

2819 Rossells, Beatriz. La mujer: una ilusión; ideologías e imágenes de la mujer en Bolivia en el siglo XIX. La Paz: Centro de Información y Desarrollo de la Mujer (CIDEM), 1988. 120 p.: bibl., ill., facsims.

Critical analysis of role of women in Bolivia in second half of 19th century. Claims that liberal and positivist ideas influenced upper-class women to demand education as a precondition for their emancipation, although most of them were not interested in improving the situation of all Bolivian women. Well-documented paper contains photographs and interesting quotes from 19th-century Bolivian magazines.

2820 Siles Salinas, Luis Adolfo. Mi palabra. Recopilación de Clemencia Siles de Vacaguzmán. La Paz: LASSER, 1991. 498 p.: bibl., ill.

Highly subjective collection of speeches and writings by former vice president and president of Bolivia deals with Latin American history, culture and politics. Includes evaluation of his five-month presidency in 1969 and sees reasons for his overthrow in both his own massive popular support and the increasing unpopularity of Gen. Alfredo Ovando.

2821 Soux, María Luisa *et al.* Apolobamba, Caupolicán, Franz Tamayo: historia de una región paceña. La Paz: Prefectura del Depto. de La Paz; Univ. Mayor de San Andrés, 1991. 363 p.: bibl., ill., maps. (Col. Historia de las provincias paceñas; 3)

Regional history from 16th century to present uses multidisciplinary approach to examine arrival of Spaniards and Franciscan missions in colonial period, economy and trade in 19th-century Caupolicán, history of Apolo (with useful information on geography and anthropology), and the colonization of Franz Tamayo after 1952. Contains maps, photographs, and statistics, as well as a list of interesting but somewhat inaccessible sources.

2822 Tandeter, Enrique. La crisis de 1800–1805 en el Alto Perú. (*in* Los Andes en la encrucijada: indios, comunidades y Estado en el siglo XIX. Quito: Ediciones Libri Mundi, 1991, p. 17–61, bibl.)

Good analysis of demographic impact and crisis of subsistence in Chayanta. Author uses parochial registers to show that crisis of 1800–05 was more severe than earlier crises because hacienda growth and mining crisis had changed consumption patterns, urban markets, and jobs for indigenous population.

Chile

WILLIAM F. SATER, *Professor of History, California State University, Long Beach*

HISTORIANS STILL SIFT THROUGH the ashes of the Moneda seeking to understand why the UP collapsed. Faúndez, who sees Allende as part of the development of the left, blames domestic forces for fomenting the 1973 coup (item **2843**); Kaufman considers the US as a major contributor to Allende's fall (item **2861**); and Angell cogently argues that generic flaws within the Chilean political system itself condemned Allende to failure (item **2824**). Meanwhile, scholars are finally focusing on the Pinochet period: the Captain-General's memoirs, while hardly enlightening, should be consulted if not perused (item **2876**), and Valdivieso's work acts as a distinctly rightist antidote to the majority of the publications (item **2889**).

Chile's pre-1891 history remains neglected; a notable exception is Bravo's collection of splendid essays (item **2878**) describing not merely Portales and his policies but the nation he molded. There is, as usual, a work on the star-crossed Balmaceda. This year's effort, however, is the particularly innovative study by Subercaseaux which explores the interaction of culture and politics in post-Balmaceda Chile (item **2887**).

Scholars still pay some attention to the traditionally-neglected post-World War I years. Covarrubias' volume tracing the early efforts of future leaders of the Christian Democratic Party is quite useful (item **2839**). Muñoz's essay on the 1932 Socialist Republic (item **2853**) provides a good, brief summary of a period which still begs for some stalwart soul to investigate more thoroughly. The Milicia Republicana, one of the results of the turbulent early 1930s, is discussed in Maldonado's welcome, albeit far from definitive study (item **2864**). Since Ibáñez's second regime seems to attract little attention, Moulian's work (item **2868**) as well as Garay's analysis of the PAL and the General of Hope's rise to power (item **2848**) are well worth reading.

Historians of the Chilean economy continue to be productive. Particularly worthy of mention is the joint effort by Julio Pinto Vallejos and Luis Ortega to explain the relationship between the growth of mining and the development of local industry (item **2877**). The late Harold Blakemore's splendid monograph on the British nitrate railroad explains that company's activities in the north (item **2830**). Two authors have concentrated on the more bucolic agrarian sector: Bengoa's superb two volumes explore Chile's various agricultural endeavors as well as the relationship between *patrón* and *inquilino* (item **2828**); and Garrido's study provides a detailed monograph on the history of Chile's agrarian reform (item **2855**). While not as graphic as Lillo's *Sub terra* (Santiago: Imprenta Moderna, 1904), Figueroa deftly describes the lot of the coal miners and their attempts to improve their lives (item **2845**). Garcés notes how the *salitre* miners' attempts to use the strike to address their grievances culminated in the infamous 1907 Iquique massacre (item **2849**).

Military history continues to enjoy some popularity. Rodríguez has compiled an exhaustive bibliography on the War of the Pacific (item **2880**). The Estado Mayor's index to its multivolume study of the Chilean Army is useful (item **2858**) and its three-tome biographical dictionary (item **2847**), while hardly analytical, provides the reader a quick sketch of various military figures as well as a good bibliography. A more successful monograph is Maldonado's examination of how the *carabineros* evolved from a military appendage into a highly efficient and professional national police (item **2863**). Naval buffs will enjoy Aguirre's article demonstrating that Chile's fleet, unlike its army, performed well in the war against the Peruvian-Bolivian Confederation (item **2890**).

Institutional history has been enriched by several scholars. Yaeger's article on the Instituto Nacional, Chile's most venerable *liceo* which educated generations of the nation's leading *laicos,* is particularly useful (item **2893**). Muñoz's workmanlike history of the Universidad de Santiago, from its inception as the Escuela de Artes y Oficios, enhances our understanding of the history of higher education in Chile (item **2869**). Huerta's analysis of the role of the Roman Catholic Church, while relying perhaps too much on clerical sources, nonetheless provides important information for understanding that seminal institution (item **2857**).

Chileans are finally paying some attention to their immigrant past. Couyoumdjian's comprehensive bibliography constitutes an excellent starting point for those interested in the pre-1930 period (item **2838**), and Norambuena's work is especially helpful because it includes material describing the various laws regulating immigration (item **2872**). Ferrer shows how Spanish Loyalists reached Chile just as the Republic collapsed (item **2844**). Díaz's work on the often-denigrated Italians widens the scope of immigrant history (item **2842**), while Capellero's autobiography provides a classic study of the sojourner (item **2837**). Olguín is one of the few to chronicle the less numerous but often vilified *turcos:* hapless refugees of the Ottoman Empire who filtered into Chile beginning at the turn of this century (item **2873**). Eventually, someone should chronicle the Italians and Arabs as Blancpain did the French.

Regional histories, long a research focus, benefit from Campos Harriet's study of Concepción (item **2835**). Worthy of special mention are the magisterial works of Martinic on Punta Arenas and Magallanes (items **2867** and **2866**). Last but not least, Romero's excellent work traces the odyssey of the displaced or ambitious *inquilinos* who moved back and forth from the supposedly bucolic *fundos* to the city in search of work (item **2882**).

2823 Allende Gossens, Salvador. Obras escogidas, 1933–1948. v. 1, El camino hacia la identidad. Recopilación, selección e introducción de Patricio Quiroga Zamora. Concepción, Chile: Instituto de Estudios Contemporáneos,: Ediciones Literatura Americana Reunida, 1988. 1 v.: bibl., ill. (Col. Teoría y sociedad)

Excellent collection of Allende's speeches and writings. This material traces development of Allende's ideas about public health, politics, international relations, and social policy up to 1948. A valuable tool not merely for understanding Allende but for his descriptions of Chile and the position of the Partido Socialista on various significant issues.

2824 Angell, Alan. Some problems in the interpretation of recent Chilean history. (*Bull. Lat. Am. Res.*, 7:1, 1988, p. 91–108)

Attributes 1973 coup to lack of strong political parties, their tendency to favor ideological purity over compromise, an alienated military, runaway inflation, ungratified expectations, and inability to institute reforms. This highly provocative article raises tantalizing questions and whets the appetite for answers. Author calls into question various cherished, and often mistaken, beliefs about Chile's political system and challenges notion of the importance of political parties, noting a hostility toward them as well as a certain discrepancy between the parties and their ideologies. This latter fact tended to make compromise difficult.

2825 Apey Rivera, María Angélica. Sociedad Nacional de Agricultura, Universidad Metropolitana de Ciencias de la Educación: proyecto de la historia de la agricultura chilena. v. 1. Prólogo y epílogo de Gonzalo Vial C. Santiago: Sociedad Nacional de Agricultura, 1988. 1 v.: bibl., ill.

Highly laudatory description of the Sociedad Nacional de Agricultura's activities. Work provides a quick overview and contains some interesting bits of data, but is more of a polemic defending the landed aristocracy than a history of the institution.

2826 Arriagada, Carmen. Carmen Arriagada: cartas de una mujer apasionada. Estudio preliminar y notas de Oscar Pinochet de la Barra. Santiago: Editorial Universitaria, 1989. 548 p.: index, ports. (Col. Fuera de serie)

Collection of letters written 1835–51 by a provincial gentlewoman to Mauricio Rugendas, a German painter who resided temporarily in Chile. Valuable insights into the lives of the "gente decente" during the first half of the 19th century as well as into author's views of Chile and the world.

2827 Avila Martel, Alamiro de et al. Estudios sobre José Victorino Lastarria. Santiago: Ediciones de la Univ. de Chile, 1988. 306 p.: bibl., port.

Series of essays on Lastarria, his personality, his career at the Univ. of Chile, his understanding of the law, his attempts to reform the legal curriculum, his intellectual development and ideas, and his relation with the English Positivist Buckle. Useful collection of articles for those interested in Lastarria's contributions and personality.

2828 Bengoa C., José. Historia social de la agricultura chilena. v. 1, El poder y la subordinación. v. 2, Haciendas y campesinos. Santiago: Ediciones Sur, 1988–1990. 2 v.

Superb, well-documented and researched study describes Chilean agriculture, the working of the *fundo,* and the relationships between *patrón* and *inquilino.* Vol. 1 examines the growth of the *fundo* system, its economic development based on cereal production, and how *terratenientes* controlled the rural work force as well as interacted with other socioeconomic elements. Vol. 2 focuses on *fundos* operating throughout the nation, providing data on workers, their salaries, and the spread and eventual decay of the Chilean *fundo* system. This work, which contains some excellent photographs, is essential reading for all scholars interested in agricultural history. For sociologist's commment, see *HLAS 53 : 5388.*

2829 Bernedo, Patricio. Prosperidad económica bajo Carlos Ibáñez del Campo, 1927–1929. (*Historia/Santiago,* 24, 1989, p. 5–105, tables)

Welcome and well-done study of the economic policies of Ibáñez's first regime. Studies various facets of the nation's economic development and Ibáñez's reorganization plan, which was completed with the assistance of his minister, Pablo Ramírez. Despite Ibáñez's best efforts, Chile remained too dependent on *salitre* whose price never recovered after 1929.

2830 Blakemore, Harold. From the Pacific to La Paz: the Antofagasta (Chili) and Bolivia Railway Company, 1888–1988. London: Antofagasta Holdings; Lester Crook Academic, 1990. 334 p.: bibl., ill. (some col.), index, map.

An elegant study by one of the field's pre-eminent scholars explains the operations of the Antofagasta and Bolivia Railway. Using company records, Blakemore provides insight into the operations of Chile's and Bolivia's mining industries, the relationships between the gringo operators, their workers, and the governments in Santiago and La Paz.

2831 Blancpain, J.P. LÞarmée chilienne et les instructeurs allemands en Amérique latine, 1885–1914. (*Rev. hist./Paris,* 578, avril/juin 1991, p. 347–394)

Account of attempts to convert Chile's army into the Prussians of the Pacific concludes that the Teutonic advisors, led by Gen. Emil Körner, may have been willing to train them but the Chileans seemed either unwilling or unable to assimilate anything more than the *paso de ganzo.*

2832 Bravo Lira, Bernardino. De Portales a Pinochet: gobierno y régimen de gobierno en Chile. Santiago: Editorial Jurídica de Chile; Editorial Andrés Bello, 1985. 185 p.: bibl.

Compilation of previously published essays demonstrates author's displeasure with the post-1925 period. He emphasizes the apparent collapse of authority and the rise of partisan politics.

2833 Bravo Lira, Bernardino. Imagen de Chile en el siglo XX: cultura, sociedad, instituciones. Santiago: Univ. Metropolitana de Ciencias de la Educación, 1988. 228 p.: bibl., ill.

Brief and not particularly successful attempt to analyze Chilean society, culture, and political developments. Emphasizes period up to end of the Parliamentary Regime rather than subsequent decades. Although the book does have some useful charts, it is filled with unrelated facts. Historians can avoid this work with a clear conscience.

Cablegramas chilenos durante la ocupación de Lima, julio-octubre 1881. See item 2704.

2834 La caída de Allende: transcripción textual de las conversaciones, a través de las líneas radiotelefónicas militares, sostenidas entre Pinochet, Leigh y otros altos mandos en las horas decisivas del golpe de estado de setiembre de 1973. Recopilación de Jorge Boldáz Aguirre. Buenos Aires: Frente Argentino Chileno por la Democracia, 1986. 38 p.: ill.

Transcription of radio conversations between the leaders of the 1973 coup (Pinochet, Leigh, and Carvajal) as they directed the assault on the Moneda. Valuable but not particularly riveting.

2835 Campos Harriet, Fernando. Historia de Concepción, 1550–1988. 4. ed. Santiago: Editorial Universitaria, 1989. 438 p.: bibl., ill., index. (Col. Imagen de Chile)

Regional study attempts to cram 300 years of Concepción's cultural, economic, political, and institutional history into one volume. Although too brief for the serious reader, it nonetheless contains some worthwhile data.

2836 Camus Argaluza, Maite. La inmigración vasca en Chile: 1880–1990. Vitoria, Spain: Depto. de Cultura, Gobierno Vasco; Santiago, Chile: Eusko Etxea-Chile, 1991. 45 p.:

Superficial but somewhat useful work includes information on immigration in general and specific facts on the number of Basques settling in Chile, their economic activities, and their organizations.

2837 Capellaro, Ernesto. Memorias de un inmigrante italiano en Chile. Recopilación de Silvia Mezzano Lopetegui. Santiago: Los Libros del Arcabuz, 1989. 97 p.: bibl., ill.

Autobiography of an Italian who settled in Valparaíso in 1885 after first traveling to New York, Buenos Aires, and then treking over the Andes. He remained in Chile, working as a hat maker, until 1919 when he returned to Italy. An excellent but brief study of the classic sojourner's experiences in the New World.

2838 Couyoumdjian, Juan Ricardo and Antonia Rebolledo Hernández. Bibliografía sobre el proceso inmigratorio en Chile, desde la independencia hasta 1930. (*in* Bibliografía sobre el impacto del proceso inmigratorio masivo en el Cono Sur de América. México: Instituto Panamericano de Geografía e Historia, 1984, p. 121–186, bibl.)

Extensive bibliography on various ethnic communities which have immigrated to Chile includes material from each group as well as from offical reports, laws, and powerful interest groups. Essential for students of immigration history.

2839 Covarrubias, María Teresa. 1938, la rebelión de los jóvenes. Santiago: Editorial Aconcagua, 1987. 141 p.: bibl, ill.

Author traces the influence of the Church's call for social justice and that of certain progressive members of the clergy on the founders of the Falange Nacional, the predecessor of Chile's Christian Democratic Party. Plodding but methodical; useful for students of political and intellectual history.

2840 Covarrubias, María Teresa. Políticos y militares: antecedentes históricos del quiebre entre los sectores civil y militar en la sociedad chilena, 1924–1932. Santiago: Centro de Estudios del Desarrollo; Editorial Atena, 1991. 232 p.: bibl.

Author uses a minimum of sources in attempt to explain military involvement in politics from the 1920s to Alessandri's 1932 reelection. She evinces a pronounced sympathy toward Ibáñez, who is described as well intentioned, but adds little new information.

2841 Devés V., Eduardo. Los que van a morir te saludan: historia de una masacre, Escuela Santa María, Iquique, 1907. Santiago: Ediciones Documentas; América Latina Libros; Nuestra América, 1988. 218 p., 37 p. of plates: bibl., ill.

Dense work describes events leading up to and including the infamous 1907 Iquique massacre. Relying heavily on newspapers, author attributes bloodshed to bad luck and to workers' mistaken reliance on passive resistance. Author's descriptions adequately capture the event but his explanations are lacking.

2842 Díaz, Carlos and Fredy Cancino. Italianos en Chile: breve historia de una inmigración. Santiago: Ediciones Documentas; Milan?: Instituto Fernando Santi, 1988. 140 p.: bibl.

Few Italians chose to immigrate to Chile due to its remote geographical location and lack of encouragement and incentives to attract them. Those who did reach Chile created an intricate web of mutual aid societies and social and cultural organizations. Superficial work does not adequately cover the Italian contribution to Chile.

Espinoza, Vicente. Para una historia de los pobres de la ciudad. See *HLAS 53:5419.*

2843 Faúndez, Julio. Marxism and democracy in Chile: from 1932 to the fall of Allende. New Haven, Conn.: Yale Univ. Press, 1988. 305 p.: bibl., index.

Traces the role of the left in the Chilean political process, from the inception of the Partido Socialista to 1973 coup. This fair, balanced work relying on secondary sources is most useful to students of the left rather than for those looking for an analysis of the Allende regime.

2844 Ferrer Mir, Jaime. Los españoles del *Winnipeg:* el barco de la esperanza. Santiago: Ediciones Cal Sogas, 1989. 202 p.: bibl., ill.

Volume commemorates the 50th anniversary of the arrival of approximately 2,000 Spanish Loyalist refugees to Chile. Author describes last days of the Spanish Civil War, the flight of the refugees to France, and the efforts of Chilean diplomat Pablo Neruda to gain them asylum. Based on personal memories, congressional debates, and newspaper editorials.

2845 Figueroa Ortiz, Enrique and **Carlos Sandoval Ambiado.** Carbón: cien años de historia, 1848–1960. Santiago: Centro de Asesoría Profesional, 1987. 306 p., 16 p. of plates: bibl., ill.

First-rate work manages to combine history of the local left-wing press, a description of various labor demonstrations, the lives of miners and their social institutions, and their attempts to achieve some social justice. Written from a leftist perspective, but bias is made clear from the start.

2846 Fuenzalida Bade, Rodrigo. Marinos ilustres y destacados del pasado: síntesis biográfica. Chile: Sipimex, 1985. 280 p.: bibl., index, ports.

Very useful biographical compilation of Chile's most influential naval figures, both famous and obscure.

2847 Galería de hombres de armas de Chile. v. 1, Períodos hispánico y de la independencia, 1535–1826. v. 2, Período de la influencia francesa, 1826–1885. v. 3, Períodos de las influencias alemana y norteamericana, 1885–1952. Santiago: Estado Mayor General de Ejército, 1987? 3 v.: bibl., ill. (some col.) (Col. Biblioteca militar)

Provides biographical sketches of the leading military figures, as well as of various foreign advisors who shaped the Chilean army. Drawn from a variety of excellent sources, the volumes contain valuable bibliographical information and are extremely useful for students of modern military history.

2848 Garay Vera, Cristián. El Partido Agrario Laborista, 1945–1958. Santiago: Editorial Andrés Bello, 1990. 245 p.: bibl., ill.

Study of the political movement which provided the vehicle for Ibáñez's 1958 return to Chilean political life, and the Moneda. Drawing on a wide range of sources, author focuses more on the PAL ideology and the various internal struggles than on the second Ibáñez regime. A welcome addition to a subject about which little is known.

2849 Garcés, Mario. Crisis social y motines populares en el 1900. Santiago: Ediciones Documentos; ECO-Educación y Comunicaciones, 1991. 263 p.: bibl.

Chilean workers began a wave of violent strikes after 1900. These demonstrations mobilized disparate workers and underscored the elite's inability to address their needs. The workers sought to change Chilean society first by supporting the Partido Demócrata, and when that party had been co-opted by the parliamentary system, by supporting socialist groups.

Garcés, Mario. Crisis social y motines populares en el 1900. See *HLAS 53:5426.*

2850 Gazmuri, Cristián. Los artesanos de Santiago en 1850, y el despertar político del sector popular chileno. (*Rev. Indias,* 5:192, mayo/agosto 1991, p. 397–416, tables)

In 1850, Chile's artisan population numbered approximately 15,000 in Santiago and about 31,000 in the provinces. This highly speculative article argues that the Chilean working class became so politically aware that it participated in the anti-Montt demonstrations. Using limited, sometimes controversial sources, author stretches to make his point and even admits that his thesis is debatable.

2851 Gómez Araneda, León. Que el pueblo juzgue: la historia del golpe. Santiago: Terranova Editores, 1988. 426 p.: bibl., ill.

Recounts story of Allende's death and the fate of those who supported him. This is a vivid, even lurid account of the Junta's trials and punishments of Allende supporters. Includes a list of those killed and their political affiliations.

2852 Góngora, Mario *et al.* Historia de las mentalidades. Palabras preliminares de Juana Muñoz Salinas. Valparaíso, Chile: EDEVAL, 1986. 146 p.: bibl., ill. (Col. Jornadas académicas; 7)

Excellent series of essays on mentalities in Chile. Particularly noteworthy are Góngora's study of the changing image of *lo civil* from the colonial to the modern period, and Ricardo Krebs' essay which uses the centenary of Chilean independence to study the mindsets of the upper class. A valuable contribution to the history of ideas in Chile.

2853 González Deluca, María Elena; Hernán Muñoz Villafuerte; and **Luis Cipriano Rodríguez.** Tres momentos del nacionalismo en Chile. Caracas: Fondo Editorial Tropykos, 1989. 179 p.: bibl. (Serie Ensayos)

Three essays of uneven quality, uncertain purpose, and strong political bias: González's study on the 1891 Revolution, Muñoz's more successful précis of the 1932 Socialist Republic, and Cipriano's stale work on Allende. Though providing a brief summary of these three events, the studies are not particularly distinguished.

2854 González Pizarro, José Antonio. Claudio Gay y la historiografía chilena: el contexto histórico-cultural en la formulación de una concepción historiográfica. (*Caravelle/Toulouse*, 55, 1990, p. 83–104)

French-born Claudio Gay brought many European ideas to his writing of Chile's history. He approached history as a positive tracing of human development, and though willingly using history to reinforce a sense of Chilean identity, he still based his research efforts on documentation and interviews.

2855 Guerrero Yoacham, Cristián and María Soledad Valdés. Historia de la reforma agraria en Chile. Edición de José Garrido R. Prólogo de Rolando Mellafe. Santiago: Editorial Universitaria, 1988. 272 p.: (Col. Imagen de Chile)

Extremely useful work based on the doctoral dissertation of María Soledad Valdés relies on extensive primary materials drawn from a variety of sources to objectively trace history of agrarian reform from its unlikely beginning under Ibáñez to the post-1973 coup government. Excellent comprehensive and analytical study of a controversial topic.

2856 Hirsch-Weber, Wolfgang. Chiles Salpetermonopol in seiner Bedeutung für Staat und Gesellschaft. (*Ibero-Am. Arch.*, 16: 2, 1990, p. 273–340, tables)

Analysis of Chilean nitrate trade (1900–25) concludes that it fostered large-scale venality within the nation's bureaucracy. State policies enriched the upper class and contributed to inflation, while depriving the State of revenue to improve the physical and social infrastructure for the nation as a whole. [C.K. Converse]

2857 Huerta, María Antonieta and Luis Pacheco Pastene. La iglesia chilena y los cambios sociopolíticos. Santiago: Pehuén; CISOC-Bellarmino, 1988. 369 p.: (Ensayo)

Authors describe role of Church as a force for Christianizing Chile and then explain its ability to adapt to a society in flux. Valuable for tracing evolution of Church and its responses to a Chile confronting the problems of the 20th century. Relies heavily on clerical sources.

2858 Indice de la Historia del Ejército de Chile: tomo I, El Ejército del Reyno de Chile, 1603–1810 al tomo XI, Historia de nuestros uniformes, 1986. Santiago: Estado Mayor General del Ejército, 1986. 246 p. (Historia del Ejército de Chile; 12)

Index for the multivolume *Historia del Ejército de Chile*. Extremely useful guide for military historians.

2859 Izquierdo Fernández, Gonzalo. Historia de Chile. v. 2–3. Santiago: Editorial Andrés Bello, 1989–1990. 2 v.: bibl., ill.

General history written by a talented historian who died prematurely. Vol. 2 includes material on Chile's political, economic, cultural, and intellectual development from 1800–91 and is excellent. Vol. 3 tries to cover too much and hence gives the 20th century short shrift, but it does provide excellent material on Chile's political parties.

2860 Jiménez, Oscar; Juan Antonio Salinas; and Enrique Zorrilla Concha. Masacre: por qué los asesinaron? Parral, Chile: Ediciones Nuestramérica, 1988. 155 p.: bibl., ill. (Col. Tierradentro)

Highly sympathetic account of participants in the abortive 1938 uprising which culminated in the massacre in the Social Security Building. Citing primary documents, author blames Pres. Alessandri and his minions. Concludes with a section attempting to whitewash Chile's Movimiento Nacional Socialista.

2861 Kaufman, Edy. Crisis in Allende's Chile: new perspectives. New York: Praeger, 1988. 414 p.: bibl., ill., index.

Somewhat tortured attempt to apply ideas about international relations in order to explain Allende's government and its overthrow. While founded on sound research, the unwarranted speculation on the role of the US as well as on Allende's motivations undermine some of the book's real merit.

2862 Laborde, Miguel. Vascos en Santiago de Chile. Vitoria, Spain: Depto. de Cultura, Gobierno Vasco; Santiago: Eusko Etxea-Chile, 1991. 106 p.:

Biographies of some of the Basque immigrants for whom streets have been named in Santiago. Hardly earthshattering but author includes meaning of the names in Spanish. A joy for Basque nationalists.

López Rubio, Sergio E. Los vengadores de Rancagua. See *HLAS 53:3016.*

Loveman, Brian. Chile: the legacy of Hispanic capitalism. See item **2474.**

2863 Maldonado P., Carlos. Los carabineros de Chile: historia de una policia militarizada. (*Ibero-Am./Stockholm,* 20:3, 1990, p. 3–31)

Modeled after the Italian Carabineros and influenced by the Chilean army, the Carabineros filled a need for a professional police force. Identified with the Ibáñez regime and its abuses, the force distanced itself from the military after 1932. Nonetheless, its increasing involvement in maintaining national security, participation in the 1973 coup, and later, service to the junta, led to a remilitarization of the Carabineros.

2864 Maldonado P., Carlos. La Milicia Republicana: historia de un ejército civil en Chile, 1932–1936. Santiago: Servicio Universitario Mundial, Comité Nacional-Chile, 1988. 160 p.: bibl.

Initially created to deter the army from attempting to regain political control, the *Milicia Republicana* espoused a corporatist and anti-leftist ideology. It collapsed when it lost the support of the Partido Radical and became a political embarassment for Alessandri. Although disjointed and lacking a broad research base, the book still has some merit.

2865 Martínez Fernández, José G. Allende: su vida, su pensamiento político. Santiago: Ediciones Palabra Escrita, 1988. 192 p.: bibl.

Short, hagiographic biography of Allende is followed by excerpts from some of his statements. Useful as a source of some of Allende's later ideas and positions but otherwise a superficial compilation devoid of analysis.

2866 Martinic Beros, Mateo. Magallanes, 1921–1952: inquietud y crisis. Punta Arenas, Chile: Prensa Austral, 1988. 386 p.: bibl.

Detailed work describes cultural, economic, and administrative changes which marked the development of Magallanes after 1921. Superb regional study, based on extensive run of newspapers. Essential study for all historians.

2867 Martinic Beros, Mateo. Punta Arenas en su primer medio siglo, 1848–1898. Punta Arenas, Chile: M. Martinic B., 1988. 329 p.: bibl., ill.

Epic study of Punta Arenas by the preeminent historian of Chile's south. Beginning with its founding in the mid-1840s, the author provides information on the city's social and intellectual life, the expansion of the local economy, and various political administrations. Excellent work necessary for understanding the role of this port in Chile's development.

2868 Moulian, Tomás. El gobierno de Ibáñez, 1952–1958. Santiago: Programa FLACSO, 1986. 83 p.: bibl. (Material docente sobre historia de Chile; 2)

Chile's tattered political parties managed to outlive Ibáñez's second administration because he could not offer a viable alternative. Although unable to restructure the nation's political landscape, changes did occur during his regime: the right lost its appeal, the left coalesced into a powerful coalition, and the Christian Democrats emerged as a potent political force. Workmanlike and welcome study of Ibáñez's second regime.

2869 Muñoz Correa, Juan Guillermo et al. La Universidad de Santiago de Chile: sobre sus orígenes y su desarrollo histórico. Santiago: Univ. de Santiago de Chile, 1987. 298 p., 16 p. of plates: bibl., ill.

The Escuela de Artes y Oficios, which began in 1849 as a center for teaching technology, became the Universidad Técnica del Estado in 1952, and, in 1980, the Universidad de Santiago de Chile. Author uses University archives to trace the University's evolution into a center for teaching liberal arts and technical subjects.

2870 Müther, Jutta. Orllie-Antoine I., König von Araukanien und Patagonien oder Nouvelle France: Konsolidierungsprobleme in Chile, 1860–1870. Frankfurt am Main; New York: P. Lang, 1990. 287 p.: bibl., ill. (Europäische Hochschulschriften. Reihe III, Geschichte und ihre Hilfswissenschaften, 0531–7320; 421)

Well-researched examination of French

citizen's bizarre claims to royal leadership of the Araucanian Indians (1860–70). Illustrates Chile's somewhat unjustified fear of French intervention as well as the government's perception of disloyalty on the part of its disaffected Indian population. Müther's study is a valuable contribution to a little-known episode in Chilean history. [C.K. Converse]

2871 Nolte, Detlef. Zwischen Rebellion und Integration: Gewerkschaften in der chilenischen Politik. Saarbrücken; Fort Lauderdale: Breitenbach, 1986. 659 p.: bibl. (Forschungen zu Lateinamerika, 0177–0918; 4)

Based on exhaustive research, this interpretation of the Chilean labor movement (1900–79), set against the nation's socioeconomic and political history, emphasizes the contradiction between tight government control and successful circumvention of legal curtailments. Includes detailed tables compiled by author. [C.K. Converse]

2872 Norambuena Carrasco, Carmen and **Guillermo Bravo Acevedo.** Política y legislación inmigratoria en Chile, 1830–1930. (*Rev. Hist. Am.,* 109, enero/junio 1990, p. 69–128, appendix, index, tables)

Despite efforts of the central government, Chile did not attract many immigrants. The opening of the southern frontier encouraged immigration but many Chileans resented the concessions given to immigrants. The Sociedad Nacional de Agricultura and Sociedad de Fomento Fabril also tried to attract people, but immigration declined after 1907, perhaps in part because of the passage of laws which required papers certifying immigrants' health and skills. Useful summary which includes the legislation regulating immigration.

2873 Olguín Tenorio, Myriam and **Patricia Peña González.** La inmigración árabe en Chile. Santiago: Ediciones Instituto Chileno Arabe de Cultura, 1990. 163 p.: bibl., maps.

For political and then economic reasons, "turcos" of the Ottoman Empire began arriving in Chile after 1880. Although they settled throughout the country, most concentrated in Santiago. Despite a hostile reception, the "turcos" entered the world of commerce, some achieving substantial success. A good first effort which merits more consideration.

2874 Orellana Muermann, Marcela and **Juan Guillermo Muñoz Correa.** Mundo minero Chile, siglos XIX y XX. Santiago: Univ. de Santiago, 1992. 190 p.

Series of original essays related to the mining industry, some emphasizing literary themes. The best rely on extensive primary sources to describe the living and working conditions of the miners in southern coal pits and the northern *salitreras.* Essential work for social and economic historians.

2875 Parker de Bassi, María Teresa. Tras la estela del *Dresden.* Santiago: Ediciones Tusitala, 1987. 212 p.: bibl., ill.

Covers battles of Coronel and Falklands in 1914 and eventual destruction of the *Dresden* in Chilean waters, off Robinson Crusoe Island. Mediocre naval history but interesting for those studying the reaction of the Chilean government, and its citizens of German extraction, to the events of WWI.

2876 Pinochet Ugarte, Augusto. Camino recorrido. v. 1, Biografía de un soldado. Santiago: Tall. Gráf. del Instituto Geográfico Militar de Chile, 1990. 1 v.: ill., ports.

Pinochet's memoirs concentrate more on his earlier years than on the events leading up to the coup. Mildly interesting, work reveals little, if anything, other than an implacable distaste for the left and the ability to survive garrison duty in the provinces.

2877 Pinto Vallejos, Julio and **Luis Ortega Martínez.** Expansión minera y desarrollo industrial: un caso de crecimiento asociado, Chile 1850–1914. Santiago: Depto. de Historia, Univ. de Santiago de Chile. 1990. 184 p.: bibl., ill.

Authors draw on an extensive bibliography to clearly demonstrate how the mining industry, and its workforce, provided the capital and the market which led to the creation and growth of Chile's industries and its transportation system from the mid-1850s to 1914. An essential and elegant work for all scholars.

2878 Portales, el hombre y su obra: la consolidación del gobierno civil. Recopilación de Bernardino Bravo Lira. Santiago: Editorial Jurídica de Chile; Editorial Andrés Bello, 1989. 539 p., 26 p. of plates: bibl., ill.

Superb collection of essays describes Portales the man, the diplomat, the statesman, and the businessman, as well as his administrative, judicial, and economic policies. Concludes with an interesting study of the image of Portales in painting and in Chilean historiography. An essential work for all historians of Chile.

2879 Pozo, José del. Les chemins vers la gauche: la socialisation politique des supporteurs de l'unité populaire chilienne. (*Can. J. Lat. Am. Caribb. Stud.*, 15:29, 1990, p. 83–104, table)

Article depends on a very narrow sampling to conclude that there were a variety of reasons, many unexpected, which influenced people to support Allende. Author encourages more work on this topic because traditional reasons such as family and social class are not the only forces which dictate political behavior.

2880 Rodríguez Rautcher, Sergio. Bases documentales para el estudio de la Guerra del Pacífico con algunas descripciones, reflexiones y alcances. v. 1–2. Santiago?: s.n., 1991. 2 v.

Superb bibliography of the various sources on the War of the Pacific, its causes, its course, and its consequences. Particularly useful because it provides a guide to the various unpublished government documents as well as the press in Chile, the territories it occupied, Bolivia, and Peru. Essential for anyone interested in the war.

2881 Rodríguez Villegas, Hernán. Historia de la Chacra Subercaseaux: contribución al estudio de la propiedad en Santiago. (*Bol. Acad. Chil. Hist.*, 55:99, 1988, p. 257–306, map)

Surveys colonial origins and traces in considerable detail post-independence history of a famous property in Santiago, the Subercaseaux estate in the Llano de Maipo. Before becoming property of Senator Ramón Subercaseaux in 1835, it belonged to Bernardo O'Higgins. [M.T. Hamerly]

2882 Romero, Luis Alberto. Rotos y gañanes: trabajadores no calificados en Santiago. (*Cuad. Hist.*, 8, dic. 1988, p. 35–71, tables)

Unskilled agricultural laborers began moving to urban centers after 1875, attracted by jobs working on public works projects, railroads, and later the *salitreras.* Although workers often changed employment, and

sometimes returned to work on the farms, competition for labor proved hard on employees, destroying the old ties binding *patrón* with workers.

2883 Sagredo Baeza, Rafael. Pragmatismo proteccionista en los orígenes de la república. (*Historia/Santiago*, 24, 1989, p. 267–286)

O'Higgins favored retaining some traditional mercantilistic doctrines, such as seeking self-sufficiency, which he had to temper in order to raise revenues. He saw the *aduana* as a source of revenue and an instrument to foment industries that would in turn provide additional sources of revenue. These policies continued under Rengifo.

2884 Salazar González, Julene and **Roberto Hernández Ponce.** Cuatrocientos años de presencia vasca en Chile. Vitoria, Spain: Depto. de Cultura, Gobierno Vasco; Santiago: Eusko Etxea-Chile, 1991. 182 p.: bibl.

Series of short biographies on important Basque-Chileans and their achievements. Includes information on various Basque organizations. Useful for genealogists.

Salazar Vergara, Gabriel. Violencia política popular en las "grandes alamedas," Santiago de Chile, 1947–1987: una perspectiva histórico-popular. See *HLAS 53:5475.*

2885 Salina Meza, René. Orphans and family disintegration in Chile: the mortality of abandoned children, 1750–1930. (*J. Fam. Hist.*, 16:3, 1991, p. 315–329, bibl., graphs, tables)

Santiago's orphan asylum provided temporary haven for orphans, most of whom died either from disease or lack of proper care. Although survival increased after 1900, people tended to accept their demise with a passivity perhaps born out of habit or a sense of fatalism.

Scherzer, Karl, *Ritter von.* Así nos vio la Novara: impresiones austríacas sobre Chile y el Perú en 1859. See item **2778.**

Scully, Timothy. Rethinking the center: party politics in nineteenth- and twentieth-century Chile. See *HLAS 53:4021.*

2886 Silva, Rosario Güenaga de. La presencia alemana en el extremo austral de América. (*Jahrb. Gesch.*, 26, 1989, p. 201–227)

Various Germans settled in the south of Chile and Argentina where they quickly became entrenched in the local economy, launching highly successful businesses as well as creating social and educational institutions which exercised an enormous influence over the area. Author concentrates on one of these clans, the Braun family, which created a livestock empire.

2887 Subercaseaux, Bernardo. Fin de siglo: la época de Balmaceda; modernización y cultura en Chile. Santiago: Editorial Aconcagua; CENECA, 1988. 323 p.: bibl.

Literature and culture increasingly reflected issues that preoccupied post-1891 Chile, such as the decline in public morality, the tendency to blindly adopt foreign customs, and the appearance of the *cuestión social.* As political life stagnated, fiction and poetry, sometimes reflecting European modernism, began to confront these issues. Interesting study analyzes the impact of politics on culture.

2888 Thomas, Jack Ray. The influence of Marmaduke Grove on the Chilean socialism of Salvador Allende. (*in* The crucible of socialism. Edited by Louis Pastouras. Atlantic Highlands, N.J.: Humanities Press International, 1987, p. 369–382)

Marmaduke Grove, the founder of Chile's Partido Socialista, did not wish to blindly implement Marxist doctrine, but rather to address Chile's problems. Allende, according to the author, shared many of Grove's ideas, including a committment to pluralism and a willingness to make change.

2889 Valdivieso Ariztía, Rafael. Crónica de un rescate: Chile, 1973–1988. Santiago: Editorial Andrés Bello, 1988. 327 p.: bibl., ill., ports.

Highly conservative account of Chile's post-1973 period attempts to combine politics, economics, and international relations. Though not deeply researched, it does provide the reader information, albeit biased, on this crucial period.

2890 Vidaurre-Leal, Carlos Aguirre. En al año del sesquicentenario del combate naval de Casma: rumbo a la gloria del triunfo marcia. (*Rev. Mar.,* 106:791, julio/agosto 1989, p. 409–431, bibl., maps)

Nationalistic but a happily brief and comprehensive study of the naval aspects of Chile's war against the Bolivian Confederation. Notes that the fleet performed better than the army. Laments that Chile so quickly forgot the importance of the fleet, an oversight which the Spanish bombardment of Valparaíso would subsequently make apparent.

2891 Villalobos R., Sergio. Breve historia de Chile. Caracas: Academia Nacional de la Historia, 1987. 188 p.: ill. (El libro menor; 121)

Somewhat superficial for scholars, work is nonetheless a useful overview of Chile by one of its more well-known historians.

2892 Yávar Meza, Aldo. El Gremio de Jornaleros y Lancheros de Valparaíso, 1837–1859: etapa de formación. (*Historia/ Santiago,* 24, 1989, p. 319–395, tables)

The need to ensure a constant flow of income from commerce forced the Moneda to organize port workers in Valparaíso and to intervene actively to reconcile the interests of labor and capital. Divergent interests in the union led workers to support anti-Montt forces in the 1859 Revolution. An interesting and well-researched article demonstrating that the Moneda was not so *laissez faire.*

2893 Yeager, Gertrude M. Elite education in nineteenth-century Chile. (*HAHR,* 71: 1, Feb. 1991, p. 73–105, tables)

The Instituto Nacional served as Chile's premier secondary school, producing graduates with an excellent education as well as sober personal habits and high moral values. Though an elite institution with a select faculty, it served the country well, providing a trained cadre of civil servants and politicians. A well-researched and interesting article.

Argentina, Paraguay, and Uruguay

JOSEPH T. CRISCENTI, *Professor Emeritus of History, Boston College*

HISTORICAL WRITINGS IN THIS BIENNIUM show the influence of the Columbus Quincentennial and reflect a tendency to challenge what some perceive to be
the myths and unsupported assumptions of earlier historiography. Case studies are
more numerous, and more research is being done in the provincial archives and
newspaper collections outside of Buenos Aires. As in the past, modern Argentina
continues to attract the attention of most scholars, but emphasis has shifted from
the post-1930 period to the years between 1880–1930. A majority of the female historians focus primarily on modern Argentina. Many scholars of 19th-century Argentina have embarked on major projects which promise to bring into better focus the
first decades of the independence era. Historians seeking statistical or economic data
continue to struggle with incomplete or absent census data, tax collection records,
and trade accounts, but are nevertheless discerning patterns that give new insights
into more obscure areas of the former Viceroyalty of the Río de la Plata.

Research results to date confirm the widespread view that independence from
Spain did not mean a sharp break with the past. Colonial agrarian practices, commercial law, social customs, and institutions remained virtually unchanged until
about 1880: not until then did the modern period truly begin in Argentina, Paraguay,
and Uruguay. Further investigations have cast doubt on the traditional image of the
gaucho and rural areas in the 18th and 19th centuries. Scholars now are seeking to
define the gaucho, and along with him, the estanciero, hacendado, and the small
farmer, but contemporary usage of these terms makes typification difficult. Economic historians are uncovering a growing body of evidence pointing to colonial and
post-independence economic competition between Buenos Aires and Córdoba, and
to an uneven economic development of the Interior provinces: Córdoba and Salta, it
now appears, were exceptionally prosperous. Palomeque has expanded our knowledge of inter- and intra-regional trade relations in the Interior provinces, and has
demonstrated that the viceregal economy was an integral part of the world economy
(item **3029**). Also apparent is the existence of an economy in which specie payments
coexisted with payments in kind.

The understanding of some well-known 19th-century issues has benefitted
from the publication of additional documents. Some attest to the mixture of political ideas that circulated after independence. For example, documentary publications
(items **2983** and **2948**) reveal that Martín Miguel de Güemes of Salta joined forces
with the Governor of Córdoba to nullify the opposition of Bernardino Rivadavia of
Buenos Aires to San Martín and the Congress of Tucumán. Güemes was a monarchist, but some Salteños—Unitarians—wanted to build the future nation on local
laws and customs, and still others—followers of José Artigas—looked to the US as a
model. French political ideas were present, but were more influential in Buenos
Aires and Paraguay than in the Argentine Northwest. Viola found additional archival
evidence to support his thesis that Paraguay's Francia admired Napoleon and the US,
and was both a defender and a builder of his own nation (items **3119** and **3099**). Debate continues on the origins and consequences of the Paraguayan War, though interpretations often reflect ideological considerations rather than new data. Tjarks
found documents that seem to confirm the partisan view of the Mitre Administration as not genuinely neutral prior to the outbreak of the war (item **3117**). He as-

sumes that Mitre was a strong president and that a body of enforceable neutrality laws existed. The diary of Silvia Cordal Gill (item **3116**) and accounts of the women accompanying Solano López (item **3114**) reflect unfavorably on Solano López but do support the view that the traditional family structure was unaffected by the war. Paraguayan economic history, with the exception of the yerba maté trade, remains relatively unexplored. Provincial caudillos continue to undergo a reevaluation which is changing their unfavorable image created by the Unitarian exiles. Perhaps the most definitive biography of Felipe Ibarra appears in Alén Lascano's impressive social and economic history of Santiago del Estero (item **2898**). An overlooked but important biography of Governor Estanislao López of Santa Fé, a friend of San Martín and Artigas, the father of Argentine federalism, and Quiroga's rival, has been reissued (item **3002**). It is based on provincial archives.

As the literature canvassed here indicates, one concern of the colonists that persisted into the 19th century was the abundance of unoccupied and mostly unclaimed land on the fluid frontier. The solution advanced by colonial theorists, Sarmiento, and others was to fill the empty space with a rural class of small landowners. Paraguay used colonial laws to encourage occupation of the border facing the Chaco, and the government sent Correntino refugees to Concepción to resist the Mbyas. Uruguay tried unsuccessfully to become a land of small farmers, but land was scarce or expensive and immigrants preferred Argentina and Brazil. In the province of Buenos Aires, few took advantage of the frontier land grants offered by Rosas. However, Danes and Frenchmen did settle in and around the frontier town of Tandil, and their experiences are depicted in the fascinating memoirs of Juan Fugl (item **2963**). The government of Santa Fé aggressively encouraged the establishment of agricultural colonies on its frontiers. Some were sponsored by the Jewish Colonization Association, others by entrepreneurs and the railroads. The result was a patchwork of ethnic settlements, each with its own historian. The most arresting of the Jewish accounts tells of the founding and growth of Moisés Ville (item **2993**). These self-governing pioneers never learned Spanish law and defended their independence from the provincial government. Their discontent with living and economic conditions led them to organize the Argentine Agricultural Federation in the 20th century. Some of the agricultural colonies eventually became manufacturing towns, but this process has received little attention from scholars.

In the modern era the national government continued the policy of welcoming all immigrants, hoping they would further economic growth by forming a class of small farmers in the Argentine "desert." A wide variety of ethnic groups arrived, some to settle in the city and province of Buenos Aires, others in thinly populated border areas, and still others in the "younger" provinces. Akmir prepared a model study of the Syrians and Lebanese who settled in the province of Santiago del Estero (item **2897**). Scholarly attention has focused primarily on the Italian immigrant, but all ethnic groups had the same basic experience. Migration, as the concept of chain migration holds, did not mean an abrupt break with the past. Each ethnic group tended to think of itself as a separate colony: to preserve its language and culture, it might organize mutual aid societies, schools, churches, and presses. Most were eventually assimilated, but few immigrants became naturalized citizens, for it would mean losing their exemption from military service and aid from their consular agents. The immigrant's refusal to acquire Argentine citizenship concerned thoughtful Argentines who wanted a more democratic society for their country, but they disagreed on an explanation for the phenomenon and its solution.

Government propaganda abroad influenced the influx of immigrants after

1880, and the newly-arrived found an agricultural state that was gradually industrializing and urban centers that still retained their colonial ways and outlooks. The tempo of change was not uniform throughout the country, nor did the immigrants experience similar economic and social conditions. Immigrants employed by the railroad and sugar refinery in Rosario lived primarily in wooden or tinplate huts and not in conventillos as in Buenos Aires and Montevideo, and they worked in the countryside at harvest time. This not uncommon link between an industrializing urban center and its surrounding rural area is currently undergoing investigation.

The studies annotated here are part of an ongoing review of the process of industrialization that took place between 1880–1930. A fresh look is being taken at a wide variety of subjects: the multifaceted intellectual climate of the period, the labor movement, the spread of farming into marginal areas, the internal divisions of the Unión Cívica Radical, the effects of the Great Depression, the nationalist movement, and the rise of peronism. This reassessment had already made clear that the Unión Industrial Argentina did not represent the industrial sector until 1957, that differential railroad freight rates distorted agricultural development, and that porteño political leaders thwarted an incipient democratic movement in Mendoza. Studies of the post-1930 years further suggest that political and labor leaders in Buenos Aires acted independently of their colleagues in the provinces, and that the provincianos saw things differently from porteños. These tentative conclusions find support in the provincial studies of Lacoste (item **2998**) and Tcach Abad (item **3075**).

Two recurring themes in Argentine historiography require little comment. One is the alleged Argentine dependence on the British government and capital (the fact that British capital competed with French capital in 19th-century Argentina is often forgotten in the debate). For instance, the relationship between British and Argentine money markets is currently being investigated. In addition, recent research in British diplomatic archives is destroying many myths concerning British policy toward British firms in Argentina and toward Argentine domestic politics. Nevertheless, the implications of the decline of British influence and the rise of the US have not yet been fully explored. The second theme concerns the role of the military. As a result of the "dirty war" and the Falkland/Malvinas War, the military and its partisans are on the defensive. Defenders of the military recall that Irigoyen and other political leaders always thought of affecting change with the military's aid, but seldom defended the military for obediently complying with their unpleasant orders. They also stress that civilian governments are equally guilty of violence and violations of human rights.

Finally, the role of women as wives, mothers, and mistresses continues to receive attention. The porteño women with ties to Rosas and Sarmiento continue to be considered fascinating subjects, but this emphasis has obscured the existence of other talented women in Buenos Aires. However, the provincial women who made notable contributions to literature and politics are emerging from anonymity. Recent studies have examined the impact of Spanish law and the concept of "honor" on the status of upper and lower class women, but have failed to clarify the issues. In Paraguay the State protected an unmarried woman's honor from her lover, whereas in Buenos Aires the State helped the husband shield his own honor by providing "houses of deposit" for his "misbehaving" wife. The contributions of urban and rural women to the local economy is also undergoing review, but the extent to which women in the Río de la Plata were educated and under what conditions are subjects which await investigation.

Few works on modern Paraguay, that is, the years after the Paraguayan War, were received during this biennium. One recurring theme is that a democratic base was established between 1870–1940. The causes, conduct, and outcome of the Chaco War, as well as the role of the military, remain favorite subjects of discussion. This often involves a defense or criticism of the Colorado party and the Stroessner Administration.

Scholars exploring developments in modern Uruguay, that is, after 1880, stress the establishment of liberal institutions in the prosperous environment of the 1880s and 1890s, the Latorre and Terra dictatorships, and the economic crisis of 1930. Caetano and Jacob argue in their detailed analysis of the Terra Administration that the liberals, satisfied with the establishment of political democracy, failed to notice the deteriorating economic situation, and that the Revolution of 1933 was a conservative reaction to unsuccessful liberal reform efforts (item **3129**). The ease with which the government was overthrown suggests that it was unpopular. The ex-president of the Socialist party recalls his transformation from an extreme radical to an extreme reformist, and the party struggles to define its own anti-fascist political strategy (item **3127**). Like Argentina, Uruguay has seen the decline of British influence and the rise of that of the US, but the phenomenon is just beginning to undergo serious study.

ARGENTINA

2894 Adelman, Jeremy. The social bases of technical change: mechanization of the wheatlands of Argentina and Canada, 1890 to 1914. (*Comp. Stud. Soc. Hist.*, 34:2, April 1992, p. 271–300, tables)

Thoughtful study compares Canadian prairie landowner and Argentine leaseholder on the pampas, and concludes that property relations determined development of their distinctive characteristics.

2895 Adelman, Jeremy. Socialism and democracy in Argentina in the age of the Second International. (*HAHR* 72:2, May 1992, p. 211–238, tables)

Close analysis of thinking of Juan Bautista Justo and other Socialists suggests that failure of democratic socialism to win an Argentine following prior to 1943 is attributable to their concept of democracy and its influence on their approach to politics.

2896 Adelman, Jeremy. State and labour in Argentina: the portworkers of Buenos Aires, 1910–21. (*J. Lat. Am. Stud.*, 25:1, Feb. 1993, p. 73–102, map)

Detailed descriptions of maritime strikes of 1911–12, 1916, and 1921, and of short-lived syndicalist movement, illustrate and reinforce thesis that decisions made by workers themselves contributed to failure of labor radicalism.

2897 Akmir, Abdelwahed. La inserción de los inmigrantes árabes en Argentina, 1880–1980: implicaciones sociales. (*Anaquel Estud. Arab.*, 2, 1991, p. 238–259)

Comprehensive study examines Syrian and Lebanese immigrants to Argentina; their reception by the *criollos* in Buenos Aires and in the northwest; their internal cultural, religious, and economic divisions; their marriage patterns within and outside the Arab community; and their integration into Argentine society.

2898 Alén Lascano, Luis C. Historia de Santiago del Estero. Buenos Aires: Plus Ultra, 1992. 640 p.: bibl., ill., maps. (Col. Historia de nuestras provincias; 14)

A prominent provincial historian presents exemplary introduction to developments in his province to 1991.

2899 Alonso de Crocco, Magdalena and Liliana Juana Ferraro. La "crisis" ganadera Argentina. (*Rev. Hist. Am. Argent.*, 15: 29/30, 1989/1990, p. 213–234, bibl.)

Attributes meat crisis of 1921–22 to British domestic policies, foreign monopoly of *frigoríficos,* indifference of the Argentine government, disorganized producers, and poor harvests.

2900 Alonso Piñeiro, Armando. Historia de la guerra de Malvinas. Buenos Aires: Planeta, 1992. 328 p.: appendix, bibl., ill., index. (Espejo de la Argentina)

Highlights logistical errors and military and diplomatic misjudgments made by both sides in the conflict. Also examines conduct of the US and other mediating powers, divisions within the Argentine military junta, and reaction of the Argentine people to both the war and its aftermath.

2901 Alonso Piñeiro, Armando *et al.* José de Sn. Martín: un camino hacia la libertad. Dirección editorial de Manrique Zago. Coordinación general de Fernando Alonso. Buenos Aires: M. Zago Ediciones, 1989. 208 p.: bibl., ill. (some col.).

Well-illustrated volume is dedicated to the memory of San Martín. Contains short essays on San Martín written by Argentine and Chilean scholars.

2902 Alvarez, Adriana *et al.* Mar del Plata: una historia urbana. Buenos Aires: Fundación Banco de Boston, 1991. 221 p.: bibl., ill., maps. (Crónicas urbanas; 1)

Provides excellent introduction to the city, its population, its political and economic history, and its social and cultural life.

2903 Alvarez Guerrero, Osvaldo. Las máscaras del poder: Lebensohn-Cooke. Buenos Aires: Centro Editor de América Latina, 1992. 2 v.: bibl. (Biblioteca Política argentina; 343–344)

Affirms that both John William Cooke and Moisés León Lebensohn wanted to replace existing governmental system that favored the traditional sectors of economic power and excluded the majority with one that was more democratic and that furthered social justice. They had philosophical differences. Cooke was anti-imperialist, a nationalist, and a revolutionary Marxist. Lebensohn was a social democrat, a humanist, and interested in modernizing Argentina.

2904 The Argentine right: its history and intellectual origins, 1910 to the present. Edited by Sandra McGee Deutsch and Ronald H. Dolkart. Wilmington, Del.: SR Books, 1993. 205 p.: bibl., index. (Latin American silhouettes)

Although each contributor studies a distinct part of the 20th century, the six essays taken together provide excellent introduction to philosophical currents that influenced the "right" or "nationalists" from turn of the century to 1983, and to this sector's strength in civilian and military circles.

2905 Arturo Frondizi, historia y problemática de un estadista. v. 4, El gobernante. Dirección de Roberto Gustavo Pisarello Virasoro y Emilia Edda Menotti. Prólogo de Julio Oyhanarte. Buenos Aires: Ediciones Depalma, 1983-. 1 v.

Contains the following articles: Roberto Gustavo Pisarello Virasoro, "Estudios Preliminares;" Carlos Regino Moreno, "Arturo Frondizi y la Convención Reformadora de 1957;" Ana Edelmira Castro, "El Camino hacia el Gobierno;" Héctor C. Sauret, "El Marco Histórico de 1958;" Emilia Edda Menotti, "Mensaje Presidencial del 1° de Mayo de 1958;" Carlos Regino Moreno, "El Programa de Estabilización Económica del 29 de diciembre de 1958;" Emilio A. García Solá, "El Presidente de Acero;" Enrique de Gandía, "El Problema del Petróleo Argentino;" Armando Ramos Ruiz, "El Petróleo y Frondizi;" Alberto R. Constantini, "Política de Obras y Servicios Públicos en el Período 1958–1962;" and Roberto T. Alemann, "La Política Económica Argentina de abril de 1961 a enero de 1962." For vols. 1–2, see *HLAS 46:3161*; for vol. 3, see *HLAS 50:2319*.

2906 Auza, Néstor Tomás. La bibliografía nacional argentina en la Exposición Universal de París, 1878. (*Anu. Estud. Am.*, 46:1, 1989, suplemento, p. 13–34, table)

Relates history of origins and nature of *Colección de obras argentinas* prepared in 1878 and now available in the Biblioteca Nacional. Collection was to include a copy of all official and other works published in Argentina, but it never did. Still it is substantial, for it includes 332 titles and 1,067 volumes.

2907 Avramov, Rumen. La emigración búlgara en Argentina, 1900–1940. (*Estud. Latinoam.*, 12, 1989, p. 225–255, tables)

Working with incomplete Argentine and Bulgarian statistical data, writer speculates on flow of Bulgarians to and from Argentina from 1900–46, on their characteristics, on their Bulgarian origins, on their geographical distribution in Argentina, and on their development of cotton agriculture in the Chaco.

2908 Baer, James. Housing and the working class in Buenos Aires: consumer issues and class identity. (*in* MACLAS Latin American Essays. Edited by Robert J. Alexander, Juan Espadas, and Vincent Peloso. Collegeville, Pa.: Ursinus College, 1991?, v. 4, p. 135–145, bibl.)

Describes housing and living conditions in a *conventillo* community of Buenos Aires at turn of the century.

2909 Barbará, Federico *et al.* Con Rosas o contra Rosas. Buenos Aires: Ediciones Federales, 1989. 212 p.

Thirty-two Argentine historians and writers express their pro- and anti-Rosas views in short, mostly original essays. Some essays are based on family oral traditions.

Barbé, Carlos. Lo stato degli studi sulle elites politiche argentine. See *HLAS 53:5495.*

2910 Bellotta, Araceli. Aurelia Velez: la independencia a ultranza. (*Todo es Hist.*, 24:285, marzo 1991, p. 26–39, ill., photos)

Presents very touching biographical sketch of a woman who was mistress and intellectual equal of Domingo Faustino Sarmiento and who influenced his political career.

2911 Bellotta, Araceli and **Julia Matesanz.** Julieta Lanteri, primera sufragista de América Latina. (*Todo es Hist.*, 278, agosto 1990, p. 76–82)

Presents brief history of a suffragist who won right to vote and was a candidate of the Partido Feminista Nacional for national deputy in 1920 and 1924.

2912 Berisso, Juan Carlos. Los Berisso en la Argentina, 1848–1987. Investigación histórica de Juana Giordano. Buenos Aires: Gaglianone Establecimiento Gráfico, 1987. 269 p.: ill., index.

Genealogical history of a family includes description of their land acquisitions and *saladeros* from the time first member arrived in Buenos Aires in 1848.

2913 Bertoni, Lilia Ana. La naturalización de los extranjeros, 1887–1893: ¿Derechos políticos o nacionalidad? (*Desarro. Econ.*, 32:125, abril/junio 1992, p. 57–77, bibl.)

Presents lucid description of contemporary setting in which Congress debated whether to grant foreigners only civil rights or civil rights *and* Argentine citizenship, and in which the Revolution of 1890 took place.

2914 Bischoff, Efraín U. Cincuenta años de vida gremial periodistica en Córdoba. Córdoba, Argentina: Editorial de la Municipalidad de Córdoba, 1986. 66 p., 10 p. of plates: ill.

Provides brief introduction to the press in Córdoba prov. and to accomplishments of the journalists' union.

2915 Bischoff, Efraín U. Historia de los barrios de Córdoba: sus leyendas, instituciones y gentes. 3 ed. Córdoba, Argentina: Lerner B Editores, 1992. 392 p.: ill.

Outstanding provincial historian presents first systematic treatment of origins and growth of the suburbs of the city of Córdoba.

2916 Bistué, Noemí del Carmen and **Beatriz Conte de Fornés.** Práctica de la justicia mercantil en Mendoza entre 1830 y 1870. (*Rev. Hist. Am. Argent.*, 15:29, 1989, p. 187–211, bibl.)

Describes commercial laws and regulations that were in effect until 1870, and gives examples of how they were applied. Based on 120 cases found in the Archivo Histórico de Mendoza.

2917 Bitrán, Rafael and **Alejandro Schneider.** El gobierno conservador de Manuel A. Fresco en la provincia de Buenos Aires, 1936–1940. Buenos Aires: Centro Editor de América Latina, 1991. 113 p.: appendix, bibl. (Biblioteca Política argentina; 338)

Explores labor policies of a conservative governor who anticipated Perón by involving the Departamento de Trabajo in labor-owner negotiations, and who otherwise was a traditional conservative.

2918 Bjerg, María M. Dinamarca bajo la Cruz del Sur: la preservación de la herencia cultural danesa en la Pampa argentina, 1848–1930. (*Stud. Emigr.*, 28:102, giugno 1991, p. 219–232, bibl.)

Summarizes experience of Danish immigrants in south-central part of Buenos Aires prov., especially their efforts to preserve their culture and their gradual assimilation into Argentine society.

2919 Blacha, Noemí M. Girbal de. Producción agraria, tarifas y fusión ferroviaria en la Argentina: los ferrocarriles Central Argentino y Buenos Aires y Rosario, 1900–1908. (*Rev. Hist. Am.*, 111, enero/junio 1991, p. 7–30, tables)

Discusses negotiations between Argentine government and new firm created by merger of the two railroads, the congressional and press debate generated by the merger, and the freight rate system that favored long over short hauls.

2920 Bollo Cabrios, Palmira S.; Hebe Mancedo de Seguí; and Alicia Otamendo Etchevertz. Sarmiento en sus escritos: sus inquietudes educacionales y progresistas a través de sus obras completas. Argentina: Instituto Sarmiento de Sociología e Historia, Filial Quilmes, 1990. 59 p.

Provides index to Sarmiento's *Obras completas* and his unedited manuscripts on education that are located in the Museo Histórico Sarmiento in Buenos Aires and in the Archivo de la Provincia de San Juan.

2921 Bonaudo, Marta; Silvia Cragnolino; and Elida Sonzogni. La cuestión de la identidad política de los colonos santafesinos, 1880–1890: estudio de algunas experiencias. (*Anuario/Rosario,* 1989/90, p. 251–276)

Authors note that foreigners who formed the colonies were frontier pioneers who governed themselves and resisted the administrative control of the provincial government. This "spontaneous democracy" led settlers to demand Argentine citizenship without surrendering their original allegiance, a demand some Unión Cívica Radical leaders endorsed.

2922 Bonzo, Héctor E. 1093 tripulantes del crucero ARA General Belgrano: testimonio y homenaje de su comandante. Buenos Aires: Editorial Sudamericana, 1992. 515 p.: bibl., ill., maps.

Describes mission of the cruiser in the Falkland/Malvinas War, its sinking by the British, and conduct of the rescue operations.

2923 Bosch, Beatriz. Sarmiento y la ubicación social de la mujer. (*Invest. Ens.,* 39, enero/dic. 1989, p. 93–105)

Describes Sarmiento's campaign for education of women.

2924 Bruno, Cayetano. Apóstoles de la evangelización en la Cuenca del Plata. Rosario, Argentina: Ediciones Didascalia, 1990. 225 p.: bibl.

Biographies of pre-1810 missionaries are based on author's major works.

2925 Bruno, Cayetano. El General Urquiza y la Iglesia. (*Invest. Ens.,* 39, enero/dic. 1989, p. 275–313, bibl.)

Emphasizes Urquiza's Catholicism and his support of the Catholic Church as reflected in his service as governor of Entre Ríos prov. and as President of the Argentine Confederation. Author consulted the Vatican Secret Archives.

2926 Cacopardo, María Cristina and José Luis Moreno. La emigración italiana meridional a la Argentina: calabreses y sicilianos, 1880–1930. (*Bol. Inst. Hist. Ravignani,* 3:3, 1er semestre 1991, p. 29–51, bibl., graphs, tables)

Presents synthesis of existing literature on immigrants from Calabria and Sicily, and concludes that these immigrants were more likely to adapt and integrate than were northern Italians.

Caputo, Dante et al. SSSR/Rossiā-Argentina: stranitsy istorii, 1885–1986; dokumenty i materialy [USSR/Russia-Argentina: pages from history, 1885–1986; documents and materials]. See *HLAS 53:4738.*

2927 Carmagnani, Marcello and Chiara Vangelista. Mercados monetarios y ferrocarriles ingleses en Argentina, 1880–1914. (*Anu. IEHS,* 3, 1988, p. 249–285)

Theorizes that Argentine money market was integrated into London money market without losing all of its autonomy, and that this connection accounts for dominance of England in Argentina.

2928 Charlton, Michael. The little platoon: diplomacy and the Falklands dispute. Oxford, England; New York: B. Blackwell, 1989. 230 p.: index.

Relates interviews with Argentine, British, and US diplomatic and military officials involved in events leading to Falklands/Malvinas War. Highlights miscalculations made by the adversaries that led to a war no one wanted, and the importance attached to the wishes of the islanders, the "little platoon." For international relations specialist's comment see *HLAS 53:4740.*

2929 Chassin, Joëlle. Comment rallier les foules à la Révolution? les discours de Juan José Castelli dans l'expédition libératrice du Haut-Pérou, 1810–1811. (*Caravelle/Toulouse,* 54, 1990, p. 153–163, bibl.)

In this well-founded essay author maintains that Castelli was more a radical than a Jacobin or Robespierrist, and that he sought to legitimatize the independence movement by associating it with the principles of liberty and equality.

2930 Ciafardo, Eduardo O. Cadenas migratorias e inmigración italiana: reflexiones a partir de la correspondencia de dos inmigrantes italianos en Argentina, 1921–1938. (*Stud. Emigr.*, 28:102, giugno 1991, p. 233–256, appendix, bibl.)

Letters to and from two brothers are used to demonstrate that chain migration could involve cooperation or exploitation and did allow the immigrant to consider more than one final destination.

2931 Ciafardo, Eduardo O. Las damas de beneficiencia y la participación social de la mujer en la ciudad de Buenos Aires, 1880–1920. (*Anu. IEHS*, 5, 1990, p. 161–170)

Argues that charitable organizations formed with middle class women that appeared after 1880 were used to further social control of the popular sectors.

2932 Ciaralli, Aldo et al. Wheelwright: nombre gringo, tierra de gauchos. (*Universidad/Santa Fe*, 101, mayo 1991, p. 221–249, bibl., tables)

Provides comprehensive history of origins and economic and social evolution of a town in province of Santa Fe, 1856–1972.

2933 Cibotti, Ema. La elite italiana de Buenos Aires: el proyecto de nacionalización del 90. (*Anuario/Rosario*, segunda época, 1989/90, p. 227–250, bibl.)

Corrects literary vision that Italians formed a "colony" and that they and their press took no part in local politics. Calls special attention to division within Italian community between those for and against the revolution of 1890, and to assimilation of Italians. Excellent analysis of the Italian press.

2934 Cirvini, Silvia. Mendoza: la arquitectura de la reconstrucción posterremoto, 1861–1884. (*Rev. Hist. Am.*, 108, julio/dic. 1989, p. 171–189, ill., photos)

Discusses architectural style adopted for rebuilding the city after the earthquake of 1861.

2935 Collier, Simon. The popular roots of the Argentine tango. (*Hist. Workshop*, 34, Autumn 1992, p. 92–100)

Informed study discusses popular dances that inspired creation of the tango in the *barrios* of Buenos Aires, the tango's

spread to the *conventillos*, its "Italianization," and its reluctant acceptance by Argentine elite.

2936 Comadrán Ruiz, Jorge. La clase dirigente mendocina y sus relaciones con D. Juan Manuel de Rosas. Mendoza, Argentina: Univ. Nacional de Cuyo, Facultad de Filosofía y Letras, 1989. 76 p.: bibl.

Small documented monograph demonstrates how elite of Mendoza first supported Juan Manuel de Rosas and then completely reversed themselves to support Justo José de Urquiza. Reproduces decrees found in provincial archives and the *Registro Ministerial de Mendoza*.

Cortés Conde, Roberto. Dinero, deuda y crisis: evolución fiscal y monetaria en la Argentina, 1862–1890. See *HLAS 53:2445*.

2937 Cremaschi de Petra, Martha. Aspectos socio-demográficos de Mendoza entre 1800 y 1840 a traves de registros parroquiales (libros de matrimonios). (*Rev. Hist. Am. Argent.*, 15:29/30, 1989/1990, p.235–254, graphs, tables)

Presents analysis of 2,752 marriage records of the Iglesia Matriz de San Nicolás, Mendoza. During period examined, population was predominantly *criollo*.

2938 Crisafulli, Gustavo. Ciudad y campaña durante el boom agroexportador: el sudoeste de Buenos Aires, 1880–1914. (*Rev. Hist./Neuquén*, 2, nov. 1991, p. 143–153, bibl., tables)

Summarizes transformation that Bahía Blanca and its hinterland underwent as local economy changed from wool to wheat production. During that process Bahía Blanca became a port through which wool and wheat were exported, began to industrialize, and became source of seasonal farm hands.

2939 Cuadernos del águila. v. 4, Barrio de Liniers [de] Emilio Juan Vattuone. Buenos Aires: Fundación Banco de Boston, 1989-. 1 v.

Provides informative introduction to a Buenos Aires suburb.

2940 Cuadernos del águila. v. 17, San Isidro: el sueño del capitán [de] Mónica G. Hoss de le Compte. Buenos Aires: Fundación Banco de Boston, 1989-. 1 v.

Provides instructive introduction to a Buenos Aires suburb.

2941 Devoto, Fernando. Italian immigrants and Argentine society: problems of models and sources. (*J. Eur. Econ. Hist.*, 20:3, Winter 1991, p. 629–643)

Provides useful discussion of conceptual models used by researchers interested in interaction of migrants and the host society, and of sources they use.

2942 Di Tella, Guido and **Eva Balbina Fernández.** Los Diarios, 1927–1930. Buenos Aires: Instituto Torcuato Di Tella, 1989. 425 p. (Serie Materiales de investigación; 2)

Reproduces editorials that appeared in *La Prensa, La Nación, La Epoca,* and *Revista de Economía Argentina,* together with selections from annual reports of the Sociedad Rural and the Unión Industrial Argentina.

2943 Díaz, Hernán. Alberto Ghiraldo, anarquismo y cultura. Buenos Aires: Centro Editor de América Latina, 1991. 126 p.: bibl. (Biblioteca Política argentina; 316)

Short biography of poet, journalist, editor, and well-known figure among the generation of intellectuals in 1890s. Author stresses connection between Ghiraldo's belief in armed struggle and in the Revolution of 1890, and his conversion to anarchism.

2944 Díaz Araujo, Enrique. Hombres olvidados de la Organización Nacional: Facundo Zuviría. Mendoza, Argentina: Univ. Nacional de Cuyo, Facultad de Filosofía y Letras, 1991. 217 p.: bibl.

Analyzes intellectual ideas of ex-Unitarian from Salta who presided at the Constitutional Convention of 1852 and who disapproved of the constitution it wrote.

2945 Dik, Evgueni. Emigración rusa a Argentina: fines del siglo XIX y comienzos del XX. (*Am. Lat./Moscow*, 7:163, julio 1991, p. 70–78, photos)

Provides clear exposition of Russian immigration to Brazil and Argentina and of Russian immigration laws then in effect.

2946 Dumrauf, Clemente I. Historia de Chubut. Buenos Aires: Plus Ultra, 1992. 573 p.: bibl., ill., maps. (Col. Historia de nuestras provincias; 15)

Excellent introduction to one of the "younger" provinces calls attention especially to European colonization efforts, creation of Indian settlements, missionary activities, and economic developments.

2947 Duval, Natalia. Los sindicatos clasistas: SiTrac, 1970–1971. Buenos Aires: Centro Editor de América Latina, 1988. 152 p.: bibl. (Biblioteca Política argentina; 235)

Contains chronological description of SiTraC activities from January 1, 1970, to October 26, 1971, and collection of SiTraC press releases, public statements, and flyers.

2948 Echazú Lezica, Mariano de. El encuentro de Güemes y Pueyrredon en Tarija y su circunstancia histórica. (*Invest. Ens.*, 39, enero/dic. 1989, p. 431–450)

Describes limited aid and protection Güemes afforded Pueyrredón while he transported gold and silver from Potosí to Buenos Aires. Includes a good description of Tarija.

2949 Edelman, Angel. Primera historia del Neuquén: recuerdos territorianos. Buenos Aires: Editorial Plus Ultra, 1991. 263 p.: ill.

Province's first governor (1958–60) recalls Neuquén's early political, economic, social, and cultural developments.

Elkin, Judith Laikin. Recoleta: civilization and barbarism in Argentina. See *HLAS 53: 5503.*

2950 Encuentro de Historia Argentina y Regional, 1st, Mendoza, Argentina, 1990. Repensando el '90: aspectos: político, social, económico, cultural, religioso, artístico y literario. Mendoza, Argentina: Univ. Nacional de Cuyo, Facultad de Filosofía y Letras, 1991. 2 v.: bibl., ill, maps.

Essays by 27 contributors focus on developments in provinces of Mendoza and San Juan in 1890, on relations with Chile, and on three historians (Agustín Alvarez, Nicolás Matienzo, and Adolfo Saldías).

2951 Endrek, Emiliano. Nicolás Avellaneda en la Universidad de Córdoba, 1850–1855. (*Rev. Junta Prov. Hist. Córdoba*, 13, 1988, p. 67–86, tables)

Presents list of Avellaneda's classmates at the Colegio de Monserrat.

2952 Favaro, Orietta and **Marta B. Morinelli.** De la crisis del 90 al golpe del 30: el reformismo liberal en el Río de la Plata. (*Rev. Hist./Neuquén*, 2, nov. 1991, p. 3–19, bibl.)

Authors maintain that the two events discussed are linked by a basic conservatism, what might be called democratic liberalism. Though neither event threatened the traditional structures, both favored political change. Expands on ideas of Carlos Ibarguren.

2953 Ferioli, Néstor. La Fundación Eva Perón. Buenos Aires: Centro Editor de América Latina, 1990. 2 v.: bibl. (Biblioteca Política argentina; 293–294)

Important work examines origins, organization, revenues, and activities of Fundación Eva Perón, as well as disposition of its assets. Based on documents and interviews with Fundación officials.

2954 Fernández, Virginia. Mujeres e imagenes femeninas en Mendoza a fines del siglo XIX y principios del XX. (*Rev. Hist. Am.*, 110, julio/dic. 1990, p. 125–131)

Divorce cases in 1890s suggest that women of the popular classes and of the dominant class interpreted the abstract and contradictory official image of the domestic woman and mother in accordance with their social class and different experiences.

2955 Fernández García, Antonio. Los círculos de emigrantes ante la guerra de España: la colonia gallega de Buenos Aires. (*Quinto Cent.*, 16, 1990, p. 121–140)

Examines divisions among the Galicians as seen in their press, social organizations, and conferences. Stresses writings of Eduardo Blanco Amor and José R. Lence.

2956 Ferns, H.S. The Baring crisis revisited. (*J. Lat. Am. Stud.*, 24:2, May 1992, p. 241–273)

In this major contribution author uses sources not consulted in the past and satisfactorily demonstrates that Baring crisis of 1890–97 was "resolved primarily by the policies of the Argentine government and secondarily by the Governor of Bank of England," with the assistance of Lord Rothschild and Baring. Crisis originated in Baring's efforts to encourage a private firm to operate the water and sewage system of Buenos Aires.

2957 Ferré, Pedro. Memorias, 1821–1845. Estudio preliminar de Isidoro J. Ruiz Moreno. Buenos Aires: Editorial Claridad; Editorial Heliasta, 1990. 241 p. (Col. Testimonios; 1)

Re-edition of 1921 original without the supporting documentation. Ferré was governor of the province of Corrientes during the Rosas years.

2958 Ferreiro Aspiroz, Hernán L. El 31 de marzo de 1933 según algunos documentos británicos. (*Bol. Hist. Ejérc.*, 279/282, 1990, p. 115–130)

Reproduces three British Embassy reports assessing reasons for the revolution of March 31, 1933, the reaction of the public, political alignments, and character of the new administration.

2959 Ferrer Vieyra, Enrique. Segunda cronología legal anotada sobre las Islas Malvinas/Falkland Islands. Prólogo a cargo del Dr. Enrique de Gandía. Córdoba, Argentina: Lerner, 1992. 643 p.: bibl.

Collection includes English, French, and Spanish legal documents that pertain to the islands; known Argentine documents are not included. These documents may not settle dispute over legal and historical ownership of the islands, but do stress strategic importance of the island group. Based on research in British, French and Spanish archives.

2960 Fittipaldi, Silvia. Santa Cruz y la historia de un barrio. Fotos de Juan Camacho, Carlos Lunghi y Archivo General de la Nación. Ed. en conmemoración del centenario de la colocación de su piedra fundamental. Buenos Aires: Ediciones Pasionistas, 1990. 83 p.: bibl., ill.

This is a well-written and informative introduction to history of a Buenos Aires suburb.

2961 Floria, Carlos Alberto and César A. García Belsunce. Historia de los argentinos. Buenos Aires: Larousse, 1992. 2 v.: bibl., ill., maps. (Referencias Larousse)

Argentine history from Age of Discovery to election of Carlos Menem in 1989 is presented in a straightforward, lucid manner.

2962 Fraga, Rosendo. El General Justo. Buenos Aires: Emecé Editores, 1993. 490 p.: bibl.

Political biography focuses on Gen. Justo's goal of creating a professional army that observed the constitution; his efforts to improve relations with the US; and the social and cultural objectives of his policies as President (1932–38). This rehabilitation of Justo is based on his archives.

2963 Fugl, Juan. Memorias de Juan Fugl: vida de un pionero danés durante 30 años en Tandil, Argentina, 1844–1875. Traducción de Alice Larsen de Rabal. Buenos Aires?: Reprografías J.M.A., s.d. 510 p.: ill.

Describes local reactions to Fugl's introduction of wheat farming and flour milling, to his encouragement of education, and to the presence of foreigners. Written from memory at the age of 73.

2964 Gallardo, Jorge Emilio. Etnias africanas en el Río de la Plata. Buenos Aires: Centro de Estudios Latinoamericano; Ultimo Reino, 1989. 37 p. (Col. Ensayos breves; 26)

Identifies ethnic groups to which African slaves introduced into Río de le Plata from 16th-19th centuries belonged, and describes their distribution in South America.

2965 Gallo, Ezequiel. El liberalismo y la actual experiencia peronista en la Argentina. (*Rev. Occident.*, 131, abril 1992, p. 122–129)

Reflects on role of classical liberalism in Argentina and its current resurgence under aegis of the former populism. Reforms are motivated by economic necessity and are made possible by concentrating more power in the executive branch of government.

2966 Gamas, Federico Manuel Julián. El otro Belgrano. Prólogo de Ricardo Miguel Zuccherino. La Plata, Argentina: Fondo Editorial Esto es Historia, 1990? 119 p.: bibl. (Col. Extensión histórica; 11)

Biography of Manuel Belgrano.

2967 Gandía, Enrique de. Historia política argentina. v. 8, Rivadavia y su tiempo. Buenos Aires: Editorial Claridad, 1988- 1 v.

Discussion of Rivadavia's activities prior to 1824 is followed by a digest of debates in the Congress of 1824–27. Views Rivadavia as a dictator and precursor of Rosas, and provincial governors as reluctant to surrender power to any central government.

2968 Garavaglia, Juan Carlos. Ecosistemas y tecnología agraria: elementos para una historia social de los ecosistemas agrarios rioplatenses, 1700–1830. (*Desarro. Econ.*, 28; 112, enero/marzo 1989, p. 549–576, bibl.)

Describes persistence until 1875 of colonial farming practices along wheat-growing ecosystem of San Isidro and cattle-cereal ecosystem of San Antonio de Areco, both in Buenos Aires prov. Concludes that abundance of unoccupied fertile public land made retention of laborers by landowners and tenant farmers very expensive.

2969 Garavaglia, Juan Carlos. ¿Existieron los gauchos? (*Anu. IEHS*, 2, 1987, p. 42–52)

Revisits and questions traditional image of the gaucho, and notes the variety of *es-*

tancieros that existed, the presence of *labradores*, and background to the *papeleta de conchabo.*

2970 García-Godoy, Christián. Tomás Godoy Cruz: su tiempo, su vida, su drama: ensayo crítico. Washington: Full Life/Vida Plena; Impressions In Ink, 1991. 811 p.: bibl., ill., indexes.

Biography of an exceptional 19th-century provincial statesman and advisor to San Martín is based on research in numerous archives.

2971 García Heras, Raúl. Capitales extranjeros, poder político y transporte urbano de pasajeros: la Compañía de Tranvías Anglo Argentina Ltda. de Buenos Aires, Argentina, 1930–1943. (*Desarro. Econ.*, 32:125, abril/junio 1992, p. 35–56, bibl., tables)

Demonstrates that the Compañía de Tranvías Anglo Argentina received little help from the British government because it was part of a Belgian company. Nor was the firm able to influence urban transportation policies of conservative nationalists in the municipal government in order to improve service and meet its financial obligations. Based on Argentine and British official correspondence.

2972 García Heras, Raúl. Las compañías ferroviarias británicas y el control de cambios en la Argentina durante la Gran Depresión. (*Desarro. Econ.*, 29:116, enero/marzo 1990, p. 477–505, tables)

Argentine and British diplomatic records reveal that neither Argentina nor Great Britain attached much importance to needs of the railroad companies during negotiation of the Roca-Runciman Treaty (1933). Britain wanted to protect its commercial, financial, and shipping interests; while Argentina used foreign exchange controls to eliminate local speculation in foreign exchange market, to service its foreign debt, to maintain its foreign credit rating, and to limit depreciation of the peso.

García Heras, Raul. Las compañías ferroviarias británicas y el control de la Argentina durante la gran depresión. See *HLAS 53:2454.*

2973 Gelman, Jorge Daniel. ¿Gauchos o campesinos? (*Anu. IEHS*, 2, 1987, p. 53–59, table)

Suggests that the peon could work on a *chacra* for cash or on an *estancia* when he was not planting or harvesting his own wheat crop. There was no labor shortage, but availability of labor on the 18th-century *estancia* depended on the wheat cycle.

2974 Gociol, Judith; Luis Felipe Lacour; and Rodrigo Gutiérrez Hermelo. Ex combatientes de Malvinas: ocho años de posguerra. (*Todo es Hist.*, 24:276, p. 26–41, photos)
Describes veterans' feeling that both government and society have forgotten them, and reviews the aims of their representative organizations.

2975 Goldenberg, Raquel. Manuel Gleizer: un editor "legendario" y el "ultimo de los románticos." (*in* Ensayos sobre judaismo latinoamericano. Buenos Aires: Editorial Milá, 1990, p. 319–338)
Author endeavors to reconstruct life of a famous Argentine publisher using only the testimony of those who remembered him.

2976 Goldman, Noemí et al. Imagen y recepción de la Revolución Francesa en la Argentina: jornadas nacionales. Palabras preliminares de Gregorio Weinberg. Buenos Aires: Grupo Editor Latinoamericano, 1990. 399 p.: bibl., ill. (Col. Estudios políticos y sociales)
Twenty-one scholars discuss impact of the French Revolution on Argentine political leaders and developments in the 19th century.

2977 González Bernaldo, Pilar. La revolución francesa y la emergencia de nuevas prácticas de la política: la irrupción de la sociabilidad política en el Río de la Plata revolucionario, 1810–1815. (*Bol. Inst. Hist. Ravignani*, 3:3, 1er semestre 1991, p. 7–27)
Convincingly maintains that informal revolutionary group formed by *colegio* students and intellectuals in 1811 had a democratic base because of its association with urban militia, whereas the Sociedad Patriótica, founded in 1812, excluded urban population from the political process. Thoughtful essay on gradual appearance in city of Buenos Aires of political associations and of public opinion as a force in politics.

2978 González Seguí, Oscar. Una experiencia de expropiación y colonización de tierras en la región pampeana argentina: la colonia Balcarce. (*Relaciones/Zamora*, primavera 1991, p. 37–66, appendix, bibl., map, tables)
Significant study examines a State experiment to create a rural class of small landowners in a fertile part of Buenos Aires prov. Author attributes experiment's failure to stop rural depopulation and decay, despite generous State investments, to the attractions of the city.

2979 Gordillo, Mónica B. Los prolegómenos del Cordobazo: los sindicatos líderes de Córdoba dentro de la estructura de poder sindical. (*Desarro. Econ.*, 31:122, julio/sept. 1991, p. 163–187)
Attributes the *cordobazo* in part to growth of local labor unions that cherished their independence from the central labor union, that had a democratic base that was anti-*porteño* and anti-bureaucracy, and that dealt with multinational firms interested only in the local labor union.

2980 Gravil, Roger. Gran Bretaña y el ascenso político de Perón: un nuevo enfoque. (*Rev. Ciclos*, 1:1, 1991, p. 41–64, table)
Essayist speculates that decision of Ernest Devin to ask Argentines to hold their 1946 presidential elections in February rather than April contributed to the victory of Perón. His analysis of complex maneuvering between Great Britain and the US for dominance in Argentina is based on research in three national archives.

2981 Grondona, Iván. Imprenta Coni: apuntes para la historia de una imprenta y una dinastía. Buenos Aires: Digital Impresiones, 1990. 80 p.: bibl., ill.
Provides brief introduction to family that owned an important publishing house in Buenos Aires.

2982 Gualco, Jorge Nelson and Alberto S.J. de Paula. Temperley, su historia, su gente. Buenos Aires?: Editorial Pleamar, 1988. 197 p., 16 p. of plates: bibl., ill.
Provides succinct description of land transactions and different ethnic groups in the community, from its origins.

2983 Güemes, Luis. Güemes documentado. v. 12. Buenos Aires: Ediciones Güemes Arenales, 1990. 1 v.: indexes.
Contains documents of or pertaining to Martín Güemes. See also *HLAS 46:2882* and *HLAS 50:2080*.

2984 Guido, Horacio J. Triple Alianza: la otra guerra: uniformes, alimentos y sanidad. (*Todo es Hist.*, 288, junio 1991, p. 84–96, facsims., ill., photos)

Surveys organization and logistical system of the Argentine military forces during the Paraguay War.

2985 Guy, Donna J. Emilio and Gabriela Coni: reformers, public health, and working women. (*in* The human tradition in Latin America: the nineteenth century. Edited by Judith Ewell and William H. Beezley. Wilmington, Del.: Scholarly Resources, 1989, p. 233–248, bibl.)

Husband and wife, both socialists, share common concern for health of women and children, but take different approaches to solving the health problem.

2986 Guy, Donna J. Oro blanco: cotton, technology, and family labor in nineteenth-century Argentina. (*Americas/Francisc.*, 49:4, April 1993, p. 457–478)

Essayist attributes failure to develop cotton production to the retreat from family farming, expensive transportation, and technical problems.

2987 Guy, Donna J. Sex & danger in Buenos Aires: prostitution, family, and nation in Argentina. Lincoln: Univ. of Nebraska Press, 1991. 260 p.: bibl., ill., index, maps. (Engendering Latin America; 1)

Attributes establishment of legalized, medically supervised prostitution in Argentina to concern for family, society, and nation, and to the presence of "marginal women" eking out a living. Notes exaggerated accounts of white slave trade which focus exclusively on immigrant prostitutes.

2988 Halperín Donghi, Tulio. La apertura mercantil en el Río de la Plata: impacto global y desigualdades regionales, 1800–1850. (*in* América Latina en la Epoca de Simón Bolívar: la Formación de las Economías Nacionales y los Intereses Económicos Europeos, 1800–1850. Edición de Reinhard Liehr. Berlin: Colloquium Verlag, 1989, p. 115–138)

Pt. 1 of this thoughtful and enlightening essay analyzes the uneven impact the 1778–82 opening of the Río de la Plata to free trade had on the former viceroyalty. Analysis notes strengths and weaknesses of current literature on the subject and singles out economic and social consequences of the innovations introduced by free trade. In Pt. 2, the notion that the Argentine experience supports the dependency theory is rejected.

2989 Heredia, Edmundo A. Sarmiento en Lima. (*Bol. Inst. Riva-Agüero*, 15, 1988, p. 199–212)

Summarizes activities of Sarmiento during his unauthorized participation in the Lima Congress (1864–1865), and his advocacy there of public education for all social classes and the establishment of agricultural colonies.

2990 Horowitz, Joel. Industrialists and the rise of Perón, 1943–1946: some implications for the conceptualization of populism. (*Americas/Francisc.*, 47:2, Oct. 1990, p. 199–217)

Maintains that Perón lacked support of the industrialists as a group in 1945, and that as a result he turned to labor for support, which did not come easily. Author calls for a rethinking of the concept of populism, as he fails to find that peronism is an example of populism even though peronism is often so defined.

2991 Iglesia e inmigración. Recopilación de Néstor Tomás Auza y Luis Valentín Favero. Buenos Aires: Centro de Estudios Migratorios Latinoamericanos, 1991. 349 p.: bibl.

Sixteen scholars discuss issues that need further study and then assess influence and activities of priests and Protestant ministers among immigrants.

2992 Infesta, María Elena and **Marta E. Valencia.** Tierras, premios y donaciones: Buenos Aires, 1830–1860. (*Anu. IEHS*, 2, 1987, p. 177–211, tables)

Classifies and minutely examines public land grants made during Rosas period and their fate after Caseros. Major work of revision.

2993 Katzowich, Noiaj. Génesis de Moisés Ville. Traducción de Iaacov Lerman, con la colaboración de Abraham Platkin. Buenos Aires: Milá, 1987. 301 p.: bibl., ill. (Testimonios = ᵋEduyot)

A colonist and delegate of the Jewish Colonization Association describes experiences of Lithuanian and Ukrainian Jews in an agricultural colony founded by the Association in province of Santa Fe. Includes interesting discussion of clashes between Association and colonists, of conflicts within the colony between Jews of different national backgrounds, and of adjustment of inexperienced colonists to farming. Memoirs were begun on 1930 and cover history of the colony only from 1894–1905. Includes memoirs of Salomón Alexenicer.

2994 Kohn Loncarica, Alfredo G. and **Norma Isabel Sánchez.** La inmigración escocesa en la Argentina en la visión de Cecilia Grierson. (*Todo es Hist.*, 286, abril 1991, p. 76–93, bibl., photos)

Grierson, a *porteña* of Scottish descent, describes founding of Scottish colony of Monte Grande and arrival of Scottish settlers and merchants. She obtained data from her father John Parish Robertson Grierson, relatives, and the British consul in Buenos Aires.

2995 Korol, Juan Carlos and **Hilda Sábato.** Incomplete industrialization: an Argentine obsession. (*LARR*, 25:1, 1990, p. 7–30, bibl.)

Essayists look at works of historical and social analysis by the Argentine academic community in the 1950s and 1960s that concern the Argentine industrial process. Works are grouped according to intellectual ideas that influenced the writers, such as the development theory, sociology of modernization, and variants of Marxism, in the attempts to explain why Argentina never became industrialized.

2996 Korzeniewicz, Roberto P. The labor politics of radicalism: the Santa Fe crisis of 1928. (*HAHR*, 73:1, Feb. 1993, p. 1–32)

Maintains that an attempt by Radical provincial officials to develop closer relations with the labor movement divided the provincial community and failed to stop labor conflict. Decision of Yrigoyen Administration to intervene as requested by business and conservative groups cost it popular support.

2997 Korzeniewicz, Roberto P. Labor unrest in Argentina, 1930–1943. (*LARR*, 28:1, 1993, p. 7–40, bibl., tables)

Maintains that in 1930s workers began to organize along industry lines, a trend which permitted the Communists to gain influence among them and which led to greater State regulation of capital-labor relations.

2998 Lacoste, Pablo. Hegemonía y poder en el oeste argentino. Prólogo de Daniel Santamaría. Buenos Aires: Centro Editor de América Latina, 1990. 2 v.: bibl. (Biblioteca Política argentina; 302–303)

Attributes victory of the Revolution of 1905 in Mendoza prov. to the rise of popular democratic forces.

2999 Lafage, Franck. L'Argentine des dictatures, 1930–1983: pouvoir militaire et idéologie contre-révolutionnaire. Préface de Emile Poulat. Paris: L'Harmattan, 1991. 191 p.: bibl., index, maps. (Recherches & documents. Amérique latine)

Maintains that peronism has replaced Catholic nationalism, and is identified with popular conservatism. This new nationalism is threatened by the military, economic chaos, and the breakdown of society.

3000 Laferrère, Alfonso de. Historia, política, letras. Buenos Aires: Cia. Impresora Argentina, 1990. 347 p.: bibl., map.

Essays on Argentine history, politics, and literature are written by a journalist who was founder of *La Opinión* and editor of both *La Nación* and *La Prensa.* The essays on the Acuerdo de San Nicolás and the plans to dismember Buenos Aires prov. are published here for the first time. A posthumous work.

Laguarda Trías, Rolando A. Apuntes sobre ingenieros militares españoles en la Banda Oriental. See item **3137.**

3001 Lanusse, Alejandro Agustín. Protagonista y testigo: reflexiones sobre 70 años de nuestra historia. Santiago: M. Lugones S.A. Editores, 1988. 394 p.: ill.

Contains reflections of a professional soldier and president of Argentina who ended military rule in 1973.

3002 Lassaga, Ramón J. Historia de López. 2da. ed. Sante Fe, Argentina: Fundación Banco Bica, 1988. 469 p.: bibl. (Col. La Región)

Reprint of sympathetic biography of Estanislao López of Santa Fé prov., originally published in 1881. Used provincial sources.

3003 Lattuada, Mario J. Política agraria y partidos políticos, 1946–1983. Buenos Aires: Centro Editor de América Latina, 1988. 136 p.: bibl. (Biblioteca Política argentina; 233)

Analyzes agrarian policies advocated by Argentine political parties from 1946–83 and factors influencing implementation.

3004 Lobato, Mirta Z. Mujeres en la fábrica: el caso de las obreras del Frigorífico Armour, 1915–1969. (*Anu. IEHS*, 5, 1990, p. 171–204, tables, graph)

Uses archives of Armour S.A. de Berisso to study the tasks assigned to women drawn from the rural area who worked in the meat packing plant, their reaction to their work assignments, and their objectives. Attributes failure to develop a class and gender identity to their diverse ethnic background, to their view that they were in the work force only temporarily, and to seasonal nature of the work.

3005 López de Borche, Celia Gladys. Cooperativismo y cultura: historia de Villa Domínguez, 1890–1940. 2. ed. ampliada. Entre Ríos, Argentina: Editorial de Entre Ríos, 1987. 135 p.: bibl., ill., maps.

Relates origins and development of a Jewish agricultural colony in Entre Ríos prov. and formation of the first cooperative.

3006 López del Amo, Fernando. Ferrocarril, ideología y política ferroviaria en el proyecto liberal argentino, 1852–1916. Madrid: Centro Español de Estudios de América Latina, 1990. 345 p.: bibl., maps. (Serie Estudios; 15)

Excellent study examines ideological basis of government railroad policies and the contribution of railroad network development to national unification.

3007 Lozier Almazán, Bernardo P. Liniers y su tiempo. Buenos Aires: Emecé Editores, 1990. 300 p.: bibl.

Sympathetic biography of Santiago Liniers stresses his commercial activities and his role during the English invasions. Documented study.

3008 Luna, Félix. El radicalismo de ayer y de hoy. (*Todo es Hist.*, 289, julio 1991, p. 8–37, photos)

Prominent Argentine historian and journalist reviews political and intellectual history of the Unión Cívica Radical, and concludes that it has evolved into a party containing many discordant views and is firmly committed to democracy.

3009 Luque Colombres, Carlos A. La Ley Saenz Peña y la primera elección de gobernador de Salta. (*Invest. Ens.*, 39, enero/dic. 1989, p. 389–397)

The first provincial elections held under the Saenz Peña law were conducted in Salta, and showed that the people were prepared for the new electoral system.

3010 Luque Colombres, Carlos A. Patrón Costas en la historia. Córdoba, Argentina: s.n., 1991. 242 p.: bibl., ill.

Provides introduction to Robustiano Patrón Costas, a prominent industrialist (sugar), ex-governor and national senator of Salta, and founder of the Partido Demócrata Nacional.

3011 Lynch, John. Foreign trade and economic interests in Argentina, 1810–1850. (*in* América Latina en la Epoca de Simón Bolívar: la Formación de las Economías Nacionales y los Intereses Económicos Europeos, 1800–1850. Edición de Reinhard Liehr. Berlin: Colloquium Verlag, 1989, p. 139–155, tables)

Provides excellent review of economic history of Buenos Aires prov. and of contributions of British capital, markets, and merchants to the local economy.

3012 Manachino de Pérez Roldán, Isabel. Aportes de la colectividad italiana a la formación de la sociedad cordobesa. (*Rev. Junta Prov. Hist. Córdoba*, 13, 1988, p. 185–202)

Provides overall description of Italian cultural, educational, and economic activities in both rural and urban sectors of the province.

Marco, Miguel Angel de *et al.* Rosario. v. 1, Política, cultura, economía, sociedad: desde los orígenes hasta 1916. See *HLAS 53:2947.*

3013 Marquiegui, Dedier Norberto. Las cadenas migratorias españolas a la Argentina: el caso de los Sorianos de Luján. (*Stud. Emigr.*, 29:105, marzo 1992, p. 69–102, map, tables)

Results of an examination of emigration from three rural towns of Spanish province of Soria to Luján are best explained by application of the chain migration theory. Brief biographies of the Soriana elite.

Martí, Gerardo Marcelo. Argentina: la crisis de 1890; endeudamiento externo y crack financiero. See *HLAS 53:2463.*

3014 Martínez, Carlos M. Alsina y Alem: porteñismo y milicias. Buenos Aires: Ediciones Culturales Argentinas, 1990. 155 p.: bibl.

Follows career of Adolfo Alsina after Caseros, and briefly that of Leandro Alem as spokesman for the Guardias Nacionales of

Buenos Aires prov. Concludes that the Partido Autonomista originated in the Guardias Nacionales.

3015 Martínez, Pedro Santos. Después del 90: la deuda externa, las inversiones inglesas y el Comité Rothschild. (*Invest. Ens.*, 39, enero/dic. 1989, p. 245–273)

Reexamines with the aid of a French diplomat's report the origins of the financial crisis of 1890, and efforts of Argentine and European governments and capitalists to save Baring Brothers from bankruptcy.

3016 Mataloni, Hugo. La inmigración entre 1886–1890. Santa Fe, Argentina: Ediciones Colmegna, 1992. 92 p.: bibl., ill.

General discussion examines the 133 colonies established in Santa Fe prov. from 1856–87, and the cultural and economic transformation of the province as it absorbed the foreigners.

3017 Matassi, Francisco Pío. La batalla aérea de nuestras Islas Malvinas. Buenos Aires?: Editorial Halcón Cielo, 1990. 320 p.: bibl., ill. (some col.).

Argentine Air Force officer evaluates planning for air operations during the war. Instructive.

3018 McKenna, Patrick. Irish migration to Argentina. (*in* Patterns of migration. Edited by Patrick O'Sullivan. Leicester, England: Leicester Univ. Press, 1992, p. 63–83, graphs, maps)

Presents overview of Irish migration to Argentina from 1536–1960 that can serve as a basis for further research.

3019 Meardi, Norma and **María Rita Corona.** El lamento de Villa Cañas: ecos no acallados de una rebelión campesina. (*Universidad/Santa Fe*, 101, mayo 1991, p. 177–194, bibl.)

Presents background to a strike by tenant farmers facing eviction in Santa Fe prov. that led the Federación Agraria Argentina to successfully seek passage of a law correcting abuses not covered by Law No. 11.170 (1912).

3020 Metz, Allan. La Semana Trágica: an annotated bibliography. (*Rev. Interam. Bibliogr.*, 40:1, 1990, p. 51–91, bibl.)

Useful multi-disciplinary research tool even mentions specific pages in which La Semana Trágica is discussed for each citation.

3021 Milia, Fernando A. The Argentine Navy revisited. (*Nav. Hist.*, 4:1, Winter 1990, p. 24–29, photos, tables)

Brief, comprehensive introduction to the Argentine Navy looks at sources of its educational system, its operational and strategic doctrines, and its equipment. Argentine Navy definitely is not a "copy of Great Britain's Royal Navy."

3022 Mirande, María Cecilia. Repercusiones de la crisis de 1930 en Santa Fe. (*Res Gesta*, 29, enero/junio 1991, p. 161–183, graph, tables)

Analysis of cereal, meat, wool and sugar production from 1895–1930 reveals commodities' cyclical nature, and that they had already declined in importance by the 1930s when national policy decisions began to stress industrialization rather than agriculture.

3023 Muñoz Moraleda, Ernesto. El gobierno de Pablo de la Torre en Salta, 1832–1834. (*Rev. Dep. Hist./Tucumán*, 1:1, 1991, p. 74–84)

Briefly describes a governor who faced simultaneously external and internal threats to his rule and who was compelled to recognize the independence of Jujuy.

3024 Neiburg, Federico B. Fábrica y villa obrera: historia social y antropología de los obreros del cemento. Prólogo de Hugo Ratier. Buenos Aires: Centro Editor de América Latina, 1988. 2 v.: bibl. (Biblioteca Política argentina; 237–238)

Case study examines living and working conditions of laborers in a factory town built by their employer, the Loma Negra cement company, and their decision to form a labor union.

3025 Nelli, Ricardo. La injusticia cojuda: testimonios de los trabajadores del azúcar del Ingenio Ledesma. Buenos Aires: Puntosur Editores, 1988. 213 p.

Members of the Ledesma labor union complain that the peronists, the bureaucracy of the Confederación General del Trabajo, and the federal government failed to represent them in 1973–75. Their conclusion is that "el peronismo no es lo que ellos proclaman."

3026 Nicolau, Juan Carlos. Correspondencia inédita sobre historia argentina: cartas entre Rosas y Parish: informe de Griffiths a

Lord Palmerston. Buenos Aires: Editorial Leviatán, 1990. 91 p.: bibl. (Col. Otra historia)

Relates interesting correspondence on French policy in South America, and on failure to replace Spanish colonial laws with those more in accordance with republican principles.

3027 Olsson, Evald Guillermo. Suecos en la selva. Buenos Aires: Ediciones La Aurora, 1991. 201 p.: bibl., ill.

Briefly describes Swedish immigration to South America between 1890–1937, first to Brazil, and finally to colonization of Oberá (also known as Yerbal Viejo), Misiones prov., Argentina. Recollections of six of the early settlers are presented.

3028 Otero, Hernán. La inmigración francesa en Tandil: un aporte metodológico para el estudio de las migraciones en demografía histórica. (*Desarro. Econ.*, 32:125, abril/junio 1992, p. 79–106, bibl., graphs, maps, tables)

Presents analysis of regional and microregional origins of French immigrants who arrived in Tandil from 1850–1914, and identifies existence of "family nets" and "chain migration."

3029 Palomeque, Silvia. La circulación mercantil en las provincias del interior, 1800–1810. (*Anu. IEHS*, 4, 1989, p. 131–210, appendix, graphs, table)

This significant examination of regional and interregional trade patterns in the interior provinces is based on incomplete tax records found primarily in provincial archives. Statistical evidence calls attention to Córdoba and Salta as major consumers of imports from Europe and from the other provinces, and to existence of an interregional trade system in which the value of goods exchanged equalled the value of imported overseas goods.

3030 Palti, Elías José. Sarmiento, una aventura intelectual. Buenos Aires: Instituto de Historia Argentina y Americana Emilio Ravignani, Facultad de Filosofía y Letras, Univ. de Buenos Aires, 1991. 130 p.: bibl. (Cuadernos del Instituto Ravignani; 3)

Review of the controversy surrounding Sarmiento's ideas is followed by a careful reexamination of those ideas to identify their basic internal logic and the modifications made in response to reality. As a result, Sarmiento's ideas seem more consistent than is generally realized.

3031 Pan, Luis. Juan B. Justo y su tiempo: apuntes para una biografía intelectual. Buenos Aires: Planeta, 1991. 286 p.: bibl.

Exceptional study examines intellectual and scientific world in which Justo developed, his contributions to science and medical practice in Argentina, his critique of Marx, and his analysis of economic and social conditions in Argentina.

3032 Páramo de Isleño, Martha S. La candidatura de Sarmiento en el 80 en las cartas de Francisco Civit. (*Rev. Hist. Am. Argent.*, 15:29, 1989, p. 159–185, bibl.)

Civit's three letters to Sarmiento reveal divisions within the Partido Liberal de Mendoza, the absence of information on political maneuvering in Buenos Aires, and the fragility of electoral alignments.

3033 Paso, Leonardo. 1930, la frust[r]ación del nacionalismo. Buenos Aires: Editorial Futuro, 1987. 274 p.: bibl.

A Marxist attributes the revolution of 1930 to a nationalist spirit that was antilabor, undemocratic, racist, and unpopular.

3034 Patroni, Adrián. Adrián Patroni y *Los trabajadores en la Argentina*. Prólogo y estudio preliminar por Víctor O. García Costa. . Buenos Aires: Centro Editor de América Latina, 1990. 2 v.: bibl. (Biblioteca Política argentina; 289–290)

Biography of a leading organizer of the Partido Socialista and the Argentine labor movement includes reproduction of his instructive 1898 book describing the oppressive social and economic conditions the workers faced. Critical of misleading press reports and Argentine capitalists.

3035 Pioli de Layerenza, Alicia and **María Isabel Artigas de Rebes.** Amado Bonpland en el Plata. (*Hoy Hist.*, 7:41, sept./oct. 1990, p. 54–63, bibl.)

Brief biography of a French scientist sheds new light on his activities.

3036 Pondé, Eduardo Bautista. Los reelegidos—Roca, Yrigoyen y Perón. Buenos Aires: Editorial Legasa, 1991. 348 p.: bibl., ill. (Ensayo crítico)

Critical review of modern Argentine history reports confirmed and unconfirmed gossip, dissects legal and political agreements, and analyzes personalities of leading political figures.

3037 Prieto, Agustina. Condiciones de vida en el barrio Refinería de Rosario: la vivienda de los trabajadores, 1890–1914. (*Anuario/Rosario*, 14, 1989/1990, p. 165–181)

Closely examines living conditions in a "workers' " quarter occupied primarily by foreigners employed by the railroads and the local sugar refinery. Workers lived in huts of wood or tinplate; worked in the fields at harvest time; and were "class conscious."

3038 Punzi, Orlando Mario. La tragedia patagónica: historia de un ensayo anarquista. Buenos Aires: Círculo Militar, 1991. 135 p.: bibl., ill., maps. (Biblioteca del oficial; 743)

Documented analysis examines mission and accomplishments of an army unit sent to quell a separatist movement in Territorio Nacional de Santa Cruz in 1921 and 1922. Also looks at misrepresentation of conditions in the region and condemnation of the army commander by the press, and government silence on the military operation. Sees a parallel with conditions in the 1970s.

3039 Quesada, Vicente Gregorio. Memorias de un viejo: escenas de costumbres de la República Argentina. Estudio preliminar de Antonio Pagés Larraya. Buenos Aires: Academia Argentina de Letras, 1990. 616 p.: bibl., ill.

Reedition of an Argentine classic first published in Buenos Aires (1888).

3040 Quijada, Mónica. Aires de república, aires de cruzada: la Guerra Civil Española en Argentina. Barcelona: Sendai Ediciones, 1991? 254 p.: bibl., ill.

Well-researched and lucid description depicts Spanish Civil War as a temporarily divisive factor within Argentina's Spanish community, where the majority favored the Republic. Work also examines the evenhanded approach of the Argentine government to the situation, and the rapid adjustment to the victory of the *franquistas*.

3041 Ramallo, Jorge María. El Colegio y la Universidad de Buenos Aires en la época de Rosas. Buenos Aires: Ediciones Braga, 1992. 181 p.: bibl.

Monographic study of faculty, educational programs, and student body corrects

myth that Rosas government was hostile to education.

3042 Rapoport, Mario and **Claudio Spiguel.** Crisis económica y negociaciones con los Estados Unidos en el primer peronismo, 1949–1950: ¿un caso de pragmatismo? (*Rev. Ciclos*, 1:1, 1991, p. 65–116, graphs, tables)

Well-researched study notes the breakdown of the Great Britain-Argentine-US triangle, which then tested the domestic and international policies of each country. Concludes that established historical tendencies and pragmatism prevailed as both the US and Argentina attempted to solve Argentina's commercial and financial problems and to bring Argentina closer to the US and into the hemispheric defense system. A complicated problem is made very understandable.

3043 Ravina, Aurora. La obra historiográfica de la Academia Nacional de la Historia, Argentina. (*Rev. Hist. Am.*, 109, enero/junio 1990, p. 19–43, table)

Presents excellent introduction to publications and activities of the Academia, and to its members and their area of scholarly expertise.

3044 Recalde, Héctor. El colera en la Argentina. (*Todo es Hist.*, 286, abril 1991, p. 12–41, photos, tables)

Comprehensive discussion considers origins and spread of cholera and other infectious diseases from the city of Buenos Aires into the provinces, and measures taken to combat them.

3045 Regalsky, Andrés M. Foreign capital, local interest and railway development in Argentina: French investments in railways, 1900–1914. (*J. Lat. Am. Stud.*, 21:1, Feb. 1989, p. 425–452, bibl.)

Excellent study examines competition between French and British investment groups interested in railroads, the role of their bankers and the local elite, and passage of the Mitre law.

3046 Rein, Raanan. The Franco-Peron alliance: relations between Spain and Argentina, 1946–1955. Translated by Martha Grenzeback. Pittsburgh, Pa.: Univ. of Pittsburgh Press, 1993. 329 p.: bibl., index. (Pitt Latin American series)

Argues convincingly that Perón's policy toward Franco was based not on ideology but on the similarities of their international positions, and on Perón's domestic policies, political and economic considerations, and the desire to reduce ties to Great Britain and the US. Based on research in the national archives, on newspapers of four countries, and on interviews with political leaders.

3047 Riquelme de Lobos, Norma Dolores and María Cristina Vera de Flachs. Crisis en el campo, 1910–1913. (*Rev. Junta Prov. Hist. Córdoba,* 13, 1988, p. 145–180, bibl.)

Description of economic hardships faced by the rural population is followed by analysis of the origins of the union movement among the tenant farmers and sharecroppers, the founding of the Asociación Agraria Argentina (1912), and the spread of the agricultural strike that began in Alcorta in 1912. Relies on newspaper accounts that appeared in Buenos Aires, Córdoba, and Rosario, and stresses support of local merchants for the striking farmers.

3048 Robles Carcedo, Laureano. Unamuno y los estudios del General Belgrano. (*Estud. Hist. Soc. Econ. Am.,* 9, 1992. p. 317–342)

Publishes names of professors and classmates of Belgrano at the Universidad de Salamanca, and describes intellectual climate at the university.

3049 Rocamora, Joan. Catalanes en la Argentina: centenario del Casal de Catalunya. Buenos Aires: Librería Fausto, 1992. 339 p.: bibl., ill., index.

Surveys Catalonian contributions to Argentine civilization.

3050 Rock, David. Authoritarian Argentina: the nationalist movement, its history, and its impact. Berkeley: Univ. of California Press, 1993. 320 p.: bibl., index.

Major study examines political ideas and basic ideological concepts of nationalist movement as seen in literary writings of its leading advocates from 1910–85.

3051 Rodríguez Fox, Alberto. Proceso al vencido: análisis crítico de los golpes de estado desde la óptica de los vencidos. Buenos Aires: Artes Gráficas Negri, 1987 157 p.: bibl.

Author analyzes Argentine Supreme Court decisions from 1930–83 on charges brought against officials of overthrown governments. Study reveals that civilian-military relations have been a crucial element in Argentine political struggles and suggests that the military, with civilian cooperation, has resorted to a coup d'état to restore democracy.

3052 Rodríguez Lamas, Daniel. La presidencia de José María Guido. Buenos Aires: Centro Editor de América Latina, 1990. 112 p.: bibl. (Biblioteca Política argentina; 295)

Author carefully analyzes relations between Guido, a reluctant president, and an internally divided military, maneuvering political parties, and united labor unions led by experienced leaders.

3053 Ruggiero, Kristin. Honor, maternity, and the disciplining of women: infanticide in late nineteenth-century Buenos Aires. (*HAHR,* 72:3, Aug. 1992, p. 353–373)

Analyzes essential elements in concepts of female honor and motherhood that determined judicial decisions in infanticide cases.

3054 Ruggiero, Kristin. Wives on "deposit:" internment and the preservation of husbands' honor in late nineteenth-century Buenos Aires. (*J. Fam. Hist.,* 17:3, 1992, p. 253–270, bibl.)

Men interned their wives to maintain their own honor, not their wife's, and to assert their marital authority over them. Describes conditions in the house of deposit and the nature of State and Church control of women. Based on actual cases.

3055 Ruschi, María Isabel de. El diario *El Pueblo* y la realidad socio-cultural de la Argentina a principios del siglo XX. Buenos Aires: Editorial Guadalupe, 1988. 146 p.: bibl. (Col. Iglesia hoy. Serie Realización eclesial)

Provides brief but useful description of contents of a Catholic newspaper that appeared from 1900–54, and from 1956–60. Newspaper articles discussed the Círculo de Obreros, la Liga Democrática Cristiana, the Church and education, and Catholics in politics.

3056 Saá, Víctor. San Luis en la gesta sanmartiniana. San Luis, Argentina: Junta de Historia de San Luis, Fondo Editorial Sanluiseño, 1991. 348 p.: bibl., ill., index.

Presents documented account of province's contributions in 1810s to the independence movement. Corrects older versions with documents from provincial archives and includes informative footnotes.

3057 Sábato, Hilda. Citizenship, political participation and the formation of the public sphere in Buenos Aires, 1850–1880. (*Past Present*, 136, Aug. 1992, p. 139–163)

Author theorizes that electoral practices in Buenos Aires during the 1860s and 1870s did little to create a political citizenry. Instead *bonarenses* used the informal means of the public sphere as a vehicle of political participation.

3058 Sábato, Hilda and Elías José Palti. ¿Quién votaba en Buenos Aires?: práctica y teoría del sufragio, 1850–1880. (*Desarro. Econ.*, 30:119, oct./dic. 1990, p. 395–424)

Thoughtful discussion explores the meaning of popular sovereignty and its implementation among liberals, who were interested in creating a stable social order. Theory and practice differed, but few voted, and those who did were recruited from the masses by the State and its clients.

3059 Sábato, Hilda and Luis Alberto Romero. Los trabajadores de Buenos Aires: la experiencia del mercado, 1850–1880. Buenos Aires: Editorial Sudamericana, 1992. 284 p.: bibl. (Col. Historia y cultura)

Studies growth and changes that took place in the free labor market as pastoral economy gave way to an emerging market economy. Based on census data.

3060 Sáenz Quesada, María. Mujeres de Rosas. Buenos Aires: Planeta, 1991. 255 p.: bibl., ill. (Mujeres argentinas)

Documented biographies of Encarnación, Manuela, Maria Eugenia Castro, Josefa Gómez, and Agustina López de Osornio reconcile different accounts of their roles in the life of Rosas and put to rest many myths.

3061 Salas, Ernesto. La resistencia peronista: la toma del frigorífico Lisandro de la Torre. Buenos Aires: Centro Editor de América Latina, 1990. 2 v.: bibl. (Biblioteca Política Argentina; 297–298)

Examines reaction of union leaders, workers, and district of Mataderos to efforts of Frondizi Administration to implement austerity program recommended by the International Monetary Fund. Based largely on oral interviews with labor leaders and workers involved in 1959–60 strike at the *frigorífico*.

3062 Salvatore, Ricardo Donato. Criminology, prison reform, and the Buenos Aires working class. (*J. Interdiscip. Hist.*, 23:2, Autumn 1992, p. 279–299, table)

Author explores emphasis of the positivist criminologists on work habits and attitudes of immigrants. He discusses criminologists' view of labor discipline, their prison reform proposals, and the effect of their analysis on the elite's perception of crime and social problems.

3063 Salvatore, Ricardo Donato. Modes of labor control in cattle-ranching economies: California, southern Brazil, and Argentina, 1820–1860. (*J. Econ. Hist.*, 51:2, June 1991, p. 441–451)

Essayist speculates that labor force differences found in three ranching economies are not attributable to their distinct modes of production but to social and political instability of the period and to changing market conditions.

3064 San Martino de Dromi, María Laura. Intendencias y provincias en la historia argentina. Buenos Aires: Editorial Ciencias de la Administración, 1990. 422 p.: bibl.

Detailed comparison of the Real Ordenanza de Intendencias (1782) with the constitutions of the Argentine provinces and the Argentine Constitution of 1853 reveals that development of Argentine federalism was strongly influenced by the colonial ordinance.

3065 Santucho, Pedro Manuel Atilio. Historia del pueblo de Río Primero. Córdoba, Argentina: Artesol Taller Editor, 1987. 373 p.: bibl., ill., maps.

Contains genealogical tables for important families, documents describing land distribution and inheritance disputes, and a list of all important government and military employees. Source book.

3066 Sarlo Sabajanes, Beatriz. Una modernidad periférica: Buenos Aires, 1920 y 1930. Buenos Aires: Ediciones Nueva Visión, 1988. 246 p.: bibl. (Col. Cultura y sociedad)

Literary critic explores the world of Argentine intellectuals living in Buenos Aires during a period of rapid urban change.

Saulquin, Susana. La moda en la Argentina. See *HLAS 53:5522.*

3067 Schvarzer, Jorge. Empresarios del pasado: la Unión Industrial Argentina. 2. ed. Buenos Aires: CISEA; Imago Mundi, 1991. 309 p.: bibl. (Col. CISEA/Imago Mundi)

Analysis of internal organization of the Unión Industrial Argentina reveals that it does not represent the industrial sector but rather very wealthy entrepreneurs who are part of the *porteño* traditional elite; are engaged in a variety of agricultural, industrial, mining, and financial activities; and are not always interested in industrial development.

Schwartz, Herman. Foreign creditors and the politics of development in Australia and Argentina, 1880–1913. See *HLAS 53:4145.*

Segato, Rita Laura. Uma vocação de minoria: a expansão dos cultos afro-brasileiros na Argentina como processo de reetinização. See *HLAS 53:5523.*

3068 Senkman, Leonardo. Argentina, la Segunda Guerra Mundial y los refugiados indeseables, 1933–1945. Buenos Aires: Grupo Editor Latinoamericano, 1991. 442 p.: bibl. (Col. Estudios políticos y sociales)

Demonstrates that Argentina's policy towards Central European refugees between 1938–45 was dictated by the view that legal immigrants should be Catholic and Latin to facilitate assimilation and should contribute to the agroexport economy. Another policy determinant was the social and popular image of Jews. Author consulted archives of the Argentine Ministerio de Relaciones Exteriores y Culto.

3069 Seoane, María. Todo o nada. Buenos Aires: Planeta, 1991. 381 p.: bibl., ill. (Espejo de la Argentina)

Well-researched biography of Mario Roberto Santucho, leader of the Partido Revolucionario de los Trabajadores, describes his personality, his intellectual formation, and his political career. Based on family archives, interviews with Santucho's relatives and companions, and research in European and Latin American libraries.

3070 Silva, Hernán A. *et al.* Historia del sudoeste bonaerense. Dirección de Félix Weinberg. Buenos Aires: Plus Ultra, 1988. 328 p.: bibl., ill.

Contains general introduction to the history and development of the region, and in particular of Bahía Blanca.

3071 Stoetzer, O. Carlos. L'influence française au Rio de la Plata à travers les règimes politiques et les textes constitutionnels, 1811–1848. (*Cah. Am. lat.*, 10, 1990, p. 65–80)

Notes that constitutional documents written on both sides of the Río de la Plata reflected the influence of the French Revolution as well as a Spanish approach to Locke.

3072 Storani, Conrado. Les doy mi palabra: 50 años en la política al servicio del país. Buenos Aires: Ediciones Astro, 1990. 309 p.: ill.

Leading politician of Córdoba and former cabinet member recalls conversations with Illia and Alfonsín, with members of the US State Department, and with the Argentine military. Praises Illia, but criticizes Alfonsín for ignoring the Unión Cívica Radical and for adhering to economic policies that led to the return of peronism to power.

3073 Sulmanas, Armando J. Yerba mate e integración regional en la frontera argentino-brasileña. (*Jahrb. Gesch.*, 27, 1990, p. 69–100)

Author compares cultivation and marketing of yerba mate in Misiones prov., Argentina, and state of Paraná, Brazil, in 1920s, and finds no basis for integration of the two economies.

3074 Tasso, Alberto. Aventura, trabajo y poder: sirios y libaneses en Santiago del Estero, 1880–1980. Buenos Aires?: Ediciones Indice, 1988. 294 p.: bibl., ill.

Excellent introduction to Arab integration into the cultural, economic, and political life of Santiago del Estero in 20th century is based on interviews and archival sources.

3075 Tcach Abad, César. Sabattinismo y peronismo: partidos políticos en Córdoba, 1943–1955. Buenos Aires: Editorial Sudamericana, 1991. 287 p.: bibl. (Col. Historia y cultura)

Maintains that cultural conservatism and absence of a democratic party tradition account for initial support of peronism in Córdoba prov. and later for emergence of an anti-peronist movement. Excellent analysis of ideas of Sabattini and of the local political parties. Based on provincial sources.

3076 Tenti de Laitán, María Mercedes. La agricultura en Santiago del Estero antes y despues del ferrocarril. (*Todo es Hist.*, 283, enero 1991, p. 47–58, bibl., facsims, map, photos, tables)

Calls attention to disasterous effect on agricultural development of railroad freight rates that favored competing provinces.

3077 Terracini, Lore. Una inmigración muy particular: 1938, los universitarios italianos en la Argentina. (*Anu. IEHS*, 4, 1989, p. 335–369)

In short biographical sketches describes activities in Argentina of 11 Italian Jewish intellectuals who fled Fascist Italy, and identifies eight others.

3078 Thompson, Andrew. Informal empire?: an exploration in the history of Anglo-Argentine relations, 1810–1914. (*J. Lat. Am. Stud.*, 24:2, May 1992, p. 419–436)

Presents carefully reasoned argument that Argentina was never part of Britain's "informal empire."

3079 Tica, Patricia Ana. Aspectos de la vida social santafesina en la época de la Confederación. (*Res Gesta*, 29, enero/junio 1991, p. 217–240)

Well-researched study describes life styles in Rosario and Santa Fe, two up-river cities which were intermediaries between Buenos Aires and the interior provinces and Paraguay, at a time when their economic and political roles were beginning to expand.

3080 Torino, Luis Arturo. Coronel José de Moldes: semblanza. Salta, Argentina: Impr. INTI, 1991/ 74 p.: bibl., ill.

Calls attention to contributions of an important *salteño* to the war of independence.

3081 Torre, Juan C. Acerca de los estudios sobre la historia de los trabajadores en Argentina. (*Anu. IEHS*, 5, 1990, p. 209–220)

Very thoughtful discussion looks at strengths and weaknesses of past and present trends in the writing of political and social history of Argentine labor.

Torre, Juan Carlos. La vieja guardia sindical y Perón: sobre los orígenes del peronismo. See *HLAS 53:5526.*

3082 Torres, Félix A. La historia que escribí: estudios sobre el pasado cordobés. Córdoba, Argentina: Lerner, 1990. 422 p.: bibl., ill., index.

Enlightening essays based on Córdoba archival records describe province's pre-1810 commercial rivalry with Buenos Aires, its slave trade and population, its economy, and its post-1810 financial and material contributions to the independence movement.

3083 Triado, Enrique Juan. Historia de la Base Naval Puerto Belgrano. Buenos Aires: Centro Naval, Instituto de Publicaciones Navales, 1991. 175 p.: bibl., ill. (Decimosexto libro de la Colección Historia. Nonagesimo segundo libro de las Ediciones del Instituto de Publicaciones Navales)

Describes construction of the naval base, its facilities, and the lives of two pre-1900 naval commanders, Félix Dufourq and Luis Luiggi.

3084 Vacante, Vicente J.N. San Eduardo, su historia y sus hombres. (*Universidad/ Santa Fe*, 101, mayo 1991, p. 37–75)

Provides comprehensive description of founding of a town that began as a railroad station for the Compañía de Tierras del Grand Sud de Santa Fe y Córdoba in 1890, and of its physical, economic, social, and institutional growth to 1957.

3085 Vera de Flachs, María Cristina and Norma Dolores Riquelme de Lobos. La educación primaria en Córdoba, 1930–1970: crecimiento y contradicciones. Córdoba, Argentina: Junta Provincial de Historia de Córdoba, 1987. 166 p.: bibl., ill. (Cuadernos de historia; 7)

Evaluates successes and failures of efforts to reform the educational system, to reduce the illiteracy and dropout rate, and to raise the level of literacy to meet the requirements of a technological age.

3086 Viguera, Aníbal. El primero de mayo en Buenos Aires, 1890–1950: evolución y usos de una tradición. (*Bol. Inst. Hist. Ravignani*, 3:3, 1er semestre 1991, p. 53–79)

Describes different attributes and meanings acquired by the May 1 celebration as it evolved from a festive occasion organized by the Partido Socialista and labor organizations in 1890 to an official celebration in which political parties or organized labor showed their strength.

3087 Vogel, Hans. New citizens for a new nation: naturalization in early independent Argentina. (*HAHR*, 71:1, Feb. 1991, p. 107–131, tables)

Describes efforts of the governments in Buenos Aires to create and implement a naturalization policy during the confusing first two decades of the independence period.

3088 Vuotto, Pascual. El proceso de Bragado: ¡yo acuso! Buenos Aires: Editorial Reconstruir, 1991. 172 p.: bibl., ill. (Col. Testimonios)

Author claims that he and two others, anarchists and militants in the Federación Obrera Regional Argentina, were unjustly condemned in 1931 for a crime they never committed. Here he reviews the trial and evidence in an effort to clear his and their names.

3089 Walter, Richard J. The impact of foreign scholarship on Argentine historiography of the post-war era. (*Estud. Latinoam.*, 13, 1990, p. 257–281)

Discusses influence of foreign scholars of Argentine history, especially of the 20th century, on Argentine historians.

3090 Ward, Sharkey. Sea Harrier over the Falklands: a maverick at war. Annapolis, Md.: Naval Institute Press, 1992. 299 p.: ill., index, map.

A RAF pilot, who was stationed aboard the *HMS Invincible,* recalls his wartime experiences.

3091 Weil, Adolfo. Origenes del judaísmo conservador en la Argentina: testimonio. Buenos Aires: Ediciones Seminario Rabínico Latinoamericano, 1988. 156 p.: ill.

Author recounts his successful efforts to revitalize Jewish life in Argentina by bringing together people of different European origins, by introducing the Movimiento Conservador, and by associating the Congregación Israelita de la República Argentina with the United Synagogues of America.

Williams, Glyn. The Welsh in Patagonia: the State and the ethnic community. See *HLAS 53:5527.*

3092 Yeager, Gertrude M. Juana Manuela Gorriti: writer in exile. (*in* The human tradition in Latin America: the nineteenth century. Edited by Judith Ewell and William H. Beezley. Wilmington, Del.: Scholarly Resources, 1989, p. 114–127, bibl.)

Fascinating biography of a *salteña* novelist who took an active part in Lima's cultural life for thirty years (1850–78) and encouraged other women writers.

3093 Zimmermann, Eduardo A. Racial ideas and social reform: Argentina, 1890–1916. (*HAHR,* 72:1, Feb. 1992, p. 23–46, bibl.)

Thoughtful discussion looks at sources of racial and social ideas in Argentina at the turn of the century, and how these ideas shaped social legislation.

3094 Zuccherino, Ricardo Miguel and **María Josefina Morena Rithner.** Manuel Dorrego, el repúblico del federalismo: ensayo sobre un pensador que aun es futuro. Prólogos de Roberto Fernández Cistac y Federico Manuel Julián Gamas. La Plata, Argentina: Fondo Editorial Esto es Historia, 1990? 113 p.: bibl. (Col. Extensión histórica; 12)

Reviews historians' evaluation of Dorrego's political career and ideas.

PARAGUAY

Abente, Diego. Foreign capital, economic elites, and the State in Paraguay during the Liberal Republic. See *HLAS 53:4157.*

Abente, Diego. The Liberal Republic and the failure of democracy in Paraguay. See *HLAS 53:4158.*

3095 Casal, Aníbal Raúl. Juan León Mallorquín, defensor del Chaco y los yerbales. Asunción: Ediciones y Arte, 1990 216 p.: bibl., ill.

Extensive quotations from editorials in *Patria* and statements of Mallorquín (Partido Colorado president from 1937–47) define party's principles and Paraguayan claims to the Chaco and the *yerbales* of the Upper Paraná River.

3096 Cooney, Jerry W. The Archivo Nacional de Asunción: an update. (*Americas/Francisc.,* 47:3, Jan. 1991, p. 349–353)

Calls attention to transfer of Coleção Visconde de Rio-Branco to Asunción from Rio de Janeiro; to the availability of microfilm reader-copiers in the archives; and to progress made in classifying documents. Scholars are welcomed, and their investigations now will proceed much more rapidly than before.

3097 Dávalos, Serafina. Humanismo. Ed. facsimilar. Asunción: RP Ediciones; Centro de Documentación y Estudios, 1990. 102 p.: bibl., ill.

Reprint of 1907 doctoral dissertation by first Paraguayan woman lawyer. Author proposes that women: 1) should have equal rights with men; 2) should have right to vote and hold public office; and 3) could have roles other than motherhood. Dávalos participated in numerous congresses and conferences concerned with status and rights of women, often as representative of Paraguay.

3098 Ferreira Pérez, Saturnino. Testimonios de un capitán de la Guerra del 70, Justiniano Rodas Benítez: parte de la historia de San Ignacio de las Misiones. Asunción: S. Ferreira Pérez, 1989. 220 p., 10 p. of plates: ill.

Reminiscences are written by a veteran of the Paraguayan War and of the political contests in San Ignacio de las Misiones to 1932. Includes excerpts from Asunción press and list of military and civilian appointments in San Ignacio. Local history.

3099 Francia, José Gaspar Rodríguez de. Cartas y decretos del dictador Francia. v. 3. Recopilación de Alfredo Viola. Asunción: Univ. Católica, 1989-. 1 v. (Biblioteca de estudios paraguayos; 39)

Collection of documents for the years 1819–21 sheds light on northern border disputes with the Portuguese, on relations and treaties with the *mbayás*, on Artigas and Francisco Ramírez, on organization of the military, and on the indigenous peoples of Misiones. Vols. 1 and 2 were annotated in *HLAS 52:2815.*

3100 Klassen, Peter P. Die deutsch-völkische Zeit: in der Kolonie Fernheim, Chaco, Paraguay, 1933–1945: ein Beitrag zur Geschichte der auslandsdeutschen Mennoniten während des Dritten Reiches. Dietzenbach, Germany: Bolanden-Weierhof; Mennonitischer Geschichtsverein, 1990. 148 p.: ill.

Author relies exclusively on Mennonite archives and experience of his youth as a Paraguayan-German Mennonite in order to describe conflict between pacifists and disciples of Nazi Germany within this religious community from 1933–45. Although short on analysis, book provides insight into ideological seduction of a minority population in South America before and during World War II. [C.K. Converse]

3101 Kleinpenning, J.M.G. Rural Paraguay, 1870–1932. Amsterdam: CEDLA, 1992. 525 p.: bibl., ill., maps. (Latin America studies; 66)

Detailed study examines fundamental changes in agricultural sector and the countryside following the Paraguayan War. Most

State land was sold to large private (and often foreign) owners. Paraguay increasingly became a supplier of primary products exported mainly to the La Plata market, Europe, and North America. [R. Hoefte]

3102 Krüger, Hildegard. Asunción . . . hace cien años, vista por un periodista. (*Hist. Parag.,* 21, 1984, p. 315–323)

German journalist gives brief description of Asunción as seen in 1882.

3103 Lezcano, Carlos María. El régimen militar de Alfredo Stroessner: fuerzas armadas y política en el Paraguay, 1954–1988. (*Rev. Parag. Sociol.,* 26:74, enero/abril 1989, p. 117–147, bibl., tables)

Essayist maintains that Stroessner's rule was based on fusion of the military with the Partido Colorado, and that Stroessner's overthrow resulted from a long economic crisis, the opposition of the Church, and the breakdown of the unity between the military and the Partido Colorado.

3104 Lynch, Elisa Alicia. Exposición y protesta. 2a. ed. Asunción: Fundación Cultural Republicana, 1987. 209 p.: bibl. (Col. documental)

This reissue of a very important document by Elisa Alicia Lynch also contains letters written by her, her children, and several members of the López family. Very informative on efforts of Lynch to secure possession of properties she acquired before 1870, and on controversy between Lynch and the López family over estate left by Solano López. Chronological data is not very accurate.

3105 Mazacotte, Alejandro. Ensayo sobre la Guerra del Chaco. v. 4. Asunción: NAPA, 1983-. 1 v.

See *HLAS 50:2471.*

3106 Olmos Gaona, Alejandro. Alberdi y dos diplomáticos paraguayos: nuevos aportes documentales. (*Hist. Parag.,* 21, 1984, p. 41–77, bibl.)

Calls attention to dependence of Alberdi on two Paraguayan diplomats for his information but not for his opinions on the Paraguayan War.

3107 Peña Villamil, Manuel. Eusebio Ayala: perfil de un ciudadano. (*Hist. Parag.,* 21, 1984, p. 131–172, photo)

Sympathetic biography of a Paraguayan diplomat and president during the Chaco War includes anecdotes taken from unpublished memoirs of Ayala's wife.

3108 Pesoa, Manuel. Documentos originales del "Centro Democratico," año 1887. Asunción: M. Pesoa, 1990. 61 p.: ill.

Reproduces first records of the Partido Liberal, written between June 26 and October 24, 1887.

3109 Pesoa, Manuel. Orígenes del Partido Liberal Paraguayo, 1870–1887. Asunción: Criterio-Ediciones, 1987. 186 p.

Chronicles political events that led to formation of the Partido Liberal.

3110 Plá, Josefina. Aventura y desventura del oro en el Paraguay. (*Hist. Parag.,* 20, 1983, p. 141–187, bibl.)

In a fascinating essay, author describes search for gold initiated in the colonial period, the sources of gold accumulated by the Paraguayan government prior to 1864, and the uses to which it was put.

3111 Potthast-Jutkeit, Barbara. The ass of a mare and other scandals: marriage and extramarital relations in nineteenth-century Paraguay. (*J. Fam. Hist.,* 16:3, 1991, p. 215–239, bibl., tables)

Argues persuasively that Paraguayan War failed to significantly alter patterns of family structures intact from colonial days. Relies on colonial and post-independence accounts and on 1846 census. For sociologist's comment see *HLAS 53:5363.*

3112 Prieto, Justo José and Arturo Bray. Ciudadano y soldado: comentarios a la correspondencia de Justo Prieto con Arturo Bray. Introducción y comentarios de Justo José Prieto. Asunción: Univ. Católica, 1988. 175 p.: bibl. (Biblioteca de estudios paraguayos; 25)

Correspondence of two exiled Paraguayans, one a professional soldier, the other a liberal professor, discusses militarism, participation of the military in government and revolutions, and whether civilians or the military conducted the Chaco War. The six letters were written between March 12 and May 14, 1953.

3113 Pusineri Scala, Carlos Alberto. Periódicos chaqueños. (*Hist. Parag.,* 21, 1984, p. 101–129, ill.)

Describes 14 periodicals published by the military at the unit and sector levels during the Chaco War. Some were informative; others were entertaining and deliberately full of misinformation. Briefly comments on Radio Prensa and press releases as instruments of psychological warfare and on a Bolivian military newspaper.

3114 Residentas, destinadas y traidoras. Recopilación de Guido Rodríguez Alcalá. Asunción: RP Ediciones-Criterio, 1991. 159 p.: maps.

Collection of documentary accounts describes Solano López's persecution of women during Paraguayan War and the fate of women in army and "concentration" camps. These accounts, included here, are confirmed by statements of judges who witnessed the inhumane treatment of women. Includes judicial decision on claims of Elisa Lynch to land Solano López gave her. Not the usual view of the war.

3115 Silva, Fernando. Mis memorias: Regimiento de Caballería no. 1 "Valois Rivarola," "listo, adelante Valois": Guerra del Chaco, 1932–1935. Asunción: Criterio Ediciones, 1989. 320 p.: ill., maps.

Relates history of an elite cavalry unit during the Chaco War.

3116 Silvia. Recopilación de Manuel Peña Villamil. Pesquisa genealógica de Roberto Quevedo. Asunción: Criterio Ediciones, 1987. 187 p.: bibl.

History of a Paraguayan family based on diary, letters, and memoirs of two women, one of them a *destinada,* relates their experiences during and after the Paraguayan War. Observes that the *residentas* were women fleeing from the enemy, not obligated or willing followers of Solano López. Includes genealogies of the following families: Cordal, Díaz de Bedoya, Decoud, García del Barrio, and Gill.

3117 Tjarks, Germán O.E. Nueva luz sobre el origen de la Triple Alianza. (*Hist. Parag.,* 21, 1984, p. 245–313, appendices)

Finds the origins of the Paraguayan War in a clash between prevailing liberal and conservative ideologies and in failure of the Mitre Administration to observe strict—that is, real—neutrality toward internal political struggles of Uruguay. Uses unedited archives of Rufino de Elizalde, and in them finds evidence that the Triple Alliance, in an informal state, was formed on June 18, 1864.

Urízar, Rogelio. Los dramas de nuestra anarquía: análisis de la evolución del Paraguay. See *HLAS 53:4187.*

3118 Vega Gaona, Ceferino. El RI Batallón 40 en la Guerra del Chaco. Asunción: Dirección de Publicaciones Militares, EMFA, 1991. 2 v.: ill., maps.

Reexamines role of a military unit in the Chaco War, and corrects earlier accounts.

3119 Viola, Alfredo. El Dr. Francia: defensor de la independencia del Paraguay. Asunción?: C. Schauman, 1992. 276 p.: bibl.

Presents well-documented thesis that Francia's policies were governed by need to provide for political and economic independence of Paraguay; to neutralize Spanish and *porteño* merchants involved in country's export-import trade; and to defend the nation from Buenos Aires and the Indians on its borders.

3120 Whigham, Thomas L. The back-door approach: the Alto Uruguay and Paraguayan trade, 1810–1852. (*Rev. Hist. Am.*, 109, enero/junio 1990, p. 45–67, map, table)

Presents able discussion of important Itapúa-São Borja trade route and disputes between Paraguay and Corrientes prov. over its control.

3121 Whigham, Thomas L. Rosa Dominga Ocampos: a matter of honor in Paraguay. (*in* The human tradition in Latin America: the nineteenth century. Edited by Judith Ewell and William H. Beezley. Wilmington, Del.: Scholarly Resources, 1989, p. 73–81)

An 1847 legal case involving two lovers reveals persistence of the Hispanic legal tradition and its successful use by a woman seeking to restore her honor.

3122 Whigham, Thomas L. and Barbara Potthast-Jutkeit. Some strong reservations: a critique of Vera Blinn Reber's *The demographics of Paraguay: a reinterpretation of the Great War, 1864–70.* (*HAHR*, 70:4, Nov. 1990, p. 667–678)

Reber's conclusions on Paraguayan family size, population, growth rates, mortality from disease, and civilian and military war casualties (see *HLAS 52:2831*) are challenged, but authors fail to resolve the issues.

3123 Whigham, Thomas L. La yerba mate del Paraguay, 1780–1870. Asunción: Centro Paraguayo de Estudios Sociológicos, 1991. 152 p.: bibl. (Serie Historia social)

Brief but fascinating revisionist study examines growth of Paraguayan yerba mate exports, misguided government policies, and competition with Brazilian yerba mate. Collection of documents.

URUGUAY

3124 Arocena Olivera, Enrique. El desgaste de las levitas: entre el Quebracho y la elección de Batlle, 1886–1903. Epílogo de Carlos Manini Ríos. Montevideo: Barreiro y Ramos Editores, 1988. 206 p.: bibl., ill.

Provides detailed description of the economic, political and social transformations that contributed to the end of the military era and the rise of civilian influence.

3125 Arteaga, Juan José. La inmigración en el Uruguay a fines del siglo XIX y principios del XX. (*Estud. Cienc. Let.*, 19, dic. 1990, p. 11–20)

Uses census figures to delineate the successive waves of immigrants from 1879–1908, and to suggest why Uruguay failed to attain its goal of becoming an agricultural country.

3126 Barrios Pintos, Aníbal. Rivera: una historia diferente. v. 2. Montevideo: Intendencia Municipal de Rivera, 1985-. 1 v. See *HLAS 50:2495.*

3127 Blixen, Samuel. José Pedro Cardoso: recuerdos cargados de futuro. Montevideo: Ediciones Trilce, 1991. 239 p., 4 p. of plates: bibl., ill., index.

Cardoso, former Secretary-General and presidential candidate of the Partido Socialista, recalls and reflects upon important political events in his 60-year career (1931–91). His comments on developments in the Partido Colorado and Partido Nacional are especially interesting.

3128 Bronstein, Abel et al. Vida y muerte en comunidad: ensayos sobre judaísmo en el Uruguay. Montevideo: Kehila, Comunidad Israelita del Uruguay, 1990. 179 p.: bibl., ill.

Informative essays consider Jewish theater (1920–60) and diversion of potential Jewish settlers from Uruguay and Argentina to Chile in the 1930s.

Bruno, Cayetano. Apóstoles de la evangelización en la Cuenca del Plata. See item **2924.**

Caetano, Gerardo. Del primer batllismo al terrismo: crisis simbólica y reconstrucción del imaginario colectivo. See *HLAS 53:4197.*

3129 Caetano, Gerardo and **Raúl Jacob.** El nacimiento del terrismo, 1930–1933. Montevideo: Ediciones de la Banda Oriental, 1989-. 3 v.: bibl. (Historia y presente; 3, 6, 8)

Detailed analysis examines effects of 1929 world economic crisis on political groups, the institutional breakdown that began in 1933, and the constitutional reform movement that led to Terra dictatorship. Absence of any broad-based demand for constitutional reform and of a break with liberalism convinces authors that Uruguay is basically conservative.

3130 Casas de Barrán, Alicia and **Susana Martínez Fuentes.** Historiografía del siglo XX uruguayo en la Biblioteca Nacional, 1900–1980. (*Rev. Bibl. Nac./Montevideo*, 27, abril 1990, p. 85–112, bibl.)

Annotated guide lists works on 20th-century Uruguayan history, most of which are published in Uruguay.

3131 Díaz de Guerra, María Amelia. Historia de Maldonado. Maldonado, Uruguay: Intendencia Municipal de Maldonado, 1988. 2 v.: bibl., ill.

Encyclopedic history of *departamento* and city of Maldonado from earliest times to 1930 is based on primary and secondary sources. Describes origins of first settlers; presents short biographies of landowners and of political, military, and religious leaders; and traces growth of the city and *departamento.* Selective bibliography at end of each chapter.

3132 Fajardo Terán, Florencia. El niño chasque. Maldonado, Uruguay: Museo Didáctico Artiguista, 1991. 90 p.: ill., maps. (Publicaciones/Museo Didáctico Artiguista; 2)

Briefly describes irregular founding of important port of Maldonado, genealogy of the Mendoza Estremera family, and events in the city during British occupation in 1806.

3133 Fernández Huidobro, Eleuterio. Historia de los tupamaros. v. 2, El nacimiento. Montevideo: Tae Editorial, 1986-. 1 v.

Tupamaro describes events of 1965 that led to formal organization of the Movimiento de Liberación Nacional. For annotation of Vol. 1 see *HLAS 52:2856.*

3134 Francia — Uruguay, historia de sus confluencias. Montevideo: República Oriental del Uruguay, Presidencia de la República, 1987. 79 p.: bibl., ill.

Brief, but excellent introduction to French influence and presence in Uruguay.

Frega, Ana. El pluralismo uruguayo, 1919–1933: cambios sociales y política. See *HLAS 53:4203.*

3135 Frogoni, Jorge. Don Domingo Ordoñana: su vida, su obra. (*Hoy Hist.*, 8: 44, marzo/abril 1990, p. 17–32, photos)

Brief biography of a founder of the Asociación Rural del Uruguay and a writer of the Código Rural del Uruguay.

3136 Harari, José. Contribución a la historia del ideario del M.L.N. Tupamaros: análisis crítico. v. 1. Montevideo: Editorial MZ, 1986. 1 v.

Sympathetic and well-documented account relates origins, composition, aims, internal divisions, and strategies of the Movimiento de Liberación Nacional-Tupumaros to 1972.

3137 Laguarda Trías, Rolando A. Apuntes sobre ingenieros militares españoles en la Banda Oriental. Maldonado, Uruguay: Museo Didáctico Artiguista, 1991. 68 p.: bibl. (Publicaciones; 3)

Contains biographical sketches of military engineers who served in Buenos Aires or Montevideo.

3138 Maggi, Carlos. Artigas y su hijo, el Caciquillo: el mundo pensado desde el lejano norte, o, las 300 pruebas contra la historia en uso. Montevideo: Editorial Fin de Siglo, 1991. 204 p.: bibl., col. map. (Col. Raíces)

Presents plausible thesis that Artigas had a *charrúa* son. This could explain presence of *charrúa* soldiers in his military campaigns to 1815, and his opposition to a policy endorsing extermination of infidel indigenous peoples. Based on the Archivo Artigas.

3139 Martínez Cherro, Luis. Por los tiempos de Francisco Piria: creador de 70 barrios en Montevideo, pueblos y ciudades en el Este. Piriápolis, Uruguay?: Asociación de Fomento y Turismo de Piriápolis, 1990. 149 p.: bibl., ill.

Excellent introduction to Piriápolis and its founder, Francisco Piria.

3140 Martínez Díaz, Nelson. La resistencia a la abolición en los países del Río de la Plata. (*in* Coloquio Internacional sobre Abolición de la Esclavitud, *Madrid, 1986.* Esclavitud y derechos humanos: la lucha por la libertad del negro en el siglo XIX. Edición de

Francisco de Solano y Agustín Guimerá. Madrid: Consejo Superior de Investigaciones Científicas, 1990, p. 625–634)

Briefly reviews Uruguayan laws on slavery that were enacted from 1825 to 1862 when the last legal obstacle to abolition of slavery was removed.

3141 Moraes, María Inés. Bella Unión: de la estancia tradicional a la agricultura moderna, 1853–1965. Montevideo: Centro de Investigaciones Económicas; Ediciones de la Banda Oriental, 1990. 323 p.: bibl.

Impressive economic study examines transition of a port and surrounding region from a pastoral to an agricultural economy. Also looks at port's short-lived role as a transit point for shipments of European and Brazilian merchandise to Rio Grande do Sul, and for Rio Grande do Sul to export its own production.

3142 Musso Ambrosi, Luis Alberto. Bibliografía de historia del Uruguay. (*Anu. Estud. Am.*, 46:1, 1989, suplemento, p. 67–176, bibl., index)

Third part of bibliographical guide to works on Uruguay published in Argentina, Brazil, France, Spain, and Uruguay itself is of special interest to historians, economists, and social scientists. English titles in Spanish translation are included.

3143 Musso Ambrosi, Luis Alberto. José María Fernández Saldaña: relación de su obra bibliográfica. Montevideo: Biblioteca Nacional, 1989. 85 p.: ill.,index.

Guide to the writings of Saldaña.

3144 Oddone, Juan Antonio. Uruguay en los años 30: los países atlánticos de América Latina y su relación con los centros hegemónicos. Montevideo: Fundación de Cultura Universitaria, 1989. 126 p.: bibl. (Cuadernos de investigación y docencia. Cuadernos de interguerras; 2)

Examines 1929 world economic crisis as it affected the local economy and inter- and intra-party struggles. Stresses that Herrerismo and Riverismo both supported Terra's opposition to the *colegiado* and the demand for constitutional reform, and contributed to establishment of the Terra dictatorship.

3145 Oddone, Juan Antonio. Uruguay entre la depresión y la guerra, 1929–1945.. Montevideo: Fundación de Cultura Universitaria, 1990. 323 p.: bibl.

Describes Uruguay's adjustment to the depression of 1929 and to political and economic realignments taking place on the eve of World War II. British and US diplomatic correspondence was consulted.

3146 Parodi, Fernando. Dr. Carlos Villaderos: un personaje olvidado de nuestra historia. (*Bol. Hist. Ejérc.*, 279/282, 1990, p. 175–195, facsim., plate, map)

Provides brief introduction to a man who represented the government of President Manuel Oribe in Rio de Janeiro (1837–38); occupied numerous cabinet positions; and edited, among others, Oribe's important newspaper *El Defensor de la Independencia Americana* (1844–51).

3147 Pollero, Raquel. Estudio de la población de Tacuarembó en base a datos histórico-demográficos. (*An. Encuentro Nac. Reg. Hist.*, 2:2, oct. 1990, p. 216–226, bibl., tables)

Analysis of available records indicates that one-fifth of region's population has an Indian ancestor, and another fifth, a Negro ancestor.

3148 Posadas, Diego A. de. Dignidad y regocijo, arriba y abajo: reflexiones de un siglo que se va: alegato histórico sobre la descentralización, la autonomía—y la gente: bases y puntos de partida para una reorganización política del Uruguay. Montevideo?: Tall. Gráf. Barreiro, 1988. 238 p.: bibl.

Attributes existence of a strong central government and suppression of popular democratic tendencies to the country's colonial heritage and to the elite of Montevideo and their merchant allies.

3149 Real de Azúa, Carlos. Los orígenes de la nacionalidad uruguaya. Prólogo de Gerardo Caetano y José P. Rilla. Montevideo: Arca; Instituto Nacional del Libro, Ministerio de Educación y Cultura; Nuevo Mundo, 1990. 472 p.: bibl.

Posthumous work is written by polemist and revisionist who questioned existing interpretations that an independent Uruguayan republic emerged by 1828. Well documented.

3150 Ricci, Maria Lúcia de Souza Rangel and Lilia Inés Zanotti de Mendrano. El papel del contrabando y la interacción fronteriza del Brasil sureño con el Estado Oriental del Uruguay, 1850–1880. (*Not. Bibliogr. Hist.*, 21:140, out./dez. 1990, p. 257–265)

Provides brief introduction to the subject.

3151 Rodríquez Ximénez, Margarita. En los albores de la Iglesia uruguaya: la relación ad limina (1888) del obispo de Montevideo Inocencio María Yéreguy. (*Quinto Cent.*, 16, 1990, p. 55–100, tables)

The second bishop of Montevideo reports to the Vatican on organization of the Church, religious activities in the diocese, relations with the State, number of religious and their geographical distribution, religious communities, Protestant activities, work of the Jesuits, and difficulties of administering the sacraments in rural areas. Notes that most priests are foreigners.

3152 Rojas Beltrán, Ramón. Historia del gremialismo médico del Uruguay. Montevideo?: s.n., 1989? 161 p.: bibl.

Brief history of the Sindicato Médico del Uruguay (1920–79) includes supporting documents and membership lists.

3153 Schonebohm, Dieter. Judíos de izquierda en Montevideo: los Bundistas. (*Hoy Hist.*, 7:41, sept./oct. 1990, p. 21–29) See item **3154.**

3154 Schonebohm, Dieter. Judíos de izquierda en Montevideo: la "comunidad progresista." (*Hoy Hist.*, 8:44, marzo/abril 1991, p. 59–70, graph)

Leftist Polish and Lithuanian Jews who arrived between 1928–48 were divided between nonzionists, socialist zionists, and procommunists. Disturbed by condition of Jewish workers and calling themselves progressives, they sought integration by joining the labor movement and simultaneously organized their own cultural associations and political parties. Based on interviews with leftist Jews. See also item **3153.**

3155 Soiza Larrosa, Augusto. Inmigración médica al Uruguay, 1839–1895. (*Hoy Hist.*, 8:47, sept./oct. 1991, p. 38–48, tables)

Describes medical background of Spanish doctors and surgeons who arrived in Uruguay, and identifies those who revalidated their foreign medical degrees in Uruguay between 1885–94.

3156 Villegas, Juan. Historia de la Iglesia en el Uruguay en cifras: V centenario de la evangelización de América. Montevideo: Univ. Católica del Uruguay Dámaso A. Larrañaga, Depto. de Investigación y Estudios Superiores de Historia Americana, 1987. 100 leaves: bibl.

Collection of Church statistics is mostly for years after 1860. Tables do include Protestants and those without a religion, and divorces.

Whigham, Thomas L. The back-door approach: the Alto Uruguay and Paraguayan trade, 1810–1852. See item **3120.**

3157 Zubillaga, Carlos. Cinco momentos en la vida de José Benito Lamas. (*Rev. Bibl. Nac./Montevideo*, 27, abril 1990, p. 67–81)

Laudatory biography of a Franciscan priest who defended independence movement by providing it with an ideological justification, and who accompanied Artigas.

BRAZIL

MARSHALL C. EAKIN, *Associate Professor of History, Vanderbilt University*
KATHLEEN HIGGINS, *Assistant Professor of History, University of Iowa*

THE QUANTITY OF PUBLICATIONS on Brazilian history continues to be impressive, with social history remaining the dominant methodological approach in the field. Studies of women, families, workers, slaves, and immigrants have been notable both in quantity and quality. A number of fine studies of the various regions, the First Republic, the 1950s, and the left have also appeared. Biographical and military works, as well as local histories, also continue to appear in significant numbers. There has been a notable decline in work by historians on the Empire and the post-1964 period since *HLAS 52.*

Several noteworthy general or historiographical works have appeared recently.

Linhares has organized and edited an excellent new one-volume history of Brazil (item **3167**); Schneider has written a text that is largely the political history of the past century (item **3427**); and the Instituto Brasileiro de Geografia e História recently published an important series of historical statistics (item **3175**). Topik reviews the key literature in the field (item **3192**), and Bom Meihy has edited a series of interviews with several generations of Brazilianists (item **3169**).

In colonial history, the emphasis clearly continues to be on social history, rather than political or economic history. Metcalf makes a major contribution to the history of settlement patterns and family history (item **3209**). Vainfas' history of sexuality and morality in colonial Brazil is also an impressive addition to the literature of this period (item **3226**). Excellent analyses of the inheritance system are provided by Silva (items **3224** and **3223**), Lewin (item **3206**), and Nazzari (item **3181**). Also to be noted is Whatley's excellent translation of Léry's 16th-century encounter with coastal Indians (item **3205**).

The number of works appearing on slavery continues to be large, but with almost overwhelming emphasis on the 19th century. For the colonial period two noteworthy statistical analyses are those of the slave family by Metcalf (item **3210**) and of the international traffic in child slaves by Gutiérrez (item **3202**). Quantitative studies are also prevalent for the national, or near-national, period (items **3349**, **3369, 3183, 3159** and **3421**). Among the historians of slavery, those who have demonstrated either quantitatively or qualitatively that slaves exercised some agency within the constraints of their oppression—a good example of the latter being Chaloub (items **3260, 3261,** and **3262**)—have been scathingly criticized by Gorender (item **3178**) and defended in a rejoinder by Schwartz (item **3188**).

In the field of Afro-Brazilian history, several noteworthy items have appeared: a biography of the black physician and politician, Dr. Alfred Casemiro da Rocha (1855–1933) by Oracy Nogueira (item **3383**); and studies of Afro-Brazilian political mobilization by Andrews (item **3231**) and Butler (items **3250**). Andrews has also published an important study of race relations and racial inequality (item **3232**).

Some of the most interesting and innovative work has been in studies of women, family, gender, and sexuality. In addition to Metcalf (item **3209**) and Nazzari (item **3181**), Borges has produced a fine study of the family in Bahia from 1870–1945 (item **3246**). Rago (item **3407**), Samara (item **3422**), Esteves (item **3282**), Engel (item **3280**), Hahner (item **3311**), and Kuznesof (item **3336**) also make important contributions to this area of research.

Labor, workers, and immigrants continue to receive a great deal of attention. Gomes' study of "trabalhismo" (item **3301**), Dutra's monograph on workers in Minas Gerais (item **3278**), and French's detailed study of workers in the ABC region are important contributions to the literature (item **3296**). In addition to some of the scholarly works on immigrants—such as those by Klein on Spaniards and Portuguese (items **3332** and **3331**), Campos on Syrians and Lebanese (item **3253**), and Vangelista on Italians (item **3446**)—the flood of works by amateur historians continues.

Regional studies, especially those with an economic orientation, form a notable segment of recent publications. Among the better works in this genre are Bittencourt for Espirito Santo (item **3164**), Mott for Sergipe (item **3377**), Pesavento for Rio Grande do Sul (items **3393** and **3391**), and Hering for Santa Catarina (item **3314**). Mattoso's magisterial work synthesizes years of research on Bahia (item **3368**).

Studies of the Empire are conspicuous by their relative paucity since *HLAS* 52, and the same is true for the post-1964 period. However, a number of fine works on the period of the First Republic have appeared. Carvalho's innovative study of republican political iconography (item **3259**) and of the 1870–1914 period (item **3258**), and

Topik's work on economic history (item **3441**) stand out. Levine has produced a major new analysis of the Canudos rebellion (item **3342**), and several studies have examined the 1950s, especially the life and times of Juscelino Kubitschek (items **3361, 3360,** and **3288**).

Some other areas that have received significant attention recently are urban history, the left, and economic history. For instance, Holloway contributes a fine study of the police in Rio de Janeiro (item **3320**) and Martins studies São Caetano (item **3365**). Reis Filho (item **3413**), Pinheiro (item **3396**), and Vianna (item **3447**) focus on the left, while economic history is examined by Topik (item **3441**) and, for Campinas, by Semeghini (item **3430**).

GENERAL

3158 **A abolição do cativeiro: os grupos dominantes: pensamento e ação.** Coordenação de Arno Wehling. Rio de Janeiro: Instituto Histórico e Geográfico Brasileiro, 1988. 198 p.: bibl.

Collection of papers delivered on topics related to abolition in Brazil examines roles of Catholic Church, political parties, and the military. Perhaps of use to specialists.

3159 **Andrade, Maria José de Souza.** A mão de obra escrava em Salvador, 1811–1860. São Paulo: Corrupio, 1988. 235 p.: bibl., ill. (Baianada; 8)

Provides quantitative study of urban slavery in Salvador in first half of 19th century. This detailed analysis may be quite useful for comparative studies.

3160 **Arquivo Público do Estado do Ceará (Brazil).** Catálogo de fontes primárias sobre a escravidão negra. Fortaleza, Brazil Secretaria de Cultura, Turismo e Desporto, 1988. 59 p.

Provides preliminary (i.e., incomplete) catalog of documents available in the archive of Ceará relating to slavery. Useful for researchers.

3161 **Assunção, Matthias Röhrig.** Pflanzer, Sklaven und Kleinbauern in der brasilianischen Provinz Maranhão, 1800–1850. Frankfurt: Vervuert Verlag, 1993. 511 p.: bibl., maps, tables.

Author uses a wealth of demographic and economic data from Maranhão provincial and municipal archives to examine a highly stratified, partially autonomous peasant economy that developed alongside plantation agriculture, but omits the historical and cultural framework of the region. The resulting conflict, known as the Balaiada Rebellion, led to a unique alliance between free peasants and slaves. [G.K. Converse]

3162 **Atualidade & abolição.** Organização de Manuel Correia de Andrade e Eliane Moury Fernandes. Recife, Brazil: Fundação Joaquim Nabuco; Editora Massangana, 1991. 198 p.: bibl. (Série Abolição; 21)

Collection of papers addresses topics relating to slavery in Brazil including abolition, slave resistance, *quilombos,* urban life, and racism. Perhaps of use to specialists.

3163 **Balhana, Altiva Pilatti** and **Cecilia Maria Westphalen.** As fontes para a história social do Brasil meridional. (*ANPOCS BIB,* 23, 1987, p. 49–56)

Provides valuable overview of sources (especially archival) for history of southern Brazil.

3164 **Bittencourt, Gabriel Augusto de Mello.** A formação econômica do Espírito Santo: o roteiro da industrialização: do engenho às grandes indústrias, 1535–1980. Rio de Janeiro: Livraria Editora Cátedra; Vitória, Brazil: Depto. Estadual de Cultura do Estado do Espírito Santo, 1987. 302 p.: bibl., ill.

Useful economic history of Espírito Santo draws largely on secondary sources.

3165 **Brasil revisitado: palavras e imagens.** Compilação de Carlos Guilherme Mota e Adriana Lopez. São Paulo: Editora Rios, 1989. 199 p.: ill. (some col.).

Beautifully produced "coffee table" book with quotes, paintings, photographs, and drawings illustrates 500 years of Brazilian history. Connected by brief comments by Mota.

3166 **Bretas, Marcos Luiz.** O crime na historiografia brasileira: uma revisão da pesquisa recente. (*ANPOCS BIB,* 32, 1991, p. 49–61, bibl.)

Useful review of literature on crime from perspective of social historians emphasizes studies related to slavery, free labor, and the "forces of order."

3167 Cardoso, Ciro Flamarion Santana *et al.* História geral do Brasil. Organização de Maria Yedda Leite Linhares. Rio de Janeiro: Editora Campus, 1990. 303 p.: bibl., map.

Well crafted general history written by a group of respected Brazilian historians.

3168 Cativeiro e liberdade: seminário do Instituto de Filosofia e Ciências Humanas da Universidade do Estado do Rio de Janeiro. Rio de Janeiro: Univ. do Estado do Rio de Janeiro, 1989. 268 p.: bibl.

Collection of papers addresses various topics relating to slavery in Brazil including racism, labor, slave trade, negritude, and slave resistance. Perhaps useful for specialists.

3169 A colônia brasilianista: história oral de vida acadêmica. Organização e revisão de José Carlos Sebe Bom Meihy. São Paulo: Nova Stella, 1990. 499 p.: bibl.

Offers fascinating look at Brazilianists and development of Brazilian studies in US. Includes oral histories and interesting introductory essays on history of the project and development of the field. Idiosyncratic selection.

3170 Cunha, Manuela Carneiro da. *On the amelioration of slavery* by Henry Koster. (*Slavery Abolit.*, 11:3, Dec. 1990, p. 368–376, bibl.)

Title work was published in London in 1816. Cunha examines Koster's ties to British abolitionist movements, and posits this connection as possible explanation for Koster's now famous misinformation on the legal right to a peculium and to paid manumission in Brazil. May be very useful for teaching about authority of travelers' accounts.

3171 Delaunay, Daniel. La fragilité séculaire d'une paysannerie nordestine: le Ceará, Brésil. Paris: Editions de l'ORSTOM, 1988. 193 p.: bibl., ill. (Col. Etudes et thèses: 0767–2888)

Brief survey focuses on household economy in Ceará from 1500–1940. Based entirely on published secondary sources.

3172 Dias, Manuel Nunes *et al.* Brasil. v. 1–3. Caracas: Academia Nacional de la Historia de Venezuela, 1991. 3 v.: bibl., ill. (some col.), indexes. (Historia general de América; 17–19. Período colonial)

Part of multi-volume history of the Americas originally conceived in the 1940s by the Pan American Union, these three volumes are written in Spanish for a general audience by very traditional historians. A number of the contributors are diplomats and politicians. Not cutting-edge material for the specialist.

3173 Eisenberg, Peter L. Homens esquecidos: escravos e trabalhadores livres no Brasil, séculos XVIII e XIX. Campinas, Brazil: Editora da Unicamp, 1989. 394 p.: bibl., ill. (Col. Repertórios)

Includes articles and essays written between 1972–87, some of which are published here for the first time.

3174 Escravidão e abolição no Brasil: novas perspectivas. Organização de Ci Flamarion Santana Cardoso *et al.* Rio de Janeiro: Jorge Zahar Editor, 1988. 112 p.: bibl. (Jubileu)

Contains two historiographical essays on slavery and abolition. Useful for specialists.

3175 Estatísticas históricas do Brasil: séries econômicas, demográficas e sociais de 1550 a 1988. 2a. ed. rev. e atualizada. Rio de Janeiro: IBGE, 1990. 642 p.: bibl. (Séries estatísticas retrospectivas; 3)

Volume is exceptionally valuable source for historical statistics on demography, the slave trade, economically active population, social indicators, prices, agriculture, industry, transportation, energy, money and banking, trade, public finances, and elections.

3176 Estudos Ibero-Americanos, Vol. 16, No. 1/2, julho/dez. 1990- . I Simpósio Gaúcho sobre a Escravidão Negra: Anais. Porto Alegre, Brazil: Pontifícia Univ. Católica do Rio Grande do Sul, Depto. de História.

Collection of papers relating to slavery in the south of Brazil examines topics such as slavery in Montevideo, slave crimes, manumission, infant mortality, and *quilombos.* Of interest to specialists.

3177 Giacomini, Sonia Maria. Mulher e escrava: uma introdução histórica ao estudo da mulher negra no Brasil. Petrópolis, Brazil: Vozes, 1988. 95 p., 7 p. of plates: bibl., ill. (Col. Negros em libertação; 4)

Very brief work exploring the lifestyle of female slaves. A clear call for further research on this topic.

3178 Gorender, Jacob. A escravidão reabilitada. São Paulo: Editora Atica; Secretaria de Estado da Cultura, 1990. 271 p.: bibl. (Série Temas; 23: Sociedade e política)

Pithy critique of nearly all current scholarship on slavery in Brazil. Gorender attacks what he sees as anti-Marxist and anti-theoretical trends in recent publications, and he decries the recent emphasis on slaves' agency and autonomy as a return to Gilberto Freyre's benign vision of Brazilian slave society. See also item **3262.**

Mauro, Frédéric. Histoire du café. See item **889.**

3179 Motta, José Flávio. O advento da cafeicultura e a estrutura da posse de escravos, Bananal, 1801–1829. (*Estud. Econ./São Paulo,* 21:3, set./dez. 1991, p. 409–434, appendix, bibl., graphs, tables)

Assesses changing structure of slaveholding from 1801–29 in Bananal where coffee agriculture was spreading. Useful for specialists.

3180 Museu Imperial (Brazil). Arquivo Histórico. Catálogo: manuscritos relativos à escravidão. Petrópolis, Brazil: Fundação Nacional Pró-Memória; Museu Imperial, 1990. 138 p.: index. (Série Arquivo histórico; 4)

Catalog of documents relating to slavery in Brazil located in the Museu Imperial.

3181 Nazzari, Muriel. Disappearance of the dowry: women, families, and social change in São Paulo, Brazil, 1600–1900. Stanford, Calif.: Stanford Univ. Press, 1991. 245 p.: bibl., index.

Important and impressive study presents controversial conclusions. Argues that the dowry disappeared as Brazil became more individualistic and market-oriented, and as marriage became a matter of love instead of a property matter.

3182 Octávio, José. A escravidão na Paraíba: historiografia e história: preconceitos e racismo numa produção cultural. Prefácio de Leda Boechat Rodrigues. Posfácio de Humberto Mello. João Pessoa, Brazil: União Superintendência de Impr. e Editora, 1988. 144 p.: bibl.

Provides very brief regional study of slavery, historiography, and racism in the state of Paraíba. Perhaps of limited use for comparative studies.

Ohlweiler, Otto Alcides. Evolução sócio-econômica do Brasil. See *HLAS 53:2549.*

3183 Oliveira, Maria Inês Côrtes de. O liberto: o seu mundo e outros, Salvador, 1790–1890. São Paulo: Corrupio, 1988. 111 p.: bibl. (Baianada; 7)

Brief quantitative analysis of 400 wills of manumitted slaves in Bahia (1790–1890) includes useful details about their lives.

Osculati, Gaetano. Esplorazione delle regioni equatoriali: lungo el napo ed il fiume delle Amazzoni. See item **2684.**

3184 Piratininga Júnior, Luiz Gonzaga. Dietário dos escravos de São Bento: originários de São Caetano e São Bernardo. São Paulo: Hucitec Editora; São Caetano do Sul, Brazil: Prefeitura de São Caetano do Sul, 1991. 257 p.: bibl., ill., map. (São Caetano do Sul: Série Histórica; 2)

Written by a direct descendent of the slaves who labored for Benedictine monks near São Paulo until 1871 (when the Order manumitted all of its captives), this impressive work utilizes family papers and photographs as well as archival records to document author's own historical roots and lives of slaves in this unique setting.

3185 O processo legislativo e a escravidão negra na Província de São Pedro do Rio Grande do Sul: fontes. Planejamento, coordenação e supervisão de Eni Barbosa. Porto Alegre, Brazil: Estado do Rio Grande do Sul, Assembléia Legislativa, 1987. 214 p.

Compilation of legislation referring to slavery in the province of Rio Grande do Sul is useful for specialists.

3186 Reunião Anual da Sociedade Brasileira de Pesquisa Histórica, 8th, São Paulo, 1989. Anais. São Paulo: Sociedade Brasileira de Pesquisa Histórica, 1989. 266 p.: bibl.

Among topics examined in this collection of papers relating to slavery in Brazil are: slave families, manumission, and abolition. Useful to specialists.

3187 Robert Bosch GmbH. Biblioteca brasiliana da Robert Bosch GmbH: catálogo. Organização de Susanne Koppel. Introdução de Hanno Beck. Tradução de Rosemarie Erika Horch. Rio de Janeiro: Livraria Kosmos Editora, 1992. 516 p.: bibl., ill. (some col.), index, maps (some col.).

Annotated catalog of private collection of rare books relating to history of Brazil.

Schneider, Ronald M. Order and progress: a political history of Brazil. See *HLAS 53:4343*.

3188 Schwartz, Stuart B. Slaves, peasants, and rebels: reconsidering Brazilian slavery. Urbana; Chicago: Univ. of Illinois Press, 1992. 174 p.: bibl., ill., index, maps. (Blacks in the New World)

In a collection of essays, some previously published, Schwartz affirms importance of two orientations in current scholarship on Brazilian slavery: 1) emphasis on the all-pervasive and oppressive nature of the institution; and 2) focus on resources within control of slaves which were used to ameliorate their situation. Fundamentally a rebuttal of Gorender (see item **3178**).

3189 Soares, Francisco Sérgio Mota. Documentação jurídica sobre o negro no Brasil, 1800–1888: índice analítico. Salvador, Brazil: Secretaria da Cultura, Depto. de Bibliotecas, 1988. 270 p.: bibl.

Compilation of legislation that refers to Afro-Brazilians (1800–88) is very useful for specialists.

3190 Souza, Laura de Mello e *et al.* História da criança no Brasil. Organização de Mary del Priore. São Paulo: Editora Contexto; CEDHAL, 1991. 176 p.: bibl., ill. (Col. Caminhos da história. Historia Contexto)

Important collection of essays considers children and changing perceptions of them in Brazilian society in all periods of Brazilian history.

3191 Targa, Luiz Roberto Pecoits. As diferenças entre o escravismo gaúcho e o das [plantations] do Brasil, incluindo no que e por que discordamos de F.H.C. (*Ensaios FEE*, 12:2, 1991, p. 445–480, bibl.)

Presents somewhat anti-*paulista* critique of Fernando Henrique Cardoso's *Capitalismo e escravidão no Brasil meridional* (São Paulo: 1962). Author underscores differences between slavery in Brazil's southernmost state and the plantation slavery of coffee and sugar-producing areas.

3192 Topik, Steven. History of Brazil: essay. (*in* Latin America and the Caribbean: a critical guide to research sources. Edited by Paula H. Covington. New York: Greenwood Press, 1992, p. 407–441)

Excellent bibliographical essay and an-

notated bibliography is divided by topic and then by period. Highly recommended.

COLONIAL

3193 Alden, Dauril. God's share or the king's?: Jesuit opposition to the payment of tithes in colonial Brazil. (*Colon. Lat. Am. Rev.*, 1:1/2, 1992, p. 185–200, bibl.)

Presents overview of history of tithe collection in colonial Brazil and opposition of the Jesuits to such taxation. A clear and useful introduction to Church/Crown conflicts and alliances.

3194 Boogaart, Ernst van den. The slow progress of colonial civility: Indians in the pictorial record of Dutch Brazil, 1637–1644. (*in* La imagen del indio en la Europa moderna. Sevilla, Spain: Consejo Superior de Investigaciones Científicas, Fundación Europea de la Ciencia; Escuela de Estudios Hispano-Americanos, 1992, p. 389–403, photos)

Governor Johan Maurits of Nassau-Siegen, Dutch Brazil, hired European painters and naturalists to create a visual and written record of the colony. Their works suggest that views of the cannibalist indigenous peoples became more specific and differentiated over time. [R. Hoefte]

Brazil and the world system. See *HLAS 53:4805*.

3195 Brioschi, Lucila Reis *et al.* Entrantes no sertão do Rio Pardo: o povoamento da freguesia de Batatais, séculos XVIII e XIX. São Paulo: CERU, 1991. 293 p.: bibl., maps.

Traditional narrative history of settlement patterns for the Rio Pardo region of São Paulo includes much useful demographic and economic data.

3196 Brown, Gregory G. The impact of American flour imports on Brazilian wheat production, 1808–1822. (*Americas/Francisc.*, 47:3, Jan. 1991, p. 315–336, tables)

Argues that imports of wheat from US (principally from Baltimore and Philadelphia) ruined commercial wheat farming in Rio Grande do Sul in early 19th century.

Calógeras, João Pandiá. A política exterior do Império. v. 2, O primeiro reinado. See *HLAS 53:4807*.

3197 Costa, Samuel Guimarães da. O último capitão-mor, 1782–1857. Curitiba, Brazil: Scientia et Labor; Paranaguá, Brazil:

Prefeitura de Paranaguá, 1988. 237 p.: ill., map.

Biography of Manoel Antônio Pereira, last *capitão-mor* and first *prefeito* of the city of Paranaguá, Paraná, written by a journalist and direct descendent. Part genealogy and part regional history, this book may serve as a preliminary source for scholars of the period.

3198 Furtado, Joaci Pereira and **Ronald Polito.** Da organização de acervos à descrição de fontes: um guia para os documentos de Mariana. (*Rev. Inst. Estud. Bras.*, 31, 1990, p. 217–227, tables)

Presents preliminary overview and description of archives in one of the most important cities of colonial Minas Gerais.

3199 Giucci, Guillermo. A visão inaugural do Brasil: a terra de Vera Cruz. (*Rev. Bras. Hist.*, 11:21, set. 1990/fev. 1991, p. 45–64)

Examines initial European perspective on encounter with Tupiniquin people of Brazil, emphasizing their immediate view of natives as barbaric lesser beings.

Gomes, Plínio Freire. O ciclo dos meninos cantores, 1550–1552: música e aculturação nos primórdios da colônia. See item **5160.**

3200 Guerzoni Filho, Gilberto. Política e crise do sistema colonial em Minas Gerais, 1768–1808. Ouro Preto, Brazil: Univ. Federal de Ouro Preto, Instituto de Ciências Humanas e Sociais, Depto. de História, 1986. 123 p.

A very brief analysis of colonial administration and economic activities in 18th-century Minas Gerais is of use to specialists.

3201 Gutiérrez, Horacio. Crioulos e Africanos no Paraná, 1798–1830. (*Rev. Bras. Hist.*, 8:16, março/agôsto 1988, p. 161–188, bibl., tables)

Provides careful demographic analysis of slave population and slave market in southern state of Paraná. Furnishing useful figures for comparison with other regions of Brazil, author also emphasizes importance of slaves born in Brazil (*crioulos*) for this area.

3202 Gutiérrez, Horacio. O tráfico de crianças escravas para o Brasil durante o século XVIII. (*Rev. Hist./São Paulo*, 120, jan./julho 1989, p. 59–72, bibl., tables)

Provides concise statistical analysis of traffic in African children (no mention of gender) to Brazil. Author found that percentage of children on ships declined in 18th century and that fewer slave children went to Brazil than to other markets in the New World.

3203 Jardim, Márcio. A Inconfidência Mineira: uma síntese factual. Rio de Janeiro: Biblioteca do Exército Editora, 1989. 415 p.: bibl. (Biblioteca do Exército Editora; 579. Col. General Benício; 268)

Very useful straightforward synthesis of information on the famous "Minas Conspiracy" of 1789 emphasizes events, participants, and main issues. Good bibliography and bibliographical essay.

3204 Kjerfve, Tânia Maria Gomes Nery and **Silvia Maria Jardim Brügger.** Compadrio: relação social e libertação espiritual em sociedades escravistas, Campos, 1754–1766. (*Estud. Afro-Asiát.*, 20, junho 1991, p. 223–238, bibl., tables)

Statistical work examines kinship among slaves in Campos dos Goitacazes (Rio de Janeiro). Argues, for yet another location in colonial Brazil, that slaves used godparentage to build social ties with one another.

3205 Léry, Jean de. History of a voyage to the land of Brazil, otherwise called America. Translated and with introduction by Janet Whatley. Berkeley: Univ. of California Press, 1990. 276 p.: bibl., ill., index. (Latin American literature and culture; 6)

Provides wonderful and long-needed translation of 16th-century encounter between Huguenot missionary Jean de Léry and native peoples of coastal Brazil. Translator's introduction is both lucid and scholarly, providing an illuminating analysis of this historic document.

3206 Lewin, Linda. Natural and spurious children in Brazilian inheritance law from colony to empire: a methodological essay. (*Americas/Francisc.*, 48:3, Jan. 1992, p. 351–396)

Provides lucid discussion and explanation of colonial and imperial succession laws. Author justifiably calls upon scholars to reexamine historical interpretations in light of specific legal provisions.

3207 Medeiros Filho, Olavo de. No rastro dos flamengos. Natal, Brazil: Fundação José Augusto, 1989. 104 p.: bibl., ill., maps.

Includes selections from expeditionary records of Dutch adventurers in Rio Grande do Norte and Paraíba during period of Dutch occupation. Relies heavily on secondary source interpretations.

3208 Memória da Amazónia: Alexandre Rodrigues Ferreira e a Viagem Philosophica pelas capitanias do Grão-Pará, Rio Negro, Mato Grosso e Cuyabá, 1783–1792. Textos de M.L. Rodrigues de Areia, Maria Arminda Miranda, e Tekla Hartmann. Catálogo de Tekla Hartmann. Coimbra, Portugal: Museu e Laboratório Antropológico, Univ. de Coimbra, 1991. 262 p.: bibl., ill. (some col.).

Catalog of the exhibit "Memória da Amazónia" which displayed parts of the collections of 18th-century naturalist Alexandre Rodrigues Ferreira that had been sent to the Museu de História Natural in Coimbra in 1806. Of interest to naturalists and ethnographers as well as to historians of science.

3209 Metcalf, Alida C. Family and frontier in colonial Brazil: Santana de Parnaíba, 1580–1822. Berkeley: Univ. of California Press, 1992. 280 p.: bibl., ill., index, maps.

Important pioneering study examines family strategies employed by inhabitants of São Paulo's rural frontier to promote family enrichment and/or family survival. Author examines archival records of planter, peasant, and slave families, carefully illustrating their varying patterns of interaction with the frontier and its resources.

3210 Metcalf, Alida C. Searching for the slave family in colonial Brazil: a reconstruction from São Paulo. (*J. Fam. Hist.*, 16:3, 1991, p. 283–297 bibl., graphs, tables)

Statistical reconstruction of slave family life in Santana de Paraíba depicts significant numbers of slaves who marry and have a high fertility rate. Author points out that slave families were vulnerable to forced separation when owners' property was divided. Analysis illustrates how slaves' experiences of family life in colonial Brazil could and did vary according to region and economic cycles.

3211 Nazzari, Muriel. Transition toward slavery: changing legal practice regarding Indians in seventeenth-century São Paulo. (*Americas/Francisc.*, 49:2, Oct. 1992, p. 131–155, table)

Clearly outlines development of laws that gradually increased the claims of creditors and consequently diminished status of captive indigenous people. Should be of interest to those who do comparative history.

3212 Nederveen Meerkerk, Hannedea van. Recife: the rise of a 17th-century trade city from a cultural-historical perspective. Assen, The Netherlands: Van Gorcum, 1989. 438 p.: bibl., ill.

English translation of Dutch-authored history of architecture in Recife focuses on the years of Dutch occupation. Useful to specialists.

3213 Nova história da expansão portuguesa. v. 7, O império luso-brasileiro, 1620–1750. Coordenação de Frédéric Mauro. Direcção de Joel Serrão e António Henrique R. de Oliveira Marques. Lisboa: Editorial Estampa, 1991. 1 v.: bibl., ill. (some col.), maps.

Useful synthesis of colonial history begins with Dutch occupation and ends in mid-18th century. Relying on published sources, including previous syntheses, work maintains historiographical emphasis on the Northeast and on institutional structures (government and the Catholic Church).

3214 Novinsky, Anita. Inquisição: rol dos culpados: fontes para a história do Brasil, século XVIII. Rio de Janeiro: Expressão e Cultura, 1992. 195 p.: bibl., ill.

Biographical dictionary lists New Christians in Brazil during 18th century as identified by Inquisition records. Annotations include disposition of each individual's case (721 women and 1,098 men).

3215 Perrone-Moisés, Leyla. Vinte luas: viagem de Paulmier de Gonneville ao Brasil, 1503–1505. São Paulo: Companhia das Letras, 1992. 186 p.: bibl., ill., index, map.

Translation of account of first Frenchmen in Brazil who arrived in 1504 consists of brief "contact" narrative and extensive textual analysis.

3216 Pires, Maria Idalina da Cruz. Guerra dos Bárbaros: resistência indígena e conflitos no Nordeste colonial. Recife, Brazil: Governo do Estado de Pernambuco, Secretaria de Educação, Cultura e Esportes/ FUNDARPE; Companhia Editora de Pernambuco, 1990. 143 p.: bibl.

History of conquest of the Tapuya in late 17th and early 18th centuries emphasizes importance of non-export regions to colonial history of the Northeast.

3217 Potelet, Jeanine. Projets d'expéditons et d'attaques sur les côtes du Brésil, 1796–1800. (*Caravelle/Toulouse,* 54, 1990, p. 209–222, bibl.)

Explains document from French naval archives describing seven naval expeditions aimed at disrupting Portuguese commerce as a part of Anglo-French wars of late 18th century.

3218 Ramos, Donald. Single and married women in Vila Rica, Brazil, 1754–1838. (*J. Fam. Hist.,* 16:3, 1991, p. 261–282, bibl., graph, tables)

Presents clear statistical analysis of childbearing practices among single and married women, as well as of the phenomena of female-headed households and child abandonment. Author emphasizes distinctiveness of household composition in comparison with European and North American communities.

3219 Reis, João José. Magia Jeje na Bahia: a invasão do Calundu do Pasto de Cachoeira, 1785. (*Rev. Bras. Hist.,* 8:16, março/agôsto 1988, p. 57–81, tables)

Account of 1785 repression of Afro-Brazilian religious practices called *calundu* is based on unique primary sources. Author mines investigation records from Cachoeira, Bahia, for clues as to ethnic origins and characteristics of this manifestation of resistance to the slave regime.

3220 Roderjan, Roselys Vellozo. Os curitibanos e a formação de comunidades campeiras no Brasil meridional: séculos XVI a XIX. Curitiba, Brazil: Instituto Histórico, Geográfico e Etnográfico Paranaense, 1992. 326 p.: bibl., ill., maps. (Estante paranista; 36)

This history of Curitiba (Paraná) from its founding until mid-19th century includes traditional narrative chronology of settlement patterns and much genealogical information.

3221 Russell-Wood, A.J.R. Frontiers in colonial Brazil: reality, myth, and metaphor. (*in* Seminar on the Acquistion of Latin American Library Materials, *33rd, Berkeley, Calif., 1988.*. Latin American frontiers, borders, and hinterlands: research needs and resources. Albuquerque, N.M.: SALALM; Univ. of New Mexico, 1990, p. 26–61)

Discusses utility of frontier concept in understanding colonial Brazil, arguing for viewing the frontier as a cultural boundary traversed from several directions.

3222 Russell-Wood, A.J.R. Society and government in colonial Brazil, 1500–1822. Aldershot, England; Brookfield, Vt.: Variorum, 1992. 1 v.: bibl., ill., index. (Collected studies series; CS382)

Reproduces six notable essays on colonial Brazil written over the past 25 years.

Sant'Ana, Rizio Bruno and **Iraci del Nero da Costa.** A escravidão brasileira nos artigos de revistas, 1976–1985. See *HLAS 53:45.*

3223 Silva, Maria Beatriz Nizza da. Family and property in colonial Brazil. (*Port. Stud.,* 7, 1991, p. 61–77, tables)

Presents clear outline of laws regarding division of family property upon marriage, divorce, and death. Includes interesting discussion of concubinage and illegitimate children.

3224 Silva, Maria Beatriz Nizza da. Herança no Brasil colonial: os bens vinculados. (*Rev. Ciênc. Hist.,* 5, 1990, p. 291–319, tables)

Outlines clearly the terms, conditions, and persistence of entailed property in colonial Brazil. Also includes thoughtful analysis of 18th-century legislation which subjected entailments to considerable oversight and regulation and restricted creation of new ones.

3225 Souza, Miguel Augusto Gonçalves de. O Marquês de Queluz e sua época. Belo Horizonte, Brazil: Editora Itatiaia, 1988. 156 p.: facsims. (Biblioteca de estudos brasileiros; 22)

Very straightforward (and brief) narrative of life of one of the most important political figures of the early empire includes facsimile reproduction of some documents.

3226 Vainfas, Ronaldo. Trópico dos pecados: moral, sexualidade e Inquisição no Brasil. Rio de Janeiro: Editora Campus, 1989. 393 p.: bibl., ill.

History of morality and sexuality in colonial Brazil is based on archival sources (Inquisition records), and is well informed as to recent secondary literature on this topic. Impressive contribution to social history of the colonial period.

3227 Vilhena, Maria da Conceição. Viagens no século XVIII: dos Açores ao Brasil. (*Studia/Lisboa,* 51, 1992, p. 5–15)

Provides brief account of voluntary immigration of impoverished residents of the Azores to Brazil in the mid-18th century, with particular emphasis on the dreadful, disease-inducing conditions of the voyages.

3228 Wolff, Egon and **Frieda Wolff.** Judeus em Amsterdã: seu relacionamento com o Brasil, 1600–1620. Rio de Janeiro: ERCA Editora e Gráfica, 1989. 100 p.: bibl., ill.

Includes brief selection of references to activities of Jews in Amsterdam who later lived in Brazil or who had commercial dealings with Brazil.

NATIONAL

3229 Alexander, Robert Jackson. Juscelino Kubitschek and the development of Brazil. Athens: Ohio Univ. Center for International Studies, 1991. 437 p.: bibl., map. (Monographs in international studies: Latin America series; 16)

Laudatory account of presidency and life of one of 20th-century Brazil's most important political figures is based largely on secondary sources and interviews. Written by a very prominent Latin Americanist.

3230 Alfredo, João. Minha meninice & outros ensaios. Prefácio de Manuel Correia de Andrade. Brasília: Ministério da Ciência e Tecnologia, CNPq, Comissão de Eventos Históricos; Recife, Brazil: Fundação Joaquim Nabuco, Editora Massangana, 1988. 98 p., 1 leaf of plates: port. (Série Abolição; 5)

Brief essays, one autobiographical, written by prominent statesman of the Second Empire who was an important figure in the process of abolition.

Alves, Castro. The major abolitionist poems. See item **5066.**

3231 Andrews, George Reid. Black political protest in São Paulo, 1888–1988. (*J. Lat. Am. Stud.,* 24:1, Feb. 1992, p. 147–171)

Valuable periodization of protest focuses on four particular moments in the history of Afro-Brazilian political mobilization. Of particular interest are the analysis of the Frente Negra Brasileira and its association with Integralism, and the discussion of Afro-Brazilians in the context of redemocratization. For sociologist's comment (on Portuguese translation) see *HLAS 53:5546.*

3232 Andrews, George Reid. Blacks & whites in São Paulo, Brazil, 1888–1988. Madison: Univ. of Wisconsin Press, 1991. 369 p.: bibl., index, map.

Chronological exposition emphasizes how official and unofficial institutions have sustained racial inequality in Brazil. Also focuses on organizations and movements through which Afro-Brazilians have mobilized to oppose and survive discrimination. A useful study, but one largely devoid of Afro-Brazilian women. For sociologist's comment see *HLAS 53:5545.*

3233 Andrews, George Reid. Racial inequality in Brazil and the United States: a statistical comparison. (*J. Soc. Hist.,* 26:2, Winter 1992, p. 229–283, graphs, tables)

Author uses statistical data (for Brazil, as recent as 1987) to compare and measure forms of racial inequality and how inequality has evolved both in Brazil and the US. Argues that since 1950 racial inequalities have declined in US and remained stable in Brazil. Today, the US record for racial equality is better than Brazil's. Excellent comparative analysis; useful for teachers of Brazilian history. For sociologist's comment see *HLAS 53:5547.*

3234 Aragão, Elizabeth Fiúza. A trajetória da indústria têxtil no Ceará: o setor de fiação e tecelagem, 1880–1950. Fortaleza, Brazil: Univ. Federal do Ceará, Núcleo de Documentação Cultural, Projeto História do Ceará, 1989. 118 p.: bibl. (Col. Estudos históricos; 2)

Provides short but informative study of vicissitudes of small textile industry in a northeastern state.

3235 Athayde, Johildo Lopes de. Salvador e a grande epidemia de 1855. Salvador, Brazil: Univ. Federal da Bahia, Centro de Estudos Baianos, 1985. 41 p.: bibl., ill. (Centro de Estudos Baianos; 113)

Brief essay on 1855 cholera epidemic is not very well developed. Rare example of medical history.

3236 Bakos, Margaret M. Regulación de los servicios de criados en el Brasil: el ejemplo de Río-Grande do Sul, 1887. (*HISLA/ Lima,* 13/14, 1989, p. 7–13, bibl.)

Provides brief account of regulations governing servants in Rio Grande do Sul near the time of abolition in Brazil. Regulations suggest that Republicans intended to deny emancipated slaves freedom in the labor market and a place among equals in the republican social order.

3237 Barbosa, Francisco de Assis. João Pinheiro e sua liderança em Minas. (*Análise Conjunt.*, 5:2, maio/agosto 1990, p. 49–64, bibl.)

Very detailed and rambling account describes career of one of the most important political figures in Minas Gerais in early 20th century.

3238 Barros, Geraldo Mendes. História da siderurgia no Brasil: século XIX. Belo Horizonte, Brazil: Imprensa Oficial de Minas Gerais, 1989. 284 p.: bibl.

Journalistic and episodic account of iron and steel industry (principally in Minas Gerais) during 19th century is based on published secondary sources.

3239 Bartelt, Dawid. Fünfte Kolonne'ohne Plan: Die Auslandsorganisation der NSDAP in Brasilien, 1931–1939. (*Ibero-Am. Arch.*, 19:1/2, 1993, p. 3–35)

Analyzes pre-World War II activities in Brazil by the Auslandorganisation (AO), the foreign organization of the Nazi Party, and by the Auswärtige Amt (AA), Germany's foreign office. AO aimed to establish a powerful fifth column in Brazil but never succeeded. AO lacked not only sufficient acceptance among German-Brazilians but also money and competence, and in addition the organization was at odds with Getúlio Vargas' nationalism. In contrast, Brazilian-German trade relations, cultivated by the traditional AA, proved mutually advantageous. [C.K. Converse]

Bastos, Aurélio Wander; Eli Diniz; and José Murilo de Carvalho. O balanço do poder: formas de dominação e representação. See *HLAS 53:4260.*

3240 Becher, Hans. O Barão Georg Heinrich von Langsdorff: pesquisas de um cientista alemão no século XIX. Apresentação de Marcos Pinto Braga. Posfácio de Nicolau Sevcenko. Brasília: Editora UnB; São Paulo: Edições diá, 1990. 223 p.: bibl., ill., index.

Detailed overview of work of one of the great German explorers of early 19th-century Brazil, written by a German ethnologist who has done fieldwork in Brazil since the 1950s.

3241 Benevides, Cezar. Camponeses em marcha. Rio de Janeiro: Paz e Terra, 1985. 140 p.: bibl., facsim. (Política)

Brief history of peasant leagues in Sapé, Paraíba, from late 1950s to early 1960s is based primarily on newspapers and interviews. Focuses on key leader João Pedro Teixeira who was assassinated in 1962.

3242 Bentes, Abraham Ramiro. Primeira comunidade israelita brasileira: tradições, genealogia, pré história. Rio de Janeiro: Gráficos Borsoi, 1989. 325 p.: bibl.

Largely genealogical reference work on Jews who arrived in Brazil after independence.

3243 Bento, Cláudio Moreira. O Exército na Proclamação da República. Rio de Janeiro?: SENAI, 1989. 135 p.: bibl., ill. (some col.), photos.

Provides very detailed description of organization and equipment of Brazilian army and its movements in coup that toppled the Empire in 1889. Includes excellent color illustrations of uniforms and black-and-white photos from November 15, 1889.

3244 Bernardes, Maria Thereza Caiuby Crescenti. Mulheres de ontem?: Rio de Janeiro, século XIX. São Paulo: T.A. Queiroz, 1989. 214 p.: bibl. (Col. Coroa vermelha: Estudos brasileiros; 9)

Sociologist analyzes portrayal of women in novels, in women's journals, and by male literary figures from 1840–90. Very descriptive but not very thorough analysis.

3245 Bittencourt, Gabriel Augusto de Mello. Café e modernização: o Espírito Santo no século XIX. Rio de Janeiro: Livraria Editora Cátedra, 1987. 139 p.: bibl.

Offers brief and superficial survey of impact of coffee cultivation on state of Espírito Santo.

3246 Borges, Dain Edward. The family in Bahia, Brazil, 1870–1945. Stanford, Calif.: Stanford Univ. Press, 1992. 422 p.: bibl., ill., index, maps.

Excellent study examines movement from a patriarchal to a more nuclear model by primarily upper- and middle-class families. Emphasizes interaction among family, law, medicine, politics, and the Catholic Church. Rich documentary base.

3247 Brazil. Congresso Nacional. Senado Federal. Subsecretaria de Arquivo. A abolição no Parlamento: 65 anos de luta, 1823–1888. v. 1. Brasília: Congresso Nacional, Senado Federal, Subsecretaria de Arquivo, 1988. 1 v.: bibl., ill., index.

Provides chronological compilation of parliamentary activity leading to abolition of slavery in Brazil, as found in the Arquivo do Senado for the period 1823–88. Includes final legislation as well as earlier proposals. Valuable record of legislative process and senatorial opinions.

3248 Bretas, Marcos Luiz. A queda do império da navalha e da rasteira: a República e os capoeiras. (*Estud. Afro-Asiát.*, 20, junho 1991, p. 239–256, tables)

Brief study of *capoeira* gangs and their repression by authorities during early years of Old Republic is based primarily on newspapers and some criminal records.

3249 Buescu, Mircea. Um estadista controvertido: Joaquim Murtinho. (*Rev. Inst. Estud. Bras.*, 362, jan./março 1989, p. 529–572, bibl., tables)

Provides extensive summary of ideas and actions of key finance minister and economic policymaker from first years of the First Republic.

3250 Butler, Kim D. Up from slavery: Afro-Brazilian activism in São Paulo, 1888–1938. (*Americas/Francisc.*, 49:2, Oct. 1992, p. 179–206, tables)

Usefully synthesizes both older and newer secondary sources on Afro-Brazilians in São Paulo, emphasizing networks of social interaction, mutual aid, communication, and activism. Using interviews and Afro-Brazilian newspapers, author also develops her own discussion of activism.

3251 Cabral, Ligia Maria Martins; Paulo Brandi de Barros Cachapuz; and Sergio Tadeu de Niemeyer Lamarão. Panorama do setor de energia elétrica no Brasil. Coordenação de Renato Feliciano Dias. Rio de Janeiro: Centro da Memória da Eletricidade no Brasil, 1988. 333 p.: bibl., ill., index.

Excellent survey of history of electrical power industry. Straightforward narrative with little analysis. Excellent bibliography, but lack of footnotes will surely frustrate serious readers.

3252 Camargo, Aspásia *et al.* O golpe silencioso: as origens da república corporativa. Rio de Janeiro: Rio Fundo, 1989. 279 p.: bibl., index.

Important collaborative study examines coup d'etat of November 1937, especially key figures and events in period leading up to the coup. Emphasizes shift from oligarchic republic to corporatist State.

3253 Campos, Mintaha Alcuri. Turco pobre, sírio remediado, libanês rico: a trajetória do imigrante libanês no Espírito Santo, 1910–1940. Vitória, Brazil: Instituto Jones dos Santos Neves, 1987. 160 p.: bibl., ill., facsims., ports. (Col. Temas capixabas; 2)

Interesting study of Lebanese immigrants to Espírito Santo, drawing on local archives and more than 100 interviews. Originally presented as a master's thesis at Univ. Federal Fluminense.

3254 Canêdo, Letícia Bicalho. Bancários: movimento sindical e participação política. Campinas, Brazil: Editora da Unicamp, 1986. 324 p.: bibl., ill. (Série Teses)

Labor history that emphasizes political chronology covers period 1923–77 and focuses on São Paulo. Originally a doctoral dissertation.

3255 Cansanção, Elza. E foi assim que a cobra fumou. Rio de Janeiro: Imago Editora, 1987. 239 p.: ill., index.

Idiosyncratic account of military nurse who served with the Força Expedicionária Brasileira in Italy during World War II. Amply illustrated.

3256 Capelato, Maria Helena. Os arautos do liberalismo: imprensa paulista 1920–1945. São Paulo: Editora Brasiliense, 1989. 258 p.: bibl.

Provides interesting analysis of liberalism as seen through *paulista* newspapers.

3257 Carone, Edgard. Brasil: anos de crise, 1930–1945. São Paulo: Editora Atica, 1991. 336 p.: bibl. (Série Fundamentos; 77)

Very detailed narrative of politics and labor movement, written by prominent historian. Follow-up volume to his *Classes sociais e movimento operário* (see *HLAS 52:2986*).

3258 Carvalho, José Murilo de. Brazil, 1870–1914: the force of tradition. (*J. Lat. Am. Stud.*, 24, Quincentenary Supplement 1992, p. 145–162)

Excellent synthesis shows how both traditional society and the modernity that arose as an alternative to it were subverted and altered through a process of "conservative modernization."

3259 Carvalho, José Murilo de. A formação das almas: o imaginário da república no Brasil. São Paulo: Cia. das Letras, 1990. 166 p.: bibl., ill. (some col.).

Stimulating and creative work analyzes iconography of the New Republic in late 19th century as liberals, jacobins, and positivists battled to shape popular imagination.

3260 Chalhoub, Sidney. Medo branco de almas negras: escravos, libertos e republicanos na cidade do Rio. (*Rev. Bras. Hist.*, 8: 16, março/agôsto 1988, p. 83–105)

Well-documented exposition examines actions of slaves and former slaves in 19th-century Rio de Janeiro which fueled whites' fears and, according to Chalhoub, informed early republican policies designed to regulate non-white behavior and "sanitize" the urban environment. Chalhoub reminds historians of non-elite role in formulation of elite-authored policies.

3261 Chalhoub, Sidney. Slaves, freedom and the politics of freedom in Brazil: the experience of blacks in the city of Rio. (*Slavery Abolit.*, 10:3, Dec. 1989, p. 64–84)

Argues that 1871 legal reform guaranteeing slaves the right to manumission was significant, and that it represented a dismantling of an ideology of manumission in which all parties had understood that the prospect for a slave attaining freedom depended entirely on the wishes of the owner. A careful and articulate essay.

3262 Chalhoub, Sidney. Visões da liberdade: uma história das últimas décadas da escravidão na corte. São Paulo: Companhia das Letras, 1990. 287 p.: bibl.

Explores historical agency of slaves in Rio de Janeiro in decades preceding abolition. Presents significant challenge to an older and still operant historiography which has emphasized authority of slaveholders and their power to determine even the slaves' vision of themselves. See also item **3178.**

3263 Chaul, Nasr N. Fayad. A construção de Goiânia e a transferência da capital. Goiânia, Brazil: CEGRAF, UFG, 1988. 174 p.: bibl., ill., maps. (Publicação; 138. Col. Documentos goianos; 17)

Valuable study of construction of Goiânia in 1930s and 1940s emphasizes politics of creation of the capital and role of the workers in the construction.

3264 Cherpak, Evelyn. Reminiscences of Brazilian life, 1834–1848: selections from the diary of Mary Robinson Hunter. (*Americas/Francisc.*, 49:1, July 1992, p. 69–76)

Intriguing glimpse of impressions of Rio de Janeiro. Numerous block quotations from this diary of an American diplomat's wife reveal observations on court life, slave punishments, and attitudes toward servants.

3265 Chevalier, François and **Jean Chazelas.** Le Brésil différent: un heritage original de la Révolution Française. (*Cah. Am. lat.*, 10, 1991, p. 205–223, bibl.)

Discusses influence of French Revolution, and more precisely of Benjamin Constant, on Pedro I and the Brazilian Constitution of 1824. Argues that much of the Constitution, specifically the "moderating power," was derived from writings of Constant. Places moderating power under Pedro II within context of other Latin American political systems in 19th century.

3266 50 anos, Federação do Comércio do Estado de São Paulo: uma história de trabalho. Organização de Jean-Claude Silberfeld. São Paulo: Federação do Comércio do Estado de São Paulo, 1988. 119 p.: bibl., ill.

Brief history of important commercial association is drawn from internal documents. Not very in-depth or revealing, but useful as introduction to the workings of the group.

3267 Corrêa, Carlos Humberto. Militares e civis num governo sem rumo: o governo provisório revolucionário de Desterro, 1893–1894. Florianópolis, Brazil: Editora da UFSC; Ed. Lunardelli, 1990. 157 p.: bibl. (Série geral)

Brief, straightforward political history of rebel government formed in Santa Catarina during military revolt of 1893–94 is based primarily on newspapers and published sources.

3268 Costa, Cruz. Pequena história da República. Prefácio de Antônio Cândido. 3a. ed. São Paulo: CNPq, Programa do Centenário da República; Editora Brasiliense, 1989. 146 p.: bibl.

New edition of brief history of Brazil

(1889–1964) by prominent historian includes memorable preface by Antônio Cândido.

3269 Costa, João Severiano Maciel da et al. Memórias sobre a escravidão. Introdução de Graça Salgado. Rio de Janeiro: Arquivo Nacional; Brasília: Fundação Petrônio Portella; Ministério da Justiça, 1988. 222 p.: bibl. (Publicações históricas; 88)

Reedition of four notable 19th-century documents (1821–37) in which merits and costs of trade in African slaves were debated. Perhaps useful for specialists.

3270 Costa, Rovílio et al. As colônias italianas Dona Isabel e Conde d'Eu. Porto Alegre, Brazil: Escola Superior de Teologia, 1992. 435 p.: ill. (Col. Fontes; 7. Col. Imigração italiana; 149)

Collection of documents examines Italian settlements in Rio Grande do Sul. Last half of book consists of detailed genealogical information on Italian immigrants to the region.

3271 Cunha, Maria Clementina Pereira. Loucura, gênero feminino: as mulheres do Juquery na São Paulo do início do século XX. (*Rev. Bras. Hist.*, 9:18, agosto/set. 1989, p. 121–144)

Wide-ranging think piece speculates on gender and sex roles in Brazil using examples of women interned in a psychiatric hospital at the beginning of 20th century.

3272 Diacon, Todd A. Millenarian vision, capitalist reality: Brazil's Contestado Rebellion, 1912–1916. Durham, N.C.: Duke Univ. Press, 1991. 199 p.: bibl., index, maps.

Revisionist analysis of important rebellion in southern Brazil links motives and views of the rebels to larger regional, national, and international context. Impressive monograph on a region that has not been well studied.

3273 Díaz, Arlene and Jeff Stewart. Occupational class and female-headed households in Santiago Maior do Iguape, Brazil, 1835. (*J. Fam. Hist.*, 16:3, 1991, p. 299–313 bibl., graphs, tables)

Shows that in this rural parish in Bahia one-third of all households were female-headed and nearly half of the free population lived in such households.

3274 Diehl, Astor Antônio. Círculos operários no Rio Grande do Sul: um projeto social-político, dos anos trinta a 1964. Porto Alegre, Brazil: EDIPUCRS, 1990. 131 p.: bibl.

Master's thesis analyzes role of the Catholic Church in organizing workers in southern Brazil. Based primarily on newspapers and published writings of key figures.

Dik, Evgueni. Emigración rusa a Argentina: fines del siglo XIX y comienzos del XX. See item **2945.**

3275 Downes, Richard. Autos over rails: how US business supplanted the British in Brazil. (*J. Lat. Am. Stud.*, 24:3, Oct. 1992, p. 551–583, graph)

Very well researched analysis shows rise of automobile industry and road network with strong backing of US business, and decline of Brazilian railway network and British business influence. Excellent use of business history to illuminate larger shifts in Brazilian economy.

3276 Duarte, Paulo de Queiroz. Sampaio. Rio de Janeiro: Biblioteca do Exército Editora, 1988. 327 p.: bibl., ill. (some col.). (Publicação; 569. Col. General Benício; 259)

Very dry and traditional biography, written by a general, of an important military figure who played key role in emergence of the Brazilian army in first half of 19th century.

3277 Dulles, John W.F. Carlos Lacerda, Brazilian crusader. v. 1, The years 1914–1960. Austin: Univ. of Texas Press, 1991-. 1 v.: bibl., index.

Very detailed authorized biography of one of 20th-century Brazil's most controversial politicians emphasizes politics. This volume covers Lacerda's life up to his election as governor of Guanabara in 1960. A concluding volume will cover period from 1960–77.

3278 Dutra, Eliana Regina de Freitas. Caminhos operários nas Minas Gerais: um estudo das práticas operárias em Juiz de Fora e Belo Horizonte na primeira república. São Paulo: HUCITEC-Editora; Belo Horizonte, Brazil: UFMG, 1988. 225 p.: bibl., ill.

Excellent comparative analysis examines rise of workers' movements in the two major industrial centers of Minas Gerais.

3279 Eakin, Marshall C. Creating a growth pole: the industrialization of Belo Horizonte, Brazil, 1897–1987. (*Americas/Francisc.*, 47:4, April 1991, p. 383–410, tables)

Presents overview of historical development of Belo Horizonte and process of city's industrialization. In this prelude to a larger project on the same unique subject, author emphasizes role of state government as promotor and guarantor of industrial development.

3280 Engel, Magali. Meretrizes e doutores: saber médico e prostituição no Rio de Janeiro, 1840–1890. São Paulo: Editora Brasiliense, 1989. 149 p.: bibl.

Excellent analysis of development of a "science of sexuality" in 19th-century Rio de Janeiro examines how physicians studied and proposed ways to control prostitution. Originally a master's thesis at Univ. Federal Fluminense.

3281 Uma epopéia moderna: 80 anos da imigração japonesa no Brasil. São Paulo: Editora HUCITEC; Sociedade Brasileira de Cultura Japonesa, 1992. 604 p.: bibl.

Very thorough and detailed collaborative work is based on Japanese and Brazilian sources. First two-thirds of book is a history of Japanese immigration to Brazil; last third looks at specific contributions of Japanese community to agriculture, commerce, industry, and culture.

3282 Esteves, Martha de Abreu. Meninas perdidas: os populares e o cotidiano do amor no Rio de Janeiro da belle époque. Rio de Janeiro: Paz e Terra, 1989. 212 p.: bibl. (Col. Oficinas da história)

Important study examines juridical and popular discourse on sexuality through analysis of court records of sex crimes in Rio de Janeiro in first two decades of 20th century. Originally a master's thesis at Univ. Estadual de Campinas.

3283 Evangelista, José Geraldo. Escravidão e abolição na Alta Mojiana: o caso da Franca. (*Rev. Inst. Hist. Geogr. São Paulo*, 83, 1988, p. 61–72, bibl.)

Largely descriptive overview of slavery in a cattle-ranching municipality in interior of São Paulo during 19th century is based on state and municipal archive sources.

3284 Expedição Langsdorff ao Brasil, 1821–1829. Text by Boris Nikolaevich Komissarov. Rio de Janeiro: Edições Alumbramento; Livroarte Editora, 1988. 3 v.: bibl., ill. (some col.), maps, ports.

Contains beautiful photographic reproductions in color of the drawings and watercolors of three artists (J.M. Rugendas, Her-

cules Florence, and Aimé-Adrien Taunay) who participated in a remarkable expedition to Brazil sponsored by the Russian Tsar. Expedition covered 16,000 kilometers in Rio de Janeiro, Minas Gerais, São Paulo, the centerwest, and the Amazon. After more than 150 years in Russian archives, this is first publication of these exceptional drawings of Brazilian flora, fauna, landscapes, and people.

3285 Faermann, Martha Pargendler. A promessa cumprida: histórias vividas e ouvidas de colonos judeus no Rio Grande do Sul: Quatro Irmãos, Baronesa Clara, Barão Hirsch e Erebango. Porto Alegre, Brazil: Metrópole, 1990. 191 p.: ill.

Roughly half of this slim volume is personal memoir of daughter of Russian Jews who immigrated to southern Brazil in 1913. Other half contains pieces from interviews with other immigrant families, all sent to Brazil with aid of Jewish Colonization Association.

3286 Falbel, Nachman. Yehuda Wilensky e Leib Jaffe e o movimiento Sionista no Brasil, 1921–1923. (*in* Ensayos sobre judaismo latinoamericano. Buenos Aires: Editorial Milá, 1990, p. 148–169)

Detailed narrative of activities of Zionists sent by World Zionist Organization to help organize chapters in Brazil uses Yiddish and Hebrew correspondence between Brazil and Zionist headquarters.

3287 Faria, Maria Juscelina de. João Pinheiro e a república em Minas. (*Análise Conjunt.*, 5:2, maio/agôsto 1990, p. 67–77, bibl., tables)

Provides very useful and detailed description of archive of important *mineiro* political figure. Documents are deposited in Arquivo Público Mineiro in Belo Horizonte and cover period from 1880s to roughly 1910.

3288 Faro, Clóvis de et al. O Brasil de JK. Organização de Angela Maria de Castro Gomes. Rio de Janeiro: Editora da Fundação Getúlio Vargas; CPDOC, 1991. 161 p.: bibl., ill.

Essays by specialists on the politics, foreign policy, economic policies, and cultural trends of the Juscelino Kubitschek presidency (1956–61).

3289 Fausto, Boris. Estado e burguesia agroexportadora na Primeira República: uma revisão historiográfica. (*Novos Estud. CEBRAP*, 27, julho 1990, p. 120–127)

Presents thoughtful review of about a dozen recent works that address relationship between the State and coffee planters during the First Republic.

3290 Fausto, Boris. Historiografia da imigração para São Paulo. São Paulo: IDESP, Editora Sumaré, 1991. 62 p.: bibl. (Série Imigração; 0103–7730)

Excellent historiographical essay stresses works since 1950 and themes of social mobility, integration, and cultural pluralism.

3291 Ferrara, Miriam N. A imprensa negra paulista, 1915–1963. São Paulo: FFLCH-USP, 1986. 279 p.: bibl., ill., facsims. (Antropologia; 13)

Examines Afro-Brazilian press in São Paulo between 1915–63, and emphasizes integrationist position of urban Afro-Brazilians in this period. In some respects a synthesis of previous publications, but also includes valuable interviews with press founders.

3292 Ferrez, Gilberto. Velhas fotografias pernambucanas, 1851–1890. 3a. ed. Rio de Janiero: Campo Visual, 1988 90 p., 1 folded leaf of plates: chiefly ill.

Includes over 100 photos of Recife, Olinda, and interior of the state from last half of 19th century. Short introductory essay discusses history of Brazilian photography and photographers who worked in Pernambuco.

3293 Fonseca, Guido. Crimes, criminosos e a criminalidade em São Paulo, 1870–1950. São Paulo: Editora Resenha Tributária, 1988. 363 p.: bibl., ill.

Veritable "crime stories" by police officer and professor at police academy in São Paulo is based primarily on newspaper and police records and presented in largely anecdotal style.

3294 Foot, Francisco. Trem fantasma: a modernidade na selva. São Paulo: Companhia das Letras; Editora Schwarcz, 1988. 291 p., 16 p. of plates: bibl., ill.

Fascinating cultural analysis of late 19th-century Brazil focuses on ill-fated Madeira-Mamoré Railway. Also explores "modernity in the jungle" theme that the railway represented, as depicted in world expositions.

3295 Forjaz, Maria Cecília Spina. Tenentismo e Forças Armadas na Revolução de 30. Rio de Janeiro: Forense Universitária, 1989. 240 p.: bibl.

Serious study of *tenentismo* in Brazilian military makes extensive use of contemporary archives of Centro de Pesquisas de Documentação da História Contemporânea do Brasil (CPDOC) in Rio de Janeiro, and of interviews with key figures. Excellent bibliography.

3296 French, John D. The Brazilian workers' ABC: class conflict and alliances in modern São Paulo. Chapel Hill: Univ. of North Carolina Press, 1992. 378 p.: bibl., index.

Significant revisionist work challenges corporatist model of Brazilian labor history. Argues that workers and unions in this key industrial region were not co-opted by the State, but rather forged alliances that made possible political and economic gains. Detailed case study utilizes variety of important (and largely unexploited) archival materials.

3297 Fundação Getúlio Vargas. Centro de Pesquisa e Documentação de História Contemporânea do Brasil (CPDOC). Memória da Petrobrás: acervo de depoimentos. Coordenação de Aspásia Camargo. Rio de Janeiro: Petróleo Brasileiro S.A., Serviço de Comunicação Social, 1988. 142 p.

Provides very valuable reference source for interviews on file at CPDOC, Fundação Getúlio Vargas, dealing with formation and history of the national oil company. Contains brief biographical sketches of those interviewed and synopses of the interviews.

3298 Garcez, Angelina Nobre Rolim. Associação Comercial da Bahia, 175 anos: trajetória e perspectivas. Rio de Janeiro: Expressão e Cultura, 1987. 106 p.: bibl., ill.

Provides brief, straightforward, and not very probing sketch of history of an important business interest group. Such groups have not been well studied for any part of Brazil.

3299 Gebara, Ademir et al. História política da República. Organização de José Roberto do Amaral Lapa. Campinas, Brazil: Papirus Editora, 1990. 214 p.: bibl., ill. (Tempo e memória)

Collection of short essays, originally written for general public, includes seven on the First Republic, six on São Paulo and the Republic, and two on Campinas.

3300 Gertz, René E. Catolicismo social no Rio Grande do Sul: a União Popular. (*Veritas/Porto Alegre*, 37:148, dez. 1992, p. 553–580)

Useful discussion of influence of German Catholic social action in regions of German colonization in southern Brazil at turn of the century focuses primarily on one Catholc organization.

3301 Gomes, Angela Maria de Castro. A invenção do trabalhismo. Rio de Janeiro: Instituto Universitário de Pesquisas do Rio de Janeiro; São Paulo: Vértice, 1988. 343 p.: bibl. (Formação do Brasil; 5)
Analysis of emergence of *trabalhismo* during period 1889–1954 is based primarily on government documents (especially from the Ministério do Trabalho) and published writings of key labor leaders and politicians. Emphasizes corporatist strategy of the government.

3302 Gomes, Danilo. Antigos cafés do Rio de Janeiro. Rio de Janeiro: Livraria Kosmos Editora, 1989. 154 p.: bibl., ill.
Provides brief descriptions and histories of cafés of Rio de Janeiro.

3303 Gouvêa, Fernando da Cruz. Joaquim Nabuco entre a Monarquia e a República. Recife, Brazil: Fundação Joaquim Nabuco, Editora Massangana, 1989. 399 p.: bibl., ill. (Série República; 9)
Hagiographic study of political life of Nabuco relies heavily on newspapers and on his writings, and speeches.

3304 Graham, Sandra Lauderdale. Slavery's impasse: slave prostitutes, small-time mistresses, and the Brazilian law of 1871. (*Comp. Stud. Soc. Hist.*, 3:4, Oct. 1991, p. 669–694)
Argues that: 1) anti-prostitution efforts in Brazil identified slave prostitutes as victims of their owners' greed and immoral abuse; and 2) in anti-prostitution court cases slaveholding authority was jeopardized, but only the least reputable of all slave owners were at risk. An insightful juxtaposition of Brazilian attitudes toward commerce in sex and slavery.

3305 Greenfield, Gerald Michael. The Great Drought and elite discourse in imperial Brazil. (*HAHR*, 72:3, Aug. 1992, p. 375–400)
Discusses parallels between elite discourse about Great Drought of 1877–79 that stressed flaws of the interior and of traditional society, and discourse of reform in late 19th-century Brazil that highlighted need to modernize the nation.

3306 Grover, Mark L. The Mormon Church and German immigrants in southern Brazil: religion and language. (*Jahrb. Gesch.*, 26, 1989, p. 295–308)
Interesting essay examines introduction of Mormonism to Brazil in 1920s via German-speaking communities in southern Brazil. Shows how the church experienced an important shift from German to Portuguese services beginning in 1939.

3307 Guerzoni Filho, Gilberto. Ocupação de escravos em Minas Gerais no século XIX. (*Ciênc. Cult.*, 41:11, nov. 1989, p. 1105–1109, bibl., tables)
Initial study of slave occupations in Minas Gerais is based on 1831 census. Includes several useful tables illustrating occupations according to sex and to slave or non-slave status.

3308 Guilhon, Norma. Confederados em Santarém: saga americana na Amazônia. 2. ed. Rio de Janeiro: Presença, 1987. 223 p.: bibl., ill., maps, photos.
Amateurish account of southern expatriates in eastern Amazon is based largely on secondary sources, published primary sources, and some unpublished accounts. Second half of book contains mostly genealogical information and photographs of families.

3309 Guimarães, Antônio Ferreira Prestes. A revolução federalista em Cima da Serra: apontamentos históricos da Revolução Civil do Rio Grande do Sul, 1892–1895. Porto Alegre, Brazil: Martins Livreiro, 1987. 91 p. (Série História gaúcha; 4)
Campaign memoirs of important politician and military figure during civil upheaval of 1890s includes brief introduction.

3310 Guimarães, Silvana Goulart. Sob a verdade oficial: ideologia, propaganda e censura no Estado Novo. São Paulo: Editora Marco Zero; MCT/CNPq, 1990. 175 p.: bibl. (Col. Onde está a República)
Analysis of main propaganda agency of Estado Novo regime is based primarily on its publications and to a lesser extent on interviews and archival material. Heavy-handed theoretical framework.

3311 Hahner, June Edith. Emancipating the female sex: the struggle for women's rights in Brazil, 1850–1940. Durham, N.C.: Duke Univ. Press, 1990. 301 p.: bibl., ill., index.
Presents straightforward and very use-

ful survey of growth of women's rights movement in Brazil. Places movement within larger context of Brazilian society and politics. For sociologist's comment see *HLAS* 53:5567.

3312 Hecker, Alexandre. Um socialismo possível: a atuação de Antonio Piccarolo em São Paulo. São Paulo: T.A. Queiroz, 1989. 225 p.: bibl. (Biblioteca básica de ciências sociais. Série 1a., Estudos brasileiros; 11)

Examines efforts of an immigrant Italian socialist to adapt democratic socialism to Brazil in first four decades of the 20th century.

3313 Heranças e lembranças: imigrantes judeus no Rio de Janeiro. Direção editorial de Susane Worcman. Coordenação e pesquisa de Aiala Feller e Karen Worcman. Rio de Janeiro: Associação Religiosa Israelita do Rio de Janeiro; Fundação Museu da Imagem e do Som; Centro Interdisciplinar de Estudos Contemporâneos, 1991. 336 p.: bibl., ill., photos. (Quase catálogo; 5)

Nicely produced volume contains oral histories of immigrants, photographs, and a few short essays which provide historical context.

3314 Hering, Maria Luiza Renaux. Colonização e indústria no Vale do Itajaí: o modelo catarinense de desenvolvimento. Blumenau, Brazil: Editora da FURB, 1987. 334 p.: bibl., ill., index, map.

Very informative study examines textile industry in Santa Catarina between 1880–1945. Focuses primarily on two important companies: Hering and Renaux. Argues that isolation of region was key factor in its local development. Rejects dependency analysis in favor of Schumpeter's emphasis on the entrepreneur.

3315 Hildén, Eva. A saga de Penedo: a história da colônia finlandesa no Brasil. Rio de Janeiro: Fotografia Brasileira, 1989. 111 p.: ill.

Brief personal memoir is by a member of a Finnish colony established in the *município* of Resende, Rio de Janeiro, in 1929.

3316 Hilton, Stanley E. A Brazilian Foreign Office look at power politics in the Southern Cone in the 1920s. (*Luso-Braz. Rev.*, 27:1, Summer 1990, p. 79–97)

Reproduces and annotates a secret document written by Ronald de Carvalho, at request of Foreign Minister Otávio Manga-

beira, for the General Staff of the Brazilian Navy. Report analyzes Brazil's relations with Spanish South America, especially Argentina.

3317 Hilton, Stanley E. A rebelião vermelha. Rio de Janeiro: Editora Record, 1986. 217 p.: bibl.

Fascinating account of 1935 abortive Communist uprising and events leading to creation of the Estado Novo in 1937 is based on archival research in Europe, Brazil, and the US.

3318 História dos metalúrgicos de São Caetano. São Paulo?: CEDI-Programa Memória e Acompanhamento do Movimento Operário no ABC, 1987? 132 p.: ill. (Contribuição ao debate; 2)

Impassioned history of *metalúrgicos* in one of the three *municípios* of the so-called ABC Paulista is based largely on oral histories; no notes or other sources cited. Published by workers who led opposition movement within the union.

3319 História e ideal: ensaios sobre Caio Prado Júnior. Organização de Maria Angela d'Incao. São Paulo: Editora UNESP; Secretaria de Estado da Cultura; Editora Brasiliense, 1989. 502 p.

Collection of articles considers one of Brazil's foremost historians in this century. Includes reminiscences of friends, critiques of his writings, a bibliography of his works, documents, and photographs.

3320 Holloway, Thomas H. Policing Rio de Janeiro: repression and resistance in a 19th-century city. Stanford, Calif.: Stanford Univ. Press, 1993. 369 p.: bibl., ill., index.

Very fine study of rise of modern police force in city of Rio de Janeiro is based on extensive and intensive examination of police and judicial records. Emphasizes dialectic between repression and resistance.

3321 Horbatiuk, Paulo. Imigração ucraniana no Paraná. Porto União, Brazil: Uniporto, 1989. 322 p.: bibl., ill. (Col. Vale do Iguaçu; 56)

Originally a master's thesis, this brief historical work on immigration to Paraná focuses on contemporary descendants of Ukrainians in *municípios* of Mallet and Paulo Frontin, and on persistence of cultural traditions.

3322 Hörmeyer, Joseph. O Rio Grande do Sul de 1850: descrição da Província do Rio Grande do Sul no Brasil meridional. Tradução de Heinrich A.W. Bunse. Porto Alegre, Brazil: D.C. Luzzatto Editores; EDUNI-SUL, 1986. 126 p.: bibl., ill.

Translation of slim volume by German military officer in Brazil in mid-19th century focuses largely on geography and promotes immigration to Rio Grande do Sul.

3323 Hutter, Lucy Maffei. Imigração italiana em São Paulo de 1902 a 1914: o processo imigratório. São Paulo: Instituto de Estudos Brasileiros, Univ. de São Paulo, 1986. 248 p.: bibl., ill.

Amply documented study of Italian immigration takes reader through the various steps in the process. Makes extensive use of state archival materials, Italian sources, and newspapers.

3324 Idéias políticas de Assis Brasil. v. 1. Organização de Paulo de Souza Pinto Brossard. Brasília: Senado Federal; Rio de Janeiro: Fundação Casa de Rui Barbosa, MinC, 1989. 1 v.: bibl., ill., indexex. (Ação e pensamento da república; 12)

Collection of documents and commentary on important diplomat and politician from Rio Grande do Sul, whose career extended from 1880s to 1930s. Organized by a former Minister of Justice using very traditional approach.

3325 Iokoi, Zilda Márcia Gricoli. Trabalho escravo no Brazil atual. (*Rev. Hist./São Paulo,* 120, jan./julho 1989, p. 109–119)

Briefly discusses condition of landless laborers in Brazil in late 1980s and proximity of that condition to slavery.

3326 Ipanema, Cybelle de. História da Ilha do Governador. Rio de Janeiro: Livraria e Editora Marcello de Ipanema, 1991. 228 p.: bibl., ill., map, photos.

Somewhat haphazard collection includes essays, documents, and photographs on history of the island in Guanabara Bay that now serves as location for Rio's international airport.

3327 Janotti, Aldo. O Marquês de Paraná: inícios de uma carreira política num momento crítico da história da nacionalidade. Belo Horizonte, Brazil: Editora Itatiaia; São Paulo: Editora da Univ. de São Paulo, 1990. 236 p.: bibl. (Col. Reconquista do Brasil; 2a. sér., 159)

Traditional biography of one of the most important political figures of 19th century focuses on 1830s.

3328 Janotti, Maria de Lourdes Mônaco. The Monarchist response to the beginnings of the Brazilian Republic. (*Americas/Francisc.,* 48:2, Oct. 1991, p. 223–243)

Detailed examination of efforts by anti-republicans during first years of the republic to restore the monarchy includes brief discussion of why monarchism failed to achieve its goal.

3329 Jucá, Joselice. Joaquim Nabuco: uma instituição de pesquisa e cultura na perspectiva do tempo. Apresentação de Fernando de Mello Freyre. Recife, Brazil: Fundação Joaquim Nabuco, Editora Massangana, 1991. 236 p.: bibl., ill. (Série Documentos; 37)

Provides institutional history of important cultural research center in Recife, created in 1949.

3330 Keck, Margaret E. The Workers' Party and democratization in Brazil. New Haven, Conn.: Yale Univ. Press, 1992. 315 p.: bibl., index.

Important analysis of origins and development of the Partido dos Trabalhadores in 1970s and 1980s relies heavily on interviews with key participants. For political scientist's comment see *HLAS 53:4302.*

3331 Klein, Herbert S. A integração social e econômica dos imigrantes portugueses no Brasil no fim do século XIX e no século XX. (*Rev. Bras. Estud. Popul.;* 6:2, julho/dez. 1989, p.17–37, bibl., tables)

Quantitative analysis places Portuguese immigration to Brazil within larger context of Portuguese immigration to other regions. The largest group of European immigrants to Brazil, the Portuguese tended to concentrate in urban areas, not to return to Portugal, and to marry within the Portuguese community.

3332 Klein, Herbert S. The social and economic integration of Spanish immigrants in Brazil. (*J. Soc. Hist.,* 25:3, Spring 1992, p. 505–529)

Highly quantitative analysis shows that the Spanish were the third largest group of European immigrants to Brazil; also, that they were the poorest and least prepared. They concentrated in the state of São Paulo and in secondary cities, and worked mainly in the agricultural sector.

3333 Klein, Herbert S. The supply of mules to central Brazil: the Sorocaba Market, 1825–1880. (*Agric. Hist.*, 64:4, Fall 1990, p. 1–25, map, tables)

Highly quantitative analysis is based on tax registers in Sorocaba, São Paulo. Shows size and extent of mule supply, and emphasizes collapse of the market in 1870s with arrival of railroads.

3334 Kornis, Mônica Almeida *et al.* A República na velha província: oligarquias e crise no estado do Rio de Janeiro, 1889–1930. Coordenação de Marieta de Moraes Ferreira. Edição de texto de Dora Rocha Flaksman. Rio de Janeiro: Rio Fundo, 1989. 316 p.: bibl.

Serious collaborative work by scholars associated with the Centro de Pesquisa e Documentação de História Contemporânea do Brasil (CPDOC). Series of essays has been revised to produce what is largely a political history. Exceptionally good bibliography.

3335 Kraay, Hendrik. "As terrifying as unexpected:" the Bahian Sabinada, 1837–1838. (*HAHR*, 72:4, Nov. 1992, p. 501–527, tables)

Provides excellent analysis of major uprising against imperial government. Shows how rebels (radical liberals and army and militia officers) lost control of revolt as lower classes, people of color, and slaves joined the rebellion.

3336 Kuznesof, Elizabeth Ann. Sexual politics, race and bastard-bearing in nineteenth-century Brazil: a question of culture or power? (*J. Fam. Hist.*, 16:3, 1991, p. 241–260, bibl., tables)

Analyzes "relationship between race, legitimacy, fertility, and residence patterns" in mid 19th-century Rio de Janeiro and São Paulo. Concludes that definitions of legitimacy and marriage were very fluid and that it is difficult to find clear patterns related to family ties or residency. Excellent bibliography and review of the literature.

3337 Lacombe, Américo Jacobina. Ensaios brasileiros de história. São Paulo: Companhia Editora Nacional, 1989. 156 p.: bibl. (Brasiliana; 385)

Series of brief essays, largely on the Empire, was published in honor of Lacombe's 80th birthday and 50th year as head of the Casa de Rui Barbosa.

3338 Lacombe, Lourenço Luís. Isabel, a princesa redentora: biografia baseada em documentos inéditos. Petrópolis, Brazil: Instituto Histórico de Petrópolis, 1989. 288 p.: bibl., photos.

Very traditional and laudatory biography relies primarily on previously unavailable correspondence of royal family. Very well illustrated with photographs.

3339 Leite, Glacyra Lazzari. Pernambuco 1824: a Confederação do Equador. Recife, Brazil: Fundação Joaquim Nabuco, Editora Massangana, 1989. 209 p., 4 folded leaves of plates: bibl., ill. (Série República; 2)

Serious and useful study examines uprising in Northeast and its complexities. Research done in Brazil and Portugal.

3340 Lesser, Jeff. Jewish colonization in Rio Grande do Sul, 1904–1925 = Colonização judaica no Rio Grande do Sul, 1904–1925. São Paulo: Centro de Estudos de Demografia Histórica da América Latina, Univ. de São Paulo, Faculdade de Filosofia, Letras e Ciências Humanas, 1991. 95 p.: bibl. (Estudos CEDHAL; 6)

Presents interesting analysis of efforts by Jewish Colonization Assocation to establish settlements in southern Brazil. Finds that experience was similar to other colonization schemes in Brazil, and that it met with little success.

3341 Levine, Robert M. Canudos in the national context. (*Americas/Francisc.*, 48:2, Oct. 1991, p. 207–222)

Argues that Canudos movement was neither messianic nor millenarian; that Antônio Conselheiro was not a fanatic; and that there was no legal reason for authorities to attack Canudos. Discusses meaning of the episode for the nation. Argument is developed in a more extended format in item **3342.**

3342 Levine, Robert M. Vale of tears: revisiting the Canudos massacre in northeastern Brazil, 1893–1897. Berkeley: Univ. of California Press, 1992. 353 p.: bibl., ill., maps.

Very important and thorough analysis examines the most famous millenarian movement in Brazilian history. Reassesses previous works on Canudos, and seeks to consider events from the perspective of the participants. Highly recommended. See also item **3341.**

3343 Levy, Herbert Victor. Viver é lutar. São Paulo: Editora Saraiva, 1990. 286 p.

Autobiographical account by one of the most powerful publishers and financiers in 20th-century Brazil is very polemical, but not very revealing.

3344 Lima, Geraldo Oliveira. Marcha da Coluna Prestes através do Ceará. Rio de Janeiro: Cia. Brasileira de Artes Gráficas, 1990? 379 p.: bibl., ill.

Detailed account of Coluna Prestes in state of Ceará is put together and published by a local amateur historian.

3345 Lima, Oliveira. O movimento da independência, 1821–1822. Belo Horizonte, Brazil: Editora Itatiaia Limitada; São Paulo: Editora da Univ. de São Paulo, 1989. 324 p.: bibl. (Col. Reconquista do Brasil: 2a. sér., 154)

Reprint of a classic work first published in 1922.

3346 Lobo, Eulália Maria Lahmeyer; Lia Aquino Carvalho; and Myrian Stanley. Questão habitacional e o movimento operário. Rio de Janeiro: Editora UFRJ, 1989. 229 p.: bibl., ill., maps.

Richly detailed study examines living conditions of workers in Rio de Janeiro during First Republic. Bibliography offers a wonderful list of archival sources as well as printed materials.

3347 Lopes Mendes, António. América austral: um viajante português no Brasil, 1882–1883: cartas. Rio de Janeiro: UNIPAR, 1988. 220 p.: ill. (some col.).

Well-produced volume contains letters and pencil drawings of a Portuguese veterinarian who traveled along most of the Brazilian coast and across the Amazon Basin.

3348 Loureiro, Antonio José Souto. O Amazonas na época imperial. Manaus, Brazil: T. Loureiro, 1989. 288 p.: bibl., photos.

Veritable compendium of information about province of Amazonas in 19th century is something of a small encyclopedia with lots of statistical data and photographs, but little analysis.

3349 Luna, Francisco Vidal and Herbert S. Klein. Slaves and masters in early nineteenth-century Brazil: São Paulo. (*J. Interdiscip. Hist.*, 31:4, Spring 1991, p. 549–573)

Provides quantitative analysis of slave labor force in three towns of São Paulo province, including São Paulo itself. Most of the data precedes coffee economy. Useful exposition of figures for comparative purposes.

3350 Lustosa, Oscar de Figueiredo. A Igreja Católica no Brasil-República: cem anos de compromisso, 1889–1989. São Paulo: Edições Paulinas, 1991. 178 p.: bibl. (Estudos & debates latino-americanos; 21)

Brief history of Church-State relations emphasizes social role of Catholic Church. Written by a priest.

3351 Macedo, Joaquim Manuel de. As vítimas-algozes: quadros da escravidão: romances. Estabelecimento do texto e notas por Rachel Teixeira Valença. 3a. ed. comemorativa do centenário da abolição. Rio de Janeiro: Fundação Casa de Rui Barbosa; São Paulo: Editora Scipione, 1991. 314 p.: ill.

Provides welcome reprint of three abolitionist novels first published in 1869 and out of print since 1896.

3352 Machado, Maria Clara Tomaz. Muito aquém do paraíso: ordem, progresso e disciplina em Uberlândia. (*Hist. Perspect.*, 4, jan./junho 1991, p. 37–77)

Looks at ways local elites attempt to impose modernity, discipline, order, and progress on this city in western Minas Gerais, primarily since 1950s.

3353 Machado, Teobaldo. As insurreições liberais em Goiana. Recife, Brazil: Governo do Estado de Pernambuco, Secretaria de Turismo, Cultura e Esportes/FUNDARPE: Companhia Editora de Pernambuco, 1990. 217 p.: bibl. (Biblioteca comunitária de Pernambuco. Ensaio; 2)

Argues that the middle sectors, not the rural aristocracy (as has been asserted), led the liberal uprisings in Pernambuco between 1817–24. Case study of municipality of Goiana, near Recife.

3354 Madden, Lori. Evolution in the interpretations of the Canudos Movement: an evaluation of the social sciences. (*Luso-Braz. Rev.*, 28:1, Summer 1991, p. 59–75)

Reviews literature on Canudos rebellion from anthropological perspective. Sees movement toward greater emphasis on symbolic and discourse analysis in more recent work. For sociologist's comment see *HLAS 53:5583.*

3355 **Maestri Filho, Mário José.** Depoimentos de escravos brasileiros. São Paulo: Icone Editora, 1988. 88 p.: bibl. (Col. Malungo: Memória)

Brief collection of documents includes two testimonies of former Brazilian slaves interviewed in early 1980s. Questions of the interviewers are included.

3356 **Maggie, Yvonne.** Catálogo, Centenário da abolição. Rio de Janeiro: ACEC; CIEC/Núcleo da Cor/UFRJ, 1989. 257 p.: bibl., ill. (Publicações avulsas; 2)

Catalogs events that took place throughout Brazil to commemorate centennial of abolition. This simple listing documents modern Brazil's continuing relationship to a major historical event and may serve as a useful resource for social scientists.

3357 **Malamud, Samuel.** Recordando a Praça Onze. Rio de Janeiro: Livraria Kosmos Editora, 1988. 119 p.: ill., ports.

Memoir and historical account of Jewish community in Rio de Janeiro in 1920s–1930s was originally published in Yiddish in 1981.

3358 **Malan, Souto.** Missão militar francesa de instrução junto ao exército brasileiro. Rio de Janeiro: Biblioteca do Exército Editora, 1988. 267 p.: bibl., ill. (Biblioteca do Exército Editora; 572. Col. General Benício; 262)

History of French military training mission in Brazil in 1920s–1930s, written by a general in the style of a report. Includes bibliography, but sources not cited.

3359 **Malatian, Teresa Maria.** Os cruzados do Império. São Paulo: Editora Contexto, 1990. 140 p.: bibl. (Série República. Biblioteca da República. Repensando a República. História Contexto.)

Interesting analysis examines antiliberal, anti-communist Catholic movement Ação Imperial Patrianovista Brasileira, a largely middle-class movement that functioned from the 1920s to 1960s.

3360 **Maram, Sheldon.** Juscelino Kubitschek and the 1960 presidential election. (*J. Lat. Am. Stud.*, 24:1, Feb. 1992, p. 123–145)

Discusses Kubitschek's political maneuvering as he attempted to select his own successor and guarantee his reelection in 1965. Stresses Kubitschek's personalistic leadership style and lack of commitment to party politics.

3361 **Maram, Sheldon.** Juscelino Kubitschek and the politics of exuberance, 1956–1961. (*Luso-Braz. Rev.*, 27:1, Summer 1990, p. 31–45, bibl.)

Article attempts to redirect studies of Kubitschek's presidency to his style and leadership qualities as an antidote to social science analyses that have emphasized structures and patterns.

3362 **Martins, Eloy.** Um depoimento político. Porto Alegre, Brazil: E. Martins, 1989. 227 p.: bibl., ill. .

Memoirs of a metalworker from southern Brazil who eventually became part of the central committee of the Partido Comunista Brasileira focuses mainly on period 1920s–early 1960s. Includes a fervent defense of Soviet model and the Cuban Revolution.

3363 **Martins, Hélio Leôncio.** A revolta dos marinheiros, 1910. Rio de Janeiro: Serviço de Documentação Geral da Marinha; São Paulo: Cia. Editora Nacional, 1988. 255 p.: bibl., photos. (Brasiliana; 384)

Very traditional and thorough history of a major naval revolt in Rio de Janeiro, written by a retired naval officer. Good photographs.

3364 **Martins, José de Souza.** A imigração espanhola para o Brasil e a formação da força-de-trabalho na economia cafeeira, 1880–1930. (*Rev. Hist./São Paulo*, 121, agôsto/dez. 1989, p. 5–26)

Interesting analysis compares Spanish and Italian immigrants to Brazil at beginning of 20th century. Emphasizes rural origins of Spaniards, their entry into Brazil at a time of few opportunities for social mobility, and their assimilation into Brazilian society.

3365 **Martins, José de Souza.** Subúrbio: vida cotidiana e história no subúrbio da cidade de São Paulo: São Caetano, do fim do Império ao fim da República Velha. São Paulo: Editora Hucitec; São Caetano do Sul, Brazil: Prefeitura de São Caetano do Sul, 1992. 363 p.: bibl., ill., maps. (São Caetano do Sul— Série Histórica; 3)

Vol. 2 of projected three-volume study of community that forms part of Greater São

Paulo. Written by a prominent sociologist and native of the community, work is a series of essays, rather than traditional historical narrative.

3366 Massi, Fernanda *et al.* História das ciências sociais no Brasil. v. 1. Organização de Sergio Miceli. São Paulo: IDESP; Vértice; FINEP, 1989. 1 v.: bibl., ill.

Collaborative project resulted in 10 essays that mainly analyze institutional and professional developments. Focus is primarily on 20th century and on states of São Paulo, Rio de Janeiro, Minas Gerais, and Pernambuco.

3367 Matos, Henrique Cristiano José. Um estudo histórico sobre o catolicismo militante em Minas, entre 1922 e 1936. Belo Horizonte, Brazil: Editora O Lutador, 1990. 502 p.: bibl., index.

Heavily documented study especially emphasizes role of Archbishop Dom Antônio dos Santos Cabral and the Catholic press in Minas. Originally a doctoral dissertation that appeared as series of articles.

3368 Mattoso, Kátia M. de Queirós. Bahia, século XIX: uma província no Império. Rio de Janeiro: Editora Nova Fronteira, 1992. 747 p.: bibl., ill.

Magisterial social history in style of the French Annales school, written by a very prominent scholar. Family, State, Church, economic organization, prices, and salaries provide framework for analysis.

3369 Mattoso, Kátia M. de Queirós. O filho da escrava, em torno da Lei do Ventre Livre. (*Rev. Bras. Hist.*, 8:16, março/agôsto 1988, p. 37–55, tables)

Using inventory records from Bahia in last three decades of slavery (1860–88), and the Lei do Ventre Livre, author discusses how owners defined childhood for slaves. As a result, slave women might have limited the number of their offspring. Important contribution to 19th-century Bahian slave life.

3370 As memórias de Joahann [sic] Carl Dreher e de Heinrich Georg Bercht. Tradução, introdução e notas de Günter Wiemer. Porto Alegre, Brazil: Escola Superior de Teologia e Espiritualidade Franciscana, 1988. 95 p.: ports. (Col. Imigração alemã)

Contains brief autobiographical sketches and genealogies of two German immigrants to Brazil in last half of 19th century.

3371 Mendonça, Sonia Regina de and Virginia Maria Fontes. História do Brasil recente, 1964–1980. São Paulo: Atica, 1988. 87 p.: bibl. (Série Princípios; 152)

Sketchy and schematic overview of recent Brazilian history inexplicably stops at 1980. Geared toward introductory college level.

3372 Mercadante, Paulo. Crônica de uma comunidade cafeeira: Carangola, o vale e o rio. Belo Horizonte, Brazil: Editora Itatiaia, 1990. 167 p., 48 p. of plates: bibl., maps, photos. (Col. Reconquista do Brasil; 2a. sér., 163)

Very traditional local history of a community in the *zona da mata* of southern Minas Gerais is based on secondary sources. Excellent photographs.

3373 Méro, Ernani. O Barão do Penedo: a missão da palavra. Maceió, Brazil: SERGASA, 1992. 205 p.: bibl., ill.

Very traditional and laudatory biography portrays one of Brazil's most important diplomats of the 19th century.

3374 Meznar, Joan E. The ranks of the poor: military service and social differentiation in Northeast Brazil. (*HAHR*, 72:3, Aug. 1992, p. 335–351)

Argues that working poor opposed expansion of base of recruitment into the army in late 19th century (and more precisely in the Quebra Quilos revolt in 1874) in order to maintain their social position as distinct from slaves and "undesirables."

3375 Moreira, Aluizio Franco *et al.* Recife, que história é essa? Recife, Brazil: Prefeitura da Cidade do Recife, Secretaria de Educação e Cultura, Fundação de Cultura Cidade do Recife; Fundação Nacional Pró-Memória, 1987. 265 p.: bibl. (Col. Tempos e espaços; 1)

Contains series of essays on diverse topics, and of varying quality, on history of Recife.

3376 Moreira, Regina da Luz. Brasilianistas, historiografia e centros de documentação. (*Estud. Hist./Rio de Janeiro*, 3:5, 1990, p. 66–74, bibl.)

Presents interesting account of emergence of first major historical archives in

1970s and of the role of "Brazilianists" in this process.

3377 Mott, Luiz Roberto de Barros. Sergipe del Rey: população, economia e sociedade. Aracajú, Brazil: Governo de Sergipe, Secretaria de Estado da Educação e Cultura, Fundação Estadual de Cultura, 1986. 204 p.: bibl. (Col. Jackson da Silva Lima)

Ten articles by prominent anthropologist/historian examine demographic history of Sergipe. Strong emphasis on ethnic groups and racial conflicts.

3378 Nabuco, Joaquim. Nabuco e a república. Organização e introdução de Leonardo Dantas Silva. Recife, Brazil: Fundação Joaquim Nabuco, Editora Massangana, 1990. 173 p.: bibl. (Série República; 6)

Introduction is followed by three essays by Nabuco: "O Povo e o Trono" (1869); "O Dever do Monarquistas" (1895); and "A Intervenção Estrangeira na Revolta da Armada" (1896).

3379 Napoleão, Aluízio. Juscelino Kubitschek: audácia, energia, confiança. Rio de Janeiro: Bloch, 1988. 95 p.: bibl., port.

Brief, anecdotal accounts written by one of Kubitschek's political confidants emphasize his personal qualities. Very laudatory.

3380 Naro, Nancy Priscilla Smith. Customary rightholders and legal claimants to land in Rio de Janeiro, Brazil, 1870–1890. (*Americas/Francisc.*, 48:4, April 1992, p. 485–517, tables)

Intensive analysis examines strategies of planters to restructure labor market following demise of slavery in two *municípios* of the Paraíba Valley (Vassouras and Rio Bonito), and responses of smallholders. Using rich archival documentation, focuses on conflicts over rights to improvements on land.

3381 Naro, Nancy Priscilla Smith. Revision and persistence: recent historiography on the transition from slave to free labour in rural Brazil. (*Slavery Abolit.*, 13:2, Aug. 1992, p. 68–85)

Carefully outlined discussion of reshaping of free labor market in post-1850 rural Brazil emphasizes regional variations in free labor arrangements, relative mobility of ex-slaves in post-emancipation period, importance of non-export agriculture to capital accumulation, and national labor market.

3382 Needell, Jeffrey D. A liberal embraces monarchy: Joaquim Nabuco and conservative historiography. (*Americas/Francisc.*, 48:2, Oct. 1991, p. 159–179)

Excellent analysis examines the continuity in beliefs and politics of this famous abolitionist and supporter of the monarchy.

3383 Nogueira, Oracy. Negro político, político negro. Prefácio de Antônio Cândido. São Paulo: Edusp, 1992. 317 p.: bibl., ill.

Fascinating account of life and career of black physician and politician Dr. Alfredo Casemiro da Rocha (1855–1933), discussed in context of the First Republic and São Paulo politics.

3384 Oliveira, José Aparecido de et al. JK, o estadista do desenvolvimento. Brasília: Memorial JK; Subsecretaria de Edições Técnicas do Senado Federal, 1991. 367 p.

In series of presentations, friends and colleagues of Juscelino Kubitschek recall their work with him. Originally presented at a conference in Brasília in 1985, on 10th anniversary of Kubitschek's death.

3385 Otten, Alexandre H. Só Deus é grande: a mensagem religiosa de Antônio Conselheiro. São Paulo: Edições Loyola, 1990. 393 p.: bibl. (Col. Fé e realidade; 30)

Makes serious effort to evaluate image of Conselheiro in previous writings and to "recuperate" his image as a religious leader. Emphasizes his religious ideas and motivations as opposed to socioeconomic interpretations of Canudos.

3386 Palacin, Luiz. Coronelismo no extremo norte de Goiás: o padre João e as três revoluções de Boa Vista. Goiânia, Brazil: Centro Editorial e Gráfico UFG; São Paulo: Edições Loyola, 1990. 245 p.: bibl., maps.

Examines system of *coronelismo* in northern Goiás (currently the state of Tocantins) between 1890s-1930s. Argues that party politics mediated between power of the state government and the local *coroneis* as shown through analysis of three rebellions (1892–95, 1907, and 1930).

3387 Palacios, Guillermo. A "Guerra dos Maribondos:" uma revolta camponesa no Brasil escravista. (*Hist. Quest. Debates*, 10:18/19, junho/dez. 1989, p. 7–75, bibl.)

Provides lengthy analysis of Pernambucan peasant revolt against an 1851 national regulation calling for civil registration of births and deaths. Author ably situates revolt in context of class conflict, elite political struggles, and Church-State relations.

3388 Parente, Josênio Camelo. Anauê: os camisas verdes no poder. Fortaleza, Brazil: EUFC, 1986. 150 p.: bibl.
Study of Integralist movement in Ceará emphasizes role of Catholic Church. Argues that movement was both working class and middle class in its origins.

3389 A participação da mulher na sociedade brasileira. Coordenação de José Antônio Segatto. São Paulo: Prefeitura do Município de São Paulo, Secretaria Municipal de Cultura, Depto. do Patrimônio Histórico, Divisão de Iconografia e Museus, 1987. 70 p.: photos. (Série Registros; 10)
Interesting set of photographs of Brazilian women, mainly in political settings, includes brief narrative text.

3390 Pedro, Joana Maria *et al.* Negro em terra de branco: escravidão e preconceito em Santa Catarina no século XIX. Porto Alegre, Brazil: Mercado Aberto, 1988. 64 p.: bibl. (Documenta-SC; 2)
Brief regional study of slavery in largely white state of Santa Catarina is perhaps useful for specialists.

3391 Pesavento, Sandra Jatahy. A burguesia gaúcha: dominação do capital e disciplina do trabalho: RS [i.e. Rio Grande do Sul], 1889–1930. Porto Alegre, Brazil: Mercado Aberto, 1988. 279 p.: bibl. (Documenta; 23 [i.e. 24])
Important study examines emergence of industrialists in southern Brazil and their power to influence but not dominate state politics. Based primarily on government documents, company reports, and journals from the period.

3392 Pesavento, Sandra Jatahy. Emergência dos subalternos: trabalho livre e ordem burguesa. Porto Alegre, Brazil: Editora da Univ. Federal do Rio Grande do Sul: FAPERGS, 1989. 84 p.: bibl.
Brief and highly theoretical analysis examines shift from slavery to free labor in Rio Grando do Sul.

3393 Pesavento, Sandra Jatahy. Os industriais da república. Porto Alegre, Brazil: IEL, 1991. 266 p.: bibl.

Highly theoretical analysis of industrial growth in Rio Grande do Sul to 1930 is based largely on published sources. Though presentation is frustrating, work contains much important data on a region whose industrialization has not been well studied.

3394 Pesavento, Sandra Jatahy. Mulheres e história: a inserção da mulher no contexto cultural de uma região fronteiriça (Rio Grande do Sul, Brasil). (*Travessia/Florianópolis*, 23, 2nd semestre, 1991, p. 54–72, bibl.)
Author discusses need to construct a history of Rio Grande do Sul that recognizes roles of women. Points out some examples of prominent women.

3395 Pilar, Fabrício Batista de Oliveira. Memórias da Revolução de 1893. Organização e apresentação de Helio Moro Mariante. Rio de Janeiro: Presença, s.d. 223 p.: bibl., ill., indexes. (Col. 150 anos Brigada Militar)
Journals of a lieutenant colonel who fought in southern Brazil (principally in Rio Grande do Sul) during the military uprising of 1893–94.

3396 Pinheiro, Paulo Sérgio de M.S. Estratégias da ilusão: a revolução mundial e o Brasil, 1922–1935. São Paulo: Companhia das Letras, 1991. 379 p., 32 p. of plates: bibl., ill., index.
Important and extensive study examines the Brazilian left, its strategies and illusions, and the repression it faced. Major work by a prominent sociologist. Excellent photographs.

3397 Pinsdorf, Marion K. German-speaking entrepreneurs: builders of business in Brazil. New York: P. Lang, 1990. 403 p.: bibl., index. (American university studies: Series XVI, Economics; 6)
Very traditional study of immigrants as innovators reads like a dissertation. About one-third of book examines Pinsdorf family that first arrived in Brazil in 1890s.

3398 Pondé, Francisco de Paula e Azevedo. Organização e administração do Ministério da Guerra no Império. Coordenação de Vicente Costa Santos Tapajós. Brasília: Fundação Centro de Formação do Servidor Público, 1986. 532 p.: bibl., ill. (História administrativa do Brasil; 16)
Part of an extensive series on Brazilian

administrative history, work is largely a compilation of laws, decrees, and bureaucratic structures. Essentially a reference work.

3399 Pontes, Heloisa A. Brasil Com Z. (*Estud. Hist./Rio de Janeiro,* 3:5, 1990, p. 45–65, bibl., tables)

Analyzes portrayal of Brazil in books by foreign social scientists and historians since 1930s. Divides nearly 150 books into two periods for analysis: 1930–68 and 1969–88. Emphasizes role of French and US Brazilianists.

3400 Porto, Walter Costa. O voto censitário no Brasil. (*Rev. Bras. Estud. Polít.,* 69/70, julho 1989/jan.1990, p. 91–104)

Provides descriptive overview of changing income requirements for voters in 19th-century Brazil.

3401 Potelet, Jeanine. Temoignages des marins français au Brésil: la "Cabanagem." (*Bol. Mus. Para. Goeldi,* 6:2, dez. 1990, p. 131–144, bibl., ill., maps)

Reveals that documents containing French sailors' eyewitness accounts of the Cabanagem revolt (1835–37) in Pará are preserved in French naval archives.

3402 A presença italiana no Brasil: atas. Organização de Luis Alberto de Boni. Porto Alegre, Brazil: Escola Superior de Teologia; Torino, Italy: Fondazione Giovanni Agnelli, 1987- . 2 v.: bibl., ill., maps. (Col. Imigração italiana; 80, 100)

Wide-ranging series of articles was originally presented at a 1985 conference in São Paulo.

3403 Presença luterana, 1990. Redação de Gottfried Brakemeier. São Leopoldo, Brazil: Editora Sinodal, 1989. 195 p.: bibl., ill., map.

Official publication of Evangelical Lutheran Church in Brazil was prepared for 1990 meeting of Lutheran World Federation in Brazil. First half of volume offers general essays orienting non-specialist to Brazil. Second half contains essays on structure and history of Protestantism, and more specifically, the Evangelical Lutheran Church in Brazil.

3404 Prestes, Anita Leocádia. A Coluna Prestes. São Paulo: Secretaria de Estado da Cultura; Editora Brasiliense, 1990. 498 p.: bibl., ill., maps. (Col. Tudo é história)

Very detailed history of military col-

umn led by Luís Carlos Prestes in 1920s, written by his daughter. Based heavily on oral histories, especially her interviews with her father.

3405 Queiroz, Suely Robles Reis de. Reflections on Brazilian Jacobinism of the first decade of the Republic, 1893–1897. (*Americas/Francisc.,* 48:2, Oct. 1991, p. 181–205)

Very useful survey examines Jacobinism—its ideology, proponents, and role in first years of the Republic.

3406 Quintaneiro, Tania. A criança brasileira no século XIX na percepção de viajantes ingleses e norte-americanos: uma análise comparada. (*Sínt. Nova Fase,* 19:58, julho/set. 1992, p. 361–390)

Intriguing essay analyzes world of children in 19th-century Brazil as seen through eyes of English-speaking travelers. Looks at slavery, motherhood, inter-ethnic relations, among other topics.

3407 Rago, Margareth. Os prazeres da noite: prostituição e códigos da sexualidade feminina em São Paulo, 1890–1930. Rio de Janeiro: Paz e Terra, 1991. 322 p.: bibl., ill.

Fascinating and sensitive analysis examines prostitution in São Paulo through legal, medical, literary, and artistic sources. Strongly influenced by work of Michel Foucault.

3408 Reis, Eustáquio J. and Elisa P. Reis. As elites agrárias e a abolição da escravidão no Brasil. (*Dados/Rio de Janeiro,* 31:3, 1988, p. 309–341, graph, tables)

Analysis of abolition in Brazil is formulated in relation to "open resource" theory. Recaps existing interpretations and attempts to synthesize and integrate them. Although sources cited are not altogether new, authors' exposition of issues is clear and possibly useful to students new to the literature.

3409 Reis, João José. "Death to the cemetery:" funerary reform and rebellion in Brazil. (*Hist. Workshop,* 34, Autumn 1992, p. 33–46)

Brief work examines rebellion that successfully maintained tradition of burying dead in churches in Salvador. Includes overview of burial traditions and customs of the period.

3410 Reis, João José. A morte é uma festa: ritos fúnebres e revolta popular no Brasil do século XIX. São Paulo: Companhia das Letras, 1991. 357 p.: bibl., ill., maps.

Work focuses on a demonstration held in Salvador, Bahia, in 1836 to protest burial laws, which became known as the "Cemiterada." Following the demonstration negotiations were held between local authorities and members of religious orders and others, during which the history of funeral rites, attitudes toward death, and popular resistance to prohibition of burials inside churches were explored. Impressive contribution to social history of 19th-century Bahia.

3411 Reis, João José. Slave rebellion in Brazil: the Muslim uprising of 1835 in Bahia. Translated by Arthur Brakel. Baltimore, Md.: Johns Hopkins Univ. Press, 1993. 281 p.: bibl., ill., index, maps. (Johns Hopkins studies in Atlantic history and culture)

Revised and expanded English translation of *Rebelião escrava no Brazil* (see *HLAS 50:2728*). Work describes one of the most successful urban slave revolts ever to occur in Brazil. Impressive contribution to history of slave resistance in the Americas.

3412 Reis, Liana Maria. Fugas de escravos e formação do mercado de trabalho livre na província mineira, 1850–1888. (*Rev. Bras. Estud. Polít.*, 73, julho 1991, p. 203–217.)

Argues that runaway slaves in 1850–88 period who were looking for work contracts (however temporary) contributed to formation of a free labor market in Minas Gerais. More documentation on magnitude of the phenomenon for this period (as opposed to earlier) is needed to sustain author's thesis.

3413 Reis Filho, Daniel Aarão et al. História do marxismo no Brasil. v. 1. Rio de Janeiro: Paz e Terra, 1991-. 1 v: bibl.

First of projected four-volume study of Marxism in Brazil includes essays by six social scientists examining impact of early Marxism, Leninism, the Comintern, Maoism, the 20th Party Congress in the USSR, and the Cuban Revolution on the left in Brazil. An important and ambitious project.

3414 Renault, Delso. O desenvolvimento da indústria brasileira: subsídio ao período de 1850 a 1939. Rio de Janeiro: Serviço Social da Indústria, Conselho Nacional, s.d. 143 p.: bibl., facsims., ill., index.

Brief, narrative overview of growth of Brazilian industry focuses on important episodes. For the uninitiated, not the specialist.

3415 A República em Pernambuco. Organização de Leonardo Dantas Silva. Recife, Brazil: Fundação Joaquim Nabuco, Editora Massangana, 1990. 179 p., 5 leaves of plates: bibl., ill. (Série República; 15)

Collection of essays includes several published at turn of the century and only two written in recent years.

3416 Rezende, Tereza Hatue de. Ryu Mizuno: saga japonesa em terras brasileiras. Curitiba, Brazil?: s.n., 1991. 113 p.: bibl., ill., map, photos.

Brief biography of a Japanese immigrant includes photographs and fair amount on history of Japanese immigration to Brazil.

3417 Ribeiro, Gladys Sabina and **Martha de Abreu Esteves.** Cenas de amor: historias de nacionales e de imigrantes. (*Rev. Bras. Hist.*, 9:18, agôsto/set. 1989, p. 217–235)

Uses criminal records of parishes of central Rio de Janeiro from second half of 19th century to study family relations, leisure, and love among lower classes. Focuses primarily on two cases of alleged rape.

3418 Ribeiro, Jalila Ayoub Jorge. A desagregação do sistema escravista no Maranhão: 1850–1888. Prefácio de Mário Martins Meireles. São Luís, Brazil: SIOGE, 1990. 188 p.: bibl.

Examines decline and abolition of slavery in the state of Maranhão. Includes descriptions of the economy and transportation system, and relates government attitudes toward ending slave trade. Useful for comparative studies.

3419 Ribeiro, Lucílio da Rocha. Pequena contribuição à história da Estrada de Ferro Vitória a Minas. Vitória, Brazil: s.n., 1986. 134 p.: bibl., ill.

Useful survey of important railway deals primarily with period 1900–45. Written by an amateur historian without footnotes.

Ricci, Maria Lúcia de Souza Rangel and **Lilia Inés Zanotti de Mendrano.** El papel del contrabando y la interacción fronteriza del Brasil sureño con el Estado Oriental del Uruguay, 1850–1880. See item **3150.**

3420 Salles, Ricardo. Guerra do Paraguai: escravidão e cidadania na formação do exército. São Paulo: Paz e Terra, 1990. 165 p.: bibl., ill., maps.

Most of volume summarizes existing secondary literature, but final chapters present interesting material on composition of Brazilian army during the Paraguayan War.

Salvatore, Ricardo Donato. Modes of labor control in cattle-ranching economies: California, southern Brazil, and Argentina, 1820–1860. See item **3063.**

3421 Samara, Eni de Mesquita. A família negra no Brasil. (*Rev. Hist./São Paulo,* 120, jan./julho 1989, p. 27–44, table)

Discusses marriages and families of blacks in São Paulo in 19th century. Concludes that slave families and marriages were more numerous than previously thought.

3422 Samara, Eni de Mesquita. As mulheres, o poder e a família: São Paulo, século XIX. São Paulo: Editora Marco Zero; Secretaria de Estado da Cultura de São Paulo, 1989. 194 p.: bibl., ill.

Sophisticated quantitative analysis of wills, parish registers, and census materials covers two years and several neighborhoods of 19th-century São Paulo. Shows very clearly that family structure was much more varied and complex than indicated by the traditional view which held that Brazil was characterized by the extended patriarchal family.

3423 Samios, Eva Machado Barbosa. Die Wohnungsbaupolitik und das Wohnungsfinanzierungssystem in Brasilien, 1964–1977: Sozialpolitik oder Finanzpolitik? Bielefeld, Germany: Ruck-Zuck-Druck, 1987? 450 p.: bibl.

Relying almost exclusively on Brazilian sources, author examines and analyzes role of Banco Nacional da Habitação (BNH) during 1964–77. Concludes that BNH legitimized the military and became an instrument of financial rather than social policy. By transferring savings of those in need of housing to projects benefiting primarily the government and upper income groups, BNH subverted its stated policy. [C.K. Converse]

3424 Sampaio Neto, José Augusto Vaz et al. Canudos: subsídios para a sua reavaliação histórica. Rio de Janeiro: Fundação Casa de Rui Barbosa; Monteiro Aranha, 1986. 548 p., 11 p. of plates: ill., indexes, maps.

Indispensable bibliography on this "rebellion in the backlands" in 1890s contains exhaustive, annotated listing of sources in Rio de Janeiro and Bahia. Lists military forces materials, maps, journals, monographs, government documents, pamphlets, memoirs, and other types of sources.

3425 Sandoval, Salvador A.M. Social change and labor unrest in Brazil since 1945. Boulder, Colo.: Westview Press, 1993. 245 p.: bibl., ill., index.

Analyzes strike activity in Brazil since 1945 especially in relation to regime changes. Concludes that "mass politics notions inherent in the analysis of Latin American populism, and more recently in analysis of authoritarian regimes, do not correspond to the complexity and extent of working-class political participation."

3426 Santos, Eloína Monteiro dos. A rebelião de 1924 em Manaus. Manaus, Brazil: SUFRAMA; Ed. Calderaro, 1985. 170 p.: map.

Solid and well-documented regional study of 1924 *tenente* rebellion was originally a master's thesis.

3427 Schneider, Ronald M. Order and progress: a political history of Brazil. Boulder, Colo.: Westview Press, 1991. 486 p.: bibl., index, map.

Excellent one-volume history of Brazilian politics in 20th century contains very little on pre-20th-century years or on topics other than politics. For political scientist's comment see *HLAS 53:4343.*

3428 Schuh, Angela Schumacher and Ione Maria Sanmartin Carlos. Cachoeira do Sul: em busca de sua história. Porto Alegre, Brazil: Martins Livreiro-Editor, 1991. 204 p.: bibl., ill., maps.

Local history of *município* in central Rio Grande do Sul is informative and well illustrated, with little analysis.

3429 Scliar, Moacyr. Caminhos da esperança: a presença judaica no Rio Grande do Sul = Pathways of hope: the Jewish presence in Rio Grande do Sul. Porto Alegre, Brazil: Instituto Cultural Judaico Marc Chagall; Riocell, 1991? 120 p.: bibl., ill. (some col.), maps. (O Continente de São Pedro; 2)

Essay by prominent Brazilian writer is accompanied by interesting photographs. Bibliography, but no notes.

3430 Semeghini, Ulysses Cidade. Do café à indústria: uma cidade e seu tempo. Campinas, Brazil: Editora da Unicamp, 1991. 197 p.: bibl. (Série Teses)

Very good study examines economic and urban development of Campinas, São Paulo. Industrial production of this *município* surpasses that of almost every state in Brazil (except São Paulo and Rio de Janeiro). Written by an economist with emphasis on 20th century.

3431 Signor, Lice Maria. João Batista Scalabrini e a migração italiana: um projeto sócio-pastoral. Porto Alegre, Brazil: Pallotti, s.d. 272 p.: bibl., ill., index, ports.

Laudatory history of Italian immigration to southern Brazil focuses on role of Bishop Scalabrini of Piacenza and the Missionary Sisters of São Carlos Borromeo (Scalabrinianas).

3432 Silva, Alberto Martins da. João Severiano. Rio de Janeiro: Biblioteca de Exército Editora, 1989. 167 p.: bibl., ill., index. (Biblioteca do Exército Editora; 580. Col. General Benício; 269)

Work is laudatory and very traditional biography of João Severiano da Fonseca, physician and general who played key role in military medical services in 19th century.

3433 Silva, Leonardo Dantas. A imprensa e a abolição. Recife, Brazil: Fundação Joaquim Nabuco; Editora Massangana; Ministério da Ciência e Tecnologia, Comissão de Eventos Históricos, 1988. 1 v.: ill. (Série Abolição; 13)

Collection of sample segments of abolitionist newspapers from Brazil may be of interest to teachers.

3434 Silva, Marcos A. da. Caricata república: Zé Povo e o Brasil. São Paulo: Editora Marco Zero; Programa Nacional do Centenário da República e Bicentenário da Inconfidência Mineira, 1990. 100 p.: bibl., ill. (Biblioteca da República. Col. Onde está a República?)

Analysis of cartoons from turn-of-the-century Brazil was originally presented as a master's thesis in social history at Univ. of São Paulo.

3435 Silva, Maria Beatriz Nizza da. Filantropia e imigração: a Caixa de Socorros D. Pedro V. Rio de Janeiro: Real e Benemérita Sociedade Portuguesa Caixa de Socorros D. Pedro V, 1990. 168 p.: bibl., col. ill.

History of a Portuguese philanthropic society in Rio de Janeiro was commissioned to commemorate its 125th anniversary in 1988.

3436 Silva, Maria Beatriz Nizza da. Movimento constitucional e separatismo no Brasil, 1821–1823. Lisboa: Livros Horizonte, 1988. 143 p.: bibl. (Col. Horizonte histórico; 17)

Collection of newspaper articles and pamphlets dates from period of Brazilian independence. Collected, edited, and introduced by prominent Portuguese historian from Univ. of São Paulo, work is addressed to a Portuguese audience.

Silveira, Joaquim Xavier da. A FEB por um soldado. See *HLAS 53:4850.*

Smith, Joseph. Unequal giants: diplomatic relations between the United States and Brazil, 1889–1930. See *HLAS 53:4852.*

3437 Soihet, Rachel. Mulheres ousadas e apaixonadas: uma investigação em processos criminales cariocas, 1890–1930. (*Rev. Bras. Hist.*, 9:18, agosto/set. 1989, p. 199–216)

Contrasts views of females as fragile, submissive, and emotional with reality of women's behavior as seen through criminal records in Rio de Janeiro during First Republic.

Sulmanas, Armando J. Yerba mate e integración regional en la frontera argentino-brasileña. See item **3073.**

3438 Sylvestre, Josué. Nacionalismo & coronelismo: fatos e personagens da história de Campina Grande e da Paraíba, 1954–1964. Brasília: Centro Gráfico do Senado Federal, 1988. 626 p.: bibl., ill., index.

Essentially a collection of documents and photographs dealing with political history of Campina Grande, Paraíba, work includes much political narrative, but little analysis.

3439 Telles, Norma. Rebeldes, escritoras, abolicionistas. (*Rev. Hist./São Paulo*, 120, jan./julho 1989, p. 73–83)

Presents short, useful discussion of abolitionist literature in Brazil, particularly the work of Maria Firmina dos Reis (b. 1859), the first female novelist in Brazil.

3440 Ternes, Apolinário. Histórica econômica de Joinville. Joinville, Brazil: Associação Comercial e Industrial de Joinville, 1986. 279 p.

Useful, but superficial, economic history of most important industrial city in Santa Catarina is written with "booster" approach for general audience, without footnotes.

3441 Topik, Steven. Brazil's bourgeois revolution? (*Americas/Francisc.*, 48:2, Oct. 1991, p. 245–271)

Excellent study examines financial and economic crisis (*Encilhamento*) of early 1890s. Argues that previous analyses have oversimplified and distorted complexity of contending interest groups. Conflict was not between backward planters and modern capitalists, but between "bourgeois factions of capital and competing subordinate classes."

3442 Topik, Steven. Los lazos que ataron: Brasil y Méjico en la economía mundial, 1880–1910. (*in* Jornadas de Historiadores Americanistas, 2nd, Granada, Spain, 1989. América: encuentro y asimilación. Edición de Joaquín A. Muñoz Mendoza. Granada: Diputación Provincial de Granada, 1990, p. 181–215, tables)

Compares trade and foreign investment in both countries. Concludes that Brazilian model allowed the State more room to maneuver than did the Mexican model which reinforced the private sector.

3443 Topik, Steven. Metrópoles macrocéfalas: uma comparação entre a primazia do Rio de Janeiro e a da Cidade do México entre 1800 e 1910. (*Dados/Rio de Janeiro*, 34:1, 1991, p. 53–77, table)

Interesting comparative analysis relates how both cities excercised political and economic hegemony. Shows that Mexico City depended more on political power, and Rio de Janeiro on economic might, to maintain their primacy.

3444 Tota, Antônio Pedro. A locomotiva no ar: rádio e modernidade em São Paulo, 1924–1934. São Paulo: PW; Secretaria de Estado da Cultura, 1990. 141 p.: bibl., ill.

Well-documented and well-illustrated history of early years of radio in São Paulo.

3445 Ullmann, Reinholdo Aloysio. A atividade dos Jesuítas de São Leopoldo, 1844–1989. Coordenação de Aloysio Bohnen. São Leopoldo, Brazil: UNISINOS, 1989. 364 p.: bibl.

Emphasizes educational role of Jesuits

in Rio Grande do Sul, beginning with arrival of Spanish and German Jesuits in mid-19th century. Study was commissioned and published by Jesuits in São Leopoldo.

3446 Vangelista, Chiara. Os braços da lavoura: imigrantes e "caipiras" na formação do mercado de trabalho paulista, 1850–1930. Tradução de Thei de Almeida Viana Bertorello. São Paulo: Editora Hucitec; Istituto Italiano di Cultura; Instituto Cultural Italo-Brasileiro, 1991. 293 p.: bibl., ill. (Estudos brasileiros; 29)

Sophisticated quantitative analysis of *Paulista* labor market emphasizes role of Italian immigration and of the state government. Originally published in Italian.

3447 Vianna, Marly de Almeida Gomes. Revolucionários de 35: sonho e realidade. São Paulo: Companhia das Letras, 1992. 413 p.: bibl., ill., index.

Most thoroughly researched analysis to date of the Intentona Comunista of November 1935. Uses archives of the Partido Comunista do Brasil (PCB), trial records, interviews (including many with Luís Carlos Prestes), and a variety of other sources. Originally written as doctoral thesis by longtime member of Central Committee of PCB. Empathizes with rebels while criticizing their mistakes.

3448 Vianna, Sérgio Besserman. A política econômica no segundo governo Vargas: 1951–1954. Rio de Janeiro: Depto. de Projetos de Comunicação, Area de Relações Institucionais-BNDES, 1987. 181 p.: bibl.

Detailed and very valuable study argues that Vargas Administration had a coherent and consistent set of economic policies. Clear explanation of policies and their failure.

3449 Viégas, João Alexandre. Vencendo o azul: história da indústria e tecnologia aeronáuticas no Brasil. São Paulo: Livraria Duas Cidades; Conselho Nacional de Desenvolvimento Científico e Tecnológico, 1989. 221 p.: bibl., ill.

Fascinating and wonderfuly illustrated volume presents history of technology as inventors and inventions with little of the larger social and political context.

3450 Vieira, Hermes. A vida e a época do Visconde do Rio Branco. São Paulo: T.A. Queiroz, Editor, 1992. 484 p.: bibl., index. (Col. Coroa vermelha. Estudos brasileiros; 22)

Traditional, political biography of important 19th-century statesman.

3451 Wilcox, Robert. Cattle and environment in the Pantanal of Mato Grosso, Brazil, 1870–1970. (*Agric. Hist.*, 66:2, Spring 1992, p. 232–256, maps)

Focuses largely on recent history and ecology, emphasizing negative impact of ranching on the Pantanal.

3452 Wilcox, Robert. Paraguayans and the making of the Brazilian far west, 1870–1935. (*Americas/Francisc.*, 49:4, April 1993, p. 479–512, map, tables)

Looks at Paraguayan immigration to Mato Grosso, emphasizing pursuit of opportunities by immigrants, their contributions to local development, and disappearance of their influence after 1940.

3453 Wolfe, Joel. Working women, working men: São Paulo and the rise of Brazil's industrial working class, 1900–1955. Durham, N.C.: Duke Univ. Press, 1993. 312 p.: bibl., ill., index, map.

Excellent study of role of class and gender dynamics in the rise of unions focuses especially on part played by the rank-and-file. Innovative use of impressive variety of sources.

3454 Wolff, Egon and Frieda Wolff. Dicionário biográfico. v. 2, Judeus no Brasil, século XIX. Rio de Janeiro: E. e F. Wolff, 1986- . 1 v.

Second of projected six volumes of valuable reference source contains 7,000 entries.

3455 Wolff, Egon and Frieda Wolff. Documentos. v. 4, Uma amostragem documentária e fotográfica. Rio de Janeiro: ERCA Editora e Gráfica, 1988- . 1 v.

Brief, idiosyncratic collection includes photographs, birth certificates, travel documents, and other papers on Jews in Brazil.

3456 Wright, Simon. Villa-Lobos. Oxford; New York: Oxford Univ. Press, 1992. 146 p.: bibl., ill., index. (Oxford studies of composers)

Provides excellent introduction to one of Brazil's most important musical talents.

3457 Wyatt, Loretta Sharon. Princess Isabel and the overthrow of the Brazilian monarchy in 1889. (*in* MACLAS Latin American Essays. Edited by Robert J. Alexander, Juan Espadas, and Vincent Peloso. Collegeville, Pa.: Ursinus College, 1991?, v. 4, p. 99–112)

Brief but useful overview of role of Princess Isabel in collapse of the empire is based on secondary sources as well as archival research.

3458 Zaidan, Michel. Comunistas em céu aberto, 1922–1930. Belo Horizonte, Brazil: Oficina de Livros, 1989. 139 p.: bibl.

Brief analysis of the political thought of the 1920s Partido Comunista Brasileiro emphasizes party's "relative autonomy" from the Communist International.

JOURNAL ABBREVIATIONS

Actas Colomb. Actas Colombinas. Univ. de la Serena. Chile.

Agric. Hist. Agricultural History. Agricultural History Society. Univ. of Calif. Press. Berkeley.

Allpanchis/Cusco. Allpanchis. Instituto de Pastoral Andina. Cusco, Peru.

Alternativa/Chiclayo. Alternativa. Centro de Estudios Sociales Solidaridad. Chiclayo, Peru.

Am. Anthropol. American Anthropologist. American Anthropological Assn., Washington.

Am. Antiq. American Antiquity. The Society for American Archaeology. Washington.

Am. Hist. Rev. The American Historical Review. American Historical Assn., Washington.

Am. Indian Q. American Indian Quarterly. Southwestern American Indian Society; Fort Worth Museum of Science and History. Hurst, Tex.

Am. Indíg. América Indígena. Instituto Indigenista Interamericano. México.

Am. Lat./Moscow. América Latina. Academia de Ciencias de la Unión de Repúblicas Soviéticas Socialistas. Moscow.

Amazonía Peru. Amazonía Peruana. Centro Amazónico de Antropología y Aplicación Práctica, Depto. de Documentación y Publicaciones. Lima.

Americas/Francisc. The Americas. Academy of American Franciscan History. Washington.

An. Antropol. Anales de Antropología. Univ. Nacional Autónoma de México, Instituto de Investigaciones Históricas. México.

An. Encuentro Nac. Reg. Hist. Anales del Encuentro Nacional y Regional de Historia. Junta Regional de Historia y Estudios Conexos. Montevideo.

An. Mus. Michoacano. Anales del Museo Michoacano. Centro Regional Michoacán del INAH; Museo Regional Michoacano. Morelia, Mexico.

Anál. Pol. Análisis Político. Instituto de Estudios Políticos y Relaciones Internacionales, Univ. Nacional de Colombia. Bogotá.

Análise Conjunt. Análise & Conjuntura. Fundação João Pinheiro. Belo Horizonte, Brazil.

Análisis/Lima. Análisis. Cuadernos de Investigación. Lima.

Anaquel Estud. Arab. Anaquel de Estudios Arabes. Univ. Complutense de Madrid, Depto. de Estudios Arabes e Islámicos. Madrid.

Anc. Mesoam. Ancient Mesoamerica. Cambridge Univ. Press. Cambridge, England.

Annales/Paris. Annales. Centre national de la recherche scientifique de la VIe Section de l'Ecole pratique des hautes études. Paris.

ANPOCS BIB. Boletim Informativo e Bibliográfico de Ciências Sociais: BIB. Associação Nacional de Pós-Graduação e Pesquisa em Ciências Sociais. Rio de Janeiro.

Anthropol. Verkenn. Antropologische Verkenningen. Coutinho. Muiderberg, The Netherlands.

Anthropologica/Lima. Anthropologica. Depto. de Ciencias Sociales, Pontificia Univ. Católica del Perú. Lima.

Antropol. Ecuat. Antropología Ecuatoriana. Casa de la Cultura Ecuatoriana, Sección

Académica de Antropología y Arqueología. Quito.

Antropol. Soc. Antropología Social. Instituto Nacional de Antropología e Historia. México.

Anu. Dep. Hist./Madrid. Anuario del Departmento de Historia. Depto. de Historia, Univ. Complutense de Madrid.

Anu. Estud. Am. Anuario de Estudios Americanos. Consejo Superior de Investigaciones Científicas; Univ. de Sevilla, Escuela de Estudios Hispano-Americanos. Sevilla, Spain.

Anu. Estud. Centroam. Anuario de Estudios Centroamericanos. Univ. de Costa Rica. San José.

Anu. Hist. Iglesia Chile. Anuario de Historia de la Iglesia en Chile. Seminario Pontificio Mayor. Santiago.

Anu. IEHS. Anuario IEHS. Univ. Nacional del Centro de la Provincia de Buenos Aires, Instituto de Estudios Histórico-Sociales. Tandil, Argentina.

Anuario/Rosario. Anuario. Univ. Nacional de Rosario, Escuela de Historia. Argentina.

Apuntes/Lima. Apuntes. Univ. del Pacífico, Centro de Investigación. Lima.

Arch. Hist. Soc. Iesu. Archivum Historicum Societatis Iesu. Rome.

Arch. Ibero-Am. Archivo Ibero-Americano. Revista de Estudios Históricos. Los Padres Franciscanos. Madrid.

Årstryck/Göteborg. Årstryck. Etnografiska Museum. Göteborg, Sweden.

Asclepio/Madrid. Asclepio: Archivo Iberoamericano de Historia de la Medicina y Antropología Médica. Consejo Superior de Investigaciones Científicas, Instituto Arnaú de Vilanova de Historia de la Medicina. Madrid.

Bol. Acad. Chil. Hist. Boletín de la Academia Chilena de la Historia. Santiago.

Bol. Acad. Nac. Hist./Caracas. Boletín de la Academia Nacional de la Historia. Caracas.

Bol. Am. Boletín Americanista. Univ. de Barcelona, Facultad de Geografía e Historia, Depto. de Historia de América. Barcelona.

Bol. Arch. Nac./Cuba. Boletín del Archivo Nacional. Editorial Academia. La Habana.

Bol. Cult. Bibliogr. Boletín Cultural y Bibliográfico. Banco de la República; Biblioteca Luis-Angel Arango. Bogotá.

Bol. Fuentes Hist. Econ. Méx. Boletín de Fuentes para la Historia Económica de México. Centro de Estudios Históricos, El Colegio de México. México.

Bol. Hist. Ejérc. Boletín Histórico del Ejército. Montevideo.

Bol. Inst. Hist. Ravignani. Boletín del Instituto de Historia Argentina y Americana Dr. Emilio Ravignani. Facultad de Filosofía y Letras, Univ. de Buenos Aires.

Bol. Inst. Riva-Agüero. Boletín del Instituto Riva-Agüero. Pontificia Univ. Católica del Perú. Lima.

Bol. Lima. Boletín de Lima. Revista Cultural Científica. Lima.

Bol. Mus. Para. Goeldi. Boletim do Museu Paraense Emílio Goeldi. Nova série: antropologia. Conselho Nacional de Desenvolvimento Científico e Tecnológico, Instituto Nacional de Pesquisas da Amazônia. Belém, Brazil.

Bol. Nicar. Bibliogr. Doc. Boletín Nicaragüense de Bibliografía y Documentación. Biblioteca, Banco Central de Nicaragua. Managua.

Bol. Pesqui. CEDEAM. Boletim de Pesquisa da CEDEAM. Comissão de Documentação e Estudos da Amazônia, Univ. do Amazonas. Manaus, Brazil.

Boletín/Bogotá. Boletín del Museo del Oro. Banco de la República. Bogotá.

Bull. Inst. fr. étud. andin. Bulletin de l'Institut français d'études andines. Lima.

Bull. Lat. Am. Res. Bulletin of Latin American Research. Society for Latin American Studies. Oxford, England.

Cah. Am. lat. Cahiers des Amériques latines. Paris.

Can. J. Hist. Canadian Journal of History. Univ. of Saskatchewan. Saskatoon, Canada.

Can. J. Lat. Am. Caribb. Stud. Canadian Journal of Latin American and Caribbean Studies. Univ. of Ottawa. Ontario, Canada.

Caravelle/Toulouse. Caravelle. Cahiers du monde hispanique et luso-brésilien. Univ. de Toulouse, Institute d'études hispaniques, hispano-americaines et luso-brésiliennes. Toulouse, France.

Caribb. Q. Caribbean Quarterly. Univ. of the West Indies. Mona, Jamaica.

Caribena/Martinique. Caribena: cahiers d'études américanistes de la Caraïbe. Centre d'études et de recherches archéologiques (CERA). Martinique.

Cent. Estud. Puertorriq. Bull. Centro de Estudios Puertorriqueños Bulletin. Hunter College, City University of New York. New York.

Chungará/Arica. Chungará. Univ. del Norte, Depto. de Antropología. Arica, Chile.

Ciênc. Cult. Ciência e Cultura. Sociedade Brasileira para o Progresso da Ciência. São Paulo.

Ciênc. Hoje. Ciência Hoje. Sociedade Brasileira para o Progresso da Ciência. Rio de Janeiro.

CLAHR/Albuquerque. Colonial Latin American Historical Review. Spanish Colonial Research Center, Univ. of New Mexico. Albuquerque.

Clio/Sinaloa. Clio. Univ. Autónoma de Sinaloa, Escuela de Historia. Culiacán, Mexico.

Colon. Lat. Am. Rev. Colonial Latin American Review. Simon H. Rifkind Center for the Humanities, Dept. of Romance Languages, City College of New York. New York.

Comp. Stud. Soc. Hist. Comparative Studies in Society and History. Society for the Comparative Study of Society and History; Cambridge Univ. Press. London.

Conjonction/Port-au-Prince. Conjonction. Bulletin de l'Institut français d'Haïti. Port-au-Prince.

Cristianismo Soc. Cristianismo y Sociedad. Junta Latinoamericana de Iglesia y Sociedad. Montevideo.

Cuad. Acad. Cuadernos Académicos. Instituto Profesional del Maule. Talca, Chile.

Cuad. Am. Cuadernos Americanos. Editorial Cultura. México.

Cuad. CENDES. Cuadernos del CENDES. Centro de Estudios del Desarrollo, Univ. Central de Venezuela. Caracas.

Cuad. Centroam. Hist. Cuadernos Centroamericanos de Historia. Centro de Investigación de la Realidad de América Latina (CIRA). Managua.

Cuad. Esc. Dipl. Cuadernos de la Escuela Diplomática. Ministerio de Asuntos Exteriores. Madrid.

Cuad. Hist. Cuadernos de Historia. Univ. de Chile, Facultad de Humanidades y Educación, Depto. de Ciencias Históricas. Santiago.

Cuad. Hist. Moderna. Cuadernos de Historia Moderna. Facultad de Geografía e Historia, Univ. Complutense de Madrid.

Cuba. Stud. Cuban Studies. Univ. of Pittsburgh, Center for Latin American Studies. Pittsburgh, Penn.

Cult. Guatem. Cultura de Guatemala. Univ. Rafael Landívar. Guatemala.

Dados/Rio de Janeiro. Dados. Instituto Univ. de Pesquisas. Rio de Janeiro.

Data/La Paz. Data: Revista del Instituto de Estudios Andinos y Amazónicos. Instituto de Estudios Andinos y Amazónicos (INDEAA). La Paz.

Dédalo/São Paulo. Dédalo. Univ. de São Paulo, Museu de Arqueologia e Etnologia. São Paulo.

Del Caribe. Del Caribe. Casa del Caribe. Santiago, Cuba.

Desarro. Econ. Desarrollo Económico. Instituto de Desarrollo Económico y Social. Buenos Aires.

ECA/San Salvador. Estudios Centro-Americanos: ECA. Univ. Centroamericana José Simeón Cañas. San Salvador.

Econ. Soc. Hist. Neth. Economic and Social History in the Netherlands. Nederlandsch Economisch-Historisch Archief. Amsterdam.

Edad Oro. Edad de Oro. Depto. de Filología Española, Univ. Autónoma. Madrid.

Ensaios FEE. Ensaios FEE. Secretaria de Coordenacão e Planejamento. Fundação de Economia e Estatística. Porto Alegre, Brazil.

Estud. Afro-Asiát. Estudos Afro-Asiáticos. Centro de Estudos Afro-Asiáticos. Rio de Janeiro.

Estud. Cienc. Let. Estudios de Ciencias y Letras. Instituto de Filosofía, Ciencias y Letras. Montevideo.

Estud. Cult. Maya. Estudios de Cultura Maya. Centro de Estudios Mayas, Univ. Nacional Autónoma de México. México.

Estud. Cult. Náhuatl. Estudios de Cultura Náhuatl. Instituto de Investigaciones Históricas, Univ. Nacional Autónoma de México. México.

Estud. Demogr. Urb. Estudios Demográficos y Urbanos. El Colegio de México. México.

Estud. Econ./São Paulo. Estudos Econômicos. Univ. de São Paulo, Instituto de Pesquisas Econômicas. São Paulo.

Estud. Hist. Mod. Contemp. Méx. Estudios de Historia Moderna y Contemporánea de México. Univ. Nacional Autónoma de México. México.

Estud. Hist. Novohisp. Estudios de Historia Novohispana. Univ. Nacional Autónoma de México. México.

Estud. Hist./Rio de Janeiro. Estudos Históricos. Associação de Pesquisa e Documentação Histórica. Rio de Janeiro.

Estud. Hist. Soc. Econ. Am. Estudios de Historia Social y Económica de América. Univ. de Alcalá de Henares. Madrid.

Estud. Ibero-Am./Porto Alegre. Estudos Ibero-Americanos. Pontifícia Univ. Católica do Rio Grande do Sul, Depto. de História. Porto Alegre, Brazil.

Estud. Latinoam. Estudios Latinoamericanos. Academia de Ciencias de Polonia, Instituto de Historia. Wrocław.

Estud. Parag. Estudios Paraguayos. Univ. Católica Nuestra Señora de la Asunción. Asunción.

Estud. Soc. Centroam. Estudios Sociales Centroamericanos. Programa Centroamericano de Ciencias Sociales. San José.

Estudios/Guatemala. Estudios. Instituto de Investigaciones Históricas, Antropológicas, y

Arqueológicas, Univ. de San Carlos de Guatemala. Guatemala.

Ethnohistory/Society. Ethnohistory. American Society for Ethnohistory. Duke Univ., Durham, N.C.

Ethnology/Pittsburgh. Ethnology. Univ. of Pittsburgh, Penn.

Etnía/Olavarría. Etnía. Museo Etnográfico Municipal Dámaso Arce. Olavarría, Argentina.

Fénix/Lima. Fénix: Revista de la Biblioteca Nacional del Perú. Biblioteca Nacional. Lima.

Fla. Hist. Q. The Florida Historical Quarterly. The Florida Historical Society. Jacksonville, Fla.

Généal. hist. Caraïbe. Généalogie et histoire de la Caraïbe. Assn. de la généalogie et histoire de la Caraïbe. Le Pecq, France.

HAHR. Hispanic American Historical Review. Conference on Latin American History of the American Historical Assn.; Duke Univ. Press. Durham, N.C.

HISLA/Lima. HISLA. Centro Latinoamericano de Historia Económica y Social. Lima.

Hisp. Sacra. Hispania Sacra: Revista de Historia Eclesiástica de España. Centro de Estudios Históricos, Instituto Enrique Flórez. Madrid.

Hispania/Madrid. Hispania. Instituto Jerónimo Zurita, Consejo Superior de Investigaciones Científicas. Madrid.

Hist. Anthropol. History and Anthropology. Harwood Academic Publishers. New York.

Hist. Crít./Tegucigalpa. Historia Crítica. Univ. Nacional Autónoma de Honduras. Tegucigalpa.

Hist. Cult./Lima. Historia y Cultura. Museo Nacional de Historia. Lima.

Hist. Espac. Historia y Espacio: Revista de Estudios Históricos Regionales. Depto. de Historia, Univ. del Valle. Cali, Colombia.

Hist. Gaz. History Gazette. Univ. of Guyana, History Society. Turkeyen, Guyana.

Hist. Mex. Historia Mexicana. Colegio de México. México.

Hist. Parag. Historia Paraguaya. Anuario de la Academia Paraguaya de la Historia. Asunción.

Hist. Perspect. Historia & Perspectivas: Revista do Curso de Historia. Univ. Federal de Uberlândia. Uberlândia, Brazil.

Hist. Quest. Debates. História, Questões e Debates. Associação Paranaense de História. Curitiba, Brazil.

Hist. Relig. History of Religions. Univ. of Chicago. Chicago, Ill.

Hist. Soc./Río Piedras. Historia y Sociedad. Depto. de Historia, Univ. de Puerto Rico. Río Piedras.

Hist. Soc./Valencia. Historia Social. Centro de la UNED, Instituto de Historia Social. Valencia, Spain.

Hist. Workshop. History Workshop. Ruskin College, Oxford Univ., Oxford, England.

Historia/Santiago. Historia. Univ. Católica de Chile. Instituto de Historia. Santiago.

Historian/Honor Society. The Historian. Phi Alpha Theta, National Honor Society in History; Univ. of Pennsylvania. Univ. Park, Penn.

Histórica/Lima. Histórica. Pontificia Univ. Católica del Perú, Depto. de Humanidades. Lima.

Historiogr. Bibliogr. Am. Historiografía y Bibliografía Americanista. Escuela de Estudios Hispano-Americanos de Sevilla. Sevilla, Spain.

Hómines/San Juan. Hómines. Univ. Interamericana de Puerto Rico. San Juan.

Homme/Paris. L'Homme. Laboratoire d'anthropologie, Collège de France. Paris.

Horizontes/Ponce. Horizontes. Univ. Católica de Puerto Rico. Ponce.

Hoy Hist. Hoy es Historia: Revista Bimestral de Historia Nacional e Iberoamericana. Editorial Raíces. Montevideo.

Hua ch'iao hua jen li shih yen chiu. Hua ch'iao hua jen li shih yen chiu [Studies on History of Overseas Chinese and Citizens of Chinese Origin]. China Institue of History of

Overseas Chinese; China Society of History of Overseas Chinese. Beijing.

Ibero-Am. Arch. Ibero-Amerikanisches Archiv. Ibero-Amerikanisches Institut. Berlin.

Ibero-Am./Stockholm. Ibero-Americana: Nordic Journal of Latin American Studies. Institute of Latin American Studies, Univ. of Stockholm.

Int. Migr. International Migration = Migrations Internationales = Migraciones Internacionales. Intergovernmental Committee for European Migration; Research Group for European Migration Problems; International Organization for Migration. The Hague, Netherlands; Geneva, Switzerland.

Invest. Ens. Investigaciones y Ensayos. Academia Nacional de la Historia. Buenos Aires.

Islas/Santa Clara. Islas. Univ. Central de Las Villas. Santa Clara, Cuba.

J. Caribb. Hist. Journal of Caribbean History. Caribbean Univ. Press. St. Lawrence, Barbados.

J. Church State. Journal of Church and State. J.M. Dawson Studies in Church and State, Baylor Univ., Waco, Tex.

J. Econ. Hist. The Journal of Economic History. Economic History Assn.; Univ. of Kansas. Lawrence.

J. Eur. Econ. Hist. The Journal of European Economic History. Banco di Roma. Rome.

J. Fam. Hist. Journal of Family History. National Council on Family Relations. Greenwich, Conn.

J. Interam. Stud. World Aff. Journal of Interamerican Studies and World Affairs. Institute of Interamerican Studies, Univ. of Miami. Coral Gables, Fla.

J. Interdiscip. Hist. The Journal of Interdisciplinary History. The MIT Press. Cambridge, Mass.

J. Lat. Am. Lore. Journal of Latin American Lore. Univ. of California, Latin American Center. Los Angeles, Calif.

J. Lat. Am. Stud. Journal of Latin American Studies. Centers or Institutes of Latin

American Studies at the Universities of Cambridge, Glasgow, Liverpool, London, and Oxford. Cambridge Univ. Press. London.

J. Negro Hist. The Journal of Negro History. Assn. for the Study of Negro Life and History. Washington.

J. Peasant Stud. The Journal of Peasant Studies. Frank Cass & Co., London.

J. Soc. Hist. Journal of Social History. Carnegie Mellon Univ., Pittsburgh, Penn.

J. Southwest. Journal of the Southwest. Southwest Center, Univ. of Arizona. Tucson.

J. West. Journal of the West. Manhattan, Kan.

Jahrb. Gesch. Jahrbuch für Geschichte von Staat, Wirtschaft und Gesellschaft Lateinamerikas. Köln, Germany.

Jam. J. Jamaica Journal. Institute of Jamaica. Kingston.

LARR. Latin American Research Review. Latin American Research Review Board. Univ. of New Mexico, Albuquerque, N.M.

Lat. Am. Indian Lit. J. Latin American Indian Literatures Journal. Geneva College. Beaver Falls, Penn.

Lat. Am. Perspect. Latin American Perspectives. Univ. of California. Newbury Park, Calif.

Latinoamerica/Rome. Latinoamerica. Edizioni Associate. Rome.

Luso-Braz. Rev. Luso-Brazilian Review. Univ. of Wisconsin Press. Madison, Wis.

Man/London. Man. The Royal Anthropological Institute. London.

Mem. Acad. Mex. Hist. Memorias de la Academia Mexicana de la Historia. México.

Mem. Mus. Nac. Arte. Memoria del Museo Nacional de Arte. Museo Nacional de Arte. México.

Merc. Peru. Mercurio Peruano. Lima.

Mesoamérica/Antigua. Mesoamérica. Centro de Investigaciones Regionales de Mesoamérica. Antigua, Guatemala.

Mex. Stud. Mexican Studies/Estudios Mexicanos. Univ. of California, Berkeley.

Mexicon/Berlin. Mexicon. K.-F. von Flemming. Berlin, Germany.

Meyibó/Tijuana. Meyibó. Centro de Investigaciones Históricas, Univ. Autónoma de Baja California. Tijuana, Mexico.

Misc. Hist. Ecuat. Miscelánea Histórica Ecuatoriana: Revista de Investigaciones Históricas de los Museos del Banco Central del Ecuador. Museos del Banco Central del Ecuador. Quito.

Mon. Rev. Monthly Review. New York.

Montalbán/Caracas. Montalbán. Univ. Católica Andrés Bello, Facultad de Humanidades y Educación, Institutos Humanísticos de Investigación. Caracas.

Natl. Geogr. Mag. National Geographic Magazine. National Geographic Society. Washington.

Nav. Hist. Naval History. US Naval Institute. Annapolis, Md.

New Repub. The New Republic. Washington.

Nieuwe West-Indische Gids. Nieuwe West-Indische Gids. Martinus Nijhoff. The Hague.

Nóesis/Juárez. Nóesis. Univ. Autónoma de Ciudad Juárez. Juárez, Mexico.

Noroeste Méx. Noroeste de México. Centro Regional Sonora, INAH. Hermosillo, Mexico.

Not. Bibliogr. Hist. Notícia Bibliográfica e Histórica. Depto. de História, Pontifícia Univ. Católica de Campinas. Campinas, Brazil.

Novos Estud. CEBRAP. Novos Estudos CEBRAP. Centro Brasileiro de Análise e Planejamento. São Paulo.

Op. Cit./Río Piedras. Op. Cit.: Boletín del Centro de Investigaciones Históricas. Depto. de Historia, Facultad de Humanidades, Univ. de Puerto Rico. Río Piedras.

Pac. Hist. Rev. Pacific Historical Review. Univ. of California Press. Los Angeles and Berkeley.

Palabra Hombre. La Palabra y el Hombre. Univ. Veracruzana. Xalapa, Mexico.

Pap. Casa Chata. Papeles de la Casa Chata. Centro de Investigaciones y Estudios Superiores en Antropología Social. México.

Past Present. Past and Present. London.

Polít. Soc./Guatemala. Política y Sociedad. Univ. de San Carlos de Guatemala, Instituto de Investigaciones Políticas y Sociales. Guatemala.

Population/Paris. Population. Institut national d'études démographiques. Paris.

Port. Stud. Portuguese Studies. Dept. of Portuguese, King's College. London.

Prínc. Viana. Príncipe de Viana. Institución Príncipe de Viana, Gobierno de Navarra. Pamplona, Spain.

Publ. Inst. Estud. Iberoam. Publicaciones del Instituto de Estudios Iberoamericanos. Instituto de Estudios Iberamericanos. Buenos Aires.

Punto Coma. Punto y Coma. Univ. del Sagrado Corazón. Santurce, Puerto Rico.

Quad. Stor. Quaderni Storici. Facoltà di Economia e Commercio, Istituto di Storia e Sociologia. Ancona, Italy.

Quinto Cent. Quinto Centenario. Depto. de Historia de América, Univ. Complutense de Madrid.

Rábida/Huelva. Rábida. Patronato Provincial del V Centenario del Descubrimiento. Huelva, Spain.

Race Cl. Race & Class. Institute of Race Relations; The Transnational Institute. London.

Radic. Hist. Rev. Radical History Review. Mid-Atlantic Radical Historians' Organization. New York.

Relaciones/Zamora. Relaciones. El Colegio de Michoacán. Zamora, Mexico.

Res Gesta. Res Gesta. Instituto de Historia, Facultad de Derecho y Ciencias Sociales, Univ. Católica Argentina. Rosario, Argentina.

Rev. Acad. Colomb. Cienc. Revista de la Academia Colombiana de Ciencias Exactas, Físicas y Naturales. Ministerio de Educación Nacional. Bogotá.

Rev. Agust. Revista Agustiniana. Madrid.

Rev. Andin. Revista Andina. Centro Bartolomé de las Casas. Cusco, Peru.

Rev. Antioq. Econ. Desarro. Revista Antioqueña de Economía y Desarrollo.

Fundación para la Investigación y la Cultura. Medellín, Colombia.

Rev. Antropol./São Paulo. Revista de Antropologia. Univ. de São Paulo, Faculdade de Filosofia, Letras e Ciências Humanas; Associação Brasileira de Antropologia. São Paulo.

Rev. Arch. Nac. Revista del Archivo Nacional. San José, Costa Rica.

Rev. Arch. Nac. Hist. Azuay. Revista del Archivo Nacional de Historia, Sección del Azuay. Casa de la Cultura Ecuatoriana, Núcleo del Azuay. Cuenca, Ecuador.

Rev. Bibl. Nac. José Martí. Revista de la Biblioteca Nacional José Martí. La Habana.

Rev. Bibl. Nac./Montevideo. Revista de la Biblioteca Nacional. Ministerio de Educación y Cultura. Montevideo.

Rev. Bras. Estud. Polít. Revista Brasileira de Estudos Políticos. Univ. de Minas Gerais. Belo Horizonte, Brazil.

Rev. Bras. Estud. Popul. Revista Brasileira de Estudos de População. Associação Brasileira de Estudos Populacionais. São Paulo.

Rev. Bras. Hist. Revista Brasileira de História. Associação Nacional dos Professores Universitários de História (ANPUH). São Paulo.

Rev. Cent. Estud. Av. La Revista del Centro de Estudios Avanzados de Puerto Rico y el Caribe. San Juan.

Rev. Chil. Humanid. Revista Chilena de Humanidades. Facultad de Filosofía, Humanidades y Educación, Univ. de Chile. Santiago.

Rev. Ciclos. Revista Ciclos en la Historia, Economía y la Sociedad. Fundación de Investigaciones Históricas, Económicas y Sociales, Facultad de Ciencias Económicas, Univ. de Buenos Aires. Buenos Aires.

Rev. Ciênc. Hist. Revista de Ciências Históricas. Univ. Portucalense. Porto, Portugal.

Rev. Cienc. Soc./Río Piedras. Revista de Ciencias Sociales. Univ. de Puerto Rico, Colegio de Ciencias Sociales. Río Piedras.

Rev. Colomb. Antropol. Revista Colombiana de Antropología. Ministerio de Educación Nacional, Instituto Colombiano de Antropología. Bogotá.

Rev. Complut. Hist. Am. Revista Complutense de Historia de América. Facultad de Geografía e Historia, Univ. Complutense de Madrid.

Rev. Cuba. Cienc. Soc. Revista Cubana de Ciencias Sociales. Centro de Estudios Filosóficos, Academia de Ciencias de Cuba. La Habana.

Rev. Dep. Hist./Belo Horizonte. Revista do Departamento de História. Univ. Federal de Minas Gerais. Belo Horizonte, Brazil.

Rev. Dep. Hist./Tucumán. Revista del Departamento de Historia. Univ. Nacional de Tucumán, Facultad de Filosofía y Letras. Argentina.

Rev. Ecuat. Hist. Econ. Revista Ecuatoriana de Historia Económica. Banco Central del Ecuador, Centro de Investigación y Cultura. Quito.

Rev. Eme-Eme. Revista Eme-Eme. Univ. Católica Madre y Maestra. Santiago de los Caballeros, Dominican Republic.

Rev. Esp. Antropol. Am. Revista Española de Antropología Americana. Facultad de Geografía e Historia. Univ. Complutense de Madrid.

Rev. Eur. Revista Europea de Estudios Latinoamericanos y del Caribe = European Review of Latin American and Caribbean Studies. Center for Latin American Research and Documentation; Royal Institute of Linguistics and Anthropology. Amsterdam.

Rev. Filos./San José. Revista de Filosofía. Univ. de Costa Rica. San José.

Rev. fr. hist. Outre-mer. Revue française d'histoire d'Outre-mer. Société de l'histoire des colonies françaises. Paris.

Rev. Hist. Am. Revista de Historia de América. Instituto Panamericano de Geografía e Historia, Comisión de Historia. México.

Rev. Hist. Am. Argent. Revista de Historia Americana y Argentina. Univ. Nacional de Cuyo, Instituto de Historia. Mendoza, Argentina.

Rev. Hist. Econ. Revista de Historia Económica. Centro de Estudios Constitucionales, Univ. Carlos III. Madrid.

Rev. Hist./Heredia. Revista de Historia. Univ. Nacional de Costa Rica, Escuela de Historia. Heredia, Costa Rica.

Rev. Hist./Managua. Revista de Historia. Instituto de Historia de Nicaragua. Managua.

Rev. Hist. Mil. Revista de Historia Militar. Servicio Histórico Militar. Madrid.

Rev. Hist. Naval. Revista de Historia Naval. Instituto de Historia y Cultura Naval Armada Española. Madrid.

Rev. Hist./Neuquén. Revista de Historia. Depto. de Historia, Facultad de Humanidades, Univ. Nacional de Comahue. Neuquén, Argentina.

Rev. hist./Paris. Revue historique. Presses Univ. de France. Paris.

Rev. Hist./San José. Revista de Historia. Centro de Investigaciones Históricas, Univ. de Costa Rica. San José.

Rev. Hist./San Juan. Revista de Historia. Asociación Histórica Puertorriqueña. San Juan.

Rev. Hist./São Paulo. Revista de História. Univ. de São Paulo, Faculdade de Filosofia, Letras e Ciências Humanas, Depto. de História. São Paulo.

Rev. Indias. Revista de Indias. Consejo Superior de Investigaciones Científicas, Instituto Gonzalo Fernández de Oviedo. Madrid.

Rev. Inst. Estud. Bras. Revista do Instituto de Estudos Brasileiros. Univ. de São Paulo, Instituto de Estudos Brasileiros. São Paulo.

Rev. Inst. Hist. Geogr. São Paulo. Revista do Instituto Histórico e Geográfico de São Paulo. São Paulo.

Rev. Interam. Bibliogr. Revista Interamericana de Bibliografía. Organization of American States. Washington.

Rev. Junta Prov. Hist. Córdoba. Revista de la Junta Provincial de Historia de Córdoba. Córdoba, Argentina.

Rev. Juríd. Univ. P.R. Revista Jurídica de la Universidad de Puerto Rico. Escuela de Derecho, Univ. de Puerto Rico. Río Piedras.

Rev. Mar. Revista de Marina. La Armada de Chile. Valparaíso.

Rev. Mex. Cienc. Polít. Soc. Revista Mexicana de Ciencias Políticas y Sociales.

Facultad de Ciencias Políticas y Sociales, Univ. Nacional Autónoma de México. México.

Rev. Music. Puertorriq. Revista Musical Puertorriqueña. Instituto de Cultura Puertorriqueña. San Juan.

Rev. Occident. Revista de Occidente. Madrid.

Rev. Parag. Sociol. Revista Paraguaya de Sociología. Centro Paraguayo de Estudios Sociológicos. Asunción.

Rev. Paramillo. Revista Paramillo. Centro de Estudios Interdisciplinarios, Univ. Católica de Táchira. San Cristóbal, Venezuela.

Rev. Rev. Interam. Revista/Review Interamericana. Inter-American Univ. Press. Hato Rey, Puerto Rico.

Rev. Soc. haïti. Revue de la Société haïtienne d'histoire et géographie. Port-au-Prince.

Rev. Tiempo Espacio. Revista Tiempo y Espacio. Depto. de Historia y Geografía, Campus Chillán, Univ. del Bío-Bío. Chile.

Rev. Univ./Alcalá. Revista de la Universidad de Alcalá. Univ. de Alcalá de Henares. Alcalá de Henares, Spain.

RIEV/San Sebastián. Revista Internacional de Estudios Vascos. Sociedad de Estudios Vascos. San Sebastián, Spain.

Runa/Buenos Aires. Runa. Archivo para las Ciencias del Hombre; Univ. de Buenos Aires, Facultad de Filosofía y Letras, Instituto de Antropología.

Santiago/Cuba. Santiago. Univ. de Oriente. Santiago, Cuba.

SECOLAS Ann. SECOLAS Annals. Southeastern Conference on Latin American Studies; West Georgia College. Carrollton, Ga.

Secuencia/México. Secuencia. Instituto Mora. México.

Siglo XIX. Siglo XIX. Facultad de Filosofía y Letras, Univ. Autónoma de Nuevo León. Monterrey, Mexico.

Signos Univ. Signos Universitarios: Revista de la Universidad del Salvador. Univ. del Salvador. Buenos Aires.

Signs/Chicago. Signs. The Univ. of Chicago Press. Chicago, Ill.

Sínt. Nova Fase. Síntese Nova Fase. Belo Horizonte, Brazil.

Síntesis/Madrid. Síntesis. Asociación de Investigación y Especialización sobre Temas Latinoamericanos. Madrid.

Slavery Abolit. Slavery and Abolition. Frank Cass & Co., Ltd., London.

Stud. Emigr. Studi Emigrazione. Centro Studi Emigrazione. Rome.

Studia/Lisboa. Studia. Centro de Estudos Históricos Ultramarinos. Lisboa.

Supl. Antropol. Suplemento Antropológico. Univ. Católica de Nuestra Señora de la Asunción, Centro de Estudos Antropológicos. Asunción.

SWI Forum. SWI Forum voor Kunst, Kultuur en Wetenschop. De Stichting. Paramaribo, Suriname.

Todo es Hist. Todo es Historia. Buenos Aires.

Torre/Río Piedras. La Torre. Univ. de Puerto Rico. Río Piedras.

Trace/México. Trace. Centre d'études mexicaines et centraméricaines. México.

Transition/Guyana. Transition. Institute of Development Studies, Univ. of Guyana. Georgetown, Guyana.

Travessia/Florianópolis. Travessia. Univ. Federal de Santa Catarina. Florianópolis, Brazil.

Univ. La Habana. Universidad de La Habana. La Habana.

Universidad/Santa Fe. La Universidad. Univ. Nacional del Litoral. Santa Fe, Argentina.

Veritas/Porto Alegre. Veritas. Pontifícia Univ. Católica do Rio Grande do Sul. Porto Alegre, Brazil.

Vuelta/México. Vuelta. México.

Wampum/Leiden. Wampum. Archeologisch Centrum. Leiden, The Netherlands.

West. Hist. Q. The Western Historical Quarterly. Western History Assn.; Utah State Univ., Logan, Utah.

Yearbook/CLAG. Yearbook. Conference of Latin Americanist Geographers; Ball State Univ., Muncie, Ind.

Z. Lat.am. Wien. Zeitschrift für Lateinamerika Wien. Österreichisches Lateinamerika-Institut. Vienna.

LITERATURE

SPANISH AMERICA
General

SARA CASTRO-KLAREN, *Professor of Hispanic and Italian Studies, The Johns Hopkins University, with the assistance of Laura Beard*

IN THE LAST TWO YEARS we have seen a flowering of the field. Several very important books have been published in Latin America, the US, and England. A distinguishing feature of the publications included in this selection is the remarkable quality and number of the books published in English, with Cambridge University Press assuming a leading role.

Interest in the "novela del dictador" continues to elicit publications which attempt periodization and groupings according to narrative rhetoric and theme. The new historical novel commands a great deal of attention. Fernando Ainsa's *La reescritura de la historia* (item **3460**) is an in-depth and comprehensive treatment of the new historical novel which takes up many of the same issues central to the discussions on parody and testimony. All the texts in question are concerned with the inscription of the forgotten voices of women and other subaltern subjects, and degradations of foundational myths of nationality. Several articles explore the double strand woven in the relationship of genre and textuality. Others such as George Yúdice (item **3514**) and Geisdorfel-Feal (item **3468**) ponder the problematic readership that postmodern theory deploys for texts authored by women such as Domitila de Chungara. Carlos Rincón writes a capital essay on the problematic fit of the narrative of the "boom" and of John Barth's appropriation of Borges and García Márquez for his characterizations of postmodernism (item **3509**).

Interest in women writers also continues to produce a large body of research. Interviews with women writers grow in length, variety, and number. García Pinto's collection of long, frank, and thoughtful interviews is probably the best of its kind (item **3474**). Too numerous to mention individually, the articles in journals or collected in books explore women's diverse relations to political, economic, and family problems. One of the most interesting of these approaches is Mary Louise Pratt's consideration of women in dialogue with masculinist ideologies (item **3508**). *El placer de la palabra* is a welcome anthology of texts which celebrate the positive power of eroticism in women's fiction (item **3507**).

The outstanding feature of this chapter is the significance of the books published in the last three years. Gordon Brotherston has written a masterpiece on the literatures of the American Indians, a book that the field has been striving towards for many years and which has finally found its proper form in this comprehensive, informed, intelligent, and sensitive study of the classics of the Fourth World (item **3462**). Martin Lienhard's history of the oral trace in texts authored by "indios letrados" also accomplishes a goal towards which the entire field has been moving (item **3493**). In the modern period we find that books by Sylvia Molloy on autobiography (item **3503**), Roberto González Echevarría on the archive of the Latin American novel (item **3478**), Carlos Alonso on the "novela de la tierra" (item **3461**), and Lucille Kerr on the "death" of the author (item **3487**) not only deal with their subjects keenly but also provide theoretical frameworks which attempt to account for the particular character and success of fiction written in Spanish America. Though persuasive and well researched, these theories or interpretations of origins are not all compatible with one another. Yet, each one of these books will become a landmark in the field. Anyone with an interest in Latin American cultural history should take the time to engage these theoretically sophisticated books.

3459 Agosin, Marjorie. La literatura y los derechos humanos: aproximaciones, lecturas y encuentros. San José: Editorial Universitaria Centroamericana, 1989. 186 p.: bibl. (Col. Signo. Col. Séptimo Día)

Collection of essays intended to establish a canon of fundamental literary texts about torture and violence in Latin America so that "la literatura de los derechos humanos o los derechos humanos de la literatura no caigan en los sistemas institucionalizados de la crítica literaria" (p. 11). Essays are personal dialogues between Agosín and the texts.

3460 Ainsa, Fernando. La reescritura de la historia en la nueva narrativa latinoameriana. (*Cuad. Am.,* 5:4, julio/agosto 1991, p. 13–31)

Surveys more than 20 new historical novels in Spanish America and divides them into four types: 1) new historical novels that offer a critical reading of established historiographical discourse (e.g., Marta Mercader's *Juana Manuela, mucha mujer,* or José Ibargoyen Islas' *La noche de espadas*); 2) texts that have abolished epic or historiographical distances in order to imitate linguistic and ideological structures of period in which novel is set (e.g., Homero Aridjis' *1492: vida y tiempos de Juan Cabezón de Castilla* and Juan José Saer's *El Entenado*); 3) works in which there is a reexamination of the myth of nationality (e.g., Fernando del Paso's *José Trigo* on the Mexican Revolution); and 4) novels in which historicism and documentary sources are allowed free play (e.g., Edgardo Rodríguez Juliá's *La renuncia del héroe Baltazar*).

3461 Alonso, Carlos J. The Spanish American regional novel: modernity and autochthony. Cambridge; New York: Cambridge Univ. Press, 1990. 212 p.: bibl., ill. (Cambridge studies in Latin American and Iberian literature; 2)

Offers systematic and brilliant critique of the concept of "indigenous" literature. Redefines our understanding of several key texts in the "novela de la tierra:" *Don Segundo Sombra, Doña Bárbara,* and *La vorágine.* Shows that the creation of an autochthonous text produces the critical displacement of the author. Should be consulted by all those interested in cultural history and the formation of regional and national identities and literatures. Carefully researched, clearly written, cogently argued.

3462 Brotherston, Gordon. Book of the fourth world: reading the Native Americas through their literature. Cambridge; New York: Cambridge Univ. Press, 1992. 478 p., 24 p. of plates: bibl., ill. (some col.), index, maps.

Comprehensive and authoritative study of the epistemology of the ancient American civilizations. Brotherston begins with a consideration of language and its several textual instances—including writing—among the Maya, the Aztecs, and in the Tahuantinsuyo. His study of maps and other spatial representations as well as configurations of time goes well beyond the customary calendric and cosmological descriptions. One of the most salient aspects of the book is the attempt to bring together, in comparative perspective, the learning which diverse disciplines—linguistics, archaeology, anthropology, narratology, ethnohistory, and art—have accumulated on the ancient American cultures. This book presents a complex and modern understanding of the intricate rationalities that organized the knowledge and cultural practices of this hemisphere's ancient peoples.

3463 Calviño Iglesias, Julio. La novela del dictador en Hispanoamérica. Madrid: Ediciones Cultura Hispánica: Instituto de Cooperación Iberoamericana, 1985. 255 p.: bibl., ill.

Quick syntheses of numerous novels form this encyclopedia on the "narrative of power" in Latin America. Organized by country, book includes a general history with a Marxist interpretation. Most extensive discussions are on Argentina, Venezuela, Ecuador, and Mexico.

3464 Carilla, Emilio. Pedro Henríquez Ureña, signo de América. S.l.: Univ. Nacional Pedro Henrúez Ureña, 1988. 151 p.

Chronological overview of life and works of Pedro Henríquez Ureña written in laudatory, generalizing, and personalistic style. Cursory description of the *maestro's* literary criticism and linguistic studies, followed by better developed account of his linguistic analyses of Alarcón and Andalusian Spanish in Latin America.

3465 Congreso Internacional de Literatura Femenina Latinoamericana, *1st, Santiago, 1987*. Escribir en los bordes. Recopilación de Carmen Berenguer et al. Santiago: Editorial Cuarto Propio, 1990. 388 p.: bibl. (Col. Bajo palabra)

Publishes texts from "el evento literario más importante producido en Chile bajo dictadura" (p. 7), which attempted to open a space for women to reflect on the construction of other political and cultural identities. Posits crucial questions about women, writing, and power. Similar conference papers are also published in *Libertad, creación e identidad* (Santo Domingo: Univ. Autónoma de Santo Domingo, 1989).

3466 El cuento feminista latinoamericano. Recopilación de Adriana Santa Cruz y Viviana Erazo. Santiago: Fempress, 1988. 138 p. (Antología Fempress)

Collected stories by women writers, mostly from Chile and Venezuela, intended to provide a space for women's voices. Good source for "discovering" new writers.

Dorfman, Ariel. Some write to the future: essays on contemporary Latin American fiction. See item **5059.**

3467 Encuentro de Escritores Judíos Latinoamericanos, *3rd, São Paulo, 1990*. El imaginario judío en la literatura de América

Latina: visión y realidad; relatos, ensayos, memorias y otros textos. Edición de Patricia Finzi, Eliahu Toker y Marcos Faerman. Buenos Aires: Grupo Editorial Shalom, 1993? 205 p.: bibl., ill., map.

En la bellísima edición que caracteriza las producciones de Patricia Finzi (Grupo Shalom), recoge los textos presentados en el encuentro. Atraviesa los testimonios de la inmigración, las experiencias agrícolas y la formación de los barrios judíos en Argentina, Brasil y México para luego pasar a una máxima concentración en la literatura y a las relaciones con y desde América Latina con el ser judío y con el Estado de Israel. Entre otros, cabe destacar los textos de Leonardo Senkman, Margo Glantz, Moacyr Scliar, Florinda Goldberg, Santiago Kovadloff y Paúl Warszawski. [S. Sosnowski]

3468 Feal, Rosemary Geisdorfer. Feminism and Afro-Hispanism: the double bind. (*Afro-Hisp. Rev.*, 10:1, Jan. 1991, p. 25–29)

Discusses common assumptions in theories of alterity which bridge the study of race and gender. Analyzes moments of unease and tension between the demands of white and black feminism. Points out that the identity search forces the post-colonial subject into an I/not-I dichotomy that nevertheless preserves the "fantasy" of a "real" self. This dichotomy requires further examination. Recommended. Also worthwhile is author's "Feminist interventions in the race for theory: neither black nor white" (*Afro-Hispanic Review*, Vol. 10, No. 3, Sept. 1991, p. 11–20).

Ferré, Rosario. El árbol y sus sombras. See item **3862.**

3469 Foster, David William. Gay and lesbian themes in Latin American writing. Austin: Univ. of Texas Press, 1991. 178 p.: bibl., index. (The Texas Pan American series)

Studies the semiotics of homosexuality and its representation in literary texts which are often more about male homosexuality than lesbianism. Good bibliography.

3470 Franco, Jean. Gender, death, and resistance: facing the ethical vacuum. (*in* Fear at the edge: State terror and resistance in Latin America. Berkeley: Univ. of California Press, 1992, p. 104–118)

States that what distinguishes the repressive military governments of the 1960s-70s from other dictatorships is their extirpation of revolutionary politics and abolition of heroic charisma. One of the techniques for abolishing charisma was the "feminization" of torture—women were submitted to torture and men were tortured in the testicles and other parts symbolic of masculinity. Resistence and endurance were possible before these practices. Argentina's "Madres de Mayo" turned out to be the most adept group in challenging the power of the State to destroy its citizens by showing that death did not intimidate them. These women also "subverted the boundaries between public and private and challenged the assumption that mothering belonged only to the private sphere." Recommended for those interested in feminist theory and the politics of terror.

3471 Fuentes, Carlos. Valiente mundo nuevo: épica, utopía y mito en la novela hispanoamericana. Madrid: Mondadori España, 1990. 288 p. (Narrativa Mondadori)

Includes essays on Bernal Díaz del Castillo, Rómulo Gallegos, Mariano Azuela, Lezama Lima, and Julio Cortázar. Provocative introduction in which Vico's cyclical philosophy of history and Bakhtin's theory of heteroglossia are seen as the most appropriate modes for understanding the past. Fuentes also writes with ease on the current postmodern debates and the position of Latin American intellectuals within them. Regards cultural criticism as a promising approach and challenge to trends towards global cultural homogeneity. *Valiente mundo* confirms Fuentes as a prolific writer and voracious and acute reader of history, philosophy, and literature.

3472 Galeano, Eduardo H. El descubrimiento de América que todavía no fue y otros escritos. Barcelona: Editorial Laia, 1986. 131 p. (El Barco de papel)

Collection of short essays (1976–86) covers three main topics: 1) writer and "culture;" 2) the Nicaraguan revolution; and 3) the "discovery" of America. Throughout Galeano argues against and reveals the poverty of the "news" and "culture" dispensed by mass means of communication. Points to the self-censure that masks cultural imperialism and to the ever present possibilities of collusion between writing and the power of the State. Writer's obligation is to "ofrecer testimonio de nuestros tiempos." Calls for a "cultura de resistencia" against the homogeneous spread of metropolitan consumerist values.

Most original section is series of snap-shots of his visit to Nicaragua in early days of the Revolution. Conveys feeling and reasons of common people's hope for change as seen in the wisdom and courage of Jesús, the bricklayer; Dennis, the volunteer soldier; and Nora, the seamstress. Recommended to those interested in cultural criticism and testimonial literature.

3473 Gallagher, Michael Paul. Liberation in Latin American fiction. (*Studies/Dublin*, 79:315, Autumn 1990, p. 281–288)

Critica el manejo sutil e indirecto de los temas de injusticia y opresión en obras de escritores latinoamericanos. Menciona a novelistas importantes pero no de fama internacional. Intenta establecer un paralelismo entre la liberación religiosa y la literaria mediante el cual se definiría la verdadera identidad latinoamericana. [D. Gerdes]

3474 García Pinto, Magdalena. Women writers of Latin America: intimate histories. Translated by Trudy Balch and Magdalena García Pinto. Illuminations by Karen Parker Lears. Austin: Univ. of Texas Press, 1991. 258 p.: bibl., ill., index. (The Texas Pan American series)

Long, frank, and thoughtful interviews with Isabel Allende, Albalucía Angel, Rosario Ferré, Margo Glantz, Sylvia Molloy, Elvira Orpheé, Elena Poniatowska, Marta Traba, Luisa Valenzuela, and Ida Vitale discussing their childhoods, countries, readings, and writings. Interviews include occasional pieces of their texts. Recommended.

3475 Georgescu, Paul Alexandru. Nueva visión sistémica de la narrativa hispanoamericana. Caracas: Academia Nacional de la Historia: Monte Avila Editores, 1989. 367 p.: bibl. (Estudios)

Starts with Ricardo Palma and ends with López Michelsen. Dedicates long chapters to Gallegos, Borges, Asturias, Sábato, Cortázar, and Vargas Llosa. Attempts to evolve a comprehensive theory of the Spanish American novel capable of going beyond present fragmentation of critical studies. Based on Lucian Goldman's genetic structuralism, author attempts a global reading that perceives the novel as a response to social phenomena.

3476 Goić, Cedomil. Historia y crítica de la literatura hispanoamericana. v. 1, Epoca colonial. v. 2, Del romanticismo al modernismo. v. 3, Epoca contemporánea. Barcelona: Editorial Crítica, Grupo Editorial Grijalbo, 1988–1991. 3 v.: bibl., indexes. (Páginas de filología)

Consists of three voluminous tomes of primary and critical introductory material to the received canon of Spanish American literature. Prepared with peninsular Spanish students in mind, work can also be consulted by American undergraduates in search of specific introductions to periods or authors. Vol. 3 covers the "boom." Contemporary writers such as Eduardo Galeano, José Emilio Pacheco, Poniatowska, and most women writers are not included. Nevertheless, this manual is recommended as a point of departure.

3477 González, Eduardo. The monstered self: narratives of death and performance in Latin American fiction. Durham: Duke Univ. Press, 1992. 275 p.: bibl., index.

Explores grounds of reciprocity and transfiguration in characters who imagine themselves between life and death. Main concern of book is the character of dying and the perfomance of death. Each chapter is an autonomous unit sustained by theme and style. Book is of special interest to close followers of Jacques Lacan.

3478 González Echevarría, Roberto. Myth and archive: a theory of Latin American narrative. Cambridge; New York: Cambridge Univ. Press, 1990. 245 p.: bibl., index. (Cambridge studies in Latin American and Iberian literature; 3)

Traces "origins" of Latin American narrative to the Spanish legal archive. Argues that the modern novel is born with Spanish picaresque which imitates the confession of a criminal interrogated by legal authorities. Author posits three fundamental movements for Latin American narrative: 1) chronicles of the conquest which mimic the rhetoric of legal documents, especially the *relación;* 2) late 18th- and 19th-century travel literature which proposes the "scientific" (positivist) model for the representation of history and society; and 3) anthropology and its study of myth. Carefully argued, meticulously researched and provocative theory of narrative and its development in Latin America. Provides powerful readings of Garcilaso de la Vega, Inca, García Márquez, Alejo Carpentier, and Euclides da Cunha. A landmark in Latin American studies. Recommended to all those interested in the novel, discursive theory, and cultural history.

3479 Gugelberger, Georg and **Michael Kearney.** Voices for the voiceless: testimonial literature in Latin America. (*Lat. Am. Perspect.,* 18:3, Summer 1991, p. 3–14, bibl.)

Defines testimonial literature and identifies basic themes of a literature "produced by subaltern peoples on the periphery or the margin of the colonial situation" (p. 4). Argues that we cannot understand Latin America without listening to the growing number of voices that speak through the genre of testimonial literature. Recommended.

3480 Gutiérrez-Girardot, Bettina. Prostituierte in der lateinamerikanischen Literatur: das Bild der Prostituierten in der lateinamerikanischen Literatur der Jahrhundertwende. Frankfurt am Main; New York: P. Lang, 1990. 200 p.: bibl. (Hispanistische Studien, 0170–8570; 21)

From a social history perspective, Gutiérrez examines eight fictional works (published 1880–1920) and authors' treatment of professional prostitution. Concludes that fictionalized fate of prostitutes became authors' vehicle for social criticism, reflecting their interpretation of morality and justice and the perceived conflict between tradition and modernity. [C. Converse]

3481 Gutiérrez Girardot, Rafael. Temas y problemas de una historia social de la literatura hispanoamericana. Bogotá: Ediciones Cave Canem, 1989. 100 p. (Serie Ensayos)

Consists of four lectures (Bogotá, 1987). Author presents his ideas on the social history of art and literature in Latin America. Follows Theodore Adorno and the French Annals School and focuses on the history of institutions and social groups. Proposes the idea of "casa grande"—as in Gilberto Freire's *Casa grande e senzala* (1933)—as an example of the type of concept that should be applied to revamp the social history of literature. Worthwhile and thought provoking.

3482 Homenaje a Alejandro Losada. Edición de José Morales Saravia. Lima: Latinoamericana Editores, 1986. 270 p.: bibl. (La Literatura en la sociedad de América Latina)

Collection of essays by Losada's students in Berlin provides significant demonstration of collective methodology based on his theory of literature as social praxis. Includes several monographic studies, but of particular interest are essays that encompass cultural periods, movements, and their production, such as the essay on the Argentine magazine *Sur* and another on the Cuban detective novel.

3483 Homenaje a Alfredo A. Roggiano: en este aire de América. Edición de Keith McDuffie y Rose S. Minc. Pittsburgh, Pa.: Instituto Internacional de Literatura Iberoamericana, 1990. 510 p.: bibl., ill.

Testimonial by Ernesto Sábato followed by essays on Latin American literature from the colonial period by critics from around the world.

3484 In the feminine mode: essays on Hispanic women writers. Edited by Noël Maureen Valis and Carol Maier. Lewisburg, Penn.: Bucknell Univ. Press; London; Cranbury, NJ: Associated Univ. Presses, 1990. 284 p.: bibl., index.

Compilation of thoughtful essays on strategies of representation and survival of Hispanic women writers are "a gift for Marina Romero," and a gift for all readers as well. Perceptive essays on Spanish and Latin American writers, their explorations into writing a feminine identity, and ways their texts have been read by critics. Recommended.

3485 Jackson, Richard. The emergence of Afro-Hispanic literature. (*Afro-Hisp. Rev.*, 10:3, Sept. 1991, p. 4–10)

Documents steady growth of Afro-Hispanic texts and their continued inclusion into the canon. Highlights publication of Zapata Olivella's *Changó, el gran putas* (1983). Regards this novel as the epic of an Afro-centric narrative which reconstructs the experience of slavery. Novel provides reevaluation of role slaves played in their own liberation. Jackson also calls attention to fact that most productive area of Afro-centric texts today is Central America. Should be read in tandem with Edward Mullen's "The Emergence of Afro-Hispanic Poetry" (in *Hispanic Review* Autumn 1988).

3486 Jitrik, Noé. Temas de teoría: el trabajo crítico y la crítica literaria. Tlahuapan, Mexico: Premià, 1987. 117 p.: bibl., ill. (La Red de Jonás. Estudios; 31)

Includes essays written between 1974–84 while Jitrik lived in Mexico. Attempts to explain the theory implicit in the critic's own

scholarly work. Major topics are reader response theory, relations between psychoanalysis and literature, and politics and literature.

3487 Kerr, Lucille. Reclaiming the author: figures and fictions from Spanish America. Durham: Duke Univ. Press, 1992. 228 p.: bibl., index.

On the basis of a casual (?) or thoughtful (?) remark—"the Spanish Americans are actually doing what the French are only talking about"—Kerr writes a probing book on the status of the author in narrative theory and in specific fictions by Donoso, Poniatowska/Palancares, Fuentes, and Cortázar. Examines deeply the author-authority relation, dynamics of fictional author in author figures such as Vargas Llosa, and paradox of author's "death." Makes good case for notion that fiction writers in Spanish America anticipated the French philosophers of the postmodern. Elegantly written. Recommended to both the specialist and general reader.

3488 Knives and angels: women writers in Latin America. Edited by Susan Bassnett. London; Atlantic Highlands, N.J.: Zed Books, 1990. 202 p.: bibl., index.

Various authors look at women writers and filmmakers in Latin America, trace roots of women's contributions to Latin American culture, and explore current and future directions of their writings. For additional essays on women writers (e.g., Cristina Peri Rossi, Julieta Campos, Luisa Valenzuela, Isabel Allende, Clarice Lispector) see *Splintering darkness* (Pittsburgh: Latin American Literary Review Press, 1990).

3489 Kushigian, Julia Alexis. Orientalism in the Hispanic literary tradition: in dialogue with Borges, Paz, and Sarduy. Albuquerque, N.M.: Univ. of New Mexico Press, 1991. 147 p.: bibl., index.

Studies "Hispanic" orientalism. Relies on Spain's territorial and cultural relations with Arabs before their loss of Granada and subsequent expulsion from the peninsula. Extends Spanish pattern to the study of Sarduy, Borges, and Paz. Differs from Edward Said's landmark study on orientalism in France and England by dismissing the fundamental knowledge/power analysis developed by Said. Book proposes idea that "Hispanic" orientalism blends the oppositions that Said identifies and deploys.

3490 Kuteĭshchikova, Vera and **Lev Ospovat.**
Ensayos sobre novelistas latinoamericanos. Prólogo de Rogelio Rodríguez Coronel.
Traducción de Anna Guinzburg, Alfredo Caballero y Viera Piñón. La Habana: Editorial
Arte y Literatura, 1987. 433 p.: bibl. (Bolsili-
bros A.L.)
Conventional introductory overview of
Asturias, Carpentier, Rulfo, Roa Bastos, and
García Márquez emphasizes socio-historical
context of their works and includes much
biographical information. Fair comparative
section on Carpentier's *Los pasos perdidos*
and Mann's *Doctor Faustus.*

3491 Lasso, Luis Ernesto. Señas de identidad
en la cuentística hispanoamericana.
Bogotá: Divulgación Cultural, Univ. Nacional
de Colombia, 1990. 369 p.: bibl. (Serie Identidad y cultura; 1)
Systematic study of the "great masters" of the Latin American short story intended to search for, affirm, and reveal the
cultural identity of Latin America. Includes
no women.

3492 Libertella, Héctor. Las sagradas escrituras. Buenos Aires: Editorial Sudamericana, 1993. 283 p.: bibl., index.
La provocación y la heterodoxia—
también la propuesta contrapelo—identifican
las lúcidas aproximaciones de Libertella a la
literatura. Textos breves e incisivos, en los
que abundan los interrogantes, abren camino
a las propuestas de Roa Bastos, Paz, Lezama
Lima, Elizondo, Lihn; atraviesan la grafía de
las vanguardias y los topetazos de escrituras
más recientes y, cargados de historia literaria,
conjugan el diseño mismo de una crítica contemporánea. [S. Sosnowski]

3493 Lienhard, Martin. La voz y su huella:
escritura y conflicto étnico-social en
América Latina, 1492–1988. La Habana: Casa
de las Américas, 1990. 407 p.: bibl.
Studies discursive production of "indígenas letrados," considered an alternative to
the established, European oriented canon in
Latin American letters. Follows the trace of
orality in a corpus fashioned by Juan Adolfo
Vásquez. Original, well-documented readings
of *Ollantay, Crónica Mexicana, Popol Vuh,*
and contemporary Quechua poetry. This very
important contribution to issues of canon formation and cultural history is highly recommended. It should be read in tandem with
Gordon Brotherston's *Book of the Fourth*

World (item **3462**) and Roberto González
Echeverría's *Myth and archive: a theory of
Latin American narrative* (item **3478**).

3494 Lindstrom, Naomi. Dependency and
autonomy: the evolution of concepts
in the study of Latin American literature.
(*Ibero-Am. Arch.,* 17:2/3, 1991, p. 109–144,
bibl.)
In this recommended work, Lindstrom
looks at concepts of cultural dependency and
autonomy in Latin American literature as a
way to understand "Latin America's literary
culture in light of the region's historical dynamic" (p. 109). Traces historical progression
from colonial period to anti-colonial resistance. Good bibliography.

**3495 Literatura hispanoamericana de pro-
testa social: una poética de la libertad.**
Prólogo, selección y notas de Armando Zárate. Córdoba, Argentina: Lerner Editor, 1990.
519 p.: bibl. (Mundi)
Topic is historical consciousness rather
than social protest. Good thematic anthology
includes texts left out by other canonical criteria. Of special interest are Bartolomé Hidalgo's "Cielito patriótico," a poem which responded to Ferdinand VII's proclamation
against Argentina's independence, and the
Chicano writer Tino Villanueva's bilingual
memories of his childhood in the harvest
fields of Texas. Welcome addition that reveals
a refreshing approach to the compilation of
texts.

3496 Marco, Joaquín. Literatura hispanoamericana: del modernismo a nuestros
días. Madrid: Espasa Calpe, 1987. 473 p.: bibl.
(Col. Austral; 17. Filología)
Something between a history of Hispanic American literature and a dictionary/
encyclopedia of chosen writers and their
works. Covers novelists Donoso, Cortázar,
Sábato, Vargas Llosa, and García Márquez.
One long section is dedicated to Neruda and
his relationships with other contemporary
poets (e.g., Jiménez and Hernández) in the
context of Spanish history and politics.

3497 Marín, Lynda. Speaking out together:
testimonials of Latin American
women. (*Lat. Am. Perspect.,* 18:3, Summer
1991, p. 51–68, bibl.)
Explores mutually constitutive relationship of gender and genre in the testimonials of four Latin American women: Domitila

Barrios de Chungara, Rigoberta Menchú, Commander Eugenia, and Elvia Alvarado. Suggests ways in which their testimony might offer the Euro-North American First World alternative theories, models, and uses of "women's writing." Recommended.

3498 Martínez-Echazábal, Lourdes. Para una semiótica de la mulatez. Madrid: J. Porrúa Turanzas, 1990? 112 p.: bibl. (Ensayos)

Semiotic study of concepts of the mulatto and "la mulatez" that seeks to unveil mechanisms in Hispanic narrative that make being a mulatto a sign of difference in Spanish-speaking Afro-America. Good bibliography.

3499 Masiello, Francine. Women, State, and family in Latin American literature of the 1920's. (*in* Women, culture, and politics in Latin America. Berkeley: Univ. of California Press, 1990, p. 27–47)

Reviews position of women in society in the 1920s. Shows how the creative literature written by men promoted a perception of women as adversaries of nationalist interests and explores how María Luisa Bombal, Norah Lange, and Teresa de la Parra subverted patriarchal discourse and the ruling logic of traditional narratives.

3500 Matamoro, Blas. Lecturas americanas. Madrid: Ediciones de Cultura Hispánica, Instituto de Cooperación Iberoamericana, 1990. 263 p.: bibl. (Literatura)

More than 30 short and intelligent pieces on major contemporary writers (e.g., Horacio Quiroga, Macedonio Fernández, Borges, Rulfo, Paz, Sábato). Touches on diverse topics: oral literature, mass market cultural production in Brazil, periodization in Argentine literary history, and Borges' sense of history. Brings recent history to bear on established topics in acessible language and style.

3501 Maturo, Graciela. Fenomenología, creación y crítica: sujeto y mundo en la novela latinoamericana. Buenos Aires: Fernando García Cambeiro, 1989. 145 p.: bibl., ill. (Col. Estudios latinoamericanos; 35)

Essays on phenomenology and literature tie together the novel, literary theory, and postmodernism. Includes readings of *El banquete de Severo Arcángelo, El túnel, El recurso de método*, and *Sombras nada más*, and thoughts on the writings of Julia Kristeva.

3502 Maturo, Graciela *et al.* Literatura y hermenéutica: estudios sobre la creación y la crítica literaria desde una perspectiva latinoamericana. Buenos Aires: F. García Cambeiro, 1986. 263 p.: bibl., ill. (Col. Estudios latinoamericanos; 32)

Collection of theoretical essays by various critics with a humanistic, philosophical view of culture as a phenomenological experience, and literature as an aesthetic encounter. Maturo's long, rambling introductory essay, a sort of hermeneutic manifesto, counters Saussurian arbitrariness of language, and formalistic and structuralist approaches as too mechanistic and dehumanizing.

Menton, Seymour. La nueva novela histórica de la América Latina, 1979–1992. See item **3764.**

3503 Molloy, Sylvia. At face value: autobiographical writing in Spanish America. Cambridge, England; New York: Cambridge Univ. Press, 1991. 273 p.: bibl., index. (Cambridge studies in Latin American and Iberian literature; 4)

Portrays brilliantly the particular ways in which Spanish Americans have attempted to contruct (them)selves by writing autobiographies. Thought-provoking examination of the meaning of self-writing includes studies on Sarmiento, Juan Francisco Manzano, Victoria Ocampo, Norah Lange, and Vasconcelos. Molloy takes exception with several current positions on the "origins" of Spanish American writing and its difference from European writing. She demonstrates the crucial importance of books and the intertextual position of all those who write. Reading of translation, in versions more than once removed from the original (e.g., Goethe in French), is underscored as a crucial factor in the constitution of difference. Shows that the whole point of Spanish American writing is to *deviate* from "its" models because of a peculiar awareness of self and culture brought on by a perpetual ideological crisis. Elegantly written, challenging, thoroughly researched, intelligently theoretical.

3504 Navarro, Márcia Hoppe. O romance do ditador: poder e história na América Latina. São Paulo: Icone Editora, 1990. 199 p.: bibl.

See item **3506.**

3505 Oyarzún, Kemy. Poética del desengaño: deseo, poder, escritura; Barrios, Bombal, Asturias y Yáñez. Santiago: Ediciones Literatura Americana Reunida, 1989. 187 p.: bibl., ill. (Col. Estudios, tesis y monografías)

Makes use of Lacan's concept of the split subject. Takes account of the antioedipal critique in order to erode concept of the writer's "creative" authority. Follows René Girard and tries to ground desire in the body as a presence intersected by social forces. Revitalizes our received understanding of *El hermano asno, La última niebla, El Señor Presidente,* and *Al filo del agua.* These novels are read as examples of the repressed.

3506 Pacheco, Carlos. Narrativa de la dictadura y crítica literaria. Caracas: Fundación Centro de Estudios Latinoamericanos Rómulo Gallegos, 1987. 157 p.: bibl. (Col. La Alborada)

This book and Márcia Hoppe Navarro's *O romance do ditador* (item **3504**) analyze the tryptic *Yo, el Supremo, El recurso del método,* and *El otoño del patriarca.* Both critics inquire into means by which dictator consolidates power, and both depart from idea that dictator is a key figure in Latin American culture. Pacheco lists 19 schematic steps towards power, but his most valuable contribution is a chart which includes date of original publication, author's elemental biobib, and historical event to which the novel refers. Both critics use and include up-to-date bibliographies.

3507 El placer de la palabra: literatura erótica femenina de América Latina; antología crítica. Edición de Margarite Fernández Olmos y Lizabeth Paravisini-Gebert. México: Planeta, 1991. 187 p.: bibl. (Mujeres en su tiempo)

Anthology celebrates the positive power of eroticism for the woman writer. Presents texts chronologically to demonstrate writers' increasing freedom of expression. Includes poetry and prose, in Spanish and Portuguese.

3508 Pratt, Mary Louise. Women, literature, and national brotherhood. (*in* Women, culture, and politics in Latin America. Berkeley: Univ. of California Press, 1990, p. 48–73)

Considers how women are situated in masculinist ideologies of nation and how such ideologies are played out in texts by José Mármol, Juana Manuela Gorriti, Gabriela Mistral, and the contributors to the Peruvian *Revista Amauta.* Places texts of women writers in dialogue with the dominant voices of their male contemporaries in critical moments of nationhood.

3509 Rincón, Carlos. Modernidad periférica y el desafío de lo postmoderno: perspectivas del arte narrativo latinoamericano. (*Rev. Crít. Lit. Latinoam.,* 15:29, 1er. semestre 1989, p. 61–104)

Attempt to place Spanish American narrative in the theoretical discussions of post-modernism. Pays special attention to *Cien años de soledad* and *Ficciones* in problems of periodization and canon formation. Post-modernism stands for allegorical, decentered, schizophrenic texts. Examines John Barth's view of Borges and García Márquez as post-moderns. Concludes that the study of Latin American literature has followed three models: Emir Rodríguez Monegal's, Angel Rama's, and Alejandro Losada's. All are insufficient to deal with the challenge of postmodern theory and the universal reception of Latin American literature. What is needed is a new framework open to new methods and a comparative vision. Highly recommended. Cogent and well documented.

3510 Sandoval, Adriana. Los dictadores y la dictadura en la novela hispanoamericana, 1851–1978. México: Coordinación de Humanidades, Dirección General de Publicaciones, Univ. Nacional Autónoma de México, 1989. 270 p.: bibl. (Biblioteca de letras)

Attempts comprehensive review of Spanish American literature on dictator and dictatorships. Uneven chapters propose *Amalia* as the founding text and provide a sound survey of the genre. Specific chapters dedicated to *Yo, el Supremo, El recurso del método,* and *El otoño del patriarca* summarize the existing literature on these three novels.

3511 Simpson, Amelia S. Detective fiction from Latin America. Rutherford: Fairleigh Dickinson Univ. Press; London; Cranbury, NJ: Associated Univ. Presses, 1990. 218 p.: bibl., ill., index.

Provides historical outline of detective fiction in Latin America, and explores how that fiction is influenced by the marketplace as well as by what some have claimed to be the genre's incompatability with Latin American reality. Includes bibliography of works in Spanish and Portuguese.

3512 Sklodowska, Elzbieta. La parodia en la nueva novela hispanoamericana, 1960–1985. Amsterdam; Philadelphia: J. Benjamins Pub. Co., 1991. 219 p.: bibl., index. (Purdue Univ. monographs in Romance languages, 0165–8743; 34)

Solid, methodical, thorough, comprehensive examination of the parodial mode in Spanish American narrative. Studies in detail contextual use of parady in prize-winning novels along with lesser known texts such as *Los perros del paraíso, Los relámpagos de agosto, El bazar de los idiotas, Lumpérica, Cuadernos de Gofa, Evangelio de Lucas Gavilán, Crónica del descubrimiento, De paso,* and *Como en la guerra.* Introduction provides good historical overview of the term "parody." Chapters on the narcissism of *Tres tristes tigres* and the historical transformation of *Pepe Botellas* are especially worthwhile.

3513 Tradition and innovation: reflections on Latin American Jewish writing. Edited by Robert Di Antonio and Nora Glickman. Albany: State Univ. of New York Press, 1993. 225 p.: bibl. (SUNY series in modern Jewish literature and culture)

Importante colección de 17 ensayos sobre una producción literaria que ha dejado de ser marginal en los estudios latinoamericanos (si bien aún porta su cuota de exotismo para los especialistas en estudios judaicos). La mayor parte de los artículos analiza obras de escritores argentinos (Aguinis, Feierstein, Fijman, Glickman, Goloboff, Gravier, Halac). Scliar, Lispector y la presencia de los criptojudíos marcan la presencia brasileña; Berman,

Muñiz y Seligson, la de México; José Kozer la de Cuba y Samuel Rovinski la de Costa Rica. Por cubrir aspectos más amplios, resultan particularmente importantes las lecturas medulares de Senkman, DiAntonio y Goldberg, así como las respuestas de autores judíos-latinoamericanos en torno a la temática que organiza este volumen. [S. Sosnowski]

3514 Yúdice, George. ¿Puede hablarse de postmodernidad en América Latina? *(Rev. Crít. Lit. Latinoam.,* 15:29, 1er. semestre 1989, p. 105–128)

Intelligently written, recommended article. Argues for deconstructing the opposition between "lo propio" and "lo foráneo." Many features of the postmodern model—combination of styles, parodic mode—are also features of Latin American culture. Yúdice's insightful conclusions are: 1) there can be no radical and plural democracy without renouncing the idea of privileged access to the truth; 2) what is left is a multiplicity of social subjects in need of articulation; 3) postmodern theory can contribute to dismantle a fossilized understanding of Latin American culture; and 4) heterogeneity is constitutive of Latin America's own modernity. Theoretically up to date.

3515 Yúdice, George. *Testimonio* and postmodernism. *(Lat. Am. Perspect.,* 18:3, Summer 1991, p. 15–31, bibl.)

Distinguishes between testimonial literature and postmodern texts: both reject prevailing frameworks of interpreting the world and place increasing importance on the marginal, but hegemonic postmodern texts do not move beyond a Western purview. Resists the absorption of Latin American writers into the postmodernist canon when that absorption is another form of colonialization. Recommended.

Colonial Period

ALVARO FELIX BOLAÑOS, *Associate Professor of Spanish, Tulane University*

UN RASGO PERSISTENTE en el creciente número de libros, artículos y ediciones sobre obras del período colonial hispanoamericano—tanto en EE.UU. como en Hispanoamérica—es la preferencia que está recibiendo aquel profuso corpus de relaciones, cartas relatorias, diarios, crónicas, tratados naturalistas, historias, catálogos, documentos forenses, mapas, ilustraciones, etc. Se trata de textos (lingüísticos y gráficos, en español y/o en lenguas nativas americanas) cuya composición se aleja de intenciones estéticas y cuyos propósitos pragmáticos se ubican dentro de aquel traumático proceso histórico iniciado por la irrupción de Europa en América, el complejo ejercicio del control militar, político y cultural de los territorios americanos y la persistente y variada resistencia de las culturas nativas y los sectores mestizos y criollos de la población. Los libros y artículos sobre estos temas han crecido tanto y tan rápidamente en los últimos años que—conviene advertir—ofrecemos en esta introducción, y en las entradas bibliográficas siguientes, una descripción de las tendencias más destacadas de los estudios de los últimos años y una muestra de los trabajos más representativos. Con una producción tan exuberante de estos estudios nuestro intento nunca podría ser exhaustivo ni exento de omisiones importantes en el limitado espacio con que contamos.

La dificultad de inscripción de estos textos privilegiados por los estudiosos dentro de los límites clásicos y renacentistas literarios (poesía épica y lírica, comedia, tratado, crónica, historia, etc.), junto con su carácter pluricultural, tradicionalmente había generado dos actitudes de estudio: 1) desprecio por parte de aquellos críticos que sólo admitían como objeto de reflexión las estrictas derivaciones americanas de tales límites estéticos (sufrido por cronistas indios y mestizos de los primeros dos siglos de colonización); y 2) forzada inclusión dentro del canon literario con el propósito de llenar supuestos vacíos en la historia del origen de la literatura hispanoamericana (ejercido sobre cronistas españoles del mismo período).

Una nueva generación de estudiosos se está acercando a estos textos coloniales, no en términos de su carácter "literario," "ficcional" o "novelesco," sino en términos de su carácter de documentos culturales. Para la gran mayoría de ellos, una aproximación "literaria"—dependiente de un limitante marco estético convencional europeo—poco ayuda a la dilucidación de las complejidades pluriculturales de su producción. De otra parte, está hoy poco favorecida la ya tradicional aproximación esteticista que tiende a ignorar en el estudio de los textos las implicaciones que en su producción tuvieron factores como los conflictos culturales propios de la imposición de la cultura europea sobre las americanas que resisten y/o se adaptan. La preferencia de este tipo de textos de difícil clasificación en las poéticas renacentistas o dieciochescas ha exigido una aproximación interdisciplinaria presente en la gran mayoría de los trabajos aquí reseñados. Ha propiciado también el frecuente enfoque de diversos aspectos del colonialismo y el postcolonialismo y, la consideración de la interconexión de temas, épocas y regiones geográficas seleccionadas para su estudio (items **3520, 3572, 3585, 3589, 3591, 3597** y **3601**). Tal aproximación es, también, responsable de una más frecuente y elaborada actitud crítica y de una menor presencia de simples intenciones celebratorias y encomiásticas de autores y obras que antes eran frecuentemente reducidos a lo estéticamente "eximio."

Walter Mignolo, en un importante artículo, ha acertadamente llamado a esta clase de texto "the darker side of the Renaissance" (item **3592**), pues su prominente producción, al margen de los ideales literarios europeos, expuso una quiebra de la tradición renacentista en las letras del Nuevo Mundo. Esa quiebra es notoria en la insistente producción de textos "anómalos" que escapaban a una fácil clasificación y que incluían obras de autores europeos o euroamericanos (*Diario* de Colón, *El carnero* de Rodríguez Freile, *Los infortunios de Alonso Ramírez* de Sigüenza y Góngora, o *El lazarillo de ciegos caminantes* de Carrió de la Vandera) u obras culturalmente híbridas de autores nativos o mestizos (como la de Guamán Poma de Ayala, Titu

Cussi Yupangui, Joan de Santa Cruz Pachacuti o Alva Ixtlilxochitl). Ese "lado oscuro del Renacimiento" se ha preferido estudiar no en términos de "literatura colonial" sino en los de "discurso colonial" ya que este último concepto coloca la producción de los textos, no en un aislamiento estético, sino en un marco de interacciones conflictivas, de apropiaciones y resistencias, de poder y dominación.

Lo anterior no significa, por supuesto, que esté desapareciendo el interés por las obras literarias del período colonial ni que se estén acabando los estudios "literarios" de ellas—porque los hay, y algunos muy significativos, como se verá en los pertinentes textos reseñados aquí (items **3575, 3531, 3547, 3548** y **3555**); significa, más bien, que aún en los casos en que el objeto de estudio lo constituyen obras de naturaleza y pretensión estéticas, la tendencia dominante es la de articular su escrutinio, y el estudio de las circunstancias en que trabajaron los autores, al contexto de la colonización y el control europeos—y sus secuelas—de los territorios americanos desde la llegada de Colón hasta el siglo XIX.

Esta tendencia ha posibilitado un fructífero diálogo entre varias disciplinas (antropología, historia, crítica literaria, historia del arte, etc.; ver items **3569, 3532, 3589, 3617, 3600, 3608** y **3551**), la saludable intersección entre diversas áreas de estudio (hispánicos, franceses, ingleses, etc.; ver items **3575, 3579** y **3585**) y la noción de que las disertaciones sobre autores y obras suponen también una comprensión de los procesos culturales producidos por relaciones de dominio político, económico y cultural y sus implicaciones en nuestra época. El resultado ha sido el de un amplio conjunto de trabajos que intenta precisar herramientas (teóricas, históricas, empíricas) para la necesaria formulación de pertinentes preguntas sobre la producción cultural de los textos coloniales. Todos estos trabajos comparten entre sí la realización de exhaustivos análisis textuales tanto en textos lingüísticos (relación, carta, historia, etc.) como gráficos (un mapa o un emblema, por ejemplo; ver items **3539, 3617** y **3578**).

En la línea de estos propósitos y metodología ha habido últimamente un decidido esfuerzo editorial de intelectuales interesados en ampliar los horizontes de la discusión sobre las letras del período colonial por medio de muy bien coordinadas y valiosas publicaciones de colecciones de ensayos (varios de ellos con motivo de los 500 años del arribo de Colón a América). Entre ellos vale la pena mencionar a Rolena Adorno y Walter Mignolo con su "Colonial Discourse," un volumen especial de la revista *Dispositio* (ver items **3560, 3520, 3541, 3591** y **3548**); René Jara y Nicholas Spadaccini, editores de *Amerindian images and the legacy of Columbus* (item **3561**); Diana de Armas Wilson con "Dissenting Views of 1992," volumen especial de la revista *Journal of Hispanic Philology* (Tallahassee: Florida State Univ., Vol. 16, No. 2, 1992, ver items **3526, 3579, 3581, 3582, 3608** y **3614**); Beatriz González Stephan y Lúcia Helena Costigan con su *Crítica y descolonización: el sujeto colonial en la cultura latinoamericana* (item **3573**); Mercedes López Baralt con un número especial de la *Revista de Estudios Hispánicos* de la Universidad de Puerto Rico (item **3602**); Stephen Hart y Brian Dendle con su "Spain and the New World," volumen doble de *Romance Quarterly* (item **3605**); y Jerry Williams y Robert Lewis con *Early images of the Americas: transfer and invention* (item **3577**). Mención especial merece la sólida fundación de Raquel Chang-Rodríguez en 1992 de la primera revista exclusivamente dedicada a los estudios del período colonial hispanoamericano titulada *Colonial Latin American Review* (New York: City University of New York) cuya excelente organización y óptimo grupo de consejeros y lectores promete una duradera y alta calidad de las contribuciones críticas.

Una característica de muchos de los trabajos publicados últimamente es la intención de reflexionar no solamente sobre los autores y/o obras, períodos o temas escogidos, sino también la crítica de las herramientas epistemológicas, históricas y teóricas con que la comunidad de críticos ha realizado sus pesquisas en esos temas. Esos esfuerzos apuntan siempre a la propuesta de nuevos derroteros críticos muy útiles en las discusiones que generan. Uno de los autores que consistente y efectivamente ha venido contribuyendo a la precisión de herramientas teóricas y metodológicas para la formulación de necesarios interrogantes sobre los textos coloniales y su proceso de producción es Rolena Adorno. Su lectura de *Naufragios*, por ejemplo, dilucida el proceso de adaptación y supervivencia de Cabeza de Vaca en su interacción con los indígenas, desvirtuando la fácil explicación de una armonía entre europeo y americano (item **3519**). Igualmente, sus recientes aportes sobre Las Casas le han permitido no solamente explorar la utilización de sus obras más controversiales por otros cronistas de la época en el contexto de la censura española (item **3557**), esclarecer contextos históricos, políticos e historiográficos de las discusiones sobre el tratamiento del indio que determinaron la escritura sobre indígenas en el siglo XVI (items **3559** y **3558**), sino también desmantelar popularizadas falacias sobre la vida, formación intelectual e impacto de la obra del dominico en su época y la nuestra (item **3518**). Sus reflexiones sobre la importancia de los conceptos de la guerra y el espíritu caballeresco en la escritura de la historia y las discusiones sobre el orden civilizado de españoles y americanos en los siglos XVI y XVII han sido también fundamentales (items **3560** y **3516**). José Rabasa, por su parte, con un amplio y riguroso estudio de un siglo de historiografía colonial, pone en cuestión conceptos y actitudes culturales presentes en la comprensión de América y vigentes desde el siglo XVI hasta hoy (item **3600**). Contribuciones como estas están estimulando nuevas y diversas investigaciones de muchos jóvenes estudiosos del período colonial hispanoamericano.

Autores de otras latitudes como Cristina Iglesia y Julio Schvartzman, en uno de los más importantes trabajos de los últimos años, emprenden la relectura del amplio cuerpo de las letras argentinas de los dos primeros siglos de colonización española para analizar el origen de algunas de las elaboraciones míticas e ideológicas que, a través de cuatro siglos de escritura de pretensiones históricas y literarias, han sustentado una ilusionada versión "blanca" —en contra de la "cobriza"— de la fundación de esta nación austral. Igualmente revisan un amplio grupo de textos misioneros que proliferaron en los rígidos esfuerzos europeos por destruir las culturas nativas y que enfocan ángulos menos positivos de autores como José de Acosta, cuya arrogancia cultural e irrespeto por las identidades de los pueblos americanos le permitió diseñar elaborados sistemas de erradicación de las lenguas indígenas (items **3586** y **3610**).

Poniendo en cuestión la posibilidad de la reconstrucción del pasado a través simplemente de fuentes documentales, Margarita Zamora, en otra de sus formidables contribuciones, analiza los textos colombinos que testifican ante los Reyes Católicos el Descubrimiento (entre ellos los recién descubiertos del *Libro copiador*) teniendo en cuenta como crucial el papel del acto de lectura y su efecto transformador de la escritura de tales documentos (item **3556**). Esta noción, que parte de la duda de la objetividad de documentos históricos tradicionalmente considerados fidedignos, la comparte, entre muchos autores, Inga Clendinnen en un brillante artículo sobre las versiones de Cortés, Bernal, Durán, y los códices aztecas del encuentro bélico entre españoles y mexicanos entre 1519–21. Para Clendinnen tanto las fuentes españolas como las indígenas son dignas de un necesario escepticismo ya que ambas responden a un humano deseo de crear versiones coherentes basadas en experiencias y evidencias ambiguas y fragmentarias (item **3572**).

Entre los estudios del contexto social, cultural, intelectual y biográfico para la explicación del acto de lectura y escritura de mujeres prominentes en las letras hispanoamericanas es de obligada referencia la excelente colección de estudios—todos de mujeres y de orientación feminista—preparada por Stephanie Merrim sobre Sor Juana Inés de la Cruz (item **3529**). Este grupo de ensayos, que va desde una historia de la bibliografía sobre Sor Juana hasta la detenida indagación de los rasgos femeninos en sus textos, es una contribución fundamental para el necesario cambio de rumbo de los estudios sobre esta monja escritora: un cambio de la simple celebración de una "monstruo de la naturaleza" americana a la ubicación precisa de su obra en la tradición hispana de la escritura de mujeres. Con este mismo espíritu, estudiosas como Emilie Bergmann y Marie-Cécile Benassy-Berling insisten en la mayor importancia que tiene el estudio de las condiciones en que se expresó el genio de Sor Juana (antes que la descripción del genio mismo) y la manera como se le ha leído en nuestra época, así como en la necesidad de revisar la ya limitante noción de una monja brillante asediada inmisericordemente por un medio hostil (items **3525** y **3524**). Dados el rigor metodológico, la variedad de herramientas teóricas y el decidido interés de relectura de textos marginados o poco conocidos, este robusto corpus de reflexiones críticas sobre las letras del período colonial hispanoamericano promete seguir desarrollándose. Quiero agradecer la colaboración de Margaret Olsen en la preparación de esta bibliografía.

INDIVIDUAL STUDIES

3516 Adorno, Rolena. Como leer "mala cosa:" mitos caballerescos y amerindios en los *Naufragios* de Cabeza de Vaca. (*in* Crítica y descolonización: el sujeto colonial en la cultura latinoamericana. Caracas: Academia Nacional de Historia, 1992, p. 87–107)

Basada en elementos antropológicos, el marco histórico de la colonización española y el examen del diseño literario del texto, Adorno propone lectura de este episodio como arquetipo hispano de tensión entre evangelización y paganismo en América. Más que un dispositivo narrativo, o ecos de la existencia de otro náufrago anterior, o rasgos de folklore en torno al diablo, este relato, inscrito en debates sobre justeza de guerra contra indios, es aquí crucial como desenlace feliz de la obra y modelo de historias posteriores representando la conquista ideal: triunfo del caballero laico misionero sobre creencias religiosas nativas.

3517 Adorno, Rolena. The genesis of Felipe Guamán Poma de Ayala's *Nueva corónica y buen gobierno.* (*Colon. Lat. Am. Rev.*, 2:1/2, 1993, p. 53–92, bibl., facsims.)

Contraste del autor del más importante texto colonial culturalmente híbrido, y del hombre inmerso en litigios legales en una pesquisa que aclara y confirma muchos datos personales de Guamán Poma y circunstancias que generaron la *Nueva corónica.* La ocasión la ofrece la publicación en 1991 de un Expediente que revela los problemas personales del autor con el intrincado e injusto sistema legal español y revela el denuedo con que luchó dentro de ese sistema por sus intereses económicos. Ver comentario del etnohistoriador en item **591.**

3518 Adorno, Rolena. The intellectual life of Bartolomé de las Casas. New Orleans: Graduate School of Tulane Univ., 1991. 24 p.

Con exhaustiva lectura de la obra de Las Casas, y a la luz de nuevos datos sobre su biografía y contexto cultural, Adorno demuestra que fue su educación en el derecho canónico, y no su menos sólida formación teológica y filosófica, lo que le da solidez y coherencia a sus planteamientos políticos, históricos y etnográficos en defensa de los indios. De obligada consulta para reevaluación de la obra del dominico.

3519 Adorno, Rolena. The negotiation of fear in Cabeza de Vaca's *Naufragios.* (*Representations/Berkeley*, 33, Winter 1991, p. 163–199)

Observando y aprendiendo prácticas indígenas (lingüísticas, curativas, guerreras, comerciales) Cabeza de Vaca manipula hábil e inmisericordemente el arma del terror entre los indios. Esto explica—mejor que la noción de feliz coexistencia entre americanos y europeos—el éxito en su adaptación y supervivencia. Recurre a elementos antropológicos, etnográficos e históricos en esta novedosa y rigurosa lectura de las dos últimas partes de *Naufragios.*

3520 Ahern, Maureen. The certification of Cibola: discursive strategies in *La relación del descubrimiento de las siete ciudades* by Fray Marcos de Niza, 1539. (*Dispositio/Ann Arbor*, 14:36/38, 1989, p. 303–314)

Examen de estrategias de certificación en la relación de Fray Marcos de Niza quien coloca diversas voces y perspectivas informativas (europeas y nativas) en un sistema de signos que busca certificarlas unas a otras creando un texto autoreferencial. El contexto y la certificación, concluye Ahern, "informan" y "forman" un texto que Fray Marcos sabía se leería con escepticismo en México. Importante perspectiva crítica alejada de reducciones literarias (mezcla de realidad y fantasía, Carl Sauer) o potenciales reducciones etnocentristas (discurso del fracaso, Beatriz Pastor).

3521 Ahern, Maureen. The cross and the gourd: the appropriation of ritual signs in the *Relaciones* of Alvar Núñez Cabeza de Vaca and Fray Marcos de Niza. (*in* Early images of the Americas: transfer and invention. Edited by Jerry Williams and Robert Lewis. Tucson: Univ. of Arizona Press, 1993, p. 215–244)

Estudio de producción y recepción de signos rituales de mediación cultural nativos (calabaza sagrada) y europeos (la cruz), en las primeras *relaciones* (de Alvar Núñez Cabeza de Vaca y Fray Marcos de Niza) sobre contactos entre europeos y americanos en regiones allende la frontera norte de la Nueva España. Con orientación interdisciplinaria, Ahern demuestra cómo la semiosis de la comunicación transcultural jugó papel crucial en la construcción de un modelo del delicado contacto cultural entre españoles e indígenas, unas veces existoso, otras trágico.

3522 Arellano, Jorge Eduardo. *El güegüence:* obra de teatro representativa de la Nicaragua colonial. (*Mesoamérica/Antigua*, 12: 22, dic. 1991, p. 277–309, bibl.)

Nueva edición anotada con bibliografía de esta farsa indígena colonial de Nicaragua en comparación con las anteriores ediciones de C.H. Berendt y W. Lehmann de 1874, D.G. Brinton de 1883 y Francisco Pérez Estrada de 1982, entre otras. Utiles notas lexicográficas, históricas y bibliográficas; la introducción de Arellano, que exagera la ingerencia europea y desconoce la indígena, aporta modestamente a la comprensión del pluralismo cultural de este drama del período colonial.

3523 Arias, Santa. Empowerment through the writing of history: Bartolomé de las Casas' representation of the *other(s).* (*in* Early images of the Americas: transfer and invention. Edited by Jerry Williams and Robert Lewis. Tucson: Univ. of Arizona Press, 1993, p. 163–179)

Este firme aporte de Arias plantea que los argumentos jurídicos y teológicos que Las Casas usó para subvertir las conflictivas descripciones satánicas de las historias oficiales constituyeron un ingenioso marco para la descripción de la superioridad moral de los indígenas y un intento de restarle legitimidad a los muy negativos estereotipos esperados por el lector renacentista.

3524 Benassy-Berling, Marie-Cécile. Algunos documentos relacionados con el fin de la vida de Sor Juana Inés de la Cruz. (*Anu. Estud. Am.*, 44, 1987, suplemento, p. 23–33, appendix)

Mediante examen de cuatro documentos (cartas, dedicatorias de libros, recibos de transacciones de dinero) Benassy sugiere, contra la opinión general, que la posición social y la independencia de Sor Juana eran más fuertes de lo que tradicionalmente se ha creído. Excelente aporte que propone estudio de Sor Juana haciendo menos énfasis en su excepcional genio y más en su calidad y condiciones reales de existencia de mujer.

3525 Bergmann, Emilie L. Sor Juana Inés de la Cruz: dreaming in a double voice. (*in* Women, culture, and politics in Latin

America. Berkeley: Univ. of California Press, 1990, p. 151–172)

Excelente propuesta de lectura de Sor Juana que supera simple recuperación, descubrimiento y celebración de su prestigio, y pasa al examen de las condiciones de ese prestigio y las maneras en que se ha leído en el siglo XX. Para ello examina el anquilosamiento de la mujer en sus autorretratos (*Respuesta, Empeños de una casa, Primero sueño*), sujeto y objeto de una representación que une voz poética y reflexión filósofica.

3526 Bolaños, Alvaro Félix. Indians at the fringe of history: Fray Pedro Simón on the "Nuevo Reino de Granada." (*J. Hisp. Philol.*, 16:2, 1992, p. 137–154)

Dilucidación de estrategias retóricas utilizadas por el franciscano español Fray Pedro Simón (1565–1628?) en sus *Noticias historiales de las conquistas de Tierra Firme en las Indias Occidentales* (1624) para la exclusión de los indios americanos del campo de la "historia verdadera" y su inclusión en el campo de la "historia natural." Tal labor retórica la logra recurriendo a tradiciones etnográficas medievales y renacentistas y categorías culturales como bárbaro, salvaje, monstruoso y afeminado.

3527 Bolaños, Alvaro Félix. El subtexto utópico en un relato de naufragio del cronista Fernández de Oviedo. (*in* Crítica y descolonización: el sujeto colonial en la cultura latinoamericana. Caracas: Biblioteca de la Academia Nacional de Historia, 1992, p. 109–126)

Señala carácter utópico del relato sobre naufragios más elaborado de Oviedo (lib. L, cap. X de su *Historia general y natural de las Indias*, 1535) para destacar contradicción entre la solución feliz e imaginaria de este relato y la indeseable—y muy criticada por Oviedo —situación político-social creada por los españoles en las colonias americanas. En contra de la popularizada visión de Oviedo como epígono incondicional del imperio español, el artículo presenta a un cronista condenando la empresa española en América.

3528 Domingo, Mariano Cuesta. La obra de Pedro Simón, de la Parrilla, en la historia y las letras hispanoamericanas del siglo áureo. (*Edad Oro*, 10, primavera 1991, p. 53–69, bibl.)

Divulgación, valoración y celebración de *Noticias historiales de las conquistas de Tierra Firme en las Indias Occidentales* (Cuenca, España: 1624) de Fray Pedro Simón. Insistiendo en su calidad de documento histórico insustituible para conocer al Nuevo Reino de Granada, y en su valor etnográfico y antopológico, el artículo se empeña en colocar esta obra dentro de la "literatura del Siglo de Oro" español.

3529 Feminist perspectives on Sor Juana Inés de la Cruz. Edited by Stephanie Merrim. Detroit: Wayne State Univ. Press, 1991. 189 p.: bibl., index. (Latin American literature and culture series)

Exploración desde perspectivas feministas de implicaciones literarias y culturales de lo que significaba para Sor Juana ser mujer y escritora en México a fines del siglo XVII. Con variadas aproximaciones críticas los ocho ensayos del volumen se ocupan tanto de cada género literario desarrollado por la monja como del contexto personal e intelectual en que ella vivió y escribió. Sólida contribución al estudio de la obra y la crítica de Sor Juana. Util para interesados en mujeres escritoras y en crítica feminista en general.

3530 Foster, David William. Ulrico Schmidel: *Relatos de la conquista del Río de la Plata y Paraguay, 1534–1554.* (*Chasqui/Williamsburg*, 20:2, 1991, p. 73–77)

Breve nota llamando la atención sobre esta relación—relativamente abandonada por la crítica—sobre la conquista española de esta región. *Relatos*, publicado en alemán en 1567, y escrito por un protestante que acompañó a Pedro de Mendoza en la fundación de la primera Buenos Aires en 1536, escapa de prefiguraciones mitológicas e ideológicas típicas de los cronistas españoles y portugueses. Eso lo convierte, según Foster, en un texto cultural menos prejuiciado y al margen del esquema Europa/el "otro" americano "as a Diabolical Enemy" (p. 76).

3531 Gimbernat González, Ester. Speaking through the voices of love: interpretation as emancipation. (*in* Feminist perspectives on Sor Juana Inés de la Cruz. Edited by Stephanie Merrim. Detroit, Mich.: Wayne State Univ. Press, 1991, p. 162–176)

Perspicaz análisis de tres sonetos de amor de Sor Juana adheridos a rígidas tradiciones poéticas (dolce stil nuovo, jarchas,

amor cortés) y filosofía escolástica. La igno-
rancia de la amada de las sutilezas de estas
tradiciones le posibilita al amante implantar
una injusta jerarquía de poder sobre ella, esencial en el discurso amoroso tradicional. Esa
voz tiránica, sin embargo, está gobernada por
el conocimiento de la mujer poeta quien cuestiona así, según Gimbernat, la dialéctica de
ese discurso.

3532 Hernández, Max. Memoria del bien
 perdido: conflicto, identidad y nostalgia en el Inca Garcilaso de la Vega. Madrid:
Sociedad Estatal Quinto Centenario, 1991?
210 p.: bibl. (Col. Encuentros: Serie Textos)

Interesante indagación psicoanalítica
de vida y obra del Inca Garcilaso consideradas
como "texto" clave para comprender cuatro
siglos de conflictos no resueltos entre la cultura hispana y la andina. Sin discutir valor y
carácter historiográfico de la obra del Inca,
Hernández destaca relación intertextual entre
el lenguaje y los mundos interno y externo de
Garcilaso para señalar la actualidad hoy de la
ambivalencia, marginación y dolor del mestizaje que vivió Garcilaso en su época.

3533 Jiménez de Quesada, Gonzalo. El anti-
 jovio. Edición y presentación de Guillermo Hernández Peñalosa. Prólogo de Jorge
Eliécer Ruiz. Estudio preliminar de Manuel
Ballesteros Gaibrois. Nueva ed. Bogotá: Instituto Caro y Cuervo, 1991. 2 v.: bibl., ill., indexes. (Biblioteca colombiana; 37–38)

Nueva edición anotada y modernizada
(con buen estudio preliminar) del alegato en
defensa de España escrito en contra de la versión de *Historias de su tiempo*, del obispo italiano Paulo Jovio, sobre el saqueo de Roma
por las tropas de Carlos V en 1528. Aunque no
trata temas americanos provee datos autobiográficos de este conquistador, humanista y
mariscal del Nuevo Reino de Granada durante su permanencia en Europa. Importante
para señalar el sustrato ideológico imperial
que subyace en los historiógrafos de Indias a
principios del siglo XVI.

Juana Inés de la Cruz, *Sor* and **Agustín de Salazar y Torres.** La segunda Celestina: una comedia perdida de Sor Juana. See item **4599.**

3534 King, Willard F. Juan Ruiz de Alarcón,
 letrado y dramaturgo: su mundo mexicano y español. Traducción de Antonio Alatorre. México: Colegio de México, Centro de
Estudios Lingüísticos y Literarios, 1989. 290

p., 2 leaves of plates (1 folded): bibl., ill., index. (Serie Estudios de lingüística y literatura;
17)

Estudio del autor "colonial" americano
instalado exitosamente en la pléyade literaria
de la metrópoli europea. Basado en comedias
selectas (*La cueva de Salamanca, Ganar amigos, La verdad sospechosa*, y otras), y una rigurosa investigación sobre antecedentes familiares, formación, maestros, amigos,
enemigos, y el ambiente social y político
tanto en México como en España, King traza
sólido perfil de este formidable dramaturgo
injustamente marginado en la historia literaria por ser "colonial," por carecer de "mexicanidad" o por su adhesión a la metrópoli.

3535 Kovacci, Ofelia. Una muestra del teatro popular en Nicaragua: *El güegüence.* (*Filología/Buenos Aires*, 21:2, 1986,
p. 179–199)

Suscintos y útiles análisis e informaciones sobre motivos, recursos expresivos, escenificación, autoría, género y fecha de composición de esta farsa indígena-colonial que,
en una combinación de español y nahua y dirigida a un público tal vez indígena y mestizo,
humorísticamente presenta una crítica de las
instituciones, la sociedad y los individuos en
el período colonial centroamericano.

3536 Lasarte, Pedro. Sátira, parodia e historia en la "Peruntina" de Mateo Rosas
de Oquendo. (*Colon. Lat. Am. Rev.*, 1:1/2,
1992, p. 147–160, bibl.)

Sugestivo y convincente examen del
carácter contestatario y subversivo del poema
satírico burlesco "La Victoria Naval Peruntina" (obra manuscrita de circulación clandestina) que parodia la celebración de Pedro
de Oña, en el *Arauco domado*, de la victoria
naval española contra el pirata inglés Haw-
kins (1594). Ilustra cómo el poema de Rosas
de Oquendo expresa una conciencia popular
opuesta a las falsificaciones propagandísticas
de poetas defensores del status quo en Perú
colonial.

3537 Lavrin, Asunción. Unlike Sor Juana?:
 the model nun in the religious literature of colonial Mexico. (*in* Feminist perspectives on Sor Juana Inés de la Cruz. Edited by
Stephanie Merrim. Detroit: Wayne State
Univ. Press, 1991, p. 61–85)

Analizando biografías, autobiografías,
sermones, cartas, libros de instrucción y me-

ditación religiosos en su contexto histórico cultural (español y mexicano), Lavrin reconstruye mundo de clausuras conventuales hispanas en los siglos XVI y XVII. El largo rechazo de Sor Juana a esta poderosa tradición conventual la convierte en monja excepcional y su adopción de ella al final de su vida (renunciando a vida intelectual), la vuelve monja típica. Importantísimo estudio sobre una Sor Juana vista más como intelectual que como religiosa.

3538 **Lerner, Isaías.** América y la poesía épica áurea: la versión de Ercilla. (*Edad Oro*, 10, primavera 1991, p. 125–140)
Contrario a la consideración del poema de Ercilla como texto de valor documental y de válidas representaciones del paisaje americano, Lerner demuestra que *La araucana* es una fusión de hechos históricos y experiencias personales narrados de acuerdo con las exigencias del género épico (mejor adaptado a intención glorificadora de Ercilla) y filtrados a través de la postura ideológica del autor, la cual se identifica con el poder imperial de Felipe II (a quien va dirigido el poema).

3539 **López-Baralt, Mercedes.** La estridencia silente: oralidad, escritura e iconografía en la *Nueva corónica* de Guamán Poma. (*Torre/Río Piedras*, 3:12, oct./dic. 1989, p. 609–649, ill.)
Estupenda y clara exploración de la prominencia de la oralidad en los textos lingüísticos y gráficos de esta obra policultural y heteroglósica. El análisis de la retórica del sermón y la tradición oral nativa, así como de ejemplos del grito de cólera, perversión, asombro, exageración (indicado físicamente en el texto a falta de signos lingüísticos para ello), le sugieren a López Baralt una lectura oral que destaca para recuperar el tono de ese discurso oral tanto en la palabra escrita como en los dibujos.

3540 **Luciani, Frederick.** The *Comedia de San Francisco de Borja,* 1640: the Mexican Jesuits and the "Education of the Prince." (*Colon. Lat. Am. Rev.,* 2:1/2, 1993, p. 121–141, bibl.)
Tres cosas busca Matías de Bocanegra con esta comedia que combina la tradición jesuítica del teatro didáctico con el género de la *de educatione principis* y una tendencia antimaquiavélica: alabar al Virrey de Nueva España (Marqués de Villena) comparándolo con

San Francisco de Borja, reafirmar la autoridad de orden jesuita, y ofrecer un modelo de buen gobierno. La loa preliminar emplea imaginería indígena, lo cual sugiere, según Luciani, una visión milenaria de esperanzada anticipación de una redención política sea para la población indígena o el gobierno de los euroamericanos.

3541 **MacCormack, Sabine.** Atahualpa and the book. (*Dispositio/Ann Arbor,* 14: 36/38, 1989, p. 141–168)
Agudo examen de versiones (españolas y nativas) de los siglos XVI y XVII de captura de Atahualpa por Pizarro en 1532 en las que el libro entregado al rey Inca prefigura subyugación de los andinos ante la autoridad escrita europea. Ninguna versión es más correcta que las demás pero todas demuestran que su respectiva representación de ese suceso de violencia, confusión y conquista poco tiene que ver con medios y razones para hacerlo inteligible. Saludable cuestionamiento de carácter fidedigno de textos históricos.

3542 **Merrim, Stephanie.** Toward a feminist reading of Sor Juana Inés de la Cruz: past, present, and future directions in Sor Juana criticism. (*in* Feminist perspectives on Sor Juana Inés de la Cruz. Edited by Stephanie Merrim. Detroit: Wayne State Univ. Press, 1991, p. 11–37)
Formidable evaluación de tendencias críticas sobre obra de Sor Juana desde el siglo XVII hasta 1982. Propone perspectiva de estudio que no feminice, domestique ni reduzca a la monja a una brillante anomalía. Aunque reconoce el gran aporte de Octavio Paz—aún útil para futuros estudios feministas—, Merrim echa de menos en él consideración del contexto de las tradiciones de escritura de mujeres al igual que de las condiciones sociales e intelectuales de sus actos de escritura en Europa y América.

Montenegro, Juan Ernesto. Fragmentos del dieciseiseno. See item **2277**.

3543 **Moraña, Mabel.** Orden dogmático y marginalidad en la *Carta de Monterrey* de Sor Juana Inés de la Cruz. (*Hisp. Rev.,* 1990, p. 205–225, bibl.)
Considerando la dialética de hegemónico vs. subalterno, el artículo demuestra como el texto de la carta, que permea varias formas retóricas (inversión, contraposición, e

ironía), reconcilia la antítesis con fórmulas totalizadoras (uso de razón para entender fe, de lo profano para entender lo sagrado, etc.) en un proceso de resistencia de un emisor marginado por ser mujer e intelectual y opuesto al receptor (Iglesia, imperio, virreinato).

3544 Mujica, Elisa. Sor Francisca Josefa de Castillo. Bogotá: Procultura, 1991. 105 p.: bibl., ill. (Clásicos colombianos Procultura; 18)

Biografía, antología, selección de juicios críticos y bibliografía de la monja clarisa del Nuevo Reino de Granada, Francisca Josefa de Castillo y Guevara (conocida como Madre Castillo ¿1617–1742?), autora de *Mi vida* y *Afectos espirituales* (Filadelfia, 1817)—obra biográfica que expresa excepcionalmente experiencias místicas. Util breviario de divulgación escolar y popular.

3545 Pagden, Anthony. *Ius et Factum:* text and experience in the writings of Bartolomé de las Casas. (*in* New World experiences. Edited by Stephen Greenblatt. Berkeley: Univ. of California Press, 1993, p. 12–41 and 85–100)

Para representar autorizadamente a América Las Casas arduamente articula su experiencia personal y exigencias del canon cultural (Biblia, Padres de la Iglesia, autores clásicos) mediante correspondencia crucial entre "hecho y Derecho" (*ius at factum*). El círculo vicioso resultante—en que texto interpreta hecho, y el hecho al texto—propicia, según Pagden, gran vulnerabilidad ante sus detractores. Poco convincente.

3546 Pardo, Isaac J. Juan de Castellanos: estudio de las *Elegías de varones ilustres de Indias.* 2. ed con emmiendas y adiciones. Caracas: Academia Nacional de la Historia, 1991. 622 p.: bibl., index. (Biblioteca de la Academia Nacional de la Historia: Fuentes para la historia colonial de Venezuela; 211)

Edición revisada y aumentada de estudio—publicado antes en 1961—de vida del autor y análisis formal (fuentes, aspectos literarios, reflejos de antigüedad clásica, aspectos novelescos, etc.) de *Elegías,* incluyendo apéndice lexicográfico y antología de la obra. Pardo se propone, con ánimo laudatorio, demostrar que esta obra fundacional es testimonio lúcido de la vida intelectual criolla como trasplante feliz de la cultura renacentista europea. Bibliografía poco actualizada.

3547 Pérez, María Teresa. El descubrimiento del Amazonas: historia y mito. Sevilla: Ediciones Alfar, 1989? 251 p.: bibl. (Alfar/universidad: 47. Serie Investigación y ensayo)

Partiendo de afirmación de Pupo-Walker de que mucha de la historiografía colonial fue motivada por "una pertinaz voluntad de creación," Pérez estudia importante texto marginado (*Relación del descubrimiento del famoso Río Grande de las Amazonas,* de Fray Gaspar de Carvajal) atendiendo a las relaciones que en él existen entre el discurso histórico y el discurso literario. Las amazonas y El Dorado simplemente son ejemplos, para la autora, de la catalización en este texto histórico de la "imaginación novelesca" española del siglo XVI.

3548 Pittarello, Elide. *Arauco domado* de Pedro de Oña o la vía erótica de la conquista. (*Dispositio/Ann Arbor,* 14:36/38, 1989, p. 247–270)

Dos elementos determinan la composición del poema de Oña según este excelente artículo: 1) tradición clásica y renacentista del relato de la guerra que superpone la pública, severa y masculina acción bélica a la privada, sensual y feminoide vida amorosa; y 2) exigencia propagandística impuesta por mecenas Hurtado de Mendoza. Tal esquema permite feminizacion del indígena (corpóreo bárbaro entregado al amor y descuidando tareas militares) y exaltación de los varoniles y ascetas cristianos que desprecian el placer mientras propagan la civilización.

3549 Rojas Bez, José. Sor Juana y *El Divino Narciso:* síntesis americanista del "matrimonio divino." (*Islas/Santa Clara,* 94, sept./dic. 1989, p. 107–121, bibl.)

Exposición de antecedentes del uso de imágenes nupciales en la cultura universal (períodos prehistórico, egipcio-mesopotámico, judaico, místico-cristiano) para colocar *El Divino Narciso* como cumbre del tratamiento del tema logrando una "síntesis americanista" del matrimonio divino. Aunque esquemático, es un interesante intento de contextualización cultural del motivo central de este auto sacramental.

3550 Sabàt de Rivers, Georgina. A feminist rereading of Sor Juana's dream. (*in* Feminist perspectives on Sor Juana Inés de la Cruz. Edited by Stephanie Merrim. Detroit, Mich.: Wayne State Univ. Press, 1991, p. 142–161)

Destacando prominencia de adjetivos, personajes mitológicos y problemáticas femeninos en el *Sueño*, y comparándolo con los imaginería y vocabulario masculino-centristas de Góngora en *Soledades*, Sabàt de Rivers demuestra cómo Sor Juana, en un mundo que obstaculiza a la mujer intelectual, conscientemente utiliza en su poema recursos retóricos propios de lo femenino y ofrece nuevas soluciones al viejo problema— considerado propio de hombres—de la comprensión filosófica del universo.

3551 Seed, Patricia. "Failing to marvel:" Atahualpa's encounter with the word. (*LARR*, 26:1, 1991, p. 7–32)

Compara versión del español Francisco de Jerez sobre entrega del libro a Atahualpa, y su subsiguiente captura, con versiones del Inca Garcilaso, Titu Cussi Yupangui y Guamán Poma. Para Jerez la noción de superioridad cultural europea sancionada por posesión del alfabeto permite celebrar la postración de los andinos. Las versiones nativas rechazan transparencia de cultura europea y cuestionan la confortable ilusión de cronistas españoles de que la superioridad universal de su sistema de creencias y rasgos culturales justifica la masacre de Cajamarca en 1532.

3552 Stolley, Karen. *El lazarillo de ciegos caminantes:* un itinerario crítico. Hanover, NH: Ediciones del Norte, 1992. 1 v.

Considerando el lenguaje como un tema subyacente del *Lazarillo*—y más prominente que los de la historiografía y la geografía coloniales tradicionalmente estudiados—Stolley examina epígrafes, diálogos, anécdotas, chistes y juegos de palabras para exponer la complejidad y múltiples posibilidades de lecturas de un texto cuyas ambivalencias, más que descuidos del autor, son expresión inevitable de una obra compuesta en una indeseable situación colonial. Es una de las más serias y sólidas contribuciones de los últimos años al estudio de la prosa del siglo XVIII hispanoamericano.

3553 Urbano, Victoria. Sor Juana Inés de la Cruz: amor, poesía, soledumbre. Edición y prólogo de Adelaida López de Martínez. Potomac, Md.: Scripta Humanistica, 1990. 227 p.: bibl., port. (Scripta Humanistica; 76)

Dándole valor testimonial a poesía, prosa y teatro de Sor Juana, Urbano intenta reconstruir biografía y demostrar que el amor no es arquetipo literario sino experiencia vivencial; la melancolía por la imposibilidad de adquirir el conocimiento, un sentimiento romántico; y su prosa un tratado de amor evangélico. Interesantes lecturas—destacando la resistencia de la monja frente al medio hostil en que vivió—menoscabadas por su exceso de conjeturas biográficas sobre la monja.

3554 Villagrá, Gaspar Pérez de. Historia de la Nueva México, 1610. Critical and annotated Spanish/English edition, translated and edited by Miguel Encinias, Alfred Rodríguez, and Joseph P. Sánchez. Albuquerque: Univ. of New Mexico Press, 1992. 367 p.: bibl., ill., index, maps. (Pasó por aquí)

Cuidadosa edición bilingüe del poema de Villagrá (1555–1620) sobre expedición de Juan de Oñate en 1596 a la frontera norte de la Nueva España en la cual aquél participó. Típica epopeya celebratoria de expansionismo europeo en regiones no europeas ceñida cronológicamente a los eventos vistos por Villagrá. Edición cotejada con las de Alcalá de Henares (1610), México (1900) y la traducción al inglés, de Albuquerque (años 20). Incluye útiles estudios preliminares sobre características literarias del poema y sobre los hechos históricos de la colonización de Nuevo México desde principios del siglo XVI.

3555 Williams, Jerry M. Anonymous satire in Peralta Barnuevo's *Diálogo de los muertos:* la causa académica. (*Hispanófila/Chapel Hill*, 108, 1993, p. 1–14)

Exposición y análisis de este interesante *Diálogo* en prosa (1720) de circulación clandestina que critica y desafía la insidiosa, poderosa e inconsistente censura oficial impuesta sobre la expresión artística e intelectual de la Lima del Siglo de la Ilustración. Rigurosa y valiosa contextualización histórico-cultural de texto—desconocido antes—que muestra tal vez la única expresión de rebeldía de Peralta contra el status quo. Excelente y necesaria propuesta de reeamen de un período cultural tradicionalmente descartado como estéril.

3556 Zamora, Margarita. Reading Columbus. Berkeley: Univ. of California Press, 1993. 1 v.: bibl., index. (Latin American literature and culture; 9)

Atendiendo a recursos retóricos, antes que a elementos referenciales, este formidable estudio de los textos más controversiales de Colón en 500 años explora la manera como el autor y sus lectores los usaron, al igual que las circunstancias y las consecuencias de tal uso. Antes que reproducir lo que pasó, Zamora aspira a comprender las maneras en que el acto de escritura de los europeos hizo de los eventos del Descubrimiento algo inteligible en el desarrollo de un discurso central en la colonización en América.

TEXTS, EDITIONS, ANTHOLOGIES

3557 **Adorno, Rolena.** Censorship and its evasion: Jerónimo Román and Bartolomé de las Casas. (*Hispania/Teachers*, 3:28, 1993, p. 812–827)

Examinando dos ediciones de *Repúblicas del mundo* (1575, 1595) de Jerónimo Román y Zamora (1536–97), Adorno demuestra como mediante un masivo plagio de la *Apologética historia sumaria* (1560) de Las Casas este lascasista desafía la censura en la época de Felip II, denuncia la brutal colonización de las Indias y augura, en consecuencia, la caída de España. Este excelente ensayo reexamina tanto la complejidad de la censura española en la época como la resistencia a ella.

3558 **Adorno, Rolena.** Los debates sobre la naturaleza del indio en el siglo XVI: textos y contextos. (*Rev. Estud. Hisp./Río Piedras*, 19, 1992, p. 47–66)

La naturaleza (bestial o racional) del indio americano no es problema filosófico sino producto del debate sobre el derecho de la Corona para conquistarlos y gobernarlos; Vitoria, al respecto, no se diferencia de Sepúlveda ni se parece a Las Casas como tradicionalmente se cree. Con estas aclaraciones Adorno destaca la modernidad del pensamiento de Las Casas quien, con base en novedosos de principios del derecho canónico medieval, propone una relación entre españoles y americanos basada en el respeto.

3559 **Adorno, Rolena.** The discursive encounter of Spain and America: the authority of eyewitness testimony in the writing of history. (*William Mary Q.*, 49, 1992, p. 210–228)

Valioso estudio de relaciones entre el valor del testimonio histórico (de testigos oculares) y de la autoridad historiográfica (de historiadores eruditos) en la composición de

la *Historia verdadera* de Bernal Díaz y la *Apologética historia sumaria* (1560) de Las Casas. La síntesis de ambas tradiciones les sirve a ambos para fortalecer su carácter veraz y la efectividad de sus propósitos políticos, ideológicos y personales. Bibliografía con nuevas fuentes primarias e interesantes fuentes secundarias.

3560 **Adorno, Rolena.** The warrior and the war community: construction of the civil order in Mexican conquest history. (*Dispositio/Ann Arbor*, 14:36/38, 1989, p. 225–246)

El examen de la noción de "milicia cristiana" en historiadores de la conquista de México (J.G. de Sepúlveda, Gómara y Cervantes de Salazar) y de las conceptualizaciones precolombinas de la guerra en el mestizo Alva Ixtlilxochitl, le sirven a Adorno para convincentemente demostrar como la figura del guerrero ingenioso, prudente y valeroso, y su correspondiente imaginada comunidad guerrera adaptada a un auditorio europeo, son utilizadas por cada historiador para identificarse con, y diferenciarse de, "los otros" y para representar culturas civilizadas.

3561 **Amerindian images and the legacy of Columbus.** Edited by René Jara and Nicholas Spadaccini. Minneapolis: Univ. of Minnesota Press, 1992. 758 p.: bibl., ill., index. (Hispanic issues; 9)

Crítica literaria, lingüística, semiótica, antropología, etnografía e historia son las disciplinas contribuyentes en las perspicaces lecturas de textos (de Las Casas, de Bry, Colón, Fray R. Pané, Guamán Poma, Motolinía, Sor Juana, Bartolomé Arzáns, etc.) del período colonial que exploran las ficciones que le dieron fidedignidad a la construcción de la historia de la América española. Los 23 robustos estudios e "Introducción" del volumen ilustran también la conformación de un imaginario americano al calor de su constante resistencia contra la colonización europea. Recomendable colección de trabajos críticos de presitigiosos especialistas.

3562 **Anadón, José.** Historiografía literaria de América colonial. Santiago: Ediciones Univ. Católica de Chile, 1988. 420 p.: bibl. (Investigaciones)

La realidad americana fue contemplada imaginativamente por varones europeos, y muchos escribieron sobre extraordinarias vidas y experiencias novelescas. Con tal premisa Anadón estudia textos marginales de las letras del período colonial (*Peregrinación de Bartolomé Lorenzo* de Acosta, *Tragicomedia de Loubayssin de la Marca, Desierto Prodigioso* de Solís de Valenzuela, *Infortunios de Alonso Ramírez* de Sigüenza y Góngora y otros) para discernir entre historia y literatura. Rigurosa documentación y lectura independiente de textos. Importante contribución a pesar de tal limitante premisa.

3563 Antología general de la poesía ecuatoriana durante la colonia española. Recopilación de Alejandro Carrión. Quito: División de Cultura e Información, Banco de los Andes, 1992. 362 p.

Selección de poemas—muchos desconocidos o de difícil acceso—de 42 autores, entre ellos cuatro religiosas, que vivieron entre fines del siglo XVI y fines del siglo XVIII. En su mayoría influidos por Góngora, los sonetos, romances, coplas, canciones, décimas, etc., tratan, entre otros, temas religiosos, elegíacos, laudatorios y amorosos, generalmente en tono celebratorio. Una nota biográfica presenta a cada poeta. Util trabajo de divulgación de la expresión menor de la poesía renacentista en el Ecuador colonial.

3564 Blanco, José Joaquín. La literatura en la Nueva España. v. 1, Conquista y Nuevo Mundo. México: Cal y Arena, 1989. 254 p.: bibl.

Recuento historicista de la vida y obra de historiógrafos (conquistadores y religiosos), poetas y dramaturgos españoles, criollos, mestizos e indígenas pertenecientes al canon de las letras de la Nueva España en el siglo XVI. Las valoraciones de cada autor dependen de su contraste con modelos europeos. Poco crítico. Bibliografía muy tradicional.

3565 Blanco, José Joaquín. La literatura en la Nueva España. v. 2, Esplendores y miserias de los criollos. México: Cal y Arena, 1989. 293 p.: bibl.

Vol. 2 de historia de las letras de la Nueva España dedicado a la llamada literatura "novohispana" de los criollos de los siglos XVII y XVIII. Las obras de escritores de diversos géneros y calidad como Juan de Palafox, Luis de Sandoval Zapata, Sor Juana, Sigüenza y Góngora, Cabrera y Quintero, Clavijero y otros, se examinan en relación con su apego o independencia de la literatura espa-

ñola de estos siglos, en un esfuerzo por buscar productos felices o malogrados.

3566 Bolaños, Alvaro Félix. Caballero cristiano y bárbaros paganos en la historia de la conquista española de América. (*Roman. Q.*, 40:2/3, 1993, p. 78–88)

Examinando ejemplos de descripciones de combates entre conquistadores e indígenas (de Gonzalo Fernández de Oviedo, Lucas Fernández de Piedrahita, Pedro Cieza de León, Fray Pedro Simón y otros cronistas), artículo plantea cómo la ética caballeresca de la España del Renacimiento validaba los códigos culturales utilizados por el historiador europeo de la época de la conquista de América para establecer campos opuestos en contienda: buenos/malos, correctores/corregibles, cristianos/paganos.

3567 Buedel, Barbara Foley. Medieval didacticism recast as Baroque satire: Juan del Valle y Caviedes' "Privilegios del Pobre." (*in* MACLAS: Latin American essays. Edited by Alvin Cohen. Bethlehem, Penn.: Middle Atlantic Council of Latin American Studies; Lehigh Univ., 1992, v. 5, p. 8–18, bibl.)

Breve y sugestiva especulación sobre las grandes similitudes entre el poema satírico de Caviedes y algunos pasajes de tres textos didácticos medievales *Calila e Dinma, Libro de los cien capítulos* y *Libro del cavallero Zifar*) y el tratamiento de la doble moral en la exaltación del rico y el pobre.

3568 Burke, Peter. Chivalry in the New World. (*in* Chivalry in the renaissance. Edited by Sydney Anglo. Rochester, N.Y.: Boydell Press, 1990, p. 253–262)

La demostración de: 1) la popularidad de los libros de caballerías entre los conquistadores y colonizadores españoles de los siglos XV a XVII; y 2) el planteamiento del problema de la supervivencia de este género literario en la cultura brasileña de los siglos XIX y XX son los dos temas de este bien documentado e informativo artículo. Lo primero reproduce las conclusiones de Irving Leonard (*Books of the Brave*, 1949); lo segundo intenta, sin éxito, explicar tal supervivencia a través de la noción de "sociedad de frontera."

3569 Castro-Klarén, Sara. Dancing and the sacred in the Andes: from the Taqui-Oncoy to Rasu-ñiti. (*in* New World encounters. Edited by Stephen Greenblatt. Berkeley: Univ. of California Press, 1993, p. 159–176)

Taqui-Oncoy es una danza ritual de resistencia surgida entre los indios del Perú en 1565 ante colapso del imperio y cosmos incaicos (cuyos rasgos perviven en danzas andinas de hoy). Detallado examen de su origen y naturaleza en el contexto de la represión colonial en el siglo XVI y la historia y la mitología andina. Señala brevemente su presencia en el cuento *La agonía de Rasa-Niti* (1962) de José María Arguedas destacando similitud con descripciones de esta danza en crónicas del Perú.

3570 Cerrón Puga, María Luisa. Fernán Pérez de Oliva, traductor de Pedro Martír de Anglería: la historia de la invención de las Yndias. (*Edad Oro*, 10, primavera 1991, p. 33–51)

Buen estudio que demuestra cómo la traducción de Pérez de Oliva al español de *De orbe novo decades* (1493–1500 de forma epistolar) es realmente una interpretación del original narrado por Mártir. Ambos textos contrastan en forma y tono. El propósito apologético de la conquista como misión imperialista llevó a Oliva a la revisión, ampliación y reorganización del texto de Mártir. Importante aporte sobre un texto injustamente poco estudiado.

3571 Chang-Rodríguez, Raquel. El discurso disidente: ensayos de literatura colonial peruana. Lima: Pontificia Univ. Católica del Perú, Fondo Editorial, 1991. 282 p.: bibl., ill., index.

Colección de importantes ensayos (algunos inéditos) sobre: 1) el rescate andino de la historia de la conquista (Titu Cusi Yupanqui, Joan de Santa Cruz Pachacuti, Guamán Poma); 2) apropiación india, mestiza o criolla (masculina y femenina) de escritura para reordenar mundo colonial y proponer diversidad en el futuro (Guamán Poma, Inca Garcilaso, Sor Juana); y 3) examen de voces diversas (europeas, criollas, indias, mestizas) en castellano y quechua del Perú del siglo XVII (J. Mogravejo de la Cerda, J. del Valle y Caviedes, Conde de la Granja, Sor Juana). Enfasis en estrategias de resistencia de los textos.

3572 Clendinnen, Inga. "Fierce and unnatural cruelty:" Cortés and the conquest of Mexico. (*in* New World encounters. Edited by Stephen Greenblatt. Berkeley: Univ. of Calif. Press, 1993, p. 12–41)

Admirable relectura de versiones más conocidas (Cortés, Bernal, Durán, códices aztecas, etc.) del encuentro bélico entre españoles y mexicanos (1519–21) para destacar existencia de mutuo sistema de lectura y asimilación de signos culturales entre los distintos bandos que modificó la conducta y la estrategia de cada uno. Destruye noción de absolutas predominancia española y postración indígena propaladas por Prescott y Todorov. Llama atención sobre complejidad de fuentes históricas por lo general poco fidedignas o nada totalizantes.

3573 Crítica y descolonización: el sujeto colonial en la cultura latinoamericana. Coordinación de Beatriz González Stephan y Lúcia Helena Costigan. Caracas: Academia Nacional de la Historia, 1992. 669 p.: bibl., ill. (Biblioteca de la Academia Nacional de la Historia: Fuentes para la historia colonial de Venezuela; 216)

Además de textos ya canónicos (de Colón, Fray R. Pané, Cabeza de Vaca, Fernández de Oviedo, Ercilla, etc.), este volumen pretende darles espacio a las manifestaciones discursivas subalternas y periféricas (de Fernando de Alarcón, Pineda y Bascuñán, Madre María de San José, Fray Francisco del Castillo, etc.) privilegiadas por nuevas perspectivas críticas. La constitución del sujeto colonial, el origen de la identidad americana, el discurso criollo, el imaginario del "otro," la resistencia a diversos niveles contra la colonización europea, los discursos disímiles y disidentes, etc., son temas que ocupan a estos 36 trabajos. Este exitoso esfuerzo editorial ofrece buena visión panorámica de la tendencia interdisciplinaria y de crítica cultural de los estudios de las letras del período colonial hispanoamericano.

3574 Cronistas indios y mestizos. v. 1. Recopilación de Francisco Carrillo. Lima: Editorial Horizonte, 1991- . 1 v.: bibl., ill. (Enciclopedia histórica de la literatura peruana; 6)

Antología de textos andinos vertidos al español a través de traducciones o transcripciones de informantes quechuas (ladinos, mestizos), y acompañados de noticias generales sobre selecciones de Collapiña, Supno y "otros quipucamayos," *Relación de la conquista del Perú* de Titu Cussi Yupanqui, *Relación de antigüedades deste Reyno del Pirú* de Juan de Santa Cruz Pachacuti, Blas Valera, *Diosos y hombre de Huarochirí* de Cristóbal

484 / Handbook of Latin American Studies v. 54

Choqiecasa, Hernando Pauccar y otros. Muy útil selección de textos importantes.

3575 Damrosch, David. The aesthetics of conquest: Aztec poetry before and after Cortés. (*in* New World encounters. Edited by Stephen Greenblatt. Berkeley: Univ. of Calif. Press, 1993, p. 139–158)

El esteticismo de los poemas aztecas prehispánicos está íntimamente relacionado con la brutal política imperial azteca. Poesía, imperio, guerra, milicia, muerte y regeneración coexisten en la imaginería de los poetas nobles aztecas epígonos del imperio. Así Damrosch confronta la supuesta ambivalencia no resuelta de sutil esteticismo/rudeza militar imperial y la existencia de poemas estéticamente "puros" según han visto Daniel Brinton, Angel María Garibay, y Miguel León-Portilla, entre otros. Formidable trabajo.

3576 Davis, Elizabeth B. "Conquistas de las Indias de Dios:" early poetic appropriations of the Indies by the Spanish Renaissance. (*Hisp. J.*, 11:1, Spring 1990, p. 45–59)

Exploración de temprana incorporación de imágenes del Nuevo Mundo en el lenguaje metafórico de poetas renacentistas (Francisco de Aldana y Alonso de Ledesma) que nunca visitaron el Nuevo Mundo. Aunque en sus obras la imagen del Nuevo Mundo como lugar de exquisitas riquezas se subvierte, no desplaza completamente la previa y similar imaginería oriental. La riqueza material de las Indias en estos poetas, según Davis, sirve únicamente como metáfora de la riqueza espiritual.

3577 Early images of the Americas: transfer and invention. Edited by Jerry M. Williams and Robert Earl Lewis. Tucson: Univ. of Arizona Press, 1993. 319 p.: bibl., ill., index, maps.

Colección de 12 ensayos interdisciplinarios, con un amplio auditorio en mente, sintetizando complejidad del discurso colonial e integrando aproximaciones contemporáneas y tradicionales. Incluye temas como íconos utópicos y bárbaros de las culturas indígenas, creatividad histórica y literaria, dimensiones simbólicas de mediaciones culturales, y la confrontación geográfica de Europa con el cambio de las fronteras de la ciencia. La introducción ofrece un excelente panorama de la historia literaria del siglo XVI.

3578 Espinosa Fernández de Córdoba, Carlos R. La mascarada del Inca: una investigación acerca del teatro político de la colonia. (*Misc. Hist. Ecuat.*, 2:2, 1989, p. 6–39, plates, table)

Interesante examen de función social de íconos (pinturas, imágenes sagradas, arengas, cartas) y su escenificación durante el breve ejercicio del poder de un corregidor descendiente de incas, Don Alonso Florencia Inca, en la Real Audiencia de Quito en 1666. Expone dos visiones del Inca gobernador colonial: 1) cliente del Rey (inmerso en comercio de mercedes con españoles); y 2) descendiente de autoridades nativas conectadas con estrategias de pacificación en el sistema colonial.

3579 Garcés, María Antonia. Coaches, litters, and chariots of war: Montaigne and Atahualpa. (*J. Hisp. Philol.*, 16:2, 1992, p. 155–183)

Exploración del viaje cognoscitivo de Montaigne al Nuevo Mundo ("coche" es para Garcés metonimia del vehículo de la mente) hasta encontrar el otro coche en que viajaba Atahualpa, antes de caer en manos de Pizarro. Montaigne hace radical y abierta investigación de la alteridad americana (para denunciar la brutalidad de la conquista española) en contraste con la cerrada investigación—de menor simpatía con diferencias culturales—de López de Gómara. Sutil examen de estrategias retóricas de exploración epistemológica del "otro" americano.

3580 Los garcilasistas: antología. Prólogo, selección y bibliografía selecta de César Toro Montalvo. Lima: Univ. Inca Garcilaso de la Vega; Consejo Nacional de Ciencia y Tecnología, 1989. 452 p.: bibl.

Edición conmemorativa de 450 años del nacimiento del Inca Garcilaso de una colección de 29 trabajos dispersos antes en libros y publicaciones periódicas sobre su vida y obra, y escritos entre los siglos XIX y XX. La selección de estudios y comentarios (de autores como William Prescott, Menéndez y Pelayo, Porras Barrenechea, Luis Alberto Sánchez, José Durand, etc.) no tiene en cuenta un tema específico y privilegia aportes de carácter encomiástico.

3581 Gaylord, Mary M. Spain's Renaissance conquest and the retroping of identity. (*J. Hisp. Philol.*, 16:2, 1992, p. 124–136)

La insistencia de los españoles en el relato de guerras entre cristianos europeos e infieles no europeos (desde el Medioevo hasta la conquista de América) revela para Gaylord un doble esfuerzo por construir identidades personal y nacional. En tal actividad política y lingüística—dependiente de nociones de superioridad étnica, religiosa y cultural aristotélicas—relatos como el de Rodrigo y la Cava, el Cid, el Abencerraje, y los de Bernal Díaz y Cabeza de Vaca establecen esquema de dominación determinado por ansiosa conquista de "otros" y de sí mismo.

3582 Gerli, Michael. Columbus and the shape of the world: authority and experience in the *Relación* of the third voyage. (*J. Hisp. Philol.*, 16:2, 1992, p. 209–222)

Buen examen de la calculada construcción retórica (religiosa y providencial con mitos y textos canónicos medievales) de la *Relación* del tercer viaje de Cólon en contraste con la simple construcción testimonial del *Diario* del primero. Con esta mediación retórica y ficticia los eventos narrados en esta *Relación*, según Gerli, adquieren validez y fidedignidad para lectores más interesados en historias con argumentaciones culturalmente más reconocibles que en la simple exposición de material testimonial.

3583 González de Eslava, Fernán. *Villancicos, romances, ensaladas y otras canciones devotas:* Libro Segundo de los *Coloquios espirituales y sacramentales y canciones divinas,* México, Diego López Dávalos, 1610. Ed. crítica, 1. ed. Introducción, notas y apéndices de Margit Frenk Alatorre. México: Colegio de México, Centro de Estudios Lingüísticos y Literarios, 1989. 530 p.: bibl., index. (Biblioteca novohispana; 1)

Edición crítica de poesía religiosa conocida antes sólo antológicamente. Util estudio preliminar (biografía, estudio de poesía en contexto de lírica española de la época, circunstancias de su producción y difusión, y características formales). En cinco apéndices incluye todos los poemas de González de Eslava—o sobre él—hasta ahora encontrados y ausentes de las poco disponibles ediciones parciales anteriores (de México en 1610 y su reedición en 1877 por García Icazbalceta). Gran aporte al estudio de la vida cultural del siglo XVI en la Nueva España.

3584 González Vigil, Ricardo. Comentemos al Inca Garcilaso. Lima: Banco Central de Reserva del Perú, Fondo Editorial, 1989. 362 p.: bibl., index.

El título confunde porque es una antología del Inca Garcilaso con motivo de 450 años de su nacimiento. La introducción es un florilegio (vida y obra de Garcilaso, comentarios del editor a fragmento de la antología) que privilegia críticos afectos a Garcilaso (Riva-Agüero, Miró Quesada, José Durand, etc.), y desautoriza otros que, según González, no lo son. Incluye fragmentos de *Diálogos de amor* de Hebreo León, *La Florida del Inca, Comentarios reales,* e *Historia general del Perú.*

3585 Greenblatt, Stephen Jay. Marvelous possessions: the wonder of the New World. Chicago: Univ. of Chicago Press, 1991. 202 p., 8 p. of plates: bibl., ill., index.

En la representación verbal y visual que los cronistas del Renacimiento hicieron de los no europeos, el asombro determina, según Greenblatt, modo de comprensión, posesión y/o desprecio de lo extraño. Ese asombro articula dos tipos de discursos: el de "la no-posesión" en predecesores de Colón como Madeville, y el de la "posesión," que justifica brutalidad de la conquista, en Colón, Cortés, Bernal Díaz, Montaigne y menos conocidos exploradores ingleses en Norteamérica (cuyos textos son analizados parcialmente). Interesantes disertaciones sobre textos y sus contextos culturales de un estudioso no hispanista.

3586 Iglesia, Cristina. Conquista y mito blanco. (*in* Cautivas y misioneros: mitos blancos de la conquista. Buenos Aires: Catálogos Editora, 1987, p. 11–88)

Hambre y derrota, en tierra carente de oro y plata y rica en conflictos bélicos, se erigen como temas estructurantes en primer siglo de escritura del Río de la Plata (en Luis de Miranda, Ulrico Schmidel, Cabeza de Vaca, Barco Centenera y Ruy Díaz de Guzmán). Es, sin embargo, el relato ficcional de pretensiones históricas de Ruy Díaz de Guzmán—sobre la cautiva española Lucía de Miranda—el que logra articular para la imaginación popular argentina una justificación de la violenta colonización española (civilización) sobre tierra y habitantes americanos (barbarie) dominante desde 1572 hasta hoy. Admirable trabajo.

3587 Leonard, Irving Albert. Books of the brave: being an account of books and of men in the Spanish Conquest and settlement of the sixteenth-century New World. New introduction by Rolena Adorno. Berkeley: Univ. of California Press, 1992. 453 p.: bibl., ill., index.

Reedición de uno de los estudios más importantes de los últimos 50 años sobre la importación de cultura impresa a las colonias españolas en América. Demuestra documentalmente la amplia circulación y lectura de la ficción literaria en estas colonias a pesar de las prohibiciones reales. Incluye—por primera vez en edición inglesa—importante apéndice de documentos. Excelente introducción de Rolena Adorno sobre contexto intelectual en que se generó y escribió el proyecto del autor, así como las razones de su perdurabilidad en actuales estudios de historia y cultura hispanoamericana colonial y contemporánea.

3588 Lewis, Tracy K. The mind of the prisoner: ancient sources and modern echoes in the literature of the Andes. (*Lat. Am. Indian Lit. J.*, 4:2, 1988, p. 151–166)

Para Lewis, la impotencia de prisioneros que postrados sufren e imploran clemencia de fuerzas superiores constituye un rasgo común en las canciones de prisión de la *Nueva corónica* de Guamán Poma, el drama quechua *Ollantay* y la novela *El sexto* de J.M. Arguedas. Su agudo y suscinto análisis de los tres textos convence; no así su presupuesto—no demostrado—de que tal impotencia caracteriza toda la literatura hispanoamericana. Incluye versiones quechua e inglesa de canciones.

3589 MacCormack, Sabine. Demons, imagination, and the Incas. (*in* New World encounters. Edited by Stephen Greenblatt. Berkeley: Univ. of California Press, 1993, p. 101–126)

La imaginación como vehículo que el demonio puede usar para minar la sociedad cristiana fue noción con la que evangelizadores y cronistas españoles admiraron adelantos culturales incas y condenaron su "erróneo" sistema religioso. Las Casas (en *Apologética*) resuelve ese conflicto señalando que tanto la imaginación europea como la americana es susceptible de manipulaciones demoníacas. Valiosa discusión sobre milagros, apariciones y prodigios en España y complejidad de ritos en los Andes resalta modernidad de Las Casas y propone relectura interdisciplinaria de cronistas peruanos.

3590 Manual de literatura hispanoamericana. v. 1, Epoca virreinal. Coordinación de Felipe B. Pedraza Jiménez. Berriozar, Spain: Cénlit Ediciones, 1991. 1 v.: bibl., indexes.

Compendioso y útil texto de referencia para datos generales sobre numerosos autores y sus obras (clasificados por géneros literarios) de Hispanoamérica desde 1492 hasta el siglo XVIII. Contrastándola con el Renacimiento, el Barroco, y el Neoclasicismo, la literatura colonial—principalmente de euroamericanos—se evalúa en relación con sus similitudes con, o su carencia de, rasgos literarios españoles. Deja, entonces, sin explicar la complejidad cultural de textos fuera de ese canon eurocentrista.

3591 Mignolo, Walter. Colonial situations, geographical discourses and territorial representations: toward a diatopical understanding of colonial semiosis. (*Dispositio/Ann Arbor*, 14:36/38, 1989, p. 93–140)

Comparación de mapas europeos y "pinturas" indígenas (entre 1550 y 1615) en contexto de "situación colonial" (minoría étnica cristiana y tecnológicamente avanzada controla mayoría étnica no cristiana y tecnológicamente atrasada). La elaboración de mapas y descripciones geográficas europeas en Hispanoamérica supone: 1) concepción de "verdad" en que "mapa" es igual a "territorio;" y 2) escamoteo de coexistencia conflictiva de descripciones gráficas nativas del mismo territorio. Reproducción de ilustraciones. Aproximación epistemológica (en vez de historicista como la de Anthony Pagden, item bi94–4604, por ejemplo) a etnografía comparada.

3592 Mignolo, Walter. The darker side of the Renaissance: colonization and the discontinuity of the classical tradition. (*Renaissance Q.*, 45:4, 1992, p. 808–828)

Valiosa revisión de aportes críticos de la última década sobre textos coloniales hispanoamericanos al margen de tradición literaria europea renacentista (épica, lírica, drama, historia) y que conforman un híbrido cultural despreciado por estética renacentista y manuales tradicionales de "literatura colonial." Tales textos, o "lado oscuro de Renacimiento,"ocupan a nueva generación de estudiosos quienes van más allá de los "estudios literarios" y entablan productivo diálogo con ciencias humanas y sociales y la historia del arte.

3593 Moraña, Mabel. Formación del pensamiento crítico-literario en Hispanoamérica: época colonial. (*Rev. Crít. Lit. Latinoam.*, 26: 31/32, 1990, p. 255–265)

Examinando obras apologéticas y de reflexión sobre la poesía del siglo XVII y catálogos historiográficos y memorialistas del siglo XVIII, la autora plantea que la tensión entre el legado cultural español (renacentista y barroco), particularidades de la cultura americana (tradición criolla, indígena), e imprecisiones disciplinarias y metodológicas, caracteriza las primeras actitudes crítico-literaria hispanoamericanas unidas a formación de indentidad de las colonias. Muy pertinente precisión de problemas del estudio de las letras del período colonial.

3594 Myers, Kathleen. The representation of the New World phenomena: visual epistemology and Gonzalo Fernández de Oviedo's illustrations. (*in* Early images of the Americas: transfer and invention. Edited by Jerry Williams and Robert Lewis. Tucson: Univ. of Arizona Press, 1993, p. 183–213)

Elocuente discusión sobre los sistemas verbal e iconográfico de representación del Nuevo Mundo utilizados por Gonzalo Fernández de Oviedo—primer cronista oficial de las Indias—en su *Historia general y natural de las Indias* (1535). Por medio de sus propios dibujos, Oviedo establece como base de la representación histórica la preeminencia de la observación y la experiencia.

3595 New world encounters. Edited by Stephen Jay Greenblatt. Berkeley: Univ. of California Press, 1993. 344 p.: bibl., ill., index. (Representations books; 6)

Excelente colección de 14 ensayos (12 de ellos previamente publicados en *Representations* entre 1989–91), y una introducción del editor sobre el complejo registro de la otredad y la representación de culturas en autores como Colón, Cortés, Cabeza de Vaca, Las Casas, Jean de Léry, Cieza de León, Walter Raleigh y otros. Modernas perspectivas alejadas de apoteósica visión de los europeos en América. Adopta visión de los vencidos pero sin reducir la imagen de indígenas o europeos

al nivel de alegorías monolíticas. La consideración rigurosa de contingencias históricas y culturales de los hechos y personajes analizados así lo permiten.

3596 Núñez Cabeza de Vaca, Alvar. Los naufragios. Edición de Enrique Pupo-Walker. Madrid: Editorial Castalia, 1992. 334 p.: bibl., ill., index. (Nueva biblioteca de erudición y crítica; 5)

Esta edición de *Naufragios* es el más riguroso intento hasta ahora de reconstrucción de texto original. Contiene estudios biográficos del autor, evolución de la composición del texto en el siglo XVI, valoración narrativa, histórica y antropológica, y su impacto en la narrativa hispanoamericana. Amplia bibliografía anotada (ediciones, traducciones y estudios) desde el siglo XVI hasta 1990. Edición basada en la edición de 1555, *Naufragios y comentarios* y cotejada con la edición *Naufragios* (Zamora, 1542). No incluye *Comentarios* por no ser texto de autoría total de Núñez.

3597 Palencia-Roth, Michael. Cannibalism and the new man of Latin America in the 15th- and 16th-century European imagination. (*Comp. Civiliz. Rev.*, 12, 1985, p. 1–27)

El carácter no europeo del americano se lo explicaron los europeos del Renacimiento identificando a aquél con un salvaje antropófago. Examinando intentos de escritores del siglo XVI por entender el fenómeno del "caníbal" (Colón, Vespucci, Montaigne, Las Casas) y el sensacionalismo moralizante de las ilustraciones sobre caníbales entre los siglos XVI y XVII (de Hans Staden, A. Thevet, de Bry), Palencia-Roth plantea que es esta iconografía la que fija una negativa imagen cultural del "otro" americano, persistente aún hoy.

3598 Pérez Blanco, Lucrecio. Discursión en loor de la poesía: el otro lazarillo ético-estético de la literatura hispanoamericana del siglo XVII. (*Quinto Cent.*, 16, 1990, p. 209–237)

Celebración de esta reflexión en verso sobre naturaleza de la poesía (Sevilla, 1608) de la autora anónima peruana Clarinda. Para ella poesía es don divino ajeno al vulgo y propio de los ilustres. Este "Arte poética," según Pérez, es una "teologización" de poesía equiparable al *Compendio apologético en alabanza de la poesía* (1604) del mexicano Bernardo de Balbuena. Bien documentado aunque poco crítico. Interesante muestra del carácter elitista de la poesía de los euroamericanos de clase alta en la sociedad colonial.

3599 Poesía colonial hispanoamericana. Selección, prólogo y bibliografía de Horacio Jorge Becco. Caracas: Biblioteca Ayacucho, 1990. 419 p.: bibl. (Biblioteca Ayacucho; 154)

Reúne—según el editor—los mejores 32 poetas (españoles y criollos en su mayoría) de Hispanoamérica desde Juan de Castellanos (1522–1607) hasta Esteban de Terralla Landa (1785–90). Incluye dos mujeres: Sor Juana Inés de la Cruz y Francisca Josefa del Castillo. Estudio preliminar clasifica selecciones poéticas en relación con modelos del Renacimiento, Barroco, y Neoclasicismo y con categorías de popular, culta, épica, descriptiva, satírica y religiosa. Acompaña a cada selección útil noticia general de autor, obra y bibliografía. Buen panorama de la producción poética de los euroamericanos del período colonial.

3600 Rabasa, José. Inventing America: Spanish historiography and the formation of Eurocentrism. Norman: Univ. of Oklahoma Press, 1993. 281 p.: bibl., ill., index. (Oklahoma project for discourse and theory; 11)

La concepción popular del Nuevo Mundo como entidad natural susceptible de ser descubierta y comprendida—así sea imperfectamente—por los europeos del siglo XVI es una ilusión. Examinando textos de Colón, Cortés, Las Casas, Sahagún (entre otros) y el *Atlas* de Mercator, Rabasa no sólo le niega al hecho histórico de la llegada de Colón a América su condición de "descubrimiento" y "encuentro," sino que cuestiona la complacencia con que se han aceptado los rudimentos históricos, cartográficos y geográficos que sustentan una imagen del mundo desde el siglo XVI hasta hoy.

3601 Rabasa, José. Writing and evangelization in sixteenth-century Mexico. (*in* Early images of the Americas: transfer and invention. Edited by Jerry Williams and Robert Lewis. Tucson: Univ. of Arizona Press, 1993, p. 65–92)

Detenida lectura de textos de misioneros españoles sobre el primer siglo de colonización española en México. Rabasa demuestra que este corpus historiográfico sienta las bases de juicios sobre práctica, naturaleza y eficacia de la conversión al cristianismo. Destaca las diversas conceptualizaciones sobre creencias religiosas indígenas y modelos de transformación de las culturas nativas juzgadas por esos textos como incorrectas. Llama la atención sobre la relatividad de un corpus historiográfico generalmente considerado objetivo.

3602 *Revista de Estudios Hispánicos.* No. 19, número especial, 1992- . Río Piedras: Univ. of Puerto Rico.

Número dirigido por Mercedes López-Baralt consiste de variada colección de 27 estudios—la mayoría interdisciplinarios—sobre: 1) crónicas, relaciones e historias de las Indias en el contexto literario, cultural y político de su producción (de Colón, Fray R. Pané, Las Casas, Fernández de Oviedo, Cabeza de Vaca, etc.); 2) la suerte de la estética renacentista y barroca (Caviedes, Sor Juana, El lunarejo, Rosas de Oquendo); 3) iconografía, teatro colonial (Guamán Poma, *Usca Paucar*) y teatro del siglo XIX; y 4) sobre reescritura de textos coloniales por autores contemporáneos (Sor Juana y Lezama Lima, Colón y Carpentier, Fray S. Teresa de Mier y Reinaldo Arenas, etc).

3603 Reynal, Vicente. Juan de Castellanos y Puerto Rico: descubrimiento y otros relatos menores. (*Torre/Río Piedras*, 5:18, abril/junio 1991, p. 189–214)

Lectura de tres pasajes marginales de *Elegías de varones ilustres de Indias* para determinar certeza de datos históricos (lugar de descubrimiento, primeros pobladores, etc.) sobre Puerto Rico. Los pasajes corresponden al Capitán Juan Salas, el descubrimiento de Borinquen, y al Gobernador Francisco Bramón de Lugo. Reduce encuentro entre nativos y españoles a "feliz suceso" en el que dos pueblos "amorosamente" se fusionan "para construir otro nuevo" (p. 214).

3604 Rodríguez Prampolini, Ida. Amadises de América: hazaña de las Indias como empresa caballeresca. México: Academia Mexicana de la Historia, 1990. 203 p.: bibl.

Reedición (agregando introducción laudatoria de Luis Weckmann) de influyente ensayo publicado en 1948 que explora la relación entre la literatura caballeresca y las crónicas de Indias del siglo XVI. Reivindicando los libros de caballerías como documentos culturales que reflejan el carácter emprendedor del español, Rodríguez se propone la imposible tarea de demostrar que el impacto de estos textos en sus lectores motivó los hechos históricos de los españoles en la conquista de América.

3605 Romance Quarterly: Vol. 40, No. 2/3, 1993- , Spain and the New World. Washington: Heldref Publications.

Número expecial dirigido por Stephen Hart y Brian Dendle que con aproximación interdisciplinaria examina diversas formas en que textualmente se han percibido la exploración y conquista de América en 10 ensayos. Vol. 1 es dedicado a primeras versiones de la conquista (en carta de Colón de 1493, Fernández de Oviedo, Fray Pedro Simón, leyes de Indias de los dominicanos, y versiones nativas de la conquista); vol. 2 a las ramificaciones ideológicas contempóraneas de la conquista.

3606 Sabàt de Rivers, Georgina. Contribución de la mujer a la lírica colonial. (*in* Simposio sobre Literatura Latinoamericana, *1st, Moscow, 1986.* Literatura colonial hispanoamericana: coloquio de URSS-USA: Actas. Montevideo: Editorial Monte Sexto, 1990, p. 57–84)

Sugestiva exposición de la condición de opresión y la resistencia de la mujer en la literatura española del Renacimiento y en la lírica colonial hispanoamericana haciendo énfasis en su manejo de la expresión y silencio de su saber (basada en influyente ensayo de J. Ludmer sobre Sor Juana). Ofrece puntos de vista críticos interesantes y útiles que van más allá del plano celebratorio de los trabajos estudiados.

3607 Sabàt de Rivers, Georgina. Estudios de literatura hispanoamericana: Sor Juana Inés de la Cruz y otros poetas barrocos de la colonia. Barcelona: PPU, 1992. 355 p.: bibl., ill. (LHU; 6: Literatura. Ediciones y estudios: Ediciones)

Bernardo de Balbuena, Domínguez Camargo, varias mujeres poetas del Perú colonial, Sor Juana Inés de la Cruz, Santa Teresa de Jesús, Dorothy Schons y Octavio Paz son los temas del período colonial y de la crítica contemporánea de que se ocupa esta excelente colección de 16 ensayos sobre la suerte de los modelos líricos europeos en escritores euroamericanos. Su énfasis en el examen de

otras escritoras (como la anónima Amarilis peruana) enriquece el contexto de apreciación de autoras como Sor Juana.

3608 Salles-Reese, Verónica. The Apostle's footprints in ancient Peru: Christian appropriation of Andean myths. (*J. Hisp. Philol.*, 16:2, 1992, p. 185–193)

Examen de la reutilización que dos criollos agustinos (Fray Alonso Ramos Gavilán y Antonio de la Calancha) hacen en 1621 y 1638 de antiguos mitos andinos en narraciones sobre cristianización prehispánica en Perú. Esta legitimación de los mitos fue una alternativa a la brutal represión religiosa propuesta por el jesuita Francisco de Avila (diseñada en concilio limense 1582–88) que perturbó el modus vivendi establecido con los indios. Enfasis en transformación del mito de Viracocha en versiones de estos religiosos aliados de la resistencia cultural indígena. Excelente ensayo.

3609 Scharlau, Birgit. Nuevas tendencias en los estudios de crónicas y documentos del período colonial latinoamericano. (*Rev. Crít. Lit. Latinoam.*, 26: 31/32, 1990, p. 365–375, bibl.)

Plantea nuevas consideraciones en reinterpretación de crónicas coloniales (como importantes fuentes históricas e historiográficas). De la crisis del racionalismo occidental y la relación entre las culturas europeas y las no europeas han surgido, según Scharlau, nuevos problemas como la valoración del "otro," la hibridez transcultural de los textos, y el asunto de la oralidad vs. literariedad. Aunque esta propuesta no es novedosa en contexto crítico americano, es útil por formularse en contexto de intelectuales alemanes.

3610 Schvartzman, Julio. Entrada misional y correría evangélica: la lengua de la conquista espiritual. (*in* Cautivas y misioneras: mitos blancos de la conquista. Edición de Cristina Iglesia y Julio Schvartzman. Buenos Aires: Catálogos Editora, 1987, p. 89–205)

Lúcido y detallado estudio de gramáticas, vocabularios y manuales de comunicación con los "paganos" indígenas de misioneros en Lima, Asunción, Córdoba y las misiones sobre los Ríos Paraná y Uruguay. Schvartzman señala las estrategias con que se violentan los idiomas indígenas (en el contexto de la agresión militar y cultural colonialista) para la erradicación de las religiones y la cultura nativas consideradas inferiores. Destaca la poca confiabilidad de estudios lingüísticos de europeos sobre pueblos nativos considerados generalmente como objetivos. Util bibliografía.

3611 Simposio sobre Literatura Latinoamericana, 1st, Moscow, 1986. Literatura colonial hispanoamericana: coloquio URSS-USA. Edición de Iván A. Schulman y Evelyn Picon Garfield. Montevideo: Monte Sexto, 1990. 116 p.: bibl. (Temas; 015)

Ocho ponencias del Primer Simposio sobre literatura latinoamericana entre EE.UU. y Rusia (Moscú, 1986). Utopías de la Edad de Oro en España, formación de la conciencia criolla en el Barroco, literatura de la ilustración brasileña, y formación de la mentalidad hispanoamericana en el Inca Garcilaso son temas de cuatro estudiosos rusos. Los cuatro representantes de EE.UU. incluyen prosa colonial, punto de vista narrativo en *La araucana*, la mujer y la lírica colonial, y el pluralismo cultural peruano de Guamán Poma. Todos, excepto los artículos de Sàbat de Rivers y J. Ortega, tratan el tema de creación de una conciencia nacional americana en oposición a España.

3612 Velasco, María Mercedes de. Rodríguez Freyle: insigne maestro. (*Rev. Estud. Colomb. Latinoam.*, 11, 1991, p. 12–19)

Compara narración original y tratamiento de personajes de la historieta sobre Inés de Hinojosa de *El carnero* con dos novelas colombianas posteriores: *Los tres Pedros en la red de Inés de Hinojosa* (1864) de Temístocles Avellaneda Mendoza, y *Los pecados de Inés de Hinojosa* (1986) de Próspero Morales Pradilla. Afirma que de fuente narrativa de Freyle "emanan hilos que han logrado llegar hasta nuestros días" (también cita poemas inspirados por esa historia), pero el estudio poco produce además de esa afirmación.

3613 Víttori, José Luis. Del Barco Centenera y "La Argentina:" orígenes del realismo mágico en América. Santa Fe, Argentina: Ediciones Colmegna, 1991. 189 p.: bibl., ill., maps.

Considerando a Centenera como "historiador" y su "La Argentina" como un poema con "verdad documental" que evoca "emociones y fantasías" propias de la literatura, Víttori explora en esta obra la inserción de "la fantasía en la historia." Llamando a eso

"realismo mágico," intenta explicar origen y éxito de la literatura hispanoamericana actual. Exhaustivo estudio limitado en sus logros por la dualidad historia/ficción con que se aproxima a este interesante poema épico de la Argentina colonial.

3614 Way-Gómez, Nicolás. Cannibalism as defacement: Columbus's account of the fourth voyage. (*J. Hisp. Philol.*, 16:2, 1992, p. 195–208)

La horrorosa—para Cristóbal y Hernando Colón, Diego Alvarez Chanca y Pedro Mártir—apariencia "desfigurada" del indio del Caribe condujo a juicios *a priori* sobre sus supuestos depravación moral y canibalismo. La descripción inaugural de Cristóbal Colón, no detenida en detalles físicos, produce un "otro" americano carente de cara y especificidad cronológica que representa, no al indio del Caribe, sino a todos los antropófagos del mundo temidos por los europeos. Excelente dilucidación de mecanismo retórico de apropiación del "otro" americano en discurso colonial.

3615 Williams, Jerry M. El teatro del México colonial: época misionera. New York: P. Lang, 1992. 162 p.: bibl., ill. (Ibérica, 1056–5000; 4)

Significativa y útil contribución al estudio de los orígenes del teatro mexicano que enfoca tres aspectos: 1) historia, cultura y formas dramáticas nativas a la llegada de los españoles; 2) origen y desarrollo del teatro misionero a principios del siglo XVI que aprovechando formas dramáticas nativas busca imponer la religión y la cultura españolas sobre los indios; y 3) el teatro criollo popular.

MISCELLANEOUS

3616 Andagoya, Pascual de. Relación y documentos. Edición de Adrián Blázquez. Madrid: Historia 16, 1986. 227 p.: bibl., maps. (Crónicas de América; 27)

Edición moderna de extensa carta a Carlos V (1540), relación (1545?) y documentos varios (capitulaciones, concesiones y cartas) sobre primer intento de conquista del Perú. La descripción de rasgos naturalistas y etnográficos y la narración de la colonización de Castilla del Oro y las costas del Océano Pacífico del hoy territorio colombiano, se alternan con las tribulaciones de Andagoya ejerciendo la gobernación de la provincia del Río San Juan (occidente colombiano) usurpada por conquistadores renegados y exitosos (Sebastián de Benalcázar desde el Perú, el Liceniado Vallido desde Cartagena, etc.). Rigurosa edición de Blázquez de textos que merecen mayor atención de los estudiosos.

3617 Mignolo, Walter. Putting the Americas on the map: geography and the colonization of space. (*Colon. Lat. Am. Rev.*, 1 : 1/2, 1992, p. 25–63, bibl., photos)

Considerando los mapas, no como representaciones "verdaderas" de la tierra, sino como artefactos cognoscitivos y culturalmente relativos utilizados tanto para representar concepciones de espacio, tiempo y estructura del cosmos, como para orientarse y colonizar espacios y mentalidades, Mignolo estudia las similitudes entre mapas europeos, asiáticos, mexicanos e incas desde la Edad Media hasta el siglo XVII. Enfasis es en mapas europeos y su papel histórico de expansión territorial y control colonial en América. Incluye 21 ilustraciones explicadas.

3618 Pérez Martínez, Herón. Estudios sorjuanianos. Morelia, México: Gobierno del Estado de Michoacán, Instituto Michoacano de Cultura, 1988. 182 p.: bibl. (Col. Literatura)

Reedición de carta de Sor Juana al Padre Núñez (publicada tres veces antes por Au-

reliano Tapia Méndez, Octavio Paz y Antonio Alatorre) y reflexiones sobre ella. Incluye edición de carta de Sor Filotea, "aprobación" del Padre Calleja, cap. 5 de *Vida* del Padre Núñez y discusión sobre composición de Sor Juana de "ovillejos" (pareados de rima interna). Tono confrontacional contra los "sorjuanistas" por desconocer papel de la "ciencia religiosa" (p. 9) en la obra de la monja. Aporte modesto que depende mucho del supuesto de que la obra literaria de la autora da claves sobre su biografía.

3619 Zamora, Margarita. Christopher Columbus's *Letter to the sovereigns:* announcing the discovery. (*in* New World encounters. Edited by Stephen Greenblatt. Berkeley: Univ. of California Press, 1993, p. 1–11)

Traducción anotada al inglés de una carta recién descubierta de Colón a los Reyes Católicos anunciando el descubrimiento. En sus comentarios, Zamora destaca detalles omitidos por Colón en otras cartas (a Luis de Santángel y Gabriel Sánchez) haciendo el mismo anuncio: información valiosa para potencias extranjeras, rencillas internas en expedición, tribulación de Colón en España antes del primer viaje y plan del uso de riqueza de las Indias para recuperar el Santo Sepulcro. Estas omisiones enriquecen posibilidades de investigación y discusión de textos colombinos.

19th Century: Spanish American Literature Before Modernism

WILLIAM H. KATRA, *Assistant Professor of Spanish, University of Wisconsin-La Crosse*

THREE OUTSTANDING BOOK-LENGTH studies published during the past biennium offer a high critical standard by which to guide future research on Spanish America's 19th-century literature: Doris Sommer's *Foundational fictions* (item **3678**), Julio Ramos' *Desencuentros de la modernidad en América Latina* (item **3671**) and Silvia Molloy's *At face value: autobiographical writing in Spanish America* (item **3503**). All three come together in their focus on the issue of self-figuration, that is to say, the ways in which 19th-century writers demonstrated their awareness of self and culture, and how they attempted to validate their respective forms of writing within the hierarchy of social discourses. It must be remembered that 19th-century Hispanic American writers wrote at a time when national cultures and literatures were just emerging and when literary genres were not differentiated or institutionalized to the extent they are today. These critical works capture well the dilemma of Hispanic America's most accomplished and self-conscious writers in the process of forging an adequate expression and defining a social space for their fabulations.

Sommer, Ramos, and Molloy excel in drawing imaginatively from the stream of recent critical and theoretical writings in constructing their respective analytical frameworks; in each case, the resulting narrative avoids dogmatism and jargon. In addition, the three exhibit intimate familiarity with foundational as well as lesser studied texts from the library canon of the past two centuries. And lastly, all succeed in drawing the links between literary discourse and society or politics.

Even more importantly, these three critics demonstrate with remarkable success the common substratum of ideas and tendencies that influenced writers from across the Hispanic American region. The magnificent dream of Bolívar to unite the different regions in political alliance had failed due to the enormous geographical distances, impediments to communication, and the strong impetus everywhere for political autonomy. Whereas local nation-builders yielded to the pressures of interregional rivalries, the intellectuals, in their writings and thought, continued nourishing an awareness of shared linguistic and cultural links.

This triad of critics, in studying the principal writings of the previous century, demonstrate important shared practices and values. Sommer, for example, explains how, in country after country, writers of "historical novels" offered similar models in both fiction and social and political foundation. Different writers in various countries followed remarkably similar writing agendas: while novelistically depicting romantic passion and desire for domestic happiness, they also provided a rhetoric that in many cases contributed to the hegemonic project of national institutionalization. Those writers were inspired by sometimes highly contrasting social and political agendas, "ranging from racism to abolitionism, from nostalgia to modernization, from free trade to protectionism." Yet noteworthy is the longevity and universality of their collective appeal to and demand for erotic/social romance: its first manifestation was in the historical novels written in the 1840s by Argentines Sarmiento and Mármol, and the Cuban Gómez de Avellaneda. Toward the end of the century (Sommer's analysis continues up through the 1940s) the same themes continued to reverberate in the writings of Zorrilla de San Martín (Uruguay), Isaacs (Colombia), and Altamirano (Mexico).

Whereas Sommer's analysis reveals the synchronic dimensions of romance's appeal, Ramos' major contribution is his delineation of literary discourse's evolving function and status vis-à-vis the sociohistorical backdrop. Echoing Sommer, he demonstrates that in the period following political emancipation from Spain, writing in the different countries was generally "una práctica racionalizadora, autorizada por el proyecto de consolidación estatal." Then he defines and documents a subsequent stage: a progression from the renaissantistic *letrado* à-la-Andrés Bello to literature's mediating function between civilization and barbarism, or writing and orality, in the works of Sarmiento. Later writings—most notably José Martí's—announced and prefigured modernity in their autonomy from sociopolitical issues. No other critic to date has treated as authoritatively as Ramos does the important transitions toward the turn of the century in the *"función ideologizante"* of writers in relation to the State, and the dramatic contrasts in the presupposed discursive fields for their writing practices.

Similarly profound is Molloy's treatment of the "narration of self" that emerged in the different countries toward the beginning of the 19th century. She explains how the contrasting sociohistorical contexts dialectically influenced the production of this particular type of autobiographical text. For example, the crisis of authority resulting from the independence movement or the diminished importance of Enlightenment values corresponded to a "self in crisis, writing in an interlocutory void." The writers' "tentative figurations of self" and "constant search for reader recognition" affected their textual representations of self and society. While not denying the validity of reading autobiographical texts as an expression of "national essence or as national allegory"—as Sommer and Ramos generally emphasize—Molloy chooses to view preoccupations with national problems or identity as one more indication of writers' struggle to forge their own "*rhetoric* of self-figuration." Her interpretive strategy therefore highlights the vacillation in much autobiographical expression between private and public selves, vanity and honor, and individual idiosyncracy and national or continental identity.

These three critics, in affirming the shared cultural values and discursive practices of Hispanic America's most accomplished 19th-century writers, answer an emphatic "Sí" to Peruvian writer, Luis Alberto Sánchez, who, some 50 years ago, skeptically inquired, "¿Existe América Latina?"

PROSE FICTION AND POETRY

3620 Anarkos: literaturas libertarias de América del Sur, 1900; Argentina, Chile, Paraguay, Uruguay. Recopilación de Jean Andreu, Maurice Fraysse y Eva de Montoya. Buenos Aires: Corregidor, 1990. 256 p.: bibl.

Latter decades of 19th and early years of 20th centuries witnessed rise of anarchist movement in southern South America that paralleled the modernization of society and the consolidation of a socioeconomic oligarchy committed to retard change and maintain its hegemony. The "poetry of urgency"—or "activist literature"—collected here first appeared in the profusion of newspapers that were founded with the purpose of elevating the political consciousness of the new urban masses and inspire them to challenge existing social authority.

3621 Argüelles Bringas, Roberto. Lira ruda. Prólogo, recopilación y bibliografía de Serge I. Zaïtzeff. Xalapa, Mexico: Univ. Veracruzana, 1986. 186 p.: bibl. (Col. UV rescate; 20)

Poetry of Argüelles (1875–1915) was published chiefly in Mexico City magazines (1900–14); it was compiled in book form for first time in 1975. His verses, "violent and crude, emanate from profound suffering and pain."

3622 Avellaneda, Nicolás. Escritos. Prólogo de Juan Carlos Ghiano. Buenos Aires: Academia Argentina de Letras, 1988. 314 p.: bibl., ill.

Reprint of 1883 text that highlights "artistic condition" of Avellaneda's prose. Born in 1836 into patriotic family, Avellaneda followed Sarmiento as Argentina's President (1874–80).

3623 Borges, Jorge Guillermo. El caudillo. Prólogo de Alicia Jurado. Buenos Aires: Academia Argentina de Letras, 1989. 155 p., 1 leaf of plates: ill.

An "excellent novel, faithful testimony of a time and a region," notes Alicia Jurado's introduction to this work by the father of Jorge Luis Borges.

3624 Cancionero rioplatense, 1880–1925. Edición, prólogo, selección, notas, bibliografía y apéndices de Carla Rey de Guido y Walter Guido. Caracas: Biblioteca Ayacucho, 1989. 583 p.: bibl., ill. (Biblioteca Ayacucho; 137)

Important anthology of popular poetry produced during a period of great cultural, social, and technological changes in Río de la Plata. Following pioneer works by O. Fernández Latour de Botas and A. Prieto, work presents unpublished materials from the Biblioteca Criolla Roberto Lehmann-Nitsche in

Berlin. Introduction provides valuable critical history of musical forms like the milonga, *vals, cifra,* and early tango. Also provides indispensable discussion of this new literature, its means of dissemination, and its working-class public from the suburban neighborhoods of Buenos Aires and Montevideo.

3625 La correspondencia de Sarmiento. Edición de Carlos A. Segreti. Córdoba, Argentina: Poder Ejecutivo de la Provincia de Córdoba, 1988. 1 v.

Reproduces many previously unpublished letters to or by Argentina's great writer-statesman.

3626 Echeverría, Esteban. Obras escogidas. Selección, prólogo, notas, cronología y bibliografía de Beatriz Sarlo Sabajanes y Carlos Altamirano. Caracas: Biblioteca Ayacucho, 1991. 318 p.: bibl. (Biblioteca Ayacucho; 170)

Introduction (50 p.) offers the most solid appraisal yet available of Echeverría's important contributions as poet, political thinker, and leader of Argentina's distinguished generation of 1837. Anthological selections are drawn equally from Echeverría's literary and ideological or political writings.

3627 Gómez de Avellaneda y Arteaga, Gertrudis. Poesías y epistolario de amor y de amistad. Edición, introducción y notas de Elena Càtena. Madrid: Castalia; Instituto de la Mujer, 1989. 362 p., 8 p. of plates: bibl., ill. (Biblioteca de escritoras; 9)

Edition prepared by Spain's Instituto de la Mujer. Combines poetry, autobiography, and intimate correspondence of Cuba's famous writer. Her letters, especially those to Ignacio de Cepeda and Antonio Romero Ortiz, highlight the mentality of a Romantic writer, over whom "love, death, and personal misfortune" weighed so heavily.

3628 González, Juan Vicente. Biografía de José Félix Ribas: época de la guerra a muerte. Caracas: Coordinación de Información y Relaciones de Petróleos de Venezuela, 1988. 259 p.: bibl., ill. (some col.)

This is the 11th edition of 1891 classic biography of Bolívar's lieutenant during 1813–14. Valuable new studies by M. Pérez Vila and C. Pacheco situate González, the passionate author, in his time and evaluate how his political passions influenced his writings.

3629 Güiraldes, Ricardo. Don Segundo Sombra. Edición, introducción y notas de Angela B. Dellepiane. Madrid: Castalia, 1990. 459 p. (Clásicos Castalia; 183)

Introduction to this fine reprinting of Argentine gauchesque classic highlights Güiraldes' identity as "nacionalista cultural."

3630 Heredia, José María. Niágara y otros textos: poesía y prosa selectas. Selección, prólogo, cronología y bibliografía de Angel I. Augier. Caracas: Biblioteca Ayacucho, 1990. 276 p.: bibl. (Biblioteca Ayacucho; 147)

Augier's fine introduction and representative selection of both poetry and prose highlight the "civic" and "revolutionary" side of Heredia's writings, without ignoring his more lyrical, philosophical, and critical contributions.

3631 Jorge Isaacs, su *María*, sus luchas. Recopilación crítica de Carlos Arturo Caicedo Licona. Medellín, Colombia: Editorial Lealon, 1989. 315 p.: bibl. (Col. Periferia; 8)

Consists of several minor essays about Isaacs (e.g., polemics about his birthplace) and his complete poetic works.

3632 La literatura de Rosario. t. 1, El siglo XIX. Ensayo preliminar y antología compilada por Eduardo D'Anna. Rosario, Argentina?: Editorial Fundación Ross, 1989? 1 v.: bibl.

Brief but solid introduction followed by an anthology of the literature written by residents of Argentina's second city during the 19th century.

3633 Marín, Ramón. Obra completa. Recopilada y prólogo de Socorro Girón. Ponce, P.R.: s.n., 1989. 600 p.: bibl., facsims., port.

Useful because it offers complete writings of Ramón Marín (1832–1902), a very early promoter of Puerto Rico's autonomy movement. Includes poetry, plays, historical studies, etc.

3634 Marroquín, Lorenzo. Pax. Prólogo de Germán Arciniegas. Ed. no abreviada. Bogotá: Círculo de Lectores, 1986. 447 p. (Joyas de la literatura colombiana)

This novel, which was actually written in collaboration with José María Rivas Groot (b. Bogotá 1863, d. Rome 1923) provoked scandals upon its publication in 1903 due to its virulent satire of Colombia's political scene.

3635 Martí, José. Poesía completa. v. 2. Ed. crítica. La Habana: Editorial Letras Cubanas, 1985. 1 v.: bibl. (Letras cubanas siglo XIX)

Vol. 2 of Martí's complete poetry is annotated, but the only dates of composition given are Martí's own infrequent indications. Contains lesser known compositions: early poems; those written in Spain, Mexico, and Guatemala; verses from *Polvo de alas de mariposa* (no publication history of the collection is given); verses published in *La edad de oro*; miscellaneous poems; and fragments of those in process of elaboration.

3636 Mejía, Epifanio. Obras completas. Medellín: Autores Antioqueños, 1989. 385 p.: bibl., ill. (Ediciones Autores antioqueños; 54)

Third edition (previous: 1939, 1960) of poetry—with some narrative writings—by this regional Medellín poet (1831–1913).

3637 Palma, Ricardo. Ricardo Palma, corresponsal de *El Comercio.* Introducción de Aurelio Miró Quesada Soto. Recopilación de Héctor López Martínez. Lima: El Comercio, 1991. 206 p.: ill., index.

Republication of articles written by Palma and published in *El Comercio* of Lima (1892–99). Most articles were written about Spain on the occasion of Palma's participation in the festivities of the 400th anniversary of Columbus' voyage to America.

3638 Paniagua, Flavio Antonio. Lágrimas del corazón: ensayo de novela histórica. 2. ed. Tuxtla Gutiérrez, Chiapas: Gobierno del Estado de Chiapas, Consejo Estatal de Fomento a la Investigación y Difusión de la Cultura, DIF-Chiapas; Instituto Chiapaneco de Cultura, 1990. 356 p. (Obras escogidas; 1)

Novel first published in 1873 situates fictional action against the historical backdrop of the conservatives' rebellion (1864–66) in Chiapas, on the Guatemalan border in the Lacandon Indians' domain.

3639 Rivera, José Eustasio. José Eustasio Rivera. Edición de Isaías Peña. Bogotá: Procultura, 1989. 142 p.: bibl., ill. (Clásicos colombianos; 2)

Very short introduction to Rivera's life and writings includes excerpts from his poetry, theatre, and narrative. Offers helpful chronology but outdated bibliography.

3640 Sierra, Justo. La hija del judío. v. 1–2. Edición y prólogo de Antonio Castro Leal. 2a. ed. Mérida, México: Univ. Autónoma de Yucatán, 1990. 2 v.:

Reprinting of this "supreme example" of 19th-century installment novel or *novela de folletín* (Mexico, 1848). Fictional intrigues are portrayed against the backdrop of colonial customs and manners of a rich merchant family in the Yucatán.

3641 Silva, José Asunción. José Asunción Silva. Edición de Fernando Charry Lara. Bogotá: Procultura, 1989. 191 p.: bibl., ill. (Clásicos colombianos; 3)

In spite of the critic's confusion over "modernism" and "modernismo," he offers a respectable introduction to Silva's poetics.

3642 Silva, José Asunción. Obra completa. Ed. crítica, 1. ed. Coordinación de Héctor H. Orjuela. Nanterre, France: ALLCA XXe, Univ. Paris X, Centre de recherches latino-américaines, 1990. 748 p.: bibl., ill., index. (Col. Archivos; 7)

Orjuela's fine introduction, textual notes, and bibliography accompanying the best compilation yet of works by of Colombia's premier modernist poet. Final 300 p. include 12 penetrating essays about Silva and his work, by various critics.

3643 Tomás Carrasquilla, autobiográfico y polémico. Recopilación, presentación y notas de Vicente Pérez Silva. Bogotá: Instituto Caro y Cuervo, 1991. 429 p.: ill. (Serie La Granada entreabierta; 55)

Work includes many texts excluded from Carrasquilla's *Obras completas* (e.g., polemics over literature, homilies, book reviews). Also includes interviews with the writer, and speeches commemorating his achievements.

3644 Zaldumbide, Julio. Poesías completas. Precedidas de un estudio crítico por Luis Cordero y ensayos de Alejandro Carrión y Luis Pallares Zaldumbide. Quito: Presidencia de la República, Comisión Nacional Permanente de Conmemoraciones Cívicas, Casa de la Cultura Ecuatoriana Benjamín Carrión, 1988. 472 p.: bibl.

Makes available in book form, for the first time, many poems by one of Ecuador's finest romantic poets, known as Quito's *poeta filósofo* (1833–87). Includes important critical essays by L. Cordero (1888) and A. Carrión (1987).

LITERARY CRITICISM AND HISTORY

3645 Amar Sánchez, Ana María. La gauchesca durante el rosismo: una disputa por el espacio del enemigo. (*Rev. Crít. Lit. Latinoam.*, 18:35, primer semestre 1992, p. 7–19)

Luis Pérez's little studied *Biografía de Rosas escrita en verso* (1830), and Hilario Ascasubi's *Paulino Lucero* and *Aniceto el Gallo* both obeyed the political and propagandistic imperative of attracting gauchos into the anti-Rosas fold.

3646 Carballo, Emmanuel. Historia de las letras mexicanas en el siglo XIX. Guadalajara, Mexico: Univ. de Guadalajara/Xalli, 1991. 380 p.: bibl., index. (Reloj del sol)

Work with more breadth than depth as author undertakes herculean task of cataloging more than 500 poets, writers, and orators. Special sections feature the chronicle, history, literary criticism, oratory, and literary magazines, and a respectable bibliography.

3647 Carilla, Emilio. Alberdi, escritor. Tucumán: Instituto de Historia y Pensamiento Argentino, 1987. 148 p.: bibl.

Alberdi, a fierce enemy of Sarmiento, Mitre, and Buenos Aires (after 1852), has rarely been studied with impartiality in Argentina. Here Carilla treats adequately several of Alberdi's literary contributions, but rarely goes beyond a clouded mythology when touching on what are (still) controversial political issues.

3648 Castro, José Antonio. Narrativa modernista y concepción del mundo. Caracas: Comisión Presidencial para el Bicentenario del Natalicio del General Rafael Urdaneta, 1988. 201 p.: bibl. (Escritores zulianos de hoy)

Penetrating study of writings by Venezuela's accomplished *modernista* writer, Manuel Díaz Rodríguez (1871–1927), takes into account biographical, social, and political influences. Castro's study of Díaz's *Idolos rotos* (1901) and *Sangre patricia* (1902) reveals the influence of Carl Jung.

3649 Castro-Klarén, Sara. Martínez Estrada, Sarmiento, and the "other:" or desire as history. (*Dispositio/Ann Arbor*, 15:40, 1990, p. 71–82)

Martínez Estrada depicted a mystical union of Sarmiento with Argentina and projected on Sarmiento his own sense of fear, solitude, and delusion.

3650 Cobo Borda, Juan Gustavo. José Asunción Silva, bogotano universal. Prólogo de Fernando Charry Lara. Bogotá: Villegas Editores, 1988. 382 p.: ill., ports. (Biblioteca de Bogotá)

Prologue highlights Silva's status not only as precursor of "modernismo," but also as one of the continent's finest poetic voices at turn of the century. Several of Cobo-Borda's 29 short essays covering various aspects of Silva's life and oeuvre are of high critical value.

3651 Contextos: literatura y sociedad latinoamericanas del siglo XIX. Edición de Evelyn Picon Garfield e Iván A. Schulman. Urbana: Univ. of Illinois Press, 1991. 107 p.: bibl.

Based on 1987 cultural interchange between scholars from the US and USSR. Important essays include: Y. Aleksandrovich Zubritski's *Juan Wallparimachi Mayta y la conciencia étnico-nacional quechua*; Palau de Nemes on J. Zorrilla de San Martín's *Tabaré* (1988) and E. Acevedo Díaz's *Soledad* (1894); E. Picon Garfield on G. Gómez de Avellaneda's *Guatimozín, último emperador de Méjico* (1846); and I.A. Schulman's essay, *La modernización del modernismo hispanoamericano*.

3652 Cussen, Antonio. Bello and Bolívar: poetry and politics in the Spanish American Revolution. Cambridge, England; New York: Cambridge Univ. Press, 1992. 208 p.: bibl., index. (Cambridge studies in Latin American and Iberian literature; 6)

Bello's pen assisted Bolívar's sword in attaining political and cultural independence for an entire continent. This authoritative study focuses closely on Bello's poems and writings which reflected—sometimes harshly—on the accomplishments of Bolívar and the unfulfilled promises of the Spanish American revolution of the early 19th century.

3653 Foresti, Carlos. Los textos "literarios" en la prensa chilena, 1813–1828: primeros pasos de la narrativa. (*Anales/Göteborg*, 2, 1990, p. 5–40, facsim.)

Short narratives published in the Chilean press in the first years after independence. Difficult to classify according to genre, 45 narratives are divided by Foresti into three groups: 1) brief ones with epigram-like form; 2) longer "proteic" texts, sometimes fragments of longer ones, that argue a position; and 3) "closed" narrations, complete and without explicit digressions.

3654 Frederick, Bonnie. A state of conviction, a state of feeling: scientific discourse in the words of three Argentine writers, 1879–1908. (*Lat. Am. Lit. Rev.*, 19:38, July/Dec. 1991, p. 48–61)

Eduardo Wilde (1844–1913), Eduardo L. Holmberg (1852–1937), and Carlos Bunge (1875–1918) shared the dual exercise of scientific and literary writing. They found in the first an optimistic discourse of power and authority, while they utilized the second to express human anguish and the failure of objective science.

3655 Gerón, Cándido. Andrés Bello: vida y doctrina. Santo Domingo: Editora Tele-3, 1989. 147 p.: bibl., ill.

Several concise essays consider Bello's varied contributions. Includes worthwhile sections reproducing his personal correspondence (40 p.) and his drawings of South American birds (20 p.).

3656 Goodrich, Diana Sorenson. The wars of persuasion: the early years of *Facundo's* reception. (*Rev. Hisp. Mod.*, 44:2, Dec. 1991, p. 177–190)

Very detailed study of the political and personal passions underlying the diverse reactions of contemporarary readers to Sarmiento's work. First critical study to use several letters published for the first time in *La correspondencia de Sarmiento* (edited by Carlos A. Segreti, 1988).

3657 Guicharnaud-Tollis, Michèle. L'émergence du Noir dans le roman cubain du XIXe siècle. Préface de Joseph Pérez. Paris: L'Harmattan, 1991. 594 p.: bibl., index. (Recherches & documents. Amériques latines)

Detailed sociological focus on Cuban literary texts from 1830–48 that mark the emergence of anti-slavery thought and, as such, the "Cubanization" of cultural discourses on the island. Other themes singled out for extended treatment are: image of nature and peasants; woman as subject and object of cultural discourse; and diverse aspects of the black population's life under a changing slave system. Author produces valuable indexes of 12 short-lived magazines published in 19th-century Havana.

3658 Hernández Prieto, María Isabel. Vida y obra del poeta argentino Rafael Obligado. Sevilla: Consejo Superior de Investigaciones Científicas, Escuela de Estudios Hispano-Americanos de Sevilla, 1989. 217 p.: bibl., ill. (Publicaciones de la Escuela de Estudios Hispano-Americanos de Sevilla: Col. Mar adentro; 20)

Ebullient biography with respectable bibliography on Argentina's national, romantic poet (1852–1920) avoids analyzing his most famous poems.

3659 Kaplan, Marina. El romance latinoamericano: el género del *Facundo* y algunas de sus proyecciones recientes. (*Dispositio/Ann Arbor*, 15:39, 1990, p. 67–84)

Studies *Facundo* as a "romance" whose plot develops under the sign of fate or evil forces, whose characters function in ritualistic patterns and with emotional extremes, and whose plot experiences surprising twists on account of fatalistic or providential forces.

3660 Katra, William H. Sarmiento de frente y perfil. New York: P. Lang, 1993. 273 p.: bibl., index. (Ibérica, 1056–5000; 7)

Compilation of 12 previously published articles and reviews that focus on the ideas and acts of Sarmiento between 1839–52. In a period of intense political and journalistic activity, the young exiled militant's ideas were often forged under political expediency. Philosophically, romantic idealism predominated, but already there were traces of the positivist doctrines that he would later embrace. Thematic thread uniting these essays is Sarmiento's untiring promotion of Argentina's (but also South America's) progressive, liberal, and urban future, and his unrelenting campaign against those who would impede the realization of that grand vision.

3661 Ludmer, Josefina. El género gauchesco: un tratado sobre la patria. Buenos Aires: Editorial Sudamericana, 1988. 320 p.: bibl. (Pensamiento crítico)

Unconventional study of the gauchesque tradition that passes from history to text, "low" (oral) to "high" (written) "shores" of the genre, frames to foregrounds, tones, discursive codes, literary theory, and philosophy. Considers primarily foundational works of Hidalgo, Ascasubi, Hernández, and del Campo, while also taking into account key texts by El Padre Castañeda, Sarmiento, and Borges. Brilliant insights and observations make this work one of the most outstanding studies of Argentine writing and society in recent years.

3662 Lugo-Ortiz, Agnes. Escritura, nación y patriciado: los "bustos" de Julián de Casal. (*Rev. Estud. Hisp./Poughkeepsie*, 26:3, oct. 1992, p. 391–412)

Study of Casal's biographical portraits—a privileged genre since the 18th century—participates in defining the emerging *comunidad letrada* of Cuba at the end of the century.

3663 Manual de literatura hispanoamericana. v. 2, Siglo XIX. Coordinación de Felipe B. Pedraza Jiménez. Berriozar, Spain: Cénlit Ediciones, 1991. 1 v.: bibl., indexes.

Best general resource to date on Latin American writers and writing. Includes detailed sections on narrative, poetry, theater, and essay, and also covers issues relevant to language, literary criticism, historical writing, and journalism. Admirably integrates the most authoritative critical opinions into its discussion, with clear bibliographical references.

3664 Martini Real, Juan Carlos. Notas sobre el padre en *Facundo*. Prólogo de Luis Gusmán. Buenos Aires: P. Menard, 1991. 90 p. (Biblioteca Teorías y discusión en la literatura argentina)

This witty confusion of the genealogies of the "narrating subject" of *Facundo* and the author of *Recuerdos de Provincia* unexpectedly highlights the genius of their real-life author, D.F. Sarmiento (1811–88).

3665 Masiello, Francine. Angeles en el hogar argentino: el debate femenino sobre la vida doméstica, la educación y la literatura en el siglo XIX. (*Anu. IEHS*, 4, 1989, p. 265–291, bibl.)

In the period immediately after the 1852 fall of dictator Rosas, several feminist educators (e.g., Rosa Guerra and Juana Manso) published their advanced opinions on the condition of women in Buenos Aires magazines. They reclaimed a role for women within the project of the nation through their occupations as housewives and mothers.

Molloy, Sylvia. At face value: autobiographical writing in Spanish America. See item **3503.**

3666 Montero, Oscar. Translating decadence: Julián de Casal's reading of Huysmans and Moreau. (*Rev. Estud. Hisp./Poughkeepsie*, 24:3, oct. 1992, p. 369–389)

Under these two influences, Casal (in "Mi Museo Ideal" and the sonnets from *Nieve*, 1892) "translates borrowed images [of decadence and decay] in order to bring forth a mythology of the self, different, and original in the context of Cuban and Latin American cultures."

3667 Noyola, Arturo. Morir entre la escarcha: sobre Manuel José Othón. San Luis Potosí, Mexico: Letras Potosinas: Consejo Estatal para la Cultura y las Artes de San Luis Potosí, 1991. 173 p.: bibl., ill.

Meandering essay examines Othón's *Poemas rústicos* (1889–1902) and the eight-sonnet poem, "En el Desierto: Idilio Salvaje" (1904).

3668 Peñalosa, Joaquín Antonio. Literatura de San Luis Potosí del siglo XIX. San Luis Potosí, Mexico: Univ. Autónoma de San Luis Potosí, 1991. 372 p.

Thorough treatment of literature and cultural life in the Mexican state, including literary societies, cultural institutions, and literary anthologies. Work singles out for special attention five writers: Mendizábal y Zubialdea, Santa Cruz, González Bocanegra, Othón, and Asís de Castro. Unfortunately, no bibliography.

3669 Pérez Huggins, Argenis. Juan Antonio Pérez Bonalde, poeta romántico. Caracas: Academia Venezolana de la Lengua, 1988. 149 p.: bibl., ill. (Col. Argos. Col. Logos)

Structuralist and semiological study of Venezuela's great poet (b. 1846) emphasizes nationalist and mytho-musical roots of his romanticism.

3670 Podestá, Guido A. La reescritura de *Juan Moreira:* la política del decorum en el teatro argentino. (*Lat. Am. Theatre Rev.*, 25:1, Fall 1991, p. 7–19)

Juan Moreira was first published in installments (1879–80) in the Buenos Aires press. Its popularity among recently literate populations is evidenced by its reelaboration in subsequent years as a novel, a pantomime, a drama, and two movies. Study traces this process of rewriting the work in light of the conflict between the *criollismo popular* of the mass public, and the *cultura letrada* of the urban elites, with their pedagogical objectives.

3671 Ramos, Julio. Desencuentros de la modernidad en América Latina: literatura y política en el siglo XIX. México: Fondo de Cultura Económica, 1989. 245 p.: bibl. (Col. Tierra firme)

Profound series of studies considers the literary response of Bello, Sarmiento, and Martí to the respective crises in cultural systems caused by an encroaching modernity. Ramos continues in the fertile tradition of Angel Rama by investigating journalism, writing, culture, and intellectuals in an emerging 19th-century society. Especially important is Ramos' treatment of Martí's aesthetic attempts to go beyond the *"no saber"* and "inability to know" that is generated by modern fragmentation to make literature a "field of social authority."

3672 Rivas, Mercedes. Literatura y esclavitud en la novela cubana del siglo XIX. Sevilla: Escuela de Estudios Hispano-Americanos de Sevilla, 1990. 317 p.: bibl., ill. (Publicaciones de la Escuela de Estudios Hispano-Americanos de Sevilla; 351)

Scholarly and solid discourse analysis of seven important anti-slavery novels published in Cuba (1838–82). Highlights "attitude of the narrator and his/her function as creator of a spatial-temporal microcosm." Also examines political, economic, and sociocultural contexts, and text as discourse.

3673 Rotker, Susana. Fundación de una escritura: las crónicas de José Martí. La Habana: Casa de las Américas, 1992. 290 p.: bibl. (Medio milenio. Ensayo)

Rigorous study of Martí's *Escenas Norteamericanas* (1880–92) as a new genre—the "Chronicle"—which united aspects of both journalism and literary discourse. Rotker views Martí's writing here as "foundational" in offering a "collective self" (not confessional or personalized) as an answer to the crisis of modernity at the end of the century (p. 156). Martí's novel view was that art recreated (rather than imitated) life in its own ambiguous but authentic order (p. 166).

3674 Ruiz Barrionuevo, Carmen. La cultura ilustrada de José Joaquín Fernández de Lizardi. (*Anu. Estud. Centroam.*, 48:2, suplemento 1991, p. 75–94)

Basing his work on the best critical studies treating Mexico's intellectual figures at the time of independence from Spain, this critic highlights Lizardi's ties to liberal European values (e.g., influences from 18th-century Enlightenment, primarily through Spanish interpreters such as Feijóo, Jovellanos, and others) as well as his repudiation of existing colonial structures.

3675 Salessi, Jorge. Tango, nacionalismo y sexualidad: Buenos Aires, 1880–1914. (*Hispamérica/Gaithersburg*, 20:60, 1991, p. 33–53)

Study of several reputedly "scientific" studies of the period helps to explain commonly held perception that Argentina's national dance is associated with prostitution, antisemitism, misogyny, xenophobia, and homophobia.

3676 Santos Molano, Enrique. El corazón del poeta. Bogotá: Nuevo Rumbo Editores, 1992. 920 p.: bibl., ill.

Exhaustive biography of José Asunción Silva also offers detailed analysis of Colombia's political history and Bogotá's society and culture during the 19th century. Author pays special attention to Silva's interaction with leading journals and newspapers. His polemical conclusion is that the poet's tragic death in 1896 was not—as is commonly believed—a suicide, but rather an assassination.

3677 Shumway, Nicolas. The invention of Argentina. Berkeley: Univ. of California Press, 1991. 325 p.: bibl., ill., index, maps.

Highly intelligent, readable study combining literary, ideological, and political history. Shumway's thesis is that Argentina's "national failure" is largely due to the violently conflicting "mind-sets" or "guiding fictions" that have typified the thought of the country's most important ideologues and leaders since the 19th century. Chapters on the *mentalités* of M. Moreno, J. Artigas, B. Hidalgo, and B. Rivadavia are excellent. Equally lucid is Shumway's treatment of late-century writers: O. Andrade, C. Guido y Spano, and J. Hernández. However, a skewed and limited selection of "cultural documents" drawn from E. Echeverría, J.B. Alberdi, D.F. Sarmiento, and B. Mitre leads to sometimes flawed conclusions.

3678 Sommer, Doris. Foundational fictions: the national romances of Latin America. Berkeley: Univ. of California Press,

1991. 418 p.: bibl., ill., index. (Latin American literature and culture; 7)

Critical tour de force demonstrates an "erotics of politics:" how a variety of national ideals (e.g., racism, abolitionism, modernization, free trade) received allegorical expression in Latin America's most canonical books of fiction. Important chapters treat *Facundo, Amalia, Sab, María, Cumandá, Tabaré, El zarco,* and *Martín Rivas,* as well as texts from Brazil and the 20th century. These "romances" share the "common project to build through reconciliations and amalgamations of national constituencies cast as lovers destined to desire each other."

3679 Subercaseaux, Bernardo. Fin de siglo: la época de Balmaceda; modernización y cultura en Chile. Santiago?: Editorial Aconcagua; CENECA, 1988. 323 p.: bibl.

Continuation of critic's important 1981 work *Cultura y sociedad liberal en el siglo XIX* (see *HLAS 50:3077*). Offers key perspective of Chile's "mapa intelectual, cultural y discursivo" in the latter decades of the 19th century when Chile underwent dramatic social and cultural changes as it emerged into modernity.

3680 Torres-Pou, Joan. Intertextualidad en el discurso patriarcal burgués: referencias literarias en *Martín Rivas* de Alberto Blest Gana. (*Explic. Textos Lit.,* 20:1, 1991/92, p. 61–71)

Emphasizes influence of Stendahl on this Chilean novel of 1862, especialy in its description of women and imitation of a medieval, chivalric world. Torres-Pou sees in it as Hispanic America's best example of "la ideología burguesa criolla," which is simultaneously both "liberal" and "conservative."

3681 Trigo, Abril. El teatro gaucho primitivo y los límites de la gauchesca. (*Lat. Am. Theatre Rev.,* 26:1, Fall 1992, p. 53–68)

Highlights the cultured elites' objective to appropriate the art of the common people and transform it into a hybrid genre straddling popular and mass cultures. The Gauchesque *sainete* (play), originating with mimo-drama *Juan Moreira* in 1884 but did not survive as a genre, unlike the gauchesque poetic production of that theme. Attributes this to elitist social groups' control of theater performances and their negative reaction to the revolutionary message of gaucho democracy.

3682 Visión actual de Manuel J. Calle. Quito: Fundación Friedrich Naumann, 1988. 196 p.: bibl.

Five essays and bibliography investigate the writings, ideas, and historical importance of Calle (1866–1918), Ecuador's polemical journalist who fearlessly combatted the abuses of both the Church and corrupt liberalism. His realist novel, *Carlota* (1897–98), is one of the finest of the period.

3683 Vitier, Cintio. Crítica cubana. La Habana: Editorial Letras Cubanas, 1988. 570 p.: bibl. (Giraldilla)

Republication of Vitier's formidable essay (200 p.) on "La Crítica Literaria y Estética en el Siglo XIX Cubano" (1971) which, unfortunately, has neither bibliography nor footnotes. Also includes essay (60 p.) "Poetas Cubanos del Siglo XIX: Semblanzas" that treats in impressionistic fashion some five poets.

3684 Vitier, Cintio. Rescate de Zenea. La Habana: Ediciones Unión, 1987. 129 p.: bibl.

Detailed analysis concords with Martí's judgement that Cuba's famous poet, Juan Clemente Zenea, was unjustly accused of treason, and that the Spaniards in 1871 executed a Cuban patriot, not a double agent.

3685 Williams, Lorna V. The feminized slave in Gómez de Avellaneda's *Sab,* 1841. (*Rev. Estud. Hisp./Poughkeepsie,* 27:1, enero 1993, p. 3–18)

Author's critique of slavery, first published in Europe, "owed less to her concern about the destiny of Cuban slaves than to her desire to displace onto the slave her own sense of marginality as an intellectually talented woman."

3686 Williams, Raymond L. Los orígenes de la novela colombiana desde *Ingermina* hasta *Manuela.* (*Thesaurus/Bogotá,* 44:3, sept./dic. 1989, p. 580–605, bibl.)

Examines sociopolitical and cultural contexts from which the first novel in Colombia emerged. Devotes special attention to *Ingermina* (1844), by Juan José Nieto—a historical novel whose action takes place during the early colonial period—and *Manuela* (1858), by Eugenio Díaz, which captures well some of the ideological conflicts of a newly independent country, especially that between oral and written cultures.

3687 Yáñez, Mirta. La narrativa del romanticismo en Latinoamérica. La Habana: Editorial Letras Cubanas, 1989. 317 p.: bibl. (Giraldilla. Ensayo)

Marxist study sometimes reduces complex issues to schematic configurations, but excels at demonstrating how Latin America's early novels arose primarily in response to trying social conflicts. Separate chapters treat *María*, indigenous narrative (*Enriquillo* and *Cumandá*); and the *costumbrismo* of Altamirano.

3688 Zúñiga y Tejeda, Arcadio. Arcadio Zúñiga y Tejeda: poeta jalisciense del siglo XIX. Introducción y recopilación de Dante Medina. Guadalajara, México: Editorial Univ. de Guadalajara, 1989. 134 p. (Col. del Centro de Estudios Literarios)

Regional poet (1858–92) wrote on religious, amorous, and patriotic themes. Chronology offers useful outline of major literary and historical events in late 19th-century state of Jalisco.

20th–Century Prose Fiction
Mexico

FERNANDO GARCIA NUÑEZ, *Professor of Spanish, University of Texas at El Paso*

LA NARRATIVA MEXICANA DE ESTE BIENIO se orienta con preponderancia a intercalar cada vez más el yo autobiográfico para desde allí filtrar el acontecer circundante en el hoy, el ayer o el anteayer, no más allá en el tiempo. Ese proceso lleva consigo un reflexionar continuo e intermitente, las más de las veces crítico, de las diversas versiones interpretativas de los supuestos resortes impulsores del suceder. Por ello los textos mejores de ordinario son complejos en su estructura, siempre mutante, e intensos en su pretensión sintetizadora provisional, sujeta a veces a revisión dentro de la composición narrativa misma.

Esta imposibilidad de asir la realidad en una interpretación firme y convincente hace que el texto sea dubitativo, elíptico y recurrente en su frecuentemente extenso desarrollo; pero también doblega la posible soberbia del yo autobiográfico y lo invita a una actitud en la que el narrador está dispuesto a reírse de sí mismo y sus tropiezos. En este contexto no sorprende para nada la conjugación narrativa con la ensayística en la novela autobiográfica.

Todos esos elementos se encuentran presentes en diversas proporciones en las dos mejores novelas del género: *A la salud de la serpiente* de Gustavo Sáinz (item **3740**) y *La mar de utopías* de Arturo Azuela (item **3699**). Pero también se hacen evidentes, en menor grado, en un proyecto de la Univ. Nacional Autónoma de México en el cual, por invitación, se ofrece al escritor un espacio no mayor de 70 páginas para su autobiografía, novelada o no: la colección De Cuerpo Entero, que incluye un número considerable de narradores reseñados en este capítulo.

Otra orientación narrativa examina el acontecer político reciente del país, a partir de 1968 en especial, asumiendo la voz narrativa una actitud mesurada en cuanto a emociones se refiere, pero sin límite alguno en la inmensa red de hipótesis supuestamente explicativas de la atmósfera propicia para la guerrilla urbana y la manipulación informativa, como sucede en *La guerra de Galio* de Héctor Aguilar Camín (item **3690**); o para la guerrilla serrana, como la expuesta por Carlos Montemayor en *Guerra en el paraíso* (item **3723**). La desmesura hipotética exige, como en los textos autobiográficos, una escritura compleja, extensa y recurrente en sus proposiciones.

Otra orientación narrativa más rastrea la historia reciente (a partir del Porfiriato) con el objeto de situar épocas, desmitificar figuras o realzarlas; todo ello con la ayuda de la bibliografía histórica disponible, pero sin garantizar que la versión ficticia sea del todo fiel a la histórica. Así proceden Elena Poniatowska en *Tinísima* (item **3727**) e Ignacio Solares en *Madero, el otro* (item **3744**). Hubo, sí, un buen número de novelas—reseñadas en seguida—que apuntaron hacia muy atrás en el tiempo, pero lo hicieron con frecuencia y éxito disparejo por motivos celebratorios del Quinto Centenario de 1492, no exigidos por la naturaleza intrínseca de la novela.

En el aspecto crítico hubo avances espectaculares en el estudio de la narrativa mexicana en este bienio, enfocados los de mayor envergadura al establecimiento crítico de las fuentes textuales sobre la base de las cuales el investigador hará su lectura. En este aspecto resalta la colosal obra verificada por la Colección Archivo que ha publicado o está por publicar la versión crítica de textos de nueve narradores mexicanos ya fallecidos, sostenida con un impresionante coro crítico sobre la obra correspondiente, superando así en pretensiones el valioso trabajo de la colección Biblioteca Ayacucho.

Pero todavía ese proyecto sería más útil si se extendiera a la obra narrativa total de cada uno de los nueve autores y la de muchos otros no incorporados al programa, como en efecto se hizo de manera maravillosa con la de Juan Rulfo en la edición crítica de *Toda la obra* (item **3769**), constituyéndose así ésta en el modelo ideal a seguir; el cual precisará -como sucedió en el caso de Rulfo—necesariamente unir las voluntades individuales de los investigadores para trabajar en equipo.

La disponibilidad de las fuentes también es ahora mayor, gracias a la edición revisada y ampliada del trabajo bibliográfico de David William Foster en *Mexican Literature: A Bibliography of Secondary Sources* (item **3758**) y del segundo tomo de la recopilación de Christopher Domínguez Michael, *Antología de la narrativa mexicana del siglo XX* (item **3749**).

Además, en el bienio se publicaron, como se verá en las reseñas siguientes, algunas antologías de literaturas regionales, libros de entrevistas y estudios monográficos y colectivos que hacen más asequibles los textos y la información sobre los autores y los artículos críticos.

PROSE FICTION

3689 Aguilar, Luis Miguel. Suerte con las mujeres. México: Cal y Arena, 1992. 220 p.

Novela evocadora de la niñez y juventud del narrador en la célebre Colonia Condesa de la Ciudad de México. Al yo autobiográfico, ingeniosamente distanciado de sí mismo por el uso del lenguaje directo y cotidiano, lo constituye más que nada la rememoración de su mundo afectivo y circunstante.

3690 Aguilar Camín, Héctor. La guerra de Galio. 1. ed. Cal y Arena. México: Cal y Arena, 1991. 590 p.

Novela que pretende narrar las inquietudes políticas, sociales y culturales de la generación, ya adulta, a la que le tocó vivir de joven la tragedia de 1968 en México; así como hurgar en los secretos mecanismos del poder que al mismo tiempo y sin contradicción alientan y reprimen de manera sutil los ideales de dicha generación, incluidos los de las guerrillas urbanas de los años 70. Tal vez su personaje más logrado sea el polifacético y ubicuo poder gubernamental cuya espeluznante grandiosidad se manifiesta con vistosidad en Galio Bermúdez, andamio escondido del acontecer político, ideológico y cultural del país.

3691 Aguilera Garramuño, Marco Tulio. Los grandes y los pequeños amores. México: Consejo Nacional para la Cultura y las Artes, Instituto Nacional de Bellas Artes; J. Mortiz, 1992. 119 p. (Premios bellas artes de literatura)

Colección de cuentos alrededor del tema obsesionante y casi único del autor en sus demás libros: las relaciones amorosas y sus múltiples variantes y obstáculos. Del presente destaca "Paso de Baile" por recrear una experiencia erótica casi onírica.

3692 Aguirre, Eugenio. Amor de mis amores. México: Plaza y Valdés, 1988. 180 p.

Novela que da licencia a los aparecidos de las leyendas populares para encarnar juguetona y fantasiosamente en el mundo real para llevar a cabo sus amores fallidos, en medio del desasosiego de los vivos quienes desearían que los muertos los dejaran en paz.

3693 Agustín, José. No hay censura. México: J. Mortiz, 1988. 131 p. (Nueva narrativa hispánica)

Colección de cuentos con definidas tonalidades picarescas y lúdicas en la voz del narrador, el cual de ese modo desentraña el acontecer cotidiano en el México contemporáneo. Este parece estar tramado alrededor de discursos moralizantes gobiernistas ("No hay Censura," es uno de ellos), cuya lectura irónica revela exactamente lo opuesto a la proposición panfletaria.

3694 Agustín, José. No pases esta puerta. México: J. Mortiz, 1992. 141 p. (Cuarto creciente)

La última de las antologías personales de José Agustín (la penúltima fue La mirada en el centro, México: Joaquín Mortiz, 1977), en la cual traza los puntos cardinales de su geografía narrativa mediante la reorganización e inclusive—en mucho menor grado—la reescritura de cuentos anteriormente publicados.

3695 Alatriste, Sealtiel. Tan pordiosero el cuerpo: esperpento. Ilustraciones y capitulares de Sealtiel Alatriste Batalla. México: Fondo de Cultura Económica, 1987. 133 p.: ill. (Letras mexicanas)

El retablo barroco colonial es el modelo prototípico de los milagros o retablos populares de santos y sus favores en la imaginería religiosa mexicana; aquéllos son también los hilos conductores de los destinos del milagrero Sebastián en esta novela, a quien en una atmósfera de ensueño sus creaciones pictóricas predicen con malicia su conducta a seguir. Alatriste, a su vez, pinta con sutil eficacia

verbal el retablo de la cultura popular mexicana de los años 50.

3696 Arana, Federico. Yo, mariachi. México: Editorial J. Mortíz, 1991. 251 p. (Cuarto creciente)

Novela que expone con humorismo e ingenio al mexicano contemporáneo al ambiente europeo (Alemania, Suiza y España) para enfatizar el conjunto de actitudes, vicios y virtudes que lo conforman en su inescapable mexicanidad.

3697 Aridjis, Homero. Memorias del Nuevo Mundo. Barcelona: EDHASA, 1991. 395 p.

La novela histórica continúa las aventuras de Juan Cabezón a partir de su travesía con Colón en la Santamaría, en 1492 (ver item **3698**), y se extiende hasta 1560 en la Ciudad de México. En la obra monumental Aridjis prosigue la relectura y reescritura de fuentes históricas concernientes al descubrimiento del Nuevo Mundo y a la conquista de la Nueva España.

3698 Aridjis, Homero. 1492: vida y tiempos de Juan Cabezón de Castilla. Barcelona: EDHASA, 1990. 315 p.

Novela histórica monumental que recrea, en la figura del judío Juan Cabezón de Castilla, las condiciones que hicieron posible y necesaria en España la aventura de Cristóbal Colón hacia tierras ignotas, así como la urgencia de muchas gentes por unirse a ella. Aridjis, reconocido poeta y estudioso, supo en la novela dar vida y pasión a la España de finales del siglo XV a través de la reescritura y relectura casi enciclopédica de las fuentes históricas más importantes, en la supuesta voz autobiográfica de Juan Cabezón.

3699 Azuela, Arturo. La mar de utopías. México: Plaza y Valdés Editores, 1991. 330 p. (Col. Platino)

Singular novela en la que Azuela incorpora una interesantísima reflexión acerca de las coordenadas esenciales de la cultura latinoamericana actual, mediante la recreación supuestamente autobiográfica de sus encuentros personales con los más destacados escritores contemporáneos, tales como Pablo Neruda, Jorge Luis Borges, Juan Rulfo, etc.

3700 Azuela, Arturo. El matemático. 1. ed. en Plaza y Valdés. México: Plaza y Valdés, 1988. 166 p.

Novela que conjuga con singular sapiencia la reflexión acerca de los logros matemáticos más notorios del siglo XX y su conexión, en el sentir del protagonista, con las azarozas leyes de las relaciones eróticas. Ambos universos se comunican con soltura y naturalidad en esta obra que los examina críticamente en la última noche del año 1999.

3701 Azuela, Mariano. *Los de abajo; La luciérnaga* y otros textos. Selección, prólogo y bibliografía de Arturo Azuela. Cronología de Jorge Ruffinelli. Caracas: Biblioteca Ayacucho, 1991. 247 p.: bibl. (Biblioteca Ayacucho; 165)

Edición expurgada de erratas, aunque no crítica, de las dos novelas de Azuela y seis cuentos breves. El ensayo de Arturo Azuela enmarca la obra de su antecesor en el ámbito de la narrativa mexicana contemporánea y, más específicamente, en el de la novela de la Revolución. La cronología de Ruffinelli rebasa su naturaleza para convertirse en un verdadero y cuidadoso bosquejo bio-bibliográfico.

3702 Blanco, José Joaquín. El castigador. México: Editorial Quinqué, 1993. 107 p.

La distancia cronológica permite que un narrador autobiográfico cuarentón se describa a sí mismo como adolescente lúmpen, en tránsito hacia las redes eróticas de una mujer madura clasemediera, y los problemas anejos a dicha situación. El yo autobiográfico adulto, con libertad y humorismo arrabalero, habla desde la cárcel directamente a un interlocutor joven y refinado, allí recluido. En su discurso está del todo ausente cualquier afán moralizante; sólo desea conversar y pasar el tiempo.

3703 Borbolla, Oscar de la. Las vocales malditas. Ilustraciones de José Luis Cuevas. México: J. Mortiz, 1991. 50 p.: ill. (Serie del volador)

Extraño e interesante libro de cinco breves composiciones narrativas en las que se utilizan exclusivamente palabras que contengan la vocal respectiva. Tal vez a nadie sorprenda que las composiciones mejor logradas en este juego correspondan a las vocales abiertas ("Cantata a Satanás," "El Hereje Rebelde" y "Los Locos somos Otro Cosmos").

3704 Boullosa, Carmen. Son vacas, somos puercos: filibusteros del Mar Caribe. México: Ediciones Era, 1991. 138 p. (Biblioteca Era)

Un filibustero narra en esta novela su vida y la de sus compañeros en el Mar Caribe, al margen de cualquier sujeción de gobierno, propiedad o matrimonio. Por ello se oponen a la colonización llevada a cabo por los grandes poderes europeos. De este modo el bárbaro mundo de los filibusteros (los puercos) parece ser el auténtico Mundo Nuevo, muy distinto al publicitado por los descubridores y conquistadores europeos (las vacas).

3705 Bradu, Fabienne. Antonieta, 1900–1931. México: Fondo de Cultura Económica, 1991. 245 p.: bibl. (Vida y pensamiento de México)

Biografía de Antonieta Rivas Mercado, personalidad eminente en la vida cultural del México de los años 20, expuesta en forma narrativa. Bradu envuelve al lector en los vaivenes sentimentales y artísticos de Antonieta, mientras su mecenazgo impulsa el desarrollo del teatro de vanguardia y de la entonces vigente generación de los Contemporáneos; asimismo el lector sufre con Antonieta poco antes de su suicidio en París, al sentirse incomprendida por José Vasconcelos.

3706 Bravo, Roberto. Vida del orate. México: Editorial Joaquín Mortiz, 1989. 132 p.

Colección de composiciones narrativas breves acompañada de uno que otro cuento, en las cuales se insiste en presentar modos de vida peculiares de los habitantes indígenas de Veracruz por medio de una prosa sencilla. Esto adquiere proporciones más desarrolladas y certeras en el cuento que da título a la colección.

3707 Curiel, Fernando. Navaja. Tlahuapan, México: Premiá, 1991. 143 p. (Tola)

Colección de composiciones narrativas breves y brevísimas (las hay de sólo dos líneas) de carácter casi epigramático, manifestado inclusive en las más extensas por la concisión de las frases. En todas persiste la intención de hacer tajos crueles de las personas o situaciones a través del juego verbal bien calculado.

3708 Debroise, Olivier. Lo peor sucede al atardecer. México: Cal y Arena, 1990. 191 p.

La estructura de la novela policíaca sirve al narrador para enmarcar en ella más que la búsqueda minuciosa e inteligente—la cual sí se da, de hecho—de la solución de los crímenes, la inquisición de las preferencias sexuales y sociales del detective, un hombre con educación refinada felizmente casado y padre de un niño. Las argucias narrativas y humorísticas lo convierten al final en amante de un muchacho, con quien vive en un pobre departamento en el centro de Acapulco.

3709 Domecq, Brianda. De cuerpo entero. México: Coordinación de Difusión Cultural, Dirección de Literatura, Univ. Nacional Autónoma de México; Ediciones Corunda, 1991. 62 p.: ill.

Ingeniosa autobiografía asumida como verdadero ejercicio narrativo desde una perspectiva irónica. Desde allí la autora se ríe de sí misma en su proceso de escribir la autobiografía y relata sus nexos familiares iberos y norteamericanos que le hacen crecer y educárse en Nueva Inglaterra, para luego tener que reajustarse mental y culturalmente al irse a vivir a México.

3710 Domecq, Brianda. La insólita historia de la Santa de Cabora. México: Planeta, 1990. 383 p. (Col. Fábula)

Novela donde la narradora contemporánea relata el proceso preparatorio de investigaciones anterior a su escritura y su gradual inserción en la persona de Teresita Urrea, la misteriosa y mística mujer que con sus sueños y curaciones intranquiliza la mirada omnipresente de Porfirio Díaz, el cual la hace exiliarse a los EE.UU. Pero ella, desde allí, prosigue su lucha contra Díaz.

3711 Dueñas, Guadalupe. Antes del silencio. México: Fondo de Cultura Económica, 1991. 69 p. (Letras mexicanas)

Colección de cuentos breves hechos con lenguaje trabajado con esmero e imaginación audaz, que proporciona nueva e insospechada vida a personajes tan manoseados como los ángeles ("El Angel Guardián") y los ancianos ("Visita al Asilo"), o a objetos de ordinario expulsados del protagonismo cuentístico ("Las Escaleras").

3712 Espejo, Beatriz. De cuerpo entero: viejas fotografías. México: Coordinación de Difusión Cultural, Dirección de Literatura, Univ. Nacional Autónoma de México; Ediciones Corunda, 1991. 58 p.: ill.

Autobiografía cuya escritura se lleva a cabo tomando como base del relato el álbum fotográfico familiar, principalmente las imágenes de los abuelos y de los padres, todos ellos gustadores de la variada cocina mexicana. Las demás son fotografías de escuelas de monjas, en las que la autora encuentra su vocación de escritora.

3713 Garibay, Ricardo. Triste domingo. México: J. Mortiz, 1991. 332 p. (Novelistas contemporáneos)

Bella novela de amor que conjunta el dibujo certero de una joven enamorada simultáneamente de un hombre mayor y de un joven, con el trazo vivaz de la rarificada atmósfera urbana correspondiente a una y otra generación. Los protagonistas ejemplificarían de una manera trágica y fallida el intento de encontrar un mundo más puro.

3714 Garro, Elena. Y Matarazo no llamó—. México: Grijalbo, 1991. 135 p. (Narrativa)

Novela extemporánea, escrita en 1960, acerca de las peripecias y fatalidad que acompañan a un simpatizante involuntario de la huelga ferroviaria de Demetrio Vallejo en la Ciudad de México en los años 50. Poco a poco se crea en la narración una atmósfera tensa y terrible que atrapa al protagonista, a la manera ya familiar en las novelas anteriores de Garro.

3715 Guzmán, Humberto. De cuerpo entero: confesiones de una sombra—o de una generación. México: Coordinación de Difusión Cultural, Dirección de Literatura, Univ. Nacional Autónoma de México; Ediciones Corunda, 1990. 63 p., 4 p. of plates: ill.

Autobiografía que enfatiza la extracción popular y urbana del autor en la Ciudad de México, así como su timidez acrecentada por la injusta estancia en la cárcel de Acapulco por varios años; también se hace mención especial de lo que para él significó el movimiento estudiantil de 1968. Casi se esquiva el planteamiento escritural, al cual dedica una o dos páginas. El subtítulo parece concordar con el miedo medular del autor que lo hace esconder su propia cara.

3716 Krauze, Ethel. De cuerpo entero: entre la cruz y la estrella. México: Coordinación de Difusión Cultural, Dirección de Literatura, Univ. Nacional Autónoma de México; Ediciones Corunda, 1990. 57 p.: ill.

Interesante autobiografía donde la autora cuenta sus peripecias para convivir simultáneamente en el mundo judío de su familia y en el mundo mexicano. Con éste, su contacto inicial fue a través de una sirvienta y su numerosa parentela que la visitaba en la Ciudad de México. El subtítulo signa la trayectoria de la autobiografía.

3717 Loaeza, Guadalupe. Primero las damas. 2. ed. México: Cal y Arena, 1990. 175 p.: ill.

Colección de cuentos sobre la mujer mexicana de hoy, sobre todo la de los altos estratos sociales de la Ciudad de México cuya conducta y habla son sabrosamente retratadas. Escapa de esa tónica, para insertarse en una perspectiva más humana y profunda, el titulado "Miroslava," sobre el trágico suicidio de dicha actriz del cine clásico mexicano.

3718 Medina, Dante. Niñoserías. México: Alianza Editorial Mexicana, 1989. 125 p. (Alianza literatura)

Libro de ejercicios narrativos surgidos de un intento por hacer uso discursivo y analítico de formas elementales de expresión semejantes a los balbuceos infantiles, pero en verdad manifestadores de inventiva e intuición lingüística y poética. Por ello su lectura exige paciente disposición lúdica e inquisitiva, como la requerida al leer hace años a Vicente Huidobro.

3719 Mendoza, María Luisa. De cuerpo entero. México: Coordinación de Difusión Cultural, Dirección de Literatura, Univ. Nacional Autónoma de México; Ediciones Corunda, 1991. 55 p.: ill.

Autobiografía donde la autora relata sobre todo sus experiencias en la política mexicana en calidad de miembro de la Cámara de Diputados y la concordancia de tal actividad con sus menesteres de escritora. En esta perspectiva pareciera haberse enriquecido su oficio con el trato tan intenso con la gente en sus diversas giras electorales por el estado de Guanajuato y el Distrito Federal.

3720 Mojarro, Tomás. Yo, el Valedor—y el Jerásimo. México: Fondo de Cultura Económica, 1985. 239 p. (Col. popular; 322)

Colección de crónicas periodísticas cuyo narrador (el Valedor) toma como lente inquisitivo y picaresco de la conducta contemporánea del mexicano al Jerásimo. No hay vicio o acontecimiento importante que caiga fuera de la prosa vivaz, humorística e irónica de ese Periquillo Sarniento finisecular.

3721 Molina, Silvia. La familia vino del norte. 2. ed. México: Océano, 1987. 155 p.: ill.

Novela surgida de la traición de un periodista quien usa sus relaciones amorosas con la hija de un importante general revolucionario para descubrir otra traición, ésta histórica: el asesinato del General Francisco Serrano, gran amigo del entonces presidente de México, el General Alvaro Obregón, por haberse opuesto Serrano a la antirrevolucionaria reelección de Obregón.

3722 Molina, Silvia. Imagen de Héctor. México: Cal y Arena, 1990. 150 p.: ill.

Novela de carácter autobiográfico por rastrear la autora, a través de ella, la imagen lejana del padre muerto cuando ella era niña; y por el relato de las funciones gubernamentales de aquél durante la época de Lázaro Cárdenas y de Miguel Alemán. La determinación de utilizar no la primera sino la tercera persona otorga distanciamiento a la autobiografía.

3723 Montemayor, Carlos. Guerra en el paraíso. México: Ediciones Diana, 1991. 380 p.

Novela armada con frialdad objetiva para reflexionar así acerca de los ideales del profesor Lucio Cabañas y sus seguidores en la sierra de Guerrero en su lucha contra el ejército y el gobierno mexicanos en los años 70 de nuestro siglo. El narrador pareciera sólo difundir con su escritura partes militares de esa lucha y sus secuelas, pero tal suposición desaparece al ver todos los partes en conjunto al final de la novela. Entonces probablemente el lector participe del sutil terror que subyace en la supuesta objetividad narrativa.

3724 Pacheco, Cristina. Para mirar a lo lejos. Villahermosa, Mexico: Gobierno del Estado de Tabasco, ICT Ediciones, 1989. 140 p. (Los que escriben la historia)

La sexta compilación de las crónicas urbanas que Pacheco publica con regularidad en periódicos y revistas de la Ciudad de México se caracteriza por enfocarse en el señalamiento de la constante nostalgia por la tierra chica que acompaña a esos personajes de Provincia avecindados por toda una vida en el Distrito Federal, pero siempre ajenos a la gran urbe.

3725 Pacheco, José Emilio. La sangre de Medusa, y otros cuentos marginales. México: Ediciones Era, 1990. 136 p. (Biblioteca Era)

Cuentario hecho principalmente de recopilaciones de revistas y publicaciones marginales, pero revisadas con minucia por un autor cuya voluntad de reescritura nunca cesa. De tal suerte se logra la paradoja de que el primer relato de Pacheco ("Tríptico del Gato") se convierta ahora quizás en uno de sus mejores textos. El libro todo reitera ya desde los primeros escritos los futuros temas dominantes del autor y se constituye en una hermosa joya de su quehacer corrector.

3726 Pérez Cruz, Emiliano. Si camino voy como los ciegos: cuentos. México: Delegación Cuauhtémoc, 1987. 113 p. (Col. Divulgación de las artes: Serie Literatura-narrativa)

Colección de cuentos acerca de los arrabales de la Ciudad de México y sus gentes, con las cuales se identifica la voz narrativa en lo emocional y en lo discursivo; pretende utilizar en la escritura su habla.

3727 Poniatowska, Elena. Tinísima: novela. México: Ediciones Era, 1992. 663 p.: ill. (Biblioteca Era)

Apasionante novela acerca de la fotógrafa Tina Modotti, italiana participante en la vida cultural y política del México de los años 30–40, desde su militancia en el Partido Comunista que la lleva también a participar en la Guerra Civil española. Para crear a su personaje Poniatowska pinta con tanto detalle las inquietudes artísticas y culturales entonces en vigencia que su obra es un ambicioso mosaico de toda una época.

3728 Poniatowska, Elena. Todo México. t. 1. México: Editorial Diana. 1 v.: ill.

Poniatowska por medio de la entrevista crea personajes y circunstancias memorables desde hace muchos años. La presente recopilación lo confirma sobre todo en las entrevistas "Las Alzadas de Cejas de María Félix" e "Ires y Venires de Yolanda Montes, Tongolele" por crear argucias verbales que en buena medida desdicen a las entrevistadas.

3729 Prieto, Francisco. Deseo. México: Joaquín Mortiz, 1989. 229 p. (Nueva narrativa hispánica)

Esta, como las demás novelas de Prieto, indaga las pulsiones más elementales y determinantes—según el autor—del alma humana. El deseo pareciera haberse agazapado en las intenciones profundas del hombre encarcelado durante años por la violación que no cometió de hecho, pero que en su interior—lo sabe el lector después de su excarcelación—deseó con vehemencia.

3730 Puga, María Luisa. De cuerpo entero: el espacio de la escritura. México: Coordinación de Difusión Cultural, Dirección de Literatura, Univ. Nacional Autónoma de México; Ediciones Corunda, 1990. 56 p.: ill.

Interesante autobiografía en la cual Puga se describe a sí misma en su anhelo de sentirse a gusto escribiendo novelas sobre México. Vivió en Londres, Roma, París, Madrid, Grecia, Oxford y Nairobi, acompañada de su inseparable cuaderno y de sus bosquejos de novela. Al final regresa a México para respirar más el aire deseado en su escritura, pero con la convicción de que un escritor siempre está afuera.

3731 Puga, María Luisa. Las razones del lago. México: Grijalbo, 1991. 180 p. (Narrativa Grijalbo)

Ingeniosa novela en la cual el narrador es un perro que habla acerca de sus experiencias con los moradores de un pueblo situado junto a un lago, los forasteros y, sobre todo, con el lago mismo. Este lago parece ser el personaje principal e imperecedero en torno a cuyo espacio y población (humana y canina) una pareja capitalina creará ciertos cambios, pero ellos también se someterán al final a la filosofía del lago.

3732 Quirarte, Vicente. El amor que destruye lo que inventa. México: Univ. Autónoma Metropolitana, Unidad Azcapotzalco, División de Ciencias Sociales y Humanidades, 1988. 106 p. (Biblioteca de ciencias sociales y humanidades) (Serie Literatura)

Cuentos de inusitada fantasía y esmero verbal testificados anteriormente en *Plenilunio de la muñeca*, del cual se recopilan tres cuentos en el presente libro. De los otros cinco cuentos, destacan por la audacia de sus vericuetos imaginativos "La Isla está Rodeada por un Mar Tembloroso que Algunos Llaman Piel" y "El Enigma del Otro" (en éste último Rimbaud se afinca en la Ciudad de México).

3733 Ramírez, Armando. Bye, bye Tenochtitlan: digo yo no más digo. México: Grijalbo, 1992. 157 p. (Narrativa Editorial Grijalbo)

Libro de crónicas de lugares y tipos en los barrios populares del centro histórico de la Ciudad de México. El cronista, consciente de la inminente desaparición de aquéllos, habla directamente al lector para guiarlo por medio de una escritura salpicada de dialecto suburbano a ese espacio extraño para el visitante.

3734 Ramírez Heredia, Rafael. Al calor de Campeche. México: Joaquín Mortiz, 1992. 199 p. (Novelistas contemporáneos)

Amena caricaturización de novela policíaca que refleja en forma de tragicomedia los penares concomitantes a los exiliados centroamericanos recientes en sus refugios transitorios en territorio mexicano. La acción, llevada a cabo en Campeche, se desarrolla en un creciente ambiente jacarandoso y dicharachero.

3735 Ramos, Luis Arturo. Blanca-Pluma. México: Grijalbo, 1993. 99 p. (Col. Botella al Mar)

Hermosa novela corta en la que se relatan las peripecias de una pluma en un mundo hostil muy semejante al circunscrito en el México de ahora y a la demás obra narrativa del autor; sólo que aquí el lenguaje de éste es más poético y simbólico, quizás para situarse más en el contexto infantil y juvenil, como quisieran los editores de la Colección Botella al Mar.

3736 Ramos, Luis Arturo. La casa del ahorcado. México: Joaquín Mortiz, 1993. 232 p. (Novelistas contemporáneos)

Las esperanzas y desilusiones de un burócrata cincuentón que sufre de impotencia sexual parecen identificarse con las ilusiones y tropiezos del México finisecular en esta novela. En ella el autor deja a un lado el cuidado casi arquitectónico de sus obras anteriores para presentar una pieza donde impera el humor negro y el lenguaje más cotidiano.

3737 Ramos, Luis Arturo. Cuentiario. México: Editorial Amaquemecan, 1988. 53 p. (Col. Nogales)

Volumen de dos cuentos ("Zili el Unicornio" y "Telésforo, el Teléfono Desocupado") dirigidos al público infantil y adolescente, pero con ingeniosa apertura fantástica, adecuada también para la mentalidad adulta. Ese es el caso en especial de "Zili el Unicornio," cuento en que se conjuga de modo natural el mundo imaginario de la mitología con el mundo cotidiano.

3738 Rascón Banda, Víctor Hugo. De cuerpo entero. México: Coordinación de Difusión Cultural, Dirección de Literatura, Univ. Nacional Autónoma de México; Ediciones Corunda, 1990. 54 p.: ill.

Autobiografía hecha en forma de entrevista por medio de la cual se conocen las raíces familiares del autor, proveniente de la sierra de Chihuahua con la cual guarda inseparables nexos personales y de inspiración en sus obras de teatro. También se habla de su rara conjunción de escritor y funcionario bancario.

3739 Ruiz, Bernardo. De cuerpo entero: las caras de las moneda; opereta para una noche de verano. México: Coordinación de Difusión Cultural, Dirección de Literatura, Univ. Nacional Autónoma de México; Ediciones Corunda, 1990. 58 p.: ill.

Jocosa autobiografía en la que el autor habla de su familia, educación, amigos, obsesiones manifiestas en sus obras y, sobre todo, su desempeño como funcionario cultural en diversas instituciones.

3740 Sáinz, Gustavo. A la salud de la serpiente. México: Grijalbo, 1991. 787 p. (Narrativa)

Ambiciosa novela barroca donde el autor recurre con reiteración calculada a la autobiografía y a la correspondencia epistolar que tuvo en ese tiempo con las personalidades más sobresalientes del mundo hispánico, con el objetivo primordial de explicarse la significación que para él mismo y para los demás tuvo el año de 1968 en México. El proceso narrativo es tan libre e intenso que logra formular una coherente filosofía de la historia de la cultura mexicana en constantes divergencias y convergencias con la norteamericana, desde cuyo territorio académico se escribe la novela. Esta es, sin duda, la mejor obra de Sáinz hasta ahora.

3741 Sáinz, Gustavo. Retablo de inmoderaciones y heresiarcas. México: J. Mortiz, 1992. 87 p. (Novelistas contemporáneos)

Libro construido con la utilización de fragmentados textos heterogéneos de todas las épocas de la literatura hispánica, pero organizados por el narrador de tal modo que en conjunto proporcionan una perspectiva de lo que podría haber sido el mundo colonial hispano un poco antes de las luchas independentistas. El narrador personalizado simula desaparecer para dar cabida sinfónica a las voces clásicas de esa tradición.

3742 Sicilia, Javier. El Bautista. Xalapa, México: Univ. Veracruzana, 1991. 241 p. (Ficción)

La novela intenta adentrarse en el proceso formativo interior de Juan el Bautista que culmina en su capacidad de precursor de Cristo. Para ello el autor no teme entrar a las consideraciones teológicas judías y cristianas que hagan más asequible al lector de ahora la dificultad de la misión impuesta a Juan, así como las vías ascéticas a recorrer como preparación a ella. El autor conforma al final un personaje trágico y conflictivo, impreciso aún en la compresión de su cometido.

3743 Solares, Ignacio. De cuerpo entero. México: Coordinación de Difusión Cultural, Dirección de Literatura, Univ. Nacional Autónoma de México; Ediciones Corunda, 1990. 55 p.: ill.

Autobiografía escrita en tercera persona con la intención de distanciarse el autor de sí mismo como objeto de narración. Sobre todo relata sus obsesiones vitales en cuanto preceden a las literarias, tales como su interés por la muerte, por las conversaciones con los muertos propiciadas por el espiritismo, y por los personajes de la Revolución Mexicana.

3744 Solares, Ignacio. Madero, el otro. México: Editorial J. Mortiz, 1989. 254 p.: bibl. (Novelistas contemporáneos)

Una voz inquisitiva formula incesantes preguntas retóricas dirigidas directamente a Francisco I. Madero, el héroe de la Revolución Mexicana, con el objeto de cuestionar las motivaciones interiores—dictadas por los espíritus, según Madero—que parecieron haberlo llevado a él y al país de nuevo a la Revolución y a la lucha caudillesca por el poder. El inquisidor, conocedor profundo de los escritos y la psicología de Madero, lo cuestiona poco después de que él ha sido herido de muerte y apenas antes de que su espíritu se separe de su cuerpo. El molde del cuestionamiento le da un dejo trágico a la novela.

3745 Solares, Ignacio. La noche de Angeles. México: Editorial Diana, 1991. 188 p.

Una voz imperativa no identificada hace que el General Felipe Angeles, gran aliado de Francisco I. Madero y de Francisco Villa, analice minuciosamente su proceder honesto, ante las intrigas que desvirtuaron el anhelo democrático de Madero con su asesinato, favoreciendo así el poderío de Victoriano Huerta y Venustiano Carranza. El pecado de Angeles, de acuerdo a dicha voz, fue su obstinada rectitud. La novela continúa, de algún modo, las inquietudes suscitadas en *Madero, el otro* (item **3744**).

3746 Su, Margo. Posesión. México: Cal y Arena, 1991. 162 p.

Novela acerca de la corrupción en los altos mandos policíacos durante el gobierno de José López Portillo, uno de cuyos oficiales simboliza con su vida doble (jefe macho y arbitrario, así como caprichoso trasvestí) la débil cimentación de la autoridad en la nación.

3747 Torre, Gerardo de la. De cuerpo entero. México: Coordinación de Difusión Cultural, Dirección de Literatura, Univ. Nacional Autónoma de México; Ediciones Corunda, 1990. 70 p.

Autobiografía en la que el autor se presenta como un escritor tardío y autodidacta que trabajó desde adolescente como mecánico en Petróleos Mexicanos, por la imposición paterna. Relata sus luchas sindicales y su asociación con el Partido Comunista Mexicano, así como su dificultosa y progresiva inserción en el mundo de las letras.

LITERARY CRITICISM AND HISTORY

3748 Los amorosos: relatos eróticos mexicanos. Selección y prólogo de Sergio González Rodríguez. México: Cal y Arena, 1993. 438 p.: bibl.

Recopilación exhaustiva—más de 60— de relatos eróticos extraídos fragmentadamente de cuentos y novelas a partir de 1900 hasta 1990. Los precede un informativo ensayo de González Rodríguez que contextualiza el difícil proceso de la escritura y lectura erótica en el país ("Lectura y Censura Sexual en México, 1900–1990"). Divide las selecciones en cinco apartados: en el de "Los antiguos" se incluyen autores tales como Alfonso Reyes y José Juan Tablada; en el de "Los renovadores," Salvador Novo y Arqueles Vela, por ejemplo; en el de "Los cosmopolitas," Salvador Elizondo y Sergio Fernández, entre otros; en el de "Los presentes," Luis Arturo Ramos y Enrique Serna, como muestra; y en el de "Los clandestinos" se reúnen textos populares—inclusive registrados en los baños públicos—de autores no conocidos en el mundo de las letras.

3749 Antología de la narrativa mexicana del siglo XX. v. 2. Selección, introducciones y notas de Christopher Domínguez Michael. México: Fondo de Cultura Económica, 1989–1991. 1 v.: bibl., indexes. (Letras mexicanas)

El segundo volumen de esta monumental obra contiene los Libros Cuarto y Quinto, es decir, los correspondientes casi en su totalidad a escritores todavía vivos. El Cuarto se organiza en torno a la figura de Carlos Fuentes, el iniciador—dice el antologador—de "La modernidad suspendida," el título del libro. Luego, haciendo a un lado la terminología ya tradicional de "la mafia," "la onda," etc., se subdivide en autores cuya obra es clasificable bajo el encabezado de "Invención de creaturas" (tales como Salvador Elizondo y Augusto Monterroso) y "Fabulación del tiempo" (como José Emilio Pacheco y Elena Poniatowska). Dentro de esta clasificación se recopila con justicia la obra de Pedro F. Miret, casi desconocida hasta ahora. El Libro Quinto agrupa a los autores preocupados por la política en su obra (como Vicente Leñero y Héctor Aguilar Camín), bajo el subtítulo de "El poder y los cuerpos;" "Pasiones y humores" agrupa a los interesados en el amor (Fernando del Paso y Luis Zapata, entre otros); "La ciudad obscura," a los narradores urbanos (José Joaquín Blanco y Arturo Azuela, por ejemplo); "Tierra baldía," a los todavía interesados en el campo y la provincia (como Jesús Gardea y Daniel Sada, aunque también es loable que incluya a Miguel Méndez, tal vez como un intento de dar natural cabida en las letras mexicanas a la literatura chicana escrita en español); y, por último "La comedia imaginaria" incluye a todos los demás (como Alberto Ruy Sánchez y Hugo Hiriart).

3750 Antología del cuento jalisciense. t. 2. Recopilación de Ernesto Flores Flores. Guadalajara, México: Ayuntamiento de Guadalajara, 1991. 1 v.

El segundo volumen de la antología reúne a los cuentistas jaliscienses más destacados a partir de 1950, los cuales han dominado en gran medida la manera de escribir el género hasta el día de hoy tanto a nivel teórico como práctico, en las publicaciones y en las instituciones culturales (escuelas, talleres, institutos, etc.). Entre ellos sobresalen Juan Rulfo, Juan José Arreola, Emmanuel Carballo, Vicente Leñero, Huberto Batis, José Agustín y Dante Medina.

3751 Bayardo Gómez, Patricio. El signo y la alambrada: ensayos de literatura y frontera. Tijuana, México: Entrelíneas, 1990. 95 p.: bibl.

Valiosa aportación teórica y crítica en torno a los conceptos fundamentales para un estudio sistemático de la literatura escrita en la frontera norte de México: la noción de frontera y la peculiaridad lingüística a ella aneja. El autor bosqueja ambos conceptos en su análisis panorámico de la literatura bajacaliforniana y de la concepción de la frontera en la novela de un narrador jalisciense ("El Norte en *Al filo del agua* de Agustín Yáñez).

3752 Chiu-Olivares, M. Isela. La novela mexicana contemporánea, 1960–1980. Madrid: Pliegos, 1990? 141 p.: bibl., index. (Pliegos de ensayo; 51)

Ensayo que analiza las características, el sentido y el alcance de "La onda" a través del estudio fundamentalmente de las novelas de José Agustín y Gustavo Sáinz publicadas entre 1960–80; una variante posterior de ese samimiento sería la obra narrativa de Armando Ramírez.

3753 Cluff, Russell M. et al. Cuento de nunca acabar: la ficción en México. Edición, prólogo y notas de Alfredo Pavón. Tlaxcala, Mexico: Univ. Autónoma de Tlaxcala; Puebla, Mexico: Centro de Ciencias del Lenguaje de la Univ. Autónoma de Puebla, 1991. 179 p.: bibl. (Serie Destino arbitrario; 6)

El simposio (1991) de la Univ. Autónoma de Tlaxcala se orientó al estudio de la obra cuentística individual publicada entre 1930–70. Se analizó la obra de Rafael F. Muñoz, Jorge Ferretis, Francisco Rojas González, Xavier Vargas Pardo, Amparo Dávila, Salvador Elizondo, Juan García Ponce, Inés Arredondo, Jorge Ibargüengoitia y Sergio Pitol.

3754 Cluff, Russell M. Siete acercamientos al relato mexicano actual. México: Coordinación de Difusión Cultural, Dirección de Lieratura, UNAM, 1987. 158 p.: bibl. (Textos de humanidades) (Crítica literaria)

Interesantes ensayos, bajo diversas perspectivas metodológicas, sobre la obra cuentística de Sergio Galindo, José Emilio Pacheco, Sergio Pitol, Salvador Elizondo y Juan Rulfo. En todos ellos el crítico enmarca el texto a estudiar en el conjunto de la obra del autor y en la generación o corriente correspondiente, y define con cuidado el acercamiento.

3755 Cuento chicano del siglo XX: breve antología. Selección, prólogo y notas de Ricardo Aguilar Melantzón. México: Ediciones Coyoacán; Univ. Nacional Autónoma de México; New Mexico State Univ., 1993. 293 p.

Cuidadosa selección de textos fundamentales de cuentistas chicanos, disponibles ahora—acaso por primera vez en estas proporciones—al público hispanoparlante gracias a la traducción al castellano de aquéllos que originalmente fueron escritos en inglés (los cuentos de Estela Portillo Trambley, Rolando Hinojosa-Smith, Benjamín Sáenz, Floyd Salas, Rudolfo Anaya, Ron Arias, Max Martínez y Lucha Corpi). La traducción permite al lector hispanohablante adquirir una visión integral del cuento chicano, del todo incapaz de llevarse a cabo en otras circunstancias. Los textos escritos en español corresponden a Sergio D. Elizondo, Miguel Méndez, Tomás Rivera, Sabine Ulibarrí, Ricardo Aguilar, Fausto Avendaño, Juan Bruce-Novoa, Margarita Cota-Cárdenas, Denise Chávez, Alicia Gaspar de Alba, Agapito Mendoza, Jim Sagel y Margarita Tavera Rivera.

3756 Cypess, Sandra Messinger. La Malinche in Mexican literature from history to myth. Austin: Univ. of Texas Press, 1991. 239 p.: bibl., ill., index. (The Texas Pan American series)

Minucioso y acertado estudio sobre la manera en que la figura de la Malinche nace con ambigüedad en las parcas menciones hechas por Hernán Cortés, es condenada por sus contemporáneos aztecas y españoles, permanece un tanto en el limbo en la época colonial, para resurgir en los proyectos nacionalistas del siglo pasado, es poco a poco exonerada y analizada como víctima, para luego constituirse en una rica figura presente en numerosas novelas, cuentos y obras teatrales de México, y, al final atraviesa la frontera norte de México en una versión reformada entre las escritoras chicanas.

3757 Domenella, Ana Rosa. Jorge Ibargüengoitia: la transgresión por la ironía. México: Univ. Autónoma Metropolitana/Iztapalapa, 1989. 183 p.: bibl. (Cuadernos universitarios; 45)

Aproximación estructuralista que busca descubrir "la visión del mundo dominante" en algunas novelas de Ibargüengoitia, para contrastarla con la ideología externa al texto. Tal visión es irónica en *Los relámpagos de agosto* y *La ley de Herodes*; grotesca, en *Las muertas*; y humorística, en *Los pasos de López*.

3758 Foster, David William. Mexican literature: a bibliography of secondary sources. 2nd ed., enl. and updated. Metuchen, N.J.: Scarecrow Press, 1992. 686 p.: bibl., index.

La obra de Foster es fuente primaria indispensable para cualquier estudioso de la literatura mexicana y de la narrativa del siglo XX en particular, por dedicar una docena de páginas exclusivamente a ese tópico en general e innumerables a alrededor de cuarenta narradores correspondientes a nuestro siglo. Los más recientes serían Arturo Azuela, Gustavo Sáinz y José Agustín.

3759 Fuentes, Carlos. Geografía de la novela. México: Fondo de Cultura Económica, 1993. 178 p. (Col. Tierra firme)

Recopilación de ensayos y ponencias de Fuentes acerca de la naturaleza de la novela y su manifestación en las lecturas de varios novelistas europeos (Juan Goytisolo, Milan Kundera, Gyorgy Konrad, Julian Barnes, Artur Lundkvist, Italo Calvino y Salman Rushdie), dos sudamericanos (Jorge Luis Borges y Augusto Roa Bastos), un centroamericano (Sergio Ramírez) y un sólo mexicano ("Héctor Aguilar Camín: La Verdad de la Mentira," sobre *La guerra de Galio*).

3760 Leal, Luis. Breve historia del cuento mexicano. Prólogo de John Bruce-Novoa. Tlaxcala de Xicohténcatl, México: Univ. Autónoma de Tlaxcala; Puebla, México: Centro de Ciencias del Lenguaje, 1990. 152 p.: bibl., index. (Serie Destino arbitrario; 2)

Reedición del ya clásico estudio panorámico (abarca desde el cuento prehispánico y termina con los jóvenes de entonces, Juan Rulfo y Juan José Arreola), pero enmarcado con sabiduría y amor en sus límites y deficiencias desde la perspectiva crítica de ahora por Bruce-Novoa, quien para ello traza una seria minihistoria de la evolución de Leal como crítico. Bruce-Novoa asevera que Leal ha querido desde sus primeros escritos hacer ver que el cuento mexicano, como el del resto del mundo, posee raíces que rebasan con mucho el siglo XIX y se remontan a la oralidad; también su visión del cuento favorecería a aquél que refleja la realidad, sobre todo asumiendo cierto compromiso social.

3761 Literatura mexicana hoy: del 68 al ocaso de la revolución. Edición de Karl Kohut. Frankfurt am Main, Germany: Vervuert Verlag, 1991. 267 p.: bibl. (Americana Eystettensia: Serie A, Kongressakten; 9)

Recopilación de las actas de un simposio celebrado en 1989 en la Univ. Católica de Eichstatt. Sorprende que la gran mayoría de las ponencias críticas hayan sido escritas por escritores mexicanos (todos ellos narradores) que de ordinario no ejercen una función crítica pública. Entre ellas destacan las ponencias de Hugo Hiriart ("Capitulaciones y Heterodoxias: Consideraciones sobre el Hecho Mexicano") y Francisco Prieto ("Constructivistas e Inconoclastas en la Generación del 68").

3762 Martínez, Rodrigo et al. México a fines de siglo. v. 1. Recopilación de José Joaquín Blanco y José Woldenberg. México: Consejo Nacional para la Cultura y las Artes; Fondo de Cultura Económica, 1993. 1 v.: bibl., ill. (Sección de obras de historia)

Atractivo libro que aborda la problemática mexicana finisecular desde variadas disciplinas. En el área de narrativa interesa la aportación de Carlos Monsiváis sobre los espacios de la cultura popular ("Los Espacios de las Masas"), verdaderas estampas de tipos y personalidades; también, el ensayo de José Joaquín Blanco acerca de los diversos estudios de los mexicanos en su proceso de modernización ("Alcanzar a Europa").

3763 Menton, Seymour. Narrativa mexicana: desde *Los de abajo* hasta *Noticias del Imperio*. Tlaxcala, Mexico: Univ. Autónoma de Tlaxcala; Puebla, Mexico: Centro de Ciencias del Lenguaje de la Univ. Autónoma de Puebla, 1991. 175 p.: bibl. (Serie Destino arbitrario; 4)

Recopilación de algunos de los muchos artículos de Menton sobre la narrativa mexicana y su relación con la del resto de Latinoamérica y el mundo. Las aproximaciones son comparativistas, temáticas, textuales o teóricas. Los estudios abarcan desde *Los de abajo* de Mariano Azuela, hasta *Noticias del Imperio* de Fernando del Paso; pero los hay también sobre la obra de José Revueltas y Juan José Arreola, entre otros.

3764 Menton, Seymour. La nueva novela histórica de la América Latina, 1979–1992. México: Fondo de Cultura Económica, 1993. 307 p. (Col. Popular)

Estudio panorámico de la novela histórica continental, sobre todo la surgida 30 años después de las reformas iniciadas por Alejo

Carpentier en *El reino de este mundo* (1949). Menton proporciona bibliografía y discusión exhaustiva sobre el tema, pero de la nueva novela histórica en México sólo estudia a fondo *Noticias del Imperio* de Fernando del Paso, dos novelas de Homero Ardijis y *La campaña* de Carlos Fuentes.

3765 Miller, Beth Kurti. A la sombra del volcán: conversaciones sobre la narrativa mexicana actual. Guadalajara, Mexico: Univ. de Guadalajara/Xalli; Jalapa, Mexico: Univ. Veracruzana; México: Consejo Nacional para la Cultura y las Artes, Instituto Nacional de Bellas Artes, 1990. 305 p.: bibl., ill., index. (Reloj de sol)

Extensas entrevistas conducidas con familiaridad y sólido conocimiento de los 14 narradores, casi todos ellos mexicanos. Destacan por su vivacidad las hechas a Guillermo Samperio, Luis Arturo Ramos y Ethel Krauze.

3766 Pavón, Alfredo et al. Te lo cuento otra vez: la ficción en México. Edición, prólogo y notas de Alfredo Pavón. Tlaxcala, Mexico: Univ. Autónoma de Tlaxcala; Puebla, Mexico: Centro de Ciencias del Lenguaje de la Univ. Autónoma de Puebla, 1991. 151 p.: bibl. (Serie Destino arbitrario; 3)

El encuentro anual (1990) sobre cuento mexicano, de la Univ. Autónoma de Tlaxcala, parece proponerse fundamentar su estudio partiendo desde la definición del género (Alfredo Pavón) y la panorámica de las décadas del 70 y del 80 (Luis Leal, Carlos Miranda Ayala y Vicente Francisco Torres), para después encuadrar estudios de la obra de cuentistas individuales (el Dr. Atl, José Revueltas, Elena Garro, José de la Colina, José Emilio Pacheco, Inés Arredondo, Esther Selingson, María Luisa Puga y Angelina Muñiz).

3767 Peden, Margaret Sayers. Out of the volcano: portraits of contemporary Mexican artists. Photographs by Carole Patterson. Washington: Smithsonian Institution Press, 1991. 256 p.: bibl., ill.

Libro de entrevistas de artistas mexicanos, precedidas de su respectiva introducción y con bibliografía básica posterior. Quince de ellos son escritores tales como Verónica Volkow, Guillermo Samperio, Margo Glantz, Angeles Mastretta, Luis Arturo Ramos, etc. Peden muestra conocimiento profundo de las obras de los autores tanto en la entrevista como en la introducción, pero sobre todo es excelente la introducción al libro donde señala algunos aspectos fundamentales de las artes mexicanas desde la perspectiva de la cultura norteamericana.

3768 Revueltas, José. Los días terrenales. Edición crítica coordinada por Evodio Escalante. Madrid: CSIC; Nanterre, France: ALLCA XXe, 1991. 360 p.: bibl., ill. (Col. Archivos; 15)

Evodio Escalante ofrece un texto cuidadosamente cotejado y anotado de esta controversial novela de Revueltas, aunado a estudios de Florence Olivier (sobre la posibilidad de que Revueltas haya debatido en la novela lo que no hubiera podido hacer en la palestra del Partido Comunista Mexicano) y de Edith Negrín y Marta Portal (acerca de la presencia del Apocalipsis, Pascal, José Alvarado, Engels, etc. en el texto de la novela).

3769 Rulfo, Juan. Toda la obra. Edición crítica coordinada por Claude Fell. Paris: ALLCA XXe; España: CSIC, 1992. 950 p.: bibl., ill. (Col. Archivos; 17)

Claude Fell precisó de un equipo de 15 estudiosos para llevar a cabo una de las tareas más urgentes en el estudio de la narrativa mexicana: establecer un texto más definido de los libros de ficción mexicana más leídos, *Pedro Páramo* y *El llano en llamas,* saturados de evidentes variantes de edición en edición. El honor y la carga de esa mayúscula tarea recayó en Sergio López Mena, quien además los anotó e hizo las mismas operaciones con otros textos de Rulfo y diseñó la filmografía correspondiente. A los textos críticos hacen dialogante compañía más de 30 estudios a cual más interesante, aparte de la minuciosa bibliografía de Aurora Ocampo. Entre los estudios sólo se destacará—por razones de espacio—el más panorámico, extenso (75 p.) e inclusivo de todos: "Visión Panorámica: la Obra de Juan Rulfo en el Tiempo y en el Espacio," de Gerald Martin. En él reconstruye la historia de la crítica acerca de Rulfo y la clasifica en los apartados de "Lecturas Globales," formalistas, temáticas y sociales. Tal vez el presente volumen constituya la aproximación crítica más completa hasta ahora acerca de la obra de Rulfo.

3770 Ruy Sánchez, Alberto. Al filo de las hojas. México: Secretaría de Educación Pública; Plaza y Valdés, 1988. 367 p. (Serie Creación El Nigromante)

Ensayos breves acerca de aspectos teóricos de la escritura y la literatura, de reseñas sobre lecturas varias (en especial de literatura francesa), de aproximaciones a la obra de pintores, directores de cine, etc. Casi todos fueron recopilados de una columna semanal en *Sábado de Uno-másuno* (1980–85). En su escritura se hacen patentes las virtudes del fino poeta y narrador que es Ruy Sánchez.

3771 Schaefer, Claudia. Textured lives: women, art, and representation in modern Mexico. Tucson: Univ. of Arizona Press, 1992. 163 p.: bibl., index.

Estudio sobre las relaciones concomitantes entre el trabajo artístico de la mujer (escritura, pintura, etc.), la persona de la artista (incluido el cuerpo) y el cuerpo social del cual la creadora forma parte. En ese contexto analiza los autorretratos de Frida Kahlo, algunos textos periodísticos de Rosario Castellanos, el recurso epistolar en *Querido Diego, te abraza Quiela* y *Gaby Brimmer* de Elena Poniatowska y *Arráncame la vida* de Angeles Mastretta.

3772 Steele, Cynthia. Politics, gender, and the Mexican novel, 1968–1988: beyond the pyramid. Austin: Univ. of Texas Press, 1992. 209 p.: bibl., ill., index. (The Texas Pan American series)

Proyecto panorámico cuyo objetivo es aplicar las teorías contemporáneas del género y las actitudes políticas a 20 años de producción narrativa en México y, luego, con más detalle a *Hasta no verte Jesús mío* de Elena Poniatowska, *Palinuro de México* de Fernando del Paso, *Las batallas en el desierto* de José Emilio Pacheco y en *Cerca del fuego* de José Agustín.

3773 Torres M., Vicente Francisco. Esta narrativa mexicana: ensayos y entrevistas. México: Editora y Distribuidora Leega, 1991. 268 p.: ill. (Leega literaria: Serie mayor)

El trabajo periodístico fue el inicio de este interesante proyecto de Torres acerca de los narradores posteriores a "La onda," aquéllos cuya obra comienza a sobresalir a partir de 1980. La lectura profunda y el diálogo inteligente permiten al autor ofrecer una visión panorámica bien fundamentada de la obra de 16 narradores mexicanos actuales, tales como Luis Arturo Ramos, Ignacio Solares, Enrique Serna y Silvia Molina.

3774 Trejo Fuentes, Ignacio. De acá de este lado: una aproximación a la novela chicana. México: Consejo Nacional para la Cultura y las Artes, 1989. 263 p.: bibl., index. (Frontera)

Serio acercamiento temático, ideológico y analítico a la novela chicana contemporánea escrita en inglés y en español. De ésta última se estudia la obra de Tomás Rivera, Miguel Méndez, Aristeo Brito, Alejandro Morales, Abelardo Delgado y Sergio Elizondo.

3775 Voces narrativas de Veracruz, 1837–1989. Selección y notas de José Martínez Morales y Sixto Rodríguez Hernández. México: Consejo Nacional para las Culturas y las Artes, 1993. 455 p.

Excelente selección, precedida de útil estudio de José Luis Martínez Morales y proseguida de minuciosas notas biobibliográficas, de una de las presencias más ricas y variadas en la narrativa mexicana: la veracruzana. Esto se nota de inmediato al ver la lista de al-

gunos de los autores correspondientes al siglo XX cuyo nombre resuena dentro y fuera del país: Rubén Salazar Mallén, Rafael Solana, Emilio Carballido, Sergio Galindo, Juan Vicente Melo, Sergio Pitol, Lazlo Moussong y Luis Arturo Ramos, entre otros.

3776 Yáñez, Agustín. Al filo del agua. Edición crítica coordinada por Arturo Azuela. Nanterre, France: ALLCA XX, Univ. Paris X, Centre de recherches latino-américaines, 1992. 406 p.: bibl. (Col. Archivos; 22)

Arturo Azuela, aparte de magnífico novelista, se está manifestando cada vez más como estudioso. En la definición del texto y la anotación de la novela de Yáñez hay ejemplo de ello, proseguido por los trabajos, entre otros, de José Luis Martínez sobre la poética narrativa en la novela y de Carlos Monsiváis sobre la conminación que el novelista hace al lector para participar en la creación de ese mundo.

Central America

RENE PRIETO, *Associate Professor of Spanish, Southern Methodist University*

COSTA RICA CONTINUES TURNING OUT a veritable avalanche of literary and critical texts. Writings of the post-1960s reveal an ever growing social awareness as well as a focus on women both as victims, and as agents of change. Among them, Carmen Naranjo continues to hold center stage, her Protean fiction serving as a perpetual source of inspiration for younger writers. As pointed out by Luz Ivette Martínez in her illuminating article (item **3806**), Naranjo's search for authenticity shines forth in her earliest poetry, and infuses life into three recent and sensitive works about man's painful isolation: *Otro rumbo para la rumba* (item **3790**), *Nunca hubo alguna vez* (item **3789**), and *El caso 117,720* (item **3786**).

Like most of its neighbors to the north and south, Costa Rica has undergone dramatic changes in the past 30 years. Both the cities and the middle class have grown by leaps and bounds. The struggles and hardships of this spreading urban population are showcased in novels and shorts stories such as Naranjo's, which are now being written in every Central American capital. The exodus from rural to urban communities and from extended to nuclear families in metropolitan centers riddled with crime, greed, and ruthless competition has led to incommunicability, isolation, and *desencanto*, all typical of the crisis of postmodernity. Seidy Araya (item **3797**) exemplifies post-1960s Costa Rican writers who regard the world not merely as aesthetes but also as reformers and sociologists. Their politically-conscious fiction is a mirror held to a society undergoing overwhelming changes. But Costa Ricans are not alone in regarding themselves as reformers. For example, the Salvadoran Nidia López (item **3780**), and the Nicaraguan Tomás Borge (item **3800**), examine at length the role of the Revolution, and make suggestions for improving living conditions in their respective countries.

This need to understand the present has led a number of Central American authors to turn to their own past, and to examine the historical and literary traditions from which such voices of change have emerged. These are exemplified by *La voz desgarrada* (item **3809**), Alvaro Quesada Soto's analysis of the political crisis that culminated in Federico Tinoco's dictatorship in Costa Rica (1917–19); Jorge Valdeperas' examination of the contribution of three generations of authors in *Para una nueva interpretación de la literatura costarricense* (item **3813**); and Rafael Martínez Lara's thorough demonstration of how the philosophy of earlier Salvadoran poets informed the work of Francisco Gavidia (item **3804**). Pondering over such contemporary innovations has inspired editors to reconsider old masters in new anthologies such as the *Antología del relato costarricense* (item **3796**), the first collection of Costa Rican short stories to be published in more than 20 years.

In addition to exploring the forces of tradition and creativity, Central American writers are drawn to examine the constancy of war, violence, and political repression in the region, a trend evident in works such as David Escobar Galindo's disturbing stories in *Gente que pasa* (item **3781**), Nicasio Urbina's finely wrought "La Voz de los Lobos" in *El libro de las palabras enajenadas* (item **3793**), and Hernán Solís' mordantly ironic *El aprendiz de Redentor* (item **3792**). Although the theme of war permeates these works, there is a marked constrast between the present-oriented battlefield literature of early revolutionary days, and the more recent reevaluations of past events such as Sergio Ramírez's *Confesión de amor* (item **3791**). No longer written in the present-tense form of guerrilla diaries, these recent works are oriented toward the future and the prospect of formulating programs that will bring about lasting social reform.

In Central America, a region of tragic and violent changes, the victims of choice have always been the indigenous populations. In *Operación Iscariote* (item **3795**), Miguel Angel Vázquez portrays the downfall of an agrarian community in a novel that brings to mind Carlos Castillo Armas' self-serving invasion of Guatemala in 1955. The men of maize play a dramatically different role in Arturo Arias' highly original *Jaguar en llamas* (item **3777**), a fascinating blend of past and present, Mayan mythology and *latifundio* that is greatly indebted to the mythical masterpieces of Miguel Angel Asturias. Asturias himself happens to be very much in the limelight after the publication of Luis Cardoza y Aragón's *Miguel Angel Asturias: casi novela* (item **3801**), Juan Olivero's *El Miguel Angel Asturias que yo conocí* (item **3807**), Rene Prieto's *Miguel Angel Asturias's archaeology of return* (item **3808**), and of engrossing new critical editions of *Hombres de maíz* (item **3778**), as well as of Asturias' own journalistic production written during his most formative years in 1924–33 (item **3798**).

PROSE FICTION

3777 Arias, Arturo. Jaguar en llamas. Guatemala: Ministerio de Cultura y Deportes, 1989. 339 p. (Editorial Cultura; 13)
Highly original new novel set in the 16th century, richly documented, and humorously told by the author of *Después de las bombas* (1979). Combines features from the *Thousand and one nights*, Bernal Díaz's *Historia verdadera*, and the *Chilam Balam*. Describes adventures of four Jewish infidels who settle in the Guatemalan highlands and stage first series of subversive acts in the New World.

3778 Asturias, Miguel Angel. Hombres de maíz. Coordinación de Gerald Martin. Ed. crítica, 1. ed. Nanterre, France: ALLCA

XX, Univ. Paris X, Centre de recherches latino-américaines, 1992. 764 p.: bibl. (Col. Archivos; 21)

Valuable and erudite edition of Asturias' most difficult novel. Critics such as Gordon Brotherston, Martin Lienhard, and Arturo Arias contribute eye-opening essays, and Gerald Martin's two long articles about the genesis and critics of *Hombres de maíz* are especially worthwhile.

3779 Cuadra, Manolo. Solo en la compañía. Selección y prólogo de Lizandro Chávez Alfaro. La Habana: Casa de las Américas, 1989. 223 p. (Col. Literatura latinoamericana; 126)

Selected passages from *Itinerario de Little Corn Island* (1937), *Contra Sandino en la montaña* (1942), *Almidón* (1945), etc. by one of Nicaragua's most gifted authors.

3780 Díaz, Nidia. Nunca estuve sola. México: Editorial Mestiza; Univ. Autónoma Metropolitana, Unidad Xochimilco, 1989. 261 p., 4 p. of plates: ill. (Col. Testimonios; 1)

Novela testimonio written by revolutionary leader who spent nine months in prison. Díaz's personal tale of struggle and survival is showcased within the larger historical frame of the People's Revolutionary Movement in El Salvador.

3781 Escobar Galindo, David. Gente que pasa: historias sin cuento de 1988. San Salvador: UCA Editores, 1989. 206 p.: ill. (Col. Gavidia; 33)

Spell-binding collection of short stories. Themes range from friends sipping beer and talking politics to lonely school teachers opening their doors to ex-students looking for a place to hide from the police.

3782 Gutiérrez, Joaquín. Obras completas. v. 1–4. Prólogo de Jorge A. Boccanera. Bibliografía de Carlos E. Granados Molina. San José: Univ. de Costa Rica, 1988–1991. 4 v.: ill. (some col.)

Consists of six novels, three anthologies of poems, three travel journals, and as many translations of Shakespearean plays by one of the most important 20th-century Costa Rican authors. Forthcoming is his autobiography. Travel journals in Book III (*Del Mapocho al Vístula, Vietnam,* and *La URSS tal cual*) are extremely candid and particularly appealing. Contains bibliography.

3783 Liano, Dante. El lugar de su quietud. Guatemala: Ministerio de Cultura y Deportes, 1990. 90 p.: ill. (Col. Narrativa guatemalteca siglo XX; 12. Serie Miguel Angel Asturias)

Elegantly written *Bildungsroman* set in author's native Chimaltenango (Guatemala). Liano dovetails past and present as he searches for meaning in a society falling to pieces before his very eyes.

3784 Lindo, Hugo. ¡Justicia, señor gobernador!: novela. 8. ed. San Salvador: Dirección de Publicaciones e Impresos, 1989. 323 p.

Penetrating study of the deranged mind and its sometimes blinding lucidity. First published in 1960 and written in the vein of Dostoevsky's *Notes from underground,* this chronicle of a schizophrenic judge leaves no doubt as to Lindo's importance as a novelist.

3785 Monterroso, Augusto. La letra e: fragmentos de un diario. Mexico: Ediciones Era, 1987. 204 p. (Biblioteca Era)

Notes, reflections, and quips about Proust, Cortázar, *Alice in Wonderland,* Kafka, and just about every literary tendency fill the pages of this memorable diary seasoned with Monterroso's unique brand of ironic transcendentalism.

3786 Naranjo, Carmen. El caso 117,720. San José: Editorial Costa Rica, 1987. 155 p.

Skillfully written from a continually shifting narrative point of view, this biting psychological novel revolves around the catatonic body of a man dying of a mysterious disease. Naranjo wastes no time in revealing the ambition, greed, and vanity that typify humankind. Uses her poetic language as a searing scalpel to reveal the protagonists' innermost thoughts, petty passions, and, above all, their profound inability to love.

3787 Naranjo, Carmen and Graciela Moreno. Estancias y días. San José: Editorial Costa Rica, 1985. 98 p.

Two-voice counterpoint addresses issues of love and death in a dialogue between Naranjo and friend. One of the most poetic and sensitive books to appear in Central America in the last few years.

3788 Naranjo, Carmen. Memorias de un hombre palabra. San José: Editorial Costa Rica, 1978. 137 p.

Loneliness and meaningful inconsequence of daily existence are disturbingly portrayed in this prose counterpart to T.S. Eliot's "The Love Song of J. Alfred Prufrock." Original handling of language and poetic conception make this painful journey through life into a truly memorable, insightful novel.

3789 Naranjo, Carmen. Nunca hubo alguna vez. Ilustraciones de Georgina García. San José: Editorial Univ. Estatal a Distancia, 1984. 75 p.: ill.

Author's fresh and vivid perception of children lends a unique glow to her stories. These sparkling moral tales, perhaps the best written by Naranjo, concern such mundane topics as busted bicycles or feverish weeks in bed devising 18 ways to draw a mental square.

3790 Naranjo, Carmen. Otro rumbo para la rumba. San José: Editorial Universitaria Centroamericana, 1989. 205 p. (Col. Séptimo día)

Arguably Central America's most original author reaches new heights in this collection of short stories in which the ridiculous turns sublime (e.g., the off-beat, "En Todas Partes se Puede" about yet another uprooted Latin American woman finding peace, comfort, and karma when she pretends to be a mannequin and moves into Bloomingdale's).

3791 Ramírez, Sergio. Confesión de amor. Prólogo de Ernesto Cardenal. Managua: Ediciones Nicarao, 1991. 192 p: bibl. (Col. Nuestra América)

Reflections on the past, present, and future of Nicaragua and the Sandinista movement. Ramírez discusses the revolution's historical program and makes suggestions for maintaining peace and stimulating economic growth.

3792 Solís Bolaños, Hernán. El aprendiz de redentor. San José: Editorial de la Univ. de Costa Rica, 1992. 145 p.

Outlandish satire about Jesus being born again and the reader meeting his parents and grandparents. One of the most unusual and best crafted books ever written on the subject of disarmament and world peace.

3793 Urbina, Nicasio. El libro de las palabras enajenadas. San José: Editorial Universitaria Centroamericana, 1991. 127 p. (Col. Séptimo día.)

Urbina celebrates life and grieves over the senseless murder that is war in these sen-

sitively wrought stories that open with a stirring description of conception and birth entitled "Nacer es Solamente Comenzar a Morir."

3794 Vallbona, Rima de. Mundo, demonio y mujer. Houston, Tex.: Arte Público Press, 1991. 320 p.

Stirring rite-of-passage novel about a career woman and the obstacles set up by a profoundly male-oriented society. One of Vallbona's more ambitious undertakings, this novel takes place in Houston, where the author resides, but the characters are Latin American.

3795 Vázquez, Miguel Angel. Operación Iscariote. Guatemala: Impreofset O. de León Palacios, 1989. 88 p.: ill.

US invades a Central American country to defend the trampled "rights" of the United Fruit Co. Novel closely echoes Carlos Castillo Armas' invasion of Guatemala in 1955. Portrayal of an agrarian community's downfall is intended to symbolize plight of Latin American countries aspiring to free themselves from feudalism.

LITERARY CRITICISM AND HISTORY

3796 Antología del relato costarricense, 1890–1930. Selección, introducción y notas de Alvaro Quesada Soto. San José: Editorial de la Univ. de Costa Rica, 1989. 204 p.: bibl. (Serie antológica)

Timely work offers wide range of styles in this anthology of short stories. First published in Costa Rica in more than 20 years. Includes some half-forgotten authors such as Rafael Angel Troyo, Rómulo Tovar, and José Fabio Garnier, as well as short stories reprinted since their original publication several decades ago. Particularly witty is Carmen Lyra's "Por qué Tío Conejo Tiene las Orejas tan Largas."

3797 Araya, Seidy. La enajenación de la mujer en los sectores medios: Los perros no ladraron de Carmen Naranjo. (Kañina/San José, 15:1/2, p. 55–65)

As of the 1960s, Costa Rican writers begin to view the world not only as aesthetes, but as reformers and amateur sociologists. Carmen Naranjo is particularly keen on transforming the world we live in. This politically oriented and elegantly written article examines 20 years of her fiction as a reflection of a society undergoing momentous changes.

3798 Asturias, Miguel Angel. París, 1924–1933: periodismo y creación literaria. Coordinación de Amos Segala. Ed. crítica, 1. ed. Nanterre, France: ALLCA XX; Buenos Aires?: Ministerio de Relaciones Exteriores; Brasil: CNPq; Bogota?: Presidencia de la República; Madrid?: CSIC; México?: SEP; Lisboa?: Instituto de Cultura e Língua Portuguesa, 1988. 981 p.: bibl., ill., index. (Col. Archivos; 1)

Fascinating and useful compilation of difficult-to-obtain newspaper articles from Asturias' most formative period. Showcases an intellectual young author during his years in Paris, and immediately after his return to Guatemala.

Beverley, John and **Marc Zimmerman.** Literature and politics in the Central American revolutions. See *HLAS 53:3399.*

3799 Borge, Tomás. El arte como herejía: la cultura en la memoria y la vida de T. Borge. Donostia, Spain: Tercera Prensa, 1991. 276 p. (Gakoa liburuak; 9)

Collection of speeches, candid interviews, and assorted writings by prize-winning author and revolutionary leader from Nicaragua. Subjects discussed include magical realism, relationship between poetry and revolution, Julio Cortázar, and Rubén Darío.

3800 Borge, Tomás. Cultura y revolución popular sandinista. (*Unión/Habana,* 5, enero/marzo 1989, p. 2–9, photos)

In this fascinating chapter from his book, *El arte como herejía y otros actos de fé,* Borge discusses how the seemingly antithetical terms—culture and revolution—are becoming analogous in today's Nicaragua (i.e., 1989).

3801 Cardoza y Aragón, Luis. Miguel Angel Asturias: Premio Lenin de la Paz 1965, Premio Nobel de Literatura 1967: casi novela. México: Ediciones Era, 1991. 247 p.: ill. (Biblioteca Era)

More enjoyable for style than objectivity, this "novel" about Miguel Angel Asturias' life showers praise on *Hombres de maíz* while deploring that its author has been unjustly forgotten. Cardoza's enormous erudition makes this book a feast for the eye as

well as the mind. Still, one wishes there would be more revelations given that Asturias took such pains to shroud his life in mystery. Unfortunately, someone who knew him intimately and for so long has chosen to preserve the legend rather than bring us closer to the man.

3802 Cuadra, Pablo Antonio. Otro rapto de Europa: notas de un viaje. San José: Libro Libre, 1986. 167 p. (Obra en prosa; 4. Serie literaria)

Fascinating little travel book written in the style of 18th- and 19th-century *carnets de voyages.* Although title mentions Europe by way of alluding to the continent, book concerns Nicaragua more than older countries. Written during several months in 1974 when Cuadra was in charge of *La Prensa's* editorials in Managua, these travel notes are well seasoned with philosophical reflections on the nature of freedom and the vagaries of history.

3803 Lara Martínez, Rafael. De la ficción como historia: el cazador, el venado y el problema de los dobles en Salarrué; hacia una política cultural de la fantasía salvadoreña. (*An. Antropol.,* 26, 1989, p. 331–363, bibl., tables)

Insightful analysis of the relation between mythology and politics and how it illuminates the symbolic role of the deer among the Pipiles from Izalco as well as Salarrué's portrayal of this animal in his fiction.

3804 Lara Martínez, Rafael. Historia sagrada e historia profana: el sentido de la historia salvadoreña en la obra de Francisco Gavidia. San Salvador: Dirección de Publicaciones e Impresos, Consejo Nacional para la Cultura y el Arte, Ministerio de Educación, 1992. 148 p.: bibl.

Examines role of tradition in the work of Francisco Gavidia (1863–1955). Notes how the narrative aims and philosophy of earlier Salvadoran poets such as Francisco Díaz and even of ancient Mesoamerican traditions inform Gavidia's conception of the historical development of Central America.

3805 La literatura de Augusto Monterroso. Introducción de Marco Antonio Campos. México: Dirección de Difusión Cultural, Depto. Editorial, Univ. Autónoma Metropolitana, 1988. 175 p.: bibl. (Col. de cultura universitaria; 48. Serie/Ensayo)

Collection of essays by the likes of Angel Rama, Saul Sosnowski, and José Miguel Oviedo on the work of one of Guatemala's most original authors. The master of narrative silence who excels in at least three different genres—satire, fable, and "perpetual movement"—is well served by these discussions of his work although one wishes for more analytical readings in an otherwise perfect collection.

3806 Martínez, Luz Ivette. Trayectoria vital de la obra de Carmen Naranjo. (*Kañína/San José*, 15 : 1/2, 1991, p. 47–53)

Elegantly written overview of Carmen Naranjo's development pinpoints her features as a writer as well as the continual evolution of her work. In Naranjo's profoundly ontological novels, modern man is torn between being and appearances. And while humanity appears to have a potential for redemption, Naranjo's characters usually fail to attain any sense of authenticity in their lives.

3807 Olivero, Juan. El Miguel Angel Asturias que yo conocí: relato anecdótico. 2. ed. Guatemala: Tipografía Nacional, 1987. 209 p.: ill.

Wealth of details—both accurate and inaccurate—about Asturias' life comes to light in this enjoyable account penned by one of his closest friends since childhood.

3808 Prieto, René. Miguel Angel Asturias's archaeology of return. Cambridge, England; New York: Cambridge Univ. Press, 1993. 307 p.: bibl., ill., index. (Cambridge studies in Latin American and Iberian literature; 7)

Asturias was the first to write a new kind of American idiom that broke away from the strictures of Western literary tradition. His most innovative works (e.g., the *Leyendas de Guatemala*, *Hombres de maíz*, and *Mulata de tal*) are informed by surrealist techniques, Mayan mythology, and his unique involvement with *Prensa Latina*. *Hombres de maíz* is comparable to a fugue, and is undoubtedly one of the 20th-century's most originally conceived works of literature.

3809 Quesada Soto, Alvaro. La voz desgarrada: la crisis del discurso oligárquico y la narrativa costarricense, 1917–1919. San José: Editorial de la Univ. de Costa Rica, 1988. 258 p.: bibl.

Study of the political crisis that culminated in Federico Tinoco's dictatorship in Costa Rica (1917–19), and of the transformations that took place in both the literature and the propaganda written during this period.

3810 Reina Argueta, Marta. Nací en el fondo azul de las montañas hondureñas: ensayo sobre Juan Ramón Molina. Tegucigalpa: Editorial Guaymuras, 1990. 262 p.: bibl.

Insightful analysis of Juan Ramón Molina's literary universe. Chapter focusing on the Honduran author's transformation of prose into poetry is particularly illuminating.

3811 Rivero, Eliana S. Testimonial literature and conversations as literary discourse: Cuba and Nicaragua. (*Lat. Am. Perspect.*, 18 : 3, Summer 1991, p. 69–79, bibl.)

Comparing Omar Cabezas' *La montaña es algo más que una inmensa estepa verde* (1982) with Cuban author Víctor Casaus' *Pablo con el filo de la hoja* (1983), Rivero explains the innovations that permeate oral literature and concludes that "testimonial literature has had a pivotal role to play in the revolutionary discourse produced in Latin America in the 1980s."

3812 Umaña, Helen. Narradoras hondureñas. Tegucigalpa: Editorial Guaymuras, 1990. 166 p.: bibl., ill. (Col. Lámpara)

Intelligently written and well-documented study of works by Honduras' most important three authors: the women Lucila Gamero de Medina, Paca Navas de Miralda, and Argentina Díaz Lozano. Examines themes that include use of stereotypes, romance, and political utopia.

3813 Valdeperas, Jorge. Para una nueva interpretación de la literatura costarricense. San José: Editorial Costa Rica, 1991. 130 p.: bibl.

Erudite and useful study of Costa Rican literature that ranges from the turn of the century to the present. After an introductory chapter in praise of naturalism (which author feels corresponds in its style and aims to the harsh reality of Latin America), Valdeperas examines the contributions of three generations of writers: 1) "generación del 90;" 2) "generación del 40;" and 3) those writing after 1948. Focuses most particularly on the last two groups whose motivation he views in terms of the fundamental opposition between capitalism and socialism.

3814 Vallbona, Rima de. Erotismo, remembranzas tropicales y misterio en *María la Noche* de Anacristina Rossi. (*in* Mujer y sociedad en América. Edición de Juana Alcira Arancibia. Mexicali, México: Univ. Autónoma de Baja California; Westminster, Calif.: Instituto Literario y Cultural Hispánico, 1988, v. 1, p. 117–135)

Illuminating interview with one of the most promising Costa Rican authors of the new generation. Dwells on influences shaping Rossi's aesthetics.

3815 Ventura Sandoval, Juan. Ficción y realidad: las mujeres en la narrativa de Rosario Castellanos. Tlaxcala, Tlax.: Univ. Autónoma de Tlaxcala, 1987. 104 p.: bibl.

Study of Rosario Castellanos' female characters based on theories of Juliet Mitchel and Claude Brémond. Ventura compares Castellanos' feminist position as expressed in essays and conferences with characters in her fiction. Of particular interest is author's approach to Castellanos from a perspective other than *indigenismo* whereby he demonstrates that this unfairly neglected author should not be pigeonholed.

Hispanic Caribbean

CARLOS R. HORTAS, *Dean of Humanities and the Arts, Hunter College-City University of New York*
ENRIQUE SACERIO-GARI, *Professor of Spanish, Bryn Mawr College*

LITERATURE HAS ALWAYS BEEN in transition. The search for new horizons, generic experimentation, and generational struggles are always at work for/against traditional confines and future expectations. What marks a moment may mark a generation; what moves an individual may transform the deepest traditions of a nation. It seems that the Caribbean has always been in crisis. Generation after generation faces up to the idiosyncrasies of the region and sets out to secure a better future, a future that is usually frustrated by chronic internal strife or by the persistent intervention of foreign powers.

The works reviewed during the past years for this section confirm that women writers are a major reason for the high quality of Puerto Rican literature. One obvious trend in Cuban prose is the publication of most works outside of Cuba. The current crisis, based on the collapse of Soviet socialism and the increased pressure by the US, has exposed all the inefficiencies of Cuba's economy and the tenuous underpinning of its cultural project. Changed priorities under the "special period" and the scarcity of paper and electricity have contributed to inactivity or further exodus of writers.

The memoirs of Reinaldo Arenas (item **3849**) and Guillermo Cabrera Infante's *Mea Cuba* (item **3821**) present stark tales of the deterioration of the individual under socialist political correctness. In a society that divides itself between revolutionaries and counterrevolutionaries, there is a tendency to identify certain persons, stigmatized by political discrimination or social prejudices, with the counterrevolutionary group. The security apparatus is prepared to monitor society by means of simple categorizations, often based on ignorance and bigotry. When it meets resistance to political conformity or opposition to a normative code, it mobilizes fiercely against the individual. Such heightened scrutiny leads to outcomes such as the ill-advised censure of the documentary *PM* (that Cabrera Infante incessantly reviews), the persecution of conspicuous homosexuality (detailed by Reinaldo Arenas), or the unforgivable battering of María Elena Cruz Valera.

Jesús Díaz (who left Cuba) and Lisandro Otero (who comes and goes) share their tales of frustration from *within* the Revolution. Díaz's *Las palabras perdidas* and Otero's *Arbol de la vida* (items **3825** and **3837**) grasp the grayish zones of those who conformed and fought for Cuban socialism, often with great idealism and sacrifice, and were ultimately disillusioned or set back by corrupt opportunists or treacherous political climbers. Miguel Barnet takes a more nostalgic approach in *Oficio de ángel* which explores his recollections from childhood to the early 1960s and devotes many pages to the recovery of images (item **3820**). Luis Manuel García's *Habanecer* (item **3828**) constitutes an experimental *tour de force* in Cuban narrative which deserves to be seriously studied. Senel Paz's "El Lobo, el Bosque y el Hombre Nuevo" (item **3838**), a complex exploration of sexual and political orientations, is perhaps the most controversial short story ever to appear in *Unión*. Its publication may mark an important transition in Cuban letters. Cabrera Infante's unexpurgated *Tres tristes tigres* (item **3822**), which recalls another era of censorship, and new printings of Dulce María Loynaz's *Jardín* and *Un verano en Tenerife* (items **3830** and **3831**) are among the important recent reeditions.

Criticism in Cuba is best represented by the work of Desiderio Navarro, who against all odds continues to produce *Criterios*. Some critics have written extensively about the demise of detective fiction (item **3871** and **3859**) and good work has also been done on women writers and intellectual history (items **3863** and **3868**). Roberto Valero's brief essay on exiled writers is an outstanding reflection on Reinaldo Arenas (item **3879**) and Antón Arrufat's analysis of *La carne de René* by Piñera is a touching tribute to the Cuban master (item **3850**). Antonio Benítez Rojo's *The repeating island* is a skillful attempt to outline Caribbean culture realities (item **3852**), while Emilio Bejel's interviews constitute a major historical document for students of Cuban cultural policies and the role of the intellectual (item **3851**). Nadia Lie analyzes the discourse about the intellectual in *Casa de las Américas* (item **3866**).

Cuba faces another end of a century with hunger at home and many writers abroad. Whether in Cuba, or residing or working temporarily in other countries (from different waves of migration and belonging to different exile communities), Cuban fiction writers holding diverse views of cultural politics and the coming transformation of Cuban society still have much to say and do.

Rosario Ferré's writings highlight literary production in Puerto Rico. As of this date, Ferré emerges as the leading Puerto Rican writer of her time and has made important contributions to various literary genres: poetry, the novel, the short story, and the literary and cultural essay. The essays in *El árbol y sus sombras* (item **3862**) are models of well-written, incisive, and provocative prose, and *Papeles de Pandora* includes excellent samples of her short stories and poems (item **3827**).

Women writers in general have achieved exceptional literary prominence in Puerto Rico in the last ten years, as is evidenced by María Solá's critical anthology of women writers, *Aquí cuentan las mujeres* (item **3816**). The work of earlier women writers is also being restored to prominence, as in Julio Ramos' edition of *Amor y anarquía: los escritos de Luisa Capetillo* (item **3823**). All in all, women writers are finally receiving their due and are being recognized for the prominent role they have always played in Puerto Rican letters.

PROSE FICTION

3816 **Aquí cuentan las mujeres: muestra y estudio de cinco narradoras puertorriqueñas.** Edición de María Magdalena Solá. Río Piedras, P.R.: Ediciones Huracán, 1990. 177 p.: bibl., ill.

Model anthology includes short stories by five of Puerto Rico's best women writers. Exceptionally good introduction and complete scholarly bibliography.

3817 **Arenas, Reinaldo.** El asalto. Miami: Ediciones Universal, 1991. 141 p. (Col. caniqui)

Novel of sharp-edged political, personal, and linguistic experimentation. Filled with intertextual exploration (the index offers an intertextual reference for each chapter), scintillating with satire and parody at the very surface of language, text aims to erase the omnipotent tyrant (el Reprimerísimo) and the ever present mother [country].

3818 **Arenas, Reinaldo.** Final de un cuento. Ilustraciones de Jorge Camacho. Huelva, Spain: Diputación Provincial de Huelva, 1991. 84 p., 13 leaves of plates: col. ill. (El Fantasma de la glorieta: Narrativas; 3)

Includes three essays and two short stories by Arenas, and 13 drawings dedicated to Arenas, by his close friend Jorge Camacho. The essays offer reflections on underdevelopment and "the exotic" in Latin America, a retelling of the 1960s as the decade of the boom of the Latin American novel, and harsh panning of New York City. "El Cometa Halley" is a hilarious parody of La casa de Bernarda Alba. Bernarda's daughters move to Cárdenas (Cuba) and become completely liberated during a last day to be seized, under the threat of Halley's comet. "Final de un Cuento" captures the tensions of the Arenas exile. The ashes of a friend are sprinkled on the shores of Key West to reach the other shore from which he fled to lead a better life, but far from which he could not live.

3819 **Arrufat, Antón.** ¿Qué harás después de mí? La Habana: Editorial Letras Cubanas, 1988. 153 p. (Giraldilla)

Since most of these short stories were written in the early 1960s, they tend to reflect on pre-revolutionary Cuba. Parody is ever present, the absurd explored at every turn of a page.

3820 **Barnet, Miguel.** Oficio de ángel. Madrid: Alfaguara, 1989. 311 p. (Alfaguara hispánica; 61)

Nostalgic recollection of the political struggle against Machado and Batista, and family structure during those years. Written in restrained style, uses various points of view to add to the tale.

3821 **Cabrera Infante, Guillermo.** Mea Cuba. Barcelona: Plaza & Janés; Cambio 16, 1992. 484 p.: index.

Timely work explores geography and history of Cuba to commemorate an event that changed history and geography. Justifiably obsessed with events surrounding censorship of the documentary *P.M.* which led to Fidel Castro's "Palabras a los Intelectuales," Cabrera Infante offers detailed description of these proceedings and interprets comments or absence of several well-known writers. Most essays appeared before in different periodicals. The last two sections, "Vidas para Leerlas" and "Vida Unica," include many inspired pieces on Cuban writers.

3822 **Cabrera Infante, Guillermo.** Tres tristes tigres. Prólogo y cronología de Guillermo Cabrera Infante. Bibliografía de Patricia Rubio. Caracas: Biblioteca Ayacucho, 1990. 388 p.: bibl. (Biblioteca Ayacucho; 151)

Definitive unexpurgated edition of *Tres tristes tigres*, with passages cut by Spanish censors restored. Appendix identifies passages in question and the original "variants." In a prologue, Cabrera Infante takes on his censors and their prudish scissors. Revised and updated chronology of GCI is also included. One must wonder how Fidel Castro, who is the proud owner and admirer of the complete Ayacucho Collection, must have felt when he received this edition, its volume no. 151.

3823 **Capetillo, Luisa.** Amor y anarquía: los escritos de Luisa Capetillo. Edición de Julio Ramos. Río Piedras, P.R.: Ediciones Huracán, 1992. 222 p.: bibl., ill. (Col. Clásicos Huracán; 5)

Excellent anthology of Capetillo's writings includes solid introduction and critical bibliography. Capetillo's work is required reading for those interested in feminism, labor history, and Puerto Rican and Latin American society and mores.

3824 Castro Mosqueda, Rafael. Verónico. La Habana: Unión de Escritores y Artistas de Cuba, 1987. 197 p.

This novel, which won the 1982 "Cirilo Villaverde Prize," takes us back to the mountains, where the rebel army began to gather to fight against Batista. Through child's eyes it shows different types of individuals who joined the struggle, the violence and the wounded, and the persistence of the revolutionaries. Not very innovative.

3825 Díaz, Jesús. Las palabras perdidas. Barcelona: Ediciones Destino, 1992. 335 p. (Col. Ancora y delfín; 684)

Three friends (El Gordo, El Flaco y El Rojo) take on the cultural bureaucracy in order to found a new magazine for their idealistic young generation. Their project is canceled at the last minute by the censors. Political ruin follows. Many years later the story is reconstructed as El Flaco eats at a luxury restaurant in Moscow with another (jealous, minor writer) friend he suspects of being the traitor of the lost project. The restaurant is in a high-rise tower, and gyrates to vary the panoramic view. El Flaco is initially confused by the turns of the restaurant because the relative placement of other buildings change slowly from left to right and vice versa. The references are obvious, the emotional setting is thoughtful, thought-provoking, and deeply rooted in real events. El Gordo is Guillermo Rodríguez Rivera, El Rojo is Luis Rogelio Nogueras, and El Flaco is Jesús Díaz.

3826 Fernández, Alfredo Antonio. La última frontera, 1898. La Habana: Editorial Letras Cubanas, 1985. 270 p.

After beginning with an epigraph from Fidel Castro, which states that no one has been able to explain the mysteries of the Maine, author proceeds to offer his own speculation within a narrative that includes Stephen Crane as a main character.

3827 Ferré, Rosario. Papeles de Pandora. Rio Piedras, P.R.: Ediciones Huracán, 1991. 1 v.

Impressive collection of poems and short stories which examine human relationships, a woman's role in the family and society, and middle-class life and social values. Exceptional prose style and insight into the human condition characterize this author's work.

3828 García, Luis Manuel. Habanecer. La Habana: Casa de las Américas, 1992. 1 v.: ill.

Novel idea to grant the Casa de las Américas short story prize to this book. A day in the life of Habana, the reader turns not the numbered pages but the *hours* of this novel and meets various characters, official forms, and *genres*. Using weather reports, official psychological evaluations, and questionnaires of the characters of a play (all included in the novel) as well as lyrical passages and poignant vignettes, and metaliterary sections entitled "pages without time," this work will certainly join the ranks of the best homages to capital cities.

3829 Laguerre, Enrique A. Por boca de caracoles. Río Piedras, P.R.: Editorial Cultural, 1990. 264 p.

Novel which brings together two half sisters previously unaware of each other's existence. An inheritance, revenge, jealousy, love . . . all these are ingredients in this latest Laguerre novel which stylistically and structurally resembles most of his previous literary efforts.

3830 Loynaz, Dulce María. Jardín: novela lírica. Precedida de "Dulce María Loynaz" por Juan Ramón Jiménez. Barcelona: Seix Barral, 1993. 318 p. (Biblioteca breve)

Re-edition of Loynaz's work, "a story of a woman and a garden" outside of time and set in any place. Includes, as a prologue, a 1937 essay by Juan Ramón Jiménez.

3831 Loynaz, Dulce María. Un verano en Tenerife. Madrid: Mariar, 1992. 408 p.

Facsimile edition of the original Aguilar edition of 1958. Original colophon is worth the effort: "Este libro se acabó de escribir a las doce y catorce minutos, pasado meridiano del jueves 10 de abril de 1958, en la finca Nuestra Señora de las Mercedes, cerca de La Habana, a los cinco años y ocho meses de haberse comenzado." This novel, obviously the work of a poet, journeys over five years to capture a summer's images.

3832 Marcallé Abréu, Roberto. Alternativas para una existencia gris: relatos de New York. Santo Domingo: R. Marcallé Abréu, 1987. 227 p.

Short stories that take place in the New York City of the *dominicanos*, or is it,

after all, just gray New York? Themes range
from monologues in subway stations to characters on park benches that routinely meet,
with growing expectations, unfulfilled desire.
Includes brief introductory essay on "Marcallé y la Literatura de la Emigración." The
text presents in bold letters words that, in English or Spanglish, are part of Latino New
York. Such typographical aid seems unneces-
sary since several are used all over the world
in many cultures, including the Dominican
Republic.

3833 Montaner, Carlos Alberto. Trama. Barcelona: Plaza & Janés, 1987. 266
p. (Literaria)

Trama is the pseudonym of protagonist Víctor Rey, a Cuban patriot who participates in an anarchist conspiracy to blow up
the Maine. Author thus seems to accept conclusions of the 1898 and 1911 investigations
which concluded that, as this conspiracy executed it, the explosion took place outside the
ship. Of course, more recent (and more sophisticated) investigations assert that it was
probably an accidental explosion inside the
ship. This novel also tells the story of a love
triangle: Víctor, Paola, and Marcus. Its presentation is chronological; chapters state the
name of a city (in Europe, the US, or Cuba)
and a date (from Sept. 26, 1878-July 20, 1898).
Interesting omission is the lack of reference
to José Martí's death. Does not cover early
Jan. 1895 to late April 1896. Montaner thick-
ens the plot of Cuban history with debatable
speculations which are presented as real
events.

3834 Navarro, Noel. El sol de mediodía. Sevilla: Ediciones Guadalquivir, 1992.
129 p. (Biblioteca Guadalquivir: Novela; 11)

This novel won the "Premio Andalucía
de Novela, 1992." Mystery tale set in late
17th-century Habana is unravelled almost
three centuries later by a clerk. Good historical and detection work are incorporated into
contemporary archival research.

3835 Nina, Daniel. El Caribe en el exilio:
anécdotas y cuentos. San Juan: Ediciones Coa, 1990. 85 p.

Uneven collection of short stories by
a writer who is still maturing. "We Are Different" is definitely worth reading, but
other stories lack good plot structure and
development.

3836 Ochart, Yvonne. El fuego de las cosas.
Río Piedras, P.R.: Editorial de la Univ.
de Puerto Rico, 1990. 173 p.

Short stories that, in the predominance
of idea and mood over narrative plot, are
reminiscent of a fledgling Borges or Cortazar.
Ochart is a promising young writer who is exploring new narrative strategies, although her
stories need greater coherence and depth.

3837 Otero, Lisandro. Arbol de la vida.
México: Siglo Veintiuno Editores,
1990. 382 p.

Counterpoint between events of the
19th century and the 20th century as experienced by several families. The protagonist,
who is being examined for entry into the
Communist Party, has a grandfather who was
a slave trader. The shift from one brief narrative to the other is often bothersome.The protagonist is betrayed by corrupt elements in
revolutionary society and in his own house.

3838 Paz, Senel. El lobo, el bosque y el hombre nuevo. (*Unión/Habana,* 1, 1991,
p. 25-35, ill.)

Ground-breaking tale about a revolutionary student's encounter with a homosexual intellectual who challenges Cuba's
cultural, political, and homophobic policies.
The film version, with many changes and additional material, is the acclaimed *Fresa y
chocolate.* The theater adaptation is entitled
La catedral del helado (i.e. Coppelia).

3839 Pereira, Manuel. La prisa sobre el papel. La Habana: Editorial de Ciencias
Sociales, 1987. 302 p. (Ediciones políticas)

In a hurry to meet a deadline, these articles were written for the magazine *Cuba
Internacional* from 1970-75 before Pereira's
debut (and success) as a novelist with *El
Comandante Veneno.* Articles range from vignettes in Havana's Chinatown to a review of
various rums to an interview with General
Máximo Gómez's son. Useful to those interested in Pereira's early prose.

3840 Pereira, Manuel. Toilette. Barcelona:
Editorial Anagrama, 1993. 232 p.: col.
ill. (Narrativas hispánicas; 136)

Adventure of a *voyageur* and a *voyeur,*
whose compulsion is to explore and possess
all "facilities" that cross his path. As a child,
artist Lucio Gaitán shared a w.c. with many
neighbors, who always seemed to be knock-
ing at the door. In Paris he is exposed to the

high culture of the toilette, whose history he researches to find the scatological/eschato-logical keys to life. The technological history of the bathroom is also included and the po-litical reasons for the deferred appearance of the toilet is explained. Lucio finds himself returning constantly to Bosch's "The Garden of Earthly Delights," where a seated figure, a bird-insect, devours and excretes people. Needless to say that this is an unusual work that demands much of the readers: a new alle-gorical Pereira.

3841 Ramos, Juan Antonio. Vive y vacila. Buenos Aires?: Ediciones de la Flor, 1986. 110 p.

Narrative chronicles, escapades, and coming-of-age of friends who pass from care-free adolescence into the workaday reality of middle age. Interesting style in which the col-loquial and the musical predominate.

3842 Sarduy, Severo. El Cristo de la rue Ja-cob. Barcelona: Edicions del Mall, 1987. 118 p.: bibl. (Mall/narrativa: Sèrie ibè-rica; 46)

Collection of essays and fragments, what Sarduy calls epiphanies (physical and "mnemic" marks): wounds and scars (an ar-chaeology of the skin leading back to the um-bilical excision), memories of places and friends, of letters received. Highlights in-clude: the section about the four stitches over the right eyebrow, which comments on the composition of Colibrí; a final postcard to Emir, which recollects Sarduy's collaboration in Mundo Nuevo; and a letter from Lezama Lima, with extensive deconstructive notes by Sarduy.

3843 Sarduy, Severo. Epitafios, imitación, aforismos. Ilustraciones de Ramón Alejandro. Miami: Ediciones Universal, 1994. 96 p.

Includes poetry (eight epitaphs and one imitation/parody of San Juan de la Cruz), prose (eight short reflexive passages), and two studies by Concepción Teresa Alzola and Gladys Zaldívar on the work of Sarduy. Beau-tifully illustrated by Ramón Alejandro.

3844 Sarduy, Severo. Pájaros de la playa. Bar-celona: Tusquets Editores, 1993. 225 p. (Col. Andanzas; 195)

Engaging novel whose language seizes the reader, plot ever shifting as the characters (consumed by youth) probe the mysteries of

the blood that lead to death. Takes place in a severo sanatorio, where the subject doubles as illness and an "I." Examines metaphor of illness, based on a life that fills up with con-tamination and impurities to erase a frighten-ing vacuum.

3845 Silén, Iván. Las muñecas de la calle del Cristo. Buenos Aires: Ediciones de la Flor, 1989. 214 p.

Symbolic and far-fetched novel in which sexual deviance plays a central part. Although there are interesting juxtapositions which have shock value, author's symbolism and purpose are too obvious and his intent too political and pretentiously didactic.

3846 Soto, Pedro Juan. Palabras al vuelo. Se-lección de Emilio Jorge Rodríguez. La Habana: Casa de las Américas, 1990. 243 p. (Col. La Honda)

Selection of Soto's short stories from Spiks (1956) and Un decir (1976). No intro-duction or bibliography.

Varia valeriana. See item **2118.**

3847 Vélez, Ana. Tropel. v. 1. Río Piedras, P.R.: Editorial Producciones Don Pedro, 1990. 1 v.

Novelistic memoirs of a family of mod-est means, which describes daily life, tradi-tions, family values and customs, politics, so-cial mores, and struggles of a couple with more than 12 children to feed, clothe, and educate. Action of the novel takes place dur-ing 1917–79 and the narrative seems more like a social documentary than a novel. Defi-nitely worth reading for author's many ob-servations and insights regarding daily life in Puerto Rico during the first half of this century.

LITERARY CRITICISM AND HISTORY

3848 Alonso Martínez, Marcia and **Marisel García Yanes.** Cuentos dispersos de Pablo de la Torriente Brau. (Islas/Santa Clara, 92, enero/abril 1989, p. 74–86)

Analyzes short stories Torriente Brau wrote during his stay in New York. Short sto-ries compiled in Humor y pólvora (1984) are reviewed and classified as to theme, narrator functions, and type of protagonists.

3849 Arenas, Reinaldo. Antes que ano-
chezca: autobiografía. Barcelona: Tusquets, 1992. 343 p.: ill. (Col. Andanzas; 165)
  Heartbreaking memoirs from early
childhood through the years of life with
AIDS, to the last few nightmarish days before
he took his own life. A mine of information
about cultural politics and figures in Cuba
during the last two decades. Painful details
about homosexual persecution, prison conditions, and the precarious life of the disaffected
in La Habana. Relates the story of Arenas'
recreation of his disappeared manuscripts. Offers distinct analysis of political and cultural
events during the revolution: UMAP, el caso
Padilla and Mariel. Contrasts homosexual
culture in Cuba and the US.

3850 Arrufat, Antón. La carne de Virgilio.
  (*Unión/Habana,* 3 : 10, abril/junio
1990, p. 44–47, ill.)
  Contrasts Virgilio Piñera's novel *La
carne de René* with *Paradiso* and *El siglo de
las luces,* emphasizing the relative loneliness
of Piñera's protagonist. Based on conversation
with Piñera, Arrufat refers to other intertextual connections: Wilde's *The portrait of Dorian Gray* and Butler's *The way of the flesh.*
Closes with comments on Piñera's style,
which narrates unusual material with seemingly common place linguistic resources.

3851 Bejel, Emilio. Escribir en Cuba: entrevistas con escritores cubanos, 1979–
1989. Río Piedras, P.R.: Editorial de la Univ.
de Puerto Rico, 1991. 387 p. (Col. caribeña)
  Outstanding and timely interviews of
Cuban authors. In addition to questions on
genre, generations, and literary criticism, Bejel presses the interviewees on touchy issues
such as censorship, persecution of homosexuals, the Padilla case, and critical thought in a
socialist country. Many of these interviews
have appeared before in periodicals; some offer unique and creative analyses.

3852 Benítez Rojo, Antonio. The repeating
island: the Caribbean and the postmodern perspective. Translated by James
Maraniss. Durham, N.C.: Duke Univ. Press,
1992. 302 p.: bibl., index. (Post-contemporary
interventions)
  Different kind of book of criticism lies
behind apparent disorder and chance selection of materials to be studied. This paradoxical, strangely attractive interpretation of Ca-

ribbean culture is based on chaotic theory.
Transitions from Marxist sociopolitical conditions must confront the ordered chaos of
capitalist systems. Benítez-Rojo has produced
an honest and successful book. For translation specialist's comment see item **5055.**

**3853 *Criterios: Teoría Literaria, Estética,
Culturología.*** No. 29, enero/junio
1991- . La Habana: Casa de las Américas.
  Opens with five essays read at II Encuentro Internacional de *Criterios* (La Habana, 1989): Manfred Pfister (Germany) on
intertextuality, Gerald Prince (US) on narra-
tivity, Viacheslav V. Ivanov ("USSR") on semiotics, Patrice Pavis (France) on translation,
Wieslaw Godzic (Poland) on cinema. Desiderio Navarro translates above texts as well
as essays from several additional languages.

**3854 *Criterios: Teoría de la Literatura y las
Artes, Estética, Culturología.*** No. 30,
julio/dic. 1991- . La Habana: Casa de las
Américas.
  Under the most difficult economic circumstances, Desiderio Navarro continues to
publish *Criterios,* an invaluable contribution
to semiotics and the theory of literature. Yuri
Lotman opens the issue with an essay "Acerca de la Semiosfera." Articles on intertextuality, postmodernity, semiotics and
iconography, mythology, cinema—many by
"Western" critics—are also included.

3855 Díaz Valcárcel, Emilio. En el mejor de
los mundos. San Juan?: Comisión Puertorriqueña para la Celebración del Quinto
Centenario del Descubrimiento de América y
Puerto Rico, 1991. 233 p.: ill.
  Excellent memoirs include anecdotes
about leading Puerto Rican writers, literary
life in Puerto Rico, and Díaz Valcárcel's experiences in the US and his travels abroad.
Quite interesting and very well written.

3856 Diego Padró, José Isaac de. En busca de
J.I. de Diego Padró. Edición de Pedro
Juan Soto. Colaboración de J.I. de Diego Padró,
Alicia de Diego y Carmen Lugo Filippi. Río
Piedras, P.R.: Editorial de la Univ. de Puerto
Rico, 1990. 392 p., 16 p. of plates:bibl., ill.
  Introduction to life and literary works
of J.I. de Diego Padró. This volume includes
an interview with him and a representative
sample of his work. Excellent introduction to
an interesting writer long undervalued and
seldom read.

3857 Domingo, Jorge. La novela cubana de los ochenta. (*Unión/Habana*, 1, 1991, p. 9–15, ill.)

Evaluates novelistic production in Cuba, with special attention to (even seasoned) writers' first novels. Playful essay pans most works, with the (possible) exception of Jesús Díaz's *Las iniciales en la tierra*, Raúl Luis' *El cazador*, and Senel Paz's *Un rey en el jardín*.

3858 Domínguez Ávila, José. Desbalances, aciertos y contradicciones en *De tierra adentro*. (*Islas/Santa Clara*, 94, sept./dic. 1989, p. 95–106)

Judges Jesús Castellanos' short story collection in rigid Marxist fashion, where class exploitation rules above all analyses. The best part of the essay examines the conditions of the female characters.

3859 Fernández Pequeño, José M. La novela policial cubana ante sí misma, 1979–1986. (*Palabra Hombre*, 70, abril/junio 1989, p. 205–216)

Condemns low quality of Cuban detective fiction from 1979–83. Identifies *El cuarto círculo* by Luis Rogelio Nogueras and Guillermo Rodríguez Rivera, *Joy* by Daniel Chavarría, and *Y si muero mañana* by Nogueras as the high points in Cuban detective fiction. Associates three factors to the decline: 1) indiscriminate selection and publication during the boom of 1980–83; 2) absence of serious literary criticism on the genre in Cuba; 3) negative impact of the Concurso Aniversario de la Revolución that guaranteed (hasty) publication of the winners. Cites extensively from Desiderio Navarro's exceptional articles on the detective novel and mass culture.

3860 Fernández Pequeño, José M. Teoría y práctica de la novela policial revolucionaria. (*Let. Cuba.*, 10, oct./dic. 1988, p. 245–261)

Although this is not the best essay in this issue of *Letras Cubanas* devoted to detective fiction, it should be consulted primarily for thorough references to important articles on revolutionary detective fiction, its pitfalls, and its political functions.

3861 Fernández Robaina, Tomás. La literatura cubana: panorama crítico. (*Rev. Bibl. Nac. José Martí*, 81:33, julio/dic. 1990, p. 63–77)

Review of bibliographical works on Cuban literature during the last two centuries. Observes that partial works devoted to particular genres (theater, poetry, etc.) tend to dominate in interest and quality. Hopes for a general bibliographical work that gathers all those partial, yet admirable, works.

3862 Ferré, Rosario. El árbol y sus sombras. México: Fondo de Cultura Económica, 1989. 146 p.: bibl. (Col. Tierra firme)

Interesting analyses of literary and critical texts from Sor Juana Inés de la Cruz to Roland Barthes by one of Puerto Rico's best prose stylists.

3863 Garfield, Evelyn Picon. La revista femenina: dos momentos en su evolución cubana 1860/1961. (*Rev. Crít. Lit. Latinoam.*, 15:30, 2do. semestre, 1989, p. 91–98)

Studies *Album cubano de lo bueno y lo bello* (1860), a magazine directed by Gertrudis Gómez de Avellaneda, and *Mujeres*, revolutionary Cuba's magazine for/about women. Author is disappointed that after more than a century, *Mujeres* ignores, or keeps silent about, problems whose scrutiny might shake up the dominant patriarchal system. Author concludes that the value of women is still based on a primary role as "married and within the home," regardless of their contributions in the work place.

3864 Henríquez Ureña, Pedro. Obra dominicana. Santo Domingo: Sociedad Dominicana de Bibliófilos, 1988. 567 p.: bibl. (Col. Cultura dominicana; 66)

Excellent collection of Henríquez Ureña's book-length essays, articles, lectures, and letters. Includes brief but informative essay by Juan Jacobo de Lara. The general index, unfortunately, does not agree with actual pagination of the essays.

3865 Jiménez, José et al. Dossier: José Lezama Lima. (*Creac. Estética Teor. Artes*, 8, 1993, p. 58–110)

Almost the complete issue is devoted to Lezama. Includes texts by Lezama: two essays ("Doctrinal de la Anémona" and "Sobre Poesía"); a poem ("El Pabellón del Vacío"); and letters to María Zambrano and José Angel Valente. Presents an excellent selection of essays, including "Imágenes del Tiempo Inmóvil" by Severo Sarduy, as well as photographs and illustrations.

3866 Lie, Nadia. Casa de las Américas y el discurso sobre el intelectual, 1960–1971. (*Cuad. Am.*, 5:5, sept./oct. 1991, p. 187–199)

Excellent analysis of transformation of the view of the intellectual from 1960–71, from Fidel Castro's "Palabras a los Intelectuales" to Heberto Padilla's self-critical retraction. Author identifies three phases: 1960–65 (muted, polemical, phase), 1965–68 (polphonic phase), and 1968–71 (unisonous phase). One can almost hear the tanks rolling over many voices to create one voice.

3867 Márquez Rodríguez, Alexis. Alejo Carpentier: profeta y oficiante de la nueva narrativa latinoamericana. (*Inti/Providence*, 29/30, primavera/otoño 1989, p. 17–27)

Traces Carpentier's theory and practice of the Latin American novel from a 1931 article "América ante la Joven Literatura Europea" (written in Paris, published in *Carteles*) to his other better known theoretical articles. Presents Carpentier as a prophet and activist of what author considers a unique Latin American narrative mode.

3868 Montero, Susana A. La narrativa femenina cubana, 1923–1958. La Habana: Editorial Academia, 1989. 88 p.: bibl.

After a review and assessment (classification, thematic, reception) of the production of women prose writers, author examines social commitment of Ofelia Rodríguez Acosta and Dulce María Loynaz's novel *Jardín*. Twenty brief biographical notes are included in the appendix.

3869 Ortega, Julio. Reapropiaciones: cultura y nueva escritura en Puerto Rico. Río Piedras, P.R.: Editorial de la Univ. de Puerto Rico, 1991. 252 p. (Col. caribeña)

Cultural and literary essays about Puerto Rican life and literature, and a number of interviews with leading Puerto Rican writers. Excellent essays which provide valuable insights and observations about Puerto Rican life and letters. Interviews are very well done.

3870 Ortega-Vélez, Ruth E. La mujer en la obra de Enrique A. Laguerre. Río Piedras, P.R.: Editorial de la Univ. de Puerto Rico, 1989. 141 p.: bibl.

Study's thesis is that feminine characters in Laguerre's novels are accurate reflections of certain epochs of Puerto Rican history. Includes interview with Laguerre, chapter on the role of women in Puerto Rican history and literature, and adequate bibliography.

3871 Padura Fuentes, Leonardo. Novela policial y novela de la revolución. (*Let. Cuba.*, 10, oct./dic. 1988, p. 55–89)

Traces development of detective fiction in Cuba from Ignacio Cárdenas Acuña's excellent first novel *Enigma para un domingo* to what author considers the best examples of the genre: *El cuarto círculo*, *Y si muero mañana*, *Joy*, and *La sexta isla*. Essay deplores low quality of most detective novels produced during the 1970s. Informative, yet not sufficiently analytical of the sociopolitical context that produced such literature during that decade.

3872 Phaf, Ineke. La nación cimarrona en el imaginario del Caribe no-hispánico. (*Rev. Crít. Lit. Latinoam.*, 26:31/32, 1990, p. 67–97, bibl.)

Detailed summary of the negritude movement and its critics' analyses of cultural and sociopolitical confrontations between "Eurocentric nation" and "maroon nation." Useful review of the literature with special attention to Haiti as "Haití/Africa/negritud en acción/nación/delirio verbal."

3873 Prada Oropeza, Renato. Estructura y significación en *Y si muero mañana*. (*Let. Cuba.*, 10, oct./dic. 1988, p. 177–191)

Takes on critics of detective fiction. Reviews Greimas' narrative analysis and applies it to Luis Rogelio Nogueras' prize-winning novel. Useful for its analytical contrasts between detective and spy fiction.

3874 Ramos, Josean. Vengo a decirle adiós a los muchachos. San Juan: Sociedad de Autores Libres, 1989. 181 p.

Interesting evocation of the legendary singer, Daniel Santos, in which slices of his life are revealed anecdotally from different perspectives to give us a dramatic, impressionistic portrait of Santos' life and times.

Rectificación por la cultura: mesa redonda. See *HLAS 53:3676*.

3875 Romero, Cira. Notas a propósito de naturalismo y literatura: repercusión en América Latina, particularmente en Cuba, y su presencia en la obra de Carlos Loveira.

(*Rev. Bibl. Nac. José Martí*, 82:1/2, 1991, p. 7–25)

Article delivers what it promises in the title: Loveira's work as naturalist is judged primarily with reference to Guillermo Ara's *La novela naturalista hispanoamericana,* which enumerates the main traits of naturalist fiction.

3876 Soto, Sara. Magia e historia en los "Cuentos negros," "Por qué" y "Ayapá" de Lydia Cabrera. Miami: Ediciones Universal, 1988. 162 p.: bibl. (Col. Ebano y canela)

After reviewing origin and evolution of slavery in Cuba, particularly in the 19th century, and Lydia Cabrera's vision of Afro-Caribbean culture, author studies magic and its social and religious functions in Cabrera's narrative.

3877 Torre, José Ramón de la. Cuatro puertas a una fábula y otros ensayos. San Juan: Publicaciones Yuquiyú; Chicago: Yuquiyu Publications, 1991. 112 p.

Collection of essays previously published in newspapers and periodicals. No unifying thread, other than the fact that essays consist of textual criticism of Puerto Rican literary texts.

3878 Torres-Saillant, Silvio. Caribbean literature and Latin Americanists. (*Caribb. Stud.,* 23:3/4, 1990, p. 131–138)

Considers the place of Caribbean literature within Latin American literature. Traces history of views that Caribbean critics hold on this issue and contrasts them with the "typical Latin Americanist" attitude toward the Caribbean. Evaluates proceedings of a conference on this topic that was held at the Univ. of Minnesota.

3879 Valero, Roberto. ¿Como limitar la literatura del exilio? (*SECOLAS Ann.,* 22, March 1991, p. 74–79, bibl.)

Excellent, succinct, reflection on what constitutes literature in exile and what it means to be an exiled writer. Contrasts various authors in different "exiled positions," concentrating on Reinaldo Arenas. Unquestionably, adds much to our understanding of

Arenas, *el otro (el mismo),* before and after Mariel.

3880 Vásquez, Carmen. *El reino de este mundo* y la función de la historia en la concepción de lo real maravilloso americano. (*Cuad. Am.,* 5:4, julio/agosto 1991, p. 90–114)

Meticulous collation of historical texts about events Carpentier recounts in *El reino de este mundo.* Successfully explains why Carpentier emphasized certain events and personages of Haitian history (Lenormand de Mézy, Mackandal, Henri Christophe) and reasons for the lack of attention to other figures (e.g., Toussaint Louverture).

3881 Vera-León, Antonio. Montejo, Barnet, el cimarronaje y la escritura de la historia. (*Inti/Providence,* 29/30, primavera/otoño 1989, p. 3–16)

Examines writing and voice within the narrative of Esteban Montejo. Contrasts Barnet's rewriting of a personal history with Cuba's historiographical struggle to relate its cultural production and invention.

3882 Vera-León, Antonio. Politics of self-narration in contemporary Cuba. (*Apunt. Postmod.,* 2:2, spring 1992, p. 3–9)

Analyzes Jesús Díaz's *Las iniciales en la tierra* and the various languages of the State and the individual that clash in the narrative. Author detects key episodes and rhetorical strategies that articulate the "conflictive negotiations" of a writer in Cuban society.

3883 Zabala Jaramillo, Luz Elena and Manuel Cofiño López. La literatura cubana: brasa que quema al fuego. Medellín, Colombia: Editorial Ediciones Gráficas, 1985. 224 p.: col. ports. (Col. América Latina en su literatura)

Biographical sketches of Cuban authors, from Tallet to Abel Prieto, who respond to three questions regarding the process of democratization in Latin America, Cuban revolutionary society and its "ideoesthetic" development, and the theme of love in Cuban letters. A representative, but far from complete, list of authors.

Andean Countries

RAYMOND WILLIAMS, *Professor of Spanish, University of Colorado*
DICK GERDES, *Professor of Spanish, University of New Mexico*

COLOMBIA AND VENEZUELA

MUCH OF THE LITERARY CRITICISM published in Colombia dealt with Gabriel García Márquez. More than a decade since his Nobel Prize, García Márquez is still the object of a vast amount of literary criticism. Several new volumes have been written on his work, including analytical studies by Robert Sims (item **3892**) and Isabel Rodríguez Vergara (item **3891**), as well as a bibliographical book by Pedro Sorela (item **3893**).

In Venezuela, scholars and critics dedicated work to a larger variety of writers. Venezuelan critics continue to dedicate studies to traditional figures, such as Rómulo Gallegos (item **3931**) and Arturo Uslar Pietri (item **3928**). They have also focused attention on writers of later generations, such as Salvador Garmendia (items **3927** and **4032**) and José Balza (items **3930** and **4031**).

A publishing boom in Colombia (headed by Tercer Mundo Editores and Planeta Editorial) continued from the late 1980s through the early 1990s, and Gabriel García Márquez (items **3888, 3887, 3953,** and **3952**) and R.H. Moreno-Durán (item **3961**) remained the two leading writers. Both continued writing fiction and essays, and in the early 1990s poet Alvaro Mutis rose to the forefront of Colombian fiction writing. Two talented younger novelists, Marco Tulio Aguilera Garramuño (item **3945**) and Fanny Buitrago (item **3946**), published volumes of short stories.

Conventional and traditional kinds of fiction, such as the products of Manuel Mejía Vallejo (item **3960**) and Mario Escobar Velásquez (item **3947**), continued to appear in Colombia. The young writers Luis Fayad (item **3949**) and José Luis Garcés (item **3951**) published new novels, but have yet to produce their major works. Promising new figures to appear on the Colombian literary scene were Juan José Hoyos (item **3955**), Fabio Martínez (item **3959**), and Bernardo Valderrama Andrade (item **3966**).

In Venezuela, Salvador Garmendia (items **3927** and **4032**) remained one of the major figures of the contemporary novel, along with writers of the later generation, such as José Balza (items **3930** and **4032**). Some Venezuelan fiction writers took a more bold and experimental approach than seen recently in Colombia. Oswaldo Trejo (item **4035**) and Alejandro Rossi (item **4034**) were two such writers.

The vitality of literature in the northern Andean region of South America was evidenced not only by the proliferation of publications, but also by the fact that a commercial and popular writer such as the Colombian Fernando Soto Aparicio (who has not written a substantive novel since the early 1970s) launched a committee in Bogotá to support his campaign for a Nobel Prize. [RLW]

ECUADOR, PERU, BOLIVIA

A poco más de 20 años de la muerte del escritor peruano José María Arguedas, ha surgido una gama interesante e importante de trabajos analíticos de su obra literaria (items **3909, 3916, 3910, 3922, 3923, 3912, 3904** y **3914**). Se ofrecen trabajos que abarcan el pensamiento filosófico arguediano, la importancia de su novela *El zorro de arriba y el zorro de abajo,* un homenaje de los profesores de la Univ. de San Marcos y estudios sobre los elementos épicos y la presencia del amor y el eroticismo en su obra. También ha habido una abundancia de trabajos sobre la literatura peruana en general (items **3925, 3918, 3913, 3919, 3902, 3911, 3906, 3924, 3905** y **3900**), o sea, historias amplias, de una época o de una generación. Uno de los trabajos más recomendados es el de un grupo de profesores de la Univ. de San Marcos cuyo marco de referencia es el período 1970–88 (item **3905**). En cuanto al análisis del fenómeno literario-cultural del Ecuador, un estudio agudo de la época que abarca desde la de los años 60 hasta nuestros días es el de Michael Handelsman (item **3897**); otro trabajo que reúne estudios de evaluación punzante y acertada es *Signos de futuro* (item **3899**). El discurso minero sigue siendo un tema de importancia para los estudiosos bolivianos y el crítico Javier Sanjinés dedica un trabajo a tradición y cambio en la crítica literaria boliviana (item **3886**).

Durante este último período en el Perú, Ecuador y Bolivia, se destaca la diversidad de formas y temas narrativos que abarca la novela histórica, el cuento psicológico, la elaboración literaria de antiguos mitos indígenas, la narrativa feminista, el diario íntimo y la memoria autobiográfica. Curiosamente, han salido casi simultáneamente las memorias de los tres escritores peruanos de más importancia de hoy: Bryce Echenique, Ribeyro y Vargas Llosa (items **3999, 4018** y **4030**); el denominador común entre las tres memorias es la estrecha relación entre vida y oficio de escribir, lo cual resulta en textos fascinantes. Alfredo Bryce Echenique y Mario Vargas Llosa también producen novelas y otros ensayos importantes (items **4029, 4028, 4000** y **3998**). Guillermo Thorndike agrega dos obras apasionantes a una lista creciente de las novela-reportajes que viene escribiendo desde hace tiempo (items **4022** y **4023**). Luis Urteaga Cabrera recoge, reelabora y rescata hermosos y valiosos mitos antiguos de los indígenas de la zona amazónica del Perú (item **4025**), Eduardo González Viaña literaturiza un tema de la creencia popular religiosa en el Perú y escribe una novela deslumbrante (item **4008**) y Gregorio Martínez recrea el mundo afroperuano de la costa sur del Perú mediante elementos culturales (la música, el folklore) de la región.

En el Ecuador se destacan novelas y colecciones de cuentos de escritores conocidos—es decir, Eliécer Cárdenas (item **3969**), Iván Egüez (item **3976**), Raúl Pérez Torres (item **3984**) y Jorge Dávila Vásquez (item **3974**)—y otros en vías de madurez narrativa. Dos narradores que merecen mención especial son Natasha Salguero y Juan Valdano, la primera por una novela de porte feminista cuyo cuestionamiento enfoca el lenguaje (item **3988**) y el otro por una novela histórica impactante por su aspecto político y recreación del ambiente colonial (item **3990**). En el campo de las letras bolivianas predomina la publicación de obras narrativas centradas en la recreación nostálgica de pasados idílicos pero ya violados y corruptos; en el caso de la obra de Renato Prada Oropeza (item **3939**), también se presentan ambientes políticos que exceden los parámetros nacionales para cuestionar la realidad latinoamericana. [DG]

LITERARY CRITICISM AND HISTORY
Bolivia

Dencker, Angela. Der Indio in der bolivianischen Gesellschaft und Literatur dea Jahrhundertwende. See *HLAS* 53:5300.

3884 Martínez Salguero, Jaime. El relato minero de Bolivia. La Paz: Ediciones Signo, 1991. 270 p.: bibl. (Serie Ensayo)
Sobre la novela social boliviana y su relación con la minería y el indio. Abarca los temas de las huelgas y las matanzas, pathos central de este tipo de literatura boliviana. La veracidad brutal de lo que se narra puede servir de fuente de información para historiadores y sociólogos.

3885 Sanjinés C., Javier. Discurso minero y lo simbólico en la recomposición popular. (*Hispamérica/Gaithersburg*, 18:53/54, 1989, p. 25–34)

Otro estudio del minero en la literatura boliviana, enfocando el tema de su relación estrecha con el capitalismo. La ganancia pecuniaria se convierte en fantasía compensatoria y elemento simbólico de la desigualdad social.

3886 Sanjinés C., Javier. Tradición y cambio en la crítica literaria boliviana. (*Rev. Crít. Lit. Latinoam.*, 26:31/32, 1990, p. 39–55, bibl.)

Analiza el período de "renovación crítica" que ha vivido Bolivia desde 1970. Anteriormente, los críticos "oficiales" producían una crítica convencional que controlaba la opinión pública bajo regímenes autoritarios. La renovación consiste en dos etapas, formalista y pragmática.

Colombia

3887 En el punto de mira: Gabriel García Márquez. Edición de Ana María Hernández de López. Madrid: Pliegos, 1985? 356 p.: bibl., ill. (Pliegos de ensayo)

Few Latin American writers have generated the volume of critical readings as the Colombian Nobel Laureate García Márquez. Another fine testimony to this phenomenon contains 29 more pieces on the Colombian writer. Prominent critics such as Julio Ortega, Jorge Ruffinelli, and Alexis Márquez Rodríguez contribute good essays. Divided into sections covering García Márquez's work chronologically; essays on early novels, short stories, *Cien años de soledad, El otoño del patriarca,* and *Crónica de una muerte anunciada;* comparative studies (including inevitable comparisons with Faulkner); and a portrait of García Márquez the person.

3888 García Márquez, Gabriel. Primeros reportajes. Caracas: Consorcio de Ediciones Capriles, 1990. 134 p.: ill.

Contains 14 journalistic pieces by García Márquez, followed by an interview. Topics range from Grace Kelly (1956), Charles De Gaulle, French tourists, Porfirio Rubirosa, the Shah of Iran, and the Suez Canal to political and human interest articles (1957). All have been published in other volumes.

3889 Jaramillo, María Mercedes; Angela Inés Robledo; and Flor María Rodríguez-Arenas. ¿Y las mujeres?: ensayos sobre literatura colombiana. Medellín: Editorial

Univ. de Antioquia, 1991. 503 p.: bibl. (Otraparte; 5)

Three authors divide women's writing into three periods: 1) women writers in Colombia before independence, including an essay on Francisca Josefa de Castillo (by Robledo, 73 p.); 2) women writers of the 19th century, concentrating on María Martínez de Nisser, Josefa Acevedo de Gómez, and Soledad Acosta de Samper (by Rodríguez Arenas, 55 p.); and 3) 20th-century authors, emphasizing the writing of Albalucía Angel and Fanny Buitrago (by Jaramillo, 101 p.). Includes ample bibliography of Colombian women writers, bibliography of pseudonyms, and general bibliography. Valuable study would have been improved with a more complete bibliography of secondary sources that these three authors have apparently ignored.

3890 Morales Benítez, Otto. Momentos de la literatura colombiana. Santafé de Bogotá: Instituto Caro y Cuervo, 1991. 483 p.: bibl., col. ill. (Serie La Granada entreabierta; 58)

Most prolific writer (more than 30 books) has been identified in Colombia as a *polígrafo* who usually writes on political, historical, and cultural topics. This book consists of 17 literary essays which provides good biographical and historical contexts on Germán Arciniegas, Jorge Zalamea, Jorge Isaacs, Eduardo Caballero Calderón, Alvaro Cepeda Zamudio, René Uribe Ferrer, and Manuel Zapata Olivella. Also comments on two writers from author's native Caldas, Adel López Gómez, and Ovidio Rincón.

3891 Rodríguez-Vergara, Isabel. El mundo satírico de Gabriel García Márquez. Madrid: Editorial Pliegos, 1991? 230 p.: bibl. (Pliegos de ensayo; 64)

Examines works of García Márquez after *Cien años de soledad,* emphasizing satire. Covers early writings (journalism and first stories); and an analysis of *El otoño del patriarca* (1975), *Crónica de una muerte anunciada* (1981), *El amor en los tiempos del cólera,* (1985) and *El general en su laberinto* (1989). Principal theoretical bases for her understanding of satire are Bakhtin's writings and Gilbert Highet's *The anatomy of satire* (1962). Rodríguez Vergara handles García Márquez's massive bibliography with expertise and offers insightful readings of his fiction.

3892 Sims, Robert Lewis. El primer García Márquez: un estudio de su periodismo de 1948 a 1955. Potomac, Md.: Scripta Humanistica, 1990. 212 p.: bibl., ill., index. (Scripta Humanistica; 78)

Sims offers one of the most scholarly and analytical accounts of the Colombian's early writings, particularly his journalism. Uses as departure point theorists such as Todorov, Bakhtin, Genette, and Prince. Analyzes early journalistic pieces in *El Universal* (Cartagena, 1948–49), *El Heraldo* (1950–52), and others (Bogotá, 1954–55). Detailed analysis of these writings also covers *Relato de un náufrago* and writings García Márquez called "La Sierpe." Last two chapters demonstrate how structures and narrative strategies of his early period set the stage for later writings. Highly recommended book for García Márquez scholars.

3893 Sorela, Pedro. El otro García Márquez: los años difíciles: biografía. Bogotá: Editorial Oveja Negra, 1989. 333 p.: bibl. (Protagonistas)

Despite renown as a novelist, García Márquez regards himself as journalist first and novelist second. This biography (1940s–80s) responds to such a self-defined identity and centers around his career as a journalist. Based on numerous interviews and journalistic writings. Valuable contribution to García Márquez scholarship. Well documented and written.

3894 Williams, Raymond L. Novela y poder en Colombia, 1844–1987. Bogotá: Tercer Mundo Editores, 1992. 279 p.: bibl., index. Traducción de *The Colombian novel: 1844–1987* (Austin: Univ. de Texas, 1991). Por el largo período abarcado, el estudio de Williams se considera el más extenso y exhaustivo sobre el tema. Tres premisas básicas son: 1) que Colombia, más que una nación homogénea, es históricamente un conjunto de regiones semiautónomas; 2) que probablemente la mayoría de las novelas colombianas "han sido vehículos de diálogo ideológico," pues lo escrito siempre se vincula lo político; y 3) que la literatura colombiana es producto de la oposición entre lo que Walter Ong llama "la cultura oral y la cultura escrita." Libro repleto de información básica (listas cronológicas de docenas de novelas) e interpretaciones astutas y acertadas de diversas teorías litera-

rias que iluminan, explican y juzgan obras clásicas, claves de la narrativa colombiana. [D. Gerdes]

Ecuador

3895 Adoum, Jorge Enrique. Sin ambages: textos y contextos. Quito: Planeta, 1989. 185 p. (Col. País de la mitad; 9)

Interesante colección de ensayos publicados en revistas literarias ecuatorianas, latinoamericanas y europeas (1970–80). Temas predominantes son la responsabilidad del artista, relación entre arte y literatura, la cultura en el tercer mundo, la poesía como oficio, el realismo literario, literatura ecuatoriana y pensamientos sobre Benjamín Carrión, Alejo Carpentier, Julio Cortázar, Juan Rulfo y Carlos Drummond de Andrade.

3896 Fernández, María del Carmen. El realismo abierto de Pablo Palacio en la encrucijada de los 30. Quito: Ediciones Libri Mundi, Enrique Grosse-Luemern, 1991. 489 p.: bibl.

Serio, minucioso y esclarecedor texto sobre Palacio logra descubrir tanto motivaciones como procedimientos narrativos de este enigmático escritor lojano (1906–47), a quien consideraban "el precursor maldito de la modernidad literaria ecuatoriana."

Una gota de inspiración, toneladas de transpiración: antología del nuevo cuento ecuatoriano. See item **3979.**

3897 Handelsman, Michael. Del tzantzismo al desencanto: un recorrido de treinta años en la crítica literaria del Ecuador. (*Rev. Crít. Lit. Latinoam.*, 26:31/32, 1990, p. 139–152, bibl.)

Resume el estado de la crítica literaria reciente en el Ecuador, ocupada exclusivamente de temas nacionales. Distingue entre la falta de difusión de la obra ecuatoriana y la escasez de su producción, ya que es un país de poca crítica seria. La crítica literaria es casi un subproducto de la actividad creadora.

Neruda, Pablo *et al.* En defensa de Manuela Sáenz: la libertadora del Libertador. See item **2678.**

3898 Pazos, Julio. Literatura popular: versos y dichos de Tungurahua. Quito: Ediciones Abya-Yala, 1991. 275 p. (Biblioteca de ciencias sociales; 35)

Interesantísimo estudio en que el poeta y crítico Julio Pazos recopila 685 "dichos" o cuartetos de la tradición oral de la provincia de Tungurahua que contienen la cosmovisión de su pueblo. Partiendo de un análisis literario, nos lleva a temas tan dispares como el amor, la muerte, la comida, la religión y la política hacia una completa interpretación sociológica de la estructura y organización de los tungurahuenses.

3899   Sánchez Parga, José et al. Signos de futuro: la cultura ecuatoriana en los 80. Madrid: Agencia Española de Cooperación Internacional, 1991. 221 p.: bibl.

Contiene ensayos profundos de importantes representantes de la intelectualidad ecuatoriana que intentan explicar el significado de la década del 80 en cuanto a literatura, arte y el pensamiento ecuatorianos. Algunos la consideran una "década perdida;" otros, no tan pesimistas, vislumbran señales de un futuro prometedor. Buena antología de un debate sobre el acontecer cultural ecuatoriano en particular y latinoamericano por extensión.

Peru

3900   Alfaro-Alexander, Ana María. Hacia la modernización de la narrativa peruana: el Grupo Palermo. New York: P. Lang, 1992. 256 p.: bibl. (Univ. of Texas studies in contemporary Spanish-American fiction; 6)

Estudio de principios teóricos eclécticos que propone analizar la relación ideológica, temática y estilística del Grupo Palermo, narradores peruanos cuyas obras produjeron en su totalidad una radiografía de la urbanidad limeña de mediados de siglo XX. Reproducen peripecias de clases sociales no privilegiadas, hasta incorporan a la mujer a su narrativa. Los autores estudiados incluyen a Congrains Martín, Reynoso, Ribeyro, Salazar Bondy y Zavaleta. Buena introducción a este grupo importante de escritores peruanos.

3901   Armas Marcelo, J.J. Vargas Llosa: el vicio de escribir. Madrid: Ediciones Temas de Hoy, 1991. 414 p., 16 p. of plates: bibl., ill., indexes. (Col. Hombres de hoy; 25)

Suerte de biografía intelectual, itinerario político personal y análisis literario de las obras principales de Vargas Llosa. Se intentó utilizar como modelo para este libro el de Vargas Llosa sobre García Márquez, *Historia de un deicidio*, pero carece de un rigor de organización y principios literarios para el análisis; sin embargo, provee información interesante del mundo literario latinoamericano de Vargas Llosa.

3902   Bravo, José Antonio. La generación del '50: hombres de letras. Lima: Instituto Raúl Porras Barrenechea, Univ. Nacional Mayor de San Marcos, 1989. 230 p.: appendices, index.

Compilación de fichas bio-bibliográficas y fragmentos narrativos y poéticos de 50 escritores peruanos que pertenecen a la llamada Generación del 50. Contiene una introducción histórica del autor, un prólogo de Manuel Jesús Orbegoso y dos apéndices (una mesa redonda acerca de la Generación del 50 y un estudio del escritor Carlos Eduardo Zavaleta sobre la misma generación de narradores). Valioso libro de consulta.

3903   Castañeda, Belén S. Mario Vargas Llosa: el novelista como crítico. (*Hisp. Rev.*, 58:3, Summer 1990, p. 347–359)

Vargas Llosa utiliza su propio vocabulario y metodología estética para describir los principales procedimientos mediante los cuales el escritor realiza su obra. No pretende crear una crítica literaria uniforme sino mostrar al lector los factores de que se vale para crear una obra de ficción.

3904   Columbus, Claudette Kemper. Mythological consciousness and the future: José María Arguedas. New York: P. Lang, 1986. 191 p.: bibl., index. (American Univ. studies: Series II, Romance languages and literature; 52)

Applies a definition of mythological consciousness mainly to Arguedas' last novel, *El zorro de arriba y el zorro de abajo*, using examples drawn from an Andean context that promote cooperation with the environment.

3905   Díaz Caballero, Jesús et al. El Perú crítico: utopía y realidad. (*Rev. Crít. Lit. Latinoam.*, 26: 31/32, 1990, p. 171–218, bibl.)

Visión panorámica pero concisa de la relación entre sociedad, crítica literaria y literatura en el Perú durante el período 1970–88, abarcando: la crítica anterior; tendencias y problemas básicos de la crítica peruana referente al indigenismo, vanguardia, la narrativa urbana y literaturas orales y populares; y perspectivas para el futuro. Se incluye una importante bibliografía de trabajos críticos publicados desde 1970. Este trabajo es imprescindible para el estudioso de las letras contemporáneas peruanas.

3906 Encuentro de Narradores Jovenes, 1st, Lima, 1989. Perspectivas para una narrativa de los noventa. Introducción de César Toro Montalvo. Lima: APPAC Ediciones, 1991. 99 p.

Antología de cuentos del Primer Encuentro de Narradores Jóvenes y auspiciada por la Asociación Peruana de Promotores y Animadores Culturales (Lima, 1989). Son 18 cuentos de escritores que prometen mucho para los años 90: Jorge Valenzuela, Carlos Espinal Bedregal, Jorge Benavides, Alicia del Aguila y Reynaldo Santa Cruz, entre otros. Junto con la introducción de César Toro Montalvo, son narraciones de expresión generalmente culta y refinada, cuentos de imaginación y realidad pero siempre temas muy de actualidad, historias de los años 90.

3907 Escobar, Alberto. El imaginario nacional: Moro—Westphalen—Arguedas; una formación literaria. Lima: Instituto de Estudios Peruanos, 1989. 1 v.

Tres escritores peruanos durante la época que abarca desde la primera a la segunda guerra mundial comparten actitudes similares: vitalidad, ética y estética. Es más: coinciden en su enunciación literaria marginal en una situación histórica dada; el cuerpo literario ha sido constituido a partir de dicha posición y no de una manifestación formal específica; y a la marginalización ideológica le sucede el desplazamiento en la actividad vital de los tres escritores.

3908 Forgues, Roland. La estrategia mítica de Manuel Scorza. Lima: Centro de Estudios para el Desarrollo y la Participación, 1991. 174 p.: bibl. (Serie Textos universitarios)

Forgues se propone examinar la doble dimensión de mito que aparece en la obra literaria de Scorza, es decir, el mito como revelación de la realidad concreta y como conciencia que aspira a superarla. Valioso estudio de "la estrategia mítica" de Scorza.

3909 Forgues, Roland. José María Arguedas: del pensamiento dialéctico al pensamiento trágico: historia de una utopía. Lima: Editorial Horizonte, 1989. 468 p.: bibl. (Crítica literaria; 4)

Uno de los trabajos más arduos y tota-

lizadores sobre la obra de Arguedas, un verdadero asedio minucioso y penetrante de los elementos narrativos significativos del universo arguediano, desde la estructura interna, coherente y significativa hasta situarla en el contexto histórico y social, cultural y psíquico. Para el autor, lo que impulsa la obra de Arguedas es la contradicción (del pensamiento dialéctico) y la exigencia absoluta de su superación (el pensamiento trágico).

3910 Forgues, Roland et al. José María Arguedas: vida y obra. Edición de Hildebrando Pérez y Carlos Garayar. Lima?: Amaru Editores, 1991. 278 p.: bibl., ill.

Conjunto de trabajos presentados por los 20 más destacados estudiosos arguedianos en 1989 y publicado por el Centro de Estudios Peruanos y Andinos (CERPA) de la Univ. Stendhal de Grenoble. Entre los invitados figuran Antonio Cornejo Polar, Roland Forgues, William Rowe y Martin Lienhard. Se destacan las ponencias por la seriedad en el estudio de la literatura, el folklore y las ciencias sociales. Un aporte más a la mayor y mejor difusión del escritor peruano a quien rindieron homenaje.

3911 García-Bedoya Maguiña, Carlos. Para una periodización de la literatura peruana. Lima: Latinoamericana Editores, 1990. 108 p.: bibl.

Reelabora una faceta del convencional estudio histórico-literario: la periodización. Analiza el concepto de periodización en la historia literaria, propuestas anteriores y bases teóricas hacia una propuesta de la periodización literaria en el Perú. Incluye una primera etapa de Autonomía Andina (hasta 1530) y una segunda de Dependencia Externa (desde 1530 hasta el presente) que consiste de cinco períodos (1530–1620; 1620–1730; 1730–1825; 1825–1920; 1920-presente).

García Calderón, Ventura. Obras escogidas. See item **4007.**

3912 González, Galo Francisco. Amor y erotismo en la narrativa de José María Arguedas. Madrid: Editorial Pliegos, 1990. 188 p.: bibl. (Pliegos de ensayo; 57)

Obra erudita analiza detalladamente relaciones de amor y elementos eróticos en Arguedas. También examina una serie de cartas, desconocidas en su mayoría, que revelan el profundo conflicto que llevó al novelista al suicidio. Se incluye una entrevista con Sybila Arredondo.

3913 González Vigil, Ricardo. El Perú es todas las sangres: Arguedas, Alegría, Mariátegui, Martín Adán, Vargas Llosa y otros. Lima: Pontificia Univ. Católica del Perú, Fondo Editorial, 1991. 419 p.: bibl., index.

Crítico literario prolífico, González Vigil ofrece una amplia visión crítica y ecléctica de textos peruanos del siglo XX con el fin de abordar una cuestión crucial: la identidad nacional como conjunto de "todas las sangres" (Arguedas), enfocado a través de dos corrientes literarias en el Perú, el indigenismo y el vanguardismo. Se dedican capítulos a Mariátegui, Adán, Alegría, Arguedas, Scorza y Vargas Llosa pero intenta rescatar la figura de Ricardo Peña en la poesía vanguardista y la de Gamaliel Churata desde la óptica indigenista. Mucho material fue publicado antes como notas periodísticas.

3914 Gutiérrez, Gustavo. Entre las calandrias: un ensayo sobre José María Arguedas. Lima: Instituto Bartolomé de las Casas: CEP, 1990. xvi, 94 p.: bibl. (CEP; 108)

Contribución valiosa por la información bibliográfica y la sensibilidad literaria del autor en su acercamiento a la vida y obra de Arguedas. Ofrece juicios interesantes de índole filosófica y teológica sobre la obra arguediana, su identificación estrecha con las clases oprimidas del Perú y las virtudes necesarias para estudiar Arguedas: sabiduría, diligencia y amor.

3915 Higgins, James. Cambio social y constantes humanas: la narrativa corta de Ribeyro. Lima: Pontificia Univ. Católica del Perú, Fondo Editorial, 1991. 176 p.: bibl., index.

Los cuentos de Ribeyro documentan los efectos de la modernización de la sociedad peruana desde los años 50, enfocando cambios históricos a través de los estragos socio-económicos que viven sus personajes enajenados de un pasado ya caduco y un porvenir poco promisorio. Para ello, Higgins analiza detalladamente ciertos cuentos claves: "Una Sociedad en Vías de Modernizarse," "El Ropero, los Viejos y la Muerte," "El Polvo del Saber" y "Los Eucaliptos," documentando los efectos del capitalismo modernizante. Otros temas analizados incluyen la crisis de identidad, el desencanto y el escepticismo.

3916 Lienhard, Martin. Cultura andina y forma novelesca: zorros y danzantes en la última novela de Arguedas. Epílogo de

William Rowe, Luis Millones y José Cerna Bazán. 2a. ed. ampliada. Lima: Editorial Horizonte; Tarea, 1990. 239 p.: bibl. (Crítica literaria; 8)

Estudio profundo y definitivo sobre la novela póstuma de Arguedas. Lienhard tiene como meta analizar el discurso narrativo que retoma la oralidad de la cultura popular para delinear el carácter de la modernidad social. Indaga, además, el aporte del diario en la novela, lo mismo que la presencia de una cosmogonía andina en la costa peruana, entre otros aspectos novelescos importantes.

3917 Menton, Seymour. La guerra de Mario Vargas Llosa contra el fanatismo. (*Cuad. Am.*, 5:4, julio/agosto 1991, p. 50–62, bibl.)

Análisis del uso del fuego y el camaleón en la obra de Vargas Llosa como símbolos de fanatismo y flexibilidad. Su visión de un mundo mágico-realista confirma la idea borgiana y de García Márquez de que la realidad es incognoscible; mayor razón para condenar el fanatismo. Es inevitable que se postule esta obra como un espejo de la opinión política del autor sobre la situación actual peruana.

3918 Núñez, Estuardo. La imagen del mundo en la literatura peruana. 2. ed., con ampliaciones. Lima: Banco Central de Reserva del Perú, Fondo Editorial, 1989. 251 p. (Col. Tierra firme)

Examina la presencia de los peruanos y lo peruano en el cmpo literario mundial a la vez que la presencia del mundo en la literatura peruana. Dividido en cinco partes: 1) Perú frente al mundo; 2) Los "Ilustrados" y contradictorios viajeros; 3) El romanticismo: impulso de expansión; 4) Los románticos transitados; 5) El siglo XX o la toma de conciencia. Señala la influencia del Inca Garcilaso en España y la presencia de un narrador peruano contemporáneo como Alfredo Bryce Echenique en los EE.UU. Obra de interés histórico y literario.

3919 Palabra viva. v. 1, Narradores. Entrevistas de Roland Forgues. Lima?: Librería Studium Ediciones, 1988. 1 v.: ill.

Colección de entrevistas breves (1982–84) que hizo el conocido peruanista francés Roland Forgues a 22 de los más conocidos narradores peruanos de los años 50. Se abarcan diversos temas: el quehacer literario; ser escritor peruano; la marginalización; el periodismo y la creación literaria; el exilio; la técnica literaria; entre otros. Interesantes respuestas.

3920 Rochabrún S., Guillermo. ¿Viviendo en vano?: una relectura de la Mesa Redonda sobre *Todas las sangres.* (*Social. Particip.*, 57, marzo 1992, p. 21–34)
Se analiza una mesa redonda sobre *Todas las sangres* de Arguedas que tuvo lugar en el Instituto de Estudios Peruanos (1965). Se comenta su impacto y múltiples consecuencias, a través de una perspectiva sociológica y en relación al socialismo, para el futuro intelectual del país.

3921 Semana de Autor, *Madrid, 1987*. Alfredo Bryce Echenique. Edición de Fernando R. Lafuente. Madrid: Instituto de Cooperación Iberoamericana, Ediciones de Cultura Hispánica, 1991. 124 p.: bibl.
Se refiere a "La Semana de Autor" sobre Alfredo Bryce Echenique en el Instituto de Cooperación Iberoamericana (Madrid, 1987). Se incluyen transcripción de sesiones en que participaron 14 literatos españoles; extensa entrevista con el escritor; cronología biográfica; y bibliografía de sus libros y artículos y de obras sobre Bryce recopiladas por César Ferreira. Temas analizados fueron el amor, el humor, Mayo del 68 y arquetipos psicopatológicos en la obra bryciana. Texto de gran utilidad para los estudiosos de este importante escritor peruano.

3922 Seminario La Cultura en el Perú, *Lima, 1989*. José María Arguedas, veinte años después: huellas y horizonte, 1969–1989. Recopilación de Rodrigo Montoya. Lima: La Escuela de Antropología, Facultad de Ciencias Sociales, Univ. Nacional Mayor de San Marcos, 1991. 144 p.: bibl.
Colección de ensayos sobre Arguedas presentados en la Univ. de San Marcos a los 20 años de su muerte (Lima, 1989). Diversas perspectivas abarcan la antropología, historia y literatura para abarcar el problema planteado por Arguedas de entender al Perú integral en toda su complejidad.

3923 Spina, Vincent. El modo épico en José María Arguedas. Madrid: Editorial Pliegos, 1986? 211 p.: bibl. (Pliegos de ensayo; 19)
Libro sobre varios temas en la obra literaria de Arguedas: la sociedad, el héroe y la epopeya. Concluye que su visión totalizante

de la sociedad y del héroe en sus obras es casi épica. Se percibe tal evolución del héroe desde sus primeras hasta su última obra.

3924 Tauzin-Castellanos, Isabelle. Medicina y sociedad a fines del siglo XIX: su representación en una novela peruana. (*in* Peruanistas contemporáneos II: temas, métodos, avances. Edición de Wilfredo Kapsoli E. Lima: Consejo Nacional de Ciencia y Tecnología (CONCYTEC), 1989, p. 147–156)
Se examinan las obras de la gran escritora peruana Clorinda Matto de Turner, enfocando su valor histórico y aportando un recurso analítico para el estudio de la sociedad a fines del siglo XIX, o sea, la mentalidad femenina, y el uso de analogías medicinales en sus obras.

3925 Toro Montalvo, César. Historia de la literatura peruana. v. 1. Lima: Editorial San Marcos, 1991. 1 v.: bibl., ill.
Vol. 1 de tres sobre la historia de la literatura peruana a través de una antología comentada de textos clásicos. Contiene cuatro capítulos con apéndices de textos de escritores y críticos literarios: 1) breve historia de la literatura peruana; 2) literatura inca y quechua; 3) literatura de la conquista y colonia; y 4) literatura de la colonia y virreinato. Texto bastante completo y útil.

Vargas Llosa, Mario. Entre la libertad y el miedo. See *HLAS 53:3963.*

3926 Vargas Llosa, Mario. La verdad de las mentiras: ensayos sobre literatura. Barcelona: Seix Barral, 1990. 261 p. (Biblioteca breve)
Colección de ensayos analiza 25 obras importantes de la literatura universal contemporánea a fin de indagar algo que siempre ha intrigado al autor: qué diferencia hay entre una ficción u otra forma de escribir como el periodismo o la historia. Para él, son sistemas opuestos de aproximación a lo real. La novela se rebela y transgrede la vida, los otros géneros no pueden dejar de ser sus siervos. Entre las obras analizadas se incluyen "La Muerte en Venecia," *Manhattan transfer, El lobo estepario, Santuario, El extranjero, Lolita* y *El tambor de hojalata.*

Venezuela

3927 Bilbao M., Alicia. Salvador Garmendia: la relación hombre-realidad en *Los pequeños seres, Los habitantes, Día de ceniza.*

Caracas: Univ. Simón Bolívar, 1990. 101 p.: bibl. (Cuadernos USB: Serie Literatura; 1)

One of several recent efforts to fill the critical vacuum on Garmendia, a well-deserving author. Concentrates on Garmendia's early fiction (e.g., *Los pequeños seres,* 1959, *Los habitantes,* 1961, and *Día de ceniza,* 1963). Devotes much space to literary theory even though such theory is marginal to the commentary on Garmendia. Concludes that Garmendia's isolated characters are hyper-sensitive to the world in an urban space that "invades" the personal. Absence of love and eroticism leads to the prevalence of the material over the spiritual and invokes nostalgia for the past.

3928 Falgairolles, Adolphe de et al. *Las lanzas coloradas:* ante la crítica. Selección, prólogo, notas y bibliografía de Domingo Miliani. Caracas: Monte Avila Editores, 1991. 178 p.: bibl.

One of the century's major novels in Venezuela and an important work of Latin American letters, Arturo Uslar Pietri's work was first published in 1931. Consists of 14 essays published over the years (1931–71). Contributors include the writers Miguel Angel Asturias and Rene Avilés Fabila and renowned essayists Mariano Picón Salas and José Vasconcelos. Also includes German scholar Ulrich Leo. Model compilation devoted to a particular novel.

3929 Márquez Rodríguez, Alexis. Relecturas: ensayos de crítica literaria venezolana. Caracas: Contexto Audiovisual 3: Pomaire, 1991. 174 p.: bibl.

Retired Venezuelan academic continues publishing cultural articles on Venezuelan newspapers. Consists of seven essays of Venezuelan literature from the colonial period to present, originally presented as lectures in German universities (1988). Topics are history, fiction, and style in Venezuelan colonial literature; Simón Bolívar's thought; Andrés Bello as poet, grammarian, pedagogue; Venezuelan 19th-century thinkers Fermín Toro, Juan Vicente González, and Cecilio Acosta; essays, theory, and style of Mariano Picón Salas; and the Venezuelan novel (1943–88). Well-written essays provide good background from colonial period through 19th century. Less reliable commentary on author's contemporaries.

3930 Mata Gil, Milagros. Balza: el cuerpo fluvial. Caracas: Academia Nacional de la Historia, 1989. 174 p.: bibl. (El Libro menor; 152)

Balza is one of Venezuela's most innovative young writers, and deserving of more criticism. Mata Gil's intelligent and well-written critical study fills the vacuum. Well acquainted with Balza's work, she examines historical and literary context, biographical background, aesthetic agenda, and use of metaphor, imagery, and language (e.g., *Marzo anterior, Largo, Ejercicios narrativos: ejercicios, Setecientas palmeras plantadas en el mismo lugar, D,* and *Percusión*).

3931 Milanca Guzmán, Mario. Rómulo Gallegos: escrituras y destierros. Caracas: Fundarte, 1990. 160 p.: bibl. (Cuadernos de difusión; 136)

Unique volume on Gallegos by Chilean scholar residing in Venezuela. Early sections, strictly biographical, emphasize Gallegos' exile. Author, also an exile, shares his personal understanding of Gallegos' experience. Discusses Gallegos' short fiction and includes selections.

Relatos venezolanos del siglo XX. See item 4033.

PROSE FICTION
Bolivia

3932 Aguirre Lavayén, Joaquín. En las nieves rosadas del Ande: la historia romántica y trágica de Manuel Isidoro Belzu, José Ballivián y Segurola, Juana Manuela Gorriti. Santa Cruz de la Sierra, Bolivia; Cochabamba, Bolivia: Distribuidor, Amigos del Libro, 1991. 296 p.: ill.

Relatos ardientes, patrióticos y sobre todo humanos en el marco imperecedero de los Andes bolivianos. En su totalidad, el texto hilvana la historia romántica y trágica de los tres personajes del título.

3933 Bedoya Ballivián, Mario. Cinco cuentos y un recuerdo. La Paz: Instituto Boliviano de Cultura, 1991. 103 p.: ill.

En seis cuentos un escritor paceño, hombre público y conocedor de su gente, muestra Bolivia y los bolivianos: campo, ciudad, vida y costumbres de personas y animales.

3934 Contreras Jiménez, Ernesto. El mundo de los sin nombre. La Paz: Alcaldía Municipal de La Paz, 1991. 94 p.

Primer libro de cuentos del autor que tienen por común denominador la soledad y un comportamiento que llega a lo patológico, en un estilo directo y preciso. Premiado en el Concurso Nacional de Literatura "Franz Tamayo."

3935 González-Aramayo Zuleta, Vicente. Juan de los indios: novela histórica; Juan Huallparrimachi en un pasaje de la Guerra de la Independencia. Oruro, Bolivia: Editora Lilial, 1991. 142 p.: ill.

Escritor abogado y cineasta, el autor es también gran defensor de los indios de su tierra. Esta novela histórica se encuentra entre sus otras siete y sus cuatro películas de ficción. La obra se basa en las guerras de la independencia y un fantasioso relato sobre Juan Huallparrimachi. Por su lenguaje sencillo y elemento histórico, se hace muy amena y recomendable como texto didáctico para jóvenes.

3936 Ortiz Sanz, Fernando. El reparo: novela. Sucre, Bolivia: Talleres Gráficos Cordech, 1990. 183 p.

Continúa con la saga novelística sobre el indígena quechua. Inició el tema de *El reparo* en *La barricada*, lo continúa en *La cruz del sur* y lo consolida en la presente novela. Se concentra en los valores éticos y míticos de la raza quechua.

3937 Padilla Osinaga, Paz. El gemido del huracán. Santa Cruz de la Sierra, Bolivia: Editora El País, 1991. 165 p.

Novela de ambiente santacruceño, época contemporánea y lengua corriente. Es la historia de un joven pasmado ante los rápidos cambios de la sociedad actual a los que se adapta para sobrevivir.

3938 Paz Soldán, Edmundo. Las máscaras de la nada. La Paz: Editorial Los Amigos del Libro, 1990. 134 p. (Col. Literatura de hoy; 649)

Se reúnen aquí casi 90 narraciones breves (1987–90). Muchas abarcan cinco líneas, otras dos páginas. Temas diversos que giran en torno a la historia del país, situaciones cotidianas, reflexiones personales, etc. La capacidad de síntesis, la sencillez y la cla-ridad del escritor resultan en un diseño que va ligando las narraciones. Se asemeja a las *Prosas apátridas* de Julio Ramón Ribeyro.

3939 Prada Oropeza, Renato. Los nombres del infierno. Tuxtla Gutiérrez, Mexico: Univ. Autónoma de Chiapas, 1985. 128 p. (Col. Maciel; 11)

Contiene siete relatos del conocido escritor boliviano radicado en México. Los une la presencia de un clima de compromiso político, la exploración y denuncia de los que manipulan la conciencia boliviana y el espíritu de solidaridad latinoamericana. A veces los relatos se tornan en seco discurso ideológico, pero el tono desgarrador crea tensiones estéticas intrigantes.

3940 Quiroga, Giancarla de. De angustias e ilusiones: cuentos. Cochabamba, Bolivia: Editorial Serrano, 1990. 59 p.

Autora laureada con el Primer Premio de la Municipalidad de Cochabamba (1989) presenta a la mujer en ocho relatos breves: la adúltera, la hija caprichosa, la desesperada por mostrarse joven, la concubina del ciego y otros. Roles múltiples y muy propios de la sociedad contemporánea.

3941 Quiroga Santa Cruz, Marcelo. Otra vez marzo. Cochabamba, Bolivia: Editorial Los Amigos del Libro, 1990. 348 p.: ill. (Obras completas)

Novela póstuma e incompleta (el autor fue asesinado en 1980), este texto es sólo parte de un vasto y ambicioso proyecto novelesco que se compone de tres novelas de las cuales sólo fue escrita la primera (*El estiércol*) y el primer capítulo de la segunda (*La sangre*). Se incluye el plan general del proyecto novelesco, notas, acotaciones y facsímiles de los originales. Excelente prólogo de Oscar Rivera Rodas.

3942 Rivadeneira Prada, Raúl. Palabra suelta. La Paz: Ediciones Signo, 1990. 279 p. (Serie Rumor del tiempo)

Extensa colección de artículos periodísticos (feb. 1987-julio 1990). Autor de diez obras ya publicadas se ha convertido en atento observador de la realidad cotidiana de su país. Crítico implacable no exento de fina ironía. Rivadeneira Prada pasa revista a todos los aspectos, anecdóticos o esenciales, que conforman el diario vivir de sus compatriotas.

3943 Vallejo de Bolívar, Gaby. La sierpe empieza en cola. Cochabamba, Bolivia: Editorial Los Amigos del Libro, 1991. 219 p. (Col. Literatura de hoy; 650)

Mezcla de humanidad, política y religiosidad, esta novela presenta facetas poco conocidas de la vida y postergaciones de la gente pobre de ciertos ambientes. En lenguaje crudo habla mucha gente que generalmente calla, ofreciendo consideraciones y definiciones de la mujer de hoy en los vastos territorios del machismo.

3944 Vargas, Manuel. Callejones: la novela de Fermín. La Paz: Impr. Artes Gráficas Latina, 1990. 146 p.

Segundo libro de relatos breves en que el niño Fermín pasa de uno a otro en forma casi imperceptible. En este, el protagonista conoce la amistad, el sexo, la escuela, seres extraños, la muerte y otros asuntos que sirven para conocerse a sí mismo y sobrevivir. "Entre cometas, niebla y callejones siempre habrá un lugar para el olvido," concluye el texto, dando unidad al relato.

Colombia

3945 Aguilera Garramuño, Marco Tulio. Cuentos para después de hacer el amor. 4a ed. México: Leega, 1988. 141 p. (Leega literaria: Narradores americanos)

Colombian author (b. 1949), Mexican resident for several years, whose first novel, the imaginative and humorous *Breve historia de todas las cosas* was widely applauded in 1975 and was followed by other successful books of fiction. This volume consists of 11 irreverent and humorous stories revealing a wild imagination regarding sexuality and human interactions (e.g., bestiality, voyeurism, eroticism, other sexual rituals). Well written in the self-conscious and cosmopolitan style that characterizes much of this talented Colombian's writing.

3946 Buitrago, Fanny. ¡Líbranos de todo mal! Bogotá: Carlos Valencia Editores, 1989. 110 p. (Col. Nueva narrativa; 8)

One of Colombia's finest short story writers of the 1970s has published impressive fiction, including several novels. Consists of nine short stories that fictionalize everyday life in Colombia (e.g., assassinations, disappeared persons, plastic women, martyrs, Bo-

gotá saints). All are written in a direct, accessible style, but with an ironic tone and a little magic.

3947 Escobar Velásquez, Mario. Con sabor a fierro y otros cuentos. Medellín, Colombia: Biblioteca Pública Piloto de Medellín, 1991. 170 p.

Author's first prize-winning novel, *Cuando pase el ánima sola* (1979), was traditional but fast-moving. Later books were well-written but conventional and usually set in his native Antioquia. These 11 stories revisit plots and places of previous works, with bold actions but timid objectives. Still, author is one of Colombia's fine story tellers, in the best tradition of Carrasquilla and Mejía Vallejo.

3948 Espinosa, Germán. Sinfonía desde el Nuevo Mundo. Bogotá: Planeta, 1990. 157 p. (Autores colombianos)

Author of 16 books prior to this novel, author's readership in Colombia is growing. Initially imitative of García Márquez (e.g., *Los cortejos del diablo*, 1970), Espinosa has developed his own voice in several historical novels, although traces of Alejo Carpentier and R.H. Moreno-Durán are distracting. Divided according to symphonic movements, *Sinfonía del Nuevo Mundo* is one of several recent Colombian novels on the historical Simón Bolívar. Although attempting to be ambitious and serious, work is fast-paced, easy to read, and intended for a mass market. Includes questionable final essay about its *not* being an historical novel. Derivative style and poor appendix make it of minor interest beyond Colombia. Of the numerous fictionalized accounts of Bolívar, García Márquez's *El general en su laberinto* is unquestionably the best; *Sinfonía del Nuevo Mundo* may be the worst.

3949 Fayad, Luis. Compañeros de viaje. Bogotá: Tercer Mundo Editores, 1991. 373 p. (Narrativa contemporánea: Col. Prisma)

Colombian intellectuals consider Fayad, author of three books of stories and one novel, one of their most talented young writers. *Compañeros de viaje* is a history of the Lucerna family and several National Univ. students during the mid-1960s, a time of guerrilla and student violence. Father Camilo Torres, a central character, decides to take up arms, and students join along with him. Careful, detailed descriptions of the National Univ. and Chapinero neighborhood in northern Bogotá. Fayad has yet to realize his promise of writing a major novel.

3950 Gallego, Romualdo. Novelas, cuentos y crónicas. Medellín, Colombia: Ediciones Autores Antioqueños, 1991. 407 p.: ill. (Ediciones Autores antioqueños; 61)

Antioquia has a long tradition of supporting its regional culture. Volume is part of fine collection of Antioquia's writers that includes Baldomero Sanín Cano, León de Greiff, Manuel Mejía Vallejo, etc. Gallego (1895– 1931), a traditional and able realist about Antioquia's customs, published numerous novels, stories, and essays. These three short novels, seven stories, and 78 *crónicas*, are nostalgic writings about an agricultural, serene, and vanished Antioquia. Unfortunately, volume's introduction is not useful for the lay reader.

3951 Garcés González, José Luis. La llanura obstinada. Montería, Colombia: Gráficas Corsa, 1988. 183 p. (Col. Lotería de Córdoba; 1)

With other young writers in northern city of Montería who called themselves Group El Túnel, author circulated a magazine. Most prominent novelist among them, Garcés gained national attention when awarded second prize in national novel contest for *Entre la soledad y los cuchillos.* This accessible and humorous novel ridicules family life in rural Colombia and portrays its families as living between traditional values and modern crisis. Members of El Túnel have yet to produce a major Colombian novel.

3952 García Márquez, Gabriel. La aventura de Miguel Littín, clandestino en Chile: un reportaje. Buenos Aires: Editorial Sudamericana, 1986. 152 p.

Chilean film director Miguel Littín— one of 5,000 political exiles—spent six unauthorized clandestine weeks in Chile in 1985. Working undercover, with false papers and the collaboration of Chilean democratic institutions, Littín filmed more than 7,000 m of film, even in the presidential palace, about the effects of 12 years of military dictatorship. Result was a four-hour television tape and a two-hour regular film. When García Márquez heard Littín's account, he recognized another story from the film. He spent a week tape-recording Littín to produce text (600 p.) which he used to write this report (150 p.), in Littín's words but with García Márquez's voice and style. An exceptional book.

3953 García Márquez, Gabriel. Notas de prensa, 1980–1984. Madrid: Mondadori, 1991. 522 p.

Nobel Laureate has often stated that he considers himself a journalist first and novelist second. And from the 1940s in Cartagena and Barranquilla to the present, he has continued writing journalistic pieces. This compilation represents an interesting period in his life when he was living in Mexico City, before the Nobel Prize. The 1980s was a time of conflicts in Central America, and a growing drug industry in Colombia, and increasing insecurity. In 1980–84, García Márquez published 168 articles on a broad range of subjects, from literature to politics and culture. Some literary pieces will be cited for many years, such as one on how to write a novel, and another on the short story genre. These are the writings of a master journalist.

3954 Hoyos, Andrés. Por el sendero de los ángeles caídos. Bogotá: Carlos Valencia Editores, 1989. 297 p. (Col. Nueva narrativa)

Novel by this talented writer is often reminiscent of the delicate and Baroque language of Cuba's Lezama Lima and Colombia's Moreno-Durán and García Márquez. Departure date is April 9, 1948, the outbreak of Colombia's civil war known as *La Violencia.* Family story divided into two parts and including several generations also experiments with other forms of writing, including chapters with pure dialogue.

3955 Hoyos, Juan José. El cielo que perdimos. Bogotá: Planeta, 1990. 530 p. (Autores colombianos)

Author's second novel is about violent Medellín. Many situations of the traditional rural *novela de La Violencia* are taken into urban spaces. After suffering through his father's stoic and noble death, the protagonist experiences many other deaths in Medellín but there are irrational and savage endings very unlike his father's. Urban space as a comfortable and dignified human environment is transformed into a place of torture, fear, and uncertainty. Hoyos' writing is traditional, deliberate, and well conceived.

3956 Illán Bacca, Ramón. Deborah Kruel.
Bogotá: Plaza y Janés Editores, 1990.
190 p. (Narrativa colombiana)
Illán Bacca's short fiction and essays
have been published in Barranquilla and ignored in Bogotá and the rest of Colombia.
First novel, *Deborah Kruel,* is an anomaly in
Colombia: a spy thriller. Set in Barranquilla
and the Caribbean during World War II, it proposes that the war's outcome might have
been different with a change of events in the
Caribbean. Swift plot and mature style, distanced enough from the spy-novel genre,
keeps the reader entertained.

3957 Jaramillo Agudelo, Darío. Guía para
viajeros. Bogotá: Planeta, 1991. 201 p.:
ill.
Known primarily as one of Colombia's
best poets of his generation, Jaramillo has
also published one novel. These 35 very
imaginative and brief pieces combine narrative of the novelist's work and language of his
poetry, concern invented beings identified as
morgualos, frusos, sásicos, tinguanos, etc.
Reminiscent of Cortázar's inventions; most
are quite amusing.

3958 Leal, Eutiquio. La hora del alcatraz. Bogotá: Plaza & Janés, 1989. 256
p. (Narrativa colombiana)
Leal, one of Colombia's most respected
short fiction writers during the past two decades, is from Tolima, center of the civil war,
La Violencia (1950), and his best short stories
deal with that topic. Also publishes in other
genres—poetry, theater, journalism, and TV
scripts. His exceptionally experimental novel
for the time, *Después de la noche* (1964), was
ignored. *La hora del alcatraz* rewrites it and
experiments with time (12 hours, 6 pm-6 am).
Various narrators relate same events occuring
each hour. Although story is not that inher-
ently interesting, novel is an important experiment in Colombian fiction.

3959 Martínez, Fabio. Fantasio. Cali, Colombia?: Ediciones Univ. del Valle,
1992. 77 p. (Col. literatura)
Martínez, one of several promising
young writers from the Cauca Valley, was fi-
nalist in several fiction competitions. This
thin volume of 14 brief stories offers series of
remembrances of people, places, and situations (Cali, 1950s). Volume's title takes name

from Cali's most famous 1950s bar. Its music
and atmosphere permeate this volume.

3960 Mejía Vallejo, Manuel. Otras historias
de Balandú. Bogotá: Intermedio Editores, 1990. 167 p.: bibl. (Literatura)
Mejía Vallejo's fiction often looks back
nostalgically at author's childhood in small-
town, rural Antioquia. Stories afford reader
this experience without particular concern
about the referent itself. Author spent lifetime remembering, and these 70 brief pieces
attest to this search for the past. More than
short stories, these are brief anecdotes and
images, very well written in the traditional
sense.

3961 Moreno-Durán, Rafael Humberto. Los
felinos del canciller. Bogotá: Planeta,
1987. 360 p. (Col. Autores colombianos)
Moreno-Durán became the most
prominent new Colombian writer of 1980s after completing trilogy of novels begun in
1970s. *Los felinos del canciller,* first novel after that trilogy and written with irony, humor, and elegant style, is his most readable
fiction to date. Relates amusing story of 20th-
century Colombian diplomatic family. One of
the most accomplished novels of the decade
by one of Colombia's most talented writers.

3962 Mujica, Elisa. La tienda de *imágenes:*
cuentos. Bogotá: Ediciones Fondo Cultural Cafetero con la colaboración del Banco
Cafetero y Almadelco, 1987. 119 p. (Ediciones
Fondo Cultural Cafetero; 13)
A special case in Colombian letters, in
the 1940s Mujica began writing fiction and
has published for several decades, but has
been virtually ignored by readers and critics.
Two fine novels, several volumes of short fiction, and some children's literature were published by the time this volume of 19 short
pieces, direct and simple in style, appeared.
Stories underline psychological but especially
female intricacies of everyday life. One of
Colombia's most accomplished writers.

3963 Restrepo, Laura. La isla de la pasión.
Bogotá: Planeta, 1989. 321 p.: bibl.
(Col. Autores colombianos)
Well-written commercial novel by au-
thor of novels of love, action, and adventure.
Young army official accepts mission to defend
national sovereignty on small desert island
and settles there with wife and 11 soldiers.

After a civil war, the government falls, and no one remembers them or the island. Abandoned on the island for nine years, they confront numerous tests to survive. Reconstruction of strange chapter of Colombia's history.

3964 Sánchez Suárez, Benhur. Memoria de un instante. Bogotá: Contracartel Editores, 1988. 117 p. (Novela colombiana)

Author of five novels and several volumes of short fiction, Sánchez Suárez has been active participant in "post-Macondo" phenomenon in Colombia. *Violencia* of his native Huila is present in his fiction's foreground or background. In this novel, the *Violencia* is in the background of Germán Trujillo and his family. As Trujillo agonizes in death, his children reconstruct his life in which his rural family settled in Bogotá and attained some stability and economic security. Sánchez Suárez chronicles Colombian history from 1950s-70s.

3965 Santamaría, Germán. No morirás. Bogotá: Editorial Oveja Negra, 1992. 189 p.

Since the volcano's 1984 eruption in Colombia which killed over 20,000 people around Armero, numerous book-length accounts of this tragedy have been published. Tragedy also serves as catalyst for this first novel by one of Colombia's best investigative journalists, Germán Santamaría. Written in the direct and conventional style of a journalist, novel fictionalizes psychological and moral aftermath of volcano's eruption. Also explores possible roots of Colombia's violence. Novel reads well but is not as compelling as Santamaría's journalism.

3966 Valderrama Andrade, Bernardo. El gran jaguar. Bogotá: Plaza & Janés Editores, 1991. 232 p. (Narrativa colombiana)

First novel by anthropologist and architect was awarded Plaza y Janés National Novel Prize. Published with map of Tairona Indian region in northern Colombia and lengthy index of Indian names, *El gran jaguar* is a cultural anomoly: could have been published in the 1930s, at zenith of *la literatura indigenista*. Detailed study of Tairona culture, with lengthy anecdotes about Tairona mythology, religion, government, customs, work, and daily life. Also indulges in lengthy descriptions of flora and fauna. Some interior monologues attempt to imitate Indian

thought. Well written, but very traditional and conventional novel.

Ecuador

3967 Andrade Heymann, Juan. 26 años de vacaciones: antología. Quito: Editorial El Conejo, 1988. 277 p. (Col. Ecuador/letras)

Recopilación y selección del autor de sus cuentos junto con 19 narraciones inéditas. Relatos breves similares a los de Pablo Palacio en la intensión subversiva y surreal de documentar y cuestionar una realidad ecuatoriana real y ficticia.

3968 Bienal del Cuento Ecuatoriano Pablo Palacio, 1st, 1991. Obras premiadas. Quito: Centro de Difusión Cultural, 1991. 214 p.

Antología de 13 cuentos ecuatorianos premiados en la Primera Bienal del Cuento Ecuatoriano Pablo Palacio a la que se remitieron 182 textos. El relato "La Caída," del cuencano Vicente Andrade Vélez, ganó el primer premio. En su mayoría tratan asuntos íntimos y familiares entre gente de ambientes modernos, aunque el fondo histórico nacional se percibe en muchos casos. Excelente muestra de la creciente calidad cuentística ecuatoriana.

3969 Cárdenas Espinosa, Eliécer. Los diamantes y los hombres de provecho. Cuenca, Ecuador: Núcleo del Azuay de la Casa de la Cultura, 1989. 232 p.

Novela de aprendizaje sobre encuentros entre tres jóvenes a través de los que se cristaliza un deterioro impulsado por numerosos acontecimientos: la guerra de Vietnam; *Los paraguas de Cherburgo*; el ejemplo del Che Guevara; patéticos y fallidos intentos de precipitar una insurrección urbana contra el orden establecido. En contraste, figura la presencia del amor y la fe en la humanidad a través de un joven artista, un rebelde y una mujer elusiva.

3970 Cárdenas Espinosa, Eliécer. Polvo y ceniza. 1. ed. Letraviva. Quito: Planeta, 1988. 219 p. (Col. Narrativa ecuatoriana; 12. Letraviva)

Novela que propone rescatar personajes escamoteados por la historia y la literatura oficial. Nuán Briones es un mito personalizado, vuelto verdad, carne, mediante: 1) la revalorización que se hace del marginado que roba a los ricos para dar a los pobres; 2) la sintaxis del personaje con sus problemas cotidianos; y 3) la identificación del lector con el héroe y las necesidades de las masas. Novela revalora la situación marginada del pobre, de tal manera que el destinario no debe ser la pequeña burguesía urbana sino, desafortunadamente, los que no leen.

3971 Carrión, Alejandro. Divino tesoro. Quito: Centro de Investigación y Cultura, Banco Central del Ecuador, 1988. 416 p. (Obras completas de Alejandro Carrión; 6)

De los 15 vols. *Obras Completas*, No. 6 contiene tres volúmenes de relatos: "Divino Tesoro" (inédito hasta ahora), "Muerte en su Isla" (relatos publicados en la revista *La Calle* y ganadores del XIV Premio Leopoldo Alas, 1969) y "La Llave Perdida" (Monte Avila, 1970). Vol. 1 recoge experiencias personales del colegio secundario y la universidad; vol. 2 abarca temas sociales mediante un estilo realista; y vol. 3 se vale de la anécdota, con todo su humor, sencillez y gracia, para recrear escenas y costumbres de la vida provincial.

3972 Carrión, Carlos. El deseo que lleva tu nombre. Quito: Editorial El Conejo; Editorial Grijalbo-ecuatoriana, 1989? 204 p. (Col. Bienal de novela ecuatoriana)

Novela que intenta captar el erotismo real e imaginado de un profesor misógino que se enamora de una alumna. En el proceso el protagonista inventa mundos novelescos de pasión donde se funden la imaginación, el deseo y la realidad. El erotismo y el estilo socarrón de esta novela prometen nuevas posibilidades temáticas en la narrativa ecuatoriana contemporánea.

3973 Cuadra, José de la. Doce relatos; *Los Sangurimas.* Estudio introductorio y notas de María Augusta Vintimilla. Quito: Libresa, 1991. 317 p.: bibl. (Col. Antares; 52)

Antología de 12 relatos y la novela *Los Sangurimas* pertenece a la conocidísima "Colección Antares." Protagonista campesino del agro costeño del Ecuador nos revela vida, costumbres, convicciones, lenguaje, mitos y convicciones del montuvio. Se incluye amplio estudio introductorio, juicios críticos, cronología y bibliografía. Excelente texto para clase.

3974 Dávila Vázquez, Jorge. De rumores y sombras: tres novelas cortas. Quito: Planeta, 1991. 163 p. (Col. Narrativa ecuatoriana; 17)

Escritor ya maduro pero aún joven, Dávila es romántico, vigoroso y realista. Se respira en sus obras el aire del Ecuador de ayer y de hoy. Presenta aquí tres novelas breves en las que exhibe su destreza acostumbrada en la descripción de personajes y paisajes y en especial en la ambientación temporal-espacial.

3975 Donoso Pareja, Miguel. Todo lo que inventamos es cierto. Quito: Editorial El Conejo, 1990. 122 p. (Col. Ecuador/letras)

Ultimos 18 relatos del conocido escritor abarcan situaciones interiores de personajes enajenados, sabiendo que a través de sus recuerdos (certezas) y presentimientos (interrogantes), van a enfrentar sus propios sueños, anhelos, dudas y miedos que reconocen en otros.

3976 Egüez, Iván. Anima pávora. Quito?: Abrapalabra Editores, 1990. 139 p.

Escritor, traductor, editor y embajador cultural, Egüez es uno de los dos o tres narradores ecuatorianos de más importancia y su habilidad narrativa lo coloca entre los más importantes de Latinoamérica. Colección excepcional de historias deslumbrantes con finales inesperados que alteran la visión normal del mundo. Cuentos que recrea diversas sensaciones, del miedo y la degradación al amor y la muerte.

3977 Encalada Vásquez, Oswaldo. A la sombra del verano. Cuenca, Ecuador: Casa de la Cultura Ecuatoriana Benjamín Carrión, Núcleo el Azuay, 1991. 118 p.

Novela corta en que el autor viaja por la infancia de tres niños, hermanos de 12, nueve y siete años. Este último confina al lector a unas vacaciones eternas de agosto en Amanta.

3978 Galarza Zavala, Jaime. Cuentos de piedra. Guayaquil, Ecuador: Univ. de Guayaquil, Vicerrectorado Académico, 1991. 165 p.

Ex-dirigente estudiantil, ex-prisionero, organizador de campesinos, el autor "sin pelos en la lengua" escribe sobre temas populares que han sido acallados. Relatos de fuerte acento testimonial e histórico.

3979 Una gota de inspiración, toneladas de transpiración: antología del nuevo cuento ecuatoriano. Estudio, selección y notas por Raúl Vallejo Corral. Quito: Libresa, 1990. 151 p. (Col. Antares; 30)

Excelente antología de 11 autores (desde los 70). Texto bien organizado de comentarios concisos pero repletos de información valiosa enfoca la importancia del lenguaje, la ausencia de la omnisciencia, el antihéroe, la sexualidad y nuevos conceptos de tiempo y espacio en el cuento. Muy útil para estudiantes y lectores interesados en comprender mejor el cuento moderno.

3980 Isacovici, Salomón and **Rodríguez, Juan Manuel.** Hombre de cenizas. México: Diana, 1990. 1 v.

Esta obra multifacética es: 1) documento histórico que narra la verdad desgarradora del holocausto judío; 2) pieza testimonial acusatoria, confesión personal, de sobrevivencia milagrosa ante el odio antisemítico de los nazis; 3) autobiografía; y 4) obra literaria. Este último factor narrativo da estructura y cohesión creando un interés conmovedor en la trama entre protagonista y lector.

3981 Larrea Borja, Piedad. Oníricos y cuentostorias. Quito: Editorial Casa de la Cultura Ecuatoriana, 1990. 119 p.: ill.

Varios relatos breves hilvanados en forma ingeniosa. Narración a veces fragmentada como en sueños. Larrea Borja, que luce aquí tan ecuatoriana como Abdón Ubidia, produce minicuentos fáciles e interesantes.

3982 Moreano, Alejandro. El devastado jardín del paraíso. Quito: Editorial El Conejo; Grijalbo, 1990. 450 p. (Col. Bienal de novela ecuatoriana)

Obra ganadora de la Primera Bienal de Novela Ecuatoriana (1989) recoge con amarga nostalgia los recuerdos de la época revoltosa y violenta del surgimiento de las guerrillas de los años 60 que luego fracasan, todo lo cual sirve en la novela de andamio para la construcción de una gran parábola de la condición humana. Con la derrota final de los guerrillos, la libertad se transforma en destino, el héroe sufrido en mártir. Intento de indagar la dimensión trascendental de la existencia humana a través de la derrota pesimista de un grupo guerrillero.

3983 Palacio, Pablo. Un hombre muerto a puntapiés. La Habana: Casa de las Américas, 1982. 204 p. (Col. Literatura latinoamericana; 109)

Primer libro de cuentos incluye dos novelas cortas, *La vida del ahorcado* y *Débora*, y otros relatos que tuvieron gran éxito por su escandalosa burla vanguardista y crítica de la realidad moderna de los años 20 y 30. Excelente prólogo de Raúl Pérez Torres explica como Palacio quiso "desacreditar la realidad, sorprenderla en su importancia efímera," de modo que estos textos caben perfectamente dentro de un realismo crítico vanguardista y agudo.

3984 Pérez Torres, Raúl. Un saco de alacranes: cuentos. Quito?: Abrapalabra Editores, 1989. 123 p. (Narrativa ecuatoriana)

Consiste de 13 cuentos escritos a principio de los 70. Desde entonces, el autor ha creado un corpus notable de novelas y cuentos. Estos demuestran un gran dominio narrativo por constituir un gran fresco del hecho cotidiano y de conflictos tanto personales como socio-políticos que aquejan al mundo latinoamericano a través de la despiadada ternura que singulariza toda la obra de Pérez Torres.

3985 Ponce, Javier. El insomnio de Nazario Mieles: novela. Quito: Ediciones Libri Mundi, 1990. 180 p. (Narrativa)

Novela que recrea el mundo misterioso, mítico y fatal de la selva latinoamericana, en cuyo ambiente el protagonista Almalepra, de simultáneas vidas, vive la de un legendario cauchero amazónico y la del fantasma de Nazario Mieles. Dos figuras más, hombre y mujer, abarcarán la problemática del amor.

3986 Rodríguez, Juan Manuel. Fricciones: doce figuras con paisaje. Quito: Ediciones de la Pontificia Univ. Católica del Ecuador, 1991. 123 p.

Ganador del Premio Nacional de Literatura Aurelio Espinosa Polít (Ecuador, 1990), este conjunto de "doce figuras con paisaje" perfilan diversas historias de seres obligados a narrar sus peripecias, miedos, amores y rarezas. Un narrador expurga libros durante la Inquisición y otro participa en cocinar a su hermano. El tono solemne de los cuentos provee humor y ironía.

3987 Rojas Hidalgo, Raúl. Una buena razón para matar. Quito: CIDEP, 1990. 286 p.

Novela polémica sobre un desgarrador tema político de actualidad, o sea, la violencia y crisis producidas por las fuerzas guerrilleras desestabilizadoras tal como Sendero Luminoso. Finalista de la I Bienal de Novela Ecuatoriana en el año 89 capta el sentido de convulsión, negatividad, teatro e hipocresía en Latinoamérica. Tono y proyección crítica recuerdan a Eduardo Galeano.

3988 Salguero, Natasha. Azulinaciones: novela. Quito: s.n., 1990. 195 p.

Ganadora del Premio de XV Concurso Aurelio Espinosa Pólit (Quito, 1989). Crea un mundo insólito de juegos de palabras para luchar contra el lenguaje convencional y lo típicamente burgués. Capta la desarticulación de valores del repulsivo mundo moderno con una perspectiva feminista que enfoca temas del sexo, la droga y la crisis de conciencia. Esta primera obra de Salguero ensancha notablemente la ficción ecuatoriana.

3989 Tobar García, Francisco. Autobiografía admirable de mi tía Eduviges. Quito: Editorial El Conejo, 1991. 184 p.

Autobiografía de la tía del autor, escrita con tal pasión, que carece de acentos y mayúsculas. Trabajo pleno de historias bien elaboradas y con humor. Puro entretenimiento de personajes que hablan la lengua del vecino vulgar, usada en la literatura de hoy, llana, directa, chistosa.

3990 Valdano Morejón, Juan. Mientras llega el día. Quito: Grijalbo, 1990. 349 p. (El Espejo de tinta)

Finalista de la I Bienal de Novela 1989, esta fascinante importante novela histórica abarca el movimiento inicial de la independencia en la América hispánica. La trama sigue hechos acaecidos momentos antes de la insurgencia popular de Quito y la masacre de los rebeldes (agosto, 1810) con el fin de explorar las causas que desencadenaron la revolución quiteña. Recrea con asombrosa exactitud la vida cotidiana de la época colonial, mediante el manejo sutil del idioma español de la época.

3991 Vásconez, Javier. El hombre de la mirada oblicua: cuentos. Quito: Ediciones Libri Mundi, 1989. 164 p. (Narrativa)

Destacado cuentista ecuatoriano presenta siete relatos bien estructurados que indagan lo más oscuro y sórdido del hombre urbano. Emplea un lenguaje narrativo poético a través del cual los personajes se pierden en la búsqueda de alguna verdad oculta a través de la locura, soledad, amor, miedo y violencia.

3992 Velasco Mackenzie, Jorge. El ladrón de levita. Quito: Planeta, 1989. 151 p. (Col. Narrativa ecuatoriana; 14)

Novela que recoge ambientes y personajes perfilados antes: lo marginal y el lumpen guayaquileño. Un delincuente agoniza al haberse desviado y tomado el camino del delito. El protagonista es un ser real y a la vez, simbólico mediante un lenguaje directo y alejado de lo directo.

3993 Viga, Diego. Mauricio Toledano en espejo cóncavo. Quito: Editorial El Conejo, 1987. 187 p. (Col. Ecuador/letras)

Novela más reciente del narrador ecuatoriano dividida en 22 capítulos a través de los cuales el pasado y el presente se fusionan y se confunden. El viejo Toledano presiente su muerte y aprovecha para reconstruir su pasado: infancia, adolescencia, actividad teatral y matrimonio con una actriz.

Peru

3994 Adolph, José B. Dora: novela. Lima: PEISA, 1989. 151 p. (Serie del río hablador)

Novela sobre Dora Mayer, personaje histórico que encabezó luchas sociales desde principios de siglo mediante la Asociación Pro-Indígena. Adolph, conocido cuentista, novelista, dramaturgo y periodista peruano, crea un diario ficticio que narra las preocupaciones intelectuales y sociales de Mayer y el choque de una relación amorosa con un joven compañero de lucha. Este diario ficticio es un vehículo narrativo fascinante que capta la esencia de un importante personaje histórico.

3995 Arguedas, José María. Relatos completos. Lima: Editorial Horizonte, 1987. 261 p. (Narrativa contemporanea; 10)

Reúne todos los cuentos escritos por Arguedas. Ordenados cronológicamente, representan la versión definitiva de cada uno, fijada por Sybila de Arguedas. La riqueza plástica de la narrativa arguediana se ve mejor en sus cuentos que en sus novelas: el bello colorido de los bailes, las canciones, los poemas y las leyendas, además del ardor de las luchas y rebeldías indígenas.

3996 Arguedas, José María. El zorro de arriba y el zorro de abajo. Coordinación de Eve-Marie Fell. Ed. crítica, 1. ed. Nanterre, France: ALLCA XXe, Univ. Paris X, Centre de recherches latino-américaines, 1990. 462 p.: bibl., ill. (Col. Archivos; 14)

Hermosa, extensa y completa, esta edición comentada de la novela póstuma de José

María Arguedas forma parte de la prestigiosa serie "Colección Archivos." Ofrece la versión definitiva e historia del texto y lecturas importantes por críticos internacionales como Rubén Bareiro Saguier, Roland Forgues, William Rowe y Martin Lienhard. Se reproduce la correspondencia de Arguedas relacionada con la novela. Texto imprescindible para los estudiosos de Arguedas.

3997 Borrero, Víctor. Nuevos cuentos tallanes. Piura, Perú: Centro de Investigación y Promoción del Campesinado, 1991. 62 p. (Serie Cuentos piuranos; 10)

Autor conocedor de los indígenas tallanes, los identifica aquí con el árbol, la tierra, la piedra y el viento. En otros relatos los localiza en nuestra civilización, pero siempre muestra su peculiar identidad.

3998 Bryce Echenique, Alfredo. "Dos Señoras Conversan;" "Un Sapo en el Desierto;" "Los Grandes Hombres son Así, y También Asá:" novelas breves. Esplugues de Llobregat, Barcelona: Plaza & Janés, 1990. 250 p. (Plaza & Janés/literaria; 21)

Sexta novela de Bryce Echenique consiste de tres novelas cortas. Las diversas tramas resultan en una clara unidad de intención. Relatos magistrales desde diversas ópticas, tanto temática como técnica, dan testimonio una vez más de la presencia de uno de los narradores más originales de la lengua castellana de hoy.

3999 Bryce Echenique, Alfredo. Permiso para vivir: antimemorias. Barcelona: Anagrama, 1993. 1 v.

Memorias de escritores, género popular hoy en día, sirven para recoger y reflexionar sobre las experiencias. Bryce Echenique aprovecha el espacio narrado para reírse de lo que podría hacerle llorar y entre dos angustias opta siempre por el humor y la paradoja. Lo lúdico y lo profundo se entreveran y el lector no puede dejar de leerla.

4000 Bryce Echenique, Alfredo. La última mudanza de Felipe Carrillo. Buenos Aires: Editorial Sudamericana, 1990. 215 p. (Col. Narrativas latinoamericanas)

En esta novela, el arquitecto Felipe Carrillo recorre diferentes lugares—París, Madrid, Roma y una playa peruana—arrastrado por los acontecimientos más que por su propia voluntad, en busca del último y más grande amor. La novela más breve del autor,

aquí la realidad impone sus duras condiciones de vida y el protagonista tiene que confrontar el último viaje: el que realiza al fondo de sí mismo para encontrar la dimensión total de su desarraigo y de su soledad. Publicado también por Plaza & Janés Editores (Buenos Aires, 1988).

4001 Castro Arrasco, Dante. Parte de combate. Lima?: Ediciones Manguaré, 1991. 98 p.: ill.

Joven narrador, cuya narrativa revela su fuerte compromiso con el cambio social, pertenece a la última promoción de escritores peruanos. Dos cuentos, "Nakay Pacha" y "Cuentero de Monte Adentro," obtuvieron premios. Ejemplos de una cuentística que se ambienta en la selva y región andina, donde la temática abarca la violencia de la zona andina o el folklore oriental. La sicología regional se contrapone al paisaje y material narrativo, tanto punzante como humorístico.

4002 Castro Pozo, Hildebrando. Sol, algarrobos y amor. Piura, Perú: Centro de Investigación y Promoción del Campesinado, 1991. 272 p.: ill. (Serie Novela regional; 1)

Novela escrita en 1940 y no publicada hasta ahora debido a prejuicios contra el texto por la crudeza del lenguaje. Capta la modalidad expresiva del criollo peruano del norte (Piura) mientras desarrolla una trama sobre la tenencia de la tierra hace cien años cuando luchaban políticos de diferentes bandos. Describe relaciones entre amo y peón, la desigualdad social, elementos folklóricos de las canciones, bailes y costumbres de la región y así crea una estampa vibrante de las resonancias y matices de otra época.

4003 El cuento peruano, 1920–1941. Selección, prólogo y notas de Ricardo González Vigil. Lima: PETROPERU, Ediciones Copé, 1990. 514 p.: bibl.

Antología del cuento peruano que propone sugerir enlaces y matices históricos amplios entre obras antiguas peruanas que forman el trasfondo de la época entre 1920–41. Largo y disperso prólogo abarca los "ismos" predominantes del período (i.e., regionalismo, indigenismo, realismo crítico, etc.) con el fin de subrayar la conciencia crítica de escritores que trataban temas sociales en sus obras.

4004 El cuento peruano, 1942–1958. Selección, prólogo y notas de Ricardo González Vigil. Lima: PETROPERU, Ediciones Copé, 1991. 593 p.: bibl.

Antología concebida para abordar la problemática de generaciones, sobre todo la de 1950 que impulsó la transición de una narrativa peruana que recogería no sólo temas de campo y provinciales sino los del ambiente urbano que formaron la nueva narrativa peruana de los 50. Sin embargo, continúa la presencia de la narrativa regional, de la costa a la selva amazónica.

4005 Cueto, Alonso. Los vestidos de una dama. Lima: PEISA, 1987. 160 p. (Serie del río hablador)

Protagonistas de cuentos, transcurridos en el Perú del joven autor, llevan su amor, soledad, frustación y venganza a la violencia. El elemento erótico y la esperanza, presente pese a todo, intensifican el interés.

4006 Freyre, Maynor. De cuello duro: cuentos. Lima: Editorial Arte y Comunicación, 1991. 88 p.

Cuentos realistas y naturalistas sobre la vida cotidiana de gente de barrios de clase media de Lima presentan sus privaciones, ilusiones y frustraciones. Escritor de tendencias variadas e ideas comprometidas capta con cierta nostalgia el sabor de estos barrios antiguos a la manera de Julio Ramón Ribeyro o José Antonio Bravo.

4007 García Calderón, Ventura. Obras escogidas. Prólogo, selección y notas de Luis Alberto Sánchez. Lima: Fundación del Banco Continental para el Fomento de la Educación y la Cultura; Ediciones Edubanco, 1986. 632 p.: bibl.

Volumen reúne lo mejor del autor con prólogo, selección y notas de Luis Alberto Sánchez. Incluyen crónicas, novelas, ensayos y apéndice epistolar. Obra valiosa para estudiar al autor.

4008 González Viaña, Eduardo. Sarita Colonia viene volando. Ilustraciones de Ana María La Rosa Sánchez Corcuera y Felipe Varela. 2. ed. Lima: Mosca Azul Editores, 1990. 293 p., 6 p. of plates: ill.

Obra mágica y fascinante trata tema de mucho interés e importancia en la religiosidad popular peruana: la reaparición de Sarita Colonia, santa popular que murió hace 50 años. Los marginales del Perú se valen de sueños, leyendas, fantasmas, amores, tristezas, vuelos y milagros para recrear su presencia en la extrema pobreza y miseria de su mundo. Los pobres forjan sus propias creencias para poder comunicarse con Dios. La prosa que recrea este mundo maravilloso es uno de los logros más notables de la lengua castellana contemporánea.

4009 Gutiérrez, Miguel. La violencia del tiempo. Lima: Milla Batres Editorial, 1991. 3 v.

Novela en tres volúmenes (1,000 p.) en la tradición del Bildungsroman. Crónica de una familia mestiza en la costa norte del Perú ofrece una visión contestaria de la sociedad, una reivindicación de un linaje humillado, según el protagonista, cuyo vasto repertorio de referencias históricas y literarias crea una enciclopedia de fuerzas antagónicas entre lo tradicional y moderno, lo autóctono y cosmopolitano. Su enfoque de la condición mestiza peruana pertenece a la tradición literaria de César Vallejo y José María Arguedas. Una de las novelas peruanas más complejas y deslumbrantes de las últimas décadas.

4010 La Torre, Iram. Las tesis de febrero. Lima: Arte/Reda, 1991. 96 p.

Entre muertes, hechizos y curaciones este médico escritor cuenta, desde su cátedra en la Univ. de San Marcos, las peripecias de sus vecinos limeños. De los cuatro, es este primer relato el que se adentran a una cruda realidad: "Todas nuestras angustias para encontrar y digerir alimentos terminan en actos orificiales: orinar, defecar, eyacular."

4011 Lauer, Mirko. Secretos inútiles: una novela. Lima: Hueso Húmero Ediciones, 1991. 129 p.

Novela paródica de poética realista que predomina en la narrativa peruana contemporánea. Dramatiza los vínculos entre ficción narrativa y discurso factual, de modo que el enfoque parece cuestionar el crear y contar historias. Ejercicio lúdico y crítico que subvierte la ilusión de un discurso que pretende recrear fielmente un referente reconocible. Como otros que se concentran en la metaficción, este relato subraya la problemática de toda representación.

4012 Maguiña Cueva, Teófilo. Taita Llupi: hizo llegar el agua y devolvió la fe a su comunidad. Lima: Editorial Impulso, 1990. 193 p.

Novela de capítulos breves, lectura rápida y placentera. Montañas, valles, ríos y paisajes peruanos desfilan a través de la colorida paleta de este escritor, casi pintor, que sirve de fondo para una historia sangrienta entre comunidades andinas, guerrilleros y fuerzas militares.

4013 Martínez, Gregorio. Crónica de músicos y diablos. Lima: Promoción Editorial Inca S.A., 1991. 264 p. (Serie del río hablador)

Como en todas sus obras, este eficaz narrador de historias orales trata de recrear y rescatar el mundo cultural (la música) de sectores afroperuanos de la costa sur del Perú. Obra contestataria que se estructura en base a relatos folklóricos en una graciosa y alegre épica de la tradición oral cuyo estilo se ensancha, hincha y engalana cautivando e hipnotizando al lector.

4014 Meneses, Carlos. Bobby estuvo aquí. Tlahuapan, Mexico: Premià, 1990. 160 p. (Red de Jonás: Literatura latinoamericana; 16)

Escritor peruano radicado en España desde hace más de 30 años penetra profundamente en la psicología del peruano común. Las múltiples historias vividas por el protagonista Bobby avivan el interés del lector e incluyen personajes tales como padre, amigo, hermana.

4015 Ortega, Julio. Diario imaginario. Medellín, Colombia: Univ. de Antioquia, 1988. 155 p. (Celeste; 9: Col. literaria)

Parecido a *Prosas apátridas* de Ribeyro, este texto se compone de lo que el autor llama "diarios de varia imaginación" (1973–83). Pequeños trozos de pensamientos sobre diversos temas: la literatura, el oficio de escribir, la amistad, el amor, su país natal. Aunque algunos invitan a pensar en lo que es escribir, otros son totalmente banales.

4016 Ribeyro, Julio Ramón. La palabra del mudo. t. 4, Cuentos 52/92. Lima: Milla Batres Editorial 1992. 1 v.

Vol. 4 reúne cuentos publicados en 1987 bajo el título *Solo para fumadores* y los inéditos *Relatos santacrucinos*. En forma de epílogo figura otro cuento "La Casa en la Playa" cuyo tema y extensión lo coloca fuera de las series mencionadas. Como siempre, son relatos extraordinarios que captan bien la agudeza ribeyriana.

4017 Ribeyro, Julio Ramón. Prosas apátridas: completas. 3ra. ed. Barcelona: Tusquets Editores, 1986. 180 p.

Compuesto de 200 brevísimas narraciones o textos (entre un párrafo y una página de extensión) que parecen ser una feliz combinación de apuntes sueltos, citas de diario íntimo o granitos de filosofía cotidiana que, en su conjunto, crean un perfil espiritual del autor mediante sus observaciones sencillas pero profundas sobre la vida, muerte, familia, hijos, vida doméstica, sexo. Concisión y pensamiento se combinan para crear una forma de narrar poco conocida en Latinoamérica.

4018 Ribeyro, Julio Ramón. La tentación del fracaso. v. 1, Diario personal, 1950–1960. Lima: J. Campodonico Editor, 1992. 1 v.: ill. (Col. del sol blanco)

Vol. 1 (de diez) del "diario" de Ribeyro cuando vivió en Lima y en Francia, España y Alemania. El diario, género poco común entre escritores de lengua española, es una colección de anotaciones breves hechas con cierta regularidad, cuya temática ribeyriana incluye el quehacer literario, el acto creativo, la crítica literaria, la soledad (del desterrado), los miedos al fracaso (del escritor) y dos amores (con una peruana que sabía del mundo y con una jovencita francesa que fue una ilusión). En total: pensamientos desgarradoras, revelaciones penetrantes, prosa perfecta. Una joya.

4019 Rumrrill, Róger. El venado sagrado: relatos de la Amazonia. Lima?: Centro de Estudios Regionales de Cultura Amazónica, 1992. 159 p. (Col. La Luciernaga)

Once relatos relacionados con la Amazonía que comprenden elementos poéticos, narrativos, periodísticos e, ineludiblemente, sociológicos, políticos, económicos, ecológicos, y geopolíticos. Prueba de la renovación de la literatura de y sobre la Amazonía a partir de los 60.

4020 Sánchez León, Abelardo. Por la puerta falsa. Lima: Ediciones Noviembre Trece, 1991. 290 p.

Primera novela de poeta y sociólogo peruano. Obra tanto lírica como analítica, o sea, intimista y objetiva. Dos jóvenes limeños de diferentes clases sociales se entrecruzan y a pesar de sus diferencias, lamentan sus vidas y el desarraigo. En fin, texto moderno convencional: tragicómico, irónico, personajes urbanos marginalizados, lenguaje de violencia.

4021 Siu, Kam Wen. La primera espada del imperio. Lima: Instituto Nacional de Cultura, 1988. 97 p. (Col. Piedra de toque)

Ocho relatos que recrean la vida diaria de intrigas, guerras, combates y cotidianos actos simbólicos de las legendarias dinastías chinas. Aunque alegóricos, comunican significados profundos sobre la era moderna. Otros cuentos se sitúan dentro de marcos históricos y contemporáneos (el mundo de las sirvientas, prostitutas, suicidio).

4022 Thorndike, Guillermo. La revolución imposible. Lima: EMI, 1988. 556 p.

Otra vez el autor se vale de la ficción periodística para relatar un posible hecho histórico peruano que gira en torno al joven Presidente Alan García y al viejo partido socialista APRA. La trama se intensifica mediante la presencia de diferentes voces: gobernantes, opositores, terroristas, generales, insurrectos, pacifistas, asesinos encapuchados y nuevas masas conscientes de la necesidad de cambio. Como siempre, la obra de Thorndike no carece de interés, acción, dinamismos, personajes interesantes y significados importantes para el Perú.

4023 Thorndike, Guillermo. Los topos: la fuga del MRTA de la prisión de Canto Grande. Lima: Mosca Azul Editores, 1991. 173 p.

Conocido autor de obras documentales o novelas de no-ficción que comprenden desde el asesinato de un magnate, la derrota peruana ante Chile hasta el fusilamiento de 5.000 apristas en Trujillo. Esta recrea la historia verídica de la excavación de un túnel por el que escaparon de una prisión en 1990 el líder y seguidores del Movimiento Revolucionario Túpac Amaru. La fuga subterránea es un tema universal y aquí adquiere la misma intensidad y drama gracias a la fuerte identificación del autor con el grupo revolucionario.

4024 Tord, Luis Enrique. Espejo de constelaciones. Ilustraciones de Susana Rosselló. Lima: Australis, 1991. 208 p.: ill. (Col. Terra incógnita)

Doce relatos acompañados de ilustraciones de Susana Rosselló que recrean el llamado "Encuentro de Dos Mundos," en los siglos XVI y XVII. Se comunica una problemática que va más allá del choque físico, abarcando aspectos del encuentro entre creencias y espiritualidades en lucha irreductible en un medio inhóspito que empequeñece la más colosal obra humana.

4025 Urteaga Cabrera, Luis. El universo sagrado: versión literaria de mitos y leyendas de la tradición oral shipibo-coniba. Lima: PEISA, 1991. 169 p.: map.

Hermoso texto que rescata mitos y leyendas orales de los Shipibo-Conibo, grupo aborigen de la baja selva peruana. Su resistencia al largo proceso de dominación europea ha fortalecido la preservación de su vasto universo mítico y cosmovisión mediante el idioma, artes, música, costumbres y, sobre todo, la literatura oral. Magnífica labor del autor que transcribe y elabora estéticamente la memoria colectiva de esta comunidad en vías de extinguirse.

4026 Valdelomar, Abraham. Obras. v. 1–2. Edición y prólogo de Luis Alberto Sánchez. Reordenamiento de textos de Ismael Pinto Vargas. Lima: Fundación del Banco Continental para el Fomento de la Educación y la Cultura, 1988. 2 v.: bibl., ill., port.

Vols. 1–2 contienen la obra completa del escritor peruano (1888–1919), que incluye poesía, dibujo, prosa (novela y cuento), teatro, biografías, ensayos, artículos, cartas y bibliografía de sus publicaciones en diarios y revistas de Lima, de las provincias y extranjeras. Prólogo recuenta, como lo haría un viejo amigo, las andanzas y publicaciones del autor.

4027 Vargas Llosa, Mario. Carta de batalla por *Tirant lo Blanc*. Barcelona: Seix Barral, 1991. 106 p.: bibl. (Biblioteca breve)

Libro breve reúne por primera vez tres ensayos de Vargas Llosa escritos a través de 20 años y dedicados a la novela de caballerías *Tirant lo Blanc*. Para el autor, sus ensayos "son hitos de una ininterrumpida, apasionada y apasionante relación" con esta novela. Deslumbrado por la contribución de esta novela al desarrollo de la narrativa de Occidente, Vargas Llosa no sólo descubre y analiza los elementos tanto temáticos como narrativos que se destacan en la misma sino que los sitúa dentro del panorama universal de la novela contemporánea.

4028 Vargas Llosa, Mario. La guerra del fin del mundo. Estudio introductorio y bibliografía de José Miguel Oviedo. Cronología de María del Carmen Ghezzi y José Miguel Oviedo. Caracas: Biblioteca Ayacucho, 1991. 518 p.: bibl. (Biblioteca Ayacucho ; 159)

Hermosa edición de una de las novelas más importantes del autor realizada por la prestigiosa serie "Biblioteca Ayacucho." Además de la versión definitiva, el volumen incluye un estudio introductorio de José Miguel Oviedo, "Vargas Llosa en Canudos: Versión Clásica de un Clásico," y una cronología y bibliografía.

4029 Vargas Llosa, Mario. El hablador. Barcelona: Seix Barral, 1987. 237 p. (Biblioteca breve)

Brillante obra narrativa que, a través de dos historias que se alternan, abarca, por un lado, la del mismo Vargas Llosa evocando los recuerdos de un compañero de juventud interesado en culturas primitivas y, por otro, la de un ser anónimo que cuenta historias sacadas de la memoria colectiva de los indios machiguengas de la Amazonía peruana, personajes que se funden en la magia, los mitos y una visión histórica y poética de lo antiguo. Dada la amenaza que sienten los grupos de la selva amazónica ante la presencia exógena de la civilización occidental, la novela cuestiona las opciones de preservación versus integración. La traducción inglesa se reseñó en *HLAS 52:5012*.

4030 Vargas Llosa, Mario. El pez en el agua. Barcelona: Seix Barral, 1993. 1 v.

Vol. 1 de sus eventuales memorias completas abarca desde la niñez hasta poco después de la derrote en las elecciones presidenciales del Perú en 1991. Se estructura el texto mediante una doble vertiente narrativa, una relacionada con el proceso de maduración como escritor (desde sus primeros intentos artísticos en el colegio hasta la publicación de *La tía Julia y el escribidor* en 1978), y la otra relacionada con su incursión en la política a fines de los años 80. Capítulos alternados entre los temas estimulan una lectura intrigante e interesante. Lo que se deja ver es como el compromiso literario al principio cede poco a poco a una posición de compromiso político con la desastrosa realidad peruana de los últimos 20 años.

Venezuela

4031 El cuento venezolano: antología. Edición de José Balza. 2. ed. Caracas: Dirección de Cultura, Univ. Central de Venezuela, 1990. 520 p.: bibl. (Col. Letras de Venezuela; 83: Serie Narrativa)

As writer, scholar, and theorist, Balza is one of the most informed literary figures in Venezuela today. This anthology spans the entire century, beginning with Pedro Emilio Coll, Luis Manuel Urbaneja Achelpohl, and Rufino Blanco Fombona, and ending with Napoleón Oropeza, Luis Barrera Linares, and Benito Yradi. He rescues the oft-forgotten Venezuelan pioneer of the modern—Julio Garmendia—and includes Venezuela's major modern writers who followed, such as Guillermo Meneses, Salvador Garmendia, and Adriano González León. Selections from a younger generation, such as stories by Carlos Noguera and Ednodio Quintero, are particularly interesting. In his prologue, Balza explains his intentions in organizing such an anthology: to afford readers the opportunity to read forgotten texts in juxtaposition with canonical ones; to observe how imagination alters reality. The implicit agenda of this anthology is Borgesian, allowing the Venezuelan writer his or her full right of invention. Very useful, well-presented, and well-conceived anthology.

4032 Garmendia, Salvador. Crónicas sádicas. Ilustraciones de Pedro León Zapata. Caracas: Fuentes/Pomaire, 1990. 161 p.: ill.

Garmendia is best known as one of Venezuela's major and most serious novelists, but this entertaining volume is neither a novel nor sober in tone. It consists of 29 hilarious *crónicas* generally two to five pages in length. He writes in praise of vulgar language ("Elogio de la Mala Palabra"), in praise of breaking wind ("Elogio del Pedo"), in praise of masturbation ("Elogio de la Paja"), and in praise of condoms ("Elogio del Condón"). He also writes nostalgically about an old prostitute and adolescent sex. A master of language and a student of words, Garmendia creates humor primarily with his juxtaposition of the academic and colloquial language, or of the refined and the vulgar. This is not one of Garmendia's canonical works, but it is one of his most irreverent and funniest.

4033 Relatos venezolanos del siglo XX. Selección, prólogo y bibliografía de Gabriel Jiménez Emán. Caracas: Biblioteca Ayacucho, 1989. 487 p.: bibl.

This massive and complete volume contains stories by 71 major Venezuelan short story writers of the 20th century. They appear in chronological order, beginning with Tulio Febres Cordero, Manuel Díaz Rodríguez, Pedro Emilio Coll, Luis Manuel Urbaneja Achelpohl, and Rufino Blanco Fombona. Modern authors such as Salvador Garmendia, Denzil Romero, Luis Britto García, José Balza, and others are included, as well as young writers. Gabriel Jiménez Emán offers a fine introductory essay on the Venezuelan short story of the century, and each story is preceded by a short introduction.

4034 Rossi, Alejandro. El cielo de Sotero. Barcelona: Anagrama, 1987. 99 p. (Narrativas hispánicas; 42)

Rossi is a special case among Venezuelan writers: a philosopher by training who has been living in Mexico for several years. In addition to philosophical essays, he has pub-

lished two volumes of fiction. *El cielo de Sotero* consists of eight short pieces written in the self-conscious and philosophical tone of much of the fiction of Borges. The style is delicate and frequently carries ironical overtones. Rossi is a superb writer of metafiction.

4035 Trejo, Oswaldo. Metástasis del verbo. Caracas: Fundarte, 1990. 149 p. (Col. Delta; 23)

Trejo has been publishing experimental fiction since the early 1950s and has authored six books. This is one of the most radically experimental works to be published in Venezuela, with experiments in sentence structure, punctuation, spelling, and typography. No plot is apparent; author is more interested in experimenting with images and sounds. Trejo certainly confirms his role as the foremost experimental writer in the Andean region.

Chile

JOSE PROMIS, *Professor of Latin American Literature and Literary Criticism, University of Arizona*

LA PRODUCCION NARRATIVA chilena se ha incrementado considerablemente a partir de 1989. A los títulos de autores ya conocidos que se incluyen en los catálogos de grandes editoriales nacionales o internacionales, se agrega un número considerable de novelas cuyos gastos de publicación corren por cuenta de sus propios autores, quienes, o bien las publican directamente, o bajo el sello de pequeñas editoriales que han comenzado a funcionar durante los últimos años. Si bien es cierto que esta situación ha favorecido el aumento cuantitativo de obras publicadas, la calidad artística no ha acompañado necesariamente al mismo fenómeno. Se trata, en la mayoría de los casos, de narraciones de corta extensión que responden a dominantes propósitos documentales o que pretenden satisfacer expectativas preestablecidas por el público. Su nivel estético es, en consecuencia, menguado. A la ausencia de altura literaria de muchas novelas chilenas publicadas en estos años han aludido con preocupación narradores chilenos de reconocido prestigio, y también algunos estudiosos del género: Goić, en el prólogo a *La novela chilena* (item **4069**), y Saldes, en "Narrativa Chilena, 1966–1991" (item **4075**) y "Literatura Joven en Chile" (item **4074**).

Dentro de este panorama destaca, sin embargo, un número considerable de relatos de sobresaliente factura narrativa. Algunos de ellos pertenecen a escritores de calidad ya establecida; otros anuncian la aparición sorprendente de escritores que ofrecen grandes posibilidades futuras. Al primer grupo pertenecen novelas como *La rebelión de los placeres* de Fernando Alegría (item **4037**), *Camisa limpia* de Guillermo Blanco (item **4042**), *Hoy está solo mi corazón* de Enrique Lafourcade (item **4052**), o

El plan infinito o *Cuentos de Eva Luna* de Isabel Allende (items **4039** and **4038**). En el segundo grupo destacan las novelas *El paraíso* de Elena Castedo (item **4043**) y *Un viejo que leía historias de amor* de Luis Sepúlveda (item **4058**), escritor desconocido en Chile hasta la llegada de su libro al país a comienzos de 1993. La adjudicación del Premio Nacional de Literatura 1990 a José Donoso ha constituído el acontecimiento más sobresaliente de estos años. Después de publicar su última novela de larga extensión, *La desesperanza* (ver *HLAS 50:3401*), Donoso ha entregado al público sólo dos relatos de corta extensión que confirman una vez más la calidad excepcional de su prosa: *Taratuta* y *Naturaleza muerta con cachimba* (item **4045**).

En general, la novela chilena de estos últimos años mantiene las motivaciones analíticas y desacralizadoras que la caracterizan desde mediados de la década de 1980 (ver *HLAS 52*, p. 536–537). A la luz de tales propósitos, pueden distinguirse cuatro orientaciones principales de las preferencias de los narradores chilenos. Tales preferencias, sin duda alguna, están determinadas por las especiales condiciones históricas que atraviesa la producción del género en un país donde se vive un proceso de transición entre dos sistemas políticos diametralmente diferentes.

El propósito de testimoniar sobre el período del régimen militar es una preferencia que se descubre en la generalidad de las novelas consideradas en este volumen, ya se trate de un propósito dominante, subordinado u oblicuo al desarrollo argumental. Dicho interés se manifiesta a través de distintas posibilidades de representación. Para citar sólo unos ejemplos, en algunos casos se pretende mostrar una visión interiorizada de los conflictos sociales o políticos, como en *El general azul* (item **4062**), donde el interés narrativo se concentra en la figura misma del dictador; en *Santiago cero* (item **4048**) se desarrolla la denuncia utilizando el motivo de la culpa; y en los cuentos de Ariel Dorfman (item **4046**) el testimonio surge con frecuencia al observar desde el exterior una condición social o humana específica.

El interés hacia una nueva forma de novela histórica corresponde a una tendencia general dentro de la novela hispanoamericana actual. Entre las novelas de asunto histórico destacan *La rebelión de los placeres* (item **4037**) y *Allende: mi vecino el presidente* (item **4036**), que confirman el interés permanente de la narrativa de Fernando Alegría por los personajes mártires o marginados de la historia; *1891: entre el fulgor y la agonía* (item **4040**) y *Maldita yo entre las mujeres* (item **4063**), relatos que tienen como referente la figura de individuos rebeldes a los cánones impuestos por la sociedad de su época. En este aspecto destaca la excelente novela *Camisa limpia* (item **4042**), cuyo asunto aparentemente remoto responde a una intención artística de iluminar situaciones de palpitante actualidad.

Un volumen considerable es ofrecido por la novela de tendencia feminista. Desde 1988 han sido publicados numerosos relatos adscritos a esta actitud narrativa. En la mayoría de ellos se destaca una función denunciativa sobresaliente, lo cual conduce a veces a un notorio menoscabo de su dimensión artística. Notable en muchos casos como, por ejemplo, en *Cuerpos prohibidos* (item **4056**) o en *Siete días de la señora K* (item **4057**) es la violencia lingüística utilizada por las narradoras para desacralizar las formas características del lenguaje narrativo masculino. Uno de los textos más interesantes en este aspecto es *El tono menor del deseo* (item **4041**), relato que produce una sorprendente conjunción con la tendencia denunciativa de carácter político.

Finalmente, puede observarse también un interés significativo hacia la novela de formación, orientada específicamente a representar los conflictos de la adolescencia en medio de una sociedad de carácter autoritario. Esta temática adquirió prestigio en la novela hispanoamericana de comienzos de los años 70, pero por razones obvias no pudo desarrollarse contemporáneamente en Chile. Surge, pues, con cierto retraso en relación con el panorama continental, pero adquiere connotaciones particulares debido a la especial situación política chilena que constituye su ambientación histórica. Ejemplos destacados de esta tendencia son, sin lugar a dudas, *Mala Onda* (item **4049**) y *Rockeros celestes* (item **4055**).

En el terreno de la crítica literaria, la obra de José Donoso, María Luisa Bombal, Antonio Skármeta e Isabel Allende continúan acaparando el interés de los estudiosos. Sin embargo, hemos consignado solamente los textos más importantes que ofrecen interpretaciones o análisis totalizadores de la situación actual del género en Chile, o de determinados momentos de su desarrollo durante el siglo XX. El libro de Walter Fuentes (item **4066**) fija las modalidades de una importante preferencia narrativa que desde los años 20 acompaña a la novela chilena; el estudio de Kenneth Fleak (item **4065**) y, sobre todo, el de Eduardo Godoy Gallardo (item **4067**), son contribuciones definitivas al estudio de la novela de mediados del siglo. El prólogo a la quinta edición de *La novela chilena* de Cedomil Goić (item **4069**) constituye un documento que ningún interesado en el tema debiera desconocer; y *La novela chilena del último siglo* (item **4073**) trata de interpretar en forma global el sentido que adquiere el género a partir de los años 30. *Conversaciones con la narrativa chilena* (item **4071**) da a conocer una visión novedosa del pensamiento poético de un grupo de destacados narradores nacionales. Finalmente, los cuatro artículos seleccionados ofrecen un interés común para fijar las notas características asumidas por el género durante el último cuarto de siglo.

PROSE FICTION

4036 Alegría, Fernando. Allende: mi vecino el presidente. Santiago: Planeta, 1989. 299 p.: bibl. (Biblioteca del sur)

Relato en que se combina la ficción, los recuerdos personales y los acontecimientos históricos para construir una imagen personal de Salvador Allende, y de los factores sociales y humanos que formaron su vocación de dirigente político. Interpretación indispensable para conocer una visión artística de la época, las circunstancias y la interioridad del fallecido presidente chileno.

4037 Alegría, Fernando. La rebelión de los placeres. Santiago: Editorial Andrés Bello, 1990. 171 p. (Club de lectores Andrés Bello; 140)

Narrador cronista se ubica en el espacio intermedio entre la ficción y la historia para relatar un episodio de las experiencias que un grupo de chilenos vive durante la época de la fiebre del oro en California.

4038 Allende, Isabel. Cuentos de Eva Luna. Barcelona, Spain: Plaza & Janés, 1990. 246 p. (Plaza & Janés/literaria; 1)

Conjunto de cuentos narrados por la protagonista de la novela homónima. Todos presentan situaciones características de la narrativa anterior de su autora. Sobresalen las que metaforizan una reflexión sobre el poder de las palabras para crear o modificar la realidad humana.

4039 Allende, Isabel. El plan infinito. Buenos Aires: Editorial Sudamericana, 1991. 359 p.

La desbordante imaginación que ha caracterizado los relatos anteriores de la autora se utiliza al servicio de mostrar la presencia de los conflictos étnicos y sociales vividos en EE.UU. durante las últimas décadas. El estilo narrativo de esta novela desconcierta al comenzar la lectura, pero termina encerrando al lector en el torbellino de los acontecimientos.

4040 Araya, Juan Gabriel. 1891, entre el fulgor y la agonía. Santiago: Editorial Universitaria, 1990. 213 p. (Col. Generación espontánea)

Primer Premio Concurso Nacional de Novela "Cámara Chilena del Libro 1989." Novela histórica que reactualiza imaginariamente el ambiente y las circunstancias de la revolución de 1891.

4041 Barros, Pía. El tono menor del deseo. Santiago: Editorial Cuarto Propio, 1991. 142 p. (Serie Narrativa)

Relato que ejemplifica una tendencia importante en la narrativa chilena actual. La narradora desacraliza el concepto de escritura como representación, al mismo tiempo que muestra la imagen de tres mujeres encerradas dentro de las normas asfixiantes impuestas por el mundo masculino. Situación de opresión sexual y política confluyen en el desenlace, creando una sola realidad de horror y tortura.

4042 Blanco, Guillermo. Camisa limpia. Santiago: Pehuén, 1989. 243 p. (Nueva narrativa)

Relato de extraordinaria calidad artística que convierte la figura histórica del médico portugués Francisco Maldonado de Silva (1592–1639), ajusticiado por la Inquisición en Lima como enemigo de la fe católica, en símbolo de la indestructible vocación libertaria del ser humano, imposible de ser subyugada aun bajo los regímenes de mayor dogmatismo y opresión.

4043 Castedo, Elena. El paraíso. 5a. ed. Buenos Aires: Grupo Editorial Zeta, 1991. 382 p.

Versión española de la novela finalista para el Premio Nacional en EE.UU. Un mundo enigmático y caricaturesco es presentado a través de la percepción ingenua de un testigo infantil. La novela destaca como sobresaliente expresión artística del manejo del punto de vista y de la perspectiva narrativa.

4044 Contreras, Gonzalo. La ciudad anterior. Santiago: Planeta, 1991. 185 p. (Biblioteca del sur)

El narrador utiliza un lenguaje de excelente construcción artística para desplegar una imagen de la realidad que pareciera sostenerse sobre un enigmático nivel previo de existencia. El tiempo lento del relato contribuye decisivamente para crear una atmósfera extraña y llena de sugerencias.

4045 Donoso, José. Taratuta; Naturaleza muerta con cachimba. Santiago: Mondadori, 1990. 159 p.

Dos relatos breves de extraordinaria factura narrativa en torno a un tema común: el poder de la expresión artística para transformar las verdades aceptadas como tales. En el primero, la experiencia histórica y la experiencia de la imaginación constituyen una sola dimensión de realidad; en el segundo, la presencia del arte otorga sentido a una vida individual hasta entonces oscura y anodina.

4046 Dorfman, Ariel. Cuentos casi completos. Buenos Aires: Ediciones Letra Buena, 1991. 279 p. (Col. Letras/cuento)

Relatos organizados en torno a dos ejes temáticos que dan nombre a las dos partes del volumen y que remiten a los dos espacios que la obra narrativa del autor ha tratado siempre de iluminar: el de la dictadura chilena y el de los exiliados políticos, en este caso, en los EE.UU.

4047 Eltit, Diamela. Vaca sagrada. Buenos Aires: Planeta, 1991. 188 p. (Biblioteca del sur: Novela)

Relato que confirma los modos narrativos y asuntos más característicos de la obra anterior de la autora. Una narración fragmentaria, compuesta casi de instantáneas, reproduce un mundo de obsesiones, principios de posesión y destrucción, construído sobre la imagen del cuerpo femenino que configura el discurso.

4048 Franz, Carlos. Santiago cero. Santiago: Nuevo Extremo, 1989. 147 p.

Historia de una traición cuyos elementos específicos quedan siempre en la penumbra y en la incertidumbre, relatada por el personaje que la comete cuando se halla encarcelado debido a su papel de delator profesional durante la época de la dictadura chilena.

4049 Fuguet, Alberto. Mala onda. Buenos Aires: Planeta, 1991. 295 p. (Biblioteca del sur: Novela)

Novela representativa de una tendencia dominante en el género durante los últimos años: la novela de formación adolescente. El narrador, alumno de una escuela aristocrática de Santiago, actualiza las tensiones de su vida bajo el régimen dictatorial chileno, con un lenguaje que refleja la violencia y la desorientación del momento. La novela consigue su objetivo de destacar la decadencia de valores que su narrador percibe en la sociedad de los años 80.

4050 Fuguet, Alberto et al. Santiago, pena capital: narraciones. Presentación de Marco Antonio de la Parra. Edición de Anto-

nio Skármeta. Santiago: Documentas, 1991.
158 p.

Interesante y útil selección de cuentos que permite conocer a algunos de los narradores jóvenes que han comenzado recientemente a escribir en Chile.

4051 Jodorowsky, Alexandro. El loro de siete lenguas. Santiago: Hachette, 1991. 341 p.: ill. (Col. Arte y literatura)

Relato que destaca por la exhuberancia imaginativa puesta al servicio de desplegar una multitudinaria imagen simbólica de la realidad actual. La denuncia de las relaciones de opresión constituye el propósito más profundo del narrador.

4052 Lafourcade, Enrique. Hoy está solo mi corazón. Santiago: Zig-Zag, 1990. 156 p. (Col. Novelas de hoy)

Novela que reitera la atracción del autor por describir espacios poblados por seres socialmente marginados, espacios donde la miseria no logra hacer desaparecer las ilusiones y las esperanzas. Esta novela confirma a su autor como el novelista más productivo de Chile y a la vez, como uno de los mejores fabuladores de la novela chilena actual.

4053 Marchant, Reinaldo Edmundo. El abuelo. Santiago: Editorial Andrés Bello, 1989. 87 p.

El autor continúa configurando el mundo fantasmagórico de sus primeros relatos, esta vez mediante la evocación de la enigmática figura de un abuelo. El relato se destaca además por la inusual riqueza del lenguaje narrativo.

4054 Muñoz Valenzuela, Diego. Todo el amor en sus ojos. Chile: Editorial Mosquito Comunicaciones, 1990. 249 p. (Col. Narrativa)

Relato finalista en el concurso Casa de las Américas. Desde dos perspectivas temporales, un narrador observa los acontecimientos previos y posteriores al golpe militar de 1973.

4055 Oses, Darío. Rockeros celestes. Santiago: Editorial Andrés Bello, 1992. 114 p.

Relato representativo del interés hacia los asuntos de formación y adolescencia que caracteriza gran parte de la novela chilena actual.

4056 Parra, Marco Antonio de la. Cuerpos prohibidos. Santiago: Planeta, 1991. 169 p. (Biblioteca del sur)

Interpretación de la realidad delincuencial de Santiago que utiliza el mito de Edipo como referente extratextual. Un lenguaje de notable violencia sexual establece una ruptura con los cánones discursivos de la novela chilena tradicional. El relato ejemplifica muy bien el carácter antidogmático y deconstructivo de gran parte de la novela chilena actual.

4057 Río, Ana María del. Siete días de la señora K. Santiago: Planeta, 1993. 151 p. (Biblioteca del sur)

Historia de la liberación de una mujer que ha vivido aplastada bajo el peso de su medio familiar. Una circunstancia favorable le permite escapar y, a través de la experiencia sexual, redescubrirse a sí misma al romper con las barreras que la habían mantenido asfixiada.

4058 Sepúlveda, Luis. Un viejo que leía novelas de amor. Barcelona: Tusquets Editores, 1993. 137 p. (Col. Andanzas; 180)

Novela sorprendente dentro de la producción narrativa de los últimos años. Su narrador maneja un lenguaje de extraordinaria calidad artística que unido a una similar capacidad de fabulación, hacen de este texto uno de los valiosos publicados en 1993. El lector se enfrenta a una singular recreación de la naturaleza americana vista como espacio de conflicto entre las fuerzas de la sabiduría natural y de la destrucción progresiva de la civilización. Como advierte su autor, la novela pretende revelar la magia de la cotidianeidad en América.

4059 Serrano, Marcela. Nosotras que nos queremos tanto. Santiago: Editorial Los Andes, 1991. 257 p. (Serie La Otra narrativa)

Las experiencias de cuatro mujeres son presentadas por una voz femenina que indaga las razones que marcan la existencia de la mujer en el mundo contemporáneo.

4060 Skármeta, Antonio. La insurrección. Santiago: Planeta, 1989. 230 p. (Biblioteca del sur)

Primera edición chilena de una de las mejores novelas escritas por el autor en su época del exilio.

4061 Skármeta, Antonio. Match ball. Buenos Aires: Editorial Sudamericana, 1989. 203 p. (Col. Narrativas latinoamericanas)

El tema de la novela—1os desenfrenados sentimientos que una tenista adolescente despierta en un hombre maduro—inscribe a este relato en una tradición representada por Somerset Maugham, Nabokov y otros. Los intereses narrativos del autor, sin embargo, proyectan este asunto galante a dimensiones más totalizadoras de significado.

4062 Subercaseaux, Elizabeth. El general azul. Buenos Aires: Ediciones B, Grupo Zeta, 1991. 228 p. (Tiempos modernos)

Reinterpretación del tipo literario del dictador latinoamericano que se obtiene al contemplar a esta figura desde el interior de su vida privada. Novela representativa de las tendencias de denuncia que comienzan a aparecer en el género desde fines de la década de los años 80.

4063 Valdivieso, Mercedes. Maldita yo entre las mujeres. Santiago: Planeta, 1991. 143 p. (Biblioteca del Sur)

Relato que focaliza la figura de Catalina de los Ríos y Lisperguer, conocida como La Quintrala, en plena época colonial.

4064 Villegas Morales, Juan. Las seductoras de Orange County. Madrid: Libertarias, 1989. 234 p. (Narrativa; 3)

Gracias a un adecuado empleo de técnicas narrativas actuales, la novela presenta un aspecto de la vida de un grupo de exiliados políticos chilenos en California, y la alteración que sufren sus comportamientos al descubrir la presencia de un perseguidor infiltrado en el grupo, todo esto a través de las peripecias de un equipo de fútbol formado por latinoamericanos.

LITERARY CRITICISM AND HISTORY

4065 Fleak, Kenneth. The Chilean short story: writers from the generation of 1950. New York: P. Lang, 1989. 251 p.: bibl., index. (American Univ. studies. Series XXII, Latin American studies; 4)

Interesante y bien documentado ensayo de interpretación del cuento chileno de la llamada Generación de 1950. Aporta útiles referencias bibliográficas.

4066 Fuentes, Walter. La novela social en Chile, 1900–1925: ideología y disyuntiva histórica. Minneapolis, MN: Institute for the Study of Ideologies and Literature, 1990. 172 p.: bibl., index. (Series towards a social history of Hispanic and Luso-Brazilian literatures)

Detallado análisis de cuatro novelas chilenas: *Casa Grande* de Augusto Orrego Luco, *El Crisol* y *Robles, Blume y Cía* de Fernando Santiván y *El roto* de Joaquín Edwards Bello, interpretándolas como ejemplos tipificadores de la tendencia reformista social de los primeros decenios del siglo XX.

4067 Godoy, Eduardo; Haydée Ahumada Peña; and Carlos Díaz Amigo. La generación del 50 en Chile: historia de un movimiento literario; narrativa. Chile: Editorial la Noria, 1991. 389 p.: bibl.

Importante resultado de una exhaustiva investigación sobre la Generación de 1950 que recoge, además, los principales artículos críticos que se publicaron a propósito de la aparición de las novelas más representativas de este grupo. Indispensable para el estudio del tema.

4068 Goić, Cedomil. Los mitos degradados: ensayos de comprensión de la literatura hispanoamericana. Amsterdam; Atlanta, Ga.: Rodopi, 1992. 368 p. (Col. Teoría Literaria: Texto y Teoría; 8)

Recoge los artículos publicados por el autor desde 1957, entre ellos todos los dedicados al estudio de la narrativa y las generaciones chilenas.

4069 Goić, Cedomil. La novela chilena: los mitos degradados. 5. ed. Santiago: Editorial Universitaria, 1991. 245 p.:bibl. 19 cm. (Col. El Saber y la cultura)

Nueva edición de este libro clásico sobre el género en Chile que trae un prólogo donde el autor califica severamente el estancamiento narrativo que a su juicio se ha producido durante los últimos años, y señala el rumbo que los nuevos narradores deberían conceder a sus relatos.

4070 Jofré, Manuel Alcides. Novela chilena contemporánea: un fragmento de su historia. (*Logos/Serena*, 1:2, 1989, p. 23–41)

Análisis de 17 novelas publicadas dentro o fuera de Chile, con el propósito de establecer las direcciones temáticas y formales más características asumidas por el género entre 1974–89. Incorpora además una útil lista de novelas.

4071 Piña, Juan Andrés. Conversaciones con la narrativa chilena: Fernando Alegría, José Donoso, Guillermo Blanco, Jorge Edwards, Antonio Skármeta, Isabel Allende,

Diamela Eltit. Santiago: Editorial Los Andes, 1991. 254 p.: bibl., ports. (Serie Diálogos)

Entrevistas que ofrecen interesante información sobre aspectos biográficos de los entrevistados, las circunstancias históricas que rodean su producción, ambiente cultural y preferencias estéticas.

4072 Promis, José. Balance de la novela en Chile, 1973–1990. (*Hispamérica*/*Gaithersburg*, 19:55, 1990, p. 15–26)

Estudio de los diferentes modos de representación utilizados en la novela escrita en Chile para referirse a la situación política bajo el régimen militar.

4073 Promis, José. La novela chilena del último siglo. Santiago: Editorial La Noria, 1993. 273 p.: bibl.

Análisis e interpretación de los diferentes programas narrativos desarrollados por el género en Chile a partir del agotamiento de la sensibilidad positivista.

4074 Saldes B., Sergio. Literatura joven en Chile: ¿generación de 1987? (*Lit. Lingüíst.*, 3, 1990, p. 71–91)

Análisis que propone algunas notas características de la producción de escritores y narradores chilenos más recientes.

4075 Saldes B., Sergio. Narrativa chilena, 1966–1991: en busca de continuidad e integración. (*Aisthesis/Santiago*, 24, 1991, p. 67–78)

Esfuerzo de interpretar el sentido global de la novela chilena durante los últimos 25 años, con énfasis en la producción de las generaciones que el autor denomina de 1972 y 1987.

River Plate Countries

MARIA LUISA BASTOS, *Professor of Spanish, Lehman College and the Graduate School, City University of New York*
MAGDALENA GARCIA PINTO, *Associate Professor of Spanish and Director of Women's Studies, University of Missouri*
MARIA CRISTINA GUIÑAZU, *Assistant Professor of Spanish, Lehman College, City University of New York*
SAUL SOSNOWSKI, *Professor and Chairman of the Department of Spanish and Portuguese, University of Maryland, College Park*

I. NARRATIVA ARGENTINA

LA PRODUCCION DE FINES de la década de 1980 y principios de la de 1990 incluye desde relatos equiparables con noticias locales de televisión por lo superficiales o insignificantes, hasta narraciones excelentes.

Vale la pena reconocer, sin embargo, que los textos carentes de interés anecdótico, sin traza de un mínimo de artificio relacionado con la literatura, por el hecho mismo de ser muestras de trivialidad en estado puro, tienen, desde el punto de vista lingüístico, una dimensión documental no desdeñable en una lengua tan difundida como el castellano. En efecto, reproducen aspectos del habla de las clases no ilustradas de la Argentina en los años recientes (e.g., items **4082** y **4153**), posiblemente transitorios muchos de ellos, otros destinados a incorporarse a la lengua general. Erratas y errores de ortografía pululan tanto en este grupo como en el que paso a considerar, que incluye algunos relatos excelentes de facturas, tonos y temas diversos.

No falta lo que podríamos llamar "buen color local," es decir textos cuya comprensión, aunque no está restringida al conocimiento del referente, depende en buena medida de la posibilidad de identificar tiempo y lugar (items **4116** y **4092**). Como no se han apagado los ecos de la dictadura militar, de la pesadilla de los desaparecidos o de la aventura demencial de las Malvinas (item **4129**), en muchos casos ese referente es la poco feliz experiencia política todavía viva en muchas memorias. Algunas novelas históricas que se remontan a épocas más lejanas, se limitan a la reconstrucción del pasado (item **4077**). En otras, en que hay claras alusiones a la actualidad, la comparación implícita entre épocas diferentes pone en evidencia la falacia del mito de la superioridad de lo remoto sobre lo próximo (items **4077, 4116** y **4144**).

La nostalgia como resultado del trasplante inmigratorio es central en muchas novelas y cuentos (items **4157** y **4125**). En otros textos, personajes paralizados por una inadaptación difusa, cuya causa no se identifica, son al mismo tiempo estridentes y resentidos (items **4105** y **4107**).

Al descubrir, poco a poco, la insensatez alimentada y disimulada por convenciones aparentemente inocuas, se va desentrañando la trama de muchas narraciones hábilmente organizadas. Es decir: los pasos de la anécdota muestran cómo el consenso social confunde amaneramiento con esencia (items **4092** y **4159**).

Isidoro Blastein (item **4088**), Noé Jitrik (item **4110**) y María Elena Walsh (item **4163**) han publicado, respectivamente, relatos testimoniales, una excelente memoria y una autobiografía novelada.

Mediante escrituras impecables y control absoluto del *tempo* narrativo, Aira (items **4079, 4081** y **4080**) y Fogwill (items **4101** y **4102**) siguen configurando sus mundos implacables: el de uno, traicionero y falazmente controlable; sibilinamente monstruoso o perverso, el del otro. Cada autor ha dedicado un cuento al fenómeno punk: es significativo que, en los dos, protagonistas femeninas tengan la dudosa prerrogativa de esa automarginación, como si los hombres jóvenes no hubiesen participado de ella.

Los cuentos de Bioy Casares (item **4087**), versiones cada vez más depuradas de la técnica del ya remoto maestro Poe, están construidos en general desde la doble perspectiva narrador lúcido/personajes entre idiosincráticos y triviales. Postulan la claridad privilegiada de la ficción: sólo *a posteriori* se advierten las junturas secretas de la trama. En los relatos notables y arduos de Elvira Orphée (item **4136**), la clave del nudo narrativo se presenta siempre como manifestación de alguna forma inusitada, sorprendente, de justicia. Marco Denevi ha publicado un volumen de cuentos (item **4097**) y una novela (item **4095**) en los que se reconoce una vez más su pericia narrativa.

Premios y distinciones diversas han contribuido a la edición de libros de autores jóvenes o menos conocidos: se leen con placer e interés una primera novela de Flaminia Ocampo (item **4133**) y una colección de cuentos, muchos inéditos, de Jorge Castelli (item **4092**). Por lo demás, antologías y reediciones mantienen en el panorama narrativo, entre muchos otros, a Aníbal Ford (item **4104**), Liliana Heker (item **4108**), Alberto Laiseca (item **4115**), Marta Mercader (item **4147**) y Dalmiro Sáenz (items **4147** y **4148**).

Silvina Ocampo murió a los 90 años en noviembre de 1993. Dos libros suyos (items **4135** y **4134**) cierran la producción notable de una voz poética y narrativa ajena a todo cliché, articulada por una imaginación compleja, una de las más sutiles y originales, y también una de las menos reconocidas, de nuestro tiempo. [MLB y MCG]

II. NARRATIVA PARAGUAYA

Este período está dominado por la figura de Augusto Roa Bastos, quien obtuvo el importante Premio Miguel de Cervantes en 1989. A raíz de este acontecimiento, se realizaron diversas publicaciones y estudios sobre este autor: *El texto cautivo* (item

4235), publicación realizada por la Fundación Colegio del Rey de la Univ. de Alcalá de Henares y *Augusto Roa Bastos: Premio Miguel de Cervantes*, un catálogo de homenaje al escritor paraguayo (item **4231**). En 1992 apareció otra novela de este narrador relacionada con el descubrimiento del Nuevo Mundo, *La vigilia del Almirante* (item **4167**). [MGP]

III. NARRATIVA URUGUAYA

En este período anotamos *Obra selecta de Juan Carlos Onetti* (item **4183**), en edición de la Biblioteca Ayacucho preparada por Hugo Verani, junto a la publicación de una nueva novela del escritor uruguayo, *Cuando ya no importe* (item **4242**). José Pedro Díaz reunió en un volumen titulado *El espectáculo imaginario: Juan Carlos Onetti y Felisberto Hernández* (item **4242**) cuatro estudios sobre ambos narradores. La "Fundación Angel Rama" reeditó una interesante novela de este escritor, pensador y crítico, titulada *Tierra sin mapa* (item **4189**), originalmente publicado en Montevideo en 1961. Celebramos la reedición de *Cuentos* del artista Pedro Figari con prólogo de Angel Rama (item **4174**). Por su parte la "Biblioteca Literaria Iberoamericana y Filipina" publicó una nueva edición de *Ismael* del destacado escritor y pensador uruguayo, Eduardo Acevedo Díaz, preparada por Arturo Sergio Visca (item **4174**).

Entre las novedades, destacamos dos publicaciones de Alejandro Paternain, *La batalla del Río de la Lata* (item **4186**), que incluye dos relatos y una novela histórica titulada *Las aventuras de Lucy Bristol* (item **4185**). La gran Cristina Peri Rossi ha publicado en este período que reseñamos un volumen de poemas *Babel bárbara* que obtuvo el premio "Ciudad de Barcelona 1991" y una curiosa novela, *La última noche de Dostoievski* (item **4187**). También en este período Híber Conteris publicó una nueva y extraordinaria novela de suspenso, *La Diana en el crepúsculo* (item **4172**).

Finalmente, Rómulo Cosse coordinó un volumen de estudios de la obra narrativa de la excepcional escritora uruguaya titulada *Armonía Somers, papeles críticos: cuarenta años de literatura* (item **4252**). Somers murió en Montevideo el 8 de marzo de 1994, a los 80 años de edad.

Se destacan en estos años dos narradores jóvenes que mucho prometen: El primero es Rafael Courtoisie, quien ha publicado libros de poemas, una colección de textos experimentales, y recientemente, cuentos y relatos que pueden considerarse en la frontera (item **4173**). La otra narradora es Mercedes Rein con una segunda novela *Bocas de tormenta* (item **4190**). Ha sido un período muy fructífero para las letras uruguayas. [MGP]

IV. CRITICA LITERARIA: ARGENTINA, PARAGUAY Y URUGUAY

Cierto balance entre la dedicación a figuras canónicas y la atención que ya merecen algunas de las voces más jóvenes apunta a un cambio en el panorama de este período y—cabe esperar—en el cuadro de años venideros. Estos textos señalan miradas retrospectivas que tienden a recuperar lo soslayado; consignan "nuevas fronteras;" buscan la incorporación de culturas plurales al corpus nacional; piensan la escritura de la mujer ya no sólo en tanto a la segmentación sino como componente integral e imprescindible para re-pensar la nación y diseñar su imaginario. En este sentido, junto al sostenido y justificado interés en Borges, Bioy Casares, Arlt, Cortázar, Puig, Sábato, Onetti, Felisberto y Roa Bastos, se sigue ampliando ese horizonte que, particularmente en el mundo académico estadounidense, ha permanecido demasiado apegado al estrellato.

Las publicaciones que le han rendido un merecido (y separado) homenaje a Angel Rama y a Emir Rodríguez Monegal, quizá deban ser leídas junto a los balances de la crítica que dan cuenta de su legado e impacto en las miradas de las dos siguientes generaciones de críticos. Junto a las ya señaladas retrospectivas narrativas, corresponde señalar la atención que están mereciendo las publicaciones periódicas como parte de análisis más generoso de la producción crítica e intelectual del continente. Tanto la uruguaya *Marcha* (items **4249** y **4243**) como la argentina *Babel*, por ejemplo, han obtenido meritorias lecturas. Observar agudamente algunas de las revistas que han marcado y que siguen marcando rumbos, es también un modo de tomar conciencia del proceso en el cual están insertos quienes ejercen esta doble lectura de las letras. Mantener la mirada sobre el canon mientras se incorpora a su predio a María Elena Walsh (item **4213**) y a Armonía Somers (item **4251**) o cuando, en otro orden, no se deja caer la insoslayable obra de Antonio Di Benedetto (item **4200**) ni el peso de la historia más reciente sobre lo que debe ser nombrado, es también un modo de afianzar la función crítica así como el pensamiento crítico que es la marca de alguien como Piglia (item **4220**) frente a tantos libros de ocasión.

En un ejercicio permanente de reencuentro con la tradición y los días que nos siguen amaneciendo, las nuevas voces de la crítica (y otras ya más maduras) historizan los textos rubricados por el "clasicismo" con que los signaron "los mayores." Esta re-lectura—ı a que siempre es una primera lectura—ha comenzado a producir una nueva red de enunciados. En algunos sectores está generando un discurso más dispuesto al diálogo y a la interpelación creativa; un discurso más agudo y a la vez más sutil, más entrañablemente comprensible que las siglas de cofradías que se deshilvanaron rápidamente en su caducidad.

Quizá se transforme en una norma saludable el hábito de tomarle el pulso a la producción crítica por medio del cuadro más amplio que mira frontalmente las dimensiones y cambios del campo intelectual. Por lo menos para este segmento, tal norma seguirá siendo un ejercicio permanente de recuperación de la memoria y de apuesta al futuro. [SS]

PROSE FICTION
Argentina

4076 Absatz, Cecilia *et al.* Antología del erotismo en la literatura argentina. Recopilación de Francisco Herrera. Buenos Aires: Editorial Fraterna, 1990. 351 p. (Bogart)

Selección de 27 cuentos y fragmentos de novelas del siglo XX. El recurso al horror, a la ironía, a la comicidad y a la explicación psicológica ilustran la gran variedad de técnicas y perspectivas posibles en torno al mismo tema. Reúne autores tan diferentes como David Viñas, Silvina Ocampo, Dalmiro Sáenz, Ana María Shua, Antonio Dal Masetto, para sólo nombrar algunos. [MCG]

4077 Aguinis, Marcos. La gesta del marrano. Buenos Aires: Planeta, 1991. 446 p.

Novela histórica investigada con minucia. Examina el período colonial desde una perspectiva nueva: la de los judíos perseguidos por la Inquisición. Con gran maestría se alternan los episodios que siguen cronológica-mente la prisión, condena y martirio del protagonista con los que narran en pasado, el acoso de su familia. [MCG]

4078 Aguinis, Marcos. Profanación del amor. Argentina: Planeta, 1989. 324 p.

La trama de la novela está constituida por los prejuicios e inseguridades de un protagonista cuya mentalidad convencional carece de interés. [MLB]

4079 Aira, César. Los fantasmas: novela. Buenos Aires: Grupo Editor Latinoamericano: Emecé Editores, 1990. 107 p. (Col. Escritura de hoy.)

Novela fantástica. Con originalidad, añade a la crítica social un nivel simbólico, sugerido por comentarios provenientes de Lévi-Strauss. [MCG]

4080 Aira, César. La prueba: novela. Buenos Aires: Grupo Editor Latinoamericano: Emecé Editores, 1992. 87 p. (Col. Escritura de hoy)

El realismo del comienzo se desliza insensiblemente y estalla en una parábola de la violencia desenfrenada y gratuita. [MLB]

4081 Aira, César. El volante. Rosario, Argentina: B. Viterbo Editora, 1992. 95 p. (Ficciones)

Nouvelle armada con las asociaciones de ideas ingenuas y triviales de una protagonista obsesionada por la ilusión del control. [MLB]

4082 Aisemberg, Isaac. No hay ojos aquí. Buenos Aires: Plus Ultra, 1992. 212 p.

Según los editores, el libro "inicia en la Argentina la literatura de espionaje." Relato confuso cuya oralidad excesiva carece de una mínima precisión que parecería imprescindible para el género. [MLB]

4083 Albertella, Jorge Luis. Crónica de dos mujeres solitarias. Buenos Aires: Editorial Galerna, 1989. 197 p.

Técnica epistolar y narración en tercera persona se alternan en la denuncia de las injusticias cometidas contra la vejez. Recuerda *Cae la noche tropical* de Manuel Puig. [MCG]

4084 Asís, Jorge. Cuaderno del acostado. Buenos Aires: Grupo Editorial Planeta Argentina, 1988. 191 p. (Serie Rivarola; 3)

Supuesto diario de un personaje a la vez insignificante y tedioso, que, según los editores, "configura un singular retrato de nuestro pasado reciente." [MLB]

4085 Bähler, Malena. La catedral sumergida. Buenos Aires: Editorial Legasa, 1990. 141 p.

Cuentos muy bien construidos: versiones narrativas de lo que se podría llamar falta de equidad metafísica, o *status quo*, en que las mujeres llevan la peor parte. [MLB]

4086 Berlín, Martha. El amor todo locura. Buenos Aires: Ediciones Ayllu, 1992. 126 p. (Col. Literatura de hoy)

Ocho relatos que exponen obsesiones y relaciones conflictivas. Con gran economía y sin abandono del humor exploran las posibilidades psicológicas de cada drama. [MCG]

4087 Bioy Casares, Adolfo. Una muñeca rusa. Buenos Aires: Tusquets Editores, 1991. 179 p. (Col. Andanzas; 140)

Nueve relatos que confirman la maestría narrativa de Bioy. [MLB]

4088 Blaisten, Isidoro. Cuando éramos felices. Buenos Aires: Emecé Editores, 1992. 200 p. (Escritores argentinos)

Consiste de 17 relatos testimoniales en primera persona que combinan recuerdos juveniles, meditaciones y comentarios de lecturas. Diseñan la trayectoria del autor y también la de su tiempo. [MCG]

4089 Boldori de Baldussi, Rosa. La morada de los cuatro vientos. Buenos Aires: Grupo Editor Latinoamericano, 1992. 205 p. (Col. Escritura de hoy)

Novela histórica. Entreteje datos históricos con elementos ficticios para construir una versión conciliadora de la conquista del Perú. [MCG]

4090 Bottini, Clara. La depresión de Minnie Mouse: novela. Buenos Aires: Torres Agüero Editor, 1989. 106 p.

Novela que en forma de diario íntimo registra la vida de una mujer. La escritura como terapia contra la fragmentación del yo fracasa con un texto circular cuyo fin envía al comienzo. Premio Fondo Nacional de las Artes, 1988. [MCG]

4091 Brailovsky, Antonio Elio. Esta maldita lujuria. La Habana: Casa de las Américas, 1991. 182 p. (Medio milenio)

La conquista de la mítica Ciudad de los Césares provee el punto de partida a la novela que parodia las crónicas de la conquista. Los sueños y las obsesiones del narrador, Ambrosio de Lara, se combinan con datos y personajes históricos de los siglos XVIII y XIX. Premio Casa de las Américas, 1991. [MCG]

4092 Castelli, Jorge. El lugar de Fanny. Buenos Aires: Torres Agüero Editor, 1989. 195 p.

Experiencias infantiles traspuestas con imaginación narrativa. Algunos cuentos incluidos en el volumen recibieron el premio del diario *La Nación* para autor inédito (1986–87). [MLB]

4093 Castillo, Abelardo. Crónica de un iniciado. Buenos Aires: Emecé Editores, 1991. 458 p. (Escritores Argentinos)

El protagonista se encuentra, sin saber cómo en la Ciudad de Córdoba, en donde vive vertiginosamente una especie de experiencia iniciática. [MLB]

4094 Castillo, Abelardo. Las maquinarias de la noche. Buenos Aires: Emecé Editores, 1992. 203 p. (Los Mundos reales; 4. Cuentos completos/Abelardo Castillo. Escritores argentinos)

Cuentos en los que se explora la posibilidad de superar la monotonía de lo cotidiano por medio de la imaginación o la busca de la aventura. [MLB]

4095 Denevi, Marco. Hierba del cielo. Buenos Aires: Ediciones Corregidor, 1991. 226 p.

Nueve cuentos en que el diestro manejo del lenguaje crea situaciones insólitas y relaciones conflictivas. Gran variedad de recursos, cambios de punto de vista, juegos coloquiales, apartes, favorecen una amplia gama que abarca desde lo cómico hasta lo trágico. [MCG]

4096 Denevi, Marco. El jardín de las delicias: mitos eróticos. Buenos Aires: Corregidor, 1992. 93 p.

Consiste de 42 textos de extensión variada. En torno a personajes mitológicos se recrean a escenas eróticas variadas. [MCG]

4097 Denevi, Marco. Música de amor perdido. Buenos Aires: Corregidor, 1990. 167 p.

La novela utiliza elementos barrocos para elaborar una trama de suspenso. Estructurada en dos partes simétricas, cada una ofrece una versión diferente pero complementaria de la misma historia. [MCG]

4098 Diaconú, Alina. El penúltimo viaje. Buenos Aires: J. Vergara Editor, 1989. 301 p. (Ventana abierta)

Estampas impresionistas, "literarias," contraponen experiencias de una familia de emigrantes de un país del Este. [MLB]

4099 Docampo Feijóo, Beda. Vender la pluma. Con una entrevista al autor. Buenos Aires: Puntosur Editores, 1988. 188 p. (Puntosur literaria)

Novela ingeniosa cuya parte central consiste en una carta de Lope de Vega a Cervantes. Con perspicacia y verosimilitud, el homenaje se torna confesión integrando la meditación con el erotismo. Provoca una revitalización de Don Quijote. [MCG]

4100 Ferraro, Diana. Las muy privadas cartas de la terrateniente María López. Buenos Aires: Editora de la Palmera, 1989. 164 p.

Novela epistolar cuya única voz fundamenta su autoridad en la tradición terrateniente que representa. Las cartas revelan una "máscara" diferente según cada destinatario y permiten a su autora formular una teoría sobre el poder político y sus alianzas. [MCG]

4101 Fogwill, Rodolfo Enrique. La buena nueva de los libros del caminante. Buenos Aires: Planeta, 1990. 248 p. (Col. Biblioteca del sur)

Novela en primera persona que pretende ser relato de viajes. La marcha del caminante se torna metáfora y espejo de la narración misma—y en esto reside su gran interés—que incluye autobiografía, comentarios y recuerdos de lecturas. [MLB]

4102 Fogwill, Rodolfo Enrique. Muchacha punk. Buenos Aires: Planeta, 1992. 187 p. (Biblioteca del sur)

Ocho cuentos de uno de los mejores escritores argentinos actuales. Crónica implacable de la Argentina de los años 1975–83. [MLB]

4103 Fogwill, Rodolfo Enrique. Una pálida historia de amor. Buenos Aires: Planeta, 1991. 192 p. (Biblioteca del sur: Novela)

La novela sigue la evolución de la protagonista quien, bajo diferentes nombres y roles, desde los ambientes marginados de cabarets y hoteles busca lograr el poder. [MCG]

4104 Ford, Aníbal. Los diferentes ruidos del agua. Estudio posliminar de Eduardo Romano. Buenos Aires: Puntosur Editores, 1987. 206 p. (Puntosur literaria)

Antología de 14 cuentos. Incluye un estudio de Eduardo Romano sobre la obra del autor. [MCG]

4105 Futoransky, Luisa. Urracas. Buenos Aires: Planeta, 1992. 189 p. (Biblioteca del sur)

Inhabilitadas para identificar sus motivaciones, las protagonistas se debaten vicariamente sin lograr desprenderse de nimiedades convencionales. Despliegue de tics verbales, mímesis de la impotencia de los personajes. [MLB]

4106 García Luna, Raúl. Bajamar: la novela del pueblo. Buenos Aires: Torres Agüero Editor, 1988. 197 p.

Combinación de *thriller* y novela costumbrista. Premio Fondo Nacional de las Artes, 1987. [MLB]

4107 Glickman, Nora. Mujeres, memorias, malogros. Buenos Aires: Mila, 1991. 109 p. (Col. imaginaria)

Son 30 narraciones de valor variado. Recuerdos de infancia, pensamientos cortos y relatos elaborados refieren, en su mayoría, las vivencias de personajes femeninos de clase media. [MCG]

4108 Heker, Liliana. Los bordes de lo real. Buenos Aires: Aguilar, Altea, Taurus, Alfaguara, S.A. de Ediciones, 1991. 286 p. (Alfaguara literaturas)

Edición que reúne los cuentos completos de la autora. Experimentan con la transformación de lo cotidiano en lo desconocido. El hábil manejo de los finales sorpresivos los duplica en versiones inesperadas. [MCG]

4109 Iparraguirre, Sylvia. En el invierno de las ciudades. Buenos Aires: Editorial Galerna, 1988. 158 p. (Col. La Rosa de cobre)

Primera publicación de la autora. Son 13 relatos que hábilmente logran describir lo inesperado en el contexto de situaciones y expectativas cotidianas. Primer Premio Municipal de Literatura 1986. [MCG]

4110 Jitrik, Noé. Los lentos tranvías. México: J. Mortiz, 1988. 120 p.: ill. (Nueva narrativa hispánica)

Atmósfera, mentalidad, ilusiones que paralizaban o movilizaban a un sector de Buenos Aires a fines de los años 30 y principios del 40. [MLB]

4111 Jurado, Alicia. Memorias. v. 3, Las despedidas. Argentina: Emecé Editores, 1992. 1 v.

Continuación y conclusión de la autobiografía comenzada a publicar en 1989. En esta crónica de los últimos 20 años, 1972–92, se destacan aparte de episodios íntimos importantes, sucesos nacionales tales como el conflicto del Beagle y la Guerra de las Malvinas. [MCG]

4112 Kacic, Carmen. Tango mío. Buenos Aires: Ediciones de la Serpiente, 1988. 95 p.

Estos 12 relatos logran adaptar bien los elementos sentimentales y dramáticos propios del tango. [MCG]

4113 Karpuj, Dany. El día que mataron a Dalmiro Sáenz. Buenos Aires: Torres Agüero Editor, 1987. 126 p.

Efectos grotescos, irónicos, cómicos y de terror surgen de los siete relatos que sin declararlo explícitamente invitan al análisis y a la crítica social y política. [MCG]

4114 Kulino, Edmundo. Bancos de neblina. Buenos Aires: Corregidor, 1988. 207 p.

Novela policial que integra elementos fantásticos. [MCG]

4115 Laiseca, Alberto. La mujer en la muralla. Buenos Aires: Planeta, 1990. 312 p.: ill. (Biblioteca del sur: Novelas)

La novela recrea la historia de la China antigua. Con un excelente manejo de la narración se integran, en ese marco, numerosos relatos de ambientación exótica en los que alternan obsesiones y rituales eróticos con intrigas y alianzas palaciegas. [MCG]

4116 Larra, Raúl. Sitiados y sitiadores: novela. Buenos Aires: Ediciones Letra Buena, 1991. 197 p. (Col. Letras/novela)

La novela alterna de modo efectivo la lectura de un documento sobre el sitio de Buenos Aires de 1852 con la crónica de un testigo de la represión de una manifestación. "La memoria de la patria" y la historia reciente coinciden en la brutalidad y el caos. [MCG]

4117 Lezama, Hugo Ezequiel. La guerra secreta de Buenos Aires. Buenos Aires: Grupo Editor Latinoamericano, 1990. 212 p. (Col. Escritura de hoy)

Novela política. La dedicatoria al Capitán Alfred Dreyfus y el prólogo pretenden acercar las acciones de un militar argentino a la situación del oficial francés del siglo XIX. La interpretación de las luchas sectarias que dividieron a la Argentina en épocas recientes se vuelve defensa de la oficialidad. [MCG]

4118 Macho Vidal de Salarano, Lina. El árbol del sol: cuentos. Buenos Aires: Editorial Vinciguerra, 1991. 78 p.

Nueve relatos fantásticos que, aunque evocan gran variedad de ambientes—1a Grecia actual, la antigua China, el mundo quechua, Buenos Aires—establecen relaciones de semejanza cultural en base a premoniciones, encantamientos y objetos mágicos. [MCG]

4119 Maiorano, Gabriela. Casi una aventura. Buenos Aires: Grupo Editor Latinoamericano: Emecé Editores, 1990. 91 p. (Col. Escritura de hoy)

Son 15 cuentos policiales estructurados en torno a un enigma que encuentra solución en un final sorpresivo. [MCG]

4120 Marimón, Antonio. El antiguo alimento de los héroes. Estudio posliminar de Beatriz Sarlo Sabajanes. Buenos Aires: Puntosur Editores, 1988. 230 p. (Puntosur literaria)

El título es parte de un verso de "Mateo XXV, 30" de Borges. Los cuentos se refieren a los componentes del "alimento de los héroes," según el poema: "la falsía, la derrota, la humillación." [MLB]

4121 Martelli, Juan Carlos. La muerte de un hombrecito. Buenos Aires: Planeta, 1992. 216 p. (Biblioteca del sur)

Novela que integra las técnicas de los relatos de terror y aventura. Como en novelas anteriores, el autor explora ambientes sórdidos en los que personajes marginados elaboran tramas de seducción y engaño. [MGC]

4122 Martínez, Carlos Dámaso. Hasta que todo arda. Estudio posliminar de María Teresa Gramuglio. Buenos Aires: Puntosur Editores, 1989. 198 p. (Puntosur literaria)

Nueve cuentos narrados desde perspectivas originales. En el estudio posliminar, María Teresa Gramuglio describe sus mecanismos: "el presente y los recuerdos, lo real y lo soñado, ensoñado o fantaseado, se alternan en sus relatos, creando rupturas del orden temporal y espacial que en algunos casos lindan con lo fantástico, sin llegar, sin embargo, a instalarse plenamente en esa dimensión." [MCG]

4123 Martini, Juan Carlos. La construcción del héroe. Buenos Aires: Editorial Legasa, 1989. 151 p. (Nueva literatura)

Novela de corte detectivesco cuyo fragmentarismo elude revelar el enigma central. Cual nuevo Ulises, el héroe recorre una ciudad y recoge historias parciales y contradictorias que permiten la creación de la ficción. [MCG]

4124 Martini, Juan Carlos. El enigma de la realidad. Buenos Aires: Altea, Taurus, Alfaguara, 1991. 121 p. (Alfaguara literaturas)

Narración que combina ensayo y novela, teoría y práctica de escritura. Investiga con maestría los bordes que separan y confunden ficción y realidad. Las influencias de Joyce, Borges y Bioy son patentes en un texto en que la escritura, como protagonista, se analiza a sí misma. [MCG]

4125 Masetto, Antonio dal. Oscuramente fuerte es la vida. Buenos Aires: Planeta, 1990. 259 p. (Biblioteca del sur: Novelas)

Novela autobiográfica. Testimonia desde una perspectiva femenina una vida de trabajos arduos, sacrificios y guerra en la Italia de la primera mitad del siglo. Ejemplifica las experiencias de miles de inmigrantes. [MCG]

4126 Masetto, Antonio dal. Siete de oro. Buenos Aires: Planeta, 1991. 204 p. (Biblioteca del sur)

Reedición de la novela de 1969. La narración en primera persona combina el relato de viaje con las memorias; traza el recorrido del protagonista en busca de sí. [MCG]

4127 Matei, Emilio. El padre del sepulturero. Buenos Aires: Ediciones Letra Buena, 1991. 100 p. (Col. Letras/cuento)

Primera publicación que reúne 13 cuentos del autor. Al modo de Horacio Quiroga, la tensión que estructura estas narraciones depende de la lucha contra el medio físico litoraleño y de la rivalidad entre los protagonistas. [MCG]

4128 Mercader, Martha. El hambre de mi corazón. Buenos Aires: Editorial Sudamericana, 1989. 205 p. (Col. Narrativas argentinas)

Son 13 cuentos narrados en torno a protagonistas mujeres. Técnicas variadas ponen en evidencia experiencias y perspectivas derivadas de las diferencias sexuales. Es de notar "Los Intrusos" que refiere una versión diferente del cuento "La Intrusa" de Borges. [MCG]

4129 Moledo, Leonardo. Tela de juicio. Buenos Aires: Cántaro Editores, 1991. 247 p. (Col. La Ranura: Narrativa)

Las debilidades del protagonista reflejan la inmoralidad oficializada que culminó en la invasión de las Malvinas. [MLB]

4130 Nicastro, Laura Diana. Intangible. Buenos Aires: Grupo Editor Latinoamericano, 1990. 110 p. (Col. Escritura de hoy)

La selva del Noreste es la protagonista principal de esta novela. La imagen mítica que surge de ella se opone a la de los relatos de Horacio Quiroga; se trata aquí de una "madre nutricia" que precisa protección. [MCG]

4131 Nicastro, Laura Diana. Pueblos de arena. Buenos Aires: Grupo Editor Latinoamericano: Emecé Editores, 1992. 94 p. (Col. Escritura de hoy)

Los 11 relatos señalan la importancia del acto de narrar en la constitución de la identidad. A la tradición post-borgeana se incorpora la de las parábolas antiguas para elaborar mitos y rituales de mundos imaginarios. [MCG]

4132 Nos, Marta. La silla. Buenos Aires: Editorial Galerna, 1987. 173 p.

Consiste de 19 cuentos elaborados con gran economía y originalidad. Cada uno de ellos recrea de manera diferente y con verosimilitud, el pensamiento secreto y los conflictos internos de los personajes. Premio Fondo Nacional de las Artes, 1986. [MCG]

4133 Ocampo, Flaminia. Siete vidas. Buenos Aires: Rosenberg-Rita, 1989. 160 p.

Metáforas de la demencia de un hombre que ha matado a su mujer y se refugia construyendo y reproduciendo ficciones. [MLB]

4134 Ocampo, Silvina. Cornelia frente al espejo. Buenos Aires: Tusquets, 1988. 227 p. (La Flauta mágica; 11)

Treinta y uno cuentos y cuatro poemas que demuestran una vez más la pericia narrativa de Ocampo en la creación de fenómenos subjetivos y extraños. La observación meticulosa y la alteración sutil de la realidad rinden honor a Lewis Carroll a quien se alude en varias instancias. [MCG]

4135 Ocampo, Silvina. Las reglas del secreto: antología. Selección, prólogo y notas de Matilde Sánchez. México: Fondo de Cultura Económica, 1991. 623 p.: bibl., ill. (Col. Tierra firme)

Antología que incluye cuentos, poemas y traducciones. Excelentes comentarios introducen cada una de las series en que se divide: "De la Crueldad," "De la Metamorfosis," "De la Ficción," "De las Miniaturas." Incluye también una bibliografía de la publicaciones de Ocampo y una cronología. [MCG]

4136 Orphée, Elvira. La muerte y los desencuentros. Buenos Aires: Editorial Fraterna, 1989. 168 p.

Personajes paradójicos: aparentemente indiferentes, cínicos o egoístas, se mueven impulsados por una ética *sui generis*, que convalida la excentricidad y anula contradicciones. [MLB]

4137 Osorio, Elsa. Reina Mugre. Buenos Aires: Puntosur Editores, 1990. 150 p.

En estos 15 relatos predomina ironía y visión crítica. [MLB]

4138 Pagano, Mabel. Lorenza Reynafé, o, Quiroga, la barranca de la tragedia. Buenos Aires: Ada Korn Editora, 1991. 301 p.

La novela narra desde la perspectiva de Lorenza Reynafé los sucesos privados y políticos que jalonaron su vida (1799–1868). Los episodios culminantes relatan el asesinato de Facundo Quiroga. [MCG]

4139 Pampillo, Gloria. Las invenciones inglesas. Buenos Aires: Editorial Sudamericana, 1992. 153 p. (Col. Narrativas argentinas)

Dos hermanas imaginan y reconstruyen la historia de sus antepasados ingleses que llegaron a Buenos Aires con las invasiones de 1806. [MLB]

4140 Paoletti, Mario. Antes del diluvio. Toledo, Spain: Servicio de Publicaciones, Junta de Comunidades de Castilla-La Mancha, 1989? 170 p. (Creación literaria; 13: Novela)

Con gran dominio de la forma autobiográfica, la novela hace la crónica de los 30 años de la vida política argentina que desembocan en la aparición de la guerrilla urbana desde el punto de vista de un "pícaro" del siglo XX. Premio Castilla-La Mancha, 1988. [MCG]

4141 Pérez, Adriana. Más allá de las estaciones—y otros calendarios exhortados. Córdoba, Argentina: Lerner, 1991. 125 p. (Córdoba nueva generación; 4)

Son 19 cuentos estructurados en torno a la falta de reciprocidad entre las expectativas personales y la "realidad." Los precede un estudio, "Notas Marginales," de Enrique Aurora. [MCG]

4142 Posse, Abel. La Reina del Plata. Barcelona: Plaza & Janés, 1990. 254 p. (Plaza & Janés/literaria; 11)

El protagonista-narrador tiene una relación amor/odio con la ciudad de Buenos Aires. [MLB]

4143 Rabanal, Rodolfo. El factor sentimental. Buenos Aires: Planeta, 1990. 220 p. (Col. Biblioteca del sur)

Según los editores, "trata sobre la felicidad escurridiza que se entrevé en el frenesí erótico, sobre las fugas y los regresos sin gloria [. . .], sobre el precio que impone la vida a quienes la persiguen a ciegas." [MLB]

4144 Rivera, Andrés. El amigo de Baudelaire. Buenos Aires: Alfaguara Literaturas, 1991. 91 p.

Anotaciones conjeturales de un individuo enriquecido en la Argentina de fines del siglo XIX. La pátina de época (nombres, hechos) apenas disimula las alusiones contemporáneas. [MLB]

4145 Rosenzvaig, Eduardo. El sexo del azúcar. Buenos Aires: Ediciones Letra Buena, 1991. 362 p.: bibl. (Col. Letras/novela)
Novela autobiográfica. En base a fragmentos de diarios, cartas y testimonios reconstruye los 100 años de un ingenio tucumano. La "memoria" recuperada critica de modo eficaz las alianzas y estrategias de sus inicios y su transformación en centro de torturas. [MCG]

4146 Saccomanno, Guillermo. Bajo bandera. Buenos Aires: Planeta, 1991. 251 p. (Biblioteca del sur: Cuentos.)
El autor construye, con buen oído para el diálogo y sentido del humor, un cuadro implacable de las aberraciones de la mentalidad militar. [MLB]

4147 Sáenz, Dalmiro and **Sergio Joselovsky.** El día que mataron a Alfonsín. Buenos Aires: Ediciones Tarso, 1986. 214 p. (Col. Política ficción)
La trama de la novela y la trama política coinciden en denunciar la fragilidad de las instituciones y de los mecanismos de poder en la Argentina de los años 80. [MCG]

4148 Sáenz, Dalmiro and **Sergio Joselovsky.** Latinoamérica, go home. Buenos Aires: Grupo Editorial Planeta, 1988. 182 p.
Novela utópica. Postula la creación de un nuevo mundo en América Latina pero sólo reemplaza los términos del antiguo sistema por equivalentes. [MCG]

4149 Saer, Juan José. El río sin orillas: tratado imaginario. Madrid: Alianza Editorial, 1991. 250 p. (Alianza singular; 4)
Propósito del narrador del texto: " . . . en este libro no hay un solo hecho voluntariamente ficticio." Autobiografía, lecturas e historia componen un relato que, con gran claridad y perspicacia desmonta símbolos, mitos y lenguajes en una revisión de la cultura argentina. [MCG]

4150 Sánchez, Rafael. Los círculos abiertos. Buenos Aires: Catálogos Editora, 1988. 406 p.
Citas de lecturas, fragmentos de memorias ajenas y meditaciones personales se juxtaponen en una relación muy individual pero que, a la vez, espeja la historia argentina de los últimos 30 años. [MCG]

4151 Sasturain, Juan. Parecido, S.A. Madrid: Anaya, 1991. 163 p. (Espacio abierto; 8)
Novela para adolescentes. En torno a la dicotomía ser/parecer, elabora episodios de aventura con gran imaginación. [MCG]

4152 Shua, Ana María. Casa de geishas. Buenos Aires: Editorial Sudamericana, 1992. 243 p. (Col. Narrativas argentinas)
Colección de brevísimos relatos de valor variado. Las cualidades que resaltan en ellos son la crítica certera, el sentido del humor sutil y la fuerza imaginativa. [MCG]

4153 Silvestre, Susana. Si yo muero primero. Buenos Aires: Ediciones Letra Buena, 1991. 277 p. (Col. Letras/novela)
Primera novela de la autora de dos libros de cuentos y una pieza de teatro. Crónica prolija de la vida de una muchacha de un barrio periférico de Buenos Aires. Premio Concurso Emecé, 1990. [MLB]

4154 Soriano, Osvaldo. Una sombra ya pronto serás. Buenos Aires: Editorial Sudamericana, 1990. 251 p. (Col. Narrativas argentinas)
El título, proveniente de una letra de tango, da el tono de la novela. El humor mordaz y el sentimiento de frustración, característicos de la prosa de Soriano, describen las relaciones de personajes innominados que recuerdan a los de Samuel Beckett. Invita a una lectura alegórica. [MCG]

4155 Steimberg, Alicia. Cuando digo Magdalena. Buenos Aires: Planeta, 1992. 216 p. (Biblioteca del sur)
Novela que explora los meandros e interrupciones de la memoria de una mujer que no logra fijarse en un relato que le otorgue identidad. Premio de Novela Planeta Biblioteca del Sur, 1992. [MCG]

4156 Tirri, Néstor. La claridad de la noche. Buenos Aires: Puntosur, 1988. 117 p. (Puntosur literaria)
En primera persona, la novela reconstruye una memoria truncada por el exilio. Particulariza los horrores ocurridos durante las últimas dictaduras. [MCG]

4157 Tizziani, Rubén. Mar de olvido. Buenos Aires: Emecé Editores, 1992. 288 p. (Escritores argentinos)
A lo largo de la novela, construida con las experiencias de varias generaciones de in-

migrantes italianos, se van produciendo cambios cualitativos en la Argentina. [MLB]

4158 Torre, Javier. El placer inglés. 1. ed. Buenos Aires: Emecé Editores, 1991. 197 p. (Escritores argentinos)

Son 21 relatos breves: registros eficaces de vivencias de personajes muy jóvenes, alimentadas por el deseo o la fantasía. [MLB]

4159 Torres Zavaleta, Jorge. El palacio de verano. Buenos Aires: Grupo Editor Latinoamericano, 1989. 155 p. (Col. Escritura de hoy)

Los protagonistas de estos relatos atribuyen a sus amaneramientos—1os de la alta burguesía—una esencialidad invariable. Esa certidumbre equivocada genera la desilusión y la soledad. Premio Fortabat, 1987. [MLB]

4160 Valenzuela, Luisa. Realidad nacional desde la cama. Buenos Aires: Grupo Editor Latinoamericano, 1990. 105 p. (Col. Escritura de hoy)

Las tintas excesivamente cargadas desmedran el impacto del sentido del humor y los juegos de palabras, característicos de la autora. [MLB]

4161 Vallacco, Héctor. El ramal estancado. Buenos Aires: Torres Agüero Editor, 1989. 141 p.

Los relatos fragmentarios que componen la novela consiguen unidad por medio del yo narrador que cuenta su propia historia. Premio Fondo Nacional de las Artes, 1988. [MCG]

4162 Vázquez, María Esther. Desde la niebla. Buenos Aires: Emecé Editores, 1988. 189 p. (Escritores argentinos)

Son 15 cuentos muy bien narrados. Los 11 primeros se acercan al género fantástico mientras que los cuatro últimos reunidos bajo el título "Crónicas del Pasado" se relacionan con la leyenda medieval. [MCG]

4163 Walsh, María Elena. Novios de antaño: 1930-1940. Buenos Aires: Editorial Sudamericana, 1990. 341 p.

Autobiografía novelada. El lenguaje poético, sin eludir sátira ni comicidad ha sido magistralmente adaptado para rememorar percepciones y episodios de la infancia. En la segunda parte titulada "Abuela Agnes (1872-1899)" se publica el epistolario de la bisabuela de la autora; son las cartas de una inmigrante inglesa a su familia. [MCG]

Paraguay

4164 Azuaga, Moncho. Celda 12. Asunción: Editorial Ñandereko, 1991. 237 p.: ill.

Novela del premiado poeta, dramaturgo y narrador paraguayo expone los recursos utilizados por el terrorismo de Estado protagonizado por personajes que representan dos realidades del país: el dictador en la figura de un militar al servicio del capital nacional aliado al capital internacional y un profesor encarcelado por el sistema, a quien se le da la orden-condena de escribir la historia de su victimario. Esta narración contribuye al genéro de la novela de denuncia ampliamente cultivada en otros países de América. [MGP]

4165 Casaccia, Gabriel. La babosa. Madrid: Ediciones de Cultura Hispánica, 1991. 403 p.: bibl., ill. (Biblioteca literaria iberoamericana y filipina; 17)

Casaccia (m. 1980), poco conocido fuera del Paraguay, es considerado uno de los novelistas más importantes de su país, junto con Augusto Roa Bastos. Esta novela ofrece una crítica dura a la realidad de la larga dictadura paraguaya. La acción se sitúa en el microcosmo de la pequeña ciudad de Aregua. Nueva edición/póstuma (la primera, 1957) va prologada por el crítico Hugo Rodríguez-Alcalá. Contiene lista de ediciones y bibliografía. [MGP]

4166 Ferrer de Arréllaga, Renée. Los nudos del silencio. Asunción: Arte Nuevo Editores, 1988. 217 p. (Serie Literatura; 8)

Poeta y narradora paraguaya cuya obra incluye 11 poemarios y dos volúmenes de cuentos. En su primera novela, una pareja de clase media va a Europa de viaje, donde se explora el despertar de la conciencia femenina en la protagonista a raíz de un acontecimiento trivial, el espectáculo de strip-tease de una mujer vietnamita. Entre las mujeres se desarrolla una relación de solidaridad por identificarse en las trampas de la sumisión. Narración innovadora en la producción literaria femenina del Paraguay. [MGP]

4167 Roa Bastos, Augusto Antonio. Vigilia del Almirante. Madrid: Alfaguara, 1992. 378 p. (Alfaguara hispánica; 96)

Premio Cervantes, 1989: "El más alto honor que se ha dispensado a mi obra," según el autor. Relato de "ficción impura, o mixta, oscilante entre la realidad de la fábula y la fábula de la historia" en palabras de Roa Bastos, ofrece una visión de Colón desde una doble perspectiva, la de los dos mundos que se contradicen en una historia forzadamente compartida, en la que la figura de un Cristobal Colón consumido por la ambición de llegar al "Nuevo Mundo" a pesar de las miserias físicas y espirituales que lo aquejan en el viaje más famoso de la historia. [MGP]

4168 Rodríguez Alcalá, Guido. Caballero. Asunción: RP Ediciones, 1986. 191 p.: maps.

Interesante novela histórica que relata la vida del General de División Don Bernardino Caballero, segundo del Mariscal Presidente Francisco Solano López, en la Guerra de la Triple Alianza. De consulta necesaria para los estudiosos del género en el Paraguay y en América Latina. [MGP]

4169 Trías Coll, Santiago. Los diez caminos. Asunción: El Lector, 1989. 174 p.

En esta narración, cada uno de los 10 caminos del título explora las diversas latitudes del planeta cuya trayectoria es protagonizada por personajes que viven acontecimientos insólitos. Primera novela de este autor paraguayo. [MGP]

Uruguay

4170 Acevedo Díaz, Eduardo. Ismael. Madrid: Ediciones de Cultura Hispánica, 1991. 373 p.: bibl., ill. (Biblioteca literaria iberoamericana y filipina; 22)

Nueva edición de *Ismael.* Prólogo de A.S. Visca incluye biografía que destaca dos facetas de este intelectual uruguayo, la política como del Partido Blanco y la del escritor, cuya importancia se reconoce en su país, pero que debe revaluarse en el contexto de la literatura hispanoamericana. Visca ofrece una revaluación de esta novela histórica que ha quedado algo relegada en los recientes estudios sobre este género. [MGP]

4171 Blixen, Hyalmar. El tiempo y sus máscaras. v. 1–4. Montevideo: Ediciones de la Plaza, 1991. 4 v. (Col. Ficciones)

Esta obra en cuatro volúmenes incluye una serie de aventuras trágicas, sentimentales y cómicas cuyos personajes atraviesan el tiempo y el espacio del planeta, transhistórica y transcultural es la textura de este ambicioso cuadro que conduce a la creación de escenarios situados en el siglo XXIV. [MGP]

4172 Conteris, Hiber. La Diana en el crepúsculo. Barcelona: Laia, 1987. 107 p. (Laia/literatura)

Narración sobre un personaje masculino, Banlor, restaurador de cuadros y pintor, que en el proceso de restaurar una tela de un pintor poco conocido, emprende un viaje sin retorno en un periplo que abarca Montevideo, Buenos Aires y San Francisco. El relato está habilmente trazado en la figura de la metempsicosis. Excelente ejemplo de la narrativa de Conteris con suspenso, tensión narrativa y notable agilidad. [MGP]

4173 Courtoisie, Rafael. El mar rojo: cuentos. Prólogo de Rosario Peyrou. Montevideo: Ediciones de la Banda Oriental, 1991. 77 p. (Lectores de Banda Oriental: Quinta serie; 19)

Autor (n. 1958) puede considerarse de rara precocidad y gran reconocimiento dentro de literatura uruguaya. Sus cuatro poemarios recibieron amplios premios. Publicó en 1990 unos textos de género híbrido, entre la poesía y la narración, titulado *Cambio de estado;* posteriormente apareció *El mar interior,* relatos, que revelan su maestría en la prosa. Estos cuentos con prólogo de Rosario Peyrou continuan esta notable trayectoria. Situados entre la ciencia y la literatura, exploran los límites a los que han llegado el avance tecnológico y el pensamiento científico al desentenderse éticamente de la responsabilidad inherente a la reflexión científica. El género al que pertenecen estos relatos es el de la ciencia ficción, cultivado por Huxley, Orwell y Burgess entre otros. [MGP]

4174 Figari, Pedro. Cuentos. Ilustrado por el autor. Prólogo de Angel Rama. Montevideo: Ediciones de la Banda Oriental, 1990. 70 p.: ill. (Lectores de Banda Oriental; 5: ser., 4) Consiste de 10 cuentos del gran pintor Figari y el prólogo del crítico/escritor Angel Rama. Escritos en 1927–28 quedaron "pasados a máquina, corregidos e ilustrados" y han sido transcriptos respetando el léxico y puntuación del maestro. Como señala Rama, la lectura de estos cuentos evoca los cuadros de Figari: la teatralidad, la superficialidad de los personajes y los temas. [MGP]

4175 García Rey, J. Manuel. Perseguido como Orestes. Montevideo: Ediciones Trilce, 1992. 230 p.

Reflexión profunda acerca del exilio, de

la ruptura con los mundos por los que debe atravesar Facundo, un personaje atormentado por su condición itinerante, como miembro integrante de la diáspora sudamericana. Novela de acción, de desplazamiento y de búsqueda por una agitada vida de amores con escenarios en Montevideo (de donde es el personaje), en México, Madrid y Barcelona. [MGP]

4176 Iribarne, Daniel. Los infiernos de la libertad. Montevideo: Vintén Editor, 1990. 257 p. (Col. Documentos)

El autor fue uno de los detenidos por el gobierno uruguayo en 1972. Después de un proceso largo que culminó con una condena de ocho años de cárcel, fue forzado al exilio, desde donde ha realizado su labor escritural. Su novelística contribuye a dar voz y forma a la experiencia trágica de la persecución y tortura políticas por parte de un estado autoritario. [MGP]

4177 Lanza, Pancho. Las mil y una hectáreas: novela. Montevideo: Descubrimiento Editores, 1991. 383 p.

Novela sobre la vida en el interior del Uruguay, tema infrecuente en la narrativa uruguaya reciente. Una familiar rural con resabios del mundo de los hacendados rioplatenses que va lentamente desapareciendo y un pueblo movido por numerosos prejuicios son los elementos centrales de esta obra de gran interés para los estudiosos de la narrativa rioplatense contemporánea. El argentino Gudiño Kieffer considera que "es la novela del Río de la Plata que Onetti no escribió." [MGP]

4178 Liscano, Carlos. La mansión del tirano. Montevideo: Arca, 1992. 185 p.: ill.

La mansión del tirano, catalogada por el autor como "novela salvaje" por haber sido escrita en la cárcel; sin embargo no hace mención de tal realidad, sino de manera abstracta. El protagonista Hans recorre un camino de encierros que se suceden con infinitas variaciones. Obra de gran exigencia, muestra las posibilidades que persigue la ficción de tema carcelario. [MGP]

4179 Mantero, Juan José. La hiedra. Prólogo de Miguel Angel Campodónico. Montevideo: Arca, 1992. 139 p.

Concurso de Narrativa Inédita, segundo premio. Una hiedra rodea una casa habitada por dos mujeres que viven aterrorizadas por el sexo, la condena perpetua y la muerte. Los laberintos de la mente humana

en una situación de tensión muestran otra fase de la desgraciada condición humana. Prologada por el escritor uruguayo Miguel Angel Campodónico, quien la caracteriza como "literatura de atmósfera, de ambientes clausurados, de espacio/tapiados, sin fisuras, que toma al lector por los pelos y lo introduce en el interior de una casona donde se encierran dos hermanas huérfanas." [MGP]

4180 Maslíah, Leo. Tarjeta roja. Buenos Aires: Ediciones de la Flor, 1991. 191 p.

Narración de ciencia ficción política sobre un país cuyo ejército ha sido derrotado por las vacas, expulsado por las Naciones Unidas del planeta, asfixiado por el olor a queso cuartirolo pasado y a cuyas queserías se dirigen en manadas las ratas citadinas. Obras previas: *Historia transversal de Floreal Menéndez, El show de José Fin, El Lado oscuro de la pelvis* y *La Tortuga.* [MGP]

4181 Narraciones breves uruguayas, 1830–1880. Recopilación, prólogo y notas de Leonardo Rossiello. Montevideo: TAE; Göteburg, Sweden; Instituto Ibero-americano, 1990. 391 p.: bibl.

Recoge narraciones de los primeros 50 años de vida independiente del Uruguay. Algunos con autor, la mayoría, anónimos, fueron seleccionados de diarios, periódicos y revistas literarias de la época de este país y de periódicos chilenos y argentinos. Son documentos importantes para estudiar la formación de la cultura y literatura nacionales, además de evidenciar la existencia de la lírica, la novela y el teatro, el ensayo, la historiografía, la crítica literaria y la nota de costumbre de esos tiempos. [MGP]

4182 Onetti, Juan Carlos. Cuando ya no importe. Madrid: Alfaguara, 1993. 205 p. (Alfaguara hispánica; 100)

Ultima novela del gran escritor uruguayo (m. 1994) escrita en forma de diario de un exiliado en Monte que vive una vida miserable y encuentra por casualidad un aviso que ofrece trabajo para un hombre con ambición desmedida y ganas de viajar. El empleo requiere embarcarse en un viaje a un lugar llamado Santamaría, sitio imaginario donde transcurren varios relatos de la obra de Onetti. [MGP]

4183 Onetti, Juan Carlos. Obra selecta. Prólogo, cronología y bibliografía de Hugo J. Verani. Caracas: Biblioteca Ayacucho, 1989. 452 p.: bibl. (Biblioteca Ayacucho; 142)

Edición del crítico uruguayo Hugo Verani, por la prestigiosa Biblioteca Ayacucho, contiene prólogo del editor, selección de cuentos cuyo orden en esta edición refleja "la cronología interna y la biografía de los personajes" de Santa María. Los textos son los siguientes: "Juntacádaveres," "Historia del Caballero de la Rosa y de la Virgen," "Para una Tumba sin Nombre," "El Astillero," "La Novia Robada" y "La Muerte y la Niña." Cierra el volumen con una cronología breve y una bibliografía de y sobre Onetti. [MGP]

4184 Palma, Jorge. Paraísos artificiales: cuentos. Montevideo: Ediciones Trilce, 1990. 147 p.

Marca de la literatura del Río de la Plata en su insistencia en el buceo interior a través de ámbitos extraños, insólitos, geografías imaginadas, espacios poco accesibles y de dificultosa relación. Los personajes son seres perseguidos por obsesiones, marginalizados, locos, artistas o abatidos por deformaciones físicas, metáfora de sus deformaciones interiores. Narrador interesado particularmente por la otra realidad, a la que se accede con dificultad y peligro. Trabaja el cuento realista, el fantástico o el alegórico. [MGP]

4185 Paternain, Alejandro. Las aventuras de Lucy Bristol. Montevideo: Signos, 1991. 170 p.

Novela que explora las aventuras costeras y marítima de la sociedad colonial del siglo XVIII. La protagonista, Lucy Britol, es capitana de un barco y en tono burlesco, se cuentan con erotismo picaresco las coloridas aventuras de esta mujer en el litoral atlántico de la entonces llamada Banda Oriental. [MGP]

4186 Paternain, Alejandro. La batalla del Río de la Lata. Montevideo: Ediciones de la Banda Oriental, 1990. 75 p. (Lectores de Banda Oriental; 4: ser., 34)

Este volumen incluye dos relatos, "El Fantasma de las Ruinas: Memorias de un Pastor de Boston" y "La Batalla del Río de la Lata." El primer relato se estructura a partir de un texto de Charles Nodier y el segundo procede de la tradición oral de Supaca. El primero está trabajado con tono irónico alrededor de aventuras del narrador, que desembarca en Montevideo. El segundo gira alrededor de la excursión del acorazado alemán "Graf Spee" en aguas uruguayas, acontecimiento que evoca la Segunda Guerra Mundial y su recepción en el pequeño pueblo uruguayo. [MGP]

4187 Peri Rossi, Cristina. La última noche de Dostoievski. Madrid: Grijalbo Mondadori, 1992. 159 p. (El Espejo de tinta)

A partir de una cita de *Diario de ultratumba* de Dostoievski, Cristina Peri Rossi construye una novela cuyo protagonista, un cuarentón y desengañado periodista, el narrador de la novela, se deja seducir por el azar sin perder su control mental. Al jugar, entra en un mundo en el que queda cancelada la moral y la razón, y donde las reglas del juego no dependen nada más que del azar; el desafío ofrece su más amplia apertura a los límites y posibilidades. La talentosa narradora uruguaya publicó en 1991 *Babel bárbara*, poemario que recibió el premio Ciudad de Barcelona, 1991. [MGP]

4188 Prego, Omar. Ultimo domicilio conocido: novela. Montevideo: Ediciones Trilce, 1990. 174 p.

Este escritor, crítico literario y periodista destaca por su habilidad para trabajar la narrativa de tema urbano. Esta novela explora la múltiple experiencia humana de la ciudad finisecular, a través de un haz de temas que convergen en un locus central, Montevideo o la ciudad latinoamericana, decrépita y renovada, sonambulesca y mágica, cruel y solitaria, contrapuntos de la contradictoria condición humana visita a través de un narrador perspicaz y observador. [MGP]

4189 Rama, Angel. Tierra sin mapa. Montevideo: Fundación Angel Rama, 1985. 130 p.

El destacado pensador y crítico uruguayo comenzó a escribir ficción hacia 1955. Estos textos van unidos por un tema central: la recuperación de la tierra materna, Galicia, a través de la construcción de la infancia del narrador en las aventuras con su madre, personaje armado con los fragmentos de la memoria y en tono de gran ternura y melancolía. Apareció primero en 1961, en Montevideo. Habiéndose agotado la primera edición, se publicó una segunda ilustrada. La Fundación Angel Rama de Montevideo publicó esta tercera. [MGP]

4190 Rein, Mercedes. Bocas de tormenta. Montevideo: Arca, 1987. 158 p.

Retoma personajes, lugares y ejes temporales que habían aparecido en su novela anterior *Casa vacía* (1983) de amplia recepción crítica y reconocida con numerosos premios. Los personajes viven una vida cotidiana constantemente asaltada por hechos insólitos, que transcurre entre una oscilación entre lo normal del sentido común y la inestabilidad de la locura, materias ambas de la que está hecha la existencia humana. [MGP]

4191 Santi, Walter. Nada más que el viento: año 2250. Montevideo: Editorial Sudamericana, 1991. 208 p.

Novela del nuevo género de la ciencia-ficción política que proyecta una visión de futuro escalofriante: un muro rodea la ciudad de Montevideo, que sirve para aislar los tres millones de habitantes del resto del territorio que ha sido vendido y gracias a dicha venta, los habitantes viven sin trabajar. Otra novela de este género es *La Reina del Plata* del argentino Abel Posse (ver item **4142**). [MGP]

4192 70/90: antología del cuento uruguayo. Selección y notas biobibliográficas de Walter Rela. Estudio preliminar de Rómulo Cosse. Montevideo: Librería Linardi y Risso, 1991. 376 p.

Selección de Walter Rela incluye estudio de Rómulo Cosse: "El Cuento Uruguayo Actual: sus Modelos Culturales y la Modernidad." Cada cuento va introducido por una ficha biobibliográfica de cada escritor. Figuran cuentos de Onetti, Armonía Somers, Benedetti, Mercedes Rein, Galeano, Cristina Peri Rossi, Estrazulas y Teresa Porzecanski entre otros. Una muestra valiosa del género en la producción literaria del Uruguay. [MGP]

LITERARY CRITICISM AND HISTORY
Argentina

4193 Adolfo Bioy Casares: premio de literatura en lengua castellana "Miguel de Cervantes" 1990. Barcelona: Anthropos; Madrid: Ministerio de Cultura, Dirección General del Libro y Bibliotecas, Centro de las Letras Españolas, 1991. 143 p.: bibl., ill. (Ambitos literarios: Premios Cervantes; 16)

"Tengo por afortunada casualidad la circunstancia de que mi primera ambición literaria no haya sido de gloria, sino de suscitar algún día en los lectores una fascinación como la que despertó en mí una novela. Quien aspira a la gloria, piensa en sí mismo y ve a su libro como un instrumento para triunfar. Sospecho que para escribir bien, debemos pensar en el libro, no en nosotros"—dice Bioy

en un pasaje del discurso de aceptación del Cervantes. Enriqueta Morillas Ventura, Francisca Suárez Coalla, Juana Martínez Gómez, Blas Matamoro y Teresita Mauro (quien también tuvo a su cargo la bibliografía y la cronología) analizan algunos aspectos de su obra. [SS]

4194 Alazraki, Jaime et al. España en Borges. Coordinación de Fernando R. Lafuente. Madrid: Ediciones El Arquero, 1990. 139 p.: bibl., port. (Textos universitarios)

Ensayos de Jaime Alazraki, Ana María Barrenechea, Nora Catelli, Teodosio Fernández, Blas Matamoro, Carlos Meneses, Sylvia Molloy, Saúl Yurkievich. [MLB]

4195 Anderson Imbert, Enrique. Teoría y técnica del cuento. Barcelona: Editorial Ariel, 1992. 283 p. bibl. (Letras e ideas: Instrumenta)

Puesta al día de la edición publicada en 1979 y revisada en 1982 en la que se combina la actividad crítica con el conocimiento internalizado de su propia práctica narrativa. Compagina la visión histórica y crítica con el magisterio. [SS]

4196 Arana Cañedo-Argüelles, Juan. El centro del laberinto: los motivos filosóficos en la obra de Borges. Pamplona, Spain: EUNSA, 1994. 183 p.: bibl. (NT lengua y literatura)

Recorre los elementos que conforma la concepción de Borges de lo eterno y concluye: "El eje que articula la filosofía de Borges es (. . .) una crítica de la eternidad pura y de la eternidad práctica." Sugiere "que sus vindicaciones de una eternidad platónico-panteísta están penetradas por una irresistible nostalgia del cristianismo al que debe renunciar como contrapartida; que también para él es excesivo el precio que hay que pagar para abolir el tiempo; que no puede resignarse a perdurar tan sólo en un abstracto y anónimo paradigma, perdido el yo y atomizado el hombre en vivencias dispersas." [SS]

4197 Arlt, Roberto. Los Complementarios. Madrid: Instituto de Cooperación Iberoamericana, 1993. (Cuadernos Hispanoamericanos; 11)

Util miscelánea publicada con motivo del cincuentenario de la muerte de Arlt (1900–42) que incluye textos de Adriana Rodríguez Pérsico, Fernando Aínsa, Aníbal Jarkowski, Gerardo Mario Goloboff, Claudia

Gilman y Blas Matamoro y que demuestra, una vez más, que las fisuras y los quiebres éticos de la Argentina contempóranea fueron anticipados por Arlt en torno a las crisis de su propia época. [SS]

4198 Barnstone, Willis. With Borges on an ordinary evening in Buenos Aires: a memoir. Urbana: Univ. of Illinois Press, 1993. 198 p.: bibl., ill., index.

El repertorio de Borges es amplio y necesariamente conocido, pero la admiración de Barnstone por Borges y su mundo, así como el compartido regocijo íntimo ante el saber, contribuyen a un gozoso recorrido por las opiniones y los motivos de un ser singular y de una obra ya clásica. [SS]

4199 Bioy Casares, Adolfo and **Fernando Sorrentino** Siete conversaciones con Adolfo Bioy Casares. Buenos Aires: Editorial Sudamericana, 1992. 268 p.: indexes.

El autor de *Siete conversaciones con Jorge Luis Borges* (1974) sostuvo éstas con Bioy Casares (agosto/sept. 1988). Ni vida ni obra le han faltado, como se verifica en esta recuperación de la memoria literaria, de la amistad, de una Argentina que a veces parece sólo libresca. [SS]

4200 Cattarossi Arana, Nelly. Antonio Di Benedetto: "casi" memorias—I, II, III, IV, V- :testimonios de vida, bibliografías, notas gráficas. v. 1–3. Mendoza: Ediciones Culturales de Mendoza; Ministerio de Cultura y Educación, 1991–1992. 3 v.: ill.

La totalidad de la obra consta de 12 memorias distribuidas en tres tomos, un capítulo de "Testimonios de Vida" en cada tomo, bibliografías y documentación gráfica. Importante como homenaje y como aporte para un mejor conocimiento del autor de *Zama* y otras memorables páginas. [SS]

4201 Congreso Nacional de Literatura Argentina, 4th, Mendoza, Argentina, 1987. La periodización de la literatura argentina: problemas, criterios, autores, textos. v. 1–3. Mendoza, Argentina: Univ. Nacional de Cuyo, Facultad de Filosofía y Letras, Instituto de Literaturas Modernas, 1989. 3 v.: bibl. (Revista de literaturas modernas: Anejo; 5)

Antonio Pagés Larraya, Ana Pizarro, Emilio Carilla, Pedro Luis Barcia, Blas Matamoro, Rafael Gutiérrez Girardot y Raúl H. Castagnino son algunos de los críticos que abordan la problemática organización del sis-

tema literario. La convocatoria del congreso sirvió, asimismo, para rendirle un merecido homenaje a Antonio Di Benedetto y, por otro lado, para dar a conocer temas y autores del interior que ocasionalmente aparecen en los encuentros bonaerenses y en las bibliografías internacionales. [SS]

4202 Domínguez, Mignon. Cartas desconocidas de Julio Cortázar: 1939–1945. Buenos Aires: Editorial Sudamericana, 1992. 297 p.: bibl., ill., facsims.

Consiste de 24 cartas enviadas por Cortázar a María de las Mercedes Arias, colega de los días en que ejerció el magisterio en el Colegio Nacional de Bolívar. El detenido análisis de las cartas—así como lo hacen explícitamente varias de las cartas más significativas—marcan filiaciones, simpatías y los pasos estéticos en las huellas de su temprana obra ensayística y poética; pasos que Cortázar retomaría unos años más tarde en su narrativa. [SS]

4203 Fares, Gustavo C. and **Eliana Hermann.** Escritoras argentinas contemporáneas. New York: P. Lang, 1993. 255 p.: bibl., ports. (University of Texas studies in contemporary Spanish-American fiction, 0888–8787; 8)

Estela Canto, María Esther de Miguel, Alina Diaconú, Angélica Gorodischer, Alicia Jurado, Jorgelina Loubet, Martha Mercader, Elvira Orphée, Noemí Ulla y María Esther Vásquez fueron las 13 escritoras seleccionadas para esta variante de la "literatura femenina" argentina. Foto, biografía, bibliografía primaria y secundaria, entrevista y una muestra de sus obras, ofrecen un cuadro uniforme para cada una de ellas. Son llamativas algunas ausencias (y no pocas presencias). [SS]

4204 Farías, Víctor. La metafísica del arrabal: *El tamaño de mi esperanza*, un libro desconocido de Jorge Luis Borges. Madrid: Anaya & M. Muchnik, 1992. 158 p.: bibl. (Actas; 3)

Al enunciar la tesis que organiza esta "metafísica del arrabal," Farías—autor de la conocida indagación *Heidegger y el nazismo*—declara: "A diferencia del Borges posterior y consagrado, que entiende lo nacional y lo singular como una pura materialización de lo verdadero, de lo absolutamente universal, en este primer Borges (*El tamaño de mi esperanza* fue publicado en 1926) el contenido y el motivo literarios van a estar esencialmente vinculados a una experiencia humanizada de la existencia singular, cotidiana y circunscrita al horizonte de la patria, considerado genéticamente horizonte histórico. Es desde allí que él va a plantear las cuestiones universales y fundamentales." [SS]

Foster, David William. The Argentine generation of 1880: ideology and cultural texts. See item **5518.**

4205 Le gaucho dans la littérature argentine.
Paris: Presses de la Sorbonne nouvelle, Univ. de la Sorbonne nouvelle, 1992. 218 p.: bibl. (América, 0982–92237; 11)
Número especial de la revista *América* destinado a ser una fuente bibliográfica para el programa de *agrégation* de 1992 y que, de este modo, otorga una visión del régimen académico francés. La primera parte—que cuenta con textos de Paul Verdevoye, Angela Dellepiane, Claude Cymerman, Gerardo Mario Goloboff, Adolfo Prieto y Marcelo Sztrum—da un panorama histórico del gaucho junto a algunas de sus proyecciones literarias y su transformación en símbolo de las letras argentinas. La segunda parte se concentra en *Facundo, Martín Fierro* y *Don Segundo Sombra;* la tercera incluye textos que se extienden hasta Payró y Borges. [SS]

4206 Gimbernat González, Ester. Aventuras del desacuerdo: novelistas argentinas de los '80. Buenos Aires: Danilo Albero Vergara, 1992. 340 p.: bibl. (Col. Crítica)
Con análisis de variada extensión y énfasis sobre autoras de diverso calibre, y haciendo hincapié en una década de fracturas y recomposición, transita las expresiones que van de la historia y los viajes al extrañamiento y la marginalidad. En este valioso ejercicio de recuperación de los orígenes a través de la literatura, que parte de presupuestos de la crítica feminista, Ester Gimbernat lee textos que en diversos grados ya han merecido la atención de la crítica internacional (Mercader, Valenzuela, Diaconú, Heker, Roffé) junto a otros que, en parte gracias a este análisis, saldrán de sus circuitos más inmediatos (Pagano, Donato, Escofet, Pozzi, Peluffo, Fabbri, Lojo). [SS]

4207 Jaén, Didier Tisdel. Borges' esoteric library: metaphysics to metafiction.
Lanham, Md.: Univ. Press of America, 1992. 230 p.: bibl., index.
Sobre la función literaria que desem-

peñan las alusiones a sistemas esotéricos. Propone que las "metaficciones" de Borges cuestionan los límites frecuentemente asignados a términos tales como "realidad" y "cultura" liberándolos—por lo menos en su dimensión textual—de compartimentos estancos. [SS]

4208 Jarkowski, Aníbal. Sobreviviente de una guerra: enviando tarjetas postales. (*Hispamérica/Gaithersburg*, 21:63, dic. 1992, p. 15–24)
Análisis de una de las novelas más beligerantes—y quizá la más compleja—de David Viñas. Escrita en el exilio, y publicada en México en 1979, *Cuerpo a cuerpo* es considerada un "modelo de biografía" que en el cruce de discursos, y montada en su eje militar, atraviesa 100 años de historia oficial argentina. [SS]

4209 Jorge Luis Borges: variaciones interpretativas sobre sus procedimientos literarios y bases epistemológicas. Edición de Karl Alfred Blüher y Alfonso de Toro. Frankfurt am Main, Germany: Vervuert, 1992. 228 p.: bibl. (Teoría y crítica de la cultura y literatura; 2)
Miscelánea de ensayos que parte de "la reconsideración del autor argentino bajo aspectos tales como la teoría de la recepción, de la intertextualidad, del palimpsesto, del rizoma y muy especialmente de la postmodernidad." Vinos y odres intercambian su novedad y alcurnia en un docto volumen que da cuenta del estado de estas vertientes críticas. [SS]

4210 Lapidot, Ema. Borges y la inteligencia artificial: análisis al estilo de Pierre Menard. Madrid: Pliegos, 1990? 163 p.: bibl. (Pliegos de ensayo; 59)
Responde al encuentro nada fortuito de Hofstadter y Dennett (*The mind's I*) y de Rucker (*Infinity and the mind*) con textos de Borges para "leer sus escritos con la entonación, la mentalidad, las imágenes y el vocabulario que la tecnología de nuestros días, la computadora electrónica y su derivada, la IA, nos proveyera." Continuación del escepticismo ante toda máquina de pensar y del "diálogo infinito" con el lector que suscitan las páginas de Borges. [SS]

Lehman, Kathryn and **Joy Logan.** Repression and reconstruction of a culture: Argentina and the *Proceso Militar.* See *HLAS 53:4106.*

4211 Lindstrom, Naomi. Jorge Luis Borges: a study of the short fiction. Boston: Twayne Publishers, 1990. 174 p.: bibl., 1 port. (Twayne's studies in short fiction; 16)

Al buen estudio introductorio de Lindstrom le siguen una entrevista a Borges realizada por Fernando Sorrentino en 1973 y dos conocidos artículos de Carter Wheelock y David William Foster. [SS]

4212 Lorenzo Alcalá, May. Manuel, María y Manuel: ensayos. Buenos Aires: Grupo Editor Latinoamericano: Emecé Editores, 1992. 117 p.: bibl., ill. (Col. Temas)

"Crónica de una Decadencia," sobre Manuel Mujica Láinez; "El Realismo Mágico en Argentina: María Granata;" "Apuntes para una Estética Pop: sobre las Tres Primeras Novelas de Manuel Puig" y un broche testimonial que porta el título del libro, recogen páginas que dan una visión personal y emotiva de sus lecturas. [SS]

4213 Luraschi, Ilse Adriana and Kay Sibbald. María Elena Walsh, o, "el desafío de la limitación." Buenos Aires: Editorial Sudamericana, 1993. 217 p.: bibl.

Mundialmente conocida por sus canciones para niños, este valioso libro presenta las múltiples dimensiones de María Elena Walsh. Desde la esfera privada de su biografía y su generosa producción poética, hasta la denuncia de la dictadura militar ("Desventuras en el País-Jardín-de-Infantes"), su vida aparece ejemplarmente definida por un enfrentamiento sostenido contra la arbitrariedad del poder autoritario. [SS]

4214 Masiello, Francine. Between civilization and barbarism: women, nation, and literary culture in modern Argentina. Lincoln: Univ. of Nebraska Press, 1992. 1 v.: bibl., index. (Engendering Latin America)

Aporte de envergadura que demuestra cómo la producción literaria de mujeres como Juana Manuela Gorriti, Eduarda Mansilla y Juana Manso, entre otras, incorpora un discurso alternativo a la versión homogeneizadora del eje "civilización-barbarie" y a la concepción misma de la nación y de la cultura nacional. [SS]

4215 Navascués, Javier de. Adán Buenosayres, una novela total: estudio narratológico. Pamplona, Spain: Ediciones Univ. de Navarra, 1992. 296 p. bibl. (Números anejos de RILCE; 9)

Sigue el modelo de Gérard Genette ("Discurso del Relato") para "desvelar, en definitiva, la *narratividad* de las novelas de Leopoldo Marechal, revisa el "contexto narrativo" de *Adán Buenosayres* (1948) y ofrece una somera lectura de su obra literaria. [SS]

4216 La novela argentina de los años 80. Edición de Roland Spiller. Frankfurt am Main, Germany: Vervuert Verlag, 1991. 324 p.: bibl. (Lateinamerika-Studien; 29)

Valiosa introducción a los rasgos definitorios de la época a cargo de especialistas argentinos (amplia mayoría) y alemanes. Ofrece un balance relativo entre autores (y algunos críticos) que ya poseían una amplia producción antes de los 80 y aquellos que se dan a conocer en los años que marcaron la transición de la dictadura a la democratización. [SS]

4217 Ocampo, Victoria. Autobiografía. Selección, prólogo y notas de Francisco Ayala. Madrid: Alianza Editorial, 1991. 224 p. (Alianza tres; 254)

Edición abreviada de los *Testimonios* que se limita—como lo advierte Ayala en el prólogo—a "presentar de manera escueta la vibrante confesión íntima de un alma apasionada." De este modo es soslayada gran parte de la dimensión histórica que el propio Ayala solicita de otros estudiosos para dar plena cuenta de esta "excepcional criatura" (1890–1979). [SS]

4218 Osorio, Elsa. Beatriz Guido: mentir la verdad. Buenos Aires: Planeta, 1991. 221 p.: bibl., ill., index. (Mujeres argentinas)

Nueva publicación en la serie "Mujeres Argentinas" que reconstruye ágilmente los mundos de Beatriz Guido, especialmente la relación con la literatura y el cine tan marcada por la colaboración con Leopoldo Torre Nilsson. [SS]

4219 Paredes, Alberto. Abismos de papel: los cuentos de Julio Cortázar. México: Dirección General de Publicaciones, Coordinación de Humanidades, 1988. 407 p.: bibl. (Biblioteca de letras)

Crítico que se incorpora a la figura del narrador, Paredes intuye (acertadamente) que en sus relatos Cortázar "se ha dedicado [entre otros propósitos, cabe suponer] a levantar el mapa de la ciudad burguesa." Luego de parafrasear las propuestas teóricas de Cortázar sobre el cuento, organiza y revisa los relatos conforme a las categorías de narrador. [SS]

4220 Piglia, Ricardo. Crítica y ficción. Buenos Aires: Siglo Veinte: Univ. Nacional del Litoral, 1990. 209 p. (Col. Entrevistas)

Las entrevistas con Piglia que integran este libro son, en un sentido, "conversaciones ficticias; este es un libro donde los interlocutores han inventado deliberadamente la escena de un diálogo para poder decir algo sobre la literatura." Y ese "algo" de uno de los narradores y críticos más lúcidos de su generación (que transita la especificidad de la ficción junto a Arlt y a Borges, a Gombrowicz y al cine, a *Sur*, al género policial y *Respiración artificial*) es un obligado punto de referencia para comprender no sólo a la literatura sino a la Argentina (al cómo se puede pensar la Argentina) de estas décadas. [SS]

4221 Puig, Manuel. Buenos Aires, cuándo será el día que me quieras: conversaciones con Manuel Puig. Entrevistas de Armando Almada Roche. Buenos Aires: Editorial Vinciguerra, 1992. 189 p. (Col. Diálogos contemporáneos)

Reúne entrevistas hechas a lo largo de varios años. Incluye las paradas obligatorias en General Villegas, frecuentes incursiones en la esfera íntima de Puig, comentarios sobre el cine y sobre sus obras que responden, en gran medida, al rechazo o a la marginación impuesta por diversos sectores de su entorno junto a declaraciones singularmente fuertes sobre la represión y la desmemoria, sobre ese "mal argentino" que "está en nuestras raíces" y sobre la mentira en la que viven sus compatriotas. [SS]

4222 Reati, Fernando O. Nombrar lo innombrable: violencia política y novela argentina, 1975–1985. Buenos Aires: Editorial Legasa, 1992. 268 p.: bibl. (Omnibus)

La posibilidad de representar la violencia y dar cuenta del horror vertebra uno de los mejores análisis realizados hasta hoy sobre la literatura argentina (1975–85). Con el registro apropiado del testigo presencial, presenta obras que van, por ejemplo, de Asís y Medina a Costantini, Dal Masetto, Rabanal y Soriano. [SS]

4223 Refour, Christel. Una identidad judeo argentina: la narrativa de Ricardo Feierstein. Traducción del francés de Clara Berman. Buenos Aires: Editorial Milá, 1992. 159 p.: bibl., ill. (Ensayo)

Apelando a la biografía de Feierstein y a una mayor contextualización histórica, analiza la trilogía *Sinfonía inocente*—compuesta por las novelas *Entre la izquierda y la pared, El caramelo descompuesto* y *Escala uno en cincuenta*—y *Mestizo*. Este texto fue presentado como tesis en la Univ. de Rouen. [SS]

4224 Romano, Eduardo and **El Seminario de Crítica Literaria Raúl Scalabrini Ortiz.** Las huellas de la imaginación. Buenos Aires: Puntosur Editores, 1990. 198 p.: bibl. (Puntosur literaria/crítica)

Estudios sobre el joven Scalabrini Ortiz, Nicolás Olivari, Fausto Burgos y Daniel Moyano enmarcados por un detenido análisis de "El *Boom* del Cuento Argentino en la Década de 1960" y por una "Lectura Sociopolítica de la Poesía" que relee la gauchesca ante las propuestas de Angel Rama. Más allá de la seriedad de los textos, el volumen en sí constituye una importante manifestación y un legado del trabajo colectivo realizado por diversos sectores de la intelectualidad argentina para responder a la represión ejercida sobre su universidad. [SS]

4225 Speranza, Graciela; Graciela Montaldo; and **Aníbal Jarkowski.** El estado de las cosas: veinte años de crítica argentina. (*Rev. Crít. Lit. Latinoam.*, 26:31/32, 1990, p. 9–37)

Excelente visión de conjunto elaborada por tres nuevos críticos a través de libros publicados en los años 80 por Enrique Pezzoni, Aníbal Ford-Jorge Rivera-Eduardo Romano, Nicolás Rosa, Noé Jitrik, Adolfo Prieto, Ricardo Piglia, Beatriz Sarlo y Josefina Ludmer. [SS]

4226 Stabb, Martin S. Borges revisited. Boston: Twayne Publishers, 1991. 151 p.: bibl., ill., index. (Twayne's world authors series; TWAS 819: Latin American literature)

Puesta al día de su *Jorge Luis Borges* (Twayne, 1970). Dedica capítulos a "The Making of a Writer" (el más biográfico); "The Canonical Texts;" "A Late Harvest;" "The Critical Trajectory;" y un brevísimo "Borges in Perspective" para ubicarlo en el contexto latinoamericano de este siglo. [SS]

4227 Tittler, Jonathan. Manuel Puig. New York: Twayne Publishers, 1993. 152 p.: bibl., ill., index. (Twayne's world authors series; TWAS 836: Latin American literature)

Se basa en las propuestas de Bakhtin

para realizar un sobrio análisis de las novelas, guiones y otros relatos de Puig. Se detiene en los motivos definitorios de su vida y producción literaria. Una de sus mayores contribuciones es la atención prestada a las páginas menos "canonizadas" por la crítica. [SS]

4228 Vázquez, María Esther. Victoria Ocampo. Buenos Aires: Planeta, 1991. 239 p.: bibl., index. (Mujeres argentinas)

Biografía, con algunas fotos memorables, de la que no está ausente el tono testimonial de M.E. Vásquez. Incluye una cronología y bibliografía de V. Ocampo y un listado mínimo de lo escrito sobre ella. Parte de la serie "Mujeres argentinas" dirigida por Félix Luna. [SS]

4229 Villordo, Oscar Hermes. Manucho: una vida de Mujica Láinez. Buenos Aires: Planeta, 1991. 318 p.: bibl., ill., index. (Biblioteca del sur: Biografía)

Admiración y amistad, caminos y simpatías compartidas, informan esta versión testimonial producida por el recientemente fallecido poeta, crítico y periodista. Respetuoso de la esfera íntima de Mujica Láinez, Villordo (autor de múltiples notas y semblanzas del autor de *Bomarzo*) no le escatima al lector el acceso privilegiado a los círculos familiares y artísticos de uno de los últimos *dandies* porteños. [SS]

Paraguay

4230 Augusto Roa Bastos: Premio Miguel de Cervantes, 1989: Biblioteca Nacional, abril-mayo 1990. Madrid: Ministerio de Cultura, Dirección General del Libro y Bibliotecas; Centro de las Letras Españolas, 1990. 95 p.: bibl., ill.

Incluye catálogo de exposición de homenaje al escritor paraguayo como ganador del Premio Cervantes 1989, Biblioteca Nacional de Madrid. Incluye un artículo de Angel Rama, "El Dictador Letrado de la Revolución Latinoamericana;" otro artículo de Wladimir Krysinski, "Entre la Polifonía Topológica y Dialogismo Dialéctico: *Yo, el Supremo* como Punto de Fuga de la Novela Moderna;" "El Pájaro Mosca: Palabra de la Madre, Escritura del Padre" de Gabriel Saad; "Una Cultura Oral" de Roa Bastos; "Roa Bastos por Roa Bastos: Cronología;" bibliografía de y bibliografía sobre Roa Bastos. Ilustrados con diseños de sus libros y fotografías. [MGP]

4231 Augusto Roa Bastos: Premio de Literatura en Lengua Castellana Miguel de Cervantes, 1989. Barcelona: Anthropos; Madrid: Ministerio de Cultura, Dirección General del Libro y Bibliotecas, Centro de las Letras Españolas, 1990. 143 p.: bibl., ill. (Ambitos literarios: Premios Cervantes; 15)

Comienza con un texto de Dónoan ("La Escritura como un Llamado a la Memoria Soterrada de un Pueblo: el Guaraní"), incluye el memorable discurso de Roa Bastos a la entrega del premio, citas estupendamente extraídas por Paco Tovar de una conversación (Toulouse, 1990), y análisis de algunos aspectos de su obra a cargo de Trinidad Barrera, Paco Tovar, Fernando Moreno Turner y Fernando Burgos. [SS]

4232 Marini Palmieri, Enrique. De la narrativa de Augusto Roa Bastos y de otros temas de literatura paraguaya. Asunción: Editorial Don Bosco, 1991. 167 p.: bibl.

Reúne textos publicados (1976–88) sobre *Yo el Supremo, Antología personal* y "Contar un Cuento" de Roa Bastos, y "Exposición Somera de Elementos sobre la Cuestión de la Identidad Nacional y la Novelística Paraguaya." [SS]

4233 Panorama del cuento paraguayo. v. 1. Selección y edición de Francisco Pérez Maricevich. Asunción: Tiempo Editora, 1988. 1 v.

Panorama histórico—merecedor de una introducción mucho más amplia—que comienza con Adriano Aguiar y termina con Carlos Gacete. Incluye, entre otros, textos de Rafael Barret, J. Natalicio González, Gabriel Casaccia, Josefina Plá y Augusto Roa Bastos. [SS]

4234 Pérez Cáceres, Lita et al. Narrativa paraguaya, 1980–1990. Recopilación de Guido Rodríguez Alcalá y María Elena Villagra. Asunción: Editorial Don Bosco; Pen Club del Paraguay, 1992. 150 p.

Muestra útil de cuentos y fragmentos de novela de 17 narradores que oscilan entre los 25 y los 50 años. Entre las tendencias de la producción paraguaya más joven se destaca "el surgimiento de una tradición femenina"—como lo constata Josefina Plá para los años 80—, el predominio del tema urbano sobre el rural, que responde tanto a la transformación del país como al abandono del color local como marca ineludible de la identidad nacional, y la llamativa presencia de la ciencia ficción. [SS]

4235 Roa Bastos, Augusto Antonio. El texto cautivo: el escritor y su obra. Alcalá de Henares, Spain: Fundación Colegio del Rey; Univ. de Alcalá de Henares, 1990. 29 p.: bibl., col. ill.

Texto de reflexión sobre la producción y lecturas de textos del novelista paraguayo es una contribución a su labor crítica que contribuye a la disquisición sobre la literatura hispanoamericana en las postrimerías del siglo. Su publicación coincide con la adjudicación del Premio Cervantes 1989 al ilustre escritor. Roa Bastos se refiere a la correlación desequilibrada que existe entre el proceso de construcción de una literatura bajo "la coacción de intereses extraños a ella como los que representan el poder cultural." Estas reflexiones se presentan como un testimonio personal y directo del autor. Documento indispensable para los estudiosos de la literatura hispanoamericana en general y de los que se interesan por Roa Bastos en particular. [MGP]

4236 Rodríguez-Alcalá, Hugo. Augusto Roa Bastos: Premio Cervantes 1989. Asunción?: Ñanduti Vive; Intercontinental Editora, 1990. 199 p.: bibl., ill.

Trabajos escritos por "un compañero de generación" (1954–86)—varios de los cuales son de índole más amplia que lo anunciado por el título del libro—que amalgaman la aproximación crítica con el tomo testimonial. [SS]

4237 Simposio sobre la Obra de Augusto Roa Bastos, *Asunción, 1990.* Actas. Asunción: Academia Paraguaya de la Lengua Española; Centro Cultural Español Juan de Salazar, 1990. 47 p.

Simposio, a manera de reconocimiento y homenaje (Asunción, abril 1989) para acompañar la entrega del Premio Cervantes. Además del texto de Pérez-Maricevich, "La Narrativa de Roa Bastos en Perspectiva," aparecen páginas de José-Luis Appleyard, Roque Vallejos, Josefina Plá, Manuel Peña Villamil y Manuel E. B. Argüello. [SS]

Uruguay

4238 Achugar, Hugo. Primeros apuntes para una historia de la crítica uruguaya, 1968–1988. (*Rev. Crít. Lit. Latinoam.*, 26: 31/32, 1990, p. 219–235)

Rama, Real de Azúa y Rodríguez Monegal serían suficientes para justificar la denominación de Achugar sobre su país: "Uruguay, País de Críticos." Selección de libros de este período precedida por consideraciones puntuales en torno a la periodización y la consiguiente división entre la producción crítica que va de los 60 al golpe y, a partir del golpe, entre la producida dentro del país y en el exilio; cierra con las tareas que cabe llevar adelante en la reconstitución del campo intelectual. Integra un número monográfico de la *Revista de crítica literaria latinoamericana* dedicado al estado de la crítica de la literatura latinoamericana en el continente y en otras latitudes del cual también se consigna aquí el texto dedicado a la crítica argentina. [SS]

4239 Ainsa, Fernando. Nuevas fronteras de la narrativa uruguaya, 1960–1993. Montevideo: Ediciones Trilce, 1993. 151 p.: bibl., index.

Los años 1973–84, que grabaron instancias de quiebre y reconstitución del Uruguay, también marcaron su producción cultural. Ainsa ofrece un panorama *crítico*, y ocasionalmente heterodoxo, de los cambios en la producción literaria de su país que incluye un capítulo dedicado a Cristina Peri Rossi. "Raíces de una Tradición Literaria" analiza las dimensiones de la novela histórica en y a partir de Acevedo Díaz, las vanguardias y la narrativa urbana en el Montevideo de los años 20, y las obras de Enrique Amorim y Juan Carlos Onetti. [SS]

4240 Angel Rama, presencia que no acaba. (*Casa Am.*, 34:192, julio/sept. 1993, p. 3–63)

Testimonios, semblanzas y análisis de la obra y el legado de Rama a cargo de Mario Benedetti, Guillermo Mariaca, Antonio Candido, Ana Pizarro, José Ramón Medina, Jorge Ruffinelli, Antonio Cornejo Polar, Ivan Schulman, Raúl Bueno, Hugo Achugar y Roberto Fernández Retamar al cumplirse 10 años de su muerte. [SS]

4241 Benedetti, Mario. La realidad y la palabra. Barcelona: Ediciones Destino, 1991. 335 p.: bibl. (Letras/Destino; 5)

Reúne materiales escritos entre 1953–90. Referidos por lo general a temas literarios y culturales latinoamericanos, complementa las recopilaciones *Subdesarrollo y letras de osadía* (1987) y *Crítica cómplice* (1988), ambas publicadas en España. Agrupados en "Cercanías," "Acuerdos, litigios" y "Lecturas," estos textos constituyen un recorrido eficaz por el repertorio de las pasiones, compromisos y predilecciones del autor, tal como lo consignan, por ejemplo, "La realidad y la Palabra" (1990) y "Rasgos y Riesgos de la Actual Poesía Latinoamericana" (1987). [SS]

4242 Díaz, José Pedro. El espectáculo imaginario: Juan Carlos Onetti y Felisberto Hernández, ¿una propuesta generacional?. Montevideo: Arca, 1986. 207 p.

Escritor y crítico uruguayo de la Generación del 45, reúne en este volumen bajo un mismo y muy apropiado título de "el espectáculo imaginario" estudios sobre las letras de dos de los "mayores" escritores uruguayos de este siglo, Felisberto Hernández y Juan Carlos Onetti. Se inicia el libro con un artículo titulado "El Tema del Espectáculo" sobre los dos escritores; y luego dos artículos sobre Felisberto, "Mas Allá de la Memoria: Propósito de Felisberto Hernández" y "F.H.: una Consciencia que se Rehusa a la Existencia." Todos estos estudios fueron escritos para otras ocasiones, y son finalmente reunidos aquí para los interesados en estas dos figuras centrales de la narrativa latinoamericana contemporánea. [MGP]

4243 Gilman, Claudia. Política y cultura: Marcha a partir de los años 60. (Nuevo Texto Crít., 6:11, primer semestre 1993, p. 153–186)

Penetrante análisis de Marcha (1939–74), "Un conjunto de discursos e intervenciones (que a lo largo de la década del 60 y el 70 se van ampliando y profundizando) orientados hacia la impugnación del orden social, económico y político vigente en el país y el mundo." Entre otros importantes rasgos señala que Marcha no sólo se definió por su antiimperialismo, nacionalismo y latinoamericanismo sino que incorporó al periodismo de izquierda la preocupación por lo municipal. [SS]

4244 Homenaje a Emir Rodríguez Monegal. Traducción del inglés por Beatriz Pereda. Montevideo: Ministerio de Educación y Cultura, 1986? 149 p.: bibl.

Este volumen parte del sentido homenaje de varios escritores y críticos—ex-alumnos algunos de ellos—realizado en The Americas Society (mayo/1986). Incluye, entre otros, textos de Sarduy, Sáinz, Cabrera Infante, Reinaldo Arenas, Haroldo de Campos y Richard Morse, junto al texto leído por Rodríguez Monegal sobre Rodó al cumplirse un aniversario de la muerte del autor de Ariel, así como dos de sus memoriosas páginas sobre "El Primer Onetti." [SS]

4245 Lockhart, Washington. Felisberto Hernández: una biografía literaria. Montevideo: Arca, 1991. 211 p.

Luego de leer la vida y la producción literaria de Felisberto Hernández desde una perspectiva altamente simpática y testimonial, Lockhart (que lo conoció en 1934) las divide en cuatro etapas: 1) 1902–25, la etapa formativa, en la que predomina su trabajo como músico; 2) 1925–40, conciertos en Montevideo y publicación de los "modestísimos folletos" Fulano de tal, El libro sin tapas, La cara de Ana y La envenenada; 3) 1940–46: publicación de Por los tiempos de Clemente Colling, El caballo perdido, cuentos en las revistas Sur y Asir; y 4) 1946–64: publicación de algunos de sus textos más citados: "Las Hortensias," "El Cocodrilo," "Lucrecia" y, en 1960, La casa inundada, su último libro. [SS]

4246 Méndez-Clark, Ronald S. Onetti y la (in)fidelidad a las reglas del juego. Lanham, Md.: Univ. Press of America, 1993. 178 p.: bibl., index.

Atinada utilización de Los adioses (1954) para examinar "los procesos de enunciación narrativa y la elaboración textual" en Onetti con el fin de derivar su concepción de la realidad y de la práctica literaria. Incluye una sólida revisión de los enunciados y silencios de la crítica en torno a esta obra medular. [SS]

4247 La obra de Juan Carlos Onetti: coloquio internacional. Madrid: Fundamentos; Centre de recherches, latinoaméricaines; 1990. 285 p.: bibl. (Col. Espiral hispanoamericana; 15)

Recoge textos presentados en el homenaje a Onetti (Poitiers, junio 1988). Entre otros, merecen ser destacados los trabajos de Fernando Ainsa ("Sobre Fugas, Destierros y Nostalgias en la Obra de Onetti"), Carmen Ruiz Barrionuevo ("La Invención del Personaje en los Relatos de Onetti"), Sabine Horl Groenewold ("El Lenguaje de lo Imposible: acerca de La vida breve de J.C. Onetti"), Sonia Mattalía ("Dejemos hablar al viento: Cita, Autocita, Autofagia") y Jaime Concha ("Cuando entonces de Onetti: ¿De contemptus mundi Contemporáneo?). [SS]

4248 Onetti, Juan Carlos. Premio de Literatura en Lengua Castellana Miguel de Cervantes, 1980. Madrid: Anthropos/Ministerio de Cultura, 1990. 1 v.

En el formato acostumbrado de esta serie, a la introducción de Dónoan le siguen una presentación general del autor a cargo de Paco Tovar, el discurso de Onetti a la entrega del premio en el que, entre otros aspectos, elogia la libertad que halló en España al verse obligado a salir al exilio ("Ubi Libertas Ibi Patria," dice al terminar), un collage de "Conversaciones de Onetti" montado por Teresita Mauro, ensayos de Fernando Ainsa y Jaime Pont, una breve bibliografía y una cronología que llega hasta 1987. [SS]

4249 Rocca, Pablo. Escritura y ambiente literario en *Marcha* y en el Uruguay, 1939–1974. (*Nuevo Texto Crít.*, 6:11, 1993, p. 3–151)

Una de las presentaciones más útiles de *Marcha* redactadas hasta la fecha. Traza sus orígenes, el clima intelectual y político en sus diversas etapas, así como las funciones que bajo la visión rectora de Aníbal Quijano desempeñaron, entre otros, Onetti, Rodríguez Monegal, Benedetti, Rama y Ruffinelli. [SS]

4250 Rocca, Pablo. Literatura y fútbol en el Uruguay, 1899–1990: la polémica, el encuentro. Montevideo: Arca, 1991. 109 p.: bibl.

Fascinante rastreo de la presencia del fútbol en un siglo de literatura uruguaya que se inicia con algunos de los rechazos de los estetas del 1900 y acaba en su entrañable consagración. El "Tiempo Adicional" que sigue al ensayo ofrece nueve muestras que abarcan páginas de Quiroga, Morosoli y Baroffio hasta llegar a Martínez Moreno y Galeano y a un poema de Elder Silva. [SS]

4251 Rodríguez-Villamil, Ana María. Elementos fantásticos en la narrativa de Armonía Somers. Montevideo: Ediciones de la Banda Oriental, 1990. 220 p.: bibl. (Ediciones de la Banda Oriental; 142)

La publicación de *La mujer desnuda* (1950), o de *Todos los cuentos* (1967), debieron haberle valido a Armonía Somers el reconocimiento continental—que a duras penas comienza a recibir en los últimos años—como una de las voces más singulares de la narrativa uruguaya. Si bien ceñido al formato de una tesis de grado, esta lectura contribuye a reconocer en Somers esa insólita línea experimental que tiene en el Conde de Lautreamont a uno de sus máximos ejemplos. [SS]

4252 Visca, Arturo Sergio et al. Armonía Somers, papeles críticos: cuarenta años de literatura. Coordinación de Rómulo Cosse. Montevideo: Librería Linardi y Risso, 1990. 299 p.: bibl., ill.

Primer volumen crítico totalmente dedicado al estudio de la narrativa de esta destacada narradora uruguaya. Reúne trabajos de 14 críticos en cuatro secciones tituladas "Enfoques Globales" con trabajos de Arturo Visca y Nicasio Perera San Martín; "El Cuento" con estudios de E. Picón Garfield, Lilia Dapaz, Noemí Ulla, Teresa Porzencanski, Elena Martínez, Ana María Rodríguez y Jorge Arbeleche; "La Novela" con la participación de María Rosa Olivera, Wilfredo Penco, Iber Verdugo, Rómulo Cosse y "Testimonio de vida y obra" con trabajos de Miguel Angel Campodónico y Alvaro Risso. De especial interés para los estudiosos de la literatura uruguaya reciente y de la producción femenina en el Uruguay, los trabajos aquí reunidos representan la labor de investigación de un grupo que ha dedicado su trabajo a esta importante obra narrativa contemporánea. [MGP]

4253 Walker, John. From *maniáticos* to *mareados:* the fictional world of Julio Ricci. (*Rev. Can. Estud. Hisp.*, 18:1, otoño 1993, p. 91–106)

Los personajes que pueblan los cuentos de *Los mareados* (1987) del uruguayo Julio Ricci—conocido fundamentalmente por *El grongo* (1976)—confirman su filiación con la línea pautada por Arlt en la otra orilla del Plata. [SS]

Poetry

FRANCISCO CABANILLAS, *Assistant Professor of Spanish, Bowling Green State University*
LUIS EYZAGUIRRE, *Professor of Spanish, University of Connecticut-Storrs*
NORMA KLAHN, *Associate Professor of Spanish, University of California, Santa Cruz*
PEDRO LASTRA, *Professor of Spanish, State University of New York at Stony Brook*
JOSE MIGUEL OVIEDO, *Trustee Professor of Spanish, University of Pennsylvania*
OSCAR RIVERA-RODAS, *Professor of Spanish, University of Tennessee, Knoxville*
ARMANDO ROMERO, *Professor of Spanish, University of Cincinnati*
LILIAN URIBE, *Assistant Professor of Spanish, Central Connecticut State University*

GENERAL

LA LECTURA CRITICA DE LA POESIA hispanoamericana ha experimentado una estimable ampliación en este período, pues a las sostenidas preocupaciones por la obra de autores establecidos, especialmente del modernismo y de la Vanguardia, ha venido a sumarse el buen resultado de una necesaria atención por poetas más cercanos en el tiempo. En el primer caso, deben mencionarse los trabajos dedicados a R. Darío (item **4494**), J. Herrera y Reissig (item **4505**), A. Storni (items **4501, 4515** y **4522**), G. Mistral (item **4534**), C. Vallejo (items **4510** y **4519**), V. Huidobro (items **4513** y **4523**), P. De Rokha (item **4524**), J.L. Borges (item **4517**) y P. Neruda (item **4535**); en el segundo, los aportes críticos sobre la poesía de E.A. Westphalen (item **4507**), N. Parra (items **4498** y **4521**), G. Rojas (items **4520** y **4532**), Julia de Burgos (item **4514**), O. Orozco (item **4527**), E. Diego (item **4492**) y A. Pizarnik (item **4529**). Entre los estudios más meritorios dedicados específicamente a la poesía femenina sobresale el libro *Las poetas del buen amor* (item **4485**), en el que se incluyen análisis de la escritura transgresora de Sor Juana, D. Agustini, J. de Ibarbourou y A. Storni. La modalidad literaria de la entrevista está muy bien representada en los libros que recogen diálogos con A. Berenguer (item **4497**), C. Soto Vélez (item **4500**), N. Parra (item **4521**) y en el volumen *Conversaciones con la poesía chilena* (item **4480**).

Un tema relevante en el período fue el estudio de los manifiestos, proclamas y polémicas de la Vanguardia. Cuatro libros notables reúnen y procesan críticamente un riquísimo material del momento de insurgencia de los movimientos renovadores en Hispanoamérica (items **4479, 4487, 4488** y **4490**). Desde luego, algunos documentos centrales de la Vanguardia se repiten en los cuatro volúmenes, pero las variadas perspectivas de los autores—tanto en los criterios de selección como en las valoraciones—acrecientan el interés de esos libros que dialogan entre sí.

Cuatro poetas recibieron importantes distinciones internacionales y nacionales: el Premio Juan Rulfo fue otorgado a Nicanor Parra en 1991 y a Eliseo Diego en 1993, y Gonzalo Rojas mereció el Premio de Poesía Reina Sofía, de España, en 1992, el mismo año en que le fue conferido en Chile el Premio Nacional de Literatura, y en México José Emilio Pacheco recibió el Premio Nacional de Literatura y Lingüística.

En el campo de la bibliografía, la contribución mayor es el libro de Jacobo Sefamí (item **4547**), un instrumento auxiliar de primer orden para el estudioso de la poesía actual. También lo son las competentes bibliografías que la revista *Inti* incluye a menudo en sus entregas periódicas: en el último tiempo han aparecido en sus páginas las de C.G. Belli, J. Gelman y G. Rojas, entre otras.

La bibliografía y las notas sobre la producción poética y crítica de Centroamérica correspondientes al período considerado en este volumen de *HLAS* serán incluídas en el volumen 56. [PL]

MEXICO

En México la poesía se mantiene viva gracias a una minoría entusiasta de lectores, editoriales y críticos, y es dentro de ese marco de referencia que resaltan aún más la calidad y la cantidad de poemarios aparecidos en los inicios de los '90. Los premios constituyen un justo reconocimiento para este género poco comercial y que según algunos autores como Homero Aridjis se encuentra cada vez más marginado. El Premio Nacional de Literatura y Lingüística otorgado a José Emilio Pacheco en 1992 es por eso doblemente significativo: no sólo destaca la importancia de una producción notable sino también la de la poesía misma como actividad creativa.

Gerardo Deniz y Vicente Quirarte compartieron el Premio Xavier Villaurrutia de 1991 por *Amor y Oxidente* y *El ángel es vampiro,* respectivamente (items **4342** y **4427**). El Premio Nacional de Aguascalientes promueve la obra de las jóvenes generaciones: lo han recibido Jorge Esquinca con *El cardo en la voz* (item **4345**), Ernesto Lumbreras con *Espuelas para demorar el viaje* (item **4384**) y Fabio Morábito con *De lunes todo el año* (item **4401**). El Premio Nacional Jaime Sabines le fue concedido en 1992 a Elsa Cross.

Las antologías siguen siendo el mejor vehículo para dar a conocer la obra de poetas ya establecidos (items **4264, 4285** y **4281**). La poesía escrita por mujeres encuentra lectores no sólo en México sino más allá de la frontera y en importantes traducciones (items **4266, 4270** y **4272**). Especial mención merecen las obras de poetas conocidas como Elsa Cross (item **4338**) y Silvia Tomasa Rivera (item **4433**) y las de autoras que empiezan a ser apreciadas por la crítica, como Isabel Quiñones (item **4426**) y Perla Schwartz (item **4450**).

Poetas mayores como Octavio Paz, Rubén Bonifaz Nuño y Jaime Sabines estuvieron muy presentes en este panorama con nuevas ediciones (items **4415, 4312, 4313** y **4446**) y en la producción crítica que suscitaron (items **4525** y **4267**). [NK]

EL CARIBE

Si bien no se puede hablar de una temática "nueva" ni de un movimiento "nuevo" en la poesía del Caribe de los últimos años, hay que subrayar que la poesía femenina y también feminista constituye lo más novedoso. Se destacan poetas de una promoción muy joven, como la puertorriqueña Mayra Santos Febre (items **4448** y **4449**), cuya poesía registra, simultáneamente con lo femenino, la autorreflexión poética. En otras escritoras más establecidas de Puerto Rico, como Olga Nolla (item **4409**) y Etnairis Rivera (item **4432**), la lectura mitológica y filosófica, respectivamente, establece una complicidad con lo femenino.

Además de la poesía femenina y feminista, hay que señalar la presencia de la poesía homosexual del puertorriqueño Manuel Ramos Otero (item **4430**), la metapoesía del cubano José Pérez Olivares (item **4418**), la "cienciapoesía" del cubano Rafael Catalá (item **4324**) y la poesía de crítica histórica del dominicano Tomás Castro (item **4322**).

Entre los poetas establecidos, cabe señalar la publicación de *Cuatro de oros,* de Eliseo Diego (item **4343**), y la de *Las pequeñas muertes,* de Francisco Matos Paoli (item **4390**). Se reeditan dos poemarios importantes de poetas fallecidos: Juan Antonio Corretjer (item **4336**) y Luis Palés Matos (item **4413**). Por otro lado, el Instituto de Cultura Puertorriqueña publica la obra poética de Clemente Soto Vélez (item **4455**), al igual que—sorprendentemente—una antología poética de Iván Silén (item **4452**). En Madrid, Emilio de Armas publica una antología de la poesía de Lezama Lima (item **4381**).

Con excepción del estudio de Vicenta Caamaño de Fernández (item **4470**), que trabaja el tema del negro en la poesía dominicana, la mayoría de la crítica publicada se vuelca hacia la recopilación de ensayos/entrevistas sobre el trabajo de un autor. Cabe señalar el trabajo sobre Eliseo Diego a cargo de Enrique Saínz (item **4492**), las conversaciones con Clemente Soto Vélez de Marithelma Costa y Alvin Joaquín Figueroa (item **4500**), y la recopilación de ensayos de Pedro Simón sobre Dulce María Loynaz (item **4503**).

Dos artículos abordan la problemática racial y genérico-sexual: Anne Marie Bankay estudia la dinámica mujer-raza entre las poetas contemporáneas dominicanas (item **4260**), mientras que Claudette Rose Green-Williams estudia la construcción de la mulata sensual entre los poetas del Caribe (item **4541**). Yara González-Monte propone un acercamiento a la poesía cubana escrita en los Estados Unidos (item **4474**).

El Premio Juan Rulfo de 1993 fue otorgado al cubano Eliseo Diego en la Casa Universitaria de Guadalajara, México, donde tuvo lugar la presentación de su obra *Libro de quizá y de quién sabe* (La Habana: Editorial Letras Cubanas, 1989). Desgraciadamente, Eliseo Diego falleció poco tiempo después, a comienzos de 1994. En el verano de 1993 falleció el puertorriqueño Clemente Soto Vélez. Ambas pérdidas han ensombrecido no sólo el panorama poético nacional sino el del continente.

Además de las editoriales cubanas que tradicionalmente han favorecido el quehacer poético, debe mencionarse la labor de difusión que han realizado en Puerto Rico la *Revista del Instituto de Cultura Puertorriqueña* y la editorial *Mairena*. En la República Dominicana merecen reconocimiento la revista *Cuadernos de Poética* y la Editorial Taller. En los Estados Unidos, aunque no dedicado únicamente a la crítica de la poesía caribeña, cabe señalar la reciente aparición de la revista *Afro-Hispanic Review*. [FC]

COLOMBIA Y VENEZUELA

Hasta el momento, la década del 90 se ha caracterizado por una necesidad de valoración crítica, en parte por las nuevas generaciones, de la obra de los poetas precedentes. En Colombia se renuevan los análisis y lecturas de los poetas de "Piedra y Cielo" (item **4530**) y "Mito" y el nadaísmo (item **4504**), y en Venezuela los del grupo "Viernes," los poetas del 50 y los de "Sardio" o "El Techo de la Ballena." En Colombia el homenaje nacional a Alvaro Mutis en 1993 al cumplir sus 70 años y en Venezuela los homenajes en la bienal "Mariano Picón Salas" a los poetas Juan Sánchez Peláez, Juan Liscano y Juan Calzadilla, entre otros, confirman esta tendencia.

Debe destacarse en Colombia el Festival Internacional de Poesía que en Medellín vienen realizando los editores de la revista *Prometeo*. La Casa Silva en Bogotá y la Biblioteca Luis Angel Arango continúan siendo las dos instituciones líderes en cuanto al movimiento poético desde Bogotá. En la labor de difusión poética es importante mencionar en Colombia a Juan M. Roca desde el *Magazin dominical* del *Espectador* de Bogotá y a Santiago Mutis y su revista *Gradiva*.

En Venezuela la nota triste es la muerte del gran poeta Vicente Gerbasi (1913–93). Integrante del grupo "Viernes," Gerbasi no sólo fue un innovador dentro de la poesía venezolana de su época sino un activista poético desde sus cargos como diplomático y editor de la *Revista Nacional de Cultura*.

La Casa de Poesía de la Fundación Rómulo Gallegos, que dirige el poeta Santos López, continúa otorgando el premio "J.A. Pérez Bonalde." En los años recientes han sido premiados los poetas Rafael Cadenas y Enrique Molina. La editorial "Pequeña Venecia" prosigue su magnífica labor de difusión de la poesía venezolana y continental. Este año los editores fueron galardonados por el gobierno como el mejor esfuerzo editorial del país. En la poesía femenina venezolana se destaca la labor de Yolanda Pantin (item **4414**), Blanca Strepponi (item **4456**) y Alicia Torres (item **4459**). [AR]

BOLIVIA Y ECUADOR

En Bolivia, el panorama de la poesía de los últimos años ha registrado la regular aparición de volúmenes de autores consagrados y nuevos. Han llamado la atención, sin embargo, los siguientes hechos: cierto intento de ofrecer una expresión poética propiamente nacional mediante publicaciones en las que sus autores tratan de recuperar voces, imágenes y conceptos de la propia tradición oral y regional, como es el caso de Suárez (item **4457**), Montaño (item **4398**) y Arduz (item **4294**). También se ha destacado el interés cada vez mayor por la obra del poeta recientemente fallecido Jaime Sáenz, de quien se ha publicado un volumen póstumo (item **4447**). No hay duda de la dimensión excepcional de este poeta boliviano no sólo en su país sino en el contexto de la poesía latinoamericana del siglo XX. El interés creciente que su obra ha ganado en su propio país se puede ver también en el homenaje poético que le rinden otros poetas bolivianos como Avila Echazú (item **4495**) y en el caso de jóvenes que desarrollan su estilo bajo la influencia de la obra de Sáenz (item **4344**). Otro hecho de los últimos años que se debe registrar, es la aparición de estudios sobre el género, particularmente del presente siglo, como el prólogo de Mitre (item **4259**) y el libro de Rivera-Rodas (item **4483**).

En Ecuador, entre publicaciones de autores consagrados como Carrera Andrade (item **4320**) o Adoum (item **4254**), aparecieron voces nuevas como la de Basantes (item **4303**). Por otra parte, la aparición de colecciones preparadas con la autoridad de especialistas (items **4279, 4481** y **4361**) demuestra el interés por incrementar las ediciones críticas, precedidas de estudios que ayudan a la comprensión de la poesía ecuatoriana por un público escolar y general. Esas ediciones abarcan la obra de autores individuales o períodos de la historia literaria nacional. Esta tarea tiene como efecto la revaloración y re-publicación de poetas ya conocidos. Del mismo modo, se alentó la publicación de trabajos de investigación, como el caso de la poesía anónima de la provincia de Esmeraldas (item **4476**). Se puede añadir asimismo cierto interés por la difusión de la obra de autores regionales que no siempre llegan a las selecciones de la poesía oficial realizadas desde la ciudad capital. [ORR]

PERU

El fenómeno más interesante de la poesía peruana de estos últimos años es la activa presencia de las mujeres en un campo creador donde, durante varias décadas, la contribución femenina se reducía casi únicamente a la excelente Blanca Varela. Hoy esta figura aparece rodeada de poetas de diversas generaciones y tendencias, que han contribuido a dar un nuevo perfil a la poesía peruana. Las que aquí se registran—M. Alvarez (item **4290**), A.M. Gazzolo (item **4359**) y G. Pollarolo (item **4422**)—representan sólo una pequeña muestra del conjunto total. Su presencia está, por cierto, asociada a la difusión de las ideas y propuestas del feminismo, pero no se agota en ellas, pues algunas voces femeninas (Ana María Gazzolo, por ejemplo) prefieren mantenerse al margen y dejarse oir sin un soporte teórico reconocible.

Hay dos aspectos que atender en el fenómeno: uno sociológico, que es el de la ruptura de ciertos hábitos intelectuales tradicionales que no hacían fácil ni orgánico el trabajo poético de las mujeres, salvo el más convencional y menos creador; el otro es el estrictamente estético, pues incorpora a la poesía una nueva sensibilidad. Esto permite ingresar al mundo privado de las mujeres y descubrir el modo concreto como perciben la realidad en la que están insertas y cómo intentan conjurarla. Así, la poesía peruana ha enriquecido su temática y abierto otros cauces expresivos. La peculiar situación de la mujer dentro de la órbita doméstica, las nuevas exigencias que le plantea la vida moderna, su conciencia de ser autónomo en un contexto social donde no siempre lo fue, la orgullosa afirmación de su sexualidad y de su propia agresividad, son algunos de los motivos que ahora presentan las nuevas poetas peruanas.

Por cierto, el predominio de los poetas no ha desaparecido, gracias tanto a la presencia de ciertas figuras de prestigio establecido, como a creadores más jóvenes y en proceso de maduración. Se nota una tendencia a mantener la continuidad del proceso poético nacional sin las rupturas violentas y las tomas de posición extremadas de décadas anteriores, creando así un espacio en el que los diversos autores, grupos y generaciones pueden dialogar fructíferamente. Por lo menos, dos de ellos, Belli (item **4305**) y Martos (items **4388** y **4389**), han publicado nuevos e importantes libros, mientras Ruiz Rosas (item **4444**) y Cisneros (item **4329**) han hecho recopilaciones de su obra poética. En cuanto a trabajos críticos dedicados al género, el último libro de James Higgins sobre Vallejo (item **4510**) y el repertorio de Américo Ferrari sobre poetas del siglo XX (item **4472**) pueden mencionarse entre lo más destacado. [JMO]

CHILE

Destacan en el período cinco poemarios: sobresaliente es *Balance de blanco en el "Angel Triste" de Durero*, primer libro de Lila Calderón (item **4317**). Original también es el mundo de Luis Correa Díaz en sus dos publicaciones: *Bajo la pequeña música de su pie* y *Rosario de actos de habla* (items **4334** y **4335**). *Sentado en la cuneta*, de Claudio Bertoni es un irreverente *ubi sunt* de una época de adolescencia (item **4306**). Belinda Zubicueta, prisionera política en Chile, expresa en *Ardiendo piedras* ansias de libertad en términos de lo erótico (item **4468**).

Entre las nuevas ediciones y reediciones deben señalarse *Tratado de sortilegios* de Oscar Hahn (item **4369**), que reagrupa aquí su obra en un orden nuevo, al parecer definitivo, y tres libros de Gonzalo Rojas: *Cinco visiones* (item **4438**), *Antología de aire* (item **4437**) y *Contra la muerte* (item **4439**), importante reedición de una obra fundamental del autor. De Pedro Lastra aparecieron la primera publicación chilena de *Noticias del extranjero* (item **4378**) y la edición de una breve antología bilingüe: *Travel Notes* (item **4379**).

En el ámbito de lo biográfico se publicaron dos libro excelentes: la cuarta edición de *Neruda* de V. Teitelboim (item **4535**) y *El amigo piedra: autobiografía* de Pablo de Rokha (item **4546**). Estudios críticos de relieve sobre dos figuras capitales de la poesía chilena son: *La poesía de Gonzalo Rojas* de Hilda R. May (item **4520**); *El espejo trizado*, de Jacobo Sefamí (item **4532**), también dedicado al estudio de G. Rojas; y *Pablo de Rokha: una escritura en movimiento*, de Naín Nómez (item **4524**), sin duda lo mejor que se ha escrito sobre este discutido poeta. En el campo de las "conversaciones" y "entrevistas" son aportes fundamentales *Conversaciones con Nicanor Parra* de Leonidas Morales (item **4521**) y *Conversaciones con la poesía chilena* de J.A. Piña (item **4480**).

La poesía chilena queda disminuida con el fallecimiento de dos de sus figuras principales, ambos Premios Nacionales de Literatura: Eduardo Anguita murió en agosto y Humberto Díaz Casanueva en nov. de 1992. [LE]

ARGENTINA, URUGUAY Y PARAGUAY

El balance de la producción poética argentina es altamente positivo. Se destacan las reediciones, nuevos poemarios, selecciones antológicas y ensayos críticos de y sobre varios autores cuya trayectoria comienza alrededor de la década del 60. De particular interés resultan la edición de la *Obra completa* de Alejandra Pizarnik (item **4421**), los poemarios de Juana Bignozzi (items **4307** y **4308**) y el nuevo libro de Enrique Molina (item **4397**).

La obra y la vida de Alfonsina Storni ha sido objeto de varios trabajos, casi todos desde una perspectiva feminista que destaca las diversas formas de marginalidad que la escritora representa (como mujer, como madre soltera, como inmigrante, como poetisa): los aportes de Gwen Kirkpatrick (item **4515**) y de Marta Morello-Frosch (item **4522**) son muy significativos.

En la joven poesía argentina predomina la tendencia neorromántica con escasos referentes políticos. El sujeto lírico, consciente de sus limitaciones, impone a menudo un tono desesperanzado y en muchos casos irónico a sus poemas. La ciudad sigue siendo el espacio privilegiado de esta poesía.

La actividad poética paraguaya de este período fue escasa, pero interesa mencionar el nuevo poemario de Susy Delgado (item **4502**) y las ediciones antológicas a cargo de Miguel Angel Fernández y Renée Ferrer de Arréllaga (item **4283**) y de Ricardo Rolón (item **4284**).

Lo más relevante de la poesía uruguaya de estos años sigue siendo el aporte de jóvenes poetas, la mayoría de los cuales ha encontrado un espacio editorial propicio a través de Ediciones de Uno y Vintén Editor. La capacidad creativa de estos escritores se ve tanto en su producción poética como en la organización de encuentros y festivales de poesía: desde el 30 de oct. al 8 de nov. de 1993 se llevó a cabo el Primer Festival Hispanoamericano de Poesía dirigido por los poetas Luis Bravo, Silvia Guerra y Laura Haiek, con la ayuda de la Intendencia de Montevideo y de Ediciones de Uno, y al cual concurrieron más de cien poetas hispanoamericanos, españoles, estadounidenses y suecos. Voces prometedoras de esta poesía son las de Sabela de Tezanos (item **4458**), Carlos E. Brandi (item **4314**), Eduardo Roland (item **4443**) y Diana Correa (item **4333**).

Notas resaltantes del período son la edición de la *Obra completa* de Humberto Megget (item **4393**) y la publicación, largamente anticipada, del primer poemario de Fernando Pereda, *Pruebas al canto* (item **4416**); el poeta, cuya poesía giró obsesivamente en torno al tema de la muerte, falleció en mayo de 1994. [LU]

ANTHOLOGIES

4254 Adoum, Jorge Enrique. Los cuadernos de la tierra. v. 1–4. Prólogo del autor. Guayaquil: Ediciones de la Univ. de Guayaquil, 1988. 4 v. in 1 (xxiv, 220 p.): bibl.;

Reedición necesaria de textos importantes aparecidos en más de 10 años. El volumen incluye "Los Orígenes," "El Enemigo y la Mañana," "Dios Trajo la Sombra" y "El Dorado y las Ocupaciones Nocturnas." Esos cuatro extensos textos son el resultado de la reflexión e interpretación de la historia ecuatoriana, desde sus orígenes a la época colonial, realizada por su autor. El volumen incluye un prólogo del propio Adoum. [ORR]

4255 Antología de la poesía hispanoamericana actual. Selección, prólogo y notas de Julio Ortega. México: Siglo Veintiuno Editores, 1987. 505 p.: index. (La Creación literaria)

Muestra de 82 autores, desde César Moro (1903–56) hasta Raúl Zurita y Coral Bracho (n. 1951). Criterio de selección impreciso y prólogo en el que a menudo impera la vaguedad. Aunque el autor invoca la actividad del lector para convalidar su propuesta de una antología "no arbitraria," ésta resulta serlo, e incluso más que otras. Poetas importantes del período aparecen, en general, bien representados. [PL]

4256 Antología de la poesía peruana: generación del 80. Prólogo, selección, notas y entrevistas de José Beltrán Peña. 2. ed. Lima: Estilo y Contenido Ediciones; J. Beltrán Peña, 1990. 232 p.: ill.

Lleno de generalidades como "el tiempo pasa y para bien o para mal deja huellas, y el Arte poético es insolayable," el valor crítico del prólogo es completamente delezable; el de la selección misma apenas es un poco mejor: incluye algunos nombres interesantes, pero la lista de 40 poetas pertenecientes a la última década es notoriamente excesiva. [JMO]

4257 Antología de la poesía religiosa chilena: lecturas escogidas. Edición de Miguel Arteche y Rodrigo Cánovas. Santiago: Facultad de Letras, Centro de Estudios de Literatura Chilena, Univ. Católica de Chile, 1989. 593 p.:

Se trata de cubrir más de 500 años de poesía religiosa en Chile en 593 p. Se incluyen por primera vez en un libro textos yaganes, onas, alacalufes, mapuches, pascuenses, aymaras, cunzas y quechuas. Tres grandes secciones son: 1) La voz indígena; 2) La voz tradicional; 3) La voz personal del siglo XVI al siglo XX. Fuente de mucha información valiosa sobre el tema. La gran inclusividad de definición de lo religioso, particularmente en el siglo XX, permite que los criterios de selección sean extremadamente latos y generosos. Bibliografía muy completa; las notas útiles y necesarias. Texto de consulta indispensable en área que necesita otros buenos estudios como éste. [LE]

4258 Antología del soneto hispano americano. Selección y prólogo de Mirta Yáñez. La Habana: Editorial Arte y Literatura, 1988. 228 p.: index (Col. Huracán)

Prólogo resume la historia de esta forma, y selección siguiente ilustra bien su práctica constante en Hispanoamérica, desde la colonia. Entre muchas posibilidades antológicas, la autora ha optado por la amplitud de la muestra: más de 200 poetas y otros tantos sonetos, en general elegidos con apreciable buen gusto. [PL]

4259 El árbol y la piedra: poetas contemporáneos de Bolivia. Selección y estudio crítico de Eduardo Mitre. Caracas: Monte Avila, 1986 263 p.: bibl. (Altazor)

Selección de 12 poetas bolivianos del siglo XX: J.E. Guerra, A. Avila Jiménez, G. Viscarra Fabre, O. Cerruto, J. Saenz, G. Medinaceli, J. de la Vega, G. Vásquez Méndez, E. Camargo, R. Echazú, P. Shimose y J. Urzagasti. Está precedida por un prólogo de Eduardo Mitre, quien con esta selección desea presentar una muestra de la poesía moderna de Bolivia. [ORR]

4260 Bankay, Anne María. Contemporary women poets of the Dominican Republic: perspectives on race and other social issues. (*Afro-Hisp. Rev.*, 12:1, Spring 1993, p. 34–41)

Estudio sucinto pero importante y necesario de la poesía femenina dominicana contemporánea. Esta poesía, que no se suscribe a las normas tradicionales, parece más dispuesta a enfrentar, desde otros ángulos, los problemas que la literatura canónica ha solapado tradicionalmente, tales como la cuestión etnocultural, la coexistencia con Haití y los problemas de la explotación económica y sexual. [FC]

4261 Breviario de poesía lunfarda. Selección y prólogo de Eduardo Romano. Buenos Aires: Andrómeda, 1990. 269 p.: (Col. Libros de cabecera)

Prólogo fundamenta su preferencia por el término "poesía lunfardesca" y no "lunfarda" y luego analiza las principales etapas de dicha poesía y sus características. Selección incluye—entre otros—a Pascual Contursi, Yacaré, Celedonio Esteban Flores, Enrique Cadícamo, Carlos de la Púa, etc. [LU]

4262 Calle C., Waldo et al. Siete poetas. Recopilación de Sara Beatriz Vanégas Coveña. Cuenca, Ecuador: Casa de la Cultura Ecuatoriana Benjamín Carrión, Núcleo del Azuay, 1990. 154 p.:

Selección de la obra de Waldo Calle, E. Crespo Reyes, A. Ordoñez Ortiz, I. Petroff Rojas, G. Salgado Espinosa, A. Vivar y de la misma compiladora. De acuerdo a la compiladora, este grupo representa la poesía de Cuenca. Las selecciones individuales están precedidas por una ficha bibliográfica del correspondiente autor. [ORR]

4263 Cinco como un puño: poesía del "Grupo de Guayaquil." Recopilación, introducción, notas y bibliografía por Alejandro Guerra Cáceres. Guayaquil: Casa de la Cultura Ecuatoriana Benjamín Carrión, Núcleo del Guayas, 1991. 158 p.: bibl., ill.

Resultado de una investigación en diarios y revistas, este volumen reúne la poesía de cinco autores ecuatorianos del "Grupo Guayaquil" conocidos tradicionalmente como narradores. Los textos poéticos corresponden cronológicamente al período 1925–30 en que fueron publicados originalmente. Los cinco autores son: José de la Cuadra (1903–41), Alfredo Pareja Diezcanseco (1908), Demetrio Aguilera Malta (1909–81), Joaquín Gallegos Lara (1909–47) y Enrique Gil Gilbert (1912–73). Incluye una bibliografía de la

edición original de los textos compilados.
[ORR]

4264 Con sus propias palabras: antología de poetas mexicanos nacidos entre 1950–1955. Selección y recopilación de Eduardo Langagne. México: Univ. Autónoma de Querétaro, 1987. 276 p.

Util introducción a 15 poetas de las más recientes promociones. Integran esta colección José Luis Rivas, José de Jesús Sampedro, Efraín Bartolomé, Alberto Blanco, Víctor Manuel Cárdenas, Angel José Fernández, Raul Bañuelos, Ricardo Castillo, Ethel Krauze, Vicente Quirarte, Carmen Boullosa, Roberto Vallarino, Verónica Volkow, y Carlos Oliva. Cada selección va precedida por breves notas sobre y de los poetas. [NK]

4265 Contra el silencio: poesía uruguaya, 1973–1988. Introducción y recopilación de Graciela Mántaras Loedel. Montevideo: Túpac Amaru Editorial, 1989. 188 p.: bibl. (Verso libre; 1)

Los 15 años que abarca esta selección están signados por el comienzo de la dictadura militar uruguaya y los albores de un nuevo período democrático. En su introducción, la autora da cuenta de los acontecimientos políticos más importantes del período y su indudable incidencia en la producción poética que estudia. Mántaras Loedel destaca también el estilo manierista y la búsqueda de racionalidad como constantes que caracterizan a la poesía de este período. Selección de autores y textos es amplia y de gran calidad. Lo único objetable sería que algunos poemas seleccionados no fueron publicados dentro del período que comprende esta muestra. [LU]

4266 El cuerpo del deseo: poesía erótica femenina en el México actual. Introducción, selección y notas de Valeria Manca. México: Univ. Autónoma Metropolitana; Xalapa, México: Univ. Veracruzana, 1989. 287 p.: (Ficción)

Interesante antología que reúne la poesía de 22 autoras nacidas entre 1943–60 cuyo tema principal es el erotismo. Poetas capitalinas que como forma de conocimiento "escriben sobre el cuerpo, y todo lo que de él emana." Cada selección va precedida de una breve biografía que incorpora material de entrevistas hechas por la compiladora. Provee interesantes observaciones sobre el quehacer poético de las mujeres y el tema del erotismo

en México. Se destaca la presencia de una escritura distinta, "una escritura en femenino" que transforma a las mujeres de objetos a sujetos del deseo. Entre las poetas incluídas están Kyra Galván, Verónica Volkow, Perla Schwartz, Sabina Berman, Myriam Moscona, Coral Bracho, Ethel Krauze, Elsa Cross, Elva Macías, y Gloria Gervitz. [NK]

4267 Festival Internacional de Poesía de la Ciudad de México, _México_, 1987. Antología. Selección de Homero y Betty Aridjis. Notas de Alberto Ruy Sánchez. México: Ediciones el Tucán de Virginia; Fundación E. Gutman, 1988. 427 p.: ports.

La breve nota introductoria de Homero y Betty Aridjis, promotores asiduos de los festivales de poesía en México, busca definir la poesía desde la consabida frase de Wallace Stevens que afirma que el género constituye la ficción suprema. Los editores seleccionan poemas leídos durante el Festival de Poesía (Ciudad de México, 18—23 de agosto de 1987) en el Teatro de la Ciudad. Participaron 22 poetas extranjeros, y 17 poetas mexicanos, entre ellos, Juan Bañuelos, Alí Chumacero, Alberto Blanco, Francisco Cervantes, Ulalume González de León, J.E. Pacheco, Octavio Paz, Jaime Sabines. Cada selección va precedida por una biobibliografía de los poetas preparada por Alberto Ruy Sánchez. [NK]

4268 _Hora de Poesía._ Nos. 83/84, sept./dic. 1992- . Barcelona: Lentini Editor.

Dossier "Poesía Hispanoamericana" en homenaje a Luis Maristany (1937–92). Introducción y selección de J.G. Cobo Borda; colaboración de Rosa Lentini, Ricardo Cano Gaviria y Javier Lentini. Muestra de 93 poetas (de O. Girondo, 1891–1967 a R. Cote Baraibar, 1963) para lectores de poesía no muy familiarizados con este proceso. Incluye un texto y breves informaciones bibliográficas de cada autor. [PL]

4269 Jaramillo Escobar, Jaime _et al._ Rostros de la palabra: poesía colombiana actual. Selección, prólogo y notas de Luis Alejandro Ramírez Orjuela, Mauricio Contreras Hernández y Rafael del Castillo Matamoros. Bogotá: Cooperativa Editorial Magisterio, 1990. 173 p.: (Col. Lecturas)

Este libro-antología surge del encuentro de poetas y educadores en el Taller de Poesía de la Casa Silva de Bogotá. Plantea buscar caminos que hagan posible un mayor entendimiento, para los lectores, del hecho mismo de la poesía y su factura. Así, los poetas antologados (Jaime Jaramillo Escobar, Juan Gustavo Cobo, Jairo Aníbal Niño, Raúl Gómez Jattin, María Mercedes Carranza, Juan Manuel Roca, Darío Jaramillo Agudelo y Jotamario) cumplen una labor didáctica desde el ángulo propio a la poesía. Acompaña al libro una muy útil referencia a la historia de la poesía en Colombia. [AR]

4270 Light from a nearby window: contemporary Mexican poetry. Edited by Juvenal Acosta Hernández. San Francisco: City Lights Books, 1993. 231 p.:

Importante antología bilingüe de 21 poetas mexicanos nacidos después de 1945. En su breve prólogo Acosta define esta poesía en relación a un espacio y tiempo concretos. Sin estar limitados o circunscritos a su realidad, estos poetas, dice el editor, "parten de una visión-de ideas e imágenes traducidos a poemas-visión que deviene versión, y que surge de las experiencias vividas en el México de fin del milenio." Entre los poetas reconocidos en México y en búsqueda de lectores de habla inglesa se encuentra Gaspar Aguilera Díaz, Alberto Blanco, Ricardo Castillo, Elsa Cross, David Huerta, Eduardo Langagne, Fabio Morábito, Isabel Quiñones, Silvia Tomasa Rivera y Verónica Volkow. [NK]

4271 Martínez Franco, Mariano et al. Viva la cuenca y sus troveros de sotavento. Veracruz, México: Instituto Veracruzano de Cultura, 1988. 169 p. (Serie Nuestra literatura)

Nueve versadores del estado jarocho mantienen viva la tradición de la décima que iniciara Vicente Espinel en el siglo XVI. Segundo libro de estos Troveros de Sotavento cuya virtuosidad técnica, e ingenio verbal, hacen de este libro un aporte al verso popular de arte menor. [NK]

4272 Mouth to mouth: poems by twelve contemporary Mexican women. Edited by Forrest Gander. Translated by Zoe Anglesley *et al.* Introduction by Julio Ortega. Minneapolis, Minn.: Milkweed Editions, 1993. 233 p.

Texto bilingue (español/inglés) que abre espacios para la voz femenina y feminista de doce poetas cuya obra cuestiona implícitamente construcciones masculinas. Las poetas buscan decirse desde un imaginario que asume la diferencia de géneros sexuales,

visión que genera originales formas expresivas, poéticas alternativas que renueven la poesía en general. Excelente selección y traducción de, entre otras, Silvia Tomasa Rivera, Kyra Galván, Gloria Gervitz, Verónica Volkow, Myriam Moscona, y Coral Bracho. Las concisas y agudas observaciones de Julio Ortega en la breve introducción sirven como guía y punto de partida para la lectura de las poetas. Véase item **4954** para comentarios sobre la traducción. [NK]

4273 Palabras de mujer: poetas latinoamericanas. Selección y prólogo de Juan Gustavo Cobo Borda. Bogotá: Siglo Veintiuno Editores de Colombia, 1991. 1 portfolio: ill. (some col.)

Ingeniosa disposición de los poemas en 30 pliegos, cuyas primeras páginas reproducen antiguas tarjetas postales: un comentario irónico sobre la percepción tradicional de lo femenino que los textos contradicen. Las autoras son M. del Mar, R. Castellanos, F. García Marruz, C. Peri Rossi, R. Jodorowsky, A. Berenguer, A. Torres, V. Volkow, B. Cuza Malé, I. Vilariño, C. Boullosa, C. Meireles, M.M. Carranza, N. Morejón, M.L. Canfield, C. Casanova, H. Ossott, G. Belli, O. Orozco, P. Bonnet, B. Varela, A. Foppa, A. Pizarnik, A.M. Vivas, C. Bracho, S. Ocampo, Y. Pantín, C. Alegría, A. Migdal y A.M. Rodas. [PL]

4274 Poesía argentina, 1940–1960. Seleção, prefácio e tradução de Bella Jozef. Ed. bilingüe. São Paulo: Iluminuras, 1990. 189 p.: bibl.

En el prefacio, la autora parte de los años 20 en la poesía argentina para centrarse en las principales características de las generaciones del 40, 50 y 60. La selección incluye, entre otros, a Aldo Pellegrini, Enrique Molina, Edgar Bailey, Alberto Girri, Olga Orozco, Roberto Juarroz, Juan Gelman y Alejandra Pizarnik. [LU]

4275 Poesía chilena de hoy: de Parra a nuestros días. Selección de Erwin Díaz. 5ta ed. Santiago: Ediciones Documentas, 1992. 327 p.: (Documentas/literatura)

Reúne textos de poetas que comenzaron a escribir después de Neruda. Esta nueva edición añade, en particular, textos de algunas poetas relativamente jóvenes con el propósito de señalar diferencias de una escritura poética "lograda desde una sujeto femenina." Esfuerzo loable que cumple objetivo de "difundir la poesía chilena actual en un espectro amplio de público." [LE]

4276 Poesía de América. Recopilación de Raúl Bañuelos y Raúl Aceves. Guadalajara: Editorial Univ. de Guadalajara, 1992. 149 p.: bibl., index. (Col. del Centro de Estudios Literarios)

Novedosa compilación, que amplía el registro habitual con una sugestiva muestra de poesía indígena. La parte latinoamericana ha sido dispuesta por R. Bañuelos (63 autores, desde J.J. Tablada [1871–1945] a L.R. Nogueras [1945–85]), incluyendo un poema de cada autor; la sección preparada por R. Aceves reúne piezas de diversas regiones y etnias, con orientadoras indicaciones bibliográficas. [PL]

4277 Poesía gauchesca del siglo XX. Selección y prólogo de Eduardo Romano. 1. ed. en esta colección. Buenos Aires: Andrómeda, 1989. 266 p.: (Col. Libros de cabecera)

Prólogo analiza las características de este nuevo ciclo de poesía gauchesca y las principales diferencias con la del siglo XIX: renovación étnico-cultural; desplazamiento del centro de producción desde las campañas hacia los suburbios; motivos y matices diferentes de versificación o acompañamiento musical; distintos lugares de difusión. La selección incluye, entre otros, a: Leopoldo Lugones, Belisario Roldán, Elías Regules, Andrés Cepeda, Romildo Risso, Fernán Silva Valdés, Ricardo Güiraldes, Alberto Vacarezza, Yamandú Rodríguez, Serafín J. García, Pedro Leandro Ipuche, Atahualpa Yupanqui, Félix Luna, León Benarós y José Larralde. [LU]

4278 Poesía puertorriqueña. Selección por Carmen Gómez Tejera, Ana María Losada y Jorge Luis Porras Cruz. México: Editorial Orión, 1990. 425 p.: (Col. Literaria Cervantes)

Util antología con fines pedagógicos (para la escuela intermedia y superior) que, a partir de un índice temático (por ejemplo, amor, patria, hogar, sentido religioso), presenta un amplia muestra de la poesía puertorriqueña (de Santiago Vidarte hasta Matos Paoli). Publicado por primera vez en 1956. [FC]

4279 Poesía viva del Ecuador: siglo XX. Recopilación de Jorge Enrique Adoum. Quito: Grijalbo, 1990. 285 p.: bibl., index. (El Espejo de tinta)

Volumen muy útil para entrar en contacto con los poemas ecuatorianos principales del siglo XX. La selección ha sido realizada por uno de los poetas latinoamericanos mayores de la actualidad, Jorge Enrique Adoum, quien aclara el título de la antología: "Entendemos por 'viva' la poesía que se lee y relee voluntariamente y no la que nos imponen textos o maestros de escuela" o la que proponen críticos e historiadores de la literatura. [ORR]

4280 Los poetas de 1942: antología. Edición de Luis Pastori. Notas bio-bibliográficas de Guillermo Alfredo Cook. Apéndice crítico de Velia Bosch, Alexis Márquez Rodríguez y Héctor Mujica. Indices de Angel Raúl Villasana. Caracas: Monte Avila Editores, 1988. 253 p.: bibl.

Muy útil antología de algunos de los poetas que en la década del 40 formaron el poco estudiado grupo "Presente," el cual se enfrentó a los esfuerzos vanguardistas del conocido grupo precedente "Viernes." Pastori, en un detallado recuento histórico, nos sitúa bien dentro de los propósitos poéticos de estos poetas. La antología que sigue es muestra de estos resultados. Entre los poetas incluidos destacamos a: Jean Aristiguieta, Juan Berroes, Rafael Brunicardi, Ida Gramcko, Pedro F. Lizardo, Aquiles Nazoa, Ana Enriqueta Terán y el mismo Luis Pastori. [AR]

4281 Poetas de tierra adentro. Presentación y recopilación de Héctor Carreto. San Angel, Mexico: Consejo Nacional para la Cultura y las Artes, 1991. 91 p. (Fondo editorial tierra adentro; 24)

Poetas que han aparecido en la revista *Tierra Adentro* que se dedica desde 1974 a difundir obras de jóvenes poetas que radican en la gran extensión mexicana, fuera del D.F., y que empiezan a resonar en revistas y primeras publicaciones. Sólida muestra de lo que hoy se escribe en el interior del país. [NK]

4282 Los poetas lunfardos. Selección de Miguel Tabares. Buenos Aires: Torres Agüero Editor, 1989. 192 p.: bibl.

Selección incluye a poetas como Juan Carlos Lamadrid, Julián Centeya, Pascual Contursi, Celedonio Esteban Flores, Carlos de la Púa, Enrique Santos Discépolo, Hector Negro, Juan Carlos Giusti, Enrique Cadícamo, Homero Espósito. Acompañan esta selección informaciones biográficas y un vocabulario que aclara el sentido que de cada palabra hace su autor. [LU]

4283 Poetisas del Paraguay: voces de hoy.
Recopilación de Miguel Angel Fernández y Renée Ferrer de Arréllaga. 1. ed. española. Madrid: Ediciones Torremozas, 1992. 95 p.: bibl. (Col. Torremozas; 89)

Util y representativa antología de la producción poética femenina desde la década del 30 hasta el presente. Se incluye una bibliografía básica de la poesía paraguaya del siglo XX así como una nota bibliográfica de cada una de las poetas representadas. [LU]

4284 Rolón, Ricardo and Oscar Rolón. 100 años de poesía paraguaya, 1889–1989: un intento bibliográfico. Asunción: Ediciones Comuneros, 1989. 68 p.: bibl.

Libro útil como índice bibliográfico de la producción paraguaya de la centuria comprendida. Sin embargo, la ausencia de una nota introductoria que señale tendencias, subraye la importancia de determinados autores o comente los lineamientos generales de los libros más sobresalientes de cada período, resta atractivo al trabajo. [LU]

4285 La rosa de los vientos: antología de poesía mexicana actual. Selección, prólogo y notas biobibliográficas de Francisco Serrano. México: Consejo Nacional para la Cultura y las Artes, 1992. 511 p.: bibl.

Excelente antología que busca insertarse en la tradición de *Poesía en Movimiento*. Reúne a 32 poetas vivos cuya obra es representativa, según el compilador, de las tendencias más significativas, caracterizada por su diversidad, de la actual poesía mexicana. El texto dividido en cuatro secciones crea cuatro agrupaciones, cuatro regiones, o rumbos, correspondientes a los cuatro puntos cardinales. En el norte encontramos a los poetas mayores (Paz, Ponce, Chumacero, Bonifaz Nuño, Sabines), cuya obra es punto de referencia obligado del quehacer poético; en el Oeste leemos a los poetas que han alcanzado plena madurez expresiva (Segovia, Lizalde, Montes de Oca, González de León, Bañuelos, Zaid, Déniz, Cervantes, Pacheco, Aridjis); en el Sur se reúne a los autores que entran a esa madurez (Elsa Cross, Francisco Hernández, Antonio Deltoro, Francisco Serrano, David Huerta, José Luis Rivas, Efraín Bartolomé, Alberto Blanco, Coral Bracho, Manuel Ulacia, Vicente Quirarte, Fabio Morábito, Verónica Volkow); y en el Este se presenta a los más jóvenes (Luis Miguel Aguilar, Jorge Esquinca, Aurelio Asiain, Julio Hubard). Una breve his-

toria de la poesía mexicana anterior precede las observaciones críticas sobre las cuatro promociones. Cada selección tiene una concisa y útil bibliografía. Aunque toda antología, dice el autor, es arbitraria y parcial, la ausencia de excelentes poetas mujeres jóvenes es notable. [NK]

4286 Salas, Alejandro Antología comentada de la poesía venezolana. Caracas: Alfadil Ediciones, 1989. 305 p.: bibl. (Col. Orinoco; 20)

Valiosa antología preparada por el poeta Alejandro Salas que incluye un gran número de poetas venezolanos, entre ellos los más sobresalientes. A pesar de que se incluyen sólo dos poemas de cada poeta, la muestra deja ver la alta calidad de la poesía de este país. Voces como las de Antonio Ramos Sucre, Vicente Gerbasi, Juan Liscano, Rafael Cadenas, Eugenio Montejo, Juan Sánchez Peláez, Juan Calzadilla, Ramón Palomares, entre otros, son ya parte fundamental de la poesía latinoamericana. La selección va desde la época de la colonia hasta nuestros días. Una muy útil bibliografía acompaña a cada poeta así como un breve comentario hecho por otro poeta o crítico sobre su obra. [AR]

4287 El '60: poesía blindada: antología. Selección de Rubén Chihade. Prólogo de Ramón Plaza. Buenos Aires: Ediciones de GenteSur, 1990. 141 p.: (Los Libros de GenteSur)

Prólogo analiza las principales características de la generación del 60 y se complementa con una extensa lista de los poetas y principales publicaciones periódicas del momento, trabajo que recuerda el conocido texto de Alfredo Andrés sobre este mismo período. La antología incluye 20 autores de los que se destacan Juana Bignozzi, Juan Gelman, Noé Jitrik, Leónidas Lamborghini, Alejandra Pizarnik, Eduardo Romano y Francisco Urondo. Aparecen, sin embargo, algunas imprecisiones en la bibliografía (Gelman) y datos biográficos (Urondo). [LU]

BOOKS OF VERSE

4288 Acosta, Agustín. Poemas escogidos. Selección, prólogo y notas de Alberto Rocasolano. La Habana: Editorial Letras Cubanas, 1988. 205 p. (Giraldilla)

Poeta de transiciones, poesía que registra esa sucesión de estéticas, los poemas aquí reunidos—publicados en la primera mitad del siglo XX—ciñen al autor como una figura de importancia en el posmodernismo y el neo-romanticismo cubanos. [FC]

4289 Alcides, Rafael. Y se mueren, y vuelven, y se mueren. La Habana: Editorial Letras Cubanas, 1988. 164 p.

Poemas, en ocasiones narrativos, que apuntan a un pasado, a un mundo dejado atrás, no para entregarse a la nostalgia sino para biografiar el recorrido de una vida, paralelo al curso de una nación: Cuba. Desde Bayamo, junto con Céspedes, se llega al presente, donde está la Revolución. [FC]

4290 Alvarez, Montserrat. Zona dark: poemas. Ilustraciones de M. Alvarez. Lima: s.n., 1991. 195 p.: ill.

Desigual, con gestos de violencia anárquica, con caídas de tono y gusto, este libro tiene sin embargo momentos de cierto mérito: surgen cuando la autora se olvida del deseo de escandalizar y habla de experiencias concretas que conoce bien y describe con vigor e ironía. [JMO]

4291 Alvarez, Nicolás Emilio. Agua de fuego. Miami, Fla.: Ediciones Universal, 1991. 60 p. (Col. Espejo de paciencia)

Dos poemas en inglés rompen la uniformidad del español, como parte del "sueño dirigido" (Borges) o de la "conciencia soñante" (Bachelard) con que se afirma lo poético. Aquí la poesía quiere ser un sistema de comunicación a muchos niveles, en el cual le toca al lector potenciar la significación de los poemas para construir el presente de la poesía. [FC]

4292 Alvarez, Virginia. Latitud del amor. Santo Domingo: Agencia Gráfica, 1990. 111 p.

Ni erótica ni explícita, aquí la poesía crea un espacio donde el amor no aclara su género; sí por otro lado, su recorrido: la palabra, el olvido, la soledad, el cuerpo, son las estaciones por las que transita esta voz poética para quien la poesía y el amor se conjugan en el espacio de lo lírico. [FC]

4293 Araujo, Orlando. Elia en azul: homenaje a Orlando Araujo. Caracas: Editorial Ex Libris, 1988. 81 p.: col. ill.

Colección de poemas amorosos de Orlando Araujo (1927–1987) donde se alternan sonetos, poemas en prosa, canciones, etc. Son ellos un homenaje al amor, a la amada; el poeta vuelca directamente sobre el papel sus sentimientos sin mayores compromisos con las tendencias contemporáneas de la poesía. La publicación de este libro es asimismo un homenaje al poeta desaparecido de parte de sus amigos pintores y poetas. Los pintores Alirio Rodríguez y Hugo Baptista ilustran la carátula y los poemas respectivamente. Como epílogo hay varias notas y poemas recordatorios donde se destacan los de Luis A. Crespo, Ramón Palomares y Adriano González León. [AR]

4294 Arduz Ruíz, Marcelo. Intihuyphypacha = Sol de invierno. La Paz: Ediciones Signo, 1991. 87 p.: ill. (Serie Tiempo de poesía)

Intenta ofrecer una poesía nativa inspirada en la tradición e historia indígena andina. Ese esfuerzo por remontarse a los orígenes de las culturas andinas y reactualizar la visión mítica regional parece ser consecuencia del escepticismo y la crisis de valores en la actualidad. El autor afirma que su intento es ofrecer una poesía desde "una visión esencialmente aymara." [ORR]

4295 Arráiz Lucca, Rafael. Almacen. Caracas: Fundarte, 1988. 59 p. (Col. Cuadernos de difusión; 120)

Nostalgia del futuro, de un viaje que sucede entre países de infancia y de sueño, presencia de la ciudad, una mirada a la vida circundante, serían algunas de las coordenadas que encierran la poesía de Arraiz Lucca (1959). Cofundador del grupo "Guaire," este poeta no sólo se destaca por su ya extensa obra lírica sino por la contribución como editor y animador de la vida cultural venezolana. [AR]

4296 Artel, Jorge. Antología poética. Medellín?: Univ. de Antioquia, 1986. 209 p.: ill. (Col. Premio nacional de poesía)

Muy merecido el reconocimiento nacional que la Univ. de Antioquia diera al poeta Jorge Artel (1909) del cual se desprende la publicación de este libro. Artel es un poeta de raigambre popular, afianzado desde sus inicios en una búsqueda que otorga al poema esa cadencia de los ritmos negros sin perder la compostura idiomática, el rigor de la preceptiva. Su obra, a diferencia de la Guillén, afirma así los ancestros españoles mientras canta y exalta los valores de la presencia afroamericana. [AR]

4297 Avilés Concepción, Jorge Luis. El perfil de un huérfano. San Juan?: Sociedad de Autores Puertorriqueños? 1990. 82 p.:ill. (Biblioteca Sociedad de Autores Puertorriqueños)

Colección de poemas y un cuento escritos por y para el autor. Lo confesional prima sobre lo literario, donde la poesía es quizás una estética del alma y la sinceridad. Poesía cerrada en un yo para quien la estética pasa primero por la ética. [FC]

4298 Aznar, Pedro. Pruebas de fuego. Buenos Aires: Planeta, 1992. 150 p.

Errante y curioso el yo lírico deambula por ciudades y países, y desde lo cotidiano de esos paisajes interroga sobre el amor, el tiempo y el lenguaje. [LU]

4299 Barba Jacob, Porfirio. Poemas. Recopilados y anotados por Fernando Vallejo. Bogotá: Procultura S.A.; Presidencia de la República, 1985. 239 p. (Nueva biblioteca colombiana de cultura)

Nadie mejor que Fernando Vallejo, el crítico y novelista colombiano, para darnos esta edición de la obra poética de Porfirio Barba-Jacob, en la cual se destacan sus pertinentes y al extremo bien documentados comentarios y análisis. Vallejo había publicado anteriormente la biografía de Porfirio titulada *El mensajero*. No hay a nuestro juicio una mejor biografía de poeta latinoamericano alguno. [AR]

4300 Barquero, Efraín. A deshora. Santiago?: Editorial Sudamericana, 1992. 131 p.

Ultimo libro que confirma, una vez más, el control que este poeta tiene del oficio. Su verso fluye sereno, sin discordancias, develando correspondencias íntimas entre los hombres y las cosas. Dice un poema: "la mujer trae la lámpara/ el hombre trae el vino/ todos beben en su copa preguntando algo/ que nadie responde/ sino después de mucho tiempo." [LE]

4301 Barrera, Alberto. Edición de lujo. Caracas: FUNDARTE, 1990. 72 p. (Col. Cuadernos de difusión; 135)

El poema en prosa ha tenido en Venezuela serios cultores, valga el caso de Antonio Ramos Sucre y Antonia Palacios, entre otros. Barrera (n. 1960), participante de los grupos "Guaire" y "Tráfico" de la década del 80, intenta seguir esta tradición utilizando ironía y humor como utensilios para lograr el poema.

No obstante, al despojar el texto de las sutilezas del lenguaje su propósito pierde fuerza poética y el poema cae lastimosamente en lo prosaico. [AR]

4302 Bartolomé, Herman Efraín. Música lunar. México: Joaquín Mortiz, 1991. 133 p.: bibl., ill.

Cantos nocturnos y hechiceros a través de los cuales el sujeto poético encantado y transformado por la musa/diosa trasciende su cotidianeidad. Imágenes sensuales y sensoriales de vuelos y caídas, que no siempre logran el efecto buscado. [NK]

4303 Basantes Vacacela, Julio. Habitante del tiempo. Quito?: Impr. Don Bosco, 1991. 66 p.

De indudable calidad y profundidad poética, los 57 textos que conforman este volumen se caracterizan por su desencanto angustioso ante la percepción de la realidad social contemporánea en crisis. Poesía que denuncia el ambiente de violencia, desconfianza e incertidumbre que la realidad ha creado para el ser humano de nuestros días. [ORR]

4304 Basualto, Alejandra. Las malamadas: poesía. Santiago?: La Trastienda, 1993. 69 p.: ill.

Sugerentes poemas de amor que con lenguaje apasionado dialogan con un amante ausente: "Podría morir / de inviernos como éste / si no supiera / que existes." Emcomiable el control con que el lenguaje comunica la pasión erótica. [LE]

4305 Belli, Carlos Germán. Canciones y otros poemas. Trujillo, Peru: Ediciones SEA, 1992. xiv, 69 p.: (Col. Homenaje al centenario de César Vallejo; 14–15)

Precedido por un excelente estudio de Roberto Paoli, el volumen contiene 14 poemas, algunos relativamente extensos, que confirman la extraordinaria habilidad formal del poeta: su pulcra pátina arcaizante que no le impide criticar agudamente el mundo contemporáneo e incorporar vulgarismos del habla limeña. [JMO]

4306 Bertoni Lemus, Claudio. Sentado en la cuneta. Santiago: Ediciones C. Porter, 1990. 59 p.

Irreverente "ubi sunt" traspasado de humor tierno. Se pregunta por suerte de larga serie de adolescentes que poblaron la vida de la voz que lamenta desaparición de esa época. En 1987, Enrique Lihn decía de este libro:

"Excomunión de la pedantería, destierro de la gravedad, color local cambiante a tono con sus obsesiones errátiles, egotismo del antiego, cachondeos del goliardo que hace la alquimia de la delicadeza con los ingredientes fecales del lenguaje." Libro que se recomienda con especial énfasis. [LE]

4307 Bignozzi, Juana. Mujer de cierto orden. Buenos Aires: Libros de Tierra Firme, 1990. 40 p.: (Col. de poesía Todos bailan; 29)

Con la reedición de este libro de Bignozzi una vez más la editorial de José Luis Mangieri permite el (r)encuentro con valiosos poetas de la llamada "generación del sesenta" cuyas características más destacadas es posible observar en este poemario: marcado tono coloquial, redescubrimiento de la ciudad, preocupación social y política en el marco de una constante reflexión sobre el quehacer escritural y el yo lírico. [LU]

4308 Bignozzi, Juana. Regreso a la patria. Buenos Aires: Libros de Tierra Firme, 1989. 82 p. (Col. de poesía Todos bailan; 21)

Fuerte ironía de los primeros poemas da lugar a una desesperada amargura en este nuevo poemario de Bignozzi que interrumpe así varios años de silencio poético. Las díadas niñez-vejez, esperanza-vacío, pasado-presente, inocencia-desengaño vertebran el libro y crean el tono del mismo. [LU]

4309 Bischhoffshausen, Alex V. Rastro/rostro ausente. Viña del Mar, Chile: Ediciones Altazor, 1992. 1 v.

Sugerente poemario que pone de manifiesto la vieja pugna entre tradición e innovación, tradición y ruptura. Epígrafe inicial de C. Pavese "Un buen punto de partida sería modificar el propio pasado," parece regir sentido de los poemas. Con otros jóvenes poetas (Juan José Daneri, Mauricio Barrientos y Sergio Madrid Siegfield), publica poemario conjunto, *Retaguardia de la vanguardia* (Viña del Mar, Chile: Ediciones Altazor, 1992) donde también se evidencia adhesión a reflexión de Pavese. Se recomienda lectura de ambos libros por proponer vías nuevas de expresión en la poesía chilena. [LE]

4310 Blanco, Alberto. Cuenta de los guías. México: Ediciones Era, 1992. 178 p. (Biblioteca Era: Poesía)

Nuevo acierto de este autor tijuanense en plena madurez poética. Dividido en cinco secciones, las primeras tres, "El Taladro del Fuego," está compuesto de poemas en prosa, y las últimas dos, "La Nueva Centinela" y "Quinto Viento," de poemas en verso. Poesía de alta tensión poética que traza caminos reveladores a partir de los límites que imponen fronteras metafóricas, o reales, del poeta. [NK]

4311 Boccanera, Jorge A. Marimba y otros poemas, 1974–1989. 3a ed. San José: Editorial Lunes, 1990. 180 p. (Col. Manatí)

Tercera edición ampliada de una recopilación de textos de diferentes libros del autor: *Los espantapájaros suicidas; Contraseña; Noticias de una mujer cualquiera; Música de fagot y piernas de Victoria; Poemas del tamaño de una naranja; Contra el bufón del rey; Oración para un extranjero; Polvo para morder.* Incluye también letras de canciones ("La poesía es un Mal Necesario") y textos de dos poemarios, *Sordomuda* y *Zona de tolerancia,* inéditos al momento de esta edición. [LU]

4312 Bonifaz Nuño, Rubén. Del templo de su cuerpo. México: Fondo de Cultura Económica, 1992. 85 p. (Letras mexicanas; 120)

Ultima entrega de este poeta que vierte lenguajes y visiones contemporáneas en formas clásicas logrando versos que desde la tradición nos sitúan en nuestro presente. En este excelente poemario la voz poética construye desde el deseo y la pasión el espacio/cuerpo de la mujer codiciada. Búsqueda de lo femenino a través de una aventura de seducción, pasión y pérdida. [NK]

4313 Bonifaz Nuño, Rubén. Pulsera para Lucía Méndez. México: Plaza Valdés Editores, 1989. 25 p.

Nueve sonetos de este gran maestro de la versificación que rinde homenaje a la cantante y artista. Texto de canto, alegre y juguetón, a la belleza, al amor, a la mujer, y a la expresión poética: "Cambia todo, tú quedas sin mudanza. / Y el tiempo es nada, y luce-ya lucía- / lo que pone de lujo mi pobreza." [NK]

4314 Brandi, Carlos Enrique. Teorema. Montevideo: Vintén Editor, 1990. 51 p. (Col. de poesía)

Primer libro de Brandi (n. 1964). Breves, lapidarios y desesperanzados, sus poemas representan cabalmente la generación a la que pertenece su autor. Su visión del amor y de la realidad está marcada por un agrio escepticismo y una no menos cruda ironía. [LU]

4315 Burgos, Julia de. Julia de Burgos. Ilustraciones de Torres Martinó. San Juan: Instituto de Cultura Puertorriqueña, 1990. 51 p.: ill. (Cuadernos de poesía; 9)

Persiguen estos cuadernos de la literatura puertorriqueña tanto la difusión como el homenaje. A pesar de lo sucinto, se consigue dar una muestra representativa de la poeta, cuya producción literaria comprende de 1938–54, cuando se publica su obra póstuma *El mar y tú*. Espacio de confluencia entre la poesía y el dibujo: las ilustraciones de Torrés Martinó reinterpretan los 20 poemas. [FC]

4316 Cabrera, Sarandy. Papeles de Volusio. Montevideo: Vintén Editor, 1990. 181 p.

Nuevo libro de Sarandy Cabrera en el que intenta—como lo indica en su Prólogo—dar "una voz para Volusio, poeta latino coetáneo de Catulo y de quién no se ha conservado ningún escrito." El poemario no ensaya ningún tipo de juego autorial, textual o contextual en esa dirección. [LU]

4317 Calderón, Lila. Balance de blanco en el *Angel Triste* de Durero. Santiago: Editorial Offset Color, 1993. 121 p.

Poemario sorprendente por complejidad del mundo poético que despliega y por poder de sugerencia del lenguaje. Del caos surgen poemas que reinventan el mundo, sin dar paso a falsos optimismos. Abre el libro "Ronda," poema que destaca la omnipresencia de la muerte. Sin embargo, viene en seguida epígrafe que apunta a la naturaleza de las tareas (poéticas) del ser humano sobre la tierra: "Aún así, las hormigas agradecidas por la vida y el ser, fueron a buscar tierra negra a las profundidades del mundo y cubrieron las áridas arenas para enterrar y rendir honor a su creador" (Relato Bantú, de Landa). Poeta con voz propia y mundo muy suyo. Sin duda, de lo mejor del período. [LE]

4318 Calderón, Teresa. Género femenino. Santiago: Editorial Planeta, 1989. 1 v. (Biblioteca del Sur)

Segundo libro de poeta que, en lenguaje lírico de buena cepa, presenta a mujer en ámbito doméstico luchando con enemigo que la elude por los contradictorios sentimientos que éste le inspira: "Me derroté a mí misma / y obtuve la única victoria," dice el poema "Ser Mujer" que inaugura el libro. Destaca so-

ledad de amantes (la mujer, en este caso) que vencidos en guerra implacable, vuelven al campo de batalla: "Esta tarde / es apenas una tarde cualquiera / herida de tiempo empantanado / donde seguimos esperando / que algo ocurra." Poemario confirma bondades de libro anterior. [LE]

4319 Cancel, Mario R. Estos raros orígenes. San Juan?: Islote, 1991. 63 p.: ill. (Puente; 2)

Poemas afropuertorriqueños que invocan deidades afrocaribeñas (Obalatá, Ogún, Changó, Yemayá, Echú y Olofi Orula Ecué). Se lamenta la historia en tanto pasado cruel, lleno de promesas rotas, a la vez que se le rinde tributo a figuras como Ramón Emeterio Betances y Luis Palés Matos. [FC]

4320 Carrera Andrade, Jorge. Antología poética. Estudio introductorio y notas de Oswaldo Encalada Vásquez. Quito: Libresa, 1990. 191 p.: (Col. Antares; 33)

Ofrece una visión del desarrollo general de la obra poética de Carrera Andrade (1903–78) a partir de su activa participación en las experiencias vanguardistas. Los primeros textos que incluye corresponden a *Microgramas* (1926) y *Rol de la manzana* (1928); los últimos a *Misterios naturales* (1972) y *Vocación terrena* (1972). La introducción incluye una "Cronología" del poeta y su tiempo. [ORR]

4321 Carriego, Evaristo. La canción del barrio. Homenaje de Arturo Capdevila. Buenos Aires: Ediciones de Aquí a la Vuelta, 1990. 149 p. (Col. Poesía de Aquí a la Vuelta)

Reedición de importante texto que marcó el descubrimiento y homenaje de esa célula de lo urbano que es lo barrial y el lenguaje que lo acompaña. [LU]

4322 Castro, Tomás. Epigramas del encubrimiento de América. Riverdale, N.Y.: Editorial Mambrú, 1992. 135 p. (Nueva poesía latinoamericana)

Si bien la temática aquí trabajada ya es una institución, en este poemario, por la economía verbal, por una agudeza sutil y en ocasiones elíptica que jamás atropella, la historia de América, así como sus protagonistas, sus proyectos y resultados, se revisita mediante un lenguaje que, a pesar de la ironía, mantiene la frescura de la revisión. En función de su ostensible latinoamericanidad, la voz poética no puede ser sino crítica ante la trayectoria de encubrimientos que registra su recuento. [FC]

4323 Castro Ríos, Eduardo. Miradores: 1984–1989. Santiago: CESOC Ediciones, 1992? 102 p.: ill.

Promisor primer libro evoca momentos de *Canto General* de Neruda y también contracanto del mismo título de Enrique Lihn. Situado en la Araucanía, fustiga a depredadores que violentan tierra y hombre: "Sobre esta colina / yo me sentaba a observar el paisaje, / ya antes de nacer / . . . / hasta que entendí en el silabario / que el grano, el heno y la manzana / no eran míos." Poesía y amor surgen como antídotos al despojo. Lectura que se recomienda. [LE]

4324 Catalá, Rafael. Ciencia poesía. Minneapolis, Minn.: Prisma Books, 1986. 126 p. (Serie de poesía guámpara; 1)

Osados pero centrados en su legitimación, estos poemas constituyen una propuesta filosófica de la latinoamericanidad en relación con el discurso de la ciencia. La "ciencia-poesía" se define como la poética de la ciencia, y se describe como un espacio donde el juego de diferencias tramita los múltiples devenires de la humanidad, cuyas voces el lector reconocerá en las diferentes tradiciones del quehacer artístico-científico-político. [FC]

4325 Cedrón, José Antonio. Actas. México: Editorial Tierra del Fuego, 1986. 127 p.: ill.

Un tono de intimidad, sobrecogimiento y sobriedad impregna el tema del exilio—y sus múltiples rostros: la nostalgia del país, el encuentro enriquecido con el otro, la ausencia, los muertos, el amor—y da unidad a estos poemas. En general, en los poemas breves el poeta logra una mayor fuerza expresiva. [LU]

4326 Chacón, Alfredo. Decir como es deseado. Caracas: Monte Avila Editores, 1990. 64 p. (Altazor)

Dividido en cuatro partes ("El Deseo Tentado," "Así Uno," "En el Amor sin Tino," "Del Rumor de mis Límites") este libro de Chacón (1937) abunda en una dirección que trata de hacer del poema voz de lo esencial y resumen de un conocimiento, un saber. La dificultad para apreciar a plenitud el hecho de la poesía reside tal vez en que la máxima vibración que requiere esta poesía mínima se diluye cuando el poeta expresa lo poético sin dejarlo que se cree por sí sólo en el poema. [AR]

4327 Chang, Pedro. El otro lado de las cosas. Cali, Colombia: Fundación para la Investigación y la Cultura, 1989. 156 p.

Epigramática, atenta a una búsqueda donde la lucidez arrastra humor y cierta sabiduría, la poesía de este poeta colombiano (n. Buenaventura, 1946) de origen chino merece particular atención. Son poemas despojados de los ropajes de la imagen y las metáforas relucientes, más bien son apólogos que intentan un profundo viaje de conocimiento interior. [AR]

4328 Charry Lara, Fernando. Llama de amor viva. Bogotá: Procultura S.A.; Presidencia de la República, 1986. 121 p. (Nueva biblioteca colombiana de cultura)

Concisión, mesura, alto rigor y profunda visión serían los primeros calificativos para la obra de Fernando Charry Lara (n. 1920). Treinticinco poemas son todos ellos luego de más de 40 años de ejercicio poético. Sólo Aurelio Arturo en Colombia pudo escribir tan pocos poemas, y a la vez, como en Charry Lara, llevar la poesía al sitio de máxima calidad y belleza. La imaginación y la libertad conjugadas en una atmósfera nocturna, casi inefable pero poblada por el ser y los seres que habitan la poesía, hacen de estos poemas lectura imprescindible. Incluye ensayo interpretativo de Rafael Gutiérrez Girardot de gran calidad y precisión, el conocido prólogo de Vicente Aleixandre al primer libro de Charry Lara, y un magnífico ensayo del mismo poeta sobre su experiencia inicial en poesía. [AR]

4329 Cisneros, Antonio. Propios como ajenos: antología personal; poesía 1962–1988. Lima: PEISA, 1989. 211 p.

A diferencia de otras antologías del autor publicadas en La Habana y México, ésta es una primera recopilación personal. Cubre desde su libro inicial (*David*, 1962) hasta dos cuadernos inéditos de fines de los años 80, y da una idea orgánica de la evolución de este poeta que fue, en los 60, un rebelde y ahora una voz bien establecida. [JMO]

4330 Cobo Borda, Juan Gustavo. Dibujos hechos al azar de lugares que cruzaron mis ojos. Caracas: Monte Avila, 1991. 82 p. (Altazor)

Dividido en tres pares: "Poeta en Utopía," "Poeta en Bogotá," "Poeta en Tokio," este nuevo libro de poemas de Cobo Borda (1948) sigue afirmando el tono menor, casi apagado de su poesía más reciente, la cual busca todavía desprenderse del carácter altisonante, soberbio, de sus poemas anteriores. La tercera parte es la más interesante, la menos previsible, dada tal vez esa innata fuerza poética que carga el símbolo de lo oriental. [AR]

4331 Cohen, Sandro. Línea de fuego. Ilustraciones de Carlos Torres. México: INBA; Ediciones Armella, 1989. 104 p.: ill. (Caballo verde)

Endecasílabos reminiscentes de la poesía de Bonifaz Nuño que esclarecen y recuperan espacios íntimos de las vivencias diarias con un lenguaje aparentemente directo que elabora imágenes de alta poeticidad. [NK]

4332 Coimbra Sanz, Germán. La canción que tú cantabas. Santa Cruz, Bolivia: Editora El País, 1990 80 p.: ill.

Poesía que se caracteriza por el empleo de la imagen y la metáfora en un enfrentamiento candoroso con la naturaleza. Un ambiente bucólico de placidez y novedad se desprende de los efectos metafóricos que, no obstante, no describen siempre la realidad de un modo naturalista, sino según los modelos dejados por las corrientes vanguardistas de la poesía hispánica. [ORR]

4333 Correa, Diana and **Aldo Mazzuccelli.** Azulalsur [de Diana Correa]. El río desconocido [de Aldo Mazzucchelli]. Montevideo: Ediciones Casa de Cultura del Partido Comunista de Uruguay, 1988. 109 p.

La necesidad de contar y a la vez de cortar—cerrar, superar—ese pedazo de historia uruguaya que fue la reciente dictadura es el pre-texto de gran parte de los poemas. El tono oscila entre la rabia, la desilusión, la nostalgia, la ironía y las imágenes van componiendo una especie de collage que acompaña y enriquece esa variedad tonal tal como se observa en el poema "Generación." Es el primer libro de Diana Correa (n. 1948). [LU]

4334 Correa Díaz, Luis. Bajo la pequeña música de su pie. Santiago: Ediciones Documentas, 1990. 85 p.: ill. (Documentas/literatura)

Con lenguaje sugerente y personal, traspasado de profundo sentido religioso, se elaboran estos bellos poemas de amor. Abo-

gan por vida en lucha desesperada con circunstancia social que quiere ahogarlos. A la amada: "Escóndete en mi corazón, dél no te van a sacar nunca sin mí / hermanita." Al padre: "Créceme viejo / como si los suyos / y los suyos / volvieran a ver / a dos que se derraman / hasta llenar el vaso roto / de mi mejor poema." Poemas proponen un "ars futura" que perdure por sobre las inhumanidades del hombre contra el hombre. "Te bajarán del árbol dormido / a la laboriosidad húmeda / de la tierra / y no saber quién, por qué / llora todavía por ti arriba / demorará tu deseo / hasta hacerte la muerte imposible." Uno de los mejores poemarios del período. [LE]

4335 Correa Díaz, Luis. Rosario de actos de habla. Santiago: Imprenta Ñielol, 1993. 99 p.

Poemas, cuentas de un rosario que registra vicisitudes de amor perdido por culpa de amante ingrata. Cargado de erotismo filtrado por tamiz de lo religioso. En "Acto de Contrición (?)" se dice: "Acaso me arrepiento, Jesús mío, / de todo corazón, / de los pecados cometidos en mi vida; / pero no siento pena de haberla ofendido / porque es tan mala; . . ." Declara Pedro Lastra, quien estampó el *imprimatur*: "he visto el libro *Rosario de actos de habla*; no contiene cosa contra el Santo Oficio; antes bien buena palabra que antiguos y modernos han juzgado necesaria y conveniente en la república poética . . ." Opinión con la que concuerda este lector-reseñador. [LE]

4336 Corretjer, Juan Antonio. Yerba bruja. Anotada por Joserramón Melendes. 3a ed. Ciales, P.R.: Ediciones Casa Corretjer, 1992. 155 p.: ill.

La poesía de Corretjer, consagrada en la literatura puertorriqueña, testimonia una estética así como una política ante las cuales la literatura más joven ha reaccionado tanto para reivindicarla como para criticarla. Esta tercera edición (1957 y 1970) está acompañada de una erudita documentación en la cual el estudioso puede rastrear el periplo de los poemas a través de sus respectivas ediciones. [FC]

4337 Cote, Ramón. El confuso trazado de las fundaciones. Bogotá: Ancora Editores, 1991. 69 p.

Cote Baraibar (n. 1963) ha desarrollado una amplia labor crítica y poética tanto en

Colombia como en España. Sus poemas tienden a buscar algo no dicho, presentido, haciendo del vocablo el constructor de imágenes transparentes, sencillas en la complejidad de su mundo. Es indudable que su obra encontrará en un próximo futuro el lenguaje, la forma que preludia. [AR]

4338 Cross, Elsa. Jaguar. México: Ediciones Toledo, 1991. 42 p.
Cross deja atrás el Oriente para ubicarse en México. Vuelta a los espacios precolombinos, reflexión sobre el pasado, sobre los enigmas de otro tiempo para siempre perdido. Creación de estados espirituales y filosóficos que sirven en la búsqueda ontológica de la persona poética. [NK]

4339 Cuesta, Jorge. Sonetos. Con un retrato escrito y un estudio preliminar de Cristina Mujica. Carta astrológica natal levantada por María Eugenia Peláez Cuesta. Interpretación de Víctor del Valle y Cristina Mujica. México: Coordinación de Humanidades, Univ. Nacional Autónoma de México, 1987. 109 p.: bibl., col. ill., plate. (Biblioteca de letras)
Interesante y nuevo texto de uno de los miembros más importantes del grupo "Contemporáneos." Un estudio preliminar precede la colección de sus sonetos. [NK]

4340 Cunha, Víctor. Artificio con doncella. Montevideo: Arca, 1986. 54 p., 1 leaf of plates: ill. (Col. Maremagnum)
Después de cinco años de silencio poético reaparece la voz de Cunha (n. 1951). Predominan las imágenes que sugieren pluralidad y movimiento pero en términos de reiteración idéntica. La realidad persiste en idénticos rostros y no hay espacio de salvación posible. El tono del poemario es altamente irónico. [LU]

4341 Curis, Antonio. Nunca pensé en un libro etcétera, etcétera, ó, Diógenes el Cínico en su barril de angustia violado: antología. Montevideo?: Impr. Rosgal, 1991. 276 p.: ill.
Si bien hay un dejo modernista en los poemas que componen la primera parte del libro, el hábil manejo del humor y la ironía impregnan las segundas y terceras partes del mismo de una manera socarrona que ataca las zonas sagradas de la "uruguayez." La segunda parte está íntegramente dedicada a la reflexión sobre la poesía y el quehacer poético. Coloquialismo y narratividad son también constantes estilísticas del poemario. [LU]

4342 Deniz, Gerardo. Amor y Oxidente. México: Vuelta, 1991. 79 p.
Poemario ganador del Premio Villaurrutia 1991. Poesía arriesgada que busca desarticular toda práctica poética anterior. Dos poemas largos—"Amor y Oxidente" y "La Inyección a Irma"—frustran expectativas genéricas. Poemas conversaciones, o conversaciones poéticas, que deforman los espacios modernos a través de una mirada y un lenguaje rebuscado, clínico, caústico y crítico. [NK]

4343 Diego, Eliseo. Cuatro de oros. Dibujos de Rapi Diego. México: Siglo Veintiuno Editores, 1991. 95 p.: ill.
Conforme a su poética, ya establecida, esta nueva incursión de Diego replantea para reabordar, y reencontrar, esas transmutaciones y sorpresas sobre las que se ha apoyado su poesía. Así, por ejemplo, el planteo de lo personal, lo familiar, lo social, aparece nuevamente hilvanando ese orbe—siempre religioso—sobre cuya base gira la poesía como principio unificador y ejercicio ético. [FC]

4344 Diez Astete, Alvaro. Abismo. La Paz: Ediciones Ojo Libertaria, 1988. 59 p.
Nueva colección de poesías de un autor boliviano que ya publicó dos poemarios. Estos textos no se despegan de manifestaciones oníricas y surrealistas. Aunque desde la tradición de la poesía boliviana del siglo XX, este autor puede ser considerado seguidor de la poesía de Jaime Sáenz. [ORR]

4345 Esquinca, Jorge. El cardo en la voz. México: JM, 1991. 76 p.
Poemario ganador del Premio de Poesía Aguascalientes 1990. El poeta experimenta con formas que borran géneros por medio de un lenguaje prosaico que desfamiliariza las vivencias diarias. Poemas en prosa y en verso que devienen parábolas, o alegorías reveladoras. Busca y logra una nueva voz, aquella que conoce "el misterio del cardo," voz que enuncia territorios ocultos de los sentimientos y las sensaciones. [NK]

4346 Estrella, Ulises. Cuando el sol se mira de frente. Quito: Casa de la Cultura Ecuatoriana, 1989. 112 p.:
Personajes y hechos históricos relacionados con la ciudad de Quito, desde su

fundación en 1534, inspiraron los textos de este volumen de uno de los poetas más distinguidos del Ecuador. La refinada elaboración discursiva permite realizar múltiples y sugerentes lecturas de la intencionalidad reflexiva sobre la historia de esa ciudad—no siempre explícita—a través de un lenguaje vigoroso y rico en imágenes así como en constante asedio a la imaginación lectora. [ORR]

4347 Estrella Vintimilla, Pablo. Poesía: dos variaciones sobre Hiroshima. Cuenca, Ecuador: Casa de la Cultura Ecuatoriana Benjamín Carrión, 1985. 105 p.

Dos poemas largos sobre el mismo tema de Hiroshima, de este poeta ecuatoriano consagrado (n. 1948). El primero ("Retorno a Cero") data de 1967 y su sentido fundamental es la destrucción. El segundo ("En Tiempos de Eclipse y Destierro") lleva la fecha de 1983 y aunque no se despoja de sentimientos y referentes de adversidad, manifiesta cierta esperanza en la renovación. El volumen permite apreciar la evolución del discurso poético de su autor a través de tres lustros. [ORR]

4348 Fernández, Guillermo. Imágenes para una piedad. Guadalajara: Univ. de Guadalajara, 1991. 134 p. (Cuarto menguante)

Excelente selección de poemas de sus cuatro libros publicados: *Visitaciones* (1964), *La palabra a solas* (1965), *La hora y el sitio* (1973), y *Bajo llave* (1983); más seis poemas inéditos. Ecos de Pellicer y Cernuda en este poeta de lenguaje directo y conversacional que no pierde el ritmo del verso para aspirar a la comunión con la naturaleza, o al amor de la mujer, desde su condición de triste solitario. [NK]

4349 Fernández Retamar, Roberto. Hacia la nueva. La Habana: Unión de Escritores y Artistas de Cuba, 1989. 61 p. (Contemporáneos)

Se reúne en este poemario una modesta colección de poemas cuya publicación abarca nueve años (1981–88). Retamar reivindica tanto su estética como su compromiso político. Algunos de los poemas, como aquellos volcados hacia Nicaragua, evocan la solidaridad revolucionaria que, junto con Cortázar, vivió el poeta cubano. [FC]

4350 Figueroa Aracena, Alexis. Vírgenes del Sol Inn Cabaret: segunda elaboración; poesía. La Habana: Casa de las Américas, 1986. 54 p.

Premio Casa de las Américas, la poesía aquí presentada, salpicada de términos en inglés, a ratos conversacional, articula la crítica ideológica a través del uso y abuso comercial de la mujer. [FC]

4351 Flores, Miguel Angel. Erosiones y desastres. México: Fondo de Cultura Económica, 1987. 158 p. (Letras mexicanas)

Este poemario reúne *Contra suberna* (México: Joaquín Mortiz, 1981), ganador del Premio Nacional de Poesía de 1980, y su producción anterior a *Saldo ardiente* (México: Villicaña, 1985). Poética del desastre, poesía que dialoga con la de José Emilio Pacheco y contiene las constantes que serán signo de su obra posterior: el discurso de un sujeto impersonal que reflexiona sobre la erosión del tiempo y del amor, y la permanencia de la memoria y la escritura. [NK]

4352 Gaitán Durán, Jorge. Amantes, y otros poemas. 4. ed. Bogotá: El Ancora Editores, 1989. 123 p.: bibl., ill.

Una valoración cada vez más justa de los poetas que Jorge Gaitán Durán acogió en su revista *Mito* ha sido tal vez el mayor acontecimiento poético en Colombia en los últimos años. Y es precisamente la poesía del mismo Gaitán Durán, muerto a los 37 años en un accidente de aviación en la isla de Guadalupe en 1963, la que despierta una de la mayores admiraciones. Dotado de un dominio exquisito de las palabras y del verso, Gaitán confirió al poema una gran dosis de lucidez, sensualidad y belleza lírica. Esta reedición de sus poemas de *Amantes*, donde lo erótico se entrelaza con una búsqueda del ser, fueron para su época un salto revolucionario y rebelde que presagiaba nuevas aperturas, mayores logros. La tragedia de su muerte es la tragedia de la poesía colombiana. [AR]

4353 Galib, Hamid. Contravida. San Juan: Ediciones Mairena, 1992. 143 p.: ill.

Este poemario, de una serenidad constante, de un lenguaje preciso en sus imágenes, conjuga el abismo de la alteridad, del vacío, con la presencia del amor—y la poesía—como recuperación parcial. [FC]

4354 Galván, Kyra. Alabanza escribo. México: Dirección de Difusión Cultural, Depto. Editorial, 1989. 97 p. (Col. Molinos de viento: 69. Serie/Poesía)

La persona poética en un proceso de autorreconocimiento en el mundo inventa un tono y un léxico que desde la mesura subvierte modelos establecidos del decir. Poesía erótica de ritmos medidos y suaves que postulan una conciencia femenina que busca entenderse en relación al otro/a: en comunión con el hombre, en solidaridad con la mujer. [NK]

4355 García, Clara A. Grímpolas de mi alma II. New York: Senda Nueva de Ediciones, 1991. 107 p. (Senda poética)

Sobresale, entre una variada gama temática que va desde lo íntimo hasta lo profesional, la voz del exilio que, tras una espontaneidad planteada desde lo biográfico, rememora como aliciente la Cuba que quedó atrás. [FC]

4356 García, José Enrique. El fabulador y otros poemas. Madrid: Ediciones de Cultura Hispánica, 1989. 127 p. (Col. Poesía)

Espacio de reunión, donde se dan cita cuatro poemarios anteriormente publicados para convocar una temática que va de lo metafísico (el tiempo, el silencio, la muerte) hasta la experiencia del acto creador. Las huellas de la vanguardia coexisten con los ecos de poetas establecidos como Pedro Mir. [FC]

4357 Garduño, Raúl. Poemas. 2a ed. aum. Chiapas, Mexico: Fonapas Chiapas, 1982. 166 p.: port. (Col. Ceiba; 12: Poesía)

Edición aumentada de la poesía de este excelente poeta chiapaneco que murió prematuramente en 1980. A la edición de 1973 se le añadieron algunos de sus poemas más logrados como "Habitación de Rosario," "Canción," "Después del Tiempo," "El Recinto donde Duerme el Oro." Ritmo inconfundible que logra integrar el lenguaje coloquial con recursos altamente poéticos como la anáfora y la rima interna. Ecos de Vallejo en una poesía que busca trascender los límites: "huyo de mis bronquios cansados, corro contra el viento del espanto, recorro la ciudad tan larga como un pan." [NK]

4358 Gatón Arce, Freddy. Andanzas y memorias. Santo Domingo: Editorial Taller, 1990. 147 p.: ill.

Varias voces, con sus respectivos registros poéticos—poemas cortos así como extensos poemas en prosa—asoman para leer, por ejemplo, los signos de las ciudades estadounidenses (Boston), construir el amor como obsesión y fantasía (Vlía) y reprochar los excesos

del miedo (la dictadura). No falta, por supuesto, la mirada del poeta que se mira a sí mismo desde la poesía: "El escriba habla de las primicias." [FC]

4359 Gazzolo, Ana María. Cabo de las tormentas. Lima: Jaime Campodónico/Editor, 1990. 65 p.

Ya sea en la primera sección que recoge impresiones de un viaje por Europa y el Medio Oriente, o en la segunda, volcada hacia lo interior y lo cotidiano, la voz de la poeta mantiene un acento delicado y melancólico que, sin mayores pretensiones, expresa bien una visión de tranquilo desencanto. [JMO]

4360 Gómez, Isabel. Pubisterio. Santiago: Ediciones Literatura Alternativa, 1989. 62 p.: ill.

Poemario interesante por desenfado del lenguaje que busca romper con maneras tradicionales de mirar y entender a la mujer. Avalan este libro juicios de dos buenos poetas chilenos. José-Christian Páez habla de una "magia tanto conceptual como de imágenes," mientras Jorge Teillier se refiere a la poeta como "dotada de una aguda búsqueda interior, sigue el camino del conocimiento, sin que los relámpagos de la intuición dejen de iluminarla." [LE]

4361 Granda, Euler. Un perro tocando la lira y otros poemas. Estudio introductorio y notas de Sonia Manzano. Quito: Libresa, 1990. 279 p.: bibl. (Col. Antares; 50)

No se trata de la reedición del volumen que este poeta ecuatoriano había publicado con el mismo nombre en 1977. Este libro es una selección de su obra total, aparecida en más de 30 años. Está precedida por un estudio introductorio de Sonia Manzano. [ORR]

4362 Greiff, Léon de. Baladas y canciones. Bogotá: Ancora Editores, 1991. 256 p.

Precedida de un ilustrativo prólogo de Otto de Greiff, esta antología de baladas y canciones del gran poeta colombiano es una magnífica contribución a la expansión y visibilidad de una obra poética que al paso de los años despierta más lectores atentos. Dominada por los sentidos en algarabía sinestésica, la poesía de de Greiff impone un aire barroco en constante movimiento de formas y fondos. Con el surgimiento de las nuevas corrientes neo-barrocas esta poesía se actualiza, y en su ser antiguo, intemporal, preludia un futuro de voces altas en poesía. [AR]

4363 Grinbank, Alicia. Curanto. Buenos Aires: Libros de Tierra Firme, 1992. 37 p. (Col. de poesía Todos bailan; 135)

Segundo poemario de esta autora argentina (n. 1949). El libro se divide en tres partes en las que la casa, sus objetos y actividades cotidianas son teñidos de un delicado erotismo que recuerda el libro *Canon de Alcoba* de Tununa Mercado. El poema que cierra el libro es, quizás, por su concreción y fuerza expresiva uno de los más logrados. [LU]

4364 Gruss, Irene. El mundo incompleto. Buenos Aires: Libros de Tierra Firme, 1987. 57 p. (Col. de poesía Todos bailan; 48)

Segundo poemario de esta autora (n. 1950). Poemas breves y delicados que cantan al mundo de la mujer, el espacio femenino del amor, la maternidad, la casa y la seducción. Poemas que afirman y cuestionan los espacios que a su vez liberan y encierran al sujeto poético. [LU]

4365 Guerra Gutiérrez, Alberto. Hálito que se desgarra en pos de la belleza: la cotidianidad por renovar la vida. Oruro, Bolivia: Editora Lilial 1989. 73 p.: ill. (Ediciones El Duende)

Nuevos textos de este poeta boliviano conocido. Esta colección señala un persistente reconocimiento de lo esencial, de lo que puede ser origen y principio, o sentido permanente en el ser humano, sus actos y sucesos del mundo. El motivo que origina este discurso poético es, como se puede desprender de lo dicho, fundamentalista: la tradición, el pasado y el origen divino. [ORR]

4366 Guillén, Nicolás. Las grandes elegías y otros poemas. Selección, prólogo, notas y cronología de Angel I. Augier. Caracas: Biblioteca Ayacucho, 1984. 454 p. (Biblioteca Ayacucho; 103)

Siguiendo la ya establecida política editorial de la Biblioteca Ayacucho, se recoge en este volumen lo más representativo de la obra de Guillén y se complementa con un esbozo cronológico en el que se conjuga la vida y la obra del poeta cubano. [FC]

4367 Gumucio Dagron, Alfonso. Sentimetros: cien poemas con sentimiento. La Paz?: Palabra Encendida, 1990. 164 p.: ill. (Col. Palabra encendida)

Este cuarto poemario de su autor reúne una colección de textos breves, escritos entre 1980–87, sobre una diversidad de motivos expuestos también con una diversidad de medidas emocionales, como parece sugerir el título del volumen. Crítica, protesta, elogio sobre hechos de la realidad cotidiana se manifiesta en tonos irónicos, humorísticos, acusatorios, afirmativos o interrogativos. Refleja la experiencia de la agitación y heterogeneidad de la vida moderna. [ORR]

4368 Guzmán Cruchaga, Juan. A media agua del sueño. Santiago: Editorial Andrés Bello, 1989. 168 p.: ill.

Texto antológico del autor de "Alma, no me Digas Nada, . . . ," poema que consagró a Guzmán Cruchaga cuando apareció en volumen *Lejana* (1921). Incluye poemas que van de *La mirada inmóvil* (1919) hasta *El niño que fue* (1975). Hay sección con reproducciones de algunos poemas y fotografías con personajes importantes de la época. Edición muy bien cuidada, como corresponde a obra que en lenguaje pulcro dice lo que se podría considerar trivial de manera nueva y profunda. Juvencio Valle, Premio Nacional de Literatura 1966, dice de esta poesía: "Un anillo en su simplicidad de líneas, una sola gota de agua podrían ser su símil." [LE]

4369 Hahn, Oscar. Tratado de sortilegios. Madrid: Hiperión, 1992. 116 p. (Poesía Hiperión; 204)

Edición muy cuidada de obra poética de este admirable poeta. Incluye *Arte de morir* (1977), *Mal de amor* (1981), *Imágenes nucleares* (1983), y *Estrellas fijas en un cielo blanco* (1989). Reagrupación de volúmenes y poemas en un orden nuevo por el poeta mismo sugiere este libro como definitivo de esta obra en este momento. El volumen así ordenado pone de relieve las muchas virtudes de esta poesía. Núcleo de preocupaciones temáticas desemboca en esos impecables 14 "sonetos" de *Estrellas fijas sobre un cielo blanco*. [LE]

4370 Harris, Tomás. Cipango. Santiago: Ediciones Documentas; Ottawa: Ediciones Cordillera, 1992. 203 p.

Volumen incluye tres primeros libros: *Zonas de peligro* (1985,) *Diario de navegación* (1986), a mi entender su mejor libro hasta el momento, y *El último viaje* (1987). *Cipango* fue finalista premio Casa de Las Américas en 1992. La ciudad moderna es el centro temático de esta poesía, si bien superpuestas a otras varias ciudades de la antigüedad. Harris es uno de los poetas más realizados de las nuevas promociones. [LE]

4371 Harris, Tomás. El último viaje. Concepción, Chile: Ediciones Sur, 1987. 58 p.

Con éste, su tercer poemario, Harris reafirma su condición como una de las voces más originales de las más recientes promociones poéticas chilenas. Continúa diálogo intertextual de su libro anterior (*Diario de navegación*, 1986), vuelta la voz ahora al alucinante último viaje de Colón y proyectada a Concepción, ciudad que el poema transforma en un espacio también alucinante. Se propone este viaje como un regreso "hacia el vacío fétido / del que nunca debí / asomar." Propicia esta aventura poética un epígrafe del poeta peruano Carlos Germán Belli: "Todo lo narrado transcurre / en las vedadas aguas cristalinas / del exclusivo coto de la mente." [LE]

4372 Hernández Alvarez, Freddy R. Memoriales del ángel bastardo. Caracas: Ediciones En Ancas, 1986. 132 p.

Siguiendo la tradición cultista que trata de preservar para la poesía el acento de lo exótico y lo geográficamente distante, Hernández Alvarez (n. 1949) nos da una poesía de alta calidad lírica a pesar de su acento narrativo. Ante el riesgo de caer en las fórmulas del poema que se cierra acentuando el otro rostro de su propia historia, Hernández recurre al humor y a la belleza de la imagen abierta que va de lo imprevisto a lo luminoso. [AR]

4373 Izquierdo Laboy, Idelys. Esmeralda perdida. San Juan?: Esmaco Printers Corp., 1990. 89 p.: ill.

Poemas donde el amor femenino convierte al objeto de su deseo en poesía; la feminidad no está dada en la respuesta contestataria sino en la capacidad para transformar al amado en objeto de un poema. Entre la mujer y el feminismo, media el arte. [FC]

4374 Jaramillo, Carlos Eduardo. Blues de la calle Loja. Loja, Ecuador: Casa de la Cultura Ecuatoriana Benjamín Carrión, Núcleo de Loja, 1991. 241 p.

Con este volumen, C.E. Jaramillo (n. 1932) reaparece después de 20 años en la actividad de las letras ecuatorianas. Hasta 1977 este autor había publicado más de 10 volúmenes de poesía. La mayor parte de los textos del presente libro tienen motivos evidentemente autobiográficos, expresados en un es-

tilo coloquial aunque no despojado de aciertos poéticos. [ORR]

4375 Jaramillo Escobar, Jaime. Selecta. Bogotá: Tercer Mundo Editores, 1987. 114 p.

Con un lenguaje popular donde a lo popular, directo, se mezclan ritmos y rimas internas deslumbrantes, este poeta nadaísta (n. 1932) ha impuesto poco a poco una obra que según algunos críticos tiene escasos antecedentes en la poesía hispanoamericana. Sin embargo, sería pertinente señalar filiaciones con poetas como León de Greiff, Alvaro Mutis, Enrique Molina y el mejor Coronel Urtecho. La presente antología, recogida por el mismo poeta como los mejores poemas de sus últimos libros, es una buena muestra de su obra. [AR]

4376 Lamborghini, Leónidas C. Odiseo confinado. Grabados de Blas Alfredo Castagna. Buenos Aires: Ediciones Van Riel, 1992. 217 p.: ill.

Ya desde el título se advierte el tratamiento paródico de esta "neo-épica;" el carácter antiheroico del protagonista es también presentado sin demora. El marcado tono grandilocuente del libro se nutre de discursos de distinto valor como el lunfardo y las letras de tango, lo cual refuerza el tono satírico del poemario tanto como la influencia de escritores disímiles: Borges, Dante, Homero, Quevedo, Estanislao del Campo, Discépolo, Pound, etc. [LU]

4377 Lamborghini, Leónidas C. Verme y 11 reescrituras de Discépolo. Buenos Aires: Editorial Sudamericana, 1988. 86 p.

Humor y constante juego con el lenguaje son las características más salientes de este poemario que se inscribe en la propuesta poética de la generación del 60. [LU]

4378 Lastra, Pedro. Noticias del extranjero. Santiago: Editorial Universitaria, 1992. 87 p. (Col. Los Contemporáneos)

Primera edición chilena de este libro (hay dos ediciones anteriores en México). Se ofrece aquí el mundo poético de Lastra en todo su poder revelador de verdades secretas: "Desde la memoria, el sueño y la extrañeza los poemas nos devuelven una mirada inocente, sin estorbos y como si fuese la única posible," dice Luis Domínguez-Vial, refiriéndose a este volumen. Edición necesaria para una más amplia difusión de una de las obras poéticas más finas y autocontenidas de la poesía chilena de las últimas décadas. [LE]

4379 Lastra, Pedro. Travel notes = Notas de viaje. Translation by Elias L. Rivers. 2nd. ed. rev. Maryland: La Yapa Editores, 1993. 45 p. (Lagniappe series)

Bella y cuidada edición bilingüe de 16 poemas de este fino poeta cuyo mundo nos revela esa otra versión de la realidad, esa versión secreta, en tono sobrio, sin estridencias. En "Paraíso" dice: "El niño que construye / en el mundo visible / su pequeño paraíso / velozmente / se adelanta a los días / e instala en su memoria / el paraíso perdido." Significativa muestra de una admirable labor poética. Muy bien logradas las traducciones al inglés de Elias L. Rivers. [LE]

4380 León, Eleazar. Reverencial. Caracas: Monte Avila Editores, 1991. 76 p. (Altazor)

Eleazar León es uno de los pocos poetas venezolanos de la generación del 70 que no se acogió al llamado minimalista, esencialista, en el poema. En él perviven las fuerzas del lenguaje que se abren en profusión para arrastrar sueños, angustias, visiones. Sensualidad y pasión podrían ser las constantes de su poesía. [AR]

4381 Lezama Lima, José. Poesía. Edición de Emilio de Armas. Madrid: Cátedra, 1992. 396 p.: bibl., ill. (Letras hispánicas; 342)

Muestra representativa del orbe lezamesco, con un excelente ensayo introductorio ("La Poesía del Eros Cognoscente") y una introducción en la que se recogen las primeras reacciones de los latinoamericanos frente al trabajo de Lezama (Cortázar, Vargas Llosa, Octavio Paz). Cumpliendo con su objetivo didáctico, los comentarios adjuntos a los poemas contextualizan y potencian la lectura. [FC]

4382 López, Julio César. Estaciones de la vigilia: obra poética, 1972–1985. Río Piedras, P.R.: Editorial de la Univ. de Puerto Rico, 1990. 308 p.: bibl.

Se agrupan en esta edición los siete poemarios que conforman el trabajo poético de López, quien ha sido ensayista, periodista y poeta de la generación del 50 puertorriqueña. Además, se incluyen cinco ensayos introductorios correspondientes a los tres primeros poemarios, escritos por José Emilio González,

Clemente Pereda, Luis de Arrigoitia y Juan Martínez Capó. [FC]

4383 Lugones, Leopoldo. Lunario sentimental. Edición de Jesús Benítez. Madrid: Cátedra, 1988. 408 p.: ill., ports. (Letras hispánicas; 285)

Reedición de este libro clásico de la literatura hispanoamericana con una amplia y útil introducción que analiza la sociedad latinoamericana a fines del siglo XIX y principios del XX, el modernismo y el contexto literario argentino y luego la situación particular de Lugones, su biografía y su obra para finalmente centrarse en el *Lunario sentimental.* [LU]

4384 Lumbreras, Ernesto. Espuela para demorar el viaje. México: Joaquín Mortiz, 1993. 67 p.

Con esta publicación ganadora del Premio de Poesía Aguascalientes 1992, Lumbreras nacido (n. 1966), y con dos libros publicados (*Clamor de agua* y *Ordenes del colibrí al jardinero*) se reafirma como uno de los mejores exponentes de la novísima poesía mexicana. Visión vertiginosa de amplitud temática, virtuosismo técnico y vitalidad imaginativa en este texto postmoderno que reta formas establecidas. Entrega que incluye poemas en prosa, poemas breves, poemas corridos, poemas huapangos, aforismos, y decires. [NK]

4385 Manzano, Sonia. Full de reinas: poesía. Quito?: Abrapalabra Editores, 1991. 59 p.

Voz crítica empeñada en mostrar la artificialidad y superficialidad de ciertas tradiciones sociales y convenciones políticas. A partir de un contexto ecuatoriano propio, abarca circunstancias comunes de la sociedad actual de cualquier otro país, particularmente latinoamericano. La escritura poética para esta autora es un instrumento de denuncia y censura. [ORR]

4386 Marinello, Juan. Poesía. Compilación, prólogo y notas de Emilio de Armas. 2. ed. La Habana: Editorial Letras Cubanas, 1989. 114 p. (Obras/Juan Marinello)

Toda la poesía Marinello, agrupada en cuatro secciones; se le ofrece al lector la posibilidad de rastrear el movimiento poético del intelectual cubano, desde los "Primeros Poemas" hasta la publicación de *Liberación* (1972), y, además, poemas posteriores en los que queda la huella de la poesía "pura" cubana promovida por la *Revista de Avance*. [FC]

4387 Martín, Carlos. Hacia el último asombro. Bogotá: Ancora Editores, 1991. 89 p.

En la actualidad Carlos Martín (n. 1914) es el único sobreviviente de la generación "Piedra y cielo" que dominó el mundo poético colombiano en las décadas del 30 y 40. Poeta, ensayista, su obra trató siempre de desprenderse de los cánones más cerrados de este movimiento, tratando de encontrar en la imagen y la actitud surreal alimento para una nueva experimentación de lo poético. Sobre él dice Eduardo Carranza en este libro: "A través de los poemas de Carlos Martín pasa un cálido soplo de humanidad. Y como todo poeta auténtico, nos da en su poesía una visión original del mundo y su misterio." [AR]

4388 Martos, Marco. Cabellera de Berenice. Trujillo, Peru: Municipalidad Provincial de Trujillo; Casa del Artista, 1991. 94 p. (Col. Homenaje al centenario de César Vallejo; 6–7)

Debe ser uno de los mejores libros poéticos del autor, pues siendo una obra reconocible como suya es, a la vez, nueva. Es un libro melancólico y luminoso, atraído por paisajes orientales y visiones extranjeras, pero calado por un profundo afecto por los contornos naturales del país, especialmente los de su tierra natal. El poema amoroso que da título al volumen es de antología. [JMO]

4389 Martos, Marco. Muestra de arte rupestre. Lima: Instituto Nacional de Cultura, 1990. 93 p. (Col. Las Voces)

Valioso conjunto de poemas que muestran la depuración artística de un poeta que surgió a mediados de los años 60 y se distinguió por el deliberado prosaísmo de sus versos y el cortante tono crítico, ambos a la manera de Brecht. Esos rasgos se mantienen todavía en esta colección, pero atemperados por un aire más reflexivo y resignado. [JMO]

4390 Matos Paoli, Francisco. Las pequeñas muertes. San Juan: Ediciones Mairena, 1989. 161 p.

Ya establecido como voz lírica, de un decir sucinto que fija la imagen en el poema, Matos Paoli replantea en esta colección de sonetos toda su poética como constancia de una poesía que también quiere estar más allá del poema, entre la palabra precisa y las certeras incertidumbres de lo religioso, lo patriótico, el compromiso, la mujer, la naturaleza, la muerte, los otros y el yo. [FC]

4391 Mayta Bazualdo, Felipe. Harapos del silencio: poesía. Santa Cruz, Bolivia: Cabildo, 1990. 93 p.

Una intención innegable por descubrir las manifestaciones más sencillas de la realidad, en la que cabe con preferencia la naturaleza rural, es una de las notas más características de esta poesía. El lenguaje se reduce, asimismo, a la estructura necesaria, generalmente breve y económica, para reafirmar esa intención. El resultado es de estimable calidad. [ORR]

4392 Mazzucchelli, Aldo. Después de 1984. Montevideo: Arca, 1988. 65 p. (Col. Maremagnum)

Desde un paisaje desolado canta el yo lírico toda su desesperanza con un tono de resonancias manriqueñas. Todo aquello en que hemos cifrado nuestras ilusiones—como la imagen del cometa Halley—ha pasado dejándonos aún más solos y más vacíos. [LU]

4393 Megget, Humberto. Obra completa: poesía y prosa. Edición crítica, introducción y notas de Pablo Rocca. Ilustraciones de Manuel Aguiar Barrios y Antonio Pezzino. Montevideo: Ediciones de la Banda Oriental, 1991. 171 p.: bibl., ill. (Ediciones de la Banda Oriental; 144. Clásicos Banda Oriental; 1)

Excelencia crítica de Pablo Rocca queda manifestada en esta edición de la obra completa de Megget (1926–51) que incorpora 18 poemas inéditos y otros éditos pero no recogidos en libro con anterioridad. La edición está acompañada de una sugestiva y completa introducción así como de numerosas notas y una bibliografía crítica. [LU]

4394 Mejía Vallejo, Manuel. Memoria del olvido. Poemas y dibujos de Manuel Mejía Vallejo. Medellín: Editorial Univ. de Antioquia, 1990. 110 p.: ill.

No son muchos los casos de novelistas que se arriesguen en los dominios de la poesía. Sin embargo Mejía Vallejo lo hace y con gran maestría. Sus poemas, poco pretenciosos desde el ángulo de su entonación, son divagaciones iluminantes sobre nuestro ser y hacer en el mundo. Sembrados en esencias son como dardos al corazón de las cosas. Sus temas, que palpan amor, olvido y muerte desde las fronteras de la noche y el sueño, tienen ese rostro de la verdad que sólo puede autenticar una vida vivida con valentía. [AR]

4395 Mendoza Varela, Eduardo. Los 18 sonetos de Roma y otros poemas rescatados. Bogotá: Litografía Arco, 1986. 157 p.: ill.

Desde sus impresiones de viaje *El Mediterráneo es un mar joven* (1965) hasta el libro que aquí nos acupa, la atención poética de Mendoza Varela (1919–86) se centró principalmente en lo romántico y helénico. Este poeta "cuadernícola," de la generación de los 40, no quiso desprenderse de los modelos neoclásicos y románticos imperantes en la tradición poética colombiana. No obstante, la pulcritud del verso y la limpieza del vocablo hacen de sus sonetos una lectura agradable. [AR]

4396 Mirabal, Mili. El jardín de Afrodita. Río Piedras, P.R.: Editorial Cultural, 1988. 145 p.

Este poemario, precedido de una trilogía premiada en 1973 por el Ateneo Puertorriqueño, se suma a la corriente de literatura erótica que, escrita por mujeres, reclama nuevos espacios en la literatura puertorriqueña. El erotismo temático, la recontextualización de una mitología apropiada para la ocasión, la ausencia de comas y puntos, los espacios en blanco y la disposición tipográfica marcan la trayectoria de una poesía que propone, sin más: "¡Existo!" [FC]

4397 Molina, Enrique. Hacia una isla incierta. Ilustrado con dos *collages* del autor. Buenos Aires: Editorial Argonauta, 1992. 98 p.: ill. (Biblioteca de poesía; 3)

En este nuevo poemario Molina intensifica una de las características más constantes de su poesía: esa mirada que encuentra en lo cotidiano el centro del absoluto, la búsqueda de un espacio que por solitario e "incierto" más se parece a la intemperie de los primeros días del mundo, o de sus últimos brillos. En muchos de estos poemas se percibe un tono desesperanzado y hasta apocalíptico por momentos. [LU]

4398 Montaño Arroyo, Germán. La dentadura de Dios: antología poética. Selección de Ebert Peredo. La Paz: Sui Generis Editorial, 1990. 151 p.: ill.

De acuerdo al subtítulo de este volumen, se trata de una antología, aunque no incluye información sobre las fuentes de las que

procede. Es una poesía que busca las imágenes propias de su medio andino-boliviano para expresar su rechazo y violencia respecto a las manifestaciones de los sistemas occidentales ajenos a la tradición regional. [ORR]

4399 Montaño Nemer, Miriam. Sentires. Oruro, Bolivia: Empresa Editorial Hill, 1989. 80 p.

Obra primeriza de una joven poeta boliviana que se suma a la nueva poesía femenina del país. La colección está precedida por una presentación de la autora por el poeta Alberto Guerra Gutiérrez. Los textos tienen como motivos experiencias subjetivas, expresadas en versos breves. [ORR]

4400 Montejo, Eugenio. Alfabeto del mundo. México: Fondo de Cultura Económica, 1988. 209 p. (Col. Tierra firme)

Magnífica colección de la obra de Eugenio Montejo (n. 1938). Ella nos permite apreciar que más allá del virtuosismo formal, la poesía de Montejo toca con claridad y precisión la imagen que hace realidad la poesía. Son 147 poemas marcados por hallazgos donde lo telúrico se entrelaza con lo humano en un esfuerzo que linda con la belleza y la sabiduría. No está por demás indicar que la obra de Montejo, dada su innegable calidad, se destaca ampliamente en el panorama latinoamericano. [AR]

4401 Morábito, Fabio. De lunes todo el año. México: J. Mortiz, 1992. 101 p. (Premios bellas artes de literatura)

Premio de Poesía Aguascalientes 1991 de este poeta urbano. Poemas del diario vivir, de las cosas circundantes, de recuerdos que son puntos de partida para precisar la realidad presente. Visión crítica a través de un estilo directo, y anti-retórico, para decir también los sueños, y las ilusiones. [NK]

4402 Morales, Andrés. Verbo. Santiago: Red Internacional del Libro, 1991. 139 p. (Serie Círculo de tiza)

Interesante aporte al bagaje de poesía chilena actual. Voz poética vuelta al origen de las palabras y las cosas, y proyectada a visión de un "universo final de apocalipsis." Al centro de este mundo está el mar, Thalassa, "exorcismo de lo nunca plenamente hallado." Reitera futilidad de esta búsqueda la voz huérfana del mítico Ismael, personaje por siempre ajeno al mundo, a las cosas, al amor. "Yo soy ese que desciende y cae siempre, a quien vencen el engaño y la desdicha." Libro de lenguaje muy cuidado que logra crear su propio espacio poético. [LE]

4403 Mutis, Alvaro. Summa de Maqroll el gaviero: poesía, 1948–1988. México: Fondo de Cultura Económica, 1990. 242 p. (Col. Tierra firme)

Una de las mayores virtudes de la poesía de Mutis es que cada poema contribuye a la lectura de un poema total que es su obra. Son ellos fragmentos de un viaje espiritual en donde el espacio recorrido es la vida con sus vicisitudes y enigmas, y cuyo tiempo es la ineluctable muerte que nos espera. Nada que no sea lo esencial le pertenece a este poeta mayor de las letras latinoamericanas. La edición de este libro que recoge su obra poética hasta 1990 es altamente valiosa. [AR]

4404 Mutis Durán, Santiago. Tú también eres de lluvia. México: Fondo de Cultura Económica, 1988. 66 p.: ill. (Cuadernos de La Gaceta; 52)

Representante de la última generación de poetas colombianos surgidos luego del nadaísmo y los movimientos del 60, Mutis (n. 1951) no sólo ha escrito una obra ya memorable sino que ha alentado esfuerzos de expansión literaria como son sus labores de editor y director de la hermosa revista *Gradiva*. Sus poemas, de alto contenido lírico, se inscriben en una encrucijada donde la imaginación, bordada por el sueño y la memoria, abre sus puertas a una aventura que del ver va al conocer. Música, pintura y poesía amalgamadas en poemas luminosos. [AR]

4405 Naranjo, Alexis. Ontogonías. Con la obra gráfica de Carole Lindberg. Quito: Impr. Mariscal, 1990. 112 p.: col. ill.

Llama la atención la excelente impresión de este libro, en el que se destaca la colección de dibujos y pinturas de Carole Lindberg que interpreta plásticamente la poesía de Alexis Naranjo. En esta reunión de textos pictóricos y literarios, los primeros logran efectos poéticos más vigorosos que los propiamente líricos. Estos discurren en un tono narrativo sobre aspectos diversos y dispersos, desde la experiencia personal hasta la mitología universal. [ORR]

4406 Navarro Harris, Heddy. Vírgenes vacantes. Santiago: Editorial Fértil Provincia, 1992? 118 p.

Poemas cargados de erotismo producto

de unión imaginada considerada la ausencia del objeto amoroso. Ante esta ausencia, las "vírgenes vacantes" (y bacanes) se vuelcan voluptuosamente en la naturaleza: "Amame torbellino / de nubes," dice un poema. Poeta interesante con obra anterior que incide en temas de éste, su último libro. [LE]

4407 Negroni, María. La jaula bajo el trapo. Buenos Aires: Libros de Tierra Firme, 1991. 107 p. (Col. de poesía Todos bailan; 97)

Resulta de especial interés en este libro la exploración genérica que en él se lleva a cabo: poesía-collage que se nutre de manifestaciones literarias de distinto valor: tangos, versos del Arcipreste de Hita, una canción de Paul Anka, Rubén Darío. Otra de sus constantes es la puesta a prueba del lenguaje en busca de realizaciones más expresivas. [LU]

4408 Neruda, Pablo. Residencia en la tierra. Santiago: Editorial Universitaria, 1992. 178 p. (Col. Los Contemporáneos)

Reproduce primera edición completa de *Residencia en la tierra*, (Madrid: Ediciones el Arbol, Cruz y Raya, 1935). Buen prólogo de Federico Schopf que sitúa muy bien esta etapa de la producción poética de Neruda dentro del contexto de toda la obra nerudiana. Hay notas que pueden ayudar al no iniciado en la difícil lectura de algunos poemas. [LE]

4409 Nolla, Olga. Dafne en el mes de marzo. Madrid: Editorial Playor, 1989. 106 p. (Biblioteca de autores de Puerto Rico)

Cofundadora de la revista literaria *Zona de Carga y Descarga*, la poesía de Nolla, junto con la literatura femenina contemporánea, constituye un necesario golpe a los esquemas patriarcales que han sustentado la literatura puertorriqueña. En este poemario, el poder del mito se hace cómplice de una feminidad que exhibe tanto su libertad como su fantasía erótica con humor e ironía. [FC]

4410 Novo, Salvador. Antología personal: poesía 1915–1974. México: Conaculta, 1991. 390 p. (Col. Lecturas Mexicanas; 37: Tercera serie)

Miembro de "Los contemporáneos" y celebrado como uno de los mejores prosistas en lengua española, este tomo reconoce la excelencia de su quehacer poético, y ofrece al lector una muestra representativa. [NK]

4411 Ossott, Hanni. Cielo, tu arco grande. Caracas: Tierra de Gracia Editores, 1989. 60 p. (Col. Rasgos comunes)

Hanni Ossott (n. 1946) es una poeta de reconocida trayectoria literaria y quien forma parte de los grupos que emergen en la década del 60, identificados ellos en una indagación de lo esencial en la palabra y en poesía. Este libro se añade a los anteriores en esta dirección estética. Lastimosamente en él la idea de lo poético prevalece sobre la poesía misma, es decir, que palabras y versos hacen explícito lo que el poema nos debería dar a través de la magia de su factura. [AR]

4412 Osuna, William. Antología de la mala calle. Caracas: FUNDARTE, 1990. 134 p. (Col. Cuadernos de difusión; 140)

Poesía de Osuna (n. 1948) se emparenta con la de los poetas rebeldes y contestatarios de la década del 60, aquellos abanderados del "Techo de la ballena." Es una poesía de ciudad, de corte violento y verso cortante, hiriente. La tendencia al descuido, al poema deshilvanado, es parte de la retórica de respuesta directa frente a una realidad ciudadana inaceptable. [AR]

4413 Palés Matos, Luis. Tuntún de pasa y grifería. Edición de Mercedes López-Baralt. San Juan: Instituto de Cultura Puertorriqueña; Editorial de la Univ. de Puerto Rico, 1993. 226 p.: bibl., ill. (Col. puertorriqueña; 4)

Con esta "tercera salida" del texto palesiano, la presente edición reconfigura lo que debió ser el texto original del puertorriqueño; se hacen ajustes para incluir, excluir, ordenar y reubicar algunos poemas que, en las dos ediciones anteriores—1) de Federico de Onís y 2) de Margot Arce—fueron incluídos, excluídos y alterados. Se incluyen, además de la introducción crítica, dos trabajos sobre Palés: uno de Angel Balbuena Prat y otro de Jaime Benítez. [FC]

4414 Pantin, Yolanda. La canción fría. Caracas: Editorial Angria, 1989. 66 p. (Col. Literatura hispanoamericana)

En el epílogo a este libro Yolanda Pantin (n. 1954), poeta afiliada al grupo "Tráfico" de finales de la década del 70, nos habla del "sueño de lo literario" como fuente inspiradora de algunos de sus poemas. No podríamos encontrar mejor definición. Ellos entremezclan realidad y ficción, así como secretas referencias a poetas, lugares y épocas: son los espacios y tiempos que ayudan a construir los castillos de amor, ilusión y sueño del poema. [AR]

4415 Paz, Octavio. Obra poética: 1935–1988. Barcelona: Editorial Seix Barral, 1990. 863 p.: ill.

Esta nueva edición amplía la de 1979 al incluir *Arbol adentro*. El poeta, en un breve *post-scriptum* añade que ha "corregido erratas y modificado levemente unos pocos poemas." Imprescindible edición del premio Nóbel que reúne *Libertad bajo palabra* (1935–57), *La hija de Rappaccini* (1956), *Días hábiles* (1958–61), *Homenaje y Profanaciones* (1960), *Salamandra* (1958–61), *Solo a dos voces* (1961), *Ladera este* (1962–68), *Hacia el comienzo* (1964–68), *Blanco* (1966), *Topoemas* (1968), *El mono gramático* (1970), *Vuelta* (1969–75), *Pasado en claro* (1974) y *Arbol adentro* (1976–88). [NK]

4416 Pereda, Fernando. Pruebas al canto: poemas; antología. Montevideo: Arca, 1990. 130 p.

Correspondió—con justicia—a la editorial Arca la publicación de uno de los libros más anunciados de los últimos 60 años: el primer poemario de Fernando Pereda. En el texto "Entrada a la Poesía" el autor da cuenta de la concepción poética que alimenta su poesía: el poema como lucha contra el caos, su combatividad inherente, la concentración y el rigor, su inseparabilidad con lo real y la música. [LU]

4417 Pérez, María de los Milagros. Música por dentro. Ilustraciones de Andrés Rodríguez Santos. Guaynabo, P.R.: Editorial Sonador, 1991. 126 p.: ill. (Col. Primeras palabras)

Una inmitigable conciencia de la poesía—de lo poético como voz de la disidencia pero también de la intimidad, siempre dialógica, de un sujeto femenino en cuyo cuerpo se registra la "libertad ganada"— sienta las pautas de este poemario que, atento a su propia musicalidad y a las relaciones que establece con la tradición, recobra el espacio doméstico de la mujer una voz de fuerza que la mujer-poeta está llamada a decantar. [FC]

4418 Pérez Olivares, José. Examen del guerrero. Madrid: Visor, 1992. 114 p. (Col. Visor de poesía; 281)

Una de las figuras "más destacadas de la última generación cubana," cuya poesía, como la de Lezama, surge de la lectura, del espacio de los libros; texto sobre texto, los poemas, como algunos cuentos de Borges, pueden ser comentarios de otros textos. El legado ori-genista, incuestionable, se da también en la insistencia de la poesía sobre la pintura, que es deseo de recorrer su plasticidad. Ritmo pro-pio, dinámico y a la vez muy seguro de sí, en este poemario el lenguaje no vacila; la temá-tica erudita no enturbia la voz. [FC]

4419 Pesantez Rodas, Rodrigo A. Atando ca-bos: poesía, 1958–1988. Guayaquil, Ec-uador: Casa de la Cultura Ecuatoriana, Nú-cleo del Guayas, 1989. 123 p.

A falta de información, este volumen puede ser una selección o la obra inédita de este poeta ecuatoriano (n. 1937). Distribuye su material en cinco secciones. La primera con poemas de los últimos años, y las siguien-tes de períodos que corresponden a 1984–85, 1969–73, 1965–67, 1960–61, y 1958–60. Estas fechas permiten realizar una lectura cronológica y apreciar la calidad de este poeta y crítico. [ORR]

4420 Piña, Cristina. Pie de guerra. Buenos Aires: Ediciones del Dock, 1990. 67 p. (Col. El Mono hablador)

Poesía de la mujer "en pie de guerra" enriqueciéndose/empobreciéndose con las cosas cotidianas. El lenguaje es percibido aquí como la única realidad posible pero igual-mente insatisfactoria. Un delicado lirismo re-corre las páginas de este texto. Cristina Piña ha publicado tres libros de poemas anteriores. Como crítica se destacan sus ensayos sobre Alejandra Pizarnik. [LU]

4421 Pizarnik, Alejandra. Poesía y prosas. Buenos Aires: Corregidor, 1990. 315 p. (Obras completas)

Excelente edición de la producción poética y en prosa de una de las voces más al-tas de la poesía hispanoamericana contempo-ránea. [LU]

4422 Pollarolo, Giovanna. Entre mujeres so-las. Lima: Editorial Colmillo Blanco, 1991. 78 p. (Col. de arena)

Usando un título pavesiano, Pollarolo (n. Tacna, 1952) reúne en este libro una serie de escenas, reflexiones y diálogos cuyo tema central es la mujer en su relación conyugal y/o erótica. Insatisfacción y desencanto, con-sigo misma o con los hombres, es la actitud más frecuente, aunque el tono, a veces dema-siado simplista, le impide saber al lector si la víctima femenina está parodiando o acep-tando los clisés que usa. [JMO]

4423 Ponce, Javier. Los códices de Lorenzo Trinidad. Quito: Editorial El Conejo, 1985. 103 p. (Col. Ecuador/letras)

Discurso poético de interrogación cons-tante ante el acaecer cotidiano como realidad de difícil entendimiento. La imagen que me-jor describe esa realidad es la oscuridad, frente a la cual el sujeto pierde su sentido de percepción y orientación. Denuncia una preo-cupación muy propia del pensamiento con-temporáneo: la alienación del sujeto debido a la falta de saber y certidumbre. [ORR]

4424 Prieto, Martín. Verde y blanco. Buenos Aires: Libros de Tierra Firme, 1988. 39 p. (Col. de poesía Todos bailan; 77)

Primer libro de este joven poeta argen-tino (n. 1961) que integra el consejo de redac-ción de la revista *Diario de Poesía*. Lo cotidia-no que se repite inalterable en el tiempo da unidad temática a este poemario. Esceptí-cismo sin resentimiento. Esas repeticiones no son vistas como negativas. No hay cuestiona-miento ni ironía en la presentación sino cons-statación lisa y llana. Tono levemente bor-geano en los primeros poemas. [LU]

4425 Pulido, Blanca Luz. Raíz de sombras. México: Fondo de Cultura Económica, 1988. 70 p. (Letras mexicanas)

Poesía reflexiva de factura clásica re-miniscente de "Los Contemporáneos." Viaje hacia el interior que busca descifrar los mis-terios del diario existir desde los cuestiona-mientos que se logran en el silencio de la noche. [NK]

4426 Quiñónez, Isabel. Esa forma de irnos alejando. Xalapa, México: Univ. Vera-cruzana, 1989. 79 p. (Ficción)

Tercer libro de esta autora que se abre un camino sólido en la poesía más reciente. A través de imágenes sensoriales y asociativas la voz poética elabora una elegía al amante muerto, cuestiona el tiempo límite que ha-bita el ser, y busca en la naturaleza un lugar que la refleje. [NK]

4427 Quirarte, Vicente. El ángel es vampiro. México: Ediciones Toledo, 1991. 84 p.

Poemario ganador del Premio Villau-rrutia 1991 de este reconocido poeta de la ge-neración de los 50. Diversidad temática y es-tilística en versos clásicos y mesurados que se tornan elegías (al padre), homenajes (a la amada y amigos poetas), elogios (al vampiro), preludios, epifanías y fábulas. [NK]

4428 Quiroga, Igor. Los ríos del aire: poesía. Cochabamba, Bolivia: Imprenta Offset Cueto, 1990. 1 v. (unpaged).

Este volumen mereció el primer premio en el Concurso Nacional de Poesía 1988 de la Municipalidad de Cochabamba, Bolivia. Se caracteriza por su meditación sobre circunstancias y objetos inmediatos a su percepción, lo que le permite descubrir sentidos nuevos en lo cotidiano. Entre los temas de esa reflexión tienen especial predilección los motivos eróticos que son expresados con refinada sensualidad. Sin duda, es una poesía con calidad. [ORR]

4429 Raful, Tony. Las bodas de Rosaura con la primavera. Santo Domingo: Taller, 1991. 138 p.: ill.

Este poemario perteneciente a la generación del 65 dominicana, de feliz trasvase a lo narrativo, polifónico y caleidoscópico, regresa al escenario de la invasión norteamericana para ofrecer un mosaico de los diferentes frentes que, simultáneamente, urden su tejido "como trofeo roto, como remordimiento compartido o como revancha anhelada." [FC]

4430 Ramos Otero, Manuel. Invitación al polvo. Río Piedras, P.R.: Editorial Plaza Mayor, 1991. 72 p. (Biblioteca de autores de Puerto Rico)

Con esta colección de poemas, Ramos Otero se juega la última carta frente al amor y la muerte para biografiar la experiencia— indistinguible en este caso—del amor que conduce a la muerte. La invitación al amor homosexual es también la invitación a la muerte—SIDA. Publicado póstumamente, este poemario es una reivindicación homosexual del amor y la literatura. [FC]

4431 Ribera Chevremont, Evaristo. Evaristo Ribera Chevremont. Ilustraciones de J.A. Torres Martinó. 2. ed. San Juan: Instituto de Cultura Puertorriqueña, 1990. 57 p.: ill. (Cuadernos de poesía; 6)

Persiguen estos cuadernos de la literatura puertorriqueña tanto la difusión como el homenaje. A pesar de lo sucinto, se consigue dar una muestra representativa del poeta, cuya producción literaria comprende de 1912 hasta 1954. Se incluyen algunos poemas inéditos. Espacio de confluencia entre la poesía y el dibujo: las ilustraciones de Torres Martinó reinterpretan los 16 poemas. [FC]

4432 Rivera, Etnairis. Entre ciudades y casi paraísos. San Juan: Instituto de Cultura Puertorriqueña, 1989. 158 p.

Este poemario, que incluye una selección de cuatro libros publicados junto con un trabajo inédito, busca, tras imágenes imantadas a un centro temático múltiple (la naturaleza, el amor, la libertad), una visión de nuestra América por tres derroteros críticos: la cordillera de los Andes, Nueva York, el Caribe—Puerto Rico. La feminidad de la voz poética establece, en lo fundamental, una complicidad filosófica. [FC]

4433 Rivera, Silvia Tomasa. La rebelión de los solitarios: el sueño de Valquiria. México: Gobierno del estado de Veracruz, 1991. 82 p.

Ultima entrega de esta excelente poeta heredera de la tradición iconoclasta de Jaime Sabines y del compromiso social de José Emilio Pacheco. Poeta comunicante que en "La Rebelión de los Solitarios" habla desde la soledad del ser. Fuerza expresiva que se logra a través de imágenes vertiginosas donde el deseo se convierte en el móvil principal para la sobrevivencia. "El Sueño de Valquiria" es la historia de "una pasión de amor que se desata." Lenguaje sensual y sensorial en esta insólita poesía erótica de encuentro y pérdida. [NK]

4434 Roca, Juan Manuel. Ciudadano de la noche. Bogotá: Fundación Simón y Lola Guberek, 1989. 58 p. (Col. literaria; 34. Primera serie)

No es extraño que los poetas caminen al borde del abismo, lo difícil es que puedan mantener un equilibrio en ese mismo lugar donde otros, tentados por lo fácil, caen a fondos que son superficies donde muere la poesía. J.M. Roca es un poeta de grandes riesgos. Con un lenguaje que el tiempo depura más y más, recurre con maestría a imágenes, que dentro de lo surreal, abren puertas a un ver y sentir la poesía con el esplendor de una sencillez que ilumina el decir del poema. Los 33 poemas incluidos en este libro así lo atestiguan. [AR]

4435 Rocha Beltrán, Juan Carlos. A e & yo tú. La Paz?: Producciones Cima, 1991. 114 p.: ill.

Uso renovado de la metáfora con un afán evidente por evadir las descripciones tradicionales de la realidad y proponer percepciones nuevas y sorprendentes. Las construcciones poéticas instalan un espacio que se opone a visión naturalista del mundo. Y aunque la modalidad de sus recursos metafóricos proceden de los modelos vanguardistas, busca incorporar experiencias y preocupaciones contemporáneas. [ORR]

4436 Rodríguez Torres, Alvaro. El viento en el puente. Bogotá: Centro Editorial, Univ. Nacional de Colombia, 1990. 53 p.

Pasado el tremendismo confesional y polémico de las décadas de 60 y 70, la poesía latinoamericana ha encontrado como uno de sus múltiples cauces, un camino de regreso al tono intimista y existencial que la precedió. Es allí donde se inserta este libro de Alvaro Rodríguez (n. 1948) y su obra anterior. Serena, la imagen va en pos de una belleza interna, casi inapresable. [AR]

4437 Rojas, Gonzalo. Antología de aire. Santiago: Fondo de Cultura Económica, 1991. 1 v.

Hermoso y consagratario volumen que recoge parte considerable (libro a libro) de la obra de este extraordinario poeta. Presenta "cursus lineal" del sistema imaginario que surge de los 10 volúmenes que van de *La miseria del hombre*, (Valparaíso, Chile: Imprenta Roma 1948) a *Desocupado lector*, (Madrid: Hiperión, 1990). Relectura que este volumen sugiere y confirma a Rojas como un gran poeta a escala continental. [LE]

4438 Rojas, Gonzalo. Cinco visiones. Salamanca, Spain: Ediciones Univ. de Salamanca, 1992. 241 p.

Título con que se inaugura colección "Biblioteca de América;" Univ. de Salamanca. Antología de obra del poeta chileno recientemente distinguido con el primer Premio Reina Sofía de Poesía Iberoamericana. Sugerente selección de obra poética que trasciende fronteras de lo chileno o latinoamericano. Muestra incluye poemas de *La miseria del hombre, Contra la muerte, Oscuro, Transtierro, Del relámpago* (1a y 2a ediciones), *50 poemas, El alumbrado, Materia de testamento, Desocupado lector* y cuatro poemas inéditos. Prólogo sugiere lectura de estas "visiones" como una reordenación de los diversos títulos de poemarios incluidos en volumen. Aporte importante a la bibliografía de este poeta. [LE]

4439 Rojas, Gonzalo. Contra la muerte. Referencias cronológicas de Jaime Quezada. Santiago: Editorial Universitaria, 1993. 96 p. (Col. Los Contemporáneos)

Nueva edición de *Contra la muerte*, publicado por primera vez en 1964. Relectura necesaria que pone de relieve la originalidad de un lenguaje poético que se hará más y más revelador en libros posteriores. Hay referencias cronológicas muy completas de Jaime Quezada sobre Gonzalo Rojas, poeta distinguido en 1992 con el Premio Nacional de Literatura en Chile y el Premio Reina Sofía de Poesía Iberoamericana en España. [LE]

4440 Rojas, Waldo. Fuente itálica. Santiago: Editorial Universitaria, 1990. 59 p. (Col. Los Contemporáneos)

Poemas convocados por encuentros con Italia, "dispersos en el tiempo, erradizos en el espacio; momentos transmutables en esa suerte de hallazgo, conmoción graduada o fortuna continua, en el que se acuerdan el hombre y el mundo, la palabra y el silencio," dice autor. La palabra que evoca establece sugerente concordancia poética con lugares evocados. Conjunto de poemas que revelan control del oficio. [LE]

4441 Rojas Guardia, Armando. Hacia la noche viva. Caracas: FabriArt Ediciones, 1989. 63 p.

"Vivo en el umbral, el vilo." Tal vez estas palabras del mismo poeta sean una guía clara si intentamos acercarnos al hecho desgarrado, desgarrante de sus poemas. Poesía al filo de los nervios, violentada por la ciudad y la cruel experiencia de una vida que pierde sentido al volverse mecánica y de hecho, marginal. Sin embargo este tono desesperanzado y sensual no impide que podamos gozar cierta belleza sutil, diáfana, en sus poemas. [AR]

4442 Rokha, Pablo de. Sátira. Prólogo de René de Costa. Ed. facsimilar. Santiago: Editorial América del Sur, 1985. 26 p.: bibl.

Reproducción facsimilar de primer libro (1918) de Pablo de Rokha. Folletín furibundo en el que, en versos adrede destemplados, el poeta arremete contra todo y contra todos esos escritores que usan ese "verso" que de Rokha rechaza: ese "lenguaje amurallado, encerrado en el límite convencional de la estrofa." Anuncio temprano y desafiante de una vanguardia todavía nonata en Chile: "El mundo se transforma, trabaja, piensa ríe / en la máquina actual, infinita y divina . . . / y no en vuestros minúsculos gritos de sabandijas." De Costa rescata documento necesario en la literatura chilena. [LE]

4443 Roland, Eduardo. Hojas en blanco y otras sombras. Montevideo: Ediciones del Mirador, 1988. 1 v.

La creación poética—su incuestionada vigencia en el amor y en la muerte— es la preocupación central de este primer libro de Roland (n. 1958). Desde el título y la edición—hojas sueltas, algunas efectivamente "en blanco" en una especie de cajita de cartón que el lector debe abrir o más bien desatar—se impone una lectura no convencional, el acercamiento a una escritura que explora y explota la palabra como espacio sonoro y sémico que nos advierte sobre la madurez poética de Roland. [LU]

4444 Ruiz Rosas, José. Poesía reunida. Arequipa, Peru: Univ. Nacional de San Agustín, 1990. 1 v.

Primera recopilación de la ya extensa obra de un poeta (n. Lima, 1928) que, tal vez por haber vivido por largos años en la provincia, es poco conocido en Lima y completamente ignorado fuera de su país. Esa situación es injusta porque se trata de un voz de considerable originalidad y fuerza lírica. El hecho de que esta edición haya aparecido en Arequipa, no parece asegurar que el desconocimiento se remedie. [JMO]

4445 Sábato, Matilde. Cenizas y plegarias. Buenos Aires: Torres Agüero Editor, 1992. 83 p.

Misteriosa y secreta, esta poesía interroga sobre la muerte y el alma al amparo de la fe. Lo interrogativo se desdibuja, sin embargo, cuando el yo lírico se dirige directamente a Dios. Precisión y brevedad caracterizan estos poemas. [LU]

4446 Sabines, Jaime. Otro recuento de poemas. México: Joaquín Mortiz, 1992. 496 p.

Nueva edición de uno de los poetas más leídos en México después de Ramón López Velarde. La novedad no reside en los poemas nuevos que este reconocido poeta coloquial añade a la edición anterior de *Nuevo recuento de poemas* de (1984), sino en el hecho de que esta nueva lectura produce otro texto nuevo. Advertimos con más agudeza el uso diverso y acertado de recursos poéticos que configuran un hablante desgarrado ante la soledad y la muerte, aquel que confiesa sus deseos y secretos a un lector, antes conmovido, ahora deslumbrado por las imágenes construidas. Texto que marcará de nuevo la poesía mexicana. [NK]

4447 Sáenz, Jaime. La piedra imán: obra póstuma; 17 Nov. 80 al 17 Jul. 81. La Paz: Editorial Huayna Potosí, 1989. 200 p.

Como señala el subtítulo del libro, se trata de la obra póstuma de uno de los poetas latinoamericanos más originales del siglo XX. A la extensa obra de este autor boliviano se añade este nuevo volumen que reúne 26 textos inéditos, escritos entre el 17 nov. 1980 y el 17 julio 1981. Es de lamentar que el libro no mencione a ningún responsable de la preparación de los manuscritos. [ORR]

4448 Santos Febres, Mayra. Anamú y manigua. Río Piedras, P.R.: La Iguana Dorada, 1991. 72 p.: ill.

Convergen en este poemario, tres líneas temáticas y una vocación: la mujer que, desde su historia colectiva, habla con todas las mujeres; la mujer negra que, desde su piel, revive su historia; la mujer negra que, desde la poesía, acomete. Una vocación: la de escribir con conciencia del simulacro literario. [FC]

4449 Santos Febres, Mayra. El orden escapado. San Juan?: Editorial Tríptico, 1991. 24 p.

Primer premio del certamen de la *Revista Tríptico* de 1988. Esta breve colección de poemas se vuelca a la reflexión del proceso de la escritura, asumido desde el cuerpo, la tradición y la transgresión, el silencio, la palabra y la cotidianeidad. [FC]

4450 Schwartz, Perla. Instantáneas de la mujer camaleón. México: UNAM, 1990. 80 p. (Serie La Huerta)

Ecos de Rosario Castellanos y otras poetas en esta entrega. Versos de excelente factura que establecen un diálogo y una genealogía con lo mejor de la poesía feminista. Su poesía es búsqueda de un espacio en el que la mujer pueda constituirse auténticamente, sin tener que cambiar de color para defenderse. "Miles de mujeres me apuntalan /

mujeres que surgen / tras el cotidiano desencuentro. / Mujeres que me amparan / tras el desconcierto y el vacío. / Acompañada por ellas / cruzo el asfalto movedizo, / busco una coartada a la desesperanza." [NK]

4451 Sicilia, Javier. Oro. México: Ediciones Toledo, 1990. 23 p.

Poesía insólita cuyo hablante místico busca la unión divina en la tradición del *Cantar de los cantares* y San Juan de la Cruz: "Oh mi Dios celebrante/en la noche interior de las criaturas,/oh Luz, oh Centellante, oh Fuego que perduras,/oh Fulgor de la sombra siempre a oscuras, permíteme encontrarme . . . " [NK]

4452 Silén, Iván. La poesía como libertá. San Juan: Instituto de Cultura Puertorriqueña, 1992. 256 p.

Esta antología recoge cinco poemarios *(Poemas de Filí-Melé; El miedo del pantócrata; Las mariposas de alambre; El último círculo; El libro de los místicos)* en los cuales se reivindica con voluntad de héroe la inamovible filosofía del "Paria" que habita toda la obra de Silén, cuya política del No-Ser reclama una voz única en la poesía contemporánea puertorriqueña. [FC]

4453 Silva Estrada, Alfredo. De bichos exaltado. Caracas: Fondo Editorial Pequeña Venecia, 1990. 40 p.

Poesía de Estrada (n. 1933) se ha manifestado siempre por lo preciso de la forma, la búsqueda de un encuentro entre la arquitectura del poema y una voz que reclama esencias, incluso más allá de los límites semánticos del lenguaje. En estos tres poemas extensos de tema zoológico, el poeta se retira un tanto de esta línea para recrear con el lenguaje movimiento y ritmo en insectos y serpientes. En ellos no falta el humor, la ironía y una visión inocente de las cosas marcadas por la infancia. [AR]

4454 Sotillo, Pedro. Obra literaria. Caracas: La Casa de Bello, 1987. 323 p., 1 leaf of plates: ill. (Col. Zona tórrida:creación y crítica; 5)

Con prólogo de Fernando Paz Castillo se recogen en este magnífico volumen, preparado por el grupo investigador de la Casa de Bello en Caracas, poemas, narraciones y ensayos de la obra de Pedro Sotillo (1902–77). Figura importante de la vida política y cultural venezolana, su obra es un documento de

época muy importante. Una extensa bibliografía cierra el volumen. [AR]

4455 Soto Vélez, Clemente. Obra poética. San Juan: Instituto de Cultura Puertorriqueña, División de Publicaciones y Grabaciones, 1989. 450 p.

Una de las figuras importantes de la poesía puertorriqueña del siglo XX, Soto Vélez testimonia el manejo singular del lenguaje, de la imagen cargada temáticamente, envuelta en un lirismo impredecible que se ampara en una mitología personal. Incluye: *Escalio* (1937); *Abrazo interno* (1954); *Arboles* (1955); *Caballo de palo* (1959); *La tierra prometida* (1979). [FC]

4456 Strepponi, Blanca. Diario de John Roberton. Caracas: Fondo Editorial Pequeña Venecia, 1990. 45 p.

Interesante y conmovedor texto-poema en donde la autora reescribe los últimos años del médico escocés J.H. Roberton, cirujano del ejército de Bolívar en la contienda libertadora. Strepponi logra, con un lenguaje casi tan directo y violento como la naturaleza que describe, darnos un cuadro preciso de este viaje a la oscuridad del trópico, así como la lucha sin esperanzas de una de sus víctimas. [AR]

4457 Suárez, Jorge. Serenata: poesía. Cochabamba, Bolivia: H. Municipalidad de Cochabamba; Los Amigos del Libro, 1990. 66 p. (Obras Completas)

Textos inspirados en tonadas, canciones y motivos de la tradición y la voz populares. De ahí que la elaboración del lenguaje muestre rasgos del habla local boliviana. No obstante esos recursos textuales, las características propias de la obra de este autor se hacen evidentes al cabo. [ORR]

4458 Tezanos, Sabela de. Desprendimientos. Montevideo: Vinten Editor, 1991. 69 p.: ill.

Presente volumen incluye *Palabras sin nombre* (1989) y *Los Desprendimientos* (1991), libros que fueron premiados por el Ministerio de Educación y Cultura de Uruguay. La dolorosa certeza de un mundo desencantado, sin magia ni futuro posible es expresada con el rigor y riqueza poéticos que ya caracteriza a Sabela de Tezanos (n. 1959). [LU]

4459 Torres, Alicia. Fatal. Caracas: Fundarte, 1989. 51 p. (Col. Cuadernos de difusión; 122)

Sorprendente primer libro de esta joven poeta venezolana. Al dominio de la palabra, que otorga precisión y fuerza al poema, Alicia Torres (n. 1960) suma una imaginación poética ejercitada en el ver y sentir. Es interesante notar que el tema de lo femenino, tan recurrido a veces por las jóvenes poetas, aquí también se manifiesta pero con gran mesura, buscando no tanto la expresión de una idea combativa como la belleza y verdad intrínsecas a la poesía. [AR]

4460 Ulacia, Manuel. Origami para un día de lluvia. Valencia: Pre-Textos, 1991. 42 p.
Inventario lírico que contiene un largo y logrado poema. En rescate del tiempo pasado, el sujeto poético se busca y se construye a través de sus vivencias y sus lecturas. [NK]

4461 Uribe, Armando. Por ser vos quien sois. Santiago: Editorial Universitaria, 1989. 60 p. (Col. Los Contemporáneos)
Poesía de corte religioso elaborada con lenguaje personal y pulcro. Adopta tono conversacional al dirigirse a divinidad a quien enrostra por no descender al espacio terreno a remediar carencias humanas. Dialoga con divinidad fustigando flaquezas del hombre y emplazando a Dios por su aparente indiferencia: "Clamo sin voz a quien no tiene oído." [LE]

4462 Veiravé, Alfredo. Laboratorio central. Buenos Aires: Editorial Sudamericana, 1991. 101 p.
Cierto tono épico y un vocabulario que acude con frecuencia a campos semánticamente asociados a las ciencias enmarcan las constantes reflexiones sobre la poesía en este libro. El sujeto poético se enriquece en el diálogo con otros poetas y en la presentación de ciertos personajes de la historia y anónimos. La quinta—y última—parte del libro es un homenaje a la realidad que rodea al poeta y que es materia primera en el "laboratorio central" donde se gesta la escritura. [LU]

4463 Verástegui, Enrique. Monte de goce. Lima: J. Campodónico, 1991. 199 p.: ill. (Col. del sol blanco)
La historia editorial de este libro es curiosa: escrito en 1972 (o sea el mismo año en que apareció En los extramuros del mundo, su primer libro), sus originales estuvieron perdidos en una imprenta durante 17 años, al cabo de los cuales ven finalmente la luz. Como todas las de su autor, ésta es enorme-

mente ambiciosa y compleja, y tiene como centro la experiencia erótica vista como una forma suprema de revelación. [JMO]

4464 Villafañe, María Juliana. Dimensiones en el amor. San Juan?: Ramallo Bros. Print., 1992. 76 p.: col. ill.
En este primer poemario, Villafañe invita al lector a redescubrir el amor; esa dimensión más allá de las sombras que es, simultáneamente, añoranza y deseo, intimidad, comunión y también herida. Una dimensión apocalíptica, en ocasiones religiosa, impulsa las "dimensiones en el amor." [FC]

4465 Villarreal, José Javier. La procesión. México: Joaquín Mortiz, 1991. 183 p. (Serie del volador)
Libro que reúne tres poemarios de este joven poeta: Estatua sumergida que se publicó en 1983 bajo el título En torno a monumentos, Mar del norte que obtuvo el Premio Nacional de Poesía Aguascaliente 1987, y La posesión que mereció el Premio Nacional de Poesía Alfonso Reyes de Monterrey, 1989. Otorga nueva fuerza expresiva a formas tradicionales para elaborar territorios exteriores e interiores, sociales e íntimos con un lenguaje coloquial de versos por lo general largos y prosaicos. [NK]

4466 Zavala Guzmán, Simón. Manifiesto del hombre: poemas. Quito?: Depto. de Cultura, Univ. Central del Ecuador, 1983? 109 p.: ill.
Discurso lírico en diálogo constante y reflexivo con su interlocutor poético que puede ser el propio yo enunciador, otro, o la persona amada. Los objetos y circunstancias de su reflexión se ubican más allá de lo meramente cotidiano y ordinario, en un mundo trascendente a veces transparente, pleno otras, invisible, incomprensible, o vacío. [ORR]

4467 Zito Lema, Vicente. Razón poética. Collages de Kirin. Buenos Aires: Ediciones Fin de Siglo, 1991. 1 v. (unpaged): ill.
Reflexiones sobre la esencia y los límites de la poesía en un tono conversacional que impone una atmósfera íntima, de entrelínea o penumbra. La poesía aparece así dueña de misterios que no excluyen la aparente contradicción de su rostro: su inutilidad frente al dolor del hombre, y a su vez, la única capaz de redimirlo; la poesía como realidad opuesta a la vida y sin embargo, llena de ella. [LU]

4468 Zubicueta, Belinda. Ardiendo piedras: poemas. Santiago: s.n., 1993. 63 p.

Poemario escrito en la cárcel de Santo Domingo, en Santiago, por la última prisionera política del régimen de Pinochet aún encarcelada. Poesía amorosa donde ansia de libertad se expresa, en términos de lo erótico, quizás como único escape de situación que de otra manera sería insostenible. Sorprende el control que la poeta tiene sobre el lenguaje, si se considera la situación límite en que ella se encuentra: "Desdoblando momentos/recojo tu figura/y tendida/con mis dientes tirando de la almohada/hago el amor/sobre una/cordillera larga," es como lo presenta uno de los poemas. Lectura que se recomienda. [LE]

GENERAL STUDIES

4469 Arráiz Lucca, Rafael. El avión y la nube: observaciones sobre poesía venezolana. Caracas: Contraloría General de la República, 1991. 132 p.: bibl., index. (Col. Medio siglo de la Contraloría General de la República: Serie Letra viva)

Realmente la preocupación de Arráiz Lucca en estos ensayos es la de darnos una visión lo más clara posible de la poesía venezolana de los últimos años. Sin embargo, abre su análisis incluyendo a poetas de generaciones anteriores (Jacinto Fombona Pachano, Antonio Arráiz, Vicente Gerbasi, Juan Calzadilla) para ampliar el cuadro y permitir una visión más actual. El análisis desde esta perspectiva se torna lúcido y esclarecedor a la vez que ampliamente informativo. Se destaca su análisis de los grupos "Guaire" y "Tráfico" de las décadas del 70 y 80. [AR]

4470 Caamaño de Fernández, Vicenta. El negro en la poesía dominicana. San Juan: Centro de Estudios Avanzados de Puerto Rico y el Caribe, 1989. 288 p.: bibl., index.

Abarca este estudio, cuya óptica general es académica, desde los primeros siglos de la conquista y la colonización hasta la primera mitad de los años ochenta. El rastreo de lo negro se da en virtud de un método "histórico-crítico-descriptivo" que permite la comparación y el contraste a tres niveles: lo afrodominicano, lo afroantillano y lo afroamericano. Imprescindible para el estudio de la poesía negra dominicana y caribeña. [FC]

4471 Cobo Borda, Juan Gustavo. Poesía colombiana, 1880–1980. Medellín, Colombia: Univ. de Antioquia, 1987. 290 p.: bibl. (Celeste; 5. Col. literaria)

Es notoria la preocupación de J.G. Cobo Borda (n. 1948) por incrementar el estudio de la poesía colombiana. Así lo atestiguan sus múltiples ensayos. Este compendio de trabajos publicados en revistas y periódicos sigue este propósito. La visión crítica de Cobo está sujeta, en mucho, a su actividad como poeta y activista intelectual. Sus ensayos, bien ilustrativos y documentados, pecan a veces de imprecisos y parciales, ya que inevitablemente expresan una opinión personal. Se recogen aquí análisis que van desde Porfiro Barba-Jacob hasta los poetas de su propia generación del 70. [AR]

4472 Ferrari, Américo. Los sonidos del silencio: poetas peruanos en el siglo XX. Lima: Mosca Azul, 1990. 104 p.: bibl.

Valioso repertorio de estudios críticos sobre poetas peruanos de este siglo, que van desde González Prada y Eguren hasta Westphalen y Blanca Varela. El autor aclara al principio que éste no es un libro orgánico, sino un catálogo de afinidades y gustos personales. Pero su enfoque crítico es penetrante y revelador. [JMO]

4473 Flores, Félix Gabriel. Rostros de la poesía latinoamericana. Buenos Aires: Corregidor, 1990. 222 p.: bibl.

Amparado en invocaciones de Eliot, Sartre y Girri al fervor, la modestia y la sensibilidad crítica, el autor propone atractivas y compartibles lecturas de C. Vallejo, J.L. Borges, P. Neruda, O. Paz, E. Molina, A. Girri y E. Cardenal. Algunos ensayos (Vallejo, Neruda, Cardenal) resultarán iluminadores y estimulantes para lectores que han decidido prescindir de bizantinismos interpretativos. [PL]

4474 González-Montes, Yara. La poesía cubana en los Estados Unidos. (in Culturas Hispanas de los Estados Unidos de América: Hacia la Nueva Síntesis, 3rd, Barcelona-Torredembarra, Spain, 1988. Actas. Edición de María Jesús Buxó Rey y Tomás Calvo Buezas. Madrid: Ediciones de Cultura Hispánica, 1990, p. 679–689)

Una vez diagramadas las diferentes olas de exilio, y los diferentes sujetos que las mismas conjugan, el artículo se acerca a la producción poética a partir de cuatro categorías: desarraigo y alienación, principio de fijación e irreversibilidad, dislocamiento de la identidad cultural y asimilación, dimensiones arquetípicas y míticas. [FC]

4475 Herrera, Ricardo H. Nueva poesía argentina, 1970–1990. (*Iberoromania/ Tübingen*, 34, 1991, p. 70–79, bibl.)

El autor define la principal tendencia de la nueva poesía argentina como una fluctuación entre el maximalismo y minimalismo. Su análisis se concentra fundamentalmente en la producción poética de autores nacidos en la década del 40 y en particular en Jorge Aulicino, Daniel Freidemberg y Elvio Gandolfo cuya actividad crítica en revistas sumamente representativas de este período (*Diario de Poesía, El Lagrimal Trifulca, Nosferatu y Ultimo Reino*) es de gran importancia. [LU]

4476 Hidalgo Alzamora, Laura. Décimas esmeraldeñas: Recopilación y análisis socio-literario. Madrid: Visor, 1990. 406 p.: ill. (Biblioteca filológica hispana; 3)

Estudio y recopilación de la poesía anónima y oral más representativa de la provincia Esmeraldas (Ecuador), cuya población es considerablemente de origen africano. La autora destaca el valor testimonial de la décima en la tradición e historia de su pueblo; la estudia en su estructura lírica, por sus temas y por su función social desde la época colonial. Este estudio está complementado por una recopilación y edición crítica de décimas esmeraldeñas. [ORR]

4477 Historia de la poesía colombiana. Bogotá: Casa de Poesía Silva, 1991. 603 p.: bibl., index.

Es apreciable el esfuerzo de los editores de este libro al compendiar por primera vez una historia de la poesía colombiana incluyendo, aparentemente, críticos de diversas orientaciones. Lastimosamente una lectura atenta deja ver que es producto de un trabajo apresurado, sin mayor rigor académico, donde las erratas, las faltas y omisiones se imponen sobre los aciertos. Muchos de los análisis pecan de ser impresionistas y superficiales y repiten sin cesar errores interpretativos y evaluativos que limitan más que expanden la visión general de la poesía colombiana. Es obvio que esta *Historia* reponde a la dirección poé-

tica de grupos parcializantes y no al juicio imparcial que puede brindar una crítica más especializada. Debemos sí destacar trabajos que escapan a esta apreciación: el de Monserrat Ordóñez sobre José A. Silva, el de Fernando Charry Lara sobre "Piedra y cielo," el de Eduardo Jaramillo sobre el modernismo y los trabajos de William Ospina, aunque parece injusta y poco precisa su evaluación de la poesía del gran barroco don Hernando Domínguez Camargo. [AR]

4478 Lugar de encuentro: ensayos críticos sobre poesía mexicana actual. Recopilación de Norma Klahn y Jesse Fernández. México: Editorial Katún, 1987. 234 p.: bibl., ill. (Ensayo; 2)

Util compilación de trabajos sobre 15 autores contemporáneos, de conocidos estudiosos del proceso. El conjunto constituye un buen panorama del estado de la poesía mexicana y de la atención crítica que suscita. Sobresalen las lecturas de Lilvia Soto (O. Paz y J.E. Pacheco), Carlos Montemayor (E. Huerta), Norma Klahn (J. Sabines), Ramón Xirau (U. González de León), José Olivio Jiménez (J.C. Becerra) y Jesse Fernández (H. Aridjis). Completan el volumen tres estudios más generales: "Sobre 'La Espiga Amotinada',""La Mujer en la Poesía Mexicana" y "Poesía Nueva de México." [PL]

4479 Manifestos, proclamas y polémicas de la vanguardia literaria hispanoamericana. Edición, selección, prólogo, bibliografía y notas de Nelson Osorio T. Caracas: Biblioteca Ayacucho, 1988. 417 p.: bibl. (Biblioteca Ayacucho; 132)

Importante volumen, que ofrece una imagen panorámica muy viva del movimiento de las ideas de renovación vanguardista en Hispanoamérica. Incluye 103 textos programáticos, reflexivos y polémicos dispuestos en orden cronológico, desde la recepción del futurismo (artículos de R. Darío, A. Nervo y Rómulo Durón, 1909) hasta el manifiesto *Total*, de V. Huidobro (1931). El recorrido es amplio y variado, pues junto a escritos muy difundidos sobre creacionismo, ultraísmo y estridentismo, por ejemplo, aparecen documentos que ilustran aspectos menos o nada conocidos del proceso. Muy útiles las notas y la bibliografía complementaria. Libro de consulta indispensable (ver items **4487, 4488** y **4490**). [PL]

Montenegro, Juan Ernesto. Fragmentos del dieciseiseno. See item **2277.**

4480 Piña, Juan Andrés. Conversaciones con la poesía chilena: Nicanor Parra, Eduardo Anguita, Gonzalo Rojas, Enrique Lihn, Oscar Hahn, Raúl Zurita. Santiago: Pehuén, 1990. 233 p.: bibl., ill. (Col. Testimonio)

Ameno y revelador conjunto de entrevistas con seis de las figuras claves de la poesía chilena: Nicanor Parra, Eduardo Anguita, Gonzalo Rojas, Enrique Lihn, Oscar Hahn y Raúl Zurita. Extensas conversaciones inciden en aspectos biográficos y testimoniales a la vez que incitan a reflexionar sobre la vida personal en relación con la obra de estos escritores así como sobre el mundo literario, político y social en que se gestan las obras respectivas. Indispensable en toda biblioteca para acceder a un entendimiento mejor del proceso de la poesía chilena actual. [LE]

4481 Poesía modernista ecuatoriana. Selección, estudio introductorio y notas de Mario Campaña Avilés. Quito: Libresa, 1991. 287 p.: bibl. (Col. Antares; 55)

Selección de la obra de 10 modernistas ecuatorianos. Aunque este volumen parece estar dirigido a los escolares, ofrece una lectura útil para quien tenga interés en la materia. Incluye un estudio introductorio, cronología y bibliografía básica de Mario Campaña Avilés. [ORR]

4482 Rey, Clara. Poesía popular libertaria y estética anarquista en el Río de la Plata. (*Rev. Crít. Lit. Latinoam.*, 15:29, 1er. semestre 1989, p. 179–206)

Partiendo del contexto sociocultural de fines del siglo pasado y principios del presente, la autora analiza las influencias del cosmopolitismo, ideas anarquistas y positivismo en la creación de una nueva estética que conjuga las dos grandes fuerzas de la tradición y de la modernización en la sociedad rioplatense. Incluye además una muestra representativa de la producción poética del período. [LU]

4483 Rivera-Rodas, Oscar. La modernidad y sus hermenéuticas poéticas: poesía boliviana del siglo XX. La Paz: Ediciones Signo, 1991. 259 p.: bibl. (Serie Ensayo; 3)

Estudio de la poesía boliviana (1920–80) a través de siete autores cuya obra es vista como un discurso único de reflexión poética sobre la historia boliviana del siglo XX. Enfoca el reflejo de la historia nacional de esos años en la poesía y la reacción de los poetas ante la misma. Examina este discurso poético nacional dentro del amplio contexto de la modernidad. [Ed.]

4484 Rodríguez Padrón, Jorge. Del ocio sagrado: algunos poetas hispanoamericanos. Madrid: Libertarias/Prodhufi, 1991. 167 p.: bibl. (Ensayo; 50)

Entre los méritos de estos 11 ensayos deben destacarse la claridad y la precisión del comentario, que llega al lector como un diálogo fervoroso y lúcido con los textos estudiados. Particularmente invitadoras a continuarlo son las páginas dedicadas a J.M. Eguren, J.L. Borges, J. Pasos, G. Rojas, J. Sologuren y A. Mutis. [PL]

4485 Rojas, Margarita; Flora Ovares; and Sonia Mora. Las poetas del buen amor: la escritura transgresora de Sor Juana Inés de la Cruz, Delmira Agustini, Juana de Ibarbourou, Alfonsina Storni. Caracas: Monte Avila Editores, 1991. 149 p.: bibl. (Estudios)

Varios son los méritos de estos excelentes comentarios compartidos: claridad expositiva, solidez de la información teórica y rigor analítico. La novedosa perspectiva contrasta con la crítica tradicional y las limitaciones de su "vocabulario axiomático," ineficaz para leer las "voces reprimidas" que aquí se releen. El estudio de los mecanismos expresivos transgresores en las obras consideradas es sugestivo y convincente. [PL]

4486 Sefamí, Jacobo. El destierro apacible y otros ensayos: Xavier Villaurrutia, Alí Chumacero, Fernando Pessoa, Francisco Cervantes, Haroldo de Campos. Puebla, Mexico: Premià, 1987. 157 p.: bibl. (La Red de Jonás: Estudios; 36)

Essays on 20th-century poets Xavier Villaurrutia, Alí Chumacero, Fernando Pessoa, Francisco Cervantes, and Haroldo de Campos, trace general themes and poetic plots in the development of each poet's work. Rather introductory and bibliographic, essays touch on some central preoccupations of contemporary literature: colonial memory, discontinuity in language, death and voyage. [S. Castro-Klarén]

4487 Las vanguardias latinoamericanas: textos programáticos y críticos. Selecciones por Jorge Schwartz. Traducción de los textos portugueses de Estela dos Santos. Madrid: Cátedra, 1991. 698 p.: bibl., ill. (Crítica y estudios literarios)

Contribución fundamental para el estudio del período. Entre sus méritos debe destacarse la ampliación del ámbito considerado, que al incluir a Brasil permite una enriquecedora visión comparativa de las corrientes de vanguardia en América Latina. Ciento treinticuatro textos seleccionados se organizan en dos partes: 1) Geográfica: situando los países donde se produjeron los respectivos movimientos, 2) Orden temático. Introducciones a los diversos capítulos son verdaderas guías de trabajo para el examen de un momento particularmente animado de la cultura continental. (Ver items **4479, 4488** y **4490**). [PL]

4488 Las vanguardias literarias en Hispanoamérica: manifestos, proclamas y otros escritos. Recopilación de Hugo J. Verani. 2. ed. México: Fondo de Cultura Económica, 1990. 285 p.: bibl., ill. (Col. Tierra firme)

Reedición, aumentada con dos textos, del sugerente libro publicado en 1986 en Roma (Bulzoni Editore). Selección de las 56 piezas incluidas responde a un criterio que privilegia lo literario, y esta característica singulariza el volumen y explica su apreciable concisión. El material ha sido ordenado por países, desde México a Uruguay. (Por error, Francisco Contreras aparece entre los autores cubanos). (Ver items **4479, 4487** y **4490**). [PL]

4489 Vargas, Rafael. Nuevas voces de la poesía mexicana: seis casos. (*Rev. Iberoam.*, 55:148/149, julio/dic. 1989, p. 1195–1207)

Estudio general de seis poetas mexicanos, que según el crítico, serían representativos de las últimas generaciones. Estos son Ricardo Castillo, David Huerta, José Luis Rivas, Luis Miguel Aguilar, Ricardo Yañez y Jaime Reyes. Aclaremos que estos seis poetas, aunque excelentes, son parte de una generación prolífica, entre la que no es menos importante la producción femenina, aquí notablemente ausente. [NK]

4490 Videla de Rivero, Gloria. Direcciones del vanguardismo hispanoamericano. Mendoza: Univ. Nacional de Cuyo, Facultad de Filosofía y Letras, 1990. 2 v.: bibl., ill.

Los subtítulos de esta obra indican con claridad que se trata de dos libros, aunque complementarios, válidos en sí mismos. El vol. 1 (*Estudios sobre poesía de vanguardia*

en la década del veinte) está constituido por nueve capítulos de interpretación global del vanguardismo. El orden en que se disponen esos ensayos hace de la suma una notable historia de la década, rigurosa e informada. El vol. 2 *(Documentos)* incluye 56 manifiestos y textos programáticos o polémicos, presentados como complemento de la primera parte; pero el volumen admite muy bien la clasificación de antología. (Ver items **4479** y **4488**). [PL]

4491 Wong, Oscar. Entre las musas y Apolo: poesía mexicana; presencia y realidad. México: Grupo Editorial 7, 1991 125 p.: bibl.

Ampliación de artículos varios sobre poesía como respuesta a "necesidades expresivas, circunscrita al gusto social, y a situaciones geopolíticas." Crónica de referencia sobre la poesía que marca hitos desde José Gorostiza a Coral Bracho, Kyra Galván y Alberto Blanco. [NK]

SPECIAL STUDIES

4492 Acerca de Eliseo Diego. Selección, palabras preliminares, cronología y bibliografía de Enrique Saínz. La Habana: Editorial Letras Cubanas, 1991. 409 p.: bibl. (Giraldilla)

Se persigue en esta colección de ensayos, "el primer intento global de comprensión" del trabajo de Diego tanto en la poesía como en la prosa. Algunas figuras representativas de la literatura cubana (Vitier, Retamar, Lezama), al igual que extranjeras (Benedetti), coinciden en la importancia que le confieren a la obra de Diego en la literatura cubana. [FC]

4493 Angulo-Arvelo, Luis Alejandro. El fauno cautivo: biografía de Alfredo Arvelo Larriva. Caracas: Monte Avila Editores, 1986. 492 p.: bibl., ill., index. (Grandes biografías)

Figura romántica, Arvelo Larriva (1883–1934) es de suma importancia para la historia política y cultural de Venezuela. Poeta activista, preso político que reúne en sí las inquietudes y necesidades de libertad de la intelectualidad venezolana de comienzos del siglo. Biografía que toca lo personal (autor es sobrino del poeta) es un buen documento de lucha contra el gomecismo. [AR]

4494 Augier, Angel I. Cuba en Darío y Darío en Cuba. La Habana: Editorial Letras Cubanas, 1989. 339 p., 14 p. of plates: bibl., ill. (Giraldilla)

Recuento de la influencia de Cuba y de los cubanos (Antonio Zambrana, José Joaquín Palma, José Martí, Julián del Casal, José María de Heredia, Augusto de Armas) en Darío, así como de éste en los cubanos (Juana Borrero, Carlos Pío y Federico Uhrbach, entre otros). Más que un estudio sistemático, de lo que se trata es de la influencia como culto a la poesía y al poeta. [FC]

4495 Avila Echazú, Edgar. Elegía para Jaime Sáenz. Santa Cruz de la Sierra, Bolivia: Horcón, 1990. 32 p.

Discurso poético de homenaje a la obra y personalidad del poeta boliviano Jaime Sáenz. Su autor, otro poeta boliviano consagrado, elaboró este discurso desde la experiencia del amigo y el lector conocedor de la poesía de Sáenz. El resultado de esa experiencia es la fusión de dos discursos en una rica y sugerente metatextualidad e intertextualidad, puesto que asume los rasgos estilísticos de la obra poética de la que trata. Poesía de calidad, que poetiza sobre otra poesía excepcional siguiendo los rasgos de ésta. [ORR]

4496 Baguer, Néstor E. Apuntes sobre un creador, José Zacarías Tallet. La Habana: Unión de Escritores y Artistas de Cuba, 1988. 258 p.: bibl., ill. (Perfil libre)

No se trata de un acercamiento crítico sino de una valoración múltiple, como poeta, como político, como periodista, donde predomina la moral combativa de la intelectualidad de la isla. Se llega a Zacarías Tallet mediante entrevistas y comentarios; de su poesía, sin embargo, se subraya su decir cotidiano, conversacional, al igual que el "aire choteón" que la caracteriza y la sumerge en su ostensible cubanía. [FC]

4497 Berenguer, Amanda. El monstruo incesante: expedición de caza. Montevideo: Arca, 1990. 162 p.

Recopilación de entrevistas hechas a la escritora en distintos momentos de su vida. De especial interés resulta la "Autobiografía" que por primera vez se edita. [LU]

4498 Carrasco M., Iván. Nicanor Parra: la escritura antipoética. Santiago: Editorial Universitaria, 1990. 259 p.: bibl., facsim.

Nuevo libro sobre este cada vez más influyente transformador de expresión poética en español. Empieza con apretadas e informativas páginas introductorias seguidas de cinco capítulos: "Teoría del Antipoema," "Clasificación y Orígenes de la Escritura Poética de

N.P.," "Los Antipoemas Metaliterarios," "La Antipoesía de lo Sagrado," y "La Antipoesía de la Cotidianidad." Incluye muy completa biografía de Parra que llega hasta 1985, año de *Hojas de Parra.* Libro importante en bibliografía sobre Nicanor Parra. [LE]

4499 Cobo Borda, Juan Gustavo. Alvaro Mutis. Bogotá: Procultura, 1989. 102 p.: bibl., ill. (Clásicos colombianos; 10)

Es indudable que Alvaro Mutis es uno de los grandes poetas latinoamericanos de este siglo. Así lo afirman su magnífica poesía y la belleza y lucidez de su prosa narrativa y ensayística. J.G. Cobo Borda ha contribuido a lo largo de los años al conocimiento internacional de su obra con precisos ensayos críticos. Lastimosamente esta corta biografía literaria (seguida de una selección de textos) no agrega nada a la obra de Mutis. Descuidada, sin mayor rigor crítico, irrespetuosa a veces, no atiende a la necesidad de una visión de la obra de Mutis que supere los clichés y los lugares comunes. [AR]

4500 Costa, Marithelma and Alvin Joaquín Figueroa. Kaligrafiando: conversaciones con Clemente Soto Vélez. Río Piedras, P.R.: Editorial de la Univ. de Puerto Rico, 1990. 157 p.: bibl., ill.

La entrevista, cuya temática conjuga lo literario y lo político, se interrumpe periódicamente tras una muestra representativa de poemas. Interesante "historia personal" de la política y la literatura puertorriqueñas de los años 20 y 30, con sus vanguardias literarias y sus movimientos de liberación. Sobre todo, buen perfil de Soto Vélez y de las propuestas del grupo atalayista en cuanto a una literatura nacional. [FC]

4501 Delgado, Josefina. Alfonsina Storni: una biografía. Buenos Aires: Planeta, 1990. 183 p., 12 p. of plates: bibl., ill. (Mujeres argentinas)

Autora destaca los aspectos biográficos de Storni que hicieron de ella una personalidad tan singular respecto a la sociedad de su época: valor, falta de inhibición o pudor en las formas y en la palabra. Quizás se podrían haber hecho más observaciones respecto a su poesía, la evolución de su quehacer poético en el contexto de la poesía de su tiempo. Recuento más anecdótico que literario. [LU]

4502 Delgado, Susy. Tesarái mboyve = Antes del olvido. Traducción al castellano de Carlos Villagra Marsal, J.A. Rauskin y la autora. Ed. bilingüe. Asunción: Alcándara, 1987. 91 p.: port. (Col. Poesía ; 60)

Segundo libro de esta autora (n. 1939). Su temática gira en torno a la problemática de la mujer paraguaya en su lucha contra un medio todavía fuertemente patriarcal que la margina. Es una edición bilingüe guaraní-español. La presencia de elementos dialógicos es una constante estilística del poemario. [LU]

4503 Dulce María Loynaz. Recopilación de Pedro Simón. La Habana: Centro de Investigaciones Literarias, Casa de las Américas, 1991. 834 p.: bibl., ill. (Valoración múltiple)

Aunque no se trata de un estudio riguroso, sino de una compilación tanto de ensayos más o menos críticos como de opiniones, el presente volumen constituye una fuente imprescindible para el estudioso de la reconocida poeta cubana. Si bien el énfasis está puesto en la poesía, donde se la considera como "máxima exponente del intimismo posmodernista," también se incluyen referencias a su novela lírica *Jardín*. [FC]

4504 Escobar, Eduardo. Gonzalo Arango. Bogotá: Procultura, 1989. 135 p.: bibl. (Clásicos colombianos; 7)

A medida que pasan los años desde su trágica muerte, la figura contradictoria y polémica de Gonzalo Arango (1931–76) se afirma con mayor precisión. Esta semblanza de su personalidad literaria, escrita por el también nadaísta Eduardo Escobar, contribuye desde lo biográfico a este propósito. Seguida de una útil aunque fragmentaria antología de poemas y textos de Arango, tiene la virtud de abrirnos una ventana de conocimiento donde lo afectivo no se contrapone con el análisis informativo. [AR]

4505 Espina, Eduardo. El disfraz de la modernidad. Toluca, Mexico: Univ. Autónoma del Estado de México, 1992. 214 p.: bibl.

El título no lo indica, pero es un estudio de la poesía de Julio Herrera y Reissig como manifestación augural de la modernidad hispanoamericana. Abundan los aciertos: el exotismo de Herrera no es escapismo ni evasión sino un modelo para enfrentar al mundo, una escritura transgresora de la realidad que instaura un universo autosuficiente. Agudos comentarios textuales corroboran su tesis. Aporte crítico muy significativo. [PL]

4506 Espinosa Domínguez, Carlos. Cercanía de Lezama Lima. La Habana: Editorial Letras Cubanas, 1986. 418 p.: bibl.

Desde lo testimonial, que no excluye lo periodístico, este trabajo ofrece una imagen de Lezama Lima, más que de su literatura, a partir de los testimonios ofrecidos por una plétora de figuras cubanas y latinoamericanas, donde, entre otros temas, se llega a Lezama a través de su patriotismo, su dedicación a la amistad y su excepcional manejo del lenguaje. [FC]

4507 Fernández Cozman, Camilo. Las ínsulas extrañas de Emilio Adolfo Westphalen. Lima?: Naylamp Editores, 1990. 124 p.: bibl.

Descontando tesis universitarias, este valioso trabajo puede considerarse el primer libro dedicado íntegramente a examinar en detalle la obra del importante poeta peruano: examina su sistema poético, su relación con el surrealismo, la presencia de arquetipos, su visión cosmogónica, etc. [JMO]

4508 Fernández Torres, Lionel. Luis Palés Matos y su poesía. San Juan?: s.n., 1990. 59 p.: ill.

Sincero deseo de establecer un diálogo literario con Palés Matos y su poesía; sin ser un aporte substancioso, puede ser útil en un primer acercamiento, tímido, a lo afropuertorriqueño. [FC]

4509 Guirin, Yuri. Cintio Vitier: de la conciencia de la poesía a la poesía de la conciencia. (*Am. Lat./Moscow*, 6:162, junio 1991, p. 66–73, 79)

Se discute en este artículo el quehacer literario de Vitier (poesía, ensayo, novela) y su relación con la cubanía y el origenismo. Particular atención recibe la trilogía novelesca (*De Peña Pobre, Los papeles de Jacinto Finalé* y *Rajando la leña está*) en cuanto al cultivo de "la prosa pura" y la incorporación de elementos musicales en la evolución literaria del cubano. [FC]

4510 Higgins, James. César Vallejo en su poesía. Lima: Seglusa Editores, 1989. 164 p.: bibl.

El autor, que ha dedicado varios trabajos anteriores a Vallejo y lo ha traducido al inglés, intenta en este libro un ángulo nuevo: estudia diversas facetas de la vida y la evolución estética del poeta ilustrándolas con uno o dos textos, que analiza cuidadosamente. Su propósito—demostrar que la experiencia vallejiana es distinta de la de un poeta europeo—queda suficientemente demostrado. [JMO]

4511 Homero, José. La construcción del amor: Efraín Huerta, sus primeros años. México: Consejo Nacional para la Cultura y las Artes, 1991. 193 p. (Fondo editorial tierra adentro; 13)

Análisis textual de *Absoluto amor, Línea del alba* y *Hombres del alba* que busca y logra delinear una poética de la etapa inicial de este miembro importante del grupo "Taller." [NK]

4512 Jiménez, David. Rafael Maya. Bogotá: Procultura, 1989. 106 p.: bibl., ill. (Clásicos colombianos; 4)

Esta antología de Rafael Maya (1897–1980) tiene la virtud de darnos en unos cuantos poemas una imagen clara del poeta. Perteneciente a la generación de "Los nuevos," década del 20, que proclamaba cambios en la poesía y la literatura, Maya sin embargo continuó fiel a una línea muy siglo XIX, incluso pre-modernista. Su fidelidad al verso neoclásico y su filiación cristiano-conservadora lo convierten en paradigma de un pensamiento que trató y consiguió impedir el florecimiento de las vanguardias en Colombia. Excelente ensayo introductorio de Jiménez en cuanto a información y precisión crítica. [AR]

4513 Jimeno-Grendi, Orlando. Vicente Huidobro: *Altazor* et *Temblor de cielo*, la poétique du Phénix. Paris: Editions caribéennes, 1989. 180 p.: bibl. (Coll. Tropismes: Série 1, Une œuvre, un auteur)

Estudio en francés de dos de los libros más conocidos de Huidobro: *Altazor* (1931) y *Temblor de cielo* (1931). Reitera conceptos claves de esta poesía. Enfoca estética huidobriana desde perspectiva de "una semantización de la imaginación," tratando de mostrar a través de una descripción sico-fenomenológica funcionamiento de la imagen al centro de una red de líneas entrelazadas. [LE]

4514 Julia de Burgos. Edición de Manuel de la Puebla. Río Piedras, P.R.: Ediciones Mairena, 1986. 175 p.: bibl., ill.

Colección de ensayos que, desde lo biográfico hasta lo crítico, pone de manifiesto las constantes de la vida y obra de la poeta. Como introducción, resulta de gran utilidad para adentrarse en la temática de la puertorriqueña (soledad, angustia, amor, política). Colaboran, entre otros, José Emilio González, Efraín Barradas y Francisco Matos Paoli. [FC]

4515 Kirkpatrick, Gwen. The journalism of Alfonsina Storni: a new approach to women's history in Argentina. (*in* Women, culture, and politics in Latin America. Berkeley: Univ. of California Press, 1990, p. 105–129)

Sugestivo análisis de la actividad periodística de Alfonsina Storni que revela los intereses de la poeta en una esfera cultural más amplia de la que contemplan sus poemas. [LU]

4516 Lluch Mora, Francisco. Tres estancias esenciales en la lírica de Hamid Galib: *Solemnidades, Revoque, Los presagios*, 1985–1991. San Juan?: Ediciones Mairena, 1991. 37 leaves.

Acercamiento sucinto, pero certero, cuya lectura mítica lleva la poesía de Galib, reconocida en las letras puertorriqueñas, por esas tres etapas de actuación que Joseph Campbell determinó en el héroe: el apartamiento, la iniciación y el retorno. Presente en ese viaje a los orígenes, "la mujer amada, quien mitiga pesares de travesía y alienta con su presencia." [FC]

4517 Madrid, Lelia M. El hilo y el laberinto: la poesía de Jorge L. Borges. (*Iberoromania/Tübingen*, 32, 1990, p. 82–91)

Inteligente análisis de las implicancias de la literatura como producto de pérdidas o carencias en la obra poética de Borges. La autora reflexiona además sobre la diferencia de este tópico en la obra narrativa y poética de Borges y concluye que sólo la poesía es capaz de reinventar el orden perdido. [LU]

4518 Márquez, Enrique. José Lezama Lima: bases y génesis de un sistema poético. New York: P. Lang, 1991. 224 p.: bibl. (American university studies: Series XXII, Latin American studies, 0895–0490; 12)

Importante estudio del sistema poético lezamesco, visto a través de la prosa y la poesía, que a partir de un "interés crítico por la vanguardia poética hispanoamericana," y pasando por los ineludibles planteamientos de la metáfora y la imagen, encarna en una "filosofía de la libertad" donde la oposición de los contrarios suministra "fuerzas creadoras de síntesis" a la vez que sustenta la tradición. [FC]

4519 Martos, Marco and Elsa Villanueva. Las palabras de *Trilce*. Lima: Seglusa Editores, 1989. 375 p.: bibl.

Trabajo lexicográfico del lenguaje hermético del capital libro vallejiano, hecho con minuciosidad y claro sentido didáctico. Tras situarlo dentro de su contexto cultural y estético, los autores reproducen los poemas respectivos y los acompañan con una explicación de su vocabulario. Puede leerse como un complemento del conocido libro de Eduardo Neale-Silva sobre *Trilce*. [JMO]

4520 May, Hilda R. La poesía de Gonzalo Rojas. Madrid: Hiperión, 1991. 496 p.: bibl. (Libros Hiperión; 137)

Fundamental para el estudio de la vida y obra de uno de los mayores poetas actuales. La autora cumple cabalmente su propósito de ofrecer *otra* lectura de la producción poética de Rojas, a partir de la descripción fenomenológica de instancias cardinales de la vida del poeta, relacionadas con su oficio literario. Luego analiza los principales libros de Rojas y establece las líneas de su sistema imaginario. Notable trabajo, por la claridad expositiva, la amplísima información y el rigor de los comentarios. [LE]

4521 Morales T., Leonidas. Conversaciones con Nicanor Parra. Santiago: Editorial Universitaria, 1990. 186 p.: bibl., ill. (Col. Testimonios)

Revelador libro incluye introducción que presenta la "entrevista" y las "conversaciones" como pertenecientes al ámbito de los "géneros discursivos." Sigue parte que transcribe grabaciones de diálogos de fechas y lugares distintos que tratan de vida y poesía de Parra desde *Cancionero sin nombre* (1937) hasta *Hojas de Parra* (1985). Segunda parte recrea imagen de Violeta Parra, hermana del poeta. Indispensable para comprensión cabal de obra de Nicanor Parra. [LE]

4522 Morello-Frosch, Marta. Alfonsina Storni: the tradition of the feminine subject. Translated by Michael Bradburn-Ruster. (*in* Women, culture, and politics in Latin America. Berkeley: Univ. of California Press, 1990, p. 90–104)

Bien documentado y sugerente análisis de las diversas y variadas formas con que la mujer se relaciona con la tradición en América Latina. A partir de los poemas "Divertidas Estancias a Don Juan" y "Tú me Quieres Blanca" la autora discute la perspectiva feminista con que Storni enfrenta y revierte dos tradicionales arquetipos y los valores culturalmente asociados a ellos: el arquetipo del don Juan y el de la mujer pura. [LU]

4523 Navarrete Orta, Luis. Poesía y poética en Vicente Huidobro, 1912–1931. Caracas: Fondo Editorial de Humanidades y Educación, Univ. Central de Venezuela, 1988. 215 p.: bibl. (Col. Ensayo)

Libro sigue muy de cerca estudios anteriores para ofrecer interpretación de textos representativos que establecerían el lugar que corresponde a este poeta fundacional en poesía de América y Europa. Los siete capítulos se cierran afirmando que con *Altazor* (1931) Huidobro accede a la buscada "concordancia de poesía y poética." Libro provee abundante información biográfica, bibliográfica y teórica sobre Huidobro sin ofrecer novedades de importancia. Muestra, eso sí, la siempre renovada atención que atrae este extraordinario poeta. [LE]

4524 Nómez, Naín. Pablo de Rokha: una escritura en movimiento. Santiago: Ediciones Documentas, 1988. 248 p.: bibl. (Crítica)

Estudio bien fundamentado que propone una visión totalizadora de obra de Rokha. Nómez desarrolla sus ideas en cuatro capítulos: 1) "Contexto de Pablo de Rokha y los Críticos." Los cap. 2, 3 y 4 periodizan la producción poética en: 2) "Primera Epoca: 1916–1929: de la Anarquía Romántica al Nacionalismo Surrealista;" 3) "Segunda Epoca: 1930–1950: Historia y Utopía: Búsqueda de una Dialéctica entre lo Individual y lo Social;" 4) "Tercera Epoca: 1951–1968, Canto del Macho Anciano: la Escritura como Aspiración Social." Buena bibliografía de y sobre De Rokha. Libro necesario para un conocimiento más completo del poeta y su obra. [LE]

4525 Octavio Paz: la semana de autor sobre Octavio Paz tuvo lugar en Madrid del 9 al 12 de mayo de 1988, en el Instituto de Cooperación Iberoamericana. Edición coordinada por Enrique Montoya Ramírez. Madrid: Ediciones de Cultura Hispánica, 1989. 136 p.: bibl.

Compilación de las breves ponencias, coloquios y entrevistas a Paz que tomaron lugar durante la "Semana de Autor" en el Instituto de Cooperación Iberoamericana en Madrid (9–12 mayo 1988). Entre los participantes se encuentran Rosa Chacel, Pere Gimferrer,

José Carlos González Boixo, Félix Grande, Blas Matamoro, Fernando Savater. Los eventos, en su mayoría coloquios alrededor del autor, se destacan por la extensa participación de Paz. [NK]

4526 Pantigoso, Manuel. César Atahualpa Rodríguez: la emoción del pensar. Lima?: Ediciones Intihuatana, 1989. 240 p.: bibl., ill.

Basado en las tesis universitarias que le dedicara en las décadas del 60 y 70, el autor estudia los temas, símbolos y otros procedimientos estilísticos del poeta arequipeño. Siendo la obra de éste muy poco conocida y de relativo valor, el libro, convencional en su enfoque y método, sólo tiene interés para los contados estudiosos del poeta. [JMO]

4527 Pellarolo, Silvia. La imagen de la estatua de sal: síntesis y clave en el pensamiento poético de Olga Orozco. (*Mester/UCLA*, 18:1, Spring 1989, p. 41–49)

Interesante estudio del proceso de transformación alquímica de la estatua como símbolo en la obra poética de Olga Orozco. Siguiendo los textos de Gastón Bachelard y Titus Burckhardt, la autora concluye que la imagen de la estatua de sal permite superar los diferentes dualismos que aparecen en la poesía de Orozco. [LU]

4528 Pickenhayn, Jorge Oscar. Trayectoria de un gran poeta, Baldomero Fernández Moreno: con un estudio, por temas, de su obra. Buenos Aires: Corregidor, 1988. 294 p.: bibl., port.

Biografía se va ilustrando con las obras de Fernández Moreno, enriquecida además con acontecimientos de orden cultural que contextualizan mejor los datos biográficos. El autor anota rápidamente la actividad literaria de los hijos de Fernández Moreno, especialmente de César. Tras hacerse cargo de diversas opiniones críticas respecto a los distintos temas de la poesía de Fernández Moreno, distingue 24 temas principales y los analiza extensamente. El libro se cierra con "juicios críticos y anecdóticos" de la obra de Fernández Moreno más una guía bibliográfica de su producción literaria. [LU]

4529 Piña, Cristina. Alejandra Pizarnik. Buenos Aires: Planeta, 1991. 254 p.: bibl., ill., index. (Mujeres argentinas)

Apasionante recopilación biográfica de Pizarnik que se organiza "en función de su obra y de su estética." Enfoque cuya seriedad y profesionalismo ilumina y facilita el acercamiento a la obra de esta gran escritora. Destaca las particularidades de la personalidad de Pizarnik, la importancia de su ascendencia de inmigrantes judíos rusos en cuanto a la percepción de la lengua como "extranjería," la importancia de sus viajes a París y Nueva York, y el contexto generacional y literario que enmarca su obra: Olga Orozco, Alberto Girri, etc. [LU]

4530 Quessep, Giovanni. Eduardo Carranza. Bogotá: Procultura, 1990. 90 p.: bibl., ill. (Clásicos colombianos; 17)

La figura de Carranza (1913–85) dentro de las letras colombianas continúa siendo altamente polémica, debido esto a que combinó un afecto sin fronteras por la poesía y todo lo concerniente a ella, al mismo tiempo que defendió una ideología que implicaba un apego parcial aunque sustantivo a la tradición conservadora de la poesía colombiana. Este libro que lleva un magnífico prólogo del poeta Quessep es una buena antología de algunos de sus más destacados poemas. [AR]

4531 Quirarte, Vicente. El azogue y la granada: Gilberto Owen en su discurso amoroso. México: Univ. Nacional Autónoma de México, Coordinación de Humanidades, Dirección General de Publicaciones, 1990. 241 p.: bibl., ill. (Biblioteca de letras)

Este texto, ganador del Premio Nacional de Ensayo José Revueltas 1990, se concentra en "Sindbad el Varado," el poema de este importante miembro de "Los Contemporáneos" publicado íntegramente por primera vez en 1948. Esclarecedor y detallado análisis sobre este texto importante y hermético que el crítico define y lee como un poema de amor. Precede el análisis textual un estudio de los contextos vivenciales y literarios de Owen, y concluye con un apéndice que comprende variantes del poema y notas adicionales. El libro termina con una sección breve de fotografías de Owen. [NK]

4532 Sefamí, Jacobo. El espejo trizado: la poesía de Gonzalo Rojas. México: Univ. Nacional Autónoma de México, Coordinación de Humanidades, Dirección General de Publicaciones, 1992. 269 p.: bibl., ill. (Biblioteca de letras)

Estudio muy completo y bien organizado de la obra toda de Rojas. Capítulos tratan

de: 1) Ejercicio respiratorio: arte poética;
2) Errar y morar: residencias y viajes; 3) Zumbidos genealógicos; 4) Autoanálisis incesante;
5) Historia y sociedad; 6) Epifanía del eros;
7) El mundo ante la muerte. Bibliografía actualizada de y sobre Rojas. Libro necesario
para comprensión cabal de este gran poeta.
[LE]

4533 Sucre Figarella, José Francisco *et al.*
Juan Liscano ante la crítica. Selección,
prólogo y notas de Oscar Rodríguez Ortiz. 1a.
ed. en M.A. Caracas: Monte Avila Editores,
1990. 266 p. (Ante la crítica)
Treintaiun trabajos sobre la obra poética de Liscano (n. 1915) recogidos por el crítico y narrador Rodríguez Ortiz conforman
este libro. La variedad de puntos de mira en el
análisis y la divergencia y convergencia de
juicios críticos hacen de este libro guía fundamental para el estudio de la poesía de uno de
los grandes poetas latinoamericanos. [AR]

4534 Teitelboim, Volodia. Gabriela Mistral
pública y secreta: truenos y silencios
en la vida del primer Nobel latinoamericano.
Santiago: BAT Ediciones, 1991. 334 p.
Necesaria biografía del primer Premio
Nobel Latinoamericano (1945) si se considera
lo escasas que son hasta el momento las noticias biográficas de Gabriela Mistral. Libro
pone énfasis en condición de alejamiento de
la poeta y sobre el peregrinaje constante que
fue su vida, su "autoexilio perpetuo." Teitelboim no logra iluminar zonas íntimas de vida
de Mistral. "Yo la vi dos o tres veces y con
ella tuve un cortocircuito," dijo Teitelboim
una vez. No obstante, apoyado en el quehacer
público y en textos representativos de Mistral, el autor consigue armar un relato ameno
que revela aspectos importantes de esta extraordinaria mujer y poeta. Material bibliográfico indispensable. [LE]

4535 Teitelboim, Volodia. Neruda. 4a ed.,
rev. y actualizada. Santiago: Ediciones
BAT, 1991. 527 p.: bibl., ill., index.
Cuarta edición revisada y actualizada
de la mejor, más completa y amena biografía
que se ha escrito sobre Neruda. Ediciones anteriores son de 1984, 1985, y 1990. De interés
para legos e iniciados por tono muy personal
del relato y por sugerente compenetración de
vida y poesía, historia y literatura que Teitelboim logra establecer. Edición incluye varios
capítulos en que se revelan por primera vez al

público episodios importantes de la vida de
Neruda. Sólo una cercanía y una amistad de
casi 40 años pudo hacer posible revelación de
gran cantidad de datos y circunstancias en la
vida del poeta. Libro de grata lectura y muy
necesario para un mejor conocimiento de
Pablo Neruda, hombre y poeta. [LE]

MISCELLANEOUS

**4536 Alicia en el país de las pesadillas y
otros poemas: márgenes de la poesía latinoamericana.** Recopilación y banda de Ana
Porrúa. Buenos Aires: Libros del Quirquincho,
1992. 95 p.: ill. (Libros para nada)
Producción muy novedosa propuesta
no como antología sino como recorte doble:
"armado de una poética" y selección de textos que permiten ponerla en escena. Las relaciones implícitas se insinúan en la banda paralela a los poemas. Drumond de Andrade,
N. Parra, I. Vilariño, A. Mutis, E. Cardenal,
E. Lihn, J. Gelman, J.E. Pacheco, A. Cisneros y
Elvira Hernández son algunos de los autores
convocados a esta aventura. [PL]

4537 Bravo, José Antonio. Biografía de Martín Adán. Lima?: Paramonga, 1988. 100
p. (Serie Perulibros)
Trata del primer registro biográfico de
Rafael de la Fuente Benavides (Martín Adán),
después de su muerte en el año 1985. La información aparece en tres planos bien definidos:
1) Familia y estudios; 2) Anecdotarios; y 3)
Publicaciones y plano histórico desde antes
de su nacimiento hasta la Revolución del
año 48. Después de César Vallejo, se considera a Martín Adán el peruano más importante de los poetas de vanguardia del siglo
XX. [D. Gerdes]

4538 Casazola Mendoza, Matilde. Estampas,
meditaciones, cánticos: prosa poética,
1984–1989. La Paz: Univ. Mayor de San Andrés, 1990. 1 v. (unpaged).
Colección de textos heterogéneos en
prosa de una autora boliviana conocida por su
obra poética. Se trata de una colección escrita
entre 1984–89. La nota común del volumen
es su carácter reflexivo, que ayuda a comprender mejor la poesía ya publicada por esta autora. [ORR]

4539 Castañeda Vielakamen, Esther. El vanguardismo literario en el Perú: estudio
y selección de la revista *Flechas*, 1924. La

Victoria, Peru: AMARU Editores, 1989. 157 p.: bibl., ill., index.

La segunda parte del título indica con más exactitud el asunto del libro que es, esencialmente, una descripción, historia e índice detallados de esta poco conocida revista vanguardista peruana. El trabajo añade una selección de los textos que se publicaron en ella. [JMO]

4540 Coronel Urtecho, José. Rápido tránsito. Managua: Editorial Nueva Nicaragua, 1985. 191 p. (Letras de Nicaragua; 15)

San Francisco, New Orleans, and New York City as seen through the eyes of Coronel Urtecho. Fleishacker's outdoor pool, Commerce High School, Huck Finn's Mississippean wanderings, and the deafening din of Gotham City all come alive in these colorful remembrances of things past. [R. Prieto]

Corrosive signs: essays on experimental poetry — visual, concrete, alternative. See item **5058.**

4541 Green-Williams, Claudette Rose. The myth of black female sexuality in Spanish Caribbean poetry: a deconstructive critical view. (*Afro-Hisp. Rev.*, 12:1, Spring 1993, p. 16–23)

Se plantea en este artículo la relación que existe entre el patriarcado blanco y la correspondiente construcción de la mulata sexual, maligna y bestial de la poesía negrista, desde el siglo XIX (Creto Gangá, Francisco Muñoz del Monte) hasta el siglo XX (Palés, Ballagas, Hernández Blanco, Lloréns Torres). Por otro lado, en la poesía escrita por el negro (Guillén, George Campbell, Lionel Attuly y León Damas), la sexualidad de la mujer es representada desde un entorno que conjuga la espiritualidad en vez de la sexualidad. [FC]

4542 Ligorred Perramón, Francisco de Asís. Poesía maya: lírica contemporánea. (*Rev. Esp. Antropol. Am.*, 18, 1988, p. 75–94, bibl.)

Presenta y analiza una muestra de poemas líricos contemporáneos en lengua maya, recogidos en Yucatán (México), en 1983–84. En la introducción de este interesante trabajo se resume el estado de las investigaciones sobre el desarrollo histórico de la poesía maya, desde la época colonial. [PL]

4543 Mistral, Gabriela. Gabriela Mistral en *La Voz de Elqui.* Santiago: Dirección de Bibliotecas, Archivos y Museos, Museo Gabriela Mistral de Vicuña, 1992. 64 p.: ill.

Curiosa publicación donde aparecen opiniones bien fundadas sobre obra de una Mistral muy joven. Incluye prosas y poemas tempranos escritos para diario *La Voz de Elqui* en 1905, 1906 y 1909. Destaca una, para ese tiempo, insólita defensa y exaltación de la mujer: "mientras la luz del progreso irradia más poderosa sobre nuestro globo, ella, agobiada, va hirguiéndose [sic] más i más." De interés para los mistralianos. [LE]

Paz, Octavio. The other voice: essays on modern poetry. See item **5065.**

4544 Pérez Só, Reynaldo. Fragmentos de un taller: ars poética. Valencia, Venezuela: Amazonia, 1990. 1 v. (unpaged).

156 reflexiones sobre la poesía, el poeta y su oficio, recoge este libro. Producto del trabajo colectivo de un taller de poesía, donde se nota la mano directora del poeta Pérez Só (n. 1945), es un libro que apunta a un ars poética general. Interesantes variaciones sobre los eternos y limitados—como diría Borges—temas de la poesía. [AR]

4545 Potelet, Jeanine; Osvaldo Fernández Díaz; and Gerardo Mario Goloboff. Literatura e identidad en América Latina: Carpentier, Borges, Vallejo. La Garenne-Colombes, France: Editions de l'Espace européen, 1991. 85 p.: bibl. (Coll. FIED, 1155–4096)

Interesantes comentarios de textos específicos que permiten proyectar los resultados del análisis a un plano mayor de significación en las obras consideradas. Fernández Díaz examina las transformaciones de la "poética explícita" de Vallejo, de *Los heraldos negros* a *Trilce*; Goloboff estudia el "problema de la identidad" en Borges, atendiendo a procesos de desdoblamiento frecuentes en su poesía. [PL]

4546 Rokha, Pablo de and Lukó de Rokha. El amigo piedra: autobiografía [de] Pablo de Rokha. Retrato de mi padre [de] Lukó de Rokha. Edición y prólogo de Naín Nómez. Santiago: Pehuén, 1990. 327 p.: ill. (Col. Testimonio)

Apasionante documento autobiográfico, hasta ahora inédito, de este importante y controvertido poeta. Recuerdos van desde primeros años en Licantén y Talca y llegan hasta década del 50. Toda una época de la literatura, historia y política chilenas se revela en estas 233 p., desde perspectiva avasalladora del poeta. Lo mejor de Pablo de Rokha—poeta y hombre público y privado—está aquí. El tono siempre vehemente y polémico aparece controlado por cierta (inesperada) ternura hacia el mundo, las cosas y las gentes. No es así como se acostumbra ver a de Rokha. Hay también emotivo homenaje de 83 p., "Retrato de mi padre" de Lukó de Rokha, hija del poeta. Dice que aceptó escribir estos recuerdos porque "Sólo deseaba sepultar todo lo triste del pasado, para dar paso solamente a los momentos buenos y luminosos." Fundamental para estudios sobre Pablo de Rokha. [LE]

4547 Sefamí, Jacobo. Contemporary Spanish American poets: a bibliography of primary and secondary sources. Compiled by Jacobo Sefamí. New York: Greenwood Press, 1992. 1 v.: bibl., index. (Bibliographies and indexes in world literature, 0742–6852; 33)

Importante trabajo bibliográfico sobre 86 poetas, nacidos desde 1910. En cada caso, Sefamí ordena las informaciones en apartados dispuestos cronológica y alfabéticamente: "Obras Poéticas," "Compilaciones y Antologías," "Otras Obras" y "Estudios Críticos," éstos subdivididos a su vez en "Bibliografías," "Libros y Disertaciones" y "Ensayos, Reseñas y Entrevistas." El resultado es notable por la amplitud y el cuidadoso registro de los datos.

C.G. Belli, E. Cardenal, R. Castellanos, A. Cisneros, P.A. Cuadra, R. Dalton, E. Diego, J. Gelman, O. Hahn, J. Lezama Lima, E. Lihn, E. Molina, E. Montejo, A. Mutis, O. Orozco, J.E. Pacheco, N. Parra, O. Paz, A. Pizarnik, G. Rojas, J. Sáenz, J. Sologuren, J. Teillier, B. Varela, E.A. Westphalen, R. Zurita, son algunos de los autores incluidos en este útil repertorio. Guías de obras generales y por países cierran el volumen. [PL]

4548 Silva, Ludovico. Dos poetas contrapuestos de la generación del 58. Maracay, Venezuela: Casa de la Cultura, 1988. 70 p.

Dos ensayos extensos sobre dos poetas contemporáneos, Juan Calzadilla y Alfredo Silva Estrada, conforman este libro del recientemente desaparecido poeta y crítico Ludovico Silva. En ellos Silva contrapone dos tendencias igualmente valiosas en poesía: la lúdica, surreal, aunque reflexiva de Calzadilla, y la ordenada, clásica, pero también lúdica de Silva Estrada. Los ensayos, escritos con una precisión crítica admirable, nos permiten ver sin obstáculos las convergencias y divergencias en las obras de estos dos poetas y su innegable contribución a la poesía venezolana actual. [AR]

Drama

MARIO A. ROJAS, *Associate Professor and Chair of Modern Languages, Catholic University of America*

EL PANORAMA TEATRAL iberoamericano se ha enriquecido especialmente con la aparición de numerosos dramaturgos jóvenes, cuyas obras se destacan de las de sus predecesores por el empleo de nuevas modelizaciones dramáticas donde, además de descartar la estructura fabular tradicional, incorporan un nuevo discurso teatral caracterizado por sus múltiples planos ficcionales, polisemia y ambigüedad. Su preocupación principal, más que la alusión contextual directa, es la subjetividad de proyección humana universal. Entre estos jóvenes figuran nombres como los de De la Parra, Garaycochea, Izcovich, Grasso, Licona, Varela. También hay que destacar nuevos textos o reediciones de dramaturgos de sobresaliente y reconocida trayectoria teatral, como Argüelles, Cabrujas, Cossa, Gambaro, Gorostiza, Griffero, Halac, Leites, Maggi, Pavlovski, Piñera, Santana, Vilalta y Viale. Así mismo, han aparecido nuevas antologías, con textos cuidadosamente seleccionados y editados, en que se compendian obras de autores individuales (items **4571** y **4581**) o de grupos de escritores de un país, o de un movimiento teatral particular (items **4557, 4612, 4644, 4630** y **4648**).

Mención aparte merece la antología de textos de mujeres preparada por Eidelberg *et al.* (item **4718**) que incluye dramaturgas de mucho talento poco conocidas o recién dándose a conocer. Una tendencia que parece acentuarse últimamente es la creación de textos dramáticos que ficcionalizan la historia a partir de un personaje central ilustre y que, en su composición, se ciñen, en general, a los principios estéticos de la denominada "metaficción historiográfica," (items **4550, 4553, 4600, 4608, 4615, 4641** y **4577**). Otra forma de drama histórico es el que ofrece un entramado en torno a un episodio histórico, que es desplegado ya sea mediante el empleo del modelo épico brechtiano, la metaficción historiográfica o la modalidad realista de directa apelación social (items **4549, 4556, 4566, 4566, 4683, 4585** y **4584**).

En cuanto a la actividad crítica, ésta ha aumentado en volumen y calidad gracias a los números regulares o monográficos de revistas como *Gestos* y *Latin American Theatre Review* o a publicaciones especiales que reúnen estudios selectos de crítica teatral tales como *Alba de América* (item **4656**), *De la colonia a la postmodernidad* (item **4669**), *Teatro argentino durante el proceso* (item **4710**) y *Teatro Iberoamericano* (item **4711**). Una publicación muy especial, por sus ambiciosos y bien logrados propósitos, es *Escenario de dos mundos* (item **4672**) que, en una esmerada edición de cuatro volúmenes, contiene una valiosa y abundante información sobre distintos aspectos del teatro iberoamericano. De los estudios críticos en que se tratan varios autores, cabe destacar el de Jaramillo y Eidelberg (item **4718**), que se centra exclusivamente en textos de dramaturgas, el de Luzuriaga (item **4684**), que hace una crítica revisión de las propuestas teóricas más importantes de Latinoamérica y el de Albuquerque (item **4657**), de carácter socio-semiótico que estudia la violencia en cuanto reflejada en el teatro. Entre los estudios de obras de autores individuales, grupos o movimientos teatrales nacionales, se puede señalar los dedicados a Usigli (items **4660, 4705** y **4715**), a Heiremans (item **4714**) al nuevo teatro colombiano (item **4679**), al teatro chileno de la dictadura (items **4661** y **4717**) al Teatro Abierto (items **4671, 4678** y **4644**), al teatro cubano (items **4686** y **4664**) y al teatro de Yucatán (item **4690**). A la crítica de textos dramáticos o espectáculos teatrales, últimamente se ha agregado aquella que asume como objeto de su hermenéutica espectáculos marginales o parateatrales, tales como fiestas religiosas populares (items **4683, 4658** y **4690**). Entre las instituciones que han contribuido más al desarrollo de actividades teatrales iberoamericanas, es encomiable la labor del Centro Latinoamericano de Creación e Investigación teatral (CELCIT) que además del Festival de Teatro Iberoamericano que tiene lugar anualmente en Cádiz, promueve la realización de encuentros, festivales y talleres regionales o nacionales en toda Iberoamérica. Los trabajos más destacados los publica en forma de libro o en la revista *CELCIT/TEATRO* la cual ha renacido en su segunda época a partir de 1991. Igualmente destacables son los encuentros sobre teatro iberoamericano que se realizan anualmente en Buenos Aires bajo la dirección de Osvaldo Pellettieri y los que ha organizado Juan Villegas, en Irvine, California, sobre temas específicos de alto interés académico. Finalmente, además de las revistas *Latin American Theatre Review, Gestos* y *Conjunto,* en los últimos años, se han impuesto en el ámbito latinoamericano las revistas *Apuntes* de Chile y *Espacio de Crítica e Investigación Teatral* de Argentina que aunque enfatizan la crítica de textos dramáticos y espectáculos nacionales, incluyen trabajos generalmente de gran calidad sobre otras áreas del continente.

PLAYS

4549 Acevedo Hernández, Antonio. *Chañarcillo.* Versión integra, 1. ed. Chile: Pehuén, 1991. 128 p.: ill. (Teatro Pehuén; 11)

Obra realista cuyo conflicto se desenvuelve en torno a mineros del Norte de Chile que no logran cumplir sus aspiraciones de una vida mejor. La acción se ve enriquecida con la incorporación de elementos populares y folklóricos.

4550 Aguirre, Isidora. *Diálogos de fin de siglo.* Santiago: Editorial Torsegel, 1989. 102 p. (Serie Teatro; 2)

Se dramatizan las circunstancias históricas y políticas en torno al suicidio del Presidente Balmaceda a fines del siglo XIX. Aunque de construcción drámatica simple mantiene la calidad técnica demostrada por la autora en obras anteriores.

4551 Alsina, Arturo. Obra teatral, 1926–1974. Introducción y notas de Jorge Aguadé. Asunción: Editorial Manuel Ortiz Guerrero, 1990. 544 p.

Recopilación de obras, la mayoría inéditas, que fueron escritas de acuerdo a las convenciones del teatro costumbrista y la ideología del socialismo utópico de comienzos del siglo XX.

4552 Antología del teatro uruguayo moderno: Novas Terra, Paredes, Varela, Prieto. Noticia y selección de Walter Rela. Montevideo: Proyección, 1988. 210 p.

Buena selección de obras dramáticas estrenadas en las dos últimas décadas que, concebidas a partir de distintas convenciones teatrales (costumbrismo, vanguardismo, absurdismo), plantean situaciones límites del hombre contemporáneo. Por su lenguaje metafórico y alegórico, la obra de Varela, *Alfonso y Clotilde*, es la mejor lograda.

4553 Arciniegas, Germán. *El Libertador y la guerrillera.* Bogotá: Editorial Milla Batres, 1990. 99 p.

Excelente texto dramático de carácter metahistórico centrado en las figuras de Simón Bolívar y Manuela Sáenz de cuyo diálogo se reinventa y profundiza un importante momento de la historia americana. El juego entreverado de otras voces indo-afro-americanas y sus diferentes escenarios visualizan una interesante puesta.

4554 Argüelles, Hugo. *Los prodigiosos.* Guadalajara, México Editorial Agata, 1991. 139 p.: ill. (Teatro completo; 1)

Tragicomedia que, con fino humor negro, satiriza las prácticas religiosas, el engaño y falsos mitos creados por la superstición y el fanatismo. Su denso diálogo, personajes bien definidos y ambientación barroca, hacen de ésta una obra de gran calidad.

4555 Arlt, Roberto. *La isla desierta; Saverio el cruel.* Estudio preliminar y notas de Mirta Arlt. Buenos Aires: Editorial Kapelusz, 1974. 114 p. (Grandes obras de la literatura universal; 125)

Ambas obras, fuertemente influidas por la filosofía existencialista, presentan personajes acosados por la frustración y alienación que buscan un escape en la ensoñación o la locura. Tiene valiosas anotaciones dirigidas especialmente a estudiantes.

4556 Arrau, Sergio. *Santa María del Salitre.* Iquique, Chile: Comité Editorial Camanchaca, 1989. 136 p.: bibl., ill. (Ediciones especiales Camanchaca; 1)

Ficcionalización de un episodio histórico sucedido en 1907 en el Norte de Chile, donde más de un centenar de mineros del salitre fueron masacrados mientras mantenían una huelga en el puerto de Iquique. Ceñido al patrón épico-brechtiano, el autor crea una obra de compleja y bien lograda estructura.

4557 Badillo, Juan Carlos et al. Teatro. Buenos Aires: Editorial Autores, 1985. 228 p.

Selección de obras de teatro argentino contemporáneo que tienen en común el uso de la ambigüedad y metáfora para aludir a un referente político-social y el rechazo a la convención teatral realista que, a nivel superficial, parecieran seguir. Todas de gran calidad.

4558 Bárcenas, Gabriel. *¡Música maestro!* y otras obras: teatro. Guadalajara, México: Editorial Univ. de Guadalajara, 1990. 169 p. (Col. Fundamentos: Serie La Vida es sueño)

Colección de seis obras breves, la mayoría de un acto. A partir de una anécdota simple, el autor ausculta la compleja psiquis de los personajes, proceso del que desprende metáforas que se proyectan a la condición humana en general. Buen teatro en que sobresalen *¡Música maestro!* y *La sala número 6.*

4559 Betti, Atilio. *Farsa del corazón.* Buenos Aires: Torres Agüero Editor, 1990. 75 p. (Col. Cuarta pared)

Obra concebida según los códigos del teatro realista vigentes en los 50. El conflicto dramático gira en torno a un adolescente crónicamente enfermo cuyas aspiraciones de independencia le conducen a un trágico fin.

4560 Boullosa, Carmen. *Teatro herético.* Puebla, Mexico: Univ. Autónoma de Puebla, 1987. 101 p. (Col. Difusión cultural: Serie Teatro; 5)

Se incluyen tres obras (*Aura y las once mil vírgenes*, *Cocinar hombres* y *Propusieron a María*) en que la autora mediante elementos fantásticos y lúdicos plantea situaciones de ruptura de convenciones y creencias.

4561 Cabrujas, José Ignacio. El teatro de Cabrujas. Caracas: Pomaire/Fuentes, 1991. 210 p.

Las cinco obras incluidas en esta colección están permeadas por el fino humor y gran imaginación del autor, quien a partir de simples anécdotas, estructura textos de gran complejidad técnica. Valiéndose de la metáfora o alusión histórico/social directa, Cabrujas aborda temas sobre la situación social de su país. Excelente teatro.

4562 Campoamor, María José. *008 se va con la murga.* Buenos Aires: Teatro Municipal General San Martín, 1986. 86 p., 8 p. of plates: ill. (Teatro Municipal General San Martín; 13)

Excelente obra en que a partir de la relación torturador/torturado, se destruyen dicotomías, polarizaciones y dogmatismos y se crean situaciones que trascienden el plano ideológico para adquirir dimensiones filosóficas y metafísicas.

4563 Cavero León, José Salvador. *Helme:* drama en 5 actos; drama bilingüe, tradición huamanguina. Huamanga, Peru: Impr. Moralo, 1989. 164 p.: bibl., ill.

Drama pasional de un tardío romanticismo. Su conflicto se desarrolla en torno a un triángulo amoroso que se resuelve trágicamente. Su mérito radica en la versión bilingüe (español/quechua) de su texto.

4564 Chocrón, Isaac E. *Asia y el Lejano Oriente; Tric-Trac; Alfabeto para analfabetos.* Caracas: Monte Avila Editores, 1990. 281 p. (Teatro/Isaac Chocrón; 4)

Incluye tres excelentes obras en que el dramaturgo venezolano, con la fina ironía y la capacidad creativa que lo distinguen, construye mundos ambivalentes y juegos dramáticos de gran calidad.

4565 Chocrón, Isaac E. *Simón; Clipper; Solimán El Magnífico.* Caracas: Monte Avila Editores, 1992. 203 p. (Teatro/Isaac Chocrón; 5)

Contiene tres obras del autor, una inédita, *Solimán, El Magnífico*, centrada en la figura de un famoso sultán del siglo XVI cuyos distintos momentos de su vida son interpretados en forma de metateatro por diferentes actores.

4566 Corleto, Manuel. *La profecía:* teatro coreográfico y musical. Música de Joaquín Orellana. Guatemala: M. Corleto, 1989. 100 p.

Obra de carácter épico que relata un episodio de la conquista protagonizado por los quichés al mando de Tucún Umán y por conquistadores al mando de Pedro de Alvarado. La ambiciosa propuesta escénica incluye grandes espacios y la incorporación de instrumentos y danzas autóctonos.

4567 Cortés, Hernando. *Tierra o muerte.* Lima: Instituto Nacional de Cultura, 1986. 63 p. (Col. Personae)

El autor ficcionaliza (al modo brechtiano) un episodio de la historia peruana que sucedió al comienzo de los 60 protagonizado por un grupo de campesinos peruanos que pretendían adueñarse de tierras del sur andino.

4568 Cossa, Roberto M. *El sur y después.* Buenos Aires: Torres Agüero Editor, 1989. 66 p. (Col. Cuarta pared)

Obra escrita a partir de imágenes y situaciones que fueron construidas, bajo la dirección de Cossa, por el grupo de actores que la llevó a la escena. En ella se dramatiza la gran ambivalencia de las acciones humanas que tienden siempre a neutralizar la oposición de contrarios.

4569 Cossa, Roberto M. Teatro. v. 3. Buenos Aires: Ediciones de la Flor, 1990. 1 v.

Contiene las obras del autor estrenadas entre 1980–87. Se incluyen *El viejo criado, Gris de ausencia, Ya nadie recuerda a Frédéric Chopin, El tío loco, De pies y manos, Yepeto,* y *El Sur y después.* Todas obras en un acto, de excelente calidad.

4570 Costantini, Humberto. *Chau, Pericles: teatro completo.* Buenos Aires: Editorial Galerna, 1986. 190 p.

Además de su obra titular en un acto, el volumen incluye dos obras en tres actos (*La traición de Viborg* y *Una pipa larga, larga con cabeza de jabalí*) y cuatro excelentes monólogos (*Estimado Prócer, La llave, Un señor alto, rubio, de bigotes,* y *¿De qué te reís?*)

4571 Discépolo, Armando. Obra dramática de Armando Discépolo. v. 2. Estudio preliminar, notas y vocabulario de Osvaldo Pellettieri. Buenos Aires: Editorial Universitaria de Buenos Aires, 1990. 1 v.: bibl. (Arte para todos)

Vol. 2 de las obras más importantes del dramaturgo. El estudio preliminar de Pellettieri y las notas de un equipo colaborador son excelentes.

4572 Donoso, José and Carlos Cerda. *Este domingo:* versión teatral de la novela homónima de José Donoso. Santiago: Editorial Andrés Bello, 1990. 156 p.: ill.

Adaptación de la novela homónima hecha por el autor y Carlos Cerda. El ensayo de Grinor Rojo, que se refiere tanto al texto como a la puesta realizada por el ICTUS, es iluminador.

4573 Endara, Ernesto. *Donde es más brillante el sol.* Panama: Editorial Mariano Arosemena del Instituto Nacional de Cultura, 1991. 92 p. (Col. Ricardo Miró: Premio teatro; 1990)

La acción transcurre en un pasado mítico anterior a la fundación de la Ciudad de Panamá. La combinación de elementos folklóricos y legendarios, unido a acompañamientos musicales, potencian una interesante puesta.

4574 Enríquez, José Ramón. *Tres ceremonias.* México: Coordinación de Difusión Cultural, Dirección de Literatura, UNAM, 1991. 193 p. (Textos de difusión cultural: Serie La Carpa)

Cada ceremonia corresponde a una obra en un acto, las tres vinculadas a textos de autores famosos (i.e., Nietzche, Carroll, Copi) que, reficcionalizados, adquieren una nueva dimensión semántica e ideológica.

4575 España, Isidro. *Manicomio:* teatro. Comayagüela, Honduras: Ediciones Grupo, 1990. 66 p.: ill.

Se recogen personajes del folklore hon-

dureño para construir una obra lúdica en que los signos escénicos adquieren un valor primordial en el proceso de semiosis. Hay metafóricas alusiones a la realidad nacional.

4576 Espinosa, Tomás. *María o la sumisión; Pasacalles con perros; Miren el sol, ¡es gratis!.* México: Obra Citada, 1989. 90 p.: ill. (Teatro de los doce; 10)

Breve volumen que contiene tres obras en un acto que se destacan por su ludicidad, sencillez argumental y la incorporación de elementos folklóricos, máscaras, coros e instrumentos musicales autóctonos.

4577 Estévez, Abilio. *La verdadera culpa de Juan Clemente Zenea.* La Habana: Unión de Escritores y Artistas de Cuba, 1987. 127 p. (Premio UNEAC de teatro José Antonio Ramos)

Recreación de la vida de un poeta cubano para aclarar su presunta complicidad con la Corona Española durante el movimiento de la independencia cubana. Texto muy bien escrito y con una interesante propuesta escénica.

4578 Fonseca Leyva, Francisco and Armando Lamas. *El compás de madera* [de] Francisco Fonseca Leyva. *Eran las tres de la tarde* [de] Armando Lamas. La Habana: Unión de Escritores y Artistas de Cuba, 1982. 180 p. (Col. David)

Dos obras de carácter pedagógico: 1) *El compás de madera* presenta a un estudiante rebelde que termina como víctima de las imperfecciones del sistema escolar; y 2) *Eran las tres de la tarde* dramatiza la desadaptación de una mujer que se resiste a integrarse al nuevo sistema social cubano.

4579 Frías y Soto, Luciano. Teatro. Estudio introductorio y notas de Jaime Chabaud Magnus. Querétaro, México: Ediciones del Gobierno del Estado de Querétaro, 1990. 195 p. (Biblioteca Frías; 7)

Incluye tres piezas que se ciñen a la convención del romanticismo y al canon moral burgués decimonónico. Los personajes son alegóricos, la ambientación fantástica o costumbrista y el conflicto dramático estructurado alrededor de un amor funesto y a partir de situaciones típicas de la comedia de enredos.

4580 Fulleda Léon, Gerardo. *Chago de Guisa.* La Habana: Casa de las Américas, 1989. 145 p.

La acción de la obra se sitúa en Guisa, región oriental de Cuba, y tiene lugar entre 1865–68. En un trasfondo legendario y folklórico se relata la fantástica aventura de un joven campesino.

4581 Galich, Manuel. La obra dramática del Doctor Manuel Francisco Galich López. v. 1. Recopilación de Víctor Hugo Cruz. Guatemala: Univ. de San Carlos de Guatemala, Dirección General de Extensión, Consejo Editorial, 1989. 1 v.: ill. (Col. Editorial Universitaria; 1)

Contiene 11 obras de la primera etapa de Galich, que el compilador caracteriza como la "prehistoria teatral" del dramaturgo, las cuales ya revelan la imagen del futuro analista político y educador que se reflejará en obras posteriores.

4582 Gambaro, Griselda. Teatro. v. 4. Buenos Aires: Ediciones de la Flor, 1990. 1 v.

Contiene las siguientes obras de la autora estrenadas entre 1963–72: *Las paredes, El desatino, Los siameses, El campo* y *Nada que ver.* Todas excelentes.

4583 Garaycochea, Oscar. *Vals lento; Amado enemigo; ¡Sálvese quien pueda!:* teatro. Caracas: FUNDARTE; Alcaldía del Municipio Libertador, 1991. 190 p. (Cuadernos de difusión; 149)

Contiene tres obras que ficcionalizan, autorreflexivamente, al proceso de creación/producción del texto teatral. *Amado enemigo* tiene como figura central el dramaturgo italiano Carlo Goldini y *Vals lento* al escritor André Eloy Blanco. Excelente teatro.

4584 García del Toro, Antonio. *Un aniversario de larga duración, o, El "longplaying" de nuestra historia:* popurrí histórico-crítico en doce bandas y diez pausas. Río Piedras, P.R.: Editorial Plaza Mayor, 1991. 91 p.

Viñetas de la historia puertorriqueña en que el autor replantea dos temas recurrentes en la literatura puertorriqueña: el problema de la identidad nacional y el encuentro/desencuentro de los distintos estamentos raciales y culturales que coexisten en la isla.

4585 García del Toro, Antonio. *Donde reinan las arpías:* traición, trampa y esperanza en tres actos. Río Piedras, P.R.: Editorial Plaza Mayor, 1991. 61 p. (Biblioteca de autores de Puerto Rico)

Drama estructurado en torno a tres episodios históricos sucedidos en Puerto Rico en las tres últimas décadas del siglo XIX y cuya evocación conduce a reflexiones sobre la situación actual de la isla.

4586 Gené, Juan Carlos. *Golpes a mi puerta.* Buenos Aires: Torres Agüero Editor, 1988. 145 p.: ill. (Col. Cuarta pared)

Ante la violencia y opresión política y económica de gobiernos autoritarios, la iglesia popular, personificada en la obra en una monja, se presenta como una poderosa alternativa en defensa de los derechos humanos de los pobres del Tercer Mundo.

4587 Goldenberg, Jorge. *Krinsky.* Buenos Aires: Teatro Municipal General San Martín, 1986. 85 p., 8 p. of plates: ill. (Teatro Municipal General San Martín; 15)

Obra excelente en que, interpolados en un diálogo central, se reviven distintos momentos de la vida de un viejo judío, bibliotecario y fotógrafo, de solitaria vida. Se plantean situaciones relacionadas con la diáspora y la integración cultural.

4588 González-Dávila, Jesús. *Desventurados.* Guadalajara, México: Editorial Agata, 1990. 107 p.: ill. (Col. Teatro)

Historia de seres marginados que luchan por sobrevivir el espacio hostil de la llanura. Hay en la obra una gran tensión dramática provocada por la violencia física y verbal.

4589 Gorostiza, Carlos. Teatro 1. Buenos Aires: Ediciones de la Flor, 1991. 260 p.

Contiene la producción dramática del autor correspondiente a la década de los 80. Incluye *Aeroplanos, El frac rojo, Papi, Hay que apagar el fuego* y *El acompañamiento.* Todas las obras son de excelente construcción dramática, de significados plurivalentes y complejos personajes.

4590 Grasso, Jorge. Teatro. v. 1. Buenos Aires: Corregidor, 1991. 1 v.

Se incluyen tres obras en que, con humor y fantasía, el autor crea textos de compleja estructura dramática, caracterizada por la fusión de distintos niveles de ficción y ambivalentes personajes.

4591 Griffero, Eugenio. *Cuatro caballetes.* Buenos Aires: Teatro Municipal General San Martín, 1986. 58 p., 8 p. of plates: ill. (Teatro Municipal General San Martín; 12)

Cuatro pintores, acosados por situaciones límites, se sobreponen a la desesperanza recreando y exorcizando en sus pinturas, como lo hace el teatro en el escenario, los signos ominosos del mundo que los acosa. Excelente obra de uno de los dramaturgos argentinos contemporáneos más innovadores.

4592 Halac, Ricardo. Teatro. v. 1–2. Estudio preliminar de Osvaldo Pellettieri. Buenos Aires: Corregidor, 1987–90. 2 v. (Col. Dramaturgos argentinos contemporáneos; 1, 3)

Usando códigos teatrales provenientes de distintas convenciones teatrales (grotesco criollo, vodevil, teatro del absurdo, expresionismo) y técnicas como *flashback* y metateatro, el autor se adentra en los conflictos psicológicos y sociales de personajes de la clase media argentina. Teatro profundo y reflexivo, siempre sensible al referente social.

4593 Halley Mora, Mario. Para el pequeño tinglado: teatro breve. Asunción: Mediterráneo, 1987. 140 p. (Serie Teatro)

Contiene 29 obras muy breves. A pesar de ser sólo viñetas teatrales de carácter anecdótico y episódico, revelan una cuidadosa construcción dramática. Pueden ser muy útiles para talleres y clases de teatro.

4594 Hernández, Luisa Josefina. *La calle de la gran ocasión.* México: Editores Mexicanos Unidos, 1985. 207 p. (Teatro)

Nueva edición de una de las obras más conocida de la autora, compuesta por breves piezas teatrales que han sido especialmente diseñadas para estudiantes de teatro.

4595 Herrera Castañeda, Manuel. *Canción del año viejo* y otras obras del teatro. Querétaro, México: Dirección de Patrimonio Cultural, Secretaría de Cultura y Bienestar Social, Gobierno del Estado de Querétaro, 1991. 168 p.: ill. (Autores de Querétaro; 19)

Incluye cuatro textos. En *Canción de año viejo* (el mejor texto) y *Doña Vida y sus hermanas,* el autor, con fina ironía y humor, desbarata la aparente armonía impuesta por convenciones sociales. *Ofidia la inconformista* y *El Gran Dragón* están dirigidas a una audencia infantil.

4596 Herrera Rodríguez, Luis. Obras completas de teatro. Guatemala: s.n., 1989. 443 p., 20 p. of plates: ill.

Contiene siete obras del dramaturgo guatemalteco, quien a través de convenciones teatrales realistas y de la comedia liviana o de enredos, presenta anécdotas cotidianas de personajes animados por la esperanza de un futuro mejor.

4597 Ibargüengoitia, Jorge. Teatro. v. 1–3 México: Joaquín Mortiz, 1989–1990. 3 v. (Obras de Jorge Ibargüengoitia)

Contiene todo el teatro escrito por el autor, conocido más como narrador que como dramaturgo. Obras bien estructuradas dramáticamente en que, mediante la combinación de humor y seriedad, fantasía y realidad, espacios recónditos y locales, se desarrollan conflictos humanos de trascendencia universal.

4598 Izcovich, Carlos. *Memorias.* Buenos Aires: Teatro Municipal General San Martín, 1986. 88 p., 8 p. of plates: ill. (Teatro Municipal General San Martín; 17)

Un escritor regresa a una plaza de su infancia, ahora muerta, que le trae a la memoria recuerdos de un ominoso pasado. La estructura circular y la mezcla de niveles ficticios crean un ambiente fantasmagórico en que se oblitera pasado y presente. Obra excelente.

4599 Juana Inés de la Cruz, *Sor* and **Agustín de Salazar y Torres.** *La segunda Celestina*: una comedia perdida de Sor Juana. Edición, prólogo y notas de Guillermo Schmidhuber de la Mora, con la colaboración de Olga Martha Peña Doria. Presentación de Octavio Paz. México: Vuelta, 1990. 225 p.: bibl. (El Gabinete literario)

Afortunado hallazgo de Schmidhuber atribuido a la pluma de Agustín de Salazar y Torres y Sor Juana. El texto sigue los moldes y convenciones de la comedia renacentista y tiene un desenlace feliz con sendos casamientos de señores y criados. Esta publicación ha provocado una encendida polémica.

4600 Leis Romero, Raúl Alberto. *Mundunción.* Panamá: Instituto Nacional de Cultura, Dirección de Extensión Cultural, 1992. 83 p. (Col. Ricardo Miró: Premio teatro)

Mediante la ajustada adopción de técnicas brechtianas y del teatro documental de Piscator y Weiss, se revisa un episodio de la historia panameña protagonizado por Pedro Prestán, una importante figura de la cultura popular del país.

4601 Leites, Víctor Manuel. *El chalé de Gardel.* Prólogo de Sergio Dotta. Montevideo: Ministerio de Educación y Cultura, Instituto Nacional del Libro, 1991. 74 p. (Col. Teatro uruguayo; 3)

Aunque el conflicto se desarrolla a partir de otro personaje, la presencia de Gardel y sus mitos atraviesan todo el texto a tal punto que ambas figuras en muchas instancias parecen, especularmente, indiferenciadas. Obra de gran calidad.

4602 Leñero, Vicente. *El infierno*: paráfrasis de "El infierno," primera parte de la *Divina comedia* de Dante Alighieri. Ilustraciones de Isabel Leñero. México: Coordinación de Difusión Cultural, Dirección de Literatura, UNAM, 1989. 153 p.: ill. (Textos de difusión cultural: Serie La Carpa)

Sátira social, que el autor califica como "una paráfrasis de *El infierno*" de Dante, en que desfilan una galería de personajes mexicanos, en especial escritores y políticos condenados al infierno. La escenificación propuesta por el dramaturgo es monumental.

4603 Leñero, Vicente. *Jesucristo Gómez.* México: Ediciones Océano, 1986. 126 p.: ill.

Una adaptación de Leñero de su novela *El Evangelio de Lucas Gavilán* en que usa como fuente directa el Evangelio Según San Lucas. El autor se inspira en la Teología de la Liberación para reactualizar la presencia histórica de Jesucristo y defender la posición de una justicia social cristiana en favor de los pobres.

4604 Licona, Alejandro. Teatro para jóvenes: *La amenaza roja, Huelum* y 4 obras más. México?: Editores Mexicanos Unidos, 1986. 255 p.: ill. (Teatro)

Contiene seis obras breves del talentoso joven dramaturgo mexicano. Se destacan *Huelum, Las tres heridas, La araña* y *La amenaza roja.* Incluye un prólogo de su maestro Emilio Carballido y una entrevista realizada por Héctor Carrillo.

4605 Luco Cruchaga, Germán. *La viuda de Apablaza; Amo y señor.* Santiago: Pehuén, 1990. 134 p.: ill. (Teatro Pehuén; 9)

En ambas obras el autor se somete a las convenciones del teatro realista, desarrollando conflictos con personajes y costumbres típicos de la realidad chilena regional y nacional. *La viuda de Aplablaza* es señalada por muchos críticos como una obra clásica del teatro chileno.

4606 Maggi, Carlos. *La noche de los ángeles inciertos.* Prólogo de Rubén Castillo. Montevideo: Ministerio de Educación y Cultura, Instituto Nacional del Libro, 1991. 74 p. (Col. Teatro uruguayo; 2)

Un boxeador retirado vive inmerso en dos realidades: la de su circunstancia y la de sus sueños. Excelente obra.

4607 Magnabosco, Ana. *Santito mío.* Prólogo de Gloria Levy. Montevideo: Ministerio de Educación y Cultura, Instituto Nacional del Libro, 1991. 78 p. (Col. Teatro uruguayo; 6)

En un mesurado humor, y sin apegarse estrictamente a la convención mimética realista, se presenta una galería de personajes y acciones prototípicas de la sociedad uruguaya, que es percibida en términos más bien negativos.

4608 Masciángioli, Jorge. *Señor Leonardo:* tragedia de los enigmas: dos partes y seis cuadros. Buenos Aires: Grupo Editor Latinoamericano; Emecé Editores, 1992. 133 p. (Col. Escritura de hoy)

En los umbrales de la ficción e historia, se recrea la figura de Leonardo da Vinci cuando mediaba sus 50 años, que aquí reaparece en toda su complejidad interior e inmerso en un complejo mundo de relaciones. Excelente texto.

4609 Matas, Julio. *El extravío; La crónica y el suceso; Aquí cruza el ciervo.* Miami: Ediciones Universal, 1990. 205 p. (Col. Teatro)

A través del diestro manejo de técnicas y entramados convencionales o de innovadores experimentos metaficticios, el autor crea piezas de gran calidad, de transparente lenguaje o complejas alusiones.

4610 Medina, Roberto Nicolás. *La larga noche de Alcestes — bajo sospecha.* Buenos Aires: Torres Agüero Editor, 1992. 62 p. (Col. Cuarta pared)

Excelente recreación de los personajes mitológicos cuyas dimensiones trágicas y profundamente humanas permiten al dramaturgo aludir a un doble referente: al ficticio de un lejano pasado y, por traslación metafórica, al contexto extraliterario de terror y muerte que padeció su país.

4611 Méndez de la Vega, Luz. Tres rostros de mujer en soledad: monólogos importunos. Guatemala: Artemis-Edinter, 1991. 72 p.: ill. (Teatro)

Tres monólogos en que se despliegan, desde una posición feminista, los conflictos familiares y sociales de la mujer frente al mundo patriarcal que la rodea. En un lenguaje de gran lirismo, la autora crea personajes de gran profundidad y trascendencia.

4612 Monólogos teatrales cubanos. Selección y prólogo de Francisco Garzón Céspedes. La Habana: Editorial Letras Cubanas, 1989. 524 p. (Giraldilla)

Antología que reúne 38 textos. Algunos fueron preparados especialmente para esta edición, otros adaptados, por sus mismos autores, de textos narrativos. En su mayoría fueron escritos después de 1959 y presentan variaciones tanto temáticas como cualitativas.

4613 Montes Huidobro, Matías. *Funeral en Teruel.* Honolulu, Hawaii: Editorial Persona, 1990. 95 p. (Serie Teatro)

Mediante el uso de la parodia, pastiche, anacronías y una patente intertextualidad, el autor crea un texto de características postmodernistas. Una de las mejores piezas del dramaturgo.

4614 Olmos, Carlos. *El eclipse:* pieza en dos actos. 2. ed. México: Coordinación de Difusión Cultural, Dirección de Literatura, UNAM, 1990. 78 p. (Textos de difusión cultural: Serie La Carpa)

Obra realista en que se entremezcla mito y superstición. Sus personajes deben enfrentar la rigidez de normas morales y sociales que menoscaban su libertad individual y la libre elección de un estilo de vida, la homosexualidad por ejemplo.

4615 Ottino, Mónica. *Evita y Victoria:* comedia patriótica en tres actos. Buenos Aires: Grupo Editor Latinoamericano; Emecé Editores, 1990. 116 p. (Col. Escritura de hoy)

Se ficcionalizan dos encuentros entre Eva Perón y la escritora Victoria Ocampo. De su tenso diálogo se hacen patentes los contrastes personales, sociales y políticos que separaban a las dos mujeres.

4616 Ozores, Renato. *El otro final:* drama en tres actos. Prólogo de Adolfo Arias Espinosa. Panamá: Star & Herald, 1991. 150 p.

Drama en torno a un gerente de empresa cuya honradez es puesta a prueba por la corrupción circundante. La obra ofrece al lector/espectador, dos posibles desenlaces, de los

cuales por su mejor construcción dramática, se impone el negativo.

4617 Palencia, Elio; Rubén Darío Gil; and **Marco Purroy.** *Camino a Kebaskén* [de] Elio Palencia. *La dama del sol* [de] Rubén Darío Gil. *El desertor* [de] Marco Purroy. Caracas: Centro de Directores para el Nuevo Teatro, Fundación Rajatabla—Ateneo de Caracas, CONAC, 1990. 167 p.: ill. (Teatro; 1)

Tres excelentes obras de jóvenes dramaturgos venezolanos, quienes con humor e ironía y empleando las técnicas del metateatro, critican las falsas aspiraciones de grupos de teatro provinciales, los arraigados mitos patróticos o nacionales y el alienante efecto de la televisión.

4618 Parra, Marco Antonio de la. *King Kong palace o El exilio de Tarzan; Dostoievski va a la playa.* Santiago: Pehuén, 1990. 171 p.: ill. (Teatro Pehuén; 10)

Excelente teatro en que se emplean códigos provenientes de distintos géneros y sistemas culturales populares. La deconstrucción y recreación de mitos, el uso de la parodia y pastiche, que caracterizan el discurso dramático del autor, persisten en estas obras.

4619 Pavlovsky, Eduardo A. *Cámara lenta; El señor Laforgue; Pablo; Potestad.* Madrid: Fundamentos, 1989. 154 p. (Col. Espiral; 133. Serie teatro)

Contiene cuatro obras del autor que comparten el tema de la represión, el cual se manifiesta de distintas formas y ejercido por diferentes agentes: un torturador, un médico, un supuesto amigo, un policía. Textos de gran intensidad dramática.

4620 Pavlovsky, Eduardo A. *Potestad.* Buenos Aires: Ediciones Búsqueda, 1987. 45 p.: ports. (Col. Literatura de hoy)

Breve obra, monologada en su mayor parte, en que el autor aborda una vez más, pero con más intensidad y hondura, las atrocidades de la dictadura: abuso de poder, asesinatos, tortura, secuestros de niños.

4621 Pavlovsky, Eduardo A. Teatro del 60. Buenos Aires: Ediciones Letra Buena, 1992. 205 p. (Col. Letras: Teatro)

Contiene piezas breves escritas en la década de los 60 que se destacan por la profunda penetración psicológica de los personajes. En ellas se siguen los europeos en boga, pero en estrecha relación con el mundo bonaerense.

4622 Paz, Octavio. *La hija de Rappaccini.* 1. ed. en Biblioteca Era. México: Ediciones Era, 1990. 59 p. (Biblioteca Era; BE 215/1)

Fue estrenada en 1956. Se trata de una original adaptación de un cuento de Nathaniel Hawthorne, derivado a su vez de un drama político hindú del siglo IX, que tiene como motivo central la doncella de cuerpo emponzoñado que es utilizada como medio para eliminar a un enemigo.

4623 Piñera, Virgilio. *Aire frío.* Ensayos de Rosa Illeana Boudet y Juan Antonio Hormigón. Madrid: Publicaciones de la Asociación de Directores de Escena, 1990? 174 p.: bibl. (Serie Literatura dramática iberoamericana; 1)

Fue escrita en 1958. El entramado dramático se construye en torno a la familia Romaguera, cuyos miembros, perdidos en sus ilusiones y frustraciones, apenas perciben y comprenden lo que sucede en el mundo exterior. El contrapunto realidad/irrealidad, interior/exterior, dinamismo/estatismo configuran una bien diseñada estructura.

4624 Plaza Noblía, Héctor. *La cerrazón.* Prólogo de Luisa Rodríguez Correa. Montevideo: Ministerio de Educación y Cultura, Instituto Nacional del Libro, 1991. 142 p. (Col. Teatro uruguayo; 1)

Excelente obra de carácter simbólico-alegórico, que alude a un contexto político-social caracterizado por el abuso del poder y el fuerte control social. A la calidad del texto escrito se añade una interesante propuesta escénica.

4625 Pujol i García, Daniel. *¡Proceda!* Santa Cruz de la Sierra, Bolivia: Cabildo, 1989. 81 p.

Obra que el autor catalán escribe cuando sirve como funcionario internacional en Santa Cruz, Bolivia. El espacio y personajes innomidados, aunque aplicables al contexto boliviano, se proyectan a otras regiones donde aún persisten formas de represión social y personal.

4626 Ramos-Perea, Roberto. *Malasangre.* Río Piedras, P.R.: Editorial Cultural, 1990. 186 p.: ill.

El conflicto se desenvuelve en torno a la crisis familiar y social que sufre un joven matrimonio puertorriqueño que emigra a El Paso, Texas. La obra contiene directas alusiones tanto al mundo chicano como a la guerra del Vietnam.

4627 Reyes, Luis Eduardo. Alrededor de la rutina: teatro. México: Consejo Nacional para la Cultura y las Artes, 1991. 139 p. (Fondo editorial tierra adentro; 10)

Contiene dos obras: *. . . De interés social* y *Vida secreta de dos cualquieras.* Las dos obras presentan personajes que con el fin de superar problemas sociales y económicos acuden a inútiles soluciones límites. De las dos, se destaca la primera.

4628 Rivas Mercado, Antonieta. Obras completas de María Antonieta Rivas Mercado. Recopilación de Luis Mario Schneider. 1a ed. en Lecturas mexicanas. México: Editorial Oasis; SEP, 1987. 466 p.: bibl. (Lecturas mexicanas; 2a ser., 93)

Volumen que contiene toda la producción literaria de la escritora mexicana: ensayos, cuentos, epístolas y dos piezas teatrales de poco valor: *Episodio electoral* que es sólo un boceto y *Un drama,* una obra inconclusa cuyo conflicto se estructura en torno a un asesinato político.

4629 Rivera, José María. Comedias. Selección, prólogo y notas de Jaime Chabaud Magnus. Querétaro, México: Dirección de Patrimonio Cultural, Secretaría de Cultura y Bienestar Social, Gobierno del Estado de Querétaro, 1991. 135 p. (Autores de Querétaro; 18)

Incluye dos comedias romántico-realistas: *¿Casarse con un difunto?* y *Capeluche y doña Urraca.* Ambas critican la clase media mexicana de mediados del siglo XIX y tiene como tema central el viejo adinerado que se enamora de una joven. La primera es una comedia de enredos.

4630 Rodríguez, Romano *et al. Vía Benetton* [de] Romano Rodríguez. *Detrás de la avenida* [de] Elio Palencia. *Divorciadas, evangélicas y vegetarianas* [de] Gustavo Ott. *El Santo Oficio* [de] Mariozzi Carmona. *Para culebra, gato* [de] René Chamorro Guerra. Coordinación de Rodolfo Santana. Caracas: Fundación CELARG, 1991. 187 p. (Voces nuevas: Dramaturgia)

Se incluyen las obras de cinco jóvenes dramaturgos formados en el Taller de Dramaturgia del Centro Latinoamericano Rómulo Gallegos, todas de gran calidad. Entre ellas se destaca *Vía Benetton* por su original propuesta escénica.

4631 Rodríguez Solís, Eduardo. Actos de magia. México: Dirección de Difusión Cultural, Depto. Editorial, 1987. 175 p. (Col. Molinos de viento; 47: Serie/Teatro)

Contiene tres piezas publicadas en 1971–73: *Agua y jabón para nuestras ventanas, El pequeño universo del Sr. Plasco* y *Una relación cercana al éxtasis.* Todas son bien contruidas dramáticamente y despliegan plurivalentes sentidos y múltiples niveles de ficción.

4632 Rosencof, Mauricio. Las crónicas del Tuleque. Presentación de Hugo Alfaro. Montevideo: Arca, 1986. 180 p.

En su mayor parte este libro está formado de breves relatos que tienen como escenario Humaitá y Garibaldi, dos barrios montevideanos reconstruidos por la memoria. Las breves piezas teatrales que se incluyen presentan escenas y personajes típicos de estos microcosmos.

4633 Salcedo, Hugo. *Arde el desierto con los vientos que vienen del sur:* teatro. Mexicali, B.C.: Instituto de Cultura de Baja California, 1991. 35 p. (Libros de Baja California)

Se basa en el mito sobre el origen de la ciudad de Tijuana. Su figura principal es la tía Juana, que con su posada, fundará y dará nombre a la ciudad.

4634 Salcedo, Hugo. Teatro. Guadalajara, México: Editorial Univ. de Guadalajara, 1990. 66 p. (Col. Fundamentos: Serie La Vida es sueño)

Incluye tres obras breves, *Vapor, Cumbia* y *Dos a uno.* Teatro de gran lirismo e intensidad dramática, con personajes que se debaten en situaciones límites de la vida cotidiana y la violencia social que los reprime. *Cumbia* es la mejor lograda del volumen.

4635 Salmón, Raúl. *Mi compadre el ministro:* comedia criolla en un acto, teatro boliviano. La Paz: Librería Editorial Juventud, 1991. 55 p.

Tragicomedia costumbrista que, a partir de una simple anécdota, dramatiza las relaciones de poder que se crean entre una empleada doméstica y sus patrones y entre un funcionario político y su superior.

4636 Salmón, Raúl. Seis obras de teatro breve. La Paz: Editorial Popular, 1990. 205 p.

Obras de cuestionable mérito sobre escenas de la vida diaria, algunas comedias, otras didácticas. *Los exiliados* relata las peripecias de una familia boliviana en Venezuela.

4637 Sánchez Delgado, Carlos. *Purísima.* 1a. ed. en M.A. Caracas: Monte Avila Editores, 1990. 83 p. (Col. Teatro)

La acción se desarolla en el sótano secreto y laberíntico de una iglesia donde se aisla una familia, cuya vida ritual y controlada es finalmente interrumpida por el mundo exterior que rechazaba. Produce la misma extraña sensación que suscita una obra surrealista.

4638 Santana, Rodolfo. Teatro. Caracas: Talleres de la Impr. Nacional y Gaceta Oficial, 1986. 577 p.: ill.

Selección de las mejores obras del dramaturgo venezolano, todas de excelente calidad. Incluye dos textos inéditos *Primer día de Resurrección* y *Crónicas de la cárcel modelo.*

4639 Schinca, Milton. *Nuestra Señora de los Ramos.* Prólogo de Eduardo Schinca. Montevideo: Ministerio de Educación y Cultura, Instituto Nacional del Libro, 1991. 62 p. (Col. Teatro uruguayo; 4)

Ambientada en el Uruguay de las últimas décadas del siglo XIX, el conflicto básico gira en torno a las ambiguas relaciones de los agentes de un triángulo amoroso.

4640 6 obras de teatro cubano. Selección y prólogo de Rine Leal. La Habana: Editorial Letras Cubanas, 1989. 418 p.

Selección de las obras más representativas de jóvenes dramaturgos cubanos contemporáneos que buscan nuevas líneas temáticas, textos multivalentes y renovadoras puestas en escena. Incluye obras de Abelardo Estorino, Rafael González, Gerardo Fernández, Mauricio Coll, Ignacio Gutiérrez y Eugenio Hernández. Excelente prólogo de Rine Leal.

4641 Tagle Achával, Carlos. *Cuando Perón llegó a la Casa Rosada.* 2. rev. ed. Córdoba, Argentina: Editora Argentina y El Mundo, 1988. 139 p.

Drama histórico sobre el primer gobierno de Perón (1943–55). Destaca los cambios producidos en la vida política argentina del período tanto a nivel nacional como familiar. Tiene un *post-scriptum* con reflexiones sobre la relación historia/ficción.

4642 Tampieri de Estrella, Susana E. *Abzurdo.* Mendoza, Argentina: Gobierno de Mendoza, Ministerio de Cultura y Educación, Subsecretaría de Cultura, Ediciones Culturales de Mendoza, 1990. 27 p. (Sección Teatro)

Ingeniosa comedia lúdica, que a partir de anécdotas simples, crea situaciones de hilarante comicidad y veladas alusiones a la manipulación y abuso del poder político.

4643 Tavira, Luis de. *La pasión de Pentesilea:* inspirado en una idea de Von Kleist. México: Dirección de Difusión Cultural, Departamento Editorial, Univ. Autónoma Metropolitana, 1988. 171 p. (Col. Molinos de viento ; 55: Serie/Teatro)

Inspirado en la obra homónima de Von Kleist, De Tavira retoma los mitos de Penteselia—1a reina de las amazonas—y de Aquiles. La propuesta escénica constituye un gran desafío por sus múltiples planos espaciales e históricos.

4644 Teatro Abierto 1981. v. 2, 21 estrenos argentinos. Edición de Miguel Angel Giella. Buenos Aires: Corregidor, 1992. V. 2.: bibl. (Col. Dramaturgos argentinos contemporáneos)

Miguel Angel Giella compendia 21 piezas estrenadas en Buenos Aires en 1981 bajo el movimiento teatral conocido como Teatro Abierto. Esta antología sigue al vol. 1 (véase item **4678**) en que Giella hace un estudio individual de cada obra.

4645 Teatro chileno en un acto. Selección y notas de Juan Andrés Piña. Santiago: Taller Teatro Dos, 1989. 151 p.

Incluye seis obras dramáticas breves, estrenadas entre 1955–85, que representan distintas tendencias dramáticas: comedia, teatro poético, social, psicológico. Por la simple escenografía que requieren son de fácil escenificación.

4646 Teatro '90: el nuevo teatro en Buenos Aires. Recopilación y banda de Jorge A. Dubatti. Buenos Aires: Libros del Quirquincho, 1992. 77 p.: ill. (Libros para nada)

Incluye una creación colectiva *Macocos: adiós y buena suerte* de la Bavda de Teatro Los Macocos y la *Pascua Rea* de Patricia Zangaro. Además de un extenso ensayo que abarca todo el texto paralelo a las obras, contiene al final cuatro estudios breves que ayudan a comprender mejor este novísimo movimiento teatral argentino.

4647 Teatro TECAL (Bogotá). Teatro contemporáneo colombiano: tres obras. Creación de Teatro TECAL. Dramaturgia de Críspulo Torres B. Bogotá: Ediciones Saltar la Piedra, 1991. 80 p.: ill.

Incluye tres obras de creación colectiva del grupo TECAL: *Domiltilo, Los gaticos* y *Preludio para andantes.* Se destaca la primera, un espectáculo callejero, en que se recoge la tradición oral y se combinan el arte juglaresco, la comedia del arte y el estilo carnavalesco.

4648 Teatro X 2. Buenos Aires: Editorial Dramaturgos, 1989? 96 p.

Dos textos excelentes (*Hay que vivir la fiesta,* de Rubén Darío Gómez y *La inolvidable dama de los lentes curvos,* de Luis José Cymlich) en que, a partir de situaciones cotidianas, se incursiona en el mundo interior de los personajes, sus ilusiones, esperanzas y frustraciones. De interés teórico es el prólogo de Ricardo Monti por su defensa del texto escrito, posición que lo diferencia de muchos directores contemporáneos que privilegian la puesta.

4649 Tobar García, Francisco. Teatro: trilogía del mar. Estudio introductorio de Luis Campos Martínez. Quito: Libresa, 1991. 341 p.: bibl. (Col. Antares; 65)

Componen esta trilogía *Una gota de lluvia en la arena, El ave muere en la orilla* y *Las ramas desnudas,* que fueron estrenadas entre 1963–64. La soledad e incomunicación, los falsos valores y las normas sociales represivas son temas que asedian al autor.

4650 Triana, José. *Ceremonial de guerra.* Honolulu, Hawaii: Editorial Persona, 1990. 64 p. (Serie Teatro)

Excelente obra dramática cuya acción se sitúa en 1895, durante la Guerra de la Independencia cubana. La atención se dirige especialmente a los problemas éticos que sufren en general los protagonistas de un movimiento revolucionario.

4651 Urueta, Margarita. Teatro. Introitos de Alfredo Leal Cortés y Marta Villaseñor de Camarena. México: M.A. Porrúa, 1992. 343 p.: ill.

Muestra representativa de las obras más importantes de la autora en que se incluye la más ambiciosa y celebrada *La Malinche.* Además figuran *El candidote, El silencio, El ruido* y *La muerte de un soltero.*

4652 Varela, Carlos Manuel. *Interrogatorio en Elsinore: Después de la ratonera.* Prólogo de Rubén Castillo. Montevideo: Ministerio de Educación y Cultura, Instituto Nacional del Libro, 1991. 76 p. (Col. Teatro uruguayo; 5)

Excelente texto que propone dos niveles de lectura o líneas isotópicas: una primera intertextual explícitamente vinculada al *Hamlet* de Shakespeare y, la segunda, que alude metafóricamente a un referente contextual y extraliterario.

4653 Viale, Oscar. Teatro. v. 1., *El grito pelado, Encantada de conocerlo, Convivencia,* y *Convivencia femenina.* Estudio preliminar de Osvaldo Pellettieri. Buenos Aires: Corregidor, 1987. 1 v. (Col. Dramaturgos argentinos contemporáneos ; 2)

Reúne cuatro obras importantes del autor que aluden elípticamente a contextos sociales en que la complicidad y el ocultamiento fomentan el abuso del poder y el crimen. Excelente el prólogo de Pellettieri.

4654 Vilalta, Maruxa. Teatro III: *Una voz en el desierto: vida de San Jerónimo;* obra en 17 cuadros. México: Fondo de Cultura Económica, 1990. 242 p.: bibl., ill., index. (Col. popular; 406)

En 17 cuadros, la autora, premunida de una exhaustiva investigación histórica, presenta diversos episodios que relatan la vida de San Jerónimo, su rectitud y el turbulento mundo que le rodeaban. Incluye un apéndice con importantes referencias.

4655 Zambrano, Oscar. *La última fiesta.* Santa Cruz de la Sierra, Bolivia: Editorial Casa de la Cultura, 1990. 83 p. (Col. Teatro)

Se critica el abuso del poder hegemónico y los prejuicios en contra del campesino indígena. Obra técnicamente bien lograda, con una propuesta escénica en que se incorpora el canto y la danza.

THEATER CRITICISM AND HISTORY

4656 *Alba de América.* Vol. 7, No. 12–13, 1988- . Edición especial a cargo de Rose S. Minc y Teresa Méndez-Faith. Westminster, Calif.: Instituto Literario y Cultural Hispánico.

Excelente selección de artículos sobre teatro hispanoamericano a cargo de Rose S.

Minc y Teresa Méndez Faith. Entre las obras estudiadas se incluyen las de O. Dragún, Griselda Gambaro, Susana Torres Molina, Samuel Rovinski, Vicente Leñeros, Maruja Vilalta y Emilio Carballido.

4657 Albuquerque, Severino João Medeiros. Violent acts: a study of contemporary Latin American theatre. Detroit: Wayne State Univ. Press, 1991. 297 p.: bibl., index. (Latin American literature and culture)

Se estudian los signos verbales y no verbales en obras de autores que tematizan diferentes formas de violencia política, social y económica en Latinoamérica.

4658 Ariza Acevedo, Maclovio. El teatro de evangelización en Chilapa, Guerrero. Chilpancingo, Mexico: Univ. Autónoma de Guerrero, 1989. 425 p.: bibl., ill.

Se recopilan textos del teatro religioso-campesino de la región de Chilapa, cuya temática (la batalla entre moros y cristianos, por ejemplo) y coreografía se remontan al tiempo de la Conquista y Edad Media. Se acompaña de anotaciones filológicas.

4659 Azor, Ileana. Origen y presencia del teatro en nuestra América. La Habana: Editorial Letras Cubanas, 1988. 304 p.: bibl. (Giraldilla)

Visión panorámica del teatro hispanoamericano desde la época precolonial hasta mediados del siglo XX. El comentario crítico es elaborado desde una perspectiva fundamentalmente socio-histórica.

4660 Beardsell, Peter R. A theatre for cannibals: Rodolfo Usigli and the Mexican stage. Rutherford, N.J.: Fairleigh Dickinson Univ. Press; London: Associated Univ. Presses, 1992. 242 p.: bibl., index.

Importante estudio de las obras más representativas de Rodolfo Usigli, que son examinadas considerando su poética teatral, las convenciones teatrales vigentes y el contexto histórico-cultural.

4661 Boyle, Catherine M. Chilean theater, 1973–1985: marginality, power, selfhood. Rutherford: Fairleigh Dickinson Univ. Press; London; Cranbury, NJ.: Associated Univ. Presses, 1992. 226 p.: bibl., index.

Excelente estudio del teatro chileno del período de la dictadura chilena. Estrechamente vinculadas al contexto sociopolítico, se examinan las actividades y propuestas de grupos teatrales y el trabajo de dramaturgos y directores. Contiene lúcidos comentarios de textos y puestas más representativos.

Bronstein, Abel *et al.* Vida y muerte en comunidad: ensayos sobre judaísmo en el Uruguay. See item **3128.**

4662 Callan, Richard. Marqués's *La muerte no entrará en palacio* and Dionysianism. (*Lat. Am. Theatre Rev.*, 26:1, Fall 1992, p. 43–53)

Callan considera que la tensión polarizante e irreconciliable entre el racionalismo apolíneo y la intuición y libertad dionisíacas es fundamental en la configuración ideológica de esta obra de Marqués. Los contrarios son simbolizados en el texto por el gobernador José y el revolucionario Rodrigo.

4663 Cánepa Guzmán, Mario. Teatro y literatura. Santiago: Ediciones Mauro, 1987. 144 p.: bibl.

Libro muy elemental destinado a escolares secundarios. Incluye 21 autores que han recibido el Premio Nacional de Literatura en Chile, de los cuales sólo dos se destacaron en el mundo teatral: Daniel de la Vega y Carlos Cariola.

4664 Carrió Ibietatorremendía, Raquel. Dramaturgia cubana contemporánea: estudios críticos. La Habana: Editorial Pueblo y Educación, 1988. 81 p.: bibl.

Colección de cinco ensayos que revisan los hitos más importantes del teatro cubano, especialmente del período post-revolucionario. Contiene reflexiones sobre alternativas metodológicas y experimentales propuestas para el teatro cubano actual.

4665 Cazap, Susan *et al.* Cronología acotada de la década del '80. (*Lat. Am. Theatre Rev.*, 24:2, Spring 1991, p. 13–24)

Fichaje de las obras estrenadas en Buenos Aires en 1980. Incluye información sobre su puesta y un breve comentario crítico sobre su contenido.

4666 Ciria, Alberto. Roberto Cossa: el teatro histórico, la historia teatral. (*Can. J. Lat. Am. Caribb. Stud.*, 15:29, 1990, p. 129–148)

Lectura sociopolítica de dos obras de Cossa—*Los compadritos* y *El sur después*— que el articulista considera como representativas del teatro más reciente del dramaturgo argentino, caracterizado por su particular tratamiento de la historia y la utilización de personajes simbólicos y temas sociales.

4667 Cuadra Pinto, D. Fernando. Un clásico del teatro chileno: *La viuda de Apablaza.* (*Bol. Acad. Chil. Bellas Artes*, 2, 1989, p. 13–39)

Discurso de incorporación a la Academia de Bellas Artes del Instituto de Chile pronunciado en Santiago (11 agosto 1977). Cuadra hace un estudio estilístico-estructural de la obra *La viuda de Apablaza.*

4668 Damasceno, Leslie. Theater: essay. Bibliography by Lionel Loroña. (*in* Latin America and the Caribbean: a critical guide to research sources. Edited by Paula H. Covington. New York: Greenwood Press, 1992, p. 589–604)

La autora selecciona y comenta las fuentes bibliográficas más importantes sobre teatro latinoamericano considerando en especial los trabajos realizados en las décadas de los 70 y 80. Contiene, además, una bibliografía de Lionel Loroña.

4669 De la colonia a la postmodernidad: teoría teatral y crítica sobre teatro latinoamericano. Edición de Peter Roster y Mario Rojas. Prólogo de Mario Rojas. Buenos Aires: Editorial Galerna, IITCTL, 1992. 405 p.: bibl. (Crítica de teatro latinoamericano; 3)

Contiene una selección de los trabajos leídos en el II Congreso del Instituto Internacional de Teoría y Crítica de Teatro Latinoamericano—IITCTL (The Catholic Univ. of America, Washington, D.C., junio 1990). Incluye crítica de textos dramáticos, puestas y una sección especial con ensayos de dramaturgos y directores.

4670 Debesa Marín, Fernando. Discurso de recepción a Fernando Cuadra Pinto. (*Bol. Acad. Chil. Bellas Artes*, 2, 1989, p. 41–51)

Discurso de recepción a Fernando Cuadra Pinto en su incorporación a la Academia de Bellas Artes del Instituto de Chile. Debesa hace una breve historia de la escritura teatral de Cuadra destacando en especial dos de sus obras: *Murallas de Jericó* y *Doña tierra.*

4671 Dubatti, Jorge A. Teatro Abierto después de 1981. (*Lat. Am. Theatre Rev.*, 24:2, Spring 1991, p. 79–86)

El autor hace un análisis de los cambios experimentados por "Teatro Abierto" desde 1982 hasta su total extinción en 1986. Para este efecto considera tanto aspectos internos de dicho movimiento como factores contextuales que determinaron su orientación y existencia.

4672 Escenarios de dos mundos: inventario teatral de Iberoamérica. v. 1–4. Edición de Moisés Pérez Coterillo. Madrid: Centro de Documentación Teatral, 1988. 4 v.: bibl., ill.

Conjunto de ensayos (vols. 1–4) sobre teatro iberoamericano en que participan destacados críticos y teatristas de Latinoamérica, España y Portugal. Además de estudios referidos al teatro convencional de escenario, se incluyen: 1) representaciones parateatrales, como las diabladas de Oruro y el Carnaval de Río; 2) el teatro de creación colectiva de diferentes grupos, como los de Enrique Buenaventura y Santiago García; 3) las nuevas tendencias en dirección teatral; 4) los dramaturgos más destacados del continente; 5) el trabajo específico de los grupos más sobresalientes; 6) un comentario de las puestas más celebradas de los últimos años; y 7) una amplia bibliografía y una lista de direcciones de los grupos y teatristas más importantes. Los cuatro volúmenes son ampliamente ilustrados con excelente material fotográfico. Los países se ordenan alfabéticamente. Vol. 1, además de una extensa y prolija introducción, contiene estudios dedicados a Argentina, Bolivia, Brasil, Colombia y Costa Rica. Vol. 2 incluye Chile, Cuba, Ecuador, El Salvador, España y Estados Unidos de América. Vol. 3 está destinado a Guatemala, Honduras, México, Nicaragua, Panamá, Paraguay y Perú. Vol. 4 se dedica a Portugal, Puerto Rico, República Dominicana, Uruguay y Venezuela. La labor del director Moisés Pérez Coterillo es encomiable y ejemplar. Se trata de un ambicioso y muy bien logrado proyecto que da una visión histórica y totalizadora de las actividades teatrales y espectáculos iberoamericanos.

4673 Foster, David William. Ideological shift in the rural images in Florencio Sánchez's theater. (*Hisp. J.*, 11:1, Spring 1990, p. 97–106, bibl.)

Foster estudia dos obras de Sánchez, *La gringa* y *Barranca abajo,* destacando el constraste ideológico (mitificación vs. demitificación) que las diferencia en su tratamiento de la sociedad rural argentina.

4674 Foster, David William. *Krinsky* de Jorge Goldenberg y la identidad étnica argentina. (*Lat. Am. Theatre Rev.,* 24:2, Spring 1991, p. 101–105)

Además de las virtudes del texto escrito y de su mundo ficticio, Foster señala las estrategias escénicas propuestas por el dramaturgo que requiere de una especial participa-

ción del público, el cual es compelido a meditar sobre la importancia de los inmigrantes judíos en la historia social y cultural argentina.

4675 Galván, Delia V. Tres generaciones de mujeres en *Te juro Juana que tengo ganas* de Emilio Carballido. (*Conjunto/Habana,* 85/86, oct. 1990/marzo 1991, p. 155–160, bibl., photos)

Desde una crítica feminista (Beauvoir, Fetterley, Moi, Rich) la autora estudia la evolución psicológica de la protagonista quien, al descubrir su propia identidad y valor de sí misma, se sobrepone a las normas patriarcales y se convierte en un modelo revolucionario para otras mujeres.

Gambaro, Griselda. Information for foreigners: three plays. See item **5001.**

4676 Gestos. Vol. 6, No. 11, abril 1991- . Irvine, Calif.: Dept. of Spanish and Portuguese, Univ. of California.

Número monográfico, producto de una conferencia organizada en por Juan Villegas y Diana Taylor (Irvine, Calif., oct. 1990) sobre la representación de la otredad en el teatro y cine latinoamericano y chicano.

4677 Gestos. Vol. 7, No. 14, nov. 1992- . Irvine, Calif.: Dept. of Spanish and Portuguese, Univ. of California.

Número monográfico con una selección de ponencias del congreso sobre escritura/reescritura de historias del teatro (Irvin, Calif., feb. 1992). Los ensayos se refieren a obras de autores iberoamericanos y latinoestadounidenses.

4678 Giella, Miguel Angel. Teatro Abierto. v. 1, Teatro argentino bajo vigilancia. Buenos Aires: Corregidor, 1991. 326 p.

Se estudian 21 piezas teatrales representadas en Buenos Aires en 1981, bajo la dictadura militar. Tanto la concepción de estas obras como su producción fueron fuertemente marcadas por variables contextuales, lo cual justifica plenamente la aproximación socio-semiótica seguida por Giella (Para una antología de las obras estudiadas, véase item **4644**).

4679 Jaramillo, María Mercedes. El nuevo teatro colombiano: arte y política. Medellín, Colombia: Editorial Univ. de Antioquia, Depto. de Publicaciones, Univ. de Antioquia, 1992. 373 p.: bibl. (Col. Teatro; 3)

Se revisa la labor de grupos teatrales

colombianos de las últimas décadas, poniendo especial atención a sus postulados metodológicos y teóricos y sus proyecciones sociales. Entre los grupos bajo examen se incluyen los de E. Buenaventura y S. García, C.J. Reyes y J.A. Niño.

4680 Jornadas Nacionales de Investigación Teatral, 3rd, Buenos Aires, 1986. Terceras Jornadas Nacionales de Investigación Teatral. Buenos Aires: Asociación de Críticos e Investigadores Teatrales de la Argentina—ACITA, 1987. 149 p.: bibl.

Selección de ponencias de las terceras jornadas sobre teatro argentino realizadas por el ACITA (Buenos Aires, 1986). Contiene estudios dedicados a textos dramáticos, períodos de la historia argentina, e informes sobre la investigación y práctica teatral de distintas zonas del país.

4681 Latin American Theatre Review. Vol. 25, No. 2, Fall 1992- . Lawrence: Univ. of Kansas, Center of Latin American Studies.

Número especial que conmemora los 25 años de existencia de esta prestigiosa revista. Está dedicado a las actividades teatrales que tuvieron lugar en la década de los 80 en la América de habla hispana y portuguesa. Colaboran destacados investigadores y teatristas de todo el continente.

4682 Leñero, Vicente. Vivir del teatro II. Portada e ilustraciones de Alberto Castro Leñero. México: Editorial J. Mortiz, 1990. 224 p.: bibl., ill. (some col.), index. (Contrapuntos)

Anecdótica y amena relación de la intrahistoria del montaje y puesta en escena de algunas de las obras del autor, las cuales, en más de una ocasión, crearon hasta crisis políticas.

4683 Lindo, Ricardo. El esplendor de la aldea de Arcilla: apuntes sobre teatro popular en El Salvador. San Salvador: Consejo Nacional para la Cultura y el Arte, 1991. 181 p.: bibl., ill.

Descripción, de interés antropológico y teatral, de las fiestas especialmente de carácter religioso que cíclicamente celebran los campesinos salvadoreños. Incluye la transcripción de algunos textos.

4684 Luzuriaga, Gerardo. Introducción a las teorías latinoamericanas del teatro: de 1930 al presente. Puebla, Mexico: Univ. Autónoma de Puebla, Maestría en Ciencias del

Lenguaje, 1990. 212 p.: bibl. (Col. Ciencias del lenguaje: Serie Estudios literarios)

El autor selecciona las figuras más relevantes del teatro latinoamericano, de los 30 en adelante, que han teorizado sobre su práctica teatral. Especial atención es puesta al teatro de producción colectiva. Una valiosa fuente de trabajo para críticos y teatristas.

4685 Márquez, Rosa Luisa. Conferencia dramatizada sobre teatro puertorriqueño. (Conjunto/Habana, 83, abril/junio 1990, p. 40–54)

Juego metateatral que recorre la historia teatral de Puerto Rico mediante el comentario y dramatización de escenas de obras señeras como Absurdos en soledad de Myrna Casas, Los soles truncos de René Marqués, La pasión según Antígona Pérez de Luis Rafael Sánchez.

4686 Martin, Randy. El teatro cubano en la rectificación: una Revolución después de la Revolución. (Conjunto/Habana, 85/86, oct. 1990/marzo 1991, p. 43–55, bibl., photos)

Se examina la evolución de grupos teatrales que, a partir de la nueva política de descentralización del arte en Cuba delineada en 1988, han logrado profesionalizarse, creando innovadoras propuestas escénicas. Martin destaca, como representativas de esta tendencia, puestas del Grupo Buendía y la obra La cuarta pared de Víctor Varela.

4687 Meléndez, Priscilla. On Leñero's Martirio de Morelos: reading the empty stage. (Gestos/Irvine, 7:13, abril 1992, p. 51–64)

Un lúcido estudio de esta compleja obra de Leñero, que la autora interpreta como contestataria al discurso histórico y a los códigos del discurso teatral documental en cuyas convenciones la obra misma parece sustentarse.

4688 Mendoza-López, Margarita; Daniel Salazar; and Tomás Espinosa. Teatro mexicano del siglo XX, 1900–1986: catálogo de obras teatrales. v. 1–4. México: Instituto Mexicano del Seguro Social, 987-1989. 4 v.: bibl., ill., index, ports.

Además de un resumen de cada texto dramático, contiene el listado de los elementos escenográficos básicos requeridos para su representación, una bibliografía, hemerografía, apéndice fotográfico y un índice de los autores. Constituye una útil e informativa referencia.

4689 Muguercia, Magaly. Lo antropológico en el discurso escénico latinoamericano. (*Conjunto*/Habana, 85/86, oct. 1990/ marzo 1991, p. 3–17, facsim., photos)

Excelente artículo sobre nuevas expresiones teatrales latinoamericanas que, liberadas del dato contextual directo y de un marco ideológico, prestan más atención a lo vivencial, humano y personal, a la ludicidad, a lo sensorial y corporal, consiguiendo un vitalismo escénico innovador que transgrede la lógica de estructuras tradicionales.

4690 Muñoz, Fernando. El teatro regional de Yucatán. México?: Grupo Editorial Gaceta, 1987. 229 p.: ill. (Col. Escenología)

Estudio diacrónico del teatro de Yucatán. Abarca el período maya precolombino, el de la evangelización, y de los siglos XIX y XX. Cada capítulo es acompañado de una síntesis de las obras tratadas, una selección de fragmentos, algunas canciones y estudios sobre obras específicas.

4691 Obregón, Osvaldo. Le théâtre latino-américain accueilli par la critique française, 1958–1977. (*Caravelle*/Toulouse, 58, 1992, p. 99–115, bibl.)

El teatro latinoamericano se hace presente en Francia gracias al Théatre des Nations y al Festival de Nancy. Obregón se refiere a este fenómeno, a la recepción crítica francesa y a la fuerte carga ideológico/política que caracteriza a la mayoría de los grupos participantes.

4692 Ordaz, Luiz. Autores del "nuevo realismo" de los años '60 a lo largo de las tres últimas décadas. (*Lat. Am. Theatre Rev.*, 24:2, Spring 1991, p. 41–48)

Ordaz postula que el teatro argentino de los 60 (Halac, Cossa, Somigliana, De Cecco, Talesnik, Viale) ha sido fundacional para la consolidación y desarrollo del teatro de los 80. Su argumentación considera como factor determinante las convenciones teatrales del "nuevo grotesco."

4693 Pellettieri, Osvaldo. Cien años de teatro argentino: del Moreira a Teatro Abierto. Buenos Aires: Editorial Galerna: IITCTL, 1990. 184 p.: bibl. (Serie Crítica de teatro latinoamericano; 2)

Una visión diacrónica del teatro rioplatense desde *Juan Moreira* hasta *El partener* de Mauricio Kartun. Empleando un marco teórico que incluye la semiótica, teoría de la recepción e historiografía, el autor percibe el desarrollo teatral como cambios y rupturas de sistemas teatrales.

4694 Pellettieri, Osvaldo. La puesta en escena argentina de los '80: realismo estilización y parodia. (*Lat. Am. Theatre Rev.*, 24:2, Spring 1991, p. 117–131)

Se discuten la evolución y fundamentos teóricos de las puestas realizadas en Argentina en los 80, en que distingue tres tendencias: una continuadora del modelo realista de los 70, otra que lo estiliza y, una última, que lo parodia.

4695 Pérez de Giuffré, Martha. El aspecto estético en el teatro jesuítico guaraní. (*Signos Univ.*, 10:19, enero/junio 1991, p. 13–31, bibl.)

La autora estudia los rasgos específicos del teatro misionero jesuítico colonial en que se combinaron formas del ritual indígena con convenciones teatrales barrocas, lo cual dio como resultado un original espectáculo sincrético muy efectivo para los fines de la evangelización.

4696 Plá, Josefina. Cuatro siglos de teatro en el Paraguay: el teatro paraguayo desde sus orígenes hasta hoy, 1544–1988. v. 2. Asunción: Univ. Católica Nuestra Señora de la Asunción, Depto. de Teatro, 1991. 1 v.: bibl., ill.

El volumen corresponde al período que la autora denomina "IV Período Independiente" (1870–1900). Se describe la actividad teatral de los grupos y compañías teatrales y su proyección sociocultural.

4697 Quackenbush, L. Howard. Pugilism as mirror and metafiction in life and contemporary Spanish American drama. (*Lat. Am. Theatre Rev.*, 26:1, Fall 1992, p. 23–41)

Interesante estudio de obras hispanoamericanas que, bajo la forma de metateatro, teatralizan el pugilismo y sus convenciones performativas para aludir metafóricamente a un contexto político-económico-social determinado.

4698 Reyes, Candelario. El movimiento teatral hondureño. (*Conjunto*/Habana, 85/86, oct. 1990/marzo 1991, p. 150–152, facsim., photos)

El autor destaca la importancia de La Comunidad Hondureña de Teatristas que, desde su fundación en 1982, ha desempeñado una importante labor organizando festivales y congresos anuales con los cuales se promueve el desarrollo del teatro regional.

4699 Reyes de la Maza, Luis. Circo, maroma y teatro, 1819–1910. México: Univ. Nacional Autónoma de México, Impr. Universitaria, 1985. 419 p.: bibl., ill. (some col.), index.

Una valiosa investigación de 100 años de espectáculo mexicano (1810–1910) que incluye teatro, circo y actos de acrobacia callejeros. El estudio considera salas de espectáculos, grupos y puestas. Incluye fotos de teatristas.

4700 Reynolds, Bonnie Hildebrand. The spectre of violence in Caribbean theatre of the eighties. (*Hisp. J.,* 12:1, Spring 1991, p. 75–85, bibl.)

Usando como fundamento teórico el conocido estudio de Ariel Dorfman sobre la violencia en América Latina, la autora estudia las obras *Huelga* del cubano Albio Paz, *Con los pies descalzos, llenos de barro* del dominicano Franz Manuel Miniño y *Cumándula* del puertorriqueño Roberto Ramos-Perea.

4701 Rodrigo, Antonina. Margarita Xirgú: su labor pedagógica y teatral en el exilio. (*in* El destierro español en América: un trasvase cultural. Recopilación de Nicolás Sánchez Albornoz. Madrid: Instituto de Cooperación Iberoamericana; Sociedad Estatal Quinto Centenario, 1991, p. 61–68)

La autora comenta la gran influencia que ejerció Xirgú como actriz, directora y pedagoga del teatro en varios países de Latinoamérica donde residió después de salir de España al exilio en 1939.

4702 Rotker, Susana. Isaac Chocrón y Elisa Lerner: los transgresores de la literatura venezolana; reflexiones sobre la identidad judía. Caracas: FUNDARTE; Alcaldía del Municipio Libertador, 1991. 129 p. (Cuadernos de difusión; 152)

Written originally as M.A. thesis (Univ. of Md.), study provides brief but insightful analysis of two major Venezuelan playwrights, Chocrón and Lerner. Introductory chapter on transgression, identity, and alienation followed by chapters on Chocrón (30 p.) and Lerner (30 p.). Appendix contains interview with Lerner and essay by Chocrón. Rotker contextualizes the Jewish identity of both writers. [R.L. Williams]

4703 Sánchez-Grey Alba, Esther. La mujer en el teatro hispanoamericano y otros ensayos. Montevideo: Univ. Católica del Uruguay Dámaso Antonio Larrañaga, 1992. 189 p.: bibl., index.

Se estudia la mujer no sólo como dramaturga sino también como personaje de obras dramáticas y narrativas escritas por autores y autoras, y como investigadora de teatro. Aunque adolece de fallas metodológicas es una útil fuente de información.

4704 Sansone de Martínez, Eneida. Orígenes del teatro nacional: el sistema del teatro histórico, 1808–1900. (*Hoy Hist.,* 7:40, julio/agosto 1990, p. 21–27)

Succinta historia del drama histórico argentino (1808–1900) en que sobresalen los textos de carácter patriótico. En un breve análisis de obras representativas, la autora utiliza el esquema actancial de Greimas.

4705 Schmidhuber de la Mora, Guillermo. Teatro e historia: parangón entre Buero Vallejo y Usigli. Monterrey, Mexico: Gobierno del Estado de Nuevo León, 1992. 86 p.: bibl. (El Mono gramático; 2)

El autor, desde la doble perspectiva del crítico y dramaturgo, estudia novedosos enlaces entre el teatro hispanoamericano y el español a través de las figuras de Rodolfo Usigli y Antonio Buero Vallejo. Aunque breve, es un serio estudio.

4706 Seibel, Beatriz. De ninfas a capitanas: mujer, teatro y sociedad: desde los rituales hasta la independencia. Buenos Aires: Editorial Legasa, 1990. 163 p. (Omnibus)

En cuatro densos capítulos se investiga la presencia de la mujer en el desarrollo del teatro argentino, desde sus orígenes precolombinos hasta 1830, teniendo en cuenta los factores contextuales que la definieron como personaje teatral, actriz o dramaturga. Cada capítulo termina con fragmentos de textos y una bibliografía mínima.

Solórzano, Carlos. Crossroads, and other plays. See item **5006**.

4707 Sotomayor Roggero, Carmela. Panorama y tendencias del teatro peruano. Lima: Herrera Editores, 1990. 120 p.: bibl., ill.

Además de una introducción muy general, incluye diez breves entrevistas a dramaturgos y actores peruanos y dos anexos, uno acerca de la historia y actividades de la Escuela Nacional de Arte Dramático (ENAD) y, otro, del programa oficial del Teatro de la Universidad Católica (TUC).

4708 Suárez Aboy, Néstor. El teatro argentino de la emancipación a Rosas, 1810–1829. (*Publ. Inst. Estud. Iberoam.*, 8:6, 1989, p. 247–274, photos)

Reseña histórica de las actividades teatrales de Argentina en los 19 primeros años de su independencia. El autor dedica especial atención a los dramaturgos Luis Ambrosio Morante y Juan Cruz Varela y a la actriz Trinidad Guevara.

4709 Tavira, Luis de. El teatro en las fronteras de la modernidad. (*Conjunto/Habana*, 85/86, oct. 1990/marzo 1991, p. 18–22)

Reflexión acerca de la relación modernidad/posmodernidad y sus implicaciones en el teatro en general. Hay una mínima referencia al teatro hispanoamericano.

4710 Teatro argentino durante el Proceso, 1976–1983: ensayos críticos, entrevistas. Edición de Juana Alcira Arancibia y Zulema Mirkin. Buenos Aires: Editorial Vinciguerra, 1992. 266 p.: bibl. (Col. Estudios hispánicos; 2)

Contiene 14 ensayos críticos de los autores más representativos del período de la dictadura, acompañados de una entrevista y bibliografía. Entre los dramaturgos estudiados figuran Cossa, Gambaro, Pavlovski, Viale, Griffero, Kartun, Monti, Gorostiza, Bortnik, Halac.

4711 Teatro Iberoamericano: historia, teoría, metodología. Edición de María de la Luz Hurtado. Santiago: Escuela de teatro de la Pontificia Univ. Católica de Chile, 1992. 337 p.

Contiene los textos completos de las ponencias presentadas al *Simposio de teoría, metodología e historia del Teatro Iberoamericano* realizado en Santiago (mayo 1991), en que participaron especialistas chilenos y extranjeros. Los textos de más interés son los que plantean nuevas propuestas teóricas y metodologías para la investigación teatral.

4712 Teatro y teatristas: estudios sobre teatro argentino e iberoamericano. Edición de Osvaldo Pellettieri. Buenos Aires: Editorial Galerna; Facultad de Filosofía y Letras (UBA), 1992. 277 p.: bibl. (Col. Estudios de teatro argentino e iberoamericano)

Incluye selección de ponencias presentadas en el I Congreso Nacional de Teatro Iberoamericano y Argentino (Buenos Aires, agosto 1991). La mayoría de los trabajos, que particularmente se refieren al teatro argentino, reflejan y ofrecen distintas perspectivas críticas.

4713 Thomas Dublé, Eduardo. El 91 en el teatro. (*Rev. Chil. Humanid.*, 12, 1991, p. 79–98)

El autor estudia cuatro obras chilenas, tres decimonónicas y una contemporánea, que comparten un mismo tema: la revolución de 1891. Se compara la producción y recepción de las obras y su particular interpretación del hecho histórico central.

4714 Thomas Dublé, Eduardo. La poética teatral de Luis Alberto Heiremans. Santiago: Red Internacional del Libro, 1992. 127 p.: bibl. (Crítica literaria)

Sistemático estudio de la trilogía de Heiremans *Versos de ciego, El abanderado,* y *El tony chico.* Una vez que sitúa al dramaturgo en su entorno socio-cultural, Thomas se concentra en lo que considera más importante: los procesos interiores de los protagonistas de la trilogía y su proyección simbólica.

4715 Vevia Romero, Fernando Carlos. La sociedad mexicana en el teatro de Rodolfo Usigli. Guadalajara, México: Univ. de Guadalajara, 1990. 185 p.: bibl.

Desde una perspectiva socio-semiótica, Vevia se propone determinar los patrones comunes que estructuran la dramaturgia de Usigli y su modo personal de registro del referente histórico-social. Dedica un capítulo especial a *El gesticulador.*

4716 Vevia Romero, Fernando Carlos. Teatro y Revolución Mexicana. Guadalajara, Mexico: Univ. de Guadalajara, 1991. 149 p.: bibl. (Col. Humanidades)

El autor selecciona y comenta las principales obras teatrales que ficcionalizan, desde distintos ángulos temáticos, los movimientos revolucionarios acaecidos en México (1910–34). Se incluyen igualmente textos de crítica social indirectamente relacionados con la revolución.

4717 Vidal, Hernán. Dictadura militar, trauma social e inauguración de la sociología del teatro en Chile. Minneapolis,

MN: Institute for the Study of Ideologies and Literature, 1991. 230 p.: bibl., index. (Literature and human rights; 8)

Provisto de un sólido fundamento teórico, Vidal reflexiona críticamente sobre las circunstancias socio-históricas que impulsaron la labor del Centro de Indagación y Expresión Cultural y Artística (CENECA) durante los años de la dictadura chilena, y su valioso aporte en el desarrollo del discurso sociológico teatral.

4718 Voces en escena: antología de dramaturgas latinoamericanas. Edición de Nora Eidelberg y María Mercedes Jaramillo. Medellín, Colombia: Univ. Antioquia, Depto. de Publicaciones, 1991. 506 p.: bibl., ill. (Col. Teatro; 2)

Contiene obras de Albalucía Angel, Patricia Ariza, Lucía Fox, Sara Joffré, Matilde Elena López, Margarita Tavera Rivera, Susana Torres Molina y Teresa Valenzuela. Todas tratan los problemas psicológicos, morales, sociales que sufre la mujer en una sociedad patriarcal.Incluye una bibliografía sobre las autoras y otra más general.

4719 Zayas de Lima, Perla. Diccionario de autores teatrales argentinos, 1950–1990. Buenos Aires: Editorial Galerna, 1991. 295 p.

Valiosa referencia que registra una completa lista de los dramaturgos argentinos de las cuatro últimas décadas. Además de datos personales de cada autor, incluye el listado de sus obras y un breve comentario de su contenido y escenificación.

BRAZIL
Novels

REGINA IGEL, *Associate Professor, Department of Spanish and Portuguese, University of Maryland, College Park*

PROFESSOR ALEXANDRINO SEVERINO of Vanderbilt University, my predecessor as contributor to the BRAZILIAN LITERATURE: NOVELS chapter of *HLAS*, died on April 25, 1993. He was diagnosed as suffering from a brain tumor, roughly one year before his death. During the years of our acquaintance we kept in touch through letters, exchange of publications, and personal meetings at congresses in this country and in Brazil. He was indefatigable in his pursuit of Brazilian and Portuguese studies in the US. I shall always remember his bright mind, his beautiful smile, his *joie de vivre*, his exceptional kindness to friends and colleagues, and his intense love of our literatures. In his honor, *Homenagem a Alexandrino Severino: essays on the Portuguese-speaking world* has been published (Austin: Host Publications, 1993, edited by Margo Milleret and Marshall C. Eakin).

The year of 1993 also marked the passing, on Sept. 13 and at age 94, of Austregésilo de Athayde, President of the Brazilian Academy of Letters. His life was almost entirely devoted to literary interests and the administration of the Academy. He became an emblematic figure at Academy gatherings and other public events.

The same year celebrated the 31st anniversary of the coveted Juca Pato Prize, awarded to the octogenarian author Rachel de Queiroz. Established by the União Brasileira de Escritores (UBE) and the newspaper *A Folha*, the prize is a tribute to the "Intelectual do Ano" who is selected by designated writers. Critic Fábio Lucas, the 1992 prize recipient, delivered the 1993 trophy to Ms. Queiroz, who began her writing career in 1930. One year earlier, Ms. Queiroz published the novel *Memorial de Maria Moura* (item **4748**), a dense narrative that constitutes the culmination of her literary career. It concerns an extraordinarily engaging woman of great determination in a world of farmers, bandits, and idle family members.

In fact, people living on farms, large tracts of land, and forests are also depicted in a significant number of novels issued during the last three years. Examples are: Carmo Bernardes' *Perpetinha: um drama nos babaçuais* (item **4722**), set in the backlands of Goiás; Francisco Dantas' *Coivara da memória* (item **4730**), a work that deals with how landowners abuse their power over the peasants in a sugarcane plantation; and Antonio Elias' *A promessa* (item **4733**), a narrative in which a man's somber memories describe his trajectory from a rural to urban setting. About the topical and tragic problems of the Amazonian region there are three strong novels: Amil Alves' *Espaço violento* (item **4721**), Paulo Jacob's *O coração da mata, dos rios, dos igarapés e dos igapós morrendo* (item **4737**), and Miguel Oliveira's *Salve o verde da esperança* (item **4746**), all of them coalescing into a collective cry of anguish that should draw attention to the destroyers of the Amazon tropical forest.

Other authors continue to pursue time-honored historical narratives such as Izaías Almada's *O medo por trás das janelas* (item **4720**), an interesting reconstruction of the intense times lived during the period of the *Inconfidência Mineira*, and Assis Brasil's two novels about foreign invasions in Brazil, *Villegagnon, paixtildeę guerra na Guanabara*, describing the French in Rio de Janeiro (item **4725**), and *Nassau, sangue e amor nos trópicos*, concerning the Dutch settlement in the region that today is part of Pernambuco state (item **4724**). Other works that are also in the spirit of reconstructing the past are Ana Maria Miranda's *O Retrato do rei* (item **4741**), a fine fictional record of the *Guerra dos Emboabas*, emboabas being Portuguese and Brazilian men who searched for gold in the colonial period. Gold diggers are also the main interest of at least one more author, Adson da Silva Costa, in *Mocororô: romance do garimpo* (item **4729**). The figure of the Martyr of Brazilian independence emerges among the gold mines to tell his story "in the first person" in Pascoal Motta's *Eu, Tiradentes* (item **4742**). The interaction of love and history is the predominant subject of Ary Quintella's *Amor que faz o mundo girar*, based on the lifestory of Giuseppe and Anita Garibaldi, the romantic Italian-Brazilian couple who fought in the *Revolução Farroupilha* (1835–45, see item **4749**).

In addition to the traditional topics noted above, Brazilian fiction also covers various other subjects that range from conflicts among Antonio Bivar's urban dwellers in *Chicabum* (item **4723**), to problems of transcontinental travelers such as those of Rubem Fonseca's protagonist in *Vastas emoções e pensamentos imperfeitos* (item **4734**), through the tribulations of Chico Buarque de Hollanda's ultrasophisticated hero in *Estorvo* (item **4726**). The latter author, one of Brazil's finest and most acclaimed composers, may, after this novel, also be recognized as a major writer.

Modern life in the US and its myriad problems are depicted in Paulo de Carvalho Neto's *Los ilustres maestros: de como a Guerra do Vietnã alienou as universidades norte-americanas* (item **4727**), a derisive record of reactions in academia to the Vietnam War while the author was a faculty member in an American university.

Also set in a foreign land is the provocative work by Ronaldo Lima Lins, *As perguntas de Gauguin* (item **4738**), which addresses various secular questions about the human condition, relationships, ideologies, and political allegiances while the protagonist travels from England to Brazil. Distant countries also serve as the setting for immigrant novels, usually in the form of memoirs about the process of adaptation to a new land. Examples are Rodolfo L. Martensen's *Danuta* (item **4740**), a love story involving the daughter of a Polish family in the south of Brazil; Fusako Tsunoda's *Canção da Amazônia: uma saga na selva* (item **4760**), a chronicle-novel about a Japanese rural community in the north of the country; and Marcos Iolovitch's *Numa clara manhã de abril* (item **4736**), a semi-biographical account of the struggle for survival of the author's Jewish family in Rio Grande do Sul.

To an extent, one can compare the anxieties and discomfort experienced by expatriates in foreign lands to the distress and alienation of certain individuals in their own countries. This is exemplified by emancipated women who have undergone the comparable uneasiness of foreigners when trying to overcome what they view as oppressive surroundings and obstacles to their personal and professional growth. Such alienation is the theme of *Celeste* (item **4731**), the *avant-la-lettre* feminist protagonist of a novel written under Maria Benedita Bormann's pseudonym "Delia." The problems portrayed in the new and revised edition of that work, a century-old novel, are still with us as attested by Judith Grossman's contemporary work *Cantos delituosos* (item **4735**). In it, a woman ruminates about the consequences of her having chosen solitude as her path. Self-evaluation is also the topic of Elisa Lispector's *Além da fronteira* (item **4739**), with the difference that here the male protagonist is the one who debates his choices in a book written by a woman; Maria Helena Póvoa's *O abismal: o nome do rosto* (item **4744**) also reports on the same process of self-exploration, but once again in a woman's voice.

In addition to the variety and skill evident in the treatment of fictional topics described above, three noteworthy books of criticism have been recently published on three important topics: Brazilian modern fiction, the formative years of our novel, and Brazilian women as writers. Modern fiction is investigated by a gathering of the most distinguished Brazilian and American critics in a book edited by Randal Johnson, *Tropical paths: essays on modern Brazilian literature* (item **4759**). Flora Süssekind, another celebrated Brazilian critic, explores the genesis of the Brazilian novel in *O Brasil não é longe daqui* (item **4753**). Finally, women are examined in Elódia Xavier's *Tudo no feminino* (item **4760a**). This anthology of critical essays includes studies that range from defining terms such as *feminina* and *feminista* to an exploration of the marginality of women in Brazilian society that sheds light on the notion of what is a "feminist identity."

Creativity in both the imaginative and critical realms is evident in the aforementioned authors who attest to the reservoir of inventiveness and originality that exists in Brazil today.

4720 Almada, Izaías. O medo por trás das janelas. São Paulo: Estação Liberdade, 1991. 256 p.

Romantic account is focused on the *Inconfidência Mineira*, an 18th-century attempt to free Brazil from Portugal. Rich in details, novel attains a sense of historical cohesiveness and an imaginative recreation of original intent to secure political autonomy, defeated at the time.

4721 Alves, Amil. Espaço violento. Rio de Janeiro: Livrarias Taurus-Timbre Editores, 1991. 141 p.

Theme is the violence and destruction prevalent in Brazilian Amazon forest. Narrative describes arrogant atmosphere of oppression imposed by landowners enjoying a lavish lifestyle in their opulent mansions, and contrasts it with the condition of a population of debilitated indigenous peoples and others living in shacks and *favelas*. Also emphasizes roles of explorers who cruised the region's great rivers and the luxuriant vegetation of the area.

4722 Bernardes, Carmo. Perpetinha: um drama nos babaçuais. Goiânia, Brazil: CEGRAF, Univ. Federal de Goiás; Editora Associada à Associação Brasileira das Editoras Universitárias, 1991. 244 p. (Publicação; 164)

History, folklore, and superstition fill the many fragmented episodes that make up this novel. Narrative reveals aspects of tightly closed world of the Brazilian *sertão* of Goiás, where a kind of palm tree (*babaçu*) grows and multiplies around shattered human lives.

4723 Bivar, Antônio. Chicabum. São Paulo: Edições Siciliano, 1991. 227 p.

Contemporary, or maybe even futuristic, version of Joaquim Manuel de Macedo's 19th-century novel *A moreninha*. Deals with young, merry partygoers in search of sex and other diversions, who are dependent on older relatives envious of their youth and fun. Replaces the romantic naïveté of the past century with the precociousness and sagacity of more recent generations who will live well into the coming century. Exposé of a segment of São Paulo society.

4724 Brasil, Assis. Nassau: sangue e amor nos trópicos; romance. Rio de Janeiro: Rio Fundo Editora, 1990. 248 p.: bibl.

This parody of the historical novel narrates Dutch conquest of Pernambuco. Filled with invented episodes based on facts familiar to Brazilians.

4725 Brasil, Assis. Villegagnon, paixão e guerra na Guanabara. Rio de Janeiro: Rio Fundo Editora, 1991. 315 p.

Historical novel revolves around the French in Brazil during period of the short-lived colony of France Antarctique (1500s). Examines and evaluates literary contributions of both Father André Thevet, a Catholic priest, and Reverend Jean de Léry, a Calvinist minister. Fictionalized account of Villegagnon's personal life and political activities attempts to establish the historical truth about his devotion to France (he was called a traitor by the two aforementioned authors); his vows of chastity (he was a member of the Order of Malta); and his love affair with Guaracy, a woman of the Tamoyo tribe.

4726 Buarque de Hollanda, Chico. Estorvo. São Paulo: Companhia das Letras, 1991. 141 p.

The accomplished author of this novel is also an acclaimed song writer and composer. Work explores the dimensions of inner isolation, solitude, and spiritual separation from others as exemplified by the male protagonist in spite of his interaction with the outside world. Translated into English (see item **5074**) and French.

4727 Carvalho Neto, Paulo de. Los ilustres maestros: de como a Guerra do Vietnã alienou as universidades norte-americanas. Petrópolis, Brazil: Vozes, 1991. 240 p. (Col. Romances Vozes)

Sarcastically depicts certain unorthodox academic activities carried out at an American university. Spanish title points to author's derision of the faculty of the Spanish department at a certain university in the US.

4728 Carvalho Neto, Paulo de. Praça Mauá: história de Alarcos e Enilda. Rio de Janeiro: F. Alves Editora, 1991. 217 p.: ill.

Stories of love among heterosexuals, homosexuals, and lesbians are interspersed with passages taken from Spanish *pliegos.* Includes numerous ironic references to the many varieties of eroticism.

4729 Costa, Adson da Silva. Mocororô: romance do garimpo. Rio de Janeiro: J. Olympio Editora, 1991. 122 p.

Narrative describes gold diggers and their paradoxical and miserable lives, a topic addressed by renowned Brazilian novelists during the last 100 years. Examples are: Bernardo Guimarães' *O garimpeiro* (1872); Herberto Sales' *Cascalho* (see *HLAS 10:3891*); and José das Neves' *Lavras diamantinas* (Salvador, Brazil: 1967).

4730 Dantas, Francisco José Costa. Coivara da memória. São Paulo: Estação Liberdade, 1991. 328 p.: ill.

Narrator's guilt underlies this memoir of times when his family ruled over plantation workers on the family's sugarcane fields and cattle farms of the Northeast. Protagonist agonizes over unpunished human rights abuses committed against these workers as he awaits his own criminal trial. Skillful use of language in the riveting and graphic descriptions of landscapes, lives of the oppressed, and acts of cruelty committed against them makes for a powerful narrative. Includes pictures of abandoned *engenhos.*

4731 Délia. Celeste. Cotejada e atualizada por Nanci Egert. Rio de Janeiro: Presença, 1988. 176 p.: bibl. (Col. Resgate; 11)

Revised re-edition issued almost 100 years after novel's publication (1893) reflects efforts of Instituto Brasileiro do Livro to revive worthy literary works from previous centuries. A precursor of the feminist novel, *Celeste* was written during the so-called Naturalist period of Brazilian fiction. From her early years Celeste rebels against the institution of marriage, having witnessed her father's physical abuse of her mother and the latter's abuse of a kind female black slave. Celeste eventually abandons her own husband and enjoys the new-found freedom of separation. This 19th-century novel addresses contemporary issues such as sex, gender, and ethnicity, topics which were unmentionable at the time either in literature or in society at large. Thus it is not surprising that the novel had an explosive impact upon publication, probably the reason Bormann hid behind the pseudonym "Délia."

4732 Dourado, Autran. Monte da Alegria. Rio de Janeiro: F. Alves, 1990. 186 p.

Another historical and engaging novel about Portugal and Brazil also includes personalities from Christian scriptures. Superficial harmony hides development of enigmatic and treacherous friendships, while ethical aspirations among family members degenerate into depraved behavior. Includes author's familiar use of symbols and allegories.

4733 Elias, Antonio. A promessa. Campinas, Brazil: Pontes, 1991. 170 p.

Concerns grim memories of a lawyer, orphaned and destitute at an early age, of his life on the farm and in the city. Wrenching tribulations tend to overwhelm an otherwise lively and interesting narrative. Novel also scrutinizes Brazilian farms and unsavory individuals such as ruthless strangers, indifferent speculators, and nasty relatives.

4734 Fonseca, Rubem. Vastas emoções e pensamentos imperfeitos. São Paulo: Companhia das Letras, 1988. 287 p.

Unusual plot, narrated in Fonseca's skeptical voice, involves filmmaker who finds a rare script and intends to convert it into a film. Combines cinematographic techniques with author's renowned narrative skills. Story takes place in Europe and Brazil.

4735 Grossmann, Judith. Cantos delituosos. Rio de Janeiro: Editora Nova Fronteira; Instituto Nacional do Livro, Fundação Nacional Pró-Memória, 1985. 253 p.

Finely crafted story deals with heterosexual love, companionship, and the choice of loneliness. From specific feelings and thoughts, narrator/author gradually and successfully attains total abstraction. Dense novel captures concept of how spiritual and physical love can coexist with solitude.

4736 Iolovitch, Marcos. Numa clara manhã de abril. Prefácio de Moacyr Scliar. 2. ed. rev. Porto Alegre, Brazil: Movimento, 1987. 114 p. (Col. Rio Grande; 87)

Author's only book describes, in bitter voice and direct style, harsh conditions experienced by immigrant family brought to Rio Grande do Sul in early 20th century by the Jewish Colonization Association. Moacyr

Scliar's preface to this revised edition emphasizes this documentary novel's importance as a chronicle of a crucial period of Jewish immigration to Brazil. Narrative attests to author's affinity with Schopenhauer's nihilism.

4737 Jacob, Paulo. O coração da mata, dos rios, dos igarapés e dos igapós morrendo. Rio de Janeiro: Nórdica, 1991. 107 p.

Novel focuses on Brazilian Amazon and ongoing destruction of its tropical forest and resources by predatory humans. Explains many regional terms.

4738 Lins, Ronaldo Lima. As perguntas de Gauguin. Rio de Janeiro: Francisco Alves, 1988. 219 p.

Reminiscent of Machado de Assis' intriguing speculations about life, novel revolves around an existential probe resulting from an act of vandalism in an art gallery and the search for the perpetrators. Simultaneously, protagonist seeks for balance in his life, or for what he refers to as "the art of living."

4739 Lispector, Elisa. Além da fronteira. Rio de Janeiro: J. Olympio Editora, 1988. 102 p.: ill.

First published in 1945, novel redeems much abused romantic search for life's meaning, as a male character awakens and evaluates his own life.

Macedo, Joaquim Manuel de. As vítimas-algozes: quadros da escravidão: romances. See item **3351.**

4740 Martensen, Rodolfo Lima. Danuta. São Paulo: T.A. Queiroz, 1988. 252 p.

Novel recounts traumatic love story set in the Polish settlement in Paraná. Protagonists Danuta and Augusto are described in the context of the community's daily activities, folkloric celebrations, religious festivals, and ethnic prejudices.

4741 Miranda, Ana Maria. O retrato do rei. São Paulo: Companhia das Letras, 1991. 375 p.

Fictional interpretation of historical events portrays emotional atmosphere surrounding 18th-century confrontation between Portuguese and Brazilian forces for control of gold mines, an episode known as the *Guerra dos Emboabas.*

4742 Motta, Pascoal. Eu, Tiradentes. Belo Horizonte, Brazil: Editora Lê, 1990. 192 p. (Romances da história)

Work is fictionalized account of Tiradentes' life and times. Caught conspiring against Portuguese colonizers, Tiradentes became known as the Martyr of Brazilian Independence. Glossary explains author's use of Baroque terms, historical references, and "personal reminiscences."

4743 Noll, João Gilberto. Hotel Atlântico. Rio de Janeiro: Rocco, 1989. 98 p.

Neither the hotel of the title nor the plot are as important as the language and narrative pace of this novel. In the course of his peripatetic and macabre story, protagonist searches for an undefined something that might be reached when his trajectory comes to an end.

4744 Nóvoa, Maria Helena. O abismal: o nome do rosto. São Paulo: Melhoramentos, 1986. 181 p.

In this highly symbolic work characters are named Fenelon, Libertad, Homero, and Olímpia. Concerns both the Brazilian political process and a woman's self-discovery made possible only after her mother's death. Awarded the Nestlé Biennial Literature Prize for 1986.

4745 Olinto, Antônio. Trono de vidro. Rio de Janeiro: Nórdica, 1987. 382 p.

Work is final volume of trilogy composed of *A casa da água* (see *HLAS 32:4762*) and *O rei de Keto* (Rio de Janeiro: 1980). All three deal with topic of return to Africa of former slaves and their descendants in Brazil. One woman becomes a political leader in the new-old country of Zorei. African mores and traditions control and surround her personal life and the society she leads.

4746 Oliveira, Miguel. Salve o verde da esperança: romance-ensaio. Belém, Brazil: Cultural CEJUP, 1990. 130 p.

Another novel about the Amazon region in which the main character is the region itself, described as an entity in need of protection from the human predators of today.

4747 Pinaud, João Luiz Duboc. Tempo de família. São Paulo: Global Editora; Brasília: Instituto Nacional do Livro, Fundação Nacional Pró-Memória/MINC, 1986. 303 p.

Exploration of time and memory notes the implacable passage of the former in an old family clock, and contrasts it with the characters' attempts to hold time in their own memory. Reminiscent of Osman Lins' *Avalovara* (São Paulo: 1973) and the *noveau roman*.

4748 Queiroz, Rachel de. Memorial de Maria Moura. São Paulo: Editora Siciliano, 1992. 482 p.

An astounding literary and commercial success, this latest novel by the renowned octogenarian author is set in the epic Northeast. Queiroz excels in her description of Maria Moura, a shrewd female chieftain-warrior with a soft spot for the destitute. In pursuing her goal of accumulating large tracts of land, she provokes both admiration and distress as she turns the *sertão* around. Novel attests to the cultural, sociological, and psychological heterogeneity of this Brazilian region.

4749 Quintella, Ary. Amor que faz o mundo girar. Belo Horizonte, Brazil: Editora Lê, 1990. 166 p. (Romances da história)

Novel describes a historical and legendary couple, Italian liberator Giuseppe Garibaldi and his Brazilian companion Anita (who died at age 28). Having left her husband for Garibaldi, Anita is portrayed as committing the preeminent act of independence, thus becoming a lasting symbol of female liberation from the conventions of her times. Based on historical documents and enriched by a glossary of southern Brazilian terms.

4750 Rodrigues, Francisco Pereira. Desumana solidão. Porto Alegre, Brazil: Martins Livreiro-Editor, 1985. 96 p.

Novel recounts the country-to-city exodus in industrialized Brazil. Encompasses the development of slums, indifference of urban dwellers, and misery and isolation experienced by a family of peasant migrants.

4751 Samuel, Heli. O médico que sonhava com Estefânia. Rio de Janeiro: Livraria Editora Cátedra, 1987. 104 p.

An extended argument for homeopathy as a form of alternative medicine, this *roman à clef* introduces as secondary characters eminent Brazilians who favor application of this medical practice as a method of prevention and cure. Novel serves as means to convey author's convictions about a controversial topic.

4752 Studart, Heloneida. O torturador em romaria. Rio de Janeiro: Rocco, 1986. 235 p.

Author continues to dwell on subject of Brazil's military dictatorship and its consequences. Depicts a repentant ex-prison torturer on his way to the shrine of Padre Cícero, in Juazeiro, in search of absolution. Mysticism and misery permeate flashbacks of the protagonist's story during his pilgrimage.

4753 Süssekind, Flora. O Brasil não é longe daqui: o narrador, a viagem. São Paulo: Cia. das Letras, 1990. 319 p.: bibl.

Renowned literary critic adopts unusual colloquial narrative voice to examine origins of Brazilian prose fiction. Uses an allegorical path to identify literature as a map charted by authors during first 40 years of 19th century. Invaluable bibliography and interesting comments in footnotes further enhance this scholarly and accessible study.

4754 Telles, Vera. Josefa do Furquim. Rio de Janeiro: F. Alves Editora, 1991. 448 p.

Farmers, priests, noblemen, planters, and slaves parade across a Brazilian colonial landscape. Protagonist-narrator alternates letters to her daughter with accounts of her family's roots and her personal views on current events, as well as with her own attempts to survive the isolation and male domination of her rural world.

4755 Tezza, Cristóvão. Juliano Pavollini. Rio de Janeiro: Editora Record, 1989. 176 p.

Young writer's *bildungsroman*, set in Curitiba, Paraná, describes two years in the life of a teenager, focusing on his debut in a world of crime, corruption, and sex. Substitutes linear telling with innovative maze of communications between author, reader, narrator, and listener.

4756 Tezza, Cristóvão. A suavidade do vento. Rio de Janeiro: Editora Record, 1991. 204 p.

Artist's proverbial solitude is intensified by demands on author, who is also a professor, painter, visionary, and dreamer. Surrounded by real people and imaginary entities, protagonist draws ideas for plots and characters for this novel, a process resulting in an intricate and paradoxical construct about the making of a novel and the actual experience of living it.

4757 Torres, Antônio. Um táxi para Viena d'Austria. São Paulo: Companhia das Letras, 1991. 180 p.

Irony and plain humor frame fictional account of urban afflictions of an unemployed advertising man who tries to control his present situation. While sitting in a taxi, he is transformed into a mythological flying object.

4758 Trevisan, João Silvério. O livro do avesso. São Paulo: Ars Poética, 1992. 213 p.: ill. (Col. Ficção: Série Modernos; 1)

Unconventional, eclectic, exotic, and yet paradoxically simple and linear narrative unfolds as a tale told by both author and character. Control of the telling by these two voices is graphically represented by the narrators starting from opposite ends of the volume and meeting at the center. Author's voice tells us about the lives of thieves, pimps, fugitives from the law, etc., whereas the character's voice tells us about great artists, poets, and writers, most of whom address the subject of plagiarism.

4759 Tropical paths: essays on modern Brazilian literature. Edited by Randal Johnson. New York: Garland Pub., 1993. 233 p.: bibl. (Latin American studies; 2. Garland reference library of the humanities; 1555)

Essays by eminent Brazilian and some American critics includes works by: Haroldo de Campos on José Alencar; João Alexandre Barbosa on Machado de Assis; Pedro Maligo on Márcio Souza; Affonso Romano de Sant'Anna on Adalgisa Nery; Walnice Nogueira Galvão on Guimarães Rosa; Massaud Moisés on Osman Lins; Fábio Lucas on Autran Dourado and Darcy Ribeiro; and Randal Johnson on film and politics in Brazil. Major contribution to literary criticism concerns the most important Brazilian works of fiction and their authors.

4760 Tsunoda, Fusako. Canção da Amazônia: uma saga na selva. Tradução de Jorge Kassuga. Rio de Janeiro: F. Alves, 1988. 185 p.

Female author used her research on Japanese immigration in northern Brazil as basis for a documentary novel. Originally written in Japanese, author emphasizes trials and tribulations as well as successes of the immigrants in the harvesting of black pepper in the Amazon. She also describes uprisings of settlers against their bosses or immigration sponsors. Kassuga's excellent Portuguese translation should be commended.

4760a Tudo no feminino. Compilação de Elódia Xavier. Rio de Janeiro: F. Alves Editora, 1991. 149 p.: bibl.

Essays suggest innovative approaches to global feminist thought. Articles advance a Brazilian perspective on women as literary subjects and authors.

Short Stories

MARIA ANGELICA GUIMARÃES LOPES, *Associate Professor, Department of Spanish, Italian, and Portuguese, University of South Carolina, Columbia*

THE NUMBER OF SHORT STORIES PUBLISHED in the last four years continues to decline, a trend that began in the early 1980s. The previous proliferation of stories attested to the reading public's interest as well as to the venturesome spirit of publishing houses. The present reduction can be attributed to Brazil's economic problems which, in turn, are having a beneficial effect in that mediocre books are no longer being published.

Established writers continue to produce fine works (items **4773, 4775, 4779, 4784,** and **4798**), many of which reveal a new mellowness and compassion mingled with humor, in stark contrast to the more judgmental stories of past years and their castigation of bourgeois sins. As can be expected, the long shadow of 20 years of military rule compounded by the 1970s economic debacle are no longer dominant; the evils of dictatorship appear only in isolated stories. However, one wonders whether the 1992 Collor operetta and its consequences will generate another wave of cynicism in future stories.

The 50 or so books selected for *HLAS 54* are of aesthetic, technical, and topical interest. They can be classified according to various criteria, including ideology, subject matter, and geography. There are fewer manifestations of ideological trends than in previous years. Feminist writers (e.g., items **4763, 4804, 4785,** and **4803**) are less "engagé" than those pursuing Afro-Brazilian themes. For example, in Vol. 14 of *Cadernos Negros* (item **4766**) the *Quilombhoje* movement (see *HLAS 52: 4581*) attests to the earnestness and vitality of Brazil's black movement today, as do the Afro-Brazilian writers Rodrigues and Assis in their stories (items **4765** and **4797**). Other collections deal with racial, sexual, and other social injustices, topics that Guimarães, in particular, examines with gravity and literary power (item **4778**).

As usual, important collections have been reprinted for use in college entrance exams and courses. Others have been issued as homages to their authors. Some contemporary ones have become classics such as Lispector's *A legião estrangeira*, now in its 10th printing (São Paulo: Editora Siciliano, 1992), and Fonseca's *Coleira de cão*, currently in its 4th printing (São Paulo: Companhia das Letras, 1991). Another scholarly edition of stories by the great Machado de Assis has been exquisitely printed and illustrated and is available as part of Livraria Garnier's *Coleção dos autores célebres da literatura brasileira*. The original editions of these works have been annotated in previous *Handbooks*. João do Rio, long considered a premodernist, has shown interest in the cultural and aesthetic aspects of early 20th-century Rio de Janeiro in his recent two volumes, one of which is a scholarly edition (item **4796**). Literary homages to outstanding living and deceased writers offer new anthologies of their work: Coutinho (item **4770**), Pólvora (item **4792**), and Ramos (item **4793**). Other successful authors who have reissued collections modified by the inclusion of new stories and new titles are exemplified by L.F.Telles (item **4805**) and J.U. Ribeiro (item **4794**).

Some new authors continue to experiment and receive literary prizes such as those from Paraná state, Nestlé, and Guimarães Rosa. The writers Capistrano (item **4767**), Ganem (item **4776**), Coelho (item **4768**), and Strausz (item **4804**) are daring and postmodernist in their approach and themes, while others succeed in presenting viable surrealistic fables (items **4802, 4786, 4787,** and **4788**). These attempts have been original and successful, a feat if one considers the pervasiveness of magic realism in the last two decades, not all of it good literature.

Stories portraying consistent violence (item **4772**) or eroticism (items **4767, 4790,** and **4771**) illustrate two other minor but significant trends

In a country where the climate ranges from tropical summer in the north to winter in the south, it would seem appropriate to organize fiction according to geographic regions. Nonetheless, regionalism is not a limiting factor as Graciliano Ramos, Guimarães Rosa, and others have shown. Even though linguistic practice and peculiarities particular to a region may hinder a reader's comprehension, the challenge should not deter his or her interest. Two Amazonian writers annotated below are of more topical than literary value. Of the two, it is the apprentice M.P. Ribeiro (item **4795**) and not the celebrated writer Engrácio (item **4772**) whose ecological concerns move readers. Several northeastern states have issued collections on their unique region, a civilization nourished by medieval lore and feudal traditions commonly celebrated in improvised song and poetry. Ceará's Maciel (item **4786**) and Pinto (item **4791**) deliver the sentiment and verve one associates with this area of Brazil. Tales by Pernambuco's Arraes (item **4764**), Felinto (item **4774**), Lemos (item **4784**), and Souto Maior (item **4802**) echo life in big cities and canefields in themes and styles that are uniquely varied. Bahia is represented by Pólvora (item **4792**) and Ribeiro (item **4794**). The *sertão*, that mythical yet real arid territory encompassing many states in addition to northeastern ones, is featured in tales by Goiás' writers Coralina (item **4769**) and Vieira (item **4808**); by Minas Gerais' writers Pereira da Silva (item **4801**), Kleinsorge (item **4782**), and Melo (item **4788**); and São Paulo's writer Junqueira (item **4780**). The Paulista writers Lygia and Sérgio Telles (items **4805** and **4806**) deal with their huge industrial city in which factory workers, corporate managers, intellectuals, and artists lead accelerated and stressful lives. The Rio de Janeiro featured in Sant'Anna's work (item **4798**), shares much with João do Rio's vision of the city. Worthy representatives of the south who convey its rich history and folklore are Faraco (item **4773**), Kiefer (item **4781**), Schlee (item **4800**), and Todt (item **4807**).

To conclude, we must register a sad note: Brazilian literature recently lost two important story writers, Ricardo Ramos and Otto Lara Resende. Both have been posthumously honored by anthologies. Resende's *O elo partido* (São Paulo: Editora Atica, 1992) consists of a selection from his magnificent, *As pompas do mundo* (see *HLAS 38:7399*).

4761 Adam, Lízia Pessin. Alfonso e eu. Porto Alegre, Brazil: IGEL; Instituto Estadual do Livro, 1989. 107 p. (Nova literatura)
Powerful, relentless, and authoritative stories develop extreme situations regarding illicit love and hatred leading to climactic deaths. Well-crafted, suspenseful, and often laden with horror, these stories are a tour-de-force and one of the strongest collections of the last three years.

4762 Aquino, Marçal. As fomes de setembro: contos. São Paulo: Estação Liberdade & Fundação Nestlé de Cultura, 1991. 86 p.

Meditative and hypothetical stories are ironic with good humor and warmth. Fine book awarded prestigious prize.

4763 Arêas, Vilma Sant'Anna. A terceira perna. São Paulo: Editora Brasiliense, 1992. 105 p.: ill. (Espaço brasileiro)
Stories by poet and novelist are as unusual as collection's title, as well as "ambiguous and grotesque" (C. Alvim). Tales are also strangely realistic, as if reader suddenly realized that next door a new universe began, with natural laws that coincide with ours. Author's stylistic innovations make for challenging reading.

4764 Arraes, Luiz. O rastejador. Recife, Brazil: FUNDARPE, 1991. 84 p. (Oficina Espaço Pasárgada; 15)

Able writer from Pernambuco encapsules incidents and characters in very short, defined, skillful and wry tales. Theme concerns change in feelings that prevents meetings between lovers and would-be lovers. *Rastejador* (tracker) from title story is unofficial detective who finds both lovers and criminals.

4765 Assis, Anatólio Alves de. Ultimo baile da Ilha Fiscal. Belo Horizonte, Brazil: Impr. Oficial de Minas Gerais, 1988. 273 p.

Collection's interest is twofold: 1) use of Brazilian history as background and narrative; and 2) portrayal of blacks and mulattoes as elite protagonists. Author's patriotism and his pride in African ancestry and culture are evident in extensive literary allusions, poetical quotes, and anecdotes. Told in traditional manner, stories recreate Brazil in the 19th and 20th centuries.

4766 *Cadernos Negros.* Vol. 14, 1991- . São Paulo: Quilombhoje.

Work includes good quality fiction by black Brazilians from *Quilombhoje* movement (see *HLAS 52:4581* and *HLAS 52: 4819*). Authors are Conceição Evaristo, Cuti, Esmeralda Ribeiro, and Oubi Inaê Kibuko. Their styles and themes are different, but all focus on dignity and richness of Afro-Brazilian life notwithstanding major social problems.

4767 Capistrano, Rui Werneck de. Máquina de escrever: contos. Curitiba, Brazil: Governo do Paraná, Secretaria de Estado da Cultura; Editora Ghignone, 1988. 184 p.: ill.

Winner of the prestigious Concurso Nacional de Contos prize for the state of Paraná, this is a witty, joyous, playful, and erotic melange. Topics range from T.S. Eliot translation to cartoon quotes to minimalist and concrete poems to actual short stories. Work is paean to traditional typewriter, as indicated by title, theme, and illustrations. Erotic story transforms typewriter into luscious black woman and writer into potent macho à la Mailer. Although original and clever, author's invention often takes precedence over organization. Collection would have benefitted from a strict editor.

4768 Coelho, Flávio. Contos que conto: contos. São Paulo: Estação Liberdade & Fundação Nestlé de Cultura, 1991. 78 p.

Author is a writer to watch. Unusual narrative angle is conveyed through stylistic minimalism. Portrays daily life as absurd and unrecognizable as if seen from the wrong end of a telescope. Some stories are surrealistic à la Buñuel (e.g., passenger is unable to leave bus, peanut bar makes male soccer player pregnant). A distinguished, accomplished, and exciting book.

4769 Coralina, Cora. O tesouro da casa velha. Seleção de Dalila Teles Veras. São Paulo: Global Editora, 1989. 98 p.

Work by famous Goiás poet who at age 91 was discovered by Carlos Drummond de Andrade in 1981. With only a second-grade education, Cora was able to write worthwhile stories of old Goiás, the Brazilian far west. All are inspired with generous insight, suspense, and good endings. More importantly, all ring true.

4770 Coutinho, Edilberto. Amor na boca do túnel: antologia. Seleção e apresentação de Silviano Santiago. Rio de Janeiro: Tempo Brasileiro, 1992. 136 p.: bibl.

Anthology by one of Brazil's finest short story tellers written with humor and compassion. Many stories deal with soccer, Coutinho's classic theme. As expected, a very good book.

4771 Cruz, Ricardo. Benditos perversos: contos. Salvador, Brazil: Fator Editora, 1990. 121 p.

These "blessed perverts" are stories about erotic situations under a magnifying glass. Cruz recreates psychological motivation and explores unusual circumstances: incest, lesbianism, and spirit possession, among others. Very well done and, true to its title, sufficiently perverse.

4772 Engrácio, Arthur. Outras estórias de submundo: contos. Manaus, Brazil: Edições Governo do Estado, Superintendência Cultural do Amazonas, 1988. 183 p.

"Underworld" in these "other" Amazonian stories is more brutal and unforgiving than the usual fictional territory of this acclaimed author. Aggressive and melodramatic, these tales resemble a journalistic *feuilleton* more than literature.

4773 Faraco, Sérgio. Majestic Hotel. Porto Alegre, Brazil: L&PM Editores, 1991. 84 p. (Col. Olho da rua)

Fine anthology attests again to author's ability. With a sure hand, and in limpid though dramatic prose, Faraco examines children and adults in different stages and circumstances. Most stories deal with family relations that are relatively harmonious; others tell of sordid situations which, thanks to author's mastery, elicit compassion. Not to be missed. One of the finest collections published within the last three years.

4774 Felinto, Marilene. Postcard. São Paulo: Iluminuras, 1991. 113 p.

Work by author of prize-winning novels is an exciting, accomplished, poetic, dramatic, and varied collection. Topics range from child meeting blind beggars in canefield to postcard sent to lover in foreign city. Extremely well-written by "the great writer of her young generation." Not to be missed.

4775 Fonseca, Rubem. Romance negro e outras histórias. São Paulo: Companhia das Letras, 1992. 188 p.

Celebrated author continues previous work with some innovations (e.g., mellowness). Title story ("negro" as in "noir") is a thriller, as are "A Santa de Schöneberg" and "O Livro de Panegíricos." These stories belong to Fonseca's turf of mystery-cum-history characteristic of his latest novels, *Bufo & Spallanzani* (translated into English by Clifford Landers, see *HLAS 52:5038*), *Vastas emoções e pensamentos imperfeitos*, and *Agosto*. "A Recusa dos Carniceiros" deals with capital punishment as a legislative issue in 19th-century Brazil. In "Labaredas nas Trevas," a mock Joseph Conrad diary concerns his envy of dead Stephen Crane's writing. Jewel among these fine tales is "A Arte de Andar nas Ruas do Rio de Janeiro," a loving, humorous portrayal of bohemian diehards in 1980s Rio as seen through a 1940s perspective.

4776 Ganem, Eliane. A medida do possível. Rio de Janeiro: Livraria Agir Editora, 1989. 99 p.

Title novella consists of lively, intriguing, puzzle in which metamorphoses and mysteries remind reader of Kafka, Lewis Carroll, and Murilo Rubião. In first story, huge man leads several lives, and is also frozen,

melted, burnt, and turned into a dwarf. Other stories are also fast paced and deal with metamorphoses. Exciting collection.

4777 Giudice, Victor. Salvador janta no Lamas: contos. Rio de Janeiro: J. Olympio, 1989. 155 p.

Superbly inventive stories by author of *Os banheiros*, who has masterful control over the fantastic and a grim view of humanity, as if watching it from another planet. Title story examines how the ordinary can be dispelled by despair and joy. Giudice is evolving stylistically and even ideologically (traces of feminism in two of the stories).

4778 Guimarães, Geni. Leite do peito: contos. São Paulo: Fundação Nestlé de Cultura, 1988. 87 p.

Title of this outstanding collection may give a clue as to Nestle's sponsorship. Nevertheless, work is much more than a La Leche catechism even if first story *is* about breast feeding. Simplicity and narrative agility such as the author's are rare indeed. Autobiographical narratives take reader through author's early childhood to schoolteaching days. Not the least of its merits is narrator's family portrait.

4779 João Antônio. Guardador: contos. Rio de Janeiro: Civilização Brasileira, 1992. 122 p.

Prestigious author specializes in lives of poor and artists. A mellower João Antônio can be gleaned in this collection. In "Tatiana Pequena," a sensual, delicate, sentimental, and effective story, narrator regrets his beloved's wedding to another and muses on a dirty, poor, and hot Copacabana. "O Guardador" is closer to author's previous tales about social injustice. Fine collection.

4780 Junqueira, Eduardo Diniz. A historia soluçada de Juvêncio Novaes e outros contos. São Paulo: Editora Uyara, 1988. 119 p.

Includes seven regional stories about the *sertão* told in elegant but picturesque style. First tale is written as a poem in which migrant worker Juvêncio Novaes talks movingly about his difficult life.

4781 Kiefer, Charles. Um outro olhar: contos. Porto Alegre, Brazil: Mercado Aberto, 1992. 140 p.

Written by prize-winning story writer and novelist, most of these tales take place in

Pau d'Arco, a fictitious *gaúcho* town whose population Kiefer examines carefully. Excellent collection reveals able writer's perception, sensitivity, and irony. First-class entertainment.

4782 Kleinsorge, Sérgio. De nonada a travessia: contos. Belo Horizonte, Brazil: Impr. Oficial de Minas Gerais, 1991. 123 p.

Work is recipient of 13th Guimarães Rosa Prize. Both titles and well-written tales evoke the great writer. Stories are hermetic, eerie, and peopled by ethereal characters.

4783 Kuyumjian Neto, Minas. Na hora agá: contos. Ilustrações de Sérgio Nakayama. São Paulo: Clip, 1990. 324 p.: ill.

Many of the stories are thematically and stylistically linked through use of monologues by different characters leading difficult lives. Author is a ventriloquist of sorts: protagonists all seem real, part of one's experience. Characters labor and suffer in an indifferent and unfair universe.

4784 Lemos, Gilvan. A inocente farsa da vingança: novelas e contos. São Paulo: Estação Liberdade, 1991. 232 p.

Four moving and lively novellas and 12 stories by distinguished author tell about children's experiences in the Northeast. Sophisticated narrative imbued with nostalgia. Title story and others end in death.

4785 Lobo, Luiza. A maçã mordida: contos. Rio de Janeiro?: Numen Editora, 1992? 158 p.

Departure for fiction writer and critic from her fantastic realm (see *HLAS 40:7443*). These tales are semi-autobiographical, longer, and told from a Latin American historical perspective. They make for good reading and are written with author's usual aplomb.

4786 Maciel, Nilto. As insolentes patas do cão. São Paulo: João Scortecci Editora, 1991. 107 p.

Competent, lively, varied, and well-written tales cover a wide range of styles from realism to magic realism as they deal with humans and with several animals other than dogs. "O Menino e o Bacamarte" is an especially good story.

4787 Mascarenhas, Alexandre. Abra a boca e cale o bico. Brasília: Thesaurus, 1992? 78 p.: ill.

Title does not convey collection's qual-

ity or subject matter. Author's explanation is more appropriate: stories are playful, meditative, and elegant, their perspective surreal. Some themes: old woman and her telepathic rocking chair; ex-acrobat becomes barber; crime perpetrated on airplane; minuscule women and men appearing at bedtime to tell stories to children.

4788 Melo, João Batista. O inventor de estrelas: contos. Belo Horizonte, Brazil: Impr. Oficial de Minas Gerais, 1991. 83 p.

Admirable collection consists of dramatic stories of metamorphoses and other portents written in a smooth style. Reminiscent of that practitioner of the fantastic, J.J. Veiga, whose epigraph is used here. Highly recommended.

4789 Moraes, Marilena *et al*. A palavra em construção. Rio de Janeiro: Carioca Engenharia; Sanenge; Christiani-Nielsen, 1992. 143 p.: photos.

Handsome volume compiles stories by six able young authors and pictures by seven fine photographers. Unusual product of collaboration between business and academia, book was subsidized by three engineering companies; thus the pun in its title.

4790 Neves, Luiz Guilherme Santos. Torre do delírio. Vitória, Brazil?: Depto. Estadual de Cultura, Secretaria de Educação e Cultura, 1992. 79 p.: ill.

Erotic collection, handsomely illustrated, consists of short, bizarre, and elegant pieces. In one, a female character visits the narrator in his tower for a dalliance. Characters are allegorical, mysterious, and ghostly. Author attributes major influence to Jorge Luis Borges, who would be surprised at the erotic content. Entertaining.

4791 Pinto, José Alcides. Senhora Maria Hermínia, morte e vida agoniada: a saga da violência; contos. 2. ed. Fortaleza, Brazil: Impr. Oficial do Ceará, 1988. 144 p.: map.

Book from Ceará, where medieval Portuguese legends survive mixed with indigenous and African lore reminiscent of the "ballads on a string" sold at fairs. Although supposedly autobiographical, characters are very colorful, especially Senhora Maria Hermínia ("Tia Véia"), the narrator's grandmother, a matriarch who has bowlegs from riding a donkey to visit relatives.

4792 Pólvora, Hélio. Xerazade. Ed. comemorativa dos 30 anos de atividade literária do autor. Rio de Janeiro: J. Olympio Editora, 1989. 103 p.

Written by one of Brazil's ablest story tellers, work exhibits fine plotting, dramatic flair, vigorous language, and author's special talent for revealing the grandeur of humble lives. Marvelous "Chico e Natália" tells of two spouses and their marriage. "Aquém do Umbral," reprinted here, is a small gem. Book is fitting celebration of author's 30th literary anniversary.

4793 Ramos, Ricardo. Matar um homem. 2a. ed. São Paulo: Editora Siciliano, 1992. 172 p.

As tribute to deceased author, his peers have compiled this anthology of stories from several decades. Son of noted Brazilian author Graciliano Ramos, Ricardo Ramos excelled in his own genre. His powerful and elegant tales depict, among others, urban intellectuals in São Paulo.

4794 Ribeiro, João Ubaldo. Já podeis da pátria filhos e outras histórias. Rio de Janeiro: Editora Nova Fronteira, 1991. 200 p.

Two new stories have been added to author's *Livro de histórias* (see *HLAS 46: 6128*) with a title change (actually, the first line of 1822 independence hymn by Emperor Pedro I). Concerns mainly Bahia, its people, cattle, and other animals.

4795 Ribeiro, Manoel Paes. O bicho-homem, esse covarde. Tradução para o inglês de Bianca Portela Lopes Chiavicatti. Brasília: Editora Menino do Mato, 1992. 147 p: photos.

Well-intentioned product of the times, work is oddity which includes extravagant English translation. Author's culprit is *bicho-homem* (translated as "worm-man"), whose greed and depravity endanger the planet. Written by earnest author with heart in the right place, who has experienced Amazonian life as milkman, rubber-tapper, mule driver, water carrier, lumberjack.

4796 Rio, João do. João do Rio. Seleção de Helena Parente Cunha. São Paulo: Secretaria de Estado da Cultura; Global Editora, 1990. 156 p. (Melhores contos; 15)

Stories by famous journalist whose pen name attests to his allegiance to his city. This is Rio in the belle époque period of modernization before World War I, a mysterious place where vices abound (gambling, drug addiction, nymphomania, among others), but where elegance and the arts are prized. Prefatory study and selection by noted critic and novelist Helena Parente Cunha.

4797 Rodrigues, Eustáquio José. Flor de sangue: contos. Belo Horizonte, Brazil: Mazza Edições, 1990. 112 p.

Realistic and well-told tales focus on black Brazilians at home and abroad. Certainly worth reading.

4798 Sant'Anna, Sérgio. Breve história do espírito. São Paulo: Companhia das Letras, 1991. 118 p.

Three novellas written by master story teller. Ironic and well constructed title novella explores dilemma of writer living in a commercial world in which many people are unemployed. Others deal with battle of the sexes, Protestant fundamentalism in modern Brazil, business practices (including funerals). Word *espírito* is used with different connotations (e.g., spirit, alcohol, wit). First two stories are superb.

4799 Sarney Costa, Ivan. Na boca da noite. São Paulo: Global Editora, 1988. 123 p.: ill. (Singular & plural)

Stories about northern state of Maranhão written in elegant, limpid Portuguese.

4800 Schlee, Aldyr Garcia. Linha divisória. São Paulo: Melhoramentos, 1988. 104 p.

For Schlee, the *"linha divisória"* lies "... entre Jaguarão [river on the Brazilian/Uruguayan border] e o resto do mundo." Compelling author creates eccentric, shady, and impressive regional characters which are also truly universal. Recommended reading.

4801 Silva, Antônio Pereira da. Sianinha e outros casos: contos. Uberlândia, Brazil?: Academia Uberlandense de Letras e Artes, 1988. 86 p.

Deceptively simple, fine stories are written with drama, humor, and inventiveness. Unsophisticated country or small-town characters ring psychologically true. Includes outstanding stories, especially "Bela" about a retarded girl dreaming up boyfriends.

4802 Souto Maior, Armando. O gato paralelo. Recife, Brazil: FUNDARPE, 1989. 146 p. (Biblioteca comunitária de Pernambuco: Conto; 01)

Stories by Pernambuco historian are a pleasant surprise. Fantastic, psychological, serious, and humorous tales unfold before a carefully crafted background.

4803 Souza, Aglaia. Vida fêmea. Brasília: Thesaurus/ASEFE, 1991. 80 p.
Collection's first part consists of tales about psychological and physiological states ably narrated by talented author. Imprecise narrative eventually focuses on remembered incidents: (e.g., automobile and other accidents, abortion, etc.) Author's social commitment to working class is clear in stories from second part; however, literary achievement here is not as evident as in the first part.

4804 Strausz, Rosa Amanda. Mínimo múltiplo comum: contos. Rio de Janeiro: J. Olympio Editora, 1990. 63 p.
Elegant, wry, and analytical, these stories were defined as "minimalist" by V. Giudice. They are the "minimal common multiple," a pun on "lowest common denominator." Excellent collection of poetical and focused prose haikus.

4805 Telles, Lygia Fagundes. A estrutura da bolha de sabão: contos. Rio de Janeiro: Editora Nova Fronteira, 1991. 203 p.
Previously published under title *Filhos pródigos* (São Paulo: 1978), work was given new title after being translated into French and receiving important prize. Tales reveal unsuspected angles in family relationships. Very fine work by one of Brazil's most durable and distinguished fiction writers.

4806 Telles, Sérgio. Mergulhador de Acapulco: contos. Rio de Janeiro: Imago Editora, 1992. 165 p. (Série Ficção e experiência interior)
São Paulo atmosphere predominates in this well-developed, meticulous, dense, and ultimately sound collection, faithful to title of its literary series. Many characters are dissident ex-university students and ex-hippies uncomfortable in their new social positions and regretting having abandoned their youthful dreams as the price of attaining power, status, and comfort. Variety of situations and characters is one of the collection's virtues. Another is the intelligence and strength of the stories.

4807 Todt, Erwin. Selos da Bolívia: contos. Porto Alegre, Brazil: Martins Livreiro-Editor, 1987. 70 p.
Profoundly humane writer tells of minor and major catastrophes befalling Rio Grande do Sul families. Conveys illness and death in natural, colloquial style. Title story is fine account of jealousy infusing a lifelong friendship between two male characters. Fine collection.

4808 Vieira, Delermando. A luz das velas de sebo. Goiânia, Brazil: Secretaria de Cultura da Prefeitura de Goiânia, 1990. 111 p.
According to title, prize-winning stories were either written, or should be read, by candlelight. Extraordinary stories rich in linguistic complexity establish delicately crafted backgrounds. Odd characters perform equally odd actions. One of the most distinguished and distinctive books written in the last three years.

4809 Yunes, Márcio Jabur. Duelo em Aguas de São Pedro. São Paulo: Secretaria de Estado da Cultura; Art Editora, 1990. 150 p.
Author's wry humor, enviable narrative skill, erudition, and knowledge of popular culture are evident in these tales. Several deal with disappointed male characters past 50. Impressive, shrewd and entertaining.

Crônicas

RICHARD A. PRETO-RODAS, *Professor of Portuguese, University of South Florida*

BRAZILIAN FONDNESS FOR the *crônica* shows no sign of abating. Once considered a minor genre, this brief composition combining elements of essay, short story, and news continues to appeal to neophyte and seasoned professional alike throughout Brazil. We can cite yet another best seller by Luis Fernando Veríssimo (item

4857) and point to a reissue of all of Rachel de Queiroz's works (item **4847**). Another master of the genre, Fernando Sabino, has recently published two new titles (items **4850** and **4851**), while his late colleagues, Rubem Braga and Carlos Drummond de Andrade, continue to spark interest as is seen in *Em torno de Rubem Braga* (item **4828**) and *Auto-retrato* (item **4811**), a collection of previously unpublished pieces by Drummond. In fact, evocation of the latter has become a popular theme among contemporary newcomers as is evident in Murilo Badaró, (item **4815**), Orlando Carneiro (item **4817**), Sindulfo Santiago (item **4853**), and others listed below. Another theme that occurs with some frequency concerns the lamentable decline of civil behavior in urban settings, a topic often coupled with a nostalgic glance back to less complicated times. That such nostalgia may be misplaced, however, is suggested by new editions of *Mistérios do Rio* (item **4820**) and *Pernoite* (item **4814**) where we find that even in the 1920s and 1950s life in Rio left much to be desired. Even so, judging from the fortunes of *A cidade mulher* (item **4842**), reason for optimism is definitely on the wane.

The *crônica's* adaptability explains its appeal to writers well known for their work in other genres. Thus, we find *crônicas* by novelists like Moacyr Scliar (item **4854**) and Clarice Lispector (item **4832**) and by poets like Vinícius de Moraes (item **4841**) and Ferreira Gullar (item **4829**), while the famous dramatist Nelson Rodrigues (item **4849**) and critic-scholar Guilherme Figueiredo (item **4826**) have also tried their hands with noteworthy success. Even a major voice from Brazilian modernism like Mário de Andrade contributed his share of *crônicas* (item **4812**). However, it is the genre's close relationship with the print media and questions concerning the significance of current events that explain the large number of journalists from virtually every major city in Brazil whose works are mentioned below. Their interests are truly diverse, even if, as writers, they often refer to the status of their vehicle, the Portuguese language, as we can see in Moacir Werneck de Castro (item **4818**), Danilo Gomes (item **4828**), Osvaldo Peralva (item **4846**), and others who decry the decline of literacy and the failure of Portugal and Brazil to agree on a uniform orthography. To be sure, there are other symptoms of modern stress in today's Brazil such as the problem of AIDS (e.g., items **4846** and **4845**), and the scandal of street children (e.g., items **4821** and **4852**). More fortunate children in dozens of guises comprise the topic in Scliar's volume (item **4854**). Other monothematic collections include Carlos Eduardo Novaes' humorous pieces on the recently divorced parent (item **4844**), Nelson Rodrigues' collaboration with Mário Filho on soccer (item **4849**), Darcy Loss Luzzatto's Italo-Brazilian experience in Santa Catarina (item **4833**), and Nelle Vellozo Fernandes' infatuation with Ilha do Mel (item **4825**). The American reader viewing Brazilian life will occasionally find him/herself under the microscope as writers like Novaes (item **4845**) and, especially, Flenora Duvivier (item **4823**) turn a critical eye northward. As final—and dubious—proof of the *crônica's* status among respected literary genres we can point to an exhaustive academic study, Adylla Rocha Rabello Almeida's slim volume on a single example (item **4848**).

4810 Alencar, José de Sousa. 70 crônicas de Alex: o exercício da fidelidade nos 70 anos do *Jornal do Commercio*. Recife, Brazil: Fundação de Cultura Cidade do Recife; Sindicato dos Jornalistas Profissionais do Estado de Pernambuco; Bompreço Gráfica Editora Ltda., 1989. 144 p. (Col. Recife; 51)

Author casts a wide net, from Xuxa as a neo-colonial phenomenon (like vanilla cake in a land of tropical delicacies) and the scourge of racial prejudice to super-moms who neglect their children. Other topics include the strange popularity of the monarchy and singer Milton Nascimento who finds inspiration in the eyes of River Phoenix.

4811 Andrade, Carlos Drummond de. Autoretrato e outras crônicas. Seleção de Fernando Py. Rio de Janeiro: Editora Record, 1989. 171 p.

Editor has selected previously unpublished columns written by the late author from 1943–70. Ever the master of gentle irony and a style both colloquial and elegant, author reflects on the famous stone in the middle of the road, prejudice, clerical and academic posturing, and poignant memories of departed friends like the young and very promising Hélcio Martins.

4812 Andrade, Mário de. Será o Benedito! Apresentação de Telê Porto Ancona Lopes. São Paulo: EDUC-Editora da PUC-SP; Editora Giordano; Agência Estado, 1992. 117 p.: bibl., ill.

Title refers to author's shock on learning of accidental death of a personable Afro-Brazilian farm boy. Most of these pieces, though, concern this important modernist's interests in the art and music world from 1937–41.

4813 Angelo, Assis. O coronel e a borboleta: e outras histórias nordestinas. São Paulo: Estúdio F, 1992. 157 p.: ill.

All these pieces deal with the Northeast as viewed through the eyes of a humorous writer with a penchant for salacious doings on the farm.

4814 Antônio Maria. Pernoite: crônicas. Rio de Janeiro: Martins Fontes; FUNARTE, 1989. 110 p.: ports. (MPB; 26: Textos)

While writing for the magazine *Manchete* in the 1950s, author, a close friend of Vinícius de Moraes, even then lamented a deteriorating urban environment. Here he also captures carnival in Recife, Bahia's Itapoã beach, and the presence of American GIs billeted in the Northeast.

4815 Badaró, Murilo. Vigésimo mandamento: crônicas. Belo Horizonte [i.e. Brasília]: Centro Gráfico do Senado Federal, 1992. 326 p. (Col. Lima Barreto)

Formal style strains the limits of the *crônica,* and there is much of Juvenal in comments concerning the likes of Zélia Cardoso de Mello and other embarrassing examples of what passes for a social elite. But author never fails to interest as he turns his attention to inflation, Drummond's *crônicas* from

the 1930s, Roberto Carlos, and the aging *machos* of his native Minas Gerais.

4816 Bueno, Terezinha Peron. Rés-do-chão. São Paulo: M. Ohno Editor, 1991. 82 p.: ill.

In her conversational style (some of these *crônicas* assume the form of a personal letter), author expresses her "ground floor" view of such topics as the ubiquitous but plucky sparrows and the gradual Americanization of Brazilian society, which nonetheless counters with a Pelé, the Bossa Nova, and the Lambada.

4817 Carneiro, Orlando. Canto de página. Belém: Cultural CEJUP, 1988. 98 p.

From *O Flash,* a daily published in Belém, come these pieces on life at the mouth of the Amazon, where parents give their children extravagant names (e.g., Penicilina) and a street urchin falls in love with a salami hanging in a shop window. But the big picture is also present, such as when (economic) "freeze" becomes a household word in this tropical city or when the passing of Carlos Drummond de Andrade saddens many.

4818 Castro, Moacir Werneck de. A ponte dos suspiros. Rio de Janeiro: Rocco, 1990. 211 p.

Here are rewarding, if troubling, glimpses of "Rambo brain" vigilantes and others with no regard for civil rights, of a middle class nutured by the Hollywood "dream factory" of violence and wishful thinking, and of declining book sales and increasing semi-literacy. Author visits a variety of linguistic issues such as the orthographic (dis)agreement involving Portugal and Brazil.

4819 Costa, Tito. Breviário: um pouco sentimental. São Paulo: Carthago Editorial, 1991. 127 p.

Genre's brevity is suggested by title of this selection from author's newspaper columns beginning in 1974. The "sentimental" is decidedly elegiac as he considers the passing of Carlos Drummond de Andrade, ecological devastation ironically encountered on a trip to a sanatorium, and the effects of technocratic jargon. Includes interesting critique of Rachel de Queiroz's division of Brazil between the Northeast and (the author's) South.

4820 Costallat, Benjamim. Mistérios do Rio. Rio de Janeiro: Prefeitura da Cidade do Rio de Janeiro, Secretaria Municipal de Cultura, Turismo e Esportes, Depto. Geral de Documentação Cultural, 1990. 108 p. (Biblioteca carioca; 14)

Originally published in 1924, these selections by a music critic for several newspapers show the influence of similar depictions of the *bas fonds* of big cities by night. Tone is predictably decadent with its scenes of prostitution (sometimes with a respectable bourgeois mother in the role of madam), opium dens, and glamorous transvestites presented against a backround of wailing jazz bands and macumba drums on the hillsides. Book was originally received with scandalized delight.

4821 Craveiro, Paulo Fernando. Prefácio da cidade: crônicas do Recife. Recife: Prefeitura da Cidade do Recife, Secretaria de Educação e Cultura, Conselho Municipal de Cultura; Fundação de Cultura Cidade do Recife, 1991. 202 p.

Another voice from Brazil's third city, author writes of the many shoeshine boys, all apparently named José and shoeless, and finds a quiet and melancholy beauty on a side street. There is a preference for scenes involving the poor, though not marginal, city dweller.

4822 Dahl, Maria Lúcia. A bailarina agradece. Rio de Janeiro: Terceira Margem Editora, 1990? 206 p.: ill.

Journalist from prestigious *Jornal do Brasil* obviously influenced by the likes of Sabino and Braga shows an occasional spark of her days as a student revolutionary and radical feminist. Too ironic for self pity, she expresses the post-modern malaise of collective isolation ("we are all in this . . . alone") as she copes with suddenly grown children and daily reminders that she resembles a woman much disliked in her childhood. The days, even awful ones, pass ever more rapidly.

4823 Duvivier, Eleonora. O anjo de óculos. Rio de Janeiro: Civilização Brasileira, 1989. 192 p.

Many of these *crônicas,* mostly culled from a stint as graduate student of philosophy at an American university, are probing analyses of her hosts' fascination with technology, risk-free living, and facile religiosity.

4824 Emediato, Luiz Fernando. A grande ilusão: crônicas. São Paulo: Geração Editorial, 1992. 214 p.

Politically *engagé* writer who suggests

the existential humanism of postwar European thinkers reflects on death of Pixote whose life was depicted in the film, and on the loss of Carlos Drummond de Andrade to Brazilian culture.

4825 Fernandes, Hellê Vellozo. Ilha do Mel, ontem e sempre. Curitiba, Brazil: Instituto Histórico, Geográfico e Etnográfico Paranaense, 1985. 223 p.: bibl., ill. (Estante paranista; 23)

Popular Curitiba journalist, social worker, and teacher explores her favorite Shangri-la, title's island off the coast of Paraná. Rickety ferry boats, fishermen, visitors (including the stray penguin drifting in from thousands of miles south), and other topics provide view of an unfamiliar Brazil.

4826 Figueiredo, Guilherme Presente de grego e outros presentes: crônicas. Rio de Janeiro?: Editora Atheneu Cultura, 1990. 368 p. (Crônicas)

Well-known writer, educator, and critic ranges far, from pitfalls of translation in producing foreign plays to an encounter with a solitary black Brazilian on a street in Leningrad. Tone is mostly wry with an occasional touch of nostalgia.

4827 Gabaglia, Marisa Raja. O sedutor da bicharada: histórias bem humoradas do quotidiano paulista. Rio de Janeiro: Editora Rosa dos Tempos, 1992. 143 p.

Author assumes role of iconoclast as she takes on pomposity of all kinds. Title piece's target, a philandering father who sodomizes the family menagerie, however, would doubtless strike the Anglo-Saxon reader as a bit too ripe.

4828 Gomes, Danilo. Em torno de Rubem Braga. Prefácio de Otto Lara Resende. Brasília?: Signo Editora, 1991. 71 p.: ill.

Volume contains four *crônicas* about the late master of the genre, pointing out his contributions to the language, to the environmental movement, and most of all, to elevation of the genre itself to a major rank in Brazilian literature. Includes interview with Braga from 1986.

4829 Gullar, Ferreira. A estranha vida banal. Rio de Janeiro: J. Olympio Editora, 1989. 125 p.: ill.

Well-known poet approaches genre with a paradoxical view of life as both odd and monotonous. Whatever the subject, from flowers and animals to apartment hunting while in Peruvian exile, there is a bite to his humor ("When a poor person eats chicken, one of them is sick."). Includes remarkable conversation involving Fernando Pessoa and his three major heteronyms.

4830 Jorge Neto, Nagib. Que zorra, camarada!: Brasil novo, vento leste, Nova República. Recife, Brazil: Comunicarte, 1991. 131 p.: ill.

Dominant note is one of lament as writer from the Northeast considers a society obsessed with security and infatuated with violence, while remaining indifferent to economic disparities and threatened civil liberties. His selections certainly document what he sees as a general cultural decline.

4831 Leão, Anilda. Os olhos convexos e outras crônicas. Maceió, Brazil: Oficinas de Serviços Gráficos de Alagoas, 1990. 162 p.

Author has chosen her best work as a journalist in Alagoas, where she writes as a feminist who manages to be lyrical even while reflecting on violence and frustration as experienced by women in a world of double standards.

4832 Lispector, Clarice. Para não esquecer. 4a. ed. São Paulo: Editora Siciliano, 1992. 188 p.

In this reissue of a collection first published in 1978 (see *HLAS 42:6190*), Lispector's unusual world view is ever present. Some of these flashes of insight are no longer than a couple of terse questions that continue to haunt the reader.

4833 Luzzatto, Darcy Loss. Ostregheta, semo drìo deventar vèci! Porto Alegre, Brazil: D.C. Luzzatto Editores; Sagra Livraria-Editora-Distribuidora, 1989. 167 p.: ill.

Author recreates the world of Italo-Brazilians growing up in Santa Catarina's interior. Theme has been treated in previous books, but this is his first written in both Portuguese and the Veneto dialect of his childhood. Assimilation explains the dominant tone (nostalgic) and theme (the past).

4834 Machado, Théo. Meninos brincando de guerra. Salvador, Brazil: Contemp, 1990. 124 p.

Writer's second anthology contains selections arranged according to mood. Humorous first part (exemplified by a wry view of a questionable childhood game) proceeds through a melancholy view of daily life in his Bahia before ending on a lyrical note.

4835 Maia, Carlito. Vale o escrito: crônicas publicadas na imprensa. Apresentação de Eduardo Matarazzo Suplicy. São Paulo: Editora Globo, 1992. 165 p.: ill.

Journalist underlines his affinity with Charlie Chaplin as reflected in his name, as he proceeds to deflate the pretensions of São Paulo society.

4836 Mello, Gustavo Bandeira de. Muito perto de nós. Brasília: Ceclira Livros e Arte, 1991. 95 p.

Author's ninth collection of *crônicas*, several of which have appeared in earlier anthologies. Adept in weaving gripping little narratives while avoiding psychological analysis.

4837 Mello, Gustavo Bandeira de. O santuário. Brasília: Thesaurus, 1989. 147 p.

Writer excels in poetic grasp of a moment adrift, glimpsed for example when a married couple separates, or when a jazz pianist from Guyana passes through Brasília, or when a young migrant worker seeks a night's shelter on the veranda. Even a stray cat comes and goes while leaving a memory. Language is old fashioned in its elegance, with an abundant use of *tu*.

4838 Mendonça, Santos. Zig-zag: crônicas. Aracajú, Brazil: Governo do Estado de Sergipe, Secretaria de Estado da Educação e Cultura, FUNDESC, 1985. 204 p.

Title refers to author's career shift from radio and newspaper reporting to writing of these pieces, where local scene in Aracajú looks very familiar with its displays of jealousy and professional rivalry. Scope of some of these *crônicas* approach the limits of minimalism.

4839 Miranda, Célio. Arte e ritual mágico. Maceió, Brazil: Secretaria de Cultura e Esportes, 1991. 72 p.

Here we have one of several new voices from Maceió. Title fails to reflect strong note of protest against urban "renewal" and disfiguration it brings about. There is also the specter of danger lurking along the familiar streets of one's own city.

4840 Moraes, Jomar. Cinza das quartas-feiras: crônicas. São Luís, Brazil: Editora Legenda, 1990. 137 p.

Collection of author's Wednesday columns from the *Gazeta* of his island city gives his viewpoint on Halley's Comet and on the national debate on changing the national anthem. He is also moved by an 11-year-old girl washing windshields on a busy corner, and is angered by the murder of Chico Mendes. Even in this little city we read of metamorphosis from "garden to garbage dump."

4841 Moraes, Vinícius de. Para viver um grande amor: crônicas e poemas. São Paulo: Companhia das Letras, 1991. 222 p.

Famous poet's first work in prose (mostly), collection was assembled by his secretary in 1954 from his best *crônicas* published in newspaper *Última Hora*. Contains illuminating insights on writer as medium. Also includes charming vignettes of Portinari, Carmen Miranda in Hollywood, and the travails of writing *Black Orpheus* while coping with a two-year-old daughter.

4842 Moreyra, Alvaro. A cidade mulher. Rio de Janeiro: Prefeitura da Cidade do Rio de Janeiro, Secretaria Municipal de Cultura, Turismo e Esportes, Depto. Geral de Documentação e Informação Cultural, Divisão de Editoração, 1991. 120 p. (Biblioteca carioca; 19)

First published in 1923, *crônicas* reflect Modernism's heyday with their blend of ironic humor and lyricism in addition to their breezy optimism about Rio de Janeiro. Author's 1958 edition, *Havia uma oliveira no jardim* (see *HLAS 23:5581*), expressed a more sober view, and the preface here by Walder Virgolino says much about nostalgia in the midst of the exasperations of 1991.

4843 Negrão, Luiz. Canção do amanhecer: crônicas de domingo. Belém, Brazil: Edições CEJUP, 1992. 240 p.

Samples of author's Sunday column from Belém's *Diário do Pará* exemplify his aphoristic style and pithy insights on surviving personal tragedy and coping with the dangers of urban living. Laments disappearance of city's greenery and resulting silence where cicadas once trilled. An elegy for Carlos Drummond de Andrade reinforces the reflective tone.

4844 Novaes, Carlos Eduardo. Homem, Mulher & Cia. Ltda. São Paulo: Editora Atica, 1987. 111 p. (Col. de autores brasileiros; 98)

A sometimes hilarious and often spicy look at being 42, divorced, and a parent of two, pieces are glimpses of new-found freedom (?) in a time of AIDS, transvestites, and bisexuals. Writer confesses mixed feelings concerning extended family of his, her, and their children, but finds no solace in family values USA-style ("the land of hypocrisy").

4845 Novaes, Carlos Eduardo. O país dos imexíveis. Ilustrações de Vilmar. Rio de Janeiro: Nórdica, 1990. 176 p.: ill.

The country is, of course, the "unmixable" Brazil of this popular writer who can evoke love among economists ("Her stocks rise when his infatuation enters an inflationary spiral"), while recognizing that a country of doting mothers ("They'll believe anything") is inhospitable to real Jacobins and Marxists. Yet its inhabitants are becoming a useful export, including the author himself who boasts of a flirtation with Benazir Bhutto while living in London.

4846 Peralva, Osvaldo. O chapéu de palhinha. Belo Horizonte, Brazil: Editora Itatiaia, 1990. 201 p. (Col. Crônicas de ontem e de hoje; 6)

Tokyo correspondent for a São Paulo newspaper, writer offers provocative comparisons between tough-minded women politicians in Asia and their male counterparts in macho Brazil who weep in public. The topic of AIDS is unavoidable, and he shows an unusually perceptive interest in the place of Portuguese in today's world.

4847 Queiroz, Rachel de. Obra reunida. v. 3–5. Rio de Janeiro: J. Olympio Editora, 1989. 3 v.

Vols. 3–5 of this five-volume collection include all of author's *crônicas* dating back half a century. As a critical appraisal in vol. 4 by the late Paulo Rónai puts it: reading these pieces, so literary despite their casual charm, never fails to evoke feelings and food for thought that make life worth living.

4848 Rabello, Adylla Rocha. Pareço-me comigo: uma aventura carnavalesca de José Américo de Almeida. Brasília: Senado Federal, Centro Gráfico, 1988. 92 p.: ill.

The industry of academic analysis is here in all its dreary splendor in this dissection of a *crônica* by the late José Américo de Almeida. Pages of charts, diagrams, graphs, and jargon culminate in ten pages of six columns each, summarizing numbing quantitative conclusions. There is no hint regarding the piece's value or of why it may elicit any literary interest.

4849 Rodrigues, Nelson and **Mário Rodrigues.** Fla-Flu:—e as multidões despertaram! Organização de Oscar Maron Filho e Renato Ferreira. Rio de Janeiro: Edição Europa; Xerox, 1987. 191 p.: ill. (some col.).

We find the Brazilian obsession with soccer in these pieces by a pioneer of contemporary Brazilian theater and a friend. There are many photographs and a contribution from Gilberto Freyre on the role of soccer in opening doors for talented Afro-Brazilians.

4850 Sabino, Fernando Tavares. De cabeça para baixo. Rio de Janeiro: Editora Record, 1989. 320 p.

Work begins with a piece from the late 1950s relating a trip to Lisbon where the young Sabino is lionized by opponents of the Salazar regime. There are other moments from a variety of foreign settings such as Mexico, Algiers, New York, and Paris.

4851 Sabino, Fernando Tavares. A volta por cima. Rio de Janeiro: Editora Record, 1990. 204 p.

This is vintage Sabino, the master of the comic and/or harrowing situation (which may include some dubious cases like a sexual assault on an elevator and the gradually inappropriate pleasures of girl-watching). He laments growing old and wonders about how to provide sex education for children all too conversant with the topic. One noteworthy piece tries to explain the genesis of the *crônica* (real *and* imagined, fact *and* fiction) to an obtuse academic editor.

4852 Sant'Anna, Affonso Romano de. A raiz quadrada do absurdo. Rio de Janeiro: Rocco, 1989. 210 p.

Presents mostly acerbic views of modern society's attempts to find the "square root of the absurd" (a futile exercise especially practised by politicians and economists) in the midst of racial tensions, technological dysfunction, and abandoned children. Author

includes directions on how to be happy in his Brazil, where a 19th-century Portuguese novelist like Eça de Queirós can provide escape from TV soap operas.

4853 Santiago, Sindulfo. Na rota dos ausentes: e outras crônicas. João Pessoa, Brazil: S. Santiago, 1988. 157 p.

Major theme—death and the loss of loved ones—is treated with lyrical charm and no morbidity. Author recalls the near, relating a brother's death in childhood, and the great, imagining a conversation with Carlos Drummond de Andrade. For the author, the champion of life, all are in some way still living.

4854 Scliar, Moacyr. Um país chamado infância. Porto Alegre, Brazil: Editora Sulina, 1989. 101 p.: ill.

Well-known novelist and short story writer finds all his themes in the pleasures and perils of parenting, from dad's turn to feed the baby at 2:00 am, to coping with little gluttons and puny eaters and hyperactive dynamos and TV-watching couch potatoes. Weightier concerns involve providing religious assurance in skeptical times and the author's own adolescence in his city's Jewish neighborhoods.

4855 Trajano, Edgard. O oitavo canal. Rio de Janeiro: Achiamé, 1989. 156 p.

Title's eighth channel is the glow of the full moon after the writer has turned off the idiocy and violence of his TV's seven channels. Thus the astronomer-columnist creates a series of incidents all pertaining to the night sky and its effect on sensitive earthlings.

4856 Trevisan, Máximo et al. Recortes do cotidiano: crônicas. Santa Maria, Brazil: A Razão, 1988? 92 p.: ill.

"Clippings from the daily" is an appropriate title for this anthology of 15 columnists from southern Brazil who display a wide range of topics (from taking out the garbage to the art of small talk in a bar), form (from dialogue to allegory), and tone (from punning to revelry). The perspective is, however, uniformly male.

4857 Veríssimo, Luís Fernando. O suicida e o computador. Porto Alegre, Brazil: L&PM Editores, 1992. 150 p.

Perennial best-selling master of the genre provides yet another collection revealing his zany, often risqué, and always satirical perspective, which here encompasses such matters as the reaction of two mothers, one Jewish and the other Italian, to the engagement of their children. We also find conversations involving Nabakov, Borges, Italo Calvino, and Benny Goodman in the Hereafter. Title piece explains why leaving a suicide note on a word processor is impractical.

Poetry

NAOMI HOKI MONIZ, *Associate Professor of Portuguese, Georgetown University*

A RENEWED INTEREST IN Brazilian poetry began in 1985 when new forums opened for this genre, a development that took poetry back to its oral origins in the tradition of the troubadours. In the late 1980s, poetry enjoyed enormous popularity and was read in public places like restaurants, bars, beaches, and "O Circo Voador" in Rio de Janeiro. The singer and actress Maricene Costa who specializes in singing and recording works of poetry enjoyed great success in her São Paulo shows. But, as of the early 1990s, this momentum declined. And even though there is much publicity about renowned authors such as Carlos Drummond de Andrade (in, for example, his posthumously published erotic poems, item **4860**) and João Cabral de Melo Neto and Carlos Nejar (in their new poetry collections, items **4868** and **4894,** respectively), there is also a slowdown in publishing and in the discovery of new talent.

Nonetheless, a number of trends detected in previous years continue today, such as: a) the activity of established women poets such as Olga Savary, Hilda Hilst, Stella Leonardos and the new wave of women poets in the wake of authors such as Cora Coralina and Adélia Prado; b) the continued increase, from the late 1970s well into the early 1990s, of works by blacks examining issues of both identity and oppression—the importance of the African heritage, racism, and the need to challenge the ongoing inequalities endured by Afro-Brazilians; c) the continued interest in the haiku mode of poetry evident in the large number of publications by authors who are established practitioners of the style as well as recent adepts; and finally, d) the considerable upsurge of concretist works such as Haroldo de Campos' new anthology of his best poems (item **4871**) and contributions by a new generation of concretist poets mostly in their 30s.

4858 Almeida, Tácito de. Túnel; e, poemas modernistas, 1922–23. Estabelecimento de texto e estudo por Telê Porto Ancona Lopez. São Paulo: Art Editora, 1987. 117 p.: bibl., port. (Col. Toda poesia; 3)

Lopez provides good, critical edition of works of this less-known modernist poet.

4859 Anchieta, José de. Poesias: manuscrito do séc. XVI, em português, castelhano, latim e tupi. Transcrições, traduções e notas de Maria de Lourdes de Paula Martins. Belo Horizonte, Brazil: Editora Itatiaia Limitada; São Paulo: Editora da Univ. de São Paulo, 1989. 835 p.: bibl., ill. (Biblioteca básica de literatura brasileira; 3)

Extremely useful critical edition of this important figure in Brazilian colonial literature includes facsimile reproduction of the manuscript.

4860 Andrade, Carlos Drummond de. O amor natural. Ilustrações de Milton Dacosta. Epílogo de Affonso Romano de Sant'Anna. Rio de Janeiro: Editora Record, 1992. 100 p.: bibl., ill.

Most poems in this collection were published posthumously at author's request.

Includes useful afterword by Affonso Romano de Sant'Anna who examines the work within context of Andrade's *oeuvre*, and argues favorably for erotic/pornographic tone of the poems. Epigraphs of poets such as Ronsard, Camões, and Apollinaire establish the theme's classical origin and point to the elegance of Andrade's language.

4861 Andrade, Oswald de. Primeiro caderno do aluno de poesia Oswald de Andrade. Prefácio de Raúl Antelo. São Paulo: Secretaria de Estado da Cultura de São Paulo; Editora Globo, 1991. 58 p.: ill. (Obras completas de Oswald de Andrade)

Originally published in 1927, book parodies and recreates poet's ambivalence in encountering two worlds: the rural and the urban, the domestic and the cosmopolitan, the local and the national. Includes very good introduction by Raúl Antelo.

4862 Andrade, Oswald de. O santeiro do mangue e outros poemas. Redação de Haroldo de Campos. São Paulo: Secretaria de Estado da Cultura de São Paulo; Editora Globo, 1991. 114 p.: bibl., ill. (Obras completas de Oswald de Andrade)

"O Santeiro do Mangue," Oswald's most censored text, is finally accessible to public at large. Good essays introduce other poems. Edition by Haroldo de Campos also provides useful notes.

4863 Andrade, Teresa Julieta. Variável serenidade: poesia. São Paulo: M. Ohno Editor, 1991. 74 p.: ill.

Blending styles and themes of other *mineiro* poets such as Adélia Prado and Carlos Drummond de Andrade, collection evokes childhood of a young girl in Minas Gerais.

4864 Azevedo, Carlito. Collapsus linguae: poemas. Rio de Janeiro: Lynx, 1991. 58 p. (Col. Serial)

Very inventive, refreshing, and original collection plays humorously with puns, sounds, semantics, and other poets' works.

4865 Balduino, el africano. Zumbalu. Vitória, Brazil: Depto. Estadual de Cultura-ES, 1989. 56 leaves. (Col. Prata da casa; 2)

Balduino, an old tambourine master (b. 1907), writes simple verses in popular language and form, and denounces injustices suffered by Afro-Brazilians. He is the only member of the older generation with consciousness of negritude movement that began in late 1970s Brazil.

4866 Bonvicino, Régis R. 33 poemas. São Paulo: Secretaria de Estado da Cultura; Iluminuras, 1990. 51 p.

In the same vein as the avant-garde poets of the 1960s, Bonvicino experiments with space, phonic and semantic associations, and foreign words, and plays intertextual games with poets such as Cesário Verde and Laforgue, and even with medieval Portuguese poetry.

4867 Brito, Ronaldo. Quarta do singular. São Paulo: Secretaria de Estado da Cultura; Livraria Duas Cidades, 1989. 54 p. (Claro enigma)

Wallace Stevens' epigraph—"poetry is a destructive force"—sums up this *carioca* poet. Brito deconstructs and reinvents the same group of images—sand, island, desert, sea, and shadow—to explore the possibilities of language. Examines *topoi* (i.e., rhetorical themes) characteristic of his poetry, and also challenges the medium and surprises the reader by his paradoxical treatment of the fixed forms of Brazilian poetry.

4868 Cabral de Melo Neto, João. Sevilha andando: poesia. Rio de Janeiro: Editora Nova Fronteira, 1989. 84 p. (Poesia brasileira)

This poet's love for Spain reappears again in this volume, divided into two parts: "Sevilha Andando" and "Andando Sevilha." Uses same contained and rigorous style of his earlier works to capture essence of the city and its inhabitants.

4869 *Cadernos Negros: Poemas.* Vol. 13, 1990- . São Paulo: S.I. Editora Pannartz Ltda.

Anthology of eight Afro-Brazilian poets (three are women) manifests influences of different trends such as concretism and postmodernism. Includes interesting experiments with language.

4870 Câmara, Eugênia Infante da. Segredos d'alma. 2a. ed. São Paulo: Editora Pannartz, 1989. 90 p.: ill.

Second edition includes some poems from newspapers of the period that were omitted from first edition. Author was playwright made famous by her liaison with poet Castro Alves.

4871 Campos, Haroldo de. Transideraciones
= Transiderações. Recopilación y traducción de Eduardo Milán y Manuel Ulacia.
México: Ediciones El Tucán de Virginia; Fundación E. Gutman, 1987. 115 p.: ill. (Los
Bífidos)
    Bilingual anthology (Portuguese/Span-
ish) of the most significant poems of Campos'
career is taken from his books *Xadrez de estrelas* (1972), *Signatia quasi coelum* (1979),
Galáxias (1984), and *A educação dos cinco
sentidos* (1985).

4872 Carpi, Maria. Nos gerais da dor. Porto
Alegre, Brazil: Movimento, 1990. 62
p. (Col. Poesiasul; 65)
    Echoing Camões' style, and in the clas-
sic tradition, Carpi's poems examine existential suffering.

4873 Casaldáliga, Pedro. As águas do tempo.
Cuiabá, Brazil: Fundação Cultural de
Mato Grosso; Amazônida, 1989. 61 p.: port.
(Col. Letras matogrossenses: Série Poetas contemporâneos ; 5)
    Another work by a Mato Grosso
writer, a controversial Catalonian-born
bishop and missionary well known for his
commitment to the poor, landless people of
the Araguaia region. The poems, with a
strong socio-political tone, reflect Casaldáliga's love of the land and people.

4874 100 haicaístas brasileiros: antologia.
Organização de Roberto Saito, Hide-
kazu Masuda e Francisco Handa. São Paulo:
Aliança Cultural Brasil-Japão; M. Ohno Editor, 1990. 141 p.: ill.
    Anthology of 100 Brazilian *haiku* poets
celebrates the tricentennial of Bashō's famous
Oku no hosomichi (Tokyo, 1933). Includes
works of earliest *haikai* practitioners, such as
Afrânio Peixoto (b. 1919) who is considered a
precursor of the genre; Luís Aranha and Guilherme de Almeida of the Modernist Movement; the concretist poets Pedro Xisto and
Paulo Leminsky; and the Japanese-Brazilian
poets of the Grupo Haikai Ipê.

4875 Colina, Paulo. Todo o fogo da luta. São
Paulo: J. Scortecci Editora, 1989. 86 p.
    Author is poet, playwright, novelist,
and critic who is committed to Afro-Brazilian
literature. His poems reflect influence of Fernando Pessoa, and express the question of negritude in Brazil in a more aesthetic and existential form.

4876 Conrado, Juarez. O grande Akuntô.
Ilustrações de Melcíades. Aracajú, Brazil: Sercore Artes Gráficas, 1990. 111 p.: ill.
    Book of poems celebrates life of
Akuntô, a fictitious African warrior from Ni-
geria captured and taken as a slave to Brazil.
Akuntô leads a plantation rebellion, flees
with other slaves, and becomes the king of a
quilombo. Author is from Sergipe, and Akuntô, not surprisingly, shows similiarities to
the famous Zumbi from Palmares of Alagoas.

4877 Costa, Horácio. Satori. São Paulo: Iluminuras, 1989. 111 p.
    Satori is the moment of illumination
and revelation for this poet and traveler who
maps his poems through Manhattan, São
Paulo, Mexico City, Lisbon, and Assisi. But,
unlike the multiple voices of an operatic en-
semble's finale, here the cacophony of voices
shows the plenitude of emptiness, like a zen
aphorism.

4878 Damasceno, Benedita Gouveia. Poesia
negra no modernismo brasileiro. Campinas, Brazil: Pontes Editores, 1988. 142 p.:
bibl. (Literatura crítica)
    Rare example of study of Brazilian
black poetry. Postulates existence of negritude poetry and tries to characterize the genre
through the study of poets such as Adão Ventura, Éle Semog, Solano Trindade, and Jorge
de Lima, among others.

4879 Dias, Antônio Gonçalves. Os melhores
poemas de Gonçalves Dias. Seleção de
José Carlos Garbuglio. São Paulo; Global,
1991. 158 p. (Os Melhores poemas; 24)
    Selection and preface by José Carlos
Garbuglio provides useful introduction to
this important poet of Brazilian romanticism.

4880 Espinheira Filho, Ruy. A canção de
Beatriz e outros poemas: poesia reunida, 1966–1990. São Paulo: Editora Brasiliense, 1990. 265 p.
    Title poem is narrated in first person
by a prostitute who relates the violence and
poverty of an extremely unjust society. Although author considers this his most "violent" poem, he still shows the same sobriety
and discipline that characterize his use of diction and language.

4881 Góes, Clara. Cinema catástrofe. Rio de
Janeiro: Livraria Taurus; Livraria Timbre, 1989. 85 p.

Poet shows affinities with Ana Cristina César's enigmatic and poignant style but in a gentler fashion. Author's work is punctuated by unexpected and very bold imagery: "eu nem/ orquídea sou/ para expor assim os meus vermelhos."

4882 Goldberg, Jacob Pinheiro. Ritual de clivagem. São Paulo: M. Ohno Editor, 1989. 76 p.: ill.

There are many well-known Brazilian novelists of Jewish origin, but Goldberg is one of the few to express his Jewish roots and culture in lyric form.

4883 Hilst, Hilda. Do desejo. Campinas, Brazil: Pontes, 1992. 112 p.

Book is divided into seven *cadernos* of poems built around themes such as *do desejo, da noite*, etc. As in her prose work, Hilst's poems convey great power but in an elegant and unique style.

4884 Ivo, Lêdo. Crepúsculo civil: poesia. Rio de Janeiro: Editora Record, 1990. 144 p.

Ivo, of the same generation as Ferreira Gullar, João Cabral de Melo, and Mário Quintana, has published about 26 books. This book is consistent with them in the style and deft use of traditional forms.

4885 Leal, José Benedito Donadon. Dô caminho. Ilustrações de Ersília Alberti. São Paulo: M. Ohno Editor; Ouro Preto, Brazil: Univ. Federal de Ouro Preto, 1992. 1 v. (unpaged): ill.

Title calls to mind the *haiku* poet Bashō's work "Long Narrow Road." Leal reveals Bashō as a master and plagiarizes humorously one of his most famous *haiku* in his lines "Velho tanque d'água/verminhos na superfície/quem os pôs alí?" Leal's poems also reflect his experience with the Japanese community in northwestern region of Paraná.

4886 Leonardos, Stella. Cancioneiro de Alcântara. São Luís, Brazil: Edições AML, 1989. 48 p.

Leonardos has distinguished herself by the lovely archaic quality to her language. The elegance, purity, and directness of medieval Portuguese poetry is again present in this appropriately titled *cancioneiro* of the colonial town of Alcântara with its landscape, indigenous legends, and the Portuguese and French battles of its history.

4887 Lins, Jaceguay. O segundo livro de Enoch. Prefácio de Carlos Nejar. São Paulo: Nemar; M. Ohno Editores, 1991. 77 p.

It is quite appropriate that Carlos Nejar should write the preface to this book. This "second book of Enoch" refers to the 11 unknown chapters of the apocryphal Book of Enoch from the Old Testament discovered in the 1930s. Lins' use of aphorism, parables, dialogues, and prophecies reminds reader of Nejar's latest work *O pai das coisas* (see *HLAS 50:4047*); both works share this mystical quality in their search for the divine.

4888 Lyra, Pedro. Desafio: uma poética do amor. Rio de Janeiro: Tempo Brasileiro, 1991. 252 p.: bibl. (Col. Tempoesia; 34)

Work marks new phase in this poet's trajectory. His *Poema-postal* (1970) searched for new directions in the avant-garde line; *Decisão* (Rio de Janeiro: 1983) presented a dialectic view of man's historical and sociopolitical struggle. Present work goes back and reexamines classic roots of poetry and reinvents a postmodern sonnet about the most traditional theme of love.

4889 Mendes, Murilo. Poemas, 1925–1929; e, Bumba-meu-poeta, 1930–1931. Organização, introdução, variantes e biobibliografia de Luciana Stegagno Picchio. Rio de Janeiro: Editora Nova Fronteira, 1989. 136 p.: appendix.

Very useful and important critical edition of Mendes' poems of late 1920s-early 1930s. Organized by Luciana Stegagno Picchio, includes appendix on the variants, of special interest to Mendes scholars.

4890 Moisés, Carlos Felipe. Subsolo. São Paulo: M. Ohno Editor, 1989. 86 p.

Elegant and consistent in his style, Moisés presents a delightful series of poems that play intertextually with works of the arcadian poet Tomás Antônio Gonzaga, with Mário de Andrade's "hallucinated" San Francisco (in "Paulicéia Desvairada"), or in the manner of the medieval *cantigas de amigo* of D. Dinis or the sonnets of Camões.

4891 Moraes, Vinícius de. Livro de letras. Texto de José Castello. São Paulo: Companhia das Letras, 1991. 253 p.: ill. (some col.), index.

Very attractive edition of complete anthology of lyrics that Moraes wrote for songs. Includes important iconography of poet's intellectual and musical partners during a most creative period of Brazilian popular music.

Moraes, Vinícius de. Para viver um grande amor: crônicas e poemas. See item **4841.**

4892 Nejar, Carlos. Amar, a mais alta constelação: sonetos. Rio de Janeiro: J. Olympio Editora, 1991. 81 p.

Book of sonnets written 1978–79 also includes others written between 1987–89. Nejar, a member of the "Geração de 60," finds his formalist concerns tested in the classical form of the sonnet. Thus work exudes a serenity that contrasts with the fierceness of his earlier epic tone.

4893 Nejar, Carlos. A genealogia da palavra. São Paulo: Iluminuras, 1989. 310 p.: ill.

Anthology of author's work over last three decades is organized by him and includes some unpublished poems. Offers very useful insight into Nejar's perception of the overall order of his poetry.

4894 Nejar, Carlos. Meus estimados vivos. Ilustrações de Jorge Solé. Vitória, Brazil: Nemar, 1991. 27 leaves: ill.

Written in 1986 and revised in 1990, poem represents the phase at which Nejar's allegiance for his fellowman acquires a very religious tone.

Nejar, Carlos. *Miquel Pampa.* See item **4921.**

4895 Oliveira, Marly de. O deserto jardim, 1989–1990. Rio de Janeiro: Editora Nova Fronteira, 1990. 71 p. (Poesia brasileira)

Author's 15th book of poems attests to consistently high quality of her diction, technique, and style over a period of 32 years: "assim sigo, sem alarde/ com aquela fidelidade/ que torna mais viva a relva/ que torna mais verde a sombra/ antes cega."

4896 Paixão, Fernando. Fogo dos rios. São Paulo: Editora Brasiliense, 1989. 78 p.

Formed by a corpus of 125 fragments, work is inspired by Heraclitus' epigrams. Title sums up author's philosophical concerns: the essence of being (fire) and the eternal flow (river).

4897 Pallottini, Renata. Praça maior. São Paulo: Roswitha Kempf Editores, 1988. 1 v. (unpaged): ill.

Pallotini, a long-established writer, has completed works in poetry, prose, and drama. This is a book of poems about Spain, her adopted country.

4898 Pereira, Abel. Haikais vagaluminosos. São Paulo: M. Ohno Editor, 1989. 1 v. (unpaged): ill.

Bahian poet presents 99 *haiku* poems divided into 33 *blocos* of three poems each. As a whole they form a nocturnal pastoral symphony around the motif of fireflies with themes ranging from the natural to the spiritual, poems in which the light of the insect is also a metaphor for the illuminating *satori.*

4899 Portela, Miriam. Doces rios do medo. Capa e ilustrações de Selma Daffrè. São Paulo: M. Ohno Editor, 1989. 80 p.: ill.

Poetry of Miriam Portela evolves around tension between awareness and celebration of physical existence and the longing for transcendence: "Um pouco mais de espaço/ e eu me perderia/ multiplicada em células/ esfacelada em átomos/ um pouco mais de tempo/ e eu reansceria/ musgo/ minério/ mágico intervalo: entre dois números."

4900 Prêmio Cora Coralina: 1986; poesias. Goiânia, Brazil: Centro Editorial e Gráfico, Univ. Federal de Goiás; Brasília: Secretaria de Atividades Sócio-Culturais, Conselho Nacional dos Direitos da Mulher, 1988. 146 p. (Publicação; 141)

Book of poems by women from Goiás is eclectic collection about traditional motifs of female childhood, fairy tales, and erotic themes (e.g., Graça Cretton). Poems play intertextually with those of Cabral de Melo Neto and Romano Sant'Anna.

4901 Queiroz, Márcia Peltier de. As ilhas de Betacam. Rio de Janeiro: Editora Nova Fronteira, 1991. 75 p.

Thematic link is opposition between nature and technology suggested by book's title. Contrary to tradition, this island is not a paradise but a metaphor for a society controlled by an all-powerful "Big Brother" ironically named J.V.C.

4902 Rozário, Denira. Palavra de poeta: coletânea de entrevistas e antologia poética. Rio de Janeiro: J. Olympio Editora, 1989. 315 p.: bibl., ill.

Very useful anthology includes poems, short biographies, and interviews with some of the most representative contemporary poets of Brazil: Murilo Mendes, Carlos Drummond de Andrade, João Cabral de Melo Neto, Ferreira Gullar, Renata Pallottini, Olga Savary, Marly de Oliveira, Carlos Nejar, José Paulo Paes, etc.

4903 Rufino, Alzira. Eu, mulher negra, resisto. Santos, Brazil: A. Rufino, 1988. 90 p.: ill.

Poetic vindication of historical role of black women from freedom in Africa to enslavement in Brazil through their present predicament. Includes introduction by Lélia Gonzalez.

4904 Sant'Anna, Affonso Romano de. Os melhores poemas de Affonso Romano de Sant'Anna. Seleção de Donaldo Schüler. São Paulo: Global, 1991. 159 p. (Os melhores poemas; 25)

Very useful anthology covers best of author's poems from publication of *Canto e palavra* (Belo Horizonte, Brazil: 1965) up to "A Catedral de Colônia" (1985). Made known and popular mostly through his poems denouncing excesses of the military dictatorship, Sant'Anna also examines intertextually the issues of art and poetry and art and the public in modern Brazil.

4905 Sant'Anna, Affonso Romano de. Que país é este? e outros poemas. Rio de Janeiro: Rocco, 1990. 161 p.

Title poem which crystallized *zeitgeist* of Brazil during the years of military dictatorship made Sant'Anna the most popular intellectual in the media. Collection of poems in a somewhat traditional form represents poet's commitment to produce art accessible to large audiences rather than aesthetic allegiance to the Vanguard movement of the 1950s-60s.

4906 Schneider, Marco André Feldman. Carta a Lilith e outros escritos sangrados. Apresentação de Antônio Houaiss. Ilustrações de Márcio Botner. São Paulo: M. Ohno Editor, 1991. 110 p.: ill.

Polarization between concrete poetry and the marginal poetry of the late 1970s-early 1980s has not affected the reflective, mythical, and mystical lyricism of Schneider's classical diction. In his "Carta a Lilith" he examines the archetypical mother figure of Lilith, recently recovered in feminist studies.

4907 Silva Filho, Hermógenes Almeida. Oríkìs. Rio de Janeiro: Grafline Editora, 1988. 156 p.: ill.

Oríkìs (a Yoruba word that means "song of honor") is second work published by this militant poet. Book is a trilogy in the form of songs, *mornas,* and chants of the African *griot* in which poet denounces social and racial oppression of Afro-Brazilians.

4908 Silvestrin, Ricardo. Bashô um santo em mim: haicais. Posfácio de Ricardo Portugal. Porto Alegre, Brazil: Tchê!, 1988. 83 p. (Lua pirata)

Title is pun on name of most famous Japanese *haiku* poet Bashō. (*Baixou* also means "to be possessed" in the popular Afro-Brazilian religions.) Word reflects Silvestrin's desire to combine Western and Eastern traditions, using the themes sun, moon, and light.

4909 Torres Filho, Rubens Rodrigues. Poros. Desenho de Nuno Ramos. São Paulo: Livraria Duas Cidades, 1989. 57 p. (Claro enigma)

Author, professor of philosophy and poet, uses exquisite language in brief epigramatic or short lyrical expressions in a heterogeneous post-Vanguard style. In his poems about poems, lyrical and narrative forms alternate as he examines with irony the dichotomy between content and form.

Drama

JUDITH ISHMAEL BISSETT, *Associate Professor of Spanish and Portuguese, Miami University, Oxford, Ohio*

BRAZILIAN THEATER PASSED THROUGH SEVERAL phases as it developed a national identity. Early in its history, European themes, dramatic structures, language, and acting styles dominated the stage. During the 1920s and 1930s, plays with a social message reflecting Brazilian reality began to emerge as theater companies interested in promoting a Brazilian cultural identity were established. European models were assimilated and adapted and Brazilian works were written (but not always produced due to censorship). Foreign influence in the 1940s arrived in the form of directors like the Polish theater practitioner, Zbigniew Ziembinsky. His 1948 production of Nelson Rodrigues' *Vestido de Noiva* is generally considered to be the moment when Brazilian theater came of age.

Social and political questions affecting the nation were addressed more frequently and more eloquently by theater companies and playwrights during the next two decades. Protest became more difficult and dangerous after 1968, but it did not disappear. After the military regime ended in 1984, protest or committed drama often took a form which could be characterized as "theater of memory." Later, playwrights like Naum Alves de Souza focused on individual, personal concerns rather than the larger social or political problems facing the country. Women playwrights such as Leilah Assunção and Consuelo de Castro, whose work expressed both social and feminist concerns, began to explore alternative approaches to their own dramatic production.

The late 1980s-1990s represent political freedom for everyone involved in the theater. However, financial constraints and the influence of television have made such creative efforts difficult, although not entirely impossible. The majority of the plays, criticism, history, and biography listed below reflect, in many ways, all of the stages Brazilian theater has undergone. Due to limited space, I will mention only a few of the works that best represent each historical moment during the 20th century.

Music hall theater is described in a very interesting manner in *Viva o rebolado: vida e morte de teatro de revista brasileiro* (item **4940**). Other works that treat theater history and discuss influences, companies, actors, directors, and styles are *Uma oficina de atores: a Escola de Arte Dramática de Alfredo Mesquita* (item **4943**) and David George's excellent *The modern Brazilian stage* (item **4932**). Oswald de Andrade's plays (items **4910** and **4911**) epitomize not only modernism but also the "devouring" (assimilation and adaptation) of universal dramatic structures and themes. Two of the collections now being published exemplify the beginning of modern theater in Brazil (Nelson Rodrigues' *Tragédias cariocas*, item **4927**) and the following years of political and social protest (*Coleção Dias Gomes*, volumes 1–3, item **4918**). The "theater of memory" is represented by *Não seria o arco de triunfo . . .* in the collection entitled *Teatro social* (item **4929**). Alves de Souza's *Suburbano Coração* (item **4928**) portrays characters' personal desires and problems. *Lua Nua* (item **4912**) is an example of the new direction Assunção's work has taken: during the summer of 1993, she stated that she was searching for a new thematic element for future plays. At that time she also said that Brazilian theater had recently been on a continuing quest for innovative forms of expression relevant to the country's present situation.

ORIGINAL PLAYS

4910 Andrade, Oswald de. *O homem e o cavalo.* São Paulo: Secretaria de Estado da Cultura de São Paulo: Editora Globo, 1990. 119 p.: port. (Obras completas de Oswald de Andrade; 5)

According to Sábato Magaldi, this play judges bourgeois civilization by codes of new Soviet society in 1934. Action takes place in nine scences and involves dozens of charac-

ters including a dog named Swendenborg, Hitler crucified on a swastika, and tourists from Mars. Extols virtues of socialism in Brechtian-like structure.

4911 Andrade, Oswald de. *O rei da vela.* Prólogos de Sábato Magaldi e Oswald por Haroldo de Campos. São Paulo: Secretaria de Estado da Cultura de São Paulo; Editora Globo, 1991. 88 p.: ill. (Obras completas de Oswald de Andrade)

Includes introductory pieces by Sábato Magaldi and Haroldo de Campos. Although play was not produced in 1930s, it could be considered first national theater. Written during emergence of modernism, work proposed a demystification of the Brazilian vision. Satirizes capitalist greed and dependence of upper class on this system.

4912 Assunção, Leilah. *Lua nua.* São Paulo: Editora Scipione, 1990. 54 p. (Col. Palco iluminado; 2)

Action in play centers around misunderstandings concerning fidelity of both characters. As married professionals they discover the pressures involved in caring for house and child when servant is fired. Once they realize there are no love affairs, they arrive at agreement concerning chores—the husband must participate.

4913 Baião, Isis. *Em cenas curtas.* Rio de Janeiro: Achiamé, 1989. 143 p.

Collection of 20 short scenes and plays, many of which focus on women. Example: In one scene, two women encounter men out on the town, but are rejected when they are aggressive in a masculine manner. Other works deal with social problems such as inflation, injustices of capitalism, crime, government corruption.

4914 Bender, Ivo. *Trilogia perversa: teatro.* Porto Alegre, Brazil: Editora da Univ. Federal do Rio Grande do Sul, 1988. 151 p.

Contains three plays depicting historical events in Rio Grande do Sul. Each play refers to a date on which significant events occurred. Playwright frames history with Greek tragedy. Example: *1941* treats German immigrants during a major flood and tells story using Electra and Orestes motif.

4915 Castro, Consuelo de. *Urgência e ruptura.* São Paulo: Editora Perspectiva; Secretaria de Estado da Cultura, 1989. 586 p.: ill. (Col. Textos; 10)

Playwright divides plays according to *urgências* (*Prova de Fogo, À Flor da Pele, Caminho de Volta, O Grande Amor de Nossas Vidas*) and *rupturas* (*Louco Circo do Desejo, Script-Tease, Aviso Prévio, Marcha a Ré*). Includes critical material by Sábato Magaldi, Décio de Almeida, and others.

4916 Cuti. *Dois nós na noite e outras peças de teatro negro-brasileiro.* São Paulo: EBOH Editora e Livraria, 1991. 151 p.

Contains five plays, four of which concern race relations. Example: *Dois nós na noite* is a monologue in which a woman addresses white mannequins, asking them why her drunken husband preferred their company. Theme: White oppression reaches even intimate relationships between men and women. Other plays address various forms of injustice.

4917 Gama Filho, Oscar. Teatro romântico capixaba: Aristides Freire, Amâncio Pereira, Ernesto Guimarães. Vitória, Brazil: Centro de Estudos Cênicos do Espírito Santo, Depto. Estadual de Cultura, Divisão de Teatro e Dança; Rio de Janeiro: Instituto Nacional de Artes Cênicas, Ministério da Cultura, 1987. 385 p.: bibl., ill.

Contains work by three 19th-century playwrights. Gives history and political implications of romanticism in Latin America and describes its Brazilian characteristics. Plays included are comedies, considered of little value by intellectual elite; yet, they present Brazilian language and customs. Includes biography and critical material on writers and history of local theater.

4918 Gomes, Dias. Coleção Dias Gomes. v. 1, Os heróis vencidos; v. 2, Os falsos mitos; v. 3, Os caminhos da revolução. Coordenação de Antonio Mercado. Rio de Janeiro: Bertrand Brasil, 1989- 3 v.: bibl., ill.

Significant collection brings together Gomes' major works and analyses of plays by critics such as Anatol Rosenfeld and Fernando Peixoto, among others. Vol. 2 includes interview of Gomes by Ferreira Gullar and Moacyr Félix; vol. 1 includes autobiographical remarks. Works also include reviews and critical bibliographies.

4919 Lopes Neto, João Simões. O teatro de Simões Lopes Neto: v. 1. Edição comentada com estabelecimento do texto, variantes e apreciação crítica segundo pesquisa de Cláudio Heemann. Porto Alegre, Brazil: Instituto Estadual do Livro, 1990. 1 v.

Includes three short critical pieces and seven plays. Provides information on discovery of manuscripts. Not all are complete. *Nossos filhos*, considered best, concerns father who returns to protect daughter from consequences of having illegitimate child. When family does not accept effort, father takes daughter and grandchild to new life.

4920 Míseri Colóni: teatro popular na região de colonização italiana. Organização de Valentim Angelo Lazzarotto. Porto Alegre, Brazil: Escola Superior de Teologia e Espiritualidade Franciscana, 1988. 79 p.: ill. (Col. Imigração italiana; 91)

Plays produced by ethnic amateur group in Rio Grande do Sul celebrate identity of Italian immigrants and present their life and difficulties in dialect. All plays are portraits of a people and protest injuries suffered. Example: *Os três recrutas* concerns attempts of German and Italian immigrants to avoid the draft.

4921 Nejar, Carlos. *Miquel Pampa.* 2a. ed. Vitória, Brazil: Nemar; São Paulo: M. Ohno, 1991. 127 p.: ill.

Dramatic poem recounts story of a man's journey and his encounters with the clergy, vendors, and the devil. He is wounded in his struggle with the devil and dies at his destination. Author is a poet.

4922 Oliveira, Juca de. *Meno male!* São Paulo: Editora Scipione, 1989. 78 p. (Col. Palco iluminado; 1)

Play produced in 1987 under direction of Bibi Ferreira is comedy concerning Italian immigrant whose daughter is having an affair with a government official. Stereotypes are used for comic effect: father speaks with accent; minister (among others) is corrupt; secretary is in love with boss. Author is also an actor.

4923 Paiva, Marcelo Rubens. *525 linhas: teatro.* São Paulo: Editora Brasiliense, 1989. 77 p.: ill.

Playwright states that play examines post-modern, endless information, hyper reality. Mixes television soaps and reality, screen images and real people, in effort to mirror interactive TV. Scenes tell story of woman who leaves scientist-husband to become famous model. In love with her image, he kills her when she returns.

4924 Porto Alegre, Manuel de Araújo. Teatro completo de Araújo Porto Alegre. v. 1. Estabelecimento de texto, notas e aparato crítico de Renata Guerra e Edwaldo Cafezeiro. Introdução de Bárbara Heliodora. Rio de Janeiro: INACEN, 1988. 1 v. (Clássicos do teatro brasileiro; 9)

Contains playwright's unpublished works in manuscript form. Introduction describes manuscripts, where they were discovered, and changes made for contemporary reader. Includes comedies, and comic and lyric operas. Example: *Os lobisomens* concerns woman whose husband convinces her he is a werewolf as cover for his escapades. Mistaken identities provide comedy.

4925 Rangel, Paulo. *Brasil de fio a pavio.* Rio de Janeiro: Editora Codpoe, 1989. 116 p. (Col. Obras premiadas)

Received Petrobrás Prize for theater in 1988. In form of satirical, political musical, covers Brazilian history from Vargas' suicide to 1964 military coup. Actors run through scenes in chronological order creating an historical review for audience/reader. Playwright includes elaborate instructions for set variations.

4926 Rocha Filho, Rubem. *Um reino por um corsário.* Recife, Brazil: Governo do Estado de Pernambuco, Secretaria de Turismo, Cultura e Esportes/FUNDARPE; Companhia Editora de Pernambuco, 1990. 155 p. (Biblioteca comunitária de Pernambuco: Teatro; 1)

Received Hermilo Borba Filho Theater Prize for 1990. In form of musical comedy, dramatizes invasion of Rio by French pirates in 1700s. Scenes alternate among all parties concerned: local government, French government, pirates. Women are depicted as courageous, while men seem to be cowards.

4927 Rodrigues, Nelson. Teatro completo de Nelson Rodrigues. v. 3, Tragédias cariocas I. Organização e introdução de Sábato Magaldi. Rio de Janeiro: Editora Nova Fronteira, 1989. 1 v.

Vol. 3 is part of series entitled *Tragédias cariocas.* Plays examine dysfunctional families in innovative dramatic structures. Sábato Magaldi summarizes and analyzes plays, pointing out thematic and structural parallels among these and others. For example, similarities exist between *A falecida* (in this volume) and *Vestido de noiva* (in another volume).

4928 Souza, Naum Alves de. *Suburbano coração: uma peça.* Letras e músicas de Chico Buarque de Hollanda. Rio de Janeiro: Civilização Brasileira, 1989. 164 p.

Produced in Rio in 1989. Series of comic scenes revolve around three friends in search of love. One, LoveMar, finds happiness through radio show that introduces her to a truck driver. Strong women characters.

4929 Teatro social: três dramas. Rio de Janeiro: Ministério da Cultura, Instituto Nacional de Artes Cênicas (INACEN), 1986. 136 p. (Col. Prêmios)

Plays, awarded Instituto Nacional de Artes Cênicas (INACEN) drama prize for 1981–82, primarily concern oppression. *De amor encarcerado, ou, a paixão de Oscar Wilde* by Murilo Dias César treats injustice suffered by Oscar Wilde. The other two focus on Brazil: *Não seria o Arco de Triunfo um monumento ao pau-de-arara!* by Licínio Rios Neto is about Frei Tito who committed suicide due to torture suffered. *O galo* by Jaci Bezarra deals with social oppression in the Northeast.

4930 Torres, Joaquim Alves. Teatro social. Pesquisa, introdução e notas de Cláudio Heemann. Porto Alegre, Brazil: Instituto Estadual do Livro, 1990. 207 p.: bibl., ill.

Three plays by 19th-century writer Joaquim Alves Torres are consideed to be precursor to social drama of Joracy Camargo. Example: *O trabalho* pits "good" labor against evils of capitalism. *O ultraje* demonstrates consequences of adultery in a male-dominant society. Introduction contains information on playwright.

HISTORY AND CRITICISM

4931 Boal, Augusto. Augusto Boal. Rio de Janeiro: Ministério da Cultura, Instituto Nacional de Artes Cênicas, Biblioteca Edmundo Moniz, do CENACEN, 1986. 44 p.: ill. (Ciclo de palestras sobre o teatro brasileiro; 1. Col. Palestras; 1)

Transcript of talk given by Boal includes questions from audience (not always clear or complete). Topics covered include responsibility of those who create theater to protest injustice, the idea of the expression of self, philosophy behind *teatro do oprimido,* and his experience with censorship.

Castro, Consuelo de. Urgência e ruptura. See item **4915.**

Gama Filho, Oscar. Teatro romântico capixaba: Aristides Freire, Amâncio Pereira, Ernesto Guimarães. See item **4917.**

4932 George, David. The modern Brazilian stage. Austin: Univ. of Texas Press, 1992. 176 p.: bibl., ill., index.

Excellent study looks at significant theater groups in Brazil. Includes information on history of Brazilian theater during 20th century, descriptions of companies and playwrights whose work had profound effect on development of the country's theater, and analyses of both text and performance of pivotal productions.

4933 Guidarini, Mário. Nelson Rodrigues: flor de obsessão. Florianópolis, Brazil: Editora da UFSC, 1990. 204 p.: bibl.

Begins with biobibliography: events in Rodrigues' life are recounted by date, with works by him included in the narrative. Biography based on books by playwright. Remainder of text analyzes 16 of his plays. Analyses study theme, and language and its effect on action. Contains Rodrigues' theoretical discussions.

4934 Lara, Cecília de. De Pirandello a Piolim: Alcântara Machado e o teatro no modernismo. Rio de Janeiro: Ministério da Cultura, Instituto Nacional de Artes Cênicas, 1987. 153 p.: bibl. (Col. Ensaios)

Brings together Machado's writings from 1923–33 and reconstructs his role as theater critic. Discusses his view of dramatic theory and posits that his writing demonstrates presence of proposals for Brazilian theater that reflected ideas of modernism. Reviews included provide information on Brazilian theater of 1920s.

4935 Ligiéro, Zeca. Teatro & comunidade: uma experiência. Uberlândia, Brazil: Univ. Federal de Uberlândia, Depto. Formação Musical, 1983. 77 p.: ill., port.

Book is result of author's experience with community theater from 1979–80. Theater developed out of a course. Research on history of town, São Gonçalo, became a show written by students using historical events and stories. Describes various phases of the course and explains how research was done.

4936 Lima, Robert. Xangô and other Yoruba deities in the plays of Zora Seljan. (*Afro-Hisp. Rev.,* 11:1/3, 1992, p. 26–33)

Explains origin and practices of *candomblé,* and provides introduction of the playwright from Minas Gerais who incorporates figures from this religion into her plays. Characters are "saints," and plays dramatize their stories.

4937 Machado, Maria Clara. Maria Clara Machado: eu e o teatro. Rio de Janeiro: AGIR, 1991. 268 p., 16 p. of plates: bibl., ill.

Contains series of letters written by

and to Machado during 1940s-50s with auto-biographical comments at beginning and end of text. Includes information about artists, writers, and actors whose acquaintance she made through her father. Final sections recount her experience with the amateur theater group O Tablado.

4938 Martins, Leda Maria. O moderno teatro de Qorpo-Santo. Belo Horizonte, Brazil: Editora UFMG; Ouro Preto, Brazil: UFOP, 1991. 88 p.: bibl., ill. (Col. Pesquisa científica)

Author's dissertation concerns 19th-century playwright whose works became universally accessible in 1969 and who was once characterized as a precursor to romanticism. Includes information on theater history and a discussion of aspects of playwright's work that did not reflect traditional dramatic structures of his time.

4939 Moraes, Dênis de. Vianinha, cúmplice da paixão. Rio de Janeiro: Nordica, 1991. 295 p.: bibl., ill., index.

Biography is based on personal interviews and extensive research. Begins with Vianna Filho's relationship with his family and recounts family history in politics, art, theater. Gives historical background for Vianna Filho's life and work, and describes history of Brazilian theater as it affected the playwright. Bibliography and sources included.

4940 Paiva, Salvyano Cavalcanti de. Viva o rebolado!: vida e morte do teatro de revista brasileiro. Rio de Janeiro: Editora Nova Fronteira, 1991. 693 p.: bibl., ill.

History of Brazilian music hall theater contains definition and information on its origin. Provides historical background for discussion of emergence, development, and decline. Conclusion analyzes why this type of theater is no longer popular. Of interest to those who study all aspects of Brazilian theater. Includes bibliography and excerpts from shows.

4941 Pontes, Joel. O teatro moderno em Pernambuco. 2a. ed. Recife, Brazil: Governo do Estado de Pernambuco, Secretaria de Educação, Cultura e Esportes/FUNDARPE; Companhia Editora de Pernambuco, 1990.

151 p.: bibl. (Biblioteca comunitária de Pernambuco: Ensaio; 5)

First published in 1960s, work concerns 1930s-60s period. Focusing on trends, movements, and groups, describes theater companies and theater activities in various cities in Pernambuco. Covers all aspects including amateurs, critics, theater schools, and courses. Final chapter reviews "popular" theater of Ariano Suassuna and Hermilo Borba Filho.

4942 Renato, José. José Renato. Rio de Janeiro: Ministério da Cultura, Instituto Nacional de Artes Cênicas, Biblioteca Edmundo Moniz do CENACEN, 1987. 32 p.: ill., ports. (Ciclo de palestras sobre o teatro brasileiro; 4)

Talk by Renato is part of series organized by Instituto Nacional de Artes Cênicas. Renato speaks on Teatro de Arena, its history, those who participated, his relationship with the theater. Describes how works were chosen, and emphasizes group's dedication to Brazilian culture whether through use of plays by Brazilians or adaptation of universal works.

4943 Silva, Armando Sérgio da. Uma oficina de atores: a Escola de Arte Dramática de Alfredo Mesquita. São Paulo: Editora da Univ. de São Paulo, 1989. 284 p.: bibl., ill. (Série Comunicações & artes: Artes, teatro brasileiro)

Interesting study surveys dramatic arts school in São Paulo founded by Alfredo Mesquita. Reviews school's profound influence on Brazilian actors and theater. Looks at courses offered, professors, and students. Discusses amateur productions, influence of foreign directors. Emphasizes Mesquita's contribution to acting technique. Well documented.

4944 Universidade de São Paulo. Escola de Comunicações e Artes. Teatro de bonecos: bibliografia. São Paulo: ECA/USP, 1986. 38 p.

Bibliography arranged in alphabetical order contains works about puppet theater, plays, and films. First section includes books, book chapters, theses, catalogs, pamphlets, and articles. Not limited to Brazil.

TRANSLATIONS INTO ENGLISH FROM THE SPANISH AND PORTUGUESE

CAROL MAIER, *Professor of Spanish, Kent State University, Ohio*
DAPHNE PATAI, *Professor of Portuguese, University of Massachusetts, Amherst*
KATHLEEN ROSS, *Associate Professor of Spanish, New York University*

TRANSLATIONS FROM THE SPANISH

ONCE AGAIN, DURING THE CURRENT PERIOD under review (Aug. 1990-June 1993), a substantial amount of excellent work has appeared in the field of literary translation. The reservation about reception and accessibility expressed in the last volume [1] must certainly be repeated, but it is also possible to note an increased attention to translation as a mediation of which readers should be made fully aware, rather than one from which they should be protected.

This attention to practice can also be considered an attention to theory, if "theory" is used to refer not to a set of abstractions but to an informed deliberate reflection on the principles that guide translation. Although there are undoubtedly many translators who would agree with Eliot Weinberger that "Translation theory . . . is useless for translating," [2] many other translators and scholars apparently believe that the interaction between translation theory and practice must be scrutinized as thoroughly as possible. Evident with respect to both the work of individual translators and the critical study of translation in the larger sense (i.e., metaphorical, cultural, or political), such scrutiny is increasingly evident not only in the commentaries and notes of individual translators but also in the work of reviewers, literary critics, and social scientists. Examples, to cite just a few in addition to the more conventional "theory" entries reviewed below, can be found in José Piedra's comments about "packaging" Latin American culture for North American readers; [3] George Yúdice's request that critics look more closely at "how writers and other cultural workers are inserted into networks of dissemination;" [4] and Ilán Stavans' observation that the US has "limited patience for Hispanic letters," with a "kind of literary I.N.S." that monitors the yearly number of translations. [5]

The *anthologies* published during the period comprise a highly diverse group. Some of them, such as *Columbus's egg* (item **4948**) or *The secret weavers* (item **4960**) have been assembled around a specific topic; others, like *When new flowers bloomed* (item **4962**) or *Gabriela Mistral: a reader* (item **4951**), bring together selections from the work of a single writer or a particular country or countries. Still others have a much broader focus, and they aim to offer an overview, either of Latin America as a whole or of a particular group of writers; examples would be *A hammock beneath the mangoes* (item **4952**) or *Women's writing in Latin America* (item **4964**).

Although the quality of translation frequently varies within individual anthologies, it is heartening to note that editors seem to be giving increased attention to issues of translation. With a few exceptions, the translations in these anthologies range from good to excellent. Translators are acknowledged in virtually all instances, and they often figure with their own bylines in the list of contributors. Theoretical issues related to translation are also engaged in some of the introductions, such as in *Scents of wood and silence* (item **4959**) or in *Tri-Quarterly's New* *writing from Mexico* (item **4961**), whose selections were determined in part on the basis of their "translatability."

Somewhat at odds, however, with the care evident in the translation of individual pieces within collections is an apparent reluctance on the part of most editors to account fully for the criteria that guided their selections. Editors often acknowledge the inevitable subjectiveness of "quality" and "taste," but few make explicit their own definitions of those terms. Perhaps more importantly, few editors seem to have considered the extent to which compiling an anthology, as Cary Nelson has pointed out with relation to North American literature is "not only an aesthetic but also a social and political project." [6] It is to be hoped that soon editors of anthologies of Latin American literature in translation will resist even further what Thomas Colchie has referred to as the "faintly addictive nature of anthologies" (item **4952**, p. xiii). A more thorough understanding of the role played by anthologies in both the representation of Latin American literature to the North American public and in the North American literary marketplace cannot but affect editorial decisions concerning selections, size, biographical and bibliographical material, etc. These questions and the closely related question of accessibility urgently need further work, as indicated recently in essays by Myriam Díaz-Diocaretz [7] and André Lefevere. [8]

Poetry is often considered the most difficult genre to translate, and one continues to find far less Latin American poetry than fiction in English. Somewhat ironically, however, translators who do accept the challenge of poetry are apt not to be praised for the attempt but reprimanded or ignored. Other than a few notable exceptions (e.g., the work of Neruda or Paz), poetry in translation is seldom reviewed, and when the reviews do appear they tend to be harsh. Whether reviewers argue that a translator should aim to duplicate or to thoroughly "recreate" an original, they frequently point to the unfortunate alterations worked by translation; when presented with multiple versions, they tend to compare them against each other in an effort to determine which is the "best."

Not all of the poetry published during this review period deserves high praise, but the work does indicate that translations of poetry are certainly possible and worthwhile. Cola Franzen's translations of Alicia Borinsky's poems (item **4967**), for example, or Clayton Eshleman's reading of César Vallejo's *Trilce* (item **4986**), or Margaret Sayers Peden's collection of Neruda's *Odes* (item **4975**) offer editions that make the work of these poets truly accessible in English. What is more, for those readers willing to entertain multiple translations of poetry by a single poet, highly nuanced readings of texts by Jorge Tellier and Vallejo are possible. In the case of Vallejo, for instance, there are as many as four new versions of some poems—in the books published by Eshleman and Rebecca Seiferle (item **4985**) and the selections translated by Próspero Saíz [9] and Magda Bogin. [10] Conventional readings are also challenged by the interaction of photographs and words in several books, of which Cecilia Vicuña's *Unraveling words* (item **4988**) is one example. In addition, translator's comments, such as Annegret Nill's reference to an argument with Gonzalo Millán about "the sex of death" in one of his poems (item **4971**), provide insights about reading in either, or both, Spanish and English.

There were few titles in the area of *theater* during the period. One notes that all three of the volumes reviewed here are carefully presented with introductions and bibliographies, reflecting both an intended audience of practical users and student readers, and the academic presses that publish these plays. It must also be said that the volumes devoted to Griselda Gambaro (item **5001**) and Carlos Solórzano (item **5006**) bring difficult authors, well-known in their own countries, to English readers for the first time.

In the area of *brief fiction*, we note the high quality and richness of the titles on the list. Besides new work by some of the best-known Latin American authors writing today (e.g., Allende, item **4992**; Bioy Casares, item **4995**; Donoso, item **4999**; and Mutis, item **5002**), translated soon after initial publication in Spanish and published by major commercial houses, we have stories by long-established writers, introduced for the first time to the English-language audience in complete volumes through small or academic presses (e.g., Anderson Imbert, item **4993**; Coloane, item **4997**; Ferré, item **5000**; and Peri Rossi, item **5003**). Notable also is the publication of short fiction by such writers as Alegría (item **4991**), Castellanos (item **4996**), and Skármeta (item **5005**), better known in English for work in other genres. It is to be hoped that all these trends will be continued, in order that authors may be appreciated individually rather than only through anthologies. We note too the prevalence of women writers, until recently woefully undertranslated, in this list. Finally, the publication of two volumes by excellent young writers (e.g., Barros, item **4994**, and Rey Rosa, item **5004**) bodes well for the continuation of the strong tradition in Latin American short fiction.

In the translation of *fiction*, trends in the work of translators are difficult to isolate. This genre is linked most closely to the commercial concerns of the large houses where many of the Latin American novels available in translation are published and marketed—frequently with no word about the translation or translator and with no more information about the author than the few words of hype printed on the cover. One has only to compare, for instance, Magritte's sheet-wrapped faces on the Spanish edition of José Donoso's *El jardín de al lado* with the naked lovers embracing amidst the flowers on the dust jacket of the English edition (item **5021**) to recognize that more than the transfer of words is involved in "producing" a novel in translation. Excellent translations of fiction have appeared during the period, however, and it would certainly have been possible to mention more than the few examples that follow, if space had permitted.

Those examples would unquestionably include work by Andrew Hurley, a highly experienced translator responsible for versions of *Abadón el exterminador* (item **5044**) and *El palacio de las blanquísimas mofetas* (item **5012**). They would also include William I. Neuman's work with the novels of Paco Ignacio Taibo II (items **5048** and **5049**) and work by newer translators, such as Kay Prichett's translation of *Jonás y la ballena rosada* (item **5034**) or Betty Ferber's version of *1492: vida y tiempos de Juan Cabezón de Castilla* (item **5013**). Nina M. Scott's translation of *Sab* (item **5028**) should also be cited, both for its quality and for making the novel and the accompanying "Autobiography" finally available in English. Other novels long "overdue" in English that have appeared as well are *Juntacadáveres* (item **5036**), and two books by Julieta Campos (items **5019** and **5018**).

Although they could not be termed trends, two phenomena associated with the translation of fiction should be noted. First, the retranslation of such "classics" as *Los de abajo* (item **5014**) and *La muerte de Artemio Cruz* (item **5026**) makes these novels available in new versions. It also makes them available (through libraries, even if only the most recent translations are in print) in multiple versions, which offer monolingual readers a glimpse beyond the limits inherent in even the best translations. The Pittsburgh Editions of Latin American Literature are to be commended in this regard for the publication of new or revised translations based on critical editions.

A second phenomenon, made possible by university presses and small presses willing to take a chance on work that might enjoy limited commercial success, is the publication of novels eclipsed by the bestsellers of the "boom" writers and others who have become well known to North American readers. These novels include *Un mundo para Julius* (item **5016**), *El libro vacío* (item **5053**), and three Colombian novels that should prompt English-language readers to recognize that fiction from Colombia, as Jonathan Tittler has remarked, [11] "cannot be summed up in the words 'Gabriel García Márquez:'" *La casa grande* (item **5020**); *En Chimá nace un santo* (item **5054**); and *Bazar de los idiotas* (item **5010**).

Titles in the category of *essay* run a wide gamut from scholarly criticism (Benítez-Rojo, item **5055**; Dorfman, item **5059**; Espinosa, item **5058**), to memoir and diary (Borge, item **5056**; Glantz, item **5061**; Núñez, item **5063**), to indigenous anthropology as in Montejo (item **5062**). We also note volumes by Cabrera Infante, a prominent writer on cinema (item **5057**), and Eduardo Galeano's book of anecdotes and vignettes, illustrated with his own engravings (item **5060**).

Octavio Paz, winner of the 1990 Nobel Prize, has been especially well-represented in English translation during the past several years; his work is inscribed within the rich tradition of the Latin American essay as a literary form. Galeano's book transforms that tradition in a blurring of generic boundaries, as does Margo Glantz's memoir of immigration and identity, and it is to be hoped that we will see more such innovative volumes in the future.

It is with great appreciation that I note the collaboration of my new co-editor Kathleen Ross. Unless otherwise noted, she is responsible for the reviews in the sections on "Brief Fiction and Theater" and "Essays, Interviews, and Reportage" and for the paragraphs in this essay that refer to those genres. We have both endeavored to provide information about the translations that will be most helpful to teachers and scholars: our reviews, as well as our definition of "success" within each category, reflect that contingency.

We extend a note of congratulations to Margaret Sayers Peden and Eliot Weinberger, who shared the first biannual translation award established in memory of the late Gregory Kolovakos, and we offer a word of remembrance and loss in honor of Anthony Kerrigan, friend and esteemed translator of work from Spain and Spanish America. [CM with KR]

TRANSLATIONS FROM THE PORTUGUESE

Since 1990, there seems to be a decrease in the number of Brazilian works appearing in English translation. It is unclear why this is occurring. On the other hand, as the listing below indicates, quite a few trade publishers (no longer primarily Knopf) are involved in bringing out individual works from Brazil. Translation is still, however, primarily a labor of love, initiated by the translator (usually an academic), rather than a predominantly commercial matter, but this situation may be in the process of changing, as suggested by the appearance of several new series which will allow translators more ready outlets for their efforts. The Latin American Literary Review Press publishes Latin American creative writing under the series title *Discoveries*. Several of this crop's translations were published in this series. The University of Nebraska Press has inaugurated a series by Latin American Women Writers, in which some very interesting works, old and new, are being brought out. Oxford University Press (with supplementary funding from the Mellon Foundation) is undertaking the publication of Brazilian classics, a project directed by Alfredo Bosi of the Universidade de São Paulo and Richard Graham of the University of Texas. The project will commission new translations (even where old ones exist) of some 19th-century works and hopes to move into the 20th century before long.

Among the translations published since 1990, the vast majority are of contemporary works (including by the indefatigable Jorge Amado). But the appearance of several older works is especially heartening: Alencar's *Senhora* (item **5072**) is long overdue. It is mysterious that a writer of such preeminence is so underrepresented in English. Another welcome translation is of Castro Alves' abolitionist poetry (item **5066**). These are only two among the dozens of fascinating 19th-century literary figures whose works are in the public domain and could well appeal to late 20th-century audiences. A new translation of Machado de Assis' *Dom Casmurro* (item **5078**) has also been published in the past few years (at about the same time as the Helen Caldwell translation was reissued, item **5077**). Finally—and far more unusual—the appearance of *Industrial Park*, Patricia Galvão's extraordinary 1933 "proletarian novel" (item **5076**), is a welcome addition to the growing number of works available in English by Brazilian women writers. [DP]

Notes

1   See *HLAS* 52, p. 685–686.

2   Eliot Weinberger, "3 Notes on Poetry." (in *Outside stories, 1987–1991*. New York: New Directions, 1992, p. 60).

3   See José Piedra's review of *Landscapes of a new land: fiction by Latin American women*, edited by Marjorie Agosín. (*Letras Femeninas*, 17:1/2, 1991, p. 154).

4   George Yúdice, "We Are *Not* the World." (*Social Text 31/32*, 10:2/3, 1992, p. 213).

5   Article by Ilán Stavans in *The Nation*, New York, Feb. 22, 1993, p. 244.

6   Cary Nelson, "Multiculturalism Within Guarantees: From Anthologies to the Social Text." (*The Journal of the Midwest Modern Language Association*, 26:1, Spring 1993, p. 48–49).

7   Myriam Díaz-Diocaretz, "Framing Contexts, Gendered Evaluations, and the Anthological Subject" in *The politics of editing*, edited by Nicholas Spadaccini and Jenaro Talens. (Minneapolis: Univ. of Minnesota Press, 1992, p. 139–155).

8   André Lefevere, "Anthology." (in *Translation, rewriting, and the manipulation of literary fame*. New York: Routledge, 1992, p. 124–137).

9   César Abraham Vallejo, "Selections from César Abraham Vallejo's *Trilce*." Translated by Próspero Saíz. (*Abraxis*, 38/39, 1990, p. 5–63).

10   Magda Bogin, "Translating Vallejo's *Trilce*." (*Massachusetts Review*, Summer 1993, p. 183–192).

11   Book review by Jonathan Tittler in *Hispania*, 75, Dec. 1992, p. 1203.

ANTHOLOGIES

4945   Being América: essays on art, literature and identity from Latin America. Edited by Rachel Weiss, with Alan West. Fredonia, N.Y.: White Plains Press, 1991. 254 p.

Consists of papers by Central and South American writers and artists, many of whom have international reputations, presented at the festival "Latinoamérica Despierta: Art, Literature, and Identity in Latin America Today," held in 1988 at Massachusetts College of Art. Includes transcriptions of some provocative question-and-answer sessions.

4946   Beyond the border: a new age in Latin American women's fiction. Edited by Nora Erro-Peralta and Caridad Silva-Núñez. Pittsburgh, Pa.: Cleis Press, 1991. 223 p.: bibl.

Consists of 14 stories by writers b. 1900–42. Editors sought "literary quality," work unfamiliar to English-language readers, diverse themes, and wide geographical representation (11 countries, including Brazil). Introductory essay points to recurring concerns in fiction by Latin American women and provides a very general historical overview. Includes brief writers' biographies and extensive bibliographies.

4947   Castellanos, Rosario. Another way to be: selected works of Rosario Castellanos. Edited and translated by Myralyn Frizzelle Allgood. Foreword by Edward D. Terry. Athens: Univ. of Georgia Press, 1990. 146 p.: bibl.

Allgood includes poetry (*en face*), short stories, excerpts from *Balún-Canán* and *Ofi-*

cio de tinieblas, essays from El uso de la palabra, introductory material, and a selected bibliography. For the most part translations, particularly the essays, are good albeit somewhat restrained. Introduction would have been strengthened by incorporation of recent critical material.

4948 Columbus's egg: new Latin American stories on the legacy of conquest. Edited by Nick Caistor. Boston: Faber and Faber, 1992. 162 p.

Consists of 12 stories, some written for this collection, in which "contemporary writers of fiction in Spanish" from Latin American engage the question of Latin American identity and "the emotions it rouses." Afterword by Juan Goytisolo contrasts commemoration of the Spanish "Discovery" with that of the French Revolution. Translations are by Nick Caistor and others.

4949 Cuvi, Pablo et al. Diez cuentistas ecuatorianos = Ten stories from Ecuador. Traducción de Mary Ellen Fieweger. Prólogo de María del Carmen Fernández. Quito: Ediciones Libri Mundi, 1990. 316 p.

A bilingual collection of works by 10 Ecuadorian writers, all male, b. 1940s-50s. Stories selected on basis of their interest and variety. Includes brief, highly general introduction and biographical information about each writer. Translations are not wholly satisfactory because English is frequently awkward and ungrammatical.

4950 The discovery of America & other myths: a New World reader. Edited by Thomas Christensen and Carol Christensen. San Francisco: Chronicle Books, 1992. 256 p.: ill., index.

Collection is centered on "the major themes and figures of the first century or so from our post-Columbian history." Many selections are translations of material from the time of Columbus written in both European and indigenous languages. Also included is work by contemporary writers from Latin America, North America, and Europe.

4951 Gabriela Mistral: a reader. Translated by Maria Giachetti. Edited by Marjorie Agosín. Fredonia, N.Y.: White Plains Press, 1993. 227 p.

Extensive English-only selection of Mistral's poetry and prose. Included are several poems from many different volumes and

prose selections from In praise of earthly things (Santiago, 1981) and other essays about politics and Latin American figures. Agosín's sketchy, eulogistic biographical summary is disappointing and includes no bibliographical information. Giachetti's translations are uneven; she conveys Mistral's "plain words" but not her spontaneity and urgency.

4952 A hammock beneath the mangoes: stories from Latin America. Edited by Thomas Colchie. New York: Dutton, 1991. 430 p.

Editor has gathered 26 stories in this anthology, most of them reprints. The majority are from Brazil, the River Plate, and the Caribbean, although editor also has included work from Chile and Mexico. Contains brief introduction for each writer. The ten stories from Brazil (some translated for the first time) include: Jorge Amado, "The Miracle of the Birds;" Murilo Rubião, "The Ex-Magician from the Minhota Tavern;" Clarice Lispector, "Love;" Machado de Assis, "The Psychiatrist; " Moacyr Scliar, "The Plagues;" Guimarães Rosa, "The Third Bank of the River;" João Ubaldo Ribeiro, "It was a Different Day when they Killed the Pig;" Lygia Fagundes Telles, "The Corset;" Rubem Fonseca, "Lonelyhearts;" and Paulo Emilio Salles Gomes, "Twice with Helena." Each story is introduced. Many translators.

4953 Manoa. Vol. 4, No. 2, Fall 1992- . New Writing from Mexico. Edited by Hernán Lara Zavala and Darlaine Mahealani MuiLan Dudoit. Honolulu: Univ. of Hawaii Press.

Fifteen selections of fiction and poetry from Mexico are interspersed throughout the issue (rather than set apart). Includes brief essay on "New Directions in Mexican Narrative" by Ignacio Trejo Fuentes, but no introduction for poetry. Information about writers is minimal. Many translators.

4954 Mouth to mouth: poems by twelve contemporary Mexican women. Edited by Forrest Gander. Translated by Zoë Anglesey et al. Introduction by Julio Ortega. Minneapolis, Minn.: Milkweed Editions, 1993. 235 p.: bibl.

Handsome book only partially lives up to its appearance. Translations by many translators range from poor to excellent. Julio Ortega's short introduction places poems in recent Mexican literature and society, but long note about Forrest Gander makes no specific reference to his selections for this anthology. Contains brief bio-bibliographical information and personal statements for each poet. For comments on the Spanish-language text, see item **4272.**

4955 New tales of mystery and crime from Latin America. Edited and translated by Amelia S. Simpson. Rutherford, N.J.: Fairleigh Dickinson Univ. Press; London: Associated University Presses, 1992. 161 p.

Even if its eight stories were not so striking, anthology would be outstanding for its introduction. Simpson's remarks are brief, but she tells reader a great deal about Latin American mystery and crime fiction, stressing ways in which genre differs radically from both the whodunit and the hard-boiled written in English. For comment on Portuguese translation see item **5069.**

4956 Pocaterra, José Rafael *et al.* Venezuelan short stories = Cuentos venezolanos. Prólogo de Lyda Aponte de Zacklin. Traducción de Seymour Menton *et al.* Caracas: Monte Avila Editores, 1992. 274 p. (Continentes)

Readers should not let poorly translated introduction deter them from sampling the 13 stories in this collection, most of which are translated quite competently. Earliest were written by authors born at turn of the century; most recent by authors now in their 40s and 50s.

4957 Poirot, Luis. Pablo Neruda: absence and presence. Translations by Alastair Reid. New York: Norton, 1990. 189 p.: ill.

Collection of Neruda's poems and photographs of his three homes (in Isla Negra, Santiago, and Valparaíso) has been assembled in such a way that one can follow either words or pictures or both at once. Poetry selections (*en face*) are from previously published translations, most of them by Alastair Reid.

4958 River Plate section. Edited by Suzanne Jill Levine. (*Fiction/New York*, 10:1/2, 1991, p. 178–298)

Special section of issue, edited and briefly prefaced by Suzanne Jill Levine, includes 14 prose selections "from the region (and perhaps the sensibility) the British call the River Plate." Writers include Adolfo Bioy

Casares, Silvina Ocampo, Leopoldo Lugones, and Mario Benedetti. Translations by Levine and others.

4959 Scents of wood and silence: short stories by Latin American women writers. Edited by Kathleen Ross and Yvette E. Miller. Introduction by Kathleen Ross. Pittsburgh, Pa.: Latin American Literary Review Press, 1991. 218 p.: bibl. (Discoveries)

Consists of 23 stories, most of them published during 1980s, by women writers from Central and South America, including Brazil. Introductory essay highlights translation and related issues. Includes extensive bibliography for each writer, for critical studies about Latin American women writers, and for anthologies that contain their work. For comment on Portuguese translation see item **5070.**

4960 Secret weavers: stories of the fantastic by women of Argentina and Chile. Edited by Marjorie Agosin. Fredonia, N.Y.: White Plains Press, 1992. 339 p.

Although Agosin argues that "the fantastic" escapes definition and genre, she does provide a brief literary, historical, and social context for this collection of more than 40 stories by 18 writers. Selections include contemporary authors, earliest of whom began to write in 1930s. Short biography for each writer.

4961 Tri-Quarterly. No. 85, Fall 1992– . New Writing from Mexico. Edited by Reginald Gibbons. Evanston, Ill.: Northwestern Univ.

Over 50 selections that "would allow for convincing and authoritative translation," most of which also "seemed to answer in part the question 'What is Mexican?'." Gibbons' introduction discusses borders within Mexican writing and between that writing and literary work in the US. Most writers included were born after 1945; very brief byline for each.

4962 When new flowers bloomed: short stories by women writers from Costa Rica and Panama. Edited, with prologue, by Enrique Jaramillo Levi. Pittsburgh, Pa.: Latin American Literary Review Press, 1991. 208 p.: bibl. (Discoveries)

Strength of this collection is its focus. Prologue surveys Central American literature, short fiction, and the two countries from which these 19 stories are drawn. Unfortunately, Jaramillo Levi has dealt only cursorily with issues related to writing by women, a subject one would expect to find discussed at length here. Quality of translations is particularly uneven.

4963 Where angels glide at dawn: new stories from Latin America. Edited by Lori M. Carlson and Cynthia L. Ventura. Introduction by Isabel Allende. Illustrations by José Ortega. New York: J.B. Lippincott, 1990. 114 p.: ill.

Collection for children "ages 10 and up" may also interest adults. Includes 10 stories (several adaptations) by writers from Central and South America. Isabel Allende's introduction is more evocative than informative, but editors provide glossary of names and terms, and one or two sentences that place each story.

4964 Women's writing in Latin America: an anthology. Edited by Sara Castro-Klarén, Sylvia Molloy, and Beatriz Sarlo Sabajanes. Boulder, Colo.: Westview, 1991. 1 v.

Unusual in scope and focus, anthology includes nearly 50 women writers from 11 countries. Selections of poetry, narrative, and nonfiction are grouped under "Women, Self, and Writing," "The Strategies of Self-Figuration," and "Women, History, and Ideology." Emphasis is on writers not already well known in English. Translations vary greatly; many are excellent.

TRANSLATIONS FROM
THE SPANISH
Poetry

4965 Agosin, Marjorie. Circles of madness: mothers of the Plaza de Mayo. Translated by Celeste Kostopulous-Cooperman. Photographs by Alicia d'Amico and Alice Sanguinetti. Fredonia, N.Y.: White Plains Press, 1992. 1 v.

Photographs and prose poems (en face) were apparently assembled expressly for this collection. Together, they commemorate the witness borne by the mothers of the Plaza de Mayo. Agosin's work is characterized by a particular immediacy and spontaneity that have proved difficult for this translator. Preface by Emilio Mignone; afterword by Julio Cortázar.

4966 Agosin, Marjorie. Generous journeys = Travesías generosas. Translated by Cola Franzen. Reno: Univ. of Nevada; The Black Rock Press, 1992. 87 p.

"Journeys" in these 15 apostrophic poems refers to travels of New World fruits that made their way to the Old World. Cola Franzen's translations extend those travels superbly, with a sensuousness and evident love of language highly appropriate to Marjorie Agosin's Spanish. En face.

4967 Borinsky, Alicia. Timorous women. Translated by Cola Franzen. Peterborough, England: Spectacular Diseases, 1992. 52 p.

In this translation of Mujeres tímidas y la Venus de China, Franzen must have determined she would counter the fear suggested in book's title. Her work conveys admirably Borinsky's irony and urgency, perhaps pushing these even further in English than they are pushed in the Spanish. Brief translator's introduction.

4968 Cardenal, Ernesto. Golden UFOs: the Indian poems = Los ovnis de oro: poemas indios. Translated by Carlos and Monique Altschul. Edited with an introduction and glossary by Russell O. Salmon. Bloomington: Indiana Univ. Press, 1992. 453 p.

Bilingual edition includes the Altschuls' revised work from Homage to the American Indians (see HLAS 38: 6926). Salmon's introduction surveys Cardenal's poetry and chronicles development of the Indian poems, all of which are published here. Salmon's extensive glossary allows translators to incorporate Indian terms in their English.

4969 Esquivel, Julia. The certainty of spring: poems by a Guatemalan in exile. Translation by Anne Woehrle. Introduction by Joyce Hollyday. Washington: Ecumenical Program on Central America and the Caribbean, 1993. 1 v. (unpaged): map.

Translation of Florecerás Guatemala is realized in close sympathy with Esquivel's work as poet and theologian. Introductory information about the poetry's political and religious context is provided by Esquivel's own words of dedication, a brief personal memoir by Joyce Hollyday, and an essay by the editors. En face.

4970 Juarroz, Roberto. Vertical poetry: recent poems. Translated by Mary Crow. Fredonia, N.Y.: White Plains Press, 1992. 117 p.

Selection from vols. 8 through 11 of *Poesía vertical* also includes two recent unpublished poems and Mary Crow's brief but informative introduction to Juarroz's work. Crow's own work here is admirable for the concision of many of her solutions to challenges posed by Juarroz's deceptively simple, aphoristic poems. *En face.*

Light from a nearby window: contemporary Mexican poetry. See item **4270**.

4971 Millán, Gonzalo. Strange houses. Translated by Annegret Nill. Ottawa: Split Quotation, 1991. 247 p.: index

Monolingual, "representative sample" from Millán's five published books includes poems from *Virus* (see *HLAS 50:3634*) and *La ciudad* (published in Canada, where Millán lived from 1974–84). Annegret Nill's work is creative and commendable, and her "Translator's Foreword" offers brief but incisive comments about translating poetry and gender.

4972 Murillo, Rosario. Angel in the deluge. Translated by Alejandro Murguía. San Francisco, Calif.: City Lights, 1992. 85 p.: ill. (Pocket poets series; 50)

Bilingual selection from *Las esperanzas misteriosas* and *Como los ángeles* includes only briefest of introductions to Rosario Murillo's role in contemporary Nicaraguan politics and culture and as first lady of Nicaragua. While not inaccurate *per se*, Murguía's translations frequently miss Murillo's subtlety of verb tense or word choice, and they follow her syntax to a fault.

4973 Neruda, Pablo. The book of questions. Translated by William O'Daly. Port Townsend, Wash.: Copper Canyon Press, 1991. 74 p.

"Close to the spirit of the *kōan*" is how translator William O'Daly describes the 316 questions in these 74 poems. O'Daly's own work in this bilingual book, which completes the Copper Canyon Press series of late and posthumous books by Neruda, has been commended for achieving "a tone that is both meditative and spontaneous" (*Publishers Weekly*).

4974 Neruda, Pablo. Canto general. Translated by Jack Schmitt. Introduction by Roberto González Echevarría. Berkeley: Univ. of California Press, 1991. 407 p.: bibl., ill. (Latin American literature and culture; 7)

Although sections of Neruda's long

poem previously have been available in English, Schmitt is first translator to offer the work in its entirety. Schmitt has received high praise for a translation that, despite its literalness, conveys full range of *Canto general*. Roberto González Echevarría provides comprehensive introduction to poet, poem, and translator.

4975 Neruda, Pablo. Selected odes of Pablo Neruda. Translated with an introduction by Margaret Sayers Peden. Berkeley: Univ. of California Press, 1990. 375 p. (Latin American literature and culture; 4)

Generous selection of *Odas elementales* (Barcelona: 1977) "bring[s] out the sensuous quality of Neruda's odes well" (*The Nation*). Some of Peden's finest work is found here, and her introduction calls attention to the principles of simplicity, sound, sense, and shape that guide her translations. *En face.*

4976 Neruda, Pablo. Spain in the heart: hymn to the glories of the people at war, 1936–1937. Translated by Richard Schaaf. Washington: Azul Editions, 1993. 131 p.

Bilingual edition of *España en el corazón: himno a las glorias del pueblo en la guerra* (1937). Fernando Alegría's introduction celebrates poet and translator, but also places the poems with respect to Neruda's work. Leonard Lamb, a veteran of the Abraham Lincoln Brigade, places them historically. Although often literal to the point of stiffness, translation conveys Neruda's images and his emotion.

4977 Neruda, Pablo. 2000. Translated by Richard Schaaf. Washington: Azul Editions, 1992. 63 p.

Work is highly literal, Latinate translation of what Fernando Alegría terms Neruda's "book of divinations." Bilingual edition; brief eulogistic introduction by Alegría.

4978 Padilla, Heberto. A fountain, a house of stone: poems. Translated by Alastair Reid and Alexander Coleman. New York: Farrar, Straus, Giroux, 1991. 109 p.

It would be possible to echo at least one reviewer and quibble with translators' occasional choice of words. Reid and Coleman, however, convey Padilla's sensibility, his memories of Cuba, and his politics. Implicitly they also have worked in consultation with Padilla. No introductory material. *En face.*

4979 Partnoy, Alicia. Revenge of the apple = Venganza de la manzana. Translated by Richard Schaaf, Regina Kreger, and Alicia Partnoy. Illustrated by Raquel Partnoy. Pittsburgh, Pa.: Cleis Press, 1992. 99 p.: ill.

Direct, literal translations convey intensity of Partnoy's poems, if not all the sharpness of her imagery. Partnoy's introduction, written mostly in the third person, explains "apple" in title as well as her experiences as an Argentine political prisoner which gave rise to lyric fermentation and revenge. *En face.*

4980 Quijada Urías, Alfonso. They come and knock on the door. Translated by Darwin J. Flakoll. Willimantic, Conn.: Curbstone Press, 1991. 61 p.

With only a few exceptions, Flakoll's translations render appropriately this bilingual selection of work by a Salvadoran poet who works in the "vein" of Roque Dalton's "sardonic poetry centered on a nation's fate" (*Literature and politics in the Central American revolutions*, Austin: Univ. of Texas Press, 1990, p. 135).

4981 Shimose, Pedro. Reflexiones maquiavélicas = Machiavellian reflections. Translated by Michael Sisson. Madrid: Editorial Verbum, 1992. 116 p.

Book is a bilingual edition of poet's previous collection (Madrid: 1980). Sisson's reading is careful, and at times his cleverness equals Shimose's. At other times his translations would have benefitted from more risks and a more idiomatic English. Includes brief introduction to life of this Bolivian poet and a list of his works.

4982 Soto Vélez, Clemente. The blood that keeps singing = La sangre que sigue cantando. Translated by Martín Espada and Camilo Pérez-Bustillo. Willimantic, Conn.: Curbstone Press, 1991. 125 p.

Bilingual collection of poetry (with two prose selections) is drawn from five books dating back to 1937. Most selections are from *Caballo de Pano* (1959) and *La tierra prometida* (see *HLAS 44:5749*). Excellent translations, particularly of the "rhythm, repetition, and alliteration" that characterize this poetry (p. 9). Includes brief informative introduction to Soto Vélez's writing and his work for Puerto Rican independence.

4983 Teillier, Jorge. From the country of Nevermore: selected poems of Jorge Teillier. Translated and with introduction by Mary Crow. Middletown, Conn.: Wesleyan Univ. Press; Hanover, N.H.: Univ. Press of New England, 1990. 73 p. (Wesleyan poetry in translation)

Bilingual edition is drawn mostly from *Muertes y maravillas* (Santiago: 1971). In general, Mary Crow's versions support her claim that Teiller's poetry is "highly translatable into English." However, the two premises cited in her introduction (that poems in translation must also be poems in English, and that virtually "everything" about the Spanish must be retained) are at times both inevitably contradictory and visibly at odds in her work.

4984 Teillier, Jorge. In order to talk with the dead: selected poems of Jorge Teillier. Translated with an introduction by Carolyne Wright. Austin: Univ. of Texas Press, 1993. 129 p. (The Texas Pan American series)

Extensive selection of poems from *Muerte y maravillas* (Santiago: 1971), *Para un pueblo fantasma* (see *HLAS 42:5838*), and *Cartas para reinas de otras primaveras* (see *HLAS 50:3668*) includes long introductory essay by Carolyne Wright on Teillier's poetics and politics. No doubt Wright is correct about Teillier's accessibility to readers in English. She underestimates the challenge that his poems present to a translator, however. *En face.*

4985 Vallejo, César. Trilce. Translated by Rebecca Seiferle. Edited by Stanley Moss. Riverdale-on-Hudson, N.Y.: Sheep Meadow Press, 1992. 171 p.: bibl.

Seiferle's introduction makes clear her conscious decision to take risks. If critics have judged her work harshly and discounted many of her solutions, the reason is doubtless that she was not able to embed those solutions in a sustained effort that would have conveyed consistently Vallejo's intense, experimental confrontation with Spanish. *En face.*

4986 Vallejo, César. Trilce. Translated by Clayton Eshleman. Spanish text established by Julio Ortega. Introduction by Américo Ferrari. Biographical and bibliographical information by José Miguel Oviedo. New York: Marsilio Publishers, 1992. 276 p.: bibl.

Readers may take issue with individual words or lines, but they certainly will agree with Jason Wilson that this bilingual edition provides "an excellent point of departure" for reading *Trilce* (*TLS*). Eshleman has worked with Vallejo for years; he includes both a translator's introductory note and afterword. José Miguel Oviedo contributes biographical and bibliographical information.

4987 Velásquez, Lucila. El árbol de Chernobyl = The tree of Chernobyl. Prólogo de Juan Nuño. Notas de Jesus Alberto León *et al.* Traducción de Jaime Tello. Dibujos de Mateo Manaure, Alirio Rodríguez y Luis Chacón. Caracas: Monte Avila Editores, 1989. 235 p., 8 leaves of plates: bibl., ill.

Intriguing and moving sequence of poems in response to the "accident" at Chernobyl is by a Venezuelan poet who in 1986 was Ambassador to Denmark. Unfortunately, Tello's awkward translation fails to make truly accessible in English Velásquez's "nuclear poetry" in which the language of nuclear fission is introduced into a highly lyric text. *En face.*

4988 Vicuña, Cecilia. Unravelling words & the weaving of water. Translated by Eliot Weinberger and Suzanne Jill Levine. Edited by Eliot Weinberger. St. Paul, Minn.: Graywolf Press, 1992. 154 p.: ill.

Poems and photos of "precarious sculptures" are by Chilean writer and artist. Translation was largely a collaboration, with translators working closely with the poet. Most of the texts were realized with an eye to performance, and their oral dimension would be critical for full appreciation and evaluation. *En face.*

4989 Villaurrutia, Xavier and Octavio Paz. Nostalgia for death: poetry [by Xavier Villaurrutia, translated by Eliot Weinberger]. Hieroglyphs of desire: a critical study of Villaurrutia [by Octavio Paz, translated by Esther Allen]. Edited by Eliot Weinberger. Port Townsend, Wash.: Copper Canyon Press, 1993. 148 p.

Weinberger can be counted on for moving and thought-provoking translations. His work here is provocative in an additional way because, as volume's editor, he uses his brief introductory remarks to identify his own work with *Nostalgia de la muerte* as an act in support of the "pornography" threatened by recent NEA cuts and conservative politicians, and to foreground Villaurrutia's homosexuality. Paz's essay, written in 1978, offers an extensive and more conventional study of Villaurrutia's writing.

4990 Zamora, Daisy. Riverbed of memory. Translated by Barbara Paschke. San Francisco: City Lights, 1992. 129 p. (Pocket poets series; 49)

Work is bilingual edition of *En limpio se escribe la vida* (see *HLAS 52: 4201*). Paschke offers a brief introduction to the life of Nicaraguan poet Daisy Zamora, emphasizing her gradual involvement with and eventual commitment to the Sandinista Party. Paschke also conveys well the many and varied faces of what Zamora defines as her "witness."

Brief Fiction and Theater

4991 Alegría, Claribel. Family album. Translated by Amanda Hopkinson. Willimantic, Conn.: Curbstone Press, 1991. 191 p.

Includes translation of three novellas by Central American writer, which were published in Spanish under title *Pueblo de Dios y de Mandinga* (México: 1985). Although stories are not directly related, each tells of a female protagonist facing difficulty in life. Fantastic, horrific, and political aspects weave into the narration. A superb translation by Hopkinson in somewhat British English.

4992 Allende, Isabel. The stories of Eva Luna. Translated by Margaret Sayers Peden. New York: Atheneum, 1991. 330 p.

Collection includes 23 stories told by the protagonist of Allende's novel *Eva Luna* (see item **4038**). Episodes set in an imaginary Latin America concentrate on human passions, in a style similar to that of Allende's longer work (see *HLAS 52: 3766*). Fine translation by Peden captures storytelling voice of the narrative. Collection has some strong stories (e.g., "Tosca"), although that level is not consistently maintained.

4993 Anderson Imbert, Enrique. Woven on the loom of time: stories. Selected and translated by Carleton Vail and Pamela Edwards-Mondragón. Introduction by Ester Izaguirre. Austin: Univ. of Texas Press,

1990. 180 p.: bibl. (The Texas Pan American series)

Collects stories from five volumes by the underappreciated Argentine writer-scholar, spanning years 1965–85. Useful locating introduction. Translations readable and accurate. Stories display a wide range of styles, from realistic to fantastic; those from *The Cheshire cat* (see *HLAS 30:3357*) are *casos*, sometimes only a paragraph in length. No notes to explain sometimes complicated references.

4994 Barros, Pía. Astride = A horcajadas. Translated and edited by Analisa Taylor, with translations by Amanda Powell *et al.* Prologue by Juan Carlos Lértora, translated by John B. Anzalone. Santiago: Asterión, 1992. 162 p.

Bilingual edition presents each version separately. Important, strong narrative is by one of Chile's best young writers. Translations are generally high-level. As suggested in prologue, Barros explores connections between female eroticism, language, and violence. Some stories reflect Chile under the Pinochet regime; others concentrate on feminine desire within that same world.

4995 Bioy Casares, Adolfo. A Russian doll and other stories. Translated by Suzanne Jill Levine. New York: New Directions Pub. Corp., 1992. 131 p.

Intriguing volume includes recent, typically cosmopolitan, somewhat fantastic stories by Bioy Casares. Title story is especially strong. Smooth translations by Levine take occasionally controversial risks, but in general translation rises to the mastery of Spanish original, carrying reader along with ease and grace.

4996 Castellanos, Rosario. City of Kings. Translated by Robert S. Rudder and Gloria Chacón de Arjona. Introduction by Claudia Schaefer. Pittsburgh, Pa.: Latin American Literary Review Press, 1993. 143 p. (Discoveries)

Translation of *Ciudad real* (Xalapa, Mexico: 1990) is excellently introduced by Claudia Schaefer who has succinctly presented Castellanos' "space of [linguistic and political] opposition." Translators wisely have transcribed key Mayan and Spanish terms, which are explained in a glossary.

Translators also convey ironies and inequalities in Castellanos' narratives, although their own register and word choices are not always appropriate. [CM]

4997 Coloane, Francisco. Cape Horn and other stories from the end of the world. Translated and with introduction by David A. Petreman. Pittsburgh, Pa.: Latin American Literary Review Press, 1991. 184 p. (Discoveries)

Tales of southernmost reaches of South America are by Chilean writer from that region. Brief introduction demonstrates Petreman's deep knowledge of the work and his feel for its stark quality. Stories alternate between realism and lyricism, communicating in sometimes powerful description the strangeness of Tierra del Fuego. Translations are well done, with descriptive passages stronger than dialogue.

4998 Cuban theater in the United States: a critical anthology. Edited and translated by Luis F. González-Cruz and Francesca M. Colecchia. Tempe, Ariz.: Bilingual Press, 1992. 186 p.: bibl., ill.

Volume collects works written in US by nine Cuban-born playwrights, including Reinaldo Arenas. Plays are all short and of generally high quality, and in some cases were written originally in English. Translations of others range from acceptable to good. Selection reflects a broad span of concerns, themes, and styles. Introduction, notes, and bibliography successfully place works in historical context.

4999 Donoso, José. Taratuta; and, Still life with pipe: two novellas. Translated by Gregory Rabassa. New York: W.W. Norton, 1993. 158 p.

Rabassa achieves wonderfully supple, splendid translations of two novellas written in late 1980s (see item **4045**). Donoso weaves complicated tales laced with mystery, set in Europe ("Taratuta") and Chile ("Still Life with Pipe"). Told in two different first-person voices, narratives include much detail from Russian history and history of art. Small masterpieces, beautifully translated.

5000 Ferré, Rosario. The youngest doll. Translated by author, in collaboration with Diana Vélez *et al.* Foreword by Jean Franco. Lincoln: Univ. of Nebraska Press,

1991. 169 p.: bibl. (Latin American women writers)

Includes 14 stories from *Papeles de Pandora* (see *HLAS 40:6686*), along with two short essays by Ferré on her work and translations. Expertly translated collection includes some of Ferré's most important work such as "Sleeping Beauty," "Mercedes Benz 220 SL," and the title story. Short locating foreword and a brief bibliography make volume attractive for classroom use.

5001 Gambaro, Griselda. Information for foreigners: three plays. Edited, translated, and with an introduction by Marguerite Feitlowitz. Afterword by Diana Taylor. Evanston, Ill.: Northwestern Univ. Press, 1992. 175 p.: bibl.

Collection of three plays spans three decades of Argentine writer's production: "The Walls" (1963), "Information for Foreigners" (1972), and "Antígona Furiosa" (1986). Translations are generally very good, although title play slips on some colloquial expressions. Accompanying essays are useful in locating these difficult works and make volume especially good for classroom use.

5002 Mutis, Alvaro. Maqroll: three novellas. Translated by Edith Grossmann. New York: HarperCollins, 1992. 289 p.

Collects three novellas published in the 1980s, all featuring Mutis' creation Maqroll the Gaviero: *The snow of the admiral* (Madrid: 1986); *Ilona comes with the rain* (see *HLAS 52:3739*); and *Un bel morir*. Challenging, highly cerebral works full of historical, geographical, and literary references. Grossman makes her way elegantly through this dense prose, occasionally clarifying references through the translation.

5003 Peri Rossi, Cristina. A forbidden passion: stories. Translated by Mary Jane Treacy. Pittsburgh, Pa.: Cleis Press, 1993. 148 p.

Highly readable and accessible volume collects stories originally published in Spain (Barcelona: 1986). Some are short vignettes; others are more developed. All treat theme of human passions and their reverberations. Peri Rossi deserves to be better known by readers of English, and this book is an excellent introduction to her work. Translations capably rendered. Brief introduction by author places work in context.

5004 Rey Rosa, Rodrigo. Dust on her tongue. Translated by Paul Bowles. San Francisco: City Lights Books, 1992. 91 p.

Twelve stories, some very short, are from volume *El agua quieta*. Powerful, bleak, sometimes violent narratives are set in his native country by young Guatemalan writer now resident in Morocco. Bowles' translations are very fine; as he briefly notes, the bare style may "bewilder" some readers. No further locating materials are supplied.

5005 Skármeta, Antonio. Watch where the wolf is going: stories. Translated by Donald L. Schmidt and Federico Cordovez. Columbia, La.: Readers International, 1991. 188 p.

Eleven stories are collected from several volumes by the Chilean writer. Translations are generally successful in capturing Skármeta's colloquial tone, playful language, and many references to popular culture. Good selection of stories, several with political overtones, shows range of topics and settings. Book as a whole is perhaps stronger than are isolated stories.

5006 Solórzano, Carlos. Crossroads, and other plays. Translated and edited by Francesca M. Colecchia. Rutherford, N.J.: Fairleigh Dickinson Univ. Press; London: Associated University Presses, 1993. 148 p.: bibl.

Eight plays are by Guatemalan-born playwright best known for his work in Mexico. Seven are one-act, somewhat absurdist works, with *The hands of God* (see *HLAS 21: 4233*) the sole three-act play. Skillfully translated by the knowledgeable Colecchia, whose useful locating introduction and short bibliography make text accessible to readers.

5007 Valenzuela, Luisa. The censors. Translated by Hortense Carpentier *et al.* Willimantic, Conn.: Curbstone Press, 1992. 255 p.

Bilingual selection includes 20 stories previously published in English in the volumes *Clara* (New York: 1976); *Strange things happen here* (see *HLAS 44:6322*); and *Open door* (see *HLAS 52:4976*). Translations range from acceptable to very good. Facing Spanish and English texts. Volume is flawed by lack of information regarding selection criteria and original publication history, and also by absence of locating material on author and her work.

Novels

5008 Alegría, Fernando. Allende: a novel. Translated by Frank Janney. Stanford, Calif.: Stanford Univ. Press, 1993. 303 p.: appendices, bibl., ill.

In this fine translation of *Allende: mi vecino el presidente* (see item **4036**), Janney has captured well book's epic tone. Foreword by Frederick N. Nunn briefly introduces Alegría and his work; Alegría's preface explains fictional dimension of his biographical novel (*novela biográfica*). Appendices include biographical information, historical chronology, and notes.

5009 Allende, Isabel. The infinite plan: a novel. Translated by Margaret Sayers Peden. New York: HarperCollins Publishers, 1993. 380 p.

Margaret Sayers Peden offers a highly readable version of *El plan infinito* (see item **4039**) consistent with her previous work with Allende's fiction. Nevertheless, this translation of Allende's first novel set in the US has not been well received by North American critics.

5010 Alvarez Gardeazábal, Gustavo. Bazaar of the idiots. Translated by Susan F. Hill and Jonathan Tittler. Introduction by Raymond Leslie Williams. Pittsburgh, Pa.: Latin American Literary Review Press, 1991. 192 p.: ill. (Discoveries)

Although the translators of *Bazar de los idiotas* (see *HLAS 38:6657*) have followed the Spanish to a degree that some would consider paralyzing, several reviews indicate that they have made Alvarez Gardeazábal's humor, sarcasm, and social criticism thoroughly accessible. Williams provides an informative introduction to the aspects of Colombian society satirized in the novel.

5011 Arenas, Reinaldo. The doorman. Translated by Dolores M. Koch. New York: Grove Weidenfeld, 1991. 191 p.

Koch provides a successful translation, particularly with respect to word choice and idiomatic expressions, of *El portero* (see *HLAS 52:3603*), Arenas' satirical Manhattan fable about human/animal nature. Work opens with a few rough paragraphs in which several constructions seem to exemplify (de-liberately?) narrator's stated discomfort as a Cuban-in-exile obliged to use English.

5012 Arenas, Reinaldo. The palace of the white skunks. Translated by Andrew Hurley. New York: Viking, 1990. 356 p.

Having previously translated four novels by Arenas, Hurley was well qualified to work with *El palacio de las blanquísimas mofetas* (see *HLAS 48:5374*). His version of this challenging "language opera" (*Book World*) is excellent, and makes available in English the third volume of Arenas' five-part autobiographical "pentagony."

5013 Aridjis, Homero. 1492: the life and times of Juan Cabezón of Castile. Translated by Betty Ferber. New York: Summit Books, 1991. 285 p.

Provides highly competent translation of *1492: vida y tiempo de Juan Cabezón de Castilla* (see item **3698.**) Ferber not only has found convincing English for the many registers in Aridjis' historical novel, but also draws the reader into the narrative through numerous untranslated words, working definitions into the text as necessary.

5014 Azuela, Mariano. The underdogs. Translated by Frederick H. Fornoff. Coordinated by Seymour Menton. Pittsburgh, Pa.: Univ. of Pittsburgh Press, 1992. 165 p.: bibl. (The Pittsburgh editions of Latin American literature. Col. Archivos)

New translation of *Los de abajo* (Madrid: 1927), the fourth into English, includes introduction by Seymour Menton and critical essays by Carlos Fuentes, Julio Ortega, and Jorge Ruffinelli. In brief note, translator offers explanation of choices that guided his work, which is deliberate and contemporary in the best sense because of decisions, for example, to retain Azuela's paragraphing and "to leave untranslated certain names and attributes."

5015 Barnet, Miguel. Rachel's song: a novel. Translated by W. Nick Hill. Willimantic, Conn.: Curbstone Press, 1991. 125 p.

Cuban testimonial novel *Canción de Rachel* (see *HLAS 34:3521*) combines life story of a cabaret dancer with other contemporaneous materials in order to recreate atmosphere of Havana in early decades of this century. Translation provides satisfactory rendering of Rachel's earthy, colloquial voice. Crucial for study of the *testimonio*. No notes or bibliography. [KR]

5016 Bryce Echenique, Alfredo. A world for Julius: a novel. Translated by Dick Gerdes. Austin: Univ. of Texas Press, 1992. 430 p. (The Texas Pan American series)

What most engages the translator of *Un mundo para Julius* (Barcelona: 1970) is the constant and highly complex presence of speech in its narration. Although some passages in English lack sufficient agility to carry novel's frequent shifts in tone and perspective, Gerdes' version is a good one and was awarded Columbia University's Translation Center Award.

5017 Calderón, Sara Levi. The two mujeres. Translated by Gina Kaufer. San Francisco, Calif.: Aunt Lute Books, 1991. 211 p.

In this intriguing translation the English seems almost clipped, even for the short chapters and straightforward Spanish found in Calderón's sensual, transgressive *Dos mujeres* (México, 1990). Kaufer's frequent use of Spanish, however, adds yet another duality to the many found in the novel and occasions continual interaction between the two languages.

5018 Campos, Julieta. The fear of losing Eurydice: a novel. Translated by Leland H. Chambers. Normal, Ill.: Dalkey Archive Press, 1993. 121 p.

North American readers may wish for more of an introduction to Campos' work than the few words provided on volume's dust jacket. Those willing to accept the challenge, however, will find that Chambers' translation of *El miedo de perder a Eurídice* (México: 1979) offers a satisfying version of this intriguing novel.

5019 Campos, Julieta. She has reddish hair and her name is Sabina: a novel. Translated by Leland H. Chambers. Athens, Ga.: Univ. of Georgia Press, 1993. 135 p.

Albeit a bit restrained with respect to the "nervous restlessness" Chambers identifies in Campos' novel (p. xvii), translation offers a careful, sensitive reading of *Tiene los cabellos rojizos y se llama Sabina* (see *HLAS 40:6564*). Introduction briefly discusses Campos' work, focusing on relation between her fiction and her literary criticism.

5020 Cepeda Samudio, Alvaro. La casa grande. Translated by Seymour Menton. Foreword by Gabriel García Márquez. Austin: Univ. of Texas Press, 1991. 109 p.: ill. (The Texas Pan American series)

Provides unquestionably competent translation; nevertheless Menton's work raises important questions for the translation of narrative, one of which concerns formal elements. For example, Menton has retained not only the title of Cepeda Samudio's original work (see *HLAS 30:3297*), but also each of its many colons; as a result, in current English the work reads quite differently from the Colombian Spanish of the 1962 original. Another question concerns the evaluation of English translated from a Spanish that itself "translates" the style of North American writers, in this case Faulkner and Hemingway.

5021 Donoso, José. The garden next door. Translated by Hardie St. Martin. New York: Grove Press, 1992. 243 p.

Provides a generally successful translation of *El jardín de al lado* (see *HLAS 44: 5471*), with a tone appropriate for its narrator(s). However, reading is slowed occasionally by some awkwardly constructed sentences and by several footnotes with information about recent Chilean history that could have been worked into the text.

5022 Dorfman, Ariel. Hard rain. Translated by George Shivers with the author. Columbia, La.: Readers International, 1990. 270 p.

Moros en la costa (Buenos Aires: 1973) "gains noticeably" in translation (*Choice*), thanks to Dorfman's alterations and his collaboration with Shivers. Dorfman explains his changes in preface, wherein he describes circumstances of book's composition and publication in the months preceding and the days immediately following Allende's fall.

5023 Elizondo, Salvador. Farabeuf. Translated and with an afterword by John Incledon. New York: Garland, 1992. 124 p.: ill. (World literature in translation)

In his afterword Incledon speaks incisively about persuasion being the prevailing impulse in *Farabeuf, o la crónica de un instante* (1965). His translation is accurate with respect to the letter of that word, but English would have been more effective had he worked more creatively with the spirit as well.

5024 Esquivel, Laura. Like water for chocolate: a novel in monthly installments, with recipes, romances, and home remedies.

Translated by Carol Christensen and Thomas Christensen. New York: Doubleday, 1992. 245 p.

Best-selling Mexican novel *Como agua para chocolate* (see *HLAS 52:3477*) tells story of a young woman growing up on a ranch near the Texas border at the time of the Revolution. Combines motif of recipes for traditional dishes with chronological narrative that includes magical elements. Translation is acceptable, but contains a few glaring errors that should be noted for students if used for courses on literature or culture. [KR]

5025 Fuentes, Carlos. The campaign. Translated by Alfred J. Mac Adam. New York: Farrar, Straus, Giroux, 1991. 246 p.

Provides adequate, if somewhat less than entirely satisfying, translation of highly praised *La campaña* (see *HLAS 52:479*). Although some of the narrative fluctuations must be attributed to Fuentes, Mac Adam's reconstructions of Spanish syntax at times make for awkward reading; also, in some places prose seems inappropriately matter-of-fact.

5026 Fuentes, Carlos. The death of Artemio Cruz. Translated by Alfred J. Mac Adam. New York: Farrar, Straus and Giroux, 1991. 307 p.

Mac Adam has produced a highly fluent new translation of *La muerte de Artemio Cruz* (see *HLAS 25:4306*). His English is confident and idiomatic; and in addition he has clarified some of the more obscure sections of Fuentes' novel, thereby increasing their readibility through use of less "experimental" punctuation and capitalization.

5027 Gambaro, Griselda. The impenetrable Madam X. Translated by Evelyn Picon Garfield. Detroit: Wayne State Univ. Press, 1991. 149 p. (Latin American literature and culture series)

Provides very successful translation of *Lo impenetrable* (see *HLAS 52:3830*). There are instances where narrative seems somewhat informal for 19th-century prose, but Garfield's consistently ingenious punning and her unfailingly humorous and bawdy dialogue appropriately match linguistic wordplay that traverses Gambaro's suggestive spoof on the erotic novel and its (sexual) connotations.

5028 Gómez de Avellaneda y Arteaga, Gertrudis. Sab [and] Autobiography. Translated and edited by Nina M. Scott. Austin: Univ. of Texas Press, 1993. 157 p.: bibl. (The Texas Pan American series)

Although she realizes that her version may strike contemporary readers as "high-flown and rhetorical," Scott has deliberately preserved "the tone and vocabulary of nineteenth-century literature" (p. x) in her translation of *Sab* (Paris: 1920) and *Autobiografía* (Madrid: 1914). The risk was a wise one, because this translation, accompanied by an informative introduction, is fluent, elegant, and accurate.

5029 Kociancich, Vlady. The last days of William Shakespeare: a novel. Translated by Margaret Jull Costa. New York: Morrow, 1991. 297 p.

The first of Kociancich's novels to appear in (British) English, *Los últimos días de William Shakespeare* (see *HLAS 50:3455*) has been well translated, mainly because Costa has worked successfully, albeit quite literally, with the various types of narratives that comprise Kociancich's allegorical satire.

5030 Leñero, Vicente. The Gospel of Lucas Gavilán. Translated by Robert G. Mowry. Lanham, Md.: University Press of America, 1991. 257 p.

Book provides a more careful and competent translation of *El evangelio de Lucas Gavilán* (see *HLAS 44:5180*) than its rather amateurish presentation suggests (it appears to be a typescript). However, work could have benefitted from the help of a good editor. A brief foreword by John Charles Cooper discusses story of Jesucristo Gómez in the context of Liberation Theology.

5031 Mastretta, Angeles. Mexican bolero. Translated by Ann Wright. London; New York: Viking, 1989. 267 p.

In *Arráncame la vida* (see *HLAS 48:5193*), the challenge for the translator lies in work's picaresque first-person female narrator. The English of Ann Wright's Cati is credible, although significantly less colloquial and colorful than Mastretta's. A brief introduction, historical chronology, and glossary provide information about pertinent Mexican dates, events, and terms found in the text.

5032 Medina, Enrique. The tombs. Translated and with an introduction by David William Foster. New York: Garland Pub., 1993. 319 p. (World literature in translation)

Although readers may wish for more information about Medina and his work, they will appreciate Foster's succinct but thorough introduction to the "constellation of reasons" given to show why world of *Las tumbas* (see *HLAS 36:4398*) cannot fail to be "repugnant." Not least of those reasons is "aggressive register of colloquial language" with which Foster works convincingly as a translator.

5033 Molina, Silvia. Gray skies tomorrow. Translated by John Mitchell and Ruth Mitchell de Aguilar. Kaneohe, Hawaii: Plover Press, 1993. 104 p.

Provides accurate but somewhat less than dynamic translation of *La mañana debe seguir gris* (see *HLAS 42:5198*). Molina's narrator offers straightforward presentation of her brief relationship with Mexican poet José Carlos Becerra. Although translators convey that directness well, a more colloquial English would have increased the immediacy of her experiences.

5034 Montes, José Wolfango. Jonah and the pink whale. Translated by Kay Pritchett. Fayetteville: Univ. of Arkansas Press, 1991. 264 p.

Jonás y la ballena rosada (La Habana: 1987) won the Casa de las Américas Prize in 1987. In this translation Kay Pritchett has done an excellent job with a highly idiomatic first-person narrator who reveals his own foibles and the corruption of contemporary Bolivian society. Brief introduction by Edgar Lora Gumiel.

5035 Montes Huidobro, Matías. Qwert and the wedding gown. Translated by John Mitchell and Ruth Mitchell de Aguilar. Kaneohe, Hawaii: Plover Press, 1992. 165 p.

Provides abbreviated version of *Desterrados al fuego* (México: 1975). If novel's plot seems "sketchy" (*Publishers Weekly*), this may be attributable to extensive cuts made in final chapters. Translators have rendered Montes Huidobro's first-person narrative in an English less than colloquial, which is not entirely inappropriate given narrator's displacement.

5036 Onetti, Juan Carlos. Body snatcher. Translated by Alfred J. Mac Adam. New York: Pantheon Books, 1991. 305 p.

Described by one reviewer as "exuberantly translated" (James Polk, *The New York Times*), *Juntacadáveres* (see *HLAS 28:2062*) finally appears in English. Mac Adam's version is indeed a good one, with only occasional rough spots where narrative passages adhere too closely to Spanish syntax, and where word choice relies too heavily on cognates.

5037 Onetti, Juan Carlos. The pit [and] Tonight. Translated by Peter Bush. London: Quartet Books, 1991. 215 p.

Provides decidedly British, highly—and appropriately—idiomatic translation of *El pozo* (1930) and *Para esta noche* (Buenos Aires: 1943). However, at times that colloquial register and Spanish sentence structure seem to work at cross purposes.

5038 Parra, Teresa de la. Mama Blanca's memoirs. Translated by Harriet de Onís and revised by Frederick H. Fornoff. Critical ed. Pittsburgh, Pa.: Univ. of Pittsburgh Press, 1993. 183 p.: bibl., ill. (Pittsburgh editions of Latin American literature. Col. Archivos)

Fornoff brings De Onís' *Mama Blanca's Souvenirs* (see *HLAS 24:5270*) into line with definitive edition of *Memorias de Mamá Blanca* (UNESCO; Col. Archivos: 1988) followed here. Translator introduces some significant changes, but for the most part retains earlier version. A foreword by Sylvia Molloy and a collection of critical essays coordinated by Doris Sommer accompany the translation.

5039 Puig, Manuel. Tropical night falling. Translated by Suzanne Jill Levine. New York: Simon & Schuster, 1991. 189 p.

In this fine translation of *Cae la noche tropical* (see *HLAS 52:3859*), Puig's last novel, Levine has worked well with book's principal challenges: the distinct yet closely related voices of two elderly sisters and their poignant and deceptively trivial conversation alternated with occasional fragments of intercalated material.

5040 Quesada, Roberto. The ships. Translated by Hardie St. Martin. New York: Four Walls Eight Windows, 1992. 184 p.

Perhaps the biggest challenge for a

translator of *Los barcos* is novel's continual, fast-paced, highly colloquial dialogue. There are occasional slips, but overall St. Martin has managed successfully to situate that dialogue in idiomatic North American English without compromising its specifically Honduran context.

5041 Rojas, Marta. Dead man's cave. Edited by Mayra Fernández. Translated by Margarita Zimmermann. La Habana: José Martí Pub. House, 1988. 146 p.

Although far closer to journalism than to fiction, Rojas' retelling of the week after Castro's attack on the Moncada barracks in 1953 could have read like fiction if English translation had achieved the immediacy of *La cueva del muerto* (see *HLAS 50:1838*). An introduction and glossary would have provided a better historical context than the numerous footnotes.

5042 Romero, José Rubén. Notes of a villager: a Mexican poet's youth and revolution. Translated by John Mitchell and Ruth Mitchell de Aguilar. Kaneohe, Hawaii: Plover Press, 1988. 223 p.

Provides unfortunately still version of *Apuntes de un lugareño* (Barcelona: 1932), in which English is sometimes awkward to the point of inaccuracy ("but well flensed she threw it into a gully"—p. 53). Given novel's historical context, readers might wish for more of an introduction than the few paragraphs about Romero.

5043 Ruy Sánchez, Alberto. Mogador. Translated by Mark Schafer. San Francisco: City Lights Books, 1992. 107 p.

Schafer has titled his translation of *Los nombres del aire* (see *HLAS 50:3119*) with the name of the city off the Moroccan coast in which Ruy Sánchez locates this novel and other works. One senses the intensity of book's acclaimed poetic prose, even though in the English that intensity is not achieved consistently.

5044 Sábato, Ernesto R. The angel of darkness. Translated by Andrew Hurley. New York: Ballantine Books, 1991. 435 p.

Andrew Hurley's highly—and justly—praised translation of Sábato's dense, difficult *Abbadón, el exterminador* (see *HLAS 38: 6767*) has been credited with, in places, reading "better than the original" (*The New York Times*).

5045 Saer, Juan José. The witness. Translated by Margaret Jull Costa. St. Paul, Minn.: Serpent's Tail, 1991. 1 v.

Costa radically altered title of Saer's *El entenado* (see *HLAS 48:5615*), and in doing so no doubt altered the reader's expectations as well. Her translation is admirable, though, for her English elegantly conveys Saer's 20th-century narrative of Solís' 17th-century expedition in which a boy's experiences are presented in the words of an old man.

5046 Soriano, Osvaldo. Shadows. Translated by Alfred J. Mac Adam. New York: A.A. Knopf, 1993. 187 p.

The pace and narrator of *Una sombra ya pronto serás* (see item **4154**) are particularly congenial to Mac Adam's strengths as a translator, although North American readers may or may not find these elements engrossing. Mac Adam has created "a strangely endearing deadpan voice" (*Publishers Weekly*) that seems just right for Soriano's protagonist.

5047 Taibo, Paco Ignacio. Calling all heroes: a manual for taking power. Translated by John Mitchell and Ruth Mitchell de Aguilar. Preface by Jorge Castañeda. Kaneohe, Hawaii: Plover Press, 1990. 113 p.: appendix.

Héroes convocados: manual para la toma de poder (México: 1982) recounts a "revenge" of the brutal defeat suffered by Mexico's 1968 student movement. In general, translation is adequate, although Taibo's work merits a more idiomatic English. Brief historical orientation provided by Jorge Castañeda's introduction and Taibo's own appendix.

5048 Taibo, Paco Ignacio. The shadow of the shadow. Translated by William I. Neuman. New York: Viking, 1991. 228 p.

Neuman's work here with *La sombra de la sombra* (México: 1986) lives up to the highly praised, idiomatic prose he developed for Taibo's fiction in *An easy thing* (see *HLAS 52:5008*). One could argue with specific decisions or question some of Taibo's characterizations, but this translation is worth studying for its energy and inventiveness.

5049 Taibo, Paco Ignacio. Some clouds. Translated by William I. Neuman. New York: Viking, 1992. 163 p.

It remains to be seen whether North American readers will be as captivated by Hector Belascoarán Shayne as were those in

Mexico, but this version of *Algunas nubes* (México: 1985) thoroughly earns the "wit" attributed to Neuman's work (*The New York Times*).

5050 Valenzuela, Luisa. Black novel with Argentines. Translated by Toby Talbot. New York: Simon & Schuster, 1992. 220 p.

Perhaps it is inevitable that in English the distinctly Argentine element in *Novela negra con argentinos* (see *HLAS 52:3874*) remains somewhat parenthetical. However, Talbot's translation conveys well Valenzuela's intense word plays, her exploration of limits, her experimentation with the detective novel, and the relationship between fiction and reality.

5051 Valle, Rosamel del. Eva, the fugitive. Translated and with an introduction by Anna Balakian. Berkeley: Univ. of California Press, 1990. 105 p.: bibl. (Latin American literature and culture; 5)

The first English version of *Eva y la fuga* (1930; pub. 1970) is preceded by an excellent introduction and is successful in various ways. However, Balakian's acknowledged lack of confidence in English as a vehicle truly adequate for ambiguity creates a drawback for her as a translator, and leads to instances of the "stasis" she cites as surrealism's "only sin" (p. 17).

5052 Vázquez Rial, Horacio. Triste's History. Translated by Jo Labanyi. Columbia, La.: Readers International, 1990. 216 p.

Author provides his own prologue to the Buenos Aires of *Historia del Triste* (1985), to his life as a dual citizen of Spain and Argentina, and to his novels of which this is the fourth. Jo Labanyi's (British) translation follows Spanish syntax closely, wisely retaining Vázquez Rial's paragraphing and punctuation. The sentences with multiple colons, however, probably have a more disconcerting effect in English than in Spanish.

5053 Vicens, Josefina. The empty book: a novel. Preface by Octavio Paz. Translated by David Lauer. Austin: Univ. of Texas Press, 1992. 123 p. (The Texas Pan American series)

Extensive introduction to Vicens' work—emphasizing particularly the use of alter-egos such as this novel's first-person narrator and the "boom" the book anticipated—precedes the careful, albeit at times overly

cautious, translation of *El libro vacío* (see *HLAS 23:5024*). Lauer also provides well-taken comments about translating gender. Includes brief preface by Octavio Paz that is contemporary to the original novel.

5054 Zapata Olivella, Manuel. A saint is born in Chimá. Translated by Thomas E. Kooreman. Introduction by John S. Brushwood. Austin: Univ. of Texas Press, 1991. 109 p. (The Texas Pan American series)

Kooreman's translation of *En Chimá nace un santo* (Barcelona: 1963) is generally disappointing. As Jonathan Tittler has noted, Kooreman's work needed further revision, and he stayed "too close to Zapata's lexicon and grammar" (*Hispania*). Brushwood's introduction places novel in the context of Colombian and Latin American narrative. For related article, see item **5093.**

Essays, Interviews, and Reportage

5055 Benítez Rojo, Antonio. The repeating island: the Caribbean and the postmodern perspective. Translated by James Maraniss. Durham, N.C.: Duke Univ. Press, 1992. 302 p.: bibl. (Post-contemporary interventions)

Benítez Rojo's complicated prose is difficult; Maraniss has successfully captured his tone, at once scholarly and intimate, with only occasional awkward moments. *La isla que se repite* (Hanover, N.H.: 1989) provides key critical study of Caribbean culture during last decade; present work is a translation of major importance. For literary critic's comment see item **3852.**

5056 Borge, Tomás. The patient impatience: from boyhood to guerilla: a personal narrative of Nicaragua's struggle for liberation. Translated by Russell Bartley, Darwin J. Flakoll, and Sylvia Yoneda. Willimantic, Conn.: Curbstone Press, 1992. 452 p.

La paciente impaciencia (Managua: 1989) is a testimonial of the Sandinista leader's personal trajectory from early childhood up through the struggle against Somoza. Present work provides excellent translation, fluid and gripping, and at times surpassing original Spanish. Includes much detail from Nicaraguan history; lack of locating material reduces accessibility for uninformed reader.

5057 Cabrera Infante, Guillermo. A twenti-eth century job. Translated by Kenneth Hall and the author. London: Faber, 1991. 371 p.: index.

Cabrera Infante's collected cinema reviews of 1954–60 (*Un oficio del siglo 20: G. Caín, 1954–1960*, Bogotá: 1987) were originally published in Cuba. Although characterized by one reviewer as "able" (G. Pérez), translation is quite splendid; difficult Spanish wordplays are rendered into English versions with no consequent loss of fun.

5058 Corrosive signs: essays on experimental poetry — visual, concrete, alternative. Edited by César Espinosa. Translated by Harry Polkinhorn. Washington: Maisonneuve Press, 1990. 129 p.: bibl., ill.

Essays by experimental poets from Latin America, Spain, and Portugal on their work were originally gathered in 1986 (*Signos corrosivos*) in conjunction with an exhibition in Mexico and accompanied by visual images. Locating introduction gives historical-cultural background. Competent translations; a valuable volume.

5059 Dorfman, Ariel. Some write to the future: essays on contemporary Latin American fiction. Translated by George Shivers with the author. Durham, N.C.: Duke Univ. Press, 1991. 255 p.: bibl.

Critical essays of 1967–90 deal with interrelationship of fiction, politics, and identity in work of writers such as Asturias, Borges, and García Márquez. Offers as well a trajectory of Dorfman's own literary evolution. Some essays originally written in English; others smoothly translated from Spanish.

5060 Galeano, Eduardo H. The book of embraces. Translated by Cedric Belfrage with Mark Schafer. New York: W.W. Norton, 1991. 281 p.: ill.

El libro de los abrazos (see *HLAS 52: 3896*) offers vignettes of daily life, often set in Latin America, that sometimes shock with an ironic tone. Text is juxtaposed with Galeano's fanciful, somewhat surreal engravings. Translated with palpable affection and characteristic grace by Belfrage; a tribute to his skill and closeness to Galeano.

5061 Glantz, Margo. The family tree: an illustrated novel. Translated by Susan Bassnett. St. Paul, Minn.: Serpent's Tail, 1990. 186 p.

Despite translation's subtitle, *Las genealogías* (México: 1981) is a moving, nonfictional memoir of the migration of Glantz's parents from the Jewish Ukraine to Mexico in 1920s, and of her own struggle with a double identity. Translation, in rather British English, is consistently sensitive and has some brilliant moments. Helpful glossary identifies Mexican and Yiddish cultural figures frequently mentioned in the narrative.

5062 Montejo, Victor. The bird who cleans the world: and other Mayan fables. Translated by Wallace Kaufman. Preface by Victor Montejo. Introduction by Allan Burns. Willimantic, Conn.: Curbstone Press, 1991. 120 p.: col. ill.

Collects oral fables of Jacalteca Maya of Guatemala, most of which have animal protagonists. Preface places fables in past and present cultural context. Illustrations from Mayan ceramics complement text. Not stated whether translation is from original Mayan language or from Spanish; no original available.

5063 Núñez, Guillermo. Diary of a voyage. Translated and with introduction, notes, and afterword by Cola Franzen. London: Spectacular Diseases, 1990. 63 p.

Diario de viaje (Santiago: 1989) is a journal kept by a prominent Chilean painter during his imprisonment under Pinochet regime in 1974. This excellent translation communicates pathos even better than original Spanish, which moves at a sometimes frantic pace. Franzen's notes and introduction, along with text of Núñez's 1975 statement read to UNESCO, frame a moving portrayal of triumph over torture.

5064 Paz, Octavio. In search of the present: Nobel lecture, 1990. Translated by Anthony Stanton. Bilingual ed. San Diego, Calif.: Harcourt Brace Jovanovich, 1990. 68 p.

In his Nobel acceptance lecture, Paz addresses a familiar topic—the search for modernity, particularly in Latin America—and also reflects on the state of humankind at the end of the 20th century. Paz's elegant prose becomes rather more prosaic in Stanton's translation.

5065 Paz, Octavio. The other voice: essays on modern poetry. Translated by Helen Lane. New York: Harcourt Brace Jovanovich, 1991. 160 p.

In *La otra voz: poesía y fin de siglo* (Barcelona: 1990), Paz rejects concept of postmodernism and continues his meditations on poetry and modernity, starting at the point where his *Children of the mire* (see *HLAS 44: 6326*) leaves off. Second section of *La otra voz* examines poetry at the present time. Lane's melodic translation does justice to Paz's own poetic voice, which permeates his prose.

TRANSLATIONS FROM THE PORTUGUESE
Poetry

5066 Alves, Castro. The major abolitionist poems. Edited, translated, and with introduction by Amy A. Peterson. New York: Garland Pub., 1990. 169 p.: bibl. (World literature in translation; 5)

Long-awaited volume at last makes Castro Alves' important abolitionist work available to English-language readers. This bilingual edition opts for blank verse and faithful renditions. While not attaining status of independent English-language poems, the volume is very valuable and useful. Includes sensitive preface and introduction, and careful annotations.

5067 Espínola, Adriano. Taxi, or, Poem of love in transit. Translated and edited by Charles A. Perrone. Critical afterwords by translator and Elizabeth Lowe. New York: Garland, 1992. 98 p.: maps. (World literature in translation; 21)

Beautifully produced volume (complete with maps) introduces Espínola's narrative poem (São Paulo: 1986), and includes some annotations by the author and others by the translator. Excellent translation is faithful to original's energy, rhythms, and typographical and expressive games.

Brief Fiction and Theater

A hammock beneath the mangoes: stories from Latin America. See item **4952.**

5068 Lispector, Clarice. The Foreign Legion: stories and chronicles. Translated with afterword by Giovanni Pontiero. New York: New Directions Pub. Corp., 1992. 219 p. (A New Directions paperback; NDP732)

Lispector's 1964 volume (see *HLAS 28:*

2676) contains 13 stories, of the caliber of those found in *Laços de família* (see *HLAS 24:5748*; for English translation, *Family ties*, see *HLAS 38:7372*). Stories are followed by over 100 short pieces including chronicles, microstories, aphorisms, anecdotes, brief meditations and snatches of conversation, and a play—all ably and evocatively translated.

5069 New tales of mystery and crime from Latin America. Edited, translated, and introduced by Amelia S. Simpson. Rutherford, N.J.: Fairleigh Dickinson Univ. Press; London: Associated Univ. Presses, 1992. 161 p.

Includes four hitherto untranslated stories from Brazil: Ignácio de Loyola Brandão, "Monday's Heads;" Paulo Rangel, "Deposition;" Rubem Fonseca, "Mandrake;" and Glauco Rodrigues Correa, "The South Bay Crime." Excellent renditions of the dry, tough, and at times parodic Chandleresque tone favored by most of these writers. See also item **4955.**

Ribeiro, Manoel Paes. O bicho-homem, esse covarde. See item **4795.**

5070 Scents of wood and silence: short stories by Latin American women writers. Edited by Kathleen Ross and Yvette E. Miller. Introduction by Kathleen Ross. Pittsburgh, Pa.: Latin American Literary Review Press, 1991. 218 p.: bibl. (Discoveries)

Includes three versions of hitherto untranslated texts: 1) Lygia Fagundes Telles' famous story "The Structure of the Soap Bubble," translated by David George; 2) Clarice Lispector's "Beauty and the Beast, or, the Wound Too Great," translated by Earl E. Fitz; and 3) Nélida Piñon's "The Heat of Things," translated by Gregory Rabassa. See also item **4959.**

5071 Steen, Edla van. A bag of stories. Translated and with introduction by David George. Pittsburgh, Pa.: Latin American Literary Review Press, 1991. 174 p. (Discoveries)

David George, who is emerging as an important translator of Brazilian works, here presents an anthology of Van Steen's stories which reveal the ample gifts that have gained her a growing reputation among contemporary Brazilian writers. Very well translated, with great sensitivity to nuances of narrative voices.

Novels

5072 Alencar, José Martiniano de. Senhora: profile of a woman. Translated by Catarina Feldmann Edinger. Austin: Univ. of Texas Press, 1994. 198 p. (The Texas Pan American series)

Alencar's important novel (Rio de Janeiro: 1875)—half critique and exposé, half endorsement of intricate interplay of money and gender in 19th-century Carioca life—is at last available in English. Edinger's competent and fluent translation largely succeeds in capturing flavor and tone of original.

5073 Amado, Jorge. The war of the saints. Translated by Gregory Rabassa. New York: Bantam Books, 1993. 357 p.

Amado's latest vehicle is vintage Amado. Work presents elaborate portrait of Bahia, with particularly detailed descriptions of region's Afro-Brazilian religious practices in the familiar (at times overly familiar) style and tone that both Amado and his able translator Gregory Rabassa can effortlessly produce. Includes lengthy glossary of Afro-Brazilian terms.

5074 Buarque de Hollanda, Chico. Turbulence: a novel. Translated by Peter Bush. New York: Pantheon Books, 1992. 164 p.

This novel, a belated example of a *noveau roman* recalling Butor, Sarraute, and Robbe-Grillet (see item **4726**), explores obsessed and surreal consciousness of its first-person narrator. Bush's translation is uneven. Though much of translation is fluent and accurate, there are repeated instances of poor word choices that stand out in the English.

5075 Coelho, Paulo. The alchemist. Translated by Alan R. Clarke. San Francisco: HarperSanFrancisco, 1993. 177 p.

Fable of a boy in search of his destiny, drawing on myth and folklore and inspirational prose reminiscent of *Jonathan Livingston Seagull*, has sold over half a million copies in Brazil since its 1988 publication. Competently translated; the belabored simplicity of the original has led the translator to some pruning.

5076 Galvão, Patrícia Parque industrial: romance proletário = Industrial park: a proletarian novel. Translated by Elizabeth and Kenneth David Jackson. Afterword by Kenneth David Jackson. Lincoln: Univ. of Nebraska Press, 1993. 153 p.: bibl., ill. (Latin American women writers)

"Pagu's" famous (and then forgotten) modernist novel, at once Marxist and feminist, was first published in 1933 (when she was 22 years old) under the pseudonym Mara Lobo. Fascinating work was challenge to translators, who have produced a very readable and evocative text and followed it with an excellent essay.

5077 Machado de Assis. Dom Casmurro. Translated by Helen Caldwell. Foreword by Elizabeth Hardwick. New York: Noonday Press, 1991. 263 p.

See item **5078.**

5078 Machado de Assis. Dom Casmurro—Lord Taciturn. Translated and with introduction by R. L. Scott-Buccleuch. London: Peter Owen, 1992 216 p.

Nearly 40 years after Helen Caldwell's 1953 translation (see *HLAS 19:5303*) (reprinted New York: Noonday Press, 1991, with foreword by Elizabeth Hardwick, see item **5077**), this new version of Machado's masterpiece has appeared. Both translations are readable and graceful in parts, but each eliminates certain passages, simplifies the original, and introduces some awkward phrases (each version differently), which suggest that a volume incorporating the best of both translations would come closer to representing Machado.

5079 Machado de Assis. Philosopher or dog? Translated by Clotilde Wilson. New York: Noonday Press, 1992. 271 p.

Work is reprint (unfortunately renamed) of the Machado classic *Quincas Borba*, first published in English in 1954.

5080 Miranda, Ana Maria. Bay of All Saints and every conceivable sin. Translated by Giovanni Pontiero. New York: Viking, 1991. 305 p.

Controversial historical/adventure story published in 1989 is set in Bahia in late 17th century, with Gregório de Matos as main character. Translation adequately reproduces original, which is written in a simple, at times plodding, style with very few subordinate clauses. It is unclear why translator has chosen to delete entire phrases.

5081 Piñon, Nélida. Caetana's sweet song. Translated by Helen Lane. New York: Knopf; Random House, 1992. 401 p.

Piñon's elegant and complex story of dreams and delusions in small town of Trindade (Rio de Janeiro: 1987) is rendered in an equally elegant English by Helen Lane, who in 1989 translated Piñon's *República dos sonhos* (see *HLAS 52: 5043*). Extremely careful and subtle translation is faithful to tone, rhythms, and turns of phrase of original.

5082 Steen, Edla van. Village of the ghost bells: a novel. Translated by David George. Austin: Univ. of Texas Press, 1991. 197 p. (Texas Pan American series)

Presents excellent translation of fascinating and mysterious 1983 novel *Corações mordidos* (see *HLAS 48:6161*), about the failure of a community on outskirts of São Paulo. George has real flair for Van Steen's deceptively simple but in fact intricate and multifaceted narrative voice. He renders her evocative style with elegance and fidelity.

Essays, Interviews, and Reportage

5083 A book of days for the Brazilian literary year. Edited by Márcio Souza and Gilberto Vilar de Carvalho. Rio de Janeiro: Fundação Biblioteca Nacional, 1993. unpaged.

Extremely useful and attractive book includes photographs, drawings, and verbal sketches providing key information about literary figures and events in Brazil for every day in the year.

5084 Lispector, Clarice. Discovering the world. Translated by Giovanni Pontiero. Manchester, England: Carcanet, 1992. 652 p.

Between Aug. 1967 and Dec. 1973 Clarice contributed a weekly column to *Jornal do Brasil.* Hybrid in form—not quite chronicles, stories, or meditations—columns were first published as a book in 1984 (see *HLAS 48:6221*). That work is now available in a competent translation by Pontiero, who has emerged as the leading English-language translator of Lispector.

5085 Paiva, Marcelo Rubens. Happy old year: an autobiography. Translated by David George. Pittsburgh, Pa.: Latin American Literary Review Press, 1991. 238 p. (Series Discoveries)

Paiva's memoir of his life before and after a 1979 swimming accident left him paralyzed (São Paulo: 1982) is imaginatively trans-lated into an informal English that well approximates, but at times exaggerates, colloquial flavor of original. Intrusive and too frequent explanations of culturally-specific items mar the translation.

BIBLIOGRAPHY, THEORY, AND PRACTICE

5086 Barnstone, Willis. With Borges on an ordinary evening in Buenos Aires: a memoir. Urbana: Univ. of Illinois Press, 1993. 198 p.: bibl., ill., index.

Although Barnstone has focused his memoir not on his translations of Borges but rather on his friendship and many meetings with him, this is unquestionably a translator's book in a much larger sense. Those meetings involve not only discussions of translation practice (both Barnstone's and that of other translators), but also shared meals, trips, readings, and numerous experiences that translators seldom recount in commentaries about their work.

5087 Beuchat, Cecilia and **Carolina Valdivieso.** Literatura para niños, cultura y traducción. (*Taller Let.,* 18, 1990, p. 55–64)

Discusses "culture-bound" terms and works in translation of literature for children. Authors cite examples of material in French, German, and English; suggest a possible classification of problems; and offer strategies for dealing with specific situations.

5088 Brotherston, Gordon. Book of the fourth world: reading the Native Americas through their literature. Cambridge; New York: Cambridge Univ. Press, 1992. 478 p., 24 p. of plates: bibl., ill. (some col.), index, maps.

Although it would be possible to discuss Brotherston's entire volume in terms of translation, several sections of the work are of particular interest to translators: "Prologue: America as the Fourth World;" Pt. 1, "Text;" and Pt. 4, "Into the Language of America."

5089 Caracciolo Trejo, E. Octavio Paz, traductor. (*Siglo XX,* 10:1/2, 1992, p. 195–209)

Examines Paz's comments about translation included in his essays, and also considers the "desinteresado papel secundario, de mediador" that author finds in Paz's translations of work by poets such as John Donne, Andrew Marvell, and Fernando Pessoa.

5090 Dingwaney, Anuradha and **Carol Maier.** Translation as a method for cross-cultural teaching. (*in* Understanding others: cultural and cross-cultural studies and the teaching of literature. Urbana, Ill.: National Council of Teachers of English, 1992, p. 47–62)

Includes extended discussion of Rigoberta Menchú's *Me llamo Rigoberta Menchú y así me nació la conciencia* (Barcelona: 1983).

5091 Englebert, Jo Anne. Neither Hades nor hell: problems of allusion in the translation of Central American poetry. (*Lang. Commun.*, 10:1, 1990, p. 57–62)

Author uses remark by Guatemalan poet Julio Fausto Aguilera to reflect on strategies for making unfamiliar allusions accessible in translation without stripping them of their poetry, their allusiveness.

5092 Kaminsky, Amy K. Translating gender. (*in* Reading the body politic: feminist criticism and Latin American women writers. Minneapolis: Univ. of Minnesota Press, 1993, p. 1–13)

Provides excellent discussion of linguistic and cultural complexities of the terms "género" and "gender;" of the impossibility of using them interchangeably; and of the care required when one attempts to translate (between) them.

5093 Kooreman, Thomas E. Translating *En Chimá nace un santo.* (*Afro-Hisp. Rev.*, 10:3, Sept. 1991, p. 33–36)

Translator of Manuel Zapata Olivella's novel (see item **5054**) explains some of his decisions and the methods of working that guided them.

5094 Levine, Suzanne Jill. Escritura, traducción, desplazamiento: un acercamiento a *Maitreya*. (*Rev. Iberoam.*, 57:154, enero/marzo 1991, p. 309–315)

Based on her translation of Severo Sarduy's novel (see *HLAS 50:4287*), author expands on her comments in *The subversive scribe* (item **5095**) about writing, translation, and displacement.

5095 Levine, Suzanne Jill. The subversive scribe: translating Latin American fiction. St. Paul, Minn.: Graywolf Press, 1991. 196 p.: bibl., index.

Levine has written candid, informative, and interesting essays about one transla-

tor's practice and her extensive work with Spanish American writers, in particular Guillermo Cabrera Infante, Manuel Puig, and Severo Sarduy.

5096 Martín-Ogunsola, Dellita L. Translation as a poetic experience/experiment: the short fiction of Quince Duncan. (*Afro-Hisp. Rev.*, 10:3, Sept. 1991, p. 42–50)

Translator discusses her work with Costa Rican writer Quince Duncan, in particular her effort to find in English a language that would be accessible but also "truly reflect the character of [the] Afro-Costa Ricans" in Duncan's stories.

5097 On the translation of Native American literatures. Edited by Brian Swann. Washington: Smithsonian Institution Press, 1992. 478 p.: bibl., ill., index.

In addition to several introductory essays that will interest students and scholars of Latin America, an entire section of this important collection of essays is devoted to Central and South America, with contributions by Miguel León Portilla, Louise M. Burkhart, Willard Gingerich, Kay Simmons, Allan F. Burns, Dennis Tedlock, Joel Sherzer, and Nancy H. Hornberger.

5098 Rodríguez Morell, Jorge Luis. La idiosincrasia cubana en la traducción poética a la lengua inglesa: análisis de dos poemas-tipo. (*Santiago/Cuba*, 72, marzo 1989, p. 31–52, bibl.)

Analyzes English-language translations of "Tengo" and "Tierra en la Sierra y el Llano" contained in *Cuban poetry, 1959–1966* (La Habana: 1967).

5099 Santaella, Lúcia. Literatura é tradução: J.L. Borges. (*Face/São Paulo*, 1:1 jan./junho 1988, p. 19–37)

Presents "uma possível teoria da tradução" to be found in Borges' work. Includes a discussion of translation with respect to transculturation, parody, invention, and literary creation itself.

5100 Schalekamp, Jean. Dos traducciones: *La route des Flandres* y *The old gringo.* (*Cuad. Trad. Interp.*, 11/12, p. 37–46)

The translator of Fuentes' work into Dutch reads Margaret Sayers Peden's translation of *El viejo gringo* (see *HLAS 48:6555*), and finds so many mistranslations that he questions the "collaboration" between translator and author announced on book's title page.

5101 **Translating Latin America: culture as text.** Edited by William Luis and Julio Rodríguez-Luis. Binghamton, N.Y.: State Univ. of New York (SUNY), Center for Research in Translation, 1991. 348 p. (Translation perspectives; 6)

Includes selected essays from "Translating Latin America: an Interdisciplinary Conference on Culture as Text" (SUNY Binghamton, April 1990). Essays are uneven in quality, but many are excellent and all relate directly to the theory, practice, or praxis of translating Latin American literature for a North American public.

5102 *Translation Review.* No. 32/33, 1990 [through] No. 40, 1992. Richardson, Tex.: Univ. of Texas at Dallas.

Several articles in this journal, devoted exclusively to translation, will be of particular interest to scholars and students of Latin America: Carol Maier, "Reviewing Latin American Literature in Translation: Time to 'Proceed to the Larger Question' "(No. 34/35, 1991, p. 18–24); Daphne Patai, "Translating Jorge de Sena" (No. 38–39, 1992, p. 7–11); and Elena C. Murray Parodi, "Mexican Spanish: a Border Within Many Borders?: Experiences of a Bicultural Translator" (No. 38–39, 1992, p. 12–15). Issues also include numerous reviews of interest.

JOURNAL ABBREVIATIONS

Afro-Hisp. Rev. Afro-Hispanic Review. Univ. of Missouri-Columbia. Columbia, Missouri.

Aisthesis/Santiago. Aisthesis. Univ. Católica, Centro de Investigaciones Estéticas. Santiago.

Alba Am. Alba de América. Instituto Literario y Cultural Hispánico. Westminster, Calif.

Am. Lat./Moscow. América Latina. Academia de Ciencias de la Unión de Repúblicas Soviéticas Socialistas. Moscow.

An. Antropol. Anales de Antropología. Univ. Nacional Autónoma de México, Instituto de Investigaciones Históricas. México.

Anales/Göteborg. Anales. Instituto Iberoamericano, Univ. de Gotemburgo. Göteborg, Sweden.

Anu. Estud. Am. Anuario de Estudios Americanos. Consejo Superior de Investigaciones Científicas; Univ. de Sevilla, Escuela de Estudios Hispano-Americanos. Sevilla, Spain.

Anu. Estud. Centroam. Anuario de Estudios Centroamericanos. Univ. de Costa Rica. San José.

Anu. IEHS. Anuario IEHS. Univ. Nacional del Centro de la Provincia de Buenos Aires, Instituto de Estudios Histórico-Sociales. Tandil, Argentina.

Apunt. Postmod. Apuntes Postmodernos: Una Revista Cubana de Crítica Cultural, Social, Política y de los Artes. Verbum, Inc. Miami, Fla.

Bol. Acad. Chil. Bellas Artes. Boletín de la Academia Chilena de Bellas Artes. Instituto de Chile. Santiago.

Cad. Negros. Cadernos Negros. São Paulo.

Can. J. Lat. Am. Caribb. Stud. Canadian Journal of Latin American and Caribbean Studies. Univ. of Ottawa. Ontario, Canada.

Caravelle/Toulouse. Caravelle. Cahiers du monde hispanique et luso-brésilien. Univ. de Toulouse, Institute d'études hispaniques, hispano-americaines et luso-brésiliennes. Toulouse, France.

Caribb. Stud. Caribbean Studies. Univ. of Puerto Rico, Institute of Caribbean Studies. Río Piedras.

Casa Am. Casa de las Américas. La Habana.

Chasqui/Williamsburg. Chasqui. Dept. of Modern Languages, College of William and Mary. Williamsburg, Va.

Colon. Lat. Am. Rev. Colonial Latin American Review. Simon H. Rifkind Center for the Humanities, Dept. of Romance Languages, City College of New York. New York.

Comp. Civiliz. Rev. Comparative Civilizations Review. Dept. of History, Dickinson College. Carlisle, Penn.

Conjunto/Habana. Conjunto. Revista de Teatro Latinoamericano. Comité Permanente de Festivales; Casa de las Américas. La Habana.

Creac. Estética Teor. Artes. Creación: Estética y Teoría de las Artes. Instituto de Estética y Teoría de las Artes. Madrid.

Criterios/Habana. Criterios: Revista de Teoría Literaria, Estética y Culturología. Casa de las Américas. La Habana.

Cuad. Am. Cuadernos Americanos. Editorial Cultura. México.

Cuad. Trad. Interp. Cuadernos de Traducción e Interpretación = Quaderns de Traducció i Interpretació. Univ. Autónoma de Barcelona. Spain.

Dispositio/Ann Arbor. Dispositio. Dept. of Romance Languages, Univ. of Michigan. Ann Arbor.

Edad Oro. Edad de Oro. Depto. de Filología Española, Univ. Autónoma. Madrid.

Explic. Textos Lit. Explicación de Textos Literarios. Dept. of Spanish and Portuguese, California State Univ., Sacramento.

Face/São Paulo. Face. Pontifícia Univ. Católica de São Paulo.

Fiction/New York. Fiction. City College, CUNY. New York.

Filología/Buenos Aires. Filología. Univ. de Buenos Aires, Facultad de Filosofía y Letras. Buenos Aires.

Gestos/Irvine. Gestos. Dept. of Spanish and Portuguese, Univ. of Calif., Irvine.

Hisp. J. Hispanic Journal. Indiana Univ. of Pennsylvania, Dept. of Foreign Languages. Indiana, Penn.

Hisp. Rev. Hispanic Review. Univ. of Pennsylvania, Dept. of Romance Languages. Philadelphia, Penn.

Hispamérica/Gaithersburg. Hispamérica. Gaithersburg, Md.

Hispania/Teachers. Hispania. American Assn. of Teachers of Spanish and Portuguese; Mississippi State Univ., University, Miss.

Hispanófila/Chapel Hill. Hispanófila. Univ. of North Carolina. Chapel Hill, N.C.

Hora Poesía. Hora de poesía. Bruguera. Barcelona, Spain.

Hoy Hist. Hoy es Historia: Revista Bimestral de Historia Nacional e Iberoamericana. Editorial Raíces. Montevideo.

Ibero-Am. Arch. Ibero-Amerikanisches Archiv. Ibero-Amerikanisches Institut. Berlin.

Iberoromania/Tübingen. Iberoromania. Max Niemeyer Verlag. Tübingen, Germany.

Inti/Providence. Inti: Revista de Literatura Hispánica. Providence College, R.I.

Islas/Santa Clara. Islas. Univ. Central de Las Villas. Santa Clara, Cuba.

J. Hisp. Philol. Journal of Hispanic Philology. Dept. of Modern Languages, Florida State Univ., Tallahassee, Fla.

Kañína/San José. Kañína. Univ. de Costa Rica. San José.

Lang. Commun. Language & Communication. Pergamon Press. New York.

LARR. Latin American Research Review. Latin American Research Review Board. Univ. of New Mexico, Albuquerque, N.M.

Lat. Am. Indian Lit. J. Latin American Indian Literatures Journal. Geneva College. Beaver Falls, Penn.

Lat. Am. Lit. Rev. Latin American Literary Review. Carnegie-Mellon Univ., Dept. of Modern Languages. Pittsburgh, Penn.

Lat. Am. Perspect. Latin American Perspectives. Univ. of California. Newbury Park, Calif.

Lat. Am. Theatre Rev. Latin American Theatre Review. Univ. of Kansas, Center of Latin American Studies. Lawrence, Kan.

Let. Cuba. Letras Cubanas. La Habana.

Lit. Lingüíst. Literatura y Lingüística. Instituto Profesional de Estudios Superiores Blas Cañas. Santiago.

Logos/Serena. Logos: Revista de Lingüística, Filosofía y Literatura. Facultad de Humanidades, Univ. de La Serena. La Serena, Chile.

Manoa/Honolulu. Manoa: A Pacific Journal of International Writing. Univ. of Hawaii Press. Honolulu.

Mesoamérica/Antigua. Mesoamérica. Centro de Investigaciones Regionales de Mesoamérica. Antigua, Guatemala.

Mester/UCLA. Mester. Univ. of California, Dept. of Spanish and Portuguese. Los Angeles.

Misc. Hist. Ecuat. Miscelánea Histórica Ecuatoriana: Revista de Investigaciones

Históricas de los Museos del Banco Central del Ecuador. Museos del Banco Central del Ecuador. Quito.

Nuevo Texto Crít. Nuevo Texto Crítico. Dept. of Spanish and Portuguese. Stanford Univ., Palo Alto, Calif.

Palabra Hombre. La Palabra y el Hombre. Univ. Veracruzana. Xalapa, Mexico.

Publ. Inst. Estud. Iberoam. Publicaciones del Instituto de Estudios Iberoamericanos. Instituto de Estudios Iberamericanos. Buenos Aires.

Quinto Cent. Quinto Centenario. Depto. de Historia de América, Univ. Complutense de Madrid.

Renaissance Q. Renaissance Quarterly. Renaissance Society of America. New York.

Representations/Berkeley. Representations. Univ. of California Press. Berkeley.

Rev. Bibl. Nac. José Martí. Revista de la Biblioteca Nacional José Martí. La Habana.

Rev. Can. Estud. Hisp. Revista Canadiense de Estudios Hispánicos. Asociación Canadiense de Hispanistas; Univ. of Toronto. Toronto, Canada.

Rev. Chil. Humanid. Revista Chilena de Humanidades. Facultad de Filosofía, Humanidades y Educación, Univ. de Chile. Santiago.

Rev. Crít. Lit. Latinoam. Revista de Crítica Literaria Latinoamericana. Latinoamericana Editores. Lima.

Rev. Esp. Antropol. Am. Revista Española de Antropología Americana. Facultad de Geografía e Historia. Univ. Complutense de Madrid.

Rev. Estud. Colomb. Latinoam. Revista de Estudios Colombianos y Latinoamericanos. Asociación de Colombianistas Norteamericanos; Tercer Mundo Editores. Boulder, Colo.

Rev. Estud. Hisp./Poughkeepsie. Revista de Estudios Hispánicos. Dept. of Hispanic Studies, Vassar College. Poughkeepsie, N.Y.

Rev. Estud. Hisp./Río Piedras. Revista de Estudios Hispánicos. Univ. de Puerto Rico, Facultad de Humanidades. Río Piedras.

Rev. Hisp. Mod. Revista Hispánica Moderna. Hispanic Institute, Columbia Univ. New York.

Rev. Iberoam. Revista Iberoamericana. Instituto Internacional de Literatura Iberoamericana; Univ. de Pittsburgh. Pittsburgh, Penn.

Roman. Q. Romance Quarterly. Heldref Publications. Washington.

Santiago/Cuba. Santiago. Univ. de Oriente. Santiago, Cuba.

SECOLAS Ann. SECOLAS Annals. Southeastern Conference on Latin American Studies; West Georgia College. Carrollton, Ga.

Siglo XX. Siglo XX. Twentieth Century Spanish Assn. of America. Lincoln, Neb.

Signos Univ. Signos Universitarios: Revista de la Universidad del Salvador. Univ. del Salvador. Buenos Aires.

Social. Particip. Socialismo y Participación. Ediciones Socialismo y Participación. Lima.

Studies/Dublin. Studies. Dublin.

Taller Let. Taller de Letras. Instituto de Letras, Pontificia Univ. Católica de Chile. Santiago.

Thesaurus/Bogotá. Thesaurus. Instituto Caro y Cuervo. Bogotá.

Torre/Río Piedras. La Torre. Univ. de Puerto Rico. Río Piedras.

Transl. Rev. Translation Review. Univ. of Texas at Dallas. Richardson.

Tri-Quarterly/Evanston. Tri-Quarterly. Northwestern Univ., Evanston, Ill.

Unión/Habana. Unión. Unión de Escritores y Artistas de Cuba. La Habana.

William Mary Q. The William and Mary Quarterly. College of William and Mary. Williamsburg, Va.

MUSIC

ROBERT STEVENSON, *Professor of Music, University of California, Los Angeles*

THE PARAMOUNT EVENT OF THE BIENNIUM was the appearance of the *Bibliografía musicológica latinoamericana: no. 1, 1987-1988-1989*, published in two successive issues of *Revista Musical Chilena* (Vol. 46, Nos. 177–178, enero-dic. 1992). A cooperative venture of the Asociación Argentina de Musicología and *Revista Musical Chilena*, under the general editorship of Gerardo V. Huseby, this bibliography enlisted the cooperation of national representatives in nine Spanish-speaking countries plus Puerto Rico. Although neither Brazil nor Haiti were represented among the members of the editorial board, both nations are represented among the total of its 650 entries. A voluminous index, exhaustive cross-references, and an abundance of annotations give this noble enterprise a cachet hitherto unknown, north or south of the Rio Grande. Doctoral dissertations, master's theses, papers read at musicological assemblies that were duplicated but not printed, and reviews give this bibliography a scope far wider than anything thus far attempted elsewhere. A panegyric of the enterprise that appeared in the *Inter-American Music Review* (Vol. 12, No. 2, Spring/Summer 1992, p. 119) itemized other virtues.

At the close of 1992, Macmillan (London) issued *The New Grove dictionary of opera* or *NGDO* in four volumes (1296 p., 1315 p., 1370 p., and 1342 p., respectively). Edited by Stanley Sadie, with the assistance of Christina Bashford, it became at once indispensable for Latin Americanists because of the inclusion of every known Latin American opera composer ranging from the Brazilian João Gomes de Araújo (1846–1943) to the Mexican Manuel de Zumaya (1678?-1755). More particularly, the plots of the chief Latin American operas from *Bomarzo* to *Yerma* are summarized, and singers born in Latin America from Alva to Vinay are awarded biographical resumes. In addition, histories of opera productions and auditoriums are provided for Belém, Bogotá, Buenos Aires, Caracas, Havana, Lima, Manaus, Mexico City, Port-au-Prince, Rio de Janeiro, Salvador (Bahia), Santiago, and São Paulo; and Argentina, Brazil, Chile, Cuba, and Mexico earn country articles.

A lexicon planned in eight volumes, *Pipers Enzyklopädie des Musiktheaters* (Munich/Zürich: Piper, 1986-), includes in the first two volumes valuable articles by Malena Kuss on Miguel Bernal Jiménez's *Tata Vasco* (Vol. 1, p. 317–318), on Juan José Castro's *Proserpina e lo straniero* (Vol 1., p. 503–505), and on Alberto Ginastera's *Don Rodrigo* and *Bomarzo* (Vol. 2, p. 380–386). The data supplied by Norbert Christen and Peter Stalder on Carlos Gomes' *Il Guarany, Fosca, Salvator Rosa,* and *Lo schiavo* (Vol. 2, p. 497–504) are far more meticulous and exact than that found in any previous lexicon.

Latin American articles in international encyclopedias will always be eagerly welcomed, provided the entries contain accurate information. *The Oxford dictionary of opera* by John Warrack and Ewan West (Oxford Univ. Press, 1992) unfortunately repeats the same errors that disfigured the articles on Latin American nations in the 1979 second edition of *The concise Oxford dictionary of opera* by Harold Rosenthal and John Warrack. The Ginastera article is now expanded but lacks any bibliography; Villa-Lobos finally creeps in but with a mere eight lines that, even so, entail inaccurate statements.

Nicolas Slonimsky's eighth edition of *Baker's biographical dictionary of musicians* (New York: Schirmer Books, 1992) continues in the same prospering vein that made his fifth, sixth, and seventh editions (1958, 1978, 1984) cynosures. Especially felicitous in his Latin American coverage, he claims the distinction of still being the only international lexicographer with a *Music of Latin America* to his credit (a work based on firsthand contacts with Chávez, Ginastera, Santa Cruz, Villa-Lobos, and their ilk; New York: Thos. Y. Crowell, 1945; also published in Spanish, Buenos Aires, 1947).

National encyclopedias, even when published as sumptuously as the 14-volume *Enciclopedia de México* (1987–88) directed by José Rogelio Alvarez, can gravely disappoint the serious music researcher. Among South American national encyclopedias, the six-volume *Enciclopedia ilustrada del Perú* edited by Alberto Tauro (1987, item **5281**), does by way of exception contain numerous musically useful articles.

Glancing forward, the multivolume music lexicon that promises to supersede all others—so far as the Spanish-speaking Americas are concerned—will be the *Diccionario de la música española e hispanoamericana*, edited in Madrid by Emilio Casares Rodicio, Ismael Fernández de la Cuesta, and José López-Calo. Funded lavishly by the Sociedad General de Autores de España, this impending dictionary has already ushered in a new epoch in Latin American musicology.

GENERAL

5103 Aretz, Isabel. Historia de la etnomusicología en América Latina: desde la época precolombina hasta nuestros días. Caracas: Fundef-Conac-OEA, 1991. 381 p.: facsims., ill., maps, music, photos.

Splendid companion contains a treasure trove of the most variegated types of information. Reviewed in *Inter-American Music Review* (Vol. 12, No. 2, Spring/Summer 1992, p. 117–118).

5104 Béhague, Gerard. Gilbert Chase. (*Lat. Am. Music Rev.*, 13:2, Fall/Winter 1992, 3 unnumbered preliminary pages, photo)

The most illustrious of Chase's pupils pays a moving tribute to the "dean of American musicologists and cultural historians of Spanish, American, and Latin American music," who died at Chapel Hill, North Carolina, Feb. 22, 1992.

5105 Fogarada: antología de la marimba. Recopilación de César Pineda del Valle. Tuxtla Gutiérrez, Mexico: Gobierno del Estado de Chiapas, Consejo Estatal de Fomento a la Investigación y Difusión de la Cultura, Instituto Chiapaneco de Cultura, 1990. 481 p.: bibl., ill. (Serie Nuestros pueblos; 2)

The compiler's purpose, in his own words, has been to include everything ever published concerning the marimba that he could lay his hands on. A full-time instructor at the Univ. Autónoma de Chiapas, he previously published a novel, *Bartolito,* and a collection of poems. The present volume contains 125 pages of poems dedicated to, or about, the marimba. Without any kind of analytic index, the volume becomes more bedside reading than a contribution to organology.

5106 Fürst-Heidtmann, Monika. Francisco Curt Lange: Pionier, Mittler, Nestor der Musikwissenschaft in Lateinamerika. (*Ibero-Am. Arch.*, 17:2/3, 1991, p. 245–258)

Encomiastic review of F.C. Lange's career and publications by a German music journalist born at Potsdam in 1940.

5107 Kazadi wa Mukuna and **Tiago de Oliveira Pinto.** The study of African musical contribution to Latin America and the Caribbean: a methodological guideline. (*Bull. Int. Anthropol. Ethnol.*, 32/33, 1990/1991, p. 47–49)

To class what is not demonstrably European in Latin American music as being African belies reality. Individuals of African descent in Latin America came from widely disparate classes and climates and their music developed differently from that of their areas of origin.

5108 Kriázheva, Irina. Qué preocupa a los musicólogos latinamericanistas. (*Am. Lat./Moscow*, 10, Oct. 1990, p. 78–85, bibl.)

Despite the title, author concerns herself exclusively with celebrities such as Carlos Vega, Vicente Mendoza, Isabel Aretz, and Rafael José de Menezes Bastos, who classify as ethnomusicologists. In her critiques she often beats dead horses.

5109 Kuss, Malena. Identity and change: nativism in operas from Argentina, Brazil, and Mexico. (*in* Musical repercussions of 1492. Washington: Smithsonian Institution Press, 1992, p. 299–335, bibl., music)

Examples drawn from the operas of Argentinians Boero, Gaito, Ginastera, and De Rogatis, Brazilian Fernández, and Mexicans Bernal Jiménez and Ortega reveal the autochthonous underpinnings of selected New World examplars. Author, the leading world authority on her subject, also includes Ginastera's *Tres danzas argentinas* and *Variaciones concertantes* in her net.

5110 Lange, Francisco Curt. El redescubrimiento de Domenico Zipoli. (*Montalbán/Caracas*, 22, 1990, p. 207–227)

Lange recounts his own contributions and those of others to the reconstruction of Zipoli's biography and the recovery of his compositions. Author's status as Agregado Cultural (Uruguay) has aided him monumentally in his international travels and access to documents.

5111 Musical repercussions of 1492: encounters in text and performance. Edited by Carol E. Robertson. Washington: Smithsonian Institution Press, 1992. 486 p: bibl., ill., index.

This handsome volume, dedicated to *La Malinche*, contains essays by 20 American and European scholars. Some articles are self-contradictory. For instance, in "Mythologizing Pocahontas" her death date is given as both 1614 (p. 289) and 1617 (p. 293), but she is reported as being alive in 1619 (p. 292). Maintaining consistency is worsened by the difficulty in interpretating such sources as the Nahuatl *Cantares mexicanos.* Although the reader is urged to add to "the list of accomplished American composers" the names of "Nezahualcóyotl, Nezahualpilli, Temilotzin, Xocoténcatl, [and] Tecayehuatzin," not one indigenous Mexican or Guatemalan composer from the 16th-18th centuries is mentioned even though "Indigenous" is capitalized every time it appears. For annotations of individual articles, see items **5109, 5113, 5115, 5226.**

5112 Nobre, Marlos. Vanguardias musicales en América Latina. (*Gaceta/Bogotá*, 13, mayo/junio/julio 1992, p. 45–47, ill.)

Not until 1963, when at age 24 he enrolled in the Centro Latinoamericano de Altos Estudios Musicales at Buenos Aires, did Nobre have any knowledge of any Latin American composers, including even the most famous. However, he had already familiarized himself with leading European vanguardists.

5113 Olsen, Dale A. Implications of music technologies in the pre-Columbian Andes. (*in* Musical repercussions of 1492. Washington: Smithsonian Institution Press, 1992, p. 65–88, bibl., ill., map, music, table)

Although fully realizing the value of exact and minute descriptions of archaeological instruments, author rises above mere description to interpretation—valuably reflecting on uses and symbolism inherent in Chimú, Chincha, Chancay, Nasca, and Tairona clay survivals.

5114 Omojola, Bode. Kiriboto music in Yoruba culture. (*Bull. Int. Anthropol. Ethnol.*, 32/33, 1990/1991, p. 121–142, photos, music)

The language of the Yoruba is tonal. The unison melodic line in Kiriboto pentatonic singing follows inflections of the language. Drums are almost exclusively played by men. Yoruba language lacks an equivalent for the European word "music" but does have a word for drumming. Although overlapping of leader and responding chorus can cause two simultaneous pitches, all song is monodic. Songs of entreaty and thanksgiving are addressed to the appropriate deities.

5115 Rawcliffe, Susan. Complex acoustics in pre-Columbian flute systems. (*in* Musical repercussions of 1492. Washington: Smithsonian Institution Press, 1992, p. 35–63, bibl., charts, ill.)

Ceramist author finds in both the interior and exterior features of archaeological clay instruments reasons for their timbre and clues to the ritualistic purposes which they served.

5116 Stevenson, Robert. Introducción al tema: documento final. (*in* Conferencia Interamericana de Educación Musical, *8th, Washington, 1991.* Actas. Washington: Consejo Interamericano de Música, 1992, p. 60–73)

Keynote address, differentiating the historical panorama in the US and in Latin America.

5117 Stevenson, Robert. La música colonial en América Latina. (*in* América Latina colonial: población, sociedad y cultura. Barcelona: Editorial Crítica, 1990, v. 4, p. 307–330, 369–370, bibl.)

Survey of colonial music in Spanish-speaking areas.

5118 Tunas-Serna, Jane. The *nueva canción* and its mass-mediated performance context. (*Lat. Am. Music Rev.*, 13:2, Fall/Winter 1992, p. 139–157, bibl.)

Author deals chiefly with lyrics of songs by Chilean and Cuban protesters—acknowledging that "it is very difficult to define *nueva canción* as a musical style."

5119 Veiga, Manuel. Transmissão e geração do conhecimento musical. (*Art Rev./ Salvador,* abril/junho 1981, p. 73–82, bibl.)

Dedicating this essay to the memory of his daughter Tina, Veiga studies processes of musical change, "a phenomenon of extreme complexity," but one which may illumine the deepest recesses of human ratiocination.

5120 Vicuña Lyon, Magdalena. Sesión de estudio en el XV Congreso de la Sociedad Internacional de Musicología. (*Rev. Music. Chil.,* 46:178, julio/dic. 1992, p. 125–126)

The International Musicological Society Study Session in question (April, 1992) was devoted to the relationships between ethnomusicology and historical musicology. Luis Merino Montero presided and seven officially invited musicologists participated: Victoria Eli (Cuba), María Ester Grebe (Chile), Gerardo

Huseby (Argentina), Francisco Curt Lange (Venezuela), Steve Loza (US), Maria Elizabeth Lucas (Brazil), and Irma Ruiz (Argentina). Interlocutors included: Manuel Veiga (Brazil), Juan Carlos Estenssoro (Peru), Julio Estrada (Mexico), Daniel Orozco (Cuba), Samuel Claro-Valdés (Chile), and from the US, Malena Kuss, T. Frank Kennedy, and Enrique Arias.

ARGENTINA

5121 Arizaga, Rodolfo and **Pompeyo Camps.** Historia de la música en la Argentina. Buenos Aires: Ricordi Americana, 1990. 119 p.: bibl., index. (Manuales musicales)

Brief handbook provides more than a mere catalog of names. The most acclaimed colonial Jesuit, Domenico Zipoli, never served as chapelmaster in any Roman church, nor did he die in 1725. Nonetheless, this is an unusually accurate volume with no scholarly pretension. Alberto Williams and Juan Carlos Paz engage authors' sympathies and Alberto Ginastera lacks the density or space that his transcendence should have guaranteed him. The mere page on Carlos Gardel will not appease his idolators.

5122 Bensusan, Harold Guy. Carlos Gardel and the tango. (*in* The human tradition in Latin America: the twentieth century. Edited by William H. Beezley and Judith Ewell. Wilmington, Del.: Scholarly Resources, 1987, p. 167–180, bibl.)

Author states that Gardel was possibly born in 1887 at Toulouse, but later abandoned to the streets by his parents in Buenos Aires. A foster mother named Bertha Gardes or Gardel took him in. Following release from jail in 1907, he used his contacts with the underworld class to help him climb the ladder to fame and fortune. Fifty years after his death at Medellín in 1935, electronic wizardry has cleansed the surface noise and imposed new, more opulent, and sophisticated harmonics on recordings that he began making in 1915.

Cancionero rioplatense, 1880–1925. See item **3624.**

Collier, Simon. The popular roots of the Argentine tango. See item **2935.**

5123 De Persia, Jorge. En torno a Manuel de Falla: músicos españoles en Argentina. (*in* El destierro español en América: un trasvase cultural. Recopilación de Nicolás Sánchez Albornoz. Madrid: Instituto de Cooperación Iberoamericana; Sociedad Estatal Quinto Centenario, 1991, p. 77–91)

Although Falla chose to spend his last years in Alta Gracia, Argentina did not bestir itself over exiled Spaniards as did Lázaro Cárdenas' régime. Author of this meticulously documented article gives welcome details concerning the Argentine years of Jaime Pahissa and Julián Bautista. He closes with an anecdote referring to Marta Argerich's first teacher, the Catalan pianist Ernestina Corma de Kussrow.

5124 Fakih, Carlos José. Gardel, perfeccionamiento en el tiempo. (*Todo es Hist.*, 24:282, dic. 1990, p. 25–45, bibl., ill.)

This excellent traversal of events in Gardel's career leaves unresolved many intimate details. His professional male associates are profiled, but his putative *novias* remain shadowy and nameless. Author catalogs Gardel's recordings and occasionally touches on the lyrics, but never gives any satisfying analysis of the music nor differentiates among the types of songs Gardel recorded.

5125 Franze, Juan Pedro. Argentina. (*in* The New Grove Dictionary of Opera. New York: Grove's Dictionaries of Music, 1992, v. 1, p. 166–167)

The first performance of *Tosca* in the Western Hemisphere took place at Rosario three months after the Rome premiere. The Colón in Buenos Aires has staged 58 premieres of Argentine operas. Felipe Boero's *El Matrero* (12 July 1929) "has been aptly described as the most Argentine opera ever composed."

5126 Franze, Juan Pedro. Boero, Felipe. (*in* The New Grove Dictionary of Opera. New York: Grove's Dictionaries of Music, 1992, v. 1, p. 513)

Seven stage works by Boero were premiered at the Teatro Colón between June 29, 1918 (*Tucumán*) and Nov. 12, 1954 (*Zincalí*), the most successful being the three-act *El Matrero*, July 12, 1929.

5127 Greco, Orlando del. Carlos Gardel y los autores de sus canciones. Buenos Aires: Ediciones Akian, 1990. 419 p., 33 p. of plates: bibl., ill.

The fruit of a 30-year effort, this alphabetized encyclopedia of "authors" whose effu-

sions Gardel had something to do with includes figures as diverse as Herb Brown, Arthur Freed, and Francesco Paolo Tosti. Greco does not sufficiently clarify who was composer and who was lyricist.

5128 Jiménez, David. Tango y literatura. (*Gaceta/Bogotá*, 13, mayo/junio/julio 1992, p. 6–8, ill.)

Early diatribe against immorality of the tango appeared in *El Diario* (Buenos Aires), Feb. 6, 1910. Jean Richepin's defense (1913) did not assuage Leopoldo Lugones' sentiments against it. Author continues with an exhaustive list of Argentines favorably inclined or hostile to the tango. Not the music, but the dancers' motions and the lyrics decided for or against the tango.

5129 Lafourcade, Enrique. Carlitos Gardel, mejor que nunca. Santiago: Editorial Bruguera, 1985. 121 p.: ill.

Not all quotations that sprinkle this reminiscence album honor Gardel. Jorge Luis Borges "did not like Gardel because he had the same smile as Perón" and "moreover the voices of Perón and of Gardel were equally melodramatic and *sentibleras*" (p. 31). Only a week before his death, Gardel, in an interview at Bogotá (*El Diario Nacional*, June 18, 1935), confessed that "due to his career, he had no intention of marrying" (p. 24).

5130 Le Pera, José. Carlos Gardel: sus amigos, su última gira. Palabras liminares de Juan Angel Russo. Buenos Aires: Corregidor, 1991. 149 p.: ill.

Despite the title announcing male friends (Razzano, Cadicamo, Aleta, Aguilar, Rafael Rossi, and others), author also lightly profiles some of Gardel's women associates.

5131 Molina, Jorge Edgard. La música contemporánea en la ciudad de Santa Fé. (*Rev. Inst. Super. Música*, 2, dic. 1990, p. 9–28)

Local composers whose works were performed Nov. 27, 1982 at the Teatro Municipal in Santa Fé included Raúl Izaguirre, Adriana Cornú, Jorge Molina, and Ricardo Pérez Miró. On Dec. 14, 1985 new names on the program of the second Reunión Universitaria de Arte Contemporánea were those of Gabriel Monje, Alberto Perducca, Damián Rodríguez Kees, and Eduardo Schlatter. In the late 1980s, Lilia Vieri, María Luisa Lens, and Osvaldo Budón surged.

5132 Payssé González, Eduardo. Carlos Gardel: páginas abiertas. Montevideo: Ediciònes Prometeo, 1990. 471 p.: bibl., ill., index, maps.

Author proposes that Gardel was the natural son of Carlos Escayola of Tacuarembó, Uruguay, and adopted by Berthe Gardes (b. Toulouse, 15 June 1865), contradicting the generally accepted version that he was born in Toulouse on 11 Dec. 1890. Nonetheless, this densely documented book is an intriguing compilation. Author, though, never attempts to explain why Gardel never married, remaining single until his death (d. Medellín, 24 June 1935).

5133 Pérez Bugallo, Rubén. Corrientes musicales de Corrientes, Argentina. (*Lat. Am. Music Rev.*, 13:1, Spring/Summer 1992, p. 56–113, bibl., music)

Author, a renowned anthropologist and ethnomusicologist, traces musical history of Misiones, Corrientes, Entre Ríos, Santa Fé, and Chaco provinces, frequently pointing out the errors of past scholarship. How acceptable the reader will find the implications of "¿Y el aporte jesuítico?" (p. 68–69) and other controversial assessments will depend on the reader's sympathies.

5134 Richepin, Jean. A propósito del tango. Buenos Aires: Academia Porteña del Lunfardo, 1988. 33 p.

Booklet contains on facing pages the original French published in the *Séance publique annuelle des cinq académies du samedi 25 octubre 1913* (Paris: Firmin Didot, 1913) and José Gobello's introduction and translation. In searching for origins of the tango, Richepin ranges from Egyptian and Chaldean precedents to a Renaissance dance described in Thonoit-Arbeau's *Orchésographie.*

5135 Rodríguez Kees, Damián. Caetano Veloso: entre la mesomúsica y la música erudita del siglo XX. (*Rev. Inst. Super. Música*, 2, dic. 1990, p. 51–110, appendix, graph, tables)

The author, a rising composer in Santa Fé, wrote article under the supervision of Omar Corrado and begins by classifying music in layers determined by intended audiences. Pt. 6 sketches Veloso's career and analyzes eight representative songs. Pt. 7 provides results of a questionnaire answered by

ten listeners of radio in Santa Fé, indicating that only a small fraction listened to *música erudita.* Three-fourths spent their time listening to popular songs and dance tunes.

5136 Roldán, Waldemar Axel. Los pardos y la sociedad colonial de Buenos Aires hacia fines del siglo XVIII. (*Lat. Am. Music Rev.*, 13:2, Fall/Winter 1992, p. 226–233)

Cristóbal Piriobi (1764–94) was born in the Jesuit mission of San Carlos (in Alto Paraná) of indigenous parents. He adopted José Antonio Ortiz as his name when he settled in Buenos Aires in 1784. While there, he made instruments, taught music, and provided entertainment at dances. His biographical data uncovered in 1980 by Roldán in the Archivo General de la Nación, Protocolos, Registro IV-1794 and Sala IX-23,.4.4., legajo 2, expediente 58, 1800, reveal that a large part of Piriobi's music library (consisting of 240 works by 35 different composers, of which 144 were symphonies) went to the mulatto violinist Hipólito Gusmán after Piriobi's premature death at age 30. Composers in Piriobi's library included Luigi Boccherlini, Muzio Clementi, Jean Baptiste Davaux, Karl Ditters von Dittersdorf, Franz Josef Haydn, Igance Pleyel, and Johann Stamitz.

Salessi, Jorge. Tango, nacionalismo y sexualidad: Buenos Aires, 1880–1914. See item **3675.**

5137 Salter, Lionel. Beatrix Cenci. (*in* The New Grove Dictionary of Opera. New York: Grove's Dictionaries of Music, 1992, v. 1, p. 364)

Synopsis of Ginastera's third opera, premiered Sept. 10, 1971 at the Kennedy Center in Washington, D.C.

5138 Sforza, Nora. La edad dorada del Colón y la búsqueda de prestigio social. (*Todo es Hist.*, 24:276, p. 64–73, bibl., ill.)

During the centenary of Argentine independence, the Colón theatre management continued to be predominantly Italian impresarios who presented even Wagner's *Das Rheingold* and *Die Walküre* in Italian, the same language being required for French operas by Gounod and Saint-Saëns. However, boxholders were not Italians but rather Argentine aristocrats. Program booklets were filled with advertisements, not musical information. The Colón was not a temple of art but an emporium where the rich could vaunt their power and wealth. During the off-season

Sept. 10 to Nov. 15, a Spanish opera company directed by José Goula presented five Spanish operas, five Italian, one German (*Lohengrin*), all in Spanish.

5139 Stevenson, Robert. Buenos Aires. (*in* The New Grove Dictionary of Opera. New York: Grove's Dictionaries of Music, 1992, v. 1, p. 633–635, ill.)

History of opera and its venues in the chief center of opera in South America.

5140 Suffern, Carlos. Aurora. (*in* The New Grove Dictionary of Opera. New York: Grove's Dictionaries of Music, 1992, v. 1, p. 257)

Synopsis of Héctor Panizza's 3-act opera which premiered at Buenos Aires, Teatro Colón, Sept. 5, 1908. Story takes place in May 1810 at Córdoba, Argentina.

5141 Veniard, Juan María. El minué: supervivencia de una danza aristocrática en el salón romántico rioplatense. (*Lat. Am. Music Rev.*, 13:2, Fall/Winter 1992, p. 195–212, bibl., music)

In league with the present growing interest in 19th-century musical achievements (shown in Spain, Portugal, and now Latin America), author is preparing a volume to be titled *Música y músicos de salón en el Río de la Plata*. Present article is an excerpted chapter. During Rosas' dictatorship (1835–52), antiquated minuet continued as favorite in then xenophobic Argentina. Even after Rosas' fall, the ceremonious and grave *montenero* (ternary form, with a faster middle section) continued in vogue. The *Minué* by Juan Pedro Esnaola (1808–78) dated Aug. 21, 1844 (musical example on p. 207) testifies to the taste and talent of a native of Buenos Aires who ought not to continue being ignored by international music lexicons.

5142 Vila, Pablo. El rock: música argentina contemporánea. (*Gaceta/Bogotá*, 13, mayo/junio/julio 1992, p. 20–24, ill.)

Overview of rock developments in Argentina, with emphasis on conflicts between proponents of tango, folklore, and "rock nacional." Reprinted from the Buenos Aires magazine *Punto de Vista*, article presumes the reader's familiarity with major Argentine *rockeros'* biographies and is by no means an introduction to such seminal figures as Luis Alberto Spinetta, León Gieco, and Charly García.

BOLIVIA

5143 Auza León, Atiliano. Historia de la música boliviana. 2. ed. La Paz: Editorial Los Amigos del Libro, 1985. 222 p.: bibl., ill. (Enciclopedia boliviana)

Despite being a "second edition," history still betrays author's bibliographical nescience. See the review in *Inter-American Music Review* (Vol. 13, No. 1, Fall/Winter 1992, p. 112).

5144 Bustillos Vallejo, Freddy. La composición musical en Bolivia. La Paz: Museo Nacional de Etnografía y Folklore, Depto. de Programas Educativos y Etnomusicología, 1989. 121 p.: bibl. (Serie biográfica; 1)

Biographical sketches averaging fewer than 100 words each of 199 composers active on what is now Bolivian soil.

5145 Lyèvre, Philippe. Les guitarrillas du département de Potosi, Bolivie: morphologie, utilisation et symbolique. (*Bull. Inst. fr. étud. andin.*, 19:1, 1990, p. 183–213, ill., map, photos)

The calendar of the northern part of Potosí dept. is divided into dry season (from Carnival to All Saints day on Nov. 1) and wet season (from All Saints day to Carnival). Charangos, *tarka* (vertical flute), *jula-jula* (pentatonic syrinx), *ɪichiwayo* (notched quena) belong to dry season; *guitarrillas* (metal strings, reentrant tuning, pentatonic scale), and *pinkillus* (vertical flute) to the wet. This encyclopedic article, profusely illustrated and equiped with a two-page glossary, is an organologist's *ne plus ultra*. All that is lacking are musical transcriptions, giving an idea of what pieces are played on the *guitarrón talachi* and other instruments. Author, who gives the French embassy at La Paz as his address, takes great interest in symbolism read into each instrument, but does not concern himself with notated repertoire.

5146 Waisman, Leonardo. Música misional y estructura ideológica en Chiquitos, Bolivia. (*Rev. Music. Chil.*, 45:176, julio/dic. 1991, p. 43–56, music)

During the 75 years between the founding of San Javier mission in 1692 and their expulsion, the Jesuits established missions in territory of the Chiquitos (northeastern zone of present-day Bolivia), with some 20 priests serving 20,000 Indians. Erudite author of this heavily footnoted article (he directs Collegium, Centro de Educación e Investigaciones Musicales, Córdoba, Argentina) brilliantly correlates the utopian sociopolitical and religious ideals of the missionaries with the music performed and produced during their régime: music now gathered at Concepción, Bolivia, in the Archivo Musical de Chiquitos (through the zeal of Swiss architect Hans Roth).

5147 Waisman, Leonardo. ¡*Viva María!:* la música para la Virgen en las misiones de Chiquitos. (*Lat. Am. Music Rev.,* 13:2, Fall/Winter 1992, p. 212–225, bibl.)
    Amplified from a paper read at the 1990 annual meeting of the Asociación Argentina de Musicología, y IV Jornadas Argentinas de Musicología, article deals with cycle of Marian music gathered at the Concepción, Bolivia, archive. Waisman belongs to a team of Argentine experts whose research at Concepción was financed by the Consejo Nacional de Investigaciones Científicas y Técnicas (CONICET). According to him, the two *Letanías Loretanas* in the archive ascribed to Zipoli (catalogued II and III, LeO2 and LeO3) differ from the other eight by reason of the greater metrical and textural flexibility, more frequent modulations, abler treatment of suspensions, and less broken-up continuity (p. 219).

BRAZIL

5148 Andrade, Valéria. Notas para um estudo sobre compositoras da música popular brasileira: século XIX. (*Travessia/Florianópolis,* 23, 2nd semestre 1991, p. 236–252, bibl.)
    Though author has not done any arduous searching in 19th-century primary sources, she decries the paucity of information available in secondary literature concerning women who were popular music composers before Chiquinha Gonzaga.

5149 Antônio, Irati *et al.* Bibliografia da música brasileira: 1977–1984. São Paulo: Univ. de São Paulo, Escola de Comunicações e Artes; Centro Cultural São Paulo, Divisão de Pesquisas, 1988. 275 p.: bibl., indexes.
    Despite the impressive array of sponsoring entities, this attempt to bring under control the holdings of five São Paulo and two Rio de Janeiro libraries "can be considered re-

liable but not exhaustive, because thoroughness is limited due to the incomplete sources consulted" (*Fontes artis musicae,* 38:3, July/Sept. 1991, p. 242–243). See the review in *Inter-American Music Review* (Vol. 13, No. 1, Fall/Winter 1992, p. 112).

5150 Béhague, Gerard. La afinidad caribeña de la música popular en Bahía. (*Del Caribe,* 19, 1992, p. 87–92, photos)
    With his accustomed sovereign authority, Béhague identifies and analyzes abundant Bahian group and individual responses to incoming Caribbean influences during the 1970s and 1980s. Samba, frevo, and ijexá joined salsa, reggae, and merengue to innovate new hybrids. This valuable article abounds in specific Bahian Africans' personal and group names.

5151 Béhague, Gerard. Fosca. (*in* The New Grove Dictionary of Opera. New York: Grove's Dictionaries of Music, 1992, v. 2, p. 265)
    Plot summary and critique of "the most Italianate of Gomes' operas."

5152 Béhague, Gerard. Guarany, Il [O Guarani]. (*in* The New Grove Dictionary of Opera. New York: Grove's Dictionaries of Music, 1992, v. 2, p. 559–560)
    Plot summary and critique of Gomes' most popular opera.

5153 Béhague, Gerard. Guarnieri, (Mozart) Camargo. (*in* The New Grove Dictionary of Opera. New York: Grove's Dictionaries of Music, 1992, v. 2, p. 561–562)
    Review of career of São Paulo's foremost composer.

5154 Béhague, Gerard. Lo Schiavo. (*in* The New Grove Dictionary of Opera. New York: Grove's Dictionaries of Music, 1992, v. 4, p. 218)
    Next to *Il Guarany,* Gomes' most admired work, *Lo Schiavo,* "is considered in Brazil to be the best of Gomes' operas."

5155 Béhague, Gerard. Salvator Rosa. (*in* The New Grove Dictionary of Opera. New York: Grove's Dictionaries of Music, 1992, v. 4, p. 151)
    Plot summary of Gomes' "least inspired " work which, nonetheless, enjoyed enormous success at its premiere in Genoa on March 21, 1874, and continued to be very popular during the rest of the century.

5156 Borges, Beatriz. Música popular do Brasil = Brazilian popular music. São Paulo: B. Borges, 1990. 292 p.: bibl., ill. (some col.).

This bilingual, coffee-table book (printed on *couché* paper with a cornucopia of full-page color illustrations) includes 286 lyrics in Portuguese scattered among the total of 170 photographs. These are sequenced by English translations (p. 251–283). Apart from a facsimile of *Pelo Telephone* (Donga and Mauro de Almeida, 1917), volume lacks music examples. Callado, Viriato, and Pixinguinha escape author's net because their inspirations were chiefly instrumental, not vocal.

5157 Chechim Filho, Antônio. Excursão artística Villa-Lobos. São Paulo?: s.n., 1987. 134 p.: ill.

Details of the composer's Brazilian tours from Jan. 1931-Jan. 1932.

5158 Encontro Nacional de Pesquisa em Música, 3rd, Ouro Preto, Brazil, 1987. Anais. Belo Horizonte, Brasil: Imprensa da Univ. Federal de Minas Gerais, 1988. 541 p.: bibl., ill.

Among 47 contributions to the Third National Music Research Encounter, 26 deal directly or indirectly with distinctively Brazilian topics. Béhague reviews the present state of ethnomusicology in Brazil, paying homage to the true pioneer, Mário de Andrade, and concludes with a seven-point list of faults and necessities that presently impede the discipline in Brazil. According to Henrique Pedrosa, musical histories by most Brazilians are far too focused on biographical accounts. Even Ary Vasconcelos' compendia of popular music result in mere compilations of popular musicians' biographies. Nevertheless, João Bosco Assis De Luca's 39-page contribution, "A Morte em Vida: Carlos Gomes na Década de 1890," avoids the pitfalls of most of his predecessors and, though the longest article in the volume, may well be the most praiseworthy. In the same class is Diniz's 23-page article, "Gregorio de Souza e Gouvea," which brings to light the career of the musician, poet, and man of the theater, who, from July 9, 1730 to the appointment of his successor António de Almeida Jordão on June 25, 1749, directed music in the Santa Casa de Misericórdia at Bahia. In his *Escola de Canto de Orgão*, Pt. 2, p. 585 (1761), re-

nowned chapelmaster of Bahia Cathedral and author of the lengthiest music treatise in Portuguese, Caetano de Mello de Jesus, classed Gouvea, then dwelling at Cachoeira e S. Amaro da Purificação, as a "professor de música prática, homem de muito boa habilidade, claro entendimento." Diniz's landmark article provides a biography of Gouvea and numerous valuable insights into his cultural ambience.

5159 Ferraz, Silvio and Maurício Dottori. Manoel Dias de Oliveira e Davide Perez: uma aproximação entre o barroco mineiro e a ópera napolitana. (*Ciênc. Cult.*, 42: 9, set. 1990, p. 662–669)

According to the authors' notes, nine copies of homophonic sacred works attributed to late 18th-century Manoel Dias (who resided at São José do Rio das Mortas) survive at São João del Rey and elsewhere. Not all bearing his name are necessarily his. Authors, who were postgraduates in the University of São Paulo School of Communications and Arts when they published this article, include six musical examples to demonstrate likenesses perceived by them between Davide Perez's simplistic "motets" and untexted short excerpts from *A Visitação dos Passos, Pange lingua, Miserere Amplius,* and *Dominus Jesus* ascribed to Manoel Dias (whom they call the *mais arcaizante dos grandes compositores mineiros*). Authors' erroneous statement in note 2 that J.J. Baldi, Marcos Portugal, and Leal Moreira came to Brazil with the Portuguese court in 1806 (!) immediately diminishes faith in what follows in their article.

5160 Gomes, Plínio Freire. O ciclo dos meninos cantores, 1550–1552: música e aculturação nos primórdios da colônia. (*Rev. Bras. Hist.*, 11:21, set. 1990/fev. 1991, p. 187–198, bibl.)

Seven boy singers selected among students in a Lisbon orphanage school played decisive role in Jesuit evangelization efforts from their arrival at Bahia in 1550 until Bishop Pedro Fernandes' arrival two years later. Scandalized by their dancing and singing in Tupi, he restrained them from any further countryside accommodation to Tupi manners and conduct.

5161 Lisboa Junior, Luiz Americo. A presença da Bahia na música popular brasileira. Brasília: MusiMed: Sóbrindes-Linha

Gráfica e Editora, 1990. 224 p.: bibl., ill., indexes.

After summarizing 19th-century Bahia and the establishment of the phonographic industry in Brazil, author proceeds chronologically from 1902, when Manoel Pedro dos Santos (who was the most popular singer in Brazil and a native of Bahia) recorded the *lundu* of Xisto de Paula Bahia, *Isto é Bom*, through 1964, in which year Sid Biá (Sebastião Alves da Cunha) recorded the maxixe *Chão Baiano*. Author, owner of 7,500 recordings (Parlophon, Victor, Columbia, Odeon, Continental, Sinter, Star, Copacabana, Lond, Bahia), transcribes and annotates lyrics that celebrate Bahia. Despite containing no music notations, this is a valuable compendium for the popular music historian.

5162 Lody, Raul Giovanni da Motta and **Leonardo Sá.** O atabaque no candomblé baiano. Rio de Janeiro: Fundação Nacional de Arte, Instituto Nacional do Folclore e Instituto Nacional de Música, 1989. 60 p.: ill. (Col. Instrumentos musicais no Brasil: Série Instrumentos musicais afro-brasileiros; 1)

Atabaques, the conical drums central to candomblé rituals, are painted different colors, according to deities that they solemnize (light blue, Oxóssi, Iemanjá; dark blue, Ogum; yellow, Oxum; white, Oxalá; and so forth). Used together, the *rum* is the head, *rumpi* the body, and *runle* the legs of the atabaque trinity. Roles of men and women vary drastically, so far as instrumental and vocal music go. The 24 full-page photos (plus the frontispiece) make this publication more a picture booklet than a documented study.

5163 Luca, João Bosco Assis de. O *Colombo* de Carlos Gomes: ópera ou cantata? (*Ciênc. Cult.*, 41:10, out. 1989, p. 969–980)

This definitive article is a condensation of a monograph that won a first prize in a competition sponsored by FUNARTE (Instituto Nacional de Música) in 1986. It brings to light circumstances surrounding Gomes' composition of *Colombo*, its first performance Oct. 12, 1892, and the subsequent reception history of this his last large work. In every sense, this article merits maximum praise.

5164 Mariz, Vasco. Villa-Lobos, 30 anos depois. (*Rev. Inst. Hist. Geogr. São Paulo*, 85, 1990, p. 59–70)

In this transcript of a brilliant discourse pronounced Sept. 20, 1989, Mariz offers a staggering array of statistics to prove the worldwide fame of Brazil's greatest composer—as attested in books in nearly all major languages, internationally-available recordings, and entries in dictionaries and encyclopedias. Mariz also tells the history of his personal association with Villa-Lobos and defends him from politically motivated onslaughts by envious compatriots.

5165 Máximo, João and **Carlos Didier.** Noel Rosa: uma biografia. Brasília: Linha Gráfica Editora: Editora UnB, 1990. 533 p.: bibl., ill., index.

Seven years of intense research into every facet of Noel Rosa's life, his genealogy, his career, his ambience, his associates, and other relevant contemporaries preceded publication of this most grandiose of books ever devoted to a Brazilian popular composer. Lacking from this extravagant volume are music facsimiles of finished works (p. 114 provides the facsimile of a textless unfinished *choro* holograph). Rosa's lyrics matter to the authors and are all here.

Moraes, Vinícius de. Livro de letras. See item **4891.**

5166 Museu da Inconfidência (Ouro Preto, Brazil). Acervo de manuscritos musicais: Coleção Francisco Curt Lange: compositores mineiros dos séculos XVIII e XIX. Coordenação geral de Régis Duprat. Coordenação técnica de Carlos Alberto Baltazar. Belo Horizonte: Editora UFMG, 1991. 174 p.: ill. (Col. Pesquisa científica)

Of 100 cataloged composers, approximately half were positively or possibly late 18th century or early 19th century *mineiros*. Joaquim Emerico Lobo de Mesquita is represented by 38 works, José Maria Xavier by 24, João de Deus Castro Lobo with 23, Jerónimo de Souza Lobo with 19, Vicente Ferreiro do Espírito Santo with 11, and Marcos Coelho Neto with 9. With few exceptions, all works are sacred, in Latin, and instrumentally accompanied (38 Ladainhas, 22 Missas, 6 Salves, for example). Because of its completeness and exactness, this catalog is a notable achievement.

5167 Paschoal da Silva, Eliane Maria and **Flávia Camargo Toni.** Instrumentos musicais da coleção Mário de Andrade. (*Rev.*

Inst. Estud. Bras., 31, 1990, p. 197–206, photos)

Among the 14 instruments in the Mário de Andrade collection cataloged using the Hornbostel-Sachs system is a Mannborg harmonium pumped with two pedals. But the majority are Brazilian: *caxixi, tikuna, cuíca, tukano,* bamboo flutes, and syrinx.

5168 Peppercorn, Lisa M. Villa-Lobos: the music: an analysis of his style. Translated by Stefan de Haan. London: Kahn & Averill; White Plains, N.Y.: Pro/Am Music Resources, Inc., 1991. 126 p.: bibl., indexes.

Superlatively useful chronology runs from 1859–1985 and covers from the birth of the composer's mother to the death of Arminda d'Almeida Villa-Lobos, "the composer's companion." Also has extremely valuable bibliography. More opinionated than ideally irenic, the analyses of works (piano, violin and cello, voice, chamber, solo instruments and orchestra, orchestral works) translated from Part 2 of author's *Heitor Villa-Lobos, Leben und Werk, des brasilianischen Komponisten* suffer because "the music here analysed are [sic] principally works written up to 1944" and "later compositions were disregarded because in the remaining fifteen years of his life . . . his style did not change or mature."

5169 Stevenson, Robert. Belém. (*in* The New Grove Dictionary of Opera. New York: Grove's Dictionaries of Music, 1992, v. 1, p. 381, bibl.)

Best epoch for opera began with the inauguration of the sumptuous Teatro da Paz (1,100 seats) Feb. 15, 1878 and lasted until Carlos Gomes' death there in 1896.

5170 Stevenson, Robert. Campos, Carlos de. (*in* The New Grove Dictionary of Opera. New York: Grove's Dictionaries of Music, 1992, v. 1, p. 706, bibl.)

Sometime director of the São Paulo Correio Paulistano and president of São Paulo state, Campos wrote two operas that reached the stage.

5171 Stevenson, Robert. Gomes de Araújo, João. (*in* The New Grove Dictionary of Opera. New York: Grove's Dictionaries of Music, 1992, v. 2, p. 484, bibl.)

Career of the composer of six operas, three of which were produced in Brazil (in São Paulo at the Teatro Sant'Ana in 1906 and the Teatro Municipal in 1910 and in Rio de Janeiro at the Teatro Municipal in 1922).

5172 Stevenson, Robert. Manaus. (*in* The New Grove Dictionary of Opera. New York: Grove's Dictionaries of Music, 1992, v. 3, p. 175, bibl.)

Opera history centers on the ornate Teatro Amazonas inaugurated Dec. 31, 1896.

5173 Stevenson, Robert. Rio de Janeiro. (*in* The New Grove Dictionary of Opera. New York: Grove's Dictionaries of Music, 1992, v. 3, p. 1346–1347, bibl.)

History of opera in Brazil's former capital.

5174 Stevenson, Robert. Salvador, Bahia. (*in* The New Grove Dictionary of Opera. New York: Grove's Dictionaries of Music, 1992, v. 4, p. 150)

Abbreviated account of stage music history in Bahia, founded in 1549 and the capital of colonial Brazil until 1763.

5175 Stevenson, Robert. São Paulo. (*in* The New Grove Dictionary of Opera. New York: Grove's Dictionaries of Music, 1992, v. 4, p. 175–176, bibl.)

Overview of opera in São Paulo lacks precise dates (which were eliminated for editorial reasons). Events after 1960 go unmentioned.

5176 Tinhorão, José Ramos. História social da música popular brasileira. Lisboa: Editorial Caminho, 1990. 327 p.: bibl. (Caminho da música; 6)

Thought-provoking survey buttressed by 321 endnotes and a formidable list of sources traces popular musical currents from the colony to the 1964 military regime. Lacks indexes. The volume includes some fruitful discussions such as "Lundus, Maxixes e Sambas em Revista," "A Montagem Brasileira da Bossa Nova e o Protesto Musical Universitário," and "O Movimento Tropicalista e o 'Rock Brasileiro,'" but the author's opinions are sometimes farfetched.

5177 Tinhorão, José Ramos. A música popular no romance brasileiro. v. 1, Século XVIII-século XIX. Belo Horizonte: Oficina de Libros, 1992. 1 v.: bibl. (Nossa terra)

Lack of both analytic and name index, and absence of bibliography detracts from this volume, but it does provide a catena of intriguing allusions to popular music in Brazilian literature (chiefly fiction) from 1728 to 1900. Nuno Marques Pereira itemized African instruments used in nightly religious ceremonies of slaves in northeast Brazil: "[a]tabaques, botijas, canzás, castanhetas, e pes de cabras" (*Compendio narrativo do Peregrino da América*, 6th ed., 1939, p. 128). Himself a guitar player (*tocador de viola*) and singer trained by Francisco da Costa Carqueja, *mestre de solfa* at Bahia, Nuno Pereira approved of instruments that he encountered in a woman music teacher's school: *violas, harpas, alaúdes, tubas, bandorillhas, rebecas e rebeções, e cítaras.* Her school also boasted: "muitos instrumentos dedais, baixões, fagotes, cornetas, flautas, charamelas," and in another salon *um organo, um cravo e um monacordio.* On one bookshelf he found "muitos papéis de solfa da mesma arte" (*Compendio,* p. 19).

Urban, Greg. Ritual wailing in Amerindian Brazil. See *HLAS 53:1112.*

5178 Vasconcelos, Ary. Raízes da música popular brasileira. Rio de Janeiro: Rio Fundo Editora, 1991. 324 p.: bibl., ill., index.

After a 28-page historical summary, author gives extremely valuable biographies of composers flourishing in the colonial epoch, in the First Empire (1822–31), the Regency (1831–40), and Second Empire (1840–89), always accompanying biographies with page-numbered bibliographical references. Since even Carlos Gomes, Rafael Coelho Machado, Artur Napoleão, and Francisco de Sá Novonha enter the biographical section, this is a compendium of highest utility: only composers who wrote exclusively sacred and concert works fail to enter the dictionary.

5179 Villa-Lobos, Ahygara Iacyra. Villa-Lobos em família. Rio de Janeiro: Cia. Brasileira de Artes Gráficas, 1990. 77 p.: ill.

Written by a niece, this traversal of Villa-Lobos' family connections starts with his baby pictures, and continues with his genealogy, an account of his personal habits, details of his relationships with parents and siblings, material concerning his marriage to Lucília Guimarães, and encounters leading to his 22 years of companionship with Arminda. After many other personal details, concludes with his last picture taken in New York in 1959. Of eight children born to the composer's parents, five died in infancy or early

childhood. Villa-Lobos, the second, was born two months prematurely. Author, daughter of Danton Condorcet and Carmen Villa-Lobos, says her first two names mean "canoe" and "moon" in Tupi-Guarani. Born in 1936, she gives her own full name as: Ahygara Iacyra Villa-Lobos da Silva Waissmann.

5180 Wehrs, Carlos. Meio século de vida musical no Rio de Janeiro, 1889–1939. Rio de Janeiro: Instituto Histórico e Geográfico Brasileiro, 1990. 118 p.: bibl., ill.

Year by year, author—who has published four histories of Niterói (1984, 1986, 1987, 1989)—summarizes notable musical events in the former capital. Although not based on original newspaper and magazine research, the present monograph pleasantly pursues a trail provided by secondary sources. With four to a page, book contains 32 reproductions, all but one taken from photographs in author's own collection. On page 30 he enumerates publishers at Rio in the 1890s, but fails to expand on the mere mention of the Casa Editora Carlos Wehrs, beyond giving its 1890s address: Ouvidor, 153.

5181 Wright, Simon. Villa-Lobos. Oxford; New York: Oxford Univ. Press, 1992. 146 p.: bibl., ill., index. (Oxford studies of composers)

Author, who is Welsh, treats Villa-Lobos as an icon. This obsequious text glosses over problematic aspects of Villa-Lobos. The index contains entries with as many as ten page numbers, but items are not classified. For scholarly use, this manual may prove a disappointment, but for the general public its euphemisms may suffice. Even the lay reader would, however, have appreciated a bibliography (not a mere anodyne "note.")

THE CARIBBEAN (except Cuba)

Alegría Ortega, Idsa E. Tras los pasos y la música de Ana Otero Hernández. See item **1968.**

5182 Benoît, Edouard. Musique populaire de la Guadeloupe: de la biguine au zouk, 1940–1980. Pointe-à-Pitre, Guadeloupe: Office régional du patrimoine guadeloupéen; Agence guadeloupéenne de l'environnement, du tourisme et des loisirs, 1990. 127 p.: ill.

Author is the son of clarinetist Stéphane Benoît, who from 1930–60 conducted one of the best popular ensembles in the is-

land, the "Esperanza" orchestra. At present
he is Conseiller Pédagogique de Education
Musicale, the highest music education post
in the island. This survey includes photos of
14 groups active in the island 1940–80, some
of which had as many as 16 members. He
next discusses "Le biguine et ses composi-
teurs," followed by a musical analysis of four
examples: "A dan ou Komba mélé" by
Georges Célestine, "Pou nou Kouri vidé" by
Joseph Lacides, "Saverda" by Abel Zenon, and
"Monsieur Kombass à Paris" by Henri Debs.

5183 Bermúdez, Egberto. La música de las
    islas. (*Gaceta/Bogotá*, 13, p. 52–53, ill.)
    Authoritative account by a leading
Colombian student of the changing styles and
genres favored by performers in the San Andrés, Providencia, and Santa Catalina archipelago. The *pasillo* (derived from the European valse) gave way in the 1940s and 1950s
to calypsos composed by such Trinidadians as
Mighty Sparrow, Roaring Lion, Attila the
Hun, and Lord Panamá. In the 1960s Harry
Belafonte's sung calypsos became staples.
During the late 1980s, *soka*, Caribbean funk,
and rap took hold—the cassettes emanating
from pirate record houses in Cartagena, Barranquilla, Caracas, and Panama.

5184 Bethel, Clement. Junkanoo in the Ba-
    hamas. (*Caribb. Q.*, 36:3/4, Dec. 1990,
p. 1–28, music)
    Splendidly erudite and sophisticated
chronicle of Junkanoo (John Canoe) parades
celebrated chiefly Dec. 26 (formerly Dec. 25)
and Jan. 1 by "fantastically costumed" dancers along Bay Street, Nassau's main thor-
oughfare, to the traditional accompaniment
of cowbells, various types of horns, whistles,
and goombay drums. Author divides his historic account into four eras: 1800–99, 1900–
19, 1920–47, and 1948–90. His sources include notices in *The Nassau Guardian*, diaries, local histories, and, for the more recent
period, songs and tales collected by himself.
As early as 1890 the Junkanoo festivals offered participants a vehicle for social protest.
After 1947, festivals gained government encouragement because they drew tourists to
the Bahamas. Author's final section on "The
Music" begins with fifes and tambourines
used in 1854 and concludes with a score transcription of interlocking rhythms produced
by Fast Beat and Hill Beat.

5185 Holguín Veras, Miguel A. Julio Alberto
    Hernández. Santo Domingo: Impresora
Industria del Sobre, 1990. 100 p.: bibl., ill.
(Col. Semblanzas)
    Born in 1900 at Santiago de Los Caba-
lleros, Julio Alberto Hernández Camejo rose
to such distinction that Columbia Phono-
graph Company contracted him in 1928 to
record four of his songs: *El primer beso*,
Dulce recuerdo, Santiago, and *Feliz eres, la-
briego*, and the US Army band played his
criolla, Por tí sola late that year. From 1932–
35 he codirected the Orquesta Sinfónica de
Santo Domingo. In 1940 he signed a contract
with Alpha Music, New York City, for publication of his works. In Dec. 1978 the Orquesta Sinfónica Nacional performed his *Tres
danzas criollas*. His diplomas and other distinctions multiplied as the years progressed.
This brochure lists his complete works and
recordings (dates, matrix numbers, genres,
performers).

5186 Jean-Louis, Marie-Paule. Musiques en
    Guyane: 29 septembre-25 novembre
1989, Cayenne, Galerie de l'ARDEC. Cayenne: Bureau du patrimoine ethnologique,
Conseil régional Guyane, 1989. 109 p.: bibl.,
ill. (some col.).
    Handsomely printed booklet contains
illustrated catalog of indigenous instruments,
reflections on the African heritage, data on
performing groups active since 1936, and a
very useful anthology of relevant historic excerpts ranging from J.P. Labat's *Voyage aux
Îsles de l'Amérique* (1693–1705) to Alfred Pa-
repou's novel *Atipa* (Paris, 1885).

Mulvaney, Rebekah Michele. Rastafari and
reggae: a dictionary and sourcebook. See
HLAS 53:1038.

Neil, Ancil Anthony. Voices from the hills:
Despers & Laventille: the steelband and its
effects on poverty, stigma & violence in a
community; a classic study of the social, political, and economic changes in a community. See *HLAS 53:1040*.

5187 O'Gorman, Pamela. An eighteenth-
    century Jamaican oratorio. (*Jam. J.*, 22:
4, Nov. 1989/Jan. 1990, p. 41–45, bibl.)
    Thurston Dox made the following dis-
coveries: born in Jamaica in 1743 of English
immigrant parents who had married at Philadelphia in 1741, Samuel Felsted published his

Jonah (the first known oratorio by an American-born composer) at London in 1775 (Longman, Lukey and Broderip). Among 243 subscribers were Jamaican elite, many of whom (Aguilar Bernal, De Silva, De Cordova, Fernandes, Furtado, Josephs, Pereira, Tavares, and others) belonged to the important Jewish community in the island. Felsted was organist of St. Andrew Parish Church from 1775–83, and from 1783, of Kingston Parish Church. He died at Kingston March 19, 1802. *Jonah*, consisted of 12 numbers and required only two tenors, a choir, and a harpsichord, and was performed at New York in 1788, 1789, and 1802, and at Boston Dec. 2, 1789. For related item, see **5188.**

5188 O'Gorman, Pamela. An eighteenth-century Jamaican oratorio. (*Jam. J.*, 23: 1, Feb./April 1990, p. 14–19, bibl.)

Author, formerly the head of the Jamaica School of Music, analyzes movement by movement Samuel Felsted's *Jonah*, recorded under the direction of Thurston Dox by the Catskill Choral Society in 1981 (Musical Heritage Society). The six short musical excerpts are facsimiles from the short score published at London in 1775. For related item, see **5187.**

5189 O'Gorman, Pamela. Marjorie Whylie's contribution to the development of drumming in Jamaica. (*Jam. J.*, 24: 1, June 1991, p. 33–37, photos)

Beginning in 1974 Whylie made the conga drum the most vital and omnipresent instrument taught in the Jamaica School of Music. Her star pupils include Mrs. Gloria Walker and Marcia Lumsden. In 1986 she left full-time teaching to pursue an independent career as jazz musician and singer, composer, and leader of a new group called "Whylie Wrhythms."

Pérez, Jorge. La *plena* puertorriqueña: de la expresión popular a la comercialización musical. See item **2200.**

5190 Ramaya, Narsaloo. Towards the evolution of a national culture: Indian music in Trinidad and Tobago. (*in* Indians in the Caribbean. Edited by I.J. Bahadur Singh. New Delhi, India: Sterling Publishers Private Limited, 1987, p. 147–166, bibl.)

Until 1935 the music of indentured servants brought from India (beginning with 225 in 1845) remained an art orally transmitted by such pioneers in Trinidad as Phiramat, Imami, Ramcharan, Dharam Gosine, Rahimtullah, Bahadoor Syne, Bel Bagai, Ali Jan, and Fakeer Mohammed. But the impact of Indian movies, beginning in 1935 when *Bala Joban* first made the local population aware of how songs and dances accompanied by Hindi talking sounded in contemporary India, made the art of the old singers obsolete. In vain, pioneers in Trinidad and Tobago shunned movie songs avidly picked up by youth from Indian imports. During World War II younger singers banded together to produce "the greatest stage show ever seen in Trinidad," *Gulshan Bahar*—with Champa Devi as its star dancer and Tarran Persad its lead singer.

Thompson, Donald and **Annie F. Thompson.** Music and dance in Puerto Rico from the age of Columbus to modern times: an annotated bibliography. See item **1839.**

CENTRAL AMERICA

5191 Anleu Díaz, Enrique. Historia crítica de la música en Guatemala. Guatemala: Artemis, 1991. 252 p.: bibl., ill. (Col. Novelas y leyendas)

Revised edition also includes further facsimiled testimonials to author's excellencies. Walter Guido's report on musical holdings in 1980 of the Museo Nacional de Arte Moderno, Instituto de Antropología e Historia (IAH), Museo Nacional de Historia (MNH), and Conservatorio Nacional de Música (p. 233–243) cites a handwritten copy at the MNH of José Herrando's violin method published at Paris in 1756. The IAH holds 180 handwritten works by 19th-century Guatemalan composers. Volume lacks indexes and other niceties, and generally fails to fulfill author's best intentions.

5192 Anleu Díaz, Enrique. Historia de la música en Guatemala. 2. ed. Guatemala: Tip. Nacional: Centro de Estudios Folklóricos, Univ. de San Carlos de Guatemala, 1986. 199 p. (Col. Centroamérica; 3)

Born in Guatemala City June 7, 1940, author joined the Orquesta Sinfónica Nacional as a first violin in 1967. During the ensuing 15 years he conducted chamber and symphony orchestras in the Guatemala National Conservatory. According to him, Jorge Sarmientos, Joaquín Orellana, and he formed a trio of Guatemalan "vanguard composers." The literary portion of his history concludes with reprints of highly laudatory newspaper notices of both his conducting and compositions. Prefacing his historical *apuntes,* author inserts in the first 60 pages four further annexes: "Enrique Anleu Díaz en el Arte Musical y Plástico de Guatemala," "Enrique Anleu Díaz en la Historia de la Música de Guatemala," "Enrique Anleu Díaz, Compositor en la Crítica Musical," and "Enrique Anleu Díaz, como Director de Orquesta." He dedicates this volume to his two daughters.

Corleto, Manuel. *La profecía:* teatro coreográfico y musical. See item **4566.**

5193 Ellison, Cori. Salazar, Manuel. (*in* The New Grove Dictionary of Opera. New York: Grove's Dictionaries of Music, 1992, v. 4, p. 140)

Insubstantial account of the Costa Rican tenor's career (b. San José, Jan. 3, 1887; d. San. José, Aug. 6, 1950).

5194 Kaufman, Tom. Guatemala City. (*in* The New Grove Dictionary of Opera. New York: Grove's Dictionaries of Music, 1992, v. 2, p. 562)

Defective article by author ignorant of bibliography cited in *Die Musik in Geschichte und Gegenwart* (Kassel: Bärenreiter, 1979), Band 16, columns 554–555, and unaware of the opera events preceding 1859.

5195 Lehnhoff, Dieter. Espada y pentagrama: la música polifónica en la Guatemala del siglo XVI. Guatemala: Centro de Reproducciones, Univ. Rafael Landívar, 1986. 154 p., 6 leaves of plates: bibl., ill., index.

Admirably equipped with chapter endnotes specifying documentary data, this is a fundamental work by a leading hemispheric musicologist.

5196 Salazar Salvatierra, Rodrigo. Instrumentos musicales del folclor costarricense. Cartago, Costa Rica: Editorial Tecnológica de Costa Rica, 1992. 228 p.: bibl., ill.

Folklore being a *passepartout,* instruments used by the commonalty are duly discussed. In addition, author gives useful data (photos, drawings) on archaeological instruments (*báculos* = rattling wands, various teponaztli relatives; *flur cue* = rasp; *gnelé* = tortoise shell; *sabak* = hourglass drum with membrane head).

5197 Suco Campos, Idalberto. La música en el complejo cultural del *walagallo* en Nicaragua. La Habana: Casa de las Américas, 1987. 105 p.: bibl., ill.

Twenty-one Spanish-named descendants of Black Caribs over the age of 62 served as informants for this detailed study of the curing ceremony called *Walagallo.* Practiced at Orinoco on the east coast of Nicaragua, the rite requires dancers in their right hands to hold chickens by their wings. Wafted aloft the chickens banish evil sprits infecting the sick woman and purify the three drums. The effectiveness of the rite depends on the sick woman's faith. When cured, she leaps up to dance, and the chickens die.

5198 Zúñiga Tristán, Virginia. La Orquesta Sinfónica Nacional: antecedentes, desarrollo, culminación. San José: Editorial Univ. Estatal a Distancia, 1992. 269 p.: indexes.

Much more than a mere history of the Costa Rican symphony orchestra, this richly illustrated volume takes account of all phases of music in Costa Rica. Author, a former member of the governing board of the Orquesta Sinfónica Nacional (1970–78), is a pianist who graduated from the Univ. of Kentucky with an M. Mus. degree. She later obtained her doctorate at Tulane Univ. and returned as a professor of English at the Univ. de Costa Rica. In Appendix 6, she records opinions of orchestral members: the greatest symphonic composer was Beethoven; the best Costa Rican composers have been Benjamín Gutiérrez, Luis Diego Herra, and Carlos Enrique Vargas; the outstanding conductors have been Edvard Fendler and Irwin Hoffman.

CHILE

5199 Cáceres, Eduardo. Homenaje a Gustavo Becerra-Schmidt en la Universidad Alemana de Oldenburg. (*Rev. Music. Chil.,* 45:176, julio/dic. 1991, p. 9–16, facsims., photo)

Appointed Agregado Cultural at Bonn by the Allende government in 1971, Chilean composer Becerra-Schmidt paid his first return visit to Chile in 1988. During the two decades 1971–91 he composed "more than 60 compositions." In homage to his teaching career in East Germany, the Universität Oldenburg offered three programs: Nov. 9, 15, and 30, 1990, the first and third devoted exclusively to his works composed between 1954–90. Facsimiles of these programs celebrating his 65th birthday occupy p. 13–15 (the second consisting of solo cello and with piano works by himself, Eduardo Luis Naun, and Gabriel Brincic).

5200 Claro-Valdés, Samuel. Bisquert (Prado), Próspero. (*in* The New Grove Dictionary of Opera. New York: Grove's Dictionaries of Music, 1992, v. 1, p. 484–485)

Sayeda, a short opera-ballet based on a tale from the *Thousand and one nights* (libretto by the composer), was produced at Santiago's Teatro Municipal on Sept. 20, 1929.

5201 González, Juan Pablo. Raíces mapuches en la música popular chilena. (*in* Congreso Nacional de Educación Musical, 4th, Santiago, 1992. Hispanoamérica 500 años: situación y rol de la música en la educación chilena. Actas. Santiago: Ministerio de la Educación, 1992, p. 60–79, bibl., music)

Fernando Lecaroz, Violeta Parra, Los Jaivas, and Sexual Democracia incorporated Mapuche musical traits in their songs. Descending thirds, equivalency of 6/8, *mapuchina* rhythmic patterns (trochees followed by syncopated iamb), melodic glissandos, shouts, and lyrics in *mapudungun* impart flavor. However, harmonizations (such as those Lecaroz provided in *Mapuche soy*) can be extremely sophisticated.

5202 Guerrero Yoacham, Cristián. Notas para el estudio de la obra historiográfica de Don Eugenio Pereira Salas. (*Cuad. Hist.*, 9, dic. 1989, p. 9–43)

Among Pereira Salas' publications, *Los orígenes del arte musical en Chile* (1941), *Historia de la música en Chile, 1850–1900* (1957), and *Bibliografía musical de Chile desde sus orígenes a 1886* (1978) form a trilogy rightly praised by Luis Merino Montero and Samuel Claro-Valdés as unexcelled pinnacles in musical historiography. Present article exalts every phase of Pereira Salas' multifaceted career and traces his life from birth at Santiago on May 19, 1904, to death there in 1979. During his later years he received every prize, award, and distinction available to a cultural historian.

5203 Merino Montero, Luis. Jorge Urrutia Blondel y Acario Cotapos: reflexiones sobre dos facetas de la música chilena. (*Bol. Acad. Chil. Bellas Artes*, 2, 1989, p. 129–162)

The first musicologist to be elected a member of the Academia Chilena de Bellas Artes, Luis Merino Montero gave a brilliant inaugural discourse June 30, 1983. He compared the careers and creations of Urrutia Blondel (b. La Serena, Sept. 17, 1903; d. Santiago, July 5, 1981) and Cotapos Baeza (b. Valdivia, April 30, 1889; d. Santiago, Nov. 22, 1969), who although both awarded the prestigious Premio Nacional de Arte (1960 and 1977), differed from each other in extremely significant ways. Only a scholar of Merino Montero's nonpareil sovereignty could have weighed the achievements of each with such acuity.

5204 Rodríguez Musso, Osvaldo. La nueva canción chilena: continuidad y reflejo. La Habana: Casa de las Américas, 1988. 267 p.: bibl., ill., index.

Texts of songs by Atahualpa Yupanqui, Víctor Jara, Patricio Manns, Angel and Violeta Parra, and other "New Song" exponents occupy p. 107–218. Pablo Neruda's *Aquí me quedo* (1973), set to music by Jara (p. 202), contains the line "Siempre los ricos fueron extranjeros / que se vayan a Miami con sus tías." Neruda's direct connection with Chilean New Song began in 1954 when Violeta Parra gave a recital in Neruda's Santiago house that he called Michoacán. In 1960, he dedicated his *Elegía para cantar* to Parra (p. 243–244). In 1967 Sergio Ortega composed music for Neruda's *Fulgor y muerte de Joaquín Murieta*. On Neruda's return from Paris in 1973, Víctor Jara organized a national tribute.

5205 Stevenson, Robert. Carnicer Blanco, Ramón. (*in* The New Grove Dictionary of Opera. New York: Grove's Dictionaries of Music, 1992, v. 1, p. 740–741)

Biobibliography of the Catalan composer of the Chilean national anthem, whose bicentennial of birth was celebrated in 1989.

5206 Stevenson, Robert. Santiago. (*in* The New Grove Dictionary of Opera. New York: Grove's Dictionaries of Music, 1992, v. 4, p. 172–173, bibl.)

History of opera in the Chilean capital. *The New Grove Dictionary of Opera* lacks an article on Domenico Brescia (1866–1939) whose opera *Salinara* enjoyed great success at Santiago.

5207 Vicuña Lyon, Magdalena. Creación musical en Chile, 1992. (*Rev. Music. Chil.*, 46:178, julio/dic. 1992, p. 109–113)

Orchestral works by five Chileans received Santiago premieres during the *temporada oficial* of the Orquesta Sinfónica de Chile performing in the Teatro of the Univ. de Chile: Carlos Riesco (*Mortal mantenimiento*, June 11, 12, and 13, with Agustín Cullell directing, soprano Myrian Singer, soloist); Santiago Vera (*Apocaliptika II* [1988], July 23, 24, and 25, Jean Louis Le Roux directing the string orchestra, Luis Alberto Latorre, pianist); David Serendero (*Carnaval en el Rhin* [1988–91], symphonic poem, Aug. 6, 7, and 8, Serendero conducting); Eduardo Cáceres (*La batalla campal*, Sept. 24, 25, and 26, Cullell conducting, tenor Héctor Calderón soloist, Metropolitan University Chorus directed by Ruth Godoy); and Hernán Ramírez (*Música para orquesta*, Op. 9, Sept. 24, 25, and 26, Cullell conducting). At the Univ. Católica, the Ciclo España América presented works by Juan Orrego-Salas, Celso Garrido-Lecca (Peruvian), Alfonso Letelier, and Leonardo García at concerts in the Centro de Extensión March 25 to June 17. Homage concerts celebrating the careers of Orrego-Salas, Carlos Botto, and Gustavo Becerra were offered May 20 and 27 and June 2 sponsored by the Fondo Universitario de las Artes. Each concert included musicological comment (Luis Merino Montero, Inés Grandela, Hernán Ramírez).

5208 Vicuña Lyon, Magdalena. Gustavo Becerra Schmidt, profesor visitante en Chile. (*Rev. Music. Chil.*, 46:178, julio/dic. 1992, p. 119–120)

At the invitation of the Instituto de Música of the Pontificia Univ. de Chile, Becerra-Schmidt (based in Germany since 1971) directed two composition courses July 27 to Oct. 11, 1992, one for beginning, the other for advanced composers. Some 40 musicians participated in his Seminario sobre la Música Contemporánea. Additionally, he gave a lecture series Sept. 2-Oct. 2 during which he showed his desire to integrate himself anew in Chilean musical life.

5209 Vicuña Lyon, Magdalena and **Fernando García.** Creación musical en Chile. (*Rev. Music. Chil.*, 45:176, julio/dic. 1991, p. 103–114)

On Nov. 27, 1991, Agustín Cullell conducted the Orquesta Sinfónica de Chile at the Teatro de la Univ. de Chile in a program consisting of the *Preludios Dramáticos* by Domingo Santa Cruz (1899–1987), *Concierto*

para piano by René Amengual (1911–54), and *Balmaceda* for narrator and orchestra by Acario Cotapos (1889–1969). On Nov. 16, 1991 at the Goethe Institut, the Orquesta de Cámara de Chile conducted by Fernando Rosas revived Celso Garrido's *Antaras* and Juan Orrego-Salas' *Variaciones Serenas*, and premiered Federico Heinlein's *Tríptico* (1989) as well as Fernando García's *Crónicas americanas* (1991). On Aug. 26, 1991 the Asociación de Compositores and Academia Chilena de Bellas Artes honored the recently retired president of the Academia Chilena de Bellas Artes, Carlos Riesco, with a retrospective of his works performed in the auditorium of the Instituto de Chile by Elvira Savi, pianist, Patricia Vásquez, soprano, and Valene Georges, clarinet. Some 16 other concerts including works by Chilean composers, many of them by youths, occurred in Santiago between July 19-Nov. 27, 1991. At Cochabamba, Bolivia, Fernando García's *Tres Bocetos* for woodwind quintet was premiered in the Teatro Acha May 21, 1991 by the Quinteto Pro-Arte (Mauricio Aibacache, horn; Pedro Sierra, bassoon; Francisco Gouet, clarinet; Daniel Vidal, oboe; Germán Jara, flute).

COLOMBIA

5210 Abadía, Guillermo. Instrumentos musicales: folklore colombiano. Bogotá: Banco Popular, Fondo de Promoción de la Cultura, 1991. 174 p.: bibl., ill. (Biblioteca Banco Popular; 138)

Closely related to material already available in author's *Compendio general de folklore colombiano* (1970, 3d ed. 1977; see *HLAS* 36:916 and 42:1227), present manual marches through various classes familiar to students of Hornbostel-Sachs divisions. Appendices include sections entitled "Five Curious Legends" and "Five Curious Myths." Most recent item in bibliography is dated 1970, when the first edition of author's *Compendio* was published.

5211 Alviar, Oscar. Puertas para la música. (*Gaceta/Bogotá*, 13, mayo/junio/julio 1992, p. 42–44, ill.)

Among the 54 Colombian composers active from 1850 to the present whose biobibliographies have been (or are being) processed by the Centro de Documentación of Colcultura, only two are women: Jacqueline

Nova (1936–75) and Catalina Peralta (1963-). Most of the article consists of an interview with Guillermo Gaviria (1954-), who in 1992, was director of the Music Dept. of the Univ. Javeriana, director of the Asociación Colombiana de Compositores (six members, organized in 1987), and *asesor* of the Colcultura administration. In New York Gaviria studied with Jeffrey Langley at Juilliard, but decided that Colombia did not need composers, but rather music teachers. Nevertheless, Gaviria's association has worked assiduously for the betterment of the Colombian composer's lot.

5212 Arias, Eduardo and **Augusto Martelo.**
Surfin' chapinero: historia incompleta, cacheca, subjetiva, irreflexiva e irresponsable del rock en Colombia. (*Gaceta/Bogotá*, 13, mayo/junio/julio 1992, p. 1419, ill.)
Rock reached Colombia via Mexico, with Elvis Presley as the godfather. The first substantial Colombian group, Los Speakers (comprising Luis Dueñas, Rodrigo García, Humberto Monroy, and two others), flourished in 1966, doing Beatles songs. The 1971 Concierto de Ancón celebrated at Medellín (echoing Woodstock) rates as a high point in Colombian rock history. James Brown performed at Bogotá Aug. 29, 1973. In 1988 the Festival Bogotá en Armonía raised hopes that Colombian rock would get off the ground. The Argentine Charly García gave a 1989 concert and the same year Colombian groups Alerta Roja, Darkness, Distrito Especial, La Pestilencia, Signos Vitales, and Sociedad Anónima recorded LPs. Article includes list of all known Colombian rock recordings 1965–92. Nevertheless, Arias and his collaborators view Colombian rock as a procession of ships passing in the night. Colombians do not take to heart their own groups and no group resonates outside Colombia.

5213 Arteaga, José. Lucho Bermúdez: maestro de maestros. Bogotá: Intermedio Editores, 1991. 127 p., 16 p. of plates: ill.
Although José Barros wrote more popular music than any other Colombian, Lucho Bermúdez (b. El Carmen near Cartagena, Jan. 25, 1912) recorded more. The 39 albums marketed between 1954–83 (p. 126–127) by 14 companies (including RCA Victor, Philips, Columbia, and Polydor) attest to an international touring career that took him through-

out the Caribbean and to Buenos Aires, Mexico, and Los Angeles.

5214 Rojas Hernández, Carlos. Sobre la regionalización en los estudios musicológicos. (*in* Historia y culturas populares: los estudios regionales en Boyacá. Recopilación de Pablo Mora Calderón y Amada Guerrero Rincón. Boyacá, Colombia: Instituto de Cultura y Bellas Artes de Boyacá, Centro de Investigación de Cultura Popular, 1989, p. 191–195)
The municipality of Sutatenga was the seat of the radio transmitter that changed musical tastes of the country folk who listened. First they succumbed to the rumba criolla, then to the *merengue valduparense* purveyed by the trio Los Isleños and especially by Guillermo Buitrago. Next to penetrate and oust local musical traditions was the *merengue guasca.*

5215 Ulloa, Alejandro. La Salsa en Cali. Cali, Colombia: Ediciones Univ. del Valle, 1992. 619 p.: bibl., ill. (Col. Crónica y periodismo)
At Cali salsa has preempted other popular music genres. The author gives five reasons: mechanization of culture; presence of blacks; industrialization that has driven out local genres; urbanization leading to impersonality; and absence of any *sui generis* traditional music in Cali. Although containing a history of Afro-Cuban music, this book belongs to the sociology of music category.

5216 Yépez Chamorro, Benjamín. La música aborigen. (*Gaceta/Bogotá*, 13, p. 45–51, bibl., ill.)
Colombia still lacks an atlas of indigenous instruments. However, some generalizations can be made. Aboriginal instrument-makers generally eschew metal. Clay aerophones of ocarina and trumpet variety abound—the most sophisticated being those made in the Sierra Nevada de Santa Marta and in Nariño dept. By far the greatest number of instruments are of vegetable substance—syrinxes and trumpets among aerophones; maracas, and *manguaré* and *yadico* used by male members of the Murui-Muinane enclave, among percussion. All aboriginal music, except for the amatory flute expressions of youthful suitors, is ritual in character, every song being an invocation.

CUBA

5217 Aguancha Jiménez, Gabriel. Memorias de Rafael Cueto y el Trío Matamoros. (*Gaceta/Bogotá,* 13, p. 29–31, ill.)

Question-and-answer interview with last surviving member (b. March 14, 1900) of a world-famous trio formed in 1925 that began recording at Camden, New Jersey, in 1928 (ten double-sided 78s). Originating in the hometown of the three, Santiago de Cuba, the trio was headed by scrupulously honest Miguel Matamoros (b. May 8, 1894; d. April 15, 1971), who always divided intake equally among the members—himself, guitarist-singer Cueto, and the singer who also did claves and maracas, Siro Rodríguez (b. Dec. 9, 1899).

5218 Ashbrook, William. Sánchez Ferrer, Roberto. (*in* The New Grove Dictionary of Opera. New York: Grove's Dictionaries of Music, 1992, v. 4, p. 162)

Describes career of this composer (b. Havana, Dec. 31, 1927) of the three-act *Ecue-Yamba-O* which premiered at the Gran Teatro in Havana, Dec. 25, 1986, and was based on his own libretto, after Alejo Carpentier's tale.

5219 Betancur Alvarez, Fabio. Presencia del bambuco en la trova cubana. (*Del Caribe,* 19, 1992, p. 78–86, music)

Author closes with six alternative hypotheses.

5220 Blanco Aguilar, Jesús. Ochenta años del son y los soneros del Caribe, 1909–1989. Caracas: Fondo Editorial Tropykos, 1992. 119 p.: ill.

According to the author, the three "best" interpreters of Cuban sones, boleros, and guarachas have been Miguelito Valdés ("Mr. Babalú"), Benny Moré, and Antonio Machin. Along with their portraits on p. 57, 94, and 103, he interposes pictures of 16 other groups or individuals. On p. 106–115, he itemizes 39 nocturnal venues where sones were heard in Havana 1920–40 and sketches careers of pioneer members of the sextet Habanero. The loose organization and anecdotal character of this book somewhat detract from its scientific value.

5221 Carpentier, Alejo. La música en Cuba. 3. ed. cubana. La Habana: Editorial Letras Cubanas, 1988. 346 p.: bibl., music. (Giraldilla)

In this republication of Carpentier's classic history (see *HLAS* 12:3396), musical examples are shabbily facsimiled from the Fondo de Cultura Económica *editio princeps* and émigrés during the Castro régime are expunged.

5222 Dotsenko, Vitali. La música de Leo Brouwer: innovación y tradiciones. (*Am. Lat./Moscow,* 12:89, dic. 1989, p. 43–47)

Before returning home to align himself with Cuban revolutionary politics, Brouwer "without finishing a semester's studies" enrolled in 1959 for his "first professional instruction in composition" at the "Gulluard" (Juilliard) School with Vincent "Pezsichetti" (Persichetti). Despite his political correctness, author does eulogize an artist of great significance.

5223 González, Jorge Antonio and **Charles Pitt.** Cuba. (*in* The New Grove Dictionary of Opera. New York: Grove's Dictionaries of Music, 1992, v. 1, p. 1022–1023)

The Festival Internacional at Havana in 1989 included the world premiere of Yuri Ghazaryan's opera *Ernest Hemingway,* but opera has languished during the Castro era.

5224 González, Jorge Antonio. Gottschalk, Louis Moreau. (*in* The New Grove Dictionary of Opera. New York: Grove's Dictionaries of Music, 1992, v. 2, p. 498)

Only the *Final e himno triunfal* have surfaced of the opera *Charles IX* composed at Havana during Gottschalk's last visit to Cuba. This extant portion was performed at the Tacón Theater, Havana, Feb. 17, 1860, the composer conducting.

5225 Hernández Balaguer, Pablo. El más antiguo documento de la música cubana y otros ensayos. Selección y prólogo de Radamés Giro. Habana: Editorial Letras Cubanas, 1986. 219 p. (Giraldilla)

Preceded by an eight-page synopsis of Hernández Balaguer's life (b. Havana, July 13, 1920; d. Havana, Jan. 31, 1966; educated at Barcelona, Prague, Budapest, Moscow), this anthology consists of 11 sections, the lengthiest of which is a reprint of his catalog of the Santiago de Cuba cathedral music archive. Compiler omits "La Capilla de Música de la Catedral de Santiago de Cuba," *Revista Musical Chilena* (Vol. 18, No. 90, oct./dic. 1964, p. 14–61).

5226 Kuss, Malena. The confluence of historical coordinates in Carpentier/Caturla's puppet opera *Manita en el suelo.* (*in* Musical repercussions of 1492. Washington: Smithsonian Institution Press, 1992, p. 355–380, bibl., music)

In 1982, author tracked down the manuscript of Alejandro García Caturla's Afro-Cuban *Mitología bufa* for marionettes, narrator, and chamber orchestra in one act and five scenes (text by Alejo Carpentier). These were reconstructed for its 15 Feb. 1985 Havana premiere (with dancers replacing the puppets) "by the Cuban composer and historian Hilario González in collaboration with Carmelina Muñoz." Work had remained in short score, except for Caturla's orchestration of the overture (danzón), interlude, and ballad, at the time of his assassination at 34. Kuss invaluably traces the origin of the story used in the libretto and analyzes the music.

5227 Martínez, Orlando. Ernesto Lecuona. La Habana: Unión de Escritores y Artistas de Cuba, 1989. 95 p., 40 p. of plates: ill.

Author, who claims to have been Lecuona's friend for almost 30 years, credits him with having "initiated Afro-Cuban music in Cuba" when at 17 he startled his teacher Hubert de Blanck by playing *La comparsa.* Concerning Lecuona's most divulged piano piece, *Malagueña,* composed when he was 24, author states that it and one other *fragmento* are the "most famous" (p. 77). At the close of his career his repertory was "lamentably reduced" to his *Danza negra, La comparsa, Malagueña,* and one other piece (p. 62). This cheaply produced "first" biography contains 33 photographs (often poorly reproduced) but no music or musical analysis.

5228 Mikowsky, Solomon Gadles. Ignacio Cervantes y la danza en Cuba. Traducción de Rubén Casado. Habana: Editorial Letras Cubanas, 1988. 332 p.: bibl., music. (Giraldilla)

Chap. 1 treats origins of the *danza* and its introduction into Cuba at the close of the 18th century, while Chap. 2 takes into account its development in Cuba during the 19th century, and Chap. 3 provides details concerning the *contradanzas* of Manuel Saumell (1817–70) and selected coetaneans. The second half of the book exhaustively surveys Cervantes' career (p. 107–141) and *danzas* (p. 143–192). In Appendix A, author registers

Cuban and foreign editions of Cervantes' *danzas.* Appendix B contains reduced, frequently illegible, facsimiles of other Cuban *danzas.* Appendix C continues with the same for Cervantes'. Born at Havana in 1936, author has lived in the US since 1956.

5229 Orozco González, Danilo. Procesos socioculturales y rasgos de identidad en los géneros musicales con referencia especial a la música cubana. (*Lat. Am. Music Rev.,* 13 : 2, Fall/Winter 1992, p. 158–178)

Augmented version of a paper solicited by Gerard Béhague for the Foro de Música del Festival Internacional de Cultura Caribeña held Nov. 1991 (Chetumal, Cancún, Mexico). Author, whose 1987 doctoral thesis (Humboldt Univ., Berlin) was titled "La Categoría Son como Componente de la Identidad Cultural de Cuba," traverses a wide range of topics. He lists at least five reasons for ascribing the genesis of the *son* to the eastern part of Cuba (p. 173–175). He ascribes the origin of salsa in the 1950s and 1960s to a mixing not only of Cuban *son, guaguancó* (rumba), *guajira,* bolero, and *canción,* but also to a tilting toward such other Caribbean genres as *cumbia, bunde, ballerengue, gaita, porro* (and much else from Colombia, the Dominican Republic, Haiti, Panama, and Puerto Rico, p. 176–177). All of the author's *referencias* are his own contributions: the 1976 *Monumentos de la cultura cubana* being an unpublished lecture, and the *Panorama introductorio de la cultura musical cubana* being still "en preparación."

5230 Palacios García, Eliseo. Catálogo de música de concierto. Havana: Centro de Información y Promoción de la Musíca Odilio Urfé, Instituto Cubano de la Música, Ministerio de Cultura, 1990. 132 p.: ill.

After briefly profiling orchestras and chamber groups active in the island, followed by directors' biographies, author does the same for choral groups and bands. Next come instrumentalists and soloists. For lack of birth dates (with places) and other vital statistics, this well-intentioned compilation forfeits confidence.

Ramos, Josean. Vengo a decirle adiós a los muchachos. See item **3874.**

Shatunóvskaya, Irina. Inspirado por la memoria del pasado: plática con Juan Almeida Bosque, miembro del Buró Político del CC del

Partido Comunista de Cuba. See *HLAS 53: 3679.*

5231 Valdés Cantero, Alicia. El músico en Cuba: ubicación social y situación laboral en el período 1939–1946. Habana: Editorial Pueblo y Educación, 1988. 108 p.: bibl., ill.

In this sociological memoir, author compares wages and perquisites afforded white and black Cuban musicians 1939–46. She concludes that musicians, whatever their color, suffered the same iniquitous capitalist exploitation as did other day laborers in the years under review. Not content with their status, they constantly politicized their struggle upward.

5232 White, Charles W. Report on music in Cuba today. (*Lat. Am. Music Rev.*, 13: 2, Fall/Winter 1992, p. 234–242)

Author was preparing a biography of Alejandro García Caturla (1906–40) when, in Oct. 1991, he attended the "Festival de la Habana de Música Contemporánea 1991." There he read a paper titled "A.G. Caturla in Barcelona, 1929." Although unapproving of the French saxophonist Daniel Kientzy's solo recital (at the Teatro García Lorca), White reported enthusiastically on nearly all other Festival events.

5233 Yedra, Velia. Julián Orbón: a biographical and critical essay. Coral Gables, Fla.: Research Institute for Cuban Studies, Graduate School of International Studies, Univ. of Miami, 1990. 93 p.: bibl., ill.

Author, a Cuban-American concert pianist with a Doctor of Musical Arts degree from the Univ. of Miami, presents first biography (with works-analyses) of the Spanish-born Orbón, who left Cuba in 1960 to assist Chávez in the composition workshop at the Mexican National Conservatory, and in 1963 took up permanent residence in the US. According to Eduardo Mata (Foreword, p. 3), Orbón is "the greatest composer Cuba has ever produced." Mata also classes him as "the closest thing to a spiritual son of Villa-Lobos and Chávez" that Latin America has engendered.

ECUADOR

5234 Guerrero, J. Agustín. La música ecuatoriana desde su origen hasta 1875. 2. ed. Quito: Banco Central del Ecuador, 1984.

54 p. (Fuentes y documentos para la historia de la música en el Ecuador; 1)

Pioneer history covers 1825–75 and was issued by the interim director of the Ecuadorian national conservatory for 18 months after Antonio Neumane's death at Quito March 3, 1871. The *yaravíes quiteños* published in 1878 as an appendix to the *Cuarta Reunión de Americanistas* (Madrid, 1875) were furnished to Marcos Jiménez de la Espada by author of this work, for which he was never given credit. For a review of the present reprint, see *Inter-American Music Review* (Vol. 13, No. 2, Fall/Winter 1992, p. 109–111).

5235 Stevenson, Robert. La música en Quito. 2a ed. Quito: Centro de Investigación y Cultura, Banco Central del Ecuador, 1989. 37 p. (Fuentes y documentos para la historia de la música en el Ecuador; 3)

Reprint of a historical survey published in *Arnahis, Organo del Archivo Nacional de Historia* (Vol. 11, No. 17, Aug. 10, 1968, p. 7–28)

MEXICO

5236 Alcaraz, José Antonio. . . . En una música estelar: de Ricardo Castro a Federico Alvarez del Toro. México: CENIDIM; DIDA, 1987. 141 p. (Col. Ensayos; 5)

Useful program notes on 44 works by sixteen 20th-century Mexicans, ranging alphabetically from Federico Alvarez del Toro to Carlos Jiménez Mabarak.

5237 Alvarez Cabrera, Hugo. Notas sobre la música huasteca. (*in* Encuentro de Investigadores de la Huasteca, *4th, Tlalpan, México, 1988?* Cuextecapan, lugar de bastimentos. Coordinación de Agustín Avila Méndez y Jesús Ruvalcaba Mercado. México: SEP, 1991, p. 201–231, ill., music)

This is an instruction manual for the use of players of instruments used in performing *huapangos.* However, author warns against anyone's assuming that "a written manual can substitute for a knowledgeable teacher."

Anderson, Arthur J.O. La *Salmodia* de Sahagún. See item **426.**

5238 Benjamin, Gerald R. Carrillo (-Trujillo), Julián (Antonio). (*in* The New Grove Dictionary of Opera. New York: Grove's Dictionaries of Music, 1992, v. 1, p. 744–745, bibl.)

None of Carrillo's three operas, *Matilde, Ossian,* or *Xulitl,* reached the stage.

5239 Bock, Philip K. Music in Mérida, Yucatán. (*Lat. Am. Music Rev.,* 13:1, Spring/Summer 1992, p. 35–55, bibl.)

Author is a professor of anthropology at the Univ. of New Mexico, Albuquerque and editor of *Journal of Anthropological Research.* He traveled to Yucatán on sabbatical leave "to survey urban music in the capital city, Mérida" from Jan.-March 1989. Author states that "the most comprehensive information about Yucatecan song" is found in *Sensibilidad yucateca en la canción romántica* (1978) by Miguel Civiera Taboada (1916–87). He equates the *jarana* of Yucatán and the *jarocho* of Veracruz with the *jarabe* of Tabasco, at least socially. "All three may be derived from the *jota,* at least rhythmically: they are in triple meter with an alternation between 3/4 and 6/8 sections. All three carry connotations of a binge or spree, or of dancing with abandon." Among events that engaged author's attention, he describes at length the seven sections of a late-night performance (at the Teatro José Peón Contreras) of the six-year-old Ballet Folklórico de la Univ. Autónoma de Yucatán (UAY); a midnight visit to the La X'tabay *centro nocturno;* a Sunday evening band concert at the hall of the main musicians' union; a meeting of "Los Amigos de la Trova Yucateca" at a downtown hotel; and an evening at a new club that ended with songs by Mexican pop star Sergio Esquivel, sung by the composer himself.

5240 Carredano, Consuelo. Felipe Villanueva, 1862–1893. México: Consejo Nacional de Investigación, Documentación e Información Musical Carlos Chavez (CENIDIM), 1992. 174 p.: bibl., music.

Both Schubert and Villanueva died at 31. After his death on May 28, 1893, Villanueva's nephew, Aurelio Villanueva, came into possession of his unpublished works and commented on the great care he was taking of them in three articles (*El Universal,* Jan. 16, 1922 and Feb. 26, 1922, and *El Universal Gráfico,* May 5, 1937). Nonetheless, 37 are not locatable. In contrast, Schubert's brother lost none inherited by him. Author has gone to great pains to provide trustworthy account of Villanueva's aborted life and works. Loss of

the score of *Keofar,* a three-act comic opera (libretto by Gonzalo Larrañaga) composed in 1887–88 and premiered July 29, 1893 in the Teatro Principal a month after Villanueva's death, cannot be sufficiently lamented.

5241 Catalyne, Alice Ray. Zumaya (Sumaya), Manuel de. (*in* The New Grove Dictionary of Opera. New York: Grove's Dictionaries of Music, 1992, v. 4, p. 1247, bibl.)

Lack of recent bibliography results in incorrect death year and in other misfortunes. Most unsatisfactory article.

5242 Dolkart, Ronald H. Angela Peralta: a Mexican diva. (*in* The human tradition in Latin America: the nineteenth century. Edited by Judith Ewell and William H. Beezley. Wilmington, Del.: SR Books, 1989, p. 161–174, bibl.)

Storybook life of diva's career demeans her latter years. While complaining that a scholarly biography does not exist, author shies away from needed research, instead contenting himself with secondary, often unreliable, literature.

5243 Dorantes Guzmán, Sergio. Arrau: el gran artista latinoamericano. Xalapa, Mexico: Univ. Veracruzana, 1991. 76 p.: ill. (Tesitura)

The one large work by a Latin American ever played by Arrau (who completely avoided compatriots) was Carlos Chávez's piano concerto (Aug. 1, 3, and 7, 1943; Sept. 8 and 10, 1944). Highly fitting therefore is this painstakingly assembled tribute that includes an Arrau discography and chronology of all his performances in Mexico from 1933–82. At his Mexico City début Oct. 11, 1933 in Teatro Hidalgo, he played the Handel-Brahms variations, Chopin's E Major Scherzo, and three movements from Stravinsky's "Petroushka" on a Bluethner provided by the capital's Casa Wagner.

5244 Dueñas Herrera, Pablo. Bolero: historia documental del bolero mexicano. México: Asociación Mexicana de Estudios Fonográficos, 1990. 293 p.: bibl., ill., index.

Author, a physician born in the capital July 10, 1959, began collecting early recordings of Mexican popular music in 1974. Since 1979 he has diffused his versatile recoveries in lectures, radio programs, articles, and books. The maximum composer of boleros, Agustín Lara, initiated his series with "Imposible," bought by a representative of Victor, the Mexico Music Company, on Oct. 2, 1928 for 48 pesos. Recorded in New York by the Trio Garnica-Ascencio, it was immediately covered by Pilar Arcos, José Moriche, Adolfo Utrera, and José Rubio. Boasting a useful name index, volume consists mostly of a sequence of photos, each accompanied by a brief biography that mentions the performer or composer's chief successes. Chronological table of boleros dated 1885 ("Tristezas-Un beso" by the Cuban Pepe Sánchez) to 1984 ("Yolanda" by the Cuban Pablo Milanés) counts among the useful appendices.

5245 Forbes, Elizabeth. Anitúa, Fanny. (*in* The New Grove Dictionary of Opera. New York: Grove's Dictionaries of Music, 1992, v. 1, p. 141)
Unsatisfactory résumé, lacking bibliography.

5246 Goodwin, Noël. Araiza, Francisco. (*in* The New Grove Dictionary of Opera. New York: Grove's Dictionaries of Music, 1992, v. 1, p. 160–161)
Imprecise résumé of the Mexican tenor's career (b. Mexico City, Oct. 4, 1958).

5247 Goodwin, Noël. Cruz-Romeo, Gilda. (*in* The New Grove Dictionary of Opera. New York: Grove's Dictionaries of Music, 1992, v. 1, p. 1021)
Born at Guadalajara Feb. 12, 1940, this Mexican soprano made her Metropolitan Opera (N.Y.) debut in 1970 as Butterfly.

5248 Goodwin, Noël. Domínguez, Oralia. (*in* The New Grove Dictionary of Opera. New York: Grove's Dictionaries of Music, 1992, v. 1, p. 484–485)
Condensed biography of the Mexican contralto born at San Luis Potosí Oct. 15, 1928.

5249 Guerrero, Héctor. Los guitarristas clásicos de México. 1. ed. Enorme. Torreón, Mexico: E. Nor. Me., 1990. 359 p.: ill., index. (Historia Enorme; 3)
Occasionally the 37 short autobiographies, each preceded by a photograph, mention a birth year (p. 125) or even month (p. 84), but the guitarists (five are women) invariably provide the kind of data that enter program notes, not encyclopedias. According to the back cover, compiler transcribed Bach's "321 chorales" for guitar quartet.

5250 Guerrero Romero, Javier. Ricardo Castro, el primer gran concertista mexicano. Durango, Mexico: Gobierno del Estado, 1990. 32 p.: ill.
Relying on data assembled and published by Jesús C. Romero, author assigns composer's birth not to 1866 but to Feb. 7, 1864 in Number 7 of the street at Durango now named P.C. Negrete. His baptismal name was Ricardo Rafael de la Santísima Trinidad Castro Herrera. His first music teacher at Durango was Pedro H. Ceniceros. He entered the national conservatory at Mexico City Jan. 4, 1878. His first teachers of piano and harmony were Juan Salvatierra and Lauro Beristain. In 1934 the Durango theatre built in 1895 was given the composer's name. In 1989 his Concerto for cello and orchestra was revived with Carlos Prieto as soloist and his Symphony No. 1, Opus 33 in C minor (1883) was premiered by the Orquesta Clásica de México conducted by Carlos Esteva in the Sala Nezahualcóyotl (Univ. Nacional Autónoma de México), followed in July 1990 with its first performance in Durango. On Oct. 10, 1990 his remains were deposited in the Rotunda de los Hombres y Mujeres Ilustres de Durango.

5251 Herrera y Ogazón, Alba. El arte musical en México. México: Consejo Nacional para la Cultura y las Artes; Instituto Nacional de Bellas Artes; Centro Nacional de Investigación, Documentación e Información Musical Carlos Chávez, 1992. 227 p.
Long-time teacher in the Mexican National Conservatory, author confided many of her personal memories to this still useful history. Her specialty was the 19th century. For a review of this landmark publication by a woman, see *Inter-American Music Review* (Vol. 13, No. 1, Fall/Winter 1992, p. 41).

5252 Jarabes y fandanguitos: imagen y música del baile popular. México: Museo Nacional de Arte, 1990. 45 p.: bibl., ill. (some col.), music.
Facsimiled music examples derive from Miguel Ríos Toledano's *Unica y auténtica colección de treinta jarabes, sones principales y más populares aires nacionales de la República Mexicana*. Booklet concludes with seven full-color illustrations, each a full page.

5253 Kaptain, Laurence. Letter to the Editor. (*Lat. Am. Music Rev.*, 13:2, Fall/Winter 1992, p. 243–246, bibl.)

Author, associate professor of percussion at the Univ. of Missouri, Kansas City, recommends visiting the Escuela de la Música Mexicana at Mexico City directed by Daniel García Blanco, and the Instituto Chiapaneco de Cultura at Tuxtla Gutiérrez directed by Andrés Fábrega Puig. He announces as "forthcoming" his book *The wood that sings: the marimba in Chiapas, Mexico* (Alexandria, Va.: Meredith Music Publications).

5254 Ladrón de Guevara, Raúl. La obra de Rodolfo Halffter. (*Palabra Hombre*, 67, julio/sept. 1988, p. 36–59, music)

Written in response to an April 1981 invitation, essay shows no signs of revision after Rodolfo Halffter's death at Mexico City on Oct. 14, 1987. Accompanying the article are 23 musical excerpts ranging from op. 1 to op. 39, but no bibliography nor profound analysis that would confirm author's acquaintance with recent Rodolfo Halffter literature.

5255 López-Calo, José. Documentario musical de la Catedral de Segovia. v. 1. Santiago de Compostela: Univ. de Santiago de Compostela, 1990. 1 v.: index. (Col. Aula Aberta: Música; 2)

Both Lázaro del Alamo and Hernando Franco, Mexico City Cathedral *maestros de capilla* 1556–70 and 1575–85, received their musical education in Segovia Cathedral. Alamo was promoted from *mozo de coro* to *seise* in March 1545, his teacher henceforth being Bartolomé Olaso. Franco, rated May 26, 1546 as having made the most progress and possessing the best voice among the *mozos de coro*, was rewarded with a yearly salary of 8 ducats. Concerning Alamo and Franco at Mexico City, see *Inter-American Music Review* (Vol. 1, No. 2, Spring/Summer 1979, p. 138–167). Fru[c]tos del Castillo, whose *Monstra te esse Matrem, a 4* is in Puebla Cathedral, Choirbook II, fols. 52–53, was a Segovia *mozo de coro* serving as cathedral *menestril* in 1576. On July 20, 1580 the cathedral chapter awarded him 8000 *maravedís* to subsidize his continued studies during the next two years.

5256 Loza, Steven. From Veracruz to Los Angeles: the reinterpretation of the *son jarocho*. (*Lat. Am. Music Rev.*, 13:2, Fall/Winter 1992, p. 179–194, bibl., ill., music)

In this excellent study of the journey to Los Angeles of the Mexican Atlantic Coast

genre expertly studied in Daniel E. Sheehy's 1979 landmark doctoral dissertation, "The Son Jarocho: the History, Style, and Repertory of a Changing Musical Tradition," author compares the version of *El Canelo* recorded and transcribed by Sheehy with its counterpart in an East Los Angeles reinterpretation by Los Lobos. Author gives substance to his analysis by incorporating revealing statements made in interviews with members of Los Lobos: Louie Pérez, César Rojas, David Hidalgo, and Conrad Lozano. "The idea of reclamation plays an essential role in Los Lobos' reliance upon Mexican-influenced musical repetoire." Their Grammy-awarded *La Pistola y el Corazón* (1989) included *El Canelo* and one other *son jarocho*.

5257 Meierovich, Clara. Especulación y verdad: novedad histórica en la biografía más temprana de Carlos Chávez. (*Lat. Am. Music Rev.*, 13:1, Spring/Summer 1992, p. 114–123)

Vicente T. Mendoza's "Carlos Chávez y la Música Mexicana," a manuscript encountered by the author in the Fondo Reservado of the Mexican Biblioteca Nacional, is not only the earliest Chávez biography, but also contains a 15-chapter panorama of Mexico's musical past from independence to Chávez's emergence as Mexico's messiah. In *Anales del Instituto de Investigaciones Estéticas* (año III, tomo II, no. 3, 1939), Mendoza continued pouring incense on Chávez's altar. His latest known tribute appeared in *El Nacional* (July 27, 1955) under the heading "Bosquejo biográfico."

5258 Melo, Juan Vicente. Notas sin música. Recopilación de Alberto Paredes. Prólogo de Eduardo Soto Millán. México: Fondo de Cultura Económica, 1990. 576 p.: bibl., index. (Col. popular; 428)

Author was born at Veracruz in 1932 and is also a novelist (see *HLAS 32:3768*) and short story writer. In 1967, author published a predecessor album, *De música y músicos* (Mexico City: Librería Madero). In the present carryover he repeats many of his reactions to Mexico City happenings during the 1960s. Now providing a valuable name index, he ranges through Mexican composers, ensembles, orchestras, musical diffusion and administration, concerts and cycles, to foreign musicians. Although giving hard-core information is still not his goal, he does document

José Raúl Hellmer's death in the capital Aug. 15, 1971. If in search of greater value, Melo should have dated each entry. To read that Mario Kuri-Aldana "received two years ago a grant to study at Buenos Aires with Ginastera (among others)" typifies resulting confusions.

5259 Navarro, Antonio. Escritos y ensayos musicales. Guadalajara, Mexico: Editorial Univ. de Guadalajara, 1989. 185 p.: bibl. (Col. Fundamentos)

In this anthology of newspaper, journal, and lecture materials dating 1979–89, author reflects in accessible fashion on the careers of Carlos Chávez, Rodolfo Halffter, Alberto Ginastera, Mario Lavista, and Julio Estrada. His catalogs of 23 Mexican musical periodicals published between 1826–1982 and of 20 books on musical periodicals published by Mexicans at Mexico City between 1902–88 have value, even when he credits Gustavo E. Campa's 1902 compilation to A. Warner y Levin (should be A. Wagner y Levien).

5260 Orquesta Sinfónica Nacional, director artístico, Herrera de la Fuente: segunda temporada, 1989, Teatro de Bellas Artes. México: Consejo Nacional para la Cultura y las Artes, Instituto Nacional de Bellas Artes, 1989. 85 p.: ports.

Handsomely produced, program booklet itemizes contents of seven concerts by the Orquesta Sinfónica Nacional given at the Palacio de Bellas Artes in Nov. and Dec. 1989. Except for Mario Lavista's *Reflejos de la noche,* written for string quartet in 1984 and transcribed by the composer for string orchestra in 1986 (program 1, Nov. 5/6), Carlos Chávez's *Zarabanda* for strings from his *La hija de Cólquide* (program 4, Nov. 24/26), and Luis Sandi's *Díptico* (world premiere, program 6, Dec. 8/10), all items were standard international fare. Sandi called the first part of his *Díptico* a desperate outburst against cruel fate, the second part a disconsolate threnody.

5261 Radomski, James. Manuel García en Mexico: part II. (*Inter-Am. Music Rev.,* 13:1, Fall/Winter 1992, p. 15–20, music)

Authoritative traversal of García's Mexican sojourn May 8-June 21, 1828 by the author of the article on Manuel (del Pópulo Vicente Rodríguez) García in *The New Grove Dictionary of Opera,* (Vol. 2, 1992, p. 345–347).

5262 Revueltas, Silvestre. Silvestre Revueltas, por él mismo: apuntes autobiográficos, diarios, correspondencia y otros escritos de un gran músico. Recopilación de Rosaura Revueltas. México: Ediciones Era, 1989. 262 p., 16 p. of plates: bibl., ill. (Biblioteca Era)

Essential for any understanding of Revueltas' career, this compilation still leaves insufficiently adumbrated his activities in Chicago, San Antonio, Texas, and Mobile, Alabama. Whatever his distaste for the US, no Mexican composer exceeded his knowledge of the US musical scene, except perhaps Chávez.

5263 Russell, Craig H. Musical life in Baroque Mexico: rowdy musicians, confraternities and the Holy Office. (*Inter-Am. Music Rev.,* 13:1, Fall/Winter 1992, p. 11–14, facsims.)

After beatification in 1664 of Pedro Arbués (1441–85) and his adoption as patron of the Mexican Santo Oficio, musicians from Mexico City Cathedral were each year contracted to perform at Santo Domingo church on his feast day. Documentation includes facsimiles of receipts signed by Antonio de Salazar Sept. 17, 1710 and by Manuel de Sumaya (Zumaya) Sept. 16, 1733, Mexico City Cathedral chapelmasters. Wax for the candles cost more than the music.

5264 Russell, Craig H. Newly discovered treasures from colonial California: the masses at the San Fernando Mission. (*Inter-Am. Music Rev.,* 13:1, Fall/Winter 1992, p. 5–9)

At least two orchestral masses by Ignacio Jerusalem, Mexico City Cathedral chapelmaster 1750–69, reached San Fernando Mission in Alta California during the Spanish period. Junípero Serra was *vicario de coro* in the Mexico City San Fernando College during three of the years between 1758–67. The two Jerusalem masses (in D and F Major) sent northward to Alta California are copies of those in the Mexico City Cathedral archive dated 1763 and 1768.

5265 Salas Viú de Halffter, Emilia. La música en el exilio: Rodolfo Halffter y los músicos españoles en México. (*in* El destierro español en América: un trasvase cultural. Recopilación de Nicolás Sánchez Albornoz. Madrid: Instituto de Cooperación Iberoamericana; Sociedad Estatal Quinto Centenario, 1991, p. 69–75)

This panegyric by the eminent composer's widow omits precise dates and skirts over embarrassing details. For decades, price of Halffter's acceptance continued being the Spaniard's subservience to Chávez and his unflinching loyalty to Chávez's interests.

5266 Saldívar, Gabriel. Bibliografía mexicana de musicología y musicografía. México: CENIDIM, 1991–1992. 2 v.: ill.

Incomparably valuable annotated bibliography, preceded by Elisa Osorio Bolio de Saldívar's introduction and a synopsis of Mexican musical foundations, covers imprints and manuscripts dated 1538–1900. Just as the author, Gabriel Saldívar y Silva (d. Dec. 18, 1980, Mexico City), was the most diligent and successful collector of Mexican musical documents in his generation (or any generation), so also his wife's brilliant editing and augmentation of the bibiliography left unfinished at his death cannot be overpraised. For a review, see *Inter-American Music Review*, Vol. 13, No. 1, Fall/Winter 1992, p. 116–117.

5267 Sosa Manterola, José Octavio and **Mónica Escobedo F.** Dos siglos de ópera en México. Presentación de Eduardo Lizalde. México: Secretaría de Educación Pública, 1988. 2 v.: ill., indexes.

These two volumes offer chronological list of operas performed, chiefly in the capital, accompanied by names of singers in principal roles and those of the conductors. Although title promises "two centuries," the list begins in 1823. Each volume contains thorough name index and other finding aids. Although authors' traversal of operas performed after 1900 can be relied on, the citing of July 23, 1852 for the first performance in Mexico of Mozart's *Don Giovanni* counts among the many serious errors that could have been avoided had the youthful compilers conscientiously read Enrique de Olavarría y Ferrari's classic *Reseña de la historia del teatro en México*.

5268 Stevenson, Robert. Bernal Jiménez, Miguel. (*in* The New Grove Dictionary of Opera. New York: Grove's Dictionaries of Music, 1992, v. 1, p. 441)

Tata Vasco, in five scenes, was composed to celebrate the fourth centenary of the arrival at Pátzcuaro of Vasco de Quiroga (1470–1565).

5269 Stevenson, Robert. Campa, Gustavo Emilio. (*in* The New Grove Dictionary of Opera. New York: Grove's Dictionaries of Music, 1992, v. 1, p. 702–703, bibl.)

Campa's *Le roi poète*, produced at Mexico City's Teatro Principal, romanticized the amours of Nezahualcóyotl.

5270 Stevenson, Robert. Castro Herrera, Ricardo. (*in* The New Grove Dictionary of Opera. New York: Grove's Dictionaries of Music, 1992, v. 1, p. 769, bibl.)

Biography and survey of his operas.

5271 Stevenson, Robert. Chávez y Ramírez, Carlos Antonio de Padua. (*in* The New Grove Dictionary of Opera. New York: Grove's Dictionaries of Music, 1992, v. 1, p. 826–827)

Despite three revisions, Mexico's most renowned composer failed in his attempt to write a viable opera.

5272 Stevenson, Robert. Mexico City. (*in* The New Grove Dictionary of Opera. New York: Grove's Dictionaries of Music, 1992, v. 3, p. 364–365, bibl.)

History of opera in the Mexican capital.

5273 Stevenson, Robert. Morales, Melesio. (*in* The New Grove Dictionary of Opera. New York: Grove's Dictionaries of Music, 1992, v. 3, p. 463)

Life and works of Mexico's leading 19th-century composer of operas.

5274 Stevenson, Robert. Paniagua (y Vasques), Cenobio. (*in* The New Grove Dictionary of Opera. New York: Grove's Dictionaries of Music, 1992, v. 3, p. 844, bibl.)

Life and works of Mexico's first opera composer in the independence era.

5275 Stevenson, Robert. Silvestre Revueltas, 1899–1940: new biographical revelations. (*Inter-Am. Music Rev.*, 12:1, Fall/Winter 1991, p. 135–138)

Revueltas married his first wife, English-speaker Julie Klarency, in 1920; their daughter Carmen was born in April 1922. These and many other hitherto suppressed biographical details enter *Silvestre Revueltas, por él mismo* (Mexico City: Ediciones Era, 1989).

5276 Torre García, Jesús Antonio de la. Cuatro valores musicales aguascalientenses. México: Editorial Jus, 1986. 69 p.: ill.

Like many family histories, this booklet tantalizes with its few hard facts mixed with frequent vagueness. Angel García Macías, born Aug. 2, 1853, died Nov. 9, 1906— but these are the only two dates in 11 pages of anecdotal biography. His son Ricardo García Mendoza, composer of the march *General Maximino Camacho* and the pasodoble *Humberto Moro*, organized an acclaimed touring group called Coros Nocturnales and conducted the Aguascalientes Band.

5277 Villancicos y cantatas mexicanos del siglo XVIII. México: UNAM, Escuela Nacional de Música, 1990. 175 p.: bibl., facsims. (Monumentos de la música mexicana; 1:3–9)

The six vernacular and one Latin works by seven 18th-century composers that beginning at p. 50 comprise the musical portion of this splendid anthology belong to cathedral archives at Durango (Francisco Rueda, *Ah de los mares*), Guadalajara (Zárate, *Quae est ista*), Mexico City (Ignacio Jerusalem y Stella, *Admirado el orbe*), Morelia (Joseph Pérez, *A tí, mi Jesús amado*), Oaxaca (Manuel de Sumaya = Zumaya, *Si va a aquella nave*), Puebla (Alonso Mallén, *Como Chamorro es alcalde*), and Zacatecas (Joseph Antonio López de Castro y Góngora, *De dolor y pena*). By far the most talented and significant Mexican-born composer included in this anthology is Sumaya (d. Oaxaca Dec. 21, 1755). In *Monumentos de la música mexicana*, Serie 1, No. 1, González Quiñones published in 1982 his transcription of Sumaya's *Como aunque culpa*, a Christmas cantata for solo tenor accompanied by two violins, viola, and continuo. Estrada preceded González Quiñones in transcribing Sumaya's *Si va a aquella nave* recorded in *Trayectoria de la música en México: época colonial* (México: UNAM, 1984). According to Aurelio Tello, González Quiñones in both instances availed himself of photocopies of Sumaya's Oaxaca works made by Gonzalo Angulo.

PARAGUAY

5278 Kaufman, Tom. Asunción. (*in* The New Grove Dictionary of Opera. New York: Grove's Dictionaries of Music, 1992, v. 1, p. 233–234)

Article on opera in Paraguay fails to note as Josefina Plá did in her *Teatro en el Paraguay* (Asunción, 1967, p. 62) that Donizetti's *Linda di Chamounix*, given in June, 1863 at the Teatro Nacional, was the first Italian opera performed by a touring company.

5279 Rodríguez, Miguel Angel. Semblanzas biográficas de creadores e intérpretes populares paraguayos. Asunción: Ediciones Compugraph, 1992. 130 p.: index.

Succinct biographies of 59 Paraguayan popular stars, accompanied where appropriate with a listing of their musical creations. On p. 60 and 97 author profiles women's groups and soloists. At his death, Dec. 1991, author left a sequel to be edited by Mario Halley Mora, who wrote the prologue and epilogue of this useful vademecum.

Sequera, Guillermo. Cȯsmofonía de los indígenas mbya del Paraguay. See *HLAS 53: 1168.*

PERU

5280 Aguilar Luna-Victoria, Carlos. La marinera: baile nacional del Perú; alcances teóricos para la ejecución del baile de la marinera; ilustraciones e informaciones folklóricas. Lima: Ministerio de Educación, 1989. 306 p.: bibl., ill. (many col.)

In a handsomely illustrated (many color photos) volume, this dance instructor slights music in favor of costumes and steps. *Marinera* replaced the name *chilena* (1879) in tribute to the valor of the Peruvian navy (p. 30).

5281 Ayarza de Morales, Rosa Mercedes. (*in* Enciclopedia ilustrada del Perú. Lima: Promoción Editorial Inca (Piesa), 1987, p. 217–218, ill.)

One of many extremely useful articles in a six-volume encyclopedia (printed in Barcelona by Logo Press) that updates all previous lexicon sources. Ayarza de Morales was a composer and folklorist. Other useful articles are: "Alomía Robles, Daniel;" "Alviña, Leandro;" "Bolognesi, Andrés;" "Duncker Lavalle, Luis;" "Garrido Lecca, Celso;" "Gerdes, Federico;" "Iturriaga, Enrique;" "Raygada, Carlos;" "Rebagliati, Claudio;" "Sánchez Málaga, Carlos;" "Valcárcel, Edgar;" and "Valcárcel, Teodoro."

5282 Borras, Gérard. La musique dans *Yawar Fiesta*. (*Caravelle/Toulouse,* 55, 1990, p. 65–81, bibl., graphs)

A few days before his death, José María Arguedas expressed his hope that music of the *sierra indígena* would break down the wall separating Lima and the rest of the West from precolumbian Peru. In his 1941 novel *Yawar Fiesta,* what is ostensibly a Puquio celebration of Peruvian independence day, July 28, in reality becomes a Quechua triumphal day during which indigenous instruments, especially the phallic *wakawak'ras* hated by the village vicar, symbolize indigenous fortitude. The effeminate harp, violin, and clarinet entertain the *mistis* with sounds that contrast utterly with the virile blasts that consume the entire souls of the *k'ayaus.*

5283 Borras, Gérard. La "musique des Andes" en France: "l'Indianité" ou comment la récupérer. (*Caravelle/Toulouse,* 58, 1992, p. 141–150, bibl.)

During the 1970s and 1980s much so-called Andean music was performed and recorded commercially by groups of poseurs calling themselves Los Incas, Perú Inca, Inca Huasi, Waskar Amaru, and the like. Most bore little or no likeness to what ethnologists accept as authentic Andean survivals. Program notes on albums reeked with gross errors.

5284 Un cancionero religioso quechua del siglo XVIII. (*Bol. Lima,* 10:60, nov. 1988, p. 5–16, facsim.)

Spanish-language rubrics for verses sung in Quechua tell in what [psalm] tones to sing them. The Joys of Mary are to be sung in the seventh tone. The angel Gabriel's salutations of the Blessed Virgin are to be sung in high fifth tone. These prescriptions of tones in the present late 18th-century Quechua collection of song texts indicate that Quechua converts had received considerable music instruction.

5285 Coloma Porcari, César. La "Canción a la Batalla de Ayacucho." (*Hist. Cult./Lima,* 18, p. 130, facsim.)

Along with all else that he composed (except the music for the Peruvian national anthem), Alcedo's *Canción a la Batalla de Ayacucho* for chorus and orchestra has been forgotten. In 1924 the director of the Peruvian Museo Nacional, Emilio Gutiérrez de Quin-

tanilla (1858–1935), had reproduced 4,586 facsimiles of the 13 pages of Alcedo's holograph score, but they remained uncollated and unbound and never circulated.

5286 Cuentas Ormachea, Enrique. La diablada: una expresión de coreografía mestiza del Altiplano de Collao. (*Bol. Lima,* 8:44, marzo 1986, p. 31–48, ill., photos)

The Devil Dance, which is offered as an annual propitiation to the Virgen de la Candelaria on Feb. 2, originated at both Puno and Oruro among miners. Brought from Puno for exhibition in the Teatro Municipal and Manuel Asencio Segura Theatre at Lima, the masks, costumes, choreography, and music entranced the public (*El Comercio,* Aug. 12, 1964) to such a degree that author decided not only to study its origins and history, but also to examine what Quechua and Aymara concepts of malevolent and benevolent spirits entailed. Sole musical example is a 2/4 *huayno.* Repetitive melody played by *sicuri* ranges from d to f in D dorian (no accidentals among 228 notes, save one B flat), and involves 16th- and 8th-notes in syncopated rhythm (M.M. 66 increasing to 84 during repetitions).

5287 Gemert, Hans van. Organos históricos del Perú = Historic organs of Peru. Hillbrow, South Africa: H. van Gemert, 1990? 181 p.: ill.

This exceptionally valuable, bilingual, densely illustrated volume owes its excellence to author's complete mastery of all details of organ building in Renaissance and Baroque epochs, the permission given to him by competent civil and ecclesiastical authorities to inspect closely and photograph 22 17th-and 18th-century instruments, and his ability to describe precisely what he encountered during those inspections that began Jan. 9, 1983 at Andahuaylas and ended at Lamay Nov. 1, 1983. Organs examined were constructed locally, usually by Indian builders. Their names survive in contracts, many of which were included in Jorge Cornejo Bouroncle's *Derroteros del arte cuzqueño* (see *HLAS* 25:1175).

5288 Harcourt, Raoul d' and **Marguerite d'Harcourt.** La música de los incas y sus supervivencias. Presentación de Luis Alberto Sánchez. Lima?: Occidental Petroleum Corp. of Peru, 1990. 605 p.: bibl., ill.

Spanish translation with no attempt at critical updating or post-1925 bibliography.

The least that could have been done to enhance its usefulness would have been an analytical index.

Pinilla, Enrique. La música de la selva peruana. See *HLAS 53:1157.*

5289 Roel, Josafat. El wayno del Cusco. Ed. rev. Qosqo, Perú: Municipalidad del Qosqo, 1991. 235 p.: bibl., ill.

Second ed. of article evaluated for *HLAS 23:844* is augmented by: 1) tributes to the author who, after a decade in Cusco, founded the Centro de Estudio y Difusión del Folklore Nacional at the Univ. de San Marcos in Lima in 1974; 2) a prologue by Oscar Núñez del Prado Castro dated at Cusco Oct. 1990; 3) a preface by Abel Rozas Aragón dated "Qusqo" = Cusco the same month; and 4) reprint of Roel Pineda's article "Hacia la Determinación de los Caracteres Típicos del Wayno Cusqueño," *Revista del Instituto Americano del Arte* (Cusco, Vol. 9, No. 9, Oct. 1959, p. 180–212). In this latter little-known article, Roel Pineda reveals that all 151 examples analyzed in his *Folklore Americano* article were collected not by himself but by Francisco Venero Umpite, a *versado músico* from the San Jerónimo district of Cusco. Then 64 years old, Venero had been singer and organist during the previous decade in his parish church. A professional from age 12, Venero had studied with "the famous popular Cuzco musician," Mariano Carmen Almanza. Roel Pineda recorded Venero's repertory March 16–21, 1958.

5290 Rosenthal, Harold. Alva, Luigi. (*in* The New Grove Dictionary of Opera. New York: Grove's Dictionaries of Music, 1992, v. 1, p. 99)

Tepid dictionary article lacks adequate bibliography and precise dates of the Lima-born tenor's accomplishments. Sample omissions: before opting for music, he was a cadet in the Peruvian Escuela Naval (1946–48). His chief music teacher at Lima was Rosa Mercedes Ayarza de Morales (1881–1969).

5291 Siancas Delgado, Augusto. Música, músicos, Melgar y fuentes del arte tawanti[n]suyano. Arequipa, Perú: s.n., 1987. 174 p.: bibl., ill.

Poorly organized scrapbook compiled by a Puno journalist from his observations concerning autochthonous and folkloric music in the Peruvian sierra. In Pt. 1, author

gives vent to his personal likes and dislikes. Biographical data on pages headed "Publicidad" (p. 61, 66, 82, 94) and remarks concerning Highland performing groups comprise Pt. 2, which author prefaces with a remark attributed by him to Aristotle, "if you would know a people, hear their music."

5292 Stevenson, Robert. Lima. (*in* The New Grove Dictionary of Opera. New York: Grove's Dictionaries of Music, 1992, v. 2, p. 1278–1279, bibl.)

Most important event in Peruvian opera history was the premiere of Tomás de Torrejón y Velasco's *La púrpura de la rosa*, Oct. 19, 1701 at the viceregal palace.

Stocks, Anthony. Tendiendo un puente entre el cielo y la tierra en alas de la canción. See *HLAS 53:1159.*

5293 Turino, Thomas. The State and Andean musical production in Peru. (*in* Nation-States and Indians in Latin America. Edited by Greg Urban and Joel Sherzer. Austin: Univ. of Texas Press, 1991, p. 259–285, bibl.)

In this cogent exposition, the brilliant Peruvianist Turino examines elitist reactions to Andean music culture in three seminal periods: 1550–1650, 1919–30, and 1968–85.

5294 Valencia Chacón, Américo. El siku o zampoña: perspectivas de un legado musical preincaico y sus aplicaciones en el desarrollo de la música peruana = The Altiplano bipolar siku: study and projection of Peruvian panpipe orchestras. Ed. bilingüe. Lima: Centro de Investigación y Desarrollo de la Música Peruana: Artex Editores, 1989. 306 p., 20 p. of plates: bibl., ill.

With a wealth of detail author elaborates his hocketing thesis already broached in four articles published from 1980–82 in *Boletín de Lima* (nos. 8, 14, 22, 23) and in numerous other outlets (see *HLAS 48:7158–7161* and *HLAS 50:4513*). In 1987 he obtained his M. Mus. degree from Florida State Univ. with a thesis entitled "The Altiplano Bipolar Sikus: Study and Projection of Peruvian Panpine Orchestras." From it much of the present book derives. Added material includes chapter on acoustical properties of the syrinx and the performance instructions his pupils received at the Peruvian National Conservatory in 1988.

5295 Virgili Blanquet, María Antonia. El nacionalismo en España y América: influencias y relaciones. (*in* Simposio Hispano-Portugués de Historia del Arte, *5th, Valladolid, Spain, 1989*. Actas. Coordinación de Juan José Martín González. Valladolid, Spain: Univ. de Valladolid, 1990, p. 287–290)

The two younger of the three Villalba brothers born in Valladolid, Luis (1873), Enrique (1876), and Alberto (1879), became Augustinian missionaries in Brazil and Peru. Alberto published numerous works after arriving in Lima in 1910. Later he directed the Conservatorio Clementi at Jujuy. His letters to Luis surviving at Valladolid open a new window on Peruvian musical life during his epoch.

URUGUAY

5296 Aharonián, Coriún. Héctor Tosar: compositor uruguayo. Montevideo: Ediciones Trilce, 1991. 143 p.: ill. (Col. Espejos)

Up-to-date biography, list of compositions, discography, and bibliography written by a pupil of Tosar. Aharonián, born at Montevideo in 1940, is himself a well-known Uruguayan composer and critic.

5297 Corps, Pablo. Música y pueblo: historia de la Banda Sinfónica Municipal de Montevideo, 1907–1987. Montevideo: Intendencia Municipal de Montevideo, 1987. 54 p., 6 p. of plates: ill., ports.

Winner of a prize for the best history of the municipal band, this booklet traces its problems and successes. After two decades of chiefly open-air concerts, the band entered the Teatro Solís during the 1929 season, with a series of symphonic-choral programs. The first director was Agesislao Gubitosi, followed in 1927 by José Valles, with trombonist Benone Calcavecchia as sub-director. Valles' death left the band's numerous contributions to the centenary in Calcavecchia's hands, 1931–40. Mario Belardi was director 1963–74, and Valdo Malán until 1985.

5298 Manzino, Leonardo. La música uruguaya en los festejos de 1892 con motivo del IV Centenario del Encuentro de Dos Mundos. (*Lat. Am. Music Rev.,* 14:1, Spring/Summer 1993, p. 102–130, bibl., facsims., music)

Although León Ribeiro (1854–1931)

composed a fourth centenary opera *Colón* (libretto by Nicolás Granada), only his symphonic summary in ten sections drawn from it reached performance at the Teatro Solís Oct. 21, 1892. The same *velada literario-musical* included also a *sinfonía original* by Antonio Camps, a Spanish-born maestro who was a long-time resident at Montevideo (death there announced in *Montevideo Musical,* May 15, 1903). This excellent article contains wealth of hitherto unknown historical details.

VENEZUELA

5299 Asuaje de Rugeles, Ana Mercedes; María Guinand; and **Bolivia Bottome.** Historia del movimiento coral y de las orquestas juveniles en Venezuela. Caracas: Depto. de Relaciones Públicas de Lagoven, 1986. 93 p.: bibl., ill., ports. (Cuadernos Lagoven)

José Antonio Abreu, one of the supreme music educators of the century, created the most significant chain of youth orchestras founded in any Latin American nation after 1964. This monograph specifies not only their history but also gives proper due to the Orfeón Lamas and other choral movement initiatives for which Vicente Emilio Sojo and Juan Bautista Plaza were responsible.

5300 Castillo Didier, Miguel. Juan Bautista Plaza, una vida por la música y Venezuela: ensayo de biografía documental. Caracas: Consejo Nacional de la Cultura, Instituto Latinoamericano de Investigaciones y Estudios Musicales Vicente Emilio Sojo, 1985. 564 p.: bibl., ill., indexes. (Col. Investigaciones; 4)

Exhaustive biography and study of works by an indisputably major musicologist.

5301 Milanca Guzmán, Mario. Los años caraqueños de Reynaldo Hahn Echenagucia. (*Rev. Nac. Cult./Caracas,* 51:278, julio/agosto/sept. 1990, p. 183–205, bibl.)

Reynaldo Hahn was born in Caracas in 1874, one of 13 children. His father, Carlos Hahn, was born at Hamburg in 1823 and arrived at Caracas in 1845. Carlos Hahn converted from Judaism to Catholicism when baptized April 20, 1853. He also had vast business interests and remained a confidant and a frequent financial advisor of Antonio Guzmán Blanco from 1864–78.

5302 Milanca Guzmán, Mario. Palabras pronunciadas en la Academia Nacional de la Historia en la sesión del 26 de mayo de 1989. (*Bol. Acad. Nac. Hist./Caracas*, 72:286, abril/junio 1989, p. 181–191)

One of the most prolific musicologists residing until 1991 in Venezuela, the Chilean-born author lists his chief publications. He rescued many data concerning Eduardo Richter (1874–1912) and Ramón de la Plaza Manrique (1831–86) before becoming a leading exponent of Teresa Carreño's career.

5303 Milanca Guzmán, Mario. ¿Quién fue Teresa Carreño? Caracas: Alfadil Ediciones, 1990. 108 p.: bibl., ill. (Col. Guarimba mayor)

Valuable summary by a leading Carreño authority concludes with a seven-page chronological synthesis.

5304 Plaza, Juan Bautista. Temas de música colonial venezolana: biografías, análisis y documentación. Exordio de José Vicente Torres. Presentación de Francisco Curt Lange. Prólogo de Miguel Castillo Didier. Caracas: Fundación Vicente Emilio Sojo, 1990. 280 p.: bibl., ill., index. (Serie Investigaciones; 8)

The essays in this welcome volume commencing at p. 27, 109, 131, and 199 were annotated in *HLAS 26:2249*, *HLAS 13:2710* (and *HLAS 24:5950*), *HLAS 9:4827*, and *HLAS 28:3138*. The name index and introductory statements add materially to the compilation, which owes its publication mainly to author's distinguished widow, Nolita de Plaza.

5305 Shatunóvskaya, Irena. Somos felices por haber estudiado en Rusia. (*Am. Lat./Moscow*, 8, 1991, p. 76–79)

The Venezuelan couple María Elena Vargas (singer) and Rafael Saavedra (guitarist), who married while students in the Moscow Tchaikovsky Conservatory, describe their route to Moscow and reflect on what their future in Venezuela portends.

5306 Stevenson, Robert. Caracas. (*in* The New Grove Dictionary of Opera. New York: Grove's Dictionaries of Music, 1992, v. 1, p. 726)

At Caracas Teresa Carreño became the first woman conductor of operas in the Western Hemisphere (1886–87).

JOURNAL ABBREVIATIONS

Am. Lat./Moscow. América Latina. Academia de Ciencias de la Unión de Repúblicas Soviéticas Socialistas. Moscow.

Art Rev./Salvador. Art: Revista da Escola de Música e Artes Cênicas da UFBA. Escola de Música e Artes Cênicas da UFBA. Salvador, Brazil.

Bol. Acad. Chil. Bellas Artes. Boletín de la Academia Chilena de Bellas Artes. Instituto de Chile. Santiago.

Bol. Acad. Nac. Hist./Caracas. Boletín de la Academia Nacional de la Historia. Caracas.

Bol. Lima. Boletín de Lima. Revista Cultural Científica. Lima.

Bull. Inst. fr. étud. andin. Bulletin de l'Institut français d'études andines. Lima.

Bull. Int. Anthropol. Ethnol. Bulletin of the International Committee on Urgent Anthropological and Ethnological Research. International Union of Anthropological and Ethnological Sciences. Vienna.

Caravelle/Toulouse. Caravelle. Cahiers du monde hispanique et luso-brésilien. Univ. de Toulouse, Institute d'études hispaniques, hispano-americaines et luso-brésiliennes. Toulouse, France.

Caribb. Q. Caribbean Quarterly. Univ. of the West Indies. Mona, Jamaica.

Ciênc. Cult. Ciência e Cultura. Sociedade Brasileira para o Progresso da Ciência. São Paulo.

Cuad. Hist. Cuadernos de Historia. Univ. de Chile, Facultad de Humanidades y Educación, Depto. de Ciencias Históricas. Santiago.

Del Caribe. Del Caribe. Casa del Caribe. Santiago, Cuba.

Gaceta/Bogotá. Gaceta. Instituto Colombiano de Cultura. Bogotá.

Hist. Cult./Lima. Historia y Cultura. Museo Nacional de Historia. Lima.

Ibero-Am. Arch. Ibero-Amerikanisches Archiv. Ibero-Amerikanisches Institut. Berlin.

Inter-Am. Music Rev. Inter-American Music Review. Robert Stevenson. Los Angeles, Calif.

Jam. J. Jamaica Journal. Institute of Jamaica. Kingston.

Lat. Am. Music Rev. Latin American Music Review. Univ. of Texas. Austin.

Montalbán/Caracas. Montalbán. Univ. Católica Andrés Bello, Facultad de Humanidades y Educación, Institutos Humanísticos de Investigación. Caracas.

Palabra Hombre. La Palabra y el Hombre. Univ. Veracruzana. Xalapa, Mexico.

Rev. Bras. Hist. Revista Brasileira de História. Associação Nacional dos Professores Universitários de História (ANPUH). São Paulo.

Rev. Inst. Estud. Bras. Revista do Instituto de Estudos Brasileiros. Univ. de São Paulo, Instituto de Estudos Brasileiros. São Paulo.

Rev. Inst. Hist. Geogr. São Paulo. Revista do Instituto Histórico e Geográfico de São Paulo. São Paulo.

Rev. Inst. Super. Música. Revista del Instituto Superior de Música, U.N.L. Santa Fe, Argentina.

Rev. Music. Chil. Revista Musical Chilena. Univ. de Chile, Facultad de Ciencias y Artes Musicales y de la Representación. Santiago.

Rev. Nac. Cult./Caracas. Revista Nacional de Cultura. Consejo Nacional de Cultura. Caracas.

Todo es Hist. Todo es Historia. Buenos Aires.

Travessia/Florianópolis. Travessia. Univ. Federal de Santa Catarina. Florianópolis, Brazil.

PHILOSOPHY: LATIN AMERICAN THOUGHT

JUAN CARLOS TORCHIA ESTRADA, *General Secretariat, Organization of American States*

PARA CONSIDERACIONES GENERALES SOBRE esta Sección remitimos a las Introducciones correspondientes a los volúmenes *HLAS 52, 50* y *46*, donde se hace referencia a los diferentes tipos de materiales que se incluyen y a la marcha del pensamiento filosófico latinoamericano desde 1940 en adelante (la Sección de Filosofía aparece por primera vez en en el *Handbook* en ese año).

De las dos grandes categorías en que tradicionalmente se ha repartido el material de esta Sección, a saber: *filosofía* (entendida en sentido estricto o como disciplina académica) e *historia de las ideas* (más amplia, considerada como expresión de "pensamiento" o de ideas generales), la segunda es sin duda la más abundantemente representada en los últimos años. [1] La filosofía más profesional, que crecientemente se ha desarrollado en los países latinoamericanos desde mediados del siglo, ha sido proporcionalmente menos atendida por la crítica. Dentro de América Latina, los autores que se dedican al pensamiento latinoamericano no se ocupan, en general, de los filósofos académicos de la región; y estos últimos, si ejercitan la crítica, lo hacen más bien sobre figuras europeas o norteamericanas, y no sobre filósofos de Latinoamérica. Esta situación que, aun con sus excepciones, reclama correctivo, no impide reconocer que la abundancia de trabajos sobre "historia de las ideas" es de todas maneras representativa, por cuanto esos trabajos contribuyen a la compresión de fenómenos históricos más amplios y representan intereses intelectuales, prácticos e ideológicos más generalizados, por lo cual tienen su lugar propio en cualquier relevamiento del pensamiento latinoamericano.

A continuación se indican los aspectos más salientes de cada una de las subsecciones en que se divide esta entrega.

GENERAL

La literatura provocada por—o relacionada con—el Quinto Centenario (del Descubrimiento de América, del Encuentro de Dos Mundos o del genocidio, según la posición de los autores) ha sido considerablemente negativa para el sentido de ese hecho histórico. El material incluido aquí, por razones de obligada selectividad, no pretende reflejar exactamente las proporciones en que las opiniones se han dividido. Representativas de la posición crítica son las obras *Nuestra América contra el Vo. Centenario* (item **5316**) y *1492-1992: the voice of the victims* (item **5333**).

Es de particular importancia la obra de Anthony Pagden, *La caída del hombre natural* (item **5355**), cuya versión española es más completa que el original en inglés. También encarados con intención de estudio se presentan los trabajos aquí recogidos de: Arturo Ardao, "El Descubrimiento de América y la Idea del Cosmos en Humboldt" (item **5311**); Rosalba Campra, "Descubrimiento de América e Invención del

'Otro' " (item **5320**); Castilla Urbano, "El Indio Americano en la Filosofía Política de John Locke" (item **5323**); Simon Collier, "Visiones Europeas de América Latina" (item **5325**); Leopoldo Zea como compilador de *El descubrimiento de América y su sentido actual* (item **5329**); y Arturo Uslar Pietri *La creación del Nuevo Mundo* (item **5370**). El mencionado libro de Castilla Urbano coincide con la obra de Pagden en el interés por los orígenes de la etnología moderna, y con los trabajos de Campra y de Collier en la referencia a las resonancias del Descubrimiento en Europa. [2]

Continuamos incluyendo materiales de teología de la liberación, aunque necesariamente en forma muy selectiva. Con variados puntos de vista en favor y en contra de esa tendencia se encontrarán: Fernando Barroso (item **5314**); Eduard Demenchónok (item **5328**); Otto Maduro (item **5341**); y Michael Novak (item **5352**). [3]

La cuestión indígena sigue siendo atendida con interés. De particular utilidad es el libro de Bernardo Berdichewsky, *Del indigenismo a la indianidad* (item **5317**). Lo mismo debe decirse de la recopilación a cargo de José Alcina Franch, *Indianismo e indigenismo en América* (item **5309**). Los mencionados y el libro de Fernando Mires, *El discurso de la indianidad* (item **5349**), destacan la "indianidad" como diferenciada del tradicional indigenismo. [4]

En materia de enfoques generales del pensamiento filosófico latinoamericano debe tomarse en cuenta ante todo la antología de Isabel Monal (item **5339**). Otras obras generales dignas de mención son la de Rafael Gutiérrez Girardot, *Hispanoamérica: imágenes y perspectivas* (item **5338**); y *Temas de cultura latinoamericana* (item **5334**), recopilación de Ernesto García Canclini, entre cuyos autores se cuentan Francisco Miró Quesada, Arturo Ardao y Arturo A. Roig. [5]

Buenos estudios de temática más acotada son los de Bravo Lira sobre Verney (item **5319**); [6] de Romero Baró sobre el positivismo (item **5365**); de Javier Sasso sobre la ética filosófica en América Latina (item **5366**); y tres cuyo tema es el siglo XVIII hispanoamericano, de los cuales son autores Horacio Capel (item **5321**), Fermín del Pino (item **5357**) y Gregorio Weinberg (item **5374**).

Sobre el marxismo latinoamericano se incluyen: una antología (item **5346**), una bibliografía a cargo de Harry Vanden (item **5371**) y el libro de José Aricó, *1917 y América Latina* (item **5313**). Este último es comentado por Pedro J. Ríos (item **5363**). [7]

El tema de la filosofía latinoamericana sigue presente. Así en el caso del libro de Mario Berríos Caro (item **5318**); en el artículo de José Luis Gómez Martínez (item **5344**); y de alguna manera también en Francisco Miró Quesada sobre la filosofía de la liberación (item **5350**), en Aníbal Quijano (item **5361**) y en Bernardo Subercaseux sobre la apropiación cultural en el pensamiento latinoamericano (item **5368**). En este orden de cosas señalamos especialmente el artículo de Javier Sasso, "Sobre el Pensamiento Latinoamericano y su Historiografía" (item **5367**), por considerarlo un giro diferente frente al enfoque habitual del tema. [8]

MEXICO

Buenos trabajos sobre historia de las ideas en México encontramos: el de Jean-Pierre Bastian sobre sociedades de ideas (item **5379**), el de Cardiel Reyes sobre Manuel María Gorriño (item **5381**), el de Jacqueline Covo sobre la Reforma (item **5382**), el de González Navarro sobre las ideas raciales de los "científicos" (item **5387**), el de Martha Robles sobre Vasconcelos (item **5394**) y el volumen *Pensamiento político de México* (item **5377**). [9] Aunque se trata de una reedición, deben recordarse las contribuciones de Silvio Zavala sobre Vasco de Quiroga (item **5398**).

Entre las obras que rescatan textos históricos o clásicos, debemos señalar la edición del *Diálogo sobre la dignidad del hombre*, de Francisco Cervantes de Salazar, realizada por Diane Bono (item **5380**); y las obras documentales *Del pensamiento esencial de México* (item **5383**) y *El pensamiento de la reacción mexicana*, este último a cargo de Gastón García Cantú. De la crítica filosófica propiamente dicha recordamos el artículo de Gómez Martínez sobre la presencia de Ortega en México (item **5386**).

AMERICA CENTRAL Y PANAMA

Lo más destacado es una monografía sobre Juan José Aycinena (item **5400**) y una obra de mayor aliento: el libro de Hodges sobre Sandino y el sandinismo (item **5402**).

CARIBE INSULAR

La gran mayoría de las entradas se refieren a temas cubanos: Martí, el Che Guevara, Medardo Vitier, Jorge Mañach, Juan Marinello, entre otros. El otro tema principal es el de Eugenio María de Hostos, de quien se reeditan obras básicas (items **5411** y **5412**).

VENEZUELA

En el caso de Venezuela encontramos tres obras documentales de valor: una dedicada a Rafael Villavicencio (item **5434**); [10] otra sobre Francisco de Miranda (item **5426**); y una tercera, titulada *Pensamiento político de la emancipación venezolana* (item **5427**), a cargo de Pedro Grases con bibliografía de Horacio J. Becco. Además, hay una buena monografía sobre Gil Fortoul, de Elena Plaza (item **5429**).

COLOMBIA

De especial valor bibliográfico en el caso de este país es *La filosofía en Colombia*, de Rafael Pinzón Garzón (item **5439**).

ECUADOR

Un volumen colectivo sobre Montalvo (item **5443**) y una antología del pensamiento pedagógico ecuatoriano (item **5447**) constituyen los escritos de mayor magnitud. Es de interés también el artículo de Carlos Paladines sobre una expresión del pensamiento del siglo XVIII (item **5445**), en tanto Benjamín Carrión fue justamente recordado en un número de la *Revista de Historia de las Ideas* (item **5448**).

PERU

Como es habitual, Mariátegui y Haya de la Torre son los temas más frecuentados entre los que aquí se recogen. Sobre el primero, destacamos un amplio trabajo de Guenther Maihold (item **5459**). Dos trabajos de estudio, útiles para la historia de las ideas, son el de Hampe Martínez sobre libros y bibliotecas en la Colonia (item **5453**) y el de Iwaski Cauti sobre Pablo de Olavide (item **5456**).

BOLIVIA

El material sobre este país se compone de dos obras de referencia: items **5462** y **5463**.

CHILE

Respecto de Chile mencionaremos tres estudios sobre autores clásicos: una obra colectiva sobre Lastarria (item **5464**); un libro sobre Valentín Letelier, de Fuentealba Hernández (item **5465**); y un artículo sobre Bilbao de Jalif de Bertranou (item **5469**).

BRASIL

Un tema muy atendido usualmente en el caso de Brasil es el de Tobias Barreto y la Escuela de Recife. Aquí se encuentra representado por una exposición general (item **5472**) y una nueva edición de sus *Obras completas* (items **5474** y **5475**). [11] En el aspecto bibliográfico, Antonio Paim ha ampliado una anterior bibliografía filosófica brasileña (item **5485**). Sobre el darwinismo en Brasil se destaca la obra de Terezinha A.F. Collichio (item **5478**), que debe ponerse en relación con materiales sobre el darwinismo en México (véase *HLAS 50:4602*) y en Argentina (item **5526**). Hallamos también dos obras de conjunto sobre el pensamiento político en Brasil (items **5476** y **5491**) y el volumen *Inteligencia brasileira* (item **5484**). Es de particular valor el hecho de que se atienda la evolución de las ideas en algunas regiones del país, como, en esta entrega, en el caso de Ceará (item **5473**), Pernambuco (item **5482**), Rio Grande (item **5486**) y Minas Gerais (item **5488**). Por último señalamos el interés por la obra de Alvaro Vieira Pinto (items **5487** y **5489**).

PARAGUAY

Se ha recogido solamente un ensayo sobre la ideología autoritaria en el país (item **5493**).

URUGUAY

Destacamos una antología del ensayista uruguayo Carlos Real de Azúa (item **5495**). Contribuyen también a la historia de las ideas un trabajo sobre masonería y educación (item **5494**) y otro sobre los antecedentes del socialismo (item **5498**).

ARGENTINA

Entre las obras colectivas encontramos: las *Actas* del Vo. Congreso Nacional de Filosofía (item **5529**); *Estado y sociedad en el pensamiento nacional* (item **5513**); las *Actas* de las Segundas Jornadas del Pensamiento Filosófico Argentino (item **5521**); un número especial de la revista *Todo es Historia* sobre la Revolución Francesa (item **5537**); y un volumen sobre Sarmiento (item **5538**). Hallamos también tres antologías: de Saúl Taborda (item **5524**), de Francisco Romero (item **5533**), y del pensamiento económico de Alberdi (item **5499**), además de una reunión de textos sobre la repercusión de Freud en Argentina (item **5502**).

Aunque lo que hemos incluido sobre el escritor argentino Jorge Luis Borges es sólo una muy mínima parte de la ingente bibliografía que su obra continúa generando, es interesante observar la atracción que suscita la relación de este escritor con la filosofía. Así lo muestran los libros: *La filosofía de Jorge Luis Borges* (item **5500**); *Borges y la filosofía* (item **5536**) y *Borges et la métaphysique* (item **5507**). También dos artículos de igual título: "Borges y la Metafísica," uno de Manuel Benavídez (item **5503**) y otro de Carla Cordua (item **5509**). [12]

Son de valor histórico dos testimonios: uno de Enrique Dussel sobre los orígenes de la filosofía de la liberación (item **5511**) y otro de Arturo A. Roig, "Tres Décadas de 'Historia de las Ideas' en Argentina" (item **5532**).

Señalamos, por último, artículos sobre filosofía cristiana, en especial sobre Alberto Caturelli (items **5516** y **5517**), y los trabajos críticos de Angel J. Cappelletti sobre Alfredo Franceschi (item **5504**), de Lértora Mendoza sobre filosofía colonial (item
5522), de Julio Orione sobre el darwinismo (item **5526**), y de Eduardo Zimmermann
sobre ideas raciales (item **5539**).

Notas

1 Esta caracterización de la "historia de las ideas" se refiere únicamente al modo en que
el concepto es usado a los efectos prácticos de esta Sección, sin pretender que sea una definición o la única caracterización posible.

2 Ver también *HLAS* 52:5313 y *HLAS* 52:5327.

3 Sobre este asunto véase también la Introducción a esta Sección en *HLAS* 50 y las entradas 5269, 5282, 5283, 5285, 5293 y 5317 de ese mismo volumen.

4 Al respecto pueden verse las observaciones incluidas en la Introducción de esta Sección en *HLAS* 52 y las entradas 5267, 5270, 5289 y 5319 del mismo volumen.

5 Ver también *HLAS* 52:5301 y *HLAS* 52:5308.

6 De este autor véase también *HLAS* 52:5272.

7 Ver también *HLAS* 52:5290 y *HLAS* 52:5314.

8 Ver también *HLAS* 52, entradas 5274, 5277, 5296, 5299, 5300 y 5318.

9 Ver también *HLAS* 52:5329.

10 Sobre Villavicencio véase también *HLAS* 52:5366.

11 Ver también *HLAS* 52:5410.

12 Ver también *HLAS* 52:5428.

GENERAL

5307 Abramson, Pierre-Luc. L'Espérance
américaine d'Elisée Reclus. (*in* Mélanges offerts à Maurice Molho. Paris: Editions hispaniques; Centre national des lettres,
1988, v. 2, p. 231–238)

Sobre la imagen utópica que Reclus se
hace de América después de su viaje a la
Nueva Granada (1855–57), que dio lugar a su
obra *Voyage à la Sierra Nevada de Sainte-
Marthe* (1861). Vincula esa experiencia con
las ideas sobre la "latinidad" que existían en
Francia en aquella época, como reacción ante
la política de EE.UU. Reclus habla de fusión
de razas, y no coincide con la idea de poblar
América con europeos para suplantar las poblaciones originarias, como fue frecuente en
América Latina. Interesan datos sobre ediciones de Reclus en Latinoamérica.

Adorno, Rolena. Los debates sobre la naturaleza del indio en el siglo XVI: textos y contextos. See item **3558**.

5308 Ainsa, Fernando. La función utópica en
América Latina y el modelo de Ernst
Boch. (*Rev. Hist. Ideas*, 8, 1987, p. 183–198)

Destaca los aspectos de la realidad latinoamericana que harían posible la aplicación
de las ideas de Ernst Bloch sobre la utopía, especialmente *Das Prinzip Hoffnung*.

5309 Alcina Franch, José *et al.* Indianismo e
indigenismo en América. Recopilación
de José Alcina Franch. Madrid: Alianza, 1990.
339 p.: bibl., map. (Alianza univ.; 628: Ciencias sociales)

Contribución importante a un tema
complejo, de validez histórica y actual. Señala
el paso desde el *indigenismo* (preocupación
por el indio por parte del Estado, la comunidad científica o diversos "protectores") al *indianismo* o *indianidad* (organización de los
propios indios en defensa de sus derechos).
Los trabajos son muy diversos, y varios corresponden al ámbito de la antropología. Util-
mente panorámico el de Oscar Arze Quinta-
nilla, "Del Indigenismo a la Indianidad."
Sintético y claro sobre la posición india: Guillermo Bonfil Batalla, "Aculturación e Indigenismo: la Respuesta India." Histórico, pero
desde un ángulo actual: José Alcina Franch,
"El *Indianismo* de Fray Bartolomé de Las Casas." Sin agotar la lista, los temas de otros
son: la mentalidad española; la identidad; la
relación entre indigenismo y política.

5310 Amado, Jorge et al. L'Amérique latine et la Révolution française. Textes réunis par Jean Mendelson. Préface de Jean-Noël Jeanneney. Paris: La Découverte; Le Monde, 1989. 221 p.: bibl., col. ill.

Intelectuales y escritores como Octavio Paz, Vargas Llosa, Uslar Pietri y otros reflexionan sobre la significación, para América Latina, de la Revolución Francesa y sus ideas.

5311 Ardao, Arturo. El descubrimiento de América y la idea del cosmos, en Humboldt. (*Rev. Nac./Montevideo*, 1:238, quinto ciclo, sept. 1992, p. 37–46)

Sobre la relación de los estudios de Alejandro de Humboldt (especialmente los que dedicó al descubrimiento de América) con la filosofía de la historia que dicho autor desarrolla en su obra fundamental, *Cosmos*. El artículo expone también el significado de esa filosofía de la historia.

5312 Ardao, Arturo. Unión y denominación antes de la insurgencia de 1810. (*Rev. Hist. Ideas*, 2:8, 1987, p. 11–25)

Sobre el sentimiento de unidad hispanoamericana y los nombres que la región recibió (América meridional, América española, América, Colombia) antes de 1810, especialmente en los escritos de Francisco de Miranda (ver *HLAS 44:7501*).

5313 Aricó, José. 1917 y América Latina. (*Nueva Soc.*, 111, enero/feb. 1991, p. 14–22)

Ensayo de reflexión sobre el efecto que la Revolución rusa de 1917 tuvo sobre la formación de la izquierda latinoamericana. Según el autor, esa izquierda adoptó dos formas: la "socialista" y la "populista." (Desestima la importancia que puedan haber tenido los partidos comunistas). Derrumbada la fuente en que se apoyó, la izquierda latinoamericana debe encontrar ahora nuevos caminos, si ha de representar la libertad y la justicia social.

5314 Barroso, Fernando. The Theology of Liberation in the light of the Catholic Church. (*SECOLAS Ann.*, 18, March 1987, p. 39–46, bibl.)

La tesis del artículo es que la teología de la liberación se sale del marco teológico y de las enseñazas de la Iglesia para convertirse en un intento político secular.

5315 Benassy-Berling, Marie-Cécile. Notes sur quelques aspects de la vision de lᴾAmérique Hispanique en France pendant la première moitié de XIXème siècle. (*Caravelle/Toulouse*, 58, 1992, p. 39–48)

Examina dos publicaciones francesas del siglo XIX: 1) la *Biographie universelle ancienne et moderne* (1a. edic 1811–28; 2a. edic. 1843–63), de Michaud, revisando los artículos que se refieren a grandes figuras hispanoamericanas de la época (especialmente un artículo sobre Las Casas de Dauxion-Lavaysse); y 2) *Des colonies et de la révolution actuelle de l'Amérique* (1817), de Dominique de Pradt, obra muy apreciada por los patriotas americanos por su defensa del movimiento de independencia. Sobre este último tema señala bibliografía hispanoamericana reciente.

5316 Benedetti, Mario et al. Nuestra América contra el V Centenario. Coordinación de Heinz Dieterich S. 2a. ed. Tafalla, Spain: Txalaparta, 1989. 229 p.: bibl., ill. (Emancipación e identidad de América Latina; 1)

Con la excepción de Augusto Roa Bastos, que aprovecha el asunto para tratar el tema de la unidad iberoamericana, la mayoría de los autores reitera las ya tradicionales acusaciones a los españoles por la destrucción de las culturas precolombinas, la explotación de los indios, etc., y rechazan la conceptualización del arribo de los europeos como "descubrimiento." Ilustra sobre la posición de ciertos grupos de intelectuales latinoamericanos frente al significado del V Centenario.

5317 Berdichewksky, Bernardo. Del indigenismo a la indianidad y el surgimiento de una ideología indígena en Andinoamérica. (*Can. J. Lat. Am. Caribb. Stud.*, 12:24, 1987, p. 25–43, appendix)

Por la información y el enfoque es un trabajo imprescindible para comprender el paso del indigenismo (la cuestión indígena vista desde otras ideologías) a la "indianidad" (la misma cuestión vista por los propios indios o sus actuales líderes). Da ejemplos o muestras de esa *Weltanschauung* indiana.

5318 Berrios Caro, Mario. Identidad, origen, modelos: pensamiento latinoamericano. Santiago: Instituto Profesional de Santiago, 1988. 164 p.: bibl.

Trata tres principales temas con referencia a América Latina: 1) el problema de la identidad; 2) el origen del filosofar; y 3) los modelos ideológicos. Este último incluye el problema de la periodización de la filosofía latinoamericana y estudia como "modelos ideológicos" el pensamiento de la Independencia (Bolívar en particular) y el tema de la ciencia y la tecnología en la región.

5319 Bravo Lira, Bernardino. Verney y la Ilustración católica y nacional en el mundo de habla castellana y portuguesa. (*Historia/Santiago*, 21, 1986, p. 55–109, bibl.)

Artículo monográfico, prolijo y atendible. Contribuye al tema de la Ilustración en Latinoamérica. Luis Antonio Verney, portugués, fue autor del célebre *Verdadero método de estudiar* (1746), obra que se expone con cierta extensión en este artículo. La intención es destacar el carácter nacional y católico del pensamiento ilustrado de Verney. El autor tiene un trabajo de orientación semejante para el caso de Feijóo (ver *HLAS 52*: 5272).

5320 Campra, Rosalba. "Descubrimiento" de América e invención del "otro." (*Torre/Río Piedras*, 5:17, enero/marzo 1991, p. 77–88)

Sobre el encuentro de culturas producido por el "descubrimiento" de América en tanto manifestación de la relación yo-otro ("otredad"). Se examinan también las consecuencias de ese hecho para la interpretación de lo americano por parte del europeo y para la autointerpretación del americano por sí mismo. Publicado anteriormente en italiano.

5321 Capel, Horacio. Sobre ciencia hispana, ciencia criolla y otras ciencias europeas: a manera de síntesis del Coloquio. (*Asclepio/Madrid*, 39:2, 1987, p. 317–336)

Visión panorámica y muy atinadas reflexiones sobre los problemas que plantea el estudio de la ciencia desarrollada durante el siglo XVIII en el Nuevo Mundo, en España y en Europa en general. Son temas del trabajo: la comparación entre América y Europa; las características de la ciencia americana; el lugar de América en la ciencia europea; el problema de la falta de instituciones en el mundo hispánico, entre otros. Artículo sumamente útil.

5322 Castañón, Adolfo. La ausencia ubicua de Montaigne: ideas para una historia del ensayo hispanoamericano. (*Vuelta/México*, 16:184, marzo 1992, p. 35–38, ill.)

Aunque se refiere al género ensayo desde el punto de vista literario, le interesará también al historiador de las ideas (ver item **5354**).

5323 Castilla Urbano, Francisco. El indio americano en la filosofía política de John Locke. (*Rev. Indias*, 46:178, julio/dic. 1986, p. 421–451, bibl.)

Trata dos temas: 1) la influencia de América en el establecimiento del concepto de "estado de naturaleza" y el papel que éste juega en la teoría política de Locke y sus consecuencias para justificar los intereses de los colonos ingleses; y 2) el uso de la idea de América (como "mundo salvaje") en el primer libro del *Ensayo sobre el entendimiento humano*. Discute por último la importancia de estos temas para la cuestión de los orígenes modernos de la antropología. En general pertenece a la literatura sobre los efectos que América provocó en el pensamiento europeo.

5324 Cayota, Mario. Siembra entre brumas: utopía franciscana y humanismo renacentista, una alternativa a la conquista. Montevideo: Instituto S. Bernardino de Montevideo, C.I.P.F.E., 1990. 539 p.: bibl., ill.

La intención—que el autor reconoce—es presentar, para el público actual, la parte bien inspirada de la colonización de América: específicamente, la labor de los franciscanos. Además, se remonta a las fuentes del humanismo renacentista, a Erasmo y Moro. No pretende ser obra de investigación, pero el autor ha debido recorrer una extensa bibliografía para cumplir con su propósito.

5325 Collier, Simon. Visiones europeas de América Latina: en busca de una interpretación global. (*Historia/Santiago*, 21, 1986, p. 146–166, bibl.)

Excelente síntesis de las interpretaciones que en Europa se dieron del hecho americano y sus gentes. Esas interpretaciones se dividen en tres grandes corrientes: la que considera a lo americano como inferior; la que lo idealiza y lo hace fuente de utopías; y la que trata de formarse una idea "científica" del Nuevo Mundo. El proceso se sigue desde el siglo XVI hasta el XIX.

5326 Dealy, Glen Caudill. The Latin Americans: spirit and ethos. Boulder: Westview Press, 1992. 230 p.: bibl., index.

Basado en testimonios de experiencia directa, de la literatura y de obras de análisis, intenta una caracterización del latinoamericano, en sus aspectos individuales y sociales. De hecho resulta también, por el uso del contraste, una caracterización de los Estados Unidos. Es un trabajo serio, realizado con cuidado académico, pero que no podrá evitar las objeciones que recaen siempre sobre las amplias generalizaciones. Los latinoamericanos no necesitarán concordar en todo para encontrarlo útil.

5327 Delgado, Mariano. Gottes Weisheit und Güte als theologischer Verstehens- und Handlungshorizont. (*Z. Miss. Relig.*, 76: 4, 1992, p. 285–300)

Draws parallels between Bartolomé de las Casas' rejection of the *ecclesia militans* and Liberation Theology. Views Las Casas as the 16th-century precursor of contemporary theology for multicultural understanding. [C.K. Converse]

5328 Demenchónok, Eduard. "Liberación" en la teología radical. (*Am. Lat./Moscow*, 7:115, julio 1987, p. 41–51, facsims.)

Aunque considera a la teología de la liberación como un "fenómeno complejo y contradictorio," y estima que los problemas a los cuales ella quiere dar respuesta sólo tienen solución "científica" mediante "la doctrina filosófica del marxismo," es un ensayo claro y comprensivo de la corriente estudiada. Señala—lo que no es frecuente—la vinculación con manifestaciones modernas de la teología europea.

5329 El descubrimiento de América y su sentido actual. Recopilación de Leopoldo Zea. México: Instituto Panamericano de Geografía e Historia; Fondo de Cultura Económica, 1989. 227 p.: bibl. (Col. Tierra firme)

El volumen recoge conferencias y trabajos presentados a un simposio realizado en México en 1984. Los artículos son los siguientes: Domingo Miliani, "Lo Fantástico en Cristóbal Colón;" Joaquín Sánchez MacGregor, "Ideologizaciones en Textos Colombinos;" Xavier Cacho Vázquez, "Sugerencia para una Lectura Historiográfica del *Coloquio de los doce*, 1564;" Luis Ramos, "*Curtam Sero?* Algunos Antecedentes Patrísticos de la Teoría Política de Francisco de Vitoria;" Patrick E. Bryan, "Jamaica y el Caribe Español;" Antonio Lago Carballo, "La Primera Sociedad Indiana;" Francisco Miró Quesada, "Conquista y Reconquista de América;" Margarita Peña, "¿Americanos o Peninsulares?;" Horacio Cerutti, "Peripecias en la Construcción de Nuestra Utopía;" José María Muriá, "El Cuarto Centenario del Descubrimiento de América;" Javier Malagón, "Hacia una Comu-

nidad Iberoamericana en 1992;" Carlos Bosch García, "Los Imperios Marinos en la Formación de América: la Identidad Dual del Siglo XVI;" Miguel León Portilla, "El Punto de Vista Indígena;" Juan A. Ortega y Medina, "La Imagen de Cristóbal Colón en la Historiografía Mexicana;" Elsa Cecilia Frost, "América: Ruptura del Providencialismo;" Beatriz Ruiz Gaitán, "Lo Moderno y lo Popular en el Descubrimiento de América."

5330 En busca de su autenticidad: Leopoldo Zea, *Filosofía de la historia americana*; destinos de América. (*Am. Lat./Moscow*, 12:108, dic. 1986, p. 81–87)

Un grupo de especialistas soviéticos comenta la traducción al ruso del libro de Leopoldo Zea, *Filosofía de la historia americana*.

5331 Espejo, Miguel. América Latina y Occidente: las esferas recurrentes. (*Rev. Cancillería San Carlos*, 5, enero 1991, p. 54–67)

Aunque con aciertos de percepción y de razonamiento, no llega a articularse en una tesis bien delimitada. Aprovechable, de todas maneras. En general el tema es la relación de América Latina con Europa (u "Occidente"), incluido el pensamiento.

5332 Fighting the war of ideas in Latin America. Edited by John C. Goodman and Ramona Marotz-Baden. Dallas, Tex.: National Center for Policy Analysis, 1990. 252 p.: bibl.

La "guerra de ideas" a que se refiere el título es el combate por imponer el liberalismo económico, contrariando la tradición estatista de América Latina. El mismo celo ideológico se aplica a aspectos como la literatura y la religión (desestima de la teología de la liberación), entre otros.

5333 1492–1992: the voice of the victims. Edited by Leonardo Boff and Virgil Elizondo. London: SCM Press; Philadelphia: Trinity Press International, 1990. 151 p.: bibl. (Concilium, 0010–5236; 1990/6)

Se trata de un número especial de la revista *Concilium*. Entre los autores que colaboran figuran Gustavo Gutiérrez, Darcy Ribeiro, Enrique Dussel, Pablo Richard, Jon Sobrino, Leonardo Boff y Virgil Elizondo. El común denominador de los artículos es el enjuiciamiento de la conquista de América y el sufrimiento de las poblaciones originarias.

5334 García Canclini, Néstor *et al.* Temas de cultura latinoamericana. Toluca, México: Univ. Autónoma del Estado de México, 1987. 255 p.: bibl. (Col. Lecturas críticas; 13)

Contiene: Néstor García Canclini, "Para una Crítica de las Teorías de la Cultura; " Francisco Miró Quesada, "La Cultura Latinoamericana;" María Elena Rodríguez Ozán, "Recreación Cultural Latinoamericana;" Arturo Ardao, "El Americanismo Literario y la Integración Latinoamericana;" Marco Díaz, "Nacionalismo y Pintura de Caballete en Latinoamérica;" y Valquiria Wey, "La Cultura Brasileña: los Ultimos Cincuenta Años." Después de examinar concepciones muy generalizadas de la cultura, García Canclini propone una definición de tono marxista, con apoyo en Gramsci. Miró Quesada se centra en lo que denomina "cultura selectiva" (la de los intelectuales, filósofos, artistas), y combina el estilo analítico propio del autor con el apoyo a la filosofía de la liberación. Roig persigue los conceptos de nacionalidad, Estado y cultura en tres etapas americanas: el "colonialismo clásico" (de España); el "imperialismo;" y el interregno entre ambos: 1824–80. El trabajo de Ardao, que tiene tangencias temáticas con el de Roig y es de importancia para seguir la línea de la integración cultural latinoamericana, está incluido en su libro *La inteligencia latinoamericana* (Montevideo: Dirección General de Extensión Universitaria, 1987).

5335 Girardi, Giulio. La conquista de América: ¿con qué derecho? Edición de Jorge David Aruj. Traducción de Alberto Morales Gastón. San José: Editorial DEI, Depto. Ecuménico de Investigaciones, 1988. 91 p. (Col. Historia de la Iglesia y de la teología)

La posición de reclamo por la injusticia de la conquista de América se presenta aquí bajo la forma de una meditación sobre la paz: la paz del imperio frente a la paz de los pueblos, y el cristianismo en relación con ambas. Teólogo de la liberación de origen europeo, el autor menciona con frecuencia el caso de Nicaragua y se expresa elogiosamente sobre la revolución sandinista.

5336 Godoy Urzúa, Hernán. La integración cultural de América Latina. (*Integr. Latinoam.*, 14:149/150, sept./oct. 1989, p. 13–24)

Afirma la conveniencia de crear una "sociología de la cultura iberoamericana,"

que tenga por objeto el arte, la religión, la literatura, los grandes momentos históricos y los más destacados intelectuales de la región. Según el autor, el ejercicio de la sociología "científica" nos privó de una "sociología cultural," que captaría "el sustrato cultural más profundo y vigente de los pueblos americanos."

5337 Góngora, Mario. Civilización de masas y esperanza y otros ensayos. Santiago?: Editorial Vivaria, 1987. 218 p.: bibl. (Col. Historia)

Góngora fue historiador chileno, católico, especializado en historia colonial de América. En este libro expresa sus opiniones sobre diversos temas históricos y contemporáneos, revelando el pensamiento del hombre que está detrás del historiador profesional. Destacamos los artículos más cercanos a la temática latinoamericana: "Qué Puede Dar el Pensamiento Histórico a la Formación Cultural Hispanoamericana" (1969); "Materialismo Neocapitalista, el Actual 'Idolo del Foro'" (1966); "Reflexiones sobre la Tradición y el Tradicionalismo en la Historia de Chile" (1979). Contiene una bibliografía de Góngora y una entrevista que le hiciera Simon Collier.

5338 Gutiérrez Girardot, Rafael. Hispanoamérica: imágenes y perspectivas. Selección y notas de José Hernán Castilla. Bogotá: Editorial Temis, 1989. 416 p.: bibl.

Reunión de estudios y ensayos de un autor sin duda importante en el campo de los estudios latinoamericanos. Se tratan asuntos latinoamericanos en general, pero también hay artículos sobre temas colombianos en particular. Destacamos en el campo de la historia de las ideas los trabajos dedicados a Alfonso Reyes, Henríquez Ureña, José Enrique Rodó, Andrés Bello y José Luis Romero.

5339 Las ideas en la América Latina: una antología del pensamiento filosófico, político y social. v. 1, pts. 1–2, Del pensamiento precolombino al sensualismo. Selección e introducción de Isabel Monal. La Habana: Casa de las Américas, 1985. 2 v.: bibl. (Col. Pensamiento de Nuestra América)

Existen antologías del pensamiento filosófico latinoamericano en épocas recientes, pero no, como la presente, que abarquen desde el siglo XVI al XVIII inclusive, por lo cual estamos ante una verdadera aportación. La parte antológica está bien representada, aunque las indicaciones introductorias para cada autor son muy breves, y algunos textos también. La mayor extensión de Pt. 1 está dedicada a una historia sintética del período que cubre la antología (denominado por la autora *Escolástica y reformismo electivo*). Previa a dicha síntesis se presenta un ensayo sobre la periodización del pensamiento filosófico en América Latina. El lenguaje de la parte expositiva refleja la terminología propia de las obras que se producen actualmente en Cuba, pero su contenido es aprovechable en cualquier ámbito, aun si en algunos aspectos se hubiera beneficiado de disponer de más amplia bibliografía, cosa que no es imputable a la autora. Se trata, pues, de una obra muy atendible y, que sepamos, única en el género antológico para el período abarcado.

5340 Lehmann, David. Democracy and development in Latin America: economics, politics and religion in the post-war period. Philadelphia: Temple Univ. Press, 1990. 235 p.: bibl., index.

Se trata de un panorama claro, cuyos principales temas son: 1) las ideas latinoamericanas sobre desarrollo a partir de la segunda mitad del siglo XX; 2) la teoría de la dependencia; 3) el pensamiento y la acción sociales de la Iglesia; 4) la teología de la liberación; 5) las comunidades eclesiales de base y otras formas de organización popular, al conjunto de las cuales el autor denomina "basismo." La información proviene, principalmente, de la situación en tres países: Chile, Brasil y Argentina.

5341 Maduro, Otto. La desacralización del marxismo en la teología de la liberación. (*Christianismo Soc.*, 26:98, 1988, p. 69–84)

La tesis central es que la teología de la liberación, al usar partes del marxismo como "herramientas," por un lado lo "des-sataniza" (ante aquellos que lo consideran un gran peligro) y por otro lo "des-sacraliza" (ante sus adherentes, acostumbrados a considerarlo como una doctrina integral). Muestra ambas características frente a diferentes problemas: concepción de la religión y de la religiosidad popular; tratamiento de la cultura popular; visión de la diversidad étnica, lingüística y de costumbres, etc.

5342 Mansilla, H.C.F. La herencia ibérica y la persistencia del autoritarismo en América Latina. (*Folia Humaníst.*, 25:291, abril 1987, p. 261–276)

Cumple con lo anunciado en el título, pero se refiere al centralismo, el burocratismo, la alta opinión sobre el Estado, el clientelismo, etc. Gran parte de la bibliografía de apoyo es de lengua alemana.

5343 Marichal, Juan. El auge del ensayo en la España transterrada. (*Rev. Occident.*, 116, enero 1991, p. 5–11)

Sobre el efecto del exilio americano en el ensayo de ideas españolas. Breve pero muy perceptivo.

5344 Martínez Gómez, Luis. ¿Existe una filosofía hispanoamericana? (*in* América, 1492–1992: contribuciones a un centenario. Edición de José Joaquín Alemany. Madrid: Univ. Pontificia Comillas, 1988, p. 455–469)

Más que referirse al problema que expresa el título en su interrogación es, en realidad, un panorama rápido—pero no exento de opiniones—del desarrollo de la filosofía en Hispanoamérica desde la Colonia hasta la actualidad.

5345 Martínez González, Humberto et al.
Hacia el nuevo milenio: estudios sobre mesianismo, identidad nacional y socialismo. v. 1–2. México: Univ. Autónoma Metropolitana, Unidad Azcapotzalco, División de Ciencias Sociales y Humanidades; Editorial Villicaña, 1986. 2 v.: bibl. (Biblioteca de ciencias sociales y humanidades. Sociología; 1)

Resultado de un simposio llevado a cabo en México en 1984, es un libro de muchos autores y variado contenido. Milenarismo, exégesis bíblica, religiosidad popular, utopía, situación de los grupos indígenas o etnias son algunos de los temas tratados. Como línea de orientación muy general podría decirse que los objetivos son semejantes a los de la teología de la liberación, pero no llevaríamos la comparación más allá de ese punto.

5346 Marxism in Latin America from 1909 to the present: an anthology. Edited and with an introduction by Michael Löwy. Translated from Spanish, Portuguese, and French by Michael Pearlman. Atlantic Highlands, N.J.: Humanities Press, 1992. 296 p.: bibl., index. (Revolutionary studies)

Divide el material en tres períodos: 1) desde los comienzos del siglo hasta 1935, época que incluye la formación de los Partidos Comunistas; 2) desde 1935 hasta la Revolución Cubana (período estalinista); y 3) de la

Revolución Cubana en adelante. De todo ese lapso la introducción destaca, entre otros temas, autores individuales, ideología y acción de partidos políticos marxistas, naturaleza e influencia de la Revolución Cubana, reciente acercamiento de grupos cristianos al marxismo, etc. El propósito declarado es proporcionar una herramienta a "investigadores y activistas." Por lo menos de los investigadores podemos decir que encontrarán una obra útil, con textos en general de no fácil acceso.

5347 Masuda, Shozo. El pensamiento de Cieza de León. (*Cuad. Hist.*, 7, julio 1987, p. 139–146)

Interesa en tanto Cieza de León, en su *Crónica del Perú*, se suma a los autores que critican la conquista. Más bien expositivo y breve.

5348 Mendoza Cubillo, Margarita. El pensamiento confederativo de Bolívar en las Naciones Unidas. v. 1–2. Guayaquil, Ecuador: Editorial Univ. de Guayaquil, 1990. 2 v.: bibl.

Aunque publicado en 1990, fue una tesis doctoral de 1967 que se reedita sin cambios. Cubre el pensamiento integracionista de Bolívar, la reunión de Panamá (1826), las Conferencias Panamericanas, la creación de la Organización de Estados Americanos (OEA) y la presencia de ideas bolivarianas en documentos de las Naciones Unidas.

5349 Mires, Fernando. El discurso de la indianidad: la cuestión indígena en América Latina. San José: DEI, 1991. 167 p.: bibl. (Col. Historia de la Iglesia y de la teología)

La cuestión indígena se ve en tres momentos: el "descubrimiento" del indio por el conquistador; el "autodescubrimiento" del indio en sus rebeliones; y el "redescubrimiento" del indio en la forma de la "indianidad," la cual, según este autor, no es solamente la praxis india sino también la de otros grupos que actúan en defensa de los indios (indigenismos peruano y mexicano, por ejemplo). El primer capítulo es una crítica a la naturaleza y el desarrollo de la etnología como disciplina de conocimiento. Libro abundante en juicios de opinión.

5350 Miró Quesada, Francisco. Filosofía de la liberación: convergencias y divergencias. (*Am. Lat./Moscow*, 11, 1988, p. 32–45, photos, bibl.)

Caracteriza y justifica la filosofía de la liberación, y señala semejanzas y diferencias entre sus representantes. Aunque publicado en 1988, toma como principal referente para el análisis la llamada Declaración de Morelia, de 1978, redactada por Leopoldo Zea, Arturo Roig, Abelardo Villegas, Enrique Dussel y el autor de este artículo. La adhesión a la filosofía de la liberación no le impide al autor—uno de los más destacados filósofos latinoamericanos de la actualidad—sentirse partícipe de la filosofía analítica, caso más bien excepcional.

5351 Mosonyi, Jorge C. Reflexiones sobre la problemática de la identidad nacional. (*Econ. Cienc. Soc.*, 26:1, enero/abril 1987, p. 111–122, bibl.)

Estableciendo como concepto central el de *etnia*, procura definir la *identidad nacional*. Entiende que la búsqueda de la identidad es "un arma insustituible en la lucha que conduce a la liberación de los pueblos."

5352 Novak, Michael. Will it liberate?: questions about liberation theology. New York: Paulist Press, 1986. 311 p.: bibl., index.

Intensa crítica a la teología de la liberación latinoamericana, aunque diferente de la que es habitual desde los sectores tradicionalistas de América Latina. Parte de la defensa del capitalismo como fuente de invención y atmósfera para lograr la creatividad humana. Objeta que la teología de la liberación tenga sus bases en el marxismo, considerando a éste como lo opuesto a la liberación. Dedica capítulos o párrafos especiales a la teoría de la dependencia, al socialismo y al concepto de "el pobre." La argumentación contra ciertos conceptos fundamentales de la teología de la liberación se hace mediante el examen de algunas obras de Enrique Dussel.

5353 Orrego Vicuña, Claudio. De la cultura que tenemos a la cultura que queremos. Quito: FESO, 1987. 72 p.

Defensa de la democracia cristiana (con abundantes citas del documento de Puebla) frente a cuatro características "culturales" latinoamericanas: catolicismo, tradición española, liberalismo y marxismo.

5354 Oviedo, José Miguel. Breve historia del ensayo hispanoamericano. Madrid: Alianza, 1990. 162 p.: bibl. (El Libro de bolsillo; 1509: Sección literatura)

Sin la exhaustividad ni la estructura de

las obras académicas, lo que caracteriza a este panorama es la inteligencia del comentario y la fluidez de la exposición. Los capítulos que más interesan a esta Sección son los referidos a "los grandes maestros del siglo XIX" y a "los intérpretes de la realidad," pero todo el conjunto es de lectura provechosa y grata.

5355 Pagden, Anthony. La caída del hombre natural: el indio americano y los orígenes de la etnología comparativa. Versión española de Belén Urrutia Domínguez. Madrid: Alianza Editorial, 1988. 297 p.: bibl., index.

El propósito de la obra es mostrar los instrumentos mentales con que los hombres de los siglos XVI y XVII dieron cuenta de la realidad del hombre americano. Los principales autores estudiados son Las Casas y José de Acosta, pero la figura clave desde el punto de vista de los medios de interpretación es Vitoria (y en general la escuela teológica de Salamanca). Este esfuerzo de comprensión constituiría el primer intento de una etnología comparada. Lo dicho no da idea de la riqueza del libro. Es decisión del autor separarse del tradicional enfoque de ver los fenómenos estudiados como "lucha por la justicia en la conquista de América." El autor declara que esta versión española es la más completa. Libro importante.

Paz, Octavio. In search of the present: Nobel lecture, 1990. See item **5064.**

5356 Pereira, Luiz Carlos Bresser. Crise e renovação da esquerda na América Latina. (*Lua Nova*, 21, out. 1990, p. 41–54)

Los análisis que el autor realiza se basan en un concepto de "izquierda" muy laxo, que podría calificarse mínimamente de "progresista." "Lo esencial en el concepto de izquierda"—afirma el autor—"es la prioridad de la justicia sobre el orden."

5357 Pino, Fermín del. Por una antropología de la ciencia: las expediciones ilustradas españoles como *potlatch* reales. pt. 1. (*Rev. Indias*, 47:180, mayo/agosto 1987, p. 533–546)

En las expediciones científicas del siglo XVIII a Hispanoamérica destaca el factor de emulación y de aprovechamiento para el prestigio político, frente a la explicación (que no excluye) por las ventajas militares o económicas. (Se denomina *potlatch* a los regalos que hacía un jefe de tribu a otro rival, como

muestra de superioridad). De interés para la historia de las ideas.

5358 Podetti, Amelia. Filosofía y filosofía americana. (*Relato Hechos Ideas*, 14: 15/16, 1987, p. 27–47)

La cuestión de la posibilidad de una filosofía nacional se resuelve haciéndose cargo de la propia realidad y expresando la oposición a la dependencia que la caracteriza. Aunque publicado posteriormente, el texto es originariamente de 1973.

5359 Primer encuentro de filósofos latinoamericanistas. (*Am. Lat./Moscow*, 8:116, agosto 1987, p. 70–72)

Aunque es un breve resumen de las intervenciones en la parte latinoamericana de una "Conferencia nacional" sobre "Problemas Ideológicos y Metodológicos de la Historia de la Filosofía," es ilustrativo del interés por el tema de la filosofía latinoamericana en la antigua Unión Soviética.

5360 Puhle, Hans-Jürgen. Nacionalismo en América Latina. (*Rev. Parag. Sociol.*, 23:67, sept./dic. 1986, p. 119–131)

Distingue dos tipos de nacionalismo en América Latina: el tradicional y "el nuevo nacionalismo antiimperialista del siglo XX." El segundo (populista, desarrollista) sería típico del Tercer Mundo en general.

5361 Quijano, Aníbal. La tensión del pensamiento latinoamericano. (*Torre/Río Piedras*, 34:131/132/133, enero/sept., 1986, p. 163–171)

Aunque en forma muy breve y muy general, el autor expresa la "sospecha" de que lo propio del pensamiento latinoamericano pueda ser una combinación de lo racional con lo mítico, de lo intelectual con lo emocional. Por ese medio podría modificarse la cultura occidental dominante y lograr una creatividad propiamente latinoamericana, superando el eurocentrismo tradicional.

5362 Rech, Bruno. Bartolomé de Las Casas und Aristóteles. (*Jahrb. Gesch.*, 22, 1985, p. 39–68)

Relaciona los argumentos polémicos de Las Casas con el pensamiento de Aristóteles, especialmente con el contenido del *De Anima*, la *Metafísica*, la *Etica a Nicómaco* y la *Política*. La autoridad de Aristóteles explica que tanto Las Casas como Ginés de Sepúlveda lo tuvieran como referencia.

5363 Ríos, Pedro Juan. Nuestra América y Marx: la crítica y superación del "desencuentro." (*Social. Particip.*, 36, dic. 1986, p. 93–97)

El "desencuentro" aludido en el título es el de Marx y América Latina, provocado por las breves referencias que aquél hizo sobre la región y especialmente sobre Bolívar. El autor comenta su trabajo *Bolívar ante Marx* (1976) y los de José Aricó, *Marx y América Latina* (1982, ver *HLAS 46:7504*) y Carlos Franco, *Del marxismo eurocéntrico al marxismo latinoamericano* (1981, ver item **5433**).

5364 Roig, Arturo Andrés. La "inversión de la filosofía de la historia" en el pensamiento latinoamericano. (*Rev. Filos. Teor. Polít.*, 26/27, 1986, p. 170–174)

Sobre la obra de Antonio de León Pinelo (1596–1660), *El paraíso en el Nuevo Mundo: comentario apologético; historia natural y peregrina de las Indias Occidentales, Islas de Tierra Firme del Mar Océano*, escrita en 1650, y el fenómeno de la "inversión de la filosofía de la historia," que el autor considera característico del pensamiento latinoamericano.

5365 Romero Baró, José María. El positivismo y su valoración en América. Prólogo de Eudaldo Forment. Barcelona: Promociones Publicaciones Universitarias, 1989. 229 p.: bibl., index. (Biblioteca universitaria de filosofía; 15)

Buena exposición. Se enfoca panorámicamente el positivismo argentino y el mexicano, señalando las apreciaciones críticas de Alejandro Korn y Antonio Caso. A este último autor se dedica la mayor extensión del libro. También se ocupa del positivismo en Brasil, Chile y Cuba, y de Vaz Ferreira entre los "superadores" del positivismo. (Señala el antecedente que "el hombre mediocre" de José Ingenieros puede ser del "hombre masa" de Ortega y Gasset).

5366 Sasso, Javier. La ética filosófica en América Latina: tres modelos contemporáneos. Caracas: Ediciones CELARG, 1987. 215 p.: bibl. (Col. La Alborada)

Básicamente se trata del análisis de tres obras: *Para una filosofía del valor*, de Augusto Salazar Bondy; *Investigaciones sobre la estructura aporético-dialéctica de la eticidad*, de Mario Sambarino; y *Etica*, de Adolfo

Sánchez Vázquez. Uno de los criterios para la selección de los autores fue dar cabida a dos tendencias de considerable presencia en América Latina: la filosofía analítica y el marxismo, criterio que se aplica claramente al primero y al último de los autores, respectivamente. Se trata de una crítica cuidadosamente argumentativa o filosófica propiamente dicha, infrecuente en Hispanoamérica a pesar del gran interés que despierta el pensamiento latinoamericano.

5367 Sasso, Javier. Sobre el pensamiento latinoamericano y su historiografía. (*Bol. Acad. Nac. Hist./Caracas*, 73:290, abril/junio 1990, p. 31–44)

Plantea cuestiones críticas sobre el modo en que se realiza hoy la historia de las ideas (o del pensamiento) en América Latina. Entre esas cuestiones están: la "sobrefilosofización" de expresiones intelectuales de poco alcance filosófico; la "sobrepolitización" de esfuerzos filosóficos que no fueron pensados con intención política (o con no demasiada); y la desfiguración de filósofos "puros" para que encajen en un esquema de filosofía de la historia latinoamericana. Novedoso y saludable como repensamiento de formas consagradas.

5368 Subercaseaux, Bernardo. La apropiación cultural en el pensamiento y la cultura de America Latina. (*Estud. Públicos*, 30, otoño 1988, p. 125–135)

Señala la existencia de dos modelos en la recepción, por parte de América Latina, del pensamiento europeo y norteamericano: 1) la *reproducción*: absorción mimética sin asimilación; y 2) la *apropiación*: el hacer propio ese pensamiento ajeno, utilizándolo para resolver los problemas de la propia circunstancia. Si bien la idea no es nueva, el enfoque del autor es genuino y el artículo se cuenta entre los más atendibles que se han escrito sobre el tema.

5369 Urbano, Henrique. La invención andina del hombre, de la cultura y de la sociedad y los ciclos míticos judeocristianos. (*Bol. Lima*, 8:46, julio 1986, p. 51–60, bibl.)

Se trata de una comparación entre ciertos mitos fundacionales del pensamiento andino y los "ciclos míticos judeocristianos." Lo que más interesa para esta sección es cómo la transmisión de los mitos andinos pudo ser afectada por la cosmovisión y los conceptos de los primeros intérpretes occidentales, miembros de la sociedad de la conquista.

5370 Uslar Pietri, Arturo. La creación del Nuevo Mundo. (*Bol. Acad. Nac. Hist./ Caracas*, 70:278, abril/junio 1987, p. 321–331, bibl.)

Sensatas y saludables reflexiones de un gran escritor sobre la discusión en torno a los conceptos de "descubrimiento," "conquista," "colonización" y en general sobre el hecho histórico recordado por el V Centenario. Reconoce que lo fundamental fue la creación de un mundo nuevo, producto del mestizaje cultural.

5371 Vanden, Harry E. Latin American Marxism: a bibliography. New York: Garland Pub., 1991. 869 p.: index. (Garland reference library of social science; 137)

Contiene más de 6.300 entradas, divididas en cuatro períodos: hasta 1920; 1921–45; 1946–60; y 1961 en adelante. Dos tercios de la obra corresponden a la cuarta etapa. Algunas entradas son anotadas. El criterio de inclusión es muy amplio, al punto de que casi podría considerarse una bibliografía sobre la izquierda latinoamericana.

5372 Vaughan, Alden T. Caliban in the Third World: Shakespeare's savage as sociopolitical symbol. (*Mass. Rev.*, 29:2, Summer 1988, p. 289–313, bibl.)

Persigue el cambio o pasaje del símbolo de Calibán desde ser representación del opresor hasta representar al oprimido. En la aplicación del símbolo se refiere tanto a América Latina como a Africa, el Caribe de habla inglesa y Canadá. Algunos autores atendidos son: José Enrique Rodó, Dominique Mannoni, Aimé Césaire, Edward Brathwaite, Fernández Retamar, Max Dorsinville. Como visión general e introducción al asunto es excelente.

5373 Vidales, Raúl. Utopía y liberación: el amanecer del indio. San José: Depto. Ecuménico de Investigaciones, 1988. 200 p.: bibl. (Col. Análisis)

El libro no tiene una estructura o secuencia de tesis que lo haga fácilmente resumible. No obstante, la posición básica es la de una teología de la liberación que considera al socialismo como una "utopía posible" y dirige sus esfuerzos a realizarlo. Podrían distinguirse dos conclusiones: 1) El "movimiento revolucionario" debe atender a los reclamos

de las etnias; y 2) debe reconocerse la función del mito en las etnias y el peculiar modo de vivir éstas lo religioso, inclusive la posibilidad de una "teología india."

5374 Weinberg, Gregorio. Ilustración y educación superior en Hispanoamérica. (*Rev. Educ.*, Número Extraordinario, La Educación en la Ilustración Española, 1988, p. 31–58)

Este excelente panorama de la Ilustración en Hispanoamérica cubre el periodismo, las expediciones científicas, las expresiones filosóficas y las llamadas "ciencias útiles." Con respecto a la Universidad, destaca: la relación entre los cambios de orientación académica y los de la sociedad; los reclamos de modernización y las críticas a la enseñanza tradicional; y el caso especial de la enseñanza de la medicina. Aunque el volumen en que aparece se refiere en su mayor parte a España, el investigador de las ideas latinoamericanas encontrará de provecho todo el contenido.

5375 Zea, Leopoldo. Encuentro hispano-mexicano de filosofía moral y política en la filosofía en lengua española. (*Rev. Univ./Tabasco*, 5:17/18, sept./dic. 1987, p. 21–28, facsims.)

En la familiar temática de Leopoldo Zea defiende la posibilidad de una filosofía auténtica en cualquier región o idioma, oponiéndose a la idea de que haya un *logos* o discurso magistral, es decir, que se considere a sí mismo como superior, dominante o con inherente condición de modelo.

5376 Zuleta Alvarez, Enrique. Santayana en Hispanoamérica. (*Rev. Occident.*, 79, dic. 1987, p. 9–25)

Tras una caracterización de la vida y la obra de Santayana, persigue el eco de este pensador y escritor en España e Hispanoamérica, en particular Argentina, dando noticia de las traducciones que se publicaron en dicho país y de cómo fue apreciado. Señala especialmente la influencia que ejerció Pedro Henríquez Ureña en esa apreciación. La resonancia en Argentina habría sido mayor que en el resto de América Latina y aun que en España, donde Santayana había nacido.

MEXICO

5377 Aguilar Monteverde, Alonso et al. Pensamiento político de México. v. 2. México: Editorial Nuestro Tiempo, 1987. 1 v. (Col. Pensamiento Político de México)

Este vol. 2 abarca el período 1824–54, etapa de gran inestabilidad política y de transición entre la reciente independencia y el período de la Reforma. Aguilar Monteverde proporciona una visión de conjunto que ocupa más de un tercio del libro. Hay capítulos especiales sobre la Iglesia, el liberalismo, el militarismo, los rasgos culturales de la época y las masas populares. En general los autores logran una narrativa clara que hace al libro aprovechable para el lector no especializado.

Alvarado, Lourdes. Porfirio Parra y Gutiérrez: semblanza biográfica. See item **1333.**

5378 Bartra, Roger. La jaula de la melancolía: identidad y metamorfosis del mexicano. México: Grijalbo, 1987. 271 p.: bibl., ill. (Col. Enlace. Cultura y sociedad)

Es una crítica a las caracterizaciones que se han hecho de "lo mexicano" desde la filosofía, la psicología y la historia. Estas críticas y otras afirmaciones del autor no dejan de ser también una contribución a ese tema. Ideas y estilo (de pensamiento y de expresión) van en el libro más allá de lo circunscritamente académico y le dan una marcada individualidad e independencia no carente además de intención literaria. Destacamos esta afirmación: "Los estudios sobre 'lo mexicano' constituyen una expresión de la cultura política dominante."

5379 Bastian, Jean-Pierre. El paradigma de 1789: sociedades de ideas y Revolución Mexicana. (*Hist. Mex.*, 38:1, julio/sept. 1988, p. 79–110, bibl.)

Interesante y bien elaborado trabajo sobre las "sociedades de ideas" (logias masónicas, clubes políticos, agrupaciones protestantes, sociedades espiritistas, etc.) en la segunda mitad del siglo XIX y hasta la Revolución de 1910, en México. Destaca sus características de democracia interna, su tipo de liberalismo opuesto al Porfiriato y su anticatolicismo, entre otros rasgos.

5380 Bono, Diane M. Cultural diffusion of Spanish humanism in New Spain: Francisco Cervantes de Salazar's *Diálogo de la dignidad del hombre*. New York: P. Lang, 1991. 161 p. (American univ. studies: Series II, Romance languages and literature, 0740–9257; 174)

Cervantes de Salazar (1518?-75), traductor de Vives y cronista de la Ciudad de México en el siglo XVI, escribió un *Diálogo sobre la dignidad del hombre*, inspirado en el homónimo de Fernán Pérez de Oliva y al cual pretende complementar. La presente obra transcribe dicho *Diálogo*, tomando en cuenta las ediciones de Alcalá de Henares (1546) y Madrid (1772). Precede al texto una extensa introducción de la editora, con noticias biográficas y comentarios sobre el *Diálogo* y la posición de su autor en el humanismo renacentista español.

5381 Cardiel Reyes, Raúl. Del modernismo al liberalismo: la filosofía de Manuel María Gorriño. 2a ed. México: Univ. Nacional Autónoma de México, 1981. 262 p., 9 p. of plates: bibl., facsims., ports. (Col. Seminarios/ Facultad de Filosofía y Letras)

En esta obra se entiende por "modernismo" la aceptación cuidadosa de algunas ideas modernas, sin dejar de reafirmar a la vez la fe religiosa tradicional; y por "liberalismo," la aceptación de la forma política democrática. De la lectura se infiere que Gorriño (1767–1831) fue más un tradicionalista católico que un hombre de ideas modernas, excepto en admitir la forma democrática de gobierno (abandono de la monarquía después de la Independencia). La obra fue publicada por primera vez en 1967 (ver *HLAS 30:5132*), pero debe destacarse por ser un trabajo único sobre el tema y estar realizada con todo el cuidado monográfico y escrita con claridad.

5382 Covo, Jacqueline. Las ideas de la Reforma en México, 1855–1861. Traducción de María Francisca Mourier-Martínez. México: Univ. Nacional Autónoma de México, 1983. 668 p.: appendices, bibl., index.

Monografía extensa y detallada sobre las ideas de la época de la "Reforma" en México, especialmente entre 1855–57. Examina el enfrentamiento entre liberales y tradicionalistas, basándose principalmente en la prensa y los debates parlamentarios de la época. La información suministrada no podrá pasarse por alto en estudios posteriores. Contiene 18 anexos con materiales de la prensa contemporánea y una bibliografía (fuentes básicas y literatura secundaria). Véase la reseña del historiador en *HLAS 50:1148.*

5383 Del pensamiento esencial de México. Recopilación de Antonio Menéndez e Iván Menéndez. México: Grijalbo, 1988. 900 p.: bibl., index.

Repertorio de testimonios, declaraciones, textos legales, pensamientos, discursos, comunicaciones, etc., a lo largo de la historia de México desde los tiempos prehispánicos hasta 1986.

5384 Fabelo, José R. and América M. Pérez.
El problema de la existencia de los valores en la concepción axiológica de Eduardo García Máynez. (*Islas/Santa Clara*, 87, mayo/ agosto 1987, p. 18–33)
Analiza el pensamiento axiológico de García Máynez (especialmente el tema de la existencia del valor y el de la jerarquía de los valores), y lo critica desde el punto de vista del marxismo-leninismo. Aun dentro de esta perspectiva reconoce aspectos válidos de la teoría del autor mexicano.

Fell, Claude. José Vasconcelos: los años del águila, 1920–1925; educación, cultura e iberoamericanismo en el México postrevolucionario. See item **1490.**

5385 Gomes Moreira, José Aparecido. Esclavitud y evangelización indígena en el siglo XVI: el pensamiento de Don Vasco de Quiroga. (*Cristianismo Soc.*, 29:110, 1991, p. 21–36)
Artículo de interés sobre varios aspectos del pensamiento de Vasco de Quiroga: su intento de reconstruir con los indios (considerados en la "Edad de Oro") la Iglesia primitiva; la crítica a la esclavitud de los indios y la reacción de los colonizadores; la "guerra justa;" y la utopía comunitaria.

5386 Gómez-Martínez, José Luis. La presencia de Ortega y Gasset en el pensamiento mexicano. (*Nueva Rev. Filol. Hisp.*, 35:1, 1987, p. 197–221)
La tesis principal es que la influencia de Ortega en México no debe juzgarse solamente en el plano de las ideas, sino examinando la circunstancia mexicana previa a esa influencia. Ciertas ideas de Ortega proporcionaban "una respuesta epistemológica al ansia de autenticidad que dominaba en todas las facetas de la vida mexicana . . . "

5387 González Navarro, Moisés. Las ideas raciales de los científicos, 1890–1910. (*Hist. Mex.*, 37:4, abril/junio 1988, p. 565–583, bibl.)
El cuerpo del artículo está compuesto por citas de personajes y periódicos de la época que expresan juicios sobre grupos étnicos: principalmente indios, pero también negros y asiáticos. Interesa la comparación con otros países latinoamericanos en lo que se refiere a opiniones sobre la inmigración más deseable.

5388 Guadarrama González, Pablo. La evolución de las ideas de Leopoldo Zea como antecedente y pilar de la filosofía latinoamericana de la liberación. (*Lateinamerika/Hamburg*, 2, 1987, p. 9–26)
Enfoque genético de la obra de Zea en sus distintas etapas. El autor percibe (acorde con sus propias simpatías filosóficas e ideológicas) un proceso de radicalización política que haría de Zea una de las figuras más progresistas del actual pensamiento social latinoamericano.

5389 Ibargüengoitia, Antonio. Pedro José Márquez, 1784–1820: primer estudioso de la estética en México. (*Rev. Filos./México*, 24:70, enero/abril 1991, p. 41–47)
Se refiere al jesuita Márquez, nacido en México, expulsado junto con la Orden y vuelto a México en 1816. El artículo expone el contenido de *Sobre lo bello en general*, publicado en Madrid en 1801 y en Italia en 1808. La Univ. de México publicó la obra en 1972.

5390 Moreiras, Alberto. Alternancia México/mundo en la posición crítica de Octavio Paz. (*Nueva Rev. Filol. Hisp.*, 35:1, 1987, p. 251–264)
Intenta determinar los fundamentos teóricos que hacen posible la actividad crítica de Octavio Paz, y la característica de ser ella, a la vez, universal y preocupada por lo específico mexicano.

5391 El pensamiento de la reacción mexicana: historia documental. v. 1–2. Recopilación de Gastón García Cantú. México: UNAM, Coordinación de Humanidades, 1987. 2 v.: bibl. (Lecturas universitarias; 33)
Obra documental sobre el pensamiento conservador mexicano, de gran utilidad para el investigador. Abarca desde 1810–1926. Cada documento (hay casi un centenar en la obra) va precedido de una introducción explicativa.

5392 Peset, José Luis. La naturaleza como "símbolo" en la obra de José Antonio de Alzate. (*Asclepio/Madrid*, 39:2, 1987, p. 285–295, bibl.)
La tesis del autor es que al lenguaje de Alzate como naturalista o científico se le

puede dar una lectura política. Ese lenguaje trasluciría un reformismo paulatino, sin cortes bruscos.

5393 Petiáksheva, Natalia. José Vasconcelos contra el positivismo. (*Am. Lat./Moscow,* 2, 1989, p. 28–35, bibl., photo)

Visión general de Vasconcelos, pero especialmente de sus ideas sobre la "raza cósmica" y su pedagogía. Le reprocha que su filosofía, basada en el hombre latinoamericano, excluye sin embargo toda explicación social o económica de las sociedades de la región.

5394 Robles, Martha. Entre el poder y las letras: Vasconcelos en sus memorias. México: Fondo de Cultura Económica, 1989. 132 p.: bibl., ill. (Vida y pensamiento de México)

Se trata de un enjuiciamiento histórico general de la compleja y contradictoria figura del autor de *La raza cósmica,* especialmente en los aspectos políticos. A ratos muy crítico, pero no carente de animación y riqueza.

5395 Torre Villar, Ernesto de la. La teología en Nueva España: apuntamientos. (*Mem. Acad. Mex. Hist.,* 34, 1991, p. 5–61)

Más que de "apuntamientos" se trata de un útil registro o inventario de cátedras y de profesores de teología en las distintas órdenes religiosas, destacándose especialmente los franciscanos, los dominicos, los agustinos y los jesuitas.

5396 Vasconcelos, José. José Vasconcelos. Edición de María Justina Sarabia Viejo. Prólogo de Antonio Lago Carballo. Madrid: Instituto de Cooperación Iberoamericana, Ediciones de Cultura Hispánica, 1989. 123 p.: bibl. (Antología del pensamiento político, social y económico de América Latina; 6)

Antología, principalmente del pensamiento político de Vasconcelos. Buena bibliografía.

5397 Villegas, Abelardo. La filosofía de lo mexicano. 3ra. edición México: Univ. Nacional Autónoma de México, 1988. 235 p.

La primera edición de este libro apareció en 1960 (ver *HLAS 23:5842*). El prólogo mira retrospectivamente la obra y reflexiona sobre caracterizaciones posteriores del hombre y la sociedad mexicanos.

5398 Zavala, Silvio Arturo. Recuerdo de Vasco de Quiroga. 2. ed., aum., 1. ed. en la colección "Sepan cuantos." México: Editorial Porrúa, 1987. 332 p.: bibl., ill., index. ("Sepan cuantos—"; 546)

Conjunto de valiosos trabajos, generales y de detalle, escritos entre 1937–86, por parte de un importante historiador de América. Hay también notas y artículos sobre esos trabajos de Zavala.

AMERICA CENTRAL

5399 Castro Aizpu, Rodolfo. Investigaciones y estudios de carácter filosófico y literario en general. (*Lotería/Panamá,* 365, marzo/abril 1987, p. 64–74)

Noticias bibliográficas sobre publicaciones filosóficas en Panamá en los últimos años.

5400 Chandler, David Lee. Juan José de Aycinena: idealista conservador de la Guatemala del siglo XIX. Traducción de Victoria Vázquez, Marina Vázquez y Lucía Robelo Pereira. Antigua, Guatemala: Centro de Investigaciones Regionales de Mesoamérica; South Woodstock, Vt: Plumsock Mesoamerican Studies, 1988. 304 p.: bibl., index. (Serie monográfica, 0252–9971; 4)

Juan José de Aycinena (1793–1865), obispo, enemigo de Morazán, representante de ideas conservadoras, fue un personaje de gran influencia en la vida política, religiosa y académica de la época. Este libro, escrito "desde fuera" de las polémicas nacionales, traza las bases para reexaminar su figura. Estudia a Aycinena, proporciona su bibliografía y reproduce (dos tercios del libro) discursos y escritos de él. Contribución seria en su factura, con independencia de los juicios que despierte el personaje estudiado. Véase la reseña del historiador en *HLAS 52:1429.*

5401 Gismondi, Michael A. Transformations in the holy religious resistance and hegemonic struggles in the Nicaraguan revolution. (*Lat. Am. Perspect.,* 13:3, Summer 1986, p. 13–36, bibl.)

Escrito desde un punto de vista marxista. Partiendo de la afirmación de que en una sociedad de clases la religión está siempre cargada de contenido político, sigue la línea de la Iglesia desde la colonia hasta el sandinismo. En la lucha contra Somoza la religión proporcionó una base común a los diferentes actores. Contiene extensa bibliografía.

5402 Hodges, Donald Clark. Intellectual foundations of the Nicaraguan revolution. Austin: Univ. of Texas Press, 1986. 378 p.: bibl., index.

Después de trazar las líneas del pensamiento de Sandino (quizás lo mejor del libro) con los elementos que aquél absorbió en México (desde el anarquismo a la teosofía), expone: 1) la conversión de ese pensamiento de Sandino en la faz autóctona de la ideología del Frente Sandinista de Liberación Nacional; 2) el "nuevo marxismo" de los sandinistas; y 3) el cristianismo de izquierda de Ernesto Cardenal. Este resumen no hace justicia a la información que contiene el libro y deja fuera los aspectos de interpretación, muchas veces muy favorables a Sandino (si Sandino es oscuro es para confundir al enemigo, por ejemplo). Muy buena bibliografía.

5403 Sandino, Augusto César. Pensamiento político. Selección, prólogo, bibliografía y cronología de Sergio Ramírez. Caracas: Biblioteca Ayacucho, 1988. 651 p.: bibl. (Biblioteca Ayacucho; 134)

Esta obra se reseñó en *HLAS 48:7561.* Luego hubo una edición de 1984 (Editorial La Nueva Nicaragua, Colección Pensamiento Vivo, 4), y ésta de 1988.

CARIBE INSULAR

Baloyra, Enrique. The frustration of Cuban nationalism. See *HLAS 53:3576.*

Cassá, Roberto. Sociedad e historia en el pensamiento de Hostos. See item **1988.**

Chevannes, Barry. Healing the nation: Rastafari exorcism of the ideology of racism in Jamaica. See *HLAS 53:5133.*

5404 Escalona Delfino, José A. Martí y la religión. (*Santiago/Cuba,* 64, marzo 1987, p. 73–86)

Rasgos de la idea de Dios en Martí y expresiones de su anticlericalismo, con textos de Lenin como fuente de interpretación.

5405 Fernández Retamar, Roberto. Caliban and other essays. Translated by Edward Baker. Foreword by Fredric Jameson. Minneapolis: Univ. of Minnesota Press, 1989. 139 p.: bibl., index.

El artículo más conocido que contiene esta versión inglesa es "Caliban: Notes Toward a Discussion of Culture in Our America" (1971), cuya tesis principal, contraria a la de Rodó, es que el símbolo que representa a la cultura latinoamericana no es Ariel, sino Calibán (la experiencia colonialista). Que esta tesis fue pensada por el autor en el contexto de su participación en la Revolución Cubana lo expresa con claridad el ensayo siguiente: "Caliban Revisited." Otros ensayos del volumen son: "Against the Black Legend" (1976); "Some Theoretical Problems of Spanish American Literature;" y "Prologue to Ernesto Cardenal."

5406 Ferrer Canales, José. Martí y Hostos. Río Piedras, P.R.: Instituto de Estudios Hostosianos, Univ. de Puerto Rico; San Juan: Centro de Estudios Avanzados de Puerto Rico y el Caribe, 1990. 197 p.: bibl., ill.

Ensayos sobre Martí y Hostos; Hostos y Henríquez Ureña; Hostos y Varona, todos de apreciación y de intenso elogio. También incluye, en la segunda parte, textos breves de los dos autores a que se dedica el libro. Véase la reseña del sociólogo en *HLAS 53:5146.*

5407 Fung Riverón, Thalia and **Pablo Guadarrama González.** El desarrollo del pensamiento filosófico en Cuba. (*Islas/Santa Clara,* 87, mayo/agosto 1987, p. 34–47)

Tras un rápido panorama del pensamiento cubano anterior a la revolución castrista (donde, como es frecuente en esta literatura, se reconocen figuras "progresistas," como el P. Varela, Martí y Varona), sigue lo que más interesa del artículo: el desarrollo de los estudios filosóficos desde la Revolución hasta la actualidad. Vale la pena destacar tres aspectos: 1) El que se considere que el punto de partida de esta nueva etapa filosófica esté en el "documento-programa" *La historia me absolverá,* de Fidel Castro; 2) La forma en que se generalizó la uniformización doctrinaria en todas las instituciones de enseñanza, "con la asesoría de filósofos soviéticos y alemanes;" y 3) La disputa interna que se desarrolló dentro del propio marxismo cubano entre marxistas-leninistas ortodoxos y los que participaban de otras modalidades del marxismo (Althuser, Marcuse, Colletti, etc.), predominando los primeros. Interesa por último que los autores ponen como elemento permanente del programa el estudio del pensamiento cubano y latinoamericano.

5408 Guadarrama González, Pablo. Los estudios sobre pensamiento filosófico cubano en la Universidad Central de Las Villas.

(*Islas/Santa Clara*, 86, enero/abril 1987, p. 55–60)

En la Universidad de las Villas, Cuba, se han realizado exposiciones y estudios sobre el pensamiento filosófico cubano (con predominio del criterio de interpretación marxista-leninista), y el autor de este artículo ha sido uno de los autores más activos. Aquí se indican los trabajos realizados, incluyendo algunos anteriores a 1959. En tal sentido el trabajo es bibliográficamente útil. La actividad, no sólo sobre el pensamiento cubano, sino sobre el latinoamericano en general, ha continuado, más allá de la fecha del artículo.

Guevara, Ernesto. A new society: reflections for today's world. See item **2166.**

5409   Guevara, Ernesto. Notas para el estudio de la ideología de la Revolución Cubana. (*Islas/Santa Clara*, 86, enero/abril 1986, p. 6–13)

Reproduce un artículo de Ernesto Guevara publicado en la revista *Verde Olivo* en oct. 1960. Es una reflexión sintética en torno a la marcha de la guerrilla hasta el momento de entrar en La Habana, más que un trabajo propiamente teórico o de análisis ideológico.

5410   Hart, Keith. German idealism and Jamaican national culture. (*Caribb. Q.,* 36:1/2, June 1990, p. 114–125)

Establece un paralelo entre la situación de las culturas nacionales de Alemania a comienzos del siglo XIX y de Jamaica en la actualidad. Recomienda para este último país inspirarse en el idealismo y el romanticismo alemanes (Kant, Hegel, Schelling, Herder), los cuales, según el autor, constituyeron la base ideológica de los avances de Prusia.

5411   Hostos, Eugenio María de. Moral social; Sociología. Prólogo y cronología de Manuel Maldonado-Denis. Caracas: Biblioteca Ayacucho, 1982. 481 p.: bibl. (Biblioteca Ayacucho; 97)

Se reúnen aquí las dos grandes obras sociológicas (o socio-morales) de Hostos: *Moral social* (1888) y *Tratado de sociología* (1904, póstuma). Como las demás obras de la Biblioteca Ayacucho, contiene un prólogo o estudio preliminar y una cronología. Incluye además una buena bibliografía. El prólogo de Maldonado-Denis es útil, señala la peculiaridad de Hostos a pesar de utilizar fuentes europeas (positivismo y krausismo) y revela el buen conocimiento que este crítico tiene de

la obra del pensador puertorriqueño. Sin embargo, el esfuerzo por justificar el pensamiento de Hostos confrontándolo con categorías marxistas resulta hermenéuticamente innecesario.

5412   Hostos, Eugenio María de. Tratado de sociología. Edición revisada y anotada por Julio César López y Vivian Quiles Calderín con la colaboración de Pedro Alvarez Ramos. Prólogo de José Luis Méndez. San Juan: Editorial del Instituto de Cultura Puertorriqueña; Río Piedras: Editorial de la Univ. de Puerto Rico, 1989. 358 p., 1 leaf of plates: bibl., ill. (some col.). (Obras completas; 8. Sociología; 1)

Al texto original de esta obra clásica de Hostos se han agregado en esta edición más de 180 notas de los editores. El volumen contiene, además, tres apéndices con sendos trabajos de Hostos: 1) "Las Leyes de la Sociedad" (1877); 2) "Reforma del Plan de Estudios en la Facultad de Leyes" (1889); y 3) "De la Influencia de la Sociología en la Dirección Política de Nuestras Sociedades" (1877, nunca recogido antes en libro, según los editores). El prólogo de José Luis Méndez señala acertadamente los aspectos de la sociología de Hostos que van más allá de la adhesión a Comte y Spencer y le dan un perfil propio por su moralismo y su raíz latinoamericana. Cierran el volumen una bibliografía y varios índices.

Hulme, Peter. The rhetoric of description: the Amerindians of the Caribbean within modern European discourse. See *HLAS 53:1013.*

5413   Le Riverend, Julio. Varela: transición ideológica en pos del futuro. (*Santiago/ Cuba*, 71, dic. 1988, p. 5–22)

El Padre Félix Varela (1787–1853) es situado en la realidad económico-social de su tiempo y en la historia político-ideológica de Cuba.

5414   Martí, José. José Martí. Edición de María Luisa Laviana Cuetos. Madrid: Instituto de Cooperación Iberoamericana, Ediciones de Cultura Hispánica, 1988. 116 p.: bibl. (Antología del pensamiento político, social y económico de América Latina; 1)

Breve antología, con predominio de los textos vinculados a temas políticos. La introducción comparte esa característica.

5415   Martínez Heredia, Fernando. Ché, el socialismo y el comunismo. La Habana: Casa de las Américas, 1989. 185 p.: bibl.

Aunque el autor está totalmente identificado con la Revolución Cubana, el libro no es pura o solamente una exaltación del Ché, sino un análisis de sus ideas, especialmente las que explican su praxis y su actuación en el gobierno.

5416 Melis, Antonio. Fernando Ortiz y el mundo afrocubano: desde la criminología lombrosiana hasta el concepto de transculturación. (*Lat.am. Stud./Nürnberg*, 23, 1987, p. 169–181)

Trayectoria de la obra del antropólogo cubano Fernando Ortiz (n. 1881), desde sus primeros trabajos lombrosianos a comienzos del siglo hasta libros como *Contrapunteo cubano del tabaco y el azúcar* (1940) y *El engaño de las razas* (1946). De interés para la historia de las ideas.

5417 Rexach, Rosario. Jorge Mañach: tributo al hombre y a su obra. (*Linden Lane Mag.*, 6:2/3, abril/sept. 1987, p. 18–20)

Semblanza de Jorge Mañach (1898–1961), intelectual cubano autor de *Para una filosofía de la vida* y de libros sobre Martí. Fue también uno de los fundadores de la vanguardista *Revista de Avance* (ver también *HLAS 50:3295*).

5418 Rojas Gómez, Miguel. El corpus filosófico de Medardo Vitier. (*Islas/Santa Clara*, 86, enero/abril 1986, p. 61–69)

A pesar de considerar a Medardo Vitier (1886–1960) como una figura representativa de la "república neo-colonial," es útil en tanto señala aspectos de opinión filosófica personal en Vitier, escritor conocido más bien como crítico e historiador de la filosofía en Cuba.

5419 Rojas Gómez, Miguel. Juan Marinello: esteta de la libertad. (*Islas/Santa Clara*, 93, mayo/agosto 1989, p. 80–94,)

Sobre Juan Marinello, considerado como uno de los forjadores de la estética marxista en Cuba. Se afirma de él que, a pesar de su posición, no veía la obra de arte como "una consigna política o de clase."

5420 Rojas Osorio, Carlos. Ideas filosóficas de Eugenio María de Hostos. (*Rev. Inst. Cult. Puertorriq.*, 26:95/96, enero/junio 1987, p. 63–70, bibl., photos)

Oportuno resumen de la posición filosófica de Hostos. Las principales características que encuentra en ese pensamiento son: 1)

racioempirismo o unidad de la razón y la experiencia; 2) idealismo personalista en la moral; 3) agnosticismo como desconocimiento de las causas y principios últimos; 4) humanismo o defensa de la identidad del hombre; 5) naturalismo; 6) iusnaturalismo en la concepción del Estado.

5421 Santí, Enrico Mario. José Martí and the Cuban Revolution. (*Cuba. Stud.*, 16, 1986, p. 139–150)

La actual utilización de la imagen de Martí por parte del régimen cubano no sería sino un caso más dentro de un proceso recurrente de apropiación de ese héroe nacional en la historia política de Cuba. Además, resultaría de una lectura "figurativa" o teleológica, según la cual Martí llevaría encapsulado y en potencia a Fidel Castro, y éste sería el final cumplimiento del significado de Martí. El autor denuncia esta lectura, en este caso y en general, por ser distorsionante de la realidad histórica (ver también *HLAS 50:3304*).

VENEZUELA

5422 Bolívar, visto por marxistas. Compilación y prólogo de Jerónimo Carrera. Caracas: Fondo Editorial Carlos Aponte, 1987. 318 p.: bibl., ill.

La primera parte es un largo estudio de Anatoli Shulgovski sobre el pensamiento político de Bolívar. La segunda y la tercera contienen artículos, entre otros, de: Adalbert Dessau, Manfred Kossok, Jerónimo Carrera, Max Zeuske, Alvaro Delgado y Yuri Zubritski. La cuarta contiene trabajos que polemizan con ideas de Germán Arciniegas sobre el Libertador. En la última hay una declaración del Partido Comunista de Venezuela ante el bicentenario del nacimiento de Bolívar.

5423 Gallegos, Rómulo. Pensamiento y acción política de Rómulo Gallegos. Introducción por Marco Tulio Bruni Celli. Caracas: AD, 1985? 131 p.

Este breve libro contiene una extensa introducción sobre la vida política de Rómulo Gallegos y una antología de textos también políticos de ese autor, célebre novelista venezolano que llegó a ser presidente de su país.

5424 García Bacca, Juan David *et al*. Significación histórica y vigencia moderna de la obra de Andrés Bello: filosofía y otros temas. Caracas: Casa de Bello, 1989. 511 p.:

bibl., index. (Anexos a las obras completas de Andrés Bello; 6)

Contiene diversos trabajos que se supone han sido previamente publicados y que son los siguientes: Juan David García Bacca, "Introducción General a las Obras Filosóficas de Andrés Bello;" Arturo Uslar Pietri, "Los Temas del Pensamiento Crítico de Bello;" Luis B. Prieto, "La Obra Educativa de Andrés Bello;" Mariano Picón Salas, "Bello y la Historia;" F.J. Duarte, "Cosmografía y otros Escritos de Divulgación Científica;" Oscar Zambrano Urdaneta, "El Epistolario de Andrés Bello." Casi todos son escritos extensos.

5425 Kilgore, William J. Un filósofo penetrante y agudo: un estudio breve de la forma moderna de la argumentación de Andrés Bello. (*Rev. Hist. Ideas*, 9, 1988, p. 123–128)

Breve exposición de las formas argumentativas en Bello, especialmente en su *Filosofía del entendimiento.*

5426 Miranda, Francisco de. América espera. Selección, prólogo y títulos de José Luis Salcedo-Bastardo. Cronología de Manuel Pérez Vila, Josefina Rodríguez de Alonso. Traducciones de Gustavo Díaz Solís, Michel R. Monner y Gilberto Merchán. Caracas: Biblioteca Ayacucho, 1982. 686 p.: bibl. (Biblioteca Ayacucho; 100)

Importante edición documental de escritos (anotaciones, cartas, manifiestos, notas autobiográficas, declaraciones, ensayos, etc.) de Francisco de Miranda. Contiene también cronología y bibliografía. El prólogo exalta la figura del Precursor y explica el contenido de la edición.

5427 Pensamiento político de la emancipación venezolana. Recopilación, prólogo y cronología de Pedro Grases. Bibliografía de Horacio Jorge Becco. Caracas: Biblioteca Ayacucho, 1988. 434 p.: bibl. (Biblioteca Ayacucho; 133)

Excelente recopilación documental. El prólogo, muy bien logrado, destaca los antecedentes del siglo XVIII. Muy buena bibliografía.

5428 Pino Iturrieta, Elías. Las ideas de los primeros venezolanos. Prólogo de Eduardo Arcila Farías. Caracas: Fondo Editorial Tropykos, 1987. 183 p.: bibl. (Serie Ensayos)

Utilizando materiales de la época (libros, notas periodísticas, declaraciones, leyes,

memorias, etc.) persigue el contenido de ideas—especialmente políticas y económicas—durante el período 1830–45, aproximadamente, que reflejan las polémicas entre liberales y conservadores en Venezuela. El denominador común habría sido, para el autor, el mantenimiento de los intereses de la clase propietaria. A pesar del apoyo documental es, por el enfoque y el estilo, un ensayo.

5429 Plaza, Elena. José Gil Fortoul: los nuevos caminos de la razón, la historia como ciencia, 1861–1943. Caracas: Congreso de la República, Oficina de Estudios Históricos y Políticos, 1985. 168 p.: bibl. (Pensamiento político venezolano del siglo XX: Análisis y crítica; 1)

Trabajo monográfico sobre la idea de historia en Gil Fortoul (1861–1943), especialmente tal como es aplicada en su obra *Historia constitucional de Venezuela.* Lo principal de la obra es la identificación de las fuentes europeas en las que abrevó Gil Fortoul, la forma en que las asimiló, y cómo ellas se reflejan en las principales ideas sustantivas y metodológicas de su trabajo histórico y de su concepción de la historia. Esta búsqueda está bien realizada por la autora, y una de sus consecuencias es mostrar la complejidad de aquellas fuentes, no reductibles sin más a rótulos clásicos como "positivismo," "evolucionismo," etc. Buena contribución a la historia de las ideas.

5430 Prieto Castillo, Daniel. Utopía y comunicación en Simón Rodríguez. Caracas: Academia Venezolana de la Lengua; Univ. Simón Rodríguez, 1987. 216 p.: bibl. (Col. Logos; 6)

Se intenta recuperar textos de Simón Rodríguez en tanto significativos para la teoría de la comunicación social. También hay comentarios sobre otros aspectos de los escritos de dicho autor, del cual se reproducen al final cuatro documentos breves.

5431 *Revista Nacional de Cultura.* Vol. 47, No. 262, julio/agosto/sept. 1986- . Caracas: Consejo Nacional de Cultura.

Este número está íntegramente dedicado a la figura de José María Vargas (1786–1854), médico y botánico venezolano, Rector de la Univ. Central de Venezuela (en la cual promovió los estudios científicos), y por breve lapso Presidente de su país. Entre los materiales incluidos se encuentran Blas Bruni Celli,

"Bicentenario del Doctor José Vargas"; Ildefonso Leal, "Cronología de José María Vargas"; Adolfo Ernst, "Vargas Considerado como Botánico"; Mariano Picón Salas, "Centenario del Doctor Vargas." Se incluyen también algunos escritos de Vargas.

5432 Ruiz, Gustavo Adolfo. Raíces hispánicas de las ideas de Don Simón Rodríguez en la época colonial. (*Bol. Acad. Nac. Hist./Caracas*, 71:281, enero/marzo 1988, p. 55–78, bibl.)

Investigación cuyo propósito es mostrar que las ideas pedagógicas de Simón Rodríguez contenidas en la memoria *Reflexiones sobre los defectos que vician la escuela de primeras letras de Caracas y modos de lograr su reforma por un nuevo establecimiento* (1794) se basan en experiencias que se llevaban a cabo en España, y no en las ideas de Rousseau, según se ha afirmado reiteradamente.

5433 Sánchez Castro, Carlos. Marx ante Bolívar. (*Rev. Hist. Ideas*, 9, 1988, p. 209–222)

Intenta explicar las razones por las cuales Marx emitió su famoso y negativo juicio sobre Bolívar—y en general sobre América Latina.

5434 Villavicencio, Rafael. Escritos del doctor Rafael Villavicencio. v. 1–2. Recopilación, notas y estudio introductorio de Rafael Fernández Heres. Caracas: Academia Nacional de la Historia, 1989. 2 v.: bibl., indexes. (Biblioteca de la Academia Nacional de la Historia: Serie Obras completas)

Se trata de los dos primeros volúmenes de una edición que aparentemente constará de cinco, de la obra de Rafael Villavicencio (1838–1920). Los escritos contenidos en los presentes volúmenes llegan hasta 1880. El "Estudio Introductorio" (un libro en sí mismo, pues ocupa más de 200 p.), sigue la evolución del pensamiento de Villavicencio en sus aspectos positivistas, monistas y espiritualistas, y destaca lo que en ese pensamiento ha ido más allá del positivismo (ver también *HLAS 52:5366*).

5435 Weinberg, Gregorio. Andrés Bello, educador y humanista. (*Rev. Inst. Invest. Educ.*, 13:59, agosto 1987, p. 3–22, bibl.)

Panorama claro y bien informado de las tres principales etapas de la vida de Bello y la obra desarrollada a lo largo de ellas, con útiles indicaciones bibliográficas.

COLOMBIA

5436 Conte Porras, Jorge. Antología del pensamiento liberal istmeñista, 1855–1899. (*Rev. Cult. Lotería*, 361, julio/agosto 1986, p. 27–43)

Se trata no tanto de una antología como de un repaso de las opiniones y de la conducta de algunas figuras del Itsmo de Panamá antes de separarse de Colombia. Las más significativas son las de Justo y Pablo Arosemena.

Gutiérrez Girardot, Rafael. Hispanoamérica: imágenes y perspectivas. See item **5338.**

López de la Roche, Fabio E. Colombia: la búsqueda infructuosa de la identidad. See *HLAS 53:1245.*

5437 Molina, Gerardo. Las ideas socialistas en Colombia. Bogotá: Ediciones Tercer Mundo, 1987. 360 p.: bibl. (Col. Ensayos políticos; 4)

Ensayo de síntesis. Recorre la historia del país desde la Colonia hasta la acutalidad, registrando las expresiones que tuvo la cuestión social y, ya en el siglo XX, exponiendo las manifestaciones socialistas políticamente organizadas. Más historia narrativa que historia de las ideas (ver también item **5498**).

5438 Naranjo Villegas, Abel. La influencia española en la secularización de la filosofía en Colombia. (*Franciscanum/Bogotá*, 28:82, enero/abril 1986, p. 63–68)

Apreciación de lo que se denomina la "generación del cuarenta" (1940), grupo de estudiosos de la filosofía al que pertenecían, entre otros, Cayetano Betancur, Rafael Carrillo, Luis Nieto Arteta, Danilo Cruz Vélez y el propio autor. Estos representaban la apertura a los nuevos horizontes filosóficos que se exponían por entonces desde la *Revista de Occidente*, dirigida por Ortega y Gasset. Estas nuevas modalidades superaban el tradicional neotomismo imperante en Colombia.

5439 Pinzón Garzón, Rafael. La filosofía en Colombia. v. 1. Bogotá: Univ. Santo Tomás, Centro de Investigaciones de la Facultad de Filosofía, 1987. 1 v.: bibl., ill., index. (Biblioteca colombiana de filosofía; 6)

Continuación de un excelente proyecto bibliográfico del cual ha aparecido ya la parte correspondiente al siglo XX (ver *HLAS 50: 4631*). La presente obra registra manuscritos de los siglos XVI, XVII y XVIII (aparentemente no todo lo de este último siglo). Se incluyen datos bibliográficos de autores y también manuscritos anónimos. Son muy útiles dos apéndices: uno sobre "Instituciones pedagógicas coloniales" (universidades y colegios mayores) y otro bibliográfico sobre filosofía colonial.

5440 Rivadeneira Vargas, Antonio José. El bogotano J.M. Torres Caicedo, 1830–1889: la multipatria latinoamericana. Bogotá: Academia Colombiana de Historia; Alcaldía Mayor de Bogotá, Insatituto Distrital de Cultura y Turismo, 1989. 241 p.: bibl. (Col. Lecturas de Bogotá; 3)

Util en cuanto aporta datos sobre la vida y la obra de Torres Caicedo y reproduce el libro *Unión Latinoamericana* (1865), de este autor. Sobre el tema véase la obra de Arturo Ardao en *HLAS 44:7501*, que también contiene pasajes de las obras de Torres Caicedo.

5441 Valderrama Andrade, Carlos. Raíces españolas del pensamiento colombiano del siglo XIX al XX. (*Franciscanum/Bogotá*, 28:82, enero/abril 1986, p. 47–61)

La principal conclusión del trabajo es que sólo Balmes en el siglo XIX y Ortega y Gasset en el XX fueron influencias españolas importantes en la filosofía colombiana. Parte de la exposición se dedica al pensamiento español, en forma panorámica.

5442 Una visión de América: la obra de Germán Arciniegas desde la perspectiva de sus contemporáneos. Compilación y prólogo de Juan Gustavo Cobo Borda. Edición dirigida por Luis Fernando García Núñez. Bogotá: Instituto Caro y Cuervo, 1990. 454 p.: bibl., ill. (Serie La Granada entreabierta; 54)

Antología de textos sobre Germán Arciniegas y su obra. Son más de 50 artículos o notas de autores colombianos y extranjeros, siendo estos últimos la mayoría. También contiene una cronología de Arciniegas y una lista de los libros que publicó entre 1932–90. El prológo del compilador versa sobre la personalidad y la significación americanista de Arciniegas.

ECUADOR

5443 Coloquio Internacional sobre Juan Montalvo, *Ambato, Ecuador, 1988.* Ponencias y actas. Quito: Fundación Friedrich Naumann, 1989. 651 p.: bibl.

Reúne 26 trabajos sobre Montalvo y re-produce diálogos resultantes de la presentación de las ponencias. Los de mayor interés para esta sección son: Osvaldo Rivera, "Esquema del Pensamiento Filosófico de Montalvo;" Arturo A. Roig, "Eticidad, Conflictividad y Categorías Sociales en Juan Montalvo;" Diony Durán, "Juan Montalvo en la Orbita de la Latinidad;" Antonio Sacoto, "Montalvo y el Pensamiento Latinoamericano del Siglo XIX."

5444 Guerra Bravo, Samuel. La Iglesia en los siglos de coloniaje hispánico: el caso de la Presidencia de Quito. (*Rev. Hist. Am.*, 103, enero/junio, 1987, p. 107–129)

De los varios aspectos que trata, interesa a esta Sección la parte correspondiente a la Iglesia y la cultura.

5445 Paladines Escudero, Carlos. Ciencia y pensamiento moderno en la Audiencia de Quito. (*Cultura/Quito*, 8:24a, enero/abril 1986, p. 77–92)

El artículo expone la obra de Juan Magnin, *Milliet en armonía con Descartes, o Descartes reformado*, de mediados del siglo XVIII, a la cual el autor califica como "puerta de entrada del pensamiento ecuatoriano a la modernidad." La obra de Magnin sería una especie de "diálogo" de este último autor con el libro del jesuita Claudio Francisco Milliet de Chales, *Mundo matemático*, y con los *Principios de filosofía* de Descartes. De indudable valor para el conocimiento de la transición de la escolástica a la ciencia y la filosofía modernas en Quito.

5446 Paz, Juan J. and **Miño Cepeda.** Eloy Alfaro y el americanismo liberal. (*Islas/Santa Clara*, 83, enero/abril 1986, p. 69–96, bibl.)

Se relatan aspectos de la vida pública de Eloy Alfaro, dos veces Presidente de Ecuador (1895–1901 y 1906–11). Se destacan de Alfaro las medidas progresistas de índole liberal, en el contexto latinoamericano de las luchas entre liberales y conservadores. De interés lo referente a la idea (no llevada a la práctica) del Congreso Internacional de 1896, promovido por Alfaro, y su relación con la Doctrina Monroe.

5447 Pensamiento pedagógico ecuatoriano. Estudio introductorio y selección de Carlos Paladines Escudero. Quito: Banco Central del Ecuador; Corporación Editora Nacional, 1988. 527 p.: bibl., ill. (Biblioteca básica del pensamiento ecuatoriano; 33)

Obra antológica. Contiene documentos que van, en el tiempo, desde la Colonia hasta comienzos del siglo XX. Algunos de los autores incluidos son José Pérez Calama, Eugenio Espejo, Vicente Rocafuerte, Simón Rodríguez, Juan León Mera, Benigno Malo, Gabriel García Moreno y Francisco Javier Salazar. El estudio introductorio es muy orientador y de buena calidad. (Al comienzo incluye un resumen de los más recientes desarrollos de la historiografía de las ideas en Ecuador).

5448 *Revista de Historia de las Ideas.* No. 9, 1989- . Quito: Instituto Panamericano de Geografía e Historia; Editorial Casa de la Cultura Ecuatoriana.

Contiene varios artículos sobre el crítico y ensayista ecuatoriano Benjamín Carrión (1897–1979), de temática latinoamericanista y fundador de la Casa de la Cultura Ecuatoriana. Los artículos son los siguientes: Edmundo Ribadeneira, "Benjamín Carrión y los recuerdos;" Michael H. Handelsman, "Benjamín Carrión: Hombre de América;" Alejandro Moreano, "Benjamín Carrión: el desarrollo y la crisis del pensamiento democrático-nacional;" y Gustavo A. Serrano, "Benjamín Carrión."

5449 **Tinajero Villamar, Fernando.** De la evasión al desencanto. Quito: Editorial El Conejo, 1987. 115 p.: bibl. (Col. Ecuador/ letras)

Apretada pero útil síntesis de la cultura ecuatoriana, y especialmente de su literatura, en el último siglo.

Visión actual de José Peralta. See item **2693.**

PERU

5450 **García Jordán, Pilar.** Catolicismo frente al liberalismo: formación progresiva del nacionalcatolicismo peruano. (*Cristianismo Soc.*, 29:110, 1991, p. 71–87)

Buena síntesis de las relaciones entre el Estado y la Iglesia en Perú entre 1821–1919, en las diversas situaciones políticas y económicas del período. Muestra un proceso de secularización, pero a la vez la persistencia en considerar, por parte tanto de religiosos como de políticos, a la religión católica como factor determinante de la unidad de la nación peruana.

Gorriti, Gustavo. The war of the philosopher-king. See *HLAS 53:3888.*

5451 **Granados, Manuel Jesús.** El PCP Sendero Luminoso: aproximaciones a su ideología. (*Social. Particip.*, 37, marzo 1987, p. 15–35)

Señala las bases ideológicas marxistas (de corte maoísta) de Sendero Luminoso, pero también sus estrategias en relación con la realidad económico-social y racial de Perú. Expone lo que es conocido del llamado "Pensamiento Gonzalo," la más alta manifestación ideológica del movimiento. Sendero y la lucha contra él han agudizado la polarización de los extremos raciales y sociales de la población de Perú, según el autor. Véase reseña del politólogo en *HLAS 51:3782.*

5452 **Guibal, Francis** and **Alfonso Ibáñez I.** Mariátegui hoy. Lima: Tarea, 1987. 225 p.: bibl.

Contiene trabajos individuales de los dos autores. Algunos son artículos y otros reseñas críticas de obras sobre Mariátegui. Francis Guibal escribió la Primera Parte, "El Hombre y sus Circunstancias," como introducción general a los artículos más específicos que vienen después. El artículo "Un Marxismo Singular" reconoce los variados aspectos que caracterizan el marxismo de Mariátegui, sin el reduccionismo con que a veces se examina este tema.

5453 **Hampe Martínez, Teodoro.** La difusión de libros e ideas en el Perú colonial: análisis de bibliotecas particulares, siglo XVI. (*Bull. hisp./Bordeaux*, 89:1/4, 1987, p. 55–84)

Contiene información general sobre libros y bibliotecas en Hispanoamérica, y en el Perú en particular, durante el siglo XVI. Para el caso de Perú analiza el contenido de 14 colecciones particulares "que han sido examinadas y publicadas durante los últimos años." Los principales campos que se encuentran representados son derecho, religión y humanidades, con predominio numérico de la primera clase. Son de particular interés los datos bibliográficos que proporciona sobre el tema en general y la mención de los autores representados en las bibliotecas analizadas. Señala la ausencia de obras referentes a la realidad americana. Trabajo muy útil. Véase reseña del historiador en *HLAS 52:2154.*

5454 **Haya de la Torre, Víctor Raúl.** Haya de la Torre en *Cuadernos Americanos.* Edición y recopilación de Luis Alva Castro. Lima: Cambio y Desarrollo, Instituto de Investigaciones, 1990. 333 p.: bibl.

Reúne los artículos publicados por Haya de la Torre en la revista *Cuadernos Americanos*, de México, entre 1943–70. El interés radica en que reflejan los aspectos más teóricos o conceptuales del autor. Por ejemplo, hay muestras de la teoría del "espacio-tiempo histórico," y varios dedicados al análisis de la obra principal de Toynbee, *A study of history.* También es de interés el artículo "Sobre la Revolución Intelectual de Nuestro Siglo."

5455 Hovestadt, Volker. José Carlos Mariátegui und seine Zeitschrift *Amauta,* Lima, 1926–1930. Frankfurt am Main; New York: P. Lang, 1987. 261 p.: bibl. (Hispanistische Studien, 0170–8570; 19)

Aunque el tema central es la revista *Amauta,* publicada por Mariátegui durante 1926–30, el libro se ocupa también de la situación del Perú en la época, de la vida de Mariátegui y de su "socialismo indigenista."

5456 Iwaski Cauti, Fernando. El pensamiento de Pablo de Olavide y los ilustrados peruanos. (*Histórica/Lima,* 11:2, dic. 1987, p. 133–162, bibl.)

Es de particular interés en este artículo la comparación entre las propuestas de reforma de la Univ. de Sevilla por parte de Pablo de Olavide (1725–1803), con las de la Univ. de San Marcos y el Real Convictorio de San Carlos, así como con el plan de estudios de la Facultad de Medicina de San Fernando, en Lima. Olavide, representante del pensamiento ilustrado, nació en Perú, pero su mayor actuación tuvo lugar en España.

López, Sinesio *et al.* Pensamiento político peruano, 1930–1968. See item **2751.**

5457 López-Chau, Alfonso. El Hayamariateguismo. (*Social. Particip.,* 39, sept. 1987, p. 61–74)

De naturaleza polémica e inscrito en las discusiones internas de la izquierda peruana. Los autores cuyas afirmaciones se discuten son Aníbal Quijano, José Aricó y Flores Galindo. En el caso de Mariátegui encuentra que la etapa 1923–28 fue la más fecunda.

5458 López-Ocón Cabrera, Leoncio. La idea de la nacionalidad continental en el pensamiento político del peruano Francisco García Calderón. (*Rev. Indias,* 46:178, julio/dic. 1986, p. 643–649, bibl.)

Aunque breve y escrito sin mayor simpatía hacia el personaje estudiado, por no encontrar en él mayores elementos para reflexionar sobre "una cultura nacional y popular latinoamericana," el trabajo es útil por tratar un tema poco frecuentado y por las alusiones al clima intelectual de la época.

5459 Maihold, Günther. José Carlos Mariátegui: nationales Projekt und Indio-Problem, zur Entwicklung der indigenistischen Bewegung in Peru. Frankfurt am Main: Athenäum, 1988. 549 p.: bibl., maps. (Athenäums Monografien: Sozialwissenschaften; 28)

Caracteriza a esta obra una gran amplitud. No se limita al estudio de los textos de Mariátegui, sino que los sitúa en un amplio contexto: consideraciones sobre las relaciones entre Estado y nación; el problema del indio en Perú y los movimientos indigenistas (incluidas las versiones literarias); la relación entre Mariátegui y Haya de la Torre; y aun comparaciones entre Perú y México en lo referente al problema del indio. El autor señala que su propósito es captar al "Mariátegui histórico," evitando la interpretación ideologizada en función de conceptos actuales.

5460 Nieto, Jorge. El proceso de constitución de la doctrina aprista en el pensamiento de Haya de la Torre. Santiago: FLACSO, 1986. 110 leaves: bibl. (Serie Tesis)

Sigue el proceso de formación de la doctrina aprista en el pensamiento de Haya de la Torre, primero en su actuación política estudiantil hasta su destierro en 1923, y luego—etapa más importante—en el exilio (1923–26). Concluye con las polémicas de Haya con Mariátegui y con el comunista cubano Julio Antonio Mella, de los años 1926–28.

Vargas Llosa, Mario. Entre la libertad y el miedo. See *HLAS 53:3963.*

5461 Vila Bormey, María Teresa. El problema de la autenticidad y originalidad de la filosofía latinoamericana en el pensamiento de Augusto Salazar Bondy. (*Islas/Santa Clara,* 86, enero/abril 1987, p. 162–170, bibl.)

Como se reitera con frecuencia en la crítica filosófica que se realiza en Cuba en esta época, el marxismo-leninismo es el referente obligado para medir el valor de lo que se estudia. Así, la actitud de Salazar Bondy se considera loable por su preocupación social y su interés en una filosofía de la liberación, pero sus ideas sobre el hombre y el socialismo se estiman erróneas (igual que su "antisovietismo") y se califican como una expresión de "revisionismo."

BOLIVIA

5462 Arze, José Roberto. Fuentes para historia de las ideas en Bolivia en la primera mitad del siglo XX. La Paz: Univ. Mayor de San Andrés, Centro Nacional de Documentación Científica y Tecnológica, 1988. 36 p.

Util bibliografía, de más de 500 entradas. Sus principales temas son: liberalismo, positivismo y modernismo y sus respectivas crisis; nacionalismo, socialismo e indigenismo; y pensamiento más reciente. Dentro de estos grandes temas se incluyen los autores individuales. (Entre las omisiones deben señalarse las contribuciones de José Luis Gómez Martínez. Ver, por ejemplo, *HLAS 50: 4668–70*).

5463 Quince años de filosofía en Bolivia. (*Yachay/Cochabamba*, 9:15, 1992, p. 139–184)

Describe el contenido de los tesis que fueron presentadas en la Univ. Católica de Bolivia en el lapso 1977–91. La característica más notable de ellas es estar orientadas hacia la filosofía de la liberación, y más específicamente simpatizar con la posición de Enrique Dussel.

CHILE

5464 Avila Martel, Alamiro de et al. Estudios sobre José Victorino Lastarria. Presentación por Marino Pizarro Pizarro. Santiago: Ediciones de la Univ. de Chile, 1988. 306 p.: bibl., port.

Publicado con motivo del centenario de la muerte de Lastarria (1888). Alamiro de Avila Martel traza una semblanza de Lastarria, seguida de su bibliografía. Además, contiene: María Fuchslocher Arancibia, "Lastarria en la Universidad de Chile;" Javier Barrientos Grandón, "Lastarria y el Derecho;" Norman P. Sacks, "José Victorino Lastarria y Henry Thomas Buckle: el Positivismo, la Historia y España." Por último se reproduce el libro de Luis Oyarzún, *El pensamiento de Lastarria* (1953; ver *HLAS 46:7619* y *HLAS 50: 3077*).

5465 Fuentealba Hernández, Leonardo. La filosofía de la historia en Valentín Letelier. Santiago: Taller Gráfico de la Editora Universitaria, 1990. 75 p.: bibl.

Exposición clara de la filosofía de la historia desarrollada por Letelier (1852–1919)

en su libro *La evolución de la historia* (1900), dentro del clima del pensamiento positivista.

5466 Gazmuri, Cristián. El pensamiento político y social de Santiago Arcos. (*Historia/Santiago*, 21, 1986, p. 249–274, bibl.)

Aunque nacido en 1822 en Santiago (Chile), Arcos vivió largos años en Francia. Con el bagaje allí adquirido realizó su crítica a la sociedad chilena de la época, principalmente en los aspectos económico-sociales y políticos. En este artículo se estudian escritos de Arcos producidos durante 1850–52, que ilustran sobre aquella crítica y las soluciones que propuso. Entre esos escritos se cuenta su *Carta a Francisco Bilbao*. Se descarta la interpretación que se ha dado de Santiago Arcos como socialista utópico, no obstante su denuncia de las desigualdades sociales en Chile.

5467 Grünwald, Myraim Zemelman and Jaime Atabales Matus. El conflicto Iglesia-Estado en el pensamiento de Balmaceda. (*Rev. Chil. Humanid.*, 12, 1991, p. 63–77)

José Manuel Balmaceda fue presidente de Chile, 1886–91. Desde una posición inicial católica y tradicionalista, giró luego hacia una postura liberal, promoviendo por ejemplo la separación de la Iglesia y el Estado. Este giro es examinado en el artículo, y los autores lo explican por el "pragmatismo político" de Balmaceda.

5468 Guzmán Brito, Alejandro. Portales y el pensamiento de Montesquieu. (*Bol. Acad. Chil. Hist.*, 54:98, 1987, p. 69–76)

El tema es la posible lectura de Montesquieu por parte de Portales, pero sobre la base de sólo dos párrafos en el epistolario del político chileno (sobre Portales puede verse *HLAS 52:5398*).

5469 Jalif de Bertranou, Clara Alicia. Esbozo de una filosofía de la historia en Francisco Bilbao. (*Cuad. Am.*, 6:3, mayo/junio 1991, p. 34–51)

El artículo destaca principalmente dos aspectos: las propuestas de democracia "no delegada" o directa, de parte de Bilbao; y el hecho de que el discurso se mueve en un nivel de generalidad que desde el punto de vista práctico no excede la expresión de deseos.

5470 Scocozza, Antonio. Filosofía, política y derecho en Andrés Bello: orígenes de la historia de la cultura civil en Latinoamérica.

Traducción e introducción de Rafael di Prisco. Caracas: Casa de Bello, 1989. 269 p.: bibl., index. (Anexos a las obras completas de Andres Bello; 8)

Estudio de crítica filosófica, cuyo tema central es la *Filosofía del entendimiento*, de Bello; pero también se atiende a las influencias recibidas por Bello en la etapa londinense, a su filosofía moral y a su producción intelectual en Chile.

5471 Walker, John. Schopenhauer, Nietzsche y la tradición alemana en la obra de Eduardo Barrios. (*Ibero-Am. Arch.*, 13:3, 1987, p. 297–306, bibl.)

Se muestra la influencia de los filósofos alemanes mencionados en el título sobre la obra del novelista chileno Eduardo Barrios.

BRASIL

5472 Aiex, Anoar. Um estudo sobre Tobias Barreto. Rio de Janeiro: Presença, 1989. 66 p.: bibl. (Col. Atualidade crítica; 15)

Exposición muy general del pensamiento de Tobías Barreto.

5473 Aragão, R. Batista. Maçonaria no Ceará: raízes e evolução. Fortaleza-Ceará, Brazil: Impr. Oficial do Ceará, 1987. 219 p.: bibl.

Proporciona noticias sobre el movimiento masónico no sólo en Ceará, sino también en el resto de Brasil. Vincula el tema con la historia política del país desde el siglo XIX.

5474 Barreto, Tobias. Crítica política e social. Ed. comemorativa. Rio de Janeiro: Editora Record; Brasília: Instituto Nacional do Livro, Ministério da Cultura, 1990. 272 p. (Obras completas de Tobias Barreto)

Parte de las *Obras completas* de Tobias Barreto. Contiene una Introducción de Evaristo de Moraes Filho y, al final, dos trabajos críticos: "Tobias Barreto," por Brasil Bandechi, y "Tobias Barreto e a Teoria Política no Brasil," de Gláucio Veiga. La organización de la obra y las notas estuvieron a cargo de Luiz Antonio Barreto.

5475 Barreto, Tobias. Estudos de filosofia. Introdução e notas de Paulo Mercadante e Antônio Paim. Ed. comemorativa. Rio de Janeiro: Editora Record; Brasília: Instituto Nacional do Livro, Ministério da Cultura, 1990. 427 p.: bibl. (Obras completas de Tobias Barreto. Biblioteca da República)

Es parte de una nueva edición de las *Obras completas* de Tobias Barreto. El presente volumen reproduce los textos de Tobias Barreto reunidos en la edición preparada por Antônio Paim y Paulo Mercadante, de 1966. La introducción, de esos mismos autores, es ampliación de la que pusieron a la mencionada edición de 1966, pero la presente agrega una bibliografía de Luiz Antonio Barreto, muy completa, y al final, dos trabajos críticos: "A Trajetória Filosófica de Tobias Barreto," por Antonio Paim, y "Nota sobre a Noção de 'Monismo' em Tobias Barreto e na Escola do Recife," por Nelson Saldanha.

5476 Barretto, Vicente. Evolução do pensamento político brasileiro. Belo Horizonte, Brazil: Editora Itatiaia; São Paulo: Editora da Univ. de São Paulo, 1989. 463 p.: bibl. (Col. Reconquista do Brasil; 2a sér., vol. 150)

Contiene los siguientes estudios: Vicente Barretto, "Primórdios e Ciclo Imperial do Liberalismo;" Antônio Paim, "As Instituções Imperiales," "Liberalismo, Autoritarismo e Conservadorismo na República Velha," "O Socialismo," "A Opção Totalitaria" y "Correntes e Temas Políticos Contemporâneos;" Ricardo Vélez Rodríguez, "A Propaganda Republicana" y "O Travalhismo Após 30;" Francisco Martins de Souza, "O Integralismo;" Reynaldo Barros, "A Formação do Pessedismo e do Indenismo no Ciclo de Reconstitucionalização de pós-Guerra."

5477 Castro, Therezinha de. Hipólito da Costa: idéias e ideais. 2a. ed. rev. e ampliada. Rio de Janeiro: Biblioteca do Exército Editora, 1985. 112 p.: bibl. (Publicação; 540: Col. General Benício; 227)

Hipólito da Costa (1774–1823) publicó, desde Londres y en 1808–22, el mensuario *Correio Brasiliense*, que contibuyó al clima de Independencia y a la difusión del liberalismo económico. Este libro es una exposición de la vida de Hipólito da Costa y su acción mediante la mencionada publicación.

5478 Collichio, Therezinha Alves Ferreira. Miranda Azevedo e o darwinismo no Brasil. Belo Horizonte, Brazil: Editora Itatiaia; São Paulo: Editora da Univ. de São Paulo, 1988. 167 p.: bibl. (Col. Reconquista do Brasil; 2a. série, vol. 120)

Obra importante y de muy buena información sobre la recepción y el tratamiento del darwinismo en Brasil. Presenta la divulgación realizada por Augusto Cezar de Miranda Azevedo (1851–1907) hacia 1874–75; las ideas de los componentes de la "Escola de Recife" (Sylvio Romero, Tobias Barreto, Fausto Cardoso, Graça Aranha, Tito Livio de Castro, Estelita Tapajós, etc.); y las de los "darwinistas independientes:" Guedes Cabral, José de Araújo Ribeiro y Carlos von Koseritz, entre otros. Excelente bibliografía.

5479 Guimarães, Aquiles Côrtes. A prática da filosofia no Estado Novo. (*Rev. Bras. Filos.*, 37:151, julho/agosto/set. 1988, p. 225–232)

Con un juicio nada favorable a varios de los filósofos que se relacionaron de alguna manera con el régimen de Getúlio Vargas, comenta los casos de Alceu Amoroso Lima, Jackson de Figueiredo, Farias Brito, Azevedo Amaral y Leonel Franca.

5480 Konder, Leandro. A derrota da dialética: a recepção das idéias de Marx no Brasil, até o começo dos anos trinta. Rio de Janeiro: Editora Campus, 1988. 222 p.: bibl.

Ilustra sobre la escasa asimilación y poco conocimiento directo de las ideas de Marx en Brasil, aun después de fundado el Partido Comunista Brasileño en la década del 20. Son de interés también la exposición de las manifestaciones anarquistas y ciertos datos comparativos sobre el socialismo de la misma época.

5481 Krauze, Enrique. José Guilherme Merquior: el esgrimista liberal. (*Vuelta/ México*, 16:182, enero 1992, p. 38–41, ill.)

Clara e inteligente semblanza de José Guilherme Merquior, especialmente en lo que se refiere a su combate por las ideas liberales. Merquior fue un intelectual brasileño de este siglo, de ingente obra sobre el pensamiento actual.

5482 Lara, Tiago Adão. Tradicionalismo católico em Pernambuco. Recife, Brazil: Fundação Joaquim Nabuco, Editora Massangana, 1988. 161 p.: bibl. (Série Estudos e pesquisas; 53)

Monografía bien elaborada sobre el pensamiento tradicionalista católico en Pernambuco, según éste se expresa en lo social, lo religioso y lo político. Algunos de los autores tomados en cuenta son: Pedro Autran da Mata Albuquerque, Aprígio da Silva Guimarães, Braz Florentino Henriques de Souza, Antonio Rangel Torres Bandeira y José Soriano de Souza.

5483 Matta, Roberto da. A originalidade de Gilberto Freyre. (*ANPOCS BIB*, 24, 1987, p. 3–10, bibl.)

Destaca en Freyre su método "ensayístico." Por esta característica habría hablado del Brasil tal como es, evitando señalar normativamente lo que le falta o pudo ser, como, según el autor, es el caso de Nina Rodríguez, Oliveira Vianna y Darcy Ribeiro. También apuntó más a lo familiar, lo cotidiano e informal que al Estado y las instituciones.

5484 Novais, Fernando A. *et al.* Inteligência brasileira. Organição de Reginaldo C. Moraes, Ricardo L.C. Antunes e Vera Lúcia Botta Ferrante. São Paulo: Brasiliense, 1986. 305 p.: bibl.

Contiene artículos sobre Caio Prado Jr.; Plínio Salgado; Gilberto Freyre; Anísio Texeira; Cruz Costa ("Cruz Costa e a História das Idéias no Brasil"); Florestán Fernandes; Celso Furtado; y Darcy Ribeiro. También sobre la *Revista Brasiliense*; la izquierda brasileña; el ISEB (Instituto Superio de Estudos Brasileiros, que representó el desarrollismo nacionalista de la década del 50 de este siglo; ver *HLAS 44:7619*); las Fuerzas Armadas; y las ciencias sociales en América Latina.

5485 Paim, Antônio and Marta Sueli Dias Santos. Bibliografia filosófica brasileira: período contemporâneo 1931/1980. Salvador, Brazil: Centro de Documentação do Pensamento Brasileiro, 1987. 123 p.

Esta misma bibliografía, pero cubriendo solamente hasta 1977, apareció en 1979 (ver *HLAS 42:7591*). Ahora se presenta extendida hasta 1980, organizada por temas exclusivamente (la anterior estaba dividida por temas dentro de cada año). El autor destaca como uno de los mayores progresos durante 1931–80, el mayor número—y calidad—de las traducciones de textos de historia de la filosofía.

5486 Pinto, Celi Regina J. Positivismo: um projeto político alternativo; RS, 1889–1930. Porto Alegre, Brazil: L & PM Editores, 1986. 111 p.: bibl. (Col. Univ. livre)

El objetivo del trabajo es seguir la trayectoria del Partido Republicano Riograndense entre 1889 y 1930, es decir, durante el período de la llamada "República Velha." La autora afirma que el proyecto político de este partido no era liberal, sino positivista. Aunque el libro se dedica principalmente a la historia política propiamente dicha, en las conclusiones finales muestra la función de la doctrina de Comte en los principios y formulaciones del partido (ver también *HLAS 50: 4687*).

5487 Rodrigo, Lidia Maria. O nacionalismo no pensamento filosófico: aventuras e desventuras da filosofia no Brasil. Petrópolis, Brazil: Vozes, 1988. 133 p.: bibl.

El tema principal es el análisis de la obra de Alvaro Vieira Pinto, *Consciência e realidade nacional* (1960). Dicho análisis se lleva a cabo en el contexto del pensamiento nacional-desarrollista de la década de los 50 en Brasil, del cual fue expresión el Instituto Superior de Estudios Brasileiros (ISEB). Uno de los principales problemas estudiados es el de las relaciones entre filosofía, ideología y praxis (ver item **5489**).

5488 Rodrigues, José Carlos. Idéias filosóficas e políticas em Minas Gerais no século XIX. Belo Horizonte, Brazil: Editora Itatiaia; São Paulo: Editora da Univ. de São Paulo, 1986. 180 p.: bibl. (Col. Reconquista do Brasil; 2a. sér., vol. 97)

Tesis de doctorado. Utiliza, además de textos filosóficos, materiales periodísticos. Entre las corrientes consideradas se cuentan el "empirismo mitigado," el espiritualismo ecléctico y el positivismo, vinculando estas corrientes con los acontecimientos políticos de Minas Gerais. La presentación es de Antônio Paim.

5489 Roux, Jorge. Alvaro Vieira Pinto: nacionalismo e Terceiro Mundo. São Paulo: Cortez Editora, 1990. 301 p.: bibl. (Biblioteca da educação: Série 6, Filosofia; 3)

Que sepamos, es el trabajo más detallado sobre el pensamiento de Vieira Pinto, quien quiso dar fundamentación filosófica al desarrollismo nacionalista brasileño de los años 50 y 60 de este siglo. Vieira Pinto fue uno de los animadores del ISEB (Instituto Superior de Estudios Brasileiros), del cual se ocupa también este libro. Pero su propósito principal es exponer el contenido de *Consciência e realidade nacional* (1960), de Vieira Pinto, y ver esta obra no sólo como filosofía para Brasil sino para el Tercer Mundo en general.

5490 Santos, Sydney M.G. dos. O legado de Vicente Licínio Cardoso: as leis básicas da filosofia da arte. Rio de Janeiro: Editora UFRJ, 1986? 652 p.: bibl., ill.

Vicente Licínio Cardoso (1889–1931)

es autor de una *Filosofia da arte* (1918), de *Pensamentos brasileiros* (1924) y *Pensamentos americanos* (1937, póstumo). La presente obra es un extenso comentario a la vida y los escritos de V.L. Cardoso.

5491 Wolkmer, Antônio Carlos. Uma interpretação das idéias políticas no Brasil. (*Rev. Bras. Estud. Polít.*, 66, jan. 1988, p. 25–45)

Dibuja los principales rasgos de las formas que han asumido en Brasil el liberalismo, el anarquismo, el socialismo, el marxismo, el nacionalismo, el populismo y el autoritarismo. En algunos casos estos grandes movimientos se han desdoblado en varias manifestaciones. Una de las conclusiones del autor es que a partir de mediados del siglo XIX han sido predominantes, en forma alternada, el liberalismo conservador y el autoritarismo modernizante.

5492 Zilles, Urbano. Grandes tendências na filosofia do século XX e sua influência no Brasil. Caxias do Sul, Brazil: EDUCS, 1987. 148 p.: bibl.

Las grandes corrientes europeas consideradas son: neotomismo, neokantismo, neohegelianismo, marxismo y positivismo de Comte. Tras una exposición de cada una, sigue una breve descripción de la influencia que ejercieron en Brasil.

PARAGUAY

5493 Rodríguez Alcalá, Guido. Ideología autoritaria. Asunción: RP Ediciones, 1987. 139 p.: bibl.

Ensayo sobre las manifestaciones autocráticas de dictadores paraguayos como José Gaspar Rodríguez de Francia, Carlos López y Francisco López, en el siglo XIX. También examina otras del siglo XX relacionadas con concepciones europeas totalitarias.

URUGUAY

5494 Fernández Cabrelli, Alfonso. Iglesia y masonería en la reforma de la escuela uruguaya. (*Hoy Hist.*, 8:44, marzo/abril 1991, p. 44–58, photos)

Recoge numerosas manifestaciones de la prensa combativa de la época que ilustran sobre la polémica entre liberales y católicos en relación con el carácter laico o religioso de la enseñanza, especialmente en el decenio

1873–83. Muestra la eficaz participación de la masonería en favor de la escuela "laica, universal y gratuita."

Panizza, Francisco. El liberalismo y sus "otros:" la construcción del imaginario liberal en el Uruguay, 1850–1930. See *HLAS 53: 4222.*

Pareja, Carlos. Polifonía y jacobinismo en la política Uruguaya. See *HLAS 53:4223.*

5495 Real de Azúa, Carlos. Escritos. Selección y prólogo de Tulio Halperín Donghi. Montevideo: ARCA, 1987. 412 p.: bibl.
　　Antología del ensayista uruguayo Carlos Real de Azúa (1916–77), quien incursionó en la literatura, la historia y la política de su país y de América Latina, y fue autor de *El patriciado uruguayo,* entre otros escritos. El prólogo de Halperín Donghi es un largo comentario a la obra de este autor. Entre los artículos recogidos se encuentran: "Ambiente Espiritual del 900;" "Partidos Políticos y Literatura en el Uruguay;" y "Prólogo a *Ariel.*" También hay, al final, artículos sobre Real de Azúa por parte de Emir Rodríguez Monegal, Angel Rama, Lisa Block de Behar y Santiago Real de Azúa. No hay indicación de procedencia o fecha de los artículos ni de los comentarios críticos.

5496 Rodó, José Enrique. José Enrique Rodó. Edición e introducción de José Luis Abellán. Madrid: Instituto de Cooperación Iberoamericana; Ediciones de Cultura Hispánica, 1991. 126 p.: bibl. (Antología del pensamiento político, social y económico de América Latina; 14)
　　La parte antológica se nutre principalmente de *Ariel,* algunos textos de *El mirador de Próspero* y ensayos de Rodó sobre Rubén Darío. Valiosa introducción.

5497 Rodríguez Alcalá, Guido. En torno al *Ariel* de Rodó. Paraguay: RP Ediciones; Criterio Ediciones, 1990. 121 p.: bibl.
　　Visión muy negativa del pensamiento de Rodó. Parte de esa visión está basada en las ideas de la teoría de la dependencia, que sin embargo el autor en la advertencia dice ya no compartir. Obra más inclinada al juicio terminante fundado en opiniones sobre temas actuales, que a la comprensión histórica del personaje estudiado en su época.

Wiliman, Claudio. Las raíces cristianas en el pensamiento del Partido Nacional del Uruguay. See *HLAS 53:4250.*

5498 Zubillaga, Carlos. El pensamiento socialista en Uruguay: la reflexión precursora. Montevideo: Facultad de Humanidades y Ciencias, Depto. de Historia Universal, 1989. 67 p.: bibl. (Avances de investigación.)
　　Repasa la presencia, en la prensa periódica de Montevideo, aproximadamente entre 1830 y finales del siglo XIX, del saint-simonismo, la prédica de Lamennais, la enseñanza de Marcelino Pareja, el fourierismo, el eco despertado por la revolución de 1848, las resonancias de Proudhon y las primeras manifestaciones marxistas. Todo como antecedentes del socialismo.

ARGENTINA

5499 Alberdi, Juan Bautista. Estudios económicos de Juan Bautista Alberdi. Prólogos de Luis Víctor Anastasía y Alejandro Vegh Villegas. Montevideo: Fundación Prudencio Vázquez y Vega, 1989. 246 p.: bibl. (Pensamiento latinoamericano)
　　Reproducción parcial de escritos económicos de Alberdi que fueron parte de sus *Escritos póstumos* (1916). Se agrega a ellos, sin embargo, el "Discurso Pronunciado el Día de la Apertura del Salón Literario" (1837), y otro de 1880, "La Omnipotencia del Estado es la Negación de la Libertad Individual." Preceden a los textos dos extensos comentarios: "Juan Bautista Alberdi: Método Histórico y Reforma de la Economía, de la Educación y del Estado," de Luis Víctor Anastasía, y "El pensamiento económico de Alberdi," de Alejandro Vegh Villegas.

5500 Alvarez de Oro, José Alberto. La filosofía de Jorge Luis Borges. Córdoba, Argentina: Editorial de la Municipalidad de Córdoba, 1987. 101 p.: bibl.
　　La segunda parte del libro está destinada a comentar los aspectos de la obra de Borges que tienen relación con la filosofía. Lo hace desde dos perspectivas: los filósofos por los cuales se sintió particularmente atraído (Hume, Schopenhauer, Spinoza); y según temas: cosmología, teoría del conocimiento, ética, etc. (ver items **5503, 5507, 5509,** y **5536**).

5501 Alvarez Guerrero, Osvaldo. El radicalismo y la ética social: Irigoyen y el krausismo. Buenos Aires: Editorial Leviatán, 1986. 192 p.: bibl.
　　Tiene por temas: 1) la situación argen-

tina desde 1880; 2) el krausismo en Alemania y España; 3) la huella krausista en el pensamiento y la praxis política de Irigoyen (Presidente de Argentina, 1916–22, 1928–30). Sin ser un estudio monográfico, tiene su lugar en la bibliografía sobre un asunto no del todo definido ni fácil de definir. De hecho es también contribución a la historia del Partido Radical argentino.

Arana Cañedo-Argüelles, Juan. El centro del laberinto: los motivos filosóficos en la obra de Borges. See item **4196.**

5502 Beltrán, Juan Ramón et al. Freud en Buenos Aires, 1910–1939. Estudio preliminar y compilación de Hugo Vezzetti. Buenos Aires: Puntosur Editores, 1989. 301 p.: bibl. (La Ideología argentina)

Se trata de una verdadera aportación, porque saca a luz expresiones de la primera y variada recepción de Freud en Argentina (1910–39), poco conocida en general. El estudio preliminar examina esas expresiones, y la parte antológica reproduce los textos, hasta ahora dispersos. Ilustra sobre cómo Freud fue visto en ese período desde la profesión psiquiátrica, y también en tanto manifestación del pensamiento contemporáneo.

5503 Benavídez, Manuel. Borges y la metafísica. (*Cuad. Hispanoam.*, 505–507, julio/sept. 1992, p. 247–68)

Son considerados los filósofos y temas filosóficos (entre estos últimos, especialmente la metafísica) que están presentes en la obra de imaginación de Borges. Ensayo bien logrado. Al final hay una apreciación del libro de Serge Champeau, sobre el mismo tema (ver item **5507**).

5504 Cappelletti, Angel J. Alfredo Franceschi y los límites de la razón. (*Rev. Hist. Ideas*, Segunda Epoca:9, 1988, p. 139–155)

Clara y perceptiva exposición del pensamiento de Alfredo Franceschi, filósofo argentino fallecido en 1942. Dedicado a temas epistemológicos, Franceschi publicó su obra *Ensayo sobre la teoría del conocimiento* en 1925. Señala el racionalismo cauto de Franceschi, y el hecho de que en la concepción del hombre haya acogido aspectos vitales y existenciales.

5505 Caterina, Luis María. Organización e ideas del nacionalismo en Rosario, 1930–1946. (*Res Gesta*, 24, julio/dic. 1988, p. 37–51)

Aunque las manifestaciones nacionalistas que estudia son de menor nivel, tanto ideológico como de repercusión política, contribuye al conocimiento de un movimiento estudiado casi exclusivamente en sus expresiones en Buenos Aires.

5506 Caturelli, Alberto. Filosofía tomista, educación y teología en Fray Alberto García Vieyra, O.P., 1912–1985. (*Sapientia/Buenos Aires*, 42:164, 1987, p. 125–138)

Expone el pensamiento del dominico Alberto García Vieyra (1912–85), cuyos principales escritos tratan de teología y pedagogía. Desde una posición tradicionalista, Vieyra enjuició la secularización de la época, incluida la teología de la liberación. Contiene bibliografía detallada del autor estudiado.

5507 Champeau, Serge. Borges et la métaphysique. Paris: J. Vrin, 1990. 253 p.: bibl. (Essais d'art et de philosophie)

Más que un estudio de los aspectos filosóficos de Borges es una visión de esa obra en clave filosófica, o una "lectura filosófica de Borges," donde la metafísica juega un papel fundamental. El libro desafía el fácil resumen. Hay específicas referencias de confrontación entre Borges y Schopenhauer, Merleau-Ponty y Wittgenstein.

5508 Ciriza, Alejandra. Un esbozo de interpretación del pensamiento de Ezequiel Martínez Estrada. (*Rev. Hist. Am.*, 107, enero/junio 1989, p. 135–145)

Sigue brevemente la trayectoria ensayística de Martínez Estrada, desde *Radiografía de la pampa* (1933) hasta *Mi experiencia cubana* (1963), pasando por varias otras obras. Sostiene que el "discurso" de Martínez Estrada, a pesar de sus variantes a lo largo de ese período, expresa "la conflictividad social de la época." El ensayista argentino representaría el "discurso opresor," sólo mitigado, al final de su vida, por su posición en favor de la Revolución Cubana.

5509 Cordua, Carla. Borges y la metafísica. (*Torre/Río Piedras*, 2:8, oct./dic. 1988, p. 629–638)

De cómo Borges parte de conceptos metafísicos (o filosóficos en general) para convertirlos en imágenes literarias, de mayor plasticidad y sugerencia. Y de cómo separa conceptualmente filosofía y arte, y desconfía de la primera, a pesar de ser uno de los autores más "filosóficos." Ensayo inteligente y logrado.

5510 Díaz Araujo, Enrique. Deodoro Roca: reforma y radicalismo. (*Rev. Hist. Am. Argent.*, 14:27/28, 1987/1988, p. 127–170)

Sin proponerse un estudio biográfico de Deodoro Roca (líder de la Reforma Universitaria de Córdoba, Argentina, 1918), ni una historia de la Reforma, niega la afirmación de Gabriel del Mazo respecto de la estrecha relación entre el radicalismo (Partido Unión Cívica Radical) y la Reforma. Para ello procede a un análisis del Partido Radical de la Provincia de Córdoba en esa época (sobre Deodoro Roca véase también *HLAS 44:7610*).

5511 Dussel, Enrique. Una década argentina—1966-1976—y el origen de la "Filosofía de la Liberación." (*Reflexão/São Paulo*, 38, 1987, p. 20–50, appendix)

Los orígenes de la filosofía de la liberación en Argentina son situados en el contexto político de la época (1966–76). Buena parte del artículo es relato de la evolución del propio autor, en diálogo con sus críticos (especialmente Cerutti Guldberg).

Echeverría, Esteban. Obras escogidas. See item **3626.**

5512 Erro, Carlos Alberto. Qué somos los argentinos. Estudio preliminar de Matilde García Losada. Buenos Aires: Editorial Docencia; Proyecto CINAE, 1983. 107 p. (Col. Perspectivas; 12)

Carlos Alberto Erro (1903–68), ensayista argentino influido por el pensamiento existencialista (*Diálogo existencial*, 1937), fue también autor de escritos interpretativos de la realidad de su país. Este libro reproduce *Medida del criollismo* (1929, texto parcial); *Posibilidad y realidad de la vida argentina* (1937); y *Qué somos los argentinos* (1945). La autora del estudio preliminar, Matilde García Losada, se ha ocupado reiteradamente de Erro y aquí presenta al lector la trayectoria de este ensayista en lo que se refiere al tema argentino.

5513 Estado y sociedad en el pensamiento nacional: antología conceptual para el análisis comparado. Introducción y compilación de textos, Waldo Ansaldi y José Luis Moreno. Buenos Aires: Cántaro, 1989. 364 p.: bibl. (Col. de Estudios Socio-políticos; 3)

El tema que se proponen los compiladores es la relación "sociedad-Estado" en Argentina. Los artículos de índole más general son: Waldo Ansaldi, "Soñar con Rousseau y despertar con Hobbes: una introducción al estudio de la formación del Estado argentino;" Leopoldo Allub, "Estado y sociedad civil: patrón de emergencia y desarrollo del Estado argentino (1810–1930);" José Carlos Chiaramonte, "La cuestión regional en el proceso de gestación del Estado nacional argentino." Otros artículos se refieren a aspectos de economía, sociedad y Estado, y entre sus autores se encuentran Juan Carlos Portantiero y Tulio Halperín Donghi.

5514 Figallo, Beatriz J. Ramiro de Maeztu y la Argentina. (*Res Gesta*, 24, julio/dic. 1988, p. 73–92)

Util para conocer las actividades culturales y políticas de Ramiro de Maeztu en la Argentina como Embajador de Primo de Rivera (1928–30). La autora señala su vinculación con los nacionalistas argentinos y la revista católica *Criterio.*

5515 Flichman, Eduardo Héctor. Racionalidad y realismo según Mario Bunge. (*Rev. Latinoam. Filos.*, 14:2, julio 1988, p. 197–217)

Análisis crítico detallado de la obra de Mario Bunge, *Racionalidad y realismo* (1985).

5516 Forment Giralt, Eudaldo. La filosofía cristiana en América. (*Sapientia/Buenos Aires*, 43:169, julio/set. 1988, p. 277–298)

Después de señalar que en América Latina existe un vigoroso movimiento de filosofía cristiana, la mayor parte del artículo se destina a exponer las ideas de Alberto Caturelli y Octavio N. Derisi—filósofos católicos argentinos—sobre la Universidad.

5517 Forment Giralt, Eudaldo. Filosofía de Iberoamérica en Alberto Caturelli. (*Sapientia/Buenos Aires*, 47:186, oct./dic. 1992, p. 281–294)

Elogiosa exposición, desde un punto de vista cristiano-católico, de los escritos en los cuales el filósofo argentino Alberto Caturelli ha expuesto sus ideas sobre América y el Descubrimiento.

5518 Foster, David William. The Argentine generation of 1880: ideology and cultural texts. Columbia: Univ. of Missouri Press, 1990. 204 p.: bibl., index.

La característica principal del libro es que se propone una lectura de obras literarias considerándolas como manifestaciones ideológicas ("If we accept the axiom that all writing is an ideological statement . . . "). Desde ese supuesto se examinan textos escogidos de autores de la Generación del 80, como *Una excursión a los indios ranqueles*, de Lucio V. Mansilla; *Juvenilia*, de Miguel Cané; *La bolsa*, de Julián Martel; *¿Inocentes o culpables?*, de Antonio Argerich, y varios más.

5519 Guglielmino, Osvaldo. Americanismo y peronismo: expresión de una cultura libre. Buenos Aires: Ediciones Noticias Ilustradas, 1990. 314 p.: bibl.

Apología del peronismo como doctrina de liberación cultural frente a lo que el autor estima como la colonización del imperialismo. En ese sentido el peronismo sería válido para toda América Latina.

5520 Halperín Donghi, Tulio. La tradición republicana. (*Rev. Latinoam. Filos.*, 12: 2, julio, 1986, p. 199–211)

Extenso estudio evaluativo del libro de Natalio Botana, *La tradición republicana: Alberdi, Sarmiento y las ideas políticas de su tiempo* (1984).

5521 Jornadas del Pensamiento Filosófico Argentino, 2nd, Buenos Aires, 1985. Actas. Buenos Aires: Ediciones Fundación para el Estudio del Pensamiento Argentino e Iberoamericano, 1987. 115 p.: bibl.

Contiene, entre otros, los siguientes trabajos: Hugo Biagini, "Un Hallazgo Doctrinario: la Revista *La Filosofía Positiva*" (útil presentación de una revista de la cual aparecieron siete números en 1898 y que es un documento de interés para el estudio del positivismo argentino); Matilde I. García Lozada, "A Propósito de la Recepción de la Filosofía de la Existencia en la Argentina" (autores considerados: C. Astrada, M.A. Virasoro, V. Fatone, C.A. Erro y H. Guglielmini); Celina A. Lértora Mendoza, "El Movimiento Positivista Argentino y el Tema de la Mujer" (interesante trabajo sobre un tema poco frecuentado); Diego F. Pro, "América en la Filosofía" (afirma que la cultura americana es "cultura occidental americana o americanizada"). Hay también un artículo sobre la filosofía en Uruguay, por Carlos Mato Fernández.

5522 Lértora Mendoza, Celina A. Fuentes científicas europeas conocidas en el Río de la Plata colonial. (*in* Jornada de Historia del Pensamiento Científico Argentino, 3rd, Buenos Aires, 1987. Actas. Buenos Aires: Ediciones FEPAI, 1987, p. 157–166)

La autora ha analizado una serie de cursos manuscritos de enseñanza de la filosofía durante el siglo XVIII e informa, entre otras cosas, sobre los autores citados (científicos y divulgadores) y los temas tratados. Buen trabajo, orientador y basado en fuentes primarias.

5523 López Velasco, Sirio. Questionamentos *endógenos* à filosofia de Enrique Dussel. (*Veritas/Porto Alegre*, 32:127, set. 1987, p. 391–395)

Plantea una serie de preguntas críticas a las afirmaciones de Dussel, centradas en el tema del "Otro," asunto que considera como "figura central da sua ética-metafísica libertadora."

5524 Montenegro, Adelmo. Saúl Taborda. Buenos Aires: Ediciones Culturales Argentinas; Secretaría de Cultura, Ministerio de Educación y Justicia, 1984. 214 p. (Col. Ensayos)

Se trata de una antología de la obra de Saúl Taborda (1885–1944), pensador argentino que cultivó la pedagogía utilizando fuentes alemanas contemporáneas. El pensamiento político de Taborda se separa de la tradición liberal de su país y se basa en "una democracia federalista, cuya base esencial es la comuna." El ensayo preliminar es excelente como exposición de la obra de Taborda.

5525 Obieta, Adolfo de. Alberdi y la no violencia. Buenos Aires: Ediciones Nereo, 1984. 200 p.: bibl.

Ensayo sobre un aspecto no desconocido, pero sí menos tratado de la obra y el pensamiento de Alberdi. El tema principal es el libro (incompleto y póstumo) *El crimen de la guerra*; pero se estudian también antecedentes del mismo. Un capítulo se dedica a lo que en el mencionado libro puede haber de anticipo de la doctrina de la "no violencia," tal como se manifestó, por ejemplo, en Gandhi. Hay también un ensayo de conjunto sobre Alberdi y algunas páginas antológicas. Ensayo atendible.

5526 Orione, Julio and Fernando Rocchi. El darwinismo en la Argentina. (*Todo es Hist.*, 228, abril 1986, p. 8–28)

Util visión de conjunto sobre la recepción del darwinismo en la Argentina, tanto en el plano científico como en su aplicación a la interpretación de la sociedad (evolucionismo y progreso; razas y racismo).

5527 Peña Lillo, Arturo. Memorias de papel: los hombres y las ideas de una época. Buenos Aires: Editorial Galerna, 1988. 189 p.

Son de interés para esta sección los datos biográficos, intelectuales y de época sobre autores argentinos de tendencia nacionalista, dentro de la etapa 1940–70, aproximadamente. Entre ellos se cuentan: Ernesto Palacio, Luis Franco, Arturo Jauretche, Juan José Hernández Arregui y Raúl Scalabrini Ortiz.

5528 Prieto, Adolfo. Martínez Estrada, el interlocutor posible. (*Bol. Inst. Hist. Ravignani*, 3:1, 1989, p. 127–133)

El artículo, en realidad, trata del historiador argentino José Luis Romero. Los aspectos que destaca son: el aprovechamiento de materiales literarios en la obra de dicho historiador, y su apreciación de intelectuales y escritores que lograron amplias visiones de la historia mediante el género ensayístico. Ezequiel Martínez Estrada fue uno de esos intelectuales y, en ese sentido, un "interlocutor" de Romero, como también lo fue Eduardo Mallea. Buena contribución a la comprensión del estilo de historiador que fue Romero.

5529 Revista de Filosofía y Teoría Política. No. 26/27, 1986- . La Plata, Argentina: Depto. de Filosofía, Univ. Nacional de La Plata.

Parte del Quinto Congreso Nacional de Filosofía fue dedicado a la figura de Alejandro Korn. Artículos sobre este tema: Guillermo Cooper, "Alejandro Korn y el Positivismo" (sobre la apreciación que Korn tuvo del positivismo en la Argentina); William Kilgore, "La Posición de Alejandro Korn entre los Fundadores de la Filosofía Latinoamericana" (principalmente una comparación entre el pensamiento de Korn y el de George Herbert Mead); Norberto Rodríguez Bustamante, "Alejandro Korn: Pensamiento Filosófico y Militancia Política" (destaca el voluntarismo y el papel de la acción en el pensamiento de Korn); Diego F. Pro, "Metafísica y Axiología en Alejandro Korn" (ofrece consideraciones críticas a los conceptos fundamentales de Korn); Enrique L. Hernández, "Filosofía y Constitución del Estado: Consideraciones sobre las Nuevas Bases de Alejandro Korn" (sobre el contenido del artículo de Korn,

"Nuevas Bases," y la relación con Alberdi); Fernando Rovetta, "Notas sobre la Democracia a Partir de la *Libertad creadora* de Alejandro Korn" (sobre el concepto de libertad—económica y ética—en Korn y sus consecuencias para la idea de democracia).

5530 Rock, David. Intellectual precursors of conservative nationalism in Argentina, 1900–1927. (*HAHR*, 67:2, May 1987, p. 271–300)

Bien elaborada exposición de la primera etapa del nacionalismo argentino (aproximadamente las primeras tres décadas del siglo XX). Las principales figuras consideradas son el novelista Manuel Gálvez (ver *HLAS 52:5429*), Emilio Becher, Ricardo Rojas, Carlos Ibarguren y el poeta Leopoldo Lugones en la última etapa de su vida.

5531 Roig, Arturo Andrés. El *Facundo:* como anticipo de una teoría del discurso y de una semiótica. (*Rev. Hist. Ideas*, 9, 1988, p. 131–138)

Aunque respondiendo al romanticismo, el motivo básico del *Facundo* de Sarmiento sería no tanto el medio o el paisaje—con su determinación del ser humano que está situado en él -, como "la experiencia histórica de lo social, vivido y visto como conflictividad." Los símbolos y las oposiciones (tales como civilización-barbarie), y su manejo por parte de Sarmiento, serían anticipo de una semiótica y una teoría del discurso.

5532 Roig, Arturo Andrés. Tres décadas de "historia de las ideas" en Argentina: recuento y balance. (*Rev. Hist. Am.*, 109, enero/junio 1990, p. 145–160)

Excelente recuento de lo producido sobre filosofía y pensamiento argentino aproximadamente entre 1950–80, sin descuidar los principales trabajos anteriores a ese período. La posición del autor—que es uno de los protagonistas principales de la historiografía que reseña—consiste en utilizar la teoría del discurso para observar las formas en que la conflictividad social se manifiesta o se oculta.

5533 Romero, Francisco. Selección de escritos. Prólogo, bibliografía y notas de Juan Carlos Torchia Estrada. Buenos Aires, Secretaría de Cultura de la Nación; Editorial Marymar, 1994. 224 p. (Col. Identidad nacional; 89)

Antología de escritos del filósofo argentino Francisco Romero (1891–1962). Contiene extensos pasajes de su obra principal, *Teoría del hombre* (1952) y otros sobre temas como el concepto de filosofía, la historia de la filosofía, el conocimiento, la interpretación de la cultura occidental y la filosofía en América. El prólogo intenta dar una idea de conjunto de la obra y el significado de Francisco Romero.

5534 Ruibal, Juan. Anticlericalismo y religiosidad. (*Todo es Hist.*, 238, marzo 1987, p. 58–67, bibl., photo)
     Se analiza un período de la vida argentina que se extiende entre fines del siglo XIX y comienzos del XX. Reseña reacciones de la jerarquía eclesiástica y de los católicos en general en el orden de la acción social, de la educación y de los partidos políticos, todo ello frente a las tendencias secularizadoras de los gobiernos liberales de entonces, al fenómeno de la inmigración y a las ideas socialistas y anarquistas.

5535 Sarría, Gustavo. El socialismo saintsimoniano y Echeverría, Alberdi y Fragueiro. Córdoba, Argentina: G. Sarría, 1989. 190 p.: bibl.
     Se trata del material de un curso, "sin pretensión hermenéutica," según el propio autor. Se expone el pensamiento político de Saint-Simon y el de los discípulos que desarrollaron su escuela. Luego se persigue la presencia de esas doctrinas en Esteban Echevarría, Juan Bautista Alberdi y Mariano Fragueiro (1795–1872), este último mucho menos conocido (sobre Fragueiro ver *HLAS 38:9535*).

5536 Serna Arango, Julián. Borges y la filosofía. Pereira, Colombia: Editorial Gráficas Olímpica, 1990. 141 p.: bibl., ill. (Col. de escritores de Risaralda; 4)
     Mientras otros trabajos sobre las incursiones de Borges en el campo de la filosofía se organizan en función de los textos de ese autor, el presente libro parte de problemas filosóficos (por ejemplo, el tiempo, la libertad) y dentro de ellos, y entre otras opciones, incluye las manifestaciones de Borges.

5537 *Todo es Historia.* Vol. 23, No. 264, junio 1989- . Buenos Aires: s.n.
     Se trata de un número dedicado a las repercusiones de la Revolución Francesa en la Argentina. Artículos: Horacio Sanguinetti, "La Revolución Francesa y Mayo" (sobre la discusión de si en la revolución de independencia en el Río de la Plata [mayo 1810] predominó el pensamiento del jesuita Francisco Suárez o las ideas de Rousseau; se inclina por lo segundo); Noemí Goldman, "Los 'Jacobinos' en el Río de la Plata" (sobre Mariano Moreno, Juan José Castelli y Bernardo de Monteagudo, que podrían ser considerados "jacobinos" por su enfoque de la lucha revolucionaria"); Amanda Celotto, Silvia Finocchio y Gustavo Paz, "La Imagen de la Revolución Francesa en el Colegio Nacional de Buenos Aires, 1880–1910" (sobre programas y manuales de historia que incluían el tema de la Revolución); Félix Weinberg, "Esteban Echeverría y la Revolución Francesa" (sobre influencia de la Revolución y el pensamiento francés del siglo XIX en Echeverría); Hugo Biagini, "Francofilia y Contrarrevolución" (muestra de las experiencias que en la prensa y en obras escritas se manifestaron, en favor y en contra, sobre la Revolución Francesa, en el siglo XIX y comienzos del XX, en Argentina).

5538 Vigencia de Sarmiento. Buenos Aires: Comisión Permanente de Homenaje a Sarmiento, 1988. 255 p.: bibl.
     Publicado con motivo del primer centenario de la muerte de Sarmiento, este libro colectivo considera la figura del autor argentino desde distintos ángulos. Señalamos, en función de los propósitos de esta sección, el artículo de Adelmo Montenegro, "El Pensamiento Filosófico de Sarmiento."

5539 Zimmermann, Eduardo A. Racial ideas and social reform: Argentina, 1890–1916. (*HAHR*, 72:1, Feb. 1992, p. 23–46)
     Trabajo bien elaborado sobre el uso de conceptos raciales y su correspondiente lenguaje. Quiere mostrar que los prejuicios resultantes de aquellos conceptos no fueron solamente expresión aristocratizante de grupos nacionalistas, sino algo muy generalizado, y con la creencia de que se basaban en datos científicos. A esta luz, son considerados: intelectuales, ensayistas y filósofos; médicos y criminólogos; representantes de partidos políticos; y juicios emitidos sobre fenómenos como la inmigración, la higiene social, la condición de los obreros, el anarquismo y la eugenesia. Las ideas se estudian en sí mismas y en sus aplicaciones.

Zuleta Alvarez, Enrique. Santayana en Hispanoamérica. See item **5376.**

JOURNAL ABBREVIATIONS

Am. Lat./Moscow. América Latina. Academia de Ciencias de la Unión de Repúblicas Soviéticas Socialistas. Moscow.

ANPOCS BIB. Boletim Informativo e Bibliográfico de Ciências Sociais: BIB. Associação Nacional de Pós-Graduação e Pesquisa em Ciências Sociais. Rio de Janeiro.

Asclepio/Madrid. Asclepio: Archivo Iberoamericano de Historia de la Medicina y Antropología Médica. Consejo Superior de Investigaciones Científicas, Instituto Arnaú de Vilanova de Historia de la Medicina. Madrid.

Bol. Acad. Chil. Hist. Boletín de la Academia Chilena de la Historia. Santiago.

Bol. Acad. Nac. Hist./Caracas. Boletín de la Academia Nacional de la Historia. Caracas.

Bol. Inst. Hist. Ravignani. Boletín del Instituto de Historia Argentina y Americana Dr. Emilio Ravignani. Facultad de Filosofía y Letras, Univ. de Buenos Aires.

Bol. Lima. Boletín de Lima. Revista Cultural Científica. Lima.

Bull. hisp./Bordeaux. Bulletin hispanique. Univ. de Bordeaux; Centre national de la recherche scientifique. Bordeaux, France.

Can. J. Lat. Am. Caribb. Stud. Canadian Journal of Latin American and Caribbean Studies. Univ. of Ottawa. Ontario, Canada.

Caravelle/Toulouse. Caravelle. Cahiers du monde hispanique et luso-brésilien. Univ. de Toulouse, Institute d'études hispaniques, hispano-americaines et luso-brésiliennes. Toulouse, France.

Caribb. Q. Caribbean Quarterly. Univ. of the West Indies. Mona, Jamaica.

Cristianismo Soc. Cristianismo y Sociedad. Junta Latinoamericana de Iglesia y Sociedad. Montevideo.

Cuad. Am. Cuadernos Americanos. Editorial Cultura. México.

Cuad. Hispanoam. Cuadernos Hispanoamericanos. Instituto de Cultura Hispánica. Madrid.

Cuad. Hist. Cuadernos de Historia. Univ. de Chile, Facultad de Humanidades y Educación, Depto. de Ciencias Históricas. Santiago.

Cuba. Stud. Cuban Studies. Univ. of Pittsburgh, Center for Latin American Studies. Pittsburgh, Penn.

Cultura/Quito. Cultura. Banco Central del Ecuador. Quito.

Econ. Cienc. Soc. Economía y Ciencias Sociales. Facultad de Ciencias Económicas y Sociales, Univ. Central de Venezuela. Caracas.

Estud. Públicos. Estudios Públicos. Centro de Estudios Públicos. Santiago.

Folia Humaníst. Folia Humanística. Editorial Glarma. Barcelona, Spain.

Franciscanum/Bogotá. Franciscanum. Univ. de San Buenaventura. Bogotá.

HAHR. Hispanic American Historical Review. Conference on Latin American History of the American Historical Assn.; Duke Univ. Press. Durham, N.C.

Hist. Mex. Historia Mexicana. Colegio de México. México.

Historia/Santiago. Historia. Univ. Católica de Chile. Instituto de Historia. Santiago.

Histórica/Lima. Histórica. Pontificia Univ. Católica del Perú, Depto. de Humanidades. Lima.

Hoy Hist. Hoy es Historia: Revista Bimestral de Historia Nacional e Iberoamericana. Editorial Raíces. Montevideo.

Ibero-Am. Arch. Ibero-Amerikanisches Archiv. Ibero-Amerikanisches Institut. Berlin.

Integr. Latinoam. Integración Latinoamericana. Instituto para la Integración de América Latina. Buenos Aires.

Islas/Santa Clara. Islas. Univ. Central de Las Villas. Santa Clara, Cuba.

Jahrb. Gesch. Jahrbuch für Geschichte von Staat, Wirtschaft und Gesellschaft Lateinamerikas. Köln, Germany.

Lat. Am. Perspect. Latin American Perspectives. Univ. of California. Newbury Park, Calif.

Lat.am. Stud./Nürnberg. Lateinamerika Studien. Univ. Erlangen-Nürnberg, Sektion Lateinamerika. Nürnberg, Germany.

Lateinamerika/Hamburg. Lateinamerika. Institut für Iberoamerika-Kunde. Hamburg, Germany.

Linden Lane Mag. Linden Lane Magazine. Princeton, N.J.

Lotería/Panamá. Lotería. Lotería Nacional de Beneficencia. Panamá.

Lua Nova. Lua Nova. Editora Brasiliense. São Paulo.

Mass. Rev. The Massachusetts Review. Amherst College; Mount Holyoke College; Smith College; and the Univ. of Massachusetts. Amherst, Mass.

Mem. Acad. Mex. Hist. Memorias de la Academia Mexicana de la Historia. México.

Nueva Rev. Filol. Hisp. Nueva Revista de Filología Hispánica. El Colegio de México. México.

Nueva Soc. Nueva Sociedad. Caracas.

Reflexão/São Paulo. Reflexão. Pontifícia Univ. Católica de Campinas. São Paulo.

Relato Hechos Ideas. Relato de Hechos e Ideas. Editorial Relato SRL. Buenos Aires.

Res Gesta. Res Gesta. Instituto de Historia, Facultad de Derecho y Ciencias Sociales, Univ. Católica Argentina. Rosario, Argentina.

Rev. Bras. Estud. Polít. Revista Brasileira de Estudos Políticos. Univ. de Minas Gerais. Belo Horizonte, Brazil.

Rev. Bras. Filos. Revista Brasileira de Filosofia. Instituto Brasileiro de Filosofia. São Paulo.

Rev. Cancillería San Carlos. Revista Cancillería de San Carlos. Ministerio de Relaciones Exteriores. Bogotá.

Rev. Chil. Humanid. Revista Chilena de Humanidades. Facultad de Filosofía, Humanidades y Educación, Univ. de Chile. Santiago.

Rev. Cult. Lotería. Revista Cultural Lotería. Lotería Nacional de Beneficencia, Dirección de Desarrollo Social y Cultural, Depto. Cultural. Panamá.

Rev. Educ. Revista de Educación. Ministerio de Educación y Ciencia. Madrid.

Rev. Filos./México. Revista de Filosofía. Univ. Iberoamericana, Depto. de Filosofía; Asociación Fray Alonso de la Veracruz. México.

Rev. Filos. Teor. Polít. Revista de Filosofía y Teoría Política. Depto. de Filosofía, Univ. Nacional de La Plata. Argentina.

Rev. Hist. Am. Revista de Historia de América. Instituto Panamericano de Geografía e Historia, Comisión de Historia. México.

Rev. Hist. Am. Argent. Revista de Historia Americana y Argentina. Univ. Nacional de Cuyo, Instituto de Historia. Mendoza, Argentina.

Rev. Hist. Ideas. Revista de Historia de las Ideas. Instituto Panamericano de Geografía e Historia; Editorial Casa de la Cultura Ecuatoriana. Quito.

Rev. Indias. Revista de Indias. Consejo Superior de Investigaciones Científicas, Instituto Gonzalo Fernández de Oviedo. Madrid.

Rev. Inst. Cult. Puertorriq. Revista del Instituto de Cultura Puertorriqueña. San Juan.

Rev. Inst. Invest. Educ. Revista del Instituto de Investigaciones Educativas. Instituto de Investigaciones Educativas. Buenos Aires.

Rev. Latinoam. Filos. Revista Latinoamericana de Filosofía. Centro de Investigaciones Filosóficas. Buenos Aires.

Rev. Nac. Cult./Caracas. Revista Nacional de Cultura. Consejo Nacional de Cultura. Caracas.

Rev. Nac./Montevideo. Revista Nacional. Ministerio de Instrucción Pública. Montevideo.

Rev. Occident. Revista de Occidente. Madrid.

Rev. Parag. Sociol. Revista Paraguaya de Sociología. Centro Paraguayo de Estudios Sociológicos. Asunción.

Rev. Univ./Tabasco. Revista de la Universidad. Univ. Juárez Autónoma de Tabasco. Villahermosa, Mexico.

Santiago/Cuba. Santiago. Univ. de Oriente. Santiago, Cuba.

Sapientia/Buenos Aires. Sapientia. Facultad de Filosofía. Univ. Católica Argentina Santa María de los Buenos Aires. Buenos Aires.

SECOLAS Ann. SECOLAS Annals. Southeastern Conference on Latin American Studies; West Georgia College. Carrollton, Ga.

Social. Particip. Socialismo y Participación. Ediciones Socialismo y Participación. Lima.

Todo es Hist. Todo es Historia. Buenos Aires.

Torre/Río Piedras. La Torre. Univ. de Puerto Rico. Río Piedras.

Veritas/Porto Alegre. Veritas. Pontifícia Univ. Católica do Rio Grande do Sul. Porto Alegre, Brazil.

Vuelta/México. Vuelta. México.

Yachay/Cochabamba. Yachay. Facultad de Filosofía y Ciencias Religiosas, Univ. Católica Boliviana. Cochabamba, Bolivia.

Z. Miss. Relig. Zeitschrift für Missionswissenschaft und Religions- wissenschaft. Lucerne, Switzerland.

INDEXES

ABBREVIATIONS AND ACRONYMS

Except for journal abbreviations which are listed: 1) at the end of each major disciplinary section (e.g., Art, History, Literature, etc.); 2) after each journal title in the *Title List of Journals Indexed* (p. 785); and 3) in the *Abbreviation List of Journals Indexed* (p. 797).

ALADI	Asociación Latinoamericana de Integración
a.	annual
ABC	Argentina, Brazil, Chile
A.C.	antes de Cristo
ACAR	Associação de Crédito e Assistência Rural, Brazil
AD	Anno Domini
A.D.	Acción Democrática, Venezuela
ADESG	Associação dos Diplomados de Escola Superior de Guerra, Brazil
AGI	Archivo General de Indias, Sevilla
AGN	Archivo General de la Nación
AID	Agency for International Development
a.k.a.	also known as
Ala.	Alabama
ALALC	Asociación Latinoamericana de Libre Comercio
ALEC	*Atlas lingüístico etnográfico de Colombia*
ANAPO	Alianza Nacional Popular, Colombia
ANCARSE	Associação Nordestina de Crédito e Assistência Rural de Sergipe, Brazil
ANCOM	Andean Common Market
ANDI	Asociación Nacional de Industriales, Colombia
ANPOCS	Associação Nacional de Pós-Graduação e Pesquisa em Ciências Sociais, São Paulo
ANUC	Asociación Nacional de Usuarios Campesinos, Colombia
ANUIES	Asociación Nacional de Universidades e Institutos de Enseñanza Superior, Mexico
AP	Acción Popular
APRA	Alianza Popular Revolucionaria Americana, Peru
ARENA	Aliança Renovadora Nacional, Brazil
Ariz.	Arizona
Ark.	Arkansas
ASA	Association of Social Anthropologists of the Commonwealth, London
ASSEPLAN	Assessoria de Planejamento e Acompanhamento, Recife
Assn.	Association
Aufl.	Auflage (edition, edición)
AUFS	American Universities Field Staff Reports, Hanover, N.H.
Aug.	August, Augustan
aum.	aumentada
b.	born (nació)
B.A.R.	British Archaeological Reports
BBE	Bibliografia Brasileira de Educação
b.c.	indicates dates obtained by radiocarbon methods

BC	Before Christ
bibl(s).	bibliography(ies)
BID	Banco Interamericano de Desarrollo
BNDE	Banco Nacional de Desenvolvimento Econômico, Brazil
BNH	Banco Nacional de Habitação, Brazil
BP	before present
b/w	black and white
C14	Carbon 14
ca.	*circa* (about)
CACM	Central American Common Market
CADE	Conferencia Anual de Ejecutivos de Empresas, Peru
CAEM	Centro de Altos Estudios Militares, Peru
Calif.	California
Cap.	Capítulo
CARC	Centro de Arte y Comunicación, Buenos Aires
CARICOM	Caribbean Common Market
CARIFTA	Caribbean Free Trade Association
CBC	Christian base communities
CBD	central business district
CBI	Caribbean Basin Initiative
CD	Christian Democrats, Chile
CDI	Conselho de Desenvolvimento Industrial, Brasília
CEB	comunidades eclesiásticas de base
CEBRAP	Centro Brasileiro de Análise e Planejamento, São Paulo
CECORA	Centro de Cooperativas de la Reforma Agraria, Colombia
CEDAL	Centro de Estudios Democráticos de América Latina, Costa Rica
CEDE	Centro de Estudios sobre Desarrollo Económico, Univ. de los Andes, Bogotá
CEDEPLAR	Centro de Desenvolvimento e Planejamento Regional, Belo Horizonte
CEDES	Centro de Estudios de Estado y Sociedad, Buenos Aires; Centro de Estudos de Educação e Sociedade, São Paulo
CEDI	Centro Ecumênico de Documentos e Informação, São Paulo
CEDLA	Centro de Estudios y Documentación Latinoamericanos, Amsterdam
CEESTEM	Centro de Estudios Económicos y Sociales del Tercer Mundo, México
CELADE	Centro Latinoamericano de Demografía
CELADEC	Comisión Evangélica Latinoamericana de Educación Cristiana
CELAM	Consejo Episcopal Latinoamericano
CEMLA	Centro de Estudios Monetarios Latinoamericanos, Mexico
CENDES	Centro de Estudios del Desarrollo, Venezuela
CENIDIM	Centro Nacional de Información, Documentación e Investigación Musicales, Mexico
CENIET	Centro Nacional de Información y Estadísticas del Trabajo, Mexico
CEPADE	Centro Paraguayo de Estudios de Desarrollo Económico y Social
CEPA-SE	Comissão Estadual de Planejamento Agrícola, Sergipe
CEPAL	Comisión Económica para América Latina y el Caribe
CEPLAES	Centro de Planificación y Estudios Sociales, Quito
CERES	Centro de Estudios de la Realidad Económica y Social, Bolivia
CES	constant elasticity of substitution
cf.	compare
CFI	Consejo Federal de Inversiones, Buenos Aires
CGE	Confederación General Económica, Argentina
CGTP	Confederación General de Trabajadores del Perú
chap(s).	chapter(s)
CHEAR	Council on Higher Education in the American Republics
Cía.	Compañía
CIA	Central Intelligence Agency

CIDA	Comité Interamericano de Desarrollo Agrícola
CIDE	Centro de Investigación y Desarrollo de la Educación, Chile; Centro de Investigación y Docencias Económicas, Mexico
CIE	Centro de Investigaciones Económicas, Buenos Aires
CIEDLA	Centro Interdisciplinario de Estudios sobre el Desarrollo Latinoamericano, Buenos Aires
CIEDUR	Centro Interdisciplinario de Estudios sobre el Desarrollo Uruguay, Montevideo
CIEPLAN	Corporación de Investigaciones Económicas para América Latina, Santiago
CIESE	Centro de Investigaciones y Estudios Socioeconómicos, Quito
CIMI	Conselho Indigenista Missionário, Brazil
CINTERFOR	Centro Interamericano de Investigación y Documentación sobre Formación Profesional
CINVE	Centro de Investigaciones Económicas, Montevideo
CIP	Conselho Interministerial de Preços, Brazil
CIPCA	Centro de Investigación y Promoción del Campesinado, Bolivia
CIPEC	Consejo Intergubernamental de Países Exportadores de Cobre, Santiago
CLACSO	Consejo Latinoamericano de Ciencias Sociales, Secretaría Ejecutiva, Buenos Aires
CLASC	Confederación Latinoamericana Sindical Cristiana
CLE	Comunidad Latinoamericana de Escritores, Mexico
cm	centimeter
CNI	Confederação Nacional da Indústria, Brazil
CNPq	Conselho Nacional de Pesquisas, Brazil
Co.	Company
COB	Central Obrera Boliviana
COBAL	Companhia Brasileira de Alimentos
Col.	Collection, Colección, Coleção
col.	colored, coloured
Colo.	Colorado
COMCORDE	Comisión Coordinadora para el Desarrollo Económico, Uruguay
comp(s).	compiler(s), compilador(es)
CONCLAT	Congresso Nacional das Classes Trabalhadoras, Brazil
CONDESE	Conselho de Desenvolvimento Econômico de Sergipe
Conn.	Connecticut
COPEI	Comité Organizador Pro-Elecciones Independientes, Venezuela
CORFO	Corporación de Fomento de la Producción, Chile
CORP	Corporación para el Fomento de Investigaciones Económicas, Colombia
Corp.	Corporation, Corporación
corr.	corrected, corregida
CP	Communist Party
CPDOC	Centro de Pesquisa e Documentação, Brazil
CRIC	Consejo Regional Indígena del Cauca, Colombia
CSUTCB	Confederación Sindical Unica de Trabajadores Campesinos de Bolivia
CTM	Confederación de Trabajadores de México
CUNY	City University of New York
CUT	Central Unica de Trabajadores (Mexico); Central Unica dos Trabalhadores (Brazil); Central Unitaria de Trabajadores (Chile; Colombia); Confederación Unitaria de Trabajadores (Costa Rica)
CVG	Corporación Venezolana de Guayana
d.	died (murió)
DANE	Departamento Nacional de Estadística, Colombia
DC	developed country; Demócratas Cristianos, Chile
d.C.	después de Cristo
Dec./déc.	December, décembre
Del.	Delaware

dept.	department
depto.	departamento
DESCO	Centro de Estudios y Promoción del Desarrollo, Lima
Dez./dez.	Dezember, dezembro
dic.	diciembre, dicembre
disc.	discography
DNOCS	Departamento Nacional de Obras Contra as Secas, Brazil
doc.	document, documento
Dr.	Doctor
Dra.	Doctora
DRAE	*Diccionario de la Real Academia Española*
ECLAC	UN Economic Commision for Latin America and the Caribbean, New York and Santiago
ECOSOC	UN Economic and Social Council
ed./éd.(s)	edition(s), édition(s), edición(es), editor(s), redactor(es), director(es)
EDEME	Editora Emprendimentos Educacionais, Florianópolis
Edo.	Estado
EEC	European Economic Community
EE.UU.	Estados Unidos de América
EFTA	European Free Trade Association
e.g.	*exempio gratia* (for example, por ejemplo)
ELN	Ejército de Liberación Nacional, Colombia
ENDEF	Estudo Nacional da Despesa Familiar, Brazil
ESG	Escola Superior de Guerra, Brazil
estr.	estrenado
et al.	*et alia* (and others)
ETENE	Escritório Técnico de Estudos Econômicos do Nordeste, Brazil
ETEPE	Escritório Técnico de Planejamento, Brazil
EUDEBA	Editorial Universitaria de Buenos Aires
EWG	Europaische Wirtschaftsgemeinschaft. *See* EEC.
facsim(s).	facsimile(s)
FAO	Food and Agriculture Organization of the United Nations
FDR	Frente Democrático Revolucionario, El Salvador
FEB	Força Expedicionária Brasileira
Feb./feb.	February, Februar, febrero, febbraio
FEDECAFE	Federación Nacional de Cafeteros, Colombia
fev./fév.	fevereiro, février
ff.	following
FGTS	Fundo de Garantia do Tempo de Serviço, Brazil
FGV	Fundação Getúlio Vargas
FIEL	Fundación de Investigaciones Económicas Latinoamericanas, Argentina
film.	filmography
fl.	flourished
Fla.	Florida
FLACSO	Facultad Latinoamericana de Ciencias Sociales
FMI	Fondo Monetario Internacional
FMLN	Frente Farabundo Martí de Liberación Nacional, El Salvador
fold.	folded
fol(s).	folio(s)
FRG	Federal Republic of Germany
FSLN	Frente Sandinista de Liberación Nacional, Nicaragua
ft.	foot, feet
FUAR	Frente Unido de Acción Revolucionaria, Colombia
FUNAI	Fundação Nacional do Indio, Brazil
FUNARTE	Fundação Nacional de Arte, Brazil

FURN	Fundação Universidade Regional do Nordeste
Ga.	Georgia
GAO	General Accounting Office, Wahington
GATT	General Agreement on Tariffs and Trade
GDP	gross domestic product
GDR	German Democratic Republic
GEIDA	Grupo Executivo de Irrigação para o Desenvolvimento Agrícola, Brazil
gen.	gennaio
Gen.	General
GMT	Greenwich Mean Time
GPA	grade point average
GPO	Government Printing Office, Washington
h.	hijo
ha.	hectares, hectáreas
HLAS	*Handbook of Latin American Studies*
HMAI	*Handbook of Middle American Indians*
Hnos.	hermanos
HRAF	Human Relations Area Files, Human Relations Area Files, Inc., New Haven, Conn.
IBBD	Instituto Brasileiro de Bibliografia e Documentação
IBGE	Instituto Brasileiro de Geografia e Estatística, Rio de Janeiro
IBRD	International Bank for Reconstruction and Development (World Bank)
ICA	Instituto Colombiano Agropecuario
ICAIC	Instituto Cubano de Arte e Industria Cinematográfica
ICCE	Instituto Colombiano de Construcción Escolar
ICE	International Cultural Exchange
ICSS	Instituto Colombiano de Seguridad Social
ICT	Instituto de Crédito Territorial, Colombia
id.	*idem* (the same as previously mentioned or given)
IDB	Inter-American Development Bank
i.e.	*id est* (that is, o sea)
IEL	Instituto Euvaldo Lodi, Brazil
IEP	Instituto de Estudios Peruanos
IERAC	Instituto Ecuatoriano de Reforma Agraria y Colonización
IFAD	International Fund for Agricultural Development
IICA	Instituto Interamericano de Ciencias Agrícolas, San José
III	Instituto Indigenista Interamericana, Mexico
IIN	Instituto Indigenista Nacional, Guatemala
ILDIS	Instituto Latinoamericano de Investigaciones Sociales, Quito
ill.	illustration(s)
Ill.	Illinois
ILO	International Labour Organization, Geneva
IMES	Instituto Mexicano de Estudios Sociales
IMF	International Monetary Fund
Impr.	Imprenta, Imprimérie
in.	inches
INAH	Instituto Nacional de Antropología e Historia, Mexico
INBA	Instituto Nacional de Bellas Artes, Mexico
Inc.	Incorporated
INCORA	Instituto Colombiano de Reforma Agraria
Ind.	Indiana
INEP	Instituto Nacional de Estudios Pedagógicos, Brazil
INI	Instituto Nacional Indigenista, Mexico
INIT	Instituto Nacional de Industria Turística, Cuba
INPES/IPEA	Instituto de Planejamento Econômico e Social, Brazil

INTAL	Instituto para la Integración de América Latina
IPA	Instituto de Pastoral Andina, Univ. de San Antonio de Abad, Seminario de Antropología, Cusco, Peru
IPEA	Instituto de Pesquisa Econômica Aplicada, Brazil
IPES/GB	Instituto de Pesquisas e Estudos Sociais, Guanabara, Brazil
IPHAN	Instituto de Patrimônio Histórico e Artístico Nacional, Brazil
ir.	irregular
IS	Internacional Socialista
ITT	International Telephone and Telegraph
Jan./jan.	January, Januar, janeiro, janvier
JLP	Jamaican Labour Party
Jr.	Junior, Júnior
JUC	Juventude Universitária Católica, Brazil
JUCEPLAN	Junta Central de Planificación, Cuba
Kan.	Kansas
km	kilometers, kilómetros
Ky.	Kentucky
La.	Louisiana
LASA	Latin American Studies Association
LDC	less developed country(ies)
LP	long-playing record
Ltd(a).	Limited, Limitada
m	meters, metros
m.	murió (died)
M	mille, mil, thousand
M.A.	Master of Arts
MACLAS	Middle Atlantic Council of Latin American Studies
MAPU	Movimiento de Acción Popular Unitario, Chile
MARI	Middle American Research Institute, Tulane University, New Orleans
MAS	Movimiento al Socialismo, Venezuela
Mass.	Massachusetts
MCC	Mercado Común Centro-Americano
Md.	Maryland
MDB	Movimiento Democrático Brasileiro
MDC	more developed countries
Me.	Maine
MEC	Ministério de Educação e Cultura, Brazil
Mich.	Michigan
mimeo	mimeographed, mimeografiado
mimeo	mimeographed, mimeografiado
min.	minutes, minutos
Minn.	Minnesota
MIR	Movimiento de Izquierda Revolucionaria, Chile and Venezuela
Miss.	Mississippi
MIT	Massachusetts Institute of Technology
ml	milliliter
MLN	Movimiento de Liberación Nacional
mm.	millimeter
MNC	multinational corporation
MNI	minimum number of individuals
MNR	Movimiento Nacionalista Revolucionario, Bolivia
Mo.	Missouri
MOBRAL	Movimento Brasileiro de Alfabetização
MOIR	Movimiento Obrero Independiente y Revolucionario, Colombia
Mont.	Montana

MRL	Movimiento Revolucionario Liberal, Colombia
ms.	manuscript
M.S.	Master of Science
msl	mean sea level
n.	nació (born)
NBER	National Bureau of Economic Research, Cambridge, Massachusetts
N.C.	North Carolina
N.D.	North Dakota
NE	Northeast
Neb.	Nebraska
neubearb.	neubearbeitet (revised, corregida)
Nev.	Nevada
n.f.	neue Folge (new series)
N.H.	New Hampshire
NIEO	New International Economic Order
NIH	National Institutes of Health, Washington
N.J.	New Jersey
NJM	New Jewel Movement, Grenada
N.M.	New Mexico
no(s).	number(s), número(s)
NOEI	Nuevo Orden Económico Internacional
NOSALF	Scandinavian Committee for Research in Latin America
Nov./nov.	November, noviembre, novembre, novembro
NSF	National Science Foundation
NW	Northwest
N.Y.	New York
OAB	Ordem dos Advogados do Brasil
OAS	Organization of American States
Oct./oct.	October, octubre, octobre
ODEPLAN	Oficina de Planificación Nacional, Chile
OEA	Organización de los Estados Americanos
OIT	Organización Internacional del Trabajo
Okla.	Oklahoma
Okt.	Oktober
op.	opus
OPANAL	Organismo para la Proscripción de las Armas Nucleares en América Latina
OPEC	Organization of Petroleum Exporting Countries
OPEP	Organización de Países Exportadores de Petróleo
OPIC	Overseas Private Investment Corporation, Washington
Or.	Oregon
OREALC	Oficina Regional de Educación para América Latina y el Caribe
ORIT	Organización Regional Interamericana del Trabajo
ORSTOM	Office de la recherche scientifique et technique outre-mer (France)
ott.	ottobre
out.	outubro
p.	page(s)
Pa.	Pennsylvania
PAN	Partido Acción Nacional, Mexico
PC	Partido Comunista
PCCLAS	Pacific Coast Council on Latin American Studies
PCN	Partido de Conciliación Nacional, El Salvador
PCP	Partido Comunista del Perú
PCR	Partido Comunista Revolucionario, Chile and Argentina
PCV	Partido Comunista de Venezuela
PD	Partido Democrático

PDC	Partido Demócrata Cristiano, Chile
PDS	Partido Democrático Social, Brazil
PDT	Partido Democrático Trabalhista, Brazil
PDVSA	Petróleos de Venezuela S.A.
PEMEX	Petróleos Mexicanos
PETROBRAS	Petróleo Brasileiro
PIMES	Programa Integrado de Mestrado em Economia e Sociologia, Brazil
PIP	Partido Independiente de Puerto Rico
PLN	Partido Liberación Nacional, Costa Rica
PMDB	Partido do Movimento Democrático Brasileiro
PNAD	Pesquisa Nacional por Amostra Domiciliar, Brazil
PNC	People's National Congress, Guyana
PNM	People's National Movement, Trinidad and Tobago
PNP	People's National Party, Jamaica
pop.	population
port(s).	portrait(s)
PPP	purchasing power parities; People's Progressive Party of Guyana
PRD	Partido Revolucionario Dominicano
PREALC	Programa Regional del Empleo para América Latina y el Caribe, Organización Internacional del Trabajo, Santiago
PRI	Partido Revolucionario Institucional, Mexico
Prof.	Professor, Profesor(a)
PRONAPA	Programa Nacional de Pesquisas Arqueológicas, Brazil
prov.	province, provincia
PS	Partido Socialista, Chile
PSD	Partido Social Democrático, Brazil
pseud.	pseudonym, pseudónimo
PT	Partido dos Trabalhadores, Brazil
pt(s).	part(s), parte(s)
PTB	Partido Trabalhista Brasileiro
pub.	published, publisher
PUC	Pontifícia Universidade Católica
PURSC	Partido Unido de la Revolución Socialista de Cuba
q.	quarterly
rev.	revisada, revista, revised
R.I.	Rhode Island
s.a.	semiannual
SALALM	Seminar on the Acquisition of Latin American Library Materials
SATB	soprano, alto, tenor, bass
sd.	sound
s.d.	*sine datum* (no date, sin fecha)
S.D.	South Dakota
SDR	special drawing rights
SE	Southeast
SELA	Sistema Económico Latinoamericano
SENAC	Serviço Nacional de Aprendizagem Comercial, Rio de Janeiro
SENAI	Serviço Nacional de Aprendizagem Industrial, São Paulo
SEP	Secretaría de Educación Pública, Mexico
SEPLA	Seminario Permanente sobre Latinoamérica, Mexico
Sept./sept.	September, septiembre, septembre
SES	socioeconomic status
SESI	Serviço Social da Indústria, Brazil
set.	setembro, settembre
SI	Socialist International

SIECA	Secretaría Permanente del Tratado General de Integración Económica Centroamericana
SIL	Summer Institute of Linguistics (Instituto Lingüístico de Verano)
SINAMOS	Sistema Nacional de Apoyo a la Movilización
SINAMOS	Sistema Nacional de Apoyo a la Movilizaci Social, Peru
S.J.	Society of Jesus
s.l.	*sine loco* (place of publication unknown)
s.n.	*sine nomine* (publisher unknown)
SNA	Sociedad Nacional de Agricultura, Chile
SPP	Secretaría de Programación y Presupuesto, Mexico
SPVEA	Superintendência do Plano de Valorização Econômica da Amazônia, Brazil
sq.	square
SSRC	Social Sciences Research Council, New York
SUDAM	Superintendência de Desenvolvimento da Amazônia, Brazil
SUDENE	Superintendência de Desenvolvimento do Nordeste, Brazil
SUFRAME	Superintendência da Zona Franca de Manaus, Brazil
SUNY	State University of New York
SW	Southwest
t.	tomo(s), tome(s)
TAT	Thematic Apperception Test
TB	tuberculosis
Tenn.	Tennessee
Tex.	Texas
TG	transformational generative
TL	Thermoluminescent
TNE	Transnational enterprise
TNP	Tratado de No Proliferación
trans.	translator
UABC	Universidad Autónoma de Baja California
UCA	Universidad Centroamericana José Simeón Cañas, San Salvador
UCLA	University of California, Los Angeles
UDN	União Democrática Nacional, Brazil
UFG	Universidade Federal de Goiás
UFPb	Universidade Federal de Paraíba
UFSC	Universidade Federal de Santa Catarina
UK	United Kingdom
UN	United Nations
UNAM	Universidad Nacional Autónoma de México
UNCTAD	United Nations Conference on Trade and Development
UNDP	United Nations Development Programme
UNEAC	Unión de Escritores y Artistas de Cuba
UNESCO	United Nations Educational, Scientific and Cultural Organization
UNI/UNIND	União das Nações Indígenas
UNICEF	United Nations International Children's Emergency Fund
Univ(s).	university(ies), universidad(es), universidade(s), université(s), universität(s), universitá(s)
uniw.	uniwersytet (university)
Unltd.	Unlimited
UP	Unidad Popular, Chile
URD	Unidad Revolucionaria Democrática
URSS	Unión de Repúblicas Soviéticas Socialistas
US	United States
USAID	*See* AID.
USIA	United States Information Agency

USSR	Union of Soviet Socialist Republics
UTM	Universal Transverse Mercator
UWI	Univ. of the West Indies
v.	volume(s), volumen (volúmenes)
Va.	Virginia
V.I.	Virgin Islands
viz.	*videlicet* (that is, namely)
vol(s).	volume(s), volumen (volúmenes)
vs.	versus
Vt.	Vermont
W.Va.	West Virginia
Wash.	Washington
Wis.	Wisconsin
WPA	Working People's Alliance, Guyana
WWI	World War I
WWII	World War II
Wyo.	Wyoming
yr(s).	year(s)

TITLE LIST OF JOURNALS INDEXED

For journal titles listed by abbreviation, see *Abbreviation List of Journals Indexed* (p. 797).

ABI/INFORM. UMI/Data Courier. Louisville, Ky. (ABI/INFORM)

Academia: Boletín de la Real Academia de Bellas Artes de San Fernando. Madrid. (Academia/Madrid)

Actas Colombinas. Univ. de la Serena. Chile. (Actas Colomb.)

Afro-Hispanic Review. Univ. of Missouri-Columbia. Columbia, Missouri. (Afro-Hisp. Rev.)

Agricultural History. Agricultural History Society. Univ. of Calif. Press. Berkeley. (Agric. Hist.)

Aisthesis. Univ. Católica, Centro de Investigaciones Estéticas. Santiago. (Aisthesis/Santiago)

Alba de América. Instituto Literario y Cultural Hispánico. Westminster, Calif. (Alba Am.)

Allpanchis. Instituto de Pastoral Andina. Cusco, Peru. (Allpanchis/Cusco)

Alternativa. Centro de Estudios Sociales Solidaridad. Chiclayo, Peru. (Alternativa/Chiclayo)

Amazonía Peruana. Centro Amazónico de Antropología y Aplicación Práctica, Depto. de Documentación y Publicaciones. Lima. (Amazonía Peru.)

América Indígena. Instituto Indigenista Interamericano. México. (Am. Indíg.)

América Latina. Academia de Ciencias de la Unión de Repúblicas Soviéticas Socialistas. Moscow. (Am. Lat./Moscow)

American Anthropologist. American Anthropological Assn., Washington. (Am. Anthropol.)

American Antiquity. The Society for American Archaeology. Washington. (Am. Antiq.)

The American Historical Review. American Historical Assn., Washington. (Am. Hist. Rev.)

American Indian Quarterly. Southwestern American Indian Society; Fort Worth Museum of Science and History. Hurst, Tex. (Am. Indian Q.)

The Americas. Academy of American Franciscan History. Washington. (Americas/Francisc.)

Anales. Instituto Iberoamericano, Univ. de Gotemburgo. Göteborg, Sweden. (Anales/Göteborg)

Anales de Antropología. Univ. Nacional Autónoma de México, Instituto de Investigaciones Históricas. México. (An. Antropol.)

Anales de Arquitectura. Secretariado de Publicaciones de la Univ. de Valladolid. Valladolid, Spain. (An. Arquit.)

Anales del Encuentro Nacional y Regional de Historia. Junta Regional de Historia y Estudios Conexos. Montevideo. (An. Encuentro Nac. Reg. Hist.)

Anales del Instituto de Investigaciones Estéticas. Univ. Nacional Autónoma de México. México. (An. Inst. Invest. Estét.)

Anales del Museo Michoacano. Centro Regional Michoacán del INAH; Museo Regional Michoacano. Morelia, Mexico. (An. Mus. Michoacano)

Análise & Conjuntura. Fundação João Pinheiro. Belo Horizonte, Brazil. (Análise Conjunt.)

Análisis. Cuadernos de Investigación. Lima. (Análisis/Lima)

Análisis Político. Instituto de Estudios Políticos y Relaciones Internacionales, Univ. Nacional de Colombia. Bogotá. (Anál. Pol.)

Anaquel de Estudios Arabes. Univ. Complutense de Madrid, Depto. de Estudios Arabes e Islámicos. Madrid. (Anaquel Estud. Arab.)

Ancient Mesoamerica. Cambridge Univ. Press. Cambridge, England. (Anc. Mesoam.)

Annales. Centre national de la recherche scientifique de la VIe Section de l'Ecole pratique des hautes études. Paris. (Annales/Paris)

Anthropologica. Depto. de Ciencias Sociales,

Pontificia Univ. Católica del Perú. Lima.
(Anthropologica/Lima)
Anthropological Literature. Tozzer Library.
Cambridge, Mass. (Anthropol. Lit./Online)
Antropología Ecuatoriana. Casa de la Cultura
Ecuatoriana, Sección Académica de Antro-
pología y Arqueología. Quito. (Antropol.
Ecuat.)
Antropología Social. Instituto Nacional de
Antropología e Historia. México. (Antropol.
Soc.)
Antropologische Verkenningen. Coutinho.
Muiderberg, The Netherlands. (Anthropol.
Verkenn.)
Anuario. Univ. Nacional de Rosario, Escuela
de Historia. Argentina. (Anuario/Rosario)
Anuario de Estudios Americanos. Consejo
Superior de Investigaciones Científi-
cas; Univ. de Sevilla, Escuela de Estudios
Hispano-Americanos. Sevilla, Spain. (Anu.
Estud. Am.)
Anuario de Estudios Centroamericanos.
Univ. de Costa Rica. San José. (Anu. Estud.
Centroam.)
Anuario de Historia de la Iglesia en Chile.
Seminario Pontificio Mayor. Santiago.
(Anu. Hist. Iglesia Chile)
Anuario del Departmento de Historia. Depto.
de Historia, Univ. Complutense de Madrid.
(Anu. Dep. Hist./Madrid)
Anuario IEHS. Univ. Nacional del Centro de
la Provincia de Buenos Aires, Instituto de
Estudios Histórico-Sociales. Tandil, Argen-
tina. (Anu. IEHS)
Apuntes. Univ. del Pacífico, Centro de Inves-
tigación. Lima. (Apuntes/Lima)
Apuntes Postmodernos: Una Revista Cubana
de Crítica Cultural, Social, Política y de los
Artes. Verbum, Inc. Miami, Fla. (Apunt.
Postmod.)
Archivo Español de Arte. Consejo Superior de
Investigaciones Científicas, Centro de Es-
tudios Históricos. Madrid. (Arch. Esp. Arte)
Archivo Ibero-Americano. Revista de Estu-
dios Históricos. Los Padres Franciscanos.
Madrid. (Arch. Ibero-Am.)
Archivum Historicum Societatis Iesu. Rome.
(Arch. Hist. Soc. Iesu)
Armitano Arte: Revista Venezolana de Cul-
tura. Ernest Armitano. Caracas. (Armitano
Arte)
Årstryck. Etnografiska Museum. Göteborg,
Sweden. (Årstryck/Göteborg)
Art: Revista da Escola de Música e Artes Cê-
nicas da UFBA. Escola de Música e Artes

Cênicas da UFBA. Salvador, Brazil. (Art
Rev./Salvador)
Article1st. OCLC Online Computer Library
Center. Dublin, Ohio. (Article1st/OCLC)
Asclepio: Archivo Iberoamericano de Historia
de la Medicina y Antropología Médica.
Consejo Superior de Investigaciones Cientí-
ficas, Instituto Arnaú de Vilanova de His-
toria de la Medicina. Madrid. (Asclepio/
Madrid)

Bibliografía Latinoamericana-Latin Ameri-
can Bibliography. Centro de Información
Científica y Humanística, Univ. Nacio-
nal Autónoma de México. México. (Bibl.
Latinoam./CD-ROM)
Boletim de Pesquisa da CEDEAM. Comissão
de Documentação e Estudos da Amazônia,
Univ. do Amazonas. Manaus, Brazil. (Bol.
Pesqui. CEDEAM)
Boletim do Museu Paraense Emílio Goeldi.
Nova série: antropologia. Conselho Na-
cional de Desenvolvimento Científico e
Tecnológico, Instituto Nacional de Pes-
quisas da Amazônia. Belém, Brazil. (Bol.
Mus. Para. Goeldi)
Boletim Informativo e Bibliográfico de Ciên-
cias Sociais: BIB. Associação Nacional de
Pós-Graduação e Pesquisa em Ciências
Sociais. Rio de Janeiro. (ANPOCS BIB)
Boletín Americanista. Univ. de Barcelona, Fa-
cultad de Geografía e Historia, Depto. de
Historia de América. Barcelona. (Bol. Am.)
Boletín Cultural y Bibliográfico. Banco de la
República; Biblioteca Luis-Angel Arango.
Bogotá. (Bol. Cult. Bibliogr.)
Boletín de Fuentes para la Historia Econó-
mica de México. Centro de Estudios Histó-
ricos, El Colegio de México. México. (Bol.
Fuentes Hist. Econ. Méx.)
Boletín de la Academia Chilena de Bellas
Artes. Instituto de Chile. Santiago. (Bol.
Acad. Chil. Bellas Artes)
Boletín de la Academia Chilena de la Histo-
ria. Santiago. (Bol. Acad. Chil. Hist.)
Boletín de la Academia Nacional de la Histo-
ria. Caracas. (Bol. Acad. Nac. Hist./Caracas)
Boletín de Lima. Revista Cultural Científica.
Lima. (Bol. Lima)
Boletín del Archivo Nacional. Editorial Aca-
demia. La Habana. (Bol. Arch. Nac./Cuba)
Boletín del Instituto de Historia Argentina y
Americana Dr. Emilio Ravignani. Facultad
de Filosofía y Letras, Univ. de Buenos Aires.
(Bol. Inst. Hist. Ravignani)

Boletín del Instituto Riva-Agüero. Pontificia Univ. Católica del Perú. Lima. (Bol. Inst. Riva-Agüero)
Boletín del Museo del Oro. Banco de la República. Bogotá. (Boletín/Bogotá)
Boletín del Museo e Instituto Camón Aznar. Museo e Instituto de Humanidades Camón Aznar. Zaragoza, Spain. (Bol. Mus. Inst. Camón Aznar)
Boletín Histórico del Ejército. Montevideo. (Bol. Hist. Ejérc.)
Boletín Nicaragüense de Bibliografía y Documentación. Biblioteca, Banco Central de Nicaragua. Managua. (Bol. Nicar. Bibliogr. Doc.)
Bulletin de l'Institut français d'études andines. Lima. (Bull. Inst. fr. étud. andin.)
Bulletin hispanique. Univ. de Bordeaux; Centre national de la recherche scientifique. Bordeaux, France. (Bull. hisp./Bordeaux)
Bulletin of Latin American Research. Society for Latin American Studies. Oxford, England. (Bull. Lat. Am. Res.)
Bulletin of the International Committee on Urgent Anthropological and Ethnological Research. International Union of Anthropological and Ethnological Sciences. Vienna. (Bull. Int. Anthropol. Ethnol.)

Cadernos Negros. São Paulo. (Cad. Negros)
Cahiers des Amériques latines. Paris. (Cah. Am. lat.)
Canadian Journal of History. Univ. of Saskatchewan. Saskatoon, Canada. (Can. J. Hist.)
Canadian Journal of Latin American and Caribbean Studies. Univ. of Ottawa. Ontario, Canada. (Can. J. Lat. Am. Caribb. Stud.)
Caravelle. Cahiers du monde hispanique et luso-brésilien. Univ. de Toulouse, Institute d'études hispaniques, hispano-americaines et luso-brésiliennes. Toulouse, France. (Caravelle/Toulouse)
Caribbean Quarterly. Univ. of the West Indies. Mona, Jamaica. (Caribb. Q.)
Caribbean Studies. Univ. of Puerto Rico, Institute of Caribbean Studies. Río Piedras. (Caribb. Stud.)
Caribena: cahiers d'études américanistes de la Caraïbe. Centre d'études et de recherches archéologiques (CERA). Martinique. (Caribena/Martinique)
Casa de las Américas. La Habana. (Casa Am.)
CD-DIS. United States Agency for International Development, Development Infor-

mation Services Clearinghouse. Arlington, Va. (CD-DIS/Arlington)
CD-ROM Directory. TFPL Publishing. London. (CD-ROM Dir.)
CD-ROMs in Print. Meckler. Westport, Conn. (CD-ROMs Print)
CDPress. CD-ROM de México. Xalapa, Mexico. (CDPress)
Centro de Estudios Puertorriqueños Bulletin. Hunter College, City University of New York. New York. (Cent. Estud. Puertorriq. Bull.)
Chasqui. Dept. of Modern Languages, College of William and Mary. Williamsburg, Va. (Chasqui/Williamsburg)
Chungará. Univ. del Norte, Depto. de Antropología. Arica, Chile. (Chungará/Arica)
Ciência e Cultura. Sociedade Brasileira para o Progresso da Ciência. São Paulo. (Ciênc. Cult.)
Ciência Hoje. Sociedade Brasileira para o Progresso da Ciência. Rio de Janeiro. (Ciênc. Hoje)
Clio. Univ. Autónoma de Sinaloa, Escuela de Historia. Culiacán, Mexico. (Clio/Sinaloa)
College and Research Libraries News. Assn. of College and Research Libraries. Chicago, Ill. (Coll. Res. Libr. News)
Colonial Latin American Historical Review. Spanish Colonial Research Center, Univ. of New Mexico. Albuquerque. (CLAHR/Albuquerque)
Colonial Latin American Review. Simon H. Rifkind Center for the Humanities, Dept. of Romance Languages, City College of New York. New York. (Colon. Lat. Am. Rev.)
Comparative Civilizations Review. Dept. of History, Dickinson College. Carlisle, Penn. (Comp. Civiliz. Rev.)
Comparative Studies in Society and History. Society for the Comparative Study of Society and History; Cambridge Univ. Press. London. (Comp. Stud. Soc. Hist.)
Conjonction. Bulletin de l'Institut français d'Haïti. Port-au-Prince. (Conjonction/Port-au-Prince)
Conjunto. Revista de Teatro Latinoamericano. Comité Permanente de Festivales; Casa de las Américas. La Habana. (Conjunto/Habana)
Creación: Estética y Teoría de las Artes. Instituto de Estética y Teoría de las Artes. Madrid. (Creac. Estética Teor. Artes)
Cristianismo y Sociedad. Junta Latinoameri-

cana de Iglesia y Sociedad. Montevideo. (Cristianismo Soc.)

Criterios: Revista de Teoría Literaria, Estética y Culturología. Casa de las Américas. La Habana. (Criterios/Habana)

Cuadernos Académicos. Instituto Profesional del Maule. Talca, Chile. (Cuad. Acad.)

Cuadernos Americanos. Editorial Cultura. México. (Cuad. Am.)

Cuadernos Centroamericanos de Historia. Centro de Investigación de la Realidad de América Latina (CIRA). Managua. (Cuad. Centroam. Hist.)

Cuadernos de Arte Colonial. Museo de América; Ministerio de Cultura. Madrid. (Cuad. Arte Colon.)

Cuadernos de Historia. Univ. de Chile, Facultad de Humanidades y Educación, Depto. de Ciencias Históricas. Santiago. (Cuad. Hist.)

Cuadernos de Historia Moderna. Facultad de Geografía e Historia, Univ. Complutense de Madrid. (Cuad. Hist. Moderna)

Cuadernos de la Escuela Diplomática. Ministerio de Asuntos Exteriores. Madrid. (Cuad. Esc. Dipl.)

Cuadernos de Traducción e Interpretación = Quaderns de Traducció i Interpretació. Univ. Autónoma de Barcelona. Spain. (Cuad. Trad. Interp.)

Cuadernos del CENDES. Centro de Estudios del Desarrollo, Univ. Central de Venezuela. Caracas. (Cuad. CENDES)

Cuadernos Hispanoamericanos. Instituto de Cultura Hispánica. Madrid. (Cuad. Hispanoam.)

Cuban Studies. Univ. of Pittsburgh, Center for Latin American Studies. Pittsburgh, Penn. (Cuba. Stud.)

Cultura. Banco Central del Ecuador. Quito. (Cultura/Quito)

Cultura de Guatemala. Univ. Rafael Landívar. Guatemala. (Cult. Guatem.)

Dados. Instituto Univ. de Pesquisas. Rio de Janeiro. (Dados/Rio de Janeiro)

Data: Revista del Instituto de Estudios Andinos y Amazónicos. Instituto de Estudios Andinos y Amazónicos (INDEAA). La Paz. (Data/La Paz)

Database. Online, Inc., Weston, Conn. (Database/Weston)

Database Searcher. Meckler Pub., Westport, Conn. (Database Search.)

Dédalo. Univ. de São Paulo, Museu de Ar-

queologia e Etnologia. São Paulo. (Dédalo/São Paulo)

Del Caribe. Casa del Caribe. Santiago, Cuba. (Del Caribe)

Delphi en Español. Innovative Telematics. Miami Beach, Fla. (Delphi Esp./Online)

Desarrollo Económico. Instituto de Desarrollo Económico y Social. Buenos Aires. (Desarro. Econ.)

Dispositio. Dept. of Romance Languages, Univ. of Michigan. Ann Arbor. (Dispositio/Ann Arbor)

DLA Bulletin. Univ. of California, Division of Library Automation. Berkeley. (DLA Bull.)

Economía y Ciencias Sociales. Facultad de Ciencias Económicas y Sociales, Univ. Central de Venezuela. Caracas. (Econ. Cienc. Soc.)

Economic and Social History in the Netherlands. Nederlandsch Economisch-Historisch Archief. Amsterdam. (Econ. Soc. Hist. Neth.)

Edad de Oro. Depto. de Filología Española, Univ. Autónoma. Madrid. (Edad Oro)

Ensaios FEE. Secretaria de Coordenacão e Planejamento. Fundação de Economia e Estatística. Porto Alegre, Brazil. (Ensaios FEE)

Estudios. Instituto de Investigaciones Históricas, Antropológicas, y Arqueológicas, Univ. de San Carlos de Guatemala. Guatemala. (Estudios/Guatemala)

Estudios Centro-Americanos: ECA. Univ. Centroamericana José Simeón Cañas. San Salvador. (ECA/San Salvador)

Estudios de Ciencias y Letras. Instituto de Filosofía, Ciencias y Letras. Montevideo. (Estud. Cienc. Let.)

Estudios de Cultura Maya. Centro de Estudios Mayas, Univ. Nacional Autónoma de México. México. (Estud. Cult. Maya)

Estudios de Cultura Náhuatl. Instituto de Investigaciones Históricas, Univ. Nacional Autónoma de México. México. (Estud. Cult. Náhuatl)

Estudios de Historia Moderna y Contemporánea de México. Univ. Nacional Autónoma de México. México. (Estud. Hist. Mod. Contemp. Méx.)

Estudios de Historia Novohispana. Univ. Nacional Autónoma de México. México. (Estud. Hist. Novohisp.)

Estudios de Historia Social y Económica de América. Univ. de Alcalá de Henares. Madrid. (Estud. Hist. Soc. Econ. Am.)

Estudios Demográficos y Urbanos. El Colegio de México. México. (Estud. Demogr. Urb.)
Estudios Latinoamericanos. Academia de Ciencias de Polonia, Instituto de Historia. Wrocław. (Estud. Latinoam.)
Estudios Paraguayos. Univ. Católica Nuestra Señora de la Asunción. Asunción. (Estud. Parag.)
Estudios Públicos. Centro de Estudios Públicos. Santiago. (Estud. Públicos)
Estudios Sociales Centroamericanos. Programa Centroamericano de Ciencias Sociales. San José. (Estud. Soc. Centroam.)
Estudos Afro-Asiáticos. Centro de Estudos Afro-Asiáticos. Rio de Janeiro. (Estud. Afro-Asiát.)
Estudos Econômicos. Univ. de São Paulo, Instituto de Pesquisas Econômicas. São Paulo. (Estud. Econ./São Paulo)
Estudos Históricos. Associação de Pesquisa e Documentação Histórica. Rio de Janeiro. (Estud. Hist./Rio de Janeiro)
Estudos Ibero-Americanos. Pontifícia Univ. Católica do Rio Grande do Sul, Depto. de História. Porto Alegre, Brazil. (Estud. Ibero-Am./Porto Alegre)
Ethnohistory. American Society for Ethnohistory. Duke Univ., Durham, N.C. (Ethnohistory/Society)
Ethnology. Univ. of Pittsburgh, Penn. (Ethnology/Pittsburgh)
Etnía. Museo Etnográfico Municipal Dámaso Arce. Olavarría, Argentina. (Etnía/Olavarría)
Explicación de Textos Literarios. Dept. of Spanish and Portuguese, California State Univ., Sacramento. (Explic. Textos Lit.)

Face. Pontifícia Univ. Católica de São Paulo. (Face/São Paulo)
Fénix: Revista de la Biblioteca Nacional del Perú. Biblioteca Nacional. Lima. (Fénix/Lima)
Fiction. City College, CUNY. New York. (Fiction/New York)
Filología. Univ. de Buenos Aires, Facultad de Filosofía y Letras. Buenos Aires. (Filología/Buenos Aires)
El Financiero. CD-ROM de México. México. (Financiero/CD-ROM)
The Florida Historical Quarterly. The Florida Historical Society. Jacksonville, Fla. (Fla. Hist. Q.)
Folia Humanística. Editorial Glarma. Barcelona, Spain. (Folia Humaníst.)

Franciscanum. Univ. de San Buenaventura. Bogotá. (Franciscanum/Bogotá)
Fulltext Sources Online. Bibliodata. Needham Heights, Mass. (Fulltext Sources Online)

Gaceta. Instituto Colombiano de Cultura. Bogotá. (Gaceta/Bogotá)
Gale Directory of Databases. Gale Research. Detroit. (Gale Dir. Databases)
Généalogie et histoire de la Caraïbe. Assn. de la généalogie et histoire de la Caraïbe. Le Pecq, France. (Généal. hist. Caraïbe)
Geobase. Elsevier/Geo Abstracts. (Geobase/Online)
Gestos. Dept. of Spanish and Portuguese, Univ. of Calif., Irvine. (Gestos/Irvine)

Handbook of Latin American Studies. Hispanic Division, Library of Congress. Washington. (HLAS/Online)
HAPI Online. UCLA Latin American Center. Los Angeles. (HAPI Online)
HISLA. Centro Latinoamericano de Historia Económica y Social. Lima. (HISLA/Lima)
Hispamérica. Gaithersburg, Md. (Hispamérica/Gaithersburg)
Hispania. American Assn. of Teachers of Spanish and Portuguese; Mississippi State Univ., University, Miss. (Hispania/Teachers)
Hispania. Instituto Jerónimo Zurita, Consejo Superior de Investigaciones Científicas. Madrid. (Hispania/Madrid)
Hispania Sacra: Revista de Historia Eclesiástica de España. Centro de Estudios Históricos, Instituto Enrique Flórez. Madrid. (Hisp. Sacra)
Hispanic American Historical Review. Conference on Latin American History of the American Historical Assn.; Duke Univ. Press. Durham, N.C. (HAHR)
Hispanic Journal. Indiana Univ. of Pennsylvania, Dept. of Foreign Languages. Indiana, Penn. (Hisp. J.)
Hispanic Review. Univ. of Pennsylvania, Dept. of Romance Languages. Philadelphia, Penn. (Hisp. Rev.)
Hispanófila. Univ. of North Carolina. Chapel Hill, N.C. (Hispanófila/Chapel Hill)
Historia. Univ. Católica de Chile. Instituto de Historia. Santiago. (Historia/Santiago)
Historia & Perspectivas: Revista do Curso de Historia. Univ. Federal de Uberlândia. Uberlândia, Brazil. (Hist. Perspect.)
Historia Boliviana. Cochabamba, Bolivia. (Hist. Boliv.)

Historia Crítica. Univ. Nacional Autónoma de Honduras. Tegucigalpa. (Hist. Crít./ Tegucigalpa)

Historia Mexicana. Colegio de México. México. (Hist. Mex.)

Historia Paraguaya. Anuario de la Academia Paraguaya de la Historia. Asunción. (Hist. Parag.)

História, Questões e Debates. Associação Paranaense de História. Curitiba, Brazil. (Hist. Quest. Debates)

Historia Social. Centro de la UNED, Instituto de Historia Social. Valencia, Spain. (Hist. Soc./Valencia)

Historia y Cultura. Museo Nacional de Historia. Lima. (Hist. Cult./Lima)

Historia y Espacio: Revista de Estudios Históricos Regionales. Depto. de Historia, Univ. del Valle. Cali, Colombia. (Hist. Espac.)

Historia y Sociedad. Depto. de Historia, Univ. de Puerto Rico. Río Piedras. (Hist. Soc./Río Piedras)

The Historian. Phi Alpha Theta, National Honor Society in History; Univ. of Pennsylvania. Univ. Park, Penn. (Historian/Honor Society)

Histórica. Pontificia Univ. Católica del Perú, Depto. de Humanidades. Lima. (Histórica/ Lima)

Historiografía y Bibliografía Americanista. Escuela de Estudios Hispano-Americanos de Sevilla. Sevilla, Spain. (Historiogr. Bibliogr. Am.)

History and Anthropology. Harwood Academic Publishers. New York. (Hist. Anthropol.)

History Gazette. Univ. of Guyana, History Society. Turkeyen, Guyana. (Hist. Gaz.)

History of Religions. Univ. of Chicago. Chicago, Ill. (Hist. Relig.)

History Workshop. Ruskin College, Oxford Univ., Oxford, England. (Hist. Workshop)

Hómines. Univ. Interamericana de Puerto Rico. San Juan. (Hómines/San Juan)

L'Homme. Laboratoire d'anthropologie, Collège de France. Paris. (Homme/Paris)

Hora de poesía. Bruguera. Barcelona, Spain. (Hora Poesía)

Horizontes. Univ. Católica de Puerto Rico. Ponce. (Horizontes/Ponce)

Hoy es Historia: Revista Bimestral de Historia Nacional e Iberoamericana. Editorial Raíces. Montevideo. (Hoy Hist.)

Hua ch'iao hua jen li shih yen chiu [Studies on History of Overseas Chinese and Citizens of Chinese Origin]. China Institute of History of Overseas Chinese; China Society of History of Overseas Chinese. Beijing. (Hua ch'iao hua jen li shih yen chiu)

Ibero-Americana: Nordic Journal of Latin American Studies. Institute of Latin American Studies, Univ. of Stockholm. (Ibero-Am./Stockholm)

Ibero-Amerikanisches Archiv. Ibero-Amerikanisches Institut. Berlin. (Ibero-Am. Arch.)

Iberoromania. Max Niemeyer Verlag. Tübingen, Germany. (Iberoromania/Tübingen)

Index FBIS Daily Report. NewsBank/Readex. New Canaan, Conn. (Index FBIS Dly. Rep./ CD-ROM)

Index to Foreign Legal Periodicals. American Association of Law Libraries. Berkeley, Calif. (Index Foreign Leg. Period.)

INFO-SOUTH Latin American Information System. North-South Center, Univ. of Miami. Miami, Fla. (INFO-SOUTH/Online)

InfoMéxico. InfoSel. Monterrey, Mexico. (InfoMéxico/CD-ROM)

Information Today. Learned Information, Inc., Medford, N.J. (Inf. Today)

Integración Latinoamericana. Instituto para la Integración de América Latina. Buenos Aires. (Integr. Latinoam.)

Inter-American Music Review. Robert Stevenson. Los Angeles, Calif. (Inter-Am. Music Rev.)

International Migration = Migrations Internationales = Migraciones Internacionales. Intergovernmental Committee for European Migration; Research Group for European Migration Problems; International Organization for Migration. The Hague, Netherlands; Geneva, Switzerland. (Int. Migr.)

Inti: Revista de Literatura Hispánica. Providence College, R.I. (Inti/Providence)

IntlEc CD-ROM: the Index to International Economics, Development and Finance. Joint Bank-Fund Library. Washington. (IntlEc CD-ROM)

Investigaciones y Ensayos. Academia Nacional de la Historia. Buenos Aires. (Invest. Ens.)

Islas. Univ. Central de Las Villas. Santa Clara, Cuba. (Islas/Santa Clara)

Jahrbuch für Geschichte von Staat, Wirtschaft und Gesellschaft Lateinamerikas. Köln, Germany. (Jahrb. Gesch.)

Jamaica Journal. Institute of Jamaica. Kingston. (Jam. J.)

Journal of Caribbean History. Caribbean Univ. Press. St. Lawrence, Barbados. (J. Caribb. Hist.)

Journal of Church and State. J.M. Dawson Studies in Church and State, Baylor Univ., Waco, Tex. (J. Church State)

The Journal of Decorative and Propaganda Arts. Wolfson Foundation of Decorative and Propaganda Arts. Miami, Fla. (J. Decor. Propag. Arts)

The Journal of Economic History. Economic History Assn.; Univ. of Kansas. Lawrence. (J. Econ. Hist.)

The Journal of European Economic History. Banco di Roma. Rome. (J. Eur. Econ. Hist.)

Journal of Family History. National Council on Family Relations. Greenwich, Conn. (J. Fam. Hist.)

Journal of Hispanic Philology. Dept. of Modern Languages, Florida State Univ., Tallahassee, Fla. (J. Hisp. Philol.)

Journal of Interamerican Studies and World Affairs. Institute of Interamerican Studies, Univ. of Miami. Coral Gables, Fla. (J. Interam. Stud. World Aff.)

The Journal of Interdisciplinary History. The MIT Press. Cambridge, Mass. (J. Interdiscip. Hist.)

Journal of Latin American Lore. Univ. of California, Latin American Center. Los Angeles, Calif. (J. Lat. Am. Lore)

Journal of Latin American Studies. Centers or Institutes of Latin American Studies at the Universities of Cambridge, Glasgow, Liverpool, London, and Oxford. Cambridge Univ. Press. London. (J. Lat. Am. Stud.)

The Journal of Negro History. Assn. for the Study of Negro Life and History. Washington. (J. Negro Hist.)

The Journal of Peasant Studies. Frank Cass & Co., London. (J. Peasant Stud.)

Journal of Social History. Carnegie Mellon Univ., Pittsburgh, Penn. (J. Soc. Hist.)

Journal of the Southwest. Southwest Center, Univ. of Arizona. Tucson. (J. Southwest)

Journal of the West. Manhattan, Kan. (J. West)

Kañína. Univ. de Costa Rica. San José. (Kañína/San José)

Language & Communication. Pergamon Press. New York. (Lang. Commun.)

Lateinamerika. Institut für Iberoamerika-Kunde. Hamburg, Germany. (Lateinamerika/Hamburg)

Lateinamerika Studien. Univ. Erlangen-Nürnberg, Sektion Lateinamerika. Nürnberg, Germany. (Lat.am. Stud./Nürnberg)

Latin America Data Base. Latin American Institute, Univ. of New Mexico. Albuquerque. (LADB/Online)

Latin American Art Magazine. Latin American Art Magazine Inc., Scottsdale, Ariz. (Lat. Am. Art Mag.)

Latin American Indian Literatures Journal. Geneva College. Beaver Falls, Penn. (Lat. Am. Indian Lit. J.)

Latin American Literary Review. Carnegie-Mellon Univ., Dept. of Modern Languages. Pittsburgh, Penn. (Lat. Am. Lit. Rev.)

Latin American Music Review. Univ. of Texas. Austin. (Lat. Am. Music Rev.)

Latin American Perspectives. Univ. of California. Newbury Park, Calif. (Lat. Am. Perspect.)

Latin American Research Review. Latin American Research Review Board. Univ. of New Mexico, Albuquerque, N.M. (LARR)

Latin American Studies. National Information Services Corporation. Baltimore, Md. (Lat. Am. Stud./NISC)

Latin American Taxation Data Base. International Bureau of Fiscal Documentation. Amsterdam. (Lat. Am. Tax. Data Base)

Latin American Theatre Review. Univ. of Kansas, Center of Latin American Studies. Lawrence, Kan. (Lat. Am. Theatre Rev.)

Latinoamerica. Edizioni Associate. Rome. (Latinoamerica/Rome)

Letras Cubanas. La Habana. (Let. Cuba.)

Libri. Munksgaard. Copenhagen. (Libri/Copenhagen)

LILACS. Centro Latino-Americano e do Caribe de Informação em Ciencias da Saude. São Paulo. (LILACS/CD-ROM)

Linden Lane Magazine. Princeton, N.J. (Linden Lane Mag.)

Link-up. On-Line Communications. Minneapolis, Minn. (Link-up/Minneapolis)

Literatura y Lingüística. Instituto Profesional de Estudios Superiores Blas Cañas. Santiago. (Lit. Lingüíst.)

Logos: Revista de Lingüística, Filosofía y Literatura. Facultad de Humanidades, Univ. de La Serena. La Serena, Chile. (Logos/Serena)

Lotería. Lotería Nacional de Beneficencia. Panamá. (Lotería/Panamá)

Lua Nova. Editora Brasiliense. São Paulo.
(Lua Nova)
Luso-Brazilian Review. Univ. of Wisconsin
Press. Madison, Wis. (Luso-Braz. Rev.)

Man. The Royal Anthropological Institute.
London. (Man/London)
Manoa: A Pacific Journal of International
Writing. Univ. of Hawaii Press. Honolulu.
(Manoa/Honolulu)
The Massachusetts Review. Amherst College;
Mount Holyoke College; Smith College;
and the Univ. of Massachusetts. Amherst,
Mass. (Mass. Rev.)
Memoria del Museo Nacional de Arte. Museo
Nacional de Arte. México. (Mem. Mus.
Nac. Arte)
Memorias de la Academia Mexicana de la
Historia. México. (Mem. Acad. Mex. Hist.)
Mercurio Peruano. Lima. (Merc. Peru.)
Mesoamérica. Centro de Investigaciones Re-
gionales de Mesoamérica. Antigua, Guate-
mala. (Mesoamérica/Antigua)
Mester. Univ. of California, Dept. of Spanish
and Portuguese. Los Angeles. (Mester/
UCLA)
Mexican Studies/Estudios Mexicanos. Univ.
of California, Berkeley. (Mex. Stud.)
Mexicon. K.-F. von Flemming. Berlin, Ger-
many. (Mexicon/Berlin)
Meyibó. Centro de Investigaciones Históri-
cas, Univ. Autónoma de Baja California. Ti-
juana, Mexico. (Meyibó/Tijuana)
Miscelánea Histórica Ecuatoriana: Revista de
Investigaciones Históricas de los Museos
del Banco Central del Ecuador. Museos del
Banco Central del Ecuador. Quito. (Misc.
Hist. Ecuat.)
Mitteilungen des Instituts für österreichische
Geschichtsforschung. Vienna. (Mitt. Inst.
österr. Gesch.forsch.)
Montalbán. Univ. Católica Andrés Bello, Fa-
cultad de Humanidades y Educación, Insti-
tutos Humanísticos de Investigación. Cara-
cas. (Montalbán/Caracas)
Monthly Review. New York. (Mon. Rev.)

National Geographic Magazine. National
Geographic Society. Washington. (Natl.
Geogr. Mag.)
National Trade Data Bank. U.S. Dept. of
Commerce, Economics and Statistics
Administration, Office of Business Analy-
sis. Washington. (Natl. Trade Data Bank)
Naval History. US Naval Institute. Annapolis,
Md. (Nav. Hist.)

The New Republic. Washington. (New
Repub.)
Nieuwe West-Indische Gids. Martinus Ni-
jhoff. The Hague. (Nieuwe West-Indische
Gids)
Nóesis. Univ. Autónoma de Ciudad Juárez.
Juárez, Mexico. (Nóesis/Juárez)
Noroeste de México. Centro Regional Sonora,
INAH. Hermosillo, Mexico. (Noroeste
Méx.)
Notícia Bibliográfica e Histórica. Depto. de
História, Pontifícia Univ. Católica de Cam-
pinas. Campinas, Brazil. (Not. Bibliogr.
Hist.)
Notimex. Agencia Mexicana de Noticias.
México. (Notimex/CD-ROM)
Novos Estudos CEBRAP. Centro Brasileiro de
Análise e Planejamento. São Paulo. (Novos
Estud. CEBRAP)
Nueva Revista de Filología Hispánica. El Co-
legio de México. México. (Nueva Rev. Filol.
Hisp.)
Nueva Sociedad. Caracas. (Nueva Soc.)
Nuevo Texto Crítico. Dept. of Spanish and
Portuguese. Stanford Univ., Palo Alto, Ca-
lif. (Nuevo Texto Crít.)

OCLC Online Union Catalog. OCLC Online
Computer Library Center. Dublin, Ohio.
(OCLC Online Union Cat.)
Online. Online, Inc., Weston, Conn. (Online/
Weston)
Op. Cit.: Boletín del Centro de Investiga-
ciones Históricas. Depto. de Historia, Fa-
cultad de Humanidades, Univ. de Puerto
Rico. Río Piedras. (Op. Cit./Río Piedras)

Pacific Historical Review. Univ. of California
Press. Los Angeles and Berkeley. (Pac. Hist.
Rev.)
La Palabra y el Hombre. Univ. Veracruzana.
Xalapa, Mexico. (Palabra Hombre)
Papeles de la Casa Chata. Centro de Investi-
gaciones y Estudios Superiores en Antro-
pología Social. México. (Pap. Casa Chata)
Past and Present. London. (Past Present)
PeaceNet. Institute for Global Communica-
tions. San Francisco, Calif. (PeaceNet)
Política y Sociedad. Univ. de San Carlos de
Guatemala, Instituto de Investigaciones
Políticas y Sociales. Guatemala. (Polít.
Soc./Guatemala)
Population. Institut national d'études démo-
graphiques. Paris. (Population/Paris)
Portuguese Studies. Dept. of Portuguese,
King's College. London. (Port. Stud.)

Príncipe de Viana. Institución Príncipe de Viana, Gobierno de Navarra. Pamplona, Spain. (Prínc. Viana)

PROMT. Predicasts. Foster City, Calif. (PROMT/Online)

Publicaciones del Instituto de Estudios Ibero-americanos. Instituto de Estudios Iberame-ricanos. Buenos Aires. (Publ. Inst. Estud. Iberoam.)

Punto y Coma. Univ. del Sagrado Corazón. Santurce, Puerto Rico. (Punto Coma)

Quaderni Storici. Facoltà di Economia e Commercio, Istituto de Storia e Sociologia. Ancona, Italy. (Quad. Stor.)

Quinto Centenario. Depto. de Historia de América, Univ. Complutense de Madrid. (Quinto Cent.)

Rábida. Patronato Provincial del V Centena-rio del Descubrimiento. Huelva, Spain. (Rábida/Huelva)

Race & Class. Institute of Race Relations; The Transnational Institute. London. (Race Cl.)

Radical History Review. Mid-Atlantic Radi-cal Historians' Organization. New York. (Radic. Hist. Rev.)

Reflexão. Pontifícia Univ. Católica de Campi-nas. São Paulo. (Reflexão/São Paulo)

Relaciones. El Colegio de Michoacán. Za-mora, Mexico. (Relaciones/Zamora)

Relato de Hechos e Ideas. Editorial Relato SRL. Buenos Aires. (Relato Hechos Ideas)

Renaissance Quarterly. Renaissance Society of America. New York. (Renaissance Q.)

Representations. Univ. of California Press. Berkeley. (Representations/Berkeley)

Res Gesta. Instituto de Historia, Facultad de Derecho y Ciencias Sociales, Univ. Cató-lica Argentina. Rosario, Argentina. (Res Gesta)

Reuter Textline. Reuters. London. (Reuter Textline)

Revista Agustiniana. Madrid. (Rev. Agust.)

Revista Andina. Centro Bartolomé de las Ca-sas. Cusco, Peru. (Rev. Andin.)

Revista Antioqueña de Economía y Desa-rrollo. Fundación para la Investigación y la Cultura. Medellín, Colombia. (Rev. Antioq. Econ. Desarro.)

Revista Brasileira de Estudos de População. Associação Brasileira de Estudos Popula-cionais. São Paulo. (Rev. Bras. Estud. Popul.)

Revista Brasileira de Estudos Políticos. Univ. de Minas Gerais. Belo Horizonte, Brazil. (Rev. Bras. Estud. Polít.)

Revista Brasileira de Filosofia. Instituto Brasi-leiro de Filosofia. São Paulo. (Rev. Bras. Filos.)

Revista Brasileira de História. Associação Na-cional dos Professores Universitários de História (ANPUH). São Paulo. (Rev. Bras. Hist.)

Revista Canadiense de Estudios Hispánicos. Asociación Canadiense de Hispanistas; Univ. of Toronto. Toronto, Canada. (Rev. Can. Estud. Hisp.)

Revista Cancillería de San Carlos. Ministerio de Relaciones Exteriores. Bogotá. (Rev. Cancillería San Carlos)

Revista Chilena de Humanidades. Facultad de Filosofía, Humanidades y Educación, Univ. de Chile. Santiago. (Rev. Chil. Humanid.)

Revista Ciclos en la Historia, Economía y la Sociedad. Fundación de Investigaciones Históricas, Económicas y Sociales, Facultad de Ciencias Económicas, Univ. de Buenos Aires. Buenos Aires. (Rev. Ciclos)

Revista Colombiana de Antropología. Minis-terio de Educación Nacional, Instituto Co-lombiano de Antropología. Bogotá. (Rev. Colomb. Antropol.)

Revista Complutense de Historia de América. Facultad de Geografía e Historia, Univ. Complutense de Madrid. (Rev. Complut. Hist. Am.)

Revista Cubana de Ciencias Sociales. Centro de Estudios Filosóficos, Academia de Cien-cias de Cuba. La Habana. (Rev. Cuba. Cienc. Soc.)

Revista Cultural Lotería. Lotería Nacional de Beneficencia, Dirección de Desarrollo So-cial y Cultural, Depto. Cultural. Panamá. (Rev. Cult. Lotería)

Revista de Antropologia. Univ. de São Paulo, Faculdade de Filosofia, Letras e Ciências Humanas; Associação Brasileira de Antro-pologia. São Paulo. (Rev. Antropol./São Paulo)

Revista de Ciências Históricas. Univ. Portu-calense. Porto, Portugal. (Rev. Ciênc. Hist.)

Revista de Ciencias Sociales. Univ. de Puerto Rico, Colegio de Ciencias Sociales. Río Pie-dras. (Rev. Cienc. Soc./Río Piedras)

Revista de Crítica Literaria Latinoamericana. Latinoamericana Editores. Lima. (Rev. Crít. Lit. Latinoam.)

Revista de Educación. Ministerio de Educa-ción y Ciencia. Madrid. (Rev. Educ.)

Revista de Estudios Colombianos y Lati-noamericanos. Asociación de Colombianis-tas Norteamericanos; Tercer Mundo Edi-

tores. Boulder, Colo. (Rev. Estud. Colomb.
Latinoam.)
Revista de Estudios Hispánicos. Univ. de
Puerto Rico, Facultad de Humanidades. Río
Piedras. (Rev. Estud. Hisp./Río Piedras)
Revista de Estudios Hispánicos. Dept. of His-
panic Studies, Vassar College. Poughkeep-
sie, N.Y. (Rev. Estud. Hisp./Poughkeepsie)
Revista de Filosofía. Univ. de Costa Rica. San
José. (Rev. Filos./San José)
Revista de Filosofía. Univ. Iberoamericana,
Depto. de Filosofía; Asociación Fray Alonso
de la Veracruz. México. (Rev. Filos./México)
Revista de Filosofía y Teoría Política. Depto.
de Filosofía, Univ. Nacional de La Plata. Ar-
gentina. (Rev. Filos. Teor. Polít.)
Revista de História. Univ. de São Paulo, Fa-
culdade de Filosofia, Letras e Ciências Hu-
manas, Depto. de História. São Paulo. (Rev.
Hist./São Paulo)
Revista de Historia. Univ. Nacional de Costa
Rica, Escuela de Historia. Heredia, Costa
Rica. (Rev. Hist./Heredia)
Revista de Historia. Instituto de Historia de
Nicaragua. Managua. (Rev. Hist./Managua)
Revista de Historia. Depto. de Historia, Facul-
tad de Humanidades, Univ. Nacional de
Comahue. Neuquén, Argentina. (Rev.
Hist./Neuquén)
Revista de Historia. Centro de Investiga-
ciones Históricas, Univ. de Costa Rica. San
José. (Rev. Hist./San José)
Revista de Historia. Asociación Histórica
Puertorriqueña. San Juan. (Rev. Hist./San
Juan)
Revista de Historia Americana y Argentina.
Univ. Nacional de Cuyo, Instituto de Histo-
ria. Mendoza, Argentina. (Rev. Hist. Am.
Argent.)
Revista de Historia de América. Instituto
Panamericano de Geografía e Historia,
Comisión de Historia. México. (Rev. Hist.
Am.)
Revista de Historia de las Ideas. Instituto Pan-
americano de Geografía e Historia; Edito-
rial Casa de la Cultura Ecuatoriana. Quito.
(Rev. Hist. Ideas)
Revista de Historia Económica. Centro de Es-
tudios Constitucionales, Univ. Carlos III.
Madrid. (Rev. Hist. Econ.)
Revista de Historia Militar. Servicio Histó-
rico Militar. Madrid. (Rev. Hist. Mil.)
Revista de Historia Naval. Instituto de Histo-
ria y Cultura Naval Armada Española. Ma-
drid. (Rev. Hist. Naval)

Revista de Indias. Consejo Superior de Inves-
tigaciones Científicas, Instituto Gonzalo
Fernández de Oviedo. Madrid. (Rev. Indias)
Revista de la Academia Colombiana de Cien-
cias Exactas, Físicas y Naturales. Minis-
terio de Educación Nacional. Bogotá. (Rev.
Acad. Colomb. Cienc.)
Revista de la Biblioteca Nacional. Ministerio
de Educación y Cultura. Montevideo. (Rev.
Bibl. Nac./Montevideo)
Revista de la Biblioteca Nacional José Martí.
La Habana. (Rev. Bibl. Nac. José Martí)
Revista de la Junta Provincial de Historia de
Córdoba. Córdoba, Argentina. (Rev. Junta
Prov. Hist. Córdoba)
Revista de la Universidad. Univ. Juárez Au-
tónoma de Tabasco. Villahermosa, Mexico.
(Rev. Univ./Tabasco)
Revista de la Universidad de Alcalá. Univ.
de Alcalá de Henares. Alcalá de Henares,
Spain. (Rev. Univ./Alcalá)
Revista de Marina. La Armada de Chile. Val-
paraíso. (Rev. Mar.)
Revista de Occidente. Madrid. (Rev.
Occident.)
Revista del Archivo Nacional. San José, Costa
Rica. (Rev. Arch. Nac.)
Revista del Archivo Nacional de Historia,
Sección del Azuay. Casa de la Cultura Ecua-
toriana, Núcleo del Azuay. Cuenca, Ecua-
dor. (Rev. Arch. Nac. Hist. Azuay)
La Revista del Centro de Estudios Avanzados
de Puerto Rico y el Caribe. San Juan. (Rev.
Cent. Estud. Av.)
Revista del Departamento de Historia. Univ.
Nacional de Tucumán, Facultad de Filoso-
fía y Letras. Argentina. (Rev. Dep. Hist./
Tucumán)
Revista del Departamento de Historia del
Arte. Univ. de Sevilla. Spain. (Rev. Dep.
Hist. Arte)
Revista del Instituto de Cultura Puertorri-
queña. San Juan. (Rev. Inst. Cult.
Puertorriq.)
Revista del Instituto de Investigaciones Edu-
cativas. Instituto de Investigaciones Educa-
tivas. Buenos Aires. (Rev. Inst. Invest.
Educ.)
Revista del Instituto Superior de Música,
U.N.L. Santa Fe, Argentina. (Rev. Inst. Su-
per. Música)
Revista do Departamento de História. Univ.
Federal de Minas Gerais. Belo Horizonte,
Brazil. (Rev. Dep. Hist./Belo Horizonte)
Revista do Instituto de Estudos Brasileiros.

Univ. de São Paulo, Instituto de Estudos Brasileiros. São Paulo. (Rev. Inst. Estud. Bras.)

Revista do Instituto Histórico e Geográfico de São Paulo. São Paulo. (Rev. Inst. Hist. Geogr. São Paulo)

Revista Ecuatoriana de Historia Económica. Banco Central del Ecuador, Centro de Investigación y Cultura. Quito. (Rev. Ecuat. Hist. Econ.)

Revista Eme-Eme. Univ. Católica Madre y Maestra. Santiago de los Caballeros, Dominican Republic. (Rev. Eme-Eme)

Revista Española de Antropología Americana. Facultad de Geografía e Historia. Univ. Complutense de Madrid. (Rev. Esp. Antropol. Am.)

Revista Europea de Estudios Latinoamericanos y del Caribe = European Review of Latin American and Caribbean Studies. Center for Latin American Research and Documentation; Royal Institute of Linguistics and Anthropology. Amsterdam. (Rev. Eur.)

Revista Hispánica Moderna. Hispanic Institute, Columbia Univ. New York. (Rev. Hisp. Mod.)

Revista Iberoamericana. Instituto Internacional de Literatura Iberoamericana; Univ. de Pittsburgh. Pittsburgh, Penn. (Rev. Iberoam.)

Revista Interamericana de Bibliografía. Organization of American States. Washington. (Rev. Interam. Bibliogr.)

Revista Internacional de Estudios Vascos. Sociedad de Estudios Vascos. San Sebastián, Spain. (RIEV/San Sebastián)

Revista Jurídica de la Universidad de Puerto Rico. Escuela de Derecho, Univ. de Puerto Rico. Río Piedras. (Rev. Juríd. Univ. P.R.)

Revista Latinoamericana de Filosofía. Centro de Investigaciones Filosóficas. Buenos Aires. (Rev. Latinoam. Filos.)

Revista Mexicana de Ciencias Políticas y Sociales. Facultad de Ciencias Políticas y Sociales, Univ. Nacional Autónoma de México. México. (Rev. Mex. Cienc. Polít. Soc.)

Revista Musical Chilena. Univ. de Chile, Facultad de Ciencias y Artes Musicales y de la Representación. Santiago. (Rev. Music. Chil.)

Revista Musical Puertorriqueña. Instituto de Cultura Puertorriqueña. San Juan. (Rev. Music. Puertorriq.)

Revista Nacional. Ministerio de Instrucción Pública. Montevideo. (Rev. Nac./Montevideo)

Revista Nacional de Cultura. Consejo Nacional de Cultura. Caracas. (Rev. Nac. Cult./Caracas)

Revista Paraguaya de Sociología. Centro Paraguayo de Estudios Sociológicos. Asunción. (Rev. Parag. Sociol.)

Revista Paramillo. Centro de Estudios Interdisciplinarios, Univ. Católica de Táchira. San Cristóbal, Venezuela. (Rev. Paramillo)

Revista/Review Interamericana. Inter-American Univ. Press. Hato Rey, Puerto Rico. (Rev. Rev. Interam.)

Revista Tiempo y Espacio. Depto. de Historia y Geografía, Campus Chillán, Univ. del Bío-Bío. Chile. (Rev. Tiempo Espacio)

Revue de la Société haïtienne d'histoire et géographie. Port-au-Prince. (Rev. Soc. haïti.)

Revue française d'histoire d'Outre-mer. Société de l'histoire des colonies françaises. Paris. (Rev. fr. hist. Outre-mer)

Revue historique. Presses Univ. de France. Paris. (Rev. hist./Paris)

RLIN. Research Libraries Group. Mountain View, Calif. (RLIN/Online)

Romance Quarterly. Heldref Publications. Washington. (Roman. Q.)

Runa. Archivo para las Ciencias del Hombre; Univ. de Buenos Aires, Facultad de Filosofía y Letras, Instituto de Antropología. (Runa/Buenos Aires)

Santiago. Univ. de Oriente. Santiago, Cuba. (Santiago/Cuba)

Sapientia. Facultad de Filosofía. Univ. Católica Argentina Santa María de los Buenos Aires. Buenos Aires. (Sapientia/Buenos Aires)

SECOLAS Annals. Southeastern Conference on Latin American Studies; West Georgia College. Carrollton, Ga. (SECOLAS Ann.)

Secuencia. Instituto Mora. México. (Secuencia/México)

SICE: Foreign Trade Information System. General Secretariat, Organization of American States. Washington. (SICE/Online)

Siglo XIX. Facultad de Filosofía y Letras, Univ. Autónoma de Nuevo León. Monterrey, Mexico. (Siglo XIX)

Siglo XX. Twentieth Century Spanish Assn. of America. Lincoln, Neb. (Siglo XX)

Signos Universitarios: Revista de la Universidad del Salvador. Univ. del Salvador. Buenos Aires. (Signos Univ.)

Signs. The Univ. of Chicago Press. Chicago, Ill. (Signs/Chicago)

SINF. Dirección General de Información, Univ. Nacional Autónoma de México. México. (SINF/CD-ROM)

Síntese Nova Fase. Belo Horizonte, Brazil. (Sínt. Nova Fase)

Síntesis. Asociación de Investigación y Especialización sobre Temas Latinoamericanos. Madrid. (Síntesis/Madrid)

Slavery and Abolition. Frank Cass & Co., Ltd., London. (Slavery Abolit.)

Socialismo y Participación. Ediciones Socialismo y Participación. Lima. (Social. Particip.)

Studi Emigrazione. Centro Studi Emigrazione. Rome. (Stud. Emigr.)

Studia. Centro de Estudos Históricos Ultramarinos. Lisboa. (Studia/Lisboa)

Studies. Dublin. (Studies/Dublin)

Suplemento Antropológico. Univ. Católica de Nuestra Señora de la Asunción, Centro de Estudios Antropológicos. Asunción. (Supl. Antropol.)

SWI Forum voor Kunst, Kultuur en Wetenschop. De Stichting. Paramaribo, Suriname. (SWI Forum)

Taller de Letras. Instituto de Letras, Pontificia Univ. Católica de Chile. Santiago. (Taller Let.)

Thesaurus. Instituto Caro y Cuervo. Bogotá. (Thesaurus/Bogotá)

Todo es Historia. Buenos Aires. (Todo es Hist.)

La Torre. Univ. de Puerto Rico. Río Piedras. (Torre/Río Piedras)

Trace. Centre d'études mexicaines et centraméricaines. México. (Trace/México)

Transition. Institute of Development Studies, Univ. of Guyana. Georgetown, Guyana. (Transition/Guyana)

Translation Review. Univ. of Texas at Dallas. Richardson. (Transl. Rev.)

Travessia. Univ. Federal de Santa Catarina. Florianópolis, Brazil. (Travessia/Florianópolis)

Tri-Quarterly. Northwestern Univ., Evanston, Ill. (Tri-Quarterly/Evanston)

UnCover. The UnCover Co., Denver, Colo. (UnCover/Online)

Unión. Unión de Escritores y Artistas de Cuba. La Habana. (Unión/Habana)

La Universidad. Univ. Nacional del Litoral. Santa Fe, Argentina. (Universidad/Santa Fe)

Universidad de La Habana. La Habana. (Univ. La Habana)

UT-LANIC. Institute of Latin American Studies, Univ. of Texas. Austin. (UT-LANIC)

Veritas. Pontifícia Univ. Católica do Rio Grande do Sul. Porto Alegre, Brazil. (Veritas/Porto Alegre)

Vuelta. México. (Vuelta/México)

Wampum. Archeologisch Centrum. Leiden, The Netherlands. (Wampum/Leiden)

The Western Historical Quarterly. Western History Assn.; Utah State Univ., Logan, Utah. (West. Hist. Q.)

The William and Mary Quarterly. College of William and Mary. Williamsburg, Va. (William Mary Q.)

World Law Index, Part I: Index to Hispanic Legislation. Hispanic Law Division, Library of Congress. Washington. (World Law Index I)

Yachay. Facultad de Filosofía y Ciencias Religiosas, Univ. Católica Boliviana. Cochabamba, Bolivia. (Yachay/Cochabamba)

Yearbook. Conference of Latin Americanist Geographers; Ball State Univ., Muncie, Ind. (Yearbook/CLAG)

Zeitschrift für Lateinamerika Wien. Österreichisches Lateinamerika-Institut. Vienna. (Z. Lat.am. Wien)

Zeitschrift für Missionswissenschaft und Religions-wissenschaft. Lucerne, Switzerland. (Z. Miss. Relig.)

ABBREVIATION LIST
OF JOURNALS INDEXED

For journal titles listed by full title, see *Title List of Journals Indexed* (p. 785).

ABI/INFORM. ABI/INFORM. UMI/Data Courier. Louisville, Ky.

Academia/Madrid. Academia: Boletín de la Real Academia de Bellas Artes de San Fernando. Madrid.

Actas Colomb. Actas Colombinas. Univ. de la Serena. Chile.

Afro-Hisp. Rev. Afro-Hispanic Review. Univ. of Missouri-Columbia. Columbia, Missouri.

Agric. Hist. Agricultural History. Agricultural History Society. Univ. of Calif. Press. Berkeley.

Aisthesis/Santiago. Aisthesis. Univ. Católica, Centro de Investigaciones Estéticas. Santiago.

Alba Am. Alba de América. Instituto Literario y Cultural Hispánico. Westminster, Calif.

Allpanchis/Cusco. Allpanchis. Instituto de Pastoral Andina. Cusco, Peru.

Alternativa/Chiclayo. Alternativa. Centro de Estudios Sociales Solidaridad. Chiclayo, Peru.

Am. Anthropol. American Anthropologist. American Anthropological Assn., Washington.

Am. Antiq. American Antiquity. The Society for American Archaeology. Washington.

Am. Hist. Rev. The American Historical Review. American Historical Assn., Washington.

Am. Indian Q. American Indian Quarterly. Southwestern American Indian Society;

Fort Worth Museum of Science and History. Hurst, Tex.

Am. Indíg. América Indígena. Instituto Indigenista Interamericano. México.

Am. Lat./Moscow. América Latina. Academia de Ciencias de la Unión de Repúblicas Soviéticas Socialistas. Moscow.

Amazonía Peru. Amazonía Peruana. Centro Amazónico de Antropología y Aplicación Práctica, Depto. de Documentación y Publicaciones. Lima.

Americas/Francisc. The Americas. Academy of American Franciscan History. Washington.

An. Antropol. Anales de Antropología. Univ. Nacional Autónoma de México, Instituto de Investigaciones Históricas. México.

An. Arquit. Anales de Arquitectura. Secretariado de Publicaciones de la Univ. de Valladolid. Valladolid, Spain.

An. Encuentro Nac. Reg. Hist. Anales del Encuentro Nacional y Regional de Historia. Junta Regional de Historia y Estudios Conexos. Montevideo.

An. Inst. Invest. Estét. Anales del Instituto de Investigaciones Estéticas. Univ. Nacional Autónoma de México. México.

An. Mus. Michoacano. Anales del Museo Michoacano. Centro Regional Michoacán del INAH; Museo Regional Michoacano. Morelia, Mexico.

Anál. Pol. Análisis Político. Instituto de Estudios Políticos y Relaciones Internacionales, Univ. Nacional de Colombia. Bogotá.

Anales/Göteborg. Anales. Instituto Iberoamericano, Univ. de Gotemburgo. Göteborg, Sweden.

Análise Conjunt. Análise & Conjuntura. Fundação João Pinheiro. Belo Horizonte, Brazil.

Análisis/Lima. Análisis. Cuadernos de Investigación. Lima.

Anaquel Estud. Arab. Anaquel de Estudios Arabes. Univ. Complutense de Madrid, Depto. de Estudios Arabes e Islámicos. Madrid.

Anc. Mesoam. Ancient Mesoamerica. Cambridge Univ. Press. Cambridge, England.

Annales/Paris. Annales. Centre national de la recherche scientifique de la VIe Section de l'Ecole pratique des hautes études. Paris.

ANPOCS BIB. Boletim Informativo e Bibliográfico de Ciências Sociais: BIB. Associação Nacional de Pós-Graduação e Pesquisa em Ciências Sociais. Rio de Janeiro.

Anthropol. Lit./Online. Anthropological Literature. Tozzer Library. Cambridge, Mass.

Anthropol. Verkenn. Antropologische Verkenningen. Coutinho. Muiderberg, The Netherlands.

Anthropologica/Lima. Anthropologica. Depto. de Ciencias Sociales, Pontificia Univ. Católica del Perú. Lima.

Antropol. Ecuat. Antropología Ecuatoriana. Casa de la Cultura Ecuatoriana, Sección Académica de Antropología y Arqueología. Quito.

Antropol. Soc. Antropología Social. Instituto Nacional de Antropología e Historia. México.

Anu. Dep. Hist./Madrid. Anuario del Departmento de Historia. Depto. de Historia, Univ. Complutense de Madrid.

Anu. Estud. Am. Anuario de Estudios Americanos. Consejo Superior de Investigaciones Científicas; Univ. de Sevilla, Escuela de Estudios Hispano-Americanos. Sevilla, Spain.

Anu. Estud. Centroam. Anuario de Estudios Centroamericanos. Univ. de Costa Rica. San José.

Anu. Hist. Iglesia Chile. Anuario de Historia de la Iglesia en Chile. Seminario Pontificio Mayor. Santiago.

Anu. IEHS. Anuario IEHS. Univ. Nacional del Centro de la Provincia de Buenos Aires, Instituto de Estudios Histórico-Sociales. Tandil, Argentina.

Anuario/Rosario. Anuario. Univ. Nacional de Rosario, Escuela de Historia. Argentina.

Apunt. Postmod. Apuntes Postmodernos: Una Revista Cubana de Crítica Cultural, Social, Política y de los Artes. Verbum, Inc. Miami, Fla.

Apuntes/Lima. Apuntes. Univ. del Pacífico, Centro de Investigación. Lima.

Arch. Esp. Arte. Archivo Español de Arte. Consejo Superior de Investigaciones Científicas, Centro de Estudios Históricos. Madrid.

Arch. Hist. Soc. Iesu. Archivum Historicum Societatis Iesu. Rome.

Arch. Ibero-Am. Archivo Ibero-Americano. Revista de Estudios Históricos. Los Padres Franciscanos. Madrid.

Armitano Arte. Armitano Arte: Revista Venezolana de Cultura. Ernest Armitano. Caracas.

Årstryck/Göteborg. Ärstryck. Etnografiska Museum. Göteborg, Sweden.

Art Rev./Salvador. Art: Revista da Escola de Música e Artes Cênicas da UFBA. Escola de Música e Artes Cênicas da UFBA. Salvador, Brazil.

Article1st/OCLC. Article1st. OCLC Online Computer Library Center. Dublin, Ohio.

Asclepio/Madrid. Asclepio: Archivo Iberoamericano de Historia de la Medicina y Antropología Médica. Consejo Superior de Investigaciones Científicas, Instituto Arnaú de Vilanova de Historia de la Medicina. Madrid.

Bibl. Latinoam./CD-ROM. Bibliografía Latinoamericana-Latin American Bibliography. Centro de Información Científica y Humanística, Univ. Nacional Autónoma de México. México.

Bol. Acad. Chil. Bellas Artes. Boletín de la Academia Chilena de Bellas Artes. Instituto de Chile. Santiago.

Bol. Acad. Chil. Hist. Boletín de la Academia Chilena de la Historia. Santiago.

Bol. Acad. Nac. Hist./Caracas. Boletín de la Academia Nacional de la Historia. Caracas.

Bol. Am. Boletín Americanista. Univ. de Barcelona, Facultad de Geografía e Historia, Depto. de Historia de América. Barcelona.

Bol. Arch. Nac./Cuba. Boletín del Archivo Nacional. Editorial Academia. La Habana.

Bol. Cult. Bibliogr. Boletín Cultural y Bibliográfico. Banco de la República; Biblioteca Luis-Angel Arango. Bogotá.

Bol. Fuentes Hist. Econ. Méx. Boletín de Fuentes para la Historia Económica de México. Centro de Estudios Históricos, El Colegio de México. México.

Bol. Hist. Ejérc. Boletín Histórico del Ejército. Montevideo.

Bol. Inst. Hist. Ravignani. Boletín del Instituto de Historia Argentina y Americana Dr. Emilio Ravignani. Facultad de Filosofía y Letras, Univ. de Buenos Aires.

Bol. Inst. Riva-Agüero. Boletín del Instituto Riva-Agüero. Pontificia Univ. Católica del Perú. Lima.

Bol. Lima. Boletín de Lima. Revista Cultural Científica. Lima.

Bol. Mus. Inst. Camón Aznar. Boletín del Museo e Instituto Camón Aznar. Museo e Instituto de Humanidades Camón Aznar. Zaragoza, Spain.

Bol. Mus. Para. Goeldi. Boletim do Museu Paraense Emílio Goeldi. Nova série: antropologia. Conselho Nacional de Desenvolvimento Científico e Tecnológico, Instituto Nacional de Pesquisas da Amazônia. Belém, Brazil.

Bol. Nicar. Bibliogr. Doc. Boletín Nicaragüense de Bibliografía y Documentación. Biblioteca, Banco Central de Nicaragua. Managua.

Bol. Pesqui. CEDEAM. Boletim de Pesquisa da CEDEAM. Comissão de Documentação e Estudos da Amazônia, Univ. do Amazonas. Manaus, Brazil.

Boletín/Bogotá. Boletín del Museo del Oro. Banco de la República. Bogotá.

Bull. hisp./Bordeaux. Bulletin hispanique. Univ. de Bordeaux; Centre national de la recherche scientifique. Bordeaux, France.

Bull. Inst. fr. étud. andin. Bulletin de l'Institut français d'études andines. Lima.

Bull. Int. Anthropol. Ethnol. Bulletin of the International Committee on Urgent Anthropological and Ethnological Research. International Union of Anthropological and Ethnological Sciences. Vienna.

Bull. Lat. Am. Res. Bulletin of Latin American Research. Society for Latin American Studies. Oxford, England.

Cad. Negros. Cadernos Negros. São Paulo.

Cah. Am. lat. Cahiers des Amériques latines. Paris.

Can. J. Hist. Canadian Journal of History. Univ. of Saskatchewan. Saskatoon, Canada.

Can. J. Lat. Am. Caribb. Stud. Canadian Journal of Latin American and Caribbean Studies. Univ. of Ottawa. Ontario, Canada.

Caravelle/Toulouse. Caravelle. Cahiers du monde hispanique et luso-brésilien. Univ. de Toulouse, Institute d'études hispaniques, hispano-americaines et luso-brésiliennes. Toulouse, France.

Caribb. Q. Caribbean Quarterly. Univ. of the West Indies. Mona, Jamaica.

Caribb. Stud. Caribbean Studies. Univ. of Puerto Rico, Institute of Caribbean Studies. Río Piedras.

Caribena/Martinique. Caribena: cahiers d'études américanistes de la Caraïbe. Centre d'études et de recherches archéologiques (CERA). Martinique.

Casa Am. Casa de las Américas. La Habana.

CD-DIS/Arlington. CD-DIS. United States Agency for International Development, Development Information Services Clearinghouse. Arlington, Va.

CD-ROM Dir. CD-ROM Directory. TFPL Publishing. London.

CD-ROMs Print. CD-ROMs in Print. Meckler. Westport, Conn.

CDPress. CDPress. CD-ROM de México. Xalapa, Mexico.

Cent. Estud. Puertorriq. Bull. Centro de Estudios Puertorriqueños Bulletin. Hunter College, City University of New York. New York.

Chasqui/Williamsburg. Chasqui. Dept. of Modern Languages, College of William and Mary. Williamsburg, Va.

Chungará/Arica. Chungará. Univ. del Norte, Depto. de Antropología. Arica, Chile.

Ciênc. Cult. Ciência e Cultura. Sociedade Brasileira para o Progresso da Ciência. São Paulo.

Ciênc. Hoje. Ciência Hoje. Sociedade Brasileira para o Progresso da Ciência. Rio de Janeiro.

CLAHR/Albuquerque. Colonial Latin American Historical Review. Spanish Colonial Research Center, Univ. of New Mexico. Albuquerque.

Clio/Sinaloa. Clio. Univ. Autónoma de Sinaloa, Escuela de Historia. Culiacán, Mexico.

Coll. Res. Libr. News. College and Research Libraries News. Assn. of College and Research Libraries. Chicago, Ill.

Colon. Lat. Am. Rev. Colonial Latin American Review. Simon H. Rifkind Center for the Humanities, Dept. of Romance Languages, City College of New York. New York.

Comp. Civiliz. Rev. Comparative Civilizations Review. Dept. of History, Dickinson College. Carlisle, Penn.

Comp. Stud. Soc. Hist. Comparative Studies in Society and History. Society for the Comparative Study of Society and History; Cambridge Univ. Press. London.

Conjonction/Port-au-Prince. Conjonction. Bulletin de l'Institut français d'Haïti. Port-au-Prince.

Conjunto/Habana. Conjunto. Revista de Teatro Latinoamericano. Comité Permanente de Festivales; Casa de las Américas. La Habana.

Creac. Estética Teor. Artes. Creación: Estética y Teoría de las Artes. Instituto de Estética y Teoría de las Artes. Madrid.

Cristianismo Soc. Cristianismo y Sociedad. Junta Latinoamericana de Iglesia y Sociedad. Montevideo.

Criterios/Habana. Criterios: Revista de Teoría Literaria, Estética y Culturología. Casa de las Américas. La Habana.

Cuad. Acad. Cuadernos Académicos. Instituto Profesional del Maule. Talca, Chile.

Cuad. Am. Cuadernos Americanos. Editorial Cultura. México.

Cuad. Arte Colon. Cuadernos de Arte Colonial. Museo de América; Ministerio de Cultura. Madrid.

Cuad. CENDES. Cuadernos del CENDES. Centro de Estudios del Desarrollo, Univ. Central de Venezuela. Caracas.

Cuad. Centroam. Hist. Cuadernos Centroamericanos de Historia. Centro de Investigación de la Realidad de América Latina (CIRA). Managua.

Cuad. Esc. Dipl. Cuadernos de la Escuela Diplomática. Ministerio de Asuntos Exteriores. Madrid.

Cuad. Hispanoam. Cuadernos Hispanoamericanos. Instituto de Cultura Hispánica. Madrid.

Cuad. Hist. Cuadernos de Historia. Univ. de Chile, Facultad de Humanidades y Educación, Depto. de Ciencias Históricas. Santiago.

Cuad. Hist. Moderna. Cuadernos de Historia Moderna. Facultad de Geografía e Historia, Univ. Complutense de Madrid.

Cuad. Trad. Interp. Cuadernos de Traducción e Interpretación = Quaderns de Traducció i Interpretació. Univ. Autónoma de Barcelona. Spain.

Cuba. Stud. Cuban Studies. Univ. of Pittsburgh, Center for Latin American Studies. Pittsburgh, Penn.

Cult. Guatem. Cultura de Guatemala. Univ. Rafael Landívar. Guatemala.

Cultura/Quito. Cultura. Banco Central del Ecuador. Quito.

Dados/Rio de Janeiro. Dados. Instituto Univ. de Pesquisas. Rio de Janeiro.

Data/La Paz. Data: Revista del Instituto de Estudios Andinos y Amazónicos. Instituto de

Estudios Andinos y Amazónicos (INDEAA). La Paz.

Database Search. Database Searcher. Meckler Pub., Westport, Conn.

Database/Weston. Database. Online, Inc., Weston, Conn.

Dédalo/São Paulo. Dédalo. Univ. de São Paulo, Museu de Arqueologia e Etnologia. São Paulo.

Del Caribe. Del Caribe. Casa del Caribe. Santiago, Cuba.

Delphi Esp./Online. Delphi en Español. Innovative Telematics. Miami Beach, Fla.

Desarro. Econ. Desarrollo Económico. Instituto de Desarrollo Económico y Social. Buenos Aires.

Dispositio/Ann Arbor. Dispositio. Dept. of Romance Languages, Univ. of Michigan. Ann Arbor.

DLA Bull. DLA Bulletin. Univ. of California, Division of Library Automation. Berkeley.

ECA/San Salvador. Estudios Centro-Americanos: ECA. Univ. Centroamericana José Simeón Cañas. San Salvador.

Econ. Cienc. Soc. Economía y Ciencias Sociales. Facultad de Ciencias Económicas y Sociales, Univ. Central de Venezuela. Caracas.

Econ. Soc. Hist. Neth. Economic and Social History in the Netherlands. Nederlandsch Economisch-Historisch Archief. Amsterdam.

Edad Oro. Edad de Oro. Depto. de Filología Española, Univ. Autónoma. Madrid.

Ensaios FEE. Ensaios FEE. Secretaria de Coordenacão e Planejamento. Fundação de Economia e Estatística. Porto Alegre, Brazil.

Estud. Afro-Asiát. Estudos Afro-Asiáticos. Centro de Estudos Afro-Asiáticos. Rio de Janeiro.

Estud. Cienc. Let. Estudios de Ciencias y Letras. Instituto de Filosofía, Ciencias y Letras. Montevideo.

Estud. Cult. Maya. Estudios de Cultura Maya. Centro de Estudios Mayas, Univ. Nacional Autónoma de México. México.

Estud. Cult. Náhuatl. Estudios de Cultura Náhuatl. Instituto de Investigaciones Históricas, Univ. Nacional Autónoma de México. México.

Estud. Demogr. Urb. Estudios Demográficos y Urbanos. El Colegio de México. México.

Estud. Econ./São Paulo. Estudos Econômicos. Univ. de São Paulo, Instituto de Pesquisas Econômicas. São Paulo.

Estud. Hist. Mod. Contemp. Méx. Estudios de Historia Moderna y Contemporánea de México. Univ. Nacional Autónoma de México. México.

Estud. Hist. Novohisp. Estudios de Historia Novohispana. Univ. Nacional Autónoma de México. México.

Estud. Hist./Rio de Janeiro. Estudos Históricos. Associação de Pesquisa e Documentação Histórica. Rio de Janeiro.

Estud. Hist. Soc. Econ. Am. Estudios de Historia Social y Económica de América. Univ. de Alcalá de Henares. Madrid.

Estud. Ibero-Am./Porto Alegre. Estudos Ibero-Americanos. Pontifícia Univ. Católica do Rio Grande do Sul, Depto. de História. Porto Alegre, Brazil.

Estud. Latinoam. Estudios Latinoamericanos. Academia de Ciencias de Polonia, Instituto de Historia. Wrocław.

Estud. Parag. Estudios Paraguayos. Univ. Católica Nuestra Señora de la Asunción. Asunción.

Estud. Públicos. Estudios Públicos. Centro de Estudios Públicos. Santiago.

Estud. Soc. Centroam. Estudios Sociales Centroamericanos. Programa Centroamericano de Ciencias Sociales. San José.

Estudios/Guatemala. Estudios. Instituto de Investigaciones Históricas, Antropológicas, y Arqueológicas, Univ. de San Carlos de Guatemala. Guatemala.

Ethnohistory/Society. Ethnohistory. American Society for Ethnohistory. Duke Univ., Durham, N.C.

Ethnology/Pittsburgh. Ethnology. Univ. of Pittsburgh, Penn.

Etnía/Olavarría. Etnía. Museo Etnográfico Municipal Dámaso Arce. Olavarría, Argentina.

Explic. Textos Lit. Explicación de Textos Literarios. Dept. of Spanish and Portuguese, California State Univ., Sacramento.

Face/São Paulo. Face. Pontifícia Univ. Católica de São Paulo.

Fénix/Lima. Fénix: Revista de la Biblioteca Nacional del Perú. Biblioteca Nacional. Lima.

Fiction/New York. Fiction. City College, CUNY. New York.

Filología/Buenos Aires. Filología. Univ. de Buenos Aires, Facultad de Filosofía y Letras. Buenos Aires.

Financiero/CD-ROM. El Financiero. CD-ROM de México. México.

Fla. Hist. Q. The Florida Historical Quarterly. The Florida Historical Society. Jacksonville, Fla.

Folia Humaníst. Folia Humanística. Editorial Glarma. Barcelona, Spain.

Franciscanum/Bogotá. Franciscanum. Univ. de San Buenaventura. Bogotá.

Fulltext Sources Online. Fulltext Sources Online. Bibliodata. Needham Heights, Mass.

Gaceta/Bogotá. Gaceta. Instituto Colombiano de Cultura. Bogotá.

Gale Dir. Databases. Gale Directory of Databases. Gale Research. Detroit.

Généal. hist. Caraïbe. Généalogie et histoire de la Caraïbe. Assn. de la généalogie et histoire de la Caraïbe. Le Pecq, France.

Geobase/Online. Geobase. Elsevier/Geo Abstracts.

Gestos/Irvine. Gestos. Dept. of Spanish and Portuguese, Univ. of Calif., Irvine.

HAHR. Hispanic American Historical Review. Conference on Latin American History of the American Historical Assn.; Duke Univ. Press. Durham, N.C.

HAPI Online. HAPI Online. UCLA Latin American Center. Los Angeles.

HISLA/Lima. HISLA. Centro Latinoamericano de Historia Económica y Social. Lima.

Hisp. J. Hispanic Journal. Indiana Univ. of Pennsylvania, Dept. of Foreign Languages. Indiana, Penn.

Hisp. Rev. Hispanic Review. Univ. of Pennsylvania, Dept. of Romance Languages. Philadelphia, Penn.

Hisp. Sacra. Hispania Sacra: Revista de Historia Eclesiástica de España. Centro de Estudios Históricos, Instituto Enrique Flórez. Madrid.

Hispamérica/Gaithersburg. Hispamérica. Gaithersburg, Md.

Hispania/Madrid. Hispania. Instituto Jerónimo Zurita, Consejo Superior de Investigaciones Científicas. Madrid.

Hispania/Teachers. Hispania. American Assn. of Teachers of Spanish and Portuguese; Mississippi State Univ., University, Miss.

Hispanófila/Chapel Hill. Hispanófila. Univ. of North Carolina. Chapel Hill, N.C.

Hist. Anthropol. History and Anthropology. Harwood Academic Publishers. New York.

Hist. Boliv. Historia Boliviana. Cochabamba, Bolivia.

Hist. Crít./Tegucigalpa. Historia Crítica. Univ. Nacional Autónoma de Honduras. Tegucigalpa.

Hist. Cult./Lima. Historia y Cultura. Museo Nacional de Historia. Lima.

Hist. Espac. Historia y Espacio: Revista de Estudios Históricos Regionales. Depto. de Historia, Univ. del Valle. Cali, Colombia.

Hist. Gaz. History Gazette. Univ. of Guyana, History Society. Turkeyen, Guyana.

Hist. Mex. Historia Mexicana. Colegio de México. México.

Hist. Parag. Historia Paraguaya. Anuario de la Academia Paraguaya de la Historia. Asunción.

Hist. Perspect. Historia & Perspectivas: Revista do Curso de Historia. Univ. Federal de Uberlândia. Uberlândia, Brazil.

Hist. Quest. Debates. História, Questões e Debates. Associação Paranaense de História. Curitiba, Brazil.

Hist. Relig. History of Religions. Univ. of Chicago. Chicago, Ill.

Hist. Soc./Río Piedras. Historia y Sociedad. Depto. de Historia, Univ. de Puerto Rico. Río Piedras.

Hist. Soc./Valencia. Historia Social. Centro de la UNED, Instituto de Historia Social. Valencia, Spain.

Hist. Workshop. History Workshop. Ruskin College, Oxford Univ., Oxford, England.

Historia/Santiago. Historia. Univ. Católica de Chile. Instituto de Historia. Santiago.

Historian/Honor Society. The Historian. Phi Alpha Theta, National Honor Society in History; Univ. of Pennsylvania. Univ. Park, Penn.

Histórica/Lima. Histórica. Pontificia Univ. Católica del Perú, Depto. de Humanidades. Lima.

Historiogr. Bibliogr. Am. Historiografía y Bibliografía Americanista. Escuela de Estudios Hispano-Americanos de Sevilla. Sevilla, Spain.

HLAS/Online. Handbook of Latin American Studies. Hispanic Division, Library of Congress. Washington.

Hómines/San Juan. Hómines. Univ. Interamericana de Puerto Rico. San Juan.

Homme/Paris. L'Homme. Laboratoire d'anthropologie, Collège de France. Paris.

Hora Poesía. Hora de poesía. Bruguera. Barcelona, Spain.

Horizontes/Ponce. Horizontes. Univ. Católica de Puerto Rico. Ponce.

Hoy Hist. Hoy es Historia: Revista Bimestral de Historia Nacional e Iberoamericana. Editorial Raíces. Montevideo.

Hua ch'iao hua jen li shih yen chiu. Hua ch'iao hua jen li shih yen chiu [Studies on History of Overseas Chinese and Citizens of Chinese Origin]. China Institute of History of Overseas Chinese; China Society of History of Overseas Chinese. Beijing.

Ibero-Am. Arch. Ibero-Amerikanisches Archiv. Ibero-Amerikanisches Institut. Berlin.

Ibero-Am./Stockholm. Ibero-Americana: Nordic Journal of Latin American Studies. Institute of Latin American Studies, Univ. of Stockholm.

Iberoromania/Tübingen. Iberoromania. Max Niemeyer Verlag. Tübingen, Germany.

Index FBIS Dly. Rep./CD-ROM. Index FBIS Daily Report. NewsBank/Readex. New Canaan, Conn.

Index Foreign Leg. Period. Index to Foreign Legal Periodicals. American Association of Law Libraries. Berkeley, Calif.

Inf. Today. Information Today. Learned Information, Inc., Medford, N.J.

INFO-SOUTH/Online. INFO-SOUTH Latin American Information System. North-South Center, Univ. of Miami. Miami, Fla.

InfoMéxico/CD-ROM. InfoMéxico. InfoSel. Monterrey, Mexico.

Int. Migr. International Migration = Migrations Internationales = Migraciones Internacionales. Intergovernmental Committee for European Migration; Research Group for European Migration Problems; International Organization for Migration. The Hague, Netherlands; Geneva, Switzerland.

Integr. Latinoam. Integración Latinoamericana. Instituto para la Integración de América Latina. Buenos Aires.

Inter-Am. Music Rev. Inter-American Music Review. Robert Stevenson. Los Angeles, Calif.

Inti/Providence. Inti: Revista de Literatura Hispánica. Providence College, R.I.

IntlEc CD-ROM. IntlEc CD-ROM: the Index to International Economics, Development and Finance. Joint Bank-Fund Library. Washington.

Invest. Ens. Investigaciones y Ensayos. Academia Nacional de la Historia. Buenos Aires.

Islas/Santa Clara. Islas. Univ. Central de Las Villas. Santa Clara, Cuba.

J. Caribb. Hist. Journal of Caribbean History. Caribbean Univ. Press. St. Lawrence, Barbados.

J. Church State. Journal of Church and State. J.M. Dawson Studies in Church and State, Baylor Univ., Waco, Tex.

J. Decor. Propag. Arts. The Journal of Decorative and Propaganda Arts. Wolfson Foundation of Decorative and Propaganda Arts. Miami, Fla.

J. Econ. Hist.   The Journal of Economic History. Economic History Assn.; Univ. of Kansas. Lawrence.

J. Eur. Econ. Hist.   The Journal of European Economic History. Banco di Roma. Rome.

J. Fam. Hist.   Journal of Family History. National Council on Family Relations. Greenwich, Conn.

J. Hisp. Philol.   Journal of Hispanic Philology. Dept. of Modern Languages, Florida State Univ., Tallahassee, Fla.

J. Interam. Stud. World Aff.   Journal of Interamerican Studies and World Affairs. Institute of Interamerican Studies, Univ. of Miami. Coral Gables, Fla.

J. Interdiscip. Hist.   The Journal of Interdisciplinary History. The MIT Press. Cambridge, Mass.

J. Lat. Am. Lore.   Journal of Latin American Lore. Univ. of California, Latin American Center. Los Angeles, Calif.

J. Lat. Am. Stud.   Journal of Latin American Studies. Centers or Institutes of Latin American Studies at the Universities of Cambridge, Glasgow, Liverpool, London, and Oxford. Cambridge Univ. Press. London.

J. Negro Hist.   The Journal of Negro History. Assn. for the Study of Negro Life and History. Washington.

J. Peasant Stud.   The Journal of Peasant Studies. Frank Cass & Co., London.

J. Soc. Hist.   Journal of Social History. Carnegie Mellon Univ., Pittsburgh, Penn.

J. Southwest.   Journal of the Southwest. Southwest Center, Univ. of Arizona. Tucson.

J. West.   Journal of the West. Manhattan, Kan.

Jahrb. Gesch.   Jahrbuch für Geschichte von Staat, Wirtschaft und Gesellschaft Lateinamerikas. Köln, Germany.

Jam. J.   Jamaica Journal. Institute of Jamaica. Kingston.

Kañína/San José.   Kañína. Univ. de Costa Rica. San José.

LADB/Online.   Latin America Data Base. Latin American Institute, Univ. of New Mexico. Albuquerque.

Lang. Commun.   Language & Communication. Pergamon Press. New York.

LARR.   Latin American Research Review. Latin American Research Review Board. Univ. of New Mexico, Albuquerque, N.M.

Lat. Am. Art Mag.   Latin American Art Magazine. Latin American Art Magazine Inc., Scottsdale, Ariz.

Lat. Am. Indian Lit. J.   Latin American Indian Literatures Journal. Geneva College. Beaver Falls, Penn.

Lat. Am. Lit. Rev.   Latin American Literary Review. Carnegie-Mellon Univ., Dept. of Modern Languages. Pittsburgh, Penn.

Lat. Am. Music Rev.   Latin American Music Review. Univ. of Texas. Austin.

Lat. Am. Perspect.   Latin American Perspectives. Univ. of California. Newbury Park, Calif.

Lat. Am. Stud./NISC.   Latin American Studies. National Information Services Corporation. Baltimore, Md.

Lat.am. Stud./Nürnberg.   Lateinamerika Studien. Univ. Erlangen-Nürnberg, Sektion Lateinamerika. Nürnberg, Germany.

Lat. Am. Tax. Data Base.   Latin American Taxation Data Base. International Bureau of Fiscal Documentation. Amsterdam.

Lat. Am. Theatre Rev.   Latin American Theatre Review. Univ. of Kansas, Center of Latin American Studies. Lawrence, Kan.

Lateinamerika/Hamburg.   Lateinamerika. Institut für Iberoamerika-Kunde. Hamburg, Germany.

Latinoamerica/Rome.   Latinoamerica. Edizioni Associate. Rome.

Let. Cuba.   Letras Cubanas. La Habana.

Libri/Copenhagen.   Libri. Munksgaard. Copenhagen.

LILACS/CD-ROM.   LILACS. Centro Latino-Americano e do Caribe de Informação em Ciencias da Saude. São Paulo.

Linden Lane Mag. Linden Lane Magazine. Princeton, N.J.

Link-up/Minneapolis. Link-up. On-Line Communications. Minneapolis, Minn.

Lit. Lingüíst. Literatura y Lingüística. Instituto Profesional de Estudios Superiores Blas Cañas. Santiago.

Logos/Serena. Logos: Revista de Lingüística, Filosofía y Literatura. Facultad de Humanidades, Univ. de La Serena. La Serena, Chile.

Lotería/Panamá. Lotería. Lotería Nacional de Beneficencia. Panamá.

Lua Nova. Lua Nova. Editora Brasiliense. São Paulo.

Luso-Braz. Rev. Luso-Brazilian Review. Univ. of Wisconsin Press. Madison, Wis.

Man/London. Man. The Royal Anthropological Institute. London.

Manoa/Honolulu. Manoa: A Pacific Journal of International Writing. Univ. of Hawaii Press. Honolulu.

Mass. Rev. The Massachusetts Review. Amherst College; Mount Holyoke College; Smith College; and the Univ. of Massachusetts. Amherst, Mass.

Mem. Acad. Mex. Hist. Memorias de la Academia Mexicana de la Historia. México.

Mem. Mus. Nac. Arte. Memoria del Museo Nacional de Arte. Museo Nacional de Arte. México.

Merc. Peru. Mercurio Peruano. Lima.

Mesoamérica/Antigua. Mesoamérica. Centro de Investigaciones Regionales de Mesoamérica. Antigua, Guatemala.

Mester/UCLA. Mester. Univ. of California, Dept. of Spanish and Portuguese. Los Angeles.

Mex. Stud. Mexican Studies/Estudios Mexicanos. Univ. of California, Berkeley.

Mexicon/Berlin. Mexicon. K.-F. von Flemming. Berlin, Germany.

Meyibó/Tijuana. Meyibó. Centro de Investigaciones Históricas, Univ. Autónoma de Baja California. Tijuana, Mexico.

Misc. Hist. Ecuat. Miscelánea Histórica Ecuatoriana: Revista de Investigaciones Históricas de los Museos del Banco Central del Ecuador. Museos del Banco Central del Ecuador. Quito.

Mitt. Inst. österr. Gesch.forsch. Mitteilungen des Instituts für österreichische Geschichtforschung. Vienna.

Mon. Rev. Monthly Review. New York.

Montalbán/Caracas. Montalbán. Univ. Católica Andrés Bello, Facultad de Humanidades y Educación, Institutos Humanísticos de Investigación. Caracas.

Natl. Geogr. Mag. National Geographic Magazine. National Geographic Society. Washington.

Natl. Trade Data Bank. National Trade Data Bank. U.S. Dept. of Commerce, Economics and Statistics Administration, Office of Business Analysis. Washington.

Nav. Hist. Naval History. US Naval Institute. Annapolis, Md.

New Repub. The New Republic. Washington.

Nieuwe West-Indische Gids. Nieuwe West-Indische Gids. Martinus Nijhoff. The Hague.

Nóesis/Juárez. Nóesis. Univ. Autónoma de Ciudad Juárez. Juárez, Mexico.

Noroeste Méx. Noroeste de México. Centro Regional Sonora, INAH. Hermosillo, Mexico.

Not. Bibliogr. Hist. Notícia Bibliográfica e Histórica. Depto. de História, Pontifícia Univ. Católica de Campinas. Campinas, Brazil.

Notimex/CD-ROM. Notimex. Agencia Mexicana de Noticias. México.

Novos Estud. CEBRAP. Novos Estudos CEBRAP. Centro Brasileiro de Análise e Planejamento. São Paulo.

Nueva Rev. Filol. Hisp. Nueva Revista de Filología Hispánica. El Colegio de México. México.

Nueva Soc. Nueva Sociedad. Caracas.

Nuevo Texto Crít. Nuevo Texto Crítico. Dept. of Spanish and Portuguese. Stanford Univ., Palo Alto, Calif.

OCLC Online Union Cat. OCLC Online Union Catalog. OCLC Online Computer Library Center. Dublin, Ohio.

Online/Weston. Online. Online, Inc., Weston, Conn.

Op. Cit./Río Piedras. Op. Cit.: Boletín del Centro de Investigaciones Históricas. Depto. de Historia, Facultad de Humanidades, Univ. de Puerto Rico. Río Piedras.

Pac. Hist. Rev. Pacific Historical Review. Univ. of California Press. Los Angeles and Berkeley.

Palabra Hombre. La Palabra y el Hombre. Univ. Veracruzana. Xalapa, Mexico.

Pap. Casa Chata. Papeles de la Casa Chata. Centro de Investigaciones y Estudios Superiores en Antropología Social. México.

Past Present. Past and Present. London.

PeaceNet. PeaceNet. Institute for Global Communications. San Francisco, Calif.

Polít. Soc./Guatemala. Política y Sociedad. Univ. de San Carlos de Guatemala, Instituto de Investigaciones Políticas y Sociales. Guatemala.

Population/Paris. Population. Institut national d'études démographiques. Paris.

Port. Stud. Portuguese Studies. Dept. of Portuguese, King's College. London.

Prínc. Viana. Príncipe de Viana. Institución Príncipe de Viana, Gobierno de Navarra. Pamplona, Spain.

PROMT/Online. PROMT. Predicasts. Foster City, Calif.

Publ. Inst. Estud. Iberoam. Publicaciones del Instituto de Estudios Iberoamericanos. Instituto de Estudios Iberamericanos. Buenos Aires.

Punto Coma. Punto y Coma. Univ. del Sagrado Corazón. Santurce, Puerto Rico.

Quad. Stor. Quaderni Storici. Facoltà di Economia e Commercio, Istituto di Storia e Sociologia. Ancona, Italy.

Quinto Cent. Quinto Centenario. Depto. de Historia de América, Univ. Complutense de Madrid.

Rábida/Huelva. Rábida. Patronato Provincial del V Centenario del Descubrimiento. Huelva, Spain.

Race Cl. Race & Class. Institute of Race Relations; The Transnational Institute. London.

Radic. Hist. Rev. Radical History Review. Mid-Atlantic Radical Historians' Organization. New York.

Reflexão/São Paulo. Reflexão. Pontifícia Univ. Católica de Campinas. São Paulo.

Relaciones/Zamora. Relaciones. El Colegio de Michoacán. Zamora, Mexico.

Relato Hechos Ideas. Relato de Hechos e Ideas. Editorial Relato SRL. Buenos Aires.

Renaissance Q. Renaissance Quarterly. Renaissance Society of America. New York.

Representations/Berkeley. Representations. Univ. of California Press. Berkeley.

Res Gesta. Res Gesta. Instituto de Historia, Facultad de Derecho y Ciencias Sociales, Univ. Católica Argentina. Rosario, Argentina.

Reuter Textline. Reuter Textline. Reuters. London.

Rev. Acad. Colomb. Cienc. Revista de la Academia Colombiana de Ciencias Exactas, Físicas y Naturales. Ministerio de Educación Nacional. Bogotá.

Rev. Agust. Revista Agustiniana. Madrid.

Rev. Andin. Revista Andina. Centro Bartolomé de las Casas. Cusco, Peru.

Rev. Antioq. Econ. Desarro. Revista Antioqueña de Economía y Desarrollo. Fundación para la Investigación y la Cultura. Medellín, Colombia.

Rev. Antropol./São Paulo. Revista de Antropologia. Univ. de São Paulo, Faculdade de Filosofia, Letras e Ciências Humanas; Associação Brasileira de Antropologia. São Paulo.

Rev. Arch. Nac. Revista del Archivo Nacional. San José, Costa Rica.

Rev. Arch. Nac. Hist. Azuay. Revista del Archivo Nacional de Historia, Sección del Azuay. Casa de la Cultura Ecuatoriana, Núcleo del Azuay. Cuenca, Ecuador.

Rev. Bibl. Nac. José Martí. Revista de la Biblioteca Nacional José Martí. La Habana.

Rev. Bibl. Nac./Montevideo. Revista de la Biblioteca Nacional. Ministerio de Educación y Cultura. Montevideo.

Rev. Bras. Estud. Polít. Revista Brasileira de Estudos Políticos. Univ. de Minas Gerais. Belo Horizonte, Brazil.

Rev. Bras. Estud. Popul. Revista Brasileira de Estudos de População. Associação Brasileira de Estudos Populacionais. São Paulo.

Rev. Bras. Filos. Revista Brasileira de Filosofia. Instituto Brasileiro de Filosofia. São Paulo.

Rev. Bras. Hist. Revista Brasileira de História. Associação Nacional dos Professores Universitários de História (ANPUH). São Paulo.

Rev. Can. Estud. Hisp. Revista Canadiense de Estudios Hispánicos. Asociación Canadiense de Hispanistas; Univ. of Toronto. Toronto, Canada.

Rev. Cancillería San Carlos. Revista Cancillería de San Carlos. Ministerio de Relaciones Exteriores. Bogotá.

Rev. Cent. Estud. Av. La Revista del Centro de Estudios Avanzados de Puerto Rico y el Caribe. San Juan.

Rev. Chil. Humanid. Revista Chilena de Humanidades. Facultad de Filosofía, Humanidades y Educación, Univ. de Chile. Santiago.

Rev. Ciclos. Revista Ciclos en la Historia, Economía y la Sociedad. Fundación de Investigaciones Históricas, Económicas y Sociales, Facultad de Ciencias Económicas, Univ. de Buenos Aires. Buenos Aires.

Rev. Ciênc. Hist. Revista de Ciências Históricas. Univ. Portucalense. Porto, Portugal.

Rev. Cienc. Soc./Río Piedras. Revista de Ciencias Sociales. Univ. de Puerto Rico, Colegio de Ciencias Sociales. Río Piedras.

Rev. Colomb. Antropol. Revista Colombiana de Antropología. Ministerio de Educación Nacional, Instituto Colombiano de Antropología. Bogotá.

Rev. Complut. Hist. Am. Revista Complutense de Historia de América.

Facultad de Geografía e Historia, Univ. Complutense de Madrid.

Rev. Crít. Lit. Latinoam. Revista de Crítica Literaria Latinoamericana. Latinoamericana Editores. Lima.

Rev. Cuba. Cienc. Soc. Revista Cubana de Ciencias Sociales. Centro de Estudios Filosóficos, Academia de Ciencias de Cuba. La Habana.

Rev. Cult. Lotería. Revista Cultural Lotería. Lotería Nacional de Beneficencia, Dirección de Desarrollo Social y Cultural, Depto. Cultural. Panamá.

Rev. Dep. Hist. Arte. Revista del Departamento de Historia del Arte. Univ. de Sevilla. Spain.

Rev. Dep. Hist./Belo Horizonte. Revista do Departamento de História. Univ. Federal de Minas Gerais. Belo Horizonte, Brazil.

Rev. Dep. Hist./Tucumán. Revista del Departamento de Historia. Univ. Nacional de Tucumán, Facultad de Filosofía y Letras. Argentina.

Rev. Ecuat. Hist. Econ. Revista Ecuatoriana de Historia Económica. Banco Central del Ecuador, Centro de Investigación y Cultura. Quito.

Rev. Educ. Revista de Educación. Ministerio de Educación y Ciencia. Madrid.

Rev. Eme-Eme. Revista Eme-Eme. Univ. Católica Madre y Maestra. Santiago de los Caballeros, Dominican Republic.

Rev. Esp. Antropol. Am. Revista Española de Antropología Americana. Facultad de Geografía e Historia. Univ. Complutense de Madrid.

Rev. Estud. Colomb. Latinoam. Revista de Estudios Colombianos y Latinoamericanos. Asociación de Colombianistas Norteamericanos; Tercer Mundo Editores. Boulder, Colo.

Rev. Estud. Hisp./Poughkeepsie. Revista de Estudios Hispánicos. Dept. of Hispanic Studies, Vassar College. Poughkeepsie, N.Y.

Rev. Estud. Hisp./Río Piedras. Revista de Estudios Hispánicos. Univ. de Puerto Rico, Facultad de Humanidades. Río Piedras.

Rev. Eur. Revista Europea de Estudios Latinoamericanos y del Caribe = European Review of Latin American and Caribbean Studies. Center for Latin American Research and Documentation; Royal Institute of Linguistics and Anthropology. Amsterdam.

Rev. Filos./México. Revista de Filosofía. Univ. Iberoamericana, Depto. de Filosofía; Asociación Fray Alonso de la Veracruz. México.

Rev. Filos./San José. Revista de Filosofía. Univ. de Costa Rica. San José.

Rev. Filos. Teor. Polít. Revista de Filosofía y Teoría Política. Depto. de Filosofía, Univ. Nacional de La Plata. Argentina.

Rev. fr. hist. Outre-mer. Revue française d'histoire d'Outre-mer. Société de l'histoire des colonies françaises. Paris.

Rev. Hisp. Mod. Revista Hispánica Moderna. Hispanic Institute, Columbia Univ. New York.

Rev. Hist. Am. Revista de Historia de América. Instituto Panamericano de Geografía e Historia, Comisión de Historia. México.

Rev. Hist. Am. Argent. Revista de Historia Americana y Argentina. Univ. Nacional de Cuyo, Instituto de Historia. Mendoza, Argentina.

Rev. Hist. Econ. Revista de Historia Económica. Centro de Estudios Constitucionales, Univ. Carlos III. Madrid.

Rev. Hist./Heredia. Revista de Historia. Univ. Nacional de Costa Rica, Escuela de Historia. Heredia, Costa Rica.

Rev. Hist. Ideas. Revista de Historia de las Ideas. Instituto Panamericano de Geografía e Historia; Editorial Casa de la Cultura Ecuatoriana. Quito.

Rev. Hist./Managua. Revista de Historia. Instituto de Historia de Nicaragua. Managua.

Rev. Hist. Mil. Revista de Historia Militar. Servicio Histórico Militar. Madrid.

Rev. Hist. Naval. Revista de Historia Naval. Instituto de Historia y Cultura Naval Armada Española. Madrid.

Rev. Hist./Neuquén. Revista de Historia. Depto. de Historia, Facultad de Humani-dades, Univ. Nacional de Comahue. Neuquén, Argentina.

Rev. hist./Paris. Revue historique. Presses Univ. de France. Paris.

Rev. Hist./San José. Revista de Historia. Centro de Investigaciones Históricas, Univ. de Costa Rica. San José.

Rev. Hist./San Juan. Revista de Historia. Asociación Histórica Puertorriqueña. San Juan.

Rev. Hist./São Paulo. Revista de História. Univ. de São Paulo, Faculdade de Filosofia, Letras e Ciências Humanas, Depto. de História. São Paulo.

Rev. Iberoam. Revista Iberoamericana. Instituto Internacional de Literatura Iberoamericana; Univ. de Pittsburgh. Pittsburgh, Penn.

Rev. Indias. Revista de Indias. Consejo Superior de Investigaciones Científicas, Instituto Gonzalo Fernández de Oviedo. Madrid.

Rev. Inst. Cult. Puertorriq. Revista del Instituto de Cultura Puertorriqueña. San Juan.

Rev. Inst. Estud. Bras. Revista do Instituto de Estudos Brasileiros. Univ. de São Paulo, Instituto de Estudos Brasileiros. São Paulo.

Rev. Inst. Hist. Geogr. São Paulo. Revista do Instituto Histórico e Geográfico de São Paulo. São Paulo.

Rev. Inst. Invest. Educ. Revista del Instituto de Investigaciones Educativas. Instituto de Investigaciones Educativas. Buenos Aires.

Rev. Inst. Super. Música. Revista del Instituto Superior de Música, U.N.L. Santa Fe, Argentina.

Rev. Interam. Bibliogr. Revista Interamericana de Bibliografía. Organization of American States. Washington.

Rev. Junta Prov. Hist. Córdoba. Revista de la Junta Provincial de Historia de Córdoba. Córdoba, Argentina.

Rev. Juríd. Univ. P.R. Revista Jurídica de la Universidad de Puerto Rico. Escuela de Derecho, Univ. de Puerto Rico. Río Piedras.

Rev. Latinoam. Filos. Revista Latinoamericana de Filosofía. Centro de Investigaciones Filosóficas. Buenos Aires.

Rev. Mar. Revista de Marina. La Armada de Chile. Valparaíso.

Rev. Mex. Cienc. Polít. Soc. Revista Mexicana de Ciencias Políticas y Sociales. Facultad de Ciencias Políticas y Sociales, Univ. Nacional Autónoma de México. México.

Rev. Music. Chil. Revista Musical Chilena. Univ. de Chile, Facultad de Ciencias y Artes Musicales y de la Representación. Santiago.

Rev. Music. Puertorriq. Revista Musical Puertorriqueña. Instituto de Cultura Puertorriqueña. San Juan.

Rev. Nac. Cult./Caracas. Revista Nacional de Cultura. Consejo Nacional de Cultura. Caracas.

Rev. Nac./Montevideo. Revista Nacional. Ministerio de Instrucción Pública. Montevideo.

Rev. Occident. Revista de Occidente. Madrid.

Rev. Parag. Sociol. Revista Paraguaya de Sociología. Centro Paraguayo de Estudios Sociológicos. Asunción.

Rev. Paramillo. Revista Paramillo. Centro de Estudios Interdisciplinarios, Univ. Católica de Táchira. San Cristóbal, Venezuela.

Rev. Rev. Interam. Revista/Review Interamericana. Inter-American Univ. Press. Hato Rey, Puerto Rico.

Rev. Soc. haïti. Revue de la Société haïtienne d'histoire et géographie. Port-au-Prince.

Rev. Tiempo Espacio. Revista Tiempo y Espacio. Depto. de Historia y Geografía, Campus Chillán, Univ. del Bío-Bío. Chile.

Rev. Univ./Alcalá. Revista de la Universidad de Alcalá. Univ. de Alcalá de Henares. Alcalá de Henares, Spain.

Rev. Univ./Tabasco. Revista de la Universidad. Univ. Juárez Autónoma de Tabasco. Villahermosa, Mexico.

RIEV/San Sebastián. Revista Internacional de Estudios Vascos. Sociedad de Estudios Vascos. San Sebastián, Spain.

RLIN/Online. RLIN. Research Libraries Group. Mountain View, Calif.

Roman. Q. Romance Quarterly. Heldref Publications. Washington.

Runa/Buenos Aires. Runa. Archivo para las Ciencias del Hombre; Univ. de Buenos Aires, Facultad de Filosofía y Letras, Instituto de Antropología.

Santiago/Cuba. Santiago. Univ. de Oriente. Santiago, Cuba.

Sapientia/Buenos Aires. Sapientia. Facultad de Filosofía. Univ. Católica Argentina Santa María de los Buenos Aires. Buenos Aires.

SECOLAS Ann. SECOLAS Annals. Southeastern Conference on Latin American Studies; West Georgia College. Carrollton, Ga.

Secuencia/México. Secuencia. Instituto Mora. México.

SICE/Online. SICE: Foreign Trade Information System. General Secretariat, Organization of American States. Washington.

Siglo XIX. Siglo XIX. Facultad de Filosofía y Letras, Univ. Autónoma de Nuevo León. Monterrey, Mexico.

Siglo XX. Siglo XX. Twentieth Century Spanish Assn. of America. Lincoln, Neb.

Signos Univ. Signos Universitarios: Revista de la Universidad del Salvador. Univ. del Salvador. Buenos Aires.

Signs/Chicago. Signs. The Univ. of Chicago Press. Chicago, Ill.

SINF/CD-ROM. SINF. Dirección General de Información, Univ. Nacional Autónoma de México. México.

Sínt. Nova Fase. Síntese Nova Fase. Belo Horizonte, Brazil.

Síntesis/Madrid. Síntesis. Asociación de Investigación y Especialización sobre Temas Latinoamericanos. Madrid.

Slavery Abolit. Slavery and Abolition. Frank Cass & Co., Ltd., London.

Social. Particip. Socialismo y Participación. Ediciones Socialismo y Participación. Lima.

Stud. Emigr. Studi Emigrazione. Centro Studi Emigrazione. Rome.

Studia/Lisboa. Studia. Centro de Estudos Históricos Ultramarinos. Lisboa.

Studies/Dublin. Studies. Dublin.

Supl. Antropol.   Suplemento Antropológico. Univ. Católica de Nuestra Señora de la Asunción, Centro de Estudios Antropológicos. Asunción.

SWI Forum.   SWI Forum voor Kunst, Kultuur en Wetenschop. De Stichting. Paramaribo, Suriname.

Taller Let.   Taller de Letras. Instituto de Letras, Pontificia Univ. Católica de Chile. Santiago.

Thesaurus/Bogotá.   Thesaurus. Instituto Caro y Cuervo. Bogotá.

Todo es Hist.   Todo es Historia. Buenos Aires.

Torre/Río Piedras.   La Torre. Univ. de Puerto Rico. Río Piedras.

Trace/México.   Trace. Centre d'études mexicaines et centraméricaines. México.

Transition/Guyana.   Transition. Institute of Development Studies, Univ. of Guyana. Georgetown, Guyana.

Transl. Rev.   Translation Review. Univ. of Texas at Dallas. Richardson.

Travessia/Florianópolis.   Travessia. Univ. Federal de Santa Catarina. Florianópolis, Brazil.

Tri-Quarterly/Evanston.   Tri-Quarterly. Northwestern Univ., Evanston, Ill.

UnCover/Online.   UnCover. The UnCover Co., Denver, Colo.

Unión/Habana.   Unión. Unión de Escritores y Artistas de Cuba. La Habana.

Univ. La Habana.   Universidad de La Habana. La Habana.

Universidad/Santa Fe.   La Universidad. Univ. Nacional del Litoral. Santa Fe, Argentina.

UT-LANIC.   UT-LANIC. Institute of Latin American Studies, Univ. of Texas. Austin.

Veritas/Porto Alegre.   Veritas. Pontifícia Univ. Católica do Rio Grande do Sul. Porto Alegre, Brazil.

Vuelta/México.   Vuelta. México.

Wampum/Leiden.   Wampum. Archeologisch Centrum. Leiden, The Netherlands.

West. Hist. Q.   The Western Historical Quarterly. Western History Assn.; Utah State Univ., Logan, Utah.

William Mary Q.   The William and Mary Quarterly. College of William and Mary. Williamsburg, Va.

World Law Index I.   World Law Index, Part I: Index to Hispanic Legislation. Hispanic Law Division, Library of Congress. Washington.

Yachay/Cochabamba.   Yachay. Facultad de Filosofía y Ciencias Religiosas, Univ. Católica Boliviana. Cochabamba, Bolivia.

Yearbook/CLAG.   Yearbook. Conference of Latin Americanist Geographers; Ball State Univ., Muncie, Ind.

Z. Lat.am. Wien.   Zeitschrift für Lateinamerika Wien. Österreichisches Lateinamerika-Institut. Vienna.

Z. Miss. Relig.   Zeitschrift für Missionswissenschaft und Religionswissenschaft. Lucerne, Switzerland.

SUBJECT INDEX

Archivo General de la Nación (Mexico), 30, 1122, 1684.
Archivo Histórico Provincial de Las Palmas (Spain), 980.
Archivo Nacional de Cuba, 1824, 1836.
Archivo Nacional de Historia (Ecuador), 612.
Archivo Plutarco Elías Calles (Mexico), 1569.
Archivo Vaticano, 1080.
Archivum Romanum Societatis Iesu, 2253.
Arciniegas, Germán, 5442.
Arcos, Santiago, 5466.
Ardijis, Homero, 3764.
Arenas, Reinaldo, 3849, 3879.
Arequipa, Peru (city). Colonial Art, 223. Colonial Painting, 216. History, 2759. War of the Pacific (1879–1884), 2708.
Arequipa, Peru (dept.). Indigenous Peoples, 717. Pictorial Works, 205.
Arévalo, Juan José, 1760.
Argentina. Academia Nacional de la Historia, 3043.
Argentina. Corte Suprema de Justicia de la Nación, 3051.
Arguedas, José María, 3569, 3588, 3904, 3909–3910, 3912, 3914, 3920, 3922–3923, 3996, 5282.
Arias, María de las Mercedes, 4202.
Arica, Chile (city). Ethnohistory, 688. Land Tenure, 2385.
Aricó, José, 5363, 5457.
Ariel, 5496–5497.
Aristide, Jean-Bertrand, 2136, 2177.
Aristotle, 5362.
Ariza, Gonzalo, 338.
Armed Forces. *See* Military.
Arms Control. Costa Rica, 1757.
Arosemena, Justo, 5436.
Arosemena, Pablo, 5436.
Arquivo Público do Estado do Ceará (Brazil), 3160.
Arráncame la vida, 3771.
Arrau, Claudio, 5243.
Arredondo de Arguedas, Sybila, 3912.
Arreola, Juan José, 3763.
Arriagada, Carmen, 2826.
Art Collections. Bolivia, 228. Brazil, 383, 391. Ecuador, 236.
Art Criticism, 245. Argentina, 323. Peru, 361. Venezuela, 371.
Art History. Argentina, 320. Mexico, 270. Venezuela, 372.
Artifacts. French Caribbean, 1842. Indigenous Peoples, 616.
Artigas, José Gervasio, 3099, 3138.

Artigas, Manuel, 3138.
Artisanry. Arab Influences, 121. Glassware, 113. Guatemala, 1679. Peru, 2696.
Artisans. Chile, 2850. Colombia, 2631, 2661. Mexico, 1463. Peru, 226, 2747, 2780.
Artists. Argentina, 315, 318, 322, 325. Biography, 246. Bolivia, 326. Chile, 327, 332, 336. Colombia, 344–346. Cuba, 5419. Dominican Republic, 305. Ecuador, 352, 354. France, 389. Mexico, 263, 1379, 3767. Peru, 360, 366. Venezuela, 370, 374. Women, 360, 404.
Arvelo Larriva, Alfredo, 4493.
Ascasubi, Hilario, 3645.
Ashaninca. *See* Campa.
Asian Influences, 3489.
Asians. Mexico, 5387.
Asociación Agraria Argentina, 3047.
Asociación General de Agricultores (Guatemala), 1696.
Assassinations, 2147. Guatemala, 1729. Mexico, 1449.
Assimilation. *See* Acculturation.
Assis Brasil, Joaquim Francisco de, 3324.
Associação Comercial da Bahia, 3298.
Astronomy. Guiana Region, 715. Incas, 818, 835–836. Peru, 819.
Asturias, Miguel Angel, 3505, 3778, 3798, 3801, 3807–3808.
Asunción, Paraguay (city). Description and Travel, 3102. Historiography, 2559. History, 2562, 2571.
Atacama Desert (Chile). Indigenous Peoples, 724, 838. Spanish Conquest, 811.
Atacameño (indigenous group). Economic Anthropology, 724.
Atahualpa, 2351, 3541, 3551, 3579.
Atienza, Juan de, 778.
Atienza, Lope de, 798.
Atlantic Coast (Nicaragua). Ethnic Groups and Ethnicity, 1783. Foreign Intervention, 1783. Social History, 1630.
Atonal, Juan, 476.
Audiencia of Buenos Aires. Law and Legislation, 2538.
Audiencia of Charcas. Biography, 2431, 2436. Bourbon Reforms, 2543. Church History, 2437. Colonial Administration, 2543. Education, 2523. Intellectuals, 2431. Libraries, 683.
Audiencia of Cuzco. Law and Legislation, 2426.
Audiencia of Guatemala, 1674. Demography, 1654. Indigenous Peoples, 1654.

Chibcha (indigenous group). Ethnohistory, 610. Religious Life and Customs, 708.
Chicago, Illinois (city). Mexicans, 1553.
Chicanos. *See* Mexican Americans; Mexicans.
Chichén Itzá Site (Mexico), 564.
Chichimecs (indigenous group). Warfare, 587.
Chiclayo, Peru (city). Economic History, 2731.
Chihuahua, Mexico (state). Banking and Financial Institutions, 1527. Biography, 1475. Church-State Relations, 1556. Indigenous Peoples, 1400. Insurrections, 1431. Labor and Laboring Classes, 1364, 1591. Land Reform, 1592. Land Tenure, 1292, 1562–1563. Minerals and Mining Industry, 1591. Political History, 1327, 1503. Popular Religion, 1431. Social Classes, 1400. Social Policy, 1364.
Chilam Balam, 516.
Chilapa, Mexico (town). Missionaries, 4658.
Childbirth. Brazil, 3218.
Children. Brazil, 3190, 3406. Chile, 2885. Slaves and Slavery, 3202, 3369.
Children's Literature. Translating and Interpreting, 5087.
Chiloé, Chile (prov.). Colonization, 2484. Discovery and Exploration, 2477. History, 2470. Insurrections, 2485. Land Settlement, 2484.
Chimalpahin Cuauhtlehuanitzin, Domingo Francisco de San Antón Muñón, 565.
Chimu (indigenous group). Pottery, 2772.
Chinandega, Nicaragua (dept.). Oral History, 1734. Social Change, 1734.
Chincha Valley (Peru). Blacks, 2698.
Chinese. Caribbean Area, 2001. Cuba, 2048, 2050. Mexico, 1369, 1420, 1604. Peru, 2775.
Chinese Academy of Social Sciences. Institute of Latin American Studies, 1109.
Chiquito (indigenous group). Ethnohistory, 755. Missions, 2442, 2450.
Chiquitos, Bolivia (prov.). Jesuits, 2442. Missions, 2442.
Chiriguano (indigenous group). Cultural Identity, 704. Ethnohistory, 631, 787. Missions, 778. Social Life and Customs, 788. Warfare, 787.
Chiriquí, Panama (prov.). History, 1636.
Chocó, Colombia (dept.). Indigenous Peoples, 649.
Chocó (indigenous group, Brazil). *See* Shocó.
Chocrón, Isaac E., 4702.
Chol (indigenous group). Warfare, 478.
Choral Music. Venezuela, 5299.

Chota River Valley (Ecuador). Sugar Industry and Trade, 635.
Christian Base Communities, 5340.
Christian Democracy, 5353.
Christianity, 5333. Blacks, 1969. Jamaica, 1969. Mexico, 1739. Nicaragua, 1739.
Chronology. Incas, 741, 836. Peru, 741.
Chubut, Argentina (prov.). History, 2946.
Chumacero, Alí, 4486.
Chumash (indigenous group). Insurrections, 1323.
Chuquihuanca Ayulo, Francisco, 630.
Chuquisaca, Bolivia (dept.). Social Conflict, 705.
Church Architecture, 85. Argentina, 179, 181, 185, 194. Bolivia, 755, 2442. Brazil, 382. Chile, 2459. Ecuador, 233. Haiti, 1802. Mexico, 100, 104, 106, 110, 114, 121, 125, 131, 139, 146, 148, 156, 163, 166. Mural Painting, 109. Peru, 235, 238. Uruguay, 192. Venezuela, 196.
Church History, 853, 870, 892, 911, 928, 950, 958, 976, 982, 997, 1000, 1032, 1080, 1156, 5352. Andean Region, 609, 634, 2259. Archivo General de Indias, 994. Audiencia of Charcas, 2437. Bibliography, 936, 1184. Bolivia, 755, 2442. Brazil, 3367, 5482. Caribbean Area, 1856. Central America, 1659–1660. Chile, 2475, 2478, 2480, 2488, 2857. Colombia, 2296, 2301, 2309, 2316, 2653. Colonial Art, 86. Congresses, 839, 858, 906, 959–960. Costa Rica, 1683, 1788. Cuba, 2189. Dominican Republic, 2214. Ecuador, 2337, 2672, 2685, 5444. Exhibitions, 1023. Guadeloupe, 2039. Guatemala, 1625. Hispaniola, 1865. Honduras, 1637–1638. Indigenous Peoples, 1011. Mexico, 149, 1061, 1184, 1263, 1268, 1340, 1365, 1458, 1554, 1660, 5385. Missionaries, 922, 1024. Nicaragua, 1623, 5401. Paraguay, 2510. Peru, 987, 2364, 2382, 2384, 2393, 2396, 2406, 2413, 2419, 2423–2424, 2727, 2746. Seventh-Day Adventists, 1105. Uruguay, 3151. Venezuela, 2280, 2595. Viceroyalty of New Spain (1540–1821), 1156, 1160–1162, 1247–1248, 1251, 5395. Viceroyalty of Río de la Plata (1776–1810), 2532.
Church Records. Costa Rica, 1639. French Caribbean, 1912. Haiti, 1864, 2007. Martinique, 1855. Mexico, 1125, 1136.
Church-State Relations, 870, 941, 1080, 1087. Argentina, 2925, 5534. Bolivia, 2811. Brazil, 3193, 3350, 3387–3388. Central America, 1765. Chile, 2857, 5467. Colombia, 2653. Colonial History, 2274. Costa Rica, 1788.

lans, 882. Central America, 1775. Colombia, 2303. Colonial History, 971, 974, 1017, 1031, 1072, 2254. Databases, 53, 60, 64, 69. French Caribbean, 1938, 1942–1943. Guadeloupe, 1929. Guatemala, 1679. Indigenous Peoples, 601, 676. Mexico, 53. Paraguay, 3120. Peru, 2392. Río de la Plata, 2572. Spanish Caribbean, 1938. Uruguay, 3120. Venezuela, 2269, 2590, 2604.
Commercial Art. Brazil, 418.
Commercial Policy. See Trade Policy.
Communication. Databases, 66. Martinique, 1827. Venezuela, 5430.
Communism and Communist Parties, 5313. Anthologies, 5346. Argentina, 2997. Bibliography, 5371. Brazil, 3317, 3362, 3396, 3413, 3447, 3458, 5480. Central America, 1731. Costa Rica, 1711. Cuba, 2220, 5415. Guatemala, 1728, 1730. Mexico, 1446, 1469. Nicaragua, 1710. Peru, 5452, 5459–5460.
Community Development. Blacks, 1977.
Compadrazgo. Indigenous Peoples, 2367. Peru, 2367.
Los compadritos, 4666.
Compañía de Tranvías Anglo Argentina Ltda. (firm), 2971.
Compañía Real del Monte y Pachuca (firm), 1361.
Compendio apologético en alabanza de la poesía, 3598.
Composers. Argentina, 5127, 5131, 5135–5136. Bolivia, 5144. Brazil, 3456, 5148, 5153, 5157, 5164–5166, 5168, 5171, 5178–5179. Chile, 5199, 5205, 5208. Colombia, 5211. Cuba, 5222, 5226–5227, 5233. Dominican Republic, 5185. Jamaica, 5187–5188. Mexico, 5236, 5238, 5240, 5250, 5254, 5258, 5262, 5265, 5271, 5273–5275, 5277. Peru, 5281. Uruguay, 5296. Venezuela, 5300, 5304.
Computer Networks. Peace, 63.
Comuneros. See Insurrection of the Comuneros; Revolution of the Comuneros.
Con los pies descalzos, llenos de barro, 4700.
Concepción, Chile (city). Church History, 2482.
Concepción, Chile (prov.). History, 2835.
Concilio Provincial del Santo Domingo, 1865.
Conductors (music). Venezuela, 5306.
Confederación de Trabajadores de México, 1607.
Confederación General del Trabajo de la República Argentina, 3025.
Confederación Nacional Campesina (Mexico), 1479.

Confederación Revolucionaria Michoacana del Trabajo, 1455.
Confraternities. Colombia, 805. Mexico, 504, 568, 584.
Congreso de las Provincias Unidas (Colombia), 2610.
Congresses. Church History, 839. Mexico, 58, 1130.
Coni, Emilio Ramón, 2985.
Coni, Gabriela Laperrière de, 2985.
Conibo (indigenous group). Legends, 4025. Myths and Mythology, 4025. Religion, 4025.
Conquerors, 1847, 3516, 3533, 3548, 3566, 3581, 3585, 3604. Argentina, 2550, 2574. Borderlands, 1324. Central America, 1643. Mexico, 1174. New Mexico, 3554. Paraguay, 2563. Río de la Plata, 3530. Sex and Sexual Relations, 989. South America, 3616. Viceroyalty of New Spain (1540–1821), 3560, 3572.
The conquest of Jerusalem, 484.
The conquest of Rhodes, 484.
Conselheiro, Antônio, 3341–3342, 3385.
Conservation and Restoration, 95. Altarpieces, 159. Bolivia, 231. Brazil, 376. Colonial Art, 204. Jamaica, 169. Mexico, 105, 122, 146. Peru, 221. Puerto Rico, 304. Uruguay, 193.
Conservatism. Argentina, 2952, 5530. Ecuador, 5446. Mexico, 1448, 5391. Venezuela, 5428.
Constant, Benjamin, 3265.
Constitutional Conventions. Venezuela, 2593, 2606.
Constitutional History, 2656. Argentina, 2944, 3064, 3071, 5513. Brazil, 3265, 3436. Chile, 2832, 2853, 2878. Colombia, 2291, 2648, 2663. Ecuador, 2691. Mexico, 1380, 1470, 1478, 1566. Venezuela, 2606.
Constitutions. Argentina, 3064. Brazil, 3265. Mexico, 1375, 1470.
Construction Industry. Mexico, 141.
Consulado de Buenos Aires, 2553.
Consulado de Lima, 2392.
Consumption (economics). Costa Rica, 1789.
Contact. See Cultural Contact.
Contadora. See Arias Peace Plan (1987); Grupo de Contadora.
Contadora Support Group. See Grupo de los Ocho.
Contestado Insurrection (Brazil, 1912–1916), 3272.
Contrapunteo cubano del tabaco y el azúcar, 5416.
Contras. See Counterrevolutionaries.

Convento de San José (México), 1261.
Convento de San Nicolás Tolentino de Acto-
pan (Actopan, Mexico), 109.
Convento del Carmen de Morelia (Mexico),
149.
Convents. Bolivia, 209. Colonial Painting,
216. Economic History, 2360. Honduras,
1651. Mexico, 109–110, 124, 147, 149.
Peru, 216, 2360. Viceroyalty of New Spain
(1540–1821), 1244, 1261, 1269.
*Conversaciones americanas sobre España y
sus Indias,* 1093.
Cooke, John William, 2903.
Cooperatives. Argentina, 3005.
Copiapó, Chile (city). History, 2461.
Coquilago Ango, Beatriz, 2351.
Cordal Gill, Silvia, 3116.
Cordell Family, 3116.
Córdoba, Antonio de, 2564.
Córdoba, Argentina (city). Catholicism, 2577.
Church Architecture, 185. Elites, 2568.
History, 2915. Radicalism, 5510. University
Reform, 5510.
Córdoba, Argentina (prov.). Church Architec-
ture, 181. Commerce, 3029. Economic His-
tory, 3082. Elementary Education, 3085.
History, 2577. Independence Movements,
3082. Italians, 3012. Newspapers, 2914.
Peronism, 3075. Political Parties, 3075.
Slaves and Slavery, 3082.
Corn. Mexico, 432, 582.
Coronelismo. Brazil, 3386, 3438.
Corporatism. Brazil, 3252, 3296, 3301.
Correio Brasiliense, 5477.
La correspondencia de Sarmiento, 3656.
Corrientes, Argentina (city). Ethnic Groups
and Ethnicity, 620.
Corrientes, Argentina (prov.). History, 2957.
Corruption. Colonial Administration, 2445.
Corruption in Politics. *See* Political
Corruption.
Cortázar, Julio, 4202, 4219.
Cortés, Hernán, 1148, 1153, 1167, 1174, 1186,
1225, 1271, 3572.
Cortes de Cádiz, 1097.
Cortés y Larraz, Pedro, *Archbishop,* 1659.
Corzas, Francisco, 267.
Cosmology. Andean Region, 797, 802. Incas,
773, 814. Indigenous Peoples, 881. Mayas,
555. Peru, 802.
Cosmos, 5311.
Cossa, Roberto, 4666.
Costa, Hipólito José da, 5477.
Costa, João Severiano Maciel da, *Marquês de
Queluz,* 3225.

Costa Rican Development Corporation. *See*
Corporación Costarricense de Desarrollo.
Costumbrismo, 3687. Ecuador, 353.
Costume and Adornment. Aruba, 1841. Peru,
5280.
Cotton Industry and Trade. Argentina, 2986.
Bahamas, 1933. Peru, 2733. Suriname,
2106.
Counterrevolutions. Mexico, 1588. Nicara-
gua, 1707.
Coups d'Etat. Argentina, 3051. Bolivia, 2804.
Brazil, 3243, 3252. Chile, 2834, 2851, 2861,
2889. Colombia, 2650. Gran Colombia,
2609. Guatemala, 1729, 1743. Sources,
2834.
Cowboys. Colombia, 2598. Venezuela, 2598.
Coyoacán, Mexico (town). Social Structure,
502.
Crafts. *See* Artisanry.
Credit. Viceroyalty of New Spain (1540–
1821), 1306.
Credit Foncier (company), 1396.
Crespo, Pedro, 1517.
Crevaux, Jules, 1994.
Criado de Castilla, Alonso, 1674.
Crime and Criminals. Argentina, 3062. Bo-
livia, 2243. Brazil, 3166, 3248, 3282, 3293,
3417, 3437. Chile, 2479. Historiography,
3166. Indigenous Peoples, 2414. Peru, 2243,
2414. Women, 3437.
El crimen de la guerra, 5525.
Criollismo. Colombia, 2294, 2301. Cultural
History, 941.
Criollos. Colonial Administration, 958.
Cristero Rebellion (Mexico, 1926–1929),
1545, 1558. Historiography, 1559.
Croix, Carlos Francisco de Croix, *Marqués
de,* 1220.
Crónica de una muerte anunciada, 3887,
3891.
Crónica del Perú, 5347.
Cronistas, 963, 1035–1036, 1074, 3517, 3527,
3570, 3585, 3602, 3609, 3614, 5369. Ama-
zon Basin, 3547. Andean Region, 643, 2353.
Bolivia, 2430. Chile, 2457, 2469, 2483. Co-
lombia, 2306. German, 3530. Historical
Geography, 1046. Historiography, 3559.
Illustrators, 3594. Incas, 766, 3584, 3589.
Mexico, 424, 535, 562. Peru, 591–592, 600,
629, 644, 651, 669–670, 761, 2399, 3532,
3541, 3574. Río de la Plata, 2506–2507.
Spaniards, 3551. Spanish Conquest, 801.
Crosby, James, 2033.
Cruz, Francisco de la, 2416.
Cruz, Laureano de la, 2329.

Diego Padró, José Isaac de, 3856.

Diglossia. *See* Code Switching.

Dioses y hombres de Huarochirí, 3574.

Diplomatic History, 883, 1100. Argentina, 2928, 3026. Bolivia, 2781, 2787. Central America, 1702. Chile, 2704, 2875. Colombia, 2615. France, 1568. Great Britain, 1702, 1771. Guatemala, 1730. Haiti, 2176. Honduras, 1689. Latin America, 1088. Mexico, 1388, 1550, 1568. Peru, 2704, 2710, 2781. Sources, 2615. Spain, 1906, 2066, 2085, 2087. Uruguay, 3145. US, 1088, 1702, 1730, 1739, 1741, 2066. Venezuela, 2600.

Diplomats. Brazil, 3373, 3450. Mexico, 1559, 1739. Nicaragua, 1739. Paraguay, 3106–3107. US, 1739.

Directories. CD-ROMs, 1–2. Databases, 3–6. Internet, 9.

Disarmament. *See* Arms Control.

Discépolo, Armando, 4693.

Discourse Analysis. Argentina, 5531–5532. Brazil, 3305.

Discovery and Exploration, 855, 871, 900, 909, 928, 945, 954–956, 978, 985, 1009–1010, 1012, 1019–1020, 1028, 1039–1040, 1051, 1058, 1070, 3556, 3561, 3582, 3585–3587, 3595, 3600, 3604–3605, 3619, 5311, 5316, 5320, 5357, 5370. Amazon Basin, 722, 2267. Aragonese Influences, 1063. Archives, 980. Argentina, 2583. Borderlands, 1948, 1960, 1962, 1965. Brazil, 3205, 3207, 3215, 3284. Catalans, 875. Central America, 1677. Chile, 2457, 2477, 2486. Colombia, 2287. Costa Rica, 1631. Diaries, 2257. Dictionaries, 930. Ecuador, 2346. Guiana Region, 1994. Hispaniola, 1044, 1872. Historiography, 979, 1042, 5329. Jesuits, 2408. Magellan Strait, 2564. Mexico, 1677. Nicaragua, 1632, 1650. Pacific Area, 2254. Paraguay, 2559. Patagonia, 2490. Philosophy, 5517. Portuguese Influences, 1082. Puerto Rico, 3603. Sources, 2486. South America, 3616. Spanish Influences, 1082. Venezuela, 2268. Viceroyalty of New Spain (1540–1821), 1164, 3596. Views of, 5325.

Discrimination. Mexico, 1369.

Diseases, 868. Argentina, 3044. Bolivia, 2433, 2452. Brazil, 3235. Chile, 2466. Colombia, 2319. Demography, 864. Ecuador, 2320, 2339, 2687. Guatemala, 1668. Historiography, 938. Indigenous Peoples, 961, 1668, 2320, 2466. Mayas, 522. Mexico, 551, 1426, 1430. Peru, 2717. Slaves and Slavery, 2417. Venezuela, 2591. Viceroyalty of New Spain (1540–1821), 1175, 1258, 1278–1279, 1312.

Viceroyalty of Peru (1542–1822), 2320, 2421.

Dissertations and Theses. Mexico, 1144.

Distéfano, Juan Carlos, 322.

Distribution of Wealth. *See* Income Distribution.

Distrito Federal, Mexico. Boundaries, 1392. Historical Geography, 1357.

Divina comedia, 4602.

El Divino Narciso, 3549.

Divorce. Argentina, 2548.

Doblas, Gonzalo de, 2507.

Doctor Faustus, 3490.

Documentaries. Guatemala, 1692.

Documentation Centers. *See* Libraries.

Domecq, Brianda, 3709.

Domestic Animals. Brazil, 3333. Colonization, 1963.

Domestic Violence. *See* Family Violence.

Domestics. Brazil, 3236, 3264.

Domingo, de Santo Tomás, *Fray*, 2258–2259.

Domínguez, Francisco Atanasio, 1298.

Domínguez, Oralia, 5248.

Domínguez Navarro, Ofelia, 2222.

Dominicans (religious order), 186, 959, 1032. Argentina, 5506. Congresses, 858. Law and Legislation, 970. Mexico, 5395. Missions, 1024. Peru, 726, 987, 2382, 2397.

Doña tierra, 4670.

Donoso, José, 4071.

Dorfman, Ariel, 4700, 5022.

Dorrego, Manuel, 3094.

Dowry. Brazil, 3181.

Dox, Thurston, 5188.

Drama. Franciscans, 484. Jamaica, 1815.

Dreher, Johann Karl, 3370.

Dresden (ship), 2875.

Droughts. Bolivia, 2452.

Drug Enforcement. Mexico, 1575. US, 1575.

Drug Traffic. Mexico/US, 1575.

Drugs and Drug Trade. *See* Drug Abuse; Drug Enforcement; Drug Traffic; Drug Utilization; Pharmaceutical Industry.

Durán, Diego, 464.

Durango, Mexico (city). Mexican Revolution (1910–1920), 1602.

Durango, Mexico (state). Congresses, 1480. Haciendas, 1438. History, 1480. Land Tenure, 1292. Revolutions and Revolutionary Movements, 1438. Rural Sociology, 1438.

Dussel, Enrique, 5352, 5463, 5511, 5523.

Dutch. Brazil, 384, 3194, 3207, 3212–3213. Description and Travel, 2490. Missionaries, 1806. Patagonia, 2490. Slaves and Slavery, 1871.

Guacamaya, Miguel Gerónimo, 2264.
Guadalajara, Mexico (city). Colonial Architecture, 117. Colonial History, 952. Education, 1140. Elites, 1398. Historians, 1552. Historiography, 1126. History, 1126. Jesuits, 1140. Photography, 1516. Social History, 1398.
Guadalupe, Our Lady of, 118. Iconography, 120. Mexico, 128.
Guajiro. See Goajiro.
Guamán Poma de Ayala, Felipe, 591–592, 643, 709, 777, 2353–2354, 3517, 3539, 3551, 3588, 3611.
Guanacaste, Costa Rica (prov.). Latifundios, 1716. Political History, 1712.
Guanajuato, Mexico (city). Archives, 1125. Church Records, 1125. Historiography, 1133. Social History, 1125.
Guanajuato, Mexico (state). History, 1133. Marriage, 1259. Minerals and Mining Industry, 1413. Public Health, 1426.
Guane (indigenous group). Ethnohistory, 737.
Guarani (indigenous group). Acculturation, 620. Ethnohistory, 807. Family and Family Relations, 2493. History, 2494, 2507. Insurrections, 2509. Land Settlement, 749. Missions, 2514, 2554, 2582. Myths and Mythology, 632. Paraguay, 752. Poetry, 4502. Theater, 4695. Uruguay, 749.
Guatemala. Juzgado Privativo de Tierras, 1633.
Guatemala, Guatemala (city). Pictorial Works, 1754.
Guayana Region (Venezuela). History, 2283.
Guayaquil, Ecuador (city). Economic History, 2328. Labor Movement, 2675, 2688. Public Health, 2687. Social History, 2674.
Guaykuru. See Guaycuru.
El güegüence, 3522, 3535.
Güemes, Martín Miguel, 2948, 2983.
Guerra, Rosa, 3665.
Guerrero, Mexico (state). Land Tenure, 1270. Mexican Revolution (1910–1920), 1574. Peasant Uprisings, 1574.
Guerrillas. Argentina, 3069. Autobiography, 2800. Bolivia, 2800, 2812. Colombia, 2638. Cuba, 5409. El Salvador, 1713, 1737, 1752, 3780. Guatemala, 1741. Peru, 2702, 5451. Saint-Domingue, 1932. Uruguay, 3133, 3136.
Guevara, Ernesto, 2147, 2166, 2226, 2800, 2812, 5415.
Guevara, Trinidad, 4708.
Guiana Region. Astronomy, 715. Discovery and Exploration, 1994. Explorers, 1994. Myths and Mythology, 715.

Guido, Beatriz, 4218.
Guido, José María, 3052.
Guilds. Colonial History, 1037.
Guimarães, Antônio Ferreira Prestes, 3309.
Güiraldes, Ricardo, 3629.
Guitar. Mexico, 5249.
Guiteras y Gener, Jose Ramon, 2012.
Guldberg, Cerutti, 5511.
Gulf of Venezuela. See Maracaibo Gulf (Colombia and Venezuela).
Guzmán, Humberto, 3715.
Guzmán Blanco, Antonio, 2594–2595.
Guzmán Reynoso, Abimael, 5451.
Los habitantes, 3927.
Hacho de Velasco, Sancho, 2336.
Haciendas. Argentina, 2539. Bolivia, 800, 2439, 2447, 2805, 2807, 2809. Chile, 2456, 2828. Costa Rica, 1716, 1769. Honduras, 1758. Jesuits, 769. Mexico, 1124, 1341, 1385, 1422–1423, 1438, 1519, 1572. Peru, 2355, 2388, 2695, 2732, 2765. Uruguay, 188. Viceroyalty of New Spain (1540–1821), 1200, 1233, 1285, 1322.
Haeften, Benedictus van, 216.
Hahn, Reynaldo, 5301.
Haiku, Brazilian, 4804, 4874, 4885, 4908.
Haitian Revolution (1787–1794), 1891, 1904, 1908–1909, 1921, 1939, 1945. Influence of, 2128.
Haitians. Cuba, 1945.
Halffter, Rodolfo, 5254, 5265.
Hallucinogenic Drugs. Mayas, 459.
HAPI Online, 26.
Hasta no verte Jesús mío, 3772.
Hato Mayor del Rey, Dominican Republic (town). History, 2143.
Havana. See La Habana.
Hay-Herrán Treaty (Panama), 1764.
Haya de la Torre, Víctor Raúl, 2710, 2738, 2757, 5454, 5460.
Health Care. See Medical Care.
Heiremans, Luis Alberto, 4714.
Henequen Industry and Trade. Mexico, 1524.
Henríquez Ureña, Pedro, 3464, 3864, 5376.
El Heraldo, 3892.
Heredia, José María, 3630.
Heredia, Costa Rica (prov.). Economic History, 1687. Sugar Industry and Trade, 1687.
Heredia Gayán Family, 2527.
El hermano asno, 3505.
Hermosillo, Mexico (city). Industry and Industrialization, 1447.
Hernández, Felisberto, 4242, 4245.
Hernández, Francisco, 1154.
Hernández, Julio Alberto, 5185.
Hernández Martínez, Maximiliano, 1759.

Leclerc, Charles, 1918.
Lecuona, Ernesto, 5227.
Ledesma, Alonso de, 3576.
Legends. Borderlands, 1948. Historical Geography, 934. Mayas, 5062.
Léger, Jacques Nicolas, 2176.
Legislative Bodies. Mexico, 1339, 1367.
Legislators. Colonial Administration, 1097. Puerto Rico, 2137.
Legislatures. *See* Legislative Bodies.
Leirner, Felícia, 403.
Leñero, Vicente, 4682, 4687.
León, Hebreo, 3584.
León, Nicaragua (city). Church History, 1623. Colonial History, 1623.
León Gómez, Adolfo, 2637.
León Pinelo, Antonio de, 5364.
Leonard, Irving, 3568.
Leonardo, da Vinci, 4608.
Lerdo de Tejada, Juan Antonio, 1238.
Lerner, Elisa, 4702.
Léry, Jean de, 3205.
Letelier, Valentín, 5465.
Letter to the sovereigns, 3619.
Levine, Suzanne Jill, 5095.
Levy, Herbert Victor, 3343.
Lexicons. *See* Dictionaries.
Leyenda de los Soles, 525.
Lezama Lima, José, 3865, 4506, 4518.
Lezana, Luis de, 226.
Liberalism, 5353. Argentina, 5534. Brazil, 3256, 3353, 5477, 5481, 5486. Chile, 5467. Colombia, 2295, 2651, 5436. Costa Rica, 1762, 1770, 1780, 1788. Ecuador, 5446. Indigenous Peoples, 1427. Mexico, 1427, 5379, 5381. Panama, 5436. Peru, 5450. Uruguay, 5494. Venezuela, 5428.
Liberation Theology, 846, 911, 984, 5327–5328, 5332, 5335, 5340, 5350, 5352, 5373, 5388, 5461. Argentina, 5506, 5511. Bolivia, 5463. Catholic Church, 5314. Marxism, 5341. Nicaragua, 1724, 5335, 5401.
Libertad, creación e identidad, 3465.
Libraries. Mexican Revolution (1910–1920), 1600. Mexico, 1434. Peru, 683, 5453. Spain, 857. US, 1600. Viceroyalty of Peru (1542–1822), 2380.
Library Catalogs. Databases, 42, 55, 62, 68, 74. Ecuador, 42. Venezuela, 74.
Library Resources. US, 879.
Libro de los cien capítulos, 3567.
Libro del cavallero Zifar, 3567.
Lienzo de Tlaxcala, 439, 527.
Liga Eleitoral Católica (Brazil), 3388.
Lihn, Enrique, 4480.

Lima, João de Sousa, 3386.
Lima, Peru (city). Blacks, 2415. Catholic Church, 2413. Church Architecture, 238. Church History, 2364. Colonial History, 952. Commerce, 2392. Compadrazgo, 2367. Cultural History, 2722. Diseases, 2417. Economic Conditions, 2766. Economic History, 2376. Elites, 2407. Encomiendas, 2410. History, 2368. Indigenous Peoples, 2410. Inquisition, 2364. Insurrections, 746. Migration, 2737. Public Health, 2717. Slaves and Slavery, 2417, 2740. Social Classes, 2376, 2763. Social History, 2367, 2393. Urbanization, 2766.
Lima, Peru (dept.). Social History, 2356.
Limón, Costa Rica (prov.). Racism, 1738. West Indians, 1738.
Lindbergh, Charles A., 1542.
Linguistic Geography. Quechua, 720.
Liniers, Argentina (town). History, 2939.
Liniers y Bremond, Santiago de, 3007.
Lisboa, Antônio Francisco, 382.
Liscano, Juan, 4533.
Liste, Alba de, *Count*, 2247.
Literacy and Illiteracy. Andean Region, 628.
Literary Criticism. Mexico, 5390.
Literature. Argentina, 5518. Brazil, 5083. Cultural History, 3461. Feminism, 5092. Historiography, 3460. Homosexuality, 3469. Human Rights, 3459. Reference Books, 5083. Women, 3465–3466, 5092.
Lithics. *See* Stone Implements.
Lithography. Mexico, 266, 1379.
Littín, Miguel, 3952.
Livestock. Argentina, 719. Jamaica, 2102. Jesuits, 769.
El llano en llamas, 3769.
Llanos Orientales (Colombia and Venezuela). Colonization, 2635. Ethnography, 2598. History, 2660.
Llanqueuma Hacienda (Bolivia). History, 800.
Loaysa, Jerónimo de, 2397.
Lobbyists. *See* Pressure Groups.
Local Government. *See* Municipal Government.
Local Transit. Argentina, 2971.
Locke, John, 5323.
Loja, Ecuador (town). Colonial Administration, 2321.
Lopes Neto, João Simões, 4919.
López, Estanislao, 3002.
López Contreras, Eleazar, 2602.
López de Gómara, Francisco, 3560, 3579.
López Medel, Tomás, 1005, 1646.
López Pesoa, Emiliano, 3104.

Loreto, Peru (dept.). Ethnic Groups and Ethnicity, 671. Jesuits, 671.
Los Angeles, California (city). Popular Music, 5256.
Los Angeles, Chile (town). History, 2489. Sources, 2489.
Los Lobos (musical group), 5256.
Los Tres Reyes (ship), 1034.
Losada Guido, Alejandro, 3482.
Loveira, Carlos, 3875.
Lower Rio Grande Valley, Texas. History, 1589.
Loynaz, Dulce María, 3868, 4503.
Loynaz del Castillo, Enrique, 2046.
Lozada, Manuel, 1395.
Lucas, Juan Francisco, 1523.
Ludmer, Josefina, 3606.
Luis, Raúl, 3857.
Luján, Argentina (town). Landowners, 2539. Social Structure, 2539.
Lumbisí Hacienda (Ecuador). Ethnohistory, 780.
Lurigancho, Peru (district). History, 2766.
Lynch, Elisa Alicia, 3104, 3114.
Lyricists. Argentina, 5127.
Macaguaje (indigenous group). Traditional Medicine, 2619.
Macate, Peru (town). History, 681.
Maceo, Antonio, 2081.
Machado, Antônio de Alcântara, 4934.
Machado, Maria Clara, 4937.
Machiganga. See Machiguenga.
Machismo. See Sex Roles.
Machu Picchu Site (Peru), 642, 785.
Madero, Francisco I., 1492, 1498, 1525, 1577.
Madero, Gustavo A., 1498, 1535.
Madero Family, 1498.
Madres de la Plaza de Mayo (Argentina), 3470.
Maeztu, Ramiro de, 5514.
Magallanes, Chile (prov.). History, 2866.
Magdalena, Peru (town). History, 2368.
Magellan Strait. Expeditions, 2564. Maps and Cartography, 2564.
Magic. Viceroyalty of New Spain (1540–1821), 1180.
Magic Realism (art). Guatemala, 299. Peru, 360.
Magic Realism (literature), 3613, 3808.
Magnin, Juan, 5445.
Maids. See Domestics.
Maine (battleship), 1979, 1983.
Maize. See Corn.
Mak'a. See Macá.
Makú. See Macú.
Makuna. See Macuna.

Málaga, Spain (city). Commerce, 974.
Malaria, 868.
Malaspina, Alessandro, 973, 1007, 1164, 2257.
Maldonado, Uruguay (city). History, 3131–3132.
Maldonado, Uruguay (dept.). History, 3131.
Maldonado de Silva, Francisco, 4042.
Mallea, Eduardo, 5528.
Mallorquín, Juan León, 3095.
Malnutrition. See Nutrition.
Malvinas, Islas. See Falkland Islands.
Mamani, García, 783.
Mañach, Jorge, 5417.
Manaus, Brazil (city). Opera, 5172. Tenentismo, 3426.
Manco Inca, 746.
Manizales, Colombia (city). History, 2664.
Manley, Michael, 2182.
Mann, Thomas, 3490.
Manso, Juana, 3665.
Manuela, 3686.
Manuscripts. Aztecs, 438, 569. Christopher Columbus, 957. Ecuador, 2326. Indigenous Peoples, 576. Italy, 957. Mexico, 1215. Mixtec, 572. Nahuas, 569–571. Spain, 935. US, 879.
Manuscrito Can Ek, 524.
Mapa de Macuilxochitl, 543.
Maps and Cartography, 972, 1081, 1091. Aztecs, 486. Colonial History, 3591. Colonization, 3617. Magellan Strait, 2564. Martinique, 1826. Mexico, 39. Peru, 237. South America, 2248.
Mapuche (indigenous group), 700, 736. Commerce, 601. Diseases, 2466. Ethnohistory, 647–648. History, 2483. Missions, 764. Pictorial Works, 645.
Mapuche Influences. Chile, 5201.
Mar del Plata, Argentina (city). History, 2902. Social Life and Customs, 2902.
Maracaibo, Venezuela (city). History, 2590.
Maranhão, Brazil (state). Abolition (slavery), 3418. Insurrections, 3161. Slaves and Slavery, 3418.
Marañón River Region (Peru). Discovery and Exploration, 2408. Jesuits, 2408. Missions, 2408.
Marcha (Uruguay), 4243, 4249.
Marco, da Nizza, 3520–3521.
Marcos de Niza. See Marco, da Nizza.
Marechal, Leopoldo, 4215.
María, 3687.
María la Noche, 3814.
Mariátegui, José Carlos, 5452, 5455, 5457, 5459–5460.

Míseri Colóni (theater group), 4920.
Misiones, Argentina (prov.). History, 2507. Indigenous Peoples, 2535. Mate (tea), 3073. Migration, 3027.
Miskito. *See* Mosquito.
Miskito Coast. *See* Atlantic Coast (Nicaragua).
Missing Persons. *See* Disappeared Persons.
Missionaries, 186, 846, 3610. Argentina, 2924, 3586. Bolivia, 2821, 5146. Borderlands, 1950. British Guiana, 2059, 2100. Chile, 623, 765. Colombia, 2649. Colonial Theater, 3615. Congresses, 960. Cuba, 2074. Dominican Republic, 2214. Dutch, 1806. Historiography, 936, 2256. Jamaica, 1969. Jesuits, 994. Mercedarians, 906. Mexico, 484, 3615. Peru, 660, 671, 2396, 3608. Protestant Churches, 2649. Uruguay, 2924. Viceroyalty of New Spain (1540–1821), 3601.
Missions, 846, 1096, 3610, 5324. Acculturation, 922. Amazon Basin, 2408. Andean Region, 2259. Argentina, 2535. Augustinians, 839. Bolivia, 2429, 2442, 2448, 2450. Borderlands, 1946. Brazil, 697. California, 1304–1305. Chile, 765, 2472. Corruption, 2405. Costa Rica, 1683. Dominicans (religious order), 1024. Ecuador, 2337. Franciscans, 1052, 2357, 2384, 2448. French Guiana, 1817. Guatemala, 1727. Honduras, 1651. Indigenous Peoples, 609, 1305, 2255, 5324. Jesuits, 218, 875, 1054, 2241, 2448, 2541. Nicaragua, 1657. Paraguay, 752, 1054, 2511, 2514, 2517–2518, 2541, 2554, 2562, 2582. Peru, 726, 778, 2357, 2396, 2405, 2408, 2726, 2728. Religious Art, 178. Viceroyalty of New Spain (1540–1821), 1286, 1296, 1299, 1301, 1310, 1315.
Mistral, Gabriela, 3508, 4534, 4543.
Mita. Bolivia, 2438. Venezuela, 2266.
Mitología bufa (opera), 5226.
Mixtec (indigenous group). Archaeological Surveys, 548. Codices, 533, 545, 548. Genealogy, 572. Land Settlement, 548. Manuscripts, 572. Monarchs, 574. Political Development, 574. Political Ideology, 545. Social Structure, 545.
Mizque, Bolivia (town). Archives, 2449.
Mizuno, Ryu, 3416.
Moche. *See* Mochica.
Mocovi. *See* Mocobi.
Modern Architecture, 253. Argentina, 319, 321. Colombia, 350. Ecuador, 356. Mexico, 257, 280, 285. Peru, 358. Puerto Rico, 1833.
Modern Art. Brazil, 379, 391, 393, 397. Carib-

bean Area, 248. Central America, 248. Cuba, 306, 308. Elites, 397. Exhibitions, 246, 255, 283. Mexico, 284. Panama, 300.
Modernism (architecture). Brazil, 416. Chile, 330. Puerto Rico, 1833.
Modernism (art), 247. Brazil, 392. Colombia, 351. Mexico, 283.
Modernism (literature). Argentina, 3066. Brazil, 4878, 4934.
Modernization. Brazil, 3294, 3305, 3444. Caribbean Area, 1981. Central America, 1704. Chile, 330, 2882, 2887. Ecuador, 2344. Guatemala, 1714. Honduras, 1637, 1758. Mexico, 1370, 1461, 1502, 1504, 1527, 1564. Peru, 2722.
Moisés Ville, Argentina (agricultural colony), 2993.
Mojo (indigenous group). Missions, 2450. Spanish Conquest, 2306.
Moldes, José de, 3080.
Molina, Gerardo, 2646.
Molina, Juan Ramón, 3810.
Monarchism, 2676. Brazil, 3328, 3378, 3382, 3457. Ecuador, 2676.
Monarchs. *See* Kings and Rulers.
Monardes, Nicolás, 1006.
Monasteries. Mural Painting, 145. Slaves and Slavery, 3184.
Monetary Policy, 1078. Colonial Administration, 1015.
Money. Argentina, 2927. Cuba, 1907.
Monopolies. Colonial History, 1029. Costa Rica, 1773.
Montaigne, Michel de, 963, 3579.
Montalvo, Juan, 5443.
La montaña es algo más que una inmensa estepa verde, 3811.
Monte Albán Site (Mexico), 553.
Montejo, Esteban, 3881.
Montero del Aguila, Victorino, 2359.
Monterroso, Augusto, 3785, 3805.
Montesquieu, Charles de Secondat, 5468.
Montevideo, Uruguay (city). Expeditions, 2522. History, 2504. Jews, 3154. Military History, 2497, 2542. Slaves and Slavery, 3176.
Montezuma II, *Emperor of Mexico*, 1167.
Monuments. Mexico, 1397.
Moquegua, Peru (dept.). Land Tenure, 2363, 2707.
Moraes, Vinícius de, 4891.
Moral social, 5411.
Moraleda, José Manuel de, 2477.
Morales, Melesio, 5273.
Morales Carrión, Arturo, 1795.

Morales Pradilla, Próspero, 3612.
Morals. See Ethics.
Morant Bay Rebellion (Jamaica, 1865), 2018.
Morante, Luis Ambrosio, 4708.
Moravians. Suriname, 2125.
More, Thomas, 5398.
Morelia, Mexico (city). Church History, 149. Inquisition, 1229.
Morelos, Mexico (state). Ethnohistory, 523. Social Structure, 1393.
Moreno, Gabriel René, 2784, 2814.
Mormons. Brazil, 3306.
Moroleón, Mexico (town). Labor and Laboring Classes, 1378.
Morrow, Dwight W., 1595.
Mortality. Mexico, 1483.
Mortuary Customs. Brazil, 3409–3410. Costa Rica, 1676. Cuba, 2055. Panama, 1627. Puerto Rico, 2055.
Mosquitia. See Atlantic Coast (Nicaragua).
Mosquito (indigenous group), 1726. History, 1630. Treatment of, 1783.
Mosteiro da Luz (São Paulo, Brazil), 383.
Mosteiro de São Bento (Brazil), 3184.
Motherhood. Argentina, 3053.
Motolinía, Toribio, 1197.
Mourier-Martínez, María Francisca, 5382.
Movimiento de Izquierda Revolucionaria (Peru), 2702.
Movimiento de Liberación Nacional (Uruguay), 3133, 3136.
Movimiento Nacional Socialista de Chile, 2860.
Movimiento Nacionalista Revolucionario (Bolivia), 2782, 2802.
Movimiento Revolucionario Túpac Amaru, 4023.
Moxo. See Mojo.
La muerte no entrará en palacio, 4662.
Múgica Velázquez, Francisco José, 1508.
Muisca. See Chibcha.
Mujeres, 3863.
Mujica Láinez, Manuel, 4212, 4229.
Mulattoes. Guatemala, 1684.
Mummies. Andean Region, 596.
Mundo matemático, 5445.
Municipal Government. Argentina, 2512. Historiography, 991. Indigenous Peoples, 488, 512, 517. Mexico, 487, 512, 517. Paraguay, 2580. Viceroyalty of New Spain (1540–1821), 1227, 1246.
Muñoz Camargo, Diego, 439.
Muñoz Marín, Luis, 2140, 2179.
Mural Painting. Andean Region, 220. Church Architecture, 109. Ecuador, 189. Francis-

cans, 129. Mexico, 129, 261, 266. Monasteries, 145. Peru, 215, 365. US, 277, 279.
Murallas de Jericó, 4670.
Murato. See Candoshi.
Murtinho, Joaquim, 3249.
Musatti, Jeanete, 402.
Museo Colonial del Carmen (México), 132.
Museo de América (Madrid), 126.
Museo de Arte Colonial (Cuba), 176.
Museo del Convento La Concepción (Riobamba, Ecuador), 236.
Museo José Luis Cuevas (México), 284.
Museo Nacional de Bellas Artes (Chile), 329, 336.
Museo Nacional de Bellas Artes (Cuba), 309–310.
Museo Nacional de Historia (Peru), 221.
Museo Nacional del Virreinato (Mexico), 101.
Museo Provincial de Salamanca, 208.
Museu de Arte Sacra de São Paulo, 383.
Museu Felícia Leirner (São Paulo), 403.
Museu Histórico Nacional (Brazil), 380.
Museu Imperial (Brazil), 3180.
Museums. Mexico, 273, 284.
Music. African Influences, 5107, 5114. Bibliography, 1839. Mexico, 5251. Puerto Rico, 1839.
Music Industry. Argentina, 5142. Trinidad and Tobago, 5190.
Musical History. Bolivia, 5143.
Musical Instruments, 5115. Andean Region, 5113, 5288. Bolivia, 5145. Brazil, 5162, 5167, 5177. Colombia, 5210, 5216. Costa Rica, 5196. French Guiana, 5186. Jamaica, 5189. Mexico, 5237. Nicaragua, 5197. Peru, 5282, 5287, 5294. Popular Music, 5237.
Musicals. Brazil, 4940.
Musicians. Argentina, 5123–5124, 5141. Chile, 5207, 5209. Costa Rica, 5198. Cuba, 5217, 5220, 5225, 5230–5231. Guatemala, 5192. Jamaica, 5187, 5189. Mexico, 5243–5244, 5249, 5276. Paraguay, 5279. Peru, 5289. Puerto Rico, 1968. Venezuela, 5303, 5305.
Musicologists, 5104, 5106, 5108. Chile, 5203. Venezuela, 5300, 5302.
Musicology, 5120. Brazil, 5158. Chile, 5202. Cuba, 5232. Ecuador, 5234. Guatemala, 5191. Historiography, 5116.
Muslims, 863. Caribbean Area, 863.
Mutis, Alvaro, 4499.
Muzo (indigenous group). Cultural Collapse, 756.
Myths and Mythology, 3478, 5373. Amazon Basin, 767. Andean Region, 668, 2256,

vador, 1713. Italians, 2933. Labor and La-
boring Classes, 1355. Mexico, 38, 43, 50,
65, 70, 1355, 1428, 1538, 1583. Nicaragua,
40. Peru, 2729. US, 2224. Viceroyalty of
New Granada (1718–1810), 2315.
Nezahualcóytl, 5269.
Nicaraguan Revolution (1979), 5402.
Nieto, Juan José, 3686.
Nietzsche, Friedrich Wilhelm, 5471.
Nieve, 3666.
Nina Qhispi, Eduardo Leandro, 718.
Nitrate Industry. Chile, 2856.
Nivaklé. *See* Ashluslay.
Nobility. Chile, 2473. Colombia, 2299. Cuba,
1971. Peru, 2407.
Noguchi, Hideyo, 1118.
Nogueras, Luis Rogelio, 3859, 3873.
Noguerol de Ulloa, Francisco, 2370.
Nonviolence. Argentina, 5525.
Nordeste, Brazil (region). Anecdotes, 4813.
Colonial History, 3213, 3216. Indigenous
Peoples, 3216. Insurrections, 3339. Photog-
raphy, 410. Social History, 3374.
Noriega Laso, Iñigo, 1389.
El Norte (Monterrey, Mexico), 50.
*North American Free Trade Agreement
(NAFTA)*, 1474.
Notaries, 1203.
Noticias del Imperio, 3763–3764.
*Noticias historiales de las conquistas de
Tierra Firme en las Indias Occidentales*,
3526, 3528.
Novara Expedition (1857–1859), 2778.
La novela naturalista hispanoamericana,
3875.
Nueva corónica y buen gobierno, 2353, 3517,
3539.
Nuevo León, Mexico (state). Caudillos, 1348.
Indigenous Peoples, 1283. Labor Policy,
1294. Political History, 1368.
Nuevo Orden Económico Internacional. *See*
New International Economic Order.
Núñez, Guillermo, 5063.
Núñez, Rafael, 2639.
Núñez Borda, Luis, 343.
Núñez Cabeza de Vaca, Alvar, 3516, 3519,
3521, 3596.
Núñez Ureta, Teodoro, 365.
Nuns. Colonial Literature, 3544. Viceroyalty
of New Spain (1540–1821), 1244, 1269,
3537.
Nutrition. Aztecs, 542.
OAS. *See* Organization of American States.
Oaxaca, Mexico (city). Church Architecture,
131. Urban History, 102.
Oaxaca, Mexico (state). Church History,

1268. Conservation and Restoration, 146.
Cultural Identity, 445. Indigenous Peoples,
1268. Political History, 1588.
Obando, José María, 2667.
Obligado, Rafael, 3658.
Obregón, Alejandro, 345.
Ocampo, Victoria, 4217, 4228, 4615.
Ocaña R., Antonio, 2193.
Ocelocalco, Mexico (town). Cacao, 474.
O'Higgins, Bernardo, 2881.
O'Higgins, Pablo, 266.
Oidores. *See* Judges.
Olavide, Pablo de, 5456.
Olinda, Brazil (city). Architecture, 377.
Ollantay, 3588.
Olmos, Andrés de, *Fray*, 503.
Omagua. *See* Carijona.
Oña, Pedro de, 3536, 3548.
Oñate, Juan de, 1324, 3554.
Onetti, Juan Carlos, 4242, 4246–4248.
Online Bibliographic Searching. *See* Database
Searching.
Opera. Argentina, 5109, 5125–5126, 5137–
5140. Brazil, 5109, 5151–5155, 5159, 5163,
5169–5173, 5175. Chile, 5200, 5206. Cuba,
5223–5224. Guatemala, 4566, 5194. Mex-
ico, 5109, 5238, 5240–5242, 5245–5248,
5261, 5267–5275. Paraguay, 5278. Peru,
5290, 5292. Venezuela, 5306.
Operettas. *See* Musicals; Tonadillas;
Zarzuelas.
Opposition Groups. Cuba, 2168. Guadeloupe,
1928.
Oral History. Bolivia, 696. Colombia, 2636.
Cuba, 2216. Nicaragua, 1734, 1745.
Oral Tradition, 3493. Incas, 727.
Orbón, Julián, 5233.
Ordoñana, Domingo, 3135.
Oré, Luis Jerónimo de, 1950, 2482.
Orellana, Francisco de, 3547.
Organization of American States (OAS), 5348.
Organs. Peru, 5287.
Oribe, Manuel, 3146.
Oriente, Cuba (prov.). Maroons, 2038.
Orinoco River Region (Venezuela and Colom-
bia). Description and Travel, 2268.
Orozco, José Clemente, 279, 286.
Orozco, Olga, 4527.
Orquesta Nacional Juvenil (Venezuela), 5299.
Orquesta Sinfónica Nacional (Mexico), 5260.
Orquesta Sinfónica Nacional de Costa Rica,
5198.
Ortega y Gasset, José, 5386, 5441.
Ortiz, Fernando, 5416.
Ortiz, Jóse Antonio, 5136.
Ortiz, Tadeo, 1337.

5476, 5481, 5484, 5486–5487. Caribbean
Area, 2045. Chile, 2823. Cuba, 5407–5408,
5414–5415, 5421. Dominican Republic,
2163, 2199. Ecuador, 2693, 5446. Guadeloupe, 2002. Guatemala, 5400. Independence Movements, 5427. Mexico, 1352,
1448, 1557, 5377, 5379, 5382–5383, 5391,
5394, 5396. Nicaragua, 5402–5403. Peru,
2751, 5452, 5457, 5460. Puerto Rico, 1988,
2023, 2063, 5412, 5420. Trinidad and Tobago, 2045. Uruguay, 5495, 5498. Venezuela, 5423.
Politicians. Argentina, 2903, 3072, 3094,
3625. Blacks, 3383. Bolivia, 2790. Brazil,
3237, 3277, 3287, 3309, 3324, 3327, 3383.
Chile, 2888. Colombia, 2625, 2633, 2639–
2640, 2642, 2646. Dutch Caribbean, 2138.
Haiti, 2136. Honduras, 1620. Martinique,
2187. Mexico, 1465–1466, 1492, 1517,
3719. Paraguay, 3095. Peru, 2738, 2757,
4030. Puerto Rico, 2137, 2140, 2145, 2179,
2210, 3633. Trinidad and Tobago, 2171.
Pollution. See Environmental Pollution.
Polvo de alas de mariposa, 3635.
Ponce, Puerto Rico (city). Economic History,
2076. Merchants, 2076.
Ponce de León, Juan, 1962.
Poniatowska, Elena, 3771–3772.
Poor, 5352.
Popul Vuh, 429.
Popular Art. Peru, 2780.
Popular Culture, 917, 3472, 5341. Argentina,
2935. Brazil, 3259. Jamaica, 2123. Mexico,
1355, 1514. Panama, 1766. Puerto Rico,
2169, 2200.
Popular Education. See Nonformal Education.
Popular Movements. See Social Movements.
Popular Music. Argentina, 5127, 5129, 5142.
Brazil, 5148, 5156, 5161, 5176–5178. Carib-
bean Area, 5183–5184. Chile, 5201, 5204.
Colombia, 5212–5214. Cuba, 3874, 5200,
5229. Guadeloupe, 5182. Mapuche, 5201.
Mexico, 5237, 5244, 5256–5257. Musical
Instruments, 5237. Paraguay, 5279. Puerto
Rico, 2200. US, 5256.
Popular Religion, 5341, 5345. Andean Region,
792. Colombia, 2316. Cuba, 1800. Guate-
mala, 1658, 1684. Haiti, 1804. Indigenous
Peoples, 5373. Mayas, 478. Mexico, 1431.
Peru, 739. Slaves and Slavery, 3219. Vice-
royalty of New Spain (1540–1821), 1199.
Population Genetics. See Human Genetics.
Population Growth. Aztecs, 473, 544.
Population Policy, 5307.
Population Studies. See Demography.

Populism, 2990, 5313. Puerto Rico, 2198.
Por qué, 3876.
Portales, Diego José Víctor, 2832, 2878, 5468.
Porter y Cassante, Pedro, 969.
Portinari, Cândido, 398.
Porto Alegre, Manuel de Araújo, 4924.
Portobelo, Panama (village). Fortifications,
1688.
The portrait of Dorian Gray, 3850.
Portraits. Mexico, 123, 294.
Ports, 974. Chile, 2867. Mexico, 1329. Nicara-
gua, 1645. Peru, 2386, 2720. Spain, 1072.
Uruguay, 3141. Venezuela, 2590.
Portuguese, 1019. Acculturation, 3331. Ar-
gentina, 182, 2567. Brazil, 3227, 3331, 3347,
3435. Paraguay, 2502.
Portuguese Influences. Discovery and Explo-
ration, 1082. Navigation, 1010.
Posada, José Guadalupe, 290.
Posibilidad y realidad de la vida argentina,
5512.
Positivism, 5365, 5429. Architecture, 1415.
Argentina, 3062, 5521, 5529. Brazil, 5486.
Chile, 5464–5465. Guatemala, 1727. Mex-
ico, 1141, 1333, 1539, 5393. Venezuela,
5434. Viceroyalty of New Spain (1540–
1821), 1141.
Postal Service. Mexico, 140.
Postcards. Guadeloupe, 2205.
Potosí, Bolivia (city). Bourbon Reforms, 2435.
Colonial Architecture, 231. Colonial Art,
232. Convents, 209. Economic History,
2446. History, 2252. Minerals and Mining
Industry, 2435, 2438, 2446, 2451. Silver,
2451.
Potosí, Bolivia (dept.). Musical Instruments,
5145.
Poverty. Central America, 1704. Peru, 2766.
Prado Júnior, Caio, 3319.
Pradt, Dominique Georges Frédéric de, 5315.
Precolumbian Civilizations, 925, 1040. Costa
Rica, 1663. Guatemala, 1634. Militarism,
492. Music, 5113. Nicaragua, 1618. Peru,
611. Political Systems, 544. Rites and Cere-
monies, 537. Social Structure, 815. Warfare,
492. Women, 423.
Precolumbian Trade. Ecuador, 2324. Mexico,
560.
Prehistory. See Archaeology.
La Prensa (Managua, Nicaragua), 3802.
Presbere, Pablo, 1683.
Presidential Systems. See Political Systems.
Presidents. Argentina, 2905, 2962, 3001,
3052, 3622, 5501. Bolivia, 2791–2792, 2802,
2820. Brazil, 3288, 3360–3361, 3379, 3384.

Separation. *See* Divorce.

Sepúlveda, Juan Ginés de, 950, 1271, 3560, 5362.

Sergipe, Brazil (state). Demography, 3377. Ethnic Groups and Ethnicity, 3377. Race and Race Relations, 3377.

Sescosse, Federico, 105.

Seventh-Day Adventists. Church History, 1105.

Sevilla, Spain (city). Commerce, 975.

Sex and Sexual Relations, 3282. Brazil, 3226, 3280, 3407. Colombia, 2313. Colonial History, 2280. Conquerors, 989. Cuba, 2223. Incas, 652. Mexico, 1346. Paraguay, 3121. Venezuela, 2280. Viceroyalty of New Spain (1540–1821), 1180, 1187. Viceroyalty of Peru (1542–1822), 2416.

Sex Roles, 2630. Argentina, 2536. Aztecs, 442, 557. Brazil, 3271. Costa Rica, 1780. Cuba, 3863. Honduras, 1758. Puerto Rico, 1834.

Sexism, 1047. Jamaica, 2157. Mexico, 1412.

El sexto, 3588.

Shamanism. Mexico, 476. Viceroyalty of New Spain (1540–1821), 1179.

Shantytowns. *See* Squatter Settlements.

Shavante. *See* Xavante.

Sheehy, Daniel E., 5256.

Shimose, Pedro, 4981.

Shining Path. *See* Sendero Luminoso.

Shipibo. *See* Sipibo.

Shipping. Central America, 1775. Chile, 750. Germans, 912.

Shipwrecks. Caribbean Area, 1062.

Shuar (indigenous group). Boundaries, 2240.

El siglo de las luces, 3850.

Siles Salinas, Luis Adolfo, 2820.

Silva, Fernando, 3115.

Silva, José Asunción, 3641–3642, 3650, 3676.

Silva, Luís Inácio da. *See* Lula.

Silva Estrada, Alfredo, 4548.

Silver, 1060. Argentina, 2549. Bolivia, 2446, 2451. Mexico, 489, 1377. Taxation, 1055. Viceroyalty of New Spain (1540–1821), 1288.

Silversmiths. Peru, 222.

Silverwork. Argentina, 182. Colombia, 203. Ecuador, 225. Mexico, 103. Peru, 226. Venezuela, 195.

Simón, Pedro, 3526, 3528, 3566.

Sinaloa, Mexico (state). AIDS, 1430. Banking and Financial Institutions, 1409. Diseases, 1430. Economic History, 1331. Haciendas, 1322. Social History, 1322. Taxation, 1320.

Sindbad el Varado, 4531.

Sindicato de Trabajadores Concord (Argentina), 2947.

Sindicato Médico del Uruguay, 3152.

Sindicato Minero (Mexico), 1590.

Sipibo (indigenous group). Legends, 4025. Myths and Mythology, 4025. Religion, 4025.

Siqueiros, David Alfaro, 268, 279, 292.

Skármeta, Antonio, 4071.

Slaves and Slavery, 1045, 1069. Antigua, 1863, 2009. Archives, 3160, 3180. Argentina, 2570, 2964, 3082. Bahamas, 1803, 1933, 1992, 2031. Barbados, 1812, 1850, 1976, 2013. Bibliography, 1993. Borderlands, 1959. Brazil, 734–735, 3158–3162, 3168, 3170, 3173–3174, 3176–3180, 3182–3186, 3188–3189, 3191, 3201–3202, 3204, 3210–3211, 3219, 3247, 3260–3262, 3264, 3269, 3283, 3304, 3307, 3349, 3351, 3355–3356, 3369, 3390, 3392, 3408, 3411–3412, 3418, 3421, 3433, 3439. British Guiana, 2059. Capitalism, 1987. Caribbean Area, 1881, 1922, 1944, 1970, 1975, 1980–1981, 1987, 1993, 1995, 1997, 2053. Catholic Church, 1882, 2546. Children, 3202, 3369. Coffee Industry and Trade, 3179. Colombia, 2298, 2302, 2314, 2334. Commerce, 1976. Cuba, 1801, 1857–1858, 1860–1861, 1907, 1923, 1972–1973, 2038, 2042, 2079, 2083, 2089–2090, 2103, 2114, 2119, 2122, 3657, 3685. Danish Caribbean, 1811. Diseases, 2417. Dutch, 1871. Dutch Caribbean, 2070. Economic History, 1031. Ecuador, 635, 2334, 2670. Education, 1970. Family and Family Relations, 3210, 3421. France, 1995. French Caribbean, 1895, 1903–1904, 1908–1909, 1999, 2070, 2097. French Guiana, 2097. Great Britain, 1997. Guadeloupe, 1928, 2002, 2060, 2062. Haiti, 1888, 1903, 1939. Historiography, 898, 3174, 3178, 3182, 3262. Honduras, 1666. Independence Movements, 1903, 1909. Indigenous Peoples, 735, 1881, 3211. Insurrections, 1870, 1904, 2302, 2388, 3411. Jamaica, 1944, 2117. Kinship, 1897, 3204. Law and Legislation, 3185, 3189, 3211, 3261. Literature, 3672. Marriage, 1860, 3421. Martinique, 1897, 2044, 2060, 2111–2113. Mayas, 2089. Mexico, 5385. Monasteries, 3184. Names, 1999. Panama, 1627. Peru, 2388, 2415, 2417, 2425, 2699, 2740. Popular Religion, 3219. Prostitution, 3304. Puerto Rico, 1867, 1870, 1882, 1973, 1986, 2056, 2065, 2098. Saint Domingue, 1923. Social Conditions, 1867. Sugar Industry and Trade, 2098. Suriname,

1911, 1925, 1937, 2000, 2040, 2069, 2106–2107. Trinidad and Tobago, 1893. Urban Areas, 2065, 3159. Uruguay, 3140. US, 1922. Venezuela, 2264. Viceroyalty of New Spain (1540–1821), 1224, 1290. Voodooism, 1908. Wars of Independence, 1939. Women, 3177, 3369.

Slavs. Argentina, 2907.

Smuggling. Brazil, 3150. Colonial History, 1002. France, 1866. Mexico, 1391. Uruguay, 3150.

Soberana Convención Revolucionaria (Mexico, 1914–1915), 1596.

Sobre lo bello en general, 5389.

Social Change. Andean Region, 2362. Belize, 1622. Bolivia, 2454, 2809, 2822. Brazil, 3181, 3258. Central America, 1704, 1731. Colombia, 2631, 2641. Cuba, 2049. Ecuador, 2344. Guatemala, 1743. Mexico, 1578. Nicaragua, 1724. Peru, 2707. Puerto Rico, 2169. Suriname, 2000. Uruguay, 3141. Women, 1104.

Social Classes. Argentina, 2908, 2931, 2954. Aztecs, 440. Bolivia, 2819. Brazil, 3246, 3273, 3374, 3417. Colombia, 2298. Costa Rica, 1717. El Salvador, 1746. Guatemala, 1671, 1785. Guyana, 2234. Indigenous Peoples, 487. Jamaica, 2182. Mexico, 1400, 1557. Nicaragua, 1630. Peru, 2376, 2763. Puerto Rico, 1991. Saint Christopher-Nevis, 2068. Venezuela, 5428.

Social Conditions, 5340, 5352, 5373. Argentina, 4214. Costa Rica, 1732. Cuba, 3866. French Guiana, 1825. Jamaica, 1919. Mexico, 1403, 1408, 1457, 1557, 5378. Peru, 2770. Slaves and Slavery, 1867. Venezuela, 2605. Women, 2605.

Social Conflict, 943. Andean Region, 790. Argentina, 5532. Belize, 1622. Bolivia, 705, 2243, 2783, 2789, 2799, 2805. Brazil, 3161, 3296, 3387. British Guiana, 2152. Chile, 2474, 2841. Colombia, 2623, 2638, 2666. Costa Rica, 1744. Cuba, 1923. El Salvador, 1713. Guadeloupe, 2109. Guatemala, 1719, 1741. Jamaica, 2021, 2105, 2123, 2157. Nicaragua, 1707. Peru, 2243, 2377, 2706, 2724, 2726, 2743, 5451. Saint Domingue, 1923. Trinidad and Tobago, 2146. Virgin Islands, 2150.

Social Customs. *See* Social Life and Customs.

Social Darwinism. Argentina, 5526. Brazil, 5478. Guatemala, 1727. Mexico, 1739. Nicaragua, 1739.

Social History, 861, 1045, 1089, 5333. Andean Region, 2255, 2356. Anthologies, 5339. Ar-

gentina, 2536, 2547, 2568, 5539. Aztecs, 454. Bolivia, 2439–2440. Brazil, 3163, 3181, 3190, 3226, 3246, 3258, 3264, 3311, 3336, 3365, 3368, 3372, 3374, 3387, 3406, 3410, 3417, 3422, 3434. Caribbean Area, 2104. Catholic Church, 853. Central America, 1685. Chile, 2460, 2473, 2479, 2481, 2826, 2874, 2885. Colombia, 2298, 2312–2313, 2318, 2624, 2628, 2655, 2662–2663, 2665, 5437. Costa Rica, 1617, 1644, 1663, 1676, 1680, 1701, 1786. Cuba, 1858, 1915, 2005. Dominican Republic, 1808. Ecuador, 2350, 2674, 2680–2683. El Salvador, 1746. French Caribbean, 2072. Guadeloupe, 2002, 2109, 2205. Guatemala, 1641, 1671, 1684, 1692, 1777. Honduras, 1758. Inquisition, 2404. Jamaica, 1815, 2018, 2021, 2105. Martinique, 2204. Mexico, 504, 1120, 1143, 1188, 1203, 1332, 1334, 1341, 1364, 1378, 1390, 1394–1395, 1398, 1439, 1443, 1504, 1547–1548. Nahuas, 518–519. Nicaragua, 1630, 1726. Paraguay, 808–809, 3111, 3121. Peru, 2355, 2367, 2370, 2379, 2398, 2403, 2407, 2416, 2737, 2741, 2746, 2761–2762, 5455. Puerto Rico, 2101, 2211. Suriname, 1843, 1931, 2000. Travelers, 923. Trinidad and Tobago, 2146, 2197. Tzeltal, 463. Uruguay, 3124. Venezuela, 2271, 2273, 2280, 5430. Viceroyalty of New Spain (1540–1821), 1145, 1149, 1188.

Social Indicators. Panama, 1627.

Social Life and Customs. Andean Region, 638. Argentina, 3039. Brazil, 3181, 3302, 3409, 3417. Chiriguano, 788. French Caribbean, 1905. Mexico, 638, 1462. Peru, 739. Quechua, 357. Viceroyalty of New Spain (1540–1821), 1213, 1218.

Social Marginality. Honduras, 1621.

Social Movements, 5340. Central America, 1723, 1731. Chile, 2849. Colombia, 5437. Ecuador, 2688. Honduras, 1691. Nicaragua, 1710. Peru, 2724, 2749.

Social Organization. *See* Social Structure.

Social Policy, 5332. Argentina, 3093. Mexico, 1364, 5387. State, The, 887.

Social Relations. *See* Social Life and Customs.

Social Sciences, 3399. Argentina, 2995, 3081. Brazil, 3366.

Social Structure. Andean Region, 790. Argentina, 2539, 2545, 2552, 2931, 3093. Aztecs, 513, 566–567. Bermuda, 1898. Blacks, 2104. Bolivia, 2808. Brazil, 3236, 3264, 3422. Carib, 1901. Caribbean Area, 2104. Central America, 1643. Colombia, 2312.

dor, 2677. Guatemala, 1736, 1749–1750, 1760, 1792. Incas, 607. Mexico, 1348, 1462, 1467, 1603, 1607, 2754. Peru, 672, 2717, 2719, 2727, 2745, 2754, 2764, 2774. Social Policy, 887. Venezuela, 2595.
State Enterprise. *See* Public Enterprise.
States of Emergency. *See* Martial Law.
Statesmen. Argentina, 2970. Brazil, 3373, 3450. Colombia, 5440. Guatemala, 1703. Mexico, 5394. Peru, 2725. Spain, 2381.
Statistics. Brazil, 3175. Mexican-American Border Region, 1608–1609. Mexico, 39.
Stedman, John Gabriel, 1937.
Steel Industry and Trade. Brazil, 3238.
Steuart, John, 2662.
Storani, Conrado, 3072.
Storni, Alfonsina, 4501.
Strikes and Lockouts. Argentina, 2896, 3019–3020, 3047, 3061. Brazil, 3318, 3425. British Guiana, 2091. Chile, 2841, 2849. Costa Rica, 1740. Ecuador, 2675, 2688. Honduras, 1691. Mexico, 1361, 1376.
Stroessner, Alfredo, 3103.
Student Movements. Peru, 2753.
Students. Mexico, 952. Peru, 952, 2767.
Subachoque Valley (Colombia). Ethnohistory, 610.
Subercaseaux, Ramón, 2881.
Subercaseaux Estate (Chile), 2881.
Subsistence Economy. Costa Rica, 1629.
Sucre, Antonio José de, 2811.
Sugar Industry and Trade. Argentina, 3025. Barbados, 1936, 2013. Caribbean Area, 1936, 1981. Costa Rica, 1687. Cuba, 1801, 1845, 1857, 1859, 1915, 1923, 1940–1941, 1972, 2014, 2061, 2090, 2103, 2235. Dominican Republic, 1974. Ecuador, 635. French Caribbean, 1894. Guadeloupe, 1796. Hispaniola, 1873. History, 888, 893. Honduras, 1666. Jamaica, 1936. Jesuits, 635. Martinique, 1826–1827, 2112–2113. Peru, 2695, 2732. Puerto Rico, 2057, 2098. Slaves and Slavery, 2098. Suriname, 2106–2107.
Sultepec, Mexico (town). Social Structure, 1393.
Sumapaz, Colombia (region). Agricultural Colonization, 2643. History, 2636.
Sumu. *See* Sumo.
El sur después, 4666.
Surrealism (art). Exhibitions, 255. Hondurans, 298. Mexico, 255.
Sustainable Development. Congresses, 72. Databases, 72.
Swedes. Argentina, 3027. Caribbean Area, 2120.

Symbolism, 5372. Argentina, 5531. Colonial History, 2274. Religion, 3521.
Syncretism. Andean Region, 634. Colonial Architecture, 168. Colonial Art, 98, 244. Colonial Paintings, 99. Cuba, 1800. Haiti, 1804. Jamaica, 2105. Maroons, 2125. Peru, 211, 739.
Syndicalism. Argentina, 2896. Panama, 1725.
Syrians. Argentina, 3074.
Szyszlo, Fernando de, 362.
Tabasco, Mexico (state). Censuses, 1266. Church History, 1263. Commerce, 1266. Inquisition, 1263. Political History, 1465–1466.
Taborda, Saúl, 5524.
Tacna, Peru (dept.). Popular Religion, 739. Religious Life and Customs, 739. Syncretism, 739.
Tacuarembó, Uruguay (dept.). Ethnic Groups and Ethnicity, 3147.
Taki Onqoy Movement (Peru), 2366.
Tallet, José Z., 4496.
Tampico, Mexico (city). Social History, 1329.
Tandil, Argentina (city). History, 2963. Migration, 3028.
Tandil Region (Argentina). Cattle Raising and Trade, 601.
Tango. Argentina, 2935, 3675, 5122, 5128, 5134.
Tapuya (indigenous group). Colonial History, 3216.
Tarahumara (indigenous group). Missions, 1310.
Tarasco (indigenous group), 424. Demography, 550. Ethnohistory, 550. Religion, 549–550.
Tarija, Bolivia (city). History, 2441.
Tata Vasco (opera), 5268.
Taxation. Audiencia of Nueva Granada, 2300. Aztecs, 496. Brazil, 3193. British Guiana, 2092. Central America, 1655, 1673. Colombia, 2305. Colonial Administration, 1055. Databases, 56. Ecuador, 2668. Indigenous Peoples, 770, 1264, 1320, 1655, 1673, 2300, 2444, 2668, 2764. Peasants, 2700. Peru, 684, 2700, 2745, 2764. Silver, 1055. Viceroyalty of New Spain (1540–1821), 1264, 1319–1320. Viceroyalty of Peru (1542–1822), 770.
Taxco, Mexico (town). Baroque Architecture, 156. Colonial Architecture, 139. Indigenous Peoples, 489. Labor Supply, 1231. Silver, 489.
Te juro Juana que tengo ganas, 4675.
Teatro de Arena (Brazil), 4942.
Technical Assistance, US. Databases, 37.
Technology. Brazil, 3449.

Universidad Católica Boliviana, 5463.
Universidad de Buenos Aires, 3041.
Universidad de La Habana, 2144.
Universidad de Salamanca (Spain), 3048.
Universidad de Santiago de Chile, 2869.
Universidad de Santo Tomás (Costa Rica), 1755.
Universidad Nacional Autónoma de México (UNAM), 1490.
Universidad Nacional Mayor de San Marcos (Peru), 2753.
Universities. Argentina, 2496. Chile, 2458. Colonial Administration, 946. Franciscans, 1052. Jesuits, 2270. Nicaragua, 1619. Puerto Rico, 2208. Venezuela, 2270. Viceroyalty of New Spain (1540–1821), 1250.
University of Puerto Rico, 2208.
University Reform. Argentina, 5510. Costa Rica, 1693. Mexico, 1543.
UNO. *See* Unión Nacional Opositora (Nicaragua).
Urban Areas. Guatemala, 1754. Mexico, 952. Peru, 952, 2722, 2766. Slaves and Slavery, 2065, 3159. Viceroyalty of New Spain (1540–1821), 1170.
Urban History, 78–79, 83. Brazil, 419. Chile, 335. Colombia, 201, 204. Cuba, 254. Dominican Republic, 173. Ecuador, 224, 355. Mexico, 102, 150, 155, 168. Peru, 237.
Urban Planning. *See* City Planning.
Urban Policy. Argentina, 2971.
Urban Sociology. Brazil, 3365. Cuba, 2049. Puerto Rico, 1991.
Urbanization. Argentina, 2915, 2938. Chile, 2882. Colonial History, 1065. Mexican-American Border Region, 1401. Mexico, 155, 1495.
Urbano Rojas, Jesús, 2780.
Urquiaga, Manuel de, 1238.
Urquiza, Justo José de, 2925, 2936.
Urrea, Teresa, 1431.
Urteaga, Mario, 366.
Uru (indigenous group). Oral History, 696.
US Influences, 1119. Brazil, 3275. Central America, 1776. Chile, 2847. Guatemala, 1727. Haiti, 2196. Independence Movements, 1088. Mexico, 1467. Peru, 2719. Philosophy, 5368. Puerto Rico, 1833, 2208, 2238.
Usigli, Rodolfo, 4660, 4705, 4715.
Uslar Pietri, Arturo, 3928.
Utopias, 5308, 5324, 5345, 5373, 5398. Chile, 2456. Mexico, 161. Peru, 2702. South America, 2267. Views of, 5325.
Valdivia, Luis de, 832.

Valdivia, Pedro de, 2486.
Valero de Bernabé, Antonio, 2118.
Valle, Rafael Heliodoro, 1638.
Valle de México. Agribusiness, 1389. Entrepreneurs, 1389.
Valle del Cauca, Colombia (dept.). Social Conflict, 2623. Violence, 2623.
Valle y Caviedes, Juan del, 3567.
Vallejo, César, 4510, 4519, 4545, 4985–4986.
Valparaíso, Chile (city). Italians, 2837. Labor Movement, 2892.
Varela, Félix, 1978, 2004, 2043, 5413.
Varela, Juan Cruz, 4708.
Varela, Víctor, 4686.
Vargas, Getúlio, 3252, 3448, 5479.
Vargas, José María, 5431.
Vargas, María Elena, 5305.
Vargas Llosa, Mario, 3901, 3903, 4030.
Vargas Lugo de Bosch, Elisa, 165.
Vargas Machuca, Bernardo de, 1157.
Vargas Vargas, Francisco, 1712.
Varinas, Gabriel Fernández de Villalobos, *Marqués de*, 1073.
Vasconcelos, José, 1490, 5393–5394, 5396.
Vásquez de Espinosa, Antonio, 1074.
Vastey, Pompée-Valentin, 1924.
Vázquez Rial, Horacio, 5052.
Vega, Daniel de la, 4663.
Vega, Garcilaso de la, 644, 651, 804, 3532, 3551, 3580, 3584, 3611.
Vega Alta, Puerto Rico (town). History, 2095.
Vega Gaona, Ceferino, 3118.
Velasco, José María, 288, 1429.
Velez, Aurelia, 2910.
Veloso, Caetano, 5135.
Venegas, Isabel, 2561.
Veracruz, Mexico (city). Labor Movement, 1532.
Veracruz, Mexico (state). Agricultural Systems, 1423. Blacks, 1201. Church History, 1340. Elections, 1367. Haciendas, 1200. Indigenous Peoples, 1436. Land Tenure, 1436. Legislators, 1367. Literature, 3775. Merchants, 1202. Modernization, 1370. Public Administration, 1370. Textiles and Textile Industry, 1495. Tobacco Industry and Trade, 1373.
Veraguas, Panama (dept.). History, 2634.
La verdad sospechosa, 3534.
Verdadero método de estudiar, 5319.
Verde Olivo, 5409.
Verger, Pierre, 412.
Vernacular Architecture. Argentina, 181. Bolivia, 218. Brazil, 415. Jamaica, 307. Mexico, 133, 154.

AUTHOR INDEX

Aruca, Lohania, 254
Aruj, Jorge David, 5335
Arvizu García, Carlos, 167
Arze, José Roberto, 5462
Arze Aguirre, René Danilo, 2783
Asesinato en Coyoacán: antología, 1449
Ashbrook, William, 5218
Ashton, Dore, 260
Asís, Jorge, 4084
Asociación de Críticos e Investigadores Tea-
trales de la Argentina, 4680
Asociación de Educación y Cultura Alejandro
von Humboldt. Comité de Investigaciones
Históricas (Guatemala), 1790
Asociación de Licenciados y Doctores Españ-
oles en E.E.U.U., 866
Asociación Peruana de Promotores y Anima-
dores Culturales, 3906
Assis, Anatólio Alves de, 4765
Associação Religiosa Israelita do Rio de Ja-
neiro, 3313
Assunção, Leilah, 4912
Assunção, Mathias Rohrig, 666
Assunção, Matthias Röhrig, 3161
Asturias, Miguel Angel, 3778, 3798
Asuaje de Rugeles, Ana Mercedes, 5299
Atabales Matus, Jaime, 5467
Athayde, Johildo Lopes de, 3235
Atondo Rodríguez, Ana María, 1149
Atualidade & abolição, 3162
Augier, Angel I., 3630, 4366, 4494
Auguste, Claude B., 1888–1889
Auguste, Marcel B., 1890
Augusto Roa Bastos: Premio Miguel de Cer-
vantes, 1989: Biblioteca Nacional, abril-
mayo 1990, 4230
Augusto Roa Bastos: Premio de Literatura en
Lengua Castellana Miguel de Cervantes,
1989, 4231
Aun, Miguel, 411
Aurrecoechea, Juan Manuel, 259
Austin-Broos, Diane J., 1969
Auza, Néstor Tomás, 2906, 2991
Auza León, Atiliano, 5143
Avellaneda, Nicolás, 3622
Avellaneda Navas, José Ignacio, 2287
Aveni, Anthony F., 428
Avila Blancas, Luis, 1425
Avila Echazú, Edgar, 4495
Avila Espinosa, Felipe Arturo, 1450
Avila Martel, Alamiro de, 2458, 2469, 2827,
5464
Avilés Concepción, Jorge Luis, 4297
Avni, Haim, 845
Avramov, Rumen, 2907

Ayala, Francisco, 4217
Ayala, José Luis, 2749
Ayala, Manuel José de, 929
Ayala, María de la Luz, 1207
Ayala Anguiano, Armando, 1451
Ayala Mora, Enrique, 745, 2669, 2679–2683
Ayarza de Morales, Rosa Mercedes, 5281
Azara, Félix de, 2494
Azevedo, Carlito, 4864
Aznar, Pedro, 4298
Azor, Ileana, 4659
Azuaga, Moncho, 4164
Azuela, Arturo, 3699–3701, 3776
Azuela, Mariano, 3701, 5014

Bacchus, M.K., 1970
Baciero, Carlos, 2358
Backal, Alicia Gojman de, 1488
Badaró, Murilo, 4815
Badejo, Fabian, 2138
Badii, Líbero, 315
Badillo, Juan Carlos, 4557
Baegert, Jacob, 1287
Baer, James, 2908
Báez, Cecilio, 2495
Baguer, Néstor E., 4496
Bahamonde Magro, Angel, 1971
Bähler, Malena, 4085
Baião, Isis, 4913
Baila, José, 2049
Bakewell, Peter, 1288, 2245
Bakos, Margaret M., 3236
Balakian, Anna, 5051
Balbina Fernández, Eva, 2942
Baldó Lacomba, Marc, 2496
Balduino, el africano, 4865
Balhana, Altiva Pilatti, 3163
Ballán, Romeo, 846
Ballesteros Gaibrois, Manuel, 847, 3533
Baltazar, Carlos Alberto, 5166
Balza, José, 4031
Banco Chase Manhattan (Brazil), 391
Banco Safra (Brazil), 380
Bancos bibliográficos latinoamericanos y de
el Caribe I., 32
Bancos bibliográficos latinoamericanos y de
el Caribe II., 33
Bancos bibliográficos mexicanos I., 34
Bancos bibliográficos mexicanos II., 35
Bandeira, Julio, 419
Bankay, Anne María, 4260
Bañuelos, Raúl, 4276
Baptista Gumucio, Mariano, 2432
Barahona, Marvin, 1621
Barahona, Renato, 1083

Buchenau, Jürgen, 1343
Buedel, Barbara Foley, 3567
Buelna Serrano, Elvira, 944
Bueno, Terezinha Peron, 4816
Buesa Conde, Domingo, 844
Buescu, Mircea, 3249
Buisson, Inge, 1084
Buitrago, Fanny, 3946
Buker, George E., 1948
Bunter, Cora V., 713
Burga, Manuel, 837
Burgos, Julia de, 4315, 4514
Burke, Marcus B., 107
Burke, Peter, 3568
Burkhart, Louise M., 442–443
Burnham, Jeff, 575
Burns, E. Bradford, 1704
Burns, Kathryn, 2360
Burón, Ximena, 328
Bury, John, 382
Bush, Peter, 5037, 5074
Bushnell, David, 2615, 2624
Bustamante, Bárbara, 317
Bustillos Vallejo, Freddy, 5144
Bustos, Hermenegildo, 294
Butel, Paul, 1895
Butler, Kim D., 3250
Buve, Raymond, 1344
Buxó, José Pascual, 151
Byland, Bruce E., 548

Caamaño, Claudia L. de, 178
Caamaño de Fernández, Vicenta, 4470
Caballero, Luis, 339
Cabán, Pedro A., 2141
Cablegramas chilenos durante la ocupación de Lima, julio-octubre 1881, 2704
Cabral, Ligia Maria Martins, 3251
Cabral de Melo Neto, João, 4868
Cabrera, Lydia, 1800
Cabrera, Sarandy, 4316
Cabrera Infante, Guillermo, 3821–3822, 5057
Cabrera Ypiña, Octaviano, 1124
Cabrera Ypiña de Corsi, Matilde, 1124
Cabrujas, José Ignacio, 4561
Cáceres, Eduardo, 5199
Cachapuz, Paulo Brandi de Barros, 3251
Cacopardo, María Cristina, 2926
Cacua Prada, Antonio, 2625
Cadernos Negros: Poemas, 4869
Cadernos Negros, 4766
Caetano, Gerardo, 3129
Cafezeiro, Edwaldo, 4924
Cagiao, Pilar, 850
Cahill, David P., 2361–2362

Caicedo Licona, Carlos Arturo, 3631
La caída de Allende: transcripción textual de las conversaciones, a través de las líneas radiotelefónicas militares, sostenidas entre Pinochet, Leigh y otros altos mandos en las horas decisivas del golpe de estado de setiembre de 1973, 2834
Caillavet, Chantal, 618
Caille, Brigitte, 1826
Caistor, Nick, 4948
Caja de Ahorros de Asturias. Obra Social y Cultural, 126
Cajías, Lupe, 2788
Calatayud, Liduvina, 1623
Calderón, Lila, 4317
Calderón, Sara Levi, 5017
Calderón, Teresa, 4318
Calderón Chico, Carlos, 2678
Calderón de Cuervo, Elena, 945
Calderón G., Fernando, 2786
Calderón Jemio, Raúl Javier, 2789
Calderón Quijano, José Antonio, 80
Caldwell, Helen, 5077
Calero, Luis Fernando, 619
Calisto, Marcela, 2705
Calixto, Benedito, 386
Callan, Richard, 4662
Calle C., Waldo, 4262
Calleia Leal, Guillermo G., 1983
Calles, Plutarco Elías, 1462
Calviño Iglesias, Julio, 3463
Calvo, Luis María, 2499
Calvo, Thomas, 1204, 1210
Calvo, Vicente, 2357
Camacho, Jorge, 3818
Camacho Navarro, Enrique, 1705
Câmara, Eugênia Infante da, 4870
Camarena, Mario, 1463
Camargo, Aspásia, 3252, 3297
Camargo, Sérgio de, 395
Cambrón Infante, Ascensión, 1984
Camnitzer, Luis, 306
Camp, Roderic Ai, 1464
Campaña Avilés, Mario, 4481
Campaña de la Breña: colección de documentos inéditos, 1881–1884, 2706
Campbell, Carl C., 1798, 1893
Campesinos: kleine boeren in Latijns-Amerika vanaf 1520 [Campesinos: small holders in Latin America since 1520.], 851
Campo del Pozo, Fernando, 1205
Campoamor, María José, 4562
Campodónico, Miguel Angel, 4179
Campos, Haroldo de, 4862, 4871, 4911
Campos, Julieta, 5018–5019

Naranjo, Carmen, 3786–3790
Naranjo Orovio, Consuelo, 1828, 2192
Naranjo Villegas, Abel, 5438
Nariño, Antonio, 2608
Naro, Nancy Priscilla Smith, 3380–3381
Narraciones breves uruguayas, 1830–1880, 4181
National Center for Policy Analysis (US), 5332
National Information Services Corporation (Baltimore), 55
The National Trade Data Bank: NTDB., 60
Nault, François, 2062
Nauman, James, 575
Navarrete, Carlos, 133
Navarrete Linares, Federico, 450
Navarrete Orta, Luis, 4523
Navarrete Pellicer, Sergio, 536
Navarro, Antonio, 5259
Navarro, Desiderio, 3853–3854
Navarro, Márcia Hoppe, 3504
Navarro, Noel, 3834
Navarro, Ramiro, 1352
Navarro Azcue, Concepción, 899
Navarro Cárdenas, Maximina, 2332
Navarro Floria, Pedro, 2553
Navarro García, Jesús Raúl, 2063
Navarro García, Luis, 2064
Navarro Harris, Heddy, 4406
Navas-Sierra, J. Alberto, 1254
Navascués, Javier de, 4215
Nazzari, Muriel, 3181, 3211
Nebel, Richard, 1138
Necker, Louis, 2554
Necoechea G., Gerardo, 1553
Nederveen Meerkerk, Hannedea van, 3212
Needell, Jeffrey D., 3382
Negrão, Luiz, 4843
Negrete, Marta Elena, 1554
Negrón-Portillo, Mariano, 2065
Negroni, María, 4407
Neiburg, Federico B., 3024
Neira, Hernán, 2395
Neira Avendaño, Máximo, 2759
Nejar, Carlos, 4892–4894, 4921
Nelli, Ricardo, 3025
Neruda, Pablo, 2678, 4408, 4973–4977
Neuman, William I., 5048–5049
Neves, Luiz Guilherme Santos, 4790
New Iberian world: a documentary history of the discovery and settlement of Latin America to the early 17th century, 1677
New tales of mystery and crime from Latin America, 4955, 5069
New world encounters, 3595
Newland, Carlos, 1094

Newson, Linda A., 1175, 1678, 2339
Neyra, Juan Carlos, 2555
Nguyen, Thai Hop, 2396
Nicastro, Laura Diana, 4130–4131
Nicholls, David, 1924
Nicholson, Henry B., 537
Nicolau, Juan Carlos, 3026
Nieto, Jorge, 5460
Nill, Annegret, 4971
Nina, Daniel, 3835
No hay caciques ni señores, 2306
Noble, Patricia, 19
Nobre, Ana Luiza, 416
Nobre, Marlos, 5112
Noéjovich, Héctor Omar, 2760
Noelle, Louise, 280, 285
Nogueira, Oracy, 3383
Noguez, Xavier, 538
Noll, João Gilberto, 4743
Nolla, Olga, 4409
Nolte, Detlef, 2871
Nómez, Naín, 4524, 4546
Norambuena Carrasco, Carmen, 2872
Noriega, Simón, 372
Nos, Marta, 4132
Notimex, 61
Nova história da expansão portuguesa, 3213
Novaes, Carlos Eduardo, 4844–4845
Novais, Fernando A., 5484
Novak, Michael, 5352
Novas Terra, Luis, 4552
La novela argentina de los años 80, 4216
Novinsky, Anita, 3214
Novo, Salvador, 4410
Nóvoa, Maria Helena, 4744
Noyola, Arturo, 3667
Nuestras raíces: muestra de arte iberoamericano, 252
Nueva arquitectura en América Latina: presente y futuro, 253
Nueva historia de Colombia, 2307
Nueva historia del Ecuador, 745, 2679–2683
Núñez, Benjamín, 1720
Núñez, Estuardo, 3918
Núñez, Guillermo, 5063
Núñez Borda, Luis, 343
Núñez Cabeza de Vaca, Alvar, 3596
Núñez Jiménez, Antonio, 900
Núñez Machín, Ana, 2185
Núñez Seixas, Xosé M., 901
Núñez Soto, Orlando, 1707
Núñez Ureta, Teodoro, 365
Nunn, Frederick M., 1117

OAS. *See* Organization of American States
Oberem, Udo, 746

menina de América Latina; antología crítica, 3507

Plaza, Elena, 2599, 5429

Plaza, Juan Bautista, 5304

Plaza Noblía, Héctor, 4624

Pluchon, Pierre, 1930

Pocaterra, José Rafael, 4956

Podestá, Guido A., 3670

Podetti, Amelia, 5358

Poesía argentina, 1940–1960, 4274

Poesía chilena de hoy: de Parra a nuestros días, 4275

Poesía colonial hispanoamericana, 3599

Poesía de América, 4276

Poesía gauchesca del siglo XX., 4277

Poesía modernista ecuatoriana, 4481

Poesía puertorriqueña, 4278

Poesía viva del Ecuador: siglo XX., 4279

Los poetas de 1942: antología, 4280

Poetas de tierra adentro, 4281

Los poetas lunfardos, 4282

Poetisas del Paraguay: voces de hoy, 4283

Pohl, John M.D., 548

Poirot, Luis, 4957

Polanco Brito, Hugo Eduardo, 2080

La polémica del arte nacional en México, 1850–1910, 289

Polito, Ronald, 3198

Polkinhorn, Harry, 5058

Pollard, Helen Perlstein, 549–550

Pollarolo, Giovanna, 4422

Pollero, Raquel, 3147

Polo de Ondegardo, 766

Poloni, Jacques, 2766

Pólvora, Hélio, 4792

Pompejano, Daniele, 1765

Ponce, Javier, 3985, 4423

Ponce Leiva, Pilar, 1038, 2345, 2689

Pondé, Eduardo Bautista, 3036

Pondé, Francisco de Paula e Azevedo, 3398

Poniatowska, Elena, 3727–3728

Pontes, Heloisa A., 3399

Pontes, Joel, 4941

Pontiero, Giovanni, 5068, 5080, 5084

Pontual, Roberto, 247

Poole, Stafford, 950

El Porfiriato en Sinaloa, 1409

Porras Cruz, Jorge Luis, 4278

Porro, Antonio, 767

Porrúa, Ana, 4536

Portales, el hombre y su obra: la consolidación del gobierno civil, 2878

Portela, Miriam, 4899

Porto, Walter Costa, 3400

Porto Alegre, Manuel de Araújo, 4924

Portocarrero Maisch, Gonzalo, 2767

Portuondo Zúñiga, Olga, 2081

Posada, José Guadalupe, 290

Posadas, Diego A. de, 3148

Posse, Abel, 4142

Postma, Johannes, 1871

Potelet, Jeanine, 3217, 3401, 4545

Potosí: catalogación de su patrimonio urbano y arquitectónico, 231

Potosí, patrimonio cultural de la humanidad, 232

Potthast-Jutkeit, Barbara, 3111, 3122

Powell, Amanda, 4994

Powers, Karen M., 768, 2341

Poyo, Gerald E., 1832

Pozo, José del, 2879

Prada, Teresa de, 326

Prada Oropeza, Renato, 3873, 3939

Prado, João Fernando de Almeida, 389

Prado Núñez, Ricardo, 139

Prato-Perelli, Antoinette da, 2282

Pratt, Mary Louise, 3508

Prechtel, Martin, 444

Prego, Omar, 4188

Prem, Hanns J., 551, 1258

Prêmio Cora Coralina: 1986; poesias, 4900

Premio Eugenio Mendoza: mención escultura, 375

A presença italiana no Brasil: atas, 3402

Presença luterana, 1990, 3403

Presencia de la Merced en América: actas del I Congreso Internacional, Madrid, 30 de abril-2 de mayo de 1991, 906

Presta, Ana María, 769, 2401

Prestes, Anita Leocádia, 3404

Preussen und Venezuela: Edition der preussischen Konsularberichte über Venezuela, 1842–1850, 2600

Price, Richard, 1937

Price, Sally, 1937

Prieto, Adolfo, 5528

Prieto, Agustina, 3037

Prieto, Francisco, 3729

Prieto, Justo José, 3112

Prieto, Martín, 4424

Prieto, René, 3808

Prieto, Ricardo, 4552

Prieto Castillo, Daniel, 5430

Prieto Reyes, Luis, 1547

I Bienal de Arte Pictórico Cervecería Nacional, Panamá 1992, 300

Primer centenario del ferrocarril en San Luis Potosí, 1888–1988, 1410

Primer encuentro de filósofos latinoamericanistas, 5359

Salafranca Ortega, Jesús F., 1268
Salas, Alejandro, 4286
Salas, Ernesto, 3061
Salas Cuesta, María Elena, 1397
Salas Viú de Hälffter, Emilia, 5265
Salazar, Daniel, 4688
Salazar, Silvana, 2776
Salazar Bondy, Sebastián, 361
Salazar de Garza, Nuria, 147, 1269
Salazar e Hijar, Enrique, 114
Salazar González, Julene, 2884
Salazar Mora, Orlando, 1770
Salazar Salvatierra, Rodrigo, 5196
Salazar y Torres, Agustín, 4599
Salcedo, Hugo, 4633–4634
Salcedo-Bastardo, José Luis, 5426
Saldarriaga Roa, Alberto, 349
Saldes B., Sergio, 4074–4075
Saldívar, Gabriel, 5266
Sale, Kirkpatrick, 908
Salessi, Jorge, 3675
Salguero, Natasha, 3988
Salina Meza, René, 2885
Salinas, Juan Antonio, 2860
Salinas Novoa, Carlos, 1421
Salisbury, Richard V., 1771
Salles, Ricardo, 3420
Salles-Reese, Verónica, 3608
Salmón, Raúl, 4635–4636
Salmón, Roberto Mario, 1321
Salmon, Russell O., 4968
Salmona, Rogelio, 350
Salomon, Frank, 781
Salter, Lionel, 5137
Salvador Lara, Jorge, 355
Salvatore, Ricardo Donato, 3062–3063
Salvetti, Patrizia, 1772
Salzano, Francisco M., 791
Samanez Argumedo, Roberto, 215
Samara, Eni de Mesquita, 3421–3422
Samaroo, Brinsley, 1837
Samios, Eva Machado Barbosa, 3423
Sampaio Neto, José Augusto Vaz, 3424
Samper K., Mario, 1773
Samudio A., Edda O., 2285
Samuel, Heli, 4751
San Agustín de Acolman, 148
San Cristóbal Sebastián, Antonio, 238–239
San José de Gracia y San Antonio de Arrona: economía y sociedad en dos haciendas mineras de Sinaloa en el siglo XVIII., 1322
San Martino de Dromi, María Laura, 3064
San Miguel, Pedro L., 2093
Sánchez, Ana, 600, 792–793, 2356
Sánchez, Efraín, 2289

Sánchez, Fernanda, 415
Sánchez, Joseph P., 3554
Sánchez, Luis Alberto, 2777, 4007, 4026
Sánchez, Matilde, 4135
Sánchez, Norma Isabel, 2994
Sánchez, Rafael, 4150
Sánchez, Sandra, 794
Sánchez-Albornoz, Nicolás, 795
Sánchez Castro, Carlos, 5433
Sánchez Delgado, Carlos, 4637
Sánchez Díaz, Gerardo, 1411, 1508
Sánchez García, Alfonso, 1587
Sánchez Gómez, Gonzalo, 2658
Sánchez-Grey Alba, Esther, 4703
Sánchez León, Abelardo, 4020
Sánchez Parga, José, 3899
Sánchez Quell, H., 2571
Sánchez Rubio, Rocío, 1218
Sánchez Silva, Carlos, 1588
Sánchez Suárez, Benhur, 3964
Sancho, José, 302
Sanchotene, Fernando Lima, 376
Sanderlin, George William, 951
Sanders, William T., 563
Sandino, Augusto César, 5403
Sandino, the testimony of a Nicaraguan patriot: 1921–1934, 1774
Sandos, James A., 1323, 1589
Sandoval, Adriana, 3510
Sandoval, Judith Hancock de, 116
Sandoval, Salvador A.M., 3425
Sandoval Ambiado, Carlos, 2845
Sang, Mu-Kien Adriana, 2094
Sanjinés C., Javier, 3885–3886
Sansone de Martínez, Eneida, 4704
Santa Cruz, Adriana, 3466
Santa Cruz, Lucía, 2469
Santa María, Andrés de, 351
Santaella, Lúcia, 5099
Santamaría, Daniel J., 2447–2448
Santamaría, Germán, 3965
Santana, Rodolfo, 4630, 4638
Santana R., Pedro, 2659
Santana Rabell, Leonardo, 2095
Santander, Francisco de Paula, 2607-
Santander y el Congreso de 1823: actas y correspondencia, 2616
Santander y el Congreso de 1824: actas y correspondencia, 2617
Santander y el Congreso de 1825: actas y correspondencia, 2618
Sant'Anna, Affonso Romano de, 4852, 4860, 4904–4905
Sant'Anna, Sérgio, 4798
Santí, Enrico Mario, 5421